THE OXFORD COMPANION TO THE THEATRE

THE OXFORD COMPANION TO THE THEATRE

EDITED BY

PHYLLIS HARTNOLL
L.-ÈS-L., M.A. (OXON.)

THIRD EDITION

LONDON
OXFORD UNIVERSITY PRESS

Oxford University Press, Ely House, London W. 1

GLASGOW NEW YORK TORONTO MELBOURNE WELLINGTON
CAPE TOWN IBADAN NAIROBI DAR ES SALAAM LUSAKA ADDIS ABABA
DELHI BOMBAY CALCUTTA MADRAS KARACHI LAHORE DACCA
KUALA LUMPUR SINGAPORE HONG KONG TOKYO

ISBN 0 19 211531 6

First edition 1951
Reprinted (with revisions) 1952
Second edition (with illustrated supplement) 1957
Reprinted 1962 and 1964
Third edition 1967
Reprinted 1967, 1970, and 1972

Printed in Great Britain
at the University Press, Oxford
by Vivian Ridler
Printer to the University

PREFACE TO THE THIRD EDITION

A REPROACH which has sometimes been levelled at this *Companion* is that it is out of date, in that the newest playwright or the latest offering of the *avant-garde* is not to be found in it. That is as it should be. If the theatre were a dead thing we could catalogue its activities down to the last gasp. But the 'fabulous invalid' is very much alive, and has made several remarkable recoveries—from the Dark Ages, the Puritan Interregnum, the Russian Revolution, the American Depression—all of which are catalogued here. In our own times the cinema, the radio, and the television set may have 'scotched the snake'; they have not killed it. An actor can still become a star overnight; a playwright can wake to find himself famous; and a cold, empty auditorium can give way to a warm, packed house. Reversals of fortune are still the commonplaces of the theatre, and we have recently seen a forgotten dramatist hailed as the father of a new movement. Countries which find their contemporary scene inadequately represented here should be glad, for it means that even in the time which it has taken to produce this book new life has flowed into their theatres, bringing into prominence new names and new faces which may soon be known well beyond the confines of their own land.

An effort has, however, been made to provide information on every aspect of the theatre at least up to the end of 1964, and even beyond that for those countries—among them England, France, and America—on which material is easily accessible to a London-based editor. It is to be hoped, therefore, that on the historical side this book will not be found wanting. And for that, credit must go not only to the contributors who have revised their earlier articles or provided new ones, but also to the many friends of the *Companion* in all quarters of the globe who have supplied details with which to build up this composite picture of world theatre.

My first word of thanks must go, as always, to the great scholars and research workers in the theatrical field, some of whom figure in the list of contributors. The latter have, as before, earned the editor's gratitude for their forbearance when their articles have had to be cut and tailored to fit the needs of the book. It was that great journalist Henry Labouchère who said that 'the making of an article requires two persons, one to write it, the other to cut it down', and I have too often had to be 'the other', mainly because of lack of space. The rapid growth of interest in the history of the theatre everywhere has necessitated the inclusion of many new articles. Among the countries dealt with here for the first time are Bulgaria, Iceland, New Zealand, Pakistan, Portugal, Rumania, Switzerland, and Turkey. New subjects include the Byzantine theatre, Flexible Staging and Theatre-in-the-Round, Modern Religious Drama in Great Britain and the U.S.A., the Théâtre des Nations in Paris, and, for Great Britain particularly, Civic Theatres, Private Theatres, and University Departments of Drama. New players and playwrights have also been included, as well as some notes on new theatre buildings.

Articles which have been replaced by new entries incorporating the results of recent research include Architecture, Ballet, Belgium, Canada, Collections and Museums, Czechoslovakia, Hungary, The Netherlands (replacing Holland), Scotland, and Spain. Germany has been brought up to date and separated from Austria, for which a new article has been provided. New sections on the contemporary theatre have been added also to China, England, France, Greece, Ireland, Italy, Japan, Jewish Drama, Scandinavia, Russia, and the United States. The article on Brecht has been rewritten, and new sections added to Ibsen and Chekhov dealing with productions of their plays in England and the United States. In addition, new information has been provided on Acoustics, Children's Theatres, Copyright, Dramatic Criticism, Incidental Music, Lighting in Great Britain and the United States, Musical Comedy, Opera, Puppets, Scenery, South America, and Shakespearian Festivals, and on the Negro in the American Theatre, while the former article on the Nationwide Theatre in the U.S.A. has been replaced by one on the Theatre Outside New York (see United States of America, 10).

All the remaining articles have been revised or corrected, and in many cases added to, and the articles in the Supplement to the Second Edition have been incorporated into the main alphabet. Some of the longer historical articles remain as they were—notably those on the *commedia dell'arte* (Italy, 2), on Jesuit Drama, on the early history of Lighting, and on Make-up. A further twenty-two pictures on sixteen pages of plates have been added to the illustrations, and the original bibliography has been replaced by a Select List of Theatre Books compiled by the Librarian of the Society for Theatre Research.

In this new edition, which has been entirely reset, the practice of signing articles by the initials of the contributor has been discarded in favour of full names, as being more helpful to the reader. For contributors who are no longer alive, a † has been appended. Unsigned articles are by the editor, often based on material supplied by the countries or institutions concerned. For the United States, which bulks most largely in the book after Great Britain, valuable help has been given by Mr. Paul Myers, Mr. Crawford K. Wright, and Miss Dorothy L. Swerdlove of the Research Library of the Performing Arts at the Lincoln Center, New York, under the guidance of the late George Freedley, for many years a friend and collaborator; and by Mr. C. Beecher Hogan and Mr. William Melnitz. For help with Canada, which since this book was first published has achieved professional status, I am grateful to Mr. Ivon Owen and to Mr. Ralph Hicklin. All aspects of the French theatre have benefited from the advice of Mademoiselle Rose-Marie Moudouès, of the Société d'Histoire du Théâtre, and of the late Monsieur Léon Chancerel. For information on Czechoslovakia I am indebted to Dr. Z. Raszewski, of the Kabinet pro Studium Českého Divadla, Prague; on Hungary, to Dr. Gyorgy Székely, of the Hungarian Centre of the International Theatre Institute, Budapest; on Poland, to Dr. Barbara Król-Kaczorowska, of the Instytut Sztuki P.A.N., Warsaw; and on Yugoslavia to Dr. Filip K. Kumbatovič, of Ljubljana.

Nor have other friends been behindhand with material help. For information on Finland I am indebted to Professor Dr. Ester-Margaret von Frenckell; on Germany, to Dr. A. Frenzel; on Greece, to Monsieur Jean Sideris; on Iceland, to Mr. Gudlaugur Rosinkranz; on Japan, to Mr. Toshio Kawatake; on Pakistan, to the High Commissioner's Office and Miss S. B. Wajid Ali. For Spain I have been glad of the advice of Professor Parker, of Edinburgh University, and of Señor R. B. Olsina, of Barcelona. For Chile I have had the help of the playwright and Cultural Attaché, Señor Fernando Debesa; for Argentina and Mexico of their respective Cultural Attachés; and for Brazil useful suggestions have come from Dr. J. E. Bloch of São Paulo and Mr. J. A. Cayton, of the British Council, Rio de Janeiro. Coming nearer home, I gratefully acknowledge the help of the late Mr. E. G. Ashton on Scotland, and of Professor Nevill Coghill and Mr. George Rylands on Oxford and Cambridge respectively. Mr. G. V. Blackstone has kindly allowed me to make use of his work on Fires in Theatres. And in London I have had cause to be grateful to Mr. Eric Johns, editor of *The Stage*, and to Miss Freda Gaye, who, as the present editor of *Who's Who in the Theatre*, has maintained the friendly interest in the *Companion* shown from its inception by her predecessor, the late Mr. John Parker; information on London and other theatres was also supplied by the late Malcolm Morley and Mr. Neville M. Bligh.

In collecting the photographs which have been added to the illustrations, I have been greatly helped by such contributors as Mr. Metin And, Dr. Suresh Awasthi, Mr. Frederick Bentham, Mr. Victor Glasstone, Mrs. Beatrice King, and Dr. Sybil Rosenfeld; also by Mr. George Nash of the Enthoven Theatre Collection, and the staff of the Photographic Sections of the Victoria and Albert and British Museums; by the Society for Cultural Relations with the U.S.S.R.; by *The Times*; by the Guildhall Librarian and Mr. John Freeman; by Monsieur René Hainaux, editor of *World Theatre* and Signor Giacinto Giancola of the Italian Centre of the International Theatre Institute; by Mademoiselle Malms of the Collection Suisse du Théâtre, Bern; and by Mr. Hugh Hunt, Mademoiselle Hélène Leclerc, and Mr. Norman Marshall.

I cannot close my list of kind friends without reference to the many people who in New York, Paris, Munich, Venice, Vienna, and many other cities have found me tickets for current productions, often with great difficulty, and procured me access backstage to observe the workings of their theatres. And I should like also to record the kindness of Mr. John Goodwin and Mr. Vincent Pearmain, of the Royal Shakespeare Company, who have helped me in so many ways. A word of thanks is also due to Miss

Gwyneth Chaney, who kindly undertook the arduous task of correcting the proofs of the present edition, and to Miss Winifred Kimberley, who continues to make smooth the editorial path. And, finally, I should like to pay tribute to the memory of those friends and contributors who have died, and whose loss I have felt so keenly during the preparation of this Third Edition, particularly William Armstrong, William Beare, Eric Blom, Hubert Foss, Hubert Griffith, W. Macqueen-Pope, and Bernard Sobel.

Numbers in the text (e.g., see No. 1) refer to the illustrations at the end of the book.

PHYLLIS HARTNOLL

London 1966

PREFACE TO THE SECOND EDITION

THE history of the theatre is now accepted in England as a reasonable subject for scholarly research. In the years since this book was first published the Society for Theatre Research, then in its infancy, has been firmly established, and one of the first-fruits of its endeavours has been the foundation of an International Federation for Theatre Research. My work in preparing this new edition has been greatly eased by the help and encouragement of members of both these bodies. I am also grateful to the many other theatre enthusiasts who have sent me material from all over the world. For particular help with the illustrations I must acknowledge my debt to Miss M. St. Clare Byrne, Mr. James Laver, and Professor Kenneth Macgowan.

PHYLLIS HARTNOLL

London 1957

PREFACE TO THE FIRST EDITION

IN compiling a book which deals with the theatre in all ages and in all countries, the difficulty has been to decide what to omit. Since completeness was not to be thought of, a representative selection of what was most likely to interest the English-speaking reader was aimed at, and the emphasis throughout has been on the popular rather than on the literary theatre. More space has been devoted to melodrama and the music-hall than to comedy and tragedy, literary quarrels have been ignored, actors have been rated above dramatists. In short, this is a companion to the playhouse, and is meant for those who would rather see a play than read it, for those whose interest is as much in the production and setting of a drama as in its literary content. For such a study of the theatre as entertainment and not as literature we have the support of the great French critic,

Ferdinand Brunetière, who said: 'Il n'est pas du tout nécessaire qu'une pièce de théâtre soit littéraire pour être "du théâtre". L'histoire est là pour nous prouver que le théâtre s'est passé plus d'une fois d'avoir aucune valeur proprement littéraire.' This, then, accounts for such entries as Boulevard du Temple, Burlesque, Gaff, Haupt- und Staatsaktionen, Music-Hall, Vaudeville, Zarzuela, and for the number of minor dramatists, low comedians, and obscure theatres that lie cheek by jowl with Shakespeare and Aristophanes, Kean and Irving, Drury Lane and the Comédie-Française.

While thus limiting our range to the theatrical theatre, it has nevertheless proved impossible to ignore completely the sister arts of music, dancing, and design. Opera and Ballet, which have vast literatures of their own, have each been dealt with in a single article, as has Incidental Music in the Theatre. No attempt has been made to include individual composers, though a few librettists have short notes, as have some ballet-dancers and choreographers. Costume and Scenery are fully dealt with in articles covering Europe and America, as are Architecture, Acoustics, Make-Up, and Lighting; but few individual names have been singled out in these fields. On the other hand, space has been largely allotted to the development of the specifically English playhouse under its component parts—Auditorium, Proscenium, Stage—and a number of technical terms, both modern and historic, have been explained at length.

The theatres of the Far East—China, India, Japan, Malay (with Java)—have each one article, as have such European countries as Belgium, Holland, and Hungary, all supplemented by cross-references. The classical theatres of Greece and Rome have, in addition to their main articles, supplementary articles on their dramatists under their own names, and on such points of interest as Didascalia, Mime, Pantomimus, Satyr-Drama; the larger countries of Europe—England, France, Germany (with Austria), Italy, Russia, Scandinavia (Denmark, Norway, and Sweden), and Spain—have each their long main article, but in addition are furnished with a large number of supplementary articles on dramatists, actors, and theatre buildings under their own names. The history of the theatre in the United States has been minutely recorded, both in its territorial expansion and in its actors and dramatists; South America is dealt with in one article; while Canada, taken in conjunction with the Amateur Theatre in Great Britain and the Nationwide Theatre in the United States, deals with the bulk of the English-speaking amateur movement. Finally, standing somewhat apart from the above classifications, are the special articles, which range from Jesuit and Jewish Drama to Marionette, Mumming Play, and Toy Theatre.

Although cross-references are plentiful in the main alphabet, they have been used sparingly in the text, and serve to direct the reader's attention to another main article, and not to biographies or short articles. Every effort has been made to give each play mentioned its date of first production. Where this was not possible, the date of publication is indicated. In the biographical articles, the years of birth and death have been given where possible. It is hoped that those that are missing may eventually be found. Brackets indicate the subject's real name, as opposed to stage or pen-name, and Christian names not in general use, as CONWAY [RUGG] and WOFFINGTON, PEG [MARGARET]. It has not proved practicable to exclude all living actors and dramatists, but as few as possible have been included, and their biographies are in the main factual rather than critical.

The Cinema has been deliberately ignored, as being a totally different art which requires a book to itself. Lack of space has been responsible for the exclusion of the Circus, except for the short period in which it mingled with the play proper. For the same reason the lighter forms of entertainment—Cabaret, Café-Chantant, Revue—outside England and the United States have been drastically curtailed. Other omissions there are which were not intended. For these the chaotic state of Europe during the last ten years, and the difficulty of communications, must be held partly responsible. It is hoped that some gaps may be filled later, and that names, dates, facts of all kinds now sought in vain may come to light. I am well aware of these deficiencies, as of many others that mar the book, and shall welcome corrections and supplementary information on any subject. And I apologize in advance for any mistakes or misstatements that may have crept in, and hope for the opportunity to amend them.

The editor of such a book as this is laid under a heavy burden of gratitude to all those scholars and theatre historians of the past whose work has made possible such a compilation. In addition, I have a pleasant duty to fulfil in acknowledging the help I have received from the many contributors whose names will be found in the contributors' index. I thank them for undertaking the work in the first place, and even more for their patience and forbearance in dealing with the many queries that arose, for constantly revising the modern sections of their articles during the ten years that have elapsed since the book was started, and particularly for allowing me to cut and alter their material in order to make it fit the pattern of the work as a whole. Uniformity was obviously desirable in a book of reference—though even now it is not completely attained, and could not be attempted (where nearly sixty persons were working independently) without some sacrifice of individuality in the writing. To those who have so patiently borne with me I am indeed grateful. Among the contributors a special word of appreciation is due to Mr. George Freedley of New York and Mr. Macqueen-Pope of London, whose help has gone far beyond the boundaries of their allotted tasks, and whose knowledge of the theatre has been unstintedly at my disposal. I also acknowledge my debt to the works of Professor Allardyce Nicoll; and thank Mrs. Gabrielle Enthoven, O.B.E., and Miss M. St. Clare Byrne, Miss Sybil Rosenfeld, and Mr. Richard Southern, contributors and fellow-members of the Society for Theatre Research, who, with the other members of the Society, have given me inestimable help in my researches.

Among those who are not contributors to the book my first thanks must go to the great modern scholars of the English and American theatres, and particularly to Sir E. K. Chambers and Professor George C. D. Odell. I am also greatly indebted to Mr. John Parker. The many editions of his *Who's Who in the Theatre* have been a constant help and guide, as they are to all who deal with the modern theatre. Nor must I forget Mr. Hubert Foss, with whom this book was first discussed and planned in 1939–40.

For help with the articles on the French theatre I am indebted to the Société d'Histoire du Théâtre, and particularly to my good friend Monsieur J. G. Prod'homme, and to Madame Horn-Monval of the Bibliothèque de l'Arsenal. The articles on the Spanish theatre have had the expert assistance of Don Alberto Jiménez, Lecturer in Spanish in the University of Oxford, and of Miss Elizabeth Watson, while my ignorance of the Russian language has led me to rely gratefully on the help of Mr. Herbert Marshall, who translated for me long extracts from manuals of Russian theatre history and memoirs; of Mr. Hubert Griffith, who revised all the articles dealing with Russia; of Mr. Joseph Macleod and Mr. André van Gyseghem, who have made available to English readers so much material on the Russian theatre; of Miss Bertha Malnick, who gave me access to her Papers on the early Russian theatre, and allowed me to quote from one of them; and of Miss Eleanor Fox, Librarian of the Society for Cultural Relations with the U.S.S.R.

My work on the American theatre would not have been possible without the generous co-operation of Dr. Van Lennep, who opened to me the treasures of the Harvard Theatre Collection; of the Director and Staff of the Drama Department of Yale; of Miss May Davenport Seymour of the Museum of the City of New York; of Mrs. Sarah Chokla Gross of the Theatre Library Association; and of Miss Mary Virginia Heinlein of Vassar. I must also express my thanks to those good friends who smoothed my path in New York: Mr. Ben Lucien Burman, who helped me with the history of the Showboat; Miss Ruth May; and Miss Elsa Shelley. Above all I must acknowledge the help given me at every point, and particularly over the bibliographies, by Mrs. Elizabeth Barrett, Mr. Paul Myers, and their helpers in the Theatre Department of the New York Public Library, where I spent many happy and fruitful hours. I also acknowledge gratefully the help given me in England by the staffs of the British Museum, the Victoria and Albert Museum, the Bodleian Library, Oxford, and the Director and staff of the Shakespeare Memorial Theatre, Stratford-on-Avon. A special word of thanks is due to Mr. R. C. Maasz, Assistant Librarian of the Taylor Institution, Oxford, for his help in preparing the bibliographies of European countries. I am indebted also to members of the staff of the Oxford University Press both in London and in New York. To the Principal of St. Hugh's College, Oxford, and to the members of the Senior Common Room, particularly my Tutor and the Librarian, my thanks are due for help and encouragement—as much material as spiritual—over a long period. And finally a more personal word of gratitude is due to my mother, who first introduced me to the theatre, and implanted in me at an early age that love of plays and players which has sustained me throughout my task; and to Miss Winifred Kimberley, whose constant care over many years has enabled me to complete it. To all these, and to the many friends, inside the theatre and out, who have borne with my ruling passion and encouraged me to give free rein to it, I here make full and heartfelt acknowledgement of many acts of unrecorded kindness.

PHYLLIS HARTNOLL

Oxford 1950

CONTENTS

CONTRIBUTORS' INDEX

*(An * indicates contributors who appear for the first time in the Third Edition)*

ACTON, C.B.E., Harold, Florence
ADAMS, Miss Mildred, New York
*ALBACH, Ben, Amsterdam
*AND, Metin, Istanbul
APPLEBEE, The late L. G.
ARMSTRONG, The late William
*ARMSTRONG, Dr. William A., London
*ARNOTT, J. F., Glasgow
*AWASTHI, Dr. Suresh, Delhi

BAGENAL, Hope, F.R.I.B.A., London
BARBER, Miss M. Elizabeth, London
BEARE, The late William
*BECKLEY, Richard, London
*BEDNALL, J. B., Bangor
*BENTHAM, Frederick, London
BICKMORE, The late C. W.
BLOM, The late Eric
BROWN, Professor Sterling A., Washington, D.C.
*BROWNE, E. Martin, London
BURROW, Professor T., Oxford
BYRNE, Miss M. St. Clare, O.B.E., London

CAHOON, Herbert, New York
CARSON, Professor William Glasgow Bruce, St. Louis
*CHINNERY, Professor J. D., Edinburgh
CLARK, The late Barrett H.
COOKMAN, The late A. V.
CURTISS, Thomas Quinn, Paris

*DE GRUYTER, Dom., Antwerp
DELP, Dr. Wilhelmina E.
*DEYERMOND, Alan, London
DISHER, The late M. Willson
*DOWNING, Robert, New York

ENTHOVEN, The late Gabrielle

FERMOR, The late Una Ellis-
FLANAGAN DAVIS, The late Hallie
FOGERTY, The late Elsie
FREEDLEY, The late George

GASSNER, The late John
GILBERT, The late Douglas
GILDER, Miss Rosamond, New York
*GLASSTONE, Victor, London
*GUEST, Ivor, London

HARRIS, E., Israel
HASLER, Miss Olivia, Addis Ababa

*JACOBS, Miss Margaret, Oxford
JEFFREY, The late William

KEMP, The late T. C.
*KENDALL, William, London
*KING, The late Mrs. Beatrice
KITTO, Professor H. D. F., Bristol

LAVER, James, C.B.E., London
LEA, Miss K. M., Oxford
LITTLEWOOD, The late Sam R.
LOEWENBERG, The late Alfred

MCCANDLESS, The late Stanley
*MCFARLANE, Mrs. L. Kathleen, Norwich

*MAY, Professor Frederick, Sydney, Australia
*MILNE, T. C. C., London
*MITCHELL, Loften, New York
*MOORE, Miss D. M., London
*MORRISON, Professor Jack, Los Angeles

NICOLL, Professor Allardyce, Malvern

*O'CONNELL, Dan, Dublin

POPE, The late W. Macqueen-
*PORTER, Andrew, London
PURDIE, The late Edna

ROSENFELD, Dr. Sybil, London
RUBEL, Miss Margaret, London
RUTTER, The late Owen

SIMONSON, The late Lee
SOBEL, The late Bernard
SOUTHERN, Dr. Richard, Southampton
SPEAIGHT, George, London
*STADLER, Dr. Edmund, Bern
SUTHERLAND, Professor J. R., London

TANNER, Lawrence E., C.V.O., London
*TRACY, Robert, Berkeley, California

*VAREY, Dr. J. E., London

WARD, A. C., London
WHITWORTH, The late Geoffrey

A

ABBEY, Henry Eugene (1846–96), American theatre manager, and one of the most courageous and consistently successful in New York in his day. He first worked as a ticket-seller in the opera-house at Akron, and within two years he was lessee of the theatre, and arranging tours of good companies. In 1876 he was in management in Buffalo, and in the following year went to New York. The elder Sothern played under him, and he brought together for the first time William H. Crane and Stuart Robson. In 1880 he visited Europe, and on his return sealed his growing reputation by presenting Sarah Bernhardt for the first time in New York. In subsequent years he was responsible for the visits of the London Gaiety company, of Coquelin, and of Irving, who with Ellen Terry played at Abbey's Theatre (see KNICKERBOCKER THEATRE) on its opening in 1893. Abbey was one of the first American managers to present good theatre and opera outside New York, and to engage Continental stars for the United States.

ABBEY THEATRE, Ireland. In 1903 Miss Horniman, who was a friend and admirer of W. B. Yeats, was brought by him into contact with the Fays' National Theatre company, which had been producing Yeats's early plays, and decided to build a theatre in Dublin to serve as a permanent home for the company. She took over the hall of the Mechanics' Institute in Abbey Street (built on the site of the old Theatre Royal, burnt down in 1880) and an adjoining building, and there erected the Abbey Theatre. The licence was issued in Lady Gregory's name (as Miss Horniman was not resident in Ireland), and she and Yeats were the only directors. On 27 Dec. 1904 the theatre opened with Yeats's *On Baile's Strand* and Lady Gregory's *Spreading the News*. In these, apart from F. J. and W. G. Fay, were Arthur Sinclair and Sara Allgood, who were both destined to play a large part in the future success of the theatre. Productions in 1905 included Synge's *The Well of the Saints* and two more plays by Lady Gregory. By 1907 the Abbey had built up a company as good as any in Europe, and had a long list of new Irish plays to its credit. It visited several towns in Ireland and England, with increasing success, and even managed to weather the storm provoked by the first night of Synge's *The Playboy of the Western World* on 26 Jan. 1907, when the police had to be called in to restore order, and the trouble caused with the authorities by Shaw's *The Shewing-Up of Blanco Posnet*, which had been refused a licence in London by the Lord Chamberlain. It was successfully produced at the Abbey on 25 Aug. 1909.

In 1908 the Fays, who were not satisfied with the way the theatre was developing, left and went to the United States. W. G. Fay's place as manager was hard to fill and several people, including St. John Ervine and Nugent Monck, came and went. The most successful was probably Fred O'Donovan, who was a handsome actor and a good producer. In 1910 Lennox Robinson took over the management and remained until his death in 1958.

The Fays' departure, which coincided with the death of Synge, marked a turning point in the Abbey's history, for less than a year later Miss Horniman, who was already deep in her Manchester venture, withdrew, making the theatre over to the company. With Robinson's arrival, plays by the younger realistic dramatists replaced the former poetic drama, and T. C. Murray and St. John Ervine had their first successful productions.

In 1911 the Abbey players visited the United States for the first time, and although their acting was much admired, once again *The Playboy of the Western World* caused riots in several towns. The company was actually arrested in Philadelphia, and brought before a magistrate on a charge of performing an immoral play. On subsequent tours in 1913 and 1914 there was trouble, but by 1932, when the company returned after 18 years, the atmosphere had completely changed and the plays formerly objected to were hailed as masterpieces.

The outbreak of the First World War and the Irish Insurrection of 1916 nearly caused the closing of the theatre, particularly as Arthur Sinclair, Sara Allgood, and several others left the company. But from 1916–17 six of Shaw's plays were given for the first time, as well as other important productions, among them Lennox Robinson's *The White-Headed Boy* (1916). Out of these troubled years came the first plays of O'Casey, which infused new life into the theatre, whose company had now been reinforced by the arrival of Arthur Shields and his brother Barry Fitzgerald. In 1924 Sara Allgood returned for a while and was the first Juno in O'Casey's *Juno and the Paycock*. As well as O'Casey, there were the new dramatists Brinsley MacNamara and George Shiels. An important member of the company was F. J. McCormick, an actor whose whole working life was spent at the Abbey. Little known outside Ireland (and the United States, through the Abbey tours), he played in many of the theatre's outstanding productions, including O'Casey, Shakespeare, and Sophocles. His death in 1947 at the age of 56 was a great loss. An even greater misfortune was to befall the Abbey in 1951, when, on the night of 17 July, the theatre burnt down. Plans for rebuilding were immediately put in hand, but the new theatre did not open until 18 July, 1966, the company meanwhile playing at the Queen's.

The Abbey received a grant from the new Government of Eire in 1924, and so became the first State-subsidized theatre in the English-speaking world. After the years of penury this enabled scenery and costumes to be refurbished and salaries to be increased, and the impetus of these changes, which coincided with the arrival of some good new plays, carried the Abbey through several successful seasons. There has since been no lack of good dramatists and actors to keep the Abbey on an even keel, even though the theatre has not developed as Yeats, and even Lady Gregory, thought it would. Most of the new dramatists were realists, and it was left to Austin Clarke to bring back poetry to the Irish scene with his founding of the Lyric Theatre in 1942. Changes in the Abbey directorate brought Ernest Blythe to the Board; owing to his influence, more plays in Gaelic were done, and the Abbey became associated with the State-aided Am Comhar Dramaiochla, which had for some years been producing plays in Gaelic. With this innovation, for the first time the theatre was able to insist on its actors being bilingual. The theatre also acquired additional space and used part of it for the Peacock Theatre, a small playhouse seating 150, which opened in 1925. It was used by Hilton Edwards and Micheál MacLiammóir before they moved to the Gate (see also IRELAND, *passim*).

ABBOT OF MISRULE, OF UNREASON, see MISRULE.

ABBOTT, GEORGE (1887–), American playwright and director, who became interested in the theatre while at the University of Rochester, and went to Harvard in 1912 to work under Professor Baker. Some success there, and a prize for a one-act comedy, led in 1913 to a job at Keith's Theatre, and a subsequent appearance in New York at the Fulton Theatre. Five years in various parts followed, and some work for John Golden, and in 1925 *The Fall Guy*, written in collaboration with James Gleason, was put on successfully. Soon after this Abbott left the stage to devote all his energies to writing, producing, and directing, and became one of the outstanding men on Broadway. He has been responsible for numerous productions, particularly of his own plays, which include *Love 'em and Leave 'em* and *Broadway* (both 1926), *Coquette* (1927), which established Helen Hayes as a star, *Three Men on a Horse* (1935), which was also a success in London, *Where's Charley?* (1948) (a musical based on *Charley's Aunt*), *A Tree Grows in Brooklyn* (1951), *The Pajama Game* (1954), *Damn Yankees* (1955), and *Fiorello* (1959). The majority of these were written in collaboration, and Abbott's reputation as a play-doctor stands high, owing to his ability to get the best out of his material, and his competent and experienced work in direction. One of his few failures was his own adaptation of *Uncle Tom's Cabin* as *Sweet River* (1936). Among his outstanding productions of other authors' plays were *Boy Meets Girl* (1935), *The Boys from Syracuse* (1938) (a musical based on *The Comedy of Errors*), which he also produced in London in 1963, *Pal Joey* (1940), and *High Button Shoes* (1947), all of which displayed the hallmarks of an Abbott show—pace, humour, and a steady level of efficient action. In 1964 Abbott published an interesting volume of autobiography, *Mister Abbott*.

ABBOTT, WILLIAM (1789–1843), an English actor of whom Hazlitt said 'he never acts ill'. He first appeared at Bath in 1806, and came to London a few years later. By 1813 he was known at Covent Garden as a successful exponent of comedy and melodrama. He played Pylades to Macready's Orestes in *The Distressed Mother* when Macready made his first appearance at Covent Garden in 1816, and created the part of Appius Claudius in *Virginius* in 1820. Two melodramas by Abbott were given at Covent Garden. It may have been he who organized the English company which visited Paris in 1827; he was certainly a member of it, and played Charles Surface. Back in London, he played Romeo to Fanny Kemble's Juliet in 1830, and then went to America, where he appeared as Hamlet in Philadelphia in 1836. He was not a success in America, and died there in poverty.

ABELL, KJELD (1901–61), Danish dramatist and artist, who worked as a stage designer in Paris and with Balanchine at the Alhambra Theatre, London, in 1931. His first play, *Melodien, der blev væk*, was produced in Copenhagen in 1935, and at the Arts Theatre, London, a year later as *The Melody That Got Lost*. None of his other plays has been seen in London, though two of them, *Anna Sophia Hedvig* (1939) and *Dronning gaar Igen* (1943) (*The Queen on Tour*, or *The Queen's Progress*), were published in English translations. The former is usually regarded as his masterpiece. The second was produced during the German occupation of Denmark, and was a protest against the loss of freedom. After Munk's murder, Abell interrupted a performance at the Theatre Royal, Copenhagen, to protest, and then went underground until the liberation. After the war he wrote several more plays, finishing the last one shortly before his death. His imagination was closely akin to that of Hans Christian Andersen, who greatly influenced him, and in his use of poetic language he somewhat resembled Christopher Fry.

ABINGTON, FRANCES (1737–1815), English actress, the daughter of a soldier named Barton. She was first a flower-girl (Nosegay Fan) and street singer, and, after a little polishing by a French milliner who employed her temporarily, she took to the stage. Her first appearance was as Miranda in *The Busybody* at the Haymarket in 1755. On the recommendation of Foote she was taken on at Drury Lane, where she found herself overshadowed by Kitty Clive and Mrs.

Pritchard. It was at this time, apparently, that she made an ill-judged and unhappy marriage with her music-master, and from Fanny Barton became Mrs. Abington. Despairing of finding success in London, she went to Dublin, where she remained for five years, returning to Drury Lane only at the express invitation of Garrick, who disliked her but judged her to be a good actress. During the eighteen years that she remained there she played a number of important roles, and was the first Lady Teazle (1777) (see No. 30). She is said to have been excellent as Beatrice. She also revived Anne Oldfield's part of Lady Betty Modish in *The Careless Husband*, and was much admired as Miss Prue in *Love for Love*, in which character she was painted by Reynolds. In 1782 she went to Covent Garden, where she remained until 1790. After her retirement she made a few appearances between 1797 and 1799, but left the stage for good in the latter year. She was an ambitious, clever, and witty woman, and in spite of her humble origins she achieved an enviable position in distinguished society, where the womenfolk paid her the supreme honour of copying her clothes.

ABOVE, see STAGE DIRECTIONS.

ACCESI, THE, a company of *commedia dell'arte* actors who are first found in 1590. Records of their early activity are scarce, but in 1600 they were led by Tristano Martinelli and Pier Maria Cecchini, who took them to France. Among the actors were Martinelli's brother Drusiano, Flaminio Scala, and possibly Diana, formerly of the Desiosi. They returned to Italy, and on their next visit to France some years later (1608) were without their Harlequin (Tristano Martinelli), who had for some time been at loggerheads with Cecchini. In spite of this they gave a good account of themselves, and were much admired by the Court and by Marie de Médicis. Shortly afterwards Cecchini joined forces with the younger Andreini (see FEDELI), but the constant quarrelling of Cecchini's and Andreini's wives caused the two parties to separate. Cecchini retained the old name of Accesi, but little is known of his subsequent activities. Silvio Fiorillo, the first Captain Mattamoras, was with the Accesi in 1621 and 1632.

ACCIUS, LUCIUS (*c.* 170–86 B.C.), Roman dramatist, and the last important writer of tragedy for the Roman stage. The titles of over forty of his plays have survived, and show that he dealt with every field of tragedy open to a Latin writer, from the translation of Greek works of the fifth century and later to the composition of two *praetextae*. The outstanding quality of his style was force; here he excelled all Roman dramatists, though inferior to Pacuvius in learning and care. Characteristic of him are plots of a violent, melodramatic nature, flamboyant personages, majestic utterance, and powerful repartee; when we can compare him with his Greek models we find that he works up the rhetorical possibilities of each situation to the highest degree. Thus, while Eteocles' command to Polynices is simply expressed in the Greek: 'Then get thee from these walls, or thou shalt die', Accius gives us four imperatives in six words: 'egredere, exi, ecfer te, elimina urbe!' The most famous example of his style is the tyrant's retort: 'oderint dum metuant' ('Let them hate me, provided they fear me'). The continual search for rhetorical effect, the eagerness to exploit each situation to the full, is characteristic of Roman tragedy as a whole, and seems to reach its culminating point in Accius. Inevitably it tends to eliminate the half-tones of nature and reduce all portraiture to glaring white and black. Still, we may admit that Accius's heroes are grand and striking, while sometimes they seem to surpass their Greek prototypes, not merely in Stoic fortitude but in a certain grave humanity and sympathy with misfortune. On the other hand, we have no evidence that he ventured to alter the structure given him by his originals, though he seems to have remodelled certain passages and occasionally to have inserted lines from other sources. In Accius we have Roman tragedy at its climax, before a change of fashion drove it from the theatre. Comparing his extant lines with the plays of Seneca we see at once that Accius is still under the salutary discipline of having to write for a real stage. Stage technique is taken into due account; rhetoric and melodrama are kept within bounds. Accius's plays may seem stiff and strained versions of their Greek originals, but they are real plays, and as such far different from the purely literary drama of the Empire. WILLIAM BEARE†

ACHURCH, JANET (1864–1916), English actress, who made her first appearance at the Olympic in 1883, and later appeared in pantomime. She toured with Benson for some time, playing leading parts in Shakespeare, and was also seen at the Adelphi in *Harbour Lights*. It is, however, as one of the first actresses in England to play Ibsen that she is remembered. She was Nora in *A Doll's House* at the Novelty Theatre in 1889, and in 1896 produced *Little Eyolf* at the Avenue Theatre with herself as Rita, Mrs. Patrick Campbell as the Ratwife, and Elizabeth Robins as Asta. She was also seen as Shaw's heroine in *Candida* and as Lady Cecily Waynflete in *Captain Brassbound's Conversion* (both Strand, 1900). With her husband, Charles Charrington, she toured extensively, and was the first English actress to appear in the Khedivial Theatre, Cairo. A beautiful woman, with a superb carriage and lovely voice, she was called by Shaw 'the only tragic actress of genius we now possess'. Some excellent descriptions of her acting can be found in his *Our Theatres in the Nineties*. She retired from the stage in 1913.

ACKERMANN, a family of actors of eighteenth-century Germany whose work was of the highest importance in the development of German theatrical art. The father, (1) KONRAD ERNST (1712–71), was nearing thirty when he joined Schönemann's company, and it is not known what made him take to the stage. He had already served with some distinction as a soldier, and was a man of parts—a good fencer and horseman, a painter, and a dancer. He was a fine-looking man, with a restless, vagabond temperament which often did him ill service, and the life of a strolling player suited him. In later years he became fat and indolent, but was on the whole popular with his actors and audience because of his good nature. He was good in comedy, and in such parts as Major von Tellheim in *Minna von Barnhelm*. After serving his apprenticeship with Schönemann he left to form his own company, taking with him Schönemann's leading lady, whom he later married. This was (2) SOPHIA CARLOTTA SCHRÖDER (*née* Biereichel) (1714–92). She was married young to a drunken organist, but left him after a few years, and supported herself by doing gold embroidery. She became friendly with young Ekhof, and was persuaded to join him in Schönemann's company, making her début at Lüneburg as Monime in an adaptation of Racine's *Mithridate* on 15 Jan. 1740. She was immediately successful and was regarded as the leading lady of the company. A handsome woman, with a majestic presence, she had enthusiasm and an artistic sense which aided her materially in her career. She was also practical and businesslike, traits which came uppermost in later life, causing her to be accused of parsimony. Soon after she had joined Ackermann's company her husband sought her out, and a short reconciliation took place, which resulted in the birth of one of Germany's greatest actors (see SCHRÖDER). But the husband was unable to overcome his intemperance, and Sophia returned to the stage, marrying Ackermann after her husband's death.

For many years the Ackermanns toured unceasingly, with no outstanding success, but equally with no overwhelming losses. They visited Russia, Prussia, and Switzerland, with a varied repertory which included a number of Holberg's plays as well as adaptations from the French and some indigenous drama. In 1764 they were joined by their old friend Ekhof, then at the height of his fame, and with a strong company, which included Sophia's son, they later played at the first German National Theatre, established at Hamburg and inseparably connected with Lessing's *Hamburgische Dramaturgie*, corner-stone of modern dramatic criticism. Unfortunately this enterprise was ruined by internal dissension, and by the antagonism between young Schröder, who, after an unhappy childhood, was proving a thorn in the flesh to his stepfather, and Ekhof, who did not care to find himself the rival and butt of a youngster, however gifted. He left, as did Schröder, but the latter returned after a time to take over the Hamburg company, supplanting his stepfather, who died shortly after. In the company, which was still financially in the grip of his mother, who had given up acting for management and for the training of young actors, many of whom owed her a great debt of gratitude, were Schröder's two half-sisters. The elder, (3) DOROTHEA (1752–1821), had been acting for many years with her parents, and at 13 had been made to play young women's parts, some of them too difficult for her. This had caused her to be adversely criticized, and although she was later much admired, when her undoubted gifts had had time to mature, recognition came too late. She was already discouraged and ready to leave the stage when her half-brother took over, and although she agreed to remain as his leading lady for a time, she abandoned her career when she married in 1778. She was a great loss to the company, and was much mourned by her audiences, who had admired her as Minna von Barnhelm, as the Countess Orsina in *Emilia Galotti*, and as the young roguish girl-lovers of French comedy. Her younger sister, (4) CHARLOTTE (1757–74), a frail and beautiful child with a touch of genius, made her first appearance on the stage at the age of 4, as Louison in an adaptation of *Le Malade imaginaire*. She rapidly obtained complete mastery of her art, matured young, and at 14 gave a most moving performance as Emilia Galotti. By the time she was 17 she was one of the greatest and most admired actresses of Germany. But her half-brother drove her too hard, and the strain of new parts and constant appearances took their toll. She died before her eighteenth birthday, and Schröder was much blamed for her death, since there was more than a suspicion that she had committed suicide.

ACOUSTICS, THEATRE. 1. ACOUSTICS AND ORATORY. Early drama was an art not of fireside conversation but of speech projected across a distance. 'Sit in a full theatre,' says Overbury (*Character of an excellent Actor*, 1614), 'and you will think you see so many lines drawn from the circumference of so many ears while the actor is the centre.' And the building has an effect on the voice. It expands some vowels to tones and suppresses others, it can add overtones, it can alter, emphasize, repeat. That is to say it is an instrument; it can be a good or bad instrument; it can be learned and made use of, or ignored. Add also that the larger the building the more marked is the acoustic effect. The response of the voice to the needs of the building has produced oratory, an art in itself, with evocative power. But it is really inseparable from stage playing in theatres of any size because it is necessary to intelligibility. The microphone in the television play, asking for no vocal effort, is tending in the theatre to cause lack of loudness, and therefore lack of intelligibility.

The form of the theatre has developed from a complex of causes in all periods. We may note the dependence of oratory in the Graeco-Roman world on a building without echo or reverberation. In an inflected language, if word-endings are obscured the sense is lost, and the sense is equally lost if the verb at the end of the sentence is obscured. In the classical theatre both loudness and distinctness were necessary and were achieved. But excessive loudness can be a serious fault. It is curious that the evidence from Shakespeare is that he feared too loud a voice—a voice that can 'split the ears of the groundlings'. Also there are the words—'O there be players . . . that have so strutted and bellowed . . .'. The passage in *Hamlet* is doubtless the dramatist's warning against over-emphasis, a plea for the use instead of the abuse of a convention, but it points also to the oratorical facility of Elizabethan drama and to the acoustics of the theatres. The Elizabethan theatre was of a shape and dimension that generally avoided echoes, and being largely unroofed there was no reverberation. Therefore sheer loudness would not have tended to the prolonging of syllables such as can occur in a modern theatre. There is another interesting passage in the *Character of an excellent Actor*: 'He doth not strive to make Nature monstrous; she is often seen in the same scene with him, but neither on stilts nor on crutches, and for his voice it is not lower than the prompter nor louder than the foil and target.' Here is set a common-sense standard of loudness very valuable both for players and for students of acoustics.

Another factor to be noted is the contribution made by verse. This can best be realized by reciting Shakespeare in the open air to a remote listener. The rhythm of the verse clearly contributes to the carrying power. The physical strain of conveying the sense is noticeable, and it is also noticeable that the reciter is relying on one or two vowel sounds in each line to convey the sense. A range-testing experiment of this kind brings home to speaker and listener alike some of the formative factors in the growth of drama. Certainly two great schools of dramatic verse, the Greek and the Elizabethan, developed in an unroofed auditorium and in response to exacting physical requirements.

But when we turn from England to France, and compare the development of French dramatic verse and the alexandrine line to the English, we must be astonished at the difference. By comparison alexandrines are inflexible and impose a much more rigid technique. The endings of the rhymed couplets must be heard, because the rhymed words are often significant for the sense; at the same time they impose a pause at the end of each line, so that lines cannot easily be run on as in Shakespeare. The French language does not carry in the open air; the modified vowels are too delicate, there is no open *i* (English *high*), and the nasal vowels (as *enfin*) seem to need the resonance of an enclosed building. One might note that French drama developed in the halls of palaces and in converted tennis-courts: but add also that Racine was performed at Versailles or St-Cloud out of doors, although it is difficult to believe that the plays were well heard. The clue to the problem is doubtless the fact that alexandrine verse as developed in the sixteenth century was an oratorical instrument so perfectly adapted to the French language and genius that it triumphed over all obstacles and has survived to this day.

2. Greek Theatre Acoustics. When we turn to the origin of the drama we might begin by looking at some of the sacred sites upon which Greek dramatic representations developed. A smooth dancing-floor, the wall of the little temple or shrine, and finally some kind of raised platform in front of it, would then give the essentials of the Greek theatre. And each of these contributes to the acoustics. A man speaking in the open air in front of a wall can be heard further away, and if the floor in front of him is hard, and if he can raise himself a little above it, his voice will be reflected upwards and the reflections will reinforce the direct sound. Also, the higher his speaking position, the greater will be the angle of impact of sound upon his audience. This was known in the classical period: we read in Thucydides that Pericles gave his funeral speech from a high platform made for the occasion 'so that his voice might carry as far as possible over the crowd'. From the interaction of these facts the Hellenistic theatre developed, with its long narrow *logeion* (platform) increasing in height in successive periods. Since the theatre was not an enclosed space, the chances of long-path echoes were small, and reverberation or inter-reflection due to the action of opposite plane surfaces did not exist. There was therefore no loss of distinctness. The value of these simple reflectors close to the source can be tested today in Athens and at Epidaurus.

3. Vitruvius and the Graeco-Roman Theatre. The Greek theatre may be said then to give open-air conditions modified and improved. Such conditions have the advantages we have noted, but they give no response to tones. Response is given in enclosed buildings by reverberation causing a prolonging of vowel sounds. And we find evidence of an attempt on the part of Hellenistic theatre-builders to provide a resonant system in the shape of *echeia* or acoustic vases. The chief evidence for the *echeia* is found in Vitruvius (*c.* 70–15 B.C.), a Roman architect who attempted to sum up the traditions of Hellenistic building. In his Book V, which treats of theatres, he recognizes that sound is propagated in waves, also that obstacles must be avoided, and he connects with this the admirable rule that the ascent of seats must be stepped in a straight incline without noticeable breaks. In the chapter on harmony he distinguishes between reciting in a monotone and reciting with modulations, and although the subject is obscure, it is clear that the *echeia* were intended for the purpose of enhancing vowel tones. The vases are described as being of bronze or earthenware, placed in cavities under the seats of the amphitheatre, and in an inverted position with an air space around them. They were tuned in response to the notes of the tetrachord and were arranged

in a certain sequence in three tiers. Vitruvius's words are: 'By the adoption of this plan the voice which issues from the *scena*, expanding as from a centre, and striking against the cavity of each vase, will sound with increased clearness and harmony from its unison with one or other of them.' They are used, therefore, to introduce into a masonry building some special resonance factor. A recent test on a resonant 'vase' giving a pure tone, placed in an anechoic chamber giving open-air conditions, showed that, when the source was switched off, the vase continued to sound and was heard several feet away. With a fairly large number of *echeia* it is quite possible that they had, in an open-air theatre, some slight but definite effect. In the same chapter Vitruvius states clearly that theatres built of wood do not need *echeia*. In the Roman theatre the orchestra floor was a semicircle (see No. 8) rather than the Greek circle (see No. 1) and was occupied by senators' seats, with a sloping roof, to protect against rain, over the stage. The Roman stage was greater in width, and there is mention in Vitruvius of *periaktoi*, a series of tall prisms set in the wings, triangular in plan, which could rotate about their axes and provide three sets of scenes. Vitruvius also notes the practice of singers to the harp turning towards the *valvas scenae* (some part of the stage scenery) in order to project their voices. If the *periaktoi* were set at an angle of about 45° they would in fact serve to reflect sound outwards to the auditorium.

We have then in the acoustics of the classical theatre some criteria of reinforcement by reflection, of absence of echo and reverberation, and of the function of resonance. These can be applied in reviewing later types.

4. THE ELIZABETHAN PLAYHOUSE. To return to the Elizabethan playhouse, the plan and section of the Fortune Theatre, reconstructed by W. H. Godfrey from the specification, which survives, strongly suggest its origin, namely the platform set up by strolling players in the inn-yard (but see also ENGLISH PLAYHOUSE). Here again is a natural auditorium. A large part of the audience is well above the players, and the floor of stage and paved yard acts as a reflector. Sound is said to rise only because the floor, if it be hard, is the first and nearest reflector, and this explains why hearing in London theatres today is often much better in the gallery than at the rear of the pit. The Elizabethan stage roof, known as the 'shadow' or 'testa', was probably intended to keep off rain and sun. It would have reinforced sound by reflection in the lower part of the house but would have tended to screen it from top side seats. Also it would have reduced the loudness of players as heard from the stage balcony for listeners in the top gallery; that is to say, in these seats Juliet would not be as well heard as Romeo. For the players on the boards the testa would have served to return tone upon the stage, enabling them to hear themselves well, a useful thing for sustained recital. The musicians in the Elizabethan theatre appear to have occupied a position immediately on one side of the stage and at the level of the first tier. Here, and on the left as seen from the house, they are shown in Van Buchell's view of the Swan Theatre (see No. 22) and are labelled 'orchestra'.

The polygonal plan of the Elizabethan Globe and Swan theatres was carried on in a theatre plan attributed to Inigo Jones (1573–1652) in the Worcester College Collection, consisting of an octagon set in a square. But the tradition actually survives today in Wren's Sheldonian Theatre in Oxford. Here we find also the wooden galleries, but combined with the classic rostrum for oratorical exercises, and with a large ceremonial entrance door.

5. THE PALACE HALL AND MASQUE HOUSE. The palace hall and the moot hall were also used for stage plays. They were medieval or Tudor buildings resembling the college halls surviving at Oxford and Cambridge. We know that *Othello* was first performed in the Old Palace Hall at Whitehall in 1604. In the Lansdowne MSS. in the British Museum there survives the plan of this building set for a pastoral. The layout closely resembles that shown in a plan for a Masque House by Inigo Jones (also in the British Museum), and the two give evidence of the general arrangement for Court performances in which movable scenery was beginning to dominate the design. Inigo Jones, Surveyor to the King, was the chief contriver of masques in James I's reign, and the masque relied upon music, upon effects produced by machines, and upon classical scenic architecture in perspective. The general arrangement, as shown in the plan, was dominated by the royal dais with a central floor space in front of it for processions of homage, or for dancing; and having a flight of steps beyond, leading to the world of the stage at a higher level. On either hand were banks of seats, and 'Musicians' are marked in a recessed position on the left of the stage. In the Whitehall plan various pens or 'boxes' are shown railed off for important persons, including 'Mr. Surveyor' (probably Inigo Jones himself). Tennis-courts were also used both in England and France for dramatic performances, their pent-house side galleries at floor level providing some side seats.

It is interesting that this general arrangement of banked seats and pens survived to 1938 in the arrangement for the Westminster play in the School Dormitory building (see WESTMINSTER PLAY). The headmaster's seat, later in a forward position, probably corresponded originally to the royal dais, in the position shown in Inigo Jones's Masque House plan. At the Westminster play the doors on the forestage were part of the Plautine tradition: the scenes were at the crossing of a city street, and the two opposite houses, with their doors, were the dwellings of the characters. This tradition may be the origin of the doors on the forestage (see PROSCENIUM DOORS and Nos. 31, 32, 35) which are a noticeable feature of English Restoration and eighteenth-century playhouses (and of early American theatres built on the English plan—see No. 28), and which survived at Drury Lane until 1822. If this is correct we have here an English tradition lingering on from Roman adaptations of Greek comedy.

In Inigo Jones's design for a Masque House we have an embodiment of the true 'art theatre' at its fullest as a plastic and acoustic instrument. The various factors are: the *scena stabile* which yet admitted of some scenic changes in the background; the stage; the processional steps; and also the floor for ritual or dancing, which was not covered with seats and therefore made a useful sound-reflector as in the Greek theatre. This arrangement was possible because the musicians, though essential to the masque and to the opera, were not as yet interposed in front of the stage (for an early French example, see No. 18).

6. THE RESTORATION PLAYHOUSE. The Restoration playhouse in London witnessed the struggle for position of the musicians, and the first domination of the stage by movable scenery. The original London playhouses were the Duke's Theatre, home of Davenant and the Duke of York's players, and the Theatre Royal or King's Theatre, home of Killigrew and the King's players.

At this formative period there must have been discussions on rival claims to space of actors, musicians, and artists in perspective, and we find that Wren, when he built the new playhouse for Davenant and the Duke's players at Dorset Garden in 1671, made a large box or small gallery, presumably for the musicians, above the proscenium opening (see No. 63). But in this position there must have been little room, though having the theatre ceiling above them they would have been well heard. By 1674 the musicians at Dorset Garden appear to have been moved down to the modern position in front of the stage, where there was room for a much larger orchestra than before, '24 strings with harpsichord and theorbos'. An impression of the interiors of the two rival Restoration playhouses can be had from Pepys. The plans as shown on maps and engravings were long and narrow: there were pit benches, boxes at various prices, and probably a top gallery. The performance was in the afternoon, and the theatre was lighted by side windows and by candles on the stage. Killigrew, telling Pepys (in 1667) about the improvements he had effected at the Theatre Royal, said:

> That the stage is now by his pains a thousand times better and more glorious than ever heretofore. Now wax candles and many of them; then not above 3 lbs. of tallow: now all things civil, no rudeness anywhere; then as in a bear garden: then two or three fiddlers, now nine or ten of the best: then nothing but rushes upon the floor and everything else mean; now all otherwise.

It is worth noting that 'rushes upon the floor', whether in church, hall, or early theatre, acted, like a carpet, as a useful sound absorbent.

7. EIGHTEENTH-CENTURY THEATRES. Meanwhile in Italy the theatre had developed from the classical reconstructions of Palladio and Scamozzi, at Vicenza (see No. 20) and Sabbionetta (see No. 21) into the large ramped spectacle-house such as Aleotti's theatre at Parma, and later into the fully developed Italian theatre with its horseshoe plan, having boxes or *loges* in tiers one above another. To this day, it might be remarked, the Italian opera-house retains something of the spectacle-house—the spectacle being the crowd, anxious to see itself, as well as to see and hear what goes on on the stage. It is likely that the floor was preserved for some time for ballet and processions. In a seventeenth-century engraving (in the Theatre Museum in Munich) a large Masque House in Florence is represented with the floor occupied by the ballet and connected with the stage by a flight of steps. Also, as late as 1745 at Versailles a temporary *Salle de Spectacles* was erected for a fête performance of Voltaire's *Princesse de Navarre*, and an engraving shows a cleared floor space in front of the royal personages. But this floor space is now, in the French example, cut off from the stage by a large orchestral enclosure (see also No. 24). The Royal Opera House at Bayreuth, built by the Bibienas in 1748, had a flat floor kept clear for ballet, and ballet doors placed to left and right in the proscenium. Above these doors were boxes resembling stage boxes, known as *trompetenlogen.* When the royal personage entered, three trumpeters appeared in each box and blew a blast. For the ballet the doors below were opened and the dancers defiled upon the floor. This theatre is a beautiful example of the art of the Bibiena family. (In a later historical period Wagner and his family would sometimes occupy the great centrally-placed royal box.) On the Continent the development of the orchestra pit tended to cut back the forestage. But in England this was not the case, and Handel made use of the forestage at Covent Garden for his choir in performances of oratorio. In England also we find the sloping auditorium ceiling, as in the surviving Theatre Royal at Bristol, built in 1766 (see No. 27).

A theatre designed by Vanbrugh in the Haymarket (see QUEEN'S THEATRE) with a high vault, concave in shape, opened in 1705, has left a record of bad acoustics. 'On the opening of this grand and superb building it was immediately discovered that almost every quality and convenience had been sacrificed to show the spectator a vast triumphal piece of architecture . . . scarce one word in ten could be distinctly heard . . . the articulated sounds of a speaking voice were drowned by the hollow reverberation of one word upon another' (*Theatrum Illustratum*, quoting Colley Cibber). Note the early use of the term 'reverberation'.

Nevertheless fortuitous circumstances produced in the eighteenth-century theatre all over Europe a good acoustical instrument and a home for the development of an art. The reverberation was short owing to the tiers of *loges* with their drapery; echoes were avoided owing to the diffusing of sound by baroque and Louis Quinze ornament and owing to the flat ceilings and absence of domes; but orchestral tone was good owing to the large amount of wood construction. In these theatres Garrick performed Shakespeare to large audiences, in them the astonishing art of *bel canto* was developed in opera, and the Italian *aria*, with its 'introduction' and accompaniment on strings, carried music forward from the church cantata to the operas of Mozart. This was made possible by the short reverberation and bright tone of the Italian theatre form. Modern acoustic studies have also shown the useful effect of the mixture of resonant, reflecting, and absorbing materials in a hall and of their equal distribution all over the interior surface, all of which are characteristic of this type of theatre. The theatres were often very large. La Scala at Milan had six tiers above floor-level, Covent Garden in 1808 seated 2,800 persons (see No. 32). For instrumental music the theatre form was generally satisfactory, and evidence of this is shown in the influence exerted by it on the form of early concert rooms. Leopold Mozart, writing from Milan in 1770, says of the Mantua concert hall:

> I wish you could see the hall where the concert took place, the so-called *Teatrino della Accademia Filarmonica*. In all my life I have never seen anything more beautiful of its kind. It is not a theatre but a hall built with boxes like an opera house. Where the stage ought to be there is a raised platform for the orchestra and behind the orchestra another gallery built with boxes for the audience.

(Anderson: *Letters of Mozart and his Family*, 2nd ed., vol. i, p. 108.) The old Gewandhaus at Leipzig (1780) was also of this shape.

But for the purpose of developing the full tone of the chorus the Italian opera-house was not good, owing to the considerable sound-absorption and consequent short reverberation. Covent Garden, under John Rich's management, was used for pantomimes, plays, operas, and oratorios. Handel opened at Covent Garden in 1734 and in his first season gave fourteen performances of oratorio. The Pugin and Rowlandson view of Covent Garden about 1808, on the occasion of an oratorio, shows Handel's organ on the stage with the orchestra surrounding it and the choir in front on the forestage. There is evidence that Handel was sensitive to acoustic effects. On one occasion, behind the scenes at Covent Garden, he was told the audience was small and replied, 'My music will sound the better.' The significance of this is that the audience is generally the chief sound-absorbing factor in a hall and therefore the smaller the audience the longer the reverberation. Handel implied that he preferred conditions which gave a fuller tone. It is probable that the characteristic theatre acoustics of Covent Garden, with its considerable sound-absorption, contributed to the broad, loud, choral tone called Handelian.

For opera, however, the short reverberation permitted the great rapidity and animation of Mozart's and Rossini's vocal music. A Mozart opera is at its best with a weight of orchestra of about 30 players, and before 1939 it could be heard performed thus at the Residenz Theater in Munich. The conductor sat at the piano and played the recitatives. The Residenz Theater was the first theatre in Europe to increase its lighting by putting little mirrors behind the candles. The acoustics remained practically as when it was built in 1751 and from the *loges* the true effect could be studied. The extreme rapidity of the vocal ensembles of 'Don Giovanni' and 'Figaro' assumes both the tripping Italian tongue and the extremely short theatre reverberation.

8. THE WAGNER THEATRE. When the orchestra in an Italian theatre increased in size, as occurred during the nineteenth century, the unresolved problem of the orchestra position became acute in opera. The weight of instrumental tone then began to screen the singers on the stage and especially so for listeners in stall seats. At La Scala in Milan in recent times during a Verdi opera the huge orchestra was found seated far out on the floor; and consequently hearing was far better in the upper galleries than in expensive stall seats. In Wagner the loudness of the brass under these conditions is often deafening. One result of this is that Wagner singers are forced to develop the reed tones of their voices and sing sharp in order to make themselves heard, and consequently accuracy of pitch is often sacrificed. Wagner recognized the failure of the Italian theatre as an instrument for his own music-dramas, and so evolved the Wagner theatre at Bayreuth. In it the ramped floor seats beginning at stage level, the double proscenium arch, the baffled side-walls, and especially the placing of an orchestra of 110 instruments in a pit extending under the stage instead of into the stalls, combine to give a characteristic interior. The boxes are situated only on the rear wall. The roof is flat, and the building is constructed largely of wood. But what gives it acoustic character is the longer reverberation, much more that of a German concert hall, namely 2·2 seconds approximately (by the Sabine formula) as compared to the 1·2 seconds of a typical Italian theatre like Covent Garden. This longer reverberation is the result of the absence of side galleries, which gives a larger cubic air-space per seat and therefore a greater volume relative to audience-absorption. This gives a 'fullness' of tone, as distinguished from 'brightness', but requires a slower tempo. Also, the mixing and subduing of instrumental tone in the concealed orchestra pit gives a balance and unity of artistic effect, impossible for Wagner opera in an Italian theatre. It is not too much to say that it is impossible to realize the dramatic and musical quality of a Wagner opera unless the enormous tone energy produced is properly controlled, as at Bayreuth. Why then, it may be asked, is the Wagner theatre at Munich (the Prinz Regent) so much criticized? The reason is clear. The reverberation is far too long to

permit the rapid tempo of Mozart or Rossini or Donizetti. It is also quite unsuited to stage plays. That is to say, it is unsuited to repertory purposes unless precautions are taken to compensate for the lack of galleries by adding special sound-absorbents and reducing the reverberation by special means.

9. Nineteenth-century Theatres. In the nineteenth-century commercial theatre the horseshoe plan was preserved (see No. 33). The plan-form suggested the domed ceiling, and there was probably a movement after the introduction of gas-lighting for better ventilation. But domes led to some notable echoes focussed from a particular stage position, such as that of the old Alhambra in Leicester Square. The 'Irving Safety Theatre' designed as an ideal auditorium for Sir Henry Irving, but not built, had a large dome which would certainly have caused trouble. Even when echoes were not noticeable, curved ceilings gave an unequal distribution of reflected sound, so that some seats were noticeably better than others, and the myth of the 'blind spot' became fashionable. But the baroque tradition of heavy theatre ornament, of stage boxes and plenty of drapery, continued, and this tended to keep reverberation short. At the same time the smaller 'comedy' theatres came to be built, in which a sentimental society could more intimately enjoy domestic rather than heroic emotions. Thus, while the larger theatres preserved an oratorical tradition in Shakespeare, in old-fashioned melodrama, and in the pantomime, there developed a greater tendency towards naturalism in gesture and voice and with it a demand for the acoustics of the fireside. Clearly domestic comedy demanded a smaller theatre than Drury Lane or Covent Garden, in which nuances of tone and of facial expression could hardly be detected in rear seats, and the standard of loudness, without an oratorical technique, tended to decline. Thus, when a drawing-room comedy by Henry Arthur Jones went on tour from the Criterion and was performed in a large old-fashioned provincial theatre, it was not well heard in the recesses of pit and gallery, but on the whole stalls and dress circle could hear well enough.

10. Acoustics and the Modern Theatre. In the twentieth century, between 1919 and 1939, a remarkable change occurred in the design of theatres. This was due to two things: (i) a style change, and (ii) the application of building acoustics to theatre design. The modern style swept away baroque ornament. Large continuous surfaces in hard plaster, ingeniously lit, took their place. At the same time the stage boxes were removed, likewise a large area of proscenium pelmets, curtains, and velvet tympana. Then the fan-shaped plan was found to seat more persons at a medium distance from the stage, and to give better sight lines both for legitimate theatre and cinema. The smooth tunnel interior with splayed walls and ceiling thus superseded the Victorian baroque building with its broken-up surfaces interspersed with curtains. At first the new acoustic studies approved the fan-shaped plan and splayed proscenium on account of the useful reflecting surfaces provided. Loudness was considerably increased by that means in rear seats. But it was also discovered that any return of sound from surfaces at the rear, including balcony fronts, ceiling coves, balustrades, &c., found its way to front seats, and the complaints registered were no longer from cheap rear seats but from expensive seats in the stalls, especially from front side seats. Now acoustic theory assumed powerful sound-absorbing material on the rear wall behind the audience to prevent any return of sound; but in practice it was found that commercial sound-absorbents, often covered with paint, were not nearly as efficient as the modern hard plasters on the reflecting walls and ceiling. Another factor is that the fan-shaped plan gives a relatively large area to the rear wall, and that this wall was often given the most dangerous curve possible, namely a curve struck from a centre near the stage front. Thus, whatever remainder of sound was returned as not absorbed, was focussed towards the front of the house, or, if touching the side walls on its return course, was not diffused by ornament, or absorbed by side galleries, boxes, and curtains. The result was not necessarily a complete echo (that is to say, a distinct repetition) but a prolonging of word-endings liable to obscure rapid speech. A parallel symptom was that coughs and noises in galleries tended to concentrate also on stall seats. The result was to show the value of the breaking-up of sound by heavy ornament, that is to say, the value of the principle of diffusion, and to impress again on modern designers the paramount importance of absorption in the theatre auditorium, where speech is often very rapid and where the syllable intervals (about one-twentieth of a second in duration) must not be obscured by any prolonging of tone.

It was clear that the fan shape needed modification. The rear wall now must not be curved on plan, but straight or polygonal; and in large theatres it is a safeguard to avoid curved parapets, curved seat risers, and gallery fronts. The early fan theatre, shorn of boxes and side galleries, gave a much larger cube per seat in the stalls than in the region of the galleries and hence caused reverberation in the stalls. This is now countered by the restored boxes, by front-side absorbents, or by well-draped proscenium areas. But a large bare forestage can increase reverberation risk in the front of the house. The value of the *convex* curve, instead of the concave, is now recognized in the profiles of reflecting canopies, and in corrugated ceilings. If the ceiling should be stepped instead of splayed it remains a useful reflector to rear galleries and also reduces risk of the return of sound to stalls. This is important in view of the rapid speed of modern speech. Any total ceiling area approaching the parabolic greatly increases the risk of short echo back to stalls, and the focussing back of coughs and audience noise. The calculated reverberation figure should be less than 1¼ sec. at middle pitch.

The modern demand for open stage, arena stage, and theatre-in-the-round marks a revolt, not by audience and actors, but by producers, against the imaginative limitations of the picture-frame stage. But theatre-in-the-round (see No. 41) has always had a serious acoustic defect. The human voice has a direction and is not equally well heard behind and at the side. Also conversational speech is not projected speech; 'natural' conversation requires the acoustics of the fireside and very limited seating. Hence the complaints made by members of the audience of either inaudibility or shouting, and by players of speaking in the void and having no target. On the other hand the adaptable theatre giving (with safeguards as to fire risk) a good forestage projection and some convertibility as to seating is a real economic demand (see No. 43). Today theatres are very frequently used for platform concerts, and serious complaints occur unless soloists and strings can come well out in front of a curtain line. Hence the value of the modern lift units to give either a forestage at high level, or an orchestra pit at low level, or stepped units at different levels. In other words a modern theatre should be a general-purpose hall like the old masque house. But an open-stage technique will alter normal theatre acoustics. If drapes and carpets and well-upholstered seats are discarded for the sake of easy convertibility then there will be all the more need for good distributed sound absorbents (of a fire-proof kind) on walls and ceilings, in order to reduce reverberation (see ARCHITECTURE). HOPE BAGENAL

ACT. The divisions of a play are known as Acts, each of which may contain one or more scenes. Greek plays were continuous, the only pauses being marked by the chorus. Horace was the first to insist on the importance of five acts, probably from experience. With the Renaissance, the division into five acts became classic, and was adopted by the great French dramatists, whence it passed into England via Ben Jonson. It should be noted that there is no proof that Shakespeare divided his plays thus. The divisions in the printed copies were probably introduced by the editors in imitation of Jonson. In comedy more licence was allowed to the individual, two or three acts being quite usual, even in Molière. Modern drama usually keeps to three acts, as being convenient for actors and audience alike, but two acts are sometimes found, and many Shakespeare revivals have had only one interval in each play. A division into four acts, once usual, is now seldom found.

ACT-DROP, the name given in the late eighteenth century to the painted cloth which closed the proscenium opening between the acts of a play (see CURTAIN).

ACT-TUNE. In the Elizabethan theatre musical interludes between the acts of plays (particularly in the private theatres) were evidently customary, as is shown by their mention in a number of stage-directions. They may have been played by pipes and tabors, or, as in Marston's *Sophonisba*, by cornets and organs, or organs mixed with recorders. In the Restoration theatre the act-tunes became very important, and composers were commissioned to write sets of such tunes, which sometimes took on an independent existence, as with Purcell's *Ayres for the Theatre*. The introductory music was sometimes known as the Curtain Tune or Curtain Music.

ACTOR, ACTRESS, ACTING. The art of acting, and the profession of actor, is as old as man, showing itself first in ritual dance and song and somewhat later in dialogue. Of the very early actors nothing is known, but in Greece, where they took part in a religious ceremony, they were evidently men of some repute (see GREECE, 4). In Rome their status was low, and they were often recruited from the ranks of slaves, a circumstance which may be linked with the decadence of the theatre there and the decline from classical tragedy and comedy to pantomime (see ROME, *passim*). With the coming of Christianity they were finally proscribed and sank into obscurity, handing on some mutilated traditions through the little bands of itinerant acrobats and jugglers who catered for the crowds at fairs and in the larger cities. The medieval minstrels, however, occupied a special place in the social scale, and were welcome at Court and in noble houses, forming themselves into Guilds for mutual help and protection and being assured of at least a decent livelihood (see MINSTREL). They were not actors, but when the revival of the theatre came in Europe, first in the church and later in the market-place (see LITURGICAL DRAMA), they may have given advice and practical help to the big amateur groups that performed the Mystery cycles.

With the emergence of a vernacular drama in each country, as distinct from the universal Latin drama, the time was ripe for the rise of the professional actor. He came slowly, and it is almost impossible to fix a date for his arrival in any particular country. In general one might safely say that he established himself in most countries during the sixteenth century, which saw the formation of the *commedia dell'arte* troupes in Italy (see ITALY, 2), the work of the first professional actor-manager in Spain, Lope de Rueda (1510–60), the building of the first permanent playhouse in London, Burbage's Theatre (1576), and, at the end of the century, the establishment of the first professional troupe at the Hôtel de Bourgogne in Paris (see FRANCE, 3). Germany, owing to internal dissension and division, had to wait longer for a settled theatre, and not until the eighteenth century were any of her actors famous enough to be known by name. Russia, whose early theatrical history is as yet imperfectly known, can hardly be said to have had a national and professional theatre much before the middle of the nineteenth century.

Women did not act in Greece at all, and in Rome only if very depraved. The medieval stage may have employed a few women, but they were still amateurs. The professional actress emerges first in Italy, the best-known being Isabella Andreini (1562–1604), and in France appears at the same time as the professional actor, Marie Vernier or Venier being a member of the company at the Hôtel de Bourgogne from the start. Elizabethan drama made no use of women at all, and all the heroines of Shakespeare and other playwrights were played by boys and young men. It was not until the Restoration in 1660 that women were first seen on the London stage. The name of the first English actress is not known; there are several claimants, but whoever she was, she played Desdemona on 8 Dec. 1660, and paved the way for the actresses of the Patent theatres. It is interesting to note, in passing, that the first great name in the annals of the German theatre is that of a woman, Caroline Neuber (1697–1760), who tried to put into effect the reforms of Gottsched. But she was probably not the first German actress, since Jolly had one in his company of English Comedians in Germany in 1654.

The position of the actor was for a long time precarious. In Catholic countries he was refused the sacraments, and an anomalous situation arose by which a man like Molière could be wealthy, respected, received by the king and patronized by the nobility, and yet be buried in unconsecrated ground. Legally even Shakespeare and his great contemporaries were still liable to be classed as rogues and vagabonds, and it was not until the nineteenth century that the actor achieved a definite place in society, which culminated in the knighthood bestowed on Henry Irving in 1895. In becoming respectable the actor no doubt lost something of his mystery and picturesqueness, qualities which may have appealed more to the non-theatrical mind than to the harassed professional, who was for many centuries at the mercy of any jack-in-office who chose to interpret the strict letter of the law, and might find his means of livelihood taken from him overnight.

Fashions in acting change as in everything else, and the whole history of the theatre shows one method giving way to another, one convention succeeding another. Only in the Far East, which lies outside the range of this article (see CHINA and JAPAN), have traditions in acting remained unbroken down the centuries, and now even they are in a state of flux. In Greece, the tragic actor was static—a voice and a presence; in Rome he was lively, and, in the last resort, an acrobat. The *commedia dell'arte* demanded above all a quick wit and a nimble body; French tragedy once again asked for a fine presence and a sonorous voice; Restoration comedy must have called for a polished brilliance and a gentlemanly insolence. The melodrama of the nineteenth century could only make its full effect when its actors 'tore a passion to tatters', and the modern comedy which replaced it gives little scope for gesture or raised voices. Yet the true actor still needs to be a little of everything—singer, dancer, mimic, acrobat, tragedian, comedian—and to have at his command a good physique, a retentive memory, an alert brain, a clear, resonant voice with good articulation and controlled breathing (see SPEECH). Some actors have achieved fame lacking one or more of these essentials, but only at the cost of much hard work, and by the impress of their personality, amounting, as in the case of Garrick and Kean, to genius. Often the price of their victory has been an early collapse. Much of an actor's art must be born in him; something may be taught. The ideal is a good balance of intuition and hard work, tempered by all-round experience.

ACTORS' THEATRE. 1. A membership group which developed from the first Equity Players' Group of New York, formed in 1922 for actor-controlled presentation of good classic and new plays. Dudley Digges was one of the first directors, and among the plays of the first seasons were *Candida* and *The Wild Duck*. In 1927 the group fused with that of Greenwich Village under Kenneth Macgowan.

2. Another group under the same name was formed in 1939, and gave plays at the Provincetown Playhouse. It was intended as a Little Theatre organization for the tryout of new plays and young actors. Most of its activities were suspended on the outbreak of war in 1941, but it continued to function intermittently until 1947.

ADAM DE LA HALLE (*c.* 1240–*c.* 1286), also known as Le Bossu d'Arras, one of the few medieval minstrels known to us by name. He was intended for the Church, but a rash marriage prevented him from taking orders, and he turned to literature. Among his works is *Le Jeu de la feuillée*, given at Puy in 1262–3, held by competent critics to mark the beginning of lay, as distinct from ecclesiastical, drama in France. A reference in it to Hellequin, king of the underworld, has also been cited as one of the sources of the later Harlequin. It was for the Court of Robert II, Count of Artois, that Adam de la Halle wrote the charming *Jeu de Robin et de Marion*, a picture of thirteenth-century rustic happiness which by virtue of its music—for Adam was as good a musician as he was a poet—may be considered the first French light opera, as it certainly was the first French pastoral. Through the medium of wandering minstrels it may have given to England some details of the Robin Hood story.

ADAMOV, ARTHUR (1908–), French dramatist, born in the Caucasus, who in 1912 left Russia and at the age of 16 became a member of the Surrealist group in Paris. His first play, *La Parodie*, written in 1947, was produced in 1952. Two later plays, *La Grande et la Petite Manœuvre* and *L'Invasion*, had been performed in 1950. His early work, including *Le Professeur Taranne* and *Tous contre Tous* (both 1953), has much in common with the 'anti-theatre' of Ionesco, though it does not make use of the puns and dislocations of language by which Ionesco expresses his view of the absurdity of life; instead, a fantastic dream world is depicted, where the nonsense element arouses terror at the cruel helplessness and isolation of man. With *Le Ping-Pong* (1955) (which in 1959 was given an amateur production in London), a satire on the world of commerce and politics, Adamov abandoned abstract fantasy in favour of social facts, turning his back on what he called drama based on 'la fausse réalité'; that is, plays in which remediable social evils are presented as the result of an immutable destiny. *Paolo Paoli*, his most important play to date, produced by Roger Planchon at Lyon in 1957, is an examination and exposure of the corruptions of the French social scene. A similar purpose informs his later work, *Les Petits bourgeois* (adapted from Gorki, 1959) and *Les Âmes mortes* (adapted from Gogol, 1960).

T. C. C. MILNE

ADAMS, Edwin (1834–77), American actor, who made his first appearance at Boston in 1853 in *The Hunchback*. He was later seen in Philadelphia and Baltimore, and toured extensively, being well received as an excellent light comedian. At the opening performance of Booth's Theatre, New York, he played Mercutio to Booth's Romeo, and remained there for some time, playing also Iago, and appearing in modern plays. His most successful part was Enoch Arden in a dramatization of Tennyson's poem, which, said Jefferson, 'so far as the character is related to the stage, was a creation entirely his own, and one too that touched the sympathy of his audience'. He toured in the part all over the United States, but made his last appearance in San Francisco, shortly before his early death, as Iago to the Othello of John McCullough. His loss was deplored by actors and audience alike. 'Everybody loved him,' said William Winter. 'He was one of the blithest spirits of the stage.'

ADAMS, Maude (1872–1953), an American actress, daughter of the leading lady of the Salt Lake City stock company. She was on the stage as a child, and at the age of 5 scored a signal triumph as Little Schneider in *Fritz* at the San Francisco Theatre. Young David Belasco was also a member of the cast. She played all the usual child-roles, including Eva in *Uncle Tom's Cabin*, and then left the stage to continue her education. In 1892 she returned to the theatre, being engaged by the Frohmans to appear opposite John Drew in *The Lost Paradise* at Palmer's Theatre, New York. She scored a great success, and remained with this management for many years. In 1899 she gave a fine performance as Juliet, but her most famous part was probably Lady Babbie in *The Little Minister*, which Barrie rewrote and enlarged specially for her. He was fortunate in his interpreter, for her quaint, elfin personality suited his work to perfection, as was later seen in *Peter Pan*, *What Every Woman Knows*, *Quality Street*, and *A Kiss for Cinderella*. She was also much admired as Viola, Rosalind, Joan of Arc, and L'Aiglon. One of the most popular actresses of her day, she was modest and retiring, and much averse to publicity, and in 1918 retired from the theatre, not returning until 1931, when she appeared on tour as Portia to Otis Skinner's Shylock. She also toured in 1934 as Maria in *Twelfth Night*. As a young girl she was not, strictly speaking, beautiful, but had a frail and wistful appearance which later matured into true loveliness, the outward sign of her gracious and endearing personality.

A.D.C., see CAMBRIDGE.

ADDISON, Joseph (1672–1719), English politician and man of letters, friend and collaborator of Richard Steele in the *Spectator* and the *Tatler*. He was also the author of two plays, *Cato* (1713), a tragedy on the French classical model, and *The Drummer* (1715), a moral comedy which obtained little success. *Cato*, on the other hand, which was well supported by the Whigs for political reasons, and the Tories for effect, was extremely successful, and exerted a powerful restraint on the natural exuberance of English drama, so powerful, says one critic, 'that it emasculated the art of play-writing and well-nigh bereft the stage of originality of thought or freedom of expression'. Written in unrhymed heroic couplets, it contains some fine polished poetry, but cannot be esteemed good theatre. The part of Cato was originally offered to Colley Cibber, who declined it, and it was finally played by Barton Booth, with Anne Oldfield as Lucia. It ran for thirty-five nights, and was then given at Oxford, Addison's university, with equal success, the actors donating £50 out of the profits towards the repair of St. Mary's Church. Addison's dramatic theories and criticisms are found in several papers of the *Spectator*, while the *Tatler*, No. 42 (1709), contains an amusing mock inventory of the properties and furnishings of Drury Lane.

ADE, George (1866–1944), an American journalist, humorist and playwright, famous for his wisecracks, whose 'fables in slang' brought a new and refreshing idiom to American literature. His plays of contemporary life were full of the homely humour and wit that had already become associated with him. Among them were *College Widow*, which added a new phrase to contemporary language, *Father and the Boys*, *Just Out of College*, and *Speaking to Father*. He was also responsible for the books of several musical comedies, among them *The Fair Co-Ed*, which made Elsie Janis a star.

ADELPHI THEATRE. 1. London. This theatre in the Strand, London, was originally the Sans Pareil, which was built and opened on 27 Nov. 1806 by John Scott (a colour-maker who had made a fortune out of his invention of a new washing-blue) for his stage-struck daughter, who gave entertainments written by herself, ending with a display of fireworks. The theatre prospered, and in 1819 Scott sold it at a handsome profit to Jones and Rodwell. They renamed it the Adelphi, opening on 18 Oct. with seasons of melodrama and burletta. They later staged successful adaptations of Scott's novels, and in 1821 the first stage version of Pierce Egan's *Tom and Jerry; or, Life in London*, by W. J. Moncrieff, had a run of a hundred performances. A sequel, *Green in France; or, Tom and Jerry's Tour*, produced at great expense, shared the fate of most sequels, though a third play, based by R. B. Peake on Egan's *Life of an Actor*, was more successful.

Rodwell died in 1825, Jones retired, and the theatre was taken over by Daniel Terry and Frederick Yates. One of their first productions was *The Pilot*, adapted by Fitzball from Fenimore Cooper's novel, in which T. P. Cooke made a hit. In 1827 the theatre was enlarged, and a year later Terry retired, being replaced by Charles Mathews. Though good plays and companies were presented, both managers were poor business men and got into difficulties. Mathews, who died in 1835, was replaced for a season by his son, who gave way to Gladstone. From 1837 to 1845 dramatizations of novels by Dickens were very successful, and in 1833 Madame Céleste made her first appearance in a speaking part. In 1842 a dramatized version of Ainsworth's *Jack Sheppard*, with Mrs. Keeley as Jack, was a great success.

In 1844 Madame Céleste and Ben Webster took over the theatre and staged a series of 'Adelphi dramas'. These were mostly written by Buckstone, the best-known being *The Green Bushes* (1845), and *The Flowers of the Forest* (1847). In 1853 Webster, who had been running the Haymarket as well as the Adelphi, decided to devote all his time to the latter theatre, with such success that in 1858 he was able to demolish the old building, and rebuild. The new theatre opened as the Royal Adelphi on 27 Dec., and had its first outstanding success with Boucicault's *The Colleen Bawn* a year later, followed by *The Octoroon*. Other successes were *Leah* (1863) with Kate Bateman, and *Rip Van Winkle* (1865) with Joseph Jefferson. Kate Terry took her farewell of the stage in Aug. 1867, on the occasion of her marriage to Arthur Lewis, and Fechter made a successful appearance in a series of romantic melodramas.

In 1879 the theatre was taken over by the Gattis who, with William Terriss as their leading man, presented a further series of successful 'Adelphi melodramas', among them *Harbour Lights* (1885) and *The Union Jack* (1888). In 1897 Terriss, on his way to appear in Gillette's *Secret Service*, was assassinated at the stage door by a madman. In 1901 the theatre was extensively altered, and renamed the Century, but popular demand caused the old name to be restored a year later. Sarah Bernhardt appeared there on two occasions, also Wilson Barrett in *The Christian King* (1902). Under the management of Otho Stuart the theatre became the home of Shakespeare and modern poetic dramas, among them *The Prayer of the Sword*, by J. B. Fagan, and *Tristan and Iseult*, by Comyns Carr. From 1908 George Edwardes made it a home of musical comedy, beginning with *The Quaker Girl*, a policy which was continued by Alfred Butt during the First World War. In 1930, after a long run of successes which included *Mr. Cinders* (1929), the theatre was gutted, only the outer walls remaining, and it reopened on 3 Dec. with *Evergreen*, the first of a number of successful productions by Cochran. Later successes have included *Bless the Bride* (1947) and *Auntie Mame* (1959). Plans are on foot to build an office block on the site, incorporating a small theatre, when the present lease runs out. W. MACQUEEN-POPE†, *rev.*

2. NEW YORK, on 54th Street between 6th and 7th Avenues. This was originally named the Craig Theatre, and opened on 24 Dec. 1928 with *Potiphar's Wife*, in which Frances Carson and Barry O'Neill played the leading parts. The play was unsuccessful, as were several that followed, and after standing empty for some time the theatre re-opened as the Adelphi on 27 Nov. 1934 with *The Lord Blesses the Bishop*, which had only seven performances. After a short session of American ballet, the theatre was taken over by the Federal Theatre Project, which on 19 May 1936 produced there *The Dance of Death*, followed by several performances of the Negro *Macbeth*, originally produced by Orson Welles at the Lafayette Theatre in Harlem, and by the anti-Fascist play, *It Can't Happen Here*. A children's play, *The Revolt of the Beavers*, condemned as Communist propaganda by those who opposed the Federal Theatre Project, was also seen in the summer of 1936, and in the early days of the following year came the overwhelming success of Arthur Arent's Living Newspaper on housing, *One-Third of a Nation*. Produced by Philip Barber, this ran for 237 performances. The last play staged at the Adelphi by the Federal Theatre Project was the ill-fated *Sing for Your Supper* (1939), whose sixty performances, only achieved after arduous and acrimonious rehearsals, were brought to an end by the dissolution of the sponsoring body. In 1947 the Adelphi came back into the news with the production of the Theatre Guild's musical version of *Street Scene*. After a few years as a radio and television studio it became a theatre again as the Fifty-fourth Street Theatre. Among productions since the re-opening have been Camus's *Caligula* (1960) and Richard Rodgers's *No Strings* (1964).

GEORGE FREEDLEY†

ADMIRAL'S MEN, the theatrical company that shared the honours of the Elizabethan stage with the Chamberlain's Men, with whom

Shakespeare was associated. Their star actor, rival of Richard Burbage, was Edward Alleyn, who probably joined them in 1587, in which case he would have been the original Tamburlaine. Lord Howard, their patron, had had a company of players in 1576–9, known as Lord Howard's Men. He became Admiral in 1585, and at Christmas in the same year the 'Admiral's players' made their first appearance at Court. In November 1587 they were concerned in a sad accident, when a bullet fired in the course of a play killed a child and a pregnant woman and severely injured a man in the audience. They are not heard of again for a year or so, but in 1590–1 they were housed in James Burbage's Theatre with Strange's Men. Richard Burbage may have appeared in small parts in some of their plays, but it is not certain. After a quarrel with James Burbage over finance, the two companies moved to the Rose, under Henslowe, whose stepdaughter married Alleyn. When the Chamberlain's Men were formed in 1594 some of the Admiral's Men joined them, while the rest formed themselves into an independent company under Alleyn, with Henslowe as their landlord and 'banker'. The fact that Henslowe kept a combined diary and account book enables us to follow the fortunes of the Admiral's Men very closely from 1594 to 1604. They were apparently very successful, and had a large repertory of new and old plays, most of which, except for Marlowe's, have been lost or forgotten. The company also performed some of Chapman's early works and plays by Dekker and Chettle. They were badly handicapped by the retirement in 1597 of Alleyn, whose roles were shared among two lesser men, neither of whom came up to his excellence. However, he returned three years later, apparently at the express wish of Queen Elizabeth, who commanded him to play at Court, and the company took a fresh lease of life, moving into Henslowe's new playhouse, the Fortune. Here they continued after the death of Elizabeth, when they were renamed Prince Henry's Men, and again lost Alleyn, this time for good, though from his retirement in Dulwich he continued to advise and assist the company. In 1612 their young patron died, and was replaced by the Elector Palatine, the company now being known as the Palsgrave's Men. In 1621 the Fortune was burnt down, and all the wardrobe and playbooks were lost, a calamity indeed. It nearly broke them, but with Alleyn's help they struggled along and a new Fortune was opened in 1623 with practically the same company as before. New plays were bought, one by Dekker, several by Rowley, and four by an actor in the company, Gunnell; but none of them proved successful, and after two difficult years the combination of plague and the death of James I proved too much. The company disbanded, after a long and honourable career, and its remnants were probably absorbed into other existing organizations.

ADOLPH, JOHANN BAPTIST (1657–1708), see AUSTRIA.

ADVERTISEMENT CURTAIN, an outer curtain or act-drop used mostly in the English provincial and smaller London theatres. It was covered with advertisements of local shops and manufacturers, whose payments helped the theatre's budget.

AE [GEORGE WILLIAM RUSSELL] (1867–1935), Irish poet, an important figure in the Irish literary revival. He was connected with the early years of the modern Irish theatre through his one play, *Deirdre*, which was first performed in a two-act version, with AE himself in the cast, at a friend's house in Dublin at Christmas in 1901. The full version was given by the Fays' National Dramatic Society in St. Teresa's Hall on 2 Apr. 1902. It was probably AE who brought Yeats and the Fays together, and so laid the foundations of the future famous Abbey Theatre.

AESCHYLUS (525–456 B.C.), Greek dramatist, son of Euphorion, was born of noble parents in Eleusis, near Athens, and died at Gela in Sicily. He fought against the Persians in the battle of Marathon; possibly at Salamis and Plataea too. Like Pindar and other poets of his time, he visited the Court of Hiero, Tyrant of Syracuse; he composed a (lost) tragedy in honour of his founding of the new city of Etna. There seems to be no reason for believing ancient statements that Aeschylus withdrew from Athens for political reasons, or that he was killed by an eagle's dropping a tortoise upon his bald head. His epitaph at Gela is recorded; it is said to have been composed by Aeschylus himself. It may be translated: 'Here, in the fertile soil of Gela, lies Aeschylus, son of Euphorion. Of his notable courage the field of Marathon could speak, and the long-haired Mede; for he knows it well.' He was commemorated as a citizen, not as a poet.

Aeschylus is said to have written 90 plays, and he gained 13 victories. The titles of 79 plays are known: only seven are extant—the *Suppliants* (*c.* 490 B.C.), the *Persians* (472), the *Seven against Thebes* (469), the *Prometheus Bound* (? *c.* 460), and the trilogy known as the *Oresteia* (the *Agamemnon*, the *Choephori* (Libation-bearers), and the *Eumenides*) (458). About a quarter of these 90 plays must have been satyr-plays, in which riotous form of drama Aeschylus was an acknowledged master. Nothing of these survives except a few fragments.

Aeschylus may reasonably be regarded as the real founder of European drama, and no one but Shakespeare can seriously be considered his equal as a dramatic poet. At the time of Aeschylus's birth the tragic festival in Athens was only 10 years old. A play was represented by a chorus of singers and dancers, and one actor only (who of course might 'double'); except that the leader of the chorus, speaking strictly in the name of the chorus, might engage in dialogue with the actor proper. Drama therefore must have been predominantly lyrical; development of plot and of character could have been only slight. Aeschylus, by introducing a second actor, made (gradually) the histrionic part as important as the lyric, and (as it has been said) turned oratorio into drama. The transition can be seen in the early plays: in the *Suppliants* the chorus is the chief actor; the *Persians* still opens with the entrance-song of the chorus, the actors still first address themselves to the chorus and not to the other actor, and it is still through the chorus that the play gets its formal unity; the *Seven against Thebes* opens with a speech from an actor, not with a choral ode, and the play is clearly dominated by the chief actor. In his later plays Aeschylus used (though in a highly individual way) Sophocles' invention of the third actor. Even so, the proportion of lyrics to the whole play remained large; in the *Agamemnon* they form as much as one-half of the play.

Aeschylus also reduced the size of the chorus from fifty. His third innovation, one which died with him, was his use of the statutory tetralogy. Competing poets had to present three serious plays and one satyr-play; Aeschylus normally made the three plays a connected 'trilogy' in the modern sense of the word: not always, for the *Persians* is an independent play, having no connexion with the two that were presented with it. In the Aeschylean trilogy each play is a complete unity, yet each is a coherent part of a larger unity. This device gave his drama an amplitude which has never been approached since—an amplitude which his vast conceptions needed, and which only his magnificent structural sense could control. The normal scheme might be very baldly summarized as the offence, the counter-offence, and the resolution; sin provokes sin, until justice asserts itself. Thus, the *Agamemnon* deals (though in no pedestrian chronological order) with the crime of Thyestes against his brother Atreus (Agamemnon's father), and the terrible revenge of Atreus; and with the crime of Paris and Helen against Menelaus. Agamemnon, by the will of Zeus, seeks a just vengeance, but his cause is stained by personal ambition: to this he sacrifices his own daughter, and he also behaves with impiety when he has captured Troy. Clytemnestra, seeking a just revenge, kills him: but her vengeance too is stained by murder and adultery, and only promises more blood. The play shows again and again how sin begets sin, and raises, with increasing insistence, the question how and where a final act of justice can be found. All this, thanks to Aeschylus's constructional skill, is brought to a brilliant focus in the crimes and death of Agamemnon. In the second play Orestes appears to avenge his father by killing his mother. After a long preparation the horrible deed is done in two or three swift scenes. Orestes, unlike the previous avengers, is disinterested; his motives are pure, and he is acting under the direct command of Delphian Apollo, who is the mouthpiece of Zeus. But for all that, he rushes out, at the end of the play, pursued by his mother's Furies. There is no solution yet. The third play shows Orestes protected by Apollo but pursued by the Furies; Apollo is acting for Zeus, the Furies claim an even more august authority. Issue is joined before Athena (embodying Divine Wisdom) on the Acropolis. She declines to judge in so weighty a case; and it is decided by a jury of Athenian citizens under her presidency. Orestes is acquitted, by her casting-vote. Apollo and Orestes disappear. The Furies, indignant, threaten Athens with ruin, but are persuaded by Athena to relent and to accept an honoured place in her city. Disinterested justice is at last achieved, and the final plan of Zeus revealed in the usages of civic life. Thus the *Oresteia* is, among other things, a drama of human civilization.

Of the other plays, the *Suppliants* and the *Prometheus* were the first plays of their trilogies, the *Seven against Thebes* the third of its; and, judging by what can be recovered, the scale of these trilogies was hardly less majestic than that of the *Oresteia.*

These conceptions were matched by a bold dramatic technique, an immense concentration, a wonderful sense of structure, and magnificent poetry. Aeschylus made the utmost use of spectacle and colour; and, in virtue of the beauty and strength of his choral odes, he might well be regarded as one of the greatest of lyric poets, as well as, possibly, the greatest of dramatists.

As a unique honour to him, it was enacted in Athens after his death not only that his plays might be revived at the festivals (to which normally only new plays were admitted) but also that anyone proposing to do this should be 'given a chorus' without question (see also GREECE, 1 *b*). H. D. F. KITTO

AESOPUS, CLAUDIUS, a celebrated Roman tragic actor of the first century B.C., much admired by Horace. He was a friend of Cicero, who speaks of him as having great powers of facial expression and fluent gesture. During Cicero's exile Aesopus would often allude to him on the stage, in the hope of swaying public opinion in his favour.

A.E.T.A., see AMERICAN EDUCATIONAL THEATRE ASSOCIATION.

AFINOGENOV, ALEXANDER NIKOLAEVICH (1904–41), Soviet dramatist, who began writing in 1926. His first important play was *Fear* (translated into English by Charles Malamuth and published in *Six Soviet Plays*, 1936), which was first performed at the Leningrad Theatre of Drama in 1931. Later in the same year it was seen at the Moscow Art Theatre, produced by Sudakov with settings by Shifrin. It was one of the earliest Soviet plays to combine good technique and dramatic tension with party propaganda, and deals with the conversion to socialism of an irritable psychologist who has propounded the theory that fear governs the U.S.S.R. This fusion of socialist propaganda with the long tradition of classical and pre-Revolutionary playwriting, whereby humanity, with its faults, foibles, courage, and idiosyncrasies, its basic lovableness and everlasting interest, is shown as being as important as the play's message, is even more clearly seen in a later play, *Distant Point*, given at the Vakhtangov Theatre in 1934. This is a fine character-study of a Far-Eastern general on his way to western Russia, who stops at a remote Siberian railway station to give its inhabitants a much-needed lesson in unselfishness, dying in the process. The play, which has been given four separate productions in London, was first seen at the Gate Theatre in 1937 in a translation by Hubert Griffith. It has been produced by many British provincial repertory theatres and several times broadcast by the B.B.C.

Shortly after the production of *Distant Point* Afinogenov was in trouble with the authorities, but returned to favour on the outbreak of war, and in 1940 had a light comedy, *Mashenka*, produced by Zavadsky at the Mossoviet Theatre. A year later he was killed in an air raid, leaving his last play, *On the Eve*, to be produced posthumously. Set in a Moscow suburb, it shows how a typical family there played their part in the stemming of the German advance. By the death of Afinogenov Soviet Russia lost one of her few early dramatists who might have had a world-wide appeal.

AFRANIUS, Lucius, writer of Roman comedies (see FABULA, 9. *Togata*).

AFRICAN ROSCIUS, see ALDRIDGE, IRA.

AFTER-PIECE, see ENGLAND, 5.

AGATE. (1) James Evershed (1877–1947), English dramatic critic who numbered among his ancestors the actor Ned Shuter. He began his journalistic career on the *Manchester Guardian* and from there moved to the *Saturday Review*. From 1923 until his death he was dramatic critic of the *Sunday Times*. Few critics have written more entertainingly for their contemporaries, and few have served posterity more extensively than he did by reprinting his newspaper articles in book form. Between the two world wars he published a dozen books of collected criticism. His later publications include *Brief Chronicles* (1943), dealing with performances of Shakespearian and other Elizabethan plays which he had witnessed; *Red-Letter Nights* (1944), dealing with the plays of later dramatists seen between 1921 and 1943; and *Immoment Toys* (1945), a survey of light entertainment on the London stage, 1920–43. In *These Were Actors* (also 1943) he edited a selection of contemporary criticism from a newspaper-cuttings book of 1811 to 1833. He also compiled *The English Dramatic Critics* (1932), an anthology of criticism written between 1660 and 1932.

In the numerous volumes of his *Ego* series Agate published the detailed diary of his life which he started in 1932. Time will show whether he will be remembered more for his diary than for his dramatic criticism. One thing is certain: he recorded the theatre of his time with more vigour and interest than any other critic, except Bernard Shaw, brought to any period.

Agate's sister (2) May (1892–1960) studied for the stage under Sarah Bernhardt, on whom she wrote an interesting volume of reminiscences, *Madame Sarah* (1945). She appeared with her in Paris and London in 1912, and in 1916 joined Miss Horniman's company at the Gaiety Theatre, Manchester. She acted in London until 1939. In 1933, with her husband, Wilfrid Grantham, she adapted Musset's *Lorenzaccio* as *Night's Candles*, in which Ernest Milton, who produced the play as well as appearing in the title-role, scored a great success. T. C. KEMP†, *rev.*

AGATHON, of Athens, a tragic poet and a younger contemporary of Euripides, won the first of his two victories in 416 B.C. He was the first to invent his own plots, instead of taking them from legend. Also, according to Aristotle, he was the first to write choral odes, unconnected with the plot, as *entr'actes*. Few fragments of his work survive, but he seems to have written romantic drama. Aristophanes laughs at him for effeminacy, but on his death laments the loss of a 'good poet and a good friend'. There is a character-sketch of Agathon in Plato's *Symposium*. H. D. F. KITTO

AGGAS, Robert (*c.* 1619–79), English scene-painter, much esteemed in the Restoration theatre. He worked for the second Theatre Royal under Killigrew, and with Samuel Towers painted the elaborate scenery used there for *The Destruction of Jerusalem* in 1677, later suing the theatre for payments overdue. His name is occasionally found with the spelling Angus.

AGRELL, Alfhild (1849–1923), Swedish dramatist (see SCANDINAVIA, 3 *a*).

AIKEN, George L. (1830–76), American actor and playwright, who made his first appearance on the stage in 1848. His first play, a dramatization of a popular novel, was done in New York in 1851, but he is chiefly remembered for his adaptation—the best of many—of *Uncle Tom's Cabin*. This was prepared at the request of George C. Howard, who wished to star in it his wife, Aiken's cousin, as Topsy, and his daughter as Eva (see No. 168). It was given at Troy in 1852, and in New York a year later, and was constantly toured, its latest revival being in 1924. Apart from its entertainment value, it is important in the history of abolitionist propaganda. Aiken wrote or adapted a number of other plays, none of which has survived, and continued to act until 1867.

AINLEY, Henry Hinchliffe (1879–1945), English actor, possessed of a remarkably fine voice and great personal beauty and charm. He was introduced to the stage by George Alexander, under whom, after a short apprenticeship with Benson's company, he made his first success. This was as Paolo in Phillips's *Paolo and Francesca* (1902), a part to which he was eminently suited in every way. He soon made a name for himself as a romantic and Shakespearian actor, and was seen in such plays as *If I were King*, *Old Heidelberg*, and *The Prisoner of Zenda*, and as Bassanio, Orlando, Cassio, Orestes, and Hippolytus. In 1912 he made a great impression as Leontes in Granville-Barker's production of *The Winter's Tale*, and a year later showed his versatility by his playing of Ilam Carve in *The Great Adventure*. A wide range of parts followed, interrupted by war service from 1916 to 1919, after which he returned to the theatre. He was for a time associated in the management of the St. James's, the New, and His Majesty's Theatres, appearing at the last as Oliver Cromwell and Hassan, the latter one of his finest parts. Ainley would undoubtedly have ranked as one of the great actors of his generation had not serious illness kept him from the stage for several years. After a long absence he returned in 1929 to score an instantaneous success as James Fraser in *The First Mrs. Fraser*, which, with Marie Tempest in the name-part, ran for eighteen months. A year later he was seen as Hamlet at a Command Performance, and he finally retired in 1932.

AKIMOV, NIKOLAI PAVLOVICH (1901–68), Soviet scene-designer and producer. Born in Kharkov, he studied in Leningrad (then Petrograd) under Dobuzhinsky from 1915 to 1919, and then returned to Kharkov to work in the Children's Theatre there. A year later he was back in Leningrad, where in 1927 he first attracted attention by his designs for the productions of *Armoured Train 14–69* and *Fear* at the Leningrad Academic Theatre. Moving to Moscow, he worked at the Vakhtangov Theatre for several years, first as a designer, later turning to production also. One of the first-fruits of this unusual combination of artist and producer was the famous 'formalist' production of *Hamlet* in 1932, in which Hamlet faked the Ghost, and Ophelia, a 'bright young thing', was not mad but drunk, drowning after a drunken orgy. This interpretation of the text aroused a storm of controversy, and the play was soon taken off in deference to public opinion. However, even in his errors Akimov was interesting, and his work was bound to be important to the Soviet theatre as he matured. In 1934 he returned to Leningrad, where a year later he became Art Director of the Theatre of Comedy. Among the many interesting productions for which he was responsible there was a beautifully staged *Twelfth Night* (1938). In the 1950s he strove to create an original repertory, and fought for the acceptance of new Soviet comedies. From 1955 until his death he taught at the Leningrad Theatrical Institute, where he was head of the Faculty of Design and Production.

BEATRICE KING†

AKINS, ZOË (1886–1958), American poet and dramatist, whose first play, *Déclassée* (1919), had a certain success. This was followed by an amusing comedy, *Papa*, in the same year, and by several more plays, including *Daddy's Gone A-Hunting* (1921) and *The Texas Nightingale* (1922). In *The Varying Shore* in 1921 she broke new ground in a desire to experiment, but it was not until 1930, with *The Greeks Had a Word For It*, that she finally achieved an outstanding success, duplicated in London four years later. In 1935 she was awarded a Pulitzer Prize for her dramatization of Edith Wharton's novel, *The Old Maid*. She adapted several plays from the French—among them Verneuil's *Pile ou Face* and Pujet's *Les Jours heureux*—and from the Hungarian, and also dramatized several American novels. Her last play, produced in 1951, was *The Swallow's Nest*.

ALARCÓN, JUAN RUIZ DE, see RUIZ DE ALARCÓN, JUAN.

ALBEE, (1) EDWARD FRANKLIN (1857–1930), an American theatre manager, who was for some years a tent boy with Barnum's 'Greatest Show on Earth'. In 1885 he joined with B. F. Keith in the presentation of variety shows in Boston and elsewhere, and did his best to improve not only the standard of the stage shows, but also the conditions of employment and housing backstage for vaudeville artists. He was concerned with the building of a number of variety theatres in the leading cities of the East and Middle West, including the Keith, erected in Boston in 1894, and also set up an agency for the engagement of variety turns. By 1920 he was accounted one of the leading purveyors of light amusement in the United States, with a vaudeville circuit of some seventy houses, and an interest in about 300 others. His adopted grandson, (2) EDWARD FRANKLIN (1928–), is an outstanding modern dramatist whose first play, *The Zoo Story*, was produced at the Provincetown Playhouse in 1960, under the aegis of two Broadway professionals, Richard Barr and Herbert Witz. With Clinton Wilder, Barr then produced Albee's *The American Dream* and *The Death of Bessie Smith* (1961) at the York Playhouse. In 1962 the Broadway production of Albee's *Who's Afraid of Virginia Woolf?* had an outstanding success, and was later well received in London. Also on Broadway, *Tiny Alice* (1964), with Gielgud and Irene Worth, caused much controversy, and was declared to be incomprehensible by six New York theatre critics. It is as yet too soon to assess Albee's place in the American theatre, but he appears to be one of the major dramatic talents to have emerged over the last few years.

ALBERT SALOON, LONDON, built in 1844, stood near the Grecian in Shepherdess Walk, City Road. It had two stages, one with an open-air auditorium.

ALBERY. (1) JAMES (1838–89), English dramatist, author of a number of plays, of which *Two Roses*, produced at the Vaudeville in 1870, provided Henry Irving, as Digby Grant, with one of his earliest successes. Albery also made a number of adaptations, including *Jingle* (a version of *Pickwick*), done at the Lyceum in 1878, and translations from the French, mainly for the Criterion Theatre, where his wife, Mary Moore (see WYNDHAM, 2), was playing leading parts. His son (2) BRONSON JAMES (1881–1971), theatre manager, made his first ventures at the Criterion, and on the death of his mother, who had married as her second husband Sir Charles Wyndham, took control, together with his half-brother Howard (see WYNDHAM, 3), of the Criterion, Wyndham's, and New Theatres. This joint management proved a vital and important influence in the London theatre of the 1930s, and many interesting productions took place at all three theatres, including *Richard of Bordeaux*, *Hamlet*, *Romeo and Juliet*, *Noah*, and *The Seagull* (all with John Gielgud) at the New, *Musical Chairs* and *French Without Tears* at the Criterion, and *Service* and *The Maitlands* at Wyndham's. In 1949 Albery was knighted for services to the theatre. His son (3) DONALD ARTHUR ROLLESTON (1914–) has been associated in management with his father, and in the 1950s continued the policy of presenting interesting new plays with such productions as *I Am A Camera* (1954), *Waiting for Godot* (1955), *The Potting Shed* (1958), and *A Taste of Honey* (1959). He was for some years manager of Sadler's Wells Ballet.

ALBION THEATRE, LONDON, in Windmill Street. This was opened in 1832. Three years later, after an obscure career, it became the New Queen's. Sally Booth, the tragedienne, appeared there, but the staple fare was melodrama. The theatre was demolished in 1836.

The Oriental Theatre in Poplar (1867) was also known as the Albion.

ALCAZAR, LONDON, see CONNAUGHT THEATRE.

ALDRICH, LOUIS (1843–1901), American actor, whose real name was Lyon. He was an infant prodigy, and as the Ohio Roscius toured in such parts as Richard III, Macbeth, Shylock, Jack Sheppard, and Young Norval. He was later known as Master Moses, McCarthy, or Kean, and after a break for schooling returned to the stage as an adult under the name of Aldrich. After five years in St. Louis he appeared in New York, playing in Charles Kean's farewell performance, and then went to Boston as a member of the stock company there. From 1873 to 1874 he was leading man of Mrs. John Drew's Arch Street Theatre company in Philadelphia. He then toured for many years in his greatest part, Joe Saunders in *My Partner*, first produced in 1879, which brought him a fortune. He was also good as Shoulders, a drunken creature in *The Kaffir Diamond* (1888). In 1897 he became President of the Actors' Fund of America, and was the first to suggest the building of a home for destitute actors. He made his last appearance on the stage in New York in 1899, and was about to appear under Belasco's management when he died suddenly of apoplexy.

ALDRIDGE, IRA FREDERICK (1804–67), the first great American Negro actor, who in 1863 became a naturalized Englishman. Little is known of his early years, but he is believed to have been born on the west coast of Africa, a member of the Fulah tribe. In New York he was in the service of Wallack, and acted Rolla (in *Pizarro*) and Romeo with a Negro company. Billed as the African Roscius, he made his London début as Othello at the Royalty Theatre in 1826. He then went on tour, and in Belfast had as his Iago Charles Kean. He was also good as Macbeth, Zanga (in *The Revenge*), and Mungo (in *The Padlock*), and was generally regarded as one of the outstanding actors of the day. He was the recipient of many honours, amassed a large fortune, and married a white woman. He was last seen in England in 1865, and then returned to the Continent, where he had first toured in 1853. He was immensely popular in Germany, where he played in English with a supporting cast playing in German. His Lear was much admired in Russia, the only country in which he appeared in the part.

ALDWYCH THEATRE, LONDON. This was opened on 23 Dec. 1905 by Charles Frohman, with Seymour Hicks and Ellaline Terriss in a revival of *Bluebell in Fairyland*. In 1909 a lurid melodrama called *The Bad Girl of the Family* had a big success, followed by *The Girl who took the Wrong Turning*. *The Ever Open Door*, a play of a different kind, prospered in 1913, as did *Sacred and Profane Love* in 1919. With the transfer of *Tons of Money* from the Shaftesbury Theatre in 1923 the Aldwych began to make theatre history, as Tom Walls and Ralph Lynn, who had brought the play there, produced a series of successful farces, mainly written by Ben Travers, in which they played together. Among these were *A Cuckoo in the Nest*, *Rookery Nook*, *Thark*, and several others, in most of which Robertson Hare, Mary Brough, and Winifred Shotter appeared. The association, which was one of the outstanding theatrical attractions of London and made the Aldwych a most popular theatre, ended in 1933. During the Second World War this theatre housed the successful productions of Lillian Hellman's *Watch on the Rhine* (1942) and the Lunts in Sherwood's *There Shall Be No Night* (1945). In 1947 Redgrave appeared as Macbeth, and two years later Vivien Leigh gave an outstanding performance in Tennessee Williams's *A Streetcar Named Desire*. Fry's *The Dark Is Light Enough*, with Edith Evans, was seen in 1954. In 1960 the Aldwych became the London home of the Royal Shakespeare company, and extensive alterations were made to the interior, including the installation of an apron stage and a completely new system of lighting. The first season opened on 15 Dec. with *The Duchess of Malfi*. *Twelfth Night* was transferred from Stratford, and subsequent productions included *Ondine*, *The Devils*, Anouilh's *Becket*, Fry's *Curtmantle*, a very successful *Comedy of Errors*, the highly controversial *Marat/Sade*, by Peter Weiss, and Livings's *Eh?* In the summer of 1964 the Aldwych housed the first of a series of World Theatre seasons which gave London playgoers the opportunity of seeing many famous foreign companies.

ALEICHEM [really RABINOVICH], SHOLOM (1859–1916), Jewish writer and dramatist. Born in Pereiaslav (Poltava), he was educated with a view to becoming a rabbi, but at 18 took to journalism, first in Hebrew, later in Yiddish. By 1888 he was owner and editor of a newspaper in Kiev. In 1905 he emigrated to America, and died while on a visit to Copenhagen. He wrote few plays, and his connexion with the stage has been through the dramatization of his numerous novels and short stories, which deal with life in the Jewish communities of the Ukrainian villages. His characters are generous, kindly, simple folk with considerable native shrewdness, the chief being Tuvia the Milkman, the dreamer, the poor, hard-working, unsuccessful little man with an infinite trust in God, and Menahem Mendel, whose dreams are of 'big business' schemes which never come off. Their wives are the practical partners. A Sholom Aleichem cult grew up in the Yiddish Art Theatres, fostered by Maurice Schwartz in America, and by the State Jewish Theatre in Moscow, both of which saw his people as national Jewish types. These offer great scope to actors of intelligence, and it is interesting to note that Mikhoels in the U.S.S.R. and Muni Wiesenfreund (known in the cinema as Paul Muni) in Germany first emerged from obscurity in Sholom Aleichem's plays. Some idea of his work may be obtained from Maurice Samuel's *The World of Sholom Aleichem* (1943). In 1959 his centenary was celebrated by a production at the Grand Palais Theatre—the last surviving Yiddish theatre in London—of his three-act comedy, *Hard to be a Jew*. In 1964 an adaptation of *The Milkman* (*Tevye*) became a successful Broadway musical as *Fiddler on the Roof*.

E. HARRIS

ALENCAR, JOSÉ MARINIANO DE (1829–77), see SOUTH AMERICA, 2.

ALEOTTI, GIOVANNI BATTISTA (1546–1636), Italian theatre architect, designer of the Teatro Farnese (see ARCHITECTURE and SCENERY, 3).

ALEXANDER, SIR GEORGE [really GEORGE ALEXANDER GIBB SAMSON] (1858–1918), English actor, and manager of the St. James's Theatre from 1891 till his death. He made his first appearance at Nottingham in 1879 and in 1881 appeared in London. At the end of that year he joined Irving's company at the Lyceum as Caleb Deecie in a revival of Albery's *Two Roses*. He remained with Irving, except for a short session under Kendal and Hare at the St. James's in 1883, until 1889, when he entered into management on his own, a venture which was to prove financially and artistically a success. Alexander had a definite policy. At a time when English dramatic literature was at a low ebb, and the stage was cluttered up with adaptations of French farces, he deliberately encouraged English writers. Of over eighty plays which he produced at the St. James's only eight were by foreign authors. A man of distinguished appearance and great charm, Alexander succeeded in investing any part he played with romance and dignity. His greatest success was in the dual role of Rudolf Rassendyll and the King in *The Prisoner of Zenda*, to which may be added the equally picturesque parts of Villon in *If I Were King* and Karl Heinrich in *Old Heidelberg*. In 1906 he produced Pinero's *His House in Order*, perhaps the most typical 'St. James's play'; but Alexander's net was widely cast, and his productions ranged from Shakespeare to Pinero, from Stephen Phillips's verse drama, *Paolo and Francesca*, to Oscar Wilde's *Lady Windermere's Fan* and *The Importance of Being Earnest*. In the latter he was admirable as John Worthing; 'he never', says A. E. W. Mason in his *Sir George Alexander and the St. James's Theatre* (1935), 'acted with a lighter or more confident touch'.

Alexander was not only a good actor, but also a good business man, as the account books of his theatre indicate. In 1907 he was elected to the L.C.C. as member for South St. Pancras, a position he held with distinction until 1912. He also contemplated standing for Parliament, and might have been equally successful there had not increasing ill-health caused him to reconsider his decision. In 1911, the year of the coronation of George V, he was knighted, and during the First World War he was indefatigable in his efforts on behalf of the Red Cross and other charities. His death, from diabetes, was a great loss to the stage which he had graced with his presence and upon which he had maintained a consistently high standard.

ALEXANDRA THEATRE, LONDON. 1. Highbury Barn, a concert hall in the grounds of an open-air pleasure resort of a kind common round London. It was converted into a theatre in 1861 by Edward Giovanelli, who staged farces and burlesques there and ruined himself. E. T. Smith, the great showman, tried to run it, but it was finally closed, with the gardens, in 1871. J. G. Tayler, Danvers, and Rachel Sanger played there.

2. Park Street, Camden Town, opened on 31 May 1873 when Thorpe Pede, a musician, staged a double bill there consisting of an operetta, 'Marguerite', composed by himself, and a play entitled *Friendship; or, Golding's Debt*, by Robert Reece. Apparently the theatre cost £20,000 to build, and it stood near two famous taverns, The Mother Redcap and The Britannia. In 1875 Walter Bentley and a Miss Clayton played there, and in 1877 an old play, *The Rake's Progress*, was revived. In the same year Madame St. Claire took over the

theatre, chiefly to show herself off in the part of Romeo, but without success. In 1879 the theatre became known as the Park Theatre, from its proximity to Regent's Park. It mostly gave straight plays, and Stella Brereton and the celebrated Odell appeared there in a version of *Jane Eyre*. The house was burnt down after a performance in 1881 and never rebuilt.

A theatre at Stoke Newington, which opened in 1897, was also known as the Alexandra.

ALEXANDRINSKY THEATRE, LENINGRAD. This theatre, which in 1937 was renamed the Pushkin Theatre, was founded in 1824, in the same year as the Maly Theatre in Moscow. It had a fine actor in Vasily Karatygin (1802–53), but it had no authors of the calibre of Gogol and Ostrovsky, then holding the stage at the Maly, and never developed a settled policy. Also its audiences were more influenced by the Court life of St. Petersburg, and had none of the liberalism and intellectual curiosity of the middle-class merchant audiences of Moscow. For this reason it staged a good deal of ballet and opera, until the former was transferred to the Bolshoi and was replaced by the popular vaudeville of the time, or by translations of French melodramas. Later the patriotic dramas written to order by Polevoy and Kukolik were seen at the Alexandrinsky, and after a long, blank period the first stirrings of realism came with such plays as *The Father*, in which the actor Mamont Dalsky (1865–1918) scored a personal triumph. But on the whole the audience did not want new works, and the theatre continued to play for safety. Its first and last attempt at Chekhov, *The Seagull* in 1896, was a dismal failure, the theatre's old-fashioned technique being unable to convey the subtlety of the author's characterization. Just before the October Revolution Meyerhold was working at the Alexandrinsky, his last production there being a revival of Lermontov's *Masquerade*.

Amid the stress of the Revolution the Alexandrinksy clung desperately to a repertory of well-tried classics, the only new play being *Faust and the City*, by the Commissar for Education, Lunacharsky, under whose care and vigilance the Alexandrinsky, like the Moscow Art and other pre-Soviet theatres, gradually found its feet in the new world. By 1924 it was ready to include new plays in its repertory, some Soviet, some from Europe. Among the producers who worked on them were Radlov, Solovyov, and Rappoport, while in 1937 Meyerhold returned, to produce *Masquerade* again. Further outstanding productions were *Antony and Cleopatra*, a revival of *The Forest*, *Lenin in 1918*, a remarkable performance of *Macbeth*, and, during the Second World War, when the theatre was evacuated and went on tour up to the front line, *Othello*, *Oedipus Tyrannus*, and two new plays, *The Russian People* and *Kremlin Chimes*. Some interesting revivals of old plays were done under Leonid Vivyen, with a somewhat more accurate historical bias than formerly, and the policy of the theatre tended to show a heightened consciousness of the social problems of contemporary life. This tendency was greatly strengthened after the company's return to Leningrad in 1944, and in 1947 successful performances were given of two modern plays, Dovzhenko's *Life in Flower* and Simonov's *The Russian Question*. The classics, both Russian and foreign, continued to figure prominently in the repertory, and in 1954 Vivyen was responsible for *The Seagull* and *Hamlet*, the latter with incidental music by Shostakovich, composed in 1931 for a production at the Vakhtangov Theatre. A revival by Tovstonogov of Pogodin's *An Optimistic Tragedy* in 1947 was well received, though criticisms were made that in its efforts to portray reality the theatre was becoming imitative rather than creative. This was found to be no longer true of the productions in 1958 of Korneichuk's *Why the Stars Smiled*, directed by A. A. Muzil, and of Bulgakov's *Flight* and Miller's *Death of a Salesman*, both directed by Vivyen. In the following year the company undertook a successful tour of Poland, Czechoslovakia, and France, and returned to continue its work in Leningrad with a company rich in eminent actors, among them A. T. Borizov, N. K. Simonov, and the actress N. S. Rashevskaya.

ALEXIS, a Greek comic poet of the period of Middle Comedy (*c.* 400 B.C.) (see GREECE, 2 *b*). He was uncle to Menander. Only a few fragments of his work survive.

ALFIERI, VITTORIO AMEDEO (1749–1803), Italian dramatist, chiefly remembered as a writer of tragedies in verse. Born in Asti of a noble and wealthy family, he had an unhappy childhood, and at an early age left home to travel widely in Europe. For a long time French was his only language, but when in his twenties his thoughts turned to literature, he went to Tuscany and worked hard to perfect himself in Italian, which he henceforth championed against the influence of French. His first play, *Cleopatra*, was given at Turin in 1775 with great success, and was followed by a number of others, on classical, biblical, or, occasionally, romantic subjects. His two best tragedies are *Saul* (1782–4) and *Mirra* (1784–6). His verse, which owes much to Cesarotti, is austere, but fits well with his conception of tragedy as a dramatic presentation of a great theme from which all lesser matters must be banished. It has been said of his tragedies that their action flies like an arrow to its mark. He also wrote half a dozen comedies, mainly satiric, which perhaps deserve more consideration than they have received, and a remarkable autobiography, in which he depicts himself more as he wished to be than as he was. For many years Alfieri was the devoted lover of the Countess of Albany, wife of the Young Pretender. He visited London on several occasions, chiefly to buy horses, for which he had a passion. He was in France at the time of the Revolution, which he first welcomed, and later abhorred. When he returned to Italy the

French treated him as an *émigré*, and confiscated his goods and practically all his money. His books and manuscripts were given to the painter Fabre by the Countess of Albany, and Fabre bequeathed them to the University of Montpellier (see also ITALY, 3 *a*).

ALHAMBRA, LONDON, a famous music-hall whose Moorish-style architecture dominated the east side of Leicester Square. It opened in 1854 as the Panopticon, and housed a variety of shows. It was here that the famous trapeze-artist and wire-walker Léotard made his great London success. The theatre was burnt down in 1882, at which time it was being used for *opéra-bouffe*, but was rebuilt the following year. Its great days as a music-hall were from 1890 to 1910, during which time it also, like the Empire, its great rival, had a resident ballet company, headed by Catherine Geltzer. In 1911 it went over to revue, and 1916 saw the success of *The Bing Boys Are Here*, with George Robey and Violet Loraine. It later reverted to variety, and also ran seasons of Russian ballet, but towards the end of its life had no settled policy. It was finally demolished in Nov. 1936 and the Odeon cinema was erected on the site. W. MACQUEEN-POPE†, *rev.*

ALIZON (*fl.* 1610–48), an early French actor who specialized in the playing of comic women-servants, particularly in farces, or of the heroine's nurse in more serious plays. He was with Montdory when he first came to Paris, but was later transferred to the Hôtel de Bourgogne. As with his equally popular companion, Jodelet, his own name was frequently given to the parts destined for him.

ALLAN, LOUISE ROSALIE (*née* Despréaux) (1810–56), French actress, and the first to discover the excellence of Alfred de Musset as a dramatist. At the age of 10 she appeared with Talma at Brussels, and was later, on his recommendation, engaged for minor parts at the Comédie-Française, where she played the page Iaguëz in the first production of *Hernani* (1830). Coming into conflict with Mlle Mars, at that time the reigning star of the company, she left the Comédie-Française in 1831 and went to the Gymnase, where she scored a notable triumph, at the same time marrying a fellow-actor named Allan. She was then engaged to appear at the French theatre in St. Petersburg, and tradition has it that while there she saw, and may have acted in, a charming trifle which she planned to have translated into French, only to find that it was a Russian translation of Alfred de Musset's *Un Caprice*. This story is now considered apocryphal, but it is certain that *Un Caprice*, with Mme Allan and Mlle Judith, was warmly received at the Comédie-Française in 1847, seven years after its publication. Mme Allan then remained at the Comédie-Française until her death. She was the contemporary there of Mlle Rachel, and maintained, even against such a rival, a claim to be considered an actress of the first rank.

ALLEN, VIOLA (1869–1948), American actress, who made her first appearance on the stage in 1882, succeeding Annie Russell in the part of Esmeralda at the Madison Square Theatre. A year or two later she was leading lady to John McCullough, and in 1886 played with Salvini. From 1891 to 1898 she was a member of Frohman's stock company at the Empire, where she appeared in many old and new parts and gained a great reputation as one of the leading actresses of the day. On leaving Frohman she toured for some time as a star, her first venture being Gloria Quayle in *The Christian*. She was also excellent as Viola in *Twelfth Night*, and appeared in *The Winter's Tale*, *Cymbeline*, and *As You Like It*. In 1915 she toured with J. K. Hackett as Lady Macbeth, and made her last appearance in 1916 as Mistress Ford in *The Merry Wives of Windsor*. In 1946 the Museum of the City of New York Drama Department organized an exhibition devoted to her, at which many of her stage costumes and other mementoes of her long and distinguished career were on view.

ALLEN, WILLIAM (?–1647), English actor, and an important member of Queen Henrietta's Men at the Cockpit, where he played leading parts in *The Renegado* and *Hannibal and Scipio*. After the dissolution of the company in 1636 he joined the powerful King's Men. He married the daughter of a fellow-actor, and may have been apprenticed as a young man to Christopher Beeston. He has sometimes been confused with a William Allen who was an army officer in the Civil War.

ALLEYN, EDWARD (1566–1626), founder of Dulwich College (originally the College and Hospital of God's Gift), and one of the first English actors of whom we have any substantial knowledge. In 1583 he was a member of the Earl of Worcester's players, and already accounted a good actor. In 1592 he married Joan Woodward, stepdaughter of the theatrical manager Henslowe, and so laid the foundations of his later fortune. He became part-owner in Henslowe's ventures, and later sole proprietor of several playhouses and places of entertainment, including the Paris Garden and the Rose and Fortune theatres. He had a high reputation, being much praised by Nashe and Jonson, and was considered the only rival of Burbage. He was the chief actor of the Admiral's Men, and may have joined them in 1587. He played at the Rose from 1594 to 1597, and at the Fortune from 1599 till his retirement, probably at the accession of James I. Marlowe was his chief dramatist, and plays in which he is known to have appeared include *Tamburlaine*, *Faustus*, and *The Jew of Malta*, as well as Greene's *Orlando Furioso*, and, no doubt, many others lost or unrecorded. Two legends —that he retired from the stage and founded Dulwich College in a fit of remorse after seeing the Devil while playing Faustus, and that he died a pauper in his own charitable institution —are now discredited. He was, in fact, a man of substance to the end, and only three years before his death he was able to settle on his second wife, the daughter of John Donne, the sum of £1,500. A Frenchman who saw him act described him as having 'a pleasing voice, a good figure and a fine presence' and credited him with having raised the art of acting to a level hitherto unknown.

ALL-RUSSIAN THEATRICAL SOCIETY. The V.T.O. (its initials in Russian) was founded as a charitable body in 1883 to help needy members of the theatrical profession. Although it could do little to improve the inferior status at that time accorded to the actor, it fought for the recognition of his civic and social rights, and also helped to protect him from exploitation by scoundrelly managers. In 1895 the progressive members, who had found themselves in conflict with Imperial officialdom when the Society became an Imperial organization, formed a separate branch, the Union of Stage Workers, which looked after the interests of dramatists and composers as well as of actors.

The Soviet Revolution of 1917 transformed the activities of the Society. The legal and professional work was taken over by the Union of Art Workers, which covered everyone who worked in the theatre in any capacity, and the Society was left free to concentrate on the artistic side, in an endeavour to raise the level of acting and production throughout the country, a task which it is still pursuing. It arranges lectures, provides a forum for the discussion of new plays, and publishes books. It is active in the provision of artistic aid to the provincial theatre, and continues its former social activity through the provision of two homes for retired theatre workers, and holiday and convalescent homes for those still working. From 1916 until her death in 1964 the great actress Yablochkina was President of the Society. She was succeeded by Mikhail Ivanovich Tsaryov (1903–), director of the Maly Theatre in Moscow. Both Georgia and the Ukraine have Theatrical Societies run very much on the lines of the All-Russian Theatrical Society. BEATRICE KING

ALLGOOD. (1) SARA (1883–1950), Irish actress, whose early career is bound up with the history of the Abbey Theatre. After studying for the stage with Frank J. Fay and his brother, with whom she toured in a repertory of short plays and farces, she joined their Irish National Theatre Society in 1903, playing Princess Buan in *The King's Threshold*, and a year later appearing as Cathleen in *Riders to the Sea*. In Dec. 1904 she appeared in the opening productions of the Abbey Theatre and remained there for some years, among her later parts being Deidre, Mrs. Delane in *Hyacinth Halvey*, and Widow Quin in *The Playboy of the Western World*. In 1914 she joined the Liverpool Repertory Theatre company, and subsequently became a member of Miss Horniman's company at Manchester, playing Isabella in the opening production of *Measure for Measure*, a part which she later repeated at Stratford. She had appeared many times in London with the Abbey Players, and in 1920, after a long tour in Australia, was seen there as Mrs. Geoghegan in *The White-Headed Boy*; but the finest performances of her career were undoubtedly Juno Boyle in *Juno and the Paycock* (1924), in which she also appeared in America, and Bessie Burgess in *The Plough and the Stars* (1926). Among her later successes were Julia Hardy in *Things That Are Caesar's*, Honoria Flanagan in *Storm in a Teacup*, and Jemima Cooney in *Shadow and Substance*. She made her last appearance on the stage in New York in 1940, and then appeared only in films. Her younger sister (2) MAIRE O'NEILL (1887–1952) was also at the Abbey Theatre, where she created the part of Pegeen Mike in *The Playboy of the Western World*. She remained at the Abbey until 1913, and Gwynn, in his *Irish Literature and Drama*, says she and her sister 'made the company stronger in its actresses than it ever had been or has been since they left'. She appeared subsequently at the Liverpool Repertory Theatre, and during a long and distinguished career was seen in London and New York, often in Irish plays in conjunction with her sister and her second husband, Arthur Sinclair.

ALMA-TADEMA, see TADEMA.

ALMQIST, CARL JONAS LOVE (1793–1866), Swedish dramatist (see SCANDINAVIA, 3 *a*).

ALPHONSINE [FLEURY] (1829–83), French actress, daughter of a flower-seller on the Boulevard du Temple. She appeared at the theatres there as a child, and at the Petit-Lazzari, where she was extremely popular; as a young girl she was the idol of the little theatres, and was nicknamed 'the Déjazet of the Boulevards'. A fine comedienne, never falling into farce or caricature, but always subtle and witty, she was a pretty woman, with an elegant figure, good voice, and abundant high spirits. She was for many years at the Porte-Saint-Martin and the Variétés, and then went to the Palais-Royal, where she was one of the company sent on 13 Nov. 1869 to play before the Court at Compiègne—the last time French actors appeared before Napoleon III. She was playing at the Gymnase when she retired owing to ill health. In private life she was an excellent woman, and in spite of her vivacity and charm she gave no occasion for scandal.

ÁLVAREZ QUINTERO, two brothers, (1) SERAFÍN (1871–1938) and (2) JOAQUÍN (1873–1944), joint authors of about 150 Spanish plays, of which the best known are *Los galeotes* (1900), *Abanicos y panderetas* (1902), *Mañana de sol* (1905), *El genio alegre* (1906), *Las de Caín* (1908), and *Doña Clarines* (1909). Their plays are a theatrical version of the perennial legend of Andalusia. In general, their work is amusing, conventionally sentimental, and suffused with kindliness and good-humoured tolerance. Their plays have a surface sparkle, an apparent spontaneity, and the window appears to have been opened on life, even though the contrasts in their plays are facile, the problems over-simplified or avoided, and the ethics simple. Many of their plays have been translated and successfully performed abroad, in England in the translations of Helen and Harley Granville-Barker—*Fortunato*, *The Lady from Alfaqueque*, *A Hundred Years Old*, and *Don Abel Wrote a Tragedy*.

ALVIN THEATRE, NEW YORK, a handsome edifice with an Adam-style interior. It opened on 22 Nov. 1927, taking its name from the first syllables of Alex A. Aarons and Vinton Freedley, partners in musical-comedy production, who retained control of the theatre until 1932. Its size made it particularly suitable for musical shows, with such stars as the Astaires, Ginger Rogers, and Ethel Merman, but straight plays were also seen there, including *The Apple Cart*, *Mourning Becomes Electra*, a revival of *Uncle Tom's Cabin* with Otis Skinner, and Maxwell Anderson's *Mary of Scotland*. Gershwin's musical adaptation of *Porgy and Bess* delighted the critics in 1935, but did not prove as attractive to the public as had been hoped. It was left to *I'd Rather Be Right* (1937), with George M. Cohan in his spirited impersonation of Franklin D. Roosevelt, to inaugurate a series of successful productions which included *Anything Goes*, *The Boys from Syracuse* (a musical version of *The Comedy of Errors*), and *There Shall Be No Night*, this last graced by the fine acting of the Lunts. In 1945 Margaret Webster produced *The Tempest* with the Negro actor Canada Lee as Caliban, and the following year Ingrid Bergman made a great success at the Alvin in *Joan of Lorraine*. Henry Fonda starred here in *Mr Roberts* in 1948, and in 1951 Sidney Kingsley's *Darkness at Noon* won the New York Drama Critics' Circle Award. Later productions have been *No Time for Sergeants* (1955) and *A Funny Thing Happened on the Way to the Forum* (1962), with Zero Mostel. GEORGE FREEDLEY†

AMATEUR THEATRE IN GREAT BRITAIN. It would be true to say that the amateur theatre in Great Britain, as in most countries, goes back to the beginnings of English drama, for the priests and choir-boys of liturgical drama, and later the artisans of the Mystery or Guild plays, were certainly amateurs. So were the part-time troupes of players attached to the Court, or to the households of great noblemen, from which the professional theatre finally emerged in the sixteenth century. But it was in the nineteenth century that amateur theatricals, as we know them today, became a favourite pastime of the upper and middle classes, and that many of the best-known amateur societies were formed. The movement has grown so rapidly that it is impossible to estimate the number of amateur groups at any one time, though it is probably not less than 30,000. Some of the oldest of them are the Old Stagers, which has given regular annual performances, closely associated with the Canterbury Cricket Festival, since 1842; the Manchester Athenaeum Dramatic Society, which started as a play-reading group and since 1854 has presented plays regularly, sometimes giving four or more productions a season; the Cambridge University Amateur Dramatic Company (A.D.C.), founded in 1855; and the Oxford University Dramatic Society (O.U.D.S.), founded in 1885 (see CAMBRIDGE and OXFORD). The dramatic societies of other universities, though founded much later, have also done much good work, as can be seen by the productions at the annual student drama festival organized by the National Union of Students. But the strength of any particular body depends often upon the presence in the university of a devoted enthusiast, and the constant change of membership usually prevents any coherent or continuous policy.

Those who wish to disparage amateur actors say that their motive is exhibitionism or a desire for the social pleasure that can be derived from the presentation of a play with, and before, their friends, and this may be true. But it does not necessarily prevent them from giving good performances in skilfully contrived and well-planned productions. Nor should it be forgotten that the amateurs are important in the social life of their community, and that they have often kept the theatre alive in places where there were no professional companies, either resident or visiting.

Amateur organizations can be of four kinds: the occasional group, with no continuous existence or overall policy, which draws its members from a particular school, church or factory for a particular purpose, often the raising of funds for charity; the small, but more permanent group, connected with a stable organization such as a Women's Institute, a Youth Club or a Community Centre, which probably puts on one or two productions a year of one-act comedies or farces, with which it may compete in a festival of one-act plays; the dramatic or operatic societies which flourish mainly in large towns and sometimes reach a high standard, though they are more inclined to play safe with a noted West-End success than to embark on the experimental drama which could come within their province; and finally the Little Theatres, which, though few in number, are important for artistic and aesthetic reasons. These last usually own or lease their own theatres, and present every season a number of productions varying from three or four to a dozen or more. Most of them are members of the Little Theatre Guild of Great Britain, which publishes an annual report of activities and news, and arranges conferences and discussions. One of the most interesting is the Maddermarket at Norwich, a replica of an Elizabethan theatre, built in 1919 by Nugent Monck to house his Norwich Players (founded 1911) and directed by him until 1952. The actors appear anonymously, and the productions range from the classics to the ultra-modern, from Shakespeare to the plays of Japan and China. Another interesting group is the Great Hucklow Village Players, founded in 1927 by L. du Garde Peach, who directed it and wrote many of its plays. This group is unique in that it functions in a small village, and draws its audiences by the coachload from Manchester, Liverpool, Sheffield and Derby. *Clive of India*, which subsequently had a long run in London, was first presented at Great Hucklow.

Other Little Theatres, in order of seniority, are the Stockport Garrick Society (1901), the oldest in existence; the People's Theatre, Newcastle-upon-Tyne (1911), which first worked in a converted chapel, but in 1959 built its own theatre as part of an Arts Centre; the Unnamed Society, Manchester (1915), run for many years by the late Frank Sladen-Smith, which has a small theatre in the Whitworth Art Gallery (opened in 1946 by William Armstrong, then director of the Liverpool Repertory Theatre); the Loft Theatre, Leamington (1921), whose theatre, owned by the group since 1945, was damaged by fire in 1958, rebuilt, and burnt to the ground in 1964; the Leicester Little Theatre (1923), whose theatre, opened in 1930, was gutted by fire in 1955, but is again in working order; the Crescent Theatre, Birmingham (1923), which also houses a school of acting and stagecraft, run by a professional staff; the Highbury Little Theatre, Sutton Coldfield (1925), whose members distinguished themselves by completing the building of their theatre with their own hands during the Second World War; the Halifax Thespians (1927), whose present theatre dates from 1929; the Newport Playgoers' Society (also 1927), which has had a theatre since 1937; the Bradford Civic Playhouse (1929), an offshoot of the now defunct Leeds Civic Theatre (whose reputation for pioneering work stood high in the 1920s), which presents plays over a wide industrial area, and draws on a large acting membership; and the Middlesbrough Little Theatre (1930), whose new theatre was opened by Sir John Gielgud in 1957. Among the groups established since the Second World War one of the most recent is the Stables Little Theatre in Hastings, whose theatre, housed in the elegant Georgian stable-block of Old Hastings House, was opened by Sir Ralph Richardson in 1959. It is interesting to note that the Nonentities' Society in Kidderminster, founded in 1933 by Kenneth Rose, which owns its theatre (opened in 1945 by Sir Barry Jackson), alternates its amateur season with a professional repertory company, which rents the theatre from it.

Although the most significant amateur activity takes place outside London, there are (since the demise of the important St. Pancras People's Theatre) three important centres there which deserve mention. These are the Questors, the Tavistock, and the left-wing Unity Theatre. The Questors, in Mattock Lane, Ealing, was founded in 1929, and in 1933 turned a disused chapel into a theatre. After the Second World War, under the enthusiastic leadership of Alfred Emmet, a large sum of money was raised for the erection of a theatre seating 350 people, with an adaptable stage which can be used for proscenium, forestage, open-stage, arena, and 'space-stage' productions, with a separate block of rehearsal and administrative rooms. Much of the work has been done by the members themselves, with professional assistance. The Shaw Room was opened in 1958, the Stanislavsky in 1960, and the theatre itself in 1964.

The Tavistock Repertory Theatre, which was founded in 1931, was originally housed in the Mary Ward Settlement. It lapsed during the Second World War, but was re-formed in 1952 and took possession of Canonbury Tower, Islington, formerly the home of, among others, Francis Bacon and Oliver Goldsmith. The hall was converted into a proscenium theatre, and opened on 15 Feb. 1953 as the Tower Theatre, while the rest of the property was equipped as a club, with living accommodation for a warden. This theatre, which has a long list of excellent productions to its credit, is licensed by the Lord Chamberlain and therefore open to the public during the week. It gives performances for members only on Sundays.

Unity Theatre is something of a hybrid, since it was for a time professional. It was, however, founded as an amateur enterprise in 1936, and opened its theatre in a converted church hall in Britannia Street, King's Cross, on 19 Feb. One of the most interesting of its early productions was *Plant in the Sun*, in which Paul Robeson played the lead. In Oct. 1937 the group moved to its present premises in Goldington Street, and a year later presented the first Living Newspaper (a technique imported from America) with a play on a London bus-strike. In 1956 Sartre showed his appreciation of the work done by Unity by allowing the theatre to give the first English production (on 6 Jan.) of his *Nekrassov*, which later had a long run at the Royal Court. In 1962 a scheme was launched for acquiring the freehold of the Goldington Street premises, and developing them as a cultural centre for the Labour movement in London.

These last three groups all have their own theatres, but others use existing buildings when available, among them the Cripplegate Institute, the Northern Polytechnic, the Rudolf Steiner Hall, the Toynbee Hall Theatre, and the Scala. At one time the Fortune was a favourite theatre with amateurs, but it was then professionally occupied for some years with revues, among them *At the Drop of a Hat*, *Beyond the Fringe* and *Wait a Minim*.

There are several organizations which form the unifying element in amateur drama, among them the British Drama League, the Scottish Community Drama Association, and the National Operatic and Dramatic Association.

The British Drama League (B.D.L.) was founded in 1919 by Geoffrey Whitworth. It has a very large membership, not entirely amateur, though its work is mainly done among amateur groups. It has a well-stocked library which contains among other things Miss Horniman's prompt copies from Manchester and the William Archer Collection. It is particularly useful to small groups for the sets of play-scripts which can be borrowed by post. There is also a Reference Reading Room. It organizes an annual Theatre Week, sends out visiting teachers to amateur groups, and runs a number of training courses. Some of these are held at its premises in London, others are residential summer courses in holiday centres. The B.D.L. also runs an annual Community Drama Festival in England and Wales (established in 1927), the finals of which are held in London, the Howard de Walden cup being presented to the prize-winning group. A Geoffrey Whitworth Cup is awarded for the best new one-act play. In 1953 a further award, for an original full-length play done in a Little Theatre, was started and has done much to encourage the writing and producing of new plays. The B.D.L. also publishes its own magazine, *Drama*, a quarterly founded in 1919, a catalogue, with supplements, of the books in the library, and a number of books on the theatre for amateurs.

The Junior Drama League, founded in 1955, aims at bringing in young members and interesting them in the theatre. Series of Christmas and Easter lectures by professional theatre people have been most successful, as have the classes run specially for children. In 1932 the Village Drama Society, founded by Mary Kelly, was incorporated in the B.D.L.

In Scotland the counterpart of the B.D.L. is the Scottish Community Drama Association (S.C.D.A.), founded in 1926. Until 1932 it co-operated with the B.D.L. in running the National Festival of Community Drama, but since then it has run its own festival, the winning group being free to take part in the London finals if it so wishes. Since 1945 more attention has been paid to three-act plays, on which the majority of groups now concentrate their attention, and also to the encouragement of Scottish playwrights. The S.C.D.A. runs drama schools and courses, and publishes a bulletin three times a year. Scotland has several Little Theatre groups. The Dundee Dramatic Society (1924) acquired its own Little Theatre in 1936. The St. Andrews Play Club (1933), whose home is the Byre Theatre, originally a cowshed, became a club theatre in 1935, a public theatre in 1937, and now has a nucleus of professional players. In 1936 the Glasgow Jewish Institute Players were formed, and two years later opened their own theatre. When activities stopped during the Second World War, some members joined the Glasgow Unity Theatre, but in 1944 the Group was re-formed. From 1939–43 the Rutherglen Repertory Theatre brought together a remarkable group, including Molly Urquhart, Eileen Herlie, Duncan Macrae, Nicholas Parsons, and Paul Vincent Carroll. Included in the record should also be Dumbarton People's Theatre; and the Greenock Players, well housed in an Arts Centre. A newcomer is the Traverse Theatre Club, opened in 1962 in James Court in the Lawnmarket in Edinburgh.

The National Operatic and Dramatic Association (N.O.D.A.) was formed in 1899 by a group of amateur societies which felt the need for combined pooling of interests and activities. Its membership has grown to well over a thousand groups, as well as a large number of individuals. Unlike the British Drama League, it is concerned entirely with amateurs and most of its member groups concentrate on the production of opera. It publishes a bulletin three times a year, and a Year Book annually. It also has a library which is particularly rich in musical and operatic items.

Amateur drama need not necessarily be connected with education, but good use can be made of it for educational purposes, not only in schools, where the tradition of organized acting goes back a long way (see, for instance, JESUIT DRAMA), but in connexion with youth centres and church organizations. Under the 1944 Education Act, Local Government Authorities are empowered to provide premises, classes, and other facilities for youth and adult dramatic work.

In 1927 the Carnegie Trust allocated a sum of money for the encouragement of drama in the rural areas of England and Wales. This resulted in the organization of County Drama Committees to arrange lectures, supply teachers, organize groups, and assist with drama in schools. In 1940 a Joint Committee for Drama was set up, grants being administered by the National Council of Social Service, and in 1945 a Standing Conference of Drama Associations was appointed to further the work of the County Drama Committees. It publishes a newsletter and holds an annual conference in London attended by interested persons from the counties and national bodies, who discuss the problems of amateur drama in their field.

The vast number of amateur actors has repercussions on the economics of playwrights, publishers, theatrical costumiers, wig-makers, and such like, as well as providing part of the revenue of the public halls and institutes which they use if they have no theatre of their own. They provide almost the only market for the one-act play today, and also offer a good source of income to writers of full-length plays which suit them and are technically within their scope. They may also provide playwrights for the professional stage with an extra source of revenue when their West-End successes are released for amateur production (see also RELIGIOUS DRAMA).

For the Amateur Theatre in the U.S.A., see UNITED STATES OF AMERICA, 10.

AMBASSADOR THEATRE, NEW YORK, on 49th Street west of Broadway. This opened on 29 Sept. 1921 with *Blossom Time*, under the management of the Shubert brothers. It had a fair measure of success, and was often used by visiting foreign actors, including Moissi in

Reinhardt's production of *Redemption*, Maurice Schwartz playing Sholem Aleichem in Yiddish, the Argentine Players in a number of Spanish plays, and the Abbey Players from Dublin in a repertory of modern Irish plays. For a time the theatre was given over to radio and television, but it later reverted to straight plays, among them *Compulsion* (1957) and *A Passage to India* (1962). GEORGE FREEDLEY†

AMBASSADORS THEATRE, LONDON, a small playhouse in West Street, near St. Martin's Lane, which opened on 5 June 1913 with *Panthea*. It had little success until Cochran took it over a year later and staged a series of intimate revues starring Alice Delysia. From 1919 to 1930 it was in the hands of H. M. Harwood, whose productions included his own very successful *Grain of Mustard Seed* (1920) and, in the same year, Lennox Robinson's fine Irish play, *The White-Headed Boy*. In 1925 O'Neill's *Emperor Jones* occasioned Paul Robeson's first appearance in London. Sydney Carroll took over the theatre in 1932, and under him Vivien Leigh made her successful West End début in *The Mask of Virtue* (1935). A later success was *Spring Meeting* (1938), with the inimitable Margaret Rutherford as Bijou. *The Gate Revue*, transferred from the Gate early in 1939, had a long run, followed by a sequel, *Swinging the Gate*, and, during the Second World War, by Melville's intimate revues, *Sweet and Low*, *Sweeter and Lower*, and *Sweetest and Lowest*. On 25 Nov. 1952 began the record-breaking run of Agatha Christie's *The Mousetrap*, which tied up this charming theatre for many years.

W. MACQUEEN-POPE†, *rev.*

AMBIGU-COMIQUE, THÉÂTRE DE L', PARIS. This was founded by Audinot, as a marionette and children's theatre, in 1769, on the Boulevard du Temple, where it remained until it was destroyed by fire in 1827. It gave all types of entertainments at first, and from 1797 onwards mainly melodrama, by Pixerécourt, Bouchardy, and others. A theatre of the same name, still in use, opened in 1828 to replace the old one, whose site was taken over by the Folies-Dramatiques, and this has since had a long and flourishing career.

AMEIPSIAS, a Greek comic poet of Old Comedy, contemporary and rival of Aristophanes (see GREECE, 2 *b*). His *Revellers* defeated Aristophanes' *Birds* in 414 B.C. One of his plays ridiculed Socrates. Only fragments of his work survive.

AMERICA, NORTH, see CANADA and UNITED STATES OF AMERICA.

AMERICA, SOUTH, see SOUTH AMERICA.

AMERICAN COMPANY, THE, a troupe of professional actors, made up of the remnants of the elder Hallam's company, and a company under David Douglass, with Hallam's widow as their leading lady and his son Lewis as their leading man. The name by which they are usually known was first used in a notice of their presence at Charleston in 1763–4, and they retained it during successive changes of management, John Henry and the younger Hallam succeeding Douglass, and being in turn succeeded by Hodgkinson and Dunlap. The American Company played an important part in the development of early American drama, being the first professional company to produce a play by an American—*The Prince of Parthia*, by Thomas Godfrey. It was also responsible for the production of several plays by Dunlap, who became one of the managers of the company in 1796, and was still with it when it went from the old John Street Theatre to the new Park Theatre, opening there on 28 Feb. 1798. Three years previously, in 1795, the elder Joseph Jefferson, grandfather of the famous actor of the same name, had become a member of the company. He remained with it until 1803. The company's identity was finally lost when, in 1805, Dunlap went bankrupt and retired, the Park Theatre being taken over by Thomas Abthorpe Cooper, who had been a member of the company for some years. The American Company had practically the monopoly of acting in the United States for many years, its only rival being Wignell's company in Philadelphia.

AMERICAN EDUCATIONAL THEATRE ASSOCIATION (A.E.T.A.). This was formed in 1936 (though preliminary efforts had begun two years before) as a branch of the Speech Association of America, largely through the efforts of the late E. C. Mabie of the State University of Iowa, who felt the National Theatre Conference did not sufficiently represent the academic theatre. Since 1950 it has been a separate organization with a board of directors and several thousands of members drawn from the staffs and students of colleges, universities, high schools, community theatres, and libraries all over the United States. It is the official organ of the educational theatre in America, and as such supervises the election of members to the Educational Theatre Panel of the Board of Directors of the American National Theatre and Academy. It also publishes the scholarly quarterly, *Educational Theatre Journal*.

GEORGE FREEDLEY†

AMERICAN MUSEUM, THE, a show-place opened by P. T. Barnum in 1842, which by 1849 had become a theatre with a good stock company and some stars, among them the Bateman children. On 17 June 1850, much enlarged and embellished, it opened with an excellent company in a highly moral play entitled *The Drunkard*, which had a record run for that time. Barnum soon found himself at the head of a reputable theatre, which gave two performances a day, and paid its actors well. He sold it in 1855, but plays were still given there, and in 1860 its former owner, being once more financially stable, was able to buy it back. He continued to present a certain number of plays, but they were gradually ousted by freaks, baby-shows, and boxing contests, until on 13 July 1865 the old Museum was burnt down. Barnum went temporarily to the Winter Garden, and on 6 Sept. opened a new Museum, also on Broadway, with a similar mixture of freaks and plays, and pantomime in the summer. In 1867 Barnum finally withdrew from management, and Van Amburgh took over with his menagerie, though evidently plays were still given occasionally, as it was during a run of *Uncle Tom's Cabin* that on 3 Mar. 1868 the second Museum was burnt to the ground. It was never rebuilt.

AMERICAN NATIONAL THEATRE AND ACADEMY (A.N.T.A.). This organization came into being on 5 July 1935 when President Roosevelt signed the Charter which Congress had just enacted. This important document permits the establishment of a nation-wide, tax-exempt institution which, in the words of its preamble, was to be:

> a people's project, organized and conducted in their interest, free from commercialism, but with the firm intent of being as far as possible self-supporting. A national theatre should bring to the people throughout the country their heritage of the great drama of the past and the best of the present, which has been too frequently unavailable to them under existing conditions.

The Charter was secured by a group of public-spirited citizens who were actuated by enthusiasm for the theatre but were not themselves connected with it. Though authorized by Congress, it carried no government grant; money was to be raised by private subscription as soon as a working plan could be proposed. At about the time the Charter was signed the Federal Theatre was in operation, and it was impractical to raise private funds for a nation-wide theatre at that juncture. The Second World War delayed action still further. After 1945, however, the Board of Directors was reorganized to include leading theatre people and the heads of such organizations as Actors' Equity, the Dramatists' Guild, the craft unions, and such non-professional groups as the National Theatre Conference, the American Educational Theatre Association, and the Theatre Library Association. A membership structure consisting of corporate, individual, and group memberships was set up, and a long-range programme was decided on. It had as its major objective the furthering of the best in the theatre, both professional and non-professional; the fostering of a decentralized theatre, that is to say, the encouragement of professional resident theatres outside New York; and the development of a National Service Department for the country at large. In 1948 it became the United States centre of the International Theatre Institute and later of the International Association of Theatre Technicians. In 1950 it acquired the former Guild Theatre at 245 West 52nd Street as its headquarters and ran it as an experimental theatre for some years. More recently, while retaining its offices in the building, it has leased the theatre as a source of income in order to meet its increasing obligations (see GUILD THEATRE). In 1963, at the request of the directors, Elia Kazan and Robert Whitehead (see LINCOLN CENTER FOR THE PERFORMING ARTS), A.N.T.A. built a temporary theatre on Washington Square, on land lent by the New York University for three years, to house the Lincoln Center repertory company pending the completion of the Vivian Beaumont Theatre. This theatre, which was epoch-making because it was the first legitimate theatre to be built in New York for thirty years, and also because it was the first to have an amphitheatre with sharply raked seats and a thrust stage, was designed by Jo Mielziner, opened on 23 Jan. 1964 with Arthur Miller's *Before the Fall*, and will probably be demolished in 1966.

ROSAMOND GILDER

AMERICAN OPERA HOUSE, NEW YORK, see CHATHAM THEATRE, 1.

AMERICAN THEATRE, NEW YORK, on 42nd Street. This opened on 22 May 1893 with *The Prodigal Daughter*. It had a somewhat chequered career, and in 1908 became a music-hall. It was closed in 1929, but shortly afterwards reopened with burlesque, which remained its staple fare until on 18 Dec. 1930 it was badly damaged by fire. It was finally demolished in 1932.

Burton's first theatre (see CHAMBERS STREET) was called the American for a season under Davenport in 1857. For the American Theatre, Bowery, see BOWERY THEATRE, 1.

AMERICAN THEATRICAL COMMONWEALTH COMPANY, see LUDLOW, NOAH, and SMITH, SOL.

AMES, WINTHROP (1871–1937), American theatre director, who used the money inherited from his father, a railroad capitalist, to back non-commercial ventures in the theatre. In 1904 he took over the Castle Square Theatre, Boston, and later made a gallant but unsuccessful attempt to establish a true repertory theatre in New York, at the New Theatre, and finally at the Little and Booth Theatres, both of which he built. Among his productions were a number of Shakespeare plays and other classics, some revivals of Gilbert and Sullivan, and such modern plays as *Prunella*, *The Betrothal*, *Old English*, and *Will Shakespeare*. In 1914 Ames offered a prize of 10,000 dollars for the best play by an American, which was won by *Children of Earth*. This was produced in the following year, but was not very successful, since the author, Alice Brown, was, according to Quinn, 'a novelist rather than a playwright'. Ames did good work for the American theatre over a long period of years, and retired in 1932.

AMPHITHEATRE (AMPHITHEATRUM), a peculiarly Roman type of building of elliptical shape, consisting of tiers of seats completely enclosing a central arena for the exhibition of combats of gladiators and wild beasts and of sea-fights. The amphitheatre was not intended for dramatic performances, which in ancient theatres were always given in front of a permanent back-scene; in outline, however, it might be called a 'double theatre', a fact which perhaps explains the fantastic account by the elder Pliny of an amphitheatre built by Curio in 50 B.C. which consisted of two revolving theatres placed back to back so as to form separate theatres, but capable of being turned (spectators and all) on their central pivots so as to meet along their straight edges and form a single amphitheatre. Pliny's account may have arisen from some attempt to explain the shape of the amphitheatre, but it is impossible to reconcile with geometry and presents hopeless problems of engineering. Probably the first amphitheatre was that built by Julius Caesar in 46 B.C. The most famous amphitheatre was the Colosseum in Rome, completed in A.D. 80, which was said to be capable of seating 87,000 spectators, and is still extant. WILLIAM BEARE†

For the Amphitheatre in London, see CONNAUGHT THEATRE; in New York, CHATHAM THEATRE, 1.

ANCEY, GEORGES [really GEORGES DE CURNIEU] (1860–1926), French dramatist, and one of the best of the naturalistic writers who followed in the steps of Henri Becque. His plays, which were produced by Antoine at the Théâtre Libre, were even franker than Becque's, but they were popular in their time. The best of them were *Les Inséparables*, in which two friends share the same mistress, and *L'École des veufs* (both 1889), in which a father and son find themselves in the same position. Ancey's plays went out of fashion with the decline of naturalism and have not been revived.

ANDERSON, JUDITH (1898–   ), American actress, born and educated in Australia, where she made her first appearance at Sydney in 1915. Three years later she was in New York, playing small parts in stock there and in other American cities. Her first outstanding success was made as Elise in *Cobra* (at the Hudson Theatre, N.Y., 1924), with which she toured Australia, returning to New York to play in *As You Desire Me* and *Mourning Becomes Electra*. In 1936 she played the Queen to John Gielgud's Hamlet in New York, and a year later made her first appearance in London, where she gave an outstanding performance as Lady Macbeth with Laurence Olivier at the Old Vic. In 1947 she electrified New York with a superb rendering of the name-part in *Medea*, in a new adaptation prepared by Robinson Jeffers and produced by John Gielgud. Rosamond Gilder in *Theatre Arts* said of her:

> Her Medea is pure evil, dark, dangerous, cruel, raging, ruthless. From beginning to end she maintains an almost incredible intensity, yet she varies her moods so constantly, she moves with such skill through unexplored regions of pain and despair that she can hold her audience in suspense throughout the evening.

She was seen again at the Old Vic in 1960, as Madame Arkadina in *The Seagull*. In the Birthday Honours of the same year she was appointed D.B.E. for her services to the stage.

ANDERSON, MARY (1859–1940), an American actress of great charm and beauty, who made her first appearance at the age of 16 at Louisville, playing Juliet. She toured the United States for some years in a wide variety of parts, being much admired as Julia in *The Hunchback*, as Pauline in *The Lady of Lyons*, and as Parthenia in *Ingomar*. It was in this last part that she made her first appearance in London, at the Lyceum in 1883. In 1885 she was seen at Stratford-upon-Avon as Rosalind, one of her best parts, and in 1887 appeared at the Lyceum in *The Winter's Tale*, in which she was the first actress to double the parts of Perdita and Hermione. She appeared in several plays by W. S. Gilbert, *Comedy and Tragedy* (1884) being specially written for her. She retired in 1889, and was not seen again on the professional stage, though during the First World War she appeared at some charity matinées, notably as Juliet in the Balcony Scene. In 1890 she married Antonio de Navarro, and settled at Broadway in Worcestershire, where she died. She was the author of *A Few Memories* (1896) and *A Few More Memories* (1936), and part-author of the play based on Hichens's *Garden of Allah*.

ANDERSON, MAXWELL (1888–1959), American dramatist, who received his early schooling in various States and, after graduating from the University of North Dakota in 1911, taught at a college for a short time and worked on three newspapers. His first-produced play was *White Desert* (1923), a failure in the theatre. Written partly in verse, it is a tragic study of a lonely woman on a farm. *What Price Glory?* (1924), written with Laurence Stallings, was a great popular hit, which portrayed realistically and sympathetically the common American soldier in action during the First World War. There followed two historical plays, also written with Stallings; then came *Saturday's Children* (1927), by Anderson alone—a mature 'serious comedy', dealing with the problem of marriage as it affects two young people. This was an outstanding popular success. Following this were a dramatization of a book about tramp life, and (with Harold Hickerson) the passionately-written thesis-play, *Gods of the Lightning* (1928), neither of which was a success in the theatre. Another realistic play of modern city life, *Gypsy* (1929), preceded a series of historical and pseudo-historical plays, idealistic in conception and on the whole effectively poetic in language. The best of these were *Elizabeth the Queen* (1930), *Night Over Taos* (1932), *Mary of Scotland* (1933), *Valley Forge* (1934), and *The Wingless Victory* (1936). But Anderson was never content to follow any one dramatic or artistic formula, and he varied his themes and styles to conform with his aims as thinker and practical playwright intent upon providing entertainment for the public. His realistic satires on political subjects and the problems of man trying to adjust himself to a modern world are among his most effective works. This is especially true of *Both Your Houses* (1933), a savage attack on political corruption which was awarded a Pulitzer Prize. He combined poetic drama with formal verse, philosophy, and political commentary, in several other plays, notably *High Tor* (1936), *The Masque of Kings* (1937) (two of his best plays), *Knickerbocker Holiday* (1938), and *Key Largo* (1939). In *Winterset* (1935), a mood piece and a study in conscience—among other things—the author sought, as he said in his preface, 'to make tragic poetry out of the stuff' of his own times. He always held that without great poetry there is no great drama. 'If we are going to have a great theater in this country somebody has to write verse, even if it is written badly.' Among his later plays were *The Eve of St. Mark* (1942), *Storm Operation* (1944), *Truckline Cafe* and *Joan of Lorraine* (both 1946), *Anne of the Thousand Days* (1948), and *The Bad Seed* (1954, London 1955). Though Anderson was loth to make public his ideas on art and life during the earlier part of his career, he later wrote and spoke at length about poetry in the theatre, and in 1929 he collected and printed a number of articles as *The Essence of Tragedy and other Footnotes.* In spite of a growing concern over the problems of contemporary civilization and his lifelong pre-occupation with poetic form, he remained a man of the theatre, a conscientious workman who knew that the theatre is basically a medium of inspiration and entertainment.

BARRETT H. CLARK†, *rev.*

ANDREINI. (1) FRANCESCO (1548–1624), one of the outstanding actors and authors of the *commedia dell'arte.* He was originally a soldier, and was captured by the Turks, spending several years in slavery. He was famous chiefly as Captain Spavento, and evidence of the way in which he played this part may be seen in the *Bravure del Capitano Spavento* (1607). Before he made the mask of the Captain his own, Andreini seems to have played a lover's part. He was one of the leaders of the Gelosi, with whom he went to Paris in 1600. He married in 1578 (2) ISABELLA CANALI (1562–1604), one of the most famous actresses of her time, unreservedly praised in many contemporary documents. She was the leading lady of the Gelosi, and went with her husband to France, dying in childbirth on the return journey. She had seven children, of whom the most famous was (3) GIOVANN BATTISTA (*c.* 1578–1654), known as Lelio. He was a great actor, very popular in France, and appeared mainly with the Fedeli company. He was also a prolific author. He was twice married, in 1601 to (4) VIRGINIA RAMPONI (1583–*c.* 1627/30), who acted with him in the Fedeli company as Florinda, and after her death to (5) VIRGINIA ROTARI, also an actress, known as Lidia.

ANDREYEV, LEONID NIKOLAIVICH (1871–1919), Russian dramatist, who graduated in the Faculty of Law in the Moscow and St. Petersburg Universities, and became a journalist on a Moscow paper. A short story published in 1897 attracted the attention of Gorky and started Andreyev on the road to success. In his early days he was attracted to the Revolutionary movement, but he drifted away, and after the October Revolution emigrated to Finland, where he died. His plays, which express the deterioration and bitterness of the period between 1905 and 1917, fall into two groups, realistic and symbolic, of which the latter are the most important. Among them are *The Sabine Women* (1911), a satire on political compromise, *The Life of Man* (1906), *The Seven Who Were Hanged* (1908), and the theatrically effective *He Who Gets Slapped* (1914), which has been produced in England and America. Himself a man who had lost his way, his work is permeated with a bitter pessimism, as of a lost soul wandering in a cruel and unpredictable world. This may be the reason for the total eclipse of all his plays, with the exception of *He Who Gets Slapped.*

ANDRONICUS, LUCIUS LIVIUS (*c.* 284–204 B.C.), founded Latin drama in 240 B.C. by producing at Rome the first Latin version of a Greek play. The only other known date in his career is 207 B.C., when he composed the state hymn celebrating the victory of the Metaurus. His name shows that he was a Greek, probably from southern Italy, who had become a dependent of the Livian *gens.* Up to his time the Roman stage seems to have known only a formless medley of dance, song, and buffoonery. The introduction of plays with a regular plot was successful, and Andronicus continued to translate and produce pieces taken from Greek tragedy and New Comedy until his death. His importance is as a pioneer; Cicero pronounced his plays unworthy of a second reading, and the fragments of his dramas and his translation of the *Odyssey* which have come down to us indicate that his style was uncouth. Nevertheless later Roman dramatists continued to work on his lines and to use the metres which, so far as we know, he was the first to employ.

WILLIAM BEARE†

ANDZHAPARIDZE, VERA IULIANOVNA (1900–   ), Georgian actress, born in Kutaissi, the daughter of a notary there. After studying in Tbilisi she went to the Rusthavelli Theatre from 1920 to 1926, and then worked in a number of other theatres, among them the Moscow Realistic Theatre, where she played the title-role in Gorky's *Mother* in 1932. From 1957 to 1959 she was the director of the Mardzhanishvilli Theatre in Tbilisi, where she gave a fine performance as the Grandmother in Kasson's *The Trees Die Standing.* Among her other outstanding parts are Cleopatra and Marguerite Gauthier. Regarded as one of the founders of the modern Georgian theatre, she has a vivid creative individuality, and even in tragic and dramatic parts can express a delicate lyricism. BEATRICE KING

ANGEL, EDWARD (*fl.* 1660–73), Restoration actor who is referred to in Wycherley's *The Gentleman Dancing-Master* (1671), where Hippolita says: 'Angel is a good fool.' He was first with Rhodes at the Cockpit, and later joined Davenant at Dorset Garden, where he paired excellently with that great comedian, Nokes. Angel specialized in parts of low comedy, particularly French valets. He is not heard of after 1673.

ANGLIN, MARGARET (1876–1958), American actress, accounted one of the finest of her day. Born and educated in Canada, she was a pupil at the Empire Dramatic School, New York, when Charles Frohman engaged her for *Shenandoah*, in which she made her first professional appearance in 1894. After touring with James O'Neill, Sothern, and others, she made her first outstanding success as Roxane in Mansfield's production of *Cyrano de Bergerac* (1898). She was later leading lady of Frohman's stock company at the Empire, where she remained for several years, appearing in a wide variety of plays, including *Mrs. Dane's Defence, Diplomacy,* and *The Importance of Being Earnest.* Among her later successes were *The Devil's Disciple* and *Camille,* in which she appeared with Henry Miller; Moody's *The Great Divide*, both under that title and in its original form as *The Sabine Woman*; new translations of *Antigone* and *Hippolytus, Iphigenia in Tauris* and *Medea, Electra* and *Iphigenia in Aulis*; and such Shakespearian parts as Viola, Rosalind, and Cleopatra, all of which she played on tour. In later years she was excellent as Mrs. Malaprop.

ANGUS, ROBERT, see AGGAS, ROBERT.

ANNAPOLIS, one of the earliest towns in America to welcome the players, and one regularly visited by the companies of Hallam and Douglass. They had at first to adapt an existing building for their shows, as Douglass did in 1759, when he produced *The Orphan* and *Venice Preserved*, but in 1771 he built a brick theatre holding 600 persons, in which a number of plays were given, including *Cymbeline*. The first permanent modern theatre was built in 1831.

ANNUNZIO, GABRIELE D', see D'ANNUNZIO.

ANOUILH, JEAN (1910–), French dramatist, whose first play to be staged was *L'Hermine*, produced by Lugné-Poë in 1932. Two earlier plays, *Humulus le Muet* and *Attila le Magnifique*, remain unperformed, but a third, *Mandarine*, was presented by Jouvet in 1933. *Y'avait un Prisonnier* followed in 1935, after which Pitoeff's productions of *Le Voyageur sans bagage* (1937) (*Traveller Without Luggage*) and *La Sauvage* (1938) (*The Restless Heart*) became the first in a long list of highly successful plays, as popular abroad as in France. *Le Bal des voleurs* (1938) (*Thieves' Carnival*) inaugurated a fruitful collaboration with André Barsacq as producer, which included *Le Rendez-vous de Senlis* (1941) (*Dinner With the Family*), *Eurydice* (1942) (*Point of Departure*), *Antigone* (1944), *Roméo et Jeannette* (1946) (*Fading Mansions*), *L'Invitation au Château* (1947) (*Ring Round the Moon*), and *Colombe* (1951). The recurring theme in these plays is the quest for purity, frustrated either by a moral flaw in the central character's own nature, or by the degradation of the society in which he lives. Anouilh has classified the plays in two groups: 'Pièces roses', in which the theme is presented with dazzling wit and comedy, and 'Pièces noires', in which it is presented with a bitter eye for sordid detail. A certain superficiality of thought, whereby awkward questions are raised only to be arbitrarily resolved in a *coup de théâtre*, is ably concealed by Anouilh's magnificent stagecraft and sense of the theatre. In 1948 he struck a deeper vein with *Ardèle*, first of the 'Pièces grinçantes'. Here, and in *La Valse des Toréadors* (1952) (*The Waltz of the Toreadors*), his gift for character and social observation dominated his theatricality to produce genuinely acid satires. His latest work, from *L'Alouette* (1953) (*The Lark*) to *La Grotte* (1961), while retaining its technical mastery, has tended increasingly and disappointingly to compromise in order to provide the conventional entertainment required by the boulevard theatres, whether in the superficial historical drama of *L'Alouette* and *Becket* (1959), or in the reactionary comedy-drama of *Ornifle* (1955), *Pauvre Bitos* (1956), and *L'Hurluberlu* (1959). In 1963 *Pauvre Bitos*, in an English translation, was given a successful production in London with Donald Pleasence as Bitos. T. C. C. MILNE

ANSKY [SOLOMON RAPPOPORT] (1863–1920), Jewish ethnologist and man of letters, whose researches into folk-lore in Russia, Paris, and Central Europe resulted in the writing of his one well-known play, *The Dybbuk, or Between Two Worlds*, a study of demoniac possession and the Hassidic doctrine of pre-ordained relationship. It is more folk-lore than drama, and owes much of its renown to the manner of its production, first in Yiddish by David Hermann for the Vilna Troupe in 1920, and two years later in Hebrew by Vakhtangov for the Moscow Habima company. It has also been played in Yiddish by Maurice Schwartz in New York, in London in Hebrew by Habima and in Yiddish by the Vilna Troupe and the New Yiddish Theatre. Ansky was also the author of an unfinished play, again Hassidic in theme, and of a satirical poem on the popular conception of Heaven and Hell. He was keenly interested in politics, but after the purge consequent on the attempted assassination of Lenin in 1918 he retired to Vilna, where he died. E. HARRIS

A.N.T.A., see AMERICAN NATIONAL THEATRE AND ACADEMY; for A.N.T.A. THEATRE, see GUILD THEATRE.

ANTHONY STREET THEATRE, NEW YORK. This famous theatre, in which Edmund Kean first appeared in New York in a succession of fine parts, was originally a circus, and in 1812 was opened as the Olympic Theatre by a company from Philadelphia, headed by Mrs. Melmoth and Twaits, after some delay caused by a carriage accident in which the leading lady broke her arm. Among the plays, interspersed with circus turns, which were given during this season was the famous equestrian melodrama *Timour the Tartar*, then seen for the first time in the United States. In 1813 Twaits again opened the theatre, redecorated and enlarged and renamed the Anthony Street Theatre, with a passable company which included the young Placides and a Mrs. Beaumont, who was excellent in tragedy. This group survived until 1814, when the theatre passed through various hands and was named successively the Commonwealth and the Pavilion, opening only for the summer. After the destruction by fire of the Park Theatre in May 1820 its company moved to the Anthony Street Theatre, which soon proved too small to hold the crowds that flocked to see Kean. He made his first appearance there as guest-artist on 29 Nov. 1820, as Richard III. When the Park Theatre was rebuilt the company moved back, and the Anthony Street Theatre closed.

ANTI-MASQUE, see JONSON and MASQUE.

ANTOINE, ANDRÉ (1858–1943), French actor, producer, and manager, and one of the outstanding figures in the theatrical reforms of the late nineteenth century. In 1887, while working for the Paris Gas Company and employing his leisure hours in amateur acting, he founded the Théâtre Libre for the production of the new naturalistic drama then coming to the fore in Europe. Here he produced in 1890 Ibsen's *Ghosts*, playing Oswald himself, and followed it with plays by Hauptmann, Strindberg, Bjørnsen, Verga, de Curel, Becque, Brieux, and Porto-Riche. Here, too, he revolutionized French acting and inaugurated a new era of scenic design. Inspired by him Otto Brahm founded the Freie Bühne in Berlin, and Grein the Independent Theatre in London. In 1894 Antoine's first venture failed financially, though it had had an immense cultural value, and in 1897, after working at the Odéon for a while, he took over the Théâtre des Menus-Plaisirs, and, renaming it the Théâtre Antoine, made it a rallying-point for young and aspiring dramatists. From 1906 to 1914 Antoine was director of the Odéon, retiring from active work in the theatre at the end of that period. His influence, not only in France, but all over Europe and in America, has been incalculable, and he helped more than anyone to deliver Europe from the domination of the 'well-made' play and to establish the reputation of Ibsen and his followers in France. Among the outstanding figures of the next generation who owed much to him was Jacques Copeau, founder of the Vieux-Colombier.

ANZENGRUBER, LUDWIG (1839–89), Austrian actor and dramatist. He was for some years a strolling player, and his first plays were written in dialect. They dealt with problems of the ordinary man, particularly of the peasants, though his *Der Pfarrer von Kirchfeld* (1870) is a plea for the exercise of a tolerant religious spirit. He also proved in his *Der Meineidbauer* (1871), where the figure of the old farmer who has cheated two orphans of their heritage assumes demonic stature, that peasant life can furnish matter for true tragedy. A comic battle for matrimonial supremacy, with a vague background of clerical dissension, is exploited in *Die Kreuzlschreiber* (1872), where a number of peasants are induced to append their signatures—in the form of crosses—to a document much resented by the village priest. Egged on by the latter and by a vagrant wag—a figure dear to this dramatist—who engineers the whole affair for his own amusement, the wives shut out their husbands, and induce them to embark on a penitentiary pilgrimage to Rome. When they find out that, in addition to taking the family purse, the men are to be accompanied by a train of virgins, the wives change their minds and each firmly leads home her erring husband.

Continuing the vein of rustic humour, *Der Doppelselbstmord* (1875) is a farcical village version of *Romeo and Juliet*. Anzengruber's last play was *Das vierte Gebot* (1877), in which he deserts his rural solitudes for the teeming life of the city, proving himself, however, as rugged a realist in one place as in the other. Eventually his unselfconscious humanity went out of favour, and his popularity waned; but he holds an important place in theatre history as the first to bring realistic peasant life on to the modern Austrian stage.

APOLLO THEATRE. 1. LONDON, in Shaftesbury Avenue. This opened on 21 Feb. 1901, under the management of Henry Lowenfeld. Its first production, *The Belle of Bohemia*, was a failure. Then Martin-Harvey took two of his assured successes, *The Cigarette Maker's Romance* and *The Only Way*, there, and in Sept. 1901 George Edwardes produced a musical version of *Kitty Grey* (previously played as a comedy at the Vaudeville) which, with Evie Greene, Edna May, Maurice Farkoa, and G.P. Huntley in the cast, was an immediate success and ran for 220 performances. *The Girl from Kays*, in the following year, under the same management, ran for 432 performances. The Apollo, although never the permanent home of a great management, has been a consistently successful theatre. It is well situated and the right size for either musical or straight plays. The Pélissier Follies were staged there, each season exceeding 500 performances, and from 1934 to 1937 Marion Lorne starred there in plays written by her husband Walter Hackett. During the Munich crisis Sherwood's *Idiot's Delight* (1938) had a great success. Among later productions were *The Light of Heart* (1940), *Old Acquaintance* (1941), and Rattigan's

Flare Path, which ran for 670 performances between 1942 and 1944. Other long runs were achieved by *Seagulls over Sorrento* (1950) and *Duel of Angels* (1958). In 1955 there was an interesting production of Giraudoux's *Tiger at the Gates*, with Michael Redgrave as Hector.

W. MACQUEEN-POPE†, *rev.*

2. NEW YORK, on 42nd Street, between 7th and 8th Avenues. It opened as the Bryant in 1910, for films and vaudeville acts, and was renamed the Apollo on 17 Nov. 1920. One of its early productions was Hopkins's revival of *Macbeth* in 1921, with a notable cast headed by Lionel Barrymore, and triangular settings by Robert Edmond Jones. A series of musical comedies followed, and for many years the house was occupied by *George White's Scandals*. It became a cinema again in 1933.

The 3rd Avenue Variety Theatre was known as the Apollo for a short time in 1885, when it opened on 5 Jan. with plays in German, as were a mixed film and stage playhouse, on Chuter Street, New York, which opened in Oct. 1926, and a burlesque house on 125th Street.

APOLLODORUS, of Carystos, a Greek comic poet of New Comedy (see GREECE, 2 *b*), of whose works only a few fragments remain. Terence modelled his *Phormio* and *Hecyra* on plays by this author.

APPIA, ADOLPHE (1862–1928), Swiss scenic designer, whose theories on the use of light in stage production govern much of the best modern work in this medium (see LIGHTING, 1 *d* and SCENERY, 6; also No. 97).

APRON STAGE, see FORESTAGE.

AQUARIUM THEATRE, LONDON. The Royal Aquarium and Winter Garden, Westminster, built as an exhibition and amusement palace in 1876, on the site of the old Westminster Theatre, once a plague pit, had an annexe which was called the Aquarium (also the Afternoon) Theatre. It soon became a regular theatre, and Labouchère seems to have had a hand in its management, as did Edgar Bruce. Jennie Lee appeared there as Jo in *Bleak House* with great success. Jennie Hill, later a variety star, appeared as a child in one of J. A. Cave's pantomimes there, in which she played the hind legs of an animal; the framework gave way, leaving her stranded on the stage. In 1878 Phelps made his last appearance on any stage at the Aquarium, breaking down in Wolsey's farewell speech, and being carried off, never to appear again. He died in the same year. The theatre was then under the management of Marie Litton. In Apr.–May 1879 the Vokes family appeared in sketches and the theatre was renamed the Imperial. Miss Litton, afterwards Mrs. Wybrow Robertson, did some excellent productions there with fine casts. In 1880 a Dutch company from Rotterdam made a success in *Anne Mie*, and two years later Mrs. Langtry appeared in *An Unequal Match* and as Rosalind. In 1885 the theatre closed. Mrs. Langtry took it over, rebuilt it lavishly on the model of a Greek temple in marble and gilt, and opened it in April 1900 with *The Queen's Necklace*, but without success. Neither Herbert Waring, who followed her, nor Ellen Terry, who in 1903 produced Ibsen's *The Vikings* there, fared better, though Ellen Terry herself appeared in the latter play and her son Gordon Craig was responsible for the production, scenery, and lighting. In Nov. 1903 Lewis Waller became actor-manager of the theatre, and did better than the former tenants, opening with a revival of *Monsieur Beaucaire*, followed by an English version of Hugo's *Ruy Blas*, which was a failure in spite of Mrs. Patrick Campbell. *Brigadier Gerard* was his greatest success during his three years' tenancy. Mrs. Langtry eventually disposed of the theatre to the Wesleyan Methodists, and on its site the Central Hall, Westminster, now stands. The theatre was pulled down in 1908, and taken away to Canning Town to be re-erected as a cinema.

W. MACQUEEN-POPE†

AQUATIC DRAMA, see CIRCUS and SADLER'S WELLS.

ARBUZOV, ALEKSEI NIKOLAYEVICH (1908–), Soviet dramatist, born in Moscow, whose first play, *Class*, was produced in 1930. This was followed by a number of other plays, including *Tanya* (1939), the story of a woman struggling to overcome her bourgeois limitations which has found a permanent place in the Soviet repertory. Arbuzov's plays in general are characterized by sharp vital conflicts and psychological complexity. In 1941, together with V. P. Pluchek, he organized in Moscow a Youth Theatre—the Arbuzov Studio—where he supervised the writing and production of plays, notably of his own *City at Dawn* (1940) in a revised version. Among his later plays are *European Chronicle* (1953), *Years of Wandering* (1954), and *Endless Distance* (1957). The last-named has been seen at a number of theatres since its first production. *The Irkutsk Story* (1960), first produced by Tovstonogov at the Gorky Bolshoi Theatre, Leningrad, further enhanced his reputation.

BEATRICE KING†

ARCH STREET THEATRE, see DREW 1. and PHILADELPHIA.

ARCHER, WILLIAM (1856–1924), a Scottish journalist who became a London dramatic critic and brought to his work what H. G. Wells called 'unscrupulous integrity'. He worked first on the staff of the *Edinburgh Evening News* and then, in 1878, settled in London. He became dramatic critic successively to *Figaro*, the *World*, the *Tribune*, and the *Nation*. Archer took the theatre seriously as an art and helped to bring in the 'new drama' of the 1890s by his translations of the plays of Ibsen, whose collected works he edited in 1906–8. He had an astringent sense of humour which was probably responsible for his long friendship with Bernard Shaw, and, like Shaw, he was antagonistic to Irving who, he maintained, had done nothing for the modern British dramatist. Archer claimed that the drama of his day was at least as fine a product of the human spirit as the Elizabethan drama—Shakespeare only apart—and that it was incomparably superior technically, intellectually, and morally, to the drama of the Restoration. He was always protesting at the critical overvaluation of ancient drama and the undervaluation of the modern, and, being more interested in drama as an intellectual product than as a vehicle for acting, he tried always to uphold the supremacy of the author's script, which he considered was being too often used merely as a working basis for the actor's display of technique.

His publications included editions of the dramatic essays of Leigh Hunt and Hazlitt, *English Dramatists of Today* (1882), *Henry Irving* (1883), *Masks or Faces* (1888), *William Charles Macready* (1890), *Study and Stage* (1899), *America Today* (1900), *The Old Drama and the New* (1923), and, with Granville-Barker, *A National Theatre: Scheme and Estimates* (1907). His dramatic criticisms in the *World*, from 1893 to 1897, were reissued in annual volumes as *The Theatrical World*. In 1923 his play, *The Green Goddess*, was produced at the St. James's Theatre. This improbable melodrama ran for 416 performances and has since been filmed. T. C. KEMP†, *rev.*

ARCHITECTURE, THEATRE. All architecture is essentially the organization of space, and theatre architecture is the organization of the spaces needed to contain the basic relationships of actor/background and actor/audience. From the beginning these have been in a constant state of flux, but no matter where the theatrical experience takes place, whether in an open-air enclosure or in a closed building, the spaces which are physically contained constitute theatre architecture.

Although theatre architecture is the result of a theatrical manifestation, it becomes itself, once translated into terms of building, an important influence. By its solidity and technical limitations, the building which has evolved from drama subsequently disciplines and inhibits the drama it contains. This may in part account for the fact that the theatre is invariably a few paces behind intellectual developments in the other arts.

Though there have been tendencies common to the whole of Western theatre, the interpretation of these tendencies has varied from place to place, even in such periods as the Baroque, or in the nineteenth century, when certain major influences were predominant. The emphasis has often been on different facets in different countries. Chronological overlapping, too, has created some confusion. Theatre buildings have a long life, and theatres of various designs may all be in use at one and the same time. This is particularly true of the present day. The curtain does not descend firmly on one period to rise again miraculously to reveal another. Then again it must be remembered that in the theatre, and therefore in its architecture, there have always been two lines of development—the popular and the formal—sometimes converging, but more often existing separately side by side, though through juxtaposition each may contain elements of the other. The first gave rise to the temporary, or semi-permanent, booth of the ambulant actor, which in its later development was responsible, among other things, for the Elizabethan theatre building, while the second—the theatre of authority—expressed itself in such elaborate, solid, and highly formalized buildings as the Teatro Olimpico or the Paris Opéra.

1. GREECE. Greek civic building is best compared to sculpture. The temple is, as it were, carved out of a single block of marble, and the theatre is sculpted out of a hillside with, in its developed state, the circular 'orchestra' as the pivot of the architectural composition. It has been suggested that its level surface and circular shape come from the form of the threshing-floor, still common in Greece. This theory is, however, rejected by some scholars, who believe that the somewhat undefined and flattened ellipse of the small provincial theatre in Thorikos, with its practically rectangular orchestra, shows the earliest form, and that the circular orchestra of the classical period was a later stylized development. It has the added advantage of being beautiful in itself, and the practical merit of giving the maximum number of spectators a good view of the action taking place within it.

Although later Greek theatres were built within the precincts of the temple of Dionysus, and were intended to hold the entire population of the town, it is possible that when Thespis was first invited to Athens by Pisistratus in 534 B.C. he played in the Agora, with the spectators seated on raised wooden benches. There are even references to the collapse of these benches in 498 B.C. The sacred precinct of Dionysus on the south slope of the Acropolis was probably dedicated in the mid-sixth century. When the City Dionysia was moved there, the spectators still sat on wooden benches perched up the slopes of the hill, with the overflow on its rocks and scrubble. This arrangement was, after many alterations and additions, interpreted in stone when the theatre was reconstructed in 338–326 B.C. by Lycurgus, at the time when Polycleitus was building the theatre at Epidaurus, considered, even in antiquity, to be the most perfect of all Greek theatres (see No. 1). But by the time these great stone theatres, which we now think of as typically Greek, were built, the plays of the great dramatists were already classics—*Plutus*, the last play of the youngest of them, Aristophanes, was produced in 388 B.C., fifty years earlier. The plays of Aeschylus, Sophocles, Euripides, and Aristophanes had been first produced in a makeshift theatre, the *theatron*, or 'seeing-place', which had no stage, and where actors and chorus appeared on the flat orchestra in front of the *skênê*, a temporary structure consisting of two *paraskênia*, or projecting pavilions, erected on each side of an equally temporary *skênothêkê*, or hall, used as a store-house and dressing-room. At first this *skênê* was outside the circle of the orchestra, and provided merely a decorative background to the action. But as the actors became more important and the chorus dwindled, the *skênê* grew in size, and was transformed into a permanent stone structure, probably in about 420 B.C. Between the *skênê* and the *theatron* were the *parodoi*, the entrances for the audience (used also by the actors when necessary), who streamed in across the orchestra and up flights of steps to their seats arranged in wedge-shaped blocks up the hillside.

Lycurgus had barely completed his reconstruction of the theatre when new ideas became fashionable. Hellenistic Greece lost its enthusiasm for tragedy, and became devoted to New Comedy. Characterization and the art of acting reigned supreme. The actor had to be 'presented', and not merely accepted as part of the cosmos. This led, from about the beginning of the third century B.C., to the development of the raised stage, or *logeion*. The *skênê* is now closer to the audience, the orchestra has diminished in size, and the *paraskênia* have been converted into ramps leading up to the stage, built over a colonnade, the *proskênion* (whence our word proscenium). It is possible that the first of such raised stages was that built at Priene (see No. 2), and traces of the ramps leading up to them have been discerned elsewhere. Forming a background to the stage were a number of large openings—*thyromata*—separated by rectangular piers carrying a pitched tile roof. The whole structure made a stage-house of great splendour with various opportunities for scene-changing.

2. ROME. Just as Greek architecture is inherently sculpture, with a traditional timber construction translated and treated sculpturally in stone, so Roman architecture is engineering. The Romans invented mass-concrete, and inherited from the Etruscans the use of vaulting. By a combination of these elements they were able to prise the Hellenistic theatre from its protective hillside and, by the excellence of their engineering, build it anywhere they chose. Previously the characteristics of each hillside and the mood of each city-state had dictated the shape of each theatre; no two were exactly alike. The Romans, however, were structurally able to choose their sites, and they methodically provided each major city of the Empire with a theatre, evolving an almost uniform type which could be speedily designed to mathematical formulae. Vitruvius (*fl. c.* 70–15 B.C.), in his *De Architectura*, was able to give rule-of-thumb directions for building a Roman theatre far more easily than for a Greek/Hellenistic one. In any case the latter were now seldom built. Many of the older buildings were being modernized in the Roman style—the Theatre of Dionysus in Athens in A.D. 61–66; that at Ephesus in A.D. 44; that at Corinth in A.D. 50—while new buildings were constructed on the Roman model—the Theatre of Marcellus, in Rome, in 11 B.C., Orange and Leptis Magna (see No. 8) some twelve years later; Timgad, Sabratha, Aspendus, the Herodes Atticus in Athens, all in the second century A.D. These theatres are still in a splendid state of preservation, and are used today for festival performances.

Although all these Roman theatres are similar in design, the pattern naturally took several hundred years to develop. And since the circus, the chariot-race, and the gladiatorial contest were the main amusements of the people, the circus building was the first to be permanently erected for public entertainment (see AMPHITHEATRE). The early theatres of Rome, like those of Greece, were of wood, and no trace of them remains. Like the scaffoldings of seats erected for the first performances of Etruscan singers and dancers in Rome in 364 B.C., they were probably removed after the performances. But each successive theatre seems to have been more elaborate than the last, fantastic with gold inlays and painted decorations. One of 58 B.C. was reputed to seat 80,000 spectators, and had a splendid three-storey *scaenae frons*, or decorated stage-wall, of marble, glass mosaic, and gilded wood. These wooden theatres were probably designed in the transitional style of *c.* 100 B.C., the Graeco-Roman, like Segesta, Tyndaris, and the earlier version of the large Pompeian theatre, with an auditorium still horseshoe-shaped, and loosely tied to a fanciful *scaenae frons*. The raised stage was never more than 5 feet high, and was separated from the auditorium by a curtain descending into a trough. It may have developed from the *phlyakes* stage of the Italian 'popular comedy' of Magna Graecia, a type differing markedly from that of Athens, and which is known to us almost entirely through a large number of extant vase paintings (see No. 12; also PHLYAX).

The first permanent theatre in Rome was built by Pompey in 55 B.C. The Roman pattern was now fully established, and for the first time the auditorium was a full semicircle reaching round and enclosing the extravagantly adorned *scaenae frons* in one structural entity (but see also VERULAMIUM). The later Theatre of Marcellus, referred to above, is particularly important because of its colonnaded exterior, expressive of its inner construction and usage. The handling of solid and void created a style, and a type, which has influenced the façade of the theatre building from the Renaissance until the present day.

3. MEDIEVAL. Although scholars now believe that the advent of Christianity, and the fall of Rome in A.D. 476, did not bring the theatre to a sudden halt, our knowledge of the period is virtually non-existent. Some of the Roman theatres remained in use, and Theodoric the Great (454–526), who ruled Italy from 493 until his death, reconstructed one in Rome, saying that it was a good way of distracting the conquered Romans, and persuading them to accept German domination.

Performances in Constantinople are recorded as late as the seventh century A.D. (see BYZANTINE THEATRE), and doubtless the popular booth-theatres, the descendants of the *phlyakes* stage, continued throughout the period. Illustrations from the late Middle Ages are so like those which we have from the fourth century B.C. that it would be churlish not to accept a continuous tradition. It was, however, the Church which brought back the formal theatre of authority (see LITURGICAL DRAMA), and it is fitting that theatrical expression and innovation should have taken place within the church building, where the technics of the performances were often of immense complexity. Special stages were erected, and complicated machines were invented which enabled the scenes of the Passion, and particularly of the Ascension and of Christ in Glory, to be presented in a manner which may be said to vie with many of the extravagances of Victorian pantomime. The architect Filippo Brunelleschi (1377–1446) was extremely successful in this direction.

The presentation and arrangement of the earliest liturgical plays had been dictated by the plan of the church itself. At the east end was the Crucifix with Heaven on its right and Hell on its left. The various places of performance demanded by the action of the play, the 'mansions', were arranged down the nave of the church, and the audience was ambulant: an arrangement which Professor Nagler calls 'polyscenic with mansions in juxtaposition'. When the drama left the precincts of the church for the market-place or the courtyard of a palace, this form of staging was at first retained. Our knowledge of these performances comes from the plays themselves, and particularly from the stage-directions, from contemporary descriptions, and from a handful of pictorial representations which, although made in the fifteenth and sixteenth centuries, may be presumed to show how things were done two or three hundred years earlier. Most important of those known to us are the Passion Plays produced at Alsfeld and Mons in 1501, and at Lucerne in 1583. At Valenciennes in 1547, and in the St. Laurentius stage erected at Cologne in 1581, the medieval polyscenic arrangement had begun to show a Renaissance influence in that it had a 'unity of place' both for the audience and for the great stage, set with its various 'mansions'. This 'unity' may have been used even earlier. The famous Fouquet miniature of *Le Martyre de Sainte Apolline c.* 1460 (see No. 15) shows the audience, together with some of the performers, grouped in a semi-circle of covered booths facing a main acting-area—in fact, the shape of the Roman theatre without the *scaenae frons*. However, here, as with all the earliest pictorial records, controversy rages. Dr. Southern believes this performance to have taken place 'in the round', as was the case in the arenas of Perranzabuloe and St. Just (see CORNISH ROUNDS), both of which are still in existence. The former, of earth, has a diameter of 130 feet, and the latter, of stone, is 4 feet smaller. Round the perimeter of the arena was a moat and a raised mound. Within it, and possibly on its slopes, the audience sat or stood. At certain symbolic points on the mound were placed the 'mansions', and in the plan of *The Castle of Perseverance* (*c.* 1425) a castle is indicated in the centre of the arena. When we come to consider the processional plays which used the whole city as an auditorium, we again find something approximating to the *phlyakes* stage; four booths were erected at various vantage points and others were mounted on wheeled carts and drawn from place to place. In England these moveable 'mansions' were known as pageants, in Italy as *edifizii*, and in Spain as *carros* (see No. 19).

4. RENAISSANCE. While this medieval activity was still continuing all over Europe, the Renaissance was in full flower in Italy. In 1452 Alberti designed a theatre for Pope Nicholas V, and by the end of the century many of the classical writers had been discovered, acted, and published. We have some indication of what the early Renaissance theatre looked like. In the Trechsel edition of Terence's plays, published in Lyon in 1493, a woodcut labelled 'Theatrum' (see No. 14) shows an elaborately decorated raised booth-stage set up within what appears to be an open first-floor loggia. The spectators face the stage and are accommodated on a tiered floor and in two higher back-balconies. They appear to be standing. In a side box between the columns which support the roof sit two 'aediles'. An illustration in another edition of Terence, printed in Venice in 1497, again shows an open loggia with a few scholars seated on the two steps of a small semicircular amphitheatre. In their essentials these two illustrations give the pattern of the entire post-medieval theatre. Thereafter features from one or the other were used and elaborated on, combined, or enlarged, until they finally developed into the myriad sub-divisions of modern auditorium design.

Throughout the sixteenth century there was a continued interest in Vitruvius. Although the first Renaissance edition of his *De Architectura* had been published in 1486, no attempt at illustrating it was made until 1511. From then onwards new illustrated editions appeared rapidly. Many of the attempted reconstructions of classical theatres bore slight resemblance to the originals, but they had a considerable influence on the design of the theatres of the Academies, and on the architectural treatment of theatre buildings during the next three hundred years. In the 1530s Sebastiano Serlio (1475–1554) built a temporary theatre in a courtyard for the Academicians of Vicenza. He utilized the new knowledge, and produced a larger version of the building shown in the Venice edition of Terence. In 1545 he published his theatrical work, including the three famous perspective settings: Satyric, Comic, and Tragic, which had such far-reaching influence (see Nos. 56, 57, 58). Serlio and his contemporaries were mainly concerned with designing temporary theatres and extravagant scenery for the many courtly entertainments which took place in the great halls and courtyards of the Renaissance palaces. From the middle of the sixteenth century it was found useful, or attractive, to contain the perspective setting within a picture-frame, and so we get the convention of the proscenium arch and eventually of the 'fourth wall'. From the picture-frame itself steps, and later a ramp, led down to the floor of the ballroom, so that the performers could descend and perform among the spectators who lined the walls and, if the performance was taking place in an enclosed courtyard, hung out of the windows and filled the balconies. Here, however, it is necessary to distinguish between the two streams of evolution in Italy during the sixteenth century—the academic, which culminated in the still-extant Teatro Olimpico at Vicenza, built by Andrea Palladio (1518–80) (see No. 20), which opened on 3 Mar. 1585 with the epic production of *Oedipus Rex*, and the spectacular balletic-operatic tradition which led to the Italian opera-house, leaving as its early monuments the little theatre by Vincenzo Scamozzi (1552–1616) at Sabbionetta (1589) (see No. 21) and the Teatro Farnese, completed by Giovanni Battista Aleotti (1546–1636) at Parma in 1619, but not opened until 1628. Although Palladio's building with its superb *scaenae frons* was much admired, it was too impractical a building to be copied. It is not, as is usually said, the first modern theatre, but one of the last and the greatest of the Renaissance academic theatres. The line of general development followed the 'Theatrum' of the Lyon Terence, absorbing on the way the lessons learned in the temporary spectacle-theatres. The sixteenth century was a time of growth and transition. Europe was moving out of the Middle Ages, and as the Renaissance spread, Italian perspective scenery and the conception of amphitheatral seating was being taken up.

The first theatre building to be erected in Paris, in 1548, was the Hôtel de Bourgogne, a public playhouse, entirely roofed. The auditorium was long and narrow, with rising tiers of benches behind an open space where spectators could stand, and one, or possibly two, side galleries. The stage, built for the presentation of Mystery plays, was large and almost square (architecturally very similar to the indoor tennis-courts, many of which were used in the following century as theatres). The Court theatre, housed from 1572 to 1660 in the Salle du Petit Bourbon, had also a long and narrow auditorium, but the open space in front of the stage, as we see from the famous engraving of the 'Ballet Comique de la Reine' of 1581 (see No. 18), was used as part of the stage floor, particularly for dancing. There were no standing spectators, the thrones of the king and queen being placed dead centre (a pattern which continued for centuries in Court theatres), and before them various pageant cars paraded.

Very elaborate versions of the Terence booth-stage are to be found in the Low Countries in the sixteenth century. Illustrations of those in Ghent (1539) and Antwerp (1561) show complicated structures fronted by a high platform. Whether these stages were erected in the open, or in an enclosed roofed building like the Hôtel de Bourgogne, seems to be unknown. Certainly the stage of the first Amsterdam Schouwburg (1637) (see No. 25) is an obvious later development, with some hindsight of Vicenza. Here the stage, a static built-up edifice without a proscenium frame, shares a ceiling with the auditorium proper, both being contained in a large, nearly square, room. Standing spectators are accommodated on the floor, and the galleries form a flattened ellipse in plan, the two lower galleries being divided into separate boxes and the top, presumably cheaper, open. The early history and the derivation of boxes in the theatres has vexed many historians. The reason usually given for their existence has been the need to tempt the nobleman and the rich bourgeois into the theatre by offering them some degree of privacy. Little attention has been paid to the structural needs of the pre-cantilever gallery, which, if it had any depth, needed frequent support. Between the supports a natural division occurred which was later boxed in. This kind of development can be seen happening all over Europe, but it is particularly noticeable in the Elizabethan theatre and in the *corrales* (inside courtyards) of sixteenth-century Spain. The first permanent theatres were set up in these *corrales* in 1579 and 1582. They were very simple, with an open stage set against one wall. Most of the audience stood in the *patio* behind the *bancas* in front of the stage. As in the Elizabethan, the Venetian, and some other theatres, the more important people, and particularly women, sat on the surrounding balconies, or peered out from behind grilled windows. This is a direct continuation of the tradition of the *carro*, pageant, or booth-stage, set up in a city square, or courtyard, or inn-yard—in fact, the forerunner of the unroofed public Elizabethan theatre, the first of which was erected in London in 1576. Important aspects of this latter theatre were its complete physical separation from other buildings and its integrated form. In Continental Renaissance theatres this was most unusual, tied as they were to, or built into, scholarly or courtly buildings. Only in the Theatrum of the Lyon Terence can we see something which may well be an earlier form of the Elizabethan building. Since the structure of the Elizabethan public playhouse has an important bearing on the study and understanding of Elizabethan drama, particularly Shakespeare, it is considered separately in detail. It should be remembered, however, that the Elizabethans had also the entirely roofed indoor theatre, as at Blackfriars, and a long tradition of indoor entertainments in halls and at Court. These were susceptible to Continental influence, and it is significant that after the Puritan interregnum it was to the form of the private theatres that a return was made (see ENGLISH PLAYHOUSE).

5. BAROQUE. When we consider this crucial and dynamic phase in the development of theatre architecture, we find an important link is missing; when and where did the combination of the horseshoe-shaped auditorium with tiers of boxes emerge? The extant documents are insufficient to give us a conclusive answer to this problem, and we know that the rectangular auditorium continued in favour even after the introduction of boxes. An excellent example of this was the vast Imperial Theatre in Vienna (1668), by Lodovico Burnacini (1636–1707), where spectators seated along the side walls must have had a poor view of the stage, seeing only one side of the scenery (though, as each side was identical, this perhaps hardly mattered). But there is no doubt that the rectangular auditorium was out of step with the flowing architectural lines so important to the Baroque, and it was probably this, as well as the functional dictates of seeing and hearing, that was responsible for the circling horseshoe. Certainly an earlier development was the U-shape, as in the Teatro Farnese, which we find translated into tiers-and-boxes in the open-air tournament theatres, such as those at Bologna in 1628 and 1639 (by Alfonso Chenda), which, but for the division between proscenium arch and the five tiers of boxes, could be almost any of the many Italian theatres of the third quarter of the seventeenth century, for example, the Venetian theatres of S. Giovanni e Paulo (1655) and of S. Giovanni Crisostomo (1678); the Roman Tordinona (1669); or the Teatro della Accademia dei Intronati, Siena (*c.* 1670). In all these, contact between stage and boxes was tight, and the tiers ran straight from the proscenium opening. Foyer and circulation space was almost impossibly minimal, and the external elevational treatment of the theatres casual; their planning in relation to surrounding buildings seems almost accidental. Little of this was changed in the plans for the second Tordinona (1670), when Carlo Fontana (1634–1714) and his students gave consideration to both horseshoe and ovoid auditorium shapes. The search for the ideal was to continue throughout the next two centuries and still, of course, goes on. Basically, the shape was the U, with variations practised on the side arms and, less often, at the back. Truncated, the auditorium could become a semicircle, as in the beautiful little opera-house in Munich, built by the local ducal *Baumeister* Marx Schinnagl (1612–81), under the supervision of the Venetian Francesco Santurini (1627–82), the first unattached building of its kind in Germany, which opened in 1657 in Salvator Platz.

After the Renaissance Italian architects spent much time abroad. At first the traffic in ideas was always from Italy into the rest of Europe, but by the eighteenth century cross-fertilization and a true internationalism was the rule. Even after the Italian horseshoe (the U with inturned arms) had come into general use, we find a wide variety of plan forms. The Bibienas, all great travellers, favoured turning the arms of the U out at the junction with the proscenium, thus forming a bell shape. Some of the theatres they built in this way are still standing, although all have been somewhat altered or restored—the Filarmonico, Verona 1720); the Opernhaus, Bayreuth (1748); the Teatro Comunale, Bologna (1763); the Delli quattro Cavalieri, now called the Fraschini, Pavia (1773); and the Scientifico, Mantua 1775).

Another interesting and practical adaptation of the basic shape was the opened U of Vigarini's Salle des Machines (1662) erected in the Tuileries, which was not a boxed theatre but a somewhat Palladian adaptation of the Teatro Farnese and Sabbionetta with amphitheatral seating round the columns which supported a single gallery. (An interesting comparison is with the Wren drawing supposedly for the second Drury Lane.) The opened U is formed entirely by the columns; the main walls still make a rectangle. However, with the Palais Royal theatre (*c.* 1674) and the first Théâtre-Français (1689), built by François d'Orbay, the auditorium girdle-wall itself has become an opened U and boxes have replaced the amphitheatral seating. As the Théâtre-Français was a public theatre, the central parterre was used for standing spectators, as in the earlier public French theatres, and not, as at Court, for the king and his leading courtiers. Like its Italian counterparts, this Théâtre-Français was squeezed in among other buildings, and had none of the grandeur which it was to achieve later. The English were altogether more lavish. Of the auditorium of Dorset Garden (1671) a Frenchman observed in 1676 that it was 'infinitely more beautiful and functional than those in the playhouses of our French actors'. Besides amphitheatral seating and a double tier of boxes, each holding twenty spectators, and a top gallery—the paradise—the building had a main façade of flourish and intricacy, more importantly treated than that of the usual Continental theatre of the period. In general, it is not until the eighteenth century that we find the theatre assuming externally the trappings of pomp and exclusivity formerly reserved for palaces and churches. Even then foyers and circulation-spaces were usually extremely restricted. Extensive front-of-house amenities are in the main a nineteenth-century development, and although in the first half of the eighteenth century Italian opera-houses were being given staircase halls, it was in Germany that a grander conception was evolving. Von Knobelsdorff's Opernhaus on Unter den Linden (1742) (now the Staatsoper) had a ceremonial hall on the *piano nobile* whose area was almost as great as that of the auditorium itself, and the entire building was planned as a free-standing structure with four elaborately designed elevations, the main entrance being up a double stair and under a splendid classic portico. Philippe De La Guêpière's Stuttgart Opernhaus (1758) was even more developed, the auditorium taking up only about one-eighth of the total area. The design, in section, was of fantastic complexity and subtlety, and its decoration was in the exquisitely fanciful rococo style which can still be seen in the recently restored Cuvilliés Theatre in Munich (1753), designed by François Cuvilliés (?1695–1768). Unlike Stuttgart, where the section achieved its effect of limitless elaboration by a succession of planes variously juxtaposed and structurally essential, the Cuvilliés is relatively straightforward, the decoration being merely applied to the tier fronts, and encrusting their vertical supports. In the original theatre the floor could, characteristically, be jacked up level with the stage, thus forming one magnificent ballroom. It must be remembered that at this period the theatre was the architectural dominant of society, and it is not without significance that baroque architecture has been described as 'frozen opera'. The audience was 'on stage' as much as the performers, and the entire architectural and social ensemble created a unity of form and function unique in the history of the theatre. As the century wore on, private theatricals became universally popular, and every great house and every city boasted its own little theatre. Although the great opera-houses of Italy were built almost to a standard pattern—a pattern consolidated by La Scala, Milan (1778), which influenced similar buildings elsewhere—the detailed architectural treatment of the little theatres varied enormously.

6. NINETEENTH CENTURY. Although the development of the baroque theatre continued until the outbreak of the First World War, it was during the nineteenth century that its forms received a somewhat more codified treatment, and architects developed a greater rule-of-thumb assurance. New technical developments led to the use of iron and steel, gas and electricity (see LIGHTING), and the growth of a solid middle class intensified the element of pomp and civic pride. Major theatres were erected on imposing sites, and designed in a manner suitable to their amplified function. The columns, porticoes, and elevational echoes of the Theatre of Marcellus, which entered into the scheme of things in the mid-eighteenth century, became in the nineteenth easy means of identification.

In the great theatres of Victor Louis (1731–1802) we can see the transition from the essential baroque to the new technology of the nineteenth century. In his Grand Théâtre de Bordeaux (1780), the last great theatre of the *ancien régime*, he used traditional structural techniques of wood-joist, post, brick, and stone, but in the Variétés-Amusantes (1790), later the Théâtre-Français (see No. 33), he plunged into the new era. The main structure was of non-inflammable materials (which did not prevent great damage in the fire of 1900); wrought-iron framing replaced all timber in the roof; flagstones, hollow tile and stone vaulting replaced timber staircases, partitions, and beams. The entire roof construction was so counterbalanced that it needed only comparatively thin walls for its support. This structural revolution had immediate repercussions all over Europe, and in 1811 Foulston, in his Theatre Royal, Plymouth, almost entirely replaced timber with cast- and wrought-iron. Stylistically, his theatre was worthy of comparison with the imposing, well-considered edifices going up all over the Continent. Gone was the carpenter's makeshift of the Georgian playhouse. After the Restoration the English had withdrawn from competition with the magnificence shown on the Continent, and their theatres, from that built in Williamsburg, Virginia, in 1718 to that in Richmond, Yorkshire, in 1788, had maintained a plainness and squareness of home-made dimensions. Now came the architect, consciously designing 'fine buildings' and pushing the journeyman-carpenter towards the stage.

The turn of the century, and a new wave of prosperity, brought hundreds of new theatres. In 1784 there were ten in Paris, by 1791 fifty-one. Few were on the scale of Bordeaux or the Théâtre-Français, but across the Continent cities vied with each other in producing ever more costly civic theatres, ever more sumptuously treated, the tendency being always towards a more complex and integrated building, with greater circulation-space. The auditorium itself, however, changed little. In Italy the opera-house horseshoe, with hen-coop boxes from floor to ceiling, still set the pattern. Elsewhere local conditions and temperaments resulted in adaptations with their own pragmatic solutions—surfaces broken by verticals, and, towards the latter part of the century, by small boxes at varying levels. The tendency in the English-speaking world was towards undivided amphitheatral balconies, with front-of-house facilities almost non-existent. But this is a generalization, for the period is immensely rich in variety and complexity. Standing as its pinnacle of achievement is Charles Garnier's masterpiece of three-dimensional planning, the Paris Opéra (begun in 1861, but not finished until 1875). Its handling and control of disparate plan elements, its subtlety and magnificence of section, combine to make it one of the greatest buildings of Western civilization. Its influence was enormous.

It is impossible to list all the important theatre buildings of the nineteenth century, but some of the outstanding ones are the Park Theatre, New York (1805); Schinkel's Schauspielhaus auf dem Gendarmenmarkt, Berlin, (1821); the Teatro Carlo Felice, Genoa, and the Alexandrinsky, St. Petersburg (both 1828); the Hoftheater, Dresden, 1842; the Opera Real, Madrid (1850); the Bolshoi, Moscow (1856) (see Nos. 34, 54); Covent Garden (1858); the Viktoria, Berlin (1859); the Hofopernhaus, Vienna (1869); the Kongelike Teater, Copenhagen

(1874); the theatre in Odessa (1887) (designed by Fellner and Helmer, who were responsible for some eighty theatre buildings all over the world); the Burgtheater, Vienna (1888) (see No. 37); and the Teatro Massimo, Palermo (1897). (Dates given are those of completion of the buildings. These elaborate theatres took many years to build.)

Most of these buildings are, it will be noted, opera-houses. Architecturally they set the pattern for the smaller theatres which mushroomed up with bewildering rapidity.

7. MODERN. The term 'modern' correctly means 'of the present time'. For theatre architecture it has too often been used to describe buildings which appear to have broken completely with tradition. This confusion in terminology echoes clearly the confusion implicit in the proliferation of styles and the splintering of objectives which have occurred in theatre design since Wagner thrust his conception of integrated staging and egalitarian seating into the long tradition of the Italian opera-house. It is convenient therefore to date the modern period from the building of Wagner's Festspielhaus in Bayreuth (1876).

Wagner, like many reformers before and since, disapproved of the frivolity of the theatre as he found it. He wanted to attract the attention of the audience away from itself and its highly ornate surroundings towards the stage on which was being presented his carefully integrated music-drama. He therefore contrived, first with the architect Gottfried Semper (1803–79) in the abortive Munich Festspieltheater scheme, and later with O. Brückwald at Bayreuth, a single, wedge-shaped, steeply-raked amphitheatre of seats which concentrated attention upon the stage, and further enhanced the illusion of the stage-picture by a double proscenium arch, within which was the orchestra, sunk in the no-man's-land of the *mystischer Abgrund* (mystical gulf). The stage, 118 feet deep, lent itself to immense vistas, but unfortunately the width of the seating-wedge was such that only those sitting directly in front of the proscenium opening could see very far in. In addition, the elimination of the overhanging galleries, in a theatre seating 1,645, meant that many spectators were a long way from the stage, further than they would have been in the highest of the old galleries, which, encircling the stalls, had induced a sense of awareness of a community placed three-dimensionally within the volume of the auditorium. The steep rake helped the retention of much of this community sense, but in later theatres, where it was flattened out, the results were disastrous. However, the influence of Bayreuth on theatre building was not immediately apparent, though eventually it was to become so preponderant that in the mid-twentieth century the average architect, indicating a theatre in a sketch-plan, would automatically draw Wagner's wedge-shape, quite unaware that in specialist circles it had long been discredited.

Some aspects of Wagner's conception appeared in Otto March's Volkstheater (Worms, 1888). Here, the wedge was combined with back balconies and fitted into a circular building, but unlike Bayreuth, where the side walls of the auditorium were at right-angles to the stage, with only the bank of seats and the exit buttresses forming the wedge, the walls at Worms were themselves splayed out. Acoustically this was a dangerous procedure, and gave rise to one of the many problems that resulted from trying to adapt a theatre designed for music-drama to straight plays. These problems became even more apparent when the next two Wagnerian theatres to be built were used for dramatic performances. These were the Prinzregenten, Munich (1901), and the Schiller, Berlin (1906), both designed by Max Littmann (1862–1931). With the Künstlertheater, Munich (1908), he discarded the wedge, but retained the flat ceiling and the steeply raked amphitheatre, confining the latter between the parallel walls of a rectangle, and thereby much improving the sightlines. Decoration was austere, and the stage little more than a narrow platform behind a proscenium arch, with no flying space, a severe reaction from the enormous and increasingly mechanized stages that were being built almost everywhere else in Europe. The Künstlertheater auditorium became a model for later Art Theatres all over the world, and was repeated from Iowa (State University) to Pretoria (Arts Centre) and Helsinki (Little Theatre of the National Theatre). The Mermaid (London, 1959) is a slight variation on this theme, without the proscenium arch, but with the seating divided by the aisles which English, though not central-European, fire regulations demand (see No. 42). Although the auditoria and stages of the Prinzregenten and the Schiller followed Bayreuth closely, Littmann increased the foyer and circulation spaces, and provided large restaurants. Externally he tidied up Brückwald's façades, whose dramatic simplicity was inconsistent with the little Palladian villa of a Royal entrance-suite. This brought his buildings more into line with the many state and civic theatres, less revolutionary, but more solidly impressive, which were still being built in Germany, France, the Austro-Hungarian and Russian Empires, Scandinavia, and South America. Something of Wagner's democratic seating was apparent in the deep amphitheatral balconies which these theatres had absorbed from the traditional buildings of the English-speaking world. Good examples of this are Carl Moritz's Civic Theatre, Katowice (1906); Littmann's Hoftheater, Stuttgart (1912); A. and G. Perret's Théâtre des Champs-Elysées, Paris (1913); and Oskar Kaufmann's Neue Freie Volksbühne, Berlin (1914). Littmann's Stuttgart building, combining as it did an opera-house, a playhouse—both with elaborate stages—and immense workshops and storage areas for the provision of everything used on them, shows how complex and established these German theatres had become by the time of the First World War. Their mechanical elaboration, coupled with the desire for scenic self-sufficiency, turned the old subsidized theatres of the central-European Courts into modern technological theatre-centres. These, designed on a monumental scale, becolumned and quietly magnificent, were set down with their factory and office-block appendages on island sites or in lavish parks—like a complex of temples in the holy precinct—twentieth-century interpretations of a classical ideal. The respectful attitude of the audience matched the grandiose conception, presenting the absolute antithesis of the desire of English-speaking audiences to be amused, a desire which resulted in the transitory commercial theatre. Furthermore, lack of subsidies, cut-throat competition, and the high price of sites in the centre of the city combined to keep the theatre in the English-speaking world squashed into the hurly-burly of crowded streets. Seldom could more than one, or at the most two, elevations be displayed. Foyer, auditorium, and stage were ingeniously, and haphazardly, fitted into the labyrinthine complexity of a city block. In London, Collcutt's Royal English Opera House (1891), now the Palace, is the only theatre to stand clear of other buildings, on an island site surrounded by streets. Her Majesty's (1897) was interesting as continuing the old English tradition of combining a theatre with an hotel (the Carlton, now demolished) in one architectural ensemble. The Waldorf Hotel, flanked by theatres with identical façades—the Aldwych and the Waldorf (later the Strand) (both 1905)—was an elaboration of this idea. But although these London theatres are combined with other social buildings, their design, like that of most theatres in the English-speaking world, continues the tradition of the English playhouse, and their decorative treatment results from the imbroglio of renaissance and baroque motifs which constitutes the 'architecture of entertainment'. This tradition attained its apogee of florid but well-integrated magnificence by the turn of the century, and was not seriously threatened until the advent of cinema architecture, which combined with a fanatical zeal for destruction and emasculation, in the name of good sight-lines and modernity, to strip the gaudy trappings from late Victorian and Edwardian theatres, leaving the hollow shells of the late 1920s and 1930s. In London, the new puritanism resulted in the Duchess (1929), the Cambridge (1930), the Saville (1931); in the United States, in the Pasadena Playhouse (1925), the Ziegfeld, New York (1927), the Pickwick, Park Ridge (1928), the Wilson, Detroit (1928), Radio City Music Hall and the Centre Theatre (1933). By the 1920s architectural firms were no longer a matter of one-man-and-a-boy, but had become vast syndicates. Concrete and steel had taken over and a new aesthetic was emerging. Gone were the boxes and encircling galleries; gone too any contact between audience and actor, any atmosphere of 'theatre'. In cinema and theatre the audience sat fair and square to the stage-picture, and as that of the cinema was bigger and more impressive—and boasted the close-up—the theatre was found wanting, and began to atrophy.

In England the central-European theatre-centre like Stuttgart attracted no attention. But in the United States it had a great influence, particularly on some of the civic groups and in the colleges, which resulted in, for example, the Cleveland Playhouse (1927) (see No. 53), the Iowa University Theater (1936), and the Hopkins Art Center of Dartmouth College (1962). Vast buildings like the Chicago Opera House (1929), which contained a large and a small theatre with an office building superimposed, brought something of the German civic conception into the commercial scene. The Opera House itself, seating 3,471, was a tamed Bayreuth, with a flattened rake and a wedge auditorium, curved slightly in the manner of the cinema, with the inevitable balconies, here subdivided into compartments. The smaller theatre was practically identical. The Shakespeare Memorial Theatre (later the Royal Shakespeare) at Stratford-upon-Avon (1932) and the Théâtre du Palais de Chaillot (1937) in Paris were in the same idiom, though different in their manner of treating the ceiling. In Chicago it was stepped up, while the Stratford ceiling flowed up in an unbroken line, from a fairly low proscenium opening to a very high back balcony. This question of profile—of how to treat the expanse of ceiling—was a vexed problem in the cinema age. The cults both of stage-realism and of grandiose scenic simplicity had swept away the sky-borders. As a result, either the proscenium arch had to be very much lowered, or a tall and expensive cyclorama had to be provided. Sometimes, as in the costly Dresden Schauspielhaus, the problem was solved by the building of a vast fixed cyclorama; at other times by the provision of a high movable canvas which could be wound in, or partly flown (in fact, bagged), a practice which has become standard in central, northern, and eastern Europe. Elsewhere, the economics of theatre management dictated a low proscenium, but the avoidance of the discredited boxes and encircling galleries meant that a large part of the audience had to be accommodated at the back of the theatre. To increase capacity, the back balconies had to be deep and steep; the ceiling had to rise to correspond. A fashion for flowing lines made the auditorium look like an airship, and cinema and theatre became indistinguishable.

Some theatres, particularly in the United States in the 1920s, and the British Commonwealth in the 1930s, took over from the cinema the fantastic styles of decoration derived from Hollywood's passion for romantic extravaganza. In the U.S.S.R., however, many of the quite unbelievably eclectic projects of the Stalinist era are due to the reactionary spirit of the mid-1930s rather than the influence of Hollywood. Their romantic façades are of another order. Unfortunately for students of the bizarre, few were actually built. The huge Theatre of the Red Army in Moscow (1940), enclosed within a forest of columns, star-shaped in plan with Corinthian capitals, surrounding a quinquangular edifice (the Red Star solidified), is a modest example of the genre.

The cinema age continued into the Second World War. The final manifestation in London was seen in the reconstruction of the second Prince of Wales Theatre (1937). After the war many buildings of the inter-war period came to be regarded by people who were concerned for the continuance of the theatre with dismay. However, similar theatres are still being built, although the once popular flowing line has given way to a brisk angularity.

Running parallel with this general stream of development emanating from Wagner's Bayreuth theatre—'modern' in the sense of 'of the present time'—was a more particular development: that referred to above as having broken with tradition. Wagner had purposely separated the actor from the audience. Innovators in the next generation tried to integrate them again, and to break the tyrannical separation set up by the proscenium arch. A first attempt to open up the stage-picture was made by the addition of two side frames, as in Van de Velde's Werkbundtheater for the Cologne Exhibition in 1914. This was a device which, when allied to a straight-sided, ramped and raked auditorium, ensured that all seats had a direct right-angular view of the stage. The Mayan Theater, Los Angeles (*c.* 1923), had similar side-stages, but framed each one heavily and elaborately, and, in a typical cinema-age theatre, merely used the area adjacent to the stage which, in other theatres, was taken by the stageboxes. A. and G. Perret, in their temporary Théâtre de l'Exposition des Arts Décoratifs, Paris (1925), developed Van de Velde's idea in a post-and-frame structure, making the triple stage-opening wider than the seating was deep. The stage now completely dominated an almost square auditorium. In effect, when the curtains were open, the proscenium vanished completely, a situation foreshadowed in the open stage of Copeau's Vieux-Colombier, Paris (1919), with its architectural décor of steps, levels, and openings—a permanent set which audiences soon found monotonous. Neither the stage of the Vieux-Colombier, nor that of Terence Gray's Cambridge Festival Theatre (1926—an open stage which replaced the proscenium stage of an old Georgian playhouse; see No. 84) attempted the 'wrap-round' effect of the triple-stage, an idea which died out in favour of a stage with no proscenium at all, like the Mermaid in London. More enduring was the decision to wrap the audiences round the stage, following the lead of Reinhardt's Grosses Schauspielhaus (see No. 39), Berlin (1919), which was converted by Hans Poelzig from a circus. Here about 3,000 spectators were seated in a steeply ascending amphitheatre round three sides of a great U-shaped forestage, which could be sunk and replaced by seats. All the spectators faced a wide letter-box proscenium opening, inconspicuously treated. Over the forestage a large dome played havoc with the acoustics. Poelzig's decoration of stalactites was a fruitless attempt at minimizing the hazards of a building which presented a very difficult acoustic problem. They have since been removed; the dome has been roofed in, and the theatre is now known as the Friedrichstadt-Palast. The stage is still the largest in Germany, and is used for variety. It was, of course, always too big for anything else. Reinhardt soon tired of his new toy, and of the whole concept of Theatre for the Masses, but elsewhere the idea persisted. In the U.S.S.R. many vast amphitheatral-type auditoria (without the apron) have been built. Apart from the Theatre of the Red Army mentioned earlier, they can be found at Rostov-on-Don (1936), Minsk (1941) (see No. 55), and Tashkent (1948), among other places.

The next step was inevitably towards the complete arena, as visualized in 1926 by Gropius in his Totaltheater for Piscator, an unrealized dream which combined the two previous 'wrap-rounds' together with the possibility of revolving Reinhardt's tongue-like apron into the middle of the auditorium, thus creating a true arena, with a subsidiary walk-way stage encircling the entire audience.

The Grosses Schauspielhaus and the Totaltheater are the two seminal designs from which have sprung the many subsequent schemes for arena theatres, amphitheatres, and adaptable theatres. Norman Bel Geddes's various schemes of the 1920s and 1930s for true arena theatres have had a great influence. Many of the drama departments of American colleges and universities now have permanent arena theatres, some with facilities for open-stage, or semi-proscenium, productions. Notable are those at the University of Miami (1950); the Teatro S. Erasmo, Milan (1953), which has a two-sided arena; Le Théâtre en Rond de Paris (1954), and Arena Stage, Washington (1961). Because of the problems inherent in arena-theatre production, these theatres have sensibly been kept small. Miami seats only 400, Washington, the largest, 750. The shortcomings of a theatre like the Grosses Schauspielhaus, which is really good only for those people seated directly in front of the apron, have not, however, prevented quite a number from being built, the most important being the Malmö Stadsteater (see No. 40), conceived in the early 1930s, with Poelzig as a member of the committee which chose the winning design, but not completed until 1944. The amphitheatral auditorium, which seats 1,700, can be adapted to various shapes and sizes, and diminished to seat 400. Unfortunately Malmö is a small town, and financial considerations make it imperative that the theatre at its largest should be filled to capacity. Consequently the movable walls which diminish the auditorium are seldom used. The deep apron is unsuited to the average production, and the 66-foot proscenium opening is too wide. Malmö is a good example of an architectural idea which has not worked out in practice. As an adaptable theatre it has proved least satisfactory in the very way in which it must be used most. The whole building, with its small theatre attached, its workshops and foyer facilities, is an elegant continuation of the pre-1914 German idea of a theatre centre, and its architecture gave 'contemporary' a validity as the descriptive word for the better theatre buildings of the 1940s and 1950s. Its influence can be seen in John English's Tent Theatre in Birmingham (1948); in the Shakespearean Festival Theatre, Stratford, Ontario, (1953, rebuilt 1957; see No. 43); in the Umeda Koma Stadium, Osaka (1956); and in the Chichester Festival Theatre (1962), all of which have abolished the proscenium completely, and make use of the forestage and apron as the only acting areas. This form has gained many adherents, and produced, in many countries, numerous smaller theatres with varying open-stage possibilities. Malmö was, however, also largely responsible for an intensive reaction against the single-ramp amphitheatre. Complaints such as those enumerated earlier have caused producers and architects to re-examine the theatrical potentialities of the traditional galleried theatre. Many have come to believe that adaptations of this form are still relevant. This was the case in many of the ninety-odd theatres built or re-built in the German-speaking countries between 1945 and 1963—more, it is said, than in the rest of the world put together. Four main approaches have been used. First, a return to the provision of galleries, yet without losing sight of the lessons learnt since Wagner: the necessity for good sight and sound; closer contact between audience and actor; avoidance of undue emphasis on the proscenium; liberal backstage, workshop, and front-of-house amenities. The best examples of all this are the theatres of Werner Kallmorgen—the Hannover Landestheater (1950), the Kiel Stadttheater (1953), the Hamburg Thaliatheater (1960)—and those of his disciples, like the Münster Stadttheater (1956) and the Gelsenkirchen Stadttheater (1959). Secondly, there have been the auditoria with boxes like drawers pulled out of a chest, influenced by London's Royal Festival Hall (1951). Among these are the Hamburg Staatsoper (1955) and the Berlin Deutsche Oper (1961). Thirdly, there are the 'contemporary' angular versions of the cinema-age theatre—the Stuttgart Schauspielhaus (1962) and the Berlin Freie Volksbühne (1963). And lastly, those which derive from Littmann's Künstlertheater, with unadorned steep rake—the Mannheim Nationaltheater (1956) and some others. The small theatres attached to Gelsenkirchen and Mannheim are adaptable to most kinds of so-called experimental work, but are seldom used for anything but straightforward productions. Many of the buildings listed above continue the theatre-centre concept. All are post-Malmö in style, ranging from a heavy 'modern' neo-classicism to purest 'contemporary'.

In conclusion it can be said that since the end of the Second World War the British, the Americans, the Italians, and others have finally attempted the open and the arena stage, finding them exciting and stimulating, while the Germans find them old-fashioned, having pioneered them in the same way. Even the external romantic-irrationalism of Jorn Utzon's Sydney Opera House, which employs shell-concrete expressively, and in marked reaction from the plain geometry which has obsessed architects in recent years, was anticipated in the 1920s by German architects. If the past is anything to go by, the four main streams of theatre building summarized above (with subsidiary variable forms for small playhouses) could become standard practice. Already it can be said that they provide an adequate cross-section of world activity in the early 1960s. VICTOR GLASSTONE

ARDEN, John (1930–), English dramatist, whose early plays, *Live Like Pigs* (1958) and *The Happy Haven* (1960), grotesque comedies of modern life, were performed at the Royal Court Theatre by the English Stage Company, as was his first historical drama, *Serjeant Musgrave's Dance* (1959) (see No. 112). In 1964 a political play, *The Workhouse Donkey*, was produced at Chichester, where another historical drama, *Armstrong's Last Goodnight* (based on the Scottish 'Ballad of Johnny Armstrong') appeared a year later. Also in 1965 the City of London commissioned from Arden a play in celebration of the 750th anniversary of the sealing of Magna Carta, *Left-Handed Liberty*, which was produced at the Mermaid. Arden's versatility has made him one of the outstanding dramatists of the 1960s. His preoccupation with moral and social problems has caused him to be referred to as the English Brecht, though he protests that, while admiring Brecht, he has not been influenced by him.

ARENA THEATRE, see OPEN STAGE.

ARETINO, Pietro (1492–1556), Italian dramatist, who began life as a lackey, and nearly ended as a Cardinal. His one tragedy, *Orazio* (1546), is probably the best of those written at that time, but as a dramatist he is chiefly remembered for his comedies, which are exceptionally free from neo-classical conventions, and thoroughly Italian in their realistic and satiric thought and presentation. Although his plays were written in haste, and lack finish, they were original and amusing, and his public asked for nothing more; hence his popularity. He provides us with much light on the less creditable aspects of the social life of his day. It has been suggested that Ben Jonson's *Epicoene* may owe something to Aretino's second comedy, *Il Marescalco* (1533) (see also ITALY, 1 *b* iii).

ARGENTINA, see SOUTH AMERICA, 1.

ARGYLL ROOMS, London, in Regent Street. These were fitted up as a private theatre and run by subscription from 1819 to 1823, for French plays under aristocratic patronage. Performances were given every Friday from March to September. Plays began at 9 and ended at midnight when the company adjourned to the public ballroom and joined the dancing.

ARION, of Lesbos (*c.* 625–585 B.C.), an important, though vague, figure in the development of Greek music and dramatic poetry. He reorganized the dithyrambic dance (see DITHYRAMB), and was the first to give literary shape both to the dithyramb and to the satyr-revel. He was also the inventor of the 'tragic mode' (? musical mode), and, according to one tradition, the first tragic poet. He is credited with a miraculous escape from death by drowning at the hands of pirates, being conveyed to land on the back of a dolphin charmed by his singing. H. D. F. KITTO

ARIOSTO, LODOVICO (1474–1533), famous Italian poet, author of the romantic epic, *Orlando Furioso*, written in honour of his patrons, the d'Este family, in whose service he spent most of his life at Ferrara. He was one of the first, and certainly the best, of the writers of early Italian comedy, and did much to establish the literary form of the *commedia erudita*. The structure of his plays is modelled upon Roman comedies; their content is of Renaissance city life. His first plays, *Cassaria* and *I Suppositi*, were given in Ferrara in 1508 and 1509, in a permanent building of classical style erected under the influence of Vitruvius's *De Architectura*, with scenery by Raphael (this building was destroyed in 1533). These were in prose, but were later re-written in verse, and *I Suppositi*, in its revised form, was given in 1513 before Pope Leo X in his new theatre in Rome. Ariosto's next play, *Il Negromante*, written in 1520, also in verse, was performed at Ferrara in 1530. A further play was left unfinished (see also ITALY, 1 *b* iii).

ARISTOPHANES (*c.* 448 – *c.* 380 B.C.), Greek dramatist, son of Philippus, of Athens. The comic poet of Old Comedy (see GREECE, 2), he wrote some 40 comedies, of which 11 are extant (the only Greek comedies to be preserved entire): the *Acharnians* (425 B.C.), *Knights* (424), *Clouds* (423), *Wasps* (422), *Peace* (421), *Birds* (414), *Lysistrata* (411), *Women at the Festival* (*Thesmophoriazousae*) (410), *Frogs* (405), *Women in Parliament* (*Ecclesiazousae*) (392), and *Plutus* (388).

Aristophanes' name is joined with those of Eupolis and Cratinus in the well-known Horatian verse (*Satires*, Book 1, Satire 4, line 1), but we have no reason to suspect the good judgement of the ancient critics who regarded him as the greatest of the Attic comic poets. His direct influence on drama has been slight, simply because both the form and the spirit of his comedy were so intensely local that they offered no models and but little material to comic dramatists of other times and places (see MENANDER); on the other hand, his purely literary influence has been great, particularly on Rabelais and Fielding.

The form of Aristophanes' comedy is in some respects exceedingly strict, in others exceedingly loose. One element was a series of scenes (in which the chorus took part) where correspondence was strict: e.g. opposing speeches were of exactly the same length. This element was derived from a traditional animal-masquerade or revel. It will be noticed how many of the plays got their titles from the disguise assumed in them by the chorus, which became wasps, clouds, frogs, &c. A second element was the *parabasis*, the 'coming-forward' of the chorus. This was a long address of the chorus to the audience, again in a most elaborately strict form. Naturally the *parabasis* is quite undramatic; in it the poet harangues the audience quite openly in his own person. A third element is a series of loosely attached scenes in a different metre (a colloquial version of the tragic iambic verse); these have no set form.

In the earlier plays, which are more characteristic of Old Comedy, there is little development of plot; rather, some fantastic situation was quickly developed—it often involved a contest or struggle between hero and chorus, or between two halves of the chorus—and then the situation was exploited in a series of loosely connected scenes. The central situation was normally one that had direct reference to the political situation of the moment or to some urgent social question; in the *Acharnians*, for example, an Athenian citizen, weary of the war, makes a private treaty with the enemy and consequently enjoys the advantages of trading with them. The iambic scenes develop the ludicrous possibilities of this invention, and enable Aristophanes to hit out right and left at people he dislikes—politicians, busybodies, philosophers, Euripides.

These earlier plays are an astonishing mixture of fantasy, unsparing (and often, to our minds, violently unfair) satire, brilliant verbal wit, literary and musical parody, exquisite lyrics, hard-hitting political propaganda, and uproarious farce. There is an uncertain tradition that an attempt was made to limit the licence of Old Comedy, but the matter and the manner of Aristophanes shows that the attempt, if made, failed.

The *Frogs* marks the transition to the much quieter Middle Comedy, in which personal and political invective plays a smaller part, the element of the fantastic is much reduced, and the plot becomes more elaborate. The chorus, in consequence, is made much less prominent. The *Frogs* is important in the history of criticism, for it stages a contest, in Hades, between Aeschylus and Euripides, as to which shall be brought back to earth to revive the dying art of tragedy. Dionysus is umpire, and Sophocles sits by to take on the winner. H. D. F. KITTO

(For the 'English Aristophanes', see FOOTE, SAMUEL.)

ARISTOTLE (384–322 B.C.) of Stagira, Greek philosopher and scientist. His *Poetics* analyses the function and structural principles of tragedy and (to some extent) of epic; a second book, on comedy, has been lost. The *Poetics* is a reply to the criticisms of Plato and of Socrates, who says (in Plato's *Apology*) that the poets are unable to give a coherent account of what they do. To the latter criticism Aristotle replies by working out a logical theory of poetic composition; to Plato, who condemns poetry and drama for what it does not do (viz. inculcate virtue), he replies by inquiring quite objectively what it does do. It aims at pleasure, but at the rational pleasure which is a part of the good life; by its representation of serious action it does indeed excite emotions, but only to purge them and so to leave the spectator strengthened; since art represents universals and not particulars, it is nearer to the truth than actual events and objects are, not further from it, as Plato maintained. 'Poetry is more philosophical than history.'

Aristotle's account of the historical development of tragedy and comedy is extremely brief. His analysis of the form of tragedy is clear and penetrating, but, because of his biological bias, it is something less than an account of the existing types of tragedy; for Aristotle regarded tragedy as an organism which, like other organisms, developed until it achieved its 'natural' form, and then decayed; its basic laws are therefore to be disclosed by an analysis of the mature, not of the immature or the enfeebled, stages of the art. The 'complete' form of tragedy, the one in which all its structural features are fully developed and most vigorously used, is the Sophoclean (see SOPHOCLES); it is, therefore, the Sophoclean tragedy, in all essentials, that Aristotle analyses, and his dicta are not necessarily true of Aeschylus or even Euripides. Within these limits his criticism is penetrating and in many ways final.

The neo-classical critics of the seventeenth and eighteenth centuries, especially those in France, were anxious to claim Aristotle's authority for their own doctrines, some of which Aristotle never thought of. Their interpretations of Aristotle were therefore often ludicrous. For example, of the famous Three Unities Aristotle mentions only one and a half; he insists on the Unity of Action, and he remarks parenthetically, comparing tragedy with epic, that tragedy (but not the early tragedy) 'tries as far as possible to confine itself to twenty-four hours or thereabouts'. About the Unity of Place he says nothing, and several extant Greek plays disregard it, if it was convenient and plausible to move the chorus from one (dramatic) place to another.

Aristotle also compiled a list of the prize-winning tragedies and comedies (see DIDASCALIA). H. D. F. KITTO

ARLECCHINO, one of the comic, quick-witted servants of the *commedia dell'arte*. The name may have been picked up by the Italians when they visited France in the late sixteenth century, where, in the form Herlequin, it denoted a personage akin to the comic devils of the medieval Mystery play. Probably the first Italian actor to adopt the name, in its Italian form, was Tristano Martinelli. As Arlequin, still a comic servant, the character crops up in later French comedy and in the dumb-shows of the fairs, while, in the familiar form of Harlequin, it survived in the harlequinade of the English pantomime, metamorphosed into the young lover of Columbine. (For a more detailed discussion of this point, see HARLEQUINADE and ITALY, 2.)

ARLISS, GEORGE (1868–1946), English actor, whose later career was almost entirely connected with films. He had, however, already made a name for himself on the stage before he went to Hollywood, some of his finest parts being Zakkuri in *The Darling of the Gods* (1902), the title-role in *Disraeli* (1911), and the Rajah in *The Green Goddess* (1921). It was in the last part that he reappeared in London after a long absence in America, where he first went in 1901 with Mrs. Patrick Campbell. He was an excellent delineator of suave villainy, but his versatility enabled him to play with equal success the elderly gentleman in *Old English* (1924). He was also seen in Pinero, Ibsen, and Shakespeare, and was the author of several plays and of an autobiography entitled *Up the Years from Bloomsbury* (1927).

ARMIN, ROBERT (*c.* 1568–*c.* 1611), an Elizabethan clown, pupil and successor of Tarleton, who was first with the Lord Chandos's Men, later with the Lord Chamberlain's. He appears in the list of actors in Shakespeare's plays, and was certainly at the Globe. He probably played Dogberry in succession to Kempe, and his name is found in the actor-list of *The Alchemist* (1610). It is as a writer, however, that Armin is best known. His *Foole upon Foole, or Six Sortes of Sottes* appeared in 1600, and on the title-page he describes himself as 'Clonnico de Curtanio Snuffe', changed in a later edition, by which time he had probably moved from the Curtain to the Globe, to 'Clonnico del Mondo Snuffe'. These publications were anonymous, but Armin's name is found on an enlarged edition published in 1608 as *A Nest of Ninnies.* He was probably the author of *Quips upon Questions* (also 1600), a collection of quatrains on stage 'themes', or improvisations on subjects suggested by the audience, and can certainly be credited with at least one play, *Two Maids of Moreclacke*, produced by the King's Revels in 1609.

ARMSTRONG, PAUL (1869–1915), American dramatist who was for a time a purser in the Merchant Navy, and later a journalist. His early plays were not successful, but in 1905 he scored a triumph with *The Heir to the Hoorah*, and became one of the most popular and prolific playwrights of the day. Among his later successes, some of which were written in collaboration, were *Blue Grass* (1908), *Alias Jimmy Valentine* (1909), the first of a long line of crook plays, and *The Deep Purple* (1910). His dialogue was crisp, with strong situations and grim humour, but his work had little literary merit, and was in the melodramatic style later exploited by the cinema.

ARMSTRONG, William (1882–1952), English actor and producer, who was for many years connected with the Liverpool Playhouse, the oldest existing repertory company in Great Britain. He began his acting career under Benson, and made his first appearance at Stratford-upon-Avon in 1908. He later toured extensively in England and America, and was successively with the Glasgow, the Liverpool, the Birmingham, and the Everyman Repertory companies. In 1922, after touring with Mrs. Patrick Campbell in *Hedda Gabler*, he went to Liverpool as director and producer at the Playhouse, and remained there until 1941, when the theatre closed owing to heavy air-raids. He did not return on its re-opening, but was responsible for a number of outstanding productions in London theatres, including *Old Acquaintance*, a revival of *The Circle*, *Uncle Harry*, and *Claudia*. In 1945 he was appointed producer and assistant director, under Sir Barry Jackson, of the Birmingham Repertory theatre. In a letter to Norman Marshall, quoted in the latter's *The Other Theatre*, he says: 'My heart has always been in repertory and the theatre with a definite policy. . . . There is a lovely spirit of adventure and excitement in repertory which one never gets elsewhere.' His work in Liverpool was of great value to the repertory movement, and to the English theatre as a whole, many of his company going on to become leading actors in London. In 1951 he was awarded the C.B.E. for services to the theatre. He was a contributor to the first edition of this Companion.

ARNAUD, Yvonne Germaine (1892–1958), an actress who, though born and educated in France, spent her entire professional life in London. Trained as a pianist, she toured Europe as a child, but at the age of 18, with no previous stage experience, she appeared at the Adelphi Theatre in *The Quaker Girl*, and was an immediate success, as she was also a year later in *The Girl in the Taxi*. She continued to appear in farce and musical comedy, her charm and high spirits, added to a most musical broken English–French accent, making her a general favourite. Among her outstanding performances were Mrs. Pepys in *And So To Bed* (1926), the Duchess of Tann in *The Improper Duchess* (1931), Mrs. Frail in *Love for Love* (1943), and Denise in *Dear Charles* (1952). She was also good in the Aldwych farces, *Tons of Money* (1922) and *A Cuckoo in the Nest* (1925). One of her few failures was Madame Alexandra in a translation of *Colombe* (1951), where her essential kindliness and good nature vanquished the cruelty and egotism of Anouilh's ageing actress. Yvonne Arnaud, who was the wife of Hugh McLellan, followed the old tradition of keeping her private life truly private, and was averse to modern methods of publicity. She lived for a long time in Guildford, where a new repertory theatre has been named after her. Designed by John Brownrigg for an island site by the river Wey, donated by the local authority, who also gave a substantial sum towards the cost of the building (the rest was raised by private subscription), this theatre opened on 2 June, 1965 under its first director, Sir Michael Redgrave, who appeared in the initial two productions, *A Month in the Country* (with Ingrid Bergmann) and *Samson Agonistes.*

ARNOLD, Matthew (1822–88), English poet, educationist, and critic, whose interest in the drama led him, as far back as 1880, to put the case for its official support. His two poetic plays, *Empedocles on Etna* (1852) and *Merope* (1858), were both written on classical lines. Arnold said that in his endeavours to learn and practise what was sound and true in poetical art he found the only sure guidance and solid footing among the ancients. His plays are for the study rather than the stage, yet he did the drama some service by arguing its claims as an important cultural influence. In one of his essays he said: 'The theatre is irresistible: organize the theatre.' In 1882 he published an essay on *The French Play in London*, and he was for a short time dramatic critic of the *Pall Mall Gazette.* T. C. KEMP†, *rev.*

ARONSON, Boris (1900–), American scene and costume designer, born in Kiev, where he studied art. Dissatisfied with the Soviet régime, he left Russia for Berlin in 1922, and in 1923 arrived in New York, where he began to design scenery for the Unser Theatre and for Maurice Schwartz's Yiddish Art Theatre. An admirer of Marc Chagall, his early work was influenced by the sets in Cubist-fantastic style designed by Chagall and Nathan Altman for the Jewish Theatre in Moscow. His later sets were more symbolic, restating by use of forms and colours the mood of the play and its characters, as in those he designed for Odets's *Awake and Sing* (1935). He has also designed a number of sets for realistic plays. In addition to a long series of stage settings, of which that for MacLeish's *J.B.* (1959) was outstanding (see No. 111), he has painted a number of bright and action-filled circus paintings, and the influence of these is seen in the lightness and spaciousness of many of his more recent sets. He is also the inventor of 'Projected Scenery', a basic permanent set of interrelated abstract shapes made of neutral grey gauze, which can easily be 'painted' any desired colour by directing spotlights upon it through coloured slides. This device, especially good for ballet and opera, was first used in the Ballet Theatre's production of Saroyan's 'The Great American Goof' (1940). ROBERT TRACY

ART, THÉÂTRE D', see LUGNÉ-POË.

ARTAUD, Antonin (1896–1948), French actor, producer and poet, whose work has been one of the great seminal influences on the contemporary French stage. Entering the theatre in 1921, Artaud acted successively with Lugné-Poë, Dullin, and Pitoëff. From 1923 to 1927

he was actively connected with the surrealist movement in literature, and with Roger Vitrac founded the Théâtre Alfred Jarry, which in 1926 and 1927 gave four productions, including Strindberg's *Dream Play*. As early as 1922 he had been impressed by the power of the Oriental theatre, and in 1931 a performance by a group of Balinese dancers stimulated him to attempt to redefine the meaning of theatre in a series of essays, collected together in 1938 as *Le Théâtre et son double*. Here he formulated his theory of a 'Theatre of Cruelty', a theatre which would have the power to disturb the spectator to the very depths of his being, employing the Oriental theatre's symbolism of gesture, movement, sound, and rhythm, rather than language. Introducing his now well-known analogy of the plague, Artaud observed that in the ravages of the great plagues of history, men were liberated from the restraints of morality and reason, and returned to a state of primitive ferocity and power. He saw the theatre as a similar catalyst, freeing the repressed unconscious, forcing men to view themselves as they are under the veneer of civilization; audiences would no longer merely observe the actions presented on the stage, but be impelled by their inner force. Two manifestos for the 'Theatre of Cruelty' were issued, in 1932 and 1933, but it was not until 1935 that he managed to give practical expression to his theories, by producing his own play, *Les Cenci*, based on Shelley and Stendhal. The production ran for only two weeks, and was Artaud's last practical work in the theatre. After travelling in Mexico and Ireland, he succumbed to a mental crisis, and spent nine years in various asylums before being released in 1946. His influence is widespread in the theatre today, notably in the productions of Jean-Louis Barrault, Jean Vilar, and Roger Blin, and the plays of such writers as Adamov, Genêt, Camus and Audiberti.

T. C. C. MILNE

ARTEF THEATRE, NEW YORK, see COMEDY THEATRE.

ARTILLERY THEATRE, LONDON. This theatre, at Woolwich, was built by subscription with the help of the War Office, and was opened by Lord Roberts in 1905. It was controlled by various people until 1909, when a lease was granted to Mrs. Agnes Littler. She continued in management very successfully up to Sept. 1940, when the theatre was taken over for use by various Service units in entertaining the troops. Many famous actors appeared there, including Lily Langtry, Belle Bilton, George Robey, Albert Chevalier, Oscar Asche, and Violet Vanbrugh. The first wounded men to arrive in this country during the First World War were entertained there by Mrs. Littler, who, with her husband, was badly injured when in Mar. 1918 a bomb was dropped just outside the theatre while they were in the foyer.

W. MACQUEEN-POPE†

ARTS COUNCIL OF GREAT BRITAIN, THE. This body is in essence a continuation of the Council for the Encouragement of Music and the Arts (C.E.M.A.), which arose out of the necessities of the Second World War. Set up at the beginning of 1940 with the aid of a grant from the Pilgrim Trust, and from the Treasury on the vote of the then Board of Education, its avowed intention was to bring concerts and plays to the crowded evacuation areas where entertainment was limited or non-existent. In 1942 the Pilgrim Trust withdrew, leaving the Treasury to provide the whole of the Council's income, and Lord Keynes was appointed Chairman. It was largely due to his enthusiasm and unceasing activity that the good work done by the Council did not end with the war, but was put on a permanent basis, the greater part of its income being provided by an annual grant-in-aid from the Treasury. The Arts Council, as it was then called, was created a Body Corporate under Royal Charter on 9 Aug. 1946 'to develop a greater knowledge, understanding, and practice of the Fine Arts, to increase their accessibility to the public, and to improve their standard of execution'. The Council directs its financial help towards the professional aspect of the Arts, assisting drama largely through 'non-profit-distributing' theatre companies situated both in London and in the provinces. These companies enjoy complete freedom in determining their artistic policies, being required only to keep the Council fully informed at all times of their activities and financial position. They are helped also, both directly and indirectly, by the Council's special schemes for training theatre managers, helping new and promising playwrights and stage designers, giving extra assistance towards the first and second productions of approved new plays and neglected plays, and by the subsidizing of transport costs incurred by theatre parties visiting their theatres. These and other activities are summarized in the annual Report and Accounts published by the Council.

ARTS LEAGUE OF SERVICE TRAVELLING THEATRE, GREAT BRITAIN, was founded on 28 Apr. 1919 as a drama section of the A.L.S. From the beginning it was linked to an art movement rather than a theatrical tradition, which allowed great freedom in choice of material and experimentation. The members of the company, among whom were the young Angela and Hermione Baddeley, toured the country, giving a varied programme of mimed folk-song, dances, short plays, sketches, etc. Props and scenery were reduced to a minimum, all being comfortably carried in a van which also served for transport. The company, although doing excellent work in bringing varied and wholesome entertainment to remote corners of rural England and Scotland, was always in financial difficulties, in spite of a grant from the Carnegie Trust, and was finally disbanded in 1937. It may be said that its very success was its undoing, for it stimulated local interest in drama, and soon found itself ousted by the amateur companies it had helped to bring into being. Among its constant supporters were Judith Wogan, Eleanor Elder, who later (1943) wrote a short history of the movement, and Hugh Mackay, well known for his singing of Hebridean folk-songs.

ARTS THEATRE, LONDON, a club theatre for the staging of unlicensed and experimental plays, which opened in 1927. Its first important production, *Young Woodley*, in 1928, was transferred to the West End, as were *The Lady With a Lamp* (1929), *Musical Chairs* (1931), *Richard of Bordeaux* (1932), and *Viceroy Sarah* (1934). In 1942 Alec Clunes took over, and for ten years made the theatre a vital centre, producing a wide range of plays and achieving, as one critic said, the status of 'a pocket National Theatre'. It was here that Fry's *The Lady's Not For Burning* had its first production, in 1948, with Clunes as Thomas Mendip. The theatre changed hands again in 1953, when Campbell Williams took charge. He continued to offer interesting productions, among them *Waiting for Godot* in 1955, and *The Waltz of the Toreadors* in 1956. The standard then somewhat declined, and in 1962 the theatre was sold to the film-producer Nathan Cohen. It was leased for six months by the Royal Shakespeare Theatre as a London home for new and unusual plays, opening on 14 Mar. with Giles Cooper's *Everything in the Garden*. This was followed by five new plays and two revivals, *The Lower Depths* and Middleton's *Women Beware Women*, of which only the last could be accounted an outstanding success. The theatre was then used for mixed programmes, including films, and for holiday matinées of plays for children, given by Caryl Jenner's Unicorn Theatre company.

ASCH, SHOLOM (1880–1957), Jewish dramatist and novelist, born at Kutno in Poland. In 1900 he was working as a journalist in both Hebrew and Yiddish, and two years later published a volume of short stories in Hebrew. He is the author of several plays in Yiddish, of which the best-known is *God of Vengeance*. This could not be performed in Russia in the original because of the ban on Yiddish plays at that time, and it was given its first production by Reinhardt in Berlin in 1907 in German, as *Gott der Rache*. It immediately attracted the attention of the literary and theatrical world to the possibilities of Yiddish drama, and has since been translated and produced in many countries. Some of Asch's Yiddish novels have also been dramatized or adapted for the stage. He was at one time President of the Yiddish Section of the P.E.N. Club, and travelled constantly between Europe and America. He was, however, in London at the time of his death. Interested in religious problems, he wrote novels based on the lives of Jesus and of St. Paul, and an Open Letter to Christians. More than anyone else Sholom Asch raised the standard of Yiddish writing and helped to place it on a literary basis. To non-Jews he is undoubtedly the best-known Yiddish author, since his works have frequently appeared in translation. E. HARRIS

ASCHE. (1) OSCAR [JOHN STANGER HEISS] (1871–1936), English actor, of Scandinavian descent, born in Australia, who is mainly remembered in connexion with his own oriental fantasy with music, *Chu-Chin-Chow*. First given in 1916, this ran for five years without a break, setting up a record for its own day. Asche appeared in it himself as Abu Hasan, and followed it by another play of the same type, *Cairo* (1921), which was not, however, so successful. Asche made his first appearance on the stage in 1893, and was for some years with Benson's company, and with Tree at His Majesty's, being himself manager of that theatre in 1907, when he produced *As You Like It*, *Othello*, and *The Taming of the Shrew*. He made several tours of Australia, playing Petruchio, Shylock, and other parts, and in South Africa added Antony to his repertoire. In 1911 he appeared as Falstaff, and in the same year made a great success in the part of Hajj in *Kismet*. He published his autobiography in 1929. His wife (2) LILY BRAYTON (1876–1953), who appeared with him in *Chu-Chin-Chow* and many other plays, and was associated with him in management in London and on tour, made her first appearance on the stage in 1896, with Benson, remaining with him for some time. In 1902 she was seen as Yo-San in *The Darling of the Gods*, and subsequently her career followed that of her husband. She made her last appearance on the stage in 1932, playing Portia in *Julius Caesar*.

ASHCROFT, Dame PEGGY (1907–), English actress, who was trained at the Central School, and made her first appearance at the Birmingham Repertory Theatre as Margaret in *Dear Brutus* in 1926. She appeared in London a year later, but first attracted attention as Naemi in *Jew Süss* (1929), a part in which she showed that simplicity and sense of poetic tragedy which have since made so many of her performances remarkable. She played a variety of parts during the next few years, some of them at the Old Vic, but it was with her Juliet in Gielgud's production at the New Theatre in 1935 that her growing reputation was finally consolidated. With a youthful gaiety and innocence she combined a strict integrity and a deepening maturity of purpose which again served to make her Nina in *The Seagull* the following year a moving experience. That she is also an excellent player of comedy was shown in her Lady Teazle, Cecily Cardew, Beatrice, and Mistress Page, while her aptitude for modern drama showed itself in *Edward, My Son*, *The Heiress*, and *The Deep Blue Sea*. In 1956 she appeared in *The Chalk Garden*, and at the Court Theatre in an amazing dual role as the prostitute and the prostitute's male cousin in *The Good Woman of Setzuan*. One of her finest roles was undoubtedly Hedda Gabler, which she played in 1954 in London and on tour in Norway. For this performance she was awarded the King's Medal by the King of Norway. She was created D.B.E. in 1956 for services to the theatre, and on 5 Nov.

1962 a theatre named after her opened in Croydon, where she was born. It housed the company under Clement Scott-Gilbert which had formerly played at the Pembroke Theatre-in-the-Round, Croydon, and its first production was *Royal Gambit*, a translation of a German play by Hermann Griessieker on Henry VIII and his wives, who are the only characters. Michael Denison played Henry, and Dulcie Gray, Katharine of Aragon. The theatre, which is part of the Croydon Civic Centre, under an artistic director, was designed by Beatty Pownall. Although an apparently conventional proscenium-arch theatre, seating just over 700, it can be converted into an arena theatre by the use of hydraulic lifts.

ASHWELL [POCOCK], LENA (1872–1957), English actress, who was studying music when, on the advice of Ellen Terry, she abandoned it for the stage. She made her first appearance in 1891, and after playing a wide variety of parts, in London and on tour, made a great success in 1900 in *Mrs. Dane's Defence*, which she frequently revived. Among her later successes were Yo-San in *The Darling of the Gods*, Leah Kleschna in the play of that name, Jacqueline in *Madame X*, and Deborah in *The Shulamite*. She made her first appearance in America in this last part, together with *Mrs. Dane's Defence*, and on her return to England took over the Kingsway Theatre, inaugurating in 1907 a season of successful repertory with *Irene Wycherley*. She remained in management until 1915, when she relinquished all her other activities in order to organize companies for the entertainment of the troops in France and later in Germany, for which work she was awarded the O.B.E. Similar companies, under the title of the Lena Ashwell Players, continued after the war to appear in halls throughout London. Miss Ashwell was also active in the foundation of the British Drama League (see AMATEUR THEATRE). In 1925 she took over the Bijou Theatre, Bayswater, renamed it the Century, and produced there several new plays, including her own adaptations of *Crime and Punishment* and *Dr. Jekyll and Mr. Hyde*. She was the author of several books, including an autobiography, *Myself a Player*, published in 1936.

ASPHALEIAN SYSTEM, one of the earliest of the modern elaborate systems controlling the stage floor; in it the whole stage area is divided into individual platforms, upon hydraulic pistons, each of which can be separately raised, lowered, or tipped.

RICHARD SOUTHERN

ASSEMBLY THEATRE, NEW YORK, see PRINCESS THEATRE.

ASSOCIATION OF BRITISH THEATRE TECHNICIANS (A.B.T.T.). This organization, which is affiliated to the Association Internationale de Théâtre, was founded in 1961, under the chairmanship of Norman Marshall, to provide a forum for discussion among theatre technicians, and through this, and through the collection and dissemination of information, to raise technical standards in the theatre. In 1961 the association played host in London to the third Biennial Congress of the International Association, when the subject for discussion was 'Adaptable Theatres'. A report on the Congress, edited by Stephen Joseph, was afterwards published.

ASTLEY'S AMPHITHEATRE, LONDON. Best known simply as Astley's, and immortalized by Charles Dickens, this curious theatre had many names. In about 1770 Philip Astley (1742–1814), who had been a sergeant-major and breaker-in of horses with the cavalry at Minden in 1759, returned home with his general's charger, which he exhibited in a roughly made 'ring' in a meadow near the present site of Waterloo Station. Proceedings were instituted against him by interested parties, but in 1779 he had the good fortune to be able to assist George III with the calming of a horse which became restive in public, and received royal support as his reward. In 1780 he moved his activities a quarter of a mile westward, near the old Westminster Bridge, and there erected a wooden building with a gallery, pit, and boxes—all constructed out of waste timber—decorated the interior so that it looked like a grove of trees, and called it 'The Royal Grove'. It remained a circus, but in 1787 Astley added burlettas and pantomime to its attractions. It was burned down in 1794, rebuilt in less than seven months, and again destroyed by fire in 1803. Astley moved to the Olympic (Astley's Middlesex Amphitheatre) in Wych Street while he rebuilt yet again, and the new house opened in 1803 with a great equestrian spectacle, for which type of performance it became famous.

Having built similar places of entertainment all over Britain, France, and Ireland (19 in all), Astley died in 1814, and was succeeded by his son, John, who retired three years later in favour of his partner Davis. The theatre was now known as Davis's Amphitheatre, and equestrian spectacle reached great heights with *The Blood-Red Knight*, *The Battle of Waterloo*, and *The Burning of Moscow*, in which the chief actor was Gomersal, enshrined by Thackeray in *The Newcomes*.

The famous Andrew Ducrow—perhaps the finest circus rider of all time—followed Davis. He was so illiterate that he seldom played a speaking part, but excelled in riding, stage management, and production. In 1841 fire again destroyed the amphitheatre, with great loss, and Ducrow died soon after. William Batty then rebuilt it, and gave it his name. He was followed by William Cooke, who made *Macbeth* and *Richard III* into equestrian dramas, giving White Surrey, Richard's horse, a leading part.

In 1863 Dion Boucicault turned the Amphitheatre into the Theatre Royal, Westminster, but the result was a dismal failure in spite of a spirited representation of *The Relief of Lucknow*, and an adaptation of *The Heart of Midlothian*, called *The Trial of Effie Deans*. Boucicault left, heavily in debt, and was succeeded by E. T. Smith, the remarkable showman who was also a patentee of Drury Lane. He drew the whole of London across the river to see Adah Isaacs Menken in *Mazeppa* (see No. 169). Later the theatre came under the control of 'Lord' George Sanger, was known as Sanger's Amphitheatre, and finally closed in 1895. No trace of it remains, but in 1951 a memorial plaque was unveiled on the site at 225 Westminster Bridge Road.

W. MACQUEEN-POPE†, *rev.*

ASTON, ANTHONY (*fl.* first half of the eighteenth century), commonly called Tony, and known also as Matt Medley, to whom, in default of more precise information, goes the honour of having been the first professional actor to appear in the New World. A wild, irresponsible Irishman, of mercurial disposition, he tried his hand at many things, but soon wearied of them. At one time he appeared at Drury Lane, and in the preface to his *Fool's Opera*, printed in about 1730, he refers to his appearances in 'New York, East and West Jersey, Maryland, Virginia (on both sides Cheesapeek), North and South Carolina, South Florida, the Bahamas, Jamaica, and Hispaniola'. He is known to have appeared in Charleston in 1703, and later in the same year in New York, but we have no knowledge of what he played, or whether he was alone or with a company of other actors. He may have given a sort of Variety entertainment like the 'Medley' in which he appeared in the English provinces in 1717. His stay in the New World was short, and he returned to tour England and Scotland. He was still alive in 1735, when he protested against the proposed bill for regulating the stage, and in 1749 Chetwood spoke of him as 'travelling still and as well known as the post-horse that carries the mail'. There are references to him in O. G. Sonneck's *Early Opera in America* (1915), and his life was written by Watson Nicholson.

ASTOR PLACE OPERA HOUSE, NEW YORK, one block east of Broadway, a house built for Italian opera, which opened on 22 Nov. 1847. During the summer of 1848 Niblo, burnt out of his Garden, leased it and put on some good plays with an excellent stock company. After this it reverted to opera, except for Macready's season, which began on 4 Sept. and, owing to the jealousy of Edwin Forrest, terminated on 10 May 1849 with the anti-British Astor Place riot, in which 22 people were killed and 36 wounded by shots fired by the militia. The theatre then closed for repairs, and reopened on 24 Sept. 1849, with Jean Davenport as Juliet. Other actors who came during the intervals of opera were Vandenhoff, Julia Dean, and Charlotte Cushman, the last as Romeo with Fanny Wallack as Juliet. The theatre was never successful, however, in spite of the efforts of Charles R. Thorne and Frank Chanfrau, and it finally closed on 4 Apr. 1854, the furniture, scenery, and props being sold at auction.

ASTOR THEATRE, NEW YORK, on Broadway at 45th Street. This opened on 21 Sept. 1906 with *A Midsummer Night's Dream*, followed by *Cymbeline*. Two musical plays proved successful in 1908, but the theatre's first long run was achieved by a melodrama, *Paid in Full*, which ran throughout 1908, followed by the equally successful *The Man From Home*. *Seven Keys to Baldpate* (1912) had 320 performances, and the theatre's record run of 680 performances was scored by *East is West* (1918). Seven years later the Astor saw its last legitimate production with a musical play, *June Days*, and then became a cinema.

GEORGE FREEDLEY†

ASTRACANADAS, see GÉNERO CHICO.

AŚVAGHOṢA, see INDIA, 1.

ATELLAN FARCE, see FABULA, 1. *Atellana* and ROME.

ATKINS, ROBERT (1886–1972), English actor and producer, whose career was spent almost entirely in the service of Shakespeare. He was a pupil at the Royal Academy of Dramatic Art when in 1906 he was engaged by Tree for His Majesty's, making his first appearance there in *Henry IV, Part I.* He later toured with Martin-Harvey in *The Only Way*, and was in the companies of Forbes-Robertson and Frank Benson. He joined the Old Vic company in 1915, and returned there in 1920, after war service, as producer. He remained until 1925, during which time he produced and appeared in a number of Shakespearian and other plays, including the rarely seen *Titus Andronicus* and *Troilus and Cressida*, and staged, for the first time in England, Ibsen's *Peer Gynt*. In later years he took his own Shakespeare company on tour, founded the Bankside Players, and with them produced *Henry V*, *Much Ado About Nothing*, and *The Merry Wives of Windsor* under Elizabethan conditions at the Ring, Blackfriars; he was also producer at the Stratford-upon-Avon Memorial Theatre, and at the Open-Air Theatre in Regent's Park, London. During Oct. 1940, at the height of the bombing of London, he continued to present Shakespeare at the Vaudeville Theatre, in the Strand. Among his outstanding parts were Sir Toby Belch, Touchstone, Caliban, Bottom, Sir Giles Overreach, and James Telfer in *Trelawny of the 'Wells'*. In 1933, after producing Mussolini's play on Napoleon in an English translation, he was made a Cavaliere of the Order of the Crown of Italy, and he was awarded the C.B.E. in the Birthday Honours of 1949 for services to the English theatre.

ATKINSON, BROOKS (1894–), American dramatic critic, born in Melrose, Mass., and educated at Harvard. He served under H. T. Parker as assistant dramatic critic for *The Boston Transcript* in 1918, and became literary editor of *The New York Times* in 1922. From

1926 to 1960 he was dramatic critic of the latter (with a brief leave of absence during the Second World War, when he went to China and later to Russia as a war correspondent), and in this position he maintained a fine record for honest and intelligent observation of the American theatre. Among his publications are *Henry Thoreau*, *East of the Hudson*, *Skyline Promenades*, and *The Cingalese Prince*. When he retired from *The Times* in 1960 the Mansfield Theatre, New York, was renamed the Brooks Atkinson in his honour.

THOMAS QUINN CURTISS

ATTA, see FABULA, 9. *Togata*.

ATTERBOM, PER DANIEL AMADEUS (1790–1835), Swedish poet (see SCANDINAVIA, 3 *a*).

ATTWELL, HUGH (?–1621), English actor, originally with the Queen's Revels. He later joined Prince Charles's Men, and remained with them until his death. An elegy on him by William Rowley tells us that he was a little man, probably with a fine speaking-voice—''Mongst living Princes it hath sweetly sung (While they have sung his praise)', and later 'his toung a silver bell'; while it ends, 'He changed his *Hugh*, yet he remains At-Well.' He had a brother George, who was probably the author of and a performer in *Mr. Attowel's Jigge*.

AUBIGNAC, FRANÇOIS HÉDELIN, ABBÉ D' (1604–76), one of the first important French writers on the drama. His *Pratique du théâtre*, published in 1657, upheld the unities, and criticized with much acerbity those who departed from them. It marks a decisive step in the formation of the French classical style, and was translated into English in 1684. D'Aubignac's own plays, of which the first was the tragedy *Zénobie* (1640), were intended as models for aspiring dramatists, but they were not particularly successful, partly owing to the mediocrity of their style, and partly to the attacks of the many enemies which d'Aubignac's criticisms had made for him.

AUDE, JOSEPH (1755–1841), French dramatist, who came of a working-class family and was educated by the kindness of his bishop. He was for some time secretary to Buffon, whose memoirs he edited, and in 1793 returned to the theatre (for which as a young man he had written a number of ephemeral plays) with a series of farces based on Cadet Roussel. These, played by Brunet in the minor theatres, particularly the Montansier, had an enormous vogue, though they are now forgotten. Aude, who was a friend of Dorvigny and equally witty, quarrelsome, penniless, and drunken, wasted what might have been an outstanding talent for comedy. He had a nephew of the same name as himself, who also wrote farces and vaudevilles, frequently attributed to the uncle.

AUDEN, WYSTAN HUGH (1907–), English poet (now an American citizen) and author with Christopher Isherwood of several plays in verse and prose, *The Dog Beneath the Skin* (1935), *The Ascent of F.6* (1936), and *On the Frontier* (1938), given by the Group Theatre at the Westminster, London.

AUDIBERTI, JACQUES (1899–1965), French dramatist, who first made his name as a poet and journalist, and was in his forties when his first play, *Quoat-Quoat*, was produced in 1946. This was a satire on nineteenth-century melodrama, and was followed by *Le Mal Court* (1947), a tale of innocence corrupted by experience, set in the eighteenth century. These are probably Audiberti's best plays, certainly the best known outside France, but he was a prolific writer—he was awarded the Prix Charles Veillon in 1955 for the ensemble of his literary work—and his later plays include *La Fête Noire*, based on the legend of the Questing Beast, *Pucelle*, a somewhat irreverent treatment of Joan of Arc's life, *La Hobereauté*, again a historical play set in mediaeval Burgundy, and, among the plays with a modern setting, a one-act *Les Femmes du Bœuf*, which was produced at the Comédie-Française. Audiberti belonged to no particular school of dramatists, but created his own world of fantasy and farce, in which his eccentricities found full scope.

AUDIENCE ON THE STAGE. The practice, common in the early English and Continental theatres, of allowing members of the audience to buy seats on the stage was a fertile source of disorder and of acute irritation to both actor and dramatist. The places were usually occupied by young fops, who took occasion to show off their fine clothes and display their insensitiveness to any form of theatrical art by their constant chatter and restlessness. The practice was first noticed in England in 1596 and in France in 1649, but at both dates was well established. The theory has been advanced that in France it helped to do away with the old multiple setting, and to confine French tragedy in a small open space, making it a series of *bravura* recitations given before a backcloth. It had a less restrictive effect on the English theatre, where its influence on dramatic convention can be seen in the Induction to *The Taming of the Shrew*, and—a final vestige—in *The Beggar's Opera*. It was the development of the 'machine' play which finally made the presence of spectators on the stage intolerable, and Voltaire, who attributed to them the failure of his early plays, was responsible for their removal in 1759 from the stage of the Comédie-Française, other French theatres following suit at intervals. When Garrick took over Drury Lane he endeavoured to remove them, but had to wait until the theatre was enlarged in 1762, when the new auditorium offered ample space for the entire audience. In other London theatres the practice continued for many years, and on special occasions privileged people were still to be seen on some stages until well into the nineteenth century. At Grimaldi's farewell performance at Drury Lane in 1828, and again in 1838 and 1840, when Queen Victoria visited Covent

Garden, there were, according to *The Times*, 'crowds on the stage, more numerous than there generally are on such occasions'. The custom was evidently not then obsolete, though it soon became so. It is said that Molière once sat on the stage of the Hôtel de Bourgogne to watch a play in which he and his company were satirized, and that the closeness of the original somewhat embarrassed the actor who was representing him, a fact which no doubt afforded Molière some quiet amusement.

AUDITORIUM, that part of a theatre building designed or intended for the accommodation of the people witnessing the play—the audience. The word in its present usage dates from about 1727, though Auditory and Spectatory are also to be found. The auditorium can vary considerably in size and shape (see ARCHITECTURE), placing the audience in front of, part way round, or entirely round the acting area. It can also be in one entity, or divided, with galleries above the main area.

AUGIER, (GUILLAUME VICTOR) ÉMILE (1820–89), French dramatist and, with Ponsard, the first to revolt against the excesses of the Romantics. He was intended for the law, but after the success of his first play, *La Ciguë* (1844), at the Odéon he devoted himself to writing, either alone or in collaboration. After a few plays in verse, he found his true vocation in the writing of a series of honest domestic dramas dealing with social questions of the moment, of which *Le Gendre de Monsieur Poirier* (1854) is the best known. Among others which were successful in their day were *Le Mariage d'Olympe* (1855), which paints the courtesan as she is, and not as the younger Dumas had idealized her in his *Dame aux camélias* a few years previously; *Les Lionnes pauvres* (1858), which shows the disruption of home life consequent on the adultery of the wife; and the political comedies, *Les Effrontés* (1861) and *Le Fils de Giboyer* (1862). Augier, who had a solid bourgeois background and a good education, came at a moment of transition in the French theatre, when Romanticism had failed with *Les Burgraves* (1843) and people, tiring of the 'well-made' plays of Scribe, were turning back to the seventeenth-century classics, ably interpreted by the great actress Mlle Rachel. From a neo-classicist he became a social dramatist, and ended his career, under the influence of the new currents of thought then running across Europe, with two problem plays, *Mme Caverlet* (1876) and *Les Fourchambault* (1879). In the latter an illegitimate son saves his father and his father's legitimate offspring from ruin. Although Augier was scorned by Zola, Jules Lemaître, a surer judge, thought well of him, and his plays, though not without their faults, were well written and well adapted to the theatrical conventions of his time. He was more of a realist than either the younger Dumas or Sardou.

AUGUSTUS DRURIOLANUS, see HARRIS (2) AUGUSTUS.

AUSTIN, CHARLES (1878–1944), a famous music-hall comedian who for many years featured a character of his own invention, Parker, P.C., in a series of sketches built round this amusing member of the police force. He was also a well-known figure in pantomime, and was very popular in his profession. On one occasion he ran a horse, named after his famous character, in the Derby, but it was unplaced.

AUSTRALIA. The early history of the Australian theatre seems to have paralleled, in broad outline and at a distance of nearly a hundred years, that of the American. Just as the Hallams in the mid-eighteenth century went from London to establish the professional theatre in the American Colonies, so in the early nineteenth century actors from England brought professional theatre to Australia. In both countries they were preceded by amateurs, since the first recorded play in Australia was *The Recruiting Officer*, given in Sydney on 4 June 1789 by a cast of convicts. A few years later *Henry IV* was produced by a semi-professional company in Sydney's first theatre building, but the venture failed, and little but amateur performances, by convicts at Emu Plains, near Sydney, are recorded for the next thirty years. On 26 Dec. 1832 a Theatre Royal was opened in Sydney by the American impresario Barnett Levey (1798–1837) with the famous nautical melodrama *Black-Eyed Susan*, and it was at this theatre that *Richard III* (doubtless in Colley Cibber's version) was first seen in Australia. The first Australian play was A. G. Geoghegan's *The Hibernian Father* (1844). This was followed by the plays of David Burn, and by such productions as Harpur's *The Bushrangers* (1853). But the staple fare was still farce and melodrama, mainly imported. These years saw a great increase in the number of theatres—Hobart, 1837, Adelaide, 1838, Melbourne, 1841, and theatre building intensified everywhere with the gold rush of the 1850s. Many of these theatres were under the control of George Selth Coppin (1819–1906), who also inaugurated the second phase of the Australian theatre by introducing the pernicious 'starring tours' by visiting celebrities which had already threatened to wreck the American theatre. They did nothing to encourage Australian playwriting and acting, and drained off much money and energy which might have been spent in the establishment of an indigenous theatre. The first European star to be imported was G. V. Brooke, followed by such diverse players as Joseph Jefferson, the Charles Keans, Mme Céleste, Ristori, and the younger Mathews. Theatrical memoirs of the period contain many illuminating glimpses of the Australian theatre in the latter half of the nineteenth century. Later the great names of the music-hall made their way to Australia, under the auspices of the English comedian Harry Rickards [really Henry Benjamin Leete] (1845–1911). In 1882 was established the managerial triumvirate of John

Cassius Williamson (1845–1913), George Musgrove, and Arthur Garner. Among the visiting stars of this period were Irving, Bernhardt, Janet Achurch with the first performances of Ibsen, companies in Gilbert and Sullivan, and the Boucicault and Brough companies, which were active from 1866 to 1895.

In 1904 the Australian Theatre Society founded repertory theatres in Melbourne and Sydney, and in 1910 an Adelaide repertory theatre opened a good programme with Synge, Ibsen, Sudermann, and Shaw. Interesting work began in all these centres, including the production of Australian plays by A. Adams and Le Gay Brereton, but the First World War and the subsequent competition of the cinema, caused the serious theatre to languish, though musical shows flourished and served to introduce Gladys Moncrieff, who became Australia's most famous music-hall star. After the war, efforts were made, notably by Steel Rudd and by Bert Bailey, to found a national folk-theatre, and there was also a Shakespeare company run by Allan Wilkie with local actors, but during the 1930s the theatre had to contend not only with the cinema, but also with the depression and a high rate of entertainment tax. It was not until the 1940s that large audiences returned to the playhouses. Meanwhile the establishment of a Little Theatre (now St. Martin's Theatre) in Melbourne in 1931, and the foundation by Gertrude Johnson four years later of the Australian National Theatre Movement, whose theatre was destroyed by fire in 1962, were hopeful auguries for the future. The 1930s saw more Australian plays being written. *A Touch of Silk* (1930), by B. Davies, was only the precursor of such later works as K. Brownville's *Sleep to Wake* (1939), C. Duncan's *Sons of the Morning* and S. Locke-Elliott's *The Invisible Circus* (both 1946), Russel Oakes's *Enduring as the Camphor Tree*, and Douglas Stewart's verse-play, *Ned Kelly*. The first Australian dramatist to make an impact outside his own country was, however, Ray Lawler, an actor who was seen in his own *Summer of the Seventeenth Doll* in London in 1957, a production which had a great success and raised the liveliest hopes for the future. Brought to London by Olivier, after his tour of Australia with the Old Vic company in 1948, it was the first Australian play with an Australian cast to be seen in London. Lawler's later play, *Piccadilly Bushman*, sponsored by Williamson's in Australia in 1959, has not yet been seen in London. However, Richard Beynon's *The Shifting Heart*, about Italian immigrants in Melbourne, was seen there in 1959. A great deal has been done since the Second World War to encourage an interest in the theatre both by professionals and by amateurs. Hobart, which still has its Theatre Royal of 1837—now the oldest playhouse in Australia—relies mainly on touring companies in imported plays, but it has a Playhouse where the local amateur group appears. Launceston has a National Theatre for visiting artists, and also a particularly strong amateur group which competes, sometimes with new one-act plays by local authors, in the Tasmanian Drama Festival, established in 1947. Melbourne has its Tin Alley Players; Sydney, apart from the Phillip Theatre, has Her Majesty's, the Pocket Playhouse, the Independent, and the Ensemble; Brisbane has the Twelfth Night Theatre and a strong amateur tradition. Nor were the universities behindhand. Adelaide University Theatre Guild, for instance, put on in 1961 an Australian play, *The Ham Funeral*, by Patrick White, and ran a seminar for playwrights and producers. Melbourne graduates in 1962 gave an excellent account of themselves in *The Cherry Orchard*; at Sydney University plays in foreign languages are regularly staged, thus continuing a tradition begun in 1886 with a production in Greek of the *Agamemnon*.

The old-established firm of J. C. Williamson Theatres, whose founder was mentioned above, is active all over the country with resident and touring companies, which, until his death in 1962, included a Shakespeare touring company under John Alden. The joint managing director is the Brisbane-born actor John McCallum (1914–   ), who studied in London and had a successful career there before returning permanently to Australia, where he had previously made two appearances in 1958. He was accompanied by his wife, the English actress Googie [Georgette Lizette] Withers (1917–   ), who toured successfully under his management in *The Constant Wife* and *Roar Like a Dove*.

Although tours by such visitors as Sybil Thorndike and Lewis Casson, Margaret Rutherford, Fay Compton, Cicely Courtneidge, and the Royal Shakespeare company are still warmly welcomed, Australia has taken a definite step towards the establishment of a national theatre by the foundation of the Elizabethan Theatre Trust, intended to assist promising playwrights and train young actors. This was first suggested in 1954 to celebrate the Queen's visit to Australia, and a Board of Trustees was appointed with Hugh Hunt as the first Director (he was succeeded in 1960 by Neil Hutchinson). Although the main work of the Trust is done on tour, a base for operations was needed and was found in the Majestic Theatre, Sydney, which had had a varied career since it was built in 1917, finally becoming a cinema. After renovations, it reopened as the Elizabethan on 27 July 1955 with a cast of guest artists from England in *The Sleeping Prince*. The Trust's first company, headed by the famous Australian-born actress Judith Anderson, made its début in Robinson Jeffers's *Medea* at Canberra in the following September, and then embarked on a long tour. In November came the first production of Lawler's epoch-making *Summer of the Seventeenth Doll*, at the Union Theatre, Melbourne. Since then a number of plays have been toured throughout the country, including Alan Seymour's play about Anzac

Day, *The One Day of the Year*, which was also seen in London, at Theatre Workshop, in 1961. The Trust, in its effort to bring young people into the theatre, has presented puppets in such local plays as *The Tintookies*, and two companies of Young Elizabethan Players have taken 'Shakespeare in jeans' to the schools. For adult audiences there are the Trust Players, a permanent repertory company at the Elizabethan in Sydney which also tours New South Wales, and the Union Theatre, run in conjunction with the University of Melbourne, which has its own small theatre. There is also a National Institute of Dramatic Art, run in association with the University of New South Wales, under Robert Quentin, formerly of the Old Vic, which offers a two-year course for actors, producers, and writers. The Trust has at present no company for ballet, which remains the province of Williamson's, whose company, founded in 1940 and formerly run by Borovansky, was after his death directed by Peggy Van Praagh (now head of the new Australian Ballet company), a former member of Sadler's Wells Ballet; but it has endeavoured to sponsor seasons of opera under Karl Rankl in preparation for the opening of a new opera-house in Sydney. The great difficulty which faces the Trust is, of course, finance, with which is bound up the problem of increasing the size of audiences and the support given by governments and city councils. Meanwhile the Trust continues to promote the development of efficient Little Theatre organizations everywhere in the hope of assisting them to reach full professional status. Though it has not presented many Australian plays at the Elizabethan, it has sponsored trial productions of new local plays in smaller independent theatres, and is always on the look-out for fresh talent. The Arts Council of Australia, formed in 1946, aims to decentralize the arts, take them out into the country, and encourage local groups.

Television has perhaps hit the straight play more than musical comedy, which has always been a favourite genre with Australian audiences, and it may be that native talent will find its feet in this form. In 1959, at an experimental theatre in Melbourne, the New, there was given with unexpected success a ballad-opera, *Ballad of Angel's Alley*, by Jeff Underhill, which was praised as being 'slick, witty and original'.

Two unconventional activities which may prove fruitful are the Emerald Hill Theatre in South Melbourne, directed by Wal Cherry, which is housed in a converted church hall and has a large open stage, and the theatre which has been built into part of the Old Darlinghurst Gaol, now the East Sydney Technical College. This has a movable stage which can be adapted for various forms of presentation, including theatre-in-the-round.

AUSTRALIAN MARIE LLOYD, see FORD, FLORRIE.

AUSTRIA. The twin foci of the theatre in the South German lands were Vienna and Munich. Here the Austro-Bavarian race's love of spectacle and gift for the expression of inner states by outward gesture combined with the ambitions and material resources of two great Catholic dynasties to produce a truly popular theatrical art. For three hundred years the Viennese theatre was not only a unique cultural phenomenon in its own right, but also, in modern times, the nursery of some of Greater Germany's finest dramatists, actors, and producers. Of the two centres, Vienna was the more important, largely for political reasons. It was the capital of the dynasty which for four centuries—from 1438 to 1806—also wore the crown of the Holy Roman Empire. The House of Hapsburg had interests which were European in extent. Rulers of Spain and the Netherlands as well as of Germany, the Hapsburgs also early acquired the crowns of Bohemia and Hungary; their possessions stretched far south into Italy and east into the Balkans; while the states of western Europe were acquiring colonies in the New World and the Indies, they were throwing back, in 1529 and again in 1683, the last Turkish thrusts into the heart of the Continent; while the remainder of the German states were suffering social and political disruption as a result of the Thirty Years' War (1618–48), Austria, although involved in the struggle as a major protagonist, remained culturally and politically intact, and thus maintained that context of social stability which is the prerequisite of a flourishing theatre. Inevitably, the culture of the Hapsburg capital was as cosmopolitan as the Empire of which it was the focal point. Nowhere else is there to be found the same fusion of Germanic, Latin, and Slav strains; but it was the Austro-Bavarian race's flair for the theatre which ensured that that culture should achieve its most typical expression in the theatrical life of the capital. The history of the Austrian theatre is the history of the House of Hapsburg.

The first stirrings of a truly indigenous theatrical art in the Austrian lands can be traced to the small town of Sterzing in the Tyrol, where from 1455 onwards theatrical troupes were formed under the leadership of Stöffl Schopfer and Vigil Raber for the performance of a Passion play with an original text and tales of chivalry drawn from the German heroic epics. Despite these ventures on the level of folk-art, however, it may be claimed with some justice that the origins of the Austrian theatre can be traced to the work of three humanists of the early sixteenth century: Konrad Celtis, Benedictus Chelidonius, and Joachim von Watt. Konrad Celtis (1459–1508), a Franconian, one of the greatest figures in the German humanist movement, settled in Vienna in 1497. As Professor of Poetry and Rhetoric he made the university (founded by Rudolph IV in 1365) a centre of classical studies, and instituted afternoon performances of plays by Terence, Plautus, and Seneca, followed by his own *Ludus Dianae* and *Rhapsodia, laudes et victoria Maximiliani de*

Boemannis, both of which were performed before the Emperor Maximilian, the former at Linz in 1501, the latter at Vienna in 1504. The later Viennese *Haupt- und Staatsaktion* can be seen here in embryo: an elevated subject glorifying the ruling house; music, ballet, and choruses; exchanges between players and audience, and clear traces of the popular Italian *commedia dell'arte* with its stereotyped figures. It was another famous humanist of the university in Vienna, Joachim von Watt (1484–1551), a pupil of Celtis, who provided in his *Gallus pugnans* (1514) the earliest example of the Viennese *Posse* (farce). Cocks and hens appear before the court to argue out the morality of cock-fighting and the rights of the sexes. Humanist advocates represent them, capons act as arbitrators and advise each party to fulfil the functions assigned to it by nature, and a Viennese lad expresses the views of the dissatisfied audience when he declares that they should be consigned to the pot: in this he appears as a prototype of the later Hanswurst, with his cynical comments upon the behaviour of his betters.

If Celtis and Watt represent the university, with its atmosphere of secular humanism, and reflect in the popular elements in their plays something of that earthy South-German realism which had already produced the Tyrolean *Neidhartspiel*, Benedictus Chelidonius (14?–15?), Abbot of the Schottenkloster in Vienna, in his *Voluptatis cum virtute disceptatio* (1515), affords an early example of the drama of the religious orders, with its tendency to present a moral debate in dramatic form: Greek gods and goddesses act out an allegorical tale in which the conflict of virtue and vice is resolved in Christian terms. The Benedictine Schottenkloster was also the setting for Wolfgang Schmeltzl's activities. Schmeltzl (*c.* 1500–*c.* 1560), a Bavarian Protestant who settled in Vienna, turned Catholic, and became an instructor in the Schottenkloster, produced seven plays between 1540 and 1551 which are in complete contrast to the humanistic works considered so far. Under the influence of Paul Rebhun (see GERMANY, 2) he turned in his plays, which are written in the vernacular, to biblical subjects: *Der verlorene Sohn*, *Judith*, *Samuel und Saul.* Vienna proved, however, an unfruitful soil for this kind of evangelical School Drama. Ironically, the year in which Schmeltzl left Vienna (1551) was the year of the Jesuits' arrival in the Hapsburg capital. A year later Peter Canisius, who more than anyone else was responsible for halting the spread of Lutheranism in the German lands, set about organizing the Austrian Province of the Society of Jesus. A school was founded in 1553; within a year it had 300 pupils, by the end of the century 1,000. Nowhere was the Society's policy of harnessing all the resources of human art to the task of education more successful than in Vienna (see JESUIT DRAMA). As early as 1562 a report from Munich (where a school had been founded in 1559) emphasized that farce was 'the best medium of winning over the Germans, of making friends of heretics, and of filling the schools'. The same insight into the theatrical propensities of the race induced the Austrian Province of the Order (which also had an important school in Graz) to depart from its own regulations by permitting vernacular interludes from 1588 on, while from 1601 female roles were allowed in the Provinces north of the Alps, i.e. the Austrian Province, and the Upper German one with important schools at Innsbruck, Munich, and Ingolstadt.

The first Jesuit play to be performed in Vienna (1555) was the *Euripus sive de inanitate rerum omnium* by Levinus Brechtanus [Lewin Brecht], a Franciscan from Antwerp. It concerns the fate of Euripus, who is consigned to perdition after being seduced by Venus and Cupid, and shows many of the characteristics which later became typical of the Jesuit drama of the golden age in Vienna in the second half of the seventeenth century: the humanistic preference for classical themes, the moral purpose (in this a continuation of the medieval morality tradition), the Christian message. The occasion of the typical Jesuit play was usually the end-of-term prize-giving, and the aim was twofold: to instruct the pupil in the arts of grammar, rhetoric, and gentlemanly behaviour, and to convey a primarily religious message to both performers and audience by means of a theatrical experience. The Christianity of the baroque age derived from the fusion of—and sometimes the tension between—two ideas: on the one hand, a Renaissance assertion of the reality and validity of the world of everyday things; on the other, an insistence that, in comparison with the supreme reality of God and the eternity of the hereafter, such things are a delusion and a dream, as shadow is to substance. The Incarnation having brought these two worlds into close relationship, the world of the everyday can now be considered as not only a testing-ground for eternity, but also, through its dependence upon the creative and conserving action of the Divine, as a cryptogram of the latter: human action, human suffering, the configurations of events and the working out of Providence are ciphers and symbols which not only signify but also are the earthly concomitants of Divine processes. (It is precisely here that the justification for dressing up Christian themes in classical garb lies: even the amours of gods and goddesses can be made to yield a religious message.) When three more ingredients are added to this characteristic Counter-Reformation ethos, we have already that unique compositum which is the Austrian theatre: first, a hierarchic view of society in which the Hapsburg ruler is the divinely constituted upholder of a divinely constituted (and thus symbolic) social order, and whose triumph and glory may therefore be fittingly celebrated in a dramatic spectacle designed to justify the ways of God to man; secondly, a tendency, derived from the gloomy splendours of the Counter-Reformation in Hapsburg Spain (and it should not be forgotten that the Jesuits were originally a Spanish Order), to emphasize the dreamlike quality of the everyday when set against the reality of the beyond (in Spain this tendency produced Calderón's *La vida es sueño* (1673), a play which had a great influence on the Austrian theatre); and, lastly, the contact with Italian opera, which gave the Jesuit drama in Vienna—and through it the Viennese theatre as a whole—its slant towards music and spectacle. The importance of this last influence cannot be overestimated, since it is true to say that the plays on classical subjects and, later, the *Kaiserspiele* of the seventeenth century developed in imitation of and competition with opera. By 1620 the Jesuits had their own theatre; in 1659 Leopold I's opera-house was built, and Lodovico Burnacini was at work. The splendours of the Jesuit play, *Pietas victrix* (1659) were rivalled by those of the opera, 'Il pomo d'oro' (1666) (these are only two titles among dozens). The medieval simultaneous setting with which the Jesuits had started was replaced, under pressure from operatic productions, by the single set with 'telari' arranged in perspective; the stage thus set out to be a second reality rivalling and transcending the real world; and this second reality could itself be transcended and thus made to underline the baroque moral—*vanitas, vanitatis vanitas*—by means of Italian stage machinery to which transformation scenes, trials by fire and water, and descents of the *deus ex machina* were child's play.

The greatest name among the writers of Jesuit drama in Austria is undoubtedly that of Nicolaus Avancinus (1612–86), whose *Pietas victrix* has already been mentioned. Professor of Rhetoric, Philosophy, and then Theology at the university of Vienna, and Austrian Provincial, Avancinus became the Court Poet of the great age of Leopold I. Subjects taken from the classics, history, and the Bible tend in his plays to issue in praise or prophecy concerning the Imperial House. Thus, in the *Curae Caesarum* (1654) the story of Theodosius ends with a prophecy of Austria's future glory, and the four corners of the earth appear with horses, gryphons, elephants, and camels to point the moral. The victory of the Cross under Constantine in *Pietas victrix* ends with praise of Leopold as Constantine's successor. The outward splendour with which these events are celebrated makes a significant contrast with, say, the purely inward spiritual realities of *Cenodoxus* (1600), by the Munich Jesuit Jakob Bidermann (1578–1639), where the outer world is shown to be all sham and hypocrisy. The Viennese baroque theatre has within it the seeds of its own decay: when the spiritual impulse flags, the spectacle will become empty rhetoric.

From another quarter, too, its ultimate downfall was being prepared; and again the factor was an internal one: that gradual inclusion of the early permitted vernacular interlude, aimed originally at the uneducated part of the audience, which became a bridgehead for Viennese humour with its love of cynical comment. The process can be seen at its apogee in the work of Johann Baptist Adolph (1657–1708), Avancinus's successor as purveyor of drama to the Court. He took his subjects where he found them: from Avancinus (*Philemon et Apollonius*), from Calderón (*Carnevale seu Voluntas de Carne Triumphans*), from the literary drama of Andreas Gryphius (*Das Prallhansenspiel*); but in Adolph the sober splendour of Avancinus is transmuted into Viennese cheerfulness and gaiety, and the plebs is catered for in scenes of contemporary peasant life. Adolph's work represents the second high-water mark of the Jesuit theatre in Vienna: after him, although it continued high in royal and popular favour, its creative impulse flagged under the rise of the rationalistic spirit which led in 1773 to the suppression of the Order.

During these centuries the popular theatre in Austria was represented by the English Comedians, who arrived late in the sixteenth century. Green's company is recorded as having visited Graz in 1608, where it alternated with seminarists from the Jesuit College in providing a characteristically mixed Whit week programme given before the Archduchess Magdalena: *The Parable of the Lost Son*, *Faustus* (after Marlowe), *Fortunatus*, *King Ludwig and King Frederick of Hungary*, etc.; the Jesuits performed *Cipriano et Justina*. Some of the texts are preserved and show the customary *Haupt- und Staatsaktion* with comic interludes from the clown (Pickelherring); the vernacular is already being used. As in the rest of the German-speaking lands, these troupes of wandering players, in which the English members were soon replaced by native-born actors, had no permanent theatre; they set up their stages in courtyards, market-places, palaces—wherever, in fact, the authorities would tolerate them. At this period in their development they were not especially characteristic of Austria; it was only when they achieved stability in Vienna early in the eighteenth century that their typical offering—the vernacular *Haupt- und Staatsaktion* with coarsely humorous comic interludes—became integrated into and gave a characteristic flavour to the Viennese popular theatre during its first great age.

The credit for this achievement belongs to Joseph Anton Stranitzky (1676–1726), a Styrian who started his theatrical career as a wandering puppeteer associated with the celebrated Hilverding family. After travelling widely he arrived in Vienna *c.* 1705/6 and together with Johann Baptist Hilverding went over to the live theatre. About the same time (1707) he qualified at the university as a dentist, and seems to have pursued both professions to the end of his career. When Hilverding left the company, Stranitzky continued alone with his 'German Comedians', as he now called them. The Vienna Corporation's decision to build a permanent theatre at the Kärntnertor, which was completed in 1710, was the occasion of a dispute as to whether it should be let to native or Italian companies. Court influence gained the Italians the victory, but the disgruntled citizenry boycotted them. They soon left the theatre and Stranitzky's company entered it in triumph in 1711. It thus became the first permanent home of German-language comedy in any of the German lands. The plays performed there did not differ basically from the *Haupt- und Staatsaktionen* of the wandering troupes; what was new—and unique—was the replacement of the comic masks of the *commedia dell'arte* and the English clown-types (Pickelherring, Johann Bouset) by Hanswurst, a completely original comic figure derived from Austro-Bavarian folk art. Hanswurst is a peasant from Salzburg, and his appearance is always the same: hair tied in a tuft on top, fool's ruff, loose red jacket, enormous blue heart on the chest with the letters 'H.W.', red braces and yellow pantaloons. To complete the costume he has a thick, short beard and heavy eyebrows, a green pointed hat, huge yellow buttons, and a wooden lath stuck in his broad leather belt—the 'Pistolese'. Hanswurst is no longer a rustic simpleton, but a typical Viennese figure: the sly, knowing servant with coarse peasant humour and a knack of finding his way unscathed through all the trials of an incomprehensible world. We know only a few titles from the Kärntnertor repertoire—a play on the Don Juan theme, *Das steinerne Gastmahl*, a *Leben und Todt Doktor Faustus*, an *Amphitruo*; but we are fortunate in possessing fourteen *Wiener Haupt- und Staatsaktionen*, in all of which the comic figure is 'der weltberühmte Sauschneider aus Salzburg' Hanswurst; and from these texts, doubtless edited by Stranitzky, we gain a clear idea of the way he adapted Italian opera libretti to make his own *Volksstücke*. Apart from alterations to text and plot, and the replacement of musical set-pieces by original songs, the most striking characteristic of these adaptations is the way in which Hanswurst is not employed merely to provide interludes of comic relief, but has his role integrated into the plot as commentator and go-between in the actions of his betters, sometimes helping, sometimes hindering, but always in his own words and deeds reflecting on a level of mundane incomprehension the elevated sentiments and gestures of the noble protagonists. It is clear also that the verbal humour—which is frequently coarse in the extreme, in this reflecting the taste of all classes at the time—was underlined by a characteristically Viennese type of visual humour, the 'lazzi', stereotyped mimic responses to stock situations. The Viennese Hanswurst was soon imitated throughout the length and breadth of Germany in forms which tended to become more and more degraded. Stranitzky, however, having his own theatre, was able to nominate his successor: Prehauser.

Gottfried Prehauser (1699–1769) had spent several years with the travelling companies, and is reputed to have been the first to play Hanswurst in Salzburg in 1720, before being summoned to Vienna by Stranitzky in 1725. In his hands the character of Hanswurst underwent a number of subtle changes, as did the form of the plays in which he appeared. The world of the *Haupt- und Staatsaktion* slowly gives way to a recognizably Viennese milieu; kings and courtiers become Viennese officers, doctors, and lawyers, embroiled in frequently nefarious dealings with quacks, astrologers, and a huge gallery of tradesmen, artisans, and social types, while Hanswurst himself—Prehauser had the advantage of Viennese birth—undergoes a mellowing process which tones down much of the wounding peasant coarseness of his early days and leaves him more sentimental, 'gemütlich', with even a touch of sophistication in his songs. With the passing of Prehauser the age of impromptu burlesque in Vienna draws to its close under pressure from within and from without.

External pressure was represented by Josef von Sonnenfels (1733–1817), the stormy petrel of the Age of Enlightenment in Vienna. He was an arch-enemy of the Stranitzky tradition, an ardent disciple of Gottsched and advocate of the latter's demands for the reform of the German theatre and abolition of the popular burlesque, views which he aired in his *Briefe über die Wienerische Schaubühne* (1767). His aim was to import the German type of serious drama, in itself a laudable enough ambition, given the poor literary quality of most contemporary writing for the theatre, but short-sighted in that it took no account of the fact that the theatrical life of the Austrian capital was a unique manifestation of the national spirit. He greeted the death of Prehauser with the triumphant cry: 'Great Pan is dead . . . the pillar of the burlesque has fallen, its kingdom is destroyed.' Sonnenfels was not the only rationalist critic to desire the death of Hanswurst; outside Austria, Frau Neuber had decreed his demise, and the Emperor himself, soon to be Joseph II of Austria, was thinking along the same lines.

The internal pressure came from the creation of new comic types and forms of popular burlesque, especially those of Kurz and Hafner. Josef Felix von Kurz (1717–83), whose father had been a member of Stranitzky's company and had later formed his own, was the typical travelling player. His Viennese career started in 1737, but was often interrupted; on his last appearance the Viennese public, ever fickle towards its favourites, would have none of him, and he died in poverty. Kurz's contribution to the popular theatre was the figure of Bernadon, the restless and impetuous youth whose adventures, in a world where magic is the normal thing, represent a last flickering of that baroque universalism in which supernatural forces war with human destiny; thereafter, it appeared in a comfortably bourgeois form in which the hero had to contend with nothing more than an array of spirits good and bad and a wizard or two. Kurz's repertoire, *Die 33 Schelmereien des Bernadon*, in which he played several parts in succession, contained a whole series of such adventures. Sonnenfels fulminated against these 'Bernadoniaden', but in vain.

Philipp Hafner (1735–64), who was born in Vienna, became a theatrical director only after several years as a civic official. A friend of Gottfried Prehauser, he was also an admirer of Gotthold Ephraim Lessing, which may account for the balance struck in his plays, of which *Megära die förchterliche Hexe* (1755), *Der geplagte Odoardo* (1762), and *Der Furchtsame* (1764) are the most famous. While defending the rights of the living theatre against the over-literary approach of the reformers, he insisted that the impromptu burlesque should be replaced by plays constructed on literary principles and acted in faithfulness to the text. He is regarded as the father of the *Volksstück*, the typical Viennese comedy of manners which, while in his case still dependent upon situation rather than character, nevertheless shows that the baroque conception of a social hierarchy with its privileged aristocracy was yielding to a middle-class ethos with a pronounced emphasis upon honesty and civic pride.

In 1776 Joseph II, who viewed the theatre as one of the most powerful educational forces in the state, decided to harness it to his schemes for reforming Austria in accordance with his rationalist principles. In this, incidentally, he was merely continuing a process started by his mother, the Empress Maria Theresa, who had introduced censorship of the theatre in the hope of improving public taste. As a step in this direction he decreed that the Burgtheater (built in 1741) should become a national theatre for the exclusive performance of serious and improving literary drama of the kind produced by writers like Cornelius von Ayrenhoff (1733–1819), whose works, written under French influence, although popular in their day—*Der Postzug* (1769) delighted Frederick the Great—had little power of survival. Sonnenfels was entrusted with the direction of the new theatre. The popular theatre was banished to the suburbs. Some may have hoped, with Sonnenfels, that this would be its death warrant, although there is reason to believe that Joseph II himself was by no means averse to it; indeed, he often visited it in its new home, and his Court archives contain records of payments made to Marinelli's company when it played before him at Schloss Laxenburg. Once established in the suburbs, the popular theatre flourished even more vigorously than before. In 1781 Marinelli erected its most famous centre, the Leopoldstädter Theater; in 1788 the Josefstädter Theater was opened by Karl Mayer, and in 1801 Emanuel Schickaneder opened the Theater an der Wien. Karl Marinelli (1744–1803) was a celebrated actor and director who also wrote for the popular theatre; it was in his play *Der Ungar in Wien* (1733) that another traditional figure first appeared on the Viennese stage: the Magyar, first of a long line of characters from the non-German nations which made up the Hapsburg Empire, as seen with affectionate (and sometimes patronizing) amusement by its Germanic citizens. Emanuel [really Johann Josef] Schikaneder (1751–1812), best known nowadays as the librettist of Mozart's 'Zauberflöte', was in fact the most dazzling theatrical figure of his age. As actor, producer, impresario, and playwright he was equally at home in the serious theatre (his Hamlet was famous), the *Volkskomödie*, where he excelled in comic parts, and the opera and *Singspiel*: with his excellent voice he made a splendid Papageno. Favoured by Joseph II and his successors, he was noted for the spectacular nature of his productions; the opening of the Theatre an der Wien was the culminating point of his career.

The age of the extempore farce was now drawing to a close, but not before two more comic types had been added to the gallery of Hanswurst's successors: Kasperle, who became famous throughout Germany as a character in the puppet-theatre (the German equivalent of Punch) and Thaddädl. The first of these was the creation of Johann Laroche (1745–1806), whose Swabian background may account for the un-Austrian form of the name Kasperle. Among the wandering troupes Hanswurst had come to be called Hanskaspar on occasion, and in Hafner's *Der geplagte Odoardo* a comic servant bears this name. Kaspar was gradually developed as a kind of second-string comic figure alongside Hanswurst, but it was left to Laroche to make him an important Viennese type. He is recorded as having played the part in Graz in 1764 before entering Mathias Menninger's famous Baden troupe and moving to Vienna in 1769. He remained in the capital with only one break until 1806, becoming the principal comedian of Marinelli's Leopoldstädter Theater. It is clear that Laroche took over many of the characteristics of Hanswurst. He wore peasant costume and the typical beard (in two plays, *Das Glück ist kugelrund oder Kasperls Ehrentag* and *Der unruhige Wanderer oder Kasperls letzter Tag*, he appeared as a Tyrolean peasant). He spoke broad Viennese dialect and entertained by tricks, jokes which some declared to be excessively coarse (his defenders denied this), and, above all, the projection of a comic *persona*: it is said that the offstage lament, 'Auwedl, auwedl!' with which he frequently began his performance had the audience in fits of laughter before ever he appeared. His forte was improvisation, not parody, and his lack of a good singing voice excluded him from the *Singspiel* that Joseph II was encouraging.

Hasenhut's Thaddädl already belongs to a different age and a different—since no longer extempore—type of theatre. Anton Hasenhut (1766–1841) was a comic actor pure and simple, one of the most popular of his day (Grillparzer loved him above all others and dedicated a poem to his art), and he depended for his success upon a series of plays written as vehicles for the comic type he had created. Taddeo is a name from the *commedia dell'arte*; as developed by Hasenhut, Thaddädl became a falsetto-voiced youth, clumsy, infantile, perpetually infatuated. The best presentation of the character is found in Kringsteiner's *Der Zwirnhändler* (1801); but as a comic type Thaddädl lived and died with Hasenhut, whose genius alone was able to give life to what, despite its roots in the Viennese comic tradition, was really a sophisticated literary conception.

The passing of the extempore farce did not, however, mean that the great age of the Viennese popular theatre was over; it was, in fact, about to dawn. The foundations were laid by three immensely productive writers, none of whom was primarily a playwright by profession: Gleich, Meisl, and Bäuerle. They were the chief purveyors of popular theatrical fare to the age of Metternich, an epoch in Austrian history with a characteristic flavour which their works convey as much by what they do not say as by what they do. They wrote for an Austria which had been severely shaken by the Napoleonic Wars, ruled over by a monarch who had lost the crown of the Holy Roman Empire (extinguished by Napoleon in 1806) and who favoured a government pledged to restore the *status quo ante* by reactionary legislation, of which a strict censorship was the feature most directly relevant to the popular theatre. Topical themes had, inevitably, to be avoided, while the *Zauberstück*, the play with magic and supernatural elements which had its roots far back in the high baroque period, received a powerful impetus: the citizens flocked to the theatre as a form of escapism. At the same time, however, the Viennese tradition of stage impromptu gave the actors, virtuosi to a man in the art of the extempore, many a chance of slipping in a topical jibe of which the text as passed by the censor was quite innocent; thus, to the pleasures of relaxation in a world of cosy magic was added the delicious thrill of a cat-and-mouse game between actors and police informers. The three chief genres of the popular theatre now became more clearly defined: farce, magic play, and parody; Gleich, Meisl, and Bäuerle provided innumerable examples of them all.

Joseph Alois Gleich (1772–1841), with 220 plays to his credit, was the most productive of the three. A minor clerk in the Civil Service, he was so poor that he had to eke out his salary by writing. Throughout his literary career he produced an unending stream of novels about knights, robbers, and ghosts. His early plays were on the same themes (he was at various times official playwright both to the Leopoldstädter Theater and to the Josefstädter Theater), but he soon recognized that, on the stage at least, the time for such things was past, and turned in consequence to local farce and parody. The type of farce most favoured by him was the so-called 'Besserungsstück', a moral tale in which the protagonist is forced by the repeated blows of fate to recognize his own errors. Perhaps the best example is *Der Eheteufel auf Reisen* (1822), in which the hero believes that his wife alone is responsible for his matrimonial difficulties: women are always to blame in these matters. His relative Schwarz, who is also a magician, transforms him into five different shapes in succession, and in each shape makes him experience a different marriage; he finally comes to the conclusion that the man is usually the guilty party. The *volte-face*, it will be seen, is not one of inner conviction but of forcible conversion. The hammering he has received leaves him punch-drunk. With Gleich, as with Meisl and Bäuerle, it is dramatic effectiveness that is all-important, with the result that their plays make arid reading; their success on the stage depended on the fact that the popular theatre was a collective achievement.

Karl Meisl (1775–1853), unlike the other two, was not Viennese by birth. He was more of a journalist than a playwright by nature, adaptable and imitative. Of his 170 plays a good half are lacking in the true Viennese spirit, and many of the others reveal a cosmopolitan and ironic attitude which contrasts with the less sophisticated productions of the popular theatre up to that time. It is not surprising that he excelled in parody, of which his *Der lustige Fritz* (1818) is the most famous example. Fritz is the good-for-nothing son of Steigerl, a junk-dealer who has come into money. He is cured of gambling and womanizing by Poros, a magician, who, in a dream-sequence in the second act, shows him the future through allegorical figures portraying various vices and reprehensible habits. As in Gleich, the conversion is purely an external one.

Adolf Bäuerle (1786–1859), author of a comparatively modest total of eighty plays, was a journalist by profession—he edited the *Wiener Theaterzeitung* from 1806 until his death. Some of his plays are among the most charming of this Congress period. He excelled both in bourgeois comedy and in the *Zauberstück*, but it was in the former that he achieved his greatest comic creation, the figure of Staberl in *Die Bürger in Wien* (1813). The play is a simple tale of the love of Kätchen, the daughter of the honest cooper Redlich, for Berg, a poet once penniless but now adequately provided for. Her mother favours a match with the rich but rascally merchant Müller. Kätchen, abducted by Müller with her mother's unwitting assistance, escapes by jumping into the Danube and is saved from drowning by Berg, whereupon Redlich consents to their marriage, and Müller is handed over to the Civil Guard. The comic figure, Staberl, is an umbrella-maker who is also a (most unmilitary) member of the 'Bürgergarde'; in an age—and a play—which exalted above all the solid patriotic virtue of its Viennese citizenry (Müller, the villain, is suspect *ab initio* because he is a *foreigner*, i.e. German), Staberl, for all his gallant efforts and fine sentiments, lacks moral solidity; and therein lies his humorous quality. As played by the popular comic actor Ignaz Schuster, Staberl was such a success that Bäuerle was obliged to write four sequels in which he dominates the action, while the most famous actor-playwright-impresario of the day, Karl Carl, wrote many more 'Staberliaden' which popularized the figure throughout Germany (and incidentally deprived Staberl of his endearingly Viennese characteristics). Bäuerle was equally successful with his *Zauberstücke*, of which *Aline oder Wien in einem anderen Weltteile* (1822) is typical. Viennese local patriotism is again given full rein. Many plays of this period show the adventures of Viennese citizens removed by magic to some strange and distant land, where they behave with admirable aplomb, as if they were still at home, commenting on all they see in the light of the basic fact that there is no place on earth like Vienna. With Gleich, Meisl, and Bäuerle, the *Volkskomödie* is ready for that shift of emphasis from a purely external popular entertainment, with no claims to profundity, towards an interior experience which, in the works of Raimund, achieves the level of great art.

Ferdinand Raimund (1790–1836), born Jakob Raimann, is a classic case of the comedian who wished—in this case quite literally—to play Hamlet. Of humble origin, he soon abandoned the trade for which he had been destined and served the traditional apprenticeship to the Viennese stage, playing at the Josefstädter Theater from 1813 and the Leopoldstädter Theater from 1817. He was director of the latter from 1828 to 1830. He became the greatest comic actor of his day, replacing Ignaz Schuster in popular favour, but soon realized that his unique combination of wistful irony and delicately sentimental pathos needed a vehicle specially created for it if it were to be fully effective. He decided to write his own plays. The first of these, *Der Barometermacher auf der Zauberinsel* (1823), a *Zauberstück* in the manner of Gleich and Meisl, was very successful; but it was not until *Das Mädchen aus der Feenwelt oder der Bauer als Millionär* (1826) that he discovered his individual style. The framework remains traditional: a moral tale with mortals learning through experience one of life's basic truths (in this case, that one must be prepared to renounce riches if one would possess true happiness), assisted and impeded by spirits good and bad, serious and comic. The new element, one derived from the intensity of Raimund's own unhappy disposition and experiences as transmuted by a genuine creative gift of a typically 'naïve' Viennese kind, lies in the way the traditional theme and machinery, and particularly the audio-visual continuum which is characteristic of Viennese theatricals, are made the vehicle of a universal experience. Spectacle, charade, transformation, song, chorus—all received new life from the genius of Raimund; the metaphysical background of the old baroque theatre appeared, for the last time, in this new form.

Perhaps Raimund's greatest play is *Der Alpenkönig und der Menschenfeind* (1828), the story of the suspicious misanthropist Rappelkopf, who is submitted to a drastic cure by Astralagus, the kindly spirit of the mountains. Rappelkopf's conversion, after his confrontation with his own unregenerate self, is a genuine change of heart. Encouraged by his success, Raimund set about educating himself by studies in Shakespeare and—typically for a Viennese playwright—Calderón. The result was a number of *Zauberstücke* which at times bordered all too consciously on the mystical and were consequently out of tune with the demands both of the audience and of his own essentially unreflective genius. It was not until he returned—in *Der Verschwender* (1834)—to his earlier style that he scored another popular and lasting success. Raimund's last years were overshadowed by the growing success of Nestroy, the actor-playwright who was to be his successor and the last great figure in the Viennese popular theatre, and he finally committed suicide.

Johann Nestroy (1801–62) belongs already to another age. If Raimund, with his sensitive, melancholy, elegiac temperament and delicately sensuous humour, is clearly a product, on the one hand of declining Romanticism, and on the other of that stable, ordered world of the *ancien régime* which endured longer in Austria than elsewhere, Nestroy, with his irreverence, his acerbity, his love of parody, his fondness for social comment, reflects the spirit of rising liberalism and dissatisfaction with the existing order which found its (albeit unsuccessful) outcome in the Revolution of 1848. Nestroy came to the stage of the popular theatre via a legal training and the opera—he sang the role of Sarastro at the Kärntnertor Theater in 1821. In 1825 he turned to comic roles, but it was not until he joined forces with Karl Carl [Karl Andreas von Bernbrunn] (1789–1854), who had taken over the direction of the Josefstädter Theater in 1826, that the foundations of his success as actor-playwright were laid. Nestroy was a child of the Viennese popular theatre in every way. With his gift for improvisation, his dazzling abilities as a character-actor, his productivity (83 plays), his facility (he could write in the morning what he had to play in the evening), his indifference to the sources of his plots (most of which are of literary provenance, whereas Raimund's are original) and to realistic verisimilitude (which, despite his fondness for topical criticism, he was always ready to sacrifice to theatrical effectiveness): with all these characteristics, he is obviously as dependent upon his antecedents as were Raimund and, before him, Gleich, Meisl, and Bäuerle. It is in the destructive quality of his satire that he represents a new age. Nothing is sacred to Nestroy. He has more wit than Raimund, but less imagination and less heart. Many of his impromptu hits at social and political targets needed considerable courage, and, indeed, he was fined more than once, and on one occasion even spent three days in jail; but these things are external to his qualities as a dramatist and actor. His first great success was *Der böse Geist Lumpazivagabundus oder das liederliche*

Kleeblatt (1833). The established formula of the *Zauberposse* is here made the occasion of penetrating shafts of social criticism; once established, the formula was repeated in endless variations. Nestroy excelled in all three of the main Viennese genres, but it is in the field of parody that some of his most inspired work was done; his parodies of Wagner, and in particular of Hebbel in *Judith und Holofernes*, are classic examples of the art. It is upon works of this kind, and plays of social comment such as *Zu ebener Erde und im ersten Stock* (1835) and political satire such as *Freiheit in Krähwinkel* (1848), that his reputation rests today. After him the forces of disintegration which he both depicted and promoted led to a decline of the popular theatre from which it never recovered. Itself a cultural phenomenon which was the product of a particular type of society in a concrete historical context, it passed with the passing of that society. It derived its strength from a homogeneity of spirit among the citizens of the Austro-Hungarian capital which transcended class barriers. The forces which disrupted that society—social conflict and fragmentation, industrialization with its new proletariat lacking a traditional folk-culture (and unable to pay higher prices for tickets)—robbed it of its audience. Without this essential ingredient, it ceased to be itself. It could still produce its idols: the actor Alexander Girardi (1850–1918), for example; but the divorce between writer and stage was, after Nestroy, final. Existing now purely as a tradition, it was watered-down, sentimentalized, cosmopolitanized, reduced to a few basic clichés masquerading as the truth about the Austrian national character, set to waltz-time and, in the form of the Viennese operetta, conquered the world.

Literary drama in Austria, which had begun to make headway under the reforming aegis of Sonnenfels, received a powerful impetus from the appointment in 1814 of Josef Schreyvogel (1768–1832) to the directorship of the three major Viennese theatres: the Burgtheater, the Kärntnertor Theater, and the Theater an der Wien. Schreyvogel, who was well-read and a great traveller, had, while living in Jena, collaborated with Schiller, Herder, and Wieland. He now set about forming and fostering what he considered to be the type of theatrical taste most consonant with the Austrian tradition. His work at the Burgtheater was aimed mainly at providing a balanced bill of fare which would avoid exposing Vienna to the exclusive influence either of Weimar classicism on the one hand or the new Romantic universalism on the other. Vienna was not Weimar. It had its own theatrical tradition based on many centuries of cosmopolitan culture, and could only lose its identity by an undue addiction to either of the German fashions of the day. Accordingly, while allowing both their due proportion, Schreyvogel was careful to balance them with indigenous works and others from Spain—also indigenous in an Austrian sense—and England. To Schreyvogel belongs the credit for making the Burgtheater what it has, despite fluctuations, remained: one of the foremost German-speaking stages, if not *the* foremost; and it is to him also that we owe the discovery, soon after he took office, of Austria's greatest dramatist, Grillparzer.

Franz Grillparzer (1791–1872) came to the theatre by way of legal studies and a career in the Civil Service which lasted until his retirement in 1856 from the post of Court Archivist. He was a man of melancholy and ironic disposition, hesistant in the face of necessary decisions, a hypochondriac living in perpetual—though unnecessary—fear of the insanity which caused the suicide of his mother and younger brother: this was one of the reasons why, despite his many love affairs and lifelong devotion to one Kathi Fröhlich, he could never make up his mind to marry. Grillparzer was not unlike Raimund (for whom he had a high regard) both in his temperament and in his instinct for the theatre; but he differed in background, sophistication, and a ratiocinative tendency which was in complete contrast to Raimund's essentially naïve genius. Grillparzer's first success was Schreyvogel's presentation at the Theater an der Wien of *Die Ahnfrau* (1817), a fate-tragedy in the then popular mould written—significantly—in Spanish trochees: Grillparzer was all his life a profound student of Spanish literature, with an especial fondness for Calderón and Lope de Vega. It was with *Sappho* (1818), however, a classical tragedy in blank verse, that Grillparzer found his own characteristic style. The story of the love of the mature poetess Sappho for a younger man, Phaon, and the latter's attraction both to her and to the young slave-girl, Melitta, is symbolic of the forces which draw human beings out of their dedicated isolation into the world of everyday experience, only to perish from the Nemesis which stalks all who so commit themselves to life: a profoundly and passively metaphysical aesthetic of tragedy which reflects the characteristic Austrian antinomy between action and reflection. *Das goldene Vliess* (1820), based on the story of Jason and Medea, is a dramatic trilogy which reveals great skill in the theatrical marshalling of rather diffuse epic material, as well as an instinctive grasp of what is visually effective; this last is a Viennese legacy which Grillparzer developed with even more telling aesthetic effectiveness as his technique improved. In *König Ottokars Glück und Ende* (1823), an historical play set in the twelfth century which shows how the Imperial Crown passed from the autocratic warrior-king Ottokar of Bohemia to the then unknown Rudolf von Hapsburg, Grillparzer's mastery of his material is still more evident. In the figure of Rudolf he gives us his ideal of the consecrated ruler as keystone of the political edifice and defender of the weak, a man utterly simple and unassuming in his own person, but imperiously immovable in what touches his duties as Emperor. Despite its complimentary attitude to the ruling house, the clear parallels between the lives of Ottokar and Napoleon Bonaparte caused difficulties with the censor which kept the play off the stage until 1825. It was then performed at the Burgtheater with Heinrich Anschütz in the title-role (Anschütz, one of the leading actors of the day, had recently been engaged by Schreyvogel). Recognition of its qualities came slowly: it needed, for example, the more spacious stage of the Theater an der Wien to reveal its opportunities for spectacle and telling visual effect; but its place as one of the masterpieces of the German-speaking theatre is now secure. With *Des Meeres und der Liebe Wellen* (1829, first performance 1831) Grillparzer returned to a classical setting which was, however, no more than an excuse for the presentation of a religious theme; for this version of the legend of Hero and Leander is concerned primarily with Hero's betrayal of her vocation as priestess of Diana. In surrendering to the experience of human love (which Grillparzer presents as both natural and inevitable) she exposes herself to life; and, like Sappho, she perishes. The play's excellence, despite certain structural weaknesses, lies in its subtle exploration of female psychology, always one of Grillparzer's greatest—and most typically Viennese—gifts. *Der Traum ein Leben* (1834), a dramatic legend with an oriental setting, reveals Spanish influence both in its trochaic metre and its theme (an echo of *La vida es sueño*): the hero escapes the tragic consequences which his excessive ambition would bring by experiencing it all in a dream. It is a play which shows more clearly than most how deeply Grillparzer's art was rooted in the Viennese popular theatre, whereas, by contrast, his next play—and only comedy—*Weh' dem, der lügt* (1838), was too sophisticated and, towards the end, metaphysical in its approach to a genre in which the audience thought themselves connoisseurs; it failed, with the result that Grillparzer turned away from the theatre and wrote henceforward only for his own amusement. Of his last three plays—*Ein Bruderzwist in Habsburg*, *Die Jüdin von Toledo*, and *Libussa*—which were all published posthumously, it must be said that they lack that theatrical effectiveness which, in his earlier works, came from day-to-day contact with the living stage. As literary dramas, however, they are among his finest achievements. In *Ein Bruderzwist* he rounds off, in pessimistic mood, his portrait of imperial power, whilst *Libussa*, which tells of the legendary founding of Prague, returns again to the theme of betrayed vocation and the contemplative life at war with that life of action upon which the movement of history depends. Meanwhile Grillparzer's earlier plays were still performed, although not as effectively as under Schreyvogel. Many of the latter's reforms continued to exercise a beneficent influence even after their originator's typically ungrateful and summary dismissal in 1832. The interregnum at the Burgtheater under Johann Ludwig Deinhardstein and Franz Ignaz von Holbein was an undistinguished one, but in 1849, with the arrival of the German playwright and producer Heinrich Laube (1806–84), an era of great distinction dawned. Brilliant performances of Grillparzer's works established his reputation as the greatest of Austrian dramatists, fit to rank with Goethe and Schiller as one of the masters of drama in the German language.

It was many decades before the Austrian theatre produced a dramatist as distinguished as Grillparzer. In the interim, his contemporary Friedrich Halm [really Eligius Franz Josef von Münch-Bellinghausen] (1806–71) provided the stage with well-made tragedies upon themes both classical and romantic which made moderately effective theatre (*Griseldis*, 1835, *Der Fechter von Ravenna*, 1857, among others) but have been rejected by posterity as thin in substance. In the hands of Eduard Bauernfeld (1802–90), the intimate of Grillparzer as well as Raimund and many other men of the theatre, the impromptu *Posse* of the suburbs assumed a bourgeois form on the boards of the Burgtheater, whence it spread throughout Germany. The Viennese liking for acid topicalities was well catered for by Bauernfeld who, as a liberal and a freethinker by temperament, knew just how close to the wind he could sail; inevitably, such sallies date, and what remains is a number of well-made comedies—*Die Republik der Tiere* (1848) and *Der kategorische Imperativ* (1851) are still appreciated—which reveal the early influence of Iffland and Kotzebue as well as that of the native *Posse*.

The trend towards realism in literature which spread throughout Europe during the second half of the nineteenth century left its mark on the Austrian theatre, too, although it never reached such an extreme form as that practised by the Berlin Naturalists. This was largely because it represented an approach to theatrical art which ran counter to the Viennese tradition of the *Gesamtkunstwerk* embracing spectators as well as stage in the creative act, and also because it conflicted with that awareness of spiritual realities, derived from the theatre of the baroque age, which lingered, albeit often reduced to mere visual technique, as an implied metaphysical background in even the most overtly modern productions. Among the earliest writers to attempt a realistic presentation of peasant life on the stage was Ludwig Anzengruber (1839–89), Viennese by birth and upbringing, who had spent some time in a travelling company before turning to dramatic composition, earning his living meanwhile as a clerk in the Vienna police headquarters. He was equally successful in tragedy and comedy, aiming at the accurate depiction of human problems as encountered by the sturdy peasantry of the Austrian provinces. In the interests of verisimilitude he employed a dialect-flavoured dialogue, philologically inaccurate, a kind of Austrian Mummerset, which lent an air of authenticity without being as difficult to comprehend as was the real dialect literature that came later. His freethinking views emerge in such attacks upon religious intolerance as *Der Pfarrer von Kirchfeld* (1870) and *Der Meineidbauer* (1871), while his mastery of comic techniques derived from the Viennese popular theatre is evident in *Die Kreuzlschreiber* (1872) and *Der Doppelselbstmord* (1875); it was here, in fact, that his strength lay: fertility in the invention of a rich gallery of authentic types and a multiplicity of comic situations, however improbable; his greatest weakness was the sparseness of his dramatic line, to which should be added a certain hedonism of outlook which accorded well with the limited image of itself that the Viennese popular stage and operetta was developing at the time, and which it has since persuaded the world to accept as representing the whole truth concerning the Austrian attitude to life. Anzengruber's successor was Karl Schönherr (1869–1943), a doctor whose powerful and realistic dramas of Tyrolean peasant life won him widespread recognition. His themes are the peasant's clinging to the soil (*Erde*, 1907), his bewilderment in the face of religious conflict (*Glaube und Heimat*, 1910), his defence of the Tyrol against Napoleon's armies (*Volk in Not*, 1915). A sound instinct for the theatre which did not shun the melodramatic was the basis of Schönherr's success.

Something of the same blend of inherited theatrical flair with modernity of spirit is found in the vastly different social dramas of Arthur Schnitzler (1862–1931), a practising physician whose interest in psychology led him to write a series of plays in which the mainsprings of his characters' actions are analysed with subtly impressionistic technique as they drift through a series of dream-states too low-toned and will-less to be called real life. The Naturalist concern with the urban proletariat (Naturalism had found its chief Viennese advocate in the early writings of the novelist, critic, and playwright Hermann Bahr, 1863–1934) coloured a few of Schnitzler's dramatic attempts, and social realism lingers in *Freiwild* (1896) and *Das Vermächtnis* (1898); but his true style had already been discovered in *Anatol* (1890), a series of impressionistic playlets about the amorous adventures of a young Viennese man-about-town, linked only by the characters of the hero and his friend, Max. In his later plays—*Liebelei* (1894), *Reigen* (1896) (filmed as *La Ronde*), *Der grüne Kakadu*(1898), *Professor Bernhardt* (1912)—he developed a technique which remained episodic even in his full-length works. Possessed of a talent which had not the staying-power to conduct an action through exposition and crisis to denouement, in one dramatic arc, but excelled instead in exposition—always a *forte* of the Austrian drama—he aimed at the creation of situation through the close observation of everyday speech and manners. His beaux, *grisettes*, lieutenants on the loose, doctors, actresses, reveal themselves in episodes which probe without comment the morass of human existence: the impermanence and essential unseriousness of the *affaire*, marital faithfulness in hopeless conflict with the promiscuous flesh, the hollow pretence of the affair of honour, the prejudice underlying professional rivalries, the dream of life from which it is better not to waken; better, as Anatol thinks in *Die Frage an das Schicksal*, not to know the truth, even when it is to be had for the asking. Schnitzler may have been influenced in his choice of forms by the causeries of French writers like Paul Hervieu; in themes, use of the stage and, above all, dialogue, he is utterly Viennese.

Schnitzler's successor in the development of impressionistic techniques and neo-Romantic themes in the direction of erotic sensationalism is Richard Beer-Hofmann (1866–1945) with his *Der Graf von Charolais* (1904); but it was Schnitzler's friend and admirer Hugo von Hofmannsthal (1874–1929) who, starting in the impressionistic and somewhat decadent atmosphere of the 1890s, led a return to moral values and the grass roots of the Austrian theatrical tradition. At seventeen Hofmannsthal was famous throughout Austria and Germany as the author of incredibly mature poetry in the neo-Romantic and symbolist vein; by the end of his life he had become the last great representative of the Austrian spirit, who saw it as his mission to gather up and hand on the spiritual and cultural heritage of the Hapsburg monarchy in the moment of its passing. The lyric poems and verse playlets—really little more than dramatic dialogues—of his late teens show Hofmannsthal as the epigone sated with the beauty of centuries of art and crushed by the weight of the past, delivered over powerless to the ancestors and living fellow-beings with whom he feels himself to be one. Nothing would be further from the truth than to interpret this as decadent aestheticism. Even in his earliest playlet, *Gestern* (1891), the ironic portrait of the young man who asserts the impossibility of living for anything more than the day, only to be shattered when his mistress deceives him, reveals a moral concern which would belie the charge; while *Der Tor und der Tod* (1893) condemns the aesthete who has selfishly destroyed all who loved him as one who has not lived because he has refused to commit himself to life. In *Der weisse Fächer* (1897), last and most deliciously ironic of these early playlets, life itself in the form of a new emotional attachment gently mocks the despairing rhetoric of two young people who think the death of their husband and wife is the end of everything. Around the turn of the century Hofmannsthal underwent a spiritual crisis, in which the moral considerations that had been merely hinted at so far combined with a growing conviction that European civilization was spiritually sick to produce a determination to devote his gifts to the rescue of what could still be saved from the impending wreck. He abandoned lyric poetry and, becoming conscious of his identity as an Austrian (with his mixture of Italian, German, and Jewish blood he could hardly have been more typically Viennese), determined to seek contact with his own nation through the artistic medium which was its greatest contribution to European culture: the theatre. The result was a series of plays, lasting right up till his death in 1929, in which all the traditional forms and resources of the Viennese theatre were devoted in turn to the unravelling of problems which, although topical, were themselves basically Austrian: communication, change and constancy, action and contemplation. First comes a series of verse dramas retelling ancient Greek myths in terms of modern psychology and revolving round the possibility of self-sacrifice as a way to break the deadlock between the existential necessity of change and the eternal human duty of loyalty: *Alkestis* (1893), *Elektra* (1903), *Ödipus und die Sphinx* (1905). Concurrently with these plays Hofmannsthal explores the possibilities of comedy in the Viennese tradition written in colloquial Austrian, in which a number of Casanova-type figures show him revolving the idea of constancy to oneself through the equilibrium of constant self-transformation: *Der Abenteurer und die Sängerin* (1898, and still in verse) and *Cristinas Heimreise* (1909). In 1911 Hofmannsthal attempted in *Jedermann* a revival of the medieval Morality play *Everyman*, adapting it so as to tone down the more explicitly Catholic features. His forerunner in this attempt to revive the religious drama of the people was Richard von Kralik (1852–1934), whose numerous revivals and imitations of such works, designed primarily for open-air performance, had been influential beyond the confines of his native Austria. It was at about this time that Hofmannsthal's collaboration with Richard Strauss began, producing the six internationally famous operas 'Elektra' (1909, an adaptation of the play), 'Der Rosenkavalier' (1911), 'Ariadne auf Naxos' (1912 and 1916), 'Die Frau ohne Schatten' (1919), 'Die ägyptische Helena' (1928), and 'Arabella' (1933, completed by Strauss after Hofmannsthal's death). These libretti were not incidental in Hofmannsthal's work, but the logical outcome of his thinking on the nature of the Viennese theatre and his acceptance of its traditions: significantly, the setting of three of them is Vienna itself. They can be—and have been—performed as plays in their own right: in them, Hofmannsthal reveals his gradual return to a traditionally Catholic and Christian morality: commitment and self-transcendence come through Divine Grace, the ancient ethical imperatives of European civilization are reasserted, marriage is defended, anarchy warned against. Two post-war comedies, *Der Schwierige* (1918, pub. 1920) and *Der Unbestechliche* (pub. 1923), show Hofmannsthal grappling with the new situation created by the collapse of the ancient Dual Monarchy. In the former, one of the greatest of all comedies in the German language, he gives a picture of the Spanish–Austrian high aristocracy at the moment of its disintegration, using this as a vehicle for an almost impossibly subtle analysis of the difficulty—and yet necessity—of communication between human beings as seen in the hesitations and fear of words of his ex-officer hero Hans Karl Bühl. Never since Grillparzer had the unique Austrian blend of speech and silence been so effectively used on the stage: and yet, such was the low ebb which had been reached by the Burgtheater, its first performance had to take place in Munich. In 1919 Hofmannsthal conceived the idea of an annual festival of drama to be held at Salzburg. Together with Max Reinhardt he planned that series of dramatic and operatic productions which has become internationally famous, and which has been revived with great success since the Second World War. A feature of the festival has always been an open-air performance of his *Jedermann* in front of Salzburg cathedral. It was for this festival that Hofmannsthal wrote *Das Salzburger grosse Welttheater* (1922), a modern version of one of Calderón's *autos*, *El gran teatro del mundo*; in this work Hofmannsthal's return to traditional Viennese religious themes and spectacular technique is even more marked. The last years of his life were spent wrestling with the tragedy—*Der Turm* (1925, second version with alternative ending 1927)—that was intended as his testament to his nation and to Europe. Once again, a play by Calderón, *La vida es sueño*, is the starting-point of an attempt to grapple with the forces of disintegration that he felt were threatening Europe. Although the setting is vaguely Polish, the play is a medley of Viennese themes, types, and techniques so disparate as to impair its theatrical effectiveness; such is the conviction of its message, however—that the brutal self-interest of the new barbarism must be spiritualized by self-surrender if the world is not to perish—that it is always moving in performance.

With Hofmannsthal, the Austrian theatre could be said to have come to an end; although distinguished playwrights followed him, and revealed their indebtedness to the achievements of the past, the new Austrian Republic of 1919 was not the diverse human ocean of the old monarchy with its richly flavoured cultural life. Tendencies in literature which derived from outside Austria—from Berlin, for example, with its vigorous postwar theatrical experiments—produced a gradual loss of identity. Worthwhile things were still, however, produced. Max Mell (1882–) continued the revival of the morality play in his *Apostelspiel* (1923) and *Das Nachfolge-Christi-Spiel* (1927), the latter set in the time of the Turkish invasions. Naturalism blending with the new German Expressionism is found in the plays of Anton Wildgans (1881–1932), who spent two short periods during the 1920s as director of the Burgtheater. This theatre, once so famous, and still at its height during Hofmannsthal's early years, when actors of the calibre of Josef Kainz and Hermann Müller trod its boards, had fallen on evil times after the war. Wildgans made heroic efforts to preserve its identity, which was fading under unimaginative ministerial control, and stopped many malpractices (such as the hiring of its priceless wardrobe to film companies), but fell a victim to intrigue and his own unpractical idealism. In the 1930s, with such fine actors as Raoul Aslan, Ewald Balser, and Paula Wessely, the Burgtheater maintained its reputation. Damaged during the Second World War, it has been rebuilt (see Nos. 37, 38) and has regained its position as a leading German-speaking stage. The contemporary writer whose plays most clearly betray his Viennese origins is Alexander Lernet-Holenia (1897–), whose predilection for the *Haupt- und Staatsaktion* is seen in *Demetrius* (1926) and *Die nächtliche Hochzeit* (1929), while the practised hand of a writer steeped in the tradition of Viennese comedy is seen in *Ollapotrida* (1926), *Die Frau des Potiphar* (1934), and *Spanische Komödie* (1948). Expressionism, which had achieved its most striking Austrian manifestation in the mythical trilogy *Der Spiegelmensch* (1920), by Franz Werfel (1890–1945), was an important formative influence on the work of Franz Theodor Csokor (1891–) whose *Die rote Strasse* (1918) contains technical characteristics still detectable in *Europäische Trilogie* (1952), plays in which he depicts the fate of Europe between 1914 and 1945. Two more Austrian dramatists deserve mention. Ferdinand Bruckner [really Theodor Tagger] (1891–1958) developed from Expressionism to the more objective style of *die neue Sachlichkeit*, and achieved an international success with *Elisabeth von England* (1930), a historical drama which analyses the English queen in psychological terms and uses an interesting technical device in showing simultaneous actions in England and Spain with complementary dialogue. Other plays on the subject of Napoleon, a play on a classical theme, *Pyrrhus und Andromache* (1951), and contemporary dramas depicting totalitarianism—*Die Befreiten* (1946)—and the dehumanization of modern life—*Fährten* (1948), *Der Kampf mit dem Engel* (1957)—have consolidated Bruckner's reputation as one of the most distinguished modern Austrian dramatists. The most internationally celebrated of this last group of Austrian dramatists is Fritz Hochwälder (1911–), who reveals his Viennese antecedents nowhere more clearly than in his assertion that the theatre is the best instrument for repairing the shattered image of the human race by showing it what it once was and could again be. This presupposes historical drama, which is his chosen field (see HOCHWÄLDER). Plays such as *Das heilige Experiment* (1943), *Der öffentliche Ankläger* (1947), and *Donadieu* (1953) reveal the inherited skill of a writer who admits to having Viennese theatrical blood in his veins, though he has chosen to live in Switzerland since 1938. He is no innovator either in technique or subject-matter. Nevertheless, his portrayal of human weakness, passion, and injustice struggling with man's nobler instincts at such times of historical crisis as the French Revolution, the suppression of the Jesuit missions in Paraguay, or the wars of religion, is gripping theatre which makes one forget the fact that his characters sometimes tend to be mouthpieces rather than living figures; but that will always be the case when powerful ideas are embodied in a logically-worked-out action under the catalytic operation of an innate flair for the living stage. J. B. BEDNALL

AUTHOR'S NIGHT, see ROYALTY.

AUTO. The origin of the *auto* is obscure. The term is first found as one of a number of synonyms for a religious play. In Castile the *auto sacramental* develops directly from the liturgical drama during the course of the sixteenth century. Towards the end of the century, the *auto sacramental* comes to be recognized as one of the main elements in the Corpus Christi celebrations, a dramatic statement of the tenets of the Catholic faith which embodies the preoccupations and ideals of the Counter-Reformation. The most distinctive feature of the *auto sacramental*, particularly in the hands of Pedro Calderón de la Barca, is found in its use of elaborate allegory. The subject-matter may be purely sacramental, or biblical, or hagiological, a distinction which Calderón himself draws when he refers to the *auto sacramental alegórico* and the *auto historial alegórico*. The *autos* were elaborately staged and accompanied by fine music (see SPAIN). The pre-eminent composer of *autos sacramentales* in the second half of the seventeenth century is Pedro Calderón. From the middle of the century up to his death in 1681 he wrote all the *autos* performed in Madrid, and even after his death his plays were nearly always chosen for performance. They continued to be given up to 1765, when their performance was prohibited by the Crown (see SPAIN, 6). J. E. VAREY

AVANCINUS, NICOLAUS (1612–86), see AUSTRIA and JESUIT DRAMA.

AVENUE THEATRE, LONDON, see PLAYHOUSE, 1.

AVIGNON. The annual drama festival at Avignon was instituted by Jean Vilar in 1947, and the first production was *Richard II*, which had not previously been seen in France. Vilar himself played the title-role. The success of the initial festival led to a yearly visit, first by a company led by Vilar and then, after his appointment as director of the Théâtre National Populaire, by that company, sometimes with guest artists. The plays were staged in the Cour d'Honneur of the Palace of the Popes, first on a temporary stage before some 2,000 spectators, later, before a still larger audience, on a permanent stage designed by Jacques Le Marquet. There was no ramp, no curtain, and very little use of built scenery. The producer was forced to rely on his text, his actors, and the imaginative use of lighting, music, and costume. These last were mainly designed by Léon Gischia, using strong colours and a certain degree of exaggeration while remaining basically true to the mood of the play. When Vilar became head of the T.N.P., he drew on his experiences at Avignon, and it is often said that the so-called 'style T.N.P.', which was unmistakable, derived from these early productions in the open air. Among the outstanding actors seen at Avignon were Maria Cesarès, who played Lady Macbeth and Maria Tudor (in Hugo's play), Daniel Sorano, an excellent interpreter of Molière, and above all the young Gérard Philipe, whose early death robbed the French theatre of a great actor. He was at his best in *Le Cid* and in a translation of Kleist's *Prinz Friedrich von Homburg*, both of which were seen at the 1951 Festival. In 1956 the tenth anniversary of the Avignon Festival was celebrated by a revival of Beaumarchais's *Le Mariage de Figaro*, with Sorano as Figaro. This served also to celebrate the 200th anniversary of the birth of Mozart. Among later revivals seen at Avignon were *Lorenzaccio*, *Ruy Blas*, *Les Caprices de Marianne*, *A Midsummer Night's Dream* and, among modern plays, Supervielle's *Shéhérazade*, Claudel's *La Ville*, Pirandello's *Enrico IV*, Brecht's *Mother Courage*, and Bolt's *A Man For All Seasons*.

AVON THEATRE, NEW YORK, see KLAW THEATRE.

AYALA, ADELARDO LÓPEZ DE, see LÓPEZ DE AYALA, ADELARDO.

AYRENHOFF, CORNELIUS VON (1733–1819), an Austrian dramatist whose serious dramas, in contrast to the light fare popular in Vienna at the time, were intended to raise the standard of the theatre. They were given at the Burgtheater, under the able management of Joseph von Sonnenfels, but proved unequal to the task of weaning the public from the light diet provided by harlequinade, farce, and operetta.

AYRER, JAKOB (*c.* 1543–1605), an early German dramatist, successor of Hans Sachs, and like him a voluminous author of long Carnival plays and *Singspiele*, of which about seventy were published in 1618 as *Opus Theatricum*. Ayrer, who was much influenced by the English Comedians, spent most of his life in Nuremberg, and was probably a Mastersinger. His *Phänicia* and *Sidea* are related to *Much Ado About Nothing* and *The Tempest* respectively by a common source, but direct influence by one dramatist on the other is not now credited. Ayrer's plays, popular in his own day, are not distinguished by any particular literary merit, being verbose and written in doggerel verse.

B

BABANOVA, Maria Ivanovna (1900–), Soviet actress who began her career under the direction of Theodore Komisarjevsky and in 1920 was taken by Meyerhold into his Theatre Workshop, where she was soon playing leading roles. In 1922 she appeared as Pauline in Meyerhold's production of Ostrovsky's *Place of Profit* for the Theatre of the Revolution, but continued to work in the Meyerhold Theatre. In 1927 she again appeared at the Theatre of the Revolution in Faiko's *The Man with the Portfolio*, working for the first time under a producer from the Moscow Art Theatre, A. Dikie. This proved a turning-point in her career, since she was able to achieve a successful synthesis of the two methods, and she has since become the leading actress of the Theatre of the Revolution, making a notable appearance as Juliet in Popov's production of *Romeo and Juliet*. She was also considered outstanding as the heroine in *Tanya*, by Arbuzov, and was awarded a Stalin prize in 1941 for her performance in this part. Since then she has appeared as Mariam in Gusyev's *Sons of Three Rivers* (1944), as Kaoru Morimoto, and as Ophelia. She also played the part of the actress Berezhkova in Ugryumov's vaudeville, *Seat No. 16*.

BACKCLOTH, a flat painted canvas which hangs at the back of the scene, suspended from the grid. It is used in combination with wings to form a wing-and-backcloth scene, now superseded by the box set and used only in ballet and pantomime.

BACKING FLAT, a canvas-covered frame, or hinged screen, set outside a door or other opening on the stage to conceal the view beyond.

BACKSTAGE, a term applied to the parts of the theatre behind the stage, such as the actors' dressing-rooms; visitors going there are said 'to go backstage'. The word is applied also to a recess in the back wall of the stage used for the last pieces of scenery in a deep spectacular vista, and at other times used as an extra storage place for scenery.

BACON, Frank (1864–1922), American actor and playwright, who made his first appearance on the stage at the age of 25, in *Ten Nights in a Bar Room*. He was for some years in San Francisco, where he played a variety of parts, and was seen in vaudeville with his wife and family. After the 1906 earthquake he went to New York, where in 1918 he scored a triumph with his play *Lightnin'*, written in collaboration with Winchell Smith, which ran for nearly three years. In this Bacon played Bill Jones, a lovable rascal with a taste for strong drink and a great gift for exaggeration, a part eminently suited to his homely simplicity and humour and quaint, engaging personality.

BADDELEY. (1) Robert (1732–94), English actor, who was first a pastry-cook and then a gentleman's gentleman, in which capacity he toured the Continent for three years, acquiring a knowledge of foreign manners and accents which he later turned to good account. He was first seen on the stage in 1760 at Drury Lane. He married (2) Sophia (1745–86), the actress-daughter of Valentine Snow the trumpeter. A strikingly beautiful woman, she first acted in 1764, and excelled in such parts as Ophelia, Desdemona, Imogen, and Mrs. Beverley. Zoffany painted her as Fanny in *The Clandestine Marriage*. Unfortunately she was very dissipated and extravagant and Baddeley soon left her, though he later fought a duel on her behalf with the brother of David Garrick. She was last seen in London in 1781, and then played in the provinces, mainly at York and Edinburgh. Her husband remained on the stage until his death, being taken ill while dressing for his most famous part, Moses in *The School for Scandal*, which he was the first to play. He was excellent in all broken-English parts, among them Fluellen, and Canton in *The Clandestine Marriage*, and in such comic parts as Brainworm in *Every Man in His Humour*, and Grumio in *The Taming of the Shrew*. He was the last actor to wear the royal livery of scarlet and gold as one of the King's Servants. On his death he left a cottage at Molesey to the Drury Lane Fund, for the benefit of four poor actors, and a sum of money for a cake and wine to be partaken of by the company in the green room annually, a custom still observed at Drury Lane on Twelfth Night.

BAHR, Hermann (1863–1934), Austrian dramatist and critic, who, after nearly twenty years of journalism and playwriting in Vienna, became producer at the Berlin Deutsches Theater in 1906. He was one of the first to rally to the naturalism of Ibsen, and has been described as a 'lesser Schnitzler, softening the sharp edges of realism by his scrupulous art'. Nevertheless, he is unmistakably Austrian in his mixture of flippant gaiety, warm-heartedness, and witty acumen, and his best play is a comedy entitled *Das Konzert* (1910), which deals with the matrimonial difficulties of a musician and his wife. Among his other plays, which amount to nearly eighty all told, *Das Tschaperl* (1898) is considered outstanding.

BAILEY, Bryan (1922–60), English actor and theatre manager, whose sudden death in a road accident was a great loss to the English theatre. He was at the time director of the newly opened Belgrade Theatre in Coventry.

Previous to that he had been director for five years of the Guildford Repertory Theatre, which under his management showed great enterprise and vitality. He was a man of immense resources, fertile in ideas, and a hard worker. After leaving Oxford he trained at the Royal Academy of Dramatic Art, acted in repertory, and formed a group for the production of new plays. Although destined to remain at Coventry for only two years, he had already shown initiative and a willingness to encourage new authors by staging the early plays of Arnold Wesker (including *Roots*) after these had been rejected by London managements. He also commissioned from John Wiles a play about Coventry, *Never Had It So Good*, which later had a successful run at Theatre Workshop in London.

BAIRD, DOROTHEA (1875–1933), see IRVING (3).

BAKER, BENJAMIN A. (1818–90), American actor-manager and playwright. Apprenticed to a saddler, he escaped to join a travelling company, and was soon playing Brabantio to the elder Booth's Othello. In 1839 he appeared in New York, and was engaged for the company which opened the Olympic. He had already written a number of plays when on 15 Feb. 1848 he produced, for his own benefit night, *A Glance at New York in 1848*, in which the actor Frank Chanfrau made a great success as the hero Mose, a New York volunteer fireman. The 'Mose' plays were burlettas in the style of Moncrieff's *Tom and Jerry* (based on Pierce Egan's book) and they soon had many imitators in New York and elsewhere, giving rise to a type of play verging on melodrama, with strong action played against a background of local conditions. Further plays by Baker in the same vein were *New York As It Is* (1848), again with Chanfrau, *Three Years After* (1849), and *Mose in China* (1850). Baker was manager successively of several theatres, including the Metropolitan in San Francisco, returning to New York in 1856 as manager of Edwin Booth's company. In 1885 he became assistant secretary of the Actors' Fund. He continued to work as manager and theatrical agent until his death. Known as Uncle Ben Baker, he was a well-loved figure in American theatrical circles.

BAKER, GEORGE PIERCE (1866–1935), one of the most vital influences in the formation of modern American dramatic literature and theatre. He was educated at Harvard, where he later became the first Professor of Dramatic Literature. Intensely interested in everything theatrical and himself a good amateur actor, he inaugurated, first at Radcliffe, in 1904, and a year later at Harvard, a course in practical playwriting. This in turn led to the foundation of his famous '47 Workshop' for the staging of plays written under his tuition. One of the immediately successful results of Baker's enterprise was the professional production by Mrs. Fiske in 1908 of *Salvation Nell*, by Baker's pupil Edward Sheldon. Among other playwrights who attended Baker's special courses were Eugene O'Neill, Sidney Howard, and George Abbott. In 1919 Baker gave a series of lectures at the Lowell Institute, published in the same year as *Dramatic Technique*, a standard work for aspiring playwrights. He had previously written *The Development of Shakespeare as a Dramatist* and edited some unpublished letters of David Garrick. In 1925, by which time he had had the pleasure of seeing his pioneer work bear fruit in many other centres of learning, often under his own old pupils, Baker left Harvard, where his practical methods were considered perhaps a little unorthodox, and went to Yale, where Edward Harkness had provided and endowed a fine little experimental theatre. Here he remained as Director of the post-graduate Department of Drama until his retirement in 1933. Combining in a rare degree the attributes of the scholar and the practical man of the theatre, he had an immense influence not only in his own country, but throughout Europe, and to the end of his life was unremitting in his industry, accuracy, and perseverance on behalf of his students.

BAKER, HENRIETTA (1837–1909), see CHANFRAU (2).

BAKER, SARAH (1736/7–1816), English theatre proprietor, whose activities in Kent covered a period of more than fifty years. The daughter of an acrobatic dancer, Ann Wakelin, who toured with her own company, she married an actor in the company in about 1761, and was widowed in 1769. Left with three small children to support, she went into management on her own account, probably with a puppet-theatre; from 1772 to 1777 she took over the management of her mother's company. When her mother finally retired, Mrs. Baker formed a new company, with an ambitious repertory which included Shakespeare and Sheridan. With this she established herself as a regular visitor to Canterbury, Rochester, Faversham, Maidstone, and Tunbridge Wells, with occasional forays to Deal, Folkestone, Sandwich, Sittingbourne, and Lewes. At first she used a portable theatre, later she played in any suitable building, but from about 1789 onwards she built her own theatres—ten in all. Among the actors who appeared early in their careers with Mrs. Baker were Edmund Kean, Thomas Dibdin, and Fawcett. Her daughter Sally married William Dowton, who, with his son William, tried unsuccessfully to run the theatres after Mrs. Baker's death.

BALE, JOHN (1495–1563), Bishop of Ossory in Ireland, and author of a number of anti-Catholic plays, of which the greater part formed a long Miracle play, now lost. His existing works, which include Morality plays and a translation of Kirchmayer's *Pammachius*, are filled with coarse and incessant abuse of popery and priests. The most important is *Kynge*

Johan (1538), which may claim to rank as the first historical drama in English literature. In its mingling of such abstract figures as Sedition, Clergy, and England, and the historical King John and Cardinal Pandolphus, the play forms a link between the medieval and the Elizabethan drama. It may have been first acted at St. Stephen's, Canterbury, and was revived at Ipswich in 1561. The only extant manuscript is in the Huntington Library. A Malone Society reprint was issued in 1931 under the editorship of Dr. Greg.

BALIEFF, NIKITA (1877–1936), deviser and compère of a Russian cabaret entertainment, La Chauve-Souris, first seen in Paris soon after the First World War. It was brought to London in 1921 by Charles B. Cochran, and though it did not immediately achieve the success he had hoped for, repeated visits (sometimes in theatres unsuited to such intimate entertainment) brought it into notice, and it became part of the London theatrical scene. In New York its success was instant and unflagging. In both places Balieff, a big burly man with a vast genial moon-face, who must have weighed at least 16 stone, and who eked out his slender store of English with most expressive shrugs and gestures, gained immense personal popularity. His 'turns', costumed and set with a richness reminiscent of the Russian ballet, consisted of short burlesques, and small, often mimed, sketches based on old ballads, folksongs, prints, engravings, the woodenness of a toy soldier or the delicacy of a china shepherdess, rendered amusing by very slight and subtle guying of the material. Agate, who called the show 'pure theatre', said of its actors: 'Barbarian ecstasy, gallantry under French Louis, naïve buffoonery, the porcelain sentimentality of Sèvres or Dresden—all come alike to these superb artists.'

BALLAD OPERA, see GAY and OPERA, 7.

BALLET, a theatrical spectacle in which the action is presented in a highly specialized form of dancing and mime to the accompaniment of music. Though dancing has its origins in remote antiquity, and is one of the fundamental components of the theatre, ballet is of much later origin and emerges only at the Renaissance, when the various princely and ducal courts in Italy, vying with one another in the splendour of their entertainments, employed professional dancing masters, who turned the dance from a pastime into an art. The *balli*, or *balletti*, as they were called, of Domenico of Piacenza, author in *c.* 1400 of the first known treatise on dancing, of his followers Antonio Cornazano and William the Jew, and of other unknown masters, became so popular that they soon formed part of every kind of spectacle. Interludes of dancing were given during the *sacri rappresentazioni*, and found a place in the rapidly developing arts of drama, pastorale and opera.

At the end of the fifteenth century the French, advancing into Italy to claim the crown of Naples, first came into contact with the splendours of Italian courtly entertainments, with far-reaching consequences in the development of ballet. Dancing had for a long time been a courtly pastime in France, where the king and his courtiers took part in the so-called *mascarades*, but these had no set form, and it was only with the appearance of Italian dancing-masters that the seeds of the French court ballet were sown. The first tangible result of the influx into Paris of Italian dancers and musicians was the famous 'Balet Comique de la Royne', devised by Catherine de Médicis' Master of Ceremonies Beaujoyeulx [Baltazarini di Belgiojoso] in 1581 as part of the festivities in honour of the marriage of Henri III's sister-in-law, Marguerite of Lorraine (see No. 18). This took place in the great hall of the Palais du Petit-Bourbon, and is important not only in the history of ballet but also in that of scenic design. A number of engravings and descriptions of the entertainment are extant, as well as the book of the words, and it is possible to reconstruct it in its entirety. It lasted for about six hours, ending at 3 o'clock in the morning with the *grand ballet*. Because the spectators were on three sides of the stage, the most important part of the choreographer's work was to ensure that the dancers made beautiful patterns as they moved. Individual dancers were not yet singled out from the main body.

The Court ballet maintained its popularity in France for nearly a hundred years and when the smaller European countries, like Denmark, adopted the form, it was to Paris and Versailles that they looked for inspiration, even though technical innovations were still originating in Italy, where virtuosity remained the prerogative of the male dancer. (England, whose courtly entertainment was the more literary masque, remained somewhat aloof from the influence of Continental dancing, though she adopted Italian stage-craft.) Henri IV, Louis XIII, and the young Louis XIV all stimulated the development of ballet by their interest in it. Under Henri IV the *ballet-comique*, with its continuous plot based usually on a mythological subject, gave place to the simpler *ballet-mascarade*, which consisted mainly of burlesque scenes, or *entrées*, often depicting comic characters from contemporary life. Louis XIII, who had a great gift for comedy, danced in a number of these ballets, one of which he devised himself. It was under him that sung recitative replaced declamation (for ballet had not yet severed its connexion with the spoken word); music played a more important part, and the *ballet à entrée*, as it was now called, was the form used by Richelieu in devising entertainments for such royal events as the birth of the Dauphin, the future Louis XIV, under whom the Court ballet entered its final and most brilliant phase. Professional dancers had by now made their appearance at these Court spectacles, at which members of the public were sometimes allowed to be present, but they appeared mainly in comic and character parts, and the *grand ballet* which closed the proceedings was still reserved for the king and his courtiers. It was in 1651 in 'Cassandre' that the 12-year-old Louis XIV made his first appearance as a dancer, and from then until 1670, when he gave up dancing, he encouraged the collaboration of such men as the librettist Isaac de Benserade, and the musician and dancer Jean-Baptiste Lully, with the professional choreographers, of whom the most famous was Charles-Louis Beauchamps, nephew of Louis XIV's teacher, Pierre Beauchamps. Louis XIV also established in 1661 the first Académie Royale de Danse with thirteen members, which gave royal recognition to dance-teaching. But the greatest name connected with these courtly entertainments was Molière, whose first *comédie-ballet*, a logical development of the sung *ballet à entrée*, was *Les Fâcheux* (1661). In 1670 came the most famous of all *comédie-ballets*, *Le Bourgeois gentilhomme*, in which Molière again collaborated with Lully and Beauchamps, as he did in his last masterpiece, *Le Malade imaginaire* (1672). Unfortunately Lully, who had in the meantime become director of the newly founded Opéra, established a monopoly over ballet, and the dance element in Molière's plays was gradually whittled away and finally disappeared completely.

In any case the *raison d'être* of Court ballet as a manifestation of absolute monarchy was declining, and the time was coming when the professional dancers whom it had called into being would have to look to the theatre rather than the ballroom for employment. This they found under Lully at the newly formed Académie Royale de Musique (today known as the Paris Opéra), dancing in the *divertissements* which formed an important part of his operas. At first all the parts were danced by men, but soon women took over the female roles, though they were still overshadowed by the male dancers, among whom were Jean Balon and Louis Dupré, until the advent of Camargo (1710–70) in 1726 and Marie Sallé (1710–56) in 1727 established the supremacy of the ballerina. This coincided with, and was greatly helped by, the reform of ballet costume. The first dancers at the Opéra had retained the elaborate costumes, masks, and high heels of the Court entertainments, and the women were hampered by long skirts. Camargo shortened hers by several inches, thus achieving the freedom necessary for the performance of the *entrechat quatre*, which no woman had previously performed in Paris, while in London, which was not so hidebound by convention as Paris, Sallé once discarded her heavy costume in favour of a simple muslin dress.

Meanwhile two events of importance in the history of ballet were taking place, one in Italy, one in England. In Italy the strong technique which had always been a feature of Italian dancing had developed to the point of virtuosity, and produced the astonishing dancing of Barberina, and in England John Weaver, ballet-master at Drury Lane, had staged, in 1717, 'The Loves of Mars and Venus', the first ballet to rely on mime and gesture to the exclusion of song or the spoken word. The idea of wordless ballet had been in the air for some time, and mimed burlesque dancing had been a feature of the *commedia dell'arte*, but it was the development of the *ballet d'action* that finally liberated ballet from opera, and gave it an independent existence as an art form. The forerunners of this development were Sallé, who, while dancing in London as a child, may have seen Weaver's ballet, Fossano, the pantomimist and teacher of Barberina, and above all Franz Hilverding, who was staging mime versions of plays in Vienna in the 1740s and 1750s.

It was, however, Hilverding's pupil Gasparo Angiolini (1731–1803), and the great ballet-master Jean-Georges Noverre (1727–1810), who finally established the supremacy of the *ballet d'action*. Although they quarrelled bitterly in their life-time, they were both working towards the same end: the establishment of ballet as a theatrical entertainment capable of profound dramatic meaning. In his 'Don Juan' (1761) (with music by Gluck), and in his later ballets, Angiolini was successful in producing works with a closer synthesis of music and movement than had been achieved before; he also showed great judgement in choosing stories that could easily be expressed in mime, and had a remarkable gift for extracting the maximum effect by the way in which he set gestures to music. But it was Noverre, whose first important ballet 'The Chinese Festival' (1754), given at the Opéra, was brought to London by Garrick, who had the greatest influence on the development of ballet, mainly through his *Lettres sur la danse et les ballets* (1760). In this classic of ballet literature, which has been translated into several languages, Noverre set down basic principles for choreographers which are still valid today, and so paved the way for the reform of ballet which is usually associated with his name. Above all he stressed the need for unity, with everything contributing to the expression of the ballet's main theme. This could best be done, he argued, by means of movements which were natural and easily understood, tailored to fit the music as the words of a song fit the melody. Once these precepts had been accepted ballet was free to develop as an independent art, with the choreographer as its presiding genius.

Although the only work to survive from the eighteenth century, 'The Whims of Cupid and the Ballet-master' (1786), was first produced in Copenhagen under Angiolini's pupil Vincenzo Galeotti (1733–1816), it was France that continued to play the leading role in the development of ballet with such choreographers as Pierre Gardel (1758–1840) and Jean Dauberval (1742–1806), whose 'La Fille mal gardée' (1789) has recently returned to the repertory, though with music and choreography of a later period. Among Dauberval's pupils were the great Italian choreographer Salvatore

Viganò (1769–1821), and Charles Didelot (1767–1836), whose most famous ballet, 'Flore et Zéphire' (1796), was first produced in London. Most of his working life was spent in St. Petersburg. Schooled in the French tradition, he followed the precepts of Noverre. His choreography was particularly notable for the beauty of its grouping, and he was the first to employ dancers 'flying' on wires. He was also a superb teacher, and reorganized the St. Petersburg ballet-school, producing many excellent dancers. Viganò, a fine musician and an outstanding choreographer, for whom Beethoven wrote his only ballet-score (for 'Les Créatures de Prométhée', Vienna, 1801), did his best work at La Scala, Milan. But his insistence on mimed drama to the exclusion of the traditional ensemble dances and *pas de deux*, even though this was not fully realized, led to a hybrid form of Italian ballet in which mime and dance were separated. Italian ballet thus remained somewhat aloof from the main stream of development.

The latter part of the eighteenth century saw great advances in ballet technique and costume. In 1772 the mask was finally discarded and by the time the French Revolution broke out the cumbersome panniers, wigs, and Roman-style costumes had disappeared, as had the heeled shoe, a development which was to have important results in the near future. The ballerina now had almost complete freedom of movement, which enabled Anne Heinel (1753–1808), for instance, to exploit the pirouette. The great dancers of the day were still men, Gaetano Vestris (1729–1808) the 'diou de la danse', his son Auguste (1760–1842), the young Louis Duport (1781–1853). But the supremacy of the male dancer was coming to an end, and in the Romantic Ballet of the nineteenth century the ballerina was to dazzle him into oblivion so completely that he was to fall out of favour almost everywhere until Diaghilev came to restore the balance.

The Romantic Ballet, which is the most familiar and appealing of all periods in ballet history, is linked with the Romantic movement of the early nineteenth century, which was a reaction against the eighteenth-century classical obsession with form. The new spirit found expression in literature, music, and painting, and in due time found its way into ballet, which became more poetic and appealed more profoundly to the emotions of the audience than it had done before. In ballet the new spirit is associated above all with the poetic dancing of the great ballerina Marie Taglioni (1804–84), but it manifested itself in other ways, particularly in the choice of subject. Classical mythology was discarded almost overnight, and choreographers sought inspiration in legends of the supernatural—sylphides, naiads, wilis—and in rustic scenes, often set in some exotic land, with stylized dances from Spain or Poland or a glamorized Far East. In some of the great ballets of the period—'La Sylphide', 'Giselle'—the two exist side by side, and since they demand different styles of dancing—realism and rapid *terre à terre* steps for the scenes of real life, poetic feeling and steps of elevation or *ballonné* for the supernatural element—ballet became richer and more complex. An important feature of the supernatural scenes was the use of *pointe* work, the development of which had followed the adoption of the light heel-less shoe. The ballerina could now rise on the tips of her toes, reducing contact with the ground to the barest minimum, and so convey the illusion of weightlessness, a wonderful asset to choreographers who were introducing the supernatural into their work.

The development of *pointe* work and other radical transformations in ballet dancing were brought about through improved teaching methods, codified in 1820 by Carlo Blasis (1795–1878) in his *Elementary, Theoretical and Practical Treatise of the Art of the Dance*. Later, as head of the Ballet School attached to La Scala, Milan, he trained many brilliant dancers; his methods were passed on by his pupils to such later teachers as Enrico Cecchetti and Carlotta Zambelli, and are still in use.

The best-known Romantic Ballet is 'Giselle' (1841), which is danced today by companies all over the world, but there exists also a wonderful collection of ballets—including 'Napoli' and 'La Sylphide'—by Auguste Vestris's pupil August Bournonville (1805–79), ballet master at Copenhagen from 1830–77, which have been faithfully preserved for a century and more by the Royal Danish Ballet. Bournonville's 'La Sylphide' (1836) was based on the earlier and historically more celebrated version made by Filippo Taglioni for his daughter Marie, which, first performed in 1832 at the Paris Opéra, where 'Giselle' was later to have its first production, launched the Romantic Ballet on its distinguished course. Taglioni produced other ballets for his daughter, as Jean Coralli (1779–1854) did for her rival, Fanny Elssler (1810–84), and these two great ballerinas were followed at the Opéra by Carlotta Grisi (1819–99) and Fanny Cerrito (1817–1909). These last two, with Marie Taglioni and Lucile Grahn (1819–1907), were the dancers in the famous 'Pas de Quatre' seen in 1845 in London, a particularly profitable field for dancers which at this time seriously challenged the supremacy of Paris. Ballet had been given at the King's Theatre (see HER MAJESTY'S) since the middle of the eighteenth century, and its popularity reached its peak in the 1840s under Benjamin Lumley and his ballet-master, Jules Perrot (1810–92), perhaps the greatest choreographer of his time. He knew better than anyone how to use the dance to express action, and some of his *pas d'action* were vital passages in the unfolding of the plot. Perhaps the most brilliant ballet he staged in London was 'La Esmeralda' (1844), based on Victor Hugo's *Notre-Dame de Paris*. Grisi, and later Elssler, both excelled in the role of the gipsy-heroine, as did Cerrito in Perrot's 'Ondine' (1843) and Grahn in his 'Catarina' (1846). Unfortunately the popularity of ballet in London waned rapidly after the appearance in 1847 of Jenny Lind, who was largely responsible for restoring the vogue of opera, and after 1850 it survived mainly in the music-halls, at the Empire and the Alhambra.

In any case the great age of the Romantic Ballet was over, and although Paris was still to see the creation of Saint-Léon's 'Coppélia' (1870), the centre of interest now shifts to St. Petersburg, where Perrot went on leaving London, remaining there as ballet-master until 1859. While western European ballet was passing through a period of decline which even such ballerinas as Virginia Zucchi (1847–1930), Pierina Legnani (1863–1923), Carlotta Zambelli (1875–1968) and Adeline Genée (1878–1970) could not arrest, and which saw the complete eclipse of the male dancer (men's parts were often danced by women *en travesti*), a tradition was being built up in St. Petersburg, and to some extent in Moscow, which was to be further consolidated by Perrot's successors, Saint-Léon (1821–70) and Marius Petipa (1819–1910).

It was at the Maryinsky Theatre, which became the home of the Imperial Russian Ballet in 1885, that Petipa first staged the great Russian ballet 'The Sleeping Beauty' with music by Tchaikovsky. His career spanned more than half a century, until his retirement in 1903 at the age of 84. As *premier danseur*, he was able to observe at first hand the methods of Perrot and Saint-Léon, and also—which was no less useful—to learn from their experience how to deal with the authorities—the director, personally appointed by the Tsar, and those self-appointed arbiters of taste, the balletomanes, a closely knit group of spectators who attended nearly every performance and gained immense influence, not only in the castings of ballets but in matters affecting production and policy. Conservative in outlook, they needed to be carefully handled, particularly when it came to producing new ballets. It was this that drove Perrot from St. Petersburg in 1859 when he was only 49. Saint-Léon, though a lesser artist, was better able to handle them and also had the great gift of being able to tailor a ballet to suit a ballerina. He produced in 1864 'Koniok Gorbunok' (The Little Hump-Backed Horse), a work which has remained popular in Russia ever since—though now given with new music and new choreography—and was the first to be based on a Russian theme. But otherwise he was unadventurous, and by the time Petipa became principal ballet-master, in 1869, ballet in Russia had reached a low ebb. Petipa at first showed no unusual originality, but with the advent in 1881 of an intelligent and cultured director, Vsevolojsky, he entered upon the most glorious phase of his career, which culminated with the production in 1890 of 'The Sleeping Beauty'. It was Vsevolojsky who persuaded Tchaikovsky to write the music for this, for after the wretched production of 'Swan Lake' in Moscow in 1877 he had become convinced that ballet was not his field. The leading part in 'The Sleeping Beauty' was danced by Carlotta Brianza (1867–1930), one of several brilliant Italian dancers who were engaged for the Maryinsky. Another Italian was Enrico Cecchetti (1850–1928) who danced Carabosse and the Blue Bird, displaying talents as mime and dancer, and doing much to restore the lost prestige of the male dancer. 'The Sleeping Beauty' was followed by 'The Nutcracker' (1892) and, after Tchaikovsky's death, by a brilliant revival, with new choreography by Petipa and Ivanov, of 'Swan Lake' (1895): the improving standard of ballet music, to which Delibes in Paris and Tchaikovsky in Russia contributed so much, is the redeeming feature of late nineteenth-century ballet. Petipa was now 75, but as active as ever, and once again, as earlier in his career, he found himself working with great Russian dancers instead of Italian. This was mainly due to the teaching of Christian Johansson (1817–1903), who, after 30 years as a dancer at the Maryinsky, became chief teacher there in 1869. He, more than anyone else, fashioned what we know today as the Russian school of dancing, but which he always insisted was the French school which the French had forgotten, and as he was the pupil of Bournonville, who was trained by the younger Vestris, this was probably true. Under him a new generation of dancers emerged which included Mathilda Kshesinska [Kshessinskaya] (1872–1971), Olga Preobrajenska (1871–1962), Anna Pavlova (1881–1931), and, among the men, Nicolas Legat (1869–1937) and Michel Fokine (1880–1942).

Unfortunately Petipa's last days at the Maryinsky were unhappy. He was forced by an unsympathetic director to produce a ballet of which he liked neither the music (by Koreshchenko) nor the sets (by Golovin). It was greeted with jeering laughter and he went into retirement thinking himself a failure.

The reversal in Petipa's fortunes was symptomatic, not only of the revolt of the younger generation against the authority he had wielded for so long, but also of the new ideas which were beginning to emerge, and which were to influence the future of ballet all over the world. Russian ballet was at a low ebb: mime had degenerated into a stereotyped sign language, costumes were meaningless, outmoded traditions prevented choreographers from developing their ideas fully and everything in a ballet was subordinated to the demands of the prima ballerina. Reforms were badly needed, and they were destined to come about through Serge Diaghilev (1872–1929), leader of a group of progressive artists and art-lovers in St. Petersburg which included Alexandre Benois and Léon Bakst, who both designed ballets for the Maryinsky. In 1909 Diaghilev, who had been promoting Russian art and music in Paris, took there a company of dancers which included Pavlova, Tamara Karsavina (1885–), and Vaslav Nijinsky (1890–1950). Their first night at the Châtelet, on 19 May, was not only a socially brilliant occasion, but a landmark in the history of the theatre. They appeared in four ballets by Fokine—the Polovtsian Dances from 'Prince Igor', 'Cléopâtre', 'Le Pavillon d'Armide', and 'Les Sylphides', which curiously enough made the least impact at the time, though it is now probably the most frequently performed ballet in the modern repertory.

From 1909 until his death in 1929 Diaghilev reigned supreme in the ballet of western Europe. His great achievement was to raise ballet from a diverting entertainment to a serious theatrical art which absorbed the creative energies of the greatest artists and musicians of his time. He gave ballet purpose, and shaped its future course everywhere except, ironically, in Russia, from which he was cut off by the First World War and the Russian Revolution. His company had its base at Monte Carlo, but spent much time on tour. It made its first appearance in London in 1911, and in 1913 toured South America. It was during this tour that Nijinsky, whose superb dancing had been a revelation to audiences in Paris and London, married and was dismissed, being replaced by Leonide Massine (1896–). A few years later Nijinsky became insane.

The outbreak of war in Aug. 1914 closed the most brilliant period of Diaghilev's work, during which Fokine had also created for him 'Carnaval', 'Schéhérazade', and 'L'Oiseau de Feu' (all 1910), the last with music by Igor Stravinsky, 'Le Spectre de la rose' and 'Petrushka' (both 1911). This last was perhaps the greatest of all the works he inspired. The music was by Stravinsky, the décor by Benois. Diaghilev was also the motive force behind Nijinsky's 'L'Après-midi d'un faune' (1912) (music by Debussy), and 'Sacre du printemps' (1913) (music again by Stravinsky), neither of which bore any relationship to classical technique. Most of these ballets have survived in the repertory—more than from any other comparable period in history. From them, and from Diaghilev's work as a whole, came the modern concept of ballet as a composite art made up of three equally balanced elements—choreography, music, and décor. They also established the supremacy of the one-act ballet, not only because it made for greater variety in the evening's programme, but also because it proved a better length for the programme planning of touring companies such as Diaghilev's.

When Fokine, who had been Diaghilev's first choreographer and ballet-master, left the company he was succeeded by Massine, who first danced for Diaghilev in Fokine's 'Legend of Joseph' (1914). The best known of the ballets he wrote for Diaghilev are 'Les Femmes de bonne humeur' (1917), 'La Boutique fantasque', and 'Le Tricorne' (both 1919), of which the last two had their first performances in London. When he left Diaghilev—for both he and Fokine were destined to continue their brilliant careers elsewhere—Massine was followed by Bronislava Nijinska (1891–1972), sister of Nijinsky, and George Balanchine (1904–), three of whose ballets had English associations—'Romeo and Juliet' with music by Constant Lambert, 'The Triumph of Neptune' with music by Lord Berners (both 1926), and 'The Gods Go A-Begging' (1928) for which Handel's music was arranged by Beecham. Balanchine also arranged what proved to be the last Diaghilev ballet—'The Prodigal Son' (1929), with music by Prokofiev and scenery and costumes by Rouault.

The title role in 'The Prodigal Son' was danced by Serge Lifar (1905–), who joined Diaghilev from Russia in 1923. He was trained by Nijinska and by the great Italian ballet-master Cecchetti, teacher of the first Diaghilev dancers, and himself an outstanding performer. Apart from his roles in 'The Sleeping Beauty' mentioned earlier, Cecchetti created the Charlatan in 'Petrushka' and the Shopkeeper in 'La Boutique fantasque'. In 1918 he opened a ballet school in London, and from 1923 to his death was at La Scala, Milan. Lifar, whose only choreography for Diaghilev was done for a revival of Nijinska's ballet 'Le Renard' in 1929, went in that same year to the Paris Opéra where with a short interval (1945–6) he has since reigned supreme. During this time he has revitalized the ballet there, infusing it artistically with something of the spirit of Diaghilev, and technically with the substitution of the Russian style of dancing for the outmoded Italian style.

In the Diaghilev Ballets' first period it was the ballets that made theatre history: the later years are now remembered more for the individual dancers who were later to be so influential. They were mainly drawn from Russia, but among them were three English ballerinas—Lydia Sokolova [Hilda Munnings] (1896–), Alicia Markova [Alicia Marks] (1910–), and Ninette de Valois [Edris Stannus] (1898–)—and one Englishman, Anton Dolin [Patrick Healey-Kay] (1904–), whose later partnership with Markova was to be of supreme importance in the dissemination of ballet.

But the dancer who had the greatest influence on the rising generation was Pavlova, trained in the Imperial Ballet School, prima ballerina at the Maryinsky in 1906, who danced for Diaghilev only in the 1909 season in Paris. After that their paths rarely crossed. In fact, their viewpoints were fundamentally opposed, for while Diaghilev's ideal was to subordinate everything to making a ballet a complete work of art in itself, to Pavlova the dance was unquestionably supreme, and she would not allow music and scenery to assume the importance Diaghilev gave them in his productions. In 1910 she appeared in London, which became her permanent home, and soon formed her own company, mainly of English dancers. With this she embarked on long tours which covered the whole world. She visited provincial towns as well as great cities and took ballet to places which had never seen it before. Her vitality was almost superhuman and she was completely dedicated to her art. This dedication, conveyed through the force of her extraordinary personality, had a magnetic effect on her audience. A learned Indian once said that to see her dance was a religious experience, and pioneers of the revival of Indian dancing, among them Uday Shankar, were directly inspired by her, as were two small boys thousands of miles apart, Frederick Ashton (1906–) in Ecuador and Robert Helpmann (1909–) in Australia. Because it was dancing that mattered to her, and dancing in its purest form that she wanted to carry all over the world, her repertory was unadventurous, and little of it has survived. Her most famous work, apart from 'Autumn Leaves' (1918), which she arranged herself to music by Chopin, was 'Le Cygne' (1905), arranged for her to Saint-Saëns's music by Fokine, with whom she had danced at the Maryinsky in her early days. It was for her that he had first arranged the little suite of dances called 'Chopiniana' from which he later created 'Les Sylphides'.

The death of Pavlova, coming only eighteen months after that of Diaghilev, was a great blow, and although the seeds of future development, particularly in England, had already been sown, it was slow and unspectacular. Meanwhile attention was once more drawn to Monte Carlo, where in 1932 Colonel de Basil and René Blum formed their Ballets-Russes. Between them they built up a strong company with Massine and Balanchine as choreographers, and Serge Grigoriev (1883–1968), who had worked for Diaghilev from the beginning, and was said to have the whole of the company's repertory in his head, as *régisseur*. Lubov Tchernicheva (1890–), Felia Dubrovska (1896–) and Léon Woizikovski (1897–), all formerly with Diaghilev, were engaged as principal dancers, and the company soon produced its own stars in the three famous 'baby ballerinas', Tamara Toumanova (1919–), Tatiana Riabouchinska (1917–), and Irina Baronova (1919–). They were trained by Preobrajenska and Kshesinska, who had settled in Paris after the Russian Revolution, and opened ballet-schools which were to be powerful factors in preserving something of the old Imperial Russian Ballet tradition in western Europe. What could not be reproduced, however, was the iron discipline of the Imperial School which Diaghilev, by the force of his personality, had to some extent been able to maintain. Unfortunately, de Basil and Blum were a very ill-assorted pair, and neither could exert his authority as Diaghilev had done. It was not long before the company split in two, between which there were constant interchanges of dancers. The history of these Ballets-Russes companies in the 1930s, which has still to be written, is chequered with intrigues, quarrels and defections. But the standards set by Diaghilev were adhered to, and composers like Auric and designers like Goncharova and Bérard helped to create the new ballets, among them Balanchine's 'Cotillon' and Massine's 'Jeux d'enfants' (both 1932). But the most important was probably Massine's 'Les Présages' (1933), which was performed to Tchaikovsky's Fifth Symphony. This was the first of Massine's symphonic ballets, which marked an important development in choreography. It was followed by 'Choreartium' (1933) to Brahms's Fourth Symphony, and 'Symphonie Fantastique' (1936) to Berlioz's work of the same name.

The rival companies which had been formed by the split between de Basil and Blum both appeared in London in 1938 at the same time, the former at Covent Garden, the latter at Drury Lane. The Second World War found them both in America, where Blum's company, after he had left it to return to Europe and death in the concentration camp at Auschwitz, continued to tour, and became virtually an American company, while de Basil's company, having survived the war years by touring in South America, returned to Europe, but gradually dwindled and finally disappeared with de Basil's death in 1951. Its last important creation, in Sydney in 1940, was 'Graduation Ball'. The choreography, to music by Johann Strauss, was by David Lichine (1910–), a young dancer who had been in Pavlova's company, and joined the original Ballet-Russe on its formation.

When the Ballet-Russe first appeared in London in 1933 it had to meet the competition of a nascent British ballet company, whose main inspiration may be said to have come from Diaghilev, but whose roots went back much further. Ballet was popular in London long before there was any thought of establishing a national company. As we have seen, in spite of the popularity of opera, ballet shared the bills at Vanbrugh's theatre in the Haymarket, and became an important feature of the programmes at the Empire and Alhambra music-halls. Later the companies of Diaghilev and Pavlova were always assured of a warm welcome, but, in spite of the founding of a ballet school by Édouard Espinosa (1871–1950) in 1900, the lack of good teaching in London made the establishment of a British tradition virtually impossible. It was not until the 1920s that the foundation of the Royal Academy of Dancing and the Cecchetti Society brought about a rapid improvement, and ensured not only a supply of good dancers but the nucleus of an informed audience.

British ballet as we know it today owes much to the hard work and devotion of three outstanding women—Genée, a Danish dancer who became prima ballerina at the Empire, and was the first President of the Royal Academy of Dancing, a position she held for more than thirty years, Marie Rambert [Myriam Ramberg] (1888–), and Ninette de Valois, who were both briefly in Diaghilev's company.

Marie Rambert, who married the English playwright and dramatic critic Ashley Dukes, opened a ballet school in London in 1920, and ten years later formed the Ballet Club, which was to be one of the most important manifestations of British ballet during its formative years in the 1930s. She had a remarkable flair for bringing out a young choreographer's talent, and Frederick Ashton, Antony Tudor (1909–), and Andrée Howard (1910–68) all learnt many valuable lessons on the tiny stage of her husband's Mercury Theatre in Notting Hill Gate: Ashton's first ballet, 'A Tragedy of Fashion', was produced as a result of her encouragement in 1926. Although her early training had been with Jaques-Dalcroze, she later studied under Cecchetti and Serafina Astafieva (1876–1934), a dancer from Diaghilev's company who opened a school in London, and from the first she kept the importance of the classical tradition well in mind. Soon the Ballet Club was producing some remarkable young dancers, among them Pearl Argyle (1910–47), Diana Gould (1913–) (later the wife of Menuhin), Harold Turner (1909–62), and Walter Gore (1910–). Though the Ballet Rambert, as the Ballet Club was eventually renamed, has never enjoyed such a large subsidy as the Royal Ballet, it has played a very important role in the development of British ballet. Marie Rambert's production of 'Giselle' received unanimous praise, and in recent years she has mothered another very talented choreographer, Norman Morrice, whose first ballet, 'Two Brothers', was acclaimed in 1958.

Parallel with the development of the Ballet Rambert went that of the group which was eventually to become the Royal Ballet. In 1926, at about the time when Ashton was preparing his first ballet, Ninette de Valois opened a ballet school and persuaded Lilian Baylis, manager of the Old Vic, to allow her to stage the dances for the plays there. This was the beginning of a close association between the two women which, when Sadler's Wells reopened in 1931, under Miss Baylis, led to the establishment of a permanent ballet company there—the Vic-Wells Ballet. Two years later this young organization was strengthened by the transference to it of the resources of the Camargo Society. Although this body existed only for three years, it had an importance in British ballet out of all proportion to its size. Founded in 1930 by Philip Richardson and Arnold Haskell with the object of filling the void left by the death of Diaghilev and presenting ballet performances in West-End theatres three or four times a year, it drew its dancers from the Rambert and Vic-Wells companies, with Lydia Lopokova (1891–) (later Lady Keynes), Olga Spessivtseva (1895–), and Markova as guest artists. Of the new ballets it commissioned from British choreographers, two are still in the repertory, Ashton's 'Façade' (music by William Walton) and Ninette de Valois's 'Job' (music by Vaughan Williams), both produced in 1931.

Throughout the 1930s the Vic-Wells Ballet, headed by Markova and Dolin, went from strength to strength. In de Valois it possessed a leader with a genius for organization and in Constant Lambert (1905–51), who became musical director in 1932, an adviser of wide interests and impeccable taste. With the help of Nicolas Sergueyev (1876–1951), formerly *régisseur* at the Maryinsky, who had produced for Diaghilev in 1921 the splendid though financially unrewarding revival of 'The Sleeping Princess', the Vic-Wells mounted 'Coppélia', 'Giselle', 'The Nutcracker' and 'Swan Lake'. Among the new ballets the most important was de Valois's 'The Rake's Progress' (1935), a masterly re-creation of Hogarth's London designed by Rex Whistler.

When Markova and Dolin left to found their own company, Ninette de Valois was able to replace them with dancers trained in the Vic-Wells School, Margot Fonteyn [Peggy Hookham] (1919–) and Robert Helpmann. With them and the Vic-Wells dancers many ballets of lasting value were created, among them de Valois's 'Checkmate' (1935) (music by Arthur Bliss) and several by Ashton—'Apparitions' (1936), 'Les Patineurs' (1937), 'Horoscope' (1938). The company was also able to put on, for a gala performance at Covent Garden in 1939, 'The Sleeping Princess' with Fonteyn as Aurora.

The company was in Holland when the Germans invaded it, and narrowly escaped capture, leaving behind most of their scenery, costumes and music. But they quickly recovered, and as the Sadler's Wells Ballet, they appeared at the New Theatre in London and all over the provinces on tour, becoming an increasingly important part of the country's cultural life. During this time Helpmann, who in 1950 retired from dancing to become a successful actor, emerged as a choreographer with 'Hamlet' (1942) (to the Tchaikovsky overture) and 'Miracle in the Gorbals' (1944) (music by Bliss). After the war the company was invited to become the resident ballet company at Covent Garden, and in 1956 it received its charter as the Royal Ballet. It now comprises a large school and enough dancers to supply two companies. As a result of its frequent tours, and particularly its triumphant visits to America, it commands admiration all over the world. Among the male dancers who have achieved prominence in the company are Michael Somes and David Blair, and although since the war it has lost Violetta Elvin, Moira Shearer, and Beryl Grey, it has a galaxy of ballerinas, Nadia Nerina, Svetlana Beriosova, Anya Linden, Annette Page, Merle Park, Lynn Seymour, and Antoinette Sibley. In 1962 the company was strengthened by the engagement, as guest artist, of the astonishing Rudolf Nureyev, who in becoming the partner of Margot Fonteyn inspired that great ballerina to new heights of artistry. Among creations of the post-war period have been Ashton's 'Symphonic Variations' (1946), 'Ondine' (1958) and 'La Fille mal gardée' (1960), a number of ballets by John Cranko (1927–) including 'Pineapple Poll' (1951) (music mainly from Sullivan's *H.M.S. Pinafore*) and

'The Prince of the Pagodas' (1957) (music by Britten), and works by Kenneth MacMillan (1930–), among them 'The Invitation' (1961), 'Romeo and Juliet' (1965), and a series of ballets to Stravinsky's music.

Besides the Royal Ballet, the Ballet Rambert, and the Markova–Dolin Company, other companies which have helped to foster and extend the range of ballet in England have been the International Ballet, led by Mona Inglesby (1918–), which toured indefatigably in classical ballets, and the Festival Ballet, founded in 1950 with Dolin and Markova as its leaders. John Gilpin (1930–) from the Ballet Rambert is its principal male dancer, while many distinguished ballerinas have led it since Markova's departure. The success it has had with Lichine's full-length version of 'The Nutcracker' is further proof of the deep-rooted love of the classical ballets that is such a feature of British ballet today.

The main centres of ballet today, apart from London, and Copenhagen, where the Royal Danish Ballet continues the tradition of Bournonville, are France, Russia, and the United States. In Paris the influence of Diaghilev was slow to make itself felt at the Opéra where, in 1930, the prestige of ballet was at a very low ebb. Lifar restored its self-respect, and in spite of the privations of the Second World War it flourished under the German occupation. Lifar was still at the height of his powers as a dancer and as a choreographer and was admirably partnered by Yvette Chauviré (1917–). Since the war the company has embarked on a number of tours, and in 1958 it was the first foreign ballet company to appear on the stage of the Bolshoi Theatre in Moscow. Two other companies of importance were the Ballets des Champs-Elysées and the International Ballet of the Marquis de Cuevas. The first was formed in 1945 by Roland Petit (1924–) with Janine Charrat (1924–) as its leading ballerina, and Boris Kochno (1903–), Diaghilev's secretary, as artistic director. During its brief existence—it was disbanded in 1950—it raised the prestige of French ballet to great heights, it introduced many dancers who were later to become famous, among them Jean Babilée, Renée Jeanmaire, Nina Vyroubova, and it produced at least one masterpiece, Petit's 'Les Forains' (1945), a study of wandering acrobats which was designed by Bérard with music by Sauguet. In collaboration with Cocteau and Wakhévitch, Petit also produced 'Le Jeune Homme et la Mort' (1946) danced to Bach's Passacaglia in C Minor by Jean Babilée and Nathalie Philippart. For the Ballets de Paris, which he founded in 1948, Petit produced 'Les Demoiselles de la nuit' (1948), in which Fonteyn created the part of the Cat, 'Carmen' (1949), and 'Le Loup' (1953).

The International Ballet of the Marquis de Cuevas was the private company of a Spanish nobleman married to a grand-daughter of John D. Rockefeller. It dated back to 1944, when, as Ballet International, it gave a season in New York at a heavy financial loss. Three years later de Cuevas took over the Nouveau Ballet de Monte Carlo, a post-war foundation which flourished temporarily under Lifar. From 1947 until it disbanded in 1962 it was headed by Marjorie Tallchief (1927–) and Skibine (1920–), who left in 1957 to go to the Paris Opéra, Rosella Hightower (1920–), and Serge Golovine (1924–), and presented many new ballets. Practically every important choreographer of the day worked for this company, from Massine to Cranko, and among its outstanding creations were 'Piège de lumière' (1952) by John Taras (1919–) and Skibine's 'Prisoner of the Caucasus' (music by Khatchaturian).

In Russia, which because of the Revolution remained impervious to Diaghilev's influence, the development has been very different from that in western Europe. Both in Leningrad (which as St. Petersburg was the main centre of ballet in Russia) and in Moscow (which has now acquired an equal prominence) the ballet schools, dating from 1738 and 1773 respectively, have maintained an unbroken tradition. In the early years of the Soviet régime there was a danger that ballet might be discarded, as being too closely linked with Tsarist times, but thanks to those teachers who lovingly and courageously preserved intact the great classical tradition—Agrippina Vaganova (1879–1951) in Leningrad and Vasili Tikhomirov (1876–1956) in Moscow—it survived, and in spite of the loss to western Europe of many of its best dancers and teachers, and of a confused period of experiment, from which only one ballet, 'The Red Poppy' (1926), survives, the classical ballet emerged unscathed and enjoyed a new popularity in Leningrad with two brilliant young dancers who came to the fore in 1925 and 1928, Marina Semyonova (1909–) and Galina Ulanova (1910–). Much of the prestige which Russian ballet enjoys today is due to Ulanova, who has only recently retired from dancing. Among her finest roles have been 'Giselle' and Juliet in Lavrovsky's 'Romeo and Juliet' (1940), a masterly adaptation of Shakespeare's tragedy, produced on a sumptuous scale to a rich score by Prokofiev. The success of this ballet underlines the fact that in Russia the full-length ballet still remains the set framework for new works, although Soviet choreographers, influenced by the West, have recently been experimenting with the one-act form. As a result, ballets in Russia invariably have a strong story which the Soviet choreographers, following the example established by Alexander Gorsky (1871–1924) at the Bolshoi in Moscow rather than that of the classical ballet-masters of the past, try to convey in a convincing manner by means of dance, mime, and realistic staging. The process of broadening ballet's appeal to the new mass audiences has also led to another distinguishing feature of contemporary Russian ballet—a much greater use of folk-dance to enrich the choreographer's vocabulary.

To the outside world Soviet ballet generally means the Bolshoi Ballet, which has gained considerable fame through its foreign tours. Among its outstanding ballerinas are, since Ulanova's retirement, Lepeshinskaya, Plisetskaya, Struchkova, Maximova, while among the male dancers—of which Russia, like Denmark, has always a plentiful supply—are Yuri Zhdanov, Nicolai Fadeyechev, and Vladimir Vassiliev. The international renown of the Bolshoi should not blind one to the importance of the Kirov Ballet from Leningrad, direct heirs to the Maryinsky tradition. After long and distinguished careers Natalia Dudinskaya and Constantin Sergueyev have retired as dancers, and the company's fortunes are now entrusted to stars of a younger generation, among them Irina Kolpakova, Alla Shelest, Alla Osipenko, and Yuri Soloviev. Another prominent Russian company is the Stanislavsky Theatre Ballet from Moscow which visited Paris in 1956. Its ballets are produced mainly by Vladimir Bourmeister (1904–71), whose version of 'Swan Lake' used the full score as Tchaikovsky originally wrote it.

Ballet is no longer confined to Moscow and Leningrad, for there are established companies all over the Soviet Union. In Tbilisi, for example, the ballet is directed by Vakhtang Chaboukiani, who in 1957 produced an 'Othello' in which he himself gave a performance of astonishing power as the Moor of Venice.

America, which has recently become a centre of ballet activity in its own right, had a somewhat belated start. In spite of isolated visits from companies during the nineteenth century, and the more frequent tours of Pavlova before and after the First World War, it was not until the impresario Sol Hurok brought over the de Basil Ballet Russe in 1933 that a real interest in ballet as an art began to develop, and it was then that the seeds of a truly American ballet were sown. The New York City Ballet, the most important American company today, developed out of a meeting between Lincoln Kirstein (1907–) and Balanchine which resulted in the opening in 1934 of the School of American Ballet under Balanchine, out of which developed the American Ballet, which became for a time the official ballet company of the Metropolitan Opera. Most of its ballets were arranged by Balanchine, but there were ballets by other choreographers, some on American themes, of which the most successful was 'Billy the Kid' (1938), by Eugene Loring (1914–) with music by Aaron Copland. American Ballet was disbanded in 1941. In 1946 Kirstein and Balanchine founded Ballet Society, which not only gave performances but sponsored lectures and publications. In 1948 Ballet Society was transformed into the New York City Ballet with a permanent home at the City Center and an indirect subsidy from that organization. It is today based on the Lincoln Center for the Performing Arts. It is still essentially an independent company under Kirstein's control, it has been very generously subsidized by the Ford Foundation, and it is better known in Europe than any other American company. In America itself its activities are confined to some of the larger towns, for the ballet public elsewhere is so scattered that single performances only would be possible and those, though no doubt financially rewarding, would be too exhausting for the dancers.

The repertory of the New York City Ballet is mainly composed of ballets by Balanchine. Although he has had a great popular success with his full-length version of 'The Nutcracker' (1954), many of his ballets are austere abstract works which have helped to produce a typically American style of dancing. Balanchine's choreography is rooted in the formal classicism of the Petipa period, but he has removed all extraneous decoration and instilled into his dancers an iron discipline and a classical purity relieved only by their natural buoyancy and loose-limbed athleticism. The new American school has already produced its own ballerinas, among them Maria Tallchief (1925–), sister of Marjorie, and male dancers, and has its own American choreographer in Jerome Robbins (1918–). Other American dancers have developed with the other important company, Ballet Theatre. Founded in 1940, it grew out of the company formed in 1937 by Pavlova's former partner Mikhail Mordkin (1881–1944). Among its early dancers were Dolin, Markova, Baronova, and Igor Youskevitch (1912–), one of the greatest *danseurs nobles* of our time, who had formerly danced for de Basil. On its formation it had no less than eleven choreographers, including Antony Tudor, who was responsible for many important ballets in the company's early years, Massine with 'Aleko' (1943), Agnes de Mille (1909–) with 'Fall River Legend' (1948), Andrée Howard, and Eugene Loring, and it was for Ballet Theatre that Fokine produced his last works, of which 'Helen of Troy' was left unfinished and completed by Lichine. One of the most successful ballets with an American background was 'Fancy Free' (1944) by Jerome Robbins, who was a dancer in the company before going to the City Center, and who forms an important link, with his choreography for the musical *On the Town*, in the development, from *Oklahoma!* to *West Side Story*, of the idea that dances arranged by distinguished choreographers should help to advance the plot of a musical and not be merely incidental.

Since the Ballet Russe de Monte Carlo (originally Blum's company) became entirely American, its most notable new ballet has been Agnes de Mille's 'Rodeo' (1942), a vigorous work set in the land of cowboys, which includes a roisterous square dance. America's latest company is Ballets U.S.A., founded in 1958 by Jerome Robbins. It has made two visits to Europe and in 1959 was awarded a prize by the Théâtre des Nations in Paris. It is a company without stars, its strength resting largely on the unusual degree of co-ordination between its dancers. Another important American company is the Robert Joffrey Ballet.

No picture of the American dance scene would be complete without mention of modern dance. The basis of this form of theatrical dance is not the classical ballet technique, but a concept of making the whole body expressive, free from technical conventions. The modern dance movement can be traced back to Isadora Duncan (1878–1927), whose free dancing expressed an inner urge that was so personal that while she had a great influence, notably on Fokine when she went to Russia, she established no definite technique that could be handed on, and to Ruth St. Denis (1877–1968) and Ted Shawn (1891–), founders of the Denishawn School. Modern dance has certainly been influenced by the ideas of the Central European schools of Rudolf Laban (1879–1958), initiator of the system of dance notation which bears his name, Mary Wigman (1886–) and Kurt Jooss (1901–), but it has evolved independently as a major force in contemporary dance. The greatest figure in modern dance is without question Martha Graham (1900–), who is accepted as one of the most important dance creators of the day and whose technique is the most highly developed form of modern dance. Other leading exponents of modern dance have been Hanya Holm (1898–), the late Doris Humphrey (1895–1958), Charles Weidman (1901–) and José Limon (1908–).

The great tradition which we have traced from its beginnings in Italy during the Renaissance has spread across the world—to Australia, Canada, Japan, Turkey, Germany, Hungary, Sweden, Finland, Yugoslavia—and is universally recognized as an important part of man's cultural heritage. IVOR GUEST

BALTIMORE, one of the first towns in America to show hospitality to theatrical companies. The first theatre building was raised there after the War of Independence by a former member of the American Company, one Wall, and opened on 15 Jan. 1782 with *Richard II* and *Miss in Her Teens*, but performances in adapted halls had frequently been given there before that date. The town continued to be visited regularly by the early companies, and today retains its position as an important date in the tours of the best American and foreign companies.

BALUSTRADE-PIECE, see FLAT.

BALZAC, HONORÉ DE (1799–1850), the great French novelist, wrote several unacted plays in his early years, and he always enjoyed visiting the theatres, where he had many friends. In the 1830s, in the hope of clearing off some of his accumulated debts, he several times thought of writing a play, and in 1839 he succeeded in persuading Harel, manager of the Porte-Saint-Martin, to put on *Vautrin* (based on *Le Père Goriot*), with Frédérick in the chief part. On the first night, 14 Mar. 1840, there was a disturbance caused by Frédérick's appearance in the fourth act, made-up to resemble Louis-Philippe. This caused the play to be banned, and Harel went bankrupt. The critics thought poorly of the play, but all admired Frédérick's acting. Balzac, deeper in debt than ever, now wrote two more plays, in collaboration with Frédérick. The manuscript of the first, which was never produced, has been lost, but *Mercadet* was finally put on in 1851, after Balzac's death, in a version by Dennery, with Geoffroy in the chief part. In 1842 Balzac produced an extravaganza, *Les Ressources de Quinola*, at the Odéon, which ran for nineteen performances. The criticisms were mainly hostile. In 1843, at the Gaîté, *Paméla Giraud* was given in a version re-written by two hack dramatists while Balzac was in Russia. It had twenty-one performances. Janin, who disliked it, was astonished that the author of such excellent novels should descend to such trash. But it helped to pay some bills. Balzac might have had a success with his last acted play, *La Marâtre*, which was produced at the Théâtre Historique in 1848, but the Revolution closed the theatres. Those who heard Balzac read his own plays say he had great powers of mimicry and a most expressive voice.

BANCROFT. (1) SIR SQUIRE (1841–1926), English actor-manager, a tall, distinguished-looking man of great ability, who, with his wife (2) MARIE EFFIE (*née* Wilton) (1839–1921), introduced a number of reforms on the British stage, both as regards acting and the type of play produced. To them is attributable the vogue of the drawing-room comedy and drama with their typical stage-setting and décor.

Marie Wilton was the daughter of provincial actors, and was on the stage from early childhood. She played with many famous actors of the time, including Macready on his farewell performance in the provinces, when she appeared as Fleance to his Macbeth. She was also much praised by Charles Kean for her Prince Arthur in *King John*. She first appeared in London in 1856, at the Lyceum, as Henri to Dillon's Belphegor in the play of that name, in which Toole, then still unknown, played Fanfaronade. As Perdita in Brough's extravaganza on *The Winter's Tale* she quickly made a success, and continued to play in burlesque, notably at the Strand in H. J. Byron's plays, until she decided to go into management on her own account.

Meanwhile Squire Bancroft, who had no family associations with the stage, had made his first appearance in the Birmingham stock company in pantomime in Jan. 1861, and for the next four years was gaining experience of all types of parts in stock and touring companies. Towards the end of this period he played with Marie Wilton, who went to Liverpool in burlesque, and on her return to London she invited him to join her company.

On a borrowed capital of £1,000, of which little remained when the curtain went up, they opened the old Queen's Theatre (now the Scala), which, situated in an unfashionable part of London, had fallen into disrepute, and was nicknamed the 'Dust Hole'. Renamed the Prince of Wales's, charmingly decorated, and excellently run, it opened on 15 Apr. 1865, with Bancroft in Wooler's *A Winning Hazard*, while Marie Wilton appeared as Alessio in a burlesque by H. J. Byron entitled *La! Sonnambula!; or, the Supper, the Sleeper, and the Merry Swiss Boy*. The venture was a success, consolidated two years later by the marriage of the joint managers. The despised 'Dust Hole' became one of the most popular theatres in London, and there the Bancrofts presented and played in the plays of Tom Robertson, domestic comedies more credible and true to life than the melodramas which had been so much in vogue previously. As Captain Hawtree in *Caste* (1867) Bancroft gave one of his best performances, only equalled by his Orloff in *Diplomacy* and his revival of Webster's old role of Triplet in *Masks and Faces*. His wife was brilliant in the leading female roles, and was accounted one of the best actresses of her day. The company was carefully chosen and the Bancrofts did much to raise the economic status of their actors. Leading players were paid £60–£100 a week, as against a previous scale of £5–£10 elsewhere, and the theatre also paid for the ladies' dresses, an unusual arrangement at that time. Among other innovations the Bancrofts adopted Mme Vestris's idea of practicable scenery—real doors and windows in solid three-wall rooms with a ceiling (see BOX-SET). In 1880 they moved to the Haymarket and continued their successful career, in spite of a first-night riot caused by the abolishing of the pit. They retired in 1885, their last appearance being on Monday, 20 July, in a mixed bill consisting of the first act of *Money*, a scene from *London Assurance*, and the second and third acts of *Masks and Faces*. In after years they both appeared intermittently under other managements, but the main bulk of their work was done before 1885. There can be no doubt that they had a great and salutary influence upon the English stage. Happily married and of congenial temperaments, they commanded the highest respect from their staff and audiences, and the knighthood conferred upon Bancroft in 1897 was a recognition of the services of both to their profession. Their collaboration extended to three plays and a joint autobiography, while Lady Bancroft was also the author of a novel.

W. MACQUEEN-POPE†

BANDBOX THEATRE, NEW YORK, originally Adolf Phillipp's, at 205 East 57th Street. This theatre opened on 23 Nov. 1912. Two years later it was renamed, and it closed on 28 Apr. 1917, a cinema being built on the site. It was here that the Washington Square Players, forerunners of the Theatre Guild, first appeared in New York from 1915 to 1916 in a series of one-act plays, mainly by American authors, under the joint direction of Philip Moeller, Lawrence Langner, Edward Goodman, and Helen Westley.

BANGS, FRANK C. (1833–1908), American actor, who was serving his apprenticeship in a newspaper office when he saw the elder Booth as Richard III and decided to go on the stage. He made his début in Washington in 1851, and worked as general utility in a number of good companies, including those of the Ravel pantomimists and of Mrs. John Drew. In 1858 he made his first appearance in New York at Laura Keene's Theatre, and then went to Wallack's, where he shared juvenile leads with Lester. During the war he was a Confederate soldier, but returned to the stage and in 1867 made a great success in *After Dark*, at Niblo's. He retired following a dispute with the management, and spent his time lecturing and teaching elocution. In 1870 he returned to the stage, and was seen in the company of many good actors, playing Mark Antony to the Brutus of Edwin Booth and the Cassius of Lawrence Barrett with great success. In later life he was less successful, and appeared in a number of ephemeral plays, his last outstanding production being a revival in 1892 of Boker's *Francesca da Rimini*.

BANKS, JOHN (*c.* 1650–1706), English dramatist, author of eight tragedies, of which the best is probably *Virtue Betrayed; or, Anna Bullen* (1682). Banks, of whose life very little is known, has been somewhat underrated, according to Allardyce Nicoll, who considers him a writer of undoubted merit, worthy to rank next to Otway 'in the imaging of emotional and pathetic scenes'. His early works were heroic dramas in the style of Dryden, but he later shows traces of pathos and intimate tragedy which mark him as a precursor of Rowe.

BANKS, LESLIE (1890–1952), English actor, who made his first appearance in the provinces with Benson's company in 1911. He later toured America and Canada with H. V. Esmond and Eva Moore, and made his first appearance in London at the Vaudeville Theatre in 1914. After the First World War, during which he served in the army, he joined the Birmingham Repertory company, and then played leading parts on tour with Lena Ashwell. He returned to the West End in 1921, and soon established a solid reputation as a player of power and restraint in a long series of successful productions. Among his best parts were Petruchio (1937, with Edith Evans), the schoolmaster hero in *Goodbye, Mr. Chips* (1938), and the Duke in *The Duke in Darkness* (1942). He appeared many times in New York, notably as Captain Hook in *Peter Pan* (1924) and Henry in *Springtime for Henry* (1931). He was also an excellent producer, usually of plays in which he was appearing. In 1948 he became President of British Actors' Equity, and in the New Year Honours of 1950 he was appointed C.B.E. for services to the stage. He had great versatility—in a season of repertory at the Haymarket in 1944–5 he played Lord Porteous in *The Circle*, Tattle in *Love for Love*, Claudius in *Hamlet*, Bottom in *A Midsummer Night's Dream*, and Antonio Bologna in *The Duchess of Malfi*—and brought a keen intelligence to bear upon his roles. Of a distinguished presence, with a fine speaking voice, he was always interesting to watch, and listen to, and seldom failed to give a performance touched with imagination and subtle humour.

BANNISTER. (1) CHARLES (1741–1804), English actor, who after some years in the provinces appeared with Foote at the Haymarket, and established an enviable reputation as a comedian and a mimic of fashionable singers. He was engaged by Garrick to play Merlin in *Cymon* (1767), and his Caliban was considered outstanding. A pleasant, easy-going man, he was often in financial trouble, and towards the end of his life was forced to rely for supplies on an annual benefit at the Haymarket, of which Colman allowed him the use. At his 1800 benefit Lord Nelson, fresh from his victory at the Nile, was present with Sir William and Lady Hamilton. Charles's modest reputation was eclipsed by that of his son (2) JOHN (1760–1836), who was in his youth an art student at the Royal Academy with Rowlandson the caricaturist. In 1778, with the encouragement of Garrick, he went on the stage, and made his first appearance at the Haymarket in a part made famous by Woodward, who had just died. Bannister, however, did well in it, in spite of his youth and inexperience, and was engaged for Drury Lane, where he appeared mainly in tragedy. In this he was soon overshadowed by the rising fame of Henderson and Kemble, and it was in comedy that he found his true bent. He was the first Don Ferolo Whiskerandos in *The Critic* (1779), in which he later played Sir Fretful Plagiary, and was also good in such parts as Sir Anthony Absolute, Tony Lumpkin, Scrub, and Doctor Pangloss. The eminence of King in first comic parts was something of a bar to his advancement, and he took to making visits to the provinces, but he later returned to London and became one of the managers of Drury Lane, where he spent most of his career. He married in 1783 Elizabeth Harper, principal singer at the Haymarket, who retired in 1793 to take care of her increasing family. Bannister remained on the stage until 1815, and retired to spend twenty-one years of calm and happy family life. He always kept his taste for painting, and was intimate with Rowlandson, Morland, and Gainsborough. On his death it was said of him: 'The stage can point to few men of more solid virtue and unblemished character.' His life was written by John Adolphus in 1838.

BANNISTER, NATHANIEL HARRINGTON (1813–47), American actor and dramatist, who had a short and somewhat tragic life. He first appeared on the stage in Baltimore at the age of 16, playing Young Norval. In 1831 he went to New York, but in spite of his popularity in the south and west of America he never seemed to get a footing there, and died in poverty at the age of 34. He wrote a number of plays, but there also bad luck seemed to dog him, and he sold the most successful, *Putnam*, for fifty dollars. Of the rest only four have survived. They are romantic melodramas in the prevailing historical style, of small literary or theatrical merit.

BANVARD'S MUSEUM, NEW YORK, see DALY'S THEATRE, 1.

BANVILLE, THÉODORE FAULLAIN DE (1823–91), French poet and playwright, son of a naval captain. It is on his poetry and on his numerous prose works that his reputation mainly rests, but he was also the author of a number of plays in verse produced at the Comédie-Française. Although written with distinction and refinement they are deficient in dramatic power, and have fallen out of the repertory. Among them were *Le Feuilleton d'Aristophane* (1852), *Gringoire* (1866), and *Deidamia* (1876). Banville, who numbered among his friends the critic Jules Janin and the great actor Frédérick, was also dramatic critic to several papers, and by his temperate judgement and great charm exercised a wise and sound influence on the writers of the time.

BARBIERI, NICCOLÒ (? – *c.* 1640), an actor and author of the *commedia dell'arte*, who played under the name of Beltrame. He is also credited with the invention of the character of Scapino. He is first found with the Gelosi at Paris in 1600–4, and then joined the Fedeli, of whom he became joint director with the younger Andreini. One of his plays, *L'Incanto, ovvero L'Inavvertito* (1629), though originally only the usual summary for improvisation, was later published with dialogue in full, and was made use of by Molière for *L'Étourdi*. Barbieri also wrote his memoirs and an account of the stage in his time, *La Supplica*, published in 1634.

BARD, WILKIE (1870–1944), a music-hall star who started work in a cotton-spinner's warehouse. He first appeared in Manchester at the famous 'Slip Inn', and afterwards at the Grand in 1893, singing coster songs. He then went to London, appearing at Collins's in a score of impersonations all featuring the high, domed forehead (modelled on Shakespeare's—whence Bard, his real name being Billie Smith) fringed with sparse hair, and the two black spots over the eyebrows, which were thereafter inseparably associated with him. He appeared in pantomime, playing Pantaloon in the harlequinade, and, with Will Evans, reviving much of its old spirit, while as Idle Jack in *Dick Whittington* at Drury Lane in 1908 he started the vogue for tongue-twister songs with his 'She Sells Sea-Shells On the Sea-Shore'.

BARKER, a character of the fairground or itinerant theatre company, whose job it was to stand at the door of the booth and by his vociferous and spell-binding patter to induce the audience to enter. He is probably as old as the theatre itself, and was known to the ancient world. He achieved notoriety in sixteenth-century France and in the later fairs and show-grounds of Europe.

BARKER, Harley Granville- (1877–1946), English author, actor, and producer who was one of the outstanding figures of the progressive theatre at the beginning of the twentieth century. In 1891, when only 14 years of age, he joined Sarah Thorne's stock company at Margate, and for the next nine years he served a useful apprenticeship to the theatre, touring with Waller, Ben Greet, and Mrs. Patrick Campbell, and appearing in such widely diverse productions as Tree's *Under the Red Robe* at the Haymarket and William Poel's *Richard II* and *Edward II* for the Elizabethan Stage Society. Then, in 1900, Shaw chose him to play Marshbanks in the Stage Society's production of *Candida*. This proved a turning-point in his career, and from then on his unique combination of intelligence, good taste, and sound scholarship was at the service of the progressive theatre. He continued to act for the Stage Society for several years, appearing in a number of plays by Shaw, notably *Man and Superman*, where his John Tanner proved the perfect foil for the Ann Whitfield of his first wife, Lillah McCarthy. In 1904 his partnership with J. E. Vedrenne at the Court Theatre made theatrical history. He acted less, but took over the direction of a repertory which included plays by Euripides, Maeterlinck, Schnitzler, Hauptmann, Hankin, Galsworthy, and Ibsen, together with several of Shaw's, and his own *Voysey Inheritance*. Two of his earlier plays, *Waste* and *The Marrying of Ann Leete*, had been produced by the Stage Society. The former fell foul of the censor, and was not licensed for public performance until 1936.

It was his experience at the Court, which was an artistic rather than a commercial success, that led Barker to espouse the cause of a subsidized theatre, where the highest artistic standards could be maintained without constant worry over finance and box-office returns. With William Archer he published in 1907 *A National Theatre: Scheme and Estimates*, the first manifesto in a conflict which has continued ever since. In 1910 he directed a repertory season for Charles Frohman at the Duke of York's, in which the outstanding productions were his own *The Madras House* and Galsworthy's *Justice*, and a few years later he was responsible for the epoch-making productions at the Savoy of *The Winter's Tale* (see No. 153) and *Twelfth Night* (see No. 77) (both 1912), and *A Midsummer Night's Dream* (1914). He also did the first production, at the St. James's in 1913, of Shaw's *Androcles and the Lion*. His approach to the problems of producing Shakespeare were coloured by his experiences with William Poel, and his productions, designed by Albert Rutherston and Norman Wilkinson, with music from English folk-tunes arranged by Cecil Sharpe, became a nine days' wonder. It seems impossible to believe that, except for a production of Hardy's *Dynasts* in 1914, these were to be Barker's last works in the theatre. He seemed at the height of his career when a visit to America diverted his activities into fresh channels. Divorced from Lillah McCarthy, he married an American, hyphenated his name, and emerged as the translator (with his second wife) of the plays of Martinez Sierra and the Quintero brothers, and a serious Shakespeare scholar. In this latter capacity he edited with G. B. Harrison *A Companion to Shakespeare Studies* (1934), and wrote the fine series of *Prefaces to Shakespeare* (in five volumes) on which his later fame chiefly rests. These, first published between 1927 and 1947, approached Shakespeare for the first time from the point of view of the practical man of the theatre combined with the literary critic, and are full of illuminating passages which cannot but prove helpful to all actors and producers concerned with the plays. They were republished in 1963 in two volumes in a paperback edition, with illustrations and notes by Muriel St. Clare Byrne.

BARKER, James Nelson (1784–1858), American dramatist, author of the first American play on an Indian theme, which was also the first play from America to be performed in England. This was *The Indian Princess*, given in Philadelphia in 1808, and as *Pocahontas; or, the Indian Princess*, at Drury Lane in 1820. Of Barker's other plays, only four have survived, among them *Tears and Smiles*, a comedy of manners played in Philadelphia in 1807, and a dramatization of *Marmion*, which was at first announced as being by an English author. It held the stage for many years, being a favourite with James Wallack, and was last revived in 1848. Barker's last play was *Superstition* (1824), again based on American history. It deals in blank verse with the story of a Puritan refugee from England who leads his village against the Indians, mingled with a tale of intolerance and persecution of witchcraft. Barker had many interests, and playwriting was only a hobby. Quinn, in his *History of American Drama*, says of him: 'He showed a sense of dramatic values and a gift of expression in verse which cause us to wonder what the result might have been if he had devoted himself, under more favorable circumstances, to the drama as a profession.'

BARNES, Charlotte Mary Sanford (1818–63), American actress and dramatist, the daughter of John Barnes (1761–1841), who went with his wife Mary from Drury Lane to the Park Theatre, New York. They were both popular players for many years, the husband as a low comedian, the wife, who was the sister of Mrs. Baldwin, also an actress at the Park, in such parts as Jane Shore, Mrs. Haller, and Southerne's Isabella. Charlotte first appeared on the stage at the age of 4, as the child in *The Castle Spectre*. In 1834 she made her adult début at the Tremont, Boston, and in

New York, in the same play. On one occasion she played Juliet to her mother's Romeo, but was never accounted such a good actress as the older woman. In 1842 Charlotte appeared in London, playing, among other parts, Hamlet, in which she was well received. Four years later she married an actor-manager named Edmond S. Connor, and became his leading lady, being also associated with him in the management of the Arch Street Theatre, Philadelphia. She wrote her first play, *Octavia Bragaldi*, at the age of 18, basing it on a recent murder case, but transferring the scene to Renaissance Italy. It was produced at the National Theatre, New York, with the author as the heroine, and frequently revived, the last time at the Bowery in 1854 under her husband's management. She also made several adaptations of French melodramas, and dramatizations of novels, but the only one of her plays, apart from the above, which has survived is *The Forest Princess* (1844), one of the many dramatizations of the story of Pocahontas.

BARNES, SIR KENNETH RALPH (1878–1957), brother of the English actresses Irene and Violet Vanbrugh, who became director of the Royal Academy of Dramatic Art in London in 1909, and remained there until his retirement in 1955, having seen the Academy prosper under his beneficial rule. He never ceased to campaign for the training of young actors, which he regarded as essential to the well-being of the theatre. He was greatly helped by the advice and practical assistance of his sisters, and by the interest shown in his work by Queen Elizabeth the Queen Mother, who in 1952 laid the foundation stone of the present Vanbrugh Theatre, built to replace the former students' theatre, destroyed by bombing in 1941. During the First World War Barnes served in India and Russia, and organized a concert party which toured Mesopotamia. In 1919 he returned to London, and in 1925 married a former student, Daphne Graham, who had acted under the name of Mary Sheridan, being a descendant of the playwright. Barnes, who was knighted in 1938 for his services to the stage, completed shortly before his death an autobiography, *Welcome, Good Friends!* (1958).

BARNES, THOMAS (1785–1841), English editor and critic, educated at Christ's Hospital. 'He might', said Leigh Hunt, who was his school-fellow, 'have made himself a name in wit and literature, had he cared much for anything beyond his glass of wine and his Fielding.' To this it should most certainly be added that he cared also for the theatre, and still more for *The Times* newspaper, which he edited soundly from 1817 until his death. His love of the theatre is manifested in his early work in the *Examiner* under the name of 'Criticus'. In the same journal, during Leigh Hunt's term of imprisonment, he described Kean's famous first appearance as Shylock at Drury Lane, 26 Jan. 1814. His account of this, though much less well known, bears comparison with that of Hazlitt.

BARNSTORMERS, a name given in the late nineteenth century to the early itinerant companies whose stages were often set up in large barns, and whose work was characterized by ranting and shouting and general violence in speech and gesture.

BARNUM, PHINEAS TAYLOR (1810–91), a great American showman, whose name is mainly connected with the circus. For fifty years he provided the world with entertainment, constantly gulling the public yet always finding them ready to be gulled again. His first great enterprise was the American Museum, known also as Barnum's Museum, which opened in 1842 and was burnt down in 1865 and 1868. Tom Thumb, Jenny Lind, freaks, giants, and curiosities of natural history were exhibited there impartially, and during most of its history it housed plays as well. In 1871 Barnum started his immense circus—'The Greatest Show on Earth'—which for twenty years began its spring season in Madison Square Gardens. He was twice married, but had no children.

BARON. (1) ANDRÉ (*c.* 1602–55), a French actor who changed his name from Boyron when Louis XIII inadvertently addressed him as 'le sieur Baron'. He was taken into Montdory's company at the Marais in 1634, to replace the actors drafted to the Hôtel de Bourgogne, where he himself went after Montdory's retirement. He played tragedy kings and peasants in comedy, and is reported to have died of a wound in the foot which he inflicted on himself with a property sword while playing Don Diègue in *Le Cid* too energetically. In 1641 he had married (2) JEANNE AUSOULT (1625–62), child of strolling players, who became an excellent actress. She was much admired in breeches parts and wore her male attire with an air. Her early death, during the run of *Manlius*, was very much regretted by Corneille, who had in his new play a role intended for her, 'plein de tendresse'.

Of her six children the youngest (3) MICHEL (1653–1729) became a famous actor. Orphaned before he was 10, he was a child-actor in the juvenile Troupe du Dauphin formed by the elder Raisin, after whose death his widow took the company into the provinces and failed completely. Molière, with that generosity towards his fellow actors so characteristic of him, offered her the use of the Palais-Royal for three days, in order that she might make some money. Chancing to visit the theatre during a performance by the children, he was so struck by the good qualities of young Baron that he took him into his own company and treated him as a son, educating and training him for the stage, and eventually giving him small parts to play, among them Myrtil in *Mélicerte* (1666). Unfortunately Molière's wife took a dislike to the boy, and on one occasion slapped his face, whereupon he ran away and joined his former companions. He remained with them until 1670, when Molière wrote and asked him to return in order to play the part of Domitian in *Tite et Bérénice*. In the following year he played Cupid to the Psyche of Molière's wife, a juxtaposition which led to some ill-natured gossip at Molière's expense. This seems to have been unjustified, since on Molière's death Baron left the company to go to the Hôtel de Bourgogne, where he married Charlotte (1661–1730), daughter of the actor La Thorillière. There he played Racine's young tragic heroes, and later became the chief actor of the newly formed Comédie-Française. He was liberally endowed by nature with a fine presence, a deep voice, amplitude of gesture, and a quick intelligence. To these gifts, ably fostered by his great teacher, he joined application, attention to detail, and a firm belief in the importance of his profession and of his own place in it. 'Every hundred years may bring forth a Caesar; but it takes ten thousand to produce a Baron.' Baron did a great deal to raise the status of actors in his day, and helped many a struggling dramatist by his rendering of a poor part. He was himself the author of several comedies, of which the best is *L'Homme à bonne fortune* (1686). *Le Rendez-vous des Tuilleries* (1685) is an amusing trifle which introduces some of the actors of the Comédie-Française under their own names, as well as a number of well-known dandies of Paris. In 1691, at the height of his powers, Baron suddenly retired. No reason for this was given, though it was thought at the time that his pride was beginning to chafe under the stigma of being 'only an actor' and that he hoped to achieve a dignified position in social and private life. He continued, however, to write plays, and occasionally acted at Court and in private theatricals until 1720, when he returned to the Comédie-Française, remaining there until his death. Except for his voice, which was a little quavery, he was as good as ever, and it says much for the hold he had on his public that he was able to play his old parts again. He initiated a number of reforms, and guided the early progress of Adrienne Lecouvreur, as well as playing the lead in Marivaux's first play. He was taken ill on the stage during a revival of Rotrou's *Venceslas*, and died shortly afterwards. He was the last actor who had known Molière to appear at the Comédie-Française. His son (4) ÉTIENNE (1676–1711) played several roles as a child, made his adult début in 1694, and died in the prime of life as the result of dissipation. He was a cold, though correct, actor, with none of the genius of his father. His daughter and one of his nephews were in the service of the Comédie-Française for many years.

BARRAULT, JEAN-LOUIS (1910–), French actor and producer, who began his career in 1931 as a pupil of Charles Dullin at the Atelier. His first stage appearance, on his 21st birthday, was as one of the servants in Jules Romains's translation of *Volpone*, in which Dullin played the title-role. He remained for several years with Dullin, and meanwhile began, with Decroux, the study of mime, which was afterwards to be so important a part of his technique. In fact, his first independent production was a mime-play based on Faulkner's *As I Lay Dying*. In 1937 he produced a revival of Cervantes' only tragedy, *Numancia*, and a dramatization of *Faim*, a novel by Knud Hamsun. He then went into the army, but in 1940, after the Occupation, was engaged by Copeau for the Comédie-Française, where his future wife, Madeleine Renaud, was already an established star. He made his début in *Le Cid*, but his most important work was done in his productions of *Phèdre*, with Marie Bell, *Le Soulier de satin*, and *Antony and Cleopatra*. In 1946 he and his wife left the Comédie-Française to found their own company. Its opening production, at the Théâtre Marigny, was *Hamlet*, on 17 Oct. 1946, in a translation by André Gide, in which Barrault later appeared at the Edinburgh Festival. This was followed by Marivaux's *Les Fausses Confidences*, *Baptiste*, a ballet-pantomime, and Salacrou's great play of the Resistance, *Les Nuits de la colère*. This mingling of French and foreign classics and modern plays set the pattern for the future development of the company, which remained at the Marigny until 1956, achieving a great artistic success. Among its important productions were *Le Procès* (based on Kafka) and *Amphitryon* (both 1947), a superb production, with Edwige Feuillière, of Claudel's *Partage de midi* (1948), which was later seen in London, Anouilh's *La Répétition* in 1950, a year which also saw Sartre's *Mains sales* and de Montherlant's *Malatesta*, and, in the following year, Gide's *Oedipe*. Barrault has done some of his finest work with Claudel, and, in addition to those of his plays mentioned above, has produced *L'Échange* (1951), *Christophe Colomb* (1953), and *Tête-d'or* (1959), all of which remain in the company's repertory, together with *Le Soulier de satin*, revived in 1958. The importance of Marivaux in the company's schedule can be attributed partly to the outstanding acting of Madeleine Renaud in this author's works, while several productions of Molière and Shakespeare testify to Barrault's abiding interest in the classics. On the lighter side he has revived several of Feydeau's farces, and he has continued to produce modern plays with Ionesco's *Rhinocéros* (1960), and Fry's *A Sleep of Prisoners* (1955) and *The Dark is Light Enough* (1962).

In 1956 Barrault left the Marigny, and after a long tour in Europe and America returned to Paris to the Théâtre Sarah-Bernhardt and later occupied the Palais-Royal. He was appointed director of the Odéon (one of the two national theatres, renamed Théâtre de France) in 1959, and in 1964 led his company on another long tour. His work at the Odéon has included new plays by Samuel Beckett and François Billetdoux, and, in 1964, three plays by Shakespeare in honour of his quatercentenary.

As an actor Barrault, elegant and outwardly nonchalant, gives the impression of strong passions firmly controlled by a disciplined intelligence and, physically, by the strenuous exercise of mime, to which he has devoted so much of his energy with the most interesting results. As a mime, he is best-known to the public through his appearance as Baptiste in the film *Les Enfants du Paradis*, but the effect of his training can most effectively be judged on-stage, where his slightest gesture speaks volumes. Among his finest parts have been Hamlet, and Jean Cordet in *Les Nuits de la colère*.

BARREL SYSTEM, a method of moving scenery (see DRUM-AND-SHAFT).

BARRETT, GEORGE HORTON (1794–1860), American actor, son of an English actor who went to New York in 1797, and of his wife, who as Mrs. Rivers had been well known in London previously. They both joined the company at the Park Theatre under Dunlap, and there, in 1798, young Barrett made his first appearance as the child in *The Stranger*, his mother playing Mrs. Haller. At the age of 11 he was seen as Young Norval, again with his parents in the cast as Old Norval and Lady Randolph. After an absence of some years, spent at school and on tour, Barrett returned as an adult actor, and became one of the best light comedians of his day. Among his finest parts were Sir Andrew Aguecheek, young Absolute, Charles Surface, and Puff. He made his last appearance on the stage in 1855. He was for a long time stage manager of the Bowery Theatre, under Gilfert, and later of the Tremont Theatre in Boston, and of the Broadway Theatre, New York, from its opening in 1847. Familiarly known, from his elegant appearance and gracious manners, as 'Gentleman George', he married in 1825 an American actress named Mrs. Henry, and had two daughters, Georgina and Mary.

BARRETT, LAWRENCE (1838–91), American actor and producer, who was on the stage as a boy of 14, and travelled the United States with many outstanding companies, including that of Julia Dean. In 1857 he was seen in New York in *The Hunchback* and other plays, and was leading man under Burton at the Metropolitan, later the Winter Garden. In 1858 he was a member of the Boston Museum company, and was in the army during the Civil War. Afterwards he travelled widely, and became extremely popular. He managed Booth's Theatre in 1871, as the friend and associate of Edwin Booth, to whose Brutus he frequently played Cassius, his best-remembered part. While Irving was in America in 1884, Barrett took over the Lyceum in London, and though his visit was not a success financially, he was made welcome and fêted on all sides. He was a scrupulous and competent man of the theatre, careful, painstaking, and dependable. Winter called him an interpreter, not an impersonator. All the standard classics were in his repertory, and many new plays, since he tried to encourage American playwrights, though he drew the line at realism and remained faithful to romantic and poetic drama. Tall, with classic features, and dark, deeply sunken eyes, he was probably at his best in Shakespeare, to whose interpretation he brought dignity, a dominant personality, and intellectual powers somewhat exceptional in an actor at that date. He was the author of several books on the theatre. Two of his grandchildren also went on the stage.

BARRETT. (1) WILSON (1846–1904), an English actor-manager, who had few equals in melodrama. After a varied career he took over the management of the Princess's Theatre in 1881, and among the successes which he produced during his five years there the first was G. R. Sims's *The Lights o' London*, which ran for 228 performances and then toured the world with unflagging vigour. Even this, however, was surpassed by the popularity of the two plays generally connected with Wilson Barrett—*The Sign of the Cross*, which he wrote himself, and Jones and Herman's *The Silver King*, in which, as Wilfred Denver, he gave an outstanding performance as a melodramatic hero, a part for which he was eminently fitted by nature. His face was strikingly handsome, his voice resonant, and his chest and arms powerfully developed; he lacked only height to make a perfect figure of a man. As Marcus Superbus (in *The Sign of the Cross*), a Roman patrician converted to Christianity by a beautiful Christian girl with whom he goes into the arena to meet death from the lions, he gave a truly remarkable performance. The play was first produced in America, at a time when Barrett was on tour there and badly in need of money. It made a fortune for him, and when brought to England, first at the Grand, Leeds (which incidentally Barrett himself built), in 1895 and then at the Lyric, London, in the next year, it created a sensation. Clergymen preached sermons about it, and people who had never before entered a theatre crowded to see it. It was perennially successful on tour. Barrett was less successful in Shakespearian roles, which he often essayed, though his Mercutio was well thought of by Clement Scott.

His brother (2) GEORGE EDWARD (1849–94) was also an actor, who made his début in the provinces in 1866. He first appeared in London in 1872, and, after a visit to India in support of C. J. Mathews, he joined his brother's company at the Princess's, and went with him to the United States. His son also joined Wilson Barrett's company, and the family was represented further by a grandson of Wilson Barrett, who spent some years in repertory with the Brandon-Thomas companies and in 1939 was manager of a repertory season at the King's Theatre, Hammersmith. He later established repertory companies in Glasgow and Edinburgh. W. MACQUEEN-POPE†

BARRIE, Sir James Matthew (1860–1937), Scottish dramatist and novelist. Born at Kirriemuir, Forfarshire, a poor handloom-weaver's son, he was educated at the Academy, Dumfries, and proceeded to Edinburgh University. While working as a leader-writer on the *Nottingham Daily Journal*, he contributed articles to Frederick Greenwood's *St. James's Gazette* and in 1888 published his first full-length work, *Auld Licht Idylls*, followed by *A Window in Thrums* (1889). *When a Man's Single* was his first notable novel. *The Little Minister* (1891) gave the first glimpse of the laughter and tears, the strangeness and the naughtiness of a writer who could be at once sentimental and impish. His earliest plays were all unsuccessful, but *Walker, London* (1892) had Toole in the cast and caught on. *The Professor's Love Story* (1894) established Barrie as a successful playwright. In 1897 the play of *The Little Minister* established him as a wealthy man. More novels, *Sentimental Tommy* and *Tommy and Grizel*, appeared round the turn of the century, and in 1904 *Peter Pan* stepped out of a story-book and took the stage. In the theatre Barrie made his way by a series of surprises. The years before the First World War saw the production of *Quality Street* and *The Admirable Crichton* (both 1902), *Little Mary* (1903), *Alice Sit-By-The-Fire* (1905), *Josephine* (1906), *What Every Woman Knows* (1908), and *Rosalind* (1912), besides a number of short plays like *Pantaloon* (1905), *Punch* (1906), *The Twelve Pound Look* and *A Slice of Life* (both 1910), and *The Will* (1913). During the war he wrote *Rosy Rapture* (1915), a revue, for Gaby Deslys, some small occasional pieces, such as *The Old Lady Shows Her Medals* (1917) and *A Well Remembered Voice* (1918), and also *A Kiss for Cinderella* (1916) and *Dear Brutus* (1917). *The Truth About the Russian Dancers* (1920) was his first piece after the war. It was followed by *Mary Rose* (1920), a play that was almost passionately liked and disliked, a strange, creepy, harrowing, exquisitely painful play of the supernatural and the natural. *Shall We Join the Ladies?*, a delicately worked one-act puzzle, appeared in 1922. His last play, *The Boy David*, was written for Elisabeth Bergner and played by her in 1936. In 1913 Barrie was created a baronet; in 1922 he received the Order of Merit and in the same year he was elected Rector of St. Andrews University.

Barrie in his great moments was a stage magician. Only a consummate craftsman could have brought off certain masterpieces of theatrical effect—the cooking-pot at the end of Act II of *The Admirable Crichton* and the boom of the gun during the dance in Act III, the opening scenes of *What Every Woman Knows* and of *Dear Brutus*, hard to equal for rousing curiosity, the disappearance of Mary Rose on the island in the second act, and the first sentence—'Mother, I have killed a lion!'—of *The Boy David*. Most of his work reveals a mind queerly compounded of fancifulness, sentimentality, and dry pessimism; but in *Mary Rose* he is no longer afraid to say that life can be dreadful. He is brave enough for the first time to make beauty out of reality, and in *The Boy David* he treats not childishness, which in *Peter Pan* was something distinct from manhood, but the childhood which is at the core of all humanity. He was something of a seer; and what he saw and showed had so little to do with time and fashion and manners that it is unlikely to fade entirely out of memory. A. V. Cookman†

BARRIÈRE, Théodore (1823–77), French dramatist, who left his work as a map-engraver after the success of a vaudeville which he had written for the Théâtre Beaumarchais. During the next thirty years he wrote over a hundred plays, of which the best are *La Vie de Bohème* (1849), based on Murger's book with the assistance of the author, *Manon Lescaut* (1851), again based on a novel, and *Les Malheureux vaincus* (1865), which was for some time forbidden by the censor. Barrière was a social dramatist, in the style of Augier, though with less vigour and more concern for the lighter side of drama.

BARRY, Elizabeth (1658–1713), the first really outstanding English actress. She played opposite Betterton for many years, and created a number of famous roles—one biographer estimates it at 119—including the heroines of Otway's tragedies and Congreve's *Mourning Bride*. Otway all his life cherished a hopeless passion for her. Her first appearances on the stage were lamentable failures, but coached and encouraged by Rochester she appeared successfully in a revival of Orrery's *Mustapha* in 1673, and continued to improve, though she did not attain the full height of her powers until she was past her first youth. She was good in comedy, but better in tragedy, in which she displayed great power and dignity. She retired in 1710. In private life, if we are to believe contemporary accounts, she was not so estimable, and many scandals are attached to her name, some perhaps undeservedly. She never married.

BARRY, Philip (1896–1949), American dramatist, who contributed to the New York stage some distinguished high comedies and unique excursions into fantasy and serious drama. Born in Rochester, New York, he graduated from Yale University in 1919, studied playwriting at Harvard under G. P. Baker, and served in the diplomatic service. His first professional production, *You and I* (1923), was a study of a father's effort to realize his artistic ambitions in his son. His next (unsuccessful) play, *The Youngest* (1924), was followed by an ingenious domestic comedy, *In a Garden* (1925), and a satirical extravaganza about people's resistance to change, *White Wings* (1926). After writing a biblical drama, *John* (1927), Barry returned to his *métier* with *Paris Bound* (1927), in which a husband wins his wife's forgiveness for an illicit affair after he overlooks her own weakness. Following a collaboration with Elmer Rice, *Cock Robin*

(1928), Barry turned out *Holiday* (1928), a bright comedy concerning the revolt of youth against parental snobbery. Diverging from brittle themes in *Hotel Universe* (1930), he wrote a probing psychological drama in which several troubled characters achieved purgation, but the play proved too elusive for its audience. Barry, however, quickly recovered his public with the domestic comedies *Tomorrow and Tomorrow* (1931), which retells the story of Elisha and the Shunammite with a psychoanalyst in the role of the prophet, and *The Animal Kingdom* (1932), which reverses the roles of a wife and a mistress by making the latter the loyal companion and therefore the true wife. After the mishaps of *The Joyous Season* (1934), *Bright Star* (1935), and *Spring Dance* (1936), Barry won prestige with the mystifying but provocative allegory of good and evil, *Here Come the Clowns* (1938), and popularity with the deft comedy of manners and character, *The Philadelphia Story* (1939). The war in Europe inspired an allegory, *Liberty Jones* (1941), concerning the dangers threatening American democracy; *Without Love* (1942), a romantic comedy that strained a parallel between politics and love; and *The Foolish Notion* (1945), an ingeniously constructed theatrical fancy concerning a husband's return from the war in Europe. Barry left unfinished a reflective comedy, *Second Threshold*, which was completed by his friend Robert Sherwood and presented in New York, with some success, in the season of 1950–1.

JOHN GASSNER†

BARRY, SPRANGER (1719–77), Irish actor, who was first seen on the stage in Dublin in 1744, playing Othello at Smock Alley Theatre. He remained there until 1746, and then went to Drury Lane, where he appeared as Othello to the Iago of Macklin. He became one of the finest young lovers on the English stage, and remained in the Drury Lane company when Garrick took over, playing Othello, Pierre, Bajazet, Henry V, and Orestes, while Garrick took for himself such parts as Lear, Richard III, Sir John Brute, Macbeth, and Abel Drugger. They both played Hamlet at different times, and proved a great attraction when they appeared together, as Jaffier and Pierre in *Venice Preserved*, Chamont and Castalio in *The Orphan*, Hastings and Dumont in *Jane Shore*, and Lothario and Horatio in *The Fair Penitent*. In 1750 Barry went to Covent Garden, where he engaged in rivalry with Garrick, playing Romeo, Lear, and Richard III. Of the first, Macklin said that Barry swaggered so, and talked so loud in the garden scene, that the servants ought to have come out and tossed him in a blanket; but Garrick sneaked in like a thief in the night. It was generally conceded that Barry was best in the garden scene and in the tomb, while Garrick was preferred in the scenes with the friar and the apothecary. As Lear Barry was impressive, dignified, and pathetic, but far inferior to Garrick in the mad scene. He also failed as Richard III, but made an excellent Young Norval, superb in white satin, to the Lady Randolph of Peg Woffington. His first leading lady was Mrs. Theophilus Cibber, who after one season, when she played Juliet, returned to Garrick at Drury Lane. Barry then engaged Miss Nossiter, who made a charming Cordelia. He fell in love with her, but she died almost immediately. In 1758 Barry ruined himself with the speculative building of a theatre in Dublin, and on his return to London went to the Haymarket, until in 1767 Garrick engaged him to play again at Drury Lane. His sister-in-law, Mrs. W. Barry, was also in the company. Barry's first wife, Anne, who was not on the stage, died shortly after. He married as his second wife (in 1768) Ann Dancer (*née* Street) (1734–1801), an actress who was good in tragedy and unsurpassed in comedy, particularly as Millamant, Mrs. Sullen, and Angelica. After the death of Spranger Barry, who was buried in Westminster Abbey, she married Thomas Crawford (1754–94), who occasionally acted with her. She retired from the stage in 1798.

BARRYMORE, an important family of American actors, allied with the Drews. The father, (1) MAURICE (1847–1905), was an Englishman named Herbert Blythe, who took his stage name from an old playbill hanging in the Haymarket Theatre, London. Born in India and educated at Cambridge, he studied law, and was already well known as an amateur boxer before he decided to adopt the stage as a profession. He first appeared with a provincial company in 1875, and in the same year went to New York, where he played in Daly's *Under the Gaslight*. A handsome, well-built man, he was engaged by many of the leading actresses of the period, including Modjeska, for whom he wrote *Nadjezda* (1886). He played in it himself both in the States and in London, where he was also seen at the Haymarket in 1886 in *Diplomacy* and *Masks and Faces*. He later accused Sardou of having plagiarized his play in *Tosca*, and obtained an injunction to prevent Fanny Davenport doing the latter play in an English translation in the United States. He gave excellent performances in *Captain Smith* and *The Heart of Maryland*, and also appeared under the management of William A. Brady in his own *Roaring Dick*. Towards the end of his life he became a star of the vaudeville stage, where he made his last appearance before succumbing to a mental malady, brought on in part by his high spirits and convivial temperament. In 1876 he had married (2) GEORGIANA (1856–93), daughter of Mrs. John Drew, and an actress of great ability. She appeared at the Arch Street Theatre, Philadelphia, then managed by her mother, at the age of 16, and remained in the stock company there for some years. She then went to New York and appeared at the Fifth Avenue Theatre under Daly. After her marriage she appeared with her husband in *Diplomacy* and in the repertory of Mme Modjeska's company, and was considered particularly good in *The Wages of Sin* and *The Senator*, the latter with William Crane. She also appeared with Lawrence Barrett and Edwin Booth, and under the management of the Frohmans, but her career was hampered by illness and she died young. Her three children were all on the stage. The eldest, (3) LIONEL (1878–1954), made his first appearance at 15, also at the Arch Street Theatre, Philadelphia, under his grandmother, and later played with his uncle, John Drew, in *The Mummy and the Humming Bird*, making a great success as an Italian organ-grinder. Other plays followed, including Barrie's *Pantaloon*, but with his career well assured he suddenly threw it up to study art in Paris. He was later persuaded to return to the stage, appeared in *Peter Ibbetson* and *The Jest*, and made an outstanding success in *The Copperhead*. He was accounted one of the leading actors of New York, but deserted the stage for film work, where he was equally successful. He was twice married, both his wives being actresses. He published in 1951 an autobiography, *We Barrymores, as told to Cameron Shipp*. His sister (4) ETHEL (1879–1959), one of the leading women of the American stage, also made her first appearance under the aegis of Mrs. John Drew, later going to London, where she appeared with Henry Irving in *The Bells* and *Peter the Great*. A tall and lovely woman, with remarkable eyes, she was as much esteemed for her acting as for her beauty, and her long career was a succession of triumphs broken only by an illness lasting three years, from which she recovered to star in a Theatre Guild production. Her first outstanding success was scored as Madame Trentoni in *Captain Jinks of the Horse Marines* (1901), after which she played a number of fashionable young ladies, including the heroine of *Cousin Kate*. She also showed her mettle in such plays as *A Doll's House* and *The Silver Box*, appeared in such classic roles as Ophelia, Juliet, Portia, and Camille, and was outstanding in modern plays, among them *Déclassée*, *Whiteoaks*, and *The Corn is Green*, which ran for four years. She played in vaudeville in *The Twelve Pound Look*, and did much film and radio work. In 1928 she opened the Ethel Barrymore Theatre in New York with *The Kingdom of God*, in which she played Sister Gracia, and later appeared there as Lady Teazle in *The School for Scandal*. Her three children are also on the stage.

The youngest of Maurice Barrymore's children, (5) JOHN (1882–1942), was, at the height of his powers, accounted one of the finest actors of the English-speaking stage. He first appeared in *Magda* in 1903 at the Cleveland Theatre in Chicago, and later successes were *Pantaloon* (1905) and *The Fortune Hunter* (1909). Aided by outstandingly good looks, inherent talent, and a debonair manner, he became a popular matinée idol and a good light comedian, but in 1916 proved himself a serious actor also by his performance as Falder in Galsworthy's *Justice*. This was followed by an excellent rendering of the title-role in *Peter Ibbetson*, by Gianetto Malespini in *The Jest*, and by Fedor in *Redemption*. He then took voice-production lessons from an opera singer, and on 16 Nov. 1922 electrified New York by his *Hamlet*, in which Blanche Yurka appeared as Gertrude and the settings were designed by Robert Edmond Jones. The play, which was given at the Sam H. Harris Theatre, ran for 101 performances. Barrymore repeated his success in London in 1925 at the Haymarket Theatre, with Constance Collier as Gertrude and Fay Compton as Ophelia. He gave a fine, meticulous, and scholarly reading of the part, whose beauty was enhanced by the depth and flexibility of his voice and the radiance of his personal appearance. Hopes for his future ran high, but he failed to maintain this standard, and for some time confined himself to films, which he had graced intermittently since 1912. His last years were feverish and unhappy, and except for a pitiful caricature of himself in a poor play, given in 1939, he appeared mainly in films and on the radio. He was four times married and divorced, and his daughter by his second marriage, Diana (1921–60), appeared on the stage and in films.

The Barrymore eccentricities, and their famous temper, as well as the majestic personality of their maternal grandmother, Mrs. John Drew, were incorporated into a play by Edna Ferber and George S. Kaufman entitled *The Royal Family* (1927), done in England in 1934 as *Theatre Royal*. Although the three Barrymores never appeared together on the stage, they were all seen in a film, and John and Lionel were together in *Peter Ibbetson* and *The Jest*. Both brothers were good artists and musicians, and John as a young man did a poster of Sothern as François Villon in *If I Were King* which was much admired. He was also a newspaper artist for some time.

There were two William Barrymores, no relation to the above or to each other, who appeared on the London and New York stages. The elder, (6) WILLIAM (1758–1830), opened the Old Vic as the Royal Coburg (see No. 35) in 1818 (see OLD VIC). The younger, (7) WILLIAM (?–1845), was esteemed 'a sound, useful actor' and wrote a number of plays. His wife also was an actress, who played in the United States for many years, dying in England in 1862.

(8) RICHARD BARRY, EARL OF BARRYMORE (1769–93), a great amateur of the theatre, maintained a private theatre in his house at Wargrave, Berks., and another in Savile Row, where he engaged professional stars to play with himself and his friends.

BARTHOLOMEW FAIR, see FAIRS.

BASOCHE, LA, see FRANCE, I.

BASSERMANN. (1) AUGUST (1848–1931), German actor, who made his début at Dresden in 1873 and later played under Laube at the Vienna Stadttheater, where he appeared in such parts as Rolla and Karl Moor, and in contemporary French comedy. He then went on tour throughout Germany, and in 1895 became manager and leading player of the Mannheim Theatre, where he appeared in both classic and modern parts, his personal preference being for the former. From 1904 until his death he was director of the theatre at Karlsruhe. He went to New York several times, and played in the German Theatre there, being much admired in classic and heroic parts. His nephew (2) ALBERT (1867–1952) made his first appearance at Mannheim at the age of 19. He was a well-disciplined actor, who studied his roles with great care. He was for a time with the Meininger company. Under Otto Brahm, whom he joined in 1899, he became the outstanding interpreter of Ibsen in Germany. He later worked under Reinhardt, and was considered one of the greatest actors of Germany until the rise to power of the Nazi party drove him to America. He went to Hollywood to play in films, and in 1944 appeared on Broadway in his first English-speaking part, as the Pope in *Embezzled Heaven*. In 1945 he returned to Europe, and died in Zürich.

BATALOV, NIKOLAI PETROVICH (1899–1937), Soviet actor, who in 1916 began his career in the Moscow Art Theatre. In 1927 he gave a lively comic performance of Figaro which added to his growing reputation, and in the same year his portrayal of Vasska Okorka in Ivanov's *Armoured Train 14–69* brought a tribute from Lunacharsky for its warmth and tempestuous gaiety. An optimist by nature, Batalov was able to use his naturally jovial temperament to give a fine satirical edge to his portrait of the anarchist-marauder in *Blockade* (1929) by V. Ivanov. He was a versatile actor, and his roles included many classical and modern parts. BEATRICE KING†

BATEMAN, a family of actors important in the history of the English stage, since it was under (1) HEZEKIAH LINTHICUM BATEMAN (1812–75) that Irving first appeared at the Lyceum, and after some initial disappointments persuaded his manager to put on *The Bells* (1871). Bateman, who was an American, married the half-sister of the famous comic vocalist Sam Cowell, (2) SIDNEY FRANCES (1823–81), actress and author, who after her husband's death continued to manage the Lyceum until Irving took over in 1878. She then assumed the management of Sadler's Wells, where she remained until her death. She had six children, her four daughters being all on the stage. The eldest, (3) KATE JOSEPHINE (1843–1917), first appeared in Louisville, Kentucky, at the age of 4, and with (4) ELLEN DOUGLAS (1844–1936) toured in adult parts which included Richmond, Portia, and Lady Macbeth to her younger sister's Richard III, Shylock, and Macbeth. They were first seen in London in 1851. Ellen retired on her marriage to Claude Greppo in 1860 and returned to the United States, but Kate, as an adult actress, made a success in *Leah* (1863), and played opposite Irving at the Lyceum in Lady Macbeth and other parts. She retired in 1892, and under her married name, Mrs. George Crowe, conducted a school of acting in London. The third Bateman daughter, (5) VIRGINIA FRANCES (1853–1940), was also on the stage as a child, and appeared at the Lyceum under her parents' management. She married the actor Edward Compton and became the mother of a distinguished progeny (see COMPTON). The youngest daughter, (6) ISABEL EMILIE (1854–1934), was also at the Lyceum, and was associated with her mother in the management of Sadler's Wells. She then toured with her own company. In 1898 she left the stage and joined the Community of St. Mary the Virgin, Wantage, Berks., of which she later became Reverend Mother General.

BATES, BLANCHE (1873–1941) American actress, daughter of the manager of a theatre in Portland, Oregon, who was murdered while on tour in Australia. Her mother, a small, dark frail woman, was an excellent actress, her Camille being highly thought of. Blanche made her first appearances on the stage in California, where she toured from 1894 to 1898, and then made a brief appearance in New York under the management of Augustin Daly. It was, however, as the leading lady of Belasco's company that she made her name, particularly by her moving performance of Madame Butterfly in 1900. She then played Cigarette in a dramatization of *Under Two Flags* (1901), Yo-san in *The Darling of the Gods* (1902), and the title-role in *The Girl of the Golden West* (1905), her last important part, though she continued to act under her own and other managements until her retirement in 1927, from which she emerged briefly in 1933.

BATH. The first theatre in Bath was built in 1705 for John Power, at a cost of £1,300. It was paid for by subscription. On the passing of the Licensing Act in 1737 the building was demolished and the players adapted a room under Lady Hawley's Assembly Rooms, which in 1745 was being managed by Simpson. In 1750 a new theatre was erected in Orchard Street, the shell of which still exists. The two theatres were rivals until 1756, when John Palmer, manager of Orchard Street, bought out Simpson's. The Orchard Street Theatre was reconstructed by Arthur in 1767, and again in 1774–5, a royal patent being obtained in 1768. The Palmers, father and son, were succeeded in management by Keasberry and Dimond. Mrs. Siddons was a member of the stock company from 1778 to 1782, at a salary of £3 a week. In 1805 a new theatre in Beaufort Square was erected by Palmer, the city architect, in conjunction with George Dance. In 1817 a long connexion with the Bristol Theatre was broken, and from 1822 a decline set in. A succession of short-lived lessees included Mrs. Macready, and J. H. Chute, who partially revived the theatre's fortunes. In 1862 it was destroyed by fire, and a new theatre opened on the same site, designed by C. J. Phipps and financed by a limited liability company. Since 1884 this theatre has been used by touring companies. SYBIL ROSENFELD

BATHYLLUS, a pantomime actor of Imperial Rome referred to by Juvenal (vi. 63) (see PANTOMIMUS).

BATTEN, a length of timber used to stiffen a surface of canvas or boards, as by 'sandwich-battening' a cloth (i.e. fixing the upper and lower edges between pairs of 3 inch or 4 inch by 1 inch battens screwed together), or by 'batten-ing-out' a section of boards, or a run of flats, with crossbars. A row of lights fixed rigidly together is also known as a Light Batten (for the American use of batten see LIGHTING, 3).

BATTY'S AMPHITHEATRE, LONDON, see ASTLEY'S AMPHITHEATRE.

BATY, GASTON (1885–1952), French producer, whose work had much influence on the theatre between 1920 and 1940. After studying production in Germany he returned to Paris, and worked in a number of theatres, where he was responsible for the production of many experimental dramas by new authors. He also travelled extensively, but in 1930 settled in Paris at the Théâtre Montparnasse, to which he gave his own name. Here he put on an imposing series of old and new plays, many of them foreign classics, and several dramatizations of novels, which he prepared himself. The best was probably his version of *Crime and Punishment*. His own play, *Dulcinée* (1938), was based on an episode in *Don Quixote*. Baty was sometimes accused of subordinating the text of his productions to the décor, which with him was all-important. This led to a tendency to substitute pictorial groupings for action, but it also gave the theatre some fine work, as in *Maya*, *Cyclone*, *Simoun*, and *Martine*. In 1936 Baty was appointed one of the producers of the Comédie-Française, where he brought his undoubted erudition and fine theatrical sense to re-animate the classical repertory.

BÄUERLE, ADOLF (1786–1859), see AUSTRIA.

BAUERNFELD, EDUARD (1802–90), see AUSTRIA.

BAX, CLIFFORD (1886–1962), English author and playwright, who trained as an artist, and retained in his writing something of the visual quality and preoccupation with form and colour of his former career. His early verse-plays, of which *The Poetasters of Ispahan* was produced in 1912, were more successful in print than on the stage, but in 1922, following the success of Playfair's revival of *The Beggar's Opera*, he prepared for the same management an adaptation of its sequel, *Polly*, and also translated Čapek's *The Insect Play* (1923). Among his later plays, which included a number of translations, notably of Goldoni, the most successful were those dealing with historical subjects—*The Rose Without a Thorn* (1932), on Catherine Howard, which is frequently revived by amateur societies, *The King and Mistress Shore* (1936), and *Golden Eagle* (1946), which deals with Mary, Queen of Scots. He was one of the founders of the Phoenix Society, which did excellent work in the 1920s in reviving masterpieces of Elizabethan and Restoration drama. In 1929 he was elected Chairman of the Incorporated Stage Society.

BAXTER, (1) RICHARD (1593–?1666), English actor who appeared at the Red Bull for some fifteen years, probably beginning as a young apprentice of about 14 years of age. He remained there until 1623, when he joined the King's Men, playing minor roles. He was acting at the Red Bull when he accidentally wounded an apprentice, presumably a member of the audience seated on or near the stage. A riot threatened, but all was smoothed over. In *c.* 1630 Baxter appeared in *The Mad Lover*, in which his son (2) RICHARD (1618–?) played a boy's part, as he did in *Believe As You List* a year later. The younger Baxter was a member of Beeston's company at the Restoration, and later joined Killigrew's company at Drury Lane.

BAYLIS, LILIAN (1874–1937), founder of the Old Vic and Sadler's Wells companies, and one of the outstanding women of the English theatre. She was appointed Companion of Honour in 1929 and was the second woman outside the university to be given an Hon. M.A. at Oxford (1924). Daughter of Newton Baylis and Liebe [Elizabeth] Cons, both singers, she was given a musical education which resulted in a life-long devotion to opera, and appeared in London, her birthplace, as a child prodigy. At the age of 16 she went with her family to South Africa, touring in a combined musical and dramatic entertainment, and later settled in Johannesburg, where she was one of the first teachers of music. Recalled to England to assist her aunt, Emma Cons, who since 1880 had been running the old Victoria Theatre as a temperance hall under the name of the Royal Victorian Coffee Music Hall, she took over the management in 1912, and from then on the history of her life must be looked for in her work. An intensely religious and single-minded woman, she brought all her forces to bear on the achievement of her object—a popular home for opera and, incidentally, drama. When drama threatened to oust opera, she looked about for another theatre, and took over, rebuilt, and opened in 1931 the Sadler's Wells Theatre, where the popularity of opera has again been equalled, if not surpassed, by that of ballet. Lilian Baylis may have had some faults, but they were offset by the fervour of her belief in the destiny of her theatres, by her tireless work for them, by her uncanny knack of inspiring enthusiasm, and by her perspicuity in choosing her collaborators, as witness her choice of Ninette de Valois as ballet-mistress, and the subsequent rise of a hitherto undreamed-of English Ballet, or her selection of Charles Corri as musical director, a position which he held for over thirty years.

Under Lilian Baylis's management all Shakespeare's plays were produced at the Old Vic, from *The Taming of the Shrew* in 1914 to

Troilus and Cressida in 1923. *Hamlet*, which was the second play to appear in the repertory, was several times done in its entirety, always at matinées, on account of its length. Plays by other dramatists were sometimes included in the programme, among them *Peer Gynt* (1922), but it was as the home of Shakespeare that the Old Vic made its name, and it is a tribute to the soundness of the foundations on which Lilian Baylis built up its reputation that it survived the shock of her death and continued its successful career until in 1963 it became the temporary home of the National Theatre company under Sir Laurence Olivier.

BAYREUTH, a German town near Nuremberg, formerly the capital of Franconia, where the famous opera-composer Richard Wagner (1813–83) settled when he was about 60, and made a festival-centre for the performance of his works. This continued after his death under his widow and children, and later under his grandchildren. The operas are given in a theatre specially built for the purpose—the Festspielhaus, which was paid for by private subscriptions and donations from various Wagner Societies. It was built by the Bayreuth architect Wölfel and the stage machinist Karl Brandt, for whose use Wagner borrowed from King Ludwig of Bavaria the plans made by Gottfried Semper for the abandoned site at Munich. It had no galleries, and made use of the fan-shaped auditorium, first employed by the English architect Edward Shepherd in 1733, with rising rows of seats all facing the stage directly. The orchestra and the conductor were out of sight in a sunk pit, and the whole attention of the audience was thus concentrated on the stage. Most of these features were planned by Wagner himself. Alterations have been made in recent years, but the main design remains the same. The Festspielhaus was opened in Aug. 1876 with a complete production, on four evenings, of 'Der Ring des Nibelungen'. Up to 1944 the six later operas and the Ring cycle were performed at varying intervals—39 festivals in 69 years. After Wagner's death in 1883, control of the festivals passed to his widow, and, from 1908 to 1930, to his son Siegfried. During this period there was a somewhat rigid adherence to the rules laid down by Wagner himself. From 1931 to 1944, Siegfried's widow, Winifred, a Yorkshirewoman, was in charge. In 1945 the U.S. army captured Bayreuth, and used the Festspielhaus for entertainments for their troops. On 29 July 1951 Wagner's grandsons, Wieland and Wolfgang, with the support of the Federal German Government, re-opened the theatre for its proper purpose. There is now an annual festival which fills the theatre to capacity. New staging, expert use of lighting, and continual experiments in production characterize the present régime, which has abolished the old 'romantic' scenery. In 1961 the score of an opera—'Tannhäuser'—was 'edited' for the first time, and also during that season the first coloured singer was heard at Bayreuth.

The Royal Opera House at Bayreuth was built by the Bibienas in 1784 (see ACOUSTICS) and has so far escaped damage. It is a perfect example of eighteenth-century rococo theatre architecture, and occasional concerts given there display its exquisite acoustics to perfection.

BEARD, JOHN (*c.* 1716–91), English singer, for whom Handel composed some of his finest tenor roles. He was also a good actor, making his first appearance at Drury Lane in 1737 in ballad opera. One of his best parts was Macheath. A happy marriage interrupted his career for a time, but after the death of his wife he returned to the stage, in about 1743, and later married the daughter of John Rich, taking over the management of Covent Garden on the death of his father-in-law in 1761. Like Garrick, he was defeated by the rioters who opposed the removal of half-prices after the third act, though he managed to hold out against them rather longer. A man of excellent character, universally popular, he was president of the Beefsteak Club, where his recitations were much admired. He retired in 1767.

BEAUBOUR. (1) PIERRE TROCHON DE (1662–1725), French actor, third husband of (2) LOUISE PITEL (*c.* 1665–1740) daughter of the Beauvals, who had been in Molière's company. His wife played only secondary roles, but Beaubour, who had been brought from the provinces in 1691 to replace Baron, was accounted good in tragedy, though somewhat noisy and declamatory. He also lacked all sense of theatrical illusion, but his good looks and excellent presence helped to compensate for the absence of real talent. His influence on French acting was unfortunate, since he tended to force it back to its former stiffness, a style later abolished by the more natural approach of his successor, Dufresne. He retired in 1718, at the same time as his wife.

BEAUCHÂTEAU. (1) [FRANÇOIS-MATHIEU CHASTELET] (*fl.* 1625–65), French actor who joined the company at the Hôtel de Bourgogne at the same time as Bellerose, and remained there until 1634, when he went with his wife, (2) MADELEINE DE POUGET (1615–83), an actress whom he had married a year previously, to the Théâtre du Marais. Both husband and wife were parodied, as the young lovers, by Molière in his *Impromptu de Versailles* (1664), but they had their admirers, though, like Bellerose, they were somewhat insipid and sentimental.

BEAUMARCHAIS, PIERRE-AUGUSTIN CARON DE (1732–99), French dramatist, among other things. The son of a watchmaker, who brought him up to his own trade, he was handsome and assured, and soon decided to turn his undoubted talents to something more lucrative. As a first step he married the young widow of a Court official, and took over her late husband's position. It was at this time that he added Beaumarchais to his original surname of Caron. A year later he was a widower, giving lessons on the harp to the daughters of Louis XV—Coche, Loque, Chiffe, and Graille, as their father called them—and directing the music of the Court concerts. He indulged in speculation under the able guidance of the financier Paris-Duverney, and after the latter's death engaged in unprofitable litigation. His interest in Spanish literature was first aroused when in 1764 he went to Madrid on behalf of his sister, entangled there in an unhappy love-affair. On his return he wrote his first play, *Eugénie*, which had a somewhat cool reception when produced at the Comédie-Française in 1767. He altered it considerably and it was then moderately successful, as was *Les Deux Amis* (1770). Meanwhile Beaumarchais had been making himself heard outside the theatre, first by his quarrels with the Duc de Chaulnes over Mlle Ménard, an actress at the Comédie-Italienne, and particularly by his sallies against Goezman in his famous *Mémoires*, whose style and humour aroused the envy of Voltaire. Beaumarchais was fighting a popular battle, and though he lost it he became the idol of the people. All this was reflected in the turmoil which greeted his first great play, *Le Barbier de Séville*. Originally intended as a play with music, and later used as the basis of an opera by Rossini, it was refused by the Comédie-Italienne, who thought its barber-hero a caricature of their leading actor, who had formerly been a barber himself. It was accepted by the Comédie-Française soon after its completion in 1772, but the author's lawsuit with the Duc de Chaulnes delayed production. A second lawsuit, with Goezman, caused further delay, as did Beaumarchais's addition of allusions to Goezman in the script. The play was finally produced in 1775 before an audience which still felt secure from the Revolution which it presaged. Nine years later, when *Le Mariage de Figaro* (1784)—used by Mozart for his famous opera—was first given, again after a hard struggle, the situation was somewhat different. The public was beginning to realize the dangers that lay before it, and Figaro, older and wiser, criticizes not an individual man, as in the earlier play, but society as a whole. No wonder it needed, as was said at the time, more wit to get it put on the stage than to write it. In 1782 Louis XVI is reported to have said, after reading it: 'It is detestable; it must never be played. It would be necessary to destroy the Bastille to prevent the production of this play being a dangerous anomaly. This man laughs at everything which ought to be respected in a government.' Whereupon the Queen said, disappointedly: 'It will not be played, then?', and the King replied: 'No, certainly not. You may be sure of that.'

These two plays sum up Beaumarchais's whole life and character. He is himself the precocious page, the handsome Almaviva—he was three times married—and above all he is Figaro, jack-of-all-trades, watchmaker, musician, financier, courtier, gun-runner, author, secret agent; in prison, ruined, embroiled with the law, libelled, harassed, hunted across Europe—all this according to his own account of his life—and yet always imperturbable, landing on his feet, clever, and unscrupulous.

His later dramatic works, *La Mère coupable*, a lachrymose play produced in 1792, and an opera, 'Tarare' (1787), which under cover of a story of Eastern despotism attacks the vices of the monarchy and the Church, are less interesting. More important was his part in breaking the stranglehold of the actors on their authors. Like many other dramatists of the day, he objected to the rules governing the financial relations of theatre and playwright, and was instrumental in getting them altered, though not as fundamentally as he wished. (He was the founder of the Société des Auteurs.) His later years were spent in the turmoil of the Revolution, of whose early utterances he had been the mouthpiece, and he was imprisoned in 1792 on suspicion of having arms hidden in his house. He was freed after six days by the intervention of a friend, M. Manuel. At the time of Robespierre's downfall in 1794 Beaumarchais was an *émigré*, in hiding at Hamburg, but his wife, daughter, and sister were all in prison in Paris. They were freed soon after Robespierre's death.

BEAUMENARD, Rose-Perrine le Roy (1730–99), French actress, wife of the actor Bellecourt. She made her début at the Opéra-Comique in 1743 with some success, and then toured the provinces, being a member of the company taken on his campaigns by Marshal Saxe. In 1749 she joined the Comédie-Française, where she excelled in the soubrettes of Regnard and Molière, being considered the perfect Nicole in *Le Bourgeois gentilhomme*. She was variously nicknamed La Rieuse and Gogo, and was a great favourite with the public. She retired from 1756 to 1761, but on her reappearance proved as good an actress as ever. After the Revolution she again retired, this time with no intention of returning, but by 1799 she was penniless, and forced to take up her former profession. She attempted to play Nicole, but was only a shadow of her former self, and died in the August of that year.

BEAUMONT, Sir Francis (1584–1616), English dramatist, whose name is so associated with that of John Fletcher (1579–1625) that they are usually spoken of in one breath, and scholars are still disentangling their separate contributions from the bulk of work that passes under their joint names. Beaumont had had some connexion with the stage, writing *The Woman Hater*, and possibly *The Knight of the Burning Pestle*, before his name was first linked with Fletcher's in laudatory verses affixed to Jonson's *Volpone*. Their collaboration began in about 1608–9, and covered, according to some authorities, not more than six or seven plays, though in collections published in 1647 and 1679 fifty-three are assigned to them. Later investigations have attributed large parts of these to Massinger, Jonson, Tourneur, Middleton, Rowley, and Shirley, either in their original form or in later revisions.

It is thought that Beaumont ceased to write for the stage on his marriage in 1613, although his work was once or twice seen at Court entertainments (for further details see FLETCHER).

BEAUPRÉ. (1) [NICOLAS LION] (*fl.* 1624–30), French actor, who with his wife (2) MADELEINE LEMOINE (*fl.* 1624–50) was in a somewhat obscure company which came to Paris in 1624. They both went to the Hôtel d'Argent and in 1630 Bellerose took the wife (the husband having just died) into his company at the Hôtel de Bourgogne, where she proved an excellent actress in both comedy and farce. At some point she returned to the company she had been with previously, which was now established at the Théâtre du Marais, for she played there in Corneille's *Cinna* (1640), and was still there when the troubles of the Fronde a couple of years later closed the theatres and sent the actors back into the provinces. She joined a provincial company, probably that of Filandre, which was going to the Low Countries, and was not heard of again in Paris. Her niece, (3) MAROTTE (*fl.* 1662–70), was in Molière's company.

BEAUVAL. (1) [JEAN PITEL] (*c.* 1635–1709), a French actor who was in the provincial troupe of Filandre in 1661. Here he met and married in about 1665 (2) JEANNE OLIVIER DE BOURGUIGNON (*c.* 1648–1720), of whose early life little is known. She is said to have been an orphan who was adopted by a kind-hearted Dutch washerwoman and taken at the age of 10 into Filandre's company as maid-of-all-work. Filandre taught her to read and write, and eventually entrusted her with small parts. After her marriage she and her husband joined another troupe, and from it went to Molière's company in 1670. Beauval was a mediocre actor, though he was apparently good as Thomas Diafoirus in *Le Malade imaginaire*, more by nature than art. His wife, however, though rather coarse-featured and bad-tempered, was an excellent comic actress, and profited much by Molière's teaching. She was given to irresistible fits of laughter, which Molière incorporated into her part of Nicole in *Le Bourgeois gentilhomme*. She also played Zerbinette in *Les Fourberies de Scapin* and Toinette in *Le Malade imaginaire*. After Molière's death the Beauvals went to the Hôtel de Bourgogne, where the wife, who was competent in tragedy, played Oenone in *Phèdre*, and Cleopatra in *Rodogune*. She also took over the part of Hermione from Mlle Champmeslé. Both she and her husband became members of the newly formed Comédie-Française, from which they retired in 1704, thus breaking the last direct link with Molière. Of Mlle Beauval's numerous children—she is thought to have had at least ten—one, (3) LOUISE (*c.* 1665–1740), was the first Louison in *Le Malade imaginaire*. She married, as her third husband, the actor Beaubour, both retiring from the Comédie-Française in 1718.

BEAZLEY, SAMUEL (1786–1851), English architect, designer particularly of theatres, among them the Lyceum, the St. James's, the City of London, that part of the Adelphi fronting on the Strand, and the colonnade of Drury Lane. He left plans for theatres in several English provincial towns, and for places abroad. His buildings, though plain and somewhat uninteresting, were good and well adapted for their purpose. A prolific dramatist, mainly of ephemeral farces and short comedies, Beazley was also responsible for the translation of several operatic libretti.

BECCARI, AGOSTINO (?–1598), Italian dramatist, author of an early pastoral, *Il Sacrifizio*, which was performed at Ferrara in 1554–5, before the Duke and his Court. Although it contains some happy imitations of classical pastoral poetry, it is mainly important as having preceded and perhaps inspired the *Aminta* of Torquato Tasso (see ITALY, 1 *b* ii).

BECHER, LADY, see O'NEILL, ELIZA.

BECK, HEINRICH (1760–1803), a German actor, born in Gotha and intended for the Church, who began his career under Ekhof in his native town in 1777, at the same time as Beil and Iffland. He was tall and slim, and eminently suitable for juvenile leads. After Ekhof's death he went with the company to Mannheim under Dalberg, and became a friend of Schiller, playing the part of Ferdinand in the first production of *Kabale und Liebe*, in which his wife, an excellent little actress (Karoline Ziegler), played Louise. He was also a life-long friend of Iffland, and was associated with him in his work at Mannheim, where he was on the administrative committee.

BECKETT, SAMUEL (1906–), Irish dramatist, novelist, and poet, who was awarded the Nobel Prize for literature in 1969. Resident in France since 1938, Beckett has written mainly in French since 1945, becoming known as a novelist before his first play, *En Attendant Godot*, was produced in Paris by Roger Blin in 1953. All his work is dominated by memories of the horror of the concentration camp and extermination plant, and contemplates with anguished humour the prospect of a society threatening itself with total destruction. In *En Attendant Godot* (staged in London in 1955, in the author's own translation, as *Waiting for Godot*), Beckett abandoned conventional structure and development, in both plot and language, to create a static form which was a perfect dramatic image of his vision of the terrible absurdity of the human situation in a world over which mankind has lost control. His two tramps, indecisive and incapable of action, simply suffer and wait hopefully for the help which never comes; at the same time, their circular, meandering dialogue illuminates the grotesque inadequacy of optimistic faith in such formulae as 'man is naturally good', or 'justice will prevail'. *Fin de partie* followed in 1957, having its first performance in London because of difficulty in finding a theatre in Paris; an English version, *Endgame*, again by the author, was produced in London in 1958, accompanied by *Krapp's Last Tape*, a one-act play written in English (and produced in Paris in 1960 as *La Dernière Bande*). In *Fin de partie*, as in *Oh, Les Beaux Jours!* (*Happy Days*) (first produced in New York, 1961; London, 1962) and *Comédie* (*Play*) (first produced in Germany in 1963; London, 1964). Beckett again expressed his vision of the moral paralysis of mankind, cutting down even further on the already minimal action and development of *Waiting for Godot*, and moving from a vision of absurdity to one of genuine pain at the prospect of man continuing to exist, blithely unaware of the increasing circumscription of his liberty and power of action. T. C. C. MILNE

BECQUE, HENRY FRANÇOIS (1837–99), French dramatist, and one of the outstanding exponents of naturalistic drama. He had a hard life, which was reflected in his plays, and was of a somewhat quarrelsome and misanthropic turn of mind. His first work was a libretto, based on Byron's *Sardanapalus*, written in 1867 for the composer Joncières. This was followed by a four-act comedy, *L'Enfant prodigue* (1868), and by *Michel Pauper* (1870), an important play which was overlooked on its first production, and only appreciated in a revival of 1886. Meanwhile Becque had written the two plays with which his name is usually associated, *Les Corbeaux* (1882) and *La Parisienne* (1885), both naturalistic dramas of great force and uncompromising honesty. They present rapacious or amoral characters who are unaware even of their own degradation, and unlike the 'well-made' play, against which they were a reaction, they leave it to the audience to draw their own conclusions, merely presenting the facts and not commenting on them. This was in the tradition of Zola's 'slice of life', of which Becque's *comédies rosses*, as they were called, were the natural outcome. Becque, who never again reached the heights of these two plays, though he continued to write until his death, was not fully appreciated until Antoine's Théâtre Libre had provided a stage for the new drama. He had a number of followers, of whom the most important was probably Georges Ancey.

BEDFORD, PAUL (*c.* 1792–1871), English actor who had already been many years on the stage as a singer in light and ballad opera when in 1838 he was engaged by Yates for the Adelphi to play second low-comedy roles. Here he made a great reputation in such parts as Blueskin in *Jack Sheppard* (1839), Jack Gong in *Green Bushes* (1845), and the Kinchin Cove in *Flowers of the Forest* (1847). Portly in later life, with a deep, rolling voice, he was a sound, reliable actor, who spent more than fifty years on the stage.

BEDLOW STREET THEATRE, NEW YORK, see GROVE THEATRE.

BEEKMAN STREET THEATRE, NEW YORK, see CHAPEL STREET THEATRE.

BEER-HOFMANN, RICHARD (1866–1945), see AUSTRIA.

BEERBOHM, SIR MAX (1872–1956), English dramatic critic and half-brother of Sir Herbert Tree. He was dramatic critic of the *Saturday Review* from 1898 to 1910, succeeding Bernard Shaw, who, in his Valedictory, spoke of the younger generation knocking at the door, 'and as I open it, there steps spritely in the incomparable Max'. Max lived up to this introduction. 'For my own part, I am a dilettante, a *petit-maître*. I love best in literature delicate and elaborate ingenuities of form and style.' Yet he realized that, without personality, artistry goes for little, and his appreciation of the art of the theatre embraced almost every type of personality, from the dignified actor of the legitimate stage to the homely humorist of the halls. The elegance of Max Beerbohm was that of the natural aristocrat which rises above snobbery. He held that vulgarity is an implicit element of the true music-hall. For all the enchanting lightness of his critical pen, it ran always to sincerity and often to wisdom. His twelve years of criticism brought distinction to the theatrical journalism of his time. Some of his best work reappeared in *Around Theatres* (1924). His one-act play, *The Happy Hypocrite*, based on one of his own short stories, was produced at the Royalty Theatre in 1900 by Mrs. Patrick Campbell, and a three-act version by Clemence Dane was seen at His Majesty's in 1936. His short play, *A Social Success*, was put on at the Palace Theatre in 1913 and in it George Alexander made his first music-hall appearance. In 1902 *The Fly on the Wheel*, which Max wrote with Murray Carson, was produced at the Coronet Theatre. Beerbohm was knighted in 1939 for his services to literature (see also KAHN, FLORENCE).

T. C. KEMP†

BEESTON. (1) CHRISTOPHER (?1570–1638), an important figure of the Jacobean and Caroline stage. He began his career as a member of Strange's Men, with whom Shakespeare was also connected. Though not named in the list of actors in Shakespeare's plays, Beeston was probably a minor member of the famous Chamberlain's Men, for Phillips, who left a legacy to Shakespeare and others of the company, left one also to Beeston. In 1602 Beeston was with Worcester's Men at the Rose and stayed with them when they became the Queen's Men on the accession of James I. He was appointed their business manager on the death in 1612 of Thomas Greene, the actor who had hitherto held this position. A few years later, in about 1616–17, he built or acquired the Cockpit in Drury Lane, also known as the Phoenix, which he leased to various companies, himself ceasing to act. He was apparently an excellent manager, but suspected of being more shrewd than honest in his dealings with the actors. In 1637 he collected and trained a young company called Beeston's Boys, some of whom later made their name in the Restoration theatre. Beeston was a life-long friend and admirer of the dramatist-actor Thomas Heywood, many of whose plays were given at the Cockpit. When Beeston died his son (2) WILLIAM (?1606–82), who had acted with his father probably from boyhood, succeeded him as head of Beeston's Boys, but soon got into trouble with the authorities for performing an unlicensed play which gave offence to James I. William was imprisoned, and his place taken by Davenant, who was later to play so important a part in the history of the Restoration theatre; but in 1641, when Davenant had to leave England owing to his political activities, Beeston returned to the Cockpit. On the closing of the theatres in the following year his activities ceased, but he managed to acquire Salisbury Court, where he trained a company of boys. This theatre was one of the first to reopen in 1660, with a licence from Sir Henry Herbert, Master of the Revels, still under the control of Beeston, who also opened the Cockpit again, leasing it to John Rhodes's company, and probably to a company under the joint control of Davenant and Killigrew. With the granting of Royal Patents to the two last, however, Beeston was put out of business, and nothing further is known about him. He left a mark on the theatre, being a link between the Elizabethan and Restoration stages, and his ability in training young actors, which is several times referred to in contemporary records, must have meant that some of the traditional business of the old actors reappeared in the work of many of the leading Restoration actors. He is suspected, perhaps unjustly, of being the 'ill Beest' who betrayed to Commonwealth soldiers the actors who were appearing secretly at Gibbon's Tennis-Court in 1652, but this may have been Theophilus Bird.

BEHN, MRS. APHRA (1640–89), playwright and novelist and the first Englishwoman to earn a living by her pen. Brought up in the West Indies, the scene of her novel *Oroonoko* (dramatized in 1696 by Southerne), she returned to England in 1658 and married a merchant of Dutch extraction. Soon widowed, she went to Holland during the Dutch war as a spy, and did good work, for which she does not appear to have been paid. In any case, she was shortly afterwards imprisoned for debt; but she was soon released, perhaps through the intervention of Killigrew. Her first play, *The Forced Marriage; or, the Jealous Bridegroom* (1670), was a tragicomedy given at Lincoln's Inn Fields with Betterton and his wife in the leading parts. (Otway, the dramatist, also made his first and last appearance on the stage in this play, with such conspicuous lack of success that he gave up all thought of being an actor.) It was, however, in comedies of intrigue that Mrs. Behn did her best work, and her first substantial success came with *The Rover; or, the Banished Cavalier* (1677), with Betterton as the hero, Belville, and Lee and Underhill as the comedians. The play, in a modified version, was often revived, the part of Willmore the Rover being a favourite one with leading actors. It was followed by several other comedies, of which *The Feign'd Curtizans; or, a Night's Intrigue* (1678), was a complicated affair dedicated to Nell Gwynn, while *The Roundheads; or, the Good Old Cause* (1681) and *The City-Heiress; or, Sir Timothy Treat-All* (1682) owed most of their success to their topicality. Her later plays were less successful, though *The Emperor of the Moon* (1687), a pantomime-farce based on a *commedia dell'arte* scenario recently given in Paris, is historically interesting. Anthony Leigh played Scaramouche and Jevon Harlequin; the play was frequently revived and was the forerunner of the many harlequinades which later led to the English pantomime.

Aphra Behn, whose plays have been edited by Montague Summers, is said to have introduced milk punch into England. Witty and high-spirited, she was the friend of Dryden, Otway, Southerne, and other prominent literary men of the time. She worked hard, and was more prolific than any dramatist of her day except Dryden, and the coarseness of her work is often compensated by excellent lyrics. It has been the fashion to consider her a loose-living creature, a scandal in a scandalous age, but her unremitting industry argues at least some time taken from the pursuit of pleasure, and on examination her plays are found to be somewhat better than those of the average playwright of the day. Much of their indecency is due to the fashion of the time, and to the necessity for writing with masculine pungency if they were to be given a hearing. Allardyce Nicoll says:

> Indecent, free, sometimes positively vulgar, she was in several of her plays; but, on the whole, when we compare her works with similar productions of D'Urfey, and Shadwell, even of Dryden, we must be prepared to admit the comparative purity of her dialogue. She has, moreover, on many occasions introduced thoughts and ideas which not only display her unconventional and modern attitude towards life's relations, but also formed the basis for not a few moralisations in the sentimental eighteenth century to come!

BEHRMAN, SAMUEL NATHANIEL (1893–), American dramatist, who combines deft characterization and sparkling dialogue in the pursuit of high comedy. Born in Worcester, he attended Clark University, Baker's playwriting workshop at Harvard, and Colombia University; then wrote criticism, read plays professionally, acted as a theatrical press agent, and collaborated with Kenyon Nicholson on the trifles *Bedside Manner* (1923) and *Love Is Like That* (1927). His apprenticeship ended with *The Second Man* (1927), a bright comedy of manners concerning a young girl's infatuation with a cynical novelist. It was followed by *Serena Blandish* (1929), a comedy based on a novel (by Enid Bagnold) about a girl's adventures in Mayfair society, and *Meteor* (1929), a tantalizing study of an egotist in the world of business enterprise. *Brief Moment* (1931) dramatized the romance and misalliance of a socially prominent young man. *Biography* (1932) provided a provocative study of contrasts of temperament in the romance of a carefree woman portrait-painter and a crusading journalist who leaves her when she proves too indulgent toward reactionary politicians. *Rain From Heaven* (1934) used conflicting viewpoints at an English house-party to establish the untenability of civilized detachment in a strife-ridden world. *End of Summer* (1936) described the bankruptcy of the idle rich. As a pleasant interlude between this play and *Wine of Choice* (1938), a wavering political comedy, Behrman adapted Jean Giraudoux's *Amphitryon 38* for the Lunts (see No. 101). With *No Time for Comedy* (1939), however, the playwright returned to a social problem in the dilemma of a writer who wants to express the tragedy of his times but has a talent only for light comedy. The problem was, in a sense, a personal one, since *The Talley Method* (1940), the study of a domestic tyrant, and *Dunnigan's Daughter* (1945), an exposé of a ruthless capitalist, proved unrewarding, whereas his next trifle for the Lunts, *The Pirate* (1942), adapted from a play by Fulda, succeeded. Behrman was able to fuse comedy and the serious subject of the fall of France in an adaptation of Franz Werfel's *Jacobowsky and the Colonel* (1944). In the fall of 1949 he presented a concise chronicle of a long marriage, *I Know My Love*, in which Alfred Lunt and Lynn Fontanne played husband and wife; the play had 246 performances in New York. In Feb. 1952 *Jane* (a dramatization of Somerset Maugham's story), first presented in England in 1947, ran for 100 performances. Great success attended the musical comedy *Fanny* (1945), based on Pagnol's trilogy, for which Behrman wrote the 'book' with Joshua Logan, while Harold Rome provided the music and the lyrics. Less successful was Behrman's touching comedy of character, *The Cold Wind and the Warm* (1958), based on his own autobiography. Behrman is also an essayist and the biographer of Duveen and Max Beerbohm. In 1964 his *But For Whom Charlie* was included in the repertory of the Lincoln Center's first season. JOHN GASSNER†

BEIL, JOHANN DAVID (1754–94), German actor who, after several years in small touring companies, went to Gotha to act under the great Ekhof in 1777, the same year as Iffland. He was excellent in comic parts, a good mimic and lively observer. In person he was round-faced and jolly. He went with the company to Mannheim under Dalberg after Ekhof's death, and played in Schiller's early works, and in the plays of Iffland, to whom he proved a loyal friend and colleague during the great days of the Mannheim stage. Unfortunately he was much given to drink and fell a victim to it at the early age of forty, much to the despair of Iffland, who had just been appointed producer to the theatre, and in addition had to take on a number of Beil's leading roles.

BÉJART, a family of actors intimately associated with Molière. The eldest daughter, (1) MADELEINE (1618–72), was already an actress of some repute in the provinces when Molière met her, and it is usually assumed that it was for love of her that he became an actor. Together they formed a company which played in Paris without success under the name of the Illustre-Théâtre. They then went into the provinces, where they amalgamated with a troupe under Dufresne, of which Molière soon became the leader. Madeleine returned to Paris with Molière in 1658, shared in his success, and remained with him at the Palais-Royal until her death a year before his. In her early years she played the heroines of classical tragedy, and in later life created a number of Molière's witty maids who ridicule the follies of their mistresses. At one time she managed the finances of the company. It is impossible to assess how much Molière owed to her constant affection and support over a period of thirty years. Associated with her in the Illustre-Théâtre were her brother (2) JOSEPH (1616–59) and her sister (3) GENEVIÈVE (1624–75). In spite of a stammer Joseph was a useful actor, and a popular member of the company. His death soon after they were established in Paris was a great blow. He was taken ill during a performance of *L'Étourdi*. Little is known of Geneviève, who was called Mlle Hervé from her mother's maiden name, beyond the fact that she was twice married and was probably better in tragedy than in comedy. During its travels Molière's company was augmented by the arrival of another brother, (4) LOUIS (1630–78), who was known as L'Éguisé on account of his sharp tongue. He also accompanied Molière to Paris, and did yeoman service in the company until his retirement in 1670. He was lame in the right leg, a trait which Molière incorporated into the part of La Flèche in *L'Avare*, where Harpagon calls him 'lame dog', and the limp has remained traditional for this character. He was the first of Molière's actors to draw a pension. The last, and in some ways most important, member of the family was (5) ARMANDE-GRÉSINDE-CLAIRE-ÉLISABETH (1641–1700), whom Molière married in 1662 in the church from which the signal for the massacre of St. Bartholomew was given. She had been brought up by Madeleine, who had herself lost a girl-child at the time of Armande's birth, and contemporary gossip believed her to be Madeleine's daughter. Molière was therefore accused of having married the child of his former mistress, and even, by the rival actor Montfleury, his own daughter by Madeleine, a calumny which has never been expressly disproved, though it is no longer credited. The marriage was an unhappy one, and after Molière's death his young widow married an actor named Guérin d'Étriché, and was apparently happy with him. She was an excellent actress, who owed all her training to Molière. She first appeared on the stage as Élise in his *Critique de l'École des femmes* and as herself in *L'Impromptu de Versailles* (both 1663). In the following year she played a gipsy woman in *Le Mariage forcé*, when she had the honour of dancing with Louis XIV, and had her first important part as the heroine in *La Princesse d'Élide*. After 1664 she played most of Molière's heroines. Whatever her faults, she was an able and energetic woman, and contemporaries admired the firm way in which she kept her company together after her husband's death. She had three children, of whom only one, a girl, survived.

BEL SAVAGE INN, see INNS USED AS THEATRES.

BELASCO, DAVID (1853–1931), American actor-manager and playwright, and for many years one of the outstanding personalities of the American stage. Born in California, of a Portuguese–Hebrew family originally named Valasco, he inherited his good looks from his father, who had been a harlequin at various London theatres, and his strong-willed and imperious temperament from his mother. His love for the stage showed itself in early days, and as a child he appeared at the local theatre in *Pizarro*, *East Lynne*, and *Richard III*, playing the little Duke of York to Charles Kean's Richard on the latter's farewell tour. Belasco later joined the stock company of the San Francisco Theatre, where he played with John McCullough, Booth, and other famous actors. He married at 20, dabbled in journalism, and for several years led the usual life of the itinerant actor, travelling the Pacific coast. He served his apprenticeship to playwriting by dramatizing novels, poems, and stories, and by adapting old plays, a task made less onerous by the lack of any copyright laws. As stage-manager at various theatres he devised some spectacular melodramas, with battles, fires, and other calamities, and produced an overwhelming Passion Play with real sheep. All this served as a useful introduction to his career in New York, where he later became the outstanding purveyor of 'sensation drama'. He first appeared there with Herne in 1879 in *Hearts of Oak* (also known as *Chums*), a joint adaptation of an old melodrama entitled *The Mariner's Compass*. It was not a success, and Belasco returned to California to continue his stage-management and play-doctoring, until in 1882 he was called to New York again by Daniel Frohman to become stage manager of the Madison Square Theatre. Here his first venture was *Young Mrs. Winthrop* (1882), and in 1884 he produced his own *May Blossom*, in which year he also made his first visit to England. On his return to New York he became Steele Mackaye's stage manager at the Lyceum, where he remained until 1890, continuing to turn out a number of plays, mainly in collaboration. Success came with *The Girl I Left Behind Me* (1893), written in collaboration with Franklyn Fyles, and *The Heart of Maryland* (1895), in which Maurice Barrymore was excellent as the hero. *Zaza* (1899), an adaptation from the French, starred Mrs. Carter, whom Belasco had launched on a spectacular career some years before. It was a success both in New York and in London, and was followed by *Madame Butterfly* (1900), in which Blanche Bates, another of Belasco's stars, gave a fine performance as the Japanese girl, a part played in London by Evelyn Millard. This dramatization of a story by John Luther Long was seen by Puccini, and used as the basis of an opera, as was *The Girl of the Golden West* (1905). Meanwhile Belasco had begun his association with the actor David Warfield, whom he took from the variety stage and starred in *The Auctioneer* (1901). He also achieved a lifelong ambition by leasing the Republic Theatre from Hammerstein. Completely rebuilt, and renamed the Belasco, it opened with a revival of *Du Barry*, with Mrs. Carter, which had previously been seen at the Criterion Theatre. This was followed by *The Darling of the Gods* (1902), another Japanese story written in collaboration with John Luther Long, in which Blanche Bates played the heroine and George Arliss the villainous Minister for War, and by *Sweet Kitty Bellairs* (1903). Other successes at this first Belasco theatre were *Adrea* (1905), with Mrs. Carter, and *The Rose of the Rancho* (1906), while Warfield scored a triumph in *The Music Master* (1904), in which he toured for many years.

In 1906 Belasco built a new theatre, known first as the Stuyvesant, under which name it opened in 1907 with *A Grand Army Man.* It took the name of Belasco in 1910, when the former Belasco reverted to its original title of the Republic. Here Belasco remained until his death, and his private rooms in the theatre, where priceless *objets d'art* were jumbled up with theatrical properties in artistic disorder, presided over by the owner with his deceptively benign and clerical appearance, have passed into legend. Here he produced *The Return of Peter Grimm* (1911) with Warfield as the old man who returns after death to rectify the errors of his life; *The Case of Becky* (1912) with Frances Starr, dealing with a dual personality and hypnotism; *Kiki* (1921) with Leonora Ulric; *Laugh, Clown, Laugh* (1923), based on an Italian play; and, his last production as well as his last play, *Mima* (1928), adapted from *The Red Mill* by Ferenč Molnár.

It will be seen that Belasco ended his career as he began it, adapting the work of another. He contributed little that was original to the American stage, and can in no sense be said to have encouraged the national American drama which was growing up round him. He belongs to the great age of American stagecraft, when the subject-matter of drama was imported from Europe, and his great contribution to the American stage lay in his elaborate scenic displays, his passion for realism, which led him in *The Governor's Lady* (1912) to place an exact replica of a Child's restaurant on the stage, and in the strong vehicles which he provided for the stars of the day, many of them becoming stars only through his efforts. He was in the widest sense a man of the theatre, though he did not act after 1880, and even his weaknesses—his vanity, his craving for admiration, his constant posturing—were products of his intensely dramatic nature. As a stage-director he was meticulous, a hard master but a just one, and he should be judged on what he did for the American stage, and not on what he failed to do. His long career covers a transition period in the history of American drama, and it was inevitable that he should give the weight of his authority to the older, romantic, flamboyant period, rather than to the less spectacular though more truly realistic drama of the new age. Yet he did not disdain the mechanical inventions of the day, and made interesting and often far-reaching experiments in the use of light. Nor should his long fight against the stranglehold of the Theatrical Syndicate, and his ultimate triumph, go unrecorded, since it involved the whole question of the freedom of the American theatre, and the independence of the artist in the theatre. His large collection of theatrical material is now housed in the New York Public Library. The second Belasco Theatre (for the first see also REPUBLIC) is still owned by his estate. It was at one time leased to Katharine Cornell, who produced there *Alien Corn* and a translation of Obey's *Le Viol de Lucrèce*. Two of Elmer Rice's plays were first given at the Belasco, while for six years the Group Theatre had their headquarters there, producing the plays of Odets. In 1945 *Trio*, a play on an equivocal theme which caused a good deal of trouble, was seen at the Belasco for a short run which was terminated by the censor. From 1949 to 1953 the Belasco was used for broadcasting, but *The Solid Gold Cadillac* (1953) was successful there, as was *All the Way Home* (1960).

BELCARI, FEO (1410–84), early Italian dramatist, author of a number of religious dramas written about 1450 (see ITALY, 1 *a* ii).

BELFAST, see IRELAND.

BELGIUM. 1. THE FLEMISH-SPEAKING THEATRE. The development of the Belgian theatre, especially in the Flemish-speaking areas, was very similar to that of the English theatre. Mystery and Miracle plays were performed by local amateurs and small bands of strolling players as early as 1275. Flemish drama in the fourteenth and fifteenth centuries may well have been responsible for the creation of the first form of secular drama with the *abele spelen* such as *Esmoreit*, *Lanceloet van Denemerken*, and *Gloriant*. The performances of Miracle plays and of *abele spelen* were nearly always followed by rough farces and short plays called *kluchten* or *sotternien* (jokes), the main theme being the battle of the sexes. The masterpiece of Flemish drama is undoubtedly the Morality play *Elckerlyc*, written by a Chartreuse monk, Petrus Dorlandus. This play, printed in Delft in 1495 under its full title, *Den Spieghel der Salicheit van Elckerlyc*, has been the subject of much scholarly discussion, the conclusion being that it is probably the original of the English Morality play, *Everyman* (see also NETHERLANDS, THE).

From the early Middle Ages to the beginning of the seventeenth century, Flemish drama grew in importance. The Flemish amateur actors, the Rederykers, were linked very closely with the master-painters' guild of St. Lucas. Through the organization of *Landjuwelen* (drama festivals), they became a national institution. In his excellent book, *From Art To Theatre*, published in 1944, George Kernodle shows that the principle of the Flemish Rederykers' stage may well have influenced the architectural form of the Elizabethan playhouses on London's South Bank, while one may also presume that the thousands of Flemish immigrants added their taste for the theatre to that of the English people with whom they were working and living.

The Rederykers, who had been growing in importance socially and culturally, playing before emperors, kings, and foreign ambassadors, were the first to suffer from the religious quarrels and subsequent war with Spain. Hundreds of them paid with their lives for their loyalty to their country and their faith, many others fled to Holland and England. Spanish rule almost put an end to the development of Flemish theatre culture, and it took more than two hundred years to revive.

In 1853 the first professional Flemish theatre came into being in Antwerp; this was the Koninklyke Nederlandse Schouwburg. Ghent followed suit in 1871. Brussels, which was mainly French-speaking, had a Flemish theatre in 1887—the Koninklyke Vlaamse Schouwburg. Started as repertory companies, drawing chiefly on French and English melodrama, they developed through hard work, and found their true form in about 1890, when classic plays and the works of the most important dramatists of the nineteenth century were added to the repertory. Of great importance, too, were the guest performances of the companies of the Duke of Meiningen and of Ernesto Rossi. The biggest change, however, took place in 1922, when Dr. Jan Oscar De Gruyter, after touring the country with his Flemish Popular Theatre (Vlaamse Volkstoneel), became, through his appointment as director of the theatre in Antwerp, the Flemish theatre's greatest renovator. He renewed the entire repertory, and under the influence of the leading French and English theatre men of his time sought to build up a team of actors working together in harmony. He eschewed all 'star nonsense', and set out to encourage talent, knowledge, and artistic integrity. Under his guidance the theatre in Antwerp was perhaps most successful in its performances of Shakespeare. J. T. Grein, founder of London's Independent Theatre, had a high opinion of De Gruyter's work, praising the unity of style and the acting qualities of his company (see the *Illustrated London News*, Oct. 1927: 'The World of the Theatre'). After De Gruyter's untimely death in 1929, two directors took over his work, endeavouring to live up to the standards set by their great predecessor.

The establishment of the National Theatre (Nationaal Toneel) in 1945, which grouped the companies of Ghent and Antwerp together, permitted the broadening of the field of activities in both cities. The new theatre became the main centre of professional work in the Flemish part of Belgium, thus realizing De Gruyter's basic idea of some twenty years earlier. Handicapped by the limitations of the Flemish theatre, a policy of alternating weekly repertory was nevertheless worked out in Ghent and Antwerp, later to be changed to fortnightly repertory, with an increasing number of one-night stands in the principal provincial towns. Plays are taken from the whole field of international drama. It was hoped that the National Theatre, receiving a large subsidy and additional grants from the state and city councils, would adhere to a policy of unswerving artistic efforts in casting, acting, and production. The situation at present, however, shows some departure from the basic principles laid down by De Gruyter. A tendency to play down to the taste of a mass audience, and a craving for easy success, has destroyed much of the earlier integrity.

The Royal Flemish Theatre (Koninklyke Vlaamse Schouwburg) of Brussels, formerly a weekly repertory theatre, now operates on a three-weekly or monthly basis. Profiting by the pioneer work of an earlier generation, this theatre is trying to awaken a new interest in Flemish drama in Belgium's capital. Its efforts seem to be being rewarded, in spite of performances which are sometimes somewhat indifferent. Here again the choice of play is international, though the work of Flemish authors has regularly been encouraged.

A remarkable part has been played in the modern development of the theatre in Belgium by the Popular Touring Theatre (Reizend Volksteater), which visits the smaller towns and villages whose theatrical horizon has so far been bounded by the local amateur groups. This company's greatest success has been achieved with its annual open-air performances, in the courtyard of Rubens' house in Antwerp, of plays by Shakespeare—*Twelfth Night*, *The Taming of the Shrew*, *The Merchant of Venice*, *Othello*, and *The Tempest*.

The Youth Theatre (Jeugdteater) in Antwerp, established in 1941, houses a regular company, playing a varied programme of fairy tales and historical plays for a devoted audience of children between 4 and 14 years of age. Popular productions recently have been Barrie's *Peter Pan* and dramatizations of Kipling's *The Jungle Book* and *The Second Jungle Book* and Mark Twain's *Tom Sawyer*.

All the Flemish theatres are officially subsidized, very much in the same way as the German civic theatres (Städtische Bühnen). Private or commercial enterprise is rare, except for one small comedy theatre in Antwerp, a few theatre clubs and some touring companies which have not yet attained full professional stature. Since the sixteenth century only a few Flemish authors have written above the level of popular demand for comic and local plays. The limitations of the Flemish theatre may be partly to blame for this state of affairs, but it is perhaps due also to the fact that most authors do not seem to have realized that in order to write a good play one must learn the basic essentials of one's craft. Literature in dialogue form is not enough—a lesson only a few have learned! During the last fifty years the most important contributions to Flemish dramatic literature have been made by Cyriel Buysse (1859–1932), who under the influence of Hauptmann and Heyermans wrote a strong social play, *Het Gezin van Paemel*; Herman Teirlinck (1879–1967), who in the 1920s wrote plays under the influence of Expressionism—among them *De Man zonder lyf*; and Gaston Martens (1891–), author of a number of popular plays, especially *Paradysvogels*, an amusing and very moving play which, translated into French and staged at the Hébertot in Paris, met with great success. Today many dramatists, inspired by their predecessors, are writing plays which may prove to be suitable not only for the Flemish theatre, but also for the international stage.

(2). THE FRENCH-SPEAKING THEATRE. The Belgian–French theatre, mainly centred in Brussels, first manifested itself in the religious drama of the Middle Ages, brought in from France. This theatre also developed through the activities of amateur societies (Sociétés d'art dramatique) and, in a more popular vein, in the Walloon theatres and fairground booths (théâtres forains). In the seventeenth century French dramatists—particularly Corneille and Racine—had a great influence, though Belgian dramatists did not achieve works of comparable importance. In spite of constant changes in the political situation, there was no real break in the development of the French-language theatre, as, unlike the Flemish, it received consideration and encouragement at the hands of subsequent governments, and by the end of the eighteenth century professional companies were established in Brussels and Antwerp. It was not until the end of the nineteenth century, however, that Belgian–French drama became internationally known, with the works of Maurice Maeterlinck (1862–1949)—*Pelléas et Mélisande* (1892), *Monna Vanna* (1902), *L'Oiseau bleu* (1909)—Henri Ghéon (1875–1944), Fernand Crommelynck (1888–), and, more recently, Michel de Ghelderode (1898–1962) with *Pantagleize* (1929), *Magie rouge* (1931), and *Hop! Signor* (1935). These playwrights have not only made a contribution to world drama, but are the inspiration behind the younger generation represented by Herman Closson, Marcel Falmagne, Charles Bertin, Suzanne Lilar, and Charles Cordier.

After the First World War Brussels became more and more the centre of Belgian–French theatrical activity, and one of the most important men in the theatre at that time was undoubtedly Jules Delacre, who at the Théâtre du Marais trained a company of actors, created an atmosphere, and played a repertory whose equivalent could probably be found only in Copeau's Théâtre du Vieux-Colombier. His main principle, well worth repeating, was: 'There is a form of theatre which is born of the free imagination of the author, existing in itself. On our new stage we make room for the author, and room only for him.' This, of course, was very similar to the idea of Sir Barry Jackson, whose Birmingham Repertory Theatre served the art of the theatre in the spirit of John Drinkwater's lines: 'Here shall the Player work, as work he may . . . in service of the play.' Mention should also be made of the work of the Groupe Libre and the efforts of the Théâtre du Parc and the Théâtre des Galeries.

Since the 1920s the number and the activities of professional companies have augmented considerably. The playgoer can now choose between the Théâtre du Parc (the oldest Belgian–French theatre), the Théâtre des Galeries, the Rideau de Bruxelles, the Théâtre Molière, the Théâtre de Poche, and, most interesting of all, the Théâtre National. To complete the picture, there are in Liège a theatre, the Gymnase, a couple of less important pocket-sized theatres, and some touring companies. A few of these theatres are subsidized, the others are commerical enterprises. The Théâtre National, Théâtre des Galeries, and Théâtre du Parc have permanent companies, though Belgian–French actors, like actors everywhere, prefer to divide their time between the theatre, the radio, and television. The run of a play in Brussels may vary from a fortnight to several months, the latter only on very rare occasions. The general standard of acting is adequate, and in some cases very high. The repertory is international, with a preponderance of French authors perhaps, though English, American, and Russian plays figure regularly on the playbills. It must, however, in all fairness be pointed out that even in the Belgian–French theatre there is a tendency to seek a doubtful originality and a 'bubble reputation' in acting and production even at the expense of the author's intentions and against the psychological meaning of the characters and the plot.

In spite of fluctuations in the economics of the theatre, there has been a definite increase in public interest. Large audiences are the rule, not only in the capital but also in the provinces, where one-night stands are usual for most touring companies. In this connexion excellent work has been done by the Théâtre National, founded in 1945 by the Huysman brothers. They had already taken their former group, Les Comédiens Routiers, up and down the country just before and during the Second World War, and well deserved the honour of being given the task of organizing the National Theatre. Since its inception this enterprise has shown Belgian–French theatre at its best, in choice of play, production, and acting. Good work has also been done under its guest producers, who have included, from England, Michael Langham, Denis Carey, and André van Gyseghem.

International recognition has come to the Flemish and Belgian–French theatres alike through their performances in Paris at the festivals of the Théâtre des Nations. The Théâtre National de Belgique also appeared in London in 1953, in a production of Giraudoux's *Ondine* and of Shaw's *Arms and the Man* as *Le Héros et le soldat*. D. DE GRUYTER

BELGRADE THEATRE, COVENTRY, the first civic theatre to be built in England, and the first new professional theatre since Dance's Oxford Playhouse, built in 1938. It got its name in recognition of a gift of timber from the city of Belgrade and of the bond of friendship between the two towns. Designed by the city architects, the theatre, which seats 911 at stall and circle levels, with a number of boxes, has a conventional proscenium stage with a fore-stage over the orchestra pit. It is run by an independent Trust largely composed of City Councillors. Under its first director, Bryan Bailey, who was killed in a motor accident on the M 1 two years later, the theatre opened on 27 Mar. 1958 with *Half in Earnest*, a musical version by Vivian Ellis of *The Importance of Being Earnest*. The present director is Warren Jenkins. Among the many new plays presented since 1958 have been several by Arnold Wesker and David Turner. The latter's *Semi-Detached*, commissioned by the Belgrade for the Coventry Cathedral Festival, was seen in London in Dec. 1962 with Laurence Olivier in the chief part. Besides encouraging new playwrights, the theatre has made serious efforts to attract a new and young audience. Its Young Stagers' Club, which offers reduced seat prices and special holiday programmes, has several thousand members, and the company, which takes part in poetry recitals in the city, also presents a programme of theatre appreciation for local schools. The building, which has excellent foyer accommodation, a restaurant, and a bar, is also used for concerts and displays the work of local artists (see No. 44).

BELGRAVIA THEATRE, LONDON, see ROYAL COURT THEATRE, I.

BELL INN, see INNS USED AS THEATRES.

BELL, JOHN (1745–1831), English publisher and bookseller, who, though quite uneducated, was a pioneer of good printing with excellent engravings. One of his most important ventures was the publication of *Bell's British Theatre*, a comprehensive selection of plays, each prefaced by an interesting character portrait. His 1773 acting edition of Shakespeare, edited by Francis Gentleman—not to be confused with the 1788 edition by Johnson and Steevens—was based on the prompt-books of the Theatres Royal, and is interesting as showing what was actually performed on the stage at the time. He was also the publisher of *Bell's Weekly Messenger*, which appeared on Sundays from 1801 until well after the accession of

Queen Victoria, and of several other papers and journals, including *La Belle Assemblée*, a monthly review of fashion. He was the first to discard the long s, and Leigh Hunt said of him: 'His taste in putting forth a publication, and getting the best artists to adorn it, was new in those times and may be admired in any.'

BELL, JOHN JOY (1871–1934), Scottish dramatist, and one of the pioneer writers of plays in the Scots vernacular. His work was represented in the repertory of the Glasgow Repertory Theatre under Alfred Wareing's management, notably by *Wee Macgregor*, a dramatization of his classic sketches of Glasgow working-class life. In *Thread o' Scarlet* (1923), Bell made a definite contribution to the series of thrillers and Grand Guignol pieces that Edgar Wallace and others supplied to the theatre in the years immediately following the First World War. His other plays include *The Pie in the Oven*, and *Courtin' Christina*. WILLIAM JEFFREY†, *rev.*

BELLAMY, GEORGE ANNE (*c.* 1727–88), English actress, rival of Mrs. Cibber in the heroines of tragedy, who received her first names from a mishearing of Georgiana at her christening. She was the child of Lord Tyrawley by a Quakeress, Miss Seal, who eloped with him from boarding school and later married a sea-captain named Bellamy. Tyrawley, however, acknowledged his daughter, had her educated, and would have done much for her had she not disobeyed him by going to live with her mother. Introduced to Rich, she appeared at Covent Garden, possibly in 1744 as Miss Prue in *Love for Love*, and certainly, as her early biographies say, two years later with Quin in *The Orphan*. Taken up by her father's relatives, she was much petted and spoiled, and at one time administered a severe snub to Garrick, who had thought her too young to play Constance with him in *King John*. Beautiful, arrogant, and extravagant, she was twice married, once bigamously, and much public scandal attached itself to her name. As an actress she was at her best in romantic and tragic parts, being an admirable Juliet to the Romeo of Garrick (see No. 162), who admired her acting sufficiently to make her one of his leading ladies at Drury Lane; but she had none of the professional probity of Peg Woffington or indeed of Mrs. Cibber, and much of her success was due to her youth and beauty. When these left her, the more quickly for her riotous pursuit of pleasure, managers were chary of engaging her, and an appearance in Dublin in 1780 was a complete failure. She continued to act intermittently until her retirement in 1785, when a benefit was organized for her at Covent Garden, but she was constantly harassed by her creditors and held in very little esteem by the public or her fellow actors. In 1785 appeared her *Apology* for her life, in six volumes, edited by another hand, a sensational affair, readable rather than reliable.

BELLECOURT [JEAN-CLAUDE-GILLES COLSON] (1725–78), French actor, husband of Mlle Beaumenard. He was in his youth a painter, and studied under Carl Van Loo. At the same time he appeared in several amateur dramatic productions with a success which, joined to a secret predilection for the stage, decided him to become an actor. He went into the provinces, and by dint of hard work made so much progress that in 1750 he was accepted by the Comédie-Française instead of Lekain, who presented himself at the same time. This was chiefly owing to his fine stage presence, for Lekain was undoubtedly the better actor. When Lekain was finally admitted to the company, Bellecourt, who had no aptitude for tragedy, was happy to hand over to him all the tragic roles, reserving for himself the fine gentlemen of comedy, in which he excelled.

BELLEROSE [PIERRE LE MESSIER] (*c.* 1600–70), French actor, first found in a provincial company in 1619 and in Paris three years later. After bitter controversy with the Confraternity of the Passion, holders of the old monopoly of acting in Paris, a company of which Bellerose was a member took permanent possession of the Hôtel de Bourgogne, where it remained until the foundation of the Comédie-Française in 1673, and some time between 1630–4 Bellerose became its acknowledged head. He was an excellent actor both in comedy and tragedy, though some critics found him insipid and sentimental. Unlike his rival Montdory, he was not a ranter. His style was quiet and rhetorical rather than declamatory, and the name-part in Corneille's *Le Menteur* (1643), with which he is particularly associated, though he was not the first to play it, was probably well suited to his style. Bellerose's acting may have helped to raise the prestige of the serious actor and oust from public favour the older generation of farce-players. He figures as himself in *La Comédie des comédiens* (1633), and created a number of roles in pastoral and tragi-comedy during the years of transition from early farce to French classical tragedy. He controlled the Hôtel de Bourgogne for many years, and his traditions were carried on by his successors Montfleury and Floridor. His wife, Nicole Gassot (?–1680), widow of an actor named Meslier, had red hair and was an excellent actress. She retired in 1660 with a pension.

BELLEVILLE, the name under which the great French comedian Turlupin played serious parts at the Hôtel de Bourgogne from 1612 to 1627.

BELLEW, HAROLD KYRLE (1855–1911), English actor, who was for some time in the navy. He made his first appearance on the stage in Australia in 1874, and in the following year went to England, appearing at Brighton under the name of Harold Kyrle. He reverted to his own name in 1878, when he joined Irving at the Lyceum, having previously been with the Bancrofts and Adelaide Neilson. In 1885 he was first seen in New York, appearing at Wallack's in old comedy, in which he was at his best, his finest parts being Orlando and

Charles Surface. He was for a long time associated with Mrs. Brown-Potter, in whose company he toured extensively, leaving it to settle in Australia, where he made money in mining. In 1902 he returned to the New York stage and remained there until his death, two of his best-remembered parts being Raffles and Brigadier Gerard. He was a man of great charm, handsome, with clear-cut features and a gentlemanly ease of address, added to an extremely beautiful voice and fine elocution.

BELLOY, Pierre-Laurent Buirette de (1727–75), French dramatist, known by one play only, *Le Siège de Calais*, given at the Comédie-Française in 1765. It owed its great and unexpected success to the acting of Lekain, Molé, and Mlle Clairon, but above all to its topicality. France had just signed a humiliating peace, and the audience were consoled by seeing themselves, on the stage, forcing the admiration of their conquerors by their moral virtues. The play itself is of little value, and shows only too clearly the continued decline of classical French tragedy. It contains little or no psychology, the speeches are trivial and narrative rather than poetic; but it came at the right moment, and after a successful start in Paris it was often revived in the provinces, being played before soldier audiences to arouse their patriotism. De Belloy, who was early orphaned and brought up by an uncle for the law, ran away and became an actor under the name of Dormont de Belloy. He was for some years in a French company at the Court of St. Petersburg. He wrote a number of other plays which had little success at the time and are now forgotten.

BELLWOOD, Bessie (1847–96), a music-hall performer, best remembered for her singing of 'What Cheer, Riah!' As Bessie Mahoney she was for some time a rabbit-skinner in the New Cut, near the Old Vic. After a riotous first appearance at the Star, Bermondsey, she was given an audition at the Holborn, and turned down as being 'too quiet', a judgement which her later career did much to disprove. She had a happy knack of indulging in repartee with members of the audience, usually in the gallery, who invariably got as good as they gave. In private life a warm-hearted, generous woman and a fervent Catholic, she was one of the most high-spirited stars of the day, both on and off the stage, and many racy stories, some probably apocryphal, are associated with her name.

BELMONT THEATRE, New York, a small playhouse on 48th Street which opened on 18 Jan. 1918 as the Norworth, with Jack Norworth, one-time husband and partner of Nora Bayes, as its owner and star. It received its present name a few months later, but its early years were not successful. Its first real hit was scored by the Pulitzer Prize-winner for 1920–1, *Miss Lulu Bett*. In the following season *The Hero* also had a respectable run, and was included by Burns Mantle among the ten best plays of the season. A more popular success was scored by *Tarnish* (1923), and in the same year the Belmont saw *You and I*, the first play by Philip Barry, fresh from study under Baker at the '47 Workshop', and later one of America's outstanding dramatists. Two more successes were *Young Woodley* in 1925 and a revue in 1926, after which the fortunes of the house declined. It became a cinema, and was finally demolished in the winter of 1951–2. George Freedley†

BELOW, see stage directions.

BELTRAME, see barbieri.

BENAVENTE, Jacinto (1866–1954), the most famous Spanish dramatist of the first quarter of the twentieth century, winner of the Nobel Prize for Literature, 1922. He brought to the stage an impeccable technique and a wide knowledge of the works of contemporary European dramatists, and translated into Spanish some of the plays of Shakespeare and Molière. The author of 168 plays, his works vary from dramas extolling the power of the will (such as *La noche del sábado*, 1903) to social criticism (*Gente conocida*, 1896) and plays for children (*El príncipe que todo lo aprendió en los libros*, 1909). His masterpiece is *Los intereses creados* (1907), done into English as *The Bonds of Interest*, a cynical fantasy based on the *commedia dell'arte* convention. In this excellent and highly theatrical play, Benavente exploits to the full the theme of self-interest, and shows how human beings can exploit for their own ends, through self-deception, their so-called virtues as well as their obvious vices. Of his other plays, the most important are *Señora ama* (1908)—a play which deals with peasant life—*El marido de la Téllez* (1897), *La malquerida* (1913), *Los malhechores del bien* (1905), and *Más fuerte que el amor* (1906)—penetrating studies of contemporary society, exposing its follies and vices with smiling irony. J. E. Varey

BENCHLEY, Robert Charles (1889–1945), American man of letters, a fine humorist turned dramatic critic. Though he wrote in a light vein, his judgement of actors and plays was very sound, and he was a discerning reporter. Born in Worcester, Massachusetts, he graduated from Harvard in 1912. He was editor of *The New York Tribune Sunday Magazine* in 1916 and managing editor of *Vanity Fair* in 1919. In 1920 he became dramatic critic of *Life*, and his witty work at once attracted wide attention, boosting the magazine's circulation considerably. In 1929 he joined *The New Yorker* as dramatic critic, but retired in 1939 to devote his time to motion-picture acting. Before this he had appeared on the stage as an actor in *The Music Box Revue of 1924*. Unfortunately, there is no collected volume of his criticisms, but many of them may be found scattered through his books: *After 1903—What?*, *My Ten Years in a Quandary*, *The Early Worm*, and *Inside Benchley*. Thomas Quinn Curtiss

BENDINELLI, Giacinto (?–1668), an actor of the *commedia dell'arte*, who played the part of a young lover under the name of Valerio. He is first noted in the Modena troupe in 1651, and went to Paris in 1660, where he married a French actress, Jeanne-Marie Poulain, retiring a few years later.

BENEFIT, a performance of which the financial proceeds, after deduction of expenses, were given to one—or at the most two—members of the company. In the days of the sharing system and the stock company an actor might rely almost entirely on his benefit night to provide him with ready money, his weekly 'share' hardly paying current expenses. Doran, in *Their Majesties' Servants*, says that the first actor's, as distinct from author's (see ROYALTY), benefit was given for Mrs. Barry on the order of King James, and that 'what was commenced as a compliment soon passed into a custom'. In France the first benefit is believed to have been given in 1735 for Mlle Gaussin after she had lost all she possessed in a fire. It was a vicious system, which exposed the actor to petty humiliations and kept him in a constant condition of financial uncertainty. It lingered on in the provinces long after it had been abandoned in London, though Macready had a London benefit as late as 1848. There is an interesting account of the benefit system in Dickens's *Nicholas Nickleby*, and its abuse in the early American theatre can be studied in Odell's *Annals of the New York Stage*. It was abolished at Wallack's in 1867–8, salaries being raised instead. A slightly more dignified method of making money was the Bespeak Performance, whereby a wealthy patron would take up most of the tickets and sell or give them to his friends, choosing his own play from the company's repertory. Exceptional benefit nights might be given for the family of an actor or actress who had recently died, or for one in retirement who had fallen on bad times; but in general the proceeds of a benefit night went to an acting member of the company, who might choose the play in which he wished to appear, and often took the opportunity of introducing one of his own (see also PROVINCIAL THEATRES, 1 *d*).

BENELLI, SEM (1875–1949), Italian dramatist, considered in some ways a successor to D'Annunzio, with less poetry, perhaps, but more strength and subtlety. Among his plays, which were first brought into prominence by the Compagnia Stabile Argentina, founded in 1906, the most successful was *La cena delle beffe* (1909), a Renaissance melodrama of jealousy and fratricide founded on a short story by Anton Francesco Grazzini which, as *The Jest*, was played in New York in 1919 by John Barrymore and his brother Lionel. It was in blank verse, as were *La maschera di Bruto* (1908), based on the life of Lorenzino, who in 1537 murdered his cousin Alessandro de' Medici, and *L'Amore dei tre re* (1910). Benelli's other, more serious works included the modern prose comedy, *Tignola* (1908).

BENFIELD, ROBERT (?–1649), English actor, who joined the famous King's Men in about 1615. He replaced Ostler, in whose part of Antonio in *The Duchess of Malfi* he appeared in the 1619 revival. Before that he had been with two or three other companies, and was probably not a young man when he joined the King's, since he regularly took such elderly and dignified parts as kings, counsellors, and noble old men. His name appears in the list of actors in Shakespeare's plays, and in those of Beaumont and Fletcher. He also played the part of Junius Rusticus in *The Roman Actor* (1626) and of Ladislaus, King of Hungary, in *The Picture* (1629), both by Massinger. Benfield was not an original shareholder in the Globe or the Blackfriars, but he later acquired some interest in both.

BENGER, SIR THOMAS, see MASTER OF THE REVELS.

BENINI, FERRUCCIO (1854–1925), Italian dramatist and actor, author of a number of plays in the Venetian dialect, acted by his own company. He himself was a comedian of repute, with an ugly, mobile face and expressive gesture, one of his best parts being the untruthful, but fascinating, hero of Goldoni's *Il Bugiardo*. His repertory extended over the comedies of Goldoni and Gallina and a few modern pieces, including his own, written specially for him.

BENNETT, (ENOCH) ARNOLD (1867–1931), English novelist and dramatist, whose reputation rests more upon his novels than upon his plays, although he enjoyed considerable success in the theatre. His plots were ingeniously constructed, and his character-drawing had vitality and was mellowed by a homely humour. *The Great Adventure* (1913) had much success and owed a great deal to the fine acting of Henry Ainley and Wish Wynne. *Milestones* (written in collaboration with Edward Knoblock) was produced at the Royalty Theatre in 1912 and ran for 607 performances. It was revived at the same theatre in 1920, and at the Yvonne Arnaud Theatre, Guildford, in 1965. Bennett's other plays include: *Cupid and Commonsense* (1908), *What the Public Wants* (1909), *The Honeymoon* (1911), *Rivals for Rosamund* (1914), *The Title* (1918), *Judith* and *Sacred and Profane Love* (both 1919), *The Love Match* and *Body and Soul* (both 1922), and *London Life* (1924), written with Edward Knoblock. T. C. KEMP†

BENOIS, ALEXANDRE (1870–1960), theatre artist, born in St. Petersburg of a family with long associations with the theatre. His great-grandfather was director of the Fenice Theatre in Venice, and his grandfather architect of the Bolshoi Theatre, Moscow (see Nos. 34, 54). Benois was the great-uncle of the English dramatist, Peter Ustinov. He began his career with designs for the ballet in St. Petersburg in about 1901, where with Diaghilev and Léon Bakst he founded a society of painters and musicians, 'The World of Art', from which the Diaghilev Ballet finally developed. It was for this company that Benois's finest work was done, including the designs for 'Petrushka',

'Les Sylphides', 'Giselle', and many other ballets. In 1957, at the age of 87, he did a superb set of designs, both costume and scenery, for a revival, in London and Milan, of 'The Nutcracker'. His work had a great influence in the theatre, and he helped immeasurably to raise the prestige of the scene-designer. He was also the author of two admirable books of autobiography.

BENSERADE, Isaac de (1613–91), French poet and dramatist, related to Cardinal Richelieu, who gave him a pension. He came of a good Norman family, and was intended for the Church. But a passion for the wife of the actor Bellerose, contracted while he was studying theology in Paris, turned his thoughts to the theatre, and in 1635 he produced his first play, a comedy of little account, followed in the next year by a tragedy, *Cléopâtre*, the best of his not very considerable output. On the death of Richelieu he gave up writing plays, and devoted himself to the composition of libretti for ballets, then much in favour at Court. He excelled at this, and collaborated with Molière and Lully in *Les Fêtes de l'Amour et de Bacchus*.

BENSLEY, Robert (1742–1817), English actor, who went on the stage after seeing service in the Marines. After some years in the provinces he appeared at Drury Lane in 1765, and was seen there and at Covent Garden, retiring in 1796. He played few new parts, since little of any value was being written at the time, and his best work was done in such characters as Malvolio, Pierre in *Venice Preserved*, and Evander in *The Grecian Daughter*, which he played, just before his retirement, to the Euphrasia of Mrs. Siddons. A man of unblemished character and a sound actor, he was often severely criticized, and seems to have had to overcome several physical disabilities. Lamb, however, speaks feelingly of him. He died at Stanmore, where a tablet to his memory can be seen in the church.

BENSON, Sir Frank Robert (1858–1939), English actor-manager, best remembered for the Shakespearian company which he founded. With this he toured the provinces, keeping the plays of Shakespeare always before the public, and at the same time providing a fine training for countless young actors and actresses, all of whom in later years were proud of being Old Bensonians. A man of breeding and culture, Benson, who was the son of a wealthy barrister, was educated at Winchester and Oxford, where he was a prominent member of the O.U.D.S. Among the parts he played there was Clytemnestra in his own production of the *Agamemnon* of Aeschylus in the original. He made his first appearance on the professional stage in 1882, at the Lyceum under Irving, as Paris, and in the following year took his own company on tour, producing in due course all Shakespeare's plays with the exception of *Titus Andronicus* and *Troilus and Cressida*. The first of his numerous London seasons took place in 1889–90, at the Globe, and in 1916, on the occasion of the Shakespeare Tercentenary celebrations at the Theatre Royal, Drury Lane, he was knighted by King George V for his services to his profession. There was nearly a disaster on that occasion because, when the King sent for Benson to come to the Royal Box for his accolade (he was the only actor ever to be knighted in a theatre), there was no suitable sword available, and one had to be borrowed from a military outfitters' shop near by. In 1933 Sir Frank was granted a Civil List pension in recognition of his work for the drama. In addition he was a Governor of the Shakespeare Memorial Theatre, a trustee of the Shakespeare Birthplace, and a freeman of Stratford-upon-Avon. His success as a manager and trainer of young actors somewhat obscured his personal performances, yet in certain parts he was more than capable. He had a noble appearance, with handsome aquiline features, and had about him much of an 'antique Roman'. He married in 1886 a member of his company, Constance Featherstonhaugh (1860–1946), who continued to play leading parts with him for many years. In 1930 he published his reminiscences, and he was also the author of a handbook on acting. W. MACQUEEN-POPE†

BENZON, Otto (1856–1927), Danish dramatist, with Edvard Brandes one of the earliest exponents of modern social drama in that country (see SCANDINAVIA, 1).

BEOLCO, Angelo (*fl.* 1520–42), one of the earliest Italian actors and dramatists connected with the origins of the *commedia dell'arte*. He was born in about 1501–2, and, though in all probability never a professional actor, is found acting in 1520 at Venice. Most of his activities occurred there in carnival season, under the name of Ruzzante, 'the gossip', a shrewd peasant who indulges in long and amusing soliloquies. His plays were written in the dialect of Padua; they have been edited by Lovarini, and translated into French by Ruzzante's biographer, A. Mortier (pub. 1925–6). Riccoboni, who probably knew very little of Beolco's work, attributed to him the invention of the *commedia dell'arte*, but modern scholarship discounts this, though rating highly his own plays, which are fully written out and not scenarios for improvisation (see ITALY, 2).

BÉRAIN. (1) Jean (1637–1711), French theatrical designer, who replaced Vigarani at the Salle des Machines and as scenic designer to the Paris Opéra. In 1674 he succeeded Gissey as designer to the King, and the costumes (see No. 146) and decorations which he prepared for Court spectacles had a great influence on the ornamentation of rooms and furniture (see COSTUME, 5). His son (2) Jean (1678–1726) succeeded him in his official functions, but though industrious and inventive, lacked his skill.

BÉRARD, Christian (1902–49), French artist and theatre designer whose work had a great influence. He began his career in 1929 with designs for Diaghilev, which were not used because of the latter's death, but he was later associated with most of the famous choreographers of his time—Lifar, Fokine, Massine, Lichine, and Roland Petit among them. Apart from ballet, he had already attracted notice by his set for Cocteau's *La Voix humaine* (1930) when in 1934 he began his fruitful collaboration with Jouvet, starting with Cocteau's *Machine infernale*, and continuing through such important productions as *La Folle Journée* (1941), *La Folle de Chaillot* (1945) (see No. 104), *Les Bonnes* and *Don Juan* (both 1947). Bérard also designed a number of productions for other theatres, including the Comédie-Française and, for the Renaud–Barrault company, *Amphitryon* (1946) and *Les Fourberies de Scapin* (1949). He died while supervising the lighting of this last play on the night before its production. He also designed the costumes for *L'Aigle à deux têtes* (1946). Jouvet said of his work that it was characterized by a wonderful feeling for the visual aspects of the theatre. He had great skill in the use of colour, was an innovator in many directions, and was always careful in his designs to serve the text to the best of his considerable ability.

BERGELSON, David (1884–1952), Russian-Jewish writer of plays on contemporary themes, produced at the Moscow State Jewish Theatre (see JEWISH DRAMA, 6).

BERGERAC, Savinien de Cyrano de (1619–55), French author, who was in the Compagnie des Gardes under M. de Carbon de Casteljaloux. He was a great duellist, ready to run through at a moment's notice anyone who dared to remark on his abnormally large nose. After being twice badly wounded in the wars, he left the army and settled in Paris, intending to cultivate his undoubted gifts for literature and science. He followed the lectures of Gassendi and wrote on scientific subjects. But his friendship with Molière and Scarron turned his thoughts to the stage, and he produced a tragedy, *La Mort d'Agrippine* (1653), which was not a success. He was also the author of a comedy, *Le Pédant joué*, written between 1645 and 1649, which does not seem to have been performed. There is no contemporary reference to it, though it is often spoken of by later critics as a great success. It was, however, given in an expurgated version in America in 1899, and deserves to be remembered, since Molière took from it a scene for his *Fourberies de Scapin*, and it is thought that Cyrano's Gareau, the dialect-speaking peasant, was the model for several of Molière's Lubins and Pierrots. Scarron may also have been indebted to Cyrano's play for some of his *Dom Japhet*. Cyrano, who thought Molière the greatest actor and dramatist of France, agreed with him in his dislike of the actor Montfleury, then the star of the rival theatre, the Hôtel de Bourgogne, and once forbade him to appear on the stage for a month. When Montfleury disobeyed, Cyrano went to the theatre and enforced obedience. He was killed by a wooden beam which fell on his head. Both these incidents are made use of by Edmond Rostand in his play, *Cyrano de Bergerac*, in which the elder Coquelin made a great success as Cyrano.

BERGMAN, Hjalmar (1883–1931), Swedish dramatist and novelist, and one of the most influential writers in the Swedish theatre from the death of Strindberg to his own death in 1931. His early work, like that of his younger contemporary Pär Lagerkvist, was strongly influenced by Strindberg, though in Bergman's case the influence of Maeterlinck and Ibsen must also be allowed for. The experiments in dramatic and theatrical technique, which characterize his work throughout, were also of great value as a stimulus to the renaissance of the Swedish theatre. Although he began his career as a playwright as early as 1905, he first became widely known by the 'Marionette Plays' of 1917, *Dödens Arlekin* and the exquisite psychological tragedy *Herr Sleeman kommer*, and their immediate successors, *Ett Experiment* (1918) and the three published in 1923, *Vävaren i Bagdad, Spelhuset*, and *Porten*. His most successful later plays were *Swedenhielms* (1925), done at the Birmingham Rep. in 1960 as *The Family First*, and *Patrasket* (1928), and in these and his final works for the stage, the dialogue, mood, and structure of comedy have replaced the tragic mood of his earlier work.

BERGMAN, Ingmar (1919–), Swedish theatre director who after a long and successful career in films was from 1963–66 director of the Royal Dramatic Theatre, Stockholm. He introduced a number of reforms, including increases in salary which attracted to the theatre some of the country's finest actors. His plans included the redecoration and refurbishing of the theatre—which already had the most up-to-date lighting control system based on a Swedish adaptation of an I.B.M. punched-card computer—while the resident company went on tour, and the encouragement of young spectators and new playwrights. Classical plays also figure largely in the repertory, among them Molière's *Don Juan* and Ibsen's *Hedda Gabler*; Bergman's production of the latter was remarkable also for the acting of Gertrud Fridh as Hedda. He was succeeded as director by Erland Josephson.

BERGOPZOOMER, Johann Baptist (1742–1804), an Austrian actor who made his début in his native town of Vienna in 1764, where he played in improvised comedy and in the old popular farces. He went to Germany with the company of Joseph von Kürz, and was with him on the arrival of the great actor Schröder, then a youngster, who played the valet to his Don Juan. The two men, who were much of an age and temperamentally suited, became fast friends, and when Schröder in after years went to Vienna he was delighted to find Bergopzoomer installed as one of the chief tragedians of the Burgtheater there. Bergopzoomer was an old-fashioned, ranting actor, but was highly thought of in his day.

BERGSTRØM, HJALMAR (1868–1914), Danish dramatist, one of the best-known of his period outside his own country. In his plays he deals, under the influence of Ibsen, with such social problems as feminine emancipation, as in *Karen Bornemann* (1907), for example, and the struggle between the classes, as in *Lynggaard & Co.* (1905).

BERINGER. (1) ESMÉ (1875–1972) and (2) VERA (1879–1964), English actresses, daughters of the composer and pianist Oscar Beringer and his wife Aimée, well known as a novelist and playwright. She was the author of *Tares* (1888), in which Vera made her first appearance shortly before her ninth birthday. Later in the same year she created the part of Little Lord Fauntleroy in Mrs. Burnett's dramatization of her book, and in 1890 was seen in the dual title roles of *The Prince and the Pauper*. In 1896 she played Juliet to the Romeo of her elder sister, who had been with her in *Little Lord Fauntleroy* and *The Prince and the Pauper*, and had then embarked on a separate and equally distinguished career. Vera, whose career was broken by intermittent absences from the stage, was last seen as the Queen in *Hamlet* at the Arts Theatre in 1938. She was author, part-author or adapter of a number of plays. Among the last were *The Blue Stockings* (1915), based on *Les Précieuses ridicules*, and *Alice and Thomas and Jane* (1932), a play for children based on Enid Bagnold's book. In both of these she herself appeared. She was for many years Professor of Elocution at the Royal Academy of Music and continued to examine for the Associated Board of the Royal Schools of Music until she was over 80. During the Second World War she and her sister toured the west of England in a series of dramatic recitals. Esmé, after her appearance as Romeo, continued a career which ran parallel to, and sometimes overlapped, Vera's, as when she appeared in several of the latter's plays. She was an excellent Shakespearian actress, and at the age of 62 played Hamlet. Among her later successes was Gran in *Whiteoaks* (1937). She made her last appearance at the Royal Court, Liverpool, as old Sarah Johnson in *Mountain Fire* (1954).

BERLIN. Up to the late eighteenth century there was no very strong theatre tradition in Berlin, but in 1786 the Komödienhaus on the Gendarmenmarkt, which had previously housed a French company, was taken over by Döbbelin. Three years later Fleck, the great Schiller actor, assumed active control, though Döbbelin remained attached to the theatre till his death in 1793, and in 1796 Iffland was summoned from Mannheim to run what was to prove the first successful German National Theatre. He brought with him the naturalistic style of acting which he had learned in Mannheim, and soon reformed the organization and repertory, producing plays by Schiller, Goethe, Shakespeare, and Kotzebue as well as his own works. By the time he died in 1814, the Berlin theatre equalled those of Hamburg and Vienna. He was succeeded by Brühl, who brought with him from Weimar a number of actors, including Ludwig Devrient. The latter soon modified the aristocratic declamatory style typical of Berlin acting at this time, and by his efforts, added to those of Brühl, he made the theatre notable for its productions of the great classic dramatists, Goethe, Shakespeare, and Calderón. He died in 1832—Brühl had retired in 1828—and the theatre, which had been destroyed by fire in 1817 and rebuilt in a neo-classical style, entered on a period of decadence and triviality.

Between the years 1850 and 1890 several new theatres were opened in Berlin. The most important was the Deutsches Theater, founded by a group of actors under Adolf L'Arronge, which established itself in the Friedrich-Wilhelmsstädtisches Theater (built in 1850). Playing a traditional repertory, the new group set out to emphasize the psychological truth of the play, revealing new possibilities of experience, and bringing back some of the poetry of an earlier day. In 1889 the Freie Bühne, founded by Otto Brahm, opened with Ibsen's *Ghosts* and followed this shortly afterwards with Hauptmann's first, crudely naturalistic, play, *Vor Sonnenaufgang*. After L'Arronge's retirement in 1894 Brahm was appointed director of the Deutsches Theater, which then became the platform of realistic drama.

In 1901 Reinhardt, who as a young actor had appeared at the Deutsches Theater and had since become known as a producer, founded the famous 'Schall und Rauch' in the Künstlerhaus, destined to become later the Little Theatre on Unter den Linden. Here, in 1905, he produced *A Midsummer Night's Dream* which became famous for its fascinating blend of realism and fantasy. In 1907 he took control of the Deutsches Theater and inaugurated a series of productions which made Berlin an outstanding theatrical centre in Europe (see No. 78). He staged *Oedipus Rex* in the Zirkus Schumann in 1910, rediscovering in a circular auditorium with no proscenium arch that intimate fusion of actor and spectator which had been a feature of classical Greek drama. Much of Reinhardt's work was done in Berlin. From 1915–18 he was director of the Volksbühne, and in 1919 he produced the *Oresteia* of Aeschylus in his newly-built Grosses Schauspielhaus, which had an open stage and every possible contemporary mechanical device (see No. 39).

Between the two world wars Erwin Piscator, producer of the theatre of the 'proletariat marching towards the revolution' was in Berlin as director of the Zentral-Theater (1923–4), the Volksbühne (1924–7), and finally of his own Piscator-Theater (1927–9), where he employed elements from other performing arts such as the cinema and the circus. After he and Reinhardt had left Germany, the Berlin theatre sank to a low level artistically, but in the years after the Second World War it rose again. In 1951, the Schiller-Theater (whose company was seen in London in 1964) was rebuilt and housed a number of excellent productions. A strong impetus to the theatrical life of Berlin was imparted by the return from exile in 1949 of Bertolt Brecht, who installed his own company, the Berliner Ensemble, at the Theater am Schiffbauerdamm, where he remained until his death, the company then being controlled by his widow and leading lady, Helene Weigel. DOROTHY MOORE

BERNARD, JOHN (1756–1828), actor and theatre manager in England and the United States. His memoirs, *Retrospections of America*, edited in 1886 by Laurence Hutton and Brander Matthews, are an important source of information on the early American theatre.

BERNARD. (1) TRISTAN (1866–1947), French dramatist, author of innumerable light farces, satires, comedies, and melodramas, of which the first was produced in 1897. Several of them have been translated into English, and *Triplepatte* (1905), adapted by Clyde Fitch as *Toddles*, was popular both in London and New York, where it was played by John Barrymore. These plays have little literary value, but are deftly constructed and amusing, and mainly serve to show man in his less heroic moments, entangled in petty intrigues from which the author extricates him with superb craftsmanship and no little ingenuity. If any moral can be drawn from this thistledown work, it is that success or failure in life depend more upon a man's character than upon his circumstances. Bernard's son, (2) JEAN-JACQUES (1888–), is also a dramatist, but in a very different style. His work, which deals with the tragedies of unrequited or unacknowledged love, derives from the *école intimiste* founded by Maeterlinck, and though contemporary in form and matter, is essentially lyric in tone. A number of his plays have been seen in translation in London and New York, among them *Le Feu qui reprend mal* (1921) as *The Sulky Fire*, *Martine* (1922), the story of the wooing and desertion of a country girl by an educated man, *L'Invitation au voyage* (1924), which deals with a woman's self-deception in love, and *L'Âme en peine* (1926), done in London as *The Unquiet Spirit.*

BERNHARDT [BERNARD], SARAH HENRIETTE ROSINE (1845–1923), French actress, and one of the best known, not only in Europe but in America, both North and South, in Australia, and in Egypt, where she frequently appeared on tour. Numerous legends about her eccentricities were in circulation, some provoked by her undoubted unconventionality, others apocryphal. She was probably one of the finest actresses the world has ever seen, and had a voice which, though likened to a 'golden bell', or the 'silver sound of running water', can never be adequately described to those who have not heard it. It constituted one of her main charms, added to a slim, romantic figure, dark eyes, and a consummate mastery of her art. She began her training for the stage at the age of 13, and in 1862 made her first appearance at the Comédie-Française, where she was destined to make many a brief and stormy appearance, her free spirit not accommodating itself easily to the traditions of that venerable establishment. She left it for good in 1880, and the rest of her career was passed in other theatres. After an unsuccessful attempt to sing in burlesque, she first attracted attention by her performance in Coppée's *Le Passant*, given at the Odéon in 1869. Her career was interrupted by the Franco-Prussian war, but in 1872 she returned to the Comédie-Française and played Cordelia in a French version of *King Lear*, and the queen in *Ruy Blas*. This double triumph brought her to the head of her profession, and she consolidated her position by outstanding performances as Phèdre, and as Doña Sol in *Hernani*, where for Hugo's sombre *femme fatale* she substituted an adorable creature, all tenderness and charm. She then set out on her travels, making her first appearance in London in 1879 in *Phèdre*, and in New York in 1880 in *Adrienne Lecouvreur*, scoring an immediate triumph in both capitals. She returned to them many times in later years, and always with success, her last appearance in London being in *Daniel*, not long before her death. In Paris she managed several theatres, including the Ambigu and the Porte-Saint-Martin, before opening the old Théâtre des Nations as the Théâtre Sarah Bernhardt (see No. 170). There she revived a number of her former successes and also appeared in some outstanding new plays. Among the plays in which she scored her greatest successes, apart from *Phèdre*, were *La Dame aux camélias*, Sardou's *Fédora*, *Théodora*, and *La Tosca*, the plays of Edmond Rostand, particularly *L'Aiglon*, with which her name is always associated, and *Hamlet*. She was an accomplished painter and sculptress, and wrote poetry and plays, appearing in the latter herself. Among them were *L'Aveu* (1898), *Un Cœur d'homme* (1909), and the unpublished *Dans les nuages*, the manuscript of which is in Harvard College library. A volume of reminiscences was published in English in 1907.

BERNINI, GIOVANNI LORENZO (1598–1680), see MACHINERY and SCENERY, 3.

BERNSTEIN, ALINE (1882–1955), American scenic designer, and founder, with Irene Lewisohn, of the Museum of Costume Art in New York. Opened in 1937, this houses actual costumes, as well as a library of books and other documents devoted to the history of costume, which are available for study by research workers. Aline Bernstein's first work for the theatre was done in connexion with the Neighborhood Playhouse, and she was then responsible for a number of important productions (see also UNITED STATES OF AMERICA, 11, and No. 82).

BERNSTEIN, HENRY (1876–1953), French dramatist, whose early plays were written under the influence of the Théâtre-Libre. His own, more distinctive, manner emerged in *La Rafale* (1906) and *Le Voleur* (1907) and other plays of action and situation, which had slight literary importance. They were ably interpreted, however, by Lucien Guitry, and were also successful on Broadway in translation. Shortly before the First World War Bernstein gave signs of greater seriousness of purpose than had hitherto been seen in him, with *Samson* (1910), *L'Assaut* (1912), and *Le Secret* (1913), a process which continued with *Judith* (1922), *Galerie des glaces* (1925), and *Le Venin* (1927). With these, and in his later plays, he endeavoured to emulate, with some success at the time, the playwrights of the younger generation who were preoccupied with 'le théâtre de l'inquiétude'; but it is in his earlier, and more genuine, plays that his true nature is revealed.

BERSENEV, Ivan Nikolayevich [really Pavlishchev] (1889–1951), Soviet actor and producer, born in Moscow. While studying law at Kiev University he became an enthusiastic amateur actor, and in 1907 appeared at the Solovtsev Theatre, Kiev, working under Mardzhanishvili. Two years later he deserted law for the stage, and appeared in many Ukrainian towns, where his undoubted gifts, allied to a handsome appearance and a beautiful voice, soon made him popular. From 1928 to 1938 he was both actor and director at the Moscow Art Theatre, leaving there to become artistic director and leading man of the Lenkom Theatre. Here he trained a talented group of actors, and created, in collaboration with their authors, a number of fine plays, among them *A Chap From Our Town* (1941), *The Youth of the Fathers* (1943), by Gorbatov, and *So It Will Be* (1944), by Simonov. His productions were notable for their precision and clarity of ideas, their profound intellectuality, and a lively feeling for contemporary life which immediately established a *rapport* with his audiences. He also taught at the Lunacharsky State Institute of Dramatic Art in Moscow. BEATRICE KING†

BERTINAZZI, Carlo (1710–83), the last of the great Arlequins of the Comédie-Italienne, where he was known as Carlin, and one of the last Italians to join the company (1741), which later became composed almost entirely of French actors. Bertinazzi was much admired by Garrick, who said that his back wore the expression his face would have shown had not the mask covered it.

BESKOW, Bernhard von (1796–1868), Swedish dramatist and dramatic critic (see SCANDINAVIA, 3 *a*).

BESPEAK PERFORMANCE, see BENEFIT.

BESSENYEI, György (1747–1811), Hungarian writer, author of *Agis Tragédiája* (pub. 1772), a play which marks the beginning of modern Hungarian literature.

BETTERTON. (1) Thomas (?1635–1710), English actor, and the greatest figure of the Restoration stage. He was apprenticed young to a bookseller, John Rhodes, who had a great love for the theatre and reopened the Cockpit as soon as the Restoration was an accomplished fact. When Killigrew and Davenant obtained patents from the king, they took over all the existing companies of actors. Rhodes's men, including the young Betterton, fell to the share of Davenant, and went with him to the theatre in Lincoln's Inn Fields. In 1671, after Davenant's death, the company, of which Betterton was now the head, moved to a new theatre in Dorset Garden, and remained there until the union of the two companies at the Theatre Royal in 1682. In 1695 Betterton broke with the management of the Theatre Royal, and reopened the theatre in Lincoln's Inn Fields most successfully with the first performance of Congreve's *Love for Love*, moving ten years later to Vanbrugh's new theatre in the Haymarket.

Cibber had a high opinion of Betterton and considered him 'without competitors'. He was admirable in both comedy and tragedy, his Hamlet and Sir Toby Belch being equally admired. Though not perhaps so well suited to the requirements of Restoration comedy, he excelled in the high-flown rhetoric of the heroic drama of the day, and created many famous parts by well-known dramatists, who, for their part, were always ready to profit by his advice. The great Dryden himself cut twelve hundred lines of his *Don Sebastian* in rehearsal, 'judiciously lopt by Mr. Betterton'. He adapted a number of plays, including some of Shakespeare's, to suit the taste of the time, and turned Fletcher's *The Prophetess* into an opera with music by Purcell (1690). This was most successful, and ended with an elaborate masque whose stage directions show to what a pitch stage mechanism had been brought by this time, influenced no doubt by the machinery of opera, and Betterton's own study in Paris of French theatrical effects.

Betterton married one of the first English actresses, (2) Mary Sanderson (?–1712), whom Pepys always refers to as Ianthe, from her excellent playing of that part in Davenant's *Siege of Rhodes*. She seems to have been at her best in Shakespearian roles, and as Lady Macbeth Cibber thought her superior to her successor, Mrs. Barry. Both she and her husband were much esteemed by their contemporaries, both as actors and as private individuals, and were noted for their kindness to young and aspiring players, particularly Anne Bracegirdle. Mrs. Betterton was buried in Westminster Abbey on 13 Apr. 1712.

BETTI, Ugo (1892–1953), Italian playwright. He was first a poet, and his work is marked by a lyrical quality which enhances its intensity of meaning and the delicacy of its statement. Most of his principal characters are concerned in a struggle against accepting the will of God: latter-day Sauls, they run from God, only to find Him at the end of the journey. Betti, a High Court judge in the last years of his life, was haunted by the inescapable tragedy implicit within the fallibility of human justice. Only one justice is true and exact, he says, God's charity. In certain aspects, Betti may be grouped with the unanimists (typical of this range of his work is *Un albergo sul porto*, 1933). In his treatment of the reality/illusion conflict he reveals the influence of Pirandello, as he does in his preoccupation with man's regret for the loss of his earthly paradise. Unmistakably personal, however, are his vision of a fully-explored and deeply-experienced sexuality as sacramental, as part of spirituality, his perception of the interweaving of good and evil, and his paradox of the beloved sinner—in which category Betti's finest example (and one of his best-drawn characters) is probably Cust in *Corruzione al Palazzo di Giustizia* (1949). Betti is not afraid of symbol and allegory, and in his mature work handles them with power, freedom, and unobtrusiveness. His strength lies in tragedy and drama, though his lighter pieces, *Una bella domenica di settembre* (1937) and *Il paese delle vacanze* (1942), are not negligible. His more important works, however, are *Frana allo scalo Nord* (1936), *Ispezione* (1947), *Lotta fino all'alba* (1949), *La regina e gli insorti* (1951), and two plays, *L'aiuola bruciata* and *La fuggitiva*, both given posthumously in 1953. Two of Betti's plays were seen in London in 1955 in English translations by Henry Reed—*L'aiuola bruciata*, as *The Burnt Flower Bed*, at the Arts Theatre in Sept. and *La regina e gli insorti*, as *The Queen and the Rebels*, at the Haymarket in Oct. *Ispezione*, as *Island Investigations*, was given an amateur production in 1956 by the University of Bristol Dramatic Society. In 1952 *Il Giocatore* (1951), as *The Gambler*, was produced in New York in an adaptation by Alfred Drake, who also played the leading role. FREDERICK MAY

BETTY, WILLIAM HENRY WEST (1791–1874), born in Ulster, a child prodigy, known as the Young Roscius, who for a season, from 1804 to 1805, took London by storm. He had already played with great success in Ireland and Scotland when he went to Covent Garden on 1 Dec. There, and at Drury Lane, he appeared in all the great tragic roles of Shakespeare and others, ousting even Mrs. Siddons and Kemble from public favour. The House of Commons adjourned on a motion of the younger Pitt to see him as Hamlet, and Northcote painted him as Norval in *Douglas*. After a brief and hectic success, however, opinion turned against him, and he was hissed off the stage when he attempted Richard III. He went to Cambridge in 1808, and three years later again attempted the stage, without success. He was ignored, his father squandered his money, and the rest of his long life—he was well over eighty when he died—was passed in complete obscurity.

BEVERLEY, WILLIAM ROXBY (*c.* 1814–89), English scene-painter, son and brother of actors, who painted his first scenery for the Theatre Royal, Manchester, then under the management of his father, William Roxby (1765–1842). He was for some time an actor on the Durham circuit, playing heavy comedy, but his chief interest lay in scenic design and in 1842 he was engaged by Knowles for the Theatre Royal, Manchester, painting for him a beautiful act drop which remained in use for twenty-five years. Some years later he did good work for the Vestris–Mathews management at the Lyceum, achieving his greatest success in *The Island of Jewels* (1849). He perfected the transformation scene in pantomime, and was engaged by the entertainer, Albert Smith, to paint the dioramic views for his 'Ascent of Mont Blanc'. Beverley's long and fruitful association with Drury Lane began in 1854 and lasted through successive managements until 1884. His best work was done in pantomime, but he worked intermittently for other theatres, and was responsible for several of the important Shakespearian revivals at the Princess's, including *King John*, *Henry IV, Part I*, and *Macbeth*, as well as for an elaborate production of *Comus*. He was a frequent exhibitor at the Royal Academy, mostly of seascapes. Next to Stanfield, Beverley may be accounted the most distinguished scene-painter of the nineteenth century in England, and much assisted the development of the art of scene-painting by his original methods and use of new inventions. A one-surface painter, he was all his life opposed to the innovation of built stuff. His last work was done in 1885 for the pantomime at Drury Lane.

BHARATA, BHĀṢA, BHAṬṬA NĀRĀYAṆA, BHAVABHŪTI, see INDIA, 1.

BIANCOLELLI, a family of actors of the *commedia dell'arte*. (1) ISABELLA FRANCHINI (*fl.* 1630–50), the daughter of an actor who played Pantalone, acted servant parts under the name of Columbina, and was a member of the troupe at Modena. She had previously married an actor named Biancolelli, who died in 1640 leaving her with a small boy. She married as her second husband Carlo Cantù, an actor who played as Buffetto. A certain Niccolò, who is said to have played the part of a young lover about 1650, may have been her brother-in-law. Her son (2) GIUSEPPE DOMENICO (*c.* 1637–88), who was also a playwright, became famous as Dominique, playing the role of Arlequin. From his youth he was accounted a good actor, and he became a particular favourite of Louis XIV when on Mazarin's invitation he joined the Italian troupe in Paris. It was under him that the Italians first began to play in French. He became a naturalized Frenchman, and in 1663 married (3) ORSOLA CORTESI (*c.* 1636–1718), an actress who was also in the Paris troupe, where she became leading lady under the name of Eularia on the death of Brigida Bianchi (see ROMAGNESI, 2). Soon after the death of her husband she retired, and later entered a convent, where she died. She had eight children, one of whom, the godson of Louis XIV, although not an actor, left a manuscript collection of *scenarii*. Two daughters and one other son are known. The eldest, (4) FRANCESCA MARIA APOLLINE (1664–1747), made her début in *Arlequino Proteo* in 1683. She acted in Paris until 1695, marrying a few years before her retirement an officer in the Guards, who died in 1706. Her younger sister (5) CATERINA (1665–1716) also made her début in *Arlequino Proteo*, as Columbina, the name under which her grandmother played. She married in 1685 an actor of the Comédie-Française, Pierre Lenoir de la Thorillière, and continued to act in Paris until her retirement in 1697. The youngest child of Dominique, (6) PIETRO FRANCESCO (1680–1734), played for a while in Paris, both as Arlequin and as Pierrot, but on the closing of the Théâtre-Italien in 1697 he went into the provinces. As Dominique le Jeune he was a member of the company which Riccoboni (Lelio) took back to Paris in 1716, and he remained with it till his death.

BIBBIENA, BERNARDO DOVIZI DA (1470–1520), an Italian cardinal, author in his youth of a comedy, the *Calandria*, freely adapted from the *Menaechmi* of Plautus. The twin brothers are replaced by twins of different sexes, and a sub-plot uses as a comic figure Boccaccio's Calandrino. In situation and language the play is more witty than decent. It was first performed at Urbino during the carnival of 1506. A year later it was given in Rome, and it made its appearance at most of the princely Courts of Italy, delighting its audiences, as is apparent from the contemporary descriptions of its productions which survive.

BIBIENA (BIBBIENA, DA BIBBIENA). A family of scenic artists and architects, originally of Florence, whose work, in pure baroque style, is found all over Europe, though Parma and Vienna probably saw their greatest achievements. The family name was Galli, and Bibiena (or Bibbiena) was added later, from the birthplace of the father of (1) FERDINANDO (1657–1743) and (2) FRANCESCO (1659–1739), who together founded the family fortunes and renown. Orphaned at an early age, they were trained first in the studio of a Bolognese painter, and later under Rivani, a stage engineer responsible for some of the machinery in Louis XIV's Court theatre at Versailles. While still a young man, Ferdinando was employed by the Dukes of Parma, for whom he worked in the beautiful Teatro Farnese built by Aleotti. Early in the eighteenth century he left Parma, at the command of the Emperor Charles VI, to go to Vienna, where, with the help of his brother and his sons, he was responsible for the decorations of the Court fêtes and theatrical performances. Of his sons (3) ALESSANDRO (1687–*c.* 1769) was an architect, but concerned himself less with theatrical work than his three brothers—(4) GIUSEPPE (1696–1757), designer of a fine opera-house in Bayreuth and the first to use transparent scenery lighted from behind (in 1723), (5) ANTONIO (1700–74), designer of the Teatro Communale in Bologna, which opened in 1763, and (6) GIOVANNI MARIA (*c.* 1704–69), who is believed to have built a theatre near Lisbon. Giuseppe's son (7) CARLO (1728–87), also a famous designer of stage settings, one of which is preserved in the old Royal Theatre at Drottningholm, was associated with his father in the decoration of the Bayreuth opera-house. The whole family worked so much in the same tradition, and so often in collaboration, that it is sometimes impossible to apportion their work individually. They introduced many modifications and reforms into scenic design and acoustics, working not only for their royal patrons, but for the powerful Jesuit colleges which included dramatic work in their educational programmes (see JESUIT DRAMA), for the Church, wherever the tradition of religious plays was continued, and for the rich municipalities of Italy. They made their home at Bologna, but were more often than not to be found in every corner of Europe, working on Court spectacles for royal weddings, accessions, and funerals, and in the public and private theatres of the time, where their new diagonal perspective, or *scena d'angolo* (see No. 64), which had taken the place of the central perspective beloved of the seventeenth century, opened up new vistas and made possible the elaborate architectural stage settings so characteristic of the family style.

BIBLE-HISTORIES, a name given by modern scholarship to the medieval plays based on Scripture and formerly known as Miracle or Mystery plays.

BICKERSTAFFE, ISAAC (1735–1812), English dramatist, considered in his day the equal of John Gay as a writer of lyric comedy. The first of these, *Thomas and Sally; or, the Sailor's Return*, described as a 'musical entertainment', was given at Covent Garden in 1760. It was followed by *Love in a Village* (1762), a ballad opera (based on *The Village Opera* (1728) of Charles Johnson) which has been described as a musical amalgamation of *The Gentleman Dancing Master* and *Le Jeu de l'amour et du hasard*. It has been frequently revived down to the present day. Another piece of the same nature, *The Maid of the Mill* (1765), based on the novel *Pamela*, also held the stage for many years, and must have been popular in the early nineteenth century, to judge from its frequent inclusion in the repertory of the Juvenile Drama. Among Bickerstaffe's later productions, many of them written in collaboration with Foote and Dibdin, the best was *Lionel and Clarissa* (1768), which again has often been revived. Four years after its production the author, who enjoyed the friendship of Dr. Johnson, Goldsmith, and Garrick, was suspected of some heinous offence, and fled to the Continent, where he led a long life of misery and exile, and died in poverty.

BIDERMANN, JAKOB (1578–1639), see AUSTRIA and JESUIT DRAMA.

BIEDERMANN, JOSEPH (1800–?), Austrian Jew, author of a number of plays in Yiddish, performed in Vienna by amateurs in about 1850 (see JEWISH DRAMA, 4).

BIJOU THEATRE. 1. LONDON. A small theatre of this name was attached to Her Majesty's (The Royal Italian Opera House) in the Haymarket. It was mostly used for concerts and light dramatic performances. Charles Mathews the younger appeared there in 1862 with his wife. It was also used by amateurs, and on one occasion Palgrave Simpson, the dramatist, staged *Macbeth* there with Clement Scott—afterwards the well-known dramatic critic—as Fleance. The theatre was burned down with the Opera House in 1867.

2. A small theatre in Bayswater, used occasionally for performances of a special nature and by amateurs, was also known as the Bijou. In 1905 Oscar Wilde's *Salome* had its first London production there. In 1925 Lena Ashwell took it over and renamed it the Century, producing plays and appearing in them herself. Among these were *A Mirror of Souls*, *The Ship*, *Crime and Punishment*, and *Dr. Jekyll and Mr. Hyde*, all of which she adapted from novels. W. MACQUEEN-POPE†

3. NEW YORK, a small playhouse devoted to operetta and light entertainment. Situated at 1239 Broadway, it opened with variety, as the Brighton, in 1878. It then became Wood's Broadway Theatre, and the Broadway Opera House. On 31 Mar. 1880 it was renamed the Bijou Opera House. Lilian Russell, coming from Tony Pastor's in 1882, appeared there in several musical plays, including *Patience*. The theatre was occasionally used for visiting companies and straight plays, until 7 July 1883, when it was pulled down and a larger one built, opening 1 Dec. 1883 with Offenbach. It was at this theatre that Julia Marlowe made her début as an adult actress. It continued in use, mainly as a home of musical and light entertainment, until 1911.

4. On 45th Street west of Broadway. This was opened by the Shuberts on 12 Apr. 1917. Its smallness and consequent heavy overhead expenses put it at a disadvantage, and in 1938 it was turned over to films, being only occasionally used after that for plays. It is, however, interesting to note that *Life With Father* ended its phenomenal run at the Bijou in 1947. Among the plays produced at this theatre during its twenty years of legitimate activity were *Sleeping Partners* (1918), *The Skin Game* (1920), *The Dover Road* (1921), *Uptown West* (1921), a problem drama of a Japanese-American marriage, and *What Every Woman Knows* (1926), with Helen Hayes. Later came Blanche Yurka in *The Lady from the Sea*, and *Springtime for Henry*, which was the Bijou's last successful production. It then became a cinema, except for 1957–8, when *The Potting Shed* and other plays were done there, and, as the Toho, specialized in Japanese films. GEORGE FREEDLEY†

BILL-BELOTSERKOVSKY, VLADIMIR NAUMOVICH (1885–1959), Soviet dramatist, whose early play, *Hurricane* (or *Storm*), written, as a Russian critic said, 'with his heart's blood', was produced in 1926 at the Mossoviet Theatre, then known as the Moscow Trades Unions' Theatre. This was a fine, stirring piece of propaganda about the struggles of a Revolutionary leader in a small village during the Civil War. Bill-Belotserkovsky's later plays were somewhat quieter, but *Life is Calling* (1934), published in 1938 in an English translation by Anthony Wixley, marked a step forward in the development of the Mossoviet Theatre, which had lost its early fervour and tended to lapse into dullness and stagnation. The plot of *Life is Calling* (or, as it is also called, *Life Goes Forward*) is somewhat conventional, on the 'eternal triangle' theme, but the tension is heightened by the conflict, not only between the characters' emotions, but between social duty and personal happiness. It is enlivened by the acid comments of the old grandfather, who, before his death at the end of the play, shows the younger generation that their trivial quarrels are as nothing beside the great tide of new life surging outside, which they must accept if they wish to survive. A later play, produced in 1936, treats of the same theme from a different angle, showing the adjustment of an old Russian intellectual to the new social order. Bill-Belotserkovsky's later years were unproductive, though he twice, in 1951 and 1953, produced new versions of *Hurricane*.

BILLY ROSE THEATRE, see NATIONAL THEATRE, 2.

BILTMORE THEATRE, NEW YORK, on 47th Street between Broadway and 8th Avenue. It was built by the Chanins as one of a chain of playhouses with which to challenge the Shubert brothers' supremacy in Broadway management, and opened on 7 Dec. 1925. It had an undistinguished career until 1929, when it found itself in trouble over Mae West's *Pleasure Man*, which was closed by the police after 3 performances. A further period of fluctuating fortunes was ended in 1936, when the Federal Theatre Project took over the theatre and presented there, with some success, their experimental Living Newspapers. A Yiddish version of *It Can't Happen Here* was the last production before the theatre was bought by Warner Brothers, to become the happy hunting ground of George Abbott. *Brother Rat* ran for 577 performances, and was followed by the equally successful *What a Life!* Among later successes at this theatre were *My Sister Eileen* and *Kiss and Tell*. It was then used for radio and television, but in 1961 reopened as a theatre with *Take Her, She's Mine*. *Barefoot in the Park* began its long run in 1963. GEORGE FREEDLEY†

BINGLEY, WARD (1757–1818), Dutch actor, born in Rotterdam of parents of English extraction. He married the sister of the great Dutch actress Johanna Cornelia Wattier-Ziesenis, who was often known as 'the Dutch Siddons'. He played opposite her many times, and among his outstanding parts were Alva,

Parma, and Nero—all tyrants cast in the heroic mould. He began his career on the Rotterdam stage, where he finally settled as director of the South Holland theatre group, but appeared also in Amsterdam and at The Hague, where he spent his last years. During the Napoleonic era he supported the House of Orange, and was exiled to England until 1813. Sometimes known as 'the Dutch Garrick', he acted also in French, and wrote and translated a number of plays.

BINYON, Laurence (1869–1946), English poet, whose verse-drama *Paris and Oenone* (1906) was produced by Gertrude Kingston. *Attila* (1907) was done at His Majesty's by Oscar Asche, while *Arthur*, written for Martin-Harvey, with music by Elgar, was given at the Old Vic in 1923. Of his other plays, *The Young King* and *Boadicea* were produced privately by John Masefield in his theatre on Boars Hill, Oxford, while the rest have been published but not produced.

BIO-MECHANICS, the name given to Meyerhold's system of production. Reducing the actor to the status of puppet, to be thrown into attitudes at the producer's whim, it calls for the complete elimination of personality, and the subjugation of mind and body to a series of acrobatic turns. It further demands the stripping of the stage to the bare bones, the elimination of 'detail' scenery, and the willing co-operation of the audience in building up the desired stage-picture by association. Meyerhold himself admitted that his system was in a large measure based on Pavlov's theory of association. It has also, in its insistence on conventional and stylized gesture, been compared to the *Kabuki* theatre of Japan. A mental rather than an emotional theatre, it served its purpose in the early days of the October Revolution in clearing away the inessentials of production which cluttered up the old theatres; but it was fated to be outstripped by the forces it had liberated, and finally became outmoded.

BIRD, Robert Montgomery (1806–54), American playwright, leader of the Philadelphia group of dramatists, and by profession a doctor. He had already written a number of unacted plays when in 1831 Edwin Forrest produced his romantic tragedy, *The Gladiator*, playing Spartacus, the hero. It was an immediate success, and Forrest selected it for his first appearance at Drury Lane in 1836, continuing to act in it until his retirement in 1872. It was also done by John McCullough, who made his last appearance in it in 1884, and it was seen on the stage as late as 1892. Bird wrote two more plays for Forrest, another romantic tragedy, *Oralloossa* (1832), and a domestic drama entitled *The Broker of Bogota* (1834), and revised for him Stone's *Metamora*. All these were popular and frequently revived, but owing to the chaotic state of the copyright laws at that time Bird made no money from their production, and Forrest would not allow them to be printed. Bird consequently withdrew from the theatre and sought a livelihood elsewhere, writing several successful novels, later dramatized by other hands, and engaging in journalism and politics. Quinn says of him: 'Had he lived in a time when the American playwright received fair treatment, it is not easy to put a limit to his possible achievements. For he had a rare sense of dramatic effect, a power to visualize historic scenes and characters, to seize the spirit of the past out of the mass of facts and, in a few brief lines, to fuse those facts into life.'

BIRD [Bourne]. (1) William (?–1624), English actor and an important member of the Admiral's Men, since he frequently figures in Henslowe's diary as their agent. Before joining them he may have been with the short-lived Pembroke's Men. He remained one of the leading figures of the Admiral's Men when they became the Palsgrave's Men, retiring a year or so before his death. His son (2) Theophilus (1608–64) may have appeared as a child with his father, but is first found playing female parts for Queen Henrietta's Men. In 1635 he was Massinissa in *Hannibal and Scipio*, and shortly afterwards he married Anne, the eldest daughter of Christopher Beeston. In 1637, when the theatres opened after the plague, he joined the King's Men at Blackfriars, remaining with them until the closing of the theatres in 1642. He still retained his interest in the theatre, however, since it was he, as brother-in-law of William Beeston, who negotiated the transfer of Salisbury Court to Beeston in 1647. Bird is named first in Downes's list of actors who appeared immediately on the opening of the theatres in 1660, and Pepys notes a rumour that he had broken his leg while fencing in *Aglaura* in 1662.

BIRMAN, Serafima Germanovna (1890–), one of the outstanding actresses of the Soviet stage, who has also a number of fine productions to her credit. She studied at the Adashev Drama School, and in 1918 joined the Moscow Art Theatre company. She became leading lady of the Lenkom Theatre in 1938, where she was responsible for the production of *The Living Corpse* and of a new translation of *Cyrano de Bergerac* with Bersenev as Cyrano. She also produced a number of new plays, including *Under the Chestnut Trees of Prague* (1946) and Simonov's *The Russian Question* (1947). In 1955 her playing of Kashperskaya in Shteyn's *Wheel of Fortune* earned her high praise. She has been guest producer at a number of theatres throughout the U.S.S.R. Her work is characterized by clarity, decision, and deep psychological insight.

BIRMINGHAM. Well known as the home of Barry Jackson's repertory theatre, Birmingham has a long theatre history, typical in its early days of many English provincial towns. Two theatrical booths existed before 1730, but the first theatre was built in Moor Street about 1740. Richard Yates brought a company from London there every season. A theatre in King

Street opened in 1751, another in New Street in 1774. This last was twice rebuilt after fires, in 1792 and 1820. The elder Macready became manager of it in 1795. In 1840 the manager was Mercer Simpson, whose son introduced touring companies into the theatre in 1849. The stock company lingered on, however, until 1878. The theatre closed in 1901, was rebuilt and reopened in 1904, but was finally demolished in 1957. Another theatre, the Prince of Wales's, was destroyed by enemy action during the Second World War.

The Birmingham Repertory, which in intention and in achievement is one of the most significant enterprises launched in the English theatre during the twentieth century, began with private theatricals at the home of Barry Jackson. From these emerged in 1907 the Pilgrim Players, who put on at local halls, up to 1913, twenty-eight productions, mainly of plays never seen in the commercial theatre. This early organization was entirely amateur, and owed its success to the enthusiasm of Barry Jackson and his associates. It soon became apparent that the conversion of Birmingham to the cause of intelligent drama would be a full-time job, demanding a permanent theatre and a professional company. Fortunately Barry Jackson was a wealthy man and, inspired by the founding of similar theatres in Manchester and Liverpool, he built and equipped a playhouse for the Birmingham Repertory company in which it made its first appearance on 15 Feb. 1913 in *Twelfth Night*. During the first ten years a wide variety of uncommercial plays was staged. Drinkwater's *Abraham Lincoln* made money; the first English performance of Shaw's *Back to Methuselah* was a landmark in theatre history. *Cymbeline* in modern dress, followed by similar productions of *Macbeth*, *Hamlet* (see No. 81), and *The Taming of the Shrew*, stressed the essential Shakespeare, who was in danger of being swamped by excess of scenery and stagecraft. These and other productions offered Birmingham a decade of comprehensive playgoing to which it was only partly responsive. Intensive support from the perceptive few was outbalanced by the indifference of the city as a whole. In 1924 Jackson threatened to close the theatre. The Birmingham Civic Society took action and guaranteed a sufficient body of season-ticket holders to keep the theatre open. The subsequent success of such plays as *The Farmer's Wife* and *The Barretts of Wimpole Street* induced Jackson to transfer the best of the Birmingham productions to London, and when he founded the Malvern Festival in 1929 it was the Birmingham company which provided the nucleus of the Malvern company until 1938. The Birmingham Rep. became known as a fine training-ground for young actors—among them Ralph Richardson, Laurence Olivier, Paul Scofield, and, more recently, Albert Finney—and the settings and costumes designed by Paul Shelving set new standards in English stage decoration (see No. 100). In 1935 Sir Barry (as he became in 1925) transferred the theatre to a Board of Trustees. He himself remained its director until his death in 1961. A year later Sir Robert Aitken, vice-chancellor of Birmingham University, became Chairman of the Board, thus implementing Sir Barry's wish that the university and the theatre should work closely together. Miss H. Nancy Burman (daughter of Mrs. Isabel Thornton, one of the theatre's most admired actresses), who joined the Birmingham Rep. in 1949 as assistant producer, coming from Stratford-upon-Avon, was appointed administrator. The theatre celebrated its jubilee in 1963.

BIRÓ, LAJOS (1880–1948), see HUNGARY.

BISHOP, GEORGE WALTER (1886–1965), English dramatic critic, who was theatre correspondent of the *Daily Telegraph* from 1932, and book editor from 1937, until his death. The theatre was first his hobby—he was for many years in the Inland Revenue Department —but in 1928 he was appointed editor of the stage newspaper, *The Era*, where he remained until he went to the *Daily Telegraph*. His enthusiasm for the theatre, his practical knowledge of it, and his retentive memory, made him an admirable correspondent, and his column was always informative and enjoyable to read. He was also an admirable organizer, and revived the tradition whereby the *Daily Telegraph* made itself responsible for special stage celebrations. These included Marie Tempest's jubilee (1935) and Irving's centenary (1938). Bishop was the author of *Barry Jackson and the London Stage* (1933) and of an autobiography, *My Betters* (1957).

BJERREGAARD, HENRIK (1792–1842), Norwegian dramatist (see SCANDINAVIA 2 *a*).

BJØRNSON. (1) BJØRNSTJERNE (1832–1910), Norwegian novelist, poet, and dramatist, was born in the bleak upland district of Kvikne and early went to live at Romsdal. The changes in the formative years of his life are thus the reverse of those in Ibsen's. His biographers have remarked upon the joy and delight with which Bjørnson, as a child, looked at the new and unexpected beauty of the world to which he found himself transferred, and something from the mood of that moment seems to have remained with him throughout his life; for Bjørnson, although his work reflected the same ideals of truth and freedom as did Ibsen's, differed widely from him as a man and as an artist, showing those very qualities of happiness and optimism, a certain sweetness and radiance of temperament, which Ibsen lacked, but lacking also Ibsen's profundity and power. His contribution to Norwegian drama is affected at every point by these factors. He was a fertile innovator, exploring territory such as the moral diseases of contemporary society before Ibsen himself actually did so. In all his work, however apparently unpropitious the theme, there is a frank and firm confidence in the love of God and the potential goodness of man, which is often explicit: 'Where good men walk, there are God's ways.' His criticism of the evil in society, though uncompromising, as befitted a Liberal leader, has that confidence in redemptive forces which in Ibsen's work is rare and seldom more than implicit. As a dramatic artist he shows the skill born of years of theatrical experience—he is a true man of the theatre—but his technique is swift and effective rather than architectural. Withal, to the foreigner, his plays seem more alien than do Ibsen's; they have in them, that is to say, more of the immediate and local and less of the ageless and universal.

His plays are too numerous to describe in detail, but they may be roughly grouped in three periods. In the earliest, to which belong also his novel *Synnøve Solbakken* and other tales of country life in Norway, besides his two years' experience (1857–9) as director of the Bergen theatre, comes the group which is mainly historical and patriotic: *Mellem Slagene* (1855); *Kong Sverre* (1861); *Sigurd Slembe* (1862); and *Maria Stuart i Skotland* (1864). From 1865 to 1867 he was a director of the Christiania Theatre, edited a newspaper, and became a leader of the Liberal party. He was away from Norway for a few years, and during and after this time wrote his second group of plays, the realistic social dramas which often treat material like that which Ibsen was to use a few years later (in the group beginning with *Pillars of Society*) and which are often compared with Ibsen's. Such a comparison, if pushed at all closely, must inevitably be detrimental to Bjørnson, who is by contrast an eager poet and an able theatre-artist, using the stage skilfully as a pulpit for his liberal, and often noble, thought. Between 1867 and 1883 he produced *De Nygifte* (1865); *Redaktøren* (1874); *En Fallit* (1875); *Kongen* (1877); *Leonarda* and *Det ny System* (both 1879); and, after an interval of lecturing in America (1880–1), *En Handske* (1883), perhaps the height of his achievement in this kind and too bold for immediate production.

The second play of that year, *Over Ævne I* (1883) (given at the Royalty in London in 1901 as *Beyond Human Power*), one of Bjørnson's greatest plays, marks the increasing interest in spiritual rather than social problems which characterizes much of his last phase and is clearly seen also in the novel *Paa Guds Veje*, published in 1889. The other plays of this period are *Over Ævne II* (1895); *Paul Large og Tora Parsberg* (1898); *Laboremus* (1901); *Daglannet* (1904); and *Naar den ny Vin blomstrer* (1905). Bjørnson, who died in Paris, was awarded the Nobel Prize for Literature in 1903.

UNA ELLIS-FERMOR†

His son (2) BJØRN (1859–1942) was a well-known actor and theatre manager. After training in Vienna, he joined the Duke of Meiningen's company in 1880, and five years later became a leading director of the Christiania theatre, where he remained until 1893. After some years abroad, in Denmark and elsewhere, he returned to Norway in 1899 to take over the newly-established Nationalteater, and for the next forty years was active in the theatre in Norway in many different capacities.

L. KATHLEEN MCFARLANE

BLACK, GEORGE (1890–1945), a Northern music-hall manager who went to London in 1928 as director of the General Theatre Corporation Ltd. In 1933 he joined Moss Empires Ltd., of which he later became joint managing-director. Next to C. B. Cochran, he was the outstanding figure in the music-hall world between the two world wars, and his Crazy Gang shows at the Palladium, with Flanagan and Allen and Nervo and Knox as their moving spirits, caused a minor revolution in the profession, bringing back some of the atmosphere of the old 'halls'. Black was also responsible for a number of shows at the Hippodrome, notably *The Fleet's Lit Up* (1938), *Black Velvet* (1939), and *Black Vanities* (1941), and after the outbreak of war in 1939 he took over the Prince of Wales's. He was excellent at spotting nascent talent, and was at all times receptive to new ideas, but in later life he became somewhat intolerant of criticism, and after the poor notices given to *Jenny Jones* (1944) he refrained from inviting the critics to his next production.

BLACKFRIARS THEATRE, LONDON. There were two Blackfriars theatres, one succeeding the other, both built within the boundaries of the old Blackfriars monastery, the site of which is now covered by the offices of *The Times* and Playhouse Yard.

1. On the dissolution of the monasteries part of the Blackfriars building was granted to Sir Thomas Cawarden, Master of the Revels for Henry VIII, and the first holder of that office, who already had the use of several rooms there for the storing of properties and costumes used at Court entertainments. He may also have used the rooms for rehearsals. In 1576 Richard Farrant, Master of the Children of Windsor Chapel, adapted part of the building, probably the frater, as a theatre which was used by the Children of the Chapel Royal and of Windsor Chapel from 1577 until Farrant's death in 1580. From 1583 to 1584 it was used by a mixed company of children from the Earl of Oxford's company, Paul's and the Chapel. It then lapsed and was let out as lodgings. Its size is unknown.

2. In 1597 James Burbage bought part of the old monastery and adapted another hall, not the one Farrant had used, as a roofed theatre, hoping to use it in the winter when inclement weather stopped his company, which included his son Richard, Lowin, Condell, Armin, Heminge, and Shakespeare, from playing in roofless playhouses like the Theatre and the Curtain.

He was, however, prevented from using it by those who opposed the establishment of yet another playhouse. On James's death in 1597 the property passed to his son Richard, who in 1600 leased it to the Children of the Chapel, and it was not until 1608 that the King's Men, as they were now called, appeared there. They remained in possession until 1642.

The dimensions of the second Blackfriars, which was bigger than the first, were 46 × 66 ft. It had several galleries and was lit by candle-light. Its prices were higher than at the open-air theatres. Jonson refers to the stools on its stage as being 'twelvepenny' seats. Seating was also provided for all patrons, in the form of benches, and there was no standing room. Music was a great feature of the plays performed here, the performers paying to play in the hope of attracting patronage from the nobility in the audience. That scenery of some sort was used is certain, for there are references to it in connexion with Suckling's *Aglaura* (1637). One of the scenes was jeered at in a contemporary play by another author. Habington's *Queen of Aragon* (1640) also had scenery, which had been in use for Court masques for some time.

In 1631 another unsuccessful effort was made to suppress the Blackfriars. It was one of the best patronized of the pre-Restoration playhouses, and from the Burbages it passed to Henry Evans, who said that the Burbages' company got 'more in one winter in the said Great Hall by a thousand powndes than they were used to get in the Banckside'. Evans obtained permission to 'sett up a company of boys . . . to play playes and interludes', but shortly afterwards he was arraigned by the Court of Star Chamber for his 'unorderlie carriage and behaviour in taking up of gentlemens children against their wills and to employe them for playes'.

In 1629 a French company played at the Blackfriars and women appeared on the stage, to the great scandal of the audience, who pelted them with apples and other missiles until they retired in disorder. The building was finally demolished in 1655.

BLAGROVE, Thomas, see master of the revels.

BLANCHAR, Pierre (1896–1963), French actor, who trained at the Paris Conservatoire, and from 1919 to 1923 played at the Odéon in a number of parts. After a short interval in films he returned to the stage, and distinguished himself in such plays as Pagnol's *Jazz* (1925), Achard's *Domino*, and Salacrou's *L'Inconnue d'Arras* (1935). In 1939 he joined the Comédie-Française, where his striking presence and impressive delivery made him outstanding in such parts as Oedipus and Julius Caesar. After leaving the Comédie-Française in 1946 he continued to appear both on the stage and on the screen, his highly successful film career running parallel to his theatre work, and among the new plays in which he was seen to advantage were Achard's *Nous irons à Valparaiso*, Montherlant's *Malatesta*, and Camus's dramatization of *The Possessed*.

BLANCHARD. (1) William (1769–1835), English actor, who in 1785 joined a travelling company under the name of Bentley. He reverted to his own name in 1789 and was for many years an actor and manager in the provinces. He made his first appearance in London at Covent Garden, playing Bob Acres, on 1 Oct. 1800, and remained there until his death, except for a short visit to the United States in 1831, when he played at the Bowery under his son-in-law Hamblin. He was at his best in heavy comedy, and in character parts, particularly those of drunkards and old men. Oxberry gives special praise to his Polonius, Pistol, Fluellen, and Sir Andrew Aguecheek. He was also good as Peachum, and as Mungo in *The Padlock*. His first wife and his daughter Elizabeth (later Mrs. Hamblin) were both on the stage, and his younger son (2) Edward Leman (1820–89) became famous as a writer of pantomime and Christmas extravaganzas. From 1844 until his death he wrote at least one pantomime a year, generally under the pseudonym of Francisco Frost. Most of them were given at Drury Lane, the others at such minor theatres as the Surrey, Astley's, and the Olympic. He was also responsible for a number of farces, some burlesques, including one of Dickens, *The Cricket on Our Own Hearth* (1846), and a comedy, *The Road of Life*, given at the Olympic in 1843. He edited the plays of Shakespeare, and was for many years (from 1863) dramatic critic of the *Daily Telegraph*. He also wrote dramatic criticism for the *Era* from 1850 to 1879. His diary, edited by Clement Scott, was published in 1891. Nothing of his work, which was mainly topical and spectacular, has survived on the stage.

Two actors, father and son, both named Thomas Blanchard, of whom the first died in 1797 and the second in 1859, do not appear to have been related to the above.

BLANCHARD'S AMPHITHEATRE, New York, see chatham theatre, 1.

BLANCHE, August Theodore (1811–68), Swedish dramatist (see scandinavia, 3 *a*).

BLAND. (1) George (?–1807), English actor, the brother of Mrs. Jordan, and the illegitimate son of Francis Bland, whose name he adopted when he went on the stage. He was not a particularly good actor, and died in penurious circumstances in Boston, Mass., where he acted under the name of Wilson at the Park Theatre in 1801 and at the Grove in 1805. His wife (2) Maria Theresa Romanzini (1769–1838) had been an actress in Dublin at the same time as Mrs. Jordan. She later became a well-known ballad-singer at Vauxhall and was attached for forty years to the Drury Lane company. She married Bland at St. Paul's, Covent Garden, on 21 Oct. 1790. Of her two sons the elder, Charles, was a singer, but the younger, (3) James (1798–1861), though he was first a singer, later appeared at the Olympic in burlesque, and played the fathers and similar parts in the extravaganzas of Planché. He died suddenly at the Strand Theatre.

BLOOD-TUB, see gaff.

BLUES, a Victorian term for plain sky borders (see BORDER).

BOADEN, JAMES (1762–1839), English playwright, critic, and journalist, who became editor of the *Oracle*, a paper started in opposition to the *World*. He was intensely interested in drama, and had several plays to his credit: *Fontainville Forest* (1794), *The Secret Tribunal* (1795), *The Italian Monk* (1797), founded on Mrs. Radcliffe's novel, *Cambro-Britons* and *Aurelio and Miranda* (both 1798).

Boaden was a keen Shakespearian and took part in the correspondence on the Ireland forgeries. In 1837 he published a pamphlet on the authorship of the sonnets in which he identified the 'Mr. W. H.' of the dedication as William Herbert, Earl of Pembroke. His knowledge of the theatre is apparent in his biographies of famous actors. His *Life of Kemble* appeared in 1825, *The Life of Mrs. Siddons* in 1827, and *The Life of Mrs. Jordan* in 1831. T. C. KEMP†

BOARDS, the component parts of the stage floor, used also as a phrase indicating the acting profession, to be 'on the boards' or to 'tread the boards' signifying 'to be an actor'. In the smaller modern theatres the boards form a level, unbroken expanse, but in earlier times, and in the larger theatres, the boards, which run up- and down-stage supported on joists running crossways, were removable to facilitate the working of traps and machinery. This meant that each joist had to be supported separately by its own system of vertical posts rising from the floor of the cellar under the stage. Thus the structure below such a stage resembled a series of independent frameworks, all parallel to the audience. With a raked stage a certain stress was exerted which tended to make the stage slide in the direction of the slope, and since the working of the traps and bridges made it impossible to counteract this by any permanent cross-bracing, there can be found, beneath old raked stages, a system of metal strap-hooks, linking one row of uprights with the next behind, and so knitting the whole together. These tie-bars could be unhooked when necessary to allow the passage of a piece of scenery.

BOAR'S HEAD INN, see INNS USED AS THEATRES.

BOAT TRUCK, a large, low platform, running on castors, on which whole scenes, or sections of scenes, can be moved on and off stage. The idea can be extended in various ways, as when two trucks are used in successive scenes, and pivoted each at the down-stage and off-stage corner, so as to swing in over the acting area, or out of sight into the wing-space at need. Sometimes such a system is known as a Scissor Stage. Or the trucks may reach a high degree of elaboration and run on a system of rails and lifts, until as many as five separate Waggon Stages are to be found in one theatre, each capable of moving aside from the acting area, or of rising and sinking in the cellar, with a full set of scenery. RICHARD SOUTHERN

BOBÈCHE [ANTOINE MANDELOT] (1791–*c.* 1840), a farce-player of the boulevards, who, with his companion Galimafré [Auguste Guérin] (1790–1870), amused the holiday crowds with his *parades*. They were both working with their fathers, Bobèche as an upholsterer and Galimafré as a carpenter, when they were taken up and trained by the acrobat Dromale. They became extremely popular, and were invited to private houses to entertain the guests, but Bobèche, whose red jacket and grey tricorne hat with butterfly antennae were familiar sights on the Boulevard du Temple, offended Napoleon by the topicality of his jokes and was banished from Paris. He returned under the Restoration, and was again successful, but he had a hankering for serious drama, and took over the management of a provincial theatre—Mlle Flore in her memoirs says it was at Rouen. He failed, and was not heard of again. Galimafré, who refused to act after 1814, joined the stage-staff of the Gaîté and later of the Opéra-Comique, and died in retirement. A play based on the lives of these two comedians, by the brothers Cogniard, was given at the Palais-Royal in 1837.

BOBO, the rustic clown of early Spanish plays, who amused the noble audiences with his naïve witticisms and malapropisms.

BOCAGE. (1) [PIERRE-FRANÇOIS TOUSEZ] (1797–1863), celebrated French actor, one of the finest of the Romantic period. He tried a wide variety of trades before joining a travelling troupe in the provinces, and had a hard apprenticeship to acting before in 1821 he went to Paris. His efforts to join the Comédie-Française proved unavailing, and he returned to the provinces for a short time and then went to the Odéon. He found his métier in the new drama and melodrama, which suited him better than the old comedy and tragedy. A forceful personality, with a fine physique and sonorous voice, he revelled in the plays of the elder Dumas, particularly *Antony* and *La Tour de Nesle*. He finally entered the Comédie-Française, but its somewhat arid atmosphere proved too confining for him, and he returned to the boulevards, where his popularity was greater than ever. In 1845 he became director of the Odéon, and died in the midst of success, much of which he owed to the dramatists of the Romantic movement. He was not as good an actor as Frédérick, but he had a huge following among the youth of the day. His nephew (2) PAUL (1824–87) was the author of several plays, mostly written in collaboration, and editor of the *Mousquetaire*, a paper founded by Dumas *père*, in much of whose work the younger Bocage is believed to have had a hand.

BODEL, JEAN (*fl.* thirteenth century), a contemporary of the minstrel Adam de la Halle, and with him one of the founders of French secular drama. He wrote a *Jeu de Saint Nicolas* which was given on the vigil of the saint.

It contains a number of contemporary allusions, some of which seem to indicate that Bodel had been on a crusade, and though from a literary point of view it is not as good as the best of Adam de la Halle's work, it is more dramatic, and probably seemed better in performance. Bodel was preparing to go on a second crusade when he was stricken with leprosy, and retired from the world. The date of his death is uncertain.

BOECK, JOHANN MICHAEL (1743–93), German actor who played young lovers in Ackermann's National Theatre company at Hamburg. He later made theatre history by being the first to play Karl Moor in *Die Räuber* when it was put on under Dalberg at Mannheim, where Boeck had gone with his wife after the death of Ekhof. He was not a particularly intelligent or subtle actor, but he had a fine presence, a passionate style, and a strong repertory of theatrical tricks which made him acceptable to the more uncritical section of the audience. He was a staunch supporter of Iffland at Mannheim, and was sadly missed when he died of drink soon after the latter had been appointed producer to the theatre. His wife (Sophia Schulze) had received her early training under Schönemann, and always retained something of the early affected style, but she was very popular, particularly in her youth in breeches parts.

BOILEAU-DESPRÉAUX, NICOLAS (1636–1711), a French critic who exercised a great influence on French literature and drama. He was intended for the Church, but studied law and in 1660 took to literature. His criticism brought a new and invigorating atmosphere into the literary debates of Paris. He was not a poet, but a writer of verse, and a good one. He had no imagination, no warmth, but plenty of common sense and an uncanny flair for the best in art. He appreciated and was the friend of the great men of his time, of Racine—whom he taught to write verse—of La Fontaine, and particularly of Molière, whose satire matched his, and whom Boileau called *le contemplateur*. It was at the height of his friendship with Boileau that Molière wrote his greatest plays, *Tartuffe* and *Le Misanthrope*, as well as *Don Juan*. It was said of Boileau that his criticisms were mordant, but always justified, and that those whom he attacked never recovered.

BOINDIN, NICOLAS (1676–1751), French dramatist and man of letters, whose lonely and delicate childhood developed in him habits of study and reflection beyond his years and a decided bent towards atheism. After a year in the army, which he left owing to ill health, he frequented the literary cafés of Paris and became a friend of Saurin and La Motte. He wrote a number of plays, of which the most successful, *Le Bal d'Auteuil* (1702), caused a tightening-up of the censorship laws by its equivocal plot. His work in other directions, which included a number of volumes on French theatre history, would have earned him a seat in the French Academy, but he was denied it owing to his irreligion, which later led the clergy to refuse him Christian burial. After quarrelling with La Motte, Boindin founded a new literary clique which had its headquarters at the Café Procope. He was an excellent talker, at his best when he was in the wrong, and Voltaire, who disliked him intensely, drew a savage picture of him as Bardon in *Le Temple du goût*.

BOISROBERT, FRANÇOIS LE METEL DE, ABBÉ (1592–1662), a great talker, a pleasant companion, a priest who preferred the pleasures of the world to the duties of his office, a friend of Richelieu, and a foundation member of the French Academy. In addition to all this he found time to be a dramatist, producing his first play at the age of 40. Since it was successful he continued to write for the stage until he had nearly twenty plays to his credit. He was one of the dramatists chosen by Richelieu to write his plays for him, and in the eyes of his contemporaries he was no doubt the most important, although his collaborators included Corneille. Boisrobert's continued success in the theatre may have done something to disgust Corneille with play-writing, especially after the failure of *Pertharite* in 1662. Yet, since Molière found some of *L'Avare*, and a hint of *L'École des maris*, in Boisrobert's forgotten comedies he cannot be said to have lived in vain. He was the younger brother of the profligate playwright d'Ouville.

BOITO, ARRIGO (1842–1918), Italian poet and composer, and the first to realize that the libretto of an opera should have some literary value. His own opera 'Mefistofele' (1868), based on Goethe's *Faust*, was not at first a success, though in a revised form it later won acceptance; but it is as the librettist of Verdi's 'Otello' (1887) and 'Falstaff' (1893) that he is chiefly remembered. His handling of the themes is excellent, and his translations keep closely to the Shakespearian originals, without sacrificing the sense to the music.

BOKER, GEORGE HENRY (1823–90), American dramatist, who imported into the early drama of the United States themes of historical romance, interpreted in blank verse. Two of these were on incidents in Spanish history, *Calaynos* (1849) and *Leonor de Guzman* (1853), but *Francesca da Rimini*, his best-known play, was based on an Italian theme. This was first given at New York in 1855, and in 1883 was revived by Lawrence Barrett with himself as Lanciotto, Francesca's husband, who in Boker's version becomes the chief character in the play. It remained in Barrett's repertory for many years and was again revived in 1901 by Otis Skinner. The text was frequently revised, notably by William Winter in 1882, and has never been acted from the printed version, since Boker himself altered it extensively for production. He later wrote two other plays in the style of *Francesca da Rimini*, but they were not produced. His comedies, of which he wrote three, are less important, and it is as one of the few successful exponents of blank verse tragedy that he is chiefly remembered. Boker was a poet of some standing, and from 1871 to 1875 and 1875 to 1878 served as American envoy to Turkey and Russia respectively.

BOLIVIA, see SOUTH AMERICA, 1.

BOLT, ROBERT (1924–), English dramatist, who was teaching when his first play, *The Critic and the Heart*, was staged at the Oxford Playhouse in 1957. He first came into prominence when *Flowering Cherry*, with Ralph Richardson in the leading part, was seen at the Haymarket, London, later in the same year. This moving study of a man foredoomed to failure gained the *Evening Standard* award for the most promising play of the year, and was later seen in New York. It was followed, in 1960, by two plays—*The Tiger and the Horse*, in which Michael Redgrave starred with his daughter Vanessa, and *A Man For All Seasons*, with Paul Scofield as Sir Thomas More, and Leo McKern as a commentator who doubles a variety of parts—a Brechtian touch which delighted the critics and public alike. Transferred to New York in 1961, this play was awarded the critics' prize for the best foreign play of the season. Bolt's next play, *Gentle Jack* (1963), in which Edith Evans appeared, was not a success, and had a very short run in London.

BONARELLI DELLA ROVERE, GUIDOBALDO (1563–1608), Italian dramatist, author of the best-known pastoral of the seventeenth century, the *Filli di Sciro*, produced at Ferrara in 1607. (See ITALY, 1 *b* ii). This, as *Scyros*, was given at Cambridge in a Latin translation by Samuel Brooke before Charles, Prince of Wales, on 2 or 3 Mar. 1613, and in an English translation about twenty years later before the Court in London. A second English translation, by Gilbert Talbot, was played in London in 1657. The first was printed in 1655, the second remains in manuscript.

BOND, THOMAS (?–1635), English actor, whose portrait is at Dulwich, somewhat surprisingly, since he does not appear to figure with any great prominence in the theatrical records of the time. He was a provincial actor in 1624, when he appeared at Norwich and Exeter, and played small parts in two London companies, at the Red Bull and Salisbury Court. Kemble was certainly mistaken in saying that Bond (or Band, as he is sometimes called) was the third actor to play Bussy d'Ambois, since he was never with the King's Men, who owned the play.

BONSTELLE, JESSIE (1872–1932), American actress and theatre manager, nicknamed 'the Maker of Stars'. Her real name was Laura Justine Bonesteele, and she began her career as a child, reciting at concerts and playing in amateur productions. In 1890 she started her professional career in a touring company under Augustin Daly. At the age of 19 she was already managing the Shuberts' theatre in Syracuse, and after several similar ventures in other towns, including Toronto, she was the lessee of the Garrick Theatre in Detroit from 1910 to 1922. She then purchased the Playhouse in the same city. She opened it in 1925, and three years later, having aroused the interest of the townsfolk, was able to make it one of America's first civic playhouses, run on the lines of the Theatre Guild. Under her many-sided control it flourished until her death. She was responsible for the fostering of much native American talent, and among her discoveries was Katharine Cornell. In 1892 she married an actor, Alexander Hamilton Stuart, who died in 1911.

BOOK-HOLDER, the Elizabethan name for the prompter, not to be confused with the book-keeper, an important functionary for whom see below. In addition to prompting the actors in their parts the book-holder saw that they were ready for their entrances, and was responsible for their props.

BOOK-KEEPER, an important member of an Elizabethan company, who was responsible for the manuscript copies of plays and of actors' parts. He might also, though not necessarily, be an actor, and was in any case likely to be concerned with the finance and management of the company.

BOOK WINGS, used on the English Victorian stage, usually four at each entrance, each quartet hanging on its own central upright spindle. This passed down through a hole in the stage, and at its lower end was a grooved wheel. By means of a connecting rope passing over these wheels, all the spindles could be rotated and all the wings of a scene changed simultaneously by means of one master handle.

BOOKED FLAT, two flats hinged together. They may also be used as a Booked Wing (not to be confused with Book Wing above).

BOOMERANG, see LIGHTING, 2.

BOOTE, ROSIE (1878–1958), one of the most celebrated of the Gaiety Girls, who in 1901 married the fourth Marquess of Headfort, and retired from the stage. She remained loyal, however, to the theatre, and became a well-known figure at all London first nights almost up to the time of her death. Born in Luton (not Tipperary, as was at one time thought), she trained as a dancer, and in 1895 joined the chorus at George Edwardes's Gaiety Theatre during the run of *The Shop Girl*. In 1898 she played the small part of Marietta, the flower girl, in *The Runaway Girl*, and two years later made a great success as Isabel Blyth in *The Messenger Boy*, singing Monckton's 'Maisie'. She was much regretted on her retirement, as a great future in musical comedy had been predicted for her.

BOOTH, a family of actors, of English origin, but important in the history of the American theatre, and indeed in world history generally, since one member of it was responsible for the assassination of President Lincoln on 14 Apr. 1865. The first of the family to achieve eminence on the stage was (1) JUNIUS

BRUTUS (1796–1852), who owed his Christian names to the republican sentiments of his lawyer father. He was given a good education and destined for the law, but went on the stage at 17. After touring for some years he appeared at Covent Garden as Richard III, and almost immediately entered into rivalry with Edmund Kean, the reigning favourite of the London stage. He was seen at Covent Garden as Sir Giles Overreach, Leonatus Posthumus, and, in 1818, as Shylock. Two years later he was seen as Lear, and shortly afterwards went to Drury Lane, where he played Iago to Kean's Othello, Edgar to his Lear, and Pierre to his Jaffier. In 1821 he deserted his legal wife, by whom he had one son, and with Mary Ann Holmes, a flower-seller in Bow Street, went to America, making his first appearance, as Richard III, at Richmond, Va. From then until his death, except for two short visits to Drury Lane, he was constantly seen in America, where he may be said to have founded the tradition of tragic acting. He made his first appearance in New York late in 1821, again as Richard III, and was seen in a number of classic, as well as modern, parts. He was also manager of several theatres. Among his other achievements was the playing, in French, of Oreste in Racine's *Andromaque*, and he is said to have played Shylock in Hebrew. He was on tour in the West when he died on board a Mississippi steamboat, and was buried at Baltimore. He made his last appearance at the St. Charles Theatre, New Orleans. He was a superb actor, rough and unpolished, but full of grandeur and eloquence, with a resonant voice and ample gesture. There was, however, a streak of insanity in him, aggravated by his intemperate habits, which he appears to have passed on to his sons. He and Mary Ann had ten children before, in 1851, his first wife divorced him and they were able to marry. Several of them died young, a fact which contributed not a little to Booth's habitual melancholy. The eldest, however, (2) JUNIUS BRUTUS junior (1821–83), survived to make the stage his profession, and though never as good an actor as his father, he was accounted an excellent manager and producer. He acted with the elder Booth in 1835, and again in 1852, playing Iago to his father's Othello. He was for many years a useful member of the stock company at the Bowery Theatre, New York, and later of that at Booth's Theatre. One of his best parts was Dan Lowrie in Frances Hodgson Burnett's *That Lass o' Lowrie's* (1878), which he also played on tour. He was three times married, and had two sons on the stage. The elder shot himself and his wife in a London hotel, but the younger, (3) SYDNEY BARTON (1873–1937), who made his début at Wallack's in 1892, was a successful leading man with such actresses as Maude Adams, Lillian Russell, Jane Cowl, Ruth Chatterton, Grace George, and Alice Brady. In 1902 he went into vaudeville for two seasons.

The second surviving son of the elder Booth was (4) EDWIN THOMAS (1833–93), one of the first great American actors, and the first to win a European reputation. He was an unhappy man, prone to melancholia and much affected by the insanity of his father, brother, and second wife. But as a tragic actor he had few equals. He made his first appearance in his father's company at the age of 16, and remained with him until the latter's death, playing Richard III at 18. He soon established a fine reputation, one of his best parts being Sir Giles Overreach. He toured Australia in 1854 with Laura Keene, and in 1861 was seen at the Haymarket, London, as Shylock, Overreach, and Richelieu. It was during this visit that his daughter Edwina was born, his wife Mary Devlin (1840–63) dying two years later. He returned to the United States, and from 1863 to 1867 was manager of the Winter Garden Theatre, where in 1864 he set up a record with a hundred consecutive performances of *Hamlet*, which was not broken until John Barrymore's one hundred and one in 1922. After the destruction by fire of the Winter Garden Theatre he built his own theatre, opening it with a fine production of *Romeo and Juliet* on 3 Feb. 1869. The actress who played Juliet, Mary McVicker, later became his second wife, dying in 1881. Both remained there with a fine company in a distinguished list of plays until 1873, when Booth went bankrupt. Nothing daunted, he embarked on a series of starring tours throughout the United States, and built up a new and enviable reputation. He was seen in England between 1880 and 1882, and also went to Germany, where his fine acting was much appreciated. In London he appeared at the Lyceum by invitation of Henry Irving, and the two actors alternated the roles of Othello and Iago. In 1888 he presented his house in Gramercy Park, where there is a statue of him, to the newly founded Players' Club, and continued to occupy his rooms there until his death. A good deal of Edwin's moodiness and despair must be ascribed to the shock consequent on the assassination of Lincoln by his youngest brother (5) JOHN WILKES (1839–65), during a performance at Ford's Theatre, Washington, of *Our American Cousin*, on 14 Apr. 1865 at 10.22 p.m. There are two conflicting theories current about this mad act. The one presents John Wilkes as a wild, undisciplined, and embittered madman, jealous of his brother's success, and seeking notoriety through crime; the other considers him an excellent actor, though eccentric, and ascribes his action to motives of mistaken patriotism. For a systematic survey of the whole question, see *The Mad Booths of Maryland* (1940), by Stanley Kimmel.

The elder Booth had two daughters, Rosalie, who was looked after all her life by Edwin, whom she predeceased, and Asia, who married the actor-manager John Sleeper Clarke (1834–99).

BOOTH, BARTON (1681–1733), English actor, of good family and well educated, whose aptitude for the stage showed itself early in a fine performance in the *Andria* of Terence while he was at Westminster School. His theatrical ambitions not meeting with much encouragement from his family, he went to Dublin, and after two seasons at the theatre there, and possibly a short tour of the English provinces, was engaged by Betterton for Lincoln's Inn Fields Theatre in 1700. Here he proved himself a fine tragic actor, worthy to carry on the traditions of Betterton, but he was slow in establishing himself, even when the company moved to Vanbrugh's new theatre in the Haymarket. This was possibly due to the jealousy of Wilks, who was, however, unable to prevent Booth's success as Pyrrhus in *The Distressed Mother* (1712), and as Addison's Cato, his greatest part, in the following year. These successes, coupled with that of his Othello, brought him money as well as reputation, and he became one of the managers of Drury Lane with Cibber and Wilks, Doggett retiring in disgust on political grounds. Booth played a wide range of tragic roles, and though not tall, was dignified in appearance, with a rich, well-trained voice. He is believed to have regretted his decision to become an actor, but persevered in his profession for many years, though in later life he proved somewhat lazy. The most striking features of his acting were his 'attitudes'—the pose, for instance, in which he listened, with appropriate gestures, to Emilia's address to her dying mistress. In these he was unexcelled, and even those who were jealous of his popularity conceded his effectiveness at such points. After the death of his first wife he married, in 1719, Hester Santlow, a dancer and actress of some repute, with whom he lived happily, though accused of marrying her for her money. She died on 21 Jan. 1773, and is buried with her husband at Cowley, Oxford.

BOOTH THEATRE, New York, on 45th Street. This was built by Winthrop Ames, and opened 16 Oct. 1913 with *The Great Adventure*, based by Arnold Bennett on his novel *Buried Alive*. Lyn Harding and Janet Beecher headed the cast, and a minor part was played by Guthrie McClintic, later to figure so prominently in the New York theatre. The Booth is still in use, and has had a fair number of successes, including *The Green Goddess* (1921) and *You Can't Take It With You* (1936), which ran for two years. Two distinguished failures were *White Wings* (1926) and *For Services Rendered* (1933). In 1925 a production of *Hamlet* in modern dress was seen at the Booth, with Basil Sidney in the title-role supported by a fine cast. Among its later successes have been *Claudia* and a fantastic production of *Le Bourgeois gentilhomme* with the comedian Bobby Clark as M. Jourdain. Later productions have been *Come Back, Little Sheba* (1950), with Shirley Booth, the two-character play, *Two for the Seesaw* (1958), and *Luv* (1964).

BOOTH'S THEATRE, New York, on the south-west corner of 6th Avenue and 23rd Street. It was built for Edwin Booth, and opened on 3 Feb. 1869, with Booth and Mary McVicker, later his second wife, as Romeo and Juliet. The stage, which was not raked (the wings were supported by braces), had a tall stage house, perhaps the first in New York, and large hydraulically-powered elevator trays for lowering three-dimensional scenery to the basement. During Booth's management box sets were occasionally used. After the opening production came *Othello*, and subsequent seasons saw Booth in many of his finest parts, as well as such outstanding actors as Kate Bateman—her last appearance in New York before her departure to London as Mrs. Crowe—Hackett, also in his last regular New York season, Jefferson in *Rip Van Winkle*, Lawrence Barrett, who played Cassius to Booth's Brutus, and Charlotte Cushman, who played opposite Booth in *Macbeth* and *Henry VIII*. Booth had hoped to establish a great national theatre for the production of poetic drama, but after a good start the venture failed, and in 1873 he withdrew from the management on which he had embarked with such high hopes. He frequently appeared at the theatre as a guest-star, in common with other outstanding actors of the day, and it was at Booth's that Adelaide Neilson made her first appearance in New York, and the younger Wallack his last. Fanny Janauschek appeared in a version of *Bleak House*, made by herself, and Minnie Maddern, later the famous Mrs. Fiske, played Arthur in *King John*. After Edwin's withdrawal, his brother, Junius Brutus, had endeavoured to manage the theatre, but on 30 May 1874 it passed out of the control of the Booth family, and was opened by Jarrett and Palmer with plays by Boucicault. Later in the same year Charlotte Cushman made her farewell appearances, ending with Lady Macbeth on 7 Nov. The great event of 1875 was the importation from the Theatre Royal, Manchester, of Calvert's production of *Henry V*, with George Rignold in the name part and Mrs. Charles Calvert as Chorus. Calvert's production of Byron's *Sardanapalus* was also seen, with scenery by Telbin, but it was much hampered by adventitious ballet and spectacle, and was not a great success, though it ran for 113 performances. The theatre continued to house visiting stars, and saw the last appearance of E. L. Davenport, as Edgar in Lawrence Barrett's *King Lear*. In 1879 Dion Boucicault became its lessee. Under him Rose Coghlan, John Brougham, Robert B. Mantell, Helena Modjeska with Maurice Barrymore, and many other stars, gave successful seasons, and Charles R. Thorne junior made his last appearance on any stage in *The Corsican Brothers*. He played only two nights, and died shortly after. The theatre was then sold, and disappeared in a blaze of glory, with Salvini, Clara Morris, and Modjeska in quick succession. Its last production was *Romeo and Juliet*, with Modjeska and Maurice Barrymore. It closed on 30 Apr. 1883, and was pulled down, a large department store being built on the site.

BORDER, a narrow strip of painted cloth, battened at the top edge only, used to mask-in, or hide, the top of the stage as seen from the auditorium. The lower edge is often cut to a shape, and the whole is then known as an Arch, Beam, Cloud, Sky, or Tree Border. The use of clouds for masking the top of almost any scene was formerly common (see CLOUDINGS). In Victorian times plain sky borders were sometimes known as Blues. Tails, or Legs, on a border, are long vertically-hanging extensions at each end, forming with the border an arch over the scene.

RICHARD SOUTHERN

BORISOVA, YULIA KONSTANTINOVNA (1925–), Soviet actress, who studied at the Shchukin Theatrical School, and in 1949 became a member of the company at the Vakhtangov Theatre. There she played a number of parts portraying the vivid personality of the contemporary Russian girl, among them Natasha in *City at Dawn* (1957) and Valya in *The Irkutsk Story* (1960), both by Arbuzov. One of her finest performances was as Nastasya Filipovna in the dramatized version of Dostoievsky's *The Idiot* (1958). Reuben Simonov wrote of her: 'She can play any role, comedy or tragedy.' Her performance as Cleopatra revealed her powers as a Shakespearian actress.

BEATRICE KING†

BØRJESSEN, JOHAN (1790–1866), Swedish dramatist, one of the first to write under the influence of Shakespeare, whose works first appeared in a Swedish translation in 1847 (see SCANDINAVIA, 3 *a*).

BOSSU D'ARRAS, LE, see ADAM DE LA HALLE.

BOSTON, a town important in the history of the American theatre, though the early companies had much opposition to contend with. Even after the building of the New Exhibition Room (1792), later the Board Alley Theatre, plays had still to be given as 'Moral Lectures'. In 1794 the Federal Street Theatre was built, rebuilt after a fire four years later, and finally destroyed, after a long and chequered career, in 1852. Two years later the present Boston Theatre was built. The Haymarket, built in 1796, was unable to rival the popularity of the Federal Theatre, and was pulled down in 1803. The Tremont Theatre, which opened in 1827, was able for a short time to take over and close the Federal, its only rival, but was itself outshone by the Boston Museum, which opened in 1841; the Tremont closed in 1843 and was used as a church, and for concerts and lectures, until destroyed by fire in 1852. Other Boston theatres were the Howard Athenaeum, opened by Hackett in 1846, and the National, which opened in 1832 as the American Amphitheatre, later became the Warren, and was destroyed by fire in 1852. The Boston Museum, which had a long and glorious history, reached the height of its popularity in 1873–83, with a fine stock company and good visiting stars. It finally closed in 1893.

BOTTOMLEY, GORDON (1874–1948), English poet, and one of the few to bring verse-plays successfully into the professional theatre. His *King Lear's Wife* (1915), *Britain's Daughters* (1922), *Gruach* (1923), and *Laodice and Danae* (1930), were all seen in London, while *Gruach* was awarded the Femina–Vie Heureuse Prize. He was in no way a neo-Elizabethan, although the influence of Shakespeare can be seen in his work, as can that of the Japanese *Nō* play. But his themes are taken mainly from Celtic and Northern legend and early history, and he introduced to England, as Yeats did to Ireland, the Celtic and Northern twilight, the old world of fear and evil. He was an important figure in the evolution of modern poetic drama; he wrote also a number of one-act plays, and the Exeter Cathedral Festival play for 1933, *The Acts of St. Peter*.

BOUCHER, FRANÇOIS (1703–70), famous French artist, who in 1744 succeeded Servandony as decorator at the Paris Opéra, remaining there until 1748 (see COSTUME, 7).

BOUCICAULT [BOURCICAULT and BOURSIQUOT]. (1) DIONYSIUS LARDNER (1822–90), actor and dramatist, whose life and works were divided between England and the U.S.A. He appeared under the name of Lee Moreton (or Morton) in the English provinces, and had his first success as a dramatist with *London Assurance*, a comedy of contemporary life first seen at Covent Garden on 4 Mar. 1841, with Charles Mathews, his wife Madame Vestris, and William Farren in the chief parts. It was frequently revived, notably by Hare in 1870, Kendal in 1873, and Wyndham in 1888. In 1913 it was chosen for the first all-star matinée in aid of King George's Pension Fund for Actors and Actresses, and was then produced by Boucicault's son Dion. After the success of *London Assurance* Boucicault wrote a number of other plays for the London theatres, including the Princess's, where he was later to stage some of his greatest successes. In 1845 he married and lived for a time in France, where his wife died. Returning to London, he continued to write plays, of which the most successful, all seen at the Princess's, were *The Corsican Brothers* (1852) and *Louis XI* (1855). It was during this period that Boucicault met and married the actress Agnes Robertson, and also made his first visit to the United States, where he wrote and produced *The Poor of New York* (also known, according to the locality in which it was being played, as *The Poor of Liverpool*, *London*, etc.), *Jessie Brown*, with himself as Nana Sahib and his wife in the title-role, and *Dot*, based on Dickens's *The Cricket on the Hearth*, in which Jefferson played his first serious part as Caleb Plummer. Boucicault was also the author of the first play to be based on the American Civil War, *Belle Lamar* (1874). In the same year he produced one of the best of his Irish plays, *The Shaughraun*. Another great success was *The Colleen Bawn* (1860). He was a prolific writer, being credited with some 150 plays, of which some remain in manuscript. Many of them were translations from the French or adaptations of novels. More than any other dramatist of the day he had 'the trick of the theatre', and his material, whatever its source, was always shaped to the taste of the time. Professor Allardyce Nicol, who has a great admiration for Boucicault's undoubted gifts, said of him (*Nineteenth Century Drama*, i. 48):

[His] importance as a dramatist rests on two things —his uncanny sense of theatrical values and his keenly observant eye. No man knew better than he just what would appeal on the stage. The construction of his plays, if we make allowance for their frankly melodramatic framework, is excellent; and of countless theatrical devices he was the eager inventor.... Crude as many of his effects may seem to us, he had an acute eye for oddity in real life, and many of his best scenes rely, not on scenic splendour, but on the depiction, through laughter or tears, of domestic interiors. It was this—the cultivation of naturalistically conceived scenes allied to melodramatic excitement—which gave him his contemporary importance.

He was also the first, and for a long time the only, dramatist to treat the American Negro seriously on the stage, in *The Octoroon; or, Life in Louisiana* (1859). It is possible that Boucicault may have been the first dramatist in England to receive a royalty on his plays, instead of a lump sum, and soon after his arrival in New York he joined Boker and Bird in their efforts to ensure the passing of the first dramatic copyright law (in 1856), more than twenty years after that of England.

Boucicault, who appeared in many of his own plays, spent his whole life in the theatre, and had no interests outside it. He finally settled in America, where he made a lot of money, and became a teacher at a drama school started by Palmer. By his second wife he had four children, but later, wishing to marry the young American actress Louise Thorndike, which he did in 1888, he repudiated Agnes Robertson, saying she was not legally married to him, but only his common-law wife. Their children were thus rendered illegitimate. Much sympathy was felt for Agnes Robertson, who was universally beloved, and kept her married name until her death.

(2) AGNES KELLY ROBERTSON (1833–1916), who married Boucicault in 1853, first appeared on the stage in Scotland as a child, and in 1850, under the aegis of the Charles Keans, was seen in London. After her marriage she accompanied her husband to America, where she was immensely popular, and, though a Scotswoman by birth, played to the life the Irish heroines of *The Colleen Bawn*, *Arrah-na-Pogue*, and *The Shaughraun*, as well as the more congenial heroine of *Jessie Brown*, based on the Relief of Lucknow, and Jeanie Deans in a dramatization of *The Heart of Midlothian*. Her four children were all connected with the theatre. Her elder son, (3) DIONYSIUS GEORGE (1859–1929), known as 'Dot', was an actor and dramatist. He made his first appearances in his father's company in New York in 1879, and in London he played with Hawtrey. He was for many years in partnership with Robert Brough in Australia, and from 1901 to 1915 he produced all the plays given at the Duke of York's Theatre, London, under the management of Charles Frohman. His best parts were Sir William Gower in *Trelawny of the 'Wells'* (1898) and Carraway Pim in *Mr. Pim Passes By* (1920). In 1901 he married Irene Vanbrugh, who appeared in many of his productions at the Duke of York's, and was Olivia to his Mr. Pim (see VANBRUGH, 2). His sister, (4) NINA (1867–1950), was born in London, but made her first appearance on the stage in her father's company in America, playing Eily O'Connor in a revival of his *Colleen Bawn*. She first appeared in London as Flossie Trivett in *The New Wing* in 1892. In 1903 she gave excellent performances as Bessie Broke in *The Light that Failed*, and as Mona Loiney in *Little Mary*, but she is chiefly remembered for her Peter in Barrie's *Peter Pan*, which she played on its first production in Dec. 1904. She continued to appear on the London stage until 1927, and in 1935 returned for a few months as Lady Bernice Jeune in *Frolic Wind*. Her last appearance was as the Countess Mortimer in *Waste* (1936).

The Boucicaults' other children, Eva and Aubrey (1869–1913), were also on the stage. Eva retired on her marriage to an actor, John Alfred Clayton [really CALTHROP] (1842–88), and became the mother of Dion Clayton Calthrop (1878–1937), author, illustrator, and dramatist, Donald Calthrop (1888–1940), actor, and Ian, theatre manager. Donald's son John and Ian's son Dion Gordon were both on the stage.

BOUFFES-PARISIENS, a theatre opened by Offenbach in 1855, first in the Champs-Élysées, in the old Salle Lacaze, and on its present site at the end of the same year. It is mainly used for light opera, of which the most successful was 'Orphée aux Enfers', and for musical plays.

BOULEVARD DU TEMPLE, a fair-ground in Paris which took the place of the earlier fairs of Saint-Germain and Saint-Laurent, and during the Revolution saw the building of a number of small permanent playhouses, of which the first was that of Nicolet, later the Gaîté. The whole area became a centre of entertainment, having also in its precincts the Ambigu-Comique, the Folies-Dramatiques, the Funambules, as well as circuses and booths for acrobats and puppet-shows. The whole picturesque scene was swept away in 1862, in the rebuilding scheme of Haussmann, and the Boulevard Voltaire now occupies most of the site. Many famous actors, including Deburau, Frédérick, Mme Dorval, and Bocage, were seen in its theatres, while Dumas *père* and Gautier were among those who wrote for it in its later years. But its main purveyors were the prolific authors of melodrama, Pixerécourt, Bouchardy, and others, from whose works it took its nickname of 'the Boulevard of Crime'. In its earlier days the two farce-players Bobèche and Galimafré revived memories of the earlier *parades*, and children's companies played in the little theatres which were later to house some of the greatest actors of France. And always there were innumerable sideshows, wild beasts, fireworks, waxworks, and museums, as well as the cafés with their concerts and the perambulating musicians and ballad-singers.

BOURCHIER, ARTHUR (1863–1927), English actor, husband of Violet Vanbrugh (see VANBRUGH, 1), whom he married in 1894. Educated at Eton and Oxford, he was one of the founders of the Oxford University Dramatic Society, playing Hotspur, Feste, Falstaff, and Brutus in its first productions. On leaving the university he joined the company of Mrs. Langtry, and made his first professional appearance as Jaques at Wolverhampton. After his marriage he toured with his wife, who played the leading parts in his farces and comedies, many of them adapted from the French. From 1900 to 1906 he was in management at the Garrick Theatre, London, playing Shylock, Macbeth, and new plays by Pinero, Gilbert, H. A. Jones, and others. In 1910 he joined Tree at His Majesty's Theatre, and was seen in a number of Shakespearian parts, being particularly admired as Henry VIII. He later appeared at the Oxford Music-hall as Old Bill in a sketch based on Bairnsfather's *The Better 'Ole.* He was devoted to the theatre, and frequently lectured on it. He was at his best in truculent, fiery, or broad, hearty parts, but had little subtlety and hotly resented criticism, spoiling much of his best work by impatience and over-eagerness. He died in South Africa while on tour. His second wife, an actress whom he married in 1918, was Violet Marion Kyrle Bellew.

BOURDET, ÉDOUARD (1877–1945), French dramatist, whose plays, written under the influence of Becque, are subtle and penetrating portrayals of social and moral disequilibrium. The first, *Le Rubicon* (1910), was a light comedy based on the complications of a wedding-night, but with his succeeding works Bourdet became more serious, until by way of *La Cage ouverte* (1920) and *L'Heure du berger* (1922) he reached his peak of analysis and penetration with a study of Lesbianism entitled *La Prisonnière* (1926). Some years later he followed this with a study of homosexuality in *La Fleur des pois* (1932), but developed his theme as comedy instead of tragedy, as previously. One of his most penetrating plays was *Vient de paraître* (1927), a satire on the modern commercialism of literature. Most of Bourdet's plays have been translated into English, and have been seen in London and New York. It has been said of him that his 'conflicts of the heart were situated often on the borderline of the forbidden, but he managed with consummate art not to overstep the line of dramatic propriety'. He brought wit and irony to his satires, which made no pretence at propaganda, and struck out at corruption wherever he found it without seeking to point the moral.

BOURSAULT, EDMÉ (1638–1701), French man of letters, who went to Paris at the age of 13, entirely uneducated, and by dint of study and application, joined to a natural aptitude for literature, soon made a name for himself. In 1661 his first play, a farce entitled *Le Médecin volant*, was given at the Hôtel de Bourgogne. It was followed by several others, and then, thinking himself attacked in the character of Licidas in Molière's *La Critique de l'École des femmes*—which was mainly aimed at d'Aubigné—he replied with *Le Portrait du peintre* (1663), in which he accused Molière of putting recognizable contemporary characters on the stage. The dispute threatened to become acrimonious, but Boursault, who really admired Molière and knew how much he owed him, capitulated, and they became friends. Boursault also attacked and then became friendly with Boileau, who at one time rated him soundly for his bad style, and congratulated him when he improved. Boursault, who was happily married and father of a large family, had none of the faults of the self-made man, but was modest, kindly, and good-mannered. For many years he was taken up with literary work for the Court, and wrote no plays, but in 1683 he reappeared with *La Comédie sans titre; ou, le Mercure galant*, which shows an immense improvement on his earlier works, as did two later plays, based on the life and fables of Aesop. They are interesting as being the first instance of direct moral teaching in French drama, forerunners of the eighteenth-century *drames sérieux.* The more successful of the two, *Ésope à la cour* (1701), was produced after Boursault's death, and was adapted in English by Vanbrugh.

BOUSCHET, JAN, see ENGLISH COMEDIANS.

BOWER SALOON, LONDON, at Stangate St., Lambeth, was built and opened in 1838 by a scene-painter named Phillips. East End actors who were afterwards to please the West End made their débuts there, and West End actors out of work were glad to find employment there in its early days. George Hodson, father of Henrietta Hodson, was an early manager; so was Biddles, father of Mrs. Calvert, who made her first appearance at the Bower Saloon as Adelaide Biddles. James Fernandez was for some time a member of the company. Eventually it sank very low, with rowdy audiences, and plays—from *Macbeth* to *Maria Marten*—done in the roughest and most barnstorming manner. It came to an end in 1879.

W. MACQUEEN-POPE†

BOWERY THEATRE, NEW YORK. 1. A theatre was first projected for the Bowery in 1823, when it was to have been called the Bull's Head Theatre, from the name of a tavern on the intended site. It finally opened on 23 Oct. 1826 with *The Road to Ruin*, as the New York Theatre, Bowery, but it was always known simply as the Bowery. Gilfert and George H. Barrett were the first managers, and they had gathered round them a fine cast. The theatre was lit by gas, not with naked jets, as previously at the Chatham, but with the flames enclosed in glass shades. One of the earliest productions at the Bowery was a fine *School for Scandal*, with Mrs. Gilfert as Lady Teazle and Barrett as Charles. Edwin Forrest, whose name is for ever associated with the Bowery, where he had many of his early triumphs, made his first appearance there as Othello, and shortly afterwards Hamblin, its manager for many years, appeared as Virginius. At first the new theatre proved stronger in comedy than in tragedy, but it later became the home of melodrama. Among highlights in its early history were the French ballet dancers introduced by Gilfert to New York, which had seen nothing like them before, and the appearance of Louisa Lane, later Mrs. John Drew, at the age of 8. Cooper and Forrest then starred in a joint engagement, but on 26 May 1828 the theatre was burnt down, and the actors had to migrate to Niblo's Sans Souci. A second Bowery Theatre opened on 20 Aug. of the same year, again under Gilfert, with Forrest as its star, but soon declined into melodrama and spectacle, as with Dunlap's *Trip to Niagara*, which was merely the excuse for the employment of dioramic scenery. On 30 July 1829 Gilfert died, and after a period during which the Bowery was managed jointly with the Park, Hamblin entered on his twenty years of management. Under him melodrama flourished, and the Bowery was the first theatre in New York to start continuous runs, in opposition to the constant changes of bill as still practised at the old-fashioned Park Theatre. Hamblin tried to rechristen the theatre, naming it the American Theatre, Bowery, but it was always referred to by its old name. Rice appeared there in his famous Jim Crow song and dance, Louisa Lane, now aged 13, came back as 'general utility', and a great success was scored by *Mazeppa*, and by Mme Céleste, appearing for the first time in her famous *French Spy*. The Bowery saw, in the season of 1835–6, the last appearance in New York of the great actor Cooper, and the first of Charlotte Cushman, as Lady Macbeth. In Sept. 1836 the theatre was once again burnt down, but a third Bowery was ready by the following New Year's Day. It was destined to have a short and uninteresting history, as it was again destroyed by fire on 18 Feb. 1838, and not reopened until 6 May 1839, once more under the management of Hamblin, who had been absent in England during the lifetime of the third Bowery. Among the successful melodramas of the fourth Bowery was *Jack Sheppard*, with Mrs. Shaw, who later appeared on her benefit night as Hamlet. John Gilbert made his first appearance in New York as Sir Edward Mortimer in *The Iron Chest*, but the fortunes of the theatre appeared to decline. Circus, boxing, aquatic drama, unsuccessful plays, and constant cuts in the price of admission, had brought the theatre to a very low ebb when on 25 Apr. 1845, for the fourth time in less than seventeen years, it was once more destroyed by fire, just prior to a benefit for the Davenports. The actors went to Tryon's Amphitheatre, and the Bowery was again rebuilt. It opened on 4 Aug. 1845, continuing its policy of melodrama, and Hamblin, still its manager, undertook also the management of the Park Theatre after the death of Simpson until it too was destroyed by fire.

In 1851 an actor who was long to be the idol of the Bowery audiences made his first appearance in a series of strong parts. This was Edward Eddy who, after the death of Hamblin in 1853 and the consequent decline of the theatre under several unsuitable managers, took over himself in 1857. He too was unable to restore prosperity to the old theatre and left after one season. On 7 Aug. 1858 the theatre (see No. 52) reopened under George L. Fox and James W. Lingard with a curious mixture of plays and pantomimes, and a series of melodramas by Boucicault. When they left to open the New Bowery in the following year the old Bowery, now the oldest playhouse in New York, was once again subjected to a series of incompetent managers. During the Civil War it was occupied by the military, and then became a circus. After thorough renovation, which it badly needed, Fox reopened it as Fox's Old Bowery, and put on a succession of novelties, including a pantomime based on the tale of Old Dame Trot and her Wonderful Cat. Long after old-fashioned farce had vanished from New York's newer playhouses it continued to flourish at the old Bowery, but melodrama was always its staple fare. On 2 Nov. 1868 Boucicault's *After Dark* was put on at the Bowery, but was stopped on the complaint of Niblo's managers, who held the American rights. The theatre then fell a victim to the prevalent craze for burlesque, and finally closed in 1878, having seen the New York début of Ada Rehan in melodrama and farce, a curious beginning for the future star of Daly's. In Sept. 1879 the old Bowery, which had spanned more than fifty years of the young American theatre, was reopened as the Thalia for plays in German, and was finally destroyed by its old enemy, fire, in 1929.

2. The New Bowery opened on 5 Sept. 1859, under Fox and Lingard, with a good company, some filched from the old Bowery, where the managers had been in office the previous year. The theatre had a short and somewhat undistinguished career, enlivened only by visits from guest-stars and the inevitable *Uncle Tom's Cabin*. When Fox returned to the old Bowery, Lingard carried on alone, with a stock company in an undistinguished repertory, and the season of 1866–7 was well under way, mainly with melodrama and pantomime, when on 18 Dec. 1866 the theatre was destroyed by fire and never rebuilt.

BOWYER, MICHAEL (?–1645), English actor, who, after several years on the stage, played leading romantic roles with the Queen's Men, a company organized at the Cockpit in 1625. He was apparently considered the leader of the company after Beeston, but some years later (about 1637) he left it for the King's Men, with whom he remained until the closing of the theatres in 1642. He was evidently a man of means, and he left a large legacy to his fellow player, Richard Perkins.

BOX, a term used for small compartments in the auditorium, now usually found only at the sides of the stage, though formerly they ran right round the pit, and could hold up to twenty people each. Modern boxes hold four or six. They are usually the most expensive but least adequate seats in the house, since from them one obtains a distorted sideways view of the stage. They were often occupied by those who wished to be seen as much as to see, and are now, even in the modern theatres which still retain them, seldom used. This does not apply to opera-houses, where they may still encircle the auditorium. In many theatres, particularly Court theatres, a large Royal, or King's, Box was placed in the centre of the first tier, over the entrance to the pit, directly facing the stage. In England, in Georgian times, it shifted to the side (see also ENGLISH PLAYHOUSE).

BOX-OFFICE, that part of a theatre devoted to the selling of seats. The name dates from the time when the majority of seats in the house, except in the gallery, were in boxes. The staff of the Box-Office may consist of from one to six persons, according to the size of the house, some of the larger theatres having separate divisions for differently priced seats, and for booking in advance. The term Pay-Box, used in the eighteenth century for the recesses at which entrance money was paid, is now generally reserved for those windows (i.e. gallery, amphitheatre, pit) which collect money at the door, and do no advance booking. But customs may vary from one theatre to another. The Box-Office is under the control of a Box-Office Manager, an important member of the theatre staff, who may remain attached to one theatre for many years and become, as it were, a repository of its history and traditions. He works long hours, and usually has three telephones to attend to at once, and half a dozen more connected to the 'libraries', or ticket-selling agencies. A quick mind, a cheerful disposition, and great patience and tact are requisites for this job, while the holder of it must be an accurate accountant and ready reckoner as well. The term 'box-office' is used metaphorically to indicate the appeal of a play to the public, and 'good box-office' may indicate a drawing-power in money incommensurate with the excellence of the fare offered. In happier circumstances the two may be combined, and good drama prove equally good box-office.

BOX-SET, a scene representing the three walls and ceiling of a room, not by means of perspective painting on wings, backcloth, and borders, as in early scenery, but by an arrangement of flats which form continuous walls, with practicable doors and windows, completely covered in by a ceiling cloth. The flats are lined-and-cleated together, edge to edge, on any desired ground plan, with reveals, or false thickness-pieces, to give solidity to the openings, and returns, or setbacks, in the walls. The bottoms of openings in a door or arch flat are strengthened by flat metal strips called sill irons. The box-set was first used in Mme Vestris's production of W. B. Bernard's *The Conquering Game* at the Olympic on 28 Nov. 1832, and brought to perfection in her production of Boucicault's *London Assurance* at Covent Garden in 1841. It is now in general use for most modern plays (for an early example, see No. 71; for later, Nos. 44, 69, 70, and some of Nos. 72–114).

BOY BISHOP, THE, a choirboy appointed to be the chief personage in the children's revels held either on St. Nicholas's Day (6 Dec.) or on Holy Innocents' (28 Dec.) in medieval cathedral and monastic schools. Earlier in origin than the Feast of Fools, with which it was sometimes amalgamated, this festival probably began as a serious church service conducted by the choirboys, but soon developed a secular, merry-making character, with plays—usually in Latin—given by the children, and considered as part of their education. It can be traced all over Europe and was extremely popular in England, where the first note of it (at York) is earlier than 1221. The custom of appointing a Boy Bishop survived till the Reformation; it was revived at Bermondsey in 1963, and later at Boston, Lincs.

BOY COMPANIES. In London during the sixteenth century plays were frequently given at Court by boy actors, particularly those attached to the choir schools and known as the Children of the Chapel and the Children of Paul's. In 1576 the former made their first public appearance at the Blackfriars, which for some time after was used exclusively as a children's theatre. The popularity of the boy players is attested by Hamlet's reference to them as 'an aerie of children, little eyases'. They achieved a quasi-professional status, and gave first performances of many important plays, including Jonson's *Cynthia's Revels* (1600) and *The Poetaster* (1601), and almost all the plays of Lyly.

BOYLE, ROGER, see ORRERY.

BOYLE, WILLIAM (1853–1923), Irish dramatist, whose first play was *The Building Fund* (1905), done at the newly established Abbey Theatre. With this, and with his later plays, *The Eloquent Dempsey* and *The Mineral Workers* (both 1906), he helped to establish the new type of 'realistic' Irish play which was soon to alter the character of the theatre as Yeats and Lady Gregory had originally conceived it.

BRACCO, ROBERTO (1862–1943), Italian playwright, whose work is only now becoming known, since he opposed Mussolini and was neglected under fascism. Though many of his plays are placed in Naples, he was not essentially a dialect writer. His weakness was over-indulgence in sentiment, his strength was acute psychological insight. He was a brilliant writer of comedy, reminiscent perhaps of Shaw in *Uno degli onesti* (1900), but unmistakably himself in the witty *Il perfetto amore* (1910), a highly sophisticated and frequently profound piece for a virtuoso actor and actress. *Don Pietro Caruso* (1895) and *Sperduti nel buio* (1901) are naturalistic studies of Neapolitan lower life, ironic and pathetic and uncompromisingly theatrical. Bracco resembles Giacosa in manifesting in his plays influences from Dumas *fils* (*Una donna*, 1892, and *Maschere*, 1893) to Ibsen (*Il trionfo*, 1895, and *I fantasmi*, 1906). Unlike him, he both established an identity that mattered and added to the techniques of serious drama. He was the first dramatist of the 'theatre of silence', well in advance of Jean-Jacques Bernard and Charles Vildrac. Major examples of this are *Il piccolo santo* (1909) and, less strikingly perhaps, *La piccola fonte* (1905) (see also ITALY, 3 *b*).

FREDERICK MAY

BRACE, see STAGE BRACE.

BRACEGIRDLE, ANNE (*c.* 1673/4–1748), one of the first and loveliest of English actresses. She first appeared on the stage as a child of 6. She was a pupil of Betterton, and was much indebted to him and to his wife for kindness and encouragement. In Downes's *Roscius Anglicanus* she is mentioned as one of the actresses of the Theatre Royal in 1688, playing young women's parts. She would then have been about 14 or 15. She made her greatest successes as the heroines of Congreve (whose mistress she was for some years), and was particularly applauded as Millamant. From 1680 until her retirement in 1707 she was universally admired and beloved, by her fellow actors as much as by the public, and deeply regretted when she left the stage at the height of her fame. But a new star had risen in the person of Anne Oldfield, and the older actress preferred to leave the field rather than be driven from it. She was buried in Westminster Abbey, and in the register of burials her age was mistakenly given as 85. The evidence in favour of her having been born *c.* 1673/4 and not *c.* 1664 is strengthened by the fact that in 1692 Captain Richard Hill (aged 19), who was madly in love with her, attempted to abduct her, and, with Lord Mohun, set on assassins to murder the actor William Mountfort, whom he suspected of being his successful rival. It is more likely that Mrs. Bracegirdle was about 18 at this time, and not 28.

BRACKENRIDGE, HUGH HENRY (1748–1816), an early American dramatist, author of two plays on the American Revolution, *The Battle of Bunkers Hill*, published in 1776, and *The Death of General Montgomery*, published in 1777. Brackenridge is perhaps more important in the history of the American novel than of the drama, but his verse is flexible and dignified, and he is faithful to the old traditions of blank verse and the three unities. His plays were probably given an amateur production at the Maryland Academy, where Brackenridge was a master. He was later a chaplain in the army.

BRADFORD CIVIC PLAYHOUSE, see AMATEUR THEATRE IN GREAT BRITAIN.

BRADY. (1) WILLIAM A. (1863–1950), American actor and theatre manager, who made his first appearance on the stage in San Francisco in 1882. He later toured successfully with his own company, and was for a considerable time seen as Svengali in *Trilby*. Among the New York theatres with which he was associated were the Forty-Eighth Street, the Manhattan, which he managed from 1896 until its demolition, and the Playhouse, which he built in 1911. He was responsible for a number of outstanding productions, in many of which his second wife, (2) GRACE GEORGE (1879–1961), appeared in leading parts. She had a long and active career in America, where she was particularly admired in such parts as Peg Woffington, Lady Teazle, Barbara Undershaft, Lady Cicely Waynflete, and the title-roles in *The First Mrs. Fraser* and *Mademoiselle*. She also adapted a number of plays from the French, in some of which she appeared. Her only appearance in London was at the Duke of York's in 1907 as Cyprienne in Sardou's *Divorçons*, which many considered her greatest achievement. By his first wife Brady was the father of (3) ALICE (1892–1939), who studied singing at the Boston Conservatory of Music, and appeared in a number of operettas, including Gilbert and Sullivan. Her first appearance as an actress was made in 1909, after which she was frequently seen in straight parts, both tragic and comic. She, like her father, was connected with the early days of the film industry, in which much of her later career was passed.

BRAHM [ABRAHAMSOHN], OTTO (1856–1912), a German literary critic with a marked interest in the theatre, who founded the journal *Die Freie Bühne* (later *Neue Deutsche Rundschau*), and in 1889 the dramatic enterprise of the same name. This was inspired by the work of Antoine's Théâtre Libre in Paris, and its main purpose, in marked contrast to that of the Devrients, was to further the work of the new naturalistic playwrights. For this a new type of actor had to be trained, and Brahm, already well known for his penetrating criticisms of contemporary acting, succeeded in getting together a noteworthy company, among whom the outstanding figure was Emanuel Reicher. In 1894 Brahm, realizing that the sporadic efforts of his new venture were insufficient, affiliated it to the larger Deutsches Theater group, established in 1883, and continued to produce both old and new plays in the new naturalistic style, brought to perfection in

Russia by Stanislavsky. This method was admirable for new plays written for this particular type of theatre, as was proved by such successes as *Die Familie Selicke* and *Vor Sonnenaufgang*. It failed when applied to older plays by classic or romantic writers, since it was inadequate to convey passion or exalted emotion or even polished comedy. Brahm, however, did good work in clearing the German stage of outmoded traditions, and bringing it into the main current of European drama.

BRAITHWAITE, Dame LILIAN (1873–1948), actress, who in 1943 was created D.B.E. for her services to the English stage. She had had some experience in amateur productions when in 1897 she appeared in a series of Shakespeare productions in Natal, and during her long and distinguished career she was seen in many revivals of the classics, as well as in a number of new plays. In her early years she was with Julia Neilson, and Frank Benson, and with Alexander at the St. James's for several seasons; she played Mrs. Gregory in *Mr. Wu*, both on its first production and in subsequent revivals, and in 1924 was Florence Lancaster in *The Vortex*. In later years she gave some excellent performances, notably as Queen Elizabeth in *La Femme sans homme*, and as Abby Brewster in the first English production of *Arsenic and Old Lace* (1942), which ran for over three years. She was the first wife of the actor Gerald Lawrence, by whom she had a daughter, the actress Joyce Carey.

BRANDANE, JOHN [DR. JOHN MACINTYRE] (1869–1947), Scottish dramatist, born of working-class parents in Bute. His father was of Highland descent, his mother of Lowland. As a boy he worked twelve hours a day in a cotton mill in Glasgow, and later, from his fifteenth to his twenty-seventh year, he was a clerk in a warehouse. During part of that time he studied medicine, qualifying as a doctor in 1901. He then became a general practitioner in various parts of England and Scotland. His interest in drama was stimulated by his visits to performances by the Abbey Theatre players during their seasons in London, and after he settled in Glasgow he began writing plays for the Scottish National players, a company formed to foster Scottish drama. He fought uncompromisingly for his ideal school of Scottish dramatists and actors who would derive sustenance from their native soil. In *The Glen is Mine* he contributed to that movement its best Scots comedy. He has also written a number of other plays, some of which have been translated into Erse, Gaelic, German, and Norse. Brandane's plays are strongly constructed and alive with acute observation and humour, while the dialogue has a natural unaffected Highland lilt. It was largely due to Brandane's influence that James Bridie became a playwright. WILLIAM JEFFREY†

BRANDES. (1) GEORG MORRIS COHEN (1842–1927), Danish critic, was an aesthetician, philosopher, and writer of articles for the contemporary Danish press, whose influence as a dramatic critic was felt throughout Denmark and beyond. He succeeded Hauch in the Chair of Aesthetics at Copenhagen in 1872 and in the same year he founded the Litteraturselskabet (The Society of Literature), gathering round him a circle of critics and writers. Among them was his brother (2) EDVARD (1847–1931), who, with Otto Benzon, was one of the earliest exponents of modern social drama in Denmark (see SCANDINAVIA, 1 *a*). Georg Brandes gathered into his mind the best of contemporary European thought and culture and eventually became famous for his *Hovedstrømninger* (*Main Currents of Nineteenth Century Literature*) (6 vols., 1872–90), in which he traced the tendencies and development of European culture. He departed from the systematic criticism of the schools of Hegel and Heiberg and developed instead the psychological criticism of Taine, maintaining that literature must be related to the problems of its time and can best be interpreted in the light of that background. This aesthetic creed made him quickly appreciate Ibsen's work and ranged him on Ibsen's side when the criticism of his work became controversial. Throughout that period Brandes was one of the most constant, as he was the most penetrating, of Ibsen's defenders, and for many modern readers he is remembered primarily as the author of a series of essays on the drama of Ibsen and Bjørnson and for his volume *Henrik Ibsen* (1898).

BRANDES. (1) JOHANN CHRISTIAN (1735–99), a German actor and playwright, whose reminiscences, *Meine Lebensgeschichte*, published in 1800, give a fairly clear idea of the organization and vicissitudes of theatrical companies during the eighteenth century. After a miserable boyhood he became a manservant, which gave him the opportunity of improving his manners and his education, and in 1757 joined Schönemann's company, of which the celebrated Ekhof was then a member. He was not successful, and when the troupe broke up was obliged to return to domestic service. His first settled engagement came later, with the company of the old harlequin-player Schuch, who was an excellent friend to him. It was while he was with Schuch that Brandes married in 1764 the sister of a fellow actor, (2) ESTHER CHARLOTTE HENRIETTA (*née* Koch) (1746–84), who soon proved herself a good actress, particularly in grand tragic parts. This brought her into continual conflict with the redoubtable Sophie Hensel, particularly at Mannheim and at Hamburg, where her husband was for a short time, during Schröder's stay in Vienna, appointed manager. His easy-going ways and weak affability helped to bring the theatre into disrepute, which was only checked by the return of Schröder. Brandes, as he confesses in his memoirs, was at best a poor actor, but he prided himself on his plays, which are now forgotten. The most successful of them were probably *Miss Fanny*, which had a thrilling shipwreck with appropriate music, and the monodrama (a genre of his own invention) *Ariadne auf Naxos*. Of his three children the eldest (3) MINNA (1765–88), who was Lessing's godchild, made her first appearance on the stage in one of her father's plays. She later developed a fine voice, and was highly thought of in opera as well as in straight plays. She died when she was only 23, and was much missed by the Hamburg audiences. Brandes, having lost his wife and only son a year or so previously, retired to Berlin, where he lived on the proceeds of his literary labours and occasionally appeared at the National Theatre under Iffland.

BRANSBY WILLIAMS, see WILLIAMS, BRANSBY.

BRAYTON, LILY (1876–1953), see ASCHE (2).

BRAZIL, see SOUTH AMERICA, 2.

BRECHT, BERTOLT (1898–1956), German dramatist and poet. He was born in Augsburg, Bavaria, but his parents were of Swabian origin. Although his father was a Catholic, Brecht was brought up in the faith of his mother, who was a Protestant. He received his secondary schooling at the Augsburger Realgymnasium, where he was nearly expelled during the First World War for expressing pacifist sentiments in an essay his class had been set to write on the subject 'Dulce et decorum est pro patria mori'. By the age of 16 he was already contributing poems to a local newspaper. According to the school registers, he left school in 1917 without matriculating because he was called to serve at the front as a medical orderly shortly before the examinations were due to be held. After the war, however, he went to Munich with the intention of studying medicine as a *Gasthörer* at the university. The dramatic movement known as Expressionism was celebrating some of its greatest successes at this time. Many of the private Court theatres had been taken over by the civic authorities, and the war-time censorship no longer operated. There were also many newly-formed experimental theatre groups and clubs, and the theatre-going public was on the whole favourably inclined towards the work of new young authors. Brecht had always shown an interest in the theatre and was at this time theatre critic for the *Augsburger Volkswille*. His medical studies were soon neglected for work on a play called *Trommeln in der Nacht*, which, with the help of the dramatist Lion Feuchtwanger, was accepted and performed by the Munich Kammerspiele in 1922. The play was about a soldier returning home after the war. Brecht set the action against the background of the German Communist revolution of 1919 and made his hero, disillusioned and tired of strife, turn his back on the revolutionaries fighting for a better future and accept the fiancée who had been sleeping with a black-marketeer in his absence. This new sober-cynical tone, which contrasted so strongly with the emotional idealism of some of the other Expressionist plays, marked the beginning of a reaction which later developed into the literary phase known as 'die neue Sachlichkeit'. It was remarked upon by Herbert Jhering, the influential theatre critic of the *Berliner Börsen-Courier*, who awarded Brecht the Kleist Prize for his play and championed him throughout his later career.

From 1922 onwards Brecht made repeated visits to Berlin, the real centre of German theatrical life in the 1920s. In 1924 he settled there permanently and spent some time as Max Reinhardt's assistant at the Deutsches Theater, together with another young dramatist, Carl Zuckmayer. In these years Brecht wrote a number of plays which are now mainly interesting as the attempts of a dramatist in an age of experiment to find and develop his own style. They show him putting into practice the now famous theories of Epic Theatre and 'alienation' (*Verfremdung*) long before he formulated them in writing. The avowed aim of this new type of theatre was to alienate the subject-matter of the drama by destroying the illusion, interrupting the course of the action, and lowering the tension, so that the audience could remain emotionally disengaged during the performance and capable of taking an intelligent and objective view of what it was offered.

Brecht's first real success with the theatre-going public was *Die Dreigroschenoper* (1928), an adaptation of John Gay's *The Beggar's Opera*, for which Kurt Weill, a pupil of Busoni, wrote music in the American jazz idiom. Like all Brecht's adaptations, it was so different from the original as to constitute virtually an original work. Macheath, the hero of Gay's opera, becomes an anti-social villain, working hand-in-glove with the foolish chief of a corrupt police force, while Peachum is seen as Macheath's victim, and the only man aware of the poverty and distress behind the facade of Victorian England's political supremacy.

Brecht was reading Marx's *Das Kapital* in the mid-1920s and the influence of this work is traceable in a *Singspiel* called *Aufstieg und Fall der Stadt Mahagonny* (1927; music again by Weill; produced as a 3-act opera in 1930). This deals with the founding and destruction of a boom-town in the chaos of a capitalistically-governed country. However, Marxism did not become an all-determining force in his work until the early 1930s, when he wrote a number of short didactic plays, the best of which are probably *Die Massnahme* and *Die Ausnahme und die Regel*. These plays have a dramatic economy, a starkness and simplicity of language, and a seriousness of tone approaching severity only occasionally found in the earlier work.

These newly acquired powers are wedded to the old exuberance in *Die Heilige Johanna der Schlachthöfe*—the most ambitious of Brecht's plays up to that time, in which he seems to have found a theme, a subject, and a conflict of such magnitude that they offer scope for all the dramatic forms and devices with which he had experimented in the ten preceding years: a poor but determined little Salvation Army girl tries to save the exploited workers in the Chicago meat factories from starvation by appealing to the feelings of the rich factory-owners, and it is not until she has helped to thwart a Communist-organized revolt, on the grounds that violence is un-Christian, that she discovers violence is the basis of the whole capitalist system. It was because of such plays as this that Brecht had to flee from Germany in 1933, on the advent of National Socialism, taking with him his wife, the actress Helene Weigel, and their two children. 'Changing countries more often than his shoes', as Brecht puts it in one of his poems written during these years of exile, he lived alternately in Switzerland, Denmark, and Finland, finally arriving, in 1941, in California, where he remained till the war was over. (The reason which has been offered for Brecht's preferring America to Russia is that Russia was Germany's ally in 1941.)

It was during these years that Brecht wrote what are generally considered to be his more important plays—*Mutter Courage und ihre Kinder*, *Das Leben des Galilei*, *Der gute Mensch von Sezuan*, and *Der kaukasische Kreidekreis*. These plays possess a maturity of vision and depth of expression combined with a wider sympathy for the human predicament than is found in any of the earlier plays. It is the human dilemma in the social or political conflict which is now stressed. Mother Courage has to make a living for herself and her children by following in the wake of the armies in the Thirty Years' War and supplying the common soldier with his daily needs; but the war really lives off her, claiming all her children one by one for its victims and finally leaving her destitute. Galileo wishes to make scientific experiments and discover secrets of the universe that will liberate mankind physically and spiritually; but his choice of patron lies between the Venetian senate, who exploit his discoveries for purposes of aggressive commercial and imperial expansion, and the Duke of Florence, with his allegiance to the Roman church, for whose obscurantist notions Galileo's discoveries are heresy. Shen-Te's greatest wish is to be the good woman of Setzuan and come to the help of all the poor and the desperate; but she discovers that human nature and the conditions of human existence are such that it is impossible to survive without exploiting one's fellow-men.

After the war, in 1947, Brecht was called before the Committee of Un-American Activities to account for certain opinions expressed in his work, and although no charge was brought against him, he left America in the same year. He first went to Switzerland, but on receiving an invitation from the East German government to take charge of a theatre and a group of actors to be maintained at the expense of the state, he moved to East Berlin and there founded the troupe called the Berliner Ensemble at the Theater am Schiffbauerdamm, where his own *Dreigroschenoper* had had its long, successful run in the 1920s. More important than his adaptations of the work of other authors (Lenz's *Der Hofmeister*, Farquhar's *Recruiting Officer*), propagandist in tone and specially made for performance by the new company, were the authoritative productions of his own plays, some of which had only received amateur or club performances up to that date. Most popular of all was the production of *Mutter Courage* (see No. 108), with Brecht's wife, at the peak of her career, playing the title-role. The high standard of acting and production, as well as the plays themselves, drew the attention of a wider audience than that of East Germany to Brecht's work. The visit of his company to Paris in 1955 was received with enthusiasm, and when he died in August 1956 his company was rehearsing for an impending visit to London (see below). Since his death, the work of the Berliner Ensemble has been continued under the supervision of his widow.

It is still too early to assess Brecht's place in the history of German drama. His fame after his death led to his work and his dramatic theories being imitated in most countries where they were known, and a great deal has already been written on both by scholars and theatre-critics. RICHARD BECKLEY

The influence of Brecht's works, and particularly of his methods of production, has been extensive both in England and in America. It has been disseminated by critics and writers, and by productions of his plays in the original and in translation. On their first visit to London in 1956 (they have not yet (1965) appeared in New York), the Berliner Ensemble were seen at the Palace Theatre in *Mutter Courage und ihre Kinder*, *Pauken und Trompeten* (based on Farquhar), and *Der kaukasische Kreidekreis*. On a second visit, in 1965, they played at the National Theatre (Old Vic) in *Die Dreigroschenoper*, *Koriolan* (based on Shakespeare), *Die Tage der Commune*, and *Der aufhaltsame Aufstieg des Arturo Ui*. In translation, the first play to be given was probably *Señora Carrar's Rifles*, produced at Unity by John Fernald as early as 1938. Other productions at this theatre were *Mother Courage*, *Simone Machard* and *The Exception and the Rule*. *Mother Courage* was also done by Theatre Workshop at the Taw and Torridge Festival in 1955, with Joan Littlewood in the title-role, and at the National Theatre in 1965, with Madge Ryan. In 1956 *The Good Woman of Setzuan*, with Peggy Ashcroft in the dual role of the prostitute Shen-Te and her male cousin, was seen at the Royal Court, which had already produced *The Threepenny Opera* (in an adaptation by Marc Blitzstein which ran for six years in New York; see THEATRE DE LYS) earlier in the year, and was to do *Happy End* in 1965. *Galileo*, first seen in English in an amateur production at Birmingham University, and in New York in 1947, was produced at the Mermaid in 1963, as was *Schweik in the Second World War*. The Royal Shakespeare company at the Aldwych in 1962 did *The Caucasian Chalk Circle*, and in 1965 *Puntila*, which, as *Herr Puntila und sein Knecht*, was written in 1940, while Brecht was in Finland, but not produced until 1948, at Zürich. In 1963 Peter O'Toole was seen in *Baal* at the Phoenix; and the operatic version of *Aufstieg und Fall der Stadt Mahagonny* was given at Sadler's Wells. In New York a programme, *Brecht on Brecht*, an anthology compiled from his works by George Tabori, had a long run at the Theatre de Lys in 1962. Other plays seen in New York in translation were *Mother Courage and her Children* (1963), with Anne Bancroft, and *Arturo Ui* (1964), with Christopher Plummer. (See also No. 108).

BRÉCOURT [GUILLAUME MARCOUREAU] (1638–85), French actor and dramatist, child of strolling players, who had an adventurous and nomadic life. He was playing in the provinces in 1659 when he married an actress, Étiennette Des Urlis (*c.* 1630–1713), whose two sisters, Madeleine and Catherine, and brother Jean, were at the Théâtre du Marais, where the newly married couple joined them. Catherine Des Urlis had been with Molière in his first venture, the Illustre-Théâtre, and in 1660 Brécourt, probably introduced to Molière by his sister-in-law, joined the company at the Palais-Royal. He remained only two years, however, and left unregretted, owing to his quarrelsome temper, going to join Floridor at the Hôtel de Bourgogne. After Molière's death Brécourt wrote a one-act play about him, *L'Ombre de Molière* (1674), in which he spoke most feelingly of the great actor-dramatist's good qualities. Brécourt, who was the first to play Britannicus in Racine's play, had the misfortune in 1680 to kill a coachman in a fit of temper, and was forced to take refuge in Holland. Pardoned by Louis XIV, whose life he is said to have saved in a boar-hunt, he entered the Comédie-Française and remained there until his death. In 1682 he was arrested for debt, and had to attend rehearsals and performances in charge of a jailer, who took him to and from his prison cell. Among his plays, some of which are lost, the best was *La Feinte Mort de Jodelet*, given at the Marais in 1659, just before the comedian named in the title left there to join Molière.

BREDERO, GERBRAND ADRIAENSZ (1585–1618), see NETHERLANDS, THE.

BREECHES PARTS, the name given to roles written for handsome young heroes in romantic comedy and played by personable young women; not to be confused with the temporary assumption of male attire for the purpose of disguise by such heroines as Rosalind or Viola, nor with the serious undertaking of such parts as Hamlet, Romeo, Richard III, or Shylock by intrepid actresses. The classic example of a breeches part is Sir Harry Wildair in *The Constant Couple*, as played by Peg Woffington and later by Mrs. Jordan. Others who wore the breeches with no little success were Nell Gwynn, Mrs. Bracegirdle, and Mrs. Mountfort, who was considered outstanding as Lothario and Macheath. This fashion for playing *en travesti* formed an essential part of Regency spectacle and Victorian extravaganza, the great exponent in the latter style being Madame Vestris, and was one of the formative elements in the development of the Principal Boy (played by a young woman) in pantomime.

BRETÓN DE LOS HERREROS, MANUEL (1796–1873), Spanish playwright. Author of more than 100 original plays, he also translated from the French and adapted seventeenth-century *comedias*. His plays are mostly comedies, and are for the most part written in easy, flowing verse. He may be said to follow in the tradition of Moratín in that his comedies have often an element of social satire, but his main intention is undoubtedly to divert his audience. Bretón's literary life spanned the period which saw neo-classicism challenged by Romanticism. Neither literary fashion had a very great impact on the theatre-going public and, in his refusal to be swept off his feet by these literary currents, Bretón perhaps reflects more correctly the taste of his times than either Moratín or Zorrilla. Among his best-known plays are *Marcela, o ¿a cuál de los tres?* (1831), *Muérete ¡y verás!* (1837), and *El pelo de la dehesa* (1840). J. E. VAREY

BRIDGE, a mechanical device for raising heavy pieces of scenery, or a tableau formed by a number of actors, from below to stage level. The joists and floor-boards were cut and framed, usually with sliders, to allow a large platform, framed and tied, to rise in corner-grooves with the aid of counterweights and a winch. Great variety is found in the design of bridges, and today the electrically-controlled bridges of a large theatre may reach a high degree of engineering complexity.

RICHARD SOUTHERN

BRIDGES, JOHN, see STEVENSON, WILLIAM.

BRIDIE, JAMES, C.B.E. [DR. OSBORNE HENRY MAVOR] (1888–1951), Scottish dramatist, born in Glasgow, where his father conducted an engineering business. Educated at the Glasgow Academy and Glasgow University, he qualified at the age of 25 as a medical practitioner. Meanwhile visits to the Abbey players, and other itinerant theatrical attractions, had aroused his latent interest in the theatre. He was invited to write a play for the Glasgow Repertory Theatre, and did so, but it was never produced. He became in turn a successful general practioner, a consulting physician at a large hospital and, during the First World War, a doctor in the army. This took him far afield in Mesopotamia, Persia, and Russia, on journeys which he has described in a whimsical book, *Some Talk of Alexander*, and from which he drew local colour for his comedy *Marriage is no Joke* (1934) and for his biblical plays. After the war he resumed his medical career in Glasgow. James Bridie's first success in the theatre was made through the Scottish National players, who, under John Brandane, were striving to nurse a Scottish drama into life (see SCOTLAND). Brandane drew Mavor into the circle as playwright and reader of plays, and so James Bridie was born. His first pen-name, however, was Mary Henderson, to whom was credited *The Sunlight Sonata*, produced by Tyrone Guthrie in 1928 with Elliot Mason and Morland Graham in the cast. Once set in motion, Bridie's pen seemed tireless, and plays followed each other in quick succession, including *The Anatomist* and *Tobias and the Angel* (both 1930), *Jonah and the Whale* (1932), *A Sleeping Clergyman* (1933), *Colonel Wotherspoon* (1934), *The Black Eye* (1935), *Storm in a Teacup* (an adaptation of Bruno Frank's *Sturm im Wasserglas*, with a Scots setting) (1936), *Susannah and the Elders* (1937), *The King of Nowhere* (1938), and *What Say They?* (1939). In addition to these plays James Bridie wrote a witty autobiography, *One Way of Living* (1939), two books of essays, and a book for children. On the outbreak of the Second World War in 1939 he rejoined the Army Medical Corps with the rank of Major, but continued to write plays, as witness *Mr. Bolfry* (1943), *It Depends What You Mean* and *The Forrigan Reel* (both 1944), and *Dr. Angelus* (1946). He returned to civilian life before the end of the war and played a leading part in the founding of the Glasgow Citizens' Theatre. In 1949 his *Daphne Laureola*, with Edith Evans in the title-role, had a great success in London, and in the following year he wrote, for the Edinburgh Festival, *The Queen's Comedy*, which many consider his best play. His last play was *The Baikie Charivari*, which was produced by the Glasgow Citizens' in 1952. As A. P. Kelloch, Bridie also had a hand in three pantomimes at the Glasgow Citizens'. He held a number of important medical posts, and continued in practice until 1938. WILLIAM JEFFREY†, *rev.*

BRIEUX, EUGÈNE (1858–1932), French dramatist, whose plays are naturalistic dramas in the tradition of Zola and Henri Becque. In him, however, bitterness and misery were tempered by a deep pity for humanity, and he railed not so much at the sins of the flesh as at the social conditions which produced them. Each of his plays is, as it were, a plea for the amelioration of some particular evil, which sometimes degenerates into a sermon lacking in dramatic action. This tendency to mistake the theatre for a pulpit was Brieux's greatest weakness, as he himself realized. But in his best plays he combined his didactic outlook with a fierce pity for individual victims which produced some fine and lasting pieces of work. Chief among them are *Les Trois Filles de M. Dupont* (1898), which portrays the dangers of a marriage of convenience; *La Robe rouge* (1900), which exposes the abuses of the judiciary system; *Les Avariés* (1902), a study of venereal disease which, as *Damaged Goods*, created a sensation in England and America; and *Maternité* (1903), which deals with the question of legalized birth-control. Most of Brieux's plays will be forgotten as the conditions he writes of pass away, but these four will probably continue to be revived, since they represent the best works of an undoubted talent, and their general interest far exceeds that of the momentary problems they attack.

BRIGHELLA, one of the *zanni* or servant roles of the *commedia dell'arte*. Like Arlecchino, he has some connexion with Bergamo, but has in him much of the Neapolitan street-corner boy. Originally a thief, a bully, and an intriguer, he gradually quietened down until he became a lackey, retaining his love of intrigue and lying. Through the influence of the Italian popular comedy in France, he may have had some part in the shaping of the French valets of Marivaux and others, and so entered into the composition of Figaro.

BRIGHOUSE, HAROLD (1882–1958), English dramatist, usually referred to as one of the so-called 'Manchester School', together with Allan Monkhouse and Stanley Houghton, though many of his later plays were not produced at Miss Horniman's Gaiety Theatre, Manchester. It was there, however, that Brighouse got his start, and he had written a number of plays before he scored an instant success with *Hobson's Choice*, which was first seen at the Apollo, London, in 1916, with Norman McKinnel as old Hobson, whose managing daughter Maggie insists on marrying her father's timid little employee, Willie Mossop. The play wears well, and has been revived frequently, notably at the National Theatre (Old Vic) in 1965. Brighouse continued to write plays, both full-length and one-act, for many years, but none of them was as successful as *Hobson's Choice*, though *The Northerners* (1914), a play on the Luddites, has been favourably compared with Toller's on the same theme. Brighouse was the author of several novels, and of an autobiography, published in 1952, and in his later years he was on the staff of the *Manchester Guardian*.

BRIGHTON, which is an important stopping-place for plays on their way into or out of London, had its first permanent theatre in 1774. This was built in North Street by a bricklayer named Samuel Paine. The first lessee, Roger Johnstone, was succeeded by Fox, who built a new theatre in Duke Street in 1790 at the cost of £500. This was later remodelled in horseshoe form, and a royal box added. It closed in 1806, when a theatre in New Road was built, opening in 1807 under Brunton. It ruined a number of managers, in spite of royal patronage, and had to be closed temporarily in 1820. Redecorated and re-opened, it staged its first pantomime in 1823. In 1854 Nye Chart became lessee of the theatre, which he bought outright in 1866, demolishing it and building another on the same site. His management lasted until his death in 1876, when he was succeeded by his widow. It was while playing at this theatre in Oct. 1891 that Fred Terry and Julia Neilson were married. Touring companies started to visit the theatre in 1868, but the stock company existed up to 1873. There was in Hove an adapted church hall, known as the Little Theatre (in Farman Street, a few yards from the Brighton boundary). Its managers were Ernest Baxter and Ruth Goddard. It opened in 1901, and closed in 1928, reverting to its former state as a parish-hall—St. Patrick's.

SYBIL ROSENFELD

BRIGHTON THEATRE, NEW YORK, see BIJOU THEATRE, 3.

BRISTOL, home of the Bristol Old Vic and of the first university in England to have a drama department, had its first theatre in 1729, built by John Hippisley at Jacob's Wells. This was used by a mixed company from London, while the Bath company, who had already obtained a foothold in the town in spite of Puritan opposition, continued to provide a spring season. In 1766 a new theatre in King Street (see No. 27) was erected at a cost of £5,000. The architect was John Paty, who had plans from Saunders, a Drury Lane carpenter, and many features echo those of the London playhouse. A royal patent was obtained in 1778. The connexion with Bath, broken in 1817, was renewed by the younger Macready in 1837. The stock company lasted until 1878. The Theatre Royal then became the home of variety and pantomime until in 1943 it reopened as the Bristol Old Vic (with a drama school attached) with the help of the Council for the Encouragement of Music and the Arts (later the Arts Council). It was thus the first theatre in England to be state-aided. In 1962 the Arts Council relinquished its lease of the theatre, which was taken over by the City Council, to be run by a Theatre Trust (for the Bristol University Drama Department, see UNIVERSITY DEPARTMENTS OF DRAMA).

SYBIL ROSENFELD

BRITANNIA THEATRE, LONDON, stood in High Street, Hoxton, on the site of an Elizabethan tavern called the Pimlico, to which Shakespeare is said to have resorted. Sam Lane (1804–71) built it as the Britannia Saloon in 1841, and ran it as a place of entertainment, charging only for refreshments, until in 1843 the abolition of the old Patents enabled him to stage complete plays, mainly farce and strong drama. The Britannia, or the Brit., as it was usually called, prospered, and in 1850 Lane enlarged and improved it, making it a true theatre. Among other attractions, James Anderson appeared in a number of Shakespeare plays at a weekly salary of £120. In 1858 the theatre was again enlarged to hold 3,000 people. After Lane's death his widow, Sara Lane (1823–99), an excellent actress related by marriage to the Lupino family, continued in management, and ran it successfully until her death, over a quarter of a century later. The Britannia was an institution, with its own traditions, and its history is unique in London's theatrical annals. No theatre has ever been for so long under one management. Authors wrote for it exclusively, actors joined it as boys and remained until old age. Its main support came from the people of the surrounding neighbourhood, who loved it and revered its manageress. In its annual pantomimes (which always ran till Easter) Sara Lane played the Principal Boy until she was in her seventies. In these magnificent spectacles the transformation scene was an outstanding feature. The Britannia was the last London theatre to give up its own local and democratic drama and take in touring companies. After the death of Mrs. Lane, mourned by the entire neighbourhood, the theatre passed into the hands of relatives and became a cinema. In 1927 three generations of the Lupino family, who had so often played there, went to the Britannia, gave a farewell show, and addressed the audience amid scenes of the wildest enthusiasm. The theatre then became a cinema, and was destroyed by bombing in 1940.

W. MACQUEEN-POPE†

BRITISH ACTORS' EQUITY ASSOCIATION, see EQUITY.

BRITISH COUNCIL, THE. Founded in 1934 for the purpose of promoting a wider knowledge of the United Kingdom and the English language abroad and developing closer cultural relations with other countries, the British Council established its Drama Department in 1937. In this field the Council's main activities are the sponsoring of overseas tours by leading British companies, the distribution of copies of British plays with a view to their performance overseas by local professional and amateur companies, the giving of advice and information on theatrical matters, and the sponsoring of visits to Britain by eminent personalities of the theatre for professional studies and contacts with representatives of the British theatre. Among the United Kingdom scholarships awarded by the Council to graduates and others of like status from overseas there are a number for studies relating to drama and the theatre. Brochures which have been specially produced by the Council for overseas readers include *Drama Since 1939*, designed to meet the demand for information in countries that were cut off during the war, *The British Theatre*, three annual surveys of *The Year's Work in the Theatre* for the years 1948–49, 1949–50, and 1950–51, *Drama 1945–50* and *The British Theatre since 1950*. Shortly before the outbreak of the Second World War the Council sponsored tours of Europe, Malta, and Egypt by the Old Vic and Dublin Gate Theatre companies, and performances of Gielgud's *Hamlet* at Elsinore, A tour of Holland by the Sadler's Wells Ballet in 1940 was cut short by the German invasion of that country. Since 1945 a number of theatre and ballet companies have toured under the auspices of the Council, particularly in 1964 in connexion with the Shakespeare Quatercentenary celebrations, visiting not only Europe but also the U.S.S.R., the Middle and Far East, West Africa, Australia, and the West Indies. In April 1961 the Council's Drama and Music Departments were amalgamated.

BRITISH DRAMA LEAGUE (B.D.L.), see AMATEUR THEATRE IN GREAT BRITAIN.

BRITISH THEATRE MUSEUM ASSOCIATION. This was founded in Oct. 1957 on the initiative of the Society for Theatre Research, which had convened a meeting of interested parties in 1955. Its objects were to preserve theatrical material in Great Britain, and to make it available to the public by the establishment of a Theatre Museum. Trustees were appointed to hold gifts and bequests, and Laurence Irving, grandson of Henry Irving, became the first Chairman of the Association. A large amount of material has already been donated, among which may be mentioned the Henry Irving archives containing some 4,000 items, the Murray Carrington and Ernest Short collections, and the archives of the English Stage Society. In order to publicize its work the Association has mounted a series of exhibitions at the Saville Theatre, including ones of Gordon Craig, *Hamlet*, Ivor Novello, and several drawn from its own collection. In 1962 premises were found at Leighton House, Kensington. Sir Hugh Casson devised a scheme of decoration, and the Museum was opened to the public on 18 June 1963.

BRITTON, HUTIN (1876–1965), see LANG (2).

BRIZARD [BRITARD], JEAN-BAPTISTE (1721–91), French actor, of good family and well educated. He had a decided talent for painting, which, like Bellecourt, he studied under Van Loo, but gave it up for the stage. He had been for ten years in the provinces when in 1756 he attracted the attention of Mlle Clairon and Mlle Dumesnil, who happened to be in Lyon during his appearance there. The following year he joined the company of the Comédie-Française and, owing to being prematurely white, could play old men's parts without a wig. Of a dignified presence, with a good voice and a natural style of acting, he was much admired, particularly as Henry of Navarre in *La Partie de chasse d'Henri IV* when in 1774 it was finally passed by the censor. Brizard was also the first French actor to play Lear, in the adaptation by Ducis, in 1782. He retired in 1786, much regretted by the public and by his companions, and employed his leisure by again taking up painting, which he had abandoned for the theatre forty years previously.

BROADHURST, GEORGE HOWELLS (1866–1952), American dramatist, born in London, who at the age of 20 went to the United States and became manager of several provincial theatres. His work marks the transition in American drama at the turn of the twentieth century from the old melodrama to modern comedy, and though his early plays were farcical comedies like *What Happened to Jones* (1897) and *Why Smith Left Home* (1899), a more serious note is struck later, notably in *The Man of the Hour* (1906), probably his best play. He did not, however, entirely desert his earlier melodramatic style, as is shown by his production in 1911 of *Bought and Paid For.* On 27 Sept. 1917 Broadhurst opened his own theatre at West 44th Street with *Misalliance.* His first outstanding venture was *39 East*, which ran for 160 performances, and then moved elsewhere to make room for the first play by Broadhurst to be seen at his own theatre, *The Crimson Alibi* (1919). Later successes at this theatre include *Beggar on Horseback*, produced by Winthrop Ames, the record-making *Broadway*, first of a long series of gangster plays, a revival of *The Merchant of Venice*, and, in 1931, a fine production of *Hamlet* with Raymond Massey and Colin Keith-Johnston, in a vast setting designed by Norman Bel Geddes. This, however, had less success than the series of light musical comedies to which the theatre was later devoted, though in 1933 the Pulitzer Prize-winner, *Men in White*, was seen there, as was *Victoria Regina*, in which Helen Hayes gave an outstanding performance as the Queen, in 1935. In 1959 *Fiorello!*, a musical based on the life of New York's mayor La Guardia, started a long and successful run, and in 1964 came London's Theatre Workshop's *Oh, What a Lovely War!*, produced by Joan Littlewood.

BROADWAY, the symbol for the commercial theatre in the United States, as the West End or Shaftesbury Avenue in London is for England, since almost from the beginning of theatre history in New York the main playhouses have been located on Broadway, or in the side-streets that lead off that famous thoroughfare (see New York theatres under their own names).

BROADWAY MUSIC-HALL, NEW YORK, see BROADWAY THEATRE, 2.

BROADWAY OPERA HOUSE, NEW YORK, see BIJOU THEATRE, 3.

BROADWAY THEATRE, NEW YORK. 1. The first Broadway was a bright, cheerful theatre, with gold and white decorations, built by Trimble, architect of the Olympic. It opened on 27 Sept. 1847 with Henry Wallack and Rose Telbin as the Teazles in *The School for Scandal*, while Lester Wallack played in the afterpiece, his first appearance in New York. The Broadway had been intended as a stock house but, after the final destruction by fire of the old Park Theatre, took its place as a home of visiting stars. Forrest was there when the Astor Place riot took place, caused, it was believed, by his jealousy of Macready. Charlotte Cushman, after four years in England, reappeared at the Broadway as America's greatest tragic actress, and in the same year, 1849, the Bateman children, Kate aged 6 and Ellen aged 4, appeared as Portia and Shylock, Richmond and Richard III, Macbeth and

Lady Macbeth. Later stars seen at the Broadway included Lola Montez, Julia Dean, and Mr. and Mrs. Barney Williams, and it was there that Boker's fine poetic play, *Francesca da Rimini*, was first seen, in 1855. Shortly afterwards, when workmen were excavating for a new building next door, the walls of the theatre fell down and had to be rebuilt, but it seemed as if the prestige of the house, which had never really taken the place of the old Park, was fatally injured, for after a poor season in 1857–8, redeemed only by a visit from the younger Mathews, it sank to circus and variety, and closed with a spectacular show on 2 Apr. 1859.

2. On 2 Sept. 1861 Wallack's old theatre opened as the Broadway Music-hall. It had a chequered career, under a variety of names, and saw one of the few appearances in New York of the assassin of Lincoln, John Wilkes Booth, in Richard III and other parts. It was for some time known as the Olympic, but finally, renovated and redecorated, it opened as the Broadway Theatre under George Wood. It had a short life, and the main incidents were the emergence of John E. Owens as a fine comedian in *The People's Lawyer*, in which he played Solon Shingle, the truly rural old Yankee farmer, and as Caleb Plummer in *Dot*, Boucicault's version of *The Cricket on the Hearth*; the farewell appearance in New York of the Charles Keans, and of Julia Dean; and the production by Florence of *Caste*. This was first seen on 5 Aug. 1867, and caused trouble, as Lester Wallack thought he held the American rights in the play. It subsequently transpired that Florence had seen and memorized the play in London and, in the absence of international copyright laws, he won the case which Lester Wallack brought against him. In later years he is known to have regretted his action. A year later the site of the theatre was required for shops, and it closed on 28 Apr. 1869, being subsequently demolished.

3. A concert hall on 41st Street, originally known as the Metropolitan Casino, which opened on 27 May 1880 and saw, among other things, the famous Hanlon-Lees troupe in their *Voyage en Suisse*, was rebuilt and opened as the Broadway on 3 Mar. 1888, with Fanny and Harry Davenport in Sardou's *La Tosca*. In 1890 Mrs. Leslie Carter made her first professional appearance at this theatre in *The Ugly Duckling*, and in 1899 came the successful run of *Ben Hur*. An English pantomime had a long run in 1901, but all previous records were eclipsed by the popularity of *Little Lord Fauntleroy* in 1907. Among the European actors who visited this theatre were Modjeska, Salvini, and Mlle Rhéa, while Helen Hayes appeared there as a child. Weber and Fields occupied the house with variety for a while, and after the failure of a Sousa operetta in the early part of 1913 it became a cinema. Closed in 1928, it was pulled down a year later.

4. On Broadway at 53rd Street. This was originally a cinema which opened in 1924, but from 1930–3 it was used for revue and for Earl Carroll's *Vanities*. After a further session as a cinema, it housed such varied productions as *This is the Army* (1942) and *Carmen Jones* (1943), and revivals of *Lady in the Dark* (1943) and *Where's Charley?* (1951), with their original stars, Gertrude Lawrence and Ray Bolger respectively. In 1959 came *Gypsy*, the musical based on Gypsy Rose Lee's autobiography, with Ethel Merman starring as Gypsy's mother.

Daly's Theatre, originally Banvard's Museum, was also known as the Broadway for the season of 1877–8, as was the Euterpean Hall for a few unsuccessful weeks.

BROCHET, HENRI (1898–1952), see GHÉON.

BROCKMANN, JOHANN FRANZ HIERONYMUS (1745–1812), German actor. He was a barber's apprentice who took to the stage and became the friend and pupil of Schröder, to whose company he belonged in Hamburg. He played Hamlet in the first production there of a German version of the play in 1776, with Schröder as the Ghost. He later went to the Burgtheater in Vienna, where he was highly thought of. He had great natural gifts but lacked control, and in the absence of a firm hand, such as Schröder's had been, he proved less successful. In spite of this, and of increasing girth, however, he remained an honoured member of the Burgtheater until his death.

BRODY SINGERS, see JEWISH DRAMA, 5.

BROME, RICHARD (*c.* 1590–1653), English dramatist, who was at one time in the service of Ben Jonson, where he no doubt learned much that later stood him in good stead. His comedies, on which his reputation mainly rests, show plainly Jonson's influence, though Brome has a greater insistence on plot than his mentor, and seems in his later work—which was interrupted by the closing of the theatres in 1642—to be working towards a more individual style. His best plays are generally thought to be *The City Wit; or, the Woman Wears the Breeches* (1628), *The Northern Lass* (1629), *The Sparagus Garden* (1635), *The Antipodes* (1638), and *A Joviall Crew* (1641). The last was often revived, and was later turned into an operetta. Brome also collaborated with Heywood, or perhaps revised some of his plays for revivals, and wrote some romantic dramas in imitation of Fletcher and Middleton.

BROOK, PETER STEPHEN PAUL (1925–), English producer, whose early work aroused much controversy, but produced interesting results. He was in his late teens when he produced *Dr. Faustus* and *The Infernal Machine* on the minute stages of the Torch and Chanticleer theatres. At 20 he was with Sir Barry Jackson at the Birmingham Rep, where his production of *King John*, with Scofield as the Bastard, attracted much attention. In 1946 he followed Sir Barry to Stratford-upon-Avon, and there did an enchanting *Love's Labour's Lost*, costumed *à la Watteau*. In the same year he produced, in London, *The Brothers Karamazov* and Sartre's *Vicious Circle*, both with

Alec Guinness. Returning to Stratford in 1947, he was responsible for a *Romeo and Juliet* which unleashed the fury of the critics, mainly on account of the clumsy cutting and handling of the verse. In the same year he continued his association with Sartre's plays by producing *Men Without Shadows* and *The Respectable Prostitute*, both at the Lyric, Hammersmith, and was appointed director of productions at Covent Garden Opera House. Here his 'Salome', with designs by Salvador Dali, again started a stimulating argument over the value and purpose of his work. He vindicated himself triumphantly with *Ring Round the Moon* (1950) in London, and with *Measure for Measure* (Stratford, 1950) and *The Winter's Tale* (1951), both with Gielgud. These were followed by a revival of *Venice Preserved* at the Lyric, Hammersmith (1953), which did honour to all concerned. Brook's later productions include Fry's *The Dark is Light Enough* (1954), Anouilh's *The Lark*, and *Titus Andronicus* (both 1955). Also in 1955 he produced *Hamlet* with Scofield, not altogether successfully. After a short tour, and a season in London, this company went to Moscow—the first English company to appear there since 1917. In 1957 Brook produced *Cat on a Hot Tin Roof* in Paris, *The Tempest* in Stratford-upon-Avon, and 'Eugene Onegin' at the Metropolitan, New York. In 1962 he was appointed co-director, with Peter Hall and Michel Saint-Denis, of the Royal Shakespeare Theatre, Stratford-upon-Avon, where he produced, among other things, *King Lear* (1962), again with Scofield, and, at the Aldwych, in the same year, *The Persecution and Assassination of Marat as performed by the Inmates of the Asylum of Charenton under the direction of the Marquis de Sade* (usually known as the *Marat/Sade*), by the German dramatist, Peter Weiss.

BROOKE, GUSTAVUS VAUGHAN (1818–66), an actor of Irish extraction, who made his first appearance on the stage in Dublin as a boy of 14, taking the place of Kean and appearing as William Tell, Virginius, Young Norval, Rolla, and Frederick. He subsequently toured England and Scotland as the Dublin (or Hibernian) Roscius. A tall handsome man, with an excellent voice and everything in his favour, he yet failed to fulfil the promise of his youth, and spent many years starring in the provinces, where he played with Macready (with whom he had quarrelled over an engagement for Drury Lane) as well as Forrest, Helen Faucit, Lester Wallack, and Charlotte Cushman. In 1848, at the height of his powers, he appeared at the Olympic in London as Othello, and had a most enthusiastic reception, being hailed as the successor of Kean. (He had previously appeared in London in 1834, with little success.) He also played Sir Giles Overreach, Richard III (in Cibber's version), Hamlet, Shylock (his only appearance in the part), and Virginius, which he had played as a boy of 14. Success seemed within his grasp but, with a careless, happy-go-lucky spirit, he dissipated himself in conviviality, fell into low water financially, and finally was ill-advised enough to refuse an offer from Webster to star at the Haymarket, returning eventually to the provinces. Here, his voice much altered and his physique impaired, he soon found himself in financial difficulties which an unfortunate experience at the New Olympic in London did nothing to alleviate, and he was twice arrested for debt. He decided to seek his fortune in New York, appearing on 15 Dec. 1851 at the Broadway Theatre in *Othello*. After a successful tour of the principal cities of the United States, he embarked on the management of the Astor Place Opera House with disastrous results. He returned to England, where he finally appeared at Drury Lane with unexpected success in 1853 in a round of his well-known parts, and was then persuaded to go to Australia. This he did, appearing in the principal cities with some success, marred occasionally by his return to old habits of insobriety. On his return to England these rapidly became worse and led him into even greater difficulties, until he finally found himself in Warwick jail. Determined to rehabilitate himself, he once more set sail for Australia and was drowned in the sinking of the s.s. London in the Bay of Biscay. His first wife, whom he married in 1851, was Marianne Elizabeth Woolcott Bray, his second (in 1863) the American actress Avonia Jones (1839–67), whose death was hastened by grief at his loss. Brooke's Life was written by W. J. Lawrence (1892).

BROOKLYN THEATRE, NEW YORK, the second playhouse in this district, which was opened on 2 Oct. 1871 by the Conways, who had previously managed the Park, Brooklyn. They continued their policy of engaging stars to play with the stock company, and gave mainly standard comedies, revivals, and some contemporary melodrama. In 1873 Daly's company, while waiting for the completion of their new theatre, came for a season. Mrs. Conway remained at the Brooklyn until her death in 1875, her husband having died the previous year. Her daughter Minnie attempted to take over the management of the theatre, but was unsuccessful, and left after a few months. On 20 Sept. 1875 it reopened under Palmer for a brief but exciting season, and on 5 Dec. 1876 it was burnt down during a performance of *The Two Orphans*. Two actors lost their lives, and about 300 of the audience. This was one of the worst theatre fires in the United States, equalled only by those at the Richmond Theatre in 1811 and the Iroquois, Chicago, in 1903.

BROOKS ATKINSON THEATRE, NEW YORK, see MANSFIELD THEATRE.

BROUGH, a family of English actors, descended from a dramatist named Barnabas Brough. Two of his sons, (1) WILLIAM (1826–70) and (2) ROBERT BARNABAS (1828–60), were also dramatists, writing alone or in collaboration a number of burlesques, extravaganzas, and pantomimes, in one of which, by William, Robert's daughter (3) FANNY WHITESIDE (1854–1914) made her first appearance on the stage in 1869 in Manchester. She appeared in the same town as Ophelia to the Hamlet of Barry Sullivan, and a year later was seen in London at the St. James's Theatre under Mrs. John Wood. During her subsequent career she was associated with all the outstanding managements of the day, and was unrivalled in certain lines of comedy. Her brother Robert was also an actor and theatre manager. Barnabas's youngest son (4) LIONEL (1836–1900) was a distinguished actor, who also made his first appearance in one of William's plays. He was for a time in journalism, being assistant publisher to the *Daily Telegraph* and the first man to organize newsboys selling papers in the street. He returned to the stage seriously in 1864, and in 1873 was the principal low comedian of the Gaiety under Hollingshead. He was not a character actor, but a clown in the best sense, his gift of improvisation and rich sense of humour making him excellent in burlesque. Two of his finest parts were Tony Lumpkin and Bob Acres, but he was also good in Shakespeare, and played with Tree at Her Majesty's. He toured extensively, and was popular in the United States and South Africa. His four children were all on the stage, two of them dying young. But (5) MARY (1863–1934) was an excellent comedy actress, particularly in later years, when she was associated with the Aldwych farces. She also had a distinguished film career. Her brother (6) SYDNEY (1868–1911) made his first appearance in 1885, and remained on the stage until his death, being seen mainly in comedy parts in London and New York.

BROUGHAM, JOHN (1810–80), American actor and dramatist, who was born in Ireland. He was intended for the medical profession, but forsook it for the stage, making his first appearance in London in July 1830 in Egan's *Tom and Jerry*. After a long engagement with Mme Vestris he became manager of the Lyceum, and in 1842 went to America. Here he made his début at the famous Park Theatre, and later was at Burton's and Niblo's. On 23 Dec. 1850 he opened his own theatre on Broadway, Brougham's Lyceum, in the hope of rivalling the success of Mitchell's Olympic. Brougham was a fine actor, an experienced manager, and a jovial, popular personality, and his venture ought to have succeeded. Unfortunately Mitchell's formula for success—a varied bill of short burlesques and farces, which had served him so well in the heyday of the Olympic—was now outmoded, and in spite of the success of Florence in his first New York hit, and of a hurried importation of such stars as Charlotte Cushman, circumstances proved too strong for Brougham. In less than two years the theatre had passed into the control of the elder Wallack, who started it on a glorious career.

Brougham continued to act, reviving *King John* at the Bowery, appearing at most of the big Broadway theatres, and spending several years in England, before he opened his second playhouse, on the site of the present Madison Square Theatre, on 25 Jan. 1869. This again was not a success. Brougham retired from management in a few months, and up to his death appeared with various stock companies in New York, his last appearance being on 25 Oct. 1879 at Booth's. He was essentially a comedian, and his best parts were the stage Irishmen of tradition, Sir Lucius O'Trigger, Dennis Brulgruddery, O'Grady, O'Callaghan, and such parts as Captain Cuttle, Micawber, and Dazzle in *London Assurance*, of which he was long believed to be part author. He wrote copiously, mainly ephemeral farces, burlesques, and adaptations of novels and stories, and none of his works has survived. He was twice married, and both his wives, who were also on the stage, predeceased him.

BROWN, IVOR (1891–   ), English dramatic critic and author who in 1913 relinquished a post in the Civil Service in order to devote himself to writing theatre criticism for the *Manchester Guardian*. In 1928 he became dramatic critic to the *Observer*. He has also written for the *Saturday Review*, *Illustrated London News*, and the *Sketch*. In 1942 he was appointed editor of the *Observer*, but continued as its dramatic critic, retiring in 1954. He was succeeded by Kenneth Tynan, and later, for a year, by Bamber Gascoigne.

Ivor Brown himself wrote in the *Observer*: 'The first business of criticism, in any art, is to assist and extend the enjoyment of that art by writing about it intelligently, agreeably, and with sensitive response to its beauties, and with a good-tempered and, if possible, witty dismissal of its follies.' He has certainly lived up to his definition. He regards the theatre as a contribution to the full life and, in looking at a play, sees it steadily and sees it whole. He brings sound judgement to the theatre and expresses his findings in lively and witty style.

In 1925 he wrote *Smithfield Preserved* (a play). His other writings on the theatre include *Masques and Phases* (1926), *First Player* (1927), *Parties of the Play* (1928), and (with George Fearon) *Amazing Monument, A Short History of the Shakespeare Industry* (1939). His excellent life of Shakespeare was published in 1949, and *Shakespeare in his Time* in 1960. He was created C.B.E. in 1957. T. C. KEMP†, *rev.*

BROWN, JOHN MASON (1900–69), American dramatic critic, born in Louisville, Kentucky. He graduated from Harvard, and in 1924 became an associate editor and dramatic critic of *Theatre Arts Monthly*. In 1929 he was appointed dramatic critic of *The New York Evening Post*, and in 1939 he went to *The World-Telegram*, a post he held until he entered the U.S. Navy during the Second World War. After the war he deserted daily reviewing to become dramatic critic of the weekly *Saturday Review of Literature*. His refreshing and vivid writings won him a large public, and for some years he also had conspicuous success on the lecture platform, delivering talks on the theatre. The best of his newspaper reviews may be found in *Two on the Aisle* (1939) while *Upstage: The American Theatre in Performance* is a rewarding and accurate picture of the American stage and its personalities in the 1920s. Among his other books are *The Modern Theatre in Revolt* (1929), *Letters from Greenroom Ghosts* (1934), *The Art of Playgoing* (1936), *Seeing Things* (1946), *Seeing More Things* (1948), and *Still Seeing Things* (1950).

THOMAS QUINN CURTISS

BROWN-POTTER, MRS., see POTTER.

BROWNE, E(LLIOTT) MARTIN (1900–), English actor and producer, who has been closely connected with the revival of poetic, and particularly religious, drama in England. He directed the Pilgrim Players, who in association with the Arts Council toured England in a repertory of religious plays, and in 1945 took over the Mercury Theatre for a series of plays by poets, among which have been *The Old Man of the Mountains*, *This Way to the Tomb*, *The Shadow Factory*, *A Phoenix Too Frequent*, and *Happy as Larry*. He had previously been associated with Ashley Dukes in the production of poetic plays at the Mercury, including *Panic* and *In Theatre Street*, and was responsible for the first production, in 1935, of *Murder in the Cathedral*, in which he played the Fourth Tempter and Knight. The play was originally given in the Chapter House of Canterbury Cathedral, and, after a run at the Mercury, was seen at the Duchess, at the Old Vic, and on tour in England. It was also given in New York in 1938. It had an unexpected and unprecedented success, and inaugurated a new era of poetry in the theatre. E. Martin Browne produced all T. S. Eliot's subsequent plays, *The Family Reunion* (1939), *The Cocktail Party* (1949), *The Confidential Clerk* (1953) (he also staged the last two on Broadway), and *The Elder Statesman* (1958). He was responsible for the revival in its native city, for the first time since 1572, of the York Cycle of Mystery Plays in 1951, and produced it again in 1954, 1957 and 1966. In 1945 he succeeded Whitworth as director of the British Drama League, and held this post until 1957, when he went to inaugurate the Program in Religious Drama at Union Theological Seminary, New York, where he was visiting professor until 1962. On returning to England he became Honorary Drama Adviser to the new Coventry Cathedral. He was created C.B.E. in 1952.

BROWNE, MAURICE (1881–1955), dramatist, manager, and actor. He was born and educated in England, but first made his name in the United States, where he is credited with the founding of the Little Theatre movement by his establishment in 1912 of the Chicago Little Theatre, which he directed for several years. After several productions in New York he appeared in London for the first time in 1927, and two years later he produced, at the Savoy Theatre, Sherriff's *Journey's End*, a play of the First World War which had a remarkable success, and with which his name is always connected. In the following year he produced *Othello* with Paul Robeson in the title-role, he himself playing Iago. He was later responsible for the management of the Globe and Queen's Theatres, presenting among other plays Gielgud's *Hamlet*, transferred from the Old Vic in 1930, and seasons of Moissi and the Pitoëffs. Among his later productions were *The Improper Duchess* (1931) with Yvonne Arnaud, *Wings Over Europe* (1932), of which he was part-author, *Viceroy Sarah* (1935), and *Quiet Wedding* (1939). He retired from management in that year, and in 1955 his autobiography, *Too Late To Lament*, which betrays a certain bitterness and dissatisfaction over his chosen career, was published posthumously.

BROWNE, ROBERT (*fl.* 1583–?1620/40), an Elizabethan actor who was well known on the Continent between 1590 and 1620. Nothing is known of his parentage or early years, and he is first mentioned as one of the Earl of Worcester's players in 1583. He may later have been a member of the Admiral's Men, with Alleyn. In 1592 he took a company of English actors to Holland and Germany with a repertory of jigs, biblical plays, early English comedies, and plays by Marlowe. In Aug. 1592 he made the first of many visits to Frankfurt Fair, and was acting there a year later when his wife, children, and servants died of the plague in London. In 1595 he and his companions were appointed players and musicians in the service of Maurice, Landgrave of Hesse-Kassel. Among them was a John Webster, who may have been the dramatist. In 1608 the actor William Sly left his share in the Globe Theatre to Browne, his second wife, and their daughter. Browne was intermittently in London at the beginning of the seventeenth century, being connected with the Earl of Derby's Men at Court, and with the Children of the Queen's Revels at Whitefriars, but he continued to visit Frankfurt and other German towns, and spent the winter of 1619 at the Court of Bohemia in Prague. The last mention of him is at the Easter Fair in Frankfurt in 1620. He may have returned to England then, and be identical with a Robert Browne who toured the English provinces with a puppet-show during 1638 and 1639. His work on the Continent was continued by his friend and pupil John Green.

BROWNING, ROBERT (1812–89), English poet, three of whose verse-plays were seen on the stage: *Strafford* (1837), written for Macready, *A Blot in the 'Scutcheon* (1843), and *Colombe's Birthday*, published in 1844, and acted in 1853, when it was seen briefly at the Haymarket. None of these was particularly successful, and they serve only to mark the great cleavage between poetry and the stage in the nineteenth century. His other plays were written to be read, and are part of English literature rather than drama.

BRUCKNER, FERDINAND [really THEODOR TAGGER] (1891–1958), an Austrian dramatist whose first play, *Krankheit der Jugend* (1926), caused something of a sensation: it dealt with a group of medical students preoccupied with the idea of suicide, death being the one certain alternative to disillusionment. A second play, *Die Verbrecher* (1928), was one of the many which, between the two world wars, discussed modern problems through historical personages, in this case Elizabeth I of England. In 1933 came *Timon*, based on Shakespeare, and in the same year, which also saw his departure from Germany, he wrote *Die Rassen*, a study of the tragedies which result from racial persecution. Two more apparently historical plays, *Napoleon der Erste* (1937) and *Heroische Komödie* (1942), were both concerned with Hitler's rise to power. Bruckner returned to Germany in 1951, and, apart from Brecht and Zuckmayer, was the only German playwright to re-establish himself in the German theatre. His later plays were *Der Tod einer Puppe* (1956), *Der Kampf mit dem Engel* (1957), which was seen in London, and an adaptation of an Indian play. DOROTHY MOORE

BRÜCKNER, JOHANNES (1730–86), German actor, a member of the company of Koch, who married his sister. He was trained for the stage by Lessing and Ekhof, and was one of the best tragedians of his time. His Mellefont in *Miss Sara Sampson* was considered superior even to Ekhof's, particularly when the latter grew too old for the part and yet insisted on playing it. One of Brückner's greatest triumphs was his portrayal of Götz von Berlichingen in Goethe's play of that name.

BRUEYS, DAVID-AUGUSTIN DE (1640–1723), French dramatist, a lawyer of good family, who later became a priest. In 1686 he met and later collaborated with Palaprat, a writer of comedies to which Brueys gave an added substance and firmness. They wrote several plays for the Comédie-Française, of which the best were *Le Grondeur* and *Le Muet* (both 1691), and their collaboration persisted until Palaprat left Paris in the service of the Duc de Vendôme. Brueys also wrote a number of plays on his own, including three tragedies of which only one reached the stage, and a new and most successful version of the farce of Maistre Pierre Pathelin. As *L'Avocat Pathelin* (1706), this remained in the repertory of the Comédie-Française for many years.

BRUN, NORDAHL (1745–1816), Norwegian dramatist (see SCANDINAVIA, 2 *a*).

BRUNELLESCHI, FILIPPO (1377–1446), Italian machinist, designer of a piece of stage mechanism known as a 'Paradiso' (see MACHINERY).

BRUNO, GIORDANO (1548–1600), Italian philosopher, author of a fine play, *Il Candelaio* (*c.* 1582), a brilliant, mordant piece of work which disclosed the corrupt customs of the time with unabated candour and for that reason was banned. During his travels through Europe Bruno went to England, and visited Oxford at the invitation of Sir Philip Sidney, to whom some of his works are dedicated. Among the contemporary English authors who were cognizant of him may perhaps be reckoned Thomas Carew, whose masque *Coelum Britannicum*, performed at Whitehall in 1634, shows traces of Bruno's influence. At one time scholars were anxious, perhaps too anxious, to find a like influence in Shakespeare, particularly in *Hamlet*. The resemblance is probably fortuitous. More informed criticism sees something in Bruno's comic genius akin to Ben Jonson's. Bruno was burnt at the stake by order of the Inquisition in 1600. In 1965, in a cut and modernized version, his play had what was probably its first professional performance, with Paolo Poli as the miserly philandering Bonifacio and Maria Monti as his wife Vittoria. The witty sets and costumes, which contributed greatly to the success of the production, were by Eugenio Gugielminetti.

BRUNSWICK THEATRE, LONDON, see ROYALTY THEATRE, 1.

BRUNTON, a family of English actors, of whom the first was (1) JOHN (1741–1822), a grocer in Drury Lane, who appeared at Covent Garden in 1774 as Hamlet. He was afterwards in the Norwich and Bath stock companies and manager of the Norwich circuit. He had three children on the stage, of whom the eldest, (2) ANNE (1769–1808), first appeared in Bath at the age of 15, and was so well received that in 1785 she was engaged to play at Covent Garden. There the future American dramatist and theatre manager, Dunlap, saw and described her début. In 1792 she retired from the stage to marry Robert Merry, but he lost his money, and a few years later she accepted Wignell's offer to go to the Chestnut Street Theatre in Philadelphia. Here she appeared on 5 Dec. 1796 as Juliet, and as Mrs. Merry was soon the leading actress of the time, equally successful in New York, where she first appeared in the season of 1797, and in Philadelphia. Many contemporary accounts testify to her beauty and success, particularly in Mrs. Siddons's great part of Belvidera in *Venice Preserved.* She was widowed in 1798 and in 1803 married Thomas Wignell, who died soon after the marriage. In 1806 she married William Warren, who had succeeded, jointly with Wood, to the management of the Chestnut Street Theatre, made several successful appearances in New York at the Park Theatre under Dunlap, and died in childbirth at the age of 40. Her loss was a great blow to the American stage.

Her brother (3) JOHN (1775–1848) first appeared on the stage at Lincoln, at the age of 18. He made his début at Covent Garden in 1800, and remained in London for some years, being at one time manager of the West London Theatre. He was also manager of several provincial theatres. He married an actress, Anna Ross (1773– ?), and was the father of Elizabeth, later Mrs. Frederick Yates. The youngest

Brunton, (4) LOUISA (1779–1860), made her début at Covent Garden in 1803. She excelled in light comedy, and was considered a worthy successor to Elizabeth Farren. Among her best parts were Beatrice, Lady Anne in *Richard III*, and Dorinda in *The Beaux' Stratagem*. She was also the original Emily in *The Wheel of Fortune* and Julia in *The School of Reform*. She retired from the stage in 1807, on her marriage with the Earl of Craven.

BRUSCAMBILLE [JEAN DESLAURIERS] (*fl.* 1610–34), a mountebank at the Paris fairs in the early seventeenth century who went with Jean Farine to the Hôtel de Bourgogne to play in farce. He won fame as a speaker of witty prologues and harangues to the rowdy audiences, which he composed himself. These are extant, and give an interesting picture of the tribulations of the actor before his profession became respectable, summed up in Bruscambille's oft-quoted epigram, 'une vie sans soucis et quelquefois sans six sous'.

BÜCHNER, GEORG (1813–37), a German dramatist who, in a general dearth of talent, stands out as one of the best playwrights of his day. His strongest and best play, *Dantons Tod* (first produced in 1916), retains its vitality today, as was proved by two revivals, one in Berlin in 1927 by Max Reinhardt, and the other in New York in 1938 by Orson Welles. It depicts Danton as a disillusioned man sickened by the bloodshed which he has helped to start, and is amazingly objective for a young revolutionary. Büchner had little in common with the romantic writers of his day, and, had he not died before his powers came to maturity, he might have been one of the earliest of the naturalistic writers. Little else remains of his work, except the dramatic fragments on which Alban Berg later based his opera 'Wozzeck' (1925).

BUCK, SIR GEORGE, see MASTER OF THE REVELS.

BUCKINGHAM, GEORGE VILLIERS, second Duke of (1628–87), English nobleman and a prominent literary figure of the Restoration. He was the original of Zimri in Dryden's *Absalom and Achitophel*. Keenly interested in contemporary drama, he satirized Dryden and the heroic verse-play in *The Rehearsal* (1671). This provided a model for many later burlesques, of which the best was *The Critic; or, a Tragedy Rehearsed* (1779). Buckingham rewrote in 1666 Fletcher's comedy *The Chances*, which Pepys saw and enjoyed at the King's Theatre (i.e. Drury Lane). It was revived by the Phoenix Society in 1922, and again at the Chichester Festival in 1962, with John Neville and Keith Michell as the twin heroes, Don John and Don Frederick.

BUCKSTONE, JOHN BALDWIN (1802–79), English actor and dramatist, who was articled to a solicitor, but left the law for the stage. He made his first appearance in the famous melodrama, *The Dog of Montargis*, in a barn at Peckham, and spent several years in the provinces, where he acquired an excellent reputation as a low comedian. Kean, who saw him act, encouraged him in his profession, and he eventually appeared in London, first at the Surrey in 1823, then at the Coburg in 1824, and, in 1827, at the Adelphi. Here he was seen in his own play *Luke the Labourer*, which had previously (1826) been given anonymously because the manager, Daniel Terry, had lost the author's name and address. He was also seen at the Surrey as Gnatbrain in *Black-Eyed Susan* (1829), and during the summer seasons of 1833–9 at the Haymarket, of which he later became manager. It was here that many of his plays were first produced, with himself and an excellent company, and his ghost is said still to haunt the theatre. As an actor he had great breadth and humour, and the mere sound of his voice, a mixture of chuckle and drawl, heard off-stage was enough to set the audience laughing. For fifty years he was one of London's most popular comedians and most prolific playwrights, writing some 200 plays of all kinds, chiefly melodramas and farces. The best were *Married Life* (1834), *Single Life* (1839), *The Green Bushes; or, a Hundred Years Ago* (1845), and *The Flowers of the Forest* (1847). He also dramatized a number of contemporary novels, and in later life wrote pantomimes.

BUEN RETIRO, see MADRID THEATRES.

BUFFALO BILL, see CODY, W. F.

BUILT STUFF, a scenic term comprising all specially carpentered, three-dimensional objects, from banks and rostrums to columns and complete scenes on trucks. The most common is perhaps the Rostrum, which may vary in size from a small throne-dais to an 8 ft. high platform, approached by steps or a ramp. Beyond this, by way of porches and mantelpieces, one reaches all the ingenious applications of light carpentry, of chicken-wire reinforcement, of glued and shaped canvas, and of papier mâché, which enable a room complete in all details, or a wood scene with every tree in the round and every leaf separate, to take shape upon the stage.

RICHARD SOUTHERN

BULANDRA, LUCIA STURDZA (1873-1961), Rumanian actress, who spent her whole life in the service of the theatre, appearing as the Mother in *The Glass Menagerie* only a few days before her death. The widow of a theatre manager who died before the Second World War, she supported the new republican régime, and appeared regularly at the National Theatre. She also acted in and managed the Bucharest Municipal Theatre, which now bears her name, and encouraged many young Rumanian dramatists by appearing in their plays. Among her most popular roles were Mrs. Warren, and the Countess Aurelia in *The Madwoman of Chaillot*. She was a woman of immense vitality, versatility and charm, and has been compared to the English actress Sybil Thorndike.

BULGAKOV, Michael Afanasyev (1891–1940), Soviet dramatist, who graduated from Kiev University in 1916 with the intention of becoming a doctor. In 1920, however, he turned to literature, and became a journalist in Moscow. He wrote a novel, *The White Guard*, dealing with the Civil War in the Ukraine, which he later turned into a play. This, as *The Days of the Turbins* (or *The Last of the Turbins*), was produced by the Moscow Art Theatre under Stanislavsky in 1926. In its delicacy and restraint, and its handling of personal rather than national problems, it was an advance on earlier Soviet plays, and was successful. But its sympathetic treatment of the bewildered White Russian aristocrats, at a time when feeling still ran high, made it suspect for a time. As *The White Guard* it was produced in London in 1938 in an adaptation by Rodney Ackland. In 1928 Bulgakov, who had joined the staff of the Moscow Art Theatre, prepared for it an excellent dramatization of Gogol's *Dead Souls*, and in 1936 wrote a play based on the life of Molière. In 1941 his last play, based on *Don Quixote*, was produced posthumously at the Vakhtangov Theatre. One of his early plays, *Flight*, was revived in Leningrad in 1958.

BULGARIA. Bulgarian drama is of recent origin. The medieval literature of the country contains neither secular nor ecclesiastical drama, and Bulgarian folk dances never progressed from the mimic to the dramatic type. During most of the long period of Turkish rule (1396–1878) foreign intercourse was rare and indigenous cultural activity of any sort nonexistent, so much so that the written Bulgarian language almost vanished. The first modern literary work, a patriotic history of the Bulgars, appeared in 1762, the first grammar of the language in 1835. About 1840 Iordan Djzinot, a schoolteacher at Veles, wrote and staged moral-patriotic 'dramatic dialogues' which were soon known all over the country. In the next fifteen years many amateur dramatic societies appeared, performing in Bulgarian the plays of such authors as Schiller, Goldoni, Fonvizin, Molière, and Hebbel. The first play in Bulgarian, *Mikhail*, was a comedy adapted from a Serbian original. It was written by S. I. Dobroplodnij (1820–94), a schoolmaster at Shumen, and staged in a café there by his pupils on 15 Aug. 1856. Two of these pupils soon became dramatists themselves: Dobri Vojnikov (1833–78), who emigrated to Brăila, in Rumania, where he founded and directed (1866–71) an amateur Bulgar theatre in exile, and wrote for its stage patriotic-historical dramas (*Princess Raina*, 1866; *Baptism of the Court of Preslav*, 1868; *The Accession of Tsar Krum the Terrible*, 1871) and a few comedies (*Civilization Misunderstood*, 1871); and Vasil Drumev (1841–1901), also an emigré to Brăila, whose *Ivanko, Assassin of Asen I* (1872), a vigorous costume drama of intrigue, is still occasionally acted.

To these early dramatists the stage was a moral and patriotic tribunal which could be used to remind their people of past glories and so inspire them to throw off Turkish rule. Plays based on the national history thus predominated, although an occasional modern comedy appeared, the best perhaps being *The Crinoline* (1864) by P. R. Slavejkov (1827–95), in which the pretences of Europeanized Bulgarians are satirically contrasted with peasant innocence.

The ten years preceding the Liberation (1878) are the period of the so-called *hayduk* drama. Hayduks were Bulgarian outlaws who lived in the forests and hills, whence they issued to attack the Turks and their collaborators. Their romantic life and their patriotism were celebrated in poems and ballads. The *hayduk* drama owes a good deal to Byron and Schiller as well as to the Hayduks themselves. Some notable examples are L. Karavelov's *Hadji Dimitar Asenov* (1871), S. Iordanov's *Golden Stoyan the Voivode* (1865), B. K. Petrov's *Poor Tanko* (1874), adapted from a story by Karavelov, K. Velichkov's *Svetoslav and Nevenka* (1874), and such post-liberation works as P. Ivanov's *Apostles of Freedom* (1884), T. Frangov's *An Incident at Drianovskaya Monastery in the Year 1876* (1885), R. Popova's *On the Day of Revolt* (1900), and I. Kirilov's *Towards the Mountain Ridge*.

As the Bulgarian repertoire thus grew, organized theatrical activity became necessary. In 1880 there were seven theatres operating in Bulgaria, the most important of which were at Sofia, where the Croatian G. Jovanović directed a company, and at Plovdiv, at that time the cultural capital of the country, where S. Popov (1846–1920) and K. Sapunov (1844-1906) formed the Rumelian Theatre Company, the first organized Bulgarian troupe (1881). In 1886 N. Kravarev formed the Plovdiv Amateur Theatre, which became a professional company on moving to Sofia (1888), where the tiny wooden Osnova Theatre was built, the first in the country. The government added an opera troupe in 1890, but in 1892 the actors withdrew from the Osnova. V. Nalburov, I. Popov, and R. Kaneli formed the Laughter and Tears Company, which lasted until 1906. This group was the first to play Shakespeare (*Othello*, 1897) and Chekhov (*Uncle Vanya*, 1904) in Bulgaria. From it derived the Bulgarian National Theatre, which opened in a fine new building on 3 Jan. 1907; this structure was burned down in 1923 and was replaced by an excellent modern theatre designed by the German architect Duelfer.

The dominant figure in Bulgarian drama, and indeed in all forms of Bulgarian literature at the end of the nineteenth century, is Ivan Vazov (1850–1921), who wrote historical-patriotic dramas (*Borislav*, 1909; *Ivailo*, 1909–11) as well as satiric social comedies (*Chorbadji Mikhalaki*, 1878; *Are You a Journalist?* 1900; *The Placehunters*, 1903), and also adapted his own novels for the stage (*Rouska*, 1883; *The Tramp*, 1894; *Under the Yoke*, 1911). Technically his dramatic works are primitive and suffer from the haste with which he composed them. They are episodic and diffuse and, in the histories especially, principally concerned with arousing patriotic fervour. Vazov's virtues, however, include sharp observation, humour, and above all the ability to fix and portray accurately the manners and customs as well as the spirit of the period of Liberation.

As the years of enforced cultural isolation ended the Bulgarian theatre became more aware of general European cultural influences, and the strictly moral or patriotic drama began to seem old-fashioned. *The Lark* (1906) by I. Kirilov (1878–1936) and *The Awakening* (1902) by Anna Karima (1872–1948) show Ibsen's influence. Symbolism and Nietzschean ethics appeared in *Babel* by K. Hristov (1875–1944) and in his tragedy *Boyan the Sorcerer* (1911), the first verse drama in Bulgarian. In the tragedy *St. Ivan Rilski* (1911) A. Strashimirov (1870–1937) explored the philosophical implications of legendary history, while his *Vampire* (1901) is a vivid study of peasant passions, *The Wedding at Bolyarovo* (1901) a rural comedy, and *Rebecca* (1908) and *The Suspension Bridge* (1912) are problem plays. French symbolism and the influence of Chekhov combine in the pessimistic poetic dramas of P. K. Iavorov (1877–1914), *At the Foot of Mount Vitosha* (1911), *When the Thunder Rolls* (1912), and *As the Echo Replies* (1912). P. K. Todorov (1879–1916) also wrote symbolic plays in which he attempted to combine the mood and techniques of Ibsen's later dramas with the motifs of Bulgarian folk-song and folk-lore (*The Masons*, 1902; *The Fairy*, 1903; *The Dragon's Marriage*, 1910). His *The First* (1912) is a social drama about the *chorbadjis*, the wealthy Bulgarians who often collaborated with the Turks.

Bulgaria's alliance with Germany in the First World War isolated her for a time from her most important sources of culture, France and Russia, but after the war writers, actors, and producers once again responded to new influences. The National Theatre, ruled (1915–20) by the brilliant actor K. Sarafov, and then by the symbolist poet G. Milev (1895–1925), was profoundly affected by the Soviet stage. Many of its actors had studied at the Moscow Art Theatre and the repertoire imitated that of Moscow, while Meyerhold's methods of staging were followed by his Bulgarian disciples, such as H. Sankiv, B. Danovski, and N. Fol. In 1925 the Russian actor N. O. Massalitinov, formerly director of the Moscow Art Theatre's Second Studio, arrived in Sofia and took charge of the National Theatre and its school. Russian influence thereafter became paramount

Between the two world wars no single school of playwriting prevailed. *Hayduk* plays and historical dramas continued to be popular, especially those by D. Syarov, S. Savov, I. Beljov, and V. Polyanov, all of which glorified national heroes. The symbolist I. Grozev (1872–1957) studied the Manichaean Bogomils, a heretical sect in medieval Bulgaria, in his mystical and supernatural *The Golden Chalice* (1922); *Borjana* (1924) by I. Iovkov (1884–1937) and *Delba* (1931) by I. Enchev were vigorous and acute studies of peasant life. Provincial stupidity and greed were satirized in Iovkov's *The Millionaire* (1930); S. L. Kostov (1879–1939) ridiculed the urban bourgeoisie in *The Gold Mine* (1925) and *Golemonov* (1928), perhaps the most finished products of the period, while S. Mikhailovski (1856–1927) wrote gently humorous domestic comedies (*When the Gods Laugh*, 1922; *The Tragedy of Conjugal Love*, 1927). R. Stoyanov (1882–1951) portrayed the lives of petty artisans in his justly celebrated *The Masters* (1927), in which caricature mingles with love intrigue and discussions of social issues.

Since 1945 the Bulgarian theatre has flourished materially, and many new companies of actors, singers, and puppet-players have been established in their own buildings, but there seems to have been something of a dearth of original playwrights. Dramatists such as K. Kyolyakov (1893–1955) and A. Rastsvetnikov (1897–1951) adapted the situations of the old *hayduk* drama to fit tales of communist partisans operating against the Nazis, and other propaganda plays included *The Tsar's Mercy* (1948) by K. Zidarov (1902–) and *The Promise* (1949) by A. Gulyashki (1914–), in which good workers and responsible communists were shown at grips with foreign saboteurs. After the death of Stalin in 1953 there was some relaxation, and such plays as *Fear* (1956), by T. Genov, which portrays a communist opportunist working himself into an important position in the Party, were able to reach the stage. Since 1957, however, controls have tightened up, and Bulgarian drama has again been standardized. ROBERT TRACY

BULL, OLE BORNEMAN (1810–80), famous Norwegian violinist, and the founder of the first National Theatre in Norway. After five years of negotiation, this opened in 1850 at Bergen, Bull's birthplace, and was the first theatre in Norway to be staffed by Norwegians, since earlier ventures had been in the hands of Danes.

BULL INN, see INNS USED AS THEATRES.

BULWER-LYTTON, see LYTTON.

BUNN. (1) ALFRED (1798–1860), English theatrical manager, best remembered for his numerous quarrels, particularly for his brawl with Macready, whom he tried to force into a triple bill in a mutilated version of *Richard III*, and for his attacks on Douglas Jerrold, Gilbert à Beckett, and Mark Lemon—as Wronghead, Sleekhead, and Thickhead—in a pamphlet, *A Word With Punch*, got up to look like *Punch*, in which he had been criticized. He was considered an adventurer and an impostor, and coming at a time when the London theatre was at a low ebb, he debased it still further by his methods and manners. Appointed stage-manager to Drury Lane by Elliston in 1823, he later went to Birmingham. In 1833 he tried to control both Drury Lane and Covent Garden, a policy which ended in failure and caused him to write his apologia in *The Stage; Before and Behind the Curtain*, published in 1840, in which year he went bankrupt. He made great efforts to establish English opera, with the help of the composers Balfe and Wallace, but defeated his own ends by the poorness of his libretti, of which 'The Bohemian Girl' is a fair sample; he also made some weak translations of foreign libretti, and of a number of Scribe's plays, now forgotten. His facile though flat versification, and his pretensions to poetry, caused him to be nicknamed derisively 'Poet Bunn'. In 1819 he married (2) MARGARET AGNES SOMERVILLE (1799–1883), an actress who had been engaged for Drury Lane three years previously by Byron and Kinnaird. She was at her best in heavy tragedy, but Macready and Kean disliked her, the latter finding her too tall and overpowering to play with. She left the stage soon after; her marriage does not appear to have been a very happy one.

BUONTALENTI, BERNARDO (1536–1608), Italian theatre architect and scenic designer, who spent all his life in the service of the Medici family. He was the architect of a theatre in Florence, which opened in 1585 (see SCENERY, 2 and No. 59).

BURBAGE (BURBADGE, BURBEGE). (1) James (*c.* 1530–97), a joiner by trade, became an actor in the Earl of Leicester's company in 1572 or thereabouts. Opposition from the Lord Mayor of London to actors playing in open inn-yards within the City boundary led Burbage in 1576 to build the Theatre—the first English building entirely devoted to the presentation of plays—an enclosed structure of wood situated outside the City boundary in Finsbury Fields. From an indictment of 1579/80, now in the Middlesex Record Office, it is clear that Burbage's father-in-law, James Braynes, not only lent him some of the money needed for building the Theatre, but was also an actor there, and probably joint proprietor of the building. In 1596 James also took over and rebuilt the Blackfriars Theatre, but died before he had obtained permission to use it. All his life he was harassed and beset by financial and other difficulties, but he never wavered in his allegiance to the theatre. In *A Note on Burbage*, Mrs. Stopes says: '[James] did more than build the first theatre; he raised and purified the stage, and honoured his profession; he selected and trained his fellow-actors, among them Shakespeare and his own son Richard.' James appears to have been a man of violent temper, stubborn and unscrupulous, but devoted to the theatre, though probably a poor actor. His eldest son, (2) CUTHBERT (*c.* 1566–1636), inherited the Theatre, and after a dispute with his rivals, Alleyn and Henslowe, dismantled it, and used the timber to build (in 1599) the Globe, on Bankside, Southwark. This was the scene of the greatest triumphs of Cuthbert's brother (3) RICHARD (*c.* 1567/8–1619), who was the first great English actor, and the original player of Shakespeare's Hamlet, Lear, Othello, Richard III, and other characters. He also appeared in plays by Jonson, Kyd, Webster, and others. His acting career began early, probably in 1584 with the Admiral's Men at the Theatre. He had a high reputation both during his lifetime and afterwards. There are numerous references to him in contemporary verse and prose (see Jonson's *Bartholomew Fair*: 'Which is your Burbage now? . . . your best actor?'), and his name long remained synonymous with all that was best in acting.

BURIAN, EMIL FRANTIŠEK (1904–59), Czech critic, actor, director, playwright, and musician. The composer of several operas and many dramatic works, he founded in 1933 the D34 Theatre in Prague, which soon became an important centre for the production of new and experimental plays, many of them from abroad. In 1941, under the Nazi régime, the theatre was closed, and Burian imprisoned, but he returned to Prague after the Second World War, and, though his health was much impaired by his sufferings, he reopened his theatre with official support, and succeeded in raising it to its former pitch of popularity. His death was a great blow to the Czechoslovak theatre.

BURKE, CHARLES (1822–54), see JEFFERSON (4) and (5).

BURLA (pl. *burle*), the longer comic interlude of the *commedia dell'arte*, usually involving a practical joke, perhaps the tripping up of one character by another, or a certain amount of horseplay. The slighter decoration of a comic touch was known as a *lazzo* (pl. *lazzi*).

BURLESQUE. 1. A satiric play, usually based on some well-known contemporary drama, or dramatic fashion, which offered elements fit for parody. The prototype of the burlesque was Buckingham's *The Rehearsal* (1671), which made fun of Dryden and the heroic drama, and set the pattern for future writers. The genre was finally crystallized in *The Critic* (1779), where Sheridan amused himself at the expense of the sentimental drama and the literary foibles of the day. In the meantime the traditions of burlesque had been worthily upheld by Gay's *Beggar's Opera* (1728), by Henry Carey, who burlesqued both opera and drama, and by Fielding's *Tragedy of Tragedies; or, the Life and Death of Tom Thumb the Great* (1730).

In the nineteenth century a new type of burlesque flourished. It retained enough consciousness of its origin to hang, where possible, its nonsense and high spirits on the convenient peg provided by some popular play, such as *The Maid and the Magpie* or *Black-Eyed Susan*; but the original impulse of criticism was lacking. This may have been due to the increase in the size of the audience and the lowering of its general educational level, since the success of the earlier type of burlesque had depended on the familiarity of the greater part of the audience with the play or prevailing mode which was under dissection. One of the best writers of the new burlesques was H. J. Byron, with such things as *Aladdin; or, the Wonderful Scamp* (1861), *The Corsican 'Bothers'; or, the Troublesome Twins* (1869), *Robert MacMaire; or, the Roadside Inn turned inside out* (1870). It was possibly Byron's execrable puns, as well as the reform of the stage initiated by Robertson, that finally killed the burlesque, though not before it had provided Londoners with a good deal of amusement at the old Gaiety, with the famous quartet headed by Nellie Farren. It survived for a time as a short scene in such revues as *The Gate* (1938–9), *The Little* (1939), and the *Sweet and Low* series (1943–6), parodying a current Shakespearian production or some long-running London success. (For the American use of the word in the sense of a variety entertainment see below, 4.)

2. EXTRAVAGANZA. It is almost impossible to disentangle the extravaganza from the burlesque, since many of the latter, so called in memoirs of the day and reminiscences of old playgoers, are listed by Allardyce Nicoll in his *Nineteenth-Century Drama* as extravaganzas. The original distinction seems to be that the extravaganza had no particular satiric object but was a fantastic affair intended solely for amusement, and that its subject was taken from mythology or fairy tale. The great purveyor of extravaganzas was J. R. Planché, who wrote a long series of them for Mme Vestris and others, while H. J. Byron also produced a number currently with his burlesques. The extravaganza has now entirely disappeared from the London theatre.

3. BURLETTA. Closely allied to both burlesque and extravaganza is the burletta, which began in the middle of the eighteenth century as 'a poor relation to an Opera' and 'a drama in rhyme, which is entirely musical'. It was the efforts of the smaller theatres to evade the licensing laws which led to a broadening of the term in the nineteenth century. This led Planché to sub-title one of his plays 'A Most Extravagant Extravaganza, or Rum-Antic Burletta'. Legally, any piece with at least five songs in each act was a burletta, and could be performed at the minor theatres. This allowed the adaptation and presentation of plays by Shakespeare and other 'legitimate' dramatists, and accounts for the odd interpolations found in some nineteenth-century productions. ED.

4. IN THE U.S.A. American burlesque, a native sex and comedy entertainment for men only, was devised by Michael Bennett Leavitt (1843–1935) in about 1868 and known popularly as 'burleycue' and 'leg show'. The comedy was reminiscent of the bawdy days of Aristophanes, and the sex feature, the display of girls in tights, was borrowed from Lydia Thompson's troupe of visiting British Blondes and the notorious 'Black Crook' extravaganza of 1866. The show opened with a 'spiel'—or pattertalk—by the 'candy butcher', who walked down to the front of the theatre just before the curtain rose, sold picture-books revealing 'woman's hidden charms', and promised fabulous prizes to purchasers of ten-cent boxes of candy. The performance which followed was divided into three parts on the pattern of the American minstrel show. Part I was a combination of chorus numbers, comedy sketches, called the 'bits', and monologues. Part II, the 'olio', was made up of variety acts: acrobats, instrumentalists, magicians, freak entertainers, and sentimental-song singers. Part III consisted also of chorus numbers, 'bits', and an occasional travesty on politics and current plays, the only claim which the show had to the title Burlesque (see above).

The final number was called the Extra Added Attraction, and was usually the 'hootchy-kootchy' or *danse du ventre*. Certain managers, however, occasionally substituted a boxing bout or some other exhibition of manly skill and prowess.

Burleycue comedy material consisted largely of monologues and the 'bits', which were identified either by the trick apparatus employed, like bladders, or by opening lines like 'I'll meet you 'round the corner'. The intervening dialogue the comedian supplied, giving it his own personal type of humour, with the aid of comic make-up—putty nose, scare wig, false feet, drooping trousers, and grotesque headgear. He was assisted also, from time to time, by two or three other comedians (known as the dude, the Chinaman, or the tramp) and by the straight man or 'feeder', dressed in faultless evening attire.

One of the most famous 'bits' was the courtroom scene. It showed a judge, lawyers, witnesses, and jury all busy considering the case of a lady guilty of a misdemeanour. As the trial progressed the judge shot peas at the jury, hit himself on the head with the gavel while calling for order, and finally collapsed in the pandemonium which he had himself created. Though the 'bits' were old and familiar, the audience loved the *double entente*, the suggestive stage business, the slapstick and bladders. Between scenes and drinks the patrons laughed, applauded, and participated actively in the performance, sang the sentimental songs, ogled the girls, dated them up, and handed them presents when they strutted down the runway. Burlesque became the natural, extemporaneous school for most of the great American stage, screen, and radio comedians, among them Al Jolson, W. C. Fields, Fannie Brice, Sophie Tucker, Jack Pearl, Jimmy Barton, Leon Errol, Bobby Clark, Willie Howard, Bert Lahr, and Weber and Fields. The training was difficult, an ordeal by fire, for the rowdy audience heckled the comedian, hurled vegetables across the footlights, and often shouted 'Get the hook!' Sometimes a fist-fight in the front aisle interrupted the comic in the midst of a monologue, but he had to carry on or get off. Sometimes the police rushed in, raided the show, and carried him off along with the other performers on charges of indecency.

About 1920 the strip-tease, an innovation

of uncertain origin, startled audiences who eventually turned the theatre into a disrobing arena by inducing the dancer to remove more and more of her scant attire by applauding and shouting 'Take 'em off!' The dance, ostensibly simple, had an involved routine, requiring skill and personality. First came the 'parade', in which the so-called dancer promenaded back and forth across the stage. Then came the 'grinds', vigorous twistings of the torso, and the 'bumps', a forward thrusting of the abdomen, and finally 'the flash', with the girl exposing herself for one moment completely nude except for a G-string. Gypsy Rose Lee broke down puritanic convention by establishing the scandalous burlesque number as a conventional Broadway revue speciality. Her subsequent career as novelist, actress, *découpé* artist, and social favourite made her, for a time, the most-talked-of woman in the United States.

Burlesque reached its peak of popularity just before the outbreak of war in 1914. At that time resident companies like Minsky's at the Winter Garden, New York, played to packed houses; and two rival syndicates, or 'wheels', the Mutual and the Columbia, had companies touring the entire United States successfully. Among the best-known companies were Rentz-Santley's, Sam T. Jack's, Billy Watson's 'Beef Trust', 'Wine, Woman and Song', and Rose Sydell's 'London Belles', which ran twenty years. Among the stars, who had large followings, season after season, were Al Reeves, 'Bozo' Snyder, 'Sliding' Billy Watson, and 'Snuffy the Cabman'.

With the enforcement of prohibition, burlesque lost its hold over the public for a time, and was finally barred from New York in Apr. 1942. The causes for the breakdown were numerous. Broadway revues appropriated the bawdy 'bits' under the title of 'black-outs', and also the exploitation of female nudity. The invention of motion pictures provided a new, cheaper, and more accessible amusement. Finally, the shows lost their male appeal when Columbia cleaned them up, and made them suitable for ladies and children.

BERNARD SOBEL†

BURNACINI. (1) GIOVANNI (? –1656), architect of a theatre in Vienna, for which he also designed the scenery. His son (2) LODOVICO OTTAVIO (1636–1707) was also a scenic designer, and a representative of stage baroque at its richest and most typical. Some of his best work was done in Vienna, where he worked for Leopold I (see also COSTUME, 7, OPERA, 2, SCENERY, 3 and No. 148).

BURNAND, SIR FRANCIS COWLEY (1836–1917), editor of *Punch* from 1880 to 1906. He was closely connected with the theatre, and in 1855 was instrumental in founding the Cambridge Amateur Dramatic Club (A.D.C.). He wrote over a hundred plays, mainly burlesques of popular drama or adaptations of French farces. He had little profundity or originality, but much wit and agility, and was a great punster and player on words. The success of his works was mainly due to their topicality, and none has survived.

BURNT-CORK MINSTRELS, see MINSTREL 2.

BURTON, WILLIAM EVANS (1804–60), an actor-manager and dramatist, born and educated in England, whose professional life was passed in the United States, where he went in 1834. Son of a printer, he inherited his father's business and became editor of a monthly magazine, but gave it up to go on the stage. He first appeared in London in 1831, and in the following year was at the Haymarket, where he played with Edmund Kean. His American début was made at the Arch Street Theatre, Philadelphia, and he first appeared in New York in 1837. After converting a circus in Philadelphia into a theatre, and running it successfully as the National, he returned to New York and took over Palmo's Opera House in Chambers Street, which had degenerated into a home of variety. Renovated and redecorated, it opened on 10 July 1848 as Burton's, and was one of the most important theatres of the day. Odell, in his *Annals of the New York Stage*, dates the beginning of modern times from the opening of Burton's, four years before Wallack's. It had a talented company, which flourished under a genial management, and Burton, himself a supreme comedian, appeared there in a number of richly characteristic parts, of which the most popular were Timothy in *Toodles*, Aminadab Sleek in *The Serious Family*, and Captain Cuttle in Brougham's adaptation of *Dombey and Son*, which was the theatre's first outstanding success. Dickens was always popular at Burton's, and Oliver B. Raymond's Toots and Johnston's Uriah Heep were both memorable, as was a series of old English comedies with Henry Placide. The arrival in 1851 of Mrs. Warner from Sadler's Wells led to a revival of several Shakespearian plays, beginning with *The Winter's Tale*. In the following year Burton began to suffer from the success of Wallack's, which took some of his best actors from him. But before Burton finally deserted his theatre in 1856 it had seen the début of Agnes Robinson in a long run of *To Parents and Guardians*, and fine productions of *A Midsummer Night's Dream* and *The Tempest*, with Burton as Bottom and Caliban. On 8 Sept. 1856 Burton took over the Metropolitan, and opened with *The Rivals*. But he was never so successful there as in his old theatre. The competition of Wallack's was too keen, and the theatre was too big to stand up to the financial crisis of 1857. In spite of some successful new plays and the appearance of such guest-actors as Booth, the Florences, Charlotte Cushman, Brougham, Mathews, and the Davenports, the theatre was put up for sale in 1858 and finally closed on 9 Sept. It reverted to its original name, and was only used intermittently (for its later history, see WINTER GARDEN, 1).

Meanwhile Burton made his last appearance

on the New York stage at Niblo's in 1859, and then went to Canada, returning to New York to die. His life was written in 1885 by W. L. Keese. He was the author of several plays, none of which has survived. On his death he left behind a substantial fortune, a splendid library, as befitted one educated at St. Paul's School, London, and a reputation as actor and manager which time has in no way diminished.

BUSKIN, the English name for the thick-soled boot worn by the Greek actor in tragedy only (see COTHURNUS), hence used to imply writing, or acting in, tragedy. The itinerant actors of the English countryside were called Buskers, a name derived from Buskin.

BUZARIO, ANTONIO (*fl.* fifteenth century), early Italian dramatist, author of the *Cauteriaria* (1469), a comedy in Latin which borders on tragedy. It turns on the misdemeanours of an erring wife, whose husband punishes her infidelity with torture, and is in turn to be tortured by her priest-lover. But on the wife's pleading he relents, and the play ends grossly (see ITALY, 1*b* iii).

BYRON, GEORGE GORDON, LORD (1788–1824), English poet, and author of several plays in verse which were staged in the hope of reviving poetry in the English theatre, but with little success. Only one was produced during his lifetime, *Marino Faliero* (1821), which was done at Drury Lane. Macready first played *Werner*, also at Drury Lane, in 1830; Phelps revived it in 1844 at Sadler's Wells, Irving at the Lyceum in 1887. *Sardanapalus* was produced by Macready in 1834. *Manfred*, a dramatic poem, and *The Two Foscari* were given at Covent Garden in 1834 and 1838 respectively. *Cain*, written in 1821, does not appear to have been produced in England. It has been six times translated into German, in which language it was produced at Frankfurt-on-Main in 1958, and at Lucerne in 1960. Byron joined the Committee of Drury Lane in 1815, and his letters are full of references to theatrical matters of the day; but his plays read better than they act, in spite of his undoubted dramatic talents, and stand somewhat apart from the main stream of nineteenth-century theatre development.

BYRON, HENRY JAMES (1834–84), English actor and dramatist, best known for his series of burlesques, of which the first was seen in 1857, the last in about 1881. They were usually given at the smaller London theatres, the Olympic, Adelphi, Strand, and others. Intended for medicine, which he hated, and then for the law, which bored him, he joined a provincial company, and in 1869 made his first appearance in London in one of his own comedies. He continued to appear almost entirely in his own plays, one of the exceptions being his last appearance on the stage in 1881, in Gilbert's *Engaged*. In 1865 he joined Marie Wilton (Lady Bancroft) in the management of the renovated Dust Hole, to whose opening programme as the Prince of Wales's he contributed a burlesque of 'La Sonnambula'. He was under contract to write exclusively for this theatre, and two of his three-act comedies, *War to the Knife* (1865) and *A Hundred Thousand Pounds* (1866), were given there, as were several burlesques and extravaganzas. In 1867 he took over the management of the Alexandra Theatre, Liverpool, where some of his best work was done, but with little financial success. He returned to management in London in 1874 at the Criterion and in the following year, on 16 Jan. 1875, produced his famous *Our Boys*, which ran till 18 Apr. 1879, and set up a record which lasted for many years—1,362 performances.

Byron's work—he was responsible for nearly 150 plays, ranging from sentimental comedy to pantomime—owed little to the prevalent pilfering from French and German drama, but can hardly be called original, for all that. His themes were taken from mythology, nursery tale, opera, legend, and topical events; his style was ingenious, but heavily overloaded with wearisome puns, and with smart repartee which somehow lacked wit. In his serious plays he tended to create stock types, which recur constantly throughout his work, and he had no profundity. At his best he reflected the prevailing taste of the day, against which T. W. Robertson rebelled, and that, and his own charming personality, accounted for much of his ephemeral success. Hibbert, in *A Playgoer's Memoirs*, says of him: 'His habit of word contortion, or punning, in burlesque is tiresome to us now, and seems laborious, but it was natural to him. His humour is homely, and even vulgar. His characters are mostly conventional creatures of the stage. But he never set up a suggestive situation, or wrote an indecorous line.' He also adds that he was 'a tall, handsome, heavily moustached man, who was hardly ever known to lose his temper, who was universally beloved for his charm and for his ready wit' and as an actor 'he rejected make-up and would step from a cab on to the stage'.

BYZANTINE THEATRE. With the fall of the Roman Empire the greater part of its dramatic achievement passed into oblivion, but some activity continued in Constantinople, which became the new capital of the Empire. Sources which cast light on the conditions obtaining on the Byzantine stage are: the sermons and writings of the Early Fathers of the Church, particularly St. John Chrysostom; reports of ceremonies and festivities by historians and writers, especially the *Anthology of Epigrams*; collections of laws; various ivory tablets of the Consuls; and two important essays, the first by Chorikios, a Rhetor of Gaza, defending the mimes of the Dionysiac cult, and the second by Libanios, defending the *pantomimus*. Unfortunately the Iconoclastic movement was probably responsible for the destruction of much early material. It is true that Byzantium did not create a genuine theatre, or any truly dramatic poetry, but there were undoubtedly dramatic elements in its festivals, games, mummings, and masqueradings. There are records of four early theatres in Constantinople, not counting hippodromes and circuses, and many other cities within the domain of Byzantine culture—Antioch, Alexandria, Brytos, Gaza, Caesarea—had at least one theatre each. According to Ioannes Lydus, a sixth-century Byzantine historian, the main types of Roman comedy (see FABULA) continued to be played in Byzantium, and although no written texts survive, it is evident that the *mimus*, *pantomimus* and *tragoedia* competed for attention with horse-racing, bear-baiting, jugglers, and acrobats. In spite of the Edict of the Trullan Council, and the active opposition of the Church, the *mimus* kept its popularity until the capture of Constantinople by the Turks in 1453. Its subject-matter varied from simple buffoonery and scenes of adultery to social satire, especially protest against corrupt state officials, taking its themes from mythology and history and even ridiculing Christian rites and beliefs. There is evidence for the playing of the *pantomimus*, in which a solo dancer, sometimes impersonating several characters, mimed the entire plot to off-stage singing, and of the *tragoedia* (in which the actor himself sang while miming the story in dumb-show, but did not dance), but not for the playing of classical tragedy and comedy. Perhaps these were reduced to simple declamation.

As for the religious theatre in Byzantium, it appears to have been closely linked with the sermon or homily, many of which contained a strong dramatic element, so much so that the scholar La Piana called them 'the dramatic homilies'. These contained fully dramatized episodes of the life of Christ which were accompanied or followed by oratorical passages. A 'homily drama', as defined in the Encomium attributed to Proclos, is one in which the dramatic elements make up a complete play to which the fundamental idea gives unity of purpose and meaning, though it remains linked with the sermon. It appears as part of the *Panegyris* reserved for the greater liturgical feasts. There seem to have been two cycles, each embracing a trilogy—The Annunciation, Nativity, and Flight into Egypt; the Baptism of Jesus, his Passion, and the Harrowing of Hell. The Byzantine homily-drama derives from three sources, the Apocrypha, the Syriac *sogitha* or homily-canticle, in which the hymn-writers tended to dramatize sacred history, and the *mimus*.

What remains controversial is the relationship between these homily-dramas and the scenario of a Greek Passion Play preserved in a Vatican manuscript of the thirteenth century. Its date is not precisely determinable. The scenario, in which the actions to accompany each speech are carefully described, is divided into the following episodes: after a poem addressed to the actors come the Raising of Lazarus, the Entry of Jesus into Jerusalem, the Last Supper, the Washing of the Disciples' Feet, the Betrayal by Judas, the Denial by Peter, Jesus before Herod, the Crucifixion, the Resurrection, and Doubting Thomas. The play was probably acted outside the church, and whether it is derived from a Western model, or whether the Greek or Cyprus Passion Cycle influenced Western plays has not yet been decided.

There is also a Syrian manuscript (in Berlin) which may possibly be a translation from a Greek original, and could be the scenario of a religious play. It is called *The Tale of the Actors*. In the first part a company of pagan actors are ridiculing the Christian religion, and in the second part they are converted to Christianity and as a result are martyred.

Some plays were written during this period, but they were closet dramas, not intended for the stage. A Jew, Ezechiel, wrote *Exagoge*, a hellenistic dramatization of a biblical story. We find also poems like that attributed to Ignatius of Nicaea (ninth century), *Verses on Adam*, which are in a dramatic form, and may have been intended for public reading, even if not for performance. We hear of a play by Stephanus Sabbaita, *The Death of Christ*. And there is the Greek drama, *Christos Paschon*, variously dated from the fourth to the eleventh century—the eleventh century is more probable—a mosaic composed of verses from the Greek tragic poets, particularly Euripides, on the passion, death, and resurrection of Jesus, which was probably read in public. There is no further evidence that Byzantium ever produced a Christian dramatic literature. All we have are a few short fragments, some vague references to doubtful authors, a few dialogues with abstract characters written for didactic and moral purposes, and some satirical, philosophical or allegorical pieces attributed to Michael Haplochira, Theodore Prodromos, and Manuel Phile, all twelfth-century writers.

As to the legacy of Byzantium, there seems to be some evidence that Western religious drama in the Middle Ages may have been derived from Byzantine material, particularly the homilies. But it is only a possibility. It is also uncertain whether the traditions of the Byzantine stage continued in Istanbul after the Turks took over. But there are certain similarities, which may derive from reciprocal exchanges or influences, in the Turkish guild processions, in certain aspects of Karagöz, the Turkish Shadow Theatre, and in the rural Dionysiac and other mysteries (notably the Eleusinian) still surviving in Anatolia and practised by Turkish peasants. More research is needed in this field, which has been neglected in favour of the hippodrome. The old translations of texts need revising and re-editing, their dates need to be verified, their provenance established, and then their true character could be ascertained (see also TURKEY).

METIN AND

C

CAECILIUS STATIUS (*c.* 219–*c.* 166 B.C.), Roman dramatist, said to have been a Gaul from north Italy. During the years between the death of Plautus and the advent of Terence, he translated Greek comedies for the Roman stage. Some 40 titles and about 300 lines have survived. Cicero thought Caecilius's latinity bad. In one of the most interesting passages in Latin literary criticism Aulus Gellius sets extracts from Caecilius's *Plocium* side by side with their original by Menander to show how inferior the Latin writer is in style, wit, simplicity, and truth to nature. It is certainly illuminating to see how widely a Latin 'translation' can differ from the original. We may grant that Caecilius has coarsened his material (the theme of the peccant husband and the jealous wife), yet claim that he has lent it a lively pungency which was probably more in keeping with Roman taste than all the subtle grace of Menander. Here as elsewhere in Latin drama we see how the translator has used every trick of rhetoric to make a situation instantaneously effective. In Menander the wife's triumph is stated in matter-of-fact language: 'Out of the house she has cast the troublesome girl'; in Caecilius we can hear her nagging accents: 'ita plor*ando* or*ando* inst*ando* atque obiurg*ando* me optudit.' We notice also that the Latin writer has introduced a broad jest (a reference to the lady's unpleasant breath) for which there is no justification in the Greek. It would seem, then, that Caecilius allowed himself considerable freedom in expression and style, just as his predecessors, Naevius and Plautus, had done; nevertheless his plays were at first unpopular and only succeeded because of the steady support given them by the famous actor-producer Ambivius Turpio. Caecilius seems to have set the new fashion of leaving titles for the most part in the Greek; he favoured Menander, the most refined of the Greek authors of New Comedy; his plots, we are told, were good, which presumably means that he chose originals with good plots and did not tamper with them; he was something of a moralist. It would appear, then, that he had at least set foot on the road which led from the careless gaiety of Naevius and Plautus to the more Hellenic and sentimental comedy of Terence and his successors. WILLIAM BEARE†

CAFÉ-CONCERT, the name given to the French restaurant where singers and orchestra amuse the diners, sometimes with a simple programme of ballads and light music, sometimes with an elaborate operetta. A number of good singers and actors have come to the legitimate stage from the cafés-concerts, which were originally known, by their Dutch name, as Musicos. They were a product of the Revolution of 1789, and flourished until their licences were restricted under Napoleon I, reappearing in the 1830s under Louis-Philippe. The destruction under Napoleon III of so many small popular theatres along the Boulevard du Temple gave new life to many cafés-concerts elsewhere. The café-spectacle was run on the same lines, but offered its clients more solid fare, with acrobats, conjuring, short sketches, and dancing.

CAFÉ FLAMENCO, a type of entertainment popular in Spain, native to Andalusia, and corresponding to the French café-concert. The patrons of the café are regaled with songs and dances, in folk-lore and gipsy tradition, which have a vaguely oriental flavour, due no doubt to the persistent influence of the Moors, comparable to that of café-singers in Algiers and Tunis. (See Sargent's painting *El Jaleo*, which was in the Paris Salon of 1882.)

CAIN, ANDREW (*fl.* 1620–1644), English actor, a goldsmith by profession, who became a player in 1622, first as one of Lady Elizabeth's Men and then as a Palsgrave's Man. He was evidently a comedian, for he is frequently referred to as 'Cane the Clown', and in 1631 (by which date he had evidently joined the Prince's Men at Salisbury Court) he played the part of Trimalchio, a humorous gallant, in *Holland's Leaguer*. He was one of the actors who continued playing surreptitiously at the Red Bull after the closing of the theatres in 1642. In 1641 *The Stage-Players' Complaint* was published, with the sub-title *In a Pleasant Dialogue between Cane of the Fortune and Reed of the Friers* (Timothy Read was another popular comedian of the day), and woodcut portraits of both men. During the Civil War Cain (whose name is found in numerous spellings, including Keyne and Kein) returned to his trade, and engraved dies at Oxford for the debased coinage of the Royalists. Thirty years later he was still remembered for his jigs at the Fortune, and at the Red Bull, where the Prince's Men spent their last active years.

CALDERÓN DE LA BARCA, PEDRO (1600–81), Spanish dramatist, successor to Lope de Vega and the most celebrated dramatist of the latter part of the seventeenth century. Many of his best-known plays date from the period 1625–40. The public theatres of Madrid were closed for five or six years from 1644, and in 1651 Calderón was ordained priest. From that date onwards he devoted himself to the writing of *autos sacramentales* and plays for the Court theatre, both of which genres make use of elaborate allegory. The *autos sacramentales* put upon the stage the abstract ideas of Catholic theology by means of a combination of intense lyricism and excellent stage-craft. A. A. Parker, in his study of Calderón's religious plays, writes:

Calderón is not a dramatist who was forced by his environment to retail theological clichés and to distort the nature of his medium. He is a theological poet and dramatist in a deep and legitimate sense, and as such his achievement is not only valuable, but also unique in literature.

Of these plays, the best known are *El gran teatro del mundo* (before 1641) on which Hugo von Hofmannsthal based his *Grosse Welttheater* (1922), written for production by Reinhardt at the Salzburg Festival, and *La cena de Baltasar* (before 1634).

One of the most famous of Calderón's secular plays is *El alcalde de Zalamea*, a study of prudent virtue and of the vices which spring from uncontrolled passions, set against the background of an idealized vision of the class-structure of contemporary society. *La vida es sueño* is a story of human regeneration, as the Prince who at the start of the play is little better than a beast, having passed all his life immured in a dungeon, comes to realize the need to keep in check his pride and brute passions and learns the value of reason and prudence. *El mágico prodigioso* has been interpreted as a variant of the Faust legend; its theme is rather the search of the human soul for God. The plays dealing with the question of *honor* (such as *El médico de su honra*, *El pintor de su deshonra*, and *A secreto agravio, secreta venganza*) have been much discussed, some critics dismissing them as barbarous, and others being concerned to show that Calderón does not by any means accept all the conventional implications of the code of honour. Calderón's Court plays have, as yet, been little studied.

Calderón lacks Lope de Vega's spontaneity but his plays are more finished, the work of a great craftsman, and have exercised a considerable influence on European drama. A number of his plays were translated into French and so found their way into Restoration England. Out of favour during the eighteenth century, Calderón was rediscovered by the German critics of the Romantic period, notably by Schlegel and Tieck. Shelley also was an enthusiastic admirer and translator of Calderón, but the best-known versions of Calderón's plays in English are the very free adaptations of Edward Fitzgerald and the more stilted translations of Denis Florence MacCarthy. J. E. VAREY

CALLIPIDES, a Greek actor of the fifth century B.C. (see GREECE, 4).

CALMO, ANDREA (1509/10–*c.* 1561), a Venetian gondolier, and an early Italian dramatist and amateur actor, contemporary and rival of Ruzzante (see BEOLCO). He seems to have exercised considerable influence on the literary development of the *commedia dell'arte.* As an actor he specialized in old men, and may have played a part comparable to Pantalone, though the name was not yet in use. His plays were edited by Rossi in 1888 (see ITALY, 2).

CALVERT. (1) CHARLES (1828–79), English actor and manager, who made his first appearances in the provinces, before going to London in 1855. In 1859 he became manager of the Theatre Royal, Manchester, and was the first manager of the Prince's Theatre there when it opened in 1864. He remained until 1875, when he went to New York to produce *Henry V.* On a previous visit to the U.S.A. in 1871 he had been responsible for the production of *Richard III* at Niblo's Garden. On his return to England he continued to appear in the provinces until his death. It was, however, at Manchester that his main work was done, with the production of a number of Shakespeare and other plays which were much admired by discerning critics of the day. In 1856 he married (2) ADELAIDE HELEN (*née* Biddles or Bedells) (1837–1921), daughter of a provincial actor, who had been on the stage since, as a child of six, she appeared with the Charles Keans, going with them to America. After her marriage she appeared in leading parts under her husband's management with great success, and also accompanied him to America. She returned there after his death and toured with Edwin Booth, Mrs. Langtry, and Mary Anderson. In 1884 she returned to England and was a prominent actress in London until shortly before her death. She was the author of two plays, *Trotty Veck* (1872), based on Dickens's *The Chimes*, and *Can He Forgive Her?* (1891). All her eight children went on the stage, but only one achieved any great eminence. This was (3) LOUIS (1859–1923), who made his first appearance in Durban, Natal, in 1879, and from there went to Australia. On his return to England in 1880 he joined Sarah Thorne's famous stock company at Margate. He appeared at Drury Lane in 1886, and at the Lyceum with Irving in the following year, and was subsequently associated with most of the leading managements of London, including that of Fred Terry and Julia Neilson, with whom he gave a splendid performance as an old actor in *Sweet Nell of Old Drury.* He was a leading member of the company at the Court Theatre during the Vedrenne–Barker management, playing Broadbent in *John Bull's Other Island* and William the Waiter in *You Never Can Tell*, with marked success. He several times formed and managed his own company, in London and on tour in England and America. He was at one time producer at the New Theatre, New York, and appeared there also in several revivals of the classics and Shakespeare. Besides being a splendid actor, robust, with a fine voice and a complete knowledge of his art, he was an excellent producer, and a successful and highly respected manager. Whether in Shakespeare, Shaw, costume plays or modern comedy, he was equally at home and always in the front rank. His Mercutio and Casca were memorable, as was his Creon in the Reinhardt production of *Oedipus Rex* at Covent Garden in 1912. At his best in parts requiring dramatic strength which gave his fine voice full play, he could also play comedy roles with ease and polish. He was the author of a handbook to acting, *Problems of the Actor*, published in 1918. W. MACQUEEN-POPE†

CALZABIGI, RANIERI DA (1714–95), Italian poet, and the librettist of Gluck, whom he encouraged in his attempts to reform opera. The first result of their collaboration was 'Orfeo' (1762), followed by 'Alceste' (1767) and 'Paride ed Elena' (1770).

CAMBRIDGE. Medieval religious drama was particularly at home in East Anglia, and plays were probably given in Cambridge churches as early as elsewhere. But the first recorded reference to a dramatic performance is in connexion with the guilds, when a husband and wife, admitted to the Guild of Merchants of Corpus Christi in 1350, gave a donation towards the staging of *The Children of Israel*. There are frequent references in the fifteenth and sixteenth centuries to the town minstrels, and the practice of singing and declamation was encouraged among the students. In 1546 a production at Christ's College of *Pammachius*, by Kirchmayer, gave great offence to the Chancellor on account of its Protestant bias, and at the same college, some years later, there was a less controversial production of the early English comedy, *Gammer Gurton's Needle*. There are also records of plays being given in 1556 in the Falcon yard and at the Saracen's Head. As in all educational establishments (see, for instance, JESUIT DRAMA) the acting of Latin plays was regarded as part of the curriculum, and Elizabeth I, on her only visit to Cambridge, in 1564, was entertained in King's College Chapel by a performance of Plautus's *Aulularia* and an original Latin tragedy on the subject of Dido written by a Fellow of King's, Edward Halliwell. A play in English, *Ezechias*, by Udall, was also given, but this was apparently not to the taste of the authorities, since a letter of 1592 from the Vice-Chancellor asks the Queen to allow a Latin play to be prepared in honour of her approaching visit—which did not materialize—instead of the English play which she had commanded, the latter not being customary and 'nothing beseeminge our students'. Certainly by 1575 there was a settled tradition of winter performances, and the records show a preponderance of Latin plays, several of them translated from contemporary Italian works, directly or through the French. St. John's seems to have been particularly addicted to play-acting, and it was there that a play in Latin verse on Richard III by Thomas Legge was performed in 1579. There, too, between 1598 and 1603, *The Pilgrimage to Parnassus* and the two parts of *The Return from Parnassus* were first acted. King's saw the first performance—in a Latin translation—of Guarini's famous *Pastor Fido*, round about the turn of the century. It was with a Latin translation of Bonarelli's *Filli di Sciro* (as *Scyros*) that Trinity men entertained Prince Charles (later Charles I), when with his sister Elizabeth and her husband, the Elector Palatine, he visited Cambridge in 1613, and the visit of James I in 1615 was made memorable by the performance, among other plays, of Ruggle's *Ignoramus* (based on Della Porta's *La Trappolaria*), which so delighted the king that, being unable to get the actors up to Whitehall, he returned to Cambridge to see it again.

There appear to have been occasional visits to Cambridge by professional companies, particularly in summer when plague closed the London theatres—the Lord Chamberlain's Men are believed to have played *Hamlet* in Cambridge in 1603—and there was also the influence of dramatic performances at nearby Stourbridge Fair to be reckoned with. These caused trouble in 1592, and on the whole non-academic acting was not encouraged. Even the college plays in Latin grow fewer as the Commonwealth approaches, and the last recorded play in English was *The Guardian* (an early version of Abraham Cowley's *Cutter of Coleman Street*) which was performed at Trinity before the eleven-year-old Prince Charles (later Charles II) in 1641–2. The Restoration brought very little theatrical activity to Cambridge, but by the eighteenth century the town was part of the Norwich circuit and the players were well received, though no theatre was allowed within the university precincts. There was, however, a commodious wooden theatre at Stourbridge, on the Newmarket road, which was occupied annually in the autumn by the Norwich company, and several successively at Barnwell, which in the nineteenth century housed a number of London companies on tour. It then became derelict until in 1926 it was taken over to become the Festival Theatre (see GRAY, TERENCE and No. 84).

In the colleges, plays were occasionally given, but there was no revival of the old traditions, and it was not until the founding of the Amateur Dramatic Club in 1855 by F. C. Burnand that acting became part of undergraduate life as a social and extra-curricular activity. There had been some earlier attempts: the Shakespeare Club, 1830, the Garrick Club, 1834, a Sheridan Society, a Dramatic Reading Society, and, in 1855 also, an Amateur Theatrical Society, which in 1864 celebrated Shakespeare's Tercentenary with a production of *The Merchant of Venice* and *As You Like It*. Its last recorded performance was given in 1868. Meanwhile the A.D.C. was gaining strength, though during its first fifty years it produced mainly comedies and burlesques. A more ambitious venture was Taylor's *The Overland Route*, which was successful enough to warrant further essays in the same style, including a version of *The Lyons Mail* with no female characters. One of the early A.D.C. actors to achieve success on the professional stage was Charles Brookfield, first seen in *Money* in 1877, while the founder of the Club went on to become editor of *Punch* and a prolific writer of light plays.

After the break in tradition caused by the

First World War the A.D.C. was re-formed in 1919, and better plays and acting became the rule, mainly through the efforts of Frank Birch, who gave up a Fellowship at King's to go on the stage. In 1933 the Club's premises, adapted in 1860 from several rooms in the Hoop Hotel, were destroyed by fire, and were rebuilt as a well-equipped theatre holding 200. Many members of the A.D.C. have made outstanding reputations on the professional stage, among them Aubrey Smith, Miles Malleson, Michael Redgrave, Robert Eddison, Peter Woodthorpe and Julian Slade. A centenary celebration performance was given on 12 June 1955.

Women are now admitted to full membership of the A.D.C., but, since this was not so in 1928, Alistair Cooke and Charles Shope founded the Cambridge Mummers, with men and women members. This company usually gives two performances annually in the A.D.C. theatre and sometimes one outside Cambridge in the vacation. An earlier and most important group was the Footlights, founded in 1883. Their first production was an extravaganza, *Aladdin*, given in May week. Their performances were given at the Theatre Royal, which William Redfern, an artist interested in scene-painting, who in 1875 had founded the Bijou Dramatic Club for Cambridge citizens, had reconstructed from the old St. Andrews Hall in 1882. (It was here that *The Private Secretary* had its first production in 1883, under Hawtrey.) When in 1896 Redfern demolished the old building and erected his New Theatre—opened in 1896 with Tree in *Hamlet*—the Footlights continued to appear there until 1926, when they moved to the Arts Theatre, built by Lord Keynes. A number of professional actors have come from the Footlights, including the brothers Jack and Claude Hulbert in the early part of the century, and more recently Jimmy Edwards, and Jonathan Miller, inspirer of the phenomenally successful quartet of *Beyond the Fringe* (1960). The annual Footlights revue has become an important feature of Cambridge theatrical life, and is often seen in London for a short season.

In 1907 a group of undergraduates who were interested in the possibilities of reviving Elizabethan plays did a preliminary production of *Dr. Faustus.* This was successful enough to warrant the founding of the Marlowe Dramatic Society in the following year, with Rupert Brooke, who had played Mephistopheles, as its first President. From the beginning the Marlowe Society has maintained a tradition of anonymity, and an outstanding feature of its work has been the fine speaking of verse. It has devoted itself mainly to Shakespeare, with such memorable exceptions as *Edward II*, *The Duchess of Malfi*, *Volpone*, *Friar Bacon and Friar Bungay*, and *The Revenger's Tragedy*. The productions of *Hamlet*, *Lear*, *Othello*, *Romeo and Juliet*, *Troilus and Cressida*, and *Coriolanus*, by George Rylands, a Fellow of King's who combines in himself the attributes of scholar and practical producer, led to the recording under his direction, on long-playing discs, of all Shakespeare's plays by past and present members of the Marlowe Society, with the support of professional players. The enterprise was completed in time for the 1964 quatercentenary celebrations. The Marlowe Society has given many actors to the professional stage, and a group of outstanding producers—Peter Hall, John Barton, Peter Wood, and Toby Robertson.

The Arts Theatre, mentioned above, was built and presented to the City and University of Cambridge by John Maynard Keynes as a memorial to his parents. Under his direction and that of his wife (the former ballet dancer Lydia Lopokova), it did much to stimulate local interest in good plays, films, ballet, opera, and concert music. During the Second World War it was used as the headquarters of the Ballets Jooss, and the Apollo Society was later founded there. In spite of rising costs and increased competition from other forms of entertainment, the Arts, under the chairmanship of George Rylands, continues to implement the policy of its founder.

An important theatrical event in Cambridge is the production of a Greek play in the original which, under the impetus of Oxford's first successful venture in 1880, began in 1882 with Sophocles' *Ajax.* A year later came the *Birds*, with music by Parry, and in 1884 a society was formed for the continued production of Greek plays, now a triennial fixture. From 1921 to 1950 J. T. Sheppard (later Sir John and Provost of King's) was responsible for ten productions, beginning with the *Oresteia* and ending with the *Oedipus Coloneus.* For each of these a modern English composer was commissioned to write or arrange the music. Dennis Arundell, who had led the chorus in 1921, wrote the music for the *Electra* in 1927, set the choruses of the *Bacchae* to music by Handel in 1930, and in 1962 directed the first production in Cambridge of the *Clouds.* Rylands directed the *Agamemnon* in 1951 and, with Alan Kerr, the *Oedipus Tyrannus* in 1965.

CAMBRIDGE THEATRE, LONDON, in Seven Dials, built by Bertie A. Meyer and opened by him on 4 Sept. 1930 with *Charlot's Masquerade*, by Jeans. Though a charming playhouse, the Cambridge has as yet contributed little to theatre history. The Chauve-Souris company played a season there soon after its opening, and other productions were *Elizabeth of England* (1931) and a revival of *Night Must Fall.* In 1943 there was a successful revival of *Heartbreak House*, and after the Second World War Jay Pomeroy took over the theatre for artistically successful but financially unrewarding seasons of opera. Menotti's 'The Consul' was first heard there in 1951, and in 1960 *Billy Liar* started a long run.

W. MACQUEEN-POPE†, *rev.*

CAMERON, BEATRICE (1868–1940), see MANSFIELD (2).

CAMINELLI, ANTONIO (1436–1502), author of the first Italian play to bear the formal name of 'tragedy'. This was *Filostrato e Panfile* (1499), and in it Caminelli, who was known as 'Il Pistoia', tried to force a story from the Decameron into the mould of Senecan tragedy, while retaining much of the tradition of the old medieval religious play.

CAMÕES, LUÍS DE, see PORTUGAL.

CAMPBELL, BARTLEY (1843–88), one of the first American dramatists to make playwriting his only profession. He even retired from journalism when his first play was given in 1871, on the ground that a playwright could not also be a critic. He wrote a number of melodramas, of which the first was *Through Fire* (1871), and directed a theatre in Chicago where many of his later works were produced, including *Fate* (1872), and a domestic drama, *Risks* (1873). It was the visit of the Chicago company to San Francisco which inspired Campbell's best play, *My Partner* (1879), a drama of the American frontier which owes much to the stories of Bret Harte. It was first played with Louis Aldrich in the chief part, and was translated into German. Among Campbell's later plays were *The Galley Slave* (1879) and *The White Slave* (1882), both emotional melodramas, which he directed and financed himself, thus losing the fortune which *My Partner* had brought him. He died insane, of overwork and worry. His plays have little literary quality, but are interesting in the history of the late nineteenth-century American stage. Some of them were published in the 1940s in anthologies of early plays.

CAMPBELL, HERBERT (1844–1904), a music-hall performer, who began his career as a member of a burnt-cork trio during the Minstrel boom, and then went on the halls as a solo turn. He appeared regularly in Drury Lane pantomimes from Boxing Night, 1882, until the year of his death, and with his large fat figure and jolly red face proved a wonderful foil to diminutive Dan Leno during the many years they played together.

CAMPBELL, MRS. PATRICK [*née* BEATRICE STELLA TANNER] (1865–1940), English actress, who made her first appearance on the stage in 1888 at Liverpool. After touring with Ben Greet, she appeared in London in 1890, playing in *The Hunchback*, *The School for Scandal*, and *As You Like It*. A season at the Adelphi was followed by her outstanding performance as Paula in *The Second Mrs. Tanqueray* at the St. James's, and she was soon considered one of the leading actresses of the day. Among her later successes were Agnes in *The Notorious Mrs. Ebbsmith*, Juliet and Ophelia to the Romeo and Hamlet of Forbes-Robertson, Mélisande in English and in French—the latter to the Pelléas of Sarah Bernhardt—and a number of leading roles in Ibsen. She also appeared in London and in New York in the title-role of *Magda*, in which Matheson Lang thought her superior to Duse. Shaw, however, in *Our Theatres in the Nineties*, pours scorn on it, as he does on her Rita in *Little Eyolf*, though he wrote for her the part of Eliza Doolittle in *Pygmalion*, which she played at the first production in 1914 and at subsequent revivals. Among her other parts were Fedora, Bella Donna, Lady Macbeth, and—one of her finest creations—Anastasia Rakonitz in *The Matriarch*, a play based on the novel by G. B. Stern. A beautiful woman—Shaw calls her 'perilously bewitching'—she had a devastating wit, and became a legend long before her death. In spite of long absences from the stage, she was one of the great theatrical figures of her generation. Her correspondence with Bernard Shaw was published after his death. An American actor, Jerome Kilty, made a dramatic dialogue out of extracts from it. As *Dear Liar*, with Kilty as Shaw and Cavada Humphrey as Mrs. Patrick Campbell, this was successful in the United States and in London in 1959–60.

CAMPDEN HOUSE, Kensington. This had a well-appointed private theatre where frequent amateur performances were given in the 1850s and 1860s.

CAMPEN, JACOB VAN, see VAN CAMPEN, JACOB.

CAMPION, THOMAS (1567–1620), English poet and musician, who at one time practised as a doctor. He was connected with Philip Rosseter, also a musician, who was lessee of Whitefriars theatre, and manager of the Queen's Revels, and may have made contact with the public stage through him, though there is no evidence that he ever wrote for it. His masques for performance at Court, however, place him next to Jonson in the history of the genre during Jacobean days. The words of these are printed in the 1909 edition of Campion's works, edited by Percival Vivian.

CAMPISTRON, JEAN-GALBERT DE (1656–1723), French dramatist who, after a stormy and precocious youth, went to Paris and was befriended by the actor J. B. Raisin. His first two plays having been produced at the Comédie-Française, Campistron was engaged on the recommendation of Racine to write the libretto for Lully's last opera 'Acis et Galatée'. Its success brought him recognition and a lucrative position with a noble house. Campistron's most important play, *Andronic*, given in 1685, is, like so many plays of the time, contemporary history under a Roman guise, and it marks the extent of the influence exercised on drama by the historical novel, to the detriment of the former. The continued decadence of classical tragedy is also apparent in its exaggerated and improbable intrigue. Of his other plays, *Alcibiade* (1685) was momentarily successful, owing to the excellent acting of Baron, but his later plays were failures, being weak in execution and overweighted with intrigue. In 1686 a play entitled *Phraate* was given four performances, but was then stopped by the authorities, possibly on account of some fancied slight to the King. No copy of it exists, and it is said that Campistron was made to burn the only manuscript copy. Though the plan and conception of Campistron's plays were good, his style was poor, owing to laziness. He also wrote two comedies, which are of no importance. The poverty of French drama at this time is revealed by the fact that from 1683 to 1693 Campistron was considered its leading tragic writer. Like Racine, he gave up the theatre to enter the King's service.

CAMUS, ALBERT (1913–60), French dramatist and novelist, who gained his first experience of the theatre in 1936 as actor and producer with Le Théâtre du Travail, a left-wing group in Algiers, for which he adapted Malraux's novel, *Temps du mépris*. In 1937, he founded the Théâtre de l'Équipe, also in Algiers, for which he adapted Gide's *Retour de l'enfant prodigue*, and produced (among other plays) Vildrac's *Paquebot Tenacity* and Copeau's version of Dostoievsky's *Brothers Karamazov*. The last production by this company, shortly before the outbreak of war in 1939, was *The Playboy of the Western World*, in which Camus played Christy Mahon. In France, during the German occupation, he edited the clandestine newspaper, *Combat*. In 1944 he returned to the theatre, as playwright, with *Le Malentendu*, produced in Paris by Marcel Herrand. In the following year he first attracted wide attention with *Caligula*, in which Gérard Philipe scored a great personal success in the title-role. Although Camus always refused to be labelled as an existentialist, *Le Malentendu* and *Caligula* are both accented heavily on the existentialist themes of 'l'acte gratuit' and the absurdity of the human condition. *L'État de siège*, produced by Jean-Louis Barrault in 1948, although a failure then, is probably his most ambitious and interesting play, using the symbol of the plague to characterize the evil (totalitarianism) that crushes man in his search for liberty. Like the later work of Sartre, the play takes on a wider philosophical breadth, but remains existentialist in that the hero, who successfully refutes the established order symbolized by the plague, is able to do so because he is a free being. Like Sartre, Camus was an 'engaged' writer, but he was more concerned with aesthetic problems than Sartre, who has been content to accept the conventional theatrical forms as he has found them. After *Les Justes* (1949) (done at the Oxford Playhouse in 1962 as *The Just*), Camus devoted himself to a series of adaptations and translations which may be viewed as experiments through which he was working towards a wider and freer theatrical technique, notably: *La Dévotion à la Croix* (from Calderón, 1953), *Un Cas intéressant* (from Dino Buzzati, 1955), *Requiem pour une nonne* (from William Faulkner, 1956), *Le Chevalier d'Olmédo* (from Lope de Vega, 1957), and *Les Possédés* (from Dostoievsky, 1959). The last three were all produced by Camus himself. His return to active collaboration in the theatre was tragically cut short by his death in a car crash. T. C. C. MILNE

CANADA. Canadians, scattered in small groups over a vast territory, and so forced to rely very much upon themselves for entertainment, became, between the two World Wars, enthusiastic supporters of the amateur Little or Community Theatre movement. But no professional theatre evolved from all this amateur activity, and the visits of touring companies from Europe and America to the larger centres seemed sufficient to satisfy the need for professionalism. Discouraged and baffled in their efforts to expand, the enthusiasm of the amateurs gradually waned, and it was not until after the Second World War that a combination of circumstances brought about the establishment of a professional Canadian theatre, strong enough to stand up to the competition of visiting companies, and able to offer its members sufficient prospects of work and some security to keep them from drifting away to America or Europe.

1. FRENCH THEATRE. The history of the French theatre in Canada goes back to the days of the first settlers, for as early as 1604 a masque, or open-air pageant, entitled *Le Théâtre de Neptune*, was produced by Marc Lescarbot on the beach at Port Royal, in Acadia. Similar spectacles followed, particularly in Quebec, and in 1646, only ten years after its first performance, Corneille's *Le Cid* was produced there by amateurs, followed by *Héraclitus* in 1651. Unfortunately, later in the century, moral objections to theatre-going arose and a performance of *Tartuffe* in 1694 had to be abandoned. This, however, as earlier in England, did not prevent the performance of plays for educational purposes, and many French classics were presented by the Jesuits in their colleges. During the eighteenth century war with England severely hampered the extension of French theatrical activity; but in 1790 a permanent playhouse, the Théâtre du Marché au Foin, opened in Quebec. In Montreal, in the same year, a performance was given of a comedy entitled *Colas et Colinette*. This was by Joseph Quesnel, an immigrant from France. In the early nineteenth century amateur dramatics flourished in Quebec and Montreal and several theatres were opened. The first Canadian-born dramatist was Pierre Petitclair (?–1860), who wrote comedies in the style of Molière, a dramatist who was already well-known through the versions of his plays given in the marionette theatres of the time. A succession of plays by French-Canadians followed, stimulated by the increasing number of professional touring companies which were, by this time, finding Canada a profitable and easily accessible market. Sarah Bernhardt visited Montreal in 1880, Coquelin in 1889; Mounet-Sully was in Quebec City in 1894. Such distinguished visitors were common until the outbreak of the First World War. After 1918 some European actors returned, notably Firmin Gémier and Sacha Guitry, but interest in the theatre was declining, partly because of the rise of the cinema. It was not as marked here as in the

English-speaking parts of the country, however, and plays by native authors continued to be written and produced. Encouraged by the foundation in 1932 of the bilingual Dominion Drama Festival, several amateur companies made solid reputations. The years immediately before the Second World War saw the emergence of two important features of French-Canadian theatre, which later received further stimulus from the arrival of Gustave Cohen, and Ludmilla Pitoëff's company.

The first portent of a new era was the establishment by Father Émile Legault, who had studied in Paris under Ghéon, of the Compagnons de Saint-Laurent, an amateur group organized on the lines of similar groups in France, such as Les Théophiliens, originally founded to produce early religious and secular plays. At the same time the first Canadian actor of star quality was emerging. This was Gratien Gélinas, known as Fridolin, after the character in the revues he wrote for production at the Monument National. These 'Fridolinons' ran from 1937 to 1946. Two years later his play *'Tit-Coq* (*Lil' Rooster*) broke all Canadian records with a run of more than 450 performances. In 1958 Gélinas founded the Théâtre de la Comédie Canadienne, housed in a former burlesque theatre, bought and redecorated with a donation from a brewery. The opening production was Anouilh's *L'Alouette*, in both French and English versions. Gelinas's next play, the immensely successful *Bousille et les justes* (1959), was also done in both languages, in Montreal and on tour. The Comédie Canadienne has also staged plays by Canadian authors, among them Marcel Dubé and Guy DuFresne, and such imported productions as *The Summer of the Seventeenth Doll*, done by the Crest Theatre of Toronto.

There were still a number of flourishing amateur groups in Montreal, notably l'Équipe, established by Pierre Dagenais, which from 1944–7 did seasons of modern plays. But the Compagnons de Saint-Laurent outgrew their amateur status and enlarged their repertory. They also found a permanent home, first in L'Ermitage in 1943, and then in the Salle Gésu in 1945. Here they gave some remarkable seasons of French plays, old and new, and established a theatre school which soon had a good reputation. In 1947 they won the Bessborough Trophy with a Flemish farce, *Les Gueux en Paradis*, and in the same year they staged their first Canadian play, Felix Leclerc's *Malunon*. A year later they moved to a new theatre, and for the first time remained open all the year round. Their first production there was a translation of *The Glass Menagerie*, followed by *Murder in the Cathedral* and *Our Town*. But their repertory was still predominantly French, particularly Molière.

Meanwhile a group of actors who had been with the Compagnons, and had then studied in France, founded a new company, the Théâtre du Nouveau Monde. The leading spirit of this enterprise was Jean Gascon, and it succeeded beyond expectation, so well, in fact, that it absorbed all the available audiences, and Les Compagnons de Saint Laurent, after a good production of Pirandello's *Enrico IV*, were disbanded.

The new company inaugurated its career at the Salle Gésu in 1951 with Molière's *L'Avare*. In 1955 it appeared in Paris at the Théâtre des Nations, the first Canadian company to appear abroad, in three one-act farces by Molière. A year later Gascon and some of his actors, with Gélinas, played the French parts in *Henry V* at the Shakespearean Festival Theatre, Stratford, Ontario and at the Edinburgh Festival. In 1959 the Théâtre du Nouveau Monde appeared at the Brussels Exhibition, visited New York, Paris, and Antwerp, and toured across Canada. In 1965 it appeared in London at the National Theatre (Old Vic) in a new French-Canadian musical, *Klondyke*, and in Molière's *École des femmes*, as part of the first Commonwealth Arts Festival. It now occupies the Orpheum Theatre where it celebrated its tenth anniversary with a highly praised production of *L'Opéra de quat' sous*, a French version of the Brecht–Weill *Die Dreigroschenoper* (based on *The Beggar's Opera*).

English theatre in Montreal has fared less well. After the demise of the long-lived Montreal Repertory Theatre only Norma Springford's Mountain Playhouse remained, but by 1961 a dozen French companies were established. Yvette Brind'Amour's Rideau Vert marked its tenth anniversary in 1958 with a powerful production of *La Reine morte*, and in 1960 moved into its own theatre. In 1965 it played in the U.S.S.R. The Théâtre-Club, founded in 1954 by Jacques Létourneau and Monique Lepage, does French and English classics, as well as Canadian plays. In 1957 Jeannine Beaubien took over a historic gunpowder storehouse on St. Helen's Island, and there founded La Poudrière, a small playhouse which does plays in English, French, and several other languages.

In 1960 the National Theatre School was founded in Montreal with backing from the Canada Council and the Province of Quebec, and thirty students were enrolled. Separate training was provided for English and French students, the former directed by the Welsh actor-teacher Powys Thomas, the latter by Jean Gascon. Michel Saint-Denis was appointed artistic adviser, and the first Chairman of the Board of Governors was Tom Patterson, founder of the Stratford, Ontario, Festival. By 1962 the school had eighty-six students taking the three-year acting course and twenty-four taking the two-year production course; classes were given from November to June in Montreal, and from July to September in Stratford. For the 1962 Stratford Festival Martha Henry, who had completed her second year, was chosen to play Miranda in *The Tempest*.

Montreal's growing consciousness of theatre has now led to the establishment of a cultural centre, the $18,000,000 Place des Arts, situated in the heart of the city on land obtained by clearing a slum. When completed, it will contain three theatres of different sizes.

2. ENGLISH THEATRE. The English-speaking theatre in Canada naturally developed later than the French, but by 1795 there were enough English colonists and officials resident in Quebec and Montreal to justify the visit of the first of many English touring companies, usually after a season in New York. In 1826 Edmund Kean spent August in Montreal and September in Quebec, playing mainly in Shakespeare. (It was during this latter season that he was 'adopted' by four Huron chiefs under the name of Alanienouidet, and given a Red Indian costume in which he later had his portrait painted, and frequently paraded the streets of London. He also had his Red Indian name engraved on his visiting cards.) Dion Boucicault and his wife were in Montreal in 1853. Sothern, the original Dundreary, ran a theatre in Halifax—the Lyceum—from 1857 to 1859, incurring heavy debts, and from the 1870s onwards a number of English and American actors toured Canada, among them Irving and Ellen Terry, the Kendals, Ben Greet, and Mrs. Patrick Campbell, from England, and Clara Norris and James Hackett (both born in Canada) from the United States.

None of this professional activity, however, encouraged the establishment of a Canadian theatre with Canadian playwrights. Native plays, in fact, in the late nineteenth century, tended to be written for reading rather than for production, like Charles Heavysege's *Saul* (1857) and Charles Mair's *Tecumseh* (1886). With the turn of the century a consciously distinctive Canadian literature began to emerge, as Canada changed from an agricultural into an industrial community; but playwriting lagged behind, and was mainly devoted to non-Canadian themes. The amateur theatre, however, flourished as a social activity, and the early years of the twentieth century saw the birth of the Little Theatre Movement in Canada. A pioneer town in this respect was Toronto, where the Governor-General, Earl Grey, encouraged music and drama festivals. There too, just before the First World War, the Arts and Letters Club under the American-trained producer, Roy Mitchell, gave a number of interesting performances. But it was only after the war, with the establishment in 1919 of Hart House Theatre as an integral part of the men students' recreation centre donated to the University of Toronto by the Massey Foundation, that an organized amateur movement can be said to have begun. This theatre, which was one of the finest Little Theatres on the North American continent, with an excellently equipped stage and an auditorium seating some 300, was organized on a semi-independent basis, with a subscription membership drawn both from the university and from the city. It had a professional producer, electrician, and stage-manager, and an amateur cast of undergraduates and townspeople, all jointly responsible for the making of scenery, costumes, and properties. The first productions at Hart House were given by the Players' Club under Roy Mitchell, but almost from its foundation the theatre was under the control of a Board of Syndics, with Vincent Massey, after whose father Hart House had been named, as its first chairman, a position he retained until 1935. In addition he directed and appeared in several plays, as did his younger brother Raymond, later a well-known professional actor.

Under a succession of directors—Roy Mitchell, Bertram Forsyth, Walter Sinclair, Carroll Aikens (who in 1920 established the Home Theatre at Naramanta in British Columbia, where he staged his own Passion Play in 1922), Edgar Stone, and Nancy Pyper—much interesting work was done. But towards 1939 Hart House Theatre fell somewhat from its high estate. At the outbreak of the Second World War it was closed, and on its reopening in 1947, under Robert Gill, it became an undergraduate theatre where students present four plays a year, mainly classics.

Except for Hart House Theatre, Toronto has never had a building which could house suitably a developing local group. The Royal Alexandra, for more than fifty years the leading playhouse, is too large and expensive for anything but touring companies. When Murray and Donald Davis, after experience at Hart House, and with their own summer theatre in Muskoka, established a theatre in Toronto, they had to make do with a converted cinema, The Crest, which will never really be satisfactory for the production of plays. It still survives, however, with varying success. It was for The Crest that J. B. Priestley wrote *The Glass Cage*. After its Toronto run, this play was transferred to London with its Canadian cast, the first to appear there.

Toronto's most important acquisition of recent years has been a beautifully appointed theatre, seating 209, in the Central Library, provided by the city's Library Board. It has proved ideal for the inexpensive production of experimental plays, and almost immediately on its opening in 1961 it was leased by the Red Barn Theatre—a former summer-theatre group run by Marigold Charlesworth and Jean Roberts—for a repertory season of Sheridan, Genêt and Simpson, followed in 1962 by Ionesco and Beckett. Shaw's *Mrs. Warren's Profession* was also produced there, in co-operation with the Manitoba Theatre Centre, and seen afterwards in Winnipeg.

In size and magnificence Toronto's leading playhouse is now the O'Keefe Centre for the Performing Arts, a gift to the city from the financier E. P. Taylor. This opened in Oct. 1961, with the world première of the big musical show, *Camelot*. Seating 3,200 (though it can be reduced by a curtain which shuts off the rear section of the stalls) it overpowers any play. It has, however, provided an excellent home for the Canadian Opera Company, and also for the National Ballet of Canada, founded in 1951 under Celia Franca of the Sadler's Wells Ballet.

Other Toronto activities which deserve mention are the Toronto Children's Players, founded in 1930, and the Margaret Eaton Theatre School, where Bertram Forsyth worked after he left Hart House Theatre. A prize-winning play by a Canadian dramatist, Isabel Ecclestone Mackay, *Two Too Many*, had its first performance here in 1928.

The company whose loss is, however, the most regretted is that formerly directed by Dora Mavor Moore, daughter of Shaw's friend, Professor James Mavor, cousin of James Bridie, and formerly an actress in Ben Greet's company. It developed from the Village Players founded by Mrs. Moore to give performances in a barn on the outskirts of the city, and as the New Play Society gave several stimulating seasons in the theatre of the Royal Ontario Museum and elsewhere. Besides developing a number of leading actors, it also gave a first hearing to several Canadian plays, among them John Coulter's fine historical drama, *Riel*, and Harry Boyle's *The Inheritance*. An offshoot of the New Play Society, the Jupiter Theatre, now defunct, also offered in its short lifetime some interesting productions, including some of Canadian plays. When the New Play Society discontinued production, its founder turned her attention entirely to the training of young actors. An annual revue, *Spring Thaw*, first produced for the society by Mrs. Moore, and then by her son, still continues to make coast-to-coast tours.

Winnipeg has for many years been a centre of theatrical activity which since 1958 has had as its focal point the Manitoba Theatre Centre founded by Tom Hendry and John Hirsch with the amalgamation of the Winnipeg Little Theatre and Theatre 77, the latter also a Hirsch–Hendry enterprise. The Centre has its own playhouse, where it presents a ten-month season of plays, and a theatre school, and it also visits schools outside the city with a programme of scenes from Shakespeare. Winnipeg is also the home of Canada's oldest ballet company, founded in 1938.

In 1933 a Winnipeg amateur company, the Masquers' Club, was awarded first prize in the first Dominion Drama Festival, an organization founded in 1932 by the Governor-General, the Earl of Bessborough. As stated in its charter, the objects of the festival are:

> to encourage dramatic art in Canada by the holding of a Dominion Drama Festival and such regional or other subsidiary festivals as may be deemed advisable, and by the granting of prizes and awards for distinctive effort in any of the arts relating to the drama, including among others the writing of plays, their presentation, mounting, costuming and lighting.

In order to cover the vast area quickly the country is divided into fourteen regions, and the winners of the regional festivals compete in the final festival in early summer. Before 1939, this was held in Ottawa. When, after an eight-year gap, the festival was resumed, it moved to various other large cities. In 1947, the first festival after the war, the finals were held in London, Ontario, whose Little Theatre, formed in 1934 by the amalgamation of four small amateur groups, now numbers 10,000 members. The group owns and operates its own playhouse, having in 1945 purchased the old Grand Theatre, which had housed its earlier productions.

Many other Canadian cities, besides London, have had good amateur groups; the Montreal Repertory Theatre, for instance, directed by Martha Allan, and the Canadian Play Society in Ottawa. Vancouver, whose stock company, flourishing during the 1920s, was disbanded after its best actors had gone to Hollywood, had nevertheless a good Little Theatre group, founded in 1922, which made intermittent use of a small theatre, the York, with a seating capacity of about 400. In 1959 the Queen Elizabeth Theatre opened, but, with a seating capacity of 2,800, proved too large for anything but the operas and ballets presented there during the Vancouver Festivals. Later, a smaller theatre was added to it. Outside Vancouver, drama in British Columbia is in the hands of the School and Community Drama Department, run by the Provincial Government. The University of British Columbia includes theatre studies in its curriculum, as does the University of Alberta, where Gordon Peacock's Studio Theatre has done good work. Both Calgary and Alberta have large theatres, but how best to use them is a vexed question. In Saskatchewan there has been a sustained theatrical tradition, inaugurated in 1912 by the formation of the Regina Amateur Dramatic Society. This was started by a group of talented new-comers from England, and lasted until the outbreak of war in 1914. Re-formed in 1923, it was reorganized three years later as the Regina Little Theatre Society, which still flourishes. Amateur clubs were then organized in other towns in the province, and in 1932 the methods of the British Drama League were used to form the Saskatchewan Drama League, under the patronage of Lord Bessborough. This organization now has well over a hundred affiliated clubs, and during the Second World War was able to run its own local festival. Since then a number of other districts have formed similar drama leagues.

In Halifax in 1962 plans were made for the establishment of a company to operate all the year round. With initial advice from Tom Patterson, founder of the Shakespearean Festival Theatre at Stratford, Ontario, a building was acquired and named the Neptune, in honour of the first theatrical performance given in Canada. Leon Major, a young and energetic Toronto director, was appointed to launch the first season.

Mention must also be made of the summer 'Straw Hat' theatres, organized by many groups. Their activities have ranged from vast productions (up to 1960) of musical shows in the Vancouver Theatre-under-the-Stars and the Winnipeg Rainbow Stage to modest performances in converted barns. Montreal has a large open-air playhouse on top of Mount Royal, where in 1952 Noel Coward's *Private Lives* had a record run (for Canada) of five weeks. Among the summer theatres which have survived their early trials are the Garden Centre Theatre, Vineland, Ontario, the Muskoka Straw Hat Players founded by the present directors of the Crest Theatre, Toronto, and the Red Barn Theatre, Jackson's Point, Ontario.

So much acting activity has not been without its effect on Canadian playwriting. In addition to the encouragement given by the Dominion Drama Festival, which resulted in twelve new plays in 1935, and sixteen in 1936, of which four reached the finals, further impetus was given by playwriting competitions sponsored by such groups as the Western Theatre Conference, the Drama League Workshop and the London Little Theatre. In 1960 the Toronto *Globe and Mail* sponsored a contest for a play to be produced at the Stratford Festival, which was won by Donald Lamont Jack with *The Canvas Barricade*. Much excellent work has been done by the universities, many of which have summer schools and festivals of dramatic art. The first of these was held at the Banff School of Fine Arts, in 1933, when an extension course in playwriting and production was sponsored by the University of Alberta. The school was modelled on that of the Carolina Playmakers, whose director, Frederick Koch, came himself to the Banff Summer School for several consecutive years, ably assisted by the first playwright trained at the school, Gwen Pharis, author of *Dark Harvest* (1945) and half a dozen other plays on Canadian themes. The Crest Theatre and the Manitoba Theatre Centre have also offered encouragement to writers. Playwrights who have emerged in recent years are Len Peterson, Patricia Joudry, and James Reaney, whose *The Killdeer* and *The Easter Egg* were done by an enterprising Toronto group, the University Alumnae. *The Killdeer* was also seen at the Citizens' Theatre, Glasgow, Scotland, as part of the First Commonwealth Arts Festival in 1965. The best known of the University Alumnae is Robertson Davies, a former Old Vic actor and now Master of Massey College in the University of Toronto. His one-act *Eros at Breakfast* won the Barry Jackson Trophy for the best Canadian play in 1948. A three-act play, *Fortune My Foe*, gained the trophy again in 1949, in a presentation by the Ottawa Drama League under the veteran W. A. Atkinson, and in 1960 he adapted one of his own novels, *Leaven of Malice*, which was seen in Toronto and New York in a production by Tyrone Guthrie.

All the amateur and semi-professional activity enumerated above paved the way for the professional companies which have emerged in recent years. Among them are the Ottawa Stage Society, later the Canadian Repertory Company, founded in 1948 by the English actor Malcolm Morley, the Totem Theatre, Vancouver, founded in 1951 by two young actors, Thor Arngrim and Stuart Baker, and the Western Stage Society, based on Saskatoon, which toured Saskatchewan.

Some stability has been given to the Canadian scene by the establishment of the Shakespearean Festival Theatre at Stratford, Ontario. There had been previous efforts to establish a Shakespeare company in Canada, notably by Earle Grey and his wife Mary Godwin, who first visited the country in 1939 as members of a company sponsored by the British Council. In 1942 they were responsible for a production of *Twelfth Night* in the garden of Trinity College, Toronto, and in 1945 they established a regular Festival there which continued until 1958. They also did good work visiting schools and colleges with a programme of carefully-chosen scenes from Shakespeare which served to introduce many young people to live theatre for the first time.

The theatre at Stratford (see SHAKESPEARE FESTIVALS) opened in 1952, and played for three months in the summer. It has exchanged its original tent-like structure for a permanent building which embodies many of the features of Shakespearian production evolved in England from the time of William Poel onwards (see No. 43). First directed by Guthrie and now by Michael Langham, it has helped to raise the standard of theatre all over Canada, and has provided a focal point for the ambitions of Canadian actors, stage-designers, producers, and playwrights. By 1962 the Festival was able to present a longer season with an all-Canadian company, with a Canadian director, George McCowan, to produce *The Tempest*.

That Canada could produce good professional actors was proved by the emergence in the past of such players as Raymond Massey, Walter Huston, Margaret Anglin, and Beatrice Lillie, to name only a few, all Canadian-born, and all forced to seek a wider sphere for the full development of their talents. In future this should not be necessary, and a hopeful sign of two-way traffic between the English and Canadian stages has been the engagement by England's Royal Shakespeare Theatre company of Christopher Plummer, born and trained in Canada, who had already been seen in leading roles at the Stratford, Ontario, theatre. An offshoot of the Stratford venture, by the same guiding spirit, Tom Patterson, was the formation of the Canadian Players, which went from Stratford on tour, doing 'platform' productions of Shakespeare, Shaw, Ibsen, and Brecht in places which had previously had no live theatre. Their first production was a simply-set *Saint Joan*, produced by Douglas Campbell, and starring his wife, Ann Casson, daughter of Sybil Thorndike and Lewis Casson. Later enlarged to two companies, the Canadian Players undertake long tours in Canada and the United States, each company producing two plays. In 1965 Marigold Charlesworth and Jean Roberts were named co-producers for the Canadian Players.

It is difficult to predict the future of anything as intangible and volatile as the theatre. But it does seem as if professional theatre, both English and French, has finally taken root in Canada, and all who have the cause of the theatre at heart must hope that what has been done so far will prove only a prelude to a stable and flourishing national art.

CANE, ANDREW, see CAIN, ANDREW.

CANEVAS, the French name for the outline plot or *scenario* of the *commedia dell'arte*.

CAÑOS DEL PERAL, see MADRID THEATRES.

CANTERBURY, THE. 1. LONDON. The Canterbury Arms, which was London's first music-hall, occupied the site of an old tavern which had stood for centuries in the Westminster Bridge Road. In 1848 it was taken over by Charles Morton, who ran popular concerts on Saturday evenings. No charge was made, and the concerts were paid for out of the profits on the drink which was consumed. The Saturday—and later Thursday—concerts became so popular that Morton was first able to hire professional entertainers and then to build a hall on the site of the tavern's old skittle-alley, for which an entrance fee was charged. Morton spared no expense to make the entertainments given there the best of their kind. The 'Chairman' was John Caulfield, and Jonghmann the musical director. Most of the famous stars of the early music-halls appeared at the Canterbury, including Sam Cowell and E. W. Mackney. After a further period of success a new hall was built round the old one and opened on a Monday, the old hall having been pulled down over the week-end. Entrance was 6*d*. downstairs and 9*d*. in the gallery. The audience still sat at small tables, as in the original tavern, and had their food and drink brought to them. Morton stayed at the Canterbury until 1867, by which time the earlier classical music and ballad-singing had disappeared and comedy predominated. Among the famous artists who appeared there were George Leybourne, The Great Vance, Fred Coyne, Arthur Roberts, and many others. Ballets were added to the bill, one of the most successful being the spectacular 'Trafalgar'. Among the royal visitors to the Canterbury in its heyday were the Prince of Wales (later Edward VII), the Duke of Cambridge, and the Duke and Duchess of Teck. For many years the Canterbury bar was a favourite place of call for the members of the music-hall profession. When its popularity began to wane a drastic reduction in prices filled it again, but it eventually had to give up and was taken over by a limited company.

W. MACQUEEN-POPE†, *rev.*

2. NEW YORK. This was originally the Canterbury Concert Hall at 663 Broadway, which opened in 1860. It was shortly afterwards destroyed by fire. On 15 Apr. 1861 it opened at 585 Broadway, in what had been the French Theatre. It was closed on 7 Apr. 1862 by legislation.

CAPA Y ESPADA, COMEDIAS DE, see CLOAK-AND-SWORD PLAYS.

ČAPEK, KAREL (1890–1938), Czech dramatist, and one of the few to be widely played in translation outside his own country. Among his plays, some of which were written in collaboration with his artist-brother, Josef, the best known are *R.U.R.* (Rossum's Universal Robots) (1920) and *The Insect Play* (1921). (The latter has also been staged as *The World We Live In* and *And So Ad Infinitum*.) Both are satires on the contemporary world, depicting the horrors of regimentation and the terrible end that awaits the regimented, and both have been extremely successful all over Europe and in America. Čapek also wrote *The Makropulos Affair* (1922), which deals with the desirability or otherwise of long life, and *Adam the Creator* (1927), which serves as a sequel to *R.U.R.* in that it shows man endeavouring to rebuild the world which the robots have destroyed. His last plays, *Power and Glory* (1937) and *Mother* (1938), deal with the rise of dictatorship and the terrible consequences of war. Čapek's plays were always a reflection of the world he lived in, and served as a comment on its grosser follies. He also wrote an amusing short monograph, *How a Play is Produced*.

CAPITANO, IL, the braggart soldier of the *commedia dell'arte*, vainglorious and cowardly. Andreini was one of the first to play him, as Captain Spavento, while Silvio Fiorillo made him a Spaniard, Mattamoros (death to the Moors, anglicized as Captain Matamore). The mask of Scarramuccia, though more properly a *zanni* role, had something of the captain in it (see ITALY, 2 and No. 138).

CAPON, WILLIAM (1757–1827), English architect and painter, who in 1791 was appointed scenic director of the new Drury Lane by John Philip Kemble. He started with a clear field, the new theatre being too large for the scenery left over from Garrick's day, and his historical scenes introduced a radical change in the scenic system, doing away with the old flats and wings. Of a plodding, pedestrian temperament, he was a painstaking antiquarian, which accorded well with Kemble's plans for scenic reform, and he designed a number of approximately correct scenes and costumes for many of the latter's productions, including streets of ancient houses copied with careful accuracy from actual remains of the period. The banquet scene in *Macbeth*, with which the new theatre opened in Apr. 1794, was spoken of as 'a thing to go and see of itself', while a later setting, in 1799, showed a fourteenth-century cathedral with nave, choir, and side aisles superbly decorated, the whole being about 56 ft. wide, 52 ft. deep, and 37 ft. high. One serious drawback to Capon's work was, incidentally, the difficulty of shifting such heavy and cumbersome pieces. He was nevertheless held in high regard, and continued to work at Drury Lane after Kemble's departure in 1802, until in 1809 the theatre was burnt down, involving Capon in a severe monetary loss, since much of the scenery destroyed in the fire had not been paid for. He then worked for Kemble again at the new Covent Garden Theatre, which became noted for the splendour of its Shakespearian revivals. Many of his sets remained in use in the theatre for years, and, with a little touching-up, served for stock pieces until the arrival of Macready. The precursor of Charles Kean in the application of archaeological studies to the stage, Capon had also something of Kean's pedantic inaccuracy, and delighted the public with his Anglo-Norman hall for *Hamlet*, which was made up of fragments from the periods of Edward the Confessor, William Rufus, and Henry I. (See also No. 164.)

CARL, KARL [really KARL ANDREAS VON BERNBRUNN] (1789–1854), Austrian actor and impresario. Born in Cracow, he used the title of baron, despite his illegitimacy, on account of his mother's noble antecedents. Dismissed from the army after a chequered career, he turned actor and was soon playing romantic leads at the Munich Court theatre, where he eventually became director. He married the actress Margarethe Lang. He excelled in comic as well as serious roles and was responsible for introducing the figure of Staberl (see AUSTRIA) to Munich; his Staberl, however, appeared in fool's costume and lost his Viennese characteristics, becoming in this cosmopolitanized form a favourite throughout Germany. Carl moved to Vienna in order to make his fortune, and in 1825 appeared at the Theater an der Wien, which he leased from 1827 to 1845. He became director of the Theater in der Josefstadt in 1826, a year which marked the beginning of his successful association with the actor-playwright Johann Nestroy (see AUSTRIA). He at first favoured spectacular productions of romantic dramas, but came to realize that there was more money to be made in the local Viennese *Posse* (farce), to which he turned increasingly. In 1847 he built a new theatre on the site of the old Leopoldstädter Theater. Karl Carl was famous for his sharpness as a business man. He paid low wages—his contracts were known as 'Korsarenbriefe'—and was ruthless in his exploitation of actors and public alike. He died a millionaire.

J. B. BEDNALL

CARLIN, see BERTINAZZI.

CARLTON THEATRE, LONDON. 1. Greenwich, built by Sefton Parry in 1864 to replace the derelict Theatre Royal, Deptford. It was well built and compact, but attained no special eminence. It fell into disuse when the Broadway Theatre, Deptford, was built in 1897.

2. Haymarket, opened on 27 Apr. 1927, with *Lady Luck*, under the management of Laddie Cliff and Edgar O'Brien. It had a short theatrical history, presenting *Good News* and *The Yellow Mask* in 1928, and a revival of *The Merry Widow* and a revue with George Robey in the following year. It then became a cinema.

W. MACQUEEN-POPE†

CARNEY, KATE (1868–1950), a much-loved star of the music-halls, who made her début on 10 Feb. 1890 at the Albert as a singer of Irish melodies. These, however, quickly gave way to the Cockney songs for which she is best remembered. She sang them dressed in a coster suit of 'pearlies' and a vast hat with towering feathers—the feminine equivalent of Albert Chevalier's costermonger. Her most popular songs, were 'Liza Johnson' and 'Three Pots a Shilling'. In 1885 she married George Barclay, a Cockney step-dancer who became one of the leading music-hall agents and a successful racehorse owner, and retired after the First World War, returning later to the halls with a mouth-organ band. In 1935, just after the celebration of her golden wedding, she appeared at the Royal Variety Performance and sang two of her old coster ditties, the audience joining heartily in the choruses.

CARPENTER'S SCENE, a short front scene, usually devoted to the sub-plot, and containing matter irrelevant to the development of the main plot, used in Victorian times to enable elaborate scenery to be prepared behind its backcloth, out of sight of the audience. With the practice of dropping the front curtain between changes it became obsolete, and was at no time anything more than a makeshift device. It is, however, still properly and effectively used in pantomime and in big spectacular musical shows.

CARPET CUT, a long narrow opening, found in many stages, stretching nearly the width of the proscenium opening, and just behind the curtain. Its aperture is closed by one or more flaps, hinged on the down-stage side. When these are lifted, the edge of any carpet or stagecloth that may be needed in the scene is dropped through for an inch or two, and the flap closed to trap it. Thus it is neatly and instantaneously fixed, and so cannot trip up the player. RICHARD SOUTHERN

CARRETTO, GALEOTTO DEL (*fl.* 1497–1530), early Italian dramatist, whose tragedies *Timon* (1497) and *Sofonisba* (1502), though influenced by Senecan models, retained much of the freedom of composition of the early religious dramas (see ITALY, 1 *b* i).

CARRIAGE-AND-FRAME, a device for changing the scenery wings, used on the Continent and occasionally in England. It was also known as the Chariot-and-Pole. In this system each wing-piece is hung on a frame (or sometimes a simple mast) so as to be suspended just clear of the stage floor. Each frame (or mast) projects downwards through a long slit in the stage, and is borne on a wheeled carriage, running on rails in the mezzanine floor. At every wing-position this arrangement exists in duplicate, and the two carriages at each position are connected by ropes, working in opposite directions, to a common shaft serving the whole series, in such a way that one carriage of each pair moves off as its neighbour moves on, thus exchanging one set of wings for another. The withdrawn wing may then be replaced by the wing for the next scene and the process repeated when required. This system was devised by Torelli, and can still be seen in operation at Drottningholm (see No. 29).

CARROLL, EARL (1893–1948), American theatre manager and producer, who began his association with the theatre as a programme boy in Pittsburgh (1903–9). After spending the next year in the box-office of the Nixon Theatre, Pittsburgh, he worked his way round the world, and then settled in New York as a songwriter (1912–17), producing, in collaboration, over 400 songs. In 1919 he established himself as an independent manager in New York, and as a playwright. He built the first Earl Carroll Theatre in 1922. From 1923 until 1936 he produced fifteen 'editions' of *Earl Carroll's Vanities*, a series of revues modelled on the *Ziegfeld Follies* and featuring chiefly comedians alternating with lines of chorus girls. The motto of his theatre was 'Through these portals pass the most beautiful women in the world'. Carroll also presented two *Sketch Book Revues* and about sixty legitimate plays, of which the most famous was *White Cargo* (1923). In 1931 he opened the second Earl Carroll Theatre; in 1938 he moved to Hollywood where he opened his third theatre, presented a number of revues, and was active in films until his death in an air accident.

ROBERT TRACY

CARROLL, PAUL VINCENT (1900–68), modern Irish dramatist. His plays take their own line, as distinctive as that of any of his predecessors in the Irish Dramatic Movement (see IRELAND). The setting of the earlier ones, the little-exploited area around Dundalk, is somewhat akin to the Midlands of William Boyle, Padraic Colum, and Brinsley Macnamara. The series of studies of priests, the profound interest in the relations of religion and daily life, the sympathy with the rebel against convention imposed from within or from without, touch upon the territory now of T. C. Murray, now of Sean O'Casey, now of Teresa Deevy. But these things apart, Carroll stands alone among Irish dramatists both in his attitude to his material and in the balance of his qualities. The sympathy, humour, and above all the discernment of subtle but significant distinctions which makes memorable his studies of priests, extend also to the other characters, so that, especially in the later plays, Carroll begins to reach the balance of genuine drama, attained only when the dramatist identifies himself not with one or two of his characters but with all.

His plays have had considerable success in Dublin, New York, London, and Glasgow. *Things that are Caesar's* was produced at the Abbey Theatre, Dublin, in 1932; *The Wise Have not Spoken* followed. *Shadow and Substance*, produced at the Abbey in 1937, had immense popularity in New York later as the best foreign play of the year. *The White Steed* was first produced in New York in 1939 and *The Strings, My Lord, are False* at the Olympia in Dublin in 1942. After that he wrote *The Old Foolishness* (1945), *The Devil Came From Dublin* (1952), and *The Wayward Saint* (1955). Carroll, who was a schoolmaster in Glasgow from 1921–37, helped to found the Curtain Theatre in that town.

UNA ELLIS-FERMOR†, *rev.*

CARROLL, SYDNEY W. [really GEORGE FREDERICK CARL WHITEMAN] (1877–1958), actor, dramatic critic, and theatre manager. Born in Melbourne, he came to England in 1896, and toured with Calvert, Ben Greet, and Wilson Barrett. He then settled in London and divided his time equally between theatre management and journalism. He was drama critic of the *Sunday Times* from 1918–23, and from 1928–39 was mainly responsible for the *Daily Telegraph*'s weekly theatre page. He also founded, in 1933, the Open Air Theatre in Regent's Park, where for many years Robert Atkins produced and acted in Shakespeare's plays, in spite of financial and climatic frustrations. Carroll managed a number of London theatres at different times, among them the Criterion, the New, the Ambassadors (where in 1935 *The Mask of Virtue* made Vivien Leigh a star overnight), the Shaftesbury, and Her Majesty's. He was part-author of several plays, and of a volume of dramatic criticism and a book on acting. In 1933 he was appointed Commendatore of the Crown of Italy, in appreciation of his production of Mussolini's play, *Napoleon*, in Drinkwater's adaptation (1932).

CARTER, MRS. LESLIE [*née* CAROLINE LOUISE DUDLEY] (1862–1937), an American actress, who is chiefly remembered for her appearances in Belasco's productions. Married in 1880 and divorced nine years later, she decided to adopt the stage as a profession, and asked Belasco to train and launch her. There was a certain amount of opposition to her on account of her divorce, but she was an able woman, and eventually achieved her object. After an arduous course of training she made her first appearance in *The Ugly Duckling* (1890), a poor play in which she achieved a moderate success. Her first outstanding part was as the heroine in Belasco's *The Heart of Maryland* (1895), in which she appeared in New York and London, as she did in *Zaza* (1899). She then played the heroine in *Du Barry* (1901), and in *Adrea* (1904) (which were not seen in London), her last appearances under Belasco's management, as two years later she remarried, touring under her own and other managements with some success.

CARTON [CRITCHETT]. (1) RICHARD CLAUDE (1856–1928), English dramatist, who had a short career as an actor from 1875 to 1885 and then turned to playwriting. His first plays were much influenced by Dickens, the best being *Liberty Hall* (1892), but in 1898 he scored a success with *Lord and Lady Algy*, and continued to write comedies, bordering on farce, which poked discreet fun at the aristocracy and were much enjoyed by the occupants of the London stalls. Elegantly staged, they served as starring vehicles for his wife (2) KATHERINE MACKENZIE COMPTON (1853–1928), who played almost exclusively in his plays from 1885 onwards, and was a great factor in their success. She was adept at portraying the society woman of shrewd wit and few scruples. The daughter of Henry Compton, she made her first appearance in London in 1877 as Julia in *The Rivals*, and was for some years at the St. James's Theatre.

CARTWRIGHT, WILLIAM. There were apparently two, if not three, actors of this name, of whom the first appears with great frequency in Henslowe's diary, and was presumably an important member of the Admiral's Men. He is thought to have died in 1650, and there is a portrait of him at Dulwich College. His son was born *c.* 1606, and may have acted as a boy at the Fortune with his father; but his first recorded appearance is in 1634, when he is noted with a band of King's Revels Men at Norwich. He was at Salisbury Court when the theatres were closed in 1642, and was one of the actors who later played surreptitiously at the Cockpit. Aubrey says of him that he was also a bookseller and that he gave a collection of plays to Dulwich College, where there are two portraits of him. He was still alive in his eightieth year.

CASINO THEATRE, NEW YORK, on the south-east corner of Broadway and 39th Street. This was for almost fifty years the leading musical-comedy house of New York, maintaining a consistently high standard in spite of financial stringency. Built in a massively Moorish style, it held 1,300 people, and was equipped with a fine staircase leading to the auditorium. Rudolph Aronson opened it on 21 Oct. 1883 in an unfinished state, which necessitated an almost immediate closing for final touches, when a fine roof garden was added for summer evening concerts. Marie Tempest was seen at the Casino in 1892, and among the musical plays produced were *Florodora* (1900), *A Chinese Honeymoon* (1902), *Wildflower* (1923), and *The Vagabond King* (1925), which, with Dennis King as Villon, ran for 511 performances. The house's last hit was *The Desert Song* (1926), and after a performance by the American Opera Company of 'Faust' on 18 Jan. 1930 it was pulled down. GEORGE FREEDLEY†

For Metropolitan Casino, New York, see BROADWAY THEATRE, 3; for the London Casino, see PRINCE EDWARD THEATRE.

CASSON, SIR LEWIS THOMAS (1875–1969), English actor, who made his first appearance in 1903, after some success as an amateur in Charles Fry's productions of Shakespeare. He was at the Court Theatre under the Vedrenne–Barker management from 1904–7, where he appeared in a number of Shaw's plays, and in 1910 at the Duke of York's in Charles Frohman's repertory season. In 1908 he became a member of Miss Horniman's company at the Gaiety, Manchester, which he directed from 1911–14. It was here that he met and married the distinguished actress Sybil Thorndike. His career was interrupted by the First World War, but he returned to the stage in 1919 and later, in conjunction with his wife, produced a season of Greek tragedy at the Holborn Empire and of Grand Guignol at the Little Theatre. For some years he concentrated mainly on production, though continuing to act, and toured widely in South Africa and Australia with his wife, being co-director with Esmé Church of the Old Vic Mediterranean tour in 1939. He accompanied Dame Sybil on her tour of the mining towns during the Second World War and was knighted in the Birthday Honours of 1945 for his services to the theatre. After the Second World War he toured extensively with his wife in dramatic recitals, and gave some excellent performances in such parts as Professor Linden in *The Linden Tree* (1947) and Sir Horace Darke in *Eighty in the Shade* (1959). One of his greatest assets as an actor was his beautiful diction and clear well-modulated voice.

CASTRO Y BELLVÍS, GUILLÉN DE (1569–1631), a Spanish dramatist of Valencia, friend and follower of Lope de Vega. His main claim to fame rests on his dramatization of the ballads celebrating Spain's national hero, *Las mocedades del Cid*, from which Corneille took the main outline of his *Le Cid* (1636). (This was a turning-point in the history of European drama, and the first play of the French classic theatre which was later to prove so detrimental to that of eighteenth-century Spain.) Its sequel, *Las hazañas del Cid*, was also successful, as were a number of other plays, including *Los malcasados de Valencia*, *El Narciso en su opinión*, and *El conde de Alarcos*, in all of which Castro followed in the steps of Lope de Vega, though with less charm and vitality. Castro's drama is almost purely national, and his style is admirably suited to his subjects.

CATHERINE STREET THEATRE, LONDON, see ROYAL PANTHEON.

CATWALK, a narrow bridge slung on iron stirrups from the grid above the stage, running from one fly-floor to another to enable the fly-men to reach and adjust any portion of the hung scenery.

CAULDRON TRAP, see TRAP.

CAUSSIN, NICOLAS (1580–1651), see JESUIT DRAMA.

CAVE, JOE ARNOLD (1823–1912), an early music-hall performer who started as a juvenile, and then became a black-faced singer and violin player. He later became a prominent music-hall proprietor and manager, running, among other places, the West London (then known as the Marylebone), where he produced many of his own plays and pantomimes, the Old Vic, and the Elephant and Castle.

CAWARDEN, SIR THOMAS, see MASTER OF THE REVELS.

CECCHI, GIOVANNI MARIA (1518–87), an early and prolific Italian dramatist, whose work ranged from religious plays (*drammi spirituali*) to comedies of which the best is possibly the *Assiuolo* (prod. 1550). The secularization of Italian drama was carried a step further by his interpolation into Bible stories of extraneous characters, usually farcical, borrowed from classical comedy, and incidents taken from contemporary life (see ITALY, I *a*ii).

CECCHINI. (1) PIER MARIA (1575–1645), an actor and author of the *commedia dell'arte*, who was apparently an amateur before he joined a professional company about 1591. After appearing in various Italian cities he went to Paris, returning there again later with his own company. His stage name was Fritellino. His wife (2) ORSOLA (*fl.* 1590–?), whom he married in 1594, may have been the daughter of Flaminio Scala. Her stage name was Flaminia, and with her husband she was associated with the Accesi troupe. She was much praised for her beauty and her acting, and seems to have been the bitter rival of Virginia Andreini (Florinda).

CEILING, a canvas stretch, battened-out and suspended flat over the top of a box-set. Ceilings were often 'booked' transversely to enable them to be the more easily flown.

CÉLESTE, CÉLINE (1814–82), a famous French dancer and pantomimist, who appeared with much success on the Parisian stage as a child, and in 1827 went with a troupe of dancers to New York. Here she was seen at the Bowery, then known as the American, Theatre, and was much admired for her exquisite dancing and expressive gesture. Shortly afterwards she made an unhappy marriage with a Mr. Elliott, but soon separated from him, and in 1830 she was seen in London and the provinces. In spite of her years in England and the United States, she was a long time learning the language, and did not attempt a speaking part until 1838, relying until then on dumb-show. She created a number of parts in new plays, few of them of any lasting value, and was manager of the Adelphi and Lyceum Theatres in London for a short time, the former in association with Ben Webster. She was frequently seen in the United States, where her farewell performances are said to have outnumbered even those of Charlotte Cushman. She made her last appearance there in 1865, and in London in 1874, reappearing for one performance as Miami in *Green Bushes*, one of her best parts, at a benefit night at Drury Lane in 1878. She was also the original Madame Defarge in *A Tale of Two Cities* (1860), and scored triumphs in *The Woman in Red* and *The French Spy*. From her photographs she appears to have been an extremely plain woman, but intelligent, and contemporary accounts leave no doubt of the beauty and expressiveness of her dancing and acting.

CELESTINA, LA, a Spanish work (first extant edition 1500) in dialogue and divided into acts, but often regarded as a novel. There is no evidence of early performance (its length and complexity would make this almost impossible, although it was probably read aloud), but adaptations have recently been successfully staged. The author of Act I and the beginning of Act II is unknown; the remainder is by Fernando de Rojas (*d.* 1541), a lawyer of Jewish ancestry, who completed *La Celestina* when young and seems to have written nothing more. The first published version is in sixteen acts and is entitled *Comedia de Calisto y Melibea*; soon afterwards Rojas added five more acts and changed the title to *Tragicomedia.* It is now called after its most forceful character, the old bawd Celestina, who helps Calisto to seduce Melibea. Celestina is murdered by her accomplices, Calisto falls to his death and Melibea kills herself. The work ends on a note of deep pessimism; the passions destroy those whom they control, and there is no defence against them. Much recent criticism, however, stresses Rojas's moral intention. The structure is based on the fifteenth-century humanistic comedy, although the tragic ending recalls contemporary Spanish fiction. There is a notable realism of characterization, presentation of popular and cultured speech, and uninhibited depiction of low-life scenes. *La Celestina* enjoyed great popularity in Spain and abroad for 150 years, but then fell from favour; interest has revived in the present century. It had substantial influence on the drama and the novel in Spain and England. The early part of the work was adapted in English verse, probably by John Rastell, *c.* 1530; the first full translation is by James Mabbe (1631). A good modern translation is that of Phyllis Hartnoll, Everyman's Library (1959). J. E. VAREY

CELLAR, the space under the stage which houses the machinery necessary for traps, scene changing, and special effects. In the English theatre the system of grooves, which allowed tall framed pieces to be slid to the sides of the stage for a scene-change, meant that the cellar could be, in general, far shallower than in Continental theatres, where any framed backgrounds (as opposed to hanging drops) had to be lowered beneath the stage. This, in a theatre or opera-house which was in any case of far greater dimensions than the more intimate English playhouse, entailed a greater depth. The Continental cellar, or *dessous*, often descended for four or five storeys, whereas the average English cellar usually consisted of a mezzanine floor below the stage floor, where most of the machines were housed, and beneath this a well in the central part of the area, into which the base of the traps and the bridges descended, and at the bottom of which were the drums and shafts which worked them. Also under the stage on the mezzanine floor is the Band Room, a retiring-room for members of the orchestra. RICHARD SOUTHERN

CELLE, a small German town, between Hanover and Hamburg, whose castle contains a private theatre, designed by Arighini. It is baroque in style, with a horseshoe-shaped auditorium, and a stage of considerable depth but with little wing space. It seats 330, with no standing room. Started in 1670, it was first used in 1674, and is thus the oldest existing playhouse in Germany. In 1692 Italian opera was given there, and the kings of Hanover, after the extinction of the dukedom of Celle, used it as a ballroom, concert-hall, and playhouse during their summer residence at the castle. When the Elector of Hanover became George I of England in 1705 the theatre was abandoned, and remained unused until 1772, when the exiled Danish Queen, Caroline Matilde, arranged seasons of plays there until 1775. Schröder, the great German actor, appeared at this theatre early in his career. During the nineteenth century it was seldom used, but was maintained in good condition. In 1935 it was restored and redecorated, its stage enlarged, and a fly-floor added, thus enabling scenery to be handled for elaborate productions. It reopened on 13 May, and was used occasionally up to 1939. It escaped damage during the Second World War, and in 1950 a permanent company was installed there to give three-weeks' runs of plays of all kinds, classical and modern.

C.E.M.A. (Council for the Encouragement of Music and the Arts), see ARTS COUNCIL.

CENSORSHIP, see DRAMATIC CENSORSHIP.

CENTLIVRE, MRS. SUSANNAH (1667–1723), English actress and dramatist, a masculine-looking woman who delighted to play men's parts. After two unhappy marriages she went to Windsor to play Alexander the Great and there met and married (in 1706) Joseph Centlivre, cook to Queen Anne. She was more successful as a writer than as an actress, and among her many comedies of intrigue, in which she rivalled the verve and ingenuity of Aphra Behn, the best are *The Busie Body* (1709), *The Wonder, a Woman keeps a Secret* (1714), and *A Bold Stroke for a Wife* (1718). All three were frequently revived, and the second later provided a vehicle for Garrick in the part of Don Felix, while its initial success was largely due to the fine acting of Anne Oldfield as Violante. The last is perhaps better classified as a comedy of manners, in which Mrs. Centlivre shows the influence of Congreve. Some of the scenes may have been written by John Mottley. Mrs. Centlivre was also the author of the sentimental drama, *The Gamester* (1705), based to some extent on Regnard's *Le Joueur* (1696), but with the moral tone of Cibber and Steele. It was closely followed by a similar play entitled *The Bassett-Table*. Mrs. Centlivre's early plays were published under her second married name, Mrs. Carroll.

CENTRAL PARK THEATRE, NEW YORK, see CENTURY THEATRE, 2.

CENTRAL SCHOOL OF SPEECH TRAINING AND DRAMATIC ART, London. This was founded in 1906 by Elsie Fogerty, C.B.E., with Sir Frank Benson as its first President. It grew out of Miss Fogerty's classes and private lessons in speech and diction which she gave in the Crystal Palace School of Art and later in the Royal Albert Hall, where the Central School was housed until 1957. It provides three-year training courses for the stage, for teachers of speech and drama, and for speech therapists. There is also a two-year technical course in stage management and allied subjects, and a one-year supplementary course for qualified teachers. Students training as teachers take the Diploma in Dramatic Art of London University. Integral to the speech therapy course is work in speech clinics, particularly that of St. Thomas's Hospital which was inaugurated with the help of Miss Fogerty in 1912. The school has always been associated with the development of poetic drama, and provided the chorus for Eliot's *The Rock*, and the Women of Canterbury for *Murder in the Cathedral*. Permission was also given for part of Fry's *The Lady's Not For Burning* to be included in one of the school's public shows before its first production in London. Two famous former students are now Vice-Presidents—Laurence Olivier and Peggy Ashcroft. From 1939 to 1942 the school was evacuated to premises at the University College of the South-West, Exeter. On its return to London in 1942 Miss Gwynneth Thurburn, herself an old student and for some years Vice-Principal, became Principal in succession to Miss Fogerty. The Central School is now situated in the Embassy Theatre, together with the John Davis Wing and a Studio Workshop.

CENTRAL THEATRE, NEW YORK, on the west side of Broadway near 47th Street. This was opened on 9 Sept. 1918 by William A. Brady, with Owen Davis's *Forever After*, starring Alice Brady and Conrad Nagel. Under the management of Weber and Fields the theatre had several successes, but from about 1920 onwards it was used for continuing runs of successful plays produced elsewhere rather than for new productions, and in 1928 it became a cinema. In 1956 it reverted to plays, and was renamed the Holiday.

CENTRAL THEATRE OF THE RED ARMY, MOSCOW, see RED ARMY THEATRE.

CENTRE THEATRE, in the Rockefeller Centre, New York. This holds 3,700 people, and was opened on 29 Dec. 1932 as a cinema, the R.K.O. Roxy. This name was already in use, and was changed a year later to R.K.O. Centre. In 1934 the stage was rebuilt and used for spectacular musical shows, and for ballet, opera, and pageant. In 1940 came the first ice-show, which was successful enough to warrant an annual edition. The theatre was demolished in the 1950s.

CENTRE 42, a cultural organization, directed by the playwright Arnold Wesker, who first had the idea of interesting the Trades Unions in the propagation of culture for their members. A series of six festivals in the provinces was planned, of which the first took place at Wellingborough in late 1962. Two new plays were given, one by Wesker, the other by Bernard Kops, and the Youth Theatre visited selected schools in *Hamlet*. These productions were financed by grants from the Arts Council and the Gulbenkian Foundation. The expenses of the festivals, however, had to be met from other sources, including the local trades councils and the municipal authorities, and they left the Centre heavily in debt. Nevertheless, in the autumn of 1964 Wesker was able to take over the Round House at Chalk Farm, formerly a railway shed, and opened it as an entertainment centre, with theatre, cinema, and art gallery, as well as administrative offices. The idea behind Wesker's project is laudable and deserves every encouragement, but it remains to be seen whether the audience aimed at will give the venture its support.

CENTRES DRAMATIQUES, Les. The French dramatic centres were founded between 1947 and 1952 with the object of fostering drama in the provinces, which had for too long been starved of live entertainment by the centralization of all theatrical activities in Paris. The idea of such a theatre in the provinces was first mooted by Gémier in 1912, with his Théâtre Ambulant, and later developed by Copeau, whose Copiaus lived and worked in Burgundy from 1924 to 1929.

The centres, supported by the State and the municipality, are based on university towns, from which a permanent professional company, with portable sets, lighting, and costumes, goes out on tour. In large towns it may play for two or three nights, elsewhere for one night only. Where there is no theatre the performance is given in a cinema or hall. The repertory consists mainly of French classics—comedy in preference to tragedy—good new plays, and translations of foreign classic and modern plays. New French plays are scarce, since most authors look to Paris for their first production, but the centres hope eventually to encourage and establish good regional playwrights.

The first centre to be founded, under the direction of André Clavé, was that in the east, covering Colmar, Haguenau, Metz, Mulhouse, and Strasbourg. It gave its first performance in Jan. 1947. It was then based on Colmar, but later moved to Strasbourg, where it also runs a drama school. Here, in a building specially designed by Pierre Sonrel, students are given a three-year training. The school opened in 1954 under Michel Saint-Denis, Copeau's nephew, who had taken over from Clavé in 1952. He, in turn, was succeeded by Hubert Gignoux from the western centre.

The centre at St.-Étienne, which serves the Lyonnais, the Valley of the Rhône, Burgundy, and the Alps, is directed by Jean Dasté, pupil and son-in-law of Copeau and a member of Les Copiaus and of the Compagnie des Quinze. In 1942 he had founded an amateur company named Les Comédiens de Grenoble, which was absorbed by the centre on its establishment in Sept. 1947.

In 1945 Maurice Sarrazin founded an amateur company called Le Grenier de Toulouse, which in 1946 won first prize in a competition held in Paris. In Jan. 1949 this became the basic company of a centre covering the area from the Atlantic at Bordeaux to the banks of the Rhône. It is still directed by Sarrazin, and is proving extremely popular. One of its most successful performances, which was seen in Paris, was a translation of *The Taming of the Shrew* as *La Mégère apprivoisée*. In 1965 the company celebrated its 20th anniversary by taking possession of the Théâtre Daniel Sorano, built specially for it by the municipality.

The western centre, originally under Hubert Gignoux, was also based on a good amateur company. It opened in Nov. 1949, and covers Brittany, Normandy, and the Valley of the Loire, with its centre in Rennes. In 1951 it gave a number of open-air performances of *Cymbeline*. Gignoux was succeeded by two members of the company as joint administrators, Georges Goubert and Guy Parigot.

A Provençal centre at Aix-en-Provence was founded by Baty in 1952, just before his death. Georges Douking was its first director, followed by René Laforgue, and by Jacques Fabbri. It serves the eastern Midi, and the coast from Perpignan to Nice.

In 1957 Roger Planchon founded the Théâtre de la Cité de Villeurbanne (Rhône), which has undertaken numerous tours, particularly in Eastern Europe. One of its best productions was Shakespeare's *Henry IV*.

In 1961 a new northern centre, based on Lille, was founded with André Reybaz as its director and in the same year one of Jean Dasté's former colleagues, Gabriel Monnet, founded the Comédie de Bourges, which soon became a Centre Dramatique. Other local groups will no doubt do the same, among them those of Caen under Jo Tréhard, Bourgogne under Jacques Fornier (which started in Copeau's old house in 1955), Grenoble under René Lesage, Nantes under Jean Guichard, Marseille under Michel Fontayne, Champagne under André Mairel, and Guy Rétoré's Théâtre de l'Est Parisien at Ménilmontant. Some of these groups already have their own theatres. There are also two touring companies, the Tréteaux de France under Jean Danet, and the Théâtre Populaire des Flandres, based on Lille under Cyril Robichez, which also visits Belgium.

CENTURY THEATRE, New York. 1. Originally the New Theatre, on Central Park West at 62nd Street, this was intended as a home of modern repertory. It opened on 6 Nov. 1909 with Julia Marlowe and E. H. Sothern in *Antony and Cleopatra*, and gave two seasons of Shakespeare and foreign plays. In spite of a large and expensive company and the reputation and experience of those connected with the enterprise—Ames and Lee Shubert—the venture was not a success. The general public felt that it was a theatre for the few, and stayed away. It closed, and reopened as an ordinary playhouse under the name of the Century on 15 Sept. 1911. Its main successes were musical shows, for which it was eminently suitable, having been planned as an opera-house; but in 1916 the Shakespeare Tercentenary was celebrated with a fine production of *The Tempest*, while in 1921 Martin-Harvey's *Hamlet*, and in 1924 *The Miracle*, with Norman Bel Geddes's fine scenery, were both successful. In 1927 Reinhardt, who had produced *The Miracle*, brought his own company to the Century in *A Midsummer Night's Dream*, *Everyman*, and *Dantons Tod*. It closed in 1929 and was pulled down a year later. There was a small theatre on the roof of the Century, known as the Cocoanut Grove or the Century Grove, where intimate revue was given, and also plays for children, under George C. Tyler.

2. On Seventh Avenue just below Central Park South, a big theatre which was opened by the Shuberts as the Al Jolson on 6 Oct. 1921. An early production was that of *The Insect Play*, given as *The World We Live In*, while in 1923 came the epoch-making visit of the Moscow Art Theatre under Stanislavsky. These fine actors, of whom three—Varvara Bulgakova, Maria Ouspenskaya, and Akim Tamiroff—remained in the U.S.A. and contributed largely to its theatrical life, were seen in Tolstoy, Gorky, Chekhov, and Turgeniev, and the influence of their productions could long be traced on the American stage. They remained for twelve weeks, and were followed later in the year by Julia Marlowe and Sothern in several Shakespearian plays. The following year saw the arrival of another great foreign actor, Firmin Gémier of the Odéon in Paris. His repertory included some Shakespeare translations, Molière's *Le Bourgeois gentilhomme*, and several modern French plays. Later came the long run of *The Student Prince*, whose 608 performances constituted a record for this house. In 1932–3 the Shakespeare Theatre occupied the Century, giving fifteen of Shakespeare's plays at low prices to an audience mainly composed of students. The theatre, which has also been known as the Venice and the Central Park, has housed a Negro operetta, an Italian company, the Federal Theatre Project, and Maurice Schwartz with his Yiddish Players, while in 1946 the Old Vic company from London, headed by Laurence Olivier and Ralph Richardson, appeared in *Henry IV, Parts I* and *II*, *Oedipus Rex*, *The Critic*, and *Uncle Vanya*. In 1948 *Kiss Me, Kate!* began its highly successful run, and in 1952 came Margaret Webster's production of Shaw's *Saint Joan*, starring Uta Hagen, transferred from the Cort. It is now used for television.

GEORGE FREEDLEY†

For the CENTURY THEATRE, London, see ADELPHI THEATRE, 1, and BIJOU THEATRE, 2.

CERVANTES SAAVEDRA, Miguel de (1547–1616), the author of *Don Quixote*, was also a dramatist of some repute. From his youth he had a passion for the theatre, and saw and much admired the famous actor-manager Lope de Rueda, who died when Cervantes was only 18. There are numerous references to contemporary actors and acting in *Don Quixote*, and in Cervantes' other writings, particularly in the preface to his published plays. These appeared in 1615, and consist of 8 comedies and 8 *entremeses* or comic interludes. Cervantes himself says that he wrote nearly 30 plays, but if so, some must be lost, since, in addition to the above 16, only one tragedy and one other comedy have survived. The tragedy, *El cerco de Numancia*, is founded on the history of the Spanish town of that name which so heroically resisted the power of Rome, a struggle which still has power to move a Spanish audience, as was proved at a revival of Cervantes' play in besieged Madrid in 1937. Of the other plays, *Los tratos de Argel* deals with the sufferings of men captured by pirates, and is based on the author's own five-year captivity at Algiers, while *El rufián dichoso* gives an excellent picture of contemporary Spanish life. The *entremeses*, of which *El viejo celoso* and *El retablo de las maravillas* are perhaps the best, are models of realistic and dramatic truth and profound satire.

ČESKÝ KRUMLOV, Czechoslovakia. The castle of Český Krumlov, which is situated about 100 miles from Prague, contains a small theatre, built in 1766—the same year as that at Drottningholm, Sweden—for the Schwarzenberg family, to replace an earlier wooden one. Approached through a ballroom whose walls are painted with gay figures in masquerade costume, dating from some twenty years earlier, the theatre has a small, horseshoe-shaped auditorium with a parterre and single narrow balcony supported on columns, in the centre of which is the private box of the reigning family. The magnificent baroque proscenium has candelabra on each side between the proscenium columns, upheld by gilded cherubs, with a painted, draped and tasselled curtain hung as though drawn up before the scene. The theatre's most exciting asset, however, is ten sets of contemporary scenery, which are probably the oldest surviving in Europe. Painted by two artists from Vienna, Jan Wetschela and Leo Merkla, who were also responsible for the decoration of the auditorium, these show how the sumptuous perspective scenes of such artists as the Bibienas were translated into the actuality of wood and canvas. The use of free-standing columns, supported by struts and topped by borders, in addition to the five sets of wings running in grooves with their borders and a backcloth painted in perspective, gives a far greater sense of depth than could be achieved with the side-wings and flat backcloth only. The sets, one of which is normally displayed on the stage, while others are set up in the adjacent riding-school, are for the usual scenes—palace, wood, harbour, and so on—and one, for a street, has for backdrop one of the angled views leading down two asymmetrical perspectives for which the Bibienas were famous (see No. 65; also No. 64). The stage machinery, installed by another Viennese, Lorenz Mackh, consists of axles, ropes, and winches for instantaneous changes of scenery, as at Drottningholm, and there are four traps in the stage-floor. The only thing which appears to have been omitted is the apparatus for the descent of the *deus ex machina*. Performances are occasionally given on this baroque stage, but, not surprisingly, the precious and indeed unique scenery is considered too fragile for overmuch handling. SYBIL ROSENFELD

CHAIRMAN. The presiding genius of the old-time music-hall, a link with the days of the public-house entertainment from which the 'halls' evolved. In full evening dress, with much flashing of imitation jewellery, he sat at a table placed below the footlights at auditorium level, with his back to the stage. A mirror enabled him to follow what was going on on stage, a clock to time each 'turn', which it was his duty to announce, and, if necessary, cut short, and a gavel helped him to keep order. Usually a large, commanding figure with a ruddy complexion and a stentorian voice, he needed a ready wit and a gift for repartee. On occasion he might sing a song—and sing it well. It was considered an honour to be invited to sit at his table and buy him a drink. There were many famous chairmen—W. B. (Punch) Fair, singer of 'Tommy Make Room for Your Uncle'; Jonghmann of the Oxford; Harry Fox; Walter Leaver, of Canning Town, who in 1905, at the age of 75, was as magnificent and imposing as ever, and perhaps the last of his kind. He outlasted the great days of the Chairman, which ended with the disappearance of the old 'free-and-easy' atmosphere at the Middlesex—the famous Old Mo in Drury Lane. When in 1937 the Late Joys revived the traditions of the music-hall, they revived too the office of Chairman, the best known being Leonard Sachs and Don Gemmell.

CHAMBERLAIN'S MEN, the theatrical company with which Shakespeare was mainly connected, and for which he wrote the bulk of his plays. It first emerges when the actors were regrouped after the disastrous plague of 1594. The repertory already included *Titus Andronicus*, *The Taming of the Shrew*, and a *Hamlet* (either an early draft or by someone other than Shakespeare, whose *Hamlet* as we know it was not given until 1601). After a joint session at the Rose with the Admiral's Men, the players moved to James Burbage's Theatre, with his son Richard as their chief actor, and for some years appeared there, later at the Curtain, and regularly at Court, giving plays by Shakespeare (for the chronology of these see SHAKESPEARE) and others, including Jonson, whose *Every Man in His Humour* was done by them in 1598. There is, however, no evidence that Jonson, who was reputed a poor actor, ever played with the Chamberlain's Men, since he was at this time concerned in the scandal over *The Isle of Dogs*, in which he appeared at the Swan. Shakespeare, who probably made his early appearances with Strange's or Pembroke's Men, played also with the Chamberlain's, in his own plays and in Jonson's *Every Man in His Humour* and *Sejanus*, his last traceable appearance being in the cast of the latter in 1603. In 1599 the company left the Theatre, and migrated to the Globe, which was built by the younger Burbages from the timbers of the old playhouse. The Globe was owned by a group of actors in the company, of whom Shakespeare was one. *Henry V* may have been produced there (or at the Theatre before the removal); *Julius Caesar* certainly was, as was Jonson's *Every Man out of His Humour*. In 1601 the actors got into trouble for performing *Richard II*, which, taken in conjunction with the Earl of Essex's unsuccessful rebellion, smacked of treason; but they got off lightly, though they may have had to take to the provinces for a while. It is conjectured that they played *Hamlet* at this period in Oxford and Cambridge. They played at Court not long before Elizabeth's death in 1603, and shortly afterwards became the King's Men, under the direct patronage of James I. A new actor who joined them at this time was Lawrence Fletcher, who had taken some English actors on tour in Scotland, and become a favourite of James I; but it was probably more in the capacity of a royal servant than as an actor, for he does not appear in any of the cast-lists, nor in the list of actors appended to the Shakespeare Folio. As the King's Men these players, who already had an excellent reputation, outshone all the other Jacobean and Caroline companies, not excepting Alleyn's, which now became the Palsgrave's Men (see ADMIRAL'S MEN). They continued to act Shakespeare's plays as they were written, but from 1608 onwards he gradually withdrew more and more from London and the theatre, his place being inadequately filled by Beaumont and Fletcher, whose earliest play for the King's Men, *Philaster*, dates from about this time. At the same period they took over Blackfriars, of which Richard Burbage held the freehold, but which since 1600 had been leased to the Children of the Chapel, and shares were allotted among the actors, Shakespeare being one of the 'sharers', together with Burbage, Heminge, Condell, and Sly (who died while the business was in hand). The company continued, however, to use the Globe, which caught fire during a performance of *Henry VIII*, Shakespeare's last play, in 1613 and was burnt to the ground. It was rebuilt in the following year, and saw the first production of Webster's *Duchess of Malfi*, in which Burbage played Ferdinand. The death of Shakespeare in 1616, and of Burbage three years later, broke up the company, and some of its members are traceable in other theatrical organizations. Taylor took Burbage's place, and Heminge and Condell, who had been the company's business managers for so long, were replaced by Lowin and Taylor. A great event in the company's history was the publication in 1623 of the First Folio of Shakespeare's plays, the largest collection of contemporary plays yet to appear in print. The following year saw the production of Middleton's *A Game of Chess*, aimed at the Spaniards, whose Ambassador took umbrage. The players were restrained from acting, admonished, and fined, and the play was shelved; but its immense popular success was long remembered in theatrical circles. The company, in spite of being in disgrace, continued to prosper, and on the death of James I, when it came under the patronage of his son, it numbered at least thirty-five men, with an unknown number of boys. During the new reign they continued to do well, though they had trouble over the lease of the Globe, which was finally extended to 1644, and with the Puritan inhabitants of Blackfriars, who tried to get the theatre closed. That this was not done was probably due to the interest which the king, and particularly the queen, took in the players. They were constantly commanded to Court, and the queen, at any rate, paid several visits to Blackfriars, which became the haunt of wit and nobility. Meanwhile the Cockpit at Whitehall had been refashioned as an indoor theatre, and the King's Men appeared there frequently. Massinger was their main dramatist, and was succeeded on his death by James Shirley. Evil times, however, were coming, and in 1642 the theatres were shut, the players disbanded, and, in spite of clandestine acting, organized theatrical activity ceased, to be resumed in 1660 under totally different circumstances.

CHAMBERS STREET THEATRE, New York. This was Burton's first theatre, originally Palmo's Opera House. When Burton left to go to the Metropolitan, his old theatre was taken by Eddy, renamed the Chambers Street, and opened with *Othello*. It soon degenerated into melodrama and farce, and on 13 Feb. 1857 it was taken over by E. L. Davenport. He rechristened it the American Theatre, and did a season there, during which Fanny Davenport made her first appearance in New York. The theatre finally closed on 30 Mar. 1857.

CHAMPAGNE CHARLIE, see LEYBOURNE, GEORGE.

CHAMPION, Harry (1866–1942), a music-hall performer who appeared originally as a black-faced comedian under the name of Will Conray, his first discoverable appearances being at the Queen's, Poplar, and the Parthenon, Greenwich, in Feb. 1888, though he may have been working before that. As Harry Champion he reappeared with a white face, and became famous as the singer of 'Ginger, Ye're Barmy', 'Enerey the Eighth I am, I am', 'When the Old Dun Cow caught fire', 'Any Old Iron', and other well-remembered ballads. He sang his songs at terrific speed and with tremendous zest and vitality right up to the day of his death, and for some years specialized in ditties about food, such as 'Boiled Beef and Carrots', 'Baked Sheep's Heart, Stuffed with Sage and Onions', 'Hot Tripe and Onions', and 'Hot Meat Pies, Saveloys, and Trotters'. At the Palladium after the First World War he appeared as himself in a scene where young actors had given imitations of old stars, and was received with riotous applause. As a side-line to his music-hall performances he ran a very successful jobmaster's business in North London.

CHAMPMESLÉ. (1) Charles Chevillet (1642–1701), French actor and dramatist, who began his career in a provincial company at Rouen. He then went to the Marais, and later to the Hôtel de Bourgogne, where he played mostly in tragedy. A handsome man, with excellent taste, he soon became popular, and many authors profited by his recommendations. He was a friend of La Fontaine, to whom several of Champmeslé's plays have been attributed. Among his many comedies the best is probably *Crispin chevalier*, a one-act version of an earlier play given in 1682, though *Le Florentin* (1685) was the most popular. It was given in Paris as late as the 1920s, as was *La Coupe enchantée* (1688). Champmeslé was one of the members of the Comédie-Française on its foundation, as was his celebrated wife (2) Marie Desmares (1642–98), the chief tragic actress of the troupe. She was already in a provincial troupe, which she had probably joined on the death of her first husband, when she met and married Champmeslé in 1665. They went to the Marais in 1669, where the husband was at first accounted the better actor. His wife, however, profited so much by the lessons of Laroque that in six months she was playing leading roles. A year later she went to the Hôtel de Bourgogne, where she replaced Mlle Desœillets, and became so popular that the rival troupes competed for her services. In 1679 she joined the amalgamated Molière–Marais company, thus depriving the Hôtel de Bourgogne of its pre-eminence in tragedy, and from there became the leading lady of the Comédie-Française, playing opposite Baron, a position which she retained until her death. She created many famous tragic roles, including Racine's Phèdre and Bérénice, and the Ariane of Thomas Corneille, and was much esteemed for her wit and charm by many famous men of her time. She had a fine figure, an expressive face, and a voice which served her equally well in tenderness, passion, or rage. La Fontaine dedicated his *Belphégor* to her, and she was the mistress, in his youth, of Racine, who owed so much to her acting. She favoured a chanting, sing-song declamation which she taught to her niece (see DESMARES) and to Mlle

Duclos, the leading actresses of the next generation. The tradition lingered on at the Comédie-Française until the time of Sarah Bernhardt. Her husband, from whom she was for some time separated on a reciprocal charge of adultery, died suddenly in a café while endeavouring to reconcile Baron and Sallé, who had quarrelled over the distribution of roles.

CHANCEREL, Léon (1886–1965), French dramatist and producer, a pupil of Jacques Copeau, whom he accompanied to Bourgogne. In 1926 he was with Jouvet at the Champs-Élysées, and from 1929 to 1939 he directed the Comédiens Routiers, a travelling company formed to bring good religious and popular plays to Boy Scout camps. In 1935 Chancerel also formed in Paris a company of young actors to play to children. It had its headquarters at Neuilly, and performed on Sunday afternoons in the Salle des Ingénieurs. This company was known as Le Théâtre de l'Oncle Sebastien, and its plays were not written but improvised, in conscious imitation of the *commedia dell'arte*, with stock characters, stock situations, and direct appeal to the children at crucial moments in the plot. Chancerel succeeded Jouvet as President of the Société d'Histoire du Théâtre. He was also French representative on the Committee of the International Federation for Theatre Research, and head of the Centre Dramatique in Paris.

CHANFRAU. (1) Frank S. (1824–84), American actor, closely identified with the success of Benjamin Baker's *A Glance at New York* (1848) and similar productions, in which he played Mose, the New York fireman. The plays had little literary value, and depended on swift action and caricature, and on the personality of the chief actor. Chanfrau played Mose to the life, and many of the Bowery Boys he impersonated were delighted spectators of his mimicry. He then wrote *New York As It Is* (1848), also for Mose, and on the profits took over the Chatham Theatre, rechristened it the National, and continued Mose's adventures in *The Mysteries and Miseries of New York* (1848) and other plays, all of which were successful. Chanfrau was henceforth identified with Mose, but he was also good as the pioneer Kit Redding in *Kit the Arkansas Traveller* (1870), which he played until 1882. His son Henry, also an actor, continued to play it until 1890. In 1858 Chanfrau married the actress (2) Henrietta Baker (1837–1909), whose real name was Jeannette Davis. She usually appeared apart from her husband, starring with most of the famous actors of the day, but they were together in *London Assurance*. She played Portia in the 1864 production of *Julius Caesar* which brought together for the only time the three Booth brothers. After her husband's death she retired from the stage, but in 1886 embarked on a tour of Europe.

CHANINS THEATRE, New York, see FORTY-SIXTH STREET THEATRE.

CHAPEL STREET THEATRE, New York. This was opened by David Douglass in 1761, in what was later Beekman Street, by which name the theatre is often called. It was at this playhouse that the first known performance of *Hamlet* in New York was given on 26 Nov., with the younger Hallam as Hamlet. The company's repertory was extensive, but contained few plays that had not been seen before. The actors, we learn from contemporary documents, were often incommoded, as in Europe earlier, by members of the audience who insisted on sitting on the stage, which must have been a small one, as the entire theatre measured only 90 feet in length by 40 feet wide. After the departure of Douglass's company in May 1762, the theatre was used occasionally by amateur companies, and possibly also by the officers of the British garrison in New York. In May 1766 a company, whether Douglass's or not is uncertain, but certainly a professional company, were playing *The King and the Miller of Mansfield* when the Sons of Liberty, an unruly band of anti-Britishers to whom all players were suspect, broke up the performance, routed the players, and greatly damaged the building, which fell into desuetude.

CHAPMAN, George (*c.* 1560–1634), English poet and dramatist, author of the translation of Homer which inspired Keats's sonnet. He is believed by some critics to be the 'rival poet' referred to in Shakespeare's sonnets, and the original of Holofernes and Thersites, but this lacks proof. Little is known of Chapman's early life. In 1596 he was accredited dramatist to the Admiral's Men, in the pay of Henslowe. Most of his early plays are lost, but enough of his later work remains to substantiate the claims which have been made for him as a fine playwright. Among his tragedies the most important is *Bussy d'Ambois*, based on the story which Dumas *père* later used in *La Dame de Montsoreau*. It was given in about 1604 by the children of Paul's, who also acted *Eastward Ho!* (1605), written by Chapman in collaboration with Jonson and Marston. This gave offence to James I and caused the imprisonment of the authors. In comedy Chapman's best work was done in *All Fools* (*c.* 1604) and *May Day* (1609), both given at Blackfriars. The former, called by Swinburne one of the best comedies in the English language, is based on Terence. Among Chapman's other plays are *Charles, Duke of Byron* (1608), which gave offence to the French Ambassador, *The Revenge of Bussy d'Ambois* (*c.* 1610), *Chabot, Admiral of France* (*c.* 1613), and *Caesar and Pompey* (*c.* 1613), all tragedies. He was also the author of a masque played by the Middle Temple and Lincoln's Inn in 1613, for which he complained he was insufficiently paid, being ranked merely 'with taylors and shoomakers and such snipperados'. Chapman was Sewer in Ordinary to Henry, Prince of Wales, on whose early death he wrote a pathetic ode.

CHAPMAN, William (1764–1839), one of the earliest and possibly the first of the American showboat managers. Born in England, he was as a young man a member of a travelling company under one Richardson, visiting the fairs. In 1803 he made his début on the London stage, and in 1827 appeared at the Bowery Theatre, New York. With his wife and large family he started on tour for the south-west, and in Pittsburgh had built for him by a Captain Brown a 'floating theatre', on which he played up and down the Ohio and the Mississippi (see SHOWBOAT). He died on board, and his widow continued to run the business for some years, finally selling it in about 1847 to Sol Smith.

CHAPPUZEAU, Samuel (1625–1701), a French man of letters, well educated and widely travelled, who wrote some mediocre and forgotten plays, and is best remembered for his *Théâtre françois* (1674), which consisted of three parts, (1) *De l'usage de la comédie*—a defence of the theatre, (2) *Des auteurs qui soutiennent le théâtre*, a dictionary of dramatists, and (3) *De la conduite des comédiens*, an apology for players, with lives of many of the best known up to the date of publication. This third part contains a long chapter on Molière, who had just died. Though somewhat inaccurate in regard to detail, particularly for the earlier history, the work as a whole remains important as a source book, indispensable to students of the seventeenth-century French theatre. There is a possibility that an early farce by Chappuzeau, published in Lyon in 1656, may have been done by Molière's company while they were touring the provinces, or alternatively that Molière may have seen or read it, since it appears to have influenced *Les Précieuses ridicules*.

CHARING CROSS THEATRE, London, see TOOLE'S THEATRE.

CHARIOT-AND-POLE SYSTEM, see CARRIAGE-AND-FRAME.

CHARLES HOPKINS THEATRE, New York, see PUNCH AND JUDY THEATRE.

CHARLESTON, a town important in the early history of American drama. It saw a production of *The Orphan* in 1735, and of *The Recruiting Officer* a year later, when the actors performed in the first theatre in Dock Street. This remained intermittently in use until 1763, when Douglass built a new theatre to house the American Company, to which they returned in 1766. After the War of Independence Charleston was one of the first towns to be visited by a theatrical company, that of Wall, which under Ryan continued to play there in opposition to the company of young Hallam and Henry. The theatre in Charleston continued to flourish, and in the early years of the nineteenth century had its own group of dramatists, writing plays which were put on under the management of Placide.

CHÂSSIS À DÉVELOPPEMENT, see TRICKWORK ON THE ENGLISH STAGE.

CHÂTELET, THÉÂTRE DU, Paris. Built in 1862, this theatre held 3,000 people and was intended for spectacular and musical shows. Among its early productions were *Les Mystères du vieux Paris, Le Tour du monde en 80 jours*, and such fairy plays as *La Poudre de Perlinpinpin*. In 1874 Colonne started his famous symphony concerts at this theatre.

CHATHAM THEATRE, New York. 1. A summer resort in Chatham Gardens, opened by a pastrycook named Barrière in 1819, with ice-cream, punch, and open-air music. Plays were first given there in 1822, and in 1823 a theatre, known as the Pavilion, was opened for a summer season with a company strong in farce and operetta. In 1824 this gave place to the Chatham Theatre, open all the year round, which soon proved a serious rival to the old-established Park Theatre. The Chatham, which seated 1,300, was the first theatre in New York to be lit by gas-jets. Its architect and scenic designer was Hugh Reinagle, its machinist George Conklin. The company included George Barrett and his future wife, Henry Wallack and his wife, formerly a dancer, and young Jefferson and his father, who made his last appearance in New York at this theatre on 4 Oct. 1825. It flourished until the death of Barrière on 18 Feb. 1826, when Henry Wallack took over. He proved unsuccessful, as did a number of other managers, among them Cooper, Hackett, who renamed the theatre the American Opera House, and Blanchard, who ran it as the Amphitheatre in 1830 with a mixture of equestrian and straight drama. It finally closed in 1832, under Hamblin, and became a Presbyterian chapel and a centre for sacred concerts.

2. On the south-east side of Chatham Street. Known as the New Chatham Theatre, it was built for Thomas Flynn and H. E. Willard from designs by Samuel Purdy, and held 2,200 people. It was first managed by James Anderson from the Bowery Theatre, and opened on 11 Sept. 1839. After a successful start, the theatre found itself in financial difficulties, until Charles R. Thorne became sole manager, and brought it a modicum of prosperity. Its bills were somewhat mixed, Booth and Shakespeare one week being followed by Rice and Negro farce the next. In 1843 Thorne retired, and a number of ephemeral managements followed. The main event of these years was the emergence as a great American comedian of Frank Chanfrau, who in 1848 took over the theatre, and renamed it Chanfrau's New National Theatre. It was henceforth known as the National, and Purdy, its next manager, kept the name. It was at this theatre that Edwin Booth made his first appearance in New York (27 Sept. 1850) and the elder Booth his last. Fanny Wallack also made her farewell appearance here. One of the greatest successes of the National was *Uncle Tom's Cabin*, which ran intermittently from 1853 to 1854. The fortunes of the theatre then began to wane, and Purdy had recourse to circus, dog dramas, and pantomime. His last success in legitimate

drama was *Ten Nights in a Bar Room*, which opened on 23 Aug. 1858, and his last production a revival of *Black-Eyed Susan* on 21 Mar. 1859. During Purdy's last season Adah Isaacs Menken made her first appearance in New York, under his management, as a young and untried actress. After Purdy's departure the National had a number of short-lived managements. A fire, on 9 July 1860, damaged much of the building, but it continued in use, as the Union Theatre, the National Concert Hall, and once again the Chatham. It finally became the National Music Hall, and in Oct. 1862 it was pulled down.

CHAUVE-SOURIS, LA, see BALIEFF, NIKITA.

CHEKHOV. (1) ANTON PAVLOVICH (1860–1904), Russian dramatist, possibly the one best known outside Russia, whose plays are in the repertory of every country. He came of humble parentage (his grandfather had been a serf), but graduated as a doctor from Moscow University in 1884. As he himself has pointed out, his study of medical science affected his approach to literature, and he always thought of himself more as a doctor than a writer. His short stories, published during his student days, caused something of a stir, and through them he became acquainted with the literary figures of his time, notably Tolstoy and Gorky, resigning his membership of the Russian Academy when the latter was dismissed from it by order of the Tsar.

Chekhov was early attracted by the theatre, particularly by the then popular vaudeville and French farce, and his first dramatic essays were one-act comedies such as *The Bear* (1888) and *The Proposal* (1889), for which he always retained an amused affection. A deeper note was struck in *On the Road*, a study in nomadic derelicts, which was banned by the censor. His first full-length play, *Ivanov* (1887), was written for the Korsh Theatre, but was not a success. A second, *The Wood-Demon* (1889), also done by a private theatre, was unremarked. And finally *The Seagull* (1896), when done by the old-fashioned Imperial Theatre, the Alexandrinsky, was a complete failure.

Chekhov now made up his mind to leave play-writing and concentrate on other things, and he would have done so, thus robbing the world of his fine later plays, had not Nemirovich-Danchenko persuaded him to let the newly founded Moscow Art Theatre revive the ill-fated *Seagull*. Nemirovich-Danchenko had realized that this new dramatist needed a new style of presentation, which the old stereotyped actors could not give him, but which the Moscow Art Theatre, with its delicate and subtle technique, could. The revival was successful, and was followed by *Uncle Vanya* (1899), *Three Sisters* (1901) (see No. 95), and *The Cherry Orchard* (1904). Chekhov died shortly afterwards, at the height of his powers.

The reasons for Chekhov's apparent failure at first are not far to seek. His plays had nothing in common with the current melodrama and grand heroic drama and were often incomprehensible to actors trained in the old tradition. They portray the constant attrition of daily life, and the waste, under the social conditions of Old Russia, of youthful energy and talent. At the same time they contain a note of hope for the future which is heavily stressed in modern Russian productions, where the characters are not presented, as they were when Chekhov was first seen in England, as wistful and pathetic creatures steeped in gloom, assisting at the disintegration of their lives. This hopefulness seems to accord with Chekhov's own view of his plays, but not with Stanislavsky's, who wrote that he wept when he first read *The Cherry Orchard*, and who conveyed to its first audience his own impressions of regret and impermanence.

But however one interprets the plays, they demand a delicacy of apprehension and a subtlety of ensemble playing by the actors which was not available in Russia until the Moscow Art Theatre developed it. Even they needed to perfect their technique, and the audience to rise to the demands made upon it, before Chekhov could be fully understood. He may still, particularly in translation, be falsified, but gradually the truth of his work, both for his own time and for ever, is imposing itself on his interpreters. As an American critic (John Gassner) has said: 'We have heard a good deal about the plotlessness and irresolution of Chekhov's work. But we have not heard enough about the secret strength and drive, the portentous hunger for life and positiveness, in his plays. We hear a great deal about Chekhov's simplicity, but overlook the terrible power that often resides in such simplicity.' And when we consider that the forces at work, however obscurely, in Chekhov's dramas are those which produced the Russian Revolution, it must be admitted that there is a great deal of truth in that summing-up. It is not without interest that the great speech by the student Trofimov at the end of Act II of *The Cherry Orchard*—the celebrated 'All Russia is our garden'—is not only a concise and accurate review of then recent Russian history, but an astonishingly and fiercely accurate prediction of the Revolution itself. ED.

The first of Chekhov's plays to be acted in English was *The Seagull*, which was produced by Alfred Wareing and George Calderon at the Glasgow Repertory Theatre in Nov. 1909. Calderon himself translated and directed the play; he also had a hand in Maurice Elvey's production of it at the Little Theatre in London in 1912, in which Gertrude Kingston played Madame Arkadina. In 1911 Shaw persuaded the Stage Society to produce *The Cherry Orchard*. Nigel Playfair, who was in the cast, said later that the actors had little understanding of their roles; most of the audience walked out, and the critics condemned the play as gloomy and formless. The Stage Society also produced *Uncle Vanya* in 1914. These early productions failed because their audiences were ill-attuned to them, but they helped to make Chekhov's work familiar to actors and critics of the time.

In 1919 and 1920 Mme Donnet [Mrs. Harold Bowen], a Russian who had seen the plays in Moscow, produced *The Seagull*, *The Cherry Orchard*, and *Three Sisters*. Many critics remained hostile, but, although excessively gloomy, the productions were popular in Bloomsbury, and marked the beginning of the so-called 'Chekhov craze', led by Katherine Mansfield and aided by Shaw. Excessive gloom also marked Fagan's production of *The Cherry Orchard* at Oxford in 1925, which was later seen in London. Some newspapers still insisted that Chekhov was 'fatuous drivel', but the play was a commercial success. Even more successful was the series of productions inaugurated by Philip Ridgeway at the Barnes Theatre (*Ivanov*, 1925; *Uncle Vanya*, *Three Sisters*, *The Cherry Orchard*, 1926), which finally naturalized Chekhov in England. Unfortunately, many of his native characteristics were lost in the process. Komisarjevsky, who produced the plays, wished to emphasize Chekhov's humour, but he often over-simplified by defining nuances, and by sentimentalizing and idealizing the characters. Some of his interpretations are still current in the English theatre.

Numerous revivals have followed, notably Guthrie's *Cherry Orchard* at the Old Vic in 1933, with Athene Seyler and Charles Laughton; Komisarjevsky's glittering version of *The Seagull* in 1936, with Edith Evans, Peggy Ashcroft, Martita Hunt, John Gielgud, and Stephen Haggard; Michel Saint-Denis's beautiful *Three Sisters* for Gielgud's repertory season at the Queen's in 1938, with Peggy Ashcroft and Michael Redgrave, which avoided any exaggeration or caricature; the Old Vic's postwar production of *Uncle Vanya* in 1946, with Ralph Richardson and Laurence Olivier, and of *The Cherry Orchard* in 1948, with Edith Evans as a nostalgic Madame Ranevsky; Gielgud's production of the same play in 1954, which managed to present the characters as both pathetic and amusing; and Olivier's superb production of *Uncle Vanya* at the Chichester Festival in 1962, in which he played Astrov, supported by an excellent cast. Although not suited to the open stage, the play came over splendidly and was the success of the season. It would be impossible to list all the provincial, repertory, and amateur productions of Chekhov, but it is perhaps worth noting that his early, unfinished play, *Platonov*, which was seen at the Royal Court Theatre in London in 1960, had its first production at the Nottingham Playhouse.

London has not often had the opportunity of seeing Chekhov in the original, but in 1928 a group of actors from the Moscow Art Theatre headed by Maria Germanova played *The Cherry Orchard* in a programme of Russian plays at the Garrick Theatre, and in 1958, at Sadler's Wells, the Moscow Art Theatre company was seen in *The Cherry Orchard*, *Uncle Vanya*, and *Three Sisters*. They returned in 1964, again with *The Cherry Orchard*.

Curiously enough, America's introduction to Chekhov was in the Russian text, as Paul Orlenev and Alla Nazimova appeared in *The Seagull* in its original language in 1905. In an English translation, this play was produced by the Washington Square Players in 1916, but American interest in Chekhov really dates from the visits of the Moscow Art Theatre in 1923 and 1924, and subsequent American productions have been strongly influenced by Stanislavsky's interpretations. They include *The Seagull* (1929), produced by Leo Bulgakov, a former member of the Moscow Art Theatre; Eva Le Gallienne's Civic Repertory series (*Three Sisters*, 1926; *The Cherry Orchard*, with Nazimova, 1928; *The Seagull*, 1929); *The Seagull* at the Theatre Guild in 1938, with the Lunts; *Three Sisters* (1942), with Katharine Cornell and Judith Anderson; Norris Houghton's production of *The Seagull* at the Phoenix Theatre in 1954; and David Ross's productions of all four of the major plays at the Fourth Street Theatre in the 1955–6 season.

ROBERT TRACY

There have been a number of translations of Chekhov's plays into English. For many years the standard acting versions were those of Constance Garnett, first published in 1923, and these have been used as the basis of new adaptations by actors and directors concerned with the productions. *The Cherry Orchard*, *Three Sisters*, and *Ivanov* were contained in a volume of the Penguin Classics in versions by Elisaveta Fen. The first three volumes of the definitive Oxford Chekhov contain all the plays translated by Dr. Ronald Hingley from the standard Moscow edition of 1944–51. Vol. I contains the short plays, Vol. II *Platonov*, *Ivanov*, and *The Seagull*, Vol. III *Uncle Vanya*, *Three Sisters*, *The Cherry Orchard*, and *The Wood-Demon*. All vols. have scholarly introductions, notes and bibliographies.

Among the first actors of the Moscow Art Theatre was a young student who had come from Nemirovich-Danchenko's class at the Moscow Philharmonic Society, (2) OLGA KNIPPER (1869–1959). She appeared in Chekhov's plays, and was married to him in 1901. After his death she remained with the Moscow Art Theatre as one of its leading actresses, and in 1943, at the 300th performance of *The Cherry Orchard*, was still playing the part of Madame Ranevsky which she created in 1904. She was one of the outstanding figures of the Soviet stage, and an important link with pre-revolutionary days (see No. 95).

(3) MICHAEL ALEXANDROVICH (1891–1955), nephew of Anton Chekhov, was also an actor and producer. He first appeared on the stage in St. Petersburg, and in 1910 joined the Moscow Art Theatre, where he became a member of the group Studio One. Here he played his best parts, Tackleton in *The Cricket on the Hearth*, Hamlet, and Erik XIV. After the departure of Vakhtangov he remained for a while as the leader of the group, but he was unable to adjust himself to the new régime,

and in 1927 emigrated to America, where he opened a studio for dramatic training.

CHELSEA THEATRE, LONDON, see ROYAL COURT THEATRE, 1.

CHÉNIER, MARIE-JOSEPH (1764–1811), French dramatist (younger brother of the poet André Chénier, who was guillotined in 1794) and one of the few important literary figures of the French Revolution. He had already produced some unimportant and unsuccessful plays when, after a battle with the censor lasting two years, his *Charles IX* was given in 1789. It had a strong republican bias, disguised as history, and was enthusiastically received. Its triumph was in some measure due to the magnificent acting of Talma, who later opened the Théâtre de la République with Chénier's *Henri VIII* (1791), following it in the same year with *Jean Calas*, and in 1792 with *Caius Gracchus*, another revolutionary play well suited to the temper of the time. Chénier was now at the height of his popularity, and was as active in politics as in drama. A member of the Convention, he voted for the death of Louis XVI, but his political career came to an end in 1802, when he opposed the rising star of Napoleon. He continued to write, but without success, and his *Timoléon*, first given in 1794, was proscribed and burnt by order of the censor. Only one copy, saved by an actress who much admired him (see VESTRIS, 2) escaped destruction. Chénier's work marks an important step in the evolution of historical drama in France, and has the merit, rare at this period, of moderation and some literary grace. Chénier has been much blamed for not using his influence to save his elder brother's life, but he had the wit to see that obscurity best served André's turn, and it was the father's ill-judged interference that brought André to the scaffold.

CHÉRI, ROSE [ROSE-MARIE CIZOS] (1824–61), French actress, daughter of actors, who played as a child in a provincial travelling company. On 6 July 1842 she made her début at the Gymnase and remained there for twenty years, marrying the director in 1847 and continuing as his leading lady, playing opposite Bressant. With a lovely face and figure she combined much intelligence and a willingness to profit by experience and teaching which soon brought her to the front, and she became one of the best-loved actresses of Paris. She was also much admired in London, where she appeared several times. She was at her best in the ingénue parts of vaudeville, had a fresh, clear singing voice, and was a good dancer. Her elder sister Anna was also in the company at the Gymnase, and proved a reliable actress, particularly when she took over elderly parts. She married an actor and retired in 1875, having made her début at the Gymnase in 1842.

CHESTER CYCLE, see ENGLAND, 1 and MYSTERY PLAY.

CHESTNUT STREET THEATRE, PHILADELPHIA, built in 1793 for the company brought from England by Thomas Wignell, formerly leading comedian of the American Company. Owing to an epidemic of yellow fever, it was not opened until 17 Feb. 1794. A copy of the Theatre Royal at Bath, it was an elegant and impressive building, holding about 2,000 people. Here Wignell remained until his death, being succeeded by Warren and Wood as joint managers, and the Chestnut Street Theatre had practically a monopoly of acting in Philadelphia until the opening of the Walnut Street Theatre in 1811. Under Warren and Wood it prospered, and its fine company, with such actors as Henry Wallack and his wife, and Joseph, John, and Thomas Jefferson, was unequalled in light comedy. From its prominent position in the American theatre world it was sometimes known as 'Old Drury'. It was one of the first theatres in the United States to be lit by gas (25 Nov. 1816) and in every way it was superior to the theatres of New York. It was not until 1828 that Wood's retirement from management, and the rivalry of the Walnut Street and Arch Street Theatres, brought about the dissolution of the company, which went bankrupt in 1829. From this time onwards the theatre had a stock company which served to support visiting stars, and the supremacy of Philadelphia passed to New York. Under Maywood in the early 1830s it started on a disastrous policy of employing foreign stars at fabulous sums which, however profitable the evening, left the management out of pocket.

The first theatre built on Chestnut Street, between 6th and 7th streets, was damaged by fire in 1820 and rebuilt in 1821. In 1856 it was completely destroyed by fire, and the new building did not open until 1863. The last performance was given in 1910, and the theatre was finally demolished in 1917 (see No. 28).

CHETTLE, HENRY (*c.* 1560–1607), a prolific playwright, who is credited by Henslowe in his diary with a long list of plays, mostly written in collaboration and now lost. Of his surviving works, the only one which he appears to have produced unaided is *Hoffman*, known also as *Revenge for a Father* (*c.* 1602), which follows the pattern of the 'revenge tragedy' set by Kyd. With Anthony Munday he wrote two plays on Robert, Earl of Huntingdon, or Robin Hood, and with Day a comedy entitled *The Blind Beggar of Bethnal Green*, to which Day subsequently wrote two sequels. Chettle, who was also a printer, was concerned with the publication of Nashe's pamphlets as well as Greene's *Groatsworth of Wit*, which he edited in 1592. From the numerous small sums lent him by Henslowe as advances on his plays he appears to have been both needy and improvident.

CHEVALIER, ALBERT (1861–1923), a music-hall performer best remembered for his coster songs. He was first an actor with the Bancrofts, Kendals, and Hare, and even appeared in grand opera. He was persuaded by Charlie Coborn, with great difficulty, to sing some of his own songs on the halls, and his début at the London

Pavilion in 1891 singing 'The Coster's Serenade' was a great success. He became the great exponent of Cockney humour and pathos in such perennial favourites as 'Knocked 'em in the Old Kent Road', 'The NastyWay 'e Sez It', 'It Gits me Talked Abaht', ''Appy 'Ampstead', and, best loved of all, 'My Old Dutch'. He wrote and appeared in a number of serious and sentimental sketches and ballads, which the audience tolerated for the sake of the coster songs, and was the author of an ill-fated musical play, *The Land of Nod*, which after a successful run of nine months in the provinces was withdrawn in London after a week. He also published a volume of memoirs entitled *Before I Forget*. He was one of the few music-hall stars who did not appear in pantomime.

CHEVALIER, MAURICE (1888–1972), French actor and music-hall artist, equally popular in Paris, London, and New York. He made his first appearance on the stage in 1906, and from 1909 to 1913 he was with Mistinguett at the Folies-Bergère. After serving in the First World War, when he was wounded and made prisoner, he reappeared in Paris, and in 1919 made his first appearance in London in *Hullo, America*. Two years later he made his first appearance in a straight play, *Dédé*, but soon returned to revue, and in 1929 gave a programme of songs from his repertoire at the New Amsterdam Roof Garden in Ziegfeld's Theatre in New York. He then had a long and consistently successful career, which he recounted in his memoirs, *The Man in the Straw Hat*, published in 1949. This straw hat was, indeed, his trade-mark, and its debonair flourish, combined with his slightly raffish appearance, quizzical smile, and the seduction of his voice, with its charming broken-English accent, made him a popular idol. He gave a large number of one-man shows, culminating in his appearance at the State Fair in Dallas in *An Evening with Maurice Chevalier*. He also had a most successful career in films.

CHIARELLI, LUIGI (1884–1947), Italian playwright, regarded as the principal representative of the *teatro grottesco* in Italy. He excels as the satirist of a bored and cynical society, in which an excess of leisure combines with moral and intellectual vacancy. The literary quality of his work is slight, but he is a skilled creator of good theatre. His major play is *La maschera e il volto* (1916—but completed in 1913), a merciless (if occasionally sentimental) exploration of the inadequacy, corruption, and total lack of authenticity of social man. *Fuochi d'artificio* (1923) is similar in approach. More ordinarily commercial and melodramatic is *K. 41* (1929), while *Il cerchio magico* (1937) is charmingly whimsical in a manner recalling Barrie or Van Druten. *Una più due* (1935), a sophisticated light comedy, has great pace and unexpected depth. Some of Chiarelli's plays have been staged in England and America, though the best-known version of *La maschera e il volto* (*The Mask and the Face*, by John Fernald, 1924; revived 1950) is a very free adaptation. FREDERICK MAY

CHICHESTER THEATRE FESTIVAL. The enterprise shown in the founding and maintaining of an open-stage theatre in Stratford, Ontario, inspired a member of an amateur dramatic society in Chichester, Leslie Evershed-Martin, to plan a somewhat similar theatre for his own town. By his enthusiasm and hard work he soon collected enough money to enable the theatre to be built, Laurence Olivier was appointed its first director, and on 3 July 1962 the Chichester Festival season of ten weeks opened with *The Chances*, a comedy by Fletcher (based on Cervantes) adapted by Buckingham. This, like the two other plays in the repertory, *Uncle Vanya* and Ford's *The Broken Heart*, was produced by Olivier, who also appeared as Bassanes in the latter play, and as Astrov in *Uncle Vanya*, with a strong supporting cast—Michael Redgrave, Sybil Thorndike, Lewis Casson, Fay Compton, Joan Plowright, and Joan Greenwood. The Chekhov, though apparently unsuited to the open-stage theatre, proved the most succesful; *The Chances*, however, which started badly, picked up and became extremely popular. In later seasons new plays were introduced into the repertory—Arden's *The Workhouse Donkey* and *Armstrong's Last Goodnight*, Shaffer's *Royal Hunt of the Sun* and *Black Comedy*—together with such classics as *The Dutch Courtesan*, *Othello*, and *Trelawny of the 'Wells'*. At the end of the 1965 season Olivier retired, and was replaced as director by John Clements. The theatre (which Olivier once referred to as a 'concrete hexagon') is set on the edge of the town among trees, has a large open stage with the audience on three sides, a semi-permanent balcony, a catwalk all round the interior wall, and access to the stage from numerous entrances in the stage wall and also from two auditorium staircases. Lighting is from lamps suspended from the spider's-web structure of the tent-like roof. There are bars in the large foyer, and a detached restaurant in the grounds. It is hoped later to add more buildings backstage, where conditions are very cramped, and also a room for meetings of the club members. In addition to a summer season of plays by a professional company, the theatre is used for Sunday concerts and poetry readings, and during the winter for performances by local amateur and visiting companies.

CHILDREN OF THE CHAPEL, OF PAUL'S, see BOY COMPANIES.

CHILDREN'S THEATRE, a term covering performances given by adult professional or amateur actors and puppeteers for young people, either in theatres or in school halls. It does not cover professional acting by children (see BOY COMPANIES), or amateur performances by school-children in public (see JESUIT DRAMA, SCHOOL DRAMA, and WESTMINSTER PLAY); nor has it anything to do with the use of drama as part of the educational curriculum.

Although it has long been agreed that the only way to build up a continuing audience for the professional adult theatre is to introduce children to the best possible expression of it and so inculcate the habit of theatre-going, in practice the great stumbling block has been finance. It is impossible for a company playing only for young people, even if the age-limit is extended to 18, to become self-supporting. Only in countries where children's theatre is fully state-supported, as in Russia and other eastern European countries, has there been steady progress. Elsewhere there has been haphazard and piecemeal development dependent on the energy and initiative of individuals, or on the uncertain assistance of local councils and educational bodies. In England one of the first attempts to provide theatres specially for children was made by Jean Sterling Mackinlay, who from 1914 to 1939 ran a six-weeks' matinées-only season over the Christmas period. Before this children had had to be content with the Christmas pantomime or the annual revival of such plays as *Bluebell in Fairyland* (first perf. 1901), *Peter Pan* (1904), and *Where the Rainbow Ends* (1911); to which may be added the later *Make Believe* (1918), *The Windmill Man* (1921), *Toad of Toad Hall* (1930), *The Silver Curlew* (1949), and the fairytale adaptations of Nicholas Stuart Gray, which date from the 1940s. These were all specially written for children. An effort to provide professional productions of Shakespeare and other classics for young spectators was made by the English School Theatre, which played in West-End theatres and drew its audiences from schools, mainly in the Home Counties, but on some occasions from as far afield as South Wales. Recognized by the then Board of Education as an educational activity, and supported by some educational authorities who paid for their children to attend, the organization began work in 1936 but had to be disbanded during the Second World War. After the war a more ambitious project was set on foot with the Young Vic, founded and directed by George Devine. Although artistically a great success, particularly on its Continental tours, this too was finally defeated by financial problems. In 1948 Caryl Jenner, so far one of the most successful producers to grapple with this problem, started her English Theatre for Children, which in 1962, as the Unicorn Theatre, achieved a certain stability with headquarters in London and holiday seasons at the Arts Theatre for matinées only. Otherwise the company still appears mainly in school halls during school time, which entitles it to support from the local education authority. Other groups developed during the 1950s, run by devoted organizers working in cramped and discouraging conditions. All believe that for the full impact of theatrical experience the child should ideally be brought to the theatre, but only in a few cases, as with Frank Dunlop's matinées at the Nottingham Playhouse (1945) and John English's Arena Theatre in Sutton Coldfield (1949), has this proved feasible. In most cases the theatre still goes to the child. The oldest surviving company (founded in 1927) is Nancy Hewins' Osiris Players, who appear mainly in Shakespeare. Bertha Waddell's Scottish Children's Theatre, also 1927, closed in 1968. Among later foundations is Brian Way's London Children's Theatre (1954). There is also La Troupe Française, run by Gaston Richer and his wife Pamela Stirling, which visits a number of schools with two French classics a year.

All the above companies are fully professional and belong to the British Children's Theatre Association, founded in 1959. To this belong also the far larger number of amateur groups, mostly founded since 1945, some of which have their own theatres and confine their activities to their own locality.

In Australia there are active children's theatre groups in the large cities, and extensive tours of Shakespeare plays for schools are undertaken by the Young Elizabethan Players under the auspices of the Australian Theatre Trust, which has also been responsible for the tours of Peter Scriven's puppets in such plays as *The Tintookies* (little people who live in the sandhills) and *Little Fella Bindi*, the story of an aboriginal boy who makes friends with the bushland creatures. New Zealand has the Canterbury Children's Theatre, founded in Dec. 1952 which opened with *The Tinder Box*. There is considerable activity in Canada, where the Winnipeg Children's Theatre dates from 1920 and the Montreal from 1933, and much good work has been done recently in South Africa and India.

In Europe, Denmark can boast of being one of the first countries to provide theatres specifically for young people. A small amateur group, founded in 1920 by a schoolteacher, Thomas P. Hejle, has grown into a complex professional organization which receives municipal help and caters for two age-groups, 11–14 and 14–18. Plays are given in the afternoons, either in theatres in the towns or in a hall or school in country districts. They are chosen from the adult repertory and performed by carefully selected adult professional actors. One of the outstanding successes was *The Hasty Heart*, by John Patrick. In Sweden the National Theatre runs performances for young people, mainly in the larger towns. In both countries young people of 14–18 are allowed to buy tickets at reduced prices for adult performances. This is the case in most European countries where the theatre is subsidized or state-aided.

In spite of the early start made by the Théâtre de l'Oncle Sebastien in Paris in 1935, France appears to have little in the way of specifically children's theatres, apart from the *matinées scolaires* at the Comédie-Française and some commercial theatres which put on weekly matinées for children. During the winter months the Théâtre Roland Pilain stages matinées on Thursday afternoons, but the company is composed of children and not of adult actors. Holland has two subsidized companies, the Arena Acting Group and the Scapino Ballet, which appear in theatres and halls in performances commissioned by the educational authorities and attended in school time. Belgium has the Théâtre de l'Enfance, directed by José Geal, which provides puppet-shows for very young children and live performances by adult professionals for older children. There are also six puppet-shows a month in a children's theatre at Antwerp, which has flourished since 1946.

Germany, which before the Second World War gave considerable official support, mainly in the way of annual subsidies, to organizations catering for children, has somewhat fallen away, and now seems to have only two companies which appear in their own theatres, one in Munich, one in Cologne. But here again young people can buy tickets for normal theatre-going very cheaply through their own organization, School Theatre. In Nuremberg, however, there is a close connexion between the theatres and schools, a factor which is said to have reduced juvenile delinquency in the city.

In East Germany, as in other Communist countries, children's companies are heavily subsidized and have their own theatres, the actors being specially trained for their work. Touring companies visit small towns and villages, and perform also in schools and children's clubs. Since the Second World War there has been a great expansion of children's theatres in Bulgaria, with a permanent company in Sofia directed by Lilia Todovova, having its own theatre and playwrights, and also one in Plovdiv. Here, as elsewhere, one of the complaints is of the lack of good suitable new plays. Czechoslovakia, which had a long tradition of puppet-plays, has now a widespread system of children's theatres, with permanent companies in Prague, Brno, Bratislava and Ostrava. The actors and technicians are specially trained for their work, which caters for three age-groups both in and out of school, and the repertory of plays, based on Czech history, folk-lore, and world drama, is rich and varied. Children's theatre is still in its infancy in Hungary: the company in Budapest began work in 1959, and a second company operates in connexion with the State Déry Theatre, in addition to its adult performances. Great expansion is hoped for, especially in provincial towns, where some performances are already being given by amateur groups. In Poland two theatres for children, one in Warsaw and one in Cracow, opened soon after the Second World War, and by 1962 twenty theatres all over the country were giving plays for children at the weekends. In Rumania, where the first children's theatre opened in Bucharest in 1944, and most adult theatres include in their annual repertory one play suitable for young people, there are plans for expansion (see Nos. 130, 131, 176).

It is, however, as one might expect, in Russia that children's theatre has reached its highest point of expansion so far. The first children's theatre opened in Moscow in 1920 under Natalie Satz, who, in 1945, became director of the Kazakhstan Children's Theatre. Then came one in Kharkhov (1921), one—the Theatre for the Young Spectator (Lentyuz) under Professor Bryantsev—in Leningrad (1922), and one in Kiev (1924). A second opened in Moscow in 1927. The growth of theatres for children intensified with the introduction of compulsory education, since they were found to be an excellent instrument of propaganda and mass education among the young, and by 1941 the number had risen to seventy, excluding puppet-theatres, situated in all parts of the U.S.S.R. and playing in the various national languages. The Second World War destroyed a number of them, including the very beautiful one at Kiev, and later reorganization reduced the total number to thirty-four in 1961. Most of the existing theatres have, in addition to a resident company, at least one touring company which serves the surrounding countryside. All this activity is, of course, fully subsidized by the state, which also trains the actors and technicians, provides orchestras, and pays the dramatists. Research into the problems of production, writing, and acting for young people, and into the educational aspect, is carried on, particularly in Leningrad, where Professor Bryantsev insisted on it from the first. He has been ably supported by Professor Makaryev, the director of productions. There are discussions after the play, both in the theatre and in school, in which the author of a new play sometimes takes part. Conferences are also held in Moscow, where representative companies from the Republics are invited to give performances (see No. 129).

In the United States, where children's theatres, as in England, are not subsidized, they are mainly run by independent groups or by individuals like the late Charlotte Chorpenning, who ran the Goodman Children's Theatre in Chicago for twenty-one years. They are much helped by the fact that at least one publishing firm, the Children's Theatre Press, founded in 1935, devotes its resources exclusively to the publication of plays suitable for performance to children. The Press was the moving spirit behind the first Children's Theatre Conference held in 1944 by the American Educational Theatre Association (A.E.T.A.), whose large membership is drawn from all types of theatre groups.

In South America the greatest enterprise in the field of children's theatre so far seems to have been shown in Brazil, where up to 1949 the only performances for children were given by amateur child groups. In that year, however, a production for young people of *The Enchanted Cloak* by Lucia Benedetti, performed by members of an important company, the Artistas Unidos, headed by Henriette Morineau, the leading actress, and produced by the company's star actor, Graca Mello, was such a success that it ousted the company's adult plays, and aroused interest all over the country. This resulted in further plays for children by the same author in one of which—*Simbita and the Dragon*—the leading part was played by Sergio Cardoso, a fine interpreter of Hamlet. In 1950 an annual prize was instituted for the best play for children, which was first awarded to Lucia Benedetti for *Little John Walks Backwards*. Subsequently a number of other dramatists concentrated on writing plays for children; the National Theatre was granted a subsidy for the provision of a new department concerned with children's theatre, and in São Paulo a permanent Children's Theatre is envisaged. Unfortunately some of the initial fervour has subsided,and the bulk of the work for children is now (1964) done by amateurs. The problems are the same as in the United States and western Europe—insufficient funds, inadequate premises, a lack of good new plays, and of good dedicated actors trained in the special problems of theatre for children. The whole matter of children's theatre has, however, now received world-wide attention—India has several established groups playing only for children—and it has been taken up by the International Theatre Institute, which made it the subject of a special issue of *World Theatre* (vol. II. No. 3).

CHILE, see SOUTH AMERICA.

CHIMNEY, an opening practised in the thickness of the side wall of the stage to house the counterweights which control the working of the scenery.

CHINA. 1. TRADITIONAL. Popular Chinese drama, perfected in Peking during the nineteenth century, is a flexible and harmonious combination of spoken dialogue, operatic singing, dancing, and acrobatics; and the play or libretto, roughly classified as civil (*wên*) and military (*wu*), is little more than a framework for skilled actors to complete. The language is a hybrid of colloquial and literary Chinese, a purely theatrical dialect which is easily acquired and understood: vocal passages are in verse; spoken dialogue breaks the tension, elucidates the plot, and gives the singer a rest. When the protagonist appears, he chants a prologue and prefatory poem and proceeds to render a full account of himself, his names, family, circumstances, motives, and intentions. A character speaks until his gathering emotions plunge him into melody, and the last word spoken is prolonged *crescendo* as a signal to the orchestra.

The same plays are performed again and again to tireless audiences far more critical than our own. They are divided not into acts but into numerous scenes of varying length. While unities of time and place are disregarded and stage properties are simplified, an elaborate set of conventions has been evolved which, like the written symbols for speech, are as logical as they are imaginative. This unlocalized drama allows the Chinese playwright, as it allowed the Elizabethan, to indulge in loose flowing construction, episodic plots, and complex action. Although incongruous changes are creeping in, the stage still mirrors the life and thought of China through the centuries: the subject-matter is mainly traditional, derived from legends, historical anecdotes, and famous novels, and always makes some pretence of pointing a moral. Goodness is rewarded, wrongs are redressed, and evil punished—eventually. There is no clear distinction between comedy and tragedy, and the majority of Chinese plays may be described as melodramas with happy endings.

As in Greece, dramatic performances were of ancient ritual origin. According to the experts, it was not until the Northern Ch'i dynasty (A.D. 557–81) that singing and dancing were combined with the dramatizing of a story. The practice of wearing masks originated in the same period, and engraved reliefs from contemporary tombs bear witness to the stylized grace of the dancers. The famous T'ang Emperor Ming Huang is credited with the foundation of the first dramatic school, known as the 'Pear Garden', in A.D. 720.

Chinese actors have developed a technique that renders scenery superfluous. To indicate change of place they have only to tread in a circle. The projecting stage is almost square with an embroidered curtain or flat painted background, flanked by two curtained doors, the left for entrances and the right for exits. Stage properties are symbolic and, like almost everything connected with the Chinese theatre, strictly conventional. An ordinary table may represent an altar, a judge's bench, a bridge, a banquet-board, etc., and can serve for climbing mountains or scaling battlements: by jumping over it the actor may be jumping over a wall. The position of chairs is also significant: circumstance and social status are conveyed by the manner of sitting, the left being invariably the place of honour. Two or three chairs covered with a curtain may represent a bed. An arched gate with bricks painted in white on a square blue cloth is held up by stage hands when characters are to enter or leave a city: this and the screen-like panels on which formal rocks are depicted for a mountain range are the nearest equivalents to scenery. Among important properties are the tasselled horse-whip which enables an actor to ride an invisible horse; the horse-hair duster which symbolizes spirituality and is held by deities and religious characters; and the oar which represents a boat. Painted flags serve many purposes: four black flags are flourished when a violent wind is required; four flags painted with waves represent water; two yellow flags with wheels a chariot. Large banners in groups of four represent armies; inscribed with characters, they denote military rank. A hat wrapped in red cloth does duty for a decapitated head, a bench with hat and robe flung over it for a corpse. A woman's diminutive red shoe represents needlework, a cube wrapped in yellow silk an official seal. A fan is usually a sign of frivolity. Other properties, such as military weapons, state umbrellas, imperial mandates, arrows of command, shop-signs, lanterns, and candles (not necessarily lighted), are mostly realistic.

Scenic problems are solved by vivid pantomime: the actor is the cynosure of the performance. Standing on a bare projecting stage, he is seen in space. Hence all his movements are sculptured to combine grace with maximum significance. He is his own producer: he must be a skilful singer, dancer, mime, and acrobat. His strenuous training begins at the age of twelve or earlier; from his physique and the talents he displays it is soon decided in which type he shall specialize, and for seven years or more he is coached in every detail of his craft.

Characters are classified under four types: *shêng*, males in general; *tan*, females in general; *ching* or *hua-lien*, robust males with faces painted like masks; and *ch'ou*, broad comedians. But these have a number of precise subdivisions. The righteous elderly bearded male role (*lao-shêng*) was the most important from about 1850 till 1910, and there were no less than four distinct schools of interpreting it. But with the meteoric rise to fame of Mei Lan-Fang (see No. 119), the role of female impersonator assumed a greater importance. As in Elizabethan England, boys had impersonated girls since the origin of drama. Neo-Confucian prejudice against the mingling of sexes on the stage encouraged this practice, facilitated by a slender build and an exiguous growth of whiskers. Until recently the actors were all of one sex, usually male, and though there is a modern tendency for women to appear in feminine roles, the finest critics prefer female impersonators, since theirs is the subtler triumph of art over nature.

Except broad comedians and those vigorous males with mask-like make-up who sing in a forced bass, most characters speak and sing in falsetto. The music must have been influenced by the open-air conditions of primitive theatres, which resembled the temporary mat-shed structures in villages and at temple fairs. The orchestra is accommodated on the stage. A hard wooden instrument like castanets beats the time; a fiddle called *hu-ch'in*, with a hollow cylindrical body of varying size, the smallest with two strings bowed horizontally, is the leading instrument of vocal accompaniment; and the volume of sound which a small Chinese orchestra can produce when the *so-na*, or clarionet, and the brass instruments of percussion are in full force, is more astonishing than agreeable to the average Western ear.

The costumes are generally adapted from the styles of the T'ang, Sung, Yüan, and Ming dynasties: they are sumptuous but seldom historically accurate. The main colours indicate social rank, character, and occasion: emperors wear yellow, high officials red, civilian worthies blue, elderly people brown, and rough characters black. For ceremonial occasions high officials don satin robes with capacious 'rippling water' sleeves, embroidered with dragons and bordered with wave-patterns, and a big jade belt dangling a little below the waist. There is a saying, 'the longer the sleeves, the better the dance', and their adroit manipulation is a salient part of the actor's technique. White silk cuffs about two feet long, left open at the seam, are sewn to sleeves which would otherwise be too heavy for rapid motion. Their flowing lines accentuate physical grace and the delicacy of hands, and enhance dramatic expression. For 'asides' the right hand is raised level with the cheek and the sleeve hangs down like a curtain between the character and his immediate neighbour. When a character weeps, a corner of the left sleeve is held up to the eyes. The stage warrior's costume could scarcely be more magnificent. Embroidered tiger heads are attached to the heavily padded shoulders and waist, long scalloped panniers sweep down between the legs, and a 'heart-protecting' mirror glitters on the chest. Four triangular pennons, fixed between the shoulders, are worn on the backs of generals, and their head-dress of brilliant pompons, spangles, and imitation jewels is often surmounted by two pheasant-plumes, which may be six or seven feet long. The swirling and twirling of these noble plumes intensifies the exuberant pride of a victorious commander.

Painted-face roles (*hua-lien*) wear the most complicated make-up and shave their foreheads to lengthen or broaden their features. Temperament is expressed by certain lines about the eyes, nose, and mouth, and by symbolical combinations of colours. Since the Ming dynasty these have increased in elaboration and decreased in significance, but the main background and predominant colours remain the same: all white indicating treachery; black, straightforwardness and tough integrity; red, loyalty and courage; blue, stubbornness and ferocity; green, outlaws, brigands, and demons; yellow, strength and hidden cunning; gold, gods and immortals; dull pink and grey, advanced age. This unique art upon which Chinese actors have lavished so much taste and ingenuity requires careful study. The great historical roles have been chiselled and polished for generations, from facial make-up to the most trivial mannerisms. Ts'ao Ts'ao, for instance, has become a classical monument of villainy. Tou Erh-tun, perhaps the most gorgeous of theatrical brigand chiefs, is made up like a ferocious monster beetle. Indigo blue is the main colour, with scarlet eyebrows and curving lines of black and white of various thicknesses about the eyes to represent the tiger-head hooks which were his most formidable weapon, and another pair of eyes are painted beneath his own to denote his remarkable powers of vision, while the forehead appears as if encrusted with gems. An enormous scarlet beard completes this masterpiece. 'Iron Face' Pao Chêng, the Sung dynasty judge who never smiled, has a jet-black make-up except for the striking silhouette of his arched eyebrows and the crescent moon on his forehead to symbolize his supernatural acumen. His diction is hard and rasping, and all his movements are calculated to inspire awe. But the awe is blended with a certain affection, and the audience revels in his fulminations against wickedness in high places. The make-up of Sun the Monkey God, 'Discoverer of Secrets', is wonderfully expressive, though hardly more than an inverted triangle of bright crimson with touches of gold about the nostrils and golden circles round the blinking, mischievous eyes. His every twitch is realistic and formal at the same time, and the result is far subtler than an imitation of monkey cunning; it is a synthesis and sublimation of the whole simian tribe. The veteran actor Hao Chên-chi gave uncanny demonstrations of metempsychosis in this fascinating role (see No. 118).

Numerous types of beard also help to indicate age and character, and owing to their prestige in ancient China, the longest and fullest, covering the mouth, denote heroism and prosperity; tripartite beards, culture and refinement; red and blue beards, supernatural beings (announced by flashes of fire), while moustaches are generally a sign of coarseness or cunning. In anger the foot is stamped and the beard swept upward.

The broad comic roles with white patches on the nose are the most realistic, and the domestic farce, equivalent to our curtain-raiser, bears a closer relation to the Western theatre than any other type of Chinese play.

The actors walk on and off stage to a tempo set by the orchestra; every movement should follow a strict convention. A small hand-gong heralds a civil play, a large gong and the clash of cymbals a military play. Naturally the difference between the sexes is emphasized by all sorts of appropriate devices. Every finger of the female impersonator must contribute to the effect of fragile femininity. A genius for doing the right thing in the right way, supreme theatrical instinct, is the final test. 'She whose movements are disciplined, she who is a living harmony, a lyric in flesh and blood', wrote Sarcey of Sarah Bernhardt. Alter the pronoun, and these words apply to Mei Lan-Fang. Fortunately the essentials of the Chinese theatre still remain intact, even in Shanghai, where actor-managers have made numerous concessions to the vulgar (see No. 117). HAROLD ACTON

2. MODERN. Two largely separate dramatic traditions coexist in the contemporary Chinese theatre. One is the traditional theatre outlined above, which includes the classical *K'un-ch'ü*, the Peking Opera (*ching-hsi*) and the various types of local theatre (*ti-fang hsi*). The other is the modern 'spoken drama' (*hua-chü*) which has developed under foreign influence since the early years of this century.

The traditional theatre, having survived the vicissitudes of war and revolution, remains firmly established as the most popular form of theatrical entertainment. The Peking Opera, which had replaced the older *K'un-ch'ü* as the dominant form of the traditional theatre early in the nineteenth century, has continued to flourish, aided by certain reforms which have enabled it to retain its popularity through a period of social change. The most notable of these reforms has been the introduction of women on to the stage to act alongside men, a practice which, as in Greece and Elizabethan England, was unknown in the Chinese theatre up to 1911. Since 1949 greatly increased state support has facilitated the revival, along with the Peking Opera, of many types of local theatre, which, while sharing the composite song–dance–mime form of all traditional theatre, have each their own repertoire and characteristic styles of music and acting. Local companies frequently visit Peking and other centres, rivalling the Peking Opera in popularity. In recent years traditional theatre companies have toured many countries of Asia, Africa, Europe, and S. America.

The 'spoken drama' originated among a group of Chinese students in Japan who in 1907 founded the Spring Willow Society in Tokyo. The first production of this society was a Chinese adaptation of *La Dame aux camélias*. However, it was not until after the beginning of the 'New Culture Movement' in 1917 that the 'spoken drama' won a serious following. During this time the works of Ibsen and other modern Western dramatists were introduced into China in translation, and the first attempts were made to write original Chinese plays along Western lines.

Prominent in this pioneering activity in the 1920s were the dramatists T'ien Han and Hung Shen, who in addition to writing plays also organized theatre companies and founded schools of drama. In the late 1930s the plays of Ts'ao Yü, notably *Thunderstorm*, *Sunrise*, and *Peking Man*, reached a higher technical level than had been attained hitherto, and they continue to be enjoyed by theatre audiences today. After the Japanese invasion of 1937 the theatre increasingly became the vehicle of patriotic propaganda, and since 1949 plays about the revolution have been favoured. As in the case of the traditional theatre, 'spoken drama' has recently received considerable state support, which has raised the standard of acting and spread its influence.

China also has an ancient tradition of puppet drama, which declined in the earlier part of this century, but has recently been revived in its various forms (marionettes, hand-puppets, and shadow-puppets). Other dramatic genres which are receiving attention include the Western ballet, an experimental troupe having been founded in 1959. J. D. CHINNERY

CHINA HALL THEATRE, LONDON. This stood in the pleasure-grounds of a public-house in Rotherhithe in the eighteenth century. George Frederick Cooke played there in 1778. The prices were Boxes, 3*s.*; Pit, 2*s.*; Gallery, 1*s.* There had evidently been a place of entertainment there long before, as Pepys mentions it in his diary.

CHIONIDES, a very early Athenian comic poet of *c.* 500 B.C. (see GREECE, 2 *b*).

CHIRGWIN, GEORGE H. (1854–1922), a famous Minstrel, originally known as the White-Eyed Musical Moke, who from 1877 was billed as 'the White-Eyed Kaffir' because of the white lozenge-shaped patch round his right eye. He made his first appearance at the age of six at the Swallow Rooms, Piccadilly, with a Minstrel troupe, and later made a name for himself as a solo turn on the halls, celebrating his jubilee at the Oxford in 1911. He sang sentimental coon songs—the two favourites being 'The Blind Boy' and 'My Fiddle is My Sweetheart'—in a high-pitched, piping voice, accompanying himself on the banjo and, later, on the one-stringed fiddle.

CHOCOLATE-COLOURED COON, see ELLIOTT, G. H.

CHOERILUS, an Attic tragic poet of the generation before Aeschylus. Beyond the fact that his first production took place about 520 B.C., practically nothing is known of him.

CHOREGUS. Under the Athenian democracy, certain specific financial burdens (liturgies) were imposed in rotation on citizens whose wealth exceeded a certain sum. These included the equipping of a man-o'-war, defraying the cost of certain religious ceremonies, and, the one that comes into question here, the equipping and paying of a chorus for a tragic, comic, or dithyrambic contest. Hence the name *choregus*, or chorus-leader. The dramatic contests were therefore contests between *choregi* as well as between poets and, later, actors. It was important to the poet that his *choregus* should not be stingy, since the proper presentation of the play depended on him; *choregi* therefore were assigned to the poets by lot (see GREECE, 3). H. D. F. KITTO

CHOREOGRAPHY, the term applied to the creating of a ballet, that is, to the choice and grouping of the various movements, with their intermediate positions, which will best interpret both the music and the drama of the subject. The creator of a ballet is known as a choreographer, and his work calls for a rare combination of talents, since he must be an expert in music, dancing, anatomy, aesthetics, and in artistic appreciation. Only thus can he adequately interpret his thought in movement. He must also be a student of human nature as well as of the theatre, and an inspired teacher. Choreography is not an art that can be taught; it is the irresistible expression of the personality of the dancer, working through the medium which he knows, understands, and can manipulate at will. The early choreographers, of whose work nothing remains but 'Giselle', were also *maîtres de ballet*, often in their youth dancers, though they may later have given up active participation in their ballets; later choreographers, among them Fokine, Massine, Ninette de Valois, Balanchine, Ashton, and Helpmann, were active dancers who appeared in the leading roles which they thus 'created' in a double sense. Choreography is a complex subject, and a part of ballet-dancing which still remains mysterious to the inquiring layman.

CHORUS, in Greek drama a group of actors who stood aside from the main action of the play and commented on it (see GREECE, 1 *c*). In Elizabethan phraseology the Chorus was the speaker of the introductory prologue, as in Shakespeare's *Henry V*, a legacy from Euripides via Seneca. In the modern theatre the word is usually taken to mean the chorus of a musical comedy, which reached its apogee in the late nineteenth century, particularly at the Gaiety Theatre. It consisted of a number of beautiful young women who could sing and dance a little, stand and move gracefully, and wear lovely clothes. As their attire became scantier their activities increased, until in the 1920s they wore practically nothing at all and reached an exceedingly high standard, particularly in the clockwork precision of their dancing. The male members of the musical comedy chorus have, on the other hand, remained almost static throughout, merely acting as foils for the women, and being entirely dispensed with in some plays and in revue. Under the influence of the modern American musical play the chorus tends to have a greater share in the actual development of the plot, and to attain, in both sexes, a good standard in singing, dancing, and acting. The use of the Chorus in the Greek sense has been revived in some modern poetic plays, notably T. S. Eliot's *Murder in the Cathedral* (1935).

CHRISTY MINSTRELS, see NEGRO IN THE AMERICAN THEATRE.

CHRONEGK, LUDWIG (1837–91), German actor, producer, and manager, who assisted Duke George II of Saxe-Meiningen in his theatrical work. After his début at the Kroll Theatre, Berlin, in 1855 as a juvenile comedian and clown, Chronegk acted in various German theatres, notably at Zürich, Königsberg, the Thalia at Hamburg, and the Leipzig Stadtstheater. In 1866 he entered the service of the Duke as an actor at the Meiningen Court theatre, specializing in comic Shakespearian roles. The Duke saw that his true talents lay in directing, and appointed him producer in 1871; thereafter he became successively manager of the company (1877), a councillor (1882), and superintendent of the Court theatres (1884). In all these positions he was essential to the successful and revolutionary activities of the Meiningen Players. Plays were chosen by the Duke, who reserved to himself the general supervision of all productions, the design of scenery and costume, and the preparation of the famous crowd scenes; his morganatic wife, the former actress Ellen Franz, studied the text of the play, adapted it to the stage, and advised on the interpretation of individual lines and related matters;

Chronegk was responsible for the actual execution of all their decisions, the conduct of rehearsals, the supervision and discipline of the company, and arrangements for tours. He served, in fact, as theatrical Prime Minister to his ducal master. His last illness, brought on by the difficulties of the troupe's second Russian tour (1890), ended the Meiningen's activities, since the aging Duke decided that without Chronegk's aid his work would no longer be possible. ROBERT TRACY

CIBBER. (1) COLLEY (1671–1757), English actor, theatre manager, and playwright, now chiefly remembered for his *Apology for the Life of Mr. Colley Cibber, Comedian*, published in 1740, and for its admirable descriptions of Restoration actors. The son of a Danish sculptor who had settled in England, Cibber was well educated and went on the stage in 1690 against the wishes of his family. He had few advantages of voice or person, but quickly improved and became an excellent comedian, particularly in the fops of Restoration comedy and of his own plays. The needs of a young family turned his thoughts to playwriting, and in 1696 his first play, *Love's Last Shift; or, the Fool in Fashion*, was given at Drury Lane with some success. Striking a happy balance between the Restoration comedy of manners and the new vogue for sentiment and morality, this is now considered the first sentimental comedy, and undoubtedly influenced Steele and Farquhar, as well as setting the pattern for Cibber's later plays. It is also worthy of note in that it inspired the young Vanbrugh to write *The Relapse*, where the elegant fop Sir Novelty Fashion becomes in Vanbrugh's hands the cynical rake Lord Foppington, a part which Cibber played brilliantly, thus establishing his reputation as an actor. Among his later plays the best was *The Careless Husband* (1704), of which it has been said 'it played an important part in the development of sentimental comedy . . . and helped to fix standards of gentility and politeness which were profoundly to influence comic writing throughout most of the eighteenth century'. With this, and the earlier *She Would and She Would Not; or, the Kind Imposter* (1702)—revived as late as 1886 by Daly in New York, with Ada Rehan and John Drew—Cibber achieved a reputation for the writing of scenes of high life, which are, however, found to be somewhat spurious when compared with those of Congreve. A snob and a social climber, Cibber was only on the fringe of the society he strove to depict, yet for a hundred years his comedies were taken as representative of English high society. His tragedies were mostly failures, but he achieved success with his famous adaptation of *Richard III* (1700), which remained the standard acting text, in Europe and later in America, until well into the nineteenth century, and with his adaptation of Molière's *Tartuffe* as *The Non-Juror* (1717). Cibber chose to think that it was his championship of the Hanoverian cause in this latter play that brought him the coveted position of Poet Laureate in 1730; but the general opinion seems to have been that it was due to his friendship with great men, and to a certain flat facility in the composition of state verse which was happily lacking in greater poets. The appointment caused no little dismay, in spite of the fact that Cibber's predecessors had included Shadwell, Tate, and Rowe, none of whom was a poet.

The greater part of Colley Cibber's life was spent at Drury Lane. He early insinuated himself into the good graces of the miserly and eccentric Christopher Rich, and later became one of the triumvirate which ruled the fortunes of the theatre—with Doggett and Wilks. This establishment of the actor-manager was not very successful, and Cibber spent most of his time trying to keep the peace between his co-partners, until the arrival of Barton Booth drove Doggett out (see DRURY LANE). Cibber himself, though the theatre prospered under him, and he was instrumental in accepting a number of good new plays—choosing them always for their theatrical effectiveness rather than their literary merit—was unpopular, and for so eminent and in many ways able a man had remarkably few friends. He was tactless, rude to minor actors and playwrights, supremely self-confident, and given to posing as an expert on subjects of which he knew little. He was savagely ridiculed by critics of the time, by Pope in *The Dunciad*, by Dr. Johnson, and by Fielding in several of his plays and again in the opening chapter of *Joseph Andrews*. He was a competent rather than an inspired playwright, good at doctoring other men's plays, and his methods can best be studied in his completion of Vanbrugh's unfinished *Journey to London*, which was produced at Drury Lane in 1728 as *The Provoked Husband*, with Anne Oldfield, the greatest actress of Cibber's period, as Lady Townley.

Cibber married young and had several children, of whom two went on the stage. His son (2) THEOPHILUS (1703–58) was born in one storm and died in another, being drowned in the Irish Sea on his way to act at the Smock Alley Theatre, Dublin. He was a wild and eccentric character, who went on the stage at 16, and seemed as if he might have the making of a good actor, especially in such parts as Ancient Pistol. But his imprudences and extravagant manner of living were his undoing. He was for some time co-manager of Drury Lane in succession to his father, but soon forfeited all claim to respect by his insolence and complacency, while the scandal of his second marriage drove him eventually from London. Having first married an actress who died young, he took as his second wife in 1734 the sister of Dr. Arne, (3) SUSANNA MARIA (1714–66), who was then known as a singer at the Haymarket. The elder Cibber, however, saw in her the makings of a good tragic actress, and coached her to such effect that she appeared in 1736 in *Zara* with much success. Unfortunately her husband embroiled her with the other ladies of the company by trying to take for her the part of Polly in *The Beggar's Opera*, hitherto the perquisite of Kitty Clive. He then, to escape his creditors, allowed her to be drawn into an intimacy with one John Sloper in return for substantial payments, all three living together in London until Theophilus was able to withdraw to France. The outcome of this affair was an unsavoury lawsuit which drove Mrs. Cibber from the stage for some years, and caused Sloper to retire to the country under an assumed name. Theophilus continued to appear in minor parts for a while, but gradually sank to the status of a hack-writer, without losing any of his effrontery and self-confidence. His wife later returned to the stage with some success, and was for a long time at Drury Lane with Garrick, who said, when he heard of her death, 'Then tragedy has expired on one side.' Though at her best in tragedy, she was sometimes seen in comedy, and her last part was that of Lady Brute in *The Provoked Wife*. She was buried in the Cloisters in Westminster Abbey.

One of Colley Cibber's daughters, (4) CHARLOTTE (1713–*c.* 1760), had her full share of her family's eccentricity, and made herself extremely conspicuous in London. She was intensely masculine and scorned all pursuits except hunting and shooting, spending most of her time in the company of the stable-boys. Married at 16 to Richard Charke, a violinist at Drury Lane, in the hope of taming her, and widowed in 1737 (Charke died in Jamaica), she went on the stage, quarrelled with the managers, and ran away, communicating with her family from time to time in order to borrow money from them. She disguised herself as a man, acted men's and women's parts indifferently in strolling companies, was a conjuror's assistant in Petticoat Lane, a puppet-master, a performer at fairs, and kept a tavern in Drury Lane. She published a remarkable *Narrative of the Life of Mrs. Charlotte Charke*. Odell believed that the Mrs. Harman who acted in New York towards the end of her life and was buried in Trinity Churchyard there, in 1773, was a daughter of Charlotte Charke. One of Theophilus's daughters by his first marriage was also on the stage for a short time, but with no great success.

CICOGNINI, GIACINTO ANDREA (1606–60), Italian dramatist, a prolific and popular provider of theatrical fare in the seventeenth century. He was much influenced by the Spanish theatre, which had come into Italy by way of Naples, where, under a Spanish viceroy, the plays of Lope de Vega and Calderón were frequently performed by visiting Spanish companies. Cicognini, who is credited with over forty compositions, of which perhaps only half were really his own, is also believed to have been the first Italian dramatist to handle the legend of Don Juan (for further details on Cicognini, see ITALY, 1 *b*).

CINQUEVALLI, PAUL (1859–1918), probably the greatest juggler the music-halls ever knew. He juggled with anything, from cannon balls to billiard balls, with equal skill, and was top of the bill for over twenty years. A Pole by birth, he was unjustly accused of German sympathies during the First World War and this, preying on his mind, is believed to have caused his death.

CINTHIO, IL, see GIRALDI.

CIRCLE-IN-THE-SQUARE, NEW YORK. In 1950 the Loft Players of Woodstock, N.Y., leased the former Greenwich Village Inn at 5 Sheridan Square, and under the direction of José Quintero, in association with Theodore Mann and Emilie Stevens, opened it as the Circle-in-the-Square for arena productions. In Mar. 1954 it was closed by the Fire Department as a fire hazard, but on 1 June 1955, after adequate safety measures had been taken, it reopened, and became one of New York's most popular off-Broadway theatres. Its first production, on 1 Dec. 1950, was *Dark of the Moon*, followed by *Summer and Smoke*, in which Geraldine Page had a great success, *The Girl on the Via Flaminia*, *The Grass Harp*, *Yerma*, and *The Cradle Song*. In 1956 it gave a production of *The Iceman Cometh*, with Jason Robards, jr., directed by Quintero, which, in the opinion of some critics, was superior to the original Theatre Guild production of 1946. In 1960 the demolition of their building forced the company to move to a new home at 159 Bleecker Street (a remodelled music-hall), where they opened with Genêt's *The Balcony*, and have since done *Under Milk Wood*, by Dylan Thomas, and Wilder's *Three Plays for Bleecker Street* (1962). GEORGE FREEDLEY

CIRCUIT, see PROVINCIAL THEATRES, 1 *b*.

CIRCUS, in Roman times a place of exhibition for chariot-racing and athletic contests. In its modern sense a circus is an entertainment of a particular kind, which lies outside the scope of this book. It is cosmopolitan and itinerant (though Europe has some permanent circuses), and is performed in the central area of a tent (known as the Big Top) or in the arena of a building specially adapted to its needs. Its programme is built up of separate turns, mainly featuring performing animals or acrobatics, loosely correlated by the antics of the Clown or Auguste. Owing to the specialized nature of their work, circus performers tend to remain a class apart, with much intermarrying. The great names of the American circus are Barnum and Sand, of the English Sanger and Bertram Mills; but the circus is universal and, since it places little dependence on the spoken word, can be at home anywhere. Its history is fully documented, and a list of books in which further information can be found is given in the Bibliography.

There was, however, a time in the late eighteenth and early nineteenth centuries when stage and circus mingled. Philip Astley, who is credited with introducing the circus to England, opened in 1770 an Amphitheatre in which both theatrical performances and displays of horsemanship were given. They were apparently kept separate, however, and it was not until the early years of the nineteenth century that Equestrian Drama, as it was called, became popular. As the spectacular side of the theatre increased in these years, so the employment of horses, and even lions, became more general. *Richard III* offered an admirable claimant for fame in the person of Richard's horse, White Surrey, but horses could be, and were, introduced everywhere, even into *Macbeth.* Two famous equestrian dramas were *Mazeppa* and *Dick Turpin's Ride to York*, but horses were used most effectively in such melodramas as *Timour the Tartar* and *The Blood-Red Knight.* The invasion was not confined to the minor theatres, but attacked Drury Lane and Covent Garden. They also succumbed to a further innovation which came from the circuses of Paris, the Aquatic Drama. For this the stage was flooded, and fine mimic sea-fights took place, particularly in plays based on the victories of Lord Nelson. The use of an entire menagerie in *Hyder Ali; or, the Lions of Mysore* also connected the theatre with the circus in its widest sense, as did the sudden craze for Dog Drama which swept England and America in the nineteenth century. This probably had its origin—though there had of course been performing dogs before—in a little afterpiece at Drury Lane where a real dog, Carlos, effected a rescue from a tank of water. The most famous Dog Drama, however, was written by Pixerécourt in 1814, and given in several English versions as *The Dog of Montargis*, or *The Forest of Bondy.* It is said that the Duke of Weimar's insistence on seeing a German version of this play, with a performing poodle, caused Goethe's retirement from the Court theatre in disgust. There can be no doubt that the admixture of circus with theatrical elements had a bad influence on the drama, and that both are far better when confined to their separate spheres.

CITÉ, THÉÂTRE DE LA, PARIS, a large playhouse for spectacle and music built during the French Revolution. It opened as the Palais-Variétés on 20 Oct. 1792, but failed to achieve its purpose and devoted itself mainly to broad farce and pantomime, one of its most popular actors being Brunet. It took the name Cité in 1793, became a circus, reopened as a theatre in 1800 under Saint-Aubin, and passed from hand to hand with constant changes of name until in 1807 it closed. It later became a famous dance hall known as Prado.

CITIZEN HOUSE, BATH, founded as a resident Community Art Centre by Councillor Helen Hope, J.P., of Bath, was also a pioneer force in the development of community and institutional drama. Its Little Theatre, founded in 1913 by Miss Consuelo de Reyes, who controlled it till her death in 1948, began in a lecture room, but is now housed in its own building, complete with simplified theatre equipment which makes ample provision for the courses in acting and production which are a feature of its activities. There is also an open-air theatre. A fine theatrical library and museum, a collection of costumes which may be borrowed for group productions (some unfortunately lost in 1944 by fire), and an advisory bureau dealing with all aspects of community drama make up a comprehensive service at the disposal of those concerned with drama whether in schools, colleges, institutions, clubs, or local societies. In 1930, hoping to establish a permanent centre in London, Citizen House purchased the Everyman Theatre, Hampstead. This was used for vacation courses in dramatic art, and for productions by amateurs attending the courses, but was later sold. After Miss de Reyes' death the work of Citizen House continued under her husband, Peter King, and Marion Radford.

CITIZENS' THEATRE, see GLASGOW.

CITY CENTER, NEW YORK. This opened in 1943 for the provision of theatrical entertainment at prices within the reach of all, and since its inception, in spite of the lack of any endowment or official grant, it has managed to maintain its policy of cheap seats, both in New York and on tour. The building, in midtown Manhattan (formerly the Mecca Temple, headquarters of the Masonic Shriners), is owned by the city and leased for $1 a year. Of the three companies—for grand opera, ballet, and light opera—which functioned for fixed seasons each year, the ballet company has now migrated to the New York State Theatre at the Lincoln Center (where musicals under Richard Rodgers are also given), but the other companies will continue at the City Center in addition to the programmes at the Lincoln Center.

CITY OF LONDON THEATRE. This stood in Norton Folgate, adjoining Bishopsgate. It was built by Beazley, architect of the Lyceum, and opened on 27 Mar. 1837 under the management of Cockerton with a version of *Pickwick* by Edward Stirling. In 1837 Mrs. Honey, a popular actress, appeared there in *Don Juan*, with Miss Pincott [Mrs. Alfred Wigan] also in the cast. In the same year Mrs. Honey became manageress. In 1838 Osbaldiston succeeded her and ran the theatre for three years. Then Cockerton returned, with Shepherd (afterwards at the Surrey) as his partner and Nelson Lee as his dramatist. In 1846 Mr. and Mrs. Honnor appeared there in Shakespeare and other plays, of which *The Battle of Life*, based on Dickens, was a success. The palmiest days of this theatre came in 1848 under Nelson Lee and Johnson, who controlled it for many years with great success and made it well known. These two men had succeeded Richardson in his famous booth, or portable theatre, and knew their business. They worked on cheap prices—the gallery was threepence and the pit sixpence—and they gave good value for money. Nelson Lee's pantomimes were a great attraction. When the Patent Theatres' rights were broken many leading actors and actresses visited the City of

London. Constance Loseby made a very early appearance there. When Nelson Lee retired the place began to decline, though Sarah Thorne was there in 1867, and Burton's Christy Minstrels later in the same year. By 1868 the house had fallen to a lowly position, and the land on which the stage stood being required for an extension of the railway, the theatre closed. The auditorium became a soup kitchen and later a Temperance Hall.

W. MACQUEEN-POPE†

CITY MUSIC-HALL, LONDON. This was originally the Dr. Johnson public-house and supper-room, a most popular place of entertainment in Bolt Court, Fleet Street. It was noted for the excellence of its brown beer, chops, kidneys, and oysters, and for the high standard of the entertainment offered to its patrons while they ate and drank. It closed in 1863. W. MACQUEEN-POPE†

CITY PANTHEON, LONDON, see CITY THEATRE, 2.

CITY THEATRE. 1. NEW YORK, a small playhouse at 15 Warren Street, which was opened on 2 July 1822 by Mrs. Baldwin. This lady, with her husband, her sister Mrs. Barnes, and her brother-in-law, left England in 1816 and became a member of the company at the Park Theatre, where she was first seen as Juliet's nurse, and later as Mrs. Malaprop. Unfortunately her first season at the City Theatre was stopped by an outbreak of yellow fever, and though for her second season she engaged Hilson and other good actors, she never recovered from her initial setback, and the theatre closed in 1823. GEORGE FREEDLEY

2. LONDON, a disused chapel in Grub Street, E.C. (later Milton Street), which in 1829–30 was converted into a theatre. Its name was afterwards changed to the City Pantheon. John Bedford, a popular comedian, was its first manager, and was succeeded by Chapman. Edmund Kean played there in 1831, and in the same year Ellen Tree and James Vining appeared in *Eily O'Connor*, a play based on Griffin's novel *The Collegians*, which supplied Boucicault with the foundation of his successful *Colleen Bawn*. *Love in a Village* and *Black-Eyed Susan* were also given there with excellent casts. In 1831 Chapman retired in favour of Davidge, and a working arrangement was come to with the Coburg (later the Old Vic) by which the same companies appeared at both theatres, being taken to and fro in hackney coaches. Harriet Smithson, who married Berlioz, appeared at the theatre in 1832, *The Rake* was produced there, and, with Webster as manager, Mrs. Waylett starred there. Moncrieff the dramatist also ran it for a while, selling tickets off the premises to evade the Patent Act. It was last used as a theatre in 1836, and then became a warehouse. W. MACQUEEN-POPE†

3. NEW YORK, in the upper part of the City Saloon on Broadway. It opened on 13 July 1837 under the management of J. J. Adams, with Joseph Cowell as Crack, his famous part in *The Turnpike Gate*. Cowell had not been seen in New York for nine years, but in spite of a good supporting company and a repertory of popular plays, the venture soon failed.

CIVIC REPERTORY THEATRE, NEW YORK, see LE GALLIENNE, EVA.

CIVIC THEATRES IN GREAT BRITAIN. There are in Great Britain over a hundred theatres, or halls used primarily for entertainment, which are owned by local authorities. About two-thirds of these are in holiday resorts and operate on a commercial basis, providing entertainment during the holiday season only. Most of the buildings date from before the Second World War, but more recent examples are the De La Warr Pavilion at Bexhill-on-Sea, which has a resident repertory company, and the Princess Theatre, Torquay, which offers a variety of programmes.

The term 'civic theatres' is applied generally, and rather loosely, to the remaining theatres, about thirty in number, which are distinguished by the fact that they enjoy, in varying degrees, support from local public funds. The campaign for civic theatres developed before and during the Second World War, and received precise expression in the *Memorandum on Civic Theatres*, prepared by a Special Committee of the British Drama League, appointed in 1942. This recommended, among other things, that theatres in the provinces, built or rented for the purpose, should be managed by local trusts (as charitable organizations), and should be subsidized out of local government funds in order to present a repertoire of classical, contemporary, and new plays. Clause 132 of the Local Government Act of 1948 empowered the local authority to provide entertainment 'of any nature' in premises 'suitable for the giving of entertainment' (which may be a theatre, concert hall, or dance hall), subject to a maximum expenditure of the proceeds of a sixpenny rate. Prior to the 1963 revaluation, this amounted to about £16 million annually, but in 1962, for instance, no more than £2½ million was spent on entertainment, with music, traditionally, the major recipient. Moreover, there is still no 'civic theatre' which conforms to the original specifications. Those that are so called vary widely in background and purpose, and the distinction between them and the municipal theatres run commercially is not always clear. In some important respects the original objectives have been realized in the Chichester Festival Theatre, but this is not generally accepted as a civic theatre, although it is managed by a local Trust, presents a season of 'true repertory' and is built on land for which the local authority accepts a pepper-corn rent. However the 'civic theatre' is regarded as having a closer connexion with civic enterprise in the field of entertainment than is the case at Chichester.

So far as the theatre is concerned, the activities of the local authority cover assistance to theatre organizations, chiefly repertory companies, and the acquisition or building of theatres, either to provide facilities for existing theatre organizations, or as part of their own entertainments programme. Of the fifty-five repertory companies in Great Britain in 1962, one-third were housed in municipally-owned theatres. For the most part they are responsible for their own artistic direction, but they may receive subsidies from the local authority, as may those companies in privately-owned theatres. These subsidies, however, are usually given as an emergency measure rather than as part of a considered policy for theatre development. Companies housed in civic theatres often receive special terms as tenants while still retaining their artistic independence. Theatres of this kind include the Cheltenham Everyman*, Chesterfield Civic, Colchester Repertory, Glasgow Citizens', Harrogate Opera House*, Leicester Phoenix, Northampton Repertory, St. Andrews Byre, and York Royal.

Direct provision of entertainment by an authority may take the form of a civic centre with buildings to house entertainments of various kinds, including a theatre. Several such centres have been proposed—in Birmingham, for instance, and in Glasgow—but the only one so far in operation is at Croydon, where the new Fairfield Halls provide for art, music, and theatre. A General Administrator appointed by the local authority is in charge, but the Ashcroft Theatre has its own Director. Other civic theatres directly managed by the local authority for general entertainment purposes, which may include visits or even seasons by repertory companies, are the Bradford Alhambra, Bristol Little*, Cardiff New*, Chelmsford Civic Centre, Crewe New, Luton Library, Malvern Festival, Manchester Library, Rotherham Civic, Scarborough Library, Scunthorpe Civic and Sunderland Empire*. The last is also an example of intervention by a local authority to save a theatre threatened with demolition. Others preserved in this way are also marked with an asterisk.

Of special interest among civic theatres, not only because it is a new theatre built by a local authority, but also because of its organization, is the Belgrade Theatre, Coventry. It is managed by a Trust appointed by the local authority, and is supported by local funds. It has, however, a policy of fortnightly runs. More recently, the Nottingham Playhouse, also built and revived by the local authority, presents a repertoire. Other civic theatres managed by Trusts with strong local-authority interest are those of Hull New*, Watford Palace*, and Bristol Old Vic (Theatre Royal)*. A Trust is also concerned with restoring the Georgian Theatre* in Richmond, Yorkshire, and another will operate the restored Theatre Royal* in Bury St. Edmunds. These theatres, like Chichester, are not owned by the local authority. Ownership of a building is not essential to the provision of theatre as a cultural amenity supported by public funds, but by building its own theatre the local authority can ensure that it is the best of its kind, and suitably serviced. It may also help in retaining a controlling interest even if a local trust is set up. As the number of civic theatres increases—they are already envisaged by more than 30 other local authorities—the idea of a 'civic theatre' may become clearer. At the moment there is no basis of agreement on its form and purpose, on its relation to the repertory movement, on the provision of a repertoire, or even on the role of civic entertainment itself (see also PROVINCIAL THEATRES, REPERTORY, and THEATRE PRESERVATION).

WILLIAM KENDALL

For civic theatres in the United States, see UNITED STATES OF AMERICA, 10.

CLAIRON, CLAIRE-JOSÈPHE-HIPPOLYTE LÉRIS (Leyris) DE LA TUDE (1723–1803), outstanding French actress. She was the daughter of a sempstress and, according to her own memoirs, which are not very reliable, had a hard childhood. At 12 she showed signs of precocious ability, and joined the troupe of the Comédie-Italienne, where she played minor roles for a year or so before going to La Noue at Rouen. Later she developed a fine singing voice, and in 1743 went to the Opéra. But her real talent was for acting, and she was transferred to the Comédie-Française to understudy Mlle Dangeville. When asked, as was customary, to choose the role for her début, she horrified the entire company by demanding to play the title-role in Racine's *Phèdre*, in which at that time Mlle Dumesnil excelled. Thinking she would fail, and that the lesson would be salutary, they allowed her to tackle it. Her performance on 19 Sept. 1743 was a triumph, and led to her being entrusted with important tragic roles. Contemporary accounts show that her first appearances were hailed everywhere with acclamation, particularly by Voltaire, in many of whose plays she was destined to appear. This early success did not, however, prevent her from studying her parts with fervour and determination. With the great actor Lekain, also a protégé of Voltaire, she was responsible for introducing some much-needed modifications into the contemporary costumes worn on the stage for any and every play, mainly by adding some historical note in keeping with the character she portrayed. The time was not yet ripe for complete historical accuracy, but she made a tentative step towards it, and also, on the good advice of Marmontel, abandoned in about 1753 her somewhat stiff and declamatory style of acting for a freer and more natural method. The naturally tragic depth of her voice prevented her from lapsing into triviality, and the new departure was a success. In 1765 Clairon, with Lekain and other members of the Comédie-Française, was imprisoned for quite rightly refusing to play with an actor who had brought disgrace on the company, and after this did not return to the theatre. Instead she took refuge with Voltaire at Ferney, and acted in his private theatre there. On her return to Paris she retired from public life and appeared only in private theatricals and at Court. She was 50 when she went by invitation to the Court of the Margrave of Anspach, and it was there that she wrote her *Mémoires et réflexions sur l'art dramatique*. On the outbreak of the Revolution her pension ceased and, the Margrave also dying about this time, Clairon found herself almost penniless. She returned to Paris, where she remained until her death, living on the proceeds of her book, published in 1799. Among her pupils were Larive and Mlle Raucourt. Garrick, on a visit to Paris in 1764, saw and admired Clairon, though there is apparently no reason to believe that they were intimately acquainted.

CLARENCE THEATRE, LONDON, see PANHARMONIUM.

CLARK, HUGH (?–1653), English actor who was probably apprenticed to the stage as a child, since he played the leading feminine roles in *The Wedding* (1626) and *The Fair Maid of the West* (1630), in between which he appears to have got married. A few years later he was playing men's parts, and transferred from the Queen's Men to the King's, with whom he signed the dedication of the Beaumont and Fletcher folio in 1647.

CLARKE, JOHN SLEEPER (1833–99), American actor, who made his début in 1851 at Boston, became the principal comedian at Baltimore, and was joint lessee of the Arch Street Theatre, Philadelphia. With Edwin Booth, whose sister he married, he managed several theatres. He was first seen in London in Oct. 1867, and in 1872 opened the Charing Cross Theatre. He later took over the Haymarket and the Strand, appearing in all three theatres under his own management. Two of his sons were on the stage.

CLAUDEL, PAUL (1868–1955), French poet-dramatist, whose work has, owing to the devotion of his many enthusiastic admirers, been performed in many countries. He was born in Picardy, but later went to Paris, where he was a disciple of Mallarmé. He joined the French consular and diplomatic service, and at 24 went to America, where he seems to have come under the influence of Walt Whitman. The scene of *L'Échange*, one of his earliest plays, is 'America: The East Coast'. While in China he wrote his *Grandes Odes*. In 1908 he was appointed French consul at Prague, and held similar posts in German cities until the summer of 1914. He was appointed French Ambassador at Tokyo in 1921, at Washington in 1927, and at Brussels in 1933. His earlier publications were anonymous; their ardent Catholicism might have proved damaging at that time to his career. Little, in fact, was known of his plays until the Théâtre de l'Œuvre staged *L'Annonce faite à Marie* in Paris in 1912. This was followed by *L'Échange*—written in 1893—at the Vieux-Colombier. When these plays were given in Germany they excited enthusiasm among the reformers of theatrical presentation. The Little Theatres of the United States also gave a number of Claudel performances. The first in London were directed by Edith Craig, whose Pioneer Players gave *Exchange* at the Little Theatre on 2 May 1915; she was also responsible for a performance of *The Tidings brought to Mary* at the Strand the following year, and for *The Hostage*, a translation of *L'Otage*—the most theatrically effective of Claudel's dramas—at the Scala in 1919, when the heroine, Synge du Coûfontaine, became one of the outstanding achievements of Sybil Thorndike's career. Among Claudel's other works are *Le Pain dur, Le Père humilié*, and the best-known, *Le Soulier de satin*. This was written between 1919–24, but was not performed until 1943, when it was done at the Comédie-Française. It was translated by John O'Connor as *The Satin Slipper*. After the outbreak of war in 1939 Ludmilla Pitoëff, who had played in many of Claudel's plays in Paris, took them to Canada and America, where they were well received. Claudel needs audiences that are familiar with his work before they come to the theatre—a demand more easily satisfied in French- than in English-speaking countries, where published translations are scarce as yet. *The Tidings brought to Mary*, the first and for a long time the only one available, has now been joined by *The Hostage, Crusts*, and *The Humiliation of the Father* (1946), in translations by John Heard. Shortly before Claudel's death *L'Annonce faite à Marie* was seen at the Comédie-Française (see No. 110). Recently Claudel's plays have achieved even greater popularity, mainly owing to their presentation by the Renaud–Barrault company, who did *L'Échange, Partage de midi*, and *Christophe Colomb* at the Marigny Theatre in Paris. The last two were seen in London during their seasons there in 1951 (at the St. James's) and 1956 (at the Palace) respectively. *Jeanne d'Arc au Bûcher*, with music by Honegger, was first performed at Basle in 1938 with Ida Rubinstein as Joan; in 1954 Ingrid Bergmann played the part in London. *L'Histoire de Tobie et de Sara*, written for Ida Rubinstein, and first performed at Hamburg, was given in French for the first time at the Avignon Festival in 1947, in a production by Jean Vilar. Five years later it was again given, in a German translation, at the Schauspielhaus, Zürich. Like so many of Claudel's plays, it has been revised and rewritten several times. Other plays which have been seen in Paris are *Le Pain dur* and *Protée*, a lyric farce with music by Darius Milhaud, who also wrote the music for *Christophe Colomb*.

CLAXTON, KATE (1848–1924), American actress, who made her début at Chicago in 1869, after which she joined Lotta on tour. From 1870 to 1873 she was a member of Daly's company at his Fifth Avenue Theatre. In 1874 she scored an outstanding success as Louise, the blind girl in *The Two Orphans*, a melodrama adapted from the French, and for the rest of her life she was identified with this part, which she acted all over the United States. She was appearing in it at the Brooklyn Theatre in 1876 when the latter was destroyed by fire, with the loss of 200 lives. In fact, she was connected with so many theatres that burned down when she was playing in them that she became known as 'the fire jinx', and many managers would not engage her for this reason, although she had a good public following. ROBERT DOWNING

CLEANDER, a Greek actor associated with Aeschylus.

CLIFTON, HARRY (1832–72), a music-hall singer of 'motto' songs of unimpeachable respectability and moral fervour, which were as popular in Victorian drawing-rooms as on the halls, especially 'Pulling Hard against the Stream', 'Work, Boys, Work', and 'Paddle Your Own Canoe'. He also sang comic songs, of which 'The Weepin' Willer', written by himself, is the best known.

CLIVE, KITTY [CATHERINE RAFTOR] (1711–85), English actress, who though not strictly beautiful was so charming and animated that she achieved a great reputation in the playing of high-spirited comedy and farce. She was early attracted to the stage and at 17 appeared under Colley Cibber at Drury Lane in minor parts. She first charmed the audience by her singing, and by 1731 was established as an actress, her first outstanding success being as Phillida in Cibber's *Love in a Riddle* in 1729. She married in 1732 a barrister named George Clive, but the marriage soon broke up, though merely through incompatibility, and no scandal ever attached itself to her name. Most of her career was spent at Drury Lane, where she and Garrick, with much admiration for each other's powers, were nevertheless constantly at loggerheads, and she is said to have been the only actress of whose temper Garrick stood in awe. She was passionate and vulgar, but always generous and quite without pride or ostentation. Her one fault was a constant desire to appear in tragedy, or even in genteel comedy, for which she was quite unfitted. Her excellence in low comedy, and in burlesques of Italian opera, endeared her so much to the public that they were willing to tolerate her as Portia, though she burlesqued the Trial Scene by mimicking famous lawyers of the day. But as Zara and Ophelia she was less successful, and much of her animosity against Garrick came from his preventing her appearing in such unsuitable parts. One of her great admirers was Horace Walpole, who on her retirement in 1769 presented her with a small house —Clive's-Den—on Strawberry Hill, where her company and conversation were much relished by his friends, particularly Dr. Johnson. Kitty Clive was frequently painted, notably by Hogarth, and was the author of several short farces.

CLOAK-AND-SWORD PLAYS (*Comedias de capa y espada*), the name given to a type of Spanish drama which has often mistakenly been assumed to be characteristic of the whole. Contemporary writers divide seventeenth-century plays written for performance in the public theatres into two main categories: machine plays (*comedias de tramoyas*, or *de apariencias*, or, more expressively, *comedias de ruido*), and plays of wit (*comedias de ingenio*), that is to say, plays which do not depend for their appeal upon spectacle but upon the nature of their intrigue. Of this latter category the *comedia de capa y espada* is a subdivision. As its name implies, the characters often wore cloak and sword; with the former they disguised themselves and thus introduced the necessary complications into the plot, and with the latter they fought the duels which inevitably resulted. The term comes, therefore, to be applied to any play of intrigue. Nineteenth-century dramatists found a great attraction in this type of play, which is often taken to mean any sort of romantic costume play with a strong love interest and a certain amount of sword-play.

J. E. VAREY

CLOSET DRAMA, see PLAY and ROME, 2.

CLOTH, a term used for any large unframed expanse of canvas or material used for scenery. A modern cloth is generally made of widths of canvas, seamed horizontally together, and attached at top and bottom to a sandwich batten, or one formed of two lengths of 4×1 in. timber, screwed together with the cloth between. A Cut-cloth is one with cut openings. The shape of the opening, if it is elaborately fretted, may need the reinforcement of a piece of netting, glued on behind. A Gauze-cloth is used for special effects, and consists of an unbroken stretch of fine net, which appears opaque when lit from the front, but transparent, almost to vanishing point, when lit from behind. Such a cloth can be painted in dye to appear as a normal cloth.

A distant cousin of the hanging cloth is the Stage-cloth, which is an expanse of painted canvas, not attached to battens but laid on the stage as a floor covering. It is painted a plain colour, or patterned to suit a scene, and further and self-describing varieties of it are known, such as Sand-cloth, for desert and other scenes.

A variant of the framed cloth is the Ceiling, a canvas stretch battened out and suspended flat over the top of the Box Set.

RICHARD SOUTHERN

CLOUDINGS, a term formerly applied to cloud borders, which were used to mask the top of almost any scene. They could be drawn off sideways by hooked poles, and are mentioned as late as 1743. The detail of their arrangement is not clear, but they recall the form of border used by Inigo Jones in his last masque, *Salmacida Spolia* (1640). This had not only 'the Clouds of ye heaven which went crosse ye sceane', and were like the modern cloud border, but also, at either end of each of these, to left and right, further independent 'peeces of Clouds which came downe from ye roofe before ye upper part of ye syde shutters whereby ye grooues aboue were hidden and also ye howse behind them'. The sectional drawing of the stage for this masque, preserved in the Lansdowne manuscripts in the British Museum, shows these to have been deeper than the borders proper, turning them into a species of arch. These 'side-clouds' were not left unchanged throughout the show as were the borders themselves, for 'these Clouds also' (like the shutters) 'went in grooues . . . and changed with ye sceanes below'. They could presumably be slid off sideways to reveal a second set behind, thus transforming a stormy sky into a calm sky, or vice versa.

RICHARD SOUTHERN

CLOWN is not as simple as he looks. No other stage figure has such complexity. 'Clod, clot, lump' explains his origin in the unconscious humour of the village idiot and in representations of this upon the stage. Just as the natural fool of real life could become the hired jester of entertainments, so the clown has always tended to be both the part and the player, which is merely one of his peculiarities among *dramatis personae*. This overlapping of life and art creates such legendary figures as Harlequin, Pierrot, Joey, and Auguste, whose gradual metamorphosis from humble butts into idols of the motley, and thence into glamorous immortals, affords a curious insight into the workings of mass imagination. Their evolution reveals in its stages the chief types of clowns, (*a*) the simpleton, such as the one upon whom Shakespeare bestows his own Christian name in *As You Like It*, (*b*) the knave, who is usually more temperate in his habits than Punch in the puppet-show, though this is his apotheosis, (*c*) the jester or professional fool, like Touchstone, invested in his motley and given leave to speak his mind, (*d*) the transcendental spirit of mirth, such ghosts of departed clowns as Harlequin. Encounters between knave and butt occur throughout the history of clowning, notably in the tricks played by the Vice upon the Devil in the religious drama of the Middle Ages. The triple partnership whereby the butt vainly tries to delude the jester with the tricks of the knave is a modern convention.

'Merry Andrew', one of the earliest nicknames for clowns in England, was derived from Andrew Borde, an ex-Carthusian monk whose amusing *Breviare of Health* was published in 1547. Thomas Heywood, court jester of Henry VIII, wrote comic interludes now studied as foundations of the drama. Richard Tarleton, first clown of the professional theatre in England, kept the Tabard in Southwark, where the young Shakespeare may have seen this fellow of infinite jest set the table on a roar. William Kempe was clown and shareholder of the Globe. Because he left the company for a time the unflattering portrait of a clown in the First Quarto, omitted in all other versions of *Hamlet*, is supposed to be his. The scene between clown and musicians in *Romeo and Juliet*, staged before he left, resembles the scene between clown and musicians in *Othello*, staged at the time of his return. In *The Travels of Three English Brothers* (1607) he appears under his own name to flout a dolt from Italy—Harlequin on his arrival in English drama. Here begins the long struggle between the British idea of individual humour and the foreign delight in perpetuated type. Harlequin was known merely as clown to travelling mountebanks who sold quack nostrums, and was so represented in the masque of *Britannia Triumphans* at Whitehall in 1637. The Italians triumphed when Tiberio Fiorillo played Scaramouche in London in 1673, and this braggart in black was the first figure of the *commedia dell'arte* to acclimatize the pattern of mirth in this country. In *Scaramouche a Philosopher, Harlequin a Schoolboy, Bravo, Merchant and Magician*, staged at Drury Lane four years later, Harlequin was a simpleton, mocked and beaten even by infants, and yet before the end he caused his opponents to hit each other when aiming blows at him—which indicates how the butt inevitably turns into the knave. As the change progressed another butt had to be provided—another clown hatched from a clod. Either Pierrot or 'a farmer's man' served the purpose, while Harlequin, imitating Dominique's Arlequin in Paris, took on the graces of a dancer. Comparison between his English and French evolutions is instructive. The sentimental Arlequin of Marivaux at last became the insipidly moral, impeccably respectable Arlequin of Florian's comedies for the propagation of domestic virtue under Louis XVI. John Rich (who billed himself at Lincoln's Inn Fields and Covent Garden as 'Lun') kept Harlequin's rascality alive while representing him in dance and dumbshow as a lover and a magician, until the vogue of virtue affected him also; in the Christmas pantomimes of England henceforward there was nothing to laugh at in Harlequin. Pierrot became the chief character of these harlequinades when he was played by Delpini, an Italian who gave him the stamp of the over-grown schoolboy which English audiences have always loved. Dubois, his humble rival, added colour to the costume, and shortened legs and sleeves in a compromise with the motley of the Merry Andrew. Hitherto Pantaloon's blundering servant had been either Pierrot or a ragged yokel (a clown in the older sense), but this mongrel had an overwhelming popularity when played by Joseph Grimaldi. The new character took Clown as his proper name, and was affectionately called Joey. In his acrobatic heyday his costume was spare; his wig was a single crest like that on the helmets, fashioned after an antique style, of the Household Cavalry. Changes in his appearance reflected changes in his character. In rebellion against the vogue of virtue he was villainous; he persecuted true love and had all the mentionable vices—particularly gluttony, covetousness, drunkenness, avarice, vanity, craft, and cruelty. His trunks were widened by pockets for stolen food, and his wig became triple-tufted, each with a frozen pigtail like the one worn by his master. Pantaloon was now the butt and Clown the knave—more cunning even than Punch, whom he outwitted when they met in the puppet-show at street-corners. Joey now had an existence outside the harlequinade where he was born. He was still in his prime when Grimaldi retired and bequeathed the part to his son, and when both were dead the harlequinade existed solely as the vehicle for his pranks. In modified forms—wearing a conical cap for juggling—but still called Clown and Joey, he was the pet of circuses in all lands, until metamorphosis overtook him. The affection lavished upon him transformed him first into the 'Shakespearian Jester' and then into a glamorous being in silk and spangles too elegant for horseplay. Blows and drenching needed a new type, and fell upon some clumsy attendant in the ring. One of these won fame under the name of Auguste; instead of his semi-military uniform he took to wearing cast-off clothes, the better to receive rough treatment—thus naturally obeying the so-called tradition that the butt wears rags. Grock took the Auguste from the circus to the music-hall. Beneath a vast greatcoat he wore dress clothes many sizes too small; inside a 'cello case was a tiny dancing-master's fiddle; his bald dome had a short fringe of hair. His inarticulate speech consisted of gurgles and growls. He exhausted himself pushing the piano towards the stool. He fell through a chair when he stood upon it to reach the spotlight for his accordion, and then played masterfully while displaying an oafish grin of beatitude. The Fratellini (three brothers, members of a veritable dynasty of clowns) established themselves as the chief clowns of the circus, mainly at the Cirque d'Hiver in Paris. These three conformed to the pattern which was customary on the Continent between 1918 and 1939; one was elegant in satin, spangles, and face-powder, another was a bulbous-nosed, doltish Auguste, and the other a shabby-genteel Auguste who blundered more through ill luck than downright stupidity. The white faces of elegant clowns in the French circus maintain an ancient Paris tradition. In Molière's childhood three clowns (Gros-Guillaume, Turlupin, and Gaultier-Garguille) made such play with their death-like pallor that they were said to have been bakers who discovered their comic powers while throwing flour at each other. Similarly Pierrot (after disappearing from the English harlequinades) fascinated Paris as a being 'pale as the moon'. Jean-Gaspard Deburau had created, before he died in 1846, a legend of sentimental romance which was carried on by his son Charles, by Paul Legrand, and by Séverin, who died in 1930.

Perpetuated type still continues in clownship. Individual humour has been equally productive, especially on the music-halls, where clowns are miscalled comedians to distinguish them from the players of Clown. The 'red-nosed' comic, being both the player and his part, is essentially a clown, which the man who doffs his mirth with his motley is not. This ingrained quality of clownship, richly possessed by Whimsical Walker and Joe Craston, has been strongly marked in those who were stars of music-hall and pantomime. They have been in real life what they are on the boards, freely giving their spirit to add to the zest in life of their duller fellows. The music-halls have not produced one definite type to be perpetuated, but the comic characters which their comedians have added to children's stories, such as Widow Twankey in *Aladdin*, Idle Jack in *Dick Whittington*, and Buttons in *Cinderella*, are worthy to be set by the side of the immortal Joey. Like him they are no author's work. Year by year they are nourished by the spirit of the clowns who pretend to be them; and they are likely—particularly the now utterly devoted Buttons—to inspire feelings too deep for laughter. What we mean by 'clown' cannot be clipped. It has grown into a magical word. M. WILLSON DISHER†

CLURMAN, HAROLD (1901–), American director, critic, and author, who has been associated with some of the most important developments in the American theatre since the 1920s. He had already worked at the Greenwich Village Playhouse for a year when in 1925 he joined the Theatre Guild, where he remained as stage manager, actor, and play-reader until 1931. He then founded the Group Theatre in association with Lee Strasberg and Cheryl Crawford. This continued functioning until 1941, and as its managing director Clurman was responsible for many notable productions, among them *The House of Connelly* (1931), *Men in White* (1933), and the early plays of Clifford Odets. Since the demise of the Group Theatre he has directed, among other things, *The Member of the Wedding* (1950), *The Autumn Garden* (1951), *Bus Stop* (1955), *The Waltz of the Toreadors* (1957), *A Touch of the Poet* (1958), and *Heartbreak House* (1959). In 1955 he was responsible for the London production of *Tiger at the Gates*, starring Michael Redgrave, which was subsequently seen in New York, and was acclaimed in both cities. He is the author of several books of essays and criticism on the theatre.

COAL HOLE, LONDON, see TERRY, EDWARD.

COATES, ROBERT (1772–1848), a wealthy and eccentric gentleman from the West Indies, who believed himself to be a superb actor. In 1810 he rented the Theatre Royal, Bath, and displayed himself as Romeo; hence his nickname 'Romeo' Coates. Taking the hilarity of the audience as a tribute to his genius, he toured the provinces and finally reappeared at the Haymarket in London, again as Romeo, wearing a sky-blue spangled cloak, tight red pantaloons, a muslin vest, a full-bottomed wig and a tall hat. He was also seen as Lothario in *The Fair Penitent*. He had a brief blaze of notoriety, but the public soon tired of his absurdities, and he relapsed into poverty and obscurity.

COBORN, CHARLIE (1852–1945), music-hall star whose real name was Colin Whitton McCallum. He was first on the halls as an Irish comedian, calling himself Charles Lawrie. A friend advising him to change his name, he adopted that of Coborn Street, Poplar, where they were standing. His most famous songs were 'Two Lovely Black Eyes' (1886) and 'The Man Who Broke the Bank at Monte Carlo' (1890). Coborn was one of the founders of the Music-Hall Benevolent Fund in 1888, and during the Second World War was indefatigable in entertaining the troops, singing almost to the day of his death with unimpaired vigour.

COBURG THEATRE, LONDON, see OLD VIC and Nos. 35, 36.

COBURN. (1) CHARLES DOUVILLE (1877–1961), American actor and manager, who at 17 was in charge of the Savannah Theatre, where he had begun his career as a programme boy. He was for some years with a stock company in Chicago, and in 1901 made his first appearance in New York, subsequently touring the United States in *The Christian.* He married (2) IVAH WILLS (1882–1937), an actress with whom he organized in 1906 the Coburn Shakespearian Players, both playing leading parts in it for many years. He was outstanding as Falstaff, but he also scored a success as Old Bill in *The Better 'Ole* (1918), which ran for nearly two years, and in 1925 he played James Telfer in an all-star revival in New York of *Trelawny of the 'Wells'*. One of his greatest successes otherwise was *The Yellow Jacket*, a play in the Chinese manner which he frequently revived, himself playing the hero Wu Hoo Git. In 1934 the Coburns inaugurated the Mohawk Dramatic Summer Festival at Union College, Schenectady, which became an annual event, and in the same year Coburn appeared in *The First Legion.* He retired from the stage on his wife's death, but in 1946 returned to play Falstaff for the Theatre Guild. He had a distinguished career in films also.

COBURN'S THEATRE, NEW YORK, see DALY'S THEATRE, 3.

COCHRAN, SIR CHARLES BLAKE (1872–1951), one of the master-showmen of his day. He began his career as an actor, playing in America with Comstock, Joseph Jefferson, and others, and was for three years personal representative for Richard Mansfield. After experience in practically every branch of popular entertainment, he went into management, and his first theatrical production was Ibsen's *John Gabriel Borkman*, given in New York in 1897. In London his first independent production was *Sporting Simpson* (1902) at the Royalty. In 1911 he promoted and managed the production of *The Miracle* by Reinhardt at Olympia, and three years later he entered the field of revue, beginning at the Ambassadors with *Odds and Ends*, followed by *More* and *Pell Mell*; but the most memorable were probably those which he presented at the London Pavilion between 1918 and 1931—*As You Were*; *London, Paris and New York*; *This Year of Grace*; *Wake Up and Dream.* He was equally successful with musical comedy and straight plays, of which *Damaged Goods* was one, and his long association with Noël Coward was responsible, among other things, for *Bitter Sweet* at Her Majesty's and *Cavalcade* at Drury Lane. In 1948 he was knighted for his services to the theatre. He wrote three volumes of reminiscences—*Secrets of a Showman* (1925), *I Had Almost Forgotten* (1932), and *Cock-a-Doodle-Do* (1941), the last title being taken from his nickname in the theatre, 'Cocky'. W. MACQUEEN-POPE†, *rev.*

COCKPIT, LONDON (later the Phoenix), situated in Drury Lane, where for many years its name was perpetuated in Pitt-Place. It should not be confused with the Cockpit at Whitehall, which was only occasionally used for the presentation of plays before the Court. The Drury Lane Cockpit was built, for cockfights, by John Best in 1609, but was converted into a roofed or 'private' theatre in 1616 by Christopher Beeston. It was about the same size as and very similar to the Blackfriars theatre. It soon met with disaster, for on Shrove Tuesday 1617 the London apprentices, in the course of their usual rowdy merrymaking on that day, sacked and set fire to it. It was quickly rebuilt and named, appropriately enough, the Phoenix, though the old name continued in use. It was very nearly the first Theatre Royal, for in 1636/7 Beeston was sworn in as Governor of the King and Queen's Young Company, popularly known as Beeston's Boys. In 1639 he died and his son William succeeded to the title. A year later William was foolish enough to produce an unlicensed play which offended the king and queen. He was arrested and lodged in the Marshalsea, and his post was given to Sir William Davenant, who was later to make his mark in the Restoration theatre.

The Cockpit was closed with all the other theatres in 1642, but illicit performances were occasionally given there, as is shown by a raid made by Parliamentary soldiers in 1649, when the audience was fined on the spot. The amount collected was £3. 11*s.* 4*d.* Two of Davenant's 'plays with music' (or early operas) were performed at the Cockpit, *The Cruelty of the Spaniards* and *Sir Francis Drake*, the former probably with the connivance of Cromwell, as political propaganda.

When the theatres reopened Rhodes, at one time prompter at the Blackfriars theatre, played at the Cockpit with a troupe of youngsters, many of whom became famous, and a joint company under Killigrew and Davenant may have played there before the granting of the two Patents. In 1661 a company of

Erench actors gave at the Cockpit Chapoton's *Mariage d'Orphée et d'Eurydice*, with a profusion of 'Great Machines', and it was occupied from 1661 to 1665 by a troupe under George Jolly, who had previously made a name for himself in Germany; but when the Theatre Royal, Drury Lane, opened in 1663 the fortunes of the Cockpit declined.

W. MACQUEEN-POPE†

COCOANUT GROVE, NEW YORK, see CENTURY THEATRE, 1.

COCTEAU, JEAN (1889–1963), a prominent figure in French intellectual life from an early age as poet, novelist, critic, and artist. He was also an outstanding dramatist. Some of his early works have proved ephemeral, but he first attracted attention as a dramatist (he was already known as a poet) with *Orphée*, produced by Pitoëff in 1924 at the Théâtre des Arts. A new version of Sophocles' *Antigone*, done by Dullin at the Atelier in 1922, was also well received. Jouvet was responsible for the production of a further excursion into Greek mythology, *La Machine infernale*, based on the story of Oedipus. But Cocteau's versatility showed also in the astounding variety of his plays, which ranged from such costumed fantasies as *L'Aigle à deux têtes* through modern problem plays—*Les Mariés de la Tour Eiffel*, *La Machine à écrire*, *Les Parents terribles*—to the one-act monodrama *La Voix humaine*, and included the 'opéra parlé' *Renaud et Armide*, and a tragi-comedy entitled *Les Chevaliers de la Table Ronde*. It is impossible in a short space to do justice to the extent and influence of his dramatic writing, which with its singular blend of poetry, irony, and fantasy proved a constant source of inspiration and controversy, and, in the period between the two wars, did much to redeem the French theatre from triviality and staleness. His career in film-making was no less distinguished and influential.

CODY, WILLIAM FREDERICK (1846–1917), American showman, better known as Buffalo Bill. Born on a farm in Iowa, he was at the Colorado gold-mines as a boy, and then became a pony-express rider and a Civil War scout. He afterwards went on the stage, playing in Western plays specially written for him. In 1883 he first embarked on the Wild West show which made him famous all over the world. This, however, partook more of the nature of the circus than the theatre, and is outside the scope of the present volume.

COGHLAN. (1) CHARLES F. (1842–99), English actor, much of whose professional life was spent in the United States. Hibbert, in *A Playgoer's Memories*, calls him 'handsome, fascinating, selfish, spendthrift Charles Coghlan, whose death was a mystery, and whose body was washed up on the Pacific shore'. He had a daughter, also on the stage in New York. He made his first appearance at the Haymarket under Buckstone in 1860, and subsequently played a number of parts, including Charles Surface, Shylock, and the name part in Burnand's *The Colonel*, before going to New York, where he was seen at Wallack's with his sister (2) ROSE (1851–1932). A distinguished actress, she had made her first appearance on the stage as a child, playing one of the witches in *Macbeth*, and in 1869 made her adult début under Hollingshead at the old Gaiety Theatre, London. Two years later she was seen in New York with Lydia Thompson, where she made an immediate success, and, after a few years in London and the provinces, returned in 1877 to settle down, becoming an American citizen in 1902. She was for many years leading lady at Wallack's Theatre, one of her most successful roles being Lady Teazle. She also appeared in such modern productions as *The Silver King*, *Masks and Faces*, and *Diplomacy*, and was good as Rosalind, and, in 1893, in *A Woman of No Importance*. Towards the end of the nineteenth century her fortunes declined somewhat, and her style was considered outmoded. But her fine voice, distinguished presence, and technical ability kept her in demand, and in 1916 she celebrated her stage jubilee. She was frequently seen in vaudeville, and in 1920 made her last appearance in Belasco's production of *Deburau*.

COHAN, GEORGE MICHAEL (1878–1942), American actor, dramatist, and manager. Son of vaudeville actors, he appeared as a child with his parents and sister in an act billed as The Four Cohans, and by the time he was 15 he was writing skits and songs for vaudeville performance. In 1901 his first full-length play was seen in New York, and he soon built up a big reputation, both as actor and author, with such shows as *Little Johnny Jones* (1904) and *Forty-Five Minutes from Broadway* (1906). In 1911 he opened his own theatre with *The Little Millionaire*, and two years later scored a success with *Seven Keys to Baldpate*, based on a story by Earl Biggers. Apart from his own plays, which included *The Song and Dance Man* (1923), in which he played the part of a second-rate variety performer who thinks himself perfect, he also appeared with success in such plays as *Ah, Wilderness!* and *I'd Rather Be Right*, and as a manager was responsible for a wide variety of productions. Cohan was essentially a man of the theatre, as he reveals in his autobiography, published in 1925, and his work had great entertainment value, though it is of little interest otherwise. It is to his credit, however, that he made full use of his gifts, and was not content to remain in vaudeville.

A statue of Cohan, in Duffy Square, New York, was unveiled on 11 Sept. 1959, he and Edmund Booth being the only American actors, so far, to be thus commemorated.

COHEN, GUSTAVE (1879–1958), French scholar, whose researches on the medieval theatre of France have materially added to our knowledge of liturgical drama as a whole. His *Histoire de la mise en scène dans le théâtre religieux français au moyen âge*, first published in 1906, was re-edited and brought up to date in 1926, after the discovery of the documents relating to the Mystery of the Passion given at Mons in 1501. These were also published separately in 1925. Appointed to the staff of the Sorbonne, Cohen formed a group of students, known as the Théophiliens, who produced in one of the lecture halls of the university a number of medieval plays, adapted and slightly modernized by Cohen himself. The first of these, from which the little company took its name, was *Le Mystère de Théophile*, by Rutebeuf, given in 1933. It was followed by *Le Jeu de Robin et de Marion*, by Adam de la Halle, and by a reconstruction of the earliest known French play, the *Mystère d'Adam*. On the outbreak of war in 1939 Cohen retired from his post and went to live in America, from where he made several visits to Canada, returning to France after 1945. He continued his work of bringing back to life the old medieval plays which had for too long been considered only as texts for examination purposes, and is also the author of numerous books on other aspects and authors of the Middle Ages and Renaissance, and on the theatre of the seventeenth century.

COLERIDGE, SAMUEL TAYLOR (1772–1834), English poet, critic, and philosopher. He was the author of several plays in verse, of which one, *Remorse*, written in 1797 as *Osorio*, was produced at Drury Lane in 1813 with moderate success. The rest, among which are several translations from the German, remain unacted, except for a Christmas entertainment which, with alterations by Dibdin, was given at the Surrey in 1818. Coleridge's chief importance in theatre history lies in his critical and editorial work on Shakespeare, though even there he was handicapped by his ignorance of Elizabethan theatre conditions, which Malone was only gradually bringing to light.

COLISEUM, THE LONDON, Sir Oswald Stoll's famous music-hall in St. Martin's Lane, opened on 24 Dec. 1904 for the presentation of variety. It was the first London theatre to have a revolving stage. In 1931 music-hall was abandoned for musical comedy, and *The White Horse Inn*, which inaugurated the new policy, had a run of 651 performances. Subsequently the Coliseum was used for musical shows and revivals—including a successful *Vagabond King* in 1937—straight plays and ice-shows. From 1936 onwards an annual pantomime was staged, but the theatre really made its mark after the Second World War with a succession of American musicals which included *Annie Get Your Gun* (1947), *Kiss Me, Kate!* (1949), and *Guys and Dolls* (1953). In 1961, after the run of *The Most Happy Fella*, the theatre closed and reopened as a cinema.

W. MACQUEEN-POPE†, *rev.*

COLLÉ, CHARLES (1709–83), French writer, of whose private life little is known. As a young man he wrote light verse, and through his friendship with some of its members became a frequenter in 1729 of the famous Société du Caveau, a drinking-club celebrated for its wit and good company. When the Caveau was dissolved in 1739, Collé entered the household of Orléans, and for the grandson of the Regent, the Duc de Chartres (1725–85) (later Duke of Orléans and father of Philippe Égalité), who was an excellent comic actor, he wrote the plays collected in his *Théâtre de société* (printed in Amsterdam and not intended for publication), and in the *Théâtre des boulevards*. These were imitations of the medieval *parade*, which survived during the eighteenth century at the Paris fairs, and though somewhat modified in tone, were still extremely licentious. Apart from these, of which the best is perhaps *La Vérité dans le vin*, Collé wrote two serious plays. The first, a sentimental comedy entitled *Dupuis et Desronais*, was given at the Comédie-Française in 1763 with some success, but the second, *La Partie de chasse d'Henri IV*, based on Dodsley's *The King and the Miller*, was forbidden by the censor on the orders of Louis XV, and was not played in public until 1774, though it had been printed and played in the provinces much earlier. It was this charming little essay in democracy, in which a king incognito is taught his duty by a humble subject, which was given by some actors from the Comédie-Française, including Préville, at the house of the retired actress, Mlle Dangeville, as a surprise for her birthday.

COLLECTIONS, THEATRE. The ephemeral literature of the theatre—playbills, programmes, pamphlets, scenic designs, even the texts of the plays themselves—was treated with scant respect in the old days, and even where it survived was often left to moulder in garrets and cellars, or on inaccessible library shelves. At the beginning of the twentieth century the fresh impetus given to the study of theatre history led to a revival of interest in these fugitive memorabilia. Libraries, museums, and theatres turned over their treasures and began systematically to docket them, to allow scholars access to them, to reprint or reproduce them, and in some cases to gather them together in a definite theatre collection. A further development was the establishment of museums devoted entirely to theatre material.

Some of the great libraries—among them the British Museum and the Bibliothèque Nationale—have no special theatre collection, items being scattered among different departments. Others, like the New York Public Library (whose dance, drama, and music collections are now housed at the Lincoln Center for the Performing Arts), the Vienna Nationalbibliothek, and the Victoria and Albert Museum, London, have gathered as much as possible in one place, thus facilitating research and study. The Birmingham Library has a department entirely devoted to Shakespeare, and in many libraries private collections which have been bought or donated are still established as entities. Among these are the Gabrielle

Enthoven Collection in the Victoria and Albert Museum (which also has the Stone Collection of Toy Theatre material, and the Guy Little Collection of miscellaneous theatrical photographs); the Douce Collection in the Bodleian, Oxford; the Rondel, Soleinne, and Gordon Craig Collections in the Bibliothèque de l'Arsenal, Paris; the Hamilton Collection of English Plays in Stockholm; and the many collections housed in the libraries of American universities, which are constantly being added to.

Old-established theatres, like the Opéra and the Comédie-Française, La Scala, and the Moscow Art Theatre, have a rich source of material in their archives, which form a collection relating to that particular theatre. One of the most interesting of these specialized museums is that attached to the eighteenth-century Court theatre at Drottningholm in Sweden; in recent years an archivist has been appointed at Covent Garden, and a determined effort is being made to collect, catalogue, and make available to scholars material relating to productions there.

Among museums devoted entirely to the theatre, though not attached to any particular institution, the oldest is probably the Bakhrushin in Moscow, which started as the hobby of a wealthy amateur and was first opened to the public in 1894. A similar collection formed the basis of the Clara Ziegler Museum in Munich. It was begun by the actress after a visit to the International Music and Theatre Exhibition in Vienna in 1892, and bequeathed, together with her house and an endowment, to the city on her death in 1909. The house was destroyed during the Second World War, but most of the collection was saved and has been transferred to new premises in the Hofburg. Many European towns possess theatre museums. That in Copenhagen (housed in the Christiansborg Court theatre) opened in 1922; the Bucardo Museum in Rome, run by the Centro di Ricerche Teatrali, in 1931; the Oslo, housed in part of the oldest house in the city, in 1939; a Dutch theatre museum opened in Amsterdam in 1960. In England a British Theatre Museum Association was established in 1957. It has as yet no premises of its own, but occupies temporarily a room in Leighton House, London, where a number of its treasures are on display. England also has the specialized libraries devoted to Shakespeare in Stratford-upon-Avon and a small museum housed in Ellen Terry's old home in Kent. Pride of place among libraries devoted to one subject must go to the Folger Shakespeare Library, Washington, but interesting collections are also to be found in the Victor Hugo Museum in Paris, in the Casa Goldoni in Venice, and in the former homes of such eminent men of the theatre as Stanislavsky, Chekhov, Lessing, Pixerécourt, and Booth. There are also museums devoted to one particular subject, among them one in Leningrad for the circus, and those in Moscow and Munich for puppets.

There are still a number of collections in private hands, some of which are very little known. Others are accessible to the serious student on application. Among such collections in England the most important is probably the Duke of Devonshire's, at Chatsworth, with its many drawings by Inigo Jones. There are also the Harry R. Beard Collection, housed at Little Eversden, near Cambridge, which deals mainly with opera; the Mander and Mitchenson Collection, in South London, rich in everything to do with the English theatre, particularly in illustrations relating to the nineteenth and twentieth centuries; the Richard Southern Collection, now in Bristol; and the Herbert Hinkins Collection of Toy Theatre material (in Oxford), part of which formerly belonged to Prior. (See also HENSLOWE.)

Most art galleries contain theatre paintings and portraits. The Garrick Club, London, and the Players' Club, New York, own fine collections. There are also a number in the drama collection of Harvard University which have been catalogued in four volumes by Lillian A. Hall (1930–2). In 1959 the Society for Theatre Research issued a *Catalogue of Theatrical Portraits in London Public Collections,* modelled on that of Harvard.

COLLIER, CONSTANCE (1878–1955), an English actress whose long and distinguished career began at the age of 3, when she played Peasblossom in *A Midsummer Night's Dream.* In 1884 she played the child Cissie (at the Theatre Royal, Hull) in *The Silver King,* with Wilson Barrett. In 1893 she made her first appearance in London at the Criterion, in the chorus of 'La Fille de Madame Angot', and she was then seen as the child Fernando in *Don Juan.* In the same year she became one of the famous Gaiety Girls, but left to further her ambition to play serious parts, and was seen as Mercia in *The Sign of the Cross* during the absence of Maud Jeffries. She scored a great success as Chiara the Gypsy in Esmond's *One Summer's Day,* and as Lady Castlemaine in *Sweet Nell of Old Drury,* with the Fred Terrys. She went to Her Majesty's under Tree, and appeared in all his major productions from 1901 to 1908. She also went with his company to Germany, playing before the Emperor. In 1908 she made her first appearance in New York, and then divided her time between London and the United States, being equally popular in both. She was Gertrude in John Barrymore's London *Hamlet,* and among her outstanding parts were Nancy in *Oliver Twist,* the Duchess of Towers in *Peter Ibbetson,* Mrs. Cheveley in *An Ideal Husband,* the Duchesse de Surennes in *Our Betters,* and Anastasia in *The Matriarch.* She was part-author with Ivor Novello of *The Rat,* and produced several plays in London. In 1929 she published her reminiscences as *Harlequinade.* She was for a time engaged to Max Beerbohm.

COLLIER, JEREMY (1656–1726), a non-juror and pamphleteer, best known for his attack on the theatre in his *Short View of the Immorality and Profaneness of the English Stage,* published in 1697–8. It strikes out most forcibly at the contemporary drama, not without reason, and Collier had many sensible and courageous things to say. His work is, however, marred by excessive pedantry and an ignorance of theatrical matters, both historical and technical. He also made the mistake of accusing the Restoration stage of corrupting English morals, instead of realizing that it was only a reflection of a corrupt society, and he laid himself open to ridicule by his lack of proportion and literary ability. Nevertheless, his work had a salutary effect, and reflected, and perhaps helped in, the reform which was in any case overdue.

COLLIER, John Payne (1789–1883), English dramatic and literary critic, the value of whose work was ruined by his forgery of entries in Elizabethan documents, many of which still persist in spite of the rectifications of later scholars. Originally a journalist and law-student, Collier was much attracted by the Elizabethan dramatists, some of whom he edited for a new edition of Dodsley's *Old Plays*, published in 1825–7. He also wrote a volume on the puppet-play of Punch and Judy, in which he gave a reconstructed text, combining several in use by puppet showmen. His three-volume history of the stage, published in 1831, seemed full of new and interesting material, for much of which he was himself responsible, and his falsifications extended to his several volumes on Shakespeare, thus rendering them useless. He also edited for the Shakespeare Society, of which he was an enthusiastic supporter, the papers of Henslowe and Alleyn, again with his additions, thus ruining what might have been an excellent and useful piece of research. It is impossible to say how far Collier's forgeries extended—he is known to have made some manuscript additions to a second folio of Shakespeare, which first aroused the suspicions of such scholars as Dyce, Knight, and Halliwell—and they are still being refuted. They extended even to the State Papers, and are all the worse in that he had access to many private collections and so abused the confidence of his employers. In everything else his behaviour was irreproachable. He seems to have had no literary conscience whatsoever, and to have been actuated merely by vanity. In consequence of his aberrations, all his statements and every document he handled are open to suspicion. Proof of his guilt, which he never admitted, was found in his papers after his death.

COLLIER'S COMEDY, New York, see comedy theatre, 2.

COLLINS. (1) Lottie (1866–1910), a well-known music-hall performer who gained fame through one song—'Ta-Ra-Ra-Boom-De-Ay'. This was written by Harry Sayers, manager of an American minstrel troupe, who died in 1934 at the age of 77, and was first sung by Thatcher's minstrels in a show called *Tuxedo* (from the Tuxedo Club, New York); but it had no great success until Lottie Collins introduced it, in an English version written by B. M. Batchelor, into the pantomime of *Dick Whittington* at the Grand, Islington, in 1891. It was then an enormous hit, so much so that while the pantomime was still running George Edwardes engaged the singer to perform it at the Gaiety Theatre as well, in the burlesque *Cinder-Ellen-Up-Too-Late*. Lottie Collins would rush from Islington to the Strand to sing this famous song and do her terrific dance, starting gently on a low note, and suddenly placing her hands on her hips and whirling into the high-kicking, swift dance. She did it for years, and was paid £200 a week for it all over America, where the song had originally failed. Her daughter (2) José (1887–1958) was a fine singer, who appeared with great success in many musical comedies, the best-known being *The Maid of the Mountains*, under which title she wrote her reminiscences in 1932. The play ran for three years, and was later revived with José Collins in her original part of Teresa. She toured the halls also, both in England and America, and occasionally appeared in straight plays. W. MACQUEEN-POPE†

COLLINS, Sam (1826–65), a chimney-sweep whose real name was Samuel Vagg. He was the original music-hall Irish Comedian, first appearing at Evans's Song-and-Supper Rooms to sing 'Paddy's Wedding' and 'The Limerick Races', and then starring at all the London halls, including the first of them, the Canterbury. He became proprietor of the Marylebone Music-Hall, and then took over the Lansdowne Arms at Islington Green. He opened it as Collins's, after a brush with the licensing authorities, on 4 Nov. 1863 and ran it till his death, when his widow took over. It was later used as a repertory theatre, and still stands. On Collins's grave in Kensal Green cemetery are carved pictures of the hat, the shillelagh, and the shamrock with which he always appeared. W. MACQUEEN-POPE†, *rev.*

COLMAN. (1) George the elder (1732–94), English dramatist, who, after a good education at Westminster and Oxford, and some legal studies, became a well-known man of letters, and by his friendship with Garrick was attracted to the stage. His first play, given at Drury Lane in 1760, was a farce, attributed to Garrick. It was not acknowledged by its author until after the success of his *Jealous Wife* (1761), one of the most popular comedies of its time, which was played by a remarkably strong cast—Garrick, Yates, Palmer, King, Moody, Mrs. Pritchard, and Kitty Clive. This, with *The Clandestine Marriage* (1766), probably represents Colman's best work, and both plays were frequently revived, and translated into French and German, the second being used also as the basis of an Italian comic opera. Colman received some help in its composition from Garrick, but its production led to a breach between the two friends, as Garrick refused the part of Ogleby, played by King. Colman, to mark his displeasure, took a lease of Covent Garden with three associates, with whom he almost immediately found himself involved in litigation, Colman and Powell against Harris and Rutherford. After many troubles, including the death of his wife and of Powell, Colman retired from Covent Garden in 1774. During his reign Spranger Barry had made his appearance, and several good plays had been put on, including those of Goldsmith. Colman also revived *Cymbeline*, and produced a *King Lear* with his own alterations instead of those of Nahum Tate; several of his own plays were produced during this time, including *The Oxonian in Town* (1767). In 1776 Colman took over the Haymarket from Foote, engaged a good company, headed by John Henderson, and did well for several seasons. He was an energetic manager of strict probity, and a good dramatist. His adaptation of *Philaster* was the first play in which Powell appeared in London, while Tattle, in his farce *The Deuce is in Him* (1763), played by King, may be considered the first of those 'patter-parts' in which Mathews was later to excel. His translations of Terence, published in 1765, also met with approval. Among the plays which he produced at the Haymarket during his managership there was the first work of his son, (2) GEORGE the younger (1762–1836), a negligible farce which had only one performance. Some later works, however, also given at the Haymarket, were more successful, and included the musical play *Inkle and Yarico* (1787). In 1794 the younger Colman succeeded his father as manager of the theatre, and remained there till 1803, though with less success. He was reckless and extravagant, and was constantly involved in lawsuits, which had a bad effect on the conduct of the theatre. He was also hampered by a secret marriage which he had contracted in 1784 with a young actress, Clara Morris. He had powerful friends, however, and from 1824 until his death was Examiner of Plays, in which capacity he showed a prudery and strictness which were unexpected from the general tenor of his own works, particularly his comic poems. He had none of the rectitude and stability of his father, but was profligate and disorderly, though some scurrilous publications have been attributed to him without cause. He was a good dramatist, excelling in comic characters, many of which have remained favourite parts with comedians—among them Dr. Pangloss and Dennis Brulgruddery. His best plays are probably *The Iron Chest* (1796), which, after an initial failure ascribed by Colman to Kemble, was later revived and supplied Kean and other tragedians with a fine part; *The Heir at Law* (1797); *Bluebeard; or, Female Curiosity* (1798); and *John Bull; or, the Englishman's Fireside* (1803), considered his masterpiece by his contemporaries, and a great favourite in America. Colman also wrote for Mathews *The Actor of All Work; or, First and Second Floor* (1817), in which two rooms were shown on the stage simultaneously, something of an innovation in those days.

Colman is believed to have married as his second wife his leading lady, (3) MARIA LOGAN (1770–1844). Of unknown parentage, she was the godchild of John Palmer, with whom she appeared at the Haymarket at the age of 13. She was first billed as Mrs. Gibbs at Goodman's Fields in 1787, and retained that name for over fifty years. Fair, plump, with blue eyes and a sweet singing voice, she had good looks, good taste, and a good temper. She played heroines at the Haymarket for many years, eventually succeeding Mrs. Mattocks in duenna parts in old comedy. She retired to Brighton on the death of the younger Colman, and died there. Peake called her 'a kind, unaffected woman, who, with very considerable acquirements and much accurate study of her art, is yet more admired for the cheerfulness of her mind and the goodness of her heart'.

COLOMBIA, see SOUTH AMERICA, 1.

COLOMBIER, MARIE (*c.* 1842–1910), French actress, who studied at the Conservatoire and made her début in 1863 at the Châtelet, going later to the Gaîté and Porte-Saint-Martin. She went with Sarah Bernhardt to tour in the United States, and on her return published a violent attack on her manageress which led to an acrimonious lawsuit. Marie Colombier then left the theatre and attracted attention as the author of a number of novels, continuing at the same time her attacks on Bernhardt (whom she called Sarah Barnum). One of the latter's supporters retaliated with a somewhat scandalous *Vie de Marie Pigeonnier* (1884). These skirmishes between the two actresses seem somewhat to have obscured Marie Colombier's gifts for the theatre, and the abrupt ending of her career gave her little time to develop them fully.

COLON, JENNY [MARGUERITE] (1808–42), a lovely little French actress, whose short career was spent in an atmosphere of gaiety and affection. She made her first appearance at the Opéra-Comique in 1822, and two years later toured England, marrying at Gretna Green a French actor named Lafont, whom she left the following year. She was seen at several Parisian theatres, and Janin, reviewing her work in a new part at the Variétés, called her 'queen and fairy compounded at once of songs and smiles'. She was capricious and self-willed, but kept her hold on the public until her early death. Her elder sister was also on the stage, and was for many years a useful member of the company at the Opéra-Comique.

COLOSSEUM, LONDON, in Albany Street, Regent's Park. This building, which opened in the early 1830s, was used occasionally for plays. From 1835 to 1838 it was run by Braham, first in partnership with Frederick Yates, later alone, but he abandoned it when he left the St. James's. It is mentioned intermittently in 1840–41, but then disappears from theatrical history. It should not be confused with the Colisseum, Regent's Park, which was not used as a theatre.

COLOSSEUM THEATRE, NEW YORK, opened on 10 Jan. 1874. Renamed the Criterion in 1882, Harrigan's Park in 1885, and the Park in 1889, it had an undistinguished career until, rebuilt as Herald Square Theatre, it opened on 17 Sept. 1894 with Richard Mansfield in *Arms and the Man*. It was for some years an important link in the opposition to the powerful Theatrical Syndicate, but was burnt down in 1908, and finally demolished in 1915.

COLUM, PADRAIC (1881–1972), though better known for his later works in other fields, contributed, in the early years of the Irish Dramatic Movement, three plays that, together with those of Boyle and Robinson, had a strong influence upon the realistic development that followed. The first, *Broken Soil*, was done by the Fays' National Dramatic Society at the Molesworth Hall in Dec. 1903, and revived at the Abbey Theatre in 1905. Colum then revised and retitled it, and as *The Fiddler's House* it was done at the Abbey in 1909. It is a moving and imaginative study of the instinct of the vagrant artist in conflict with the practical demands of the life of the small farmer. The sympathy felt for all the characters simultaneously gives tragic balance to the play, and makes it probably the finest Colum wrote. His second play, *The Land* (1905), is a firmly drawn study of farming life in the grip of the agrarian problem. There is a double conflict, on the one hand between the older and the younger generations, and, on the other, between the love of Irish soil and the longing for the adventure of emigration in the minds of the young. The characters are memorable and though the speech is plain and literal, the poetry that is never wholly absent in the Irish dramatist is revealed in the passion of the conflict. In Colum's last play, *Thomas Muskerry* (1910), the setting is small-town life and the play, though it has less power than the earlier ones, shows that the author could reveal the drab life of such towns as clearly as he could the more powerful passions of those who live on the land. His work gave a strong impetus to the second phase of the movement and when he abandoned the theatre for other forms of literature, one of the leaders of the realistic drama was lost to the Irish theatre.

UNA ELLIS-FERMOR†

COLUMBINE, the young girl of the English harlequinade, usually the daughter, ward or wife of the old man Pantaloon, in love with Harlequin, with whom she eventually elopes. She was a late mask in the *commedia dell'arte*, and the name, Columbina, was used by several actresses of the Italian company in Paris in the latter half of the seventeenth century. Originally she was not one of the pairs of stage lovers, but was classed among the maid-servants, with Rosetta, Fiammetta, Pimpinella, or Puparella, as the counterparts of the *zanni*, one of whom, Harlequin, has turned into her youthful lover. Columbine is usually dressed in a conventional ballet dress, the *tutu*, with a wreath of small roses on her hair, and came into England in the eighteenth century with the growing popularity of pantomime (see ITALY, 2 and Nos. 139 & 140.

COLUMBUS CIRCLE THEATRE, NEW YORK, see MAJESTIC THEATRE, 1.

COMBEROUSSE, ALEXIS DE (1793–1862), a French dramatist, typical in his facility, his contemporary successes, and his later oblivion, of the many indefatigable vaudevillists of his day—Mélesville, Dupeuty, Bayard, Ancelot, Théaulon, Miéville, and, greatest of them all, Scribe—whose names crop up in different combinations throughout the lighter side of French theatrical life in the first half of the nineteenth century. Comberousse's love for the theatre was said to have been kindled when, at the age of 14, he played truant from school to see Talma in *Britannicus*. While studying law in Paris he had several plays put on with some success, and, encouraged by Picard, gave up the law for literature. He wrote more than seventy-five plays, in which many of the outstanding actors of the day—outside the Comédie-Française—appeared with marked success, including Frédérick, Léontine Faÿ, Mlle Déjazet, and Mlle Dorval. But, like all his contemporaries except Scribe, he was first submerged in the torrent of Romanticism and then outdistanced by the social drama of Augier and the younger Dumas, and it is doubtful if any of his plays would bear revival. The best of them were collected in three volumes and published in 1864 with a preface by Jules Janin.

COMÉDIE-FRANÇAISE, LA. This national institution, which is at once the glory and despair of the French theatre, was officially founded in 1680 by the fusion of the company of the Hôtel de Bourgogne with the already amalgamated troupes of Molière, who had died in 1673, and the Théâtre du Marais. In honour of France's great actor-dramatist the theatre is also known as La Maison de Molière. Its other name is the Théâtre-Français. It was apparently first called the Comédie-Française to distinguish it from the Italian actors at the Hôtel de Bourgogne, usually referred to as the Comédie-Italienne. At first the new company continued to play in the theatre of the rue Guénégaud, with Mlle Champmeslé, Mlle Guérin (formerly Molière's wife) and her husband, Baron, Hauteroche, and the elder Poisson as its chief members. In 1689 they moved to a new theatre, specially built for them by François d'Orbay in the tennis-court of the Étoile, rue Neuve des Fossés, St-Germain-des-Prés, where they remained until 1770, the chief actors of that period being Beaubour, Mlle Duclos, Mlle Desmares, Mlle Dangeville, Adrienne Lecouvreur, and Legrand, followed by Mlle Clairon and Lekain, whose partnership made theatre history, with Préville, Grandval, Bellecour, the Dugazons, and Molé. After some years in the Salle des Machines at the Tuileries the company, which now included Mlle Raucourt and Louise Contat, again moved to a new theatre on the present site of the Odéon. The Revolution caused a split, the more revolutionary actors, headed by the great Talma, going to the Palais-Royal as the Théâtre de la République, while the others under Molé remained *in situ* as the Théâtre de la Nation. The second group soon lost the favour of the public, who considered them 'aristos', and first Laya's *Ami des lois* and then Neufchâteau's *Paméla*, based on Richardson's novel, caused riots, which culminated in the arrest and imprisonment for nearly a year of the actors concerned. For the next few years the history of the theatre in Paris is confused and the actors were dispersed over many stages. But in 1803 the company of the Comédie-Française was reconstituted in the theatre occupied by Talma and has since remained stable, though in the upheaval it lost the monopoly which it had enjoyed for so long.

The organization of the Comédie-Française is interesting, as being the last remaining example of the system on which all French theatrical companies were organized from the far-distant days of the medieval Confrérie de la Passion. On its formation it was minutely regulated by royal command, and through all its vicissitudes the essentials have remained unchanged. The company, whose constitution was redrafted by Napoleon on his way to Moscow, is a co-operative society in which each actor holds a share, or, in the case of younger or less important actors, a half or quarter share. Admission depends on merit, and the aspiring actor is allowed to choose his own part in tragedy and comedy for his first essay. If successful, he is then considered to be 'on probation' and is called a *pensionnaire*, drawing a fixed salary. After a time, which may vary from weeks to years, he may be admitted to the company as a full member, or *sociétaire*, taking the place of a former member who has resigned or died. On retirement, which is not usually permitted under twenty years' service, the *sociétaire* is entitled to a pension for the rest of his life. The oldest actor, in years of service, not in age, is the head of the company, and known as the *doyen*. The green-room is a meeting-place for actors and distinguished visitors, where each member of the company in turn performs the duties of host. Its library and archives house a rich collection of theatre material.

The value of the Comédie-Française lies in the stabilizing influence of tradition, the keeping alive of a varied repertory, representing all that is best in the history of French dramatic literature, and the excellent team-work which results from the working together of a number of actors who know each other's ways and who are securely placed at the head of their profession. Its disadvantages lie in the numbing weight of that same tradition, which tends to lie heavily on young and aspiring talents and discourages initiative and the trying-out of new methods, whether of acting or production, the retention of a number of outworn plays, and the carelessness that security sometimes brings in its train. Yet, weighing the good against the bad, it must be agreed that on the whole the influence of the Comédie-Française has been beneficial to the development of the French theatre. At times its inertia and pontifical attitude have caused a sudden uprush of young life in some other part of Paris, but the great talents thrown to the surface in such an upheaval, as with Antoine's Théâtre Libre and Copeau's Théâtre du Vieux-Colombier, have usually ended by placing themselves at the service of the National Theatre, to the ultimate benefit of both (see No. 33).

COMÉDIE-ITALIENNE, LA. The Italian *commedia dell'arte* companies (for a history of the *commedia dell'arte* see ITALY, 2) were often in France, and naturally included Paris in their itinerary. The first mention of them there is in 1570–1, when Ganassa and his company paid a short visit, succeeded in 1571 by the Gelosi. In 1577 the Gelosi, who had been summoned to Blois by Henri III during the assembly of Parliament there, again came to Paris, and probably had with them the famous Isabella and Francisco Andreini. Other companies followed, for long or short stays, playing either at the Hôtel de Bourgogne, or at the Petit-Bourbon, on payment of a levy to the Confraternity of the Passion, holders of the monopoly of acting in Paris. They were popular at Court, where Italian was in the ascendant, and also with the populace, whom they amused by their antics in spite of playing in a foreign tongue. It was on returning from a visit to Paris in 1604 that Isabella Andreini died at Lyon in childbirth. Many years later her son, Giovann Battista, known as Lelio, was leader of the Fedeli when at the invitation of Louis XIII they also went to Paris and made a long stay. In the company at that time were Tristano Martinelli, known as Arlequin, and Niccolò Barbieri, known as Beltrame, both popular with Parisian audiences.

The Italian actors first became prominent in French dramatic history when in 1658 Molière obtained permission to settle in Paris, and was allowed to share the Petit-Bourbon with an Italian company already settled there, paying them a yearly rental for the theatre, which he used on Mondays, Wednesdays, Thursdays, and Saturdays, while the Italians kept their usual days, Tuesdays and Sundays. Little is known of Molière's relations with the Italians, whose leader was the famous Tiberio Fiorillo (or Fiorilli), better known as Scaramouche, but they were evidently cordial. It is unlikely, however, that Molière profited, as has been said, from watching the Italians, since he was already an experienced actor when he came to Paris; any profit he may have gained from contact with Italian acting, and such influence as his plays show of *commedia dell'arte* scenarii and methods, must date from the earlier years of touring, when he would no doubt have had many opportunities of seeing the various *commedia dell'arte* companies that regularly visited the larger provincial cities.

In 1660, after the destruction of the Petit-Bourbon, the Italians, who had been away from Paris, returned and found themselves obliged to pay rent to Molière for a part-share in his theatre, the Palais-Royal. Here they remained until the foundation of the Comédie-Française in 1680, when they were allowed sole possession of the now vacated Hôtel de Bourgogne, playing there every day except Friday. In the company, besides Scaramouche, now an old man but still incredibly active, were Domenico Biancolelli, known as Dominique, and, like Scaramouche, a naturalized Frenchman, and his two daughters, together with Romagnesi, and Angelo Costantini, known as Mezzetin.

The Comédie-Italienne, is it was now called, to distinguish it from the Comédie-Française, had for some years before 1680 begun to interlard its Italian with French songs and phrases, and even whole scenes. This innovation was opposed by the French actors, but Dominique, who was popular with Louis XIV, persuaded him to allow the Italians a modicum of French in their performances. This soon led to the acting of some plays entirely in French, and contemporary dramatists, led by Fatouville, Dufresny, Regnard, and Palaprat, were not slow to take advantage of this new market for their wares. The acting, however, continued to be purely that of the *commedia dell'arte*, and even in French plays the actors figured under their own names and were allowed ample scope for improvisation. They fell victims ultimately to their high spirits, and after having been warned several times for transgressing, they were expelled from France in 1697 because, it is said, they offended Mme de Maintenon by playing *La Fausse prude*, which the audience took the greatest delight in applying to her.

While Louis XIV lived the Italians stayed away from Paris, but in 1716 they returned under the leadership of the younger Riccoboni. The Hôtel de Bourgogne was put in order, and the company set to work to regain their former status. They found, however, that the time for harlequinades was past, while Italian was definitely out of favour. Even the French plays of their earlier repertory seemed old-fashioned, and the company, afraid of being forced to leave Paris again, looked round for fresh material. They lighted on the first play of an elderly painter, Jacques Autreau. This was a comedy entitled *Le Port-à-l'Anglais*, with musical interludes by Joseph Mouret. It was an immediate success, and once more the Italians had a permanent place in French theatrical life. The younger dramatists were ready to write for them, and they gave, among other things, many of Marivaux's finest plays. It was, however, no longer even remotely the true *commedia dell'arte* that they played, but a mixture of foreign art and native material which produced a specialized type of play and player. Seeking to extend their popularity, they leased, in the summer of 1721, a newly built theatre at the Foire St-Laurent, where they found the holiday crowd in the humour for them. Two years later, on the death of the Regent, they were given the title of *comédiens ordinaires du roi*, with a yearly grant from public funds, paid today to their successors, the Opéra-Comique. From this time they were Italian only in name, and shared the theatre-going public with the Comédie-Française. They produced an astonishing variety of shows, from true comedy to ballet-pantomime, last relic of the harlequinade, and the newly fashionable vaudevilles. Gradually French actors joined the company and ousted the Italians, of whom the last—and incidentally the last Arlequin—was Carlin Bertinazzi, whom Garrick considered one of the best actors in Paris. The arrival in 1752 of an Italian *opera buffa* company (see OPERA, 5), and its success, together with that of its imitator, the Opéra-Comique de la Foire under Monnet, led the Comédie-Italienne to venture into this new territory. This they did with such success that they were able to absorb their rivals, but at the expense of their former repertory and individuality. The rest of their history belongs to the domain of music. In Apr. 1783 they left the Hôtel de Bourgogne and opened a fine new theatre on the Boulevard des Italiens, to which they gave its name. In 1789, soon after their change of policy, a danger threatened them in the success of the Théâtre de Monsieur (later, under the Revolution, the Théâtre Feydeau, while the Italians were known as the Théâtre Favart), which was being run by Viotti and Léonard, hairdresser to Marie-Antoinette. The intense rivalry between these two theatres produced many excellent works at both, but nearly ruined them. In 1801 they amalgamated as the Opéra-Comique, a name that was given to the new theatre, built in 1835 after the destruction of the older one by fire, and the Comédie-Italienne, which had held an important place in French theatre history, then ceased to exist in name as well as in fact.

COMEDY, a term which, in its modern use, covers a wide variety of plays. These differ from tragedy in that they have a happy ending, and from farce in that they contain some subtlety and character-drawing. The word, of Greek origin (see GREECE, 2), was applied to the satiric plays of Aristophanes and to the works of Terence and Plautus (see FABULA, and ROME, *passim*), but by medieval times had lost its connexion with drama, and merely indicated any tale with a happy ending, particularly one written in a colloquial style and dealing with the love-affairs of lesser folk. The Renaissance brought back the term to the theatre, but without its former satiric connotation; it also lost in course of time its connexion with 'comic' and 'comedian', terms now reserved for low humour, though on the Continent the latter term in the generic sense of actor was used later than in England, where from the eighteenth century onwards it was applied to players of farcical parts, as in the stock companies.

It has been said that comedy is, by its very nature, incapable of translation. Its appeal depends, far more than with tragedy, on local and topical interest and on its preoccupation with the immediate concerns of its audience. Thus, the greater its appeal to its contemporaries the less its impact on future ages, and the history of the theatre shows innumerable instances of comedies enormously successful in their own day and soon forgotten. This handicap is, of course, subject to the overriding force of genius, and the comedies of Aristophanes, Shakespeare, and Molière can still be enjoyed, though they demand from the audience a certain amount of co-operation in recapturing the spirit of their time, and in translation suffer a loss which it is impossible to assess.

Students of dramatic literature group comedies under various headings, as Comedy of Character, of Humours, of Intrigue, of Manners, and of Morals. The Comedy of Humours, as practised by Ben Jonson and Fletcher, might have developed into a truly native English comedy, had it not been deflected by the Commonwealth and Restoration, for it is the type most congenial to the English temperament. The Comedy of Intrigue, which subordinates character to plot, originated in Spain, and was practised in England by Mrs. Aphra Behn. With it may be classed Romantic Comedy, which also came from Spain and reached its highest point in France during the Romantic Revival. It is marked by exaggeration and violence, and by an overpowering use of local colour, costume, and scenery. In the hands of a great poet it may give an illusion of greatness, but easily degenerates into melodrama. The Comedy of Manners originated in France with Molière's *Les Précieuses ridicules* (1658), and Molière himself defined it when he said 'correction of social absurdities must at all times be the matter of true comedy'. Pushing it to its logical extreme, he adventured into the Comedy of Morals—the correction of abuse by the lash of ridicule—of which the greatest exemplar is *Tartuffe*, a play which could not be written or understood outside its own country. The Comedy of Manners, however, proved fertile in Restoration England, and gave us the plays of Congreve. This artificial comedy, or Old Comedy, as it was later called, was at its best delicate and disarming, at its worst equivocal and indecent, but always witty and intellectually remote from reality. It has been called 'the sublimation of the trivial', and after seeming to vanish from the English stage with the death of Farquhar in 1707, it revived under Sheridan with much wit and less indelicacy. But even Sheridan tended to be influenced by the prevalence of Sentimental Comedy, a type of pathetic play which reflected the false sensibility of the rising eighteenth-century middle class. In France this led to the *comédie larmoyante*, which reached its height in the plays of Nivelle de la Chaussée, and, after blurring the distinction between tragedy and comedy and ousting them from the stage, was in its turn eclipsed by the *drame bourgeois*.

Modern comedy turns mainly upon the trivial complications of sex, and has lost both its robust humour and its wit. The last true writers of English comedy were Wilde and Coward. Some of the best elements of comedy have, however, been imported into the modern serious play, which deals lightly and yet persuasively with social problems of the day. The playing of Old Comedy makes heavy demands on the actor, who must be able, without affectation or pedantry, to suggest elegance, leisure, and a nimble wit. Its broader forms may demand great mobility of countenance and a command of dialect. In the nineteenth century the acting of comedy was regarded as a separate branch of the art, and comedian and tragedian rarely trespassed on each other's territory, but the distinction is now seldom maintained.

COMEDY, OLD, MIDDLE, AND NEW, see GREECE, 2 and OLD COMEDY.

COMEDY THEATRE. 1. LONDON. In Panton Street, Haymarket. It opened on 15 Oct. 1881, under the management of Alexander Henderson, with Audran's light opera 'La Mascotte', the cast including Lionel Brough and Violet Cameron. It was a great success, as were the productions which followed it. In 1884 Violet Melnotte, soon to build her own theatre, took over the management and produced, among other things, *The Silver Shield* with Arthur Roberts and Kate Rorke, and a comic opera 'Erminie' with Marie Tempest in the title role. In 1887 Tree ventured into management for the first time at the Comedy, producing one of his greatest successes, *The Red Lamp*. He then went to the Haymarket, and from 1887 to 1892 Charles Hawtrey was at the Comedy. He was succeeded by Comyns Carr, under whose management Winifred Emery made a great success in *Sowing the Wind* (1893) with Cyril Maude and Brandon Thomas, as she did also in *The New Woman* (1894) and *The Benefit of the Doubt* (1895).

Ada Rehan made one of her last London appearances at the Comedy in 1896. Charles Hawtrey controlled it for some time, producing several of H. V. Esmond's plays, but it fell upon bad days, until on 28 Oct. 1902 Lewis Waller went there with a play which, intended as a mere stopgap, proved a big success—*Monsieur Beaucaire*. Arthur Chudleigh, who had been manager at the Court Theatre, ran the Comedy for many years. Gerald du Maurier made a hit there in 1906 with *Raffles*, in which he played the title-role, and on 10 Oct. 1914 Alfred Butt presented Laurette Taylor in *Peg o' My Heart*. This had a long run and was then transferred to the Globe. From 1914 to 1918 Charlot produced revue at the Comedy, and afterwards Norman McKinnel had a short managerial season there. Among the successful plays of later years was *Busman's Honeymoon*, produced in 1936. The theatre was one of the last in London to keep its old-time green baize act-drop. It was for a short time the headquarters of the New Watergate Theatre Club, which in 1956 staged there, for members only, Miller's *View from the Bridge*, followed by Anderson's *Tea and Sympathy*, and Tennessee Williams's *Cat on a Hot Tin Roof*, all plays which would have had difficulty in obtaining the Lord Chamberlain's licence. It then reverted to use as a commercial theatre, and housed, among other things,

Five Finger Exercise, A Passage to India, The Tenth Man, Bonne Soupe, An Evening of British Rubbish, and Spike Milligan in *Son of Oblomov.* W. MACQUEEN-POPE†, *rev.*

2. NEW YORK, on West 41st Street, between 6th Avenue and Broadway. Built by the Shuberts as a small, intimate playhouse, it opened on 9 Sept. 1909. It was leased to the comedian William Collier for three years, and later saw the first production in New York of *Fanny's First Play*, produced by Granville-Barker, fresh from his guest directorship at Yale's Department of Drama. It was at this theatre that the Washington Square Players, forerunners of the present Theatre Guild, made in 1917 some of their early appearances, and in the same year Ruth Draper first appeared there in her one-woman show. She returned in 1928 and 1929, creating a record of five months' solo playing. An exciting moment in the history of the Comedy was the brief but stimulating management of Orson Welles in 1937, when, as the Mercury, the theatre saw the modern-dress production of *Julius Caesar*, a revival of *The Shoemaker's Holiday*, and an interesting production of *Heartbreak House*. In Sept. 1939 the theatre was taken over by the Artef Players for the production of Yiddish dramas, but reverted to its original name on their departure. It was demolished in 1942.
GEORGE FREEDLEY†

COMELLA, LUCIANO FRANCISCO (1751–1812), Spanish dramatist, extremely prolific and very successful in his own day, whose works are now forgotten. His plays, which number over a hundred, range from falsifications of contemporary history to one-act satires. The latter have best stood the test of time and can still hold our attention as sketches of contemporary customs Moratín heavily satirizes Comella in *El café*, a play which attacks the absurdities of Comella's over-written historical pieces. J. E. VAREY

COMMEDIA DELL'ARTE, the name usually given to the Italian popular improvised comedy which flourished from the sixteenth to the early eighteenth centuries. Its history is somewhat obscure and must be pieced together from fragments, but its influence was felt all over Europe and penetrated even to England, where its ebbing tide left behind the harlequinade of the Christmas pantomime and the perambulating Punch and Judy show. Other names for this particular style of acting are *a soggetto*, since it was acted in accordance with a *scenario* or pre-arranged synopsis; *all'improvviso*, since the actors made up some at least of their speeches as they went along; *dei zanni*, from the comic servants who later gave us Harlequin and Punch; *dei maschere*, since most of the actors wore masks; and *all'italiana*, since its home was Italy. *Dell'arte*, the only phrase to survive in general use, is hard to translate exactly, but means substantially 'of the profession', since its actors were trained professionals (see ITALY, 2 for a detailed account of the *commedia dell'arte*; also COSTUME, 6).

The *commedia dell'arte* had a great influence in France, and the company which settled in Paris produced what was virtually a separate genre, the *comédie-italienne*. Through successive French playwrights, particularly Molière and Marivaux, many of the features of the *commedia dell'arte* became naturalized and passed into French literary drama (see COMÉDIE-ITALIENNE, FRANCE, MARIVAUX, and MOLIÈRE).

To distinguish it from the improvised comedy, the written drama of this period in Italy was known as the *commedia erudita*.

COMMONWEALTH, see THEATRICAL COMMONWEALTH.

COMMONWEALTH THEATRE, NEW YORK, see ANTHONY STREET THEATRE.

COMMUNITY THEATRE, U.S.A., see UNITED STATES OF AMERICA, 10.

COMPAGNIE DES QUINZE, see COPEAU, OBEY, and SAINT-DENIS.

COMPAGNONS DE JEUX, DE NOTRE-DAME, see GHÉON.

COMPTON, a family of English actors, allied with the Batemans, which has given many notable players to the English and American stages. The family name was originally Mackenzie, but when Charles, a collateral descendant of the actor-manager David Ross (1728–90) and the son of a Scottish minister, decided to go on the stage, he took his grandmother's maiden name, and it was as (1) HENRY COMPTON (1805–77) that he embarked on his new profession. He married an actress and had nine children, all connected with the theatre, his daughter Katherine being the wife of the dramatist R. C. Carton. His memoirs were published in 1879 by two of his sons, of whom (2) EDWARD (1854–1918) was an elegant and subtle actor whose talents received insufficient recognition. He was the moving spirit of the Compton Comedy Company, which from 1881 until his death toured the provinces, and sometimes appeared in London, in a repertory of Foote, Sheridan, Goldsmith, and other standard comedies. He married in 1882 (3) VIRGINIA FRANCES BATEMAN (1853–1940), who made her first appearance on the stage at the age of 12, and later, as Virginia Francis, was seen at the Lyceum under her parents' management, with her sisters Kate and Isabel, and young Henry Irving. She was her husband's leading lady in the Compton Comedy Company, and continued to manage it after his death. She was the mother of the novelist Compton Mackenzie, and had four other children on the stage, of whom (4) FAY [VIRGINIA LILLIAN EMMELINE] (1894–) has had a long and distinguished career. She made her début in 'The Follies' of her first husband, H. G. Pélissier. Among her later successes were the name-part in Barrie's *Mary Rose* (1920), written specially for her, Phoebe

Throssel in *Quality Street* (1921), the Lady in *The Man With a Load of Mischief* (1925), Fanny Grey in *Autumn Crocus* (1931), Dorothy Hilton in *Call It a Day* (1935), and Martha Dacre in *No Medals* (1944). This ran for two years. She then toured Europe for the British Council in Shaw and Shakespeare, appeared as the Virgin Mary in *Family Portrait* in 1948, and was with the Old Vic for the season of 1953–4. In 1959 she was seen as Lady Bracknell in a revival of *The Importance of Being Earnest*, and at the first Chichester Festival she gave an interesting performance as Maman in *Uncle Vanya*, appearing also as Penthea's attendant Grausis in *The Broken Heart*. In both parts her fine elocution was noticeable in a company whose younger members tended at times to be somewhat inaudible. In the course of her varied career she played Ophelia to the Hamlet of John Barrymore (1925) and of John Gielgud (1939), and was seen in a number of Shakespearian parts at the Open-Air Theatre, Regent's Park. She also appeared in pantomime and variety. In 1926 she published a volume of reminiscences, *Rosemary*. After the death of Pélissier in 1913 she married Lauri de Frece, who died in 1921. Her third husband was the actor Leon Quartermaine, and her fourth Ralph Michael.

CONCERT THEATRE, New York, at 202 West 58th Street. This was originally the John Golden—the first to bear that name. Seating 900 people, it opened on 1 Nov. 1926, and shortly afterwards was taken over by the Theatre Guild, who staged there two plays by Sidney Howard, *Ned McCobb's Daughter* and *The Silver Cord*. In 1927 the Guild was also responsible for the production of O'Neill's *Strange Interlude*, directed by Philip Moeller. Lynn Fontanne played Nina Leeds and the décor was designed by Jo Mielziner. The play reached 426 performances, and was the Theatre Guild's greatest success up to that time. After a short period as the 58th Street Theatre in 1935–6, the Concert Theatre, as the Film-arte, became the home of foreign films, making a brief return to live entertainment in 1942 with intimate revue, for which it was eminently suitable. It is now used for radio and television shows. GEORGE FREEDLEY†

CONDELL, Henry (?–1627), Elizabethan actor, first mentioned in 1598 as playing in *Every Man in His Humour*. His only other known role was the Cardinal in *The Duchess of Malfi*, but he is believed to have played in Shakespeare's plays in such parts as Horatio in *Hamlet*. He was one of the original sharers in the Blackfriars theatre in 1608, and by 1612 had acquired, with his fellow actor Heminge, a large part of the Globe shares. These two men are noted in the list of players who were granted a licence by Charles I in 1625, and to them we owe the printing of Shakespeare's complete works, since the author made no provision for it himself, and the quarto copies of single plays were more often than not incomplete and badly mutilated. The complete collection of thirty-six plays was published in 1623, price twenty shillings. Although there is no record of how many copies were first printed, a second edition was not called for until 1636, by which time both editors were dead. Though Condell was not an outstanding actor—he left the stage to devote himself to business matters in about 1616—it has been surmised that he was a well-known and respected figure of Jacobean theatre society (see also HEMINGE).

CONFIDENTI, The. There were at least two *commedia dell'arte* troupes of this name. The first seems to have been associated in some way with the Uniti, and the same actors are frequently found in both. The first definite mention of the Confidenti, who may have been in existence then for some years, is found in 1574. Some years later Vittoria Piissimi and Pellesini (Pedrolino) (who may have been husband and wife) became the leaders of the Confidenti, whose wanderings took them all over Italy and into France and Spain. Towards the end of the century little is heard of them, though some of the Gelosi actors may have joined them on the death of Isabella Andreini. The second Confidenti troupe, which emerges about 1610, had Flaminio Scala (Flavio) at its head, more as business manager and author than as actor. In the company were Domenico Bruni (Fulvio), Marc' Antonio Romagnesi (Pantalone), Niccolò Barbieri (Beltrame), and two actresses whose rivalry caused a lot of trouble, Lavinia and Valeria. It seems likely that the Confidenti travelled chiefly in Italy, and after the break-up of the company around 1621 a number of the actors are found with the younger Andreini in Paris.

CONFRATERNITY OF THE PASSION (Confrérie de la Passion), an association of the burghers of Paris, formed in 1402 for the performance of religious plays. Their first permanent theatre was in the disused hall of the Guest-House of the Trinity outside the walls of Paris, in the direction of the Porte Saint-Denis. In 1518 they were confirmed in their privileges and given a monopoly of acting in Paris which later proved a serious hindrance to the establishment of a permanent professional theatre there. When the Confraternity, who had abused their position by an increasing licence in the matter of farce and innuendo, were driven from their first home, they built themselves a theatre in the ruins of the palace of the Dukes of Burgundy, ornamenting its doors with the emblems of the Passion (see HÔTEL DE BOURGOGNE). No sooner was it ready for their occupation in 1548 than they were forbidden to act religious plays, though still retaining their monopoly. Thus deprived of the major part of their repertory, they gave up acting, and from about 1570 onwards leased their theatre to travelling and foreign companies, always retaining, however, a couple of boxes and the right of free entry. The Confraternity kept a jealous eye on any company that tried to establish itself in

Paris, and usually succeeded in having it sent away. When the pressure of circumstances grew too strong for them, and the actors of the Hôtel de Bourgogne became their permanent tenants, they still insisted on the payment of a levy for every performance, and were constantly engaged in recriminations and lawsuits with outside companies as well as with their own tenants. The first breach in their privileges was made when in 1595 the fairs of St-Germain and St-Laurent were thrown open to provincial actors, but the monopoly lingered on until 1675, after the death of Molière and only a few years before the foundation of the present Comédie-Française.

CONGREVE, WILLIAM (1670–1729), the greatest English writer of the Restoration comedy of manners. He was educated in Ireland, first at Kilkenny, where Swift was his schoolfellow, later at Trinity College, Dublin, where he frequented the theatre in Smock Alley more than the lecture-halls. In 1689 he went to England, and spent a couple of years in the country, writing his first play, *The Old Bachelor*. This, revised by Southerne and Dryden, was produced at Drury Lane in Mar. 1693, with a fine cast headed by Betterton and Mrs. Bracegirdle. The play, which gave a sharper edge of wit to the theatrical conventions of the time, was well received, and was followed by *The Double-Dealer*, given in 1694 by the same company. This was less successful, perhaps because of the intricacies of the plot, but the commendation of Queen Mary improved its reception. The following year saw Betterton's secession from Drury Lane and his reopening of the old theatre in Lincoln's Inn Fields with *Love for Love*, with himself as Valentine and Mrs. Bracegirdle as Angelica. This was Congreve's most successful play. It contains some of his best writing, and calls for a high degree of skill in the acting. It continued to hold the stage, and still does. On the tide of good fortune Congreve made his one essay in tragedy, *The Mourning Bride* (1697). It was a success with the public and the actors—the part of Almeria, first played by Bracegirdle, was long a favourite with tragedy queens—but not with the critics. Congreve now became entangled, not very successfully, in controversy with Jeremy Collier. This, or some caprice on the part of the public, caused his best, and last, play, *The Way of the World* (Lincoln's Inn, 1700), to be coldly received. Pique, laziness, or ill health, or a combination of all three, drove Congreve from the theatre, and, except for some words for a masque and a translation of Molière in collaboration with Vanbrugh, he wrote no more. In 1707 he was for a short period manager of the Haymarket Theatre, again with Vanbrugh, opening with an opera in deference to the public demand for this 'prevailing Novelty'. The last years of his life were clouded by ill health and failing sight. He died of injuries received when his coach overturned on the way to Bath, and was buried in Westminster Abbey.

CONNAUGHT THEATRE, LONDON. This opened as the Amphitheatre, Holborn, in 1867. It became a playhouse in 1873, under John Hollingshead, at cheap prices. He mixed his attractions in a curious manner, staging pantomime with *The Maid's Tragedy*, and companies of straight actors with some of his burlesque artists from the Gaiety. George Rignold produced a version of *Adam Bede*, and the career of the theatre, which had meanwhile been known as the Alcazar, ended in 1886.

CONNELLY, MARC(US) COOK, see KAUFMAN and UNITED STATES OF AMERICA, 8.

CONQUEST, a family of English actors and pantomimists, the first of whom, (1) BENJAMIN OLIVER (1805–72), adopted the name Conquest when he first went on the stage. He was lessee of the Garrick Theatre in Leman Street from its opening in 1830, with brief intervals, until its destruction by fire in 1846. In 1851 he acquired the Grecian Theatre, which he managed until his death. He married a dancer and ballet-mistress, Clarissa Ann Bennett, by whom he had three daughters and a son, who were all on the stage. His step-daughter Clara (1825–88) married the tragedian Charles Dillon. His only son, (2) GEORGE AUGUSTUS (1837–1901) (who established his father's stage-name of Conquest as the family surname by deed poll in 1883), acted as a child at the Garrick Theatre. He was then educated in France, where the famous French actor Coquelin was his fellow-pupil. Originally intended for the musical profession, George preferred to be an acrobat and pantomimist. In collaboration with Henry Spry he wrote and produced nearly fifty pantomimes, celebrated for their brilliant acrobatic effects (on one occasion no less than thirty traps were used). In these pantomimes the flying ballet was brought to perfection. George also wrote, alone or in collaboration (often with Paul Meritt or Henry Pettitt), over one hundred melodramas for production at the Grecian, and later at the Surrey. Many of these were translations or adaptations from the French. He was also a competent artist, designing and painting stage scenery, properties, and masks. He was a powerful character actor and an excellent animal impersonator. Off-stage he stammered badly, but this defect was not apparent in his acting. When his father died he succeeded to the management of the Grecian, which he sold in 1879 to T. G. Clark. He then visited America, intending to make a lengthy tour, but a serious accident at the outset obliged him to abandon the project and return to England. In Aug. 1881 he took the Surrey Theatre (see No. 49), which he made famous for its melodramas and pantomimes. His eldest son, (3) GEORGE (1858–1926), was known as a good comedian and a pantomime Dame. In 1904 he sold the Surrey Theatre, which he had inherited from his father, but in 1910 for a short time managed the Britannia, Hoxton. His younger brothers, (4) FRED (1871–1941) and (5) ARTHUR (1875–1945), were competent actors and notable animal impersonators, the former being especially remarkable for his pantomime Goose, and the latter (who played for nearly twenty years in pantomime at Covent Garden and Drury Lane) for his music-hall act 'Daphne, the Chimpanzee'. Another distinguished member of this family was the grand-nephew of the elder George, Francis Lister (1899–1951), for thirty years a leading man in the West End and on Broadway.

CONTAMINATION is a term used in modern literary criticism to denote the combining of two original works so as to make one borrowed work, and it is generally supposed that both this sense of the word and the practice of combining originals are Roman. In fact *contaminare* means 'to stain', 'to spoil', never 'to combine'. Terence was accused of 'spoiling' Menander's *Andria* (evidently by departing from it in his translation). His reply was that all he had done was to add certain suitable material from a very similar play by Menander; he adds that the charge against him is a charge against earlier Latin translators also, but that he prefers the 'carelessness' of Plautus, etc., to the dull carefulness of his critics. Donatus, in his commentary, shows that Terence made other changes involving independent work—for example, the addition to the *Andria* of three characters *not* in Menander. It is evident that Terence is misleading his audience (1) in saying that the only changes he has made consist of borrowings, (2) in implying that the changes he had made are of the same kind as those introduced by his 'careless' predecessors. Clearly 'combining' is a process which requires care. Of course Terence does not admit that he has 'spoiled' his originals, and it is ironical that the injurious term used by his critics of his freedom in translation should have come to be applied to the very process of which (whether honestly or not) he boasts. Donatus defines *contaminare* as 'stain'; his later remark about 'making one play out of two' is derived from the words of Terence.

WILLIAM BEARE†

CONTAT, LOUISE (1760–1813), French actress, who first appeared at the Comédie-Française in 1776. She was not at first considered remarkable, and in tragedy was, like her friend and tutor Préville, distinguished but cold. Her real bent was for comedy, at that time in the capable hands of Mlle Dangeville. Beaumarchais, however, gave her the role of Suzanne in *Le Mariage de Figaro*, which set the seal on her growing reputation, and she continued to play coquettes with intelligence and grace, particularly in the plays of Marivaux when they eventually reached the stage of the Comédie-Française. She retired at the age of 50, much regretted by her companions and by the public, having for some years previously given up youthful parts in favour of elderly matrons owing to her increasing size. During the Revolution she narrowly escaped being guillotined, the pretext for her arrest being a phrase in a letter she had written to Marie-Antoinette in 1789. Having, to please the Queen, learnt a long part in twenty-four hours, she says, in mentioning this fact: 'J'ignorais où était le siège de la mémoire; je sais à présent qu'il est dans le cœur.' She was the daughter of a linen-draper who served the actresses of the Comédie-Française, and had many opportunities in her youth of watching them from the wings. Her younger sister was also an actress, making her first appearance as Franchette in *Le Mariage de Figaro* at the age of 13.

CONTI, ITALIA (1874–1946), English actress, founder of the school for training stage children which bears her name. She made her first appearance on the stage in 1891 at the Lyceum, and was later with Benson, playing small parts in Shakespearian repertory and gaining useful experience. After a long tour of Australia with the Robert Brough company, she returned to London and was seen in a variety of parts, which included Mirra in *Paolo and Francesca*, Rosalind in *As You Like It*, Marie Gaubert in *Maternité*, and Tulpe in *Hannele*. It was, however, her engagement by Charles Hawtrey in 1911 for the training of the children in *Where the Rainbow Ends*, in which she appeared as Mrs. Carey from 1929 to 1938, that decided her future vocation, and although she was later seen intermittently on the stage, she devoted most of her energies to the work of her theatre school, from which came a succession of notable theatre personalities, including Noël Coward, Gertrude Lawrence, June, and Anton Dolin, as well as several film stars. In 1918 she was asked by the Ministry of Education to advise on the drawing-up of regulations for the licensing of children on the stage. In 1961, the school, which continues her work, celebrated its jubilee, and a plaque to Miss Conti was unveiled in the entrance hall of the London premises.

CONWAY [RUGG]. (1) WILLIAM AUGUSTUS (1789–1828), English actor, known as 'Handsome' Conway, from his exceptional good looks and fine carriage. He was first seen on the stage in Dublin in 1812, and later went to England. He was a good actor, but morbidly sensitive, and is said to have thrown up his part in London because of adverse criticism. In 1824 he went to New York and appeared at the Park Theatre as Hamlet, Coriolanus, Romeo, and Othello, with great success. He also played Edgar to the Lear of Cooper, then at the height of his fame, Faulconbridge to his King John, and Joseph Surface to his Charles. An actor of the Kemble school, Conway seemed on the threshold of a brilliant career; but his morbidity increasing, he threw himself overboard on the way to Charleston and was drowned. His son (2) FREDERICK BARTLETT (1819–74) was also an actor, who with his wife (3) SARAH CROCKER (1834–75), the sister of Mrs. Bowers, was important in the development of the theatre in Brooklyn, since in 1864 they took over the Park, the first theatre erected there, and in 1871 opened the larger Brooklyn

Theatre. Here, with a good stock company and frequent visits from stars, they provided excellent entertainment until they died within a year of each other. Their daughter (4) MINNIE (MARIANNE LEVY) (1854–96) made her first appearance on the stage under their management in 1869. She married the actor Osmond Tearle, and was the mother of Godfrey (see TEARLE).

COOK, EDWARD DUTTON (1829–83), English dramatic critic, who was on the *Pall Mall Gazette* from 1867 to 1875 and the *World* from 1875 to 1883. His writings on the theatre include *A Book of the Play* (1876), *Hours with the Players* (2 vols., 1881), *Nights at the Play* and *On the Stage* (both 2 vols., 1883). He also contributed articles on actors and dramatists to the *Dictionary of National Biography*, and with Leopold Lewis was the author of a play entitled *The Dove and the Serpent*, which was produced at the City of London Theatre in 1859.

Nights at the Play contains many of Cook's notices of the early London appearances of Irving and Ellen Terry. Of Irving's first Hamlet he wrote: 'Mr. Irving's Hamlet is the conscientious effort of an intelligent and experienced player, and presents just claims to respectful consideration and a fair measure of approval . . . his voice seems somewhat artificially treble in quality and to be jerked out with effort: his movements are angular, and his bearing is deficient in dignity and courtliness, though not without a certain refinement of its own.' T. C. KEMP†

COOKE, GEORGE FREDERICK (1756–1812), an eccentric and unstable English actor, who made his first appearance at Brentford in 1776, and then, except for a fleeting engagement at the Haymarket two years later, spent twenty years as a strolling player in the provinces. In 1786 he found himself playing opposite Mrs. Siddons, and later he was with John Philip Kemble in Dublin. He had already contracted the habit of intemperance which was to be his ruin when, on 31 Oct. 1800, he appeared at Covent Garden as Richard III. He was immediately successful, and it is said that after this Kemble never appeared in the part again, for fear of invidious comparisons. Cooke remained at Covent Garden for ten years, playing a wide range of parts, and constantly in trouble with the management, who never knew whether he would arrive in time, or be sober enough to go on the stage. When he played, he played well, but he was undisciplined and dissipated, usually in debt and often in prison. He seemed to play better when drunk, and was probably somewhat insane with constant inebriation. In 1810 he went to New York, appearing at the Park Theatre before a crowded and enthusiastic audience who, however, fell away during his second season when he proved himself as undependable as in England. With Dunlap as his travelling manager, he toured America, but he was already a dying man, and but for his good constitution would not have lasted so long. He was buried in New York, where Edmund Kean, who though his rival had a high opinion of his capabilities, erected a monument to his memory. Cooke was a powerful but coarse actor, at his best in villainous parts—Richard III, Iago, Stukely, the hypocritical Sir Archy MacSarcasm, or the impudent Sir Pertinax MacSycophant, in which he was considered the equal of the original interpreter, Macklin. He had a deeply lineed face, with a long and somewhat hooked nose, an uncommon breadth between the eyes, which were fiery, dark, and tremendously expressive, a lofty forehead, and a powerful voice of great depth and compass. He had no grace or nobility, but was unequalled at expressing the worst passions of mankind. Careless in studying his parts, he picked them up quickly, and played them intuitively. He had great gifts, and an earlier success in London might have given him the opportunity of conquering his bad habits and developing his genius to the full.

COOKE, THOMAS POTTER (1786–1864), an English actor who in his youth was a sailor. He was at sea in 1796, but in 1804 left the Navy and appeared on the London stage at Astley's, the Surrey, and Drury Lane. He then went into the provinces, but was re-engaged by Elliston for the Surrey, where in 1829 he appeared as William in the 400 consecutive performances of *Black-Eyed Susan*, the part with which his name is always associated. As William, and as Harry Halyard in *Poll and My Partner Joe* (1857), he frequently figures in the theatrical portraits and tinsel pictures of the time. A man of strong physique and great energy, he was at his best in such parts as Ruthven in *The Vampire* (1820), his first outstanding success, and the Monster in *Frankenstein* (1823). It was in this latter play that little Louisa Lane, later the famous American actress Mrs. John Drew, appeared with Cooke on tour, playing Frankenstein's young brother. Cooke, whose nickname was 'Tippy', made his last appearance at Covent Garden in 1860.

COOKMAN, ANTHONY VICTOR (1894–1962), English dramatic critic, who in 1939 succeeded Charles Morgan in that capacity on *The Times*, where he had been working since 1925, first on the parliamentary reporting staff, and then, in 1928, as Morgan's assistant. Born in Salisbury, Cookman served his apprenticeship to journalism on the *Salisbury and Winchester Journal*. After four years as a gunner in the First World War he joined the staff of the *Manchester Guardian* under C. P. Scott, and remained there until he went to *The Times*. From 1945 until his death he was also dramatic critic of the *Tatler*. His obituary notice in *The Times* said of him:

> Widely read in literature and in political history, gifted with a keenly fastidious sense of style, and relishing the good things of life, he brought to the theatre the critical attention of an all-round civilized man of the world. His capacity for enjoyment was catholic, and nothing in drama was

alien to him, except pretension and bad workmanship. He had the background of knowledge against which to see the success or failure of playwrights and of actors in cool appreciative perspective.

Cookman was a contributor to the first edition of this Companion.

COON, see MINSTRELS.

COOPER, THOMAS ABTHORPE (1776–1849), an English actor, son of a surgeon, who made his début at Edinburgh in 1792, appearing in London three years later at Covent Garden, where he played Hamlet, Macbeth, and Lothario in *The Fair Penitent*. In 1796 he went with Wignell to Philadelphia, and spent the rest of his life in the United States, except for visits to Drury Lane in 1803 and 1827. He soon became a firm favourite with the American public, and, having quarrelled with Wignell, joined Dunlap's American Company, in which he played a number of tragic parts. In 1806 Cooper, who had taken a lease of the Park Theatre, New York, on the bankruptcy of Dunlap, employed the latter as his assistant stage manager, and with Stephen Price as his partner toured the eastern circuit—New York, Philadelphia, and Charleston, S.C. He appeared in most of the big tragic roles of Shakespeare, his best part being Macbeth. He was also outstanding as Jaffier in *Venice Preserved*, in which he made his New York début in 1797. A handsome man, with a fine voice and much eloquence and dignity, he unfortunately continued to act too long, and towards the end of his life his popularity declined. He holds an important place in the early history of the American theatre, and was one of the first outstanding English actors to become an American citizen.

COPEAU, JACQUES (1879–1949), French actor and producer, whose work had much influence in the European and American theatres. Although interested in the work of Antoine at the Théâtre Libre, Copeau was as antagonistic to the realist theatre as to the 'well-made' plays of Scribe's emulators, and in 1913, after being associated with André Gide in the foundation of *La Nouvelle Revue Française*, he opened his own theatre, the Vieux-Colombier, in an effort to bring back truth, beauty, and poetry to the French stage. Among his actors were Louis Jouvet and Charles Dullin, and later Valentine Tessier, while the main strength of his repertory lay in his productions of Molière and Shakespeare. The latter's *Twelfth Night* proved to be one of his greatest successes, but he was also instrumental in bringing before the public the work of a number of young dramatists. He instituted major reforms in scenic design, which he simplified to the point of symbolism, and in acting, training his company himself. Indeed, after his return from New York, where his troupe had been installed in the Garrick Theatre from 1917 to 1919 as part of France's propaganda programme, he tended to concentrate more and more on the training of his students, finally giving up the direction of the Vieux-Colombier and retiring in 1924 to Burgundy with a group of young actors, known as 'les Copiaus', some of whom later became members of the famous Compagnie des Quinze, directed by Copeau's pupil and nephew, Michel Saint-Denis, a key figure in the history of English and American theatre-production (see SAINT-DENIS). In 1936 Copeau, whose work was at last beginning to bear fruit, was appointed one of the producers at the Comédie-Française, retiring in 1941. Copeau wrote a number of articles and books on the theatre, translated some of Shakespeare's plays, and published an annotated edition of the plays of Molière.

COPYRIGHT IN A DRAMATIC WORK. 1. GREAT BRITAIN. Medieval law recognized virtually no distinction between a literary work and the material upon which it was written. The underlying Common Law principle that a man should be allowed undisturbed enjoyment of his property applied equally to both. When the invention of printing, however, made it possible for a literary work to be appropriated without theft of the manuscript, a revolution in the practical and legal aspect of the position began which, accelerated as each new method of reproduction came into being, led finally to the abstract legal conception now known as 'copyright'. Today the manuscript of an author's work is but the outward symbol of a network of rights and interests—rights of publication in any form in any language; stage, film, broadcasting, and television rights —which time and the law have brought into being.

The law always lags a little behind events, and the branch of the law governing the protection of literary property is no exception. The first Act to concern itself with copyright in the modern sense was passed in the reign of Queen Anne. For two centuries previously there had been legislation governing the publication of literary works, but its primary purpose was to enforce State control over freedom of expression. From 1556, with short intermissions, until 1694, no book might be published without a licence from the Stationers' Company. As entry on the register of the Company of the work to be published was necessary as an indication of ownership, the public was, it is true, gradually familiarized with the idea of ownership of a literary work as distinct from ownership of the manuscript, but as such entries could be made only in the name of a member of the Company, which consisted exclusively of printers and publishers, the author himself was not directly protected.

However, it was in the general interest of authors to see that there was some more effective safeguard against piracy than their cumbersome and ill-defined Common Law property right, so that, when the Licensing Act of 1662, which had been revived in 1685 and continued in 1693, expired in 1694, authors joined with booksellers and publishers in an agitation for statutory protection against

COPYRIGHT IN A DRAMATIC WORK

printers who were 'stealing' their 'copies'. The result of their efforts was a bill 'for the Encouragement of Learning, by vesting the Copies of printed Books in the Authors or Purchasers of such Copies during the Time therein mentioned', drafted, it is said, in its original form by Dean Swift, which took its place on the Statute Book in 1709 as 8 Anne, c. 19.

Under this Act the authors of books already printed who had not transferred their rights, and booksellers or other persons who had acquired copies of books with a view to reprinting them, were given the sole right of printing those books for a period of twenty-one years from 10 Apr. 1710; in the case of books not already printed the right endured for only fourteen years, but was extended for a further fourteen years if the author were living at the end of the first period. The title of every book printed had still to be registered at Stationers' Hall, but registration could now be taken out in the author's name. Copies had also to be deposited at certain libraries, and a fine and forfeiture of the infringing copies were the penalties provided for a breach of the Act.

As soon as the twenty-one year period granted under the Act expired disputes arose as to whether an author's proprietary right at Common Law was extinguished with the statutory right acquired under the Act, and for the next forty years there followed a series of lawsuits on this point, culminating with the case of *Donaldson* v. *Becket* (1774), 4 Burr 2408, in which the House of Lords decided by a bare majority that so far as published works were concerned the Common Law right had been destroyed by the Act of Anne, the Common Law right in the case of unpublished works being unaffected.

In 1810 the civil remedy of damages was made available in cases of infringement and in 1814, by 54 Geo. 3, c. 156, the period of protection was extended to twenty-eight years from publication or the life of the author, whichever was the longer.

Thus, by the beginning of the nineteenth century, Parliament had recognized the right of the proprietor of a literary work, dramatic or non-dramatic, to prevent for a limited period any unauthorized person from making copies of it. As the performance of a dramatic work did not necessitate the making of a copy of it, there was no statutory protection as yet against an unauthorized stage production, and although the author of an unpublished play could theoretically at Common Law prevent its production without his consent, there does not seem to have been any case where this argument was used successfully.

In 1833, however, the position was regularized by the Dramatic Copyright Act of that year (3 & 4 Will. 4, c. 15), commonly known as Bulwer Lytton's Act, which gave to the author of 'any tragedy, comedy, play, opera, farce or other dramatic piece or entertainment' the sole liberty of representing it 'or causing it to be represented at any place or places of dramatic entertainment whatsoever' in Great Britain and the Dominions for twenty-eight years from publication, with a reversionary period to the author for the rest of his life.

In 1842 the Literary Copyright Act (5 & 6 Vict., c. 45) consolidated the law relating to the protection of literary, dramatic, and musical property and brought within the terms of a single statute the two rights so far recognized, 'copyright' or the right of 'multiplying' copies and 'performing right' or the right of representation.

It provided that copyright should endure for forty-two years from publication or for the life of the author and seven years, whichever was the longer, and laid down that 'the sole liberty of representing dramatic pieces' should last for a similar period. A 'dramatic piece' was now defined as 'every tragedy, comedy, play, opera, farce, or other scenic, musical or dramatic entertainment'.

Under Bulwer Lytton's Act an unauthorized presentation in order to constitute an infringement of copyright had to be given in a 'place of dramatic entertainment'; the Literary Copyright Act made no such condition, but in *Russell* v. *Smith* (1848), 12 Q.B. 217, it was held that a building 'when used for the public representation and performance of "a dramatic piece" for profit, became a place of dramatic entertainment'. The term of protection in the case of an unpublished play was still left open.

A play had to be registered before an action for infringement of copyright could be brought. No registration, however, was necessary as a condition precedent to an action for infringement of the performing right.

Although the Act was in general a great advance on earlier legislation, a number of flaws in its drafting soon came to light.

In the first place, 'the sole liberty of representing' a work attached only to 'dramatic pieces'. Unauthorized performances of dramatizations of non-dramatic works could therefore be given with impunity and were judicially sanctioned in such cases as *Reade* v. *Conquest* (1861), 9 C.B. (N.S.) 755, although the multiplication of copies of such dramatizations where passages were copied verbatim was held to amount to an infringement of copyright (*Warne & Co.* v. *Seebohm* (1886), 39 Ch.D. 73).

In *Reade* v. *Lacy* (1861), 1 J & H 524, it was decided that an author could protect himself against these unauthorized dramatic representations of his non-dramatic works by himself making dramatizations of them before they were published, and so acquiring the sole liberty of representation in them as 'dramatic pieces'. This practice was, therefore, followed by many authors as the only practical safeguard against such exploitation of their work.

Another cumbersome institution brought into being by ambiguous phrasing in the Act was the 'copyright performance'. It was generally believed, though the belief seems to have had no clear legal support, that if a play was published before it was performed, the

COPYRIGHT IN A DRAMATIC WORK

performing right in it was irretrievably lost. Actors were therefore hired to give what amounted to public readings of manuscript plays. Normally no costumes were worn and no scenery used.

These and other inconsistencies and ambiguities in Statute and Common Law forced a Commission, appointed to investigate the position, to report in 1878 that 'the law is wholly destitute of any sort of arrangement, incomplete, often obscure and, even where it is intelligible upon long study, it is in many parts so ill-expressed that none who does not devote study to it can expect to understand it'.

It was not, however, until some thirty years later that any steps were taken to remedy the position.

In 1908 a Committee was appointed to recommend changes in the law to enable Great Britain to keep abreast of the trend of international opinion and legislation, and in particular to give effect to the Revised International Convention signed at Berlin in the previous year. Three years later a new Copyright Act was passed—the Copyright Act 1911—which incorporated in modified form the more important of the Committee's recommendations. In this Act, which repealed with one or two minor exceptions all previous legislation, the two separate rights—the right of multiplying copies and the right of representation—were merged for the first time in the general term 'copyright'. For the first time no formalities were necessary to obtain copyright or as a condition precedent to the institution of proceedings.

The introduction of broadcasting and television, and developments in films, recording and other fields in the next thirty years or so, began to make the 1911 Act seem out-moded, and if the United Kingdom was to be in a position to adhere to the 1948 Brussels Convention and ratify the Universal Copyright Convention signed at Geneva in 1952, revision of the 1911 Act became essential.

A Committee was therefore appointed in 1951 to make recommendations, most of which were included in a new Copyright Act passed five years later—the Copyright Act 1956—which repealed (except for certain provisions relating to delivery of copies to the British Museum and other libraries) the Act of 1911.

Under the 1956 Act copyright subsists in *inter alia* every original dramatic work written by a British subject or other 'qualified person'. Section 2 (5) lists the 'acts restricted by copyright' as reproducing the work in any material form; publishing the work; performing the work in public; broadcasting the work; causing the work to be transmitted to subscribers to a rediffusion service, and making an adaptation of the work. 'Reproduction' is defined as including, in the case of a dramatic work, reproduction in the form of a record or cinematograph film and 'performance' as covering 'any mode of visual or acoustic presentation' (Section 48). 'Adaptation' in the case of a non-dramatic work means 'a version of the work (whether in its original language or a different language) in which it is converted into a dramatic work' and, in the case of a dramatic work, means 'a version of the work (whether in its original language or a different language) in which it is converted into a non-dramatic work' (Section 2 (6)).

'Dramatic work' includes 'a choreographic work or entertainment in dumb show if reduced to writing in the form in which the work or entertainment is to be presented but does not include a cinematograph film, as distinct from a scenario or script for a cinematograph film' (Section 48). The phrase '*original* dramatic work' is, however, not defined and its interpretation has, therefore, been a matter for the Courts. Judges have emphasized in a number of cases that the word 'original' must be given a much wider meaning than it has in everyday use. A work need show no originality of thought in the ordinary sense in order to be entitled to copyright protection. It is sufficient if it is the product of 'labour' and 'skill', as, for example, in the case of modifications or modernizations of a Mystery or Miracle play.

'In public' is another phrase which is given no statutory definition so that, again, judicial decisions have to be relied on. For example, in *The Performing Right Society Ltd.* v. *Gillette Industries Ltd.* and *Ernest Turner Electrical Instruments Ltd.* v. *The Performing Right Society Ltd.* (1943), Ch. 167, it was held that the relaying of wireless programmes to workers in factories were performances in public. In these cases, and in previous cases where the same point was at issue, the courts made it clear that the question to be decided narrows down to an analysis of the nature of the audience before whom the performance is given. Whether performers are paid, whether admission is charged and whether the hall in which the performance is given is part of a private house or is a public building are now held to be irrelevant except in so far as these facts are a guide to the nature of the audience. Lord Justice Romer in *Jennings* v. *Stevens* (1936), 1 Ch. 469, where a performance to a Women's Institute of Gertrude Jennings's play, *The Rest Cure*, was held to be a performance in public, said that the difference between a performance in public and a performance in private is that 'in the latter case the entertainment forms part of the domestic or home life of the person who provides it, and none the less because of the presence of his guests. They are for the time being members of his home circle. In the former case, however, the entertainment is in no sense part of the domestic or home life of the members of the audience. It forms part of what may be called, in contradistinction, their non-domestic or outside life. . . . The home circle may, of course, in some cases be a large one. The section of the public may in some cases be a small one. But this can make no difference, though it may sometimes be difficult to decide whether a particular collection of persons can properly be regarded as constituting a domestic circle.'

'For the avoidance of doubt' about the nature of school performances, Section 41(3) clearly states that where a dramatic work

(*a*) is performed in class, or otherwise in the presence of an audience, and

(*b*) is so performed in the course of the activities of a school, by a person who is a teacher in, or a pupil in attendance at, the school

the performance shall not be taken for the purposes of this Act to be a performance in public if the audience is limited to persons who are teachers in, or pupils in attendance at, the school, or are otherwise directly connected with the activities of the school.' A parent or guardian of a pupil is 'not connected with the activities of the school' for this purpose (Section 41(4)).

It should also be noted that 'The reading or recitation in public by one person of any reasonable extract from a published literary or dramatic work, if accompanied by a sufficient acknowledgement' (Section 6(5)) does not constitute an infringement of copyright. This subsection does not apply to broadcasting.

In addition to the general liability for infringement by public performance, a special liability falls upon the person who lets for hire a place of entertainment. Section 5(5) provides that 'The copyright in a literary, dramatic or musical work is also infringed by any person who permits a place of public entertainment to be used for a performance in public of the work, where the performance constitutes an infringement of the copyright in the work' but the subsection does not apply if the 'person' 'was not aware, and had no reasonable grounds for suspecting, that the performance would be an infringement of the copyright' or 'gave the permission gratuitously, or for a consideration which was only nominal or (if more than nominal) did not exceed a reasonable estimate of the expenses to be incurred by him in consequence of the use of the place for the performance'. There need be no express permission or authorization, but a general authority to use a theatre for public performance is not sufficient (*The Performing Right Society Ltd.* v. *Ciryl Syndicate* (1924) *I.K.B.I.*).

The acts 'restricted by copyright' under Section 2(5) apply as much to 'a substantial part' of a work (Section 49(1)) as to a complete work. The phrase 'substantial part' is a third phrase which is not defined in the Act. In the various cases that came before the courts when the identical phrase in the 1911 Act was under consideration, stress was laid on the fact that quantity is not the sole criterion by which to judge whether a substantial part of a work has been copied. The quality and importance of the passage taken must also be given consideration. For this reason, four lines from Kipling's thirty-two-line poem *If* were held to amount to a substantial part of the poem in *Kipling* v. *Genatosan Ltd.*, Macg. C.C. (1920), 203, and in *Hawkes & Son Ltd.* v. *Paramount Film Services Ltd.*, Macg. C.C. (1933), 473, twenty-eight bars, the playing time of which was twenty seconds, were held to amount to a substantial part of a musical work, the playing time of which in its entirety was four minutes.

Where there is no verbatim copying 'both the plot (including in that word the idea and the arrangement of the incidents) and the dialogue and working out of the play must be regarded in order to see whether one play is a reproduction of the other or of a substantial part of it, and regard must also be had to the extent to which both plays include stock incidents' (*Rees* v. *Melville*, Macg. C.C. (1911–16), 168). In this case, it was decided that the basic idea of a young man marrying a beggar girl to comply with the terms of a will and acquire a fortune did not constitute a substantial part of a play.

It has been emphasized in many cases that, particularly in the field of melodrama, there are certain stock characters and stock situations the inclusion of which in two plays does not of itself give the author of the earlier play a good cause of action against the author of the later play, 'though the combination of these ordinary materials may nevertheless be original, and when such combination has arrived at a certain degree of complexity it becomes practically impossible that they should have been arrived at independently by a second individual' with the result that there is a presumption that there has been infringement.

As copyright is not a monopoly, proof that a later author had no knowledge of an earlier author's work and arrived at his results independently of it will be a good defence, however similar the two works may be.

The normal period of copyright protection is fifty years from the end of the calendar year in which the author dies. In the case of works of joint authorship, the period of protection dates from the end of the calendar year of the death of the author who dies last (Schedule 3, para. 2). If the work has not been published, performed in public, offered for sale on gramophone records, or broadcast during the author's lifetime, the period of protection is fifty years from the end of the calendar year which includes the earliest occasion on which one of these acts was done (Section 2).

The first owner of the copyright in a dramatic work is normally the dramatist. However, in those rare cases where a dramatic work is made in the course of the dramatist's employment by another person (who is not the proprietor of a newspaper or magazine) under a contract of service or apprenticeship, that other person is entitled to the copyright in the work in the absence of agreement to the contrary.

Infringement of copyright is primarily a civil offence for which the remedies are an injunction and damages. Proceedings must be instituted within six years of the date of the infringement. Criminal proceedings lie only against a person who makes, sells, lets for hire, exhibits by way of trade, imports or distributes articles which he knows to be infringing copies of the work (Section 21 (1) and (2)) or 'causes a literary, dramatic or musical work to be performed in public' knowing that copyright is infringed thereby.

2. THE UNITED STATES OF AMERICA. The Copyright Law of the United States of America is a direct legacy from Great Britain. The differences which today exist between the Copyright Laws of the two countries are largely due to the fact that American theory and practice in the copyright field have changed and developed in their essentials very much less than have our own during the two centuries that have elapsed since America won her independence. The Copyright Act in force in 1783 was the Statute of 1710 and it is the characteristics of that Act—the formalities of registration and deposit of copies—which still underlie American Copyright Law today.

Shortly after the end of the American War of Independence, twelve of the American states passed laws giving protection to their authors based on that afforded by the statute of Anne. These state laws gave no protection outside the boundaries of each state. In 1790, however, a clause in the United States Constitution empowering Congress 'to promote the progress of science and useful arts, by securing for limited times to authors and inventors the exclusive right to their respective writings and discoveries' was put into effect.

On 31 May 1790 the first United States Copyright Act was passed 'to encourage learning'. Its substance, no less than its preamble, followed very closely the Statute of Anne. Protection was given to the author of any 'book, map or chart' for fourteen years from the registration in the Register Book of the local District Court renewable for a further fourteen-year period if the author were living at the end of the first period.

During the next sixty years the scope of the Copyright Act was enlarged to cover wider categories of literary and artistic material, but the general basis and period of protection remained the same, until in 1831 the first term was extended to twenty-eight years, renewable for a further fourteen years at the request of the author, his widow, or his children.

In *Wheaton* v. *Peters*, 8 U.S. 591 (1834), the American courts reached the same decision as that to which the British courts came in *Donaldson* v. *Becket*, namely that an author lost on publication whatever Common Law rights he had in his unpublished manuscript.

It was not until 1856 that dramatic compositions with the right of performance in public were brought under statutory protection (11 St. L. 138), and in 1870 registration formalities were transferred from the local district courts to the Library of Congress at Washington.

By the early years of the twentieth century the mass of piecemeal copyright legislation and case law had reached very much the same confused state as that obtaining in Great Britain in the latter part of the nineteenth century, and a report on the position was made by the first Register of Copyrights in 1903. This paved the way for the passage of the Copyright Act of 4 Mar. 1909—the statute which, with certain amendments, is the law in force today.

The principal improvements made by this Act were the extension of the term of copyright protection, a slight relaxation in the copyright formalities and the expansion of copyright protection to 'all the writings of an author' (Copyright Act 1909, Section 4).

The Act also provided, as previous United States copyright legislation had done, that all books and periodicals written in the English language, with the exception of dramatic or dramatico-musical compositions, seeking copyright protection in the U.S.A., should be manufactured in the United States.

During and after the Second World War there were modifications of the regulations governing the 'manufacturing clause' requirements but now the 'manufacturing clause' has been removed altogether in the case of new works by British authors. All that is now necessary is for British authors to comply with the provisions of the Universal Copyright Convention which both the United States and the United Kingdom have ratified (see below).

Plays published or unpublished by British authors may, however, still be registered at the Library of Congress, Washington D.C., from which details about fees, copies for deposit etc. may be obtained. Proceedings for infringement of the copyright in a play cannot be instituted in the United States if the play has not been registered. There are other advantages in registration, both as regards duration of protection and otherwise, too complex to go into here.

3. THE CONTINENT OF EUROPE. The history of the development of legal protection for intellectual property on the continent of Europe follows very closely in its general outline that of the development of British Copyright Law.

A number of countries were readier than was Great Britain to dispense with registration formalities and to provide for automatic copyright protection. Most European countries now grant protection for the author's life and fifty years thereafter.

The Berne Convention of 1886, amended in 1896, 1908, 1914, 1928, and 1948, established the International Copyright Union and is responsible for assimilating the basic principles of copyright protection in all the European countries. Today (1966) the Union has more than fifty members and includes in its membership all the European countries, their colonies and mandated territories and the United Kingdom and the British Commonwealth. Although individual countries in joining the Union have made certain special reservations and stipulations, all adhere to the principle that a national of any member-country of the Union enjoys in every other country of the Union the rights and privileges of a national of that country.

The most prominent absentees from the

Union are the United States of America and the U.S.S.R. The United States has, however, joined the Universal Copyright Convention which came into force in Sept. 1957 and now (1966) has nearly fifty member countries. The minimum period of copyright protection which it requires is twenty-five years from the death of the author and no formalities are necessary beyond the publication on all copies of works claiming protection of the symbol © accompanied by the name of the copyright proprietor and year of first publication 'Placed in such manner and location as to give reasonable notice of claim of copyright'. This Convention is supplementary to and not in substitution for the International Convention. Countries, therefore, which are members of both Conventions are bound in their relations with each other by the International Convention which provides for more comprehensive protection and for a longer period.

M. E. BARBER

COQUELIN. (1) CONSTANT-BENOÎT (1841–1909), French actor, known as Coquelin *aîné* to distinguish him from his brother (see below, 3). A pupil of Régnier at the Conservatoire, he first appeared at the Comédie-Française in 1860, and remained there until 1886, when he left for a prolonged tour of Europe and America. After a further session at the Comédie-Française, he left it finally in 1892, went to the Renaissance, and later became director of the Théâtre de la Porte-Saint-Martin, where he first played the part always associated with his name, that of Cyrano de Bergerac in Rostand's play. His son (2) JEAN (1865–1944), also an actor, appeared in this play as Ragueneau, the pastrycook, having previously been with his father at the Comédie-Française, where he first appeared in 1890. In 1900 Coquelin *aîné* toured with Sarah Bernhardt, with whom he appeared at her own theatre in *L'Aiglon*. Towards the end of his life he was much in London, where he was extremely popular. He died suddenly during rehearsals for Rostand's *Chantecler*, in which he was to have played the leading role. A big man, with an expressive face and an excellent voice, Coquelin *aîné* was outstanding in the great comic roles of Molière and other classics, and in modern parts of a romantic, flamboyant type. He was also the author of a number of books on the theatre, including *L'Art et le comédien* (1880) and *Les Comédiens par un comédien* (1882). His younger brother (3) ERNEST-ALEXANDRE-HONORÉ (1848–1909), known as Coquelin *cadet*, first appeared at the Comédie-Française in 1868, and remained a member of the company until his death. He was at his best in secondary comic parts, and in 1881 appeared with Gôt in a modernized version of the old farce of Pierre Pathelin with much success. He was the author of several amusing books, some of which he published under the pseudonym of Pirouette, and his monologues were also very popular. He died insane about a fortnight after his elder brother.

CORCORAN, KATHARINE (1857–1943), see HERNE, JAMES A.

CORNEILLE. (1) PIERRE (1606–84), France's first great tragic dramatist. He wrote his first play, *Mélite*, a comedy, for a strolling company under Lenoir, with Montdory as its star, which was appearing in Rouen, Corneille's birthplace, in some of Alexandre Hardy's plays. In 1629 the company was in Paris, and *Mélite* was given in a converted tennis-court near the Porte-Saint-Martin. After a slow start it was a success, in spite of the fact that it contained none of the stock personages of farce, and that it violated the unities, then coming into fashion under the influence of Jean Mairet.

Piqued by some of the criticisms levelled at *Mélite*, Corneille next wrote a tragicomedy, *Clitandre* (1631), and it was said 'the critics were then ready to implore him to return to his earlier style'. This he did, and his next four plays were comedies—*La Veuve* (1631–2), *La Galerie du Palais* (1632), *La Suivante* (1633), and *La Place Royale* (1633). In 1635 came his first tragedy, *Médée*, written probably as a result of the success of Mairet's *Sophonisbe* at the Marais the previous year, followed by *L'Illusion comique* (1636), again a comedy. Meanwhile Corneille, who had settled in Paris, had been chosen by Richelieu as one of the five authors commissioned to write his plays for him, probably on account of his success as an author of comedies. But he was not temperamentally fitted for such servitude, and after incurring the wrath of Richelieu by altering some part of the plot allotted to him, Corneille retired again to Rouen. He had as yet done nothing to justify any extravagant hopes being placed on him, and ranked merely as one among a number of good contemporary dramatists who were experimenting with new forms in French dramatic literature. Back in Rouen, however, Corneille dipped again into Spanish literature, with which he had already shown himself familiar in *L'Illusion comique*, and on *Las mocedades del Cid* by Guillen de Castro y Bellvis he based *Le Cid*, which has been described by George Saintsbury as 'perhaps the most epoch-making play in all literature'. Certainly it has become the custom to date the great age of French dramatic literature from its production in 1636 (though modern research indicates the first days of 1637 as a more likely date). Like its predecessors, this play was first given at the now flourishing Théâtre du Marais, with Montdory in the name-part. It was an immediate success, and was translated into English by Joseph Rutter, tutor to the Duke of Dorset. The English version was played by Beeston's Boys in 1637. Madrid also saw and admired a translation, though Spaniards were amused at the scene being laid in Seville, which at the time of the play's action was in the hands of the Moors. According to Corneille's nephew, Fontenelle, Turkey was soon the only country to lack a translation of *Le Cid*, a want now supplied.

The success of *Le Cid* raised up a number

of enemies for Corneille, chief among them Mairet and Scudéry, and a fierce pamphlet war raged round it, in which Richelieu played a part which later laid him open to a charge of jealousy. This was possibly a calumny, since two performances of the play were given in Richelieu's private theatre, later to be the stage of Molière. In any case the public, and Rotrou, to his credit, remained faithful to Corneille, and were ready to applaud his *Horace* (1640), *Cinna* (1641), and *Polyeucte* (1642). These were all given at the Marais, but with Floridor in the name-parts, since Montdory had retired from the stage in 1637, owing to ill health.

In 1643, which saw the production of another tragedy, *La Mort de Pompée*, Corneille produced his finest comedy, *Le Menteur*, based on Alarcón's *La verdad sospechosa*. Floridor played Dorante, with Jodelet as Cliton. It had a great success, which unfortunately was not repeated with its sequel in the following year, *La Suite du menteur*.

The place of production of Corneille's next group of plays—*Rodogune*, *Théodore* (both 1645), and *Héraclitus* (1646)—is uncertain, and depends on the date of Floridor's removal to the Hôtel de Bourgogne, which took place somewhere between 1643 and 1653. Corneille was now established as France's major dramatist, and in 1647 was elected a member of the French Academy. *Nicomède* (1651), one of his best and most popular plays, which Molière chose for his reappearance in Paris in 1658, was preceded by the rather weak *Don Sanche d'Aragon* (1649), and by *Andromède*, a spectacle-opera written at the request of Mazarin to show off the machinery of Torelli. This was produced by the actors of the Hôtel de Bourgogne at the Petit-Bourbon in 1650. By now Corneille was showing signs of that fatigue which led to the poor productions of his later years, and this, added to the troubles of the Fronde, probably accounted for the disastrous failure of *Pertharite* (1652), after which Corneille abandoned the theatre for some years.

It was not until 1659 that Paris again saw a play by its veteran dramatist. This was *Oedipe*, done at the Hôtel de Bourgogne, where Floridor was now firmly established in succession to Bellerose. Tradition has it that the subject was suggested to Corneille by Fouquet. It was a moderate success, and Louis XIV enjoyed it, while it was sufficiently well known for Molière to quote from it in his *Impromptu de Versailles*. It was followed by another spectacle-play, *La Toison d'or*, written for the marriage of Louis XIV, and played by the actors of the Marais at the castle of the Marquis de Sourdéac in Nov. 1660. Later, having been given the scenery and machines by their generous patron, the actors were able to put the play on in their own theatre. *Sertorius* (1661) was also given there, though *Sophonisbe* (1663) and *Othon* (1664) were done at the Hôtel de Bourgogne, without much success.

In 1663 Corneille finally deserted Rouen for Paris, but his plays became less and less successful, partly because of the increasing popularity of Racine. *Agésilas* (1666) was hampered by the author's employment of a new verse-form, while *Attila* (1667) was overshadowed by the success of Racine's *Andromaque* in the same year. It was done by Molière, who had a great admiration for Corneille and is reported to have said that without *Le Menteur* he might have written *L'Étourdi*, but never *Le Misanthrope*. He followed it by a production of *Tite et Bérénice* (1670), given at the same time as Racine's play on the same subject at the rival Hôtel de Bourgogne. This circumstance gave rise to much gossip, particularly as it was said that Henrietta, sister of Charles II and sister-in-law of Louis XIV, had deliberately suggested the same subject to both authors in order to enjoy their rivalry. There is no evidence for this, but the two men certainly were rivals, and may have been seeking to outshine each other. It was in Corneille's play that the young Baron, later to be so famous an actor, had his first adult part, as Domitien. La Thorillière played Tite, and Molière's wife Bérénice. The play was moderately successful, and was followed by some of Corneille's most charming work, done for *Psyché* (1671) in collaboration with Molière and Quinault. *Pulchérie* (1672), done at the Marais, and *Suréna* (1674), done at the Hôtel de Bourgogne, are Corneille's last plays, and both, though successful for a short time, soon fell out of the repertory.

Corneille was not an easy person. He was brusque and shy with strangers, had none of Racine's easy graces—but was probably a far finer character—and was sometimes too pleased with himself and his work. His domestic life was happy, and he had not to wait for posterity to give him his due, since in his lifetime he was successful (though never wealthy), honoured, fêted, and called *le grand Corneille*. Even Racine at his best could not easily prevail against the popularity of Corneille in his decline, which did not prevent his making a memorable eulogy of the older dramatist at the Academy on the reception of Thomas Corneille in his brother's stead. Corneille's fame was a little eclipsed in the eighteenth century, but the nineteenth restored him to his true place. His work is unequal, and it may be that he would have been happier working for a freer theatre. He had not, as Racine had, the art of making an asset out of the limitations imposed on him. It is ironical that the form of French tragedy which he adopted and did so much to further was not really suited to his genius. But he rightly ranks first among French dramatists, and the best of his plays still hold the stage.

His brother (2) THOMAS (1625–1709), referred to above, was also a playwright. He had undoubted talent as a poet, great facility, and untiring industry. He was also more attractive in manner and conversation than his elder brother, and a favourite in Parisian drawing-rooms. He married a younger sister of his brother's wife, and nothing is more charming than the account of their lives, the two families living in the same or adjoining houses, completely in harmony. All the evidence goes to show that Pierre rejoiced in his younger brother's popularity, and never showed to him the anxious jealousy with which he sometimes regarded another's success. Thomas wrote over forty plays, all successful and all forgotten. He had not his brother's genius. The first of his productions was a comedy, *Les Engagements du hasard* (1647), based on a Spanish play, and given, in the year of Pierre's election to the French Academy, at the Hôtel de Bourgogne. His first tragedy, *Timocrate* (1656), was done at the Marais, and helped to restore the genre to popularity after the troubles of the Fronde. Altogether the younger Corneille is an interesting person, and deserves a little pity for having had such a famous brother, beside whom his fires naturally pale. His best plays are usually considered to be *Ariane* (1672), in which Mlle Champmeslé and later Rachel were outstanding, and *Le Comte d'Essex* (1678), given at the Hôtel de Bourgogne, again with Champmeslé.

To distinguish him from Pierre, Thomas was known as Monsieur Corneille de L'Isle.

CORNELL, KATHARINE (1898–), one of the leading actresses of the United States. The daughter of a theatre manager in Buffalo, she made her first appearance in *Bushido* with the Washington Square Players in 1916, and remained with them for two years. In 1919 she was seen in London as Jo in *Little Women*, with great success. She returned to New York, and was seen in a wide variety of parts, among them Mary Fitton in *Will Shakespeare* (1923) and Candida (1924). In 1931 she appeared under her own management as Elizabeth Moulton-Barrett in *The Barretts of Wimpole Street*, a part which she has played many times, and with which her name is always associated. It was produced by her husband, Guthrie McClintic, whom she had married in 1921 (and who died in 1961), and who was responsible for many other productions in which she appeared, notably *Alien Corn*, *Romeo and Juliet*, *Antony and Cleopatra*, *The Dark is Light Enough*, and *Dear Liar*. They formed an admirable partnership, their gifts being complementary, and together they brought rare skill and a fine sense of theatrical values to the service of the American theatre. Miss Cornell, who has been the recipient of many honours from American universities, was awarded the Drama League Award for her performance of Juliet in 1935, the Woman of the Year Award from the Friends of the Hebrew University in 1959, after her performance in New York and Tel Aviv as Anath Bithiah in *The Firstborn*, and a Medal for Good Speech on the Stage in the same year. In 1943 she published a volume of reminiscences.

CORNISH ROUNDS. There are in Cornwall, particularly in the west, remains of circular earthworks which are believed to have been open-air theatres used for annual performances of Mystery plays. These could accommodate, on banks (usually seven) cut in the rising ground, and sometimes faced with granite, a large number of spectators grouped round a central area or 'playing-place' (*plen an gwary*). Some of them were still in use in the seventeenth century. The surviving plans for a trilogy consisting of a play on the Creation, one on the Passion, and one on the Resurrection, and for a two-day play on the life of St. Meryasek, show that Heaven was at the eastern end, with Hell on the north. This is probably a survival from the days of church performances. There must also, from the stage directions, have been rostrums or stages of varying levels on the central area.

One feature of the Cornish playing-place which has given rise to some controversy is the 'conveyour', which Chambers took to be a person, i.e. a stage-manager, charged with the duty of shepherding or 'conveying' a character to his appointed place. R. Morton Nance, however (see *Journal of the Royal Institution of Cornwall*, vol. xxiv, pp. 190–211), thinks that by 'conveyour' is meant a central covered pit with a tunnel running to it from the side of the 'playing-place', by which characters could 'appear' unexpectedly, as from a nineteenth-century trap, and he equates it with the so-called Devil's Spoon at Perran Round, a long shallow trench running from a depression in the first bank of seats to a central pit.

CORONET THEATRE, NEW YORK. This opened as the Forrest on 24 Nov. 1925 with a musical play which had a moderate run of some eighty performances. It was followed by a series of unremarkable plays, and in May 1927 the theatre housed a brief season of the Spanish Art Theatre, under Crosby Gaige. The first production to achieve a hundred performances was *Women Go On Forever*, a melodrama of dubious morality which had a number of outstanding actors in its cast. A spate of thrillers was followed by revivals of recent successes, until on 17 Sept. 1934 *Tobacco Road* moved to the Forrest—having opened on 4 Dec. 1933 at the Masque Theatre—and remained until 31 May 1941, setting up a record which was later broken by *Life With Father*. The theatre received its present name in 1945, when it was taken over by the City Playhouses Inc., and remodelled. Miller's *All My Sons* (see No. 105) was seen there in 1957 and O'Neill's *Great God Brown* in 1959. The theatre was then renamed the Eugene O'Neill, in honour of America's foremost playwright, opening with Inge's *A Loss of Roses*. GEORGE FREEDLEY†

CORRAL DE COMEDIAS, see MADRID THEATRES.

CORREA, JULIO, see SOUTH AMERICA, 1.

CORRIE, JOE (1894–1968), Scottish dramatist, who supplied the modern Scottish dramatic movement, and especially that branch of it associated with the Community Drama Festivals (see AMATEUR THEATRE), with some of its most representative one-act plays. He began writing while working in the coal-mines in Fife, and had his first plays, *The Shillin'-a-Week*

Man and *The Poacher*, performed by the Bowhill village players during the General Strike in 1926. This group of actor-miners, of which Corrie himself was one, toured the music-halls of Scotland and the north of England with Corrie's plays during 1929–30, and for the first time in the history of the music-hall succeeded in putting on a three-act play there (*In Time o' Strife*). During the next ten years Corrie's plays were welcome additions to the repertory of the amateur stage. They include kitchen comedy, tragedy, and history. Many have been festival prize-winners, and some have been translated into French and Russian. Corrie also wrote a full-length play on Robert Burns, another entitled *Master of Men*, produced by the Glasgow Citizens' Theatre in 1944, a novel, and several volumes of poems.

WILLIAM JEFFREY†

CORSICAN TRAP, a piece of stage mechanism first used for the apparition in *The Corsican Brothers*, by means of which it rose slowly, at the same time appearing to drift across the stage. It was also known as the Ghost Glide (see TRAP).

CORT THEATRE, NEW YORK, opened 20 Dec. 1912 with Laurette Taylor in the immensely successful *Peg o' My Heart*. After several successes, the theatre was taken by Charles Coburn and his wife, who appeared in revivals of *The Yellow Jacket* and *The Better 'Ole*. A notable event in the history of this theatre was a successful production there in 1919 of Drinkwater's *Abraham Lincoln*. A series of unremarkable plays followed, though *Behold the Bridegroom*, with Judith Anderson, was listed by Burns Mantle among the ten best plays of 1927. In the following year Katharine Hepburn made her first appearance on Broadway at the Cort, and in 1930 came a magnificent revival of *Uncle Vanya*, superbly acted by a fine cast. Other successes were *Five Star Final* (1930) and *The Green Bay Tree* (1932), the latter with Laurence Olivier and Jill Esmond and an elegant setting by Robert Edmond Jones; *Boy Meets Girl* (1935) and *Room Service* (1937), both of which had long runs; the fine war-play *A Bell for Adano* (1944); and a translation of Anouilh's resistance play, *Antigone*, with Katharine Cornell in the name-part. Later successes were *The Shrike* (1952), and *The Diary of Anne Frank* (1955). In 1958 *Sunrise at Campobello*, with Ralph Bellamy as Franklin D. Roosevelt, had a successful run.

GEORGE FREEDLEY†

CORT'S SIXTY-THIRD STREET THEATRE, NEW YORK, see DALY'S THEATRE, 3.

COSMOPOLITAN THEATRE, NEW YORK, see MAJESTIC THEATRE, 1.

COSSA, PIETRO (1830–81), Italian playwright. Liberal, anti-clerical, and ineluctably middle class, he domesticated tragedy, evolving a supremely Italian romantic realism. Apart from *Pushkin* (1870), his plays are in poor verse. There is, however, considerable forcefulness in his writing, and a lively sense of the theatre. *Nerone* (1871) is his most successful piece, revealing beneath the fustian a shrewd psychological insight and exact feeling for drama. Vigorous, attacking drama is to be found in *Giuliano l'apostata* (1877), and *Cola di Rienzo* (1874), where Cossa vents his anticlericalism. *Messalina* (1875) is remarkable for its evocation of period and of the necessary atmosphere of lasciviousness. Cossa is at his best with Roman subjects, and his central characters, such as Messalina and Nero, are excitingly alive. *Nerone* was translated into English by Frances E. Trollope.

FREDERICK MAY

COSTANTINI. A family of actors of the *commedia dell'arte*, of whom (1) COSTANTINO (*fl.* 1668–96) played under the name of Gradelino, and was for some time in Paris. He married (2) DOMENICA (*fl.* 1675–?), also an actress, and was the father of the famous Mezzetino, (3) ANGELO (*c.* 1655–1729), author of a life of Tiberio Fiorelli (Scaramuccia). Angelo was in Paris from 1683 to 1697, and after the death of Dominique took over the role of Arlequin, retaining however his own sobriquet. While appearing in Brunswick he had the misfortune to be the successful rival in love of the Elector of Saxony, which cost him twenty years in prison. His brother (4) GIOVAN BATTISTA (?–1720) was also an actor, and played second young lover parts under the name of Cintio. He was in Paris in 1688, and succeeded Marc'Antonio Romagnesi when the latter abandoned the part of the young lover for that of the pedant-doctor.

COSTELLO, TOM (1863–1945), a music-hall performer who went to London from Birmingham in 1886 and played in melodrama at the old Surrey. He later made his name on the halls with a song 'Comrades', but is probably better remembered as the hen-pecked husband singing 'At Trinity Church I met me Doom'. He was also a fine singer of stirring patriotic ballads, often in naval officer's uniform. He retired from the halls at the time of the First World War but returned with the Veterans of Variety in the 1920s.

COSTUME, THEATRICAL. Theatrical costume is of much more ancient date than theatrical scenery. It is possible for the theatre to do without a stage, but 'acting' *must* mean 'assuming a character', and assuming a character means dressing up. Every ritual dance (and what people are so primitive as to have no ritual dances?) involves its appropriate costume, its animal disguise, its dignifying feathered headdress, or its appropriate mask. The actor assumes the god, impersonates the hero, or affects the garb of men like himself. This descent to realism, which is that of the drama itself, is necessarily reflected in the history of stage costume.

1. GREEK. We must, however, attempt to distinguish in a field where distinction becomes progressively more difficult the earlier we take up the story. We must attempt to strip

theatrical costume of its religious and magical elements at a time when the theatre itself was still full of both. The point of departure must be an arbitrary one, and perhaps none better can be found than the Greek theatre of Aeschylus on the one hand and Aristophanes on the other. For tragedy and comedy, having different origins, had different systems of dress, both quite different again from the ordinary dress of the day. The costumes worn by the actors in tragedy seem to have been fully established by the time of Aeschylus and to have long persisted. The long *chiton* had sleeves (unlike that worn in ordinary life) and was coloured and patterned. It was once thought that the tragic actors derived their clothes from those worn by the priests of Eleusis, but Margarete Bieber (*The History of the Greek and Roman Theatre*, 1939) lends her great authority to the view that it was 'rather the Eleusinian priests who borrowed this costume from the actors'. Both actors and chorus wore the mask (see Nos. 3, 4, 5, 13).

In Old Comedy the actors all wore clothes grotesquely padded, and each was provided with an enormous phallus of red leather. In the *Clouds*, Aristophanes declares that his characters will not wear it, which seems to imply that it was usual to do so. No doubt it was still popular with the less refined part of the audience. Several of Aristophanes' plays demanded a chorus of beasts, birds, or allegorical figures, and these were represented not by complete disguises but by suitable accessories such as feathered wings or horses' heads and tails.

The Attic New Comedy, represented by Menander, abandoned the phallus and the mythological elements. Its intention was to reflect the life of the day, and the clothes worn were those of the ordinary citizens of Athens, except that a regular tradition seems to have grown up of colouring the clothes differently for the different characters. The masks also were stereotyped in a regular series of character parts, and used over and over again for different plays.

2. ROMAN. Greek tragedy and comedy were imported into Rome in the middle of the third century B.C., and with them the whole system of Greek stage costume, including the cothurnus in its most exaggerated form. When the Romans developed a drama of their own they naturally added such typically Roman garments as the toga and the *stola*. By the time of the Caesars stage costumes, especially in tragedy, had become very gorgeous. The same colour symbolism was adopted as the Greeks had used to express the characters or the moods of the players.

Pantomime and mime were very popular in Rome. In the former very scanty clothing was worn, and when women began to take part in it the effect must have been something similar to a modern revue or cabaret. In mimes, or farces played without masks, women appeared from the beginning, and these entertainments soon became more popular than the regular drama. The most interesting dress in the mimes was the patchwork garment worn by the Fool, an interesting parallel with the Harlequin costume to be worn in the Italian Comedy more than a thousand years later.

Similar parallels with the characters, if not with the costumes, of the *commedia dell'arte* are to be found in the Atellanae, the improvised farces of the Roman Campagna, in which we find five permanent types or characters closely corresponding with the Capitano, the Dottore, the Pantalone, etc. of the sixteenth century. The strolling Atellan players were masked, like their later counterparts.

The mimes became ever more popular as the Empire moved towards its dissolution, and the costumes of the players steadily more gorgeous. We hear in the sixth century of actresses' dresses adorned with pearls and enriched with cloth of gold. These extravagances excited the hatred of the Church, and after the collapse of the Empire public performances in regular theatres ceased altogether, although some of the traditions must have been carried on by strolling players throughout the Dark Ages.

3. MEDIEVAL. Drama was reborn in the Mystery and Miracle plays of the Church. The earliest of these performances were given inside the sacred edifice itself, and were performed by the priests wearing their usual sacerdotal robes. These, since the ninth century, had become very elaborate. Female characters were indicated by the simple expedient of placing a kerchief on the head and draping a cloak over the shoulder. Secular costumes, however, and even false beards, soon began to creep in, and with the progressive secularization of the plays, this tendency was accentuated. Finally the priests were forbidden to take part and the drama moved out of the church, first to a place in front of the great doorway, and then into the markets or other open spaces of the towns (see LITURGICAL DRAMA).

Once the plays had been abandoned to the laity, some of the minor roles, played in the ordinary costume of the day, took on a new importance, and very soon developed into comic characters. The devils too were comic. This obviously gave some scope for fantasy in costume, and there is plenty of evidence to show that the opportunity was eagerly seized. Some of the performances of the later Middle Ages were most gorgeously mounted and extremely expensive, but, except for a slight orientalism in some of the costumes, there was, of course, no attempt at any kind of historical or geographical accuracy, the necessary knowledge being completely lacking. Realism, however, in so far as it could be obtained by such devices as painted wounds or tights of white leather, was much in vogue. Towards the end of the medieval period martyrs or damned souls were sometimes presented quite naked (see No. 16).

In the Morality plays, which dealt with

allegorical figures of Virtues and Vices, the costumes were sometimes extremely rich. The characters were clothed in fantasticated contemporary dress, with the exception of the Devil, taken over with all his accessories from the Miracle plays, and the 'Vice', a new character usually clothed as a fool or jester. The French *soties* were regular fool-plays, the costumes being contemporary dress with certain fantastic or archaic elements such as long donkey's ears on the hood, cockscombs, and bells. Some of these details, together with the deformity which former ages considered comic, have survived into our own day in the costume of Punch.

4. Renaissance. By the middle of the sixteenth century the medieval theatre was in full decay. Its place was taken by attempts in academic circles to revive the classical drama, and also by that astonishing flowering of the Elizabethan stage which culminated in the achievement of Shakespeare. The same period was the Golden Age of the Spanish drama, but very few records have survived of either its costume or scenery. It is probable that both followed the same course as in the presentation of Shakespeare. The Elizabethan theatre took over some of the elements of the Miracle and Morality plays. Its stage was as bare as theirs, its costumes no less gorgeous. Little attempt was made at historical accuracy, the players wearing contemporary costume with such minor modifications as might be suggested by the knowledge that orientals were in the habit of wearing long robes and turbans. The players' wardrobes were enriched by gifts from aristocratic patrons, so that the stage kings and queens were almost if not quite as finely clad as their counterparts in real life.

It was impossible, however, for the public theatres to compete in magnificence with the masques presented at Court. Elizabeth was fond of such shows, but very few records of them have survived. James I had a passion for them, and for the entertainments at Whitehall under him and under Charles I we have a mass of material preserved in the library of the Duke of Devonshire at Chatsworth. Inigo Jones (1573–1652) was the architect-designer in charge, and it was through him that all the recent Italian developments were reproduced in England. As in Italy, mythological subjects were highly in favour and gave considerable scope to the artist's fantasy. The male costumes were, in general, of the 'Roman' pattern, the Roman breastplate moulded to the form of the body and some variation of the Roman kilt being an essential part of it, modified by elements of contemporary fashion. The female costumes (see No. 144) followed the dress of the period more closely, but strove for a looseness and transparency supposed to be typical of 'classical' dress. Every advantage was taken of décolletage, and some of the dresses, with their low-cut bodices or bosoms veiled with gauze, would not be out of place in a modern revue. The grotesque characters show elements of costume continued from the Morality plays or borrowed from the ever more popular *commedia dell'arte*. The cost of the dresses being borne by the wearers (the lords and ladies of the Court) there was almost no limit to their magnificence and luxury.

5. Seventeenth Century. This splendour, however, was as nothing compared with that of similar shows on the Continent. At the Courts of Italy, of Germany (up to the outbreak of the Thirty Years' War), and of France the most extravagant entertainments were used with the deliberate policy of enhancing the prestige of the Prince, and they reached a new height of elaboration in France in the early years of the reign of Louis XIV. Italian scenography had by this time spread almost all over Europe, and Mazarin had called in numerous Italian artists, of whom the most celebrated was Giacomo Torelli (1608–78). It is possible that he was responsible for the splendid costumes in the *Noces de Thétis et de Pélée*, given by the Cardinal at the Petit-Bourbon in 1654, but the French, with their innate talent for anything relating to costume, soon had this field in their own hands. The *Grand Carrousel* of 1662, a kind of mock-tournament in fantasticated *habits à la Romaine*, was designed by Henri Gissey (1621–1673), and the appearance of the costumes has been preserved in an admirable series of engravings by Chauveau (see No. 146). So great was the enthusiasm and emulation provoked by this entertainment that every monarch in Europe wished to stage something of the kind, the most notable being the fête given in Vienna a few years later. After his death Gissey was succeeded as *Dessinateur du Cabinet du Roi* by the great Jean Bérain the elder (1637–1711). The influence of this artist was not confined to the restricted area of theatrical costume but extended over the whole field of the decorative arts. In fact it would not be much of an exaggeration to say that the *style Louis XIV* is the *style Bérain*. Numerous examples of his designs have been preserved in the Louvre, in the Musée de l'Opéra in Paris, in the Library of Versailles, in the Victoria and Albert Museum (see No. 147) and elsewhere. It is possible that many of these are copies or tracings by the pious hand of Jean Bérain the younger (1678–1726), but they enable us to gain a very complete idea of the evolution of theatrical costume during the greater part of the reign of the *Roi Soleil*. The most striking characteristic of Bérain's work is the complete blend of fantasy and contemporary taste. Even when the costumes are those of Romans, Turks, or mythological personages, the exotic elements are, as it were, absorbed and digested into one supreme manifestation of style. There was no attempt at realism or archaeological reconstruction. Bérain's style is at once intensely personal and completely contemporary, and perhaps this makes him the greatest designer of stage costume that has ever lived. His influence both on his contemporaries in other European countries and on his successors in France was immense.

6. COMMEDIA DELL'ARTE. Before dealing further with this, however, it is necessary to say something of the costumes of the *commedia dell' arte*, that astonishing manifestation of theatrical activity which swept over Europe and spread its influence everywhere during the whole of the seventeenth century. As a dramatic form the improvised Italian Comedy is dealt with elsewhere (see ITALY, 2). We are concerned merely with its traditional costumes. Some of the elements of these go back, it is thought, to the Atellanae of Roman times, but when the Comedy re-emerges, towards the end of the sixteenth century, we find certain definite traditional types. While the plays changed (indeed, as they were improvised, no two performances could be exactly alike), the characters remained constant. The most famous of these were il Capitano, il Dottore, Brighella, Pantalone, Pulcinella, and, of course, Arlecchino. It is one of the curiosities of the *commedia dell'arte* that all the characters (with the exception of the 'straight' parts, the lovers and the female servants, who played in contemporary dress) wore the costumes of different Italian towns or provinces. Pulcinella was a Neapolitan, Brighella and Arlecchino were from Bergamo, Pantalone was a Venetian, il Capitano a swaggering Spaniard—for the Spaniards still held considerable territory in Italy. Arlecchino's costume was 'a thing of shreds and patches', but these patches gradually became stylized and decorative, until we reach the familiar lozenge-shaped pattern of parti-coloured cloth (see No. 140) which has survived to our own day (see No. 176). Pierrot represented a French development of a minor character, and his traditional costume was stereotyped by Watteau. But Watteau or anyone familiar with the Italian Comedy would have been astonished at the notion of a 'troupe' of Pierrots, for Pierrot was essentially one character among others of strongly contrasting types. The characters of the *commedia dell'arte* have a long history, and have found their way into many unexpected places, but they were too traditional and unchanging to have much influence on the evolution of theatrical costume in general (see Nos. 132–9 and 149).

7. ROCOCO and EIGHTEENTH CENTURY. So long as the desire for historical accuracy played an altogether minor part in the minds of theatrical designers, that evolution followed the main lines of the taste of the time. The Austrian equivalent of Bérain was the great Italian designer Lodovico Burnacini (1636–1707) (see No. 148), who flourished at Vienna under the cultivated Emperor Leopold I. In France the work of Bérain was carried on by his son and other disciples, but the *style Louis XIV* gradually merged into the *style Régence* and was dissipated in the fantasies of rococo. Claude Gillot (1673–1722) (see No. 149), the master of Watteau, was responsible for some of the costumes of the Court ballets in the early years of the eighteenth century, but the great name of the middle of the century is that of François Boucher (1703–70). As early as 1734 we find him designing a whole series of theatrical costumes to illustrate a new edition of the works of Molière. It may have been these which brought him to the notice of the authorities. He was certainly working for the Opéra in 1737, and in 1744 he succeeded Jean Nicholas Servandony (1695–1766) as official decorator. His style is sufficiently familiar to need no description, and his painting and non-theatrical work in general seems to have absorbed more and more of his time, for in 1748 he abandoned his post at the Opéra to Jean-Baptiste Martin (*fl.* 1748–57), chiefly remembered for his rococo shepherds and shepherdesses. The rococo style was to find its completest development, however, in the designs of Louis René Boquet (*fl.* 1760–82), who worked both for the Opéra and the Menus-Plaisirs, that is, the Court entertainments at Versailles and Fontainebleau. A good many of his designs have been preserved, and they show that he was, like Bérain, content to suggest character or period by some small decorative accessory and, for the rest, brought everything under the domination of the contemporary style. His designs have great charm and his costumes, both male and female, are characterized by his use of wide paniers, forming a kind of ballet-skirt covered with rococo detail.

These wide paniers haunted the stage not only in France, and not only in ballet or opera. The English actor Quin played Coriolanus in just such a ballet-skirt as we find depicted in the drawings of Boquet, and one of Garrick's most 'realistic' reforms was the abolition of such garments. England could offer, in the eighteenth century, no such opportunities for the theatrical designer as were enjoyed on the Continent, and of what records may have existed very few have come down to us. The main story of development still lies in France.

Boquet worked for the Opéra from about 1760 until 1780, and towards the end of his reign a notable change in taste began to make itself felt. In classical plays at any rate a real effort was made to approximate more closely to what was known of the costumes of antiquity. The first real costumes *à l'antique* are said to have been due to the collaboration of the famous singer Mlle Saint-Huberty and the artist Moreau le Jeune (1741–1814). This was in 1782. By 1785 it was possible to find quite a number of correct classical costumes on the French stage, and the French Revolution, with its passion for the Ancients, powerfully reinforced a tendency that had already set in.

The reform of stage costume had been advocated for many years previously by authors of the calibre of Voltaire and Diderot, and the actress Mlle Favart and the actor Lekain had made efforts in the same direction. In Voltaire's *L'Orphelin de la Chine* in 1755 the famous Mlle Clairon appeared with bare arms and without paniers, although how this made the costume more 'Chinese' than it would otherwise have been it is difficult to say.

However, she played the part of Roxane in a fairly close approximation to Turkish costume.

In England Garrick's reforms consisted in abandoning the traditional stylization of costume, and playing Shakespeare, for example, in contemporary dress (i.e. the dress of Garrick's day, not Shakespeare's). It is odd to reflect that he acted Macbeth in the scarlet of the King's livery. Komisarjevsky, in his *Costume of the Theatre*, has recorded that when Garrick, in 1758, was playing the part of 'the ancient Greek, Aegis,'[1] 'he wore the costume of a Venetian gondolier, on the ground that the majority of Venetian gondoliers at that time were of Greek origin'. It is perhaps sufficient commentary on the accuracy of eighteenth-century stage costume to say that Garrick passed as a realist. English tragic actresses of the same period wore contemporary dress with a few accessories, such as a turban, a crown, or a veil. Engravings have survived of an Electra in the high headdress of the 1770s, and in her hand an elegant urn in the taste of the period, purporting to contain the ashes of her brother.

8. NINETEENTH CENTURY. As we have seen, France was in the van of the reforming movement, and the first step forward was taken by the famous Talma, supported by the painter David. When, however, in the very year of the Revolution, he appeared as Brutus with bare arms and legs, the reaction of the public was anything but favourable. But by the end of the century classical costumes, at least for women, were the fashion in ordinary life, and so appeared less incongruous on the stage.

It is the same story in the first quarter of the nineteenth century. There was considerably more interest in 'historical' costume, and following the success of the novels of Scott, 'Elizabethan' details began to take their place in ordinary fashions. Planché, in 1823, did some pioneer work for Charles Kemble's production of *King John* at Covent Garden (see No. 150). The Restoration period in France is marked by an outbreak of ruffles *à la Marie Stuart*, somewhat incongruously attached to dresses which still followed in their main outlines the 'classical' Empire modes. The same was true of stage costumes, which indeed were hardly distinguishable from those of the street and the ballroom. The new rage for historical plays merely meant the addition of a jumble of sixteenth- and seventeenth-century details to early nineteenth-century dress. The resulting mixture is not without its charm (the charm we are beginning to discover in late eighteenth- and early nineteenth-century Gothic), but it bore, it is perhaps needless to say, very little relation to any kind of historical accuracy.

It is of course arguable that the quest for historical accuracy is a mistake. As Carlos Fischer remarks, regretfully, in his *Costumes de l'Opéra*, 'le costume d'opéra, étant désormais consacré à l'Histoire, n'a plus d'histoire'. But this is not quite true. It was not until the very end of the nineteenth century that historical costume on the stage made any very close approximation to reality. During the whole of the crinoline period, at least, the forms of stage dress followed the contemporary mode. As Hermione in Charles Kean's production of *The Winter's Tale* in the 1850s, Mrs. Kean wore a perfectly correct Greek costume, but she wore it over a crinoline! None the less the archaeological research undertaken by Charles Kean had its effect, and his work in England was paralleled by that of Paul Lormier in France. Lormier's long reign as designer for the Paris Opéra lasted forty-five years, and he strove unceasingly to make the costumes of the principal singers and *figurantes* as accurate as possible.

However successful he was with these, he was completely defeated as regards the ballet by the curious convention of clothing the *danseuses* in the *tutu*, the short powder-puff skirt of many layers of gauze or tarlatan, which lasted as the inevitable ballet costume until the reforms of Diaghilev. This dress was very convenient for dancing in, but it owed its origin to the enormous success of Taglioni in 'La Sylphide'. Her costume in this was perhaps designed by Eugène Lorris Lami (1800–90), but in essentials it was merely the dress of the day, white and somewhat shortened. Its persistence in every ballet whatever the theme or period made any attempt at historical verisimilitude quite impossible.

It is necessary when considering female stage costume of past periods to remember how difficult it is to escape, even with the best intentions, from the prevailing mode. The Bancrofts prided themselves upon their realism, and Mrs. Bancroft twice played Peg Woffington in what she fondly imagined was eighteenth-century costume. To the modern eye the photographs which have come down to us bear no suggestion of eighteenth-century costume at all. They show merely the dress of the different dates of production. It is particularly difficult for any actress to abandon an attractive (i.e. a contemporary) style of hair-dressing, and this alone is sufficient to throw the most painstakingly 'accurate' costume out of focus.

Towards the end of the nineteenth century, realism took on a new meaning. On the one hand it was an attempt, as with the company of players organized by the Duke of Saxe-Meiningen (see No. 151), at an almost pedantic degree of accuracy in historical plays; on the other an abandonment of historical themes altogether and a concentration upon the problems of everyday modern life. In the plays inspired by this ideal there was obviously no place for the costume designer at all. The actresses had dresses made for them by fashionable dressmakers and the men wore their own clothes.

The designer, excluded almost entirely from the 'legitimate' stage, let his fancy run riot in the lighter musical productions. In England

[1] In fact, Garrick was playing Lysander in Home's *Agis*.

such men as Attilio Comelli (1858–1925) and Wilhelm—whose real name was William John Charles Pitcher (1859–1925) (see No. 152)—designed innumerable dresses for *figurantes* in the early years of the twentieth century, and large collections of these have survived. They are valuable social documents, indicating as they do the whole erotic-aesthetic of the day; the elaborate plumed hats, the ample bosoms dripping with lace and jewels, the tight-clad thighs, the open-work stockings. Much earlier in France, *La Vie Parisienne* artists, men like Alfred Grévin (1827–92), had been called in for a similar purpose. From the point of view of the history of manners, 'show-girl' costumes have perhaps hardly received the attention they deserve. The 'Empire' ballets of the Edwardian epoch provide an almost complete summary of the taste of the time.

9. BALLET. For the history of stage costume much more important was the movement inaugurated by Diaghilev. He had at his command all the resources of the 'classical' ballet, but he broke completely with the traditional manner of presentation, in particular with the slavery to the *tutu*, the flounced white ballet skirt which had lasted so long. In Alexandre Benois (1870–1960) and Léon Bakst (1866–1924) he had two giants of theatrical art, and if the talents of the former were shown most effectively in décor, those of Bakst were pre-eminently those of the costume designer. Bakst brought to western Europe a riot of oriental colour which first dazzled and then delighted audiences in London and Paris. His costumes were not historically 'accurate', and his stylized treatment was influential not only in his own field but in every department of theatrical costume.

In addition to Russian artists like Larionov, Roerich, and Goncharova, Diaghilev brought in French painters of the stature of Braque, Derain, and Picasso. The drawings of Picasso for 'The Three-Cornered Hat' are among the masterpieces of costume design. His cubism found its way on to the stage in the much-criticized 'Parade'. Juan Gris, Marie Laurencin, Rouault, and G. de Chirico also designed costumes for the Russian Ballet; the last named worked also for the Swedish Ballet, as did Fernand Léger and Irène Lagut.

10. MODERN PERIOD. (*a*) *European.* The French state theatres commissioned costumes from Valdo Barbey and Maxime Dethomas; the Théâtre des Arts employed Desvallières; the Vieux-Colombier, Luc-Albert Moreau and others; the Atelier, Barsacq and Jean-Victor Hugo. The last named, however, had his greatest success with his costumes for *Romeo and Juliet* (in Cocteau's adaptation) for the Soirées de Paris, some of which are reproduced in the Folio Society's edition of the play. The number of French experimental theatres in the period between the two wars gave ample scope for the talents of designers of theatrical costume.

In Germany Ernest Stern continued, at the beginning of the same period, the traditions of stylized realism instituted by Reinhardt (see No. 154). The movement known as Expressionism had perhaps more effect on stage settings than on stage costume. Artists like Oscar Schlemmer inaugurated some interesting experiments of an abstract-mechanical kind, but the human figure places very definite limits to the process of abstraction; the actors themselves always tend to rebel against too rigid a style, and so-called cubist costumes tend when worn to become merely the fantastic–historical. A production such as that of *Saint Joan* at the Kamerny Theatre, Moscow, showed this clearly enough. At the same theatre the Sternberg costumes for *All God's Chillun Got Wings*, and those of I. Nivinsky for Puccini's opera 'Turandot', showed the breadth and variety of the Russian approach to the problem of stage-costuming. Very interesting work was also done in Moscow by Varpekh for the Theatre of the Young Spectator.

(*b*) *American.* In America as elsewhere the 'modern movement' found expression more easily in décor than in costume. The costumes of Norman Bel Geddes for *Lysistrata* were considerably less abstract than his settings. His method, as also in *Boudoir* and *The Miracle*, was a witty commentary on the styles of the past. Many plays in which the setting was highly formalized clothed the actors in the dress of every day, and indeed it is difficult to see how they could have done anything else. Historical plays, especially where the scene represents a period the dresses of which are more or less known to the public, allow a certain fantastication or formalization of Elizabethan or 'classical' dress, and this fact was soon taken advantage of by such artists as Woodman Thompson (*Iphigenia in Aulis*), Robert Edmond Jones (*Othello*), and Walter René Fuerst (*The Oresteia*). Robert Edmond Jones made some interesting experiments by way of showing one age through the eyes of another, as when he set and costumed *Lucrèce* in terms of Renaissance Rome. As in other countries, the American lighter stage gave the designers of costume opportunities for which they would have waited long elsewhere. Some of the great spectacular 'musicals' provided almost a cross-section of all the aesthetic impulses of the contemporary theatre.

(*c*) *English.* In England one of the most talented of the designers of stage costume during the early years of the twentieth century was Charles Ricketts (1866–1931). Even before the appearance of Diaghilev, Ricketts was already a pioneer in the protest against an unimaginative realism. Some of his costumes were devised for the sheer love of imagining a stage picture, and many of them were never used, but already in 1906 we find him decorating *Salome* and *A Florentine Tragedy*. *Don Juan in Hell* and *The Man of Destiny* were among the first of his professional tasks, but it was not until some sixteen years later that he really caught the attention of the public with his costumes for *Saint Joan* (see No. 98). Then followed *Henry VIII* and *Macbeth*. His attempt to re-dress *The Mikado* had a less favourable reception. His last work was for *Elizabeth of England* in 1929.

A much shorter but almost equally brilliant career was that of Claud Lovat Fraser (1890–1921). His fame rests chiefly on his designs for the costumes (as well as the scenery) of the Hammersmith revival of *The Beggar's Opera*. So successful was his stylizing of the period that a Lovat Fraser influence can be traced in almost all eighteenth-century plays produced in England since. His early death deprived the English theatre of one of its major artists (see Nos. 156, 174).

Norman Wilkinson of Four Oaks (1882–1934) first attracted attention with his designs for Granville-Barker's productions of Shakespeare at the Savoy Theatre in 1913. In the following year he was concerned in the production of *The Dynasts* at the Kingsway; and under Playfair's management of the Lyric Theatre, Hammersmith, he decorated *Lionel and Clarissa*, *The Rivals*, and *The Would-be Gentleman*. The same management employed no less an artist than Sir William Nicholson for *Polly*, the sequel to *The Beggar's Opera*. Other artists who were tempted into occasional work for the theatres were James Pryde, F. Cayley Robinson, Paul Nash, E. McKnight Kauffer, and Albert Rutherston (see No. 153).

George Sheringham (1884–1937) employed his delicate talent for Playfair and other managements; Paul Shelving worked mostly for Barry Jackson at Birmingham and elsewhere (see No. 100); the more naturalistic style of George W. Harris (1880–1929) found scope in a wide variety of plays. Among the most successful scenic designers of the 1920s was Aubrey Hammond, who decorated, among other plays, *The Man with a Load of Mischief* and *The Circle of Chalk*. Some excellent work was done by Michael Weight (see No. 157) and Stewart Chaney (see No. 159).

The period between the two World Wars was marked by the emergence of a number of talented women designers: Gladys Calthrop (who did much work for Noël Coward's productions); the Motleys, three young women who did some of their best work for John Gielgud; Nadia Benois (the niece of the great Alexandre), Molly McArthur, and Doris Zinkeisen. The lighter stage often gave opportunities to the imaginative designer, and C. B. Cochran, with such productions as *Helen!*, did much to launch the fame of Oliver Messel. Rex Whistler (1905–44) was an admirable stage-designer whose death in action was a great loss to the English theatre.

The reopening of Sadler's Wells in 1931 and the building up of a permanent company for opera and ballet gave designers a whole new field of which advantage was taken by, among others, William Chappell, Leslie Hurry, Roger Furse, and John Stevenson. After the Second World War a new non-realistic drama offered scope to such designers as Edward Delaney, Sophie Fedorovitch, Osbert Lancaster, Michael Ayrton, and Alan Barlow. Cecil Beaton's work for *Lady Windermere's Fan* and *My Fair Lady* contributed much to their success. In addition, those who have done excellent work for the theatre include John Gower Parks (1905–55), James Bailey, Reece Pemberton, Tanya Moiseiwitch, Leonard Rosoman, Osborne Robinson, Robert Medley, Franco Zeffirelli, Anthony Holland, Peter Rice, Audrey Cruddas, Felix Kelly, Lila di Nobili, Sean Kenny, Alix Stone, Desmond Healey, Jocelyn Herbert, and Mariano Andreu (see No. 160). JAMES LAVER

COTHURNUS (*Kothornos*). This word meant in Greek a woman's boot; thus in the *Frogs* of Aristophanes the effeminate Dionysus wears cothurni. They were loose-fitting and came high up the calf. In his *Dramatic Festivals in Athens*, p. 233, Pickard-Cambridge says: 'There is no evidence that in the classical period the tragic boot was specifically named Kothornos.' Nor is there any evidence that the actor's boot had thick soles; these were a device of the late Hellenistic and Roman period, when tragic acting had become very stiff and artificial. WILLIAM BEARE†

The word is occasionally used to describe an elevated, high-flown style of acting, particularly in tragedy (see also BUSKIN).

COULDOCK, CHARLES WALTER (1815–98), American actor. Born in London, he decided to adopt the stage as a profession after seeing Macready. In 1836 he made his début in a provincial company, later playing in Birmingham and Liverpool with most of the leading actors of the day. Among them was Charlotte Cushman, who engaged him for her New York company, where he made an immediate success in *The Stranger*. After several seasons at the Walnut Street Theatre, Philadelphia, he went on tour, making a great reputation in *The Willow Copse* (1853) and *The Chimney Corner* (1861). He played Abel Murcott in *Our American Cousin* (1858), and was outstanding as Dunstan Kirke in *Hazel Kirke* (1880). He was for more than sixty years on the stage, and was the friend of Booth, Macready, and Jefferson, a man of great vitality and energy, and a witty, genial companion.

COUNCIL FOR THE ENCOURAGEMENT OF MUSIC AND THE ARTS, see ARTS COUNCIL.

COUNSELL, JOHN (1905–   ), actor and theatre manager, who in 1938 took over the Theatre Royal in Windsor, which he still manages. This was first run on the usual lines of a weekly repertory theatre, but it has evolved into a unique type of provincial theatre, in that, being so near London, it can draw on actors for one production only, and has therefore done away with its permanent company. Each play is separately cast, and runs for two weeks. This has only been possible owing to the Windsor Theatre's unusual position in an area which can provide a good mixed audience, can supply local support, and yet is conveniently near the capital. John Counsell, who was a member of the O.U.D.S. while at Oxford, and later director of the repertory company there, was an actor before going to Windsor, and has since directed plays in other theatres, among them *Anastasia* (1952), *Grab me a Gondola* (1956) and *How Say You?* (1959). With his wife Mary Kerridge (1914–), an accomplished actress who often appears in his productions, he has built up a strong and independent organization, and been responsible for a number of interesting productions, some of which have later been seen in the West End.

COUNTERWEIGHT HOUSE, the name given to a theatre where the scenery is worked by a modern system of endless lines and counterweights, as opposed to the traditional system of lines from a fly-floor used in a Rope, or Hand-worked, House. In the counterweight house the sets of lines, generally of wire rope, are attached to a steel barrel, and the scenery is strapped to this barrel. The lines, after leaving the headblock, are clewed together and attached to a Counterweight Cradle, which may be loaded to balance the weight of the scene piece, and which is raised and lowered by means of an endless, line passing over pulleys and working (generally) from the floor of the stage, where a system of brakes is installed for each line. Since no great lengths of spare rope have to be accommodated, the counterweight house need not have a fly-floor. RICHARD SOUTHERN

COURT THEATRE, LONDON, see ROYAL COURT THEATRE.

COURTELINE [MOINEAUX], GEORGES (1858–1929), French dramatist, author of a number of amusing farces, some of which were produced by Antoine before finding their way eventually into the repertory of the Comédie-Française. They deal with the humours of military life, as in *Lidoire* (1891) and *Les Gaietés de l'escadron* (1895), and of the law, as in *L'Article 330* (1901); or, as in what is perhaps his best play, *Bourbouroche* (1893), with episodes in the life of ordinary people, salted with much wit and a certain gross brutality which recalls the farces of the early French theatre.

COURVILLE, ALBERT PIERRE DE (1887–1960), one of the earliest producers in London of spectacular revue. He had had a variety of jobs before he visited New York in 1909, where a visit to the Ziegfeld Follies led him to suppose that a similar form of entertainment might be acceptable to English audiences. Returning to London, he entered the theatre, and shortly afterwards was entrusted with the task of engaging Continental artists for the Hippodrome and Edward Moss's Empires. From this he graduated to the production of full-time spectacles, and was responsible for *Hullo Ragtime* (1912) and *Hullo Tango* (1913), in both of which his first wife, the American jazz singer Shirley Kellogg, appeared. De Courville was also responsible for the first appearance in London of Violet Lorraine. During the First World War his spectacular revues became famous, and in 1918 he took *Zig-Zag* to the Folies-Bergère. During the 1920s he produced at least one new show every year, including the intimate revue *Pins and Needles* (1921), and in later years he turned to the presentation of straight plays. His last production in London was *Lute Song* (1948), an American musical with a Chinese setting. In 1928 de Courville published a volume of reminiscences.

COVENT GARDEN THEATRE, LONDON. There has been a theatre on this site since 1732, when John Rich, holder of the Patent granted by Charles II to Davenant (see PATENT THEATRES) built the first Theatre Royal, Covent Garden, on a piece of land leased from the Duke of Bedford, which had formerly been part of a convent garden (hence the name). With his company from Lincoln's Inn Fields, headed by James Quin, Rich opened his new theatre on 7 Dec. 1732 with a revival of *The Way of the World*. The early years were uneventful. In 1740 Peg Woffington made her first appearance in London at Covent Garden, playing Sylvia in *The Recruiting Officer* on 8 Nov., and on 20 Nov. electrifying the town with her famous 'breeches part', Sir Harry Wildair in *The Constant Couple*. It was here also that she made her last appearance, in 1757. Among other famous actors seen under Rich, who performed only in his own pantomimes, were George Anne Bellamy, Spranger Barry, and, for a short time, Garrick. Rich died in 1761, and was succeeded by his son-in-law, John Beard, who was mainly interested in opera. In 1767 he disposed of the Patent to George Colman the elder and three partners, one of whom, Harris, after a good deal of wrangling and some physical violence, became sole manager in 1774. During this period *She Stoops to Conquer* was produced (15 Mar. 1773) on the recommendation of Johnson, and Macklin appeared as Macbeth, dressed in roughly realistic Scottish garb, though not actually a kilt. He was to be seen again, as a very old man, in his own play, *The Man of the World*, in 1781, and he made his last appearance here, as Shylock, in 1789.

In 1784 and 1792 the theatre was so extensively altered that it may be said to have been virtually rebuilt. Some years later Cooke made his London début as Richard III, and during his meteoric and short-lived career was mainly associated with this theatre. In 1803 John Philip Kemble, after quarrelling with Sheridan at Drury Lane, bought a sixth share of the Covent Garden Patent, and appeared there with his sister, Sarah Siddons. One of his first importations was the child prodigy, Master Betty, a 13-year-old tragedian. He had a prodigious success, and on the motion of the younger Pitt Parliament adjourned to see him act Hamlet.

On 20 Sept. 1808 the theatre was burnt down, twenty-three firemen losing their lives. In this fire perished Handel's organ and the manuscript scores of some of his operas, which had been produced at Covent Garden in the

1730s and 1750s. A new theatre, designed by Robert Smirke and modelled on the Temple of Minerva on the Acropolis, arose on the site, and opened on 18 Sept. 1809 with *Macbeth*. Owing to the high cost of building (£150,000) Kemble increased the prices of the seats, but this, and his engagement of Madame Catalani, who was unpopular with a section of the audience, caused the famous O.P. (Old Prices) Riot. After continual disturbances every night for about two months, he was forced to submit, apologize to the public and return to the old prices. (For an interior view of this theatre, see No. 32.)

Between 1809 and 1821 most of the famous actors of the day, and many singers, appeared at Covent Garden, as did famous pantomimists like Byrne, Farley, Bologna, Ellar, and Grimaldi. On 29 June 1812 Mrs. Siddons made her farewell appearance, and on 16 Sept. 1816 Macready his first. Kemble retired on 23 June 1817 (in which year the theatre was first lit by gas), and his brother Charles took over. It was under Charles's management in 1823 that a production of *King John* took place, with 'historically accurate' costumes and scenery designed by Planché after a great deal of research (see No. 150). This was probably the most important innovation in costuming since Macklin's *Macbeth*. Soon after, the theatre found itself in financial difficulties, which were only alleviated when Charles Kemble's daughter Fanny stepped into the breach and appeared as Juliet, with immense success. By this and subsequent appearances she enabled her father to pay off a load of debts, and for a time the theatre prospered. Edmund Kean made his last appearance on 25 Mar. 1833, and the management passed into the hands of Alfred Bunn, who was already installed at Drury Lane. He lasted only a short time, however, and was succeeded by Osbaldeston, who engaged a strong company with Charles Kean and Macready, and introduced Helen Faucit to London. Audiences, however, remained unmoved, and Osbaldeston gave way to Macready, who first introduced limelight on the stage many years before it became a regular lighting effect (for his *Othello*, see No. 71).

Unfortunately Macready's reign was marked by much internal dissension, and his obstinacy and determination to have his own way eventually ruined him. He left in 1839 and was succeeded by Mme Vestris, with her husband Charles Mathews. She put on some beautiful productions of Shakespeare, but financially her greatest success was Boucicault's *London Assurance* in 1841. After she left in 1842 the theatre fell on hard times, and was finally closed, to reopen on 6 Apr. 1847, after extensive alterations, as the Royal Italian Opera House. From this time the story of Covent Garden is the story of opera in London, and it ceased to be a home of 'legitimate' drama. On 5 Mar. 1856, after a Bal Masqué, it again burnt down, and the present theatre, designed by Sir Edward M. Barry, was built in six months. Although the frontage remained on Bow Street, the building covered extra ground leased by Frederick Gye, now sole manager, from the Duke of Bedford, and was laid out from east to west, instead of from north to south as before. The only further theatrical entertainments were a handful of pantomimes, some revues, and in 1912 Reinhardt's production of *Oedipus Rex* starring Martin-Harvey.

W. MACQUEEN POPE †, *rev.*

COVENTRY CYCLE, see ENGLAND, 1 and MYSTERY PLAY.

COVENTRY HOCKTIDE PLAY, see HOCKTIDE PLAY.

COWARD, NOËL (1899–), English actor, producer and composer, and a prolific dramatist, who has been on the stage since childhood, making his first appearance on 27 Jan. 1911 in a fairy play, and later playing with Charles Hawtrey at the Prince of Wales's. His early plays, which include *The Young Idea* (1922), *The Vortex* (1924), and *Fallen Angels* (1925), aroused a great deal of controversy and were considered typical of the post-war generation, as was the successful *Hay Fever* (also 1925). They were, however, well suited to the taste of the time and in 1925 Coward had five plays running in London, including the revue *On With the Dance*, for which he wrote most of the music as well as the words, as he later did for *This Year of Grace* (1928). The inevitable reaction to his sudden success came with a riot on the first night of *Sirocco* (1927), but in 1929 Coward was winning golden opinions with the romantic sentiment of *Bitter Sweet*, and two years later he consolidated his position with the patriotic *Cavalcade*. Among later successes have been *Design for Living* (1932), the nine one-act plays of *To-Night at 8.30* (1935), *Blithe Spirit* (1941), which set up a record run for a non-musical play in England with 1,997 performances and was made into a musical as *High Spirits* (1964), *Present Laughter* (1942), *Peace in Our Time* (1947), *Nude With Violin* (1956), *Waiting in the Wings* (1960), and *Sail Away* (1962). He has appeared in many of his own plays, some of which have been successfully revived, and has written two volumes of autobiography, *Present Indicative* (1937) and *Future Indefinite* (1954). In 1964 he directed a revival of *Hay Fever* in which Edith Evans made her first appearance with the National Theatre Company, playing Judith Bliss, while in 1965 *Present Laughter* was also given a successful revival at the Queen's Theatre.

COWELL. A family of actors in England and America, of whom the first was (1) JOSEPH LEATHLEY [WHITSHED] (1792–1863), born in England and intended for the navy, which he joined at 13. He went on the stage in 1815, making his first appearance in Plymouth as Belcour in Cumberland's *The West Indian*. After a period at Richmond, Yorks, under Beverley, where he was noted as a fine low comedian, he went to York, and appeared in *The Turnpike Gate* as Crack—a part ever after associated with his name. After further appearances in the provinces, he joined the company at Drury Lane. He was later at Astley's, where the American impresario Stephen Price saw him and engaged him for New York, where he made a great success as Crack at the Park Theatre, on 24 Oct. 1821. He was later in Philadelphia with William Warren, and from 1826 until his return to England in 1844, in which year he published his autobiography, he was one of the most popular comedians in the United States, though a short venture into management in 1837 proved unsuccessful. In 1850 he reappeared in New York, making his final appearance as Crack, and he then returned to England for good, dying at Putney in 1863.

Cowell was married three times. Through his first wife, a Miss Murray, he was connected with the Siddons family, one of his wife's sisters being the wife of Sarah Siddons's son Henry. By this marriage he had three children, Joseph, Maria, and Samuel. Joseph, who died young, was for a time a scene-painter at Covent Garden. By his second marriage, to Frances Sheppard, Cowell had a daughter, Sidney Frances (1823–81), who married the actor-manager H. L. Bateman, under whom Irving first appeared at the Lyceum (see BATEMAN). Cowell's third wife, Harriet Burke, whom he married in 1848, outlived him, dying in 1886.

Cowell's second son (2) SAMUEL HOUGHTON (1820–64) was one of the earliest stars of the English music-halls. Born in London, he grew up in America, and at the age of 9, billed as the Young American Roscius, he played Crack at a benefit performance for his father in Boston. Father and son also appeared together as the two Dromios in *The Comedy of Errors*. In 1840 Sam appeared in Edinburgh under his uncle, W. H. Murray, and he made his first appearance in London at the Surrey in 1844. He had already made a name for himself as a singer of comic songs during the intermissions of a play, and he had been 'chief comic singer' at Cremorne in the summer of 1846 before he deserted the legitimate theatre for the halls. He soon became popular at the Grecian and later at the Canterbury. He wrote a number of his own songs, but is best remembered for 'Villikins and his Dinah' (first popularized by Robson) and 'The Ratcatcher's Daughter'. In 1860 he embarked on a strenuous starring tour of America which led to his premature death from tuberculosis. His wife, an actress named Emilie Marguerite (Emma) Ebsworth, whom he married in 1842 while playing in Edinburgh, kept a detailed diary of this tour, which was edited and published by M. Willson Disher in 1934 as *The Cowells in America*. There were nine children of this marriage. Two girls, (3) SYDNEY (1846–1925) and (4) FLORENCE (1852–1926), were both well-known actresses. After appearing in London and the provinces, they went with Wyndham to America, and Sydney remained there, later marrying an American. She was at her best in such parts as Maggie MacFarlane in Gilbert's *Engaged* and Dolly Dutton in MacKaye's *Hazel Kirke*. In 1900 she retired, but returned to the stage five years later, playing small parts. Florence, who is best known under her second married name as the wife of the actor and stage manager Alfred B. Tapping, was for many years with the Kendals. She was also a member of Miss Horniman's Manchester company, and the first actress to play Mrs. Jeffcote in *Hindle Wakes*. She celebrated her stage jubilee in 1914, while appearing in Manchester. By her first husband, the actor John Parselle (1820–85), she had a daughter, (5) SYDNEY (1872–1941), who appeared under her great-grandmother's name of Fairbrother. She was successsful in a wide variety of parts, from Wally in *Two Little Vagabonds* to Mahbubah in *Chu-Chin-Chow*. In her later years she was a fine character actress, one of her best parts being Mrs. Badger in *The Young Person in Pink*. She also toured the music-halls with the elder Fred Emney in the sketch *A Sister to Assist 'er*.

COWLEY, ABRAHAM (1618–67), English poet and Royalist, who was also the author of a play which, as *The Guardian*, was given at Cambridge before Prince Charles (later Charles II) in 1642. As *Cutter of Coleman Street*, this was one of the first plays performed publicly at the Restoration. It was given at the Duke's House by Davenant's company at the end of 1661. A comedy of contemporary manners, it satirized both the Puritans and the Cavaliers, and was much enjoyed by Pepys, who was present at the first London performance. Its satire was not, however, everywhere acceptable, and it aroused a good deal of controversy. In spite of this it was played at Court, and was revived in 1668, 1702, and 1723. Cowley, whose first volume of verse was published when he was only 15, was also the author of a pastoral comedy, *Love's Riddle*, written when he was 18 and published in 1638. It was not acted until 1723, when it was 'arranged' for performance at a boarding school for young ladies. Cowley also wrote a Latin play, *Naufragium Joculare*, based on Plautus, which was given at Trinity College, Cambridge, in 1638, and translated in 1704 by Charles Johnson as *Fortune in Her Wits*.

COWLEY, HANNAH (*neé* PARKHOUSE) (1743–1809), one of the first women playwrights of England, whose work marks the transition from Restoration to eighteenth-century comedy, though without too strong an infusion of sentimentality. She was at her best in the comedy of manners, and her first play, *The Runaway*, given at Covent Garden in 1776, is said to have been improved by Garrick. Of her later plays, which include *Which is the Man?* (1782), *A Bold Stroke for a Husband* (1783), and *The Town Before You* (1794), all given at Covent Garden, the best is *The Belle's Stratagem* (1780), based on *La Fausse Agnès*, by Destouches. This was revived several times, notably by the Kembles and by Irving, Ellen Terry playing Letitia, one of Mrs. Jordan's finest parts. It was last seen in London at the Court Theatre in 1913, and was one of the earliest comedies to be given in the New World, being in the repertory of the Hallams and Hodgkinson in New York in 1794. There also it was frequently revived, Ada Rehan playing Letitia to Arthur Bourchier's Doricourt in 1893. In 1813 a number of Mrs. Cowley's plays were published with a biographical notice.

COWLEY, Richard (?–1619), an Elizabethan actor who was the first man to play Verges, probably to the Dogberry of Kempe. He was one of Lord Strange's Men in 1593, and joined the Lord Chamberlain's Men on their formation in the following year. He is in the actor-list of Shakespeare's plays, but does not appear to have been a sharer in either the Globe or Blackfriars.

COX, Robert (?–1655), an English actor of the time of Charles I, who was probably on the stage before 1639, when he is noted as a member of the Cockpit company. On the closing of the playhouses in 1642, he managed to evade the ban by playing drolls, or short farcical pieces, with himself in the chief parts, interspersed with rope-dancing and conjuring. He appeared at country fairs, and at the Red Bull playhouse in London where, with several companions, he was apprehended in 1653 by Commonwealth soldiers, and imprisoned. Apart from one or two drolls which he is presumed to have written himself, his repertory consisted mainly of extracts from popular plays (e.g. 'Bottom the Weaver' from *A Midsummer Night's Dream*). These were published by Francis Kirkman as *The Wits; or, Sport upon Sport* (1662, new ed. 1672) with a laudatory preface and an illustrated frontispiece (see No. 23). Cox was a great favourite with his audiences, and apparently a good actor, upon whom the closing of the theatres fell heavily.

CRABTREE, Charlotte (1847–1924), an American actress, known on the stage simply as Lotta. Born in New York, she was taken to California at the age of 6, where she was taught to dance by the famous Lola Montez. An attractive child, tiny, with black eyes and a mop of red hair, she toured the mining-camps from the age of 8, singing, dancing, and reciting, and becoming, in ten years of this nomadic and often dangerous life, a well-known and much-loved figure. In 1865 she went to New York, and there made her first success in Brougham's dramatization of *The Old Curiosity Shop* (1867), in which she played Little Nell and the Marchioness. Throughout her career she preserved a look of youth and innocence, even in her most daring dances and by-play. She was outstanding in burlesque and extravaganza, and in slight plays specially written to give scope for her comic powers, among which were *Zip* and *Musette*, in which she toured indefatigably. She retired in 1891, having amassed a large fortune, which she left to charity. She never married.

CRAIG. (1) Edith (1869–1947), daughter of Ellen Terry and E. W. Godwin. She appeared on the stage as a child, and as a young woman played with her mother and Irving at the Lyceum. She also appeared with the former in *The Good Hope* and *Alice Sit-by-the-Fire*. During Ellen Terry's tour in America in 1907 she acted as her stage-manager, and later studied music in London and in Berlin. She then turned her attention to production and from 1911 directed the Pioneer Players, for whom she also designed costumes and scenery. In 1929 she inaugurated an annual Shakespeare matinée on the anniversary of Ellen Terry's death, when performances were given in the converted barn adjacent to the house at Small Hythe where Ellen Terry spent her last years. This has now been made into an Ellen Terry Museum. Her brother (2) (Edward Henry) Gordon (1872–1966) was also on the stage as a child, and in 1889 joined Irving's company at the Lyceum, where he remained for nine years. During this time he played also many leading parts on tour, and in 1897 gave six performances of Hamlet at the Olympic. In 1903 he designed three scenes for Fred Terry's production of *For Sword or Song*, with some interesting and unusual lighting effects, and with, in one scene, a curious and most effective appearance of mist rising from the ground. He also did the designs for his mother's productions of *The Vikings* and *Much Ado About Nothing*, and from that time deserted the stage for design and production. Among his productions were *Venice Preserved* (1905) in Berlin, *Rosmersholm* (1906) for Eleonora Duse in Florence, and *Hamlet* (1912) at the Moscow Art Theatre. In 1908 he settled in Florence, where he founded and edited *The Mask*, a journal devoted to the art of the theatre, and also ran a school of acting in the Arena Goldoni. He had an immense influence on production methods in Europe and America, more by his originality and prodigality of ideas than by his actual achievements. His theories, which cannot be briefly summarized, are best studied in his publications, *The Art of the Theatre* (1905); *On the Art of the Theatre* (1911), incorporating the previous book and frequently translated; *Towards a New Theatre* (1913), which contains forty plates of scenic designs; *The Marionette* (1918); *The Theatre Advancing* (1921); *Books and Theatres* (1925). He has also written a volume on Irving and one on Ellen Terry, and published an edition of *Hamlet* with woodcuts. In 1957 he published a volume of autobiography, *Index to the Story of My Days, 1872–1907*. His theory of acting has been much criticized as reducing the actor to the status of a puppet working under the instruction of a master-mind 'capable of inventing and rehearsing a play; capable of designing and superintending the construction of both scenery and costume; of writing any necessary music; of inventing such machinery as is needed and the lighting that is to be used'. In 1926 he produced *The Pretenders* at Copenhagen, his designs for the production being subsequently published in portfolio. His influence has been most marked in Germany and America, but he has been somewhat overlooked in England. Shortly before his death his vast theatrical library was bought by the French Government for the Rondel Collection. (For an example of his work, see No. 75).

CRAIG THEATRE, NEW YORK, see ADELPHI THEATRE, 2.

CRANE, RALPH (*c.* 1550/60–after 1621), in early life a household servant to the Osbornes, and later an underwriter in the Privy Seal Office. He added to his income by copying plays, either for their authors or for the actors. His copy of *Sir John van Olden Barnavelt*, made for the King's Men in 1619, was used as a prompt copy, and his two copies of *A Game of Chess* are in the Bodleian and the British Museum respectively. He also made the copy of *The Witch* which is in the Bodleian. There must have been an immense amount of this work done for the playhouses, and it is curious that more names and facts are not known in connexion with it. It was probably poorly paid, and done by hacks and hangers-on of the literary profession.

CRANE, WILLIAM HENRY (1845–1928), American actor, who had had some amateur experience before joining a light-opera company. He had a fine bass voice, and intended to become an opera singer, but he proved so good in comedy that he finally devoted himself to it. In 1877 he joined forces with Stuart Robson, and they appeared as the two Dromios in *The Comedy of Errors*. Among their other successful plays were *Our Boarding House*, *Our Bachelors*, and *The Henrietta*, the last being specially written for them. Crane also played Falstaff and Sir Toby Belch, and after parting amicably from his companion in 1888 he continued to appear in bluff, kindly American parts. Among his later successes were *David Harum* and *Business is Business*. He retired in 1916.

CRATES, of Athens, one of the masters of Old Comedy, who won his first prize in 450 B.C. He was a contemporary of Aristophanes, who praised him in the *Knights* for his wit and graceful style. Fragments of his work survive (see GREECE, 2 *b*). H. D. F. KITTO

CRATINUS (*c.* 520–*c.* 423 B.C.), of Athens, Greek dramatist, one of the masters of Old Comedy, and an elder contemporary of Aristophanes. Only fragments of his works survive. In the *Knights* Aristophanes makes fun of Cratinus as a worn-out drunkard; in the following year (424 B.C.) Cratinus had his revenge by defeating Aristophanes' *Clouds* with his own *Wine-Flask*, probably his last play. Aristophanes also speaks of Cratinus's torrential style, and of the popularity of his lyrics.
H. D. F. KITTO

CRAVEN, FRANK (1880–1945), American actor, dramatist, and producer, who made his first appearances on the stage as a child in Boston, where his parents were members of the stock company. He returned to the stage after some years' schooling, and toured extensively. His first New York success was James Gilley in *Bought and Paid For* (1911), in which he was also seen in London for the first time. During the long run of this play he wrote his first comedy, *Too Many Cooks*, in which he appeared himself in 1914. The most important of his later works was *The First Year* (1920), a comedy of domestic life which has been called 'a milestone in the American theatre', in that the 'matter and the manner, characters, dialogue and situation were all treated with a like gaiety and understanding'. He appeared in it himself, and was also seen as the Stage Manager in *Our Town*. Much of his later work was done in films.

CRAVEN, HAWES [HENRY HAWES CRAVEN GREEN] (1837–1910), English scene-painter, son of a pantomime actor and an actress. As a young boy he played in the provinces, but showed a preference for art and was apprenticed to the scene-painter of the Britannia, Hoxton. His first outstanding work was done for *The Lighthouse*, given at the Olympic in 1857. Befriended by Stanfield and Beverley, he worked at Covent Garden and Drury Lane, and from 1862 to 1864 was at the Theatre Royal, Dublin. He is, however, chiefly remembered for his connexion with Irving at the Lyceum, and his finest work was done there for *Faust*, *Hamlet* (see No. 79), *Romeo and Juliet*, *Becket*, and *Coriolanus*, the last from designs by Alma Tadema. He was much admired, being considered the equal of Stanfield and Beverley in craftsmanship, and their superior in his grasp of theatrical essentials. As an innovator he ranks with de Loutherbourg, and was held by a contemporary critic to have 'carried scenic realism and stage illusion to their utmost limits, much helped by the recent introduction of electric lighting'. Ellen Terry, who knew his work well from her connexion with the Lyceum, called him 'dear Mr. Craven, who so loved his garden and could paint the flicker of golden sunshine for the stage better than anyone'.

CRÉBILLON, PROSPER JOLYOT DE (1674–1762), French dramatist, who in his own day enjoyed enormous prestige, no one being considered worthy to figure between him and Racine, thus conveniently forgetting Pradon, Longepierre, Genest, Campistron, and La Fosse, who were, perhaps, not worth remembering. Crébillon was 32 when his first play was given at the Comédie-Française. It was followed by three more, the last of which, *Rhadamiste et Zénobie* (1711), is usually considered his best. By this time he was lauded as the French Aeschylus, and it was commonly said that he had revived the great days of Corneille and Racine. But he had his detractors. Boileau called him 'Racine drunk' and 'a Visigoth in an age of good taste'. His poetry was certainly crude, but the audience bore with it for the sake of the romantic element and the atmosphere of terror which he succeeded so well in imparting. His plays are, strictly speaking, not tragedies but melodramas, and they remained popular up to the time of the Romantics, when they were ousted by the works of the elder Dumas, on the principle that one corpse is good, but two are better. Crébillon's early plays, in spite of their success, brought him little money, and his later ones were failures. Continually hampered by poverty and by the consequences of an imprudent marriage, Crébillon became embittered and a recluse. He used his position as dramatic censor to oppose Voltaire, while the latter, to prove his superiority in verse-writing, took for the subjects of five of his tragedies plots already treated by Crébillon. The only good thing Crébillon got from his rivalry with Voltaire was a pension, granted him at the age of 72 at the instance of Voltaire's enemies, who chose to exalt the work of the older man at the expense of the younger.

CREPIDATA, see FABULA, 2.

CRISPIN, a character of French comedy who derives from the *commedia dell'arte* mask Scaramuccia (Scaramouche). As originally played by Raymond Poisson, he had in him something of the braggart captain, as witness his enormous rapier, and a good deal of the *zanni* or servant. Succeeding generations of Poissons played the part until 1753, making him more and more a quick-witted unscrupulous valet. Molière used the character but not the name, which was introduced by Scarron. It later figured largely in French comedy, as in *Crispin rival de son maître*, *Crispin musicien*, *Crispin gentilhomme*, and as a character in *Le Légataire universel* and *Le Chevalier à la mode*.

CRITERION THEATRE. 1. London, in Piccadilly Circus. The theatre was originally an adjunct to Spiers and Pond's restaurant, and opened on 21 Mar. 1874 with H. J. Byron's *An American Lady*, in which Mrs. John Wood played the title-role. It is an underground theatre, and at the time was considered a great novelty, as air had to be pumped into it. Success did not come until 1877, with *Pink Dominoes*, adapted by James Albery from a French farce. In the cast was Charles Wyndham, who in 1879 took over the theatre, inaugurating his management with *Truth*. Among later successes were *Betsy* (also 1879) and *Little Miss Muffet* (1882). The theatre was reconstructed and greatly improved in 1883–4, when electricity was installed. It was at the Criterion that many of Henry Arthur Jones's plays were first produced, including *The Case of Rebellious Susan* (1894) and *The Physician* and *The Liar* (both 1897); another success of this period was *Rosemary* (1896). Wyndham left in 1899 to go to his own theatre (see WYNDHAM'S), but he remained lessee of the Criterion until his death, when it passed to his widow, Mary Moore, who made many outstanding appearances there from 1886 onwards.

The theatre was again remodelled in 1902, and five years later Wyndham returned to it to score a success in *The Mollusc* (1907). One of the greatest successes of the First World War, *A Little Bit of Fluff*, began its long run here in 1915, and post-war successes were *Lord Richard in the Pantry* (1919), *Ambrose Applejohn's Adventure* (1921), and *Advertising April* (1923), a farcical comedy mainly remarkable for the presence of Sybil Thorndike in the title-role. From 1926 to 1929 Marie Tempest made several successful appearances, and in 1932 John Gielgud and Frank Vosper appeared in *Musical Chairs*, by Ronald Mackenzie, who was killed in a car accident in the same year. *French Without Tears* began its record run in 1936, followed by *Tony Draws a Horse* (1939); during the Second World War the theatre became a B.B.C. studio, but it reverted to use as a theatre in Sept. 1945 with a revival of *The Rivals* in which Edith Evans played Mrs. Malaprop. Among later successes have been *Traveller's Joy* (1948) with Yvonne Arnaud, *Waiting for Godot* (1955), *Waltz of the Toreadors* (1956), and *A Severed Head*, dramatized from Iris Murdoch's novel by J. B. Priestley. W. MACQUEEN-POPE†, *rev.*

2. NEW YORK, opened as the Lyric on 25 Nov. 1895, as part of Hammerstein's Olympia. It seated 2,800 and had a roof garden for promenading. In 1899, having been sold at auction, it reopened as the Criterion under Charles Frohman. Among its early productions were Julia Marlowe in *Barbara Frietchie* (1899), John Hare and Irene Vanbrugh in *The Gay Lord Quex* (1900), and Mrs. Leslie Carter in *Zaza* (1901). In 1903 Charles Hawtrey opened the season with *The Man from Blankley's*, while the following year *The Dictator*, with William Collier and John Barrymore, ran for three months. In 1908 Isadora Duncan was seen at the Criterion; Laurette Taylor was successful in *Happiness* (1917) and *One Night in Rome* (1919), and the last production, before the house became a cinema, was a version of Brieux's *La Robe rouge* as *The Letter of the Law*, with Lionel Barrymore.

The Herald Square Theatre, New York, originally the Colosseum, was named the Criterion from 1882 to 1885. GEORGE FREEDLEY

CRITICISM, see DRAMATIC CRITICISM.

CROSS KEYS INN, see INNS USED AS THEATRES.

CROTHERS, RACHEL (1878–1958), American dramatist, whose first short plays were produced while she was a student at a dramatic school. She subsequently appeared on the stage, and was responsible for the production of all her own plays. These include *The Three of Us* (1906); *A Man's World* (1909), an attack on the 'double standard of morality' which has been regarded as one of the most significant plays of its time; *He and She* (also known as *The Herfords*) (1911), in which Rachel Crothers herself played the lead in a revival in 1920; *A Little Journey* (1918); *Nice People* (1920), a study of post-war youth;

Expressing Willie (1924); *As Husbands Go* (1931), which contrasts the English and the American conception of marriage; *When Ladies Meet* (1932), a deft study of feminine psychology; and *Susan and God* (1937). Miss Crothers, who had a long and distinguished career in the American theatre, was always in the vanguard of public opinion, yet never allowed her feminist viewpoint to weaken the theatrical effectiveness of her writing. Quinn, who calls her a 'craftsman' of the theatre, says of her:

> Without inventive power of the highest order, she is a keen observer of life, especially in the concrete, and her plays are filled with minor characters who indeed at times attract attention more easily than the major ones. Her view of life is sane and progressive. . . . This ability to progress, to keep abreast of the fashions of the theatre and the conditions of life, reveals the flexibility and adaptability which are her most characteristic traits.

CROW STREET THEATRE, see DUBLIN.

CROWNE, JOHN (?1640–1703 or 1714), a Restoration dramatist and a favourite of Charles II, whose birth, death, and parentage are all equally obscure. His best work was done in comedy, with the creation of Sir Courtly Nice in the play of that name (1685) based on Moreto—a favourite part with many actors; but he also contributed a two-part *Destruction of Jerusalem* (1677) to the contemporary spate of heroic drama. This was given at the Theatre Royal, with most elaborate scenery and dresses, at vast expense. The scenery was probably painted by Aggas and Towers, who later sued the theatre for payment. Indeed, it is possible that many of Crowne's successful but forgotten plays owed much to the resources of scenic art. Crowne was also the author of a masque, a tragedy in rhyme, and a verse comedy which, in the opinion of competent critics, shows a return to a late Elizabethan style. He may therefore be regarded as a synthesis of the dramatic styles and types prevalent in his day. He was part author, with Dryden and Shadwell, of the satirical *Notes and Observations* on Settle's *Empress of Morocco.*

CRUGER'S WHARF THEATRE, NEW YORK, built in 1758 by David Douglass, who appeared there with a company formed of the remnants of that of the elder Hallam, whose widow he had married, and some English actors brought to Jamaica by Moody. The younger Hallam was leading man, and his brother and sister were also in the company. They opened in *Jane Shore,* probably with Mrs. Douglass as the heroine, and after a season of two months ended with *Richard III,* after which 'the Theatre on Mr. Cruger's Wharff' was used no more. It was sometimes referred to as the Wharf Theatre.

CRUMMLES, VINCENT, see LANDER, JEAN.

CRUZ, SOR JUANA INÉS DE LA (1651–95), see SOUTH AMERICA, I.

CRUZ CANO Y OLMEDILLA, RAMÓN FRANCISCO DE LA (1731–94), a Spanish dramatist noteworthy for his lively one-act *sainetes,* vivid farces or satirical sketches which stand out against the prevailing neo-classical literary fashion. He said of his own *sainetes* that they copied what his eyes saw: the dramatist's role was 'to portray men, their words, their actions, and their customs'. These short pieces, then, can be seen at one and the same time as the descendants of the *pasos* and *entremeses* of the sixteenth and seventeenth centuries, and as the forerunners of the nineteenth-century sketches of customs and realistic drama. Ramón de la Cruz also wrote libretti for *zarzuelas,* the Spanish operetta. His plots again turn to popular life, to the depiction of the customs of the lower classes of Madrid, a decided innovation in a genre which had hitherto concerned itself largely with the more complicated love intrigues of the classical gods and goddesses. J. E. VAREY

CSIKY, GERGELY (1842–91), Hungarian dramatist, and the first to put on the stage the social problems of the Hungarian middle class.

CSOKOR, FRANZ THEODOR (1891–), see AUSTRIA.

CUEVA, JUAN DE LA (*c.* 1550– *c.* 1610), Spanish dramatist and the chief writer for the Sevillian school of drama, where his most important plays were produced between 1578 and 1581. Writing in the period when classical influences were still of some importance in the Spanish theatre, Cueva owes a considerable debt to Seneca. Apart from plays on classical themes and comedies of intrigue, Cueva turned also to Spanish history, being one of the first dramatists to put the subject matter of the ballads upon the stage. Bernardo el Carpio, King Sancho, and the tragedy of the *Siete infantes de Lara* paved the way for the great Spanish dramas of Lope de Vega and his contemporaries. Cueva drew freely on popular poetry to enliven his historical plays. He was also an innovator in the comedy of manners with his *Comedia del viejo enamorado* and *El infamador.* J. E. VAREY

CUMBERLAND, RICHARD (1732–1811), English dramatist, well educated, and a grandson of the great Richard Bentley, Master of Trinity College, Cambridge. He had spent some years in politics before in 1761 he embarked on a career as a prolific playwright, mainly because he was in need of money. He wrote a number of poor tragedies, including reworkings of *Timon of Athens* with a new fifth act and of two plays by Massinger, but it is in sentimental domestic comedy that his most characteristic work is found. He first achieved recognition with *The Brothers* (1769), but his best-known play is *The West Indian* (1771), produced with great success by Garrick, and typical of the whole school of sentimental comedy. Among his later plays were *The Fashionable Lover* (1772) and *The Jew* (1794), the latter one of the earliest plays to plead the cause of Jewry. It was frequently revived, and translated into several languages, providing a fine part for outstanding actors of the day. Cumberland, whose success made him an important figure in the literary world of London, was extremely sensitive to criticism, and figures in *The Critic* as Sir Fretful Plagiary, a portrait which his own memoirs, published in 1807, show to be substantially true. A study of his life and works by S. T. Williams was published in 1917 by the Yale University Press. With Hugh Kelly he is perhaps the most typical exponent of the eighteenth-century style which received its death-blow at the hands of Goldsmith and Sheridan.

CUREL, FRANÇOIS DE (1854–1929), French dramatist, whose plays belong to the naturalistic movement, and were first produced at Antoine's Théâtre Libre. A wealthy man of good family, he was trained as a scientist, and brought his analytical faculties to bear on the problems of social life. His first three plays dealt with feminine psychology, and were somewhat limited in scope, though giving promise of the excellence shown in his later works, of which the best was *Le Repas du lion* (1897). This was a study of the struggle between tradition and socialism, which he later returned to and revised. De Curel, who was a somewhat remote and unconventional playwright, never became popular, but his work ranks high for its integrity and its subtle delineation of souls in torment.

CURTAIN. Within the proscenium opening (see PROSCENIUM) hangs the curtain, unknown in the Elizabethan theatre. In the Restoration theatre it rose at the conclusion of the prologue (spoken on the forestage) and remained out of sight till the play was ended and the epilogue spoken, when it fell to mark the finish of the performance. During the play the end of an act was marked by an empty stage, and the end of a scene merely by the changing of the scenery, often with the actors still on the stage ready to walk straight into the next action and so sustain the flow of the play. This curtain was at first, and remained for many decades, green. Its commonest form was probably that of the 'french valance', in which a series of lines descend at the back through rows of rings. When the lines are pulled the curtain rises vertically in a series of bunching, shallow festoons. It might occasionally, and for special effects, be dropped during a performance, but it was not until about the mid-eighteenth century that it began to be used regularly to mark the end of the act, and to hide the stage during an interval. Shortly after, this function was transferred to the Act-Drop, a painted cloth descending in the proscenium opening, and bearing some decorative picture which became associated with the theatre and was not directly related to the play being performed. By 1895 the act-drop had become such a recognized feature of the theatre that popular articles were written about its proper design.

This drop, however, only marked the acts; the scene-transitions were still at this time unconcealed. It was not till Irving's revival of *The Corsican Brothers* in 1880 that a crimson velvet curtain was set in the proscenium to hide scene-changes, and even then the master-manager saw to it that the heaviest change was so well organized as to be performed in only 38 seconds.

The Front Curtain, often called the House Curtain, has today a variety of possible forms of working, including straightforward 'flying', or vertical ascent; side-parting on the traverse principle; and bunching up sideways to the outer top corners—a form often called Tabs (short for Tableau Curtain). This name is now applied to any front curtain, and is sometimes misapplied to the curtain setting on the stage itself.

Another curtain in the proscenium opening is the Safety or Fireproof Curtain, sometimes nicknamed the Iron, of which an example was present at Drury Lane as early as 1800. The Advertisement Curtain made its appearance as an act-drop in the smaller theatres, and bore, in various panels, painted notices of local manufacturers and their wares.

RICHARD SOUTHERN

CURTAIN-RAISER, a one-act play, usually farcical, which in the nineteenth century served to whet the appetite of the audience before the main five-act drama of the evening. It continued into the early years of the twentieth century, and was the last relic of the days when a full evening's entertainment included several plays to which late-comers were admitted on payment of a reduced fee. Together with the After-piece (see ENGLAND, 5), a one-act farce intended to mitigate the horrors of the preceding tragedy, it is now seldom seen, owing to the modern professional theatre's determined adherence to the single bill, and the one-act play survives mainly in the productions of the amateur theatre in England and America.

CURTAIN SET, the simplest method of dressing the stage for a performance. It consists of Side Curtains, a Back Curtain, and Borders, which latter are narrow, hanging strips to mask-in the top. It may also include a Traverse Curtain, one centrally divided and running off to the sides of the stage on a wire or railway. The Curtain Set is a favourite stand-by of amateurs and Little Theatres, and can be used with remarkable ingenuity. It has, strictly speaking, no scenic function, but achieves one if, for the playing of a given scene, a small set-piece is placed on the stage before the back curtain. The set then becomes characterized by that additional modification, and remains so until it is removed or changed (for the varieties of front curtain, see CURTAIN).

CURTAIN THEATRE. 1. LONDON. The first Curtain was London's second playhouse, opened in 1577, the year after the Theatre. There is no definite information as to who built it, how much it cost, or the actual date of its opening. It may be that Burbage was responsible for it as well as for the Theatre, for the two stood very close together. The Curtain seems to have been a more peaceful house than its neighbour. It took its name, not from a theatre curtain or act-drop, but from the fact that it stood on a piece of land called the Curtain, or Curtain Close, and later Curtain Court. The name survives today in Curtain Road, Shoreditch. The choice of Finsbury Fields was a wise one. It was the playground of London. The citizens practised archery there, train-band musters were held there, and the Artillery Company (now the H.A.C.) was near by. This place of public resort was the very spot for theatres.

In shape, form, and design the Curtain was the same as the Theatre, but its dimensions are not known. That it was crowded more often than not is proved by numerous entries in the legal records concerning pickpockets caught there red-handed, lifting the purses of members of the public gaping at the show; and at first it was probably a venue, as was the Theatre, for exhibitions of swordplay, fencing, quarterstaff, and the like. Theatrically it has a much more distinguished record than its older rival. Some of the most notable companies of the time appeared there under Elizabeth, including the Lord Chamberlain's, which on the accession of James I became the King's. Pope, who had a share in the theatre, was a member of this company, as were Tarleton and Armin, under the control of Burbage. They were specially licensed to appear at the Curtain in 1603. There were many attempts to suppress the Curtain, and it was seriously threatened with extinction when the Fortune was opened in 1600. The opponents of theatres, having succeeded in abolishing the Theatre itself, suddenly realized that the Fortune, another playhouse, was to be erected. They petitioned the Privy Council, who replied that it was not proposed to increase the number of theatres, and that should the Fortune arise, it would be in lieu of the Curtain. But nothing came of that, and the Curtain continued its existence. Its greatest glory is that it was associated with Shakespeare. It is claimed, with some justification, that *Henry V* was first played at the Curtain, and that it was 'the wooden O' referred to by the Chorus. *Romeo and Juliet* may also have had its first production there, and Jonson's *Every Man in His Humour*, as it was by that time (1600) a home of legitimate drama.

In 1615, in spite of the opposition of the City Fathers, certain young men of the City, presumably talented amateurs, gave a performance of *Hector of Germany* at the Curtain. At that time it could be hired for such performances, or by any company who so desired. In 1617 the Prince's Company occupied it. In *Vox Graculi, or The Jackdaw's Prognostications for 1623* it is said: 'about this time new plays will be more in request than old, and if company come current to the Bull and Curtain, there will be more money gathered in one afternoon than will be given to Kingsland and Spittle in a whole month.'

The last traceable reference to the Curtain is none too happy—a prosecution in 1627 of one Richard Burford 'for defiling a sewer near the Curtain Playhouse'. After that reference it vanishes from knowledge, but it is quite likely that it stood until the general suppression of theatres in 1642. W. MACQUEEN-POPE†

2. GLASGOW. This was founded in 1933 by a group of amateurs, led by Grace Ballantine, who was to direct most of their productions, Norman Bruce, a journalist and dramatist, and Paul Vincent Carroll, then a school-teacher in Glasgow. The group began in their own miniature theatre in a Victorian terrace house in the west end of the city. After nearly three years' work there, regular public presentations began at the Lyric Theatre in the autumn of 1935, and continued until the spring of 1940. The principal aim of the group was the encouragement of Scottish playwrights, and a number of interesting new plays were presented, including works by Norman Bruce, Paul Vincent Carroll, and Robins Millar. But the most promising young playwright found by the Curtain was Robert MacLellan, who in *Jeddart Justice*, *Toom Byres*, and *King Jamie the Saxt* displayed a remarkable control of the humour and raciness of the vernacular. Among the actors who played for the Curtain were Duncan Macrae, Brown Derby, and James McKechnie. Although the Curtain was a victim of the Second World War, its pioneer work was not wasted. In Jan. 1941 John Stewart, who had been music adviser to the Curtain, opened in the house next door his Park Theatre, which he directed for ten years before moving to Pitlochry and founding the Festival Theatre there.

3. The name 'Curtain Theatre' was taken by a small professional touring company under Ann Casson, younger daughter of Sybil Thorndike and Lewis Casson, which toured the camps and civilian halls of the Orkneys, Scotland, and the north of England in the winter of 1943–4. Among the actors was Frank Baker, whose book, *Playing with Punch*, describes the tour and gives the text of his new version of the Punch and Judy play which was used by the company.

From 1866 to 1880 the Holborn Theatre, London, was called the Curtain.

CUSHMAN. (1) CHARLOTTE SAUNDERS (1816–76), American actress, outstanding in tragic or character parts. She made her first appearance in opera, but had the misfortune to lose her singing voice and turned to acting. She made her first appearance on the legitimate stage in 1836, as Lady Macbeth, in which she was considered to be unequalled. At the Park Theatre, New York, she played a number of parts, including Romeo, but was at her best as Meg Merrilies in a dramatization of Scott's *Guy Mannering*, and as Nancy in *Oliver Twist*. She later played Oberon, and Lady Gay Spanker in the first American production of *London Assurance* (1841). A turning-point in her career came with a season in New York when she played opposite Macready, who noted in his diary: 'The Miss Cushman who acted Lady Macbeth interested me much. She has to learn her art, but she showed mind and sympathy with me; a novelty so refreshing to me on the stage.' According to a contemporary critic, her acting improved enormously after this experience, and on Macready's advice she went to London, where she was well received. She made her first appearance at the Princess's on 13 Feb. 1845, being seen as Lady Macbeth, Rosalind, Mrs. Haller, Beatrice, Meg Merrilies, and Portia. At the Haymarket later in the same year she was seen as Romeo to the Juliet of her sister (2) SUSAN (1822–59), who, after an unhappy marriage with a Mr. Merriman, had joined her sister on the stage. They played together in the provinces and in Dublin, and in 1848 Susan was married again, to an Englishman named Muspratt. Before returning to America in the following year Charlotte was seen as Queen Katharine to Macready's Wolsey at Drury Lane, for his benefit night. She repeated this part in New York, and also played Claude Melnotte. In 1852 she gave the first of many farewell performances, but remained before the public until a year before her death, being seen in 1857 as Cardinal Wolsey. Among the other great parts attempted by this intrepid woman were Hamlet, Phèdre, and Bianca. But her greatest part was undoubtedly Meg Merrilies, which she practically created, being criticized by some purists for her departures from the original novel. Dutton Cook wrote of her: 'Her performances lacked femineity, to use Coleridge's word; but in power to stir an audience, to touch their sympathies, to kindle their enthusiasm, and compel their applause, she takes rank among the finest players.' Joseph Jefferson, who admired her very much, praised her warm and charitable disposition, and described her as 'tall and commanding in person, with an expressive face, whose features might have been called plain but for their strength and character'. During the last years of her life, though she continued to act intermittently, she was mainly occupied with Shakespeare readings, which proved very successful. In 1907 a Charlotte Cushman Club, which still flourishes, was established in Philadelphia. Its club-room contains many interesting theatrical relics, paintings, and material contemporary with her career.

CUT, a division practised in the floor-boards of a stage to allow the passage of flat scenery up from the cellar.

CUT-CLOTH, see CLOTH.

CYCLORAMA. This scenic device has had a short and not entirely happy history. In principle it is the solution to half a scene-designer's difficulties, but in practice its design and accommodation on any given stage are matters demanding the greatest forethought. The cyclorama is, in essence, a curved wall, or section of a dome, built at the back of the stage, and demanding one quality—an absolutely unbroken surface. Upon it light can be thrown, and the effects thus achieved are amazing; but to present that perfect surface a cyclorama has to be rigidly and heavily built, and it should generally be of hard cement. Thus it becomes a completely immobile part of the stage, and so a potential obstacle when not needed. Movable cycloramas have been invented, but never widely adopted. A full cyclorama interferes with access to the stage from the sides and with the suspension of scenery from above. It thus tends to limit the scenery used on the stage to one given style only, and to restrict or forbid the use of other, traditional, types of scene arrangement. A partial, or shallow, cyclorama—even a plain, uncurved, distempered back wall—is often used instead of a full cyclorama, and has proved effective and less restrictive. A well-planned cyclorama may considerably reduce the amount of scenery needed to mask a stage, but only if the types of scenes are such as can widely include the cyclorama effect. In most other cases it is useless, and the scenery must stand in front of it and hide it (see also LIGHTING and SCENERY).

RICHARD SOUTHERN

CZECHOSLOVAKIA. Owing to the bilingual character of Czechoslovakia the history of her theatre divides into two main currents, Czech and Slovak.

1. CZECH. The Czech language is found in liturgical plays as early as the thirteenth century, and Czech actors also were not lacking, bringing into the plays secular satirical scenes like that of the quack doctor. The tradition of the native Passion play was, however, submerged in the Hussite wars of religion in the early part of the fifteenth century. A fresh start was made in the next century, but though plays by such writers as Pavel Kyrmezer portrayed scenes from contemporary life in the vernacular, and historical plays were also written, drama was mainly educational, as with the Latin plays of J. A. Comenius. The promising beginnings of humanist drama were smothered by the onset of the Thirty Years' War and by the tyranny of the Hapsburgs. After the battle of Bílá Hora (1620) the Czech nobility and intelligentsia were either executed or forced to emigrate. For more than 150 years the Czech theatre seemed dead, while Italian opera and German or Jesuit plays reigned supreme. The itinerant companies of English, German, or Italian comedians did, however, occasionally play in Czech, while the tradition of the vernacular Christmas play, or comedies of peasant life, continued in the villages.

The earliest theatres—the first in Prague was built in 1737—were destined for the use of foreign companies, and, although a few plays in Czech were produced in Prague and Brno between 1767 and 1783, it was not until 1785 that František Bulla, manager of the theatre built in 1783 by Count Nostitz-Rieneck (now the Tyl Theatre, see No. 94), managed to put them on more frequently, with the intention of contributing to the revival of Czech national culture by means of the spoken word. From this period of enlightenment, which lasted half a century, dates the prevalent idea of the theatre as an important instrument in the furthering of new ideas, and that awareness of responsibility which is one of the main reasons for the high standing of contemporary dramatic art in Czechoslovakia. The outstanding theatre men of the first phase of the period of enlightenment were the Thám brothers, whose work was connected more especially with the Bouda or Hut Theatre from 1786 to 1789. The second period, 1812–30, had perhaps less driving force, but among the outstanding writers were J. N. Štěpánek and V. K. Klicpera, whose popular plays took their subjects from the daily life of the peasantry and lower middle classes who had done so much to keep the Czech theatre alive under oppression. There can be no doubt that Czech drama owes much of its charm and vivacity to this source of strength. It was in 1839 that a new generation came to the fore, led by J. K. Tyl, from whose unassuming play *Fidlovačka* (1834) (portraying a fair), with music by František Škroup, came the Czech national anthem, 'Kde domov můj?', (Where is my home?). In 1848 came the pioneers of the bourgeois theatre, Josef Jiví Kolár (1812–96), who was also an actor and producer, F. B. Mikovec and others. In Prague there were by now semi-professional companies of Czech actors, as there were also in some provincial towns, beginning with Brno, and in 1859 the first Czech touring company, Prokopš, set out on its travels. Other potent influences were the famous Czech puppeteers, like M. Kopecký, who performed all over the country, and the established amateur groups. But it was not until 1862 that a separate independent Czech theatre building—the Provisional Theatre—was erected, paid for by private subscriptions. On the same site, twenty-one years later, arose the National Theatre, seating 1,500 and paid for by contributions from the whole nation. On the frieze above the stage ran the proud inscription 'Národ Sobě' (The nation to itself), and to this day the Czechs consider this so-called 'little golden chapel' one of the highest symbols of their national independence and culture. Although Czech drama, unlike Czech opera under Smetana, had not yet reached international standards, the efforts of those who, like Jan Neruda (1834–91), wanted to combine artistic development with national aspirations, were beginning to bear fruit. The first generation of eminent actors and actresses, which included O. Sklenářová-Malá, K. Šimanovský, and J. Seifert, still modelled their style on the powerful rhetoric of the Vienna Burgtheater; but they were soon joined, and in some cases superseded, by the advocates of dramatic realism, among them J. V. Slukov, J. Mošna, F. Kolár, J. Šmaha, V. Budil, and M. Bittnerova, under F. A. Šubrt, the dramatist who was director of the National Theatre from 1883 to 1900. During this time a generation of realistic dramatists arose, who combined the new technique with subjects of the national renaissance—as in L. Stroupežnický's *Naši furianti* (1887)—or transformed rural comedies into broad pictures of contemporary life with social undertones—as in A. Jirásek's *The Father*, the Mrštík brothers' *Maryša* (both 1894) and G. Preissová's *Její pastorkyňa* (1800), which last provided the libretto for Janáček's opera 'Jenůfa'.

Against this realistic movement the romantic and poetic dramatists such as Julius Zeyer and Jaroslav Vrchlický could not prevail, though the latter translated a number of foreign plays. Another poet of the same generation, J. V. Sládek, made admirable Czech translations of all Shakespeare's plays, to which have now been added the modern prose versions of E. A. Saudek and others. The presentation of Shakespeare on the Czech stage began with the actor and producer J. J. Kolár, and found its outstanding interpreter in Jaroslav Kvapil (1868–1950), who worked at the National Theatre from 1900 to 1918. The climax of his work was his production of twenty-one of Shakespeare's plays, of which fifteen were performed in 1916 to mark the tercentenary of the dramatist's death. Under Kvapil a new generation of actors was formed, led by the overwhelming personality of E. Vojan, accounted by some the best tragedian of his time, and by Hana Kvapilová, Kvapil's wife and his most delicate and subtle interpreter. He also discovered and developed such dramatically opposed talents as those of Marie Hubnerová (1862–1931), unsurpassed exponent of the women of the people in popular drama, and Anna Sedláčková (1887–), one of the most elegant and entrancing leading ladies of the Central European stage of her time.

Kvapil, who was more occupied with theatrical than social questions, was succeeded in 1921 by Karel Hugo Hilar (1885–1935), who stressed the role of the producer. Since 1910 Hilar had been director of the Municipal Theatre of Královské Vinohrady (situated in one of the sections that make up the city of Prague), founded in 1907 by Šubrt and V. Štech. Under Hilar it became one of the most important theatres in the country.

During his active career, Hilar did much to encourage contemporary dramatists, of whom the most important was undoubtedly Karel Čapek (1890–1938), author of *The Insect Play* and *R.U.R.*, both well known in English. In scenic design Vlastislav Hofman, the first modern Czech stage designer, worked closely with Hilar.

Meanwhile, under the influence of the U.S.S.R., the foundations were being laid for a socialist theatre of the working class. The leader of the movement was Jindřich Honzl, whose activities culminated in the First Workers' Spartiakiade held in Prague in 1921, at which time the first socialist theatre also came into being. During the 1920s two original comedians, J. Voskovec and J. Werich, put on at their Free (or Unfettered) Theatre (Osvobozené Divadlo), under the mask of ingenious clowning, satiric programmes which, after Munich, led them to transfer their activities to New York.

Of the other progressive theatre leaders—among them A. Kurš, a pupil of the Moscow Art Theatre, and J. Frejka—the outstanding figure was E. F. Burian (1904–59), who in 1934 founded his own small experimental theatre, where he trained actors in his own methods. Unfortunately the Second World War intervened and destroyed much that had been accomplished. Many people died or emigrated and in 1944 all the theatres were closed, the personnel being sent into industry. The years of occupation marked the end of the Czech theatre as it had been before 1938. When the theatres reopened in 1945 they were nationalized, and a law passed on 20 Mar. 1948 made it the concern of the State to provide theatres, not only in the towns, but also in the villages. It is as yet too early to say what the results will be. The large increase in the number of theatres, most of them with excellent backstage accommodation, but otherwise undistinguished, testifies to the enthusiasm of the Czech people for the drama, but new beginnings have had to be made in playwriting, production, and interpretation. To begin with the repertory was based mainly on classical dramas capable of forming a link with the present-day situation and on topical foreign plays. The newer dramatists were most successful when, like J. Drda, they worked in the tradition of the folk-tale, or, like M. Stehlík, turned to the realistic portrayal of village life. Only recently have writers taken as their province the problems of the urbanized working man. New plays have contributed to the development of a fresh approach to the problems of production, and individual theatres are evolving their own characteristic styles. But the greatest advance has probably been in scenic design, with the use of new materials and techniques, of which J. Svoboda is the leading spirit (for set designs by Czech designers see Nos. 83, 94). Satire still flourishes, as do puppets and children's theatres. There has also been an interesting upsurge of small experimental theatres run by young actors, among them the Zábradlí (or Balustrade) Theatre in Prague, with L. Fialka's mime company and Jan Grossman's drama group, the Semafor, a musical cabaret which specializes in popular songs by J. Suchý and J. Šlitre, the Rococo Theatre, and, in Brno, the Evening Theatre, devoted to political satire.

2. SLOVAK. Although German biblical plays were presented in Slovakia in the fifteenth century, and Protestant 'school dramas' in the sixteenth, while Jesuit plays (in Latin) and religious folk drama in the vernacular flourished side by side in the seventeenth and eighteenth centuries, the Slovaks were not able to build up a theatrical culture of their own before the founding of the Republic in 1918, since the Hungarians suppressed any sign of cultural activity on their part. There was, however, some amateur activity linked with the growing national movement in the early nineteenth century. The moving spirit in this was Fejérpataky-Belopotocký in Liptovský Mikuláš, where, on 22 Aug. 1830, he presented *Chalupska's Kocúrkovo*, which was not only the first amateur performance in Slovak, but also the foundation of the great Slovak tradition of social satire, a tradition continued in the 1860s and 1870s by J. Palárik with *Incognito* and J. Záborský with *Najdúch*. But the main trend of the repertory was in accordance with official policy, and only Gregor-Tajovský portrayed the realities of the Slovak situation.

In 1920 the municipal theatre in Bratislava, which had formerly housed companies playing in German or Hungarian, became the Slovak National Theatre. The actors at first were Czech in a bilingual Czech and Slovak repertory. Victor Šulc (who died in a German concentration camp) led the Czech company, and Jan Borodáč, who was later to be important in the development of the National Theatre, the Slovak. With the establishment of a touring company, and of a permanent Slovak company in Košice, Slovak actors soon took over entirely, creating their own tradition of acting and production, and in the late 1930s and early 1940s gained a notable satirist in the dramatist Ivan Stodola. But artistic progress was impossible in the conditions created by the division of Czechoslovakia in 1938, and the period of the so-called Slovak State from 1939 to 1945, though new theatres were opened in Nitra and Martin, and the Frontline Theatre was active in 1944, during the Slovak uprising.

A new epoch in the Slovak theatre began in 1945. Three new playhouses were opened in Bratislava, one at the University Drama School, four in regional cities and two, one Hungarian in Komárno and one Ukranian in Prešov, for non-Slovak national minorities.

At first the new dramatists, apart from Stodola, in trying to portray the revolutionary traditions and the turbulent changes in their country, which was rapidly becoming industrialized, limited themselves to externals. Only later was it possible to probe more deeply. One of the best modern playwrights is Petr Karvaš (1910–), whose play *Pulnoční mše*, set in the period of the Slovak uprising of Aug. 1944, represents the peak of Slovak dramatic art. In the same way staging and production no longer concentrate on external realism, but, as in productions at the National Theatre by Josef Budský and Tibor Rakovský and in settings by Ladislav Vychodil, seek to express the inner truth of the play. (For an 18th-century Court Theatre in Czechoslovakia, see No. 65).

D

DAHLGREN, FREDRIK AUGUST (1816–95), Swedish dramatist (see SCANDINAVIA, 3 *a*).

DALBERG, BARON WOLFGANG HERIBERT VON (1750–1806), a wealthy and aristocratic amateur of the theatre who was also a playwright. His interest in theatrical matters led to his appointment in 1777 as honorary director of the newly opened Mannheim National Theatre. Here his inexperience led to his making a bad start by engaging Seyler and his redoubtable wife Sophie Hensel at the same time as her bitter rival, the wife of Brandes. Their quarrels led to the speedy departure of both couples, and a new democratic rule was instituted. After the death of Ekhof in Gotha in 1778 Dalberg arranged for his actors to be transferred to Mannheim, and with a fine company headed by Iffland the theatre flourished. Iffland's first plays were given there, as was *Julius Caesar* for the first time in Germany in an adaptation by Dalberg. But the chief glory of this period was the production of the young and then unknown Schiller's first play, *Die Räuber*, and his appointment as theatre poet from 1783 to 1784, during which time *Fiesco* and *Kabale und Liebe* also appeared. The enterprise continued to prosper until the rigours of war reached Mannheim in 1796, when it was disbanded and Iffland left to go to Berlin.

DALIN, OLOF (1708–63), Swedish dramatist, the first to introduce contemporary French classic tragedy to the Swedish stage. He was also the author of a number of comedies, which show the influence of Molière and Holberg.

DALY, (JOHN) AUGUSTIN (1839–99), American dramatist and manager. At 21 he became a dramatic critic, and by the time he was 30 had served in that capacity on several leading papers. He also wrote and adapted a number of plays, among them the London melodrama, *Under the Gaslight*, and *Leah the Forsaken* (from Mosenthal's *Deborah*). In 1869 he went into management, opening the Fifth Avenue Theatre, New York, where he produced a season of Shakespearian and other plays. In 1873 the theatre was burned down, but he rebuilt it, retiring from its management in 1878. He then spent a short time in England, but returned to New York to open his own theatre (see below, 1.) with a fine company headed by John Drew and Ada Rehan, which in 1884, under the management of William Terriss, played at Toole's Theatre in London. Although previously unknown, Ada Rehan scored such a success there that the company became welcome visitors, returning to the old Strand Theatre in 1886, to the Gaiety in 1888, and to the Lyceum in 1890. Daly then decided to have his own theatre in London (see below, 2). Returning to New York in 1894, Daly made one more visit to London before his death. Both in New York and in London his first nights were important events, and he was one of the outstanding managers of his day on both sides of the Atlantic. He accomplished much, and had a high standard, in spite of his tendency to tamper with the text of established classics.

W. MACQUEEN-POPE†

DALY, (PETER CHRISTOPHER) ARNOLD (1875–1927), American actor, who had already had some success on the stage, where he made his first appearance in 1892, when in 1903 he came into prominence with his production of *Candida*, in which he played Marchbanks. This was the first production of one of Shaw's plays in the United States since Mansfield's tour of *The Devil's Disciple* in 1897, and Daly, who was intensely interested in Shaw's work, and ready to further it by every means in his power, followed the success of *Candida* with a production of *Mrs. Warren's Profession* which led to an uproar and prosecution by the police. In spite of this Daly produced *You Never Can Tell*, *Arms and the Man*, and a double bill consisting of *The Man of Destiny* and a trifle written specially for him by Shaw, *How He Lied to Her Husband*. He also played this last sketch in vaudeville. Opposition eventually proved too much for him and he became soured by ill usage and the attacks of prudish journalists and city fathers. An effort to run a 'theatre of ideas' failed financially, and Daly, who was a good actor, though inclined to be somewhat temperamental, went back to the usual run-of-the-mill life of the theatre, dying in a fire in his early fifties.

DALY'S THEATRE. 1. NEW YORK (for Daly's first theatre in New York, see FIFTH AVENUE THEATRE). Daly's last theatre was originally Banvard's, and later Wood's, Museum. Plays were first given there in 1867, and under Wood in 1868 Lydia Thompson and her Blondes started the vogue for British burlesque. It was at this theatre that Laura Keene made her last appearance, on 27 Apr. 1872, dying the following year, but in spite of a sprinkling of stars in straight plays, it relied mainly on extravaganza, burlesque, variety, and melodrama. Odell, in his *Annals of the New York Stage*, calls it 'a Broadway Bowery' and says that its early history is but the 'cluttered story of a humble house'. A series of revivals in the season of 1874–5 was notable for the first appearance of Ada Rehan at the theatre she was afterwards to adorn for so long. This was on 26 Apr. 1875, in *Thoroughbred*. After the removal of the museum exhibits, the theatre, as the New Broadway, was rented to travelling companies, and from 1877 to 1878, under James Duff, it had a good season as the Broadway. Finally, on 17 Sept. 1879, entirely remodelled and redecorated, it opened as Daly's, of glorious memory, and in spite of a slow start became one of the leading theatres of New York, particularly after the burning of the Park and the break-up of Wallack's and Union Square. By 1882–3 Daly was firmly established as the most enterprising and successful manager on Broadway. The same season saw Ada Rehan, who with John Drew was the star of Daly's fine company, as Donna Hypolita in a revival of Cibber's *She Would and She Would Not.* She was also extremely good in an expurgated edition of *The Country Girl*, but scored her greatest triumph in the revival of *The Taming of the Shrew*, given on 17 Jan. 1887. This was only one of Daly's great revivals of Shakespeare. Other notable productions were *The Merry Wives of Windsor* on 14 Jan. 1885, and a lovely *Midsummer Night's Dream* with scenery by Henry Hoyt. Daly remained at this theatre until his death, and it still retained his name until it was demolished in 1920, having for the last five years of its life been a cinema. GEORGE FREEDLEY†

2. LONDON, in Cranbourn Street, Leicester Square. This was built for Daly by George Edwardes at a cost of £40,000. The foundation stone was laid by Ada Rehan on 30 Oct. 1891, and on 12 Mar. 1893 she appeared as Katharina in the opening production, *The Taming of the Shrew*, supported by Daly's own company—sixty-one strong and nineteen walk-ons—with a special ode of welcome written by Irving. Daly, who believed in frequent changes of programme, then revived Sheridan Knowles's *The Hunchback* and presented, among other plays, Tennyson's *The Foresters.* This was not a success, but is notable as being the first play in this theatre to be lighted entirely by electricity. Before he left in 1894 Daly put on a number of other plays, including Shakespeare, with whom, be it said in passing, he took almost as many liberties as Colley Cibber had done. George Edwardes then took over the theatre and presented Duse in *La Dame aux camélias.* The critics, however, preferred Bernhardt in the part. The first production of 'Hansel and Gretel' in London was given by the Carl Rosa Opera Company in 1894, and after a visit from Bernhardt and Lucien Guitry, Daly's became the home of musical comedy, beginning with *An Artist's Model* (1895), followed by *The Geisha* (1896). In the cast was Huntley Wright, who spent nearly a lifetime at this theatre. During the next fifteen years Daly's became one of the most fashionable and successful theatres in London, being rivalled only by the Gaiety, Edwardes's other home of musical comedy. Among the eleven productions which occupied the theatre during this period were *San Toy* (1899), *A Country Girl* (1902), *The Merry Widow* (1907) with Lily Elsie and Joseph Coyne, and *The Dollar Princess* (1909). Edwardes's last production at Daly's was *The Marriage Market* (1913). War broke out a year later, and he died in the following year. In 1917 Oscar Asche produced *The Maid of the Mountains*, in which José Collins made a great hit, and *A Southern Maid* followed in 1920. *The Lady of the Rose* (1922), with Harry Welchman and Phyllis Dare, and *Madame Pompadour* (1923), with Evelyn Laye and Derek Oldham, were given under the management of James White, ex-bricklayer and millionaire, who had bought Daly's for £200,000. He lost a lot of money, for the tide of success was now flowing away from Daly's, and the theatre was involved in the crash which led to White's suicide on 29 June 1927. A production of Noël Coward's *Sirocco* led to a riot, but the resultant publicity did the theatre no lasting good, and a succession of new plays, revivals, and even pantomime, failed. Finally, on 25 Sept. 1937, the curtain fell for the last time on a play about the Jesuit Order entitled *The First Legion.* There was no ceremony, not even a speech, to mark the passing of this famous theatre. It was pulled down and a cinema erected on the site.

W. MACQUEEN-POPE†

3. NEW YORK, on 63rd Street. This was built as the Davenport in 1909, but became a music-hall in 1919, and was a home of musical comedy when in 1922 it was rechristened Daly's. Its first important production was a revival of *Love for Love* in 1925. It was known successively as the Coburn, as the Recital, when *Lady Windermere's Fan* was seen there, as the Park Lane, and in 1935 as Gilmore's, with Paul Gilmore and his daughter Virginia in popular and cut-rate revivals. It became the Experimental on 4 Mar. 1936, when the Federal Theatre Project leased it and produced there a number of new plays and revivals, including Shaw's *On the Rocks* for the first time in New York. The Yiddish Theatre Project also occupied the house for a time, but with the passing of the Federal Theatre Project in 1939 the theatre closed, to open again in 1941 under its old name of Daly's. It stood empty for many years, and was used by the Shuberts for storage before being demolished in 1957.

GEORGE FREEDLEY†

DAME, a female character in the English pantomime which is traditionally played by an actor. Although, as with Principal Boy (played by an actress), efforts have been made to derive this tradition from the Roman Saturnalia, a more obvious source can be found in the fact that in an all-male company (as in the classical Greek theatre and in Elizabethan England) women's parts must be played by men, and even when the actresses had taken over the young women's parts they were often reluctant to appear as old (particularly comic old) women. Such parts therefore remained in the male repertory both in seventeenth-century France (see ALLARD) and in England as late as the eighteenth century, when Woodward, Samuel Foote, and Tate Wilkinson played comic old women parts in farce. The tradition, like so many others, lingered on in the pantomime, which, as V. C. Clinton-Baddeley has so well said in *All Right on the Night* (1954), 'has become a repository for traditions of the English stage which have died out everywhere else'. Among the Dame parts are Aladdin's mother, Widow Twankay (a name invented by H. J. Byron in an extravaganza, taken from the name of a Chinese tea-exporting port), Jack's mother, Dame Durden or Dame Trot, and usually Cinderella's ugly sisters. If they are played by women, then their mother, the Baroness, is played by a male comedian. Other Dame parts are the Cook in Dick Whittington, the Queen of Hearts, Mother Goose, and Mrs. Crusoe. Among famous players of Dame parts have been Dan Leno, George Robey, Will Fyffe, Barry Lupino, Shaun Glenville, and Clarkson Rose.

D'AMICO, SILVIO (1887–1955), Italian theatre scholar, who inaugurated and, until his death, edited the monumental *Enciclopedia dello Spettacolo.* Born and educated in Rome, he first studied law, and in 1911 entered the Ministry for Fine Arts, where he remained, with an interval for service with the Italian Army during the First World War, until 1923, when he was appointed Professor of the History of the Theatre at the St. Cecilia Academy in Rome. In 1935 he founded the Academy of Dramatic Art, of which he remained President until his death, lecturing there on the history of the theatre. The Academy is now named after him. From 1918 D'Amico was dramatic critic of the Roman daily paper *Idea Nazionale*, and of *Tribuna* when the former was amalgamated with it in 1925. From 1941 to 1943 he was dramatic critic of the *Giornale d'Italia*, and, from 1945 until his death, of *Tempo*. He was also drama critic for Rome Radio. In 1932 he helped to found the theatre review *Scenario*, which he edited till 1936, and he was also the founder, and from 1937 to 1943 editor, of the *Rivista italiana del Dramma* (later *del Teatro*). He wrote many books on the theatre, of which the most important was undoubtedly his *Storia del teatro drammatico* (1939–40; 3rd edition in 4 vols., 1953). A great lover of the living theatre, he did not confine his attention to the academic side only, but encouraged his students to act. They performed abroad, and in 1940–1 formed a professional company.

DANCE, SIR GEORGE (1858–1932), English theatrical manager, author, and song-writer, whose early song, 'Girls are the Ruin of Men', was one of Vesta Tilley's successes. From composition he turned to the writing of libretti for musical plays, and his 'books', which include *The Nautch Girl* (1891) and *A Chinese Honeymoon* (1899), are models of their kind. The former immediately succeeded the series of Gilbert and Sullivan works at the Savoy, while the latter, first seen at Hanley, had a long run at the old Strand Theatre in 1901. Dance became one of the most successful and most powerful theatre managers in the United Kingdom, and often had as many as twenty-four companies on tour at once. He was behind the scenes financially at many of the big West-End theatres in the days preceding the First World War, and had a keen eye for a rising man or woman of talent, either artistically or managerially. He was a tireless worker, a forceful personality, and a man of vision. He was knighted in 1923 in recognition of his services to the theatre, which included a gift of £30,000 for the reconstruction of the Old Vic. His son, Eric, who died in a prison camp during the Second World War, was responsible for the building of the Oxford Playhouse, which opened in 1938. W. MACQUEEN-POPE†

DANCHENKO, VLADIMIR NEMIROVICH-, see NEMIROVICH-DANCHENKO.

DANCOURT. (1) FLORENT CARTON (1661–1725), French dramatist and actor. He was studying law in Paris when he fell in love with the actress (2) MARIE THÉRÈSE LENOIR (1663–1725), daughter of La Thorillière and god-daughter of Molière. He married her in 1680 and adopted her profession. He had a good face and figure, and a natural liveliness of disposition which was an asset in comedy, though in the playing of tragedy he was judged cold and monotonous. After some years in the provinces Dancourt, with his wife, joined the Comédie-Française and remained there until 1718. During this time he wrote more than fifty comedies, many of them ephemeral, based on small scandals or topicalities of the day. But his better plays, though never approaching the true comedy of Molière, show wit and observation, and much skill in etching the contemporary scene. He was particularly good in his delineation of the rising middle class, with its love of money, its desire for political power, its shrewdness in taking advantage of a corrupt government, and its avidity for easy pleasure. There is no bitterness in Dancourt's writing, but under the superficial wit and good humour much brutality and selfishness are apparent. His best play is *Le Chevalier à la mode* (1687), written in collaboration with Saint-Yon, an excellent portrait of contemporary life with much satire at the expense of parvenu financiers. Others worthy of note are *La Maison de campagne* (1688), and the one-act *Vendanges de Suresnes* (1695), the most frequently revived of all his works. In *La Foire de Bezons*, also given in 1695, Dancourt's two daughters, (3) MARIE-ANNE-ARMANDE (1684–1745), known as Manon, and (4) MARIE-ANNE-MICHELLE (1685–1780), known as Mimi, made their first appearance on the stage. They were both precocious, talented children, and their father continued to write plays for them in which they were much admired. In 1701 they became members of the Comédie-Française. Manon retired a year later on her marriage, but Mimi remained, and was still drawing her pension at the age of 95. Dancourt was not as versatile as Dufresny, nor as poetic as Regnard, but more than anyone after Molière he was a dramatist who was also a man of the theatre. His dialogue was easy and humorous, and he was a keen observer of contemporary manners, either in town or in the country.

DANE, Clemence [Winifred Ashton] (1888–1965), English playwright and novelist, who took her pseudonym from the church of St. Clement Danes in the Strand, and also acted for a few years as Diana Cortis. She made her first appearance in 1913 as Vera in *Eliza Comes to Stay*. The success of her first play, *A Bill of Divorcement* (1921), which deals sympathetically with the problem of divorce on the grounds of insanity, led her to devote herself entirely to writing. Among her later plays the most remarkable were *Will Shakespeare* (also 1921), which Darlington ranked as 'the most distinguished failure of its time', *Naboth's Vineyard* and *Granite* (both 1926), *Wild Decembers* (1932), a play on the Brontës in which Diana Wynyard played Charlotte, Beatrix Lehmann Emily, and Emlyn Williams Branwell, and *Eighty in the Shade* (1958), written for Sybil Thorndike and Lewis Casson. Her love for the theatre, and her knowledge of it, was shown also in her novels, *Broome Stages*, the history of a theatrical family, and *The Flower Girls*. She was appointed C.B.E. in the Coronation Honours List of 1953 for her services to the theatrical profession. She was also an excellent sculptor, and her bust of Ivor Novello stands in the foyer of Drury Lane Theatre.

DANGEVILLE, Marie-Anne Botot (1714–96), French actress, and the most important member of a family of actors who served the Comédie-Française for three generations. She was on the stage at an early age, playing child-roles with much success, and in 1730 joined the company for comedy roles, in which she excelled. She occasionally attempted tragedy, but without much success. Some of her greatest triumphs were gained in Marivaux's plays, in which she was ably supported by Préville, and Garrick considered her the leading French actress of the day, ranking her even above Mlle Clairon. She was a woman of great integrity. No breath of scandal ever touched her private or public life, and she was as kind-hearted as she was virtuous. In old age she adopted a granddaughter of the great actor Baron, whom she found living in poverty. Her retirement in 1763 was much regretted by the public and by her fellow actors, who lost no opportunity of testifying their fondness for her by arranging parties and surprise visits for her birthdays and other festive occasions. It was at her house in Vaugirard that some of the actors of the Comédie-Française first performed Collé's *Partie de chasse d'Henri IV*, which Louis XV had banned from the public stage.

DANIEL, Samuel (*c.* 1563–1619), English poet and dramatist, author of an unacted tragedy in the classical manner on the subject of Cleopatra, and of *Philotas* (1604), which got him into trouble on account of some fancied resemblance to the unhappy fate of the Earl of Essex. Daniel was at this time in charge of the Children of the Queen's Revels, and was implicated in the trouble over their production of *Eastward Ho!* (1605), where a reference to Scotland annoyed James I. He was also the author of two pastorals, and of a number of Court masques which contain some excellent poetry, little relished by Jonson, Daniel's rival in this field, but highly praised by many of his contemporaries and later by S. T. Coleridge.

DANIELS, Frank Albert (1856–1935), an American musical comedy star, who, after a successful début in light opera in 1879, became second comedian of the Gaiety, Boston. He first sprang into prominence with a farce entitled *The Electric Doll* (or *Spark*), with which he visited London, returning to New York to star as Old Sport in Hoyt's first success, *The Rag Baby* (Tony Pastor's Theatre, 14 Apr. 1884). He later went into management. In 1887 he had another long run in *Little Puck* (based on *Vice Versa*), and in 1895 appeared in *The Wizard of the Nile*, by Harry B. Smith, with music by Victor Herbert, dancing, singing, and clowning. The same authors supplied him with *The Idol's Eye*. Daniels continued to appear in a series of similar productions, including *Miss Hook of Holland*, the last being *The Pink Lady*. In 1913 he retired. He had a round, irresistibly comic face, a short, stout body, and most expressive eyebrows. He was a good dancer and singer, and a fine exponent of patter songs.

D'ANNUNZIO, Gabriele (1863–1938), Italian poet, novelist, and dramatist, whose real name was Rapagnetta. He was one of the most discussed and controversial figures of his day. His first volume of poems was published when he was 15, and in 1919 he figured largely in politics when he raided and captured the port of Fiume for Italy, relinquishing his authority a year later. His plays, which are simple in structure but rich in poetry and sensuality, have been both praised and condemned; though few critics would now attempt to justify him as a playwright. None of his plays reflects a mature mind, none—except perhaps *La figlia di Jorio* (1904), which D'Amico finds classically perfect and sincere—is truly dramatic. His stage directions, written with a wealth of detail, reveal the extent and accuracy of D'Annunzio's archaeological knowledge. But his people are puppets, driven by elemental passions, and his works live by their poetry rather than their humanity. Among the best known, in addition to that mentioned above, are *La città morta* and *La Gioconda* (both 1898), *Francesca da Rimini* (1902), and his last play, *La Piave* (1918). Many of his heroines were first played by Eleonora Duse, wasting her talent and virtually destroying her art in the process, as Pirandello so acutely observed. She achieved an outstanding success in *La città morta* and *La Gioconda*, contributing not a little to the author's success as a dramatist (see also ITALY, 3).

DANVERS, Johnnie (1860–1939), a music-hall performer, uncle of the famous Dan Leno, who was a month younger than himself. Danvers made his first appearance at the Alexandra, Sheffield, then toured with the Leno family, and later went into pantomime with Dan Leno at the Surrey. After this he joined the Mohawk Minstrels, and remained with them for twenty years, during which time he also appeared in many Drury Lane pantomimes, in musical comedy, and in light opera. He was a masterly performer on the tambourine, and despite his size—for he was a heavily built man—remarkably light on his feet.

DARLINGTON, William Aubrey (1890–), English dramatic critic, on the *Daily Telegraph* since 1920. He was appointed examiner for the Diploma of Dramatic Art, University of London, in 1929, and member of the Advisory Committee for the Diploma in 1931. In 1919 he wrote *Alf's Button*, an extravaganza which was first produced in 1924 at the Prince's Theatre, and has been twice filmed; it was filmed again in 1937 in a modernized version, as *Alf's Button Afloat*.

W. A. Darlington is also the author of the following plays: *Carpet Slippers* (1930), *A Knight Passed By* (1931), a burlesque version of Boucicault's *The Streets of London* (1932), and *Marcia Gets Her Own Back* (1938). In 1932 appeared his *Sheridan* (Great Lives Series), and in 1938 *J. M. Barrie* ('Order of Merit' Series). His critical works on the theatre include *Through the Fourth Wall* (1922) and *Literature in the Theatre* (1925). In 1947 he published a volume of reminiscences entitled *I Do What I Like*.

W. A. Darlington looks at the drama with a clear objective eye, and writes on what he sees with wit and understanding. T. C. KEMP†

DAUBENY, Peter (1921–), English impresario and theatre manager, to whom London is indebted for the importation, often under great difficulties, of many foreign ballet companies and such important theatrical groups as the Barrault–Renaud company, Vilar's Théâtre National Populaire, Edwige Feuillère, Marie Bell, the Berliner Ensemble, the Chinese Classical Theatre of Peking, and, in 1958 at Sadler's Wells, the Moscow Art Theatre in three plays by Chekhov. In 1964 he inaugurated at the Aldwych a season of visits by foreign companies which proved very successful, and became an annual event. Daubeny, who was originally an actor under William Armstrong at the Liverpool Repertory Theatre, lost an arm during the Second World War, and gave up acting for management. In addition to the foreign companies listed above, he has been responsible for a long series of London productions, among which the most successful have been *Jacobowsky and the Colonel* (1945), *The House by the Lake* (1956), *The Aspern Papers* (1959), and *Chin-Chin* (1960). Although not all his importations have met with general approval—witness the uproar which greeted *The Connection* in 1961—he has certainly helped to widen the horizon of London playgoers, and in a tribute to him Peter Ustinov said that alone and unaided he has performed in London the functions of the government-aided Théâtre des Nations in Paris.

DAUVILLIERS. (1) Nicolas Dorné (? –1690), French actor who went from the provinces to the Marais in 1670. Two years later he married (2) Victoire-Françoise (*c.* 1657–1733), daughter of the famous comedian Raymond Poisson. They both joined the depleted company at the rue Guénégaud after Molière's death, but the wife retired from the stage on the foundation of the Comédie-Française on account of ill health. Dauvilliers continued to play until his death. It was said of him that he was not a good actor in comedy, and had no advantage of person, but in tragedy he sometimes showed a genius akin to madness. He was evidently a somewhat wild and undisciplined actor, and tradition has it that he went mad on the stage, and tried to kill himself with a property sword while playing Eros in *Cléopâtre*, subsequently dying in an asylum. His daughter Anne was also an actress, and married an actor.

DAVENANT, Sir William (1606–68), English dramatist and theatre manager. Born and educated at Oxford, he was reputed to be the natural son of Shakespeare by the hostess of the Crown Inn, Cornmarket. There is no proof of this, though Shakespeare was certainly well acquainted with his family and may have been his godfather. Davenant had a great love for the theatre, and before the closing of the playhouses in 1642 had written a number of plays, of which the first, *A Cruel Brother*, was seen at Blackfriars in 1627. He also wrote and produced Court masques in the style of Ben Jonson, whom he succeeded as Poet Laureate in 1638. During the Civil War he fought on the king's side, and was knighted by Charles I in 1643. After spending several years in exile he returned to London and managed to evade the ban on stage-playing by presenting it as 'music and instruction'. By this means he got permission to put on *The Siege of Rhodes* (1656), considered by some the first English opera, *The Spaniards in Peru* (1658), and *Sir Francis Drake* (1659).

As soon as the Restoration was an accomplished fact, Davenant and Killigrew obtained, from Charles II, patents giving them a monopoly of acting in London. While Killigrew took most of the veteran actors into his company at the Theatre Royal, or King's House, Davenant recruited his actors mainly among the younger generation, and took them to Lincoln's Inn Fields, to the Duke's House. Among his youngsters was Thomas Betterton, destined to become the foremost actor of his day, Mrs. Sanderson, later Betterton's wife, the comedians Jevon and Nokes. A new theatre in Dorset Garden (see No. 63) was built for the Duke's Men, but Davenant died before it opened.

With Dryden, Davenant was responsible for adaptations of Shakespeare to suit the new tastes of the day, thus, according to one irate critic, turning Shakespeare into pantomime. Hand in hand with the new proscenium stage, with its greater reliance on scenery and its lack of intimate action, went the new taste for elaborate machinery, ballet, and music, which Davenant had been one of the first to foster. There can be no doubt that the English theatre received a great impetus from the work of Davenant and Killigrew, even if it was not always in a direction favoured by later critics. In founding a training school for young actors at Hatton Garden, Davenant continued the work begun by Burbage in apprenticing young actors to the stage. He was originally the person aimed at in the character of Bayes in Buckingham's *The Rehearsal*, transferred after his death to Dryden.

DAVENPORT, a family of American actors, of whom the father, (1) EDWARD LOOMIS (1815–77), was the son of an innkeeper. He made his first appearance on the stage in 1837, playing at Providence, R.I., with Junius Brutus Booth in *A New Way to Pay Old Debts*, billed as Mr. E. Dee. After some years on tour he appeared in New York in 1843, supporting Mrs. John Drew in a series of Shakespearian and other revivals. He visited England in 1848 with Mrs. Anna Cora Mowatt, remaining for some years and being accounted a fine actor in such parts as Othello, Richard III, Sir Giles Overreach, Claude Melnotte, and the Corsican Brothers. Returning to New York, he appeared as Hamlet, engaged in theatre management, and starred at a number of theatres with his own company. A distinguished actor and an indefatigable worker, he seemed destined for great things. William Winter said of him: 'Davenport was an actor of extraordinary versatility. I have seen him act, in one evening, Shakespeare's Brutus and Roaring Ralph Stockpole. . . . He was massive and weird in Macbeth. His Duke Aranza in *The Honeymoon* was peerless. . . . His Sir Giles Overreach was a sinister and grisly embodiment of worldly craft and insensate villainy. His Othello was, in construction, as nearly perfect as a work of art may be. Mind, grace, force, variety, and occasional flashes of fire were characteristic of Davenport's acting.' Yet with all these gifts he failed to attain the eminence which seemed his due, and some lack of sympathy between himself and his audiences led him to pass the greater part of his career outside New York. He made his last appearance as Dan'l Druce at the National Theatre, Washington, D.C., in Apr. 1877. While in England he married, in Jan. 1849, (2) FANNY ELIZABETH VINING (1829–91), member of a famous theatrical family. She was on the stage as a child, and was already an accomplished actress when she accompanied her husband to New York. She appeared with him in leading parts until his death. Of her nine children, five went on the stage. The most distinguished of them was (3) FANNY LILY GYPSY (1850–98). Born in England, she played child parts with her father at the Howard Athenaeum in Boston, and at 15 made her adult début as Mrs. Mildmay in *Still Waters Run Deep*, also in Boston. In 1869 she joined Augustin Daly's company in New York, and was his leading lady until 1877, when she formed her own company, starring with it in the principal theatres of the United States. Her range of parts was wide, including Shakespeare's heroines and such modern women as Polly Eccles and Lady Gay Spanker, while between 1883 and 1895 she produced and played in four of Sardou's plays, *Fédora*, *La Tosca*, *Cléopâtre*, and *Gismonda*. Of her sisters Blanche was an opera singer, while (4) MAY (1856–1927) made her first appearance on the stage at the age of 6 playing the Duke of York in *Richard III*. She then went to school until 1872, and made her adult début at 16 at the Chestnut Street Theatre, Philadelphia, under her father's management. At the same theatre she created the part of Libbie Ray in *The Mighty Dollar* (1876), and later joined Daly's company. She retired on her marriage to William Seymour, returning to the Boston Museum in 1885, and making her last professional appearance at a benefit for the Actors' Fund in 1894. Her daughter May was also on the stage (see SEYMOUR). Fanny's younger brother, (5) EDGAR LONGFELLOW (1862–1918), made his first appearance as a child at the Chestnut Street Theatre. He was at the Walnut Street Theatre from 1878 to 1879, supporting his sister Fanny in a season there, and for several years toured as leading man with a number of companies, including those of Kate Claxton and McKee Rankin. From 1887 to 1892 he was leading juvenile at the Boston Museum, appearing with Julia Marlowe, Viola Allen, and other great actresses of the day. His brother (6) HARRY GEORGE BRYANT (1866–1949) made his first appearance at the age of 5 under his father's management, playing Damon's son in *Damon and Pythias*. He continued to play children's parts in the companies of Jefferson, McCullough, and Frank Mayo, and in 1879 made his first appearance in New York as Sir Joseph Porter in a children's production of *H.M.S. Pinafore*. As an adult actor he played leading parts in New York and on tour, and in 1898 made his first appearance in London in *The Belle of New York*. He married Phyllis Rankin, who was with him in this play, and for many years appeared with her in vaudeville. He was one of the first actors to appear in films, being engaged by the Vitagraph Picture Company in 1912, and his later career was mainly in Hollywood.

DAVENPORT, JEAN and T.D., see LANDER.

DAVENPORT THEATRE, NEW YORK, see DALY'S THEATRE, 3.

DAVIS, OWEN (1874–1956), American dramatist, who as a young graduate from Harvard, finding no market for his tragedies in verse, turned to more remunerative branches of the theatre and wrote over a hundred ephemeral melodramas for the popular-priced circuit. Prompted, however, by Ibsen and the new spirit abroad in the theatre, he wrote in 1921 a sincere and moving play, *The Detour*, which was recognized as one of the best of the year, in spite of its lack of financial success when compared with his earlier works. This was followed by *Icebound*, a study of New England farming folk which was awarded the Pulitzer Prize for 1923. Davis's later work hardly maintained the promise of these two plays, though in 1936 he made, with his son, a good dramatization of Edith Wharton's novel, *Ethan Frome*. In 1931 he published his autobiography, *I'd Like To Do It Again*.

DAVIS'S AMPHITHEATRE, see ASTLEY'S.

DAY, JOHN (*c.* 1574–*c.* 1640), English dramatist, noted in Henslowe's diary as writing plays for the Admiral's Men and later for Worcester's, mainly in collaboration with Chettle, with whom he wrote the first part of *The Blind Beggar of Bethnal Green*. To this he later added two further parts, possibly with a different collaborator. This play is also known as *Thomas Strowd*, and is all that survives of Day's early dramatic work. His later plays, which Chambers says 'are of finer literary quality than his early record would suggest', include *The Travels of Three English Brothers* (1607), *The Parliament of Bees* (1608), and the ill-fated *Isle of Gulls*, given in 1606 by the Children at Blackfriars. This, because of its satire on English and Scottish relations, caused the imprisonment of those connected with its production.

DE ANGELIS, THOMAS JEFFERSON (1859–1933), an American actor, son of one of the original members of the San Francisco Minstrel Company. With a younger sister he appeared on the stage as a child, and travelled extensively, giving performances at small cities and mining camps from St. Louis to the coast. He has vividly portrayed this life in his autobiography, *A Vagabond Trouper* (1931). He was never a great actor, but always a reliable and likeable one, who appeared in light opera, musical shows, straight plays, and vaudeville with equal facility. He was the first American to sing the part of Sir Despard Murgatroyd in *Ruddigore* and his greatest personal success was the song 'Tammany', which he sang in his own production of *Fantana*. In 1927 he was in *The Royal Family* (*Theatre Royal*) and his last part was in *Apron Strings* in the same year.

DE BERGERAC, CYRANO, see BERGERAC.

DE BRIE. (1) EDMÉ VILLEQUIN (1607–1676), a mediocre actor who was in Molière's company in the provinces and later in Paris. He played various small parts, such as the fencing-master in *Le Bourgeois gentilhomme* and the river-god in *Psyché*. His main claim to fame is that he married, in about 1651, the charming actress (2) CATHERINE LECLERC DU ROZET (*c.* 1630–1706), who as Mlle de Rose had joined Molière a year previously. A gentle, affectionate woman, and a fine actress in comedy, she was destined to create many of Molière's best women's parts, and remained his friend and companion all his life, though there is no proof that she was ever his mistress. Her first important part was Cathos in *Les Précieuses ridicules*, and among her many fine performances Agnès in *L'École des femmes* was considered the best. She continued to play it for over twenty years, and when in later life she was replaced by a younger actress the audience clamoured for her return. Tradition has it that she was sent for after the curtain had risen, in such haste that she had to play the part in her ordinary clothes. She retired on pension in 1685, having been one of the original members of the Comédie-Française.

DE FILIPPO, a family of Neapolitan actors and playwrights which consisted of (1) TITINA [ANASTASIA] (1898–1963), (2) EDUARDO (1900–), and (3) PEPPINO (1903–). Children of actors, they were all on the stage from their early years, and in 1929 appeared together on tour, with the Molinari company. In 1931 they settled in Naples and opened a theatre there, where they soon achieved a high reputation in a series of productions which had much in common with the work of the *commedia dell'arte*. In 1945 the two brothers formed their own separate companies, Titina going with Eduardo, with whom she remained until her death. Although all three wrote plays, Titina and Peppino confined themselves mainly to one-act sketches or scenarios in which they appeared themselves, and the outstanding dramatist of the family was Eduardo. He began to write in the early 1920s, but it was not until after the Second World War that he emerged as one of the most important figures in the Italian theatre today. In a sense he may be called the Pirandello of the dialect play, in the tradition of that author's *Liolà* and *Il berretto a sonagli*, the portrayer of the new age of crisis, the analyst of Italy's emergence from the widespread chaos of the 1940s and 1950s. His major works are probably *Napoli milionaria* (1945), *Questi fantasmi* (1946), *Filomena Marturano* (1946), *Le voci di dentro* (1948), *La grande magia* (1949), *La paura numero uno* (1950), *Bene mio e core mio* (1955), and *Il figlio di Pulcinella* (1959). Although some of his plays have been translated and acted in English, he has not as yet made an impact on the English or American theatre, though he has undoubtedly great skill in construction, fostered by his training as a farce-player. In 1964 Peppino brought to London, as part of the World Season at the Aldwych Theatre, an Italian company in his own play, *The Metamorphoses of a Wandering Minstrel*, a gallimaufry of farcical jokes, acrobatic tricks, miming, and buffoonery which won the Young Critics' Award at the Paris Théâtre des Nations in 1963. Peppino is, however, something more than a farce-player, and is seen at his best in such parts as Harpagon in Molière's *L'Avare*.

DE LOUTHERBOURG, Philip James, see LOUTHERBOURG.

DE VILLIERS, see VILLIERS.

DEAN, Basil (1888–), English actor, dramatist, and theatre director, who first appeared on the stage in 1906. He was for four years a member of Miss Horniman's Repertory company at the Gaiety, Manchester, and in 1911 became first director of the Liverpool Repertory Theatre. From there he went to Birmingham under Barry Jackson, and during the First World War organized entertainments for the troops. He was later active in the London theatre, both as manager (with Alec Rea as ReandeaN from 1919 to 1926) and as producer. Among the many plays which he produced, under his own and other managements, were *A Bill of Divorcement* (1921), *A Midsummer Night's Dream* (1924), *The Constant Nymph* (1926), *Young Woodley* (1928), *Autumn Crocus* (1931), *Johnson Over Jordan* (1939). He was also a pioneer of stage lighting, importing much new equipment from America and Germany, and devising some of his own. During the Second World War he was again called on to organize entertainments for the troops, becoming director of the Entertainments National Service Association (E.N.S.A.), an assignment he later described in his book *The Theatre at War* (1955). He returned to the West-End theatre after the war with *An Inspector Calls* (1946), and among his later productions have been *The Diary of a Nobody* (1954) and *The Aspern Papers* (1959), the latter with Michael Redgrave, Flora Robson, and Beatrix Lehmann. He also organized the first British Repertory Theatre Festival in 1948. In 1947 he was awarded the C.B.E. for his services to the theatre, having already been given the M.B.E. in 1918.

DEAN, Julia (1830–68), American actress, granddaughter of the English actor Samuel Drake (1769–1854), who went to the United States in 1810 and became a pioneer theatre manager in Kentucky. With her father and step-mother (her mother, Julia Drake, also an actress, having died when she was 2) Julia Dean appeared as a child under the management of Ludlow and Smith, and in 1846 made her adult début in New York as Julia in *The Hunchback*. A beautiful woman, with a gentle personality and great charm of manner, she had a few years of immense popularity, though she was not perhaps a great actress. She could on occasion rise to great heights of passion, but was at her best in roles of tenderness and pathos, such as Adrienne Lecouvreur and Mrs. Haller. She made an unhappy marriage in 1855, and her acting declined. A tour of California in 1856 was a success, but she never regained her position in New York, where she returned after her divorce. In 1867 she married again, dying the following year in childbirth. It was with Julia Dean that Belasco, as a small boy, made his first appearance on the stage in 1856 when he was carried on as the child in *Pizarro*. Later he played Little Willie in her production of *East Lynne*.

DEBURAU. (1) Jean-Gaspard (1796–1846), famous French pantomimist, creator of the long, pale, lovesick Pierrot who has since remained a popular figure in the public imagination. He was born in Bohemia, member of an acrobatic family with whom he toured the Continent. In 1811 they played at the Parisian fairs, and Deburau was engaged for the Funambules on the Boulevard du Temple, a home of tumblers and tight-rope walkers. His subsequent history is bound up with that of this theatre, where he remained until his death. He was at first an inconspicuous member of the company, but as he developed, with great subtlety and many delicate touches, his conception of Pierrot as the ever hopeful and disappointed lover, as the child, the prince, the poet, and the eternal seeker, all Paris flocked to see him, and his praises were sung by all the critics, particularly by Jules Janin, who devoted a whole volume to his work. He died a few days after his last appearance on the stage, some said from the effects of a fall, others of consumption. His son (2) Charles (1829–73) carried on the tradition of the white-faced white-robed Pierrot after his creator's death, without his father's genius, but with a vast store of goodwill and popularity to draw on. He remained at the Funambules until it was destroyed, and then opened a theatre under his own name. It was not very successful, and he took to the provinces until his death.

DÉJAZET, Pauline-Virginie (1798–1875), French actress, who made her first appearance on the stage at the age of 5. Gardel, the ballet master, would have made a ballerina of her, but her real aptitude was for acting, and, after appearing with several children's companies, she went for her training to the Théâtre des Jeunes Élèves. In 1807 she was at the Vaudeville, and later at the Variétés under Brunet, where her success in the part of a young boy so displeased the reigning star that her engagement was terminated. She then went into the provinces, and dropping the name of Virginie, by which she had hitherto been known, she used that of Déjazet for the first time. In 1821 she returned to Paris and appeared with some success in a vaudeville by Scribe at the Gymnase, where she remained for some time, playing male roles. The arrival of Jenny Vertpré from the Vaudeville robbed her of the parts she considered hers by right, and she left. Her reputation really dates from the opening of the Palais-Royal in 1831. She stayed there thirteen years, and became one of the most popular actresses in Paris. After an argument over her salary she continued her triumphant career at the Variétés and the Gaîté, still playing masculine roles—soldiers, collegians, students—as well as great ladies and pretty peasant girls. Some idea of her versatility is given by the fact that her parts included Voltaire, Rousseau, Napoleon, Henri IV, Ninon de l'Enclos, Sophie Arnould, Mlle Champmeslé, and Mme Favart. In 1859 she took over the Folies-Nouvelles, which she renamed Théâtre Déjazet, and appeared there in a number of new plays under the management of her son Eugène. At the age of 62 she made a great hit in a male part in Sardou's *Monsieur Garat*. She made her last appearance in Paris in 1870, and in the same year was seen in London at the Opéra-Comique in a season of French plays. Her last years were unhappy, and, harassed by financial difficulties, she played continuously in the provinces to support her children and grandchildren. Two of her sisters were also on the stage, one as a singer, one as a dancer (for the Théâtre Déjazet, see FOLIES-NOUVELLES).

DEKKER, THOMAS (*c.* 1572–*c.* 1632), English dramatist, about whose life very little is known. He was working for Henslowe towards the end of the sixteenth century, and had a hand in more than forty plays, of which about fifteen survive. The most important, which has an honoured place in the evolution of English comedy, is *The Shoemaker's Holiday*, which tells how one Simon Eyre, a master shoemaker, became Lord Mayor of London. It was first given at the Rose towards the end of 1599, and at Court on the following New Year's Day. Robust and full-blooded, this play of London characters reveals a promise which Dekker's later work unfortunately did little to fulfil. His other plays include *Satiromastix* (1601), written in collaboration with Marston, in which Jonson, who had satirized the authors in his *Poetaster*, is ridiculed as Horace; *The Honest Whore* (1604), and *The Roaring Girl* (1610), both with Middleton; and two plays which he apparently wrote by himself—*If It be not Good, the Devil is in It* (1610) and *Match Me in London* (*c.* 1611). With Massinger he also wrote a tragedy, *The Virgin Martyr*, given at the Red Bull playhouse in 1620, but probably dating in a different version from some ten years earlier. Dekker is also believed to have had a hand in *The Witch of Edmonton* (1621). In his later years he wrote a number of pamphlets in imitation of Nashe, and in 1609 published *The Gull's Handbook*, a satiric account of the fops and gallants of the day, which gives some interesting information about the contemporary theatre. It has been said of Dekker that he was of a sunny and sympathetic nature, with much simplicity, and an unusual feeling for the poor and oppressed.

DELAUNAY, LOUIS-ARSÈNE (1826–1903), French actor, son of a wine merchant, who entered the Conservatoire as a student in 1844 and a year later, impatient of further study, made an unauthorized début (as M. Ernest) in a vaudeville at the Gymnase. This experience taught him that he was not yet ready for the stage, and he returned to the Conservatoire, making his proper début at the Odéon, where his youth and precocity in classical comedy caught the attention of the Comédie-Française. He appeared there on 25 Apr. 1848 and had a long and brilliant career, playing young lovers till he was nearly 60, seldom knowing failure and becoming the idol of the public. His first outstanding success was made in a little one-act play, *Le Moineau de Lesbie*, in which he appeared with Rachel, and he was the original Fortunio in Alfred de Musset's *Le Chandelier*. He was also good in *Les Caprices de Marianne*, which went out of the repertory for many years after his retirement in 1886. He played in Marivaux, Regnard, in Hugo's *Hernani* when it was first given at the Comédie-Française, and in new plays by Augier, Ponsard, Legouvé, and Pailleron. His son was also a member of the Comédie-Française.

DELLA PORTA, GIAMBATTISTA (1538–1613), a Neapolitan scientist and philosopher, who amused himself in his leisure hours by writing plays, fourteen of which survive out of a possible thirty-three. These are all in prose, and take their subjects from authors both of classical Rome and the Italian Renaissance, particularly Plautus and Boccaccio. His *Il due fratelli rivali* is taken from a tale of Bandello's which supplied Shakespeare with the plot of *Much Ado About Nothing*. In all his plays, the dates of which are unknown, the dialogue is vivacious and the satire keen. This *commedia erudita* was much imitated by later seventeenth-century dramatists, none of whom, however, brought to their material the freshness and deft handling of their original. Della Porta is accessible in excellent critical editions. His *La Cintia*, *La Fantesca*, and *Astrologo* were given in Latin translations at Trinity College, Cambridge, between 1598 and 1615. *La Trappolaria* was used as the basis of *Ignoramus* by Ruggle, which was the success of the day when James I visited Cambridge in 1615.

DELPINI, see CLOWN.

DELYSIA [LAPIZE], ALICE (1889–), French actress and singer, who made her first appearance in 1903 at the Moulin Rouge under Flers, being engaged by him for the chorus of *The Belle of New York*. She was later seen at the Variétés, and at the Folies-Bergère with Yvonne Printemps, and in 1905 made her first appearance in the United States at Daly's. In 1914 Cochran engaged her for London. Her success in the revue *Odds and Ends* was immediate, and she continued to appear under Cochran's management for many years, usually in revue or spectacle, returning for a time to New York in 1920. Among her outstanding parts were Zaydee in *Agfar* (1919), Suzy Courtois in *Topaze* (1930), and Pavani in *Mother of Pearl* (1933). A beautiful and witty woman, she was the mainspring of many of Cochran's most successful enterprises, and in his volumes of memoirs he constantly pays tribute to her loyalty and good nature.

DENMARK, see SCANDINAVIA, 1.

DERWENT, CLARENCE (1884–1959), actor and producer. Born and educated in London, he made his first appearance on the stage, after studying at the Birkbeck Institute, in 1902, and was for five years with the Benson company.

He subsequently spent two years at the Gaiety, Manchester, under Miss Horniman's management, and then appeared in London in 1910 under Tree. In 1915 he went to America, where he had a long and distinguished career on Broadway, making only one further appearance in London, in *The Late Christopher Bean* (1933). His last appearance was in *The Mad Woman of Chaillot* at the Belasco Theatre, N.Y., in Dec. 1948. He was responsible for many productions, and instituted the Clarence Derwent awards given in London and New York annually for the best performances by players in supporting roles. He was the author of several plays, and in 1946 was elected President of the Actors' Equity Association of America.

DES URLIS, see BRÉCOURT.

DESCLÉE, AIMÉE-OLYMPE (1836–74), French actress, who studied at the Conservatoire, but, finding the discipline irksome, left it to make her début at the Gymnase in 1855. After appearing at several other Parisian theatres and meeting with little success, she retired and went to Italy and elsewhere, appearing in a repertory of French plays. Dumas *fils*, seeing her in his *Diane de Lys* at Brussels in 1867, brought her back to Paris and persuaded the Gymnase to re-engage her. The hard years of touring bore fruit, and she was an immediate success in *Frou-Frou*, becoming overnight the idol of the Parisian public. Her gratitude to Dumas knew no bounds, but, he being at this time a fervent moral reformer, she could show it only by her excellent performances in his plays, being particularly good as the heroines of *Visite de noces* (1871) and *La Femme de Claude* (1873). She died suddenly at the height of her success.

DESEINE, MLLE (?–1759), see DUFRESNE (2).

DESIOSI, THE, a company of *commedia dell'arte* actors led by Diana (da Ponti) which first emerges in 1580. In 1595 Tristano Martinelli is found with them, after breaking away from Pellesini's troupe. The company appears to have broken up some years later, when the two chief actors are found with the Accesi.

DESJARDINS, MARIE-CATHERINE-HORTENSE (1632–83), one of the first women playwrights of France. She left home after a love-affair with a cousin, and may have become an actress, possibly in Molière's provincial company. She was later taken under the protection of the Duchesse de Rohan, and wrote poetry, novels, and plays, of which *Manlius*, a tragedy, was first produced at the Hôtel de Bourgogne in 1662. It was while appearing in this play that the mother of the famous actor, Michel Baron, died and was replaced by Mlle Desœillets. Mlle Desjardins was also the author of a comedy, *Le Favory* (1665), given by Molière at the Palais-Royal. As Mme de Villedieu, bigamous wife of an absconding officer, Mlle Desjardins became a figure in Parisian society, and later married the aged Marquis de Chasté, giving him a son whose godparents were the Dauphin and Mlle de Montpensier. After the death of the Marquis she reverted to her first married name, retired to the country, and died, it is said, of over-indulgence in drink. *Manlius*, which had been consistently successful since its first appearance, remained in the repertory of the Comédie-Française until the time of the French Revolution.

DESLYS, GABY [GABRIELLE] (1884–1920), a celebrated French singer and music-hall artist, around whom some fantastic stories have accumulated, particularly the tale of her famous pearls, said to have caused a revolution in Portugal from which she escaped in a hay-cart. She appeared in Paris and New York, and was first seen in London at the Gaiety in 1906 under George Edwardes. She had no great stage talent, but any amount of glamour, being a blonde with a small but perfect figure and large appealing blue eyes. She had a short and successful career, making her last appearance in London in 1917. On her death she left a considerable sum of money to the poor of Marseille, where she was born.

W. MACQUEEN-POPE†

DESMARES. (1) NICOLAS (*c.* 1645–1714), French actor and dramatist, brother of the celebrated actress Mlle Champmeslé. He spent some years in a French company at the Court in Copenhagen, and was also a member in 1680 of a provincial company under the patronage of the great Condé. Five years later he became a member of the Comédie-Française, where he remained until his retirement in 1712. His range was somewhat limited, but he was unsurpassed in the playing of peasant characters. His plays are forgotten. He married a granddaughter of the actor Montfleury, and his daughter (2) (CHRISTINE ANTOINETTE) CHARLOTTE (1682–1753), profiting by the tuition of her aunt, Mlle Champmeslé, to many of whose parts she succeeded, became an excellent actress, sharing feminine roles with Mlle Duclos. She retired in 1721, having seen herself surpassed by the young and lovely Adrienne Lecouvreur. Charlotte Desmares was at her best in pathetic and tender roles, and was particularly admired in Voltaire's *Œdipe*, in which she played opposite Quinault-Dufresne.

DESMARETZ DE SAINT-SORLIN, JEAN (1595–1676), French novelist, poet, and dramatist, one of the original members of the French Academy, and a frequenter of the Hôtel de Rambouillet. Urged by his patron, Richelieu, to attempt the theatre, he wrote *Aspasie* (1636), a somewhat mediocre play given in the same year as *Le Cid*. Desmaretz, who helped Richelieu in his extensive systems of reform, is best remembered, however, for his comedy, *Les Visionnaires* (1637), probably the most important before Corneille's *Le Menteur*. A witty comment on the foibles of fashionable society, it was produced at the Marais with Montdory as the hallucinated old-fashioned poet who believes himself to be a great modernist. It had some influence on Molière, who revived it twice at the Palais-Royal. Desmaretz wrote several other plays, including the greater part of *Mirame* (1641), the first production to be staged in Richelieu's new private theatre.

DESŒILLETS [ALIX FAVIOT], Mlle (1621–70), French actress, who served a long apprenticeship in the provinces, where she married an actor, before she was seen in Paris in her late thirties. She was for a short time at the Marais, where Corneille admired her acting as Viriate in his *Sertorius* (1662), and later in the same year she joined the company at the Hôtel de Bourgogne, taking the place of Mlle Baron, mother of the famous actor, Michel Baron. Neither young nor pretty, and of short stature, Mlle Desœillets was nevertheless an excellent actress, most moving in tragedy, and in high favour with the audience. She created a number of tragic roles, among them Corneille's Sophonisbe and Racine's Hermione. During an illness she was replaced in the latter part by the young Mlle Champmeslé, who was so good that the elder actress retired from the theatre in tears, and never acted again.

DESTOUCHES, PHILIPPE NÉRICAULT (1680–1754), French dramatist, and an important link in the development of eighteenth-century *drame* from seventeenth-century comedy. He was an imitator of Molière, but spoilt his plays by emphasizing the moral, which Molière had allowed to emerge naturally in the course of the action. Even his titles—*L'Ingrat*, *L'Irrésolu*, *Le Médisant*—read, as it has been said, 'like sub-titles to Molière'. There is a tradition that Destouches was, in his youth, an actor, but proof of this is wanting. He must, however, have left the stage fairly soon for diplomacy, for in 1716 he was at the French Embassy in London, where he was well received. He also contracted at this time a secret marriage with an Englishwoman, which later supplied material for one of his best plays, *Le Philosophe marié* (1727). Before his visit to London he had written several moderately successful comedies, and on his return he retired to the country and gave himself up wholly to writing. His stay in England had helped to heighten his taste for gothic romance, and accounts for the mingling of sentiment and tragedy with comedy in his later plays, though many of them, particularly towards the end of his career, were spoilt by sententiousness. His most important play is undoubtedly *Le Glorieux* (1732), which was translated into English in 1791. It pictures the struggle between the old nobility and the newly rich who are rising to power, and some traits of the central character are said to have been taken from the actor Dufresne, who played the part. Destouches became a member of the French Academy in 1723, in succession to Campistron. He was a man of a serious, even a religious, turn of mind, and at 60 he turned his attention entirely to theology, though he left several plays in manuscript, of which one, *La Fausse Agnès*, was given after his death with some success.

DETAIL SCENERY, the name given to small, changeable pieces of scenery used for a particular scene in or before a formalized setting.

DEUS EX MACHINA, see GREECE, 6.

DEUTERAGONIST, see PROTAGONIST.

DEUTSCHES THEATER, a private play-producing society founded in Berlin in 1883 for the purpose of staging a repertory of good plays, old and new, as a protest against the deadening effect of long runs and outmoded theatrical tradition. Under its chief promoters, Adolf L'Arronge and Ludwig Barnay, ably assisted by the actors Josef Kainz and Agnes Sorma, it presented classical historical plays in the style inaugurated by the Meiningen company. In 1894, by which time the enterprise was well established and flourishing, it was given a new direction by its affiliation with the Freie Bühne, under the latter's founder and director Otto Brahm. He brought to it the naturalistic methods which had proved so excellent with Ibsen and Hauptmann, less successful with the classics and romantics. The Deutsches Theater knew another period of fame under the direction of Max Reinhardt, who went there in 1905 from the Neues Theater with a band of keen young actors trained in his methods. Here he was able to realize some of his ambitious schemes of production, in which music, scenery, ballet, and mime all played their parts. In the crisis following on the First World War the company collapsed, but was later revived under Heinz Hilpert.

DEVINE, GEORGE ALEXANDER CASSADY (1910–1965), English actor and theatre director, who in the early part of his career was closely associated with John Gielgud and Michel Saint-Denis. As President of the O.U.D.S. in 1932 he was instrumental in inviting Gielgud to Oxford to produce *Romeo and Juliet*, a memorable production in which Peggy Ashcroft and Edith Evans played Juliet and the Nurse, Christopher Hassall was Romeo, and Devine himself Mercutio. Making his professional début later in the same year, in *The Merchant of Venice* at the St. James's, he spent a season with the Old Vic, was again associated with Gielgud from 1934 to 1938, and from 1936 to 1939 was a teacher and producer at Michel Saint-Denis's London Theatre Studio. After six years in the army he returned to the theatre, and joined Saint-Denis again at the Old Vic School, being also director of the Young Vic company, two enterprises whose early demise was a great loss to the English theatre. Among the parts played by Devine mention must be made of his outstanding Tesman to Peggy Ashcroft's Hedda Gabler in 1954. In 1955 he was at Stratford-upon-Avon, where he produced *King Lear* (see No. 91). A year later he was appointed director of the newly formed English Stage Company at the

Royal Court, which proved a galvanizing force in the London theatre, particularly with its sponsoring of young playwrights. In addition to directing the company and producing a number of plays seen there, Devine gave some excellent performances, particularly as Mr. Shu Fu in *The Good Woman of Setzuan*, Mr. Pinchwife in *The Country Wife*, and the Old Man in *The Chairs*. He was appointed C.B.E. in the Birthday Honours of 1957 for his services to the theatre. In the early 1930s he was associated as business manager with the firm of Motley, and in 1940 married Sophia Harris, one of the partners.

DEVRIENT, a family of German actors of whom the first, (1) LUDWIG (1784–1832), of Dutch origin, was a brilliant actor, but of a fiery temperament, unamenable to discipline. An inimitable comedian, he was considered at his finest as Falstaff, but he himself preferred tragedy, and Franz Moor, Shylock, and King Lear were his favourite parts. He appeared in the chief theatres of Germany until 1815, when he took Iffland's place in Berlin, remaining there until he died. He had three nephews on the stage. The eldest, (2) KARL (1797–1872), excelled in heroic and character parts—Wallenstein, Faust, Lear, Shylock. He was for many years attached to the Court theatre in Dresden and later joined the companies of Karlsruhe and Hanover. In 1823 he married the opera singer Wilhelmine Schröder-Devrient (1804–60), from whom he was divorced five years later. The second nephew, (3) EDUARD (1801–77), began his career as a singer, and with Mendelssohn-Bartholdy revived Bach's St. Matthew Passion, himself taking the part of Christ. In 1852 he was appointed director of the Hoftheater at Karlsruhe, and was the first professional man of the theatre to be appointed to such a post. Of conservative tastes, but thoroughly competent and reliable, he made good team-work his first aim, and brought his company to a high pitch of excellence. He also induced his public to accept a number of German classics and Shakespearian plays in the repertory, and his German versions of Shakespeare—*Deutscher Bühnen-und Familien-Shakespeare*—published from 1869 to 1871, though somewhat bowdlerized, proved more suitable for the stage than Schlegel's and other literary translations. He was also the first to write a detailed account of the development of the German stage in his *Geschichte der deutschen Schauspielkunst* (1848). His youngest brother, (4) EMIL (1803–72), was a handsome and polished actor, at his best in youthful heroic parts. He was for nearly forty years attached to the Dresden Court theatre, but was frequently given leave of absence to star elsewhere, including London, where his Hamlet was well received. His excellent acting was somewhat marred by virtuoso mannerisms, but his Tasso, Egmont, and Essex were considered outstanding. His son (5) OTTO (1838–94) played under him in Karlsruhe in the 1850s and 1860s, and in 1873 went as character actor to the Weimar Court theatre. Here, in 1876, his staging of both parts of Goethe's *Faust* as a Mystery play, on a stage on three levels, aroused much interest. Seven years later he was at Jena, where, for a festival in honour of Luther, he wrote and staged a pageant play. From 1884 until his death he was in Oldenburg. He was the author of several tragedies.

One of the outstanding members of the family was (7) MAX (1857–1929), son of Karl and his second wife Johanna Block, who made his début in Dresden in 1878 as Bertrand in *Die Jungfrau von Orleans*. He played extensively all over Germany, and was for many years at the Vienna Burgtheater, joining the company in 1882, and making his first appearance there in *Die Räuber*. A handsome man, of commanding presence, he excelled in big tragic roles, particularly in Goethe, Schiller, and Shakespeare. He was also considered good in comedy, and was much admired as Petruchio in *The Taming of the Shrew*. Another member of the family, (8) HANS (1878–1927), though not on the stage, became editor of the *Archiv der Gesellschaft für Theatergeschichte*.

DIAGHILEV, SERGE (1872–1929), see BALLET, COSTUME, 9 and SCENERY, 6.

DIBDIN. (1) CHARLES (1745–1814), English dramatist, actor, and song-writer, whose ballads of ships and sailors, among them 'Tom Bowling' and 'The Lass that Loved a Sailor', were said to have 'brought more men into the Navy in war than all the press-gangs could'. They were probably inspired by Charles's brother Thomas, a naval captain for whom he had a great affection. Charles was a good actor, though he preferred light opera to straight comedy, and made a hit as Mungo in *The Padlock*. He wrote a number of ballad operas, of which *The Waterman* (1774) long remained a favourite and passed into the repertory of the Juvenile Drama. He quarrelled constantly with the managers, and his relations with Garrick are dwelt on at length in his autobiography, *The Professional Life of Mr. Dibdin*. From 1788 to 1793 he gave one-man entertainments, playing, singing, and reciting monologues. Handsome, but quarrelsome and bad-tempered, he left his wife after he had spent all her money, and by his association with the actress Harriet Pitt had three children, of whom the eldest (2) CHARLES ISAAC MUNGO PITT (1768–1833) was a popular and successful writer of plays and pantomimes, and was for some time proprietor and manager of Sadler's Wells Theatre. He also wrote a history of the London theatres, published in 1826, and had two children who were both musicians. His younger brother (3) THOMAS JOHN PITT (1771–1841) first appeared on the stage at the age of 4, as Cupid to the Venus of young Sarah Siddons. He was a choirboy at St. Paul's, and later ran away from his apprenticeship to an upholsterer to become an actor, occasionally a scene-painter, and always 'a dramatist of a fatal facility'. When he was first on the stage he called himself S. Merchant, but in about 1800 took the name of Dibdin, much to his father's annoyance. Thomas, who in his early years was genial and good-tempered, was devoted to his mother, and though proud of his father's work was resentful of his neglect. In later life he became sour and embittered. He was the composer of some 2,000 songs in the style of the elder Dibdin, to whom they are often attributed, and his most successful dramatic work was the pantomime of *Mother Goose*, done at Covent Garden in 1806–7 with Grimaldi as Clown. His theatrical glorifications of the Navy, as in *The Mouth of the Nile* (1798) and *Nelson's Glory* (1805), were also extremely popular. He was the author of one of the many translations of *La Pie voleuse*, as *The Magpie, or the Maid of Palaiseau* (1815) (see No. 32). He married an actress named Nancy Hilliar, who died in 1828, and had four children, who under their grandmother's name of Pitt were all connected with the stage. Some of their children went to the United States, where there are still several Pitts in theatre management.

DICKENS, CHARLES (1812–70), the great English novelist, was all his life intimately connected with the stage, and had an immense influence on it through the numerous dramatizations of his books. As a young man he had serious thoughts of becoming an actor, and there is a stubborn tradition, unsupported by any evidence, that he was at one time in the company of T. D. Davenport at the Portsmouth Theatre, where he obtained the material which later went to the fashioning of the Crummles family, little Jean Davenport being the original of the Infant Phenomenon. This has been hotly disputed, but there is no doubt that both in *Nicholas Nickleby* and in *Great Expectations* he showed an intimate knowledge of the details of an actor's life between 1837 and 1844. Early in his career he wrote several operatic burlettas which he did not later wish to see revived.

Those who saw Dickens in his many amateur appearances, notably as Captain Bobadil and Shallow, considered that he would have made a fine eccentric comedian, and his famous readings from his own works were in a way solo dramatic performances, as has been clearly shown by the outstanding success of Emlyn Williams's reconstruction of them, in which he portrays Dickens at the height of his success. Dickens had a small theatre, perfectly fitted up, where with his friends and family he gave private performances before a distinguished audience. Two of Wilkie Collins's plays were given there before their professional productions at the Olympic. Dickens also collaborated with Collins in *No Thoroughfare*, which was given in 1867 with Fechter and Ben Webster in the cast.

It would be impossible to catalogue here the plays based on Dickens's novels, many of which were done before the books had finished appearing in fortnightly parts. The most persistent adapters were W. T. Moncrieff and Edward Stirling, but Dickens entrusted Albert Smith with the Christmas Books, and himself dramatized *Great Expectations*, hoping Toole would play Joe Gargery. His version was not acted, however, and the first to appear on the stage was that prepared by W. S. Gilbert and given at the Court Theatre in May 1871. Owing to the absence of copyright laws, Dickens's novels were pirated for the American stage, and he received nothing from the numerous adaptations in common use.

Dickens's characters are so vivid, his plots so dramatic, that it is not surprising that they found favour with actors and audience alike. At Christmas 1845, versions of *The Cricket on the Hearth* were being given at twelve London theatres, all of which were later surpassed by Boucicault's excellent adaptation entitled *Dot* (1862). Among the outstanding actors who appeared as Dickens's characters were Toole as the Artful Dodger and Bob Cratchit, Mrs. Keeley as Oliver Twist, Smike, Little Nell, and Dot, Joseph Jefferson as Newman Noggs and Caleb Plummer, George Fawcett Rowe and John Brougham as Micawber, the latter in his own version of *David Copperfield*, Lotta as Little Nell and the Marchioness, Mme Céleste as Mme Defarge, Irving as Jingle, Tree as Fagin, Seymour Hicks as Scrooge in a music-hall sketch, and, most famous of all, Sir John Martin-Harvey as Sidney Carton in *The Only Way*, a dramatization of *A Tale of Two Cities*. Bransby Williams had a whole gallery of Dickens characters, while Betsey Prig and Sairey Gamp were for a long time acted by men, the most popular exponent of the latter being John Clarke. In the 1960s a new turn was given to adaptations of Dickens's novels (many of which have been serialized as radio and television plays) by the conversion of *Oliver Twist* and *The Pickwick Papers* into musicals, as *Oliver!* (see No. 113) and *Pickwick*.

DIDASCALIA, from the Greek *didaskalos*, meaning teacher, and, by extension, dramatic poet, since in the earliest times of Greek drama the poet 'taught' his chorus its part and produced his own play. Hence *didascalia* meaning production, while *didascaliae* was the title given to catalogues, made by Aristotle and others, of dramatists, plays, and victories. Fragments of these survive in the ancient Arguments prefixed, in the manuscripts, to most Greek plays.

H. D. F. KITTO

DIDEROT, DENIS (1713–84), French man of letters. Compared with his labours over his Encyclopaedia, and his numerous writings on any and every subject, Diderot's plays are but a minor feature of his busy literary life. Yet they are important, as is his *Paradoxe sur le comédien*, for they helped to diffuse the new ideas of the time, and had a great influence on Lessing, and through him on the European drama of the nineteenth century. Diderot was an exponent of bourgeois drama, that offshoot of *comédie larmoyante* whose mixed sentiment, virtue, and sheer priggishness appealed so strongly to the middle-class audiences of the eighteenth century. The titles of his plays—

Le Fils naturel, *Le Père de famille*—are sufficiently revealing, and, in spite of some feeling for dialogue, they degenerate all too quickly into didactic expositions of philosophical theories. They were in some cases published years before they were acted, while some, like *Est-il bon, est-il méchant?*, were seen only on private stages. Yet the extent of his influence may be gauged by the fact that during his lifetime they were translated into German, English, Dutch, and Italian. But the best of Diderot's work for the theatre must be looked for elsewhere; in his *Observations sur Garrick*, his *Essai sur la poésie dramatique*, and his *Entretien avec Dorval*, which tell us, far better than his somewhat weak and confused plays, what he is aiming at. Among other things he endeavoured to place the actor as a member of a united company, and pleaded for greater unity between actor and dramatist.

DIDRING, Ernst (1868–1931), modern Swedish dramatist, whose *Elna Hall* (1917) was given with much success throughout Europe (see SCANDINAVIA, 3 *a*).

DIGGES, Dudley (1879–1947), Irish actor, who made his first appearances with the Irish National Players in 1901–3. He was trained for the stage by Frank J. Fay, and was in the original production of *Deirdre* and other plays, being particularly good as the Wise Man in *The Hourglass*. After the second visit of the Irish company to London Digges, with two other members, accepted an invitation to America, where he spent the rest of his life, becoming one of the outstanding actors of New York, and a potent force in the theatre there. His departure was a great loss to the Irish players, since he had a good presence and was equally at home in comedy and romance. He began his New York career in 1904 in *John Bull's Other Island*, and was later with Ben Greet, Mrs. Fiske, and George Arliss, acting as stage manager for Arliss for seven years. He was in the first productions of the Theatre Guild in 1919, and remained with it until 1930, playing a wide variety of parts, and producing some of the plays, notably *Pygmalion* and *The Doctor's Dilemma*. He later produced the all-star revival of *Becky Sharp*, and in 1937 was seen as Franz Joseph in *The Masque of Kings*. His last, and one of his finest, parts was Harry Hope in *The Iceman Cometh* (1946).

DIGGES, (John) Dudley West (1720–86), English actor, who served his apprenticeship in Dublin and Edinburgh, where he remained from 1749 to 1764, and was the first to play Young Norval in *Douglas* (1756). By a curious twist of fortune he played Old Norval at the Haymarket in 1780. Meanwhile he had been seen at the same theatre between 1777–81 as Macbeth, Lear, Shylock, Wolsey, Cato, Sir John Brute, and Lord Townley, showing a remarkable versatility. He then went to Dublin and acted there till incapacitated by paralysis in 1784. In his prime he had a noble presence, and a fine resonant voice.

DIKIE, Alexei Denisovich (1889–1955), Soviet actor and producer. The son of a peasant, he began his theatrical career at the Moscow Art Theatre in 1910, where he came under the influence of Stanislavsky. After the Revolution he concentrated mainly on production, being responsible at various theatres for productions of such plays as Faiko's *The Man with the Portfolio* and Wolf's *Sailors of Cattaro*. He also produced the first version of Shostakovich's opera 'Katerina Ismailova' (under the title of 'Lady Macbeth of Mtsensk'). But he continued to act, and in 1942 gave an unforgettable performance as Ivan Gorlov in Korneichuk's *Front* at the Vakhtangov Theatre. Two years later he went to the Maly Theatre, where he produced Sofronov's *Moscow Character* (1948) and a revival of Ostrovsky's *The Warm Heart*. In 1951 he went to the Pushkin (formerly Kamerny) Theatre, where he produced in 1953 a revival of *Shadows* by Saltykov-Shchedrin. He was also well-known as a film actor.

DILLINGHAM, Charles Bancroft (1868–1934), American theatre manager who, through his friendship with Charles Frohman, became the manager of Julia Marlowe, and of many other famous actors, some of them making their first visit to New York under his aegis. In 1905 he introduced Shaw's *Man and Superman* to America, and later the comedies of Frederick Lonsdale. In 1910 he opened the Globe Theatre (see GLOBE, 3), and for the next twenty years was responsible for all the productions there, mainly musical shows and revues, in most of which Fred Stone appeared. He also managed other New York theatres, and at the height of his prosperity had as many as six plays running at once. In 1914 he took over the Hippodrome for lavish vaudeville shows, which included trained elephants, Anna Pavlova on her first visit to New York, Gaby Deslys, and performing seals. He produced over 200 plays, but later failed, and in 1933 became bankrupt, dying a year later.

DIMMER, see LIGHTING.

DINGELSTEDT, Franz (1814–81), German theatre director, who was appointed to the control of the Munich theatre at the time of the big industrial exhibition held there in 1854. Here he made theatre history by his elaborate productions, for which he imported actors from all over the country. The experiment, however, ended disastrously, owing to a combination of cholera and slighted native talent, and Dingelstedt withdrew to Weimar. Later he was appointed director of the Vienna Burgtheater, and in both places staged remarkable productions of some of Shakespeare's historical plays.

DIONYSUS, a Greek nature-god (Bacchus being a roughly equivalent name), who was associated particularly, but by no means exclusively, with wine. His worship took many forms. The most remarkable was the orgiastic revels in which his votaries, women in particular, withdrew for a time into the wild and experienced a mystical communion with Nature (see Euripides' *Bacchae*). As Dionysus was a vegetation-spirit, who died and was reborn each year, he was associated not only with all kinds of rites designed to promote fertility but also with mystery-religions, of which an important part was teaching about death, purgation, and rebirth. The death and 'sufferings' of Dionysus were commonly presented in quasi-dramatic ritual; his rebirth, presumably, in ritual of a more cheerful kind; while as god of plenty, and of wine, intoxication, and ecstasy, he was honoured with rites that may be mildly described as jolly.

In so dynamic a worship there are obviously all sorts of contacts with every form of drama, and in fact drama in Athens, whether tragic, satyric, or comic, was always strictly associated with the festivals of Dionysus (see GREECE). In Old Comedy the phallus (as a symbol of fertility) and the Dionysiac *comus* or revel (whence 'comedy') are constant features; and another element, the 'contest' (*agôn*), is by some scholars derived from the 'agony' of Dionysus. In the satyric-drama too, direct Dionysiac influence is obvious; the satyrs, or 'horse-men', imaginary creatures of the wild, came to be regarded as attendants on Dionysus, though apparently they were not that originally.

With tragedy the connexion is less clear, and may be more indirect. Attempts have been made to trace, in the basic form of tragedy, a Dionysiac ritual-sequence, but they are not very convincing. It is possible, though it cannot be proved, that the earliest tragedy in Athens dealt exclusively or mainly with Dionysiac subjects; but when we begin to have knowledge of it, some thirty years after its inception, it certainly does not. Dionysiac subjects are common (though only one Dionysiac play, the *Bacchae*, happens to have survived), but not more common than the dramatic nature of the Dionysus-legends would lead us to expect. When Aristotle says that tragedy originated in the dithyramb (a type of hymn to Dionysus), he is obviously thinking of the form of tragedy, that it grew out of a choral performance with dialogue interspersed; he cannot be held to mean that the new art was Dionysiac in spirit or content, though it may have been. He states also that tragedy developed 'out of the satyr-drama' (which was undoubtedly very closely connected with the more boisterous side of Dionysus-worship) by discarding its rollicking metres, its ridiculous diction, and its insignificant plots; it might therefore be argued that tragedy became itself actually by getting rid of Dionysiac elements. The whole question remains obscure because, though there is an abundance of analogies and possibilities, there is little direct and trustworthy evidence; but at the very least it is certain that the worship of Dionysus stimulated, in a most catholic way, the lively dramatic sense of the Greeks, and gave to the Athenians, in its festivals, a congenial home in which diverse forms of the drama could grow to maturity.

H. D. F. KITTO

DIPHILUS (*d.* 290 B.C.) of Sinope, Greek poet of the New Comedy, contemporary with Menander (see GREECE, 2 *b*). He was frequently imitated by Plautus and Terence. Only fragments of his work survive.

DIRECTOR, see PRODUCER, 2.

DISGUISING, a term used in the fifteenth and sixteenth centuries in England to cover any sort of entertainment which included mummery or dice-play and the wearing of masks. The word was later (1512) replaced by mask, or masque, and was obsolete by 1544. 'Disguise', says Ben Jonson, 'was the old English word for a mask.'

DITHYRAMB, a type of hymn in honour, originally, of the Greek god Dionysus, then of other deities. It was performed by a chorus of fifty, and would normally relate some incident in the life of the deity to whom it was addressed. The leader of the chorus later became semi-detached, as a soloist; and in the question-and-answer that might pass between him and the rest of the chorus lies, almost certainly, the origin, or one of the origins, of drama (see further GREECE, 1).

H. D. F. KITTO

DMITREVSKY, IVAN AFANASYEVICH (1733–1821), one of the first important actors in the Russian theatre. He appeared with the amateur company founded by Fedor Volkov, and went with him to play before the Court in Jan. 1752. He was then sent to the Cadet College to be trained for the Court theatre, and was a member of the company organized by Sumarokov. After the untimely death of Volkov in 1763 Dmitrevsky was appointed Inspector of Theatres, and took a leading part in the running of the State playhouses. Between 1765 and 1768 he twice went abroad to complete his theatrical education, and spent most of the time in Paris with the leading French actors of the day. On his return he occupied the highest position in the St. Petersburg theatre, both as actor and administrator, being known as 'the ornament of the Russian stage'. He was extremely gifted, and appeared with equal success in tragic and comic parts. His best performances were considered to be the title-roles of *Le Misanthrope* and Sumarokov's *Dmitri the Impostor*, and Starodum in *The Minor* by Fonvizin. He wrote and translated plays, prepared a history of the Russian theatre, and was elected a member of the Russian Academy. These activities set him apart from the general run of Russian actors, who at that time were usually lacking in education. Dmitrevsky played a big part in the development of the theatre in Russia. As head of the State theatres he determined its artistic development, chose its repertory, formed its companies, and rehearsed the actors in their parts. Among his pupils was Alexei Yakovlev.

DMITRI OF ROSTOV, SAINT (1651–1709), Russian bishop and author of religious plays, whose original name was Daniel Tuptalo.

Born near Kiev of a Cossack family, he was educated as a monk at the Kiev Academy and rapidly became well known as a preacher and hagiographer. Peter the Great summoned him to Moscow in 1701 and in 1702 made him Metropolitan of Rostov, where he defended Peter's westernizing reforms against conservative churchmen. He died at Rostov in 1709 and was canonized in 1757. His six sacred dramas are very similar to medieval European Mystery and Morality plays, and are based on the sacred 'school dramas' or dialogues acted at the Kiev Academy in his time, which in turn were based on Jesuit drama. In rhyming syllabic metre, they include *The Nativity Play*, *The Penitent Sinner*, *Esther and Ahasuerus*, and *The Resurrection of Christ*. Biblical characters appear together with such allegorical figures as Jealousy, Hope, Earth, and Death, and humorous peasants who comment irreverently on the sacred action. Some of the dialogue is vivid and natural, and the speeches of the shepherds in *The Nativity Play* bear comparison with those in the *Second Shepherds' Play*. It was in St. Dmitri's *Esther and Ahasuerus* that Ivan Dmitrevsky made his first appearance before the Russian Court in 1752.

ROBERT TRACY

DÖBBELIN, KARL THEOPHILUS (1727–93), German actor-manager, who started his career in the company of Caroline Neuber and later of Ackermann; he found his true vocation, however, in the several troupes of wandering harlequin-players which he afterwards joined. He was a boastful and unscrupulous man, who started his own company on money won at cards, and kept it going by blatant publicity and somewhat underhand means. He settled in Leipzig, and for some time proved a serious rival to Koch, who was established there. Döbbelin was a great noisy cheerful creature who played all his parts, whether tragic or comic, in the same style, thundering out his lines in a roar, and rushing about the stage to the great danger of the scenery and his fellow actors. This pleased the groundlings mightily, and for the rest he was indifferent. It should, however, be said in his favour that he had a good repertory of plays and kept his company well under control. None of his actors was outstanding, with the exception of his wife, a gentle, charming woman, whose quiet, subtle style was a great contrast to her husband's. Nevertheless Döbbelin, by sheer personality, carried his company to the point where it was taken seriously by contemporary critics. In 1765 he took over the management of Schuch's company, which had gone to pieces under the management of the old harlequin-player's three sons, took it to Berlin, re-formed it, and again forced it and himself on the attention of the critics. On the opening of the National Theatre in Berlin he was replaced by Fleck, though he retained a nominal position as stage-manager till his death.

DOBUJINSKY, MSTISLAV (1875–1957), Russian artist and stage designer, a member, with Benois and Bakst, of the group Mir Iskusstva (The World of Art) whose ideas were introduced to western Europe by Diaghilev. He was a versatile artist in many mediums, but is best remembered for his stage designs. Before leaving Russia he worked with Stanislavsky at the Moscow Art Theatre, and also with Meyerhold, but his finest work was probably for the ballet—'Petrushka', 'Coppelia', 'Nutcracker', and 'Swan Lake' among others. His work showed an unusual combination of accuracy of atmosphere with profound imagination, and his work was always dramatic and artistically satisfying.

DOCKSTADER, LEW [GEORGE ALFRED CLAPP] (1856–1924), American blackface minstrel and vaudeville star. Beginning as an amateur minstrel in and around Hartford, he turned professional about 1873, travelling with Bloodgood's Comic Alliance, Emmett and Wilde, and similar plantation groups. In 1876 he and Charles Dockstader organized their own troupe, the Dockstader Brothers, and Clapp retained the name for himself when Dockstader retired in 1883. He opened his own theatre on Broadway in 1886, and entered vaudeville about 1890. In 1898 he went into partnership with George Primrose (1852–1919) to form Primrose's Minstrels, an organization which lasted until 1913. From 1913 to 1923 he travelled on the Keith circuit. Big and lumbering, in a 'Taft-sized' ten-yard tailcoat and shoes two feet long and one foot wide, Dockstader combined elements of the blackface minstrel and the clown. He gave new scope to the declining plantation show by turning it into an instrument of political and social satire. His blackface characters abandoned the singing of plantation songs to parody aviators, politicians, polar explorers and other figures in the news, while he himself provided blackface replicas of Cleveland, Theodore Roosevelt, and other well-known men. His basic innovation was to portray not comic Negro characters but comic whites in blackface.

ROBERT TRACY

DOCK STREET THEATRE, see CHARLESTON.

DÓCZY, LAJOS (1845–1919), Hungarian dramatist, and with Rákosi founder of the neo-romantic drama, which abandoned the realistic social problems of the day for fantasy and legend. His best play was probably *A Csók* (*The Kiss*), which had a great success on its production in 1874.

DODD, JAMES WILLIAM (1734–96), English comedian, the last of the fops who started with Cibber, all lace, frills, and snuff-boxes. After a hard apprenticeship in the provinces he joined the company at Drury Lane in 1765, and was the original Sir Benjamin Backbite in *The School for Scandal* (1777). One of his finest parts was Sir Andrew Aguecheek, of which Lamb has left an excellent description: 'Dodd was *it*, as it came out of nature's hands.... In expressing slowness of apprehension this actor surpassed all others. You could see the first dawn of an idea stealing slowly over his countenance, climbing up little and little, with a painful process. . . . The balloon takes less time in filling, than it took to cover the expansion of his broad moony face over all its quarters with expression.' Boaden described him as 'the soul of empty eminence'. He was good as Lord Foppington, as Tattle, as Bob Acres, and in such parts as Fribble. Off-stage he was serious and a great student, leaving at his death a fine library which was bought chiefly by the King, the Duke of Roxburghe, and John Kemble.

DODD, Lee Wilson (1879–1933), American man of letters, who, in addition to poetry and novels, wrote several plays. Among them the most important were *Speed* (1911), a satire on the early motor-car craze, and *The Changelings* (1923). A satiric comedy, *A Stranger in the House*, met with disaster when its leading man, Henry Miller, died during rehearsals in 1926. After some financial losses in the slump of 1929, Dodd turned successfully to the teaching of English, and at the time of his death had just been invited to succeed Professor Baker, whose assistant he had been for some time, in his playwriting course at Yale.

DODSLEY, Robert (1703–64), an interesting figure in the English literary world of the early eighteenth century. The son of a Mansfield schoolmaster, he was apprenticed to a weaver, but ran away and went into domestic service. While working as a footman in London he attracted notice by some occasional verses, was taken up and patronized by the nobility, and became the friend and protégé of Defoe and Pope. He appears to have been a charming and attractive young man, whose head was in no way turned by his success, though he knew how to profit by it. On the proceeds of his first play, *The Toy Shop* (1735), and other literary works, he established himself as a bookseller and publisher at the sign of Tully's Head in Pall Mall, where he issued works by Pope, Dr. Johnson, and his own important *Select Collection of Old Plays*, later revised and edited by Hazlitt. His best-known play was *The King and the Miller of Mansfield* (1737), which, with its sequel, *Sir John Cockle at Court* (1738), was given at Drury Lane, and frequently revived. It provided the basis for Collé's *Partie de chasse d'Henri IV*, and is still obtainable in the repertory of the nineteenth-century Juvenile Drama. Dodsley's last play, *Cleone* (1758), was a tragedy which owed much of its success to the acting of George Anne Bellamy, and was revived by Mrs. Siddons in 1786. He also wrote the libretto of a ballad opera, *The Blind Beggar of Bethnal Green* (1741).

DOG DRAMA, see circus.

DOGGETT, Thomas (*c.* 1670–1721), English actor, who first appeared in London after some years in the provinces, and soon made a reputation in the playing of low comedy. Congreve admired him exceedingly, and wrote for him the parts of Fondlewife in *The Old Bachelor* and Ben in *Love for Love*. Doggett, of whom Cibber has left an excellent pen-portrait in his *Apology*, had the good sense never to step outside his own line of characters. He was joint manager of Drury Lane with Cibber and Wilks, retiring in disgust when Barton Booth, whose politics he disliked, was allowed a share in the Patent. In 1696 he wrote a farce which was played at Lincoln's Inn Fields Theatre, and later revived in an adaptation by Colley Cibber. He also instituted the Doggett Coat and Badge for Thames watermen, a race which is still rowed, in honour of the accession of George I. It takes place on 1 Aug., and figures in *The Waterman* (1774) by Dibdin. Doggett was the friend of Addison, Steele, and Pope, whom he met daily at Button's Coffee-house, where he had also to encounter Cibber, whom after his retirement from Drury Lane he ignored for a year. They eventually became friends again, and made common cause against the insufferable and extravagant Wilks.

DOLCE, Lodovico (1508–68), Italian dramatist of whom Walker, in his *Historical Memoir on Italian Tragedy* (1799), says scathingly 'little is known that can be related with pleasure'. He was one of those who 'supped full of horrors', and his tragedies, drawn from classical drama, are only a degree less distasteful than the famous *Canace* of Speroni. One of the most successful, which was given to great applause in 1565, was *Marianna*, a rehandling of the story of Herod and Mariamne which is, for its period, unusually subtle. By some critics it is considered the most representative tragedy of the sixteenth century. His *Giocasta*, based on Euripides' *Phoenician Women*, was given in translation at Gray's Inn in 1566.

DOMINION DRAMA FESTIVAL, see canada.

DOMINION THEATRE, London, a large playhouse on the site of a famous brewery at the junction of Tottenham Court Road and Oxford Street. It opened on 3 Oct. 1929 with *Follow Through*. Other productions there were Julian Wylie's pantomime *Aladdin*, and a musical play called *Silver Wings* (both 1930). It became a cinema in 1932.

DOMINIQUE, see biancolelli (2).

DONAT, Robert (1905–58), English actor, whose last years were a struggle against ill-health, which kept him off the stage for long periods. This was all the more unfortunate in that, at his best, he was an outstandingly moving and sincere actor, with a fine voice and presence, and an uncompromising integrity. In his early years he was with Benson's company, where he proved himself a good Shakespearian actor, and he also played leading parts at the Festival Theatre, Cambridge, under Terence Gray. Among his greatest successes were Sarn in *Precious Bane* (1931), Charles Cameron in *A Sleeping Clergyman* (1933), and Captain Shotover in *Heartbreak House* (1943).

He was with the Old Vic in 1939 and again in 1953, when he played Becket, most beautifully, in *Murder in the Cathedral*—his last appearance on the stage. He was for a time manager of the Queen's Theatre and of the Westminster.

DON JUAN, a character derived from an old Spanish legend, who first found vital expression in Tirso de Molina's *El burlador de Sevilla y Convidado de piedra* (before 1630), and has since become a constantly recurring figure in European literature. There is no evidence for the existence of Don Juan as an historical figure, though tradition usually connects him with Seville. Tirso's play is in two parts, the first concerned with the character and activities of the hero, the second with his mocking invitation to dinner given to the marble statue, who accepts it and brings retribution by supernatural means upon Don Juan in punishment of his many crimes. Each part derives from a separate source, but is so linked with the other as to present a convincing whole. Don Juan is not portrayed merely as a sensual man; he is the embodiment of self-will, unable to curb his desires although he knows they are evil. There is no lack of Catholic belief in him, as there is in Molière's version of the story. He does not doubt that retribution will come, but he continually puts off repentance, hoping through God's mercy and long-suffering to remain immune as long as possible.

Among the many works on the same theme are Mozart's opera 'Don Giovanni', Byron's poem *Don Juan*, Molière's *Festin de Pierre*, Goldoni's *El dissoluto*, a Russian version by Pushkin, and frequent versions in Spanish, the best being Zorrilla's *Don Juan Tenorio*. Don Juan also appears in the third act of Shaw's *Man and Superman*.

DOORS OF ENTRANCE, see PROSCENIUM DOORS.

D'ORGEMONT [ADRIEN DES BARRES] (?–*c.* 1665), French actor, who was at the Théâtre du Marais with Montdory and succeeded him as Orator of the troupe. Little is known of his acting, though he was favourably compared with Bellerose and was a good comedian. In 1638 he married the widow of the farce-player Turlupin and went to the Hôtel de Bourgogne, where he remained until his death. He is believed to have played Don Diègue in the first production of *Le Cid*.

DORIMOND [NICHOLAS DROUIN] (*c.* 1628–*c.* 1664), a French provincial actor-manager, whose early career bears some resemblance to that of Molière, though, unlike his famous contemporary, he never succeeded in establishing himself in Paris. With his wife, who after his death appeared at the Marais, he directed the Troupe of Mademoiselle, in which the son of Floridor also played for a short time. Dorimond was the author of nine plays, including one on the subject of Don Juan, which were given by the above company, probably between 1657 and 1660, and his farces may have been seen by, and had some influence on, Molière, who no doubt encountered Dorimond's company on his wanderings.

DORSET GARDEN THEATRE, LONDON (the second Duke's House), was planned by Davenant, who died before it was completed. Designed by Wren, it cost £9,000, the money being subscribed by people known not as 'backers', the term in use today, but much more picturesquely as 'adventurers'. It stood by the river, just to the south of Salisbury Court, and was larger than either Davenant's old house in Lincoln's Inn Fields or the Theatre Royal, Bridges Street (Drury Lane). It had a river frontage and steps for those landing by boat, called Dorset Stairs. Over the front were the arms of the Duke of York, for he was its patron, and its players were known as the Duke's Men. The building, which was of a magnificence never before seen in a London theatre, was decorated with statues of Melpomene and Thalia, and had a striking proscenium arch (see No. 63). Over the theatre were apartments, where lived Betterton, the chief actor—known as the Keeper. He and Harris were the artistic directors of a fine company, while the business arrangements were in the capable hands of Davenant's widow, Dame Marie de Tremblay Davenant, and later of her sons.

The theatre opened on 9 Nov. 1671 with *Sir Martin Mar-All*, a tried favourite. The first new play was *King Charles VIII of France*, which, says Downes the prompter in his *Roscius Anglicanus*, though 'all new cloathed, yet lasted but 6 days together'. *Mamamouchi; or, the Citizen turned Gentleman*, the next new play, had Harris, Haines, Nokes, Sandford, Underhill, Mrs. Betterton, and Mrs. Leigh in the cast. The critics described it as foolish, but it ran nine days to full houses. Opera, for which the theatre later became famous, began with Davenant's adaptation of *Macbeth*. Shadwell's operatic version of *The Tempest* was given a spectacular revival, with great success, and his *Psyche*, with music by Matthew Locke, ran for eight days and proved very remunerative. Two dramatists made unsuccessful appearances as actors during this time, Lee in *Macbeth*, Otway in *The Forced Marriage*. Betterton's reputation was much enhanced by his performance in Shadwell's version of *Timon of Athens*, and his *Libertine* and *Virtuoso*, while Otway's *The Orphan* and *Venice Preserved*, with Southerne's *The Fatal Marriage*, made the name of the famous Mrs. Barry, for whom Otway's plays were written.

Under Betterton's skilful direction the theatre proved a thorn in the side of Drury Lane, and from 1672, when the latter was burnt down, until 1674, when it was reopened, Dorset Garden was the only first-class theatre in London. Although most of Dryden's plays were done at Drury Lane, his *Spanish Friar* and *Mr. Limberham; or, the Kind Keeper* were first done at Dorset Garden. Other dramatists who wrote for this theatre were D'Urfey, Settle, Aphra Behn, Etherege, and Ravenscroft.

Things got bad for both houses eventually, and in 1682 the two companies combined, making Drury Lane their headquarters, with Betterton as leading man, displacing Hart and Mohun. After the union Dorset Garden declined. It gave operas occasionally, and in 1689 was called the Queen's Theatre, out of compliment to Queen Mary (William and Mary). But it descended the scale gradually, and was finally used for acrobatic and wild beast shows. The last mention of it is in 1706.

W. MACQUEEN-POPE†

DORVAL, MARIE-THOMASE-AMÉLIE (*née* DELAUNAY) (1798–1849), French actress, illegitimate daughter of strolling players, orphaned at 15, married in the following year, and soon widowed. She was on the stage from her earliest years, and made her début in Paris at the Porte-Saint-Martin in a poor melodrama to which her excellent acting gave a momentary sparkle. It was as Amélie in *Trente Ans, ou la Vie d'un joueur*, in 1827, that she made her first great success, playing opposite Frédérick. At the same theatre, with Bocage, she was superb in the elder Dumas's *Antony* (1831). On 21 Apr. 1835 she made her first appearance at the Comédie-Française, giving a performance as Kitty Bell in *Chatterton* which long remained in the memory of those who saw it. Gôt, in later life, put it on a level with Mlle Mars's Célimène and Rachel's Camille (in *Horace*). The play was written by Alfred de Vigny, whose mistress Dorval was at that time. She later appeared in Hugo's *Angélo* (1835), and might have remained at the Comédie-Française until her retirement, but she found the restrictions irksome, and the jealousy of Mlle Mars insupportable. She preferred to return to the popular theatres, where she was several times seen again with Frédérick. In 1842 she played *Phèdre* at the Odéon with marked success, but her health was already failing. She was taken ill during an unsuccessful provincial tour in 1847, and returned to Paris to die in poverty.

DORVIGNY [LOUIS-FRANÇOIS ARCHAMBAULT] (1742–1812), French actor and dramatist, a reputed son of Louis XV, whom he certainly resembled in looks. He played for some time on the boulevards under Nicolet, but being idle and dissipated he soon turned to playwriting as a less arduous occupation, and turned out some 300 light comedies and farces, many of which were never printed. Most of them were done at the Foire Saint-Laurent in the 1770s, and his Janot, played by Volange, and Jocrisse, played by Brunet, delighted uncritical audiences for years. The Comédie-Française, hoping to profit by his success elsewhere, finally did two of his plays, but the academic atmosphere of this great theatre was not suited to them, and they were comparative failures. Usually penniless, often drunk, a bohemian and a wit, Dorvigny was a friend of the dramatist Aude, who became his boon companion in dissipation. His life was written by Charles Monselet.

DOSTOIEVSKY, FEODOR MIKHAILOVICH (1821–81), distinguished Russian novelist, several of whose novels have been dramatized, notably *The Idiot* and *The Brothers Karamazov*. Both these were done before 1917, and have been revived since. *The Insulted and Injured* (also known in English as *The Despised and Rejected*) was adapted for the Moscow Art Theatre by V. A. Solovyov, and in 1946 an adaptation of *Crime and Punishment* was given with some success in London.

DOTTORE, IL, the pedant and second agèd parent of the *commedia dell'arte*. He was usually depicted as a Bolognese lawyer, and frequently confused with the Pedant. His name was often Graziano (see ITALY, 2). Unlike his companion, Pantalone (Pantaloon), he has left no trace in the English harlequinade, though he passed into French dramatic literature via Molière.

DOUBLE MASQUE, see MASQUE.

DOUGLASS, DAVID (?–1786), the first American actor-manager, who in 1758 met and married the widow of the elder Hallam in Jamaica, where he was touring with a company. He took her and her family, with his own actors, back to New York, later calling them the American Company. He was an excellent manager, and seems to have found his work most profitable, in spite of some opposition from the more Puritan elements of the population in New York and Philadelphia. He built a temporary theatre on Cruger's Wharf, another in Beekman Street, and a third in John Street, all in New York, and was also responsible for the erection of the first permanent theatre in the United States, the Southwark, in Philadelphia, which opened in 1766. It was under Douglass's management that the American Company did *The Prince of Parthia*, the first American play to have a professional production, and that John Henry, later to succeed Douglass as manager, first joined the company in New York.

DOWNES, JOHN (*fl.* 1662–1710), author of *Roscius Anglicanus*, a volume of scattered theatrical notes which is one of the rare sources of information on the early Restoration theatre. Downes, who was connected with the theatre all his life, wanted to be an actor, but his first appearance on the stage, in Davenant's *Siege of Rhodes* in 1661, was such a fiasco that he gave up, and worked backstage. He was connected with Davenant's company, and later with Betterton's at Lincoln's Inn Fields, as prompter and book-keeper, in which capacity he had charge of the play scripts, copied the actors' parts, and attended all rehearsals and performances. His *Roscius Anglicanus* was first published in 1708. It was edited in 1886 by Joseph Knight, and in 1930 by Montague Summers.

DOWNSTAGE (the acting area nearest the audience), see STAGE DIRECTIONS.

DOWTON, WILLIAM (1764–1851), English actor, who was intended for architecture but was led by some successful appearances in amateur theatricals to take to the stage. In 1791 he joined Sarah Baker's company and soon became her leading man, marrying her daughter Sally (1768–1817) in 1794. Two years later he was playing Sheva in Cumberland's *The Jew* when he was seen by Sheridan and engaged for Drury Lane, where he made his début shortly after. He was soon recognized as an outstanding player of such elderly characters as Sir Anthony Absolute, Dr. Cantwell, Hardcastle, and Old Dornton. He was also extremely good as Falstaff, in which part he made his New York début at the Park Theatre in 1836. He was later seen there as Shylock also. A thorough artist, of the Garrick school, he was considered by Leigh Hunt to be one of the finest comic geniuses of the day, while Hazlitt described him as 'a genuine and excellent comedian'. He continued to act with Mrs. Baker's company during the summer months and in 1815 took over the company. He was not very successful, possibly because his main interests lay in London, and soon relinquished the management to his son William, who, in 1832, also went to Drury Lane; a final attempt to revive the Kent circuit in 1838 ended in failure. By 1840 the elder William was destitute, and a benefit performance for him was organized at Her Majesty's. The younger William abandoned the stage and became a Brother of the Charterhouse. His younger brother Henry (?–1827) was also an actor.

D'OYLY CARTE, RICHARD (1844–1901), theatrical impresario, who encouraged the early collaboration of Gilbert and Sullivan and with the profits which accrued to him therefrom built the Savoy Theatre, London, the first to be lighted by electricity. It opened with *Patience*, and became a home of light opera. D'Oyly Carte also built the Royal English Opera House, Cambridge Circus (now the Palace Theatre), in an endeavour to encourage the writing and production of English opera. He did much to raise the musical taste of his generation, gave employment to young singers, and founded the company for the production of Gilbert and Sullivan which still bears his name.

DRACHMANN, HOLGER HENRIK HERHOLDT (1846–1908), Danish poet and dramatist, was born in Copenhagen, went to the university and the Academy of Fine Arts, and for many years was simultaneously a writer and a painter. He came for a time under the influence of Georg Brandes, travelled widely in England and on the Continent, and wrote a good deal of prose and verse before he attempted dramatic work. When he did so his wide experience of men and nations gave him a wealth of material, though his form remained to the end lyrical rather than dramatic. His poetry was already famous (from the time of *Dæmpede Melodier* in 1875) when he began writing plays in 1882. Three plays were written between 1882 and 1884 and then the well-known *Der var en Gang* in 1885. Two dramatic poems and two more plays followed and then, in 1894, *Vølund Smed*, the first of his melodramas, a collected volume of which appeared in 1895. His popularity as a playwright was now very high and it was increased by his *Brav Karl* in 1898. Two more plays followed in 1898 and then the last plays, *Gurre*, a romantic play, in 1899, *Hallfred Vandraadeskjald*, a lyrical drama, in 1900, and *Det grønne Haab* in 1903. UNA ELLIS-FERMOR†

DRAMA. 1. A term applied loosely to the whole body of work written for the theatre, as English drama, French drama, or to a group of plays related by their style or content, as Restoration drama, realistic drama.

2. A term applicable to any situation in which there is conflict and, for theatrical purposes, resolution of that conflict with the assumption of character. This implies the co-operation of at least two actors, and rules out narrative and monologue. The dramatic instinct is inherent in man, and the most rudimentary dialogue with song and dance may be classed as drama. In a narrower sense the word is applied to plays of high emotional content, which at their best may give us literary masterpieces, and at their worst degenerate into melodrama. The term dramatist is not necessarily restricted to a writer of such dramas, but serves, like playwright, to designate anyone writing for the theatre.

DRAMATIC CENSORSHIP. 1. GREAT BRITAIN. The wide powers of supervision and control over the stage in this country which are today vested in the Lord Chamberlain are an elaboration of the functions of the Master of the King's Revels of Tudor times. He was appointed in the reign of Henry VII to supervise the entertainments of the Court, his duty being, in part, to ensure that such entertainments were carried on in an orderly manner and contained no matter offensive to the king. With the growth of the Tudor and Stuart policy of suppressing in the drama, as elsewhere, opinions which were unorthodox or tended to heresy or sedition, the work which devolved upon him outgrew his administrative capabilities and was gradually taken over by his superior officer in the Royal Household, the Lord Chamberlain, whose primary duty it became to give effect to the royal will in these matters as it varied from reign to reign. His appointment depended upon no statutory enactment and there were no statutes defining the extent of his authority in the theatre. The first statute directly concerned with control over the stage was passed in the reign of James I (3 Jac. I, c. 21) —'an Act to restrain the abuses of players . . . for preventing and avoiding of the great abuse of the Holy name of God in Stage Plays, Enterludes, May-Games, Shews, and such like.'

For over two centuries there was little change in the general situation. The Lord Chamberlain concerned himself almost exclusively with political and religious issues, paying attention to the moral aspect of the theatre only to the extent of prohibiting riotous or immoral conduct at dramatic performances.

With the emergence of the theatre from its extinction under the Commonwealth, the reaction towards a general unruliness in the theatre became pronounced and resulted in the passing of an Act in 1713 (12 Anne, stat. 2, c. 23) 'for reducing the laws relating to rogues, vagabonds, sturdy beggars and vagrants, into one act of Parliament; and for the more effectual punishing such rogues, vagabonds, sturdy beggars and vagrants, and sending them whither they ought to be sent'. 'Common players of Interludes' were deemed under the Act to be 'rogues and vagabonds'.

In 1737, however, a development occurred. For the first time the Lord Chamberlain's prerogative powers received statutory recognition and his dual function in the theatre was clearly defined. Under Section 1 of 10 Geo. II, c. 28, any person acting 'for hire, gain or reward' in any place where they have not a settlement, or 'without licence from the Lord Chamberlain of His Majesty's Household for the time being, shall be deemed a rogue and vagabond'; while under Section 2 no new plays or additions to old plays might be acted unless and until a copy of such plays or additions had obtained the approval of the Lord Chamberlain.

In 1843, matters were taken a stage further, when the Theatres Act of that year (6 & 7 Vict., c. 68) repealed all previous acts relevant to the control of the stage, and consolidated the law on the whole subject. Under this Act, which is still in force, detailed regulations are laid down as to the structural and other requirements necessary before premises can be licensed by the Lord Chamberlain as suitable for the production of stage plays. The Lord Chamberlain is the licensing authority for this purpose for all theatres in Windsor and London other than Drury Lane and Covent Garden. Over these two theatres, his control derives from other than statutory sources. Elsewhere the licensing of theatres comes under the jurisdiction of the local authorities.

As this article is concerned with the Lord Chamberlain's second function—as Censor of plays—it is to Section 12 of the Act and the sections which amplify it that the reader should refer. Section 12 provides that:

> One copy of every new stage play, and of every new act, scene, or other part added to an old stage play, and of every new prologue or epilogue, and of every new part added to an old prologue or epilogue, intended to be produced and acted for hire at any theatre in Great Britain, shall be sent to the Lord Chamberlain of Her Majesty's household for the time being, seven days at least before the first acting or presenting thereof, with an account of the theatre where and the time when the same is intended to be first acted or presented, signed by the master or manager, or one of the masters or managers of such theatre; and during the said seven days no person shall for hire act or present the same, or cause the same to be acted or presented; and in case the Lord Chamberlain, either before or after the expiration of the said period of seven days, shall disallow any play, or any act, scene, or part thereof, or any prologue or epilogue, or any part thereof, it shall not be lawful for any person to act or present the same, or cause the same to be acted or presented, contrary to such disallowance.

The term 'stage play' is defined by Section 23 of the Act as including 'every tragedy, comedy, farce, opera, burletta, interlude, melodrama, pantomime or other entertainment of the stage, or any part thereof'.

The application of any definition gives rise to disputes in borderline cases and the interpretation of Section 23 has led to a certain amount of litigation during the century since the passing of the Act. In *Wigan* v. *Strange* (1865 L.R. I.C.P. 175) where a *ballet divertissement* in contradistinction to a *ballet d'action* was held not to constitute a stage play, Erle, C.J., in dealing with the particular issues involved, gave a general indication of the position. He said 'the *ballet divertissement* involves no consecutive train of ideas, but consists merely of poses and evolutions by a number of persons, elegant in shape and graceful in action. On the other hand, the *ballet d'action* has a regular dramatic story which may give rise to all manner of emotions incident to tragedy, comedy, or farce, accompanied by elegance of form and grace of motion.' Willis, J., in the same case, in associating himself with the Lord Chief Justice's decision, said of the *ballet divertissement*: 'In strictness, it is not an entertainment of, but on the stage.'

Provided that a performance is a performance 'of the stage' and has 'a regular dramatic story' it is not necessary for all the performers to be 'on the stage'. In *Day* v. *Simpson* (1865 18 C.B.N.S. 680) only two of the characters were 'on the stage'; the rest were below the stage, their reflections only appearing in front of the footlights.

As Section 12 relates to every 'new stage play', plays written before the passing of the Theatres Act need not be submitted to the Lord Chamberlain. Such plays, however, can be suppressed by the Lord Chamberlain under powers vested in him by Section 14 of the Act. This section reads:

> It shall be lawful for the Lord Chamberlain for the time being, whenever he shall be of opinion that it is fitting for the preservation of good manners, decorum, or of the public peace so to do, to forbid the acting or presenting any stage play, or any act, scene, or part thereof, or any prologue or epilogue, or any part thereof, anywhere in Great Britain, or in such theatres as he shall specify, and either absolutely or for such time as he shall think fit.

Under the terms of the same section the Lord Chamberlain can also withdraw a licence already granted. This power is, however, exercised only in exceptional cases.

Paragraphs 88, 89, and 90 of the *Rules and Regulations with regard to Theatres in the Jurisdiction of the Lord Chamberlain* lay down that no profanity or impropriety of language; no indecency of dress, dance, or gesture; and no offensive personalities or representations of living persons are permitted on the stage, or anything calculated to produce riot or breach of the peace.

At the time of writing the Lord Chamberlain has three English readers and one Welsh reader of plays, who read and report upon the works submitted. Although his power to withhold or withdraw a licence is absolute and he is under no legal obligation to disclose the reasons which led his readers to come to their decision, as a matter of practice the Lord Chamberlain's office when refusing a licence is normally ready to indicate changes in the text that would enable a licence to be issued. There is no appeal against the Lord Chamberlain's decision in such matters.

The penalty for performing an unlicensed play is a fine not exceeding £50 for every offence, and, in addition, Section 15 of the Act, now amended by Section 43 of the Criminal Justice Act 1925, gives discretionary power to the court dealing with the case to suspend the licence of a theatre where an unlicensed play is produced. Prosecutions for such offences must begin within six months after the offence is committed and may be brought against any persons who 'for hire shall act or present or cause, permit or suffer to be acted or presented' the unlicensed play. This definition covers the licensee of the theatre, the manager, producer, and actors.

The Lord Chamberlain's power over the licensing of plays is not territorially limited as is his authority to license theatres. He is the sole authority in Great Britain with power to give or withhold his licence for a play intended for 'presentation for hire'. 'Presentation for hire' is defined under Section 16 of the Act in the following way:

> In every case in which any money or other reward shall be taken or charged, directly or indirectly, or in which the purchase of any article is made a condition for the admission of any person into any theatre to see any stage play, and also in every case in which any stage play shall be acted or presented in any house, room, or place in which distilled or fermented excisable liquor shall be sold, every actor therein shall be deemed to be acting for hire.

Although within the strict terms of the Act the Lord Chamberlain has control over plays produced by play-producing societies who draw their income indirectly in the form of annual subscriptions, rather than directly from the sale of tickets for each performance, the Lord Chamberlain does not always exercise his full powers in such cases and has always shown himself inclined to lenience in this respect in the case of societies 'bona fide established for the private performance of stage plays' where tickets are issued to members of such societies and 'no payment, directly or indirectly, beyond an honorarium' is paid to the actors.

The formalities necessary to apply for the Lord Chamberlain's licence are as follows:

One copy of the work to be performed must be sent to the Lord Chamberlain's office at least seven days before the first performance, accompanied by the appropriate fee—£1. 1*s*. 0*d*. in the case of 1-act plays, or single additional scenes, £2. 2*s*. 0*d*. in the case of other plays—and a statement giving the name of the theatre where, and the time when, the work is first to be presented. Manager, producer, author, or anyone interested in a particular production may submit a play to the Lord Chamberlain for a licence. The licence is, however, always sent by the Lord Chamberlain to the licensee of the theatre.

The controversial question of the desirability or the reverse of any form of dramatic censorship lies outside the scope of this article. It should, however, be noted that in 1853, 1866, and 1892, Select Committees of the House of Commons investigated the position and reported that the system was working satisfactorily. There was no protest from any individual or organization at either of the first two investigations, but in 1892 one dramatic critic put forward the case against censorship in the form prescribed under the Act of 1843. In 1909 a Joint Committee of the House of Lords and House of Commons again looked into the question, and on that occasion most of the leading dramatists individually and through their representative organization asked for drastic modifications in the existing machinery. Some of the witnesses who appeared before the Committee asked for the total abolition of any form of pre-production censorship, while others asked either for the censorship of plays to be optional only or alternatively for there to be an appeal from the Lord Chamberlain's decision.

Although the Lord Chamberlain has absolute power to decide whether any play shall or shall not be 'presented for hire', he has no powers of censorship whatsoever over the *publication* of dramatic works, which are in this respect treated in exactly the same way as any other literary work: that is to say, they are subject to no pre-publication censorship whatsoever, but are liable to suppression if they contain anything which is in the eyes of the law blasphemous, seditious, or obscene. Prosecutions for sedition and blasphemy are so rare nowadays that they can be ignored for the purpose of this article, but a word must be said about the crime of publishing an obscene libel.

Until the end of the eighteenth century the law took notice of only those forms of immorality which tended to a breach of the peace, and criminal proceedings brought in a number of cases against the publishers of obscene literature were unsuccessful.

By the beginning of the nineteenth century, however (the Society for the Suppression of Vice was founded in 1802), public opinion was changing and, with it, the law. In 1857 the Obscene Publications Act (commonly called Lord Campbell's Act) was passed. Its intention was largely to create machinery for the more effective enforcement of the Common Law as it then stood, and it was passed by Parliament only on Lord Campbell's assurance that 'the measure was intended to apply exclusively to works written for the single purpose of corrupting the morals of youth and of a nature calculated to shock common feelings of decency in any well-regulated mind'. The test of obscenity was to be 'what was indictable under the present law'. Under Lord Campbell's successor in office, Lord Chief Justice Cockburn, however, the Act was given a very much more 'puritanical' interpretation. In *R.* v. *Hicklin* (1868 L.R. 3. Q.B. 360) he said: 'The test of obscenity is this, whether the tendency of the matter charged as obscene is to deprave and corrupt those whose minds are open to such immoral influences and into whose hands a publication of this sort may fall.' This dictum remained the test of obscenity until the coming into force of the Obscene Publications Act, 1959, which laid down that a work should be deemed obscene if 'taken as a whole' its effect were 'such as [tends] to deprave and corrupt persons who are likely, having regard to all the relevant circumstances, to read, see or hear the matter contained in it'. The Obscene Publications Act, 1959, repealed the Obscene Publications Act, 1857. Censorship was abolished in England by the Theatres Act, 1968.

2. THE UNITED STATES OF AMERICA. There is no office in the United States corresponding to that of the Lord Chamberlain in this country and no pre-production censorship of any kind. The law relating to dramatic works is, therefore, to be found in the Federal and State laws dealing with literary works as a whole. The Federal Acts are principally concerned with the prevention of the importation of obscene literature into the United States, and the sending of obscene literature by post, while the State Acts, although varying in detail, contain provisions similar in substance to the dictum of Lord Cockburn in *R.* v. *Hicklin.* A typical State law makes it a crime

> to sell, lend, give away, or show, or have in possession with intent to sell, lend, or give away, or to show, or advertise in any manner, or to otherwise offer for loan, gift, sale, or distribution any obscene, lewd, lascivious, filthy, indecent, or disgusting book, magazine, pamphlet, newspaper, story paper, writing, paper or any written or printed matter of an indecent character.

M. E. BARBER

DRAMATIC COPYRIGHT, see COPYRIGHT IN A DRAMATIC WORK.

DRAMATIC CRITICISM. If one considers dramatic criticism in a broad sense, as anything said or written about the theatre, the earliest surviving example dates back to a time before 3000 B.C. It is the testament inscribed at Abydos by the Egyptian actor, I-kher-nefert, giving a personal impression of the Passion Play of Osiris, which he himself produced. Herodotus's account (Book II, ch. 63) of the ritual drama at Papremis, as it was in the fifth century B.C., may also claim to be dramatic criticism; and so might the Biblical record of the exhibition of Samson in the temple at Gaza (Judges xvi. 27).

The *Poetics* of Aristotle (384–322 B.C.), vulnerable as it is, remains the first known attempt at analytical and comparative criticism. It is one of the ironies of history that this 'salvaged' assortment of lecture-notes, evolving supposed laws for the theatre by impersonal deduction from incomplete data, should have been for so many centuries regarded as infallible. Of the three unities ultimately put forward on Aristotle's authority as essentials to drama, those of time and place had in view the Attic theatre, where the scene could never be entirely changed and the same chorus was to be seen all the while. A 'unity', or coherence, of action remains obviously desirable, as each drama is still framed by its beginning and its end—now, as then, the source of countless conventions. Opinion continues divided over the exact meaning of Aristotle's definition of tragedy as effecting, 'through pity and fear', a 'purge of like passions'. The points in question are as to whether actual fright is meant, what are the 'like passions', and how and why they should be purged.

The *Ars Poetica* of Horace (65–8 B.C.) extended Aristotle with arbitrary maxims in undying verse. Juvenal, Martial, Lucian, and Petronius have useful references to the theatre of their time. Plutarch and Quintilian give critical surveys. But the father of dramatic criticism as an art was Longinus (*c.* A.D. 220–73), doubtfully identified with Queen Zenobia's adviser. His demand for sincere expression on the part of dramatist and critic alike has only recently found full appreciation, though Boileau translated him in 1674 and Burke owed him some points in his *Essay on the Sublime and Beautiful* (1756). Amid the chaos of the enslaved world of the third century A.D., Longinus tempers the onslaughts made upon the theatre by Tertullian—and afterwards by St. Augustine—as the temple of false gods, which it most certainly was, both officially and otherwise. For the rest, the Dark Ages were as barren of enlightened criticism as they were of good drama, save for Hroswitha, the nun of Gandersheim, who has left a revealing note upon her plays.

With the awakening of drama at the Renaissance came the awakening also of criticism—primarily in Italy, with Scaliger (1484–1558), Minturno (?–1574), and not least Castelvetro (1505–71), who first formulated the unities out of Aristotle. Erasmus and Sir Thomas More both wrote with insight upon the theatre. Sir Philip Sidney's *Apologie for Poetrie* (pub. 1595) has its disappointments. He did not foresee the romantic outburst which was at hand. Stephen Gosson's *School of Abuse* (1579), which provoked him, was a vigorous and, at heart, sympathetic satire—a far better work than William Prynne's dreary *Histriomastix* (1632). Thomas Coryate, in 1611, gave a vivid description of the Venetian theatre, with a sidelight upon the Italian 'impromptu comedy' (see ITALY, 2). John Dryden's *Essay of Dramatic Poesy* (1668), with his *Defence* of that essay, and the *Discours* and *Examens* of Pierre Corneille (1606–84), flog the dead horse of the *Poetics*. Jeremy Collier's *Short View of the Immorality and Profaneness of the English Stage* (1698) stands out in its period as a well-reasoned call for good taste, to be echoed ten years later by Steele in the *Spectator*.

From Jonson's ode and Heminge and Condell's First Folio preface down to the last of several thousand volumes, criticism has been on the whole helpful to the true life of Shakespeare's plays—this, even at the cost of such controversies as the Baconian and Oxfordian. Hazlitt, Coleridge, Leigh Hunt, and De Quincey did much to rescue Shakespeare from eighteenth-century travesty, towards which Dr. Johnson, and Mrs. Inchbald in her *British Theatre*, had been complacent. Goethe, Lessing, Schlegel, and a host of laborious successors spread the light of a closer understanding in Germany. The later work of Dowden, Furnivall, Ward, Chambers, Lee, Gollancz, Dover Wilson, Boas, and others in England, and Bradley and Brander Matthews in America, kept Shakespeare as man and dramatist faithfully and intimately before the minds of readers and playgoers. Hence it is probable that English and American productions during their time were—with some freakish exceptions—nearer Shakespeare's intentions than those of any intervening period or even of the present day (see SHAKESPEARE, 2).

With the eighteenth century, criticism of the individual actor began to be conscious of its value in the survival of the written word. The genius of Charles Lamb (1775–1834), who had already revived interest in the lesser-known Elizabethan dramatists, graced the very falsity of the later eighteenth-century theatre with the charm of his own style. Thanks to this, the art of Munden and other old actors has won immortality, deserved or not. Colley Cibber's *Apology* (1740) gives us the best idea of Betterton, Lichtenberg of Garrick, Hazlitt (in conjunction with Crabb Robinson) of Kean. Churchill's *Rosciad* (1761) makes Quin live in satiric verse. The account in the *English Review* of Mrs. Siddons's performances at Drury Lane in 1782 by Thomas Holcroft, author of *The Road to Ruin*, was one of the earliest critical heraldings of its kind. Victorian criticism also, for the most part, centred upon the actor. George Henry Lewes's *On Actors and the Art of Acting* set a fruitful example. The rise of Henry Irving had a stimulating effect upon criticism in the 1870s, as did the visit of the Comédie-Française to London in 1879. In the same year was published George Meredith's *Essay on Comedy*, with its illuminating tributes to Congreve and Molière.

On both sides of the Atlantic criticism benefited in some respects from the fact that it became a recognized branch of journalism for practical news-purposes. At the same time it developed as an art far beyond the demands of its immediate professional task. The critics who brought a vast new public into the English theatre in the 1880s and 1890s did so by their own self-expression rather than as reliable judges. Clement Scott's utterly unfair abuse of Ibsen did not prevent him from being of immense use to the romantic stage of his time. William Archer's invaluable work as Ibsen's champion and translator was coupled with a certain lack of sympathy for popular farces and conventional dramas, which were human and not necessarily without merit in their own kind. Walkley and Shaw both attracted by their own idiosyncrasies of wit and of purpose, sometimes quite regardless of the play under consideration. None the less, they helped to foster interest in the theatre. J. T. Grein is to be remembered for his passionate enthusiasm, faith, and breadth of sympathy. Nor should Max Beerbohm be forgotten, nor C. E. Montague and the Mancunian tradition.

The saying of Anatole France, that criticism tells of 'the adventures of a soul among masterpieces', entails a reservation that adventures cannot always be among masterpieces for the professional critic. No critics survived this hazard more adroitly than his countrymen. Sainte-Beuve, when he turned his attention to the drama, Janin, Sarcey, Lemaître, Faguet, Filon, and other Parisian critics of the nineteenth century, though often limited in their outlook, were past masters in the art of enticing the reader to join in their own spiritual experiences, whatever the theme. They were the first 'columnists'.

It may have been largely due to the existence of the Comédie-Française that French criticism kept a tradition of its own through all political changes. The dicta of Horace and Aristotle, as approved by Boileau and Voltaire, did stifle the drama, but they afforded a perpetual topic for critical discussion. The influence of Rousseau made itself felt through Sébastien Mercier, author of *Le Tableau de Paris* (1781–9), who made a candid comparison between the hidebound state of the French theatre and the freedom of the English. Diderot's *De la poésie dramatique* (1758), and his critical upholding of domestic drama and comedy—*larmoyante* and otherwise—and Beaumarchais's *Essai sur le genre dramatique sérieux* (1767) signalled a more popular appeal, quite apart from their work as dramatists. In 1827 came the Romantic outburst, with Victor Hugo's famous preface to *Cromwell*. In 1873 Zola claimed that 'naturalism' was 'stammering its first accents'. In 1894 Ferdinand Brunetière, in *La Loi du théâtre*, was discovering yet another formula, based on the 'quality of will'; but he was careful to call it a 'law' and not a 'rule'.

Without the stabilizing focus of a central theatre like the Comédie-Française, criticism in Italy was more volatile and sporadic, but extremely alive. The duel of words between Carlo Goldini (1707–93) and Carlo Gozzi (1720–1806) over the *commedia dell'arte*—to which both, as well as the world's theatre, were so profoundly indebted—still affords bright reading. Also, political events had a far closer relation in Italy than in France both with the theatre itself—from Alfieri to D'Annunzio—and with dramatic criticism. The national struggles were the direct and confessed inspiration of Francesco de Sanctis (1817–83) and his fellow-romanticists of the latter half of the nineteenth century. For the same reason, to some extent, criticism in Italy tended to be philosophic rather than technical. It has been said of Benedetto Croce (1866–1952)—whose importance to Italian drama, as to every side of Italian culture, cannot be doubted—that for him neither theatre nor actor nor audience exists. His belief in the intuitive nature of dramatic genius remains none the less sound. It has a bearing upon Wagner's suggestion that all true dramatic art, whether expressed in verse or prose or no words at all, and with music or without, is at its birth an improvisation—unconcerned with any conscious technique. Neither the 'futurism' of Marinetti nor the 'expressionism' which still has to seek its critical classic in Nietzsche has founded any enduring school of criticism. External events have been, possibly, too absorbing. The psychological masks of Pirandello are tantalizing; but the despair for humanity that lies behind them hardly invites their removal by others than himself.

During the twentieth century the possibility of professional criticism in England having something more than a news-value has lessened considerably so far as daily journalism is concerned. There are fewer newspapers, but these have a much larger circulation, and news is drawn from a much larger area. The result is that time and space on daily papers have been minimized to a point at which a full and considered over-night criticism of a first performance is seldom feasible. In these circumstances the average daily-paper dramatic critic has become little more than a paragraphist. None the less, in some weekly and monthly journals dramatic criticism still endeavours to maintain a high level of sincerity and scholarship.

One of the characteristics of early twentieth-century criticism was the extent to which it was combined with dramatic authorship, though, as we have seen, the combination was in itself no new thing. Generally speaking, it is good for the critic to have had some experience as a dramatist. At the same time it has proved bad for the dramatist, as such, to relapse in any large degree upon the easier method of expression. Shaw's critical habit, continued in his prefaces, sometimes made him less careful over the creative content of the plays themselves. The prefaces of Hugo and the younger Dumas can no longer transfuse life into many of their plays. Henry Arthur Jones's value as a dramatist noticeably declined when he took to prose of a different kind—fine prose though it was. Somerset Maugham announced the end of his career as a dramatist in bringing out his critical book, *The Summing Up*. St. John Ervine, as manager, critic, and novelist, and Ashley Dukes, who forsook regular criticism before entering management, divided their energies, not always to the benefit of their work as dramatists. Among other English critic-dramatists must be numbered James Agate, Horace Horsnell, Charles Morgan, W. A. Darlington, Ivor Brown, Willson Disher—all of them also novelists—and Herbert Farjeon, manager, dramatist, and lyricist, who left novel-writing to other members of his family.

S. R. LITTLEWOOD†

During the decade after the Second World War, most British critics would have endorsed the liberal conception of their function proclaimed by J. C. Trewin when he asserted that the good critic should be able to take pleasure in 'anything between Sophocles and Max Miller'. In recent years, however, the controversial plays of Brecht, Beckett, and the so-called New Movement have severely tested this ideal. J. C. Trewin, A. V. Cookman, and J. W. Lambert have maintained it with some reservations, whereas other critics have frankly declared a preference for certain types of play. Harold Hobson has zealously endorsed Beckett's innovations. Convinced that the best drama distils 'the living essence of societies and their problems', Kenneth Tynan has been a trenchant interpreter of the New Movement and has given short shrift to plays with little or no social significance. One result of the current concern with dramatic themes and techniques has been that critics have given more attention to plays and producers than to individual performances, though recordings have done much to remedy this deficiency.

WILLIAM A. ARMSTRONG

In America between the wars daily criticism did not suffer anything like so disastrous a reduction as in England—indeed, it improved greatly, alike in style, purpose, and opportunity. The official interest in drama shown by the American universities was important—particularly the stimulus given by Professor Baker and his English successor at Yale, Professor Allardyce Nicoll. Such critics as Brooks Atkinson and John Mason Brown in New York dailies, and George Jean Nathan in weekly reviews—not to mention Robert Benchley and particularly Alexander Woollcott, both well known in England—had a scope and power appropriate to the advancing value of American drama. Some excellent critical and historical work was done by American women, e.g. Winifred Smith's study of the *commedia dell'arte*, Hallie Flanagan's *Shifting Scenes of the Modern European Theatre*, and criticism in *Theatre Arts Monthly* (up to 1948) by Rosamond Gilder.

The retirement of Brooks Atkinson of the *New York Times* in 1960, the decision of John Mason Brown no longer to cover the theatre for the *Saturday Review*, the final disappearance of *Theatre Arts Monthly*, which ceased publication in Jan. 1964, and the deaths of George Jean Nathan and Stark Young, changed the New York critical scene completely. Howard Taubman, music critic of the *New York Times*, was switched to the drama post. Henry Hewes has emerged as the successor to Brown on the *Saturday Review* and shows great promise, with a predilection for the off-beat in the theatre. Kenneth Tynan served two brilliant years on the *New Yorker*, to be succeeded by John McCarten. Richard Watts, Jr., of the *New York Post* and Whitney

Bolton of the *Morning Telegraph* are the only ones of the Old Guard left. Walter Kerr, sometime educator, playwright, and stage director, and drama critic of the *New York Herald Tribune* until its demise in 1966, is usually considered New York's major critic.

GEORGE FREEDLEY†

Some intensely valuable dramatic criticism has come from theatrical producers and from some actors and dramatists. The books written by Gordon Craig, William Poel, Granville-Barker, Stanislavsky, Komisarjevsky, Jacques Copeau, Jean-Louis Barrault, Vilar, Gielgud, Redgrave, Emlyn Williams, Moss Hart, to name only a few, are rich in suggestion as well as record.

DRAME BOURGEOIS, a type of play which arose in eighteenth-century France from the blending of the hitherto incompatible forms of tragedy and comedy, and may be defined as 'tragedy in low places'. It differs, however, from the earlier *tragédie bourgeoise* in that its prevailing tone is serious rather than tragic, and it may end happily, after extolling the virtues of home life and leading the erring to repentance. It eschews comedy, however, and appeals purely to the emotions. Its popularity had much influence on the art of acting, causing the break-up of the declamatory line, and the toning-down of gesture. It also led to the adoption of dress and scenery conforming to time and character.

DRAPER, RUTH (1884–1956), American actress who achieved world-wide fame as a speaker of dramatic monologues which she wrote herself. Daughter of a well-known doctor, she grew up in easy social circumstances, but early discovered in herself a remarkable gift for mimicry. In her twenties she began to employ this talent, composing short sketches based on the people she met in New York and on her travels abroad, and soon found herself much in demand at private parties and charity performances. But it was not until 1920, at the age of 36, that she made her first professional appearance, performing a number of her monologues at the Aeolian Hall, London, on 29 Jan. and 17 May. She had in 1916 had the small part of a lady's maid in an American production of *A Lady's Name* starring Marie Tempest, but realized from this experience that she worked better on her own. She quickly established herself as an international figure, and for the rest of her life toured continuously, elaborating and adding to her repertory, but never changing the basic formula, a bare stage, a minimum of props, and herself as one person responding to invisible companions (as in 'Opening a Bazaar' or 'Showing the Garden') or as several people in succession (as in 'Three Generations', 'Mr. Clifford and Three Women' or 'An English House Party'). She had to an extraordinary extent the power of altering her appearance on stage with no other help than a shawl or hat, merely by thinking herself into the character; she had, too, the ability to conjure up a crowd, its component parts reflected in the mobility of her features, the turn of her head, or the modulations of her voice. Her career was a long series of triumphs. She was commanded to the White House in 1921, to Windsor in 1925, to Mussolini's Palazzo Chigi in 1928, introduced to Paris by Lugné-Poë (1921), to Germany and Austria by Max Reinhardt (1927), to Poland by Arthur Rubenstein (1928). Her longer runs were in New York, where she remained in the same theatre for four or five months. But she was also immensely popular in England, playing often in London and in the main provincial cities. She made her last appearance in London at the St. James's Theatre in July 1956, and died in her sleep on 29–30 Dec. of that year, after appearing at the New York Playhouse. The basic texts of some of her best-known monologues, including those mentioned above, together with a short memoir by Morton Dauwen Zabel (*The Art of Ruth Draper*), were published in 1960, but they are *aides-mémoire* only, since she varied her dialogue at every performance, working entirely from memory.

DRESSLER, MARIE (1871–1934), an American actress probably best remembered for her work in the cinema. But she served a long apprenticeship to the stage, and at 14 joined a succession of light opera companies, taking the name of an aunt because of family opposition to her stage career. Her real name was Leila Koerber. She toured for many years, and in 1892 appeared in New York in Maurice Barrymore's *The Robber of the Rhine* (Fifth Avenue Theatre, 28 May), and when it failed remained to sing in vaudeville. In the following year she joined Lillian Russell's company and later made a great success as Flo Honeydew in *The Lady Slavey* (1896). In 1905 she was again in vaudeville and in 1907 had a great success in London, appearing at the Palace, though later her American humour failed to get across. After further tours she found fame with the part of Tillie Blobbs, a boarding-house drudge in *Tillie's Nightmare* (1909), in which she sang 'Heaven will Protect the Working Girl', a song ever after associated with her. The play had a phenomenal run and incidentally led to her first appearance in films in 1914 under Mack Sennett, in which from 1927 till her death she had an outstanding career.

DREW, a family of actors important in the history of the development of the American theatre, and allied by marriage with the Barrymores. The first outstanding member of the family was (1) LOUISA LANE [really CRANE] (1820–97), daughter of English actors who could trace their theatrical ancestry back to Elizabethan days. Born in Lambeth, she went on the stage as a small child and played with such actors as Macready, Cooke, and Maria Foote. In 1827, her father having died, she was taken by her mother to New York, where she appeared as many characters in one play, in the style of Clara Fisher, with much success. She was also seen with the elder Booth, with the first Joseph Jefferson, then a very old man, and with Edwin Forrest, who much admired her precocious talent. She spent practically the whole of her long life on the stage, playing Lady Macbeth and the Widow Melnotte at 16, and appearing all over the United States in a variety of parts. From 1860 to 1892 she was manageress of the Arch Street Theatre, Philadelphia, which flourished under her firm rule, and from 1880 to 1892 was constantly seen on tour as Mrs. Malaprop, one of her best parts, with Joseph Jefferson as Bob Acres. A woman of strong, almost masculine, personality, she ruled her theatre and family with an unwavering rectitude and energy, and contributed not a little to the establishment of the American theatre during the nineteenth century. She had already had three or four husbands, being first married at 16, before in 1850 she married (2) JOHN DREW (1827–62), and it was as Mrs. John Drew that she was generally known. John Drew was an Irish actor who in his brief career was considered an excellent portrayer of Irish and eccentric characters, among them Sir Lucius O'Trigger and Handy Andy.

Mrs. John Drew had three children, of whom the youngest became an actress and the wife of Maurice Barrymore (see BARRYMORE, 2). A son, (3) JOHN (1853–1927), was one of the outstanding actors of his day. He had already appeared in his mother's stock company in Philadelphia when in 1875 he was engaged by Augustin Daly to play opposite Fanny Davenport in *The Big Bonanza*, in which he appeared as Bob Ruggles, the young lover. Under the same management he later scored a success as Alexander Spinkle in *An Arabian Night; or, Haroun al Raschid and his Mother-in-Law*. He remained with Daly for many years, playing opposite Ada Rehan, and visited London several times in the 1880s, being seen in such classics as *As You Like It*, *The School for Scandal*, and *The Taming of the Shrew*. His Petruchio was considered remarkable. In 1892 he agreed to appear under the management of the Frohmans, for which Daly found it hard to forgive him, and appeared in many modern comedies, often with Maude Adams, making frequent visits to the larger cities of the United States. In 1893 his *Twelfth Night* had a long run in London. One of his finest performances in later life was as Major Pendennis in a dramatization of Thackeray's novel, and he was last seen in a tour of *Trelawny of the 'Wells'*. A handsome man, of distinguished presence, he was for many years president of the Players' Club, and in 1903 presented the library of Robert W. Lowe, which he had acquired, to Harvard University, thus inaugurating the fine theatre collection there. He was the author of *My Years on the Stage* (1922). His daughter Louise who died in 1955 was also an actress. She married an actor, Jack Devereaux, and their son John went on the stage.

An adopted son of Mrs. John Drew, (4) SIDNEY WHITE (1868–1919), was also on the stage, and appeared in vaudeville with his first wife in sketches written by her. She was also the author of several melodramas and farces. With his second wife he appeared on the stage, but his later career was mainly in films.

DRINKWATER, JOHN (1882–1937), English poet and dramatist, whose work did much to strengthen and popularize the modern poetic play. He was one of the foundation members of Barry Jackson's Pilgrim Players, which later gave rise to the Birmingham Repertory Theatre, where he was for some years producer, actor, and general manager. His early plays in verse were taut and economical in dialogue, without false romanticism; the most successful was *X = O*, an episode of the Trojan War. But it was in his prose play, *Abraham Lincoln*, that Drinkwater did his finest work. Transferred to the Lyric, Hammersmith, in 1919 under the management of Nigel Playfair, it ran for a year, and has been frequently revived. It was also well received in New York, where Drinkwater, who had appeared in the original production, played the Chronicler. Later, but less successful, chronicle plays were *Mary Stuart* (1922), *Oliver Cromwell*, and *Robert E. Lee* (both 1923). In 1927 Drinkwater's first comedy, *Bird in Hand*, opened the season at the Birmingham Repertory Theatre. It was revived there in 1931 and again for the theatre's silver jubilee. It also had a long run in London.

DROLL, the name given to a short, comic sketch, usually a scene taken from a longer play. Its origin must be looked for during the lean years of the Puritan interregnum (1642–60), when the actors, deprived of the right to act, of scenery, of costumes, and often of their playhouses, nevertheless managed to give a certain amount of entertainment. For their illicit purposes long plays were useless, so they invented or hashed up these 'drolls'—the term is short for Droll Humours or Drolleries—rounding them off with dancing in the manner of the Jig. Some of the most famous are 'Bottom the Weaver' from *A Midsummer Night's Dream* and 'The Grave-diggers' from *Hamlet*. Others were from biblical sources. The actor Robert Cox was a noted player of drolls, and his repertory was printed in 1662 by Kirkman as *The Wits; or, Sport upon Sport*. Droll was also the name applied to early puppet shows, and was given to collections of humorous or satiric verse, not dramatic, as in 'Westminster Drolleries' (1672). It was sometimes used to designate actors, particularly players of humorous parts, and men of quick wit and good company. Pepys uses it in this sense of Killigrew.

DROP, an unframed piece of scenery, first used about 1690, usually a canvas backcloth. It had the advantage of offering an unbroken plain surface for painting, free from any central join such as marked the alternative 'pair of flats'. Initially it had the disadvantage that no doors or practicable windows could be used with it. Today a cloth or drop can be made into a framed cloth by the addition of battens at the back, with the doors hinged to the framing so afforded, thus making the piece, in a sense, a large single flat which can be flown like an ordinary cloth. The early theatre, however, possessed no height for such flying of an entire cloth, which had to be rolled. The framed cloth was, therefore, impossible.

The early method of handling a loose drop was to roll it on a bottom roller, which ascended by means of lines, furling up the cloth as it went. This system had a disadvantage in that, as records show, the ends of swords and cloaks, or even the hem of a petticoat, might be snatched by the ascending roller and swallowed in the turns, to the detriment of dramatic dignity.

Another method of getting rid of a cloth was by 'tumbling'—when a batten was fixed across the back a third of the way up, and the cloth taken away in bights, with a loose roller, or tumbler, inside the bight to weight the cloth, and keep the bend straight. RICHARD SOUTHERN

DROTTNINGHOLM THEATRE AND MUSEUM, Sweden. The Drottningholm Theatre, situated on an island not far from Stockholm, was built in 1766 by C. F. Adelcrantz as part of the palace of Queen Louisa Ulrika. Until 1771 it was used by a French company resident in Stockholm, and, during the summer months which the royal family spent at the Palace, by Court amateurs. In 1777 the Palace, and so the theatre, became State property. The theatre continued in use until about 1800, but had its heyday during the reign of Gustaf III (1772–92), when Louis-Jean Desprez came from Paris to design scenery and costumes. It was during this time also that Baron Tessin and his son collected the seventeenth- and eighteenth-century French stage designs which now form one of the most important deposits of the Drottningholm Museum. A selection of these designs, together with a model of the theatre, was shown in Paris and London (by the Arts Council) in 1956. In the nineteenth century the Drottningholm Theatre fell into disuse, but its employment as a lumber-room saved it from demolition or modernization, and in 1921 it was restored to its former glory. As Dr. Agne Beijer, its first director, said: 'Nothing was needed in the way of restoration except to remove the accumulated dust, and to replace, as a safeguard against fire, the old wax candles by electric lighting which would give as nearly as possible the same effect of illumination.' The stage is about 57 feet deep, and 27 feet wide at the footlights. The eighteenth-century machinery is still in working order, and there are more than thirty sets of usable scenery of the same period. The theatre is now used for occasional summer seasons of early opera. The museum exhibits are housed in the former royal apartments. Its present director is Dr. Hilleström. (See No. 29.)

DRUM-AND-SHAFT, an early system, based on the principle of the lever, used for the moving of theatre scenery. It is also known as the Barrel System. Its purpose is to draw in, or let out, a rope actuating some piece of scenery. The rope is fixed to the cylindrical shaft. In order to turn this shaft a lever was sometimes inserted through the shaft and the whole twisted thereby like a corkscrew. A more apt arrangement, however, was to build a circular drum round part of the shaft, but of a diameter considerably greater than that of the shaft. Then the shaft might be rotated by pulling on a line wound round the drum, and in this way the lever principle would be the more easily and steadily applied.

Where a number of pieces have to be moved simultaneously the drum-and-shaft system has many advantages, and applications of it are found in many parts of the stage—below, for working traps, bridges, and sloats; above, for working borders and cloud machines, and, later, cloths. It may be varied by drums of different diameters used on the same shaft, and separate pieces of scenery attached to the different drums, when, upon the rotation of the shaft, the individual pieces move at various speeds. This is exemplified in gradually unfolding cloud effects, where a number of clustered cloud-pieces expand to a great aureole.

Today, when visible scene-changes are no longer made, simultaneity of movement is not necessary and the drum-and-shaft system has been abandoned, all pieces of flown scenery now being worked independently.

RICHARD SOUTHERN

DRURIOLANUS, AUGUSTUS, see HARRIS (2) AUGUSTUS.

DRURY LANE THEATRE, LONDON. This is London's most famous theatre, and the oldest still in use. The first theatre on the site (which was formerly a Riding Yard) was built by Killigrew under a Charter granted by Charles II in 1662 (see PATENT THEATRES). Known as 'the Theatre Royal in Bridges Street', it opened on 7 May 1663 with a performance of *The Humorous Lieutenant*, the company being led by Charles Hart and Michael Mohun. The whole theatre was about the same size as the stage of the present Drury Lane; the pit benches were covered in green cloth, and the floor was steeply raked so that people at the back could converse with the occupants of the boxes behind. There were six proscenium doors and an apron stage. A Frenchman who visited the theatre soon after it was opened said it was the best he had ever seen, with a well-equipped stage, charming decorations, and gilded upholstery. Pepys, however, in his diary for June 1663, complains of catching cold there because of the draught and rain from the glazed cupola over the pit. Refreshments were in the hands of Orange Moll (see MEGGS) but she was not allowed to sell her oranges (for which the regulation price was 6*d.* each) in the upper gallery, probably because they were such handy missiles.

For ten years the theatre prospered, in spite of having to be closed on account of plague from June 1665 to Nov. 1666, during which time Killigrew made some useful alterations. In 1665 Nell Gwynn, who had been trained for the stage by Hart, made her first appearance in *The Indian Queen*. It was at Drury Lane that Charles II in 1669 heard her speak the epilogue to *Tyrannic Love* and fell in love with her, taking her from the stage in the same year to become his mistress.

On the night of 25 June 1672 the theatre was partly destroyed by fire, with the loss of the entire wardrobe and stock of scenery. Richard Bell, a member of the company, was accidentally killed when some houses in the vicinity were blown up to prevent the fire from spreading.

Killigrew took his company to a deserted theatre in Lincoln's Inn Fields while the new theatre, designed by Sir Christopher Wren, was being built. It was larger than the first theatre, and its foundations can still be seen under the present stage. It opened (as the Theatre Royal in Drury Lane) with *The Beggar's Bush* on 26 Mar. 1674, in the presence of the King and Queen. With Dryden as its playwright, the theatre prospered for a while, but Killigrew, Hart, and Mohun were getting old, younger actors were lured away to the rival theatre at Dorset Garden, and in 1676 it closed. After Killigrew's death his sons, both useless fellows, tried to run it, but without success. Finally it closed again, and the two companies, Drury Lane's and Dorset Garden's, merged under Betterton. Times were changing; Charles II, a great patron of the playhouse, was dead, audiences were apathetic, and London could support only one theatre. So Betterton settled at Drury Lane in 1682, and Davenant's son Charles took over the Patent. Unfortunately, he sold it in 1690 for £80 to a rascally lawyer named Christopher Rich, father of the John Rich who built the first Covent Garden. Rich's one idea was to make money, and he treated his actors, who included Verbruggen, Powell, and the young Colley Cibber, so disgracefully that Betterton broke away, and obtained a licence from William III to act at Lincoln's Inn Fields. He took the best players with him and Drury Lane sank very low. In 1709 Rich, who had been constantly in trouble, lost his Patent, and the theatre closed (for a mock inventory of the sale that then took place, see *The Tatler*, No. 42). It was at this juncture that the famous triumvirate—Cibber, Wilks, and Doggett—took over. They formed an excellent combination, each supplying what the others lacked. All were first-class actors. Cibber was a fop and fine gentleman, happy in the company of a lord, and the only actor for many years to be a member of White's Club. Wilks was the best light comedian of his day. Doggett was a master of make-up and character parts. With Anne Oldfield as their leading lady the triumvirate prospered, and inaugurated in 1711 one of the brightest periods in the annals of the English stage.

The first split came when Barton Booth joined the triumvirate and Doggett, on political grounds, left it. Booth took Betterton's place, and Anne Oldfield succeeded to the throne of Mrs. Bracegirdle. Wilks died, and Cibber, now Poet Laureate, retired, a man called Highmore buying his share of the Patent, and also Wilks's, from his widow. But Theophilus, Colley Cibber's worthless son, caused so much trouble that Highmore failed, and was glad to sell out at a loss to Charles Fleetwood, who had also managed to get Booth's share of the Patent from his widow, and so held the whole. A gambler with no money sense, he soon ran into debt, and threw away a golden opportunity. Drury Lane sank to a very low level indeed. The one bright spot was Macklin, who pressed for a revival of *The Merchant of Venice*, which had not been seen for many years, with himself as Shylock. At length Fleetwood consented, and on 11 Jan. 1741, with considerable trepidation on the part of everyone save himself, Macklin took the stage as the Jew. It was a revelation, for Macklin threw over the accredited idea that Shylock was a comic part and played it as we know it now. His performance was of such intensity that he thrilled his audience where they were accustomed to laugh, and so impressed George II that he could not sleep after seeing it. Pope immortalized it in the couplet, 'This is the Jew, That Shakespeare drew'. It put Macklin, a very great actor, in the front rank. Had he been of a less quarrelsome nature he might have been the leader of the stage. As it was, he was the forerunner of a new school of acting which Garrick was to glorify.

It was under Fleetwood that a riot took place on 5 May 1737, caused by the abolition of the custom of allowing free admission to the gallery for footmen attending their masters (see FOOTMEN'S GALLERY). Incidentally, it was from Drury Lane that the news of the defeat of Prince Charles Edward at Culloden on 16 Apr. 1746 was first made known. The news was brought to George II, who was in the Royal Box. He attempted to address the audience, but his English was not equal to the task, and he could only shout and wave the dispatches, until an equerry finally made the announcement. One good thing Fleetwood did was to engage Garrick for Drury Lane after his phenomenally successful season at Goodman's Fields Theatre. He made his first appearance as Chaumont in *The Orphan* in 11 May 1742, and was then seen as Lear and Richard III. Five years later, when Fleetwood had brought the theatre to the verge of bankruptcy and lost the services of Macklin by his ill treatment of the company, Garrick, with John Lacy, took over. He instituted a number of reforms—regular rehearsals, careful casting, better lighting, more accurate texts, especially of Shakespeare; he even managed, with difficulty, to remove the audience from the stage. He surrounded himself with a good company (Kitty Clive, Peg Woffington, Mrs. Cibber, Mrs. Pritchard, Spranger Barry, Macklin, Yates, Shute), and opened on 15 Sept. 1747 with Macklin as Shylock. For the next thirty years Garrick brought credit and renown to Drury Lane. His capacity for work was remarkable, and he did not hesitate to add spectacle and ballet, as well as pantomimes, some of which he wrote himself, to the usual repertory of comedy and tragedy. In 1776 he announced his retirement, and appeared in a series of his most famous roles. On his last night his farewell speech moved the packed house to tears. He had served the theatre with dignity and left it far richer than he had found it, not only in reputation, but in outward appearance, for in 1775 it had been extensively altered and refurnished by the Adam brothers. There had, of course, been setbacks and disappointments, not least the failure of the lavish *Chinese Festival* in Nov. 1755, which had, however, brought Noverre to London for the first time, and of Mrs. Siddons, making her first appearance in London in December of the same year, after which she retired to the provinces until 1782.

When Garrick left Drury Lane the playwright Sheridan, with his father-in-law Linley, took over. His first outstanding production was *The School for Scandal* on 8 May 1777 (see Nos. 30, 166). In the Gordon Riots of 1780 the theatre suffered damage, and a company of Guards was thereafter posted nightly to protect it. This custom was not abolished until 1896. Sheridan re-engaged Mrs. Siddons to play the heroine in *Isabella; or, the Fatal Marriage* on 10 Oct. 1782, when she instantly achieved the success she deserved. As Lady Macbeth she even effaced the memory of Mrs. Pritchard, hitherto considered incomparable in the part. Her brother, John Philip Kemble, joined her the following year, making his first appearance as Hamlet on 30 Sept., and in 1788 Sheridan, who was busy with politics and other ploys, was glad to hand over the active management of the theatre to him.

By 1791 the theatre was in such a bad state of repair that it was decided to rebuild it. Holland was responsible for the new design, and it opened on 12 Mar. 1794 with a concert of sacred music by Handel (because it was Lent). Plays began again on 21 Apr. with John Philip and Mrs. Siddons in *Macbeth*. An epilogue, spoken by Miss Farren, who, with Mrs. Jordan, was now a member of the company, informed the audience that they were safe from fire, and an iron safety curtain was lowered upon which a man beat with a hammer. Fifteen years later on 24 Feb. 1809 the theatre was burnt down! Before that happened there had been an attempted assassination of George III during a performance of *She Would and She Wouldn't*. Sheridan had so mismanaged his affairs that Kemble had left for Covent Garden in 1802, taking his sister with him; melodrama and spectacle had brought real elephants and performing dogs on the stage.

After the fire there were no funds available for rebuilding, but the situation was saved by the prompt action of one of Sheridan's sharers in the Patent, the brewer Samuel Whitbread, who raised £400,000 to pay for the new theatre. Designed by Wyatt, it opened on 10 Oct. 1812, under the management of Samuel Arnold, with *Hamlet*. Two years later, on 26 Jan. 1814, a bitter winter's night, with the theatre half-empty, Kean made his first appearance, playing Shylock, and the theatre embarked on a further period of prosperity (for a view of the interior at this time, see No. 31; see also No. 165). For six years Kean carried on but even his success could not keep pace with the rising costs of the theatre. Whitbread committed suicide in 1815, and Elliston, under whose management gas lighting was first installed, the portico was added, and the interior was remodelled, went bankrupt. He was succeeded by an American impresario, Stephen Price, under whom Charles Kean made his first, and Grimaldi his last, appearance. Finally, in 1831, Alfred Bunn took over, and the theatre sank to the level of a fairground booth, in spite of the efforts of the young actor Macready, who at Christmas 1841 took over himself. Although he had a good company, and some initial success, he too was forced to give up, and for a time the resilient Bunn returned. He engaged Charles Kean as his leading man, but he really preferred opera and spectacle to straight drama, and in 1845 he had a great success with 'The Bohemian Girl'. But even Bunn was powerless to stop the rot which seemed to have attacked Drury Lane, and, ruined, he retired to Boulogne. Managers came and went; Anderson was ruined by the Great Exhibition of 1851, in which year Macready, on 26 Feb., an impressive but not emotional evening, said farewell to the stage as Macbeth; Gye was unsuccessful with opera; E. T. Smith took possession, at a greatly reduced rental—Drury Lane was going at bargain prices! Beginning with *Uncle Tom's Cabin*, he managed to survive for seven years, sandwiching G. V. Brooke and Charles Mathews between Chinese conjurers and the Human Fly, and following Rachel with a circus. Eventually he too went bankrupt, and in 1862 Dion Boucicault took over. He was followed by Falconer, who had made a fortune at the Lyceum and lost it at the Lane. The whole unhappy period ended finally with the defeat of F. B. Chatterton, in spite of good actors, the Vokes family in pantomime, and Beverley's scenery. It was Chatterton who, from sad experience, laid it down that 'Shakespeare spells ruin, and Byron bankruptcy'.

The theatre was now closed, and a young and ambitious man, with less than five pounds in his pocket, proposed himself as a tenant. He was told he would be accepted if he deposited £1,000. He got the money within twenty-four hours, and starting with a revival of *Henry V*, followed by a pantomime, he began a new page in the history of Drury Lane. He was Augustus Harris, who soon became known as 'Augustus Druriolanus'.

Harris pinned his faith to big shows and pantomime. He brought over distinguished foreign companies, like the Saxe-Meiningen, the Comédie-Française, and Ristori herself. In 1886 he gave opera with the De Reszkes, Melba, Lassalle, Nordicaa, and others; and always he did his vast realistic melodramas with big spectacular scenes, and always his gigantic pantomimes. (see No. 134) He had other interests, but it is as the impresario of Drury Lane that he is remembered. It was under his management that Dan Leno—who first appeared at the Lane in 1889—and Herbert Campbell played together in pantomime. He staged explosions, earthquakes, avalanches, chariot races, shipwrecks, and, in *The Whip*, a horse-race with real horses. He died in 1896, at the age of 45, and his right-hand man, Arthur Collins, who almost deserves to be called Druriolanus II, took over. Pantomimes and dramas became more and more elaborate, sensation was piled on sensation. Prosperity reigned, and the theatre once more held a high position. Irving's last London season and Ellen Terry's Jubilee in 1905, Forbes-Robertson's farewell, when he mingled with the audience, Beecham's great opera season in 1913, and the first appearance of Diaghilev's Ballets Russes, all took place at Drury Lane, and the Shakespeare Tercentenary in 1916 was celebrated by a performance of *Julius Caesar*, after which Frank Benson, who played Caesar, was knighted by George V in the Royal Box with a property sword. In 1919 peace was celebrated by the *Pageant of Drury Lane*. Pavlova danced there for a season. In 1921 the auditorium was rebuilt and Collins retired two years later, his last production being appropriately named *Good Luck*. He had reigned for twenty-seven years.

Sir Alfred Butt then took charge, and for a short time Basil Dean was associated with him, but it was not until the policy of great musical shows, starting with *Rose Marie*, was inaugurated that fortune smiled once more. Pantomime, banished since 1919, came back to its traditional home in 1929, when Julian Wylie presented *The Sleeping Beauty*. In 1931 Butt retired and *The Land of Smiles* introduced Richard Tauber to this country. It was followed by Noël Coward's *Cavalcade*, produced by himself and C. B. Cochran. After that, luck seemed to desert Drury Lane again until pantomime in 1934 revived it. Then came Ivor Novello, who, understanding the needs of the great house, wrote, composed, and acted in a series of successful plays with music—*Glamorous Night*, *Careless Rapture*, *Crest of the Wave*, and *The Dancing Years*. This last, presented by Tom Arnold, who had also been responsible for *Henry V* with Ivor Novello in the title-role, was still running when the theatres were closed for a brief period on the outbreak of war in 1939. On their reopening it ran elsewhere for six years, the longest run of any Drury-Lane-produced show.

On 8 Sept. 1939 Drury Lane was taken over as E.N.S.A. headquarters, and in spite of being bombed in 1940 continued to be used. After the war it was again used as a theatre, and housed a series of American musicals, beginning with *Oklahoma!* in 1947 (see No. 46), followed by *Carousel* (1950), *South Pacific* (1951), *The King and I* (1953), and *My Fair Lady*, which opened on 30 Apr. 1958, and broke all existing records for the theatre. It was followed by *The Boys from Syracuse* (1963), first produced in New York in 1938, which had only a short run, by *Camelot* (1964), and by *Hello, Dolly!* (1965).

Like the Haymarket, Drury Lane has its ghost, an eighteenth-century gentleman in a long grey riding cloak, riding boots, sword, three-cornered hat, and powdered hair, who walks in at one wall of the upper circle and out at the other, but only at a matinée and when the house is full. He may have some connexion with the skeleton found bricked up in one of the walls, with a dagger in its ribs—the murderer or the murderee?

W. MACQUEEN-POPE†, *rev.*

Little Drury Lane was the name given by Elliston to the Olympic Theatre in 1813.

DRUTEN, JOHN VAN, see VAN DRUTEN.

DRYDEN, JOHN (1631–1700), English writer, critic, poet, and satirist, and the outstanding dramatist of the Restoration stage, though his best work was done in other fields. He was very prolific, being responsible, alone and in collaboration, for nearly thirty plays of all kinds. Of his comedies the most successful were *Sir Martin Mar-All* (1667), *Marriage à la Mode* (1671), in which the part of Melantha was finely played by Mrs. Mountfort, and yet another version of *Amphitryon* (1690). His wit was mordant, but lacked humanity. *Marriage à la Mode* was revived by the Phoenix Society in 1920, and by the Birmingham Repertory Theatre in 1928. Two other comedies, *The Spanish Friar*, in which Antony Leigh later made a great hit, and *Mr. Limberham; or, the Kind Keeper*, are perhaps better left in oblivion.

Dryden's tragicomedies include *The Rival Ladies* (1664), from the Spanish, and *Secret Love* (1667), based partly on Madeleine de Scudéry's famous novel *Le Grand Cyrus*. The parts of Florimel and Celadon, played by Nell Gwynn and Charles Hart, have sometimes been considered the prototypes of Congreve's Millamant and Mirabell. Dryden's most characteristic work, however, was done in the heroic drama, a new development in the history of the English theatre which rose, flourished, and fell with him. Written in rhymed couplets, and dealing with the conflict in noble bosoms between love and honour, on the lines of Corneille's *Le Cid*, this genre had perhaps been foreshadowed by Davenant, and to a certain extent by Fletcher and Quarles. But Dryden was its greatest exponent, though his contemporaries shared in its vogue.

His first serious essay in rhymed verse, *The Indian Queen* (1664), was written in collaboration with Sir Robert Howard, whose sister, Elizabeth, Dryden had married in the previous year. This was followed by *The Indian Emperor* (1665), by Dryden alone, by *Tyrannic Love* (1669), and by the greatest of his heroic dramas, *Almanzor and Almahide*, usually called, from its sub-title, *The Conquest of Granada*. This vast and complicated play, in two parts (1670, 1671), contains all the elements, good and bad, of the heroic drama—rant, bombast, poetry, vigour, battle, murder, and sudden death. It was guyed unmercifully in Buckingham's *The Rehearsal* (1671), and soon died a natural death. Dryden's last play in this style was *Aureng-Zebe* (1675), and from the restraints of rhyme he then turned to blank verse for the play which, in the opinion of posterity no less than in that of his contemporaries, was his masterpiece—*All for Love* (1677), a retelling of the story of Antony and Cleopatra, which takes only its plot from Shakespeare: all the rest is Dryden's own. It is well constructed, contains some fine poetry, and observes more strictly than any other English tragedy the unities of time, place, and action. It has been called 'the happiest result of French influence on English tragedy'. Above all, it provides excellent theatrical material, and was frequently revived in the eighteenth century, with such actors as Mrs. Oldfield and Booth (1718), Mrs. Yates and Holland (1766), Mrs. Hartley and Smith (1773). In 1922 the Phoenix Society gave two performances of it, with Edith Evans and Ion Swinley.

Dryden's last play was a tragi-comedy, *Love Triumphant* (1694). He also, in the course of his lifetime, wrote numerous prologues and epilogues, then very much in fashion, both for his own and other people's plays. These are not only a mine of theatrical information, but a notable contribution to English poetry. Less admirable are the adaptations of Shakespeare in which Dryden had a hand. He helped Davenant to make a perversion of *The Tempest* (1667), and in later years rewrote *Troilus and Cressida* (1679), but without the success which attended *All For Love*. In his prefaces and critical writings Dryden contributed largely to literary and theatrical controversies which need not detain us here; nor need his pamphlet war with another popular dramatist, Elkanah Settle.

DU CROISY [Philibert Gassot], (1626–95), French actor, who may have been related to the tragedian Bellerose. After touring the provinces he joined Molière at the Petit-Bourbon in 1659, with his wife, a mediocre actress who retired a few years later. It seems from some remarks in *L'Impromptu de Versailles* that Molière disliked her. Du Croisy, however, remained with the company until 1689, and was the first to play Tartuffe, both in 1667, when the character was called Panulphe, and, under its original name, in 1669. A handsome man, though somewhat fat, he was a good comedian, and played poets and pedants in Molière's comedies. He was also good in tragedy. After Molière's death he remained with the company, retiring in 1689. He had two daughters, both actresses, of whom one married Paul Poisson, and in her old age wrote articles on Molière and his company for the *Mercure de France*, 1738.

DU MAURIER. (1) George Louis Palmella Busson (1834–96), English artist, best remembered for his work on *Punch*, and for his novels *Peter Ibbetson* and *Trilby*. The latter was dramatized by Salter and produced in 1895 with much success. Of George's two sons, the elder, (2) Guy (1865–1916), a soldier by profession, was killed in action in France. He was the author of *An Englishman's Home*, produced anonymously in 1909, a patriotic play which provided a great stimulus to the recruiting of the Territorial Army; the younger son, (3) Sir Gerald Hubert Edward (1873–1934), who was responsible for the production of his brother's play, was a famous actor-manager. He made his first appearance at the Garrick in 1894, went on tour with Forbes-Robertson, and in 1895 appeared under Tree at the Haymarket in a small part in *Trilby*. He remained with Tree for some years, both at Her Majesty's and in America, but his real talent became apparent when he went to the Duke of York's Theatre under Charles Frohman. There, in *The Admirable Crichton* and as the original Mr. Darling and Captain Hook in *Peter Pan*, he did excellent work. His great success, however, came in 1906 with *Raffles*, where he destroyed all the old traditions of drama by making the villain of the piece the hero. As the gentleman crook his performance was memorable, and the part is always associated with his name. Following it with *Arsène Lupin* and *Alias Jimmy Valentine*, he seemed doomed to crook-plays for the rest of his career; but in 1910 he broke away, and took over the management of Wyndham's Theatre in association with Frank Curzon, making it a home of light comedy for many years. At this time du Maurier, who was a great exponent of natural acting and of the art that conceals art, was virtually the leader of the English stage. Striking rather than good-looking, with a strongly marked face, gaunt and thin, he had compelling power and great charm. His voice was not strong, but he knew how to use it. His style tended to be somewhat monotonous, and his range of parts limited; but within those limits he was seldom excelled, and he could on occasion step beyond them, as was proved by his portrayal of Harry Dearth in *Dear Brutus* in 1917. A more typical part, and one which brought him solid success, was *Bulldog Drummond* in 1921. A year later du Maurier was knighted for his services to his profession, and shortly afterwards left Wyndham's for the St. James's Theatre, where his last two outstanding appearances were in *The Last of Mrs. Cheyney* and *Interference*. A memoir, *Gerald, a Portrait*, was published in 1934 by his daughter (4) Daphne (1907–), novelist, and author of the stage version of her novel *Rebecca*, and of two plays, *The Years Between* (1945) and *September Tide* (1949). Gerald's wife, (5) Muriel Beaumont (1881–1957), was on the stage for a time, making her first appearance at the Haymarket in 1898. She and du Maurier were together in the original production of *The Admirable Crichton* (1902), and married five months later. She retired in 1910.

W. MACQUEEN-POPE†

DU PARC. (1) [RENÉ BERTHELOT] (*c.* 1630–64), French comic actor, known as Gros-René, who was with Molière in the provinces and went to Paris with him. He was a good actor, but was overshadowed by his wife, (2) MARQUISE-THÉRÈSE DE GORLA (1633–68), who had already had some experience in a travelling company before she married Gros-René and joined Molière. A woman of great beauty and majestic presence, she was excellent in tragedy, less good in comedy, and probably for this reason left Molière in 1666 to join the company at the Hôtel de Bourgogne, where she played the title-role in Racine's *Andromaque* (1667). She died suddenly, and Racine, whose mistress she had been, was later accused of having poisoned her to make way for Mlle Champmeslé. According to contemporary gossip, Mlle du Parc was loved by Corneille and by his younger brother Thomas, by Molière, whom she disdained, by Racine, and by La Fontaine.

DUBLIN. The first theatre in Dublin was built in 1635, and closed under the Commonwealth, as did the London theatres. After the Restoration the famous Smock Alley, known also as the Orange Street Theatre, was opened, but it was not until the eighteenth century that Dublin society became enamoured of playgoing. Even then all the plays and most of the chief actors were imported from London, and it was the Irish Literary Movement that first gave the country an indigenous drama (see IRELAND).

The first outstanding actor to appear at Smock Alley was Wilks, in 1692, but it reached its heyday, after extensive rebuilding, in the 1730s and 1740s, when Quin and Woodward, Garrick and Peg Woffington, gave extensive seasons, followed by the ten-year management of Thomas Sheridan, father of the dramatist, and himself an excellent actor. Towards the end of the eighteenth century Smock Alley fell into disrepair and was finally converted into a corn store. Almost its only rival was the Crow Street Theatre, opened in 1758 by Spranger Barry, who had at one time as partner in his enterprise the Irish actor Macklin. Another Irish actor, Henry Mossop, was in control of both theatres for some time, and after the disappearance of Smock Alley he remained at the Crow Street Theatre in sole charge of all professional enterprises in Dublin until in about 1819 Harris, an actor from Covent Garden, opened the Theatre Royal. The Crow Street Theatre then closed and was pulled down in the early 1830s. ED.

The Theatre Royal perished by fire in 1880. A much larger Theatre Royal, now a cinema, was then built, which housed touring companies from England in spectacular drama. The Gaiety, in which the Irish Literary Theatre performed in 1900, before the building of the Abbey Theatre, was a smaller, more intimate, playhouse for 'drawing-room' plays. The Queen's Theatre in Brunswick Square was also used for melodrama, and it was there that J. W. Whitebread's company appeared in plays on Irish themes by Dion Boucicault. There were also two music-halls. In 1918 the Dublin Drama League was formed, and in the ten years of its existence introduced the plays of outstanding Continental authors—Pirandello, Lenormand, D'Annunzio—and also the early plays of O'Neill. These were done by the Abbey company once a week, and formed a useful adjunct to the normal run of Irish plays (see ABBEY THEATRE and IRELAND).

In 1942 Austin Clarke founded the Lyric Theatre, to bring back poetry to the Irish stage, from which it seemed to have been banished by the current realistic plays of the Abbey Theatre dramatists. Some excellent revivals of Yeat have been given, and many poetic plays by Irish and European dramatists.

In 1957 it was decided to hold a Dublin Festival, *An Tostal*—on the lines of an earlier effort at Easter 1953—as part of an effort to attract more visitors to Ireland in the early part of the year. The first was held in May, and one of the attractions was an important production at the Pike Theatre. This was the European première of Tennessee Williams's *The Rose Tattoo*. After the production opened, complaints were made and the director of the theatre, Alan Simpson, was arrested. In 1958 the Festival was abandoned, after an unofficial censorship had demanded cuts in an O'Casey play and in *Bloomsday*, an adaptation of part of Joyce's *Ulysses* by Alan McClelland. In 1959, however, the Festival, held in September, was a great success, mainly because of a genuinely Irish quality in the acting and the plays chosen. Among them were a new version of *Dreaming Dust* by Denis Johnston, Cecil Beaton's *Landscape with Figures*, and a revival of Goldsmith's *The Good-Natured Man*. A committee was then established under Lord Killanin to create interest in the Festival and give it a good civic standing. Since then it has become an annual event, with perhaps twenty new productions in two weeks. It soon became evident that the Festival should stress the work of Irish authors, and among the interesting productions have been a splendid revival of Synge's *Playboy of the Western World* and MacLiammóir's *The Importance of Being Oscar* (on the life and works of Wilde). Both of these were seen in 1960, and have since toured Europe. In 1961 there was *The Voice of Shem*, based by Mary Manning on Joyce's *Finnegan's Wake*, which also went on tour, as did *Mrs. Warren's Profession*, with Eithne Dunn in the lead. The same year was the production of Brecht's *Saint Joan of the Stockyards*. In 1962 O'Neill was the great attraction, with *A Touch of the Poet* and *A Long Day's Journey into Night*, together with *Othello*, *Stephen D*, adapted by Hugh Leonard from Joyce's *Portrait of the Artist as a Young Man*, and *An Evening with Samuel Beckett*. The Festival has had its troubles and its critics, but in spite of slender resources it has survived, for Ireland loves the theatre, and even if no visitors came, the Festival would still be a lively affair.

DAN O'CONNELL

DUBOIS, see CLOWN and GRIMALDI.

DUCHESS THEATRE, LONDON, in Catherine Street, a medium-sized playhouse which opened on 25 Nov. 1929 with Hubert Griffith's *Tunnel Trench*, under the management of Jack de Leon and his sister Delia. Soon after the opening the theatre changed hands, and for a few months in 1932 housed productions by Nancy Price's People's National Theatre Company, among them *The Merry Wives of Windsor* with Baliol Holloway as Falstaff, and *The Rose Without a Thorn*, with Frank Vosper as Henry VIII. This was followed by a successful run of the all-woman play, *Children in Uniform*, in which Jessica Tandy gave an outstanding performance. In 1934 J. B. Priestley, whose *Laburnum Grove* had had a successful performance at the Duchess the previous year, took over the management of the theatre, which was redecorated by his second wife, Mary Wyndham Lewis, and produced there his *Eden End* and *Cornelius*. In 1935 Emlyn Williams appeared in his successful thriller, *Night Must Fall*, which ran for a year, and was followed by the first West-End appearance of *Murder in the Cathedral*. Another Priestley play which had a long run was *Time and the Conways* (1937), and Emlyn Williams returned in *The Corn is Green*, which was still playing when the outbreak of the Second World War closed the theatres. The Duchess reopened in 1942 and soon had another long run with the transfer of *Blithe Spirit* from the Piccadilly. It has since had a number of successful productions, *The Linden Tree* (1947), *The Holly and the Ivy* (1950), *The Deep Blue Sea* (1952), *The Caretaker* (1960), and *Boeing-Boeing* (1962). This theatre holds the record for the shortest run of any production, when in 1930 *The Intimate Revue* failed to finish its first performance.

W. MACQUEEN-POPE†, *rev.*

DUCIS, JEAN-FRANÇOIS (1733–1816), French dramatist, best known as the first adapter of Shakespeare for the French stage. He was the son of a linen-draper, and remained all his life a sturdy, independent bourgeois of simple tastes, having nothing to do with the Revolution, refusing the overtures of Napoleon, and welcoming with pleasure the re-establishment of the monarchy. As a young man he served in the Seven Years' War, and returned home to live quietly and amuse himself with plays and poetry. His *Amélise* (1764) was not successful, but he consoled himself with the plays of Shakespeare, which he probably read in the deplorable translations of Le Tourneur and Laplace, since there is no proof that he himself knew English. Profiting by the vogue for all things English he adapted Shakespeare for the Comédie-Française, often so drastically that nothing remained of the original but the title. He well understood, however, the temper of his audience, and knew that they would only accept Shakespeare with modifications. Beginning with *Hamlet* in 1769, in which Molé appeared in the title-role, he dealt faithfully, after his own methods, with *Romeo and Juliet*, *King Lear*, *Macbeth*, *King John*, and *Othello*. This last, given in 1792, owed much of its success to the fine acting of Talma. When we remember that none of Ducis's own plays have survived, it is interesting to note that in connexion with his adaptation of *King John* a contemporary critic deplored his wasting his undoubted talents on such rubbish. Ducis became a member of the French Academy in succession to Voltaire, and after the failure of his last play in 1801 retired quietly to Versailles.

DUCLOS [MARIE-ANNE DE CHÂTEAUNEUF] (1668–1748), French actress, who, after an unsuccessful attempt to join the company at the Opéra, was accepted by the Comédie-Française in 1693 for tragic roles, in which she later replaced Mlle Champmeslé, sharing feminine leads with Mlle Desmares. Her strength lay in declamation, and her acting was stiff and artificial, in opposition to the traditions of Molière and Baron. Mlle Duclos was not at all popular in the theatre on account of her violent temper and strong passions, which she vented freely on the young and lovely Adrienne Lecouvreur when the latter was allotted some of her roles. She was also most undisciplined in her private life, and at the age of 55 married a young boy, who soon left her. This involved her in a lawsuit, the speeches in which make curious reading. She retired at 72, by which time the artificiality of her acting seemed sadly old-fashioned beside the freer methods of the younger generation.

DUFF, MARY ANN (*née* DYKE) (1794–1857), American actress, born in London. With her sister Elizabeth, later the wife of Tom Moore, she appeared in Dublin as a dancer, and then married William Murray of the Theatre Royal, Edinburgh, brother of Mrs. Henry Siddons. He died almost immediately, however, and his widow re-married, her second husband being an Irish actor, John Duff (1787–1831), with whom she went to America. They appeared in Boston in 1810 as Romeo and Juliet, and were both considered excellent actors. It was in Boston, and later in Philadelphia, that Mrs. Duff made her reputation, for in spite of the approbation of the critics she was never wholly accepted by audiences in New York, where she made her first appearance in 1823, as Hermione in *The Distressed Mother* to the Orestes of the elder Booth. A tall, dark, graceful woman, she was at her best in tragedy—Ophelia, Constance, Lady Macbeth, Jane Shore—and in the pathetic heroines of such plays as *The Maid and the Magpie* and *The Innkeeper's Daughter*. The early death of her second husband left her with seven small children, of whom one, also Mary, became a good actress, and the wife of J. J. Addams. In spite of constant tours throughout America Mrs. Duff's financial distress became acute, and in a moment of mental aberration she married the actor Charles Young. The marriage was never consummated and was soon after annulled. Mrs. Duff retired into obscurity for some time, but eventually returned to the stage, and in 1835 married a lawyer of New Orleans named Seaver, making her last appearances there in the following year as Jane Shore and Portia.

DUFRESNE. (1) [ABRAHAM-ALEXIS QUINAULT] (1693–1767), French actor, whose father, brother, and three sisters were members with him of the Comédie-Française (see QUINAULT). He is sometimes referred to as Quinault-Dufresne. He made his début as Oreste in Crébillon's *Électre* in 1712, and was engaged to play young heroes and lovers. He was extremely handsome, and, as a contemporary said of him, had the good fortune to please the ladies in an age when they took little trouble to fight against their inclinations. At first the simplicity of his acting was against him, and it was not until the retirement of Beaubour, a somewhat pompous actor, that Dufresne came into his own. He had a fine voice, and a good presence, reminding many of the great Michel Baron, whose traditions he had inherited through the teaching of Ponteuil. Dufresne was the first to play the name-part in Voltaire's *Œdipe* (1718), and Destouches wrote for him his best comedy, *Le Glorieux* (1732), in which Dufresne hardly had to act, so completely was he the person Destouches was satirizing. His companions, who had suffered much from his arrogance, must have got a good deal of quiet amusement out of seeing him as the hero of this play. His wife, (2) CATHERINE-MARIE-JEANNE DUPRÉ (?–1759), known as Mlle Deseine, was a good actress, overshadowed by several outstanding actresses of the period. She first appeared at Fontainebleau in 1724, and from there went to the Comédie-Française. She had much charm and a delightfully natural style of acting, but a weak voice. She was delicate in health, and after several prolonged absences from the stage finally retired in 1736, four years before her husband.

DUFRESNE, CHARLES (*c.* 1611–*c.* 1684), a French actor-manager, first found in the provinces in about 1643, as leader of a company under the patronage of the Duc d'Épernon. A year or two later he was joined by the remnants of the ill-starred Illustre-Théâtre, and soon ceded his leadership to Molière, with whom he returned to Paris in 1658, retiring a year later. Son of a Court painter, Dufresne played second lead in tragedy, but does not appear to have shone in comedy. Even before the arrival of Molière and the Béjarts his company was considered one of the best in France.

DUFRESNY, CHARLES-RIVIÈRE (1654–1724), French dramatist, reputed to be a great-grandson of Henri IV, a relationship which procured him many privileges at Court. His inveterate habit of gambling, however, and his light-hearted lack of thought for the morrow, not to mention two imprudent marriages, kept him poor all his life. But he was always happy, had no great ambitions, and no enemies. He began his dramatic career by writing for the Italian actors established at the Hôtel de Bourgogne, and after their departure from Paris in 1697 turned his undoubted talents to the service of the Comédie-Française. Of his numerous plays the best was the one-act *Esprit de contradiction* (1700). Others, successful when first produced, were *Le Double veuvage* (1702), *La Coquette du village* (1715), and *Le Mariage fait et rompu* (1721), all of which kept their place in the repertory for some time. Dufresny was very conscious of the weight of tradition in comedy, and made some effort to shake it off, as may be seen from his prologue to *Le Négligent* (1692), in which he complains that a good comic writer is blamed for copying Molière, and a bad for not. Dufresny shrank from hard work, however, and with all his qualities his plays were never more than witty and superficial. Many of them, in accordance with the fashion of the time, had a number of interpolated songs, which he composed himself.

DUGAZON. (1) MARIE-MARGUERITE GOURGAUD (1742–99), French actress, daughter of a provincial manager who had aspired unsuccessfully to the Comédie-Française in 1739. She made her first appearance there in 1767, playing secondary soubrette roles. With her was her younger sister, who had married the brother of the celebrated dancer Vestris (for her career, see VESTRIS (2), and a younger brother (2) JEAN-BAPTISTE-HENRI GOURGAUD (1746–1809), who joined the company in 1771. He was a most amusing comedian, at his best in somewhat farcical roles, particularly in the comedies of Scarron and Legrand. With Préville, Molé, and Fleury, he was appointed to the newly founded School of Declamation (1786), which in 1793 became the Conservatoire. He was one of the teachers of Talma, whom he later supported in the upheavals consequent on the Revolution, and followed him to the Comédie-Française when it was reconstituted under Napoleon.

DUKE OF YORK'S THEATRE, LONDON, in St. Martin's Lane; this was built for Frank Wyatt and his wife Violet Melnotte, and opened on 10 Sept. 1892 as the Trafalgar Square Theatre with a comic opera, 'The Wedding Eve', which was not a success. It was at this theatre that the first performances of Ibsen's *The Master Builder*, with Elizabeth Robins, were given in 1893, for matinées only. Two years later the theatre took its present name, and had its first success with *The Gay Parisienne*, with Ada Reeve, in which that quaint droll, Louie Freear (1871–1939), who had been on the stage since early childhood, first made a name for herself. Produced on 4 Apr. 1896, it ran for 369 performances. Nothing further happened of note until in 1897 Charles Frohman, the American theatrical manager, took a long lease of the theatre, and with the younger Dion (Dot) Boucicault as his resident manager, began a successful tenancy, introducing many well-known American actors to London, among them Maxine Elliott and her husband Nat Goodwin. Many of Barrie's plays were first produced here—including *The Admirable Crichton* (1902), *Peter Pan* (1904), which was revived annually for ten years, *Alice Sit-By-The-Fire* (1905), and *What Every Woman Knows* (1908). In 1910 Frohman tried to introduce the repertory system to London with an outstanding programme of modern plays, which included Shaw's *Misalliance*, Galsworthy's *Justice*, Granville-Barker's *The Madras House*, and revivals of *Trelawny of the 'Wells'* and *Prunella*. But the time was not yet ripe, and the venture failed. The theatre reverted to straight runs of Pinero, Barrie, Shaw, and Somerset Maugham, whose *Land of Promise* was the last new play put on by Frohman before he died in the Lusitania disaster in 1915. Two later successes at this theatre were *Daddy-Long-Legs* (1916) and *Brown Sugar* (1920). In 1923 Violet Melnotte assumed active control, her first success being Charlot's review, *London Calling*, written mostly by Noël Coward, whose *Easy Virtue* was produced here three years later. *Such Men Are Dangerous*, *The Chinese Bungalow*, and *Jew Süss*, all with Matheson Lang, followed, Peggy Ashcroft making an early appearance in the last-named, and in 1931 Van Druten's *London Wall* had a successful run. A year later a season of non-stop Grand Guignol occupied the theatre, but up to the outbreak of the Second World War nothing further of note happened. Violet Melnotte died in 1935, and various managements came and went. As a result of enemy action the theatre was closed for three years, reopening in May 1943 with *Shadow and Substance*. Since then it has had a fairly stable career, numbering among its successes *Is Your Honeymoon Really Necessary?* (1944), with Ralph Lynn, *The Happy Marriage* (1952), with John Clements and Kay Hammond, *The House by the Lake* (1956), with Flora Robson, and a translation of Anouilh's *Pauvre Bitos* (1963), with Donald Pleasence. It also had two of the shortest runs on record—*All the Year Round*, which played for three nights in Oct. 1951, and *Thirteen for Dinner*, which survived only one performance, on 17 Dec. 1953. W. MACQUEEN-POPE†, *rev.*

DUKE'S HOUSE, LONDON, see DORSET GARDEN and LINCOLN'S INN FIELDS THEATRE.

DUKE'S THEATRE, LONDON, see HOLBORN THEATRE.

DUKES, ASHLEY (1885–1959), English dramatist, theatre manager, and dramatic critic, in which last capacity he worked for the *Star* and the *Illustrated Evening News*. He was also English editor of the American *Theatre Arts Monthly* for many years. In 1933 he opened the Mercury Theatre, a small playhouse in Notting Hill Gate in which he did excellent work with the production of new and foreign plays, particularly poetic drama. The theatre also housed a ballet company directed by his wife Marie Rambert, which played an important part in the development of British ballet. Dukes's wide knowledge and appreciation of Continental drama was turned to good account in the adaptations of French and German plays which he did for the London stage. The best known of these are *The Man Who Married a Dumb Wife*, and *Mozart*, both from the French; *From Morn Till Midnight*, *The Machine Wreckers*, *Such Men are Dangerous*, and *Jew Süss*, all from the German. He also adapted from the Italian Machiavelli's *Mandragola*, and from the Spanish part of *La Celestina*, which, however, he considerably falsified. As *The Matchmaker's Arms* it provided a humorous vehicle for Sybil Thorndike, with a romantic sub-plot. Of Dukes's own plays the most successful was the charming *Man with a Load of Mischief*, in which Fay Compton scored a great success as the Lady. He was the author of several books on the theatre, including *Drama* in the Home University Library, and of an autobiography, *The Scene is Changed*, published in 1943.

DULLIN, CHARLES (1885–1949), French actor and producer, pupil of Gémier, who, after some appearances in melodrama, became one of the original actors of Copeau's company at the Vieux-Colombier, remaining with him until the return of the troupe from America after the First World War. He then collected his own company, and after some preliminary training, took it on a long tour in the provinces. Back in Paris, confronted by many difficulties, and always short of money, Dullin nevertheless succeeded finally in establishing himself and his actors in the Théâtre de l'Atelier, which soon gained a reputation as one of the outstanding experimental theatres of Paris, worthy to rank with the Vieux-Colombier. The list of plays produced at the Atelier covers the classics of France, the comedies of Aristophanes, translations of famous foreign plays, including Shakespeare and Ben Jonson, Pirandello for the first time in France, and the works of some new authors. Dullin sought first in his productions to engender that current of sympathy between actors and audience without which no play can come to life, and then to bring to the stage, with the help of dancing, décor, and, above all, poetry, the sense of wonder and imagination which the 'well-made' play had banished for so long. Himself an excellent actor, he ran a school of acting connected with his theatre, and in 1936 was invited to become one of the producers at the Comédie-Française. During the occupation of France he toured the unoccupied zone with Molière's *L'Avare*.

DUMAS. (1) ALEXANDRE *père* (1803–70), a prolific writer, of Creole parentage, who is now mainly remembered for his novels, but whose plays were an important part of the Romantic movement in the French theatre. He began by writing vaudevilles, but in accordance with the contemporary orientation, and influenced in part by the visit to Paris of an English company in Shakespeare, turned to historical romance, and his *Henri III et sa cour* (1829) was the first triumph of the Romantic theatre. In the prevailing decadence of the stage the colour and movement of Dumas's plays delighted the audience, and brought the author the friendship and admiration of Alfred de Vigny and Victor Hugo. A play on Napoleon was followed by *Antony* (1831), given at the Théâtre de la Porte-Saint-Martin, where many of Dumas's more melodramatic pieces were first produced. It was extremely successful, owing in part to the excellent acting of Bocage and Mlle Dorval. The Porte-Saint-Martin saw also the first production of Dumas's most famous play, *La Tour de Nesle* (1832), which for terror and rapidity of action—not to mention the number of corpses—surpassed anything seen on the French stage since the days of Alexandre Hardy. When Dumas had run the gamut of history, alone or in collaboration, from Roman times to the contemporary scene, he turned to his own novels and made them into plays, of which in all he wrote nearly a hundred. Some of them were given at the Théâtre Historique, which he built and financed himself, and which nearly ruined him when it failed in 1850, for in spite of his enormous earnings Dumas was continually harassed by his creditors, and a prey to harpies and hangers-on. He was finally rescued by his daughter, who came to live with him in 1868. Meanwhile his natural son (2) ALEXANDRE, known as Dumas *fils* (1824–95), had also turned to the theatre. He was a complete contrast to his father, who seems to have had practically no influence on his literary career, though they lived in harmony together, the younger man often supporting and shielding the elder from the consequences of his own folly. The younger Dumas approached the theatre by way of a dramatization of his own novel, *La Dame aux camélias*, which, first acted in 1852, became one of the outstanding theatrical successes of the second half of the nineteenth century, and is occasionally revived today. But this romantic presentation of the repentant courtesan was destined to remain unique among his dramatic works, for he later turned to social questions, and became the leading exponent of what has been called 'the useful theatre', which regards the stage as a pulpit for the expounding of moral principles. Himself an agnostic, he sought to enforce Christian virtues and conventional morality by dramatic examples. He had little liking for the bohemian society in which his childhood had been passed, and to which he gave a permanent label in the title of his play *Le Demi-Monde* (1855). The bitterness of his illegitimacy found expression in *Le Fils naturel* (1858) and *Un Père prodigue* (1859), while social problems of the day were ventilated in such plays as *La Question d'argent* (1857), *L'Étrangère* (1876), and his last play, *Francillon* (1887). The sanctity of home life was his constant theme and, by a curious reversal of ideas, the prostitute became his main target. Unlike his father, he had no thought of rebelling against society, but sought to ameliorate conditions by the inculcation of moral standards. Much of his theatre has disappeared with the conditions which gave rise to it, and later enactments on paternity and illegitimacy have outdistanced many of his arguments. In his own day a popular and powerful social dramatist, he is now only remembered by his least typical work, mainly because the consumptive and pathetic figure of Marguérite Gautier offers a fine part for an ambitious and passionate actress.

DUMB BALLET, see TRICKWORK ON THE ENGLISH STAGE.

DUMESNIL, MARIE-FRANÇOISE (1713–1803), French actress, rival and contemporary of Mlle Clairon. She first appeared in the provinces, and joined the company of the Comédie-Française in 1737. She was a fine actress, excellent in passionate roles, and was by some critics acclaimed above Mlle Clairon, who with more art had less range. Voltaire attributed much of the success of his *Mérope* (1743) to the acting of Mlle Dumesnil, who, unlike Mlle Clairon, had no interest in the reform of theatrical costume, and aimed at magnificence rather than correctness, being always robed in rich stuffs, made in contemporary styles, and loaded with jewels. She retired in 1775, and passed the rest of her long life at Boulogne. She remained in full possession of her faculties until the end, and was able to remember and pass on to younger actors many traditions temporarily lost during the upheavals of the Revolution. Towards the end of her life she published a book of memoirs, mainly in reply to the many injurious references made to her in Mlle Clairon's *Mémoires*. It is not particularly interesting, though some passages have a technical value. There are also some useful notes on the theatrical slang of the time, which constituted a language of its own, and in which, says Dumesnil, Préville excelled.

DUMFRIES. The Theatre Royal (first called Royal in 1811) opened in 1792 under the management of Williamson, formerly of the Haymarket, London. The architect was Thomas Boyd, whose design was based on that of the Theatre Royal, Bristol (see BRISTOL and No. 27); the scenery was by Alexander Nasmyth, and Robert Burns was an active supporter. Thereafter, the history of the theatre was very much that of any provincial theatre in Scotland or the north of England. Later managers included Stephen Kemble and the elder Macready. Phelps was a member of the stock company in the 1834–5 season. A frequenter of the theatre in the 1870s was J. M. Barrie, then a schoolboy at Dumfries Academy. By 1909 audiences had declined, and the theatre closed. It was used as a cinema from 1911 to 1954. In 1959 the Dumfries Guild of Players, a long-established amateur group, bought it, and after carrying out some internal reconstruction, reopened it as a theatre the following year. Each season they present six productions of their own interspersed with plays, concerts, and ballet by touring professional artists sponsored by the Arts Council. J. F. ARNOTT

DUNDREARY, see SOTHERN (1).

DUNLAP, WILLIAM (1766–1839), one of the first outstanding figures of the American stage, and its dominating force from 1790 to 1810. He at first intended to become a painter, and went to England in 1784 to study under Benjamin West (for one of his paintings, see No. 163). But he neglected his work for the theatre, with which he had first made contact through the productions of British officers in New York. He soon saw most of Shakespeare's plays, a good many contemporary comedies, and the work of such actors as Charles Kemble and Mrs. Siddons. It was at this period that Dunlap imbibed that sense of dramatic and theatrical values which was later to stand him in good stead. Late in 1787 he returned to the United States, and, inspired by the success of Tyler's *The Contrast*, wrote a comedy for the American Company. This was accepted but never played, owing mainly to the lack of suitable parts for the manager, John Henry, and his wife. A second comedy, *The Father; or, American Shandyism*, remedied this defect, and was produced at the John Street Theatre, New York, on 7 Sept. 1789.

Dunlap continued to write for the American Company, and in 1796 became one of its managers in partnership with Hallam and Hodgkinson, whose joint management had led to constant bickering between themselves and their wives. Dunlap strengthened the company by the inclusion of the first Joseph Jefferson, and did all he could to keep the peace among his co-partners. In 1797 Hallam withdrew from active management, and Hodgkinson and Dunlap opened the Park Theatre, New York, on 29 Jan. 1798, with *As You Like It*. One of the first plays to be done there was *André*, a tragedy which Dunlap based on an incident in the War of Independence, thus making it the first native tragedy on American material. Hodgkinson played André, and the part of Bland, his friend, was taken by a newly imported young English actor, Thomas Abthorpe Cooper, who was later to succeed Dunlap as lessee and manager of the theatre.

In 1798 Hodgkinson left the management of the Park Theatre, and Dunlap continued alone, producing a number of his own plays, many of them translations and adaptations of the highly popular Kotzebue. Among these the most successful were *The Stranger*, which has not survived, *Lovers' Vows*, *The Wild Goose Chase*, *The Virgin of the Sun*, and its sequel *Pizarro*. Dunlap also translated a number of French plays, and wrote some original works, of which the early ones mentioned above were the best, though *Leicester* and *The Italian Father* have much to recommend them. Many of them were performed also in Boston, where Dunlap had leased the Haymarket Theatre, and in Philadelphia under Warren and Wood at the Chestnut Street Theatre. Meanwhile Dunlap struggled on at the Park Theatre, hampered by the temperaments of his actors and recurrent epidemics of yellow fever, until in Feb. 1805 he went bankrupt and was forced to close down. He returned to painting, but a year later agreed to become assistant stage manager of the Park under Cooper, in which capacity he engaged in 1809 Mr. and Mrs. Poe, the parents of Edgar Allan Poe, for parts in Monk Lewis's *Castle Spectre*. In 1812 he accompanied George Frederick Cooke on his American tour, and then retired finally from the stage to devote himself entirely to literature and painting. He contemplated the publication of his plays in a uniform edition, but produced only the first volume, and in 1832 published his invaluable *History of the American Theatre*. Quinn, who devotes a chapter of his *History of the American Drama from the Beginning to the Civil War* to the career of William Dunlap, sums him up as follows: '[He] had the soul of an artist and the intrepidity of the pioneer, and his place in our dramatic literature will remain secure.'

DUNLOP STREET THEATRE, see GLASGOW.

DUNSANY, EDWARD JOHN MORETON DRAX PLUNKETT, LORD (1878–1957), a man of wide interests who in his capacity as a dramatist was connected with the early years of the Abbey Theatre (see IRELAND), where his first plays were produced—*The Glittering Gate* (1909) and *King Argimenes* (1911). These were also seen in London, as were *The Gods of the Mountain* (1911) and *The Golden Doom* (1912), both at the Haymarket. Most of his later plays were seen only in Ireland, or in amateur productions, but *If* had a long run at the Ambassadors' in 1921. A versatile writer, his plays range from one-act farces (*Cheezo*), fantasy (*The Old King's Tale*), and satire (*The Lost Silk Hat*) to full-length tragedy (*Alexander*) and comedy (*Mr. Faithful*).

DUNVILLE, T. E. (*c.* 1870–1924), an eccentric music-hall comedian whose real name was Wallon. He specialized in songs made up of short terse sentences, which left much to the imagination and were delivered in an explosive manner. A typical one was 'Little boy, Pair of skates, Broken ice, Heaven's gates'. He became stage-struck as a youngster after seeing a performance of Pepper's Ghost at Coventry Fair. After practising high kicks in the counting-house of a silk merchant where he was employed he joined a local Minstrel troupe, and then went into pantomime at obscure theatres. He and a partner gained their first success through their carefully rehearsed act going wrong and causing the audience to laugh so much that they continued the mistakes as the real act. It was when appearing as an extra turn at Bolton in 1899 that Dunville first caught the eye of an enterprising manager, and his luck turned. For years he was top of the bill, wearing the extraordinary make-up—

long black coat, small hat, baggy trousers, big boots, and ugly face with red nose—which he often tried vainly to alter. His bills always announced him as 'Sticking Here for a Week', and showed him suspended from the wall. When the music-halls began to slump after the First World War it preyed on his mind. One night in 1924, in a saloon bar, he overheard someone referring to him as a 'fallen star'. Some days later his body was recovered from the Thames near Reading.

W. MACQUEEN-POPE†

D'URFEY, THOMAS (1653–1723), Restoration dramatist and song-writer, a favourite with Charles II and James II, whom he ardently supported in his writings. He wrote a number of plays, mainly based on earlier English or foreign dramatists, none of which has survived on the stage. The earlier ones are purely farcical, but later ones are tinged with the sentimentality which was soon to bulk so large in English drama. D'Urfey was one of the writers most savagely attacked for indecency by Collier in his *Short View*, and in 1698 he was prosecuted for profanity. In 1719 he published a collection of songs and ballads called 'Wit and Mirth, or Pills to Purge Melancholy'.

DÜRRENMATT, FRIEDRICH (1921–), Swiss dramatist, who has made his name in the post-war German-speaking theatre. His work shows the influence of Brecht in its epic quality, and also of Wedekind and the Expressionists, particularly in his first play, *Es steht geschrieben*. His first big success in the theatre was gained with the mock-heroic *Romulus der Grosse* (1949), in which the action takes place on a single day, the Ides of March A.D. 476, when the Emperor in his country home hears with complete calm the news of the barbarians' victory, and, deserted by his followers, goes out alone to surrender his crown to the invader. He has for twenty years tried to bring about the destruction of Rome by his passivity, so as to avenge the men killed in her imperial wars. But, by the irony of fate, those who deserted him are killed, while he is condemned to live. Of Dürrenmatt's other plays, the two produced in 1954—*Ein Engel kommt nach Babylon* and *Die Ehe des Herrn Mississippi* (done at the Arts Theatre in 1959)—are not well known outside the German-speaking world, but *Der Besuch der alten Dame* (1956) has been done in England and the United States by the Lunts as *The Visit*, while *Die Physiker* (1962), as *The Physicists*, was a great success at the Aldwych Theatre in 1963 in a production by the Royal Shakespeare company. Dürrenmatt is interested in exploring the possibilities of dramatic technique, and although he has written in *Theaterprobleme* (1955) that our disintegrating world is a subject for comedy and not for tragedy, fundamentally his plays are deeply pessimistic and reflect the uncertainty of the times.

DOROTHY MOORE

DUSE, ELEONORA (1858–1924), famous Italian actress, and one of the great tragediennes of the international theatre. She had a hard and unhappy childhood, much saddened by the death of her mother. Daughter and granddaughter of strolling players, she was on the stage from her earliest years, playing Cosette at the age of 4, and Juliet at 14, a performance immortalized by D'Annunzio in his novel, *Il Fuoco*. In 1878, after a popular success as the heroine in *Les Fourchambault*, she was engaged by Ernesto Rossi as his leading lady, and went on tour with him, soon taking her place as one of the greatest actresses of the day. In 1885 she toured South America, and appeared in the United States in 1893, 1903, and again just before her death. In 1881 she acompanied the Città di Roma company to Russia, where Chekhov saw her as Cleopatra and was captivated by her art, which was a revelation to him. It has been suggested that he had her in mind when he wrote *The Seagull*, and that she may have inspired also some of the ideals which led to the founding of the Moscow Art Theatre. In London in 1895 she and Sarah Bernhardt both appeared as Magda, an event which caused much excitement among public and critics alike. Shaw, at that time dramatic critic of the *Saturday Review*, unhesitatingly proclaimed the supremacy of Duse, while Clement Scott preferred Bernhardt. Duse had a certain statuesque way of playing, a slowness and subtlety which was not always to the taste of her audience. A slender woman, with a dark, mobile face, melancholy in repose, and long slender hands and arms, she was noted for the beauty and expressiveness of her gestures, but her excessive nervousness and overwrought temperament led at times to too much restlessness on the stage, and it was in her rare moments of immobility that one best realized her greatness. She was probably at her best in big emotional parts—Tosca, Fédora, Théodora, Camille—though she was much admired, even by Clement Scott, as the Hostess in *La Locandiera*, one of the most popular pieces in her repertory, in spite of her inability to present a buxom, vigorous woman, as the part demands. She was also outstanding in Ibsen, as Hedda Gabler, Nora, Rebecca West (in *Rosmersholm*) (see No. 96), and Ellida (in *The Lady From the Sea*). In her late thirties, when she stood in the forefront of her profession, she ardently championed the cause of D'Annunzio's poetic drama, and made him famous as a dramatist by her playing in *La Gioconda*, *Francesca da Rimini*, and *La città morta*. Even after the failure of his *Gloria* at Naples in 1899, she continued to appear in his plays, often with much loss of money and reputation. She retired shortly before 1914, but returned to play in London and New York in 1923, dying in Pittsburgh the following year.

Shaw, who always had the greatest admiration for her, much to the fury of those who preferred Sarah Bernhardt, said, with reference to her Magda:

> When it is remembered that the majority of tragic actors excel only in explosions of those passions which are common to man and brute,

there will be no difficulty in understanding the indescribable distinction which Duse's acting acquires from the fact that behind every stroke of it is a distinctively human idea. In nothing is this more apparent than in the vigilance in her of that high human instinct which seeks to awaken the deepest responsive feeling without giving pain. (See *Our Theatres in the Nineties*.)

Unlike Bernhardt, Duse professed a great hatred of publicity, but in seeking to avoid it made herself even more conspicuous. She was an enigmatic personality, who captured the imagination of the theatre-going public and even in her own lifetime became a legend. Yet, with all her faults, she was a superb actress, and it was finally the sterling truth of her representation which fired public imagination. She disdained the use of make-up on the stage, and was noted for her ability to blush or turn pale at will.

DUST HOLE, see SCALA THEATRE.

DUTCH DRAMA, see NETHERLANDS, THE.

DYBWAD, JOHANNE (1867–1950), Norwegian actress, who made her first appearance in 1887 in Bergen. After the opening of Norway's National Theatre in 1899 she became its leading actress, a position she retained for the next forty years. She appeared frequently in other Scandinavian countries, and also in Hamburg, Berlin, and Paris, and was particularly esteemed for her roles in Ibsen, which included Lady Inger, Hjördis, Solveig, Aase, Nora, Mrs. Alving, Rebecca West, Hilde Wangel, Asta Alving, and Maja Rubek.

L. KATHLEEN MCFARLANE

DYMOV, OSSIP (1878–1959), see JEWISH DRAMA, 6.

E

EAGLE THEATRE, New York, see STANDARD THEATRE, 2.

EARL CARROLL THEATRE, NEW YORK, see CARROLL, Earl.

EARL OF DERBY'S MEN, see STRANGE'S MEN.

EARL OF LEICESTER'S MEN, see LEICESTER'S MEN.

EARL OF LINCOLN'S MEN, see LINCOLN'S MEN.

EARL OF OXFORD'S MEN, see OXFORD'S MEN.

EARL OF PEMBROKE'S MEN, see PEMBROKE'S MEN.

EARL OF SUSSEX'S MEN, see SUSSEX'S MEN.

EAST LONDON THEATRE, see EFFINGHAM SALOON and ROYALTY THEATRE, 1.

ECCLESIASTICAL DRAMA, see LITURGICAL DRAMA.

ECCLESTON (Eglestone), William (?–?1625 or 1652), an actor in the lists of those who played in Shakespeare's plays, and a member in 1610 of the King's Men, with whom he remained, with one break, until about 1623. Baldwin, in his *Organization and Personnel of the Shakespearian Company* (1927), assigns to him the roles of sprightly youths with a penchant for sword-play. He also assumes that he played, as an apprentice, a number of Shakespeare's female roles, but there is no proof of this. Eccleston may have died in 1625, when his name disappears from the actor lists, or may conceivably have lived to be the W. E. who contributed some verses to the 1652 edition of *The Wild Goose Chase*, in which Lowin acted in 1632.

ECHEGARAY, José (1832–1916), the most important Spanish dramatist of the later nineteenth century, who was awarded the Nobel Prize for Literature in 1905. His plays, which retain the verse-form and much of the fire and imagery of the Romantics, deal nevertheless with questions of social import, which often arise indirectly in the unfolding of the plot. They caused fierce controversy, but were enthusiastically received, and had a great influence, not only in Spain, but on the European theatre generally. Echegaray's best-known plays are *O locura o santidad* (1877), *El loco Dios* (1900), *El hijo de Don Juan* (1892), a study of inherited disease which owes something to Ibsen's *Ghosts*, and, most important of all, *El gran Galeoto* (1881), given in England as *Calumny* and in the United States as *The World and His Wife*. Its theme is that slanderous tongues may cause the downfall of the most virtuous, since a woman wrongfully accused of being a poet's mistress, finally becomes so driven to it by the oppression of unfounded scandal.

ECHEIA, see ACOUSTICS, 3.

ECKENBERG, Johann Carl (1685–1748), a German strolling actor, an acrobat and juggler of great dexterity, who with his wife, a rope-dancer, led a company of acrobats and actors up and down Europe. He was once the successful rival of the great actress Caroline Neuber at Hamburg, his varied entertainment proving more acceptable to the public than her classic plays.

EDDY, Edward (1822–75), American actor, long popular at the Bowery Theatre, where he first appeared on 13 Mar. 1851 as Richelieu. He followed this with such parts as Othello, Claude Melnotte, and Belphegor, and with his greatest success of this first season, Edmond Dantès in *The Count of Monte Cristo*. Tall, handsome, and extremely vigorous in his acting, he was at his best in youthful, melodramatic parts, and, though he never attained great eminence in New York, he was a good actor with a wide range. He appeared occasionally in Shakespeare, but was also seen in less reputable works, even taking part in the Dog dramas which were such a feature of the popular stage at this time, and earning for himself the sobriquet of 'robustious Eddy'. He was at Burton's in 1855 with Chanfrau and Holland, and also at the New Metropolitan, but his style was not suited to the fashionable theatres, and he went back to the Bowery as Richard III. Further ventures into management ended in the same way, with a return to the Bowery and pure melodrama. Towards the end his popularity waned and he was seen fleetingly at a number of theatres.

EDESON, Robert (1868–1931), American actor, whose later career was in films, but who spent many years on the stage. Son of an actor-manager and his wife, Marion Taliaferro, he started work at 16 in the office of the Park Theatre, appearing there a year later as an understudy. By 1892 he was leading man at the Boston Museum, where he was seen and engaged by Charles Frohman during a performance of *Our Boys*. Frohman took him to the Empire in New York, where he played for many years, making a great hit as the Rev. Gavin Dishart in *The Little Minister* (1897) with Maude Adams. Two years later he made his first appearance in London, as David Brandon in *The Children of the Ghetto*, and appeared there again in 1907 in his most successful part, Soangataha in *Strongheart* by William C. de Mille. After a further series of successes, including two plays by himself, he made his last appearance as the Vagrant in *The Insect Play* (done as *The World We Live In*) in 1922. Edeson was one of the earliest stage stars to go into motion pictures, in which he was most successful. He had four wives, the third, 1917–24, being the actress Mary Newcomb. In person he was quiet and friendly, and a man of fine presence.

EDINBURGH. 1. There appear to be indications that Edinburgh might well have developed as the centre of an indigenous Scottish drama during the sixteenth century, had not the Kirk adopted the attitude of the English Puritans, or the Court been too weak (and after 1603 too remote) to afford patronage. The scanty records indicate a succession of performances in Edinburgh and nearby towns between 1663 and 1689, including the first known Scottish performance of *Macbeth* in 1672. Thereafter there is a gap in our knowledge until an advertisement of 1715 reveals a company established in Edinburgh. The best documented of early managements is Tony Aston's, from 1725 to 1728. By 1733 advertisements refer to 'The Edinburgh Company of Players'. In 1736 the poet Allan Ramsay, who had been a patron of Aston's, opened a theatre in Carubber's Close, only to have it closed in six months by the Licensing Act of 1737. From 1741 there were theatrical seasons every year, the law being evaded by the device of charging, not for the play, but for an introductory concert. In 1747 the Concert Hall in the Canongate was opened, which, on the granting of a patent in 1767, became the first Theatre Royal. Here, under the management of Digges, *Douglas*, by John Home, was first performed in 1756.

In 1767 David Ross, a well-known London actor whose father had been a lawyer in Edinburgh, became manager, and within two years built a new Theatre Royal on a site now occupied by the General Post Office at the east end of Princes Street. The next manager of note was John Jackson, actor and author. Stephen Kemble took over the theatre from 1791 until 1800, when Jackson returned for a second period of control. Mrs. Siddons made two sensational visits to the Scottish capital in 1784 and 1785. Other distinguished players in this era were Samuel Foote, Mrs. Bellamy, Tate Wilkinson, Mrs. Hartley, Mr. and Mrs. Inchbald, Mr. and Mrs. Yates, Shuter, Mr. and Mrs. Barry, and John Kemble. In 1809 the theatre went dark, the new manager, Henry, son of Sarah Siddons, preferring the building then known as Corri's Rooms, and earlier as the Circus and Sadler's Wells, which he called the New Theatre Royal. In 1811, however, he was forced by law to return to the original Theatre Royal in Shakespeare Square. While Siddons was artistically successful, financially his management was ruinous. When he died in 1815, his widow and her brother, William Henry Murray, found that they were left heavily in debt. Despite this they elected to keep the theatre going, and from then until 1851, when Murray, who was then the patentee, gave up, it had a period of almost unbroken success. Adaptations of Scott's novels were immensely successful, and a Royal Command Performance in 1822 before George IV set the seal on the theatre's popularity in Edinburgh. The theatre was pulled down in 1859, but before its final disappearance it had a further period of greatness under R. H. Wyndham, who gave Henry Irving many opportunities as a member of his stock company from 1857 to 1859.

Meanwhile a second theatre, known successively as the Pantheon, Caledonian, and Adelphi, had emerged from the earlier Circus mentioned above; burnt down in 1853, this was reopened in 1856. To it the patent of the Theatre Royal was transferred, and it was known as the Royal through all its vicissitudes, being burnt down in 1865, 1875, and 1884, and always rebuilt on the same site. Other theatres in Edinburgh included the Princess's, which was first a music-hall and flourished from 1860 to 1888, and the Edinburgh, which had a short life, 1875 to 1877, but saw Salvini's first appearances in the United Kingdom. The Lyceum opened in 1883, and the King's Theatre in 1906 (see also SCOTLAND).

2. THE EDINBURGH INTERNATIONAL FESTIVAL OF MUSIC AND DRAMA, which lasts for three weeks from, roughly, the middle of August to early September, started in 1947. Drama has always been the weakest side of the programme, but some interesting events have taken place. The practice of inviting foreign companies to appear at the Royal Lyceum Theatre was begun in the Festival's first year, when Jouvet's company from the Athenée was seen in *L'École des femmes* and Giraudoux's *Ondine*. In 1948 the company formed by Jean-Louis Barrault and his wife Madeleine Renaud appeared in Gide's translation of *Hamlet* and in Marivaux's *Les Fausses Confidences*; and in 1957 in Anouilh's *La Répétition*. Since then the Dusseldorf company, the Atelier, the Comédie-Française, the Théâtre National Populaire, the Piccolo Teatro of Milan, the Teatro Stabile of Genoa, and the mime-artist Marcel Marceau, have all been seen in Edinburgh. In 1955 Edwige Feuillère appeared in *La Dame aux camélias*. New plays which have had their first productions during the Festival include T. S. Eliot's *The Cocktail Party*, *The Confidential Clerk*, and *The Elder Statesman*, Charles Morgan's *The River Line*, Wilder's *The Matchmaker* and *A Life in the Sun*. This last was produced on a specially constructed stage in the Assembly Hall, where Tyrone Guthrie directed in 1948, 1949, and 1959, in an adaptation by Robert Kemp, Sir David Lindsay's *Ane Satyre of the Thrie Estaits*, last performed nearly four hundred years before. Other performances at the Assembly Hall have included Jonathan Griffin's *The Hidden King*, Sydney Goodsir Smith's *The Wallace*, and the

Old Vic in *Bartholomew Fair*, *Romeo and Juliet*, and Schiller's *Mary Stuart*, translated by Stephen Spender; and the Stratford Ontario Festival Company in *Oedipus Rex*. In 1960 the candle-lit Regency hall of the Royal High School was the setting for an enchanting production by Guthrie of Ramsay's *Gentle Shepherd*. In 1950 the Glasgow Citizens' Theatre gave Bridie's *The Queen's Comedy* and revived the famous *Douglas* by John Home, with Sybil Thorndike and Lewis Casson as Lord and Lady Randolph. The Edinburgh Gateway company appeared regularly, its productions including the première of Robert McLellan's *Young Auchinleck*. Other repertory theatres which have appeared at the Festival are those of Birmingham, Dundee, and Perth, and the Bristol Old Vic. The English Stage Company has made several appearances, presenting the British première of O'Casey's *Cock-a-doodle Dandy* and of Ionesco's *Exit the King*; and the première of Dennis's *August for the People*. In 1962 the Royal Shakespeare Company made its début at the Festival with a programme which included the first performance in English of Fry's *Curtmantle*. From the beginning the Festival attracted to Edinburgh a 'Fringe', as it came to be known, of plays and revues not included in the official programme, of which the best-known and most successful has been *Beyond the Fringe*.

3. The Edinburgh Gateway Theatre, previously the Broadway cinema, was opened in 1946 by the Church of Scotland, which had received it from an anonymous donor. To begin with, the programme presented consisted of both films and plays, the plays being provided by visiting companies (the Pilgrim Players, for instance) or by a company engaged directly by the theatre management. From 1953, however, the theatre was rented for some eight months of each year to an independent company whose first chairman was Robert Kemp. Responsibility for the choice of plays lay with a board of management, subject to the proviso that, if there was any doubt about the suitability of a play, the director of the theatre, as representing the Church, should be consulted. In fact there were few clashes, the policy laid down by the Church for the theatre being liberal, rejecting plays with a 'religious' message but without artistic value, accepting those of artistic and human value if their aim was 'to deepen man's understanding of his own true nature and his compassion for others', and welcoming the inclusion of comedy. The conduct of the Gateway was approved by the General Assembly in 1961 after a debate which recalled the *Douglas* controversy of two centuries ago. In 1965 the company was wound up, passing to the newly formed Edinburgh Civic Theatre Trust 'its limited assets and its unlimited good wishes.'

4. The Edinburgh Civic Theatre Company opened its first season in October 1965 at the Royal Lyceum Theatre under the artistic direction of Tom Fleming with a Scots version by Victor Carin of Goldoni's *Servant of Two Masters*. The theatre is administered by a Trust consisting of representatives of Edinburgh Corporation (which owns the theatre) and other members formerly on the board of the Gateway. J. F. ARNOTT

EDOUIN, Willie [William Frederick Bryer] (1846–1908), English comedian, son of a dancing-master. With his five brothers and sisters he gave children's shows in Brighton and London, and appeared in pantomime. As an adult actor he played in Australia and in New York, and was associated with Lydia Thompson and her burlesque troupe, one of whom he married. At Wallack's in 1871 he appeared in a burlesque of Bluebeard, in his famous character of Wishee-Washee. He then returned to London and made his first adult appearance there in 1874, at the Charing Cross Theatre. After a further visit to America, he opened Toole's Theatre, London, in 1884, with Brough as his co-manager. He was also at one time manager of the Strand, but was not successful financially, being a poor business man. He was excellent in certain grotesque and whimsical parts, but his main successes were made in burlesque and extravaganza.

EDWARDES, George (1852–1915), London theatre manager, to whom we owe the form of entertainment known as Musical Comedy. Even if he did not invent it, it was through him that it came into being and his influence that gave it its final form, while his name is indissolubly linked with its history. Edwardes was intended for the army, but drifted into theatre management in Ireland, his native country, at the Gaiety Theatre, Dublin, in 1875. He became business manager of the Savoy Theatre, London, when D'Oyly Carte opened it in 1881, but left there in 1885 to go into partnership with John Hollingshead at the old Gaiety. In the following year Hollingshead retired, and Edwardes ran the theatre on his own account. His flair for what the public wanted, his genius in finding talent and bringing out the best in it, his imagination in supplanting burlesque by musical comedy, made the Gaiety even more famous than it had previously been, while a 'Gaiety Girl' from his carefully chosen and well-trained chorus was a recognized type of beauty and ability. In 1893 Edwardes built Daly's for Augustin Daly, afterwards taking control of it himself, and making it as great a theatrical landmark in London as the Gaiety. He made stars by the score, his chorus-girls married into the peerage, and he made few mistakes in the choice of plays and casts. His list of successes at Daly's, the Gaiety, the Prince of Wales's, the Apollo, and elsewhere, is remarkable, and includes most of the musical comedies whose titles and tunes are still known today—*The Geisha*, *San Toy*, *The Merry Widow*, *A Country Girl*, *The Shop Girl*, *The Runaway Girl*, *The Quaker Girl* (he always maintained that there was magic in the word 'girl'). To his staff and companies, who adored him, he was always known as 'The Guv'nor'. Tall, good-looking and burly, he had a curiously sleepy, almost complaining, voice, that was very characteristic, as was his disregard of expense. He wanted the best for his theatres, and cared little what it cost. He was rewarded by packed houses and almost constant prosperity, and his popularity with the public was as great as with his own profession. W. MACQUEEN-POPE†

EDWARDS, HILTON (1903–), see IRELAND.

EDWIN. (1) JOHN the elder (1749–90), English actor who was appearing in amateur theatricals when he made the acquaintance of the comedian Ned Shuter. This led to an engagement in Manchester to play Shuter's parts, and to further work in the provinces and in Dublin. Edwin was naturally unable to establish himself in London while Shuter was there, but he became a favourite actor in Bath. Later he was extremely successful at the Haymarket during the summer seasons, appearing in a number of plays by O'Keefe, who also wrote the comic songs for which Edwin became famous. A good, reliable actor, with a face which contrived to be both humorous and handsome, he was accounted the best burletta singer of the day, his voice being naturally good. He was not a buffoon, and seems to have played with great subtlety, in spite of a sad propensity to over-indulgence in drink. Among his best parts in comedy were Dogberry, First Gravedigger, Launcelot Gobbo, Sir Hugh Evans, and Sir Anthony Absolute. His son, (2) JOHN the younger (1768–1803), was the child of a Bath milliner, and was first on the stage as a youngster, playing with his father at Bath and at the Haymarket. As an adult, he made his début at Covent Garden in 1788, and was taken up by Lord Barrymore, for whom he devised private theatricals at Wargrave. He died young as a result of dissipation, which prevented him from realizing his full powers as an actor. He married (3) ELIZABETH REBECCA RICHARDS (*c.* 1771–1854), an actress who had played with her parents in Dublin while still quite young. She returned to the stage after some schooling, and was in Tate Wilkinson's provincial company, being excellent in comedy and farce. After her husband's death she was at Drury Lane and other London theatres, and retired early. The loss of her money caused her to return, when, being too old for her previous parts, she appeared in such characters as Sheridan's Duenna. She was small, fair, with an expressive face, and had some of the charm and vivacity of Mrs. Jordan, though without her excellence.

EFFINGHAM SALOON, LONDON. This opened as a music-hall in the 1840s. In 1867 it was rebuilt and became the East London Theatre, with one of the roughest audiences on record and plays to suit their taste. It was burnt down in 1879, and later a building called Wonderland rose on the site, which housed plays in Yiddish and then became a boxing saloon.

EGAN, PIERCE (1772–1849), English journalist and reporter of sporting events, author of *Life in London*, first published in shilling parts in 1821 with illustrations by the Cruikshank brothers. It was an immediate success, and was at once dramatized by many hands as *Tom and Jerry; or, Life in London.* Versions by Barrymore at the Royal Amphitheatre, and by the younger Dibdin at the Olympic, were superseded by that of Moncrieff, first given at the Adelphi and later frequently revived. This version was also popular in America. Egan himself prepared a version for Sadler's Wells, and wrote a sequel, *Finish to the Adventures of Tom, Jerry and Logic*, both books doubtless suggesting to Dickens the rough idea of *The Pickwick Papers*. Egan was also the author of *The Life of an Actor*, an amusing survey of the progress of young Peregrine Proteus from poverty and the provinces to the honour of a performance before royalty. Dedicated to Kean, it was published in 1824 with illustrations by Theodore Lane, and proved almost as popular as *Tom and Jerry.*

EGRESSY, GÁBOR (1808–66), Hungarian actor, the leading man, with Szerdahelyi, of the company of the first Hungarian National Theatre opened in Budapest in 1837.

EICHELBAUM, SAMUEL (1894–), see SOUTH AMERICA, 1.

EKHOF, KONRAD (1720–1778), great German actor who did more than anyone, after Caroline Neuber, to raise the status of the professional actor in Germany, and to prepare the way for the reforms and triumphs of the great F. L. Schröder. He was originally a clerk, but an overwhelming love of the theatre led him to go on the stage. He joined Schönemann's newly formed company in 1740, taking with him Sophie Schröder, at that time separated from her drunken husband. Being short and ungraceful, with a plain face, he was not at first thought much of, and made himself generally useful. But he had a fine speaking voice, which later developed into a mighty organ of which Iffland said 'the like was never heard on the German stage'. He made his début in a small role in *Mithridate* on 15 Jan. 1740, and remained with Schönemann for seventeen years, deepening and perfecting his art by study and observation, till from the wooden declamation and stiff posturings of Caroline Neuber's school he had evolved a supple and natural style of acting, which, though already known elsewhere in Europe, was something new in Germany. During this time he married a young actress in the company, the daughter of Frau Spiegelberg-Denner, and trained her in his own methods. He was the first professional theorist on German dramatic art—since Gottsched was no actor—and the first to think of giving young actors formal training, for which purpose he founded, in 1753, a short-lived Academy of Actors for classes in reading and discussion of plays. As Schönemann became more and more immersed in horse-dealing, which was his passion, he left the running of the company to Ekhof, who was unable to stave off disaster. He left, but after a short tour with a harlequin company, which was not at all suitable for him, returned to take over the remnants of the old company. He had no taste or talent for business management, and soon called in the actor-manager Koch to take control. They spent six years together, but there was continual friction, and in 1764 Ekhof left to join the Ackermann company. He was now at the height of his powers, with a flexible voice, expressive gesture, and a fully controlled technique. He was a great asset to Ackermann, who had just taken over the newly opened National Theatre—Germany's first—at Hamburg, and he remained with them five years, leaving only because he could not stomach the rudeness and bad manners of the youthful and arrogant Schröder. He spent several miserable years touring in the company of Abel Seyler, husband of the redoubtable Sophie Hensel, who tormented him with her professional jealousy, until he found a permanent home at the Court theatre of Weimar. Here he pursued a cautious but acceptable policy, gaining the affection and esteem of his audience, until a disastrous fire at Weimar caused a removal to Gotha. There, as chief actor and stage director, he spent his last happy and honoured years, dying in 1778, the year after he had taken Iffland into the company. Just before his death he went to Weimar to appear in private Court theatricals with Goethe, when he probably imparted to him some of the reminiscences which were incorporated in *Wilhelm Meister*, and he made his last appearance on the stage at Gotha as the Ghost in *Hamlet*, in an adaptation made by his old enemy, Schröder, now the uncontested head of his profession. To Schröder Ekhof also entrusted the organization of an Actors' Benevolent Fund which he had been instrumental in starting.

Ekhof excelled in the mingled tragicomic and pathetic roles, the rough but good-natured, crusty but noble, characters which the new drama had brought in its train. His best parts were Old Barnwell in Lillo's *London Merchant*, the father in Diderot's *Père de famille*, and Odoardo in *Emilia Galotti*. In spite of his physical shortcomings he was also outstanding in tragedy, as Schröder found when, expecting some travesty of the part, he first saw Ekhof play Oedipus. In comedy Ekhof was subtle and discreet, and his portrayal of north-German peasants was good enough to wring a tribute from one of them. In his early days he was adequate in juvenile leads, but unfortunately continued to play them until late in life, which called forth some caustic remarks from contemporary critics. This, however, was a minor blemish in a man who commanded the respect and affection of audiences all over Germany, and lived to see his fellow actors, in great part through his own exertions, raised from the misery of strolling players to the dignity of an assured profession under noble patronage.

EKKYKLEMA, or 'wheel-out', see GREECE, 6.

ELECTOR PALATINE'S MEN, see ADMIRAL'S MEN.

ELECTRIC LIGHTING, see LIGHTING, 1 *d*, 2 and 3.

ELEN, GUS [really ERNEST AUGUSTUS] (1862–1940), a music-hall performer who first appeared in the old taverns of the 1880s. He became famous as the singer of London cockney ditties, especially 'Never Introduce yer Donah to a Pal' and 'You Could Almost Shut yer Eyes and 'ear 'em Grow'. His presentations of Cockney character were true to life, whereas those of Chevalier had been idealized. Elen's songs were the true songs of London, and his characters had a Dickensian touch. ''E Dunno Where 'E Are', 'Down the Road', 'If It Wasn't For the 'ouses in Between', and 'Wait Till the Work Comes Round' are music-hall classics. Elen retired a successful man, but came back to the London Palladium to a Command Performance in 1935 to show a delighted audience that he was as good as ever.

W. MACQUEEN-POPE†

ELEPHANT AND CASTLE THEATRE, LONDON, at the northern end of the New Kent Road. This was built in 1872, and staged 'transpontine melodrama', with pantomime at Christmas. It is said to stand on the site of the old theatre at Newington Butts, of which little is known. The Elephant and Castle closed in 1928. After reconstruction, it opened as a cinema in 1932.

ELIOT, THOMAS STEARNS (1888–1965), poet and dramatist. American by birth, but British by adoption, Eliot initiated an important revival of poetic drama by writing *Murder in the Cathedral* for production in the Chapter House of Canterbury Cathedral in 1935. Based on the martyrdom of Thomas à Becket, it uses liturgical forms and a chorus to present Eliot's basic theme of inner development from despair to an awareness of the nature of Original Sin and thence to a capacity for self-redemption. It was subsequently revived several times with great success in commercial theatres in Britain and the United States. In his later plays he worked in accordance with an idea outlined in *The Sacred Wood* (1920) by attempting to adapt popular modern forms of drama to his poetic and religious purposes. In *The Family Reunion* (1939) he placed his Oresteian hero in a modern country house, but, as he acknowledged in *Poetry and Drama* (1950), he failed to integrate the ritualism of his chorus with the realism of his setting. In his last three plays he discarded the chorus and moved ever closer to a patterned naturalism. *The Cocktail Party* (1949) has obvious affinities with the modern comedy of manners and takes place in a drawing-room and a psychiatrist's consulting-room, but it owes more to Euripides' *Alcestis* in its concern with spiritual guardianship, altruism, and self-sacrifice. In *The Confidential Clerk* (1953), the coincidences and dénouements of a farcical plot reminiscent of Wilde are uneasily related to the spiritual development of the hero. *The Elder Statesman* (1958) resembles Ibsen's *Ghosts* in its tight structure and probing of guilty secrets, though the serenity which its hero achieves by confessing his sins to his daughter makes clear its acknowledged connexions with Sophocles' *Oedipus at Colonus*. For all their limitations, however, these plays effectively demonstrated the dramatic potentialities of a line of variable length with three strong stresses divided by a caesura as an alternative to blank verse as a medium for poetic drama.

WILLIAM A. ARMSTRONG

ELIZABETHAN STAGE SOCIETY, see POEL, WILLIAM.

ELIZABETHAN THEATRE TRUST, see AUSTRALIA.

ELLIOTT, GEORGE HENRY (1884–1962), a music-hall comedian, known as the Chocolate-Coloured Coon. Born in England, he was taken young to America, where he appeared as a child in straight plays. Later he joined a Minstrel troupe, but returned to England and toured the music-halls. His first appearance in London was at Sadler's Wells in 1902. A fine singer and dancer, and an excellent pantomime performer, he was the successor of Eugene Stratton. Until his death he continued to work, being particularly admired for his soft-shoe dancing. One of his best-known songs was 'I Used to Sigh for the Silvery Moon'. He was twice married, first to a singer, Emily Hayes, and in 1943 to a variety artiste, Florence May Street.

ELLIOTT. (1) MAXINE (1868–1940), an American actress, and a woman of great personal charm and beauty. Born in Rockland, Maine, the daughter of a sea-captain, her real name was Jessie Dermot. She made her début on the stage in *The Middleman*, with E. S. Willard, adopting her stage name at the suggestion of Dion Boucicault. From Willard's company she went to that of Rose Coghlan, playing, among other parts, Dora in *Diplomacy*. In 1895 she became a member of Augustin Daly's company, appearing in his Shakespearian and other productions, both in London and New York. Some years later she married the comedian, Nat Goodwin, with whom she toured Australia, and appeared with him in a number of plays by Clyde Fitch. It was in the latter's *Her Own Way* that she made her first independent starring venture in 1903, following it by *Her Great Match* (1905). In 1908 she built and managed her own theatre in New York (see MAXINE ELLIOTT THEATRE). A personal friend of Edward VII, she was extremely popular in England, and retired there shortly before the First World War. During the war she was active in war-work both in England and Belgium, for which she received official recognition. In 1920, impoverished by her relief work for Belgium, she returned to the films and stage, and was once again one of the best-loved stars of the American theatre. One of her first appearances was with William Faversham in a revival of *Lord and Lady Algy*. She was later able to retire definitively, and spent the rest of her life in England and France. Her sister, (2) MAY GERTRUDE (1874–1950), made her first appearance in 1894 in Rose Coghlan's company at Saratoga in *A Woman of No Importance*. She appeared in New York at the Star Theatre in the same year, and was engaged by Nat Goodwin for his company; she appeared at the Duke of York's Theatre in London in 1899, as Midge in *The Cowboy and the Lady*, supporting her sister. In 1900 she was engaged by Forbes-Robertson, with whom she went on tour, marrying him at the end of the year. She appeared subsequently as her husband's leading lady, toured with him in America, Canada, and the English provinces, and was with him during his farewell season at Drury Lane in 1913. After her husband's retirement she appeared in London under her own management, and undertook extensive tours of South Africa, Australia, and New Zealand. She was not seen in New York after the First World War until 1936, when she played the Queen in Leslie Howard's production of *Hamlet* at the Imperial Theatre. (For her husband and daughter, see FORBES-ROBERTSON.)

ELLISTON, ROBERT WILLIAM (1774–1831), English actor, who was intended for the Church, but, after a taste of amateur theatricals, left home in 1791 and went to Bath, playing there and on the York circuit. At some point he was reconciled with his family, met Kemble, who encouraged him in his ambitions, and eloped with a teacher of dancing, making his London début in 1796 at the Haymarket under Colman while still retaining his position as leading man at Bath under Dimond. Dibdin wrote a number of entertainments for him, and he was frequently seen at Drury Lane, being one of the most popular actors of the day. Leigh Hunt placed him second only to Garrick in tragedy, and accounted him one of the best lovers on the stage. He was also good as Doricourt, Charles Surface, Ranger, Hamlet, Romeo, and Hotspur, and one of his greatest parts in later life was Falstaff. He was an eccentric and extravagant man, much given to drink, of whose odd behaviour many entertaining stories are told, and he had a passion for management. After trying unsuccessfully to open a theatre in Oxford, he took over innumerable provincial theatres, and in 1809 became lessee of the Surrey, London. Ten years later he achieved his ambition of managing Drury Lane. He opened with Kean in *King Lear*, put on Byron's *Marino Faliero* (1821) in the face of much opposition, and engaged Clarkson Stanfield and David Roberts, whose work gave the theatre a great reputation for scenery. He also surrounded himself with a fine company, and engaged Kean both before and after his visit to America. His resources could not, however, stand up to his extravagances and his outside speculations, and in 1826 he went bankrupt. A year later he re-instated himself with the production at the Surrey of *Black-Eyed Susan*, starring T. P. Cooke, an immediate success which netted him a large sum. His last appearance on the stage was made about a fortnight before his death. All contemporary critics were loud in his praise. He had a fine voice, noble face, and gallant bearing, and was unrivalled as gentlemanly rakes and agreeable rattles. A brilliant, fascinating personality, of whom Lamb said: 'Wherever Elliston walked, sat, or stood still, there was the theatre.'

ELTINGE, Julian [really William Dalton] (1883–1941), American actor, chiefly known as a female impersonator. At the age of 10 he played a female role in a school play in Boston, and his first professional appearance, in *Mr. Wix of Wickham* (1904), was also as a woman. Five years in vaudeville as a female impersonator followed, during which he toured Europe and the United States. In 1911 he acted a difficult dual role (Mrs. Monte and Hal Blake) in a play written for him, *The Fascinating Widow* (Liberty Theatre, New York), with which he toured until 1914. A series of successful plays followed, as well as several films, until he went into virtual retirement in 1930. In 1940 he returned briefly to the stage and to night-club work. His impersonations were an extraordinarily accurate reproduction of the walk and mannerisms of a beautiful young woman; extreme fidelity to detail and a rigorous avoidance of anything in poor taste were the bases of his art. In 1910 he and his partners built the Julian Eltinge Theatre on 42nd Street, New York, which opened on 11 Sept. 1912 with a melodrama, *Within the Law*, sponsored by the American Play Company. It ran for 541 performances, and established Jane Cowl as a star. The theatre housed a number of interesting straight plays, as well as farces, before, in 1930, it became a home of burlesque, notorious for the daring and vulgarity of its strip-tease acts and its dubious jokes. It was closed in 1942 and later became a cinema.

ROBERT TRACY

ELTON, Edward William (1794–1843), English actor, whose real name was Elt. His father, a schoolmaster, was interested in acting and staged several productions by his pupils, in some of which young Elt appeared. This gave him a taste for the stage, and in a short time he had changed his name to Elton and joined a company of strolling players. In 1823 he was seen at the Olympic, but it was not until he had been brought back to London from the provinces by Charles Mayne Young that he really established himself. At the Garrick Theatre in Whitechapel under Conquest he played Richard III, and was seen at several minor theatres before in 1837 he made an outstanding success in the name-part of *Walter Tyrrell* at Covent Garden. He was the original Beauséant in *The Lady of Lyons* (1838), and from 1841 to 1842 was at Drury Lane under Macready, playing Romeo, Rolla, and Rizzio. He then went to Ireland, and on his way back was drowned in the wreck of the *Pegasus*, leaving seven small children for whom a benefit was later given at the Haymarket. Elton, who was excellent as Edgar in *King Lear* and in the plays of Sheridan Knowles, also wrote a little and lectured on the theatre.

ELVIN, Joe (1862–1935), the son of an old actor named Matthew Keegan. He specialized in music-hall sketches, some of which, like *'Appy 'Ampstead*, were most spectacular. He was a quaint, eccentric comedian, with a white face and red wig, whose uncouth antics, in his constant stage battles with misfortune, made him extremely popular. He did much for his profession, and was a man of great integrity and goodness of heart. First President of the Variety Artistes' Benevolent Fund, he gave £300 towards the purchase of a home for old music-hall performers at Brinsmead, and was one of the founders of the music-hall institution, the Grand Order of Water Rats. In later years he was himself in need of assistance, and on the fiftieth anniversary of his début a matinée was organized for his benefit which resulted in an annuity of £5 a week.

EMBASSY THEATRE, London, at Hampstead. This opened as a try-out theatre for new plays on 11 Sept. 1928, with *The Yellow Streak*, under the management of Herbert Jay and Sybil Arundale. From 1930 to 1932 Alec. L. Rea ran it as a repertory theatre. It sent many successful plays to the West End, including *The Dominant Sex* and *Ten Minute Alibi*. It was damaged by enemy action during the Second World War, but was repaired and reopened, and did good work under the management of Anthony Hawtrey. After his death in 1955 it closed, and two years later was taken over by the Central School of Speech and Drama.

EMERY. (1) John (1777–1822), English actor, son of Mackle Emery (1740–1825), himself a competent player, whose wife (*c.* 1755–1827) took small parts at Covent Garden. Even as a youngster John had a remarkable faculty for portraying old men, and at 15 was considered by Tate Wilkinson to be already an outstanding actor. In 1798 he was engaged for Covent Garden to take the place of the comedian Quick, and played every sort of stage countryman, making good use of his knowledge of the Yorkshire dialect, and of 'the loutish cunning of the three Ridings'. After a short engagement at the Haymarket, he returned to Covent Garden and remained there until his sudden death. Hazlitt said of him: 'In his line of rustic characters he is a perfect actor. His Hodge is an absolute reality . . . his Robert Tyke the sublime of tragedy in low life.' His Caliban was highly praised, and he was good as Sir Toby, the First Gravedigger, and Dogberry. He was also an artist, and between 1801–17 exhibited frequently at the Royal Academy. His son (2) Samuel Anderson (1817–81), inherited much of his father's talent. After some years in the provinces, he was at the Lyceum with the

Keeleys, where he was the first to play Jonas in *Martin Chuzzlewit*, Will Fern in *The Chimes*, and John Peerybingle in *The Cricket on the Hearth*. In 1853 he went to the Olympic, and in the following year became lessee of the Marylebone Theatre, making his last appearance in London in 1878. He was good as Sir Peter Teazle and Robert Macaire, and in many new plays of the period.

His daughter, (3) (ISABEL) WINIFRED (1862–1924), began her long and distinguished career in 1870 in Liverpool, when she appeared as the child Geraldine in *Green Bushes*. Four years later she was in London in pantomime, at the Princess's, and made her début as an adult actress at the Imperial in 1879. She appeared with Wilson Barrett, Hare, and Irving—with whom she went to America—and in 1888 married Cyril Maude, becoming his leading lady when he went into management at the Haymarket in 1896. A beautiful woman of great charm, Winifred Emery adorned every part she played, and was one of the most versatile and popular actresses of her generation. Among her best parts were Lady Windermere in Wilde's comedy and Lady Babbie in *The Little Minister* (see also MAUDE, CYRIL). W. MACQUEEN-POPE†

EMNEY. (1) FRED (1865–1917), English actor, who, after many years in light opera and musical comedy, toured the music-halls with the famous sketches *A Sister to Assist 'er* (with Sydney Fairbrother), *Getting Over a Stile*, and the riotous *Plumbers*. He also appeared in many Drury Lane pantomimes, and was the supreme exponent of the 'Dame'. He died of injuries received on the stage in *Cinderella* when he slipped on the soap-suds in a knock-about comedy scene. His son (2) FRED (1900–), starting on the halls with a partner and a piano (he is a fine pianist), made for himself a definite place as a leading comedian on the musical comedy stage and in revue. His heavyweight personality, his imperturbable face and manner, his eyeglass and his eternal cigar, make up an unforgettable character—and his comic powers equal those of his father.

W. MACQUEEN-POPE†

EMPIRE, LONDON, in Leicester Square, a famous music-hall, originally a theatre which opened on 17 Apr. 1884. It had no success until Hollingshead brought his Gaiety company there in a burlesque entitled *The Forty Thieves*. Later productions were *Round the World in Eighty Days* and *The Palace of Pearl* (1886). It then became a music-hall, and was soon famous as a home of ballet. Katti Lanner was its ballet-mistress, and its leading dancers were Adeline Genée, Lydia Kyasht, and Phyllis Bedells. A famous male dancer who appeared there was Fred Farren, a master of mime, whose sensational apache dance thrilled London audiences. One of the great features of the Empire was its promenade, which was attacked as a haunt of vice by Mrs. Ormiston Chant in her Purity Campaign in 1894. Revues were staged at the Empire shortly before the First World War and in 1918 it became a theatre again with *The Lilac Domino*. *Irene* followed in 1920. Later successes were *Henry VIII* (1925) with Sybil Thorndike as Queen Katharine, and *Lady, Be Good!* (1926), a musical comedy with music by Gershwin. A year later the Empire was demolished and a cinema built on the site.

EMPIRE THEATRE, NEW YORK, a handsome edifice with a rococo red and gold interior. It was for many years New York's oldest surviving playhouse. Built for Charles Frohman, it opened on 25 Jan. 1893 with *The Girl I Left Behind Me*, which ran for 288 performances. This was followed by *Liberty Hall*, in which Viola Allen, Henry Miller, and May Robson, names always associated with this theatre, all appeared. During the next few years the theatre built up a reputation for sophisticated comedy, with occasional incursions into sentiment and whimsy. Three permanent companies shared it, the Empire stock, the John Drew, and the Maude Adams, while in the summer the theatre was let to travelling companies. Few outstanding plays were presented at the Empire during its first thirty years, but whatever came was sure of an adequate run. They were mainly by Henry Arthur Jones, Haddon Chambers, or Paul M. Potter. In 1899 Maude Adams appeared as Juliet to Faversham's Romeo, and in the same year John Drew scored a great personal success in *Richard Carvel*. One of the most popular plays ever seen at the Empire was *When Knighthood was in Flower*, with Julia Marlowe, while 1905 brought Maude Adams in *Peter Pan*. *Captain Brassbound's Conversion* was seen in 1907 with Ellen Terry, for whom it was written, followed by *The Good Hope*, in which Edith Craig and Beatrice Forbes-Robertson also appeared. Ethel Barrymore was seen at this theatre in *Mid-Channel* (1910) and *Déclassée* (1919). Further interesting productions were *Mary Rose* with Ruth Chatterton, *Blood and Sand* with Otis Skinner and his daughter, and Doris Keane in *The Czarina*. It was in 1923 that a name frequently associated with the Empire first appeared on its bills—Katharine Cornell, who was seen there later in *The Age of Innocence*, *The Barretts of Wimpole Street*, and *Candida*. Judith Anderson in *The Dove* (1924) and Jane Cowl in *Easy Virtue* (1925) also made their names at this theatre, which in 1926 found itself in trouble over *The Captive*, a translation of Édouard Bourdet's *La Prisonnière*. Although seriously designed and intended, and graced by a superb performance by Helen Menken, this was considered disturbing in its implications, and was closed by the authorities. Two important productions of later years were the socially significant *We The People* (1933), with settings by Aline Bernstein, and a startling revival of *Ghosts*, with sets by Stewart Chaney and fine performances by Nazimova and Harry Ellerbe. One of the outstanding events in the life of this theatre was its first *Hamlet*, in 1936, with John

Gielgud, Lillian Gish, Judith Anderson, and Malcolm Keen. The play was directed by Guthrie McClintic, and its 132 performances broke the records set up by Booth and Barrymore. On 8 Nov. 1939 came the first night of the record-breaking *Life With Father*, which occupied the theatre for six years. On its removal to the Bijou, the Empire saw the Lunts in Rattigan's *O Mistress Mine* (done in London as *Love in Idleness*). It was demolished in 1953. The last full-scale production there was *The Time of the Cuckoo*, by Arthur Laurents, with Shirley Booth. This closed on 30 May 1953. The previous Sunday evening a memorial programme, *High Lights of the Empire*, was presented by the American National Theatre and Academy with Cornelia Otis Skinner as compère. GEORGE FREEDLEY†

ENCINA, JUAN DEL (*c.*1468–*c.* 1537), known as the 'patriarch of the Spanish theatre'. With his later contemporaries Naharro and Vicente, he was the founder of Spanish drama, which he helped to secularize. Little is known of his life, though he was in Italy in the early part of the sixteenth century, and was at one time a chorister in the chapel of Pope Leo X. His *églogas*, or pastoral dialogues between shepherds and shepherdesses, are based on Christmas, Easter, and biblical themes, and, though they contain vivid scenes of daily life, with characters speaking a rustic dialect, they were intended for performance at Court and in the private houses of the nobility, not for the people, who still found their amusement in the spectacles provided by the clergy, either in the church or the market-place. Encina's plays may originally have been given by talented amateurs of high rank or by their servants, but they were also the first serious plays to be acted by the professional actors of the strolling companies which were by now beginning to travel the countryside. Apart from religious dramas, reminiscent of the medieval Mystery and Morality plays, Encina also wrote on mythological subjects. One of these plays, probably the *Égloga de Plácida y Vitoriano*, was given in Italy in 1513 before a brilliant audience which included the Spanish ambassador. In all his plays Encina introduced *villancicos* or rustic songs, and his work in general owed much to his musical talent.

ENFANTS SANS SOUCI, see FRANCE, 1.

ENGLAND. 1. MEDIEVAL. If English drama, like that of other European countries, may be said to have originated in the dramatic presentation of certain elements in the Church service (see LITURGICAL DRAMA), it had little freedom for growth in such a soil, and was cultivated only for its usefulness in strengthening the faith of humble worshippers. The priest, after all, was bound to handle his material in much the same spirit as a scholar deals with his sources; he was not really free to invent, to draw upon his imagination, or to depart very far from the words of scripture. The opportunities for acting were limited, and while the liturgical play remained within the church and the words spoken were not English but Latin there was no chance of humanizing the biblical story by means of humour or of idiomatic and colloquial expression. The real opportunity came when the plays passed out of the hands of the priests into those of the people. The change was gradual: from the church to the churchyard, and later, when the crowds became too large, to the market-place. Once in the market-place the plays were no longer under the direct control of the Church, and the process of secularization could begin. (The clergy were forbidden by a papal edict of 1210 to appear on a public stage.) Without losing their religious significance the plays, in which the priestly Latin had been replaced by the vernacular, now began to reflect the purely secular interests of medieval folk, and were often vitalized by a broad humour in which it would have been indecorous for priests to participate.

In the well-ordered life of the Middle Ages it would have been surprising if the religious plays, after leaving the Church, had not come under the control of some other authority. In fact they were taken over by the Trade Guilds of the various towns all over England, and as far north as Aberdeen in Scotland. They became linked, too, to one particular day in the Church calendar: in 1311 the Council of Vienne had ordained that Corpus Christi Day, on the Thursday after Trinity Sunday, should be strictly observed as a feast day, and it was accordingly with Corpus Christi Day (one of the longest days in the year, when the weather was most likely to be fine) that the religious plays became associated. Starting about sunrise, performances continued till sunset. These plays have been variously referred to in the past as Miracle and Mystery plays; they are best described (a modern scholar has suggested) as 'Bible-histories', since they invariably deal with some part of the Bible story. Plays based on the lives of saints were also written and performed, but they can be left out of account here, since only one seems to have survived (on St. Mary Magdalene in the Digby Mysteries). Of Bible-history plays, on the other hand, we possess five collections (or 'cycles'): the York (with 48 pieces), the Chester (25), the Towneley (32), the Coventry (42), and the Digby. The Towneley plays are so named because the manuscript in which they are preserved was for long in the possession of the Towneley family; the plays themselves probably belong to the Wakefield (Yorks.) cycle. The Coventry plays may be wrongly designated: they appear on linguistic grounds to belong to some town in the north-east Midlands, though a Latin inscription on the fly-leaf assigns them to Coventry.

These guild plays were at their height from about 1300 to 1450. In an important town such as York each of the larger guilds made itself responsible for the performance of one play; the smaller guilds would combine their resources in groups of anything up to half a dozen. The plays were performed on pageants, that is, large timber structures on four wheels that could be drawn through the streets from one place to another, so that spectators gathered at different points in the town had a chance of seeing many different plays during the course of the day (for an example of a pageant stage, see No. 19). The often-quoted account of Archdeacon Rogers, describing a performance in Chester as late as 1594, will clear up some obscurities:

Every company had his pagiant or parte, which pagiants weare a high scafolde with two rowmes, a higher and a lower, upon four wheeles. In the lower they apparelled themselves, and in the higher rowme they played, being all open on the tope, that all behoulders mighte heare and see them. The places where they played them was in every streete. They begane first at the abay gates, and when the firste pagiante was played it was wheeled to the highe crosse before the mayor, and so to every streete: and so every streete had a pagiant playing before them at one time, till all the pagiantes for the day appointed weare played.

It will be realized that considerable organization was required to get through the day's programme on time. Discipline was maintained by the guilds, and we hear of players being fined for not having memorized their parts satisfactorily. Details from the accounts of expenses incurred show that costume ('God's coat of white leather'; 'jackets of black buckram with nails and dice upon them for the Tormentors') and stage properties ('The cross with a rope to draw it up, and a curtain hanging before it') formed an important part of the dramatic appeal. Actors were paid, and so too was the author of the 'book'.

The Chester plays dealing with Noah's Flood and the Sacrifice of Isaac are good early examples of the humour and pathos which the medieval playwright had always at his command. The Towneley *Secunda Pastorum*, dealing with the three shepherds at the Nativity, develops into the delightful comedy of Mak the sheep-stealer and his wife. The process of secularization is here almost complete.

2. TUDOR. Side by side with the Bible-history plays there developed another form of religious drama, the Morality play, which appears to date from the late fourteenth century. In this the characters are for the most part personified virtues and vices, such as Ignorance, Humility, Covetousness, Good Deeds, Riot, and so on, and these (sometimes with the aid of Good Angel and Bad Angel) are shown characteristically as contending for the soul of Man (variously referred to as Mankind, Humanum Genus, Everyman). Here, in however wooden a fashion, we have a dramatic action: a struggle between irreconcilable adversaries, a human soul wavering in the balance, a choice to be made between two lines of conduct, a climax to be reached when the decision is at last taken. To the medieval spectator, delighting in allegory and familiar with personification, the Morality plays offered an intellectual entertainment to which the twentieth-century reader is probably slow to respond. Some of them, such as the anonymous *Castell of Perseverance* and Skelton's *Magnyfycence* (both of considerable length), are indeed heavy going; but the well-known *Everyman* (an English version of a Dutch original) is far more interesting and moving than any summary of its simple action would be likely to suggest. The fact is that in spite of the personified abstractions the Morality play at its best contains many touches of human nature; the abstractions (as in Bunyan's *The Pilgrim's Progress*) come to life, and we find that we are listening not to Poverty or Sensual Appetite, but to Englishmen of the fifteenth and sixteenth centuries. The deep seriousness of the issue involved, too, can hardly fail to impress anyone whose religious instincts are not atrophied. As we might expect, the vices rather than the virtues provide the most lively examples of character-drawing. In *Hickscorner* (*temp.* Henry VIII) Freewill and Imagination are two rollicking and shameless characters, coarse and vigorous, speaking in the idiom of the early sixteenth century. By 1550 the Morality play had developed so far that we get a play such as *Nice Wanton* (on the theme of 'Spare the rod and spoil the child'), in which some of the characters are still abstractions and others have become fully individualized.

A very faint line divides the Morality play from the Moral Interlude; and if any distinction may properly be made it is that the Moral Interlude introduces more mirth than the Morality play proper. The *Interlude of Youth* and *Lusty Juventus* may be cited as examples. The latter (*c.* 1550) has a further interest: it was an anti-Catholic play. There are several other extant Morality plays which were written to propagate either Protestant or (as in *Respublica*, 1553) Catholic views.

If the distinction between Morality plays and Moral Interludes is almost imperceptible, that between Morality plays and Interludes is easier to define. The precise significance of the term 'interlude' has long been in dispute; it may indicate, as the word suggests, a play given in the pauses between other entertainments during a banquet. At all events a distinct genre of dramatic entertainment was produced in the late fifteenth and early sixteenth centuries to which the term is usually applied: this was a development of the Morality play in which the matter treated is of intellectual rather than moral interest, and so reflects the new stirring of thought among the English humanists of the Renaissance. Several writers of these Interludes are known to us. John Rastell, who had a little theatre built in the grounds of his house and possessed a stock of players' costumes, wrote an Interlude called *The Four Elements*, in which he sought to impart both learning and entertainment in dramatic form. John Redford's *Wit and Science* follows the same lines. The liveliest writer of Interludes was undoubtedly John Heywood (?–1580). His best-known work, *The Four PP.*, a dialogue between a Palmer, Pardoner, Poticary, and Pedlar, turning on the question of which can tell the greatest lie, and his *Play of the Wether* (in which various people with contending interests pray to Jove for the weather they would like) are designed more for pure entertainment than instruction. Heywood's Interludes have few purely dramatic qualities, but they do at least progress to a climax or conclusion, and the dialogue is animated and natural. Rather earlier than any of these last-mentioned writers is Henry Medwall, whose *Fulgens and Lucrece* (*c.* 1500) came to light in 1919 in a London sale-room. This odd and, for its time, remarkable play has been dated by its editors 1497; it is an example of the purely secular drama at a date considerably earlier than anything hitherto known. For this Interlude, performed in two parts as an entertainment at a banquet, Medwall dramatized the story of Lucretia, a Roman lady, who was wooed by two very different suitors, an idle patrician and a virtuous young man of humble birth. To this story he added a comic sub-plot, involving two servants and Lucretia's maid. Medwall's play, in fact, foreshadows that mixture of a serious with a comic plot which was to be a feature of Elizabethan romantic comedy.

From what has been said it will be seen that the Interludes were written for a more educated audience than the plays performed by the Trade Guilds. Heywood's little plays were all written for performance at Court. The Morality plays, too, were probably acted for the most part in the halls or gardens of noblemen's houses, though there is evidence that they were also performed by professional actors in country towns. By the early years of the sixteenth century there was a considerable number of companies of players in the service of the Court or of the great noblemen: in the account books of Thomas Cromwell (*c.* 1530) we read of the King's players, the Queen's, the Lord Chamberlain's, the Marquis of Exeter's, the Lord Cobham's, and several others. A generation earlier Cardinal Morton had his company of players, and we learn that young Thomas More would sometimes 'slip in among the players' and 'make a part of his own' *ex tempore.* Under the Tudors, bands of actors who were not the servants of some nobleman were looked upon as 'rogues and vagabonds', and subject to severe penalties when found performing plays. These restrictions were still in force in Shakespeare's time; the company of which he was a member came under the protection of the Lord Chamberlain in 1594, and in 1603 was reconstituted as the King's Men.

3. ELIZABETHAN. The development of the drama in the early years of Queen Elizabeth's reign has to be pieced together from such imperfect evidence as still remains. Not many plays found their way into print, and of those that did by no means all have survived. The influence of classical comedy had begun to appear in Nicholas Udall's *Ralph Roister Doister*. Written between 1534 and 1552, this was probably intended for performance by schoolboys. So, too, was *Jacke Jugeler*, described on the title-page as 'A new Enterlude for Chyldren to playe', and derived from the first scene of Plautus's *Amphitruo.* The classical influence appears at second hand in Gascoigne's *Supposes*, acted at Gray's Inn in 1566; this play was based on Ariosto's *I Suppositi*, which in turn was derived from the *Captivi* of Plautus. *Gammer Gurton's Needle* (*c.* 1560) is an entirely English farce, though the author (his identity is uncertain) has learnt something of plot construction from classical comedy. Writers of academic tragedy were also turning to classical models, though not to the tragedy of ancient Greece, at this time almost unknown in England, but to the Latin tragedies (written to be read or recited rather than acted) of Seneca. In *Gorboduc*, first acted in 1562 in the presence of Queen Elizabeth by members of the Inner Temple, Thomas Norton and Thomas Sackville produced what is by common consent the first English tragedy; a five-act drama in blank verse, it has many features of the Senecan play. These 'classical' plays, it will be noticed, were for the most part performed in the Inns of Court before an audience of lawyers and their friends, or in schools and universities; in no sense were they popular. For popular drama we must go rather to such tragicomedies as the *Cambyses* (*c.* 1570) of Thomas Preston. This 'lamentable tragedie, mixed full of plesant mirth' is the sort of play that the classically minded Sidney objected to in his *Defence of Poesie*; it was 'neither right tragedy, nor right comedy, mingling kings and clowns'. Equally objectionable in Sidney's eyes was another popular type of play, the chronicle history. As early as 1538 John Bale had written *Kynge Johan*, a kind of cross between the Morality and the history play; and in the second half of the sixteenth century many more plays loosely dramatizing the reigns of English kings were written and produced. Shakespeare's Histories, while still dramatizing a series of historical events which may stretch over a number of years, are much more artistically constructed; the events are knit together into a genuine plot, and though the hero is still apt to tower in importance above the other characters he is not (as in the old chronicle histories) the sole means of giving the play unity.

The sudden leap forward which English drama made in the last two decades of the sixteenth century is phenomenal; perhaps the nearest parallel to it is the advance made by the cinema between 1910 and 1930. Right up to the time of Marlowe and Kyd the English drama, for all its earnestness and animal vigour, had shown little sign of growing up; there is much that is not fully adult about such a play as *Cambyses*, much that is naïve, and home-made, and hopelessly awkward. The crudeness is partly due to the metrical form (the 'jigging veins of rhyming mother wits'), which in itself makes any real dignity of expression almost impossible, but partly also to the jerkiness of the dramatic movement, the spineless plot, and the rapid and haphazard alternation between tragedy (or, more precisely, bloodshed) and farcical comedy. Of *Gorboduc*, it is true, such complaints cannot be made. But though *Gorboduc* is indeed adult, we may perhaps be excused for feeling that it was born old. There is dignity in its stiff, unyielding blank verse, in its grave, sententious speeches, in its coherent plot; but it is the dignity of a marble monument. The characters are wholly without interest, and the dialogue has not the accent of living speech.

It was, however, from those two oddly assorted parents—the crude popular tragedy like *Cambyses*, and the academic tragedy like *Gorboduc*—that the tragedy of Christopher Marlowe (1564–93) sprang. It might be enough to account for the great gap that lies between *Tamburlaine* and those earlier plays by saying that Marlowe was a great poet and dramatist, while his predecessors were only well-meaning purveyors of entertainment. But though this is true enough, it is not quite the whole truth. The great advance made by Marlowe had been rendered easier by what is certainly not a comparable, yet none the less a real, advance in the physical conditions under which plays were performed. The first regular London playhouse, the Theatre, had been built by James Burbage in 1576. It was erected in Shoreditch, outside the jurisdiction of the City magistrates; and it was in this neighbourhood or on the Bankside, south of the Thames, that the sixteenth-century London theatres were built. For various reasons, but chiefly because they regarded them as detrimental to public morality, the civic authorities, among whom the Puritan element was strongly represented, were hostile to the theatres. By 1587—the year in which *Tamburlaine* was first performed—two other houses, the Curtain and the Rose, had been built, and by 1600 their number had been increased by the Swan (see No. 22), the Globe, and the Fortune. All of these were open to the air, unlighted, and unheated. Up to this time the players had been forced to play wherever they could find a pitch, most commonly in the yards of inns. Among London inns the Red Lion in Stepney, the Bell and the Cross Keys, both in Gracechurch Street, the Bull in Bishopsgate Street, and the Bel Savage on Ludgate Hill were all being used for the performance of plays before Burbage built his theatre. An inn-yard, after all, is a kind of natural theatre, enclosed on all sides and therefore reasonably quiet, with room for a platform or 'scaffold' round which the spectators can group themselves, and with more comfortable accommodation for the better-class auditors at windows and balconies overlooking the courtyard. If any plays came to Stratford when Shakespeare was a boy it was probably in such surroundings that he saw them acted. Those surroundings were good enough in their way, but they were undeniably crude. No doubt great drama does not depend on the existence of luxuriously equipped theatres, but to put the issue so is beside the point. There was no question of luxury here; the English drama was contending with primitive staging and makeshift accommodation which almost necessarily retarded its growth and kept it on an amateur footing. Now at last buildings specially adapted for the performance of plays were being erected, though with their platform stage and seating arrangements they reproduced the main features of the inn-yard. A regular play-going public was already in being and steadily increasing in numbers, a public that no longer looked on a play as a rare event but that could, and did, attend the theatre frequently. With the growth of this public (at once metropolitan and sophisticated) the dramatist had not merely a less casual audience; he had one that was more experienced and more critical, for whose entertainment it was worth exerting himself seriously, and who could respond by appreciating his fine things. Marlowe and Kyd certainly gave much to the English theatre, but the influence was reciprocal: a new audience (which could hardly be said to have existed in the 1560s) called forth their powers and encouraged them to do still better. Almost certainly, too, this audience exercised a similar influence on the acting and producing of plays; it expected more, and got it.

Tamburlaine is a real landmark. With the sound of Marlowe's blank verse in their ears—that 'great and thundering speech'—the Elizabethans could never again be content with the homelier rhythms of the earlier drama. There was, too, a grandeur in Marlowe's Scythian warrior, a feeling of inevitability in his triumphant progress, a sense of vastness in the events and their setting, that gave the English drama a new importance. No less significant than the confidence of Tamburlaine is the confidence of Marlowe himself: the fumbling and uncertain workmanship that gave the older drama the atmosphere of amateur theatricals has almost entirely disappeared; the professional writer has arrived, perfectly sure of himself, and making the effects that he intended to make. In *Dr. Faustus* (1589–92) Marlowe found an even finer tragic theme; and in *Edward II* (*c.* 1592) he revealed a hitherto unsuspected interest in character, and also showed his ability to handle a more intricate plot.

Thomas Kyd (1558–94) was not, like Marlowe, a thinker, but he was a born playwright. In *The Spanish Tragedy* (*c.* 1585–9; the date is uncertain), he adopted and popularized some of the main features of the Senecan play, and with this full-blooded drama, with its revenge motive, its ghost, its murders, and its madness, he not only delighted the Elizabethans but gave to later dramatists a successful prototype for the Revenge play.

What Marlowe did for tragedy, John Lyly (*c.* 1554–1606) did in some degree for comedy. For doggerel verse he substituted a delicate and sensitive prose, and for rollicking humour a refined wit and fantasy. His plays, which were performed by the Children of the Chapel Royal and the Children of Paul's between 1584 and

1595, are a unique blending of the classical and the Elizabethan, the fantastic and the real; we get the impression that we are listening to an echo coming back from life rather than looking on at life itself. Lyly's world is oddly Arcadian; his characters have almost the remoteness of fairies, whose movements may delight us but whose concerns do not touch us. He left no direct descendants; but he taught his successors the value for comedy of wit and repartee, and of disguise and mistaken identity for complicating a plot. Above all, he refined comedy, and showed the possibility of combining humour with sentiment, the witty with the romantic. In *The Old Wives' Tale* (*c.* 1590) of George Peele (*c.* 1558–*c.* 1597) we meet again with fantasy and humour, and something of the same effect reappears later in the *Old Fortunatus* of Thomas Dekker (*c.* 1572–*c.* 1632). In *Friar Bacon and Friar Bungay* (*c.* 1589) by Robert Greene (*c.* 1560–92) we have a prototype of that romantic comedy which Shakespeare was to make peculiarly his own. In Greene's play an upper-class world of refinement and a lower-class world of comedy alternate and occasionally mingle, the scene shifting between Court and countryside. Into this fabric Greene also weaves magic, poetry, and a romantic love story.

When, therefore, William Shakespeare (1564–1616) began writing for the stage about 1590, he found several types of drama already firmly established. In *Titus Andronicus* (*c.* 1594) he offered his own version (still crude) of the Revenge play, and recurred in his maturity to this genre in *Hamlet* (1601). The influence of Marlowe can be seen in *Richard III* (*c.* 1593), whose hero is a superman of the Machiavellian kind, and in *Richard II* (*c.* 1595), which has some resemblance to *Edward II*. Lyly's influence can be traced in Shakespeare's nimble-witted young women, often wandering about disguised as boys, and in his fondness for word-play. Shakespeare's history plays, as we have seen, are a development of the old rambling chronicle history. Indeed, his vast contribution to English drama was made rather by example than by technical innovation. Time after time he showed what might be done with a form of drama which had hitherto yielded only moderate results. Towards the end of his career, in the group of plays which closed with *The Tempest* (1611), he was experimenting with a new kind of tragi-comedy in which the clouds of grief and misfortune which have gathered about the heads of an erring generation are dispersed by the mutual love and reconciliation of the next. This, then, may be Shakespeare's own special contribution to the dramatic 'kinds'; though even here we cannot be certain that he was not at his old practice of doing better what had already been attempted by others.

The theatre for which Shakespeare wrote was in the fullest sense a place of popular resort. The audience at the Globe about 1600 was a representative cross-section of the London population, with no important absentees except the growing body of Puritans, whose hostility to the theatres was made abundantly clear in sermons and pamphlets. No doubt, therefore, Shakespeare's audiences were a very mixed lot; but it is a common mistake to rate their intelligence too low, and to think too exclusively of the 'groundlings', whistling, cracking nuts, shouting, and caring only for blustering rhetoric and bawdy jokes. Recent research has tended to suggest that the Elizabethan playgoer was a trained listener, that a considerable part of the audience consisted of people of some education, and that if it was predominantly male there was nevertheless a considerable sprinkling of respectable women present, citizens' wives and the like. There is surprisingly little on record to suggest riots or disturbances of any kind at the Elizabethan theatre; indeed there is good evidence that the audience was normally attentive and well behaved, and in many ways more civilized than English audiences in the eighteenth and nineteenth centuries. The fact that plays were generally performed in the afternoon (and therefore in broad daylight) may have had something to do with this good behaviour; the play had not yet become the prelude to a night's debauchery. Prices, too, though relatively 'popular', were not particularly low when related to the average wages of the period, and no reasonable man will refuse to listen to a play that he has paid good money to hear, or permit his neighbours to ruin it by their interruptions.

For this mixed audience the Elizabethan dramatist had to cater as best he could, and the varied appeal of Elizabethan tragedy and comedy reflects the composition of the audience at the Globe and the Swan. Romance, realism, intellectual comedy, rough humour, bawdry, satire, horror, pathos, ghosts and fairies, kings and clowns, poetry, patriotic sentiment, social and political problems, fantasy, history, murder, love, brawling, melancholy gentlemen, and plain country wenches—all this and much more we meet in the drama of the period; in the same play curiously mixed (and, to all but the Elizabethan, incompatible) effects are constantly to be found. Clearly the Elizabethans retained some of that medieval facility for passing easily from one emotional state to another; they loved variety, they were not interested in decorum, or unity of action, or any of those classical restraints and decencies that a Sidney or a Jonson thought so important. They wanted plenty of action, too, but they also enjoyed rhetoric, and they could stand a good deal of poetry. Sometimes they got a play like *Othello*, in which the action moved steadily and consistently to a tragic climax; but next week they might get a play like *Antony and Cleopatra*, in which the interest was split up between world history and the passion of a man and a woman, in which Lepidus got drunk, and Cleopatra's ladies talked bawdry with a eunuch, Antony died upon his sword, and Cleopatra put the asp to her bosom. If one thinks only of the infinite variety of Cleopatra

—passionate, witty, dreaming romantically of the absent Antony, striking the messenger, rising at last to tragic grandeur, 'everything by starts and nothing long'—one has the very soul of the Elizabethan drama. It was a drama vibrating with action and passion, racing along in witty badinage or dawdling delightfully in scenes of slow and almost bovine humour: a brief abstract of life, heightened for the purposes of an afternoon's entertainment, and so (like life) very rarely all tragedy or all comedy, but a blending of both.

If Shakespeare may be said to have gone with the tide, Ben Jonson (1572–1637) spent much of his energy in swimming against it. In an age which cared little for dramatic rules and found it so easy to reconcile opposites, Jonson is rather a lonely figure. It was his aim in comedy to 'sport with human follies, not with crimes', but to sport with them in such a way as to render them contemptible. He set himself, therefore, to write a realistic comedy (with 'deeds and language such as men do use') in which he could expose and correct the follies of the day. In *The Alchemist* (1610), for instance, he lays bare greed and credulity in different walks of life: these are the particular 'humours' in this comedy on which he has chosen to concentrate his satire, and he shows their results in a series of highly effective scenes which culminate in the wholesale exposure of the last act. For all his realism Jonson has also a strain of fantasy and extravagance which occasionally lands him in absurdity; but his ingenious plotting, his clear characterization, and his conscientious craftsmanship are in striking contrast with the 'sluttish incoherence' of some of his less painstaking contemporaries.

By the end of the first decade of the new century certain changes began to make themselves felt. While Shakespeare's company still played at the Globe, they had also come into possession of another theatre at Blackfriars, considerably nearer to the Court. At the Blackfriars, which was roofed in, prices were higher; the atmosphere, too, was more intimate, and a quieter type of acting was possible. In time the roofed-in theatres (known to the Elizabethans as 'private' theatres) ousted the open-air or 'public' theatres altogether, and the decline of the latter coincides with a gradual change in the composition of the audience. In the Jacobean and Caroline period it becomes less representative of the middle classes, and the drama begins to reflect increasingly the tastes of the more sophisticated upper class. It was for this audience that Francis Beaumont (1584–1616) wrote *The Knight of the Burning Pestle* (1607), in which the citizen and his wife come in for good-humoured ridicule. For this audience, too, were written the tragicomedies in which he collaborated with John Fletcher (1579–1625), John Ford's (1586–1639) *'Tis Pity She's a Whore* (c. 1627), which turns on the incestuous love of a brother and sister, and James Shirley's (1596–1666) fashionable comedies of wit and intrigue. An air of gallantry creeps into the drama which was absent from the plays of Shakespeare and Jonson; the honest bawdiness of the Elizabethans is transformed into a more furtive indecency; the high argument and the ruthless facing of facts of Elizabethan tragedy—still to be met with in the work of Marston, Webster, Tourneur, and the early Middleton—give place to a shirking of tragic issues, or an excess of pathos, or the exploitation of unnatural vice. The dish has now to be more highly seasoned. In the work of Beaumont and Fletcher or of Philip Massinger (1583–1640) there is much ingenuity of construction and plenty of entertainment, but there is a new willingness to subordinate everything to excitement. Effects become theatrical rather than dramatic; character is sacrificed to plot, and plot is anything the dramatists care to make it. One ceases to anticipate the behaviour of characters when the only certainty is that they will do something unexpected. A typical example of the new drama is Beaumont and Fletcher's *Philaster* (1610), in which the hero rushes impetuously from one unpremeditated action to another, until in the end we care very little what happens to him. In Massinger's *Duke of Milan* (1620) there is more consistency of character and a more natural development of the action; yet here too the chief character seems to be an entirely different person in the second part of the play from what he was in the first.

The contemporaries of Shakespeare and Jonson—Chapman, Marston, Dekker, Massinger, Middleton, Webster, Tourneur, Heywood, Ford, Shirley, and the rest—are dealt with separately. Here it is sufficient to indicate some of the main types of drama which the age evolved. The Revenge play enjoyed a new lease of popularity in the early seventeenth century; the action was often set in Italy, which to the Elizabethans was the proper milieu for poisonings and stabbings and deeds of horror of all kinds. Among the finest plays of the period which turn on revenge or bloody deeds leading to retribution are Chapman's *Revenge of Bussy D'Ambois* (*c.* 1610), Webster's *The White Devil* (1612) and *The Duchess of Malfi* (1614), and Middleton's *The Changeling* (1622). Elizabethan and Jacobean tragedy concerned itself usually with the misfortunes of the great, but a minor genre in this period was Domestic tragedy, as seen in *Arden of Feversham* (*c.* 1591) and Heywood's *A Woman Killed with Kindness* (1603). Tragicomedy has already been noted as a form increasingly popular in the Jacobean period. The History play lost some of its popularity as the years passed; Ford's *Perkin Warbeck* (*c.* 1630) is an interesting late example. Romantic comedy continued with some modifications (e.g. with a strong infusion of middle-class manners in *The Shoemaker's Holiday* of Dekker) throughout the period, but some of the best comedy written by Jacobean dramatists comes nearer to the Jonsonian satirical kind, as Chapman's *All Fools* (*c.* 1604), Massinger's *A New Way to Pay Old Debts* (1625), and Middleton's *A Trick to Catch the Old One* (*c.* 1605). Some of the plays of Beaumont and Fletcher also belong to this kind, while others again are closer to the upper-class comedy of intrigue which Shirley was writing in the 1630s. Among minor genres the Pastoral play is represented by Fletcher's *The Faithful Shepherdess* (1608) and Jonson's *The Sad Shepherd* (*c.* 1637). Many plays, of course, fall outside any category, for the dramatists were fertile in invention and not browbeaten by critical canons. A word may be said, in conclusion, of the masques. These elaborate entertainments, performed at the Court of James I and Charles I by ladies and gentlemen for their own diversion, left their mark on the drama. There is, for instance, a masque in *The Tempest.* Apart from Milton's *Comus* (1634), written for performance at Ludlow Castle to celebrate the inauguration of the Earl of Bridgewater as Lord President of Wales, the highest achievement of the English masque was reached in the collaboration of Ben Jonson and Inigo Jones. The scenes and machines designed by Jones for performances at Court were often elaborate, and he introduced many innovations which ultimately affected the setting and production of stage plays (see ENGLISH PLAYHOUSE, SCENERY, and No. 61). Here William Davenant should be remembered, for Davenant, who had been associated with the production of masques for the Court of Charles I, was also the first to introduce scenery on the English stage. When the Civil War broke out in 1642 the drama was one of the first casualties. The London theatres, so long frowned upon by the Puritans, were closed by Act of Parliament, and dramatic performances practically ceased in England. Towards the end of the Commonwealth period, however, there was a partial relaxation of the ban, and Davenant, for instance, was permitted in 1656 to stage a musical play, *The Siege of Rhodes,* at Rutland House (see PURITAN INTERREGNUM).

4. RESTORATION. With the return of Charles II in 1660 the drama was quickly revived, but with a difference. It was no longer in any important sense a national drama. For the rest of the century the theatrical needs of Londoners were met by two playhouses and two companies of players, and even so the theatres often had difficulty in showing a profit. Less than three months after his return the King had issued patents to Thomas Killigrew (1612–83) and William Davenant (1606–68) enabling them to form two companies of players, and forbidding any other company to act in London. Killigrew was the first in the field: on 8 Nov. his company, the King's Players, opened at Gibbon's Tennis-Court in Clare Market, and in May 1663 he moved to the newly built Theatre Royal in Bridges Street—the site of the present Drury Lane Theatre. Davenant, who had taken the old Salisbury Court Theatre as a temporary house, moved with his actors (the Duke's Players) into his new theatre in Lincoln's Inn Fields in the summer of 1661. The most striking innovation since the closing of the theatres was the introduction of female actors in place of the former boy players; and several of them, such as Nell Gwynn, and, rather later, Mrs. Barry and Mrs. Bracegirdle, became celebrated either for their acting, or for less professional reasons, or for both. How well they must sometimes have acted may be seen from Colley Cibber's description in his *Apology* (1740) of Mrs. Mountfort playing the part of Melantha in Dryden's *Marriage à la Mode*: the whole scene lives before us, as it had lived in Cibber's memory for fifty years. Of the men the finest actor (and one of the great English actors) was Thomas Betterton (? 1635–1710), who also exercised a steadying influence on the theatre. Considerable advances were made at this time in scenic effects and stage machines, and the old Elizabethan platform stage was being gradually modified to a less prominent apron stage, which still jutted out, however, for a good distance beyond the proscenium.

Among large sections of the community the habit of theatre-going had been lost, and was not in fact to be recovered during the next two centuries. In the Restoration period the theatres became almost exclusively a rendezvous of the fashionable class and their hangers-on, the rakes and bullies, the ladies of pleasure, the young inns-of-court men, and a smattering of the *nouveau riche* class. For this specialized audience a specialized drama was required, and in a year or two the dramatists were meeting the demand. For the first few years the managers had to draw upon the pre-Commonwealth drama for most of their plays, and it is significant that the dramatists who proved most acceptable to this new audience were not Shakespeare and Jonson, but Beaumont and Fletcher and others of their type. 'They understood and imitated the conversation of gentlemen much better', is one of Dryden's explanations (*Essay of Dramatic Poesy*); and no doubt Shakespeare's dialogue had a rather old-fashioned ring in the ears of up-to-date young men in the 1660s, whereas Fletcher and Shirley were nearer to their own time. But there were other, and perhaps deeper, reasons. This new age (much influenced by French standards) found the Elizabethans altogether too poetical; Shakespeare's metaphor was too rich for the modern taste, and the liberties he took with language offended against the new standards of correctness. In Fletcher and Shirley the stream of metaphor is much thinner, and the metaphor itself is often of a conventional kind and therefore much easier to assimilate; intellectually, too, they made smaller demands on an audience anxious only to be easily amused and not made to think.

The most important contribution made by the Restoration theatre to English drama was the comedy of manners; here it found its liveliest and most natural expression. It should not be forgotten, however, that only a small part of this comedy falls within the Restoration period proper; it reached its highest expression in the plays of William Congreve (1670–1729) (written and produced in the reign of William and Mary), and came to an end in the first decade of Queen Anne's reign with the death of George Farquhar (1678–1707). Congreve wrote nothing for the stage after 1700, and John Vanbrugh (1664–1726) nothing after 1706 (though he left an unfinished play which Colley Cibber completed in 1728 as *The Provoked Husband* and produced at Drury Lane with great success, Wilks and Anne Oldfield playing Lord and Lady Townly). This early drying up of their dramatic productivity cannot be dissociated from a change in the tastes of the public, which by 1700 was beginning to be shocked by, or otherwise dissatisfied with, the dry intellectual comedy of Congreve and his predecessors. At its best that comedy had wit and poise, delicacy of phrase, and an engaging impudence; it held the mirror up to one small and incorrigible segment of the London scene. In *Love in a Tub* (1664), and still more in *She Would if She Could* (1668), by George Etherege (1634–91), we meet with early examples of those gay young men and witty, assured young women who are going to reappear with little variation or distinction of personality in the comedies of the next forty years. Etherege has an air of innocence that disarms criticism; it is all so obviously fun for him that we scarcely consider the moral implications of what is going on. But with *The Country Wife* (1675) and *The Plain Dealer* (1676) of William Wycherley (1640–1716) we do. In his plays cuckolding has become almost the serious business of life; we are in a world of inverted moral values, with the dramatist not quite certain whether to accept or satirize it. Congreve, the most accomplished artist of the group, works the same vein, but with greater detachment. Here again we have the battle of the sexes, the successful management of an intrigue, the ridicule of marriage, the nice discrimination between fools and men of sense—all this reaching its culmination in his last and subtlest play, *The Way of the World* (1700). His aristocratic detachment, his flawless style, and a certain remoteness from reality enable Congreve to skate over the thinnest of ice; this is the intellectual comedy at its best. He is not a satirist, but he is always, however unemphatically, a critic of life. Vanbrugh, a jollier man, is more of a realist; his situations (as in *The Relapse*, 1696; *The Provoked Wife*, 1697) are no more and no less indecent than those of Congreve, but we feel the indecency more because his characters are made of flesh and blood and are not the exquisitely artificial phantoms that Charles Lamb would persuade us *all* the characters in this artificial comedy are. He has, however, genuine humour, and his dialogue is delightfully easy and natural. Farquhar has little of Congreve's deliberate perfection; he is boisterous and high-spirited rather than witty or critical. In *The Recruiting Officer* (1706) and *The Beaux' Stratagem* (1707) the intellectual comedy is beginning to dissolve; his young men are still rakes and scamps, but they are not heartless. The change is no doubt mainly due to Farquhar's warm-hearted Irish temperament; but it is probable, too, that the celebrated attack by Jeremy Collier, *A Short View of the Immorality and Profaneness of the English Stage* (1698), was having its effect. At all events, with the turn of the century comedy becomes progressively more decent, if also a good deal less witty.

Of the other types of comedy written in the period just surveyed the most interesting is Shadwell's revival of the comedy of humours. Thomas Shadwell (*c.* 1642–92), who never tired of announcing himself as a follower of Jonson, has been unduly disparaged ever since Dryden ridiculed him in *MacFlecknoe*; but he was a shrewd observer of contemporary life, and his comedies, such as *The Squire of Alsatia* (1688) and *Bury Fair* (1689), have point and sense. The comedy of intrigue (often borrowed from Spanish sources) was the speciality of Mrs. Aphra Behn (1640–89). This comedy of cuckolding and closets, of midnight assignations and panting lovers, becomes excessively tedious; it is rarely leavened with much wit (though it has plenty of impudence), and relies for most of its interest on the comic vicissitudes of the plot. The lower levels of the drama at this period are best forgotten, and indeed are singularly easy to forget. An occasional comedy such as Sir Samuel Tuke's *Adventures of Five Hours* (1663), or Otway's *The Soldier's Fortune* (1680), or Crowne's *Sir Courtly Nice* (1685), stands out from the rest, but only the specialist is likely to interest himself today in the D'Urfeys and Tates who wrote so industriously in the manner of the period.

The late seventeenth century was not a heroic age, and it is not surprising to find that its tragic drama is on the whole inferior to its comedy. The period produced a form peculiar to itself, the rhymed Heroic play, so wittily satirized in Buckingham's *Rehearsal* (1671). The author who had most success with this form of drama was John Dryden (1631–1700), whose *Conquest of Granada* (two parts, 1670/1) gave the English stage the celebrated boasting hero, Almanzor. The Heroic play reverberates with rant and hyperbole; it is characterized, too, by the constant juxtaposition of Love and Honour, between which the hero must decide, and by violent action and startling reversals of fortune. Read in a cool hour in the scholar's study, these plays are no doubt sufficiently absurd; but in justice to them we ought to see and, still more, hear them, for their appeal is mainly rhetorical. Besides writing several plays of this type, Dryden turned out a number of comedies, the worst of which rank as low as anything written in the period, but one of which, *Marriage à la Mode* (1671), is among the more memorable Restoration plays. In tragedy he had at least two successes, *All for Love* (1677), based on *Antony and Cleopatra*, and *Don Sebastian* (1689). Both these are in blank verse, the fashion for rhymed plays having passed after only a few years. He also wrote a number of operas, the best known of which, 'King Arthur', owes its fame to the composer, Henry Purcell: the libretto is not much above the usual level of such things.

In the general dearth of good tragedy two plays, *The Orphan* (1680) and *Venice Preserved* (1682), by Thomas Otway (1652–85), stand out prominently; they continued to move English audiences well into the nineteenth century. The new note in Otway, pathos, must have been welcome after much heroic bluster. Rant and hyperbole blow as furiously as ever in the plays of Nathaniel Lee (*c.* 1653–92) (*The Rival Queens*, 1677), but Lee keeps a precarious hold on immortality by reason of a daring imagination which flames out fiercely from time to time in an age which was growing more and more rationalistic. Mention may also be made of John Banks (*c.* 1650–1706), whose plays were rather looked down upon by the critics, but who succeeded in *The Earl of Essex* (1681) in writing a tragedy which long held the stage on account of its dramatic rather than literary qualities.

5. Eighteenth Century. Entering the eighteenth century we find that London playgoers are still restricted to their two houses (both rebuilt), the Theatre Royal and the new theatre in Lincoln's Inn Fields. In 1705 another theatre, built by Vanbrugh, opened in the Haymarket; it was found acoustically unsuitable for plays, however, and became the home of opera. The Covent Garden theatre dates from 1732. It opened under the management of John Rich, famous as the producer of *The Beggar's Opera* (1728), and much satirized in his own day for his highly successful development of pantomime, in which many people saw a serious threat to the regular drama. Rich himself was a popular Harlequin. Equally gloomy misgivings were aroused in many quarters by the growing taste for Italian opera, which became popular in the reign of Queen Anne and was supported by large numbers of the nobility and the people of fashion. According to Addison, 'Arsinoe' (by Motteux, 1705) 'was the first opera that gave us a taste of Italian music'. Handel, who came to London in 1710, was promptly commissioned to write an opera for the Haymarket. The opera which he wrote, 'Rinaldo', had a phenomenal success, and ran from 24 Feb. 1711 to the end of the season, June. Joseph Addison's English opera, 'Rosamund' (1707), was written with the intention of making English lovers of opera take some interest in the words, since to the great majority of the audience Italian was unintelligible. But the public cared only for the music and continued to patronize Italian opera, or sometimes (strangely enough) opera in which the chief parts were sung in Italian and the less important parts were performed by Englishmen in English. Italian singers—Nicolini, Margharita de L'Épine, and (in the next generation) Cuzzoni, Faustina, and Farinelli—made vast sums of money and quarrelled like cats. Not all the singers were foreign: Mrs. Katherine Tofts shared the honours in the first decade of the century with L'Épine. Opera under the management of the Swiss, John James Heidegger, was carried on successfully at the Haymarket in the reigns of the first two Georges; but the prices charged (seats cost as much as a guinea) kept the audience select, and prevented opera from becoming widely popular.

The early part of the century saw another interesting development: the introduction of after-pieces. These were generally short comedies or farces. From the beginning of the century and even earlier the play notices contain references to 'entertainments of singing and dancing' which were often thrown in as an additional attraction to the playgoer. Such supplementary entertainments point to competition for a public which was willing to be easily amused, or which relished some light diversion after sitting through a five-act tragedy. The after-piece may be looked upon as a development from this light diversion. But it must also be related to the contemporary social background: the customary hour for a performance to begin in the theatre was six o'clock—in the first years of the century even five o'clock—and this was altogether too early for the middle classes and for anyone else who had business to do. It had long been the practice to charge a second price at the close of the third act of a five-act play, and at that later hour a number of additional spectators would drop in. The after-piece is therefore to be regarded as a bid to attract the middle-class public to the theatre by providing them with a solid entertainment, and not with a few musical scraps or odds and ends of farce, at an hour at which they could attend. The after-piece was often a five-act comedy cut to the required length, but many short plays were specially written by Garrick, Murphy, Foote, and others.

The eighteenth century's contribution to English drama is various, but if we compare it with that of the previous century it shows a sharp decline. Tragedy in the first decade was represented most favourably by the plays of Nicholas Rowe (1674–1718), who followed at a respectful distance behind Otway. In *The Fair Penitent* (1703) and *Jane Shore* (1714) Rowe concentrated on heroines and was more successful at moving pity than fear. Joseph Addison's (1672–1719) celebrated *Cato* (1713) is a good example of that French neo-classical tragedy which found favour all through the century; the action was slight, the speeches were long, and 'Declamation roar'd while Passion slept'. Edward Young, James Thomson, David Mallet, Aaron Hill, and many other contemporary poets, often with little knowledge of the theatre, contributed their quota to the tragic pool; but most of their plays are now forgotten. Dr. Johnson is not remembered for his *Irene* (1749), but *Irene* for Dr. Johnson, and Home's *Douglas* (1756) is preserved rather by the enthusiasm of the anonymous Scotsman who shouted 'Whaur's your Wully Shakespeare noo?', and by the popularity as a recitation of the passage beginning

'My name is Norval', than by its own vitality. A more interesting development was that of bourgeois tragedy in the plays of George Lillo (1693–1739) (*The London Merchant*, 1731) and in *The Gamester* (1753), by Edward Moore (1712–57). In these there is a good deal of the sentiment noted below in the comedies of Steele, and a strong insistence on the middle-class virtues; but no great dramatist arrived to lift this genre above interesting mediocrity.

In comedy the record is not quite so depressing. At the beginning of the century Mrs. Centlivre (*c.* 1667–1723) was writing slightly chastened comedies of intrigue such as *The Busybody* (1709) and *A Bold Stroke for a Wife* (1718), and Colley Cibber (1671–1757) was allowing the rake in *Love's Last Shift* (1696) to run the old course for four acts, but pulling him up in the fifth act and dismissing him as a converted character. Societies for the Reformation of Manners, started in the reign of William and Mary, give evidence of a new, if modified, Puritanism, and in the reign of Queen Anne the moral tone of the drama is distinctly less libertine. Sir Richard Steele (1672–1729), whose *Tatler* and *Spectator* did so much to amend contemporary morals and manners, did not shrink from using comedy for the same ends. His four sentimental comedies, culminating in *The Conscious Lovers* (1722), were all written to render vice contemptible and virtue attractive. They suffer, however, from the faults of the genre: virtue becomes too much a matter of pious sentiments, laughter is drowned in tears of forgiveness or repentance, and while the characters are all breathing good resolutions reality unobtrusively escapes. Yet Steele's comedies are robust when compared with the mawkish plays of Hugh Kelly (1739–77) and Richard Cumberland (1732–1811) in the 1770s. Here eighteenth-century sentimentalism sobs itself out; and the success of *She Stoops to Conquer* (1773) by Oliver Goldsmith (1730–74) is some indication that public taste was willing to react from such sentimental refinements. In his first comedy, *The Good-Natured Man* (1768), Goldsmith had shown rather tentatively the dangers of excessive delicacy, but in his later comedy he ridicules it unsparingly in the person of Tony Lumpkin. In the plays of Richard Brinsley Sheridan (1751–1816) we return to the comedy of manners, with all the traditional wit and perfection of phrase, but with none of the indecency. In characterization and in management of plot and situation Sheridan loses nothing in comparison with Wycherley and Congreve: what he does in *The Rivals* (1775) and *The School for Scandal* (1777) could hardly be done better. *The Suspicious Husband* (1747) of Benjamin Hoadly (1706–57), and *The Jealous Wife* (1761) of George Colman the Elder (1732–94), are favourable examples of the more ordinary run of eighteenth-century comedy.

Among the minor things which this century did well are the burlesque play—Carey's *Chrononhotonthologos* (1734), Fielding's *Tom Thumb* (1730), above all, Sheridan's *Critic* (1779)—and the ballad opera (see OPERA, 7). A word should be said, too, of the continuing popularity of the prologue and epilogue throughout the century; they point to an age in which the theatre was still very much a social rendezvous and the audience could still be addressed directly and made pleasantly conscious of itself.

The eighteenth century brought some interesting changes in theatrical representation and acting, some of which must be credited to David Garrick (1717–79). After a long struggle playgoers were finally banished from the stage, where they had sat intermittently from Elizabethan times. Under Garrick's management a new system of lighting the stage from the wings was introduced (see LIGHTING). Actors and actresses were regularly dressed in contemporary costume whatever part they might be playing, but towards the end of the century period costumes had begun to supplant the hooped petticoat for Juliet and the wig and velvet breeches for Romeo (see No. 162). In the early part of the century tragic acting was still declamatory and formal, but under the influence of Garrick (and perhaps of the improved lighting) it became much more naturalistic.

6. NINETEENTH CENTURY. At the beginning of the nineteenth century there were still only the same two theatres (both rebuilt) licensed for the performance of legitimate drama (see Nos. 31, 32). These were so large that a critic of 1840 complained that it was difficult 'to see the countenances of the performers without the aid of a pocket telescope', and hard to hear anything 'except the ranted speeches'. In such conditions intimate or naturalistic acting was almost impossible, and plays with frequent and violent action and comparatively little dialogue—in short, melodrama—flourished in the early decades of the century. The theatres tended, too, to concentrate on spectacular effects; and such attractions as Mount Vesuvius in eruption or the Grand Falls of Tivoli were offered to the gaping spectators. Tragedy and comedy could hardly thrive in this environment, and the dramatist gave place to such journeyman entertainers as Charles Dibdin (1743–1814), J. R. Planché (1764–1841), and Frederick Reynolds (1796–1880), who kept turning out farces, burlesques, operettas, pantomimes, and extravaganzas. Besides the two licensed theatres there were various unlicensed houses in London and the suburbs, and these were permitted to stage musical plays, for musical plays did not infringe the monopoly held since 1660 by Drury Lane and Covent Garden (see ASTLEY'S, OLYMPIC, SADLER'S WELLS, SURREY). More and more, however, those secondary theatres were contriving to circumvent the law by putting on 'straight' plays with a few pieces of incidental music and not less than five songs added, and calling them 'burlettas'. In 1812, for instance, the Surrey (see No. 49) included among its burlettas *Antony and Cleopatra, The Beaux' Stratagem, A Bold Stroke for a Wife, The Merry Wives of*

Windsor, *King Lear*, and *Richard III*. Finally, in 1843, as a result of prolonged agitation, came an Act for Regulating the Theatres, and the old cramping monopoly came to an end. If there was little immediate effect on the quality of the plays produced, the lifting of the monopoly undoubtedly contributed to the dramatic revival in the later decades of the nineteenth century (see COPYRIGHT and DRAMATIC CENSORSHIP).

Among the more serious dramatists of the first half of the century were Lord Byron, James Sheridan Knowles, Thomas Noon Talfourd, and Sir Henry Taylor, but they were working in an outworn convention. Yet Sheridan Knowles (1784–1862), and, still more, Bulwer Lytton (1803–73) in *Money* (1840), were feeling their way towards a more naturalistic drama in which real human issues were at least raised. Apart from such plays as were written for performance, there were many others intended to be read rather than acted. Wordsworth, Coleridge, Scott, Shelley, Keats, Landor, and Beddoes all tried their hand at poetic drama, and later in the century Browning, Tennyson, Arnold, Swinburne, and many others, dwindling at last to the once celebrated Stephen Phillips (1864–1913), continued the practice of writing for the Victorians as if they were Elizabethans or ancient Greeks. When such plays had any success on the stage it was due rather to actor and producer than to the dramatist, as when Irving put on Tennyson's *Becket* (1893) and Alexander staged Phillips's *Paolo and Francesca* (1902). Contrary to popular belief, too, people are willing to be bored—for some time, at least—by what they have been led to believe is great drama, and as few people expect to enjoy poetic drama few people can tell if it is good or merely bogus.

In the work of Dion Boucicault (1822–90) there was at least some character study and some technical skill. But more important are Tom Taylor (1817–80) (*The Ticket-of-Leave Man*, 1863) and Thomas William Robertson (1829–71) (*Caste*, 1867), who both deal with life as it was being lived in their own day, and put contemporary characters on the stage involved in contemporary dilemmas. About this time the influence of the French dramatist Sardou was making itself felt in the London theatre; the 'well-made' plays of Sardou and other French playwrights were acted in English versions, and for some time dominated the work of English dramatists. Two of those, Henry Arthur Jones (1851–1929) and Arthur Wing Pinero (1855–1934), were now bringing a good deal of fresh air into the theatre; at least they had opened a window or two, and one could hear the authentic sounds of life coming in from outside. Jones in particular (his work is most unequal) was a serious dramatist, a conscious pioneer, who not only wrote plays that were intended to startle his contemporaries, but followed them up with a considerable amount of dramatic criticism. Jones startled the Victorians in 1884 with *Saints and Sinners*, a play which (in spite of some melodramatic features) introduced them to a naturalism that they had not known in the theatre, though they were perfectly familiar with it in prose fiction. Pinero's *The Second Mrs. Tanqueray* came in 1893 as another delightful shock to them, and it was followed two years later by *The Notorious Mrs. Ebbsmith*. In the work of both Jones and Pinero, however, there is a tendency (as Shaw pointed out) for them to run away at the last moment from the issues which they have raised, and the behaviour of their characters is still usually governed by the conventions of the theatre rather than by life itself. They had, in fact, the sort of success that comes to men of talent who walk ahead, but not too far ahead, of their contemporaries. The success of Bernard Shaw (1856–1950), who made a more absolute break with the past, was harder to achieve, but more decisive and valuable when it was finally won.

While Jones and Pinero were sailing rather tentatively down the main stream of the intellectual drama in the 1890s, Oscar Wilde (1854–1900) was writing in quick succession a number of brilliant artificial comedies, of which *The Importance of Being Earnest* (1895) is the most likely to survive. Wilde had impudence and gaiety and epigram at his command, and (what seems to come naturally to Irishmen) an ear for the rhythms of speech which enabled him to write the most sparkling dialogue in English drama since Sheridan. Victorian wit found a more typical expression in the comic operas which William Schwenck Gilbert (1836–1911) wrote with Arthur Seymour Sullivan (1842–1900), beginning with *Trial by Jury* in 1875. Besides irradiating the English theatre with his fantastic humour and good-natured satire, Gilbert set new standards of precision for acting and producing. J. R. SUTHERLAND

7. THE MODERN PERIOD. During the 1870s and 1880s the English theatre began to attract a more intellectual public, and in the 1890s some enthusiasts for serious drama were able to institute a reaction against the despotism of actor-managers, the policy of the long run, the fetish of scenic spectacle, the escapism of romantic melodrama, the stereotyped form and conventional morality of the well-made play. In 1891 J. T. Grein founded the Independent Theatre and in 1897 William Archer helped to organize the New Century Theatre. These club theatres staged private performances of controversial plays by Shaw, Ibsen, and others. Neither survived the 1890s, but Shaw propagated their ideals with great eloquence in the *Saturday Review*, and in 1899 Grein and his followers were able to establish the Stage Society, which for the next forty years arranged Sunday performances of experimental plays in West-End theatres.

Encouraged by these pioneer ventures, Harley Granville-Barker staged a series of brilliant productions between 1904 and 1907 at the Royal Court Theatre, setting a new standard in ensemble acting and in the use of simple but significant décor. Though some poetic plays were performed, the enterprise was chiefly devoted to the new drama of Ibsen, Shaw, Galsworthy, Granville-Barker, and St. John Hankin, with its radical innovations in plot-construction, moral ideas, and characterization. Long runs were barred and an approximation to repertory presentation was achieved by performing thirty-two plays by seventeen authors in two and a half years. The repertory ideal quickly spread to the provinces. In 1907, Miss A. E. F. Horniman established a repertory company in Manchester, with weekly changes of programme and a liberal policy which brought into being a school of Manchester playwrights, notably Allan Monkhouse, Stanley Houghton, and Harold Brighouse, who applied the moral and structural ideas of the new drama to Lancashire characters and problems. In 1911, local enthusiasts started a repertory theatre in Liverpool, and in 1913 Barry Jackson built a theatre for his repertory company in Birmingham, where he staged the best of the old and the new drama.

Shaw stands apart from the other creators of the new drama. His range of interest was much wider than theirs, embracing socialist propaganda in *Widowers' Houses* (1892), mock heroics in *Arms and the Man* (1894), the marriage relationship in *Candida* (1898), the Irish question in *John Bull's Other Island* (1903), the Life Force in *Man and Superman* (1905), the unconventional hero in *Caesar and Cleopatra* (1906), and art and science in *The Doctor's Dilemma* (1906). His characters are intensely animated and his plots are frequently enlivened by touches of the fantastic and the absurd. The characteristic incisiveness of his dialogues is blended with the soaring but finely organized rhetoric of his long speeches. The methods of Galsworthy, Granville-Barker, and St. John Hankin were more naturalistic than Shaw's. *The Silver Box* (1906), *Strife* (1909), and *Justice* (1910) show how deeply Galsworthy probed the injustices of the written law and the class prejudices of contemporary society, and how compassionately he represented both sides of the questions that he raised. Granville-Barker's *The Voysey Inheritance* (1905) and *Waste* (1907), and Hankin's *The Return of the Prodigal* (1905) and *The Cassilis Engagement* (1907), on the other hand, appeal more to the intellect than the heart, and are especially concerned with the emancipation of women and the influence of money on moral principles.

Though J. M. Barrie commented ironically on class distinctions and essayed an alternative structure to that of the 'well-made' play in *The Admirable Crichton* as early as 1902, he was not of the new school of drama. His was an ingratiating not a reforming genius, in which fantasy and sentiment were curiously blended with a pessimism which in *Quality Street* (1903) and *Peter Pan* (1904) represents the passing of childhood as essentially tragic and in *Dear Brutus* (1917) finds an incorrigible foolishness in adults. Alfred Sutro is a more classifiable playwright; he wrote light comedies of manners well suited to the Edwardian taste for epigrams. So, too, did W. Somerset Maugham, though he later became a penetrating satirist.

The various experiments in poetic drama attempted during the early twentieth century suffer by comparison with the influences which inspired them. The work of Stephen Phillips abounds in Shakespearian pastiche: J. E. Flecker's *Hassan* (1923) lacks the unity of Wilde's *Salome*: Gordon Bottomley's dramatizations of Celtic and Northern legends fall short of the symbolic wisdom of the *Nō* theatre and the plays of W. B. Yeats. In *Nan* (1908) and *A King's Daughter* (1925), John Masefield toiled in the different tracks beaten by J. M. Synge and Euripides. The poetic dramatist had to break away from the Shakespearian tradition and the trammels of romantic diction before he could speak for the new century instead of echoing its past.

Though the actor-managers gave little encouragement to the new drama or the best poetic plays, they maintained a certain continuity of policy in their theatres and preserved drama proper against the competition of musical comedy and the music hall. During the First World War, however, theatre rents and the cost of production quadrupled, and the actor-manager was ousted by groups of investors intent upon exploiting a public increased by large numbers of colonial and American troops. Musical comedies, melodramas, and farces became the staple entertainment of the London and provincial theatres. In Liverpool, the repertory theatre survived with difficulty, but in Manchester declining support obliged Miss Horniman to disband her repertory company in 1917. In Birmingham, however, Jackson continued to subsidize a repertoire of plays far superior to that of any other British theatre, and during the war the Old Vic became a Shakespearian repertory theatre under the thrifty but idealistic management of Lilian Baylis.

Between 1918 and 1939, the practice of sub-letting the principal London theatres made production more costly than ever before. Their managements, with a few honourable exceptions, preferred long-running plays of obvious appeal to serious drama. In the 1920s such actor-managers as F. R. Benson, Fred Terry, and Matheson Lang still toured the provinces successfully, but the popularity of the talking film caused many theatres to be converted into cinemas and the touring system declined drastically in the 1930s. More and more the staging of recent or new drama of the better kind devolved upon the idealists in charge of club or suburban theatres in London, and upon a few repertory theatres in the provinces. Few modern plays were presented at the Old Vic, but there were memorable productions of Strindberg, Shaw, and O'Neill at the Everyman Theatre (Hampstead), of German expressionist drama and new English plays at the Gate Theatre, of Chekhov at the Barnes Theatre, and of poetic drama by Eliot, Auden, and Isherwood at the Mercury Theatre, thanks to the enterprise of Norman Macdermott, Malcolm Morley, Peter Godfrey, Norman Marshall, Theodore Komisarjevsky, and Ashley Dukes. At Oxford, J. B. Fagan's revivals of European classics deserved better support than they received, and at the Festival Theatre, Cambridge, Terence Gray subsidized a series of highly experimental productions on a stage of revolutionary design between 1926 and 1933 (see No. 84). The greatest benefactor of the stage, however, was Barry Jackson, who not only maintained his adventurous policy at the Birmingham Repertory Theatre, but organized summer festivals of drama at Malvern (see No. 100) between 1929 and 1937, and presented plays continuously in London between 1922 and 1935, including the full cycle of Shaw's *Back to Methuselah*.

A wide public could now appreciate Shaw's earlier work, but he continued to experiment with new themes and forms. In *Heartbreak House* (1919) he contemplates the generation which preferred war to wisdom with Chekhovian pity and mirth, and in *St. Joan* (1924) his tone shifts from the tragic to the inquisitorial when he ends by asking his audience whether it is worthy of the noblest embodiments of the Life Force. In most of his subsequent plays, disquisitions on the post-war generation and its politics are combined with a strain of apocalyptic fantasy; in *Geneva* (1938), for instance, the discussion on the League of Nations and the morality of aerial bombardment ends with the news that mankind is doomed to freeze because the orbit of the earth has shifted. Though Shaw was prescient of the dilemmas and fears of the atomic age, his ultimate faith was strong. Uniting five plays into one in *Back to Methuselah* (1923), he sees longevity as a means by which man will learn from his mistakes, and looks forward to the time when the Life Force will be freed from the bondage of matter, when 'there will be no people, only thought'.

Shaw's visionary moments were not entirely in harmony with the disillusioned and iconoclastic temper of the 1920s. The post-war audience was out of sympathy with the flamboyant style of acting favoured by Beerbohm Tree and other Edwardian actor-managers, and with the picturesque melodramas which they had produced. It preferred the adroit understatement of Gerald du Maurier's acting and the critical realism of the problem play and the drama of social purpose. Schooled by the cinema, it found no fault with the episodic structure of Galsworthy's last important play, *Escape* (1927), and applauded the characters who defied the law by helping a convict on the run. The indictment of the inhuman laws governing the marriage-bond in Clemence Dane's *A Bill of Divorcement* (1921), the disquisition on eugenics in James Bridie's *The Sleeping Clergyman* (1933), and the discussion of Christianity and birth-control in St. John Ervine's *Robert's Wife* (1937) were likewise to its taste. The conflict between younger and older generations was a favourite theme for problem plays, notably in Noël Coward's *The Vortex* (1924) and Maugham's *For Services Rendered* (1932), both of which show the moral chaos resulting from the frustration of the young and the fallibility of their parents.

More than any other dramatist, Maugham set the pattern for the cynical tone and destructive satire of the post-war comedy of manners. In *Our Betters*, written in 1913 and produced in London in 1923, he creates modern counterparts to the gigolo and the dancing-master of Restoration comedy to expose the lust and vanity of titled American expatriates in London. The title of his next and greatest comedy, *The Circle* (1921), is ironical because its young lovers are incapable of learning from the cautionary example of their elders, and he pessimistically concludes that this failing is congenital to mankind. Frederick Lonsdale and Noël Coward were likewise deft craftsmen who mocked bourgeois morality, but in Lonsdale's *On Approval* (1927) and Coward's *Private Lives* (1930) the business of the comedy of manners has dwindled to the permutations of the sleeping arrangements of men- and women-about-town.

Naturalism was the prevailing dramatic technique of the inter-war period, but some of the ablest playwrights of the time searched for a method which would permit a more imaginative presentation of life without succumbing to the exaggerations and sentimentalities of Edwardian romanticism. In this spirit, John Drinkwater wrote *Abraham Lincoln* (1918), a history play with ideas relevant to contemporary problems of war and peace, using verse commentaries by two choric characters between the acts. Other reactions against naturalism took the form of allegory in Sutton Vane's treatment of life after death in *Outward Bound* (1923), and fantasy tinged with irony in James Bridie's *Tobias and the Angel* (1930). Bolder experiments came in the 1930s, though only Sean O'Casey and J. B. Priestley risked sustained experiments with the techniques of expressionism. Aided by Augustus John's stylized setting, the second act of O'Casey's tragedy *The Silver Tassie* (1929) blended poetry, song, and expressionist devices more successfully than any of his later plays. Priestley moved away from the efficient naturalism of *Eden End* (1934) to the dramatization of novel theories of the serialism and circularity of Time in *I Have Been Here Before* (1937), and thence to a mixture of morality and expressionist techniques in *Johnson over Jordan* (1939), where he used music, masks, dances, symbolic settings, and allusive prose, to represent the problems of the soul after death.

An even more important development in the 1930s was the creation of a new idiom in poetic drama. In *The Dog Beneath the Skin* (1935) and *The Ascent of F6* (1936), Christopher Isherwood and W. H. Auden used conversational forms of verse to express a highly topical criticism of bourgeois family life, imperialism, and fascism, in episodic plots which were influenced by German expressionism and the narrative technique of Bertolt Brecht. In many respects the anti-naturalistic movement of the inter-war period reached its climax in T. S. Eliot's *Murder in the Cathedral* (1935), which expresses historical fact in a ritualistic form, concentrates on the suffering and redemption of an archetypal character, and shows that verse of variable syllabic length can serve the purposes of conversation, catechism, choric incantation, and impassioned introspection just as effectively as the iambic pentameter. In *The Family Reunion* (1939), Eliot made another important experiment by putting an Aeschylean theme of sin and expiation into a modern setting and imposing an unobtrusive rhythmical pattern upon modern idioms. His characters are skilfully grouped around his Oresteian hero, but, as he has admitted, he failed to make the choruses and the Furies organic parts of the play.

Though air raids caused many theatres in London and large provincial cities to be closed for lengthy periods between 1939 and 1942, there was an important revival of dramatic art in Britain during the Second World War, chiefly because the state began to subsidize productions for the first time in the history of the British theatre. In 1940, Parliament made a substantial grant to the Council for the Encouragement of Music and the Arts, whose monetary aid was limited at first to touring companies in the provinces. By 1945, however, it was organizing its own companies, managing the Theatre Royal, Bristol, and sponsoring excellent repertory seasons by the Old Vic company and Tennent Plays, Ltd., at the New and Haymarket Theatres in London. Memorable short runs of English and foreign plays of high quality were also staged by Alec Clunes during his management of the Arts Theatre between 1942 and 1953. During the same period, however, a process of economic rationalization placed most of the best theatre-buildings in London and the provinces in the control of a small group of investors. The high rents of these theatres and the high costs of production after the war greatly increased the hazards of producing-managements and obliged them to rely more and more on players of long-established popularity and long runs of plays of obvious appeal like Agatha Christie's *The Mousetrap*, which opened at the Ambassadors Theatre on 25 Nov. 1952, and was still running in 1966.

Since the war the cause of the experimental play and the repertory ideal have been supported chiefly by idealistic or non-commercial groups who have succeeded in creating a new audience and several schools of playwrights. In a series of seasons at the Mercury Theatre between 1945 and 1948, E. Martin Browne staged some lively experiments in poetic drama by Ronald Duncan, Norman Nicholson, and Anne Ridler. Formed in 1945 under the direction of Joan Littlewood, Theatre Workshop endeavoured to bring proletarian culture back to the theatre and presented significant work of this kind by Ewen MacColl, Brendan Behan, and Shelagh Delaney. Managed by George Devine at the Royal Court Theatre from 1956 to 1965, the English Stage Company also accepted the dramatist as the fundamental creative force in the theatre and was largely responsible for the current interest in the work of John Osborne, Arnold Wesker, and Harold Pinter. New plays also form part of the repertoire of the Mermaid Theatre (opened in 1959), where important experiments in the use of the open stage have been essayed by Bernard Miles. Though the attractions of television have led to the closing of hundreds of theatres and a drastic decline in the touring system, the best provincial repertory theatres have won more support for their work, and at Birmingham, Bristol, Nottingham, Coventry, and Oxford they have regularly staged new plays as well as classics. This spirit of enterprise in London and the provinces is partly the result of annual subsidies given to non-profit-distributing companies by the Arts Council, which in 1945 replaced the Council for the Encouragement of Music and the Arts, and partly the result of aid from local authorities, who have been empowered since 1948 to levy a rate of up to sixpence in the pound for entertainments. The future of the best British drama thus seems largely dependent on enlightened state and municipal patronage (see CIVIC THEATRES).

The conditions of the Second World War favoured revivals rather than new plays, but Peter Ustinov and Terence Rattigan emerged from it as young dramatists of some promise. In *The Browning Version* (1948) and *The Deep Blue Sea* (1952), Rattigan treated disrupted marital relationships with psychological and theatrical skill, but he showed little interest in the moral and ideological conflicts peculiar to the post-war world. In this respect such older dramatists as Bridie, Priestley, and O'Casey were in closer contact with the anxious spirit of the age. In *Daphne Laureola* (1949), Bridie related the aberrations of a lonely and haunted woman to current uncertainties about the permanence of order and justice, though he characteristically left final decisions to his audience. Priestley, on the other hand, was a more positive moralist, who gave optimistic answers to family and international problems in *The Linden Tree* (1948) and *Home is Tomorrow* (1948), and even presaged a better life in Britain as the outcome of an atomic war in *Summer Day's Dream* (1949). Though Priestley constantly aspires to poetic vision, he has not achieved more than a heightened naturalism in these plays. The use of symbolism, music, and impassioned speech came more naturally to O'Casey, and his last plays illustrated two aspects of his basic theme of the struggle between life- and death-forces. In *Red Roses for Me* (1946) and *Oak Leaves and Lavender* (1947) he challenged the destructive powers of capitalism; in *Cock-a-Doodle Dandy* (1949) and *The Bishop's Bonfire* (1955) he derided the forces of superstition at work in modern Ireland.

Memorable Shakespeare productions during and after the war quickened interest in poetic drama. T.S. Eliot and Christopher Fry were the most notable experimenters in this kind. In *The Cocktail Party* (1950), *The Confidential Clerk* (1953), and *The Elder Statesman* (1958), Eliot blended Christian ideas with themes from Greek tragedy, showing how personal relationships can lead to increased self-knowledge, crucial moral choices, and, ultimately, salvation. He abandoned the formal chorus and subordinated poetic devices more and more to strict dramatic utility. Fry, on the other hand, experimented with lyrical and flamboyant blank verse, though he, too, essayed religious themes in *A Sleep of Prisoners* (1951) and *The Firstborn* (1952). In *The Lady's Not for Burning* (1948) he infused a comic spirit into verse drama, though his characters tended to speak the same ornate idiom. His latest play, *Curtmantle* (1961), makes more sparing use of adjective and image.

Since 1955 interest has shifted from the poetic dramatists like Fry to a group of playwrights who have reacted violently against the stereotyping processes of mass civilization, the regimentations of the welfare state, and the anxieties of the atomic age. They suspect that contemporary democracy is a façade concealing an oligarchical establishment, which they associate with an effete middle-class morality, imperialism, the use of nuclear weapons, and capital punishment. Hence they have created a drama of protest and satire, which exalts the non-conformist, the misfit, and the martyr, and sympathizes at times with the frustrations and fears of the common man. The movement began with John Osborne's *Look Back in Anger* (1956), in which the hero is a provincial graduate turned street vendor who hurls invective at class distinctions, Kiplingesque patriotism, suburban ennui, Sunday newspapers, and his mother-in-law. Correspondingly, the older generations of provincial families were criticized in Shelagh Delaney's *A Taste of Honey* (1958) and Arnold Wesker's *Roots* (1959), and the patriotic shibboleths of the Irish establishment were mocked in Brendan Behan's *The Hostage* (1958) in a Brechtian sequence of dialogues, songs, dances, and direct addresses to the audience. Brecht's influence is also seen at work in the episodic narrative method of such plays as Robert Bolt's *A Man for All Seasons* (1960), John Whiting's *The Devils* and Osborne's *Luther* (both 1961), which dramatize the lives of historical characters who defied established powers. In *The Caretaker* (1960), on the other hand, Harold Pinter made discriminating use of the techniques of Samuel Beckett and Eugène Ionesco to show the cosmic absurdity of modern man, his imperfect powers of communication with his fellows, and his inevitable fears and loneliness. This new movement has brought a refreshing variety of contemporary idioms and dialects to the stage, and has made effective use of functional and symbolic settings, breaking the barriers of the fourth-wall convention. Its future development seems to depend upon whether its leaders can think constructively as well as critically about the human dilemma in the atomic age. WILLIAM A. ARMSTRONG

ENGLISH ARISTOPHANES, THE, see FOOTE, SAMUEL.

ENGLISH COMEDIANS, THE. During the late sixteenth and early seventeenth centuries a number of English actors went abroad, and soon made a name for themselves, especially in Germany, where the so-called *Englische Komödianten* had a great influence on the development of the German theatre, the prose form of their dialogue indicating the break with tradition. The first records of English players abroad is of a company of instrumentalists at the Danish Court in 1579–80, while five years later English actors appeared at Elsinore under Kempe. In the following year they were invited to Dresden, and thereafter they crop up in the archives of many German towns. They probably performed short comic musical sketches or jigs, whose humour was broad enough to be obvious even to a foreign audience, and acrobatic and other feats. Though they played in English, their clown pattered in Low German. The outstanding name in connexion with later English companies is Robert Browne, who made a short visit to Leyden in 1590 and in 1592 took a company on an extended tour, in the course of which he played some of Marlowe's plays, *Gammer Gurton's Needle*, and several biblical plays at Frankfurt fair. A company, probably under Sackville, one of Browne's companions, was at Wolfenbüttel, capital of Heinrich Julius of Brunswick, himself author of several plays in which an English influence is apparent, particularly in the character of the Fool, played by Sackville under the name of Jan Bouschet (Posset). Sackville later went into business in Frankfurt and prospered exceedingly. Meanwhile Browne continued his tours, and stayed for some time at the Court of Count Moritz of Hesse, another princely enthusiast of the drama, who in 1606 built a private theatre for the amusement of his guests. Browne was succeeded on tour by a company under John Green, and at Cassel by a company under Ralph Reeve. The next notable name to crop up in these records is that of Robert Reynolds, who made a great reputation as a clown under the name of Pickelherring, while John Spencer, known as Stockfisch, with headquarters in Berlin, went as far afield as The Hague and Dresden.

The repertory of all these companies was in the main similar. The titles of many of their plays are known, but as the names of the authors conveyed nothing to the audience they were usually omitted. Two collections of texts were printed, one in 1620, one in 1630, the first being plays of English origin, while the second is wholly German. Some idea of the English

ENGLISH FAIRGROUND THEATRES

Comedians in action can be gained if the following points are borne in mind: subtlety and poetic language could not be appreciated by a foreign audience, and are therefore dropped; pirated editions and older versions of plays are often used; since visual action alone could convey the plot there was a strong incentive to exaggeration, horseplay, and lurid horrors; the audience was kept amused by music and ballet interpolated into the action for the benefit of the more sophisticated spectators, and by the introduction of fooling for the groundlings; the actors who sought employment abroad, though obviously adventurous spirits, were perhaps not in the front rank of their profession. Their acting would therefore tend to be violent and declamatory, with much boisterous action and broad effects in comedy. From the literary point of view therefore the influence of the English actors was on the whole deplorable; but it must be admitted that they first acquainted the German public with passion on the stage, and so paved the way for an appreciation of tragedy; and further, they counteracted the German tendency to excessive discussion; for them the play was the thing, to the exclusion of all else. In these respects they revolutionized German drama in a manner long overdue.

The Thirty Years' War baulked their activity somewhat, but a number of English companies continued to play on the Continent, particularly during the Puritan Interregnum of 1642–60. The last authenticated record of an English troupe is in 1659, but such was their prestige that the name *Englische Komödianten* was used for publicity purposes as late as the eighteenth century. The constant passage of actors to and from the Continent, and the consequent interchange of ideas and subjects for drama, produced some interesting problems of comparative literature, of which the theme of Faustus is a case in point.

ENGLISH FAIRGROUND AND PORTABLE THEATRES. The provision of an adequate stage has always been one of the chief difficulties of theatrical touring companies. It is said that Thespis acted on a cart; and, in essence, this solution has often been adopted since. The medieval pageants, upon which incidents from the Mystery plays were performed, were, in fact, built-up carts, usually of two storeys, that were drawn round the streets of a town from one assembled audience to another. The tableaux displayed in carnivals and the Lord Mayor's Show are, to a certain extent, relics of the same tradition.

By the end of the sixteenth century there were several companies of players touring the country towns and villages of England, and in the seventeenth century their number was greatly increased; but as theatrical productions grew more ambitious, and the London theatres more elaborately fitted up, the actors and the audiences must have grown dissatisfied with the meagre stage accommodation provided at country inns and rustic barns; there were, of course, at this period no such things as provincial theatres. The creation of portable theatres, as completely self-contained units, was a natural growth to satisfy an obvious need.

The earliest travelling theatres in England seem to have grown up in the fairs during the seventeenth century; at first they were probably little more than tents, housing a small stage, and presenting crude popular drolls, intermixed with turns of juggling and rope dancing. Later some of these became more elaborate, and by the eighteenth century quite ambitious stage productions were being presented at Lee and Harper's and Fielding's Theatrical Booths, and many good actors served their time upon their boards; besides these there were many smaller companies—Hippisley's, Yeates's, Mme Violante's, and so on. At least one 'Great Theatrical Boothe' always attended Bartholomew Fair, and the London theatres used to close down during its celebration, lending their audiences and sometimes their actors to the fairground (see also FAIRS).

Between the great London fairs of Bartholomew, Smithfield, Southwark, Mayfair, and Greenwich, the theatrical booths would spend the summer making the round of the country wakes. This tradition was sustained for over 200 years; during the nineteenth century Richardson's Theatre was by far the largest concern on the road, but there were dozens of other 'portable theatres' that continued to cover the country after that great enterprise was broken up in the middle of the century—'Johnson's Thespian Temple', 'Baker's Pavilion', 'Douglass's Travelling Shakespearean Saloon', Holloway's, Wadbrook and Scard's, Maggie Morton's, and many another. With the spread of the cinema the old 'portable fit-ups' lost their importance, but even today an obscure theatrical road-show may still occasionally be found trouping the English countryside.

The fairground theatres of the eighteenth and nineteenth centuries seem to have conformed to a general pattern; the stage itself was solidly constructed, sometimes upon the carts that carried the show round, and was furnished with a few simple backcloths and properties; the auditorium consisted of a canvas tent that could be easily rolled up and transported on the wagons; the seats were almost always plain wooden planks. If the show was at all pretentious there might be a built-up front of gaudily painted canvas flats, and a platform outside upon which some of the performers would parade as an advertisement for the marvels within. These parades were often very elaborate, and sometimes even superior to the actual performance.

The performances themselves were often conducted with the main idea of getting through the piece as quickly as possible and clearing the seats for another audience; on a busy day a play might be run through as often as a dozen times. The plays were, for the most part, strong dramatic stuff, based on popular legends and stories from the classics, the Bible, or English history; sometimes they dramatized sensational topical murders (Maria Marten is, of course, the most famous example), presented pantomimes, or adapted current theatrical successes. There was hardly ever any written script; the actors were given the stock situations and were expected to improvise the stock speeches, and the result usually bore very slight verbal resemblance to any dramatic original. Like the puppet-show, whose repertory was very similar, the fairground theatre preserved some interesting elements of the Elizabethan stage tradition.

Despite their crudities the theatrical booths and the portable theatres played a great part in carrying the English drama throughout the English countryside to the English people, and they deserve a fuller recognition than they have received from theatre historians. The ordinary stage histories ignore them almost entirely, but some information may be gleaned from Morley's *Bartholomew Fair*, Frost's *Old English Showmen*, Peter Paterson's *Glimpses of Real Life*, and similar theatrical reminiscences.

There are indications that the travelling theatre has not exhausted its usefulness today; for several years the Arts League of Service toured the country with an easily portable entertainment of traditional English song and drama, and later the Century Theatre undertook extensive tours to theatreless provincial towns. Well-appointed provincial theatres and village halls will reduce, but never perhaps entirely destroy, the scope of genuine portable theatre. GEORGE SPEAIGHT

ENGLISH OPERA HOUSE, see LYCEUM THEATRE, 1, PALACE THEATRE, and ROYALTY THEATRE, 2.

ENGLISH PLAYHOUSE. The history of the English playhouse as a building specially designed for the accommodation of a professional company begins with the erection of James Burbage's Theatre in 1576. Before this actors appeared in inn-yards (see INNS USED AS THEATRES), or on temporary stages set up in the open-air or in the hall of a nobleman or civic dignitary. The Theatre was quickly followed by the Curtain (1577); then came Henslowe's Rose (*c.* 1587) and Fortune (1600), and in *c.* 1596 the Swan, which served as a model for the Hope, converted by Henslowe from the old Bear Garden in 1613. In 1599 Burbage's sons built the most famous of all Elizabethan playhouses, the Globe on Bankside, from the timbers of the original Theatre. It was here that many of Shakespeare's plays were first performed. There was also a theatre at Newington Butts, but very little is known about it, and one on the site of the Red Bull Tavern, built *c.* 1605. This was used surreptitiously during the Commonwealth, and for a year or two after the Restoration. Pepys visited it in 1661.

The above were all public theatres, unroofed, and charging a very small entrance fee. But the Elizabethans, and more particularly their successors, the Jacobean and Caroline playgoers, had also a number of so-called private theatres, roofed and charging higher prices. If the public theatres may be said to have developed from the open-air and inn-yard performances of earlier times, the private theatres continued the tradition of the performance in a nobleman's hall. Although both types of theatre had features in common, they differed in some important respects, and a knowledge of their structure and functioning is helpful for the understanding, and especially the production, of the plays of the period. Particularly with regard to Shakespeare's plays, a knowledge of the Elizabethan public theatre is essential, and for this reason it has been widely studied. Nothing structural remains, and the extant documents are few and confusing. They consist of the Swan drawing (see No. 22), the builder's contract for the Fortune Theatre, and one or two maps of London showing theatre exteriors (see No. 48). All the rest must be deduced from the texts and stage directions, if any, of contemporary play-texts, and from scattered references and descriptions in contemporary writings. Unfortunately all the information available lends itself to several interpretations, and has caused constant controversy. But it seems probable that the main features of the Theatre, for instance, were based on the inn-yard, with its open space surrounded by balconies and windows. Recent research, however, tends to show a greater influence from the triumphal arches and stages erected on ceremonial occasions, both in England and on the Continent, and from the Dutch Rederijker stage, than was formerly realized. Apart from being open to the air, the Elizabethan public theatre had a large open platform stage jutting out into the centre of the yard, with the audience standing on three sides (sometimes on all four sides). Round the interior ran one or two galleries, divided into sections known as rooms, with a narrow thatched roof above. At the back of the stage (in those theatres where the audience was on three sides of the stage only) was a tiring-house, which provided a permanent architectural feature, pierced with doors. Above this the first gallery provided an open balcony (or possibly only windows) which could be used by the actors for scenes involving their appearance on city walls, in upper rooms, etc. This corresponded roughly to the layout of the inn-yard, and also to that of the nobleman's Great Hall, which usually had a musicians' gallery over the screen which divided it from the kitchen. Over the rear part of the stage was a roof (the Heavens) supported on pillars. Above the balcony at the back of the stage was a hut used to house the machinery for raising or lowering actors or properties, the thunder-run, and other necessities for special effects—fireworks, cannon, etc. In the stage itself, which had a curtained or boarded-in cellar below it, were trapdoors, used for apparitions and for such things as the witches' cauldron in *Macbeth* and the burial of Ophelia in *Hamlet*.

One of the fiercest controversies has raged round the question of the inner stage. This was formerly thought of as a large curtained recess behind the tiring-house wall in which interior scenes could be played, or as a structure projecting on to the roofed part of the stage from the wall. Certainly there was a recess, since stage-directions in some plays demand a 'discovery' by the drawing of a curtain (for example, Ferdinand and Miranda playing chess in *The Tempest*). But it is now thought that this inner recess was nothing more than part of a narrow corridor behind the wall which could be made visible through an opening usually closed by a door or curtain. Certainly it would not have been possible for many people to see a scene played inside this recess under the Heavens. It seems probable that actors so 'discovered' came forward on to the main stage to take part in the action of the play. But there may also have been small structures—caves, tents, monuments, even simple rooms—either standing free on the stage, or abutting on the back wall. Some such arrangement would, for instance, be necessary for the monument scene in *Antony and Cleopatra*.

The original public theatres were either round (like the Bear Pit) or octagonal (like the Globe), and the first rectangular theatre was the Fortune. The audience, admitted by one door only (the actors had a second door leading to the back-stage area) on payment of one penny, could then stand round the stage as 'groundlings' in close proximity to the actors, or, on payment of a further penny or two-pence, go up into the galleries, where stools and benches were provided, the best places costing as much as sixpence. In all parts of the house people amused themselves by cracking and eating nuts, and munching apples and pears, often throwing the cores at any actor who displeased them.

Performances were given during the afternoon, beginning at 2 p.m., and though at first they were countenanced on Sundays, much to the disgust of the already vociferous Puritan element, this was later discontinued, and they were limited to weekdays. The audience was summoned by a trumpet blown from the highest point of the building, above the stage, and during the performance a flag was flown there. Scenery on the stage was kept to the minimum—a throne, a bench, a tree—but costumes, many of which came to the players from their courtly patrons, might be gorgeous, though often inappropriate, since contemporary dress was used for any place or period. There were, however, some conventional touches which served to distinguish foreigners, such as a breastplate for a Roman or a turban for a Turk, and most plays needed music (see WAITS), and called for processions and bouts of most realistic fencing or fisticuffs.

It is obvious that these can only be general remarks (for further details see the theatres, under their own names), and that each playhouse must have differed, not only from the others, but even from itself at different times, and also from the private theatres. The first of these was set up in the Almonry House of St. Paul's in 1575. A year later the first Blackfriars opened under Farrant, and in 1596 Burbage established the second Blackfriars. In 1615 the short-lived Porter's Hall opened, and in 1616 came the Cockpit (later the Phoenix), which, with Salisbury Court, the last private theatre to be opened, survived the Commonwealth. Both were used for a short time after the Restoration.

The early roofed playhouses, which, unlike the public playhouses, were adapted from existing buildings and not specially built, were used mainly by the Boy companies, the 'little eyases' who caused the adult companies so much uneasiness, but later the men took over, and the Burbages' company, for example, used both the Globe and the second Blackfriars, according to the season and the state of the weather.

The general design of the stage in the private theatre had obvious affinities with the public one, since it also had a platform stage against an architectural façade complete with doors and windows and an upper stage. But it almost certainly had also an inner stage. It used at different times the old simultaneous or fixed settings which had come down from the medieval cycles via the Court play, the unlocalized successive staging of such theatres as the Globe, and the movable painted scenery of Inigo Jones's masques, which does not appear to have reached the public stage. Added to this, the stage and the auditorium were lit by artificial light (candles, either of wax or tallow), and all spectators were seated, the standing groundlings being replaced by pittites on benches. With the closing of the theatres in 1642 the Elizabethan public theatre vanished, and it was along the lines of such private theatres as the second Blackfriars that the Restoration theatre developed after 1660.

The financial affairs of the Elizabethan stage were so involved that it is impossible to give details here; but each company, which took its name from the great lord under whose protection it existed (as the Earl of Pembroke's, the Earl of Leicester's, Lord Strange's, the Lord Admiral's, the Lord Chamberlain's), was an association of partners, or 'sharers', who acted together, and had a joint stock of plays and clothes. One man might be appointed to act as manager for the rest, but all received a share in the profits, though some might be full sharers, others only half- or quarter-sharers. The owner of the playhouse was allotted part of the entrance-money, usually the takings in some particular part of the house, and for this purpose he appointed 'gatherers', or money-takers, to collect up his due portion. Certain actors might also have a share in this entrance-money, and they were then known as 'housekeepers'. This at any rate was the method used by the Burbages and their chief rivals. A different system was in force at the Rose, where Henslowe was virtually an 'outside capitalist', since he paid all the bills on behalf of the actors and frequently made loans to them and to their playwrights, reimbursing himself from the takings in all parts of the house.

Not all actors were necessarily 'sharers', since the boys, who in the absence of actresses played the women's parts, were usually apprenticed to the older men, while extra actors could be hired by the sharers; and it was possible for a man to be a 'housekeeper' in a playhouse at which he did not necessarily act. Also the shares could be bought and sold, or left as legacies, which enabled Heminge and Condell, for instance, to buy up those Globe shares which were not held by the Burbage family. The housekeepers were responsible for the upkeep of the building, while the sharers met all other incidental expenses, the minor ones of lights and music, and the major charges of playwrights and wardrobe.

When the theatre was re-established in London after the Puritan interregnum (1642–60), the effects of the long interruption were profound and far-reaching, and Restoration London had only two playhouses as against the earlier proliferation. These were Killigrew's Theatre Royal (later to be Drury Lane) and Davenant's Duke's House in Lincoln's Inn Fields. They were indoor roofed theatres, like the Blackfriars, with seated spectators and a company which included actresses for the first time, and they made a much greater use of scenery than had been the case previously. They also replaced the large Elizabethan platform stage with an apron or forestage which, though it curved out into the auditorium, was much smaller and was placed in front of a proscenium arch in imitation of the Continental, and particularly Italian, theatres. The rectangular auditorium was probably influenced by the shape of the converted tennis-courts which both managers had used initially (see TENNIS-COURT THEATRES). Characteristic of the Restoration theatre were the Doors of Entrance (see PROSCENIUM DOORS) which opened on the forestage, the Musique Room, as Pepys called it (a gallery projecting from above the top of the proscenium arch), and the division of the auditorium into pit, boxes, and galleries. These last were to remain almost continuously part of the English playhouse through its successive changes, which may perhaps be attributed to the fact that the English theatrical genius was dramatic rather than operatic, and the playhouses therefore escaped, at least for a time, the prevalent influence of the Italian opera-house. Pathé, in an *Essai sur l'architecture théâtrale* (1763), remarked on the unusual planning of the English Georgian theatre with its fan-shaped auditorium, on the three tiers of boxes along the side walls holding only four boxes in each tier, on the pit, on the three galleries or amphitheatres, and on the sloping ceiling—all indigenous features which had developed successively from the two earliest theatres mentioned above through Dorset Garden (1671) (see No. 63) and the 1674 Drury Lane, through Betterton's Lincoln's Inn Fields (1695) to Vanbrugh's Queen's Theatre in the Hay (1705), which led off in a new direction, and through two theatres which form a link between the Restoration and Georgian periods—Rich's Lincoln's Inn Fields Theatre (1714), and Covent Garden Theatre (1732).

The first of the typically Georgian theatres appears to have been Potter's Little Theatre in the Haymarket, but we know little of its early years, or of those of the two theatres of the 1730s in Goodman's Fields. It was at this time that the orchestra finally moved into the pit, or well, in front of the stage which it continues to occupy (when the theatre has an orchestra). Killigrew had tried it at Bridges Street, but the time was not ripe for such a change. From *c.* 1752 dates the use of the term 'Gods' for the topmost gallery, or its occupants.

Towards the end of the century several new theatres were built—the Pantheon and the King's Concert Rooms (later the Scala) in 1772, the Royal Circus (later the Surrey) in 1782, Astley's in 1786, the Royalty in 1787—and Covent Garden, Drury Lane, and the Queen's Theatre extensively altered. Characteristic of this period was the simplification of the architectural treatment of the side boxes, and the increase in the number of galleries. In Holland's Drury Lane, which in 1794 replaced Wren's, there were no less than five towering above the pit. But most characteristic of all was the tendency to carry the lowest tier of boxes right round the pit to increase the number of side boxes, and to run the tiers of boxes up three or four storeys. In most theatres the two top galleries were strictly isolated from the side boxes and a profusion of spiked railings kept members of the audience from climbing on to the stage or to superior parts of the house. One development which must have exerted a strong influence on English theatre buildings was the custom which arose from 1785 onwards of covering over the excavated pit so as to provide an unbroken expanse of floor-space, at stage and first-tier box levels, for balls and masquerades.

One feature of the English playhouse which owed little to Continental influence was the method of scene-changing (see GROOVES) which began with Inigo Jones and continued into the late nineteenth century. This method was still being built into the Regency theatres, of which the two extremes were probably Wyatt's Drury Lane, which replaced Holland's in 1812 (see No. 31) after the fire of 1809, and the Sans Pareil (later the Adelphi) of 1806, which marked a fresh trend in theatre design. Wyatt was preoccupied above all with the social aspect of the theatre, and introduced an increasing number of saloons, coffee-rooms, lobbies, and rotundas where the audience, deprived of some of its social activities by the new fashion of darkening the auditorium by the manipulation of a gas chandelier, could parade in full splendour. Among the other theatres built at this time—the new Covent Garden (1809) (see No. 32), the Lyceum (1816), the Haymarket (1821)—the tendency was luckily towards smaller auditoriums, away from the mammoth size of Holland's Drury Lane, where the comfortable range for the capacity of an actor's voice seems to have been over-reached.

If Wyatt's Drury Lane appeared as the apotheosis of the Georgian theatre, the Sans Pareil in the Strand took the first step towards its transformation into the nineteenth-century style we know today. The bond between boxes and pit is finally broken and the first circle is raised over the pit, which is pushed back under it by the spread of the orchestra well, and the stalls emerge as the best places nearest the stage with individual seats instead of the old benches. Among the theatres built in this new pit-under-balcony style were the Coburg (later the Old Vic) (see No. 35) in 1818 and the rebuilt Olympic (1850) and Surrey (1861). Other theatres followed the fashion until the box-tier directly flanking the pit became a rare curiosity where it was once a Georgian commonplace. It is seen today in the Theatre Royal, Bristol (1766) (see No. 27), the Richmond Theatre, Yorks., and to some extent in the Theatre Royal, Bath.

A slight lull in theatre building in the first half of the nineteenth century was followed by unprecedented activity, and in the seventy years from 1866 to 1936 no fewer than eighty new theatres were built in London, as well as countless music-halls. A proportionate increase took place in the provinces. A new feature was the removal of the columns supporting the tiers. These had been a characteristic feature of the earlier playhouse, but they must always have seriously obstructed the view of the stage for the spectator who sat behind them; yet to do away with them was to leave the circles unsupported. The first solution was to build one very shallow Dress Circle with only two or three rows of seats and a row of boxes directly behind, and then to set back the upper circles and galleries to the level of the box façades, thus leaving the Dress Circle projecting, free and unobstructed, like a half-open drawer from a chest. Phipps's theatres—the Queen's (1866), the Gaiety (1868), and the Vaudeville (1870)—all give evidence of a move in this direction, and from that it was a short step to the abolition of columns in other parts of the auditorium. By the 1880s such theatres as the Savoy (1881), the Prince's (1884), Terry's (1887), and the Garrick (1889) had done away with most or all of them. In 1901 Wyatt's old Adelphi was transformed by Runtz into the Century, and all traces of supporting pillars were removed. The modern era in playhouse design had begun, to be confirmed in 1921 by the reconstruction of the interior of Wyatt's Drury Lane, when the columns were replaced by cantilever construction.

Another characteristic of the Victorian theatre was the increase in comfort for the playgoer, with padded and sprung seats, velvet upholstery and thick carpets—a far cry from the backless benches covered in green baize of the Georgian era. Many of these nineteenth-century theatres are still in use, but architects, actors, and dramatists are in search of new forms of theatre which must eventually influence the design of the playhouse. Smaller, more intimate auditoriums are likely, with massed ranks of seats in one single spreading tier, and open stages, as at the Mermaid or at Chichester, will replace the proscenium-arch stage picture. More use will probably be made of arena theatre or theatre-in-the-round techniques (see No. 41), and of the adaptable stages which have so far been built, only privately, for Bristol University, for the London Academy of Music and Dramatic Art, and for an amateur company, the Questors. The eventual building of the National Theatre on the South Bank may lead to a new era in English playhouse design, perhaps under the influence of the new Continental theatres (for a more general survey of theatre building, see ACOUSTICS and ARCHITECTURE; see also London and other theatres under their own names and PROVINCIAL THEATRES).

ENGLISH STAGE COMPANY, an organization formed in 1956 to present modern plays, both English and foreign, and to encourage young dramatists. After an unsuccessful attempt to reopen the bomb-damaged Kingsway Theatre, the company, under the artistic direction of George Devine, with Tony Richardson as assistant director, opened at the Royal Court Theatre in Sloane Square on 2 Apr. 1956 with Angus Wilson's *The Mulberry Bush*, previously produced at the Bristol Old Vic. Its first outstanding success, after a slow start, was Osborne's *Look Back in Anger* in May. In pursuance of its avowed aims, the company has presented plays by Beckett, Brecht, Frisch, Genêt, Ionesco, Sartre, Tennessee Williams, and others from abroad, and, of the new English dramatists, Arden, N. F. Simpson, Christopher Logue, Ann Jellicoe, Willis Hall, Arnold Wesker, and others. It also sponsors Sunday-night 'productions without décor' as a means of bringing untried dramatists before the public. It occasionally stages a revival of a classic—*The Country Wife, A Midsummer Night's Dream*—and once lapsed so far from its somewhat austere principles as to present a farce—Feydeau's *Look After Lulu* in an adaptation by Noël Coward. But on the whole it remains faithful to its ideals, and has done invaluable work in breaking down old prejudices, widening the theatrical horizons of London, and forming a useful counterblast to the more complacent offerings of the commercial theatre (see also ROYAL COURT THEATRE, 2).

ENNIUS, QUINTUS (239–169 B.C.), one of the greatest of Latin poets, and an important figure in the history of Latin drama. Born at Rudiae in the south of Italy, he went to Rome in 204 B.C. A man of versatile genius and broad human sympathies, he brought into Latin literature a fresh impulse of Hellenism. In the absence of a reading public at Rome it was inevitable that Ennius should turn to drama; here the death of Andronicus and the disgrace of Naevius left the way clear for him in tragedy, and fragments from no fewer than twenty of his tragedies have come down to us. He seems to have taken many of his plays from Euripides, a writer in whom he found a questioning spirit and humanitarian outlook like his own. Like other Roman dramatists Ennius kept, or tried to keep, close to the sense of the Greek he was translating, though allowing himself considerable freedom in expression and in metre; of original construction we have no evidence, except that in his *Iphigenia* he introduced a chorus of soldiers. The fragments illustrate his poetic power; compared with the Greek they may strike us as rhetorical, but they are free from the excesses of later Roman tragedy in this respect, and they contain much that is beautiful and moving. The influence of his tragedies on the Romans of his generation must have been great. His contemporary Plautus burlesques his style—a proof that his plays were well known—and in the next generation Terence refers to him as one of the 'careless' but nevertheless admirable dramatists of the past. His plays continued to be read down to the end of the Republic, though Roman opinion seems to have ranked Pacuvius and Accius higher as writers of tragedy. He also attempted comedy, though, it would appear, without much success, and two *praetextae* are doubtfully assigned to him—the *Sabinae*, dealing presumably with the Rape of the Sabines, and the *Ambracia*, which perhaps told of the conquest of that region by Ennius' patron, M. Fulvius Nobilior. There are few losses in Latin literature which we have to regret more than the disappearance of the tragedies of this gifted and warm-hearted man.

WILLIAM BEARE†

E.N.S.A., see ENTERTAINMENTS NATIONAL SERVICE ASSOCIATION.

ENTERS, ANGNA (1907–), an American mime-actress, whose programme as a one-woman entertainer consists of a series of wordless mime and dance sketches, in appropriate costume, which she writes herself. They now amount to some 200 items, among them the 'Queen of Heaven', 'Boy Cardinal', 'Pavana', 'Little Sally Waters', 'Pierrot', 'Harlequin'. Her range is wide, and with a gesture she can evoke an Impressionist picture of a wood on a hot summer's day or the sad ennui of provincial life in France in 1910, an ageing prostitute or a Byzantine ikon. She made her first appearance in New York in 1924, and was seen in 1927 in London, where she has returned many times in between extensive tours of America and other parts of the world. An accomplished painter, she has also written a number of books, in one of which, *Artist's Life* (1958), she describes her professional life in the theatre, and shows how much thought and hard work have gone into the making of her apparently effortless entertainment.

ENTERTAINMENTS NATIONAL SERVICE ASSOCIATION, THE, commonly known as E.N.S.A., an organization formed in 1938–9 to provide entertainment for the British and allied armed forces and war-workers during the Second World War. It was directed by Basil Dean, and had its headquarters at Drury Lane Theatre, London. Working closely in collaboration with the Navy, Army, and Air Force Institute (N.A.A.F.I.), which was responsible for the financial side, it provided all types of entertainment, from full-length plays and symphony orchestras to concert parties and solo instrumentalists, not only in the camps, factories, and hostels of Great Britain, but on all war-fronts, from the Mediterranean to India, from Africa to the Faroes.

ENTHOVEN, MRS. GABRIELLE, O.B.E. (1868–1950), English theatre historian, who in 1924 presented to the Victoria and Albert Museum in London the vast collection of theatre material which bears her name. This included innumerable playbills, engravings, prints, books, models, and newspaper cuttings, covering the history of theatrical production in London from the eighteenth century onwards. Mrs. Enthoven continued to administer and work on it for the benefit of research students, constantly revising and adding to its resources. She was herself an amateur actress and a dramatist, appearing for many years with such companies as the Old Stagers and the Windsor Strollers, and writing several plays, including an English adaptation of one of D'Annunzio's poetic dramas.

ENTREMÉS, a Spanish term which derives originally from the French *entremets*, applied to a diversion, dramatic or non-dramatic, which took place between the courses of a banquet. In Catalonia such diversions were termed *entrameses* and this name was transferred to the dramatic interludes which enlivened the Corpus Christi procession. In Castilian the term was applied in the sixteenth and seventeenth centuries to a short comic interlude, often ending in a dance, which was performed in the public theatres between the acts of a play. Most of the well-known dramatists of the period wrote *entremeses*, among them Cervantes, Lope de Vega, and Calderón. Luis Quiñones de Benavente (*c.* 1589–1651) is remembered chiefly as an *entremesista.* In the eighteenth century the term *sainete* is found, applied to much the same type of entertainment, whilst the nineteenth-century *género chico* has often been recognized as the lineal descendant of the *entremés* of the Castilian theatre.

J. E. VAREY

EPIDAURUS. The ruins of the splendid Greek open-air theatre on this site (see No. 1) are now used for an annual festival. Casts from the Greek National Theatre, headed by Katina Paxinou and Alexis Minotis, perform such plays as the *Oedipus Rex* and *Hecuba*, *Phoenissae* and *Hercules Furens*. In 1960 Menander's *Dyskolos* was added to the repertory, with music by Skalkottas. The production was by Alexis Solomos, who was also responsible for *Lysistrata*.

EPICHARMUS (*c.* 550–460 B.C.) of Syracuse, Greek comic poet and the most important figure in Sicilian-Greek comedy, which influenced the Old Comedy of Athens (see GREECE, 2 and MIME, 1 *b*). His work survives only in a few fragments and in some doubtful traditions; the traditions make him something of a philosopher, and the fragments suggest that mythological burlesque was an important element in his comedy. According to Horace (*Epistles*, ii. 1. 58) Plautus was said to have imitated the fast-moving style of Epicharmus ('dicitur . . . Plautus ad exemplar Siculi properare Epicharmi'). H. D. F. KITTO

EPILOGUE, see PROLOGUE.

EPISODE, see GREECE, 1 *c*.

EQUESTRIAN DRAMA, see CIRCUS.

EQUITY, the professional actors' association in England and America. British Actors' Equity was founded on 1 Dec. 1929, on a proposal by Ben Webster at a meeting held at the Duke of York's Theatre. It regulates all questions of actors' salaries, working conditions, and terms of employment, in London and in the provinces, and advises the Ministry of Labour on the issuing of work permits for foreign actors. Before its foundation there had been various attempts at organizing theatre workers in the hope of improving salaries and back-stage conditions, which by the end of the nineteenth century, after the collapse of the stock company in 1880, were often horrifying, particularly on tour. Irving was president of the first Actors' Association, formed in 1891, but, like the first Actors' Union, founded in 1905 by H. B. Irving and Seymour Hicks, this had a short life and made little impression. It was in 1906 that the suggestion was first made that the Actors' Association should become a trade union and work to improve the minimum rates of pay and to raise the status of its members. It took nearly twenty-five years of hard work, including the first actors' strike in 1920, before Equity emerged. It still has to exercise the utmost vigilance in securing advantageous terms for its members working in the theatre and films, and on radio and television. Variety artists, however, have their own Federation, though the same person can belong to both.

Unlike British Equity, American Equity (The American Actors' Equity Association) deals only with performers in the legitimate theatre. It is affiliated to the American Federation of Labor, and was founded on 12 Dec. 1912. In 1919 it called its first strike and was successful in gaining better conditions. It has also worked to implement a policy of racial non-segregation in theatres, for which purpose it boycotted for a time the National Theatre in Washington, D.C. In 1943 Sam Jaffé, representing Equity, and George Freedley, representing the New York Public Library, founded the Equity Library Theatre as a showcase for actors, directors, and technicians. A year later John Golden joined them, and helped to finance the enterprise, which is now run by Equity itself in the Master Institute on Riverside Drive.

ERCKMANN-CHATRIAN, the pseudonym of two French authors, Émile Erckmann (1822–99) and Louis-Gratien-Charles-Alexandre Chatrian (1826–90), who wrote a series of novels dealing with the French Revolution and the Napoleonic period seen from the point of view of the private soldier. Some of these were dramatized, but the collaborators are best remembered for their play, *Le Juif polonais*, which, in an English adaptation by Leopold Lewis as *The Bells*, provided Irving with a fine part in which he made his first great success.

ERLANGER THEATRE, NEW YORK, see ST. JAMES THEATRE.

ERNST, PAUL (1866–1933), German dramatist, a writer of great austerity who forsook naturalism because it did not satisfy his innate sense of form. In his tragedies, which he wrote for the Düsseldorf theatre, where he was employed for a time, he isolates the inner action and reaction in a timeless sphere, and is inclined to reduce drama to dialogue. There is more movement in his comedies, *Eine Nacht in Florenz* (1904), *Der heilige Crispin* (1910), *Pantalon und seine Söhne* (1916), where the characters, though traditional, are seen from a new angle, while the comic situation, often arising out of a confusion of identity, provokes reflection rather than laughter.

ERVINE, JOHN ST. JOHN GREER (1883–1971), Irish dramatist and critic, whose early work was produced at the Abbey Theatre, Dublin, where he was for a short time manager. He later settled in England. He served as dramatic critic on a number of papers, notably the *Morning Post* and the *Observer*, while from 1928 to 1929 he was guest critic of *The New York World*. A controversial and outspoken writer, he has not hesitated to use the theatre for the furtherance of his ideas on social problems, as in *Robert's Wife* (1937), in which Edith Evans gave a fine performance, and *Private Enterprise* (1947). He has also written a number of light comedies, including *Antony and Anna* (1926), and *The First Mrs. Fraser* (1929), which ran for two years with Marie Tempest in the title-role. More serious themes are dealt with in *Mixed Marriage* (1911) and *John Ferguson* (1915), which were both given originally in Dublin, and *Jane Clegg*, given at Manchester in 1913 with Sybil Thorndike in the title-role. Ervine has written several books on the theatre, including *The Theatre in My Time* and *How to Write a Play*; he has received honorary degrees from St. Andrews and Belfast, and in 1937 became President of the League of British Dramatists.

ESLAVA, FERNÃN GONZÁLEZ DE, see SOUTH AMERICA, I.

ESLAVA THEATRE, see MADRID THEATRES.

ESMOND, HENRY V. (1869–1922), English actor-manager and dramatist whose real name was Henry Jack. The son of a doctor, he was born at Hampton Court and educated privately. He went on the stage in 1885, and after gaining experience on tour was seen in London in 1889, appearing at the Opera Comique, the Globe, the Princess's, and several other theatres which have now vanished. He was for a time associated with E. S. Willard and Edward Terry, and then joined George Alexander at the St. James's, where he scored a big success as Cayley Drummle in *The Second Mrs. Tanqueray* (1893). He was also Little Billee in the first production of *Trilby* (1895). While at the St. James's he began writing plays, sentimental comedies of the period which had a great vogue, and in which he toured with much success, his wife, Eva Moore (1870–1955), whom he married in 1891, playing opposite him. The best known of these are *One Summer's Day* (1897), *The Wilderness* and *When we were Twenty-One* (both 1901), *My Lady Virtue* (1902), *Billy's Little Love Affair* (1903), and *Eliza Comes to Stay* (1913). His last play, which had a considerable success, was *The Law Divine*, produced at Wyndham's in 1918. W. MACQUEEN-POPE†

ESPAÑOL THEATRE, see MADRID THEATRES.

ESPY, L' [FRANÇOIS BEDEAU] (*fl.* 1610–64), French actor, the elder brother of the clown Jodelet, with whom he is usually found, first in Lenoir's company at the Hôtel d'Argent, then at the Hôtel de Bourgogne, and finally at the Théâtre du Marais. He joined Molière's company in 1659, but was already somewhat old and soon gave up acting in favour of management. It was he who was responsible for the alterations made in Richelieu's old theatre, the Palais-Royal, before Molière took possession of it in 1661. He retired in 1664, being then well over 60.

ESSLAIR, FERDINAND (1772–1840), German actor, of good family, whose passion for the theatre declared itself at an early age. He made his début at Innsbruck and for many years travelled from one town to another, poor, overworked, early married, and soon widowed. As his second wife he married a young actress, with whom he continued to tour until, after a short period as manager of the theatre in Stuttgart, he was in 1820 appointed leading actor and manager of the Court theatre in Munich. Here he remained for a long time. He relied more on inspiration than on study, but his passionate acting allied to exceptional graces of person and voice made him one of the most popular actors in Germany. At the height of his fame he again undertook a tour of the chief towns in the country, being everywhere fêted and applauded. He was at his best in Schiller, particularly as Wilhelm Tell and Wallenstein.

ESTCOURT, DICK (1668–1712), a Restoration actor immortalized by Steele in *The Spectator*. He does not appear to have been a particularly good actor, but he was an amazing mimic, and his natural good humour and vivacity made him a favourite with any company. Shortly before his death he became landlord of the Bumper Tavern in St. James's Street. For an excellent account of Estcourt, see *The Spectator*, No. 468, which also records his death.

ETHEL BARRYMORE THEATRE, NEW YORK. This was built by Lee Shubert, and opened on 20 Dec. 1928 with *The Kingdom of God*. It seats 1,100 people, and its history, though not sensational, has almost invariably been one of success. The actress after whom the theatre was named first appeared at it as Lady Teazle in a brief revival of *The School for Scandal*. Among outstanding productions there were Noël Coward and the Lunts in *Design for Living*, the latter pair in *Point Valaine*, and Margaret Rawlings in *Parnell*. Emlyn Williams, with May Whitty and Angela Baddeley, in his own play, *Night Must Fall*, was followed by Clare Boothe's scathing comedy, *The Women*, which set up a record for the theatre of 657 performances. In 1947 *A Streetcar Named Desire* won both the Pulitzer Prize and the New York Drama Critics' Circle award, a feat repeated ten years later by Ketti Frings's adaptation of Wolfe's *Look Homeward, Angel*. GEORGE FREEDLEY†

ETHEREGE, SIR GEORGE (1634–91), English dramatist, the first to attempt the social comedy of manners developed by Congreve and later perfected by Sheridan. Etherege spent part of his early years in France, and was doubtless influenced by memories of Molière when he came to write his first play, *The Comical Revenge; or, Love in a Tub* (1664), a serious verse drama with a comic prose sub-plot. It was this latter style that Etherege explored further in his two later comedies, *She Would if She Could* (1668) and *The Man of Mode* (1676). The latter, which may be taken as typical of Restoration comedy, is Etherege's best play, a picture of a society living exclusively for amusement, with a tenuous plot of entangled love-affairs offering an opportunity for brilliant dialogue and character-drawing. It contains the 'prince of fops', Sir Fopling Flutter, and the heartless, witty Dorimant, often considered a portrait of Lord Rochester, just as the poet Bellair is supposed to be Etherege himself.

ETHIOPIA. In Ethiopia, as in Europe, drama grew out of the rites of religious festivals. The Hamites, the original inhabitants of the country, worshipped the sun and stars, trees, and the spirits of earth and water. Their earliest dramas were probably mimes, acted in the open under trees, beside rivers, or on mountain tops. Later they were transferred to temples. The remains of such a temple, with inscriptions that reveal the worship of south-Arabian deities, has been found in Aksum, an ancient city in the north of the country.

These early rites appear to have died out when the Semitic tribes, and particularly the Amhara, penetrated into Ethiopia and took over its political and cultural affairs. Ancient Ethiopian traditions say that their Queen Mekeda (the Biblical Queen of Sheba) visited Jerusalem and had a son by Solomon. This son, Menelik I, returned to Ethiopia in 1000 B.C. to found the first Amharic-Ethiopic dynasty. With him went the first-born sons of the high priests and nobles of Israel, bearing with them the sacred Ark of the Covenant. On arriving at Aksum they built a temple to house the Ark, and in the courtyard the priests performed Semitic dances which they had learnt at King Solomon's court. From these developed a form of dance-drama, to the accompaniment of drums, staves, and percussion instruments, whose influence is still apparent today. Later, rudimentary forms of drama began to develop, with choral speaking accompanied by the beating of a gong, drum, or other instrument. Each ceremony had its own mime—the Burnt Offering, the Meal Offering, the Peace Offering, the Guilt Offering, the Sin Offering—while three times a year the male members of the community performed open-air religious dramas in which women had no part. One of these commemorated, in a procession of brightly clad priests, the bringing to Ethiopia of the Ark of the Covenant.

Early in the fourth century missionaries from Egypt and Syria brought Christianity to Ethiopia, and in A.D. 334 it became the State religion of the Empire. New ceremonies were introduced in an endeavour to combine Christian dogma with Jewish and pagan rites. Among these was the annual three-day dance-drama of *Timket*, which took place in the third week of January. This retained the ceremony of the Ark, but added to it the Baptism of Christ.

Another drama of this time was *Kadam Souarir*, which celebrated the giving-up of the Jewish Sabbath for the Christian Sunday. *Maskal*, which took place in Sept. at the end of the rainy season, also shows a blending of pagan, Jewish, and Christian elements. It began with the actors collecting the bright yellow flower called Maskal which grows in profusion at this time of the year, and presenting it to the audience as a reminder of the beginning of spring. This was probably a survival of early nature-worship. It was followed by a Jewish episode based on the belief that the smoke of sacrifice ascends to heaven and returns to bless the earth. The actors collected dry branches and tied them together in bundles. Then, with songs and dances accompanied by musical instruments, they cast the bundles into a fire kindled round a tall pole stuck in the ground. The Christian interpretation of this episode is based on an old legend which says that an Ethiopian queen named Helena went with other Christians to search for the cross on which Christ was crucified. When the search proved successful, the queen commanded that a long pole should be erected and set fire to, so that the Christians in Constantinople could see it and learn the good news. These early church dramas were acted in Ge'ez, which belongs to one of the southern groups of Semitic languages, but as time went on, and secular drama developed, this was replaced by Amharic, the language of the ruling tribe.

Secular drama first developed when people gathered together to act plays, improvising their dialogue and action on a given plot, usually an episode from their own tribal history. Scenery was rarely used, except for leaves and branches to denote out-door scenes. Most of the plays began at sunset and lasted for two to four hours.

Through the centuries music, dance, and drama played an ever-increasing part in the social life of the Ethiopians, but it was not until the reign of the present Emperor Haile Selassie I that an organized movement, sponsored by the Government, came into being. A National Theatre was opened in Addis Ababa, in which only Ethiopian artists are employed, to preserve and stimulate the folk-art of the country. No make-up is worn, except by clowns and comic characters. The programme, made up of variety turns, lasts about three hours, during which time the audience can enter and leave freely, and refreshments can be obtained. National songs and dances are performed, and sometimes comic dramatic sketches on current events. In these the actors improvise round a given plot, and the actor usually plays the same character in a number of different sketches—the young heroine, her lover, the rogue, the comedian, and the clown. The clown always wears a white wig, eyebrows, moustache and beard, and a long black cloak, which he wraps round himself when making his entrances and exits. He is often a skilled acrobat and contortionist.

In 1956, to commemorate the Silver Jubilee of the Emperor Haile Selassie I, a magnificent theatre of contemporary design, seating about 2,000 people, was opened in Addis Ababa. Since its inception artists of international fame from many countries have performed in it, and at other times it is used for the production of modern Ethiopian plays in Amharic. These are not, as at the National Theatre, improvised on a set plot, but written out in full, and carefully rehearsed and produced, with full use of the elaborate stage lighting, and of costume, scenery, and make-up. A regular State company of sixty actors is attached to the theatre. Among the modern playwrights of Ethiopia are Berhanu Denqé, author of a verse-play on the Queen of Sheba's visit to Solomon entitled *Negest Akeb* (1951); Makonnen Endelkachew, former Prime Minister of Ethiopia, who has written several historical plays; and Kabbada Mika'el, former Minister for Education, who has written some plays in verse, of which *Ya-tinbit qutaro* (1946) has been translated and published in English as *Fulfilment of Prophecy*; he has also made a translation and adaptation of *Romeo and Juliet* (1953). Another playwright, Germanchau Takla-Hawaryat, is the author of a verse-drama *Tewodros* (1950), which tells the story of the nineteenth-century Ethiopian Emperor Theodore, who fought against the English and later committed suicide. Among the women playwrights Senedu Gabru has written two verse-dramas, published in her book *Yalibbe Mashaf* (1949)—The Book of My Heart; and Romana-Warq Kasahun has written, among other works, *Mahtota Tebab* (1951)—The Lamp of Science—on the subject of Princess Tsahai, the daughter of the present emperor, who was trained as a nurse and died in the service of her profession.

Through the advance of education, and with the help and encouragement given to writers and actors by the Imperial family and the Government, a new era for the theatre is beginning in this ancient land. OLIVIA HASLER

ETHIOPIAN OPERA, a turn in the minstrel show, consisting of burlesques on Shakespeare and opera, with Negro melodies inserted. It was modelled on the early burlesques of T. D. Rice (Jim Crow), of which the best were *Bone Squash Diavolo* (on 'Fra Diavolo'), *Jumbo Jim*, *Jim Crow in London*, and a burlesque of *Othello*.

EUGENE O'NEILL THEATRE, NEW YORK, see CORONET THEATRE.

EUPHORION. (1) The father of Aeschylus. (2) The son of Aeschylus, and himself a tragic poet, apparently of some merit.

EUPOLIS (*c.* 446–*c.* 411 B.C.), of Athens, one of the leading poets of Old Comedy, and a contemporary of Aristophanes (cf. Horace: 'Eupolis atque Cratinus, Aristophanesque poetae'). Eupolis is said to have won seven victories. Many fragments of his work survive, but no complete play.

EURIPIDES (484–406/7 B.C.), Athenian tragic poet, son of Mnesarchus (or Mnesarchides), born, probably, in the Athenian island of Salamis. His parents were well-to-do, his mother apparently of good family. Aristophanes' standing joke that she was a greengrocer was funny perhaps because it was so remote from the truth. Of Euripides' life little is known, and still less can be believed. Thus, statements that he had matrimonial troubles may be based only on the supposed misogyny of his plays; and the story that he had a study fitted up in a cave on the coast of Salamis sounds like a plausible invention. He is said to have been morose; he was certainly deeply interested in the philosophic and scientific movements of his day. He seems to have played little part in public life, being in this respect an interesting contrast with Aeschylus and Sophocles, for in many ways Euripides was a forerunner of the greater individualism of the next and following centuries. He is said to have written ninety-two plays, of which there survive seventeen tragedies, one quite entertaining satyr-play, the *Cyclops*, and a very large number of fragments (an indication of his later popularity), which include substantial parts of the *Hypsipyle* (on papyrus). The extant plays are: *Cyclops*, *Alcestis* (438 B.C.), *Medea* (431), *Hippolytus* (428), *Children of Heracles* (? *c.* 428), *Andromache*, *Hecuba*, *Heracles Furens*, *Suppliants*, *Ion*, *Electra*, *Trojan Women* (415), *Iphigenia in Tauris* (? 414), *Helen* (412), *Phoenician Women* (411), *Orestes* (408), and the *Bacchae* and *Iphigenia in Aulis*, both produced posthumously. Included with these plays in the manuscripts is a weak play, *Rhesus*, sometimes thought to be an early play by Euripides, more probably a fourth-century work.

Euripides gained five victories (compared with Sophocles' eighteen). In 408 he visited (like Agathon) the Court of Archelaus, King of Macedonia, much as Aeschylus visited Hiero of Syracuse; and he died there soon afterwards. Sophocles, who outlived him by a few months, is said to have dressed his next chorus in mourning as a mark of respect. Aristophanes, in the *Frogs* (405 B.C.), compares Euripides very unfavourably with Aeschylus, but he obviously felt that the death of Euripides and Sophocles had left Athens with no worthy successors to them.

Though contemporaries, Sophocles and Euripides seem to belong to different ages. Sophocles is the last of the 'classics', carrying into a democratic age the traditions and outlook of an aristocratic society; Euripides is critical, sceptical, individualistic, in a sense cosmopolitan. His drama deals less with the community than with the individual, less with broad questions of religion and morality than with the emotions and passions—love, hate, revenge—and with specific social questions, like war. In this respect he looks forward to the thought and art of the cosmopolitan Hellenistic age and of Rome; Seneca could imitate the emotionalism, sententiousness, pathos, and rhetoric of Euripides, but very little in Aeschylus or Sophocles. In his lifetime Euripides aroused great interest and great opposition; his realism, his interest in abnormal psychology, his portraits of women in love, his new and emotional music, his unorthodoxy, his argumentativeness, all gave offence; on the other hand, Aristophanes, by continually parodying not only his manner but also particular scenes and verses, is good evidence for the great interest that he aroused. His immense fame did not begin until after his death; he soon eclipsed both Aeschylus and Sophocles, for he was the only one of the great three who could speak directly to the new world established by Alexander's conquests. In modern times his reputation has fluctuated. He has been unduly disparaged by critics of a neo-classic turn of mind, perhaps overpraised by 'advanced' thinkers. His work is uneven, his manner can become tiresome; few would put him on a level with Aeschylus or Sophocles, but many would echo Aristotle's description of him as 'the most tragic of the poets'.

His plays fall into two clearly marked kinds, tragedies (in the modern sense) and plays which may variously be called tragicomedies, romantic drama, melodrama, or high comedy. The tragedies are of unequal merit; in most of them Euripides' episodic plot-construction is —at any rate at first sight—a stumbling-block. The best are the *Medea*, *Hippolytus*, *Bacchae*, *Trojan Women*, and *Hecuba*. The *Children of Heracles* and the *Suppliants* are weak, and the *Heracles Furens* is hardly a success. It is in the tragedies that most of the puzzling features of Euripides' work are to be found—episodic plots, irrelevant philosophizing, over-simplified characterization, a poetic style that sometimes becomes tediously rhetorical. Of the other plays, the *Electra* and the *Orestes* (completely misunderstood by many critics of the nineteenth century) are powerful studies in morbidity and insanity; the *Alcestis*, *Ion*, and *Iphigenia in Tauris* are excellent tragicomedy or romantic drama—the *Alcestis* was the fourth play of its tetralogy, taking the place of the usual satyr-play; the *Helen* is most delightful high comedy, and the *Phoenician Women* is a kind of pageant-play. All these plays (except the last) show a skill in construction, and a delicacy and wit both in the dialogue and in the characterization, which are of the very highest order. Euripides was the earliest master in this non-tragic genre, and remains unsurpassed. It is through these plays that he, and not the contemporary writers of Old Comedy, points forward to the New Comedy of the fourth century (see GREECE, 2 *b* and MENANDER).

Euripides continued to use the three actors and chorus as finally established by Sophocles, but one innovation of his, the 'prologue', has been important in the history of the drama. Early Greek tragedies began with the entrance-song of the chorus; Aeschylus's later plays, and all the extant plays of Sophocles, begin with a histrionic scene, whether in dramatic soliloquy or dialogue, the chorus entering later. Any such scene was, in Greek, a 'prologos'; what Euripides did was to invent a quite formal 'prologue', spoken sometimes by a character in the play, sometimes by an external god, which did little more than summarize the story up to the point where the action begins. This, via Seneca, is the origin of the 'prologue' in Elizabethan drama.

Another development in Euripides' drama was that the chorus came to be less closely connected with the action. This was inevitable when plays began to deal with private rather than public issues (e.g. the conjugal difficulties of Medea and Jason); and when the plot was very largely intrigue (as in the *Iphigenia in Tauris* and *Helen*) the presence of a chorus might be a positive embarrassment. It therefore tended to become (and in the younger dramatist Agathon did become) a quite conventional lyrical decoration, having no close connexion with the plot. A similar thing happened to the comic chorus (see GREECE, 2 *b*). Hence the Elizabethan idea of an extraneous person called the 'Chorus' speaking a 'prologue'.

H. D. F. KITTO

EVANS, DAME EDITH MARY (1888–), English actress, created D.B.E. in 1946 for her services to the theatre. She made her first appearance on the stage in 1912 as an amateur, playing Gautami in William Poel's production of *Sakuntala*, and Cressida in his *Troilus and Cressida* for the Elizabethan Stage Society. She then became a professional actress and toured with Ellen Terry. After varied experience—mainly in modern plays, though in 1922 she played Cleopatra in *All for Love*, and other seventeenth-century parts, for the Phoenix Society—she first came prominently before the public with her fine performance of Millamant in *The Way of the World* at the Lyric, Hammersmith, in 1924. She was with the Old Vic for the 1925–6 season, playing among other characters Portia, Cleopatra, Beatrice, Rosalind, and the Nurse in *Romeo and Juliet*, and in 1927 went back to Hammersmith to play Mrs. Sullen in *The Beaux' Stratagem*. Other outstanding parts of her distinguished career have been the Serpent and the She-Ancient in *Back to Methuselah*, Florence Nightingale in *The Lady with a Lamp*, Orinthia in *The Apple Cart*, which she first played at the Malvern Festival, Irela in *Evensong*, the name-part in *Viceroy Sarah*, Agatha Payne in *The Old Ladies*, and Sanchia Carson in *Robert's Wife*. She was also excellent as Lady Bracknell in the 1939 revival of *The Importance of Being Earnest* and as Mrs. Malaprop in *The Rivals*. In 1936 she was again with the Old Vic company, playing Lady Fidget in *The Country Wife*, Rosalind, and the Witch in *The Witch of Edmonton*. In 1946, after extensive tours abroad entertaining the troops, she was seen as Katerina Ivanova in *Crime and Punishment*. Among later outstanding performances were her 'old peeled wall' of a Lady Wishfort in *The Way of the World* and her Madame Ranevsky in *The Cherry Orchard* (both 1948), Lady Pitts in *Daphne Laureola* (1949), the Countess Rosmarin in *The Dark is Light Enough* (1954), the Queen in *Henry VIII* at the Old Vic (1958) and, at Stratford-upon-Avon, the Countess Rousillon in *All's Well That Ends Well* (1959). In 1963 she returned to modern drama to play Violet Lazara in Bolt's *Gentle Jack*, which had, however, an unusually short run.

EVANS, MAURICE (1901–), English actor, whose first appearances on the stage were in amateur dramatizations of Hardy's novels. His début on the professional stage was made at Cambridge, but he first came prominently before the public with his performance as Raleigh in *Journey's End* in 1928. He joined the Old Vic company in 1934 and was seen in a variety of parts, including *Hamlet* in its entirety, which he later played in New York with great success. He first went to America in 1935, and has since remained there, becoming an American citizen in 1941. Among his outstanding parts have been Romeo, with Katharine Cornell, Richard II, Falstaff, Malvolio, and Macbeth in productions by Margaret Webster. During the Second World War he entertained the troops with the so-called

G.I. version of *Hamlet*, which he subsequently published.

EVANS, WILL (1875–1931), one of the funniest comedians of the London stage, both on the halls and in pantomime, was the son of Will Evans, a clown in the Grimaldi tradition. The younger Will, who made his first appearance at Drury Lane in 1881, was particularly good in kitchen scenes in pantomime, where he performed small tasks with an immense amount of superfluous energy, bungling them thoroughly, and accompanying them with a lot of spilling and slopping about of soft dough or flour paste. Among his most amusing music-hall sketches were *Building a Chicken House*, *Whitewashing the Ceiling*, and *Papering a House*. He was part-author of the successful farce, *Tons of Money*, which was produced in 1922, ran for nearly 800 performances, and has since been revived.

EVERYMAN THEATRE, LONDON, at Hampstead. This small playhouse, which is mainly known as a cinema, had a brief blaze of theatrical glory in the 1920s, under the management of Norman MacDermott. He opened there on 15 Sept. 1920 with a translation of Benavente's *Los Intereses creados* as *The Bonds of Interest*, and closed on 30 Jan. 1926 with Chesterton's *The Man Who Was Thursday*. During the intervening years seasons of Shaw and Ibsen were given, and first performances of such plays as Pirandello's *Henry IV*, Bjørnsen's *Beyond Human Power*, and Chiarelli's *The Mask and the Face*, while O'Neill was first introduced to England with *Diff'rent* and *The Long Voyage Home*. Among plays first seen at the Everyman, and then transferred for long runs to the West End, were *At Mrs. Beam's* and *Outward Bound* (both 1923) and Coward's *The Vortex* (1924). The scenery and costumes of most of the productions were designed by MacDermott himself, a notable exception being Randolph Schwabe's costumes for *Twelfth Night*. Among the actors who appeared at this theatre early in their careers were Felix Aylmer, Leslie Banks, Noël Coward, Raymond Massey, and Claude Rains, while Angela Baddeley, Jeanne de Casalis, Isabel Jeans, and Elissa Landi had their first major successes there.

EVREINOV, NIKOLAI NIKOLAIVICH (1879–1953), Russian dramatist, a symbolist who was an able exponent of non-realistic stagecraft. He held that each play should be a projection of the inner self, a theory which he exemplified in *The Theatre of the Soul*, a 'monodrama' in which various aspects of the same person appear as separate entities. The idea was further expanded in his controversial book, *The Theatre for Oneself*. A later play, *The Chief Thing* (1921), which has some affinity with Pirandello, affirms the healing power of illusion. It was the best of Evreinov's work, as his later output was negligible, and was in any case quickly submerged in the new 'socialist realism' of the Soviet era, in which Evreinov's theories had no place. Two short plays, translated by C. E. Bechhofer, *A Merry Death* and *The Beautiful Despot*, were published in *Five Russian Plays* (1916).

EWALD, JOHANNES (1743–81), Danish lyric poet and dramatist (see SCANDINAVIA, 1 *a*).

EXIT, 'he goes out', see STAGE DIRECTIONS.

EXPERIMENTAL THEATRE, NEW YORK, see DALY'S THEATRE, 3.

EXPRESSIONISM, the name given to a movement which embraced all the arts and which began in Germany about 1910. The term is generally supposed to have been suggested by some paintings which Auguste Hervé exhibited in 1901 at the Salon des Indépendants in Paris under the title of 'Expressionismes', probably because he wished to indicate that they were conceived in reaction to the currently popular Impressionist art. The theoretician of the movement in Germany was Kasimir Edschmid, who defined the aims of the movement in a lecture given in Berlin in 1917, when the term 'expressionistisch' had already gained currency among critics of art and literature. As far as literature in general is concerned, Expressionism was a young man's revolt against the specializing tendencies in Naturalism, Neo-Romanticism, and Impressionism, and the aims and attitudes with which these movements had become associated. In particular, the 'passive' role of the artists of the previous generation—the Naturalist observation of the minute details of everyday life, and the Impressionist recording of every mood and movement of the soul—were rejected by the Expressionists for a 'vision' of life that came from within the artist. The basically pessimistic attitude to life which was associated with this factual or psychological observation was also rejected for a belief in mankind's ability to undergo a spiritual rebirth, which the younger generation, in opposition to the narrow-mindedness and materialism of their elders, were to be instrumental in bringing about. It follows that the drama in particular was favoured by the Expressionists, both as a means of propagating and disseminating their ideas and as a medium which lent itself to their forceful, urgent, and emotionally charged style of utterance, and that one of the main concerns of the Expressionist dramatist was man's inner struggle to achieve his spiritual transformation into 'der neue Mensch'. Visionary or dream-like scenes frequently presented this process against a background of actuality which was often distorted to the point of grotesqueness. Georg Kaiser (1878–1945) is considered the leading dramatist of the movement, mainly on account of his vast output and his experiments with Expressionist techniques. With his sense of the theatre, as opposed to literary drama, and his preference for presenting an argument in dramatic terms rather than for creating character, he gave to modern German drama a lightness, colourfulness, and tempo suited to the exploration of contemporary forms of consciousness. Among the other dramatists, Fritz von Unruh (1885–) gave expression to a sense of frustration with the older generation and its outmoded code of values, while the sense of mission and hope is strongest in the work of Reinhard Sorge (1892–1916). These early Expressionists are considered to have been influenced by the later visionary plays of Strindberg, particularly *Ett Drömspel* and *Till Damaskus*, but the influence of such 'cosmic' plays as Ibsen's *Peer Gynt* and Goethe's *Faust, Part Two*, may be traced both in technique and subject-matter.

The idea of spiritual renewal could not help but touch on social and political reform, and towards the end of the First World War there was a general change of emphasis in this direction, in the work of Ernst Toller (1893–1939) and Walter Hasenclever (1890–1940). Some dramatists, among them Franz Werfel (1890–1945) saw the dangers attendant on such a change, without, however, being able to alter the trend. What is generally considered the decline of Expressionism in the mid-1920s was in fact only the failure of one aspect of Expressionism—its enthusiastically expressed idealism—to meet the needs of a new and disillusioned age. The bold experimentation in search of new forms continued into the 1930s in the work of Bertolt Brecht (1898–1956); and in the sphere of the theatre itself, it was not until the mid-1920s that such producers as Erwin Piscator (1893–1966) and Leopold Jessner (1878–1945) were able to challenge the tradition established by Max Reinhardt and develop styles compatible with Expressionist modes of conception. Indeed, it might be said that post-Expressionism initially owed as much to its producers as to its playwrights, and that they were in a large part responsible for the continued treatment and modification of Expressionist themes in the years that followed. RICHARD BECKLEY

EYSOLDT, GERTRUD (1870–1955), German actress, who made her first appearance on the stage at Meiningen in 1890 in *King Henry IV*. After touring in Germany and Russia she appeared in Berlin in 1899, and later played under Reinhardt. An extremely clever and subtle player, she was at her best in modern realistic parts, particularly in the works of Wedekind, in which she played opposite the author. She was also good in Ibsen, in such parts as Salome and Cleopatra, and in the plays of Maeterlinck.

F

FABBRI, Diego (1911–   ), Italian playwright. Italy's major dramatist since the death of Ugo Betti in 1953, Fabbri is undoubtedly influenced both by him and by Pirandello. His drama is markedly symbolic and concerned passionately with 'tragic Christianity'. Socially he stresses man's need to care, reminding us that we are all responsible for evil. He disregards his early works (from 1932 to 1941), though they are important to his development of a technique for modern religious drama. Probably his most significant works are: *Inquisizione* (1950), *Il seduttore* (1951), *Processo di famiglia* (1953), *Processo a Gesù* (1955), and *La bugiarda* (1956). The versions he has made of Dostoievsky (*The Devils* and *The Karamazov Trial*, published in the volume *I demoni*, 1961) are held by some critics to be his best works for the theatre. Fabbri's plays are well known in Europe and South America, but English-speaking audiences have had little opportunity of seeing them, though four at least have been translated. In 1965 the Compagnia dei Giovani appeared at the Aldwych, London, during the World Theatre season in *La Bugiarda*. Produced by Giorgio de Lullo, this starred Rossella Falk as the 'liar' of the title (see ITALY, 3 *b*).

FREDERICK MAY

FABBRICHESI, Salvatore (1760–1827), see MODENA.

FABRE D'ÉGLANTINE, Philippe-François Nazaire (1755–94), French dramatist and revolutionary who took the name 'Églantine' after winning a prize at the Floral Games of Toulouse for his verses. His origin is unknown, but he was for some time an actor. Although he had a good voice and presence, he was unsuccessful, and soon forsook the stage in order to devote himself to the Revolution. In this he took an active part, being a member of the Convention with Danton, Marat, and Robespierre. His excesses led to his downfall, and he was guillotined in Apr. 1794. He wrote several poor plays and a number of libretti for the little theatres. In 1790 he produced *Le Philinte de Molière*, which showed what he could do, and gave promise of great things in the future. But he had time for nothing more. He was very much a child of the Revolution which destroyed him, and his faults were more those of his age than of his character.

FABULA. 1. Atellana. Like their Neapolitan descendants at the present day, the inhabitants of the pleasant land of Campania had in antiquity a reputation for love of jest and merriment. At an early period there grew up here a rustic farce which displayed certain traditional characters in ridiculous situations. This farce seems to have been designed to suit the taste of the crowds which gathered on market days in country towns, and its Latin name is traditionally connected with the small town of Atella, nine miles from Capua on the road to Naples. Greek influence was widespread along the Campanian coast, but the Campanian farce was always sharply distinguished by the Romans from Greek performances of a farcical nature such as the mime. The essential feature of the *atellana* was the appearance of certain traditional characters, Maccus and Bucco, both clowns, Pappus the Old Fool, Manducus the Ogre, Dossennus. All these have a family resemblance as coarse, greedy clowns (see No. 11 *a*), whose characteristics were such as might amuse a primitive and rustic audience, ever ready to laugh at guzzling and drunkenness, horseplay, and obscene jest. Manducus was certainly an ogre with champing jaws; *manducare*, to champ the jaws, is the slang word for 'to eat' from which is derived the French *manger*. It has been thought that Bucco means 'Fat-cheeks' (*buccae*) and Dossennus 'Hunchback' (*dorsum*), but this is uncertain. These stock roles would require stock costumes and masks. Indeed, a recurring motif of the *atellana* was disguise and masquerade. Hence arose those complications, *tricae atellanae* (the origin of our word 'intrigue'), indicated by such titles as *Maccus the Maiden*. Atellan pieces were apparently of no great length; the number of characters is said to have been small. The use of *atellanae* as *exodia* or interludes would suggest that in length they corresponded to our curtain-raisers, and they were in all probability impromptu performances until they received literary form in the time of Sulla. Originally given in the Oscan tongue, they assumed Latin dress when they came to Rome. The performers must have been professionals; Plautus makes a character, whose teeth are chattering with cold, propose to 'hire himself out as a Manducus at the games'. Plautus also uses the word *bucco* in the sense of fool, and the prologues to the *Mercator* and *Asinaria* give the author's name as Maccus. Livy's account of theatrical origins in Rome seems to be largely theorizing, but he does assert that in his own day the Atellani (professional performers of Atellan plays) were of citizen status. Most of our information about the *atellanae* is derived from the literary *Atellanae* of Pomponius and Novius, who belong to the opening decades of the first century B.C. But the very assumption of literary form must necessarily have altered the character of this type of farce; though Pomponius and Novius strove to retain the traditional characters and the rustic style of jest, the surviving titles and fragments remind us at times of other forms of drama, the *palliata*, the mime, the

Greek satyric play, and the mythological burlesque of Tarentum, the so-called *rhinthonica* or *hilarotragoedia*. At the beginning of the first century B.C. farce seems to gain at the expense of higher forms of drama; from now on we hear of no writer who made a living by writing tragedy or comedy for the stage. From Pomponius we have the titles of 70 *atellanae*, with fragments amounting to 200 lines or parts of lines; from Novius we have 44 titles with over 100 lines of fragments. To distinguish between the styles of these two writers seems impossible, so meagre is our information. The stock characters frequently appear. Maccus appears to be the most popular; we hear of *Maccus the Soldier*, *Maccus the Innkeeper*, *Maccus the Maiden*, *Maccus in Exile*, and even *The Twin Macci*. We have also such titles as *Bucco the Gladiator*, *Bucco Adopted*, *Pappus the Farmer*, *The Bride of Pappus*, *Pappus Defeated at the Poll*, and *The Two Dossenni*. Other titles point to the maintenance of the primitive rustic atmosphere: *The Pig*, *The Sow*, *Hog(g) Sick*, *Hog(g) Well* (companion pieces these, one would imagine), *The Farmer*, *The Woodpile*, *A-Hoeing*, *The Vine-Gatherers*, *The She-Ass*, *The She-Goat*. Others suggest the life of the town: *The Candidate*, *The Fullers*, *The Inspector of Morals*, *The Pimp*. Such characters might easily be imagined in any fair-sized town of Campania, and indeed some of the fragments remind us of the scribblings on the walls of Pompeii. Here, then, the *atellana* approached the boundaries of the *togata* (see below, 9); other titles remind us of the *palliata* (see below, 3)—*Synephebi*, *Adelphi*, *Hetaera*; yet others of the *hilarotragoedia* (see below, 5)—*The Counterfeit Agamemnon*, *Marsyas*, *Phoenissae*. That Maccus might be dressed up as a maiden is shown by the title *Maccus Virgo*; and the feelings of someone who is deceived by such a trick are expressed in a fragment of the *Macci Gemini* of Pomponius. Elsewhere we find someone being coached to adapt his voice to a woman's role; this kind of impersonation must have been popular with the Romans, witness the concluding and very Roman scenes in the *Casina* of Plautus. Bucco's clownish wit appears in his over-literal interpretation of a request to 'Handle the job cleanly', to which he replies 'I have already washed my hands'. In Pappus the disadvantages of old age were satirized without mercy; whether as a candidate for election, a lover, or a husband, he is sure to be unlucky. We cannot tell how many of these stock characters appeared in any one piece. The language is homely; a peasant defines wealth as 'a short-lived blessing, like Sardinian cheese'. As contrasted with the *palliata*, the *atellana* was vulgar and rustic; this rustic quality, as well as the use of masks, differentiated it from the equally vulgar mime. There were plenty of jokes; Cicero, when discussing the subject of jest, turns for examples to the *Atellanae* of Novius. The scantiness of literary fragments from *atellanae* after the days of Pomponius and Novius suggests that the *atellana* returned to its improvised character. We have a few lines of Atellan songs from the early Empire, e.g. Datus, an Atellan actor in the time of Nero, sang in Greek a song containing the words 'Health to you, father; health to you, mother', at the same time indicating by gestures the acts of drinking and swimming—the point being that Claudius, Nero's stepfather, had been poisoned, and Nero had tried to bring about Agrippina's death by drowning. Songs of this kind would no doubt have to be written down, and so might outlive the dialogue, which may have consisted largely of 'patter'. The line quoted also illustrates the perennial, often fatal, interest of the Atellan performers in politics. In spite of all extraneous influence which acted on it, this masked farce seems to have retained something of its primitive, rustic, Italian character, and on the stages of the early Empire its performers, though social outcasts, enjoyed considerable popularity. Eventually, it would seem, they had to yield place to the mime.

2. CREPIDATA. The meaning of this rare term is not clear, but as the *crepida* was a Greek shoe, regularly worn with the *pallium*, the word was probably a synonym for *palliata* (see below, 3). The *cothurnus*, or boot worn by tragic actors, was quite different from the *crepida*.

3. PALLIATA, a play translated from Greek New Comedy (see GREECE, 2 *b* and MENANDER), from *pallium*, the Greek cloak of everyday wear. For authors of *palliatae* see Andronicus, Caecilius, Naevius, Plautus, and Terence. The last writer of *palliatae* for the stage was Turpilius, who died in 103 B.C.

4. PRAETEXTA or PRAETEXTATA, an original Latin play of serious character on a theme taken from Roman legend or contemporary history; from *toga praetextata*, the purple-bordered toga worn by Roman magistrates. This form of drama was created by Naevius, but we know of only about half-a-dozen fairly certain examples from the time of the Republic. It may be that those *praetextae* which dealt with recent events were intended for production at the funeral games of the heroes whose victories they celebrated, thus avoiding a violation of the general principle that the names of living men must not be mentioned on the stage. To deal with affairs and personalities fresh in the minds of all present must have been a delicate matter, as we see from the fate of Naevius himself. Accius, Ennius, and Pacuvius are thought to have written *praetextae*. In 43 B.C. L. Cornelius Balbus illustrated his lack of good taste by producing at Gades a *praetexta* on his own achievements in the civil war. Other *praetextae* intended for reading only were written under the Empire; we possess only the *Octavia*.

5. RHINTHONICA, a burlesque of tragedy, named after the Greek writer Rhinthon of Tarentum (*fl. c.* 300 B.C.). Another name for it was *hilarotragoedia*, or 'merry tragedy'. The popularity of such plays among the Greeks of southern Italy is illustrated by the so-called phlyax vases, which show, for example, Zeus

on a love-adventure about to climb a ladder to the window from which a lady is looking out, while Hermes holds a lantern to assist him (see No. 12). Our nearest example in Latin is the *Amphitruo* of Plautus.

6. RICINIATA, a synonym of mime (see MIME, 2), from *ricinium*, the hood worn in the characteristic mime-costume.

7. SALTICA, a 'play for dancing', that is, the libretto to be sung by the chorus in a pantomime (see PANTOMIME, 1 and PANTOMIMUS).

8. TABERNARIA, apparently a synonym for *togata* (see below), from *taberna*, a poor man's house.

9. TOGATA, or Roman comedy, arose out of the irrepressible Italian instinct for social satire and topical allusion—an instinct which failed to find satisfaction in the imported *palliata*, especially in its later and more strictly Hellenic form. But as the ruling classes at Rome would have reacted vigorously to any political or personal attacks on them, the *togata* seems to have found its themes in the life of ordinary folk in Italian towns or among the lower classes in Rome. We have the names of three writers of *togatae*—Titinius (15 titles of his and 180 lines are preserved), Atta (11 titles, 20 lines), and Afranius (44 titles, 400 lines); they all seem to have lived in the second century B.C. Afranius seems to have been the ablest; we hear further that he introduced into his plays the theme of homosexuality; but the material does not enable us to distinguish very clearly between the three writers. The extant titles bring us into a brisk world of business, amusement, matchmaking, and family relationship: *The Weavers*, *The Games the Aedile Gave*, *The Matchmaker*, *The Aunt*, *The Mother-in-Law*, *The Clown's Adoption*, *The Divorce*, *The Hairdresser*, *The Butler*, *Tit for Tat*, *Neck or Nothing*, *Fire!* It would seem that the plot might be fairly complex. The *Vopiscus* of Afranius introduces the parents of the 'twin that lived', a newly married pair (scarcely to be identified with these parents), a husband whose wife has left him, a woman who feigns submission while really playing on the violence of a man's temper, a trusted parasite, a pampered slave, a door-keeper, a lady's maid. The *Fullonia* of Titinius shows us a wrangle between fullers and weavers, a wife who complains that her husband is squandering her dowry, and a philanderer who, in fear of capture by an angry husband, is about to commit himself (like brave Horatius) to the Tiber. On the other hand, we have a statement by a scholiast that the cast of a *togata*, like that of an *atellana*, was smaller than that of a *palliata*; and on general grounds we should suspect that an average *togata* would be both shorter and simpler than a comedy taken from the Greek. We are told by Donatus that in the *togata* slaves were not allowed to be cleverer than their masters; it would seem, then, that in the *togata* we must have none of those swindling slaves who extract money from their old masters and assume control of their young masters' affairs. The wheels of the *palliata* were set in motion by love; yet, as Athenian convention prevented young women of good class from appearing in public, the dramatists have to employ various devices—midnight festivals, kidnapping, exposure of children, recognition scenes—if a love-plot, leading to marriage, is to be at all possible. In Roman life women of the citizen class had much more freedom; and indeed in the fragments of the *togata* we find that they can appear in public, can meet eligible suitors, and can accompany their fiancés on social calls. It would seem, then, that the typical plots of the *palliata* would be out of place in the *togata*, in which we find an atmosphere of family life not altogether unlike our own, where marriage is to some extent based on mutual attraction, and where relatives, male and female, express their opinions about a projected match. There is no sign of a romantic interest in Afranius's *Setina*, where the reluctant suitor doubts the wisdom of aspiring to a maiden of superior fortune, or in the family councils of the *Fratriae*, where it is calculated that a pretty girl will need less dowry, and a hope is expressed for possible advantages in kind if she marries the confectioner. In general we should suspect that the *togata* was not sentimental but lively, amusing, and satirical. The opening scene of Afranius's *Epistula* shows some eager gallant or belated reveller, bareheaded and be-slippered, out of doors in the cold air of a winter's dawn; the other fragments of this play give us glimpses of a drinking-party, of someone escaping from a street-bully, of someone dressed up as a girl, of a girl who can hardly restrain her laughter while her mother storms in fury, and of a general state of domestic turmoil. In *The Divorce* a father forces his daughters to leave their husbands, in *The Pretender* another father is advised to follow a similar course. Elsewhere we hear of husbands trying to play the gallant —a stock theme in the *palliata*, it is true, but in the *togata* there is this curious difference: the erring husband chooses not the town but the country for his amours. Afranius's use of sodomy as a theme shows that the *togata* was unfettered by the sexual conventions which the *palliata* had taken over from New Comedy. In the *palliata* a man may love anyone except 'maiden, wife or widow, youths or boys' (*Curculio*, ll. 37–38)—in other words, love-affairs can only occur between the hero and a girl who for some reason is not regarded as his social equal. In the *togata* we hear of adultery involving women of respectable position. What the fragments do not tell us is how a coherent plot was built up around such themes; indeed, in the whole range of Latin stage-drama, we have no knowledge of the course of so much as one plot invented by a Latin writer. The *togata* must have enjoyed some popularity, at least during the lifetime of its authors, for we have the titles of seventy pieces. Revivals at a later period are not often recorded. The purely literary *togata* continued to be written down to Juvenal's day.

10. TRABEATA, a form of *togata* dealing with Roman knights, from *trabea*, the official robe

of the equestrian order. Invented by Melissus, the freedman of Maecenas, it was probably short-lived; at all events we know nothing else about it. WILLIAM BEARE†

FAGAN, JAMES BERNARD (1873–1933), playwright and producer, who in 1923 founded a repertory theatre in the old Big-Game Museum on the Woodstock Road, Oxford, and for two seasons produced there a series of excellent plays with a young company which included at various times Flora Robson, Dorothy Green, Molly McArthur, John Gielgud, Tyrone Guthrie, and Raymond Massey. Fagan, who was born in Ulster, began his stage career in Benson's company, making his first appearance in 1895; he then played two seasons under Tree at Her Majesty's and after some years in retirement took over the management of the Court Theatre, where he gave some notable productions of Shakespeare, including *The Merchant of Venice* (1919) with Moskovitch as Shylock. In 1929 he became director of the Festival Theatre, Cambridge, and he was also responsible for many productions by the Irish Players. Among his own plays the most successful were *The Wheel* (1922), *And So To Bed* (1926), and *The Improper Duchess* (1931). He also made an excellent dramatization of *Treasure Island* (1922). A kindly, lovable man, widely read and extremely cultured, he worked tirelessly for the betterment of the English theatre, on which his unobtrusive work had a profound influence.

FAIKO, ALEXEI MIKHAILOVICH (1893–), early Soviet dramatist, whose most important play, *The Man with the Portfolio*, produced in 1928, dealt for the first time with the problem of the intellectual at odds with the new régime. Its chief character, a professor at a Moscow college, tries to make the best of both worlds by conforming in public and abusing the Government in private, but finally, a spiritual bankrupt, he commits suicide. The play has its melodramatic moments, and the ending is somewhat contrived, but its production marked an immense step forward in Soviet dramatic history. It was revived several times after the Second World War in Leningrad and in Moscow. In 1957 a new comedy, *Don't Set Yourself up as a God!*, was produced in the Lenkom Theatre, in Moscow, but on the whole Faiko has confined himself in later years to writing in theatre journals.

FAIR, WILLIAM B. (1851–1909), music-hall performer. He is best remembered as the singer of 'Tommy, Make Room for your Uncle', with which he made a fortune, singing it at as many as six halls a night. With the money thus earned he bought the Surrey Music-Hall (renamed the Winchester), lost every penny, returned to the halls as Chairman, and ended as link-man outside the Coliseum.

FAIRBROTHER, SYDNEY (1872–1941), see COWELL (5).

FAIRS. In England and Europe the big fairs, held usually in the spring and autumn, were from the beginning associated with theatrical enterprise, just as the small country fairs were never without their little groups of acrobats, dancers, and singers. The assembling of a number of people in one place for a definite time provided a ready-made audience for the travelling companies of the fifteenth and sixteenth centuries, and finally provided them with a site on which to build a permanent theatre. This was most noticeable in the case of the Parisian fairs, particularly that of Saint-Germain in early spring, and that of Saint-Laurent in August and September. Some of the best-known farce-players of seventeenth-century Paris are believed to have graduated from the fairs, or to have been the children of fairground actors, but the main development of the *forains*, as they were called, came at the end of the seventeenth and in the eighteenth centuries, when they gradually extended their season beyond that of the fairs proper, and replaced their wooden booths with permanent playhouses. Their popularity, and the fact that during the fairs provincial companies were allowed to play in Paris without further permission, gave constant annoyance to the Comédie-Française and the Comédie-Italienne. The latter finally made common cause with the enemy and combined with the *forains* to form the Opéra-Comique, occupying during the summer months the Théâtre de la Foire Saint-Laurent, built in 1721 and finally destroyed in the rebuilding of the Opéra-Comique in 1761.

The old French farce survived at the fairs in the form of the *parade*, a rough sketch played on a long narrow balcony, traditionally the one overlooking the courtyard of the Foire Saint-Germain. This was destroyed in 1756, but the plots of the *parades* were printed in a volume entitled *Théâtre des Boulevards*, in which the genre is explained. They were meant to arouse the interest of the spectator in the play to be given inside the booth or, later, playhouse, and by the names of the characters show their affinity with the *commedia dell'arte*. After the French Revolution the freedom accorded to the theatres led the *forains* to settle permanently on the Boulevard du Temple, where Bobèche and Galimafré revived the *parade*, and where a number of small but important playhouses were built, including Deburau's Funambules, the Gaîté, the Ambigu-Comique, and the Cirque Franconi, as well as innumerable small booths of acrobats and marionettes. The whole thing was swept away at the height of its success by Haussmann in his rebuilding scheme in 1862, thus breaking the last link between the modern theatre and the old fairground actor.

In England the fairs of Saint Bartholomew, Smithfield, and Southwark, as well as the smaller Greenwich and May fairs, were always connected with theatrical entertainments, particularly puppet shows, and there were also booths for the accommodation of living actors. The dramatist Elkanah Settle is believed to have ended his days as a green dragon in Mrs.

Myn's booth at Southwark, and he also wrote drolls and short sketches for Bartholomew Fair. The theatrical development of the English fairs was, however, less noticeable than in France, perhaps owing to the greater inclemency of the weather, which must often have precluded open-air entertainment, and there is no record of any permanent playhouses being built on fair-sites. The English fair is portrayed in Jonson's *Bartholomew Fair* (1614) and in some of the plays of Shadwell (see also ENGLISH FAIRGROUND AND PORTABLE THEATRES).

Of the German fairs, held in different towns, those of Leipzig and Frankfurt are best known in connexion with theatrical matters. It was at Frankfurt that the English Comedians appeared most frequently and had, if anywhere, a permanent home, while Leipzig saw the reforms of Gottsched first put into action by the great actress Caroline Neuber. Fairs also played a big part in the history of the early Russian theatre, which, however, developed somewhat differently from the rest of Europe. Little information seems to be available on the fairs of Italy and Spain, but no doubt the *commedia dell'arte* in the first, and the travelling companies of such actor-managers as Lope de Rueda in the second, were to be found wherever they saw the chance of a ready-made audience.

FALLING FLAPS, see TRICKWORK ON THE ENGLISH STAGE.

FALSE PROS., a name given to an arrangement of wings and top border, often painted to simulate drapery, which serves to diminish the stage opening in a proscenium arch (see INNER PROSCENIUM). The term is also used of a device to save scenery, consisting of a pair of wide flats, usually with a door, which stand facing each other on either side of the stage behind the proscenium arch. A third special flat, or ceiling piece, is suspended face-down between their tops. Thus a sort of tunnel or bridge is formed, and the scenery is set beyond, with a consequent saving of all the more forward, or down-stage, pieces. Considerable additions may be made to such a system until the result bears the appearance of an elaborately modelled piece of built architecture, or the false proscenium is treated in bare simplicity and associated with a cyclorama behind in such a way that a complete stage-setting is provided, and the scenery reduced to a single small set piece, on the system of 'detail setting'.

RICHARD SOUTHERN

FAN EFFECT, a method of scene-changing used in the Transformation Scene (see TRICKWORK ON THE ENGLISH STAGE).

FARCE, an extreme form of comedy in which laughter is raised at the expense of probability, particularly by horse-play and bodily assault. It must, however, retain its hold on humanity, even if only in depicting the grosser faults of mankind; otherwise it degenerates into travesty and burlesque. Its subject is the inherent stupidity of man at odds with his environment, and it belongs in its origins to the great submerged stream of folk-drama of which little written record remains. It stands at the beginning of classical drama (see GREECE, 2 and FABULA, 1) as of modern European, and was most popular in France, where in the seventeenth century the great farce-players, Turlupin, Gros-Guillaume, and Gaultier-Garguille, kept alive the old traditions. These gradually died out, and the farce was last seen at the Théâtre du Marais, in the lifetime of Jodelet. It had a great influence on Molière, who must often have seen and played in old farces, particularly in the districts round Lyon and whose own early plays followed the old pattern. Among the many that were long current, of which the greater part no doubt were never written down, the best known is *Maître Pierre Pathelin*, which has survived revision, adaptation, and even translation, without losing its savour and robust humour. There were elements of farce in early English biblical plays, and later farcical interludes were written by scholars for production in schools and other places, but, as in Italy and Germany, it was the influence of the French farce that was paramount in its development, culminating in the works of John Heywood.

In the eighteenth and nineteenth centuries short one-act farces were popular on the English and American stages, usually as part of a bill which included also a five-act tragedy. They were ephemeral productions, though some of them achieved a great success, mainly through the acting of some particular comedian. A few might bear revival. In modern usage the word farce is applied to a full-length play dealing with some absurd situation hingeing generally on extra-marital relations—hence the term bedroom farce. Farce has small literary merit but great entertainment value, and owing to its lack of subtlety can be translated from one language to another more easily than comedy.

FARINE, JEAN (*fl.* 1600–35), a mountebank in the style of Tabarin, who is believed to have been originally a travelling quack doctor. After having served his apprenticeship at the Paris fairs he went to the Hôtel de Bourgogne with Bruscambille, and together they played improvised farces in the manner of Turlupin and his associates, with whom they are often mentioned approvingly in contemporary doggerel.

FARJEON, HERBERT (1887–1945), see JEFFERSON (7).

FARQUHAR, GEORGE (1678–1707), English dramatist, usually classed among the writers of Restoration comedy, though chronologically and spiritually he stands a little apart from them, showing more variety of plot and depth of feeling, and, in his later and best plays, a more conscious effort to adapt the licentiousness of the early comedy of manners to the changing taste of the time. Born in Ireland and educated at Trinity College, Dublin, Farquhar was for a short time an actor, but left the stage after accidentally wounding a fellow actor in the last act of Dryden's *The Indian Emperor* by attacking him with a real instead of a property sword. He may also have had some doubts as to his abilities, and believed himself more fitted for writing than acting. With the assistance of Wilks, who remained his firm friend in later life, he went to London, where his first play, *Love and a Bottle* (1698) was produced at Drury Lane. With *The Constant Couple; or, a Trip to the Jubilee* (1699), Farquhar established his reputation as one of the outstanding dramatists of the day, and the play held the stage throughout the eighteenth century, the hero, Sir Harry Wildair, first played by Wilks, being a favourite breeches part with Peg Woffington and Dorothy Jordan. A sequel to it proved less successful, as did a revision of one of Fletcher's comedies, and a melodrama entitled *The Twin Rivals* (1702), and Farquhar left London for some time, after a sudden marriage with a penniless lady whom he believed to be an heiress. He bore this misfortune with what his contemporaries regarded as noble resignation, and appears to have been happy in his family life, though always harassed by financial entanglements and two daughters. He returned to the theatre in 1706 with a fine comedy entitled *The Recruiting Officer*, based on his own experiences in that capacity in Shropshire, where he was sent to get together a company for the War of the Spanish Succession. This was an immediate success, and was followed by what many critics regard as Farquhar's finest play, *The Beaux' Stratagem*, given at Drury Lane in 1707 with Wilks as Archer, and Anne Oldfield —with whom the dramatist was at one time in love—as Mrs. Sullen. It has since been frequently revived, notably at the Lyric, Hammersmith (1927), and at the Royalty (1930), with Edith Evans as Mrs. Sullen. The play has a wholesome, open-air humour in which, says Professor Strauss in his study of it, Farquhar 'blended the essentials of character, plot, and situation in juster proportions than any previous writer of realistic comedy. . . . The result was a form of comedy unsurpassed for naturalness and fidelity to life: the form adopted and perfected by Sheridan and Goldsmith.'

This was Farquhar's last work, written in six weeks while he was lying ill and harassed in mean lodgings, with no encouragement but that of the faithful Wilks. His early death was a great loss to the stage, since *The Beaux' Stratagem* shows clearly the way in which he might have developed, with subsequent benefit to the history of English comedy.

FARR, FLORENCE [MRS. EDWARD EMERY] (1860–1917), British actress, producer, and manager. She began acting in entertainments at William Morris's house in the 1880s, and also at the *avant-garde* Bedford Park Theatre. Soon after, she produced and played the lead (as a 'New Woman') in the first English performance of *Rosmersholm* (1891). In 1892 she was Blanche in *Widowers' Houses* at the Royalty, for the Independent Theatre Society, the first Shaw play to be acted. Two years later Miss Horniman financed for her a season at the Avenue Theatre, where she produced *Arms and the Man* and Yeats's first acted play, *The Land of Heart's Desire*. In 1899 she created the part of Aleel the minstrel in *The Countess Cathleen* on its first production in Dublin, a role that allowed her and Yeats to test their theories of reading or intoning verse to the psaltery in a monotonous chant-like manner and 'a rhythmic dreaminess of movement and gesture'. She arranged the music and choruses for the Vedrenne–Barker productions of *The Trojan Women* (1905) and *Hippolytus* (1906), but her desire to emphasize the archaic qualities of the Greek dramas clashed with Granville-Barker's and Gilbert Murray's desire to make them natural and modern. A novelist of some talent, she was for many years a follower of Mme Blavatsky and a student of theosophy and Indian philosophy. In 1912, learning that she would soon die of cancer, she went to Ceylon and spent her last years there as principal of a Hindu girls' college.

ROBERT TRACY

FARREN, ELIZABETH (1759–1829), English actress, child of strolling players, with whom she appeared from her earliest years. She made her first appearance in London on 9 June 1777 at the Haymarket, as Miss Hardcastle, and then went to Drury Lane. She was not immediately successful, owing to the popularity of Mrs. Abington, but she soon became recognized as the outstanding player of fine ladies, for which her natural elegance, tall, slim figure, and beautiful voice rendered her particularly suitable. Horace Walpole considered her the best actress he had ever seen, and was enchanted by her keen wit. She was received everywhere on an equal footing with women of birth and fashion, and at one time organized private theatricals for the Duke of Richmond. The Earl of Derby was in love with her for many years, and married her on the death of his wife in 1797, in which year she made her last appearance on the stage as Lady Teazle. She was much regretted, and Boaden considered that her loss 'produced the degeneracy of comedy into farce'. Her younger sister was also an actress, known as Mrs. Knight.

FARREN. (1) WILLIAM (1725–95), English actor, head of a distinguished theatrical family, who was at Drury Lane from 1776 to 1784, and then at Covent Garden until his death. He was the first to play Careless in *The School for Scandal* and Leicester in *The Critic*, and also had some success in Shakespeare in such parts as Hotspur, the Ghost in *Hamlet*, and Buckingham in *Henry VIII*. His sons, (2) PERCIVAL (1784–1843) and (3) WILLIAM (1786–1861), were also on the stage, though the elder afterwards deserted the boards for stage-management. He was the friend and tutor of Helen Faucit, whom he prepared for her first appearance in 1833, by which time a severe asthmatical condition had caused his retirement from the theatre. William made his début at Plymouth, under his brother's management, and first appeared in London at Covent Garden in 1818 as Sir Peter Teazle, always one of his finest parts. Vandenhoff, writing of him in this role, said: 'I have never seen any representation of Sir Peter that could compare with him in animation, ease, naturalness of manner and piquancy of effect.' He was equally good in such parts as Lord Ogleby, and during his long career he appeared also in a number of Shakespearian roles, Aguecheek, Shallow, Malvolio, Polonius, and Dogberry being perhaps his best. He retired in 1853, his last years on the stage having been overshadowed by the effects of a stroke. Contemporary critics were loud in his praise, Lewes going so far as to compare him for quickness of apprehension and natural elegance to the best French actors of the day. William's two sons, (4) WILLIAM (1825–1908) and (5) HENRY (1826–60), were both actors, the former being connected with the Haymarket from 1853 to 1867. He played a number of original roles in Tom Taylor's plays, and was the first Sir Geoffrey Champneys in *Our Boys*. His son (6) WILLIAM PERCIVAL (1853–1937) was also an actor and dramatist. Henry made his London début under his father before going to America, where he remained until his early death while managing the theatre at St. Louis. Of his three daughters, all actresses, one married the brother of Mary Moore, while the most famous was (7) ELLEN (1848–1904), known as Nellie, a favourite at the old Gaiety Theatre, London, from 1868 until her retirement in 1891. She was a member of the famous burlesque quartette with Edward Terry, Kate Vaughan, and Edward Royce. She specialized in the playing of boys' parts—Smike, Sam Willoughby in *The Ticket-of-Leave Man*, and the Cockney and cheeky boys in Byron's burlesques and extravaganzas. A contemporary critic said of her: 'Miss Farren may be a wife and a mother, but she is certainly one of the best boys in existence.' Her husband, Robert Soutar, was an actor, and for a long time stage-manager at the Gaiety. Her two sons were also on the stage, Joseph, whose career stretched over fifty years, dying in 1962 at the age of 91. Towards the end of her life Nellie contemplated a return to serious comedy, but ill health forced her to retire before she had achieved this ambition.

FASTNACHTSSPIEL, the German Carnival or Shrovetide play of the fifteenth century, performed mainly by students and artisans. It shows, in its somewhat crude couplets, a mingling of religious and popular elements interesting in the light of later developments in German drama, and is somewhat akin to the French *sotie* (see GERMANY, 1).

FATE DRAMA, the name given to a type of early nineteenth-century German play, inaugurated by Werner's *Der vierundzwanzigste Februar* (1809), in which a malignant fate is shown to be dogging the footsteps of some unfortunate and fear-ridden mortal, driving him, by a chain of fortuitous circumstances, to commit a horrible crime. In Werner's play, for instance, a father unsuspectingly kills his own son, the fatal instrument, a dagger, falling from the wall at the fatal moment. The genre was further exploited by Adolf Müllner in *Der neunundzwanzigste Februar* (1812), and by the young Grillparzer in *Die Ahnfrau* (1817), his first play, which has been described as having 'all the *frissons* of Gothic romance'.

FATHER OF THE HALLS, see MORTON, CHARLES.

FAUCIT, HELEN [HELENA SAVILLE] (1817–98), English actress of great beauty and charm, whose best work was done in revivals of Shakespeare and in new verse dramas, many of them written specially for her. She first appeared in London in 1836, in *The Hunchback*, and was much admired, though some critics found her acting somewhat exaggerated. In the dearth of fine actresses at that period she shone even more brightly, and appeared with Macready and Phelps, one of her finest parts being Pauline in *The Lady of Lyons*. She appeared in several other plays by Bulwer Lytton, and in Browning's *Strafford* (1837), *A Blot in the 'Scutcheon* (1843), and *Colombe's Birthday* (1853). It is said that her refusal to appear in Matthew Arnold's *Merope* caused him to abandon its production. She appeared in Paris with great success, and embodied her experiences as an interpreter of Shakespeare in a volume entitled *On Some of Shakespeare's Female Characters* (1885). She married in 1851, becoming Lady Martin when her husband was knighted in 1880. In later life she acted almost entirely on behalf of various charities and was a friend and guest of Queen Victoria.

FAUST. A medieval legend of a man who sells his soul to the devil became linked in the sixteenth century with the name and adventures of a wandering conjuror, Johann Faust (*c.* 1488–1541). His story was published in a chapbook produced in Frankfurt in 1587, and found its way to England in translation, to provide the material for Marlowe's *Tragical History of Doctor Faustus* (*c.* 1588, publ. 1601 or 1604). It returned to its country of origin via the English Comedians, and lived on until the eighteenth century in a popular puppet show which greatly disgusted the literary precisian, Gottsched. It was first taken up seriously in Germany in 1759 by Lessing, who saw in it a reflection of his own problem, that of a scholar's inquiring mind in conflict with the limits imposed by the Almighty. Only two scenes of Lessing's version appeared during his lifetime, but it is clear from fragments and from accounts of it published posthumously that Faust's soul was to be saved. One account speaks of an angelic voice declaring that man's noblest impulse was not given him in order to lead him to eternal pain.

During the *Sturm und Drang* period the legend made an instant appeal, and was taken up by Goethe, Müller, and Klinger, each treating it in the light of his own temperament.

The scenes Müller wrote have an unromantic realism, Faust being driven to make his pact with the devil largely through pecuniary difficulties. In Klinger's novel Faust attempts to use his powers to right the wrongs of this world, only to find that he has caused more evil than he has countered. He ends in the deepest confines of hell, cursing the Almighty.

In Goethe's version, of which Part I was begun about 1774 and published in 1808, while Part II did not appear until 1832, the year of his death, Faust is possessed by a thirst not only for knowledge but for experience. Mephistopheles fosters his illicit relations with Gretchen (Margaret), an innocent, loving girl, who perishes on the scaffold for child-murder (end of Part I). Mephistopheles had reckoned that Faust's impulse to action would be choked by despair and remorse; but Goethe's Faust, who, far from striking a bargain with hell, had defied the devil to bring him satisfaction, never flags. His energies are directed to wider spheres, and he finally embarks on the reclamation of land from the sea, an enterprise which will benefit mankind. The initiative has passed from Mephistopheles to Faust, and though in the closing scene of his life the latter declares himself satisfied, this satisfaction is not the result of the devil's efforts. Consequently hell has no power over his soul, and by the grace of God it is borne away to heaven.

Since Goethe's *Faust* the subject has been treated again by Lenau, Heine, Grabbe, and others. It has also formed the subject of operas by Gounod and Boito (based on Goethe) and by Spohr and Busoni (in new versions).

FAVART. (1) CHARLES-SIMON (1710–92), French dramatist, the son of a pastrycook, and the first man to make a solid reputation out of the writing of libretti for light opera, in which genre he was the mentor and forerunner of Marmontel and Sedaine. He had much in common with La Fontaine as regards style and easy versification and also something of his wit and good humour. Favart's best works are written to be sung, and read poorly. His one straight play was an amusing trifle entitled *L'Anglais à Bordeaux*, given at the Comédie-Française in 1763. He married a charming actress, (2) MARIE-JUSTINE-BENOISTE DURONCERAY (1727–72), known before her marriage as Mlle Chantilly. She played for many years at the Comédie-Italienne, and is credited with the first introduction there of historical and local details into her costume, a practice soon to be inaugurated at the Comédie-Française by Lekain and Mlle Clairon. She and her husband were at one time members of the private company maintained by the Maréchal de Saxe.

FAVART, THÉÂTRE, see COMÉDIE-ITALIENNE.

FAVERSHAM, WILLIAM (1868–1940), American actor-manager, who was born in London and studied for the stage under Carlotta Leclercq. After a brief appearance in London he went to New York, and made his début there in 1887. He played small parts at the Lyceum with Daniel Frohman's company, and was for two years with Mrs. Fiske. In 1893 he was engaged by Charles Frohman for the Empire Theatre company, and remained there for eight years, playing a wide variety of parts, including Gil de Bérault in *Under the Red Robe*, Lord Algernon in *Lord and Lady Algy*, Henry Beauclerc in *Diplomacy*, and Romeo to the Juliet of Maude Adams. He then starred in a number of modern plays, and in 1909 made his first independent venture with the production of *Herod*, in which he played the name-part. It was, however, his production of *Julius Caesar* in 1912, in which he played Mark Antony, that set the seal on his growing reputation both as actor and director. With a fine cast, the play ran for some time in New York, and then went on tour, being followed by productions of *Othello* and *Romeo and Juliet*. After a further series of new plays, Faversham toured Australia, and on his return was seen in several more Shakespeare plays, and as Jeeter Lester in *Tobacco Road* (1933).

FAY. (1) FRANK J. (1870–1931) and (2) WILLIAM GEORGE (1872–1947), Irish actors who were important in the early history of the Abbey Theatre. They began their careers at the Dublin Dramatic School, run by Mrs. Lacy, wife of a touring manager. In 1898 they formed the Ormonde Dramatic Society and played in Dublin and the surrounding country in a repertory of sketches and short plays and farces. Among their actors were Dudley Digges and Sara Allgood, who were both to be associated with them in the Irish National Theatre Movement which later gave rise to the Abbey Players. The Fays produced and acted in *Deirdre* and *Cathleen ni Houlihan* (with Maud Gonne in the title-role) in Apr. 1902, and in four plays, including Yeats's *Fot of Broth*, in October of the same year. A number of other productions followed until in 1904 the company took possession of the Abbey Theatre, built for it by Miss Horniman, who admired the brothers' enthusiasm and persistence. Both the Fays appeared in the plays produced there, Frank, who was interested in verse-speaking, being responsible for the company's speech, and W. G. for stage direction. Stephen Gwynn, in *Irish Literature and Drama*, says of these first productions: 'The style of acting identified with the Abbey Theatre is due to the genius of the Fays—and of W. G. Fay especially.' It was a style which Fay himself defined when he wrote that he had endeavoured 'to enforce the most rigid economy of gesture and movement, to make the speaking quite abstract, and at the same time to keep a music in it by having all the voices harmonized'. Both brothers appeared in the most significant production of this period, *The Playboy of the Western World* (1907), W. G. playing Christy Mahon, and Frank his rival Shawn Keogh, as well as in most of the other plays seen at the Abbey. They left in 1908 and went to America, where they were responsible for the production of a repertory of Irish plays for Charles Frohman, in which they also appeared. Back in London in 1914, W. G. was seen in several new parts, and was successively producer at the Nottingham and the Birmingham Repertory theatres. Among his later parts were the Tramp in a revival of Synge's *The Shadow of the Glen*; Mr. Cassidy in *Storm in a Teacup* (1935), which he also produced; Johnny Mahoney in *Spring Meeting* (1938); and the name-part in *Father Malachy's Miracle* (1945). He produced a number of plays at the Arts Theatre, and in 1940 was seen as Stephano in the Old Vic production of *The Tempest*. He was the author of *The Fays of the Abbey Theatre* (1935), and of a volume of reminiscences, *Merely Players*, and in 1932 published *A Short Glossary of Theatrical Terms*. After some years abroad, Frank returned to the Abbey to play in a revival of *The Hour-Glass*, and finally settled in Dublin as a teacher of elocution.

FEAST OF FOOLS, see FOOLS, FEAST OF.

FECHTER, CHARLES ALBERT (1824–79), an actor who played in French and English, in Europe and America, with equal success. He first appeared in Paris at the Salle Molière in 1840, and made his début at the Comédie-Française in the same year. He soon left there, however, and his reputation was made at the smaller theatres, including the Porte-Saint-Martin. He was the first to play Armand Duval in *La Dame aux camélias* (1852). At this time he was the leading *jeune premier* of Paris, and co-director of the Odéon, but, chafing at the restrictions imposed on him by the Government in favour of the Comédie-Française, he came to England, where he had already appeared some years earlier, and played Ruy Blas in an English translation. Although his accent was never very good, he had confidence and fluency, and was much admired in London. It was his revolutionary Hamlet in 1861, however, which first brought him into prominence. Joseph Knight said of his performance that 'the text gained greatly in beauty and intelligibility by the abandonment of old traditions'. Fechter's reading brought out the subtlety and depth of the part, and even those who clung to the older view of Hamlet were impressed by his interpretation, while his admirers were fervent in his praise. His next venture was not so successful, and Lewes remarked that while his Hamlet was one of the best, his Othello was one of the worst he had ever seen. In a subsequent revival Fechter played Iago. In 1863 he took over the management of the London Lyceum, and appeared in a series of melodramas in which he proved himself a powerful actor and one of the best exponents of youthful heroes on the English stage. He went to America in 1869, and after a successful tour opened the old Globe Theatre in New York as Fechter's. He was responsible for a number of improvements and innovations there, and appeared in a number of his old successes as well as in new plays; but his imperious and quarrelsome nature made him many enemies. He left for a short visit to England, and on his return to New York appeared only in revivals. In 1876 he retired to die on a farm near Philadelphia. He was the author of several dramatizations of novels, which he produced himself.

FEDELI, THE, a company of *commedia dell'arte* actors, formed probably by the younger Andreini in the last years of the sixteenth century, and always connected with him. Early records are scanty, and the company first comes into prominence in 1603. It was later strengthened by the inclusion of some of the actors from the disbanded Gelosi company, and between 1606 and 1608 several attempts were made to fuse the Fedeli with Cecchini's company, the Accesi, but without success, mainly owing to quarrels between the two men's wives and their mutual jealousies. These animosities continued to embitter relations between the two companies, and finally the Fedeli, without Cecchini, but with Tristano Martinelli as their Harlequin, returned to Paris for a long stay. Andreini (Lelio,) Barbieri (Beltrame), and Gabrielli (Scapino) were particular favourites of the Parisians and their king, Louis XIII. The company continued for some years, under the direction of Andreini, to tour Italy, but he and his companions were ageing, and the Fedeli seem to have been disbanded before Andreini, in his old age, made a final visit to Paris to play with Mazarin's company in 1644. The Fedeli had made for itself a fine reputation during the first quarter of the seventeenth century, and was accounted one of the best troupes of its time.

FEDERAL STREET THEATRE, see BOSTON.

FEDERAL THEATRE (1 Oct. 1935–1 July 1939). This was the first nation-wide federally sponsored theatre in the United States. It was a project of the Works Progress Administration to give employment to needy professional theatre people in socially useful jobs.

Directed nationally from Washington, it operated through regional assistants throughout the country. Payment at the security wage was less than prevailing pay for corresponding work in industry, but was adjusted through hours to meet that wage in order not to lower standards in the theatrical unions to which most of its personnel belonged. Nine out of ten of its members came from relief rolls, and nine dollars out of ten were spent for wages. In the beginning the Government paid, in addition to labour costs, all non-labour costs; by the end of the project, admissions (never higher than a dollar) totalled approximately $2,000,000 and were paying the equivalent of all non-labour costs—scenery, costumes, royalties, rentals, advertising—although 65 per cent. of the productions were free. At its peak employment Federal Theatre employed 10,000 people, 2,600 of whom were returned to private industry; operated theatres in forty states; published a nationally distributed theatre magazine; conducted a play and research bureau serving not only its own theatres but 20,000 schools, churches, and community theatres throughout America; and played to audiences totalling many millions.

From the first Federal Theatre offered an ambitious programme of classical and modern plays, dance drama, musical comedy, children's plays, religious plays, marionette shows, and cycles of plays by distinguished dramatists and by young playwrights. Dramatic critics gave increasing approval and between 1936 and 1939 the Federal Theatre had successful plays running simultaneously on Broadway and throughout the country.

Drawing on various techniques, Federal Theatre invented the Living Newspaper, a terse, cinematic type of production dealing with such social and economic subjects as agriculture, flood control, and housing. *Triple-A Plowed Under*, *Power*, and *One-Third of a Nation* were pioneer works in an art form still widely used in theatrical, cinematic, and radio production.

Other artistic achievements of the Project included the development of a Negro theatre responsible for such productions as *Macbeth*, *Haiti*, *The Swing Mikado*; classical revivals such as *The Tragical History of Doctor Faustus*, Miracle and Morality plays, and a long line of Shakespeare revivals; an international cycle of plays from Euripides to Ibsen; simultaneous production in twenty-one cities of Sinclair Lewis's *It Can't Happen Here*; over national networks, such well-known series as *The Epic of America*, *Men Against Death*, *Women of America*; nation-wide productions of plays by Elmer Rice, Eugene O'Neill, and Bernard Shaw, including the American première of *On the Rocks*; regional productions, such as *The Sun Rises in the West* in Los Angeles, and Paul Green's *The Lost Colony* on Manteo Island in North Carolina, which is still played to thousands of people each summer. From *Treasure Island*, at the San Francisco Exposition, Federal Theatre built and equipped out of its own box-office receipts a modern theatre.

Sponsorship of Federal Theatre was wide and varied: theatre and other unions; schools and universities; churches—Catholic, Jewish, and Protestant; civic and community groups; industrial and philanthropic organizations; a great following of youth never before (or since) able to afford theatre-going. In *Federal Theatre Magazine* this audience speaks:

> We're a hundred thousand kids who never saw a play before. We're students in colleges, housewives in the Bronx, lumberjacks in Oregon, sharecroppers in Georgia. We're rich and poor, old and young, sick and well. We're America and this is our theatre.

And in the same article:

> We're the Caravan theatre in the parks, Shakespeare on a hillside, Gilbert and Sullivan on a lagoon, the circus under canvas, Toller on a truck. We're the theatre for the children of the steel mills in Gary; we're the theatre for the blind in Oklahoma. We're dramatic companies and vaudeville companies and marionette companies touring the C.C.C. camps, touring the flood areas, playing in schools, playgrounds, prisons, reformatories, hospitals. We're the Living Newspaper; we're the Negro theatre, the Yiddish theatre and theatres throughout America playing not only in English but in French, German, Italian, and Spanish; we're the file, we're the record, we're theatre history.

Emphatically a people's theatre, the candour of its comment on economic issues, especially in the Living Newspapers, led to criticism by witnesses before the House Committee to investigate un-American activities and before the sub-committee of the House Committee on Appropriations. All major units of screen, stage, and radio, many schools, churches, and sponsoring bodies spoke in favour of Federal Theatre. There was a struggle in Congress. The House voted to liquidate the project; the Senate voted to restore it. On 30 June 1939 the Federal Theatre was ended by Congressional action (see also NEGRO IN THE AMERICAN THEATRE). HALLIE FLANAGAN†

FEDOROVITCH, SOPHIE (1893–1953), stage designer, who came to England in 1924, and from 1926 onwards designed settings for most of the leading ballet companies of the time, including Sadler's Wells. The keynote of her art was simplicity, and she had a great gift for creating atmosphere by skilful lighting and an uncluttered set which left the imagination free to roam. Her last work was done for Gluck's 'Orpheus', presented at Covent Garden after her death.

FELLOWES, AMY, see TERRISS (1).

FEMALE IMPERSONATION. In the Greek and Elizabethan theatres female parts were always played by boys and men, as they were for centuries in China and Japan, where the actress is still a comparatively recent importation. Some actors have become renowned for their excellent portrayal of women—Bathyllus in Rome, Alizon in Paris, Ned Kynaston in London, Mei Lan-Fang in China. In English pantomime the Dame is always played by an actor, but this is less impersonation as an art than burlesque or caricature, as was the work of the American actors Harrigan and Hart, Weber and Fields, and Wallace Beery. The 'woman' in the Negro minstrel troupes was always played by a man. The greatest modern exponent of the art of female impersonation was probably the American actor Julian Eltinge, who starred in *The Fascinating Widow* in 1911. His deft satire was appreciated by the women in his audiences as well as by the men. In the *Passing Show* and the *Ziegfeld Follies* in the 1920s Bert Savoy played the part of a vulgar but good-natured young 'gal about town'. The tradition, which does not appear to have flourished so well in England, in spite of Charley's immortal Aunt, is being carried on today in New York by T. C. Jones, who differs from his predecessors in that he imitates, not womankind, but specific women.

GEORGE FREEDLEY†

FENN, Ezekiel (1620–?), a boy actor who at the age of 15 played Sophonisba, the chief female part in *Hannibal and Scipio*. He must already have had a good deal of experience, since at about the same time he played Winifred, an even more exacting role, in a revival of *The Witch of Edmonton*. He was with the Queen's Men at the Cockpit, and stayed on with Beeston after their removal, possibly as one of the older members of Beeston's Boys. He must have had a good reputation and been very popular with his audience, since Henry Glapthorne wrote him a prologue in 1639 'at his first Acting a Man's Part'. It is not known what happened to Fenn on the closing of the theatres in 1642.

FENNELL, James (1766–1816), an English actor, intended for the law, who went on the stage in 1787 at Edinburgh as Mr. Cambray, his first part being Othello. Later in the same year he was at Covent Garden, but he was not outstandingly successful in London, and preferred to tour the provinces. In 1792 he went to America, where he was very popular. He was a member of the American Company, and also of Wignell's company in Philadelphia. His best part was always considered to be Othello, though he appeared in most of the tragic roles of the current repertory, including Jaffier. This he played at the Park Theatre, New York, in 1799, in company with Cooper and Mrs. Melmoth. He speculated heavily in salt, and fell into debt, retiring, after several farewell performances, in 1810. A fine man, six feet tall, with an expressive face, he was an excellent actor, and was also the author of a comedy and editor of a theatre magazine. In 1814 he published his autobiography, entitled *An Apology for the Life of James Fennell*.

FENTON, Lavinia (1708–60), English actress, and the first to play Polly Peachum in *The Beggar's Opera*. She was the daughter of a naval lieutenant named Beswick, but took her name from her widowed mother's second husband, a coffee-house keeper in Charing Cross. She made her first appearance on the stage at the Haymarket in 1726, as Monimia in *The Orphan*, followed by Cherry in *The Beaux' Stratagem*, and was an immediate success, being pretty, witty, and only 18. Her appearance as Polly at Lincoln's Inn Fields on 29 Jan. 1728 sealed her reputation, and she became one of the most talked-of women of the London stage. She made her last appearance on 28 June 1728, and retired to live with the Duke of Bolton, whom she married in 1751.

FERBER, Edna, see KAUFMAN and SHOWBOAT.

FERNALD, John Bailey (1905–), English producer, who from 1955–65 was Principal of the Royal Academy of Dramatic Art in succession to Sir Kenneth Barnes. Educated at Marlborough and Oxford, he was President of the Oxford University Dramatic Society in 1927, and in 1929, after some experience with amateur productions, did his first professional production at the Arts Theatre. He has since had a long and successful career as a producer, broken only by war service at sea from 1940–5, after which he went to the Liverpool Playhouse for three years, 1946–9. During this time he was Shute Lecturer on the Art of the Theatre at Liverpool University (1948). In 1949 he was associated with Roy Rich in the direction of the Arts Theatre, London. He is the author of *The Play Produced: An Introduction to the Technique of Producing Plays* (1933), and, with his second wife, the actress Jenny Laird, of a play, *And No Birds Sing* (1955). He produced at Unity, in its early amateur days, the first translation of a play by Brecht to be done in England, *Señora Carrar's Rifles*. His daughter Karen is also on the stage.

FERNÁNDEZ DE MORATÍN. (1) Nicolás (1737–80), a Spanish dramatist of the eighteenth century and a staunch upholder of the neo-classical theories expounded in Spain by Ignacio de Luzán. In support of these theories he wrote several unsuccessful plays. His son, (2) Leandro (1760–1828), was the most successful of the Spanish neo-classical dramatists. He combined the contemporary neo-classicism of France and the Venetian comedy of Goldoni with traditional Spanish elements, both in the presentation of character and of social background. One of his early successes was a brilliant satire on the type of extravagant drama then delighting the public. The victim of this play (*El café* or *La comedia nueva*, 1792) was recognizable as Comella, whose plays, though of no great value, were at that time popular. Moratín's most famous play, however, was *El sí de las niñas* (1806), a piece of lively dialogue and excellent characterization in which the author defends the principle of a woman's freedom to marry the man she loves, a situation reminiscent of Goldoni's amusing *I rusteghi*. Moratín, unlike his predecessor García de la Huerta, was a great admirer of Molière, of whose *École des maris* and *Médecin malgré lui* he made spirited translations. He also translated *Hamlet* into Spanish. Moratín was the author of a study of the theatre, *Los orígenes del teatro español* (published posthumously in 1830).

J. E. VAREY

FERRARI, Paolo (1822–89), one of the most popular Italian dramatists of his time. He studied law, and was engaged in its practice when his first plays were produced. He won fame when in 1853 his play about Goldoni, *Goldoni e le sue sedici commedie*, won a prize offered by a Florentine dramatic academy. It was followed by several other plays, of which *Il suicidio* (1875) held the stage for many years; but his best-known work is undoubtedly *La satira e Parini* (1856), of which one character, Marchese Colombi, is as familiar to Italian audiences as Mrs. Malaprop to English.

FERRAVILLA, EDOARDO (1846–1915), Italian actor, trained by Modena, in whose company he played young lovers. He later developed as a great comedian and character-actor, and although he could when he wished play in pure Italian, it was in the comic exploitation of the Milanese dialect that he made his reputation, frequently writing his own plays. In 1870 he was joint founder with Arrighi of a theatre in Milan.

FERREIRA, ANTÓNIO, see PORTUGAL.

FERREIRA, PROCÓPIO, see SOUTH AMERICA, 2.

FESTIVAL THEATRE, see GRAY, TERENCE.

FESTSPIELHAUS, see ACOUSTICS, 8, BAYREUTH and OPERA, 11.

FEUILLÈRE [CUNATI], EDWIGE (1907–), French actress, who studied at the conservatoires of Dijon and Paris, and then appeared in light comedies at the Palais-Royal and Bouffes-Parisiens under the name of Cora Lynn. In 1931 she made her début at the Comédie-Française, unofficially in *Le Sicilien* and later as Suzanne in *Le Mariage de Figaro*, in which, says Robert Kemp, she showed 'grace et pétulance, mais pour une soubrette un excès d'autorité et une beauté provocante'. In 1933 she left to go into films, but a year later returned to Paris, though not to the Comédie-Française. In 1937 she appeared in *La Parisienne*, and in the same year played Marguérite Gautier in *La Dame aux camélias*, in which she was seen in London in 1955. She appeared as Lia in the first production of Giraudoux's *Sodome et Gomorrhe* (1943), and as the Queen in Cocteau's *L'Aigle à Deux Têtes* (1946), and a year later joined the Barrault–Renaud company to play Ysé in Claudel's *Le Partage de midi* with general acclamation. In this too she was seen in London, in 1951. Among her later roles have been the Queen in Betti's *La regina e gli insorti* (1957). A superb actress and a beautiful woman, she has a particularly lovely voice, with a warm vibrant quality which adds to the impact of her personality.

FEYDEAU, GEORGES (1862–1921), French dramatist, son of the novelist Ernest-Aimé Feydeau (1821–73). The author of more than sixty farces, some written in collaboration, he had his first success with *Tailleur pour dames* (1887). Among his later plays were *Le Système Ribadier* (1892), *Un Fil à la patte* (1894)—which had an enthusiastic reception in London in 1964 when performed by the Comédie-Française with Robert Hirsch as Bouzin and Feydeau's grandson Alain as Fontanet—*Le Dindon* (1896), and *La Dame de Chez Maxim* (1899), seen in London in 1902 as *The Girl from Maxim's*. After a brief excursion into more serious comedy with *La Main passe* (1904), he returned to his earlier vein with *Occupe-toi d'Amélie* (1908) (adapted by Noël Coward in 1959 as *Look after Lulu*, with Vivien Leigh and Antony Quayle), and some one-act farces, among them *On purge bébé* (1910), *Mais n'te promène donc pas toute nue!* (1912), and *Hortense a dit: J'm'en fous!* (1916).

FEYDEAU, THÉÂTRE, see COMÉDIE-ITALIENNE.

FIABE, LE, the name given by Gozzi to his 'fairy-tale' plays (see ITALY, 2 vi).

FIELD, NATHAN (1587–1620), English actor and playwright, the son of a preacher who fulminated against the players. He was a scholar at St. Paul's in 1600, when the Master of the Children of the Chapel Royal, abusing the powers conferred upon him to impress singing-boys, snatched him away to become a boy actor. He went to Blackfriars, where he appeared in *Cynthia's Revels*, and later in the *Poetaster* and *Epicoene*. He also continued his education under Ben Jonson, reading Horace and Martial with him. Nat, or Nid Field, as he was commonly called (the modern form of Nathaniel is incorrect), was a wild and dissolute young man, constantly in debt, from which he was more than once rescued by Henslowe, but apparently an excellent actor, playing the parts of young lovers, and noted as excelling in the title-role of *Bussy d'Ambois*. He was absorbed into the company of the Lady Elizabeth's Men in 1613, and two years later joined the King's Men, possibly in succession to Shakespeare. He was the author of two plays, *A Woman is a Weathercock* (1609) and *Amends for Ladies* (1611), and collaborated in several works with Massinger and Fletcher. A portrait of him in Dulwich College shows him as a dark and handsome young man.

FIELDING, HENRY (1707–54), famous English novelist, who in his early years played an important part in the history of the London theatre, since it was mainly owing to his satirical attacks on governmental and other abuses that the Licensing Act of 1737 was passed. His first three plays were fairly harmless, being comedies aimed at some contemporary and mainly literary follies, as was *Tom Thumb the Great*, which satirized the conventions of heroic drama. It was with a ballad-opera, *The Welsh Opera; or, the Grey Mare the Better Horse*, done at the Haymarket in 1731, that Fielding openly attacked both political parties, and brought the Royal Family, thinly disguised, on to the stage. The repercussions were sufficiently alarming for Fielding to drop politics for the moment and write for Drury Lane five plays dealing light-heartedly with the social scene. He might not have meddled with politics again, had it not been for the repercussions of the hated Excise Bill, combined with the opportunities offered by the announcement of a parliamentary election. The combination was too good to miss, and in *Don Quixote in England*, again done at the Haymarket, in 1734, Fielding returned to the attack on Walpole and on corrupt electioneering practices. Encouraged by success, Fielding took over the management of the Haymarket and put on his two most audacious satires, *Pasquin* (1736) and *The Historical Register for the Year 1736* (1737). The former had almost as great a success as *The Beggar's Opera*. In addition to his own plays, Fielding staged several other plays in which Walpole's administration came under fire, and it was probably the cumulative effect of these which finally decided the Government to curtail the liberty of the theatres. Adopting as a pretext the scurrility of a play entitled *The Golden Rump*, which probably had nothing to do with Fielding and was submitted to Giffard at Goodman's Fields Theatre, from where it found its way to Walpole's desk, the Government rushed through the Licensing Act, which limited the legitimate theatres in London to two, Covent Garden and Drury Lane, a monopoly which lasted until 1843, and created a regularized and strictly enforced censorship of plays which is still in force. The closing of the unlicensed theatres, among which was the Haymarket, hit Fielding hard. Having a wife and growing family to support, and knowing that the censor would not license, nor the legitimate theatres accept, plays written by him, he turned his attention to the more lucrative field of the novel. It may perhaps be laid to the credit of the unfortunate Licensing Act that it indirectly produced *Tom Jones* and *Joseph Andrews*.

FIELDING, TIMOTHY (?–1738), a small-part actor who in 1733 became landlord of the Buffalo Head Tavern in Bloomsbury. For some years he had a booth at Bartholomew Fair, and by a confusion of names it was said at one time time that the booth had belonged to Henry Fielding. Timothy acted the part of Mr. Furnish the upholsterer in Henry's play *The Miser* (1733).

FIELDS, GRACIE [GRACE STANSFIELD] (1898–), a Lancashire comedienne and singer of popular ballads, and a much-loved entertainer of the music-halls in their closing phase. She was on the halls as a child, and worked also in a cotton mill in Rochdale, where she was born. In 1923, while touring in his *Mr. Tower of London*, she married Archie Pitt [Selinger], a Cockney comedian, and scored a notable success when the revue reached London. She was invited to appear in a straight play with Gerald du Maurier, *S.O.S.*, but her heart was in vaudeville, and during the run of the play she appeared nightly in the second house at the Alhambra. She was also in cabaret at the Café Royal, in *The Show's The Thing*, which ran for eighteen months, and in *One Week of Grace*. She toured the United States and South Africa, and was received everywhere with acclamation. She appeared in numerous Command Performances, and recorded many of her most popular songs and monologues. Her marriage with Pitt, who was much older than herself, was not a success, and she left him, later marrying the film producer, Monty Banks. During the Second World War she gave numerous concerts for the troops, and to help the war effort (and incidentally to remain with her husband who, as an Italian, would have faced internment in England) she undertook a concert tour in America which raised nearly £500,000 for the Navy League. Banks died in 1946, and five years later Gracie Fields, who was living in semi-retirement in Capri, married Boris Alperovici. In the early part of her career she was joined on the halls by her sisters Betty and Edie, and her brother Tommy. She was appointed C.B.E. in the Birthday Honours of 1938 for services to the stage, and received the Freedom of the City of Rochdale.

FIELDS, WILLIAM CLAUDE [really DUKINFIELD] (1879–1946), American comedian. Born in Philadelphia, he left home at the age of 11 and lived in great privation for some years. He made his first professional appearance as a 'tramp juggler' in July 1897 at an open-air theatre near Norristown, Pennsylvania. For his New York début in 1898 at the London Theatre he juggled and acted a slapstick comedy routine, and soon became a vaudeville star on the Keith circuit. In 1900 he appeared at the Palace Theatre, London, and thereafter toured Europe. He gradually began to introduce a comic monologue into his juggling and established himself as a comedian, appearing in *The Ham Tree*, a series of loosely connected vaudeville sketches, in 1905. He was in pantomime at Manchester in the same year, toured with *The Ham Tree* from 1906 to 1907, and juggled at the Folies-Bergère in 1908. Evolving slowly from juggler to eccentric comedian, he abandoned vaudeville permanently to appear as a comedian in seven editions of the *Ziegfeld Follies* (1915–21) and in George White's *Scandals* (1922). In 1923 he played a strolling carnival swindler in *Poppy*, a type of character he had been portraying in sketches for some time. He began to act in films after 1925 and turned exclusively to film work in 1931. Stout, with small, cold eyes and a bulbous nose, a rasping voice, and a grandiloquent vocabulary and manner, his pose was generally that of a petty and inept crook, an anarchist devoid of any conventionally decent feeling. ROBERT TRACY

FIFTH AVENUE THEATRE, NEW YORK. 1. This was originally the Fifth Avenue Opera House, on 24th Street near Broadway, home of Negro minstrelsy. On 2 Sept. 1867 it opened as a theatre with light entertainment and burlesques, of which the best was Talfourd's *Shylock; or, the Merchant of Venice Preserved*, with Leffingwell as Shylock. The theatre closed abruptly after a dispute in the auditorium which ended in the death of a member of the audience, and did not open again until 25 Jan. 1869, when John Brougham appeared there in one of his own plays. After another interval of idleness it finally opened on 16 Aug. 1869 as Daly's Fifth Avenue Theatre, with a good company which included Mrs. Gilbert and Fanny Davenport. A number of plays by Robertson, some old comedies, and Boucicault's *London*

Assurance, with Fanny Davenport as Lady Gay Spanker, were seen in the first season, as was Mrs. Scott-Siddons as Viola and Rosalind. Daly's first outstanding success at this theatre was *Frou-Frou*, but he was anxious to encourage American dramatists, and on 21 Dec. 1870 produced Bronson Howard's first play, *Saratoga*, which had a long run. The theatre was by now firmly established, and in 1872 was redecorated and much improved. Some fine productions followed, but on New Year's Day 1873 it was burnt down. The company went to 728 Broadway temporarily, where *Alixe*, with Clara Morris, was produced.

2. On 3 Dec. 1873 Daly opened his second Fifth Avenue Theatre at Broadway and 28th Street but with little success. Among other failures was that of a costly and elaborate production on 21 Feb. 1874 of *Love's Labour's Lost*, which had not previously been seen in New York. The financial panic of 1873–4 had a bad effect on the theatre, but success came with the production on 17 Feb. 1875 of *The Big Bonanza*, in which John Drew made his New York début as Bob Ruggles. The following season saw the popular London success, *Our Boys*, with Maurice Barrymore, Fanny Davenport, Mrs. Gilbert, and Sydney Cowell, while Daly's *Pique*, in which Fanny Davenport had her first big starring role, was also a success. It was during the run of this play that Georgiana Drew, later the wife of Maurice Barrymore, made her first appearance in New York.

The season of 1876–7 was memorable for the first appearance of Charles Coghlan in New York as a leading man of distinction and charm. He played Orlando to Fanny Davenport's Rosalind, and appeared in a revival of *The School for Scandal* on 5 Dec. 1876, whose opening-night success was marred by the disastrous Brooklyn Theatre fire in which over 300 people lost their lives. In 1877 Adelaide Neilson was seen at the Fifth Avenue as Viola, as Imogen, new to New York audiences, and as Juliet. Daly was now finding the financial loss on his theatre too great, and in 1878, after several failures, he found himself unable to pay the rent, and so left. The Fifth Avenue was taken over by Stephen Fiske, and Mary Anderson, at the age of 18, made her début there, followed by Helena Modjeska. The theatre was then leased to various travelling companies, and frequently housed light opera, including several by Gilbert and Sullivan under D'Oyly Carte. After many changes of name, this famous theatre was pulled down in 1908.

FIFTY-EIGHTH STREET THEATRE, NEW YORK, see CONCERT THEATRE.

FIFTY-FIRST STREET THEATRE, NEW YORK, see HOLLYWOOD THEATRE.

FIFTY-FOURTH STREET THEATRE, see ADELPHI, 2.

FILANDRE [JEAN-BAPTISTE DE MOUCHAINGRE] (1616–91), a French actor-manager whose long and active life was spent entirely in the provinces, where he led a company which toured northern France, Holland, and Belgium. He is believed to have served as a model for Léandre in Scarron's novel, *Le Roman comique*. Floridor, the actor, who took a company to London in 1635, and was subsequently one of the stars of the Hôtel de Bourgogne, was for a short time associated with Filandre, as was Mlle Beauval, creator of some of Molière's most charming feminine roles.

FINLAND. The first attempt to introduce the theatre into Finland seems to have been made at the Academy of Åbo Turku in 1640, when a student company acted translations of Renaissance dramas, Moralities, and Latin comedies on a raised stage with classical columns and tapestry hangings. With the prevalence of war and plague, however, this had little effect, and during the eighteenth century Finland depended mainly on Swedish travelling actors for dramatic entertainment. In the early nineteenth century, after the annexation of Finland by Russia, German influence was particularly strong.

As in many countries today, Belgium and Switzerland for instance, the theatre in Finland is bilingual, and the two halves, the Finnish-speaking and the Swedish-speaking, develop independently, with occasional shifts of actors and technicians from one to the other. There are also two National Theatres. The Finnish-speaking one was founded in 1872, the Swedish-speaking in 1916, though the theatre and company on which this latter is based were founded as early as 1867. The moving spirit in the foundation of the Finnish-speaking National Theatre was Kaarlo Bergbom (1843–1906), who gathered round him a company which included the great actress Ida Aalberg (1857–1915). Bergbom was a great lover of Ibsen, and the first performance of *John Gabriel Borkman* was given at his theatre in 1897. The acquisition of Adolf Lindfors (1857–1929), an excellent actor in Molière, who had previously been with the Swedish-speaking company, established the tradition of Molière-acting which eventually led to the appearance of the Finnish National Theatre in a translation of *L'Avare* at the Paris International Theatre Festival in May 1955. The history of the Finnish-speaking theatre, from its inception to 1902 (the date of the company's installation in its present theatre) has been written by Eliel Aspelin-Haapkylä (in 4 vols.). A further volume, by Rafael Koskimies, brings the story down to 1917. The father of Finnish drama was Kivi [Aleksis Stenvall] (1834–72), whose statue, outside the Finnish National Theatre, was unveiled on 10 Oct. 1939. The production of his *Lea* in Helsinki on 10 May 1869 marks the inauguration of Finnish dramatic literature. He also wrote a play on Kullervo (a character in the great Finnish epic *Kalevala*), but his most important plays are undoubtedly his comedies of village life, of which *Nummisuutarit* (1864) is still in the repertory. Other important Finnish dramatists are Minna Canth (1844–97), whose realistic plays deal with contemporary problems, particularly those of the emancipation of women, and two poetic dramatists, Juhana Henrik Erkko (1849–1906) and Eino Leino (1878–1926). The former drew on the *Kalevala* for his two most important plays, the latter on Finnish history. Later dramatists include Maria Jotuni (1880–1943), author of satirical comedies of rural life, Lauri Haarla (1890–1944), and Hella Vuolijoki (1888–1954). There are a number of good dramatists writing today whose work it is not yet possible to evaluate.

The Swedish-speaking stage in Finland owes much to the Swedish actor Carl Gottfried Seuerling (1727–92) who, with his wife, brought Shakespeare to Finland, beginning with *Romeo and Juliet* in 1780, as well as Racine, Molière, Voltaire, Calderón, and Holberg. Marie Silfvan (1802–65) was the first outstanding Finnish-born actress. The leading actor of the Swedish company today is Erik Lindström (1906–), who played Hamlet at Elsinore in July 1947 and was seen in 1950 in Stockholm as Petruchio in a production of *The Taming of the Shrew* directed by Tyrone Guthrie, which had opened previously in Helsinki. In a playwriting competition held in 1955, for which scripts were received from Denmark, Sweden, Norway, Iceland, and Finland, the first prize was won by a Finnish Swedish-language author, Walentin Chorell, with his *Systrarna*. Of the older dramatists J. J. Wecksell, Mikael Lybeck, and Runar Schildt deserve mention.

There are in Finland (with a population of 4½ million, of which one-tenth is Swedish-speaking) 30 professional Finnish theatres (8 in Helsinki) and 5 Swedish (2 in Helsinki, 1 at Åbo, 1 at Vasa, and a travelling company which tours the provinces). There are also innumerable amateur groups. Of the director-producers the most notable are Eino Kalima, Arvi Kivimaa, who succeeded Kalima as director of the Finnish National Theatre, Eino Salmelainen, and, of the younger generation, Vivica Bandler, who runs Helsinki's second Swedish-language playhouse, the 'Lilla Teatern', Sakari Puurunen, director of the Helsinki City Theatre, Jack Witikka and Rolf Långbacka, who in 1965 took over the direction of the Swedish National Theatre.

FINN, HENRY JAMES (*c.* 1790–1840), American actor and playwright, who studied law at Princeton University, but deserted his profession to go on the stage. He was at the Charleston Theatre for some time, and in management in Boston with Thomas Kilner. After the burning of the Park Theatre, New York, in 1820, where he was a member of the resident company, he appeared at the Anthony Street Theatre as Hamlet, a part which he also played at Chatham Garden Theatre in the great season of 1824. He was also seen as Andrew Aguecheek, and finally deserted tragedy for comedy, in which he was inimitable. In 1825 he played Sergeant Welcome Sobersides in his own play *Montgomery; or, the Falls of Montmorency*, an amusing Yankee character who was later incorporated into *The Indian Wife* (1830), and played by James H. Hackett. Finn, who was also the author of a good farce, died in the destruction by fire of the s.s. *Lexington* in Long Island Sound.

FINN [KHALFIN], KONSTANTIN YAKOVLEVICH, (1904–), Soviet dramatist, whose comedies have a light ironic and lyrical touch while dealing with the conflict of individual and environment, social outlook, and personal feelings. His greatest success to date has been *Nonsense*, produced in 1933 by V.Ts.P.S., which ridicules those who make love the only thing in life, while pointing the moral that hard work will go far to assuage a man's emotional pangs. Finn's later plays, particularly those produced during the Second World War, such as *Peter Krymov*, have made him a playwright of considerable importance.

FIORILLO. A family of actors of the *commedia dell'arte*, of whom (1) SILVIO (?–*c.* 1632), the original Capitano Mattamoros, was probably the first Pulcinella. He had a company of his own in Naples, his birthplace, in the last years of the sixteenth century, and later appeared with other companies. He was the author of several plays, and of *scenarii* in the *commedia dell'arte* tradition. He had a son, (2) GIOVAN BATTISTA (*fl.* 1614–51), who played the parts of Trappolino and Scaramuccia and was married to (3) BEATRICE VITELLI (*fl.* 1638–54), also a *commedia dell'arte* actress.

It is now thought unlikely that (4) TIBERIO (1608–94) was Silvio's son. His surname is sometimes found as Fiurelli and Fiorilli. One of the most famous actors of his day, he was first in a poor company, but left it to make a name for himself elsewhere. He paid many visits to Paris, and was one of the Italian company at the Petit-Bourbon in 1658, when Molière's company was playing there on alternate days. He was the greatest, if not the first, actor of Scaramuccia (Scaramouche), which he played unmasked. His life was written by Angelo Costantini (Mezzetin) in 1695, and edited from the original impression, with introduction and notes, by Louis Moland in 1876. He visited London several times, notably in 1673, when he became the rage, displacing French puppets and English actors in the affections of fashionable society. He was a fine dancer and acrobat, and at the age of 80 was still so supple that he could tap a man's cheek with his foot.

FIRES IN THEATRES. Fire has always been a major hazard in theatres, and many theatre buildings have perished because of it, sometimes with heavy loss of life. Drury Lane and Covent Garden have both been burnt down twice, the first in 1672 and 1809, the second in 1808 and 1856. The first recorded theatre fire in America was that of the Federal Street Theatre in Boston in 1798, and between then and 1876, when the Brooklyn Theatre went up in flames during the last act of *The*

Two Orphans with the loss of about 300 lives, including two members of the cast, over seventy-five serious fire disasters were reported. In Richmond, Virginia, on 26 Dec. 1811 seventy persons, including the Governor of the State, lost their lives when the candles of a stage chandelier set fire to the scenery. But it was the introduction of gas-lighting, with its naked flames in close proximity to inflammable scenery and costumes, coupled with the vogue for very large theatres, that caused the heavy death-rolls in nineteenth-century disasters: in the Lehman Theatre in St. Petersburg in 1836, 800 casualties; in Quebec in 1846, 100; in Karlsruhe a year later, 631; in Leghorn in 1857, 100. The greatest disaster of all time, however, was probably the fire in a Chinese theatre in 1845 which killed 1,670 persons. These and other tragedies caused a tightening-up of fire regulations. A theatre fire in Liverpool in 1878 led to the passing of the Act under which English provincial theatres are still licensed. This, however, did not prevent the double tragedy of the Theatre Royal, Exeter, which was burnt down in 1885, rebuilt and burnt down again in 1887, with 186 people killed. In America, where strong safety measures were taken after the Brooklyn fire, the futility of stringent regulations without equally stringent enforcement procedures was demonstrated on 30 Dec. 1903, when the supposedly fireproof Iroquois Theatre in Chicago became the scene of the worst such catastrophe in the history of the American theatre. During a performance of *Mr. Bluebeard*, starring Eddie Roy, and played to an overcrowded house with too many people standing, a fire, which was quickly controlled, led to a panic which resulted in the loss of over 600 lives. Subsequent investigation showed that while a building may be structurally fireproof, poor maintenance and inadequate safety facilities can turn it into a death-trap. With the introduction of electric lighting, fireproofing of stage materials, and a comprehensive code of fire regulations which laid the onus for prevention of fire squarely on the theatre managers, conditions improved, and fires in theatres are now comparatively rare, though the evasion of the fire regulations caused 492 deaths at the Cocoanut Grove Night Club in Boston on 28 Nov. 1942, and two years later, on 6 July, a circus fire at Hartford, Conn., caused 168 deaths, mostly of children.

FIRST PIPE, see LIGHTING, 3.

FISHER, CLARA (1811–98), a child prodigy who made her first appearance on the stage at the age of 6, being much admired as Richard III, Shylock, and Young Norval, as well as in such parts as Young Pickle and the Actress of All Work, in which she impersonated a series of characters. Having appeared at Drury Lane, Covent Garden, and in the provinces, she went in 1827 to New York, making her début at the Park Theatre as the four Mowbrays in *Old and Young*. For the next few years she toured in light opera and vaudeville, and in 1834 married a musician, James G. Maeder. She continued to act, however, though with less than her former success, and was seen in a number of classic parts, such as Ophelia, Viola, Lady Teazle, and in modern comedies and musical comedy. She retired from the stage in 1844, but later returned to star in *opéra bouffe*, finally retiring in 1880. Her brother John, and two sisters, Jane (Mrs. George Vernon) and Amelia, were also on the stage, appearing at the Park Theatre, New York, in the late 1830s. Jane, who died in 1869, was also at Wallack's, where she played old ladies and elderly secondary roles.

FISKE, MINNIE MADDERN (1865–1932), one of the outstanding women of the American stage, daughter of a theatrical agent in New Orleans. At the age of 3 she appeared on the stage, billed as Little Minnie Maddern, a name which she afterwards retained, her real name being Marie Augusta Davey. At 5 she was in New York, where her early appearances included Little Eva in *Uncle Tom's Cabin*, the Duke of York in Cibber's version of *Richard III*, Little Alice in *Kit the Arkansas Traveller*, and Arthur in *King John*. At 13, after some schooling and several tours in the South and Mid-West, she played the Widow Melnotte in *The Lady of Lyons*, and reappeared in New York on 15 May 1882, in a poor play in which she was much admired for the vivacity and naturalness of her acting. Several later productions served only to enhance her success, but in 1890 she retired from the stage on her marriage to Harrison Grey Fiske (1861–1942), editor of *The New York Dramatic Mirror*. The theatre at this time was in a state of transition, and in 1893 Mrs. Fiske, as she was now called, returned to the stage to star in her husband's *Hester Crewe*, an attempt to establish the new tradition in play-writing. She also appeared in *A Doll's House*, but it was her Tess in a dramatization of Hardy's novel by Stoddard, on 2 Mar. 1897 at the Fifth Avenue Theatre, that again won over the public. Mrs. Fiske's versatility embraced Dora, Magda, and both light and musical comedy, one of her great successes at this time being in Langdon Mitchell's *Becky Sharp*, with Maurice Barrymore as Rawdon and Tyrone Power as Steyne. Since her husband's opposition to the powerful Theatrical Syndicate prevented her from appearing in their theatres, the Fiskes rented the Manhattan in 1901. For six years she played there with a splendid company, putting on a series of fine plays which were not equalled until the early years of the Theatre Guild. Among them were *Hedda Gabler* and *Rosmersholm*. Mrs. Fiske was also responsible for the first professional production of a play from Professor Baker's 'English 47 Class', *Salvation Nell* (1908) by Sheldon. She also starred in his *High Road* (1912). A short but unsuccessful attempt at films resulted in her return to New York, where for some years she appeared in light comedies, followed by a long tour as the finest Mrs. Malaprop since Mrs. John Drew.

In 1927 she toured as Mrs. Alving in *Ghosts*, and one of her last productions was *Much Ado About Nothing*, in which she played Beatrice. In her last years she seldom appeared in New York, but revived her early successes on tour. Her acting was instinctively natural, and from 1893 on she was one of the most potent forces in the battle for realism on the New York stage. Even those who detested Ibsen had to admire her greatness in playing him, while she was, significantly, much admired by members of her own profession. During her six years in her own theatre she gave proof of great ability as a director, and she was always encouraging to young playwrights. In tragedy she was good, though not universally admired, but in comedy she had no peer among her contemporaries.

FITCH, William Clyde (1865–1909), one of America's best-loved and most prolific dramatists, who before his death at the age of 44 had written fifty plays. He began his career with *Beau Brummell*, commissioned from him by Richard Mansfield, who produced it in 1890 with himself in the title-role and retained it in his repertory until his retirement. Once launched, Fitch continued to pour out plays, the best of his early ones being *Nathan Hale* (1898) and *Barbara Frietchie* (1899), based on American history and showing in their mingling of personal and political problems a strength which might have taken Fitch far had he not been content to dabble in light comedy. He was at the height of his popularity in 1901, when *The Climbers* and *Lovers' Lane*, social comedies of life in New York, and *Captain Jinks of the Horse Marines*, in which Ethel Barrymore first appeared as a star under Charles Frohman, were running simultaneously in New York, while in London Tree was producing *The Last of the Dandies.* Among Fitch's other plays, many of which were written to order for certain stars, were *The Moth and the Flame* (1898) and *The Cowboy and the Lady* (1899), both melodramas, *The Stubbornness of Geraldine*, dealing with the American abroad, *The Girl with the Green Eyes*, a drama of jealousy (both 1902), *The Truth* (1906), which is sometimes considered to be his best play, and *The Woman in the Case* (1909). Fitch, who was one of the first American playwrights to publish his plays, was excellent at seizing certain phases of contemporary and domestic life, but his work as a social historian was spoilt by the introduction of melodrama in deference to the prevailing fashion.

FITZBALL, Edward (1792–1873), English dramatist, author of a vast number of melodramas given at the minor theatres of London, and now forgotten. He dramatized most of the novels of Sir Walter Scott, and is credited with the development of Nautical drama, which had as its hero a typical Jolly Jack Tar. His *Jonathan Bradford* (1833), based on a sensational murder case, made a fortune for the managers of the Surrey, where it was first produced. Fitzball was appointed dramatist to Covent Garden under Osbaldiston, and later went to Drury Lane, where he provided libretti for the light operas staged by Alfred Bunn. In 1859 he summed up his years of hack-work in *Thirty-Five Years of a Dramatic Author's Life.* A master of theatrical trick and artifice, and the creator of many terrifying devils, villains, murders, conflagrations, and suicides, he was in private life a mild little man, whose facility prevented his bothering much about good terms for his plays, since he could always earn more money with little effort. Several of his melodramas, notably *The Red Rover* (1829) and *Paul Clifford* (1835), passed into the repertory of the Juvenile Drama. In 1827 he wrote a version of *The Flying Dutchman* which was given at the Adelphi, full, says its author, 'of horrors and blue fire'. He had little originality, and wrote too quickly, but his work suited the taste of the time, and for over fifty years he was a prodigal purveyor of what the public wanted.

FITZROY THEATRE, London, see scala theatre.

FLANAGAN, Hallie [Mrs. Philip H. Davis, *née* Ferguson] (1890–1969), theatre historian and organizer, author of *Shifting Scenes of the Modern European Theatre* (1928), and *Arena* (1940), a full account of the Federal Theatre Project. In 1925 she was appointed Professor of Drama and Director of the Experimental Theatre at Vassar, leaving there in 1941 to occupy the same position in Smith College, Northampton, Mass., where she remained until her retirement in 1955. In 1935 she became Director of the Federal Theatre Project of the Works Progress Administration, in which capacity she was responsible for the working of the project in some forty towns, and for the overseeing of more than a thousand productions up to 1939, when the organization was disbanded (see federal theatre project). She was also a prolific contributor on theatrical topics to many leading American magazines.

FLANDERS, Michael Henry (1922–), English actor, lyric-writer, and entertainer. He made his first appearance on the professional stage at the Oxford Playhouse in 1941, playing Valentine in *You Never Can Tell.* He then went into the Navy, and in 1943, while on active service, contracted poliomyelitis. He has since been confined to a wheelchair, but this has in no way hindered his theatrical career, which ranges from collaboration in the writing of such revues as *Penny Plain* (1951) and *Airs on a Shoestring* (1953) to opera libretti, an English version of Stravinsky's 'The Soldier's Tale' (1956) in which he appeared at the Festival Hall, and an appearance in the London production of Brecht's *The Caucasian Chalk Circle* (1962). He is, however, probably best known for the revues *At the Drop of a Hat* (1956) and *At the Drop of Another Hat* (1965), a two-man entertainment in which he appeared with Donald Swann, his contemporary at

Westminster School and Christ Church, Oxford. They had already collaborated in the writing of songs for revues when in Dec. 1956 they appeared together at the New Lindsey in a programme of their own devising, Flanders providing the lyrics and dialogue and Swann the music. This was scheduled for a fortnight, but when transferred to the Fortune in the following January it ran for over two years. It was equally successful in New York, and on tour throughout the world, as was the second version, first seen at the Haymarket.

FLAT, a frame, made of 3 in. × 1 in. timber, generally covered with canvas (though modern stage designers have introduced a variety of surfaces). It is possibly the most important single element of the designer's equipment, and is the solution to the problem that scenes must be made up of separate parts, which should be as light as possible. The standard full-sized flat is 18 ft. high; in small theatres it may be lower, and in large ones may reach 24 ft. Its width may vary from 1 to 6 ft., or more rarely 8 ft. For widths above this, two or more flats, hinged together, are used; these are known as Booked Flats. Flats may be plain, or may contain openings; they may be straight edged, or may bear profiling boards of wood ¼ in. thick, fixed to the side of the frame and sawn to a required shape. They may be used as one of a set of wings (or a Booked Flat may be used as a Booked Wing), and may then carry on their on-stage edge an extension of profiling known as a Flipper. This is hinged so that it may face the audience even if the flat is set at an angle, and so that it may be folded in for packing. Flats may be used to form the three walls of a Box Set. Those at the back may be battened together, and the whole wall is then flown like a cloth (see DROP) in a scene change. Such a group is termed a French Flat.

Variants of the flat are the Groundrow, which may be likened to a flat on its side, lying across the stage, and the Set Piece. This latter is a low flat, profiled all round and probably cut to the silhouette of some representational or decorative shape. The term is, however, applied also to similar 'built' pieces (see SET PIECE, 2). A flat, when standing separately, is supported by a Stage Brace—a rod, generally extensible, hooked to the back of the flat at one end, and screwed into the floor at the other by means of a Stage Screw (a sort of corkscrew), or weighted with a Braceweight (a weight shaped to fit over the foot of the brace). Sometimes, however, the support of the flat takes the form of a framework of wood shaped like a right-angled triangle and hinged to the back of the piece, to be opened out and weighted as it is needed; this is termed a French Brace. A flat forming a wall with others is connected with its neighbours by a Throwline, a 16-ft. length of sashcord, fixed at the back of the left-hand stile near the top, and tossed over a cleat in a similar position behind the right-hand stile of the next flat. The line is then brought across the join and made off below by taking a turn round a pair of cleats, one on either flat, and finished in a 'slippery hitch'. The join between the two flats may then be 'broken', when it is required to 'strike' them, by a single tug at the end of the line and an upward toss to clear the cleat at the top, the operation being practically instantaneous.

A Backing Flat is a small flat, or booked flat, set outside a door or other opening to stop the view beyond.

There remain a number of small pieces that belong to the 'flat' family in that they are canvas-covered frames—such as rostrum-fronts, balustrade-pieces, staircase-sides, and raking pieces (that is, pieces with a sloping top edge, used either independently as small groundrows, or as fillings before ramps).

Since no full account of the construction of the traditional English flat is readily available, the following description may be of interest, and may serve as a record of a nice piece of traditional design which the commercial speed of modern production-methods may soon render obsolete. (For American flat see Burris-Meyer and Cole's *Scenery for the Theatre*, 1939.)

The frame of an English flat consists of four 3 in. × 1 in. timbers, of which the two vertical side-pieces are the Stiles, and the others, the top and bottom Rails. The corners are morticed-and-tenoned. It is essential that the stiles always bear the tenons, and the rails the mortises, since the Running, or sliding of the flat on its lower edge during shifting, would split up the foot of the stile if it were carried through to form the mortise with the bottom rail tenoned into it. The mortises on the rails are of the 'closed' variety; the tenons on the stiles are 'shouldered' and the mortises made to fit. No glue or screws are used in the assembly; the parts are put together and 'dry-pinned' with wooden pins. Thus, any flat can be altered, transformed into a door flat, or shortened, without the waste of cutting away glued joints. The canvas is laid back, the pins struck out, and the parts then easily separated for alteration. It is vital to keep the stiles dead straight, or adjacent flats will not join properly, and in that case the edges will need to be shot with a plane. Since the contracting draw of size paint on the canvas of the flat when drying is so powerful as to pull the sides concave, two or three horizontal Toggle Rails are 'jumped in' between the stiles as stays. These are of timber slightly thinner than the outer frame, so as not to touch the back of the canvas and cause a ridge under the pressure of the painter's brush. Each rail is tenoned and pinned, at either end, into the mortise of a triangular Toggle, or cross-piece, about 18 in. long. These toggles fit just between the inner edges of the stiles, and are screwed into their thickness. This method of inserting the rails tends both to resist the twisting strain exerted when the flat is handled, and to avoid any cutting into the material of the stile, which is a prime fault, since every such cut becomes a point of weakness that may eventually break in handling. To preserve squareness at the corners, a diagonal, cross-corner brace, about 3 ft. long, is shouldered across at one, or two, of the corners, but here again the outer frame is not cut, and the brace is halve-jointed at the ends, planted on, and screwed from the back face, from which it now stands proud by about ½ in. If the flat is to be profiled, the necessary profile board (or, nowadays, fireproof plywood) is attached to the stile at this stage. The flat is then canvased by tacking the canvas to the face, keeping the tacks near the inner edge of the frame. The waste canvas is roughly trimmed off, and the edges beyond the tacks are laid back while the frame is glued. The edges of the canvas are then pressed back in position on the glue. Finally a sharp knife is run round ⅛ in. from the edge of the flat, cutting the canvas clean, and at the same time making a slight incision into which the cut edge of the glued canvas tends to be pressed, and so sealed. If the flat is to be used in a box set it is provided with a Throwline, fixed near the top of the left-hand stile, and a cleat of special pattern in a corresponding position on the right-hand stile. The flat is now ready for priming and painting. So closely is this piece of carpentry adapted for the work it has to do, for the considerable strains of twisting that it must suffer in changes, and for the highly essential requirement of lightness and good balance consistent with strength, to ease the labour of those changes, that tall flats in big productions are sometimes made with the stiles slightly tapering in thickness throughout their whole length, so that they balance more easily in 'running'. Many quicker or cheaper alternatives are known for various parts of the construction, but none gives a lighter, stronger, finished article than the above traditional method.

Historically, the word Flat is perhaps one of the most interesting in stage parlance. Its present meaning is explained above; in the mid-nineteenth century, however, it had a different application. It was then used in the phrase 'a pair of flats', and was confined to the two separate halves of a back scene, which then, unlike ours today, parted centrally in the middle of the picture, and drew off to either side. Farther back, the word is used only adjectivally, and the full term is Flat Scene. Formerly, scenes were divided into two sorts, of which the flat scene, consisting of a painted cloth, or of a pair of painted 'flats', was distinguished from the Scene of Relief (a word found in many spellings). To discover the origin of this distinction, it is necessary to go back to the Court masques of Inigo Jones. The scenic system of the masques—the origin of our modern scenery—was in its final form briefly this: behind a decorative frontispiece, or Proscenium Arch, was placed a set of wings, called Side Scenes or Side Shutters, to frame the back scene on either side. These were masked-in with borders, or Clouds. The wings were either permanent throughout the performance, or were in groups working in grooves, and changeable with the changing back scenes, which consisted of centrally divided pairs of shutters, from two to four in number, sliding in grooves about the middle of the stage. A point to note here is that, very early in the later Restoration theatre, the position of the back shutters was extended beyond their old central position, for there are indications that they could be closed at other positions further down-stage—there was possibly provision made for them behind every pair of wings—thus permitting shallow Front Scenes as well as the deeper scene. Behind such front scenes it was possible to set furniture, or groups of players, for discovery at the opening of the flats.

In some masques the shutters were further divided horizontally into two storeys. The Upper Back Shutters might then open independently to show a view beyond into heaven, or on to a mountain-top, while the Lower Back Shutters parted to disclose a distant landscape beneath, or the interior of a cave in the mountain. This system may have persisted well into the next century, for in 1736 Fielding has an interesting allusion to an imaginary scene-painter named Mynheer Van Bottom-Flat.

Most scene changes in the masques were achieved by the opening and closing of the shutters described above; but, at specially dramatic moments, the shutters might all be opened to disclose the deeper half of the stage, and so reveal what came to be known as the Scene of Relief—that is, a scene which was not flat. It was composed of cut-out pieces in various planes, set, like modern groundrows, before a backcloth, and often framed by a narrow pair of wings, set in a special groove immediately behind the shutters. That these 'groundrows' were made in wood is suggested by a note on the back of one of Inigo Jones's drawings (No. 286 in the Duke of Devonshire's collection) where there is an account for 'putting bourdes togeather for sceanes of releaue'. This joining of boards edge to edge to make a continuous sheet is so like the method of making old-fashioned profiling (as described for instance in F. Lloyds's *Practical Guide to Scene Painting*, c. 1875) that it seems likely that the scenes of relief were constructed in a manner similar to the Set Scenes, with their successive, profiled groundrows, of a modern pantomime.

Such a scene could not be neatly changed before the eyes of the audience, as the shutter scene could be. Its component pieces were set in place beforehand, and revealed, as a discovery, by opening a pair of shutters upon them; it was, in short, a previously set scene, or, to give it the name which eventually became one of the principal terms in the stage vocabulary, it was a Set Scene. Today a 'set' is any complete scene, and the true meaning of the word is thus obscured, since it was originally a verbal adjective applying only to a scene previously prepared, as against a flat scene whose two simple parts slid on and off in view of the audience, according to the method of visible scene-change normal in the English theatre up to the time of Irving.

The flat scene, as far back as the Restoration, might be either plain, or a Cut Flat or Open Flat Scene—that is, its two halves might each be a plain painted surface, or might contain openings for doors, windows, arches, or the interstices between the trees of a Cut Wood Scene. With such open flats another piece of scenery was needed behind, to mask the opening. Any small scene behind a central opening was later termed an Inset, or an Inset Scene.

In Chamber Scenes, or room interiors, which might have to travel on circuit, the pairs of central flats might be comparatively narrow. A pair still in existence in Oxfordshire is only 8 ft. wide in all. If need arose, additional pieces could be pushed in from either side as Close-Ins. Such an arrangement is apparently visible in Hogarth's painting of the juvenile performance, at Mr. Conduit's, of *The Indian Emperour*. This system of a back-wall in several pieces approaches the box-set of today, and in both a perfect join between the pieces is very important. Frequent references are found in literature to lights showing through the cracks of bad joins. RICHARD SOUTHERN

FLAT SCENE, see FLAT and SET.

FLAVIO, see SCALA, FLAMINIO.

FLECK, JOHANN FRIEDRICH FERDINAND (1757–1801), an excellent German actor who forsook theology for the stage and was stage-director at the Berlin National Theatre shortly before Iffland went there in 1796. He was a gifted but eccentric personality and first made his mark as Gloucester to Schröder's Lear. His fine presence, resonant voice, and fiery artistic temperament made him eminently suitable to interpret the stormy heroes of the *Sturm und Drang* period. In such parts as Karl Moor and Don Carlos he excelled Schröder, and was the idol of the young Romantics. But his capricious and unstable character, which caused him to act well one night and badly another, was often a sore trial to his fellow actors, and an irritation to his audience, who never knew if they would, as they said, see the 'little' or the 'big' Fleck. Such was his magnetism, however, that he could in a moment win over an audience which he had previously alienated by his behaviour. He died at the comparatively early age of 44, and was a sad loss to the Berlin theatre, where he might have helped to counterbalance Iffland's cautious and old-fashioned repertory, and satisfy the young Romantic generation who railed against it. The last part he played was his greatest—Wallenstein in Schiller's trilogy.

FLECKER, (HERMAN) JAMES ELROY (1884–1915), English poet, and author of the fine poetic plays *Hassan* and *Don Juan*. The first was brilliantly produced at His Majesty's in 1923, with music by Delius, and proved a success, owing as much to the splendour of its oriental costumes and scenery, and the excellence of a fine cast, as to its inherent poetic beauty. Had Flecker lived longer he might have proved an important influence in the renaissance of poetic drama, but *Don Juan* (written 1910–11), more modern and realistic than *Hassan*, had only a private production by the Three Hundred Club, and *Hassan* remained for many years the only poetic play to have a full-scale West-End production without a preliminary production in the provinces or at one of the smaller London theatres. Both *Don Juan* and *Hassan* have been revived, the former as an unofficial venture at the Gateway Theatre, Edinburgh, during the 1950 Festival there, the latter by Basil Dean, with much splendour but little success, at the Cambridge Theatre, London, during the Festival of Britain in 1951.

FLEETWOOD, CHARLES (?–*c.* 1745), a wealthy gentleman who took an interest in the theatre and became manager of Drury Lane, first with Cibber and later with Macklin, who was also his leading man. They were both gamblers by temperament, and eventually ruined each other and everyone who came into contact with them. It was, however, under the management of Fleetwood that Macklin played his epoch-making Shylock in 1741, and that Garrick came from Goodman's Fields, where his success had been endangering the receipts of Drury Lane. Fleetwood also abolished in 1737 the free entry of lackeys into the Footmen's Gallery, thus doing away with a constant source of annoyance and disorder. He was always in the hands of money-lenders, but by his charm and his repentant manner he continually staved off disaster and wheedled his actors into playing with their salaries still unpaid. He finally gave up, and sold his Patent in about 1744 to two city men, Green and Amber. It was said of Fleetwood that he was 'a gentleman by birth, a coarser Sheridan, pleasant and fascinating, but addicted to low company, a gambler and a spendthrift'. He certainly played havoc with the finances of Drury Lane, in spite of Garrick's popularity.

FLESCHELLES, the name under which the great French comedian Gaultier-Garguille played serious parts at the Hôtel de Bourgogne from 1621 until his death in 1633. He was good in light comedy, and made an excellent tragedy king.

FLETCHER, JOHN (1579–1625), English poet and dramatist, who spent most of his life actively writing for the stage, either alone or in collaboration. His name is so indissolubly linked with that of Sir Francis Beaumont (1584–1616) that more than fifty plays have been ascribed to their joint authorship, of which Chambers believes only some six or seven are authentical. The rest were either by other hands, by Fletcher alone, or by Fletcher in collaboration with other contemporary dramatists, particularly Massinger.

Fletcher had already written for the Queen's Revels *The Woman's Prize* and *The Faithful Shepherdess*, both given in the early years of the seventeenth century, before his name was first linked with Beaumont's in some commendatory verses prefixed to Jonson's *Volpone*. The chief plays of Beaumont and Fletcher were *Philaster* (1610), *The Maid's Tragedy* (1611), *A King and No King* (1611), and *The Scornful Lady* (1613). It has been said of the collaborators that Beaumont, influenced by Jonson's comedy of humours, shows a more conservative and moral outlook in style and versification, together with greater power in tragedy, while Fletcher, starting from Middleton's comedy of manners, was the finer poet and more inventive mind. Together they stand as the chief exponents in English literature of the romantic tragicomedy. Beaumont seems to have ceased writing on his marriage in 1613, but Fletcher continued with such comedies as *Monsieur Thomas*, *Wit without Money*, and the tragedy, *Bonduca*, in which Burbage played the lead. Fletcher has been credited with collaboration with Shakespeare in *The Two Noble Kinsmen* and *Henry VIII*. The former is doubtful, and Beaumont or Massinger has been substituted for Shakespeare, but there seems reason to believe that Fletcher had a hand in parts of *Henry VIII*. He is noted in the Stationers' Register (1653) as having collaborated with Shakespeare in *The History of Cardenio*, now lost. One play assigned to him, *The Chances* (1623), was adapted by Buckingham in 1666, and acted with some success. It was revived in 1922 by the Phoenix Society and in 1962 at the first Chichester Festival.

FLEURY [ABRAHAM-JOSEPH BÉNARD] (1750–1822), French actor, son of the manager of a theatre at Nancy, where he made his first appearances. He was at first considered to be fit only for minor parts, but with his sister, who with her husband was on the stage under the name of Sainville, he went to Geneva and was invited to play at Ferney. Encouraged by Voltaire, who discerned great promise in him, he made his first attempt at the Comédie-Française in 1774, helped by Lekain, who had known his father. He was thought promising, but was advised to return to the provinces for further practice, which he did, playing chiefly at Lyon. In 1778 he made a second, successful, attempt, and remained at the Comédie-Française until his retirement in 1818, being its seventeenth *doyen*. During the Revolution he was imprisoned, together with a number of his companions, but after his release returned to the stage, and was one of the members of the company reconstituted in 1799. An excellent actor, he owed his position to hard work and a certain innate feeling for the theatre, being almost totally uneducated. He had a natural nobility of carriage and character, and was a master of polished comedy, being particularly fine as Alceste in *Le Misanthrope*.

FLEXIBLE STAGING. In an effort to break away from the conventions of the proscenium, or picture-frame, stage, producers have been experimenting for many years with various types of staging which go back, in essentials, to the Greek and Elizabethan theatres. The aim of these experiments has been to re-create a sense of intimacy and immediacy between actors and audience by abolishing the proscenium arch, as Terence Gray did at Cambridge in 1926 (see No. 84), and by building out a forestage so that the audience is seated on three sides, or even by placing the stage in the central area, as Robert Atkins did at the Ring, Blackfriars, in 1936. The advantage of such methods for the new or experimental group lies in the fact that they need not rely on acquiring or building a conventional proscenium-type theatre, but can adapt to their own purposes any convenient or easily obtainable hall.

Theatre-in-the-round had already been envisaged by Robert Edmond Jones in 1920, but he was not able to put it into practice. It was left to Glenn Hughes to show the efficacy of the idea in the Penthouse Theatre (see No. 41) which he created for the University of Washington, Seattle, in 1940. An interesting post-war development of this idea was Margo Jones's theatre in Dallas (see her book, *Theatre-in-the-Round*).

In Europe Meyerhold and Reinhardt were pioneers of theatre-in-the-round, as was Okhlopkov in some of his productions at the Realistic Theatre, Moscow, during the 1930s. In England Jack Midgley in Norfolk and Stephen Joseph in Scarborough proved how successful the form can be even with plays written for a proscenium stage. London had an opportunity of seeing Joseph's work when he brought his company, The Studio Club, from the Library Theatre, Scarborough, to the Mahatma Gandhi Hall to give arena-type productions. Another interesting venture was the short-lived but excellent Pembroke Theatre, Croydon, where some remarkably vivid and exciting productions of plays, old and new, showed what could be done in this medium. There is, however, still something to be said for limiting the audience to three sides of the acting area, as was done by Ann Jellicoe at the Portcullis with great success for such different types of play as *The Comedy of Errors* and *Rosmersholm*. This is the form of the Chichester Festival Theatre. Large forestages have been built at the Old Vic (for the National Theatre Company) and at Stratford-upon-Avon; and the Mermaid Theatre, at Puddle Dock, though it has the audience seated in front of the stage only, in the conventional manner, has nevertheless done away with the proscenium arch and produces its plays on an open stage (see No. 42).

These, and other experiments too numerous to mention, have led to the evolution of the all-purpose theatre which can be used for theatre-in-the-round, for productions with the audience on three sides, possibly in a horseshoe-shaped formation, for staging at one end of a hall, usually with a large forestage, or for proscenium productions. The university theatre at Bristol, designed by Richard Southern, is adaptable, as are the Questors' Theatre at Ealing and the experimental theatre at the London Academy of Music and Drama.

FLIES, the name given to the space above the stage, hidden from the audience, where scenery can be lifted clear from the stage or 'flown' by the manipulation of ropes. The men in charge of these are known as Fly-men, and they work on a Fly-floor, while the railing to which the ropes are attached is known as the Fly- or Pin-rail.

FLIPPER, a hinged extension at the on-stage edge of a wing, usually with a cut profile (see FLAT).

FLOATS, see LIGHTING.

FLORENCE, WILLIAM JERMYN (or JAMES) (1831–91), American actor, whose real name was Bernard Conlin. He began his career as call-boy at the Old Bowery, but his excellent powers of mimicry and exceptional memory soon took him on to the stage, and he made his New York début in 1849 at Niblo's Garden in dialect impersonations. Two years later, while appearing at the Broadway Theatre, he married the actress Malvina Pray, sister of Mrs. Barney Williams, and with her toured the United States in a repertory of Irish plays. Husband and wife were first seen in London in 1856, when they appeared at Drury Lane in *The Yankee Housekeeper* with great success. Among Florence's best parts were Captain Cuttle in *Dombey and Son*, in which he followed and reproduced with some fidelity the acting of W. E. Burton, Bob Brierly in *The Ticket-of-Leave Man*, which he was the first to play in America, and Bardwell Slote in *The Mighty Dollar*, a play which remained in his repertory for many years. He was good in burlesque, and as a comedian ranked with Jefferson, appearing with the latter as Sir Lucius O'Trigger in *The Rivals* and Zekiel Homespun in *The Heir-at-Law*. He also gave the first production in New York of *Caste*, which he had memorized while in London, staging it at the Broadway Theatre on 5 Aug. 1867 with all the realistic scenery and atmosphere of the Bancroft production. He himself played D'Alroy, one of his best parts, with his wife as Polly, Mrs. Chanfrau as Esther, Davidge as Eccles, and Mrs. Gilbert as the Marquise de St. Maur, her first important part in New York. The production caused a good deal of controversy, as Lester Wallack had bought the American rights of the play, but in the absence of copyright laws had no redress against piracy, and did not put it on himself until 1875, probably fearing to challenge comparison with Florence's excellent production. Florence, who was at first inclined to justify his behaviour on the score of expediency, later regretted it, but maintained that he did not know Wallack had already bought the play for New York. His feat of memory, which extended to the words and business, recalls that of Holcroft in memorizing for translation Beaumarchais's *Mariage de Figaro* nearly a hundred years before.

FLORIDOR [JOSIAS DE SOULAS, SIEUR DE PRIMEFOSSE] (1608–72), French actor, of good family, who left the army to join a company of strolling players. He soon became their leader, and in 1635 took them to London, where they appeared before the Court and at a theatre in Drury Lane. Three years later Floridor toured the provinces with Filandre, and shortly before or after that joined the company of the Théâtre du Marais, becoming Orator of the troupe after the departure of d'Orgemont. He had all the attributes of a good actor, aided by an excellent education, and was equally good in tragedy and comedy. Some of his best performances were given in the plays of Corneille, who was godfather to one of his children, and it may have been Floridor's move to the Hôtel de Bourgogne, which took place some time between 1643 and 1653, which induced Corneille to give his later plays to that theatre rather than the Marais. At the Hôtel de Bourgogne Floridor took the place of Bellerose and soon became leader of the company. His quiet, authoritative acting was in marked contrast to the bombastic style of his colleague, Montfleury, and he was the only actor spared by Molière in his mockery of the rival troupe in *L'Impromptu de Versailles* (1663). In 1671 he fell ill, and on the advice of his confessor renounced the stage, dying shortly afterwards.

FLY-FLOOR, a gallery running along the sides of the stage above the wing space, to supply a working area for the Fly-men engaged in handling the lines from the grid which are attached to the scenery, and also to keep the rope-ends from cumbering the stage-space below. The gallery itself is protected by a heavily built railing, carrying two rows of cleats, an upper and a lower. The lines are made off to the cleats on the lower rail when a cloth or border is trimmed, or 'deaded', that is, hung squarely at its correct height. When the cloth is 'flown', the lines are not taken off the lower cleats, but pulled in from above until the scenery is at a sufficient height, when they are made off, in a bight, upon the upper rail. Thus, when the cloth has to be lowered into position, the lines have only to be detached from the upper rail and lowered out, and their attachment to the lower rail will ensure the cloth being roughly in its correct position (roughly, because variations in temperature and humidity noticeably affect the length of the ropes).

There may be a fly-floor on either side of a stage, though generally one side (the prompt side) is chiefly used for tying-off. Between these floors there were formerly Catwalks, or narrow communicating bridges, slung on iron stirrups from the grid, so that the fly-men might get out to any point over the stage to see to the proper working of scenery. Generally there was one catwalk above each set of grooves.

Often the borders in an eighteenth-century and early nineteenth-century theatre were a simple stock of three types—arch borders, sky borders, and tree borders. These could, of course, be supplemented upon occasion, but the stock borders were so commonly used that in Foulston's Theatre Royal, Plymouth, in 1811, the borders of each set were all connected with their own shafts, and these three shafts, together with a fourth from which the groove-arms worked, were situated over the stage-left fly-floor, and worked by hanging endless lines, round drums at the extremities of the shafts.

The greater complexity of the large Continental theatres and opera-houses meant that there might on occasion be three fly-floors before the grid was reached, but English theatres rarely had more than one on either side of the stage. RICHARD SOUTHERN

FLYING EFFECTS. Since the first days of the theatre, the ingenuity of mechanists has been directed to flying effects. Of these, the simplest is a direct descent, where four lines over pulleys in the grid suspend a platform decorated with clouds and bearing a figure. The lines are taken to a windlass on the fly-floor. But such a merely vertical rise or fall was not enough, and the flying figure was moved across the stage as well as up or down. Many ingenious systems may be found, whose basis was usually as follows: a small 'carriage' was arranged—either on a taut rope, or on a specially built railway—capable of moving across above the stage from side to side at the level of the fly-floors. The motive power was manual, or supplied by counterweight and check-line. The 'carriage' was situated above one side of the stage, and carried pulleys, down past which ran the lines bearing the flying car or figure. These lines ascended straight from the object to be flown, through the carriage above, directly up to points in the grid. To begin the flight, these suspending lines were not touched, but the carriage through which they ran was drawn across the stage, so that the pulleys in the carriage bore against the vertically hanging lines as it moved and pushed them sideways, thus progressively raising the object from the stage as the carriage was drawn across, and thereby achieving a diagonal cross-ascent. A reverse movement of the carriage achieved a descent. A rearrangement of the parts, and an alteration of the points of suspension, would produce a sweeping curve, where the figure descended to the centre and rose again to the other side. A different arrangement produced a similar flight, but in two straight lines, down and up, so that the path of the flight was in the shape of a V. A further arrangement would produce an undulating flight.

Such ingenuities were well known in the theatre by the Restoration period, where frequent references to 'flyings' are found. Actual diagrams exist of English procedures at the end of the eighteenth century. By the mid-nineteenth century many elaborations are found, including a most complicated machine for controlling the circulatory gyrations of a pair of flying figures. Individual flying artists, too, can be traced about this time and immediately following. One of the most famous was Mlle Aenea, with her husband, W. P. Dando, who used a simple windlass with stout, stretched, rubber cords, which allowed Mlle Aenea to achieve the famous act of *La Mouche d'Or* on the Continent in the 1890s, and at the Palace Theatre, London, in 1894. The fascinations of flying continue into the present century where, for instance, in the pantomime *Red Riding Hood*, at Covent Garden in 1938, Kirby's Flying Ballet gave a brilliant and graceful performance in which two figures, suspended by lines worked from a winch above the centre of the auditorium, rose from the stage—their lines shortening on the winch as they swung forward, so that their level was controlled—flew hand in hand directly over the heads of the audience in the stalls, turned at the limit of their travel by a neat movement of exchange of hands, and, as gracefully, swung back to the stage and lightly stood upon it again.

In these effects, where no chariot or cloud is used to bear the figure, the line is attached to a hook at the player's back which forms part of a harness worn under the costume. It is easily fixed or discarded, but a safety device prevents the line leaving the hook in flight.

Many forms of motive power are used, from the manual or the counterweight in earlier times, to the stretched rubber of Dando, and the electric motor of today. An article published at the beginning of the nineteenth century says of flying effects: 'The cords are very slender and painted black, to elude the eye of the spectator. The lights also are strong in front, and dim behind, to assist the optical deception. To give the cords sufficient strength without increasing their diameter, they are spun of the best hemp, mixed with brass wire well annealed. Those used at Covent Garden for the flying horse, in the Pantomimic Spectacle of *Valentine and Orson* . . . although less in diameter than a common quill, were said to possess sufficient strength to suspend a ton weight' (see also TRICKWORK ON THE ENGLISH STAGE). RICHARD SOUTHERN

FOGERTY, ELSIE, C.B.E. (1866–1945), English actress, who trained for the stage in London and Paris, and made her first appearance in 1879. She was, however, keenly interested in the problems of diction, which led her to lecture on elocution and speech-training, and finally to found the Central School of Speech Training and Dramatic Art which she directed until her death. In pursuance of her efforts to further the study and adoption of choral speaking she adapted and produced a number of Greek plays, and was the author of several manuals of speech-craft and of *The Speaking* *of English Verse.* She was closely concerned with the development of the British Drama League, and was a member of the Advisory Committee for the Diploma in Dramatic Art established by the University of London in 1923. In 1936 she was awarded the C.B.E. for services to the English language.

FOIRE SAINT-GERMAIN, SAINT-LAURENT, PARIS, see FAIRS.

FOLGER, HENRY CLAY (1857–1930), American business man, founder of the great Shakespeare Library in Washington which bears his name. As an undergraduate at Amherst he heard Emerson lecture on English literature, and was led through him to take an interest in the works of Shakespeare. From a modest set of the plays in thirteen volumes he went on to make the finest collection of Shakespeariana in the world, which after his death was donated to the nation. Under Dr. Joseph Quincy Adams, the great Shakespearian scholar who became its first director, the collection, administered by Amherst College, increased rapidly in size and scope. It now contains a series of English manuscripts from 1475 to 1640 which is exceeded in value and rarity only by those in the British Museum and the Bodleian. Fellowships were established in connexion with work on Shakespeare and his contemporaries, exhibitions arranged, lectures given, and a series of Folger Shakespeare Reprints inaugurated under the general editorship of Dr. Adams.

FOLIES-BERGÈRE, a famous music-hall in Paris, built in 1869 on the site of a livery-stable, and intended as a vast café-spectacle. It opened on 1 May with a mixed bill of light opera and pantomime in which Paul Legrand appeared as Pierrot, and soon became the rendezvous of the young men of the town, who either watched the successive turns on the stage, or loitered in the immense promenade which was one of the attractions of the house. It caters to a large extent for visitors, whether French or foreign, and one of the main features of its programme is a bevy of young and beautiful women, either stark naked or clad only in inessentials. For the rest its turns consist of acrobats, singers, and sketches, the last extremely vulgar or surpassingly beautiful, the scenic resources of the theatre being immense though its stage is small. Many of the greatest names of the entertainment world have appeared on its bills.

For the Folies-Bergère, New York, see FULTON THEATRE.

FOLIES-DRAMATIQUES, THÉÂTRE DES, PARIS, on the Boulevard du Temple. This was built on the site of the first Ambigu-Comique (destroyed by fire in 1827) and opened with melodrama on 22 Jan. 1831. Under its first proprietor, Mourier, it had twenty-five years of unbroken success, catering mainly for a local audience and playing each new piece about thirty times. Many young actors found the theatre a convenient stepping-stone to higher things, since Mourier would only pay them a certain sum and when they asked, or deserved, more was ready to let them go elsewhere, taking on in their place a new batch of youngsters. The repertory consisted mainly of patriotic and melodramatic plays, written by the Cogniard brothers, Comberousse, de Kock, Théaulon, and others. In 1834 the great actor Frédérick had one of his first successes at this theatre in *Robert Macaire.* It continued to be one of the best-conducted and most popular theatres in Paris until Mourier's death in 1857. Harel then took over, and when the Boulevard du Temple was demolished in 1862 built a new Folies-Dramatiques in the rue de Bondy. It ruined him, however, and under new management became a home of light musical shows, rival of the Bouffes-Parisiens and Variétés.

For the Folies-Dramatiques in London, see KINGSWAY THEATRE.

FOLIES-MARIGNY, THÉÂTRE DES, PARIS, a small playhouse, originally the Salle Lacaze, used by the Bouffes-Parisiens. In 1858 the son of the great pantomimist Deburau opened it under his own name, but it was not a success, and became the Théâtre des Champs-Élysées and finally the Folies-Marigny under the director of the Délassements-Comiques, who had lost his own theatre in the demolition of the Boulevard du Temple. It became a home of vaudeville, and was fairly successful until 1869. It then passed from hand to hand, and was finally destroyed in 1881. A circular building for a panorama was erected on the site of this theatre and is still standing. It became a music-hall in 1896, Marigny-Théâtre in 1901, Comédie-Marigny in 1913. In 1925 it was bought by Léon Volterra, whose widow still owns it. From 1946 to 1956 it housed the Renaud–Barrault company in a distinguished repertory of plays.

FOLIES-NOUVELLES, THÉÂTRE DES, PARIS, a small theatre which had a short but brilliant career. It opened in 1852 and under several successive names was a home of pantomime, with Paul Legrand as Pierrot and Vauthier as Punch. It also put on light opera with good singers and dancers and a small but adequate orchestra. Two years later it became the Folies-Nouvelles, and was given a licence which allowed it to use four people in operetta instead of the original two. Its programmes were like those of the old fairground theatres, simple, crude, and naïvely charming. It had a great vogue until 1859 and then became an ordinary theatre under the son of the great actress Virginie Déjazet, opening with plays by Sardou and others as the Théâtre Déjazet.

FOLK FESTIVALS, connected with the activities of the agricultural year, must have existed from the time of the first organized communities. In Europe they survived the rise and fall of Greece and Rome, and the coming of Christianity, but lost much of their significance, and were often kept up merely 'for fun' or 'for luck'. The Church, considering them an undesirable pagan survival, tried either to suppress them or to graft them on to its own festivals. But they were irrepressible, and constantly broke out again, often under the aegis of the parish priest. Wandering minstrels may have had some slight share in them, but they depended mainly on local talent, and the details varied from one district to another. The main folk festivals of England, and elsewhere, were Plough Monday, May-day, Midsummer Day, and Harvest Home, of which May-day longest retained its importance, with its May Queen, Maypole, garlanded processions, its Morris dancers, Jack-in-the-Green or Jack-a'-lantern, and its Hobby Horse, often with the addition of Robin Hood and his Merry Men. Most of the festivities were athletic rather than dramatic, but traces of a rudimentary play can be found (see PLOUGH MONDAY and MUMMING PLAY). The folk element in modern literary drama is very slight.

FOLK PLAY. Under this heading may be grouped the rough-and-ready dramatic entertainments given at village festivals by the villagers themselves. These were derived, with the minimum of literary intervention, from the dramatic tendencies inherent in primitive folk-festivals, and should not be confused with the productions of professional minstrels. They were given either at the May-games, at Harvest Home, or at Christmas, and to the central theme of a symbolic death and resurrection were added the names and feats of local worthies. Later, though not before 1596, these were replaced by the Seven Champions of Christendom, or other heroes, probably under the influence of the village schoolmaster (cf. Holofernes). St. George may have figured in them from the earliest times, as patron saint of England. With some dramatic action went a good deal of song and dance, of which the Sword Dance and the Morris Dance are the main survivals, except for the Mumming Play, usually given between Christmas and Twelfth Night, at Easter, or on Plough Monday (for further details see MUMMING PLAY). Practically no written records of the folk play survive, as is to be expected of an unliterary and impromptu form of drama, and it contributed only a small stream to the main current of modern drama; but its influence should not on that account be entirely disregarded.

FOLLIES, see PÉLISSIER and ZIEGFELD.

FOLLOWING SPOTS, see LIGHTING, 2.

FOLLY THEATRE, LONDON, see CHARING CROSS THEATRE.

FOLZ, HANS (*fl.* fifteenth century), a writer of German popular farces (see GERMANY, 1) who lived in Nuremberg, and was a Mastersinger of that town.

FONTANNE, LYNN (1887–), see LUNT (2).

FONTENELLE, BERNARD LE BOVIER DE (1657–1757), French man of letters, and nephew of Corneille, to whom we are indebted for many, mostly inaccurate, anecdotes of his famous uncle. He wrote with ease in many styles but, having failed in tragedy and comedy, he wisely retired from playwriting. His libretto for the opera 'Thétis et Pélée', written in 1689, was much admired by Voltaire, but has not otherwise survived.

FONVIZIN, DENIS IVANOVICH (1744–92), early Russian dramatist who forms the link between the neo-classical literary plays of Sumarokov and the social comedies of Ostrovsky. Son of a nobleman, he was educated at Moscow University, and his first work, a translation, appeared in print when he was 18. In the same year (1762) he went to St. Petersburg, where he became an official translator, and was later attached to the staff of the Supervisor of Theatres. His first attempt at play-writing was a comedy, *The Minor*, contrasting the crude provincial nobility, with their lack of education, with the cultured nobility of the city. He put it aside unfinished in favour of a second play, *The Brigadier-General*, which he himself, being a fine elocutionist, read before the Court in 1766 with great success. It satirized the illiterate newly rich men who were filtering into Russian society, and at the same time attacked the existing fashion for praising everything from western Europe at the expense of everything Russian.

It was not until 1781 that Fonvizin took up *The Minor* again and rewrote it, sharpening the satire on the landowners and their politics. As this party was then predominant in the government, Fonvizin's daring was his downfall. After the death of his patron Panin in 1783 he was forced to retire from public life, and his works were refused publication. Nevertheless, *The Minor* remains a small classic in its own way, and is still in the repertory of the Soviet theatre. Although Fonvizin wrote in the comic tradition of Molière and the French eighteenth century, he infused into his work a native Russian element of folk comedy which was to come to fruition in his successors.

FOOL. The licensed buffoon of the medieval Feast of Fools, and later a member of the French *sociétés joyeuses*; not to be confused with the Court Fool or King's Jester, a permanent member of the Royal Household, whose origin has been variously traced to the Court of Haroun-al-Raschid, to the classical dwarf-buffoon, or to the inspired madman of Celtic and Teutonic legend. The traditional costume of the fool, adopted by the Court Fool at some unknown date in imitation of his humbler rival, is a cap with horns or ass's ears, and sometimes bells, covering the head and shoulders; a particoloured jacket and trousers, usually tight-fitting, and occasionally a tail. He carries a marotte or bauble, either a replica of a fool's head on a stick, or a bladder filled with dried peas; exceptionally a wooden sword or 'dagger of lath', a relic of his predecessor the Vice (or buffoon) in medieval drama (see *Twelfth Night*, 'Like to the old Vice, . . . Who with dagger of lath, In his rage and his wrath, Cries, Ah, ah! to the devil'). It is surmised that this costume is a survival of the head and skin of the sacrificial animal worn by the worshipper at the primitive folk festival, while the ass's ears were imported from the ass used in the procession of the Feast of Fools. The grotesque fool of the Morris dancers and of village festivities invariably had a tail. Shakespeare's fools have nothing to do with the Feast of Fools or with the Folk revellers, but derive from the Court Fool, already by his time a tradition in Europe and England. In dramatic use fools are vehicles of social satire (see also CLOWN and No. 152).

FOOLS, FEAST OF, the generic name given to the New Year revels of the minor clergy in cathedrals and collegiate churches, which Chambers summarizes as 'the ebullition of the natural lout beneath the cassock'. The feast seems to have originated in France in about the twelfth century, and may have had in it some dim remembrance of the festivities of the Roman Kalends. During the feast the minor clergy usurped the functions of their superiors and gave free rein to their turbulence and high spirits. The entertainments from the beginning seem to have included some form of crude drama, with much tippling, noise, and burlesque ceremonies. A 'king' was appointed from among the participants (in schools his function was usurped by the Boy Bishop), and the ceremonies included a procession headed by the 'king' riding on a donkey, an innovation taken over by ecclesiastical drama with the introduction of Balaam's ass and the Flight into Egypt into the liturgical plays. The Feast of Fools, which is known to have been held in England at Lincoln, Beverley, Salisbury, and St. Paul's, died out in the fourteenth century, though it continued intermittently in France until the sixteenth century, by which time it had passed from the church to the street, and was finally absorbed into the *compagnies des fous* or *sociétés joyeuses* (see FRANCE).

FOOTE, LYDIA (1844–92), see KEELEY (3).

FOOTE, MARIA (*c.* 1797–1867), English actress, daughter of a Samuel Foote who claimed some relationship with the dramatist (see below). He was manager of the theatre at Plymouth, where his daughter made her first appearances as a child, playing Juliet while still quite young. In 1814 she was at Covent Garden, playing Amanthis in *The Child of Nature* with such success that she was engaged permanently, playing Miranda and, in 1815, Statira to the Alexander the Great of Master Betty. She was not a great actress, but beautiful and talented enough to secure steady engagements, travelling constantly to Ireland, Scotland, and in the provinces. Her love affairs, particularly her breach of promise case against Haynes, caused much scandal, but she had powerful friends who secured her preferment at both Patent Houses until in 1831 she retired to marry the Earl of Harrington.

FOOTE, SAMUEL (1720–77), English actor and dramatist, well born and well educated but so extravagant that lack of money drove him to adopt the stage as a profession in 1744. He had had some experience as an amateur, but his first appearances at the Haymarket were not particularly successful, and he went to Ireland, where he was well received. On his return he went to Drury Lane, but seemed fit neither for tragedy nor for comedy. Yet it was in the latter that his strength lay, as he discovered when he took over the Haymarket in 1747. Here, with great ingenuity, he evaded the Licensing Act by inviting his friends to a dish of tea or chocolate, their invitation-card giving admittance to an entertainment in which Foote mimicked his fellow actors and other public characters. In 1749, having inherited a second fortune, he went to Paris, spent it, and returned to take up in earnest a life of hard work as actor-manager and playwright. He had already written a few farces, but his first success was *The Englishman in Paris* (1753), with its sequel, *The Englishman Returned from Paris* (1756). After acting at both Patent Houses, in Dublin, where he was always welcome, and in Scotland, Foote again took over the Haymarket. He staged there, in the summer of 1760, his best play, *The Minor*, which had had its first performance earlier in the year at the Crow Street Theatre, Dublin. In this satire on Whitefield and the Methodists he himself played Shift, a character intended to ridicule Tate Wilkinson. Foote remained at the Haymarket, appearing in his own comedies in afternoon performances until in 1766 he lost a leg through some ducal horseplay and the Duke of York, who was present at the accident, procured him a Royal Patent in compensation (see HAYMARKET). With this he was able to present summer seasons of 'legitimate' plays, the first in 1767 with Spranger Barry and his wife in leading parts.

Foote had a bitter wit, and his plays were mainly devised with the idea of caricaturing one person, which he did most successfully, judging to a nicety how far he could go without chastisement or open rebuke. He disliked Garrick, and missed no opportunity of lampooning him, though Garrick disdained to reply to his shafts. He had such wonderful powers of mimicry and repartee that even his victims found themselves bound to laugh at him. He was often in trouble, but evaded it for many years, until Nemesis finally overtook him, and he disposed of his Patent to the elder Colman, dying shortly after on his way to France. His plays were successful through their topicality, and have not survived. He had a keen eye for character, and wrote brilliant sketches of contemporary manners, which caused him to be nicknamed 'the English Aristophanes'. Short, fat, flabby, with an ugly but intelligent face and a bright eye, he was at once feared and admired by his contemporaries,

Dr. Johnson being one of the few who despised him without any wish to placate, though he said of him: 'Sir, he was irresistible.' Foote's portrait was painted by Zoffany and Reynolds.

FOOTLIGHTS, see LIGHTING.

FOOTLIGHTS TRAP, a long rectangular opening at the front of the stage before the curtain, with a post below at either end. Between the posts a framework slid up and down, and upon this the lamps of the footlights were arranged. They were lowered (according to an account of 1810) not only to enable a stage hand in the cellar to trim them, but so that the stage might, upon occasion, be darkened. For this purpose a pair of lines was taken up from the ends of the framework over pulleys at the heads of the posts and down again to the drum of a central shaft in the cellar. A line led from this same drum in the opposite direction to a counter-weight, designed to balance the framework, and from the shaft an endless line was brought by pulleys to a point at the side under the stage floor, where it ascended to a winch in the prompter's corner, so that the whole operation of dimming the footlights could be conducted from the stage without going into the cellar (see also LIGHTING). RICHARD SOUTHERN

FOOTMEN'S GALLERY. At the Restoration the usual charge for the Upper Gallery was a shilling, but footmen waiting for their masters were admitted free at the end of the fourth act, at any rate at Dorset Garden, and probably at the Theatre Royal also. The latter theatre, however, under Christopher Rich, hoping to curry favour with the rougher element, allowed the footmen from 1697 onwards to occupy the gallery gratis from the opening of the play, which led to much noise and disorder. This abuse was finally abolished, not without much rioting and opposition, by Fleetwood in 1737.

FORBES-ROBERTSON. (1) SIR JOHNSTON (1853–1937), English actor-manager, son of an art critic and journalist. Educated at Charterhouse, he first studied art, but abandoned it for the stage, learning his perfect elocution from Samuel Phelps. He made his first appearance in 1874, and from then until his retirement in 1913 he had a long and varied career. His first big success was at the Haymarket in *Dan'l Druce, Blacksmith*, in 1876. Two years later he joined the Bancrofts at the Prince of Wales's, scoring a great success in *Diplomacy*, *Duty*, and *Ours*. Wilson Barrett then engaged him to play opposite Madame Modjeska at the Court and Princess's Theatres, where he appeared as Romeo, as Armand Duval in *Heartsease* (a version of *La Dame aux camélias*), and as Maurice de Saxe in *Adrienne Lecouvreur*. In 1882 he went to the Lyceum under Irving. Then followed a tour in England and America as leading man to Mary Anderson, with whom he made his first appearance in New York—as Orlando—at the Star Theatre in 1885. He went into management in 1895 at the London Lyceum, playing Romeo to the Juliet of Mrs. Patrick Campbell. At the same theatre he appeared in *Hamlet* (see No. 79), and made a deep impression, proving to be one of the greatest Hamlets of his time. It is indeed doubtful if modern times have seen a better. Forbes-Robertson had one of the finest voices ever heard on the stage, and was an actor of great sensibility and delicacy of imagination. His ascetic fine-featured face made him a notable figure, while his repose, his power, and his understanding of his art placed him in the forefront of English actors. His performance as the Stranger in *The Passing of the Third-Floor Back*, with which he opened his season at the St. James's in 1908, was considered by many to be memorable—reverent, yet exciting. That, with his Hamlet, Buckingham (*Henry VIII*), Mark Embury (*Mice and Men*), and Dick Helder (*The Light that Failed*), made up a gallery of exquisite stage portraits. Forbes-Robertson was knighted in 1913, during the last week of his farewell performances at Drury Lane Theatre. Those privileged to be present at his final appearance long remembered the emotion of the evening, and his coming down among the audience to say his last farewell.

Sir Johnston's younger brothers, (2) IAN (1858–1936), (3) NORMAN (1859–1932), and (4) ERIC (1865–1935), were also actors. Norman was seen on the stage for the first time at the Gaiety in 1875, under the name of Norman Forbes. He appeared under most of the outstanding managements of the day, and was at one time manager of the Globe. He was the author of several plays, and of dramatic versions of *The Scarlet Letter* and *The Man in the Iron Mask*, himself playing Louis XIV and Marchiali in the latter. His son Frank was also on the stage. Eric, who was also a painter, took the name of John Kelt.

In 1900 Sir Johnston married Gertrude Elliott, an American actress (see ELLIOTT, 2), a beautiful and accomplished woman who was on many occasions his leading lady. They had three daughters, of whom the second, (5) JEAN (1905–62), was also an excellent actress. She first appeared on the stage in South Africa, in her mother's touring company, assuming the name of Anne McEwen. She appeared in London in 1925, and a year later was seen as Sonya in Komisarjevsky's production of *Uncle Vanya*. Her success in this part was followed by an outstanding Juliet (1926) and Viola (1927). For eight consecutive years, from 1927 to 1934, she played Peter Pan, her slight boyish appearance and extraordinary likeness to her father being admirably suited to the part, as also to Puck, Oberon, and Jim Hawkins in *Treasure Island*, which she played in 1945. She was excellent in Ibsen, particularly as Rebecca West and Hedda Gabler, and in such parts as Lady Teazle, Mary Rose, and the Lady of the Camellias. She appeared in a number of modern plays, being particularly successful as Helen Pettigrew in *Berkeley Square* (1926), as Jenny Lyndon in *Strange Orchestra* (1932), and as Kay in *Time and the*

Conways (1937). She was twice married, her second husband being the actor and producer André van Gyseghem.

W. MACQUEEN-POPE†, *rev.*

FORD, JOHN (1586–1639), English dramatist, four of whose plays are lost, destroyed by Warburton's cook. Little is known of his life, except that he was born and died in Devonshire, and was admitted to the Inner Temple in 1602. It has been said that the prevailing note of his work is 'the powerful depiction of sorrow and despair', which caused him to be named 'the melancholy John Ford'. He is believed to have been part-author with Dekker and Rowley of *The Witch of Edmonton* (1621) and *The Sun's Darling* (1624), but his own work, which is more important, includes the four romantic and somewhat effeminate dramas which contributed to the continued emasculation of the English stage before the closing of the theatres in 1642—*The Lover's Melancholy* (*c.* 1625–6), *Love's Sacrifice* (*c.* 1627), *The Broken Heart* (1629) (revived at the first Chichester Theatre Festival in 1962) and, his best-known work, *'Tis Pity She's a Whore* (*c.* 1625–33), which was revived in 1661, given by the Phoenix Society in 1923, by Donald Wolfit at the Strand Theatre in 1941, and in 1961 was again revived at the Mermaid Theatre. In all his plays Ford shows a totally different attitude towards morality from that of Shakespeare or Jonson, and his more modern point of view makes it difficult to assess his originality. He has been called a romantic rebel, a believer in the divine impulse of human passion which leads in the end to self-destruction.

FORD, JOHN THOMSON (1829–94), American theatre manager, who was in charge of the theatre in Washington where Abraham Lincoln was assassinated on 14 Apr. 1865 by the actor Wilkes Booth. With his brother he was imprisoned for thirty-nine days, but was later acquitted of complicity in the crime, and continued his career, managing a number of other theatres, and being for some forty years an active and honourable member of the American theatrical profession.

FORDE, FLORRIE (1876–1940), music-hall singer, who came from Melbourne, where she appeared in pantomime and was known as the Australian Marie Lloyd, her real name being Florence Flanagan. She appeared in London on August Bank Holiday 1897, and was particularly good at putting over a chorus. On one occasion the audience made her repeat an old favourite thirty-three times. A massive woman, she was in her time a famous Principal Boy and a great star. 'Down at the Old Bull and Bush', 'Has Anybody Here Seen Kelly?' 'Hold Your Hand Out, Naughty Boy', and 'Oh, Oh, Antonio' are her best-remembered songs. Her voice and delivery matched her ample figure.

W. MACQUEEN-POPE†

FORESTAGE, a term applied in the modern theatre to the small area of the stage in front of the proscenium arch and the front curtain. This is the final vestige of what was once the main acting area, the apron stage of the English Restoration theatre, itself a modified form of the Elizabethan platform stage. It served the purpose of an unlocalized 'platea', the actors approaching it from the inner stage or through the proscenium doors. Its loss proved a great handicap in staging revivals of Elizabethan and Restoration drama in modern theatres, and in some new theatre buildings, particularly those intended for experimental or academic work, forestages have been built out in front of the proscenium arch. They have also, as at Stratford-upon-Avon and the Old Vic, been built on to existing stages.

FORK, a device used in the English nineteenth-century theatre to replace the upper groove by which a wing of scenery was supported.

FORMALISM, the name given to a theatrical method popular in Russia soon after the October Revolution, and put into practice by Meyerhold, Akimov in his earlier period, and, to a lesser degree, Taïrov. It implies a negation of humanity, the schooling of the actor so that he becomes the producer's puppet, and the insistence on exterior symbolism at the expense of inner truth. Though in its origin it served its purpose in helping to clear the stage of the old falsities and conventions of pre-Revolutionary days, when pushed too far it resulted in a complete lack of harmony between stage and audience. Joseph Macleod says of Formalist producers: 'Their brains are in front of their eyes', and in the long run intellectual isolation so cut them off from the new audiences that they had either to return to the warmth and intimacy of normal human relationships or leave the theatre.

FORMBY, GEORGE (1905–61), son of the famous Lancashire music-hall comedian of the same name who died in 1921, was first a jockey, and then went on the halls after his father's death, under the name of George Hoy. His act consisted of songs and patter to the accompaniment of the ukelele. He reverted to his own name after a year or so, but his act never varied. He was a great success in films, and in 1951 he starred in the stage show, *Zip Goes a Million*, at the Palace Theatre, London. During the Second World War he entertained the troops in France, Italy, North Africa, India, and Burma, with his wife Beryl as his partner. He toured Canada in 1950, visited South Africa and Australia in 1955, and in 1956 was seen in pantomime. He was a highly paid and extremely popular comedian.

FORREST, EDWIN (1806–72), one of the finest American tragic actors of the nineteenth century. He appeared in an amateur performance at the age of 10, and four years later played Young Norval at the Walnut Street Theatre in Philadelphia, his birthplace. His early years were hard, and overshadowed by poverty and thwarted ambition, but in the end he triumphed and became the acknowledged head of his profession for nearly thirty years, and the idol of the public. Yet even then the defects of his character made him as many enemies as friends, and no one received more abuse mingled with the praise which was his due. William Winter, who characterized him as 'utterly selfish' and said that the motives of his conduct were 'vanity, pride, self-assertion, and avarice of power, praise and wealth', also called him a 'vast animal, bewildered by a grain of genius', and his portraits show him as a heavy, brooding man with a sombre expression. Yet Mrs. John Drew, who appeared with him in *William Tell* at the age of 8, spoke feelingly of his good qualities, and praised his unselfishness in allowing other actors to gain the attention of the audience during their important moments. He certainly had great advantages of person, expressive features, and a powerful voice, which he used unsparingly, but his acting, though bold and forceful, lacked delicacy, and in his early years he was much criticized for 'ranting'. This he later cured to some extent, and was then outstanding as Lear, Hamlet, Macbeth, and Richelieu. Among his other parts were Spartacus and Metamora, written specially for him and well suited to his art and personality, Jaffier, Othello, Rolla, Mark Antony, and Virginius. He appeared in London in 1836 with some success, but on a later visit in 1845 was received with marked hostility, which he attributed to the machinations of Macready. Their quarrel led eventually to the fatal Astor Place riot in New York in 1849, when Macready barely escaped with his life. This caused Forrest to be ostracized by the more sober members of the community, but he was the idol of the masses, who looked on him as their champion against the tyranny of English superiority.

In 1837 Forrest married Catharine Norton Sinclair (1817–91), who was on the stage and later became manager of a theatre in California. The marriage proved an unhappy one, and he was divorced in 1850. In his last years Forrest knew again the bitterness of failure, and died a lonely, unhappy man. He last appeared on the stage at the Globe Theatre, Boston, on 2 Apr. 1872, as Richelieu.

FORREST THEATRE, New York, see CORONET THEATRE.

FORSTER, John (1812–76), English historian, biographer, and editor, who from an early age took a keen delight in the theatre. While still a youth, he wrote a play, *Charles at Tunbridge; or, the Cavalier of Wildinghurst*, which was performed at his native Newcastle. He became dramatic critic of the *True Sun* in 1832. In the same year he began editing a weekly collection of essays called *The Reflector*, to which Lamb and Leigh Hunt were contributors. In 1833 Forster became chief literary and dramatic critic to the *Examiner*, and in 1846 he succeeded Dickens as editor of the *Daily News*. In the general run of literature, Forster is remembered principally for his biographical writings; but he brought to dramatic criticism a well-stored mind and a warm enthusiasm for the theatre. T. C. KEMP†

FORTUNE THEATRE, London. 1. The first Fortune Theatre was built by Henslowe in Golden Lane, Cripplegate, after Burbage had invaded the territory south of the river with the Globe. It was modelled on the Globe, and its dimensions were almost similar (the builders' contract for the theatre still exists), but it was built of plain unpainted timber. It cost £550 and took its name from a statue of the Goddess of Fortune over the entrance. It opened in the autumn of 1600 with a performance by the Admiral's Men, who occupied it continuously for many years, first as the Admiral's Men, then as Prince Henry's Men, and after his death in 1612, as the Palsgrave's Men. In 1621 the theatre was burnt down, but rebuilt in brick and reopened two years later. After the closing of the theatres in 1642 the Fortune was used occasionally for surreptitious performances until in 1649 Commonwealth soldiers entered and dismantled it. It was finally pulled down in 1661.

2. A small intimate theatre in Russell Street, Drury Lane, built by Laurence Cowen, who opened it on 8 Nov. 1924 with his own play, *Sinners*. Externally it was intended to resemble the old Fortune, but the likeness was based upon a print of doubtful authenticity. The theatre had few successes in its early years, except for Lonsdale's *On Approval*, and a season of O'Casey plays presented by Fagan, both in 1927. For some years it was used mainly for amateur productions and Sunday shows. In 1946, after a period of fluctuating fortune, it finally housed the successful show, *At the Drop of a Hat*, with Flanders and Swann. This ran for over 700 performances; and in 1961 *Beyond the Fringe* started its long and successful career.

W. MACQUEEN-POPE†, *rev.*

FORTUNY, Mariano (1871–1949), Italian scenic designer and lighting expert, and inventor of the diffused-lighting system which bears his name (see LIGHTING, 1 *d* and SCENERY, 6).

FORTY-EIGHTH STREET THEATRE, New York. This opened on 12 Aug. 1912, and housed opera and musical comedy, including Gilbert and Sullivan, as well as a number of successful straight plays. In 1922 came Kelly's delightful satire on Little Theatres, *The Torch Bearers*, which ran for 17 weeks, and was transferred elsewhere to make room for the Equity Players in *Malvaloca*. Later successes were *The Squall* (1926) with Blanche Yurka, which had 444 performances, a revival of *The Streets of New York* in 1931, the Pulitzer Prize-winner, *Harvey* (1944), and *Stalag 17* (1951). *Tea and Sympathy*, which opened at the Ethel Barrymore Theatre in 1953, finished its run here in June 1955. Two months later, when the theatre was unoccupied, a water tank fell through the roof, causing considerable damage to the auditorium. The building was demolished in 1956. From 1937 to 1943 it was known as the Windsor. GEORGE FREEDLEY†

FORTY-FOURTH STREET THEATRE, NEW YORK. This was built by the Shuberts, and opened on 21 Nov. 1912 as the Weber and Fields New Music-Hall. Seating 1,463 people, the building housed in its basement for some time the famous Little Club, while on its roof was a smaller theatre, later known as the Nora Bayes. This little playhouse had few successes, which led to its being considered unlucky, but Little Theatre Tournaments were held there, and in Dec. 1922 some of Gershwin's first tunes were heard in a 'musical melodrama'. In 1935 it was occupied for a short time by the Yale Puppeteers, and two years later it was taken over by the Federal Theatre Project. It was scheduled for demolition in 1945, together with its parent house, which in 1914 had housed a successful revival of *The Geisha*. In 1915 Robert B. Mantell appeared in his classical repertory, which showed, among other things, what the nineteenth century demanded of an actor's memory. Mantell's parts in this season included Lear, Richelieu, Louis XI, King John, Macbeth, Hamlet, Shylock, Richard III, and Romeo. After this excursion into the classics, the theatre returned to light opera and musical plays, varied by the Marx Brothers in a long run of *Animal Crackers*. An outstanding production seen in 1930 was that of Gilbert Seldes's adaptation of *Lysistrata*, played by an excellent cast. Other plays seen at this theatre included *The Good Companions* (1931), a fleeting glimpse of Pierre Fresnay and Yvonne Printemps in *Conversation Piece* in 1934, Walter Hampden in a four-weeks' classical repertory, the shortlived but memorable *Johnny Johnson* (1936), and, in 1943, *Winged Victory*. GEORGE FREEDLEY†

FORTY-NINTH STREET THEATRE, New York, on the north side between Broadway and 8th Avenue. This was opened by Lee Shubert on 26 Dec. 1921. Early in the following year Morris Gest presented the Chauve-Souris for a season which continued during the summer on the roof of the old Century Theatre. A series of successful new plays followed, though Wedekind's *Lulu* was a failure, as was Coward's *Fallen Angels*. In 1928 came a fine revival of *The Wild Duck* with Blanche Yurka, followed by *Hedda Gabler*, and a year later the public were delighted by the great Chinese actor, Mei Lan-Fang. Among later productions were *Marigold*, *Bird in Hand*, a revival of *The Father* with Robert Loraine, a season of Yiddish plays with Maurice Schwartz, and three productions by the Federal Theatre Project. The last play seen here was a modern-dress revival of *The Wild Duck* in Apr. 1938, after which the theatre became a cinema. GEORGE FREEDLEY†

FORTY-SIXTH STREET THEATRE, NEW YORK, west of Broadway. This was built by the Chanins, whose name it bore until 1932. It was intended for musical shows, and opened on 24 Dec. 1925, since when it has been consistently successful. Among the straight plays produced at this theatre have been *The First Legion* (1934), a sensitive portrayal of Jesuit life, and a Group Theatre production of *Weep for the Virgin* (1935) which, though not particularly successful, first brought into prominence a young actor named Jules (later John) Garfield. The theatre is, however, mainly associated with such musical hits as *Hellzapoppin* (1938), *Du Barry Was a Lady* (1939), *Panama Hattie* (1940), *Finian's Rainbow* (1947), *Guys and Dolls* (1950), *Damn Yankees* (1955), and *How to Succeed in Business Without Really Trying* (1961). In 1958 Gielgud occupied the theatre with his one-man recital of passages from Shakespeare, *Ages of Man*. GEORGE FREEDLEY†

FOURTEENTH STREET THEATRE, NEW YORK, see LYCEUM THEATRE, 2.

FOWLER, RICHARD (?–1643), English actor, and one of the chief players at the Fortune Theatre from 1618 until the closing of the theatres in 1642. He figures in two anecdotes of a later date, which represent him as playing heroic parts—conquering captains and mighty fighters—which helped to give the theatre a bad reputation for noisy plays, and apparently noisy audiences, since on one Shrove Tuesday they rioted, and threw nuts, apples, and oranges at the actors.

FOX. (1) GEORGE WASHINGTON LAFAYETTE (1825–77), American actor and pantomimist, who at various times used several variants of his name, but is generally known as G. L. Fox. He was on the stage as a child, and from 1850 to 1858 was a stalwart member of the National Theatre company. While there he persuaded the management to put on Aiken's adaptation of *Uncle Tom's Cabin*, which ran for a year, and was the best of many versions. In 1858 he went into partnership with Lingard, and took over the management of the Bowery, the New Bowery, and in 1862 the Lyceum, which he rechristened Fox's Olympic. From 1862 to 1867 he staged a long series of successful pantomimes at the Old Bowery, and in 1867 gave a fine performance as Bottom in James E. Hayes's production of *A Midsummer Night's Dream* at Laura Keene's old theatre. A year later he produced at the same theatre his pantomime *Humpty-Dumpty*, and a travesty of *Hamlet* which Edwin Booth is said to have seen and enjoyed. He continued to appear in successive editions of *Humpty-Dumpty* until his death, and was accounted a competent actor, and 'the peer of pantomimists'. Much of the pantomime 'business' in his shows was devised by his brother (2) CHARLES KEMBLE (1833–75), who with his parents and brothers and sister played as a child in the Howard-Fox company. He was also in Aiken's version of *Uncle Tom's Cabin*, as was his mother, and played Pantaloon in his elder brother's pantomimes.

FOX WEDGES are those used under the side flats of a Box Set on a raked stage.

FOX'S BOWERY, New York, see bowery theatre, 1.

FOX'S BROADWAY, New York, see new york theatre, 1.

FOY, Eddie (1856–1928), American actor and vaudeville player, whose real name was Edwin Fitzgerald. He was a singer and entertainer from childhood, and in 1878 sang and danced in the Western boom towns with a minstrel troupe. Later he was seen in comedy and melodrama, and from 1888 to 1894 he played leading parts in a long series of extravaganzas in Chicago. He was acting in the Iroquois Theatre there in 1903 when fire broke out, and did his best to calm the audience, but without success, the panic resulting in the loss of 600 lives. Foy, who was an eccentric comedian with many mannerisms and a distinctive clown make-up, played in musical comedy until 1913 and then went into vaudeville, accompanied by his seven children, with whom he made his last appearance in 1927. He subsequently wrote his autobiography as *Clowning Through Life* (1928).

FRAGSON, Harry (1869–1913), a music-hall performer, whose real name was Potts. He was as popular in Paris with his Cockney accent as in London with his French accent. His songs were witty and well-observed, the best-remembered being 'Billie, Billie Brown of London' and 'The Other Department'. He appeared before Royalty on several occasions, and played in pantomime at Drury Lane. When he played Dandini in *Cinderella*, the character, out of compliment to his Anglo-French reputation, was rechristened Dandigny. Fragson was shot by his father in a fit of insanity. W. MACQUEEN-POPE†

FRANÇA JUNIOR, Joaquín José da, see south america, 2.

FRANCE. 1. Medieval. In France, as elsewhere in Europe, national drama evolved from the drama of the Christian Church (see liturgical drama), with some slight but definite accretions from the folk-play and the minstrel tradition. The evolution of the play based on the liturgy, and performed wholly or mainly by the clergy inside the church, was complete by the middle of the thirteenth century, and any further development was bound to intensify the secular elements which had already crept in. This process began when exigencies of space, and a growing sense of the limitations imposed by the church walls, forced the play from the nave and choir to the churchyard and, eventually, to the market-place. In France this move was made early, for a twelfth-century Anglo-Norman play on the subject of Adam was clearly intended for outdoor performance, and while plays continued no doubt to be given in churches long after this date, they were gradually overshadowed and replaced by their secularized open-air offspring.

Once the drama escaped from the church it grew and altered rapidly. The details of the transition period are confused and obscure, and must be studied in the works of scholars who have collected and collated the scattered fragments which are all that remain to us. It is, however, clear that from the early days of secularization the plays were taken over by the guilds, that important feature of medieval civic life, who first supplied the extra actors needed, and later were entirely responsible for the financing and production of the plays. These fell into two main groups—those based on the Old and New Testament stories, a series of episodes strung together to cover the whole span of creation from the Fall to the Last Judgement; and those based on the lives of the saints and, in France particularly, on that of the Virgin Mary (see miracle play). These still remained linked with the Church festivals, and could be played either on a stationary platform raised against the church wall or in the market-place (see No. 15), or in procession, when each scene was enacted on a wheeled stage, or pageant (see No. 17), which visited different parts of the city in turn. It would seem that the stationary stage was more common in France, while England favoured the succession of pageants. In both countries the practice of acting in the open air, at the mercy of the elements, caused the plays to be given mainly in the summer, since, as Chambers says in his *Mediaeval Stage*: 'Even in sunny France, Christmas is not exactly the season to hang about the market-place, looking at an interminable drama.' So Whitsun, and particularly the Feast of Corpus Christi (the Thursday after Trinity Sunday), were the favourite times for theatrical activity.

The staging of medieval plays developed from that of liturgical drama, where various sites in the church had symbolized the different scenes of the action. As many localities as were needed—and these might range from four to forty—were denoted by booths, or 'mansions', grouped behind or around a central, unlocalized acting space, which for the stationary stage was merely the unencumbered front of the platform, but for the perambulating pageants included also a roped-off portion of the street. The most ornate and elevated mansion represented Heaven, while Hell, as far removed from Heaven as possible, was usually shown in the shape of a dragon's mouth (see Nos. 15, 16). In between were the earthly 'mansions'—houses, shops, rooms, gardens—appropriately draped and furnished. Pulleys, trap-doors, and other mechanical devices were freely used, costumes were elaborate and brightly coloured, singing and dancing had their place in the general scheme. A few plays might be given on one day, or the whole cycle might be spread over a week, the latter perhaps at intervals of several years, a reasonable supposition when one considers the time and energy that must have been expended in rehearsals, carpentry, and dressmaking, as well as the heavy expense involved.

The outstanding results of the passing of drama from the hands of the clergy into those of the laity, and the most important for the future of the theatre, were the extended use of the vernacular, already present in the twelfth-century play on Adam referred to above, which inevitably produced a national, as opposed to a cosmopolitan, drama, and an intensification of the comic and rowdy elements which had already begun to make their appearance inside the church, and were later strengthened there also by a reciprocal influence from the secular plays. There were plenty of opportunities for comedy in these early productions, mainly in connexion with the extraneous personages grafted on to the Bible story—wives, merchants, servants—and with the imps and devils attendant upon Satan. By the thirteenth century, as can be seen from the *Jeu de Saint Nicolas* by Jean Bodel (*fl.* thirteenth century), scenes of everyday life were already being incorporated into the religious plays, thus further weakening their original liturgical character. A further influence at work in the direction of humour was that of the purely secular farce, a twofold inheritance from the almost submerged traditions of the classical *mimi* preserved in the repertory of the minstrels, and from the licensed buffoonery of the Feast of Fools. Just as the serious religious play became the concern of the town guilds and literary societies, so the farcical horseplay of the minor clergy became the perquisite of the *sociétés joyeuses*, those bands of light-hearted, irreverent youths who, when the ecclesiastical merry-making fell into disrepute and desuetude, took it upon themselves to provide amusement for their fellow townsmen. They, and such similar societies as the *clercs de la basoche*, formed by the law-students in the universities under Philippe le Bel, and the student society of the Parisian *enfants sans souci*, formed under Charles VI, were primarily associations of amateurs, and must not be confused with the professional corporations of minstrels. These latter, however, were not excluded from participation in the revels and, though there is no proof of their association with them, professional entertainers may have been employed by the guilds to assist in the religious plays, particularly in the domain of music. They certainly played a part in the production of the non-religious plays, where their experience and ready pens would be most welcome. To a minstrel, Adam de la Halle (*c.* 1240–*c.* 1286), goes the honour of having written in the late thirteenth century the earliest-known French secular plays—a link between folk-song and drama—the *Jeu de Robin et Marion* and the *Jeu de la feuillée*. Another thirteenth-century minstrel whose work is extant is Rutebeuf (*c.* 1230–*c.* 1285). He, Adam, and Bodel, are lone figures surging above the sea of anonymity which covers most of medieval drama.

2. THE PERIOD OF TRANSITION. These various influences, working together, shaped the early destiny of French drama, which by the fifteenth century emerges as a national entity, capable of classification and of more detailed study than was possible in the earlier confused period. Drama has now utterly forsaken the Church, and been forsaken by it. The Confraternity of the Passion, a guild of amateur actors formed in 1402 for the performance of Mystery plays in and around Paris, probably indoors and for a small entrance fee, was the model for many similar associations up and down the country. The literary societies (the *puys*) and the student companies had their allegorical drama (see MORALITY PLAY) and their topical satiric drama (see SOTIE), the first a fourteenth-century offshoot of the religious play, whose characters were abstractions of vice and virtue dealing not specifically with religion, but with morality in general, the latter a short topical skit, spiced with pungent wit, often political and wholly irreligious. The best-known writer of these *soties*, as they were called, was Pierre Gringore (*fl.* sixteenth century), the *mère-sotte*, or chief fool, of the Parisian *enfants sans souci*, in whose *Jeu du Prince des sots* (1511) may be seen a fusion of the Morality and the *sotie* pure. The *sotie* was not a farce, though it had elements in common with it, for its plot was weak, and its content mainly topical, which may account for the frequency with which its actors found themselves in trouble with the authorities. The farce, that perennial and unliterary form of popular drama, flourished also, the most famous example being the anonymous fifteenth-century *Maître Pierre Pathelin*, done by the *enfants sans souci* in 1470, whose robust humour survives modernization and even translation. During the whole of the fifteenth and sixteenth centuries in France Mystery, Miracle, and Morality plays, *soties* and farces, continued to be performed, often by the same actors and on the same programme. On the whole the actors were probably still amateurs, though modern critics incline to the view that *soties* may have been done by semi-permanent bands of actors, who thus take on a somewhat professional air.

This mingling of the genres had its dangers, the most obvious being the final swamping of the religious element by the secular. That the actors of the Confraternity of the Passion did not escape this snare is proved by a decree of 17 Nov. 1548, which, while confirming the brotherhood in its monopoly of acting in Paris, at the same time forbade the performance of anything but secular pieces, on the ground that the admixture of sacred and profane elements, and the consequent disorder and licence, brought religion into disrepute. The Confraternity was thus deprived of the greater part of its repertory, and with the ban the history of early religious drama in France comes to an end. The secular theatre is now free to develop in its own way along literary and popular lines.

3. THE ESTABLISHMENT OF A NATIONAL AND PROFESSIONAL THEATRE. Owing to the ravages

of civil war, however, the secular theatre took a long time to establish itself, and the sixteenth century, which saw the emergence of a fine national drama in Spain and England with Lope de Vega and Shakespeare, was still in France a period of confusion and experiment. It is interesting, though useless, to speculate on what direction the popular element in drama might have taken had it not been caught up and overwhelmed by the tide of new learning sweeping in from Italy. The influence of the Renaissance triumphed in the end over the old farces and *soties* as much as over the complicated and out-moded Bible-histories. Drawing not only their inspiration but also their form and content from classical antiquity, the writers of the French Renaissance were students first and playwrights almost by accident. Étienne Jodelle (1532–73), whose tragedy, *Cléopâtre captive*, given in 1552 together with a comedy on classic lines, is generally held to be the first neo-classic drama of France, opened the way for the great drama of the seventeenth century. Among his contemporaries, who all looked to Greece and Rome for their models, the best was probably Robert Garnier (*c.* 1535–*c.* 1600), a fine poet and scholar, who made good use of the chorus, but hampered himself by slavish adherence to the drama of antiquity, which he envisaged through Roman eyes. A later dramatist, Antoine de Montchrétien (*c.* 1575–1621), continued the vogue for tragedy. He was also a fine poet and one of the first playwrights to deal with modern history, making Mary, Queen of Scots the heroine of his *L'Écossaise* (1603).

True to what they believed to be the principle of their Greek models—a view since somewhat modified—these early French dramatists allowed themselves no mingling of the serious and the gay. The old medieval mixture of high tragedy and low farce was no longer permissible, and the genres were sharply defined. The same author might adventure in both, as Jodelle himself did, and as did Jacques Grévin (*c.* 1538–*c.* 1570), whose tragedy on Julius Caesar is overshadowed by the popularity of his comedy *Les Esbahis* (1560); but this owes nothing to the popular farce of old France, nor do the comedies of Pierre Larivey (*c.* 1540–*c.* 1612), an Italian turned Frenchman, who saw the Italian *commedia dell'arte* company, the Gelosi, play at Blois in 1577, and was inspired to write a number of comedies in French based on Italian models. This early association of French with Italian comedy is interesting, since it foreshadows the connexion between the *commedia dell'arte* scenarii and the early plays of that great writer of French comedies, Molière. Also from Italy came the Pastoral, the delight of a courtly society, which shared the popularity of tragedy.

The years which saw the gradual shaping and perfecting of French drama in a form which was to reach its height in the plays of Corneille and Racine saw also the emergence of a body of professional actors to interpret them. The early writers, Jodelle, Garnier, Grévin, relied on amateurs, on themselves and their friends, or on the schools, particularly those run by Jesuits, where Latin plays and occasionally comedies in the vernacular formed part of the educational curriculum (see JESUIT DRAMA). Jodelle himself played the heroine in his *Cléopâtre captive*, while Grévin's plays were given at the Collège de Beauvais. While the new drama was thus establishing itself as literature, the old discredited drama was still played in the provinces by bands of strolling actors who were, by the 1570s, beginning to form permanent professional companies. They had as yet no foothold in Paris. Apart from the monopoly still held, and jealously exercised, by the Confraternity of the Passion, the country was in too troublous a state to allow of the establishment of permanent theatre-buildings. Peace came with the accession of Henri IV in 1594, but it was not until Richelieu came into power some thirty years later that the theatre could flourish in the capital, and Paris achieve that pre-eminence which she has since retained. Until then she had to be content with visits from foreign companies, mainly Italian, brought in expressly for the amusement of the Court, and from French provincial companies which included the town in their itineraries, and took the old theatre of the Confraternity of the Passion, the Hôtel de Bourgogne, on a short lease. One such company is noted in 1578 under Agnan Sarat (?–1613), an actor-manager who became the comedian of the first professional company which can really be said to have established itself in Paris. Led by Valleran-Lecomte (*fl.* 1590–*c.* 1613), this company has two other claims to distinction. Its leading lady was Marie Venier (*fl.* 1590–1619), the first French actress to be known by name, and it had as its dramatist Alexandre Hardy (*c.* 1575–*c.* 1631), a prolific dramatist who, with a spark of genius, might have changed the course of French dramatic literature. His numerous plays, which subordinated character to action, were mainly tragicomedies. They were extremely popular, and many future dramatists of the great age of French drama, including Corneille, owed their first glimpse of the theatre to Hardy.

The Hôtel de Bourgogne was at this time in much the same state as when the Confraternity of the Passion had used it for their medieval Bible-histories. A long, narrow room, it had rising tiers of benches at one end, opposite the stage, and boxes on each side. A pit, for standing spectators only, ran half the length of the room, and the stage and auditorium alike were lit by candles, which had frequently to be snuffed during the performance. The old system of simultaneous, or multiple, settings was still in use, at least during the early seventeenth century, and each actor played his part as a solo, advancing to the edge of the stage to declaim, and retiring to make way for his successor.

Since the Confraternity of the Passion still clung to their monopoly of acting, it followed that only companies to whom they leased their theatre at the Hôtel de Bourgogne could legally act in Paris. A breach was, however, made in their privileges by an edict of 1595, which permitted other companies to play at the fairs, at that of St-Germain in the spring and of St-Laurent in the autumn. The father of Valleran-Lecomte's leading lady, himself a provincial actor-manager of long standing, was quick to profit by this, and took his company from the spring fair to the Hôtel d'Argent, where he was allowed to remain on payment of a levy to the Confraternity. On a later visit there he was joined for a time by his daughter and her husband, also an actor, and author of some lost plays, under the name of Laporte.

The opening years of the seventeenth century thus found Paris with two semi-permanent and wholly professional companies. The fortunes of both fluctuated, as did their composition, for actors constantly migrated from one group to another, while a political upheaval, such as the assassination of Henri IV in 1610, was sufficient to uproot them all and send them back into the provinces again. But by 1629 the *Comédiens du roi*, as the company once headed by Valleran-Lecomte was now called, had established itself firmly at the Hôtel de Bourgogne, while a rival company under Charles Lenoir (*fl.* 1610–37) was competing for public favour elsewhere.

The establishment of the French professional actor in the capital led to an increase in the number of plays written, but little of permanent value was produced. Some of the plays that survive, many of them anonymous, have scenes of merit but little form. They are intended to entertain or amuse, and are not yet subject to criticism or bound by laws of dramatic composition. In spite of a slight ascendancy, Paris has not yet attained complete control of theatrical activity, and good companies are still found in the provinces, particularly in Normandy, while an increasing number of plays are published in Rouen. A study of the repertory, where indications of it can be found, discloses a curious mingling of the old medieval play with those written under classical or Italian influence. The actors who leased the Hôtel de Bourgogne in the early years of the century showed a marked preference for plots derived from medieval romance epics. Scenes of violence, later to be banned by the purists, are often found, and were apparently much enjoyed by the audience. The pastoral continued in high favour, with tragicomedy not far behind. Comedy is practically non-existent. Hardy's neglect of it may have caused others to disdain it also. Farces were no doubt abundant, but as they were seldom printed, perhaps hardly even written down, few have survived. We can, however, judge of their popularity by the fact that the outstanding actors of the period are farce-players. Some of them are reputed to have come to the professional theatre from the booths of the fairs, among them Bruscambille (*fl.* 1610–34), famous for his amusing prologues and epilogues; his partner Jean Farine (*fl.* 1600–35), and the famous trio Turlupin (*c.* 1587–1637), Gaultier-Garguille (*c.* 1573–1633), and Gros-Guillaume (*fl.* 1600–34), delight of the audiences at the Hôtel de Bourgogne for many years, and actors, under the names of Belleville, Fleschelles, and Lafleur, of serious parts also. An actor who never achieved the dignity of the Hôtel de Bourgogne, but whose clowning on the Pont-Neuf was long a feature of Paris life, was Tabarin (?–1626), whose name passed into the colloquial language of France, while one of his jokes was later used by no less a person than Molière.

The leader of the company at the Hôtel de Bourgogne, whose acting in pastoral and tragicomedy did much to raise the status of the profession and oust the farce-players from public favour, was Bellerose (*c.* 1600–70). Under him such clowns as Guillot-Gorju (1600–48), though still popular, were content with a secondary place, while an interesting feature of this period is the sudden flowering of feminine talent with such actresses as Mlle Beauchâteau (1615–83) and Mlle Beaupré (*fl.* 1624–50), both wives of actors. At the newly established Théâtre du Marais, too, where the great actor Montdory (1594–1651) was building up a fine reputation in tragedy, there was an excellent actress, Mlle de Villiers (?–1670). She and Montdory, with an able and experienced company, were called upon to interpret the early plays of the French classical period, which Corneille is generally held to have inaugurated with his tragicomedy, *Le Cid* (1636), in which they played Chimène and Rodrigue respectively.

4. The Great Age of French Drama. (*a*) *Corneille*. Many influences had been at work, however, before Corneille produced his masterpiece, the most important being the establishment of the unities of time, place, and action. These unities, codified by French logic from the precepts of Aristotle, were destined to have a great influence on French drama and to lead to much argument, both at the time and in succeeding generations. Their history belongs mainly to the domain of literature, where they are represented either as a code imposed on dramatists against their will, which thwarted their natural development, or as a formulating of theatrical devices which had already proved successful in action, and were therefore adopted by contemporary dramatists. It has been remarked, in support of the latter theory, that plays of the early classical period written in accordance with the unities were more successful in performance than those that were not, a fact which would provide sufficient incentive for their adoption by other writers.

The unities were first adhered to in the Pastoral, a genre which had proved popular ever since the publication in 1584 of a translation of Tasso's *Aminta*, and which was to achieve a sudden blaze of glory before it disappeared for ever. Courtly poets, like the Marquis de Racan (1589–1670) and Théophile de Viau (1590–1626), had already brought to the art of playwriting some distinction in style and versification, and a greater insistence on emotion than on action, while raising at the same time the prestige of the dramatist, when a young writer, Jean Mairet (1604–86), influenced and encouraged by them, brought out his *Sylvanire* (1630). The success of this play induced other writers to adopt the rules which Mairet had set out in his preface, and the triumph of the unities was assured by the reception given to his *Sophonisbe* (1634). This play, which provided Montdory with a fine part as Massinisse, brought about a return to popular favour of the tragedy after its partial eclipse by tragicomedy, and had a marked influence on other writers of the period. One of the best plays written under its influence was the *Mariamne* (1636) of Tristan l'Hermite (1601–55), who followed it with a number of other plays without again equalling its excellence. It, too, gave scope for Montdory's powers in the part of Herod, which he was playing when paralysis of the tongue caused his premature retirement from the stage.

Before this melancholy event, however, Montdory had been instrumental in introducing to the public the plays of Pierre Corneille (1606–84). He had already given eight of them at the Marais, mainly comedies of intrigue, of a type new to the Parisian stage, when he put on *Le Cid* (1636). This tragicomedy, based on the story of Spain's national hero, proved popular, as did many others of the same type written at this time; but, unlike its emulators, *Le Cid* had a permanent value, and is today recognized as one of the outstanding works of French literature.

Its present position, however, and the popular acclaim with which it was first received, should not blind us to the fact that contemporary criticism of it was not wholly favourable. Corneille was accused of violating the unities, and a fierce quarrel broke out among the literary figures of Paris. Mairet, possibly through jealousy, stood firm for his beloved rules, as did such lesser writers as Georges de Scudéry (1601–67), who nevertheless violated them in his own plays, and Jean Gombauld (1570–1666), while those who had already some perception of Corneille's stature argued that genius makes its own rules and may discard those of lesser men where it pleases. The question was finally brought for arbitration to Cardinal Richelieu (1585–1642), who added an interest in the theatre, an urge to organize it, and a desire to shine as a playwright, to his many other preoccupations. The point never was, indeed never could be, settled, but posterity has given the verdict to Corneille against his opponents.

Undeterred by the storm of criticism he had aroused, Corneille continued to write, but it is interesting to note that his next plays, among them *Horace* (1640) and *Cinna* (1641), were mainly tragedies, as though he wished to prove that he could beat his opponents at their own game. Tragedy was now established as the recognized vehicle for classical French drama, and many fine ones were written at this period, among them those of Pierre du Ryer (*c.* 1600–58) and Jean Rotrou (1609–50). The former had been an early adherent to the theory of the unities, and had followed some early tragicomedies in the style of Hardy with tragedies written strictly in accordance with the rules of Mairet. The best of these was *Scévole* (1644), which remained in the repertory of the Comédie-Française until the middle of the eighteenth century, as did Rotrou's *Venceslas* (1647). Rotrou was an excellent dramatist, whose first play was produced when he was only 19. His popularity, and also his industry, can be judged from the fact that he had four plays produced in the year of *Le Cid*, and throughout his career he never failed to provide good parts for Bellerose and the company of the Hôtel de Bourgogne, to which he was attached as official dramatist in succession to Hardy.

An interesting dramatist, contemporary with Corneille's early years, was Gautier de Costes de La Calprenède (*c.* 1610–63), who, unlike his companions, looked to English rather than Roman history for the subjects of his tragedies. The best of these, and certainly the most interesting, was *Le Comte d'Essex* (1637), in which he introduces for the first time the episode of the ring given by Elizabeth to Essex. An earlier play by La Calprenède had dealt with Lady Jane Grey. La Calprenède later deserted the theatre for the novel, and his success in that genre has somewhat overshadowed his reputation as a dramatist.

Tragedy was still in the ascendant when the troubles of the Fronde overwhelmed France, and caused a slowing-down of theatrical activity, and a slight but noticeable change in the development of drama. Among Corneille's plays at this time are *Rodogune* (1645), with which is associated the name of a much lesser dramatist, Gabriel Gilbert (*c.* 1620–*c.* 1680), who was later accused, with some justification, of having plagiarized Corneille's play in his own *Rhodogune*, done early in the following year; *Andromède* (1650), the first 'machine-play', embellished by the mechanical inventions of Torelli; and the unfortunate *Pertharite* (1652), whose failure, added to the troublous times, led Corneille temporarily to abandon the theatre. His retirement coincided with that of du Ryer and the death of Rotrou. The public taste was for lighter fare, and new dramatists came forward to satisfy it, among them Corneille's younger brother, Thomas Corneille (1625–1709), whose first play was produced in 1647, Philippe Quinault (1635–88), friend and protégé of Tristan l'Hermite, and the prolific and elderly Abbé Boisrobert (1592–1662), who had already contributed a number of plays to the repertory, the first at the age of 40, but whose main activity was confined to the 1650s.

Although all the later dramatists mentioned above wrote tragedies, their work in the period under review was mainly done in comedy, a genre which for the first time comes into prominence, and seeks to rival and even outdo tragedy and tragicomedy. Its development through the first half of the seventeenth century was to culminate in the work of the actor-dramatist, Molière, one of France's greatest dramatists and perhaps one of the greatest writers of comedy in the history of the European theatre.

(*b*) *Molière.* In the early years of the seventeenth century playgoers relied for humour mainly on the rough horseplay of the farce, or on the incidental comic scenes and characters in the pastorals and tragicomedies. The 1630s saw a few isolated examples of comedy by such established authors as Rotrou, du Ryer, and Scudéry, but it was Corneille, with the series of plays which preceded *Le Cid*, who liberated true comedy from the entanglements of farce and melodrama, and made it a genre worthy of serious attention. Later, having proved himself a great writer of tragedies, he returned to this earlier form, and produced in *Le Menteur* (1643), based on a play by Alarcón, the best French comedy of the period. Its success, however, was not repeated by its sequel in the following year, and the failure of *La Suite du Menteur* may have decided Corneille to return to tragedy. Whatever the reason, he wrote no more comedies; but he had blazed a trail which others were not slow to follow.

Among the few notable comedies before *Le Menteur* was *Les Visionnaires* (1637) by Jean Desmaretz de Saint-Sorlin (1595–1676), one of Richelieu's protégés, in which plot is subordinated to the study of a series of comic characters, monomaniacs who think of themselves as brave, rich, poetic, or adored, when in reality they are cowardly, poor, prosaic, or ridiculous. French comedy might, after this, have concentrated on character rather than intrigue, had it not been for the influence of Antoine d'Ouville (*c.* 1590–1656/77), brother of the Abbé Boisrobert, and like him a dramatist. He had lived much in Spain, and most of his comedies were based on Spanish models, as were those of his brother, and of Paul Scarron (1610–60), friend of Corneille and first husband of the future Mme de Maintenon. Better known for his novels, which included one on the life of a travelling company, *Le Roman comique*, Scarron nevertheless ranks high in the history of French comedy, since to him is due the introduction, in his *L'Écolier de Salamanque* (1654), of the valet Crispin. Another writer who owed much to Spain was the younger Corneille; like his brother, he began by writing a series of comedies, but since they are drawn from Spanish sources they are all comedies of intrigue. For a revival of true French comedy, as indicated by Corneille, but with its roots in the indigenous farce, we must turn to Molière.

Jean-Baptiste Poquelin, known as Molière (1622–73), came of a good family of the upper middle class and, as far as is known, had no affiliations with the stage. Yet before he was 21 he had renounced his succession to his father's position as Court upholsterer, and gone off with a family of young actors, drawn perhaps by love for the eldest girl, but more probably by the irresistible attraction of the theatre, which he never again deserted. After an unsuccessful start in Paris, where they were billed as the Illustre-Théâtre, the young company left for the provinces, and remained there until 1658, playing stock Italian farces, knockabout comedies written by Molière himself, who had soon become the leader of the troupe, and tragedies by contemporary dramatists, particularly Corneille, whom Molière much admired. Little is known of these years in the provinces, but the experience gained in them proved useful when Molière brought his company back to Paris in 1658. In addition to himself and the Béjarts, Madeleine (1618–72), Joseph (*c.* 1620–59), Geneviève (*c.* 1622–75), and Louis (1625–78), remnants of the original company, he had two good actresses in Mlle du Parc (*c.* 1633–68) and Mlle de Brie (?–1707), a staunch veteran in Charles Dufresne (*fl.* 1643–60), once leader of the troupe and soon to leave it, and a good comedian in Gros-René (*c.* 1600–64), husband of Mlle du Parc.

The company first appeared at Court, before the king, in *Nicomède*, but without much success. They redeemed themselves, however, by a splendid performance of one of Molière's early farces, *Le Docteur amoureux*, now lost. In consideration of their success they were allowed to remain in Paris and share the stage of the Petit-Bourbon with an Italian *commedia dell'arte* company established there under Scaramouche (Tiberio Fiorillo), where they remained until their removal to the Palais-Royal in 1660.

Paris now had three permanent troupes of actors—the Hôtel de Bourgogne, which, under the successors of Bellerose, Floridor (1608–72) and Montfleury (*c.* 1600–67), had achieved supremacy in tragedy; the Marais, fallen from its high estate but still able, under Laroque (*c.* 1595–1676), to tempt away two of Molière's best actors, the du Parcs, and already beginning to specialize in 'machine-plays'; and Molière's company, which, after another abortive attempt at tragedy, found its true vocation in the acting of Molière's comedies. These, which range from the one-act *Précieuses ridicules* of 1658 to the three-act *Malade imaginaire* of 1673, mark the development and flowering of French comedy of character, and added a number of masterpieces to the repertory of French dramatic literature. It is almost impossible to overestimate the influence of Molière, not only in his own country, but on European literature in general. Before him comedy had been a neglected art, too often relegated to the status of a farce in a fair-booth; he made it a genre worthy to rank with tragedy. His genius was peculiarly his own, and though like Shakespeare he borrowed freely, yet he adorned everything he touched. In spite of the speed with which he wrote, and his many other preoccupations as actor and leader of a company, his comedy is in no way superficial. His most ridiculous characters have about them some touch of pathos, some sense of lost and bewildered humanity which gives them a universal appeal. He was never deliberately malicious, though his satire cut deep; it was directed against those who sought to dupe or entangle the ordinary man, in whose innate goodness and kindliness he firmly believed. He attacked hypocrisy and pretension wherever he found it and did not scruple to bring down on himself the wrath of those in high places, as when he attacked the false piety of the religious hypocrite in *Tartuffe*, whose stormy history shows the forces he had to contend with.

Apart from his straightforward plays, which were usually given for the first time on the public stage, and included such light-hearted comedies as *L'École des maris* (1661), *L'École des femmes* (1662), *Le Médecin malgré lui* (1666), *Le Malade imaginaire* (1673) (see No. 20) and two comedies of character, *Le Misanthrope* (1666) and *L'Avare* (1668), Molière was also responsible for a large number of entertainments written for the amusement of the Court. These, known as *comédies-ballets*, show a judicious mingling of speech, song, and dance, and many of Molière's plays, including *Le Bourgeois gentilhomme* (1671), were originally written for these elaborate spectacles in which the king and his courtiers took part as dancers and actors. Though Molière cannot claim to have invented the *comédie-ballet*, which was much in vogue at Court before his day, he extended and developed it, and gave it a literary, as well as a musical, importance. His collaborators were Lully, who eventually obtained a monopoly of music in Paris which effectually put an end to the development of plays with music, and hastened the overwhelming popularity of opera and operetta, and Isaac de Benserade (1613–91), protégé and kinsman of Richelieu, whose inconsiderable early plays were overshadowed by the later popularity of his libretti; and, on one occasion, in *Psyché* (1671), the great Corneille himself, who had returned to the stage in 1659 with *Œdipe*.

Molière's work for the Court and for his own theatre completely filled his life, and from his arrival in Paris in 1658 until his untimely death in 1673 he had no interests and no affiliations outside. He even took a wife from among his actors, marrying in 1662 Armande Béjart (1642–1700), youngest sister of Madeleine, and an excellent actress who was the first to play many of Molière's delightful heroines. It was an unhappy marriage, and many critics have sought in Molière's plays a reflection of his domestic troubles. The parallel does not seem to have struck contemporary audiences overmuch. As with many authors, Molière's plays through the centuries have gathered an accretion of interpretation and application perhaps foreign to his original intention. He was too good a judge of what was theatrically effective to risk boring his audience with a purely personal problem, and it may be coincidence that his situations and speeches, with their universal appeal, apply also to his own life.

(*c*) *Racine.* Although he was sufficient in himself to sustain the burden of writing for his own theatre for many years, Molière did not neglect the work of contemporary dramatists, and among the plays which he imported into the Palais-Royal was the first tragedy of a young man whose fame was soon to overshadow that of Corneille himself. This was *La Thébaïde* (1664), by Jean Racine (1639–99). Early orphaned, educated at the Collège de Beauvais and at Port-Royal, Racine was already known as a poet, and had made the acquaintance of the actors of the Marais and the Hôtel de Bourgogne, was a friend of La Fontaine, and at some point met Molière.

His first venture was a success, and it is interesting to see that, in spite of its somewhat brutal subject and the inexperience of its author, the play contains already the germ of Racine's future theatre. Though it lacks the poetic charm and psychological insight of some of his later work, its Greek theme, its technical excellence, and its insistence on the love-interest, show the way he is going.

At the time of Racine's début French tragedy was becalmed. Comedy flourished under Molière, whose success had raised up a host of imitators, some of them actors also. But to the new names in comedy, tragedy could oppose only such established authors as the ageing Corneille; his brother Thomas, whose *Timocrate* (1656) heralded the return of tragedy after the upheaval of the Fronde, and was followed by a number of other tragedies, mostly on classical themes; the mediocre works of Jean Magnon (1620–62) and Claude Boyer (1618–98); the one classical tragedy, *Manlius* (1662), of Mlle Desjardins (1632–83), one of the few women dramatists of the period; and Quinault, who after four successful comedies and a number of tragedies, of which *Astrate* (1665) is usually considered the best, gave himself up entirely to the writing of libretti for opera, mainly set to music by Lully. The time was therefore ripe for a new talent, and Racine came at his hour. *La Thébaïde* was followed by *Alexandre et Porus* (1665), which Racine, with a callous disregard of Molière's kindness that cost him the older man's friendship, gave to the actors at the Hôtel de Bourgogne a fortnight after it had opened at the Palais-Royal. Molière's insufficiency in tragedy has been advanced as the cause of this double-dealing; whatever the explanation, Racine's plays were henceforth given at the rival theatre, which also took from Molière his leading actress, Mlle du Parc, now the mistress of Racine. She was at the Hôtel de Bourgogne in time to play the title-role in *Andromaque* (1667), a fine play which established Racine as the leading dramatist of the day, superior even to the great Corneille, whose *Agésilaus* (1666) and *Attila* (1667) had been coolly received. The rivalry between them came to a head when in 1670 both authors produced plays on the same subject, Racine's *Bérénice* being given at the Hôtel de Bourgogne a week before Corneille's *Tite et Bérénice* at the Palais-Royal. Racine's play, with its simplicity and fine poetry, and the added attraction of the great tragic actress Mlle Champmeslé (1642–98) in the title-role, was judged the better of the two, in spite of the excellence of Molière's wife as Corneille's heroine, and the fine Domitien of young Michel Baron (1653–1729), later to be the foremost actor of France, and now appearing in his first adult part after a childhood spent on the stage.

While Corneille was bringing his honourable career to a close with two rather frigid tragedies, which showed to great disadvantage against the warmer, more passionate, works of his young rival, Racine turned to oriental subjects in his *Bajazet* (1672) and *Mithridate* (1673), treating them in a contemporary style that was purely French, and then went back, as his only rivals Thomas Corneille and Quinault were doing, to Greek mythology. *Iphigénie* (1674) was followed by Racine's masterpiece, *Phèdre* (1677), which has been acclaimed as one of the greatest plays ever written. The success Racine might well have looked for at this culminating point in his career was, however, vitiated by the efforts of a powerful cabal. Jealous of his growing prestige, this group extolled a mediocre play on the same subject by a second-rate dramatist, Nicolas Pradon (1644–98), author of a number of tragedies which suffer by comparison with Racine's. Pradon's temporary success, however, added to Racine's official appointment at Court, and perhaps some private scruples, combined to make the latter forsake the theatre. He retained an interest in it for many years, but his only connexion with it after *Phèdre* was through the two biblical plays, *Esther* (1689) and *Athalie* (1690), written at the request of Mme de Maintenon for private performance by the young ladies of Saint-Cyr, and never publicly produced in Racine's lifetime.

Unlike Corneille, Racine wrote only one comedy, *Les Plaideurs* (1668), a satire on the law, based to some extent on Aristophanes' *Wasps* and intended for the Italian *commedia dell'arte* troupe. Owing to Scaramouche's absence from Paris, it was given at the Hôtel de Bourgogne with some success, and it has often been regretted that Racine did not further develop his undoubted comic vein. Perhaps he hesitated to enter into competition with Molière, whose chief rivals in comedy were his brother-actors. Claude de Villiers (1600–81), husband of the first Chimène, wrote farces and a version of Don Juan. A better actor and dramatist was Raymond Poisson (*c.* 1630–90), whose numerous plays were successfully performed at the Hôtel de Bourgogne, where the author appeared as a farce-player under the name of Philipin, and was the first to immortalize the valet, Crispin. Of his plays, several of which deal with theatrical people or situations, the most interesting is *Le Baron de la Crasse* (1663). It portrays a provincial nobleman being entertained by a travelling company, whose leader may be intended as a caricature of Molière. Poisson, even more than Molière, was influenced by the form and content of the old French farce, with its short lines, violent action, and elementary humour. He understood his audience, and his plays proved most successful in performance, having a more individual stamp than those of most of Molière's imitators. Like Molière, he was a good comic actor, a tradition carried on through several generations by his numerous children and grandchildren.

A restless actor, Guillaume Brécourt (1638–86), who is found in all three Parisian troupes and in the provinces, wrote several comedies, of which *L'Ombre de Molière* (1674) was a tribute to the great dramatist, and owed perhaps more to him than to its author. *La Feinte Mort de Jodelet* (1659) was one of a series intended to give scope for the comic powers of the actor Jodelet (*c.* 1604–60), who had appeared in *Le Menteur* and its sequel, and was for a year before his death in Molière's company at the Palais-Royal. The plays of Charles Champmeslé (1642–1701) were for a long time attributed to La Fontaine or the Abbé Abeille, but have recently been restored to him. Those attributed to La Fontaine, *Le Florentin* (1685) and *La Coupe enchantée* (1688), were still being given in Paris in the early twentieth century. Champmeslé's main claim to fame, however, is that he was the husband of the outstanding tragic actress of her day, who was the first to play Racine's later heroines, and replaced Mlle du Parc in the dramatist's affections.

Of the many writers of comedy at this time the only one to approach Molière, either in quantity or quality, was an actor at the Hôtel de Bourgogne, Noël de Hauteroche (*c.* 1616–1707). He was at his best in simple, often one-act, sketches based on a single humorous situation, and among his most successful plays were those that gave the chief part to the valet Crispin, played by his colleague Raymond Poisson. Another author closely connected with the stage, though not himself an actor, was Antoine de Montfleury (1639–85), son of the great tragedian, a lawyer and dramatist, who found himself in continual competition with Molière, mainly owing to the pressing need for the actors at the Hôtel de Bourgogne to put on a comedy each time Molière produced one. Even the titles are similar, as in *L'École des jaloux* (1661) and *L'Impromptu de l'Hôtel de Condé* (1663), the latter intended as a counterblast to the satire of *L'Impromptu de Versailles*, in which Molière had hard things to say of the elder Montfleury and his associates.

Apart from Boisrobert and the younger Corneille, the only other writer of comedies at this period who deserves a passing mention is Edmé Boursault (1638–1701), who at various times found himself quarrelling with Molière and with Boileau, two redoubtable enemies. His attack on Boileau was not acted, but that on Molière—*Le Portrait du peintre*—was given at the Hôtel de Bourgogne in 1663. Boursault, however, was destined to do his best work after Molière's death, with *La Comédie sans titre, ou Le Mercure galant* (1683) and two comedies based on the life and fables of Aesop.

The great age of French drama, which opened with *Le Cid* in 1636, closed with *Phèdre* in 1677. Corneille had gathered up the strands woven by those who preceded him, and of them fashioned the French classical drama, seen at its best in the conflict of love and honour in *Le Cid*, and in the lofty and noble diction of such tragedies as *Horace*, *Cinna*, and *Nicomède*. Racine, taking up the challenge of the older man, narrowed the range of tragedy but deepened it immeasurably with the introduction of passion and poetry. He also made extensive use of the theatrically effective device of raising the curtain on a situation which is about to be resolved, and then handling with consummate art the various pretexts which delay the catastrophe until the end of the fifth act. It is idle to compare Corneille and Racine. They are two different facets of the same jewel. Between them stands Molière, who chose for his début in Paris one of Corneille's tragedies, and was the first man of the theatre to recognize and encourage the genius of Racine. He was never their rival, since he never adventured into tragedy himself; but his comedies form the perfect pendant to their tragedies, and all three together represent the summit of French dramatic art.

During his lifetime Molière saw great changes come over the French theatre, some of which he helped to bring about. Apart from assisting in the literary development of farce into comedy, and the evolution of French tragedy, Molière lived through three eras of stage-craft. In his early days he saw, and may have used, the medieval system of simultaneous or multiple settings, which long continued to be popular at the Hôtel de Bourgogne, and may have been employed, in a modified form, for *Le Cid*. This gradually gave way to an unlocalized set scene suitable for the formal acting of French tragedy, usually summed up as *palais à volonté*. During this period, as in England, the actors were hampered by the presence on the stage of a number of spectators, who were not finally dislodged until the eighteenth century. The setting of comedy was influenced by the scenery of the *commedia dell'arte* troupe with whom Molière had to share his stage. This showed a street or square in perspective, with houses grouped round from which the actors issued to transact their most intimate affairs in the open air—domestic quarrels, signing of wills, consultations with doctors, and so on. This fairly simple setting, which employed stylized scenery of painted and folding screens, was at first taken by Molière to Court, but he was soon influenced by the spectacular effects necessitated by Court spectacles and by the fashionable opera, and one of the last things he did was to rebuild the stage of the Palais-Royal to accommodate elaborate scene-shifting and machines. *Psyché* (1671) was the first play to be given there with all the effects which had been possible at Court. Earlier elaborate plays of this type had been Corneille's *Andromède* and *Toison d'or*, and the Marais had specialized in such spectacles. After Molière's death his new stage proved very useful to the wily Lully, who managed to get it assigned to him, under his monopoly of music, for the production of opera.

It is more difficult to assess the changes which had come over acting during this period, but there can be no doubt that great advances had been made, and that the early unpolished hit-or-miss methods of the itinerant companies had given way to a more studied technique. Bellerose and Montdory, the one gentle and somewhat insipid, the other forceful and declamatory, had raised the art of acting to a high level, and their work was continued by Floridor and Montfleury, both excellent actors in their different styles. Molière, though never a good actor in tragedy, excelled in comedy, and it was doubtless a far cry from the horseplay and acrobatic buffoonery of the early farces to his subtle and more natural style of acting, while his discarding of the mask, which he originally wore in imitation of the *commedia dell'arte*, as did all the farce-players, allowed full play to facial expression. Some of his company have already been mentioned. Others worthy of note were La Grange (1639–92), Molière's close friend, editor of his works, and keeper of a daily register of the theatre which has proved invaluable to later students of the period; Philibert Gassot du Croisy (*c.* 1630–95), who with his wife joined Molière soon after his arrival in Paris, and was the first to play the part of Tartuffe; and François Lenoir de La Thorillière (1626–80), who played a number of important roles in Molière's comedies, went to the Hôtel de Bourgogne after his death, and by the marriages of his sons and daughters, all on the stage, became the founder of a big theatrical family. Lesser parts in Molière's plays were taken by André Hubert (*c.* 1634–1700), a good impersonator of old women, and the first to play Mme Jourdain in *Le Bourgeois gentilhomme*; by L'Espy (*fl.* 1610–64), the brother of Jodelet; and by Beauval (*c.* 1640–1709), a mediocre actor whose one great success, more by nature than by art, was the part of Thomas Diafoirus in *Le Malade imaginaire*. His wife, Mlle Beauval (*c.* 1649–1720), was, however, an excellent actress, both in comedy and tragedy, worthy to rank with Mlle de Brie and Mlle du Parc, mentioned above. The former played the part of Agnès in *L'École des femmes* for nearly fifty years, from its first production, while the latter, who died at the height of her powers, had the distinction of being admired by Corneille, trained by Molière, and loved by Racine.

At the Hôtel de Bourgogne two actors not yet mentioned were Jean de la Tuillerie

(1650–88), a fine actor in tragedy, who married a daughter of Raymond Poisson, and wrote comedies about the valet Crispin for his father-in-law; and Mlle Desœillets (1621–70), who took the place of Michel Baron's mother at the Hôtel de Bourgogne, and created a number of tragic roles, including Corneille's Sophonisbe and Racine's Hermione. She was replaced in the latter part by Mlle Champmeslé.

Although Paris had, by the end of the century, attained complete supremacy in theatrical matters as in all else, provincial companies continued to circulate, and some of their actor-managers achieved a certain reputation. Among these was Filandre (1616–91), who is credited with the early training of Mlle Beauval and possibly of Floridor; Dorimond (?–*c.* 1664), whose career resembles that of Molière in his early years (though he never attained Paris), in that he headed his own company on their wanderings, and supplied them with farces and comedies written by himself; and Rosimond (*c.* 1640–86), who eventually came to the Marais, and afterwards joined the remnants of Molière's company, playing a number of Molière's roles. He, too, wrote several plays, among them one on Don Juan.

5. AFTERMATH AND EIGHTEENTH CENTURY. After Molière's death his company, under the leadership of his widow and La Grange, amalgamated with the actors at the Théâtre du Marais, and in 1680, as a result of Louis XIV's passion for centralization and monopolies, was again amalgamated with the actors of the Hôtel de Bourgogne to form what was eventually called the Comédie-Française (also known as the Théâtre-Français and the Maison de Molière). The name seems to have arisen in an effort to distinguish the French actors from the Italian (see COMÉDIE-ITALIENNE) who, after intermittent but increasingly lengthened visits to Paris during the past hundred years, took complete possession of the now disused Hôtel de Bourgogne, and began to mingle French with their Italian.

The Comédie-Française, which is still the national theatre of France, had the sole right of acting and producing plays in Paris, and first call upon the services of provincial actors. Its constitution was in the main that of the old Confraternity of the Passion, on which Molière's first abortive venture, the Illustre-Théâtre, had also based its articles of association. Roughly speaking, it is a co-operative enterprise, in which each member is entitled to a certain share in the proceeds and to a pension after some fixed period of service, has definite rights and obligations, and is subject to a discipline administered by general agreement in the common interest.

The most important members of the Comédie-Française on its foundation were Baron, Raymond Poisson, Hauteroche, Mlle Beauval, and Mlle Champmeslé, with the latter's husband, the widow of Molière and her second husband, Guérin d'Étriché (*c.* 1636–1728), whom she had married in 1677. A newcomer who was to prove so good in comic parts that he was nicknamed 'le petit Molière' was Jean-Baptiste Raisin (1655–93), whose brother, sister, and wife were also members of the company. A few years later a second generation of actors was represented by Paul Poisson (1658–1735), son of Raymond, by his wife, daughter of Molière's du Croisy, and by Pierre Lenoir de La Thorillière (1659–1731), whose father's death in 1680 is generally held to have accelerated the formation of a single troupe, to which he had been strongly opposed. This younger La Thorillière married the daughter of Dominique, leader with Scaramouche of the Italian actors at the Hôtel de Bourgogne, while his sisters were the wives respectively of Baron and of the actor-dramatist Dancourt (see below).

At the one theatre with which they now had to be content, Parisian audiences could see revivals of Molière, Corneille, and Racine, together with some older plays, and a host of inferior imitations. Some of the blame for the aridity of this period must lie with the authors, who were afraid to venture into new paths; some with the actors, who used their monopoly as an excuse to avoid anything but variations on an old theme. Tragedies on classical and exotic subjects continued to be written, often by those whose aptitudes were for some other form of art, but began to lose their hold on the public, who looked for something new. In the same way, comedy, while appearing to flourish in new hands, is no longer the fine comedy of character perfected by Molière, but a superficial imitation, a comedy of manners which no longer holds an audience whose milieu has altered.

Among the few writers of tragedy who make some small showing in the period are Jean de La Chapelle (1655–1723), whose *Cléopâtre* (1681) provided Baron with an effective part, and Hilaire-Bernard de Roqueleyne Longepierre (1659–1731), whose only successful play was a re-writing of Corneille's *Médée*, done in 1694. La Chapelle might have kept classical tragedy alive after Racine's retirement, but he soon became immersed in politics and wrote no more, while Longepierre's main interest lay in criticism. A more prolific dramatist was Jean-Galbert de Campistron (1656–1723), several of whose plays dealt with contemporary history under a Roman guise. The most successful were *Virginie* (1683), *Arminius* (1684), and *Andronic* (1685), all early works in which Baron and Mlle Champmeslé were excellent. Campistron's later tragedies were weaker in structure, and the subjects were unfortunately chosen.

A writer whose best tragedy marks the end of the seventeenth century was Antoine de La Fosse (1654–1708). His first play was not produced until he was over 40, and it was often said that had he turned to playwriting earlier he might have rivalled Racine. As it was, only one of his plays, *Manlius Capitolinus* (1698), based to some extent on Otway's *Venice Preserved*, remained in the repertory, after a resounding initial success. La Fosse's later plays were less interesting and were overshadowed by the works of the infant prodigy Joseph de La Grange-Chancel (1677–1758), whose first play was written at the age of 13, and who, by 1700, had had four tragedies performed at the Comédie-Française. This young author was helped and encouraged by Racine, but does not seem to have profited by his advice as he might have done, and his plays, of which *Amasis* (1701) and *Ino et Mélicerte* (1713) were the most successful, could only have appealed to an audience that had lost the taste for grand tragedy. Yet La Grange-Chancel had good qualities, and might have kept tragedy from some of its later excesses had he continued writing. Unfortunately he came into conflict with the authorities and was exiled from France for many years. Meanwhile, in the hands of Prosper Jolyot de Crébillon (1674–1762), tragedy was turning to melodrama, its force and dignity to the horrors of incest and child-murder, its psychological realism to the puerilities of intrigue and romance. All these traits are observable in Crébillon's early works, of which the best, and perhaps the best of his long career, was *Rhadamiste et Zénobie* (1711).

Unlike Crébillon, who devoted himself entirely to tragedy, La Grange-Chancel and Campistron both produced comedies. But these were isolated examples and it is to two actors that we must look for the largest output in comedy. Baron, famous for his acting in tragedy, wrote only comedies, of which the best was *L'Homme à bonne fortune* (1686). This study of contemporary life, in which Baron himself played the leading part, Moncade, shows an adventurer living by his wits in a society where love is no longer a passion but a pastime. In this, and in *La Coquette* (1686), there is a part for a precocious boy, written for and acted by Baron's son Étienne (1676–1711), who later joined the Comédie-Française and proved a difficult and undisciplined actor, dying in the prime of life as the result of dissipation. Baron's plays owe much to Molière, with whom he was so closely associated in his youth, but he tended to concentrate too much on his main role at the expense of the rest. His lesser personages have nothing of the life and individuality of Molière's.

Baron's attempt to keep alive in some measure the comedy of character was frustrated by the concentration of his fellow-actor and brother-in-law, Florent Carton Dancourt (1661–1725), on the comedy of manners. Dancourt's plays cover a wide field, and though they are, on the whole, superficial and lack permanence, they give an interesting picture of Parisian life at the time. The best is *Le Chevalier à la mode* (1687), which shows the penniless aristocrat at grips with the newly rich. This was one of the few occasions when Dancourt ventured on a full-length play. The success of his *Maison de campagne* (1688) and *Opéra du village* (1692)—the latter the first of a long series of *comédies-vaudevilles*—induced him to confine himself mostly to one act. Of these shorter plays, many dealt with seasonal amusements and in one, *La Foire de Bezons* (1695), Dancourt's two young daughters first appeared on the stage. The younger, known as Mimi (1685–1779), later joined the Comédie-Française and remained a member of it all her long life.

While Dancourt was dramatizing with much skill and gaiety something of the social struggle implicit in the changing conditions of his day, and his fellow actor Marc Antoine Legrand (1673–1728) was basing his ephemeral comedies on contemporary events, other writers were catering for the Italian actors, who were becoming increasingly important in the theatrical life of Paris as their use of French was extended. Permission to use French at all had only been achieved with a struggle, and was strenuously opposed by the Comédie-Française. With the help of Dominique, who himself wrote several plays for his companions, the Italians won their case before no less a person than Louis XIV, and looked increasingly to French dramatists to supply them with material. In course of time they evolved what was virtually a new method, foreign art working on native material, a combination which was destined to have important results in the later history of French comedy. Among their collaborators the most important were Charles-Rivière Dufresny (1654–1724) and Jean-François Regnard (1655–1709), who both contributed largely to the repertory of the Comédie-Française also. Their first plays, however, were written for the Italians, and they might have continued to work there had not Louis XIV dismissed the company in 1697, annoyed at some fancied slight to Mme de Maintenon, and also, perhaps, not unwilling to lighten his budget by withdrawing the large subsidy which the Italians had enjoyed for so many years, often at the expense of their French rivals.

Deprived of their Italian interpreters, Regnard and Dufresny were forced to depend entirely on the Comédie-Française, where they had already made a start. The best of Regnard's comedies were *Le Joueur* (1696) and *Le Légataire universel* (1708), but Dufresny, who was the reputed great-grandson of Henri IV, wrote little of permanent merit. He had good qualities, but grudged the time given to playwriting, preferring to gamble. His light comedies, however, many of them interspersed with songs which he wrote himself, were successful, and appealed to the light-minded audience of the time.

Two authors who collaborated in comedy for the French actors, though one at least wrote for the Italians also, were Jean de Bigot Palaprat (1650–1721) and David-Augustin de Brueys (1640–1723). The finest result of their joint labours was *Le Grondeur* (1691), a comedy of character worthy to rank with some of Molière's. Brueys, who also wrote several tragedies on his own account, was the author of a refurbishing of the old farce of Pathelin, which, as *L'Avocat Pathelin* (1706), became one of the most popular plays in the repertory of the French theatre.

With such comedies as these, dramatists succeeded for a time in persuading their contemporaries that the great art of Molière was still flourishing. But the finest comedy of the time was to come from a novelist, Alain-René Le Sage (1668–1747), whose early plays had been drawn from Spanish cape-and-sword dramas, and proved little to the taste of the audience. He then turned to more native themes, and made a success with *Crispin rival de son maître* (1707). But his most important contribution to drama was undoubtedly *Turcaret* (1709), a scathing attack on the financiers and *nouveaux riches* who embittered the last years of the reign of Louis XIV. Its production was delayed by the machinations of those it satirized, and either this or quarrels with the actors of the Comédie-Française over a later play led Le Sage to waste his great talents in writing for the ephemeral productions of the fair-booths.

Two writers of slight comedies were Nicolas Boindin (1676–1751), whose *Bal d'Auteuil* (1702) caused a tightening-up of the censorship laws through its somewhat equivocal plot, and Antoine Houdard de La Motte (1672–1731), who also made one notable contribution to post-classical tragedy with his *Inès de Castro* (1723). The last outstanding writer of tragedy, however, was Voltaire (1694–1778), whose universal genius applied itself to the theatre as to every other aspect of eighteenth-century thought. His first play, *Œdipe* (1718), and such later tragedies as *Brutus* (1730) and *Zaïre* (1732), which both owe something to Shakespeare, are classical in form, and continue the illusion of greatness. But Voltaire had a far more disintegrating influence on tragedy than his lifelong enemy Crébillon, now censor of plays and still a prolific dramatist. Crébillon kept, in however pedestrian a style, to the old ways in form and content, while Voltaire, whose sense of tradition led him to follow Racine for the form of his plays, found no difficulty in reconciling that form with the liberal ideas of his time, which looked on the theatre as a school of morals. At the same time his use of spectacular effects and the intrusion of sentiment and emotion contributed to the development of the *drame* (or *tragédie bourgeoise*) which, with the *comédie larmoyante*, constitutes the main offering of the eighteenth century to the evolution of the French theatre. Both are the logical outcome of the influx into the theatre of the middle class, with its toleration for moral teaching and its desire for strong emotional situations, placed in a recognizable décor of modern society. The doctrine of the equality of man brought the heroes of tragedy from the palace to the parlour, while the sensibility of the age needed something to weep at even in comedy. This in itself was not fatal to the theatre, but it was France's misfortune at this time to have no dramatist of genius capable of making great drama out of the material to hand.

The germ of *comédie larmoyante*, and so of *drame*, can be found in the plays of Philippe Néricault Destouches (1680–1754), who detracted from the vigour of his comedies by too much insistence on the moral virtues. In spite of the humour of his valet Pasquin, and a gift for comic situations, he was too anxious to move his audience to be able to impart a cutting edge to his satire. His best play is *Le Glorieux* (1732), which dramatizes once more the struggle between the old nobility and the wealthy parvenu. It provided an excellent part for Abraham-Alexis Quinault, known on the stage as Dufresne (1690–1767). This illustrious member of a family which gave many actors to the Comédie-Française was one of the few outstanding players of his time. Beaubour (1662–1725), though good in some parts, could not adequately take the place of Baron, while Mlle Champmeslé had been replaced, but not equalled, by her niece Charlotte Desmares (1682–1753) and her pupil Marie-Anne Châteauneuf, known as Mlle Duclos (1664–1748). The Comédie-Française had also to suffer the competition of the unlicensed actors in the well-built, permanent theatres of the fairs, open nearly all the year round, where the plays of Le Sage, and other less eminent dramatists, were put on by enterprising managers, among them the widow of Étienne Baron, herself the daughter of a German fairground actor. In spite of constant complaint and litigation, the *forains*, as they were called, flourished, and evaded each new law as it was passed with an ingenuity which merely served to enhance their popularity. The early history of the fair-theatres is obscure, and little is known of their actors and managers beyond a few names and anecdotes, but they could not be suppressed, and by the 1770s had fused with the Comédie-Italienne to form the Opéra-Comique, whose history belongs to the domain of music. The Italian actors were recalled by the Regent in 1716, and returned under Lélio and the younger Dominique to reap new triumphs, and to become completely assimilated into the theatrical life of France; how completely can be realized when we remember that the finest plays of Pierre Carlet de Chamblain de Marivaux (1688–1763) were written for and performed at the Comédie-Italienne. He did, at times, write for the Comédie-Française; but he found the actors there overbearing and narrow-minded, and much preferred the gaiety and freedom of the Italians, whose acting, in any case, was more suited to the quick wit and subtlety of his dialogue. His plays are fine, penetrating analyses of young love, a restricted subject from which he drew a remarkable amount of material. His characters often have the same names, taken from the actors who played them, as was the tradition of the Italian company. The heroines of *La Double Inconstance* (1723) and of *Le Jeu de l'amour et du hasard* (1730) are both Silvias, while the hero of the second is Mario, from the stage-names of the actors who took the parts, the enchanting Rosa Zanetta Benozzi and her husband. But in spite of a similarity of name, they are all clearly defined, presenting to the audience innumerable facets of the stock pair of lovers, whose difficulties, though usually of their own making, are poignant enough for the moment, and universally applicable. No one ever laid bare with greater insight and delicacy than Marivaux the fluctuations of the proud, foolish, wilful, human heart.

Yet, in spite of wit, gaiety, and good humour, aided by fine acting, Marivaux was not much appreciated by his contemporaries. He belonged to no stream of tradition, he had no imitators. His style, which was so much his own that the word *marivaudage* was coined to describe it, though it looked easy, was a pitfall to the unwary, and few ventured on it. Marivaux remains an isolated phenomenon in French dramatic literature, the one great exponent of that fusion of French and Italian art which arose from the acclimatization of the *commedia dell'arte*.

Much more to the taste of eighteenth-century audiences were the tearful comedies of Pierre-Claude Nivelle de La Chaussée (1692–1754). Pathos was *à la mode*, and reached its summit in the plays of a wealthy, middle-aged man whose own tastes were decidedly more libertine and scabrous than those of his virtuous stage parents and children. Equally averse to classical tragedy and to the wit and characterization of comedy, he sought to amalgamate the two in a form which brought tears to the eyes of the audience, particularly of the women, who now frequented the theatre in far greater numbers than in the previous century. They brought their husbands to be edified by the spectacle of a patient wife in *Le Préjugé à la mode* (1735), and laughed and wept alternately at *L'École des mères* (1744). Later they were to forgo even a modicum of amusement in favour of an excess of sensibility, for La Chaussée's later plays, though still called comedies, are more allied to those moral effusions which went under the name of *drame*.

Although La Chaussée's name is always associated with the *comédie larmoyante*, others essayed the genre, notably Alexis Piron (1689–1773), best known for his comedy *La Métromanie* (1738), Jean-Baptiste-Louis Gresset (1709–77), and even Voltaire with *L'Enfant prodigue* (1736) and *Nanine* (1749). Voltaire, however, continued to write tragedies in his own manner, and was fortunate in being able to call on a new generation of actors to appear in them. First among them was the lovely and ill-fated Adrienne Lecouvreur (1692–1730), who died in his arms, and who was, like Molière, refused Christian burial, a fact not calculated to soften Voltaire in his attitude to the Church. Her early death was a great loss, but she was replaced by Mlle Dumesnil (1711–1803), for whom Voltaire wrote *Mérope* (1743), and by Mlle Dangeville (1714–96), who, with Préville, excelled in the plays of Marivaux when they eventually attained the boards of the Comédie-Française.

The greatest players of the period were, however, Hippolyte Clairon (1723–1803), an actress from childhood, and Henri-Louis Lekain (1728–78), friend and protégé of Voltaire. They played opposite each other in many of Voltaire's plays, and were instrumental in effecting some slight reforms in the theatre, notably in the adoption of a modified form of historical costume. After Mlle Clairon had played Roxane in oriental draperies instead of in panniers and seventeenth-century head-dress, Lekain appeared as Orestes with some attempt at Greek costume, and in *L'Orphelin de la Chine* (1755) both made a determined effort to simplify clothes, acting, and scenery. Under the influence of Jean-François Marmontel (1723–99), in whose *Denys le tyran* she played in 1748, Mlle Clairon dropped her declamatory style for a more natural tone, and induced her companions to do likewise. Lekain and Voltaire were also responsible jointly for the long-overdue clearance of the stage, which had been cluttered up with audience for nearly a hundred years. This encroachment on the acting space, which had been tolerated by French classical tragedy, had already proved impossible in the 'machine' plays, and matters finally came to a head with the introduction, under the influence of Shakespeare, of crowd scenes and spectacular effects in some of Voltaire's later tragedies, when, in opposition to his old enemy Crébillon, he took up the subjects of six of the latter's plays and rewrote them, the best being *Sémiramis* (1748).

Another actor associated with Voltaire was Jean de La Noue (1701–61), director of a provincial company in which Mlle Clairon played for a short time. He had had a play on Mahomet accepted by the Comédie-Française, and Voltaire acknowledged what his own *Mahomet, ou le fanatisme* (1741) owed to it by allowing La Noue to put it on at Lille before it was done, without much success, in Paris. La Noue later joined the Comédie-Française for secondary roles. Among his companions were Grandval (1711–84), preferred by some to Lekain, and Bellecour (1725–78), excellent in comedy.

Voltaire, though living in exile, was still writing for the French stage, and had just sent *Tancrède* (1760) to the Comédie-Française when Denis Diderot (1713–84) saw his first play in production. This was *Le Père de famille*, written and published two years earlier. *Le Fils naturel*, Diderot's other important play, though published in 1757, was not acted until 1772, a curious reversal of the earlier practice by which plays were not seen in print until some time after their first production. Both these plays, typical of the *drame bourgeois*, as was the *Brouette du vinaigrier* (1784) of Sébastien Mercier (1740–1814), are written in an exalted, declamatory prose, weighed down with moral sentiments, which now appears somewhat ludicrous in connexion with its homely application. Yet both Diderot and Mercier brought something to French drama which even La Chaussée had not adumbrated—man in relation to his social life. Grimm thought it likely that Diderot would bring back morality to France by force of dramatic examples, but he had to wait for his successors until the rhetoric of the Romantics had had its day. Mercier's plays were technically better than Diderot's, and his translation of Lillo's *London Merchant* as *Jenneval* (1768) reduced it to some order and unity of purpose. But his quarrels with the actors, and his unpopular political ideas, militated against his success, though his plays, when read, seem not to deserve the oblivion which has overtaken them.

The plays of Michel-Jean Sedaine (1719–97), though equally moral, are written with greater simplicity. Most of his work was done for the Opéra-Comique, and consisted of libretti for rustic comedies, sprung from the fashionable cult of the simple life. His best work, however, was *Le Philosophe sans le savoir* (1765). It has several dramatic moments, and even some touches of humour, a quality noticeably lacking in the *Béverlei* (1768) of Bernard-Joseph Saurin (1706–81), a *drame bourgeois* based on Moore's *The Gamester*. A tragedy by this author, *Blanche et Guisard* (1763), was expected to do well, but Mlle Clairon, who acted in it, says it was coldly received. The actors were, however, consoled for their disappointment by the sudden success, on patriotic grounds, of a poor play entitled *Le Siège de Calais* (1766) by Pierre-Laurent Buirette de Belloy (1727–75). Another dramatist who had some success at this time was Jean-François de La Harpe (1739–1802), who is, however, mainly remembered as a critic.

The Comédie-Française now decided to move, and leaving in 1770 the theatre which they had occupied since 1689, they went first to the Tuileries and, in 1782, to a new theatre on the present site of the Odéon. Mlle Clairon retired shortly before the first removal, and was replaced by two sisters, one known as Mlle Dugazon (1742–99), the other as Mlle Vestris (1743–1804), sister-in-law of the famous dancer. Her husband was an actor at the Comédie-Italienne. In 1786 was founded the École de Déclamation, which in 1793 became the present Conservatoire. Among the first pupils was Talma (1763–1826), later the outstanding actor of the Revolutionary period. One of his teachers, soon to become a close friend and supporter, was Molé (1734–1802), the chief actor of the time in comedy, who, by a curious irony, was destined to be the first French Hamlet. Struck by the overwhelming popularity of everything English, an unsuccessful dramatist, Jean-François Ducis (1733–1816), conceived the idea of refashioning the plays of Shakespeare, probably from an existing translation, to the taste of the time. This he did so successfully that *Hamlet* was produced in 1769, and was followed at short intervals by *Roméo et Juliette*, *Le Roi Lear*, *Macbeth*, *Jean sans terre*, and *Othello*.

In the welter of tears, piety, blood, sentimentality, and sheer dullness that characterizes most of the theatre of the second half of the eighteenth century, one writer of comedy stands out, Pierre-Augustin Caron de Beaumarchais (1732–99). This extraordinary man, whose life would provide material for half a dozen picaresque novels, was destined to be the one memorable name in the theatre of his time. This, however, was not immediately apparent. His first play, *Eugénie* (1767), written under the double influence of Diderot and Spain, was only moderately successful, as was *Les Deux amis* (1770), a somewhat arid financial drama. Then Beaumarchais, fresh from his encounters with Goezman and the French judicial system, wrote a light opera which he offered to the Comédie-Italienne. It was refused; the leading actor of the company had been a barber, and thought Beaumarchais's hero, also a barber, was intended as a caricature of himself. Rewritten as a five-act comedy in prose, *Le Barbier de Séville* was accepted by the Comédie-Française in 1772, but had to wait three years before it could be produced. It roused a storm of criticism such as the French theatre had not known since the days of *Tartuffe*. Complaints of its length, among other things, caused Beaumarchais to shorten it by one act, and in its final form it continued to be played successfully. It led Beaumarchais into arguments with the actors, however, since he had the temerity to question their traditional system of payments to authors, and the tenacity to get it altered. In spite of this first attack on their privileges, forerunner of many shocks which the established monopolists of the theatre were to suffer before the end of the century, the actors accepted *La Folle journée*, better known as *Le Mariage de Figaro*, which again had to wait three years, from 1781 to 1784, before it could be produced. It was read in the salons and at Court, and even asked for in Russia, before permission could be obtained for a public production. Its first night, with Dazincourt (1747–1809) as Figaro, and the charming Louise Contat (1760–1813) as Suzanne, assisted by Molé and Préville (the original Figaro), was a triumph. Dazzled by its wit, attracted by curiosity, and perhaps a little defiant, blind to its political significance, the audience that applauded it represented the very people who were later to suffer under the Revolution it presages.

Against the blaze of notoriety achieved by Beaumarchais, other writers of comedy stood little chance; but one charming little play deserves mention, *Les Châteaux en Espagne* (1789) by Collin d'Harleville (1755–1806), who might have written more and even better comedies had he not been overwhelmed by the Revolution, and persecuted by his rival, the revolutionary Fabre d'Églantine (1755–94), who paid for his excesses under the guillotine.

6. Revolution, Romanticism, and Realism. The Revolution, which produced only one

playwright, Marie-Joseph Chénier (1764–1811), whose historical dramas were contemporary events in disguise, first closed the theatres and then opened them to all comers. It did not cause as great a shock to theatrical life as did the Puritan interregnum in England. The French theatre was too firmly established for that, and had a longer tradition behind it. It did, however, put an end to the monopoly of the Comédie-Française, which had already suffered much, in the latter part of the century, from the activities of the unlicensed theatres, particularly those on the Boulevard du Temple, where even Nicolet with his performing monkey drew greater audiences than the king's players. The activities of Mlle Montansier (1730–1820), friend of Marie Antoinette and manageress of numerous provincial and suburban theatres, also caused the Comédie-Française some concern, particularly when she opened her own theatre in the grounds of the Palais-Royal. With the removal of all restrictions, theatres sprang up in every corner of Paris, and soon numbered nearly forty. The most important of the newcomers was the Odéon, which now ranks second only to the Comédie-Française. Founded and managed by Louis-Baptiste Picard (1769–1828), a capable man of the theatre who wrote most of its repertory himself, the Odéon provided light amusing plays which suited the taste of its audience and avoided giving offence to the censorship, re-established in 1804. Napoleon, though interested in the theatre, was too ready to suppress any manifestations of originality, and did not allow his authors that liberty accorded to Molière by Louis XIV. Consequently his Empire proved singularly barren in playwrights, and the one man who might have adorned it, Népomucène Lemercier (1771–1840), who tried unsuccessfully to establish historical romance, broke with his patron when he saw where ambition was taking him. Satire and comedy could not flourish, tragedy was out of date. The chief and most popular genre of the time, apart from operetta, was the vaudeville, child of the old theatres of the fair. Given at the secondary theatres, the Gaîté, Ambigu-Comique, Variétés, and Vaudeville, it provided light entertainment for the vast new theatre-going public, and at the same time served as the echo and mirror of the times. Under the Republic, the Empire, and the Restoration it continued undisturbed, its authors adapting their subjects to the prevailing ideology, with many a backward glance to the seemingly heroic ages of the past. But the great delight of the new, often illiterate, audiences who crowded the popular theatres were the melodramas of the prolific Guilbert de Pixerécourt (1773–1844), which delighted the uncritical with their swift, violent action, their mingling of bloodshed and sentimentality, their elaborate settings and stage effects, and their expert manipulations of well-worn themes, in which, after the pleasurable excitements of villainy, virtue rose triumphant. Many of Pixerécourt's works, which were influenced by the contemporary German theatre, found their way to London in adaptations, often without acknowledgement, and became the staple fare of the smaller theatres, and so of the Penny Plain, Tuppence Coloured Toy Theatre.

Pixerécourt wrote, as he himself said, for those who could not read. Meanwhile the elderly and learned formed a fast-diminishing audience for the frigid tragedies and dull comedies which were all that the Comédie-Française could offer. The time was ripe for a revival of French literary drama, and it came with the onslaught of Romanticism. The leader of the new movement was Victor Hugo (1802–85), its manifesto was contained in the Preface to his *Cromwell*, published in 1827, and its battle-cry was his *Hernani* (1830), whose first night was one of the most tempestuous the Comédie-Française had seen for a long time. *Ruy Blas* (1838), first seen at the Théâtre de la Renaissance, set the seal on the triumph of the new drama. But Hugo was more a poet than a dramatist. His plays pleased by their fine verses, by the audacity of their challenge to the unities and the outmoded restrictions of the classical theatre, and by their appeal to the youthful adherents of Romanticism. A far better dramatist, and the first to see his work on the stage, was Alexandre Dumas (1803–70), whose *Henri III et sa cour* was given in 1829. It was followed by a number of others, on subjects taken from all sides, from history, from legend, from the English stage (Kean), and finally from his own novels. Among them the best and most characteristic of Dumas's varied styles are the melodrama, *La Tour de Nesle* (1832), and *Antony* (1831), a study of the Romantic hero, *l'homme maudit*, driven to murder by the conventions of an unsympathetic environment.

Among the other dramatists of the Romantic period must be reckoned Alfred de Vigny (1797–1863), whose translation of *Othello* (1829) marked a step further in the acclimatization of Shakespeare in France, and yet another triumph for the Romantics. His best-known play, *Chatterton* (1835), based on the short life and tragic death of the English poet Thomas Chatterton, is a play of the emotions. It has little action, but appeals by its imaginative and psychological insight, showing, as it does, the anguish of the poet at grips with society.

The plays of Alfred de Musset (1810–57), charming trifles often based on popular sayings —*Il ne faut jurer de rien*, *Il faut qu'une porte soit ouverte ou fermée*, and *On ne badine pas avec l'amour*—together with such lyric fantasies as *Lorenzaccio* and *Fantasio*, were written at this time, but after the failure of his first play, *La Nuit vénitienne* (1830), were not acted. They had to be translated into Russian and discovered by the actress Mlle Allan-Despréaux (1810–56), who brought them back to Paris, before the French theatre would accept their delicate wit and melancholy, their mingling of imagination and caprice. Once acted, they proved popular, but they were written with no thought of the stage, and de Musset, child of Romanticism in his prose and poetry, had no influence on the drama of his time.

In any case the life of the Romantic theatre was short. It left behind it some fine works, but on the whole it was antipathetic to the true genius of France. The public, once so enthusiastic, wearied of its excesses, and in 1843 Hugo's *Les Burgraves* failed completely, while the calm neo-classicism of *Lucrèce*, by François Ponsard (1814–67), was acclaimed. It seemed as if there might be a classical revival, but the real taste of the time was shown in the popularity of the *comédie-vaudeville*, the light opera, and the 'well-made' plays of that prolific dramatist, Eugène Scribe (1791–1861), who, during the whole of the Romantic period, continued to turn out an inexhaustible supply of bourgeois comedies, beautifully constructed, optimistic, platitudinous, and no longer acted. Unlike the Romantics, who made high tragedy of everyday events, Scribe excelled in bringing great historical events down to the level of a second-rate boarding-house. Witness his *Verre d'eau* (1820), where the struggle of Whig and Tory under Queen Anne is reduced to an amorous intrigue more suited to a back drawing-room than to an English Court. Yet Scribe should not be despised. His technique was superb. He had none of the lavish disregard for probability and the general untidiness of the Romantics. His plots are so closely knit and so well dovetailed that no single incident can be omitted, and when the curtain comes down all the loose ends are gathered together and tied off. This was a great satisfaction to an audience which had been somewhat hurriedly introduced to the splendid irrelevancies of Shakespeare and his imitators, and brought Scribe and his numerous collaborators, of whom the best was Ernest Legouvé (1807–1903), a vast fortune and an undisputed eminence in the theatre of their time.

During the nineteenth century the French theatre slips away in all directions. The old signposts have gone. No longer can one follow the steady evolution of tragedy and comedy. Their component parts are broken up and scattered among a hundred different genres, ranging from the flamboyant historical romances of the early Romantics, through the staid bourgeois comedies of Scribe, to the farcical productions of the *théâtres des boulevards*. No longer is the Comédie-Française the only theatre whose actors are worthy of notice. Great reputations can be made elsewhere, as witness the careers of such actors as Frédérick (1800–76), the first to play Ruy Blas, Jean Gaspard Deburau (1796–1846), beloved Pierrot of the Funambules, of Mlle Dorval (1798–1849), star of the Porte-Saint-Martin, and many other favourites of the Parisian public too numerous to mention. Even the members of the Comédie-Française itself were not averse to seeking more remunerative employment elsewhere. Samson (1793–1871) signed a contract with another theatre which he was not, however, allowed to implement, and the greatest actress of the day, Rachel (1821–58), who had succeeded Mlle Mars (1779–1847), the Desdemona and Doña Sol of the Romantic theatre, as leading lady of the Comédie-Française, was more often in the provinces or abroad than in Paris. Yet her influence was considerable, and she revived the fine tradition of French classic acting which had almost been lost sight of in the upheavals of the Revolution and the vagaries of Romanticism. She was not immediately successful, but helped by the notices of the great critic and theatre historian Jules Janin (1804–74) in *Le Journal des débats*, she finally triumphed and brought a modicum of prosperity to the tottering fortunes of the French National Theatre. Reviving *Phèdre*, she revived at the same time the glories of French classical literature for an audience that had never known them. She could not, however, sustain alone the burden of a classic repertory, and received little support from her comrades, many of whom were jealous of her prestige, and not a little sarcastic over her frequent absences, and the Comédie-Française was glad to take over plays which had proved popular elsewhere. This was done in the case of *Le Gendre de M. Poirier* (1854), the best-known play of Émile Augier (1820–89), which had made a successful début at the Gymnase.

The Revolution of 1848 brought new preoccupations to the theatre, and the comedies of Scribe were replaced by a more serious type of social drama, though it was long before French dramatists broke away from the tradition of the 'well-made' play in matters of form. The first exponent of the new drama was Augier, who had been associated with Ponsard in the short-lived classical reaction against Romanticism. After writing a few plays in verse, he turned to prose and, basing his work on the doctrine of common sense, produced a number of *pièces à thèse* which glorified the virtues of the *bourgeoisie* and attacked the social problems of the day. It was in his political plays, many of them based on contemporary problems, that he scored his greatest triumphs. There was much in the régime of the Second Empire that merited his attention, and he was not slow to profit by his observations. *Les Effrontés* (1861) is an attack on contemporary journalism, *Le Fils de Giboyer* (1862) on contemporary politics. The latter, which is usually ranked as Augier's best play, had important repercussions, and was considered to be the manifesto of the liberal party. Of his other works, the best was probably *Les Lionnes pauvres* (1858), which dealt with the current social phenomenon of the wealthy courtesan, a subject taken up in a different spirit by the younger Dumas (1824–95) in his *Dame aux camélias* (1852). He, too, with perhaps even more success in his own day than Augier, treated social problems, and in *Le Demi-Monde* (1855), *Une Question d'argent* (1857), *Le Fils naturel* (1858), and right on to his last play, *Francillon* (1887), accustomed his audience to discussions of social and ethical problems, a habit which proved useful to later exponents of social drama.

It might be said of Augier and the younger Dumas that they set out to reform society by showing morality in action. They were seconded, rather faintly, by Octave Feuillet (1821–90) and Théodore Barrière (1823–77), while farcical comedy was kept alive by Eugène Labiche (1815–88), who set out frankly to amuse, and succeeded admirably, so well, in fact, that he was compared by his grateful contemporaries to Molière. The best of his plays, *Le Chapeau de paille d'Italie* (1851) and *Le Voyage de M. Perrichon* (1860), are still amusing, and bear revival. Their continued success may have been a tacit protest against the serious preoccupations of his rivals. But without doubt the spirit of the Second Empire finds its truest expression in light opera and in the musical burlesques of Henri Meilhac (1831–97) and Ludovic Halévy (1834–1908), whose collaboration produced *La Vie parisienne* (1866) and *Frou-Frou* (1869), as well as operettas like 'La Belle Hélène', with music by Offenbach. Better than anything they sum up the light-hearted, corrupt, and amusing world which came to an end in 1870.

Meanwhile the work of Scribe was continued by Victorien Sardou (1831–1908), who was at home in all types of play. Comedy of contemporary manners, historical romance, political satire, social drama—he brought to all of them the same technical ability and the same poverty of thought. In his hands any subject lost whatever depth it might have, and became simply a vehicle for a series of complicated intrigues. Yet Sardou must be credited with having provided some excellent parts for that incomparable actress Sarah Bernhardt (1845–1923), who, like Rachel, was a member of the Comédie-Française but had her greatest triumphs elsewhere. Indeed, much of the history of the French theatre from this time onwards must be sought outside the Comédie-Française, which tended to lag further and further behind the times, in spite of the excellence of such actors as Edmond Gôt (1822–1901) and the elder Coquelin (1841–1909) who appeared together in an amusing comedy by Édouard Pailleron (1834–99), *Le Monde où l'on s'ennuie* (1881), and who were responsible for the first visit of the Comédie-Française to London; the younger Coquelin (1848–1909); Jean Mounet-Sully (1841–1916), the outstanding tragic actor of his day; and Gustave-Hippolyte Worms (1836–1910), together with many excellent actresses. From time to time the venerable National Theatre suffered the shocks of modernization, and its opponents became its directors, but in the main it served as a repository of tradition. Like others before her, the fine comédienne Gabrielle Réjane (1857–1920) carried the glories of French art and acting all over Europe and America without ever setting foot in the National Theatre. The full tide of theatrical life must be looked for elsewhere, particularly in the experimental theatres of the end of the nineteenth century which heralded a new era.

7. THE THEATRE UP TO 1945. It is noticeable that during the nineteenth century the outstanding dramatists are not wholly addicted to the theatre, but are also poets, like Hugo, or, above all, novelists, like Dumas. Drama is no longer the pre-eminent literary genre as it was in the seventeenth and to a certain extent in the eighteenth century. It is therefore not surprising that the impulse towards a new realism in the theatre should have come from the novelists. Balzac, Flaubert, and the Goncourts had made tentative efforts in this direction, but it was Émile Zola (1840–1902) who first put their ideas into practice. He rejected with equal fierceness the problem plays of Augier and the younger Dumas, and the well-conducted intrigues of Scribe and Sardou, substituting for their artifices the naturalistic slogan of 'a slice of life'. His dramatization of his own novel, *Thérèse Raquin* (1873), was the first consciously naturalistic play, and paid for its temerity by being hissed off the stage. Yet the seed had been sown, and the harvest was reaped by Henri Becque (1832–99), whose plays were uncompromisingly naturalistic, the best known being *Les Corbeaux* (1882) and *La Parisienne* (1885).

Becque's work might, however, have rested without result had it not been for the efforts of André Antoine (1858–1943), who in 1887 founded the Théâtre Libre, and later the Théâtre Antoine (previously the Théâtre des Menus-Plaisirs), for the production of the new drama. Here, with actors trained in a new style of acting and with a new type of stage setting, he produced the plays of such great contemporary foreign dramatists as Ibsen, Strindberg, Hauptmann, and Tolstoy, as well as of his own countrymen, notably Georges Ancey (1860–1926), Octave Mirbeau (1850–1917), author of *Les Affaires sont les affaires* (1903), a sordid study of the lust for money, and Eugène Brieux (1858–1932). Antoine had a great influence on the European theatre, and his Théâtre Libre was a model for the Freie Bühne founded in Berlin in 1889, and the Independent Theatre which was established in London in 1891.

Of Antoine's authors the most important was Brieux, who was primarily a moralist and a reformer. His plays deal with specific problems and offer concrete remedies. This concentration on actualities dates many of them, but since most of the problems he treated are always with us, the best of his plays will bear revival. Among them are *Les Trois Filles de M. Dupont* (1897), which deals with the dangers of a marriage of convenience, and *Les Avariés* (1901), a study of the ravages of venereal disease. The latter, given in England and America as *Damaged Goods*, aroused much controversy on its first production.

Among the other exponents of naturalism in

France, albeit in a somewhat diluted form, were François de Curel (1854–1929), who brought an austere intellect to bear on social problems; Paul Hervieu (1857–1915), a writer in the tradition of the younger Dumas; and Henri Lavedan (1859–1940), whose work shows a curious mingling of realism and fantasy.

As was inevitable, a wave of reaction against naturalism soon set in, in which the Belgian poet Maurice Maeterlinck (1862–1949) was the leading figure. His symbolic dramas, which include *Pelléas et Mélisande* (1892) and *L'Oiseau bleu* (1908) (well known in English as *The Blue Bird*, with its sequel, *The Betrothal*), brought back poetry and a sense of wonder to a theatre which was in danger of losing both. The reaction was intensified by the distinguished talent of Edmond Rostand (1868–1918), whose fine verse plays, intensely theatrical and full of vitality, ensured him an enormous popularity which seems in no danger of diminishing. The best known are *Cyrano de Bergerac* (1898), a swashbuckling romance written for the elder Coquelin after he had left the Comédie-Française, and *L'Aiglon* (1900), a poignant evocation of Napoleon's young son, in which Sarah Bernhardt gave a most moving performance.

An author of the early twentieth century whose work defies classification, and who only became widely known after the Second World War, is Paul Claudel (1868–1955). Among his plays, which bear traces of symbolist influence, but are deeply impregnated with his fervent Catholicism, are *L'Otage* (1911) and *L'Annonce faite à Marie* (1912), while his *Soulier de satin*, written between 1919 and 1924, was given at the Comédie-Française in 1943 and has since been revived (see BARRAULT).

The production of *Amoureuse* (1894), by Georges de Porto-Riche (1849–1923), in which Gabrielle Réjane gave an outstanding performance, set the fashion for plays dedicated to the penetrating analysis of love and marriage, among them those of Maurice Donnay (1860–1945), Henri Bataille (1872–1922), and Henry Bernstein (1877–1953), while a more light-hearted approach to the subject is to be found in the comedies of Alfred Capus (1858–1922), of Georges Feydeau (1862–1921), and of Tristan Bernard (1866–1947), author of *L'Anglais tel qu'on le parle* (1899). A master of French farce was undoubtedly Georges Courteline (1861–1929), whose first plays were put on by Antoine, while Lucien Guitry (1860–1925) and his son Sacha (1885–1957) continued the tradition of many French actors by appearing in their own light comedies. Sacha in particular was the author of a number of amusing trifles, in which Yvonne Printemps (1895–), at one time his wife, appeared with him.

Shortly before the outbreak of the First World War, Jacques Copeau (1879–1949) started an experimental theatre known as the Vieux-Colombier, where fine work was done in the production of new authors, among them Charles Vildrac (1882–), whose *Paquebot Tenacity* was given in 1922, and in new productions of Shakespeare and other classics. An offshoot of this venture was the foundation of the Compagnie des Quinze under Michel Saint-Denis (1897–1971) for which André Obey (1892–) wrote *Noé* and *Le Viol de Lucrèce* (both 1931), the latter serving as the basis for Benjamin Britten's opera. At the same time the work of Antoine was being carried on by Aurélien-François Lugné-Poë (1869–1940) at the Théâtre de l'Œuvre, and by Georges Pitoëff (1886–1939), a Russian refugee who, with his wife Ludmilla, enriched the French stage with a number of productions of foreign authors, and some fine performances in his own subtle and delicately nuanced style.

The partnership of the actor Louis Jouvet (1887–1951) with the playwright Jean Giraudoux (1882–1944) produced some fine work, including *Amphitryon 38* (1936), in which the American actor Alfred Lunt and his wife Lynn Fontanne were later extremely successful in an English translation. It was at Jouvet's theatre too (formerly the Comédie des Champs-Élysées) that *La Machine infernale* (1934) by Jean Cocteau (1892–1963) was first produced. Cocteau, a versatile author, wrote also *Les Parents terribles* (1938) and symbolist dramas which turn to surrealism, while the work of Maeterlinck was developed and intensified in the expressionist plays of Henri René Lenormand (1882–1951) and the subtle psychological dramas of Jean-Jacques Bernard (1888–1951). Three important events of the late 1930s were the appointment of Jouvet to a professorship at the Conservatoire, the invitation to Jouvet and Édouard Bourdet (1887–1945) to produce at the Comédie-Française, and the formation, with financial assistance from the State, of a combination of theatre directors known as the Cartel, and including, with Jouvet and Pitoëff, the actor Charles Dullin (1885–1949) and the producer Gaston Baty (1885–1952). It seemed as if the Comédie-Française might once more take a leading part in the theatrical life of Paris, and although the German occupation of France from 1940 to 1945 shattered a great many hopes, this one was in part realized.

ED.

8. THE THEATRE SINCE 1945. The production at the Comédie-Française in 1943 of Claudel's *Le Soulier de satin* was the first of a series by Jean-Louis Barrault (*Partage de midi* in 1948, *L'Échange* in 1951, *Le Livre de Christophe Colomb* in 1953, *Tête d'Or* in 1959) which did much to establish this long-neglected dramatist's work on the stage. The novelist Henri de Montherlant (1896–), whose play *Pasiphaé* had been performed in 1938, turned seriously to the theatre after the success of *La Reine morte* at the Comédie-Française in 1942; his subsequent plays include *Le Maître de Santiago* (1947), *Celles qu'on prend dans ses bras* (1950), *Malatesta* (1950), *Port-Royal* (1954), and *Don Juan* (1958). Both Claudel and Montherlant are essentially Christian dramatists, concerned mainly with

theological issues, and a note of greater immediacy came with the work of the Existentialist philosopher, Jean-Paul Sartre (1905–), the one outstanding talent to emerge during the war. His first play, *Les Mouches* (1943), dealt with the contemporary situation of occupied France through the legend of Orestes and Electra. *Huis-clos* (1944) (known in English as *Vicious Circle* or *No Exit*), *Les Mains sales* (1948), *Le Diable et le Bon Dieu* (1951), *Nekrassov* (1955), and *Les Séquestrés d'Altona* (1959), established him firmly as a major dramatist. Jean Anouilh (1910–), noted before the war as a promising young playwright, put on under the German occupation an *Antigone* (1944) which provided a rallying-point for the aspirations of insurgent youth. A steady stream of successful plays followed, all brilliantly stageworthy but increasingly revealing a certain shallowness in inspiration. For several years following the end of the war, Anouilh was France's most popular and frequently produced dramatist abroad. His only real rival in popularity has been André Roussin (1911–), prolific author of gay comedies, notably *La Petite Hutte* (1947) and *Les Œufs de l'autruche* (1948) (done in English as *The Little Hut* and *Hippo Dancing*), *Nina* (1949), *Bobosse* (1950), *L'Amour fou* (1955), and *La Mamma* (1957). The most important figure in the immediate post-war years was undoubtedly the actor-director Jean-Louis Barrault (1910–), who with his wife formed in 1946 the Compagnie Madeleine-Renaud-Jean-Louis Barrault. From 1946 to 1956, at the Théâtre Marigny, Barrault mounted a memorable series of productions, carrying on the traditions of the Cartel, not only in his intelligent choice of repertoire from classical and modern plays, but in his boldly experimental use of staging and lighting. Even Barrault, however, was unable to stimulate any real creative surge in playwriting, and most of his best work was done in classical revivals, or in work with writers who, like Claudel and Montherlant, were already established in the theatre or in other fields of literature: Anouilh (*La Répétition*, 1950); Albert Camus (*L'État de siège*, 1948); Armand Salacrou (*Les Nuits de la colère*, 1946); André Obey (*Lazare*, 1951); and Jean Cocteau (*Bacchus*, 1951). In 1951, the actor-director Jean Vilar (1912–71), who had attracted attention in particular with his productions of Strindberg, was appointed to the directorship of the Théâtre National Populaire, and soon turned it into one of the best companies in Paris, supplementing Barrault's work at the Marigny, but tapping an entirely new, young, and popular audience, and staging his productions with startling simplicity. He resigned in 1963.

Two dramatists of importance did, however, emerge at this time, in Jean Genet (1910–) and Jacques Audiberti (1899–1965). Genet's first play, *Les Bonnes*, was produced by Louis Jouvet in 1947 without much success; but with *Le Balcon* (Paris, 1960, but performed in London three years earlier as *The Balcony*), *Les Nègres* (1959), and *Les Paravents* (1961), the exceptional brilliance and clarity of his use of language became evident, and he managed to impose his conception of theatre as masquerade. Audiberti's first play, *Quoat-Quoat*, was produced in 1946, and already showed the curious and highly personal mixture of farce, melodrama, parody, and poetry which he was to develop further in *Le Mal court* (1947), *La Hobereauté* (1958), and *L'Effet Glapion* (1959).

After the war the restriction of production, and the disappearance of the provincial theatres and old touring system, had meant that theatrical activity became centred almost entirely on Paris. The Théâtre National Populaire's movement to secure a new audience was greatly aided by the formation, between 1946 and 1961, of seven 'Centres Dramatiques', all run with state and local financial aid with the intention of providing genuinely regional theatres and cultural centres, at Strasbourg, St-Étienne, Rennes, Aix-en-Provence, Toulouse, Lille, and Bourges. To these should be added the Théâtre de la Cité de Villeurbanne, founded by Roger Planchon (1931–) in 1957 with the aid of of a municipal subsidy. Greatly influenced by the work of Bertolt Brecht and Jean Vilar, Planchon is now generally recognized as one of the most stimulating directors in the French theatre, particularly for his work in presenting classical plays in a new light. In 1959, when the Minister of Culture, André Malraux, announced his plan to reorganize the national theatres in the hope of improving the theatrical climate, the Théâtre de la Cité was awarded a state subsidy, and Planchon became the director of the first 'Théâtre Populaire de province' (i.e. the provincial equivalent of Jean Vilar). At the same time, the two theatres of the Comédie-Française were separated. The Comédie-Française, accused of neglecting classical tragedy to concentrate on farce and light comedy, retained the Salle Richelieu; while the Salle Luxembourg (or Odéon, annexed to the Comédie-Française in 1946; now renamed the Théâtre de France) was given to Jean-Louis Barrault, whose company had toured or been temporarily housed in various theatres since he had lost the lease of the Marigny in 1956. The Comédie-Française's subsidy was cut by approximately one quarter, this sum being awarded to Barrault. In order to stimulate new and experimental writing, which he had been unable to attempt in the enormous and costly Palais de Chaillot (home of the Théâtre National Populaire), Jean Vilar was given a second theatre, the Théâtre Recamier, seating 600. As his subsidy was not increased, he was forced to abandon this second theatre within eighteen months, though not before he had initiated several interesting experiments, notably *Le Crapaud-buffle* (1959) by Armand Gatti (1924–), *Les Bâtisseurs d'Empire* (1959) by Boris Vian (1919–1959), and *Génousie* (1960) by René de Obaldia (1918–). After 1950, French playwriting took a sudden step forward with the development of what has come to be called the Theatre of the Absurd, which developed partly out of the Existentialist philosophy of the absurdity of the human condition in a world where purpose has been destroyed and values devalued, and partly out of the surrealistic tradition and dislocation of language which has descended from Alfred Jarry, and particularly his play, *Ubu Roi* (1896). The earliest manifestations on the stage came from Arthur Adamov (1908–) (*La Grande et la Petite Manœuvre* and *L'Invasion*, both 1950; *Le Professeur Taranne* and *Tous contre tous*, both 1953) and Eugène Ionesco (1912–) (*La Cantatrice chauve*, 1950; *La Leçon*, 1951; *Les Chaises*, 1952; *Victimes du devoir*, 1953). Adamov, who made less use of puns and dislocation of language than Ionesco, changed styles in 1955 with *Le Ping-Pong*, and turned to reality and social satire; Ionesco has been unable to sustain the style fully in his full-length plays, *Tueur sans gages* (1959) and *Rhinocéros* (1960). It is too early to be sure where this development will lead, except to say that in Samuel Beckett (1906–) it has produced at least one major dramatist. *En Attendant Godot* (1953), *Fin de partie* (1957), and *Oh, Les Beaux Jours!* (1961), reveal an unequalled theatrical power, depth of vision and mastery of language. T. C. C. MILNE

In a brief survey of the French theatre during the last fifty or more years, no space has been given to those lesser but typically Parisian amusements, the revue, the *café-chantant*, the cabaret. They deserve a whole volume to themselves, and have produced a number of stars, like Mistinguett (1875–1956), Yvette Guilbert (1865–1944), Maurice Chevalier (1889–1972), and many others, known and loved far beyond the confines of Paris. They are an integral part of the theatre, though they stand a little outside the main stream which we have been considering here, and their work is often so much a matter of improvisation and atmosphere, their material, in its topicality, so ephemeral, that it would seem an impossible task to pin down their excellence on paper. They should be remembered, however, since they represent the quintessence of that Gallic wit and gaiety which is one of the outstanding characteristics of the French theatre.

FRANK, BRUNO (1887–1946), modern German playwright who, in reaction from the extreme drama of the realists and expressionists, wrote a number of light, sophisticated comedies. Of these *Sturm im Wasserglas* (1930) was successfully given in England in an adaptation by James Bridie as *Storm in a Teacup* and in America as *Storm over Patsy*. Frank has also written some historical dramas, of which the best and most characteristic is *Zwölftausend* (1927). In an English translation this was successful in New York, and was seen in London in 1931.

FRANKLIN THEATRE, NEW YORK, a small building at 175 Chatham Street, holding about 600 people. It opened on 7 Sept. 1835 with a good company in *The School of Reform*, followed by some classic comedies. It soon degenerated into melodrama and farce, however, in spite of a long visit by Booth in 1836–7; but this theatre is memorable as being the first at which the famous Joseph Jefferson, then aged 8, appeared on a New York play-bill. It closed for a time in late 1837 and reopened under a succession of managers, who were never able to achieve its initial popularity. It was finally vanquished by the success of the New Chatham Theatre, and in 1840 was taken over by a semi-professional group of German actors. It later housed variety, and was run for a short time by the great Yankee actor Hill. Early in 1841 the actors from the Park, which was at that time given over to balls and concerts, gave a successful season at the Franklin Theatre, which also saw the first productions in New York of *Fifteen Years of a New York Fireman's Life* and *Money*. It then struggled along under various names, but forsook legitimate drama and ended up as a home of pantomime and minstrel shows.

FRANZ, ELLEN, see MEININGER COMPANY.

FRASER, CLAUDE LOVAT (1890–1921), English artist and stage-designer, many of whose early and most imaginative designs were published in *Flying Fame* (1913). The first of his settings to impress the theatre-going public were those for *As You Like It* and *The Beggar's Opera*, at the Lyric Theatre, Hammersmith, in 1920. The latter, in particular, may be said to have inaugurated a new era in stage design. He also worked extensively for ballet and opera. Albert Rutherston, who in 1923 collaborated with John Drinkwater in a memoir of Fraser, said of him that his inspiration came 'especially from the 18th and early 19th century. His work stands for a gay, brightly coloured romanticism.' His early death was a great loss to English art and to the theatre, and his influence, when one considers how brief was his career, has been phenomenal (see Nos. 156, 174).

FRÉDÉRICK [really ANTOINE-LOUIS-PROSPER LEMAÎTRE] (1800–76), celebrated French actor, who embodied in himself all the glory and excesses of the Romantic drama, many of whose heroes he created. Usually known as Frédérick (his grandfather's name, which he took when he went on the stage unbeknown to his family), he was a unique personality, his art proceeding from a judicious blending of application and intuition. He never appeared at the Comédie-Française, which was then in the hands of elderly and incompetent actors clinging to the last vestiges of the classical tradition soon to be reanimated by Rachel, and he spent most of his career in the theatres of the Boulevard du Temple, living long enough to see Haussmann pull them all down in his rebuilding of Paris. It was on the Boulevard du Temple, at the Variétés-Amusantes, that he made his first appearance at the age of 15, as the lion in *Pyrame et Thisbé*. He then went to the Funambules, where he was a contemporary of the great mime Deburau, and was successful enough to be admitted to classes at the Conservatoire. At the same time he appeared at the Cirque-Olympique, where melodramas were given in between the circus acts, and soon became one of the most popular actors in Paris. From the Conservatoire he was admitted to the Odéon in 1820, but he found the audiences apathetic and opportunities for sustained acting too few, and he was glad to return to the popular stage, replacing Fresnoy at the Ambigu-Comique. It was here that he made his first appearance as Robert Macaire in *L'Auberge des Adrets* (1823) a part ever after associated with him, and one which he frequently revived. The play had been written as a serious melodrama, but Frédérick, sensing that the public were beginning to tire of the genre, carried it to an unexpected success by burlesquing it. He was equally successful in a sequel, *Robert Macaire* (1834), much of which he wrote himself. Like Figaro, Macaire had political repercussions, and it was said that the plays in which he appeared contributed not a little to the downfall of Louis-Philippe. Frédérick, who was always at his best in strong parts, whether melodramatic or comic, made a tremendous impression at the Porte-Saint-Martin in *Trente Ans, ou la Vie d'un joueur* (1827), a powerful play on the evils of gambling in which he literally terrified his audiences. After this and other successes he returned to the Odéon, where, in spite of a more critical audience, he was an outstanding success, rising nobly to the demands made upon him, and shedding some of his earlier crudities. All his life he combined to an unusual degree the power to move the masses while retaining the respect of the critics. Among his later successes were Othello, in Ducis's translation, and several of the leading roles in Dumas's plays, notably in *Kean, ou Désordre et génie* (1836), which was specially written for him, as was Balzac's *Vautrin* (1840). When in 1838 Dumas and Hugo took over the old Théâtre Ventadour and renamed it the Théâtre de la Renaissance, Frédérick opened it as the home of Romantic drama with an electrifying performance of Ruy Blas, the lackey who falls in love with a queen. This play gave great offence to Queen Victoria when Frédérick played it in London in 1852, though she had been one of his greatest admirers on his previous visits, enjoying his Don César de Bazan in 1845, and commenting favourably in her diary in 1847 on his performance in *Le Docteur noir*. He had been seen in London even earlier, making his first appearance at the Tottenham Street Theatre in 1828 in *Trente Ans, ou la Vie d'un joueur*, and in 1835 in a repertory which included *Robert Macaire*. Frédérick's last years were unhappy. The taste of the public had changed, and though he continued to act until almost the end of his life with little diminution of his powers, he could find only trivial or unsuitable plays to appear in. But he left his mark on the theatre, and when Bateman first saw Irving in *The Bells* he could bestow no higher praise on him than to say that 'the acting was equal to Lemaître's'. One of Frédérick's nicknames was 'the Talma of the Boulevards' which he considered a great compliment, as he had the highest opinion of his famous predecessor's gifts. It was therefore ironic that Talma should have died on Frédérick's wedding day.

FREDRO, Aleksander (1793–1876), Polish poet and playwright. Son of an aristocratic family, he served in Napoleon's Grand Army from 1809 to 1814, and then settled down on his estates. His comedies, which are written in strict classic form and in impeccable verse, deal with the life of the country gentleman as he knew it, or had heard of it from his elders. Among them the best are *Husband and Wife* (1822), which deals boldly with the problems of marriage, *Maidens' Vows* (1833), and *Vengeance* (1834). An English version of the lively farce *Ladies and Hussars* (1825) was acted in New York in 1925. His plays are still in the Polish repertory, and in 1964 his comedy, *The Life Annuity* (1835), was done by a visiting Polish company, in the original, at the Aldwych.

FREEDLEY, George (1904–67), American theatre historian, founder and director of the Theatre Collection of the New York Public Library, which in 1956 celebrated its twenty-fifth anniversary. On this occasion Freedley was awarded the Kelcey Allen Award for distinguished services to the American theatre. A graduate of the Baker Workshop at Yale, he became an actor for a short time, and was then associated with the Theatre Guild. In 1931 he joined the staff of the New York Public Library. In addition to the Theatre Collection there, he founded the Theatre Library Association and the Equity Library Theatre, and from 1946–64 was secretary of the New York Drama Critics' Circle. He lectured and wrote extensively on the theatre, and was at one time dramatic critic of the New York *Morning Telegraph*, for which he later became feature writer and book editor. He was part-author of *A History of the Theatre* (with John Reeves), of *A History of Modern Drama* (with Barrett H. Clark), and of *Theatre Collections in Libraries and Museums* (with Rosamond Gilder).

FREIE BÜHNE, Die, was founded by Otto Brahm in 1889 on the lines of Antoine's Théâtre Libre in Paris, for the production of the plays of the new naturalistic school of writers inspired by Ibsen. The society had no fixed theatre, and gave only matinées. Its first production was Ibsen's *Ghosts*, followed by translations of plays by Tolstoy, Strindberg, and Zola. The first German play to be given was Hauptmann's *Vor Sonnenaufgang*, but the real manifesto of the new movement was *Die Familie Selicke*, a sordid picture of lower middle-class life, played in a realistic manner against an equally realistic background. The actors of Brahm's company had to be trained anew to interpret characters so far removed from the conventional heroes and heroines of the contemporary theatre, and this led to the formation of a permanent company, whose chief actor was Emanuel Reicher. This in turn led to a growing desire for something more stable than the sporadic employment afforded by the Freie Bühne, and the consequent amalgamation in 1894 with the older and well-established Deutsches Theater. The movement, however, had achieved its object and its impulse continued to be felt.

In 1890 the Freie Volksbühne was founded for the purpose of bringing good plays at low prices within the reach of the working-class population. Admittance was limited to subscribers, who drew lots for their seats.

FRENCH BRACE, see STAGE BRACE.

FRENCH FLAT, the name given to a series of flats battened together and 'flown' as one piece (see FLAT).

FRENCH PLAYERS' THEATRE, a temporary playhouse fitted up in a riding school in Drury Lane, kept by a Frenchman, N. Le Febure. It was used in 1635 by a company of French actors under Floridor [Josias de Soulas].

FRESNEL SPOTLIGHT, see LIGHTING, 3.

FREYTAG, GUSTAV (1816–95), German writer. Best known as the author of sociological and historical novels, he began his literary career as a dramatist. He was the German exponent of the 'well-made' play of France, and two somewhat artificial serious plays, exalting the sterling qualities of the *bourgeoisie* in contrast to the flightiness of the gentry, were followed by an excellent comedy, *Die Journalisten* (1852), a good-humoured portrayal of party politics in a small town during an election. This can still be read with pleasure, but his attempt at an historical tragedy in verse is less attractive. In 1863 Freytag published his *Technik des Dramas*, with its famous pyramid, or diagrammatic plot of a 'well-made' play.

FRIDOLIN, see CANADA.

FRISCH, MAX, (1911–   ), playwright, born in Zürich. Frisch is one of the few followers of Brecht who recognizes what he owes to him. His first play, *Nun singen sie wieder* (1945), evokes, in a series of scenes, all the sorrows and squalor of war. In the course of the action the dead, singing of their hopes for peace, mingle with the living, although the latter remain unaware of their presence. *Die chinesische Mauer* (1946) was a comment on the atom bomb, again in the form of a loosely connected series of scenes—almost an historical pageant. Cleopatra, Columbus, Romeo and Juliet, Napoleon, and many others appear, and their actions are commented on by 'Der Heutige' who realizes finally that he cannot change the course of history, and that all his warnings will go unheeded. *Als der Krieg zu Ende war* (1949) is set in Berlin at the end of the war in Europe. A woman finds herself in love with a Russian billeted in her house. At the same time she manages to keep her husband concealed in the basement, unknown to her lover. When she discovers that her husband is guilty of war crimes, and that he has been willing to turn a blind eye to her infidelity in order to save himself, she decides that the only way out is for her to commit suicide. In *Graf Öderland* (1951), Frisch tries to show the chaos of life today—a judge suddenly abandons his former respectable way of life and takes to crime, becoming the leader of a terrorist band with its headquarters in a city sewer. They terrorize the government and eventually defeat it; but at this moment the judge decides to restore the government and to die himself, as death is the only freedom. At no point in this cynical drama can one be sure if the judge is mad or sane, but a certain nightmarish logic proves the close affinity between order and chaos in man and the community.

In complete contrast to these moral dramas Frisch has also written plays of a more romantic flavour, such as *Santa Cruz* (1946) and *Don Juan, oder Die Liebe zur Geometrie* (1953). The former concerns three characters, a man, his wife, and Pelegrin. Many years ago they had met abroad when the wife was Pelegrin's mistress. His reappearance causes the husband and wife to relive the past in their minds, but this time the result is different—the roles of the husband and wife are reversed. The whole play is a blend of dream and reality. In *Don Juan* Frisch gives a new twist to the old legend. Don Juan's only interest in life is geometry; he has no time for women. Therefore they are attracted to him and in the end he finds that his only way of escape is marriage. In 1958, after devoting the intervening years mainly to writing fiction, Frisch produced two short plays, *Biedermann und die Brandstifter*, which he termed a 'Lehrstück ohne Lehre', and *Die grosse Wut des Philipp Hotz*, which is nothing more than a farce. Both plays have a running commentary, provided in the first by a chorus of firemen, in the second by the husband who sometimes steps out of his part to address the audience, very much as in the Brecht plays. As *The Fire Raisers*, the first had a successful run at the Royal Court in 1961. Frisch's *Andorra* (1961) has had a resounding theatrical success. An illegitimate child is brought up by his father as a Jew and is so influenced by public opinion that when he learns the truth about himself he is unable to discard his Jewishness. He finally accepts martyrdom at the hands of an anti-semitic invader. During the play the citizens of Andorra (an imaginary State) change from easy-going pleasant people to a rabble lusting for revenge. In 1964 this play was given twice in London, in German by the Schiller Theater, and in English at the National Theatre.

DOROTHY MOORE

FROHMAN. (1) DANIEL (1851–1940), American theatre manager. In his early days he was a journalist, but in 1880 became business manager of the Madison Square Theatre, where he remained for some years. He first went into management on his own account in 1885, when he took the old Lyceum Theatre, New York. Here he brought together an excellent stock company, and was responsible for a number of outstanding productions, including plays by Pinero and H. A. Jones. It was under Daniel Frohman's management that E. H. Sothern scored his earliest successes. When the old Lyceum closed in 1902, Frohman became owner of the new theatre bearing the same name. He was also manager of Daly's New York Theatre from 1899 to 1903. In 1911 he published a volume of reminiscences, *Memories of a Manager*, and followed it in 1935 by *Daniel Frohman Presents*. On the death of his youngest brother (see below (3) CHARLES) he took over the administration of his affairs in America. He was also active in the film world. His brother (2) GUSTAVE (1855–1930) was also a theatre manager. The best known of the family, however, is the youngest brother, (3) CHARLES (1860–1915), who was as well known and as well liked in England as in America. Like his brothers, he inherited a love of the theatre, and made it his life. From selling souvenirs and programmes he graduated to walking-on, and then to various grades of executive rank, learning all there was to know about theatrical business, and storing it away in his extremely alert and lively mind. He first visited England in 1880 as business manager of Haverley's Minstrels, for whom he achieved great things, including Royal patronage. He liked England, and decided to return. Back in America he became a manager, a dramatic agent, and an organizer of touring companies. His first great success came in 1888–9 with the production of *Shenandoah*. This had a long run and laid the foundations of his fortune, since he had had the acumen to purchase the American rights. In 1893 he opened the Empire Theatre with a fine stock company, which he maintained for many years, and he soon had a controlling interest in many other theatres, in New York and elsewhere. His first venture in London was not a success, but his second, when he produced *A Night Out* at the Vaudeville in 1896, made up for it. He then joined forces with the Gattis, with George Edwardes, and with Barrie, taking Edwardes's musical comedies and Barrie's plays to America. Feeling the need for a permanent theatre in London, he leased the Duke of York's from Violet Melnotte, and made many notable productions there, including Barrie's *Peter Pan* (1904). At one time he had five London theatres under his control, but his efforts to establish a repertory theatre at the Duke of York's in 1910 were unavailing. He was drowned when the *Lusitania* was torpedoed in 1915. A memorial to him was later erected in Marlow churchyard. A small, odd-looking man, very like a little Buddha, he was charming, kindly, helpful to everyone, and never had a contract with anyone; his word was good enough. He was sincerely mourned in England, a country to which he was deeply attached, and left behind him a name for honour and fair dealing, and a record of remarkable achievements in both London and New York. W. MACQUEEN POPE†

FRONT OF HOUSE, a term applied to those parts of a theatre which appertain to the audience as distinct from the performers. These include the auditorium, the passages, lobbies and foyers, the bars, cloakrooms, and refreshment-rooms, and the box-office or pay-box for the booking of seats, the whole being under the supervision of a front-of-house manager.

FRY, CHRISTOPHER [really HARRIS, Fry being his mother's maiden name] (1907–), English dramatist who achieved a great success with his poetic plays from 1949 to 1956. In his early days he was a schoolmaster, actor, and theatre director. He first came into prominence with a one-act *jeu d'esprit*, *A Phoenix Too Frequent*, based on Petronius's story of the widow of Ephesus, which was produced at the Mercury Theatre, and later transferred to the Arts. He had previously written a couple of pageants and a religious play about St. Cuthbert entitled *The Boy with a Cart* (1937). In 1948 *Thor, With Angels* was produced at the Canterbury Festival, and in 1950 *The Firstborn* was given a professional production at the Winter Garden with Alec Clunes as Moses. It was, however, with the production, first at the Arts, and later at the Globe Theatre, in 1949, of *The Lady's Not For Burning* that Fry sprang into the limelight. With Gielgud and Pamela Brown heading a distinguished cast, the play had a long run, and seemed to herald a renaissance of poetry on the English stage (see No. 107). It was said at the time that Fry's main achievement consisted 'in the long-needed reinstatement of the Comic Spirit in English poetic drama'. His next play, written for Laurence Olivier, was *Venus Observed* (1950), and in the same year he translated Anouilh's *Invitation au Château*, which, as *Ring Round the Moon*, with Scofield in the dual role of the twin hero and villain, had a long run. In 1954 Edith Evans starred in *The Dark is Light Enough*. In the meantime Fry had reverted to his earlier biblical vein with *A Sleep of Prisoners* (1951), a play planned for performance in churches. It was seen at St. Thomas's, Regent Street, in 1951, and frequently revived. After the production of *The Dark is Light Enough*, which, in spite of Edith Evans's superb acting, did not have the success that was hoped for, Fry remained quiescent for some time except for translations (Anouilh's *L'Alouette* (on Joan of Arc) as *The Lark* and Giraudoux's *La Guerre de Troie n'aura pas lieu* as *Tiger at the Gates*, both 1955. The latter, with Michael Redgrave as Hector, had successful runs in London and New York). It was by now obvious that the trend of the time was away from, rather than towards, poetry, and his next play, *Curtmantle* (on Henry II and Becket), had its first production in translation at the opening on 1 Mar. 1961 of the Stadsschouwburg Theatre, Tilburg, Holland. It was seen in London a year later, in a production by the London company of the Royal Shakespeare Theatre. A 'summer comedy', *A Yard of Sun*, was performed at Nottingham in 1970.

FULL SCENERY, that system of setting where all the parts of the stage picture belong to the current scene only and must be changed for another scene, as against Detail Scenery or Permanent Setting, where the scenic element amounts only to a part of the whole picture, the rest being a neutral or generalized background remaining in place for the whole of the performance.

FULLER, ISAAC (1606–72), English scene-painter, who studied in Paris under François Perrier, probably at the new Academy there. He worked for the Restoration theatre, and in 1669 painted a scene of Paradise for the Theatre Royal's production of *Tyrannic Love*, later suing the company for payment. He was awarded £335. 10*s*. 0*d*.—a large sum in those days—but his scene may have been utilized for other plays.

FULLER, ROSALINDE (1901–), English actress who made her first success in America, where, after touring with her sisters in a programme of folk-songs, she appeared on Broadway and in 1922 played Ophelia to John Barrymore's Hamlet. After a season with the Provincetown Players and further appearances on Broadway, she made her first appearance in London in 1927. Among her outstanding parts were the Betrothed in *The Unknown Warrior* and Irina in *Three Sisters*. She was also seen in a number of Shaw plays, and in 1940 she joined Donald Wolfit's company, playing Viola, Katharine, Desdemona, Portia, and Beatrice. In 1950 she first appeared alone in a programme entitled *Masks and Faces*, consisting of her own adaptations of a number of short stories. She has since toured in this, and in a similar programme, *Subject to Love*, under the auspices of the British Council, visiting the Middle East in 1958, South Africa in 1960 and 1961, Australia in 1962, and the Far East in 1964. She has also made several tours of the United States. Her slight figure and mobile expressive face lend themselves well to her various impersonations, which she performs in costume and with a minimum of scenery. They range from Dickens to de Maupassant, Henry James, and Katherine Mansfield.

FULTON THEATRE, NEW YORK, originally the Folies-Bergère, the first theatre-restaurant on Broadway. It opened on 26 Apr. 1911, but its prices were considered too high, and it soon closed. Remodelled as a regular playhouse, and renamed the Fulton, it opened again on 20 Oct. 1911 with a series of short-lived comedies. Its first hit was *The Yellow Jacket*, which ran for ten weeks. Equally good, though in a more serious vein, was Brieux's *Damaged Goods*. A record for the theatre of 411 performances was set up by the farce *Twin Beds*. A revival of *A Woman of No Importance* in 1916 was moderately successful, while in 1921 *Abie's Irish Rose* started its record run here, before moving to the Republic. Among later interesting productions were *The High Road* (1928) with Edna Best and Herbert Marshall, *Oscar Wilde* (1938) with Robert Morley, and *Arsenic and Old Lace* (1941), which set up a new record with 1,437 performances. A moving play on the Negro problem, *Deep are the Roots*, was seen at this theatre in 1945. In 1955 it was renamed the Helen Hayes, in recognition of that celebrated actress's fifty years on the stage, and in 1958 she appeared there herself as the mother, Nora, in O'Neill's *A Touch of the Poet*. The theatre's longest run to date—three years—has been Jean Kerr's *Mary, Mary*, which opened in 1962. GEORGE FREEDLEY†

FUNAMBULES, THÉÂTRE DES, PARIS, situated on the Boulevard du Temple. The name of this theatre was derived from the Latin name for rope-dancers, and it began as a booth for acrobats and pantomime. In 1816 the booth was replaced by a permanent playhouse which, under the existing laws, had to have a barker outside, while the actors, even in slightly serious roles, had to indulge in somersaults and handsprings. In 1820 Deburau was in the company, but had not yet made his name as Pierrot, and most of the pantomimes still had Arlequin as hero. It was in them that the great actor Frédérick made his first appearances. In 1830 the new liberty of the theatres allowed the Funambules to play vaudeville and to do away with the tight-rope and acrobatics. Then came the great vogue of Deburau as Pierrot, celebrated by Jules Janin and visited by all Paris, and by other great actors, who were not ashamed to admire this unique pantomimist. The Funambules offered to its patrons no other star but Deburau until his death, though he was always surrounded by a good company. Fairy-plays were given with wonderful scenery, transformations, and tricks. The stage was excellently equipped, and even had apparatus for the production of a real waterfall. When Bertrand, the original owner, retired, his son took over until 1843, when the theatre was rebuilt, with 500 more places, and the prices raised. It continued to flourish, still with Deburau, for whom good writers turned out pantomimes, mimes, and fairy-plays. Everything was going well when Deburau died on 17 June 1846. Luckily the theatre was able to continue, with Charles Deburau and Paul Legrand successively as Pierrot, until it was demolished by Haussmann in 1862.

FURNITURE STORE, a room opening from the stage, where stage furniture, as distinct from scenery or properties, is stored.

FURTENBACH, JOSEF (1591–1667), see JESUIT DRAMA, LIGHTING, 1 *a* and SCENERY, 2.

FUZELIER, LOUIS (1672–1752), French author, whose plays were written mainly for the small theatres of the Paris fairs, with Piron, Dorneval, and Le Sage. The Comédie-Française having tried to stop their performances, regarding them as an infringement of their monopoly, Fuzelier and his companions solved their difficulties by writing the verses on long placards, held up by two children dressed as cupids, so that the audience could sing them to a popular air while the actors mimed the action. Many of Fuzelier's plays, written for this convention, are very charming and have been reprinted in numerous collections. He also wrote several serious plays, done at the Comédie-Française, of which none has survived. He was editor of the *Mercure* from 1744 to 1752, and wrote widely for it on the theatre and other subjects.

FYFFE, WILL (1885–1947), music-hall comedian, who was born in Dundee and as a boy toured Scotland in a stock company run by his father. Here he played all sorts of parts, including Shakespeare, but made his first appearance as Little Willie in *East Lynne*. He played Polonius at the age of 15. He then went into revue, and when some ideas for Scottish character sketches had been refused by Harry Lauder and Neil Kenyon, he decided to go on the halls and use them himself. He was a great success, and by 1921 was at the top of the bill, where he remained till his death. His art lay in his grasp of character and his really fine acting. His people lived, whether they were an engineer on a liner, a guard on a Highland railway, or a centenarian desiring to ride a motor-bicycle. He was also one of the best pantomime comedians of his day. During the Second World War he was created C.B.E. in recognition of his tireless war work.

W. MACQUEEN-POPE†

G

GABRIELLI. A family of actors of the *commedia dell'arte*, of whom the father, (1) GIOVANNI (*c.* 1588–*c.* 1635), played under the name of Sivello. He was a whole company in himself, taking each personage of a comedy in turn, either with or without a mask. His son (2) FRANCESCO (?–1654), the creator of Scapino, played with most of the important companies, and is first found in the Accesi in 1612. For many years he was one of the outstanding members of the Confidenti, but went with the younger Andreini and the Fedeli to Paris in 1624, later rejoining the Accesi. He appears to have been a skilful musician, and also a maker of musical instruments. A number of his letters, which have been preserved, give interesting information on the internal affairs of the companies, and on the theatrical life of the time. He had a daughter, (3) GIULIA (*fl.* 1639–45), who appeared as Diana with the company in Paris, and possibly a son, (4) GIROLAMO (*fl.* 1687), who played Pantalone. It is not certain that two other actresses, Luisa, who married Domenico Locatelli, and Ippolita, were related to the above. They may have been daughters of Francesco.

GAELIC DRAMA, see IRELAND, 6.

GAFF, a nineteenth-century term for an improvised theatre, in the poorer quarters of London and other large towns, on whose stage an inadequate company dealt robustly with a repertory of melodrama. The entrance fee was a penny or twopence. The lowest type of gaff was known as a blood-tub. In Scotland it was called a 'geggie'.

GAIETY THEATRE. 1. LONDON, stood in the Strand (now part of the Aldwych) on the site formerly occupied by the Strand Musick-Hall, which opened in 1864 and had a short and inglorious career, though Jolly Johnnie Nash was its Chairman. The man who opened it and made it famous was John Hollingshead. He wanted a restaurant under the same roof, so that diners could go straight to the play, but the authorities refused to allow a connecting door between theatre and restaurant.

Many troubles were encountered during the erection of the theatre, but Hollingshead overcame them all. He lost all his scenery by fire shortly before the opening date, Monday, 21 Dec. 1868, and only got possession of the stage three hours before the curtain went up on the first night. Much of the paint was still wet, and some eighty workmen who had not quite finished their jobs took possession of the front rows of the upper circle and refused to move, demanding to see the theatre they had helped to build launched on its career.

The theatre opened with a successful triple bill, a comedy, *On the Cards*, an operetta, 'The Two Harlequins', and an extravaganza, *Robert the Devil*. Hollingshead had a fine company, with Nellie Farren and Madge Robertson (Mrs. Kendal) as leading ladies and Alfred Wigan as leading man, and he began his reforms by paying salaries large enough to make the old-fashioned system of benefit nights unnecessary. He had a flair for success and, though he made mistakes, his reign was on the whole a prosperous and exciting one. Dickens, that inveterate playgoer, saw his last play at this theatre—*Uncle Dick's Darling* in 1869, the year before he died—and prophesied the future greatness of a young actor in it, Henry Irving. Mr. Gladstone visited it and made an exhaustive tour behind the scenes. Phelps played Shakespeare, and a company came from France under the Commune to play to the many French refugees in London. But the great feature of the Gaiety was its burlesques, many of them written by Burnand and Byron, in which appeared the famous quartette, Edward Terry, Kate Vaughan, E. W. Royce, and Nellie Farren, who first played together in 1876 in *Little Don Caesar de Bazan*. They became steadily more and more popular, as did the Gaiety girls, famous for their looks.

In 1885 Fred Leslie joined the company. He was the perfect foil to Nellie Farren, with whom he first appeared in *Little Jack Shephard*, the only joint production of Hollingshead and George Edwardes, who was to be his successor. In 1886 Hollingshead retired and Edwardes, who had come from the Savoy, took over. His first production was *Dorothy*, which became a success when Hayden Coffin sang an interpolated song, 'Queen of My Heart'. Burlesques continued, one, *Ruy Blas; or, the Blasé Roué*, containing the famous *pas de quatre*, with Fred Leslie, C. Danby, Ben Nathan, and Fred Storey dressed as ballet girls and made up to look like Irving, Toole, Edward Terry, and Wilson Barrett. Irving protested and the make-up was altered. In 1891 Nellie Farren left the Gaiety through illness, and her place in *Cinder-Ellen* was taken by Kate James, while Lottie Collins joined the cast to sing and dance 'Ta-Ra-Ra-Boom-De-Ay'. In 1892 Fred Leslie (whose real name was Frederick Hobson) died suddenly of typhoid fever, aged 37, and was replaced by Arthur Roberts.

Edwardes transferred from the Prince of Wales's a new type of show called *In Town*, now considered the first musical comedy. It was followed by many similar, and successful, shows, most of which had the word 'girl' in their titles. The end of the old Gaiety was now approaching; the site was required for the Aldwych reconstruction. The last production there, on 17 June 1901, was *The Toreador*, which introduced a new star, Gertie Millar. The passing of the old theatre was celebrated by a special show written by George Grossmith, jun., entitled *The Linkman*, in which many of the great stars who in their early days had played at the Gaiety returned to say farewell. It was a wonderful cavalcade, and Irving, forgetting his previous displeasure, gave the farewell address on 4 July 1903.

2. LONDON. The New Gaiety Theatre was built by Edwardes on the Aldwych–Strand corner, and opened on 26 Oct. 1903, with *The Orchid*. The early first-nighters lined up at 5 a.m. and King Edward VII and Queen Alexandra occupied the Royal Box. The cast included Gertie Millar, George Grossmith, jun., Edmund Payne, Connie Ediss, Arthur Hatherton, Robert Nainby, and Gabrielle Ray, who formed what was practically a stock company. Gaiety composers were Lionel Monckton, Ivan Caryll, Leslie Stuart, and Paul Rubens, whose musical shows ran successfully, especially *Our Miss Gibbs*. When George Edwardes died the fortunes of the Gaiety declined somewhat and the company split up. Things revived in 1915 when *To-Night's the Night* was put on, and a new comedian, Leslie Henson, burst upon London. When he, with Grossmith and Laurillard, went to the Winter Garden, much of the old Gaiety spirit went with them, though Butt had some success with Evelyn Laye as his leading lady. The Gaiety became more its old self when Henson returned under the management of Firth Shephard with a new team consisting of himself, Richard Hearne, and the younger Fred Emney. They were still in possession of the theatre when it closed in 1939, the last play there being *Running Riot*.

W. MACQUEEN-POPE†

3. NEW YORK, a most attractive playhouse on Broadway's west side at 46th Street. It opened on 4 Sept. 1909 with John Barrymore in *The Fortune Hunter*. This and the productions which followed, including one with the then novel setting of a Pullman car, had good runs, as did the popular *Daddy-Long-Legs* in 1914, *Turn to the Right* in 1916, and *The Country Cousin* in 1917. A year later came the house's record run with the 1,291 performances of *Lightnin'*, which brought stardom to old Frank Bacon, and proved to be his last part, as he died during the Chicago run which followed. Among later successes at this theatre were *Loyalties*, *Aren't We All?* a revival of *Rain* with Jeanne Eagels, and *The Youngest*, which passed the century mark. In 1932 the Gaiety was given over to burlesque and films, and renamed the Victoria. GEORGE FREEDLEY†

For the Gaiety, Manchester, see HORNIMAN, A.E.F. and REPERTORY THEATRE MOVEMENT.

GAÎTÉ, THÉÂTRE DE LA, PARIS, the first of the French theatres which was not state-aided. It stood on the Boulevard du Temple, and was originally Nicolet's marionette theatre, and then a theatre for living actors which, after the upheaval of the Revolution, became the Gaîté. From 1808 until its destruction in 1862 it flourished, sharing the vast output of melodrama with the Ambigu-Comique, and putting on elaborate fairy-plays, pantomimes, and vaudevilles. Pixerécourt was its manager from 1825 to 1834, and in 1835 it was rebuilt after a disastrous fire. When the Boulevard du Temple was pulled down in 1862 the Gaîté took its old name to a new building, which under Offenbach became the home of light operetta and big spectacular musical shows.

GALANTY SHOW, see SHADOW SHOW.

GALDÓS, see PÉREZ GALDÓS, BENITO.

GALIMAFRÉ, see BOBÈCHE.

GALLERY, in the nineteenth-century theatre the highest and cheapest seats in the house, usually unbookable. The seating generally consisted of wooden benches, in some cases without backs. The occupants of the gallery, from their elevated position, were nicknamed 'the Gods', and often formed the most perceptive and certainly the most vociferous part of the audience (see also FOOTMEN'S GALLERY).

GALLIARI FAMILY, see SCENERY, 3.

GALLI-BIBIENA, GALLI-BIBBIENA, GALLI DA BIBBIENA, see BIBIENA.

GALLIENNE, EVA LE, see LE GALLIENNE.

GALSWORTHY, JOHN, O.M. (1867–1933), English dramatist and novelist. Born into an old and well-to-do Devon family, he was educated at Harrow and at New College, Oxford. He was called to the Bar in 1890, but did not engage in serious practice; instead he travelled widely. *The Island Pharisees* (1904) was the first work fully to reveal his gifts as a novelist, which came to maturity and power in *The Forsyte Saga*, his great claim to abiding importance. He entered the theatre in 1906, when Shaw's plays and the brilliant Vedrenne–Barker season at the Court had just brought the drama of social discussion into fashion. His first play, *The Silver Box* (1906), which draws a disquieting contrast between the treatment given by the law to a poor man and a rich man guilty of theft, impressed itself as a masterpiece of realistic observation. *Joy* (1907), his second play, was only a qualified success, but *Strife* (1909), giving tense and moving dramatic form to the meaning of a great strike, at once established Galsworthy among the first dramatists of the day. The sombre tragedy of *Justice* (1910), with the famous scene depicting the torture of solitary confinement when endured by a nervous prisoner, led to a reform of prison practice, and its success in this respect may have encouraged the reformer in Galsworthy at the expense of the dramatist. At all events, his next group of plays, *The Pigeon* and *The Eldest Son* (both 1912), *The Fugitive* (1913), and *The Mob* (1914), hardly marked an advance of his talent, and it was not until after the First World War that, with *The Skin Game* (1920) and *Loyalties* (1922), he recovered an impulse as purely dramatic as his nature would allow. Though he continued to write plays as well as novels, *Windows* (1922), *The Forest* (1924), *Escape* (1926), and others all fell some way below his own high standard. He began, like his Forsytes, to 'date'.

There were qualities of greatness in Galsworthy the dramatist. They may be seen in the first and last acts of *Justice*, in the masterly control of the whole action of *Strife*, and in many other well-remembered scenes. His dialogue, significant, clean, actual without ever being trivial, dramatically characteristic and emotionally rich, is the dialogue of enduring drama. Yet there is somehow a lack of vitality in the *corpus* of his work for the theatre. He renders the errors, the cruelty, and the ugliness of life as it is, but seems to withhold his own vision of what life might be, as though he lacked confidence in that side of his sensibility. The hiatus is filled with indignation and pity which, though sometimes noble, is often rooted in squeamishness. The beauty which is a pervading presence in the finer novels is absent from the plays and, perhaps for that reason, his dramatic vision of life seems incomplete. A. V. COOKMAN†

GALWAY THEATRE, see IRELAND, 6.

GAMMER GURTON'S NEEDLE, see STEVENSON, WILLIAM.

GANASSA, ZAN [real name probably Alberto Naseli] (*fl.* 1568–83), one of the earliest actors of the *commedia dell'arte* to take a company abroad. He was in Paris in 1571–2, but his most successful tours were in Spain, where he is found frequently during the 1570s. A curious painting in the Bayeux Museum, reproduced in Duchartre, *The Italian Comedy* (p. 84), is believed by him to represent a performance by Ganassa's troupe assisted by some French courtiers (see SPAIN, 4).

GARCÍA DE LA HUERTA, VICENTE (1734–87), a Spanish dramatist who revolted against the eighteenth-century neglect of the Spanish classics in favour of French translations, though in his own edition of forgotten plays (1785–6) he did not always choose the best, and entirely omitted Lope de Vega, Tirso de Molina, and Alarcón. He was in spite of himself much influenced by the unities imposed on Spain by the *Poética* of Luzán (1737), and among his own plays the one which enjoyed the greatest success, *La Raquel* (1778), was modelled on French lines; but its inspiration was entirely Spanish, and it stands out, in the general poverty of eighteenth-century Spanish drama, as a worthy successor to the plays of the Golden Age.

GARCÍA GUTIÉRREZ, ANTONIO (1813–84), Spanish dramatist of the Romantic period, whose somewhat inferior play *El trovador* (1836) achieved world-wide popularity when it was used by Verdi as the basis of his opera 'Il Trovatore'. García Gutiérrez was also the author of a number of other plays, including *Juan Lorenzo* and *Venganza catalana*, both superior in conception and execution to his better-known *El trovador*. His work shows the influence of Dumas *père*, two of whose melodramas he translated into Spanish. He also translated several plays by Scribe.

GARCÍA LORCA, FEDERICO (1898–1936), a Spanish poet and dramatist, assassinated during the first days of the Spanish Civil War. As a child, Lorca had played with puppets and shown a keen interest in make-believe, and as a young man he produced puppet performances in his native Granada. His first play, *El maleficio de la mariposa*, was produced in 1920 by Martínez Sierra during his management of the Teatro Eslava. *Mariana Pineda* (1927) has a historical subject, but Lorca, in his endeavour to limit the scope of a work of art, and in conformity with the contemporary tendency to dehumanize art, turned back to the theme of the puppet with his *Amor de Don Perlimplín con Belisa en su jardín* (1931). Lorca's fame rests securely on his three great tragedies. In *Bodas de sangre* (1933) implacable forces sweep men to their doom and natural impulses are frustrated by the dead hand of convention, themes which are parallelled poetically by contrasting sets of images. *Yerma* (1934) again contrasts the desire for freedom and the forces of convention, seen in terms of fertility and sterility, life and anti-life, but also brings into prominence the contrast between outward reputation and inner rectitude, a theme which underlies *La casa de Bernarda Alba* (1936), a play of frustration from which there is no escape. Lorca's own career was to be ended abruptly, and the manner of his death made his name famous throughout the Western world, whilst misguided attempts were made to turn him into a political dramatist. During his lifetime Lorca's influence on the reviving Spanish theatre was most important, both through the medium of his own plays and productions and through La Barraca, an itinerant amateur company which Lorca directed and which did much to familiarize the common people of Republican Spain with their great dramatic heritage. Many of his plays have been translated into English, but no translation has yet succeeded in conveying the haunting poetic intensity of its original. J. E. VAREY

GARDEN THEATRE, NEW YORK, at 61 Madison Avenue. This opened on 27 Sept. 1890 and in the following year saw the reappearance in New York of Sarah Bernhardt in *La Tosca*, in its original French form as a play. Other interesting productions were *The Mountebanks* (1893), *Under Two Flags* (1901), and Hauptmann's *The Weavers* (1915) in a translation by Mary Morrison, while in Jan. 1910 the Ben Greet Players from England were seen in a number of Shakespeare's plays. In 1919 the theatre became the Jewish (later Yiddish) Art Theatre (see JEWISH DRAMA, 6) and it was demolished in 1925.

GARDIN, VLADIMIR (1877–1965), Russian actor who at the age of 21, after some experience in amateur theatricals, became a professional, playing in a number of provincial theatres. Among his best parts at this time were the President in *Kabale und Liebe* and Fedya in *The Brothers Karamazov*. His work attracted the attention of Vera Komisarjevskaya, who engaged him for her theatre in St. Petersburg, where he made an outstanding success in such parts as Krogstad in *A Doll's House* and Shalimov in Gorki's *The Summer Guests*. In 1907 he opened a small private theatre in Finland for the production of plays banned by the Russian authorities, among them Hauptmann's *The Weavers* and two plays by Andreyev. A year later he went to Paris, London, and other capital cities with a company in a repertory of plays in Russian, and in 1912 returned home to join the Korsh Theatre, where his finest and favourite part was Potrassov in Tolstoy's *The Living Corpse*. His later years were almost entirely devoted to films, in which he was a pioneer in Russia.

GARNIER, ROBERT (*c.* 1535–*c.* 1600), a lawyer who by his adaptations of Greek plays prepared the way for French classical tragedy. He began writing for the theatre in 1568, and produced eight tragedies, all on Greek models, which give proof of wide reading, keen perception, and great lyric power. The best was *Sédécie*, usually known by its sub-title as *Les Juives*, which was also his last. He had a vigorous and supple style, which occasionally reads like Corneille. To scholarship he united imagination and a deep sense of moral dignity. His choruses are particularly fine, and he made many important innovations adopted by later dramatists. But he suffered, as did his contemporaries of the French Renaissance, from a belief that to follow the best models was necessarily to excel, and he saw Greece through Roman eyes.

GARRETT, JOÃO BAPTISTA DA SILVA LEITÃO DE ALMEIDA, see PORTUGAL.

GARRICK, DAVID (1717–79), one of the greatest of English actors, of whom Burke said that 'he raised the character of his profession to the rank of a liberal art'. He was responsible for a radical change in the style of English acting in his day, and during his long management of Drury Lane instituted many reforms before and behind the curtain, the most important being the introduction of stage-lighting concealed from the audience (see LIGHTING, 1) and the banishment of the audience from the stage, a measure long overdue and achieved at about the same time by Voltaire in Paris. Garrick has also been credited with the revival of Shakespeare's texts, freed from the gross corruptions of the seventeenth century, but this assertion must be taken with caution. He was himself responsible for a production of *Hamlet* with the Grave-diggers omitted, a bad precedent followed in our own day by Maurice Evans in his *G. I. Hamlet*; a *Lear* without the Fool; and a *Romeo and Juliet* which allowed the lovers a scene together in the tomb before dying (see No. 162). He also concocted a *Katherine and Petruchio* and a *Florizel and Perdita* (both 1756) from *The Taming of the Shrew* and *The Winter's Tale*, and did not scruple to add to, or alter, scenes and speeches in any play by Shakespeare which he put on. He had, however, to contend with the taste of the time, and the ignorance and lack of appreciation of Shakespeare's genius which was then prevalent, and even in his worst excesses he seems to have had a deep and sincere appreciation of the dramatist he was tampering with.

Garrick, who was of Huguenot descent, early showed an inclination for the stage, and at 11 appeared with some success as Sergeant Kite in a schoolboy production of *The Recruiting Officer*. Later, being sent to study under Dr. Johnson at Lichfield, he accompanied the latter to London, and there indulged in amateur theatricals at the expense of his business career in the wine trade, which he soon abandoned. Some obscurity surrounds his early appearances on the professional stage, but in 1741 he was playing small parts at Goodman's Fields Theatre, and went with the manager, Giffard, to Ipswich. There, under the name of Lyddal, he was received in a variety of parts with sufficient acclaim to justify his continuing on the stage, and he looked forward confidently to an engagement in London. Being rejected by the managers of both Drury Lane and Covent Garden, he again fell back on Goodman's Fields, and there, on 19 Oct. 1741, made his formal début as Richard III, with such success that playgoers crowded to see him, leaving the Patent Theatres to repent of their obtuseness. Garrick's first biographer, Davies, says of this performance that the actor at first took the audience by surprise, his 'easy and familiar, yet forcible style in speaking and acting' and the 'concurring expression of the features from the genuine workings of nature' being novelties for which the declamatory and laboured manner of Quin, then the greatest exponent of tragedy, had not prepared them. They were soon won over, however, and Garrick embarked on a triumphant career which suffered no serious check until his retirement in 1776. In person he might have seemed unsuited to tragedy—he is described as being 'a small man of middle height, with good mobile features and flashing expressive eyes' and a clear but not particularly resonant voice. But his genius rose superior to all disadvantages, and he was unsurpassed, not only in the tragic heroes of the contemporary theatre, but in such parts as Hamlet, Macbeth, and particularly Lear—which he apparently played in a scarlet coat. Murphy, who published a life of Garrick in 1801, said of him: 'It was in Lear's madness that Garrick's genius was remarkably distinguished. His movements were slow and feeble; misery was depicted in his countenance. . . . During the whole time he presented a sight of woe and misery, and a total alienation of mind from every idea, but that of his unkind daughters.' Garrick himself has related how he modelled the madness of Lear on that of an unfortunate man who had accidentally killed his two-year-old child by dropping it from a window. It was to this 'copying of nature' that much of Garrick's success was due, and with it he brought a fresh lease of life to the English stage, which at the time of his first appearance was at a very low ebb. He was equally admired in comedy, one of his earliest parts being Abel Drugger in *The Alchemist*; he was good as Benedick, and as Ranger in *The Suspicious Husband*, in which part he was much admired by Fanny Burney, while as Bayes in *The Rehearsal* he scored a signal triumph with his mimicry of well-known actors of the time. He exempted from his mockery his rival Quin, however, and was always careful to give the older actor his due, admitting his greatness in Falstaff and in such heroic parts as Cato, while he filched from him the great parts in which he had hitherto reigned supreme. Garrick was also generous in his admiration of Spranger Barry, often his rival for public favour, and in later years resigned to him the parts of Romeo, in which he excelled, and Othello, a part in which Garrick was not successful, chiefly, says Murphy, because the blacking of his face deprived him of that marvellously expressive play of features which constituted one of his greatest assets and made him intelligible even to a spectator who was deaf. With Macklin, another great actor of the day, Garrick's relations were less happy, an unfortunate quarrel at the outset of his career preventing any close friendship.

Garrick's fiery temper, vanity, and snobbishness, as well as his sudden rise to fame, naturally brought him many enemies. The worst of these was the malicious Samuel Foote, to whom many bitter criticisms of Garrick are due; it may possibly be from that source that Garrick got his somewhat undeserved reputation for meanness; he had also to contend with the petulance of unacted authors and disappointed small-part actors. He was not always responsible for the quarrels in which he found himself involved, notably those with Dr. Johnson over the failure of *Irene* (1749) and with Colman the elder, whom he offended by refusing to play the part of Lord Ogleby in *The Clandestine Marriage* (1766), a comedy in which they collaborated. As a result Colman took his later plays to Covent Garden, of which he assumed the management in rivalry with Garrick at Drury Lane.

Apart from his collaboration with Colman, and his adaptations of Shakespeare, Garrick was also the author of several plays, of which the farces *Miss in her Teens* (1747), in which he played Fribble, and *Bon Ton; or, High Life Above Stairs* (1775) were the most successful. He was a vivacious and competent dramatist, at his best about equal to Colley Cibber, but much of his work was mere hack-writing and adapting of old plays. His rewriting of Wycherley's *The Country Wife* as *The Country Girl* (1766) was most successful, and held the stage for many years. Garrick was also a prolific writer of epilogues and prologues, published with his other works in a three-volume edition in 1785. One of his most publicized achievements, and the one which has occasioned much malice at his expense, was his Shakespeare Jubilee at Stratford in 1769, to which, it was said, 'the wits and the weather were equally unkind'; it was remarkable for a number of odes, songs, speeches, and other effusions by David Garrick, of which the manuscript has been lost, and for the complete absence of anything by Shakespeare.

It was in 1747 that Garrick first took part in the management of Drury Lane, where the major part of his career was spent. On the death of Lacy he became sole manager, resigning his share of the Patent on his retirement to Sheridan, Linley, and Ford. During his time many reforms were introduced, and he gathered round him a good company, his leading ladies being Peg Woffington (also his mistress for some years), Kitty Clive, Mrs. Cibber, who resembled him like a sister, Mrs. Bellamy, who played Juliet to his Romeo (see No. 162), and Mrs. Abington. Among the men, apart from intermittent appearances by Quin and Barry, his chief supports were the unfortunate Mossop, Woodward, who wrote the Drury Lane pantomimes and appeared in them as Harlequin, Yates, a fine comedian and character actor, and Tom King, who took over Lord Ogleby when Garrick refused it, and was the original Sir Peter Teazle of *The School for Scandal*. Garrick's management was marred by two serious riots, one caused by the abolition of half-price at the end of the third act, a time-hallowed concession which the manager was forced to restore, and the other by his importation of French dancers into *The Chinese Festival* shortly before the outbreak of war with France. The former caused Garrick, described as 'a peaceful, long-suffering man, petted and rather spoilt by the distinguished men to whose society he was admitted, who shrank from dependence upon the mob', to retire for a time, and from 1763 to 1765 he travelled on the Continent with his wife, Eva Marie Violetti (1724–1822), a dancer at the Haymarket whom he had married in 1749. He was well received everywhere, particularly in France, and his reputation shed much lustre upon the contemporary English stage. He returned, greatly refreshed, and a public surfeited with musical spectacles was glad to see him in a succession of his greatest parts. He made his farewell appearance on 10 June 1776 as Don Felix in *The Wonder, a Woman never Vexed*, and retired to Hampton to enjoy the society of his friends until his death, which was felt as a personal loss by many, and called from Dr. Johnson the memorable epitaph: 'I am disappointed by that stroke of death which has eclipsed the gaiety of nations and impoverished the public stock of harmless pleasure.' He was buried in Westminster Abbey (where Henderson and Irving later joined him), and the carriages of the mourners reached as far as the Strand. His brother George, who had been his right-hand man at Drury Lane for many years, died a few days later, because, said the wits of the time with rueful humour, 'Davy wanted him'.

Garrick was several times painted by Sir Joshua Reynolds, one of whose portraits of him hangs in the Garrick Club, named in honour of the great actor, as was the Garrick Theatre, London. A fine portrait by Gainsborough, done in 1766, and said by Mrs. Garrick to be the best ever painted, was lost when the Stratford-upon-Avon Town Hall was destroyed by fire in 1946.

GARRICK CLUB, LONDON, which has numbered among its members many great names of the English stage, owes its inception to the Duke of Sussex, who, according to T. H. Escott, 'recognized the need for furthering the literary industry in England by the formation of a Club on less formal lines than the Athenæum, recruited from the most active caterers for the public taste with pen and pencil, in the studio and on the stage'. The first committee consisted of Colonel Sir Andrew F. Barnard, equerry to George IV, Lord Kinnaird, Samuel James Arnold, manager of Drury Lane Theatre, Francis Mills, Henry Broadwood, and Samuel Beazley. Most of the work necessitated by the formation of the club was done by Mills and Broadwood. The first committee meeting was held on 17 Aug. 1831, and the club, with the Duke of Sussex as its patron, opened in November of the same year, though its premises (Probatt's Family Hotel, King Street) were not ready for the use of members until Feb. 1832. The present club-house, opened on 4 July 1864, stands on part of old Rose Street and in that warren of crowded alleys which lay between King Street and St. Martin's Lane, home of Curll, the bookseller at the 'Pope's Head'—associated too with Samuel Butler and Samuel Johnson. The club, which is restricted to 700 members, has a fine collection of theatrical portraits, of which an annotated catalogue was prepared in 1908 by Robert Walters. In 1896 the Rev. R. H. Barham, author of *The Ingoldsby Legends*, published a collection of short biographies of 135 of its former members (see also Percy Fitzgerald's *History of the Garrick Club*).

GARRICK THEATRE. 1. LONDON, at Leman Street, E.1, opened in 1831 and took its name from its proximity to the old theatre in Goodman's Fields where Garrick made his début. Freer Wyman and the elder Conquest were its first managers. In 1846 it was burned down and rebuilt. It held a very low position, even among East-End theatres, and was practically a 'gaff'. In 1873–4 J. B. Howe, a great local favourite, took it, and with redecoration and better companies made a gallant bid for popularity. He went bankrupt in 1875 and the theatre remained empty for a time, but in 1879 Tree appeared there, under the management of Miss May Bulmer, and made a great success as Bonneteau in *A Cruise to China*. Shortly afterwards the building was demolished and a police-station erected on the site.

2. LONDON, in the Charing Cross Road, opposite the statue of Irving and the National Portrait Gallery. This was opened on 24 Apr. 1889 by Hare, with himself, Forbes-Robertson, Lewis Waller, and Katie Rorke in *The Profligate*. *La Tosca* followed, with Mrs. Bernard Beere, and then in 1890 *A Pair of Spectacles*, which ran for 335 performances. Five years later *The Notorious Mrs. Ebbsmith*, with Hare and Mrs. Patrick Campbell, caused a sensation, and a woman of that name was found drowned in the Thames with the counterfoil of a ticket for the play in her pocket; she had written to a friend that the play had preyed on her mind. When Hare left the theatre its standing declined until in 1900 Arthur Bourchier and his wife, Violet Vanbrugh, leased it and inaugurated a long and brilliant period, with productions ranging from Shakespeare to farce. Oscar Asche and Lily Brayton occupied the Garrick in 1911, notable productions being *Kismet* which ran for 328 performances, and a revival of *The Merry Wives of Windsor*. For some years the theatre had no regular policy or management, and in 1934 it ran a season of Old Time Varieties. It was used for revues. In 1935 *Love on the Dole* established Wendy Hiller as a star, and ran for 391 performances. Closed from 1939 to 1941, the theatre reopened but had nothing noteworthy until *Uncle Harry* (1944), in which Michael Redgrave made a great success, playing opposite Beatrix Lehmann. In 1960 Theatre Workshop's *Fings Ain't Wot They Used T'Be* started a long run and was followed by *Rattle of a Simple Man* (1962). In 1965 an unexpectedly popular revival of the farce, *Thark*, was transferred to this theatre from the Yvonne Arnaud at Guildford.

W. MACQUEEN-POPE†, *rev.*

3. NEW YORK, in 35th Street between Fifth and Sixth Avenues. It opened as Harrigan's Theatre on 29 Dec. 1890 with a play by Harrigan in which he himself appeared. In 1895 Richard Mansfield took it over, renamed it the Garrick, and appeared there with his wife in repertory. He was not particularly successful, and the theatre housed other attractions, the longest run under Mansfield's management being that of William Gillette in his own play, *Secret Service*, which lasted for five months. The same actor appeared later at the Garrick as Sherlock Holmes, a part always associated with the last years of his life. Among later productions at the Garrick were *Captain Jinks of the Horse Marines*, which made Ethel Barrymore a star, *The Stubbornness of Geraldine*, and *Her Own Way*, all by Clyde Fitch, while 1905 saw a successful run of *You Never Can Tell*. A distinguished failure was Percy Mackaye's fine drama, *The Scarecrow*, which had only twenty-three performances in 1911, and was followed by Paul Orleneff and his company in a repertory of Russian plays. In 1919 a great

American subscription theatre was established at the Garrick when the Theatre Guild opened there on 19 Apr. with Benavente's *Bonds of Interest*, in a new translation by J. G. Underhill. This was followed by *John Ferguson* and by *Jane Clegg*, both by St. John Ervine. Among later productions were *Heartbreak House*, *Mr. Pim Passes By*, *Liliom*, *He Who Gets Slapped*, *R.U.R.*, *Peer Gynt*, and *The Adding Machine*. In 1924 came the Lunts in *The Guardsman*, and *They Knew What They Wanted* with Pauline Lord. The Theatre Guild moved into its own playhouse in 1925, and the Garrick had only two more important productions, *The Mystery Ship* and the modern-dress *Taming of the Shrew* (both 1927), before it was pulled down in 1929. It was at this theatre that the Provincetown Players made their last appearance, shortly before its demolition. GEORGE FREEDLEY†

GASCOIGNE, GEORGE (*c.* 1535–77), a scholar of Cambridge, and a versifier of some reputation, who helped to prepare the entertainments given before Elizabeth I at Kenilworth and Woodstock in 1575. He was also the author of a translation of Lodovico Dolce's *Giocasta* (based on Euripides' *Phoenician Woman*), and of Ariosto's *I Suppositi* (based on Plautus's *Captivi*), both done at Gray's Inn in 1566. The latter was also given at Trinity College, Oxford, in 1582.

GAS LIGHTING, see LIGHTING, 1 *b*.

GASSMANN, VITTORIO (1912–), Italian actor-manager, born in Switzerland, son of an actress married to a German. After some training, he made his first success in a production of *The Beggar's Opera*, and from 1947 to 1949 appeared in *All My Sons*, *Antony* (by the elder Dumas), *L'Aigle à deux têtes*, as Orlando, and as Stanley Kowalski in *A Streetcar Named Desire*, under Visconti. He also appeared in Alfieri's *Oreste*, probably his finest part so far, and was an excellent Troilus in a production of *Troilus and Cressida* in the Boboli Gardens in Florence. In 1950 he founded the Teatro Popolare Italiano—somewhat on the lines of Vilar's T.N.P.—which he brought to London in 1963 in a programme which consisted of excerpts from his repertory under the general title of *The Heroes*. Among his productions, in most of which he starred himself, have been *Peer Gynt*, *Romeo and Juliet*, Betti's *Il Giacatore*, Dumas's *Kean*, revivals of Aeschylus (the *Persians*), Euripides (the *Bacchae*), and Sophocles (the *Oedipus Rex*). He has also appeared as Hamlet, and in 1956 alternated the parts of Othello and Iago.

GATE THEATRE, LONDON, a club which between the two world wars gave theatregoers the opportunity of seeing many plays, both English and in translation, which would not have found their way into the commercial theatre or been given a licence by the censor. Some of these were later transferred to West-End theatres, but on the whole the Gate catered for an intelligent minority. The first Gate Theatre was in premises on the top floor of a warehouse in Floral Street, Covent Garden. It opened on 30 Oct. 1925, under the management of Peter Godfrey, with Susan Glaspell's *Bernice*, and had its first success with Toller's *From Morn To Midnight*, after a favourable review by Agate. In 1927 the theatre moved to Villiers Street, off the Strand. It opened on 22 Nov. with Gantillon's *Maya*. From then until 1931 Charles Spencer was joint manager with Godfrey. In 1934 Norman Marshall took over, and reopened with Toller's *Miracle in America*. Among his successful productions were *Parnell*, *Oscar Wilde*, *The Children's Hour*, *Distant Point*, *Elizabeth La Femme sans homme*, and the witty Gate Revues. In 1941 the Gate was extensively damaged by bombing, and it has not been reopened (see also EDINBURGH and IRELAND).

GATHERER, a functionary of the Elizabethan playhouse whose task it was to collect the money from that part of the house, usually the upper gallery and the boxes, allotted to the owner of the building.

GATTI'S MUSIC-HALL, LONDON. This stood in the Westminster Bridge Road, and began as a restaurant opened by Carlo and Giovanni Gatti in 1862, after the demolition of their premises in Hungerford Hall because of the building of Charing Cross station. It was granted a licence in 1865, and it was here that Harry Lauder made his first London appearance, in 1900. It was sometimes known as Gatti's-in-the-Road, or over-the-Water, to distinguish it from Gatti's-under-the-Arches, in Villiers Street, Strand. The latter was underneath the new station, and opened as a restaurant under Carlo Gatti in 1868; but by 1875 it was one of the recognized music-halls of London. Later known as the Hungerford Music-Hall, but more often referred to as Gatti's, it flourished until 1903. Part of its extended premises later became a theatre, as did the original portion, after some years as a cinema (see PLAYERS' THEATRE).

GAULTIER-GARGUILLE, [HUGUES GUÉRU] (*c.* 1573–1633), French actor and chief farce-player, with Gros-Guillaume and Turlupin, of the company at the Hôtel de Bourgogne, to which he may have graduated from the Paris fairs. He was a tall, thin man with a dry humour, much appreciated by Parisians. As Fleschelles he also played serious parts, but it is as a low comedian that he is best remembered. He figures as himself, with other members of the company, in Gougenot's *La Comédie des comédiens*, given at the Hôtel de Bourgogne in 1633, the year of his death. He married Aliénor Salomon, who was at one time thought to be the daughter of the mountebank Tabarin. This, however, is not certain.

GAUSSIN, JEANNE-CATHERINE (1711–67), French actress, daughter of Antoine Gaussem, valet to the great actor Baron. As a child she had the opportunity of watching Adrienne Lecouvreur and other actresses from the wings of the Comédie-Française, and profited so well from what she saw that while quite young she was taken on tour by a travelling company. She made her first appearance at the Comédie-Française in 1730, later succeeding Mlle Duclos in tragedy. She was particularly good in roles demanding tenderness and grief rather than the portrayal of the sterner passions, which had to await the arrival of Mlle Dumesnil and Mlle Clairon. Dark, with languorous eyes and a rich voice, which, as La Harpe said, 'had tears in it', she never lost her youthful look, and at the age of 50 could still play young girls. She appeared in several of Voltaire's plays, notably *Zaïre* (1732), and was considered outstanding in the sentimental comedies of La Chaussée. In 1759 she made an unhappy marriage with a dancer at the Opéra, and retired from the stage four years later, at the same time as Mlle Dangeville. Off-stage Mlle Gaussin was modest, amusing, kind, and most generous. While playing Bérénice in 1752 she was so heart-rending that a soldier on guard in the wings dropped his musket and burst into tears, a tribute to the pathos of her acting which was commemorated in numerous poor verses of the time.

GAUZE-CLOTH, see CLOTH.

GAY, JOHN (1685–1732), English poet and satirist, friend of Pope, to whom he dedicated his first book, and author of the famous ballad-opera, *The Beggar's Opera*, first given at Lincoln's Inn Fields in 1728 under John Rich, thus, as it was said, 'making Gay rich and Rich gay'. A light-hearted mixture of political satire and burlesque of Italian opera, then a fashionable craze, it has frequently been revived, notably at the Lyric, Hammersmith, in 1920 and 1925. In 1929 it was done into German by Bertolt Brecht as *Die Dreigroschenoper* with music by Kurt Weill. Its sequel, *Polly*, was not produced for many years owing to political censorship, but was finally given at the Haymarket in 1777 with alterations by Colman. Gay was also the author of several comedies and of the libretto of Handel's 'Acis and Galatea', but his fame rests almost entirely on *The Beggar's Opera*.

GEDDES. (1) NORMAN BEL (1893–1958), American scenic designer, and a pioneer of décor in the American theatre. As early as 1915 he had the idea of a theatre without a proscenium, and in 1923 he won instant recognition with his magnificent designs for Reinhardt's American production of *The Miracle*. In 1931 he designed a complex of steps and rostrums for a production of *Hamlet* far in advance of anything that had so far been seen. Another of his successful experiments was the multiple setting for *Dead End* (1935). His monumental production of Dante's *Divine Comedy* for which he planned an immense circular stage in Madison Square Garden was unfortunately never carried out, nor was his plan for a 'theatre-in-the-round' in 1930. But these, and other seminal ideas, had a great influence on the development of the modern American theatre. His period of activity in the theatre was at its height during the 1930s, after which he concentrated mainly upon industrial design. By his first wife, he was the father of (2) BARBARA (1922–), who first appeared on the stage in 1940, and in New York a year later. In 1943 she made a great success in the long run of *Deep Are the Roots*. Among her later parts were Rose Pemberton in *The Living Room* (1954) and Margaret in *Cat on a Hot Tin Roof* (1955).

GELOSI, THE, one of the earliest and best-known *commedia dell'arte* companies. After an initial visit to France in 1571, it was summoned to play before the French King, Henri III, at Blois in 1577, and from there went to Paris, thus inaugurating the visits of the Italian players which later had such a marked influence on the French theatre. In the company at this time were Franceso Andreini and his beautiful and talented wife, Isabella, accounted one of the best actresses of her day. Vittoria Piissimi, later of the Uniti and Confidenti troupes, was also with it in its early days, and reappeared with it intermittently in after years, indulging in much rivalry with Isabella. After constant travelling and much shifting of personnel, the Gelosi, with the Andreini in charge, returned to Paris in 1602, and it was on their return journey to Italy that Isabella died and her husband disbanded the troupe.

GÉMIER, FIRMIN (1865–1933), French actor and producer, pupil of Antoine, whom he succeeded as director of the Odéon in 1906. After walking-on in one of Antoine's productions in 1887, he spent four years in the suburban theatres of Paris, and then joined Antoine at the Théâtre Libre, where he proved himself an excellent actor, both in classic and modern roles. He was also a good producer, but it was as a teacher that his influence made itself felt in the modern French theatre, since he was the first to emphasize the importance of improvisation and systematic exercises in the training of young actors, in the style of Stanislavsky, whose contemporary and disciple he was. One of his most famous pupils was Charles Dullin, who, after developing his methods still further, passed them on to those outstanding figures in the Parisian theatre today, Barrault, Vilar, and Valde. The germ of the present Centres Dramatiques and the Théâtre National Populaire was implicit in Gémier's early tentatives, both before and after the First World War, to found such a theatre, with his Théâtre National Ambulant (1911–12) and his Théâtre National Populaire (1920). An excellent life of Gémier, by Paul Blanchart, was published in 1954.

GENERAL UTILITY, see STOCK COMPANY.

GÉNERO CHICO, or *teatro por horas*, a generic term applied in Spain to the lesser and lighter types of dramatic entertainment. In its present form it dates from about 1868, when the performance of one-act pieces became popular. It has its own authors, too numerous to mention, and was at its best in the late nineteenth century, being now practically defunct. The first productions of this genre were short comic scenes of daily life, usually in Madrid, heightened to the point of caricature, but the fashion developed for mucical accompaniments, until *género chico* became synonymous with one-act *zarzuela*. It was treated with scorn by academic critics and the more conventional dramatists, but was nevertheless a living and popular entertainment, with a distinguished ancestry, since it derives from the old *sainete* or *entremés*, and is thus connected with the earliest traditions of drama in Spain. It has been superseded by the *astracanadas*, or sketches with wildly improbable plots and a dialogue thick with untranslatable puns and plays on words (see also ZARZUELA).

GENET, Jean (1910–), French dramatist, novelist, and poet, whose view of theatre as an act of revolt against society has been conditioned by an early life spent largely in correctional institutions and prisons. Often compared to the work of other outcast writers like Villon, Sade, and Rimbaud, his plays are characterized by the frenzied rebellion of the characters against being pigeon-holed by conventional morality. At first attacked as scandalous and obscene, his work is now generally recognized as important, not only for its extreme beauty of language, but also for its creation of a form capable of embodying the 'Theatre of Cruelty' dreamed of by Antonin Artaud: a theatre freed from the restrictions of society, and therefore restored to its true power as an instrument in revealing man's metaphysical reality. Genet's first play, *Les Bonnes*, produced by Louis Jouvet in 1947, introduced his conception of the play as ceremony and masquerade. Through the masquerade, or impersonation, the characters enact their dreams and secret desires, thus demonstrating the nullity of what is usually termed 'reality'. The ceremony, or ritual, imposed on the masquerade is designed, on the analogy of the Catholic mass, to unite the spectators in a metaphysical experience beyond 'reality', and beyond normal conceptions of good and evil. This conception, implemented by the brilliant use of language, is developed and strengthened through all his plays: *Haute Surveillance* (1949), *Le Balcon* (first produced, as *The Balcony*, in London, 1957; not performed in France until 1960), and *Les Nègres* (known in English as *The Blacks*) (1959). This had a very long run from 1960 in an off-Broadway production. His latest play, *Les Paravents*, dealing with the Algerian situation, had a stormy reception in Paris at the Odéon in 1966. Genet has also published novels and poems; a ballet, 'Adam Miroir', with choreography by Janine Charrat and music by Darius Milhaud, was produced in 1948.

T. C. C. MILNE

GENGENBACH, Pamphilus (*fl.* sixteenth century), a Swiss printer of Basle whose *Totenfresser* (1521) is a savage attack on the Roman Catholic Church (see GERMANY, 2).

GENTLEMAN, Francis (1728–84), who was born and died in Dublin, is best remembered by his dramatic criticism, which appeared in 1770 in two anonymous volumes called *The Dramatic Censor*. The first volume is dedicated to Garrick, the second to Foote. As a critic Gentleman dealt judiciously but verbosely with various plays of Shakespeare and of his own day. His remarks on actors, at the end of each article, are more valuable and informative. He was for some years a soldier, and then became a player, succeeding in spite of what he himself called 'an unconsequential figure and uncommon timidity'. On his way to London from his native city he acted with Macklin at Chester, and had two tragedies of his own composition presented at Bath, where from 1752 to 1755 he acted as 'Mr. Cooke'. It is known also that he acted Othello in Edinburgh, met James Boswell at Glasgow, and appeared in the first production of the best of his own plays, *The Modish Wife* (1761), at Chester. Among many other adaptations *The Tobacconist* (*c.* 1760), watered down from Ben Jonson's *The Alchemist*, was the most successful and was reprinted in the collections of Dibdin and Oxberry. Gentleman appears to have been prone to self-pity and ingratitude towards his benefactors. Garrick called him a 'dirty dedicating knave' on that account. In his forties Gentleman retired to Yorkshire for five years, and married there. His wife died in 1773, leaving him with two infants. He repaired finally to Dublin, and the last seven years of his life brought him nothing but sickness and abject poverty. Professor C. H. Gray justly says of Gentleman's *Dramatic Censor*: 'He wrote much as other men of his day wrote and with many echoes of Dr. Johnson's criticisms, except that here and there he expressed opinions that have an air of fresh discovery about them. . . . His criticisms of the actors are full of vivid descriptions of the way certain parts were played by different men.'

GEORGE, Grace (1879–1961), see BRADY (2).

GEORGE M. COHAN THEATRE, New York, on Broadway at 43rd Street. This opened on 25 Sept. 1911 with Cohan's play *The Little Millionaire*, the author and his parents being in the cast. It was followed by a revival of *45 Minutes from Broadway*, while the following year saw *Broadway Jones*, again with the three Cohans. Among later successes were *Potash and Perlmutter*, which had 441 performances, *It Pays to Advertise*, *Come Out of the Kitchen*, and a number of musical shows, including *Two Little Girls in Blue* in 1921. Clemence Dane's *Bill of Divorcement*, in the same year, established Katharine Cornell as a star, and was moved to Times Square to make way for Ed Wynn in *The Perfect Fool*, by which sobriquet he has continued to be known.

The last years of the theatre were uneventful, and its swan-song was *The Dubarry* (1932) with Grace Moore. A year later it became a cinema, and has since been pulled down.

GEORGE FREEDLEY†

GEORGE, Mlle [MARGUERITE-JOSÉPHINE WEYMER] (1787–1867), French tragic actress, and one of the best of her day, in spite of the handicap of a wilful and imperious temper which made her many enemies and spoilt her acting. Daughter of the conductor of the Amiens theatre orchestra, she was befriended by Mlle Raucourt of the Comédie-Française, and made her début there in 1802 as Racine's Iphigenia. Her majestic bearing and fine voice assured her instant success in tragic parts, but in 1808 she eloped suddenly with a dancer named Louis Laporte and went to Russia, where she acted with a French company for five years. Back at the Comédie-Française, she was again successful until her fellow actors, tiring of her temper and her caprice, asked her to resign in 1817. She then went to London and on tour, and in 1822 returned to Paris to star at the Odéon. She was reputed to have been successively the mistress of Napoleon, Talleyrand, Metternich, and Ouvrard, and for many years lived with the manager Harel, following him into the provinces and to the Porte-Saint-Martin, where she acted with great success in romantic drama. Increasing stoutness led her to retire, and she became a teacher of elocution, but her extravagance forced her back to the stage, where she found herself outmoded and forgotten. She struggled on for some time, and finally retired to die in obscurity.

GEORGE II OF SAXE-MEININGEN, see MEININGER COMPANY.

GERMANOVA, MARIA NIKOLAEVNA (1884–1940), Russian actress, who entered the Moscow Art Theatre School in 1902. In 1904 she made her début as Calpurnia in *Julius Caesar*, and soon attracted the attention of Nemirovich-Danchenko, who found her intensity and delicate appearance ideal for the more expressionist dramas with which he hoped to counterbalance Stanislavsky's naturalism. Passionate and vivacious, she excelled in the portrayal of sultry and tempestuous *femmes fatales*, but the deeper tones of tragedy were often beyond her range. Her chief roles were Agnes in *Brand* (1906), Marina in *Boris Godunov* (1907), the Fairy in *The Blue Bird* (1908), Grushenka in *The Brothers Karamazov* (1910), Lisa in *Redemption* (or *The Living Corpse*) (1911), and the title role in Andreyev's *Katerina Ivanovna* (1912), which was written for her. With several other members of the Moscow Art Theatre she left Russia in 1920, and in 1922 founded the Prague Group of the Moscow Art Theatre. She appeared with this group in Paris in 1926 and in London in 1928, playing (among other roles) Medea and Mme Ranevsky. After the group disbanded in 1929 she played Olga in Pitoëff's production of *Three Sisters*, acted briefly in the United States, and retired in 1930.

ROBERT TRACY

GERMANY. 1. PRE-REFORMATION DRAMA. The precise origin of secular drama in Germany, as elsewhere, is still under discussion. Direct descent from the ancient classical theatre through the *mimi* is no longer claimed, and recent criticism in Germany tends to regard the indigenous pagan rites as being of far greater importance in the growth of religious as well as of secular drama than was formerly conceded, a theory which affords a convenient explanation for the presence of grotesque and comic elements in religious plays. Thus the *Fastnachtsspiel* (originally a Carnival play, later acted at any season) which emerges in the fifteenth century, far from being a mere offshoot of the Church play (see LITURGICAL DRAMA), frequently shows cognate native elements in an unchristianized form. No doubt the wandering minstrel was also instrumental in the propagation of medieval farce, at any rate before it became the preserve of the burghers, while the Church, by admitting the practice of the Feast of Fools, in which young clerics were allowed to vent their high spirits, and their grievances, also furthered its development.

The Carnival plays, which form the pre-Reformation secular drama of Germany, were governed by the taste of the audiences before which they were performed. They attack what the burgher dislikes or despises, but they lack the satirical pungency and the political element of the French *sotie*, as well as the charm of the English Interlude, for they had little contact before the sixteenth century with either School Drama or with Courts, petty or imperial. This is, perhaps, an early instance of the way in which German drama has always been affected by the absence of a central focus of culture such as Paris or London.

Religious subjects still appear in these secular farces, as for example in the *Debate between Church and Synagogue*, but the punishments meted out to the losing party are so revolting as to preclude ecclesiastical patronage. The learned Aristotle on all fours with a lady on his back preserves a trickle of classical tradition. Contemporary events are reflected in a play about the Turkish wars. There are also links with ancient pagan festivals, as in the Austrian *Neidhartspiel*, in which the *Minnesinger* Neidhart von Reuental, having seen the first violet of the year, herald of spring, marks the spot with his hat and hastens to call his lady so that she may admire it, and the courtiers dance round it. He has been spied on by some peasants, who hate him for mocking their ways and decoying their women. They pick the flower and, after putting something offensive in its place, tie it to a pole and caper round it. Neidhart, utterly discomfited in the presence of his mistress, suspects the trick and, with a few followers, pounces on his foes. A scrimmage ensues in which the peasants are routed, whereupon Neidhart leads his lady to the dance.

In all these plays the weaknesses of lawyers and their clients, doctors and their patients, are drastically portrayed, and the illicit relations of the clergy with women are shown up with gusto. But by far the most popular themes were those within the experience of the spectators themselves. All the human failings that undermine domestic peace—unfaithfulness, quarrelling, gluttony, avarice, bullying, lack of physical self-control—are described with disconcerting frankness. In the fifteenth-century farces these family crises are not usually shown in action. The problem is ventilated before a magistrate or some other person of authority; or else the help of a doctor or a friend is sought, in which case the advice given often redounds upon the adviser.

A delightful example of the former type is found in *Rumpolt und Marecht*. It is a breach-of-promise case, in which Rumpolt desires to rid himself of Marecht, who declares that she has just cause to demand marriage. Rumpolt is staunchly supported by his father, even to the extent of financial aid; Marecht by her nimble-tongued mother and a hussy, her friend. Each party pays cash down—heavily—for legal assistance. Rumpolt stoutly denies Marecht's insinuations, but unfortunately gives himself away. His attempts to turn upon his lawyer are unavailing, and he is about to submit with a bad grace when, on the banns being called, an earlier claimant to Marecht's favours appears. Rumpolt's possessive instincts are aroused; he champions his lady, and the warring parties join in a dance. This witty little sketch is a masterpiece of characterization, and shows dramatic qualities to which few of these plays attain.

A variable feature of many fifteenth- and sixteenth-century German farces is the *Narr* or fool. The word originally meant those who live foolishly, that is, not as befits their hope of salvation or their true interest, a conception immortalized by Brandt in his *Narrenschiff*. This personage is not necessarily funny, but in the Carnival plays is usually made to appear so. He may also stand for the quality of folly regarded as a disease which may be cured by exorcism, by purging, or by the use of the knife. This *Narr* is always the central figure of the action. A secondary form of the type is the dullard who cannot see the sun at noonday. Further, assumed stupidity may cover slyness, and the *Narr* may either hoist his master with his own petard, or in some way succeed in feathering his own nest. Lastly the existence of the Court fool leads to the introduction of the *Narr* in plays where the scene is laid in high places. Here he may simply be vulgar, but he may have a certain gravity, and in one fifteenth-century farce at least he shows far more sense than his betters.

These early farces were probably acted by youths, usually artisans, from the neighbourhood, and their jokes were doubtless largely personal. Gradually the plays assumed a more general significance, and groups of such actors, having gained a certain competence, occasionally visited other places; but no organized companies on the scale of the Parisian *enfants sans souci* are recorded in Germany. At first the presentation of the plays must have been extremely simple, performers and audience being almost one, both joining in the final round dance. A 'precursor' or crier begs for hospitality and a hearing, and gives instructions for a space to be cleared. He, or another, afterwards conveys the thanks of the company, and craves pardon for any licence of speech. In the most primitive form of farce, which resembles the modern revue, the actors step forward one by one from a row or semicircle, usually addressing an authoritative central figure who comments on each person in turn, and winds up the discussion (see MUMMING PLAY for a parallel English production). There is no setting, but there must have been some rudimentary indication of character by costume, gesture, speech, or perhaps by masks. When action was introduced, properties such as chairs, tables, and so on would be required, and as soon as there was something to see as well as to hear it became more convenient to raise the actors above the level of the floor on tables and trestles, thus setting the play at a greater distance from the audience; but the practice of having all the actors on the stage from start to finish continued, and as the action grew more elaborate accommodation had to be found for more than one group of actors at a time. The stage was therefore erected in the open, or, if permission could be obtained, in the halls of public buildings. With few exceptions the medieval farces are in one act only, though they vary greatly in length, and the scene is not localized. The *Neidhartspiel* has two actions going on simultaneously, one with courtiers, one with peasants, the speeches coming sometimes from one group, sometimes from the other. As the process of elaboration continued there was no doubt some idea of emulating the magnificence of the religious plays or the richer setting of the School Drama, but it must have been held in check by lack of funds, for the performance of popular farces was not for some time an institution which had any claim on public money, and only small contributions could be collected from the audience. Not until the middle of the fifteenth century, when the guilds undertook the performances, was more money forthcoming under the stimulus of local pride. The most active of these guilds were the Mastersingers, who flourished in the large towns of southern Germany. Two of the few authors of fifteenth-century farces known by name, Hans Rosenblüt and Hans Folz, lived in Nuremberg about the middle of the century, and Folz was certainly a Mastersinger. Serious secular drama was hardly known in Germany at this period. The *Tellspiel* from Uri, celebrating the winning of Swiss independence, probably belongs to the sixteenth century (see SWITZERLAND).

2. THE REFORMATION AND LATER SIXTEENTH-CENTURY SECULAR DRAMA. Since the days of Hroswitha of Gandersheim (*c.* 970), who wrote

plays on the model of Terence, but of Christian content, Latin drama had lain fallow in Germany; but in 1450 the University of Heidelberg acquired some manuscripts of Terence and Seneca, and intensive study of these authors ensued. For a time admiration for the early Renaissance drama in Latin as it developed in Italy, and the use of the Dialogue for argument, retarded the adoption of classical dramatic form. In 1497, however, Reuchlin, in his *Henno*, dressed up a popular farce (on the theme of *Maistre Pierre Pathelin*) in five acts, complete with prologue and choruses. The neo-Latin drama is of its nature international, and there was considerable give and take in it all over western Europe. The most notable contributions by German humanists were probably those pertaining to the religious struggle (see below). Latin comedy and its derivatives were first in the field. Tragedy, it may be said, did not on the whole flourish in sixteenth-century Germany. Seneca was republished, commented on, and translated, but purely for educational purposes. Of the Greek tragedians Euripides was the first to evoke interest, Erasmus and Melanchthon making translations of which performances are recorded. The contemplative mind of Sophocles could find no echo during the turmoil of the Reformation. The humanist drama is thus important rather as a model of form, and for the importation of classical themes, than for positive achievement, though Nicodemus Frischlin, an alert mind, gained fame and imprisonment for his spirited but indiscreet comedies.

By the end of the fifteenth century religious drama, though widespread, had largely deteriorated into pageantry, and was beginning to yield to the onslaught of the Reformation, while the old farces were also losing their vitality. Though still popular, they relied on a rehandling of old material, and gave increasing offence by their coarseness. The Reformation brought new life and fresh material. Certain practices of the Church were attacked, particularly in the free cities of Switzerland, with a violence as yet unknown in German drama. In Basle the printer Pamphilus Gengenbach in his *Totenfresser* (1521) shows the Church battening on the dead, growing rich on the money paid by credulous relatives in order to save the souls of the departed from purgatory. The Pope, a bishop, a lay brother, a monk, and a nun sit round a table carving up a corpse, while the devil plays the fiddle. In the foreground the laity, led by a parson, cry for deliverance. The play, if it can be so called, is primitive in form, but anger imparts fire to the uncouth speeches.

In the same year the painter-poet Niklas Manuel of Berne used an even simpler but no less effective device. Two men, a naïve peasant and his more knowledgeable town cousin, are watching two processions entering the market-place. On the one hand are seen richly caparisoned horses, their crowned mitred riders wearing costly cloaks and gazing disdainfully upon the crowd. On the other is seen One riding upon an ass, meanly clad and attended by rough fishermen, while the poor and humble throng round Him. The country lad is dazzled at first by the display of wealth and power, but his companion soon draws the moral. Here pageantry and dialogue are happily combined, and the words are plain-spoken but restrained.

In a later play, *Der Ablasskrämer* (1525), Manuel gives us almost a foretaste of the French Revolution. A certain Ricardus Hinterlist (Dick Trickster), a seller of indulgences, unwarily returns to a former field of action. His female customers have, however, seen through him, and supported by their husbands they arrive armed with shovels, distaffs, and rusty weapons, setting upon him with torrents of abuse. His entreaties and his threats are alike unavailing. Having thrashed him they tie his hands together and hoist him up repeatedly until he has confessed all his tricks one by one, and disgorged his ill-gotten gains. For concentrated fury this little sketch, which was acted in the market-place of Berne, would be hard to beat.

Elsewhere in Germany too the old dramatic forms were used in support of the Reformation. In Riga the former monk Burkhart Waldis points the parable of the prodigal son against the Catholics. The prodigal is robbed of his fortune in a papist house of ill repute, at the instigation of the devil. His brother, trusting in the virtue of his own good works, represents a doctrine Luther seeks to frustrate. The wicked are converted and in a final chorus join in Luther's hymn. This play in two acts, written in a Low German dialect, is not without its lively moments, but action is subordinated to argument. It was performed on a stage similar to that required for the *Neidhart-spiel*, with the two actions located on opposite sides of the available space; but they do not in this case proceed simultaneously.

It was only to be expected that Protestant dramatists would make use of the *mise en scène* of the Passion Plays. A striking example of this occurs in the *Pammachius* (1538) of the humanist Naogeorg (1511–63) [really Thomas Kirchmayer]. Originally written in Latin, this play was soon translated into racy German and performed at Zwickau. The first act opens in heaven, the second in hell. Pope Pammachius is shown to be utterly perverted by the acquisition of secular power. St. Peter, who had believed in him, and the emperor Julian, who had sponsored him, are much distressed. His deeds cry to heaven. Christ, having sent Truth and her outspoken maid, Bold, to investigate matters, comforts them on their return by pointing to the little town of Wittenberg in Germany where a certain 'God's Word' will shortly arise and set matters right. For the concluding fifth act Naogeorg bids his audience look around them. This play, inordinately long, was doubtless cut for performance. It was played in Latin at Christ's College, Cambridge, in 1545, and was translated into English by John Bale.

The greatest zest in the struggle was clearly

displayed by the attackers. Nothing of comparable vigour was produced by the Catholics until the second half of the sixteenth century, when the Jesuit schools instituted play-acting as an effective method of training and propaganda (see JESUIT DRAMA). In plays such as *Pammachius* the stage is clearly used as a pulpit, while many others, without so definite an argument, show unmistakable Protestant, or more rarely Catholic, bias. The increasing number of printed copies shows too that their authors could now count on a reading public.

The early dramatists of the Reformation had been content to use popular or traditional forms, but sporadic division into acts and scenes reveals the influence of classical studies. The humanist movement had been gaining ground in Germany towards the end of the fifteenth century, and though the religious upheaval hindered anything like a renaissance of poetry for the time being, the mere fact that Latin plays were acted in the schools and universities with much pomp and ceremony led to a wider acquaintance with the form of classical drama, and incidentally to somewhat novel staging. In the *Fastnachtsspiel* any stage there was was neutral; it could represent any place, and did not alter, though the introduction of a throne, for example, might underline the locality. The religious drama had required a far more elaborate structure, and the action moved from one part of the stage to another. For the performances of Terence, however, a special type of stage had been evolved in Renaissance Italy, ostensibly on a classical pattern: the back of the stage showed a number of curtained openings, or cells, flanked by pillars, leading to the various localities required for the action, and from these the characters entered and departed. This arrangement, known as the Terence-stage, marks a deliberate attempt to counteract both elaboration and naturalism. Later in the sixteenth century the desire for realism again prevailed, and a series of scenic houses on both sides of a sharply converging central prospect was used, terminating in a painted backcloth. This technique also was of Italian origin, and it was rendered more flexible by the use of *telari* or triangular prisms revolving on pivots (see SCENERY). Such a stage may have been used by Paul Rebhun (*c.* 1500–46) when in 1535 he presented his *Susanna,* written with direct encouragement from Luther, though the intimacy of many scenes suggests rather an approximation to the medieval stage with its multiple setting as the characters come and go from their several houses. The action falls naturally into five acts, each followed by a lyrical chorus in varying measures; in the body of the play Rebhun uses lines of different length and rhythm, according to the effect he wishes to create. The play has a delightful simplicity and homeliness combined with dignity.

Although Rebhun had imitators, no other sixteenth-century dramatist rose to such a height; in most of the longer plays (the Carnival play meanwhile retaining tenaciously its one-act anecdotal character) the division into acts is purely mechanical and rarely corresponds to any break in the organic structure. This applies also to Hans Sachs (1494–1576), the master-cobbler, mastersinger, and master of ceremonies of the Carnival play in Nuremberg. He was probably stimulated to his more ambitious dramatic efforts by witnessing academic entertainments in his native town. He recognized no virtue in the five-act play as distinct from the two-, seven- or even eleven-act play, and frequently begins his new act precisely where the previous one left off. His four-beat doggerel verse contrasts oddly with the attempted dignity of many of his productions. But to Hans Sachs belongs the honour of having instituted the first German theatre building. In 1550 he took over the Marthakirche, disused since Nuremberg had adopted Protestantism. There has been much speculation as to the detailed arrangement of his stage. It was certainly a simple one. Curtains with slits screened the sides and back; visible steps led from the floor-level to the sides, hidden steps to the back; there was a floor trap and a pulpit, and existing steps may have been incorporated. Isolated features such as doors were probably of painted wood. Incidental properties were brought on to the stage and removed by the characters in the course of the play. It should be noted that here, as in the case of School Drama, the audience sat facing the stage, and not on three sides of it. As Hans Sachs staged his own plays, his methods, ascertainable to some extent from his stage directions, are of interest. In the Carnival play, which he purged of indecency without abating a jot of its fun, the acting must have been fairly realistic. Not so in the serious plays. Here he could hardly follow the example of the School Drama, which laid its principal emphasis on delivery and facial expression, and so probably fell back on the stylized gestures of the old religious plays. As his stage was small, mass scenes must have been resolved into single incidents. In the case of persons of exalted rank the costume seems to have been traditional, while the lesser characters wore their ordinary garments. Hans Sachs clearly gave some training to his actors but they can in no sense be regarded as professionals.

Thus, by the 1580s German drama was gropingly making headway, hampered by tradition. There is evidence that by slightly raising a portion of the stage and using a partition with an exit to a lower level, interior scenes were made practicable alongside the usual scenes in public places; there were other experiments too. In the *Comedi vom Crocodilstechen* (*c.* 1596) a stone crocodile in effigy on a wall scares the beholders, and sets the whole of Nuremberg, including authentic notabilities, by the ears. If this racy little satire was actually performed, it must have necessitated quite elaborate scenery. Apart from its personal element, it is well in the Hans Sachs tradition. It is a Carnival play in two parts, though the use of the term *comedi* implies that the earlier name was being dropped.

The real quickening of dramatic life in Germany came, however, from the English Comedians whose first performances of plays in Germany under Robert Browne are recorded in 1592. Many German princes, among them Heinrich Julius, Duke of Brunswick, engaged these strolling players for periods varying in length, and undertook their remuneration and lodging. Otherwise, for performances in towns, permission had to be obtained from the authorities, usually after much bargaining as to the price to be charged for entrance and seats. Town halls, school halls, fencing grounds, and, as a last resort, inn yards were hired. The players carried all their apparatus with them, so the scenery must have been modest; but their costumes were colourful and picturesque, and their devices manifold. The characteristic features of their Shakespearian stage, which had to be constructed locally, were the projecting apron stage, the space to the rear which could be used for interior scenes, and, when practicable, the gallery above either for the musicians or for balcony and window scenes. This clearly gave a stage which had more possibilities than that used by Hans Sachs. Their repertory, in which most of the Elizabethan dramatists were represented, is characterized by the complete absence of the moralizing tendency so prevalent in contemporary German drama, and by the element of excitement it provided, translated into more energized dramatic form. The actors had quickly learned Low German, which they used for comic interludes, and were soon acting in German entirely, helped by local men who gradually took over the whole concern. The original companies were small, which meant that doubling was frequent and crowd scenes had to be cut, but the vivid acting of these professionals, masters of gesture and facial expression, supported by superb fooling, expert dancing, fencing, and acrobatics, carried the day. Sackville evolved Jan Bouschet (John Posset), who has all the characteristics of the late sixteenth-century *Narr*. He was by no means squeamish, got plenty of humour out of linguistic misunderstandings, and was a master of repartee; he is always commenting on or parodying the main action, or taking part in it with exaggerated zeal. Though a secondary character, he doubtless held the stage and was given free rein to improvise. Similar types were created by other leading actors—Hans Stockfisch by John Spencer, Pickelherring by Robert Reynolds—and eventually the native Hanswurst or Kasperle (see AUSTRIA) came into being, with his likeable clumsy ingenuousness. The vivaciousness and self-assurance of these English players, enhanced by the practice of improvisation which came from the *commedia dell'arte*, raised the standard of acting in Germany for all time.

Clearly German authors could no longer afford to ignore this new importation. In the south Sachs still had a great following, and Jakob Ayrer (*c.* 1543–1605), his successor, retained much of his manner, including the doggerel verse and the old verbosity; but several of his subjects are of English origin, and a certain increase in pace shows that he had profited by the visits of the English Comedians to his native town from 1593 onwards. The English fool, recognizable under his many disguises by his first name of Jan, appears in a number of the longer plays, and is even the hero of a few Carnival sketches. Although Ayrer's actors were amateurs, he aimed at big spectacular effects. He learned many tricks of the trade from the English Comedians, and his stage must have been of a fair size to accommodate his large casts.

Heinrich Julius of Brunswick (1564–1613), reigning Duke from 1589 till his death, was less influenced by tradition than Ayrer. He wrote to supply his English company with plays, and adopted their prose form and manner of staging. Like them, he shrank from no horror.

Given the popularity of the English Comedians, and the slow progress of the Renaissance in Germany owing to the Reformation and the strife of religious wars, it is not surprising that the general trend of drama about 1600 was towards noisy hilarity or gory sensationalism. It was not until the turn of the century that comparison with the achievements of other countries opened the eyes of patriots to the backwardness of the German stage.

3. THE SEVENTEENTH CENTURY. The opening years of the century, however, even before the outbreak of war in 1618, were a period of growing disintegration in which nothing of value could flourish. The well-meant efforts of numerous literary societies modelled on the *Accademia della Crusca* were unavailing until a handbook of poetics by Martin Opitz (1597–1639) bade the budding poet look to the classics, to France, and to Italy for guidance. His almost unchallenged authority resulted in a complete break with national tradition, and in an academic literature, smooth, not ungraceful at times, but devoid of all life and action. His translations from Seneca into monotonous, if stately, alexandrines awakened no echo. Once again the element of passion was lacking, and the genre primarily affected was the lyric. Towards the middle of the seventeenth century, however, under the stress of suffering and religious perplexity, the more highly coloured exuberance of the Italian *seicento* gained ground in Germany, mainly through the influence of the Jesuit Counter-Reformation. It produced a rhetorical style, expressive of pent-up emotion controlled by rationalistic stoicism, and this baroque mentality, as it may be termed, whatever its merits or demerits, produced in its turn German tragedy.

A taste for the serious plays of Andreas Gryphius (1616–64), the chief dramatist of this time, needs to be acquired, yet they are epoch-making and reveal an inner life of great depth. In five usually well-balanced acts, separated by allegorical lyrical choruses, they relate the clash of imperious desires and stoic endurance. They deserve respect as the first literary

German dramas, however much they may try the patience of the modern reader by their sustained loftiness of language, by pages of stichomythia, and by the all too rhythmic ebb and flow of the rhymed alexandrines. Although a staunch Protestant, Gryphius owes much to the Jesuit productions, as well as to performances of plays by Corneille and others which he witnessed during his travels from 1644 to 1646, while a double comedy of intrigue, in which four scenes of a musical play of Italian flavour alternate with four richly comic prose scenes in Low German, prove that he had had contact with the strolling players. This is even more noticeable in two other comedies closely allied to the popular repertory in form and subject-matter, though distinguished by their well-pointed dialogue.

Gryphius is the first German dramatist to handle his material with conscious artistry. He wrote at a time when high and low, after the strain of war, craved entertainment as never before. Yet—and this is the tragic element in his career—there was no permanent theatre in which his plays could be given to the public, and only sporadic performances, mostly by schoolboys, are recorded.

There were at this time three main types of theatrical performances in Germany, though no very sharp line of demarcation can be drawn between them, since their conditions were governed by circumstances. At the lower end of the scale the strolling players struggled on, being rapidly eclipsed by their more moneyed rivals, the Court opera and operetta, and the Jesuit school productions. Their decline is indicated by the significant fact that the middle of the seventeenth century saw the managers resorting to marionettes. The most splendid productions of the day were those at the Courts. Here the Italian machines, and scenic devices painted by famous artists, were much in favour. Of almost equal importance were the Jesuit school plays, mostly given in Latin, and forming part of the regular educational curriculum. Apart from religious propaganda they were considered useful for training in deportment and articulation for public occasions. No efforts were spared to create powerful effects. The austere Terence-stage no longer sufficed and was replaced by a deep stage divided into three sections by curtains, sometimes painted, or by shutter-like flats carrying painted scenery, and moved on ropes. The full depth of the stage was used for important scenes which demanded elaborate settings; the two front sections allowed the use of a restricted number of properties, while the foremost section was used for undefined localities and the less important scenes. A front curtain was not in regular use. The Protestant School Drama, also active, could not allow itself to be entirely outshone by its Catholic rivals, but it evinced greater sobriety, both of necessity and on purpose. It was for this stage that Gryphius's plays were written.

With the increased interest in the past and in other countries characteristic of this age, costumes were more carefully differentiated, and lighting effects were freely used. The prevalent martyr-plays demanded flaming stakes, descending clouds, and so on. Opera was even more exacting. Music, especially vocal music, was then of a high standard, and was freely used, even outside opera, for choruses and arias supported by instrumentalists. Gryphius, avoiding in his tragedies the ultra-rhetorical gestures of the Jesuits, appears to have aimed at as much expressiveness as was consistent with dignity. Comedy allowed of more realistic acting. Women now appeared in opera, and in a few strolling companies. Generally speaking the aim of the theatre in the seventeenth century was to create an illusion as far removed as possible from drab reality.

The baroque drama proper reached its peak in the work of Daniel Caspar von Lohenstein (1635–83) and his imitators. His *Cleopatra* (1661, rev. 1680) and *Sophonisbe* (1666, pub. 1680) have theatrical qualities, but their bombastic language, overburdened with far-fetched similes and interlarded with erudite references, covers no depth. It is not surprising to find towards the close of the century a sharp reversal of taste in the direction of realism on the one hand and simplicity on the other.

The former tendency is manifest in the productions of Christian Weise (1642–1708), headmaster of a large school at Zittau. He is the author of a prodigious number of lengthy plays with enormous casts, written for his pupils, in which all the characters, whether historical, biblical, fanciful, or farcical, are made to speak in the same vein of home-spun prose. His *Böse Catherina* (1702) is a crude version of the main plot in Shakespeare's *Taming of the Shrew*. Weise used a simple stage, and readily admitted the fool into his plays. In place of declamation he demanded clear delivery and individualized characterization.

The second tendency is marked by an increasing number of translations and adaptations from French classical drama, and culminates in the plays of Gottsched in the following century. It is first revealed in the work of Johannes Velten (1640–*c.* 1692), who strove to improve the status of actors by raising their standard of living, both social and moral, and to educate them and the public by the performance of plays derived from French classical drama. He wanted to do away with improvisation and to make the play an artistic entity, and he insisted that female parts should be played by women. Like many such attempts made without sufficient financial backing, Velten's failed, and he had to turn again to the popular plays—the *Haupt- und Staatsaktion*—to replenish his coffers. Nevertheless in the last decade of the century French classical tragedies were performed at the Court of Brunswick in imitation of the Parisian style.

4. The Eighteenth Century. The seventeenth century had seen the emergence of the professional actor whose improvisations invaded the domain of the dramatist; in contrast the eighteenth century sees the dramatist reinstated,

and an advance made towards the establishment of the German theatre on a permanent basis. The theatre formed only part of the vast programme in which Johann Christoph Gottsched (1700–66) joined forces with the philosopher Wolff and other advocates of enlightenment in their endeavours to educate the German public. In the 1720s he had launched some periodicals on English models, and when in 1730 he issued his *Critische Dichtkunst* he had every reason to think himself the dictator of German letters. A thorough-going rationalist, he saw salvation only in the application of reason—in his case a synonym for common sense. His bugbears were the disorderly popular plays with their improvisations, their Hanswurst, and their rowdy fooling. Boileau was his lodestar and the French theatre with its decorum and its easily formulated rules his ideal. French actors were at that time much in favour with all the emulators of Versailles at petty German Courts, and in Berlin, where Voltaire had brought in a French company for Frederick the Great. Owing to their detachment from Paris these actors were largely uninfluenced by the more natural style of acting instituted by Molière, and adhered to the declamation suitable to the works of Corneille.

The German theatre as Gottsched found it was undoubtedly in a poor way. The public was dazzled by the splendour of opera, and its taste vitiated by crude dramatic fare. In the absence of satisfactory German plays, Gottsched, assisted by his wife, tried to fill the gap with works in the French classical style, both translations and original plays, all written in sober prosaic alexandrines. Good fortune brought him into contact with the best theatrical company of his day—that of Caroline Neuber (1697–1760)—'die Neuberin', as she was called. Their alliance dates from 1727, when her company was playing during the Leipzig fair, and was strengthened by a later visit to Strasbourg, where the actress had the opportunity of studying the work of a French company. She was greatly impressed by their style, and resolved to emulate it—a decision which fitted in well with Gottsched's reforms. It was, however, not an easy task to convert the largely mercantile public of Leipzig to high-brow drama; her temporary success was due partly to Gottsched's authority, partly to the regard in which all things French were held at that time, but largely to her own vivacious charm. The collaboration could not, however, last, for Gottsched was a stickler for detail, Caroline Neuber a temperamental woman with a good sense of theatre and a desperate need of funds. Her famous enactment of Harlequin's banishment from the stage was not so much a tribute to Gottsched as a thrust at an inconvenient rival—the harlequin-player Müller; she had the audacity to reject Frau Gottsched's translation of Voltaire's *Alzire* for one less polished but more lively; they bickered over the costumes in *Der sterbende Cato* (1731)—in brief, the rift between them was inevitable. She came to Leipzig again in 1741 and was heartened by the enthusiasm of the young Lessing, but he had as yet neither fame nor influence, and with the passing of time her star waned. It must, however, be said in her favour that in combining French stateliness with German emotion she inaugurated a new era in German acting.

Gottsched found compensation for her loss in the companies of Heinrich Koch (1703–75) and Johann Schönemann (1704–82), both of whom had worked under Caroline Neuber; but his day too was over. By 1740 his overbearing arrogance had alienated even his own Leipzig followers, and his Zürich opponents were acclaiming the superiority of English imaginative poetry. The most gifted of his disciples, Johann Elias Schlegel (1719–49), cautiously compared *Julius Caesar*, recently translated into German and condemned by Gottsched as a wretched thing, with the work of Andreas Gryphius, and while conceding all the 'faults' of Shakespeare's play, firmly declared the latter to be superior in character-drawing. A new star had arisen on the horizon, destined to eclipse Gottsched's life-work. Lessing's oft-quoted remark that it would have been better if Gottsched had never meddled with the German theatre need not be accepted nowadays. The discipline he imposed was necessary and salutary, and first induced in the German public some recognition of artistic form; and if Schlegel later urged that the theatre should be regarded as a civic institution, his high conception of its value may ultimately be traced back to the influence of Gottsched. How firmly the latter had impressed himself on the German theatre may be gauged by the fact that Schlegel himself in his plays adhered strictly to Gottsched's ideal of French classical drama, and also by the violence with which Lessing, Herder, and others attacked it.

Schlegel's comedies are pleasant; his tragedies are remarkable chiefly for the fact that several, such as *Hermann* (1743), deal with episodes from German history. This vein was also exploited by the poet Klopstock, who celebrated Hermann and his victory over Quintilius Varus in A.D. 9, and his struggle against disunion among his own people, in a trilogy (1769–87) in the bardic, that is Ossianic, style. Written in rhythmic prose of studied simplicity, interspersed with lyrical choruses, these richly emotional scenes lack dramatic life, but the theme is symptomatic of a rising national consciousness.

Though Gottsched had all unsuspectingly signed his own death-warrant in damning *Julius Caesar*, Shakespeare was neither the first nor the only factor which militated against the stilted heroes and heroines of French origin; the play-going public was being further deflected from them by the converging streams of the *comédie larmoyante*, the *drame sérieux*, and the domestic tragedy, in all of which a strong middle-class element was asserting itself. In the domestic tragedy the moralizing sentimentality of Richardson's novels, then very popular in Germany, fused with the sterner accents of Lillo's *London Merchant* to produce, in the hands of Lessing, Schiller, and others, a type of drama truly German in character, and of vivid actuality. In all these plays verse gives way to prose.

The first milestone on this journey was the *Miss Sara Sampson* (1755) of Gotthold Ephraim Lessing (1729–81), which drew many tears, much to the satisfaction of the author, and had many equally tearful successors. Lessing himself made no further concession to Richardsonian soulfulness, and when he later returned to this genre with *Emilia Galotti* (1772) he imbued it with a far greater robustness. Sentimentality has vanished, and the main emphasis falls on the difference of outlook between the licentious despot and the commoner. If Emilia chooses to die for fear of her own weakness, and if the libertine is punished only by remorse, we may still see in Lessing, not indeed a revolutionary, but none the less an audacious critic of contemporary social conditions. Certain characters in this play, the stern, upright father, the more worldly-minded mother, the virtuous daughter, the high-born seducer, and the discarded mistress, set the pattern for this type of tragedy until our own day.

Between *Miss Sara Sampson* and *Emilia Galotti* appeared *Minna von Barnhelm* (1767), a comedy in which laughter results from humour rather than from ridicule, and in which the middle classes are made to inspire affection and respect. For the first time in German drama the characters are truly three-dimensional, and German to the core. The play is new also in that it deals with a topical subject, the aftermath of the Seven Years' War.

Lessing's last play, *Nathan der Weise* (1779), is the first to voice the great humanitarian message of this epoch, and fitly ushers in the blank-verse form.

As a dramatic critic Lessing demolished Gottsched and all he stood for in his *Briefe die neueste Litteratur betreffend* (1759), when he declared Shakespeare to be essentially nearer to the ancients than Corneille, in spite of the latter's classical form, and more likely to kindle indigenous talent. Nevertheless, in his *Hamburgische Dramaturgie* (1767–8) he seeks only to rid German drama of outworn conventions, and not to substitute for it the Shakespearian form, the inner scaffolding of which he does not seem to have understood. He insists on close logical linking of every scene, so much so that his *Emilia Galotti* drew from a Romantic critic the witty criticism: 'An excellent example of dramatic algebra.'

Comments on acting appear only in the earlier sections, but they are enough to show that he was a connoisseur, and could have given helpful advice. He sought grace and dignity rather than statuesque stylization, expressiveness rather than naturalism. Here as elsewhere the law of beauty must not be transgressed. Lessing believed with Riccoboni that the actor must never be carried away by his part, and also that the simulation of emotion may engender enough feeling to give warmth to the performance.

From the time of Caroline Neuber until the late 1760s the German theatre presents in its development a confused picture of companies formed, broken up, and reshuffled, all homeless, all dependent on the whim of the public or a patron, all wandering incessantly from Court to town, and town to Court, mostly in Germany but with excursions abroad to Zürich, Vienna, Russia. Entertaining glimpses of this way of life may be gained from the autobiographies of the actors Brandes and Iffland, or from Goethe's *Wilhelm Meister*. There were bitter feuds among the actors, but also much healthy emulation, and the standard of acting was continually being raised. After Schönemann and Koch, who mainly carried on the work of Caroline Neuber, came a number of eminent actors who in the course of the century brought the German theatre to the front rank of European art.

Konrad Ekhof (1720–78) was successful in overcoming the tendency to declamation imported from France, and by 1767 he had acquired a natural style which delighted Lessing. To Ekhof falls the honour of having founded the first academy of acting in Germany, in 1753, thus raising his calling to the status of a profession. The programme included lectures, discussions, and analyses of plays to be performed. Guiding principles were laid down to ensure high standards, collaboration between actors, and social recognition. Ekhof laboured unceasingly for this, and shortly before his death was busy with a scheme of pensions and insurances for actors. What he accomplished may be measured by the fact that while in 1692 a priest refused the sacrament to Velten because he was a comedian, Ekhof was accorded something resembling a public funeral.

Konrad Ackermann (1712–71) deserves a place in the history of the German stage because he first sought to establish in Germany a 'national' theatre, one, that is, that eschewed private, profit-making ownership, and set itself a high standard of plays and productions. In 1765 Ackermann settled in Hamburg which, on account of its active literary life and its contact with English letters, was rapidly outstripping Leipzig, formerly the intellectual centre of Germany. Here, prompted by his own needs and by the recent posthumous publication of Schlegel's thoughts on the theatre, he sought to establish a permanent playhouse, backed by a number of prominent business men and notabilities of the town. Only plays of repute were to be performed, preferably by German writers. Ballet, hitherto a sure source of revenue, was to be curtailed. Lessing, foremost critic and playwright of the day, was to be the mouthpiece of the new order, and in support of it a certain F. L. Löwen wrote the first history of the German theatre.

Much of this ambitious programme went unrealized. Ackermann was not a good business man and, disheartened by numerous cabals and lack of public appreciation, soon lost interest; his second-in-command, the aforesaid Löwen, had no control over the actors. The repertory proved inadequate, ballet inevitably reappeared, and Lessing, having failed to enlist general interest in the art of drama, gave up the attempt, and in his last Hamburg article of 4 Apr. 1768 scoffed at the naïve idea of giving the Germans a national theatre when they were not yet a nation. Nevertheless the idea lived on and bore fruit in Gotha, Mannheim, and Vienna, though not under municipal patronage.

It was at Gotha that the great actor August Wilhelm Iffland (1759–1814) got his first serious training for the stage. A group of writers, musicians, and connoisseurs had gathered there at the Court of Duke Ludwig Ernst, a man of taste and a patron of the arts. In 1774 a fire gutted the Weimar theatre where a company which included Ekhof and other actors of repute was then installed under Abel Seyler (1730–1801), and they were invited to Gotha, where they gave great satisfaction. The actor-dramatist Johann Christian Brandes (1735–99), developing the lyrical element introduced into German drama by Klopstock and intensified by the influence of Rousseau's *Pygmalion*, devised the monodrama, incidentally creating effective parts for his wife. For some five years these short *tours de force*, useful because with ballet they eked out the then customary triple bill, had an immense vogue. Libretti were provided for them by many leading writers, including F. W. Gotter, one of the outstanding literary men of Gotha. The fame of the theatre spread abroad, and there was general consternation when Seyler announced that he was going permanently to Dresden. At this point the composer Johann Friedrich Reichardt (1752–1814), an able schemer, suggested to the Duke that a 'national' theatre should be formed under his royal patronage, independent of private enterprise. Reichardt succeeded in detaching some of Seyler's company, and with Ekhof as his partner became managing director of the concern. This second 'national' theatre aroused much interest at first, Reichardt's *Theaterkalender* was widely read, and the introduction of a pensions scheme was felt to meet a great need among actors. After two years, however, enthusiasm died down. The somewhat conservative repertory—only two of the least stormy of the *Sturm und Drang* plays were given—quarrels between the management and the actors, the death of Ekhof in 1778, and the danger inherent in a repertory company playing continuously to the same limited public, all combined to wreck the scheme, and in 1779 the theatre closed.

Iffland, who had done excellent work at Gotha, and two of his companions there, Heinrich Beck (1760–1803) and Johann David Beil (1754–94), were engaged by Count Dalberg to go to Mannheim, then embarking on the third German 'national' theatre. The Duke of the Palatinate, having succeeded in 1778 to the kingdom of Bavaria, was obliged to remove his court to Munich, and, by way of compensation to his Mannheim subjects, had decided to equip a theatre for them under the direction of Dalberg. It was a happy choice, for the Count was a man of culture, energy, and resource. For two years the actual work of production was in the hands of Seyler, but in 1781 Dalberg himself took over, and the theatre forged ahead. Some memorable performances by Schröder in 1780 established Shakespeare in the repertory, and the theatre opened its doors to the younger generation. In 1781 *Die Räuber* by Friedrich Schiller (1759–1805), its turbulence somewhat toned down but its vitality unimpaired, was staged there. There was no lack of variety. Iffland, by his writing and acting in the genre, established the domestic drama, while Dalberg leaned to the polished French style, which accounts somewhat for the uncongenial atmosphere the young Schiller found there.

Friedrich Ludwig Schröder (1744–1816), mentioned above in connexion with the Mannheim theatre, is important in the history of German drama as the manager who first established Shakespeare in Germany. He alone was an actor of sufficient calibre to undertake such parts as Lear, Falstaff, and Iago. Herder, an earlier admirer of Shakespeare, had not wished to see him acted, and indeed the German stage at that time was not ready for him. Some attempts had been made to force *Hamlet* and *Romeo and Juliet* into the prevailing mould, but it was not until the *Götz von Berlichingen* (1773) of Johann Wolfgang Goethe (1749–1832) had broken the barriers of the 'regular' play that Shakespeare could be acted and appreciated. Schröder, who had seen *Hamlet* in Austria, though arranged *à la viennoise*, took the bold step of putting it on for an astonished Hamburg audience in 1776. It was much adapted, Hamlet being allowed to survive, as was Cordelia in a later version of *King Lear*, but an initial success had been gained, and other German theatres followed it up.

By now the *Sturm und Drang* movement, unleashed as far as drama was concerned by *Götz von Berlichingen*, was in full swing. The boldness with which the characters are sketched, their wide range, the utter disregard of the unities, the historical perspective, all proclaim the influence of Shakespeare. In this picture of the sixteenth century, 'natural man', hearty, healthy, staunch, stands out against the encroachment of civilization and its shams, while in Schiller's *Die Räuber* (1781) and *Kabale und Liebe* (1784), which close the movement, the author challenges the perverted social order of his day. The Faust legend is dramatized no less than three times, proof that the divine order is no longer accepted submissively. The younger generation, resentful of the tyranny of reason over aspiration and fervent ardour, rebels against regimentation and restraint. The tragic implications of rebellion—inescapable guilt and its retribution—are squarely faced, and it may be said that a new sense of tragedy is dawning, that of the tragedy inherent in the march of progress.

In many of these productions the poetic licence of Shakespeare is outdistanced, and even where the form is not irregular, the quickened pace sweeps the audience into a different world. In short, vivid scenes the action is spotlighted, or a mood reflected. Reinhold Lenz (1751–92) uses this technique with good effect in order to stress successive aspects of whatever evil he happens to be attacking in such plays as *Der Hofmeister* (1774) and *Die Soldaten* (1776). The break with classicism is complete, and it is obvious that the informality, even slovenliness, of the language called for increased realism in acting. An incidental change brought about in theatres by *Götz von Berlichingen* and the historical dramas (see RITTERDRAMA) which followed it was the acquisition by a number of companies of wardrobes of medieval costumes, which led to a greater use of the picturesque element in production.

By the time of the French Revolution the literary upheaval in Germany had spent itself. In *Egmont* (1788) Goethe abandoned the practice of scrappy scenes and rough-hewn language, and having achieved serenity in Italy, and a love of artistic shapeliness, returned in *Iphigenie* (1787) and *Tasso* (1790) to a regular form and blank verse of exquisite mellowness. Schiller, still avid for freedom, sought it now in the realm of thought and conscience, and gave it expression in verse even more vibrant than Goethe's. *Don Carlos* (1787), structurally the weakest of Schiller's plays owing to the shifting of emphasis from personal suffering to political and humanitarian issues, nevertheless heralds a change of outlook. During the subsequent ten years, a period of ill health but concentrated study, Schiller gained objectivity and aesthetic insight. His friendship with Goethe, which began in 1794, inaugurated a decade of intensive production. The year 1799 saw the completion of *Wallenstein*, a trilogy in which the turmoil of the Thirty Years' War is woven into a lucid pattern. *Maria Stuart* (1800) followed, equally well knit, and with an impressive array of finely contrasted personalities. Here, for the first time, is explored the theme of the soul freed by the acceptance of suffering. It appears again in the romanticized setting of *Die Jungfrau von Orleans* (1801), the most operatic of Schiller's plays, and in *Die Braut von Messina* (1803), the closest approximation of the age to the form of ancient drama. Fate, or Nemesis, assails a princely house; two hostile brothers are drawn to the same woman, who, too late to avert catastrophe, is discovered to be their sister; death is the penalty of fratricide. In this distillation of human passions, written in chiselled verse with superb lyrical choruses, Schiller's characteristic conception of tragedy is clearly portrayed; adverse fate is seen as a stepping-stone to sublimation, leaving a final sense of victory in defeat. His last completed play, *Wilhelm Tell* (1804), is not a tragedy, but for sheer stagecraft it surpasses its predecessors. This tale of the liberation of the Swiss cantons from the Austrian yoke by unity and singleness of purpose is told with dignified simplicity, in language which has cast off the last trammels of rhetoric.

The 'classical' dramas of Goethe, unlike Schiller's clarion calls, make an intimate and personal appeal. *Iphigenie* is bathed in a cool and tranquillizing light; in *Tasso* the characters quiver at a touch. Here staging can add little, and rarely satisfies, while Schiller's personages gain when the actor fills them out. It was Iffland, ably assisted by Johann Ferdinand Fleck (1757–1801), who first presented Schiller's later work to the public beyond Weimar. In the 1790s the campaign against the French revolutionaries had caused much disorganization in the Mannheim theatre. Iffland, then in charge of production, went on tour. In 1796 he appeared with great success in Berlin, until then much in the rear of theatrical development, and was promptly appointed director, by royal decree, of a National Theatre, the culminating honour of his career. The public flocked to his productions, and a better building had to be provided, more worthy of Schiller's masterpieces. During the French occupation Iffland, bereft of his state subsidy, had to adapt his repertory to the demands of the authorities, but loyalty led him to refuse a flattering summons to Vienna. The return of the royal family assured him once again of financial support, and music and ballet, as well as drama, were entrusted to his care. Overwork and the hostility of the rising Romantic generation undermined his health, and he died in harness in 1814.

In the meantime an experiment of great importance and interest was being carried out in Weimar. Goethe's dramatic work of the 1790s and after, though dealing with problems made actual by the French Revolution, is highly stylized; the characters have paled to symbols. This development finds its parallel in his work as director of the Weimar theatre. When in 1792 Goethe was entrusted by the Grand Duke with the entire responsibility for the Weimar Court theatre, he went to work with his usual thoroughness and circumspection. By this time the naturalism fostered by the domestic conversation-piece and the *Sturm und Drang* plays had become popular among actors, to the exclusion of all else. Goethe regarded this as a degradation of the theatre, and resolved to combat it with the same determination with which he and Schiller opposed all pandering to the public taste in the literary sphere. The worst offender in both respects was August von Kotzebue (1761–1819), a prolific writer and master of stage effect, whose clever but shallow and often risqué plays outshone their own in public favour. He was a great thorn in Goethe's flesh, as his works had perforce to be included in the Weimar repertory to swell the box-office takings.

As the years went by Goethe's horror of realism increased. The Greece of Sophocles became his mental refuge. His essay *Shakespeare und kein Ende* (1815, pub. 1826) relegated Shakespeare from the visual scene to the realm of the inner eye. He sought to inculcate in his actors a technique of dignified gesture, differing from the French style prevalent at the beginning of the century by the absence of rhetorical declamation. Already in 1785 J. J. Engel, in his treatise *Ideen zu einer Mimik*, had defined gesture as 'music for the eye', and had worked out elaborate patterns of movements conveying every shade and grade of emotion without transgressing the laws of beauty. Engel, however, had no belief in verse drama, and Goethe could only use him as a starting-point. The actors, speaking in cadenced phrasing, were not allowed to turn away from the spectator, nor to diverge from carefully prescribed groupings, nor to attract undue attention to themselves. Thus an artistic ensemble was for the first time made the prime purpose of dramatic presentation, and it is much to be regretted that the tendency to artificiality increased after Schiller's death, so that the rugged humour of such a play as Kleist's *Der zerbrochene Krug* was smoothed out. Goethe's aim, however, if not the manner of its execution, commands respect, and the Weimar tradition was taken to Berlin by Pius Alexander Wolff (1782–1828), the most accomplished actor of this school.

5. THE NINETEENTH CENTURY. The achievement of the eighteenth century in the German theatre had been the employment, in the absence of centralization in the country, of drama as one of the main vehicles of culture, and as a potentially great factor in social and literary life. On the other hand, the profession of acting was still hampered by insecurity and lack of funds, with all their attendant evils, and there was a disquieting cleavage between the intellectual leaders and the general public. Nor could the Romantic school, which arose in about 1798, be looked to to bridge the gap. The highly intellectual and individualistic outlook of its writers was not favourable to drama. The Schlegels, Arnim, Brentano, Fouqué, Eichendorff, produced no dramatic work of lasting value; the recurring features of their work are the frequent use of the supernatural, the mythical, and the mysterious, the accentuation of abnormality and indefiniteness of form. The ironical twist which Ludwig Tieck (1773–1853) gave to his dramatized folk-tales robbed them of their vigour, while the not unattractive church-window transparency of his more ambitious medieval plays denied to his characters the attributes of flesh and blood. His intensive study of Elizabethan drama bore no dramatic fruit, though his public readings from Shakespeare's plays probably did more than all the Romantic theorizing to make the latter's genius appreciated in Germany. As critical adviser to the Dresden theatre Tieck stimulated artistic endeavour as far as the prevailing conditions would allow, though a performance of *A Midsummer Night's Dream* on a specially constructed Shakespearian stage, as Tieck imagined it to have been, remained an isolated experiment.

Meanwhile the authors of the so-called Fate Dramas—Zacharias Werner (1768–1823) with his one-act tragedy *Der vierundzwanzigste Februar* (1810, pub. 1815), Adolf Müllner (1774–1829) with *Der neunundzwanzigste Februar* (1812) and the successful *Die Schuld* (1813), and the young Grillparzer with *Die Ahnfrau* (1817)—wallowed in morbid perversions, and turned into sheer malignancy the power Schiller had revered in Sophocles. Yet one dramatist of genius did appear—Heinrich von Kleist (1777–1811), who pursued his lonely way determined to unite in his work the grandeur of the fate element in antiquity with Shakespearian character-drama. In *Penthesilea* (1808) the warring impulses in the heroine of the amazon and the woman brought Kleist very near his goal, though the savagery of her passion has no parallel in classical tragedy. In this play, and in his comedy of village life, *Der zerbrochene Krug* (1808), Kleist sought to increase the pace by substituting the ebb and flow of action for the conventional division into acts, an experiment which he later abandoned. His highly nervous temperament led him to create heroes of a like mould, self-willed, excitable, equally capable of collapse or heroism. The supporting characters were of tougher fibre; only in some of his women did he prove that he could use a softer touch. He showed himself a true Romantic in his use of sleep-walking scenes, dreams, and second sight. His *Prinz Friedrich von Homburg* (1810, pub. 1821), with its gallery of brilliantly characterized military types, reveals most clearly his gift of individualization with the utmost economy of effort. Kleist's language is terse and pregnant, bursting into vivid imagery at moments of heightened emotion. During his lifetime he failed almost entirely to establish contact with the stage; neither Goethe, averse by nature to tragedy, nor his Romantic contemporaries suspected his quality.

The German theatre in the opening decades of the nineteenth century seemed to be in a state of stagnation. The Napoleonic wars hampered enterprise, and the nation that was soon to rise in arms against the invader could slake its thirst for freedom on nothing more 'actual' than Schiller's plays. After the battle of Waterloo the reactionary Metternich régime, which excluded social, political, and religious subjects from public discussion, reduced the theatre to a mere place of entertainment; importations from France—'well-made' plays by Scribe, Delavigne, and the vaudevillists—and from Denmark—the dramas of Oehlenschlaeger—occupied a considerable place in the repertory. The chief German purveyors of light refreshment were Eduard von Bauernfeld (1802–90) with his conversation pieces, Roderich Benedix (1811–73) with his bourgeois domestic interiors, Ernest Raupach (1784–1852) with plays in the Kotzebue tradition, and Friedrich Halm (1806–71), would-be successor to Schiller. To these must be added

Elias Niebergall (1815–43) in Frankfurt, and Charlotte Birch-Pfeiffer (1800–68), wholesale purveyor of other people's goods (her *Die Waise von Lowood* of 1856 is based on *Jane Eyre*), who outshone even Bauernfeld in popularity. The only people to rebel against this emasculation of the stage were the politically minded members of the 'Young Germany' movement, with the result that vigilance in high quarters increased until the troubles of 1848 produced some relaxation. The movement produced at least two dramatists who, without writing masterpieces, showed at any rate vigour and vitality—Christian Dietrich Grabbe (1801–36) and Georg Büchner (1813–37). Both rebels, one by temperament, the other by disillusioned conviction, they have some affinity in form and style with the *Sturm und Drang* writers. Karl Gutzkow (1811–78) also connected with the movement, aired his political views in lengthy novels; Gutzkow's plays, except for *Uriel Acosta* (1847), are of little account. His contemporary Gustav Freytag (1816–95) marks the transition from unrest to constructive endeavour on a bourgeois basis, characteristic of the so-called *Biedermeierzeit*.

If drama in Germany during the inter-revolutionary years was on the whole mediocre, some enterprise is visible in the theatrical field. There was able and even brilliant acting by Ferdinand Esslair (1772–1840) and Ludwig Devrient (1784–1832), but the individual actor still tended to display his powers to the detriment of artistic unity. Moreover, the dispersion of German theatrical companies among many small states meant that only in a few large towns possessing several theatres could they cultivate a style of their own. Tieck's work in Dresden has already been mentioned. In Düsseldorf Karl Immermann (1796–1840) founded a little colony of artistically-minded men, convinced of the potential influence of a good theatre. From 1834 to 1837 he was director of the Stadttheater, and provided a number of 'subscription performances' of standard plays, intended to serve as models and show what could be achieved. He laid the main stress on delivery, emulating in this respect Goethe, whose results at Weimar had impressed him, but avoided the latter's exaggerations. The press and the bulk of the public were, however, indifferent to his efforts, and to his intense disappointment his experiment ended in bankruptcy. Certain technical improvements were also made at this time. Scenery was lighter and more easily moved, gas-lighting was introduced after 1830—though Cologne still considered it too dazzling in 1837—and in Berlin, most highly subsidized of the Court theatres, Iffland's successor, Count von Brühl, insisted on greater accuracy than hitherto in historical costume.

Richard Wagner (1813–83) belongs mainly to the domain of music, but the texts of his operas, all written by himself, have considerable merit. His works may be regarded as the fulfilment of the Romantic ideal—the perfect fusion of poetry, music, and the pictorial arts. The buried treasures of medieval myth and epic, unearthed during the Romantic period, were fused into a clear-cut action, working up to a sublime close, and imbued with some moral or philosophical ideal which ensured their appeal to a modern audience. In his revival of Old High German alliterative verse Wagner skilfully made use of sound and rhythm to convey both thought and mood.

His greatest contemporary in the field of pure drama was Friedrich Hebbel (1813–63), whose first play, *Judith*, was produced in 1840, and his last, *Die Nibelungen*, in 1861. Hebbel's style lacks the mellow clarity of Grillparzer's. It is allusive, syncopated, image-laden, and leaves the reader still searching for motive and implication beneath the words. In this, as in his questioning mind, his sense of the complexity of life, his understanding of women, Hebbel is essentially modern, and Ibsen and many others are greatly in his debt.

Less successful was Hebbel's contemporary, Otto Ludwig (1813–65). His characters, magnificently alive and self-willed, were often unamenable to the demands of dramatic structure; hence his plots tended to become involved and even obscure, and a number of promising first drafts came to nothing. His best play, *Der Erbförster* (1850), is linked by some of its characters to traditional domestic tragedy while anticipating the future in its vigorous realism, as seen in the tricks of speech by which the characters betray themselves.

By the time Hebbel and Ludwig died a great change was coming over Germany. Successful wars had brought her political supremacy, unification had stimulated industrial enterprise, and the all too sudden rise in prosperity created extravagant hopes, naïve national self-conceit, and rampant materialism. This was poor soil for serious drama. The nation's mentality was expressed in the plays of Ernst von Wildenbruch (1845–1909). An ardent admirer of the Hohenzollerns, and proud of his nation's past, he wrote historical dramas which proved extremely popular, mainly on account of his great gift for effective crowd scenes, racy dialogue, and picturesque lower-class characters. Wildenbruch's work is undoubtedly sincere, and it is to be deplored that he descended at times to sheer claptrap, as in his trilogy on the story of Canossa, *Heinrich und Heinrichs Geschlecht* (1896).

No dramatist of outstanding merit marked the opening years of the new empire in Germany, but a number of theatrical enterprises deserve mention at a time when the commercial spirit invaded the artistic as well as every other sphere. Duke George II of Saxe-Meiningen (1826–1914), an artist of considerable talent, and a devotee of the theatre, took to designing for his Court company scenery and costumes depicted with the utmost accuracy after exhaustive study. Inspired by the actress Ellen Franz, later his second (morganatic) wife, and by the productions of Charles Kean which he had seen in London, he concentrated on continuous rehearsal in costume, particularly of crowd and battle scenes, and on silent by-play, in which the leading characters, if not otherwise occupied, were obliged to share. The scene-painter and the stage mechanic, supplied with first-class material, came into their own. The result of all this was that many historical and romantic plays came to life for German audiences for the first time. The earlier endeavours of von Brühl in Berlin and Dingelstedt in Weimar were combined with a new desire for verisimilitude, consistent with beauty of effect, and for historical accuracy of scenery and costume. The fame of the Meininger players spread. From 1874 onwards they visited Berlin and other capitals (including London in 1881) and within a few years the reforms popularized by the Meininger so influenced the theatre in Germany that it rapidly advanced to a leading position in Europe. In 1890 the indefatigable director, Ludwig Chronegk, broke down, and the tours, having accomplished their mission, were discontinued. The greatest actor trained in this company was Albert Bassermann (1867–1952), who later supported Otto Brahm. In course of time the Meininger players were accused of excessive attention to detail, but there is no doubt that they set a standard of ensemble playing and pictorial effect which was new to the European theatre (though not to the English), and had great and far-reaching results. The chief difficulty of their method was the necessity for avoiding frequent changes of scenery, and this was not finally overcome until Karl Lautenschläger introduced the revolving stage in 1896.

Although in 1876 the opening of the new opera-house at Bayreuth had been hailed as an important event which raised high hopes of artistic progress, by 1883, in Berlin at any rate, there was a feeling of stagnation, intensified by the increasing practice of long runs. The new movement in drama, known as naturalism, being a movement of revolt, was naturally in bad odour politically and socially. Yet the more thoughtful of the younger generation were shocked by the national complacency and by the misery of the working class under the new industrialism. Ibsen's plays gave further impetus to their discontent. The Deutsches Theater, founded by Adolf L'Arronge and Ludwig Barnay, with the actors Josef Kainz and Agnes Sorma, would have opened its doors to the new dramatists, but there was trouble with the censor, and in 1889 a private company, the Freie Bühne, modelled on Antoine's Théâtre Libre in Paris, came into being under the aegis of the critic Otto Brahm. It had no fixed habitat, and played at matinées only. The campaign opened with Ibsen's *Ghosts* and plays by Tolstoy, Strindberg, and Zola. The first German play to be performed was *Vor Sonnenaufgang*, but the real manifesto of the new school was *Die Familie Selicke* (1890), by Arno Holz (1863–1929), a sordid picture of mental, moral, and physical decay, in which man appears as the helpless plaything of circumstance. The fame of the movement rests, however, on the work of the young Gerhart Hauptmann (1862–1946). He did not disdain squalor but neither did he seek it. His early plays vibrate with actuality, but the comparative failure of his historical drama, *Florian Geyer* (1895), whose violent and stirring action was not well served by the naturalistic approach, caused him to forsake naturalism for symbolism, as in his next play, *Die versunkene Glocke* (1896). His subsequent work, tending sometimes to one style, sometimes to the other, conformed more and more to normal dramatic procedure. It opened up no new avenues, but served to confirm the excellence of his gift for creating characters in the round and dialogue that rings true.

Hauptmann's chief rival in popularity was Hermann Sudermann (1857–1928), a clever playwright with an unfailing sense of the theatre. His plays reflect the problems of contemporary society from a progressive angle. His manner is realistic, but submits to no scientific discipline; compared with Hauptmann his situations often appear forced in order to ensure an effect.

The founding of the Freie Bühne was followed, when the need for providing good plays at low prices for the working class was realized, by the Neue Freie Volksbühne in 1890, limited to subscribers who drew lots for their seats, and by the Schillertheater in 1894. In the new drama that was sweeping across Europe Berlin was well to the fore. The Meininger methods of staging could be adapted to the requirements of naturalism, provided such conventions as facing the audience, speaking standard German, and so on, were scrapped. The stress laid on the darker side of life and on the endless frailties of human nature demanded from the actor, as from the dramatist, the most minute observation; all self-expression was an offence against the first principles of naturalism, which demanded the subordination of the actor to his role, and made of the whole play 'a slice of life'.

A reaction against naturalism originated in Munich, and is a sign of the gradual ascendancy of the southern capital. Frank Wedekind (1864–1918), in flouting the philistine with such plays as *Frühlings Erwachen* (1891), and also *Erdgeist* (1895), gave his characters the significance of types rather than individuals, and thus pointed the way to expressionism. This Bohemian, with his predilection for animal passions, however amoral, and his eye for the grotesque, acted his own heroes, ably supported by Gertrud Eysoldt (1870–1955), with flamboyant irony, in garish settings which suggested the cabaret, that product of modernity which was about to become a serious rival to the theatre. W. E. DELP, *rev.*

6. THE TWENTIETH CENTURY. No new dramatist of more than passing interest appeared in the early years of the twentieth century. It was rather a period in which the dramatists of the previous decade consolidated their reputations. Hauptmann enriched the tradition of the *Bürgerliches Trauerspiel* with

Rose Bernd (1903). The heroine of this play differs from her literary predecessors in that she is a working-class girl and is to a greater degree than they a victim of her environment and the physical demands of her own nature. Wedekind's sequel to *Erdgeist*, *Die Büchse der Pandora* (the two plays together are known as *Die Lulu-Tragödie*), appeared in 1904. In this the amoral and irresistible heroine meets a gruesome end in a Whitechapel garret at the hands of Jack the Ripper.

By the turn of the century neo-Romantic drama, written mostly in verse and offering opportunities for spectacular scenery and gorgeous costumes, was ousting the naturalistic drama on which it had gradually been gaining in popularity for the past ten years. This was due in part to the European success of the plays of Maeterlinck and of Oscar Wilde's *Salomé*. Herbert Eulenberg's *Ritter Blaubart* (1905), Ernst Hardt's *Tantris der Narr* (1907), and Wilhelm Schmidtbonn's *Graf von Gleichen* (1908), are examples of the German equivalent of this genre. A 'neo-classicism' which began to manifest itself in these years seems to have been an offshoot of neo-Romanticism rather than a reaction to it, although Paul Ernst (1866–1933) in his *Demetrios* (1905) and *Canossa* (1908), and Wilhelm von Scholz (1874–) in *Der Jude von Konstanz* (1905), follow their models, Schiller and Hebbel, in writing plays classical in form and with a clearly expressed ethical content.

With the greater opportunities for scenic variety and splendour offered by these differing types of drama, and with the invention or increased efficiency of various technical devices (electric lighting, spotlighting, revolving and sliding stages, etc.), the role of the producer as a co-ordinator in the theatre became of the utmost importance. The age found its man in Max Reinhardt (1873–1943), who was director of the Deutsches Theater in Berlin from 1905 to 1920 and again from 1924 to 1932. His production of *The Merchant of Venice* in 1905 marked the beginning of one of the most brilliant eras in Berlin's theatrical history, and culminated, as one after another of Shakespeare's plays were taken into the repertoire, in the two Shakespeare 'cycles' of 1912 (see No. 78) and 1915. The maximum of colour and movement compatible with the demands of the individual drama was Reinhardt's self-confessed aim at this time, though later in his career he conducted many progressive theatrical experiments.

Towards the end of the first decade of the twentieth century two dramatists appeared whose work is indicative of a coming change in the dramatic climate. Two attempts at neo-Romantic drama by Carl Sternheim (1878–1942), *Ulrich und Brigitte* (1900) and *Don Juan* (1910), were failures because their author's talent was essentially comic, but a year later he turned to social satire and achieved fame with *Die Hose*, which constituted a merciless attack on the selfishness and vulgarity underlying the pseudo-romantic affectation and hypocritical morality-mongering of the German bourgeoisie From now on Sternheim regarded himself as 'der Arzt am Leib seiner Zeit' and followed up his first success with a series of similar satires, to which he later gave the collective title *Aus dem bürgerlichen Heldenleben*. The dialogue was at one and the same time distorted and flat, conveying the dehumanized or devitalized nature of his characters. In its partial disregard of the laws of grammar and syntax and the habits of colloquial speech it foreshadows the linguistic experiments later undertaken by writers of the Expressionist movement.

If Sternheim may be said to have elaborated on the element of savage social satire found in the plays of Wedekind, Sternheim's contemporary, Georg Kaiser (1878–1945), could be described as the inheritor of Wedekind's glorification of sex as representative of the life-force in a decadent world—at least in his early plays. It is combined with a lightly irreverent attitude to the scriptures and the German classics (Hebbel's *Judith*) in *Die Jüdische Witwe* (1909). Kaiser's Judith goes out against Holofernes because her impotent old husband has made her frustrated; she returns to be rewarded with the office of high-priestess and the promise of clandestine joys with the handsome high-priest in the inner sanctum of the temple.

Kaiser is generally considered to have been the leading dramatist of the Expressionist movement, which began in about 1912. He was possibly the most popular, and certainly the most prolific dramatist of the time, but the pioneer of the movement, as far as drama is concerned, was Reinhard Johannes Sorge (1892–1916). His first play, *Der Bettler* (1912) has all the elements later considered to be characteristic of Expressionist drama. It presents the struggle of a young man to find both his true vocation in society and a meaningful inner existence which will establish a bond between himself and the rest of mankind and reveal the short span of his own life as a link in the chain of eternity. The form and structure of the play is determined by the subject-matter: the inner development of the main character provides the interest which unites a series of otherwise very loosely connected incidents, and in this respect Sorge's play approaches the epic form of the novel. (One is reminded of Aristotle's remarks on the undramatic nature of the *Odyssey*, in which the character of Ulysses is the main unifying element.) Also reminiscent of the epic form are the short scenes faded in and out by means of spotlighting; these tend to produce an even flow of movement at a relaxed state of tension rather than a taut action building up to a climax. There is also a wide variety of mood and style: scenes in verse representative of the hero's spiritual struggle alternate with crassly naturalistic scenes of domestic life in which sequences typical of the Symbolists' use of words and gestures have been boldly placed. In fact, the fundamental nature of the theme is matched by a technique which soars above the limitations which the medium of the stage usually sets.

A whole host of writers, mostly of Sorge's generation, now wrote drama approximating more or less to the tendencies found in *Der Bettler*. In Kaiser's *Die Bürger von Calais* (1914) the idea of 'der neue Mensch' is developed: the hero is the representative of a new and better generation in that he teaches his fellow men the way to a nobler life by the rejection of violence as a means of solving human conflicts and by willingly sacrificing himself for the sake of the community. The language of this play is already highly experimental and typical of general Expressionist practice. Short explosive phrases separated by dashes replace grammatically constructed sentences. Articles and pronouns are omitted as unessential, and verbs and nouns stand starkly without adjectives.

In the plays of Fritz von Unruh (1885–) these linguistic experiments develop out of an attempt to convey the mood peculiar to the clipped speech of army officers. The atmosphere of frustration generated by this means in *Offiziere* (1911) and *Louis Ferdinand, Prinz von Preussen* (1913), illustrates the tension between the older and the younger generations at this time in their attitude not only to war but also to material, as opposed to spiritual, progress. In Unruh's most celebrated play, *Ein Geschlecht* (1916), this theme is universalized by making the characters types, such as mother, son, coward, soldier, etc., who wear costumes reminiscent of no particular age, speak in verse, and make stylized gestures against the background of a bare landscape suggesting metaphysical dimensions. The sculptor-cum-dramatist Ernst Barlach (1870–1938) achieves something of the same effect in *Der arme Vetter* (1917) by using the opposite means of a localized setting—that of his own north German landscape—as a background for semi-humorous characters who talk in dialect. The awed consciousness of a spiritual reality dwarfing the mundanities of life, and the way his characters conflict in their experience of both, give to all his plays their peculiar tension.

In *Seeschlacht* (1918), by Reinhard Goering (1887–1936), the contemporary problem of whether, in wartime, one should obey orders or one's own conscience is isolated and elevated to reveal its significance for man's spiritual development by setting the action in the turret of a warship before and during the Battle of Jutland in May, 1916, and making the participants a group of sailors whose dialogue is reminiscent of the exchanges of the chorus in Greek drama.

The choice of a contemporary incident for the subject of Goering's play indicates a tendency among expressionist dramatists in these war years to divide into two camps—those mainly interested in the spiritual rebirth of the individual, and those more concerned with the concrete problems of political and social reform thrown up by the Russian revolution of 1917. The first tendency, in an already well developed form, is represented by the *Himmel und Hölle* (1919) of Paul Kornfeld (1889–1942). The idea expressed in this drama is that the soul must struggle out of the world of sin and darkness into purity and light, and Kornfeld shows the spiritual progress of his characters from devils to angels in a series of stages—a form already present in embryo in earlier expressionist plays but now earning the description of *Stationendrama*.

This technique was also employed by the main representative of the opposite or 'activist' tendency, Ernst Toller (1893–1939), though with very different results. In *Die Wandlung* (1919), which really goes back to Sorge's *Bettler* for its inspiration, the hero, after encountering the horrors of modern existence, finds his true vocation in leading the people to a social revolution whose aim is mass spiritual rebirth rather than simple material gain. Realistic scenes alternate regularly with symbolic or 'dream' sequences in a way which suggests that the author is exploiting the resources of a technique, the possibilities of which have already been well tried out and defined. The contemporary political and social scene was more specifically criticized in the adaptation of Sophocles' *Antigone* by Walter Hasenclever (1890–1940), an anti-war play in which the figure of Creon is intended as a satirical picture of the German emperor.

These plays were in fact indicative of a coming change in the tone and mood of expressionist drama. The idealism expressed, sometimes grimly, in the adverse years of the war, and the high hopes placed in the future and a new generation of men, barely outlasted the peace of 1919, which was followed by social upheaval, political revolution, and anarchy in many walks of public life. In Kaiser's *Gas, Part I* (1918), the contemporary problem of the inevitable march of material progress, after social revolution, bringing with it the spiritual disintegration of mankind fills the whole play with gloomy foreboding, and the promise of the Girl at the end of the play that she will give birth to one of a generation less materialistically minded than the last does not carry much conviction. In *Gas, Part II* (1920), the incidents of Part I are brought into historical perspective and shown to be a stage of doubtful idealism which had negative results. The new man is unable to prevail over his own generation, which is no less materialistic than the last, and the play ends with mankind annihilating itself by losing control of the vast technical resources which it has developed without thought for the adverse effects on its spiritual existence.

The second part of *Gas* is typical of the pessimistic turn taken by expressionist themes from 1920 onwards and prepares the way for the decline of the 'ecstatic' kind of expressionist drama. In the work of lesser dramatists the elements of experimentation, stylization, and expressiveness led to formlessness, gross exaggeration, and crudity for its own sake; even the work of dramatists of merit was affected by this critical period in the history of German drama. The belief in the approaching dawn of the Kingdom of Love in *Die Gewaltlosen* (1919) of Ludwig Rubiner (1882–1920) is somewhat too starry-eyed; the treatment given by Hanns Johst (1890–) to the subject of the *poète maudit* in *Der Einsame* (1919) was very popular at the time, but now appears ranting and emotional; the *Spiegelmensch* (1920) of Franz Werfel (1890–1945) complicates the stages of a soul's journey to redemption by giving it a reflection and having it play hide-and-seek with itself; while Toller's genius for conveying the physical horrors of reality is carried to extremes beyond the point of mere embarrassment in *Der deutsche Hinkemann* (1924).

By this time, however, a generation of writers too young to have taken part in the inception of the movement was beginning to produce its first plays. In the *Vatermord* (1920) of Arnolt Bronnen (1895–1960) and the *Krönung Richards III* (1921) of Hans Henny Jahnn (1894–1959) the excesses of expressionism in decline become an end in themselves. The subject-matter—sexual vagaries coupled with murder and torture—suggests that the elements of expressionism which interested them most were mainly those of chaos and anarchy found in the early experimental plays of the painter Oskar Kokoschka (1886–), whose theme of the revolt of man's animal nature in a society ordered with an unnatural severity bordering on hysteria really belongs to the pre-expressionist period of Wedekind. It is probable that they reflect the moral and social chaos of post-war Germany, and the emotional frigidity with which their authors pile horror on horror (also reflected in the thriller-films *The Cabinet of Doctor Caligari* and *Doctor Mabuse*) is another indication of the growing change of mood.

After these years of crisis the need was felt for a return to a more realistic, less subjective style of drama coupled with a more orthodox approach towards the problems of dramatic form and technique, and the name of *die neue Sachlichkeit* was soon found for the new tendency. (Sternheim was already satirizing it in 1926 in *Die Schule von Uznach.*) Most of the expressionist writers of the previous decade were affected by it, but the works of the new generation give it its authoritative note. Thematically, the *Heimkehrerdrama* (drama of the home-coming soldier) is a genre representative of the new movement. Two years before the appearance of *Der deutsche Hinkemann*, Toller's play on the subject, Bertolt Brecht (1898–1956) had been awarded the Kleist Prize for his first play, *Trommeln in der Nacht* (1922), in which the home-coming soldier unheroically turns his back on the idealism of the Communist revolutionaries of 1919 and decides to make the best of the situation by marrying the fiancée who has been sleeping with a black-marketeer during his absence at the front. This acceptance of the bleak reality of the present was followed by the early attempts of the comic dramatist (comedy had not thrived with expressionism) Carl Zuckmayer (1896–) to place the spectacle of a world run mad in its proper perspective by aiming at sanity and sobriety of vision. In *Schinderhannes* (1927), this resulted in his showing a robber and his band in eighteenth-century Germany as no worse than the grasping merchants and inhuman officers of the law who are his natural enemies. All this without resort to the grotesque, which had been one of the essentials of expressionist technique. A year later Brecht, more cynically inclined than his contemporary, produced a version of Gay's *Beggar's Opera* called *Die Dreigroschenoper*, in which the robber Macheath, in league with a corrupt chief of police, battens on the poor, whom Brecht sees as the real victims.

Historical drama was extremely popular in this period, particularly in the late 1920s when a historical setting was used to present contemporary political problems and crises. The rise, marked by extreme violence, of dictators or dictatorial elements in various European countries was the occasion for a series of plays in which the problems of the power of the tyrant, of nationalism and mass feeling, and of how violence should be met, are variously treated. Unruh's *Bonaparte* (1926) presents Napoleon as the one man who in his age had the unique opportunity of forgiving his enemies and becoming 'der neue Mensch', but he succumbs to the temptation of personal glory and prefers to be elected emperor. In Werfel's *Paulus unter den Juden* (1926), the Jews as a nation fail to overcome their age-old prejudices and, misled by an unprincipled priesthood, reject the new prophet in their midst. *Der weisse Heiland* (1920) is the ironic title given by Gerhardt Hauptmann to a play about Montezuma, pious king of the Aztecs, who discovers all too late that the white men arriving from over the sea are no saviours, but invaders bent on the merciless extinction of his people. This irony becomes savage a few years later in *Die heilige Johanna der Schlachthöfe* (1929), where Brecht, with more overt reference to the contemporary, social, and political situation than had been made by Hauptmann, shows a young Salvation Army girl being destroyed in a conflict between big-businessmen and their starving employees whom she is trying to help without resorting to violence. It was at this time, too, that Zuckmayer produced the bitterest (and most successful) of his comedies, *Der Hauptmann von Köpenick* (1931), in which a desperate out-of-work cobbler, whose prison-record is against him, steals a captain's uniform and, because of the cringing obedience accorded to even the mere outward signs of power and authority in a Prussia run mad with militarism, is able to arrest the Mayor of Köpenick and abscond with the civic funds.

This outburst of pessimism, with its urgent sense of the dangers imminent in a Europe already drifting towards another war, was suddenly silenced shortly before 1933, when many German writers fled from the advent of National Socialism. Most of the dramatists who remained, or made a name for themselves in the period up to the close of the Second World War, wrote ideological drama nationalistic in tone. The favourite subjects were incidents in German history which lent themselves to showing the German people in righteous conflict with the materialistic English or the perfidious French. Johst's *Schlageter* (1933), which shows patriotic German resistance to the French occupation of the Ruhr after the First World War, represents the first of a long line of such plays, the most celebrated of which were perhaps those by Erwin Kolbenheyer (1878–1962). In *Gregor und Heinrich* (1934) the Pope and the Kaiser fight against each other as representatives of politico-philosophical opposites. The ageing Hauptmann was one of the few dramatists who, probably because of his popularity, managed to continue writing without toeing the ideological line. His *Atridentetralogie* (1941–6), in which the high priest who persuades Agamemnon to sacrifice his daughter is a thinly disguised portrait of a modern dictator, ends with the self-immolation of Iphigenia in a world of bloodshed and violence.

Understandably, the volume of drama written in exile did not equal that of novel-writing and poetry, and yet it was during these years, and as he fled from country to country before the invading German armies, that Brecht's art reached its summit in four plays already considered by some to be the most important in the German drama of the twentieth century. *Das Leben des Galilei* (1942) appears to be a development from the historical drama of the 1920s, with Venice and Florence representing Capitalism and Communism respectively and Galileo the socially conscious artist who must choose between them. The army-victualler in *Mutter Courage und ihre Kinder* (1942) who tries to live off the, war which takes from her all her children, is Brecht's most famous creation. Brecht not only continued and developed the themes of post-Expressionism: he also developed the formal experiments of the Expressionists into a theory of 'epic theatre' with a device called *Verfremdung* (alienation), which enabled him to take advantage of the new possibilities opened up by the Expressionist liberation of dramatic form while imposing a unity on his material by means of his tendentious or didactic attitude. A more orthodox Communist than Brecht, but a lesser artist, the prolific Friedrich Wolf (1888–) continued while an exile in Russia in the footsteps of Ernst Toller with *Die Matrosen von Cattaro* (1930), a drama of social revolt, and was one of the first to attack the Nazi persecution of the Jews, in *Professor Mamlock* (1935).

The immediate post-war years produced no new names in German drama. The kind of play propagated by National Socialism naturally ceased to be written or performed, and the plays Brecht wrote while in exile, which might have provided an inspirational link with the past, were at first only performed in Switzerland or East Germany. A minor exception was Wolfgang Borchert (1921–48), whose *Draussen vor der Tür* (1947) was originally written as a radio-play. Borchert conveys the returning soldier's sense of isolation by presenting his former friends and relatives as phantoms of his imagination, and by making the river into which he throws himself an actor in the drama. Zuckmayer returned to Germany and wrote again for the stage, but his one considerable success, *Des Teufels General* (1947), was really a war-time play in the sense that it dealt with a war-time problem from a war-time point of view: a German pilot is finally convinced by a friend whom he has caught in the act of sabotage that he is fighting for an evil cause, and as a result he commits suicide by crashing his plane.

The continuity in the German dramatic tradition seems to have been provided by Switzerland, where Brecht's *Mutter Courage* was performed during the war and where this dramatist first produced his plays on returning to Europe after the years spent in exile. Max Frisch (1911–) had in fact begun writing plays during the war, but it was not till some time afterwards that he scored a success in German-speaking countries with *Die chinesische Mauer* (1946, revised 1955), an ambitious attempt in the style of Brecht's *Der kaukasische Kreidekreis* (1943), but with the addition of cabaret-like scenes interrupting the action of a simple Chinese fable to present famous figures from European literature and history. Frisch's description of the play as a farce indicates the tendency towards grotesque comedy or 'comedy of menace' to be found in post-war German drama, including Frisch's successful radio-play *Herr Biedermann und die Brandstifter* (1956, stage version 1960), in which what looks like the rise of the Nazis in pre-war Germany is presented in terms of a conflict between a timid civilian and two fire-raisers. A later play, *Andorra* (1961), once again reflects the preoccupation with Germany's more recent past. It is a parable in which the anti-semitism of the war-years is seen both historically and from a peculiarly Swiss standpoint, which, because of the close cultural and racial connexions between the two countries, affords a view of the problem from both inside and outside. Frisch's compatriot Friedrich Dürrenmatt (1921–), who did not begin writing until after the war, scored his first real success with *Romulus der Grosse* (1951, new version 1957), in which the literary cliché of the great hero from legend or history is debunked with more wit and sophistication than by Kaiser or Brecht, but also without the earnestness of purpose found in the latter. Dürrenmatt showed the real extent of his talent in *Der Besuch der alten Dame* (1956), which deals with the origins and growth of evil and the processes which bring retribution—a problem that has an important history in the Swiss literary tradition. A millionairess returns after many years to the place of her birth, and demands from the impoverished town the judicial murder of the man who seduced her as a young girl, in exchange for a large sum of money that will bring prosperity to all. As the town gradually succumbs to the lure of the bribe, and the figure of the old woman takes on mythical proportions, one realizes that, although again the action may be taken as symbolic of Germany's recent past, the parable is conceived with a clarity, depth, and precision which light up the whole problem of personal guilt and social responsibility in our time. Although Dürrenmatt has not so far repeated this success, the immediate future of German drama probably rests in his hands.

RICHARD BECKLEY

GHELDERODE, Michel de (1898–1962), Belgian dramatist, writing in French. His first play, the one-act *La Mort regarde à la fenêtre*, produced in Brussels in 1918, was followed in 1919 by the three-act *Le Repas des fauves*. His first work of importance, *La Mort du Docteur Faust*, written in 1924–5, was performed in Paris in 1928. From 1927 to 1937 most of his major work was written, including *Escurial* and *Christophe Colomb* (1927), *Les Femmes au tombeau* (1928), *Barabbas*, *Fastes d'enfer*, and *Pantagleize* (1929), *Magie rouge* (1931), *Sire Halewyn*, *La Ballade du grand macabre*, and *Mademoiselle Jaïre* (1934), *La Pie sur le gibet* and *Hop! Signor* (1935), and *L'École des bouffons* (1937). The world created in these plays recalls the grotesque cavalcade of the Flemish fairs and the paintings of Pieter Breughel and Hieronymus Bosch, peopled by deformed puppets, walking dead, tormented kings and jesters, masked executioners, cripples, dwarfs, sadistic monks, lecherous and drunken men and women. The wild, rank, and decaying décor, often suggesting the crumbling remains of Gothic architecture, sets the scene for his recurrent theme: an agonized appraisal of man's condition, seen as a crude and violent burlesque, where purity is engulfed by the obscene deformities of the flesh, and which ends in the eternal mystery of death. Although produced fairly frequently in Belgium, sometimes in Flemish translations, Ghelderode's work was little known in France, apart from productions of *La Mort du Docteur Faust* and *Christophe Colomb* in 1928 and 1929, until the production of *Hop! Signor* in Paris by Catherine Toth and André Reybaz in 1947, which aroused considerable interest. Productions of *Escurial*, *Mademoiselle Jaïre*, and *Fastes d'enfer* followed. The last caused a furore and scandal when performed at the Théâtre Marigny in 1949, and was withdrawn: Ghelderode's plays then retreated from the Right Bank of Paris to their natural home in the little theatres of the Left Bank. In England, his work is almost unknown; a production of *Mademoiselle Jaïre* in Oxford had little success.

T. C. C. MILNE

GHÉON, Henri (1875–1943), French dramatist, and leader of the modern revival of religious drama in France. His plays, though written after those of Claudel, were performed before them, and were the first to combine the reforms envisaged by Copeau with the expression of a newly awakened Catholicism. The early ones, of which the most important was *Le Pauvre sous l'escalier* (1913), were given at the Théâtre du Vieux-Colombier, but it was not until after the First World War, during which Ghéon returned to the Church, that he embarked on the work with which he was afterwards associated, the writing and production of plays on religious and biblical themes in provincial parishes, colleges, and schools. Among the many works which he produced for this purpose, running into nearly a hundred, the best-known outside France is *Le Noël sur la place* (1935), which, as *Christmas in the Market Place*, in a translation by Eric Crozier, has had many productions in England by professionals and amateurs. It was originally played by Les Compagnons de Jeux, a semi-amateur company organized in 1932 by Henri Brochet (1898–1952), himself an excellent actor and religious dramatist, to take the place of Ghéon's earlier troupe, Les Compagnons de Notre-Dame. In recent years a number of Ghéon's plays, which combine fine poetry and an excellent theatrical sense with great simplicity and religious feeling, have been given in the smaller theatres of Paris, and, on one occasion, at the Odéon.

GHERARDI. (1) Giovanni (*fl.* 1675–?), actor of the *commedia dell'arte*, whose great accomplishment was his imitation of a flute, from which he took the name of Flautino. He joined the company in Paris in 1675, but his misdemeanours caused him to be imprisoned and later expelled. He was the father of (2) Evaristo (1663–1700), a famous Harlequin, whose professional career was spent entirely in Paris, where he made his début in 1689 in Regnard's *Le Divorce forcé*. He is chiefly remembered now for his collection of plays given by the Italians in Paris.

GHOST GLIDE, another name for the trap first used in *The Corsican Brothers*, by means of which the apparition appeared to drift across the stage while rising slowly from beneath it (see TRAP).

GIACOMETTI, Paolo (1816–82), Italian dramatist, whose plays are of a homely popular type, known as *teatro da arena*—a phrase which may be said to cover drama appealing to 'simple minds and honest hearts'. His reputation is widespread in his own country. His best play is probably *La morte civile* (1861), a dramatization of a social theme, which has as its hero an escaped convict who, unable to return to his wife and daughter, commits suicide.

GIACOSA, Giuseppe (1847–1906), Italian playwright and librettist. After Verga he is Italy's most important realistic dramatist. An accomplished craftsman and alert observer of the middle-class, his range is narrow, his psychological insight limited, and his world of ideas essentially derivative. The very facility which made it possible for him to write successful verse melodrama, sentimental 'proverbs', Ibsenite bourgeois drama, and libretti for Puccini, seems to have prevented his making any significant statement. His *Diritti dell'anima* (1894) is typical of his limitations: the theme and analysis of *A Doll's House* are diluted to furnish a new twist to the adultery-triangle-play. *Tristi amori* (1887), *Come le foglie* (1900), and *Il più forte* (1904), are considerable social comments, the last play being reminiscent of *Mrs. Warren's Profession* in the parent-child estrangement. Giacosa graduated in law and practised for a short time, until his growing popularity in the theatre enabled him to concentrate on writing. A kindly and humane man, he sought to assert the value of middle-class morality, but his greatest achievement is that unconsciously he painted an accurate and pathetic portrait of the decadence of the bourgeoisie. He enjoyed great success with such charming and well-turned comedies as *La zampa del gatto* (1883), the pseudo-medieval *Una partita a scacchi* (1871), the historical *Signora di Challant* (1891)—which provided a vehicle for both Duse and Bernhardt—and the libretti for 'La Bohème', 'Tosca', and 'Madame Butterfly' (written in collaboration with Luigi Illica). Many of his plays have been staged in England and America.

FREDERICK MAY

At his death Giacosa left four unpublished comedies, which have now been added to his complete works. One of them, *L'onorerole Ercole Malladri*, first seen at the Carignano Theatre on 20 Oct. 1884, and the following year in Milan, was revived by the Piccolo Teatro della Città di Torino for the fiftieth anniversary of his death (1956).

GIBBON'S TENNIS-COURT, see VERE STREET THEATRE.

GIBBS, MRS. (1770–1844), see COLMAN (3).

GIBBS, WOLCOTT (1902–58), American dramatic critic, born in New York City. He worked as an architect's apprentice, as a railroad conductor, and as a rural newspaper reporter before becoming a copy-reader on *The New Yorker* in 1927. In 1939 he replaced Robert Benchley as drama critic of that magazine and soon became recognized as a most valuable addition to the ranks of American critics. A shrewd and alert playgoer, he often wrote more brilliantly of bad plays than of good ones; but his irony was a tonic Broadway badly needed. Sometimes he erred in judging a play by its production, but he was never to be won over—as were so many of his colleagues—by the 'sincerity' of inept and bogus dramas dealing with vital problems, and though he wrote with humorous and sardonic detachment, he never descended to 'wise-crack' reviewing. He was an excellent parodist—admiring Max Beerbohm above all other models—and his book, *Season in the Sun*, contains a dozen biting burlesques of contemporary novelists and playwrights. THOMAS QUINN CURTISS

GIDE, ANDRÉ (1869–1951), French novelist, who also made several important contributions to the theatre. His early plays, *Le Roi Candaule* and *Saül*, made little stir, but *Œdipe* (1932), which dramatized a situation often found in Gide's writing—the conflict between individualism and religious submission—was favourably received. It was, however, with his translations of Shakespeare that he became best known in the theatre—*Antony and Cleopatra* and *Hamlet* in particular. The latter was in his mind for many years. He published a brilliant first act in 1928, but it was a chance meeting with Jean-Louis Barrault in 1942 that led him to finish the play, with which the Renaud–Barrault company opened their first season on 17 Oct. 1946. Two years later Barrault was seen in this translation at the Edinburgh Festival. It was also for Barrault's company that Gide dramatized Kafka's *The Trial*, which opened on 10 Oct. 1947. It was revived by Barrault at the Odéon in 1962.

GIELGUD, SIR (ARTHUR) JOHN (1904–), English actor and producer, grand-nephew of Ellen Terry. After studying under Lady Benson and at the Royal Academy of Dramatic Art, he made his first appearance on the stage at the Old Vic in 1921 as the Herald in *Henry V*, returning there some years later to star in a fine series of Shakespeare productions. He was by then accounted one of the most promising young actors of the English stage, but his first popular success came with *Richard of Bordeaux* (1932), which he also produced An actor of commanding presence, with a fine speaking voice, he is at his best in Shakespeare, and his Hamlet, which has achieved record runs in London and New York, is accounted by some critics the finest of his generation. He has, however, also given a good account of himself in such plays as *Love for Love* (see No. 102), *The School for Scandal*, and *The Importance of Being Earnest*, and has appeared in some modern plays, among them *Noah* (1935), *The Lady's Not for Burning* (1949) (see No. 107), *A Day by the Sea* (1953), *Nude With Violin* (1956), and *The Potting Shed* (1958). He has produced many plays besides those in which he himself appeared, and was responsible for two important repertory seasons, at the Queen's Theatre in 1937–8, and at the Haymarket in 1944–5. At the opening of Sadler's Wells Theatre in 1931 he appeared as Malvolio, and played Hamlet at the Lyceum in 1939, subsequently taking his company to Elsinore. In 1950 he was at Stratford-upon-Avon, proving a memorable Angelo in *Measure for Measure*, a good Benedick, and a suitably sardonic Cassius. Back in London, his Leontes (in *The Winter's Tale*) (1951) was also outstanding, and he appeared with great success as Jaffier in a revival of *Venice Preserved* (1953). In 1955 he was seen as Lear in a production with a Japanese setting by Isamu Noguchi (see No. 91). His Othello for the Royal Shakespeare company in 1961 was not a success. In 1958 he first appeared in a solo recital of passages from

Shakespeare entitled *Ages of Man*. This was immediately successful, and he has since toured widely in it in Europe, America, and Australia. He is the author of a volume of autobiography, *Early Stages* (1938), and of a collection of essays and speeches, *Stage Directions* (1963). He was knighted in 1953 for services to the English stage.

GIFFARD, HENRY (1694/9–1772), English actor and manager, of Irish extraction, in whose company Garrick made his first appearances on the stage. Giffard, who at 17 was a clerk in the South Sea Company, became an actor at 20, and played first at Bath. He then joined Rich at Lincoln's Inn Fields, and subsequently became manager of the theatre. In 1729 he went to Goodman's Fields Theatre under Odell, and two years later took over the management, opening with *George Barnwell*. He remained at this theatre with a good company, headed by Yates, until 1737, in which year he took to Walpole, who rewarded him with £1,000, the script of a scurrilous play entitled *The Golden Rump*, which was used by the Government as an excuse for passing the Licensing Bill of 1737. Since this led to the closing of all unlicensed playhouses, Giffard found himself without a theatre; but he subsequently managed to reopen Goodman's Fields, and it was there in 1741 that Garrick first played small parts and later triumphed as Richard III. When Fleetwood engaged Garrick for Drury Lane, he took on also Giffard and his wife, a fine actress who played Lady Macbeth and other leading parts opposite Garrick. Little, however, was subsequently heard of Giffard. He held for a short time part of the Patent of Drury Lane, but relinquished it because he could not stomach Fleetwood's extravagances.

GILBERT, GABRIEL (*c.* 1620–*c.* 1680), French dramatist, author of numerous plays, but best known through Fontenelle's accusation that his *Rhodogune* was stolen from the *Rodogune* of Corneille. It is certain that he must either have seen Corneille's play, or heard it read, since the resemblances between the two are too obvious to be the result of chance. *Rhodogune* was probably given in 1646, a year later than Corneille's play, and is a very inferior piece of work, particularly in the fifth act. Gilbert's other plays are equally negligible, though *Téléphonte* (1641) may have been given in Richelieu's private theatre. Gilbert's origins are obscure. Well educated and patronized by several women of high rank, including Queen Christina of Sweden, whose secretary he was for a short time, he nevertheless died in poverty in the house of a kindly benefactor, M. d'Hervart, where La Fontaine also subsequently found shelter.

GILBERT, MRS. GEORGE H. (*née* ANN HARTLEY) (1821–1904), a much-loved American actress, who in her later years was extremely popular as a player of eccentric spinsters and aristocratic dowagers. She was in her youth a ballet dancer in London, where in 1846 she married George Gilbert, an actor, with whom she toured England and Ireland. Having saved enough to emigrate, they went to Wisconsin, but failed to make a success of farming and in 1850 returned to the stage, touring the larger cities. Gilbert, who was pre-eminently a dancer, injured himself falling through a trap, and though he continued to work in the theatre, he was unable to appear on the stage, and died in 1866. His wife had already given up dancing in favour of straight acting, and almost immediately found her niche in the playing of comic elderly women, in which capacity she was with Mrs. John Wood's company at the Olympic, New York, in 1864. Her first important part was the Marquise de St. Maur in Florence's pirated production of *Caste* in 1867. The period of her greatest fame, however, was from 1869 to 1899, when she was in Daly's company, and with Ada Rehan, John Drew, and John Lewis formed a unique combination of artistic and technical skill. When Daly died she was engaged by Frohman, with whom she remained until her death. During her long career she played with most of the famous actors and managements of her time. Her angular body and homely features prevented her from attempting tragedy, but proved assets in comedy. She played well and carefully every part she was given, and to the end of her days was conscientious in studying and rehearsing, being a reliable as well as a rare and distinguished actress.

GILBERT, JOHN [really GIBBS] (1810–89), American actor, who made his début in Boston in 1828. He then toured the Mississippi river towns until 1834, and returned to the Tremont Theatre, Boston, until it closed, playing the parts of elderly men, in which he later became a great favourite in New York as a member of Wallack's company. He was particularly good as Sir Anthony Absolute and Sir Peter Teazle. In 1847 he had a successful season in London, and studied for a while in Paris, returning to play at the Park Theatre, New York, until it was destroyed by fire. He first joined Wallack's in 1861, and remained until the company was disbanded in 1888, dying the following year during a tour of *The Rivals* with Jefferson. Although an excellent comic actor, and exceedingly popular both with the audience and his fellow players, off-stage he was somewhat formal and unhumorous. He was a man of some erudition, and after his death his widow presented his fine collection of books to the Boston Public Library.

GILBERT, SIR WILLIAM SCHWENCK (1836–1911), English dramatist whose name is always associated in the public mind with that of Sir Arthur Sullivan, for whose music he wrote the libretti of their famous light operas. As a young man he was called to the Bar and was also a journalist, contributing regularly to many of the humorous papers of the day. He was encouraged to write for the stage by T. W. Robertson, and his first play was a burlesque commissioned for a Christmas entertainment. He also wrote dramatic sketches for the entertainers, Mr. and Mrs. German Reed. In 1870 Buckstone produced his *Palace of Truth* at the Haymarket with himself, Madge Robertson, and W. H. Kendal in the cast. It was followed by *Pygmalion and Galatea* (1871), a somewhat artificial classical romance which was nevertheless a great success. The part of Galatea was played by many lovely young actresses of the day, including Mary Anderson and Julia Neilson. Gilbert then embarked on a series of comedies for Marie Litton, which were given at the Court Theatre. Among his more serious plays may be cited *Sweethearts* (1874), *Broken Hearts* (1875), *Dan'l Druce, Blacksmith* (1876), long a favourite part with character actors, and *Engaged* (1877). His collaboration with Sullivan began with *Thespis; or, the Gods Grown Old* (an operatic extravaganza) given at the Gaiety on 26 Dec. 1871. The first of the well-known light operas, however, was *Trial by Jury* (1875). Their partnership continued for over twenty years and ended with *The Grand Duke* (1896), though *The Gondoliers* (1889) was the last of those which still hold the stage. The others are: *The Sorcerer* (1877), *H.M.S. Pinafore* (1878), *The Pirates of Penzance* (1880), *Patience* (1881), *Iolanthe* (1882), *Princess Ida* (1884), *The Mikado* (1885), *Ruddigore* (1887), and *The Yeoman of the Guard* (1888). *Utopia Limited* (1893) has not been revived.

Gilbert wrote libretti for other composers, but with little success, just as Sullivan wrote music for other dramatists but failed to recapture the brilliance of the Savoy operas—so called because the later ones were given at the Savoy Theatre. Their partnership was not happy, Gilbert being a man of irascible temperament and a martinet in the theatre. He believed in long and arduous rehearsals and in the dominance of the playwright, which led him into many disagreements with his actors, particularly Miss Hodson. He used the profits from his plays to build the Garrick Theatre, which was opened by Sir John Hare in 1889, and he was knighted in 1907. He was an outstanding figure among the playwrights of the Victorian era, having much literary grace and finish, and a wit second to none. Yet of all his theatrical work only the libretti for Sullivan have survived (see also PLANCHÉ, J. R.).

GILCHRIST, CONNIE (1865–1946), English actress, a very lovely woman, who made her first appearance on the stage as a child in pantomime and in later years was at the Gaiety as a skipping-rope dancer. In 1880 she made a hit as Libby Ray in *The Mighty Dollar*, but she preferred burlesque to straight comedy and had a brief but glorious career before she left the stage in the late 1880s to become the Countess of Orkney. Her name is best remembered in connexion with the supreme example of 'judicial ignorance', when Mr. Justice Coleridge in *Scott v. Sampson* asked 'Who is Miss Connie Gilchrist?'

GILDER, ROSAMOND (1900–), American dramatic critic and a tireless worker in the cause of good theatre everywhere. Born in New York City, she is the daughter of Richard Watson Gilder, the celebrated editor and poet of the 1890s, whose letters she has edited. From 1924 to 1948 she was on the staff of *Theatre Arts*, the outstanding American theatre magazine of its time, being appointed its dramatic critic in 1938, and editor in 1945. Her monthly report on Broadway was a valuable record and contained excellent criticism of plays and players. She has written *Enter the Actress*, *A Theatre Library* (notes on 100 books), and *Gielgud's Hamlet* (the record of a performance she greatly admired). She was director of the Playwrights' Bureau of the Federal Theatre in 1935–6, and is now Secretary of the American National Theatre and Academy, and President of the International Theatre Institute.

THOMAS QUINN CURTISS

GILLETTE, WILLIAM (1855–1937), American actor and dramatist, author of a number of adaptations from foreign sources and dramatizations of novels, in most of which he appeared himself. The most important of these were *Esmeralda* (1881), which ran for a year, and *Sherlock Holmes* (1899), with which Gillette's name is usually associated. He played it with outstanding success both in England and America, and frequently revived it up to his retirement in 1932. Of his original plays the best were the spy-stories of the Civil War, *Held by the Enemy* (1886) and *Secret Service* (1895), strong melodramatic plays of action in which his own forceful personality found a suitable medium. He also wrote a comedy, *Too Much Jonson* (1894). He appeared in *The Admirable Crichton* and *Dear Brutus*; but his best work was done in his own plays, which remained on the stage while he played them, but would probably not bear revival.

GILMORE'S THEATRE, NEW YORK, see DALY'S THEATRE, 3.

GILPIN, CHARLES SIDNEY (1878–1930), American Negro actor, who spent many years as a minstrel in vaudeville. From 1903 to 1913 he toured with various companies, and in 1916 became manager of the first all-Negro stock company in New York, at the Lafayette Theatre, Harlem. Among his later Broadway parts were the Negro clergyman in *Abraham Lincoln* (1919), and Brutus Jones in *The Emperor Jones* (1921), which ran for three years and was frequently revived. It provided Gilpin with a great emotional part, in which he was at once powerful, terrifying, and extremely moving. He retired in 1926, but occasionally reappeared in revivals of *The Emperor Jones* until his death.

GIPSY THEATRE, MOSCOW. This was founded in 1930 from among a band of enthusiastic amateurs at a time when the authorities were trying to influence the nomadic gipsy population of the U.S.S.R. (which now numbers about 132,000, mostly Romany-speaking) towards a more settled way of life. The theatre had a considerable part to play in this campaign, and the school which was established at the same time as the acting and rehearsal classes did a great deal to raise the standard of literacy. Problems of the early years were the dearth of good plays about gipsy life, one of the few available being *Life on Wheels*, by Alexander Hermano, a gipsy dramatist, and the finding and training of new talent. Many of the present members of the company came from the travelling gipsy groups, among them Nadezhda Mikhailova, Konstantin Ananyev and Raya Udakovo, who have all been trained in the theatre's own school. The theatre—the Romen—has a permanent company of about seventy, with a repertory of some sixteen plays, two or three new ones being added each year. In addition to gipsy plays, it includes Russian and foreign classics, both in Russian and in Romany. The theatre is very popular, and its productions usually average about 300–400 performances, though an outstanding success like Shtock's *Grushenka* may run to 1,000. The theatre building in Moscow seats only 400, but on tour the company plays to many thousands of spectators. Many of the original company still work in the theatre as actors or playwrights, among them Lyalya Chernaya, Ivan Rom-Lebedev, Ivan Khrushulev, and Valeryan Polyakov. BEATRICE KING†

GIRALDI, GIAMBATTISTA (1504–73), an Italian writer of the Renaissance, better known as 'Il Cinthio'. His collection of short stories, or 'novelle', entitled the *Hecatonmiti*, is chiefly remembered, but he was also a dramatist, whose 'horror' tragedies are modelled on Seneca. The first, and most violent, was acted before the Duke of Ferrara and his Court in 1541, at the author's house. Music was specially composed for the occasion and the scenery was designed by Carpi. His later plays, commissioned also by the Duke, were not quite so blood-thirsty, and some were conceded a happy ending (see also ITALY, 1 *b*).

GIRAUDOUX (HIPPOLYTE) JEAN (1882–1944), French novelist and dramatist, whose fruitful collaboration with the actor Louis Jouvet produced some of the finest plays of the period. He was 45 before his first play, *Siegfried* (1928), was produced by Jouvet at the Champs-Élysées and already known as a somewhat esoteric novelist. As a dramatist, his reputation grew with each succeeding play. *Siegfried* was followed at the same theatre by *Amphitryon 38* (1929), a witty and elegant retelling of the old legend in which Jouvet played Mercury, Pierre Renoir, Jupiter, and Valentine Tessier, Alcmena. In an English adaptation by S. N. Behrman the play had a great success in England and America, with the Lunts as Jupiter and Alcmena. After the comparative failure of *Judith* (1931), a biblical tragedy, at the Pigalle, Giraudoux returned to the Champs-Élysées with the enchanting *Intermezzo* (1933), a mixture of fantasy and realism in which all his imagination and skill as a writer were happily blended. The play was seen in London in 1956 in a production by the Renaud–Barrault company. With his next play (if one omits *Tessa* (1934), a French version of *The Constant Nymph*) Giraudoux had a resounding success. This was *La Guerre de Troie n'aura pas lieu* (1935), a paradoxical examination of the fateful moments leading up to the Trojan war, which is on the point of being averted when it breaks out owing to a lie and a misunderstanding—a sad commentary on the ageless misery of man. As *Tiger at the Gates* (with Michael Redgrave as Hector) the play made a belated but successful appearance in London in a translation by Christopher Fry in 1955, going on to achieve an equal success in New York. Its poignancy was perhaps reinforced for English audiences by the intervention of the Second World War between the French and English productions.

Giraudoux's next full-length play, which was preceded by a divertissement, *Supplément au Voyage de Cook* (also 1935), was a retelling of the story of Electra. Although not a failure, it was nevertheless a disappointment, due perhaps, as Inskip says in his *Jean Giraudoux* (1958), to the fact that the play is 'devoid of the unity essential to real theatrical effect'.

After an attack on contemporary drama critics in the style of Molière, *L'Impromptu de Paris* (1937), written as a curtain-raiser for a revival of *La Guerre de Troie n'aura pas lieu*, and a slight one-act play, *Cantique des Cantiques* (1938), Giraudoux produced what many believe to be his finest work, *Ondine* (also 1938), a retelling of the legend of the water-nymph on which he brought to bear all the poetry and imagination of which he was capable, and (in the second act) all the theatrical tricks which he knew Jouvet could stage for him. The combination, together with Madeleine Ozeray as Ondine and Jouvet as Hans, proved irresistible. To quote Inskip again:

> The naïve and the ultra-sophisticated are blended here in such a manner as to blur the frontiers of human experience. . . . The technical skill with which the author accomplishes his tight-rope passage from mood to mood is only equalled by the virtuosity of his scene-construction and the certainty of his delineation of character.

The play, produced on 27 Apr. 1939, was to have continued its run in the autumn after the usual summer break, but it was one of the casualties of the Second World War, and it had only a short revival in 1940, before the German occupation. It was not revived again until 1949, five years after Giraudoux's death. The French version was seen in London (at the Lyric, Hammersmith) in a production by the Théâtre-National de Belgique in 1953, and, in an English translation, was one of the successes of the Royal Shakespeare's London season at the Aldwych in 1961, Leslie Caron playing Ondine.

It was not until 1943 that Giraudoux returned to the theatre, with *Sodome et Gomorrhe*, in which Lia, the leading role, was played by Edwige Feuillère. In the absence of Jouvet on tour, the production was by Douking. The play, a study in conjugal incompatability, was not wholly successful in spite of the beauty of the language. It was with *La Folle de Chaillot* (1945) (see No. 104), performed by Jouvet on his return to Paris at the end of the war after Giraudoux's death, that Giraudoux's magic re-established itself. The play was an instant success, as it was in New York in 1948, with Martita Hunt. Her performance in London in 1951 was praised, too, but the play had only a short run.

Giraudoux's last two plays were seen posthumously in Paris—*L'Apollon de Bellac* (1947), which Jouvet had produced in Rio de Janeiro in 1942, and *Pour Lucrèce* (1953), which was done by Barrault at the Marigny with Edwige Feuillère as Paola. Lacking the hand of the author for revision and that close collaboration which he had known with Jouvet, the play, in spite of moments of great beauty, was not as successful as had been hoped. But revivals of earlier plays from the 1930s, even in the very different atmosphere of the 1950s and 1960s, have shown that they have qualities which will endure in the theatre.

GIRL. George Edwardes was of the opinion that there was magic in the word 'girl', and this seems to have been borne out by the titles of many successful productions of the late nineteenth and early twentieth centuries—the melodrama *The Girl Who Took the Wrong Turning*, the musical play *The Girl in the Taxi*, the musical comedy *The Girls of Gottenberg*, the music-hall song 'The Girl in the Clogs and Shawl'. In the 1920s the word was usually applied to the chorus, especially to well-trained precision dancers like the Tiller Girls. An exception to this rule was C. B. Cochran, who billed his beautiful and talented chorus at the Pavilion politely as 'Mr. Cochran's Young Ladies'. Many of them later became famous in the theatre, among them Florence Desmond and Anna Neagle.

GISSEY, HENRI (1621–73), see COSTUME, 5.

GITANA, GERTIE [really GERTRUDE MARY ROSS] (1889–1957), one of the best-loved stars of the old English music-hall. She joined a children's troupe at the age of 4, and was 8 when she first appeared as a single turn, at the Tivoli, Barrow-in-Furness. At 15 she made her first appearance in London, at the Lyceum, then being used as a music-hall; but it was at the Holborn Empire shortly after that she scored her first outstanding success. By the time she was 16 she was topping the bill all over the country, and her success was enhanced when she first sang the song always connected with her name, 'Nellie Dean'. She married in 1928 Don Ross, who in 1947 was responsible for the production of an 'old-time' music-hall bill 'Thanks for the Memory' in which she appeared with her friends, Nellie Wallace and Ella Shields, and many other stars. A year later she was seen at a Royal Variety Performance. She took her name Gitana from the fact that the first troupe she played with wore conventional gipsy costumes.

G.I.T.I.S.,—the Lunacharsky State Institute of Theatre Arts in Moscow—is the oldest and most important official body concerned with the teaching of theatre art in the Soviet Union. Founded on 22 Sept. 1878 by Shostakovsky as a music and drama school, it was given the status of a Conservatoire in 1886. In 1891 Nemirovich-Danchenko joined the teaching staff, his pupils including Moskvin and Knipper-Chekhova, later members of the first Moscow Art Theatre company. The Institute underwent many changes of name and status before reaching its present pre-eminent position. It was given the name of the Soviet Union's first Minister for Education in 1934 (see LUNACHARSKY), and has expanded its activities until it now covers all aspects of theatrical training. Its staff is drawn from the leading members of the major Soviet theatres, many of them themselves graduates of the Institute, which confers degrees, runs a post-graduate school, publishes text-books, and has a large library. It has at present about 1,000 students, representing at least forty nationalities, of whom roughly half are external, taking correspondence courses while working actively in cultural and theatrical institutions. In recent years more emphasis has been placed on practical work, which is done mainly in the Institute's own theatre, opened in 1958.

BEATRICE KING†

GLASGOW. Like Edinburgh, with whom she shared theatrical managements until the early years of the nineteenth century, Glasgow had a long struggle before she achieved a permanent playhouse. The first, erected in 1753, was dismantled by the owner after Whitfield had preached against it. A fire was started in the second on the eve of the opening performance in 1764. Damage was slight, and this theatre survived until burnt down in 1780. The famous Dunlop Street Theatre was built by John Jackson and opened in 1782. It underwent an eclipse when the Queen Street Theatre Royal was built in 1805, and was sold to a merchant as a warehouse. Part of the building was, however, used for miscellaneous entertainments, and in 1824 it was all brought into use as the Caledonian Theatre by John Henry Alexander, who rebuilt it twice during his long management. It became the Theatre Royal in 1829, when he acquired the Queen Street patent. In 1849 occurred the disastrous panic, caused by a false alarm of fire, in which sixty-five persons lost their lives. Burnt down in 1863, the theatre was rebuilt, but demolished in 1869. The Queen Street Theatre, opened in 1805 under a royal patent obtained by the Corporation, and according to Ryley 'the most extensive and superb out of London', was designed by David Hamilton, with stock scenery by Alexander Nasmyth, and advanced machinery. After fluctuating fortunes, it was burnt down in 1829. Here Edmund and Charles Kean first played together, to a packed house with 250 of the audience on the stage. Other theatres were the Adelphi, which opened in 1842, and was destroyed by fire in 1848, the City, which opened and was burnt down in 1845, the Prince's, opened in 1849, and the Royalty, opened in 1879. In 1867 a music-hall was built which in 1869 became the Theatre Royal, Glasgow, and was rebuilt on the same site after its destruction by fire in 1879 and 1895. It is now the headquarters of Scottish Television. Surviving Glasgow theatres include the Princess's, opened as Her Majesty's in 1877, the King's (1902), and the Alhambra (1912).

When the stock companies were superseded by touring companies in the 1860s, the theatres provided mainly English fare, but a desire for a purely national theatre found expression with the founding in 1909 of the Glasgow Repertory Theatre, under the direction of Alfred Wareing. It opened with a production of Shaw's *You Never Can Tell* in the Royalty Theatre, where from 1909 to 1914 it produced plays by many English and Continental dramatists, including *The Seagull* (1909), claimed as the first British performance of Chekhov. In its prospectus it announced a desire to foster a purely Scottish drama and it did in fact produce a few Scottish plays, the most notable being John Ferguson's *Campbell of Kilmohr*. The venture was well on its way to success when the outbreak of the First World War forced it to close down. The remaining funds were transferred to the St. Andrew Society, and later used to launch the movement that produced the Scottish National Players. The two streams in the Glasgow theatre have continued, with the creation of a Scottish drama a major concern successively of the Scottish National Players, the Curtain, Park, Unity, and Citizens' Theatres, and with current British fare presented by touring companies, or by the series of resident companies shared with Edinburgh between 1928 and 1955, though the best of these, the Masque Theatre company, drew on Scottish talents (see SCOTLAND). No account of the theatre in Glasgow would be complete without a reference to the vigorous tradition of variety and pantomime (see SCOTTISH COMEDIANS).

The Glasgow Citizens' Theatre was founded in 1943 by a directorate led by James Bridie and including Dr. T. J. Honeyman and Paul Vincent Carroll. Until his death in 1951, Bridie gave himself unsparingly to the creation of the new theatre. He believed that it must draw on English as well as Scottish theatrical resources, as he had learned to do in his own career as a playwright, a policy which involved him in controversy. It is probably true, however, that only a figure of Bridie's eminence could have built up a company in five years to the level of achievement represented by Tyrone Guthrie's Edinburgh Festival production of *The Three Estates*. Nevertheless, some of the best-remembered successes under Bridie's chairmanship had a purely Scottish character, like his *Forrigan Reel* (1946), or *The Tintock Cup* (1949), which he wrote with George Munro. The production of new plays, especially those by Scottish authors, and of modern plays in preference to classics (except Shakespeare) were other principles of Citizens' policy evolved in this period.

Since 1951 later boards of directors have endorsed the policy worked out in the early years. With the establishment of a College of Dramatic Art (see SCOTLAND), they have found it easier to form a company able to present both English and Scottish plays. Notable first productions have been of Bridie's last play, *The Baikie Charivari* (1952) and of John Arden's *Armstrong's Last Goodnight* (1964). The company celebrated its twenty-first birthday with a revival of Bridie's *A Sleeping Clergyman*. In 1965 the establishment of the Close Theatre Club, under the same roof as the Citizens' and run in association with it, provided a second theatre designed for experimental work.

J. F. ARNOTT

GLASPELL, SUSAN (1882–1948), American novelist and dramatist, one of whose early plays was given by the Neighborhood Playhouse. She was also active in the formation of the Provincetown Players, who produced several of her one-act plays and, in 1919, her first three-act play, *Bernice*, in which she herself played the devoted servant, Abbie. Her finest work for the theatre was *Alison's House* (1930), prompted partly by the life of Emily Dickinson. This deals with the efforts of the family to keep back from publication the poems of one of its members who has recently died, and with the impact of a love-affair with a married man on an older and a younger woman. This play, produced by Eva Le Gallienne at the Civic Repertory Theatre, was awarded the Pulitzer Prize.

GLEEMAN, the singer of songs and teller of tales in Anglo-Saxon England. He went underground at the Norman Conquest, but reappeared in the fourteenth century, when he descended somewhat in the social scale, becoming more of a buffoon or itinerant minstrel. In early days the gleeman was a privileged person, and partook of some of the respect accorded to the Teutonic *scôp* or bard.

GLEICH, JOSEPH ALOIS (1772–1841), see AUSTRIA.

GLOBE THEATRE. 1. LONDON. Of all the old theatres of London the Globe has the strongest hold on the popular imagination. It was certainly in its time a very important playhouse, and its Shakespearian associations have made it famous. Yet Shakespeare was as intimately connected with the Blackfriars, whose name is less well known.

The Globe was built in 1599 on the Bankside, Southwark, by Cuthbert Burbage with timber from London's first playhouse, the Theatre, built by his father, James. Chambers says 'it was almost certainly round', while Mrs. Thrale, who later lived near the site, says that 'though hexagonal in form without, it was round within'. The cost of erection was £600. The stage was 43 ft. wide, and, including the 'tiring house' or dressing-room at the back, the depth was 39½ ft. Although the structure was only 32 ft. high from floor to ceiling it had three tiers of galleries. The Globe was painted —in contrast to most other playhouses, which were of plain timber. It was an open theatre, and such roof as there was, over the stage and galleries, was thatched. Being only partly roofed, it was a 'summer' house. The company played at the Blackfriars in winter.

On the roof over the stage was a tower or penthouse, with a flagstaff from which a flag was flown when the theatre was open, and from which trumpets were blown to announce the beginning of the play or the opening of the doors. At the Globe, as elsewhere, a spectator who paid a penny and stood in the pit was referred to as a groundling; a further penny would admit him to a gallery; and for yet another penny he could have a seat. The stools on the stage were for privileged people, who were allowed to enter through the stage door. (Jonson refers to the stage stools at the Blackfriars as 'twelvepenny' seats.) In common with most other theatres, the Globe had two doors only, a front entrance which served the whole of the auditorium, and a stage door.

The glamour which surrounds the Globe comes from the fact that its actors and its playwrights were the finest of their time. Led by Richard Burbage, a strong company presented most of the plays of Shakespeare for the first time, as well as those of other contemporary dramatists. Their chief rivals were Henslowe's company under Alleyn at the Fortune.

In 1613 the original Globe was burnt down, owing to the thatched roof taking fire from the wadding in a gun discharged during a performance of what is thought to have been Shakespeare's *Henry VIII*. It was rebuilt with the help of public subscriptions and a royal grant, and reopened in 1614, this time with a tiled roof. For many years it continued as a flourishing theatre, but in 1644 it was pulled down by the ground landlord, Sir Matthew Brand. Globe Alley perpetuated its memory, and its site is now occupied by a brewery.

2. LONDON. Sefton Parry, who had a hand in many London theatres, built a Globe Theatre in Newcastle Street, Strand, which was swept away by the Aldwych alterations. It stood on the site of Lyon's Inn, an old Inn of Court dating from Henry VIII which had become the centre of a very disreputable neighbourhood. The new building was close to the Opera Comique, the two theatres being known as the Rickety Twins. It opened in Dec. 1868 with H. J. Byron's *Cyril's Success*, which lived up to its name. But it was a solitary success.

In 1871 Harry Montague, having left the Vaudeville, took over the Globe, but none of his productions succeeded, and he left England for America. He was succeeded by Edgar Bruce, who transferred *Bleak House*, in which Jennie Lee made a great success as Jo, from the Aquarium. Edward Righton followed, presenting revivals with excellent companies. In 1882 *Far From the Madding Crowd*, with Mrs. Bernard Beere, failed to emulate the success of the novel on which it was based. Mrs. Beere later became manageress of the theatre, presenting *The Promise of May*, which failed. There was a sensation on the second night of its run when the Marquess of Queensberry rose in the stalls and, proclaiming himself an agnostic, denounced the characterization of one of the people in the play who was similarly described. In 1884 Charles Hawtrey transferred *The Private Secretary* to the Globe from the Prince's, where it had not done well. With Penley in the lead it was a success, and became one of the classic stage farces.

The Globe changed hands frequently. Richard Mansfield was there in 1889, F. R. Benson played his first London season there in 1890. *Charley's Aunt*, transferred from the Royalty in 1893, ran for four years. Lewis Waller, John Hare, and Wilson Barrett all appeared there with varying success, and in 1902 the old theatre finally closed its doors. Its last production was a revival of *Sweet Nell of Old Drury*, originally produced at the Haymarket, with Fred Terry and Julia Neilson. The Globe was a badly built house, and had fire broken out it would have been a death-trap. It held about 1,000 people.

3. LONDON. The present Globe Theatre in Shaftesbury Avenue was originally called the Hicks (after Seymour Hicks). It opened on 27 Dec. 1906 under the management of Charles Frohman with *The Beauty of Bath*, transferred from the Aldwych with Hicks and his wife Ellaline Terriss in the cast. *Brewster's Millions* was produced there in the following year and *The Waltz Dream* in 1908. The theatre was then renamed the Globe, and was Charles Frohman's headquarters during the last years of his London management. After his death Alfred Butt acquired it and transferred *Peg o' My Heart* there. In the following year Gaby Deslys made her last London appearance in a musical play called *Suzette*, which had a disturbed first night but was eventually a success. From 1918 to 1927 the theatre had a number of successful productions under the joint management of Marie Löhr and her husband Anthony Prinsep, in most of which Marie Löhr appeared. Among these were A. A. Milne's *The Truth about Blayds* (1921), Lonsdale's *Aren't We All?* (1923), Somerset Maugham's *Our Betters* (also 1923—it had been seen in New York five years previously), Noël Coward's *Fallen Angels* (1925), and *All the King's Horses* (1926). After Prinsep's retirement from the management of the theatre it changed hands several times, Maurice Browne bringing here Moissi in *Hamlet* and the Pitoëffs in *Saint Joan* (1930). A year later came *The Improper Duchess* with Yvonne Arnaud, and in 1935, under Harold Gosling, *Call it a Day* ran for 509 performances. In Feb. 1937 H. M. Tennant took over the theatre, opening with a revival of *Candida*. Among the successful

productions of this management were *Robert's Wife* with Owen Nares and Edith Evans (also 1937), and all-star revivals of *The Importance of Being Earnest* (1939) and *Dear Brutus* (1940). Emlyn Williams's *Morning Star* ran for nearly the whole of 1942, and in 1943 Rattigan's *While the Sun Shines* started its long run of 1,154 nights. Later successes were *The Lady's Not for Burning* (1949; see No. 107) and *Ring Round the Moon* (1950). Gielgud, who had been in the former, returned in Coward's *Nude with Violin* (1956), his part being played subsequently during the sixteen-months' run by Michael Wilding and Robert Helpmann. Gielgud returned again in *The Potting Shed* (1958), by Grahame Greene, whose *Complaisant Lover* had a long run from June 1959, and in 1960 came Bolt's outstanding play about Sir Thomas More, *A Man for All Seasons*. Two further successes were Anouilh's *The Rehearsal* (1961) and Shaffer's double-bill, *The Private Ear* and *The Public Eye* (1962). W. MACQUEEN-POPE†, *rev.*

4. NEW YORK, an attractive playhouse on Broadway just north of 46th Street, which was opened on 10 Jan. 1910 by Charles Dillingham, whose name was always associated with it. In the main it housed musical shows, many of them extremely successful, though early in its career it saw five weeks of Sarah Bernhardt, with Lou Tellegen. Among other things seen at this theatre were Ziegfeld's *Follies* and several editions of George White's *Scandals*. The final legitimate production at the Globe was *The Cat and the Fiddle*, on 15 Oct. 1931, which set up a record for the house of 395 performances. It then became a cinema, but in 1958 it reopened as a completely remodelled legitimate theatre, renamed the Lunt–Fontanne in honour of Alfred Lunt and Lynn Fontanne, who appeared in the initial production, Dürrenmatt's *The Visit*. In 1963 the theatre housed a brilliant but short-lived production of Brecht's *Arturo Ui*. GEORGE FREEDLEY†

GLOVE-PUPPET, see PUNCH AND JUDY and PUPPET.

GLOVER. (1) JULIA (*née* BUTTERTON) (1779–1850), English actress, daughter of a respectable provincial actor who made several appearances at Sadler's Wells, and died in 1834. She first appeared on the stage at Bath on 9 May, 1795, and after spending some time on the York circuit was engaged for Covent Garden in 1797. She married Samuel Glover three years later. Her whole life was spent in the theatre, and she appears to have been an excellent actress, much admired for her fine voice and her serious approach to her work, being completely dependable—'a rare thinking actress' said Macready. She appeared with Kemble at Covent Garden, and in June 1832 played Hamlet at her benefit, being congratulated on her performance by Edmund Kean. Her last part was Mrs. Malaprop. Her son (2) EDMUND (1813–60) was for many years manager of the Theatre Royal, Glasgow, and his wife and three children were also connected with the stage, one being a scenic artist, one an actor, and one a musician.

GNESSIN, MENAHEM (1882–1953), Jewish actor and producer, born in the Ukraine. He began early to take an interest in the theatre, and in 1903 emigrated to Palestine, where he worked as a teacher. During this period he organized amateur productions, mainly in the settlement of Rehovot. His first full-length production, Gutzkow's *Uriel Acosta*, in which he himself played the chief part, was done in an Arab café in Jaffa. He also produced plays by Gogol, Asch, and Ibsen. In 1912 Gnessin joined a Jewish company in Poland, where he met Zemach and began the conversations which led eventually to the founding of Habima. In Berlin in 1922 Gnessin founded the Palestine Theatre (usually known as the 'Tai'), which he took to Palestine in 1923, building in Tel Aviv the first proper theatre building in the country. When Habima arrived in 1928 Gnessin at once joined it, and remained a member of the company until his death. Apart from appearing in Shakespeare, Gnessin's chief roles were in Jewish plays by Ansky, Gutzkow, Hirschbein, Aleichem, and others. He also wrote numerous articles on various aspects of the Hebrew theatre.

E. HARRIS

GODFREY, CHARLES (1851–1900), a music-hall singer whose real name was Paul Lacey. He started his career in melodrama at the Pavilion, Whitechapel, but later went on the halls and became famous as a singer of stirring patriotic ballads—'The Royal Fusiliers', 'On Guard', 'Nelson', and 'The Last Shot'. He also sang 'After the Ball', and one of his most popular songs in a more frivolous vein was 'Hi-Tiddley-Hi-Ti!'

GODFREY, THOMAS (1736–63), the first playwright of the United States. Apprenticed in his youth to a watchmaker, he was befriended and educated by Provost William Smith of the College of Philadelphia, who also encouraged his love of poetry and the drama by various college and academic productions. In 1759 Godfrey wrote a tragedy entitled *The Prince of Parthia*, which he sent to Douglass, manager of the American Company. It was received too late for production during the season in Philadelphia, and Godfrey died before it was either acted or printed. Douglass gave it for one night at the Southwark Theatre in 1767, and it was then not acted again until its revival at the University of Pennsylvania in 1915. It was issued in 1765 with other poems by Godfrey, and shows plainly the influence of Shakespeare and of the plays which were in the repertory of the elder Hallam in about 1754.

GODS, THE, a term, dating from 1752, used of the upper gallery of a theatre and, by extension, of its occupants (see also GALLERY).

GODWIN, EDWARD WILLIAM (1833–86), archaeologist, architect, and theatrical designer, father of Edith and Gordon Craig. By the age of 25 he was already well known and had designed several important buildings. While living in Bristol he met the 15-year-old Ellen Terry, and it was at his house, she says in her memoirs, that 'for the first time I began to appreciate beauty, to observe, to feel the splendour of things, to aspire'. After the breakdown of her early marriage with G. F. Watts she lived in retirement with Godwin from 1868 to 1875, during which time her two children were born (see CRAIG). Later, in London, Godwin supervised the Bancrofts' production of *The Merchant of Venice* in which Ellen Terry played Portia, and from then on was much absorbed by work for the theatre. He wrote a good deal on archaeology in relation to the theatre, and for a production of a Greek play designed a classical theatre which was built inside the existing structure of Hengler's Circus. In 1908 Gordon Craig reprinted in *The Mask* his father's articles on 'The Architecture and Costumes of Shakespeare's Plays', first published in *The Architect* in 1875.

GOETHE, JOHANN WOLFGANG VON (1749–1832), Germany's greatest man of letters, was the son of a well-to-do and respected Frankfurt family. He was educated chiefly by his father, who gave him an excellent grounding in languages, while the presence in the house of a French officer during the occupation of 1759–62 gave him the opportunity of acquiring complete fluency in that language. At the same time a French company whose performances he regularly visited instilled into him that admiration of French dramatic literature which survived his later enthusiasm for Shakespeare. Leipzig, that 'miniature Paris', where he went to continue his studies, confirmed this taste. Here Goethe, like his prototype the young student in *Faust*, wanted to learn 'all about everything', but this mental orgy, added to the strain of a hectic love affair, brought on a severe illness. A long rest at home followed, during which time his inquiring nature sought orientation in mystic speculation and the study of alchemy, seed of his later scientific research. When he was finally restored to health he was sent to Strasbourg to study law, in which he eventually took his degree, though medicine and, above all, literature absorbed his interest. It was at Strasbourg that Goethe had his momentous meeting with Herder. The latter, then burning with enthusiasm for Shakespeare and folk-song, was confined to a darkened room with eye trouble, and the young poet, visiting him, drank inspiration from his lips. The trappings of the rococo period fell from him; nature, truth, spontaneity, became his watchwords. Already *Faust* and *Götz von Berlichingen* were germinating, and in the meantime he poured his love for the village parson's daughter, Friederike, into lyrics which have all the simplicity and lilt of folk-song. The tie between the lovers was broken when Goethe found himself on the threshold of a wider life into which she could not have fitted, but the remorse which he felt at this desertion colours his portrait of the unfaithful lover in his first play *Götz von Berlichingen* (1773). This play, the first to be written in Germany in a Shakespearian manner, and the first of the *Sturm und Drang* pieces, is a somewhat idealized portrait of a robber baron, who is shown as an honourable and upright man in revolt against tyranny. The play suffers from diffuseness and the action is badly broken in the middle, but it became the spearhead of revolt for the *Sturm und Drang* movement, and a pattern for young dramatists, including Klinger, Lenz, and Schiller.

Goethe's next plays—which were preceded by the epoch-making *Die Leiden des jungen Werther*—were *Clavigo*, *Stella* (first version), and *Egmont*, the last dealing with the revolt of the Netherlands against Spain. Lessing had declared the poet to be under no obligation to historical fact, and Egmont in Goethe's hands becomes not a circumspect Fleming of heroic mould—portrayed in the play by William of Orange—but a warm-hearted believer in the fundamental goodness of man and of life. With sublime indifference he walks into the snare set for him and goes to the scaffold dreaming of his country's liberation. A captivating personality, he reflects Goethe's belief in his own 'daimon' at this turning-point in his career, when he was about to accept an invitation to Weimar, given by the young Duke, against the advice of his friends and family. Goethe has been blamed for the riotous gaiety at the Court of Weimar which shocked more sedate minds in Germany, but in fact he was the first to tire of it, and to endeavour to restrain the young Duke. The projected visit developed into a permanent sojourn, and finding Goethe unwilling to act as Court entertainer his master, recognizing his outstanding energy and ability, entrusted him with one office after another. Gradually he found himself responsible for agriculture, mining, forestry, with a seat in the Cabinet and the Chairmanship of the Treasury, all in the teeth of the old ministerial guard, whom he succeeded in propitiating by tact and efficiency. The poet in him chafed, however, in spite of the outlet afforded by the writing of the earlier drafts of later poetic plays and the companionship of Charlotte von Stein, a woman of sensitive discernment. At last he could bear it no longer, and in 1786 went to Italy, where he remained nearly two years. The fruits of this sojourn in the land of art and sunshine were *Iphigenie auf Tauris* and *Torquato Tasso*. The former, inspired by the *Iphigenia* of Euripides, and covering the same episode, has a definitely eighteenth-century flavour. Iphigenia owes her position as priestess and adviser to King Thoas to her personality and not to her rank. Believing in the goodness of the gods, she avoids human sacrifice until the time comes when her brother Orestes is to be killed. Then, staking all on her trust in the fundamental humanity of Thoas, and in divine clemency, she reveals their situation, and wins from the king an unequivocal pardon. The play, which is one of the masterpieces of European literature, is an expression of Goethe's belief that the salvation of mankind can come only through renunciation and humanity.

In *Torquato Tasso* Goethe portrays the difficulties of the poetic temperament in conflict with the world of action. Introspective self-pity and other shortcomings are not glossed over, nor the limitations of the man of action. In the princess whom Tasso loves can be discerned traces of Charlotte von Stein. She is depicted as an intellectual woman, of delicate health and reserved disposition. The poet brings her happiness, but she would never contemplate marriage with a commoner, and imposes on him an intolerable strain. He breaks into her reserve, and loses her. Apart from this the action is inconclusive, a cross-section of life rather than an elucidation, but it serves to show Goethe's idea of the place of the poet in the scheme of things.

During Goethe's visit to Italy his nature had expanded and consolidated. The feverish element, which had troubled him, but had made him feel akin to all things human, was eliminated, and the first signs of Olympian aloofness, very marked in his old age, began to appear. A sense of isolation came upon him, and he turned to scientific research, seeking always the inner unity of nature in the various fields in which he has left his mark. The first draft of *Wilhelm Meister*, written at Weimar, is taken up again, and becomes an illustrated treatise rather than an echo of life. In the new version, *Wilhelm Meisters Lehrjahre* (1796), the quest for the perfect stage has given place to the quest for true citizenship; the events of 1789 had put theatrical problems in the shade.

It was Schiller who won Goethe back to poetic creation, if not to drama. *Faust* (Part I) was published in 1808; the completed version appeared only after his death. As a drama it defies classification. It is the precipitate of a long life and a great man. Its language and style vary from harsh prose and lively four-beat doggerel to radiant iambics, flamboyant alexandrines, and stately trimeters. It has scenes of undying comedy and heartrending tragedy in Part I, of detached satire and philosophical symbolism in Part II. It has been successfully staged in its entirety, but it cannot adequately be contained in the theatre, in spite of the greatness (from a dramatic point of view) of several episodes, such as the prison scene in Part I and the blinding of Faust in Part II; Gretchen, and Faust himself, are fine dramatic figures, but the vastness of the conception, and strength of the execution, of this panorama of man's spirit make it impossible to judge it from the point of view of an ordinary play.

The last twenty years of Goethe's life were taken up with his autobiographical retrospect and with the writing of a fine novel, *Die Wahlverwandtschaften*, while a continuation of *Wilhelm Meister* served as the mouthpiece of an old man's garnered wisdom. In his last years he was, as it were, the mirror of intellectual life far beyond the borders of Germany. He dreamed of a world-literature in which the contributions of all nations could take their place. He had long ago outgrown the *Sturm und Drang* phase to which his own early play gave the impetus, and whose reverberations can be studied in the life and work of his contemporaries, not only in Germany, but all over the Continent and in England. W. E. DELP

GOGOL, NIKOLAI VASILIEVICH (1809–52), Russian writer and dramatist, and the first great realist of the Russian theatre. In his youth he attempted to go on the stage, but without success, and he turned to literature. His early work was highly praised by Pushkin, and in 1832 he made the acquaintance of the actor Shchepkin, a friendship which was of value to them both. It was at this time that Gogol began work on his first play, a satire on bureaucracy which he abandoned because he knew it would not pass the censor. Some scenes, slightly altered, were later published. The complete manuscript was destroyed by Gogol during the mental illness which overshadowed the end of his life. Two other plays, both satires, were started and left, to be finished in 1842, but Gogol's dramatic masterpiece, *The Inspector-General* (or *The Government Inspector*; Russian title, *Revizor*), had a curious history, since it was actually produced at the Court theatre, in the presence of the Tsar, in 1836. The authorities were disposed to be lenient to it, since it amused the Tsar. It dealt with official corruption in a small town, where an impecunious impostor is mistaken for a government official and treated accordingly, and so came opportunely at a moment when the authorities were engaged in reorganizing municipal affairs. But it proved too biting in production and was viciously attacked, as a result of which Gogol left Russia, not to return till 1848, already broken in health. He himself said of *The Inspector-General*: 'I decided to gather into a heap all that was wrong inside Russia, as far as I knew of it, all injustice committed in those places and in those cases where more than anywhere justice is demanded of man, and to deride them all at once.' This play, in its unsparing realism, had a great influence in Russia, and has been translated and produced in Europe and America. An English translation of an amusing but less important comedy as *The Marriage Broker* was seen at the Mermaid Theatre in 1965.

In 1928 Gogol's novel, *Dead Souls*, dramatized by Bulgakov, was presented by Stanislavsky at the Moscow Art Theatre. In 1959 the Moscow Transport Theatre was renamed the Gogol in honour of the dramatist's 150th anniversary.

GOLDEN THEATRE, NEW YORK, see CONCERT THEATRE, JOHN GOLDEN THEATRE, and ROYALE THEATRE.

GOLDFADEN, ABRAHAM (1840–1908), the first important Yiddish dramatist, and founder of the Yiddish theatre. Born in Russia, at Old Constantine (Volhynia), the son of a watchmaker with literary ambitions who gave him a good education, he was first apprenticed to his father's trade, but later entered the Rabbinical college in Zhitomir. Here he took part in the memorable first public performance of Ettinger's *Serkele*, in 1862, playing the title-role—a foreshadowing of his later life-work. Before he left college in 1866 he had published volumes of poetry in Hebrew and Yiddish, and was already known as a writer of popular folk-songs. A volume of dramatic sketches which appeared in 1869 went into a second edition, and one of its pieces was successfully performed by the Brody Singers, the itinerant Jewish musicians of Poland (see JEWISH DRAMA, 5) who were destined to play so large a part in Goldfaden's later work. He essayed several professions, including teaching, but after a short stay in Munich in 1875 with the intention of studying medicine, he turned to journalism. Several failures brought him at last to Jassy, where he found his songs well established in the repertory of the Brody Singers, and it was there, in Simon Marks's Wine Cellar, some time between 5 and 8 Oct. 1876, that he produced the two-act musical entertainment on which his claim to be the founder of the Yiddish theatre chiefly rests. The Brody Singers had formerly confined themselves to one-act sketches. The success of this attempt encouraged Goldfaden to collect a company, to train actors, and to produce a succession of his own works, ranging from the early farces to full-length plays, liberally interspersed with songs. A man of imperious temper, he frequently quarrelled with his actors, who left him to form their own troupes, and so spread the idea of a Yiddish theatre. He toured Rumania, Russia, and Poland, and in 1887 went to America, where he found a Yiddish theatre already established in New York, from which he encountered strong opposition. In 1889 he was in London, where he reorganized the Yiddish theatre established a year previously, but found that the actors refused to put on his plays, preferring those of other Yiddish dramatists, of whom there were now a number in Europe and America. After further travels on the Continent he settled in New York in 1903 and opened a dramatic school. One of his students was the great Jewish actor, Maurice Moskowitz (1871–1940). In later life he adopted Hebrew as his medium, and wrote in that language *David at War*, which was given an amateur production in 1904 by members of a Zionist Club, and was the first Hebrew play to be seen in the United States. Goldfaden, who died in New York and was buried in Washington Cemetery there, was the author of about four hundred plays. Among the best-known are *The Recruits* (1877), *The Witch* (1879), *The Two Kune Lemels* and *Shulamit* (both 1880) (the latter is usually considered his masterpiece, and has been translated into many languages, including Hebrew and English), *Dr. Almosado* (1882), and *Bar Kochba* (1883). His last play, *Son of My People* (1908), was running in New York at the Yiddish People's Theatre under Thomashefsky at the time of Goldfaden's death. E. HARRIS

GOLDONI, CARLO (1707–93), Italian dramatist, born in Venice, and destined by his parents for the law. He showed, however, from childhood a predilection for the theatre, and spent much of his spare time in reading classical plays. Although he took his lawyer's degree in 1731 and began to practise, he soon turned to the theatre, and his first play, *Belisario*, was acted by Imer's company in the Arena at Verona on 24 Nov. 1734. Although this, in imitation of much that he had read, was a tragicomedy, Goldoni cherished hopes of reforming Italian comedy by substituting for the improvised scenarios of the *commedia dell'arte*, now only a shadow of its former self, fully written comedies of character based on observation of daily life. He was bitterly opposed by Carlo Gozzi, who for his part was trying to reform the contemporary stage by making use of what was left of the *commedia dell'arte* and adapting it to his own ends (see ITALY, 2 vi).

Goldoni began his reforms in 1738 with *Mòmolo Cortesan*, which had one part fully written out. In 1746 he signed a five-year contract with Medebac, whose company was playing in Venice at the Teatro Sant'Angelo, and wrote for him, among other plays, *La vedova scaltra* (1748), *La buona moglie* and *Il cavaliere e la dama* (both 1749), and *Il teatro comico* (1750), a polemical play in which he sets out his plans for reform. Like Pirandello's later *Sei personaggi in cerca d'autore* (1921), this sends up its curtain on a bare working stage, and has for its cast a troupe of actors about to rehearse.

The years 1748–53 saw Goldoni at the height of his fame, beloved by all Venice, from doge to gondolier. Among the plays produced then were *Il bugiardo* and *La bottega del caffè* (both 1750) and Goldoni's masterpiece, *La locandiera* (1751), a picture of feminine coquetry which later delighted audiences all over Europe and America, particularly when the heroine, Mirandolina, was played by Eleonora Duse.

In 1753 Goldoni left Medebac to join Vendramin's company at the Teatro San Luca, where he remained until 1761. But difficulties arose almost at once. The theatre was larger and more suited to spectacular plays than to Goldoni's comedies, and the open hostility of Pietro Chiari, a mediocre dramatist who had taken Goldoni's place at the Teatro Sant'Angelo and used his position to parody his predecessor's works, soon divided Venice into two camps. Nevertheless, though embittered by strain and strife, Goldoni wrote some of his best plays during this period, among them *Gli innamorati* (1759), *La casa nova*, *I rusteghi* and *Le baruffe chiozzotte* (all 1760).

In April 1761 Goldoni went to Paris, where he wrote a number of plays in French for the Comédie-Italienne. He remained there until his death. In Paris fresh problems confronted him, not least the old struggle against actors who clung to improvisation, and resented change. Among the plays of this period which were at first not well received were *Sior Tòdero Brontolon* (1762), *Il Ventaglio* (1763), and *Le Bourru bienfaisant* (1771). Hard times then overtook him. He became tutor to the royal family and was granted a pension, but the French Revolution deprived him of it, and he died in poverty. He left behind him his autobiography, a number of comedies estimated at between 150 and 200 (some of these may be duplicates, since the same play was often given under different titles in French and Italian), ten tragedies, and eighty-three libretti for *melodrammi*. He has been called the Italian Molière, but the title does not suit him, for his excellence was of another kind. He excels in comedy of manners or 'ambiente'. He was struck by the ridiculous in human beings, and was content to draw his comedy from that, without attempting deeper commentary in the form of satire. He has been admirably summed up by Browning in his sonnet on the erection of Goldoni's monument in Venice in 1833:

> Goldoni good, gay, sunniest of souls,
> Glassing half Venice in that verse of thine,
> What though it just reflects the shade and shine
> Of common life nor renders, as it rolls,
> Grandeur and gloom? Sufficient for thy shoals
> Was Carnival. . . .

It is perhaps inevitable that after being so much admired, Goldoni's reputation should now be somewhat blown upon, particularly in an age which has little use for the lighter arts in which he excelled (for a more critical estimate of his work see ITALY, 3, *a*).

GOLDSMITH, OLIVER (1730–74), English poet, novelist, and dramatist, whose two plays, *The Good-Natured Man* (1768) and *She Stoops to Conquer* (1773), stand, like the works of Sheridan his contemporary, far in advance of the drama of his time. The first, produced by Colman at Covent Garden, had a cool reception, and was overshadowed by the success of a forgotten comedy, *False Delicacy*, at the rival theatre; but the second, also given at Covent Garden, made amends by its instantaneous appeal, Dr. Johnson, who had been instrumental in getting the play put on, leading the applause. This masterpiece has little in common with the genteel comedy of the day, or even with that of the Restoration dramatists, to which it has often been compared, but, says Nicoll (*Eighteenth Century Drama*), 'is close to the mood which is prevalent in the works of Greene and Lyly, and the young Shakespeare'. It has been constantly revived, and has a sure place in the affections of the English playgoer. Goldsmith wrote no more for the theatre, but in 1878 his novel, *The Vicar of Wakefield*, was made into a charming play with Ellen Terry as Olivia.

GOLIARD, a name given to the wandering scholars and clerks of the early Middle Ages, who, unamenable to discipline, joined themselves to the nomadic entertainers of the time, and were often confused with them, as in an order of 1281 that 'no clerks shall be jongleurs, goliards or buffoons'. They imparted a flavour of classical learning to the often crude performances of their less erudite fellows, and even when, as happened in the fourteenth century, the word was used for 'minstrel' without any clerical association, the goliard is still shown rhyming in Latin (cf. *Piers Plowman*).

GOMBAULD, JEAN (1570–1666), one of the original members of the French Academy, and a frequenter of the Hôtel de Rambouillet. He was also well received at Court, being in favour with the Queen-Mother. Among his literary works was a pastoral, given in 1630; it was of little account, but helped by its example to enforce a regard for the unities which Mairet had recently been advocating. Its success at the time of its production was probably due more to its author's reputation on other counts than to its own merits.

GONCHAROVA, NATHALIE (1881–1962), painter and scenic designer, most of whose work was done for the ballet. Born in Russia, of aristocratic parentage, she studied art in Moscow, and then travelled widely in Europe. In 1914, with her husband the artist Michel Larionov, she settled in Paris, where she was associated for many years with the Diaghilev ballet, designing the décor for Fokine's version of 'The Golden Cockerel', and Stravinsky's 'Les Noces'. She also designed 'Bolero' for Ida Rubinstein, and several sets for the Chauve-Souris. In 1926 she designed the sets and costumes for the second version of 'The Firebird', the only example of her work in the current British repertory. There are, however, a large number of her ballet designs at the Victoria and Albert Museum.

GONCOURT. (1) EDMOND-LOUIS-ANTOINE HUOT DE (1822–96) and (2) JULES-ALFRED HUOT DE (1830–70), French novelists and men of letters, whose careers cannot be separated, since they lived and wrote in collaboration. The theatre held an important place in their work, although their own plays are negligible. *Henriette Maréchal* (1865) failed in an atmosphere of political recrimination, and *La Patrie en danger*, written in 1873, had to wait until 1889 before it was put on at Antoine's Théâtre Libre. Several plays taken from their own novels fared no better, and it would seem on the face of it as if their influence on the French theatre was very slight. Indeed, they themselves considered the theatre inferior to the novel, but they were nevertheless fascinated by it, and it is in the field of ideas that their influence must be sought. They were the apostles of realism, and Zola, among others, owed much to them. They were also interested in the history of the French theatre and wrote a number of books on the actresses of the eighteenth century.

GOODMAN, CARDELL (or CARDONNEL) (*c.* 1649–99), an actor in Killigrew's company at Drury Lane, whose less endearing attributes were probably responsible for his nickname of

'Scum'. His manners and habits seem to have been reprehensible, and he was the acknowledged pet of the notorious Duchess of Cleveland, repaying her by trying to murder two of her children. The son of a clergyman, 'Scum' turned to the stage after he had been expelled from Cambridge, and was first seen in 1677, his best parts being apparently Julius Caesar and Alexander. He later turned highwayman, was captured, and pardoned by James II; in return for this magnanimity he became implicated in a plot to kill William III, and fled to Paris, where he died in obscurity.

GOODMAN'S FIELDS THEATRE, LONDON. There were two, or possibly three, theatres of this name. In 1729 Thomas Odell, having been made Deputy Licenser of Plays, converted a shop in Leman Street, Whitechapel, into a theatre. Here Fielding's second play, *The Temple Beau*, was first produced. Odell made Henry Giffard, an actor from Dublin, his stage manager, and, not having much knowledge of theatrical affairs, soon retired. He transferred his rights to Giffard, who, according to Chetwood, 'in the year 1733 caused to be built an entirely new, beautiful, convenient theatre, by the same architect with that at Covent Garden; where dramatic pieces were performed with the utmost elegance and propriety'. This theatre stood in Ayliffe Street.

A play called *The Golden Rump* being sent to Giffard frightened him so much by its abuse of the King and his Ministers that he sent it on to Sir Robert Walpole. This resulted in the passing of the Licensing Act of 1737. Giffard was given £1,000, but lost the licence of his theatre under the new Act.

He had had a good company, which included Walker, the original Macheath, Yates, later of Drury Lane, Bullock, a low comedian, and Woodward, then a boy but afterwards famous. Giffard tried a season at Lincoln's Inn Fields, but returned to Goodman's Fields, and to evade the law issued tickets of admission at 1*s*., 2*s*., and 3*s*. for a concert 'at the late theatre in Ayliffe Street'. He then performed a play, for which there was no extra charge, between the two halves of the concert. In this way he revived *The Winter's Tale*, which had not been seen for 100 years.

It was at this theatre that young David Garrick deputized for Yates, and then made his professional début on 9 Oct. 1741 as Richard III, being billed as 'a young gentleman who never appeared on any stage', though, under the name of Lyddal, he had previously played for Giffard at Ipswich. At the end of this season, in 1742, the theatre closed, never to reopen. Meanwhile at Odell's theatre in Leman Street exhibitions of rope-walking and acrobatics had been given. It now tried its fortune as a theatre again, but very obscurely, and it closed in 1751. It became a warehouse, and was burned down in 1802.

There would seem to have been yet another and older theatre hereabouts, for a periodical called *The Observator* stated in 1703 that 'the great playhouse has calved a young one in Goodman's Fields, in the passage by the Ship Tavern, between Prescot Street and Chambers Street'. But of this there is no other record.

W. MACQUEEN-POPE†

GOODWIN, NAT [NATHANIEL CARL] (1857–1919), American actor, who was born in Boston and made his début there in 1874 at the Howard Athenaeum, playing a newsboy in Joseph Bradford's *Law in New York*. His career as a vaudeville comedian began at Tony Pastor's Opera House, New York, in 1875, and the following year he scored an immense success in *Off the Stage* at the Lyceum with imitations of the popular actors of the day. Although best known as an actor of light comedy, he was also successful in such serious plays as Augustus Thomas's *In Mizzoura* (1893) and Clyde Fitch's *Nathan Hale* (1899), which was written for him and in which he played opposite his third wife, Maxine Elliott. In 1901 he played Shylock to her Portia and in 1903 appeared as Bottom, but Shakespeare proved beyond his range and he returned to modern comedy. The trade-mark of his mature years was a drily humorous manner which made him popular as a comedian and as a vaudeville raconteur. A book of reminiscences, *Nat Goodwin's Book*, appeared in 1914.

ROBERT TRACY

GORCHAKOV, NICOLAI MIKHAILOVICH (1899–1958), Russian producer, who began his career as a student of Vakhtangov at the Third Studio of the Moscow Art Theatre, soon after the Revolution. In 1924 he joined the company of the Moscow Art Theatre, and was assistant producer under Stanislavsky. Among his early productions were Katayev's *Squaring the Circle*, Kron's *An Officer of the Fleet*, and a translation of *The School for Scandal*. From 1933 to 1948 Gorchakov was director of the Moscow Theatre of Drama, and also for two years, 1941–3, artistic director of the Theatre of Satire. In 1939 he was appointed to the Chair of Theatre Production at the Lunacharsky State Institute of Theatre Art in Moscow, and was responsible for the choice and training of many of the producers now working in the Russian theatre. He wrote widely on theatrical subjects, and one of his books, based on shorthand notes taken during Stanislavsky's rehearsals, was published in an American translation as *Stanislavsky Directs* (1962). He was the producer of Rakhmanov's *The Troubled Past*, which the Moscow Art Theatre company performed in London during their visit in May 1958.

GORDIN, JACOB (1853–1909), Jewish dramatist, born in the Ukraine, the son of a well-to-do merchant, who gave him a good education on liberal principles. At 17 he became a journalist and a member of a Jewish community run on Tolstoyan lines, which advocated manual labour and a return to the land. This proved unsuccessful, and in 1891 Gordin emigrated to America in the hope of continuing its work there. He was, however, soon drawn into the orbit of the newly founded Yiddish theatre in New York and within a year had seen his first play produced there. Its success encouraged him to continue, and in all he wrote some eighty plays, of which *The Jewish King Lear* (1892), *Mirele Efros* (1898), a feminine pendant of Lear, and *God, Man and Devil* (1900), based to some extent on Goethe's *Faust*, are the best known. Although, like his contemporaries, Gordin took much of his material from non-Jewish plays, adapting and rewriting them with Jewish characters against a Jewish background, his work marks a great advance on that of such men as Hurwitch and Lateiner, in its simplicity, seriousness, and characterization. A man of strong character, with a clear conception of the problems of the Yiddish theatre, and also of what he wanted that theatre to become, Gordin opposed improvisation, and insisted on strict adherence by the actors to the printed texts. He was one of the directors of Goldfaden's dramatic school in New York, and towards the end of his life fought the 'star' system which he foresaw would be a danger to the theatre. E. HARRIS

GORKY, MAXIM [ALEXEI MAXIMOVICH PYESHKOV] (1868–1936), one of the greatest Russian dramatists, and the only one to belong equally to the Tsarist and Soviet epochs, between which he serves as a bridge. Of his plays the two most important were staged under the different régimes, *The Lower Depths* in 1902 and *Yegor Bulichev* in 1932. By temperament and conviction, however, Gorky belongs whole-heartedly to Soviet Russia, and by his work helped to bring about the establishment of the new régime. In acknowledgement of the debt owed to him his grateful country has renamed his birth-place, Nizhny-Novgorod, after him, and also the Moscow Art Theatre and the Bolshoi Dramatic Theatre in Leningrad (see GRAND GORKY THEATRE).

Gorky had a hard, unhappy childhood, and a youth overshadowed by brutality. His pseudonym of Gorky—the Bitter—well typifies his attitude at this time. Painfully (encouraged first by a ship's cook, and later by the writer V. G. Korolenko) he educated himself and began to write. His first short story was published in 1892, and was followed by a succession of works in which he became the outspoken champion of the under-dog, and the bitter opponent of 'man's inhumanity to man'. This led to his imprisonment and banishment. He spent many years in Italy, and organized a Bolshevik Party School on the Isle of Capri to which Lenin and Lunacharsky came to lecture. To such a man the October Revolution could mean nothing but good, and though he deplored some of its early excesses, he was always a whole-hearted advocate of its constructive work. A realist in his view of the worst in human nature, he was a romantic in his faith in the brotherhood of man and the hopefulness of the new generation. In 1929 he returned to Soviet Russia for good, and took a keen interest in the work of the younger writers, whom he befriended on all occasions.

It was Chekhov who was instrumental in bringing together Gorky and the Moscow Art Theatre, which in 1902 produced his first play. Since Gorky was already in the bad books of the authorities, this was given in a cut version, but even so it was sufficiently outspoken to get him into trouble, particularly when it was followed by that masterpiece of Russian realism, *The Lower Depths*, depicting the life of the Moscow underworld, huddled in a cellar. It is not surprising that Gorky's election to the Imperial Academy of Russian Artists was annulled. The performance of *The Lower Depths*, in Dec. 1902 (it has also been produced in England and America), was one of the glories of the Moscow Art Theatre's history, and to Stanislavsky, who produced it, it came to mean 'Freedom at any price!' It was followed by a number of lesser plays, all dealing with the class struggle (of which *The Enemies* was produced at the Moscow Art Theatre in 1935), but not until Gorky began his trilogy on the decay of the Russian bourgeoisie did he again attain the dramatic stature reached by *The Lower Depths*. Of this projected trilogy only two parts were completed, *Yegor Bulichev*, produced at the Moscow Art Theatre in 1934 by Nemirovich-Danchenko, and *Dostigayev*, produced at the Vakhtangov Theatre.

Gorky's work is not as well known outside Russia as it should be, but it is to be hoped that adequate translations, and careful production, will make him accessible to those who cannot read Russian.

GOSET, see JEWISH DRAMA, 6 and MOSCOW STATE JEWISH THEATRE.

GÔT, EDMOND-FRANÇOIS-JULES (1822–1901), French actor, who passed the whole of his long and honourable career at the Comédie-Française, of which he was the twenty-ninth *doyen*. He made his début on 17 July 1844 in comedy roles, playing Mascarille in *Les Précieuses ridicules*, and became a member of the company in 1850. He was one of the finest and most dependable actors of his day, and played innumerable new parts, as well as most of the classic repertory.

GOTHA, the home of Germany's second attempt at a National Theatre (see EKHOF and GERMANY, 4).

GOTTSCHED, JOHANN CHRISTOPH (1700–66), German literary critic, who endeavoured to reform the German stage and remodel it on the lines of the French classical theatre. In this he was much helped by the actress Caroline Neuber, who put his theories into action, and replaced, as far as she was able, the old plays and farces, and particularly the clowning of Hanswurst, by translations of French classics. Gottsched, who had become Professor of Poetry at Leipzig in 1730, although he had no great talent for literature or criticism, prepared a model repertory for her, which was later published as the *Deutsche Schaubühne nach den Regeln der alten Griechen und Römer eingerichtet.* This consisted of adaptations from the French by himself, his wife, and some picked collaborators, and a few original plays, of which by far the best were the comedies and tragedies of J. E. Schlegel. Of Gottsched's own plays, *Der sterbende Cato* (1732) was successful with Kohlhardt in the title-role, but was later discredited by Gottsched's Swiss opponents, who claimed that it was an amalgamation of Addison's *Cato* with one by Deschamps on the same subject. His *Agis*, which makes dreary reading, is important as the first treatment of a social problem on the German stage.

One of Gottsched's first periodicals, *Die vernünftigen Tadlerinnen*, contained an article on the theatre—probably the first of its kind in Germany—with a favourable allusion to Neuber's company. Unfortunately trouble arose between him and the actress who had done so much to further his ideas, and they parted company. By 1740 Gottsched had ceased to exercise any determining influence on the German theatre, or on German literature in general, but he laboured on undaunted to the end. His *Nöthiger Vorrath zur Geschichte der deutschen dramatischen Dichtkunst*, which appeared from 1757 to 1765, is a well-documented bibliography of German drama from the sixteenth century onwards. W. E. DELP

GOUGH. (1) ROBERT (?–1625), English actor and the brother-in-law of Augustine Phillips. He first appears in about 1592, playing a woman's part. It has been conjectured, on slender evidence, that he played a number of Shakespeare's female parts, including Juliet and Portia, and with greater probability that he succeeded to Phillips's share in the company. He was one of the earliest King's Men, and his name appears in the actor-list in the Shakespeare Folio. His younger son, (2) ALEXANDER (1614–?), was evidently apprenticed to the stage at an early age, since he appeared in an important female role in *The Roman Actor* at the age of 12. He continued to play women's parts up to 1632, but on graduating to men's roles he seems to have lost his excellence, since he is scarcely mentioned in the company's casts, and a reference to him after the Restoration, saying that he was responsible for giving the word to 'Persons of Quality' when the actors were going to perform surreptitiously under the Commonwealth, refers to him as the 'Woman Actor'. He appears to have been a publisher of plays during the 1650s.

GOZZI, CARLO (1720–1806), Italian dramatist, who endeavoured in the eighteenth century to adapt the masks of the *commedia dell'arte*, then in its decline, to the purposes of a written and literary theatre. In this he was partly inspired by his hatred and jealousy of Goldoni, who was trying to reform the stage by substituting written comedy of character and intrigue for the old improvised plays.

Gozzi's first play, performed in 1761, when Goldoni was just taking leave of Venice before settling in Paris, was *L'Amore delle tre melarance*, which was partly written, partly improvised. This, and his later plays, were given by the troupe of Sacchi, one of the best-known actors of the day, whose leading lady was Teodora Ricci.

Gozzi's *fiabe*, or fairy-tale plays, gained more applause in Germany and France, where he was regarded as a harbinger of Romanticism, than in Italy, where, though he succeeded in capturing the attention of his audience for a short time, he was considered extravagant and fantastic. In his desire to parody Goldoni he was led into absurdities which critical opinion long considered must rule out any possibility of his revival. Since the war, however, there have been some notable productions of *Il Corvo* (freely treated), *Turandot*, and *L'Augellin belverde*, while *Il Re cervo*, as *The King Stag*, was given (in Carl Wildman's adaptation) by the Young Vic, and (in Frederick May's translation) by several Children's Theatre companies. Gozzi's fantastic vein, anticipating the Pirandellian concern with myth and the workings of the subconscious (especially with respect to the reality/illusion conflict), is increasingly sympathetic to our age. The best of his plays is perhaps *L'Augellin belverde* (1764), though *Turandot* (1762), which was used as the basis of an opera by Puccini, proved extremely successful when given a fine production at the Vakhtangov Theatre in Moscow in 1922. It was also produced in America a few years later (see also ITALY, 2 vi).

GRABBE, CHRISTIAN DIETRICH (1801–36), German poet and dramatist, who with Büchner was the dramatic mouthpiece of the 'Young Germany' movement. His ambitious *Don Juan und Faust* (1829), which strives to emulate both Mozart and Goethe, has some striking scenes. A later play, *Napoleon, oder die hundert Tage* (1831), consists of little more than a long series of sketches, loosely strung together. Grabbe led an unhappy, harassed life and died young. He was later made the hero of a play, *Der Einsame* (1925), by Hanns Johst.

GRACIOSO, the comic servant in the Spanish drama of the Golden Age, corresponding to the valet in France, or the Elizabethan fool in England. According to Menéndez y Pelayo, he first appears sketchily in the character of Lenicio in Torres Naharro's *Comedia Serafina*, but his immediate ancestor is the *bobo* of Lope de Rueda's interludes (*pasos*). In the plays of Lope de Vega the *gracioso*'s actions often burlesque or parody those of his master and his language is generally lively and popular. With Calderón the *gracioso* is used to present yet another facet of the moral or doctrinal lesson implicit in the play, whether *comedia* or *auto sacramental*. In the comedies of Moreto the complicated intrigue is set on foot and maintained by the *gracioso* and his female counterpart; masters and mistresses lose all personality and our interest is centred on the ingenious shifts and stratagems of the comic figures. From the *bobo*, and even perhaps from the comic rustics of the Christmas play, a line can be imagined leading towards Figaro, but this development was not to come in Spain, for the comic figures of the first half of the eighteenth century are only pale reflections of their seventeenth-century forebears, and those of the second half weak imitations of French and Italian originals. J. E. VAREY

GRAFTON THEATRE, LONDON, a playhouse in Tottenham Court Road which opened in 1931 with a revival of *The Lilies of the Field* under Helena Pickard (Lady Hardwicke) and Beatrix Thomson. A few plays were revived and then the venture was given up. Productions were occasionally seen there in the next few years, and from 1939 to 1945 the theatre was occupied by the B.B.C. It is no longer in use.

GRAMATICA. (1) IRMA (1873–1962) and (2) EMMA (1874–1965), Italian actresses, daughters of actors. Irma was on the stage from her earliest years, appearing with her parents in Monti's company. She then studied in Florence, and joined Duse for a tour of South America. Returning to Italy, she became known for her skilful playing of the young heroines of the popular French plays of the time, though her finest part was perhaps the young Thérèse in *Thérèse Raquin*. She was also excellent in *The Taming of the Shrew*. After a few years in retirement, she returned to the stage in 1923, and some years later toured in company with her younger sister. Her last appearance was as Lady Macbeth to the Macbeth of Ruggeri in 1938, after which she retired.

Her sister Emma, though originally less promising as an actress, soon became an exceptionally fine portrayer of the women of Ibsen, Pirandello, and particularly Shaw. She played in *Mrs. Warren's Profession*, *Pygmalion*, *St. Joan*, and *Caesar and Cleopatra*, and was also seen as Marchbanks in *Candida*. A romantic actress, less lyrical than Irma, but stronger, she was an excellent linguist, and acted in both German and Spanish.

GRAND GORKY THEATRE, LENINGRAD. This theatre was founded in 1919, under the direction of the poet Alexander Blok, by amalgamating the two independent but short-lived ventures, the Theatre of Artistic Drama and the Theatre of Tragedy. Gorky took a great interest in it, advised it on policy, and guided it through its early troubles. Its first production was *Don Carlos*, followed by a number of classic and a few modern plays. Then came a period of expressionism, when Toller, Kaiser, Shaw, and O'Neill were produced in the constructivist style. From 1925 onwards Soviet plays were introduced into the repertory, and in 1933 Gorky's *Enemies* was given its first production. All Gorky's plays were first done in Leningrad at this theatre. It continued to waver between different styles, and to flirt with every novelty, until the appointment in 1938 of B. A. Babochkin as its director. Among its early scenic designers were Alexandre Benois, who left Russia to join Diaghilev's Russian Ballet company, and Akimov, who remained and made a name for himself later as a producer. During the war the theatre was evacuated, and returned to find its buildings damaged. These, however, were soon repaired, and the theatre embarked on an ambitious programme, including a revival of a fine production of *King Lear*, which had been cut short by the outbreak of war.

GRAND GUIGNOL, see GUIGNOL.

GRAND OPERA HOUSE, NEW YORK, opened on 9 Jan. 1868 by Samuel J. Pike of Cincinnati. Its early years were somewhat unsuccessful, and it was often closed between short visits from travelling stars. Daly took it over for two seasons, 1872–4, and under him Mrs. John Wood made her last appearance in New York, as Peachblossom in *Under the Gaslight*, Fechter was seen as the Count of Monte Cristo, and Fay Templeton, later a star of variety under Weber and Fields, played Puck. In 1875 E. L. Davenport was seen in the parts then being played by Barry Sullivan at Booth's, and the theatre closed, to reopen under Poole and Donnelly after redecoration, with seats at greatly reduced prices, as a local 'family' house for the visits of Broadway successes with a generous sprinkling of stars—a policy which proved successful for many years.

GRAND THEATRE, LONDON, in Upper Street, Islington. This started its career as a music-hall called the Philharmonic. At the end of 1870 it became a theatre under the management of Head, a bookmaker, and Charles Morton, the 'father' of the halls. It became the home of *opéra bouffe*, with Emily Soldene as the star, and West-End audiences, even royalty, flocked to North London to see her. The theatre burned down in Sept. 1882. One notable event in its life had been the temporary loss of its licence through the introduction of the can-can. Rebuilt, redecorated, improved, and enlarged, the theatre reopened in the autumn of 1883 as the Grand, but was burned down again in Dec. 1887. Rebuilt more elaborately still, it reopened on 1 Dec. 1888 to perish by fire once more in 1900. Again reopened, it became a theatre which relied on touring companies, though many West-End stars included it in their circuits. Its Christmas pantomimes were famous, and Harry Randall played in them for many seasons. After becoming a music-hall, and then a cinema, it was demolished. W. MACQUEEN-POPE†

GRANDVAL, CHARLES-FRANÇOIS RACOT DE (1714–84), French actor, who made his début at the Comédie-Française at the age of 19 as Andronic in Campistron's tragedy of that name. He had one great fault—he rolled his r's badly; but the public soon got used to that, and he became a great favourite with them. He played some of Baron's roles, and succeeded Dufresne in tragedy with a force and intelligence considered by some to be the equal of the great Lekain himself. Grandval retired at 52, but lack of money brought him back to the stage, where he was again successful. This, however, was his undoing, and some of his fellow actors, jealous of his return, were suspected of hiring a gang of toughs to howl him down in *Alzire*. In disgust Grandval again retired, and went to live near Mlle Dumesnil, enjoying her company, and that of his many friends, until his death. He wrote a certain amount of witty verse, and some scurrilous but amusing comedies are attributed to him.

GRANOVSKY, Alexander [really Abraham Ozark] (1890–1937), Jewish actor and producer, who received his theatrical training in Germany. In 1919 he founded in Leningrad the Jewish Theatre Studio, which later moved to Moscow and became the State Jewish Theatre (known also as Melucha and Goset). Granovsky's first production was Maeterlinck's *Les Aveugles*, with the text freely adapted to his own theories of dramatic effect. His opening evening in Moscow in 1921 was, however, devoted to short sketches by Sholom Aleichem, and the theatre then concentrated on the production of plays by Yiddish dramatists. Granovsky's methods were perhaps most clearly shown in his own dramatization of Peretz's poem, *Night in the Old Market* (1925). With no more than a thousand words of text to work on, he made music the basic element, while a subtle use of lighting evoked the presence of the dead, who, with the market people and the *badchan*, or professional jester, made up the characters of the play. In 1928, while on a European tour, Granovsky resigned his directorship of the theatre, being succeeded by his chief actor, Mikhoels, and in 1930 produced *Uriel Acosta* for Habima in Berlin.

E. HARRIS

GRANVILLE-BARKER, Harley, see BARKER.

GRASSO, Giovanni (1875–1930), a Sicilian actor, son and grandson of puppet-masters, who was encouraged to go on the stage by the great Italian actor, Rossi, under whom he trained. He was seen all over Europe, and was considered a fine actor of the realistic school, being at his best in the plays of Pirandello. He was several times seen in London, where his Othello was considered excellent.

GRAVE TRAP, see TRAP.

GRAY, Terence (1895–), founder, with Harold Ridge, of the Festival Theatre, Cambridge, which, though it remained under his management only a short time, had an influence, particularly on the Continent, out of all proportion to the work actually done there. Gray may indeed, like Craig, be said to have fertilized the theatre more by his ideas than by his achievements. He was profoundly influenced by Craig's ideas on lighting and stagecraft, and in his twenties wrote a number of wordless mime plays, and plays on Egyptian themes in which the words were to be subordinated to the movement and lighting. For these he designed settings composed of cubes, columns, and luminous screens. In order to try out his theories on staging, he took over an old Georgian playhouse, the Barnwell, which had fallen on evil days, and opened it as the Festival Theatre in 1926, with a performance of the *Oresteia*. In revolt against the cramping conditions of the proscenium arch, he abolished it, together with the footlights, and built out a forestage connected with the auditorium by a staircase, broken by platforms on different levels, which offered exceptional opportunities for grouping (see No. 84). Here, with the young Maurice Evans as leading man, and with interesting experiments in lighting by Ridge, who later became an authority on stage lighting, were produced plays ranging from Greek tragedy and comedy to modern English and foreign importations, with incursions into Shakespeare and Restoration drama. Some of these were produced, in an iconoclastic and highly individual manner, by Gray himself, others by such men as Norman Marshall (who in 1932 ran his own season at the Festival Theatre). The choreography was by Ninette de Valois, Gray's cousin, using dancers who later formed the nucleus of the Vic-Wells Ballet. After three years Anmer Hall brought a company, headed by Flora Robson and Robert Donat, to the theatre, with the young Tyrone Guthrie as producer, and profited by the experience gained there to build the Westminster Theatre in London. Gray returned intermittently, but finally abandoned his project in 1933, after the first performance in English of Aeschylus's the *Suppliants*, when the theatre was bought by a commercial management and restored in a conventional style. It is now owned by the Trustees of the Arts Theatre, and used as a workshop and costume store. Gray certainly gave a shake-up to the fossilized theatrical fashions of the time; that he did not do more was in part due to the limitations of his own personality. He was not an easy person to work for, and those concerned with him in his erratic progress through a vast cosmopolitan repertory of plays no doubt suffered accordingly; but, as Ridge was to remark many years later, 'it was fun while it lasted'. In the 1930s Gray bought the site of the old National Sporting Club with the intention of building an open-stage theatre there, but had to abandon the idea because the L.C.C. insisted on a fire curtain, which was impossible in the type of theatre he had in mind.

GRAZIANO, the most usual name of the Pedant-Doctor of the *commedia dell'arte* (see ITALY, 2).

GREAT QUEEN STREET THEATRE, London, see KINGSWAY THEATRE.

GRECIAN THEATRE, London, built in the grounds of the Eagle Saloon, in Shepherdess Walk, City Road (a summer resort for al fresco entertainment). It opened as a concert hall in 1832 under Thomas, nicknamed 'Brayvo',

Rouse. He had good actors, singers, orchestra, and chorus, and presented light opera, himself sitting in a box every night to maintain order. He lost much money in his endeavours to improve musical taste, recouping himself, however, by the profits on the tavern. Robson had his first London engagement at the Grecian in 1844, remaining there for five years before being discovered by managers and playgoers further west. Sims Reeves sang in the Grecian chorus. In 1851 Benjamin Conquest succeeded Rouse and obtained a theatre licence. The huge building with its enormous pit was then used for Shakespeare, comedy, and tragedy, but money was lost. The Grecian was rebuilt, with two tiers instead of one, and a gallery, and held 3,400 people. Ballet was given under the direction of Mrs. Conquest, herself a fine dancer, and there was still al fresco entertainment in the grounds. All through the Conquest management drama and pantomime played a big part. Conquest was a superb pantomimist and the Grecian pantomimes became one of the Christmas attractions of London. In 1876 the theatre was rebuilt at a cost of £8,000 by Conquest's son George, who in 1879 sold it for £21,000 to Clark, a marine-store dealer and one-time lessee of the Adelphi. Clark managed to lose a fortune and finally sold out to the Salvation Army in 1881. Among the actors who appeared at the Grecian were Kate Vaughan, Harry Nicholls, Herbert Campbell, and Arthur Roberts. W. MACQUEEN-POPE†

GREECE. Classical Greek drama is in fact Athenian drama; for although every Greek city and many a large village came to have its theatre, and although some dramatic forms (see MIME) originated and flourished elsewhere, Athens established and maintained a complete preeminence among the Greek states both in tragedy and in comedy, and all the Greek drama that we possess was written by Athenians for Athens. The question of the origin of tragedy, and of comedy too, is obscure and difficult, but of little practical importance when compared with the major fact that both forms of drama were, from their inception, a part of a religious festival; that is (since the word 'religious' in this context can be misleading to modern ears), a serious and splendid civic and national celebration. Both arts were, from the beginning, addressed to a whole community which came to the theatre as a community, not as individuals; and to a community which was its own political master and its own government.

Tragedy was formed while the Athenian democracy was being formed; it ennobled itself while the Athenian people were ennobling themselves by the part they played in repelling the Persians (490–479); it lost its vigour at the end of the fifth century, under the double strain of the long Peloponnesian War and an age of criticism and self-consciousness. During this century it moved, on the whole, from communal to individual or private themes. The typical Aeschylean theme, shown in his earliest surviving play, the *Suppliants* (*c.* 490; part of a lost trilogy), and his latest, the Orestes-trilogy (458), is the moral government of the universe; sin produces suffering and counter-sin, that produces more sin and suffering, until a resolution is reached in Justice. Sophocles (first victory, 468) brought to perfection the tragedy of the individual hero—this being the form of tragedy that Aristotle analyses in the *Poetics*; in Euripides, and in some of Sophocles' later work, we find the study of the abnormal, and the exploitation of dramatic situation for its own sake (romantic drama, melodrama, even high comedy, as in Euripides' *Helen*, 412).

Comedy followed a roughly parallel course, but some fifty years later. Old Comedy (*c.* 435–405) was a riotous burlesque and criticism of current personalities and movements in political life (this is represented for us by the first nine plays of Aristophanes). Middle Comedy was still strongly satirical, but quieter, more coherent, and with a social rather than a political background. New Comedy (*c.* 350–292, death of Menander) was a delicate, sometimes sentimental, comedy of manners.

The stylistic reflection of this is that in both forms of drama the chorus, that is, the communal element, is originally very prominent, and the movement of plot restricted; and in both forms the histrionic element and plot grow in importance, while the chorus becomes more and more out of place and finally disappears.

1. TRAGEDY. (*a*) *Origins.* It is beyond question that tragedy developed out of the choral lyric, an art which, during the sixth century, reached a high degree of perfection, particularly among the Dorian peoples of the Peloponnese; this was a poem, religious or otherwise, which was sung and danced by a chorus. Beyond this, nothing can be said without qualification. Aristotle's authority must stand high; unfortunately, his account of the origin of tragedy, and of comedy too, is bald and perfunctory. He derives tragedy from the 'leaders of the dithyramb'; it was, he says, at first an improvisation; then, passing out of the satyric stage (see SATYR-DRAMA), and abandoning short plots and ludicrous diction, gradually attained dignity. These statements accord with the facts that in Athens, the home of tragedy, it was performed only at festivals of Dionysus, to whom the dithyramb belonged, and that the statutory tragic trilogy ended regularly with a satyr-play. It has indeed been suggested that what Aristotle says is only an inference drawn from these facts. In modern times many detailed theories have been advanced; the whole world has been scoured for 'ritual-sequences' similar to those of Dionysus; the plays themselves have been diligently read and misread to yield evidence; but little that is secure has emerged. The Dionysiac origin is generally accepted. Dionysus was a nature-god, connected particularly, though not exclusively, with wine. As a nature-god, he died and was reborn each year, and these events were celebrated in a variety of ritual; but attempts to

trace the outlines of any such ritual in existing tragedy must be pronounced a failure. We cannot profitably look further back than the dithyramb, originally a hymn to Dionysus, performed by a chorus of fifty. It would be a natural development, and in accord with Aristotle's statement, if the leader of this chorus engaged in a simple form of dialogue with his fellows (compare the soloist and chorus in oratorio); here would be the germ of the histrionic element in drama. But if ever tragedy had a special association with Dionysiac subjects (as distinct from the Dionysus-festival), this association was lost before tragedy reached maturity.

Since the worship of Dionysus celebrated the rebirth of the god in the spring as well as his death in the autumn; since the wine-god had his jovial aspect; and since Greek ritual was tolerant of features which seem to us undignified, even indecent, it would not be surprising if the developing art of drama was now serious, now comic; and in fact the burlesque and often indecent satyr-drama was associated with tragedy from at least 500 B.C. onwards. (The origin of comedy was quite distinct; see below.) In spite of this, Aristotle's statement that tragedy itself went through a satyric stage is difficult and has been called in question.

The word tragedy means 'goat-song'. The role of the goat is also obscure; probably it was a prize—'a song for a goat'.

(*b*) *Development.* The sixth century B.C. was the formative period, but we know very little about it, as the evidence is scanty, and most of it very late. For example, ancient authorities state variously that the first tragic poet was Epigênes of Sicyon (*c.* 590 B.C.) or Thespis of Athens, or that Thespis was the second or the sixteenth. Such mathematical statements are obviously derived from earlier histories of literature, and they reflect also the difficulty of defining the term 'tragic poet' in the period before 534, when Pisistratus first instituted the regular contests (see below, 3, FESTIVALS).

At the first of these contests Thespis won the prize, appropriately, since it was he who had taken the decisive step of introducing an actor, as distinct from the chorus-leader. Aeschylus introduced a second actor; he is already in use in our earliest extant play, Aeschylus's *Suppliants*, so that we have no specimen of the earlier one-actor tragedy. It happens, however, that during a considerable part of the *Suppliants* one of the actors, playing Danaus, is quite idle on the stage; for all practical purposes therefore we do possess here drama composed for a single actor (the King) and the chorus (the Suppliants), and—if we can overlook the uselessness of Danaus—the scene is extremely dramatic. It is long, and formal, and contains practically no development of plot, but it does contain a most effective intensification, on quasi-musical lines, of the already existing situation. The early drama is often compared to oratorio, and indeed it must have consisted very largely of singing and dancing, with only the very simplest and shortest of plots, but obviously it could be intensely dramatic.

It was Aeschylus (525–456 B.C.), still the world's grandest dramatist, who brought tragedy to its maturity. His introduction of the second actor made the histrionic part of the play as prominent and significant as the choral, and the chorus gradually lost its primacy. It enabled him also to develop plot, though length and complexity of plot was never one of his objects. Aeschylus knew better than to try simply to dramatize a myth: he dramatized certain implications of the myth. He did not use his highly individual trilogy-form (see AESCHYLUS) to tell a story; each of the three plays was, in all essentials, the dramatization of a crisis, with but little movement of plot. His dramatic resources (especially the chorus), and the material that the myth could be made to provide, were so deployed as to intensify steadily the significance of that crisis. The *Agamemnon* is a very long play, but its actual plot is extremely short; in spite of the new histrionic possibilities, half the bulk of the play is lyrics. Characterization is not subtle, but catastrophic: there is little interplay between the characters, only head-on collisions, though minor characters, like the Watchman and the Nurse in the *Oresteia*, are drawn with a vividness quite Shakespearian.

At some time, perhaps after he wrote the *Suppliants*, Aeschylus reduced the number of the chorus from fifty to twelve, perhaps by simply dividing the original fifty among the four plays of the tetralogy. As we know so little about this aspect of Greek drama, we do not know why he did this, nor what the effect was. Though Aeschylus's music and dances are lost, the metrical rhythms of the odes remain, and often suggest something of the original effect: for instance, the odes in the *Agamemnon* are pervaded by variations on a slow iambic rhythm which by its sheer persistence becomes very dramatic and moving.

It should be observed that each of the actors could play more than one role. In the *Agamemnon*, using three actors, Aeschylus has six characters—an unusually large number for him. Further, apart from the statutory two, later three, actors who were paid by the city, the dramatist could employ any number of 'supers' (dumb persons) who were paid by the *choregus*. Thus, if the chorus in the *Suppliants* was still the old dithyrambic chorus of fifty, as seems probable, then there were in one scene the fifty daughters of Danaus (the chorus), fifty suitors, the two actors, and probably the King's bodyguard.

In Sophocles (496–406 B.C.), above all others the 'classical' dramatist, a new balance is struck between chorus and actors, and a very different type of drama appears. Sophocles was interested in the tragic interplay between different characters, or between a character and circumstance, or between the different aspects of a single character—a quieter, less catastrophic, but even more tense type of drama. He needed therefore much more complex characterization, a much more subtle plot, and a much more detailed and naturalistic treatment; these were made possible by his introduction of a third actor (borrowed by Aeschylus in his later plays). His plots are masterpieces of construction: complex, beautifully controlled, with every detail made to contribute to the central idea of the play. The same is true of his characterization, which is subtle, strong, and never merely decorative. Working in this more detailed way, Sophocles naturally abandoned the vast canvas of the Aeschylean trilogy, and always presented three separate plays.

He both reduced and altered the scope of the chorus. It plays a very small part in the action, though it is always relevant to it, and may intervene effectively. Its chief function is now purely lyrical; it is used between histrionic scenes, which now begin to resemble 'acts', to carry on the dramatic rhythm—to emphasize a climax, or to prepare the way for a sudden change of mood. See, for example, the ecstatic ode in the *Antigone* which stands immediately before the messenger's tale of death.

Sophocles also increased the number of the chorus from twelve to fifteen, at which number it remained. This seems to have been a purely technical development.

After Sophocles there were no important changes in the externals of tragedy, though it seems that in the (late) *Oedipus Coloneus* he employed a fourth actor. The innovations of Euripides (484–406/7 B.C.) were concerned with style and treatment—more realism and pathos, a new and more emotional style of music. In his non-tragic plays plot becomes more elaborate and important; in some plays indeed the interest lies almost entirely in the succession of the events, not in their moral or intellectual significance. The actors therefore gain still more ground at the expense of the chorus. The number of roles tends to increase. In the *Phoenician Women* there are eleven. The choral odes are sometimes only decorative, and there are fewer of them—notably in the *Helen* and in the (late) *Philoctetes* of Sophocles. The chorus was now becoming an encumbrance. The last we hear of it is Aristotle's statement that it was Agathon—a younger contemporary of Euripides—who first introduced odes that had no connexion with the plot, and were mere lyrical interludes.

(*c*) *Form.* A Greek tragedy had traditional features rather than a set form, and these are most easily understood when its choral origin is borne in mind. Originally a play was a series of choral odes on a dramatic theme, punctuated by histrionic interludes (called 'episodes', literally 'additional entrances', because the actor, as it were, came in on top of the chorus). In the classical period a balance was attained between the lyrical and the histrionic parts; the dramatic ideas presented through the action were caught up and amplified in the successive odes. The odes therefore knit the play together; there was no question of the division of the play into 'acts'. This came with the decadence, when the chorus provided only interludes, which separated rather than linked scenes. Hence the 'five acts' recognized by Horace.

Our earliest plays begin with the entrance-song of the chorus, the 'parodos'. This was written in anapaests, the marching-rhythm. (Not always, however. The chorus in the *Seven against Thebes* of Aeschylus comes pouring in to the most uneven dochmiac rhythm. The idea that Greek tragedy was always statuesque is a delusion.) Soon, as the histrionic element increased in significance, there was prefixed to the parodos a scene for the actor or actors; this was the 'prologos'. (The 'prologue' in the modern sense of an introductory monologue was a convention first adopted by Euripides.) As tragedy became more realistic, the formal parodos was replaced by lyrical conversation between members of the incoming chorus, or between the chorus and the actor on the stage. Formal odes after the parodos were (later) given the name 'stasimon', the exact interpretation of which is uncertain. The number of stasima, and therefore of the episodes which came between them, varied considerably; Sophocles wrote five (besides the parodos) in the *Antigone*, only three in the *Electra*. Everything that followed the last stasimon was called the 'exodos' (exit).

A stasimon consisted of one or more strophes with the corresponding antistrophes, and might end with an independent 'epode'. Antistrophe corresponded to strophe exactly in metre, therefore in the music and dance too, but no strophe ever corresponded with another. (The choral strophe was, in fact, not a literary but a musical form.) As the rhythms were music- and not speech-rhythms, it is rarely possible to represent them at all in translation.

But the lyrics were by no means confined to the stasima, or to the chorus. Lyrical dialogue between actor and chorus was common; this was a 'commos' (lament); or, at a crisis, a striking effect might be got by making the actor sing and the chorus reply in spoken verse. (When the chorus engaged in spoken dialogue, the chorus-leader only spoke, that is, the chorus-leader spoke for it; the Greek chorus never attempted the preposterous feat of speaking in unison.) Again, an actor might be given a solo to sing (a 'monody') before the chorus had appeared. In the decadence, such solos became much commoner and purely decorative.

Another constant feature, lyrical in origin, was strict line-by-line dialogue, 'stichomythia'. The iambic verse of ordinary dialogue was never divided between two speakers, except occasionally, and for special dramatic reasons, by Sophocles.

Of the three unities, the only one that has any essential connexion with Greek tragedy is the unity of action—and Euripides disregarded even that. The unity of time was entirely overlooked, and although unity of place was normally imposed by the continuous presence of a chorus, if circumstances made it necessary and possible to move the chorus, it was moved, and the unity of place disappeared.

The scene of the *Eumenides* shifts from Delphi to Athens, and the change of place implies also an interval of about a year.

2. COMEDY. (*a*) *Origins*. Attic comedy had a much stricter and more complex form than Attic tragedy, but its origins are not less obscure. Like tragedy, it was a blend of two elements, the choral and the histrionic; but while in tragedy it is easy to see how the histrionic part may have grown naturally out of the leader of the chorus, in comedy we seem to have rather a fusion of two separate elements. For Old Comedy (represented now only by Aristophanes *c.* 448–*c.* 380 B.C.) exhibits, with variations, a complex and elaborate form. There is, on the one hand, a succession of scenes in which form is strict; the chorus enters; there is a dispute between the chorus and an actor, or between two actors each supported by a semi-chorus; there is a formal 'contest' (*agon*) or debate; and finally an address made by the chorus direct to the audience (the parabasis—'coming-forward'). All this, but especially the parabasis, tends to be elaborately symmetrical in structure, and the contest is usually composed in metres other than the iambic trimeter of ordinary dramatic dialogue.

Besides this element, essentially choral in form, there is another; scenes for actors alone precede the entry of the chorus and follow the parabasis, these using the iambic trimeter and showing no trace of symmetrical structure.

It seems clear then that comedy had a dual origin. Without going into detail, we may say that the histrionic scenes have an obvious affinity with such things as the Sicilian mime and the burlesque performers whose masks or representations of them have been dug up in great numbers at Sparta; while the formal part must have been developed out of some ritual performance by a chorus. The name comedy means 'revel-song' (*cômos* and *ôdê*). One form of revel was associated with fertility-rites; it was a mixture of singing, dancing, scurrilous jesting against bystanders, and ribaldry. Aristotle derives comedy from this, and certainly comedy contained all these elements, including the use of the phallus, the symbol of fertility. Another form of *cômos*, well represented on vase-paintings, was the masquerade, in which revellers disguised themselves as animals or birds. Since the comic chorus was often of this type (cf. Aristophanes' *Wasps*, *Birds*, *Frogs*), the influence of this kind of revel on comedy seems clear enough. Our evidence does not enable us to say which, if either, of these forms was the lineal ancestor of comedy.

(*b*) *Development*. Aristotle says that it was not until late that comedy was taken seriously enough to be admitted to the civic festivals. The first contest seems to have taken place in 486, some fifty years later than the first tragic contest. Among the early masters were Chionides, Magnes, and Crates. Crates is said by Aristotle to have been the first to abandon the 'lampoon-form' and to write 'generalized plots'. This, emphatically, does not mean that Crates gave up direct personalities and built his plays on neatly contrived plots. Comedy did not reach this degree of sophistication until well on in the fourth century, and Aristophanes was always lampooning individuals (Cleon in the *Knights*, Socrates in the *Clouds*). It means, probably, that until the time of Crates comedy had kept up the atmosphere and style of the original revel, with its sudden and disconnected attacks on members of the audience, and that Crates reduced this to order by introducing the elements of plot and a unifying theme.

Comedy came to maturity during the second half of the fifth century and continued vigorous until the death of Menander (*c.* 342–292 B.C.). Ancient critics divided it into Old, Middle, and New. Old Comedy was the comedy of Athens in her prime, as represented by Aristophanes. (Other masters of whom only fragments survive were Eupolis and Cratinus.) These plays often baffle the modern reader, who is disconcerted by their lack of plot and by their extreme topicality. Old Comedy is the most local form of drama that has ever reached literary rank; it was, to speak very roughly, a national 'rag', in which anything prominent in the life of the city, whether persons or ideas, was unsparingly ridiculed; it was a unique mixture of fantasy, criticism, wit, burlesque, obscenity, parody, invective, and the most exquisite lyricism. Today much of it would be obnoxious to the laws of libel, blasphemy, or decency, and of the rest, a great deal would be rejected as too 'high-brow'. The atmosphere of the whole is well suggested by the story that during the performance of the *Clouds* Socrates rose from his seat to give the audience an opportunity of comparing the mask of the stage-Socrates with the appearance of the real Socrates.

Instead of plot Aristophanes uses a single fantastic situation, which is quickly developed and then exploited in a series of loosely connected scenes. The most remarkable feature is the parabasis, for in it the dramatist drops all dramatic illusion, suspends the plot, and speaks directly to the audience on matters—sometimes purely personal—which are quite unconnected with the play. Thus, in the parabasis of the *Knights* Aristophanes gives a brilliant account of his predecessors and of his rival Cratinus.

Aristophanes' last two plays, the *Ecclesiazusae* (392 B.C.) and the *Plutus* (388 B.C.), mark the transition to Middle Comedy. In this, little is left of the strict form of Old Comedy, and not much of its spirit of revelry. Plot grows, and the chorus shrinks; in particular, the parabasis disappears, and dramatic illusion is taken more seriously. These plays are still strongly political—they ridicule feminism and communism—but they are less personal and fantastic. Judging from the remaining fragments, Middle Comedy in general was social rather than political, with a background of private life. By the middle of the fourth century it had passed into New Comedy.

New Comedy is of the highest importance in the history of the drama, as it became the model and the quarry for Roman comedy. Its greatest exponent was Menander, who had an enormous fame in antiquity, but was little more than a name to us until considerable portions of several of his plays (but no complete play) were discovered among papyri from Egypt. New Comedy was pure comedy of manners. It used stock characters—the testy old man, the interfering slave, and so on—and conventional turns of plot—the foundling was a constant figure—but these, at least in Menander's hands, are treated with a delicacy of feeling and observation which make a drama of great charm. The chorus survives, but has nothing to do with the plot; Menander sometimes treats it as a band of tipsy revellers who come in singing songs.

As always in Greek drama, the scene represented a public place, usually a street, with houses as the background. This led to many conventions which were used with great discretion—e.g. that two persons can be on the stage and yet not be able to overhear each other. These were taken over by Roman comedy, including one which in Athens was topographically true, that the right-hand exit led to the town, the left-hand to the harbour or country. In general, New Comedy was much less boisterous than its Roman counterpart and paid much more attention to elegance of plot.

3. The Festivals. As was said above, it was of decisive importance in the development of Greek drama that, except in its extreme infancy, it was never a private venture, given to attract a crowd or to please a coterie. It was always part of a festival. Originally, tragedy was played at the City Dionysia, comedy at another Dionysiac festival, the Lenaea. The former was a spring festival, held in the month March–April, when the sailing-season had begun and Athens was normally full of visitors; the latter was a winter festival, January–February, and therefore a more domestic affair. Early in the fifth century contests in comedy were added to the City Dionysia, and later contests in tragedy to the Lenaea. As the arrangements for all the contests were similar, it is unnecessary to do more than outline those for tragedy at the City Dionysia.

Early in the official year, which in Athens began soon after midsummer, the magistrate in charge of the festivals had to choose from among the applicants three poets who should compete at the ensuing festival. As it was already an honour to be chosen, there was a prize, first, second, or third, for each poet. It is conjectured that the lesser-known poets had to submit their script, and established poets only a scenario; certainly Aristophanes makes one or two topical references which could only have been inserted at the last minute. Young poets would have had opportunities of learning their complex trade and making their reputations at local festivals in Attica.

To each selected poet a 'choregus' was assigned by lot. He would be one of a rota of wealthy citizens on whom the State laid from time to time special, and very honourable, burdens, such as equipping a warship, or the annual state-representation at Delphi, or a play. The chorus and the three statutory actors for each play (five for a comedy) were paid by the State; the other expenses, including the payment of supers, fell upon the choregus. It was an advantage to the poet to have a generous choregus; hence the use of the lot.

The poet wrote his own music and invented his own dances. He also produced the play and originally trained the chorus and acted as well, but the last two functions were early handed over to specialists. In the early days of the fifth century individual actors seem to have been associated with particular poets, but when the importance of the actor increased, it was considered fairer to distribute the actors too, or at least the three chief ones (the 'protagonists'), by lot.

The festival lasted for five or six days, it is uncertain which. The first day was taken up by a solemn and splendid procession, parts of which are represented on the Parthenon frieze. On the next three days (apparently) a tragic trilogy with its satyr-play was given in the morning, and a comedy later in the day; on the last day, or two days, the dithyrambic contests were held. The contest was a double one, between the choregi and the poets. After the middle of the century contests between the chief actors were added. The prizes were awarded on the vote of a small jury.

The seat of honour, in the centre of the bottom row, was assigned to the priest of Dionysus. (In the *Frogs* Dionysus, from the edge of the orchestra, makes frantic appeals to him for help.) A few other seats were reserved for state officers and such foreigners as Athens wished to compliment; between the other seats no distinction was made. Originally all seats were free; then, to prevent abuses, a charge of 2 obols (say ninepence) was made; and later still a state theatre fund was instituted to provide the admission fee to any who cared to ask for it.

During the fifth century original plays only were performed in Athens, except that in compliment to Aeschylus it was decreed, after his death, that anyone might compete by offering to revive one of his plays. Plays which had been a success at the festival were commonly reproduced in the local theatres of Attica.

4. The Actors. Very little is known about individual Greek actors. In early tragedy, in which only one actor was employed, the poet was his own actor; acting as a profession began when Aeschylus introduced parts for a second actor. For some time individual actors were associated with individual poets—Cleander and Mynniscus with Aeschylus, Cleidimides and Tlepolemus with Sophocles. Later, actors were assigned to the poets by lot.

With the decline of tragedy in the fourth century, actors became more prominent. The most famous was Polus, who is said to have taught Demosthenes elocution. In the scene in Sophocles' *Electra* in which Electra receives an urn supposed to contain her brother's ashes,

Polus is said to have used, on one occasion, an urn containing the ashes of his recently deceased son, with excellent effect. Other names of actors to which anecdotes are attached are Theodorus, Aristodemus, Neoptolemus, Thessalus, and Athenodorus. Little is known, however, of individual styles and methods. Aristotle (*Poetics*, c. 26), speaking of overacting, whether by actors, members of the chorus, or the flute-players, records that Mynniscus used to call a younger actor, Callipides, an 'ape' because of his extravagant style. A degree of specialization is suggested by the fact that a certain Nicostratos became proverbial for his excellence in delivering messenger-speeches.

The profession of acting was confined to men, and was of good repute. Since the drama had religious associations, actors enjoyed immunity of person, and because of this were often used as diplomatic envoys in disputes between Greek states. During the fourth century, to protect their privileges and interests, they organized themselves into a guild, the 'Craftsmen of Dionysus'.

About actors in Greek comedy nothing is known beyond a few names and the fact that they were quite distinct from tragic actors. Women never appeared on the Greek stage.

5. CENSORSHIP. A censorship on Greek plays did not in fact exist, though a dramatist who seriously offended might be punished by special decree. Thus Phrynichus the tragedian was fined for his *Capture of Miletus*, a play based on a recent event very painful to Athens, and it was decreed that the play should never be revived. Similarly, the demagogue Cleon prosecuted Aristophanes for denouncing the policy of Athens towards the subject-allies, and apparently had some success. A scholiast records a decree that comic poets should not satirize individuals by name; if such a decree was ever made, it had singularly little effect, for, until the spirit went out of it, Old Comedy was often extremely libellous. It should not be overlooked that since a magistrate chose the tragedies and the comedies that were to proceed to the competition, he could in fact exercise a censorship; but we never hear that he did, and it seems that the choice was made purely on literary grounds. H. D. F. KITTO.

6. THEATRE, COSTUME, AND MACHINERY. From a very early period it seems to have been the custom for actors to appear in front of a building which served as their dressing-room. The front wall of this building was necessarily the background to the action. It must, from earliest times, have contained at least one door, which, in tragedy, had to do duty now for the entrance to a palace, now for the opening into a tent or cave. When the regulation three doors were first used is much debated, but attempts to stage fifth-century comedy with only one door are very unsatisfactory. The roof of the scene-building was practicable, being reached, presumably, by means of a ladder inside the building. There were two side entrances formed by the passages between the building and the auditorium, which were also used by the audience when assembling and dispersing. The endless debate as to whether there was or was not a stage for the actors, raised some feet above the orchestra, must take into account the undoubted fact that in classical drama the chorus and actors could intermingle freely. On the whole it seems that a raised stage, however easy of access, would have been more of a hindrance than a help. The high stage of the later Greek theatre presumably reflected the decline in importance and numbers of the chorus, whose members, one may conjecture, now appeared with the actors on the raised stage. As far as we can trace the history of Greek drama (well into the imperial period) there was a chorus; and the references to it in the plays of Menander nowhere suggest that it was separated from the actors by a barrier (see also ARCHITECTURE, 1, also Nos. 1 and 2).

The question of costume in classical Greek plays has been hotly disputed, since most of the evidence dates from later periods. Many former theories have now been discarded. The use of masks, both in comedy and in tragedy, is generally agreed upon, though whether they were survivals of ritualistic elements from primitive times, or a device adopted by Thespis in imitation of the worshippers of Dionysus, is not known. Made of linen, cork, or wood, they were realistically painted, and served, in an all-male company, to differentiate between men and women, and to show something of the age and temper of the persons represented (see Nos. 3, 4, 5). The use of greatly exaggerated masks, with, in tragic masks, the peaked elevation above the forehead (the *onkos*) was a later development. It is no longer considered feasible that the mouthpiece of the mask should have served as an amplifier, nor, given the excellent acoustics of the Greek theatre, would it have been necessary. From later evidence it is believed that the tragic actor wore a long under- and short upper-robe, one or the other with sleeves, and both richly decorated. They may have been voluminous, to give the actor presence, but padding was not worn until a much later date. It is conjectured that the tragic robe, with its unusual sleeves, may have been copied from the dress of the priests of Dionysus (but see COSTUME). The chorus appears to have been dressed according to its supposed nationality and occupation. The use of the *kothornos*, or eight-to-ten-inches-high boot, by actors in classical tragedy has now been discounted. It is a later importation used in the Hellenistic and imperial periods (see No. 11), and the classical actor probably wore a soft boot with an upper reaching some way up the leg. It is probable, but not certain, that Aeschylus first put his actors into shoes.

Not much more is known about the actor's costume in Old Comedy, except that he too wore a mask and a short *chiton*, or tunic, which allowed the red leather phallus to be seen, and that he was grotesquely padded. The chorus was dressed in accordance with the needs of the play—in Aristophanes its members might represent, by means of token accessories, wasps, clouds, birds, etc. Later the costumes in comedy approximated more closely to those of daily life, and by the time of New Comedy the phallus had been discarded.

The classical Greek drama had no scenery, in the modern sense, since the action was played out against a permanent background which remained in view of the audience throughout the performance. 'Scene-painting' (*skenographia*), attributed by Aristotle to Sophocles, probably meant that painters were employed either to furnish an architectural background on the stage-wall, or to paint architectural scenes in perspective on panels which could be placed against the wall. Theoretically, these could be changed during the play, but there does not appear to be any evidence that they were. It is more likely that each play had its permanent background—temple, palace, sea-shore, country—which was changed between the plays by stage-hands in full view of the audience.

One device which was used by the classical theatre was the crane (*mechane*) which could raise persons or gods into the air so that they appeared to be flying. Its use to enable a god to appear suddenly and unravel the complications of the plot (which gave rise to the expression *deus ex machina*) was parodied by Aristophanes.

The *periaktoi*, or revolving prisms, once thought to have been used in the classical period for scene-changing, are now considered to have come into use much later, in Hellenistic times. They were triangular prisms of wood, each face of which carried a different decoration, and by the revolving of the prisms changes of scene could be indicated (for their use by San Gallo in the sixteenth century, see MACHINERY). Machines for simulating thunder (*bronteion*) and flashes of lightning were also used in the Hellenistic theatre, but not in classical times.

A machine which has caused a great deal of discussion is the so-called *ekkyklema*, or 'wheel-out', which was at one time thought to have been used for displaying interior scenes by means of a pre-arranged tableau on a movable platform. This was either pushed on stage or revolved on a turn-table to show an interior scene. It is now thought to have been nothing more than a couch on wheels, or a grouping arranged within a pair of double doors which opened to reveal it.

WILLIAM BEARE†

7. HELLENISTIC AGE. In the Greek or Hellenizing cities which sprang up everywhere in the Near and Middle East in the wake of Alexander's conquests, a theatre was an indispensable public building, and it was often of great beauty. It is from this period that most of the extant remains date. Little original drama of any merit was produced, except, early in the period, the continuation of New Comedy in Athens. In Alexandria there was an artificial revival of tragedy among a group of seven writers known as the Pleiad (from the seven bright stars in the Pleiades), of whom Lycophron is the best-known figure. The greatest contribution of this age to drama, and indeed to literature as a whole, was the work of Alexandrian scholars in collecting, purifying, annotating, and preserving texts of the great dramatists of the fifth century. The tragic drama of the fifth century (not the comedy, which was too purely Athenian) became classical and was regularly performed. More attention was given to acting, and purely spectacular productions became common. The characteristic and only vital form of dramatic art was the mime. H. D. F. KITTO

8. MODERN GREECE. A renascence of the Greek theatre began with the struggle for independence in the early nineteenth century, typified in the plays of Jacob Rizos Nerulos (1778–1850), and the first modern Greek play, by Ath. Christopoulos, was given in 1805 in Jassy. But it took a long time to overcome the handicaps of poverty and a dual language, and it was not until well into the nineteenth century that the vernacular triumphed over the earlier literary language, though an open-air theatre and an indoor theatre were built in 1840 and 1854 respectively. There are models of these in the Theatre Museum, housed in the offices of the Authors' Society, under the curatorship of Jean Sideris. The influence of Ibsen was important, particularly in the plays of Joannes Kambisis (1872–1902). A Royal Theatre, a small playhouse in the style of the late nineteenth century, opened in 1901 under the auspices of King George I. It was not, however, very successful, and closed in 1908. It was not until 1930 that the then Minister for Education, Georges Papandreou, was instrumental in putting through an act for the founding of a National Theatre subsidized by the State. This opened in 1932 in the old Royal Theatre building, which it still occupies, with the *Agamemnon*, produced by Photos Politis (1890–1934), who was the theatre's first director. In 1939 the Greek National Theatre company visited London, where their interpretation of *Hamlet*, with Alexis Minotis in the title-role, and Katina Paxinou and Emile Veakis as Gertrude and Claudius, was much admired. Katina Paxinou also gave an outstanding performance as Electra in a modern Greek version of Sophocles' tragedy.

In the 1930s it was realized that revivals of ancient comedies and tragedies should be given in the open air, and as far as possible under the original conditions. *Electra*, in 1936, was the first play to be so given, in a production by Dimitrios Rondiris. Similar open-air performances in the Roman theatre of Herodes Atticus at the foot of the Acropolis are now an integral feature of the annual Athens summer festival. In 1954 Rondiris produced *Hippolytus* in the ruins of the theatre at Epidaurus, which now has its own festival, with plays produced by Alexis Minotis, lately assisted by Takis Mouzenidis. In 1956 the first of a series of comedies by

Aristophanes was given in the Roman theatre. These were all produced by Alexis Solomos, who studied after the Second World War in London. All the productions listed above are given under the aegis of the National Theatre company, now directed by Emile Hourmouzios, which also goes on tour, and has appeared successfully several years running at the Théâtre des Nations in Paris. It has a permanent company of fifty actors (to which must be added those needed for the choruses of classical plays) and four producers, and a Conservatoire which serves as a training school. The high standards envisaged by Politis have certainly been attained, particularly in the production of the classical repertory, and have undoubtedly influenced the whole of Greek theatrical life, which is mainly centred in Athens. Apart from classical plays, and many of Shakespeare's, the National Theatre also stages an international repertory of modern plays (the success of the 1962 season was Pirandello's *To-Night We Improvise*) and plays by such Greek authors as Ant. Matessis (1791–1873), Kostis Palamas (1859–1943), and Greg. Xenopoulos (1867–1951). Musical plays are especially popular, and a musical version of Shaw's *Caesar and Cleopatra*, with music by Hatzithakis, opened successfully in 1962. Although Athens has a population of only 1½ million, it supports, in addition to the National Theatre, more than twenty playhouses, which are open from October to May, among them the Acropole, the Attikon, the Art (founded in 1942 by Karolos Koun), the Alfa, the Athens, the Bournelli, the Kosta Mousouri, the Kotopouli, the Elsa Vergi, the Xadzikristos, the National Gardens, the Porea, the Metropolitan, the Park, and the Samartzi. The Piraikon Theatre, in the Piraeus, is now directed by Rondiris, who was for so long director of the National Theatre. In 1964 Karolos Koun brought his company to London in a production of the *Birds*, which had previously been acclaimed in Paris.

In 1961 a National Theatre of Northern Greece, based on Salonika, was established, and began its summer season with *Oedipus Rex*, played in the ruins of the old theatre at Philippi. During the following winter, indoor performances were given of Wilde's *Florentine Tragedy*. Salonika also has one other permanent company, and three touring companies. Cyprus has also its professional Greek theatre, which recently presented *Romeo and Juliet* and *Othello*.

GREEN, John, an English actor, well known on the Continent from 1606 to 1627. He first went there with Robert Browne, and later succeeded to Browne's position as chief of the English actors abroad. He and his company played jigs, farces, short episodes from longer plays, and a number of plays by Shakespeare, Marlowe, and others (see ENGLISH COMEDIANS).

GREEN, Paul Eliot (1894–), American dramatist, who studied under Professor Koch at the University of North Carolina and had his first plays produced by the Carolina Playmakers. These were mainly in one act, and dealt with the problems of the Negroes and poor whites in the South, as did his later full-length plays, of which the most outstanding is *In Abraham's Bosom*. This, based on two earlier one-act plays done by the Carolina Playmakers, was awarded the Pulitzer Prize when it was given a professional production at the Provincetown Theatre in 1926. It deals with the attempts of an ambitious but illiterate Negro, son of a white man, to found a school for Negro children, and portrays poignantly the heartbreaks and disappointments which harass him until his violent death at the hands of an infuriated mob. Other full-length plays are *The Field God* (1927), a study of religious repression among the farmer folk of eastern North Carolina, *Tread the Green Grass* (1929), *Roll, Sweet Chariot* (1934), another Negro play based on the earlier *Potter's Field*, and *The House of Connelly* (1931), which presents a vivid contrast between the decadent southern planter family and the vigour of the new generation of tenant farmers. *Johnny Johnson*, with music by Kurt Weill, was given in 1936, and was a forerunner of Green's symphonic plays with music, which have not yet been seen in the professional theatre. In spite of a certain tendency to propaganda, and to epic rather than dramatic situations, Green remains the most significant figure in the drama of the American provinces. His best one-act plays of Negro life were published in 1926 in *Lonesome Road*, with a preface which shows a deep and unfailing sympathy for the Negro in his struggle with life. A further collection of plays was published in *Out of the South* (1939). In 1941 Green dramatized *Native Son*, by the Negro novelist Richard Wright, which was produced by Orson Welles (see also NEGRO IN THE AMERICAN THEATRE).

GREEN ROOM. The name given to the room behind the stage in which the actors and actresses gathered before and after the performance to chat or entertain their friends. It is regrettable that the green room has almost disappeared from the modern English theatre, actors preferring to receive their friends in their dressing-rooms. It still exists, in a modified form, at Drury Lane. The first reference to a theatre green room occurs in Shadwell's informatory *A True Widow*, given at Dorset Garden in Dec. 1678. In Cibber's *Love Makes a Man* (Drury Lane, 1700), Clodio says: 'I do know London pretty well . . . ay, and the Green Room, and all the Girls and Women-actresses there.' It seems probable that the green room was so called simply because it was hung or painted in green. It was also known as the Scene Room, a term later applied to the room where scenery was stored, and the theory has been advanced that 'green' was a corruption of 'scene'. In the larger early English theatres there was sometimes more than one green room, and they were then strictly graded in use according to the salary of the player, who could be fined for presuming to use a green room above his rank.

GREEN-COAT MEN, footmen in green liveries who, in the early Restoration theatre, placed or removed essential pieces of furniture in full view of the audience.

GREENE, (HENRY) GRAHAM (1904–), distinguished English novelist, who later turned to the theatre as a means of giving expression to certain strongly-held opinions. A Roman Catholic, his work bears the strong impress of his faith, though his expression of it is not always acceptable to the authorities. His first contact with the theatre was through the successful dramatization of his novel, *Brighton Rock*, by Frank Harvey, produced in 1943 with Richard Attenborough as Pinkie. With Basil Dean, Greene then made his own adaptation of another novel, *The Heart of the Matter*, in 1950. A third novel, *The Power and the Glory*, was adapted by Denis Cannan in 1956. These last two, however, were not as successful as Greene's own plays, written directly for the theatre. The first was *The Living Room* (1953), in which Dorothy Tutin gave a fine performance as Rose Pemberton; this was followed by *The Potting Shed* (1958) with John Gielgud, and *The Complaisant Lover* (1959) with Ralph Richardson.

GREENE, ROBERT (*c.* 1560–92), English dramatist, who studied at Oxford and Cambridge, travelled widely on the Continent, and returned to London to lead a wild and dissipated life. He was the author of numerous pamphlets and prose romances, and of some autobiographical sketches which describe with pungent detail the London rogues and swindlers of his time. Shortly before his early death from overindulgence he wrote his famous recantation, *A Groatsworth of Wit bought with a Million of Repentance*, chiefly remembered now for its attack on Shakespeare—the earliest allusion to his standing as a dramatist. This malicious remark was: 'An upstart crow beautified with our feathers, and in his opinion the only Shake-scene in the country.' It may have been prompted by Greene's consciousness of his own failings as a playwright, and of his own wasted gifts, or he may sincerely have believed that Shakespeare had profited by the work of other men, including Greene himself. He is thought to have had a hand in the *Henry VI* which Shakespeare later rewrote, as well as in Kyd's *Spanish Tragedy*, and many other plays of the time. Among those plays which can definitely be ascribed to him—these include a chronicle play on James IV of Scotland, an *Orlando Furioso*, and a romantic drama, *Alphonsus, King of Aragon*, influenced by Christopher Marlowe's *Tamburlaine*, and probably given soon after it—the most important is the charming *Honorable History of Friar Bacon and Friar Bungay*, a study of white magic probably intended as a counterblast to the black magic of *Dr. Faustus*. This comedy, important in the development of the genre in English dramatic literature, was first published in 1594, and was probably acted a few years previously. It was constantly revived up to 1630, at least, and is still occasionally given by amateur and university societies, when it proves as popular with its audiences as its early stage history shows it to have been before the closing of the theatres in 1642. Although much of Greene's work suffers from carelessness and poor construction, it has many merits, chief among them an excellent portrayal of the English scene, passages of great poetic beauty, and characters of interest and vitality. With a little more application and a little less wastefulness he might have ranked high among the dramatists of the day, and proved a formidable rival to Shakespeare. As it is, he can be regarded only as a precursor of the great age of Elizabethan drama.

GREENWICH VILLAGE THEATRE, NEW YORK, see PROVINCETOWN PLAYERS and MACGOWAN, KENNETH.

GREET, SIR BEN [really PHILIP BARLING] (1857–1936), English actor-manager, knighted in 1929 for his services to the theatre, one of the greatest being his work on behalf of Shakespeare. He first appeared on the stage at Southampton in 1879 as Philip Ben (from the nickname 'Benjamin' bestowed on him as the youngest of eight children, and later adopted as his first name, though his family called him 'Phil'). After three years in Sarah Thorne's company at Margate he went to London, where he appeared with a number of outstanding actors, including Lawrence Barrett and Mary Anderson. It was in 1886 that he gave the first of his many open-air productions of Shakespearian plays, and formed the company with which he toured the United Kingdom and America, many stars making their early appearances with him. As a training-ground for young actors his company rivalled that of Benson, while many school-children owe their introduction to the theatre to his visits in the 1920s and 1930s to L.C.C. and other centres with a repertory in which Shakespeare predominated. He was for many years in New York, but returned in 1914, and was one of those responsible for the founding of the Old Vic, where between 1915 and 1918 he produced twenty-four of Shakespeare's plays, including *Hamlet* in its entirety, and a number of other classics. In his later years he concentrated mainly on production of plays for schools and open-air performances, but was seen as the First Grave-digger at the Lyceum in 1926 in aid of the Sadler's Wells Fund, and as Egeus in a charity matinée of *A Midsummer Night's Dream* (1927). In 1929 he celebrated his jubilee, but continued active until his death. A capable, hard-working, and essentially practical man, he achieved a great deal in an unobtrusive way, and left the theatres of England and America very much in his debt.

GREGORY, AUGUSTA, LADY (1852–1932), entered the theatre in middle age with an unsuspected gift for comedy-writing, which, but for her contact with Yeats and the Irish Dramatic Movement (see IRELAND), would presumably never have been realized. She had a wide experience of life and literature and, as a great landowner, of the west of Ireland peasants out of whose lives her best comedies were made and whose way of speech she acclimatized in the Irish theatre. She proved an indefatigable and spirited worker in the movement whose early years she described in *Our Irish Theatre* (1914). In 1909 she won a notable victory for the Abbey by frustrating the attempts which were made to suppress the production of *Blanco Posnet*, and in 1911 she took the company on its famous, stormy, and triumphant visit to America. She withdrew from active theatre work in 1928 and died in 1932 on her estate at Coole in Galway, a close friend to the end of Yeats and of Irish drama.

Her plays are numerous, but the greater number are short. The most widely known are her comedies of peasant life based on what she herself calls 'our incorrigible genius for myth-making': *The Pot of Broth* (with Yeats, 1902), *Spreading the News* (1904), *Hyacinth Halvey* (1906), and *The Workhouse Ward* (1908). But she is also known for two fine, short, patriotic plays, *Cathleen ni Houlihan* (with Yeats, 1902) and *The Rising of the Moon* (1907), and for one brief peasant tragedy, *The Gaol Gate* (1906). Later, she wrote fantasies of mingled humour, pathos, and poetic imagination: *The Travelling Man* (1910), *The Dragon* (1919), *Aristotle's Bellows* (1921), and others. She also wrote plays on Irish history or legend which are still esteemed by many readers. These are all full- or nearly full-length plays: the three 'tragic-comedies', *The Canavans* (1906), *The White Cockade* (1905), and *The Deliverer* (1911), and the tragedies, *Grania* (not produced), *Kincora* (1905), *Dervorgilla* (1907). She also contributed to the Abbey repertory many translations, of which *The Kiltartan Molière*, a version of several of Molière's plays in west of Ireland speech, is the best known.

UNA ELLIS-FERMOR†

GREGORY, JOHANN GOTTFRIED (1631–75), German Lutheran pastor in Moscow, who staged the first dramatic representations at the Russian Court and thus began organized dramatic activity in Russia. Born at Marburg, he probably studied at the university there, and later served as a soldier in Sweden and Poland. In 1658 he came to the foreign quarter of Moscow as a teacher and pastor of the Lutheran church, and in 1668 founded a free school open to all. The students probably acted in plays, as was the contemporary German custom. About this time the pro-Western boyar Artamon Matveyev aroused Tsar Alexei's interest in the drama, and in 1672 the Tsar, assured by his confessor that the Orthodox Byzantine emperors had attended plays, ordered the formation of a dramatic troupe. Efforts to recruit actors abroad failed, and Alexei turned to the foreigners in Moscow. On 4 June 1672, six days after the birth of the future Peter the Great, Gregory was ordered to stage a comedy based on the story of Esther and to build a theatre in the summer palace at Preobrazhenskoye. Gregory adapted a play from a piece in the repertory of the English Comedians, sixty young Germans suddenly became actors, Matveyev provided an orchestra, and a Dutch painter, Peter Engles, painted the scenery. On 17 Oct. 1672 the *Play of Artaxerxes* was acted in German before the delighted Tsar and his Court in a hastily constructed wooden 'House of Comedy', the Tsaritza and her ladies watching through a lattice. The performance lasted ten hours and was enlivened by songs, music, dancing, and comic interludes. Gregory later prepared *The Comedy of Young Tobias* (1673) and *The Comedy of Holofernes* (1674). In 1673 a number of Russian boys were turned over to him to be trained as actors, and thereafter his plays were staged in Russian, or in a mixture of Russian and German. He died in February 1675; his theatre survived until the Tsar's death in the following January. Gregory is portrayed in Ostrovsky's *A Comedian of the Seventeenth Century* (1872).

ROBERT TRACY

GREIN, JACK [really JACOB] THOMAS (1862–1935), a Dutchman who became a naturalized Englishman in 1895, and who, as playwright, critic, and manager, did much to further the production of the new 'plays of ideas' in London at the turn of the century. He began his career as a critic by writing articles on the modern English stage for the *Dutch Art Chronicle*, and from sheer enthusiasm acted as an international intermediary for the exchange of plays between England and the Continent.

Inspired by the example of Antoine and his Théâtre Libre, Grein founded the Independent Theatre of London in 1891. The declared object of the Independent Theatre was 'to give special performances of plays which have a literary and artistic rather than a commercial value'. It was launched at the Royalty Theatre with an 'invitation' performance of Ibsen's *Ghosts*. The critics, with few exceptions, turned every gun they had upon the play and its sponsor, and Grein became the 'best abused man in London'. The Independent Theatre continued to produce 'literary and artistic plays', and in 1892 put on *Widowers' Houses*, the first of Bernard Shaw's plays to be seen in London. Grein's interest extended also to the Stage Society, and out of the Stage Society sprang the Vedrenne–Barker management at the Royal Court Theatre.

Grein was dramatic critic of *Life* from 1889 to 1893. He followed this by writing in French, German, and Dutch for Continental journals. He was also critic to the *Sunday Special*, which afterwards merged with the *Sunday Times*, for which Grein wrote until 1918. He also wrote for the *Illustrated London News*. Five published volumes of *Dramatic Criticism* cover the years from 1898 to 1903. Two other books of criticism appeared in 1921 and 1924. His wife ('Michael Orme') wrote his biography, *J. T. Grein; the Story of a Pioneer*, published in 1936.

T. C. KEMP†

GRENFELL, Joyce (1910–), English *diseuse* who first appeared at the Little Theatre on 21 Aug. 1939 in a programme of monologues written by herself. These arose out of the entertainments which she had for some time been giving privately for her friends, in which she had proved herself an excellent mimic and a wickedly accurate observer of contemporary *mores*. After touring service hospitals extensively during the Second World War, she returned to London in the revue *Sigh No More* (1947). She made her first appearance in New York on 10 Oct. 1955, at the Bijou Theatre, in *Joyce Grenfell Requests the Pleasure*, and has since been seen all over the world in her one-woman entertainment. Among her characterizations Shirley's Girl-Friend is probably the best known. A number of her lyrics have been set to music by Richard Addinsell. She has made a number of appearances in films and on radio and television.

GRESSET, Jean-Baptiste-Louis (1709–77), French dramatist, and author in his youth of a charming poem, *Vert-Vert*, published in 1734, dealing with the adventures of a parrot in a convent, which he spent the rest of his life in regretting. It was considered impious, particularly as the author was an abbé, and he was expelled from the Jesuit order on account of it. Thrown on his own resources in Paris, Gresset wrote several plays, not of any great importance, and intended mainly for the amusement of a small literary circle. The best of them is *Le Méchant* (1754), which some critics consider superior even to Piron's *La Métromanie*. An earlier play, *Édouard III* (1740), though subtitled 'a tragedy', is really a sentimental bourgeois drama, and, like all Gresset's other works, shows the influence of the artificial cult of the day for the simple life. This is particularly noticeable in *Sidneï* (1745), which takes place in an English village. The hero, in love with the unresponsive Rosalie, drinks poison, as he thinks. But his valet—sole survivor of the old French comedy in this morass of sentiment—has substituted some harmless beverage, and all ends well. The play is worth reading for amusement, though it would probably not bear revival. It was well received at the time of its first production and is yet another manifestation of the anglomania of eighteenth-century France.

GRÉVIN, Jacques (*c.* 1538–*c.* 1570), one of the precursors of French classical tragedy. His serious plays, however, have been overshadowed by his one comedy, *Les Esbahis*, given before the Court at the Collège de Beauvais in 1560 in honour of the marriage of the young Duchess of Lorraine, who was present at the performance with her father, Henri II. Grévin was also the author of a number of poems. He was a doctor by profession, and at the time of his death was attached to the household of the Duchess of Savoy.

GRIBOYEDOV, Alexander Sergeivich (1795–1829), Russian dramatist, who was educated at home and later went to Moscow University. He served in the army against Napoleon and in 1815 went to St. Petersburg, where he associated with writers and became interested in the theatre. He joined the diplomatic service and went abroad, but in 1826 was arrested for his friendship with the Decembrists. Released for lack of evidence, he resumed his career, and participated in the drawing up of the Russo-Turkish treaty of 1829. He was then appointed ambassador to Persia, where he was assassinated during an attack on the Russian embassy.

Griboyedov's literary works were the fruit of his leisure time, and with one exception were comedies translated from the French or written in collaboration with his friends. The exception is the classic play *Woe From Wit* (also known as *Wit Works Woe*, *Too Clever by Half*, *The Misfortunes of Reason*, and *The Disadvantages of Being Clever*, though *Woe to the Wise* would perhaps be nearer the mark, since the original word represented by 'wit' contains the sense also of sincerity, intelligence, far-sighted liberalism). The play's title gives a clue to its contents, for it deals with the struggle of a young man, arriving in Moscow full of liberal and progressive ideas, against the stupidity and trickery of a corrupt society. Hounded and derided by the self-seekers, reactionaries, and petty-minded officials, he is labelled mad, and even his fiancée, as superficial as her associates, turns against him, driving him away from a society which has nothing to offer him. This play, which has remained in the repertory of the Soviet theatre and is frequently revived, was the first dramatic protest against the rotten structure of Tsarist society, against corruption, bribery, ignorance, and cupidity in high places. Human and dramatic, classic in form yet realistic and satiric in content, written with sparkling wit and sympathetic insight, it is one of the great plays of the Russian theatre. Griboyedov worked on it all his life, perfecting and augmenting it until it became as it were a poetic diary which he was always bringing up to date. It was banned during his lifetime, but circulated in manuscript, and was printed four years after his death. It was first performed by the Bolshoi Theatre in St. Petersburg in 1831, and no doubt the audience regarded the hero, Chatsky, as a peculiar young man with dangerous ideas, who deserved all he got. It was produced by the Moscow Art Theatre in 1906, and when it was revived in 1938 Kachalov and Moskvin again played their former parts in it. At the same time it was revived at the Maly. The part of Chatsky is to young Russian actors what Hamlet is to English, and Famusov, the conservative father, has long been a favourite role with all the older actors of Russia.

GRID, an open framework above the stage from which suspended scenery or lights can be hung. It can be of wood or metal (see STAGE).

GRIEG, NORDAHL (1902–43), Norwegian dramatist, whose early death in action was a great loss to the European theatre. His outstanding works are *Vår Aere og Vår Makt* (1935), an anti-war play, and *Nederlaget* (1936), dealing with the Paris Commune, which inspired Brecht's play on the same subject (see SCANDINAVIA, 2 *a*).

GRIEVE, a family of English scene-painters, of whom the father, (1) JOHN HENDERSON (1770–1845), was long associated with Covent Garden, and was responsible for the scenery of spectacle plays and pantomime under the Kemble régime. Of his two sons, (2) THOMAS (1799–1882) was principal scenic artist at Covent Garden under the Vestris–Mathews management in 1839 and later went to Drury Lane, while (3) WILLIAM (1800–44) was in his youth employed at Covent Garden, but did his best work for Drury Lane. After the retirement of Stanfield he was considered the finest scenic artist of the day, and his early death was a great loss to the theatre. His moonlit scenes were particularly remarked, and he was the first theatre artist to be called before the curtain by the applause of the audience. Thomas was for a long time assisted by his son (4) THOMAS WALFORD (1841–82), whose work was remarkable for the brilliance of its style and the artistic beauty of its composition.

GRIFFITH, HUBERT (1896–1953), English dramatic critic and dramatist, who began his journalistic career on the *Daily Chronicle* in 1922, and was subsequently connected with the *Observer* and the *Evening Standard*. In 1945 he became dramatic critic of the *Sunday Graphic* and of the *New English Review*, remaining with them until his death. His first play, *Tunnel Trench*, which dealt with the First World War, was tried out by the Repertory Players in 1925 and was the opening play at the Duchess Theatre in 1929. Later plays included *Red Sunday* (1929), and *Youth at the Helm* (1934), an adaptation from the German of Paul Vulpius. Among a number of other adaptations were *Return to Yesterday*, *Young Madame Conti* (both 1936) with Benn W. Levy, and *Distant Point* (1937) from the Russian of Afinogenov. An interest in Soviet Russia led to the publication of several books on the subject, including *Seeing Soviet Russia* (1932). Griffith was also the author of *Iconoclastes, or the Future of Shakespeare* (1928), and of a translation of the memoirs of Mistinguett, published in 1938.

GRILLPARZER, FRANZ (1791–1872), Austrian dramatist, who inherited from his father his shrewd intelligence, and from his mother his love of music and a tendency to melancholy. His first play, written at the height of German romanticism, was *Die Ahnfrau* (1817), a sombre tragedy which brought him to the notice of the public. It was followed by *Sappho* (1818), a retelling of Sappho's love-story which combines dignity with warmth, and shows in its heroine the poetic temperament at odds with the everyday world, the mature woman fighting a losing battle against rosebud maidenhood. In *Das goldene Vliess* (1820), a trilogy dealing with the story of Jason and Medea, only the last section corresponds to Euripides' *Medea*, the earlier parts showing Medea before the arrival of Jason. In spite of a slightly sentimentalized portrait of the heroine, Medea towers over her ineffectual husband, and their relationship is shown in acuter form than that of Sappho to her lover Phaon. Grillparzer next attempted historical tragedy in the style of Schiller with the story of a Bohemian king's arrogant aspiration to the Empire in *König Ottokars Glück und Ende* (1823); though less vicious, Ottokar is reminiscent of Shakespeare's Richard III, while his successful opponent Rudolf von Hapsburg has something of the blunt simplicity of Bolingbroke in *Richard II*. As with Medea, the impact of the character is deliberately lessened towards the end. A positive counterpart to Ottokar is given in the unassuming and ultra-scrupulous regent in *Ein treuer Diener seines Herrn* (1826), where Grillparzer skirts the ridiculous in order to exemplify his ideal of humble heroism. With increasing frequency Grillparzer chooses to cheat expectation by unconventional methods. Thus Hero, in his retelling of the story of Hero and Leander, *Des Meeres und der Liebe Wellen* (1829), has a distinct element of tartness in her composition which eliminates sentimentality. In the same tragedy Grillparzer introduces slight comic elements, not in contrasting scenes, as in Shakespeare, but embedded in the main action, and fading away before the approaching catastrophe. For his next play Grillparzer turns to Spain, whose dramatists had much influence on him, and in his *Der Traum ein Leben* (1834), based on Calderón's *La vida es sueño*, a young man is cured of ambition by seeing the results of it in a dream. His most whimsical comedy, *Weh' dem, der lügt* (1838), shows an early Christian bishop, an idealist of the front rank, entrusting a ticklish mission to his scullion, a near relative of Figaro, with strict injunctions to tell no lies. This play failed, after a preliminary production at the Vienna Burgtheater, and Grillparzer renounced the theatre, writing for his own pleasure and interest a further play on the Hapsburgs, *Ein Bruderzwist in Habsburg*, in which the Emperor Rudolf II is depicted as an aged philosopher, of deep humanity, wearily conscious of his own impotence to prevent the outbreak of the Thirty Years' War which he clearly foresees. To this period belongs also *Libussa*, dealing with the mythical origins of Bohemia, which is considered by some critics to be Grillparzer's best work. It was produced at the Burgtheater in Vienna two years after his death, with Charlotte Wolter in the title-role. W. E. DELP

GRIMALDI, JOSEPH (1778–1837), is traditionally the funniest of clowns. His surname, that of an illustrious family of Genoa, where it is common, was borne on the English stage in the time of *The Spectator* by Nicolini Grimaldi, but this operatic falsetto was nobody's ancestor. Neither should an eminent dentist of this name be dragged into the story. It begins with Giuseppe Grimaldi, a pantomimist noted for his sardonic humour on and off the stage, who was ballet-master at Drury Lane from 1758 until his death thirty years later. He lived with Mrs. Brooker, a dancer, and they had two sons and a daughter. Joseph, born on 18 Dec. 1778 (though the date given by himself was a year later), danced at Sadler's Wells when he was two years and four months of age. In his boyhood he played dwarfs and old hags in pantomimes which had Dubois for the chief comic character. It was Dubois who changed the clown in harlequinades from a country bumpkin into a colourful Pierrot. At the Lane in winter and at the Wells in summer Joe was becoming noted for his silent acting in dramatic spectacles, particularly when broadsword combats evidenced his powers in grim fights to the death. What changed his fortunes was a quarrel with the Lane and an engagement at Covent Garden in the autumn of 1806, when he took over from Dubois the part of the bear-suckled Orson. At Christmas *Harlequin and Mother Goose; or, the Golden Egg* gave Joe full scope to display his comic powers as Clown—the type who has been called Joey ever since. This must not be judged by dwindled survivals of his tradition that have been cherished for old time's sake. Grimaldi was the most popular comic singer of his day, a finished dancer qualified to burlesque ballerinas, an acrobat of astonishing agility, an actor and a serious pantomimist admired by actors, and a past master in the 'wit of goods and chattels', as well as the inexplicable personality that because of him is called Clown. Knave and butt, stupidity and cunning, were fused by him; he feared and was feared, he was criminal and innocent dupe in one. Later Joeys were plain rascals, but Grimaldi was more of a mischievous schoolboy mounted, to borrow Lamb's phrase, into the firmament. The clue to his humour is in the new jokes he invented. Old harlequinades made much of transformations. The Bank of Paris would be changed into a balloon, and the clown who stole into a hothouse would become a water-melon. In place of such magic Joe would painfully and laboriously, in a mood of profound thought, construct a post-chaise out of basket and cheeses, or a hussar's uniform out of coal-scuttles, a pelisse, and muff. Despite these leisurely jokes the essence of his humour was dynamic energy. When his strength began to fail men waited in the wings to massage his legs directly he came off; he shook with sobs from exhaustion. At Christmas 1823 he retired, and Clown in Covent Garden's next pantomime was his son, Joseph S. (1802–32), whose easily won success was soon destroyed by debauchery. The father took his farewell of the public at Sadler's Wells on 17 Mar. 1828. Covent Garden denied him a benefit, but Drury Lane came to his rescue, and there, on the following 27 June, a crowded audience heard him sing while he was seated at the footlights. His son drank himself to death. Then Grimaldi lost his wife and was alone in the world. He moved to Southampton Street, Pentonville Hill, and spent his evenings by a tavern fireside surrounded by old cronies. The landlord carried him home pick-a-back. On the evening of 31 May 1837 he called, 'God bless you, my boy, I shall be ready for you tomorrow night', then went to bed and 'died by the visitation of God' in his sleep. He was buried by St. James's Chapel on Pentonville Hill, where his tombstone has been cared for though the ground has become a public garden. 'Hot Codlins', his song about an old woman who sold roasted apples and drank too much gin, was regularly sung in pantomimes for thirty years after Grimaldi's death, by command of 'the Gods'. M. WILLSON DISHER†

GRIMM, FRIEDRICH MELCHIOR, BARON VON (1723–1807), a German turned Frenchman, who, through his friendship with Rousseau and the Encyclopædists, and his voluminous correspondence on every possible literary and philosophical subject with at least three crowned heads of Europe and innumerable friends, is an important factor in the development of European drama in the eighteenth century. He did much to diffuse the ideas of his time, both by his admiration of bourgeois tragedy and by his championship of Italian as opposed to French opera. A man of great integrity, he brought to his observation of life and literature an excellent critical faculty and an unbiased judgement.

GRINGORE, PIERRE (*fl.* sixteenth century), one of the best-known writers of *soties*, or medieval French topical farces. He was master of ceremonies for most of the plays given in Paris from 1502 to 1515, in collaboration with the master-carpenter Jean Marchand, who built the stage while Gringore was writing or adapting the play destined to be performed on it. Practically nothing is known of Gringore's origins or early life (the spelling Gringoire, often found, proceeds from an error in Victor Hugo's *Notre-Dame de Paris*), and he had already a number of works to his credit before he became associated with the student society of the *enfants sans souci*. His best-known play, *Le Jeu du Prince des sots* (a political satire on Pope Julius II), was given in the Halles on Shrove Tuesday 1511, with Gringore himself playing second lead, *la mère-sotte*. Successful under Louis XII, Gringore was regarded with suspicion by François I as a political agitator. He therefore left Paris and attached himself to the household of Lorraine, producing only one more play, a *Mystère de Saint Louis*, the first to be written on a national theme. The place and date of his death are uncertain.

GRIPSHOLM, SWEDEN. In one of the round towers of Gustavus Vasa's fortress at Gripsholm, built in 1535, there was opened, in

1782, a small but extremely beautiful theatre, whose scenery and machinery still remain intact. One set of scenes reproduces exactly the pillared décor of the semicircular auditorium, and when it is in position the audience seems to be enclosed in a circular jewel-box, glowing with colour. The theatre, which has been carefully restored, is used for occasional performances in the summer months.

GROCK (1880–1959), whose real name was Adrian Wellach, was the supreme clown of his generation. He was born in Switzerland, the son of a watchmaker, and at 12 joined a circus. Later he toured with his sister and his parents, who were fine Tyrolean singers, and after innumerable jobs and much hardship became the partner of a clown named Brick, and changed his name to Grock. That was in 1903. For some years they toured Europe, and when Brick married, Grock joined Antonnet. It was in Berlin that they first appeared on a music-hall stage instead of in a circus, and at first were a complete failure. But they soon got the measure of their new medium, and were seen there by Cochran, who engaged them for the Palace Theatre in 1911, after which Grock appeared almost continuously in London for many years up to 1924, mainly at the Coliseum. His clowning was magnificent, wordless but so expressive that no one had any doubt what he meant. Although he was an expert performer on 24 instruments, his 'act' consisted in failing in everything he did. He would sit on a chair to play a concertina, and the chair would collapse and entangle him. A massive portmanteau would hold the tiniest violin. If he attempted to play the piano—and he was a fine pianist—the stool was too far away. It never occurred to him to move the stool. The piano must be shifted and he exhausted himself pushing it towards the stool. He slid over the piano in an attempt to stop his hat falling off and so revealing his baldness; his woe when this became apparent was one of the most impressive pieces of tragicomedy the stage has seen. Grock kept his head shaved specially for this 'gag', and wore a wig in private life. W. MACQUEEN-POPE†

GROOVE, a characteristic of English, as opposed to Continental, stage machinery, which enabled wings and flats to be slid on or off the stage sideways in view of the audience, as required by the system of visible scene-changing obtaining up to the 1880s. The wings of the old scene went off to right and left and new wings came on to replace them, the borders rose upwards and others were substituted, and the back scene parted centrally, the two parts sliding outwards, to be replaced by another pair of halves closing in. To support and guide the parts of the scenery in these movements, grooved timbers were used, built into the skeleton of the stage structure. The design, number, and placing of these grooved timbers varied greatly at various periods, and they were capable of a high degree of complexity and ingenuity.

The system is seen in its infancy in Inigo Jones's designs for masques at Court. In these shows, there was fixed to the stage floor, at the position of the back scenes (called Backshutters), a number of strips of wood, an inch or so apart, making a row of grooves across the stage, one groove for each pair of shutters. Similarly, at the level of the shutter-tops, there was suspended a flat timber, bearing corresponding grooves on its under face. The shutters stood in the bottom grooves, and were supported at the top by the upper grooves, and they were opened or closed at need by being pulled off, or pushed on, in their grooves, which were soaped to lessen friction. Such a system was used for the pastoral *Florimène* in 1635. By the time of the last and greatest of the masques, *Salmacida Spolia*, in 1640, not only was such a set of long grooves across the stage used to take the back scenes, but further sets of short grooves were to be found, one set at each wing-position, and hence the wings might also be slid on or off, to change with the changing back scene. In *Salmacida Spolia* there were four parallel grooves above and below each wing-position, and also at the position of the back scenes, so supplying means to accommodate the scenery for four complete changes of back scene and four corresponding changes of wings.

Moreover, the Side Borders and Upper Backshutters were all hung from special top grooves, and could be drawn off, or on, in a similar way.

All grooves were parallel to the front of the stage, consequently all pieces of scenery had to face the audience directly, and this later became one of the limitations of the groove system, since an oblique setting of scene pieces was made impossible owing to the difficulty of adjustment arising in any attempt to use oblique grooves on a raked stage. The parallel position imposed by the groove system also led to a very low regard for the proper masking of the sides of the scene, and spectators in side boxes must have regularly seen far more of the waiting actors than is possible today.

In the early arrangements the opposite pairs of wing-groove groups were fixed to converge as one went up-stage, so that the avenue of wings might form a perspective vista. Similarly the upper wing-grooves were successively placed lower as one approached the back, a shorter wing being used at each position, again in accordance with perspective effect. Thus, no wing could be used at any position of grooves other than the one it was built to fit, and interchangeability was impossible.

During the Commonwealth a considerably simplified system of grooves was used by John Webb, to work the backshutters only, for his scenery in *The Siege of Rhodes* in 1656.

Following the Commonwealth, evidence for the use of grooves in the Restoration public theatre is obtainable at first only from play-directions. The first direct mention of them is in 1743, at Covent Garden. Both top and bottom grooves are referred to, the top grooves being fixed to the under side of the fly-floor. There were probably six sets a side, numbered from the front of the stage—1st grooves, 2nd grooves, and so forth—and the position of a piece of scenery might be described by specifying the number of the groove it occupied, as 'Palace, 3rd groove'.

About the end of the eighteenth century several criticisms were made of the groove system, and of the rigid form of setting which it enforced, but it persisted because, better than any other, it permitted the swift, succession of scenes which suited the contemporary British drama. Several innovations were made to surmount some at least of the limitations of the grooves. Some of the fixed bottom grooves, which might trip the actor when not in use, were made removable, and the upper grooves, which intruded on a high arch-bordered scene, were cut and hinged so as to give two 'arms' easily lifted out of sight by attached lines.

Sometimes the two lines working the pair of groove-arms in each set were brought together to a cleat on the fly-rail, in which case any pair of groove-arms could be dropped at need; and sometimes all the lines from all the groove-arms on the stage were taken to one long shaft, and upon the rotation of this each groove-arm rose or fell simultaneously with the others in one operation (see DRUM-AND-SHAFT SYSTEM). The plans for the Theatre Royal, Plymouth, in 1811, well exemplify these arrangements.

The number of individual grooves in each group varied, but since it was clearly impossible to allow for the maximum number of wings which might be needed in any one performance, it seems likely that it was dependent on the total number of varieties of stock scene most likely to be used in the individual theatre. Thus at Ipswich, in the first half of the nineteenth century, there were four types of wing kept in readiness at each position—Palace interior, Wood or Tree wing, Cottage interior, and Cave or Rock wing. Plymouth, at the beginning of the same century, appears to have stocked three wing sets—Palace, Tree, and Chamber wings.

Objections continued to be raised against grooves. Sometimes the scenes stuck, and it was difficult to move all the pieces in a scene-change at the same time (though as early as 1776 we hear of the upper grooves being connected to a system of 'barrels' or shafts), which led to ragged variations in the movement. When, in about 1820, the bottom grooves became isolated single strips and finally disappeared altogether, the upper grooves only remained as supports and it became of the utmost importance that an exactly correct level should be maintained for the hinged arms. This was achieved by a chain, suspended from above and acting as a check to their fall—a chain being less subject to alteration with atmospheric changes than a rope. These chains, and the heavy falling arms, made a characteristic noise in the scene-changing of the time.

By 1857 the Continental method of scene-changing (see CARRIAGE-AND-FRAME) had replaced grooves at Covent Garden. In 1863 Charles Fechter did away with the groove system at the Lyceum, and installed the Continental method, but the innovation was not maintained, and grooves returned. In 1880 Irving again removed the grooves from the Lyceum, to use instead what became the modern method of scene-support by braces, and, incidentally, at the same time initiated the custom of dropping the curtain for scene-changes.

Grooves remained, however, for some years in smaller theatres, and a pivoted variant is found in the 1880s which surmounted the objection to their rigidly enforcing a position parallel to the footlights on all wings, for wing and groove could now be twisted to any angle. Eventually even this modification was superseded by Forks, in which the tops of the wings were held as by an inverted garden-fork. This idea is still occasionally to be found, for instance in a form where the prongs are replaced by short, vertical, rubber-covered rollers projecting down from a headboard. But the device is rarely used today, though ingenious examples of it are to be found in the late nineteenth century.

It is perhaps worth mentioning that a passage in Chetwood's *General History of the Stage* (Dublin, 1749) reports his importation in 1741 to Smock Alley Theatre, Dublin, from Drury Lane, of a 'Machine to move the Scenes regularly altogether', which involved altering the stage 'after the manner of the Theatres in *France* and *England*'. It may well be then that, before the middle of the eighteenth century, an alternative method to grooves was known. Some writers have gone so far as to ask whether Betterton himself might not have brought back something of the principle in 1673, when he returned to the Duke's Theatre after a study of machinery in France. This, however, has still to be substantiated, and however frequent and early the intermissions, the groove system was the standard English system till the end of the nineteenth century.

The groove system was also employed in the American theatre, where it was quoted as old-fashioned by 1897. Otherwise it is unknown in any other country in the world (with the possible exception of Holland) after the Renaissance period. RICHARD SOUTHERN

GROS-GUILLAUME [ROBERT GUÉRIN] (*fl.* 1600–34), one of the great farce-players, with Turlupin and Gaultier-Garguille, of the permanent company at the Hôtel de Bourgogne. He was already an actor in 1600, though he is said to have been originally a baker, and he may have appeared at the Paris fairs before going to the Hôtel de Bourgogne. He was a fat man, with black eyes and a very mobile face. After being associated with Laporte and Valleran-Lecomte in the early years of the seventeenth century he became one of the leading members of the company and was its acknowledged head from 1622 until his death.

Tradition says that, having mocked a magistrate in one of his parts, he was thrown into prison, where he died. He was known as *le fariné* from his habit of covering his face with flour, and was much admired by Henri IV. He figures as himself in Gougenot's *La Comédie des comédiens* (1633). As La Fleur he also played serious parts, but it is as a low comedian that he is best remembered.

GROSSMITH. (1) GEORGE (1847–1912), English actor, primarily an entertainer, who is best remembered for his sketches at the piano, and for his connexion with Gilbert and Sullivan. He was at the Savoy from its opening in 1881 until 1889. He was the author of an autobiography, *A Society Clown*, and with his brother, (2) WALTER WEEDON (1852–1919), of the inimitable *Diary of a Nobody*. The younger Grossmith was also an actor, making his first appearance on the stage at Liverpool in 1885. He then went to America, but returned to London in 1887 and was at the Lyceum with Irving, and at the Royalty with Alexander. In 1901 he made a great hit in his own play, *The Night of the Party*, in which he toured England and the United States. He was also the author of *The Duffer* (1905), and was an excellent artist, exhibiting at the Royal Academy and contributing frequently to the *Art Journal*. George's two sons, (3) GEORGE (1874–1935) and (4) LAWRENCE (1877–1944), were both on the stage, the latter, originally an engineer, making his first appearance in 1896 at the Court Theatre, London. He had a long and distinguished career in London and New York, and was the brother-in-law of Vernon and Irene Castle. George junior made his first appearance in 1892 at the Criterion, and became famous as the impersonator of the 'dude' or man-about-town in musical comedy. He was often seen in revue, and was part-author of *The Bing Boys* and *The Cabaret Girl*, being associated with Laurillard in the management of several London theatres. His son and daughter were both connected with the stage.

GROTO, LUIGI (1541–85), Italian dramatist and poet, known as the blind man of Adria (*il cieco d'Adria*). He was possibly the first to put on the stage the story of Romeo and Juliet, from a *novello* of Bandello, as *Adriana* (1578). He also wrote tragedies such as *Dalida* (1572), in which horrors abounded, much to the taste of his time, and is credited with a number of pastorals and comedies. *Dalida* was given at Cambridge in 1592 in a Latin translation by William Alabaster.

GROUNDROW, originally a strip of gas lights, laid flat along the stage to illuminate the foot of a back scene, and then, by transference, the low, cut-out strip of scenery placed in front to mask them. It is now applied to all long, low pieces of scenery, made of canvas stretched on wood, cut along the upper edge to represent, for example, a hedge with a stile in it, or a bank topped by low bushes (see FLAT).

RICHARD SOUTHERN

GROUP THEATRE. 1. NEW YORK, an organization formed by Harold Clurman, Lee Strasberg, and Cheryl Crawford, which evolved from the Theatre Guild, under whose auspices it produced *Red Rust* at the Martin Beck Theatre in 1929. Two years later, after a production of *The House of Connelly*, it became an independent entity, and during the 1930s was responsible for some of the most interesting plays seen in New York, including *Night Over Taos* (1932), *Men in White* (1933), *Thunder Rock*, and *My Heart's in the Highlands* (both 1939). The Group also sponsored the work of the young dramatist Clifford Odets. A permanent repertory company was built up dedicated to the principles of group acting as formulated by Stanislavsky and practised at the Moscow Art Theatre. This was disbanded in 1940.

2. LONDON, a private play-producing society founded in 1933 with the object of presenting modern non-commercial plays and experimental revivals. It had its headquarters at the Westminster Theatre, where most of its productions took place. These included the poetic plays of Auden and Isherwood (*The Dog Beneath the Skin*, 1936; The *Ascent of F.6*, 1937; *On the Frontier*, 1939), T. S. Eliot's *Sweeney Agonistes* (1935), Stephen Spender's *Trial of a Judge* (1938), and a revival of *Timon of Athens* in modern dress (1935), produced by Nugent Monck. In the same year Saint-Denis produced for the Group Theatre Jean Giono's *Sowers of the Hills*, but otherwise the plays were produced by Rupert Doone (1904–66), on a bare stage, with little or no scenery or props, and with an occasional use of masks. Incidental music to some of the plays was written by Benjamin Britten. During the Second World War the society lapsed, but in 1950 it was reformed, with some of its original promoters, and gave its first production (a translation of Sartre's *Les Mouches*, as *The Flies*) on 2 Dec. It continued spasmodically for a couple of years, but finally disintegrated in about 1953.

GROVE THEATRE, NEW YORK, a small playhouse in Bedlow Street, which opened in 1804 with a company of little-known actors, including Bland, the brother of Mrs. Jordan, and Mr. and Mrs. Frederick Wheatley, who later joined the stock company at the Park, together with several of their associates. The Grove Theatre, which gave chiefly farce and light comedy, was open only on the nights when the all-powerful Park Theatre was closed, and it lasted only a couple of seasons. Among its attractions was a pantomime staged by Signor Bologna, from London's Covent Garden, in which he himself played Clown.

GRÜNDGENS, GUSTAF (1899–1963), German actor and producer, one of the outstanding men of his time in the German theatre. He was famous not only for his acting in such parts as Mephistopheles (in Goethe's *Faust*) and Hamlet, but for his ability to reconcile theatre tradition with reasonable innovation, his fidelity to his author, and his insistence on clear musical speech. He first came into contact with the theatre when he directed an army group at the end of the First World War. He then went to the Düsseldorf Academy, and after acting in Berlin and Hamburg he joined Max Reinhardt's Deutsches Theater in 1931. This laid the foundation of his future career. Tall, blonde, and extremely good-looking, he made a striking Hamlet when in 1938 he appeared with a German company at Elsinore. By this time he was General Superintendent of the Prussian State theatres, but during the Second World War he proved himself sufficiently anti-Nazi to warrant his release from a Soviet internment camp after a brief stay in 1946. He returned to Düsseldorf, where during the next seven years he made the Düsseldorf Ensemble one of the outstanding German companies. His last seven years were spent at Hamburg, where he produced a number of important modern plays, including Lawrence Durrell's *Sappho*, Brecht's *St. Joan of the Stockyards* and Shaw's *Caesar and Cleopatra*, in which he played Caesar. One of his finest achievements was the production, after a long period of neglect in the theatre, of both parts of Goethe's *Faust*, which he played with acclaim in Edinburgh, New York, Moscow, and Leningrad. He was investigating the possibilities of a tour in South America when he died suddenly in Manila.

GRUNDY, SYDNEY (1848–1914), English dramatist, who was for some years a barrister in his native town of Manchester. His first play was a short comedy entitled *A Little Change* (1872), which was done at the Haymarket under Buckstone with the Kendals in the leading parts. Encouraged by its success Grundy continued to write comedies and farces, many of them adapted from the French, but in later years he became infected with the prevailing taste for melodrama and sentiment, and his more serious plays, of which the best are *The Silver Shield* (1885) and *Sowing the Wind* (1893), show a curious mingling of old and new fashions. He lacked the skill to handle realistic situations with any depth of insight, cramping them into the conventions of an outworn method, and the only play of his which has survived is his adaptation of a French farce as *A Pair of Spectacles* (1890). This was immensely successful, and provided Hare, as Benjamin Goldfinch, with a part which he played to perfection and revived many times, both in London and on tour.

GRYPHIUS, ANDREAS (1616–64), a seventeenth-century German dramatist (born in Silesia, where he returned in 1647) who grew up in the shadow of war. He is notable as a lyric playwright, and his religious poetry, much of which dates from his early years, reveals a soul obsessed to the point of morbidity by a sense of sin, and reaching out incessantly to the Eternal. The conviction that earthly existence is vanity pervades his work. Catherine, Queen of Georgia, a martyr for her faith, Charles I of England, Papinianus, the righteous counsellor of Caracalla, are his heroes, in their passive, but unshakable, fortitude. Yet greater interest is aroused by their opponents, who grow in complexity until in the Emperor Bassanius (Caracalla) Gryphius depicts the mixed character so essential to true tragedy. Having stabbed his half-brother in a fit of anger, he is caught in the meshes of his crime until he is forced to commit his incorruptible mentor to the executioner, knowing all the time that his conscience will never let him rest. *Papinianus* (1659) is a well-knit play with firmly contrasted personalities, in which we may discern tenderness, passion, and forthright integrity. *Carolus Stuardus, oder die ermordete Majestät* (pub. 1657), though interesting as a treatment of a contemporary event viewed with strong royalist sympathies, is the weakest of Gryphius's plays. Much in advance of his time, Gryphius also wrote a middle-class play, *Cardenio und Celinde* (1647), in which, despite visions and churchyard horrors, the characters are human, and resolve their conflicting desires by abnegation. Gryphius's comedies are all in prose, except for the doggerel of the Pyramus and Thisbe scenes in *Peter Squentz* (pub. 1663). The best of them, *Horribilicribrifax* (pub. 1663), gives a lively picture of contemporary follies—bombastic conceit, pedantry, self-seeking—as seen by a naturally austere mind with a sense of humour.

W. E. DELP

GUAL, ADRIÀ (1872–1943), Catalan dramatist and producer. Gual's first plays were written under the influence of Maeterlinck and he himself produced symbolist drama at the turn of the century in his Teatre Intim. After a period of study in France he returned to Barcelona in 1903 and aspired to the creation of a national theatre which at the same time would present in translation masterpieces of world drama. In 1903–4 the Teatre Intim presented plays varying from Beaumarchais to Ibsen, from Benavente to Aeschylus. The main unifying factor in the repertoire was Gual's own artistic approach to the theatre, his concern for the careful training of his actors, and the technical and artistic innovations in his productions. His influence in the rest of Spain was indirect, as his company played only in Catalan, but without Gual's innovations and his introduction of foreign dramatists to peninsular audiences the dramatic renaissance of the 1920s and 1930s in Madrid would have been more parochial and technically less exciting.

J. E. VAREY

GUARINI, GIOVANNI BATTISTA (1537–1612), Italian dramatist, author of *Il Pastor Fido*, a pastoral tragicomedy which stands with Tasso's *Aminta* as the outstanding achievement of the Italian pastoral drama. It was begun in 1569, but not published until 1590; it was first produced at Mantua in 1598, with much splendour and success. Frequently reprinted and translated, it had a great influence on the pastoral and romantic literature of England and France in the seventeenth century, and was given in English in 1601, and in a Latin translation at

Cambridge, by King's College men, in 1605 (see ITALY, I *b* ii and PASTORAL).

GUÉRIN D'ÉTRICHÉ, ISAAC FRANÇOIS (*c.* 1636–1728), French actor, who in 1677 married Molière's widow. Son of an actor, he was a member of the troupe at the Théâtre du Marais when it fused with that of Molière, and was already known as a good actor in light comedy. He became a member of the Comédie-Française on its foundation, and was its third *doyen*, continuing to act until he was well over 80. He was much admired in elderly parts, as in *L'Avare* and *Le Grondeur*. He also created a number of roles in early eighteenth-century plays. He was stricken with paralysis in 1717 while waiting in the wings to go on.

GUIGNOL, the name of a French marionette, originating in Lyon, with the local characteristics of the peasant and provincial man of the Dauphiné. He probably dates from the last years of the eighteenth century, and may have been invented by a puppet-master named Laurent Mourquet (1744–1844), grafting native humour on to Polichinelle (Punch). By some twist of nomenclature, perhaps because of the horrors and general heartlessness of the puppet-show, as exemplified in our Punch and Judy, the name attached itself in Paris to cabarets which catered for an over-sophisticated and decadent taste, later centralized in the Théâtre du Grand Guignol. This specialized in short plays of violence, murder, rape, ghostly apparitions, and suicide, all intended to chill and delight the spectator. In a modified form it made its appearance in England in 1908, and has appeared sporadically ever since, apart from Grand Guignol elements in such plays as *Gaslight* and *Duet for Two Hands*. Subtlety, psychology, love interest, all must be sacrificed to the overriding considerations of pain and terror. English Grand Guignol has never reached the intensity of the French, however, and its true home is in the small theatres of Montmartre. In the French theatre a 'guignol' is also a small room just beside the stage, with mirror and washbasin, used for quick changes or hasty repairs.

GUILBERT, YVETTE (1869–1944), French 'diseuse', whose wit, vivacity, and charm made a profound impression in London, Paris, and New York. She made her début at the Théâtre des Variétés in 1889, and was heard at various cafés-concerts in songs specially written for her. Tall, thin to the point of emaciation, with a voice to match, she became the rage of Paris, and her long black gloves, originally a result of her poverty, became a mark of distinction which she retained till the end. She was a favourite at the old Empire, London, and at the Coliseum, and reappeared in London in the 1920s, after a long stay in America, in a series of recitals. She was the author of a volume of reminiscences entitled *The Song of My Life*.

GUILD THEATRE, NEW YORK, on W. 52nd St. This was built to house the activities of the Theatre Guild, and opened on 13 Apr. 1925, with Helen Hayes in *Caesar and Cleopatra*. This ran for 129 performances, but was not a great success, many of the audience coming as much to see the new playhouse as the play. Later productions included the Lunts in *Arms and the Man*, and the controversial *Goat Song*, considered by some critics the outstanding venture of the Theatre Guild. Another play by Werfel, *Juarez and Maximilian*, was an artistic though not a commercial success, and was followed by a revival of *Pygmalion* with Lynn Fontanne as Eliza Doolittle. This was the first play to be produced by the Theatre Guild outside New York, with a success that justified a continuance of the policy. Other outstanding productions at this theatre were *The Brothers Karamazov* (1927), adapted and directed by Jacques Copeau, *Porgy*, *Marco Millions* (the first O'Neill play to be done by the Theatre Guild), and revivals of *The Doctor's Dilemma* and *Volpone*. *Faust, Part I*, with a German director, proved unsuccessful, as did *Major Barbara*. In 1929 Alice Brady appeared for the first time under the auspices of the Guild, which later presented Nazimova in *A Month in the Country*. The following year saw the first musical play at the Guild Theatre, and the poetic *Elizabeth the Queen*, again with the Lunts, who, after *Green Grow the Lilacs* and *Mourning Becomes Electra*, the latter with Alice Brady and Nazimova, were seen again in *The Taming of the Shrew*. Later productions were *Too True to be Good*, with Beatrice Lillie, Behrman's *Biography* and *End of Summer*, and O'Neill's *Ah, Wilderness!*

In 1950, renamed the Anta Theatre, it housed for a time productions by the American National Theatre Association, but although it still serves as a centre for this organization, it has reverted to commercial use with *Say, Darling!* (1957), Archibald MacLeish's *J.B.* (1959) (see No. 111), Bolt's *A Man for All Seasons* (1961), *Blues for Mr. Charlie* (1964), and *The Owl and the Pussycat* (1965).

GEORGE FREEDLEY†

GUILLOT-GORJU [BERTRAND HARDOUIN DE ST. JACQUES] (1600–48), French actor, originally a medical student who had abandoned his studies and earned a precarious living as a 'barker' for quack-doctors at the Paris fairs. He had great wit and powers of repartee, and Bellerose, seeing in him the makings of an actor, took him into the company at the Hôtel de Bourgogne, where he played in farce in succession to Turlupin and his companions. He was excellent as the pedantic doctor, which he played masked. He married the sister of Bellerose in 1636, and in 1641 retired from the stage to take up his old profession of medicine.

GUIMERÀ, ÁNGEL (1847–1924), a Catalan dramatist, who with Galdós represents the impact of realism on the Spanish stage. His plays were first produced in Barcelona, where he spent most of his life. They fall into two groups, the first, influenced by Shakespeare and the French Romantics, being historical dramas, a genre to which Guimerà returned in later years, while the plays of his intervening period are realistic representations of contemporary life, often with a working-class setting, and showing clearly the influence of the Scandinavians, particularly Ibsen. The best known of these is *Terra baixa* (1896).

GUINNESS, SIR ALEC (1914–), English actor, knighted in 1959, who after training at the Fay Compton Studio of Dramatic Art, where he won First Prize at the annual Public Show, made his first appearance in *Libel?* in 1934, and later in the same year played Osric in Gielgud's *Hamlet*, a part which he played again at the Old Vic in 1936–7. It was during this season that he first attracted notice by his Sir Andrew Aguecheek. He then joined Gielgud's company at the Queen's, playing Aumerle in *Richard II* with great simplicity and pathos, Snake in *The School for Scandal*, Fedotik in *Three Sisters*, and Lorenzo in *The Merchant of Venice*, the last with a magically poetic quality which seemed to foreshadow a career in romantic parts. Much of the same quality was apparent in his modern-dress Hamlet (produced by Tyrone Guthrie in 1938), a remarkably sincere, straightforward performance which had in it some unforgettable moments. It contrasted admirably with his Arthur Gower (in *Trelawny of the 'Wells'*) and his extremely amusing Bob Acres in the same season. Among his later parts have been Herbert Pocket and Mitya in his own adaptations of *Great Expectations* and *The Brothers Karamazov*, Garcin in Sartre's *Vicious Circle* (*Huis-clos*), and, with the Old Vic, an outstanding Fool in *King Lear*, and two excellent performances as Abel Drugger in *The Alchemist* and Hlestakov in *The Government Inspector*; he also appeared at Edinburgh as Harcourt Reilly in *The Cocktail Party*. In 1951 he appeared in his own production of *Hamlet*, an effort to break with tradition and present Hamlet in Shakespeare's own image which failed, but even in its failure left some of the audience more stirred and interested than by other less unorthodox Hamlets. In 1953 he played in the opening season of the Shakespearean Festival Theatre at Stratford, Ontario, and in 1954 was seen in London in the title-role of Bridget Boland's *The Prisoner*. In 1956 he gave a light-hearted performance in *Hotel Paradiso*, and in 1960 made a great impression by his portrayal of T. E. Lawrence in Rattigan's *Ross*. In 1963 he played Béranger in Ionesco's *Exit the King* at the Court Theatre. His success in films, which cannot be dealt with here, has been as great as on the stage. He is an unpredictable and protean creature, who constantly delights his audience with his wit and mimicry, or chills them with his revelations of the abysses in the mind of man. No one can say what he will do next. But whatever he does is worth watching.

GUISARD, GUISER, another name for the Christmas mummer (see MUMMING PLAY), probably from 'disguise'. The slang term 'geezer' may be derived from it.

GUITRY. (1) LUCIEN-GERMAIN (1860–1925), French actor and dramatist, trained at the Conservatoire, who made his first appearance as Armand in a revival of *La Dame aux camélias* in 1878, at the Gymnase. He was later in Russia, and toured the Continent for many years, returning to the Odéon in 1891, and appearing with Sarah Bernhardt at the Porte-Saint-Martin in 1893. He was for several years manager of the Renaissance, where he also appeared in many of his own productions and plays. His son (2) SACHA (1885–1957) was also an actor and a most prolific author, who wrote nearly a hundred plays, mainly light comedies, many of which were translated into English. He first appeared under his father's management in St. Petersburg, where he was born, and was seen in Paris at the Renaissance, again with his father, in 1902. He came to London in 1920 and proved extremely popular, appearing in a number of his own plays and sketches with (3) YVONNE PRINTEMPS (1895–), a charming French actress, the second of his four wives, who delighted English audiences with her performance in *Nono*, a play written by her husband when he was 16. She has since had a distinguished career in Paris, where she directs her own theatre.

GUNNELL, RICHARD (?–1634), one of the outstanding personalities of the English theatre from about 1623 to his death. He was with the Palsgrave's Men on their taking that name in 1612, and was a friend of Alleyn, in whose diary he often figures. He held shares in the new Fortune, rebuilt in 1618 after the disastrous fire, and he appears later as a dramatist for the company there, since two plays by him, both lost, were licensed in 1623 and 1624. At this time he seems to have given up acting and taken over the management of the Fortune, but does not appear to have prospered, since he was several times in debt. In 1629 he was associated with Blagrove in the building of Salisbury Court, where he remained in management until his death.

GUSTAV III (1746–1792), King of Sweden, took a great interest in the theatre, and had much influence on its development in Sweden in the latter part of the eighteenth century. Himself the author, or part-author, of a number of plays given at Court, he also supported the National Theatre opened in Stockholm in 1773, and encouraged the work of young dramatists (see SCANDINAVIA, 3 *a*).

GUSYEV, VICTOR MIKHAILOVICH (1908–44), Soviet dramatist, whose early plays were written for the Red Army Theatre, and were about soldiers. *Friendship*, which was in rhyme, and dealt with the unselfish affection of five friends on the Soviet frontier, was produced in 1938. During the war Gusyev came to the fore with several plays, of which *A Moscow Girl*, also in rhyme, was considered outstanding. The author's sudden death at the early age of 35 was a great loss to the Soviet stage.

GUTHRIE, SIR TYRONE (1900–71), English actor and producer, who through his mother Norah Power was the great-grandson of the Irish actor Tyrone Power. Guthrie made his first appearance on the stage in 1924 with the Oxford Repertory Company under Fagan. Relinquishing acting for production, he directed the plays given by Anmer Hall at the Festival Theatre, Cambridge, from 1929 to 1930, and for the same management produced his first play in London, James Bridie's *The Anatomist*, with which the Westminster Theatre opened in 1931. Much of Guthrie's finest work has been done in Shakespeare; he was twice appointed producer at the Old Vic, in 1933 and in 1936, and from 1939 to 1945 was Administrator of the Old Vic and Sadler's Wells Theatres. He was also producer of plays at the Shakespearean Festival Theatre, Stratford, Ontario (which was largely his creation—see No. 43) from 1953 to 1957, and has worked in many European countries, including Finland, and in Israel. A creative and experimental artist, he is not afraid to approach his material from a new angle, often with unexpected success, as in his delightful *Midsummer Night's Dream* and a modern-dress *Hamlet* starring Alec Guinness. Among other notable productions were a more orthodox *Hamlet* (1937), with Laurence Olivier, which was later seen at Elsinore, *Measure for Measure*, with Charles Laughton (1933) and Emlyn Williams (1937) as Angelo, *Peer Gynt* in 1944, all for the Old Vic; and, for the Edinburgh Festivals of 1948 and 1949, the old Scottish plays, *The Three Estates* by Lindsay and *The Gentle Shepherd* by Ramsay. He was one of the first to write plays specifically for broadcasting, and is the author of *Theatre Prospect* (1932), and of *A Life in the Theatre* (1960). He was knighted in the New Year Honours List of 1961 for services to the theatre. In 1963 a theatre named after him, and designed somewhat on the lines of Stratford, Ontario, and the Chichester Festival Theatres, opened in Minneapolis. Its avowed aim was the establishment outside New York of a permanent, professional, and classical repertory company, and the intention is to do each year three established classics, including Shakespeare, and one American play. The success of the first season, which included also a modern-dress *Hamlet*, a new version of Molière's *L'Avare* and Miller's *Death of a Salesman*, was Guthrie's own production of Chekhov's *Three Sisters*. Later productions there by Guthrie included *Henry V*, *Volpone*, and *Richard III* with Hume Cronyn as Richard. Other successful productions were *The Glass Menagerie* by the American director, Alan Schneider, and *The Way of the World* by Douglas Campbell from Stratford, Ontario.

GUTZKOW, KARL FERDINAND (1811–78), German writer, and a prominent member of the 'Young Germany' literary movement. He is, however, mainly remembered as the author of the great Jewish play, *Uriel Acosta*, written in 1847, which has become a recognized classic of world drama, and is in the repertory of the main Soviet and Jewish theatres. Dealing with the tragedy of a Jewish heretic, it is a moving and terrible picture of the struggle for intellectual freedom. It was first seen in England in 1905, and has been played, both in the original and in translation, in most European countries and in America.

GWYNN, NELL [ELEANOR] (1650–87), English actress and, during her short stage career, one of the best-loved of her day. After a stormy childhood she became an orange-wench at Drury Lane, perhaps under the redoubtable Mrs. Meggs, and with the help of Charles Hart made her first appearance on the boards at the age of 15 in *The Indian Emperor*. She was not a good actress; in tragedy she was a failure, and in comedy she owed her success more to her charm and vivacity than to her histrionic powers. Her best part seems to have been Florimel in Dryden's *Secret Love*, where she was much admired in male attire. She was much in demand as a speaker of prologues and epilogues and took Charles II by storm when she spoke the witty epilogue to *Tyrannic Love* (1669). She then became his mistress, and made her last appearance on the stage in *The Conquest of Granada* (1670), as Almahide to Hart's Almanzor. Tradition has it that the founding of Chelsea Hospital was due to her influence. She is the subject of a number of plays, including Paul Kester's *Sweet Nell of Old Drury*, a part indissolubly linked with the name of Julia Neilson.

GYLLENBORG, CARL (1679–1746), Swedish dramatist, author of *Den Svenska sprätthöken*, the first play to be given at the newly opened Royal Swedish Theatre in Stockholm in 1737.

GYMNASE-DRAMATIQUE, THÉÂTRE DU, PARIS. This opened on 23 Dec. 1820 under Delestre-Poirson, a mediocre actor but a good manager, who ran it successfully until 1844. Scribe was its dramatist, and its company included Virginie Déjazet and the 11-year-old Léontine Fay. It was at first intended as a nursery for young talent coming from the Conservatoire, and was licensed to play classical plays if condensed into one act. That soon proved impracticable, and the theatre turned to vaudevilles. The Gymnase, as it was usually called, was one of the first theatres in Paris to be lit by gas. For a short time it was known as the Théâtre de Madame, under the patronage of the Duchesse de Berry, but in 1830, the Revolution having taken away its title, it was closed for repairs and reopened under its old name. During the next few years it saw the débuts of Madame Allan-Despréaux, Rachel, and Rose Chéri, the last marrying its second director Monsigny and remaining as its leading lady for twenty years. Under Monsigny the theatre, which had suffered from Poirson's dispute with the Society of Authors, once more established itself, and gradually came to accept more serious plays. In 1852 *La Dame aux camélias* was given there, followed by other plays by Dumas *fils*, and by Sand, Augier, and Feuillet. The Gymnase now became a serious rival of the Comédie-Française, and under successive directors has retained its position among the important theatres of Paris.

There was a small children's theatre known as the Gymnase-Enfantin, founded by Joly in 1829, which was burnt down in 1843.

H

HABIMA, a company formed in Moscow in 1917 for the production of plays in Hebrew (*habima* meaning the stage). Its first members came from the short-lived Warsaw and Bialystok Hebrew theatres, and soon attracted the attention of Stanislavsky, who entrusted their training to his assistant, Vakhtangov. The company's first public performance, in 1918, consisted of four one-act plays by various Jewish writers, and proved so successful that Habima became one of the four studios affiliated to the Moscow Art Theatre. Vakhtangov's best work for Habima was done with the production of the Hebrew version of *The Dybbuk* in 1922; already a sick man, he died a few months later. In 1925 Habima played *The Eternal Jew* and *The Dybbuk* in Leningrad for three weeks; Riga was visited in 1926, and the company then went on tour in America. It had always been the intention of Habima to settle in Israel, and a first visit there was made in 1928. In the following year an extended European tour was made, during which the company was seen in the last two plays to be produced abroad, *Twelfth Night* and *Uriel Acosta*, the latter directed by Granovsky. Since 1931, except for four tours abroad, Habima has been permanently resident in Israel. Its theatre building, which also comprises a dramatic school and library, was opened in 1945 in Tel Aviv, and in 1953 Habima was officially declared a National Theatre. E. HARRIS

HACKETT. (1) JAMES HENRY (1800–71), American character actor, who made his first appearance in 1826, and became famous for his portrayal of Yankee characters, many of which he interpolated into new or existing plays. In this way he rewrote Finn's *Montgomery* as *The Indian Wife*, and turned the French comic character in *Paul Pry* into a Yankee, rechristening the piece *Jonathan in England*. One of his finest parts was Nimrod Wildfire in James Kirke Paulding's *The Lion of the West*, a play which owed much of its success to his acting. The manuscript, which was believed lost—Hackett objected to the printing of plays in which he starred, in case other actors should emulate his success in them—was found and published in 1954.

Long before Jefferson made *Rip Van Winkle* his own, Hackett had appeared in a version of it which he continued to play for some years after Jefferson's début. He was the first American actor to appear in London as a star, which he did in 1833, playing Falstaff, one of his best parts, and several of his Yankee characterizations, which were well received. By his encouragement of American dramatists, and his offer of prizes for new American plays, he had a definite influence on the development of a native drama in the United States. He was also a keen student of Shakespeare, and published his correspondence with Quincy Adams on the subject of Shakespeare's plays. Hackett was manager of the Astor Place Opera House on the occasion of the Macready riot. He was always a scholarly, genial, and hard-working actor, handsome in his youth, who served the theatre conscientiously, if not with overmuch genius. His first wife was the actress (2) CATHARINE LEE SUGG (1797–1845), who came from the Theatre Royal, Birmingham, to the Park Theatre, New York, in 1818, and proved herself a good versatile actress, with an excellent contralto voice. She appeared with her husband for a short while after her marriage in 1819, and then retired. By his second wife Hackett had a son, (3) JAMES KETELTAS (1869–1926), who became a fine romantic actor, playing leading Shakespeare and Sheridan roles under Daly in 1892. In 1895 he joined Daniel Frohman's company at the Lyceum, where he appeared in *The Prisoner of Zenda* and similar plays. In his youth he was a tall, slim figure, with dark hair and fine features, exactly suited to the heroes of dashing melodrama and romance; a certain picturesque artificiality and lack of training, however, prevented him from doing serious work later in his career, though with the profits of his production of *The Walls of Jericho* he opened his own theatre in New York, and later, with the proceeds of a legacy, put on an *Othello* with sets by Urban which marked an important step forward in the history of American stage-craft and scenic design.

HAFNER, PHILIPP (1735–64), see AUSTRIA.

HAINES, JOSEPH (?–1701), English actor, was an excellent comedian, an inveterate practical joker, and a writer of scurrilous verse and lampoons which on several occasions got him into trouble. He was a dancing-master in France, but went to England and set up a booth at Bartholomew Fair. He eventually joined Killigrew's company at the Theatre Royal, and played clowns and buffoons. He was one of the first English Harlequins, in Ravenscroft's adaptation of *Les Fourberies de Scapin*, which, being forestalled by Otway's at Dorset Garden, was renamed and remodelled on the lines of Fiorelli's *commedia dell'arte* productions in Paris. Haines made a special journey to Paris to study the methods and machinery of the French stage.

HALE, LOUISE (*née* CLOSSER) (1872–1933), American actress and author, whose later career was entirely in films. She was, however, on the legitimate stage for many years, first appearing at Detroit in *In Old Kentucky* in 1894. Her first great success came as Prossy in

Candida with Arnold Daly in 1903. In 1907 she appeared in London as Miss Hazy in *Mrs. Wiggs of the Cabbage Patch*, and before she left the stage to go to Hollywood she appeared in many other excellent productions, including *The Blue Bird* (1910), *Ruggles of Red Gap* (1915), *Beyond the Horizon* (1920), and *Peer Gynt* (1923). She wrote a number of novels, many of them dealing with theatrical life, and some travel books, the latter illustrated by her husband, Walter Hale (1869–1917).

HALL, PETER REGINALD FREDERICK (1930–), English producer and theatre manager. While at Cambridge he directed a number of plays for the A.D.C. and the Marlowe Society, and in 1953 he did his first professional production, for the Theatre Royal, Windsor. A year later he was appointed assistant producer, and in 1955 producer-in-chief, at the experimental Arts Theatre, where he was responsible for several interesting new productions, among them *South*, the controversial *Waiting for Godot*, *The Burnt Flower-Bed*, and *Waltz of the Toreadors*. At the New Theatre in 1956 he directed *Gigi*, with his first wife Leslie Caron in the title-role, and in the same year was responsible for an enchanting *Love's Labour's Lost* at the Stratford Memorial Theatre, where he was later to produce *Cymbeline* (1957), *Twelfth Night* (1958), *A Midsummer Night's Dream* (1959), and *Two Gentlemen of Verona* (1960). In 1960 he succeeded Glen Byam Shaw as Director of the Memorial Theatre at Stratford (now the Royal Shakespeare), and in 1961 he took over the Aldwych to provide a London home for the Stratford-upon-Avon company where plays other than those by Shakespeare could be done (see ALDWYCH). A year later the Arts Theatre (where in 1959 Hall returned to produce two of Anouilh's plays, *Madame de . . .* and *Traveller Without Luggage*) was added to the Stratford resources to provide an intimate playhouse for new and experimental productions, but this venture lasted only for six months. It was under Peter Hall that the Royal Shakespeare Theatre withdrew from the preliminary organization set up to establish the National Theatre.

HALLAM, a family of English actors, closely connected with the earliest beginnings of a professional theatre in the United States. The first was (1) LEWIS (1714–56), son of Adam Hallam, who was at Covent Garden from 1734 to 1741, and later at Drury Lane, and brother of William, manager of a theatre in Leman Street called the New Wells. William's wife, formerly Mrs. Parker, then Mrs. Berriman, was a well-known actress.

In 1752 Lewis took his wife and children, with a company of ten actors, to Williamsburg, Virginia, and on 15 Sept. gave *The Merchant of Venice* and *The Anatomist*. A year later, in New York, he refurbished the first theatre there, on Nassau Street. In it his company, in the face of some opposition, appeared in a fine repertory which included Shakespeare, Rowe, Lillo, Moore, Farquhar, Addison, Cibber, Vanbrugh, Steele, and Gay, together with a number of farces and after-pieces. Later, in Philadelphia, Hallam's company played in a building previously occupied by Kean and Murray, which was not demolished until 1849, and then, after a visit to Charleston, went to Jamaica. There the elder Hallam died, and his widow married David Douglass, also manager of a company touring there. The remnants of Hallam's company joined that of Douglass, and with the younger (2) LEWIS (*c.* 1740–1808) as leading man went back to New York. They were billed as the American Company, and played in a temporary theatre on Cruger's Wharf where, in 1759, the younger Hallam played Romeo to his mother's Juliet, his younger brother being also in the cast. Lewis was an excellent actor, and appeared in *The Prince of Parthia*, the first American play to be given a professional production, in the same year. Some time later he took over the management of the American Company, in partnership with John Henry. Bringing it back from the West Indies, where it had taken refuge during the War of Independence, he reopened the Southwark Theatre in Philadelphia and the John Street in New York, playing also in Baltimore and Annapolis. Hallam remained a manager of the American Company, first with Henry and later with Hodgkinson and Dunlap, until 1799, when he became merely a salaried actor, continuing on the stage until his death. He married, as his second wife, an actress named Miss Tuke, who became an important member of the company, but caused much trouble by her intemperate habits and quarrelsomeness. By a former marriage he had a son Mirvan, who was on the stage till his death in 1811, but was accounted a mediocre actor.

One of the elder Lewis's children, (3) ISABELLA (1746–1826), left behind in London when the family embarked for Williamsburg, became well known on the English stage as Mrs. Mattocks.

Two younger members of the Hallam family were Nancy, who played children's parts in Philadelphia in 1759–61, and Sarah, who became leading lady of the company in 1770 and in 1775 opened a dancing-school in Williamsburg. She was much appreciated during her short reign, and many poems were addressed to her. She is believed to have been a niece of the elder Hallam, and therefore cousin to the younger Lewis.

HALLS, a generic term for the music-halls, including those in London and in the provinces.

HALLSTRÖM, PER (1866–1960), Swedish dramatist who in the course of his career wrote lyric and romantic poetry, novels and studies, drama, essays, and some significant aesthetic criticism. His plays belong almost entirely to the twentieth century: *Grefven af Antwerpen* (1898); a tragedy, *Bianco Capello* (1900); *En veneziansk komedi* (1901); a comedy, *Erotikon* (1908); two legend-plays, *Alkestis* and *Ahasverus* (also 1908); two saga-plays, *Önskningarna* and *Tusen och en natt* (1910): *Karl XI* and *Gustaf III* (both 1918); *Nessusdräkten* (1919). Hallström's chief contribution to drama after 1919 was his translation of the plays of Shakespeare, made between 1922 and 1931.

UNA ELLIS-FERMOR†

HALM, FRIEDRICH [ELIGIUS FRANZ JOSEF VON MÜNCH-BELLINGHAUSEN] (1806–71), see AUSTRIA.

HAM, a term of derision used by actors today of the old-fashioned rant and fustian which they believe to have characterized nineteenth-century acting, particularly in melodrama. The derivation of the word is uncertain—among the suggestions offered have been 'h'amateur'; ham fat used in the 1860s to remove grease-paint; the American actor Hamish (1834–85), younger brother of John McCullough, who toured Illinois with a 'fit-up' troupe; hams as, mistakenly, common-land where such actors might set up a booth; and the American word 'hamfatter' as the equivalent of our own 'barnstormer'. The term seems to have originated in America in about 1912, and to have found its way to England after the First World War. In essence, 'ham' acting is tragic or dramatic acting which reproduces only the external characteristics and is devoid of inner truth or feeling, covering its deficiencies with a veneer of overworked tricks of technique, empty bombast, and showy but meaningless gestures.

HAMBLIN, THOMAS SOWERBY (1800–53), actor and theatre manager, who is chiefly remembered as manager and leading man of the Bowery Theatre, New York, in its most successful years. He was born in London and, after some years in the provinces, appeared at Drury Lane in leading parts. He went to America in 1825, and made his first appearance at the Park Theatre as Hamlet, later touring the United States as a tragedian. He was a fine, though somewhat melodramatic, actor, but in later years his acting was hindered by frequent bouts of asthma. He became lessee of the Bowery in 1830, rebuilt it after the disastrous fire of 1836, and only relinquished it in 1850 after further fires in 1838 and 1845. Ill luck seemed to dog him, for in 1848 he rented and redecorated the old Park Theatre and opened it on 4 Sept., only to see it destroyed by fire three months later. He then retired, and lived quietly until his death. He was twice married, his first wife Elizabeth being the daughter of the English actor William Blanchard. She was herself a good actress, and was for many years her husband's leading lady.

HAMBURG. The history of the theatre in Hamburg begins with performances of *Fastnachtsspiele* in the sixteenth century, and with performances by travelling players. In 1765 the Deutsches Nationaltheater, to which Lessing was the accredited dramatic critic, was established. The first performances there took place in 1767, but the intrigues of the actors, a poor response from the public, and the lack of a first-class national repertory, prevented the theatre from being a success. The one outstanding event of these years was the initial production of *Minna von Barnhelm* (1767), the first masterpiece of German comedy, but in 1769 the theatre was obliged to close. Later, under F. L. Schmidt, pupil of F. L. Schröder (1744–1816), it revived as the Stadttheater and had some moments of splendour. The repertory improved and guest artists like Emil Devrient, Theodor Döring, and Christine Enghaus were engaged. In 1820 Schmidt produced Kleist's popular comedy, *Der zerbrochene Krug*, a play which Goethe had been unwilling to risk doing in Weimar. When Schmidt retired in 1841 the repertory was again confined to popular pieces, similar to those given at the Thalia-Theater, founded in 1843. In fact, from 1849 to 1854 both houses presented a very similar programme. A fresh impulse to theatrical life in Hamburg came in 1900–1 from the Deutsches Schauspielhaus whose repertory, which included many foreign plays—Ibsen, Shaw, Molnár—made it the most active theatrical centre in the city.

DOROTHY MOORE

HAMMERSTEIN, OSCAR II (1895–1960), grandson of the impresario Oscar Hammerstein I, who built the Stoll Theatre, Kingsway, London, and two theatres in New York, and incidentally invented a cigar-rolling machine. The second Oscar was also the son and nephew of theatrical managers, and he began his career in the theatre as stage-manager of his uncle's shows on Broadway and on tour. He had already, while at college, tried his hand at writing lyrics and libretti for musical items, and he soon deserted stage-management for writing. He was probably the most prolific and successful lyric writer of his generation. He first came into prominence with *Wildflower* (1923), followed by *Rose Marie* (1924), *The Desert Song* (1926), *Show Boat* (from the book by Edna Ferber, 1927), *The Gang's All Here* (1931), and *Music in the Air* (1932). It was in 1943 that he began his collaboration with Richard Rodgers which resulted in the epoch-making musical play *Oklahoma!* This was followed by the equally sparkling and successful *Carmen Jones* (1944), *Carousel* (1945), *South Pacific* (1949), *The King and I* (1951), and, his last libretto, *The Sound of Music* (1960). He was twice awarded the Pulitzer Prize (*Oklahoma!* and *South Pacific*). He had many ties with England, and in his will left £2,000 to Southwark Cathedral for the upkeep of two choristers. A plaque to his memory, at the entrance to the Harvard Chapel in this Cathedral, was unveiled by his widow in 1961.

HAMMERSTEIN'S OLYMPIA, NEW YORK, see NEW YORK THEATRE, 2.

HAMMERSTEIN'S THEATRE, NEW YORK, see MANHATTAN THEATRE.

HAMMERTON, STEPHEN (*fl.* 1630–47), English actor of whom it was said that he 'was at first a most noted and beautiful Woman Actor, but afterwards he acted with equal Grace and Applause a Young Lover's part' (Wright). He is known to have been an excellent boy-actor, and must have appeared at Salisbury Court, for in 1632 Beeston, the manager, and Blagrove, one of the landlords, petitioned for his return from the King's Men, who had inveigled him away. There is no record of whether they got him back or not, and he next appears in adult male parts, as King Ferdinand in *The Doubtful Heir*, and Orsabin in *The Goblin* (both Shirley, 1640). He signed the dedication of the Beaumont and Fletcher folio in 1647, but nothing more is known of him.

HAMMOND, PERCY (1873–1936), American dramatic critic, for fifteen years on the staff of *The New York Tribune* (later *The Herald-Tribune*), where his predecessors had been Heywood Broun, and before him William Winter. Hammond's love of the theatre dated from a visit at the age of 13 to a tent performance in Cadiz, Ohio (his birthplace), of *Little Nugget*. After leaving college he worked as a journalist and newspaper editor in Ohio, and a few years later went to Chicago, where he became drama editor of *The Evening Post*. In 1909 he was appointed dramatic critic of *The Chicago Tribune*, where his outspoken criticisms were responsible for some stormy sessions with theatre managers and owners, which resulted in his being barred from certain theatres for two years. He remained with *The Tribune*, with an interlude as war correspondent during the First World War, until 1921, when he became dramatic critic of *The New York Tribune*, remaining there until his death. Again the integrity of his criticisms prevented his immediate acceptance, but gradually his honesty, which often showed itself in frank disapproval, won him an audience. He once described dramatic criticism as 'the venom of contented rattlesnakes'. Deploring whatever seemed to him vulgar and in bad taste in the theatre, he is credited with the unequivocal dictum that 'the human knee is a joint, not an entertainment.' He was always a meticulous stylist, and after his death Brooks Atkinson wrote: 'What discouraged his colleagues was the quiet choice of untarnished words that turned his reviews into fragments of literature'.

HAMPDEN, WALTER (1879–1956), American actor, whose full name was Walter Hampden Dougherty. He made his first appearances on the stage in England, where he was for some years a member of Benson's company, and played leading parts at the Adelphi, London. In 1907 he returned to the United States, and made his début in New York (his birthplace) when he appeared with Nazimova in a season of Ibsen and other plays. Among his later successes were Manson in *The Servant in the House*, Hippolytus, and a number of Shakespearian parts which included Caliban, Oberon, Macbeth, Romeo, Hamlet, Othello, and Shylock, while in 1923 he first played in *Cyrano de Bergerac*, which he several times revived. In 1925 he took over the Colonial Theatre, which he renamed Hampden's, and appeared there in an interesting repertory of Shakespeare, Ibsen, and other plays, including *Henry V*, *The Bonds of Interest*, and *Richelieu*. He remained in his own theatre until 1930, and then toured, mainly in revivals of his previous successes. In 1939 he played the Stage Manager in *Our Town*, and in 1947 was associated with the American Repertory Theatre, playing Cardinal Wolsey in *Henry VIII*.

HAND-PROPS, see PROPS.

HAND-PUPPET, see PUNCH AND JUDY and PUPPET.

HAND-WORKED HOUSE, see ROPE HOUSE.

HANKIN, EDWARD CHARLES ST. JOHN (1869–1909), English dramatist, of whom it was said that 'his plays, shot through with a cynical pessimism, made even Ibsen seem good-humoured'. He had great talent, but in revolt against the sentimentalism of the nineteenth-century theatre he renounced all faith in human nature, attacking abuses but in no way suggesting remedies for them. Among his plays were *The Two Mr. Wetherbys* (1903); *The Return of the Prodigal* (1905), in which the central figure, a young wastrel, is supported by his father and brother in case he should damage their reputations; *The Charity that Began at Home* (1906), a bitter attack on indiscriminate benevolence; *The Cassilis Engagement* (1907), where a misalliance is avoided when the bookmaker's daughter is invited to visit her fiancé's country-house family, and breaks off her engagement because of the dullness of their lives; and *The Last of the De Mullins* (1908), which deals with the opposition of her family to the New Woman of the period, who chooses to earn her own living.

HANLON-LEES, a troupe of acrobatic actors, composed originally of the six sons of an actor named Thomas Hanlon, manager of the Theatre Royal, Manchester. They worked in combination with the famous acrobat, 'Professor' John Lees, and in 1889, after some thirty years of work, the three surviving brothers, George (1839– ?), William (1844–1923), and Edward (1854–1931), were in New York with a show called *Fantasma*. This was first produced at the Fifth Avenue Theatre in 1883, at which time William Hanlon's home at Cohasset was said to resemble a museum, so crowded was it 'with curios and the models of their many productions'. Their most famous show was possibly the *Voyage en Suisse*, presented at the Théâtre des Variétés in Paris in 1879, and at the Gaiety, London, in 1880. 'It included a bus smash, a chaotic scene on board a ship in a storm, an exploding Pullman car, a banquet transformed into a wholesale juggling party after one of the Hanlons had crashed through the ceiling on to the table, and one of the cleverest drunk scenes ever presented on the stage.' *The Times*' critic was moved to describe the drunken scene as 'so dreadfully true to nature and withal so genuinely diverting, that one gazes on it with an enthralled interest more fittingly applied to some burst of passion at the Lyceum'. An account of the performance, from which the above is quoted, is given by Dr. Thomas Walton in an article entitled 'Entortillationists' in *Life and Letters To-day* for April 1941, and an analysis of the technical trickwork of the drunken scene, by Richard Southern, in the September 1941 number of the same journal.

HANS STOCKFISCH, see ENGLISH COMEDIANS and SPENCER, JOHN.

HANSEN, CHRISTIERN (?–post 1545), early Danish dramatist (see SCANDINAVIA, 1 *a*).

HANSWURST, see AUSTRIA.

HARDWICKE, SIR CEDRIC WEBSTER (1893–1964), English actor, knighted in 1934 for his services to the stage. He made his first appearance on the stage in 1912, joining Benson's company on tour a year later. In 1914 he was at the Old Vic, but his career was interrupted by war service, and he was not seen again on the stage until 1922, when he was with the Birmingham Repertory. Here he laid the foundations of a notable career with a variety of performances, of which the most important were Churdles Ash in *The Farmer's Wife* and Caesar in *Caesar and Cleopatra*, in both of which he was subsequently seen in London. Some of his best work was done at the Malvern Festival, where he played Magnus in *The Apple Cart* (1929) and, among other parts, Edward Moulton-Barrett in *The Barretts of Wimpole Street* (1930), which he continued to play during a long run in London and on tour. Later parts were the Burglar in *Too True to be Good* (1932), Dr. Haggett in *The Late Christopher Bean* (1933), and Mikail in *Tovarich* (1935). He then went to New York and was seen in the title-role of *The Amazing Dr. Clitterhouse*, which he had played in London in 1937, and as Canon Skerritt in *Shadow and Substance* (1938). After several years in Hollywood he returned to England to tour the country in a revival of *Yellow Sands* (1945). In 1948 he joined the Old Vic company, and was seen as Sir Toby Belch, Faustus, and Gaev in *The Cherry Orchard*. Returning to New York, he continued to act and direct, and scored a notable success as Koichi Asano in *A Majority of One* (1959). He is the author of two volumes of reminiscences, *Let's Pretend* (1932) and *A Victorian in Orbit* (1961). His first wife was the actress Helena Pickard, by whom he had a son Edward, also an actor.

HARDY, ALEXANDRE (*c.* 1575–*c.* 1631), an early French dramatist, and perhaps the most important before Corneille. Very little is known of his life, and his date of birth is variously given as 1560, 1569, and 1575, the latest research inclining towards 1575. He was of good family, born in Paris, and well educated. Although there is no evidence that he was ever an actor, he was certainly attached as paid dramatist to a provincial company, that of Valleran-Lecomte, which was in Paris in the early years of the seventeenth century. He had begun to write in about 1595, and was a most prolific author, turning out between 600 and 700 plays, of which about 41 survive. They were of every conceivable type, and would serve to illustrate the catalogue of Polonius, but because of their mixture of genres they are generally classed as tragicomedies, though many of them verged on melodrama. Action rather than narrative was Hardy's aim, which he achieved with a complete disregard for the unities of time and place. With a spark of the genius of Shakespeare or Lope de Vega he might have changed the course of French dramatic literature, but his facility and easy successes told against him, and he lived just long enough to see the unities triumph. Ironically enough, Corneille's first contact with the theatre was through Hardy, whose plays he saw in Rouen. In view of Hardy's definite connexion with a professional company of actors, and of the fact that unlike most contemporary dramatists he did nothing but write plays, he may perhaps be called the first professional playwright of France. His plays were given with the old-fashioned simultaneous setting of the medieval religious drama, and called for the presentation of many different localities.

HARE [FAIRS], SIR JOHN (1844–1921), English actor-manager, knighted in 1907 for his services to the stage. He made his first appearance in Liverpool in 1864 and was first seen in London on 25 Sept. 1865 at the Prince of Wales's in *Naval Engagements*, under the management of H. J. Byron and the Bancrofts. He made a success in Robertson's *Society* (1865), and stayed at the Prince of Wales's for many years, being mainly identified with the plays of Robertson. He left to assume the management of the Court Theatre, where he produced, but did not play in, *Olivia*, and appeared in a series of successful new plays from 1875 to 1879. He then went into partnership with Kendal at the St. James's for eight years, producing and playing in Pinero's *The Money Spinner* (1881). Hare then went on to the Garrick, which W. S. Gilbert built for him, and opened on 24 Apr. 1889 with *The Profligate*. It was at this theatre, where he remained until 1895, that he made such a success as Benjamin Goldfinch in *A Pair of Spectacles*, a part with which his name is always associated. He made his first appearance in New York on 23 Dec. 1895 in *The Notorious Mrs. Ebbsmith*, and then revived several of his successes. He toured as Old Eccles in *Caste*, in which he had originally played Sam Gerridge, and made his farewell performances in 1907–8, retiring finally in 1911.

HARLEQUIN, the young lover of Columbine in the English harlequinade. His name, though not his status, derives from the Arlecchino of the *commedia dell'arte*, where he was one of the *zanni* or quick-witted, unscrupulous serving-men; and so he remained in Italy. But Marivaux turned him into a pretty simpleton, while in the harlequinade he was first a romantic magician and later a languishing, lackadaisical lover, foppishly dressed in a close-fitting suit of bright silk diamonds (derived from the patches on his original rags), sometimes with lace frill and ruffles. He retains from his origins the small black cat-faced mask, and a lath or bat of thin wood, which in English pantomimes served, when slapped lightly on the floor or wall, as a signal for the transformation scene (see ARLECCHINO and HARLEQUINADE; also No. 135).

HARLEQUINADE, as distinct from *Arlequinade*, which means a sample of Arlequin's wit, is used as the label for scenes acted by Harlequin, although *the* harlequinade refers to a special kind (see CLOWN and PANTOMIME). In Ravenscroft's *Scaramouche, a Philosopher* (1677) and Mountford's *Dr. Faustus* (1685/6), Harlequin and Scaramouche already show how the *commedia dell'arte* is translated into horseplay by the English theatre. Another change originated in restrictions upon dramatic performances at Paris fairs (see COMÉDIE-ITALIENNE). Arlequin, forbidden dialogue when acting in booths, invented a new style of comic dancing which the Patent Theatres of London billed as 'Italian Night Scenes'. Thus Harlequin became permanently a dancer, who was voiceless except in freakish pieces. His bat or slapstick was replaced by a magic wand of similar pattern; in Paris Arlequin had been armed, in parodies of fairy-tales, with the conjurer's *baguette*, and the uses of this were exploited in London when Harlequin was demonstrating the latest devices of transformation scenes. The two 'hand-props' were fused into one because the pliant bat gave an effective slap upon side-wing or stage as a signal to scene-shifters. There was a still more curious translation. At the Hôtel de Bourgogne Arlequin had the licence x enjoys in mathematics of presenting himself as any number of other personages, usually leading characters in contemporary plays which the Italians were burlesquing. In London this convention was not understood. Thurmond's *Harlequin Dr. Faustus* (1723) and *Harlequin Sheppard* (1724), which duplicated characters without burlesque, established a tradition that Harlequin must be someone other than himself. In the harlequinade-pantomimes which developed from the Italian Night Scenes it was customary for Harlequin and Columbine, as eloping lovers, to be pursued by her father (Pantaloon) and his blundering servant (at first Pierrot and then Clown) (see No. 140). There had to be an 'opening' scene for Harlequin to receive his magic wand from some immortal, and this part of the plot had to be new. Towards the end of the eighteenth century it was established that the 'opening' should tell a well-known story of persecuted lovers rescued by a good fairy and changed by her into Harlequin and Columbine. In the early years of the nineteenth century Grimaldi made Clown the chief character of the harlequinade, and so began the tendency which later diminished the love scenes into an occasional *pas de deux* by Harlequin and Columbine between bouts of horseplay—shop-lifting, with Pantaloon as a weak-witted accomplice whom the policeman caught red-handed, the buttered slide for angry shopkeepers to fall upon, the pail of paste emptied over a dandy's head, the red-hot poker frequently laid upon unsuspecting trousers, and the 'spill and pelt' when vegetables were flung in battle. Throughout Victoria's reign the 'opening' increased in length, and when fairy-tales were regularly dramatized for this purpose the older delights dwindled into a plotless epilogue known as the harlequinade because it was no longer the pantomime. Harlequin was not allowed to be the hero in the fairy-tale (who had become even before this the Principal Boy for an actress to play), although for some years there was a pretence of changing one character into the other by means of traps to lower the hero out of sight and set Harlequin on the stage at the same instant. Children of the *fin de siècle* had no interest in this hocus-pocus; the harlequinade, all links severed, was usually an advertising medium after the grand finale (though introduced mid-way in one or two pantomimes). There were still vestiges of the harlequinade in London up to and during the Second World War.

M. WILLSON DISHER†

HARLEVILLE, (JEAN-FRANÇOIS) COLLIN D' (1755–1806), French dramatist, who was intended for the law, but haunted the Paris theatres and got into debt. His family called him home, and he was over 30 before he again succeeded in escaping. Back in Paris, he was brought to the notice of Marie Antoinette by Mme Campan, who persuaded the queen to allow his first play, *L'Inconstant*, to be performed at Versailles. It was then given at the Comédie-Française (1786), and was followed by *L'Optimiste* (1788), in which d'Harleville criticizes Rousseau's *homme sensible*, showing that such a man can be happy only if he closes his eyes to facts. D'Harleville's best-known play is *Les Châteaux en Espagne* (1789), an amusing study of a man who, like Candide, thinks everything is for the best in the best of all possible worlds. Its success nearly cost d'Harleville his head, for it aroused the jealousy of Fabre d'Églantine, who had just failed with a play based on a similar idea, and d'Harleville was arrested as an enemy of the Republic. But he escaped the guillotine and lived to write several more plays, none of them as good as his earlier ones. The best is *Le Vieux célibataire* (1792), which again deals with the pitfalls that beset *l'homme sensible*. D'Harleville was a popular, though not a particularly good, dramatist, and his light-hearted comedies were much appreciated by an audience caught up in the toils of the Revolution.

HARRIGAN, EDWARD (1845–1911), American actor, manager, and dramatist, who was born in New York, but ran away from home to go on the stage, and first appeared in San Francisco. It was his partnership with Tony Hart (1855–91), a female impersonator whose real name was Anthony Cannon, which first brought him into prominence, and as the comedy team of Harrigan and Hart they established themselves in New York in 1872. Here, under their own management at various theatres, they produced many successful shows, particularly the 'Mulligan Guards' series in which Ned Harrigan played Dan Mulligan and Hart his wife Cordelia. They parted company after a fire in 1884 had destroyed their theatre, but Harrigan continued to act, appearing in revivals of a number of his own plays, such as *Old Lavender* (first produced in 1877) and *The Major* (first produced in 1881). He made his last appearance on the stage in 1908. He is credited with the composition of over eighty vaudeville sketches in ten years, on which some of his later full-length plays were based. His characters are recognizable types of old New York life, chiefly Irish- and German-Americans and Negroes, and he wrote for his own productions a number of delightful songs, set to music by David Braham, his father-in-law. Edward's son William was also an actor, making his first appearance as a child of 5 with his father in the latter's *Reilly and the Four Hundred* (1890). He was first seen in London in 1934 and twice toured Australia. Edward's daughter Nedda was on the stage and became the wife of the director and producer Joseph Logan.

HARRIGAN'S THEATRE, New York, see GARRICK THEATRE, 3.

HARRINGTON, Countess of, see FOOTE, MARIA.

HARRIS. (1) Augustus Glossop (1825–73), English theatre manager, son of an opera singer known as Madame Féron, and of the Joseph Glossop who built the Coburg Theatre (later the Old Vic). Augustus first appeared on the stage in America at the age of 8, in *Cinderella*. He went to London and played at the Princess's under Maddox, and became manager of the theatre when Charles Kean retired, opening in Sept. 1859 with *Ivy Hall*. His management lasted until Oct. 1862, and during it he introduced Fechter to London; but it is as a manager of opera and ballet that Harris is chiefly remembered. He was for twenty-seven years connected with Covent Garden, and directed opera in Madrid, Paris, Berlin, and St. Petersburg. He had a good eye for colour, and was an excellent stage-manager. His son (2) Sir Augustus (1852–96), nicknamed Druriolanus from his connexion with that famous theatre, was knighted in 1891, not for his services to the theatre, but because he was a Sheriff of the City of London when the German Emperor paid a visit there. He took over Drury Lane in the 1880s, and made a success of spectacular melodrama and elaborate pantomimes. Although his efforts in the latter direction were by some held responsible for the vulgarizing of pantomime, he had a feeling for the old harlequinade, and always made it a feature of his shows, with such clowns as Whimiscal Walker and others. He also equipped his pantomimes with lavish scenery and machines, and was the first to import into them tried favourites from the music-halls as Principal Boys, Dames, and knockabout comedians.

HARRIS, Henry (*c.* 1634–1704), English actor of the Restoration period, by some accounted superior even to Betterton. Before becoming an actor he was a painter and seal-cutter. In 1661 he joined Davenant's company (the Duke's), and played a variety of parts, including Aguecheek, Romeo, Wolsey, and Henry V (in Orrery's play). In this last part his portrait was painted by Hales, but is now lost. A pastel drawing of him as Wolsey, by Greenhill, hangs in Magdalen College, Oxford. Chappuzeau, the historian of the French theatre, saw Harris act, and was much struck by his energetic playing of the name part in Orrery's *Mustapha*, first produced in 1665. Pepys, though he thought him proud and overweeningly conceited, admired him immensely, and took great delight in his company, calling him 'a man of fine conversation'. In 1663 he was appointed Yeoman of the Revels, and in 1668, on the death of Davenant, he became joint manager of the Duke's Theatre with Betterton. He was also a shareholder in the new Duke's Theatre, built in 1670–1. He had never lost his interest in seal-cutting, and in 1670 he was appointed Chief Engraver of Seals. His preoccupation with this work, though lucrative, lost him his pre-eminence in the theatre, and his place next to Betterton was taken by Smith. Harris played his last part in 1681, a Cardinal in Crowne's *Henry VI, The First Part*. He is buried in St. Paul's, Covent Garden.

HARRISON, Richard Berry (1864–1935), an American Negro actor, son of slaves who escaped to Canada. Returning to Detroit, Harrison, who had always shown a great love for the theatre, was befriended by L. E. Behymer, and after some training in elocution, toured the Behymer and Chautauqua circuits with a repertory of Shakespearian and other recitations. He was working as a teacher of dramatics and elocution when he was persuaded to play De Lawd in *Green Pastures* (1930), in which he immediately made a great success. He appeared in the part nearly 2,000 times before his death, and in 1931 was awarded the Spingarn medal for his performance. A man of medium build, with a soft, resonant voice, he was for the greater part of his life a lecturer, teacher, and arranger of festivals for Negro schools and churches. An intensely humble man, his one great regret was that he had never appeared in any of the plays of Shakespeare, whose works he knew so well.

HARṢA, see INDIA.

HART, CHARLES (?–1683), English actor who was in Killigrew's company at the Theatre Royal with Mohun. He was on the stage as a boy, playing the important role of the Duchess in *The Cardinal* in 1641, apparently with much success. He later became a soldier, returning to the stage at the Restoration. He was the original Celadon in Dryden's *Secret Love*, in which he played opposite Nell Gwynn as Florimel. He excelled in heroic parts, particularly as Alexander in *The Rival Queens*, and when on the stage became so absorbed in his parts that it was almost impossible to distract his attention. He retired on pension when the two companies amalgamated in 1682, being perhaps unwilling to enter into competition with Betterton, and died shortly afterwards.

HART, MOSS (1904–61), American dramatist and director. He began as office boy to Augustus Pitou, theatre impresario, to whom he sold his first play, *The Beloved Bandit*. Sam Harris bought his next, *Once In a Lifetime*, which, after extensive rewriting by George S. Kaufman, was produced in 1930 with marked success. This led to a long collaboration between the two men which resulted in such successes as *Merrily We Roll Along* (1934); *You Can't Take It With You* (1936), which was awarded a Pulitzer Prize; *I'd Rather Be Right* (1937); *The Man Who Came to Dinner* (1939). Hart also wrote a number of plays on his own, of which the most interesting were *Face the Music* (1933), *Lady in the Dark* (1941), *Winged Victory* (1943), *Christopher Blake* (1946), and *Light Up The Sky* (1948). His last play was *The Climate of Eden* (1952), adapted from a novel. He produced a number of his own plays, and also, among others, *Dear Ruth* (1944), *Anniversary Waltz* (1954), *My Fair Lady* (1956, London, 1958), and *Camelot* (1960). In 1959 Hart published an autobiography which carried him up to the production of *Once in a Lifetime*. Entitled *Act One*, it was an outstanding success, and it is much to be regretted that he was not able to continue the story in a second volume. Hart was married to the actress-singer Kitty Carlisle, by whom he had a son and a daughter. ROBERT DOWNING

HART, TONY (1855–91), see HARRIGAN, EDWARD.

HART HOUSE THEATRE, a small but excellently equipped playhouse which forms part of the central students' building, Hart House, built by the Massey Foundation for the University of Toronto, Canada. The theatre owed its inception to the enthusiasm of Vincent Massey, who was Chairman of its Board of Syndics from 1919 until his appointment as Canadian High Commissioner in London in 1935. Both he and his brother Raymond, later a professional actor, acted and produced at Hart House Theatre, which was founded 'to provide an experimental art theatre for the use of the University of Toronto and the wider community'—a function which it continued to perform until well into the 1930s, under a succession of able directors. It closed on the outbreak of war in 1939, and reopened in 1947 on a new basis, having relinquished its former semi-independent status and become an integral part of the university (see also CANADA).

HARTLEY, ELIZABETH (*née* WHITE) (1751–1824), English actress of such remarkable beauty that she was the favourite model of Sir Joshua Reynolds. He used her frequently for his paintings, and three professed portraits of her are in the Mathews Collection in the Garrick Club. After her death an unknown admirer wrote of her: 'Her complexion was beautifully fair, her hair was auburn, and her eyes more like those of doves than any I remember to have seen.' As an actress, she was best in pathetic and tender parts, and her Elfrida, Jane Shore, and Rosamund were more highly praised than her Lady Macbeth, Desdemona, or Cleopatra (in *All for Love*). She was very reticent about her personal affairs, and little is known of her life. She is believed to have been born in Berrow, Somerset, where her younger sister Mary was born in 1755. Her parents were married in Wells Cathedral in 1747, her father being descended from a brother of Sir Thomas White, founder of St. John's College, Oxford. Nothing is known of her husband, and it may be that the 'marriage' was a convenient fiction, as she was buried at Woolwich, where she had retired after a successful career to live on her savings, under her maiden name, which also appears on her will. She made a first fleeting appearance in London, at the Haymarket under Foote, in 1769, but went into the provinces for several years, and in 1772 made her first appearance at Covent Garden as Jane Shore, remaining there for the rest of her career. She appears to have been good in comedy, and was the original Lady Touchwood in *The Belle's Stratagem* (1780).

HARTZENBUSCH, JUAN EUGENIO (1806–80), the son of a German cabinet-maker, born and brought up in Spain, who translated many foreign plays into Spanish and adapted for the contemporary theatre a number of old Castilian dramas. He worked for a long time without success, until the production in 1837 of his masterpiece, *Los amantes de Teruel*, a romantic drama on a traditional Spanish theme which remained in the repertory of the Madrid theatre for many years. Hartzenbusch followed up his success with many others, though none of his later plays deserves to rank with *Los amantes*. He was also the author of several comedies, and of plays of magic, of which the most successful was *Los polvos de la madre Celestina* (1841).

HARVARD. Plays were given at Harvard in its very early days, since a graduate of the college records in his diary several amateur and no doubt surreptitious performances by students between 1758 and 1761 of such plays as *Cato*, *The Roman Father*, and *The Orphan*. Later a certain amount of amateur acting was encouraged by the authorities, and the Hasty Pudding Club was formed, its productions now being mainly musicals. The Harvard Dramatic Club was started in 1908, and for many years produced only plays written by students or graduates of Harvard or Radcliffe (the women's college). It later concentrated on outstanding foreign plays. It was at Harvard that Professor Baker first gave, in 1905, his famous course of play-writing 'English 47' which later developed into the extra-mural '47 Workshop', moving to Yale in 1925. Harvard possesses one of the finest theatre collections in the world. It was started in 1903 by John Drew, who presented to the university the library of Robert W. Lowe, theatre bibliographer of London. In 1915 it was increased by the collection of Robert Gould Shaw, who became the first (honorary) curator of the collection, for which he later left a liberal endowment. It is now housed in the Houghton Library and is constantly being added to by purchase and bequest. A descriptive catalogue of the engraved portraits in the collection was issued in four volumes (1930–4) under the editorship of Mrs. Lillian A. Hall, and a comprehensive system of filing, which is continually being improved, makes the material, on which much work remains to be done, easily accessible to research workers.

HARVEY, SIR JOHN MARTIN- (1863–1944), English actor-manager, who in 1921 was knighted for his services to the theatre. He made his first appearance on the stage in 1881, and in the following year joined Irving's company at the Lyceum, where he remained for some fourteen years. During that time he made rapid strides in his profession, and was already marked out for eminence when in 1899 he inaugurated his own management of the Lyceum with an adaptation of *A Tale of Two Cities* as *The Only Way*, in which he played Sydney Carton, a part with which he was associated for the rest of his life. He had previously toured in several plays of Irving's repertory, including *The Corsican Brothers* and *The Lady of Lyons*, and had made a success as Pelléas to the Mélisande of Mrs. Patrick Campbell; but it was the production of *The Only Way* which started him on his career as a romantic actor and an outstanding manager. Among his later productions were *A Cigarette Maker's Romance* (1901), *The Breed of the Treshams* (1903), *The Burgomaster of Stilemonde* (1918), and *Everyman* (1923); *Hamlet*, which he played for the first time in 1904 and frequently revived; *Richard III*, *The Taming of the Shrew*, and *Henry V*. In 1912 he gave a magnificent performance as Oedipus Rex in Reinhardt's production of this play, and toured all over the world in a repertory of his favourite parts. Harvey, who was a handsome man with clear-cut sensitive features and a distinguished presence, was regarded by many as the lineal descendant of Irving, and his death broke the last link with the Victorian stage. His acting in *Oedipus Rex*, which Macqueen-Pope called 'savage in its stark horror and relentlessness, heart-moving in its sorrow and grief', showed to what heights he might have risen had he not been so closely identified with the somewhat melodramatic role of Sydney Carton, which he was constantly forced to revive in order to satisfy an adoring public. He was, however, a man of scholarly and scrupulous taste, and on the occasion of his seventy-fifth birthday received the degree of Hon. LL.D. from Glasgow University. He published his autobiography in 1933. He married in 1889 Angelita Helena de Silva (1869–1949), known as Nina, who was his leading lady for many years. Their daughter Muriel (1891–   ) was also on the stage.

HARWOOD, HAROLD MARSH (1874–1959), English dramatist and theatre manager. He was first a doctor, but in 1912 his first play, *Honour Thy Father*, was produced, and he deserted medicine for the theatre. With his wife, Fryniwyd Tennyson Jesse (1889–1958), a great-niece of Lord Tennyson, he wrote a number of successful plays, among them *The Mask* (1913), *Billetted* (1917), *The Pelican* (1924), and *A Pin to see the Peepshow* (1951), based on the Bywaters–Thompson case. He is best known however for *The Grain of Mustard Seed* (1920), and *The Man in Possession* (1930); the latter is frequently revived by repertory companies. From 1919 to 1932 Harwood was lessee of the Ambassadors Theatre, where he put on some of his own plays, and also such works as *The White-Headed Boy*, *If*, and *Deburau*.

HARWOOD, JOHN EDMUND (1771–1809), American actor, celebrated for his portrayal of Falstaff, which he first played at the Park Theatre, New York, in 1806, with Cooper, manager and leading man of the company, as Hotspur. Harwood was for some years at the Chestnut Street Theatre, Philadelphia, under Wignell, and was with the company when it appeared in New York in 1797, being much admired in low-comedy parts. He was engaged by Dunlap for the Park Theatre in 1803, and made his first great success there as Dennis Brulgruddery in the younger Colman's *John Bull; or, an Englishman's Fireside*. Dunlap, in his *History of the American Stage*, characterized this as 'one of the richest pieces of comic acting we have ever witnessed'. He later changed his style of acting, appearing as polished gentlemen, for which his fine presence and handsome countenance made him eminently suitable. He remained at the Park Theatre until his death, except for a short session in Philadelphia after Dunlap's bankruptcy, and the company, as well as the public, felt his loss keenly. He married the granddaughter of Benjamin Franklin.

HASENHUT, ANTON (1766–1841), see AUSTRIA.

HAUCH, Johannes Carsten (1790–1872), Danish dramatist. He succeeded Oehlenschlaeger as Professor of Aesthetics at Copenhagen University, and in his youth attacked the romantic poetry and philosophy of the school of the dramatist Ingemann. While thus exerting influence at most periods of his life through his criticism, he was at the same time an active and, at the height of his power, a highly esteemed dramatist. His admiration for Oehlenschlaeger was strong from his early years. His first plays were remarkable rather for their psychological insight than for their dramatic structure; *Bajazet* (1828), *Tiberius* (1828), and *Gregorius VII* (1829) perhaps represent the best of his first phase. He reached the height of his popularity in *Søstrene paa Kinnekullen* (1849), *Marsk Stig* (1850), and *Tycho Brahe's Ungdom* (1852).

UNA ELLIS-FERMOR†

HAUPTMANN, Gerhart (1862–1946), German dramatist, a Silesian by birth, who often used his native dialect in his plays. He first intended to become a sculptor, and attended art schools in Germany and Italy, but he was attracted by the activities of the Freie Bühne in Berlin, and his first play, *Vor Sonnenaufgang*, a grim naturalistic drama, was given by that organization in 1889. Its central character was the herald of naturalistic truth, a dogmatist and purist voicing the 'progressive' slogans of the day, who in the end stands revealed as a prig, while the full weight of the tragedy falls upon the girl whose life he has callously destroyed. Even in this first play, with all its faults and its overtones of angry revolt, were revealed Hauptmann's humanity and his compassion for the suffering, qualities which pervade all his writing.

Vor Sonnenaufgang was followed by other plays in much the same style. They included *Einsame Menschen* (1891), a study of marital incompatibility which had its echoes in his own life, since he had recently separated from his wife, whom he had married in 1885. The first period of his activity ended with *Die Weber* (1892)—a drama of social comment based on the revolt of the Silesian weavers in 1844. It has been called 'a play without a hero', since the weavers as a whole form the central character, individuals emerging and submerging as the action develops. This play, which is probably a masterpiece, was revived during the 1960s, when it seemed even more powerful than on its first production. It was broadcast in an English translation in 1962.

Hauptmann's next play, *Der Biberpelz* (1893), was a satiric comedy on Prussian officialdom and bigotry, but he was at heart a romantic, and the fantasy of *Hanneles Himmelfahrt* (also 1893) led to essays in the then-fashionable symbolic style with *Die versunkene Glocke* (1896) and other, less successful, plays. In the same year his historical drama on the Peasants' War in the time of Luther, *Florian Geyer*, was not successful, though it has since been acclaimed for its portrait of Goetz von Berlichingen, very different from Goethe's portrayal of the same man. Hauptmann continued to write for many years, with constant shifts from realism to fantasy and excursions into history. He was awarded the Nobel Prize in 1912. His last dramatic work, written under the shadow of the Second World War, was a cycle of four plays on the doom of the Atrides. These, telescoped into a long evening's playing, were staged by Piscator in 1962 as part of the Hauptmann centenary celebrations, his first production on his return to work in Berlin from the United States.

Although Hauptmann never again reached the heights of *Die Weber*, many of his plays will live through the excellence of his style, and because a keen eye, a feeling heart, and a creative imagination enabled him to endow his characters with life. In his best period, the naturalistic, he deliberately subordinated action to circumstances, and his characters are more often sinned against than sinning. In his comedies he displays human foibles with engaging benevolence—his Mutter Wolffen, in *Der Biberpelz*, has been thought worthy to rank with those plausible rogues, Falstaff and Autolycus—and in such a play as *Fuhrmann Henschel* (1898) he evokes compassion for suffering humanity without compromising with reality.

W. E. DELP, *rev.*

HAUPT- UND STAATSAKTION, see AUSTRIA.

HAUTEROCHE, Noël-Jacques le Breton de (*c.* 1616–1707), a French actor and dramatist, believed to have been of good family and certainly well educated. He was at the Marais for some time, probably joining the company there in about 1654 and leaving in 1663, when he went to the Hôtel de Bourgogne. A man of upright character, he was tall and elegant and a good actor, though Molière satirized him in *L'Impromptu de Versailles*. He succeeded Floridor as Orator of the troupe, and was one of the original members of the Comédie-Française, retiring in 1684 and being later stricken with blindness. He was the author of a number of successful comedies, reminiscent of Molière, some of which remained in the repertory until late in the nineteenth century. Among them were *Crispin médecin* (1670) and *Crispin musicien* (1674), written perhaps for Raymond Poisson, and *La Dame invisible* (1684), a rewriting of d'Ouville's adaptation of *La Dama Duende* by Calderón, given over forty years previously as *L'Esprit folet*. Many years later this play provided the actor Préville with one of his greatest successes.

HAWTREY, Sir Charles Henry (1858–1923), English actor-manager, a fine light comedian. The son of a clergyman who was a master at Eton, where he himself was educated, Hawtrey was typical of the English gentleman and man-about-town of his time. He always wore a moustache (on the only occasion when he shaved it off the play failed), he had perfect poise and sang-froid, and was, on the stage, naturalness itself. He excelled in parts where he had to tell lies, which he did with such ease and brilliance that he afforded the audience, in the secret, the most unbounded delight. He was a much better actor than his public would allow him to be, since he was so popular in what were known as 'Hawtrey' parts that he seldom had the opportunity to play anything else. But in his particular line he had no equal. He made his first appearance on the stage, under the assumed name of Bankes, at the old Prince of Wales's Theatre in 1881, and soon went into management on his own account. Among the many successful plays which he produced and appeared in were *Lord and Lady Algy*, *The Man from Blankley's*, *A Message from Mars*, and, in later life, *General John Regan* and *Ambrose Applejohn's Adventure*. In 1883 he adapted a play by Von Moser as *The Private Secretary*, and tried it out in Cambridge, playing the part of David Cattermole himself. When first brought to London (at the old Prince's Theatre, 1884) it was not a success, but Hawtrey believed in it, and transferred it to the Globe, returning to the cast himself, and replacing Tree, as the Private Secretary, by W. S. Penley. It ran until 1886, and was frequently revived, rivalling even *Charley's Aunt* in popularity.

In spite of his many successes Hawtrey was often in distress financially, for money meant little to him. Always immaculate and well dressed, he was a man of great charm and culture and a keen student of the Bible, with a text for every occasion. He was knighted in 1922 for services to his profession.

W. MACQUEEN-POPE†

HAY, IAN [JOHN HAY BEITH] (1876–1952), English playwright and novelist, who also had a distinguished military career. He was awarded the M.C. and the C.B.E. during the First World War, and at the time of his death he was a Major-General and Public Relations Officer at the War Office. He was the author of a number of official works on the British Army. His first plays were dramatizations of his light novels *Happy-Go-Lucky* (as *Tilly of Bloomsbury*, 1919), *A Safety Match* (1921), and *Housemaster* (1936). Much of his work was done in collaboration with other writers or with actors, among them Seymour Hicks (*Good Luck*, 1923), P. G. Wodehouse (*A Damsel in Distress*, 1928; *Leave it to Psmith*, 1930), Anthony Armstrong (*Orders are Orders*, 1932), Stephen King-Hall (*The Middle Watch*, 1929; *The Midshipmaid* 1931). He also dramatized Edgar Wallace's novel, *The Frog* (1936). He never attempted to sound a serious note in his plays, which often bordered on farce, but his high spirits and good humour carried the plot along without a hint of offensiveness, and added much to the gaiety of the London stage during the interval between the two world wars.

HAYE, HELEN (1874–1957), English actress, who did some of her best work at an age when most actresses have retired or are dead. She was on the stage for nearly sixty years, making her first appearance in 1898 at Hastings in *School*, and her last, as the Dowager Empress of Russia, in *Anastasia*, in 1953. After touring extensively in the provinces, part of the time in Benson's company, she made her first appearance in London in 1910, in which year she also played the Queen in *Hamlet* and Olivia in *Twelfth Night*. In 1921 she toured Canada, and she made her first appearance in New York in 1925 in *The Last of Mrs. Cheyney*. She excelled in costume and aristocratic parts, such as Lady Sneerwell in *The School for Scandal*, which she played at the Old Vic in 1935, and the Dowager Lady Monchensey in *The Family Reunion* (1939). She was for many years a teacher of acting at the Royal Academy of Dramatic Art, where her pupils included Flora Robson, Celia Johnson, Charles Laughton, and John Gielgud. She was a highly accomplished technical actress of the old school, with a superb carriage and clear audible diction.

HAYES, HELEN (1900–), American actress who was on the stage as a child, making her first appearance in Washington at the age of 5. Three years later she was seen in New York under the management of Lew Fields. Among her successful child-roles of this period were Pollyanna, in which she toured extensively, and Margaret in *Dear Brutus*. She continued her career without a break, stepping easily into adult roles from about 1920 onwards. She made a great success in the long-running *To the Ladies* (1922), and appeared at various times for the Theatre Guild as Cleopatra, Viola, and Mary, Queen of Scots. Her greatest triumph, however, was the name-part in the American production of *Victoria Regina* (1936), in which she was seen in New York and throughout the United States, being awarded the medal of the Drama League of New York for the most distinguished performance of the year. She later appeared in *Harriet* (1943), *Happy Birthday* (1946), *The Wisteria Trees* (1950), *Mrs. McThing* (1952), and *Time Remembered* (1957).

She made her first appearance in London in 1948 as the Mother in *The Glass Menagerie*, produced by John Gielgud at the Haymarket. Back in New York in 1958, she played Nora Melody in *A Touch of the Poet*, by Eugene O'Neill, at the Helen Hayes Theatre (formerly the Fulton), named after her in 1955 to celebrate her fifty years on the stage. In 1961, under U.S. State Department sponsorship, she led the Theatre Guild American Repertory Company on a tour of Europe, the Middle East, and Latin America, with *The Glass Menagerie*, *The Skin of Our Teeth*, and *The Miracle Worker*. In the summer of 1962, she and Maurice Evans appeared at the Shakespeare Festival Theatre, Stratford, Connecticut, in *Shakespeare Revisited*, a programme of scenes from the plays, which they then took on a nation-wide tour. GEORGE FREEDLEY†

HAYMARKET THEATRE, LONDON. The first theatre on this site was built in 1720 by a carpenter named John Potter, who erected a small theatre on the site of an inn called 'The King's Head'. The whole building, including decorations, fittings, scenery, and wardrobe, cost £1,500. It had no licence or Patent, it stood in what was still almost a rural district, and its first few years were uneventful. The first recorded performance there was on 29 Dec. 1720, by a French company under the patronage of John, 2nd Duke of Montagu. In 1726 it was occupied by acrobats, including Madame Violante, the rope-walker who discovered Peg Woffington. In 1729 a dancing-master, Samuel Johnson of Cheshire, put on a wild, extraordinary burlesque called *Hurlothrumbo; or, the Supernatural,* which proved most popular and ran for thirty nights. In 1730 Fielding, who had already had one farce performed at 'the Little Theatre in the Hay', as it was called, brought out his satire on heroic drama, *Tom Thumb the Great.* A year later, in *The Welsh Opera,* he openly attacked the leaders of both political parties, and caricatured the King, Queen, and Prince of Wales. He returned to the attack in 1734 with *Don Quixote in England,* which satirized the conduct of parliamentary elections. This was successful enough to warrant Fielding taking over the management of the theatre, where, as well as satires by other hands, he produced his own *Pasquin* (1736) and *The Historical Register for the Year 1736* (1737). The cumulative effect of these and other attacks resulted in the passing of the Licensing Act of 1737, which reinforced the monopoly of the Patent Theatres. Forced to close, the Haymarket became practically derelict, except for a short season by Macklin in 1744. In his company was Samuel Foote, a clever actor and playwright and a master mimic, who took over the theatre himself in 1747 and started a new phase. He invited people to attend 'The Diversions of the Morning'—tickets for which could be obtained at the coffee-houses. As his diversions included an act of *The Old Bachelor,* Drury Lane intervened, and he was forced to close after the second performance. But nobody could defeat Foote. He had set his heart on making the Haymarket a great theatre, and on rivalling Garrick as a Patent-holder. So he invited his friends to come and take a cup of chocolate with him (tickets at George's Coffee House, Temple Bar), and this time he pretended to be training young people for the stage. He made his own imitations the great feature of the entertainment, which soon became the rage. Foote carried on with variations of this scheme for some years, making the theatre prosperous, but never getting any nearer his heart's desire, a Royal Patent, until in 1766, when he was the guest of Lord Mexborough, his host and friends, amongst whom was the Duke of York, mounted him for a joke on an unmanageable horse. It threw him and broke his leg. The limb had to be amputated, and to make amends his tormentors begged the King to grant him a Patent for the Haymarket. This was done, but only for the summer months, and only for Foote's lifetime. So the little theatre finally became a Theatre Royal.

Foote sold the theatre in 1776 to the elder George Colman, who re-roofed it and carried out many improvements, after which it entered upon a second period of prosperity. All the great actors of the day played there during the summer months, when Drury Lane and Covent Garden were closed. In 1794 Colman handed over the management to his son, in which year there was a great calamity, for when on 3 Feb. their Majesties commanded a performance there—the first in the history of the Haymarket—such an enormous crowd collected that fifteen people were trampled to death and many injured.

Elliston made his début at the Haymarket in 1796, Charles Mathews the elder in 1803, Liston in 1805. That year was marked by another curious riot. The tailors of London took exception to a revival of Foote's satire *The Tailors,* in which Dowton was the star, and they attended in vast numbers, howling him down, throwing shears on the stage, and rioting outside until dispersed by the Life Guards.

In 1807 the tragedian Charles Mayne Young made a big success at this theatre, and in 1810 'Romeo' Coates, an eccentric amateur, caused the loudest laughter the theatre had ever heard by his attempted portrayal of Romeo.

Although the theatre was prosperous Colman was always in difficulties, and finally he was imprisoned for debt. The theatre closed, and David Morris, Colman's brother-in-law, who had been his partner since 1805, took over alone in 1817. In 1820 he left the old building, which became shops and a café, and built the present Haymarket, designed by Nash, a little to the south. It opened on 4 July 1821 with *The Rivals.* In 1825 the farce *Paul Pry* was produced with Farren, Mrs. Waylett, Mrs. Glover, Mme Vestris, and Liston. It ran for fourteen nights; but Morris relied mainly on revivals of old favourites with excellent casts, Farren in the lead, and Liston, always a success, in comedy. It was at the Haymarket in 1833 that the actress Julia Glover, who had previously played Hamlet at the Lyceum, appeared as Falstaff in *The Merry Wives of Windsor.*

In 1837 Benjamin Webster, who had been a member of the company since 1829, became manager. Under him the theatre was again successful. Phelps made his London début there in 1837, Barry Sullivan in 1853, and between those two dates all the great players of the day appeared there. Among many fine plays was *Masks and Faces* (1852), in which Webster and Mrs. Stirling made a success. Webster brought the theatre to a very high level. Under him it was substantially altered: gas lighting was installed (the Haymarket was the last theatre in London to give up candles), and the forestage and proscenium doors were abolished. Webster was succeeded in 1853 by

Buckstone, a magnificent comedian, whose ghost is still said to haunt the theatre he loved. Drury Lane at this time was little better than a showbooth and Covent Garden was given over to opera, so the Haymarket became the foremost playhouse in London. Buckstone gathered a fine company round him, and in five years the theatre was not closed on any night when the law allowed it to remain open. It frequently kept open until 1 a.m., people flocking in after other shows to see Wright in a farce.

In 1861 Edwin Booth made his first London appearance at the Haymarket, in which year also Edward Sothern, coming from America, was first seen in his famous part of Lord Dundreary in *Our American Cousin.* He made a further success in *David Garrick* in 1864 by the then unknown T. W. Robertson.

Buckstone retired in 1879, and in 1880 Mr. and Mrs. Bancroft took possession. They remodelled the interior of the theatre, doing away with the pit (which led to a first-night riot on 31 Jan. 1880, when they opened with a revival of *Money*), and also contained the stage entirely within the proscenium arch, thus making it the first London picture-frame stage. They ran the theatre splendidly for five years, adding to its prestige, until they retired in July 1885. In September of that year Bashford, who had been their manager, took over in partnership with Russell, but with little success, and in the autumn of 1887 the theatre passed into the hands of Herbert Beerbohm Tree. His most striking success there was *Trilby* (1895) with himself as Svengali and Dorothea Baird in the title role.

In 1896 Tree moved to his own theatre—Her Majesty's—across the way, and Frederick Harrison and Cyril Maude became managers of the Haymarket, the former attending to the business, and the latter to the artistic side. Opening on 17 Oct. 1896 with *Under the Red Robe*, they continued in association for nine years, with magnificent plays, casts, and settings. In 1905 Cyril Maude left, and Harrison carried on until his death in 1926 with the same regard for tradition, being succeeded by Horace Watson, and he in turn by his son Stuart Watson. The theatre escaped damage from enemy action during the Second World War; in 1944–5 it housed a brilliant company in repertory under John Gielgud, and in 1948 a production of *The Glass Menagerie* in which that fine American actress Helen Hayes made her London début. In 1949 *The Heiress*, with Peggy Ashcroft and Ralph Richardson, was a great success, as was *A Day By the Sea*, with a strong cast headed by John Gielgud, whose production of *The Chalk Garden*, starring Edith Evans, was seen in 1956. Ralph Richardson gave a fine performance a year later in *The Flowering Cherry*, and in 1960 Alec Guinness appeared as Ross in Rattigan's long-running play about T. E. Lawrence. A revival of *The School for Scandal* with an all-star cast, including Richardson, occupied the theatre in 1962.

W. MACQUEEN-POPE†, *rev.*

HAZLITT, WILLIAM (1778–1830), English essayist and critic, and the first of the great dramatic critics, who wrote in an age when literary criticism was flourishing at the hands of a group of masters which included Leigh Hunt, Coleridge, and Lamb. From 1813 to 1818 Hazlitt reviewed plays for the *Examiner*, the *Morning Chronicle*, the *Champion*, and *The Times*, and although this period coincided with the dearth of new dramatic writing that fell on the English theatre during the first quarter of the nineteenth century, it was his good fortune to survey a distinguished period of acting exercised chiefly in revivals of Shakespeare, on which the theatre relied during the lean years. A selection of his criticisms was collected in *A View of the English Stage* (1818). In *The Characters of Shakespeare's Plays* (1817) and *The Literature of the Age of Elizabeth* (1820) Hazlitt took the conceit out of his own age by pointing to the glories of the past: 'Pavilioned in the glittering pride of our superficial accomplishments and upstart pretensions, we fancy that everything beyond that magic circle is prejudice and error, and all before the present enlightened period but a dull and useless blank in the great map of Time'. In his zeal for bygone dramatists Hazlitt was once led to say he loved the written drama more than acted drama: but no one who has read his essay *On Actors and Acting* will be misled by that temporary reaction which at times comes to most dramatic critics, tethered to their stalls year in and year out. Whatever may have been Hazlitt's pleasure at performanaces taking place in the theatre of his own mind, there is no doubt that he also took a vivid delight in acting, and in writing about it. 'There is no class of society whom so many persons regard with affection as actors. We greet them on the stage: we like to meet them on the streets; they always recall to us pleasant associations; and we feel our gratitude excited without the uneasiness of a sense of obligation.'

But Hazlitt's affection for actors never prejudiced his opinions as a critic. His knowledge of plays enabled him to assess a player with unerring accuracy, as he assessed Macready in *Macbeth*: 'There is not a weight of superstitious terror loading the atmosphere and overhanging the stage when Mr. Macready plays the part. He has cast the cumbrous slough of Gothic tragedy, and comes out a mere modern, agitated by common means and intelligible motives.' There was no one like Hazlitt for finding the right word for the wrong action. No wonder he has been called 'the critics' critic'.

T. C. KEMP†

HEAVY FATHER — LEAD — WOMAN, see STOCK COMPANY.

HEBBEL, FRIEDRICH (1813–63), German dramatist, was the son of a poor North German mason, and the bitter struggles of his youth left their mark on his work. Obsessed by the tragedy of life, Hebbel probed ceaselessly for its cause; he found it less in the realm of guilt and human frailty than in the very process of life and progress. What the *Sturm und Drang* writers had rebelliously suspected became in his case philosophical conviction. The consciousness of his own imperious nature led him to analyse the reactions of the woman wronged. Hence a gallery of subtle portraits in *Judith* (1840), his first play, in *Maria Magdalena* (1844), a powerful middle-class tragedy which anticipates the later naturalism of Ibsen, in *Herodes und Mariamne* (1850), a fierce tragedy of jealousy, in *Gyges und sein Ring* (1856), and in the trilogy of *Die Nibelungen* (1861), his last work. Hebbel was fortunate in finding an excellent interpreter of his heroines in his wife, Christine Enghausen. W. E. DELP

HEBREW DRAMA, see JEWISH DRAMA.

HEDBERG, TOR (1862–1931), Swedish dramatist, son of Franz Hedberg, a popular dramatist of the mid-nineteenth century whose interest in the lives of the working population of Stockholm the younger man shared and continued to use in his work. Tor's earliest works were novels and stories, but he began writing plays in 1886, the best of these early efforts being perhaps *En Tvekamp* (1892). His work shows great variety, ranging from comedies like *Nattrocken* (1893) to dramatic poems—*Gerhard Grim* (1897)—and tragedies—*Johan Ulfsjerna* (1907) and *Borga gård* (1915). In 1910 he became a director of the Royal Dramatic Theatre in Stockholm, but continued a steady output of plays, of which the most notable was probably *Perseus och vidundret* (1917). Hedberg also wrote a certain amount of dramatic criticism, which was collected, together with other essays and articles, and published in 1912 (see also SCANDINAVIA, 3). UNA ELLIS-FERMOR†, *rev.*

HEDGEROW THEATRE, THE. This organization, which is based on Moylan, Pennsylvania, was founded in 1923 by Jasper Deeter, and is the oldest repertory company in the United States. It has a repertory of approximately two hundred classical and modern plays of Europe and America, based mainly on Chekhov, Shaw, and Ibsen. But it has also given the first world performances of such plays as *Cherokee Night* (1932), *Winesburg, Ohio* (1934), and *In the Summerhouse* (1951), as well as the first American performance of many foreign plays. It has been seen in New York and Philadelphia, and toured throughout the United States. Under the direction of Jasper Deeter, who still controls the organization, the Hedgerow Theatre School offers students a three-year course of study for the stage.

HEIBERG, GUNNAR (1857–1929), Norwegian dramatist, whose work shows the influence of Ibsen's later style. He was for a time director of the Norwegian theatre at Bergen, and wrote some volumes of dramatic criticism. He was the author of a number of light, satiric comedies, but his best-known works are *Balkonen* (1894) and *Kjaerlighedens Tragedie* (1904), both serious studies of contemporary social problems (see also SCANDINAVIA, 2 *a*).

HEIBERG. (1) JOHAN LUDVIG (1791–1860), Danish poet, dramatist, aesthetic critic, journalist, and theatre director. His influence on the Danish drama to some extent counteracted Oehlenschlaeger's, much as Oehlenschlaeger's had that of Holberg before him. Though he was capable of writing romantic drama, especially romantic comedy, he was strongly influenced by the French and Spanish theatres and transmitted much of their thought and ideas through his comedy, his vaudevilles, and his dramatic criticism. Heiberg was simultaneously a practising dramatist and an active critic. He defined the nature of the vaudeville, which he had himself fostered in Denmark, in his *Om Vaudevillen som Dramatisk Digtart* in 1826, and, in 1827, founded the *Kjøbenhavns flyvende Post* in which appeared those criticisms of the dramatic art of Oehlenschlaeger and his school which had a stronger influence than any similar body of work before Brandes'. Heiberg's importance as a critic in dramatic aesthetics is considerable.

The titles of a few only of his plays can be listed. His vaudevilles began in 1825 with *Kong Salomon og Jørgen Hattemager*, which was followed, between 1826 and 1836, by eight others. The last of these, *Nej*, is a masterpiece of miniature technique and fine witty vaudeville-monologue. His longer and more traditional dramatic writing extends over the whole of his life, beginning with *Dristig vovet halvt er vundet*, a romantic drama written under the influence of Calderón, and *Psyche*, a mythological play, in 1816. After the period of the principal vaudevilles come *Elverhøj* (1828), a highly popular romantic play; *Fata Morgana* (1838); *Syvsoverdag* and *En Sjael efter Døden* (both 1841); *Nøddeknakkerne* (1845), a satire on newspapers and critics and the new tendencies in politics and literature; and *Valgerda* (1849), a comedy.

UNA ELLIS-FERMOR†

Heiberg married an actress, (2) JOHANNE LUISE PÄTGES (1812–90), who made her first appearance at the Royal Theatre, Copenhagen, in 1826. She was extremely versatile, ranging from high tragedy—she was a famous Lady Macbeth—to comedy and even vaudeville. In her own generation she was supreme among Danish actresses. She gave up acting in 1864, but for the next ten years remained active as a producer. L. KATHLEEN MCFARLANE

HEIBERG, PEDER ANDREAS (1758–1841), Danish dramatist (see SCANDINAVIA, 1 *a*).

HEIJERMANS, HERMAN (1864–1924), see NETHERLANDS, THE.

HEINRICH JULIUS, DUKE OF BRUNSWICK (1564–1613), noble playwright whose favourite theme was matrimonial discord, usually with the onus on the female side, unless the husband, through sheer stupidity, deserved his punishment. The Duke, who succeeded to his title in 1589, was much attracted to the English

Comedians, who may have visited his capital of Wolfenbüttel some time early in the 1590s, and a company of English actors, under Sackville, was definitely attached to the royal household from 1596 intermittently until the Duke's death. His plays show considerable English influence. The first of them, *Susanna* (*c.* 1590), with its large cast, its wailings, and the manifold activities of the fool Jan Clant or Bouschet (from the English Clown and Posset respectively), marks the complete change which has taken place in the approach to religious subjects since Rebhun. In all the Duke's plays the fool is endowed with sound common sense, and talks humorously in Low German. One of his most successful comedies was *Vincentius Ladislaus* (1594), in which the braggart soldier of the *commedia dell'arte* is tripped up by the fool.

HELEN HAYES THEATRE, New York, see FULTON THEATRE.

HELLMAN, Lillian (1905–), American dramatist, born in New Orleans, but educated at Columbia and New York universities. She entered the theatre as a press agent and as a play-reader for the Broadway producer Herman Shumlin. Her first play, *The Children's Hour* (1934), aroused extraordinary interest with its story of a neurotic schoolgirl's defamation of her teachers, whom she accuses of lesbianism, and compelled attention on both psychological and social levels. Miss Hellman failed with her next play, *Days to Come* (1936), a penetrative if also unwieldy study of a labour strike, but fulfilled the promise of her début with *The Little Foxes* (1939) and *Watch on the Rhine* (1941). The former exposed a predatory family of industrial entrepreneurs, comparable to the little foxes that destroy the vineyards. *Watch on the Rhine* dramatized the mortal struggle of an anti-Nazi leader against his betrayer, a Rumanian aristocrat living with the hero's American mother-in-law near Washington, and implied that America could not long remain neutral in the struggle against Fascism. *The Searching Wind* (1944), an incompletely integrated chronicle, reviewed the errors of an American career diplomat whose moral fibre was no stronger in his private life than in his public policy of appeasement. In *Another Part of the Forest* (1946) Miss Hellman returned to the antecedent history of her 'little foxes' with a Jonsonian picaresque comedy of villains outsmarting one another. *The Autumn Garden* (1951) was a powerful group study in frustration, and *Toys in the Attic* (1960) a searing study of failure and possessiveness. It was later seen in London, but with less success than on Broadway. Miss Hellman's preoccupation with the problem of evil drew accusations of misanthropy, and her tightly knit plots caused her to be charged with the outmoded technique of the 'well-made' play of Sardou. Her work is, nevertheless, invigorated by sharp characterization and by respect for active idealism. JOHN GASSNER†

HELPMANN, Robert Murray (1909–), ballet dancer and choreographer who has successfully achieved the transition to actor and play producer, bringing to both careers the same meticulous attention to detail and artistic integrity. Born in Australia, he made his first professional appearance at Sydney, as a dancer, in 1927. In 1933 he joined the Vic-Wells Ballet, and was principal dancer of the Sadler's Wells Ballet from its inception till 1950, though he subsequently made appearances as guest-artist in London and abroad. He became well known as a choreographer, having been responsible for such important ballets as 'Comus', 'Hamlet', 'Miracle in the Gorbals', and 'Adam Zero', in which he also danced. In 1937 he made his first appearance in a leading acting role, as an impressive Oberon at the Old Vic. In 1944 he was seen as Hamlet, again with the Old Vic, and he later appeared with that company in such diverse parts as Shylock, Petruchio, Angelo, Richard III, and Launcelot Gobbo. He also played Shylock and Hamlet, as well as King John, during the Stratford-upon-Avon season of 1948. Among other parts in which he has appeared are Flamineo in *The White Devil*, the Doctor in *The Millionairess*, Georges de Valera in *Nekrassov*, and Sebastien in *Nude With Violin*. He devised the choreography for a number of productions in London and elsewhere, and directed *Murder in the Cathedral*, *The Tempest*, *Antony and Cleopatra*, and *Romeo and Juliet* for the Old Vic. He also directed *The Marriage-Go-Round* in London (1959) and *Duel of Angels* in New York (1960). He was knighted in 1968 and is now director, with Peggy van Praagh, of the Australian Ballet, which visited London in 1965.

HELTAI, Jenő (1871–1957), Hungarian dramatist, well known for his light comedies, which show the gayer side of life in Budapest. One of them, *Jó Üzlet*, has been translated into English as *A Good Bargain*, while a verse-play, *A Néma Levente*, given in Budapest in 1936, was translated into verse by Humbert Wolfe, and given in London at the St. James's Theatre in 1937 as *The Silent Knight*.

HEMINGE (Heminges, Hemmings), John (1556–1630), English actor, was in Burbage's company, and probably the first player of Falstaff. When this company became the King's Men, he probably acted as their business manager. He held considerable shares in the Globe and Blackfriars playhouses. He lived in the parish of St. Mary, Aldermanbury, near the theatre in Shoreditch. In his will he describes himself as 'citizen and grocer', but his wife probably ran the business while he was off play-acting. To him, with Condell, we owe the printing of the Shakespeare Folio. Fault has been found with these first editors for their arbitrary division of the plays into five acts, regardless of sense, on the classic model of Ben Jonson, and for many sins of omission and commission which have given headaches to literary historians and caused much ink to flow. But since Shakespeare himself made no efforts to get his plays printed, they would probably have been lost entirely or survived only in mutilated fragments—for no complete Shakespeare manuscript has ever come to light—had it not been for the labour of love undertaken by his friends and fellow-actors (see also CONDELL).

HENDERSON, JOHN (1747–85), English actor whose early passion for the stage was fostered by Garrick, who had recently retired, and to whose literary gatherings in Beckett's bookshop the young Henderson, at that time apprenticed to a jeweller and silversmith, was a frequent visitor. He got an introduction to Garrick's brother George at Drury Lane when he was 21, but was refused on account of his weak voice and unprepossessing appearance, due in great part to his extreme poverty. However, he was determined to act, and after several amateur appearances, in which he imitated Garrick to the life, the latter gave him a letter of recommendation to Palmer at Bath, where he was engaged at a guinea a week. He made his first appearance on 6 Oct. 1772 as Hamlet, and was successful. Several years of hard work followed, during which he was painted by Gainsborough as Macbeth, a portrait which shows him to be a stoutly built, fair-haired man with a strong, determined face —not handsome, but commanding. In 1777 his years of labour were justified, as he was engaged by Colman to appear at the Haymarket in London, which he did on 11 June as Shylock. His success was instantaneous, and even Macklin, that great player of Shylock, congratulated him. He returned to Bath, but in the following year Sheridan wanted him for Drury Lane, which had three times shut its doors to him, and to induce Palmer to release him gave the latter the sole right of playing *The School for Scandal* in Bath. Henderson stayed at Drury Lane for two years, going from there to Covent Garden, and never again left London except on tour. One of his greatest parts was Falstaff. He died young, before his fortieth birthday, of overwork and early privation, and was buried in Westminster Abbey near Garrick. It was his rendering of *John Gilpin* at a series of readings in the Freemasons' Hall in 1785 that first launched Cowper's poem on its successful career. W. MACQUEEN-POPE†

HENRY, JOHN (1738–94), an actor who was for many years one of the leading men of the American Company, which he joined in 1767 at the John Street Theatre, New York, under Douglass. He was an Irishman, and had already appeared in Dublin and London before he sailed for the New World. On the return of the American Company from the West Indies, where they took refuge during the War of Independence, Henry assumed the management, jointly with the younger Hallam. He accepted and played in Dunlap's first play, and was responsible in 1792 for the importation from England of that excellent actor John Hodgkinson, by whom he was soon forced into the background, retiring from management and acting shortly before his death. He was twice married. His first wife, an actress named Storer, was lost at sea before the company came back from the West Indies, and was never seen in New York. After living for some time with her sister, Ann or Nancy (1749–1816) (later Mrs. Hogg), by whom he had a child, Henry married a younger member of the Storer family, Maria (*c.* 1760–95). She was first on the stage as a child, and later became a member of the American Company, where her imperious temper caused much trouble. She retired from the theatre at the same time as her husband, and went mad after his sudden death on board ship, surviving him by only a year. Yet another Storer, Fanny, was also an actress, though not a very remarkable one. Later, as Mrs. Mechtler, she gave concerts in New York.

HENRY MILLER'S THEATRE, NEW YORK, on 43rd Street east of Broadway. This opened on 1 Apr. 1918. Its first successes were Mrs. Fiske in *Mis' Nelly of N'Orleans* (1919) and Blanche Bates and Henry Miller in *The Famous Mrs. Fair* (1920). A succession of moderate successes, with strong casts, followed, and in 1922 Mme Simone gave a short season of French plays. Soon after this the theatre embarked on the production of the sophisticated drama with which its name is now connected, including *The Vortex* (1925). In 1929 came the overwhelming success of *Journey's End*, and in 1932 Pauline Lord in *The Late Christopher Bean*. The Theatre Guild produced *Days Without End* (1934), destined to be O'Neill's last play for many years, and in 1936 came a revival of *The Country Wife*, with Ruth Gordon, and settings and costumes by Oliver Messel. *French Without Tears* followed, but failed to repeat its London success, and in 1938 *Our Town* opened on 4 Feb., subsequently moving to the Morosco for a long run. In 1944 the theatre broke its own records with the 680 performances of *Dear Ruth*. Other successful productions have been *The Cocktail Party* (1950), *Witness for the Prosecution* (1954), *The Andersonville Trial* (1959), and the Royal Shakespeare Theatre's recital, *The Hollow Crown* (1963). GEORGE FREEDLEY†

HENSEL, SOPHIE FRIEDERIKE (*née* Sparmann) (1738–89), a German actress, and one of Ackermann's company at the Hamburg National Theatre. She had an adventurous girlhood, and at 17 married a comedian, from whom she later separated to live a dissipated life. Built on generous lines, with a face and figure of majestic beauty, she was much admired, and filled admirably the roles of noble heroines in German classical drama. Even Lessing, who detested her, had to admit that she was, in her own line, a fine actress, and Schröder too thought well of her. In private life she was a malicious and intriguing character, who caused trouble wherever she went, and was undoubtedly one of the factors which brought about the downfall of the Hamburg enterprise. She then married Abel Seyler, who had for a short time been one of the managers of the theatre, and set out on tour, taking Ekhof with her. Her jealousy of his acting was so profound, however, that when he took over the leadership of the company she left and went to Vienna. Returning to Germany, she found herself at Mannheim, and later at Hamburg, confronted with her bitterest enemy, the wife of the actor-playwright Brandes, against whom she continued to intrigue until her death. She was known and feared all over Germany, but the infatuated Seyler remained faithful to her, though she was a constant source of anxiety and financial failure to him, and it was only after her death that he retired to the peace of Schröder's country estate.

HENSLOWE, PHILIP (?–1616), important in the history of the Elizabethan stage as being the owner of the Rose, Fortune, and Hope playhouses. He may also have been the lessee of Whitefriars. He married the wealthy widow of a dyer to whom he had been apprenticed, and his stepdaughter Joan married Alleyn, the great actor and rival of Burbage. Henslowe was a shrewd business man, and gradually amassed a good deal of property in London, in addition to the playhouses. On his death his papers (with other property) passed to Alleyn, and are now housed in Dulwich College. Among them is his diary, a basic document for the study of Elizabethan theatre organization. In it he entered accounts for his various theatres, loans made to actors, payments made to dramatists, and various private memoranda. Unlike other outstanding theatre men of this period, Henslowe was not an actor. Greg, to whom we owe most of our knowledge of him, calls him the 'banker' of the company. He did not take a fixed rent for his playhouses, but a sum allotted from the daily takings, originally half the proceeds of the galleries and later the whole. He appears to have paid all bills, including the purchase of plays, and of clothes and properties, for the companies acting in the theatre for the time being. These varied from time to time, but the Admiral's Men were at the Rose from 1594 to 1600, and when they moved to the Fortune were succeeded by Lord Worcester's Men. The upkeep of the structure, and the licensing fees paid to the Master of the Revels, appear to have been Henslowe's only liabilities as landlord, and it follows that the players were constantly in his debt. Since some of the individual actors were contracted to Henslowe personally, and not, as was usually the case in Elizabethan companies, to their fellow actors, and as he paid the dramatists for their work, it follows that he had a large say in the policy of the company. That his relations with his actors were not always cordial is proved by a document headed *Articles of Grieuance, and Articles of Oppression, against Mr. Hinchlowe*, drawn up in 1615, in which he is accused of embezzling their money and unlawfully retaining their property. He is even accused of having bribed Nathan Field, who was acting as the company's representative, to testify in his favour. There is no note of how the controversy ended, and apart from this document there is no evidence of Henslowe's having done more than keep the actors in his debt in order to retain his hold over them. There can be no doubt that such an arrangement was not so good, nor did it make for such stability, as that in force in the Burbages' company, where the actors were joint owners of their own theatre, and responsible to each other and not to any 'outside capitalist', as Chambers calls Henslowe.

HENSON, LESLIE (1891–1957), English actor and producer, who, after a short business career, made his first appearance in a concert party at Bath in 1910. His early career was mainly in musical comedy, and he appeared in *To-Night's the Night*, based on *The Pink Dominos*, with music by Paul Rubens, both in New York in 1914 and in London in 1915 with equal success. He returned to the stage, after serving in the army during the First World War, in *Kissing Time* (1919), and was later much appreciated in *Funny Face* (1928) and in the farces *It's a Boy* (1930) and *It's a Girl* (1931). After the death of Sid Field he appeared in the title-role of *Harvey* (1950), and was also an engagingly amusing Pepys in the musical version of *And So To Bed* (1951). He was a stimulating producer, and in association with Tom Walls was responsible for *Tons of Money* (1922) and *A Cuckoo in the Nest* (1925). During the Second World War he toured continuously, playing to the troops in every possible and impossible place. A generous and warm-hearted man, he did a great deal for theatrical charities, and for nearly twenty years was President of the Royal General Theatrical Fund. In 1926 he published a volume of reminiscences as *My Laugh Story*. He appeared several times in pantomime and at the time of his death was rehearsing as Widow Twankey for a pantomime at Windsor. He had a most amusing india-rubber face, and could keep a theatre in gales of laughter without saying a word—a true comic.

HERALD SQUARE THEATRE, NEW YORK, see COLOSSEUM THEATRE.

HERBERT, SIR HENRY (1596–1673), Master of the Revels from 1623, in which capacity he controlled the actors and licensed the theatres. He was also responsible for the censorship of plays, which he read personally, and for collecting the fees due for each performance of licensed drama at the official playhouses. The extant passages taken from the lost manuscript of his office book, which he kept from 1622 to 1642, have been collected in Professor J. Q. Adams's *Dramatic Records of Sir Henry Herbert* (1917), and form a precious deposit of material on the stage history of the period. At the Restoration Sir Henry made strenuous efforts to recover the powers of his office, and issued licences to William Beeston for the Cockpit and also to Mohun for a company at the Red Bull; but he was routed by the royal monopoly granted to Killigrew and Davenant, and although he kept up a continual skirmishing with them until his death, his importance in stage matters was constantly whittled away until he was left with nothing but a token payment from the players and no real authority over them. Killigrew, who was more amenable to Sir Henry's attempts at discipline than Davenant, inherited his title of Master of the Revels on his death, and later passed it on to his son, but the office was of no importance, and, with the Licensing Act of 1737, its main function, the censorship of plays, passed to the Lord Chamberlain, where it still remains (see DRAMATIC CENSORSHIP).

HERCZEG, FERENC (1863–1954), one of Hungary's leading dramatists, author of many excellent comedies and satires on contemporary life, and also of historical dramas on subjects taken from Hungarian history.

HER MAJESTY'S THEATRE, LONDON. 1. This stood on the site of Vanbrugh's opera-house in the Haymarket (see QUEEN'S THEATRE, 1). It opened on 26 Mar. 1791 as the King's, and was renamed on the accession of Queen Victoria in 1837. It had a somewhat chequered career at first but as the Italian Opera House it became famous during the period 1830–50 for its productions of opera with international stars, and also for its association with the Romantic Ballet. Jenny Lind made her début here on 4 May 1847; 'Fidelio' was given its first English performance in 1851. It was burnt down in Dec. 1867, and although it was reopened two years later it never regained its former prosperity. In spite of such isolated events as the first complete performance of the Ring cycle in England in 1882, and seasons by Sarah Bernhardt in 1886 and 1890, it was often dark or used for non-theatrical activities. In 1890 it closed and a year later it was demolished, only the Royal Opera Arcade being left standing.

2. A new theatre was built on the site by Tree, who always referred to it, with some justification, as 'my beautiful theatre'. He had always wanted his own playhouse, and this was made possible by the success of *Trilby*, which provided the money necessary for the new building. It opened on 19 Apr. 1897 with *The Seats of the Mighty*, by Gilbert Parker, which ran until the following June, when Tree revived several of his former successes, including *Trilby*. Then followed a succession of excellent productions, including Shakespeare and new plays, which formed a distinguished repertory. Tree disliked long runs, and referred to his production of *Henry VIII* (see No. 76), which ran for nine months, as 'an obstinate success'. His rooms in the dome of the theatre were a centre for artistic London, and it was there that in 1904 Tree instituted a drama school which eventually moved to other premises to become the Royal Academy of Dramatic Art. The theatre was renamed His Majesty's on the accession of Edward VII in 1901, and kept this name until the accession of Elizabeth II, when it again became Her Majesty's. It was while managing this theatre that Tree received a knighthood, in 1909. He played there for the last time in 1915, dying two years later. With his departure the theatre lost that eminence which he had given it, but in 1916 it saw the phenomenal run of *Chu-Chin-Chow*. Later successes were *Cairo* (1921), *Hassan* (1923) with incidental music by Delius, *Bitter Sweet* (1929) with Peggy Wood, *The Good Companions* (1931), *The Dubarry* (1932) with Anny Ahlers, *Henry IV, Part I* (1935) with George Robey as Falstaff, *The Happy Hypocrite* (1936). Jack Hylton later took over the theatre, and was responsible for a number of interesting productions there, including *Anna Lucasta* (1947). In 1954 *The Tea House of the August Moon* began its long run, and four years later *West Side Story*, which began a new chapter in the history of American musicals, opened and ran until June 1961. After that a long run was achieved by a transfer from the Mermaid of *Lock Up Your Daughters* (1962).

W. MACQUEEN-POPE †, *rev.*

HERMANN, DAVID (1876–1930), see JEWISH DRAMA, 6, and VILNA TROUPE.

HERNÁNDEZ, ANTONIO ACEVEDO Y, see SOUTH AMERICA, 1.

HERNE, JAMES A. (originally AHEARN) (1839–1901), American actor and dramatist, who made his first appearance on the stage in 1859, and was later leading man for Lucille Western, his sister-in-law. He was for some time stage manager of Maguire's New Theatre in San Francisco, where he appeared in a number of adaptations of Dickens's novels, which later had a great influence on his own writing. He was leading man of the Baldwin Theatre in the same town, where he worked with Belasco, collaborating with him in a number of plays, including *Hearts of Oak* (see BELASCO). This was purely melodrama, but Herne's later works show a deflexion towards realism and sobriety, mainly under the influence of his wife, Katharine Corcoran (1857–1943), a fine actress who played most of his heroines. His first important play was the sombre drama of marital infidelity, *Margaret Fleming* (1890), which was at first too far ahead of its time to appeal to the public, in spite of the fine acting of Mrs. Herne in the title-role. It was revived in 1894, in 1907, with Herne's daughter Chrystal as Margaret Fleming, and in 1915. It was followed by *Shore Acres* (1892), which had a hard struggle to establish itself, but ended by being one of the most popular plays of the day, mainly through the character of Uncle Nathaniel Berry. *The Reverend Griffith Davenport* (1899), a tale of the Civil War of which no complete copy remains, and *Sag Harbor* (1900), a rewriting of the old *Hearts of Oak*, in which Herne was acting when he died, complete the number of his works. They have little literary value, but, particularly in *Margaret Fleming*, they mark a great advance on the American plays of their day, which led to the best of them being unsuccessful at first.

This was due mainly to the realistic treatment of even the most conventional types, like Uncle Nat, and to the simplicity and sincerity with which Herne approached his subjects.

HERODAS (or HERONDAS) (*c.* 300–250 B.C.), Greek dramatist, a writer of semi-dramatic mimes, nine of which were discovered, whole or in part, on an Egyptian papyrus in 1891. They represent very vividly, and with some coarseness, scenes from ordinary life (see also MIME, 1 *b*).

HEROIC DRAMA, a type of play in rhymed couplets, in vogue in England from 1664 to 1678. Influenced by the French classical forms, and dealing with the theme of 'love and honour' from Spain's Golden Age, it found its greatest exponent in Dryden, though it could be stretched to include Davenant and some earlier writers. The heroic play was satirized by Buckingham in *The Rehearsal* (1672).

HERON, MATILDA AGNES (1830–77), American actress, who made her début in Philadelphia in 1851, and after a brief visit to New York went to California, where she made an immediate success in such parts as Juliet, Mrs. Haller, Juliana in *The Honeymoon*, and Bianca in *Fazio*. It was, however, as Marguerite Gautier that she achieved widest recognition, though she was not the first to play the part in America, Jean Davenport having forestalled her with an innocuous adaptation entitled *Camille; or, the Fate of a Coquette*. In 1855 Matilda Heron, while on a visit to Paris, saw *La Dame aux camélias* in its original form, made a fairly accurate version of it herself, and played it all over the United States. It was particularly successful in New York, and the author-actress made a fortune out of it, most of which she spent or gave away. She later played Medea, and Nancy in a dramatization of *Oliver Twist*, and was seen in several of her own plays. It was said of her that in a few good parts she displayed a 'strange wild beauty and elemental passion, and much influenced the actresses of her time'. Among those whom she trained for the stage was her daughter by her second marriage, Hélène Stoepel, known as Bijou Heron, who married Henry Miller.

HERRERA, ERNESTO (1887–1917), see SOUTH AMERICA, 1.

HERTZ, HENRIK (1798–1870), a Danish dramatist of Jewish parentage, who is chiefly remembered for his highly popular *Kong Renés Datter*, for his comedies, his national, romantic, and historical dramas, and for his dramatic criticism in defence of and collaboration with J. L. Heiberg. In his early work he reverts to Holberg, against the tendencies of the 1820s, and throughout his life some of his most popular work was character-comedy after the tradition of French drama. In all, he wrote some twenty-five plays, of which the best known are: *Herr Burchardt og hans Familie* (1827); *Amor's Geinstreger* (1830); a number of vaudevilles produced between 1827 and 1835; *Sparekassen* (1836), a popular and highly skilful comedy; *Svend Dyrings Hus* (1837), a romantic tragedy; the lyrical drama *Kong Renés Datter* (1843), seen in London in 1908; *Ninon* (1848); *Den Ingste* (1854); *En Kurmethode* (1861), and *Tre Dage i Padua* (1869), his last play. UNA ELLIS-FERMOR†

HERVIEU, PAUL (1857–1915), French dramatist, whose plays resemble those of Brieux in their preoccupation with social problems, but are free from the somewhat didactic tendencies of the latter dramatist. Realizing that the sorrows of human life, though no longer expressed in the grandeur of classic verse, are as poignant and immutable as ever, he sought to introduce into a modern setting the ancient elements of tragedy. He was concerned not so much with the fugitive inequalities of social custom as with the unchangeable vices of individuals—egotism, vanity, indifference, deceit. He was constantly preoccupied with the problems of divorce and the child, as in *Les Tenailles* (1895) and *La Loi de l'homme* (1897), usually considered his best plays, and in *Le Dédale* (1903) and *Connais-toi* (1909). One of his most interesting plays is *Les Paroles restent* (1892), which traces the destructive course of a slanderous rumour which ruins several lives, while his *La Course du flambeau* (1901) is devoted to the perennial problem of maternal love and filial ingratitude.

HEVESI, DR. SÁNDOR (1873–1939), Hungarian producer and theatre manager, who in 1904 founded his own company, Thalia, and produced a number of modern Hungarian plays and translations of foreign dramatists. He was much influenced by the theories of Gordon Craig, which he endeavoured to put into effect when he was appointed director of the State Theatre in Budapest.

HEWES, HENRY (1917–), American drama critic who in 1952 became associate dramatic critic of the *Saturday Review of Literature* in New York, and in 1955 the senior drama critic of that publication, a position he currently holds. His many theatre activities include adapting *La Belle Aventure* of Caillavet, de Flers, and Rey, which was produced in 1954 at the Saville Theatre, London, under the title of *Accounting for Love*, and also the adaptation and direction of an experimental version of *Hamlet* produced at the Theatre de Lys in New York in 1957 with Siobhan McKenna. He has been active in the Greater New York Chapter of the American National Theatre and Academy, serving as executive director from 1953 to 1958, as well as serving as executive secretary of the Board of Standards and Planning for the Living Theatre in New York since 1956. From 1958 to 1961 he edited the Off-Broadway section of the Best Plays Series, and, with the edition for 1961–2, succeeded Louis Kronenberger as over-all editor of the series. He is a vital and respected figure in the contemporary American theatre scene.

HEYWOOD, John (*c.* 1497–1580), early English dramatist, author of a number of interludes which mark the transition from the medieval Morality and Mystery plays to the comedy of the Elizabethans. Heywood, who was an accomplished singer and player of the virginals, much in favour at Court, married Elizabeth Rastell, niece of Sir Thomas More, and there is little reason to doubt that he owed much to the influence of More, whose love and encouragement of acting are well known. His most famous play is *The Playe called the foure P.P.; a newe and a very mery enterlude of a palmer, a pardoner, a potycary, a pedler*, each of whom tries to outdo the others in lying. The palmer wins when he says that in all his travels he never yet knew one woman out of patience. This was given in about 1520, probably at Court, and was published some twenty years later by his brother-in-law, William Rastell, as were *The Play of the Wether* and *The Play of Love* (both 1533). *The Dialogue of Wit and Folly*, which probably dates from the same year, remained in manuscript until 1846, when it was issued by the Percy Reprint Society. Two further interludes are sometimes attributed to Heywood, *The Pardoner and the Frere* and *Johan Johan*, which were both published anonymously by Rastell in 1533, while A. W. Pollard considers him a likely author of *Thersites*, also attributed to Udall. Heywood left England on the accession of Elizabeth and died at Malines.

HEYWOOD, Thomas (*c.* 1570–1641), English actor and dramatist, who may be connected with the older dramatist, John Heywood (see above), though there is no certain proof of this. Thomas Heywood worked for Henslowe, and was a member both of the Admiral's Men and of Worcester's until their dissolution in 1619 on the death of Queen Anne, to whose patronage Worcester's Men had been transferred. After a period of retirement, during which he wrote a good deal of non-dramatic prose and poetry, including the *Apology for Actors* (pub. 1612) and a lost and unfinished collection of *Lives of All the Poets*, Heywood returned to the theatre, and produced a number of new plays and revivals of his older ones, as well as pageants for the Lord Mayor's Show for many years. He says himself that he had a hand in 220 plays, most of which are lost. He wrote entirely for the moment, and did not trouble to print his plays until driven to it by piracy and, possibly, the growth of a demand for plays in print for reading. Of those that survive the best is undoubtedly *A Woman Killed with Kindness* (1603), a domestic tragedy whose excellence may almost entitle it to rank with some of Shakespeare's work. Other plays by Heywood are *The Fair Maid of the West*, *The English Traveller*, *The Wise Woman of Hogsdon*, and *The Rape of Lucrece*, all of which appear in a volume in the Mermaid Series edited by Verity in 1888. Heywood's *Four Prentices of London* (*c.* 1600), a somewhat absurd romantic drama, was satirized by Beaumont in his *Knight of the Burning Pestle*. In spite of his many excellences Heywood undoubtedly contributed to the decadence of the later Elizabethan drama, particularly by the almost complete separation between his main- and sub-plots and by the weakness of his poetic diction. His industry was applied to many types of drama, including the chronicle play *Edward IV* and the rambling *If You Know Not Me, You Know Nobody* (1605), a two-part survey of the 'Troubles of Queen Elizabeth'; but it was in the drama of everyday life that he was most successful.

HIÄRNE, Urban (1641–1724), early Swedish dramatist, author of a School Drama, *Rosimunda* (1665).

HICKS, Sir (Edward) Seymour (1871–1949), English actor-manager and dramatist, who has been described as the 'Admirable Crichton' of the British stage. He was the author of a number of plays which included *Bluebell in Fairyland*, *The Gay Gordons*, and *Sleeping Partners*, and part-author of others, including adaptations from French drama such as *The Man in Dress Clothes*. With Charles Brookfield he produced the first revue seen in London, *Under the Clock*. He published several volumes of reminiscences, and was the first actor to take a party of entertainers to France in the First World War and again in the Second. In 1931 he received the Legion of Honour from the French Government in recognition of his services to French drama in London, and he was knighted in 1935. He began his career in 1887 by walking-on at the Grand, Islington, and was for a long time with the Kendals, both in England and America. In the course of his long and varied life he topped the bill in the music-halls, and appeared with equal success in musical comedy and straight plays. Among the latter will be remembered his performances in *Sleeping Partners*—a *tour de force* of silent acting—and in *Quality Street*. He married Ellaline Terriss, who appeared with him in many of his plays (see terriss, 2), and together they formed an ideal couple, both on and off stage.

w. macqueen-pope†

For Hicks Theatre see globe (3).

HILAROTRAGOEDIA, see fabula, 5.

HILL, Aaron (1685–1750), English playwright, satirized by Pope in the *Dunciad*, whose plays are now forgotten but who in his own day had a certain success. He is now chiefly remembered for his adaptations of three of Voltaire's plays (*Zaïre*, *Alzire*, and *Mérope*) and for his connexion with Handel, whose first London opera 'Rinaldo' was produced at the Haymarket while Hill was briefly in management there. He also had a hand in the libretto. Hill's own plays include *Elfrid* (1710, later rewritten as *Athelwold*, 1731), *The Fatal Vision* (1716), *The Fatal Extravagance* (1721), all tragedies in the style of the time, and a successful farce, *The Walking Statue; or, the Devil in the Wine Cellar*, first produced in 1710 and frequently revived up to 1745. Although Hill was later stigmatized as 'a solemn prig' and 'an old windbag', he had many good qualities. He was generous towards his friends, giving them the proceeds of many of his plays, and towards the actors, allowing them the profits on his benefit night. A man of a restless and inventive turn of mind—he was constantly involved in commercial enterprises which finally disposed of the handsome fortune brought him by his wife—he left in his letters and journals a good deal of entertaining information about the theatre of his time.

HILL, JENNY (1851–96), early music-hall performer, the daughter of a Marylebone cab-driver. She first worked in a North Country public-house, where, in the intervals of serving the beer, she amused the customers by her songs and dances. She married an acrobat, who nearly killed her by trying to teach her his trade, and who then deserted her, leaving her with a child to support. She went to London and, after heartbreaking delays and poverty, got an audition at the Pavilion, where she was an immediate success. Billed as 'The Vital Spark', she sang and danced and did male impersonations, eventually earning enough to buy a large estate in Streatham, where she gave extravagant parties, and where she eventually retired, broken in health, to lead the life of an invalid until her death at the early age of 44.

HINDU DRAMA, see INDIA, 1.

HIPPODROME, LONDON. This opened on 15 Jan. 1900 as a circus with a large water-tank which was used for aquatic spectacles. It later became a music-hall, and in 1909 was reconstructed internally, the circus arena being covered by stalls. Ballet and variety were seen there, and in Dec. 1912 Albert de Courville began a series of successful revues which lasted until 1925. This was followed by an equally successful run of musical comedies, among them *Sunny* (1926), *Hit the Deck* (1927), *Mr. Cinders* (1929), and *Please, Teacher* (1935). Among the stars of this period were Jack Buchanan, Elsie Randolph, Binnie Hale, Bobby Howes, and Cicely Courtneidge. Among later productions were the revue *The Fleet's Lit Up* (1938), Novello's musical comedy *Perchance to Dream* (1945), and the play *The Caine Mutiny Court Martial* (1956). Later, after complete interior reconstruction once more, the building opened on 11 Sept. 1958 as a combined restaurant and cabaret, The Talk of the Town, and was no longer used as a theatre. W. MACQUEEN-POPE†, *rev.*

HIPPODROME THEATRE, NEW YORK. This theatre, the largest in America, seating 6,600 people, was situated on 6th Avenue between 43rd and 44th Streets. It opened on 12 Apr. 1905 with a lavish spectacle entitled *A Yankie Circus on Mars*, and a year later was taken over by the Shuberts, who were succeeded in management by Dillingham. Every kind of entertainment was given, including grand opera. In 1923, as B. F. Keith's Hippodrome, it became a vaudeville house, and in 1928, as the R.K.O. Hippodrome, a cinema. Closed in 1932, it reopened in 1933 as the New York Hippodrome, and in 1935 was taken over by Billy Rose. His spectacular *Jumbo* failed, and closed on 18 Apr. 1936. This marked the end of the Hippodrome as a theatre. It was used for miscellaneous purposes, and finally demolished in Aug. 1939. GEORGE FREEDLEY†

HIRSCHBEIN, PERETZ (1880–1949), Jewish actor and dramatist, and founder of the first Yiddish Art Theatre in Odessa (see JEWISH DRAMA, 6). Born near Grodno, in Poland, he spent his early years in the country, and in 1905 published his first play, *Miriam*. This was written in Hebrew, as were his early poems. His company was formed in 1908 for the production of plays in Yiddish, however, as the Russian ban against them had just been rescinded, and Hirschbein wrote thereafter in Yiddish, translating his plays into Hebrew himself. Among the most important of them are *The Smith's Daughters* (1915) and *Green Fields* (1916), both idylls of Jewish country life. The latter is considered one of the finest plays in Yiddish literature, and Samuel J. Citron, in an article on Yiddish and Hebrew drama in *A History of Modern Drama* (1948), said of Hirschbein that 'his simple and honest treatment of his subjects have endeared to theatre audiences the country Jew, the simple man of the soil, a type which has been all too rare in Jewish life until the recent return to the land in Palestine'. E. HARRIS

HMELEV, HMELYOV, see KHMELEV.

HOADLY, BENJAMIN (1706–57), a well-known English physician, son of a bishop, who had a certain partiality for the stage and in 1747 offered Garrick a comedy entitled *The Suspicious Husband*. With Garrick in the part of Ranger—in which he was much admired by, among others, Fanny Burney's Evelina—the play made an unexpected success, and was often revived, though it reads poorly. Nicoll, in his *Eighteenth Century Drama*, says of it: 'It shows the weakening of the genteel comedy inaugurated by Cibber when that genteel comedy had become transfused with sentimental emotions.' This is Hoadly's only important contribution to the theatre, though he is believed to have written another comedy, now lost, and to have collaborated in a third.

HOBBY-HORSE, a character common in folk festivals throughout Europe, and probably a survival of the primitive worshipper clad in the skin of a sacrificial animal. He rode a wooden or wicker framework shaped like a horse, usually with a green saddle-cloth. In England the hobby-horse became a necessary accompaniment of the Morris dancers, and sometimes of the Mummers. By Elizabethan times he was already beginning to be 'forgot', as Shakespeare and Ben Jonson bear witness (for his survival in the company of the Christmas mummers, see MUMMING PLAY). Hobby-horses were also used to represent horsemen, as in the Coventry Hocktide play.

HOCHWÄLDER, FRITZ (1911–). Born in Vienna, Hochwälder has lived in Switzerland since 1938, and it was there that he had his first success in the theatre with *Das heilige Experiment* (1943), later done in London as *The Strong are Lonely*, with Donald Wolfit. The play deals with the destruction of the Jesuits in Paraguay in the eighteenth century, and Hochwälder showed considerable theatrical gifts in making a dramatic situation out of a moral issue. His second play, *Der Flüchtling* (1945), founded on a scenario by Georg Kaiser, concerns a frontier guard, his wife, and a fugitive who seeks refuge in their house. In the end the guard is left alone, ready to die for his new-found faith in freedom, while the fugitive escapes with the woman. *Der öffentliche Ankläger* (1947) is set in the period of the French Revolution; the Public Prosecutor conducts a case against an unknown enemy of the people who turns out to be himself. *Donadieu* (1953), like *Das heilige Experiment*, has a religious theme. The action takes place during the Huguenot wars and involves a moral conflict. A Huguenot noble recognizes a stranger who seeks shelter in his castle as the man who had murdered his wife, and is overcome with a desire for vengeance. After a struggle with himself he conquers his desire and resigns the punishment to God. *Die Herberge* (1956) is set in a country inn and the drama concerns the theft of a bag of gold. In the course of investigations the past history of the characters is gradually unfolded and a much greater crime exposed. *Der Unschuldige* (1958) is a comedy of a respectable citizen in whose garden a skeleton is dug up and who, as a result, finds himself suspected of murder. Eventually the skeleton is found to be that of a Napoleonic soldier, but meanwhile the man's whole view on life has been changed, as he realizes that he might have committed a crime, though in this case he was innocent. Although he has not written conventional historical plays, Hochwälder has used historical settings for many of his works, with characters who give voice to conflicts of ideas. These are emphasized not by the use of modern stage techniques, but rather by a strict adherence to the classical unities. DOROTHY MOORE

HOCKTIDE PLAY, COVENTRY, given on Hock Tuesday (the third Tuesday after Easter Sunday), and revived as a pleasant antiquity in the Kenilworth Revels prepared for the visit of Queen Elizabeth in July 1575. It began with a Captain Cox leading in a band of English knights (on hobby-horses) to fight against the Danes, and ended with the leading away of the Danish prisoners by the English women. It was intended to represent the massacre of the Danes by Ethelred in 1002, but this is probably a late literary assimilation of an earlier folk-festival custom, traceable in other places (Worcester, Shrewsbury, Hungerford), by which the women 'hocked' or caught the men and exacted a forfeit from them on one day, the men's turn coming the following day. The practice was forbidden at Worcester in 1450. This ceremony may in its turn be merely a survival of the symbolic capture of a victim for human sacrifice.

HODGE, WILLIAM THOMAS (1874–1932), American actor and playwright, who after some years on tour appeared in New York in 1898, and had his first success in *Sag Harbour* (1900). Several years later he made a great personal success as the Indiana lawyer, Pike, in *The Man from Home* (1907), and based all his future parts on this character, writing his plays himself. These were pleasant homely tales of American life, in which Hodge figured as the slow but shrewd countryman, and though they proved too unsophisticated for Broadway they had a faithful audience elsewhere. Hodge, who married a musical comedy actress, retired in 1931.

HODGKINSON, JOHN (1767–1805), an English actor, son of a publican in Manchester named Meadowcroft. At an early age he ran away from home and joined the Bristol stock company, later touring the Midland circuit. He appeared several times in support of Mrs. Siddons, but in 1792 accepted an offer from John Henry to join the American Company, and spent the rest of his life in America. With him in the company were his wife and her sister, Arabella Brett. Hodgkinson soon became extremely popular, ousting the younger Hallam and Henry himself from management as well as from public favour, and he was joint manager with Hallam of the Park Theatre, New York, when it first opened. A handsome man, with a good memory and a fine stage presence, Hodgkinson excelled both in tragedy and comedy (see No. 163). Among his best parts were André in Dunlap's tragedy of that name, and Rolla in an adaptation of *Pizarro*, also made by Dunlap. His early death from yellow fever was a great loss to the American stage. Under him the John Street Theatre, New York's first permanent playhouse, had its most brilliant period, and it had been hoped that he would long prove an ornament to the Park Theatre. His wife, who was accounted a charming actress, died in 1803 of consumption, as did her sister. His two daughters, Rosina and Fanny, were both on the stage. Hodgkinson had also a brother, Thomas, who was licensee of the Shakespeare Tavern, New York.

HODSON, HENRIETTA (1841–1910), English actress, who made her first appearances on the stage in Glasgow and Greenock, where she was in the same company as the young Irving. They went together to Manchester to join the stock company of the Theatre Royal under Knowles, and she then went to Bath and Bristol, where she appeared with Madge Robertson, later Mrs. Kendal, and Kate and Ellen Terry. She retired from the stage on marriage, but, being soon widowed, returned, and in 1866 was seen in London in extravaganza. She then went to the Queen's Theatre, and in 1868 married Henry Labouchère, one of the proprietors. She continued to act, however, under her maiden name, and in 1871 appeared as Imogen in *Cymbeline*. She later took over the management of the Royalty, and engaged in some skirmishes with W. S. Gilbert, whose dictatorial manner, when she produced some of his plays, she much resented. A good singer and dancer, and an actress of highly individual style and technical accomplishment, she was at her best in demure humour or the farcical characters of burlesque, pathos and deep sentiment lying outside her range. She retired in 1878, and three years later was instrumental in introducing Mrs. Langtry to the stage.

HOFFMAN, François-Benoît (1760–1828), French dramatist and man of letters, chiefly remembered as an incorruptible critic. His plays were not important, being mainly libretti for light opera, but he was the author of an excellent one-act comedy, *Le Roman d'une heure, ou la folle gageure*, given in Paris in 1809.

HOFMANNSTHAL, Hugo von (1874–1929), Austrian poet and playwright, who, as a young man, was in the forefront of the reaction against naturalism at the end of the nineteenth century, contributing with his poems and verse plays to the new imaginative movement which turned away from external reality and the social scene to the more inward, withdrawn aspects of life. The verse plays of this period, such as *Gestern* (1891), *Der Tod des Tizian* (1892), *Der Tor und der Tod* (1893), *Das kleine Welttheater* (1897), *Der weisse Fächer* (1897), *Der Kaiser und die Hexe* (1897), and *Das Bergwerk zu Falun* (1899), reveal Hofmannsthal's delight in beauty and in poetic and mystical intuitions, but also his early awareness of the problems raised by this kind of experience and of its dangers. They show him to be a critic of aestheticism from the inside. In certain passages they bear a remarkable resemblance to the early plays of Yeats. (There is no evidence that Yeats's plays were known to Hofmannsthal.) Hofmannsthal's exquisite poetry is diluted in the later plays of the group by his attempt to write more dramatic dialogue, and at the turn of the century he began to experiment with subjects which were more dramatic and theatrical. There was no single line of development. Plays like *Der Abenteurer und die Sängerin* (1898), *Die Hochzeit der Sobeide* (1899), *Elektra* (1903), *Das gerettete Venedig* (1904) (based on Otway's *Venice Preserved*), and *Ödipus und die Sphinx* (1905) indicate a range of interests from pagan mysteries and Dionysian experience to moral themes of love and loyalty.

The works which followed this exploratory period gained access to the theatre more easily, and Hofmannsthal's collaboration with the composer Richard Strauss and the producer Max Reinhardt dates from about 1908. His aim was still to avoid flat realism, and he also shunned expressionist techniques, preserving a poetic and symbolic language of the theatre even when he wrote realistically. In 1909 *Elektra* became the libretto of Strauss's opera, and there followed a number of libretti for Strauss: in *Ariadne auf Naxos* (1912 and 1916), *Die Frau ohne Schatten* (1919), and *Die ägyptische Helena* (1928) Hofmannsthal used subjects from myth and *Märchen*, whereas *Der Rosenkavalier* (1911) and *Arabella* (staged 1933) were close to his comedies in their form and tone. Hofmannsthal's affection for Austrian comedy (Raimund, Nestroy, and Bauernfeld), and his love of Molière and Calderón, led to translations and adaptations, some of which, for example his rewriting of Molière's *Les Fâcheux* (*Die Lästigen* of 1915), can be regarded as completely new plays. Amongst Hofmannsthal's other comedies—*Cristinas Heimreise* (1909), *Der Schwierige* (1918), and *Der Unbestechliche* (1922)—*Der Schwierige* stands out as the masterpiece, combining high comedy of subtle human relationships with irony and social satire. *Jedermann* (1911) was Hofmannsthal's first allegorical Morality play—a rehandling of the old play of *Everyman* incorporating some elements from Hans Sachs. When Hofmannsthal and Reinhardt together created the Salzburg festival, this play was produced in front of the cathedral as a famous annual event. It was for these festivals that *Das Salzburger grosse Welttheater* (1922) was written, based on Calderón's *El gran teatro del mundo*. The two plays were partly an allegory of a modern spiritual crisis in Europe, and so prepared the way for Hofmannsthal's last drama, *Der Turm* (1925 and 1927), based on Calderón's *La vida es sueño*. Its setting is seventeenth-century Poland, but the complex realistic and symbolic action is legendary rather than historical. Here Hofmannsthal took up the theme of the conflict between material power and spiritual integrity, ending the first version of 1925 with a Utopian picture of a new and purified world; the second version (1927) closes in tragedy, showing the spirit as indestructible, but powerless and isolated in a tyrannical world.

MARGARET JACOBS

HOLBERG, Ludvig (1684–1754), was born at Bergen, in Norway, studied at the University of Copenhagen and then at Oxford, travelled through Europe on foot, came into close and sympathetic contact with the culture of England, France, and Italy, and returned to Denmark to become Professor of Metaphysics in Copenhagen University and to reach fame as an historian, philosopher, and man of letters throughout Scandinavia and beyond.

His connexion with the theatre was relatively brief, but of immense effect in Dano-Norwegian literature, for he created a native comedy in the native language, bringing to it a mind disciplined by his love of Plautus, Molière, the *commedia dell'arte*, and contemporary English prose-writers. His art is in the tradition of the first three of these; his material he sought at home in native Danish and sometimes Norwegian types, which had not appeared upon the stage before. It can indeed be said of him, more truly than of many writers to whom the words are applied, that his plays call no man father but himself.

When, in 1721, he became director of the Danish Theatre in Copenhagen, French and German drama was habitually played there. There was no Danish drama, the vernacular School Drama having died out, at least in the cultural centres (see SCANDINAVIA, 1). But he resolved that Denmark, like other countries, should have a drama in its own language and with new material peculiar to Denmark and Norway and never used before. He was by now a man of considerable experience and clearly defined tastes; his letters show him, in an age which worshipped Terence, placing Plautus far above him and believing he had no equal again until Molière. He was, admittedly, a moralist in dramatic form, but, in an age which enjoyed this tendency and in general practised its moralizing with grace, this in no way hindered his immense popularity; Holberg's comedies were known not only in Denmark, but in Sweden, Germany, Holland, and even France. The greater number of them were written during the six years of his directorship (1721–8). These, with five that had not been acted, were published in 1731, four years after the closing of the Danish Theatre. When the theatre was reopened in 1747, he returned for a time to his earlier interests and wrote six more. The first play in Danish, a translation of *L'Avare*, was performed on 23 Sept. 1722, and a week later came Holberg's first original play, *Den politiske Kandestøber*. His rapidity of production in his newly found and congenial art was remarkable. He wrote in all thirty-three plays. The best, after *The Political Tinker*, are probably *Jeppe paa Bjerget eller den forvandlede Bonde* and *Erasmus Montanus*. The former, under its sub-title, *The Transformed Peasant*, was published in 1957 in an English translation by Reginald Spink, together with two one-act plays, *The Arabian Powder* (*Det arabiske Pulver*, 1724) and *The Healing Spring* (*Kilderejsen*, 1725), preceded by an admirable introduction.

UNA ELLIS-FERMOR†, *rev.*

HOLBORN EMPIRE, LONDON. As Weston's, from the name of its founder, this was the first music-hall to challenge the supremacy of the Canterbury. It had a consistently successful career, and as the Royal Holborn saw the début of many famous stars, including J. H. Stead and Bessie Bellwood. Its chairman for many years was W. B. Fair, singer of the popular 'Tommy, Make Room for your Uncle'. Its popularity declined at the beginning of the twentieth century, but it continued in use, and as the Holborn Empire became occasionally a theatre. Annually from 1922 to 1940 Italia Conti staged Christmas matinées there of *Where the Rainbow Ends*, and in 1920 Sybil Thorndike appeared in a season which included *The Trojan Women* and *Medea*. But it continued to stage variety and was the last West-End hall to do so. It was destroyed by bombing in 1941.

W. MACQUEEN-POPE†, *rev.*

HOLBORN THEATRE, LONDON, erected in 1866 by Sefton Parry on the site of what had been stables and was later to become the First Avenue Hotel. It opened in October with *The Flying Scud*, in which George Belmore scored a success; but subsequent productions failed, and in 1868 Fanny Josephs took over the theatre from Parry, with equal lack of good fortune. Barry Sullivan followed and, with Mrs. Hermann Vezin, played a round of old plays which ended in 1871. In 1875 Horace Wigan assumed control, and renamed the theatre the Mirror. His management saw the production of the first of the plays based on *A Tale of Two Cities*, which was called *All For Her*, and in which John Clayton made a hit; but though an artistic success it made no money. The house was again renamed, this time the Duke's Theatre, but remained unsuccessful, though in 1879, under Holt and Wilmot, *The New Babylon* was well received. On 4 June 1880 the building was burned down.

W. MACQUEEN-POPE†

HOLCROFT, THOMAS (1744–1809), English dramatist who is usually credited with the introduction of melodrama on the London stage with his *Tale of Mystery* (1802), an adaptation of Pixerécourt, though the main ingredients of the mixture had been used before (see MELODRAMA). The son of a shoemaker, he became an actor and had a hard struggle until in 1777 he reached Drury Lane. After the success of his first play, *Duplicity* (1781), a sentimental comedy on the evils of gambling, he gave up acting and devoted himself to literature. His most famous play is *The Road to Ruin* (1792), with its excellent roles of Goldfinch, first played by Lewis, and Old Dornton, a favourite part with many elderly character actors, both in London and in America, where the play was frequently revived. It was last seen in London in 1937. Holcroft, who was entirely self-educated, was a very good French scholar and had a phenomenal memory, a combination which enabled him while in Paris to learn by heart *Le Mariage de Figaro*, and to put it on the London stage in 1784 as *The Follies of a Day*. He also translated Destouches's *Le Glorieux* as *The School for Arrogance* (1791). Among his other comedies the most successful was *Love's Frailties* (1794), based on a German original. Holcroft, who was a friend of Lamb, was editor of the *Theatrical Recorder*, which appeared monthly from 1805 and contained play-texts translated from French and Spanish. A somewhat irritable man, but extremely hard-working and one of the few good dramatists of his day, he was four times married, his last wife surviving him and marrying the actor Kenney. Holcroft's *Memoirs* were edited by Hazlitt and published posthumously in 1816.

HOLIDAY THEATRE, New York, see CENTRAL THEATRE.

HOLLAND, see NETHERLANDS, THE.

HOLLAND. (1) George (1791–1870), an English actor, son of a dancing-master, who after seven years on the London stage went to New York and founded a family of American actors. He made his first appearance in New York at the Bowery in 1827, and became a popular comedian. He travelled extensively, and was well known in the South, was for some years in management with Ludlow and Sol Smith, and was for six years at Mitchell's famous Olympic in burlesque. From 1855 to 1867 he played character parts in Wallack's company, being outstanding as Tony Lumpkin, which he was still playing at the age of 75. In 1869 he was with Daly. Jefferson, who knew him well, writes feelingly of his 'bright and cheerful spirit' and says that he was 'an actor of the old school, introducing even into modern characters its traditions and conventionalities; his effects were broadly given, and his personality was essentially comic'. It was in connexion with his funeral that the famous New York 'Little Church Around the Corner' first received its name, since Jefferson was directed to it under that title by a clergyman who refused to bury an actor in his own churchyard. By his second wife Holland had three sons, and a daughter who died just as she was beginning her career under Daly. Of his sons, (2) Edmund Milton (1848–1913) made his first appearance on the stage as a child, and was call-boy at Mrs. John Wood's Olympic. He was with Jefferson in the first New York production of *Rip Van Winkle*, and as E. Milton became a member of Wallack's, where he stayed for thirteen years, later reverting to his family name. He was excellent in comedy, and in the parts of elderly men. In 1879 he was seen in London with McKee Rankin, playing the Judge in *The Danites*. He was later at Madison Square under Palmer, with Frohman at the New York Lyceum, and for three years with Kyrle Bellew in *Raffles*. He had just joined Belasco's company when he died. A clean-shaven man, with thin mobile features and a high forehead, he was a comedian of a dry and subtle humour, who relied on gait, gesture, and expression for his effects. He had two children on the stage. His brother, (3) Joseph Jefferson (1860–1926), named after his famous godfather, was also on the stage as a child, and in spite of partial deafness made his adult début in 1878, playing in Daly's company from 1886 to 1889, and touring with many famous actors and with his elder brother. In 1904 he became paralysed, but for the rest of his life remained in close touch with the stage, being responsible for the direction of several amateur societies. In his heyday a versatile light comedian, dignified and attentive to detail, he made light of his subsequent disabilities, and was respected and loved by his many friends both within and without the theatrical profession.

HOLLINGSHEAD, John (1827–1904), English theatre manager, who in his young days was a journalist, an early contributor to the *Cornhill*, and on the staff of Dickens's *Household Words*. He also succeeded Edmund Yates as dramatic critic of the *Daily News* and wrote for *Punch*. He was a staunch upholder of the reform of copyright laws, particularly those intended to prevent the dramatization of novels without the author's consent, from which Dickens suffered so severely, and was against the closing of the theatres on Ash Wednesday. He became stage manager of the Alhambra in 1865, but it was with the Gaiety that his name was chiefly associated. He opened this newly built theatre on 21 Dec. 1868. He was there for eighteen years, and was succeeded by George Edwardes, who was to make the theatre a home of musical comedy. Under Hollingshead it had been used mainly for burlesque. Hollingshead is credited with the introduction of matinées, and with being the first manager to use electric light both outside and inside his theatre, which was well conducted and had always a good company. In 1880 at the Gaiety Hollingshead staged a translation by Archer of Ibsen's *Pillars of Society* as *Quicksands; or, the Pillars of Society*, the first Ibsen play to be seen in London.

HOLLYWOOD THEATRE, New York, on 51st Street. Originally a cinema, this was opened by Warner Brothers on 22 Apr. 1930. It ventured into legitimate drama, as the 51st Street Theatre, and in 1936 saw the production of *Sweet River*, George Abbott's new version of *Uncle Tom's Cabin*, with fine settings by Donald Oenslager. This can best be described as a distinguished failure, since it was taken off after five performances, and the theatre reverted to its old name and policy, except for a short run of *Romeo and Juliet*, with Laurence Olivier and Vivien Leigh, in 1940. In 1949 the theatre was renamed the Mark Hellinger, and was occupied for many years by *My Fair Lady* (1956–62).

HOLZ, Arno (1863–1929), German novelist and dramatist, whose *Die Familie Selicke* (1890), written in collaboration with his friend Johannes Schlaf, was the manifesto of the new school of naturalistic drama. Given by the recently founded Freie Bühne, this dreary catalogue of misery, rape, disease, and death, set against a sordidly realistic background, and devoid of all theatrical tricks, proved a rallying point for the younger dramatists. Among them was Gerhard Hauptmann, whose first play, *Vor Sonnenaufgang*, was the first German play to be produced by the Freie Bühne. Holz wrote a number of other plays, but, lacking the collaboration of Schlaf, without success.

HOME, The Rev. John (1722–1808), a Scottish minister, author of the famous tragedy, *Douglas* (1756), given in Edinburgh with Digges as Young Norval and Sarah Ward, who had encouraged the author in its production, as Lady Randolph. The play caused much controversy, many of the clergy and elders of the Church of Scotland being against the theatre, censuring any ministers seen there, and horrified that one of their number should write for it. But Home had the support of David Hume, Adam Smith, and other literary men, and his play was a triumph with the audience. On the first night a voice from the pit cried: 'Whaur's yer Wully Shakespeare noo?' Offered to Garrick at Drury Lane, but refused, possibly because Garrick feared that Mrs. Cibber would be too good as Lady Randolph, it was accepted by Rich for Covent Garden where Barry, 'six feet high and in a suit of white puckered satin', says Doran, played Young Norval to the Lady Randolph of Peg Woffington. The play was constantly revived, Lady Randolph being a favourite part with Sarah Siddons, while many young actors in England and America, including Masters Betty and Howard Payne, delighted in Young Norval. The speech beginning 'My name is Norval' was always to be found in recitation books and in the repertory of youthful elocutionists, while the play found its way into the stock of the Juvenile Drama, and can still be given on a Toy Theatre stage. It was revived at the Edinburgh Festival in 1950, with Sybil Thorndike as Lady Randolph and Douglas Campbell as Young Norval. Its author wrote other tragedies, but they were not successful, and *Douglas* remains his one claim to fame.

HONYMAN. (1) JOHN (1613–36), one of the most important boy-actors of the King's Men, with whom he is found playing female parts as early as 1626, when he appeared in *The Roman Actor*. For the next few years he continued to appear in actor-lists, graduating from women to adult parts in about 1630. He died before he had the opportunity of showing whether he would do as well as was expected, but his contemporaries appear to have considered him an actor of great promise. Some later references to him indicate that he may have written a play, but so far it has not been found. Honyman had a younger brother, (2) RICHARD (1618–?), who also acted with the King's Men, though probably in a minor capacity only, since he was not a member, but a hired man. He died some time in his thirties, since his widow remarried in 1657.

HOPE THEATRE, LONDON, started life as the Bear Garden, an amphitheatre in which bulls and bears were baited. In or about 1613 Henslowe and Jacob Meade, a waterman and Henslowe's partner, entered into an agreement with Gilbert Katherens, a carpenter and builder who seems to have been kept busy on theatre construction at that time, to convert the Bear Garden into the Hope—or, as the agreement states, 'into a game place or plaiehouse'. It was to have a dual use, both for plays and for bull- and bear-baiting. The form and size were to be the same as the Swan, but with a movable stage which could be dismantled for the baitings; and there was to be a bull house and stable capable of holding six bulls and three horses.

Henslowe and Alleyn, who were already Masters of His Majesty's Games of Bulls, Bears, and Dogs, were probably desirous of getting all the custom which could not go to the burnt-out Globe, and thereby stealing a march on their theatrical rival, Burbage. They engaged the company known as the Lady Elizabeth's Men, headed by Nathan Field, who played at the Hope in 1614–15, presenting, among other plays, *Bartholomew Fair*. John Taylor, the water-poet, challenged William Fennor, who called himself 'The Kings Majesties Riming Poet', to a trial of wit at the Hope in Oct. 1614. Fennor paid Taylor 10*s*. in earnest of the contest, and Taylor had 1,000 bills printed announcing it. He got a full house for this very popular form of entertainment, but Fennor failed to appear, and Taylor had to face a disappointed audience—and audiences in those days had a way of speaking their minds. He himself said: 'Then this companion for an Asse ran away and left me for a Foole, amongst thousands of critical censurers, where I was ill thought of by my friends, scorned by my foes . . . besides the summe of Twenty Pounds in money I lost my reputation amongst many and gained disgrace in stead of my better expectations.'

Henslowe died in Jan. 1616, and a new agreement was executed between Edward Alleyn, Jacob Meade, and others, probably actors in the company, now known as the Prince's Men. Matters did not prosper, for Meade quarrelled with the actors and also with Alleyn, and legal business and disputes occupied them until 1619, to the detriment of the Hope. The Globe had meanwhile been rebuilt, and the Hope now reverted to bull- and bear-baiting. It was dismantled in 1656, but the building may still have been standing in 1682–3.

W. MACQUEEN-POPE†

HOPKINS THEATRE, NEW YORK, see PUNCH AND JUDY THEATRE.

HOPPER, DE WOLF [WILLIAM D'WOLF] (1858–1935), an American actor, who at 21 deserted the study of the law to tour in his own company. He then played in light opera for some years, establishing a reputation as an eccentric comedian with a fine bass voice. In 1891 he produced and appeared in musical comedy, being responsible five years later for Sousa's *El Capitán*, in which he also appeared in London in 1899. After a couple of years at the first Weber and Fields Music-Hall he returned to light opera, and was excellent in Gilbert and Sullivan, where his clear diction made him outstanding in the patter songs, notably the Nightmare song in *Iolanthe*. His favourite part, however, was the Jester in *The Yeomen of the Guard*. From 1918 onwards, the vogue for light opera having waned, he mainly toured in revivals. He was famous for his recital of *Casey at the Bat*, which he first gave at Wallack's on 13 May 1888, and thereafter repeated some 10,000 times. He was married six times. In 1927 he published his memoirs, *Once a Clown, Always a Clown.*

HORNIMAN, Annie Elizabeth Fredericka (1860–1937), theatre manager and patron, one of the first to organize and encourage the modern repertory theatre movement, and a seminal influence in the Irish and English theatres at the beginning of the twentieth century. The daughter of a wealthy Victorian tea-merchant, she had no connexions with the theatre, but was from 1882 to 1886 at the Slade, during which time she began her travels on the Continent. Then and later she recognized the important part played in the cultural life of various countries, particularly Germany, by the subsidized repertory theatre, and also saw a number of modern plays, including those of Ibsen, which had a strong influence on her. Unable to participate actively in theatrical matters, she secretly subsidized in 1894 a season at the Avenue Theatre run by Florence Farr, during which were performed Shaw's *Arms and the Man*, the first of his plays to be seen publicly, and Yeats's *Land of Heart's Desire*. This not only marks the beginning of what may be called the 'modern theatre' movement of the time, but also aroused Miss Horniman's interest in the new Irish Theatre Movement (see IRELAND) and in the plays of Yeats, to whom she acted for some time as unpaid secretary. In 1903 she went to Ireland and there built and equipped at a cost of £13,000 the Abbey Theatre, with which she remained connected until 1910, when she disposed of it to a board of trustees for £1,000 freehold. In the meantime she had bought and refurbished the Gaiety Theatre, Manchester—now a cinema—where from 1908 to 1917 she maintained an excellent repertory company, and put on some 200 plays, of which more than half were new. Her first producer was Iden Payne. He was succeeded by Lewis Casson, who married a member of the company, Sybil Thorndike, thus inaugurating one of the most famous stage partnerships of the English theatre. Among the plays seen at the Gaiety were many of the so-called Manchester School—Brighouse, Houghton, Monkhouse—a few classics, some translations, and some by such contemporary authors as Shaw and Galsworthy. A memorable production was that of St. John Ervine's *Jane Clegg* in 1913. The Gaiety company, which contained a number of excellent players, appeared several times in London and undertook tours in Canada and the United States, and by its example materially assisted the establishment of similar ventures in other English provincial towns. Unfortunately the theatre was not as successful financially as it was in reputation, and by 1917 it had become something of a burden to its founder. The company was disbanded, and the theatre was leased to an outside manager, though until 1921 Miss Horniman continued to read and criticize all plays put on there. It then became a cinema. Miss Horniman went into retirement until her death, presenting her library of plays to the British Drama League, and taking no further active part in the theatre, though she lived long enough to see her pioneer work bear fruit in other provincial cities (see REPERTORY THEATRE MOVEMENT) and the players who had served their apprenticeship under her at the head of their profession in London. In the end she was forced to concede that though the Manchester experiment might from some points of view be accounted a failure, it was nevertheless a fruitful failure.

HOSTRUP, Jens Christian (1818–92), Danish dramatist (see SCANDINAVIA, 1 *a*).

HÔTEL D'ARGENT, THÉÂTRE DE L'. In the early days of the professional theatre in Paris the only building duly licensed for the performance of stage-plays was the Hôtel de Bourgogne, whose owners, the Confraternity of the Passion, put down all opposition with a heavy hand. But towards the end of the sixteenth century a breach had been made in their privilege by allowing provincial companies to play at the Paris fairs, and in 1598 an actor-manager from the provinces, Pierre Venier, father of the first French actress to be known by name, appeared at the Foire St-Germain and then took his company to an improvised theatre in the Hôtel d'Argent in the rue de la Verrerie. He was allowed to remain there for a short time, on condition that he paid a tax to the Confraternity for every performance. This theatre must have remained in use intermittently for many years, for in 1607 Venier is found there again, this time with his daughter and her husband, who had temporarily left the company at the Hôtel de Bourgogne where they had been acting under Valleran-Lecomte. The assassination of Henri IV in 1610 caused both troupes to leave Paris, and on their return they all went together to the Hôtel de Bourgogne, while a new company, later to be famous, leased the Hôtel d'Argent. This was the troupe of Montdory, then led by the Lenoirs. Later they are found in different quarters of Paris, and in 1634 Montdory opened the famous Théâtre du Marais. The history of the Hôtel d'Argent has been dwelt on at some length, as it was thought, before the careful researches of the theatre historian Rigal, that it was synonymous with the Théâtre du Marais, whose foundation was wrongly assigned to 1600.

HÔTEL DE BOURGOGNE, THÉÂTRE DE L', the first and most important theatre of Paris, and one of the components of the later Comédie-Française. When in the mid-sixteenth century the Confraternity of the Passion, who held the monopoly of acting in Paris, were turned out of their old quarters in the guest-house of the Trinity, they built themselves a new theatre in the ruins of the palace of the Dukes of Burgundy, which had been uninhabited since the death of Charles the Bold. Situated in the rue Mauconseil, it was ready for occupation in 1548, but the

Confraternity got little good from it, for in the same year they were forbidden to act religious plays and so saw themselves deprived of the greater part of their repertory. They struggled along as best they could with productions of farces and with secular plays drawn from the *chansons de geste* and the romances of the Middle Ages, but they gradually lost their audiences, and towards the end of the sixteenth century were glad to hire out their hall to travelling companies from the provinces which included Paris in their itinerary. As early as 1578 Agnan Sarat was there, while twenty years later an English company under Jean Sehais (possibly Shaa) is traditionally believed to have played there. The first more or less permanent company to occupy the theatre was that of the provincial actor-manager Valleran-Lecomte, usually known as the King's Players. Among its members were Marie Venier, the first French actress to be known by name, and her husband Laporte. For many years the relationships between the actors and the proprietors of the theatre were troubled, and the hall was often let to rival French or visiting Italian companies. But the King's Players gradually asserted their pre-eminence, and for a time reigned supreme in Paris, with Belleville as their star, until in 1634 a second theatre, that of the Marais, was established under Montdory. The two theatres were bitter rivals, but Montdory's early retirement again left the Hôtel de Bourgogne, under Belleville's successors, Floridor and Montfleury, in an unchallenged position until the arrival of Molière in Paris in 1658. Many of the outstanding plays of the seventeenth century, with the exception of *Le Cid*, were first seen at the Hôtel de Bourgogne, until the company was finally merged with the other actors of Paris to form the Comédie-Française in 1673. The new company moved to the theatre in the rue Guénégaud, and the stage of the Hôtel de Bourgogne was occupied intermittently by the Italian actors until 1783 (see COMÉDIE-ITALIENNE).

HOUGHTON, (WILLIAM) STANLEY (1881–1913), English playwright, and the best of the so-called Manchester School of realistic dramatists, much influenced by Ibsen. He was in cotton, and practised literature in his spare time, writing for the *Manchester Guardian* on theatrical matters. His plays, which deal with the revolt against parental authority and the struggle between the generations, were mainly given in Manchester, except for his best piece of work, *Hindle Wakes*, which was first seen at the Aldwych, London, in 1912, in a production by Lewis Casson for the Stage Society. In it Fanny Hawthorn, a working girl, refuses to marry the cowardly, vacillating, rich man's son who has seduced her, a reversal of things which took contemporary playgoers by surprise. This, with Houghton's other plays, particularly *The Dear Departed* (1908) and *The Younger Generation* (1910), has proved popular with amateur and repertory companies.

HOUSEKEEPER, the term used to denote an Elizabethan actor, or other person, who owned part of the actual playhouse building, as distinct from the sharer, whose 'share' was in the clothes and playbooks of the company only.

HOUSMAN, LAURENCE (1865–1959), English author and playwright, brother of the poet A. E. Housman. He suffered in his dramatic career from the heavy hand of the censor, several of his plays being banned, among them his one-act playlets on Queen Victoria. Some of these, under the title of *Victoria Regina*, were seen privately at the Gate Theatre in 1935, with Pamela Stanley in the title-role, but it was not until 1937, on the intervention of Edward VIII, that they were licensed for public performance. They were then seen at the Lyric with Pamela Stanley repeating her successful impersonation of the Queen. Several selections were published at various times in *Palace Scenes*, *The Golden Sovereign*, and *Happy and Glorious*, together with other scenes from Victorian life. A further series of one-act plays was *The Little Plays of St. Francis*, which have been frequently performed by amateurs, though never professionally or in the West End. Housman's first play, *Bethlehem*, was produced by Gordon Craig in 1902, and in 1904 Housman was responsible, with Granville-Barker, for the play with music (by Joseph Moorat) *Prunella*. This was first seen at the Court, and was revived several times. In 1930 it was seen at the Everyman. Most of Housman's work, however, has been done in one-act and religious plays, and *Victoria Regina* remains his most successful venture into the commercial theatre. In 1937 he published a volume of reminiscences, *The Unexpected Years*.

HOWARD, BRONSON (1842–1908), American playwright, and one of the first to make use of native material with any skill and assiduity. He had no social purpose in writing, and never forgot the necessity of amusing his audience, but his work is significant in the development of the modern American theatre. He was also the first American dramatist to make his living solely by play-writing, since his predecessors, like Bird and Boker, had other sources of income. He was originally a journalist in Detroit, where his first play was produced in 1864. He continued in journalism in New York while waiting for success in the theatre, which came finally in 1870 with the production of *Saratoga*, a farcical comedy produced by Daly which ran for over a hundred nights. As *Brighton* (1874) it was adapted for the English stage, with Wyndham in the chief part of Bob Sackett. Howard then wrote several other comedies, including *The Banker's Daughter* (1878), which, as *Lilian's Last Love*, was first performed in 1873 and as *The Old Love and the New*, with revisions by Albery, was successfully given in London in 1879. But his most important play was probably *Young Mrs. Winthrop* (1882), in which, says Quinn in his *History of the American Drama*, he 'placed on the stage for the first time in America a group of characters whose actions are determined by the power of social laws and the interruption of social distractions without making the prevailing note one of satire'. It marks a great advance in Howard's own development as well as in that of the American stage, and was the first of its author's plays to be done in England without alteration or adaptation. The most successful of Howard's later plays were *The Henrietta* (1887), a satire on financial life, and *Shenandoah* (1888), a drama of the War between the States. The latter was at first a failure, but in a revival by Charles Frohman it established itself as an outstanding success, both in New York and on tour. Howard worked hard for the betterment of the lot of American playwrights, and in 1891 founded the American Dramatists' Club, which later became the Society of American Dramatists and Composers, and was instrumental in amending the copyright laws of the period. He encouraged younger writers, and on his death bequeathed his library to the society he had helped to found.

HOWARD, SIDNEY COE (1891–1939), American dramatist, born at Oakland, California, of pioneer parents. After his graduation from the University of California in 1915 he studied playwriting under Professor G. P. Baker at Harvard. Early during the First World War he went overseas and served in many capacities, finally becoming captain of an American air squadron. He returned to his native country and by 1919 was busily engaged in newspaper and editorial work. He had done a good deal of writing in his student days, including drama and poetry, but his first play to be produced professionally was *Swords* (1922), a romantic drama in verse on an Italian Renaissance theme. It failed. His first popular success was *They Knew What They Wanted* (1924), a comedy that combined the writer's immense zest for life and his tolerant philosophy toward human beings seeking happiness within themselves. The background he chose was the grapegrowers' country in his native state. Both before and after the production of this comedy, Howard was constantly at work, alone or in collaboration, adapting, translating, or dramatizing plays from novels and stories. Among the best of these products were *Sancho Panza* (1923), *s.s. Tenacity* (1922) (from the French of Vildrac), and *Salvation* (1928), the last-named in collaboration with Charles MacArthur. *Lucky Sam McCarver* (1925), a more serious work than *They Knew What They Wanted*, was memorable chiefly as a study in character, being the portrait of a night-club proprietor in New York. Two other successes followed: *Ned McCobb's Daughter* and *The Silver Cord* (both 1926). The first is a sympathetic study of a New England woman at odds with rum-runners, while the second, though largely concerned with character, is something of a thesis play, being based on a 'mother complex'. *Half-Gods* (1929), a failure in the theatre, is the author's most deliberate attempt to preach a sermon. It is a passionate, and in places vastly amusing, protest against the idea that woman's fundamental place is anywhere but in the home. *Alien Corn* (1933) is another dramatic plea, or rather the exposition of a problem, in which the position of an artist in an unsympathetic community is made the basis of a somewhat melodramatic and unconvincing drama. But the play was an outstanding success, perhaps by reason of the incidental details and the acting of Katharine Cornell, who starred in it. Two adaptations belong to the period now under discussion: *The Late Christopher Bean* (1932), an amusing character-comedy derived from the French of Fauchois (*Prenez garde à la peinture*); and *Dodsworth* (1934), a clever dramatic condensation of the Sinclair Lewis novel. *Yellow Jack* (1934), based on scientific data furnished by De Kruif and dealing with the heroic story of the 'discovery of the means by which yellow fever is carried and controlled', was not a success when first produced, but it is one of the most distinguished dramatic works of our time. Several adaptations followed, none of them very successful, though *Paths of Glory* (1935), based on a novel, revealed Howard's attitude toward war and war-mongering. *The Ghost of Yankee Doodle* (1937), though only moderately successful on the stage, is one of the most satisfactory of Howard's plays. Here, though he is ostensibly concerned over the chaotic state of the world on the eve of global conflict, he seems to have returned to what was always his chief concern as a playwright, what he once said was of paramount importance to him, 'the value and significance of flesh'. He had determined, he claimed, to ask of the life he was reporting no more concessions than 'my limited skill as a reporter forced me to ask'. Howard had just finished work on his play, *Madam Will You Walk?*, when he was killed in an accident. The piece was tried out briefly on the road, and then withdrawn. The manuscript would, of course, have been drastically revised if Howard had lived a few weeks longer. It is an entertaining fantasy on good and evil, and shows the playwright to have been in complete control of his vigorous talents.

BARRETT H. CLARK†

HOWE, HENRY (1812–96), English actor, whose real name was Hutchinson. He had appeared several times as an amateur before he made his professional début in Oct. 1834, playing a round of small parts. In 1837 he was with Macready at Covent Garden, and played an officer in the first production of *The Lady of Lyons*. He then went to the Haymarket under Webster, and remained there without a break for 40 years. He soon rose high in his profession, and was excellent in such parts as Malvolio, Jaques, Macduff, Old Absolute, Sir Peter Teazle, Dornton, and others. In 1881 he was at the Lyceum, playing elderly parts, and went with Irving on tour in the United States, where he died. Known as 'Daddy' Howe, he was universally beloved, a conscientious actor and a most worthy man, who took great pride in his lovely garden at Isleworth.

HOYT, Charles Hale (1860–1900), American dramatist, whose numerous and forgotten plays were mainly farcical comedies depicting characters of the cities and small towns of the day. They all have large casts, improbable but infectious humour, and a rapid succession of incidents, often only faintly connected, with a generous smattering of songs, sometimes written by other hands. They have little literary quality, and their wit evaporates in print, but in their day they gave pleasure to thousands, and were an important part of New York's entertainment in the last twenty years of the nineteenth century. Among the most popular were *The Texas Steer; or, Money Makes the Mare Go* (1890), first given in 1882 as *A Case of Wine*; *A Trip to Chinatown* (1891), whose 650 consecutive performances set up a record for the day; and *A Day and a Night in New York* (1898).

HROSWITHA (Hrotsvitha, Roswitha), a Benedictine abbess of Gandersheim in Saxony, who in the tenth century, finding herself drawn by the excellence of his style to read the pagan plays of Terence, much esteemed at that time as a scholastic author, and fearing their influence on a Christian world, set out to provide a suitable alternative. This she did in six original prose plays modelled on Terence, but dealing with subjects drawn from Christian history and morality—*Paphnutius*, *Dulcitius*, *Gallicanus*, *Callimachus*, *Abraham*, and *Sapientia*. These were intended for reading rather than production, but the use of miracles and abstract characters links this isolated survival of classical drama with the later Mystery and Morality plays. The Latin is poor, but the dialogue is vivacious and elements of farce are not lacking. The plays were published in 1923 in an English translation by H. J. W. Tillyard, and *Paphnutius*, which deals with the conversion of Thaïs, was produced in London in 1914 by Edith Craig in a translation by Christopher St. John.

HUBERT, André (*c.* 1634–1700), French actor who after serving his apprenticeship in the provinces was at the Théâtre du Marais, and joined Molière's company in 1664, taking the place of Brécourt. After playing a number of secondary young lovers and other parts, he created Mme Jourdain in *Le Bourgeois gentilhomme*, playing also the Music-Master. In Molière's last play, *Le Malade imaginaire*, Hubert played M. Diafoirus. He was evidently a dependable, though not outstanding, actor, but he was not a very brave man, for on one occasion when the musketeers rioted at the Palais-Royal he vanished, and was later found stuck fast in a hole in the back wall. After Molière's death he became responsible, with La Grange, for the finance and administration of the company, and retired in 1685. His wife also served the theatre in a minor capacity, probably in the box-office.

HUDSON THEATRE, New York, on West 44th Street. Built by Henry B. Harris, this opened on 19 Oct. 1903 with Ethel Barrymore in *Cousin Kate*. It was handsomely furnished in sober taste, and was considered a fine example of the new theatre architecture of its day. Among its early productions were *The Marriage of Kitty* with Marie Tempest, Pinero's *Letty*, a short version of *Man and Superman* with Robert Loraine, and the world première of Henry Arthur Jones's *The Hypocrites* (1906), with Jessie Milward and the young Doris Keane. In 1908 came the success of *Lady Frederick*, with Ethel Barrymore and Bruce McRae, and in 1910 Belasco filled the theatre with *Nobody's Widow*. Among further productions were the sharply contrasted *Pollyanna* and *Our Betters*, and a record for the theatre of 440 performances was set up by a popular sentimental comedy, *Friendly Enemies*, which made a fortune for Al Woods. *Clarence*, a delightful comedy by Booth Tarkington, almost equalled its success, but had only 300 performances. Its cast included Helen Hayes and Alfred Lunt. *The Plough and the Stars*, with Arthur Sinclair, Maire O'Neill, and Sara Allgood, ran only a month, but success attended a Negro musical, Cedric Hardwicke in *The Amazing Dr. Clitterhouse*, and Ethel Barrymore in *Whiteoaks*. In 1940 the Players staged an interesting revival of *Love for Love*. The Pulitzer Prize-winner, *State of the Union*, opened at the Hudson in 1945, and in 1949 *Detective Story* was seen there. The theatre then became a broadcasting studio, but reopened as a theatre in Dec. 1959 and in the following year housed Hellman's *Toys in the Attic*. In 1963 the Actors' Studio Theatre presented their initial production, a revival of *Strange Interlude*. GEORGE FREEDLEY†

HUGO, Victor-Marie (1802–85), one of France's greatest lyric poets, and leader of the French Romantic movement. He was also a dramatist, of whose plays it has been said that they are masterpieces in all but their fitness for the stage. Indeed, the first, *Cromwell*, was not intended for production, and would take six hours to act. It was a battle-cry, and its preface was the manifesto of the new movement. A second play, *Marion Delorme*, intended for the stage, was forbidden by the censor on political grounds, and not acted until 1831, a year later than *Hernani*, whose first night at the Comédie-Française led to a riot in the theatre. This play, with *Ruy Blas* (1838), is the best known of Hugo's dramatic output, which includes also the prose melodramas *Lucrèce Borgia*, *Marie Tudor* (both 1833), and *Angelo, tyran de Padoue* (1835). All alike suffer from overloading, from a plethora of words and details, from too much erudition and not enough emotion. The characters fail to come to life, and even when one is under the spell of the rhetoric of *Hernani* and *Ruy Blas* one still sees them as puppets, jerking uneasily against their rich historical background. Yet by their vigour, and by the new life which they brought into the theatre, they operated a revolution in French theatre history. They are plays of youth—a young man and a young movement—and must be judged as such. Of them all *Ruy Blas* is the most theatrical, with two excellent acts, the second and the fourth, and a superb ending. But it fails to convince, since Ruy Blas kills himself because he is a lackey, yet has nothing of the lackey in his composition, which is purely that of a well-born romantic hero.

Hugo's plays mark the entry of melodrama into the serious theatre. His plots come from the boulevards, but his language is that of the author of *Les Quatre Vents de l'Esprit*, breaking like a trumpet-call into the fusty atmosphere of outworn classicism. Yet it is difficult, even in Hugo's finest dramatic moments, to disentangle the dramatist from the poet, and both from the novelist and politician. The Romantic theatre carried in itself the germ of its decay, and its vogue was bound to be short. The failure of *Les Burgraves*, in 1843, showed that the tide had turned in favour of prose and common sense, and Hugo withdrew from the stage. His later plays were written to be read, and form part of his poetic works. Of them all *Ruy Blas* and *Hernani*, and the ill-fated *Le Roi s'amuse*, forbidden after one performance in 1832, can still bear revival. The first particularly, given sincerity and force in the actors, allied with impeccable technique, retains the power to move and enthrall by the passion of its lyric poetry.

HUNEKER, JAMES GIBBONS (1860–1921), American dramatic critic, and a pioneer of immense importance. Beside him such popular educators of the 1890s as Brander Matthews and William Dean Howells fade away completely. He was not particularly concerned—as George Jean Nathan later was—with upsetting the theatre's apple-cart of prosperous mediocrity; he was a reformer only indirectly. He wrote chiefly of what interested him and what he found of value in the theatres of America and Europe, and maintained a determined silence about the second- and third-rate. He was perhaps more of an interpreter than a critic, an impressionistic ambassador of belles-lettres. In drama his tastes were very catholic, and it is difficult to discover his sympathies. Maeterlinck, Sudermann, Hervieu, and Wedekind—he praised and explained them all and taught Americans more about foreign literature than any other man of his time.

Huneker was born in Philadelphia, of Irish-Hungarian extraction. He studied law for a short period, but gave it up to become a concert pianist. This he never achieved, but he later became a music critic of international renown, writing definitive biographies of Chopin and Franz Liszt. As a young man he lived in Paris and it was there he learned his trade. Both in style—he was an admirable stylist—and in his approach there are obvious traces of French influence. His critical essays, composed in the Parisian manner, are packed with gossip about the private lives of artists, for he believed that a man's private life is often the key to his work.

In 1890 he became the music and drama critic of *The Morning Advertiser* and *The New York Recorder*. In 1902 he joined the staff of *The Sun* and in 1912 left it for *The New York Times*. As a journalist he touched on everything from architecture to zoology, and his learning—though he carried it lightly—was extraordinary. He battled in print with William Winter over Ibsen and Shaw, and his gusto and worldly knowledge shocked the Puritans of the day. He edited a two-volume edition of Shaw's criticisms from the *Saturday Review* and acted as advance man for Richard Strauss, then unheard-of in America. His own books are still remarkably alive, and his studies of Becque, Hauptmann, D'Annunzio, and other dramatists are keen, thorough, and very entertaining. Though an excessively modest man, he could never resign himself to being 'a mere critic'. On various occasions he tried becoming a musician, a novelist, and a short-story teller, but in the end he always returned to criticism. 'I am Jack of the Seven Arts, master of none', he wrote in his amusing autobiography, *Steeplejack*.

Among his critical books are *Iconoclasts*, *A Book of Dramatists*, *Egoists*, *Mezzotints in Modern Music*, *Promenades of an Impressionist*, *Bedouins*, and *Ivory, Apes, and Peacocks*. He also wrote a novel, *Painted Veils*, the biography of an imaginary prima donna, and a volume of short stories, *Melomaniacs*.

THOMAS QUINN CURTISS

HUNGARY. In Great Britain and the United States the theatre has always been regarded primarily as a medium of entertainment. In Hungary it is regarded also as a matter of public importance, and a valuable instrument for the preservation and dissemination of cultural ideas. Modern Hungarian drama dates from about the nineteenth century, but the oldest written survivals of Hungarian dramatic art are the liturgical texts in Latin, which date from about the beginning of the eleventh century. There are also references in old documents to the acting of Mystery and Miracle plays in the larger towns, and to the visits of troupes of dancers and musicians. In the fifteenth century, entertainments by Italian actors were given at the magnificent feasts at the Court of Matthias I. In the sixteenth century a number of tragedies, comedies, pastorals, and political satiric plays were given. Some of them survive, though almost nothing is known about the manner of their presentation. During this time the Hungarians' natural feeling for the theatre was also fostered by plays performed in schools, which were allowed mainly because they encouraged the study of Latin (see JESUIT DRAMA). While the Jesuit productions contributed to the development of stagecraft, the plays given in Protestant and Piarist schools encouraged the emergence of a drama in the vernacular. The first Hungarian dramatist to be known by name, Péter Bornemisza (1535–84), made an adaptation, according to the Protestant ideas of the time, of Sophocles' play in his *Magyar Elektra* (1558). Soon plays ceased to have a purely educative aim. The dramatic element developed, and national peasant types were introduced. Some fifteen play-texts from the seventeenth century have survived in manuscript, and in 1695 György Felvinczi (*c.* 1650–*c.* 1710), author of a *Comico Tragoedia*, made an attempt to form a professional company. But the chief actors of the time were still students and schoolboys, the authors priests or university professors. The first plays which were not written for student performances were those by György Bessenyei (1747–1811), author of *Ágis tragédiája* (1772), and *A filozófus* (1777).

There were, in the seventeenth and eighteenth centuries, private theatres in many princely and noble dwellings, with German or Italian actors, but these, like that of the Eszterházys, were mainly used for imported operas and concert music. The first professional Hungarian company was established in Buda in 1790, on the initiative of Ferenc Kazinczy. It was directed by László Kelemen (1762–1814). Unfortunately it did not last very long, but in 1792 another company, which opened in Kolozsvár, the capital of Transylvania, was more successful, and by 1801 was already touring the country. The great Hungarian actress Róza Déry-Széppataki (*née* Rozalia Schenbach) (1793–1872) was later a member of this company. At the same time Hungarian play-writing flourished, as if to keep pace with the development of the art of acting. Among the outstanding works of this period were the satiric comedy *A méla Tempefői* (1793) and a musical farce, *Özvegy Karnyóné* (1799) by Mihály Csokonai Vitéz (1773–1805).

The first permanent theatres were erected in the provinces in 1820–30, but it was not until 1837 that the first Hungarian theatre opened in Pest, with the support of the leading authors and actors of the day. The first play to be performed was *Árpád ébredése*, by the poet, essayist, dramatist, and translator Mihály Vörösmarty (1800–55), whose later plays, the fairy-tale *Csongor és Tünde* and the historical drama *Czillei és a Hunyadiak*, were also seen there. In 1840 the Pest theatre received a state subsidy, and became the National Theatre. The musical director was Ferenc Erkel (1810–93), composer of the music to *Bánk bán* (1826). This, a tragedy by József Katona (1791–1830), dealt with Hungary's eternal problem, the national attitude to the foreign ruler, and is of great importance. It was revived many times at the National Theatre. Meanwhile touring companies in the 1820s and 1830s were performing the plays of Károly Kisfaludy (1788–1830), the 'father of Hungarian comedy', who was the first professional playwright to bring on the stage the peasant types which were later so popular. Among his most successful plays were *A kérők* and *A pártütők* (both 1819), and *Csalódások* (1829).

The whole life of Ede Szigligeti (1814–78) was spent in the service of the National Theatre. He was its secretary when it opened, and later he became its director. He was a prolific playwright, author of about a hundred plays which he produced himself. Among them were historical, folk, and social dramas; but his best work was done in plays of village life, like *A szökött katona* (1843) and *Csikós* (1847). He may be considered the founder of the Hungarian popular play, pleasant musical comedies in which the peasants are idealized. Other playwrights of this time were Gergely Csiky (1842–91), the first playwright to study the problems of the Hungarian middle class in such plays as *Ingyenélők* (1880), *Cifra nyomorúság* (1881), *Szép leányok* (1882), *Buborékok* (1884), and Imre Madách (1823–64) whose great dramatic poem, *Az ember tragédiája*, though published in 1862, was not staged until 1883, many years after his death. It was translated into many languages (twice into English as *The Tragedy of Man*), and gained its author an international reputation, the first accorded to a Hungarian playwright.

While the number of playwrights was increasing and more and more Hungarian plays were being written, the theatre had not stood still. Early in the 1860s a second Hungarian-language theatre opened in Buda, the People's Theatre, directed by György Molnár (1830–91). In 1864 the first School of Dramatic Art opened, and among the outstanding actors of the end of the nineteenth century were Lujza Blaha (1850–1926) and Vidor Kassai (1840–1928). In 1884 the opera company left the National Theatre and moved to its own home in the first Hungarian Opera House. Under Ede Paulay (1836–94), the National Theatre became known throughout Europe; its leading actresses at this time were Mari Jászai (1850–1926) and Emilia Márkus (1860–1949).

At the turn of the century a number of new theatres were established in Budapest—the Vigszínház in 1896, the Magyar Színház in 1897, the Király Színház in 1903. The Vigszínház became particularly important at the beginning of the century with actors who excelled in the new naturalistic style of acting, among them Irén Varsányi, Gyula Hegedüs, Sándor Góth, and Frigyes Tanay. On the other hand, the Király Színház specialized in the production of operetta. From 1904 to 1907 the Thalia Company under Sándor Hevesi (1873–1939) did good experimental work.

An important playwright at the turn of the century was Sándor Bródy (1863–1924), creator of the modern bourgeois dramatic literature in Hungary. Among his plays the most significant were *A dada* (1902), *A tanitónő* (1908), *A medikus* (1911). Mention should also be made of Jenő Rákosi (1842–1929) and Lajos Dóczy (1845–1919), who together founded the neo-Romantic school in

Hungary, attempting to escape from materialism into a world of legendary heroes and fantasy.

In the years before the First World War there were two distinct trends in dramatic literature, the one represented by Zsigmond Móricz (1879–1942), and the other by Ferenc Molnár (1878–1952) and Ferenc Herczeg (1863–1954). The first is perhaps better known for his novels, but his plays are truly representative of Hungarian town and country life, among them *Sári bíró* (1909), *Ludas Matyi* (1911), *Nem élhetek muzsikaszó nélkül* (1928), and *Légy jó mindhalálig* (1929). Molnár and Herczeg, who are both well known outside their own country, are perhaps more cosmopolitan and sophisticated in their approach to drama. Molnár's best-known play is *Liliom* (1909), on which Rodgers and Hammerstein based their outstanding *Carousel* (1945). Many of his other plays have been translated into English, and been acted in England and America, among them *The Good Fairy*, *The Glass Slipper*, *The Guardsman* (in which Lynn Fontanne and Alfred Lunt made a great success in New York in 1924), *The Swan*, *Carnival*, and *Olympia*. Herczeg has written excellent comedies and historical tragedies, among them *Gyurkovits lányok* (1899), *Bizáncz* (1904), *Kék róka* (1917), and *A Híd* (1925), a study in national problems.

A remarkable playwright of this pre-war period was Dezső Szomory (1869–1944), who wrote both on general human problems and on Hungarian historical themes. Of the plays of Frigyes Karinthy (1888–1938), the great Hungarian humorist and satirical writer, the most important is his tragicomedy, *Holnap reggel* (1915).

The First World War was followed by economic depression, and by a period of decline in Hungarian theatrical life. Nevertheless there was no dearth of good actors, among them Gyula Csortos and Arthur Somlay at the Vigszínház, where they were later joined by Pál Jávor, Margit Makay, and Gábor Rajnay (1885–1961). At the National Theatre Sándor Hevesi was in charge, with Gizi Bajor (1893–1951) and Árpád Ódry (1876–1937). Among the writers of this period was Jenő Heltai (1871–1957), the poet of city life, whose long career as a playwright began in 1914 with *Tündérlaki lányok* and closed in 1955 with *Szépek szépe* (1955). He is best known in England for his verse-play *A néma levente* (1936), which was seen a year later in London as *The Silent Knight*, in a version by Humbert Wolfe. The literary career of Gyula Illyés (1902–) began before the Second World War, but his best work as a playwright was done in the 1950s, when several of his plays were seen at the National Theatre. One of the plays of Lajos Bíró (1880–1948), *Our Katie*, was seen in London in 1946. Two other playwrights of this period were Lajos Zilahy (1891–) and János Kodolányi (1899–), whose greatest success was the realistic folk play *Földindulás* (1939). László Németh (1901–) also had his greatest success in the 1950s and 1960s with *Galilei* (1956) and *A két Bólyai* (1961).

In 1949 the theatres in Hungary were nationalized, and theatrical art flourished all over the country. Budapest in 1962 had twenty theatres, and there were another dozen in the provinces. New audiences are crowding into them, the young people, the peasants, the artisans. The Déryné (or Village) Theatre (named after the great actress) takes plays into remote hamlets, and there too the size of the audiences is rapidly increasing. The status of the actors has been revolutionized. They are permanently employed, on a fixed salary, and after a certain lapse of time they qualify for a state pension. The Academy of Dramatic Art was reorganized in 1957, and in the same year the Institute of Theatrical Studies was founded. There is no lack of excellent actors and directors, and among the playwrights of today mention should be made of Lajos Mesterházi (1916–), whose *Pesti emberek* (1957) has been performed by many theatres in Europe, József Darvas (1912–) and Miklós Hubay (1918–). A number of European and American authors figure in the Hungarian repertory, among them Shaw, Brecht, Miller and Tennessee Williams. Among the producers are Tamás Major (1910–), who is also the chief actor of the National Theatre, and Kálmán Nádasdy (1904–), director of the Hungarian Opera House.

Attached to the National Theatre is a small theatre named after the great dramatist József Katona, who also has a theatre named after him in his birthplace, Kecskemét. Other theatres in Budapest are the Madách, the Petőfi, the Jókai, and the József Attila. There is an open-air theatre-in-the-round, and a marionette theatre. National Theatres have been established at Pécs, Debrecen, Miskolc and Szeged. Other important centres are the Kisfaludy Theatre in Győr, the Szigligeti in Szolnok, the Gárdonyi Géza in Eger, the Csiky Gergely in Kaposvár, and the Jókai in Békés.

Apart from professional companies, there are in Hungary some 3,000 amateur troupes, sponsored by factories or social organizations.

HUNT, (James Henry) Leigh (1784–1859), English poet, essayist, and critic, and one of the pioneers of modern dramatic criticism. He probably had a keener appreciation of acting than any of his contemporaries, and today his criticisms re-create the art of the great players who brought acting distinction to the theatre of his day. He took his profession as seriously as he expected the players to take theirs, and insisted that the player could not express passion perfectly unless that passion had first been felt. 'It is from feebleness of emotion that so many dull actors endeavour to supply passion with vehemence of voice and action, as jugglers are talkative and bustling to beguile scrutiny.'

But with all his knowledge of actors' work, Hunt maintained an unusual honesty and independence: 'To know an actor personally appeared to me a vice not to be thought of; and I would as lief have taken poison as accepted a ticket from the theatres.'

Leigh Hunt was the first regular critic of quality who made it his business to report upon all the principal theatrical events of the day. He was critic of the *News* from 1805 to 1807. He and his brother John ran their own paper, the *Examiner*, and Leigh wrote criticisms for it from 1808 to 1813. His play, *A Legend of Florence*, was produced at Covent Garden Theatre in 1840. In the same year he published the dramatic works of Sheridan, and those of Wycherley, Congreve, Vanbrugh, and Farquhar, with biographical notes. These drew from Macaulay, in the *Edinburgh Review*, the famous essay 'The Comic Dramatists of the Restoration'. Macaulay wrote of Hunt: 'We have a kindness for Mr. Leigh Hunt. Unless we are mistaken, he is a very clever, a very honest, and a very good-natured man.' The cream of Leigh Hunt's theatre criticism is contained in a volume prepared by William Archer—*Dramatic Essays* (1894)—with a long and valuable introduction by the editor. T. C. KEMP†

HURLEY, ALEC (?–1913), a music-hall singer, with a remarkably fine tenor voice, who specialized in bright and breezy coster songs of a more robust style than those of Albert Chevalier. One of the most famous was 'The Lambeth Walk', not to be confused with the later song of that name featured in *Me and My Girl*. He was the second husband of Marie Lloyd. W. MACQUEEN-POPE†

HURRY, LESLIE (1909–), English stage designer, whose first work was done for Helpmann's ballet of 'Hamlet', produced by the Sadler's Wells company at the New Theatre in 1942. He has since done the décor for a number of ballets, including 'Swan Lake' in 1943 and again in 1952; operas, among them 'Turandot' (1947), the 'Ring' cycle (1954), and 'The Moon and Sixpence' (1957); and plays. Apart from his work for Shakespeare plays at the Old Vic and the Royal Shakespeare Theatre in Stratford-upon-Avon, he was responsible for the décor of *Tamburlaine the Great* (1951), *The Living Room* and *Venice Preserved* (both 1953), *Cat on a Hot Tin Roof* (1958), and *The Duchess of Malfi* (1960). His work is characterized by a sombre magnificence which imparts a brooding air of tragedy to his productions, shot through with sudden gleams of gold and red. He is at his best in plays which call for the conjuring-up of mystery and a sense of space, together with poetic imagery.

I

I.A.S.T.A., see INSTITUTE FOR ADVANCED STUDIES IN THE THEATRE ARTS.

IBSEN, HENRIK JOHAN (1828–1906), Norwegian dramatist, born at Skien of wealthy parents who soon lost their wealth, so that his early years were spent in poverty and his youth in a slow fight for recognition.

The reputation of Henrik Ibsen is recovering from the reaction liable to occur in the half-century after a great poet's death, and the more sober judgement of a later generation now finds less perishable matter in his work than was once supposed. What will endure (all the work, that is, of his maturity and much of that of his youth) will probably be found to place him among the greatest dramatists of the world. His interpretation of life, even when it speaks in terms of the parochial and immediate, is, in fact, concerned with the universal and the unchanging; his art, which has the economy and stability of architecture, having outlived its host of imitators, can now be seen for what it is, the inevitable expression in form of profound and passionate poetic thought. Never, even in the most seemingly prosaic pictures of small-town life (with which his name is all too closely associated in England), does Ibsen speak otherwise than as a profound, passionate, and meditative poet. He himself asked that his readers should look at his works as a whole, should read them chronologically, and should leave none out. And indeed it is only by so doing that we can hope to see the continuity and breadth of his estimate of human experience, his profound apprehension of its significance. A few only of his plays are tragic in form; most of them are tragic in mood, if we include in the tragic mood the solemn, the stern, and the prophetic. It is sometimes said that his lack of humour brings him short of ultimate greatness. He had, it is true, less than Shakespeare. But he had more than Milton or Dante or Aeschylus; and it is as they see it that he sees man's nature.

His first play, *Catilina* (1850), is a melodrama full of crude strength, and of promise easier for us to recognize than for his contemporaries. In 1851 he went to the Bergen theatre as Ole Bull's assistant and travelled to Denmark and Germany to study theatrical techniques. In 1854 he wrote *Fru Inger til Østraat*, a play set in medieval Norway with a theme that, nevertheless, bears closely on the history of his own time. Already Ibsen sees the life and national policy of his country against a background of European culture and thought. In 1855 he wrote *Gildet paa Solhaug*, a medieval play, romantic and poetic this time, and full of the past glories of Norway. It was the first to have any measure of success. *Haermaendene paa Helgeland* (1857) is set in the world of the sagas, the greatest age of Norway. It is a severe, simple, and moving tragedy, and structure, character, and dialogue reveal the remarkable artistic progress made in these seven years. After this he only twice used the past as a setting for his plays and then primarily for the light thrown by it upon his own times.

In 1862 the theatre at Bergen went bankrupt and Ibsen, who had married in 1858, became artistic director of the Norwegian theatre in Christiania (Oslo). *Kjaerlighedens Komedie* was produced there in the same year, a satirical verse play on contemporary life, revealing a totally different side of Ibsen's power. Though received with some hostility it made a sharp impression. *Kongsemnerne* was produced in 1863, an impressive historical play whose interest is psychological and poetic. In 1863 also he received a travelling fellowship which allowed him to visit Italy and Germany and removed the worst of his financial difficulties. Two years later, after the appearance of *Brand* (1865), he received a state pension and his future as a poet was assured. Although he spent much of the rest of his life abroad, his interest in Norwegian politics remained keen, fierce, and often critical. He never, in any essential respect, ceased to be a Norwegian.

After the political events of 1864 he went south, and settled in Rome, where *Brand* was written. This great poetic drama, the first of his major works, established his fame throughout Europe. For the first time we meet in their full power his characteristic sternness, strength, and searching questioning of motive and deed. The method, which he never wholly forsook after, of implying the nature of truth by a series of unanswered questions and seeming negations, is here felt in all its bleakness. It is a play of unsurpassed grandeur and of profound understanding. *Peer Gynt* (1867) is in some ways a complementary study of Norwegian character (and through that of universal humanity); much of it is happy, gay, and even humorous poetry; the mountain landscape, grim in *Brand*, is often radiant with sunshine. Few plays have bewildered more critics or led to more discussion; the truths it tells are not always comfortable to live with.

After *Peer Gynt*, Ibsen wrote no more plays in verse. *De Unges Forbund*, finished in 1869, is an unexpectedly light-hearted satire on a theme on which Ibsen usually showed himself implacable—dishonesty and insincerity. The colossal *Kejser og Galilaeer*, begun in 1869, was finished in 1873. It is a highly interesting and complex study of the struggle between paganism and early Christianity under the Emperor Julian. It reveals a powerful historical imagination, but is the last play of Ibsen's to be set in the past.

The four plays that follow are realistic pictures of the small-town life of Ibsen's own day, revealing mercilessly the lies upon which certain societies, self-righteous and self-contained, are and always have been founded. They are the images of ageless and universal parochialism. *Samfundets Støtter* (1875–7) is a study of public life rooted in a lie and, by implication, of the truth that finally frees it; *Et Dukkehjem* (1878–9), of the insidious destruction worked by a lie in domestic life; *Gengangere* (1881), of the lingering poison of another marriage rooted in a lie; *En Folkefiende* (1882), of the man of truth in conflict with a corrupt society. All have the structural economy and simplicity that is reached only by a skilled and experienced artist concentrating all his powers. Their influence, both in thought and technique, was probably greater than that of any other group of Ibsen's plays.

On the threshold of the last group stands *Vildanden* (1883–4), a group in which symbolism plays an increasingly large part and the interest shifts gradually from the individual in society to the individual exploring strange areas of experience, isolated and alone. *Rosmersholm* (1885–6) traces the growth of a mind in contact with a tradition of nobility; *Fruen fra Havet* (1888), the overcoming of obsession by freedom and responsibility. *Hedda Gabler* (1890) is a subtle and skilful study of the effects of artificial society and, by contrast, of the virtue of nature and normality. The symbolism of *Bygmester Solness* (1891–2) is stronger than that of any earlier play, and much of it is concerned with the relation of the artist and the man within an individual. *Lille Eyolf* (1894) is a study of marital relations, of the nature of love and the distinctions between its kinds; *John Gabriel Borkman* (1895–6), of unfulfilled genius and of the relation of the genius to society. *Naar vi Døde Vaagner* (1897–9) is Ibsen's last pronouncement on the artist's relation to life and to truth.

UNA ELLIS-FERMOR†, *rev.*

Ibsen's grandson, Tancred, one of Norway's leading film directors, married a ballet dancer, Lillebil (1899–) who in her twenties became an actress. From 1928 to 1956 she was closely associated with Det Nye Teater in Oslo, and thereafter with the National Theatre. She has appeared in Paris, London and elsewhere in Scandinavia. L. KATHLEEN MCFARLANE

The impact of Ibsen on the English and American theatres has been so decisive that it seems worth while to summarize here some of the important productions of his plays in both countries.

1. IBSEN IN ENGLAND. The first of Ibsen's plays to be produced in London was *Samfundets Støtter* in a translation by William Archer entitled *Quicksands*. This was seen at the Gaiety on 15 Dec. 1880. It was not until 1889 that the play was done under its better-known title, *The Pillars of Society*. It was last seen on the London stage in 1926.

In 1884 a version of *Et Dukkehjem*, as *Breaking a Butterfly*, was seen at the Princes, with Tree as Krogstad (renamed Dunkley). The first production as *A Doll's House* was that of Charles Carrington at the Novelty in June 1889. He himself played Dr. Rank and his wife, Janet Achurch, was Nora. This production was revived several times. At Terry's Theatre in 1891 Elizabeth Robins, who, with Janet Achurch, was responsible for much of the early interest in Ibsen, played Mrs. Linden. She had previously appeared as Martha in *The Pillars of Society*. An important revival of *A Doll's House* was that of Nov. 1925 at the Playhouse, with Madge Titheradge as Nora. Other actresses to play the part have been Gillian Scaife (1928), Gwen Ffrangcon-Davies (1930), Lydia Lopokova (1934), Lucie Mannheim (1939), Angela Baddeley (1945) and, the last production to date, Mai Zetterling at the Lyric, Hammersmith, in 1953.

Gengangere, as *Ghosts*, was first produced privately in English in 1891 and aroused a storm of abuse, particularly from Clement Scott. It was revived several times before its first licensed production at the Haymarket on 14 July 1914. An important later revival was that of 1928, when Mrs. Patrick Campbell and John Gielgud appeared together as Mrs. Alving and Oswald for eight special matinées. Other revivals have starred Sybil Thorndike (1930), Nancy Price (1935) with Glen Byam Shaw as Oswald, Marie Ney (1937), Katina Paxinou (1940), Beatrix Lehmann (1943 and 1951), and Flora Robson (1958) at the Old Vic.

Rosmersholm had its first performance in English at the Vaudeville in 1891, the same year as *Hedda Gabler* (with Elizabeth Robins) and *Fruen fra Havet* (as *The Lady from the Sea*). Two years later came the first translation of *Bygmester Solness* as *The Master Builder* and of *En Folkefiende* as *An Enemy of the People* (with Tree as Stockman). *Vildanden* (*The Wild Duck*) followed in 1894, *Lille Eyolf* (*Little Eyolf*) in 1896, and *John Gabriel Borkman* in 1897. *De Unges Forbund* (*The League of Youth*) was seen for the first and only time in 1900, and in 1903, in which year *Naar vi Døde Vaagner* (*When We Dead Awaken*) was also given, Ellen Terry appeared in *The Vikings of Helgeland*, a translation of *Haermaendene paa Helgeland* staged by her son Gordon Craig. This play has only once been revived, at the Old Vic in 1928. Other first productions were those of *Fru Inger til Østraat* as *Lady Inger of Ostraat* in 1906; *Olaf Liljekrans* in 1911; *Brand* (and *Kæmpehøien* as *The Hero's Mound*) in 1912, the former being seen again in 1959; *Kongsemnerne* (*The Pretenders*) in 1913; *Sancthansnatten* as *St. John's Night* in 1921, and *Catilina* in 1936.

Peer Gynt was first seen in 1911 at the Rehearsal Theatre. It was given its first commercial production, in a translation by William Archer, at the Old Vic in 1922, with Russell Thorndike as Peer. Later productions there have been in 1935, in a new translation by R. Ellis Roberts; 1944 (see No. 103) with

Ralph Richardson as Peer, Sybil Thorndike as Åse and Laurence Olivier as the Button-Moulder; and 1962.

In the early days many of Ibsen's plays were produced by small experimental theatres, often for one performance only, and by far the larger number of productions have been by small enthusiastic groups. There have, however, been some remarkable revivals, apart from those enumerated above. *Rosmersholm* was revived in 1893 with Elizabeth Robins and Lewis Waller; in 1926 with Edith Evans; and in 1948 with Lucie Mannheim and her husband Marius Goring. In 1959 Peggy Ashcroft gave a fine performance as Rebecca at the Royal Court Theatre, in a new adaptation by Ann Jellicoe. The latter was also responsible for a new version of *The Lady from the Sea* (1961), with Margaret Leighton as Ellida.

Hedda Gabler was seen with Mrs. Patrick Campbell in the name-part in 1907 and 1922; with Laura Cowie in 1928; with Jean Forbes-Robertson in 1931 and 1951; with Sonia Dresdel in 1942; and, in a new translation by Max Faber, with Peggy Ashcroft in a superb performance ably supported by George Devine as Tesman, in 1954.

Other plays which have been revived with some frequency are *The Master Builder*, *The Wild Duck*, and *John Gabriel Borkman*. The last was given on the open stage of the Mermaid Theatre in 1961.

This list is of London productions only, and takes no account of numerous provincial and amateur performances. It should, however, be noted that in 1909 *Love's Comedy*, a translation of *Kjærlighedens Komedie*, was given its first English performance at the Gaiety, Manchester.

Archer was the first translator of Ibsen, but with the lapse of time his versions have been found not always adequate. Professor Ellis-Fermor translated some of the plays for the Penguin Classics series, but these, though scholarly, were not theatrical. A translation of *Brand* (1959) by Michael Meyer had an unexpected success at the Lyric, Hammersmith. His version of *An Enemy of the People* was seen at the Nottingham Playhouse in 1962, again with much success, and of *The Pretenders* at Bristol in 1963. It is to be hoped that he will continue. A new translation of all the plays has been undertaken by J. W. McFarlane. These have introductions, commentaries, and notes on earlier drafts, where they exist. Each play is also published separately in an acting version, without the scholarly apparatus.

ED.

2. Ibsen in America. The influence of a large immigrant population from Scandinavia, and the lack of effective censorship, prevented the emergence in America of the opposition which Ibsen's plays had to face in England. The first to be done in English was *Et Dukkehjem* (1882) as *The Child Wife*. The adapter, William Laurence, transferred the scene to England, added a comic Irish maid, and used Ibsen's happy ending. Helena Modjeska appeared in another version, entitled *Thora*, in 1883, also with the happy ending. *Gengangere*, which was not performed in Europe until 1883, had its world première in Chicago the previous year, in Norwegian.

The first production to arouse widespread interest in America, where echoes of the Ibsen controversy in England were beginning to be heard, was that of *Et Dukkehjem* as *A Doll's House* with Beatrice Cameron as Nora. First seen in Boston and New York in 1889, this went on an extended tour of the major American cities. *Ghosts* was first seen in English in New York in 1894, and was a success with most of the critics, though some found it 'unwholesome'. William Winter, like Clement Scott in England, emerged as the opponent of Ibsen, with William Dean Howells and James Huneker as his defenders. American enthusiasm for Ibsen's work increased with New York productions of *John Gabriel Borkman* (1897) and *Hedda Gabler* (1898), and with productions of other plays by visiting artists, among them Janet Achurch (the first English Nora) Tree, Réjane, and Agnes Sorma.

In 1900 Florence Kahn appeared in New York as Hilda in *The Master Builder*. She was also seen as Rebecca West in 1904, and as Irene (in *When We Dead Awaken*) in 1905. Mrs. Fiske, who had toured extensively as Nora from 1894 onwards, was also seen in New York as Hedda in 1903 and Rebecca West in 1907. She played her last Ibsen part, Mrs. Alving, in 1927. Other important productions at this time were those of *Hedda Gabler* with Blanche Bates (1900), Nance O'Neill and Mary Shaw (both 1904), and Ethel Barrymore's Nora in 1905. In this same year the Russian actress Alla Nazimova emerged as one of the leading interpreters of Ibsen in America. She began with Mrs. Alving and Hilda Wangel, in Russian (with Paul Orlenev). Her first English-speaking part was Hedda in 1906. Subsequently she appeared with Walter Hampden in *A Doll's House* and *The Master Builder* (both 1907), as Rita in *Little Eyolf* (1910), as Hedda in 1918 and 1936, and as Mrs. Alving in 1935. Richard Mansfield presented a new aspect of Ibsen's work to the American public in 1906 by producing and acting in *Peer Gynt*, the first performance of the play in English.

The next decade saw a falling-off of interest in Ibsen, but in the 1920s he became popular again. In 1923 Duse appeared in New York as Ellida (in *The Lady from the Sea*) and as Mrs. Alving, and the Theatre Guild staged an elaborate production of *Peer Gynt* with Joseph Schildkraut in the title-role. Eva Le Gallienne played Hilda Wangel in *The Master Builder* (1924) and Ella Rentheim in *John Gabriel Borkman* (1926); later, as director of the Civic Repertory Theatre (1926–33), she produced and acted in both plays, and also appeared as Hedda, a part she has frequently acted since. She also played Rebecca West in 1935 and

Mrs. Alving in 1948. Walter Hampden, who played Oswald in 1924, scored a great success in 1927 as Dr. Stockman in *An Enemy of the People*. Blanche Yurka's Gina (in *The Wild Duck*) and her Hedda and Ellida (both 1929) were also notable.

There were few performances of Ibsen's plays during the 1930s and 1940s, when most actors and directors considered him old-fashioned. Thornton Wilder's adaptation of *A Doll's House*, produced by Jed Harris with Ruth Gordon as Nora and Paul Lukas as Dr. Rank, was, however, a great success, and Katina Paxinou, the famous Greek actress, appeared as Hedda in 1942, playing in English. This period of comparative indifference ended with Arthur Miller's successful adaptation of *An Enemy of the People* in 1950 and Lee Strasberg's production of *Peer Gynt* in 1951. These productions initiated something of an Ibsen revival in the off-Broadway theatre. In recent years the Phoenix Theatre has presented *The Master Builder* (1955) and *Peer Gynt* (1960), and at his Fourth Street Theatre David Ross began an Ibsen cycle with *Hedda Gabler* (1960), *Ghosts* (1961), and *Rosmersholm* (1962).

ROBERT TRACY

ICELAND. A National Theatre building, to plans by the architect Guðjon Samúelsson (1887–1950), was begun in Reykjavik in 1930, but owing to financial and other difficulties it was not completed until 1950. It opened on 20 Apr. with a repertory season which included a number of European plays in translation, as well as three plays by Icelandic authors, among them the Nobel Prizewinner Halldór Kiljan Laxness, who adapted his novel *Islandsklukkan* for the occasion. Although the theatre relies heavily on imported plays, efforts are made to include at least one play by an Icelandic author in each season. Among the Shakespeare productions have been *As You Like It* (1952), *A Midsummer Night's Dream* (1957), and *Julius Caesar* (1959). A number of contemporary English and American plays have also been seen. Opera and ballet are included in the repertory, and visiting opera companies have come from Scandinavia, Finland, Germany, China; ballet companies from India, Japan, Spain, and Russia. Guest producers are also invited to stage single plays. The permanent company consists of about fifteen actors on long-term contracts, but other actors can be engaged either for a season or for a single performance. Attached to the theatre is a School of Dramatic Art, a Ballet School, and a Choir. Although the population of Reykjavik is only about 70,000, attendances at the theatre have averaged 100,000 a season. The National Theatre is the only official theatre building in Iceland, but there is a good deal of amateur activity up and down the country.

IFFLAND, August Wilhelm (1759–1814), German actor and playwright, was a member of a cultured middle-class family, and was intended for the Church. An irresistible attraction, however, drew him to the stage, and caused him to leave home, wandering from place to place in search of an opening, pursued everywhere by his father's anger. In 1777 he was taken on by Ekhof in Gotha, and a year later went with the company, on Ekhof's death, to Mannheim, where Dalberg had recently taken charge of the newly opened National Theatre. Iffland was given a large part in the management of theatrical affairs, and his first plays were produced with much success. He played the part of Franz Moor in the first production of *Die Räuber* (1781), always one of his best parts, and one in which he was warmly praised by the author. At the same time his own plays, now forgotten, were more popular than Schiller's. Their simple, unsophisticated characters, well-made plots, and superficial nobility and ecstasy caught the taste of public and critics alike. He toured in them with much success, and even acted at Hamburg with the great Schröder, who, however, thought little of him. Iffland, conscious of this, was not at his best, and preferred the atmosphere of Weimar, where, inspired by the kindness of Goethe, he played sixteen of his best parts to great applause. As an actor he developed a fine technique, but no depth. It was said of him that he was a virtuoso, capable of great moments but not of sustained effort, and he had an unfortunate predilection for tragic parts—Lear and Wallenstein—for which he was not suited. He was at his best in dignified comedy, in the parts of retired officers, elderly councillors, indulgent parents, reverend and witty old men. His character, unlike his acting, never changed, and the faults and virtues of his youth were those of his old age. He was a curious mixture—a *bon viveur* yet fond of solitude, eager for money yet always in debt, indolent yet a prolific playwright, companionable yet sensitive. He left his mark on the German theatre by his work at Mannheim, which he practically controlled throughout its heyday. He then went to Berlin, where he remained until his death. His policy was cautious, and his repertory restricted. This led to trouble with the extremists among the rising generation, and Iffland was often embittered by their attacks. But he trained a number of young actors, not in his own virtuosity, but in the serious, sober style of Schröder, and shortly before his death took on Ludwig Devrient, destined to be the greatest German actor of the Romantic period.

ILLICA, Luigi (1857–1919), Italian writer, author with Giacosa of the libretti for some of Puccini's operas (see GIACOSA and OPERA, 15).

ILLINGTON, Margaret (1879–1934), an American actress who made her first appearances in Chicago. Engaged by Daniel Frohman, who coined her stage name—her real name being Maude Ellen Light—she first appeared at the Criterion Theatre, New York, in Sept. 1900. Three years later she married Frohman, from whom she was divorced in 1909. She remained on the stage, and later toured under the management of her second husband, Major Bowes, making her last appearance in 1919. A woman of strong personality, she was at her best in forceful, passionate parts, and one of her biggest successes was Marie Louise Voysin in *The Thief*.

ILLUSTRE-THÉÂTRE, the name taken by the company with which Molière, drawn into it by his friendship with Madeleine Béjart, made his first appearance on the professional stage. The contract drawn up between the first members, among whom were three of the Béjart family, is dated 30 June 1643, and was modelled upon that of the Confrérie de la Passion. In essentials, it has remained the basic constitution of the Comédie-Française. The company leased a tennis-court in Paris, and while alterations were in progress there, played for a time in the provinces, possibly at Rouen, where they may have given a play by Corneille, a native of that town. On 1 Jan. 1644 they opened in Paris, but without great success. It was early in the course of that year that Poquelin first signed himself 'Molière', a choice of name for which no explanation has been given. The company, all young and inexperienced, led a harried and precarious life, and in Jan. 1645 changed their quarters in the hope of improvement. Financial affairs, however, went from bad to worse, and in the end Molière found himself imprisoned for debt, a predicament from which he was rescued by his father. By Aug. 1645 the Illustre-Théâtre had come to an ignominious end, and vanished without leaving a trace in contemporary records. Its repertory included plays by Corneille, du Ryer, and Tristan l'Hermite, and some specially written by a member of the company, Nicholas Desfontaines, all of which had the word *illustre* in the title. There was a marked lack of comedy, in which the company, after a provincial tour which lasted until 1658, was later to excel in Paris, under the leadership of Molière, and with several of its original members.

ILYINSKY, IGOR VLADIMIROVICH (1901–), Soviet actor, outstanding in roles of satirical comedy. He began his career in 1917 under Theodore Komisarjevsky. In 1920 he joined the Meyerhold Theatre, where, according to André van Gyseghem in *Theatre in Soviet Russia*, he was the one good actor, 'as near to genius as anyone content to work under the heavy firing of Meyerhold's terrific personality and barrage of ideas could ever be'. When the theatre was closed in 1938 Ilyinsky went to the Maly, where he played leading roles, among them Arkashka Neschastlivstev in *The Forest*, Prisipkin in *The Bug*, Raspluev in *The Wedding of Krechinsky* and Khlestakov in *Revizor*. In 1950 he appeared as the sailor Shibayev in Vishnevsky's *The Unforgettable 1919th*. His reputation has grown considerably in recent years, and he has also become a notable producer, being responsible for *Vanity Fair* in 1958 and Sofronov's *Honesty* in 1961.

IMMERMANN, KARL (1796–1840), director of the Düsseldorf theatre from 1834 to 1837. Under the influence of Goethe's work at Weimar he tried to raise the standard of theatrical performance, insisted on clear diction, and made many technical improvements in scenery, costume, and lighting. The public, however, was apathetic, and his experiment ended in failure.

IMPERIAL THEATRE, NEW YORK, on 45th Street between Broadway and 8th Avenue. One of the most consistently successful theatres in New York, this was opened by the Shuberts on 24 Dec. 1923. It has mainly been used for musical shows, but in 1936 it had its first Shakespeare production with Leslie Howard in *Hamlet*, settings by Stewart Chaney. This, however, was no match for the Gielgud *Hamlet*, which was running at the same time, and soon took to the road. It was followed by further musicals, and in 1946 came the successful *Annie Get Your Gun* with Ethel Merman, who also starred in *Call Me Madam* (1950). Later successes were *The Most Happy Fella* (1956), *Carnival* (1961), *Oliver!* (1963), and *Fiddler on the Roof* (1964).

GEORGE FREEDLEY†

INCHBALD, ELIZABETH (*née* SIMPSON) (1753–1821), English actress and one of the earliest English women dramatists. She had a brother George on the stage, and decided to join him, in spite of an impediment in her speech which she never wholly overcame. A very beautiful and spirited young woman, though without any money, she ran away from home and had many adventures before she married Joseph Inchbald (? –1779), an inoffensive little man who painted and acted indifferently, and only survived his marriage by seven years. He was at his best in old men. His wife was first seen on the stage in the provinces, where she acted Cordelia to his Lear; she became the friend of Mrs. Siddons and Tate Wilkinson, and was acting with the latter when her husband died. She later appeared at Covent Garden, but in 1789 retired from a profession in which she had made little mark, and devoted herself to the more lucrative employment of playwriting. A tall, fair woman, beautifully dressed, with a somewhat angular figure, she was extremely popular in private life, and had many opportunities of remarriage. She refused them all, but in spite of high spirits and a witty tongue no scandal attaches itself to her name. She was a capable writer of sentimental comedy, and though none of her plays has survived, they were successful in their own day, being mainly adaptations of contemporary French or German models. The best were probably *I'll Tell You What* (1785), *Wives as They Were, and Maids as They Are* (1797), and her last comedy, *To Marry or Not to Marry* (1805). She had a good sense of humour and some wit, but her plays, which are very characteristic of their time, are spoilt by an obvious moral purpose and too much sentiment. She was also the author of a number of novels, and edited several important collections of English tragedies and comedies. Among her many activities she made notable contributions to the *Edinburgh Journal*. An account of her life and times was written by S. R. Littlewood in 1921.

INCIDENTAL MUSIC. Strictly speaking, any music written for and used in the production of a spoken play is in the nature of incidental music, even if not technically so described. Such music may amount to too little for such description, or to too much. Thus, for example, Linley's song 'Here's to the Maiden' in *The School for Scandal* or Beethoven's 'Coriolan' Overture, the only piece of music written by him for Collin's play, come technically under the head of incidental music, but would hardly be so called; nor would, on the other hand, such works as those in which Lully collaborated with Molière, which amount to intermezzi, indeed almost to *opéras-ballets*, where the music is as important as the play; and the same is true of eighteenth-century English musical stage pieces, of French vaudevilles and of German *Singspiele*. These, although not operas—which even the English ballad operas are not—are sufficiently important types of musical composition, as distinct from dramatic pieces with added music, to have acquired names of their own.

Incidental music, then, may be defined as any kind of stage music expressly written for use in a dramatic performance that would still be in its essentials complete without it (even the songs could be spoken as poetry without damage to the dramatic context), music that would not have come into existence independently of the play to which it is attached, though portions of it may afterwards be extracted for use at concert performances, especially in the form of suites. Mendelssohn's *Midsummer Night's Dream* overture, written at the age of 17, was not in itself incidental music, but rather a symphonic poem for concert performance based on the subject of Shakespeare's play; but the pieces Mendelssohn wrote for the play later are incidental music properly speaking, and the overture became part of it.

From what has been said it will have become obvious that the historical origins of incidental music are complicated and indefinite. Courtly Italian spectacles, before the rise of opera in Italy at the opening of the seventeenth century, were full of music for singing and dancing; but they were distinctive types of stage entertainment with music as an integral part. The same is true of the seventeenth-century English masque. Milton's *Comus*, for instance, although it may be regarded as containing music merely as an adjunct, cannot be imagined to have been written in the first place as a self-sufficient play to which music could subsequently have been added by way of an expedient or for greater effectiveness—if not by Henry Lawes, then by any other competent composer. Up to a point it was distinctly a musical entertainment, and indeed would have become an opera if opera had by its time taken a firm foothold in England.

Plays with incidental music are in no sense primarily musical works except, precisely, 'incidentally'. Thus we must not look for the rise of incidental music in the stage entertainments of Renaissance Italy, nor in those which plainly derived from them in England (see MASQUE). We see traces of it, however, in the independent English drama of the Elizabethans, and also in the classical Spanish drama. It is clear that Shakespeare's plays asked for a good deal of music, not only interpolated songs, which the poet fortunately made an integral part of his work by himself providing the words for them, nor merely the sennets (a word probably derived from *sonata*) and tuckets (from *toccata*) he prescribed, but also interludes and dances. It is evident that there must have been music, perhaps for a consort of viols, if not a 'broken consort' of wind and strings for greater effectiveness in the theatre, at the opening of *Twelfth Night*; and since a Bergomask is called for in the last act of *A Midsummer Night's Dream* and Benedick asks the pipers to strike up for a dance at the end of *Much Ado About Nothing*, there must have been players provided. In Spain the plays of Cervantes, Lope de Vega, Calderón, Moreto, and many other classics continually called for music of various sorts; yet they have too much action and dialogue and self-sufficient verse to become anything like operas. Their music is not casual, but it is plainly incidental.

In English Restoration plays it has been said to be casual. Nevertheless, it is difficult to maintain that the contributions to the playhouse made by so important a composer as Purcell are to be ignored as contributions to the development of theatre music, and no doubt J. A. Westrup, in his book on Purcell, is justified in cataloguing the comedies and tragedies coming into this category under the head of 'Plays with Incidental Music and Songs'. These plays include works by Beaumont and Fletcher, Dryden, Congreve and others, as well as four adaptations from Shakespeare. Forty-four of Purcell's fifty stage works decidedly remain literary dramatic pieces: their music, which as such has a classical importance, must therefore be called incidental music and marks, indeed, an important historical advance in that domain.

The fact that this advance was made in England and not in any other European country of comparable musical culture is unquestionably due to two interdependent causes: the flourishing condition of the spoken drama and the failure of opera to thrive, as it was by that time doing in Italy and France, and was soon to do in Austria and Germany as well. Nowhere else had incidental music resulted in anything as fine as it had done in Purcell's hands. It might have done so in Spain if the only condition in its favour had been the drying-up of early sources of opera; but it failed there because the Spanish drama too had declined by that time.

There was not much call for incidental music anywhere during the eighteenth century. The five chief musical countries, Italy, France, Germany, Austria, and England, now developed light operatic types of stage entertainment of various sorts, in which the music, though often very flimsy, was still essential, not incidental. Handel, however, provided music for a London revival of *The Alchemist* and later for *Alceste*; Haydn for Bicknell's *Alfred* (but not, as was once thought, for *King Lear*); and Mozart for an obscure play called *Thamos, King of Egypt*, which is now of interest only because his score for it in some ways foreshadows his later great 'Egyptian' opera, 'The Magic Flute'. But the eighteenth century did something to nourish a rich soil for developments in the next. It enlarged and improved the orchestral resources, and, through the intermediary of opera on a more or less grand scale, established the orchestra in the theatre. The opera orchestras in London and Paris were the best obtainable in their time and place, while in Italy, except perhaps at one or two Courts, they were the only existing ones.

The German Courts all had their operatic establishments, and therefore their orchestras. But here conditions were rather different and, as it happened, most favourable to the development of incidental music. Although the Courts vied with each other in keeping opera going lavishly, the majority of them were situated in quite small provincial towns, such as Mannheim, Weimar, Bonn, Brunswick, Kassel, or Karlsruhe. However great their cultural ambitions, they were, on the whole, confined to the Courts and sometimes the universities. Even the few princely residences which happened to be in large centres, like Berlin, Dresden, and Munich, were still restricted in size as seats of culture, for the Court theatres were wholly inaccessible to the masses and almost as much so to the middle classes. This meant that the princes who wished to cultivate both opera and the drama were obliged to do so in a single Court theatre, with very few exceptions, one of which was Vienna, where the Court theatres kept open house more democratically.

Now an operatic establishment meant a large and good orchestra, whereas a dramatic one did not necessarily call for anything of the kind. But the latter sometimes required music of sorts, if only accompaniments for songs or some dance measures; and as on play-nights the opera orchestra was necessarily kept idle where there was only one theatre, intendants and managers naturally began to think of using it when music was called for in a play. Such a generous supply could not fail before long to lead to increasingly greedy demands. If a large orchestra was used for songs and dances in plays, it might as well be employed to the full to perform an overture and interludes between the acts. This in turn led to commissions given to composers to write such overtures and interludes and, again, it was not long before it occurred to playwrights to make the most of these orchestral opportunities by inserting into their new plays scenes actually requiring musical accompaniments, such as processions and what they called 'melodramas'—particularly exciting or moving scenes in which the spoken words were accompanied by an orchestral undercurrent. The later English 'melodrama', where attempts at robbery or murder were accompanied by appropriate music provided by a theatre composer like Jimmy Glover, was nothing else than a debased offspring of such scenes (see MELODRAMA).

The German theatre now developed along two lines in this field. There was incidental music written for plays, as for instance when the Burgtheater in Vienna, intending to produce Goethe's *Egmont*, asked Beethoven to write an overture and to provide the music Goethe specified for his final scene; and there were plays written with the intention of using incidental music, as when Helmina von Chézy turned out her preposterous *Rosamunde* (also for Vienna) and the Theater an der Wien called on Schubert to provide music for it, with the result that we are left with some delicious music by that master for a play which has vanished off the face of the earth.

Not all the German princes were necessarily enlightened, but they all felt it incumbent on them to live up to the obligations of Courts. There was much vainglorious rivalry, but it did result in a serious cultivation of opera and classical drama, the latter including translations of Greek tragedy, Shakespeare, and other non-German classics. The competition spread to the municipal theatres of some of the cities which had no Court, such as Hamburg and Leipzig, where there was probably less ostentation and more genuine endeavour.

By chance or design the greater Germanic masters of the first half of the nineteenth century wrote incidental music more conspicuously for translations than for the indigenous classics, Lessing, Goethe, Schiller, Grillparzer, and the rest. Goethe's *Faust*, for instance, was for a long time furnished with nothing better than music by an aristocratic amateur, Prince Radziwill. On the other hand, Weber contributed music to Schiller's version of Gozzi's *Turandot*, including an earlier overture on Chinese themes. Nearer the middle of the century, Schumann's score for *Manfred* appeared, and Mendelssohn was commissioned by the Prussian Court to write music for translations of Sophocles' *Antigone* and *Oedipus Coloneus*, Racine's *Athalie*, and Victor Hugo's *Ruy Blas*, as well as his extensive additions to the *Midsummer Night's Dream* overture.

By the second half of the nineteenth century incidental music was established as a musical category of some importance. It was not to be cultivated as systematically by other countries as by Germany and Austria until the present century, but important works of the kind appeared sporadically here and there. In France,

Bizet's music for Alphonse Daudet's *L'Arlésienne* comes next in importance to 'Carmen' among his works, and it is a remarkable example of what may be called 'regional music'. That is true also of Grieg's congenial, if not quite commensurate, contribution to the success of Ibsen's *Peer Gynt*, the original production of which was so exceptional an event in the Norwegian theatre as to justify the unusual extravagance of a full orchestra. Another commission for music to one of Ibsen's poetic dramas, *Gildet paa Solhaug*, was issued later in Vienna to Hugo Wolf. Ibsen's sociological plays, of course, attracted no composers, and indeed they are unimaginable with music; and it is noticeable that everywhere poetic drama—which does not necessarily mean verse drama—was the type of play that called for music and most often had its call answered by famous composers. It is not to be wondered at that, for example, Bernard Shaw's plays were left without incidental music, though it seems almost unbelievable now that, by way of exception, *Saint Joan* was not provided with a score from the hand of a distinguished British composer at its original production.

Other poetic plays that may be singled out in this connexion from the stage history of about the turn of the nineteenth century are Rostand's *Cyrano de Bergerac*, with music by Jean Nougès, and Maeterlinck's *Pelléas et Mélisande*, for which both Fauré in France (though the commission came from the Prince of Wales's Theatre in London) and Sibelius in Finland wrote music that has remained valuable in the concert-room in the form of suites, even if they are less familiar than those from the music to *Peer Gynt* and *L'Arlésienne*. In the theatre *Pelléas et Mélisande* as a play has been eclipsed by Debussy's setting of it as a music-drama.

In France many remarkable scores have been drawn from Florent Schmitt, Darius Milhaud, Arthur Honegger, and many more composers of distinction. Imperial Russia produced some interesting work, beginning rather humbly and obscurely with Glinka's music for Count Kukolnik's drama of *Prince Kholmsky*. Balakirev's music for *King Lear* and Tchaikovsky's for *Hamlet* were later examples of good work produced under the old régime, which could afford large orchestras as well as great actors and lavish productions. But the U.S.S.R., too, is generous in this matter, and it is evident from the catalogues of living Russian composers that orchestral music is expected as a matter of course in the theatre of Soviet Russia. Not many of these numerous composers—who cannot all be good, but who are at any rate all kept busy—have failed to produce at least one score of incidental music, and among these, again, every other one seems to have been composed for the production of a Shakespeare play. In America the most interesting examples of modern incidental music are those written for the new indigenous drama of Eugene O'Neill and others. But the cinema has claimed the best of American incidental music.

In England incidental music was rarely taken seriously until the present century. In the eighteenth century such slender things as Arne's delightful Shakespeare songs were exceptional, though these were written for stage productions. Nothing much of importance emerged during the nineteenth century; but something in the nature of a false start was made towards its close. It began with music commissioned from Sullivan for productions of *The Tempest*, *The Merchant of Venice*, *The Merry Wives of Windsor*, *Henry VIII*, and *Macbeth*, as well as for *The Foresters* and *King Arthur*. All this has now gone to waste, though a London production of *The Tempest* in the early 1920s, which used some of Sullivan's pieces and Arne's songs incongruously with new and very striking music by Arthur Bliss, showed how good Sullivan could be in his own much milder way at theatre music of this kind. He was certainly superior to Edward German, whom later actor-managers discovered as a purveyor of all they conceived incidental music to need—a talent for easy entertainment and agreeably picturesque, if distant, period imitation. Of German's scores for plays nothing has survived but his dances for Shakespeare's *Henry VIII* and those for Anthony Hope's romanticized *Nell Gwynn*. Little else produced before 1900 can be taken much more seriously than Glover's music, which provided stealthy undercurrents for the villain's exploits in the Drury Lane melodramas, though exceptions could be mentioned, such as Stanford's music for the *Eumenides* and *Oedipus Tyrannus* and for *Queen Mary* and *Becket*.

After that date things began to improve. Norman O'Neill's contributions to many plays produced at the Haymarket Theatre, where he was musical director, were still slight, but they showed a special aptitude for the requirements of the stage combined with graceful, sometimes fanciful, invention. But on the whole the dramatic societies at the universities were quicker in the uptake than the professional theatres. The undergraduates at Oxford and Cambridge were encouraged to have high-brow fun (in Greek) with Aristophanes, and some of the foremost composers took pleasure in writing music for these ephemeral productions, Parry being among the earliest, Vaughan Williams coming later. However, for a London production, though hardly a commercial one, Elgar was invited to write music for *Grania and Diarmid*, and thereafter interesting things happened periodically. Elgar again appeared with lovely music for *The Starlight Express*, a play based on Algernon Blackwood's fantasy-novel, *A Prisoner in Fairyland*, and later with a rather insignificant *Beau Brummell*. Bliss's music for *The Tempest* has been mentioned; Bantock's for *Macbeth*, Goossens's for Maugham's *East of Suez*, Armstrong Gibbs's for Maeterlinck's *The Betrothal*, and Frederic Austin's for Čapek's *The Insect Play*, should be referred to. Delius had a more than ordinary success with what was once again music for the poetic drama, *Hassan*, of which some has been saved for the concert-room. William Walton's music for John Gielgud's production of *Macbeth* (1942) was played on gramophone records—a wartime expedient that today would be approved neither by audiences nor by the Musicians' Union. The cinema claimed Walton for *Henry V* (1945) and *Hamlet* (1947), but these distinguished scores must have a place in any account of incidental music.

ERIC BLOM†, *rev.*

Modern producers, if they consider incidental music at all, are increasingly inclined to take it seriously. The Royal Shakespeare Theatre, which ought as a matter of course to have maintained international festival standards in every respect, for a long time kept nothing that a professional musician would call an orchestra at all, but since Peter Hall became its director and Raymond Leppard its music adviser (in 1960) it has maintained a band of some 14–16 wind players, and has commissioned incidental music from many of England's leading composers, among them Lennox Berkeley (*The Winter's Tale*, 1960), Humphrey Searle (*Troilus and Cressida*, also 1960), Alan Rawsthorne (*Hamlet*, 1961), and Roberto Gerhard (*Macbeth*, 1962)—his earlier Stratford scores for *Romeo and Juliet* and for *Cymbeline* were exceptional. The London branch of the Shakespeare company, at the Aldwych Theatre, relies for its music on a small flexible chamber ensemble of about six players. A small expert ensemble, of varying constitution but usually containing such 'evocative' instruments as trumpet, guitar, harpsichord, and recorder, is the only practical solution for a theatre company which cannot afford to maintain an orchestra; in any case, full-scale incidental music of the nineteenth-century kind accords ill with most modern productions. In 1944 the Old Vic Theatre and Sadler's Wells Opera companies were both at the New Theatre, and so the orchestra of the latter could provide the former with Grieg's incidental music for *Peer Gynt*. But Grieg's picturesque score has dated as Ibsen's play has not: Grieg's trolls now sound merely quaint and endearing, not at all grim or alarming. In 1948 the National Theatre in Oslo commissioned from Harald Saeverud a new 'de-romanticized' *Peer Gynt* score; and for the Old Vic production of 1962 an ensemble of nine musicians (including harp, xylophone, clavioline, flute, violin, and percussion) provided incidental music written by George Hall, the company's resident composer, which would not throw the audience back to the 1870s. The Old Vic also maintained up to its closing in 1963 a small flexible musical ensemble, and in its last years its musical record was as distinguished as Stratford's, including scores by such composers as Elisabeth Lutyens (*Julius Caesar*, 1962; also the *Oresteia* for the Oxford Playhouse company at the Old Vic, 1961); Michael Tippett (*The Tempest*, 1962); Peter Racine Fricker (*King John*, 1961); John Gardner (*Tamburlaine*, 1951; *Hamlet*, *King John*, 1953); Malcolm Arnold (*The Tempest*, 1954); Peter Maxwell Davies (*Richard II*, 1959); and Thea Musgrave (*A Midsummer Night's Dream*, 1960).

Contemporary incidental music, however distinguished, seldom escapes from the theatre to lead an independent life in the concert hall. Cinema producers can afford full orchestras, and incidental music for films is often refashioned in the form of suites or tone-poems. Chamber music written for curious combinations, often set down in a few spare telling strokes, tends to be too closely linked with a particular production, and to die with it. Few of Benjamin Britten's numerous admirers know his music for some thirteen plays, including *Timon of Athens* (Westminster Theatre, 1935), Priestley's *Johnson Over Jordan* (New Theatre, 1939), and *The Duchess of Malfi* (New York, 1946). Even more ephemeral are the tape-recorded scores which come somewhere between 'sound-effects' and incidental music. The new mediums of 'musique concrète' (natural sounds modified by electrical means) and electronic music (assembling sounds of electronic origin) have proved specially effective in creating 'atmosphere' of many kinds; Peter Brook's spine-chilling accompaniment to his production of *Titus Andronicus* (Stratford, 1957) and Raymond Leppard's 'enchanted' music for *The Tempest* (Stratford, 1963) are notable examples.

ANDREW PORTER

INCORPORATED STAGE SOCIETY, see STAGE SOCIETY.

INDEPENDENT THEATRE, LONDON, see GREIN, J. T.

INDIA. 1. SANSKRIT DRAMA. The origin and early history of the classical Hindu (Sanskrit) drama remain matters on which little reliable information can be found. When, about A.D. 100, the first surviving dramas were composed, the form of the drama had already developed to that which was stereotyped for later times, and the period of growth and development lies before this date. Mention of actors (*naṭa*) and other kinds of performers appears sporadically in earlier texts, but few details are available as to the nature of their performances. It would seem, from what slight evidence is available, that the drama proper developed fairly rapidly in the centuries immediately preceding the Christian era, growing out of earlier dramatic dances and mimetic representations, the tradition of which may go back indefinitely. Controversy as to whether its origin was religious or secular has little meaning in a country like India, though it is certain that it had nothing to do with the official Vedic religion of the ruling orders. The suggestion that its origin is due to Greek influence has no evidence to support it; nevertheless it is convenient in point of time, and it is possible that knowledge that plays were performed at the Courts of Greek invaders may have stimulated Indians to develop their own drama, though direct influence of classical models is certainly out of the question.

The earliest dramatist of whom anything has survived is Aśvaghoṣa (*c.* A.D. 100). Fragments of three of his plays have been found in the sands of Central Asia. They are interesting because in them we find the drama being used for purposes of propaganda for the Buddhist religion. Since this was far from being the original purpose of the drama, it is an indication that the drama had been established for some considerable time. Later come Bhāṣa and Śūdraka (fourth century) and Kālidāsa (fifth century). In the three plays of Kālidāsa, particularly in the *Śakuntalā*, the Sanskrit drama reaches its highest state of perfection. It was the translation of this play by Sir William Jones (Calcutta, 1789) that first awoke an interest in Sanskrit literature in Europe, and in particular stirred the admiration of the poet Goethe. Later works of merit are the *Mudrārākṣasa* of Viśākhadatta, based on a story of complicated political intrigue, and the *Veṇisaṃhāra* of Bhaṭṭa Nārāyaṇa who draws his inspiration from the Mahābhārata, the national epic of India. King Harṣa of Kanauj wrote two comedies of Court intrigue and one play with a Buddhist theme. Second in order of merit to Kālidāsa comes Bhavabhūti, whose works are more exalted but less spontaneous than those of his predecessor. Later dramas are more artificial and often have the appearance of literary exercises meant to be read rather than performed. By A.D. 1000 the drama is in a full state of decline, and little of value is produced after that date.

The earliest treatise on the theory and practice of the drama is the *Nāṭya-śāstra* of Bharata, which is probably to be dated in the third century A.D., that is to say, earlier than the bulk of the existing dramas. It is an extensive work dealing exhaustively with every branch of the subject, the erection of theatres, the production of plays, the composition of plays, music, dancing, costume, and so forth. The rules of this work were quickly accepted as canonical, and the practice of all later dramatists and performers is dominated by it. Later treatises on the drama contain essentially the same material and add little that is new. Some are valuable as preserving fragments of lost dramas which otherwise would be unknown. Some of the commentaries on the dramas contain useful details about the production of the plays.

Regular theatres do not appear to have existed. Bharata's account implies that the hall and stage were erected specially for the performance. This would take place in connexion with some festival or public celebration, or the king, or some rich patron, would summon the actors to perform for his benefit. Temples and palaces were frequently adapted for the occasion, and we even hear in an inscription of a cave being used for this purpose. The playhouse was constructed in accordance with certain specified measurements, divided into the two sections: stage and auditorium. The latter was divided by pillars into sections to be occupied by the four castes. The rows of seats were made of either brick or wood. In front was the seat of honour occupied by the patron and his entourage. The stage (*ranga*) was decorated by pictures and reliefs. At the back of the stage was the curtain which separated it from the dressing-rooms of the artists. Behind the curtain were performed various noises off, sounds of tumult and rejoicing, and the voices of gods, who could not suitably be represented on the stage.

It was not the general custom to represent on the stage the scenery of the action. The curtain remained the background and the rest was for the most part left to the imagination of the spectators. To indicate that certain actions were being performed, the actors would go through various conventional gestures. Thus, when a character representing a king had to mount a chariot, instead of a chariot being brought on to the stage, he would indicate by a particular set of gestures, with which the audience was familiar, that a chariot was being mounted; similarly when an actress went through the operation of watering flowers, and so on. At the same time use was made of certain minor stage properties, some accounts of which are available. Thus we hear that the toy cart which gave its name to the *Mṛcchakaṭikā* actually appeared on the stage. In another performance an artificial elephant was constructed in connexion with a certain scene in the story of Udayana, which was a popular subject of drama.

Great care was taken with costume to indicate the class, profession, and nationality of the characters. Princes wore elaborate and many-coloured garments; ascetics, garments of bark or rags. Maidens of the cow-herd class wore garments of dark blue, and so on. Dirty and ragged clothes indicated madness, distraction, or misery; sober and uncoloured garments were worn by people engaged in religious service; while gods, demigods, etc., appeared brightly arrayed like kings. For the same purposes paint was regularly employed. Peoples of the north-west were painted reddish-yellow, as also were brahmins and kings. Those of the Ganges valley as well as the two lower castes, Vaiśyas and Śūdras, were painted dark brown. Men from the south and representatives of primitive tribes appeared as black. In the same way different kinds of decorations, jewellery, garlands, etc., were adapted to the varying types of character.

The actors (*naṭa*) formed a distinct caste of their own and, to judge from numerous references, their social status was not very high, nor their morals much esteemed. At the same time instances are on record of actors enjoying the friendship of distinguished personages. Their life was to a large extent itinerant and they would wander about in troupes with their repertory of plays, seeking patronage from city to city. These troupes worked under a leader called the *sūtradhāra*, whose business it was to supervise the construction of the theatre and the production of the play, as well as acting one of the principal parts. He always appeared first on the stage to introduce the play with a few remarks on its author, the occasion of its production, etc., to which a few complimentary remarks about the audience, as being men of good taste, were usually added. He was usually married to one of the actresses (*naṭī*) with whom he appears in conversation in the introduction of the play, with reference as a rule to the domestic arrangements of his household. The *sūtradhāra* was assisted by his deputy or right-hand man (*pāripārśvika*), and we also hear of a figure called the *sthāpaka* whose duties seem to have been connected with the construction and management of the stage. The other actors and actresses worked under these. Normally male parts were taken by men, and female parts by women.

The production of the play was preceded by a series of introductory performances (*purvaranga*). This consisted of a programme of instrumental music, song, and dance, by which the spectators were entertained before the play began. To judge by the description this programme was long and complicated, and must have formed a considerable part of the day's proceedings. In addition certain ritual acts of worship and prayers to the gods had to be performed. These were brought to an end by the *nāndī* or benedictory stanza, which heralded the approach of the play proper, and was followed by the appearance on the stage of the *sūtradhāra* in the introductory scene.

Characters were early stereotyped into certain well-recognized types. First comes the *nāyaka* or hero, usually a king or some other exalted personage. He was of various types but must be noble, handsome, brave, etc. The enemy of the hero (*pratināyaka*) is represented as courageous and resourceful, but violent, stubborn, and wicked. The heroine (*nāyikā*) could be of various kinds—goddess, queen, lady of noble birth, and, in certain types of drama, courtesan—with various characteristics according to her position, but always beautiful and accomplished. Other types frequently mentioned are the *piṭhamarda*, companion or hanger-on of the hero, the *viṭa* or rake, who assists the hero in any less reputable ventures, the *ceṭa*, manservant, and so on. Curious is the *vidushaka*, who appears as a disreputable and illiterate brahmin, with an insatiable appetite for food, providing the comic relief of the piece.

The drama was divided into acts which varied in number but were not usually more than ten. The plays were written partly in prose, partly in verse. The background of the dialogue is prose, but verse is introduced when anything is to be said that appears deserving of poetic expression. The language of the characters differs according to their rank and station. Kings and brahmins speak Sanskrit; people of lower stations and women speak Prakrit, that is to say, the ordinary vernacular current in the early centuries A.D. This accurately represents the prevailing social conventions of the time. The subject-matter of the play was most frequently based on heroic and religious legend, though in certain types the story could be invented by the author. A happy ending was the rule and tragedy was never developed in India.

A large number of types of drama are classified, not all of which are represented among the surviving texts. In the most important, the *nāṭaka*, the story was based on mythology or heroic legend, its hero a king or divine person. It should have not less than five acts and not more than ten; not more than five main characters should appear in the play. The *prakaraṇa* or bourgeois comedy dealt with the activities of less exalted people, such as ministers, brahmins, and merchants, and the subject of the plot could be invented by the author. The *samavakāra* was a play dealing exclusively with the activities of gods and divine persons. The *nāṭikā* is like the *nāṭaka*, but slighter in subject and extent. It is usually a comedy dealing with the amours of the hero. The *prahasaṇa* is usually a short piece, and specializes in the tricks and intrigues of low characters of various kinds. The *bhāṇa* is a monologue, in which one character, the *viṭa* or rake, walks through the less respectable part of the town, and holds imaginary conversations with the people he meets.

After the onset of the Mohammedan invasions the drama in India underwent a rapid decline. We still hear of its being popular in eleventh-century Kashmir, but after that date the tradition of dramatic performances gradually began to die out. The new rulers were naturally averse to such things, and to an art which depended so largely on patronage this was a fatal blow. In the end the tradition almost totally vanished, so that we are dependent for our knowledge of it on books, and to some extent on artistic representations. Only in remote Malabar has some trace of the old tradition been preserved, among the Cākkiyar, a caste of actors and performers, but that is not a great deal. T. BURROW

2. MEDIEVAL THEATRE. After the breakdown of the classical tradition during the ninth and tenth centuries, there arose the 'variety' theatre of medieval times, which developed with the rise of the vernacular languages. Though it preserved some of the elements of the earlier periods, it was essentially a popular, secular theatre, as were the lyric and operatic dramas, and the emerging forms of farce.

One of the ways in which the medieval theatre expressed itself was dramatic recitations from the great Indian epics and narrative poetic works, which, though not written for performance, nevertheless bordered on drama, and could easily be adapted for presentation. These provided admirable material when, during the cultural renaissance of the fifteenth and sixteenth centuries, which released great creative forces in all the literary and performing arts, the temples began to reshape drama in a more formal manner. Plays based on the legends of the Rama and Krishna were first acted in the temples, and then moved outside into the streets on pageant wagons.

Other forms of medieval theatre were the singing of ballads to the accompaniment of dancing, and dramatic monologues and sketches, farces and skits, presented by itinerant actors.

3. Folk Theatre. The folk theatre of India is much more varied and colourful, and richer in themes and styles of presentation, than the literary theatre. There is an amazing variety of forms, ranging from the simple dramatic dance, found in all regions, to the spectacular pageantry of the Rama and Krishna play-cycles of northern India. Folk theatre incorporates elements of the literary, mimetic, and pictorial arts, and reflects the customs, beliefs, rituals, and social life of the people. It cuts across regional and linguistic boundaries, and has a pan-Indian character. It is the last repository of all the medieval arts—music, dance, pantomime, poetry, ballads, epic recitation, painting, pageantry, and the decorative arts. It provides the material for a partial reconstruction of the theatrical history of India, in which there are many gaps, and gives illuminating glimpses of the old dramatic traditions. On the one hand it contains many of the conventions of the classical theatre, often changed or adapted, but still recognizable, while, on the other, it is the direct descendant of the picturesque medieval 'variety' theatre. Practices and conventions of the Indian folk theatre which are directly related to the medieval tradition are the unlocalized platform or multi-level stage, multiple settings, stylized acting, and costume, the use of a narrator (*sūtradhāra*) with chorus, the introduction of the clown (*vidushaka*) and other stock characters, the lavish use of songs and dances, the close relationship between actor and audience, loosely constructed plots with a mixture of narrative and dramatic elements, and freedom for improvisation.

The major folk forms, however, are the Rama and Krishna play-cycles referred to above, which combine spectacle in pageantry and procession with dramatic dialogue interspersed with songs. Of these, *Raslila*, depicting episodes in the life of Krishna, is a localized operatic ballet. *Jatra*, of Bengal, has the oldest tradition, and from being purely operatic has developed into a prose drama with songs. *Yakshagana*, of South India, is operatic in character, with choreographic acting, and deals with themes from the epics and *puranas*. The actors wear fantastic and gorgeous costumes. The *Bhavai* of Gujarat, the *Tamasha* of Maharashtra, and the *Nautanki* of Uttar Pradesh, are all secular plays, some dealing with contemporary social themes, others based on historical romances or medieval legends, with songs and dances, and stylized speech. *Naqal*, *Swang*, and *Bhandaiti* are short plays, lighter in character, dealing with topical events, and dependent for much of their effectiveness on improvisation and ready wit.

4. Modern Drama. It was in the middle of the nineteenth century that modern drama arose in India, partly as a result of the direct impact of the West, though even in the early years the Indian playwrights combined the picture-frame stage and the structural patterns of the West with the dramatic conventions and practices of the classical medieval and indigenous folk drama. Shakespeare and Molière, translated and adapted into all Indian languages, inspired, guided, and nourished the Indian theatre. The professional Parsi companies which flourished during the latter half of the nineteenth century and the early twentieth century showed an amalgam of European theatre with local farces and dramas. The outstanding playwrights of the Parsi theatre—Agha Hashar Kashmiri and Radheshyam, both prolific writers—used alliterative prose, rhyming couplets, and a Shakespearian plot-structure with Indian classical and folk-stage conventions.

In the early years of the twentieth century the main influences on the modern drama were Shaw, Ibsen and Chekhov. The foundations of realistic historical drama were laid in the nineteenth century by the actor, writer, and producer, Girish Chandra Ghosh, and the playwright D. L. Roy in Bengal, by Khadilkar and Gadkari in Maharashtra, and by talented writers and actors in several other regions. Rabindranath Tagore (1861–1941), poet and author of over forty plays, successfully assimilated the influence of Western drama while exploiting the classical and folk traditions of his own country. His operas, dance-dramas, and lyrical plays are modelled on indigenous forms. Some of the better known among them are *Visarjan*, *Dak-ghar*, *Raktakarabi*, and *Muktadhara*, and the dance-dramas *Chandalika*, *Shyama*, and *Chitrangada*.

Theatrical activity in India today, apart from the folk troupes and dance-drama companies, is mainly amateur, though with the vast expansion of the amateur movement there is a shift towards professionalism, and there are already a few fully professional companies. The best-known are T. K. S. Brothers and Seva Stage (Tamil), Rangnekar's Natya Niketan (Marathi), the Little Theatre Group and Bohurupee (Bengali), and the Gubbi Veeranna company (Kannada). In Hindi, the official language of India, the only professional group, Prithvi Theatre, founded in 1944, closed in 1960 after a successful career, during which the actor-director Prithvi Raj Kapoor bridged the gap between the Hindi literary drama and the demands of a popular audience with such long-running plays as *Deewar* and *Pathan*. Other leading directors are Sombhu Mitra and Utpal Dutt (both of Calcutta), Sahasranamam (Madras), and E. Alkazi, head of the National School of Drama, and Habib Tanvir (both of Delhi).

One important aspect of the contemporary theatre is the revival of Sanskrit and folk drama. The Brahman Mahasabha Group of Bombay has been performing plays in Sanskrit since about 1950. Dr. V. Raghavan, Professor of Sanskrit at Madras University, has organized a theatre group, Sanskrita Ranga, which performs plays old and new in Sanskrit (see No. 125). A number of old plays have also been translated into Hindi and other modern Indian languages. In all these productions both new and traditional approaches have been tried. This renaissance of India's great theatrical heritage is matched by the growing popularity of dance- and music-dramas (see No. 124). Uday Shankar, the pioneer of modern Indian dancing, Rukmini Devi, Mrinalini Sarabhai, who all produce dramas in classical dance styles, the late Shanti Bardhan, who created the immortal *Panchatantra* and *Ramayana*—dance-dramas with puppet-movements and masks—Narenda Sharma and Sachin Shankar, were all leading choreographers and pioneers in this medium. In Bengal there are a number of troupes which have specialized in the presentation of Tagore's dance-dramas and lyrical plays in a distinctive style evolved by the poet himself.

With the ferment of life in the post-Independence period, theatrical activity has greatly increased, and the theatre is taking its rightful place in the cultural life of India. But the absence of a vital professional theatre has meant that dramatic literature has tended to lag behind other literary forms such as fiction and poetry. Contemporary playwrights, while attempting a more creative assimilation of Western techniques, are also exploring indigenous dramatic forms, and some, like Adya Rangacharya in Kannada, P. L. Deshpande in Marathi, Mohan Rakesh in Hindi, and Balwant Gargi in Punjabi, are trying to achieve a true synthesis which may in time lead to the evolution of a new dramatic form. Dramatic activity throughout India is coordinated by the Bharatiya Nāṭya Sangh (The Indian Theatre Centre) which is a member of the International Theatre Institute, in Delhi. The Sangh has organized several dramatic seminars, and conducted theatrical surveys and research projects on a pan-Indian basis. It runs a workshop for the production of costumes, puppets, masks, and other theatrical material, and publishes, in English, a quarterly journal on the theatre, *Nāṭya*.

5. PUPPETS. India is traditionally the home of puppetry, and there are references in early literary works which suggest the prevalence of some form of puppet-theatre in India in the first centuries of the Christian era. Puppets are of four types—shadow, string, rod, and hand (or glove) puppets. Of these the string puppets are the most common. Rod puppets are found occasionally in Bengal, as well as among the aboriginal and primitive tribes. Hand puppets are extremely rare, though in some regions they are used by beggars. For all types of puppets, themes are taken from the epics, *puranas*, and legends of India. In carving, colouring, and costuming of the various kinds of puppets the traditional folk arts and crafts of the country are fully exploited. Since Independence efforts have been made to revive and revitalize the puppet theatre. New amateur groups have emerged in the principal towns, and plays on modern themes have been produced, using new methods and techniques of production. Some experimental work has also been done with the aim of improving the design, carving, and costuming of the puppets themselves. Some government departments have organized puppet-theatre units to give puppet plays dealing with plans for national development.

SURESH AWASTHI

INGE, WILLIAM (1913–), American dramatist, who in 1953 was awarded the Pulitzer Prize for *Picnic*. He had previously scored a success with *Come Back, Little Sheba* (1950) with Shirley Booth in the lead, and he has since written *Bus Stop* (1955), *The Dark at the Top of the Stairs* (1957), and *A Loss of Roses* (1959). This last play, which was Inge's first failure on Broadway, was seen in England—at the Pembroke Theatre, Croydon—in 1962, in a production by Peter Cotes, who also produced *Come Back, Little Sheba* at the Golders Green Hippodrome in 1952. For some reason Inge does not seem to have been successful with English audiences, perhaps because he is so essentially American. He has a vivid sense of the theatre, and his dialogue is easy and uninhibited, but his approach to the psychological problems raised in his plays is perhaps somewhat elementary, and his obsession with sex quickly palls.

INGEGNERI, ANGELO (*c.* 1550–*c.* 1613), see LIGHTING, 1 *a*.

INGEMANN, BERNHARD SEVERIN (1789–1862), Danish dramatist, whose sentimental dramas were extremely popular in his day. The best of his many works—he was a prolific writer—is *Sulamith og Salomon* (1839).

INNER PROSCENIUM, a temporary and variable structure which can be put behind the proscenium arch to diminish the size of the opening. It is particularly useful on tour, when scenery has to be accommodated on stages of varying sizes and consists usually of a pair of booked wings opened to a right-angle or more and set on either side of the stage. The on-stage side of each is profiled and cut to the shape of a draped curtain, and connecting the two sides across the top is a deep border, its edge similarly cut. The whole is an elaborately painted composition of hanging drapery, decorative but suitable for any set of scenery, with folds, swags, fringes, cords, and tassels. In France it is known as the *manteau d'Harlequin*.

An interesting variation of subject appears at Rich's new Lincoln's Inn Fields Theatre and at his subsequent Covent Garden, where the proscenium wings had certain architectural features added. These consisted of changeable proscenium statues, either of draped female figures or of animals. In the modern proscenium theatre the wings are often replaced by a fixed pair of narrow flats covered in black velvet. These are known as tormentors (see also FALSE PROS).

INNS USED AS THEATRES, LONDON. These may have been converted, or merely equipped with a trestle stage at one end of the yard. The best known were:

1. The Bell Inn, in Gracious (Gracechurch) Street in the City of London. It was used for plays in 1576, and by the Queen's Men in 1583.

2. The Bel Savage Inn, on Ludgate Hill in the City of London. Plays were performed there from 1579 to 1588 and later. The Queen's Men also played there.

3. The Boar's Head Inn, in Aldgate, where a play called *A Sack Full of News* was suppressed in 1557. The players were under arrest for twenty-four hours, and thereafter all plays to be performed had to be submitted first to the Ordinary. This was the first act of real censorship the English theatre had known. Another Boar's Head Inn or playhouse somewhere in Middlesex was in use between 1602 and 1608.

4. The Bull Inn, in Bishopsgate Street, in the City of London. It was used for plays before 1575 and until after 1594. The Queen's Men played there in 1583 and probably later.

5. The Cross Keys Inn, also in Gracious Street. Plays were performed there before 1579 and up to about 1596. Lord Strange's Men played there in 1589 and 1594.

6. The Red Lion, in Stepney. A play called *Samson* was performed there in 1567.

INSET, a small scene set behind a central opening (see FLAT); also a small set, such as a triangular room or attic, lowered from the flies, or set inside (i.e. in front of) a full set that does not have to be struck.

INSTITUTE FOR ADVANCED STUDIES IN THEATRE ARTS. This educational venture, founded in 1958 by Dr. John Mitchell and his wife, is dedicated to the enrichment of the American theatre through greater knowledge of world theatre past and present, and aims to bring to New York outstanding foreign producers to work with the members of the Institute, who are all professional theatre workers. The first import was Willi Schmidt from Berlin, who directed a performance of Schiller's *Kabale und Liebe* in a new English version. Subsequent productions have been *The Misanthrope* by Jacques Charon, *The Cherry Orchard* by Yuri Zavadski, *The Way of the World* by George Devine, and *Electra* by Dimitrios Rondiris. There have also been visits from a *kabuki* actor, an Italian mime, and a choreographer from India. Courses are given at the Institute on fields relating to the play which is being produced.

INTERLUDE, the early English name for a short dramatic sketch, from the late Latin *interludium*. It is often taken as the starting-point of English drama, and seems to have some affinity with the Italian *tramesso*, signifying something extra inserted into a banquet, and so an entertainment given during a banquet. By extension it passed to short pieces played between the acts of a long play, for which Renaissance Italy adopted the term *intermedio* or *intermezzo*, the latter exclusively for musical entertainments (see below), while the former gave rise to the French *entremets* or *intermède*, meaning a short comedy or farce. In Spain the *entremes*, while having a somewhat similar origin, became a distinct dramatic genre. The first to make the English Interlude a complete and independent dramatic form was John Heywood (*c.* 1497–1580) (see also ENGLAND, 2). The Players of the King's Interludes (Lusores Regis) had half a century of history behind them when Elizabeth came to the throne. They are first recorded under Henry VII in 1493, and then consisted of four or five men, who were paid an annual fee by the Exchequer, with additional sums for performances. They later increased in number. They went up to Scotland with Princess Margaret to play at her wedding festivities when she married James IV. They also played in private houses, and may be the company referred to in *Sir Thomas More* (1595). They dwindled away during the later years of Mary and disappeared entirely under Elizabeth, the last survivor dying in 1580. During their last years they were sometimes referred to as the Queen's Players, but should not be confused with Queen Elizabeth's Men, the best-known London company of the 1580s, founded in 1583.

INTERMEZZI (INTERMEDII), interpolations of a light, often comic, character performed between the acts of serious drama or opera in Italy in the late fifteenth and early sixteenth centuries. They usually dealt with mythological subjects, and could be given as independent entertainments for guests at royal or noble festivals, on the lines of the English 'disguising' and dumb-show, or the French *momeries* and *entremets* and the Spanish *entremeses* (see also ARCHITECTURE, INTERLUDE, OPERA, 5 and SCENERY, 2).

INTERNATIONAL FEDERATION FOR THEATRE RESEARCH. A meeting of delegates from over twenty countries, held in London in July 1955 at the invitation of the Society for Theatre Research, resulted in the formation of an international body devoted to the collection, preservation, and dissemination of theatrical material throughout the world. At a meeting in Paris a year later a Constitution was drafted, which was accepted at a World Conference in Venice in 1957. The Federation, which publishes a bi-lingual journal, *Theatre Research/Recherches Théâtrales*, admits to full membership institutions engaged wholly in theatre research (those only partly so engaged can become Associate members) and has also a category of individual members. Meetings of its committee are held annually in various European cities (Paris, Vienna, Stockholm, Munich, Prague, etc.), and are accompanied by a symposium at which experts are invited to speak on a subject chosen by the host country. Every four years a world conference open to the public is held, the proceedings of which are published in volume form. The Federation has established an international centre for theatre research in the Casa Goldoni, Venice, where work on the cataloguing of theatre material in libraries, museums, and collections is being carried on, and where international summer courses are held.

INTERNATIONAL THEATRE, New York, see MAJESTIC THEATRE, 1.

INTERNATIONAL THEATRE INSTITUTE (I.T.I.). This body, which exists to promote international co-operation and exchange of ideas among all workers in the theatre, was founded as a branch of Unesco in July 1947, at a meeting in Paris presided over by J. B. Priestley. It works through 48 national centres, with headquarters in Paris, and publishes a bi-monthly illustrated journal, *World Theatre*. A world congress is held every two years in a capital city—Helsinki, Vienna, Warsaw, Tel Aviv—as well as conferences and colloquiums on such specific problems as the training of the actor or theatre architecture. The English Centre, which was one of the first to be founded, helps those who come from abroad to study the English theatre, and those going from this country to study the theatre abroad. It also serves as a central information bureau for all workers in the theatre at home and abroad. The American Centre works through the American National Theatre and Academy, and covers much the same ground as that outlined above, as do all the other centres, some of which are extremely active.

ION, of Chios, a tragic poet of some note, who lived in the fifth century B.C. Longinus compares him with Sophocles, saying that he was elegant and faultless, but not powerful. He wrote, besides tragedies, other forms of poetry, and a volume of memoirs often cited by later writers.

IONESCO, Eugène (1912–), French playwright of Rumanian origin, and one of the most popular and frequently performed exponents of the 'Theatre of the Absurd' which dominated the French theatre after 1950. The philosophical mainspring of Ionesco's work is the proposition that all human life and endeavour is essentially absurd, and therefore terrifying, and that language as a means of communication is equally absurd. His first play, the one-act *La Cantatrice Chauve*, presented in Paris in 1950 under the label of 'anti-play', is a brilliant parody of the naturalistic theatre, ridiculing the logic of its speech and conventions in a barrage of *non sequiturs*, false syllogisms, puns, *reductio ad absurdum* distortions, and totally arbitrary conclusions which turn 'truth' and 'reality' upside down. In his two subsequent one-act plays Ionesco returned to the attack on language, demonstrating in *La Leçon* (1951) its efficacity as a physical weapon, and in *Les Chaises* (1952) its total uselessness as a means of communication. Drawing on the theories of Antonin Artaud, Ionesco rejected the literary theatre, the theatre of ideas, the theatre of psychological truth: instead he sought to return to a more primitive theatre which would simply be theatrical, and which through its exaggerations and illogicalities might penetrate beyond reality. Hence the importance in his plays of bizarre objects or events which take on a significance unconnected with the words spoken on the stage. Ionesco, however, has never displayed the poetic imagination or power which has enabled Jean Genêt to fulfil Artaud's dream of a primitive, visceral theatre freed from social restrictions, and his work is closer to Surrealism in its prolific use of puns, bizarre juxtapositions, dream sequences, and grotesque situations. As his characters are mainly caricatures or abstractions, Ionesco has never really solved the problem of developing a play to three-act length, and apart from the only partially successful *Amédée, ou Comment s'en débarrasser* (1954), he devoted himself for several years to the one-act form, notably in *Victimes du devoir* (1953), *Jacques ou la soumission* (1955, but written in 1950), *L'Impromptu de l'Alma* (1956), and *Le Nouveau Locataire* (1957, but written in 1953 and first performed in Finland, 1955). In his second full-length play, *Tueur sans gages* (1959), he tried to counter the problem by introducing a more conventionally sympathetic hero—the Bérenger who reappears in *Rhinocéros* (1960), *Le Roi se meurt* (1963), and *Le Piéton de l'air* (1963): even so, all these plays give the impression of containing unnecessary padding, and fail to achieve the mastery of form which distinguishes the one-act plays. There are signs in *Le Roi se meurt*, however, particularly in its use of some of the elements of ritual which characterize Genêt's work, that Ionesco is attempting to break out of the constricting limits of his own style. Most of Ionesco's plays have been performed in England, the first being *The Lesson* in 1955, and *The Bald Prima Donna* and *The New Tenant* in 1956. *The Chairs*, in which Joan Plowright and George Devine gave excellent performances, was done at the Royal Court in 1957, as were *Rhinoceros*, with Laurence Olivier, in 1960, and *Exit the King*, with Alec Guinness, in 1963.

T. C. C. MILNE

IPSEN, Bodil Louise Jensen (1889–1964), Danish actress who made her first appearance at the Royal Theatre, Copenhagen, in 1909, and soon became an outstanding figure in the Danish theatre. She is particularly remembered for her creation of the parts of Rosaline, Nora, Mrs. Alving, Miss Julie, and Alice (in Strindberg's *Dance of Death*).

L. KATHLEEN MCFARLANE

IRELAND. 1. General Survey and Abbey Theatre. The history of Irish drama may be said to begin with the Irish Literary Movement, itself a part of the National movement, at the end of the nineteenth century. There are, it is true, certain medieval manuscripts (of liturgical plays) which are of Irish origin, and this suggests that Ireland had a share also in the composition of those religious dramas of the Church which spread over the greater part of Europe (see LITURGICAL DRAMA). But there is no continuity of tradition, and at the end of the nineteenth century the Dublin theatre depended upon English touring companies who brought over the current London successes (see DUBLIN).

But the Irish Dramatic Movement, begun by William Butler Yeats (1865–1939) and Lady Gregory (1852–1932) in 1899, offered from the beginning plays by native dramatists upon native subjects, though performed at first by English actors. After the union with the Fays' company, the Irish National Dramatic Society, in 1901 the players were Irish too. In 1904 Miss Horniman built the now famous Abbey Theatre to house them, and in 1910 they became financially independent. The Abbey won and maintained a world-wide reputation as a repertory theatre of a specialized kind, comparable with others in England, on the Continent, and later in America, but differing from them in being wholly or mainly national in its repertory. Its international fame began in 1903 with two performances given in London and was rapidly extended by other English tours and by the American tours of 1911 and later (see ABBEY THEATRE). After 1904 the Ulster Theatre (see below, 4) formed an important part of the movement; its aims and methods, though independent, were fundamentally akin.

The ideals of the movement were revolutionary; though fervently and fundamentally national, it was to be independent of all political parties; though a literary theatre, it was to be independent of European fashions; though only scantily subsidized (if at all), it was to be independent of the box-office and popular control. 'We went on giving what we thought good until it became popular', said Lady Gregory, and Yeats declared, 'Literature must take the responsibilities of its power and keep all its freedom.' While honouring Ibsen himself, the leaders of the movement had no illusions as to the value of 'Ibsenism' and determined that their material, whether tragedy or comedy, prose or verse, contemporary or historical, should be native and poetic. Besides Yeats and Lady Gregory, John Millington Synge (1871–1909), AE [George William Russell] (1867–1935), Edward Martyn (1859–1924), and many writers of the Ulster Theatre, drew upon the legendary and historical material which the great Gaelic scholars of their own and the preceding generation had made accessible by translation from Old and Middle Irish, while Lady Gregory's comedies, most of the work of Martyn, and later of Synge, drew also from contemporary Irish life. Lady Gregory, followed in this by Synge, used from the first in her dialogue the 'language of the folk', the English idiom of the Irish-speaking peasants of the West. Here, Yeats too believed, could be found the 'living language', a way of speech which did not stifle the 'living imagination' as did contemporary English speech. This principle of realism in dialogue (which was yet essentially poetic, since the speech from which it was drawn was rich in poetry) has been adopted by a long succession of Irish dramatists down to the present day, and the dialects of nearly all parts of Ireland have by now been acclimatized upon the Irish stage.

Producing, setting, and acting were also revolutionary and have, in their turn, established a fine tradition. The actors were at first amateurs (the Abbey company has continued to the present day to carry a proportion of these); their acting was that of a naturally dramatic people unspoiled by the conventions of the European stage. It has had a wide influence, reaching far beyond Ireland. Setting and dressing were necessarily strictly economical, but this economy was exercised both in Dublin and Ulster by highly intelligent artists and craftsmen and resulted in beauty and simplicity little known at that time, though, again, widely appreciated since.

Some of the original leaders—AE, Martyn, George Moore, and Padraic Colum—were either men of letters who contributed an occasional play, or writers who began as playwrights and afterwards developed along other lines. As the movement gathered power, new writers were drawn to it and some, like Synge, remained. When Yeats drew up his well-known 'Advice to Playwrights' he was able to define clearly the aesthetic principles reached in the workshop of the theatre during those early years: criticism of life or a vision of life as the substance, the logic of carefully wrought form as the means, and, in general, freedom from all conventional aesthetic prepossessions. The movement eventually developed into something quite other than its original founders foresaw, but it has never abandoned these principles, and if its standards wavered for a time during the difficult years 1916–22, they recovered as soon as conditions made it possible.

It was a sign of the vitality of the movement that the mood of its drama began to change within the first ten years of its life. With the entry of new writers—William Boyle (1853–1923), T. C. Murray (1873–1959), Lennox Robinson (1886–1958), Padraic Colum (1881–1972) in Dublin, St. John Ervine (1883–1971), and Rutherford Mayne (1878–1967) in Belfast—naturalism and objectivity, sometimes gay, sometimes bitter, sometimes satirical, began to find their place in the new drama. Between 1903 and 1912 some twenty plays by these six writers were produced; original, independent, clear-sighted plays, ranging wide in mood and subject, finding their material no longer in the heroes of a splendid mythology and the primitive tragedy or fantastic comedy of the life of the Western peasant only, but in the hard fight of the peasant everywhere in Ireland, in the world of the small farmer and the small-town man, in the people of the Dublin or Belfast suburbs. With Colum's *The Land* (1905), Boyle's *The Building Fund* (1905), Robinson's *The Clancy Name* (1908), Murray's *Birthright* (1910), St. John Ervine's *Mixed Marriage* (1911), and Rutherford Mayne's *Red Turf* (1911) added to the work, to that date, of Yeats, Lady Gregory, and Synge, little more pioneering in extending the setting remained to be done except for the inclusion of the Dublin slums, later to be made his own by Sean O'Casey (1884–1964), whose first play, *The Shadow of a Gunman*, was produced at the Abbey in 1923.

To the names of these dramatists should be added those of certain others who wrote before 1916. (And 1916 is the natural pausing-place for any survey of recent Irish affairs.) These, though taking each his own line in theme and setting, tend in general to belong to the later tradition rather than the earlier one of the original founders, though both Lady Gregory and Yeats, it should be remembered, continued to take an active part in the direction of the theatre and from time to time to contribute plays until their deaths in 1932 and 1939. Between 1907 and 1916 we may notice, as also representative of their authors, George Fitzmaurice's *The Country Dressmaker* (1907), Conal O'Riordan's *The Piper* (1908), W. F. Casey's *The Suburban Groove* (1908), R. J. Ray's *The White Feather* (1909), Seumas O'Kelly's *The Shuiler's Child* (1910), John Guinan's *The Cuckoo's Nest* (1913), J. B. MacCarthy's *Kinship* (1914), and Bernard Duffy's *The Coiner* (1916), and this list could be extended to include several more playwrights who contributed one play apiece. During these years, also, Lord Dunsany (1878–1957) began his connexion with the Irish theatre with *The Glittering Gate* (1909) and Bernard Shaw (1856–1950) his—when *Blanco Posnet* was produced in Dublin in 1909 while still forbidden by the censor in England.

The history of the Irish drama since 1916 is one of inevitable retardation during the years 1916–22, of slow recovery after, and of continued progress since.

In 1928 the Gate Theatre (see below, 2) opened in Dublin, bringing in a fresh range of drama and a different type of technique. Certain new playwrights appeared at one or other of the two theatres after 1916 with plays which, in every case, marked the beginning of an original and sometimes of a long-continued series of contributions. Brinsley MacNamara (1890–1963) wrote *The Rebellion in Ballycullen* (1919); George Shiels (1886–1949), *Bedmates* (1921); Denis Johnston (1901–), *The Moon in the Yellow River* (1931); Paul Vincent Carroll (1900–68), *Things that are Caesar's* (1932). The work of Lennox Robinson, with its variety of mood, theme, and subject, continued to bridge the gap between the periods, no less than did his lifelong association with the Abbey Theatre either as playwright, actor, manager, producer, or director.

The years immediately before the Second World War saw Teresa Deevy's *Katie Roche* (1936)—perhaps the most popular of a number of plays which include *Reapers* (1930), *A Disciple* (1931), *Temporal Powers* (1932), *The King of Spain's Daughter* (1935), and *The Wild Goose* (1936)—and the work of Margaret O'Leary (*The Coloured Balloon*), Joseph Tomelty (*The End House*), Ralph Kenny (*The Railway House*), Louis D'Alton (*The Money Doesn't Matter*), Roger McHugh (*Rossa*).

In 1942 Austin Clark, author of several successful plays in verse, founded the Lyric Players for the purpose of reviving Irish poetic drama, which had suffered somewhat from the Abbey's preoccupation with realistic drama. Revivals were given of Yeats (*The Herne's Egg*, *The Death of Cuchula n*) and of a number of other poetic dramatists.

In 1940 Abbey tradition had been broken by the box-office success of George Shiels's *The Rugged Path*. It ran for three months, and many theatre-goers felt that the Abbey was becoming commercialized. Certainly it has been the policy since then to let a success run on, and this has in some ways led to plays being produced with an eye to box-office returns. However, the new policy has never seriously hampered the production of new plays by Irish authors, among them Walter Macken's *Mungo's Mansion* (1946), M. J. Molloy's *The Visiting House* (also 1946) and *The King of Friday's Men* (1948), and Seamus Byrne's *Design for a Headstone* (1950).

In 1951, the Abbey Theatre was destroyed by fire, and after finding a temporary home in the Rupert Guinness Hall (owned by the famous brewery) the company moved to the Queen's Theatre, which had previously been used mainly as a music-hall. With government help a new theatre was built on the site of the old, and opened in 1966. There is a smaller theatre in the same building to replace the Peacock, which was also destroyed in the fire.

Although no great new plays appear to have been presented at the Queen's while the Abbey company was there, some which made an impression were Macken's *Home is the Hero* (1952) and *Twilight of a Hero* (1955), M. J. Molloy's *The Paddy Pedlar* (1953), Joseph Tomelty's *Is the Priest at Home?* (1955), Denis Johnston's *Strange Occurrence on Ireland's Eye* (1956) and *The Scythe and the Sunset* (1958), and *The Country Boy* (1960) by John Murphy.

Perhaps the most welcome innovation in the Abbey company's work was seen in 1959, when they gave an uncut version of Eugene O'Neill's *Long Day's Journey into Night*, which proved to most critics of Abbey policy that they could still give Dublin first-rate production and acting. They successfully revived this play for the 1962 Dublin Theatre Festival. Meanwhile the Abbey, if not theatrically exciting, offers a new Irish playwright the opportunity to try out his work, and is the only permanent repertory company in Dublin.

2. Dublin Gate Theatre. Because of its slightly different aims and technique separate

mention must be made of the work of the Dublin Gate Theatre. This was founded in 1928 by Hilton Edwards (1903–) and Micheál Mac Liammóir (1899–), playing first at the Peacock Theatre and opening at the Rotunda in 1929. Its work is distinct from that of the Abbey; indeed, the two theatres are complementary, the Abbey presenting a picture of Irish life in all its phases while the Gate programmes include drama of every period and every country from Aeschylus to the present day—Shakespeare, Goethe, Ibsen, Strindberg, Chekhov, Shaw, O'Neill, Čapek, Elmer Rice, and many others. The aim of the founders was twofold, to create a standard of presentation comparable with that of the best in Europe and to lay the foundations of a new Irish school of writers different in subject, style, and setting from those of the Abbey; such, for instance, as were Denis Johnston's in *The Old Lady Says No!* (1929), *A Bride for the Unicorn* (1933), *Storm Song* (1934), and *The Dreaming Dust* (1940). This twofold aim has been widely recognized by critics and audiences. When the time came for the company to travel abroad, the brilliance of their presentation and technical skill was immediately acknowledged in successive visits to England, Egypt, and the Balkans. And the growing list of Irish dramatists first produced by them indicated the need and welcome for such a theatre: Denis Johnston, Lord and Lady Longford, An Philibín, Hazel Ellis, Robert Collis, Mary Manning (with *Youth's the Season*, 1931; *Storm over Wicklow*, 1933; *Happy Family*, 1934), David Sears (with *Juggernaut*, 1929; *The Dead Ride Fast*, 1931; *Grania of the Ships*, 1933), and Ulick Burke (with *Bride*, 1931).

In 1936 a second company, 'Longford Productions', having similar aims and scope, began to alternate at the Gate at six-monthly intervals with the earlier company. For many years this arrangement worked well. When it was not playing at the Gate 'Longford Productions' toured the provinces, bringing to many small towns for the first time excellent productions of Shakespeare, Chekhov, Eliot, Wilde, Sheridan, and Shaw. The Gate has never received a grant from the government, and Lord Longford, who managed 'Longford Productions', financed the work himself. His policy was that a good play must be staged irrespective of its box-office appeal. In 1956 the Dublin Corporation insisted on extensive reconstruction work being done to the theatre in the interests of fire-safety. With the theatre closed down for alterations, and a huge debt to be faced, Hilton Edwards and Micheál Mac Liammóir relinquished all claims to the Gate. Lord Longford managed to raise about £30,000 for the reconstruction work, but with the theatre in the hands of builders and debts mounting, 'Longford Productions' came to an end, though from time to time Lord Longford presented a company at the Gate; his death in 1961 deprived the Irish theatre of one of its greatest patrons. The theatre still exists, and Lord Longford's widow Christine, Countess of Longford, manages it. No permanent company plays there, and it is let to small companies, who continue along almost the same lines as those of the earlier companies. Recent dramatists presented there have included John Osborne, Harold Pinter, and T. S. Eliot. There was also a successful adaptation of James Joyce's *Portrait of the Artist as a Young Man* under the title *Stephen D.*

In the beginning, as Lady Gregory said, 'What we wanted was to create for Ireland a theatre with a base of realism and an apex of beauty', and even in the subsequent drama, which she and Yeats had not foreseen, this was, paradoxically, achieved. For the realism of the Irish dramatists has never, by reason of the poetic imagination of the people it draws, lost the beauty inherent in its content. Out of Easter week of 1916, as Yeats himself said, 'A terrible beauty is born'. And though this was not immediately apparent in the theatre, it became clear in the mature work of Sean O'Casey and others. In some of the later Irish drama, whether in the Abbey repertory or at the Gate, beauty took new forms. Despite Denis Johnston's implication (*The Old Lady Says No!*), something like a full revolution of the circle seems to have taken place, not only in his own plays and in those of Lennox Robinson, but in the work of such writers as Paul Vincent Carroll and Teresa Deevy. The 'apex of beauty' again dominated, without destroying, the 'base of realism'. The achievement of half a century in Irish drama may still be summed up in Lady Gregory's judgement part-way through its career: 'They have won much praise for themselves and raised the dignity of Ireland'. Not once, but several times, Irishmen of genius have given to this movement their work, their names, and in some cases the chance of prosperity elsewhere, because it was Irish. UNA ELLIS-FERMOR†, *rev.*

3. Pike Theatre. A number of small theatres, seating thirty to fifty people, opened in Dublin during the 1950s, on the lines of similar theatres in Paris. They were known locally as Basement Theatres, and a number of them were literally housed in the basements of Georgian houses. Their resources were very limited, but they managed to give Dublin audiences off-beat plays that would never have been staged in the bigger theatres. The most important, and the only one to survive, is the Pike Theatre, founded by Alan Simpson and his wife, Carolyn Swift, in a converted Georgian mews. It was in this small theatre in 1955 that Samuel Beckett's *Waiting for Godot* was first seen in English and that Brendan Behan's *The Quare Fella* was first produced. Alan Simpson was probably the first theatrical producer in Ireland to be arrested for putting on a play. This occurred when he presented the European première of Tennessee Williams's *The Rose Tattoo* for the first Dublin Theatre Festival (see DUBLIN). As there is no official censorship of plays in Ireland this caused wide concern, and after some months' trial the case

was dismissed. Unfortunately the common informers' names were never disclosed.

4. ULSTER THEATRE. Though essentially a part of Irish drama, the Ulster Theatre (since 1939, the Ulster Group Theatre) has so nearly independent a history that it claims a separate notice. The work of several dramatists well known in Ireland and outside, such as St. John Ervine, Rutherford Mayne, Patrick Hamilton and George Shiels, is closely associated either with its earlier or with its later years. In the fundamental ideals from which it grew it was so closely allied to the Dublin movement that what has been said earlier of that is in general true of the parallel development of Belfast. Like the Dublin movement, it has produced its own group of actors and drawn into its service some notable dramatists. Its history has been nearly as long. Its contribution to the picture of Irish life forms a necessary complement to that of the Dublin group. There has been, too, a frequent interchange of plays and playwrights, so that the two movements may be considered aesthetically as two aspects of one.

The beginnings of the Ulster Theatre are contemporary with those of the Dublin movement; Yeats, Lady Gregory, and Edward Martyn lent their support to an Ulster branch of the Irish National Theatre and members of the Dublin company took part in a performance of *Cathleen Ni Houlihan* in 1902.

The history of the actual Ulster Theatre, however, starts in 1904 with the production of Lewis Purcell's *The Reformers* and Bulmer Hobson's *Brian of Banba*, and thereafter the Theatre continued to produce plays written by its own group of authors for its own company, treating Irish subjects and in general representing the life of the North as the Abbey plays in the beginning represented that of the South. In all, it gave first productions of nearly 100 plays, and had support and encouragement from artists and men of letters in both parts of Ireland and in England. It made a number of visits to Dublin and also to London, Liverpool, Manchester, and the United States. The impression left in every case was of a movement original and individual in its material and approach. Some of the most notable of its plays were those of Rutherford Mayne and George Shiels, and, later, those of Lynn Doyle (*Turncoats*, *Love and Land*, *The Lilac Ribbon*) and of Bernard Duffy (*Paid In His Own Coin*, *The Old Lady*).

In 1939 the Ulster Theatre was merged with other dramatic groups to become the Ulster Group Theatre in Belfast. The new organization soon became a significant regional theatre, and was acclaimed when it visited Glasgow, Liverpool, and the Edinburgh Festival. In essence it was a players' theatre, served mainly by local playwrights, all sound in craftsmanship. But by the 1950s a serious situation had arisen, in that the theatre no longer had enough experienced actors to call on—they had gone mainly to films or television. This resulted in smaller audiences, and the theatre was many times threatened with closure. Only the prompt action of the Arts Council in coming to its aid with financial help enabled the doors to be kept open. But the situation was impossible, for a live theatre needs not only money but a living audience to communicate with. The chairman of the Group Theatre Company therefore invited James Young, a local actor in revue and variety who had a large following, to become joint managing director with his partner Jack Hudson. This was a wise move, for it made the Belfast audience aware that what had been mainly a literary theatre could now give them pleasure, since two of their favourite comedians were to play there.

Since then the Group Theatre has played an important part in the life of Belfast. Its productions are well attended, and a demand is being created for lively regional plays, well presented and well acted. It would be foolish to pretend that they are all masterpieces; but they are full of good craftsmanship, and reflect much of the distinctive humour of the Ulster man and woman. This new prosperity has meant that the theatre is now completely independent. Profits have been ploughed back into improving not only the front-of-house, but also the backstage area, where new equipment is always being added. Most important of all, the theatre has proved that long runs of six to ten months are possible. It may be that from all this a distinctive new playwright will emerge. Meanwhile the Group's activities have provided a good training ground and some measure of security for many actors in Northern Ireland.

5. BELFAST ARTS THEATRE. This organization corresponds to the Dublin Gate Theatre, and has very similar aims, being concerned with both local and world drama. Founded by Hubert Wilmot in 1947, its first production, given in an improvised theatre in a loft in a back street of Belfast, was Ibsen's *The Master Builder*. The idea of an Arts Theatre in an industrial city interested many people, and audiences, though necessarily small, were stimulated by seeing first productions in Ireland of exciting, intelligent European and American plays, among them Sartre's *Huis-clos* (1950). Kingsley's *Darkness at Noon* and Van Druten's *I am a Camera* had their first European productions there, and Anouilh's *Waltz of the Toreadors* its first production in English.

In 1961 Hubert Wilmot, helped by the Arts Council, opened the first new theatre to be built in Ireland for fifty years with a production on 19 April of *Orpheus Descending*. Seating 500, it has a comfortable auditorium, a workshop and good facilities both backstage and front-of-house. The run of a play may be from three weeks to three months, and every Christmas there is a production of a Victorian melodrama. Like the Group Theatre, the Belfast Arts Theatre offers continuous employment and training to actors in Northern Ireland.

6. GAELIC DRAMA. A special branch of

modern Irish drama is the drama in the Irish language. Some of its plays were originally produced at the Abbey Theatre, but the greater part of its history belongs to the work of the Gaelic Drama League in Dublin, Galway, and the provinces and country districts. Among the first plays to be performed in country halls in the provinces were those by An-t-Athair Peadar O Laoghair, whose *Tadhg Saor* was produced in Macroom, County Cork, in 1900. This was the first production of a play in the Irish language. The pioneer of Irish Drama in Dublin was Douglas Hyde, one of the original founders of the Gaelic League in 1893, whose *Casadh an tSugáin* (The Twisting of the Rope), produced at the Abbey in 1901, was the first play in Irish to be done on a professional stage. His dramatic work and that of his followers became well known throughout Ireland. Once established, the drama in Irish never flagged, and some half-dozen later names may be mentioned: Piaras Béaslaoi (*An Danar* and *An Bhean Chrodha*), Séamus O h-Aodha (*An Luch Tuaithe*), Micheál Breathnach (*Cor in Aghaidh an Chaim*), Micheál O Siochfradha (*Cuchulainn agus Aoife*), Micheál Mac Liammóir, one of the founders of the Gate Theatre in Dublin (*Diarmuid agus Gráinne*), and Seamus Wilmot (*Barabbas*).

An interesting feature of this drama in recent years has been the Taibhdhearc na Gaillimhe (Galway Theatre), founded in 1928 by a group of enthusiasts, headed by the Professor of Romance Languages at Galway's University College, Liam O'Brien, who obtained a grant from the government. The enterprise was directed by Micheál Mac Liammóir from 1928 to 1931, opening with his *Diarmuid agus Gráinne*, and producing about twenty-five plays, either original Irish works or translations into Irish of such authors as Shaw. Several European dramatists have also been translated into Irish for An Comhar Drámuíochta. Mac Liammóir was succeeded by Professor Murray, and it was during the latter's term as director, in 1936, that de Valera visited the theatre, to see a translation of *The Marvellous History of St. Bernard*, after which the theatre's subsidy was raised. Walter Macken, who had acted in the company, took over as leading actor and producer from 1939 to 1949, during which time some of his own plays were produced. Another member of this company was Siobhan McKenna, who appeared in her own translation of Shaw's *St. Joan*. This was an immediate success, and was seen also in Dublin and London. Liam O'Flaherty and Padraig O'Conaire have also written plays in Irish for this theatre.

In Dublin, Gael Linn has produced a number of plays in Irish at the Damer Hall with great success. One play which they commissioned, by Brendan Behan, *An Giall*, was translated into English, and as *The Hostage* was successfully produced in Dublin, London, and New York. It has been translated into many European languages, and in 1962 was done in French at the Odéon, directed by Barrault.

To further interest in Gaelic Drama the Abbey Theatre has staged one-act plays in Irish after the main production of the evening, and in 1945, with *Muireann agus an Prionnsa*, by Micheál O h-Aodha, they began a series of annual Abbey pantomimes in Irish.

6. Amateur Drama. There is a good deal of amateur acting in both Eire and Northern Ireland. In Belfast the most important group is the Lyric Players, founded in 1951 by Mrs. Mary O'Malley for the furtherance of poetic plays and closely-associated arts. Although a number of Greek classics and modern European plays have been given, the main emphasis has been on Irish plays, some of them new. The first production was a new poetic play, *Lost Light*, by Robert Farren. This and all subsequent productions were directed by Mary O'Malley. In 1961 a fine production was given of *Brand*, with a professional actor in the chief part. The Lyric Players also run a drama school, in which actors are trained before joining the company.

In Eire amateur drama is centralized in Athlone, where the Amateur Drama Council of Ireland has its headquarters. This was formed in 1952, and consists of representatives from each of the fourteen area drama festivals which compete annually in the All-Ireland Drama Festival for both one-act and full-length plays. In 1961 fifty-four companies competed in the festival, and there were thought to be as many as 700 amateur companies actively engaged in production of at least one play a year. Some of their plays are original, and one, *Sive*, written by John Keane of Listowel, and acted by a group from County Kerry, was an outstanding success. Among the active amateur groups in Ireland are the St. Philomena's Drama Group (1941) in Drogheda, the Runners' Dramatic Society (1949) in Tullamore, and the Clones Dramatic Society (1951). DAN O'CONNELL

IRELAND, William Henry (1775–1835), a brilliant but eccentric Englishman who, at the age of nineteen, forged with the greatest ease and accuracy a number of legal and personal documents relating to Shakespeare. These, he explained, he had found in the house of a friend who wished to remain anonymous. Ireland successfully deceived his father, a dealer in prints and rare books, and also a number of scholars and experts. The crowning achievement of his career was the forging of an entire Shakespeare play, *Vortigern and Rowena*, which after many difficulties and delays was put on at Drury Lane on 2 Apr. 1796 by Sheridan, with Kemble and Mrs. Jordan in the cast. The play was already suspect, and was damned by a riotous audience. This failure prevented Ireland from going on with a series of similar forgeries, of which *Henry II* was already written and *William the Conqueror* nearly completed. Ireland's forgeries were published by his father, who never ceased to believe in them, maintaining that his son was too stupid to have composed them. They were easily demolished by the great Shakespearian scholar Malone, and Ireland found himself forced to confess his ingenious deception. After this short blaze of glory he lived for another forty years in ignominious retirement, doing nothing but hackwork. The whole story has been well told in John Mair's *The Fourth Forger* (1938).

IRISH LITERARY THEATRE. This, founded by Lady Gregory and W. B. Yeats in 1898, was the first manifestation in drama of the Irish literary revival of the end of the nineteenth century. The first performances were given, with English actors, on 8–9 May 1899 at the Antient Concert Rooms, Dublin, and consisted of Yeats's *The Countess Cathleen* and Martyn's *The Heather Field.* A year later, in Feb. 1900, the Gaiety Theatre was hired for the production of George Moore's *The Bending of the Bough*, Martyn's *Maeve*, and Alice Milligan's *The Last Feast of the Fianna.* On 21 Oct. 1901 a cast headed by Frank Benson was imported from England to appear in *Diarmuid and Grania*, by Yeats and Moore, and the first Gaelic play, Douglas Hyde's *Casadh an tSugáin*, was performed by Gaelic-speaking amateurs. The Irish Literary Theatre was then replaced by the Irish National Dramatic Society, a professional company run by the Irish actors, W. G. and Frank Fay.

IRISH NATIONAL DRAMATIC SOCIETY. Founded by W. G. and Frank Fay, this company performed in 1902 *Deirdre* by AE, *Cathleen Ni Houlihan* and *The Pot of Broth* by Yeats, and four other plays, including one in Gaelic. These were given in small halls, one of which, 34 Camden Street, was later used as a workshop when the company went to the larger Molesworth Hall, where in 1903 and 1904 they did Yeats's *The Hour Glass, The King's Threshold*, and *The Shadowy Waters*, as well as Lady Gregory's *Twenty-Five*, Synge's *In the Shadow of the Glen* and *Riders to the Sea*, and Padraic Colum's *Broken Soil.* The company was invited to London, and appeared in two performances of five plays on 2 May 1903. It is probable that Miss Horniman saw these productions and that they contributed to her decision to build a permanent theatre in Dublin—the Abbey—for the company.

IRON, The, see SAFETY CURTAIN.

IRVING. (1) SIR HENRY [JOHN HENRY BRODRIBB] (1838–1905), English actor-manager who dominated the London stage for the last thirty years of Queen Victoria's reign. Of Cornish extraction, he was born at Keinton Mandeville, near Somerton, the ancient capital of Somerset. At the age of 10 he went to London, and while at the City Commercial School in Lombard Street worked hard at elocution lessons to help overcome a stutter. In a school production of Talfourd's tragedy *Ion* he took the part of Adrastus. Shortly before his twelfth birthday he saw his first professional production, Phelps in *Hamlet* at Sadler's Wells. At 14 he became a clerk in a Newgate Street counting-house, and in his spare time frequented the theatres. He also took lessons from a Mr. Henry Thomas at the City Elocution Class, and appeared with other pupils in *The Rivals*, playing Captain Absolute. In 1855 he appeared in *The Honeymoon*, and in 1856, on payment of a fee of three guineas, he played Romeo at the Soho Theatre, taking Irving as his stage name for the first time.

Irving made his first professional appearance on the stage at the Lyceum Theatre in Sunderland, on 29 Sept. 1856, and in Jan. 1857 he went to Edinburgh, where he remained until the autumn of 1859. He then returned to London, to appear at the Princess's under Augustus Harris. Among the four small parts allotted to him was Osric. Conscious of failure, he returned to the provinces, where he remained until 6 Oct. 1866, when he appeared at the St. James's Theatre, London, as Doricourt in *The Belle's Strategem* and as Rawdon Scudamore in Boucicault's *Hunted Down*—a part he had previously played in Manchester, when the play was entitled *The Two Lives of Mary Leigh*, with Kate Terry in the title-role. Louisa Herbert, manageress of the St. James's, played the part in London. Irving's success in these two parts was sufficient to keep him in London, and it was from the St. James's that on 26 Dec. 1867 he went to the Queen's, Long Acre, to play for the first time with Ellen Terry, in *Katherine and Petruchio*, Garrick's popular one-act adaptation of *The Taming of the Shrew.* In 1869 he made a hit with Toole at the Gaiety as Mr. Reginald Chevenix in *Uncle Dick's Darling*, by H. J. Byron, and at the Vaudeville in 1870 he was equally successful as Digby Grant in Albery's *Two Roses.* At this time he was considered a player of heavy villains and farcically comic characters.

On 11 Sept. 1871 he appeared for the first time under the Bateman management at the Lyceum Theatre. This theatre had long been unlucky, and Irving's Jingle, in Albery's adaptation of *The Pickwick Papers*, did nothing to restore its fortunes. The management, almost in despair, allowed him to force upon them *The Bells*, an adaptation by Leopold Lewis of Erckmann-Chatrian's *Le Juif polonais.* The audience on the first night was scanty, but by the next morning Henry Irving was famous.

The Polish Jew, a study in terror, was succeeded by Charles I, a figure of pathos which allowed Irving to make noble and restrained use of all the romantic, pitiful, and tender associations of the Stuart legend. Then *Eugene Aram* repeated the triumph of *The Bells.* The brilliant new actor had found himself, and as Richelieu he deliberately pitted his own conception of acting against that of

Macready and his school. Although everything about his performance was by some accounted wrong, there were influential critics who perceived in him a genius struggling powerfully for self-vindication. Comedy was being regenerated by the Bancrofts at the Haymarket; here at the Lyceum, it seemed to Clement Scott and John Oxenford, was the champion tragedy had been waiting for. In 1874 Irving played Hamlet. He presented him as a gentle prince who failed to do the great things demanded of him not so much from weakness of will as from excess of tenderness. The reading, so different from the popular method of illumining tragic character by flashes from a dark lantern, puzzled the audience and was hotly contested by the coteries.

It was Irving's fate to gain immense prestige and never to be free from critical attack. He was not easily and in his nature popular. Few of his performances in classic parts were universally accepted. At the height of his renown there were people who found his mannerisms unsympathetic and even slightly ludicrous. Yet they also were drawn to see him, and they discussed him eagerly, because the acting he chose to give them was overwhelming in its intensity. Superseding the heavily pointed style of his predecessors, his own style was equally far removed from the subjective quietness of a Duse. To Irving acting was movement. He drew a character in sharp, sudden, delicate, superb movements, each guided by a craftsmanship on which he had worked with what seemed to his associates almost inhuman concentration. There is the ring of truth in Ellen Terry's account of his qualities. 'He was', she wrote, 'quiet, patient, tolerant, impersonal, gentle, close, crafty, incapable of caring for anything outside his work.' The picture he drew of a Louis XI, a Dubosc, a Shylock, or a Vanderdecken, challenged rather than reproduced nature. It had the splendid liberating madness of a dream in the remembered light of which the world's sanity looked drab and unreal. The tall figure, the beautiful, intense, ascetic face angled by nature for tragedy—now embodying a noble pride, now malignant horror, now sardonic impudence, now the grotesque at that point where it turns grim—threw a spell over his audience. It was a spell not so much of emotional sympathy as of intellectual curiosity; and under this spell it seemed that his peculiar pronunciation, his crabbed elocution, his halting gait, the queer intonations of his never very powerful or melodious voice, were the right and true expression of a strange, exciting, and dominating personality. Occasionally the homely and tender charm of a Dr. Primrose would solicit his imagination, and he kept an equable level of good acting, but nearly always his native grandeur would out. Even his Macaires became quasi-regal in their villainy, and when he played a Charles I, a Richelieu, a Wolsey, or a Becket, the irresistible impression was that greatness was impersonating greatness. Dominating spirit called to dominating spirit across the centuries, hidalgo to hidalgo.

Irving's management of the Lyceum began on 30 Dec. 1878 with a revival of *Hamlet* (see No. 79). It did little for the original work of contemporary English playwrights, but Irving was a great manager as well as a great actor. He was not content until he had enlisted in the service of his theatre some of the finest archaeologists and painters and musicians of the day. All he did was done with a certain magnificence. Ellen Terry was only one of the glories of a theatrical reign that melted away the remains of Puritan prejudice against the playhouse and made each new production a universal topic of late-Victorian conversation. The chief of these productions were *The Lady of Lyons* and *The Merchant of Venice* (both 1879), *The Corsican Brothers* (1880), *The Cup* and *Two Roses* (both 1881), *Romeo and Juliet* (see No. 73) and *Much Ado About Nothing* (both 1882), *Twelfth Night* (1884), *King Henry VIII* and *King Lear* (both 1892), *Becket* (1893), *King Arthur*, *A Story of Waterloo*, and *Don Quixote* (see No. 173) (all 1895), *Cymbeline* (1896), *Madame Sans-Gêne* (1897), and *Peter the Great* (1898). In 1899 Irving nominally gave up the Lyceum, and for the first time since 1878 appeared under another management, as Robespierre; his tenancy expired in 1901, in which year he appeared as Coriolanus, and in 1902 he made his last appearance at the Lyceum, in *The Merchant of Venice*. In 1903 he was at Drury Lane in *Dante*, and it was there that he gave his last London season in 1905, from April to June, playing Becket, Shylock, and Louis XI. He made his final appearance in London on 15 June, at Her Majesty's Theatre, in Lionel Brough's Testimonial Matinée, as Corporal Gregory Brewster in *A Story of Waterloo*.

Irving made several Canadian and American tours—in 1883, 1887, 1893, 1899, 1901, and 1903. His first appearance in New York was at the Star Theatre on 29 Oct. 1883, as Mathias in *The Bells*, and his last at the Harlem Opera House on 25 Mar. 1904, as Louis XI. His final provincial tour in England began at Sheffield on 2 Oct. 1905, and from there he went to Bradford, where he died on 13 Oct., after playing Becket.

Irving was the recipient of many honours during his lifetime, and was the first actor to be knighted for services to the theatre, in the Birthday Honours of 1895. On 15 July 1869 he had married Miss Florence O'Callaghan, but the marriage was not a happy one, and they eventually separated. There were, however, two sons of this marriage, both of whom went on the stage. The elder, (2) HENRY BRODRIBB (1870–1919), studied law, but after appearing with the O.U.D.S. made his first appearance on the professional stage under Hare in 1891. In the course of his career he revived many of his father's famous parts, both in England and America. His wife, (3) DOROTHEA BAIRD (1875–1933), also made her first appearance on the stage with the O.U.D.S., and was later with Ben

Greet. She made her first outstanding success in the name part of *Trilby* (1895), and later accompanied her husband to America and Australia. Irving's younger son, (4) LAURENCE SIDNEY (1871–1914), was in the diplomatic service before taking to the stage, where he made his first appearance in 1891 in Benson's company. Later performances, among them Skule in Ibsen's *The Pretenders* in 1913, indicated that he would have developed into a great actor but for his untimely death by drowning (with his wife, Mabel Hackney) when the *Empress of Ireland* sank after a collision in the St. Lawrence. He was the author of a number of plays, of which the most successful was *The Unwritten Law* (1910), and he translated for his father Sardou's *Robespierre* and *Dante*. He also wrote for Irving the tragedy *Peter the Great*, which opened at the Lyceum on 1 Jan. 1898. Though it contained some fine passages, it was an epic poem rather than a play, and it was also somewhat lacking in action and humour. It was withdrawn after thirty-eight performances, and has not since been revived.

The son of H. B. Irving, (5) LAURENCE HENRY FORSTER (1897–), is an artist who, in addition to illustrating a number of books, has been responsible for the décor of an impressive list of plays, mostly in London. His work was first seen in 1926, for *Vaudeville Vanities*, and among his later settings were those for *The Good Companions* (1931), *Evensong* (1932), *Murder in the Cathedral* (1935), and *I Have Been Here Before* (1937). After serving in the R.A.F. from 1939 to 1945, he returned to the theatre, and was responsible for the décor of *The First Gentleman* (1945) and of many subsequent productions. He is a governor of the Royal Shakespeare Theatre and was the first chairman of the British Theatre Museum Association, to which he presented the papers of his grandfather and other documents used in the preparation of his monumental work, *Henry Irving: The Actor and His World* (1951). A. V. COOKMAN†, *rev.*

IRVING, WASHINGTON (1783–1859), born in New York City, was the first American author to gain recognition abroad. Chiefly remembered as an historian and as the writer of romantic sketches and tales, he also served as a diplomat. In 1802–3 he published, in the New York *Morning Chronicle*, a series entitled 'The Letters of Jonathan Oldstyle', several of which give a vivid picture of the contemporary New York stage. Together with his brother William, and with J. K. Paulding, he wrote *Salmagundi* (1807–8), which includes a number of satiric letters on the state of the theatre. He later collaborated with John Howard Payne in a number of plays. Their *Charles II* (1824) and *Richelieu* (1826), both adapted from French originals, were particularly successful. His short story 'Rip Van Winkle' (first published in 1819) was adapted for the stage by James Hackett in 1825. Other adaptations followed, the most successful being that of Joseph Jefferson and Dion Boucicault in 1865, in which Jefferson scored his greatest success, playing the title-role regularly until his retirement in 1904.

ROBERT TRACY

ISAACS, EDITH JULIET (*née* RICH) (1878–1956), for a quarter of a century one of the leading forces in the American theatre. Born in Milwaukee, Wisconsin, she went to live in New York in 1904, the year of her marriage to Lewis M. Isaacs, and in 1913 was drama critic for *Ainslee's Magazine*. As editor of *Theatre Arts* from 1919 to 1945 (and for many years its chief stockholder), she exercised a unique and beneficial influence on the American theatre as a whole. Through *Theatre Arts* she exercised not only her remarkable editorial faculties, but also her own very keen faculties as a critic. She wrote with discernment on the theatre, dance, and music, and was an excellent judge of the graphic arts. She was also a clear-headed business woman who understood the economic as well as the aesthetic problems of the theatre, and was in the forefront of the theatre's practical as well as spiritual battles. Among the manifold activities in which she took a leading part were the founding of the National Theatre Conference, of which she was executive head from 1932 to 1936; the campaign for better theatre buildings in New York which led to improvements in the building code; assistance in the difficult first days of the Federal Theatre, when the offices of *Theatre Arts* were guest headquarters for the newly appointed director, Hallie Flanagan; assistance in organizing the first Board of Directors and professional advisory committee of the American National Theatre and Academy, of which she was first Vice-President.

The many theatre artists whose early work appeared in *Theatre Arts*, and to whom its editor gave encouragement and often practical guidance at a crucial stage, cannot be listed here. The pages of the magazine are the best record of a rich and fruitful life which was prolonged after her retirement as editor by her activities as critic and author. *Theatre Arts* contributors, from Bernard Shaw and D. H. Lawrence to Robert Sherwood and William Saroyan, included writers from many of the sixty-seven lands to which the magazine found its way. Among the books she herself edited or wrote are *Theatre* (1927), *Architecture for the New Theatre* (1935), and *The Negro in the American Theatre* (1947). ROSAMOND GILDER

ISRAEL, see JEWISH DRAMA.

ITALY. Italian drama is here dealt with in three sections:

1. The literary drama from the beginning to the eighteenth century.
2. The improvised drama or *commedia dell'arte*.
3. The literary drama from the eighteenth century to the present day.

The first section may be regarded as

subdivided into the drama of (*a*) the Middle Ages, and (*b*) the Renaissance, a term which is here very broadly taken as stretching from the early sixteenth to the late seventeenth century and even, for a special reason, in Section 2 extending to cover Gozzi's quixotic use of the *commedia dell'arte*, which is strictly eighteenth century work.

1. From the Beginning to the Eighteenth Century. The main medieval drama was liturgical; such lay forms as have survived were sporadic and rudimentary and consisted chiefly of the semi-dramatic entertainment provided by minstrels and tumblers, by verse dialogues, by festival celebrations and dances. The Renaissance represents an enormous process of expansion and secularization by which the ecclesiastical gives way to academic, courtly, and popular patronage. The changes occur roughly in this order, but no exact date can or should be given to the overlapping phases. It is significant and perhaps slightly sinister that by the seventeenth century Italian drama has three masters; scholars and, in league with them, the critics, with their passionately pedantic concern for classical precedent; the Courts, with their avidity for spectacle and subsequently for music; and thirdly, the common people feeding fat on the scraps from both these tables, served up by the genius of two or three generations of actors professing a distinctive method of improvisation.

The sixteenth and seventeenth centuries will be taken together because of the more real distinction to be made between the two styles, known as the *commedia erudita* and the *commedia dell'arte*; for this contrast Shakespeare through Polonius provided the most neatly descriptive terms when he referred to the visiting players as 'for the law of writ and the liberty'.

Medieval religious drama is anonymous; in the Renaissance period there is many a fine, rather than one superlative, figure, form, place, or phase upon which to focus. Critics have worked along various lines, concentrating now upon an individual, now on a city, a period, or a form, in each case with profit and limitation; their peaks of interest will not coincide. Warned of this we may make use of their researches, and choose the division by 'kinds'.

The history of Italian drama does not begin or end in Italy; it is important to conceive of it in relation to European drama to appreciate its full significance. It transmits the ancient to the modern stage, so that it is impossible to account for the development of the greater drama of France, and partly for that of England, without allowing for the influences, theoretical or practical, good or bad, of Italy. Spain too takes, and later repays, in fair measure. This can only be indicated in passing, but it is fundamentally important. During the Renaissance especially Italy is the exchange and mart of dramatic forms. She has not many golden pieces. Her wealth is mainly in silver and in bonds.

(*a*) *Middle Ages*. (i) *Laudi*. There is evidence that something was known indirectly, and a little perhaps directly, at least of Latin comedy during the Middle Ages, but the references do not indicate any activities or compositions that can properly be called dramatic. Writing that has more real affinity with drama is found in such collections of stories as the *Decamerone*, and in the graver counterpart that Boccaccio provided in *De Casibus Virorum Illustrium*, but here impersonation, the determining factor of drama, is only invited.

In the opinion of D'Ancona what instances survive of the liturgical drama in manuscripts of Italian provenance do not suggest anything distinctively national. This was still the drama of the Church, and it can be viewed best in Professor Karl Young's comprehensive work on the drama of the medieval Church (see liturgical drama). The first impulse that is unmistakably Italian in origin and issue comes in the middle of the thirteenth century, and is due to the amazing penitential movement of the Flagellanti. The *laudi* or praises which they and their followers sang were primarily devotional and in form lyric at first and then narrative, using almost literally the stories and phrases of the Gospels; but it is easy to understand how recitation led to dialogue, and then to dramatic impersonation. A list of the properties possessed by the Company of the Disciplinati in Perugia shows how far the process had gone by 1339.

The choice of episodes, their elaboration and grouping, were designed to follow the seasons of the Church's year. Manuscripts, mainly of the sixteenth century, preserve the cycles of *laudi* for districts of Umbria and the Abruzzi. The authors remain anonymous and their purpose was still religious rather than artistic. A recent critic, M. Apollonio, illustrates his study with reproductions of contemporary paintings, assuming some connexion between the arts in their graphic, naïve representation of incidents, but he insists that the trend of the *laudi* was choral and by this distinguishes it from the second medieval form, the *sacre rappresentazioni*, which developed later with special spectacular splendour.

(ii) *Sacre Rappresentazioni*. These constitute the religious and subsequently the artistic expression of the fifteenth century, and were particularly the pride of Florence. In 1454 M. Palmieri described the festival for St. John's Day, with its procession of clergy and religious companies involving twenty-two 'edifizi' for the enacting of episodes from the Old and New Testaments. In Siena there was a sequence in honour of Santa Caterina. While the *sacre rappresentazioni* are comparable to the French and English Mystery plays, Sanesi claims for them a Florentine sense of form and moderation. They were played by religious and educational 'companies' of young citizens in churches, refectories, or in the open, on a multiple stage. D'Ancona shows how comic and realistic characters gradually intruded to relieve the sameness of the traditional or stiffly typed figures; such chances were taken in exploiting brawls, grotesque names, the caricaturing of foreigners and certain professions, and even with satire of convent life. Occasionally there emerge individual authors such as Feo Belcari (1410–84) or Lorenzo de' Medici (*c.* 1449–92) with his *San Giovanni e Paolo* (1489). In plays based on the lives of saints some romance material is incorporated.

The simple episodic method could not hold its own against the pressure of the conscious revival of classical forms, but critics are reminded of the tradition of the *sacre rappresentazioni* as they find the early humanists plotting according to narrative sequence in defiance of the classical unities, or again when Poliziano [Angelo Ambrogini] (1454–91) substitutes a mythological for a scriptural theme, and yet again, but this time in intention rather than in form, with the *drammi spirituali* of Giovanni Maria Cecchi (1518–87) and with Counter-Reformation plays; in convents and in some seasonal country festivities other traces remain.

The *sacre rappresentazioni* gave scope to the related tastes and capacities for music and spectacle, and for two kinds of acting, grave and ribald, and so seem to have absorbed the talents which can otherwise only be descried in undeveloped arts and diversions of the Middle Ages.

(*b*) *Renaissance and Seventeenth Century*. (i) *Tragedy*. In recognition of its debt of the dramatic artists of the Italian Renaissance Europe might say 'they gave us patterns' and 'they set us bounds', and then proceed to reckon more precisely the cost of the tragic, comic, and pastoral patterns, and the bounds of the neo-Aristotelian criticism. It is easy to imagine how desirable the acquisition of some standard, form, rule, or model, must have seemed to the generation of Petrarch, and how hard to foresee was the imminent tyranny of this benevolent classical rule.

The first signs of the tragic form as well as the term in Italy are found at the end of the thirteenth century when Albertino Mussato (1261–1329), Giovanni Manzini (*fl.* 1387), and Laudivio de' Nobili (*fl.* 1464) [these latter are the dates of their tragedies], sharing Boccaccio's conception of tragedy as concerned with the fall of princes, attempt to give to the full stories of Ezzelino, Antonio della Scala, and Piccinino respectively at least the external features of Senecan tragedy; but they come short of the rigorous selection needed for classical unity. Other plays, also in Latin, still only half out of the *sacre rappresentazioni* tradition, use medieval history and ancient mythology more for moral and literary than for dramatic purposes.

In 1472 Poliziano took a turn away from scriptural drama by using its method to present the story of Orpheus, and twenty-three years later an unknown author (? Antonio Tebaldeo) gave his work another classical twist by refashioning it into *Orphei tragedia*. The two significant facts are that anyone should have wished to make the formal changes and yet not have attempted any fundamental reconception.

Apart from these experiments the first work in the vernacular said to bear the title of tragedy is *Filostrato e Panfile* (1499) by Antonio Caminelli, called 'il Pistoia' (1436–1502). It is shaped from Boccaccio's story of Tancred and Gismond, but neither Caminelli nor his successor Galeotto del Carretto (*fl.* 1497–1530) really forsook the older method.

During the second decade of the sixteenth century the rare, scholarly pleasure of direct contact with Greek drama made its mark on the vernacular in the *Sofonisba* (prod. 1524) of Gian Giorgio Trissino (1478–1550). It is a frigid and famous play, achieving unity of time by formal redisposition of the material drawn from Livy by means of narration, chorus, and act-division. It has the form, but not the pressure, of its models. As a play there seems to be no life in *Sofonisba*, but as a sign-post it has a commanding position.

Trissino stimulated Giovanni Rucellai (1475–1525) to press Gothic material and turn out *Rosmunda* (1516) and then to squeeze from Greek mythology an *Oreste*. Meanwhile the work of translating Aristotle's criticism and the tragedies themselves went on parallel to the free imitations, but for a very limited public. It is hardly surprising that it needed the ulterior attraction of spectacle and inter-act dancing to draw an audience to plays in which horror was held to be indispensable, and rhetoric came before action. If an English reader could realize what Sidney saw and admired in *Gorboduc*, he would presumably be drawn into sympathy with what Italian humanists sought to provide.

In the middle of the century Giambattista Giraldi, called 'il Cinthio' (1504–73), faced and dealt with this depressing situation, theoretically in treatise and preface, and practically in nine plays. When his public had been sated with distended Senecan atrocities in *Orbecche* (1541), Giraldi began to find his own style. There is said to be less of Seneca in *Dido* and *Cleopatra*, but there is never any retraction from the Senecan conception of a moral function and sententious speech. In *L'Altile* (1543) Giraldi presented a dramatic version of one of the medieval stories from his own *Eccatonmiti*, where the persons were noble but not royal, with the further concession of a happy ending to encourage his audience. Here too he asserts a modern independence of Aristotle, but he did not care to take much advantage of the freedom he claimed. In this respect his practice is typical of the period. Stories drawn from widely varied sources, mostly but not exclusively old, were pulped down and poured into the mould which had been made carefully and patiently to Aristotelian specifications, and in the process much, if not all, of what was the spirit of drama evaporated. To see how the rich dramatic potentialities of Giraldi's store of *novelle* could be exploited by another method it is instructive to turn to Greene and Shakespeare, and to compare *James IV* with

Giraldi's *Arrenopia*, *Measure for Measure* with *Epizia*, and *Othello* with its narrative source. For English dramatists Giraldi opened up chivalric sources and romantic situations by broaching sentiment for tragedy and tragicomedy, but for Italy, in Bertana's estimate, he consolidated the neo-classical model. He was content to further the moral and sensational purposes of tragedy, holding his public by minor concessions of novelty and sentiment, relaxing the imitation of the classical chorus a little, treating his women with unusual sympathy, and observing strict poetic justice. His tragedy asks no ultimate questions, and it seems, at least to an English reader, that he is too ready to supply his own answers. It is exasperatingly competent.

Giraldi's work was so central, comprehensive, and influential that one has the illusion of being able to predict what was to follow. Since it was his ambition to give tragedy greater currency on the Renaissance stage he must be called successful. It would be a penance to read all that was written; even so thorough a critic as Bertana finds it hard to make a satisfactory classification of the productions of the second half of the sixteenth and the seventeenth centuries, and attempts a grouping only according to historical, romantic and classical, and a characterization of the themes as horrific.

What happened may be illustrated by another method by leaping forward to Giacinto Andrea Cicognini (1606–60), who was probably the most popular provider and generally representative playwright of the next generation. It is symptomatic that he is credited with over forty compositions, but the list varies and much published in his name is palpably made over from Spanish drama. Giraldi's achieved purpose had been to adapt the classical form just so much and no more as would commend it to his own age; Cicognini's was to cater for his public by excitement in more exotic styles. Giraldi provides the concentration of neo-classical serious drama, Cicognini touches the bounds of its diffusion and dissipation. Giraldi's style is plain, Cicognini's cheaply coloured.

But Cicognini does not travel thus far on his own; along the lines of protraction from Giraldi lie scores of other tragedies, and some more correctly termed *tragicommedie* and *opere sceniche*. The range of material is considerable; *argomenti* are drawn from myths, or from ancient and modern history, frequent use is made of Ariosto, Tasso, and the *novelle*. The apparent variety is enormous, but once the stories have been 'processed' they taste much the same. It is interesting, at least to the critic, to see how the pressure of the content combining with the general temptations of popularity, and in certain cases a special pressure of religious propaganda, gradually affect the neo-Aristotelian rigidity. First one and then another of the classical conventions is ruptured, but the freedom gained is rarely used creatively; it is won as expedience and has the effect of licence. Authors go on writing, but have little to say, and they produce, as other generations before and since, only nominal tragedies. In some, however, the dynamic force of the dramatist's conception gives him a truer claim to independence.

To return to Bertana's thematic classification: among those plays drawn from Roman history the *Orazio* (1546) of Pietro Aretino (1492–1556) stands out. To a modern Italian this Renaissance presentation of ancient Rome rings true, at least in the main and in the treatment of the crowd. The style is more direct and figurative than is usual.

Occasionally the drama latent in a modern story has its way, as, for instance, when Giovanni Francesco Savarro (*fl.* early seventeenth century) takes his chance with Anne Boleyn or Mary Stuart, and Girolamo Graziani (1604–75) is nerved to refuse to be bound by Aristotle's rule in *Comuele* (*c.* 1671).

Among the horror tragedies the notorious *Canace* (1543) of Sperone Speroni (1500–88) shocked his age and it shocks ours, but not for the same reasons. It was attacked and defended in the name of Aristotle until Speroni's death, and meanwhile others, Luigi Groto (1541–85) especially, and rather less grossly Lodovico Dolce (1508–68), waded on in blood.

Those who risked romance material found the attractions and the dangers of love as a tragic motive. Erotic tragedies were popular at the turn of the century. One of the most elaborate is that of Torquato Tasso (1544–95), but it is with deference to his poetic rather than to his tragic gift that *Torrismondo* (1586) is famous. In the *seicento* many minister to this taste. Some concede to love-plots a happy ending; some venture to let the lovers speak for themselves.

As a general rule, however, care was devoted to plotting, to the impoverishment of characterization and the delineation of the more inward conflicts of motive and passion. To judge from the topics of critical controversy this was not felt as a loss. Few can pretend now that the result was very acceptable. Tragedy was expensive, and the displays in the great theatre at Vicenza were exceptional. The comparative unpopularity of the style was openly acknowledged by Ingegneri in 1598.

In the seventeenth century, at the price of concessions to popular taste and by subserving propaganda purposes, the Jesuits found uses for the form and gave it some temporary support. Since the connexion with *Paradise Lost* has been mooted, *L'Adamo* (1613) of Giambattista Andreini (*c.* 1578–1654) is probably the religious drama of the seventeenth century that an Englishman would wish to have seen, but *L'Adamo* is entitled *sacra rappresentazione* and is not typical. In itself it is more suggestive of the coming *melodramma*. Spain led the way for most playwrights, and martyrdom was more to their purpose. Massinger's *Virgin Martyr* would bring an English reader nearest to the general effect. The combination of sensation, emotion, and piety makes a nauseating mixture with a distinct flavour, but no form, of its own. One of the most prolific exploiters was Ortensio Scammacca (1562–1648), who has nearly fifty plays to his credit. Others did not trouble to develop plots beyond the 'scenario'.

Italian Renaissance tragedy had great possessions; good stories, good models, some patronage, much critical attention, much practice, but it lacked one thing, the power to make contact with the imagination. Its weaknesses are as various and sporadic as its merits. It is tempting but useless to speculate on its prospective promise or its retrospective dreariness. One plea remains. We are ill-placed to judge. We read too much and see too little. But the fact that there is no acting tradition is not encouraging.

(ii) *Pastoral.* If we are tempted to plead specially for Italian Renaissance tragedy, some consideration, though in another kind and degree, may be claimed for its rival the pastoral. According to contemporary critics the pastoral drew attention from the severer mode; that is easily understood, but if we then find it hard to appreciate the new form we may apply a rough analogy, and think of it as the cinema of the age. It was largely because it *was* new that it was rated so highly. The parallel is, of course, very rough. The novelty was apparently the result of crossing Renaissance eclogue and drama, not, as in the modern case, of the application of a new technique. It was, primarily at least, a courtly, sophisticated entertainment with a limited scope, not for the populace; but it was the age's own invention and gave it a sense of superiority over the ancients, its betters.

The exact stages of the development of pastoral as a third dramatic form have been disputed. Dr. Greg's admirable summary will be found in Appendix I of his *Pastoral Poetry and Pastoral Drama* (1906).

It is generally agreed that the chief pattern was Tasso's and its enlargement Guarini's, but there were earlier experiments in lyrical, spectacular, and rhetorical entertainments which should be mentioned. If we return to Poliziano's *Orfeo* (1472) and follow its lead we come to the *Cefalo* (1487) of Niccolò da Correggio (1450–1508). The mythological drama is in a sense a sidetrack. Looking back, some would prefer to regard it as a shoot from the old wood of the *sacre rappresentazioni*, and not as radically related to the new growth. Looking forward and reading the *libretti* it is tempting to descry *melodramma* before its time. Whatever the relations in conscious artistic experiments may have been, the affinities are obvious, and these three forms, and with them perhaps the Carnival masques, Triumphs, and such semi-dramatic shows, may be reckoned together as several ways of ministering to the delight in any sensuous blending of music, movement, impersonation, and lyrical speech.

A Jacobean who could remember seeing plays by Peele, Lyly, and Daniel, and some masques, would have understood the Renaissance variety in Italy, and perhaps suspected that England owed Italy many small debts. The relative popularity of the various forms is different, and the opera is a separate story. Only the Italian pastoral realized to the full its dramatic possibilities, and it is tempting to describe it as drama pastoralized rather than pastoral dramatized.

Guarini reckons that the *pastorale favola, Il Sacrifizio* (1554–5), by Agostino Beccari (?–1598), was the first of the new kind. It was followed by *Lo Sfortunato* of Agostino Argenti (?–1576) in 1568. This Tasso saw, and his own *L'Aminta* was acted in Ferrara in 1573. From Tasso's delicate single flower Battista Guarini (1538–1612) cultivated a rich double variety. *Il Pastor fido* (prod. 1598) is more than three times as long as *L'Aminta*, and Guarini is as proud of its complicated plotting as Tasso might be of his own simplicity. No attempt is made here to do justice either to *L'Aminta*, which is of a poet's substance, or to the artfulness of Guarini's contrivances. There are plenty of good versions and critiques of both, and summaries of the pamphlet war between the author and the critics which opened in 1587, three years before Guarini published, and went on until 1602. Superficially these plays are easy to imitate, fatally easy. The marvel is that the small Arcadian world of nymphs, shepherds, satyrs, rustics, and enchanters, with the artificiality of its sentimental concerns, its dependence upon oracles, metamorphoses, and other 'ancientry', should have stood up to so many repeats and re-combinings. The best of these, and the representative pastoral of the next generation, is the *Filli di Sciro* (1607) of Guidobaldo Bonarelli (1563–1608). Its admirers liked to regard the pastoral as the third dramatic form, but it is hardly on a level with tragedy and comedy, and has not the monopoly of the tragi-comic modification. It is rather the most prolific of period forms, and in addition to the intrinsic value of a few of the plays it can claim some part in the *melodramma* which was the great contribution of the *seicento*. The pastoral slips quietly into the stronger current and is hardly missed.

(iii) *Comedy.* What the humanists attempted for the promotion of classical form in tragedy they achieved rather more congenially with comedy. Petrarch's contribution is not extant, so that pride of place is given to the *Paulus* (*c.* 1389) of Pier Paolo Vergerio (1370–1444), where the presentation of medieval university society is intended for the correction of youth; it is only superficially classical. The content of these Latin plays is chiefly students' follies, light or gross, sharpened by national or personal satire, or, in the *Cauteriaria* (? 1469) of Antonio Buzario (*fl.* fifteenth century), by brutal realism. Others use the comedy of matrimonial misfits, as in *Comedia Bile* (first half of fifteenth century). One Dominican friar, in *Comoedia sine nomine* (? 1450–60), attempts to use a more romantic theme, but hardly with success. For some, comedy was a graver affair, and intended for moral improvement; a few, but only a few, were adroit enough to maintain the burlesque style while discharging this purpose. It is not until the turn of the century that the formative influence of classical models is apparent, but Sanesi claims that in the *Chrysis* (1444) of Enea Silvio Piccolomini (1405–64) (later Pope Pius II) the Latin types are recognizable. Slowly but surely the Romans came back,conquered, and were seen.

Alongside this more creative work there was a steady increase in the acquisition, mastery, and translation of classical comedy. Glosses and commentaries were recovered, and in 1429 twelve of Plautus's plays were added to the eight already known. There was also some attention paid to Aristophanes.

For educational purposes acting was encouraged. Isabella d'Este admits in a letter of 1502 that the *intermezzi* had compensated for the play which had bored her. It is clear that what was decorative and complimentary was used to make the more intellectual provision acceptable. The character and splendour of such display depended upon the resources in money and talent at the various Courts.

When Lodovico Ariosto (1474–1533) comes into view what had shone before now seems tentative and dim. He occupied himself with comedy for the Court of Ferrara twice, in the first decade with *Cassaria* (1508) and *I Suppositi* (1509), and in the third when he re-wrote these in verse, worked out an earlier idea in *Il Negromante* (written 1520, prod. 1530), added *La Lena* (written 1529), and left *Gli Studenti* to be finished by his brother as *La Scolastica*, and by his son as *L'Imperfetta*. Comedy was evidently a congenial, though not his favourite, form for the expression of that 'sunlight of the mind', that 'mental richness' which Meredith might have claimed for him in virtue of *Orlando Furioso*.

Ariosto used the classics with masterly freedom, and there are credible legends of how he took copy from his own father while the latter reprimanded him; ancient and modern materials are creatively welded. Even in the bareness of reading, deprived of Raphael's scenery and all the social circumstances, when we can no longer test the excitement of finding what was recognizably old made realistically new, the quality of his comedy is evident.

The proper preparation for the *commedia erudita* as it was instituted by Ariosto and his generation is to acquire a taste for Plautus and Terence, a good working knowledge of the *Decamerone* and other *novelle*, a relish for realism in the close representation of men and manners, and a callous, quick enjoyment of human folly. It is a critical comedy worked by intrigue, and showing types, if not caricatures, of city life.

In the interval between the two periods of Ariosto's activity others were discovering what could be done with the good method and rich resources now released and encouraged by patronage. *La Calandria* was published in 1521, a year after the death of its author Cardinal Bernardo Dovizi da Bibbiena (1470–1520), but it was seen at Urbino in 1506. This gross, boisterous, witty comedy is famous to us because of contemporary descriptions of its reception which make it live in the terms of the society which it delighted. To read it is another admirable way of initiation into the fashion for playing variations upon the stage twins (real or faked) and the traditional booby (Boccaccio's Calandrio). It is coarser fare than Ariosto's and more clumsily served, but it had immense popularity then, and it has some substance and flavour still.

Niccolò Machiavelli (1469–1527) is said to have worked on an Aristophanic model at first in his lost *Le Maschere*; he too reverted to Terence in *L'Andria* (date unknown) and to Plautus's *Casina* in *La Clizia* (after 1513), but in *La Mandragola* (? 1513) all is his own. It made no mould for his own use or anyone else's. No formula can be drawn from it, its form is vital, and consists in that apparently effortless fitting of means to an end which Henry James called the artist's 'deep-breathing economy'. Machiavelli's touch is so wickedly nice that each remark betrays its speaker to us. They give themselves away, so that in doing all the author seems to be doing nothing. We think we are seeing life for ourselves, but we are seeing it with his eyes, appraising it with his intellect, shirking nothing and yet not unduly shocked. Only the deft ironic verses between the acts remind us of his invisible presence. His detachment disinfects the noisome theme so that in reflection we proceed beyond it, until, imperceptibly, his Fra Timoteo, Messer Nicia, Callimaco, and Lucrezia come to count for more than types, stage or social, and are found to possess baffling but unmistakable individuality. They are not conceived as Shakespeare or Molière or Congreve would have conceived them, but they are of the same order of imaginative being. Machiavelli can only be judged by his peers, though among such he is himself and no other. Such individuality comes again in *Il Candelaio* (*c.* 1582), by Giordano Bruno (1548–1600), where the form is used effectively once and once only. Meanwhile to provide patterns Ariosto was more useful, with his imitable blending of common materials and forms.

Machiavelli's style is curt Tuscan, 'expurgate and sober, with scarcely an "issimo".' *La Mandragola* stands up like a rock-needle, emphasizing the contrast with the gross fertility of Pietro Aretino (1492–1556). We may marvel with how few words Machiavelli can say so much, and how much Aretino can find to say about so little. He had a knack for finding real life racier than fiction, and used its flavour and substance five times: in *La Cortigiana* (1525, prod. 1534), *Il Marescalco* (1526–7, prod. 1533), *La Talanta* and *L'Ipocrito* (1541–2), and *Il Filosofo* (1544, prod. 1546). Fantastic situations are accepted as his means, but the end is the presentation of men and women, mostly foolish with love or greed, but vividly alive. Practical jokes old and new, romantic complications, sustained burlesques, actual scandals—nothing was safe with Aretino about, and nothing was dull when he had worked it up. Only Jonson working at a great figure such as Subtle or a huge scene such as Bartholomew Fair can compete with Aretino as a comic artist, but as artist and man Jonson had a conscience and Aretino had not.

The originality of these plays moves Sanesi to contend that Renaissance comedy was not so formalized as to make it inflexible for the expression of vehement individual power, but no one could deny that by the mid-*cinquecento* there were already enough standard patterns to support the many who had some talent and a few who had none. The first quarter-century provided models, and later critics reduced to rules what the artistic sense of this generation had found to be expedient. This was only too helpful for mediocrity. It is hard to test the real merit of this supply; the conformity of so much that is second-rate is apt to dull the wits of the reader, still more of the modern reader, and, most of all, the foreign reader, but the plays to be mentioned below are good in their kind and very fairly representative of the favourite situations of amorous intrigue, of the chief comic types, and of the dexterous, firm way in which they had trained themselves to plot. Alongside the Italian efficiency the homeliness and romance of the English method seems naïve in all but the best of Elizabethan comedies, and yet, for this very quality, they are refreshing. Gosson has a damaging summary of the content of Italianate comedies which, allowing for his Puritan malice, is not inaptly phrased: 'Love, cosenedge, flatterie, bawderie, slye conveighance of whordome; the persons, cookes, queanes, knaves, baudes, parasites, courtezannes, lecherous old men, amorous young men with such lyke of infinite varietie.'

Trading with plots, sub-plots, situations, devices, and types was brisk. Anyone might draw upon Plautus and Terence, and much of the modern work was pooled in a common stock to which most of the chief cities had something to contribute. Venice has less to offer at this stage than, as we shall see, she had earlier and in other kinds, but Dolce, Bentivoglio, and later Loredano were productive. Brescia had Niccolò Secchi; Adria its blind playwright, Luigi Groto; Ricchi, who wrote *I Tre Tiranni* at the age of 18, came from Lucca. Florentines were the most prolific, with Giannotti, Firenzuola, Lorenzo de' Medici, Landi, Gelli, d'Ambra, Razzi, Varchi, Salviati, Cini, Borghini, while Cecchi and Grazzini even strike out, or protest that they will strike out, on lines of their own. Siena's output was more select: three comedies for the Accademici Intronati, *Gl'Ingannati* (anon., 1531), and *L'Amor Costante* (1536) and *L'Alessandro* (1543–4), both by Alessandro Piccolomini (1508–78), are excellent and particularly interesting to an English reader because of the likeness that the first bears to *Twelfth Night*, and the relation between the third and Chapman's *May Day*. Belo, a Roman, may have preceded Aretino in satirizing pedants, in *Il Pedante* (1529). Sanesi is full of admiration of the vivid realistic detail and the adroit handling of a most complicated intrigue drawn from Tatius by A. Caro in *Gli Straccioni* (1544). In Perugia, Sforza degl'Oddi also uses Tatius, and pursues more sentimental issues in *L'Erofilomachia* (1572) and *Prigioni d'amore* (1590); tears, he argues, are not incompatible with laughter when comedy chooses noble themes. Naples, with Giambattista Della Porta (1538–1613), seems to sum up the first phases and lead the way into the seventeenth century.

Giambattista Della Porta, in spite of all his other preoccupations (he was also a scientist), is said to have composed three tragedies, one tragicomedy, and twenty-nine comedies; fourteen plays survive. Wherever he finds anything good he takes it. If you want the best plots, Della Porta has them, and deserves them. He contrives capital situations, and handles disguises, substitutions, misconceptions, talk at cross-purposes, with an exhilarating deftness. His plays were packed tight with good things, and if he used stock figures he did it so well that he gave them a new lease of life. He creamed the sixteenth century, and many a seventeenth-century dramatist lived on him. The best way of testing how far and in what directions comedy had expanded since Ariosto's time is to read Della Porta. He has been admirably edited by Spampanato; *Albumazar*, Tomkis's Latin version of *L'Astrologo* (1606), done for the amusement of Cambridge in 1615, has now had the attentions of H. G. Dick. Where many are so good it is hard to choose as between *L'Olimpia*, *La Fantesca*, *La Cintia*, *La Turca*, *La Trappolaria*, *La Carbonaria*, *Il Moro*, *La Furiosa*, *I due fratelli simili*, but perhaps the most rewarding and illuminating essay in comparison would put *I due fratelli rivali* alongside *Much Ado About Nothing* and summon Bandello, whose tale it is, to judge between them.

Yet we would give all that Della Porta has in silver for the one gold piece of Bruno's *Il Candelaio*, which probably never saw the stage. Here is comedy which is truly critical of life. It is almost incredible that the familiar situations and types could be made to tell so differently. Bruno's comedy is still read by critics looking for Shakespeare's footprints, but it would be more to the purpose to match him boldly with Ben Jonson. The difference of tone between Shakespeare's treatment of the pedant and Bruno's is more striking than the butt they have in common: the likeness between Jonson and Bruno is inward. It is not suggested that anything passed between them, but there is the same fluency, trenchant accuracy of terms, and authentic ring. Manfurio's quotations have roots, his absurd etymologies are freshly drawn, the alchemical jargon is genuine; mockery goes home. Bruno can make more comedy out of two rogues recounting a gross story than many more practised playwrights with a handful of disguises. We have an uneasy feeling that the animus is personal, and for this reason obscurities must be given the benefit of the doubt; but the satire goes beyond personalities, and seems to express the author's restless brilliant intelligence. He is more interested in character than plot; an *argomento* takes the form of an analysis of the three chief persons—Manfurio, Bonifacio, and Bartolommeo. At a glance one might be in danger of dismissing *Il Candelaio* as another tangle of worn threads. Here are pedant, alchemist, and amorous old man; here are rogues dressed as officers, a serving-maid touting for the penurious courtesan, a wife dressed as her husband's mistress to catch him at his tricks; here are beatings and brawls; and yet, what is faded elsewhere, and much that is crude anywhere, has been transformed by vigorous realism and by the direction of a critical purpose. This is not a comedy of relaxation. It is for exercising the mind. If we think, Bruno tells us, we may either weep with Heracleitus or laugh with Democritus. *Il Candelaio* is primarily for those who are interested in genius and Bruno; meanwhile *commedie erudite* continued to come from the talent and industry of more ordinary men.

2. Commedia dell'arte. In so far as it was improvised it is impossible to recover an accurate impression of the *commedia dell'arte*. We lack a vital part of experience; we have not seen it. A plea which has already been hinted must now be urged with emphasis: 'Piece out' its 'imperfections with your thoughts'. Yet there is danger that our thoughts may be too kind. The only safeguard is an informed imagining, and there is much left for our instruction, given patience to recover and connect the fragments.

The separate treatment accorded here to the improvised comedy underlines the most important point about it: it was a distinct style; as soon as this is said it is essential to remark certain exceptions which bring the generalization nearer to the truth. The players who came to Elsinore had two styles—'for the law of writ and the liberty'—but were one company. So with Italy's drama; she has one drama, not two, but that one, in comedy at least, is twofold. Unless the difference and the relationship are recognized it is impossible to account for the nature, development, and effect of the *commedia dell'arte*. Several other terms are used to describe it: *a soggetto* or *all'improvviso, dei zanni, dei maschere, all'italiana.* They remind us of its distinguishing marks, but each is subject to an occasional exception. Thus, it was 'of the profession' (*dell'arte*) but it was also cultivated by academic amateurs; it was improvised, but it had its documents and discipline; it used masks, mainly but not invariably; it was Italian, but it also flourished abroad, and at the end of the seventeenth century was at least half French; between it and the *commedia erudita* there were many transactions. Puzzling as this may be to its critics and historians, it is in reality easily explained on practical considerations.

(i) *Origins.* There are three possible ways of investigating the origins of the *commedia dell'arte*: by seeking for it a tradition, or an inventor, or by studying the dramatic conditions at the time of its appearance. Neither the first nor the second inquiry has yielded a fully satisfactory answer, but they have not been unprofitable. It seems impossible to establish continuity between later Roman, and especially Atellan, mimes and the Renaissance buffoons; and it is hardly consistent with the character of what is being studied that it should have a single founder if it is, as its names indicate, the way that was devised by professional actors for making a living out of the art of the theatre. But there is something to be gained from both these researches into its heredity which may supplement the attempt to account for it by re-imagining the Renaissance conditions which encouraged the experiment.

Advocates of the more far-fetched connexions in time and space (Riccoboni, Quadrio, de Amicis, and Reich) make it clear that something like the *commedia dell'arte* has amused mankind before and elsewhere, but they do not prove that these manifestations were identical or connected with it. The slightness of the evidence from the Middle Ages weakens their case. Those who have sought to find it a 'father' have at least promoted the study of a body of drama which has not so far been mentioned, the record in literary form of the vigorous rustic or semi-rustic farce of districts round Naples, Asti, Siena, and Padua. It is time that we recognized the talent of Carracciolo, Braca, Alione, Calmo, Beolco, and the importance of small associations of enthusiasts such as the *Rozzi* of Siena and friendly groups playing in Venice.

From among these actor-dramatists two stand out—Calmo, because his work and reputation suggest some close connexion with what was soon to become the dominant form of popular comedy, and Beolco (Ruzzante) for the same reason, and still more for the quality of what survives of his work. 'Ruzzante' was the stage-name of Angelo Beolco (*fl.* 1520–42), who invented for himself the character-mask of a loquacious Paduan countryman and used it with immediate and lasting success to rejuvenate old Plautine material in *La Piovana* and *La Vaccaria*, and a neo-classical plot in *L'Anconitana*, and to support the slighter but more original compositions such as *La Commedia Senza Titolo* and two 'dialoghi'. In the Carnival season Ruzzante would take a holiday from managing the family estates and entertain his patron, Alvise Cornaro, and other friends. He collected a few companions, and devised parts for them. Thanks to the work of Lovarini, his Italian editor, and Mortier, his French translator, the Paduan dialect, in which much of the attraction lay, is less of an obstacle than it used to be. His plays have the appearance of farce, but they leave the impression of comedy, and for this reason their intrinsic excellence transcends the interest of their reputed connexion with the *commedia dell'arte*. From a distance, in synopsis or by a summary account, it is true that they seem to have everything in common with the professional comedy, and it is no wonder that Maurice Sand (following Riccoboni) was tempted to proclaim him as its 'father'. But the more Ruzzante's work is known in detail the more individual and inimitable it appears. It is arguable that by improvisation such born comedians as Martinelli, Cecchini, or Biancolleli gave performances of comparable excellence, and that this is why they were so much in general and royal demand. This can neither be denied nor proved; it is indeed very probable, but one difference remains. These men were content with their functions as actors. Their secret died with them, or was committed only partially and privately to the inheritors of their masks. Ruzzante's was also a literary gift, and we can judge for ourselves. Some of his plays were printed in his lifetime, Cornaro had access to manuscripts for a posthumous publication in 1551, Lovarini added one in 1894. No true critical purpose is served by drawing the work of Ruzzante and the professional companies too closely together. His example as an improviser was undoubtedly a contributory but not a determining factor.

When Beolco died his mantle fell upon Andrea Calmo (1509/10–*c.* 1561), but only with half a portion of Ruzzante's art. They had, it seems, been friendly rivals and Calmo had other literary ambitions. Some of their work was confused by contemporaries, but when it is sorted out it is plain that Calmo's is of a coarser grain. The likeness between Calmo's old Venetians and the mask of Pantalone has tempted many to identify them, but the proper name does not appear. Again Calmo's is mainly premeditated work, and there is no direct succession of *persona*, but nobody could deny that in its use of farcical situation, dialect, buffoonery, the caricatures of local types, and possibly, in the original instance, even of some improvisation, it is certainly as close as anything we could expect to find to the *commedia dell'arte*. He had collected stuffs and designs, and perhaps experimented with the method which others were to popularize and, in a sense, perfect, but we do not know that he intended or envisaged what was to follow so soon. When it is closely examined there is not one of these farce-writers whose work exhibits simultaneously or in true proportion all the distinguishing characteristics of the *commedia dell'arte*.

(ii) *Acting Companies*. The determining factor is the rise of companies of professionals who sought and found enough encouragement to make modern comedy their livelihood. Their method was devised as they went along; they felt out their way, using whatever talent and luck they had. Their talents were the very talents their predecessors the Atellan mimes and medieval jesters had had, they were recruited from their counterparts, the strolling tumblers and the charlatans' boys, as well as from adventurous enthusiasts of better education. Their chances were the demand for entertainment by all classes, in Italy and abroad; the comic vulnerability of certain common types or of droll individuals as they were detected by the first Arlecchino or Pulcinella; and finally the prevailing taste for a comedy with plots that could be easily and cheaply imitated. They might also reckon that their necessity was part of their luck; they had to be quick-witted, tough, and adaptable, or they perished. For a generation or two enough of them found the risk stimulating and throve on it. If we refuse to believe that there was a single founder we may acknowledge many benefactors. Each of those mentioned has some responsibility for it, no one, it seems, has it all. The *commedia dell'arte* was the major theatrical experiment of the age, combining the minor experiments in a collective effort. In its simplest form it is represented by the single actor playing many parts, as old Giovanni Gabrielli (*c.* 1588–*c.* 1635) continued to do, but in its most developed form by such a company as the one to which his son Francesco (?–1654) belonged, in which each player knew the others' ways so well that all could collaborate harmoniously.

No attempt will be made here to follow the intricacies of the make-up and itineraries of the companies. Two principles seem to have determined their constitution: the need for unity within, among themselves, to make smooth and intelligible improvisation possible, and the temptation from without when patrons bribed the best from several groups to make an 'all-star' cast to grace a special season. The intrigues and complications that resulted when actresses were making their reputations and were jealous of them may be imagined or amply illustrated from documents—letters, licences, ecclesiastical and civil protests—collected by Luigi Rasi in his biographical dictionary, *I Comici Italiani*. The earliest notice of a travelling professional company is for 1545. The chief companies of the sixteenth century were the Gelosi, with the Andreini (Francesco, 1548–1624; Isabella, 1562–1604) as their mainstay; the Desiosi, led by Diana da Ponte (*fl.* 1582–1605) and sometimes including Tristano Martinelli (*c.* 1557–1630); the Confidenti, with Vittoria Piissimi (*fl.* 1575–94) and 'Pedrolino' (Pellesini) (*c.* 1526–1612); the Uniti, under Drusiano Martinelli (?–1606/8) and his wife Angelica (*fl.* 1580–94). These gradually give place to the next generation, who carried on the tradition in the competing groups of the second Confidenti, directed by Flaminio Scala (*fl.* 1600–21); the troupe of Pier Maria Cecchini (1575–1645), the Accesi; and the Fedeli, giving scope to the many talents of the younger Andreini, 'Lelio' (*c.* 1578–1654) (all of which see also under their own names).

The patronage of Mantua continued, and later in the seventeenth century companies associated with Modena and Parma came to the fore and were in demand even beyond Italy. The earliest records of professional companies show that they were often in Paris.

Their frequent journeys thither gave place to the permanent establishment of an Italian company in 1661, which flourished until in 1697 the actors trespassed upon a royal scandal and were evicted for their impertinence. In 1716 Italian comedians came back and stayed until the end of the century. The mingling of languages, styles, and resources, and especially the connexions with the art of Molière, make this phase of the *commedia dell'arte* as much a part of the history of French as of Italian drama, and much critical research has been lavished upon it (see COMÉDIE-ITALIENNE, FRANCE, and MOLIÈRE).

(iii) *Economy of the Companies*. Takings and expenses seem to have been shared between the leading members, while a few younger actors were hired. In some cities *stanze* or public rooms could be rented for a few weeks at a time. Some patrons provided better stage accommodation now and then, including the reversion of the equipment of the *commedia erudita*. On such occasions the leaders looked for individual rewards in money, goods, and personal favours. The better companies are often found at the French Court. There are traces of their visits to Bavaria, Spain, and England, but Paris was their second home, especially towards the end of the seventeenth century.

The average company needed as a minimum two who could take old men's parts, two lovers and their ladies, two *zanni* for servants, a braggart captain, a serving-maid, and one or two extras for minor parts. Doubling was also possible, but the main masks were fixed.

(iv) *Masks*. The peculiarity of a 'mask' character is that it is transferable from one company and one generation to another while at the same time it is also subject to modification. Since it is still a matter of dispute who were the inventors of many of the chief masks, and the succession of their changes is partly conjectural, it is only possible here to remark the best-known impersonators without trying to record the individual and period modifications of dress or behaviour. They may be grouped according to their functions in the plots as parents, lovers, servants, and miscellaneous caricatures or 'oddities'.

The toughest of the parents was Pantalone de' Bisognosi, in dress and dialect a Venetian Magnifico given to reprimands, tirades, and long-winded advice; according to Cecchini it should be taken as a grave part, relaxing into absurdity only when treating of love and feasting with the servants. This was a counsel of perfection, and the comical possibilities of an amorous and avaricious old man were freely exploited. Variants were introduced as time went on, and the roles of fathers and counsellors were sometimes taken by Coviello, Pincastro, Pandolpho, Ubaldino, Prospero, Lattanzio, and others, but they had little staying power. Pasquati and Braga in the sixteenth century, Ricci, Romagnesi, and Riccoboni in the seventeenth, are known to have made the mask their own.

The favourite mask for the second parent was of a Bolognese lawyer, usually Dr. Graziano. Here, as elsewhere, an origin in a personal skit is suspected, but it was soon submerged in the professional type. He too was amorous and gullible, but grosser than Pantalone. There were two levels of caricature; when the better Graziani expounded, what they said made sense; but the cheaper imitations lapsed into *Spropositi* and tongue-twisters that were sheer nonsense. The local dialect gave way to the habit of 'saying everything the wrong way round'. Strictly, the doctor was distinct from the stage pedant, who belonged to the *commedia erudita*, but they had many characteristics in common and were confounded by foreigners. 'Luz' Burchiella, Lodovico de' Bianchi, and a certain 'Andreazzo' (? Zenari) used the mask with credit in the sixteenth century. Bongiovanni, Bruni, and Lolli were among their distinguished successors.

The lovers, usually the lost or erring children of Pantalone and Graziano, did not use masks, and their parts were hardly characters, still less caricatures. Some stylization was convenient, but their behaviour was determined by the situations of the love intrigues, and their attraction was left to their personal eloquence and grace. They were recommended to read good authors to form a style for the laments, addresses, dialogues, conceits, soliloquies for several occasions, and for the *pazzie* (ravings). It was said of Antonazzoni by a fellow actor that he was too lazy to study for the lover's part and so changed to the captain's. Many had literary ambitions, but for those who could not compose there was provision made in the *zibaldoni* or commonplace books.

It was among the professionals that actresses came into their own. The *commedia erudita* concealed, the *commedia dell'arte* displayed, their talents, and tragicomedies and pastorals gave them many chances. When the first and second ladies conducted their own affairs in public the part of the 'confidante' dwindled, but a waiting-woman, often Franceschina or Olivetta, still found enough to do pairing off with the *zanni* servant. This was sometimes a man's mask.

The captain was often used as a rival, but he had also an independent role. As a braggart and coward he went as near as he dared in satirizing the alien soldier, chiefly the Spaniard, but in Venice the Greek *stradiotto*. Francesco Andreini made this mask his own, and during the first three years of his widowhood (Isabella died in 1604 and he retired from the stage) he collected and published his famous *Bravure del Capitano Spavento del Vall'Inferno*. From this it is plain that Andreini preferred to play to the height of a literary fancy and not realistically. The *Bravure* were republished, translated, and worked into plays by later admirers such as Belando. Fornaris as a *capitano* was Andreini's contemporary, a certain 'Cardone' seems to have been his successor, and in the seventeenth century Silvio Fiorillo (?–*c.* 1632) played as Mattamoros, and Tiberio Fiorillo (1608–94) as Scaramuccia, a part which to some is more comparable to that of the *zanni*. Its fame was individual.

The servants who gave the comedy one of its names, *dei zanni*, took over the functions of the slaves of classical comedy, and discharged them with the physical skill of acrobats and the impudence of their immediate prototypes, the Bergomask *facchini*, odd-jobbers in the piazza, witty rogues and literally jacks-of-all-trades. Zanni is the Bergomask pronunciation of Gianni, diminutive of Giovanni. It became a common prefix, and individuals made themselves reputations within the group, as Panzanino, Zan Ganassa, Buratino, Francatrippe, Arlecchino, Pedrolino, Scapino, Fritellino, Beltrame, Brighella, Mezzetino, and Trappolino. They found it convenient to pair off wit against stupidity, with infinite possibility for surprise and reversal in the *burle* or practical jokes, and the smaller pieces of comic business known as *lazzi*, which were their stock-in-trade.

Greed and shrewdness were their staple characteristics; beyond this it is impossible to generalize. For a few we can recover from contemporary references or illustrations some idea of their individuality, but many are merely names now. Not all handed on their masks, but of those which persisted the luckiest were Arlecchino (Harlequin), and Pulcinella (Punch), who represents the droll wit of the countryside near Naples as it was exploited for the stage early in the seventeenth century by some genius, probably Silvio Fiorillo. Much has been written of and for these two masks, conjecturing their origins, recovering their characteristics, marvelling at their adaptability. They have lost all but a savour of local caricature, and survive as symbols of the humour of their acquired nationalities. They are perhaps the most tangible and also the subtlest part of our inheritance from the *commedia dell'arte.*

The most exhaustive study of Arlecchino's origins is Driesen's, of Pulcinella Dieterich's and Croce's. Tristano Martinelli, if he was not actually the first, was certainly the dominant Arlecchino of the sixteenth and early seventeenth centuries; to judge by his letters he could turn Their Majesties of France round his little finger. Giuseppe Domenico Biancolleli (Dominique) (*c.* 1637–88) and Evariste Gherardi (1663–1700) were among the last Italian Arlecchini flourishing in Paris.

Pulcinella developed into as distinct a person among the *zanni* as the captain among the lovers. He stole many of the jokes and devices that the doctors had used, but gave them a new twist, and specialized in animal noises. Uncertainty was his chief characteristic; no one ever knew where to have him, in what disguise he would turn up, or how he would wriggle out of outrageous situations. His sweetheart or wife was a Rosetta, a Pimpinella, a Colombina, his *zanni* pair usually Coviello.

Some plays needed a few tradesmen or peasants or foreigners, but these parts, though repeatable, can hardly be counted as masks. Often variety enough was provided by doubling and disguise. There were a number of Neapolitan skits and considerable play with dialects other than those monopolized by the main masks. (See also Nos. 132–139.)

(v) *Repertories of scenarii and miscellanies.* Since the licences and letters use masks as often as proper names it is comparatively easy to work out the membership of a company, but it is harder to determine their repertories exactly, because the surviving collections of *scenarii* more often represent the taste of private and non-professional admirers of the art of improvisation. We can only imagine in general terms what plays were given.

Flaminio Scala's *Teatro* (1611) is exceptional in many ways; it is printed, and it represents his taste, if not always his invention, and is closely associated with the Gelosi. It contains thirty-nine comedies, one tragedy, a tragicomedy, a mixed entertainment, a pastoral, and a few fairy-tale plays.

Other *scenarii* are in manuscripts in libraries in Rome, Florence, Naples, Venice, Perugia, Modena, Paris, and some even in Leningrad. In the larger collections comedy, or more properly farce, has the largest provision; much is drawn at second- or third-hand from classical and neo-classical plays, and, in the seventeenth century, the taste for Spanish drama enlarges the proportion of melodramatic and sentimental plots. Pastorals with a strong infusion of buffoonery did well.

The resources might be more neatly reckoned by breaking up the plays into stock situations, allowing for variety and for the ingenious shuffling and renovation by minor changes. This was notoriously part of the economy of improvisation. The *scenarii* are often referred to as 'skeleton-plays'; they would be better described as dried plays. How they were put to soak and swell is explained by Perucci in his *L'Arte Rappresentativa* (1699), an invaluable handbook much of which has been reprinted by Petraccone in his *La Commedia dell'arte, storia, tecnica, scenari* (1927). Perucci's manual is the best of its kind, but not unique. Several *zibaldoni* have turned up which assemble the necessary equipment of spare prologues, speeches, jokes, and *lazzi* provided by the ingenuity and industry of the more literary members of the companies, often for their general use. One of the amplest and most informative was the property of an amateur enthusiast, D. Placido Adriano. It is now in Perugia.

Other hints come in semi-critical treatises of such players as Cecchini, Barbieri, and Riccoboni. If we hesitate or flag in piecing the parts together, it is possible to find models in a number of plays, some by actors such as Fornaris, Cecchini, Fiorillo, Andreini, Barbieri; some by interested amateurs, among them Bricci, Verucci, and Locatelli. These may be used to control our conjectural reconstructions.

(vi) *Decadence; a revival. General estimate.* In the eighteenth century Goldoni's way of meeting the reproach of the decadence of Italian drama was to struggle to substitute premeditation for improvisation. He was for reforming the actors by the dramatist's control (see below, 3). Carlo Gozzi (1722–1806), in an animated opposition to Goldoni, took another way, and blew upon the ashes of the *commedia dell'arte* by using its masks and methods for his own purposes. The rough opportunist bargain was fair enough. Gozzi gave Sacchi's company their chance in 1761, when he provided them with the first of a series of plays—*fiabe*—in which in a bold, ingenious way he mingled fairy-tales with farce. He used the professionals' talents, and even allowed them some scope for improvisation, while he parodied his rivals, shot his satire, and, most important, rediscovered the attraction of this blend of fooling and fantasy. He followed up *L'Amore delle tre melarance* (1761) with *Il Corvo* in the same year; in 1762 came *Il Re Cervo*, *Turandot*, and *Donna Serpente*; *Zobeide* came in 1763, *Pitocchi fortunati*, *Nostro Turchino*, and *L'Augellino belverde* in 1764, and finally *Zeim, re dei Genii* in 1765.

A precedent for this mixed kind might be found in a few of the *scenarii* of Scala's *Teatro*, but it is not necessary to suppose that Gozzi looked back. He was bent on meeting an occasion, he wanted to worst Goldoni, and for a time he did so. Parody and satire served his present purpose, but they are perishable. The fairy-tales, and his way of touching on reality by forsaking realism, still stir the imagination if they do not satisfy it. Many have felt that in the *fiabe* is achieved a kind of imaginative release not only for the irascible author but for audiences otherwise sad and sober. Inadvertently perhaps Gozzi gave the *commedia dell'arte* its final flourish; with him it 'made a good end'. It was invented for gaiety—as Il Lasca had it 'per passatempo, burla, giuoco e festa, e fare il mondo star lieto e beato'—and its last triumph was in the true style. It is impossible at this distance to generalize fairly about the extent and quality of the improvisation, but we may mark the extremes. At its best it was, as Barbieri insisted, a serious art, a corporate discipline chosen by men and women of remarkable talents, but, as Riccoboni, another player, regretfully observes, by the eighteenth century it was a lost art, and consisted too often of a mere piecing together of stock material. The danger of the declension of a comedy into a series of practical jokes is obvious. The *commedia dell'arte* could originate farcical episodes, but in everything else it was dependent upon the support of literary forms. Unashamedly it borrowed, cut, twisted, stretched, and finally wore out all that the drama of the Renaissance had to offer; in return it gave a longer life and greater popularity to much that would otherwise have been merely literary drama. Its importance lay in the economy of its method, which made the best use of histrionic talent of several varieties. At its highest it was the actors' art *par excellence*; at its lowest, mere clowning. It survives now in reputation; in an attenuated form in puppet-shows; in mask names; and in the memory of the harlequinade. There are traces of it in the work of the pantomime company which plays in the Tivoli Gardens, Copenhagen, and in some Neapolitan troupes, notably that of Peppino de Filippo, which in 1964, in *Metamorphoses of a Wandering Minstrel*, gave London audiences some idea of what a *commedia dell'arte* performance might have been like. There have been efforts to revive it. Masks have been revived, *scenarii* prepared, actors with an extempore faculty have collaborated. It happened so with Maurice Sand (see Nos. 132–9) and his family. Experiments have more recently been made in Prague and at Queen Mary College, London. And in 1965 members of the Bristol Old Vic Theatre School and the University Drama Department gave an improvised performance on the translated scenario of Goldoni's *La Vedova scaltra*, as *The Wily Widow*. But all these efforts, though enjoyable, are not the *commedia dell'arte*; the tradition has gone.

Basilio Locatelli, in a preface to his collection of *scenarii*, remarks that 'the player's function is one thing, and the poet's another'. This states half the truth; but if drama is to be great and lasting it is necessary that the player and poet should meet on honourable terms. The plays of Ruzzante, and for some those of Gozzi, are evidence of one kind; the mirth of which we have only echoes is evidence of another kind, testifying to this hard truth.

K. M. LEA

3. Literary Drama from the Eighteenth Century to the Present Day. (*a*) *Eighteenth Century.* As has been implied in the article above, tragedy during the Renaissance and the seventeenth century was in Italy the 'failed art'. Little that is kinder can be said of it during the eighteenth and nineteenth centuries, although in Maffei, and more markedly in Alfieri, there are welcome signs of a recognition that tragedy, no less than comedy, must derive immediately from life, and that it calls for more than ample plot and lofty sentiments. It is to Verga that Italy is indebted for her first authentic tragedy, but it is not until Pirandello that she can claim works in this field worthy of the rest of her drama.

It is arguable that Italy's history till 1870—some would say till 1918—necessarily inhibited the growth of tragedy; certainly the artificiality of its language, with its subservience to rhetoric and imitation, served only to emphasize its remoteness from the needs of normal man. Where comedy, which so often drew upon a vernacular taken straight from an identifiable area, was incisive, and where the pastoral at its best could frankly avow man's weakness, tragedy was either melodrama on stilts, or propaganda for a conflict between such implausible opposites as 'love' and 'duty', 'tyranny' and 'freedom', 'self' and 'country'.

From among the earliest dramatists one

can select only a handful who contributed a positive element to Italian tragedy. Federigo della Valle (*c.* 1565–1628) is the author of two plays on biblical themes, *Judit* and *Ester*, and one on Mary, Queen of Scots, *La reina di Scotia*, all probably written before 1600 but published in the last years of his life. Their quality as theatre is negligible, their saving grace being their lyricism and sincerity. Similarly worthy of consideration is the *Aristodemo* (1657) of Carlo Dottori (1618–86). Pier Jacopo Martelli (1665–1727) is remembered chiefly for the rhyming couplet ('versi martelliani') which he devised in an attempt to create an equivalent for the dignified alexandrine, but which achieved its greatest success when used by writers of comedy. Martelli's tragedies have a certain bourgeois realism, and he has the virtue of being anti-Aristotelian. His comedies suggest that his gifts lay more in that direction. Gian Vincenzo Gavina (1664–1718) is an admirable theorist, acute in his criticism of contemporary failings, and perceptive of the true nature of the *Poetics*. He rightly sees that thought and language must be appropriate to the character; he advocates proper research into *milieu*; he distinguishes the spectacular from the theatrical. Nevertheless, his own tragedies are failures, since he is deficient in language and lacking in all sense of the stage. Scipione Maffei (1675–1755) is a greater figure than any of these. With his *Merope* (1713) he brought imagination and a certain poetic power to his task. His blank verse, not copied until Alfieri 'rediscovered' it, and his exquisite sense of dramatic equilibrium reveal the man of the theatre. He eliminated the chorus and the encroaching fringe of intrigue, cut down the cast, and moved with vigour, restoring classical measure and proportion.

The only writer of Jesuit drama of this period who calls for a note is Saverio Bettinelli (1718–1808) (see JESUIT DRAMA). Antonio Conti (1677–1749) is a gifted critic—the first one on the Continent to appraise Shakespeare—and in a limited sense a forerunner of both Alfieri and Manzoni. But his plays fail, even when he shows signs of comprehending the psychological demands of Shakespearian tragedy.

From the confluence of tragedy and the pastoral emerged the *melodramma*, where poetry and music are given equal weight. Apostolo Zeno (1668–1750), for all his mediocrity as a poet, is important for his reformation of the libretto, and his *Griselda* (1701) and *Ifigenia in Aulide* (1718) are not wholly derisory (see also ZENO). Pietro Trapassi (1698–1782), best known by his academic name of Metastasio, is the supreme exponent of the form. He enjoyed remarkable success and his work was set by all the most distinguished composers of the day. Purists found the ending of his *Didone abbandonata* (1724) too sensational, but modern critics tend to see a vital quality in Dido which is not found in Metastasio's other works. He is an economical artist, with a subtle control of words, especially in lyric passages, but a natural gift for characterization—he is no mean psychologist—is nullified by his conformism and his fashionable classicism. Typical are his walking embodiments of *virtus* and *pietas*—Titus in *La clemenza di Tito* (1734), Aeneas in *Didone abbandonata* (1742), Attilius in *Attilio Regolo* (1750). Apart from the *melodrammi* cited, Metastasio's most significant works are *Achille in Sciro* and *Temistocle* (both 1736) and, with reservations, *Olimpiade* (1733) (see also METASTASIO).

Comedy at the beginning of the eighteenth century was virtually hamstrung by the dying *commedia dell'arte*, but before Goldoni attempted to reform it, three lesser writers were to make a not inconsiderable donation to it. Despite his 'academic' posturing, Giambattista Fagiuoli (1660–1742) brings a certain naturalism into comedy. He excludes the masks, draws on contemporary life, and shrewdly appraises such institutions as *cicisbeismo*. Girolamo Gigli (1660–1722) is rather more important, and has probably been underrated hitherto. It is easy to talk of his debt to the French, but his *La sorellina di Don Pilone* (1712) is a work of clear-cut originality and verve. There is close observation of life and sound psychology. The earlier *Don Pilone* (1707) suffers from the inevitable comparison with *Tartuffe*. Tonelli sees Jacopo Angelo Nelli (1673–1767) as taking Gigli's work a stage further and bringing us to the threshold of Goldonian comedy. He certainly has an eye for a scene, but little psychological insight, his characters seeming to stand at one remove from life.

Carlo Goldoni (1707–93) reigned for so long as the towering genius of Italian drama that it was perhaps inevitable that his work should have been somewhat overrated. His limitations lie in his social inertia. He is too tolerant of social evils; he accepts the values of the decaying society to which he belongs: too many of his comedies deal with worthless people, without demonstrating their worthlessness; and he too often abandons plot for a theatrical effect. We can admire the forcefulness of his stagecraft—the opening of *Il ventaglio* (1763) is a perfect example—and the accuracy with which he gauges the tolerable length of each stretch of dialogue. He has, almost consistently, pace of a highly professional kind. His middle-class and working-class characters are his best; his aristocrats are intentional or unintentional caricatures. His language is undistinguished save when he is writing in dialect. Comic invention comes naturally to him, though he is equally adept at improving on a model, as in *Il bugiardo* (1750). Such is his gift for observation that when, as so often, he wrote 'automatically', he evolved characters of a complexity transcending his own rather limited vision of human behaviour. His satire against *cicisbeismo*, *Il cavaliere e la dame* (1749) misfires badly; the knight is a stick, the lady a moral coquette. So too are the iniquitous and sermonizing Pamela (based on Richardson's heroine) of *Pamela nubile* (1750) and its sequel *Pamela maritata* (1757), and Mirandolina in *La locandiera* (1751), Goldoni's masterpiece, a tormented creature to be compared with Lelio in *Il bugiardo*; she has wit, energy, imagination, tactical brilliance, and not a shred of genuine emotion!

Goldoni was a conscious reformer, anxious to purify Italian comedy, in much the same way as Addison and Steele had done in England. He aimed at restoring a fully scripted drama, one in which the slapstick element would be drastically reduced, but his keen sense of theatre saved him from too rigorous a suppression of *lazzi*. His desire 'to come ever closer to Nature' he only partially attained, for so many of his characters remain types. He provides effective, and frequently engaging, pictures of peasant and fisherfolk life, an attractive presentation of the virtues of the trading middle class, and a warm-hearted appraisal of that community 'in and on the square' which characterized eighteenth-century Italy, and Venice in particular.

Goldoni's struggles with rival dramatists, with recalcitrant actors who saw little point in scripts and rehearsals, and with grasping managements, were a great strain, and may well have conditioned him to a facility detrimental to the enduring quality of his work. Much of it will survive, notably the plays in Venetian dialect, *I rusteghi* (1760) and *Sior Tòdero Brontolon* (1762). Choral works—all of one piece—like *Il campiello* (1756) and the magnificently vital *Le baruffe chiozzotte* (1760) show his gifts to the best advantage. From the rest of his 120 comedies—he wrote over 200 plays in all—the following may be chosen as important: *La vedova scaltra* (1748); *Il teatro comico* (1750), a Pirandello-like piece in which he propounds his 'new' drama at the same time as he presents a *commedia dell'arte* piece; *Il vero amico* and *La bottega del caffè* (also 1750); *Le smanie per la villeggiatura* (1761); and *Le Bourru bienfaisant* (1771) (see also GOLDONI).

Pietro Chiari (1711–85), one of Goldoni's major rivals, is deservedly forgotten; the other, Carlo Gozzi (1720–1806), survives as a masterly inventor of *fiabe* (see above, 2. vi and GOZZI). Goldoni founded no school, and after him comedy had virtually to make a fresh start with the so-called Goldonians: Francesco Capacelli Albergati (1728–1804), a cautious satirist; Giovanni Gherardo de Rossi (1754–1827), an imitative writer with a measured sense of the comic, author of one play still worth the reading, *Il calzolaio inglese in Roma* (pub. 1707); Alberto Nota (1775–1847), remarkable for the hints of nineteenth-century insecurity and sensuality pervading his apparently gracious comedy; Giovanni Giraud (1776–1834), who used a formidable theatrical technique to mirror a worn-out and decrepit society; and Francesco Augusto Bon (1788–1858), the creator of the *simpatico* and highly comic Ludro—something of a Figaro of Venice—who dominates *Ludro e la sia gran giornata* (1832), *Il matrimonio di Ludro* (1836), and *La vecchiaia di Ludro* (1837).

Tragedy in the eighteenth century reached its highest expression with Vittorio Alfieri (1749–1803). Undeniably he is an author of great intensity of feeling, vigour, and power, but he seldom bothers to equip himself with a substantial plot, or to elaborate critically on his subject matter. It was enough for him to be preoccupied with tyranny and freedom, and to paint in thunderous blacks and whites. Now we tend to dismiss his 'tragedies of liberty' and to find adequate only those one or two which reveal a concern for the inwardness of man. His purism is fanatical; he is more exactingly classical than his classical sources. He almost always observed the unities; he used a mere handful of characters; he wasted no time on local colour; he cut out peripheral scenes, and sent his action scudding along; he eliminated as much movement as he could—only essential historical detail survived—while his pitiless blank verse was pruned to an all but rebarbative concision and hammered into a rapidity hitherto unknown in tragedy. But he is monotonous, and his Italian not remarkable. It is generally agreed that his best plays are *Saul* (1782–4) and *Mirra* (1784–6). Yet, concede as one will their thrust and emotional strength, it is impossible to feel that Alfieri has annihilated the limitations of his age and surveyed the peaks and depths of human experience. *Saul* is a lopsided drama, for there is no character who measures up to the hero. We cannot withold compassion from him at the end, but it is the compassion we reserve for the wilfully eccentric who, like Lear, build themselves illusions from a vanished past. Here again we have a 'failed tragedy'; but this time the failure is distinguished. It falls short because it is irrelevant to a newly felt wholeness of man. Alfieri strikes magnificent attitudes, but there is only triviality in the tableaux. Tragedy is impossible, for tragedy in the modern world (and men were modern in Alfieri's day) demands policy, implications, thought, beyond the day. At the time the paladins of resurgent nationalism lauded Alfieri's use of the theatre to wage war on tyrants. It was an absurd and touching gesture, but too late in the day. Neo-classical tragedy is as nonsensical as neo-Romantic tragedy. We can admire with detachment Alfieri's nobility, and his personal achievement in giving purpose to an undirected life—his autobiography is his real masterpiece—while remaining thankful that Verga and Pirandello are to come. It would, however, be ungenerous to suppress all mention of the high regard in which other critics hold not only *Saul* and *Mirra*, but *Agamennone* and *Oreste* (both 1776–8), or the excellencies they find in *Filippo* (1775–81) and *Ottavia* (1779–81). Alfieri also wrote a number of comedies, some of which reveal no mean skill in using the form. Emphatically, they call for reassessment (see also ALFIERI).

(*b*) *Nineteenth Century to Modern Times.* With a few exceptions, the plays of the early nineteenth century belong to the history of literature rather than to that of the theatre. Drama at this time is a lesser activity of writers whose best work was done in other fields, among them the poets Vincenzo Monti (1754–1828) and Ugo Foscolo (1778–1827), the novelist Alessandro Manzoni (1785–1873), and the prose-writer Silvio Pellico (1789–1854). Monti gained the Duke of Parma's prize for tragedy in 1786 with his *Aristodemo*—an Alfierian treatment of the Pausanias material used earlier by Carlo Dottori. He himself thought *Galeotto Manfredi* (1788) more representative of his originality, but critical opinion tends to view *Caio Gracco* (1800) as his best work. Monti, a fluent lyricist, shifted ably from attitude to attitude as fortunes varied under Napoleon, and his plays are valuable, within a narrow compass, as analyses of his times. He knew Shakespeare (through the French) and learnt something from him. Technically he is strongest in his creation of female characters and, in *Caio Gracco* especially, in his juxtaposition of scenes. Foscolo greatly admired Alfieri, and modelled his own tragedies on those of his famous predecessor. Alfieri is reported to have said that Foscolo would outstrip him in fame, but though a writer of great vigour, whose lyric concentration has given us the poetic masterpieces *Dei sepolcri* and *Le grazie*, Foscolo had little aptitude for the theatre. A rarer, more fugitive beauty informs Pellico's *Francesca da Rimini* (1814). Deriving in manner from Alfieri and in matter from Dante, it is a romantic treatment of the story, locked within a classical structure. It is more dramatic that the later, and more exquisitely lyrical, play by D'Annunzio, but remarkably uneven in development, moving from the painstaking to the violently theatrical. It is to Manzoni, the creator of the finest of Italian novels, *I promessi sposi*, that Italy looks for her master tragedies in the romantic manner. There is some breaking away from classical rules (though the chorus is reinstated), and an obvious indebtedness to Goethe, Schiller, and Shakespeare. Manzoni has little capacity for universalizing experience, despite a relative subtlety in communicating inward conflict in his noble characters. His perception of the 'true' nature of history, reaching forward to the modern school of social history, is most acute, but is only faintly realized in his tragedies. The crypto-romantic, as we learn from the *Conte di Carmagnola* (1820) and *Adelchi* (1822), is no advance dramatically on the neo-classical. In all his work, Manzoni aimed at expressing the poetry implicit in history; as a novelist he succeeded, as a playwright he failed.

Of the minor writers Ippolito Pindemonte (1753–1828) is memorable for the theoretical *discorso* he linked with his *Arminio* (1804), a romantically inflected tragedy with hints of Shakespeare, rather than for the play itself. Giambattista Niccolini (1782–1861), on the other hand, is significant for the popularity enjoyed by his robustly pamphleteering tragedies, for he saw drama as a vehicle for politics and patriotism in all their most unsubtle neo-Ghibelline vehemence. *Giovanni da Procida* (1817), *Lodovico Sforza* (1834), and *Filippo Strozzi* (1847) are undistinguishable onslaughts on despotism and exaltations of Italian nationalism. *Antonio Foscarini* (1823) crosses a love/death drama in the high romantic style with a conflict between the *ragion di stato* and love, while *Nabucco* (1815), overtly Alfierian in its portrait of the struggle between absolute power and the ideal of freedom, is an allegory on the life of Bonaparte. Niccolini's finest work for the stage—a dramatic poem rather than a play—is *Arnaldo da Brescia* (1843), a vigorous assault on the temporal power of the Pope and the corruption of the clergy. As a theorist he inveighed against the romantics, conceding Shakespeare's genius, but rightly seeing that his rhetoric was unsuited to Italian drama. The essential poverty and triviality of Niccolini may be said to exemplify the artistic bankruptcy of tragedy when it degenerates into propaganda, a lesson which is later to be driven home by D'Annunzio.

It is opera which triumphs in the nineteenth century. Even romanticism can be made tolerable within the conventions of opera, though in the majority of cases the libretti are greatly inferior to the music. Straight theatre, generally speaking, is virtually unimportant until the end of the century. There is the occasional good play, but too much is derivative from the French, and too many false starts are made. There were potential moments of departure for a native Italian naturalistic theatre in two plays which anticipate the incursion of Augier and Dumas *fils*: *Il cavaliere d'industria* (1845; performed 1854) by Vincenzo Martini (1803–62), whose *Una donna di quarant'anni* (1853) hints at bourgeois realism and is a substantial comedy of lasting effect, and *Il poeta e la ballerina* (1841) by Paolo Giacometti (1816–82). Both dramatists are concerned mordantly to satirize the prevailing society, and both were to attain popularity and an appreciable artistic seriousness with their examinations of social problems: Martini in *Il marito e l'amante* (1855)—the first approach to a properly formulated and deeply searching treatment of adultery since Machiavelli and Bruno—and in *Il misantropo in società* (1858); Giacometti in the enduring *La morte civile* (1861), a trenchant analysis of the case for divorce when one of the partners is condemned to prison for a long time.

Paolo Ferrari (1822–89) is the first playwright of any consequence to adapt French realism to the Italian stage, but ironically his reputation derives more from his historical reconstruction, *Goldoni e le sue sedici commedie nuove* (1851), than from his thesis dramas on current social questions such as *Il duello* (1868), *Cause ed effetti* (1871), and *Il suicidio* (1875). Skilful in the delineation of character, sane, expert in intrigue, and sentimental, Ferrari maintained comedy in being and suggested a way forward for drama. With Achille Torelli (1841–1922) he lays the foundation for the work of Giacosa. Torelli gained success early with *I mariti* (1867), a study of four married couples and the nature of love in marriage. He is shrewd psychologist, with a light touch and the power of handling his scenes so that they flow naturally. His later plays reveal his limitations, though they are not lacking in sound theatre, *La moglie* (1868) and *L'ultima convegno* (1898)—a sensitive study of an understanding husband—being typical of them. Akin to Martini, if a less significant writer, is Tommaso Gherardi del Testa (1814–81), whose craftsmanship is aptly illustrated by his series of works for the mask Stenterello and such plays as *La carità pelosa* (1879). Leopoldo Pulle (1835–1917), writing as Leo di Castelnuovo, is more emphatically moralistic. Elegance and liveliness, however, mark his most enduring work, *O bere o affogare* (1872).

As the unification of Italy is gradually achieved, a new drama emerges. Comedy frees itself from the influence of Goldoni and dependence on France, tragedy shakes off the influence of Alfieri. Of the new dramatists, Pietro Cossa (1830–81) has been unjustly neglected, and may soon be reassessed more highly. He created a new kind of tragedy by applying the realistic formula to the plots he evolved from Italian, and more specifically Roman, history. As the essentials of his art he postulated historical truthfulness, a direct observation of man in society, and immediately communicating verse, which admirably fulfils T. S. Eliot's aspiration that it shall obtrude no more than prose. His outstanding work, which could probably hold the stage today, is undoubtedly *Nerone* (1871)—it was translated into English by Frances E. Trollope. Here we are completely emancipated from the high-flown rhetoric of Alfieri, and immersed in a swiftly moving portrayal of Nero in action. Technically, the play is important for the way in which Cossa elaborates conflict in an almost cinematic way, by cutting from one area of experience to another. By no means negligible are his *Cola di Rienzo* (1874) and *Messalina* (1876).

Posterity has treated Giuseppe Giacosa (1847–1906) far more kindly. In many ways he epitomizes the decent bourgeoisie of newly unified Italy. His language, lucid, elegant even, unencumbered, and persuasive, indicates the man—good, sympathetic, alert, and mediocre. He moves from historical comedies in which fantastic narratives are tricked out with romantic medieval settings, such as *Una partita a scacchi* (1871) and *Il Trionfo d'amore* (1875), through 'proverbs'—typical is *Chi lascia la via vecchia per la nuova sa quel che lascia, non sa quel che trova* (1873) (which may be roughly translated as *Better the Devil you know* . . .)—to a *verista* psychological and social drama exemplified by *Tristi amori* (1888), *Come le foglie* (1900), and *Il più forte* (1904). Giacosa is an excellent artisan of the theatre, with an acute sense of what will be effective on the stage, and how far he may trespass beyond the prejudices of his audience. He is sentimental, though not unaware of sexual anguish. His defects, as much as his good qualities, made him, in collaboration with Illica, an apt librettist for Puccini (see also GIACOSA).

That Giacosa should be linked with Verga as one of Italy's finest exponents of *verismo* is a sad commentary on the drama of the time. Though his output was restricted to a few plays, and he himself hardly regarded the theatre as his natural sphere of activity, Giovanni Verga (1840–1922) towers above Giacosa. He knew the latter's world, but chose deliberately to deflate its value by searching for true drama in the lives of the obscure and humble. His Sicilian peasants, observed with compassion, have a dignity, a reserve of power, and an unsullied humanity which bind them to the heroes of all great tragedy. *Cavalleria rusticana* (1884) shows that tragedy has no need of a lofty style and a high-bred protagonist. It is its author's masterpiece, but almost matching it is *La lupa* (1896), an austere and penetrating depiction of uncontrollable lust in a woman and the doom which it provokes.

Unification, all but complete in 1870, has as its counterpart an enhanced regional culture. Verga, the Sicilian, wrote in Italian, providing a variety of the language which could give adequate expression to the unliterary world of experience of his characters, a task which was to be carried further by Pirandello. To some lesser, but still considerable, dramatists the richness and immediacy of dialect seemed more fitting, even if it restricted their area of communication. For Venice, Giacinto Gallina (1852–97) provided comedies and dramas in her own tongue, at first in the manner of Goldoni, later in a personal, romantic, and optimistic style, and finally in the key of realistic pessimism. Typical of his development are the early *Barufe in famegia* (1872), the bitter yet sympathetic *Così va il mondo, bimba mia* (1880), and the acrid *Serenissima* (1891). Gallina moves towards an awareness of and hatred for a materialistic society. He expresses the struggle in terms of the conflict between succeeding generations, and indicates that his sympathies lie with the past. His major work is now considered to be *La famegia del santolo* (1892), a grey, personal tragedy, tender in its melancholy, reminiscent of Giacosa's *Tristi amori* (1888) as an exploration of cuckoldry accepted in strength. Critics join these two plays with Praga's *La moglie ideale* (1890), discovering in them an importance for Italy comparable to Becque's *La Parisienne* in France.

From Piedmont one comedy is of high calibre, *Le miserie d'monsú Travet* (1863), by Vittorio Bersezio (1828–1900), with its optimism, its generous realism, and its firm assertion of unpretentious courage. In Milanese there is the indestructible *El nost Milan* (1893) by Carlo Bertolazzi (1870–1916), a presentation of lower- and upper-class life in the city, comparable to *L'acqua cheta* (1908), written for the Florentine stage by Augusto Novelli (1868–1927), which provides an early example of a triumphant socialist hero in a domestic drama. Finally there is *Assunta Spina* (1909), by Salvatore di Giacomo (1860–1934), which is the major Neapolitan play before De Filippo.

The drama in Italian of unified Italy has no clear voice of its own; it is seldom we hear anything but the slightly modified tones of foreign authors—French, Scandinavian, Russian. The fragmentation and corruption which were the inevitable concomitants of success—so powerfully transmuted into art by Pirandello, whose childhood and adolescence were passed in the crumbling world of which the natural outcome was Fascism—are suppressed, even by the most responsible of writers. As late as 1901, Girolamo Rovetta (1851–1910) could gain success with the romantic historical play *Romanticismo*, in which he dealt with the heroism and suffering of Mazzini's followers in the struggle for independence. Once considered to have come closest to the ideal of verist art—the impersonal exposition of reality—he is now adjudged to have cluttered up with unnecessary detail an admirable capacity for clear narrative. Typical of his work are *La trilogia di Dorina* (1889), in which a marquis who would only accept Dorina as his mistress when she was pure is driven by jealousy to propose marriage to her once her virtue is gone, and *I disonesti* (1892), which makes the point that the shattering of belief in your wife's chastity may turn you into a thief. *Il poeta* (1897) is an interesting, if Yellow-Book-ish, study of evil.

The work of Luigi Capuana (1839–1915) in some ways continues, yet dilutes, what Verga had achieved. He has none of Verga's power to comprehend the significance of primitive Sicilian violence, but, with the collaboration of the great dialect actors Grasso and Musco, the Sicilian theatre was kept alive by Capuana and by Nino Martoglio (1870–1921), whose hilarious masterpiece is unquestionably *L'aria del continente* (1915), a play of some insight on that oldest of themes, the conversion of an islander to sophisticated 'mainland' ways, and his attempts at regenerating his neighbours back home. Martoglio collaborated in dialect plays with Pirandello, and in the latter's work one can see the *aria del continente* motif taken up and refashioned again and again. Both Capuana and Martoglio are verists, concerned less to examine the implications of broad social movements and philosophies than to iterate a belief in the profound psychological abyss separating the north from the south in general, and from the islands in particular. Not the least of Pirandello's merits is that, though a Sicilian by birth, he stands aloof from regionalism. His problems are universal, and his so-called Sicilian plays are indistinguishable from his Roman, seaboard, provincial, or unlocalized dramas.

Marco Praga (1862–1929) is less important as a dramatist than for his generally creative attitude towards the theatre. Apart from *La moglie ideale* mentioned above, he is the author of the bitingly ironical *Le vergini* (1889), which may have influenced Pirandello's *Questa sera si recita a soggetto* (1929), and of a number of psychological dramas of no great importance.

Verist drama has one virtue, its recognition of the linked power of sex and money. Its weakness lies in its acceptance without question of the established social conventions of its time. Verga alone possesses the virtue and transcends the weakness. Other dramatists of his day appear unable to learn from him. *Le Rozeno* (1891) of Camillo Antona-Traversi (1857–1934), for instance, is an admirable pamphlet on the licensed bawdry and prostitution of marriage, cheaply finished off as a piece of 'sardoodledom'; Carlo Bertolazzi's *Lulù* (1903), a sensitive delineation of compulsive and neurotic sexuality in woman, is rendered frivolous by the mob-oratory of the murder with which it ends. Verga understood the sublime inevitability of sexual murder, but his contemporary verists used it either as a substitute for policy, or as an aphrodisiac, a situation which alone makes possible the plays of Gabriele D'Annunzio (1863–1938). D'Annunzio is a lyric poet of unchallenged if derivative strength; as a novelist he is a master of erotic sterility; but as a dramatist he is merely tiresome. Even his most effective piece, *La figlia di Jorio* (1904), a pastoral tragedy, is nothing more than a rationalization of the author's adolescent sexual cosmos. In all his plays—*La città morta*, *La Gioconda* (both 1898), *Francesca da Rimini* (1902)—he portrays women as bodies to be exploited by the Nietzschean 'superman'. He lacks all the fundamental virtues of a good dramatist, in construction, in dialogue, in pace. He typifies Italy's all but total artistic, moral, and political collapse after 1870. But he has the power to evoke a voluptuous mood that in a conventional world may pass for sinful. On this perhaps, more than on any other feature of his work, rests his once-inflated reputation (see also D'ANNUNZIO).

It is now possible to distinguish three main streams in twentieth-century Italian drama—a trickle from D'Annunzio; the broad sweep of the emasculated so-called realistic theatre; and the authentic flow which has Pirandello as its major exponent. Sem Benelli (1875–1949) staggers after D'Annunzio, especially in his very successful *La cena delle beffe* (1909) (see BENELLI). This is a pretentious affair which offers for serious consideration the kind of material Max Beerbohm satirized in *Savonarola Brown*. Yet, as Nicoll has suggested, there are hints of Pirandello's world in *Tignola*, *La maschera di Bruto* (both 1908) and *L'amore di tre re* (1910). In Giovacchino Forzano (1883–) the historical play finds a superb craftsman but a trivial artist, his best work going into the tetralogy on the French Revolution, the concluding play of which he wrote in collaboration with Mussolini: *Campo di Maggio* (1931). This was translated into English by John Drinkwater.

Before reaching back to the beginning of the century, to deal with the theatre of ideas, it is necessary to look at Futurism, a movement which is of increasing relevance in appraising what has happened in the theatre during the first half of the twentieth century, not only in Italy, but in Europe as a whole. If it is true that the theatre of the absurd can claim its descent from Pirandello, it is also true that its attitude towards language reflects the denunciations of the Futurist manifesto, published in Paris (in *Figaro*) in 1909. Futurism is a paradox, a right-wing revolt against right-wing decadence. Fundamentally, the movement is childishly romantic. Its chief fallacy derives from its nineteenth-century glorification of the machine while believing that it speaks for the twentieth century. Its value lies in its having accidentally brought about an examination of several neglected aspects of theatre—the role of the fragment—the function of the arena, especially the circus ring—the use of white light (reaching forward to Brecht)—the interpenetration of spheres of consciousness and desire, actuality and vision; the masks provided by parts of the body other than the face; the tonality of colour; the codes of syntax, by no means thoroughly explored by the verists; and the deployment of disintegrated humanity in search of a unified whole, however transitory and illusory.

In some things we can see the debt to D'Annunzio, in others the anticipation of Pirandello. Preposterous and apocalyptic, Futurism is a blast blown through the theatre just when it was needed, though having apparently no immediate effect. The creator of the movement was Filippo Tommaso Marinetti (1876–1944), who, after a brush with the authorities, left Milan for Paris, and wrote most of his plays in French. In 1909 his *Le roi Bombance* (*Re Baldoria*) had a lively first night at Lugné-Poë's Théâtre de l'Œuvre. There are obvious affinities between it and Jarry's *Ubu Roi*. More pertinent, if less proselytizing, are his short plays, some of which are not without a beauty and supple vigour which call for a serious appraisal of his work, and reinforce Pirandello's doctrine of evolutionary chaos.

If D'Annunzio made Marinetti inevitable, it may be that the influence of Ibsen on Giacosa, Praga, and Rovetta, casual though it was, may have led the more perceptive Butti, Bracco, and Pirandello to deal more honestly with him. But there is no subservience; certainly not in the plays of Enrico Annibale Butti (1868–1912), who is a constructive pessimist in the Ibsenite sense. While recognizing the integrity of the progressives, and sharing their views, he nevertheless shows the triumph of the conservationists. In such plays as *Il vortice* (1892—the year in which the first Italian version of *Ghosts* was produced), *L'utopia* (1894), a consideration of mercy-killing, *La fine d'un ideale* (1898), in which he contraposes free love and the security of marriage, *Lucifero*, on agnosticism, and *La corsa al piacere* an indictment of an aimless life, (both 1900), and in *La tempesta* (1901), a study of social reform through revolution, Butti reaches the conclusion that man does better to acquiesce in society's rules rather than struggle unavailingly against them. But at least he has arrived at his answer through fearless debate, and not cravenly through inertia and timidity.

Roberto Bracco (1862–1943) has yet to be assessed critically, partly because of his neglect under Fascism, which he abhorred, and partly because his output is so bewilderingly varied. He is, in Luciani's phrase, 'a brilliant eclectic', a natural genius of the theatre, who united technical expertise with forcefulness and integrity of vision. He had wit as well as an acutely developed social conscience—a rare combination anywhere, but especially in the theatre. His most accomplished play, and the most significant historically, is *Il piccolo santo* (1909), remarkable for having anticipated the 'theatre of silence' of Bernard and Vildrac. Bracco is a feminist and a compassionate observer of the underdog. His ease in presenting the complexity of the subconscious has led to his being underrated as an artist, just as his matter-of-fact freedom from labels has served to disguise the full impact of his technical solutions. It is worth emphasizing that without Bracco, the *teatro grottesco*—the Italian aspect of the European phenomenon which unites Synge's *The Playboy of the Western World*, Barrie's *Dear Brutus* and *Mary Rose*, Benavente's *Los intereses creados*, and Schnitzler's *Der grüne Kakadu*—could hardly have struck home so forcibly (see also BRACCO).

The cult of the anti-hero has taken many forms. Inevitably D'Annunzio's 'superman' evoked a sharp redefinition of 'serious' theatre, and resulted in the *teatro grottesco* and the plays of the *intimisti* and *crepuscolari* (the 'twilight' school). There is very little difference between them, but the atmosphere of the 'twilight' plays is more subdued and almost completely free of the paradox which kicks so powerfully in the *teatro grottesco*. Benelli's *Tignola* can be assigned to the *crepuscolari*, so too can the scathing anti-myths of the greatly talented Ercole Luigi Morselli (1882–1921), who seems to anticipate later psycho-analytical restatements of classical fables with his *Orione* (1910) and *Glauco* (1919). The principal 'twilit' dramatist is Fausto Maria Martini (1886–1931), though his later works are, more strictly, intimist. In *Il giglio nero* (1913) he deals with the disturbing effect of city attitudes on a quiet, self-deceiving, provincial couple, and in *Il fiore sotto gli occhi* (1921) he preaches the value of monotony and drabness. With *L'altra Nanetta* (1923) Martini came under the influence of Pirandello, and in *La facciata* (1924) and *La sera del 30* (1926) he becomes an intimist. If these last works place him with Vildrac and Bernard, *Ridi, pagliaccio* (1919), a commonplace tale of frustration leading to suicide which enjoyed enormous public success, places him dangerously near Sardou. But a fine craftsman always, Martini did much to restore conscience to Italian drama. Of the *intimisti*, Cesare Vico Lodovici (1885–1968), the highly regarded translator of Shakespeare, was outstanding. Deriving mainly from Chekhov, he exploited to the full the range of communication with which silence is instinct. Especially forceful is *La donna di nessuno* (1919). *L'incrinatura, o Isa, dove vai?* (1937) is a sensitive portrayal of the tragedy of non-communication resulting from unfounded jealousy. Of interest are *L'idiota* (1915), based on Dostoievsky, and—though he was clearly uneasy in writing historical dramas—*Vespro siciliano* (1940) and *Caterina da Siena* (1949).

That the *teatro grottesco* should survive as the regenerative force in the Italian theatre is due less to the pre-eminence of its playwrights—though a strong case could be made out for Rosso di San Secondo (see below) as a writer of unusual power and beauty—than to the sheer theatricality of its main theses. Again, a movement which finds its artistic fulfilment in Pirandello is to a certain extent protected against oblivion. The movement takes its name from the description of *La maschera e il volto* given to it by its author, Luigi Chiarelli (1884–1947)—*grottesco in tre atti*. Written by 1913, it was not staged until 1916, in the middle of the First World War. In starkly colloquial dialogue—which approaches very near to the disillusion of T. S. Eliot and our own war poets—it exposes the tragedy of social man, to whom only the mask is relevant. Hypocrisy is the supreme virtue, because it is the universal solvent. Yet the face will occasionally rebel against its masks, and so much the worse for it. Chiarelli never repeated the success of *La maschera e il volto*, but *La scala di seta* (1917), *Chimere* (1919), *Fuochi d'artificio* (1923), and *Il cerchio magico* (1937) repay study.

If Chiarelli is astringent, Luigi Antonelli (1882–1942) is acrid. The most immediate of his *avventure fantastiche* is *L'uomo che incontrò se stesso* (1918), which, less whimsically and with more force than *Dear Brutus*, propounds that man is a fool to hope to correct the errors of his youth by the wisdom (or experience) of maturity, a theme which Pirandello was to explore with such subtlety in his *Sei personaggi in cerca d'autore*. Of Antonelli's other plays *L'isola delle scimmie* (1922) ironically flays the squalor of human civilization, *La bottega dei sogni* (1927) analyses man's use of dreams, and *Il maestro* (1933) is a neatly anti-Pirandellian answer built upon Pirandellian foundations. The world of these plays is sombre, yet visionary, and always scrupulous.

It is tempting to see in Enrico Cavacchioli (1885–1954) a technical innovator and nothing more. Certainly he is fertile in his use of abstractions, symbolism, and the allegorized puppet-show. Nevertheless there is a definite weightiness in his *L'uccello del paradiso* (1919); echoes, too, of Andreyev, whose influence on Italian dramatists of this generation must be allowed for. Massimo Bontempelli (1878–1960) is a dramatist whose complexity has not as yet been fully assayed. He must be ranked with Rosso di San Secondo for his musicality and for his reformulation of man's creative need for enchantment, and with Pirandello for his vigorous reassertion of the looking-glass world. *Nostra Dea* (1925) is based on the satirical concept that woman derives her personality from the clothes she wears; scantily clad, she means nothing; through her various changes of costume she acquires meaning. In *Minnie la candida* (1929), the heroine is driven to suicide by her belief that human beings are literally puppets, and that she, too may be one, a theme used earlier by Pier Maria Rosso di San Secondo (1887–1956) in his finest play, *Marionette, che passione!* (1917), where the characters are 'puppets' known only by their clothing; each typifies a different stage along the path of despair; from their interaction we comprehend the suppressed hell of their daily life. The 1963 edition of Rosso's plays underlines the growing appreciation of his importance, not only as the best of the 'grotesque' dramatists, but as the architect of a new mythology, realistic, unflinching, and of poetic lucidity. Though a Sicilian, he is cosmopolitan; there is no restrictive provincialism about his plays. It is manifest that he participated in the twentieth century's overwhelming preoccupation with the legend of Persephone; much of his work (which includes *La bella addormentata* (1919); *Una cosa di carne* (1924) and *La scala* (1926), his greatest success commercially) can be seen as a series of new and subtle versions of the myth, issuing finally in *Il ratto di Proserpina* (written in 1933, but not produced until 1954). Rosso helped to bring Italian tragedy to maturity, substituting poetry for rhetoric, the dance of life for the dance of death, and compassion for the obtuseness of self-pity.

With Luigi Pirandello (1867–1936), who was awarded the Nobel Prize for Literature in 1934, Italian drama achieved a status it had never had before, and for the first time became a force to be reckoned with in European drama. The unaffected self-revelation in his plays, contrasting with the retiredness of his private life, had a shattering effect on a community that still took refuge in a decent reticence (or hypocrisy, as he roundly called it). It was in 1921, with *Sei personaggi in cerca d'autore*, that he won his decisive battle, but by then he had already made his major assertions. Alone among Italian playwrights he had grasped the full tragedy of an age of decay and fragmentation, evaluated the general significance of relativity, and applied, as early as his first poems and stories in the 1880s and 1890s, those techniques which we now associate with modern psychology. He understands and debates with us—for all Pirandello's work is argument—man's despair at being unable to communicate, even with himself; he obliges his audience to participate in the experience of the multiple identity, and consequent non-entity, of every one of us; and he involves it in the process of sentient man—self-discovery, self-evasion, self-construction, regeneration, and even destruction. If the Theatre Trilogy (*Sei personaggi in cerca d'autore*, 1921, *Ciascuno a suo modo*, 1924, and *Questa sera si recita a soggetto*, 1929) is his most striking contribution both to practice and theory in the theatre, his tragic masterpiece is undoubtedly *Enrico IV* (1922), though *Non si sa come* (1934), based on his own short story, *Il gorgo* (1913), challenges it very closely. In *Liolà* (1916), a realistic Sicilian peasant idyll, he produced a biting, hauntingly lyric, comedy. Its urban counterpart is *L'uomo, la bestia e la virtù*, the first genuine comedy of manners in Italian dramatic literature since Machiavelli's *Mandragola* and Bruno's *Candelaio*. *Vestire gli ignudi* (1922) deals poignantly with Pirandello's peculiar obsession, human 'aloneness', for the heroine, striving to find reality for herself, is forced to the conclusion that death is her natural dress. Though we find in his plays disquisitions on the nature of art, on the quality of belief, on man's inhumanity to man, Pirandello is never a cold-hearted manipulator of puppets. He writes about men and women caught in the universal dilemma of living. It is significant that, after Shakespeare, Pirandello found Ibsen most congenial. Among his most important plays, apart from those already mentioned, are *Così è (se vi pare)* (1917), where tragedy dances to the tune of farce, *Il giuoco delle parti* (1918), a practical exercise in the game of life, *L'uomo dal fiore in bocca* (1923), which debates the nature of time for a man suffering from incurable cancer, and *Lazzaro* (1929), a reworking of the New Testament miracle in terms of the conflict between religion and science. Nor should his collaboration with Martoglio in plays in Sicilian dialect be forgotten (see also PIRANDELLO).

Pirandello's influence can be seen in much that has been written since the 1920s, in Giraudoux, Wilder, Miller, Tennessee Williams, Priestley, Beckett, and the dramatists of the Absurd. In Italy he has been a stimulus to fruitful opposition. Ugo Betti (1892–1953), the outstanding Italian since Pirandello, and influenced by him initially, rapidly came to speak with his own voice. His plays are fables, parables of man's coming to God, unwillingly and inevitably; the prodigal son blends in the kaleidoscope with the conversion of Saul to Paul, and, with a twist in the image of the two Maries, Mary Magdalene relives the affirmation of the Virgin Mother. For Betti, the world is on trial. He is the Kafka of the drama. His characters butt against intangible frontiers, the boundaries of private nightmares, the visions of a lost Earthly Paradise, and, running away, they arrive at what they are flying from. His most important play is possibly *Corruzione al Palazzo di Giustizia* (1949), an investigation and judgement of those who judge, where the guilty man becomes the new Chief Justice. Other plays by Betti which have enhanced his stature are *Frana allo scalo Nord* (1936), *Il paese delle vacanze* (1942), *Ispezione* (1947), *Delitto all'isola delle capre* (1948), *Lotta fino all'alba* (1949), *La regina e gli insorti* (1951), *La fuggitiva* and *L'aiuola bruciata* (both 1953), a powerful and lyric example of Christian existentialism. Betti, in spite of his realistic portraits of degradation, is an optimist; for him man's journey is the discovery of Christ (see also BETTI).

After Betti the Italian scene is dominated by two playwrights—Eduardo de Filippo (1900–) and Diego Fabbri (1911–). De Filippo is perhaps the more challenging, for Fabbri has neither the thrust of Betti, to whom he is nearest in subject-matter, nor that freedom from bourgeois preoccupations which made Pirandello so original. De Filippo is an actor-manager-playwright, who, writing in the Neapolitan dialect, has succeeded in transcending the barriers created by that choice. *Questi fantasmi* (1946), *La grande magia* (1949), and *Il figlio di Pulcinella* (1959) stress his vision of the conflict between reality and illusion, while *Napoli milionaria* (1945) and *Filomena Marturano* (1946) are compassionate and realistic social studies.

If De Filippo's theatre has much in common with Pirandello's, to Fabbri (who writes in Italian) the problems of personality, separation, and regeneration present themselves as critically religious dilemmas. Though without the lucidity of Betti, and generally more sentimental in his approach, Fabbri is nonetheless well-endowed with humour. A symbolist, and a passionate exponent of the tragedy of Christianity, much of his work turns on the concept of evil, or what may be construed as evil. By some he has been set down as a Christian existentialist, but it is doubtful whether such a label fits his romantic talent. Typical of his inquiry into spiritual man are *Inquisizione* (1950), *Il seduttore* (1951), and *Processo a Gesù* (1955). *La bugiarda* (1956) (seen in London in the 1965 World Theatre season) is a comedy, with an unobtrusive complexity of deeper meaning. Some discerning critics find Fabbri's best work yet for the theatre in his dramatizations of Dostoievsky, published in the volume *I demoni* (1961).

It is useless to speculate on the future of the drama in Italy, whose cultural *risorgimento* has acquired a new cogency in recent years. But although so much creative endeavour is being directed into the art of the cinema, there are many indications that the theatre intends to preserve and capitalize the maturity bequeathed to it by Pirandello. The only question is—from which direction will it come, among the many now writing who have perforce been excluded for lack of space? FREDERICK MAY

IVANOV, VSEVOLOD VYACHESLAVOVICH (1895–1963), Soviet dramatist, who, after running away from home at the age of 15, had a hard and adventurous youth. He began writing in

1915, served first in the White Army and then in the Red, and in 1920, with the help of Maxim Gorky, settled in Leningrad. His first play, *Armoured Train 14–69*, is an important landmark, since it was the first Soviet play to be successfully produced by the Moscow Art Theatre (see No. 99). This was in 1927, by which time this pre-Revolutionary theatre had made the necessary adjustments to the new régime and was able to go ahead with confidence. The play, which deals with the capture of a trainload of ammunition during the Civil War, is a melodramatic but effective piece of propaganda, which perhaps suffered a little from the determined naturalism of the Moscow Art Theatre production. It has been revived since, and retains its place in the repertory. Ivanov produced nothing comparable to it, though a later play about events in the Far East, *The Doves See the Cruisers Departing*, had some success, as did *Lomonosov* (1953), also produced at the Moscow Art Theatre. It is based on the life of the 'father' of Russian science.

J

JACK-IN-THE-GREEN, see FOLK FESTIVALS, MORRIS DANCE, and ROBIN HOOD.

JACKSON, SIR BARRY VINCENT (1879–1961), founder of the Birmingham Repertory Theatre and of the Malvern Festival, knighted in 1925 for services to the theatre. Though originally trained as an architect, Sir Barry's dramatic mission soon showed itself, and his father's house became the rallying-place for the Pilgrim Players, a company of ardent amateurs who assumed professional status when Sir Barry built the Repertory Theatre in 1913. For twenty-two years he maintained this creative playhouse in the face of local indifference to the fact that a miracle of high patronage was being performed by one who was willing to back his faith in the intelligent theatre with his own money. The varied fare he provided bears witness to his liberal view of the function of the theatre. Classics and new plays, tragedy and farce, pantomime and ballet, opera, and even marionettes were presented on the Repertory Theatre stage. Sir Barry was always on the alert for worthy material and himself adapted several foreign pieces, including *The Marriage of Figaro* and *He Who Gets Slapped*. In addition to these, he translated Ghéon's *The Marvellous History of St. Bernard* for presentation in Birmingham and London, where it was hailed as 'one of the loveliest productions in the modern theatre'. He wrote *The Christmas Party*, a real children's pantomime, adapted Wyss's *The Swiss Family Robinson*, and contributed revue sketches to Birmingham's Christmas entertainment. Sir Barry always regarded the theatre as a workshop for artistic experiment rather than as a museum for the preservation of tradition. His productions of Shakespeare in modern dress (see No. 81) were a sincere and on the whole successful attempt to break free from convention. For Shaw (on Shaw's own admission) Sir Barry did what no commercial manager could have done by the production of *Back to Methuselah* in Birmingham and in London. By founding the Malvern Festival in 1929 he initiated the English theatre into the festival habit, and provided an entertaining month of drama in enchanting surroundings (see MALVERN and No. 100). From 1945 to 1948 Sir Barry was Director of the Memorial Theatre at Stratford-upon-Avon, and of the Shakespeare Festival plays given there. (See also BIRMINGHAM REPERTORY THEATRE.)

T. C. KEMP†

JADOT, JACQUEMIN (*fl.* 1610–60). French actor, who played serious parts under the name of La France, and farce as Michau. He was originally with the company headed by Lenoir which went to Paris in 1610, and was transferred with Lenoir, Jodelet, and others to the Hôtel de Bourgogne in 1643, where he replaced Gaultier-Garguille as a clown. Little is known about him, but he was still acting in 1658.

JAMES, DAVID (1839–93), English actor, brother of the harlequin Humphrey Belasco, and so uncle of the famous American manager, who was called after him. James made his first appearance as a super at the Princess's Theatre, London, in 1857, under Charles Kean, and then went into burlesque at the Strand and elsewhere, being much admired as Mercury in *Ixion* (1863) at the Royalty. In 1870 he built and opened the Vaudeville Theatre, in partnership with Montague and Thomas Thorne. Their intention was to make it a home of burlesque, but their first productions having proved unsuccessful they put on *Two Roses*, in which young Henry Irving, as Digby Grant, attracted the attention of Colonel Bateman and was engaged for the Lyceum, thus inaugurating his brilliant career as London's outstanding actor-manager. James was also responsible for the production of the phenomenally successful *Our Boys* (1875), which made a fortune for him and his associates. After leaving the Vaudeville, which in 1891 was taken over by the Gattis, James was seen at a number of theatres, and eventually returned to burlesque—in *Little Jack Sheppard* at the Gaiety. One of his best parts in later years was Old Eccles, in *Caste*, and he was also good as Stout, in *Money*. His son David was also on the stage.

JAMES, HENRY (1843–1916), who was born in New York, spent most of his life in England, and in 1915 became a British subject. Though he is chiefly remembered as a novelist, he had an ardent love for the theatre, as can be seen from his correspondence, and from the essays contributed to various journals, reprinted in 1949 in one volume as *The Scenic Art*. He wrote a number of plays, but few of them were produced during his lifetime, and those unsuccessfully. After the hostile reception given to *Guy Domville* (1895), which George Alexander put on in London at the St. James's, he had no more plays produced. The success he longed for came later with the production of dramatizations of his works made by other hands—notably *Berkeley Square* (1928), suggested by his unfinished novel *The Sense of the Past*; *The Heiress* (1947), based on *Washington Square*; *The Innocents* (1950), based on *The Turn of the Screw*, and *The Wings of the Dove* (1964). James's own plays were published in a one-volume edition in 1948 with an excellent introduction and notes by Leon Edel.

JAMES, LOUIS (1842–1910), American actor, who made his début in 1863, and was for some years with Mrs. John Drew at the Arch Street Theatre, Philadelphia. In 1871 he joined Daly at the Fifth Avenue Theatre, and during the next four or five years appeared there in a wide variety of parts, being good in light comedy. From 1880 to 1885 he was leading man with Lawrence Barrett, with whom he first appeared in London as Master Heywood in *Yorick's Love.* With Marie Wainwright (1853–1923) as his leading lady he toured extensively in a repertory of Shakespearian and other classics, and remained on the stage until his death, which occurred while he was dressing to play Wolsey in *Henry VIII.*

JAMES STREET THEATRE. This small eighteenth-century theatre or amusement hall stood between the Haymarket and Whitcomb Street. It was used mostly for variety, but pantomimes were given there, and occasionally plays. Its prices seem to have been 3*d.*, 4*d.*, 6*d.*, and 1*s.*

JANAUSCHEK, FRANCESCA ROMANA MADDALENA (1830–1904), Czech actress, who made her début in Prague in 1846, and two years later became leading lady of the Frankfurt Stadttheater. She remained there for some years, and then went to Dresden, building up a great reputation as an interpreter of tragic drama in such parts as Medea, Iphigenia, Maria Stuart, and Lady Macbeth. She toured extensively in Europe, and in the United States, where she was highly thought of. In 1873 she undertook to play in English, appearing in a number of Shakespearian and other roles. Her later years were spent mainly in America, where she died four years after suffering a stroke which paralysed her. She was one of the last of the great international actresses in the grand tragic style.

JANIN, JULES-GABRIEL (1804–74), French journalist and dramatic critic, most of whose best work was done for the *Journal des Débats*, where he succeeded Geoffroy. For forty years he wrote a Monday article which dealt as much with personal and national affairs as with the theatre, and his outspokenness frequently landed him in lawsuits and quarrels. But his enthusiasm for good acting, wherever he found it, made him a powerful advocate, and it was his articles that first drew the attention of the Parisian public to Rachel and to Deburau. A prolific writer, he published lives of both these actors, and also a history of French dramatic literature, as well as innumerable works of criticism and several novels. Celebrated and feared during his lifetime, he was soon forgotten, but his books are useful sources for contemporary theatrical and social history.

JAPAN. 1. CLASSICAL. The classical Japanese theatre takes three distinct though related forms—the *Nō* or lyrical drama, the *ningyo-shibai* or puppet-play, and *kabuki*, the popular theatre (from *ka* = singing, *bu* = dancing, *ki* = acting).

The first printed texts of the *Nō* date from about 1600, but their composition is attributed to Kwanami and his son Zeami, who lived at the end of the fourteenth and beginning of the fifteenth centuries. The language in which they are written is, however, the Court colloquial of the fourteenth century and they represent an art already mature; the *Nō* must therefore have been an established art-form soon after the Ashikaga line of Shōguns began to rule at Kyōto (in 1334) and may even date from the later years of the first shogunate, set up at Kamakura, thirty miles south of the modern Tōkyō, at the end of the twelfth century. The language of the *kyōgen* or comic interludes which accompanied the performances is the vernacular of the second half of the sixteenth century. The puppet theatre and the popular drama were established art-forms by the time the centre of power had shifted once more to the east with the setting up of the Tōkugawa shogunate (which lasted until the Restoration in 1868) at Edo, the modern Tōkyō, at the beginning of the seventeenth century. They reached their highest point of development in the second half of the century, and remained more or less static for some time. Since 1945 the many small *kabuki* troupes which used to tour the countryside have been disbanded, and performances are given only in the larger cities.

The *Nō*, which also reached its point of perfection in the seventeenth century, drew its forms and materials from the ritual dances of the temples and the folk dances of the countryside; from the Buddhist scriptures, and from the abundant sources of Chinese and Japanese poetry, myth, and legend. It is essentially a drama of soliloquy and reminiscence, and has no development through conflict, as in Western drama. It was from the first an aristocratic art, and with the passage of time this tendency grew until it became a close preserve of the ruling caste. On the overthrow of the shogunate in 1868 and the consequent disappearance of the feudal system, the *Nō* survived precariously at first, but has since taken a new lease of life; its enjoyment, however, is still confined to the upper classes of society and its audiences tend to be made up of elderly and middle-aged people and foreign visitors. The puppet-plays, although their sources were ultimately the same, were influenced more directly by the *katari-te* or story-tellers; their appeal was to the populace, but with the development of the popular stage, which appropriated their best dramas, interest in them has dwindled until there is only one stage for their exhibition, the Bunraku-za at Ōsaka, the commercial metropolis of Japan, not far from Kyōto. The popular stage drew not merely on the *Nō*, but more extensively on the range of marionette drama, especially in the *jōruri* form in which the chanting of the story by a chorus accompanies the action. It has from early days been the apanage of the Edo (Tōkyō) townsfolk; indeed, access to it was forbidden to the *samurai*, the warrior caste of old Japan.

The marionettes are displayed on a wide,

shallow stage of no great height; although it does not reach the same pitch of realism as on the *kabuki* stage, the scenery is elaborate, and cunningly contrived to allow for the movements of the puppets and their handlers on different planes of depth and height. The puppets are two-thirds life size and the principal characters need for their display a chief handler, who wears a ceremonial costume and is not masked, and two assistants in hoods; the minor characters are handled by a single hooded assistant. All these handlers are visible to the audience; the technique of manipulation from above by strings, although it has its exponents in Japan, has not succeeded in establishing its right to a stage of its own. The action is accompanied by the chanting of the story, usually by one singer, to the music of a *samisen*, or Japanese guitar; sometimes the chorus sings in unison, and the music has no independent existence apart from the chanting to which it forms a rhythmical background.

The *kabuki* stage (see No. 120) is also wide, shallow, and not very high; its depth is limited by the adoption of the revolving stage which dates from *c.* 1760, and is an integral part of the scenic presentment. Another special device characteristic of the *kabuki* stage, although adopted from the *Nō*, is the *hana-michi*, the 'flower way', running on the left-hand side from the back of the hall to the stage at the level of the spectators' heads. Along this the characters make their entrances and exits, and to it they sometimes withdraw for an aside; it is sometimes duplicated by a similar though narrower passage on the right-hand side. The curtain does not rise but rolls back to one side. The scenery is elaborate and complete to the last detail; but since the scene is Japan, where simplicity to the point of asceticism is the rule, this over-elaboration does not serve to distract the attention. The costumes are similarly fitted to the part; rich brocaded silks in historical subjects, plain where the scenes are drawn from common life. The performers are not masked, unless for performance of an actual *Nō*, when a replica of the *Nō* stage is sometimes constructed on the stage; but in the classical plays they are heavily made up in conventional style appropriate to the character represented. Female parts are taken exclusively by male actors who specialize in these roles. Music and sound-effects are provided by a small party of instrumentalists inconspicuously placed behind a lattice on the left of the stage; where the play is adapted from the marionette theatre a *jōruri* reciter and a *samisen* player sit in open view on the right; if from the *Nō*, in addition to the chorus and a number of *samisen* players seated on the stage, there will be the special *Nō* musicians seated in front of them. Finally, mention may be made of the stage assistants, the *kurogo* and *kōken*, the one hooded and the other not. Like the handlers of the marionettes they are conventionally invisible; they survive from a time when the actor had a 'shadow' who crouched behind him with a light on the end of a bamboo to illuminate the play of his features.

As in the Chinese theatre, it is the rule for individual scenes from several plays to be acted in the course of one performance; these scenes have their own names and enjoy a semi-independent existence apart from the play of which they form a part. The *kabuki* theatre recognizes three main classes, the *jidaimono* or histories, with a subdivision composed of scenes of exaggerated action, the *aragoto* (it is of these last that the '18 masterpieces' of the Ichikawa school of actors consist); the *sewamono* or domestic melodramas; and the *shosagoto* or dances. A typical programme would thus consist of a selection of scenes from one of the histories followed by a dance; and a second half consisting of a melodrama followed by another dance.

The *Nō* stage (see No. 121) has a floor of polished cypress 18 feet square, raised 3 feet from the ground; it projects into the auditorium so that it is surrounded by the audience on two sides, separated from them only by a narrow path of loose pebbles. Four stout pillars support a temple roof, the eaves of which are some 12 feet from the ground and the ridge 20 feet. The front pillar on the right is the pillar of the Second Actor (*waki*) and diagonally across from it at the left rear is the pillar of the First Actor (*shite, shtay*). On the right a balcony some 3 feet wide accommodates the chorus of ten singers; at the back a transverse back-stage half the width of the main stage accommodates the four musicians and the two stage assistants; from its left-hand edge runs at a backward slant a passage of the same width, some 40 feet long, the *hashi-gakari*, by which the performers enter and leave the stage, closed at the far end by a narrow curtain.

There is no scenery; on the back wall of the rear stage is painted a stylized pine-tree, and along the bridge railing are three small pine-trees or branches. The properties are equally exiguous, a frame 2 feet square from which spring four light posts to support a roof representing a house, a temple, or a palace, as the play may require. The costumes are of a great richness, and the First Actor, especially in the second part where he performs the dance which is the kernel of the play, wears a mask. None of the other players is masked; essentially there are only the two actors, of whom the second occupies a minor role, but they have companions, *tsure*, so that there may occasionally be as many as ten performers on the stage at once. The music, consisting of a transverse flute, two hand-drums—of which the smaller, held on the right shoulder, is played with a thimble, the other on the knee with the flat of the hand—and a larger flat drum resting on the floor and played with two sticks, provides a rhythmical background only.

The play normally opens with a short introductory chant delivered by the Second Actor from the bridge, indicative of the 'order' to which the play belongs. Advancing to the traditional position he recites his name or description and purpose; then follows the journey-song, at the close of which he retires to his pillar. This is the cue for the entrance of the First Actor in his first impersonation, with a chant similar to the Second Actor's, but more developed. As he enters the stage after this chant the Second Actor addresses him, and the theme of the play and the emotions it evokes are developed in exchanges between the two; the first part of the play is rounded off by a chant, more or less prolonged, by the chorus, at the close of which the First Actor (his real character now made known) retires.

Then follows an interlude during which an actor in ordinary costume, and bearing the same name as the performers in the four comic interludes which separate the individual plays, once more relates the story of the play in a prose recitative. The second part of the play opens with the Second Actor's waiting-song; the First Actor then reappears in his real person as god or hero, and performs the great dance or dances for which the rest of the play provides a setting.

Although there are special movements within it which are more animated and even exaggerated, in general the dance is a stately gliding to and fro, without raising the heel, in a series of three, five, or seven steps in a line, accompanied by gestures, of which the most striking is the throwing up of the great brocade sleeve. The dancer is in stockinged feet, the floor is highly polished and specially constructed for resonance; the tapping, beating, and stamping of the feet, accompanied by the syncopated rhythm of the drums, the piercing notes of the flute, and the sharp ejaculations of the musicians, all go to make up the total effect. The dance normally is composed of five movements, each accompanied by the use of a special accessory such as a fan, a sword, or a sacred wand.

Between the individual plays which go to compose a *Nō* sequence there are interposed, in order to relieve the emotional tension, short comic interludes or farces, *kyōgen*, performed in ordinary dress and without masks. That is not to say that there are not parts which call for costume or a wig, that the use of a mask is not sometimes the point of a scene, that parodies of the *Nō* and its masks are not common. Nothing is sacred to the *kyōgen*, the *daimyō* or feudal lord, the monk, the friar, not even the dread ruler of the lower regions; and every object of popular fun finds a place, the drunken or impudent or dishonest or stupid servant, the boaster, the glutton, the shrew, the gallant; almost it might be said that every precept of the classical canon of education is turned to ridicule. If the purpose of the *Nō* is magical, here is counter-magic.

The modern classification of the *Nō*, on which is based the selection of pieces to form a programme, divides them into:

(1) The god piece;
(2) The battle piece;
(3) The wig piece; woman's dance;
(4*a*) The mad piece;
(4*b*) The historical piece;
(5) The finale; demon's piece.

The ordinary day's programme of five pieces contains in addition four *kyōgen*, and lasts for six or seven hours, beginning at nine or ten in the morning or at one in the afternoon. Although not selected to form a programme, the following summaries will give some indication of the content of the individual classes:

Oimatsu, or The Ancient Pine. The ninth-century poet-minister Sugawara no Michizane, unjustly exiled through a palace intrigue, was miraculously followed into exile by his favourite trees. He was subsequently deified as the god of calligraphy. In the first part the spirits of the trees are represented by their attendant gardeners; in the second the spirit of the aged pine tree performs the solemn, stately *Shin no jo* dance.

Atsumori. In the great war of the twelfth century which has furnished the Japanese stage with so many of its themes the young hero turned back to face the gnarled veteran and was slain; but the slayer shaved his head and became a monk. In the first part the monk appears in person and the hero as a young reaper. The first dance of the second part is symbolic of the dance and song with which the elegants of the defeated clan whiled away the night before the battle; the second mimes the hand-to-hand fight, ending with the absolution of the monk.

Ha-goromo, or The Feather Robe. A fisherman finds an angel's feather robe, without which she cannot return to heaven, and is persuaded reluctantly to return it to her. In gratitude she performs the 'dances that are danced in heaven'.

Aoi no Ue, or Lady Aoi. Drawn from the eleventh-century romance of Genji, the Japanese Don Juan, another fertile source of inspiration for the stage, Aoi is possessed by the jealous spirit of a rival. In the first part the incantations of a sorceress evoke the jealous spirit in her natural form; in the second she is incarnate as the devil of jealousy.

Ataka, or The Barrier of Ataka. The youthful hero on the opposing side in the battle in which Atsumori lost his life quarrelled with his brother, the founder of the Kamakura shogunate, and was forced to flee in disguise. Led by his faithful supporter, the gigantic monk Benkei, the party come to a barrier, which they are allowed to pass on the production by Benkei of a subscription list, *kanjinchō*, in proof of their bona fides as mendicant friars. When they are called back for a second scrutiny, Benkei dances the *Ennen no mai*, the dance of longevity, one of the temple dances from which the *Nō* form descends.

Ko-kaji. The swordsmith Munechika is commanded to forge a blade for the emperor and invokes the aid of Inari, the god of rice cultivation, whose symbol is the fox. In the second part the god mimes the forging of the sword in the *hataraki*, a dance of agitated movement. C. W. BICKMORE†, *rev.*

2. MODERN. Although the *kabuki* and the *Nō* are still valid forms of drama in modern Japan, there has developed, in the twentieth century, a new theatrical art, the *shingeki* or modern drama. This exists side by side with, though entirely distinct from, the classical *kabuki* theatre. Actors in one form do not act in the other, nor is there any similarity in the techniques of acting and production. This dichotomy arises from the fact that when, in about 1904, the founders of the modern theatre movement in Japan, Shōyō Tsubouchi and Kaoru Osanai, tried to introduce Western drama into Japan—the first with Shakespeare, the second with Ibsen—they found it impossible to combat the strength of tradition in the old forms, and had no choice but to create a new form. Their first tentatives failed, just as the Shimpa (Modern Drama) Movement, started in 1888, had failed, mainly because their actors were trained in the old classical style.

In 1924, in a second attempt to resolve the problem, Osanai founded the Tsukiji Little Theatre, in which modern foreign plays were performed as far as possible in their original style. (This theatre was destroyed during the Second World War.) At the same time, Dr. Tsubouchi founded at Waseda University the first Japanese Theatre Museum, which incorporates a small Elizabethan-style playhouse, modelled on the Fortune, where productions of Shakespeare are sometimes given. Although the power of traditional drama is still strong, it has weakened somewhat since the end of the Second World War, and is gradually losing its hold over the general public. In spite of economic and other difficulties, among them the shortage of good modern Japanese plays, the modern drama movement has, in the last forty years, made substantial progress. There is, however, only one theatre in the country for the adequate presentation of *shingeki*—the Haiyūza-Gekijo (Actors' Theatre) (see No. 122). This is in Tōkyō, where there are three *kabuki* theatres (one restored after serious damage by fire) and several *Nō* theatres. As there are as many as forty *shingeki* groups in Tōkyō alone, they are forced to present their plays in halls which are often too small, and unsuitable for dramatic performances. This limits their repertory. Molière, for instance, is possible in such conditions; Shakespeare is not.

Japan has as yet no state-aided or National Theatre, though a proposal for the erection of the latter, first put forward at the end of the nineteenth century, was included in the national budget in 1956 and a sum of money allocated for the purpose.

One interesting development has been the organization in various towns of groups supporting the theatre. This means that in order to put on a local production of a new play a *shingeki* company no longer has to seek the support of an outside interest—a school, a business firm, a national newspaper—but can usually rely on a local audience-group. There seems to be some hope here for the future financial stability of the modern Japanese drama movement.

The main problem of the modern theatre is how to discover and produce plays dealing realistically with the everyday life of the people in Japan today. The older methods of actor-training are not adapted to the modern play, and although Stanislavsky's *An Actor Prepares* was translated into Japanese in 1930, it had had very little effect before the *shingeki* troupes were disbanded by the authorities in 1940. When they were re-formed, the Method became extremely popular, and efforts were made to acclimatize it in Japan. But although this may solve the actors' problems, dramatists have still other problems, not least that of creating a verse-drama based on folklore, thus enabling them to communicate with the people through their myths, as is done in Europe through the revivals and adaptations of Greek myths. Until recently no such assimilation had been attempted, but several writers, among them Junji Kinoshita, have been experimenting with *minwa-geki* (plays based on folklore) with some success. Finally, the modern theatre must decide what to take over and preserve of the *kabuki* theatre, a problem intensified by the fact that in the *kabuki* the actor is paramount and the play serves as a vehicle for him, while the modern theatre seeks to subordinate the actor to the play, which he interprets tor the audience (for a modern production of *kabuki*, see No. 123). A more hopeful line of approach to the classical theatre will perhaps be through the *kyōgen*, the comic interlude of the *Nō* plays which reflects the life of the medieval countryside. It cannot be denied that the modern theatre, in its efforts to assimilate and imitate Western drama, has somewhat neglected the study of the traditional Japanese forms, and is still, in spite of recent advances, in a transitional period.

Although the Bunraku puppet-show continues to be popular, efforts have been made to establish other puppet-theatres and other forms of puppetry. But most of the new companies still use hand-puppets. Among other new forms of theatre, plays for children are beginning to be considered important. They were first given at the beginning of the twentieth century, but really came into prominence for the first time with performances at the Tsukiji Little Theatre in the 1920s, when such European plays for children as *The Blue Bird* were given. Although few of the pre-war children's companies survived after 1940, others have been formed, and there are now about forty groups which visit schools. There is, however, no official encouragement of Children's Theatre in Japan, though drama is beginning to be used in the schools. There are a number of amateur groups also, mainly of recent formation. Some of the most active are in the villages, where they function from November to March, and are beginning to produce their own plays, based on local material. There is a Society for Theatre Research, based on the Waseda University Museum, which is affiliated to the International Federation for Theatre Research. In 1950 graduates of Waseda University founded the Modern Theatre (Kindai Gekijo), which has presented a number of Shakespeare's plays. A young literary critic, Tsuneari Fukuda, plans to translate all Shakespeare's plays into colloquial modern Japanese. His *Hamlet* and *Macbeth*, staged by the Bungaku-za troupe, have delighted young audiences by their freshness and vivacity.

JARRY, ALFRED (1873–1907), French poet and playwright. Although only one of Jarry's plays, *Ubu Roi*, may be said to have survived today, it is often considered to be the founder-play of the modern avant-garde theatre, and is in any case of great importance as a seminal influence on the French surrealist movement. Written when Jarry was 15 years old, first performed in 1888 as a marionette play, and first produced on the stage by Firmin Gémier at the Théâtre de l'Œuvre in 1896, *Ubu Roi* represents a savagely funny, anarchic revolt against society and against the conventions of the naturalistic theatre, which scandalized audiences in 1896 and still has considerable contemporary relevance, as Jean Vilar's successful revival demonstrated at the Théâtre National Populaire in 1958. André Breton, the surrealist writer, has described the play as 'the great prophetic, avenging play of modern times', and its hero, Père Ubu—vicious, cowardly, coarse, pompously cruel, and unashamedly amoral—is the exact prototype of the anti-hero in contemporary literature of the nuclear age. Many of the marionette elements in the play, expressly demanded by Jarry in his stage instructions to Gémier, have become common currency in the work of playwrights like Genêt and Ionesco, and directors like Brecht and Planchon: the use of masks, skeleton sets, crude pantomime and stylized speech to establish character, gross farce and slapstick elements, placards indicating scene changes, cardboard horses slung round actors' necks and similar unrealistic props. Jarry returned to Mère and Père Ubu in several other plays, notably *Ubu enchainé* (1899) and *Ubu sur la butte* (1901), but without recapturing the same creative spark. *Ubu Roi*, 1896, was published in an English translation by Barbara Wright in 1951, and produced in an adaptation by Iain Cuthbertson at the Royal Court Theatre in 1966.

T. C. C. MILNE

JAVA. The theatre of the Javanese embraces the dance-drama, which lies outside the scope of this volume, the shadow-show, and the puppet-play. The shadow-show is of great antiquity the first reference to it dating from the seventh century, when it was already an established art-form. It has had a wide-spread influence throughout the East (see also MALAYA, PUPPETS and Nos. 126, 128).

JEFFERSON, a family of actors, of English origin, but important in the history of the American stage. The first to be known by name is (1) THOMAS (1732–1807), who was at Drury Lane under Garrick, and was accounted a good actor. He was for some time manager of a theatre in Plymouth, and was twice married, having a large family, most of whom were on the stage. By his first wife, a charming and beautiful woman who died young, he had a son, (2) JOSEPH (1774–1832), the first of that name. This son was trained for the stage by his father, and in 1795 went to America. After a short stay in Boston he was at the John Street Theatre, New York, and later at the Park (see No. 163), where he was popular with the company and the public alike, particularly in comedy and in the parts of humorous elderly gentlemen. He was, however, somewhat held back by the pre-eminence of Hodgkinson, and in 1803 went to the Chestnut Street Theatre, Philadelphia, where he remained until a few years before his death. He then fell on hard times, and from about 1830 was seen mostly on tour in the big cities. Yet his career as a whole had been successful, and his influence on the stage was salutary. Walter Prichard Eaton in the *Dictionary of American Biography* says of him: 'He brought to the theatre the best traditions, and to private life dignity and kindliness and virtue.' He and William Warren married two sisters, thus connecting two families of importance in American stage history. Jefferson had a large family, all of whom were on the stage, including a second Thomas and four daughters. The best-remembered of them is, however, (3) JOSEPH (1804–42), the second of the name, who inherited his father's happy nature and strong sense of integrity, but not his genius. He was on the stage, but had a decided bent for art, and did a good deal of scene-painting. He married (4) CORNELIA FRANCES THOMÁS (1796–1849), an actress and singer of great ability who by her first marriage was the mother of the actor Charles Burke (1822–54), and had by her two children, of whom (5) JOSEPH (1829–1905), third of the name, was destined to become one of the outstanding figures of the American stage. He made his début at the age of 4, in Washington, being tumbled out of a sack by the famous Jim Crow, whose song and dance he then mimicked. With his family he toured extensively, living the hard life of pioneer players. He had little schooling outside the theatre, and at 13 lost his father. Long years of labour with little reward at last bore fruit, and in 1849 he achieved some eminence. By 1856 he was able to afford a trip to Europe and on his return joined Laura Keene's company, where he made a great success as Dr. Pangloss in *The Heir-at-Law* and as Asa Trenchard in *Our American Cousin*. This proved a turning-point in his career, as in that of E. A. Sothern, who played

Lord Dundreary, and after a short starring tour he went to the Winter Garden under Boucicault, where he played among other parts Caleb Plummer in *Dot* and Salem Scudder in *The Octoroon*. On the death of his first wife in 1861 he went on a four-year tour of Australia, and it was on his return that he first played the part with which he is always identified—*Rip Van Winkle*. There had already been several dramatizations of Irving's story, notably by Kerr, and by Jefferson's half-brother Charles Burke in 1850, in which Jefferson himself played the innkeeper. He based his own version partly on the above and partly on the original tale, and produced it in 1859, but found it unsatisfactory. The final version was done by Boucicault in 1865, while Jefferson was in England, but during the many years in which the latter appeared in it he made so many alterations that in the end the character became his own creation, and the play lived only as long as he did. He first played it in Boucicault's version at the Adelphi in London in 1865, and in New York a year later. It was during this visit to London that Jefferson was entertained by the son of his great-uncle Frank, and went with twenty-four relations to see the pantomime at Astley's. The size of the party gives some idea of the ramifications of the family, whose members in America were even more numerous. Until 1880 Jefferson played little but *Rip Van Winkle*, which was acknowledged everywhere to be a masterpiece; he then revived *The Rivals*, making Bob Acres a little more witty and a little less boorish than his predecessors in the part had done. With Mrs. John Drew as Mrs. Malaprop, and a good supporting company, this toured successfully for many years. Jefferson, whose charming, humorous personality made him typical of all that was best in the America of his time, made his last appearance on 7 May 1904, as Caleb Plummer, and then retired after seventy-one years on the stage. In 1893 he had succeeded Booth as President of the Players' Club, and so became the recognized head of his profession. He did a good deal of lecturing, and in 1890 published a delightful autobiography, from which many of the above details are taken. He strengthened the family tie with the Warrens by marrying as his second wife the granddaughter of the first William. The eldest of his children, (6) CHARLES BURKE (1851–1908), was for many years his manager, and was also an actor, as were three other sons, among them a third Thomas. His only daughter, by her marriage with the novelist B. L. Farjeon, was the mother of the composer Harry, the novelists and playwrights Joseph Jefferson and Eleanor, and of (7) HERBERT FARJEON (1887–1945), actor, author, and dramatic critic, pre-eminently a writer and producer of intimate witty revues, staged mainly at the Little Theatre, London. He was a scholarly man, editor of the Nonesuch and other editions of Shakespeare, and of the *Shakespeare Journal* from 1922 to 1925, and had much of the charm and geniality of his famous grandfather.

JEROME, JEROME KLAPKA (1859–1927), English humorist, novelist, and playwright, who was also for a short time an actor. It was no doubt his experiences then that led to the compilation of his *Stageland: Curious Habits and Customs of its Inhabitants*, which was published in 1889 with amusing illustrations by Bernard Partridge. He also wrote *On the Stage and Off* (1888), and several plays which have not survived, the first being *Barbara* (1886), produced by Charles Hawtrey at the Globe. Jerome's theatrical fame, however, rests mainly on *The Passing of the Third Floor Back* (1908), in which Forbes-Robertson scored a signal triumph as the mysterious and Christ-like stranger whose sojourn in a Bloomsbury lodging-house changes the lives of all its inhabitants. The play has been several times revived.

JERROLD. (1) DOUGLAS WILLIAM (1803–57), English man of letters, whose early experiences in the navy, where he was a shipmate of the scene-painter Stanfield, were turned to good account in his best-known play, *Black-Eyed Susan; or, All in the Downs* (1829), in which the actor T. P. Cooke made a great hit. Jerrold was then engaged by Elliston as dramatic author to the Surrey Theatre, a position he had formerly held at the Coburg Theatre under Davidge, where his farce, *Paul Pry* (1827), and his melodrama, *Fifteen Years of a Drunkard's Life* (1828), were produced. Some of his later plays, notably *The Rent Day* (1832), were given at Drury Lane, while in 1836 he took over the management of the Strand Theatre and produced his own plays there. He also acted occasionally, but had little taste or talent for it. He was associated from its foundation in 1841 with *Punch*, and in later years was more engaged in journalism than play-writing; none of his plays has survived on the stage, though in the lighter forms of burlesque and comedy, and occasionally in melodrama, he had a good deal of contemporary success. Jerrold's son, (2) WILLIAM BLANCHARD (1826–84), was also a prolific writer, and his farce, *Cool as a Cucumber* (1851), gave the younger Mathews one of his best parts. His other plays are negligible.

JESSNER, LEOPOLD (1878–1945), German producer and theatre manager, who abandoned the use of scenery in his productions in favour of different levels connected by stairways (*Spieltreppe*). A man of stern purpose and high intelligence, Jessner was a staunch republican. In art he was an expressionist, and during his years as director of the Berlin State Theatre (1919–25) he was considered one of the most advanced exponents of that creed. Among his most notable productions were *Wilhelm Tell*, *Richard III*, and *Der Marquis von Keith*.

JESSOP'S HALL, LONDON, see ROYAL PANTHEON THEATRE.

JESTER, see CLOWN and FOOL.

JESUIT DRAMA. In origin, the drama of the Jesuit schools and colleges is similar to other forms of scholastic drama; it was the product of a didactic purpose. The aim of the Jesuit plays was both educational and theological; they were directed to the improvement of the pupils who acted them and of the audience that watched them. At the same time, the degree of emphasis laid on those visual means of conveying purpose which are characteristic of the theatre differentiates Jesuit dramas to a very considerable extent from such scholastic dramas as relied mainly on the power and argument of the spoken word.

In the curriculum of study for the numerous educational institutions of the Society of Jesus, the staging of a drama, or at the least a dialogue, in Latin was laid down as an appropriate public exercise at the beginning or end of the school year; by this means the study of grammar and rhetoric was to be enlivened, the pupils were to be given an opportunity of showing their progress and abilities, and the doctrines of true religion and morals were to be effectively shown forth. In the first full *Ratio atque Institutio Studiorum* of 1586, the acting of comedies and tragedies was included among the aids to the study of the humanities, but it was to be in moderation, and without undue elaboration; an earlier rule (1577) had already laid down that plays might be acted, infrequently, and only in Latin, that they must be decorous, and in no case performed in church. In the revised *Ratio Studiorum* of 1599, Rectors were charged to see that the subject-matter of tragedies and comedies—which must only be acted rarely, and in Latin—was of a sacred and pious nature, that nothing intervened between the acts which was not in the Latin tongue, and decorous, and that no female character or feminine costume was introduced on to the stage (*nec persona ulla muliebris vel habitus introducatur*). Between the lines of these regulations and prohibitions, something of the relationship between the drama of the Jesuit schools and contemporary developments may be read; and also something of the conflict between scholastic principle and the need for adaptability. The history of drama in Jesuit institutions is in some measure a history of the transformation of a school exercise into an almost professional spectacle, showing a high degree of technical skill.

The earliest mention of the acting of a Jesuit play appears to date from 1551, only three years after the establishment of the first Jesuit college in Europe solely designed for the instruction of outside pupils—the Collegio Mamertino at Messina. A tragedy was performed there in 1551; but we know nothing of its character, and it is possible that it may in fact have been little more than a dialogue. But in 1558 a comedy by a Spanish Jesuit, P. Francesco Stefano, was acted at Messina: *Philoplutus, seu de misero avaritiae exitu*; and this was followed in 1561 and subsequent years by other plays (*Hercules, Nabuchodonosor, Goliath, Juditha*, etc.). Meanwhile, the first performance of a play by the pupils of the Jesuit College in Vienna took place in 1555 (*Euripus sive de inanitate rerum omnium*, by a Franciscan, Levinus Brechtanus of Antwerp), and this inaugurated a long series of performances of Jesuit dramas in Vienna; at Córdoba in 1556 a play by P. Pedro de Acevedo, *Metanea*, was acted. Performances of plays were given early at Ingolstadt (1558), and Munich (1560).

At this period Jesuit colleges had been and were being established in great numbers throughout Europe—in Spain, Portugal, Italy, Sicily, France, Germany, Austria, Poland, Switzerland, and the Netherlands. At the death of Ignatius of Loyola in 1556 there were already 33 colleges open for the instruction of pupils; the number catering for outside pupils had increased to 148 by 1587, and this number was nearly doubled before the seventeenth century was far advanced. In these numerous colleges of Europe, for over two centuries, at least one play—and for the most part more than one—was performed by the pupils each year. Only the best of them were allowed to be published; for by far the greater number of performances only programmes, or *periochae*, were printed, of which numerous examples survive in various European libraries. Within the last sixty years, however, the researches of scholars in many countries have brought to light manuscript versions of Jesuit plays; some of these have been published, of others detailed descriptions have been given, and a considerable number still await adequate investigation.

Records of early dramatic performances are to be found in the histories of all the better-known Jesuit colleges. In 1568 a play on the martyrdom of St. Catherine was given at the Collegio Romano in Rome; two years earlier the second great college in Rome, established for students from the German-speaking lands, had staged a drama, *Saul*. In 1561 at Ocaña there was a play on the subject of Judith, at Seville in 1562 a representation of great magnificence was given at Corpus Christi (*Comœdia habita Hispali*), and at Medina in the same year a drama, *Absalon*. At Trier a play was acted in 1562, and one at Innsbruck in 1563. The famous Collège de Clermont in Paris, founded in 1564, was the scene of a representation of a *Herod* tragedy at the opening of the session in 1579. In 1578 *Achab* was acted in the college at Pultusk; in 1581 a Faust drama was given at Liège, in 1596 *Philopater seu Pietas* at Vilna, in 1599 a play on St. Elizabeth of Hungary at Antwerp, in 1601 *Philomusus Aquisgranensis* at Aachen. These are only a few examples of the practice which by the end of the sixteenth century had become well established, indeed practically universal, in the Jesuit schools and colleges.

The last quarter of the sixteenth and the whole of the seventeenth century was a period of development in Jesuit drama which was very important both from a dramatic and a theatrical standpoint. There was a continuous process of elaboration of the technical aspects of production; moreover, in the different countries and regions where it flourished, interesting divergences within the general type can be observed. On the one hand, a degree of approximation to the characteristics of indigenous drama was combined with the maintenance of a general international pattern; on the other, changes of emphasis in the different regions led to new variations of the pattern. Such an approximation can be observed, for example, in Spain, where the characteristic verse-forms of the national drama soon found an entry into the Jesuit plays; while the development of the ballet-interlude and of the mechanism of décor reinforced the evolution of ballet in France and of opera in South Germany and Austria. In England religious policy precluded the development of Jesuit scholastic drama; but it flourished on the Continent through the seventeenth century into the eighteenth; and indeed its development was only cut short at the suppression of the Order in 1773.

The early pattern of Jesuit drama was simple in outline and purpose. There were two main types of play: *tragœdiae* in five acts, on the classical model, which were generally performed either at the opening of courses after the reassembly of pupils for the session, or at a final prize-distribution at the end of the scholastic year; and shorter plays, which were acted at Carnival time or on other suitable occasions. There were also in many places special performances of plays in connexion with royal or princely festivities. The tragedies (*ludi solemnes*) were performed by the senior classes, the less exacting plays (*ludi priores*) by the younger boys. Normally the play was written by the professor of rhetoric; and it was deliberately constructed in order to afford the pupils exercise in the Latin tongue, in declamation, and in gesture and deportment. (Sometimes, however, the pupils themselves composed, or partially composed, the play, as for example at Medina in 1562, when *Absalon* was performed.) The number of actors was large, and choruses and arias gave opportunity to many who were not chosen for individual parts. *Juditha*, by the Sicilian, P. Stefano Tuccio (1564), has 32 characters (apart from an angel, a demon, and the chorus); in the *San Hermenegildo* play performed at Seville in 1580 there were likewise 32 personages (including abstract characters), together with soldiers, pages, etc.; in the *Theseus* (acted at Paris in 1663) there were 25, and in the *Mauritius* tragedy at Aachen (1716) 67 in all. In the later period of Jesuit drama, the addition of ballets and interludes of various kinds also swelled the list of performers: in the *Tartaria Christiana* performed in Paris in 1657 there were 28 characters and 13 in the accompanying ballet (entitled *drama mutum* in the programme). In the *Pietas victrix* of Avancinus (Vienna, 1659) there was a grand array of 36 personages and 10 abstract characters, together with the Senatus, members of the army and the fleet, operatives, choruses of soldiers, youths, Roman citizens, Naiads and Tritons, and angels, *gloriae* and masks.

The early prohibition of female personages and costumes was modified in a revision of the rules in 1591; female roles were to be limited to what was absolutely necessary. In the final *Ratio* of 1599 the general prohibition remained, but in reply to comments submitted by the Provinces of the Rhine, Upper Germany, and Austria, pointing out the difficulty of such a rule both for secular and religious plays, a dispensation was granted in 1602, as long as the women characters were modest and serious and were only very rarely introduced. An exception to the general rule must indeed always have been made for the numerous dramas on Judith (of which there are early examples in the sixteenth century) or on Esther, and for some of the martyr tragedies (e.g. St. Catherine). Other roles gradually came to be accepted. In Tuccio's *Juditha* (1564) there had been five female parts besides that of the heroine. In *San Hermenegildo* (1580) there were five feminine roles; in a play on William the Pious of Aquitaine performed at Graz in 1612 in the presence of the Duke of Bavaria, there were as many as ten. Eight nymphs appeared in *Dapiferi* (Constance, 1629); of the 45 characters in *Tabropana Christiana* (Paris, 1650) two were women; and in *Athalia* (Paris, 1658) there were three. The increasingly frequent introduction of abstract characters (Felicitas, Castitas, Pietas, Fides, Industria, Pax, Fama, Ecclesia, etc.) no doubt contributed also to a modification of the regulation against feminine costume; thus gradually in practice the rule came to imply simply the absence of love interest in the plays.

The names of the actors were usually appended (with the list of *dramatis personae*) to the programmes which were prepared for distribution to the audience. These programmes contained a general summary of the plot, together with brief summaries for each of the acts, indications of the scene, and frequently the text of arias or choruses. From a scrutiny of the very numerous extant examples an idea of the prevailing pattern of Jesuit drama can be gained; but the more interesting details of its adaptation to various regions and traditions must be sought mainly in the manuscripts and reprints of complete plays.

That the themes chosen must be sacred and of a pious nature was a rule which in general governed the choice of subjects, but it was interpreted more or less widely at different stages. The Old Testament and biblical history, and the lives of saints and martyrs, provided a large number of themes which were constantly treated. Such figures as those of Joseph, Saul, Herod, Nebuchadnezzar, Judith, Esther, familiar to early scholastic drama, appear again and again, as do those of numerous saints and martyrs. The great drama of the New Testament and the Apocalypse inspired an early trilogy—Stefano Tuccio's *Christus Natus, Christus Patiens, Christus Judex*. It was recorded that at the performance of the third of these plays at Messina in 1569 the spectators

JESUIT DRAMA

were in tears; and that contrition and miraculous conversions were experienced there, and in other places where the drama was acted. The history of antiquity and the Middle Ages also provided many subjects, especially later—as for example Pompey, Brutus, Croesus, Cyrus, Alexander, Damocles, Constantine the Great, Theodoric, Hermenegildus. Subjects were drawn from national or regional history and given appropriate moral colour—*Messina liberata*, for example (acted in 1594), celebrated the victory over the Saracens at Messina in 1060; at Regensburg in 1598 a drama, *Tragœdia de infelicis Herodis obitu*, acted in the presence of the Archduke of Austria, showed Herod as a symbol of Turkish tyranny and gave encouragement in the epilogue to resist the Turks; and the liberation of Vienna in 1683 was the subject of dramas acted at Cologne in 1684 and Münster in 1689. They were drawn also from mythological sources, which were then reinterpreted allegorically (e.g. *Partus Iovis, sive ortus Palladis* at Messina in 1585). The heroic aspect of the religious ideal was increasingly emphasized. Characters in such plays as *Theophilus* (Munich, 1582), *Faust* (Liège, 1581), or *Cenodoxus* (Augsburg, 1602), showed the tension between good and evil, between this world and the next; dramas celebrating the founder of the Society of Jesus gave opportunity to display the victory of religious fervour and spiritual purpose over the forces of this world. The Christian virtues were exalted in such plays as *Clementia christiana*, or P. Acevedo's *Bellum virtutum et vitiorum*; pictures of impenitent sinners or a late repentance were drawn, as in *Udo*, or Bidermann's *Jacobus Usurarius*.

There were, however, in addition to the *tragœdiae* and *comœdiae* of serious intention, a smaller number of comic plays, usually performed by the *secundani*, or members of the lower school classes. There was a certain hesitancy over the adoption of the comic form; P. Jouvancy, for instance, in the treatise *De ratione discendi et docendi* (1703), expressed the view that it should only be used with great discretion in Christian schools, since the buffoonery proper to this genre was incompatible with the pious and liberal education of youth. Moreover—and the argument is worth noting—the gestures, customs, and jests of servants (*valets de comédie*) were unsuitable for the pupils whose education was confided to the care of the Society. But there were, nevertheless, some discreetly composed comedies—as for example *Adolescens poenitens* (MS. preserved at Messina), *Conaxa* (acted at Rennes, probably in 1710), or *Les Incommodités de la grandeur*, a five-act comedy in French verse by P. du Cerceau (performed at Paris in 1721). In France in the eighteenth century there was a considerable increase in the number of such comedies.

A Spanish farce, *Triumphus Circumcisionis* (acted at Medina del Campo) throws light on the social customs of students in Spain in the sixteenth century; and in Germany as well as Spain a mixed genre is to be found: *Ambitio infelix sive Adonias . . . oppressus* (Hildesheim, 1669) is described in the synopsis as 'Comico-Tragoedia, Vermischtes Frewden- und Trawr-Spiel'. Interludes related to the main action in substance but contrasting in mood are described on the programme of a drama on Boleslaus II, King of Poland (Jülich, 1699). A comic scene would likewise be interpolated on occasion in a serious play (as in *Rogerius, sive Panhormus liberata*, acted at Palermo in 1599, or in *Faustinianus*, Milan, 1610). Frequently there were comic interludes or entr'actes contrasting in mood with the main play; a burlesque of the classic canon is inserted in an anonymous drama at Salamanca, *Comœdia quae inscribitur Margarita*, and in P. Acevedo's *Athanasia* (Seville, 1566) there is a dialogue in Spanish popular verse-form between a rustic character and the *Parcae*. In the German Provinces, interludes in German of a character contrasting with the tragedy are found frequently in the later period (as, for example, *Von einem hintergangenen Schornsteinfeger* in a drama, *Felicitas*, at Aachen, 1771).

The rule concerning Latin prevailed in general during the sixteenth century, but with some notable modifications and exceptions. The humanistic trend of the Jesuit system of education, and in particular the regulation that Latin should be the medium of communication between masters and pupils, ensured its general observance; moreover, the models from which most of the plays were derived were Latin. But certain concessions, to the audience if not to the actors, crept in early. The Latin drama by Tuccio, *Christus Judex* (1569), was translated into Italian verse at Bari in 1584; a second translation of 1596 was reprinted at Venice in 1606, and a further much-revised version appeared at Rome in 1698. This last translation was adapted into a sacred drama set to music, in three acts with intermezzi, *L'ultima scena del mondo*, in 1721; while a more faithful rendering in Italian prose was made by a Jesuit Father in 1727. A German version of *Christus Judex* was acted at Olmütz in 1603; a Polish one at Warsaw in 1752.

The *tragœdiae* produced in the French colleges were generally in Latin, as were most of the comedies—and, as in Italy, not only the language of the dialogue but also the different lyric metres of the choruses followed classical patterns. But as early as 1580, at Pont-à-Mousson, a *Pucelle d'Orléans* is recorded, by P. Fronton du Duc, and, there also, a French *Conversion de Saint Ignace* in 1623. P. Le Jay's *Joseph venditus a fratribus* (1698) was translated into French and performed at Paris in 1704. During the seventeenth century, interludes in French became the rule; and in Italy there were plays in Italian. In the eighteenth century, both in France and in Italy, dramas were more frequently written in the native tongue. In the Netherlands likewise exceptions to the rule are recorded; dramas in Flemish were represented at Ghent and Hal in

1640. In that same year, with obvious intention, a tragedy in Spanish, *Joab*, was played by the pupils of the college at Tournai.

In Spain the mixture of Latin and Spanish appears early. Not many of the Jesuit dramas in Spain seem to have been wholly in Latin; some indeed were wholly in Spanish. The mixture conformed to medieval precedents; and it is interesting evidence for the incorporation of indigenous dramatic tradition. A Prologue in Spanish, or in Spanish and Latin (with two 'interpreters'), is sometimes found; in the *Actio quae inscribitur Examen Sacrum* acted in Salamanca in the sixteenth century there is even a discussion, mainly in Spanish, as to the language in which the play should be performed. On occasion, the compromise of a hybrid language was adopted. In the dramatic dialogue, both languages were sometimes used, with the object of distinguishing serious and noble personages from secondary and plebeian characters—again a notable instance of adaptation to a dramatic tradition. Spanish, Italian, and Latin are all used in the drama *San Hermenegildo* represented at Seville in 1591. The earliest well-known Spanish Jesuit dramatist, P. Acevedo, observed in the main the Latin rule; but as early as 1556 the mixture of Latin prose and Spanish verse which was to become the prevalent mode is to be found in his *Metanea*; while in his *Comœdia habita Hispali in feste Corporis Christi* of 1562 the prologue and arguments are translated into Spanish hendecasyllables. Four years later his *Athanasia*, written in Latin prose, had three entr'actes in Spanish verse. The evolution of the Jesuit drama in Spain shows in fact both an early admixture of the vernacular tongue and a progressive diminution of the Latin and learned elements under the influence of the native tradition of drama; in Acevedo's *Bellum virtutum et vitiorum* quintillas and redondillas are to be found; and in the *Tragœdia de San Hermenegildo* a great variety of Spanish verse-forms appears.

In the German-speaking lands the process of gradual modification of the Latin rule can also be observed. As early as 1582 a request was made on behalf of Lucerne for a play in German, if necessary a translation of a Latin drama; and the reply gave reluctant consent. In 1588 the Austrian Province was allowed to produce interludes in the vernacular, on condition that no unsuitable buffoonery was admitted. The Rhine Province petitioned in 1600 for a relaxation, which was granted on condition that liberty was sparingly used. At first the relaxation may well have been made in respect of the open-air performances which catered specifically for a mass audience, and only later in respect of the plays acted in the college buildings. Prologues in German, however, were prefixed to each of the five acts of a *Tragœdia de regibus Achab et Jezebel* given at Paderborn in 1604. Gradually the practice grew up of inserting German arias into the Latin text, and plays wholly in German are extant from the end of the seventeenth century (in 1697 a 'musical tragedy' in German, *Julius Maximinus*, was acted at Cologne).

In addition to the lyric airs which were an integral part of the plays in all regions from the beginning, there was a development of the interlude, intermezzo, or other forms of entr'acte which varied in kind and in frequency in different areas. Music and dance formed part of the earliest dramatic performances in the colleges of Spain; *entretenimientos de música y danza* are recorded of the production of the *tragicomœdia* of *Joseph* at Ocaña in 1558. Elsewhere, the intermezzo came to flourish rather later. An intermezzo was given in Scammacca's *Amira* acted at Palermo in 1610 for the festival of St. Ignatius. In France, both intermezzo and ballet became very important elements in the Jesuit drama. The great vogue of dancing at the Court and among the nobility no doubt contributed to the cultivation of the ballet in the dramatic performances of the French Jesuit schools, where young noblemen were being educated. P. Menestrier in 1682 and P. Le Jay in 1725 both wrote important treatises on the ballet; the latter observes that it need not conform to the strict rules of drama, the only requirement being that all its parts should conform to the general idea which is the design of the whole. Thus the ballet rested on allegory; and where there was a link between it and the tragedy the link was one of allegorical interpretation (e.g. a tragedy on the fall of the Assyrian Empire was accompanied by a ballet 'Les Songes', because that fall was predicted in dreams; *Cyrus* was embellished by a ballet on the Empire of the Sun). Sometimes, however, the ballet would be topical; the marriage of Louis XIV in 1660 was the occasion for one entitled 'Mariage du Lys et de l'Impériale'; the Peace of Nijmegen in 1679 was alluded to in a 'Ballet de la Paix'; and Louis le Grand was glorified in many ballets on the stage of the college which came to bear his name. Décor and costumes were of immense importance in these elaborate ballets, and P. Menestrier (*Des ballets anciens et modernes*, Paris, 1682) gives details of the costumes proper to Roman, Greek, Persian, Moorish, Turkish, Saracen, 'American', and Japanese personages, as well as to many allegorical figures. The historical accuracy thus demanded for the ballet at the height of its popularity on the college stages in France was of a piece with the elaborate conditions of décor and production in contemporary opera. The scenery and effects of the theatre at the college of Louis-le-Grand in the seventeenth century are stated to have been considerably more varied and numerous than those of the Théâtre-Français, even if they fell short of those of the Opéra.

The ballet was of course by no means confined to the French productions. It appears early in the records of performances at Munich (an elaborate one was inserted in the drama *Samson* acted there in 1568), and its popularity is attested in many of the *periochae* of plays in the German Provinces. But it is the parallel with opera, which had begun to penetrate from Italy in the early period of the seventeenth century, that is perhaps most characteristic of the Jesuit drama in South Germany and Austria. In these regions Jesuit plays, operas in the Italian style, and the popular melodramas of the *Englische Komödianten* were all being offered to the public—sometimes side by side. In the year 1608 the Archduke Ferdinand in Graz attended performances both by the pupils of the Jesuit college and by John Green's troupe of English players. In Munich, where Jesuit plays had been acted since 1560, the conjunction of their performance of the music-drama of *Philothea* in 1643 with the building of an opera-house in 1657 may be noted. In 1666, at a time when performances of great splendour were being given both at the Court theatre and at the Jesuit college in Vienna, the Imperial opera-house was erected.

With equal and characteristic skill, the Jesuit theatre accommodated itself to the mentality of the masses or to the customs of a Court while consistently pursuing its own purposes. Influences of many kinds thus bore upon its development, and its practitioners sprang from many lands. The works of the Spaniard Pedro de Acevedo (*fl.* 1560), the Italian Stefano Tuccio (1540–97), the German Jakob Bidermann (1578–1639), the Frenchman Nicolas Caussin (1580–1651), the Englishman Joseph Simon (Simeon), writing in Rome (1594–1671), the Austrian Nicolaus Avancinus (1612–86)—to name only a few representative authors of plays—all bear witness to an early expansion and elaboration of the theatrical aspects of drama; the rapid development of the means for change of scene and transformation was matched by the increased variety of visual and musical adornments. As early as 1573, a play on the Last Judgement acted at Rome made so deep an impression with its strange apparitions and fearful vistas of destruction and damnation that it was repeated the next year. A sumptuous décor is recorded of the play of *San Hermenegildo* given at Seville in 1580 to celebrate the solemn opening of the extended college; a great frontispiece represented the city of Seville, with two high towers on each side, one of which served as the saint's place of imprisonment, the other as a '*castillo de los entretenimientos*'—which appear to have consisted of fireworks and varied mechanical devices. The high degree of technical development reached in the Jesuit theatre in Vienna in the seventeenth century is shown by the nine illustrations to an edition of *Pietas victrix* by Avancinus (Vienna, 1659). It is clear from these that the play was acted on an elaborate transformation-scene stage. A comparison with the staging of earlier Jesuit plays at the end of the sixteenth century in the German Provinces reveals striking developments in the variety of scene and decoration, and in the possibilities of change of scene within the acts. In 1653, indeed, the stage of the college in Vienna was equipped with seven transformation scenes. The new technical means influenced the structure and composition of the plays themselves; they may well account in part for the prevalence of dream scenes, which could be effectively combined with music, dance, and mechanical effects of all kinds. In its luxuriance of decoration the seventeenth-century Jesuit theatre affords clear evidence of its approximation to contemporary taste; and the influence exerted by its widespread dramatic activities in the development of that taste has come to be recognized. The links with plastic and pictorial art are obvious. It is interesting in this connexion to note the prevalence in the *tragicomœdiae* of landscape as well as architectural settings; and the spectacle of the sea in movement, decorated with ships, marine creatures, Naiads, or Tritons, rivalled the effects of fire and lightning, flying machines, and suspense mechanisms which were almost universal in seventeenth-century Jesuit plays. *Dum mare turbatum fremit, et coelum fulminat, apparet Xaverius naufragus* is a stage direction in Avancinus's *Zelus, sive Franciscus Xaverius* (IV. 3); and in the huge drama acted at Lisbon for Philip II of Portugal in 1619, the sea was a constant motif both in the text and in the elaborate décor. In a play produced for the festival of the canonization of St. Ignatius at Pont-à-Mousson in 1623, the figure of the saint appeared on the stage, and by a sudden transformation changed into a tower, from which fireworks issued. At the end of the play, the saint appeared above a neighbouring roof and, descending by a mechanism as if from the sky, set fire to a castle filled with fireworks.

In the course of the seventeenth century, lighting effects were increasingly used. While it seems clear that the plays were most frequently performed in daylight—one or two o'clock in the afternoon was a favourite time for the performances to begin, just after the midday *prandium*—their length frequently made it necessary to conclude them by the light of torches. (The duration seems to have varied from two to seven hours—a regulation for the Rhine Province set a limit of four, but there was no consistent practice in the matter.) Large windows often let in light upon the stage, so that artificial light should not be needed. [Cp. the plan and description of this kind of stage in J. Furtenbach: *Mannhafffter Kunst-Spiegel*, Augsburg 1663, p. 113.] But necessary or not, it was used, and was regarded as an additional attraction to the spectacle. Lighting effects were frequently indicated in the plays; concealed lamps would irradiate the clouds, a 'gloria' would appear in the empyrean, the light of sun, moon, stars, comets would be thrown by mechanical means upon the stage. Similarly, auditory effects were achieved: thunder and other terrifying noises were used to sharpen the susceptibilities of the audience. Gruesome deeds were not always carried out behind the scenes; in the German-speaking Provinces during the seventeenth century executions and murders took place upon the stage as they did in the popular dramas of the wandering players. In *Judith* dramas, the head of Holofernes was a regular stage effect;

in the drama of Avancinus (v. 9) it is a target for the insults of the chorus of Bethulians. A puppet figure of Jezebel, decked out in realistic detail, was torn to pieces by dogs upon the stage in Graz in 1640. Costumes and stage adornments corresponded in magnificence to the customs of the particular environment—in those cities which were also Court residences, the theatre at the Jesuit college was often the recipient of munificent gifts such as were commonly made at this period to the Court operas and theatres. There were conventional costumes for the different categories of personages, but within this convention the producers aimed at accuracy. The numerous allegorical characters afforded scope for decorative invention; much of the detail was naturally borrowed from contemporary paintings.

The musical element was present in the Jesuit dramas from the beginning, but, like the other embellishments, it grew in importance as the productions became more elaborate. The presence of a chorus, on the classical model, gave rise from the outset to lyric passages which took the form of arias; while the *tableau* or *scena muta*, always a frequent accompaniment to the action, was often suitable for choreographic treatment. The influence of Italian opera can be argued from the inclusion (particularly in South Germany and Austria) of solo singing in the action of the plays. (An Italian *Singspiel*, *Tobias*, is recorded as having been given at the Innsbruck college as early as 1582.) But the powerful tradition of church music in the Order itself must not be forgotten. The songs of the different choruses in the more ambitious plays frequently approximated to the form of cantata or oratorio. They required, in their developed form, the accompaniment of instrumental music, and many of the schools had a school orchestra trained to a high degree of proficiency. At the performance of *Theophilus* in Munich in 1643 there were thirty-two instrumentalists as well as forty singers. It is probable that on some occasions professional musicians also assisted in the performances.

The elaborate nature of these arrangements made it necessary to have adequate accommodation for actors and audience alike. In the early period of any given institution, plays were frequently performed in the open—partly, no doubt, in order to attract the mass of spectators so frequently recorded. The splendid *Esther* drama given at Munich in 1577 was acted in the market-place with great magnificence of décor, the play lasted three days and 300 persons took part in it. In Vienna, the courtyard of the college served as stage until 1650, when a large interior theatre and a small rehearsal stage were opened. When an established school gave performances within its own precincts, the accommodation would vary from a simple hall—such as that in the college at Pau, where a curtain was let down to separate the audience from the stage—to such ample provision as the stage in the college at Vienna built on Italian models, or the three separate theatres at the college of Louis-le-Grand. Here there was a large theatre, a smaller theatre for the less important spectacles given in the course of the school year, and finally an interior theatre, used for the plays given in winter and for rehearsals for the grand August performances. At these last there was always a large public audience, with a high proportion of exalted personages. Jean Loret writes in 1651 (*La Muse historique*, II, letter 32):

La Reine et messieurs ses deux fils,
Lundy dernier, à jour préfix,
Allèrent, avec grandes suites,
Au collège des Jézuites,
Pour, sur un téâtre fort beau
Voir un poëme tout nouveau
Que pluzieurs jeunes philozofes,
Vêtus de brillantes étofes,
Reprézentèrent en latin,
Moitié figue, moitié raizin.
On y vit aussi pluzieurs dances,
Balets, postures et cadances,
Où maint fils de prince et seigneur
Y parurent avec honneur. . . .

The same chronicler records two years later that not only Louis XIV and his mother and brother, but also the exiled king of England, Charles II, and his younger brother, Henry, Duke of Gloucester, then aged 14, were present at the Jesuit play. In addition, he adds, there were many blonde and brunette Court beauties. Eminent personages such as cardinals, legates, and members of other religious orders, were also frequently among the spectators.

In Vienna also the Jesuit plays in the seventeenth century attracted an audience of high rank. Leopold I would be present not only at the grand performances but even at the minor plays, thus attending six or seven performances in the school year. Indeed, the Jesuit theatre during the reigns of Leopold I and Joseph I, and in the early years of Charles VI, fulfilled many of the functions of a Court theatre.

The composition of the audience varied in different regions and periods. Especially in the matter of admitting women to the performances, the practice appears to have been adapted to current social usage. Where there was a Court in residence (or even when members of a Court were passing travellers), its customs were decisive. The visits of the Queen to the performances at Louis-le-Grand clearly were enough to determine the usage in Paris. Elsewhere, the question was variously solved. As early as the late sixteenth century there was a relaxation in the German Provinces—at the discretion of the Superior and if custom demanded it—of the rule prohibiting the attendance of women; and although difficulties frequently arose, this relaxation clearly continued. (In 1680, at Hildesheim, for example, the presence of *viri et foeminae honoratiores* was recorded.) Sometimes the dress rehearsal was turned into a special performance for an audience of women (as at Freiburg in Switzerland in 1644). In the French Provinces at the end of the seventeenth century there seem frequently to have been two performances of the main play of the year, the first for a feminine, the second for a masculine, audience (the programmes of a performance at La Flèche in 1680 refer to this as the established practice).

That the Jesuit form of drama with its peculiar combination of entertainment and moral purpose, of classic pattern and flamboyant execution, was an integral part of the life of a Jesuit school is abundantly clear. But if further evidence were needed, it could be gathered from an examination of the comments that were made upon it within the Order itself, and of the attacks launched against it from without. Protests against luxuriance of décor were made in Spain in the sixteenth century. In the German-speaking Provinces, throughout the seventeenth century, decrees issued at intervals sought to curtail the number and diminish the extravagant splendour of performances; the frequency of these decrees attests the strength of the impulses which they endeavoured to control. The work of the school was said to suffer through the excessive labour and concentration on preparations for acting the plays; the expenditure on production was censured as excessive and unsuitable. (In Vienna in 1659 *Pietas victrix*, for example, cost between three and four thousand florins—defrayed on this occasion by the Emperor. At the jubilee celebrations in 1640, a great allegorical drama on St. Francis Xavier with many accompaniments of music and pageantry had cost about 13,000 gulden.) In 1714 interludes were forbidden because of their satiric and sometimes unsuitable allusions; in 1770 in Hildesheim a decree prohibited music and dancing. The number of performances had steadily increased, until it was not unusual to have as many as five repetitions of a successful play, or even, on occasion, to arrange for performances to be repeated in other places—as when the Rector and the Professor of Rhetoric at Emmerich took all the actors to Cleves in 1647 to act a play before the Elector of Brandenburg. In France also, the college pupils might be called on to give a performance at Court, or in the house of some great personage, and in the age of Louis XIV the elaborate setting and accompaniments of the plays were in close conformity with prevailing taste. It was perhaps for this reason as well as for others that the opponents of the Jesuits in France seized upon their cult of the theatre and attacked it fiercely. The highly developed ballet in particular was sharply criticized, and plays and ballets alike were severely censured by the University of Paris, and in numerous polemical writings. The attempt to depict and defend the theatre in a didactic ballet, *L'Homme instruit par les spectacles ou Le Théâtre changé en école de vertu*, by P. Charles Porée (Paris, 1726), failed to convince such confirmed opponents; and in 1762, when taking possession of the college after the Jesuits had had to give it up, the Rector of the University openly rejoiced at the cessation of such entertainments.

While controversy was thus acute in France, Jesuit dramatists in Italy during the eighteenth century had fewer rivals. The name *teatro gesuitico* appears indeed to be rather generic than specific; the Jesuit dramas of the period were written in a recognized form—a variant, subject to the general principles and particular dramatic aims of the Jesuit system, of the accepted classical pattern, under the dominant influence of France. The Jesuit authors Giovanni Granelli and Saverio Bettinelli (writing in Italian) have a recognized place among the not over-numerous pseudo-classic dramatists of this period in Italy; the *Sedecia, Manasse, Dione* of the former, the *Demetrio* and *Serse* of the latter, certainly enjoyed in their own day great popularity—not only on the scholastic stage—and they find a place in histories of Italian literature.

It is not easy to make any precise estimate of the direct contribution made by the Jesuit cult of the dramatic art to the general development of drama and the theatre in Europe—not easy to determine exactly how far it helped to form taste at any given period, or simply conformed to it and developed it further. In content and form the dramas appear on the whole conservative; though in the matter of the preservation of the unities of time and place, or where they adopt and adapt characteristic features of indigenous drama, they do not in the main follow rigid pseudo-classic conventions. But their prevailingly allegorical form and their consistently didactic purpose perpetuated through two centuries modes of approach to life which secular drama had in many regions abandoned before the first of those centuries had come to an end; and the discouragement of women's parts—even though it was by no means consistent—tended to limit both range of subject and mode of treatment. Yet it was perhaps just the allegorical element in the plays which stimulated advance in another direction. The desire to present abstract conceptions in visually attractive and therefore easily acceptable form was a powerful factor in the development of technical methods of production. And in this aspect of the art of the theatre the Jesuit drama was pre-eminent, its only contemporary rival being the opera. To what degree each of these two forms influenced the other is a question to which different answers might be given in respect of different countries; but at least their interaction is clear. Technical devices and elaborate transformations, the development of music and dancing as integral parts of a dramatic whole, were common to both; setting and costume were also of paramount importance in the artistic ensemble. If in Paris the college of Louis-le-Grand provided spectacles which rivalled those of the *Académie de danse* founded by its royal patron, in Vienna during the seventeenth and earlier eighteenth centuries the stage of the Jesuit college was the scene of *ludi caesarii* whose only counterparts in splendour of production were the operas given at the Court theatre. And in the smaller Court cities of the

German-speaking lands a similar parallel could be drawn. The music-dramas, cantatas, and oratorios of the Jesuits dating from the first half of the seventeenth century were the forerunners of the cult of opera which developed at the German Courts; opera in its turn suggested some of the more potent scenic and auditory effects of the later Jesuit dramas. At the least, the plays at the Jesuit colleges may be said to have constituted in the seventeenth and early eighteenth centuries a link between opera and drama, and to have furthered technical advances in the production of both. It is of some interest also to note the number of well-known dramatists who were educated in Jesuit schools. Some doubt has been cast, it is true, on statements that Lope de Vega was for a time at the college at Madrid, and that Cervantes studied at Seville when P. Acevedo's plays were being performed there. But Maffei and Goldoni (as well as Tasso) were pupils of the Jesuits; and so were the two brothers Corneille, Molière, the elder Crébillon, Dancourt, Le Sage, and Voltaire. Thomas Corneille acted in a play on Jezebel at the college at Rouen about 1642; Pierre Corneille and Voltaire both received prizes for Latin verse during their school-days, and it is tempting to think that they were rewarded by parts in the Latin play at the prize distribution. Voltaire indeed, in a letter to Dr. Bianchi of 1761, recalled the dramatic performances given by the pupils at the college in Paris as the best thing in the education he received there from the Jesuits. EDNA PURDIE†

JEVON, THOMAS (?–1688), one of the first English Harlequins, playing the part at Dorset Garden in *The Emperor of the Moon* (1687). He was an excellent dancer, and was credited in a contemporary satire with 'heels of cork and brains of lead'. He wrote a farce, *The Devil of a Wife; or, a Comical Transformation*, which was given at Dorset Garden in 1686 with some success. In 1731 it was made into a three-act play with music as *The Devil to Pay*, and later, curtailed to one act by Theophilus Cibber, it became one of the most popular of English ballad operas.

JEWISH DRAMA. Jewish drama has no territorial limits. Its sole boundaries are linguistic—Hebrew, the historical and religious language which has never ceased to be written and has now been reborn as a living tongue; Yiddish, the vernacular of the vast Jewish communities lying between the Baltic and Black Seas, one which emigrants have spread over the world; and Ladino (Judaeo-Spanish), the speech of the Jews who live round the Aegean Sea. Even the linguistic frontiers are not clearly defined. Israel Zangwill (1864–1926) wrote Jewish plays in English; Alexander Granach (1890–1945) began as a Yiddish actor, won fame in the German theatre, and, after 1933, returned to the Yiddish stage in Poland. Thus any study of Jewish drama must be viewed in the light of the Jewish approach to the theatre in general.

1. THE BACKGROUND. Drama was not indigenous to the Jew. The commandment in Deuteronomy xxii. 5, 'A man shall not put on a woman's garment', and the connexion between early drama and the rites of idol-worship, were strong arguments against the establishment of a theatre, and were invoked by many leading Jews as late as the nineteenth century. Yet the classical theatre, low as it had fallen by the time the Jew came into contact with Hellenism, exercised an immediate attraction. Jewish actors were found in Rome under the Empire, and Ezekiel of Alexandria, who flourished in the second century A.D., taking Euripides as his model, wrote a Greek tragedy in hexameters on the Exodus, though there is no reason to suppose that this was ever acted or indeed intended for the stage.

2. THE ORIGINS. It was from the Jewish jugglers, dancers, and mimics of the Middle Ages, and from the emphatic intonation of the Cantor and the questions and responses in the synagogue services, that the Jewish theatre slowly evolved. Itinerant musicians and professional jesters (the *badchans* of modern Yiddish literature) also played their part in its development. A more serious contribution can be found in the Hebrew philosophical dialogues, dating back to Ibn Ezra (*fl.* 12th century) and popular down to the end of the eighteenth century—Beer's *Conversation of the Spirit of Poverty with that of Good Reputation* (1674), Fiammetta's *Duet between Grace and Truth* (1697), with musical accompaniment, and Norzi's *Conversation with Death* (1800).

The travelling minstrels were much in demand at Jewish festivals, and by the fifteenth century their vernacular songs were already being dramatized under the influence of German Court drama and the plays of the Nuremberg Mastersingers. Typical examples are *The Play of the Devil, the Doctor and the Apothecary*, the farce *A Play of Food- and Drink-loving Youth*, and a fragment of a burlesque, *The Beggar's Wedding*. Philosophical dialogues, after the style of those mentioned above, were performed in the vernacular, and religious plays appeared, on such subjects as Adam and Eve, the sacrifice of Isaac, or the death of Moses, modelled on the lines of the South German Carnival play. The earliest extant manuscript of such a play is one on the Prophet Jonah, based on a similar work by the Mastersingers Simon Rothen and Balthasar Klein, and dating from 1582.

Play-acting at festivals gradually centred on Purim, the holiday observed on 14 Adar (very roughly about early March) to celebrate the events recorded in the Book of Esther—the downfall of the anti-semite Haman through the intercession of Queen Esther. The plays given then (for further details see PURIM PLAYS), with their set plots, costumes, and characters, continue to the present day. Their extensive use of interpolated songs, and their mixture of tradition and improvisation, provide elements which can be traced in contemporary Jewish drama.

3. Early Hebrew Drama. Yiddish drama was born in Germany, Hebrew in Italy and among the Spanish Jews in Holland. The first Hebrew play was *The Comedy of a Marriage*, ascribed to Leone di Somi (1527–92), which shows very clearly the influence of the *commedia dell'arte*; the *dramatis personae* consist of the pining lover, his beloved, her crafty maid, the broad-humoured servant, and the unscrupulous lawyer. The introduction to the earliest extant manuscript (1618) states that the play was intended for presentation at Purim.

It was, however, in Amsterdam, in the early seventeenth century, that Hebrew drama first became established. Marrano refugees filled the city, and their leaders saw in the drama one way of restoring their self-respect. They knew no Dutch, and Spanish was suspect in recently liberated Holland. The medium of the new drama had therefore to be Hebrew. Its content was borrowed from the religious plays of the Dutch dramatist Joost van den Vondel, its form from the *comedia* and *auto* of Lope de Vega and Calderón. It was the use of the *auto* which permitted the dramatization of the allegory inherent in the philosophical dialogues referred to above.

Throughout the whole of the seventeenth and eighteenth centuries the Dutch and Italian communities were closely connected. *Yesod Olam*, an *auto* by Moses Zacuto (1625–97), an Amsterdam Kabbalist, may have been performed in Italy, where Jewish actors could be found. It describes Abraham's rescue by an angel from the furnace into which he had been thrown after destroying his father's idols, and shows strongly the influence of van Vondel. Zacuto's *Tofteh Aruch*, a mystery-play dealing with a journey to the next world, was certainly acted by synagogue worshippers in Ferrara about 1700. It was imitated by Jacob Olmo (1690–1755) in his *Eden Aruch* about 1720. The first Hebrew play to be printed was a Morality play by Joseph Penço de la Vega (1650–1703), *Asiré Hatiqva*, published in 1673 at Amsterdam, and reprinted at Leghorn in 1770. In it a serious-minded king is led astray by Satan, by his wife, and by his passions; his reason and an angel guide him back to virtue. Songs are included in this play, which is believed to have been intended for a festivity at a religious school.

Moses Hayim Luzzatto (1707–47), the outstanding figure of the period, was an Italian Jew resident in Amsterdam. His *Migdal Oz* (1727), a pastoral play in four acts modelled on Guarini's *Pastor Fido*, compares the Law of Moses to a king's daughter who, hidden in a strong tower (the Migdal Oz of the title), shows herself only to her lover. The language and style of this drama, written for his uncle's wedding, have placed Luzzatto among the great Hebrew poets. His other important play, *Tehilla Layesharim* (pub. 1743), written for the marriage of one of his pupils, tells how Pride tries, with the help of Falsehood, to win Praise (Tehilla), who, however, weds Righteousness. Luzzatto was also the author of a third play, dating from 1724, which deals with Samson among the Philistines, and of a book of grammar in which he devotes a section to the definition of drama—an early attempt at dramatic criticism.

Eighteenth-century Italy saw a great increase in the number of Hebrew playwrights. Samuel Romanelli of Mantua (1757–1814) translated the works of several Italian authors, including Metastasio, and took the plots of his own plays from Ovid. There was a general tendency to utilize classical mythology under Hebrew names. But in spite of the increased output plays were still performed only on religious holidays and on special occasions. The widespread imitations of outside sources did not result in the establishment of a permanent theatre, and drama in general remained a literary exercise remote from stage presentation.

4. The Haskala (Enlightenment) Movement. As a result of the period of religious tolerance which followed the Thirty Years' War, the German Jews were able to enjoy a fairly normal life. This fostered the rise of the Haskala Movement in the second half of the eighteenth century, under the influence of the German-Jewish philosopher Moses Mendelssohn. It aimed at introducing the Jew to the language, literature, and science of other nations, while stimulating a revival of his own culture. The principles of the Haskala Movement spread eastward slowly, reaching the more remote regions only in the second half of the nineteenth century, and for over a hundred years provided the dominating feature in the history of Central and Eastern European Jewry.

One of the results of the movement was a renewed interest in the writing of Hebrew plays. Imitations of Luzzatto are to be found in such works as *Yaldut Ubahrut*, by Menahem Mendel Bresselau (1760–1827), written in 1786 for performance at a Barmitzva (or confirmation), and in *Amal and Tirza* (1812), written by Shalom Cohen (1772–1845) for a wedding. Knowledge of the drama was also increased by translations. Racine's *Esther* and *Athalie* were frequently translated, both on account of their subjects and because the choral structure of the plays appealed to the Jewish love for combined dialogue and song. Goethe's *Faust*, and the plays of Schiller and Lessing, were also drawn on, as were those of Metastasio, Molière, and others. Even Shakespeare was imitated by Joseph Ephrati of Toplowitz (1770–1840) in his *Reign of Saul*, which, first published in 1794, was often reprinted.

These plays were, however, still mainly intended for reading or occasional private performance. The day of the Hebrew theatre had not yet dawned, and the Yiddish theatre was destined to be established first, mainly in an attempt to check the growing vulgarity of the Purim play. Two of these early Yiddish plays were written by followers of Moses Mendelssohn in Germany: *Reb Henoch* (*c.* 1793), by Isaac Euchel (1756–1804), and *Leichtsin und Frommelei*

(1796), by Ahron Halle [Wolfsohn] (1754–1835); others by Joseph Biedermann (1800–?) in Vienna, where they were performed by amateurs about 1850. But they flourished best in Russia, with such writers as Israel Axenfeld (*c.* 1795–1868), Solomon Ettinger (*c.* 1803–56), whose *Serkele*, written in about 1825, long remained popular, Abraham Ber Gottlober (1811–99), and Ludwig Levinsohn (1842–1904).

5. The Permanent Yiddish Theatre. While the above playwrights were laying the foundations of a Yiddish repertory, an audience for the future theatre was being created by the Brody Singers, wandering musicians who took their name from the Polish town of Brody. These lineal descendants of the medieval professional jesters became extremely popular in Galicia and the Carpathians about 1850, and during the next twenty years evolved a new type of entertainment, with popular comic and sentimental Yiddish songs linked by dialogue and dance, evolving finally into one-act sketches. They provided almost all the theatrical entertainment available until in 1876 Abraham Goldfaden (1840–1908) founded the first permanent Yiddish theatre. The date is usually given as between 5 and 8 October, when, with the help of two Brody Singers, he presented a two-act musical sketch in a tavern in Jassy (Rumania). Its title, if it had one, has not been preserved. Its songs were written by Goldfaden, who also provided the scenario on which the actors improvised their dialogue. From these humble beginnings the new theatre progressed rapidly. Goldfaden, who was actor, dramatist, song-writer, producer, and manager, enlarged his company, trained his actors, employed women on the stage for the first time in Jewish history, and from the slight skits of his early days passed to the writing of full-length plays, some of which—*The Witch* (1879), *The Two Kune Lemels*, and the historical drama *Shulamit* (both 1880)—still remain in the repertory of the Yiddish theatre. He gave his audiences what they wanted, and what they could at that time assimilate—a mixture of song and Purim play, with plots and music borrowed from all over Europe, racy dialogue and broad characterization, much action and little analysis. He lacked what the established theatres of Europe could have given him—training, tradition, and experience—and much of his undoubted genius was wasted in the struggle to establish and maintain a theatre under primitive conditions. This he did, in the teeth of all opposition, and even raised up rivals in his own field. While he was in Bucharest, the Russian headquarters during the Russo-Turkish War, one of his original actors, Israel Gradner, broke away and established his own company. Its playwright was Joseph Lateiner (1853–1935), who was later to be one of the founders of a Yiddish theatre in New York. Another troupe formed at this time found a playwright in Moses Hurwitch (1844–1910), who also emigrated to New York. In Odessa, where Goldfaden went at the end of the war in 1879, his plays were considered too rough by the more sophisticated members of the Jewish community, to whom the theatre was no novelty, and they found a more congenial playwright in Joseph Yehuda Lerner (*c.* 1849–1907). He sought his material in non-Jewish works dealing with Jewish heroes, and is chiefly remembered for his translation into Yiddish of *Uriel Acosta*, by Karl Ferdinand Gutzkow (1811–78).

All this activity was brought to a sudden close by the anti-semitic measures taken in Russia after the assassination of the Tsar Alexander II. In Sept. 1883 all plays in Yiddish were expressly forbidden, and the Yiddish theatre existed precariously until the Revolution of 1917. Many actors and dramatists left the country for England and America, and New York became the centre of Yiddish drama. The first attempt at its establishment there was made by Boris Thomashefsky (1886–1939), and it found its feet with the arrival of Lateiner and Hurwitch, both prolific but unoriginal dramatists, under whom the Yiddish theatre lost much of the ground it had gained in Russia. Playing mainly to a bewildered and illiterate immigrant audience, it tended to rely on the stock themes of the old Jewish life in Europe, which became increasingly out-moded as americanization proceeded, as did the alternation of broad farce and sentimental melodrama which had proved acceptable in the early days of immigration. Even Goldfaden, who had emigrated to New York in 1887, found himself out of touch with the new audiences, and it was left to a newcomer, Jacob Gordin (1853–1909), to revitalize the American Yiddish theatre. Realizing that its weak point was the use of unsuitable material, he endeavoured to broaden its outlook by free adaptations, into Jewish terms, of the plays of the great European dramatists from Shakespeare to Ibsen. He also tried to raise the standards of the Yiddish stage by discouraging improvisation and insisting on respect for the dramatist's text as given to the actors. Among his many plays the best known are his *Jewish King Lear* (1892), *Mirele Efros* (1898), a feminine pendant to Lear, and *God, Man and Devil* (1900), based on Goethe's *Faust*. Gordin has been criticized for failing to make his plays Jewish in spirit as well as in setting, but his work is important in the development of the Yiddish theatre in America. Among those who followed him in the path of social drama, concerned mainly with the breakdown of the traditional Jewish family, may be mentioned Leo Kobrin (1872–1946), whose *Riverside Drive* was produced by Maurice Schwartz in 1927, and Solomon Libin (1872–?), author of some fifty plays dealing with the life of the immigrant Jewish worker in New York, of which *Broken Hearts* (1903) was the best.

6. The Art Theatre Period. Meanwhile in Europe the Yiddish theatre had been making headway. In 1907 Max Reinhardt's production of *Gott der Rache*—a German translation of *God of Vengeance* by Sholom Asch (1880–

1957)—and of one of the plays of David Pinsky (1872–1959)—later done as *The Treasure* by the New York Theatre Guild—had called the attention of the general theatre public to the possibilities of Yiddish drama. The Russian ban on plays in Yiddish had been relaxed in 1908, thus enabling the dramatist Peretz Hirschbein (1880–1949) to found in Odessa the first Yiddish Art Theatre for the production of his own and other plays, notably those of Gordin, Asch, and Isaac Leib Peretz (1852–1915), poet and symbolist, and author of a number of one-act sketches which have proved very successful on the stage.

Hirschbein's venture failed after two years, but it was not forgotten, and early in 1916 the Vilna Troupe, founded by David Hermann (1876–1930), endeavoured to carry on his ideas. Like Hirschbein, Hermann was preoccupied with folk-drama—Jewish themes treated in a Jewish spirit, as with Sholom Asch—and respected the printed word, without improvisation. The acting of his young company was influenced by the methods of Stanislavsky; but much of its initial success was doubtless due to the fact that it was working in harmony with a Yiddish background, and not against an alien one, as in America. When the Vilna Troupe finally split, one section remained in Europe with Hermann, while the other went to New York. There it associated itself with Maurice Schwartz (1889–1960), who in 1905 had emerged from an amateur dramatic society to re-form and re-fashion the New York Yiddish theatre, then at a low ebb. Entirely ignorant of theatre management and production, he started once again from the popular theatre. The turning-point in his career came when he first encountered the idyllic folk-romances of Hirschbein, but his greatest discovery was the work of Sholom Aleichem (1859–1916), the quintessence of Jewish folk-humour and characterization. Schwartz also introduced to the stage the works of Ossip Dymov (1878–1959), author of *Bronx Express* (1919), of Harry Sekler (1883–   ), author of *Yizkor* (*In Memoriam*), of Moses Nadir (1885–1943), author of *The Last Jew* (1919), and of Halper Levick (1888–1962), considered by some critics the outstanding Yiddish literary figure of modern America. Some of his most important plays are *The Golem*, which has been translated into Hebrew, Yiddish, Polish, and English and also made the basis of an oratorio; and his social dramas, *Rags* (1921), *Shop* (1926), and *Chains* (1930). In 1945 he produced his *Miracle of the Warsaw Ghetto*, which dealt with the struggle of the Polish Jews against the Nazis.

Schwartz's example brought into being other smaller Art Theatres, including that of Rudolf Schildkraut (1862–1930), founded in 1925; Our Theatre, founded in the same year; the New York Dramatic Troupe of 1934; and the workmen's studio, Artef, which adopted the methods of the Jewish State Theatre in Moscow (see below), and staged works by Soviet-Jewish writers. Wherever young actors were able to provide topical ideas there was a temporary revival of the American Yiddish theatre, but the widespread adoption of English in Yiddish homes and the slackening in immigration were potent factors in its continued decline. Schwartz's efforts to enlarge his repertory by playing European classics in Yiddish, which took him from Second Avenue to Broadway, was not successful; nor was his playing of Yiddish plays in English.

The third important Yiddish Art Theatre (the other two being the Vilna Troupe's and Schwartz's) is the Moscow State Jewish Theatre, known in Yiddish as Melucha, and in Russian as Goset. Its first director was Alexander Granovsky (1890–1937), and, like the Vilna Troupe and Maurice Schwartz, it found its most suitable material in the plays of Sholom Aleichem. Granovsky re-introduced the *commedia dell'arte* methods of improvisation, adapting tales of Jewish life in the Ukrainian villages to the current Soviet doctrines without losing touch with the work of such modern producers as Meyerhold. In 1927, when new trends of political thought in Russia affected literature and drama equally, Granovsky's leading actor, Salomon Mikhoels (1890–1948), became director of the theatre. He continued much of Granovsky's work, but also produced a number of new plays including those of David Bergelson (1884–1952) and Peretz Markish (1895–1955). This theatre ceased functioning a few months after Mihkoels' death, but was later revived and taken on tour.

7. Other Jewish Theatres. The Ladino-speaking Jews emigrated from Spain after the first expulsion of 1491, before the Golden Age of Lope de Vega and Calderón. Consequently they had no dramatic tradition, nor did they achieve one. Purim and other festival plays appear to have been performed for popular amusement, but no records were kept. In modern times there has been a certain amount of printed drama—the poetical plays of Yakim Behar, the one-act comedies of Alexander Ben Giyat, and a fantasy and two biblical plays, on Deborah and Jephthah respectively, by Joseph Jaen. Where plays have actually been performed, it has always been by amateurs, mostly at Salonica previous to 1939. There are translations in Ladino of some European classics, including *Le Malade imaginaire* and *Esther*, and two versions of Sholom Aleichem's *Mazal Tov*.

The period between the two world wars was a flourishing one for the Yiddish theatre. The Argentine, home of a large Jewish community, had two permanent Yiddish theatres in Buenos Aires. London, which had its first Yiddish theatre in 1888, then had two, both in the East End, and both playing the Yiddish classics. Paris, where Goldfaden founded a company in 1890, with Anna Held (1865–1918) as its leading lady, had a company which played the more popular operettas from the New York Yiddish stage, giving one performance a week. Vienna, home of the Biedermann theatre, had several notable companies, including the Free Jewish Folk Theatre, which flourished from 1918 to 1919. It worked on the lines of the Vilna Troupe, under two directors, I. Deutsch and E. Brecher, who later organized the Jewish Ensemble Art Theatre in New York. In the 1920s New York had twelve Yiddish theatres, apart from others scattered over the United States.

The Nazi holocaust of Jews on the European continent, and the progress of assimilation in Western countries not so affected, led to the decline of the Yiddish theatre. Actors and directors took to the national stage or to the films; a few, like Maurice Schwartz (1889–1960), started Yiddish theatres elsewhere, playing to immigrants of Eastern European origin plays mostly of a popular type. New York today has three, at most four, Yiddish theatres, and their future is uncertain. A similar position obtains in London, Buenos Aires, and Bucharest (where earphones are provided for simultaneous translation into Rumanian). Poland, scene of the activities of the Vilna Troupe, has always maintained a Yiddish theatre. Its Jewish Miniature Theatre, usually known as Mikkt, was evacuated to Russia in 1941, and became part of the Moscow State Jewish Theatre (as did the Yiddish theatres of the Baltic States). The most flourishing Yiddish theatre today, the Polish Jewish State Theatre, was founded in 1948 in Warsaw by Ida Kamińska, daughter of a distinguished actress. In 1953 it moved to Łódz, then to Wrocław, and finally returned to Warsaw, from where it now tours the country. Its repertory consists of forty plays drawn from Yiddish and European classics. In 1956 it visited Belgium, Holland, and France, in 1958 Germany, France, and England, and in 1959–60 Israel. It is the last of the Yiddish Art Theatres, and, in assessing its future, one must remember that today the Jewish population of Poland has been much depleted.

8. The New Hebrew Theatre. The popularity of the Yiddish theatre among the Jewish masses made it clear that the revival of spoken Hebrew aimed at by Zionism could be encouraged by the provision of a permanent company for the production of plays in Hebrew. In 1907 Isaac Katzenelson (1886–1943) founded a Hebrew theatre in Warsaw, followed by that of Nahum Zemach (1887–1939), which functioned in Białystok from 1911 to 1914. In 1917 Habima (The Stage) was founded in Moscow with the intention of transferring eventually to what was then Palestine. After a performance of four one-act plays, its first full-length production, in 1922, was *The Dybbuk*, by Solomon Ansky (1863–1920). It had already been given in Yiddish by the Vilna Troupe, and in the form in which it was produced by Vakhtangov, Stanislavsky's assistant, who was in charge of the training of Habima, it served more than anything else to set the Habima style. The décor was by Nathan Altman, Granovsky's scenic designer.

It was 1928 before Habima first appeared in Palestine, and efforts had already been made to found a theatre there. Under the Ottoman régime, before 1918, plays were produced in the Judaean settlements, and one of the pioneers, Menahem Gnessin (1882–1953) founded in 1922 in Berlin the Tai (the Hebrew mnemonic for 'Palestine Theatre'), taking it to Tel Aviv in 1923 and building there the first theatre building in the country. When Habima arrived, first for a visit in 1928, and then to take up residence in 1931, Gnessin, who had been one of its founders in Europe, joined the company. Isaac Daniel (1895–1935) had also, with very limited resources, been active on lines suggested by Reinhardt and by the French stage. And in 1926 Ohel (The Tent), founded by Moshe Halevy (1895–) and affiliated to the Labour Federation, started giving performances.

Initially the contemporary Hebrew theatre was solely a theatre of production, playing international and Jewish classics, without presenting any original works. At first the whole movement lay under the shadow of Vakhtangov's production of *The Dybbuk*. Although the style of acting appeared to be related to that of Stanislavsky it actually, in its local form, approximated more to Meyerhold's ideas as enunciated by him before the Russian Revolution, the proof thereof lying in the fact that Gordon Craig became an enthusiastic supporter of Habima. In the 1930s original plays began to appear, and by 1939 plays on Jewish themes written by Bistritzky, Silman, and Ashman had been performed. Original work of a different kind came from the 'Matate' (1928–54), a satirical theatre whose productions consisted of short sketches making gentle fun of everyday life, interspersed with interludes of song. 'Matate' has had no true successor.

By 1939 the so-called Stanislavsky style was degenerating into mere formalism, and at the end of the Second World War a new orientation was considered necessary. The success of the Kameri (Chamber) Theatre, founded by Joseph Millo (1916–) in 1944, showed that the public wanted entertainment from the theatre, and that there was a demand for contemporary successes both from the European and the American stages.

Since the establishment of the State of Israel in 1948 there have been further changes in the development of the theatre there. All three companies, Habima, Ohel, and Kameri, at different dates, have tightened up and improved their internal administration. Guest producers, among them Tyrone Guthrie, Harold Clurman, Michael Macowan, John Moody, and Peter Coe, have been invited to produce plays, while acting and producing talent has been sought for and found among the new immigrants. One difficulty common to all arises from a relatively small population which necessitates a large turnover of plays, thereby augmenting the costs of production, wear and tear, and touring. This problem has led to the successful appearance of a group of 'Little Theatres'—Zuta, Zavit, etc.—or of weak imitations of the defunct 'Matate'. Such companies prove very popular; they attract local producers and their expenses are comparatively slight.

The provision of contemporary international works has not provided a complete solution, however, as many of the plots do not apply to Israeli life, which, in a developing country, has its own particular problems. Since 1948 progress has been slow but steady, and about 20 per cent of the total repertory now consists of new plays by Israeli writers. Thus, Moshe Shamir, in *He Walked Through the Fields*, portrayed the period of the War of Independence. Igal Mossinsohn, in *Casablan*, dealt with the difficulties of a Moroccan immigrant in adapting himself to his new surroundings, while humour in daily life provided the material for Ephraim Kishon's *The Marriage Contract*. Other popular dramatists include Nathan Alterman, Aharon Meged, Nathan Schacham, and Nissim Aloni. An actors' school opened at Ramat Gan in 1961. Habima, Kameri, and Ohel now have their own permanent theatre buildings in Tel Aviv; and in northern Israel Haifa has a Municipal Theatre (1961) and Kiriyat Hayim a Community Theatre (1964).

E. HARRIS

JIG, an Elizabethan after-piece, given in the public theatres only, consisting of a rhymed farce, sung and danced by three or four characters, of whom the clown was usually one. The best-known exponents of the jig are Tarleton and Kempe. The songs were sung to existing popular tunes, and the subject-matter was often libellous or lewd. The jig disappeared from the legitimate theatre with the Restoration, but remained in the repertory of strolling players and actors in fair-booths, while it became increasingly popular in Germany from the late sixteenth century onwards, being taken there by the various companies of English comedians who toured the Continent. Some critics have inclined to see in it a formative element in the development of the German *Singspiel*, as well as in that of the English ballad opera.

JIM CROW, see RICE, T. D.

JODELET [JULIEN BEDEAU] (*c.* 1600–60), a French comedian who was in the company of Montdory shortly before the opening of the Théâtre du Marais. With several of his companions he was transferred by Louis XIII to the Hôtel de Bourgogne, but at some point he returned to the Marais, since he played Cliton in *Le Menteur* (1643) and its sequel. He then appeared in a series of farces written for him, mostly with his name in the title—as *Jodelet, ou le maître-valet*, *Jodelet duelliste*, *Jodelet astrologue*. He was extremely popular, and had only to show his flour-whitened face to raise a laugh, while he frequently added gags of his own to the author's lines. When Molière first established himself in Paris he induced Jodelet to join him at the Petit-Bourbon, thus assuring the co-operation of the one comedian whose rivalry he had reason to fear, and gave him the part of the valet in *Les Précieuses ridicules*. He may have intended the role of Sganarelle in his next play for Jodelet, but unfortunately the comedian died before its production, and Molière took the part himself. Jodelet's brother was also an actor, and was usually to be found in the same company (see ESPY).

JODELLE, ÉTIENNE (1532–73), French Renaissance writer, and a member of the famous Pléiade to which Ronsard belonged. He was intended for the army, but escaped, and divided his time equally between pleasure and literature. His *Cléopâtre captive* was the first French tragedy to be constructed on classical lines. Together with a comedy, also on a classical model, it was given before Henri II and his Court in 1552, with Jodelle, not yet 21, as Cleopatra. Remi Belleau, Jean de la Péruse, and other distinguished amateurs were also in the cast. It was a great success, and was subsequently given by a professional company at the Hôtel de Bourgogne, as were some later plays, of which only *Didon* (1558) survives. The Pléiade, overjoyed at the dramatic success of one of its members, organized a festival in Jodelle's honour, at which he was presented with a goat garlanded with ivy. The Church, suspecting nameless orgies, took umbrage at this revival of paganism, and Jodelle bore the brunt of its displeasure. He died in poverty, having successfully blazed the trail for Corneille and Racine.

JODRELL THEATRE, LONDON, see KINGSWAY THEATRE.

JOG, the American term for the narrow flat used in a Box Set to produce a 'return' or break.

JOHN GOLDEN THEATRE, NEW YORK. Built by the Chanins as the Masque Theatre, this opened on 24 Feb. 1927 with a translation of an Italian play which had only 12 performances. It was at this theatre that on 4 Dec. 1933 *Tobacco Road* had its first night in New York. It was transferred to another theatre for its record run, and in 1937 John Golden took over the theatre, named it after himself and opened with *And Now Good-bye*. Success eluded him until 1938, when Carroll's *Shadow and Substance* won the Critics' Prize for the most distinguished foreign play of the season. This intensely moving drama of the Catholic faith had Cedric Hardwicke, Sara Allgood, and many other fine actors in its cast, and set up a record for the house of 274 performances. Another hit was *Angel Street* (1941). Since 1959 a series of revues starting at 9 p.m. (instead of the usual 8.30 p.m.) have been successful. These included Flanders and Swann in *At the Drop of a Hat* (1959), and the Edinburgh Festival 'fringe' revue *Beyond the Fringe* (1962).

GEORGE FREEDLEY†

For an earlier John Golden Theatre, see CONCERT THEATRE.

JOHNSON, ELIZABETH (*fl.* 1790–1810), American actress, who made her first appearance in Boston in 1795 with the American Company, and went with them to the John Street Theatre, New York, the following year. A tall, elegant woman, she played Rosalind on the opening night of the Park Theatre, and was later seen as Juliet and Imogen to the Romeo and Iachimo of Cooper. In 1798 she appeared in London, but returned to the Park Theatre in 1802, and made a great success in fashionable ladies of high comedy, quite ousting Mrs. Whitlock, who had joined the company in her absence. Among her best parts were Lady Teazle, Beatrice, Rosalind, and Imogen. She was one of the first actresses in New York to play male parts seriously, appearing in 1804 as Young Norval. Her husband, John, was a good utility actor, specializing in old men, and he was for a short time joint manager of the Park, where his daughter Ellen, later the charming Mrs. Hilson, made her first appearance as a child of 5.

JOHNSON, Dr. Samuel (1709–84), the great English lexicographer, was the author of a five-act tragedy, *Irene*, which his friend and fellow townsman David Garrick produced at Drury Lane in 1749, with little success. After its failure Johnson never again essayed the stage, though he made more money from the proceeds of the third, sixth, and ninth nights of his play than by anything he had previously done. His edition of Shakespeare is valuable for the light it throws on the editor rather than on the author, since Johnson had little knowledge of Elizabethan drama or stage conditions, and was not temperamentally a research worker. He should not be confused with Samuel Johnson of Cheshire, author of *Hurlothrumbo* (1729) and other burlesques.

JOHNSTON, Henry Erskine (1777–1845), Scottish actor, who at 17 played Hamlet, with no training and no previous experience, at the Theatre Royal, Edinburgh. He then created a profound sensation as Young Norval, and was called the Scottish Roscius; unqualified adulation, which he had done little to deserve, much of his success being due to his youth and beauty, turned his head, and he suffered in after life from an excess of complacency. This prevented him from taking his work seriously, and he relied almost entirely on his external abilities to carry him through his parts. Leigh Hunt, who regretted seeing his good qualities going to waste, said of him that he was 'always on stilts'. He went to Covent Garden in 1797 and was the original Henry in *Speed the Plough* and Ronaldi in *A Tale of Mystery*. He was at his best in melodrama, where his graceful and effective acting made up for his lack of intelligence and humility.

JOHNSTON, (William) Denis (1901–), Irish dramatist of originality and versatility whose work has been received with interest in Ireland, England, and America. He is equally at home in direct delineation of character, essentially and distinctively Irish, the analysis of the conflicting moods of a difficult transition period (the years succeeding the war of 1922–3) and in the revelation of the more obscure territories of the mind bordering upon the unconscious, after the manner of Toller, Kaiser, and their forerunners. He has produced a good many plays, Continental and American, in Dublin and was at one time a director of the Dublin Gate Theatre (see IRELAND, 2). He has also written much broadcast drama and was well known as a war correspondent.

The first of his plays to be produced, *The Old Lady Says No!* (1929), is a satiric review of certain dominant elements in Irish life, thought, political history, and literature, and an acute exposure of the sentimentality inherent in some of them. The author has said that, for a non-Irish audience, the play 'requires in a sense to be translated', but this in fact cannot be done, for it is not knowledge of fact but association that is required to appreciate the significance of the social criticism in its rapid allusions. His second play, *The Moon in the Yellow River* (1931), earned wide popularity for the richness of its characters and the preciseness with which the author diagnosed the mood of the middle nineteen-twenties in Ireland. Though much of the material was so recent as to be used here for the first time, there was mastery and harmony in form and grouping. In *A Bride for the Unicorn* (1933) he produced one of the most original pieces of dramatic technique in modern English. The play, as he expressly states, is 'not an expressionist or constructivist drama'. If it suggests a preceding dramatist at all, it is Strindberg at the period of *The Dream Play*, but in general it appears rather to carry dramatic technique towards that of music. *Storm Song* (1934) is, like *The Moon in the Yellow River*, a straightforward play on an original theme. Later plays are *The Golden Cuckoo* (1939) and *The Dreaming Dust* (1940), to which must be added *Blind Man's Buff* (1936), from Toller's *Die blinde Göttin*, *Strange Occurrence on Ireland's Eye* (1956), and *The Scythe and the Sunset* (1958). UNA ELLIS-FERMOR†

JOHN STREET THEATRE, the first permanent playhouse of New York. It was opened by David Douglass in Dec. 1767, and is described in some detail by Dunlap in his *History of the American Stage*, where he says that its stage was equal in size to that of the Haymarket, London, under Colman. There is extant a print of the theatre dated 1791, now known to be a forgery. There is also a reference to it in *The Contrast*, performed at the John Street Theatre in 1787, where Jonathan, the country bumpkin, describes his first visit to the playhouse.

The first play to be given at the John Street Theatre was *The Beaux' Stratagem*, with the younger Hallam as Archer, and John Henry, making his first appearance in New York, as Aimwell. Up to the outbreak of the War of Independence the theatre was used intermittently for winter seasons by the old American Company under Douglass, and saw the first productions in New York of such plays as *The Merchant of Venice*, *Macbeth*, *King John*, *Every Man in His Humour*, and *All for Love*, as well as a large repertory of contemporary plays and after-pieces. During the war the playhouse was rechristened Theatre Royal, and was used for productions by the officers of the English garrison, among them Major John André—later the subject of a play by Dunlap—whose scene-painting was much admired. Just before the British evacuated New York a professional company under Dennis Ryan came from Baltimore and stayed for a time at the John Street Theatre, but without much success.

Two years after the British evacuation, in 1785, the American Company, now under the control of the younger Hallam and John Henry, returned to New York and took possession of the theatre again. The company was shortly afterwards reinforced by Thomas Wignell and the second wife of Owen Morris, who proved herself a fine actress. During the next few years the company gave regular seasons, and produced for the first time in New York *The School for Scandal*, *The Critic*, *Much Ado About Nothing*, and *As You Like It*. This theatre also saw the first productions of two works important in the history of the American drama—Royall Tyler's *The Contrast* (1787) and Dunlap's *The Father; or, American Shandyism* (1789). The American Company also gave a performance of Garrick's version of *Hamlet*, omitting the Grave-diggers and Osric, which had been done in London in 1772, but dropped after Garrick's death. Washington, who was fond of the theatre, visited John Street three times in the year of his inauguration (1789). On 6 May he saw *The School for Scandal* and a popular farce entitled *The Poor Soldier*, in which Wignell was much applauded as Darby; on 5 June he saw *The Clandestine Marriage*; and on 24 Nov. he attended Wignell's benefit night, and heard himself alluded to on the stage in *Darby's Return* by Dunlap.

After this Wignell and Mrs. Morris left the company to found one of their own (see CHESTNUT STREET THEATRE), and when the American Company returned to the John Street Theatre in 1791 a new period in its history was inaugurated with the arrival of John Hodgkinson. This actor, fresh from England, soon became so popular, and so grasping, that he ousted both Hallam and Henry from management and from the affections of the public. Henry and his wife withdrew from the company in 1794, Hallam in 1797, leaving Hodgkinson in command with Dunlap, who had been added to the management in 1796. The previous year had seen the first appearance with the company of the first Joseph Jefferson, who remained until 1803, when he went to Philadelphia.

In the autumn of 1797 Sollee, a theatre manager of Boston and Philadelphia, rented the John Street Theatre, and there entered on an intense rivalry with Wignell's company from Philadelphia, established for a season in Ricketts's Circus. In the company were Miss Arnold, later the mother of Edgar Allan Poe, and Mrs. Whitlock, sister of Sarah Siddons. In spite of this, the season was not a success, and the old company returned while waiting to move into their new Park Theatre, built by Dunlap. The theatre was used for the last time on 13 Jan. 1798, and was later sold by Hallam for £115.

JOLLY, GEORGE (*fl.* 1640–73), English actor, the last of the English strolling players who exerted so great an influence on the German theatre (see ENGLISH COMEDIANS). An entry in the St. Giles's parish register of the birth and death of his son John in 1640 suggests that he may have been employed at the Fortune Theatre near by, where Prince Charles's Men were playing at that time, and it is possible that he was apprenticed to Matthew Smith, one of their outstanding members. He was certainly in Germany in 1648, and may have gone there earlier to escape the rigours of the Commonwealth. He was particularly active in Frankfurt, where Prince Charles (later Charles II) probably saw him act. He appears to have anticipated Davenant's use of music and scenery on the public stage, and already had women in his company in 1654. He returned to England at the Restoration, and in spite of the monopoly granted to Killigrew and Davenant, got permission to open a theatre. He went to the Cockpit, where the French theatre historian Chappuzeau saw him in 1665, but by some chicanery on the part of Davenant and Killigrew he was deprived of his patent, and had to content himself with the overseeing of their training school for young actors, the Nursery.

JOLSON THEATRE, NEW YORK, see CENTURY THEATRE, 2.

JONES, HENRY ARTHUR (1851–1929), English dramatist, born at Grandborough, Buckinghamshire, the eldest son of a farmer of Welsh descent. At the age of 12 he was sent to work in a draper's shop kept by his uncle at Ramsgate. Six years later, after a spell with another draper at Gravesend, he found employment in a London warehouse, and subsequently became for ten years a commercial traveller in the London, Exeter, and Bradford districts, his leisure being devoted to private study and widely varied reading. After the rejection of several one-act plays as well as a novel, Jones's *It's Only Round the Corner* was performed at the Theatre Royal, Exeter, in Dec. 1878. Thus encouraged, he abandoned business for playwriting, and on 16 Oct. 1879 *A Clerical Error* was put on at the Court Theatre in London by Wilson Barrett, who afterwards had one of his most successful parts as Wilfred Denver in *The Silver King* by Jones and Henry Herman, produced at the Princess's on 16 Nov. 1882. The run of 289 performances of that melodrama established Jones's reputation. He then turned to plays with a more serious intention, but there continued to be a strong melodramatic current in his work, even though his contemporaries accepted him as one of the new school of dramatists who in the closing decades of the century were propagating the drama of ideas and using the stage as a platform for social criticism. Among Jones's very numerous pieces, public attention was attracted chiefly by *Saints and Sinners* (1884), *The Dancing Girl* (1891), *The Case of Rebellious Susan* (1894), *The Triumph of the Philistines* (1895), *Michael and His Lost Angel* (1896), *The Liars* (1897), and *Mrs. Dane's Defence* (1900). Beerbohm Tree, Charles Wyndham, Forbes-Robertson, George Alexander, Fred Terry, Marion Terry, Violet Vanbrugh, Julia Neilson, and Sybil Thorndike appeared with success in first productions and revivals of Jones's works. The withdrawal of Mrs. Patrick Campbell from the role of Audrie Lesden before the opening performance at the Lyceum on 15 Jan. 1896 of *Michael and His Lost Angel* was symptomatic of the wide antagonism provoked by that play, which was withdrawn after ten performances, mainly on account of the church scene in which the priest, standing before the altar, makes public confession of adultery, after having some years before exacted a similar penance from a girl member of his congregation.

With Pinero and Bernard Shaw, Henry Arthur Jones was one of the three most considerable playwrights in the period when Ibsen's influence was penetrating the English theatre, but there is no reason to doubt Jones's insistence that he was not a conscious disciple of Ibsen. Ibsenism was in the air and established a climate of opinion to which all serious and would-be serious playwrights were susceptible through either attraction or repulsion. Though Shaw praised Jones at the expense of Pinero in the 1890s, on the ground that he drew faithful portraits of men and women in society whereas Pinero merely flattered them with reflections of their own imaginings, the verdict of time on Jones's plays has been harder. His exceptional skill in naturalistic dialogue and in the creation of dramatic tension remains impressive (in these respects Act III of *Mrs. Dane's Defence* is a classic fragment), but his social and moral criticism lacked a firm philosophical basis. Towards the end of his life he ventured rashly upon sustained controversy with Bernard Shaw and H. G. Wells. He was also the author of *The Renaissance of the English Drama* (1895), *Foundations of a National Drama* (1913), and *The Theatre of Ideas* (1915).

JONES, Inigo (1573–1652), English architect and artist, and the first to be associated with scenic decoration in England. Before his day the designing and decorating of Court masques had pertained to the Office of the Revels, who employed for the purpose any artist who happened to be about the Court. Jones, having studied in Italy and worked in Denmark, was in 1604–5 attached to the household of Prince Henry, and, in addition to his work as an architect, took entire control of the masques. Of the thirteen given at Court from 1605 to 1613, nine were certainly of his devising, the others probably, the first being Jonson's *Mask of Blackness*. He was also in charge of the plays given at Oxford in Christ Church Hall in Aug. 1605, where he first used revolving screens in the Italian manner. He later used as many as five changes of scenery, with backcloths, shutters, or flats painted and arranged in perspective. These ran in grooves and were supplemented by a turn-table (*machina versatilis*) which presented to the audience different facets of a solid structure. Jones also introduced to England the picture-stage framed in the proscenium arch. His increasing power and responsibility brought him into conflict with the Court poets, particularly Jonson, who satirized him in many of his plays. The smouldering hostility between them broke out under Charles I. During the Civil War Jones was heavily fined, fell out of favour, and died in poverty. Many of his designs have been preserved in the library of the Duke of Devonshire at Chatsworth (see Nos. 61, 144).

JONES, Joseph Steven (1809–77), American actor and author, creator of a number of Yankee characters, of whom Solon Shingle in *The People's Lawyer* (1839) was the most popular. It was played by Hill, Charles Burke, and John E. Owens, the last making his final appearance in it in New York in 1884. The Honorable Jefferson S. Batkins, another Yankee character, in *The Silver Spoon* (1852), was first played by William Warren at the Boston Museum, and the play survived until well into the twentieth century. Jones wrote a number of other plays, some of them wildly improbable melodramas, and was for a time manager of the Tremont Theatre, Boston, where he had made some of his earliest appearances on the stage.

JONES, Margo (1913–55), American director and producer, founder of an experimental theatre in Dallas. After an academic education from which she emerged with a degree in psychology, she turned to the theatre which she had loved since childhood, and after studying at the Southwestern School of the Theatre in Dallas she worked with the Ojai Community Players, and at the Pasadena Playhouse in California. In 1939 she was associated with community and university drama in Houston, Texas, and in 1943 she staged an early play by Tennessee Williams, *You Touched Me*, at the Cleveland Playhouse. Two years later she established the theatre which will always be associated with her name in Dallas. Here she encouraged the work of new playwrights, and gave experimental productions of older plays, which she has described in her book, *Theatre-in-the-Round*, published in 1951. Her work was first seen on Broadway in 1945, when she directed, with Eddie Dowling, Tennessee Williams's *The Glass Menagerie*. Later productions included *Summer and Smoke*, *Joan of Lorraine*, and *Southern Exposure*. She died at the height of her powers, and her early death was a great loss to the American theatre, which she had sought to revitalize, on and off

Broadway, both by her own abounding energy and by a new approach to the problems of staging plays.

JONES, RICHARD (*fl.* 1590–1615), English actor, who was with the Admiral's Men from 1594 to 1602, and had probably been an actor before he joined them. In about 1610 he went to Germany with Robert Browne, leader of the first company of English Comedians to become popular on the Continent, and remained there until a few years before his death (see ENGLISH COMEDIANS).

JONES, ROBERT EDMOND (1887–1954), one of the outstanding men of the American theatre. He was not only a scene-designer, but a writer, lecturer, director, and an all-round scholar and artist. It was said of him that his first designs (for the New York production of *The Man Who Married a Dumb Wife*, 1915) 'sounded the note that began the American revolution in stage scenery'. In his approach to the problems of stage design, he endeavoured to include all facets of the production, and this, particularly when he also directed the actors, as with *The Great God Brown* (1926) and *Othello* (1937), made his work memorable. He was associated with all the productions of O'Neill's plays, a number of Shakespeare productions, and such modern plays as *The Jest*, *The Lute Song*, *The Green Pastures*, and *Night Over Taos*. With Kenneth Macgowan he wrote a book entitled *Continental Stagecraft*, and he was also associated with him in the running of the Provincetown Players and the Greenwich Village Playhouse (see No. 87).

JONSON, BEN(JAMIN) (1572–1637), English dramatist, and one of the outstanding men of his day, possibly the only one who may claim to rank with Shakespeare. His life was eventful and he was several times in prison or in danger of imprisonment for his outspokenness. Much of his energy was consumed in literary wrangles—usually summarized as the 'war of the theatres'—with contemporary dramatists, most of whom, always excepting Shakespeare, he despised as uneducated hack-writers. He himself was at Westminster School, but was deprived of the university education his attainments warranted by the action of his stepfather, who apprenticed him to his own trade of bricklaying. Finding this intolerable, Jonson went soldiering in the Netherlands, and returned in about 1597 to connect himself with the London stage. As actor and part-author he was probably involved in the production at the Swan of the lost *Isle of Dogs*, a play which so incensed the authorities that they closed the theatres and put Jonson in prison. He is not henceforward found as an actor, but his first comedy, *Every Man in His Humour* (1598), had Shakespeare in its cast playing Knowell. It was followed by some fine satiric plays which left an enduring mark upon the development of English comedy. These include *Every Man Out of His Humour* and *The Case is Altered* (both 1599), and *Cynthia's Revels* (1600), done at Blackfriars by the Children of the Chapel. They also did *The Poetaster* (1601), in which Jonson vents his spleen on some of his contemporaries, ridiculing Marston as Crispinus and Dekker as Demetrius Fannius, while Horace represents Jonson himself. The play also contains a generalized criticism of actors, and a side hit at lawyers and soldiers respectively. It provoked a reply in *Satiromastix*, by Dekker, possibly with some help from Marston, with whom (and with Chapman) Jonson however collaborated in *Eastward Ho!* (1604). This again landed him in prison, owing to some reflections in it on James I's Scottish policy. He had already been in trouble over his first tragedy, *Sejanus* (1603), which the authorities judged seditious and full of popery.

Jonson's best work was done in the ten years from the production of *Volpone, or the Fox*, in 1606 to that of *The Devil is an Ass* in 1616, the failure of the latter causing his retirement from the public stage for some years. The intervening period saw the production of *Epicoene, or the Silent Woman* (1609), *The Alchemist* (1610), a second tragedy, *Catiline* (1611), and the farcical *Bartholomew Fair* (1614), whose slight plot strings together a number of scenes laid in a typical London holiday crowd. The first three of these plays are those which have been most frequently revived in recent years, *Volpone* having almost a permanent place in the repertory of Donald Wolfit, and providing one of his best parts. In 1945 Guthrie produced *The Alchemist* in modern dress at the Liverpool Playhouse with some success, and again at the Old Vic in 1962. In 1947, also at the Old Vic, Alec Guinness gave an excellent performance as Abel Drugger (a part which was a favourite with Garrick). *Bartholomew Fair* was seen at the Old Vic in 1950, and in an open-air student production from Oxford at Stratford-upon-Avon in 1959. The only other production in this century was that by the Phoenix Society in 1921, the first recorded since 1731.

It was not until 1625, when he had lost Court patronage, that Jonson again wrote for public presentation, with the four comedies, *The Staple of News* (1625), *The New Inn* (1629), *The Magnetic Lady* (1632), and *A Tale of a Tub* (1633). These were not on a level with his previous works and are little known. There is, however, a further aspect of Jonson's dramatic work which cannot be ignored—the fine series of Court masques, an entertainment which in his hands reached the summit of its excellence, foreshadowing Milton's *Comus*, and to which he added the anti-masque, often a scene of Aristophanic comedy. Jonson had already introduced a masque into *Cynthia's Revels* with some success, and on the strength of it hoped to become Court poet, a position temporarily filched from him by Daniel. His genius was not to be withstood, however, and between 1605 and 1612 he was responsible, with the collaboration of Inigo Jones (see No. 144) on scenic design and costume, for some eight Court masques. The young Prince

Henry appeared in the title-role of one of these —*Oberon, the Faery Prince*—shortly before his death in 1611.

It has been said of Jonson by his great critic and editor, C. H. Herford, that he is 'probably the most signal example in literature of power without charm. He impresses, without greatly attracting, posterity; and his dominating position in the contemporary theatrical world was won in the teeth of hostile currents of opinion which almost always had a germ of reason on their side. . . . Jonson's services to English comedy were beyond question great, though his very reforms contained an element of decadence and tended to hasten its decay.' In person he was arrogant and quarrelsome, a good fighter but a staunch friend, warm-hearted, fearless, and intellectually honest. His merits are best summed up in the epitaph by one of his contemporaries, 'O rare Ben Jonson'.

JORDAN, Dorothy [Dorothea] (1761–1816), English actress, supreme in the realm of comedy, and, as Byron said, superlative in hoyden, or high-spirited tomboy, parts. She was the illegitimate daughter of an actress, Grace Phillips, and a gentleman, Francis Bland, and was originally billed as Miss Francis, since the Bland family had made her mother an allowance for some time on condition that the children did not use their father's name. When the allowance ceased, Dorothy's brother George took his father's name (see BLAND).

Mrs. Jordan's first recorded appearance was at the Crow Street Theatre, Dublin, on 3 Nov. 1779, in *The Virgin Unmasked*, and she was first billed on 20 May of the following year, when *The Governess* was given for O'Keefe's benefit. She was a great success, especially in breeches parts, and sang interpolated songs in most of the plays to great applause. In 1780 she was engaged by Daly for Smock Alley Theatre, but in 1782, after being seduced by him, she left secretly and fled to England with her mother and sister. Here she was befriended by Tate Wilkinson, who had acted with her mother in Dublin, and he agreed to give her a trial. She changed her name to Jordan, some say at the suggestion of Wilkinson himself, and on 11 July 1782 appeared at Leeds as Calista in *The Fair Penitent*, continuing to appear at the theatres in Wilkinson's circuit up to, and after, the birth of her first child (Daly's) at the end of the year. While playing at York during race week she had the good fortune to be seen and admired by 'Gentleman' Smith of Drury Lane, who was later responsible for her move to London. There she was engaged by Sheridan to play second to Mrs. Siddons, who had thought poorly of her on a visit to Hull. In spite of the preference of audiences at that time for tragedy, Mrs. Jordan chose to make her first appearance at Drury Lane as Peggy in *The Country Girl*, which she did with great success on 15 Oct. 1785. This became one of her most celebrated parts, and Leigh Hunt has left an excellent description of her in it in his preface to Wycherley's works. Realizing that her true métier lay in comedy, she wisely abandoned tragedy, and continued to delight her audiences in such parts as Priscilla Tomboy in *The Romp*, in which Romney later painted her, Miss Hoyden in *A Trip to Scarborough*, Sir Harry Wildair in *The Constant Couple*, and Miss Prue in *Love for Love*.

During her early years at Drury Lane Mrs. Jordan became entangled with a young man named Richard Ford, who promised marriage at some future date, but baulked after several years of intimacy, during which she bore him four children. In 1791 she at last left him to become the mistress of the Duke of Clarence, later William IV, by whom she had ten children, continuing to act, however, intermittently, either in London or on tour. She was one of the company which performed Ireland's Shakespeare forgery, *Vortigern and Rowena*, in 1796, and in 1800 she appeared as Lady Teazle. She was painted by Hoppner as the Comic Muse, and by Chalmers as Sir Harry Wildair. In 1811 she was separated from the Duke, to whom she had proved a faithful and affectionate companion, and the last years of her life were overshadowed by anxiety about her children and financial difficulties. Her last appearance in London was at Covent Garden on 20 April 1814, when she played in *Debtor and Creditor*, a new play, and in a revival of *As You Like It*, and in August of the following year she made her final appearance, at Margate. She was then involved in the financial ruin of her son-in-law, Edward Marsh, who had married one of her Ford daughters, and fled to France, where she died. Her grave in Paris vanished during rebuilding in the early 1930s.

JORNADA, the name given in Spain to each division of a play, corresponding to our act. It probably comes from the Italian *giornata*, found occasionally in the *sacre rappresentazioni*. The word in its present form was first used by Torres Naharro: 'The division (of comedy) into five acts is in my opinion not only good, but absolutely necessary, although I call them *jornadas* (and not acts) because they seem resting-places more than anything else.' After some initial experiments, Lope de Vega finally established the three-act *comedia*, the standard secular dramatic form of the late sixteenth and seventeenth centuries.

JOSEPH, Stephen (1921–66), actor and producer, and the leading exponent in England of theatre-in-the-round. Son of the actress Hermione Gingold, he trained at the Central School, where he was later on the staff, and then served in the navy. On coming down from Cambridge in 1948 he became producer at the Lowestoft Repertory Theatre, and then obtained a degree in drama from the State University, Iowa. In 1955 he formed the Studio Theatre Club, which gave Sunday performances in London, for the express purpose of presenting plays old and new 'in the round'. Later, basing his company on

Scarborough, he toured theatreless towns in the neighbourhood, making occasional appearances in London, usually at the Mahatma Gandhi Hall. He was the author of the booklet, *Planning for New Forms of Theatre*, which deals with the end stage (as at the Mermaid) and the three-sided stage (as at Chichester) as well as theatre-in-the-round or arena stage. In 1962 he was appointed to the first Fellowship in Drama at the newly organized Department of Drama at Manchester University, a post which involved both teaching and research. Meanwhile his former winter seasons at Newcastle-under-Lyme were abandoned for a permanent home at Stoke-on-Trent, where the old Victoria Theatre was adapted to his needs.

JOUVET, Louis (1887–1951), French actor and producer, and one of the most important figures of the French theatre in the years before the Second World War. He had already had some experience of acting and management when, in 1913, he joined Copeau's Théâtre du Vieux-Colombier as actor and stage manager. In both capacities he proved invaluable, his best work being done in Shakespeare, as Aguecheek and Autolycus. Jouvet went with Copeau to America in 1917–19, and in 1922 left him to establish his own theatre. After several tentatives he settled at the Comédie des Champs-Élysées, going in 1934 to L'Athénée, to which he added his own name. He joined the staff of the Conservatoire in 1935, and a year later was appointed one of the producers of the Comédie-Française. To Jouvet goes the honour of having first shown to the public the plays of Jean Giraudoux (see No. 104) in which he gave some of his finest performances, as well as being responsible for some excellent décor, where his own methods of lighting proved a revelation. In 1939 he published a volume entitled *Réflexions du comédien*. He had a passion for Molière, which amounted almost to an obsession, and one of his finest parts was Géronte in *Les Fourberies de Scapin*. He was also responsible for the success of Romains's *Knock, ou le Triomphe de la médicine*, which he produced, playing the chief part himself, in 1923.

JUDAEO-SPANISH DRAMA, see JEWISH DRAMA, 7.

JUDEU [António José da Silva] (1705–39), see SOUTH AMERICA, 2.

JUGGLER is the lexicographer's nightmare. Many English dictionaries stress its strictly secondary meaning of deceiver, which may be implied in such phrases as *juggling with finance*, or *juggling with words*. What it means in everyday life is explained by Hazlitt in his essay 'The Indian Jugglers', but who could reduce his opening paragraph into a phrase? During the First World War objection was raised to it in Germany as a foreign word; showmen who tried to replace it on their programmes could invent nothing better than the equivalent of 'knowing-how-to-play-at-throwing'. The juggler is not concerned with the conjurer's principle, 'the quickness of the hand deceives the eye'. When his quickness is not noticed by the eye, his effects are spoilt. To keep balls or clubs or plates or batons passing through the air from one hand to the other is the most familiar of his feats, and the expert wishes his audience to observe how many more of these objects he keeps moving than his less dexterous rivals. What were once known as the feats of the 'Balance Master', later called 'polandric tricks' owing to the success of the Little Polander over a hundred years ago, have become part of the repertoire of the juggler. Likewise 'Antipodean' displays on the soles of the feet while he lies on his back with legs in the air are often included in his performance, but only when inanimate objects are so balanced, rotated, or bounced. (If the bounced object is a child, this is known as a 'Risley' act.) Paul Cinquevalli, a favourite in British music-halls from the 1880s onwards, was a strong man and a humorist as well as a juggler. In popularity he was never surpassed, but Rastelli had greater skill in pure juggling. His experience was that British audiences were unable to observe the exceptional skill of his performances. Comedians who use simple feats to offset their humour have been credited with expert dexterity. Rich Hayes, who wore a Robinson Crusoe costume in a scene set to represent a tropical island, had both humour and uncommon skill. W. C. Fields used juggling as the medium for his humour on the halls before he became a film star. The accidental discovery on the Californian coast of the sea-lion's natural aptitude for catching things on his snout, and tossing and catching them in play, brought 'performing seals' into music-halls and circuses as rivals to the human juggler towards the end of the nineteenth century. M. WILLSON DISHER†

JUVARRA, Filippo (1676–1736), Italian architect who, while working in Rome in 1708, came to the notice of the influential Cardinal Pietro Ottoboni (1667–1740), a lover of plays and operas. For him Juvarra designed and built a small theatre (probably for rod-puppets) in his Palazzo della Cancelleria. Two designs for this are extant, and it is not known which was finally used. The theatre was demolished on Ottoboni's death, and no trace of it remains. There are, however, still in existence a number of scene-designs which Juvarra made for productions of opera there between 1708 and 1714, among them an album now at the Victoria and Albert Museum in London which has tentatively been identified as containing set-designs for the opera by Adami, 'Il Teodosio', produced in 1711 (see No. 66). Juvarra also designed sets for one or two other private Roman theatres, but his main work was for Cardinal Ottoboni, and after leaving Rome in 1714 he devoted himself entirely to civil and church architecture.

JUVENILE DRAMA, see TOY THEATRE.

JUVENILE LEAD, see STOCK COMPANY.

K

KABUKI, see JAPAN.

KACHALOV, VASILI IVANOVICH [SHVERUBOVICH] (1875–1948), Russian actor, and one of the original members of the Moscow Art Theatre. He studied at the university of St. Petersburg, and began his stage career as a super at the Suvorin Theatre. From 1897 onwards he worked in the provinces, where he played every kind of role from tragedy heroes to vaudeville ancients, until in 1900 he made his début at the Moscow Art Theatre, playing in *Tsar Feodor Ivanovich.* His talent was quickly recognized and he became a permanent member of the company, playing the leading roles in many of their outstanding productions, including Julius Caesar, Brand, Hamlet, Ivan Karamazov, Vershinin in *Armoured Train 14–69* and the Reader in the dramatization of Tolstoy's *Resurrection,* one of his best parts. Possessed of a fine voice and an excellent presence, Kachalov was one of the actors whose career marked the transition from Imperialist to Soviet Russia. For the revival of *Woe from Wit* by the Moscow Art Theatre in 1938 he again played Chatsky, the part he had taken in the same theatre's production in 1906.

KAHN, FLORENCE (1877–1951), American actress, wife of Sir Max Beerbohm. Born in Memphis, Tennessee, she first came into prominence as leading lady to Richard Mansfield. She later became a notable player of Ibsen's women, and was seen as Rebecca West, Mrs. Elvsted, the Strange Lady in *When We Dead Awaken,* and other parts. In 1908 she played Rebecca West at Terry's Theatre in London, giving an outstanding performance. It was then that she was first seen by Beerbohm, who was dramatic critic of the *Saturday Review.* He said of her:

> It is difficult to write about Miss Florence Kahn's impersonation of Rebecca; for it is never easy to analyse the merits of great acting.... Miss Kahn betrays the fact that she has a voice of great power and resonance, and a face that will eloquently express the soul.... In its appeal to the emotions, Miss Kahn's acting is not more remarkable than in its appeal to the sense of beauty.

They were married shortly afterwards, and Florence Kahn left the stage, but she made one of her rare reappearances as Åse in the Old Vic production of *Peer Gynt* in 1935.

KAINZ, JOSEF (1858–1910), German actor, famed for the richness and beauty of his voice, and the purity of his diction. He was trained with the Meiningen company and made his first appearance on the stage in 1874, in Vienna, where in 1899 he returned to end his days as a leading member of the Imperial Theatre. He was for some time in Munich, where he was the friend and favourite actor of King Ludwig II of Bavaria, and in 1883 played opposite Agnes Sorma in the newly founded Deutsches Theater in Berlin. He toured extensively in America, where he appeared in many of his best parts, which included Romeo, Hamlet, and the heroes of Grillparzer. He was also good as Tartuffe, Oswald in *Ghosts,* and Cyrano de Bergerac.

KAISER, GEORG (1878–1945), one of the most important German dramatists of modern times, and the leader of the so-called expressionist school of drama. His early plays, of which *Die jüdische Witwe* (1911) is typical, were satirical comedies directed against Romanticism. The First World War led him, however, to question the ethical foundations of a society blindly rushing to perdition, and his *Von morgens bis mitternachts* (1916) satirizes both the futility of modern civilization and the robot-like men who are caught in its meshes. This sombre history of a bank clerk whose bid for freedom led to suicide was followed by the powerful trilogy, *Gas,* Parts I and II, and *Die Koralle* (1920), a symbolic picture of industrialism crashing to destruction, and taking with it the civilization which it has ruined. Kaiser, whose other plays include the melodramatic *Der Brand im Opernhaus* (1919) and the historical drama *Die Bürger von Calais* (1914), had a great influence on the European and American theatres between the two wars.

KĀLIDĀSA, see INDIA.

KAMERI THEATRE, ISRAEL. This theatre (The Chamber Theatre) was founded in 1944 by Joseph Millo (1916–   ), who ran it until 1961, when he became artistic director of the newly opened Haifa Municipal Theatre, and was succeeded at the Kameri by Isaiah Weinberg. It began its activities with four actors, who formed themselves into a 'One-Act Play Group'. The venture not proving successful, an attempt was made to establish a Young People's Theatre, and finally the Kameri Theatre opened on 10 Oct. 1945 with Goldoni's *Servant of Two Masters.* This was followed by Čapek's *Insect Play,* and by Lorca's *Blood Wedding.* The Kameri Theatre had now embarked on the policy which has created a special niche for it in the Israeli theatre, namely, the breaking down of stylistic rigidity and the recognition that the purpose of a theatre is the provision of high-class entertainment. To this end it undertook the production of good contemporary international successes in Hebrew translations, and, since 1948, the production of original Israeli plays. In 1956 it appeared at the Théâtre des Nations in Paris in Moshe Shamir's *He Walked Through the Fields* (incidentally the first Israeli play to be produced by this group) and Brecht's *Good Woman of Setzuan* and in 1965 it achieved a great success there with Nathan Alterman's dramatization of Sammy Gronemann's *The King and the Cobbler*. E. HARRIS

KAMERNY THEATRE, Moscow. This theatre, whose name means Chamber, or Intimate, Theatre, was founded in 1914 by Alexander Taïrov, and rebuilt in 1930 with a seating capacity of 1,210. It was intended as an experimental theatre for those to whom the naturalistic methods of the Moscow Art Theatre and the conventional classics of the Maly no longer appealed. In it, particularly after the October Revolution, Taïrov sought to work out his theory of 'synthetic theatre', in which all theatrical arts and forms were to be fused into an organic whole. This, in contradiction to Meyerhold's 'conditioned theatre', where the actor was a puppet, made him the centre of everything, and demanded in his person an acrobat, singer, dancer, pantomimist, comedian, and tragedian. Although Taïrov's work caught and held the attention of the theatrical world outside Russia, he was not completely successful in Moscow until the production in 1934 of *The Optimistic Tragedy*, in which his wife, Alice Koonen, played the part of the heroine. The theatre then became important for its productions of non-Russian plays, providing a link with Western drama at a time when it was much needed. Taïrov even made the interesting if not entirely successful experiment of linking a version of Shaw's *Caesar and Cleopatra* with Shakespeare's *Antony and Cleopatra* in a single evening, with a fragment of Pushkin thrown in for good measure. Like other Moscow theatres, the Kamerny was evacuated during the Second World War, but returned with two new plays, *Moscow Skies* and *At the Walls of Leningrad*, and an imposing list of revivals, and in 1947 Taïrov gave a successful production of Jacobson's *Life in the Citadel*. After his death in 1950 the theatre was reorganized and its identity lost. Many of the company joined the newly opened Pushkin Drama Theatre, which replaced it.

KARAGÖZ, see TURKEY.

KARATYGIN, VASILY ANDREYEVICH (1802–53), famous Russian tragedian, son of an actor and producer at the St. Petersburg Dramatic Theatre. His father opposed his wish for a theatrical career, but he played with an amateur company at home and later at the Cadet College. His performance in a production of *Oedipus Rex* was so remarkable that he was invited to join the Imperial company. He refused, and continued his studies, finally making his début as a professional actor in May 1820, as Fingal. All his life he was noted for the care with which he studied his roles, returning where possible to the original sources, and labouring for historical accuracy in costume and décor, though he was opposed to the realistic style of acting and the innovations of Shchepkin. In contrast to Mochalov he developed a subtle and calculated technique which enabled him to play the most varied roles, though his preference was always for classical tragedy. He was also much admired in the patriotic drama of the day, and the tradition of his personal style persisted on the Russian stage until modern times.

KARNO, FRED (1866–1941), a notable figure in the music-halls, whose 'Jail Birds' and 'Mumming Birds' will be remembered as the training-ground of many well-known stars, including Fred Kitchen, Harry Weldon, and Charlie Chaplin. Born at Exeter, he worked as a child in a Nottingham factory, and then became a plumber's boy. His real name was Wescott. With two friends he went on the halls as an acrobatic turn billed as the Karno Trio. But his most original contribution to music-hall history was the elaboration of the 'sketches' or wordless plays mentioned above. Karno ruined himself in an attempt to popularize a Thames-side resort under the name of Karsino, and started life again in trade, but not before he had left his mark on the history of the music-hall, and, through Charlie Chaplin, on the cinema. W. MACQUEEN-POPE†

KASPERLE, see AUSTRIA.

KATAYEV, VALENTIN PETROVICH (1897–), Soviet dramatist, who was born in Odessa, the son of a school-teacher. He took part in the Civil War, and since 1922 has lived in Moscow. His most successful play, which has been produced in many countries, was *Squaring the Circle*, an amusing comedy about two ill-assorted married couples who, owing to the housing shortage, are compelled to live in one room and finally change partners. It was produced at the Moscow Art Theatre in 1928 under Nemirovich-Danchenko, and was done in English in 1938 at the Mercury in a translation by N. Goold-Verschoyle. Katayev is the author of a number of other plays, mostly light-hearted comedies like *The Blue Scarf*, an amusing trifle about a soldier at the front who receives a blue scarf from a bundle of comforts, and is all prepared to fall in love with the youthful donor, only to discover when on leave that it is a schoolboy. This was produced in 1943, in the rear of the front line. In 1946 a dramatization of his novel *Son of the Regiment* was well received at the Central Children's Theatre, and in 1951 an earlier play, *Lone White Sail*, was revived. Another play based on a novel, *All Power to the Soviets* (1954), which deals with the defence of Odessa, was successfully given at the Moscow Art Theatre. Katayev writes extensively on theatre problems.

KATONA, JÓZSEF (1791–1830), Hungarian dramatist, author of a number of historical dramas dealing with Hungarian history, and of an important play, *Bánk Bán* (*The Viceroy*), which is concerned with Hungary's eternal problem, the national attitude to the foreign ruler.

KAUFMAN, GEORGE S. (1889–1961), American journalist and dramatist, whose first plays were written in collaboration with Marc(us) Cook Connelly (1890–), the most successful being *Beggar on Horseback* (1924), in which a satire upon existing conditions is worked out in a dream-sequence. Their collaboration then ended, and Kaufman alone wrote *The Butter and Egg Man* (1925), a clever farce, but otherwise insignificant, while Connelly wrote the fine negro play, *The Green Pastures* (1930). Kaufman then wrote a number of light-hearted plays which include several collaborations with Moss Hart (1904–1962), among them *Once in a Lifetime* (1930), *Merrily We Roll Along* (1934), *You Can't Take It with You* (1936), *I'd Rather Be Right* (1937), and *The Man Who Came to Dinner* (1939), a portrait of Woollcott in which Woollcott himself appeared on tour. Kaufman, who was known as 'the Great Collaborator', was also the author, with Edna Ferber, of *The Royal Family* (1927), a play of the theatre based apparently on the lives of the Drews and the Barrymores, and done in England as *Theatre Royal.* An expert technician and an excellent director, Kaufman had a keen sense of satire and a thorough knowledge of the theatre.

KAYE, DANNY (1913–), American actor and entertainer, who began his career at the age of 15, performing in resort hotels in New York State. Two years later he toured the United States and Asia in a road-company revue. He made his first appearance on Broadway in *The Straw Hat Revue* (1939), and in 1941 was acclaimed for his success in the part of Russell Paxton in *Lady in the Dark*, which starred Gertrude Lawrence. In the same year he played Jerry Walker in *Let's Face It.* He first appeared in London in 1938, playing in cabaret at the Dorchester Hotel. He attracted little attention then, but on his return in 1948 to play at the Palladium, where he also appeared in a Variety Command Performance, he was hailed as one of London's favourite artistes. He is highly thought of for his untiring work on behalf of the United Nations International Children's Emergency Fund, and since 1954 has made a number of world-wide trips, inspecting medical and nutritional facilities, and entertaining children in all countries. The filmed record of his travels, *Assignment: Children*, has won international recognition, and he is perhaps even better known for his work in films than for his stage career.

KAZAN, ELIA (1909–), American actor and director, born in Turkey of Greek parents. His first appearance on Broadway was at the Martin Beck Theatre, in 1932, when he played Louis in *Chrysalis* for the Group Theatre, for whom he subsequently played Agate Keller in *Waiting for Lefty* (1935) and Eddie Fuselli in *Golden Boy* (1937). This latter part he also played on his first appearance in London a year later. In 1940 he played Ficzur (the Sparrow) in a revival of *Liliom.* Kazan, who has also had a distinguished career as a producer of films, has been responsible for the direction of a number of outstanding plays, including *The Skin of Our Teeth* (1942), *Deep Are the Roots* (1945), *A Streetcar Named Desire* (1947), *Death of a Salesman* (1949) (see No. 106), *Cat on a Hot Tin Roof* (1955), and *J.B.* (1958). In 1959 he directed *Sweet Bird of Youth.* In association with Cheryl Crawford, Lee Strasberg, and Robert Lewis, with whom he had been associated in the Group Theatre, he founded in 1947 the Actors' Studio, as a workshop where professional actors could experiment and study their art. He worked closely with the Studio until 1962, when he was appointed co-director of the Lincoln Center Repertory Theatre, a position he resigned in 1965 (see LINCOLN CENTER).

KEAN. (1) EDMUND (1787/90–1833), English tragedian, who appeals more strongly to the imagination than almost any other actor. The sympathy excited by his sufferings and the glamour of his meteoric success are dangerous to critical judgement. He should not be set above Garrick, whose wide range he lacked; nor should Kemble, exponent of virtue, suffer by false comparison with the exponent of villainy. Kean's was the fierce flame of crime exultant, and the true contrast is with Irving's baleful glow of crime repentant. To separate fact from fiction in Kean's life seems wasted labour. What is known to be true is so bizarre that legends cause no astonishment. The fantastic novels of his time had no stranger hero. The mysterious circumstances of his birth have been described in a biography by Giles Playfair. Was he descended, as Macaulay declared, from George Savile, Marquis of Halifax? The story, more easily believed than disbelieved, is that Halifax's natural son, Henry Carey, passed on the spark of genius to George Savile Carey, whose daughter Anne inherited little more than the wildness in their blood. At 15 she turned strolling player. As a hawker in London she caught the eye of Aaron Kean—architect, tailor, or stage carpenter—who took just enough interest in her to tell her friends when she was with child so that they should find clothes and take her to George Savile Carey in Gray's Inn. They had—supposing we may believe their story that she was the mother—only her word for it that Kean was the father. No record of the birth (Hawkins's date is 4 Nov. 1787) has been found and nothing is known of 'Master Carey's' infancy until he was found in a doorway by a kindly pair who brought him up in Frith Street, Soho. Soon Anne Carey dragged him off to be a wage-earner, and he posed as Cupid in a Covent Garden ballet. Fantastic stories of his infancy on the stage cannot be ignored; they chime with known facts. At length he found a guardian in Moses Kean, once a tailor, now a mimic and ventriloquist, the brother of Aaron. Anne Carey's friend, Miss Tidswell, also helped in gaining for the boy the freedom of the stage, which meant that he was given expert training in dancing, fencing, singing, and acting by its generous spirits. Well-meaning people adopted him and dropped him. Instinctive vagabondage drew him to the fairs. As 'The Pupil of Nature' he was a successful infant prodigy before he had to face the bitter trials of a strolling player, tramping the country with his wife, two small sons (until the elder died), and 'props' for their performance. On 26 Jan. 1814 he played Shylock at Drury Lane discarding the traditional red wig and beard which even Macklin had not dared to alter. The audience acclaimed the genius of his performance, and Hazlitt recorded it for posterity. The technical novelty of his acting is revealed in the statement that by-play was one of his greatest excellences; he relied less on his voice, so harsh that at times it 'creaked', than on facial expression. In spirit the change was still greater. While Kemble was 'the statue on the pedestal that cannot come down without danger of shaming its worshippers', Kean was deficient in dignity, grace, and tenderness; his acting was not of the patrician order. He was 'one of the people, and what might be termed a *radical* performer'. These were contemporary comments. At this distance of time a more vital difference becomes plain. That Kemble excelled in nobility and virtue was evident in all his favourite parts, from Hamlet and Coriolanus to Earl Percy and Rolla. That Kean failed when he tried to assume such qualities, or when he essayed suffering innocence, was admitted. There had to be a touch of the malign, of murderous frenzy, to inspire him. His Lear caused very considerable disappointment. As Romeo he stood beneath Juliet's balcony like a lump of lead. His Hamlet, no 'sweet prince', showed a severity amounting to virulence. Abel Drugger, Garrick's favourite comic part, he played but three times. As for polished comedy, he would have none of it. When offered the part of Joseph Surface he returned it 'with the just indignation of insulted talent'. Mild villainy made no appeal to him. At his first London appearance as a star he caused the vast, half-empty auditorium of Drury Lane to vibrate with the shouts of those who now saw Shylock as a swarthy fiend with a huge butcher's knife in his grasp and blood-lust in his eyes. Richard Crookback and Iago were the finest performances of this 'little ill-looking vagabond' magnetized by an anarchy of passions. Even his magnificent Othello was 'too often in the highest key of passion, too uniformly on the verge of extravagance, too constantly on the rack'. As Macbeth he was heart-rending. On coming to himself after the murder, his voice clung to his throat at the sight of his bloody hands. Two of his greatest masterpieces were Sir Giles Overreach, with his ruthless frenzy of miserliness, in Massinger's *A New Way to Pay Old Debts*, (see No. 165), and that barbarous fiend, Barabas, in Marlowe's *Jew of Malta*.

Biographers who whitewash Kean must surely miss the clue to his art and his character. His spirit was untamably wild. Unpublished diaries kept by Winston, Elliston's house-manager at Drury Lane, give a day-to-day account of uncouth exploits. The scandal caused by Kean's amour with the wife of Alderman Cox turned playgoers against their idol, but not before his frequent non-appearances had forfeited their respect. He played Othello at Covent Garden on 25 Mar. 1833 to the Iago of his son. 'I am dying—speak to them for me' he moaned as he fell into Charles Kean's arms. His wife came to his house at Richmond, and they were reconciled before he died on 15 May 1833. He was buried in Richmond Old Church in a vault difficult to discover. On the church wall is a memorial with a medallion portrait set up by his son. This son, (2) CHARLES JOHN (1811–68), was sent to Eton with the idea of detaching him from the stage, but Drury Lane engaged him at the time of his father's break both with that theatre and with his home. Father and son acted together finally on that memorable occasion referred to above. With his wife, (3) ELLEN TREE (1806–80), Charles rose to the head of his profession at the Princess's Theatre, 1851–9, where he set his stamp upon a style of management which lasted for the rest of the century. Praises of Charles's style in 'gentlemanly melodrama' have tended to damn him as an actor, but his place in theatre history cannot be ignored. Following in the wake of Charles Kemble, he set and costumed his productions, whether of *Macbeth* (see No. 72), *Pizarro*, or *Sardanapalus*, lavishly but with some semblance of historical accuracy. This, and his staging, had an important influence on the development of the Meininger company, whose director, George II of Saxe-Meiningen, was familiar with Kean's work through his visits to London with his first wife, a niece of Queen Victoria (see MEININGER COMPANY; also No. 167). M. WILLSON DISHER†

KEAN, THOMAS (*fl.* mid-eighteenth century), manager of a troupe which in 1749 acted *Cato* and other plays in a converted warehouse in Philadelphia, later the home of Hallam's company. Kean, who was partnered by Walter Murray, also took his troupe to New York in 1750 and, in a theatre in Nassau Street, gave a number of plays which included *Richard III*, *Love for Love*, *The Orphan*, and *George Barnwell*. From there he went to Virginia with a company of comedians, who played in Williamsburg. No information is available at present about the composition of Kean and Murray's company, or about the exact status of its members, who may have been amateurs acting for pleasure, or the first professional players of the New World. Nor is anything known of their history after 1752–3.

KEDROV, MIKHAIL NIKOLAYEVICH (1893–1972), Russian actor and producer, a leading authority on Stanislavsky, who occupied the Chair of Acting at the Moscow Art Theatre Teaching Studio for many years. He was a pupil of Stanislavsky, whose works he edited, and he spent his whole life in the service of the Moscow Art Theatre, accompanying the company to London in 1958, and being responsible for the production of the *Uncle Vanya* seen during that season at Sadler's Wells. Among his many other productions for this theatre was *The Winter's Tale*, which was three years in rehearsal.

KEELEY. (1) ROBERT (1793–1869), English actor, who ran away from his apprenticeship to join a strolling company in Richmond. His early days are obscure, but in 1818 he was at the Olympic, and later at the Adelphi, where he made a hit as Jemmy Green in *Tom and Jerry*, and played Jerry in the sequel, *Life in London*, at Sadler's Wells in 1822. In later years he was a fine low comedian, his stolid look and slow, jerky speech adding much to the humour of his acting. Dickens said of his Dogberry:

> The blunders of the old constable fell from his lips with the most immovable and pompous stolidity. . . . As we write, we see again the wonderful expression of his face at the supreme moment when he was called an ass. No other catastrophe on earth . . . could have aroused in living man such an amazing exposition of stupendous astonishment, indignation, and incredulity, as that insult wrung from Dogberry as Keeley drew him. But his Verges was even finer.

He was also a master of pathos and, Dickens continues, 'our most delightful memories of him are connected with characters into which, by a few words or a little touch, he threw a certain homely tenderness quite his own'. Among his most famous parts were Jacob Earwig in *Boots at the Swan* and Sairey Gamp. He was, however, somewhat overshadowed by the excellence of his wife, (2) MARY ANN GOWARD (1806–99), who was trained as a singer and appeared in 1825 at the Royal Opera House, London (later the Lyceum). She soon took to the stage, however, and had already made a name for herself when in 1829 she married Keeley, and thereafter appeared with him. She was a small, neatly-made person, at her best in pathetic, appealing parts like Nydia in *The Last Days of Pompeii* and Smike in Stirling's adaptation of *Nicholas Nickleby*. But her greatest part was the title-role in *Jack Sheppard*, in which the highwayman was portrayed as a wild youngster, defrauded of his heritage and driven to bad ways by the animosity of Jonathan Wild the thief-taker. From 1844 to 1847 the Keeleys managed the Lyceum; they were with Charles Kean and Webster at the Haymarket, and for five years played at the Adelphi. Mrs. Keeley retired on the death of her husband, whom she survived by thirty years. She had two daughters of whom one, Mary, married the humorist and entertainer, Albert Smith. The other, (3) LOUISE (1833–77), was on the stage from childhood, and in 1857 was Toole's leading lady in London and on tour. She married the dramatist Montague Williams, most of whose work was done in collaboration with Burnand. Louise played with Irving in the provinces, and was responsible for his first appearance in London under Harris's management at the Princess's. A niece of the Keeleys, (4) LYDIA ALICE LEGGE (1844–92), was also on the stage, as Lydia Foote, and proved herself a good actress, particularly in pathetic parts.

KEENE, LAURA (?–1873), actress and theatre manager, born in England. The date of her birth has been variously given as 1820, 1826, 1830, and 1836, and her real name may have been Moss, Foss, or Lee. She is said to have been trained for the stage by an aunt, Mrs. Yates, and to have made her first appearance at the Richmond Theatre, Surrey, as Juliet on 26 Aug. 1851. If this was so, it seems likely that she was born in 1830 or 1836 rather than earlier. Shortly after her first appearance she was seen at the Olympic, and in 1852 she went to New York on her way to tour Australia. She returned there in 1855 and spent the rest of her life in the United States, where she was the first woman to become a theatre manager. On 18 Nov. 1856 she opened her own theatre, a beautiful playhouse with a white and gold interior, upholstered in gold damask. The first production was *As You Like It*, in which she herself played Rosalind, supported by a good company. She remained at this theatre until 1863, and but for the outbreak of the Civil War might have continued to flourish. She presented good foreign and American plays with a well-balanced stock company, eschewing the destructive practice of importing visiting stars, and among her actors were Joseph Jefferson and Sothern. The latter finally brought the theatre an outstanding success in 1858 with *Our American Cousin*, whose long run, in the opinion of Odell, established New York as the metropolitan theatre centre of the United States. By July 1861 Laura Keene's was the only theatre open in New York, owing to the war, but she was forced to lower her standards and give poor, showy spectacles. She never recovered her prestige or buoyancy and, leaving genuine comedy to the newly established Wallack's Theatre, she relied more and more on melodrama and spectacle. Her last season opened in 1862, and in the autumn of the following year the theatre reopened under Mrs. John Wood (for its subsequent history, see OLYMPIC, 3). Laura Keene, who was a good melodramatic actress and an excellent manager, continued to tour, and was seen at most of the important theatres of New York, but never again attained the heights of her previous management. Her company was playing *Our American Cousin* at Ford's Theatre, Washington, on the night Abraham Lincoln was assassinated there, 14 Apr. 1865.

The Fourteenth Street Theatre, formerly the Théâtre Français, was known as the Laura Keene from 1871 to 1873, but its history is negligible.

KEENE, THOMAS WALLACE (1840–98), American actor, whose real name was Eagleson. He started his career at the Old Bowery Theatre, and made his first success while with Hackett. He toured England and the United States in support of most of the outstanding stars of the time, and from 1875 to 1880 was in the stock company at the California Theatre, where he proved his value during the engagement of Edwin Booth. He then went on tour as Coupeau in *Drink* with much success, and was seen up to the time of his death in a varied repertory, Richard III being one of his best parts. A big, florid man, of a kindly and quiet nature, he had little liking for modern plays or methods, and was somewhat old-fashioned in his acting, being most popular in the smaller and less sophisticated cities.

KEITH, BENJAMIN FRANKLIN (1846–1914), American theatre manager, who as a young man was connected with Barnum's and other circuses. He then took small shows on the road himself, and in 1883 began a long career as a vaudeville promoter. He was first active in Boston, where he inaugurated the original 'continuous performances', and eventually had a chain of popular-priced vaudeville theatres throughout the country. He paid good salaries, engaged good actors, and endeavoured to raise the standard of vaudeville and its working conditions.

KELLY, FRANCES MARIA (1790–1882), English actress and singer, who made her first appearance on the stage at the age of 7, with her uncle Michael Kelly, composer and singer, at Drury Lane. In 1800 she played Arthur in *King John* and the Duke of York in *Richard III* with great success. As an adult actress she revived some of the parts associated with Mrs. Jordan, and was for thirty-six years a favourite at Drury Lane, making occasional appearances elsewhere. In 1812 she acted with Kean at the newly built Drury Lane, being seen as Ophelia to his Hamlet. She also played leading roles in contemporary melodrama. On her retirement she endeavoured to found a school for the training of actresses, and built a theatre in Soho, later the Royalty, for this purpose. It was not, however, a financial success, and after several years of struggle and hardship she fell heavily into debt and lost her theatre. She then confined her activities to Shakespeare readings and the tuition of private pupils. She is the subject of the essay 'Barbara S——', by Charles Lamb, who was in love with her, proposing marriage in a letter of 20 July 1819.

KELLY, GEORGE (1887–), American dramatist, who gave the American stage a number of penetrative and austerely moralistic plays. Kelly entered the theatre when he became a vaudeville actor at the age of 21. His first full-length play, *The Torchbearers* (1922), was a satire on the pretentiousness of amateur theatricals. Two years later, he expanded his vaudeville skit *Poor Aubrey* into the comedy *The Show-Off* (1924), a hilarious satire on braggart philistinism as exemplified by the pompous success-worshipper Aubrey Piper. Next Kelly turned to the subject of home and marriage in the Pulitzer Prize-winner, *Craig's Wife* (1925), a relentless exposé of feminine possessiveness and lovelessness. The less successful *Daisy Mayme* (1926) was another study of selfishness, and applied the scalpel to an indulgent man's relatives. After writing an unimportant series of musical skits, the playwright composed the curiously moralistic drama *Behold the Bridegroom* (1927), in which a flighty 'modern' woman is punished with the contempt of her bridegroom, the first man she ever really loved. In *Maggie the Magnificent* (1929) Kelly treated the theme of integrity of character with unattractive coldness, and *Philip Goes Forth* (1931) exposed the limitations of a would-be playwright who fails to escape from the vulgar business world and becomes a phenomenally successful salesman. When this play failed, its author withdrew from the theatre, to which he returned unsuccessfully with *Reflected Glory* (1936), the comedy of an actress who makes a lame attempt to leave the stage The discouraged playwright again retired from the theatre and was not heard from until he produced *The Deep Mrs. Sykes* (1945), a penetrative, if rather crabbed, satire on the follies of feminine 'intuition'. It was followed by *The Fatal Weakness* (1946), a knowing if not altogether unsympathetic treatment of feminine romanticism, in which a wife loses her husband when she becomes sentimentally absorbed in his romance with another woman.

JOHN GASSNER†

KELLY, HUGH (1739–77), English writer, whose sentimental comedy, *False Delicacy* (1768), was done by Garrick to offset Goldsmith's *Good-Natured Man* at the rival theatre, which it eclipsed for a short time, though it is now forgotten. It was played in the provinces, several times revived, and translated into French and German. Kelly wrote several other plays, of which *The School for Wives* (1773) was the least sentimental and almost approached the true spirit of the comedy of manners.

KEMBLE, a famous family of English actors, of whom the first, (1) ROGER (1722–1802), was a strolling actor-manager, formerly a hairdresser. He married Sarah, the daughter of a provincial manager named Ward, who outlived him by five years, dying in 1807 at an unknown age. With her, Roger toured the country, his company being soon augmented by his numerous children, of whom the eldest became the great Sarah Siddons and is dealt with under her own name. Roger's eldest son, (2) JOHN PHILIP (1757–1823), after a childhood spent on the stage, was sent to Douai to train for the priesthood, his father being a Roman Catholic. He abandoned his studies to return to the theatre, but not before he had acquired a certain habit of severity and asceticism which never left him. He became a stately, formal actor, at his best in heavily dramatic parts, and after several years in the provinces he made his London début at Drury Lane in 1783 as Hamlet, in which character he was painted by Lawrence. He gave an unusual reading of the part which at first puzzled the audience, but later captivated them by its gentleness and philosophy. Hazlitt, who had not at first appreciated him, spoke later of 'the sweet, the graceful, the gentlemanly Hamlet. . . . Later actors have played the part with more energy . . . but Kemble's sensible, lonely Hamlet has not been surpassed.' During his long career Kemble steadily improved, and the great tragic parts became linked with his name —Wolsey, the Stranger, Rolla, Brutus, Cato, and above all Coriolanus, in which he took leave of the stage on 23 June 1817. He was successively manager of Drury Lane and of Covent Garden, causing the O.P. Riots at the latter theatre when he raised the prices of admission after the disastrous fire of 1808 in which he and his sister Sarah suffered heavy personal losses. In 1787 he married Priscilla Hopkins (1755–1845), herself an actress and widow of the actor William Brereton (1751–87). Her parents, Elizabeth and William Hopkins, were both on the stage, the latter acting in Edinburgh and the provinces before coming to London in 1761 to appear at Drury Lane, where he later worked as prompter till his death in 1780. His wife died in 1801 at a great age. She was proud of having been a member of Garrick's company in her early years. Kemble had a short and not very happy retirement. His years in management had not been a success financially, and he was forced to part with his fine library, the Duke of Devonshire buying his collection of old plays. Much troubled by gout, he went abroad and finally died in Lausanne. He had been a great actor in the grand manner, with no unexpected bursts of pathos or passion, but a steady and studied intensity of feeling. Walter Scott said of him that he was 'great in those parts where character is tinged by some acquired and systematic habit, like stoicism or misanthropy; but sudden turns and natural bursts of passion are not his forte'. He was ideally handsome, but had a harsh voice and laboured breathing, and his movements and gestures were stiff and unyielding. His somewhat pedantic approach to his work made him unfit for comedy, which he rarely attempted, and Lamb seems to have been the only critic who liked his playing of Old Comedy. It was said of him that 'even in his most convivial hours he was solemn and funereal'—a legacy of his priestly studies, no doubt. When he first took over Drury Lane from Sheridan he introduced a number of important reforms, both in the management of the theatre and in costumes and scenery. He was also responsible for the introduction of spectacular shows, with real animals and aquatic effects. He did much to improve the status of his profession, however, and on the whole his influence was salutary, (for a portrait of the Kemble family, see No. 164).

His younger brother, (3) STEPHEN (1758–1822), who married the actress Elizabeth Satchell (1763–1841), was born practically on the stage, his mother having just finished the part of Anne Boleyn. He played as a child in his father's company, became a chemist, returned to the stage when his sister Sarah became famous, and was always overshadowed by his elder brother. With reference to his great girth, which in later life enabled him to play Falstaff without padding, it was said that Covent Garden had the big, and Drury Lane the great, Kemble. Stephen had a somewhat roving life, being manager of a provincial company, of a theatre in Edinburgh, and of a company in Ireland. In 1818 he returned to manage Drury Lane, with little success, and retired after introducing his son Henry as Romeo. The latter soon sank to the Coburg and was heard of no more. Stephen also had a daughter, Frances Crawford (1787–1849), who began her career under her father's management. In 1805 she married the son of Sir Richard Arkwright and retired from the stage.

The youngest of the Kemble children was (4) CHARLES (1775–1854), who after the usual itinerant childhood became a civil servant, but left his job to return to the stage. At 17 he played Orlando at Sheffield, and first appeared in London as Malcolm in John Philip's revival of *Macbeth* for the opening of the new Drury Lane Theatre. He was not at first successful on the stage, being somewhat awkward, and having a weak voice. But in time he became an accomplished player of such parts as Mercutio, Mirabell, Orlando, Young Absolute, Charles Surface, Benedick, and Romeo, which was considered his best role. Poetic rather than emotional, he was quite unfitted for tragedy, which he wisely left to his elders. He adorned the English stage for some 25 years, and was the first to endeavour to bring some historical accuracy into costume and setting (see No. 150). He then retired, troubled by increasing deafness, to give Shakespeare readings and to become Examiner of Plays, a post which he held until 1840. In private life he was affable and much liked, and in America, which he visited in 1832, he was considered a typical 'English gentleman'. He married, in 1806, (5) [MARIA] THERESA (or Marie Thérèse) DE CAMP (1773–1838), an actress who had been a leading dancer at the Royal Surrey. She first appeared at Drury Lane in 1787, and in her twenty years on the stage created two parts always associated with her, Edmund in *The Blind Boy* and Lady Elizabeth Freelove in *The Day after the Wedding*, which she wrote herself. She was also good as Madge Wildfire in *The Heart of Midlothian*, and in all parts in which pantomime was needed. Her brother Vincent was manager in 1830 of the Montreal Theatre. He died in Texas in 1839. Her sister Adelaide, singer and actress, went to America with Charles's company in 1832, and died in Boston two years later.

Charles's daughter, (6) FRANCES ANNE (1809–93), usually known as Fanny, had no particular desire for a theatrical career, but in 1829 she appeared at Covent Garden in order to save her father, who was then managing the theatre with little success, from bankruptcy.

She was an immediate success, and for three years filled Covent Garden, bringing prosperity to everyone connected with it. She was first seen as Juliet following this with Lady Teazle, Portia, Beatrice, and Bianca, as well as with Mrs. Siddons's great parts, Isabella, Euphrasia, Calista, and Belvidera. Unlike the other members of the Kemble family, Fanny appears to have been equally at home in tragedy and comedy. She was also the original Julia in *The Hunchback*. In Sept. 1832 she went with her father to America, and was received everywhere with acclamation. She left the stage in 1834 to marry Pierce Butler of Philadelphia, but the marriage proved unhappy, and she divorced him in 1845. For some time she travelled with her sister, the singer Adelaide Sartoris, and in 1857 began a series of popular readings in England and the U.S.A. She gave the last in New York in Oct. 1868 and then settled with her daughter in London and died there. In her youth she was a most beautiful girl, with dark eyes and hair, a wistful expression, and a slender, graceful figure. In later life her face retained its beauty, but with the added charm of a mature and thoughtful cast of countenance.

Fanny's nephew, (7) HENRY (1848–1907), for whose education she made herself responsible, was also on the stage, making his first appearance at Dublin in 1867. He was for some years in the provinces, playing old men and character parts, and in 1874 he first appeared at Drury Lane. He was later with John Hare at the Court Theatre, and had a long association with the Bancrofts. He made his last appearance shortly before his death, in Apr. 1907. A short, stout man, he was an excellent comedian, particularly in strong character-parts, and an amusing and much-loved companion.

Three of Roger Kemble's daughters were also on the stage, Elizabeth (1761–1836) becoming well known, as Mrs. Whitlock, in America, where she first appeared in 1794. Her sister Anne, later Mrs. Hatton, settled in New York and became poetess to the Tammany Society. She was the author of an operatic spectacle entitled 'Tammany', done at the John Street Theatre on 3 Mar. 1794. Dunlap has left a description of it, and the songs and scenario have been preserved. Henry Mason, who with his sons John Kemble and Charles Kemble, played at the Park Theatre, New York, in 1835, married Jane Kemble, Roger's youngest daughter; their daughter married a scene-painter named Henry Hillyard.

KEMP, ROBERT (1885–1959), outstanding French dramatic critic, whose whole career was spent in journalism of the best kind. He was first attached to *L'Aurore* (1909), and after the First World War became music and drama critic of *Liberté*, transferring in 1929 to *Le Temps*, where he devoted himself entirely to drama. He was also Reader of Plays to the Comédie-Française, and wrote a number of books on music and the drama. After the Second World War he was responsible for dramatic criticism in *Le Monde*. In 1956 he was elected a Member of the French Academy.

KEMP, THOMAS CHARLES (1891–1955), dramatic critic, who from 1935 until his death was on the *Birmingham Post*, where his work was characterized by impartiality, sound scholarship, and good judgement. His criticisms, even when unfavourable, were generous and penetrating. He was born in Birmingham, and became an important figure in its theatrical life, being for some time chairman of the Crescent Theatre. He wrote several plays for the company there, and was active in Shakespearian and dramatic activities, as lecturer and writer, both in Birmingham and at Stratford-upon-Avon. He was a great admirer of Sir Barry Jackson, and of the work of his theatre, which he celebrated in a volume published in 1944 (*Birmingham Repertory Theatre: the Playhouse and the Man*), and he collaborated with J. C. Trewin in a history of the Shakespeare Memorial Theatre, *The Stratford Festival* (1953). He contributed a number of articles to the first edition of this Companion.

KEMPE, WILLIAM (?–1603), a famous Elizabethan clown, the original Dogberry in *Much Ado About Nothing*, and a great player of jigs. He was a member of the company which went with the Earl of Leicester to Holland in 1585–6, and was at the Danish Court in Elsinore in the latter year. His reputation in London was already made by 1590, and he became one of the Chamberlain's Men on the formation of the company in 1594, remaining with them until 1600, in which year he danced his famous morris from London to Norwich. He then went to the Continent, but returned, and in 1602 is noted in Henslowe's diary as having borrowed some money. He may then have been with Worcester's Men at the Rose.

KENDAL. (1) WILLIAM HUNTER [really GRIMSTON] (1843–1917), English actor-manager, who made his first appearance on the stage on 6 Apr. 1861. He played in the provinces for some years, appearing with the Keans, G. V. Brooke, and Helen Faucit, and was a member of the Glasgow stock company. In 1866 he was engaged by Buckstone for the Haymarket, where he remained for eight years, playing leading parts in Shakespeare, Sheridan, and Gilbert. It was here that he married (2) DAME MADGE [MARGARET] ROBERTSON (1848–1935); and from then on his career is inseparable from that of his wife. The twenty-second child of an actor-manager, and sister of the dramatist T. W. Robertson, she was on the stage from her early years, and had already made a name for herself before her marriage. She then went with her husband on tour and to the Court Theatre under John Hare, where by the excellence of her acting she gave a new lease of life to the old play *A Scrap of Paper*. With the Bancrofts at the Prince of Wales's she played Dora in *Diplomacy*, and appeared with Kendal in a revival of *London Assurance*. The Kendals then went into partnership with Hare at the St. James's and played leading parts in many notable productions, Kendal being somewhat overshadowed by the brilliance of his wife, but proving himself a fine actor and a good business man. His last years were uneventful and he retired in 1908, as did his wife. He was better in comedy than tragedy, and one of his finest parts was Frank Maitland in *The Queen's Shilling*. His wife was also a fine comedienne, but she could on occasion play in a more gentle mood, as witness her success in *The Elder Miss Blossom*, a play which she frequently revived and took on tour. Clement Scott said of her in this part: 'We . . . can recall no creation at once so delicate, sympathetic and faultless as Dorothy Blossom. The artist speaks in every line, gesture, and movement. She has humour, change, variety; and when she wants to touch the human heart she crushes it with an infinite tenderness and truth.' In 1926 Mrs. Kendal was made Dame Commander of the British Empire and in 1927 received the Order of the Grand Cross (G.B.E.). She and her husband were long held up as a pattern of partnership, both on the stage and in their private lives, and with Sir Squire and Lady Bancroft did much to raise the status of the acting profession. The companies with which they were connected were admirably managed, and proved an invaluable training-ground for many young actors and actresses.

KESTER, Paul (1870–1933), American playwright, whose first play, *The Countess Roudine*, was produced by Minnie Maddern Fiske in 1892. Kester's wide knowledge of European languages proved of great value to him when he came to adapt plays by foreign authors, which, in accordance with the practice of his time, he did prolifically. Among his original plays his first great success was *Sweet Nell o, Old Drury* (1900), done first in London by Fred Terry and Julia Neilson and later in the United States by Ada Rehan. It was taken on tour to Australia and the Far East, and often revived. Many of Kester's plays were written for particular players of the period, including Salvini, Janauschek, Julia Marlowe, Mrs. Langtry, Marie Tempest, E. H. Sothern, Margaret Anglin, and others, and some of the most successful—*Guy Mannering*, *When Knighthood was in Flower*, *Dorothy Vernon of Haddon Hall*, *Lady Dedlock*, *Don Quixote*—were based on novels. Kester was fond of romantic and picturesque plots, and his hobby was the study of gipsy lore.

KHMELEV, Nikolai Pavlovich (1901–1945), Soviet actor and producer, who joined the Moscow Art Theatre in 1919, where his first role was Fire in *The Blue Bird*. Here he subsequently played many important parts, including Firs in *The Cherry Orchard* and Tusenbach in *Three Sisters*. He also worked at the Second Studio and was a producer at the Yermolova Theatre, of which he became director in 1937. In 1943, on the death of Nemirovich-Danchenko, Khmelev replaced him at the Moscow Art Theatre. Among his productions there were *The Russian People* and a revival of Ostrovsky's *The Last Sacrifice*, while at the Yermolova Theatre he directed a production of Fletcher's comedy, *The Woman's Prize; or, the Tamer Tamed*.

KILLIGREW. (1) Thomas (1612–83), English dramatist, theatre manager, and, from the death of Sir Henry Herbert in 1673, Master of the King's Revels. He had already written several plays before the closing of the theatres in 1642, among them *Claricilla*, *The Princess*, and *The Prisoners*, all tragicomedies. Another, *The Parson's Wedding*, based on Calderón and first given in 1640, was revived in 1664 with a cast of women only and made even Pepys blush. It is not, however, as a dramatist that Killigrew ranks high in the history of the English theatre, but as a manager and administrator. He founded the present Drury Lane Theatre, as the Theatre Royal or the King's House, under a Charter from Charles II. With Davenant, holder of a Charter for the Duke's House, later transferred to Covent Garden, Killigrew held the monopoly of acting in Restoration London, and after a brief sojourn in a converted tennis-court in Vere Street, he opened the first Theatre Royal with a fine company, which included Mohun, Hart, and, for a short while, Nell Gwynn. The theatre was burnt down in 1672, but two years later a new theatre, designed by Wren, was ready for occupation. In it the company formed by the amalgamation of the two existing companies played from 1682. Killigrew also established a training school for young actors at the Barbican. He was, according to Pepys, 'a merry droll', and a great favourite of Charles II. He was not so good a business manager as Davenant, and was often in financial difficulties. His brother, (2) Sir William (1606–95), and his son, (3) Thomas (1657–1719), both wrote plays, while another son, (4) Charles (1665–1725), took over the management of the Theatre Royal in 1671, assisted by his half-brother Henry, and became Master of the Revels on his father's death.

KINCK, Hans (1865–1926), Norwegian dramatist, author of a number of scholarly plays on Italian subjects, and of a two-part drama which is sometimes compared to *Peer Gynt* (see SCANDINAVIA, 2 *a*).

KING, Tom (1730–1804), English actor, member of Garrick's fine Drury Lane company, and the original Sir Peter Teazle (see No. 30), and Puff in Sheridan's plays. At 17 he was a strolling player with Ned Shuter, and first appeared at Drury Lane under Garrick in Oct. 1748. He was ready to turn his hand to anything, but he was not suited to tragedy, and, deciding to confine himself entirely to high comedy, he went to Dublin, worked under the elder Sheridan, and returned a finished comedian. His Malvolio and Touchstone were both admirable, but it was as Lord

Ogleby, in *The Clandestine Marriage*, a part written for Garrick and refused, that he made his mark. He made his last appearance on the stage which he had so excellently served in 1802, again as Sir Peter. Hazlitt wrote a fine appreciation of him. 'His acting left a taste on the palate sharp and sweet like a quince. With an old, hard, rough, withered face like a sour apple, puckered up into a thousand wrinkles... he was the real amorous, wheedling or hasty, choleric, peremptory old gentleman... and the true, that is pretended, clown in Touchstone.' He amassed a great deal of money, but a passion for gambling, and an unfortunate venture into management of the Bristol and Sadler's Wells Theatres, caused him to die poor.

KING OF MISRULE, see MISRULE.

KING'S CONCERT ROOMS, LONDON, see SCALA THEATRE.

KING'S HOUSE, see DRURY LANE.

KING'S MEN, see CHAMBERLAIN'S MEN.

KING'S THEATRE, LONDON, see QUEEN'S THEATRE, I.

KINGSLEY, SIDNEY (1906–), American dramatist, who made his mark as a meticulous artist, social critic, and democratic idealist. After graduating from Cornell University in 1928, and a brief acting career, he wrote his first play, *Men in White*, in 1930. Produced in 1933, it won the Pulitzer Prize. It deals with an interne's wavering between private distractions and the exalted vocation of medical science, and provided a vivid picture of hospital life. The economic depression of the 1930s moved Kingsley to write *Dead End* (1935), a bleak but provocative study of crime-breeding slum conditions. His *Ten Million Ghosts* (1936) excoriated the international munitions cartels that had profited from the First World War. *The World We Make* (1939), a dramatization of a novel by Millen Brand, gave a moving account of a neurotic rich girl's discovery of comradeship and hope among the poor. Kingsley won the New York Drama Critics' award with *The Patriots* (1943), a chronicle of the formative years of American democracy in which Thomas Jefferson and Alexander Hamilton compound their differences in order to defend the nascent republic. Kingsley also wrote a powerful indictment of excessive righteousness in his *Detective Story* (1949), and dramatized Arthur Koestler's anti-Communist novel, *Darkness at Noon* (1951).

JOHN GASSNER†

KINGSTON [KONSTAM], GERTRUDE (1866–1937), English actress and theatre manager, for whom Bernard Shaw wrote *Great Catherine* (1913). She made her first appearance, after some amateur experience, in 1887, with Sarah Thorne's company in Margate, and a year later was seen in London at the Haymarket under Tree. After a long and varied career she built the Little Theatre in John Street, London, and opened it with *Lysistrata* in 1910, intending to make it a home of repertory. The venture was not an outstanding success, but her efforts, like those of Lena Ashwell at the Kingsway, later bore fruit in the establishment of the repertory system, mainly outside London. She then appeared in a number of plays by Shaw, including *Captain Brassbound's Conversion*, *The Dark Lady of the Sonnets*, and *You Never Can Tell*, and was several times seen in New York. She was the author of several plays, some of which she herself produced, and wrote a number of books, including a volume of reminiscences.

KINGSWAY THEATRE, LONDON. This opened on 9 Dec. 1882 as the Novelty Theatre, with a comic opera 'Melita; or, the Parsee's Daughter', and closed the same month. Renamed the Folies-Dramatiques, it opened again in 1883 with Nellie Harris's name on the bills. Ada Cavendish appeared there in a revival of *The New Magdalen*, and Willie Edouin, Lionel Brough, and others tried plays there, but all without success. In 1888 it was again renamed, this time the Jodrell, after a lady so called who sought theatrical fame. The Russian National Opera Company appeared there, and then the theatre, which had been renamed the New Queen's Theatre in 1890, and the Eden Theatre in 1894, remained closed for some time, until in 1900 Penley took it, reconstructed and redecorated it, and opened it as the Great Queen Street Theatre with *A Little Ray of Sunshine*, transferred from the Royalty, followed by a revival of *The Private Secretary*. But still no good fortune attended the theatre. In 1907 Lena Ashwell took it over, and after more reconstruction and redecoration it opened as the Kingsway on 9 Oct. with *Irene Wycherley*. This was successful, as were *Diana of Dobson's* and other plays that followed. Notable Kingsway productions were *The Great Adventure*, with Henry Ainley and Wish Wynne, in 1913, which ran for 673 performances, Granville-Barker's version of Hardy's *The Dynasts* in 1914, and a revival of *Fanny's First Play* in 1915. In 1932, when the theatre was under the management of Jay and Littler, a group of theatrical enthusiasts took it over, surrendered the Lord Chamberlain's licence, and made it into the Independent Theatre Club for the production of unlicensed plays. In spite of a distinguished beginning the venture was not a success, and the Kingsway resumed its career as an ordinary theatre. It suffered damage by enemy action in 1940–1 and was demolished in the 1950s.

W. MACQUEEN-POPE†

KIRCHMAYER, THOMAS (1511–63), German humanist and Protestant author, under the pseudonym of Naogeorg, of several anti-Catholic plays of which the most important is *Pammachius* (1538). It was written in Latin, in which language it was acted at Cambridge in 1545, and was translated into racy German for performance at Zwickau. It was later translated into English by John Bale of Ossory.

KIRKE, JOHN (?–1643), English actor who was at the Red Bull Theatre with Parry and Weekes, and later became one of Prince Charles's Men. He has been identified by W. J. Lawrence with the John Kirke who was a dramatist, since both men were attached to the Red Bull. His *Seven Champions of Christendome*, published in 1638, was given at the Red Bull and the Cockpit, and Herbert notes in his diary in 1642 that Kirke brought him two other plays; but this may have been in his capacity as bookholder, or as manager of the company. Kirke evidently ceased to act on the closing of the theatres, and may have gone into business.

KIRSHON, VLADIMIR MIKHAILOVICH (1902–1938), Soviet dramatist, and author, with Ouspensky, of a play dealing with the problems of Russian youth at odds with the new régime. This was produced at the Mossoviet Theatre in 1926, and later in America, as *Red Rust*, in a translation by V. and F. Vernon which was published in 1930. Though discursive, and somewhat melodramatic, it is an interesting study of a transitional epoch. It was, however, too superficial to be of lasting value, a criticism which seems to apply to all Kirshon's later plays.

KISFALUDY, KÁROLY (1788–1830), Hungarian writer and dramatist, author of several historical tragedies, also of a number of successful comedies in which he first introduced to the Hungarian stage the peasant types which afterwards became so popular. The Kisfaludy Society, named after him, is Hungary's most important literary society, and was responsible for the translation and editing of a complete edition of Shakespeare's plays published in 1864. The translations were done by Hungary's outstanding poets and writers, and are still in general use on the Hungarian stage.

KJAER, NILS (1870–1924), Norwegian dramatist, author of satirical comedies and plays on contemporary themes (see SCANDINAVIA, 2 *a*).

KLAW THEATRE, NEW YORK, on 45th Street between Broadway and 8th Avenue. It opened on 2 Mar. 1921 with Tallulah Bankhead, Katharine Cornell, and a fine supporting cast in *Nice People*. This was followed by William Hurlbut's *Lilies of the Field* and *Meet the Wife*, by Lynn Starling, while Henry Hatcher's *Hell-Bent for Heaven*, a mountaineering drama which won the Pulitzer Prize, was first seen at the Klaw for four matinées. In 1925–6 the Theatre Guild occupied this house with its Shavian double bill, *Androcles and the Lion* and *The Man of Destiny*. The theatre was later renamed the Avon, and on 15 Nov. 1931 Cornelia Otis Skinner appeared there in her monodrama, *The Wives of Henry VIII*, followed by Constance Collier and a fine cast in a revival of *Hay Fever*. The last legitimate production at this theatre was *Tight Breeches* (1934). It then became a broadcasting studio, and in Jan. 1954 it was pulled down. GEORGE FREEDLEY†

KLEIN, CHARLES (1867–1915), American dramatist. Born in London, he went to the United States at the age of 15, and was for some time an actor, his short stature enabling him to play juvenile parts. His first writing was done when he was asked to revise a play he was appearing in, but it was with *Heartsease* (1897) (not to be confused with Mortimer's version of *La Dame aux camélias*, done for Modjeska in 1880 under the same title) that he first came into prominence. Two later plays which had an enormous success were *The Auctioneer* (1901) and *The Music Master* (1904), both written for and produced by Belasco. They were quite trivial and unoriginal, and owed their success to the acting of David Warfield, for whom they were designed. Klein's later plays were mainly melodramas, which had a contemporary but ephemeral success. He was play-reader for Charles Frohman and was drowned with him in the sinking of the *Lusitania*.

KLEIST, HEINRICH VON (1777–1811), German dramatist, born of an East Prussian military family, who soon forsook the army for philosophy and literature. His first play, *Die Familie Schroffenstein* (1803), a gloomy fate-tragedy involving the destruction of two families, showed promise, but a more ambitious effort, *Robert Guiskard*, defied his powers, and he burnt the manuscript, of which only one beautifully written fragment survives. His best-known play, *Der zerbrochene Krug* (1808), is considered one of the finest comedies in the German language. In it a village magistrate with Falstaffian virtuosity in lying is made to try, in the presence of a visiting magistrate, a case in which he himself is the culprit. In its technique of progressive revelation in unbroken action it is a comic counterpart to *Oedipus Rex*. A similar form is used in *Penthesilea* (1808), a tragedy centring round the Amazon who, believing herself scorned by her lover Achilles, tears him limb from limb, and finds release only in death from the fatal dualism of her nature. Next came *Das Käthchen von Heilbronn* (1810), a study of a Griselda-like devotion in which supernatural and folk-tale elements are grafted upon the realistic medievalism of *Götz von Berlichingen*, but all imbued with Kleist's usual intensity. Here the continuous action of the earlier plays has given place to a Shakespearian interchange of verse and prose. By 1810 lack of recognition, and his own deep-seated pessimism and morbid introspection, had brought Kleist to the verge of suicide; only his ardent patriotism, at this dark period of Germany's history, stayed his hand while he completed *Die Hermannsschlacht*, dealing with the defeat of the Romans by the Germans under Arminius, but aimed at Napoleon, and *Prinz Friedrich von Homburg*, in which the hero, carried away by impulse, disobeys a military command in an hour of national peril, but by wise handling is brought to accept before execution the necessity of discipline.

W. E. DELP

Der zerbrochene Krug was produced by Goethe at Weimar, and has been translated into English, in a very much abbreviated form, as *The Broken Pitcher. Das Käthchen* was first seen at the Vienna Burgtheater. *Prinz Friedrich von Homburg*, in a French translation, was one of the outstanding successes of the Avignon Festival, with Gérard Philipe in the name-part. It has also been used for the libretto of an opera by Hans Werner Henze (1960).

KNEPP, MARY (?–1677), one of the first English actresses. She was trained by Killigrew and appeared under him at the first Theatre Royal. She was a friend of Pepys, in whose diary she often figures, usually as the source of back-stage gossip. According to him, she was a merry, lively creature, at her best in comedy. She was also much in demand for the speaking of the witty prologues and epilogues in which the fashion of the time delighted, and was a good dancer. She was a friend and fellow-player of Nell Gwynn.

KNICKERBOCKER THEATRE, NEW YORK, a large playhouse on the north-east corner of 38th Street and Broadway. It was long a favourite home of big musical shows, but it was opened on 8 Nov. 1893 as Abbey's Theatre by no less a person than Henry Irving, on his fourth visit to New York. With Ellen Terry, Kate Phillips, and William Terriss, he appeared there in Tennyson's *Becket*. Later stars who were seen at Abbey's were Coquelin, Lillian Russell, the Kendals, and Sarah Bernhardt, while Mounet-Sully as Hernani, Réjane as Madame Sans-Gêne, and John Hare in *The Notorious Mrs. Ebbsmith* with Julia Neilson and C. Aubrey Smith, all made their New York débuts at this theatre. On 14 Sept. 1896 the theatre was taken over by Al Hayman and re-christened, but it continued to offer hospitality to visiting stars, notably Wilson Barrett in his famous melodrama *The Sign of the Cross*, and Beerbohm Tree in *The Seats of the Mighty*. Among later interesting productions were Maude Adams in *L'Aiglon* and *Quality Street*, Ada Rehan in *Sweet Nell of Old Drury*, Otis Skinner in *Land of Heart's Desire*, and Rostand's *Chantecler* in a translation by Louis N. Parker. *Kismet*, which opened on Christmas Night, 1911, was an instantaneous hit and was followed by many successful musical shows, while in 1929 the Players selected the Knickerbocker for the revival of *Becky Sharp*, with a superlative cast. The last production at this famous theatre was *Sweet Land of Liberty*, by Philip Dunning, which opened on 23 Sept. and closed after eight performances. In 1930 the theatre was demolished. GEORGE FREEDLEY†

The Bowery Amphitheatre was called the Knickerbocker when for a short time in 1844 it was run as a theatre.

KNIGHT, JOSEPH (1829–1907), English dramatic critic and historian who wrote for the *Athenaeum* from 1867. We are indebted to him for detailed notices of the early work of Irving and Ellen Terry. Of Ellen Terry's performance as Pauline in *The Lady of Lyons*, at the Princess's Theatre in 1875, Knight wrote: 'One of the pleasantest, inasmuch as it is one of the rarest, tasks the critic is called upon to discharge is that of heralding to the world the advent of genius.' He had also a keen eye for the work of the Comédie-Française, and for the genius of Sarah Bernhardt.

Knight contributed many biographies of actors and actresses to the *Dictionary of National Biography*. A selection of his criticisms was published as *Theatrical Notes* in 1893. T. C. KEMP†

KNIPP, MARY, see KNEPP.

KNIPPER-CHEKHOVA, OLGA (1870–1959), see CHEKHOV (2).

KNOBLOCK [KNOBLAUCH], EDWARD (1874–1945), a dramatist who, though born and educated in the United States, spent much of his life in England and on the Continent. He was for a short time an actor, and had a thorough knowledge of the stage which he applied to the dramatization of novels with a skill which made him an admirable and reliable 'play carpenter' rather than an original dramatist. Of his own plays the most successful were *Kismet* (1911), an Arabian Nights fantasy done by Oscar Asche in England and Otis Skinner in New York and frequently revived, and *Marie-Odile* (1915), a tale of the Franco-Prussian war beautifully produced by David Belasco. Much of Knoblock's best work was, however, done in collaboration. With Arnold Bennett he wrote *Milestones* (1912), with Seymour Hicks *England Expects* (1914), with J. B. Priestley *The Good Companions* (1931), and with Beverley Nichols *Evensong* (1932), the last two from their novels. He also dramatized *Princess Priscilla's Fortnight* (1909), *Simon Called Peter* (1924), *Grand Hotel* (1931), and *Hatter's Castle* (1932). He translated a number of French plays, and in 1938 supervised the Irving Centenary Matinée at the Lyceum.

KNOWLES, JAMES SHERIDAN (1784–1862), member of a literary family and friend of Hazlitt, Coleridge, and Lamb, was successively attracted by the army, medicine, and the teaching profession before, in emulation of his cousin Sheridan, he turned his attention to the stage. At 24 he was in the company at the Crow Street Theatre, Dublin, where he proved himself a passable comedian and singer. His first play, a melodrama now lost, was written for Kean, who was in the same company. Knowles later wrote a tragedy, *Virginius*, for the same actor, who refused it, allowing Macready to triumph in the part in 1820. Knowles was a prolific dramatist, who interpreted his classic tragedies in the light of nineteenth-century domesticity, and was more concerned with his characters' feelings than with their actions. In his own day he was much admired, but nothing of his work has survived in performance. His most successful play was *The Hunchback* (1832), whose heroine, Julia, was a favourite part with many young and lovely actresses. He reappeared in this play after many years off the stage, playing Master Walter, a part in which he made his first appearance in New York in 1834. He was not, however, a good actor, and it is as a dramatist that he is remembered. Allardyce Nicoll, in *Nineteenth Century Drama*, says of him: 'If only Knowles could have escaped from melodrama on the one hand and from Elizabethanism on the other, he might have done something notable for the stage. As it is, many of his plays are but glorified tales of black evil and white innocence. . . . Success, in Knowles's work, is near, yet is not attained.'

KNOWLES, Richard George (1858–1919), an outstanding figure of the old music-halls, who billed himself as the 'very peculiar American comedian' (he was born in Canada). He started his career in a variety theatre in Leadville, Colorado, in about 1875, and then toured the smaller theatres. He was at the Olympic, Chicago, before going to New York, where he appeared in vaudeville, in plays, and in a minstrel troupe. In 1891 he went to London, and remained a firm favourite there until his death. He had a curiously quiet style, always wore a black frock coat, opera hat, and white duck trousers, and walked up and down across the stage. His best-remembered songs are 'Girlie, Girlie' and 'Brighton'.

KOCH, Frederick Henry (1877–1944), a university professor who is important in the history and development of the American theatre through his work with the Dakota and Carolina Playmakers. Like Professor George Pierce Baker, he introduced the serious study of playwriting and play production into the curriculum of the university student, but his main concern was with the 'folk-play' based on the regional life of the south. The Dakota Playmakers were founded in 1910, and did good work in the writing and production of plays on native themes, but it was with the Carolina Playmakers that Koch was able most fully to carry his ideas to fruition. The actors, drawn from the undergraduate body of the University of North Carolina, toured from Georgia to Washington, carrying their scenery and props with them, and produced plays, mainly in one act, written by themselves and their fellow students of the drama, on themes of Southern folklore, superstition, and local history. Although the acting of the students was less important than the plays they produced, which have been collected and published in several volumes, Koch's influence on the commercial theatre was probably greater than would at first appear, in spite of the fact that, unlike Baker, he did not aim to prepare playwrights for Broadway. But the first good plays about the Southern States, which began to appear about 1923, are probably due to him, and he can be credited with the training of at least one outstanding playwright, Paul Green, while the novelist Thomas Wolfe is also represented in the series of Carolina folk-plays. Nor should the influence of the Carolina Playmakers on the amateur and Little Theatres be forgotten, nor the impetus which Koch's work gave to the teaching of dramatics in American schools and colleges. Koch was also instrumental in founding and directing a Canadian school of playwriting at Banff, which has done interesting work.

KOCH, Heinrich Gottfried (1703–75), German actor, who in 1728 joined Caroline Neuber's company, and soon proved his value, being most versatile and adaptable. He was a good scene-painter, a good translator and adapter of plays, and a competent actor. He adopted the new style of acting which Gottsched and Caroline Neuber were sponsoring, and was particularly popular in classical comedy, which he had an opportunity of studying at its best when he frequented the performances of a French company in Strasbourg. He was also acceptable in tragedy as long as the declamatory style favoured by Caroline Neuber remained in fashion. One of his best parts was the title-role in *L'Avare*. After the break-up of the Neuber company he started on his own, quarrelling violently in the process with his old companion Schönemann, who had also broken away to start on his own. Some years later he took over the management of Schönemann's company, which included Ekhof, but after continual dissensions Ekhof left to join the Ackermanns. This gave Koch a free hand, and he continued steadily, in a quiet, old-fashioned way, gaining the respect of his audiences wherever he played, experiencing no great reverses of fortune and no spectacular successes. His actors, who included his wife, Christiane Henriette, *née* Merlick, the sister of his best tragic actor, were good. He treated them well, and was one of the few managers of his time, apart from Ackermann, to be esteemed generally. He travelled continuously, but made Leipzig his headquarters, where towards the end of his life he had the mortification of finding himself eclipsed by Döbbelin.

KOCH, Siegfried Gotthelf [really Eckardt] (1754–1831), German actor who, having served his apprenticeship in a number of small travelling companies, was engaged by Iffland at Mannheim in 1790 to replace Boeck in tragic parts. He did well, and became one of the outstanding members of the company, being particularly active on the administrative side. His daughter Betty, who later married an actor named Rose, or Roose, was also a good actress, and appeared at Mannheim as Iphigenia with much success.

KODOLÁNYI, János (1899–), see hungary.

KOMISARJEVSKAYA, Vera Fedorovna (1864–1910), Russian actress and producer, daughter of a well-known opera singer, Fyodor (1838–1905), who was one of the teachers of Stanislavsky, and sister of the producer Theodore Komisarjevsky (see below). She made her début in 1891 as Betsy in Tolstoy's *The Fruits of Enlightenment* in a production by Stanislavsky, and then toured the provinces. In 1896 she went to the Alexandrinsky Theatre, where she soon occupied a leading position. She played Nina in the first production there of *The Seagull*. The atmosphere of a Court theatre, however, was not to her taste, and she left to found her own theatre. There, in the midst of the social upheaval of 1905, she gave expression to the most advanced phases of Russian artistic life. Her early productions included plays by Gorky, Chekhov, and Ibsen. In the years of reaction which began in 1906 Komisarjevskaya came under the influence of the symbolists, and invited Meyerhold to produce in her theatre. Disagreeing with his attitude to the actor, whom he regarded as a mere puppet, she soon broke with him, and in her later years decided, like Duse, to leave the stage and become a teacher of dramatic art. In order to settle her theatrical debts she embarked on a last tour, during which she caught smallpox and died. She never appeared in England, but in 1908 she played a season at Daly's in New York. In spite of the excellence of her European repertory, and good critical notices, the venture was a financial failure. She was at her best in such parts as Gretchen (Margaret) in Goethe's *Faust*, Rosy in Sudermann's *The Battle of the Butterflies*, and Ibsen's Nora and Hedda Gabler. She was a woman of great charm, with a magnetic personality.

KOMISARJEVSKY, THEODORE [FEDOR] (1882–1954), brother of the famous actress Vera Komisarjevskaya (see above), and an outstanding personality in the European theatre of his time. Born in Venice, he was brought up in Russia, and gained his initial experience in the pre-Revolutionary theatre there, where from 1907 to 1919 he was a prolific producer of plays and operas, first at his sister's theatre, then at his own. In 1919 he came to England, where his productions had a remarkable influence which has become more apparent with the lapse of time. His first work was as a designer, and he first attracted general notice by his association with the production of Russian plays at the little Barnes Theatre in the 1920s. Although his best work was perhaps done in productions of and designs for Russian plays, particularly Chekhov, he was also responsible for a number of controversial productions of Shakespeare at Stratford-upon-Avon, notably *Macbeth* (1933), with its aluminium scenery and vaguely modern uniforms, and *The Merry Wives of Windsor* (1935), which took place against a Viennese background, with fairies wearing lighted candles on their heads. But it was with his *King Lear* (1936) that he finally won over his critics. In London he produced a wide variety of plays, including *Escape Me Never* (1933), *Magnolia Street* (1934), and *The Boy David* (1936). Disappointed at the poor reception of this last play, he went to America, where he remained until his death. He produced plays and operas there, and also in Paris and Italy. He was also the author of numerous books on the theatre, including one on theatrical costume, and one on Stanislavsky, whom he revered, but refused to follow slavishly. He was for a short time the husband of the English actress Peggy Ashcroft.

KOONEN, ALICE, see TAÏROV.

KORNEICHUK, ALEXANDER EVDOKIMOVICH (1905–72), Ukrainian dramatist, who started writing at an early age. The first play to bring him into prominence was *The Wreck of the Squadron* (1934), which dealt with the sinking of their fleet by the Red sailors to prevent its capture by the White Russians. It was first produced at the Red Army Theatre, and was awarded a prize in a nation-wide competition. This was followed by *Platon Krechet* (1935), the story of a young Soviet surgeon, and by *Truth* (1937), which shows a Ukrainian peasant led by his search for truth to Petrograd and Lenin at the moment of the October Revolution. Even more successful than these, however, was a historical play, *Bogdan Hmelnitsky* (1939), dealing with a Ukrainian hero who in 1648 led an insurrection against the Poles. Another play about his own country was *In the Steppes of the Ukraine* (1940), to which he later wrote a war-time sequel, *Partisans in the Steppes of the Ukraine* (1942). A war-play which has proved very popular is *The Front* (1943), while a satirical comedy, *Mr. Perkins' Mission to the Land of the Bolsheviks*, in which an American millionaire visits Russia to discover for himself the truth about the Soviet régime, was produced in 1944 by the Moscow Theatre of Satire. Later plays include *Come to Zvonkovo* (1946), *Makar Dobrava* (1948), an inimitable portrait of an old Donetz miner, and *The Hawthorn Grove* (1950). *Wings*, produced in 1954 by K. A. Zubov at the Maly Theatre, aroused great controversy at the time, but has now been accepted into the repertory, as have *Why the Stars Smiled* (1958) and *On the Dnieper* (1961).

KOSTER AND BIAL'S, NEW YORK, on 23rd Street. Originally the St. James's and Dan Bryant's Opera-House for minstrel and variety shows, this opened on 5 May 1879 as a concert hall. In 1881, after a distinguished musical history, it began to import outstanding vaudeville stars from abroad, and became a famous house of light entertainment. The original theatre closed on 26 Aug. 1893 and Koster and Bial moved to a site on 34th Street previously occupied by the Manhattan Theatre. There they successfully continued the policy of the earlier house until on 21 July 1901 the theatre finally closed, all the interior fittings being auctioned and the site sold to Macy's for their department store. GEORGE FREEDLEY†

KOTHORNOS, see GREECE, 6.

KOTZEBUE, AUGUST FRIEDRICH FERDINAND VON (1761–1819), German dramatist, who in his day was more popular than Schiller. From 1781 to 1795 he was a civil servant at St. Petersburg. Then followed several years devoted largely to drama and the theatre in Vienna. On his return to Russia he was arrested and sent for a time to Siberia, but was later released and became director of the Court theatre in St. Petersburg. On the death of his patron Paul I he went to Weimar, and after the downfall of Napoleon, whom he had denounced violently, he became Russian Consul-General in Königsberg. His antipathy to the Youth Movement at German universities earned him the hatred of the students, one of whom, Karl Ludwig Sand, a fanatic, stabbed him to death in 1819, an ending as melodramatic as in any of his plays.

Kotzebue, who was vain and injudicious, but by no means without literary gifts, had an unerring flair for what the public wanted, and gave it to them. He wrote over 200 plays, and his vogue, not only in Germany but all over Europe, was immense. The most successful of his plays was possibly *Menschenhass und Reue* (1789), in which an erring wife gains forgiveness from her husband, turned misanthropist, by a life of atonement. It now dates badly, but as *The Stranger* it was successfully translated and adapted for Drury Lane in 1798 by Benjamin Thompson, who did the same for a number of other plays by Kotzebue. Sheridan himself adapted *Die Spanier in Peru* in the following year, with much success, under the title of *Pizarro*. Kotzebue provided excellent parts for the great actors of his day, including Mrs. Siddons and Kemble in England, and his plays arrived in America by way of adaptations made by America's first professional dramatist, William Dunlap. A delightful skit on provincialism, *Die deutschen Kleinstädter* (1803), is the best of Kotzebue's comedies, and still provides entertainment, but on the whole he appealed to the grosser instincts of his audience, and cheapened the major virtues in his endeavour to provide thrills and excitement. His influence on the development of melodrama was unfortunate, tending to lead it further down the path of sensationalism, and as a result his plays, lacking any depth of feeling or literary grace, have disappeared with the fashion that gave them contemporary popularity.

KRASIŃSKI, Zygmunt (1812–57), Polish poet and playwright. The youngest of the three great Polish romantic poets—the others being Mickiewicz and Słowacki—he was probably the most enlightened and cosmopolitan of them all. Son of a noble family, he spent much of his time abroad. His masterpiece, *The Undivine Comedy*, written in 1833 but not acted until 1902, is a modern tragedy in poetic prose, dealing with an abortive revolution of 1832. Although his own sentiments were anti-revolutionary, the young author managed in a curious way to portray the situation impartially, and his work retains its actuality. An English version, by H. E. Kennedy, was published in 1924, and it has been acted in translation in Russia (1923) and Vienna (1936). Among Krasiński's other plays the most important is *Iridion*, written in 1836 and first acted in 1908, which was inspired by observations made at the Russian Court. In a third-century Roman setting, it shows the decadent but still powerful Empire triumphing over an internal revolution.

KRASNYA PRESNYA THEATRE, Moscow, see REALISTIC THEATRE.

KRAUSS, Werner (1884–1959), Austrian actor, who made his first appearance on the stage in 1904. He soon came to the fore, and appeared in Berlin and Vienna in many leading classical roles, including Macbeth, Richard III, Julius Caesar, King Lear, and in modern parts, among them the Crippled Piper in Reinhardt's *Miracle*, both in Germany and in New York, King Magnus in *The Apple Cart*, and Napoleon in *The Hundred Days*. He was seen in London in 1933 as Matthew Clausen in Miles Malleson's adaptation of Hauptmann's *Vor Sonnenuntergang*.

KROG, Helge (1889–1962), contemporary Norwegian dramatist, author of a number of fine plays (see SCANDINAVIA, 2 *a*).

KRONES, Therese (1801–30), Viennese actress. In her short life she rose, after a somewhat undistinguished début, to become the first woman genius of the Viennese popular theatre. Her father was a furrier of Freudenthal who turned actor. The family led a wretched existence with travelling companies in various parts of the Empire before settling in Vienna in 1809, when Hensler took pity on her father and engaged him for the Leopoldstädter Theater. Not until 1821 did Therese secure a contract there, having been discovered by Raimund, who saw her playing Ophelia at Oedenburg (Sopron) in Hungary. Small in person and in voice, and lacking the refinement and subtlety of interpretation of the well-loved Johanna Huber, upon whom she modelled her performances in the burlesque and whose successor she became, Therese Krones nevertheless more than compensated for these disadvantages by her dynamism, overflowing temperament, and a genius for provocative improvisation delivered in a disarmingly innocent style which, according to contemporary reports, enabled her to sail far closer to the wind than a male actor could have done. She did not hesitate to make indirect allusions to her own notoriously hectic private life, and by this means, and by her inspired creation of a series of comic roles from Gleich, Meisl, Bäuerle, and, above all, Raimund (her playing of Youth in *Der Bauer als Millionär* to the author's Fortunatus Wurzel was one of the great moments in the history of the theatre), she became a legend within her own short lifetime, and the idol of Vienna. She died, burnt out, before reaching the age of 29.

J. B. BEDNALL

KRUTCH, Joseph Wood (1893–1970), American dramatic critic. He was born in Knoxville, Tennessee, and attended Columbia University, where he later became an instructor in English and journalism. He was for thirty-five years (from 1924) dramatic critic of *The Nation*, and was one of the most scholarly and penetrating of the American writers. His standards were of a high order and he did not change the fundamental principles of his criticism with the passing of the years. He was a critic of the drama—and the drama as literature—rather than a reporter of the playhouses, and his introduction to *Nine Plays* contains perhaps the fairest evaluation of O'Neill's work. His *American Drama Since 1918* (1939) is a useful guide to the American stage between the two world wars.

THOMAS QUINN CURTISS

KUMMERFELD, KAROLINE (*née* Schultze) (1745–1815), a German actress who in 1758 joined the Ackermann company, and made her début as Iphigenia—as she relates in her memoirs—without rehearsals and without having read more than her own part. She remained with the Ackermanns until they went to Hamburg, where her talents and popularity excited the animosity of Sophie Hensel, who soon engineered her dismissal. She and her brother, a ballet-master, then joined Koch in Leipzig, where she was much admired by the young Goethe. Later she went to Gotha under Ekhof, and was esteemed by him as a good actress and a loyal colleague. After his death she accompanied her colleagues to Mannheim, at the invitation of Dalberg. Her memoirs, referred to above, give an interesting picture of the theatrical life of the period, and contain many sidelights on the great Ekhof, whom she blames in part for the controversy with Schröder at Hamburg.

KUPPELHORIZONT, see LIGHTING, 1 *d*.

KURZ, JOSEPH FELIX VON (1715–84), Austrian actor, who developed the typical Viennese peasant-clown Hanswurst into a personal type to which he gave the name Bernardon. He was the staunch champion of the old improvised comedy in its battle against the newly imported regular classic drama, and when the latter proved victorious he and his wife, an Italian, with a mixed company of Italians, Austrians, and South Germans, mostly young, took themselves off to the Rhineland. There they were joined by the young Schröder, who had just left Ackermann's company in Hamburg in disgust. He proved a great asset, but left after a year, harassed by the conflicting jealousies of the women of the company. Later von Kurz was divorced by his wife, and she continued to lead the old company while he returned to the Burgtheater in Vienna. The time for his 'Bernardoniades' had, however, gone by, and the new drama had obtained so strong a hold that he was forced to retire before it (see also AUSTRIA).

KYD, THOMAS (1558–94), English dramatist, author of *The Spanish Tragedy* (*c.* 1585–9), one of the most popular plays of its day, and prototype of many succeeding 'tragedies of revenge'. It was constantly revived and revised, in one instance by Ben Jonson, and survived into Restoration days, being seen by Pepys in 1668. Some scholars have noted in it a strong relation to the later tragedy of *Hamlet*; it has also been suggested that Kyd was the author of an earlier *Hamlet*, now lost, which Shakespeare used as the basis of his play, written for the Lord Chamberlain's Men at the time when Jonson was revising *The Spanish Tragedy* for the Admiral's Men. Kyd is also one of the contemporary authors credited with *The Taming of a Shrew* (1589), again a lost play believed to have been used by Shakespeare. Apart from his translation of Garnier's *Cornélie* (1574), no other plays can be definitely assigned to him, since *A First Part of Ieronimo* (printed in 1605), whose action precedes that of *The Spanish Tragedy*, is probably by someone else, and *Soliman and Perseda* (*c.* 1590) has by some been given to Peele. Traces of Kyd's work have been looked for in *Titus Andronicus* and *Arden of Feversham*. He was an intimate friend of Marlowe, with whom he was implicated in accusations of atheism, extricating himself in a not altogether creditable manner.

KYNASTON, EDWARD (NED) (*c.* 1640–1706), English actor and one of the last boy-players of feminine roles. Pepys said of him 'He made the loveliest lady that ever I saw', and it was the delight of fashionable ladies to take him, in his petticoats, driving in the Park after the play. Cibber recounts that Charles II had once to wait for the curtain to rise at the theatre because Kynaston, who played the tragedy queen, was being shaved. In later life he fulfilled the promise of his youth, and made many fine dignified appearances in heroic roles. He was particularly admired in *Henry IV*.

KYŌGEN, see JAPAN.

L

LABERIUS, DECIMUS, see MIME, 2 *b*.

LABICHE, EUGÈNE (1815–88), French dramatist, who between 1838 and 1877 wrote, alone or in collaboration, more than 150 light comedies. Of these the most successful were *Un Chapeau de paille d'Italie* (1851), *Le Voyage de M. Perrichon* (1860), *La Poudre aux yeux* (1861), and *La Cagnotte* (1864). The first two are still revived from time to time, and all have been translated into English. The first was done in New York in 1936 as *Horse Eats Hat*. Some of Labiche's contemporary success, which was so great as to cause him to be compared, somewhat extravagantly, with Molière, may be looked for in a secret revolt of the lighter-minded audiences of Paris against the serious problem-plays of the younger Dumas and others. Labiche's humour is broad, his jokes time-worn, but acceptably presented and embellished. He raised French farce to a height which it has since attained only with Feydeau, and gave new life and gaiety to the vaudeville inherited from Scribe.

LABOUCHÈRE, MRS. HENRY, see HODSON, HENRIETTA.

LABOUR STAGE, NEW YORK, see PRINCESS THEATRE.

LA CALPRENÈDE, GAUTIER DE COSTES DE (1614–63), a French nobleman, well received at Court, author of several successful novels, and also a dramatist. He wrote several excellent tragedies, the first while still in the army. It was produced at the Hôtel de Bourgogne in 1635, and met with the approval of Richelieu. La Calprenède was rather ashamed of his plays, thinking playwriting beneath the dignity of a soldier and a courtier, but he was consoled by their success and by the plaudits of the polite world. Three of his subjects were taken from English history, the most interesting being *Le Comte d'Essex* (1637), in which he introduces the episode of the ring given by Elizabeth to Essex, based on current tradition. La Calprenède was one of the little group of dramatists contemporary with the early plays of Corneille, and his work contributed to the moulding of the classical tradition in France.

LA CHAPELLE, JEAN DE (1655–1723), French nobleman who in his youth wrote plays, the first being a farce, followed by four tragedies. The latter were much influenced by Racine, and were given by the newly formed company of the Comédie-Française with Baron and Mlle Champmeslé. The most successful of them was probably *Cléopâtre* (1681), in which Baron gave an outstanding performance as Antony. It was sufficiently well known to be parodied a year or two later, and remained in the repertory of the theatre until 1727. In 1684 La Chapelle abandoned dramatic composition for politics and history, but later wrote the libretto for an opera, which was considered a more elegant pastime for a gentleman than the writing of plays. La Chapelle, who helped to keep alive classical tragedy after Racine's retirement, might have done much for the French theatre had he continued to write, and taken his work seriously.

LA CHAUSSÉE, (PIERRE-CLAUDE) NIVELLE DE (1692–1754), French dramatist, and the chief exponent of eighteenth-century *comédie larmoyante*. He was 40 before he produced his first play, *La Fausse Antipathie* (1733), though he was already a well-known figure in literary society. This and his *Préjugé à la mode* (1735) were both well received, and may be said, with their mingling of tragedy and comedy, to mark the end of old French comedy and the beginning of the *drame bourgeois*. La Chaussée was himself a wealthy man, with somewhat frank and licentious tastes, and it is obvious from his prologue to *La Fausse Antipathie* that he wrote as he did deliberately, because he saw that that was what his audience wanted. His pictures of moral virtue and of the trials of domestic life exactly suited the new middle-class audience, with its preponderance of women and its disposition to indulge freely in sentimental tears. Having proved the success of his new method, La Chaussée produced some forty plays in the same vein, of which the most successful were *Mélanide* (1741), perhaps the most typical *comédie larmoyante*, *L'École des mères* (1744), and *La Gouvernante* (1747), a foretaste of *East Lynne*. If La Chaussée's plays are forgotten today it is not so much because their subject-matter dates, as because their simple central situations are involved in a conventional network of intrigue, and their action is impeded by much narrative. Also they are written in verse, which, though the finest medium for high tragedy, seems somehow wasted on domestic interiors. Yet in his own day La Chaussée was immensely successful and, in the wave of sentimentality which was sweeping across Europe at the time, his plays were translated into Dutch, Italian, and English.

LACKAYE, WILTON (1862–1932), American actor who was intended for the Church, but adopted the stage after a chance visit to Madison Square Theatre on his way to Rome. He was in an amateur company when Lawrence Barrett gave him a part in *Francesca da Rimini* at the Star Theatre, New York, on 27 Aug. 1883. He later appeared many times with Fanny Davenport, and in 1887 made a success in *She*. He was constantly in demand, being equally good in tragedy, comedy, romance, and melodrama. He appeared in a number of Shakespeare plays, and in many new productions. He was also Jean Valjean in his own dramatization of *Les Misérables*. But his greatest part was undoubtedly Svengali, which he played for two years and in many revivals. He retired from the stage in 1927, returning only once in support of Mrs. Fiske, two years later. A handsome man of fine presence, he founded the Catholic Actors' Guild, and helped to organize the Actors' Equity Association of New York. Though intolerant of indecency on the stage, he was opposed to censorship, and his caustic wit made him an opponent to be feared.

LACY, JOHN (?–1681), English actor, originally a dancing-master, went on the stage at the Restoration, and soon became a great favourite with Charles II. His portrait by Michael Wright, showing him in three different parts—as Teague in *The Committee*, Mr. Scruple in *The Cheats*, and Mr. Galliard in *The Variety*—still hangs in Hampton Court. He was the original Bayes in Buckingham's *The Rehearsal*, and was judged to have hit Dryden off to the life. Pepys admired his Teague exceedingly, and he was considered an excellent Falstaff. He was the author of four plays, of which one was based on *Le Médecin malgré lui* and another on *The Taming of the Shrew*.

LADINO DRAMA, see JEWISH DRAMA, 7.

LADY ELIZABETH'S MEN, a company of players formed in 1611, under John Townsend and Joseph Moore, which, after a provincial tour, appeared at Court in 1612. In the following year they were joined with the Revels Company, under Rosseter, and the joint company, of which Henslowe was manager, played together for some years. It was for them that Daborne wrote, and they appear to have acted at the Swan, the Rose, and Whitefriars. In 1614 the actor Nathan Field was their chief player, and in the same year they were established at the Hope, where they found they had much to complain of in Henslowe's treatment of them (see HENSLOWE). On his death in 1616 four of the chief members of the company joined Prince Charles's Men, a company newly formed by Alleyn; Field had already left them, as had other outstanding men, and the depleted group was reduced to the status of a provincial company. For four or five years they appear only in civic records, but some time in 1621–2 a new London company, known as the Lady Elizabeth's Men, but containing none of the provincial actors, appeared at the Phoenix. Beeston was one of the organizers of the new company, which prospered exceedingly for a short time, with a distinguished list of dramatists—Middleton, Rowley, Massinger, Ford, Dekker, Heywood, and Shirley—and some outstanding actors. In 1625, however, the company was finally broken by a disastrous epidemic of plague, and disappears, its place being taken by the new Queen Henrietta's company. A later company, formed in 1628 as the Queen of Bohemia's players, seems to have had something fraudulent about it, but continued to exist intermittently until 1641.

LAFAYETTE THEATRE, NEW YORK. This was a circus, then an amphitheatre with spectacular drama, mainly equestrian, and in 1826 it opened as a regular playhouse, with newly installed gas-lighting. It had a good company, and in the summer some of the Chatham Theatre company joined it, Mrs. Duff appearing as Juliet and Mrs. Haller. The reopening of the Chatham, and the appearance of Macready and Kean at the Park, took away the Lafayette's audiences, and the theatre closed. In Sept. 1827 it reopened, enlarged and redecorated, with a company headed by Henry Wallack. It failed to maintain a high standard, however, and had sunk again to circus and melodrama when on 11 Apr. 1829 it was totally destroyed by fire and never rebuilt.

LA FLEUR. (1) The name under which the great French farce-player Gros-Guillaume played serious parts at the Hôtel de Bourgogne from 1621 to 1624. His wife and daughter were both actresses, and the latter married an actor, (2) FRANÇOIS JUVENON (*fl.* 1623–59), who also took the name of La Fleur. He played kings in tragedy in succession to Montfleury, Gascons and ranting *capitanos* in comedy. He appeared in some of Racine's plays (for his son, see LA TUILLERIE).

LA FOSSE, ANTOINE D'AUBIGNY DE (1653–1708), French dramatist, nephew of a painter, by whom he was brought up. In his youth he went to Italy as secretary to Foucher, and later, in the service of Créqui, in company with another contemporary dramatist, Campistron, was present at the battle of Luzzara, where his master was killed. La Fosse was over 40 when he produced his first play, *Polixène* (1696). The style was accounted better than the subject, but a second play, *Manlius Capitolinus* (1698), was most successful, and remained in the repertory of the Comédie-Française until 1849. Talma, in particular, was later very good in the name-part. The play was a frank imitation of Corneille and Racine, and under the guise of Roman names treated of contemporary history, being an account of the conspiracy of the Spaniards against Venice, a subject used some years earlier by Otway in *Venice Preserved* (1682). La Fosse's later plays were not successful, but many of his contemporaries thought he might have rivalled Racine had he begun his dramatic career earlier.

LA FRANCE, see JADOT.

LAGERKVIST, PÄR FABIAN (1891–), Swedish dramatist and poet, is probably the most remarkable playwright of the modern Swedish theatre. Devoted as he is to Strindberg and sharing the profound despair implicit in Strindberg's early reading of life, he is nevertheless an independent and highly imaginative artist, original both in thought and technique. Characteristic of this side of his work are the early plays, *Sista människan* (1917), *Himlens hemlighet* (1919), and *Den osynlige* (1923). Like Strindberg's before him, his mood and technique change in his second phase, though not necessarily in the same direction, for, while the gloom of his mood relents, his manner moves towards, not further from, realism. Characteristic of these later plays are *Han som fick leva om sitt liv* (1928); *Konungen* (1932); *Mannen utan själ* (1936); and *Seger i mörker* (1939). *Midsommardröm i fattighuset* (1941) is a realistic play with symbolic overtones; *De vises sten* (1947) has a Renaissance setting and deals with problems of faith and knowledge; *Låt människan leva* (1949) is his last substantial dramatic work. In 1951 he was awarded the Nobel Prize for literature.

UNA ELLIS-FERMOR†, *rev.*

LA GRANGE. (1) CHARLES VARLET (1639–92), a French actor, who joined the company of Molière from the provinces in 1659. He was young and handsome, of good presence and address, and played all Molière's young lovers, as well as the hero of Racine's *Alexandre.* A methodical man, he kept a register of the plays presented at the Palais-Royal and the receipts from each, interspersed with notes on the domestic affairs of the company which have proved invaluable to later students of the period. In 1664 he took over Molière's functions as Orator to the troupe, and was active in forwarding its affairs after Molière's death. As an act of piety to the memory of his friend he edited and wrote a preface to the first collected edition of Molière's works, published in 1682. He married (2) MARIE (1639–1737), daughter of the famous pastry-cook and lover of the theatre, Cyprien Ragueneau, immortalized by Rostand in *Cyrano de Bergerac.* She was already a member of the company, and probably played the part of Marotte in *Les Précieuses ridicules*, by which name she was known on the stage. She also created the part of the Comtesse d'Escarbagnas; she retired from the amalgamated troupe of the Comédie-Française on the death of her husband. La Grange's eldest brother, (3) ACHILLE (1636–1709), was also an actor, under the name of Verneuil, first at the Marais and later with the newly formed Comédie-Française. He, too, married an actress, Marie, nicknamed Marotte.

LA GRANGE-CHANCEL, JOSEPH DE (1677–1758), French dramatist, writer of tragedies which rank with those of Campistron and Crébillon. He was a precocious child, whose first play was written when he was about 13. With the help of Racine, who was a friend and counsellor of the young writer, it was put on in 1694, but was not a great success. It was followed by several more tragedies, in which La Grange-Chancel again had the help and advice of Racine, but his work shows the continual decline of the classical ideal, and the tendency, which later becomes more marked, to make sensationalism and not emotion the mainspring of the plot. The most successful of his plays were *Amasis* (1701) and *Ino et Mélicerte* (1713). A few years later he wrote some satirical verses about the Regent, and was imprisoned. He escaped and went into exile, not returning until after the Regent's death, when he settled in his native town of Antoniat and spent his time in alienating his friends and family by malicious epigrams. He also indulged in controversy with Voltaire. He seems to have been an embittered man, who suffered from his own precocity and failed to redeem the promise of his youth.

LA HARPE, JEAN-FRANÇOIS DE (1739–1802), French dramatist, whose plays, modelled on those of Voltaire, show the continued decline of classical tragedy during the eighteenth century. The first, *Le Comte de Warwick* (1763), is usually accounted the best, though *Philoctète* (1783) and *Coriolan* (1784) were well received. It is, however, as a critic that La Harpe is best remembered. His *Cours de littérature ancienne et moderne,* based on lectures given in 1786, is a standard work, full of interesting ideas and information, which has, however, to be corrected in the light of later literary judgements. He is at his best when dealing with the French seventeenth century, and wrote excellent commentaries on the plays of Racine. La Harpe also made a translation of Lillo's *London Merchant,* with alterations which entirely falsified the purpose and meaning of the plot. It was never acted.

LAMB, CHARLES (1775–1834), English critic and essayist who wrote about drama and dramatists with a warm affection which threw as much light on Lamb himself as upon his subject. He admits in *Imperfect Sympathies* that his mind was desultory, sadly lacking in system, 'suggestive merely, and content with fragments and scattered pieces of truth'. Yet on those 'fragments' for which he had a fondness Lamb held decided views.

Although he wrote four plays, none of them had any great success. His *John Woodvil* (1802) shows the influence of the Elizabethans, especially of Beaumont and Fletcher. His *Mr. H.*, a farce, was produced at Drury Lane in 1806 with Elliston in the title part. The play was soundly hissed, and was not revived until 1822, when it was performed at the Opera House in the Strand. It was revived also by the Society of Dramatic Students at the Globe Theatre in 1885. Lamb also wrote *The Wife's Trial; or, the Intruding Widow,* a play in poetic form which appeared in *Blackwood's Magazine* (1828), as did also his last play, *The Pawnbroker's Daughter* (1830). Neither was acted.

Lamb's dramatic essays were of more enduring stuff. His *Specimens of English Dramatic Poets who lived about the time of Shakespeare* appeared in 1808, and was designed to 'illustrate what might be called the moral sense of our ancestors'. In the essay *On the Tragedies of Shakespeare* he made out his famous case for reading Shakespeare's plays in preference to witnessing their performance on the stage. Yet the *Essays of Elia* recall more than one pleasure of playgoing. His references to old actors are tinged with the affection of one who has enjoyed the busy traffic of the stage as well as the calm seclusion of the study. His regard for Shakespeare led him to write the *Tales from Shakespeare* (1807) on which he worked with his sister Mary. In spite of his inability to see more in Lear on the stage than 'an old man tottering about the stage, turned out of doors by his daughters on a rainy night', Lamb was a man of the theatre. Put an old Drury Lane playbill before him, and 'how fresh to memory arise the magic and the manner of the gentle actor'. T. C. KEMP†

LAMBS, THE, a London supper club founded in the 1860s by a group which included the actors John Hare, Harry Montague, Henry Irving, and Squire Bancroft. It consisted of twenty-four members, under a chairman called the Shepherd, who wore a badge with the motto 'Floreant Agni', and carried a crook surmounted by a silver bell. The club had no regular premises, but met for many years at the Gaiety Restaurant and subsequently at the Albemarle Hotel. It survived until the 1890s. Meanwhile, Montague, who had returned to America, founded a similar club in New York in 1875, with himself as the first Shepherd. At first the club had no regular premises, but in 1880 a clubhouse was acquired at 34 West 26th Street. The first Gambol took place in the same year, with Edmund S. Holland, one of the original five members, as the Collie. The present constitution was adopted in 1893, a new club-house taken in 1897, and on the dissolution of the London Lambs the Shepherd's crook, bell, and badge were presented to the American Shepherd. The surviving London members were elected honorary members of the New York club, and Hare was designated Shepherd Emeritus. In 1904 the club moved to its present (1972) premises at 128 West 44th Street, which have been several times enlarged to accommodate a growing membership which now stands at over a thousand. The first Ladies' Day was held on Saturday, 6 Jan. 1952. In 1956 women, though not admitted to membership, were given the right to dine at the club on any night of the week if accompanied by a member. The Lambs in its present form is roughly the equivalent of the London Savage Club, as the Players is of the Garrick. ROBERT DOWNING

L.A.M.D.A., see LONDON ACADEMY OF MUSIC AND DRAMATIC ART.

LA MOTTE, ANTOINE HOUDARD DE (1672–1731), French dramatist, who was to have been a lawyer, but preferred literature. The failure of his play in 1693 so disgusted him that he almost decided to become a monk, but the call of the theatre was too strong, and a few years later he was writing opera-libretti and lyrics for ballets, some of them the best since Quinault. His verses were graceful and charming, though lacking in vigour. His one important work is a tragedy, *Inès de Castro*, which was given with great success at the Comédie-Française in 1723, but he was also the author of several comedies, among them *La Matrone d'Éphèse* and *Italie galante*, and his works were well enough known to be parodied at the unlicensed theatres of the Parisian fairs. He was an excellent conversationalist, witty and warm-hearted, and was much sought after in society. But, having been preferred to J.-B. Rousseau in the contest for Thomas Corneille's seat in the French Academy in 1710, he made many enemies, and died friendless and in poverty.

LANDER, JEAN MARGARET DAVENPORT (1829–1903), the daughter of an English actor named Thomas Donald Davenport (1792–1851), who is believed to have been the model for Vincent Crummles, in which case his talented little daughter, who at 8 was playing Richard III, would be the original Infant Phenomenon. She went with her family to the United States in 1838 as a child prodigy, playing a number of unsuitable parts like Shylock, Sir Peter Teazle, and Sir Giles Overreach, was then privately educated, and made her adult début in 1844 as Juliet. She toured the Continent, and in 1849 returned to the United States with such success that she settled there. She was the first actress in America to play Adrienne Lecouvreur and Marguerite Gautier, the latter with young Edwin Booth as Armand. Her repertory also included *The Wife*, *The Hunchback*, *Love*, *Ingomar*, *The Lady of Lyons*, and the roles of Charlotte Corday and Peg Woffington, in all of which she appeared during her successful tours. These were interrupted in 1860 by her marriage to General Lander, but after his death in the Civil War two years later she returned to the stage, being billed for the first time as Mrs. Lander at Niblo's Garden in 1865 in her own adaptation of *Mésalliance*. On 1 Jan. 1877 she made her last appearance on the stage at Boston, again in her own dramatization, this time of *The Scarlet Letter*. A small, well-formed woman, with a sweet face, clear voice, and graceful figure, she was an actress of great talent and intellectual judgement, but lacked fire.

LANDRIANI, PAOLO (1770–1838), see SCENERY, 4.

LANE, LUPINO, see LUPINO (3).

LANE, SARA (1823–99), see BRITANNIA THEATRE.

LANG. (1) (ALEXANDER) MATHESON (1879–1948), actor-manager and dramatist, son of a clerical family, cousin to Cosmo Lang, late Archbishop of Canterbury, and himself destined for the Church. As a boy, however, he was much attracted by the theatre, and his determination to go on the stage was strengthened by visits to Benson's and Irving's companies when they were on tour in Scotland. He first appeared with Calvert in Wolverhampton in 1897, and later joined Benson, being with him when the Theatre Royal, Newcastle, burnt down and all the company's wardrobe and properties were lost. After a visit to the United States with Mrs. Langtry, an English tour with Ellen Terry, and a Benson tour to the West Indies, he returned to London, where he had first appeared with Benson in 1900, and played under the Vedrenne–Barker management at the Court in Ibsen and Shaw. His first outstanding success, however, was scored in *The Christian* (1907) at the Lyceum, where he also gave fine performances as Romeo and Hamlet. He then took his own company on tour to South Africa, Australia, and India, playing Shakespeare and modern romantic drama with much success. It was on his return in 1913 that he appeared in a play with which his name was for a long time associated, *Mr. Wu*. First produced in Manchester, it ran for over a year in London, was subsequently seen all over the world with Lang as Wu Li Chang, and gave its title to his autobiography, *Mr. Wu Looks Back*, published in 1940. With his wife (2) HUTIN [NELLIE] BRITTON (1876–1965), who had been with him in Benson's and Ellen Terry's companies, and had subsequently toured as his leading lady, he inaugurated the Shakespeare productions at the Old Vic in 1914 with *The Taming of the Shrew*, *Hamlet*, and *The Merchant of Venice*. Among his later productions the most famous were *The Wandering Jew*, first produced in 1920, which ran for a year and was subsequently revived many times, *The Chinese Bungalow* (1925) in his own dramatization from a novel, *Such Men are Dangerous* (1928) and *Jew Süss* (1929), both dramatized by Ashley Dukes. Lang himself was the adapter of *The Purple Mask*, with which he opened his management at the Lyric Theatre, London, in 1918, and part-author of *Carnival*, seen at the New Theatre two years later. A tall, heavily built man, he was exceedingly handsome and had a fine, resonant voice. He attained eminence in the theatrical world through industry and application, making his way steadily, though without hardship, from the daily routine of the touring company to the cares of management, supported and assisted always by his wife, and by the constant affection and interest of his audiences.

LANGNER, LAWRENCE (1890–1962), who had a distinguished career as a patent agent in New York, was also a potent force in the American theatre. Born in Wales, educated in London, he emigrated to the U.S.A. in 1911 and soon after became an American citizen. In 1914 he helped to organize the Washington Square Players, who produced his first play, and after the First World War was instrumental in helping the group to re-form as the Theatre Guild, of which he was a director. He was also the founder and first president of the American Shakespeare Festival at Stratford, Conn. With Teresa Helburn he supervised the production of over 200 plays for the Theatre Guild. He also founded and directed from 1931 to 1933 the New York Repertory Company, and built for it the Country Playhouse, Westport, Conn. He was the author of an autobiography, *The Magic Curtain*, and a book on the theatre, *The Play's the Thing*, and of a number of plays, some written or translated in collaboration with his wife, Armina Marshall, who with her son Philip continues the association with the Theatre Guild.

LANGTRY, LILLIE [EMILIE CHARLOTTE] (1853–1929), English actress, daughter of the Dean of Jersey, the Rev. W. C. le Breton, who from her surpassing beauty was known as the Jersey Lily. She married at the age of 22 Edward Langtry, a wealthy Irishman, and became prominent in London society, being an intimate friend of Edward VII, then Prince of Wales. She was one of the first English society women to go on the stage, making her début under the Bancrofts at the Haymarket, as Kate Hardcastle, on 15 Dec. 1881. She caused a great sensation, but more on account of her looks and social position than by her acting, which for many years was not taken seriously by the critics. She organized her own company, being accounted a good manageress, and with it played at the Imperial and other London theatres and also toured the provinces and the United States. Although never a great actress, she was a pleasing one, being particularly acceptable in such parts as Rosalind. She maintained a large racing stable, and married as her second husband Sir Hugo de Bathe.

LA NOUE, JEAN SAUVE DE (1701–61), French actor who for many years toured the provinces successfully with his own company. In 1739 he wrote a play, *Mahomet II*, which was given at the Comédie-Française, and Voltaire, who thought well of it, was indebted to it for some of his own *Mahomet, ou le fanatisme*. He acknowledged his debt by allowing La Noue to perform the play at Lille before it was given at the Comédie-Française, and then only allowed the latter to have it if La Noue were imported into the company to play the title-role, subject to his making a satisfactory début. This he did in 1742, remaining with the Comédie-Française until 1757. In the year before his retirement he wrote a comedy, *La Coquette corrigée*, given first at the Comédie-Italienne, which showed plainly the influence of Marivaux. Some critics indeed rank it above Marivaux's work, mainly on account of its greater realism. It was his last play, and La Noue then left the stage to become director of Court theatricals, a post he held until his death.

LAPORTE [MATHIEU LE FEBVRE] (*c.* 1584–*c.* 1621), early French actor-manager, husband of Marie Venier, the first French actress to be known by name. With her he was a member of Valleran-Lecomte's provincial company which established itself at the Hôtel de Bourgogne in 1607–8, and was also for a time a member of his father-in-law's company. In 1610 he and his wife got into trouble for acting at the Hôtel d'Argent, thus infringing the monopoly of the Hôtel de Bourgogne, and soon after Laporte retired. Little is known of his acting ability, but he was a good organizer and the author of a number of plays written for the travelling company to which he originally belonged.

LARIVEY, Pierre de (*c.* 1540–*c.* 1612), an early French dramatist, who may possibly have been born of Italian parents and formed his name from a translation of theirs, Giunti. In 1577 he saw the Italian *commedia dell'arte* company, the Gelosi, play at Blois, and inspired by them he wrote nine comedies, six of which were printed in 1579, the other three not until 1611. There may have been others, but if so they are lost. All those that survive are based on Italian models, but they are in no sense of the word translations, being adaptations which often contain much new material. They were played extensively in the provinces and also in Paris. Molière drew largely on Larivey, which is indeed the chief reason for the latter's importance in the history of French drama.

LAROCHE, Johann (1745–1806), see AUSTRIA.

LAROQUE [Pierre Regnault Petit-Jean] (*c.* 1595–1676), French actor, a member of the company at the Marais under Montdory, and later its leader. When Floridor left to go to the Hôtel de Bourgogne Laroque took over his position as Orator to the troupe, and it was he who adroitly deprived Molière of the Du Parcs when they first came to Paris, though he was unable to keep them more than a year. Little is known of Laroque's abilities as an actor, but he was much esteemed as a fearless and efficient man of the theatre, and he piloted the Marais through many difficult years. He could not, however, stand up against the combined rivalry of Molière and the Hôtel de Bourgogne, and in the end his theatre was mostly given over to the newfangled 'machine' plays. On Molière's death he and his companions amalgamated with the company at the Palais-Royal, and so formed part of the original Comédie-Française. Laroque was the first to recognize and foster the talent of Mlle Champmeslé, whom he put through a systematic course of instruction when she first joined his company in 1669.

LARRA, Mariano José de (1809–37), a famous Spanish journalist and satirist, author of many dramatic adaptations and translations of contemporary French plays by Scribe, Ducange, Delavigne, and others, and of one outstanding original play, *Macías* (1834), which reflects contemporary literary preoccupations. Whilst still neo-classical in form, the emotions exhibited in it are clearly Romantic: violent, disordered, and a reflection of Larra's own emotions. Passion overrides the bounds of honour and even of religion. Larra's theatrical criticism is of great interest, reflecting not only his own personal preoccupations, the deepening of his despair which was to end finally in suicide, but also the contemporary association of literature and political and social progress, the key to this interesting period of Spanish theatrical history. J. E. VAREY

L'ARRONGE, Adolf (1838–1908), German dramatist and theatre director. He began his career as an orchestral conductor, and in 1869 took over the control of the *Berliner Gerichtszeitung*. From 1874 to 1878 he was director of the Breslau Lobetheater, and during these years wrote popular theatrical successes such as *Meier Leopold* (1873), *Hasemanns Töchter* (1877), and *Doktor Klaus* (1878). In 1883 he founded the Deutsches Theater in Berlin. This venture, run as an entirely private enterprise, was destined to become one of the leading German theatres, and L'Arronge helped to prepare the way for the future by building up a highly-trained group of players, although he was not in sympathy with the new naturalistic drama which was gradually becoming popular. Nevertheless, his work for the theatre was important, and for many years he made Berlin a flourishing theatrical centre.

DOROTHY MOORE

LATEINER, Joseph (1853–1935), writer of plays in Yiddish, and founder of the first regular Yiddish theatre in New York in 1883 (see JEWISH DRAMA, 5).

LATE JOYS, see PLAYERS' THEATRE.

LA THORILLIÈRE. (1) François Lenoir de (1626–80), French actor, who had already played in the provinces when he appeared at the Marais in about 1658–9, where he married the niece (or daughter) of the head of the company, Laroque. He later joined Molière at the Palais-Royal, played important parts in most of the latter's comedies, and himself composed a tragedy on the subject of Cleopatra which was given by Molière's troupe. On the death of Molière he went to the Hôtel de Bourgogne, and it was his death that precipitated the amalgamation of the companies to form the Comédie-Française, a course to which he had been opposed. His son (2) Pierre (1659–1731) was also an actor, and joined the Comédie-Française in 1684. As a child he had appeared in Molière's *Psyché*, and he later replaced J. B. Raisin in some of Molière's parts, gaining a good reputation as a comic actor, and occasionally replaced Champmeslé in tragedy. He married Caterina, daughter of Dominique of the Comédie-Italienne. Their son (3) Anne-Maurice (*c.* 1697–1759) was also an actor, and *doyen* of the Comédie-Française at the time of his death, having made his début there in 1722. He first played in tragedy, but later made an excellent reputation in romantic roles and in serious comedy. One of François's daughters, Charlotte, married the great actor Baron in 1675, while another, Thérèse, became the wife of Dancourt.

LATIN-AMERICAN THEATRE, see SOUTH AMERICA.

LATIN DRAMA, see FABULA, MIME, 2 and ROME; LITURGICAL DRAMA, JESUIT DRAMA and SCHOOL DRAMA.

LA TUILLERIE. (1) JEAN-FRANÇOIS JUVENON (1650–88), French actor and dramatist, son of actors at the Hôtel de Bourgogne and grandson of the farce-player Gros-Guillaume (see LA FLEUR). He himself was an actor at the Hôtel de Bourgogne by 1672, in which year he married (2) LOUISE CATHERINE (*c.* 1657–1706), daughter of the celebrated comedian, Raymond Poisson. He was a tall, stately man, at his best in tragedy, where he often replaced Champmeslé, while in comedy he played minor roles, usually those requiring a fine physique. He was, for example, the statue in *Le Festin de pierre.* His plays included tragedies which were mainly rewritings of older dramas, and farces, of which two, *Crispin précepteur* (1680) and *Crispin bel esprit* (1681), were produced at the Hôtel de Bourgogne with La Tuillerie's father-in-law in the title-roles. On the foundation of the Comédie-Française La Tuillerie's wife retired, but he remained with the company until his death a few years later. His plays were often attributed to the Abbé Abeille, author of some undistinguished works.

LAUBE, HEINRICH (1806–84), German theatre manager, who, after an undistinguished interregnum which lasted from 1832 to 1849, became director of the Vienna Burgtheater. He had been a member of the 'Young Germany' movement, and a prolific novelist, while his plays, though uninspired, were effective in production. He brought to his task a profound knowledge of the European stage, and was insistent on good acting, careful rehearsal, and strict adherence to the author's text. Laube was a friend of Wagner, who in 1843 wrote for a journal which Laube was then editing, the *Zeitung für die elegante Welt*, the autobiographical sketch which is reprinted in vol. i of his collected works.

LAUDER, SIR HARRY [HUGH MACLENNAN] (1870–1950), one of the most famous stars of the music-hall stage, whose essentially Scots humour never failed to awaken a response in the most English bosom from his first appearance in London in 1900. He first gained fame at the Argyle, Birkenhead, as an Irish comedian. When, in response to the demand for encores, his Irish songs ran out, he sang Scots ones and from then on remained faithful to them. He was knighted in 1919 for his services during the First World War, and for the work he did in entertaining the troops on the French front. He made numerous tours of the United States, South Africa, and Australia, and wrote several volumes of reminiscences. Among his most famous songs may be mentioned 'I love a lassie', 'Roamin' in the Gloamin'', 'A wee Deoch-and-Doris', 'It's nice to get up in the morning', and 'Stop yer tickling, Jock'. He invariably wore a kilt and glengarry, and carried a crooked stick. He appeared in revue, and in at least one straight play, *A Scrape o' the Pen* by Graham Moffat.

W. MACQUEEN-POPE†

LAUDI, see ITALY, 1 *a* i.

LAUDIVIO, see NOBILI, LAUDIVIO DE'.

LAURA KEENE'S THEATRE, NEW YORK, see KEENE, LAURA, and OLYMPIC, 3.

LAVEDAN, HENRI (1859–1940), French dramatist, whose plays deal with social problems and contemporary manners, somewhat in the style of Becque and the naturalistic writers, but in a less downright and drastic manner. His best play is *Le Prince d'Aurec* (1894), in which a decadent young nobleman is saved from the consequences of his folly by the sacrifices of his bourgeois mother. It was followed by a sequel, *Les Deux Noblesses* (1897), in which the hero restores the family fortunes by going into trade. Among his other plays the comedies of manners, *Le Nouveau jeu* (1905) and *Le Goût du vice* (1911), were less serious, but had a breezy vitality which made them popular.

LAVER, JAMES (1899–   ), English theatre historian, lecturer, dramatist, and novelist. In 1922 he joined the staff of the Victoria and Albert Museum, and from 1939 to 1959 was in charge of the theatre collections there as part of his duties as Keeper of the Department of Prints and Engravings. During this time he produced a number of illustrated volumes on costume, one of his main interests, and also on stage design. He has lectured widely on these and kindred subjects, and was also an examiner for the London University Diploma in Dramatic Art. He adapted the plays *The Circle of Chalk* (1928) and *La Marquise d'Arcis* (1929) from the German, and *Monsieur Trouhadec* from the French, and has himself written several plays, including *The House that Went to Sea* (1936) and *The Heart was not Burned* (1938), a study of Shelley. His novel, *Nymph Errant*, was successfully dramatized by Romney Brent in 1933. He is married to the actress Veronica Turleigh (1903–   ), who made her first appearance on the stage with Fagan's company at the Oxford Playhouse, playing Salome in *Dandy Dick*, since when she has had a consistently successful career which has included seasons at the Old Vic and Stratford-upon-Avon.

LAVINIA, see PONTI, DIANA DA.

LAWLER, RAY (1921–   ), Australian actor and playwright, whose *Summer of the Seventeenth Doll* had a great success in London in 1957, he himself playing the chief part. Born in Melbourne, he left school at 13, and after a few years drifted on to the stage by way of variety in Brisbane, after which he joined the National Theatre in Melbourne as actor and producer. He had already written a number of light comedies, much influenced by English plays of the 1930s, when his *Cradle of Thunder* was awarded first prize in a national competition.

He was director of the only professional repertory company in Australia at that time, at Melbourne University, when the newly founded Elizabethan Theatre Trust, looking for a purely Australian play, took and, after some delay, produced *Summer of the Seventeenth Doll.* A later play, *Piccadilly Bushman*, sponsored in Australia by Williamson's, has not yet been seen in London, but was done at the Liverpool Repertory Theatre and at the Watford Civic Theatre in 1965 as part of the first Commonwealth Arts Festival.

LAWRENCE, Gerald (1873–1957), romantic English actor, who made his first appearance with the Benson company at Stratford-upon-Avon, in 1893. After a tour in South Africa he appeared in London for the first time in 1898 in *Macbeth*, and subsequently joined Tree's company at Her Majesty's. He remained there until 1903, when he went to the Lyceum with Irving, with whom he remained until the latter's death in 1905. Lawrence had the greatest admiration for Irving, and remained devoted to his memory. He was playing Henry II the night Irving made his last appearance as Becket. He then went to America for a time, returning to produce Shakespeare at the Court Theatre, London, in 1909, repeating some of his productions at the Kroll Theatre, Berlin. He continued to appear, mainly in such parts as Hamlet, Romeo, and Orlando, but also as an outstanding Captain Brassbound, until the outbreak of war, when he joined the armed forces. In 1919 he reappeared on the London stage in *Cyrano de Bergerac*, as de Guiche, and a few years later he revived *Monsieur Beaucaire*, playing the name-part in London and on tour. He was also good as David Garrick in the play of that name. He appeared on the stage for the last time in 1938, and spent his last years in retirement, though he continued to take a great interest in theatrical affairs, and every year presented a prize at the Royal Academy of Dramatic Art for which he himself acted as judge. He married Lilian Braithwaite, by whom he had a daughter, Joyce Carey (1898–), who has had a distinguished career on the London stage. His second wife was Fay Davis (1872–1945), an American actress who came to London in 1895 and made a great success as Flavia in *The Prisoner of Zenda.* She subsequently became well known both in London and New York, and appeared with her husband in many of his productions.

LAWRENCE [Klasen], Gertrude (1898–1952), English actress, who studied under Italia Conti and made her first appearance in pantomime at the age of 12. She continued her career uninterruptedly, mainly as a dancer and later as a leading lady in revue, appearing in several editions of Charlot's Revue both in London and in America in 1924–6. She had, however, been seen in several straight parts before making an outstanding success as Amanda Prynne in *Private Lives* (1930). She was again associated with Noël Coward in his programme of nine one-act plays, *To-Night at 8.30* (1935–6). A vivacious and much-loved figure, she appeared in a succession of plays which included *Susan and God* (1937), *Lady in the Dark* (1941), *Fallen Angels* (1942), *Blithe Spirit* (1945). She spent her later years in America, where she married the theatre manager Richard Aldrich. In 1945 she published a volume of reminiscences entitled *A Star Danced*, which gave an excellent description of her humble beginnings and the hard work which took her to her final eminence. She was at the height of her powers when she died, and was a great loss to the English and American theatres. During the Second World War she toured the Pacific Ocean area with her own company, and did a great deal of work for the benefit of the theatrical profession.

LAWRENCE, Slingsby, see lewes (2).

LAZZO (pl. *lazzi*), a word used for the byplay of the comic masks of the *commedia dell'arte.* It consisted in small items of comic decoration on the main plot, and there is no satisfactory etymology or translation of the word, which, says one authority, 'needs to be variously rendered as antics, gambols, tricks, actions, comic turns, according to the context'. The longer comic episode, usually involving a practical joke and some horseplay, was known as the *burla* (pl. *burle*), from which are derived the terms burletta and burlesque.

LEAP, the supreme test of an acrobatic player, by which he appears on or vanishes from the stage with magical effect (see trickwork on the english stage).

LECOUVREUR, Adrienne (1692–1730), French actress, the daughter of a poor hatter who settled near the Comédie-Française. She was thus brought into close contact with the actresses of the day, among them Mlle Duclos and Mlle Desmares, and, inspired by their example, she appeared in some amateur productions with no little success. She was then taken in hand by the actor-dramatist Legrand, and after a season at Strasbourg made her début at the Comédie-Française in 1717. The public took her to its heart at once and never wavered in its allegiance, though she had much to suffer from the jealousy of her fellow-actresses, particularly Mlle Duclos. She is said to have been better in tragedy than in comedy, but it is difficult to assess her art, for her charm and beauty were such that even her faults were forgiven her, and the public looked with an indulgent eye on her love-affairs. She was for some time the mistress of Marshal Saxe, whose desertion of her in favour of the Princesse de Bouillon is said to have hastened her death. Her short but glorious reign lasted only thirteen years. She died suddenly, and was refused Christian burial, being interred secretly at night in a marshy corner of the Rue de Bourgogne. Voltaire, in some of whose plays she appeared, was with her when she died, and wrote a bitter poem on the attitude of the Church, which seemed to him even more monstrous when compared with the funeral of Anne Oldfield in Westminster Abbey in the same year. In 1849 Scribe and Legouvé wrote a play on Adrienne Lecouvreur, which, though hardly accurate, supplied Rachel, and later Sarah Bernhardt, with an excellent part.

LEE, NATHANIEL (*c.* 1653–92), English dramatist, author of a number of tragedies on subjects taken from ancient history—Nero, Mithridates, Sophonisba, Theodosius, Constantine—treated with much extravagance and bombast, though with occasional gleams of true poetic fire. The son of a clergyman, and well educated, he went to London with the intention of becoming an actor, but in spite of a fine voice and good elocution he was not successful. He turned to playwriting, confining himself entirely to tragedy, and that of the deepest dye, leaving his stage strewn with corpses and many of his characters lunatic. He had a streak of morbidity, which later turned to insanity, and was towards the end of his life confined in Bedlam. His best and most successful play was *The Rival Queens; or, the Death of Alexander the Great*, dealing with the jealousy between Alexander's wives, Roxana and Statira. First produced in 1677, with Betterton and Mrs. Barry, it held the stage for over a hundred years, and was in the repertory of Kemble, Kean, and Mrs. Siddons. Cibber, in his *Apology*, attributes much of its original success to the splendid ranting of Betterton. Lee, who twice collaborated with Dryden, was one of the most popular writers of his day, and both his rhymed heroic dramas and his blank-verse tragedies, which sought to combine the passion of Shakespeare with the classical tradition of France, were frequently played and printed.

LEE SUGG, CATHARINE (1797–1845), see HACKETT (2).

LEFFLER, ANNE CHARLOTTE (1849–92), Swedish dramatist (see SCANDINAVIA, 3 *a*).

LE GALLIENNE, EVA (1899–), American actress and producer, daughter of the poet Richard Le Gallienne. Born in London, she studied at the Royal Academy of Dramatic Art, and after playing several small parts went to New York in 1915, where she has since remained. She made a great success as Julie in *Liliom* (1921), and among her later parts were Hannele in Hauptmann's play, Hilda Wangel in *The Master Builder*, and Ella Rentheim in *John Gabriel Borkman*. In 1926 she opened the Civic Repertory Theatre and during the next six years presented there a programme of foreign and American plays (see No. 82), appearing in most of them herself. She was also associated with the founding of the American Repertory Company, playing the Queen in the initial production of *Henry VIII*. She has been one of the outstanding interpreters of Ibsen in America, and by her acting and direction has done much to further the cause of international playwrights, and widen the horizon of the theatre-going public. In 1934 she published her autobiography, and is also part-author of a popular version of *Alice in Wonderland* for the stage, in which she gave an excellent performance as the White Queen.

LEGITIMATE DRAMA, sometimes abbreviated to 'the legit.', a term which arose in the eighteenth century during the struggle of the Patent Theatres—Covent Garden and Drury Lane—against the upstart and illegitimate playhouses springing up all over London. It covered in general those five-act plays (including Shakespeare) which had little or no singing, dancing, and spectacle, and depended entirely on acting. In the nineteenth century the term was widespread, and was used by actors of the old school as a defence against the encroachments of farce, musical comedy, and revue.

LEGOUVÉ, ERNEST-GABRIEL-JEAN-BAPTISTE (1807–1903), son and grandson of French writers, himself poet, novelist, and lecturer. He is best remembered for his collaboration with Scribe and Labiche, among others. With the first he produced in 1849 *Adrienne Lecouvreur*, a fictionized account of the life of the celebrated French actress, mistress of Marshal Saxe. By himself Legouvé wrote a tragedy on Medea, which he intended for Rachel. Refused by her, it was translated into Italian, and in 1856 provided a great part for Ristori. Legouvé also wrote a number of charming one-act comedies which held the stage for many years.

LEGRAND, MARC-ANTOINE (1673–1728), French actor, the son of an army surgeon, who is traditionally said to have been born the day Molière died. He gained his experience in a French company under Sallé which played in Warsaw, and in 1702, having previously been refused, joined the Comédie-Française to play rustic and comic parts. Short and ugly in appearance, his wit made him popular. He sometimes insisted on playing tragedy, for which he was quite unsuited. He was author as well as actor, and his numerous plays, given at the Comédie-Italienne and the Comédie-Française, were mainly based on contemporary events. The most successful was *Cartouche*, which dealt with the career of a notorious footpad. It was hurriedly written after the man's arrest, and the actor who played the name-part visited the condemned man in his cell to take lessons from him in the technicalities of his profession. The play was produced on 21 Sept. 1721, and performed thirteen times, its last production being on the day before Cartouche was executed. It was revived nearly a hundred years later, as a vehicle for Frédérick. The contemporary aspect of Legrand's plays, in which he sometimes had the collaboration of Dominique, means that they have fallen out of the repertory, but they were highly successful in their day, and helped to bring back to the Comédie-Française the audiences which were drifting away to the unlicensed theatres of the fairs. Legrand's stagecraft was good, though his dialogue was occasionally highly-flavoured.

An obscene play, *Le Luxurieux*, published in London in 1738, is attributed to him (*Pièces libres de M. Ferrand*). If it is his, it corresponds to what is known of his morals. He was the teacher of Adrienne Lecouvreur, and his son and daughter were both members of the Comédie-Française.

LEGS, see BORDER.

LEG-SHOW, a slang term for a spectacular musical play, largely designed to display the charms of the chorus-girls in a series of scanty costumes and energetic dances.

LEGUIZAMÓN, MARTÍNIAN (1858–1935), see SOUTH AMERICA, I.

LEICESTER'S MEN, the earliest organized company of Elizabethan players, first mentioned in 1559. The actors were apparently on tour, having previously played in London, though not before the Queen, which they did at Christmas in the following year. They counted as Leicester's household servants, and among them was James Burbage, who in 1576 built the first theatre in London. From 1570 onwards they were in great favour at Court, and continued so until the formation in 1583 of the Queen's Men, in which many of the best actors from Leicester's company were incorporated. In 1585 the company was probably re-formed, as it accompanied Leicester to the Low Countries. Among the players was William Kempe, who with some others went to play in Elsinore before Frederick II of Denmark. The company continued to play in Leicester's name until his death, when many of its members joined the company of the Earl of Derby (see STRANGE'S MEN).

LEIGH, ANTHONY (?–1692), an actor in Davenant's company at Dorset Garden, much admired by Charles II, who called him 'his' actor. He created the part of Father Dominic in Dryden's *Spanish Friar* and took over the part of Teague in Howard's *The Committee*, originally created by Lacy. He was an excellent foil to the comedian Nokes, with whom he often played. Cibber writes of him as 'of a mercurial kind . . . in humour, he loved to take a full career . . . he had great variety in his manner and was famous in very different characters. . . . Characters that would have made the reader yawn in the closet, have by the strength of his action been lifted into the loudest laughter on the stage.'

LEIGH, VIVIEN [VIVIAN MARY HARTLEY] (1913–67), English actress, second wife of Sir Laurence Olivier, whom she married (as her second husband) in 1937 and divorced in 1960. After a short period of study in Paris and in London, a few appearances in films and one small part at the 'Q' Theatre in 1935, she made a sensational success in May of the same year as Henriette in *The Mask of Virtue*. In 1936 she played Jenny Mere in *The Happy Hypocrite*, and in 1937 went with the Old Vic to Elsinore, playing Ophelia to Olivier's Hamlet. After appearing as Titania at the Old Vic and Serena Blandish at the Gate, she went to America, where she was seen as Juliet. Later successes included Jennifer Dubedat in *The Doctor's Dilemma*, Sabina in *The Skin of Our Teeth*, and a number of parts with the Old Vic. It was, however, with her Blanche du Bois in *A Streetcar Named Desire* (1949) that she gave proof of greater powers as an actress than she had hitherto shown (her work in films, which cannot be considered here, was already outstanding), and she became one of London's leading actresses. During the Festival of Britain in 1951 she appeared with Olivier in Shaw's *Caesar and Cleopatra* and Shakespeare's *Antony and Cleopatra*, both in London and New York, the general consensus of opinion being that she was more successful in the former play. In 1953 she again appeared with Olivier, in Rattigan's *The Sleeping Prince*. She was at Stratford-upon-Avon in 1955, appearing as Viola, Lady Macbeth, and Lavinia, playing the last part in London and on a Continental tour. She had a further outstanding success as Paola in *Duel of Angels* (1957), both in London and New York, and in 1961 she undertook an extensive tour for the Old Vic with a repertory which included a new version of *The Lady of the Camellias*. In 1963 she made her first appearance as a singer and dancer in a musical version of *Tovarich*, which toured the United States before opening to great critical acclaim in New York.

LEIGH HUNT, see HUNT, (JAMES HENRY) LEIGH.

LEIGHTON, MARGARET (1922–), English actress, who first appeared on the stage at the Birmingham Repertory Theatre in 1938. After gaining experience there and on tour, she joined the Old Vic company and made her first London appearance in Aug. 1944 as the Troll King's Daughter in *Peer Gynt*. During the next few years she played a wide range of parts, and in 1950 emerged as a leading West-End actress with her Celia Coplestone in Eliot's *The Cocktail Party*. A season at Stratford-upon-Avon was followed by an excellent performance as Orinthia in a revival of *The Apple Cart* (to Coward's King Magnus), and she also won much applause for her interpretation of the widely-differing parts in the two halves of *Separate Tables*. Among her later parts were Rose in *Variations on a Theme* (1958) and Elaine in *The Wrong Side of the Park* (1960). She also gave an excellent performance in a new version by Ann Jellicoe of *The Lady from the Sea* (1961).

LEKAIN [CAÏN], HENRI-LOUIS (1729–78), famous French actor, the son of a goldsmith, who brought him up to his own trade. But the boy's passion for the stage declared itself early, and he frequented the Comédie-Française, afterwards declaiming the plays for the benefit of his fellow-apprentices. In 1748 he organized some amateur productions, playing the leading parts himself, with much success. While appearing in a poor play, at the author's request, he was seen by Voltaire, who was much struck by his acting. In spite of this he attempted to dissuade the young man from making the stage his profession. When that proved impossible, however, he did all he could to help him; invited him to his house, built a theatre for him, and played there himself with his two nieces. The little company soon achieved an enviable reputation, and society clamoured for admission. Lekain stayed six months with Voltaire, and always said he owed him everything. Before Voltaire left Paris for Berlin in 1750 he was able to see Lekain's début at the Comédie-Française as Titus in a revival of his *Brutus*. Lekain was much applauded, but through intrigue and jealousy was not received as a member for a further eighteen months, the more spectacular but less gifted Bellecourt and the elegant Grandval being preferred to him. The public wanted Lekain, however, though he was small, ugly, and had a harsh voice, for he knew how to overcome his faults, and on the stage they were forgotten. Like Kean and Rachel, he had that essential spark of genius which triumphs over disabilities. Lekain worked feverishly at his parts (for an account of his acting see Clairon's *Réflexions sur l'art théâtral*) and wore himself out playing them. He was one of the most popular actors of the day, and when he fell ill the bulletins of his progress were as eagerly awaited as those of a film star today. When he reappeared in 1770 it was remarked by many critics that he acted better than ever, as though the enforced leisure had led to a deepening of his talents. He went to Berlin on the invitation of Frederick II, and Voltaire, whose memories of French acting went back to Baron, called him the only truly tragic actor. He was highly praised also by Grimm and La Harpe, and frequently compared to Garrick. He was responsible for many reforms in the theatre, notably for the introduction of some trace of historical costume, in which he was nobly supported by Mlle Clairon. Together they did away with hip-pads and paniers, and on 20 Aug. 1755 introduced some touches of *chinoiserie* into Voltaire's *Orphelin de la Chine*. Lekain was three times in prison on account of his profession, once because, with a number of his colleagues, he refused to act with a man who had brought disgrace on the company. He suffered much from the ignominious status accorded to actors in his day, thought often of retiring, but loved his work too much. His death was tragic. After giving a magnificent performance as Vendôme in Voltaire's *Adélaïde du Guesclin*, he went out into the chill night air, took cold, and died just as his great benefactor and admirer was returning to Paris after thirty years of exile. The news of his funeral was the first thing Voltaire heard on his arrival.

LELIO, see ANDREINI (3) and RICCOBONI (2).

LEMAÎTRE, see FRÉDÉRICK.

LEMAÎTRE, JULES-FRANÇOIS-ÉLIE (1854–1914), French author and dramatic critic, who was for many years attached to the *Journal des Débats* and *Le Temps*. One of his early works was a book on Molière. As a critic he was capable of extreme kindness, as in his appreciation of Victor Hugo, or of great cruelty, as in his treatment of Georges Ohnet; his opinions were usually sound, however, and taken as a whole his work was beneficial to the theatre. His articles were published in volume form as *Impressions de théâtre*. He was also the author of several plays, none of which proved successful, and his reputation rests mainly on his critical works.

LEMERCIER, (LOUIS-JEAN) NÉPOMUCÈNE (1771–1840), French dramatist, who at one time seemed destined to be the great literary name of the Napoleonic era. Godson of the Princesse de Lamballe, he was befriended in his youth by Marie-Antoinette, and was later a protégé of Napoleon, the friend of Josephine, intimate with Cambacérès and Talleyrand. He had great gifts, and his first play was produced when he was only 16; but he was handicapped by bad health and by his position, caught between the eighteenth century, which was no longer fashionable, and the nineteenth, which he lacked the power to comprehend. His plays belong to both epochs. His *Agamemnon* (1795) might be called the last French tragedy on a classical theme, while *Pinto* (1800), with its lackey who liberates Portugal, seems to anticipate Hugo's *Ruy Blas*. *Christophe Colomb* (1809), inspired by readings of Shakespeare, also seems, by its flagrant disregard of the unities, to belong to the Romantic school. But Lemercier lacked the force and vitality which might have given life to his work, and is now totally forgotten. He apparently took no steps to safeguard his plays by printing them, and they have gradually been recovered in manuscript from various libraries and private collections, though one, which seems to have been an attack on the new Romantic school for which Lemercier had unwittingly opened the way, has not yet been found.

LEMON, MARK (1809–70), English man of letters, best remembered as the first editor of *Punch*, which he established financially in its difficult early years on the money he received for his numerous and now forgotten plays, mainly farces and melodramas. Lemon was a good amateur actor, and made his first appearance at Miss Kelly's theatre in Soho, later playing in Dickens's private theatricals at Tavistock House, and giving public dramatic readings.

LENKOM THEATRE, Moscow. This theatre, whose full name is the Moscow Theatre of the Leninist Komsomol, or Young Communist League, was founded in 1922 as the Theatre of Working Youth, known by its initials as T.R.A.M. Its original company was formed by a band of enthusiastic amateurs who trained themselves to become professional actors, writing their own topical plays dealing with such contemporary themes as life in a factory. The theatre passed through a difficult phase when success first came its way, and it seemed to be heading up a blind alley. Its reconstruction in 1933 under the leadership of the Moscow Committee of the Young Communist League, and the importation from the Moscow Art Theatre of experienced producers, including Simonov, gave it a new impetus, and with time it mellowed and matured. Under Ivan Bersenev and Serafima Birman it has given many notable productions, particularly of *My Son* (1939), a study in Fascist oppression in which Serafima Birman gave a moving performance as the mother of the condemned man. During the war the theatre was evacuated, but returned with a programme which included *The Winter's Tale* and a new play on the history of the Komsomol.

LENO. (1) DAN (1860–1904), one of the best-loved and most famous stars of the English music-hall, whose real name was George Galvin. He was the epitome of Cockney comedy, of domestic humour, and resignation. His parents sang at early music-hall concerts as Mr. and Mrs. John Wilde, and when his father died his mother married a William Grant whose stage name was Leno. Dan Leno appeared at the age of 4 with his brother Jack and with his uncle Johnny Danvers, the same age as himself, dancing in public houses all over England. At 20 Dan blossomed out as a champion clog-dancer, and in 1886 he was engaged by Conquest, with his wife, a music-hall artiste named Lydia Reynolds, for pantomime at the Surrey. In 1889 he went to Drury Lane under Augustus Harris, and appeared in pantomime there, returning for many years as Sister Anne, the Widow Twankey, Cinderella's stepmother, the Baroness, and other parts. He continued to appear on the halls, mostly at the London Pavilion, where he told, in quick, staccato style, long rambling anecdotes of incidents involving himself or some other member of his family, with frequent mutterings and asides, but always with an eager, startled look and wide smile. For his success when commanded by King Edward VII to Sandringham in 1901 he was called 'the King's Jester', and a comic paper was named after him. In 1901 he wrote a burlesque autobiography called *Dan Leno—His Book*. Towards the end of his life he broke down from overwork and became insane. His son (2) SYDNEY PAUL GALVIN (1892–1962), known as Dan Leno junior, was a good dancer and comedian, but never achieved the fame of his father, to whom he bore a strong facial resemblance. His best work was done as a writer of pantomimes.

LENOBLE, EUSTACHE (1643–1711), a French lawyer who was imprisoned for forgery, and later became a hack-writer. Among his miscellaneous works were some unsuccessful plays, including three done at the Hôtel de Bourgogne by the Italian actors there. One of them, *La Fausse prude*, was taken as a reflection on Mme de Maintenon, and was used as an excuse for the banishment of the Italian troupe from Paris in 1697.

LENOIR, CHARLES (*fl.* 1610–37), early French actor-manager, who in 1610 was a member of a company fined for playing in Paris without the permission of the Confraternity of the Passion. He became the leader of a provincial company under the patronage of the Prince of Orange which appeared intermittently in Paris from 1622 to 1626, and had as one of its members the young actor Montdory, later to play the heroes of Corneille and rival the glory of Bellerose. The two men parted company in about 1624, but were together when in 1630 they brought a troupe, not that of the Prince of Orange, and settled permanently in Paris, where they were the first actors to appear in a play by Corneille. Just before this company settled, with Montdory at its head, at the Théâtre du Marais in 1634, Lenoir, his wife (an actress who had appeared in Mairet's plays), and several other actors were transferred to Bellerose's company at the Hôtel de Bourgogne. This was due to a sudden whim of Louis XIII, who thus revenged himself on Richelieu for a number of petty indignities which culminated in the Cardinal's marked preference for Montdory's troupe over the official King's Players. Little more is known of Lenoir, and his name is not mentioned after 1637, when his wife, who outlived him, retired from the stage.

LENSKY, ALEXANDER PAVLOVICH (1847–1908), Russian actor, and one of the leading members of the Imperial Maly Theatre company, which he joined from the provinces in 1876. He spent the rest of his life there, and eventually became its director. Lensky was a many-sided man, being at once actor, producer, teacher, artist, and sculptor. He trained many actors for the Maly, and introduced Ibsen to Russian audiences. Although he supported Yermolova and her companions in their efforts to revive the fortunes of the theatre in its difficult days at the beginning of the twentieth century by renewing the old classic repertory, he was enlightened enough to further many of Nemirovich-Danchenko's reforms, notably the introduction of more rehearsals and of a dress-rehearsal, and the abolition of the old-fashioned style of stilted acting in favour of a more natural and supple approach.

LENSOVIET THEATRE, Moscow. This theatre, which takes its name from a part of the city named after Lenin and governed by its local council, the Leninsky Soviet, was organized in 1926 by a group of graduates of the State Institute of Theatrical Art. Its first productions were classics studied by the young actors previously during their training, but later it included new Soviet plays in its repertory. It was successful enough to draw not only local audiences but people from the centre who found it worth while to pay a visit to this suburban theatre. Actors from the central theatres joined its company, and L. A. Zubov became its artistic director. Under him the theatre made great strides, combining realism with experimental production, not only of classical plays, but of plays on contemporary events and problems of Soviet life.

LEONIDOV, LEONID MIRONOVICH (1873–1941), Russian actor and producer, and one of the leading members of the Moscow Art Theatre. He entered the school of the Maly Theatre in 1894, but did not finish there, preferring to leave it two years later to work in the provincial theatres of Kiev and Odessa. In 1901 he joined the Korsh Theatre in Moscow, and finally, in 1903, the Moscow Art Theatre. His most brilliant performance as a tragic actor was given in the part of Dmitri Karamazov in the dramatization of Dostoievsky's great novel. Among other parts he played Peer Gynt, Lopakhin in *The Cherry Orchard*, Solyony in *Three Sisters*, Professor Borodin in the early Soviet play *Fear*, and Plushkin in the dramatic version of *Dead Souls*. At the time of his death he was engaged on the production, with Nemirovich-Danchenko, of a new play about Lenin, *Kremlin Chimes*, given by the Moscow Art Theatre in Jan. 1942.

LEONOV, LEONID MAXIMOVICH (1899–   ), Soviet dramatist, born in Moscow, the son of a self-taught peasant poet. He began writing very early, mostly poems, and was one of the outstanding Russian dramatists of his day, gaining in strength and popularity by the work he did during the Second World War. His *Untilovsk* (1926) was the first Soviet play to be produced by the Moscow Art Theatre, but it was not entirely successful. *Skutarevski*, which followed, was more promising, and dealt with the problems of an old scientist torn between his work and his family, and between the old and new régimes, as typified by his wife and his ward, complicated by the counter-Revolutionary activities of his son. This play was produced by the Maly Theatre in 1934. Other interesting plays on contemporary themes are *The Orchards of the Polovtsi* (1938), done in 1948 by the Bristol Old Vic company as *The Apple Orchards*, and *The Wolf* (1939), which deals with the impact of the Soviet régime on personal problems; but the play which set the seal on Leonov's growing reputation was *Invasion* (1942). Owing to the difficulties caused by the evacuation of the theatres it was first produced in a provincial theatre near Moscow. Later it was produced by Sudakov at the Maly Theatre. It tells, with great force and pathos, the story of a Soviet village under Nazi rule, the reactions of the villagers, and their contribution to freedom and final victory. The play, which has been published in an English adaptation, was one of the most successful of the Soviet war-plays. Leonov seems to have written little since, but in 1957 his *Gardener in the Shade* was produced at the Mayakovsk Theatre by Okhlopkov, and a revised version of an earlier play, *Golden Chariot*, was seen at the Moscow Art Theatre.

LÉOTARD, JULES (1830–70), a famous wire-walker and trapeze-artist, born in Toulouse, who was originally trained as a gymnast. He made his début in Paris in 1859 and had a triumphant career in Europe. His success in London, where he appeared at the Alhambra under Hollingshead, led to the writing of the popular song 'The daring young man on the flying trapeze'. In spite of the risks he took he never had an accident, and died in his bed of tuberculosis at the age of 40. In marked contrast to the gaudily-spangled costumes favoured by other trapeze-artists of the period, he wore a sober one-piece garment, and his name has been given to the similar costume worn as a practice-dress by ballet dancers. Shortly before his death he published a volume of memoirs.

LERMONTOV, MIKHAIL YUREVICH (1814–41), famous Russian lyric poet, who also wrote three romantic plays, and had most of his work banned by the Tsarist censorship. He had a short and stormy life, being sent down from Moscow University in 1832, and exiled for his denunciation of contemporary society in his poem on the death of Pushkin in 1837. A year later he was pardoned and returned to St. Petersburg, but was again exiled in 1840 after a duel. While on active service in the Caucasus he quarrelled with a former student-friend and was killed at Pyatagorsk in the resultant duel.

He became interested in the theatre at a very early age. Writing to his aunt from Moscow when he was about 15 he said: 'You said that our Moscow actors were worse than the St. Petersburg ones. What a pity you didn't see *Die Räuber* done here. You would change your mind. Many St. Petersburg gentlemen agree that plays are better here than there, and that Mochalov in many ways is better than Karatygin.' He had no sympathy with the rules of French classical tragedy. His models were Schiller, and Shakespeare, whom he called 'that immeasurable genius'. His first play, a verse-tragedy, written in 1830, though it deals ostensibly with the Inquisition in Castille, is in reality aimed at the despotism of the Tsar, and was suppressed. It was first performed in Russia after the 1917 Revolution. His next play, in prose, was originally given a German title, to stress its kinship with the plays of the *Sturm und Drang* writers, particularly Schiller. Based on a family conflict which recalls Lermontov's own unhappy home life—his mother died when he was young, and he was brought up by his grandmother, who was constantly at odds with his father—it is again an indictment of contemporary society. He returned to this play later and rewrote it, making it a 'romantic drama' in which, he said, 'all the characters are taken from life, and I want them to be recognized so that some repentance may come to their souls'. In the second version he emphasized the conflict of good and evil and the struggle of the rebellious hero confronting a hostile world.

Lermontov's greatest play, and the only one by which he is now remembered, is *Masquerade*.

It was written in 1835, and again deals with the problem of good and evil, which Lermontov had begun to realize is no longer the problem of an individual only, but of the forces ranged for or against that individual. The climax of the play, in which a man poisons his wife whom he loves, is not the result of intrigue, but of the psychological state of the husband, driven to crime by the corrupt society in which he lives. In deference to the censor, Lermontov substituted a happy ending, but the play was not produced until 1852 at the Alexandrinsky Theatre and even then only in a mutilated text. The full version was given in 1864, but its history in the theatre may be said to have begun only in 1917, with Meyerhold's production at the Alexandrinsky, where it was the last play to be produced before the October Revolution. He later produced it at his own theatre, and again at the Alexandrinsky in 1938, and this 'masterpiece of sophisticated sarcasm', as it has been called, has found its way into the repertory of most Soviet theatres. It has not yet been seen in England or the United States.

LERNER, JOSEPH YEHUDA (*c.* 1849–1907), Jewish playwright, translator of *Uriel Acosta* into Yiddish (see JEWISH DRAMA, 5).

LERNET-HOLENIA, ALEXANDER (1897–), see AUSTRIA.

LE SAGE. (1) ALAIN-RENÉ (1668–1747), French novelist and dramatist. He was orphaned at an early age and confided to an uncle who soon dissipated his ward's fortune. Left penniless, Le Sage managed to make a living somehow, though his early years are obscure. By 1694, however, he was established in Paris, and married. His fellow-student Danchet had already encouraged him to try his hand at literature, and Le Sage's brilliant career begins with a mediocre and not very successful translation. He also studied Spanish literature, and, inspired by it, wrote the novels, *Le Diable boiteux* and *Gil Blas*, which constitute his main claim to fame. But though pre-eminently a novelist, Le Sage is by no means negligible as a dramatist. His early plays were adaptations from the Spanish of Lope de Vega and Rojas, but his first success, in 1707, the year of the publication of *Le Diable boiteux*, was undoubtedly *Crispin rival de son maître*. Two years later a slight play, called *Les Étrennes*, which the actors refused, was remodelled as *Turcaret* (1709), Le Sage's masterpiece and one of the best comedies in the history of French drama. The play satirizes the gross, purse-proud parvenu, the financier battening on the miseries of the poor, who was in the ascendant at this time, and reflects that bitterness against taxation which came to a head under Louis XVI. Like many another good play, it met with great opposition, and those whom it attacked tried to bribe Le Sage and the actors to suppress it. But, with the support of Monseigneur, it was put on, and was successful. Some obscure quarrel between Le Sage and the actors of the Comédie-Française, due perhaps to arguments over another play, *Tontine*, then led Le Sage to break off his association with the official theatre, and for many years he wrote for the theatres of the Paris fairs, alone, or in collaboration with Piron, Autreau, Fuzelier, Dorneval, and others. He wrote 100 or more sketches, which had a purely ephemeral interest, since it was left to Piron to establish the 'play with one actor' called for by the various decrees promulgated against the fair-ground playhouses.

Le Sage's life, though laborious and unremunerative, since he was too proud to accept patronage, was mainly a happy one, as he had a devoted wife and four children, and enjoyed the esteem of his fellow-writers. His greatest sorrow was the decision of two of his sons to become actors, a profession he disdained. The eldest, (2) RENÉ-ANDRÉ (1695–1743), took the name Montménil, and after some years in the provinces played at the Comédie-Française with great success. He was deservedly popular with the public, and was eventually reconciled with his father, after, it is said, the latter had seen him play Turcaret, one of his best parts. Father and son then became the best of friends, and Le Sage was heartbroken when Montménil died suddenly at the age of 48. Le Sage's third and youngest son (the second became a canon of Boulogne Cathedral), (3) FRANÇOIS-ANTOINE (1700–?), took the name of Pitténec, but was not as good an actor as his brother. Two plays by him were given at the Foire St-Germain, but they were only re-hashes of his father's works, and were not successful. On Le Sage's death Pitténec left the stage and retired to Boulogne, to be near his brother the canon, and the rest of his history is lost in obscurity.

LESSING, GOTTHOLD EPHRAIM (1729–81), German playwright and dramatic critic, one of the most acute intelligences of the eighteenth century. Descended from a long line of Protestant pastors and theologians, he deserted theology for literature while a student at the University of Leipzig. This later critic and reformer of the German stage intended at first to become an actor-playwright like Molière, one of his heroes. He spent much time behind the scenes at Caroline Neuber's theatre, acquiring valuable knowledge when his first light comedies were produced there. Written in the traditional French style, these nevertheless reveal an alert, inquiring mind and a readiness to flout current opinions. He also embarked on various journalistic enterprises connected with the theatre, and translated several French and English treatises on acting and the drama, including Dryden's *Essay of Dramatic Poesy*. His own combative middle-class consciousness led him to prefer works in which such a milieu was studied, and he was well versed in English novels of this kind, as is apparent in his first important dramatic work, *Miss Sara Sampson* (1755), in which the influence of Richardson is particularly noticeable. This tragedy of a middle-class heroine, which with all its faults is superior to the 'bourgeois drama' of Diderot and Lillo, was the first modern German play to be taken from life and written in natural, unstilted dialogue. It was produced by Ackermann in Berlin. It tells the story of Sara, a virtuous girl, who has eloped with an unscrupulous lover and waits in vain for marriage. Her father traces her to an inn just as her lover's former mistress, a virago, is trying to regain his affections. The latter rebuffs her, but foolishly allows her to visit Sara, whom she poisons. Whereupon the conscience-stricken lover kills himself on Sara's corpse in the presence of the lamenting father.

In 1759 Lessing with two collaborators launched the *Briefe die neueste Litteratur betreffend*, which set a new standard for literary criticism. Lessing's criterion was excellence, and with pungent wit he dissected those whose aim was low, insincere, or misguided. After serving for some years as secretary to the governor of Breslau, General Taudenzien, and so viewing the Seven Years' War at close quarters, he returned to literature with his treatise on aesthetics, *Laokoon, oder die Grenzen der Malerei und der Dichtkunst* (1766), in which, countering inferences drawn from Horace's *ut pictura poesis*, he differentiates sharply between the sphere of art (space) and that of poetry (duration); in poetry he allows discreet use of ugliness, in art almost none. Only Part I of this work was completed, which is all the more regrettable since he might later have dealt fruitfully with acting as a combination of both spheres.

In 1767 appeared Lessing's first great play, a prose comedy which still retains much of its verve, *Minna von Barnhelm*. The heroine, hearing that her fiancé Tellheim intends to renounce her, he being penniless and under a cloud, pursues him, and finds him obdurate. She resorts to various subterfuges, but in the nick of time a letter from Frederick the Great clears Tellheim's name and all ends happily. The action, as in *Miss Sara Sampson*, takes place on one day, in various rooms of an inn. In view of this regularity it is not surprising that when in 1767 Lessing became official critic to the Hamburg theatre, and made many onslaughts on the conventions of French classical tragedy in general and Corneille in particular, he nowhere advises wholesale imitation of Shakespeare, though he repeatedly acknowledges his supreme craftsmanship, his truth to nature in character-drawing, and his unerring sense of the theatre. The upshot of the *Hamburgische Dramaturgie* is that Aristotle's view of drama, provided it be intelligently interpreted, still holds good. In a discussion on catharsis and the aim of tragedy Lessing insists that both the fear and the pity, intimately linked, are felt by the onlooker as though he himself were in the place of the hero. He is clearly approaching tragedy from the angle of a predominantly middle-class audience, and rules out the admiration which heroic tragedy should evoke.

Unfortunate complications ruined the Hamburg theatre, and in 1769 Lessing became keeper of the Duke of Brunswick's library at Wolfenbüttel. He set to work on a tragedy which should elucidate his arguments. The result was *Emilia Galotti* (1772), in which a young girl is abducted by a licentious prince on her way to her wedding. When her father finds that she is not insensible to the charms of her betrayer, he stabs her, at her own request, to preserve her honour. The story, in fact, is that of the middle-class Virginia brought up to date.

Lessing's last years were taken up with a prolonged struggle against narrow-minded orthodoxy, and with philosophy, which finds expression in his final work, *Nathan der Weise*, a noble plea for religious tolerance, written in blank verse. It was not produced during Lessing's lifetime. Two years after his death it met with little success. It was not until Goethe produced it at Weimar in 1801 that it received the acclamation which was its due. It was translated into many languages, and, except during periods of dictatorship, has continued to form part of the German theatre's repertory. W. E. DELP

LEVICK, HALPER (1888–1962), writer of plays in Yiddish on modern themes, produced in New York by Maurice Schwartz (see JEWISH DRAMA, 6).

LEWES. (1) (CHARLES) LEE (1740–1803), English actor, whose first important part was Young Marlow in *She Stoops to Conquer* (1773), when he spoke an epilogue specially written for him by Goldsmith. He was at Covent Garden until 1783, creating the part of Fag in *The Rivals*, and then went to Drury Lane, where he played a number of Shakespearian parts, including Touchstone and Falstaff. He was for some time assistant to Stephen Kemble at the Dundee Theatre, and from there went to Dublin, where he was not a success. Falling into financial difficulties, he was imprisoned for debt, and spent his enforced leisure in writing his memoirs. He was three times married: to a Miss Hussey, who died in 1772, to Fanny Wrigley, who died in 1783, and to Catharine Maria Lewes, who died in 1796. Genest is mistaken in saying that Lewes played Bardolph at Covent Garden on 26 Sept. 1763, as he did not appear at that theatre until the season of 1767–8. Bardolph was played by Philip Lewis, uncle of W. T. Lewis (see below).

Lewes's grandson, (2) GEORGE HENRY (1817–78), was a philosopher, dramatist and dramatic critic. He also had some pretensions towards being an actor, and was one of the group of amateur actors connected with Dickens, playing such parts as Sir Hugh Evans in *The Merry Wives* and Old Knowell in *Every Man in his Humour*. In 1849 he appeared in Manchester as Shylock with some success, anticipating, according to a contemporary critic, Irving's conception of the part as that of 'a noble nature driven to outlawry by man'.

He then played the chief part in his own tragedy, *The Noble Heart*. He does not appear, however, to have acted professionally in London.

Under the pseudonyms of Lawrence Slingsby and Frank Churchill, Lewes wrote about a dozen other plays, most of them adapted from the French; *A Chain of Events* (1852) and *A Strange History in Nine Chapters* (1853) were written for and in collaboration with C. J. Mathews and produced at the Lyceum, as were Lewes's other plays, except for *Buckstone's Adventure with a Polish Princess* (1855), which was done at the Haymarket, and *Stay at Home* (1856), seen at the Olympic.

Lewes was one of the founders of *The Leader*, for which he wrote leading articles, and, as 'Vivian', from 1850 to 1854, dramatic and musical criticism. In the former capacity he sometimes reviewed his own plays. In 1854 began his life-long liaison with George Eliot. He left London and was succeeded on *The Leader* as dramatic critic by E. F. S. Piggott ('Chat-Huant'). Lewes had a keen eye for acting, and in 1875 republished several of his critical articles under the title of *On Actors and the Art of Acting*. A further selection was republished by William Archer and Robert W. Lowe in Vol. III of their *Dramatic Essays* (1896). In his analysis of Edmund Kean, Rachel, Macready, the Keeleys, and Salvini, he exhibited a sharp discernment between what the actor had to say and his method of saying it: 'It is the incalculable advantage of the actor that he stands in the suffused light of emotion kindled by the author, and is rewarded, as the bearer of glad tidings is rewarded, though he has had nothing to do with the facts which he narrates.' Lewes, who was one of the first to perceive the growing genius of Irving, had a particular dislike for Charles Kean, whom he harried on every possible occasion.

LEWIS, MATTHEW GREGORY (1775–1818), English novelist and dramatist, usually known as 'Monk' Lewis from the title of his most famous novel, *Ambrosio, or The Monk* (1795), written in ten weeks while Lewis was residing abroad. This provided material for a number of sensational plays, which, together with *The Castle Spectre* (1797), a musical play of little literary merit which was immensely popular, and the famous equestrian melodrama *Timour the Tartar* (1811), found their way into the repertory of the nineteenth-century Juvenile Drama. Lewis's work, which was deliberately concocted to appeal to the prevailing taste for melodrama and spectacle, was somewhat crude, but offered great scope for effective acting and lavish scenery enhanced by incidental music. His characters were all of a piece—villain, hero, romantic lover, or distressed maid—and his speeches, however much they may have moved or horrified audiences at the time of their production, read thinly on the printed page. He was of the school of Kotzebue, two of whose plays he translated, and most of his work has vanished with the fashion which gave rise to it.

LEWIS, WILLIAM THOMAS (1749–1811), English actor, whose elegance and affability earned him the sobriquet of 'Gentleman Lewis'. He made his first appearance on the stage at Dublin in 1770, and three years later went to Covent Garden, where he remained for the rest of his career. For twenty-one years he was acting-manager, and on his retirement in 1809 John Philip Kemble purchased from him his one-sixth share in the patent. He was the airiest and most mercurial of comedians, succeeding the famous Harlequin Harry Woodward in comedy parts. Boaden, in his memoirs of Kemble, calls him 'Lewis the sprightly, the gay, the exhilarating, the genteel. . . . The charm of this really fine actor was in his animal spirits.' He was the first to play nearly all the rattling, hare-brained, and impossibly lively heroes of Reynolds and O'Keefe, and was the creator of Jeremy Diddler in Kenney's *Raising the Wind*. He sometimes played tragedy in his early years, but his staccato utterance, restless gesticulation and light voice were totally unsuited for it, and he soon confined himself to comedy. He was a conscientious and hard-working manager, and was much liked by the company. He married Henrietta Amelia Leeson (1751–1826), an actress who first appeared at Covent Garden on 3 Nov. 1775.

LEWISOHN, ALICE and IRENE, see NEIGHBORHOOD PLAYHOUSE.

LEYBOURNE, GEORGE (1842–84), a music-hall performer and the original 'lion comique'. His real name was Joe Saunders, and he was a mechanic from the Midlands. He first sang in East-End tavern 'free-and-easys' and was then engaged by Morton for the Canterbury at £25 a week, rising eventually to £120. He appeared always immaculately dressed as a man-about-town with monocle, whiskers, and fur collar, singing the delights of dissipation, an art which unfortunately he did not fail to practise in his spare time. His last years were a constant struggle with disillusionment and ill health, and he died at the age of 42, after a last appearance at the Queen's, Poplar. He was popularly known as 'Champagne Charlie' from his singing of the song of that name.

LIBERTY THEATRE, NEW YORK, on the south side of 42nd Street, between Seventh and Eighth Avenues. This theatre was for a long time famous for its farces. It opened on 14 Oct. 1904, and among its early productions were *Polly of the Circus*, which ran for nearly six months, and the great horse-racing drama *Wildfire*, with Lillian Russell. The season of 1909–10 included two important productions, Tarkington's *Springtime* and *The Arcadians*, while a few years later *Milestones*, with 215 performances, and *The Purple Road*, with 136 performances, filled a successful season. Several musical successes were seen at this theatre, where the great negro musical, *Blackbirds of 1928*, had part of its long run, and the last legitimate production was given on 18 Mar. 1933, after which the building became a cinema. (See also No. 80.) GEORGE FREEDLEY†

LIBRETTO (*pl.* libretti or librettos), 'little book', from the Italian, used mainly to denote the words, as distinct from the music, of an opera or musical play. Though often the work of second-rate writers, with little to recommend them but their adaptability to the needs of the composer, some operatic libretti have been written by fine poets and dramatists, who successfully overcame the difficulties of combining the requirements of composer and singer with true poetic fervour and lyric beauty. Such were the early Italian librettists Rinuccini and Apostolo Zeno, and the great Metastasio, whose thirty-odd texts were set more than a thousand times, by many different composers. In France the dramatists Quinault, Sedaine, and Favart were excellent librettists, while the popular and prolific Scribe, like many of his contemporaries, added the writing of operatic texts to his other activities. Since opera never became acclimatized in England, no great names are connected with it, except that of Gay in ballad opera, for Nahum Tate, Alfred Bunn, and Edward Fitzball were never more than competent; but England can boast of the perfect collaboration of Gilbert and Sullivan in light opera. Dramatists in their own right whose plays have served as opera texts are Hugo von Hofmannsthal, Maurice Maeterlinck, and Oscar Wilde. Wagner avoided the dangers of collaboration by writing his own texts. Verdi was fortunate in having Boito as librettist for his 'Otello' and 'Falstaff'.

Even greater than the difficulty of writing a good libretto is the difficulty of translating it. In England, where poor translations for long did great disservice to the cause of opera, efforts were made by two distinguished music critics—Ernest Newman and Professor E. J. Dent—to raise the standard, and both were responsible for new versions used at Sadler's Wells and Covent Garden before and after the Second World War.

LICENSING ACT, 1737, see DRAMATIC CENSORSHIP and PROVINCIAL THEATRES, 1 *c*.

LICENSING LAWS, see COPYRIGHT and DRAMATIC CENSORSHIP.

LIGHTING, STAGE. 1. HISTORY. (*a*) *From the beginning to the introduction of gas.* In dealing with the history of stage lighting it is necessary to distinguish between the artificial illumination of theatre interiors and the use of lights on the stage. In all periods candles, torches, lamps, and lanterns have been used as stage properties to indicate night and darkness in performances given by daylight. For the unroofed theatres of Greece and Rome, for the open-air pageant stages of the religious drama in medieval Europe, and for the ordinary unroofed theatre of Elizabethan and Jacobean England, the practical problem of illumination to secure visibility was virtually non-existent. Until the advent of the so-called 'private' or indoor theatre, the Elizabethan stage demanded nothing beyond some kind of artificial light for the last part of the performance on a short winter afternoon, more especially when the time of opening was put on from 2 to 3 o'clock. For this purpose, apparently, cressets were used. Cotgrave's definition of the French *falot* in his 1611 *Dictionarie* is 'cresset light (such as they use in playhouses) made of ropes, wreathed, pitched and put into small and open cages of iron'.

When discussing the lighting resources of the sixteenth- and seventeenth-century theatres it may prove somewhat misleading to use the phrase 'stage lighting' if we think only in terms of the modern stage installation, which differs completely in principle and equipment from that required for front-of-house illumination. Until the increased size of both stage and auditorium in the latter part of the eighteenth century created a new set of conditions, the specific problem was not primarily how to light the stage, but how to light the interior of the theatre regarded as a whole. In normal theatre practice there was no question of extinguishing the 'house lights' during the performance; lighting was a matter of so many candelabra and candle-sconces for the auditorium and so many for the acting area; remembering that until the stage lost its apron and retreated behind the proscenium arch neither theory nor practice kept the action within the picture frame. For the most important parts of the action the actor deliberately came outside the effective range of the special stage lighting—footlights excepted.

The distinctive feature of the Elizabethan or Jacobean private playhouse was the roofed auditorium; but these buildings were well lighted by good-sized windows; such evidence as there is indicates that daylight was used whenever possible, and that the use of artificial light was matter for comment. As W. J. Lawrence originally pointed out, there is only one way to make sense of the *locus classicus* in Dekker's *Seven Deadly Sins of London* (1606), which describes the shuttered city, at the entry of Candlelight, looking 'like a private playhouse, when the windows are clapt down, as if some *Nocturnal*, or dismal *Tragedy* were presently to be acted'. The inference is, not that the private playhouses preferred or were compelled to use artificial light, but that it could be employed, on these special occasions, to create a more realistic impression of night or gloom, in contrast to the purely symbolic representation which was all the ordinary theatres could manage. A genuine drawback to artificial light, when not necessary, was the expense—a drawback of which the theatre itself remained very conscious until the introduction of gas.

That torches were sometimes used in the private theatres is evident from the reference in Lenton's *Young Gallant's Whirligig* (1629) to 'the torchy Friars', that is, the Blackfriars theatre. Normally, however, chandeliers (branches) and candle-sconces provided the general illumination. The more usual form appears to have been that shown in the frontispiece to Francis Kirkman's 1672 edition of *The Wits; or, Sport upon Sport*, consisting of eight twisted branches each carrying one candle (see No. 23). In the eighteenth century this gave way to the simpler loop or ring.

Apart from the very vague possibility that such a stage direction as 'Ici faict tenebres' (*Mystère de la Passion*, 1474) may indicate that some kind of smoke-screen effect was used in the medieval religious drama for the Crucifixion scenes, stage lighting proper, designed exclusively to enhance the stage spectacle, began in the theatre of Renaissance Italy, where it was considered an integral part of the sumptuous entertainments with which the rulers and princelings of that country amused themselves. For the sixteenth and the first half of the seventeenth centuries, scenic precept and practice are embodied in the writings of Sebastiano Serlio (1475-1554), Leone di Somi (1527–92), Nicola Sabbattini (1574–1654), and the German architect Josef Furtenbach (1591–1667). Taken together, they give a reasonably comprehensive idea of the lighting methods and resources of courtly entertainment.

Serlio, in his *Second Booke of Architecture* (English translation, 1611), says the stage is 'adorned with innumerable lights, great, middle sort and small', cunningly set out to counterfeit precious stones. 'You place great part of the lights in the middle, hanging over the scene', and to add to the brilliance of the spectacle the windows of the lath and canvas houses of the tragic and the comic scenes should contain glass or paper, and have lights set behind them. Coloured lights are contrived by filling glasses or bottles with coloured liquids and placing 'great lamps' behind them, or—for extra brilliant illumination—torches with barbers' basins behind them for reflectors. Natural phenomena, such as the rising moon, can be admirably counterfeited.

Di Somi's *Dialogues on Stage Affairs*, translated by Allardyce Nicoll in the 1937 edition of his *Development of the Theatre* (Appendix B), gives the fullest early account of lighting as practised by an expert in the 1560s. He insists upon the careful placing of candles and lamps, upon the necessity for shading or concealing most of the lights, and upon reducing the amount of light in the auditorium. In common with others he uses small mirror reflectors fixed to the backs of his wings, and also set at the judiciously selected spots where concealed lights shone forth from behind columns and in the openings between the wings. He renders the stage as bright as possible, places only a few lamps in the auditorium, and deliberately sets these towards the back of the hall, because a man standing in the shade sees a distant and illuminated object much more clearly. Bright lighting helps to engender a mood of gaiety, and he has made experiments with the contrast between light and darkness to create atmosphere. Once, when he produced a tragedy, he says, he illuminated the stage brightly so long as the episodes were happy in key. Then, with the first tragic incident—the death of a queen—he contrived (by prearrangement, of course) that at that very instant most of the stage lights not used for the perspective were darkened or extinguished'. This made a profound impression of horror and won universal praise from the spectators.

Angelo Ingegneri (*c.* 1550–*c.* 1613), whose *Della poesia rappresentativa e del modo di rappresentare le favole sceniche* was printed in 1598, regards lighting as of 'supreme theatrical importance'. He goes even further than di Somi, and would darken the auditorium completely. He believes in concealing the stage lights, and, to light the faces of the actors and cast a glow over the scene, recommends the equivalent of a concert batten screened from the audience by a valance, and 'fitted with many lighted lamps, having tinsel reflectors to direct the beams upon the actors'. Care must be taken that none of this light is spilled over the auditorium (see Allardyce Nicoll: *Stuart Masques*, 1937).

Sabbattini in his *Pratica di fabricar scene e machine ne' teatri* (1638) points out from experience that lighting from either side of the stage gives more brightness and greater contrast than lighting from in front or behind. For obscuring the scene instantaneously he has tin cylinders suspended on wires over every lamp. These must be dropped simultaneously, and there must be very little light in front of the scenery or the effect will be lost. He also makes it clear that the equivalent of concealed footlights with reflectors were habitually used, but allows that smoke and smell are drawbacks to these lamps at stage level. They were screened from the audience by a parapet or wall—corresponding to the front of the modern orchestra, but a foot or so higher than the stage and built at a distance from it of anything from 1 to 10 feet. Furtenbach, in his *Architectura Civilis* (1628), gives a similar description of footlights, and further vouches for the use of a sunk strip, 6 feet wide, at the very back of the acting area,

> in which also many oil lamps hang unseen, throwing their radiance up into the scene and thus causing many beautiful effects, particularly if the lamps are set on poles and are turned by appropriate means—a device by which very wondrous flashes of lightning and flames can be produced.

This could be used, in fact, both for effects of light and for lighting shutters or backcloths at the back of the scene behind the perspectives, and was also adapted 'to the passage not only of supposed coaches, horses, processions, marching of military formations, but also of ships, galleys, and suchlike'.

The Italian theatre used both candles and lamps. Sabbattini describes metal lamps with drip-pans and hooks to be attached to the lustres; and there were two kinds used for the scenes—the one a simple cruse lamp with a floating wick, the other specially made for theatrical use, specimens of which can still be seen in the Teatro Olimpico at Vicenza. This latter, the *bozze*, was a glass globe, blown so that it had a short handle opposite the hole left for the wick which was carried in a metal holder. The handles could be thrust into ring holders or holes drilled in a board, and two *bozzi* could be used as described above to give coloured light. Burnished reflectors and mirrors were used, both singly and in lengths.

From these writers we can establish the existence in the sixteenth- and seventeenth-century Italian theatre of the following stage lighting units: (1) chandeliers hung over the stage and in the auditorium, and standing candelabras; (2) concealed overhead and side lighting, including a No. 1 batten; (3) concealed or exposed footlights; (4) concealed sunk lighting comparable to the cyclorama trough; (5) exposed, shaded, and coloured lights on the stage. The lighting of the English masque of the seventeenth century was definitely based on Italian practice, and it is noticeable that foreign observers, when commenting on courtly entertainments, make it clear that for display and beauty England could hold her own with the European stage. Inigo Jones (1573–1652) used an abundance of coloured light, and the term he employs—'jewel glasses'—as well as the descriptions, shows that he aimed at the effect advocated by Serlio. He liked to conceal the source of his lighting, and was fully aware of the beauty and effectiveness of all kinds of reflected light. He also used transparencies, and such effects as moons, sunrises, sunsets, etc. The question is —at what period and how completely did the English playhouse stage adopt or adapt equipment similar to that used in the masque? Given the modified Elizabethan structure which was the early Restoration theatre, what evidence have we that the new conditions of 1660 definitely fostered the adoption and development of real stage lighting?

We can clear the ground at once by two statements. We know that until 1765 unconcealed chandeliers, hung over the stage, were the main source of lighting, and that *The Wits* frontispiece, which is the earliest English illustration to suggest the use of footlights, belongs to the year 1672. The placing of the chandeliers and the numbers used varied, naturally, from time to time in different theatres. For the pre-Restoration playhouses we have no pictorial evidence, unless we accept the above frontispiece as relating to that time. The second Drury Lane, designed by Wren and opened in 1674, had in Garrick's day a great central chandelier over the middle of the auditorium, and 'six chandeliers hanging over the stage, every one containing twelve candles in brass sockets' (Tate Wilkinson's *Memoirs*). Rich's Lincoln's Inn Fields theatre (1714–31) had six chandeliers, apparently iron rings hung on chains. Most theatrical prints of the eighteenth century show either a small chandelier or two-branched candelabra over the proscenium doors, and double branches at regular intervals round the fronts of the circles. The better known of the two 'Fitzgiggo' illustrations of the Covent Garden stage in 1763 shows double branches between each of the stage boxes, a lofty central chandelier over the middle of the stage carrying six candles, and four rings of some sixteen candles each hung level with the tops of the proscenium doors well to the sides of the stage, the two in front being hung, apparently, in the actual arch of the proscenium. The other two illuminate the scenic area and hang upstage of the central lustre.

Similar conditions prevailed in the French theatre at the end of the seventeenth century. Dubech (*Histoire générale illustrée du théâtre*, 5 vols. 1931–4) has several good illustrations which show the arrangement of the chandeliers. One, depicting the stage of the Hôtel de Bourgogne in 1688, shows six large chandeliers hung in front of the proscenium arch over the apron, and six more to light the scenic area behind the arch, hung three on each side in line with the perspectives, so that each wing was illuminated (op. cit. ii. 288). Two others (1664 and 1674—for the latter, see No. 24) show the stage and auditorium at Versailles, with five chandeliers hung in a line in the deep arch, illuminating the front of the stage very brightly and leaving the rear only dimly lit. Even more interesting is the reproduction of an anonymous painting of about 1670 in the Museum of the Comédie-Française, showing a stage illuminated by six chandeliers and a row of thirty-four footlights (op. cit. iii. 126).

Flecknoe, in his *Short Discourse of the English Stage* (1664), asserts that the stages of France and Italy have the advantage of us in the matter of spectacle, 'we especially not knowing yet *how to place our lights* for the more advantage and illuminating the scene'. The drawbacks to unconcealed chandeliers hung over the stage—more particularly in a line in the proscenium arch—were that they impeded the view from the second circle of any upstage action, and that the glare from the naked candle-flames was very trying to the eyes. After a visit to the Duke of York's playhouse, where he sat in a side gallery 'over against the musick', Pepys records that 'the trouble of my eyes with the light of the candles did almost kill me' (12 May 1669). An improvement of the existing arrangements was the real substance of Garrick's famous lighting reforms of 1765 at Drury Lane. It used to be said that his 'innovation' was the introduction of footlights to the English theatre. Tate Wilkinson in his *Memoirs*, however, makes it quite clear that footlights—he calls them 'the lamps'—which could be raised or lowered were in use at Drury Lane in 1758. Odell confirms Tate Wilkinson with a number of examples of the use of footlights in the English theatre between 1735 and 1765 (*Shakespeare from Betterton to Irving*, 1921, i. 281–2, 404–8); and W. J. Lawrence (*Stage Year Book*, 1927) cites *The Gentleman's and London Magazine* for Oct. 1765, which states explicitly that Garrick removed 'the six rings that used to be suspended over the stage in order to illuminate the house', indicating that though he took the hint from the French theatre he avoided its mistake of 'extremely faint and disagreeable lighting' and illuminated Drury Lane with 'a clear strong light'. Covent Garden, it adds, has been similarly improved, 'but not with the same success: instead of wax, they have given oil', which smells; and the stage is inadequately lit, having 'more of the gloom of the Comédie-Française than of the cheerfulness of Drury Lane'.

Perhaps the most helpful description of the new Drury Lane lighting, however, is that given by the *Annual Register* (Sept. 1765) which explains that it is done 'by the disposition of lights behind the scenes, which cast a reflection forwards exactly resembling sunshine'. This passage, cited by Odell, does not seem to have been noted by Lawrence, nor yet to have had its real significance sufficiently stressed. It does not tell us *how* the new lighting was done, but it certainly tells us *what* was done, and the well-known engraving of the 'screen scene' from *The School for Scandal* as performed at Drury Lane on 8 May 1777 (Enthoven Collection) undoubtedly records the artist's impression of the kind of effect which could be achieved with the 'new' lighting. It shows, first, brilliant lighting of the apron stage by footlights well masked from the pit; secondly, directed lighting on the prompt side, falling upon a considerable area of the main stage; thirdly, the absence of directed light on the O.P. side; and fourthly, the general all-over quality and amount of light still provided both for stage and auditorium by the house-lighting (see No. 30).

We are not told, either by this engraving or by contemporary accounts, whether Garrick retained any of the chandeliers for hidden overhead lighting of the scenic area: what we know is that from 1765 onwards all the stage lighting proper, except for the floats, came from behind the proscenium arch, and that it is the side-lighting which is stressed. Side-lighting, however, was no new thing in the English theatre. Garrick did not invent wing-ladders (perpendicular battens), nor did he take the idea from the French stage. An inventory of Covent Garden properties taken in Jan. 1744 lists '12 pairs of scene ladders fixt with ropes', with 24 scene blinds and 192 tin candlesticks for the same—items which make it clear that wing-ladders equipped with eight candles each were in use in England at least twenty years earlier. It is possible that besides the hint about removing the chandeliers, Garrick may have obtained from France some brighter and more effective lamps, both for his floats and for his wing-ladders. His correspondence with Monnet in June and July 1765 makes it clear that the latter sent over from Paris specimens of a 'réverbère' (a lantern with reflectors), and two different kinds of lamp for the floats (see Boaden: *Private Correspondence of David Garrick*, 1831). There is no evidence that Garrick adopted any of these, but he was obviously looking for some means of increasing the strength of his concealed lighting to compensate for the removal of the chandeliers, and contemporary comment makes it clear that he succeeded.

Although Garrick did not introduce floats to the English theatre, it seems likely that he began the process of intensification which eventually gave us 'the glare of the footlights', and before leaving eighteenth-century stage lighting it is necessary to catch up on their earlier history. The float-wick lamp, best known today as the sanctuary lamp, is at least as old as the Mycenaean period. The wick can float in the oil or be threaded through a floating disk. For stage purposes it appears to have developed in two ways: as a spout-lamp with two or more wicks, and as a long narrow tin trough filled with fish-oil on which wicks threaded through broad pieces of cork were floated. Boaden called this 'the trap or floating light' and from at least the first half of the eighteenth century the floats were suspended on counterweights and could be lowered or raised through traps in the floor of the stage.

In the earliest known illustration of footlights candles take the place of lamps. This is a water-colour drawing in Harleian MS. 4325 showing the arrangement of a temporary stage in the Salle de la Diana at Montbrison in 1588, which was lighted from above by four three-branch chandeliers and a row of twelve smaller candles on flat bases attached to the tops of a row of framed portraits which embellished the back scene. In front it was lighted on stage level by six large candles like altar candles (see Sylvia England: 'An unrecognised document in the history of French Renaissance staging', *The Library*, Sept. 1935). How far this particular instance justifies us in assuming others in sixteenth-century France it is impossible to say; but Dubech (op. cit. iii. 139) reproduces an illustration of an early seventeenth-century French stage-setting showing a row of ten unscreened candles, and Molière at the Palais-Royal (1640–50) used a *rampe* of 48 small candles weighing eight to the livre. By the middle of the century the Hôtel de Bourgogne had a *rampe* of 'petits lampions espacés' and the painting of *c.* 1670, already mentioned in connexion with the chandeliers, depicts a row of thirty-four footlights divided into three groups, the one in the middle being made up of eighteen lamps. From the Dubech reproduction it looks as if the traps have been indicated by the painter. For a performance of *Psyché* at the Comédie-Française in 1703 there was a *rampe* 'formée par 80 lampions de 6 onces de cire à trois lumières chacun'; while at Versailles in 1704 there was one of forty *bougies*.

The evidence, in fact, points to the same continuity for footlights in the French seventeenth-century public theatre as is assumed for chandeliers, both being a direct inheritance from the Italian tradition by way of the French sixteenth-century courtly entertainment. It is generally thought, however, that in England the footlights were not used for the Jacobean and Caroline masques, which tended to retain traces of their original form and bring the masquers down to the floor of the hall for the concluding dance. This entailed the use of steps or ramps, and obviously precluded the use of the parapet advocated by Sabbattini and Furtenbach, to which, in foreign practice, the footlights were attached. For Court entertainments from 1670 onwards, however, there is evidence for their use in England. The accounts for a masque of 1670–1 have an entry 'for making a trough at the foot of the stage for lights to stand in'. Further entries show that candles were generally used, though one for 1679 is worded 'putting up a long trough to set the lamps in at the end of the stage against the Pit there' (see Boswell: *The Restoration Court Stage*, 1932).

The earliest English pictorial representation of footlights is *The Wits* frontispiece (1672) mentioned above. This, however, gives us neither a firm date nor an actual stage. It has been suggested that it probably represents the kind of makeshift stage which might have been used for surreptitious performances, possibly by strolling players, during the Commonwealth period. To whatever date previous to 1672 it should be assigned, the only clear implication of the drawing is that by then chandeliers and footlights were what was expected in a picture of a stage, however crude. There is no evidence whatever to suggest that it shows the stage of the old Red Bull Theatre. For the footlights, six lamps, each with two wicks, are shown: they are of the enclosed bowl type, with wick apertures but not spouts (see No. 23).

There is no definite evidence for the general assumption that footlights came to England from France, but it would be reasonable to believe—in the absence of any certainty about the use of them earlier—that they were introduced to the Restoration playhouse by men who knew the French stage and its mid-seventeenth century resources, and were bent on employing the scenery, decoration, and machinery already well established there. W. J. Lawrence (op. cit.) makes out a good case for 1671–4 as a probable date for their introduction. In 1671 the new Duke's Theatre in Dorset Garden was equipped with up-to-date French machinery, Betterton having previously visited Paris to pick up useful hints. In 1674 Wren's new Drury Lane was opened; and from then on both these theatres were able, on the evidence of actual plays, to manage scenes of 'sudden darkness' not merely at the beginning of an act but during the course of the action. Given the chandeliers as the only source of controlled light this was obviously impossible, and Lawrence therefore infers some auxiliary source of controlled lighting which could be used to achieve this effect, provided the chandeliers had been put out or left unlighted. The natural inference is that the footlights with traps, vouched for in the early eighteenth-century English theatre, had already been adopted. There is no need to dispute this reasoning, but it does not, of itself, prove that footlights were the only source of concealed lighting in the late seventeenth century. The Court entertainments used lights attached to the backs of the wings (Boswell, op. cit.); and if the traps of the 1744 inventory are to be antedated for footlights, why not the scene-blinds of the scene-ladders for these earlier wing lights?

To sum up: the late seventeenth- and early eighteenth-century English stage was illuminated by the general theatre lighting, by the stage chandeliers, and by controlled stage lighting provided apparently by floats and wing-ladders. After 1765 the house lights and concealed footlights on traps cover the area in front of the proscenium; and controlled and directed side-lighting, with possibly some concealed overhead lighting, deals with the scenic area behind the arch. The lighting achievements of Garrick's scenic designer, Philip James de Loutherbourg (1740–1812), belong more properly to the history of stage effects, and include such things as fogs and the ever-popular conflagrations. The next milestone is the introduction of gas.

In passing, it is interesting to note that the floats, the lights beyond all others purely of the theatre, have always been the target of professional as well as critical abuse, and even in 1790 they were called 'that tormenting line of lamps at the front of the stage which wrongs everything it illuminates'. This early reformer, George Saunders (*A Treatise on Theatres*), recommended instead the use of M. Patte's reverberators (reflector lamps) fixed to each tier of the boxes at the front extremity of the stage to light the apron area, and asserts that they have been successfully used in small theatres, notably at Blenheim. Incidentally, he also recommends another set, again fixed to the boxes, immediately in front of the proscenium pillars, and others on the stage side of the arch, at the first and second shutters, to light the rest of the stage.

The argument that lighting from below is unnatural—Appia once described footlights as 'the monstrosity of the theatre'—that it calls attention to the soles of the actors' boots and the undersides of tables, and creates glare, does not condemn footlights but merely the unskilful use of them. If we light our actors entirely from above and ignore the 'under' lighting, then we get an unnatural effect. Footlights were born of experience—theatrical experience: of the desire to get more and better balanced lighting: and it is interesting to find no less an authority than Stanley McCandless asserting that in 'legitimate productions footlights should be used to illuminate the shadows on the actors' faces and to tone the setting at low intensity.... The practice of omitting them from a layout only limits the flexibility of lighting the stage for all occasions' (*A Method of Lighting the Stage*, 1932).

(*b*) *Gas to electricity*. It would appear that by a narrow margin of two days Drury Lane was the first English theatre to be entirely lighted by gas, when on 6 Sept. 1817 it re-opened for the autumn season. The Lyceum, however, was the first to light the *stage* by gas;

its bill for 6 Aug. 1817 is headed 'The Gas Lights will this Evening be introduced over the whole Stage'. On 8 Sept. the bill announced that

> the complete Success which, after a Trial of several Weeks, has attended the Experiment of Lighting the stage by Gas, has induced the Proprietors of this Theatre still further to consult the Improvement of the Public Accommodation; and this evening a new and brilliant Mode of illuminating the Audience Part of the Theatre by means of Gas Lights will be submitted to the Observation, and, it is respectfully hoped, to the Approbation of the Visitors of the English Opera House.

The statement made by Fuchs in *Stage Lighting* (1929) that gas was installed at the Lyceum by F. A. Winsor in 1803 rests upon a misunderstanding of the facts clearly given in Wm. Matthews's *An Historical Sketch of the Origin, Progress, and Present State of Gas Lighting* (1827):

> In 1803 and 1804 Mr. Winsor publicly exhibited his plan of illumination by coal-gas at the Lyceum Theatre in London. Here he delivered lectures on the subject, which he illustrated by a number of entertaining and appropriate experiments. Among others he shewed the manner of conveying the gas from one part of a house to another.... Afterwards Mr. Winsor removed his exhibition to Pall Mall, where, early in 1807, he lighted up a part of one side of the street, which was the first instance of this kind of light being applied to such a purpose in London.

Covent Garden began to use gas in 1815, but not for the stage or auditorium. The playbill for the opening of the season on 11 Sept. 1815 announces that 'The Exterior, with the Grand Hall and Staircase, will be illuminated with Gas'. It is possible that the Olympic was actually the first theatre to use gas in the auditorium, as the playbill for 30 Oct. 1815 announces that 'The Exterior, the Saloon, and part of the Interior, will be lighted with Gas'.

On 6 Sept. 1817 *The Times* gave the following account of the Drury Lane installation:

> A very considerable improvement, we think, will be found in the introduction of *gas*-lights on the sides of the stage, on which there are 12 perpendicular lines of lamps, each containing 18, and before the proscenium a row of 80. The advantage anticipated from these lights consists mainly in the facility with which they can be instantly arranged so as to produce more or less of illumination, according to the particular description of the scene.

The Examiner, on the following day, praises the effect as being 'as mild as it is splendid—white, regular, and pervading', and describes the lights as being 'enclosed in glasses and blinded from the audience by side scenes and reflectors'.

Covent Garden Theatre was not far behind Drury Lane, and gave a preliminary demonstration on 6 Sept. *The Times* on the 7th reports that 'all the former chandeliers are removed, and a great central light descends from the centre of the ceiling, but not so far as to intercept the view of the stage, even from the one shilling gallery'; five magnificent five-armed branches, one on each side of the stage and three round the circle, supplement the central lustre; and 'the gas lamps have also been fixed upon the edges of the first wings on each side of the stage'. It comments that although gauze screens can be used, or the light diminished at will, 'it is not improbable that the whole illumination may prove too brilliant'. From this description it would appear that the stage was only partially lit by gas. This is confirmed by *Bell's Weekly Messenger* (7 Sept.), which repeats *The Times* description of Drury Lane's lighting almost verbatim, but adds that at Covent Garden the gas is only to be used in the front part of the house 'as yet'.

The Times review of the opening night (in the issue for 9 Sept.) was somewhat captious about the retention of the floats, and considered that the only advantage of the famous chandelier

> that of throwing the light on the countenances of the actors from above instead of from below (which last method inverts the natural shadows of the face and distorts the expression) is defeated by the gas lights which are still retained between the stage and the orchestra. Nor do we know how these can well be dispensed with, as it is by raising or withdrawing them that the stage is enlightened or darkened as the occasion requires it.

The decade from 1817 to 1827 saw gas established, either partially or throughout, in all the more important theatres in London and the provinces. There were exceptions, of course. The Olympic, after being one of the first in the field, went back to wax-lights, and announced in 1822 that, among other improvements, the gas had been entirely removed from the interior (playbill, 28 Oct.). The rebuilt Haymarket of 1820 was lighted with oil lamps and spermaceti candles—the former in patent lamps round the upper circle, the latter in cut-glass chandeliers over the dress circle. Benjamin Webster introduced gas into the auditorium there in 1843. The playbill for 17 April announces that 'among the most important improvements is the introduction (for the first time) of GAS as the medium of light'. When the new Royal Coburg was opened in 1818 it was lighted by oil lamps. By 1832, however, and probably earlier, its stage was lighted by gas; but the playbill for 1 July 1833 announces that new lustres, to be lighted with wax, have been added to the dress circle; and it is not until 15 Aug. 1836 that we are informed that 'a set of new and splendid chandeliers has been added to the dress-circle, lighted with gas'. In 1832 the Garrick, in Leman Street, Whitechapel, possessed five handsome cut-glass chandeliers for gas.

In the provinces, Liverpool, Edinburgh, and Manchester appear to have led the way in the adoption of gas-lighting, the first in May 1818, the second in December of the same year, the third in Dec. 1819. Gas was in use by 1820 for the auditorium of the Exeter Theatre, as *The Times* for 10 Mar. 1820, describing the fire which entirely destroyed the building on the 7th, says it is thought to have been caused 'by the concentration of gas lights in the centre, which were necessarily near the ceiling or the view of the stage from the gallery would have been impeded'. In its bill for 1 Jan. 1829 the Theatre Royal, Greenock, advertises 'the whole [house] Brilliantly Lighted with Gas'; while the theatre at Gloucester, opening after re-decoration in 1830, announces in its playbill of 14 Dec. that 'the Gas Fittings have also undergone considerable Improvement—the whole of the Burners having been regulated—escapes stopped—and the *Footlights supplied with Glasses and Shades* to prevent the evil effects of so dazzling a body of light upon the eyes of the Auditors'.

The article on *The Theatre* in the 1867 edition of *Chambers's Encyclopaedia* gives a very succinct account of the gas-lighting system of the London theatres of the middle of the nineteenth century:

> The prompter has command of all the lights of the house . . . he has a large brass plate in which a number of handles are fixed, with an index to each marking the high, low, etc. of the lights; and as each system of lights has a separate mainpipe from the prompt corner each can be managed independently. . . . The proscenium is lighted by a large lustre on each side and by the footlights which run along the whole of the front of the stage. These are sometimes provided with glasses of different colours, called mediums, which are used for throwing a red, green, or white light on the stage. The stage is lighted by rows of gas burners up each side and across the top at every entrance. The side-lights are called *gas-wings* or *ladders*; and the top ones *gas battens*. Each of them has a main from the prompt corner. They can be pushed in and out or up and down like the scenery. There is also provision at each entrance for fixing flexible hose and temporary lights, so as to produce a bright effect wherever required. The mediums for producing coloured light in this case are blinds of coloured cloth.

The gas battens, the writer explains, are hidden by borders, and are hoisted into position by ropes which pass over drums in the barrel loft and are worked from the flies.

As a rule the mains for lighting the stage and the front of house were entirely independent of each other. At the control, or 'gas-table', the main divided into smaller branch mains, each controlled by its own valve or stop-cock. Each of these branches was then carried to a 'water-joint' or stage-pocket, and thence by flexible rubber tubing to each separate piece of apparatus. 'In the French Opera-House', Percy Fitzgerald tells us, in his *World Behind the Scenes* (1881), 'there are no less than twenty-eight miles of gas-piping, while the controlling "*jeu d'orgue*", as it is called, comprises no less than 88 "stops" or cocks . . . controlling 960 gas jets, etc.' That control of gas lighting was well established and genuinely adequate to theatrical needs by the 1860s is confirmed by an article in *The Builder* (13 Oct. 1866) in which the lighting equipment of the new Prince of Wales's Theatre in Liverpool is described. It obviously included a universal black-out 'switch': 'a single person, placed in front of a system of taps, effectually controls all the gas-lights of the stage and of the house, and he can, by a touch of an electric button, relight instantly, if needful, every burner in the house.' But if control was adequate, safety measures were not. Fitzgerald (op. cit.) gives some appalling statistics, which show theatre fires exactly doubling their number in the first decade following the introduction of gas—a total of 385 between 1801 and 1877, America, Great Britain, and France heading the list, in that order. As *The Builder* (5 Apr. 1856) gloomily remarks: 'The fate of a theatre is—to be burned. It seems simply a question of time.' Early gas floats were enclosed in glass chimneys and later ones were sometimes protected by ground glass or coloured glass mediums; but the open jets (generally fish-tail burners) used for wing lights were not always fenced even by wire guards (see FIRES IN THEATRES).

From the first it was universally recognized that the great advantage of gas in the theatre was its susceptibility to control, but it is difficult to say how far, in its early years, it improved upon the artistic effects which had been achieved with candles and lamps. From criticisms of early gas lighting one might be inclined to think that it had brought the stage little except even more glare and brilliance. *The Theatrical Observer* (No. 1493) in 1826 complained of the lack of contrast in the stage-picture: 'The disposition of the lamps at present is such that no shadow whatever can be presented to the audience, everything upon the stage and in the audience part is a glare of undistinguished lights, painful to the eye. . . . A more concentrated light would be truly refreshing . . . and would give the objects on the stage the utmost beauty of which they are capable, by allowing them some degree of shadow.' In 1892 Percy Fitzgerald is still complaining that 'modern stage lighting is opposed to the exhibition of facial expression. There is such a flood of light, and the face is so bathed in effulgence, from above and below, that there is little relief. There are no shadows. The eye is distracted by the general garishness.... You cannot see the face for the light.' The glare is fatal to all illusion: 'with battens and footlights, each with two or three hundred jets all in one blaze, the figures seem part of a glittering tissue, and do not stand out' (*Art of Acting*).

These are not isolated complaints; they are representative. Are we then to believe that those who worked with gas in the theatre completely lost or destroyed an earlier subtlety of light and shade? Was Dutton Cook (*A Book of the Play*, 1881) right to say that since Garrick's time little had been done 'beyond increasing the quantity of light', so that, as Bram Stoker claims, until Irving's reforms and experiments at the Lyceum in the 1880s, stage lighting by gas was 'crude and only partially effective'? Yes, in so far as the average fully illuminated scene in any large theatre was concerned; the theatres were larger than ever: gas was the first really powerful light the stage had acquired, and the obvious thing to do was to exploit its strength and brilliance. No, however, when certain specific lighting effects were the aim; as, for example, the moonlight, sunrise, and the coming of the morning light so 'exquisitely presented' in Phelps's 1853 *Midsummer Night's Dream* (see Odell, op. cit. ii, for many quotations from contemporary journals). In the 1860s, moreover, efforts were made to combat glare by sinking the floats below stage level—an innovation generally credited to Fechter (see *Illustrated London News*, 7 Nov. 1863). On occasion, too, the auditorium was darkened for the sake of stage effect, as in Charles Kemble's 1832 Covent Garden production of *The Fiend Father*.

Gas, in fact, provided the theatre with means for achieving beautiful lighting effects, but until Irving nobody gave real thought or artistry to its general use, only to its use for the special effect. Bram Stoker claimed that because, under Irving's management, all gas could be regulated from the prompt corner, this in itself made a new era in theatrical lighting. Control, as we have seen, had been there since 1817; and by 1849, probably earlier, the gas-table had put the gas 'wholly under the control of the prompter' (*Theatrical Journal*, 13 Dec. 1849). It was not mechanical control which brought about the Lyceum lighting reforms; Irving was a creative lighting artist who made valuable experiments and gave personal superintendence to the whole business of lighting his productions. The foundation of his method was the consistent darkening of the auditorium throughout the performance—advocated by Ingegneri in 1598. Thanks to Irving, playhouse practice, after three centuries, caught up with Renaissance theory; though needless to say it took some time for the reform to become general.

The difficulty of knowing precisely which of the advances in lighting technique made by Irving relate to gas and which to electricity is increased by the directly conflicting evidence offered by Ellen Terry in her *Memoirs* (1933) and by Bram Stoker in his article on 'Irving and Stage Lighting' in *The Nineteenth Century* for May 1911. Stoker states that in 1891 Irving began to install electricity, beginning with the floats. Ellen Terry says, however:

> We never had electricity installed at the Lyceum until Daly took the theatre. When I saw the effect on the faces of the electric footlights, I entreated Henry to have the gas restored, and he did. We used gas footlights and gas limes there until we left the theatre for good in 1902 . . . The thick softness of gaslight, with the lovely specks and motes in it, so like *natural* light, gave illusion to many a scene which is now revealed in all its naked trashiness by electricity.

It is generally said that after gas-floats and battens were abandoned in most theatres, Irving took his own gas jets and apparatus with him on tour. His use of colour, both with gas and electricity, marked a genuine advance. In the 1870s the thin silk or 'scrim' mediums, used over wire guards, could be had in a few simple colours to give a dominant tone to the lighting, but little more. Irving broke up his floats into separate sections to get greater control of colour, intensity, and distribution; he also experimented with the mixing of colour on the stage, and consequently achieved a subtlety and delicacy 'hitherto unknown'. In his early experiments he used blue paper bags to dim his floats, and for fear of not being able to procure the exact shade even took a supply of these bags with him on his American tour. He is generally considered to have been the first to use transparent lacquers for the glasses of his limes and his electric-light bulbs.

His lighting was at times severely criticized by his contemporaries. The *Quarterly Review* (Apr. 1883) censured his sacrifice of truth and fitness to scenic effect, and quoted as 'a flagrant instance' the 'blaze of light in which Juliet's bedchamber was filled, when even the moon's light was waning, in order that the fierce ghastly livor of the limelight might fall upon the parting caresses of Romeo and Juliet'. The *Pall Mall Gazette* considered that the 'besetting sin' of his famous 1888–9 *Macbeth* was 'the arbitrary and unnatural disposition of the lights', and objected to the courtyard being lighted by 'a strong shaft of limelight obviously proceding from nowhere at all'. Against such English comments, however, must be set the tribute of Antoine of the Théâtre Libre, who saw the production on 9 Feb. 1889, and noted in his journal that the lighting was beyond anything known or thought of in France at that time. Impartial and professional contemporary criticism of this kind lends valuable support to Bram Stoker's contention that Irving's lighting effects were far ahead of anything generally known in the American theatre, where in 1883 only the Boston Theatre had equally good appliances. Whether Irving's partiality prolonged the life of gas in the theatre, and retarded the general adoption of electricity, it is impossible to say, but there can be little doubt that in him this medium found its most remarkable pioneer artist.

(*c*) *Limelight*. Associated with the era of gas lighting is the limelight which outlived it. The lime or calcium light, as developed by Drummond in 1816, gave a brilliant white light of a quality so excellent for stage purposes that nowadays we tend to associate it with the theatre and nothing else. 'It was the application of the limelight', says Fitzgerald, 'that really threw open the realms of glittering fairyland to the scenic artist.' It was at once radiant yet mellow, 'and by crossing the rays of different lamps and of different tints, strange twilight and soft moonlight effects' could be produced. In its early days it was much used for 'realistic' beams of sun, moon, or lamplight, directed through windows, doors, etc. A special limelight, invented by Frederic Gye, was used by Macready to give extra effect to the diorama by Clarkson Stanfield (1793–1867) of Continental views used in his 1837–8 pantomime. It gave very good results, especially for moonlight, but was discontinued after a week's trial, as Macready considered that Gye's charge of 30*s*. a night was excessive. Ordinary limelight established itself in general use after the middle of the century, and is known to have been employed in the 1851 production of *Azael* at Drury Lane, which received high praise for its beautiful spectacular effects. Although the electric arc apparently gave the earliest lens-equipped spotlight apparatus, the lime was used for spotlighting and following actors about the stage, and also for experiments with front-of-house lighting in the 1870s.

(*d*) *Electricity.* Gas had a run of over sixty years in the theatre before it was even challenged by electricity, although the latter had been used for arc-lighting, to counterfeit the disk of the rising sun, at the Paris Opéra as early as 1846, while the arc was used for spots and floods in its 1860 production of Rossini's 'Mosè in Egitto'. The arc, equipped with an enclosed hood, lens, and standard, was the prototype of the modern electric spotlight; and used with a parabolic mirror it could flood certain portions of the stage more intensely than others. It gave a brilliant incandescent light, but it never superseded the lime, because it needed just as much attention, and, moreover, was noisy in operation and apt to flicker. For spotlighting, both limes and arcs continued in use long after the introduction of the electric bulb.

Like gas, electricity was tried out for entrances, staircases, and foyers before it was introduced to the stage and auditorium. It was the invention of the incandescent bulb which ensured its adoption for theatrical purposes, and the first public building in London to be illuminated throughout in this manner was the Savoy Theatre, built by D'Oyly Carte for the Gilbert and Sullivan operas. *The Times* (3 Oct. 1881) gave the new venture some excellent publicity:

> It is worthy of notice that an attempt will be made here for the first time in London to light a theatre entirely by electricity. The system used is that of the 'incandescent lamp' invented by Mr. J. W. Swan, and worked by an engine of Messrs. Siemens Bros. & Co. About 1200 lights are used, and the power to generate a sufficient current for these is obtained from large steam engines, giving about 120 horse power, placed on some open land near the theatre. The new light is not only used in the audience part of the theatre, but on the stage for footlights, side and top lights etc.... This is the first time that it has been attempted to light any public building entirely by electricity. What is being done is an experiment, and may succeed or fail.

The theatre should have opened on 6 Oct. with a transfer of *Patience*, but owing to the difficulties involved by 'the application of electric light to theatrical purposes' this was postponed to 11 Oct., when for the 170th performance the electric lights of the auditorium were turned on and 'cheered to the very echo'. Clement Scott described the light as 'soft and pleasant', but found the glare too powerful and the audience illuminated at the expense of the stage. 'The Lyceum plan', he added, 'of a darkened auditorium and a brilliant stage is, I feel sure, the correct one.' At last, on 28 Dec., *The Times* carried a special notice: 'Electric Light on the Stage. Special Matinée this day at two o'clock. On this occasion the stage will be entirely lighted by incandescent lamps. This will be the first time that any theatre or any public building will have been illuminated in every part by electricity alone. . . .' On the following day *The Times* reported the complete success of the new lighting, and described how a resistance of 'open spiral coils of iron wire' was used in order to get gradations between full light and total darkness not possible with 'ordinary' electrical apparatus, but now made practicable by the Swan lamps. Dimmers, therefore, were used from the first with electrical stage-lighting in England, as also in France, according to Lefèvre's *L'Électricité au théâtre* (1895), a volume containing valuable illustrations of early electrical apparatus and installations, which should be consulted for further information.

It is necessary to distinguish between the lighting of theatres by electric arcs and lighting by incandescent bulbs. It is sometimes stated that the Paris Hippodrome was the first theatre to be lighted by electricity, and the date given is 1878. Actually, it was lighted by the Jablochkoff candle—an arc light with two side-by-side carbons insulated by kaolin. According to a contemporary account twenty of these 'candles', in globes, were used along the line dividing the audience from the arena, reinforced by another sixteen (with reflectors) and three twenty-burner gaslights; 'but with all these powerful lights the result was poor compared with the rich radiance we are accustomed to in the theatre' (J. T. Sprague: *Electric Lighting*, 1878). The Opéra was not completely lighted by incandescent bulbs until 1886. The Brünn Theatre in Austria had electricity by 1882; so had several theatres in America. According to Belasco (see his *Life* by W. Winter, 1918), who was playing there at the time, the first American theatre to use electricity was the California in San Francisco, from 21 to 28 Feb. 1879. Generally speaking, it may be said that between 1880 and 1887 electricity was installed in most of the important theatres of Europe, England, and America, and that after 1887—largely because the two disastrous theatre fires of that year, at the Opéra-Comique and the theatre at Exeter, had once again demonstrated the terrible risks of gas—it quickly gained favour everywhere.

Before leaving the nineteenth century we may notice in passing some of its anticipations of modern lighting practice. The abolition of the floats and front-of-house lighting go back to the first half of the century in England, and to 1872 in America; and in Mar. 1879, in San Francisco at the Grand Opera, David Belasco began the experiments which were to lead to the lighting of *The Darling of the Gods* and *Peter Grimm*, when he got rid of the floats and for his production of *The Passion Play* by S. Morse lighted his stage from the front with old locomotive bull's-eye lanterns, thus anticipating the methods of Reinhardt and Granville-Barker by a quarter of a century. Even more unexpected, perhaps, are the mid-nineteenth-century experiments—again generally involving the abolition of the footlights—in which illusions of space and depth now associated with the cyclorama were to some extent realized. It looks as if they were developments of the panoramic and dioramic background effects popular on the London stage in the early years of the century. The most interesting of these occurred in the French ballet, 'Le Corsair', staged at Her Majesty's in July 1856, in which for the storm scene when the Corsair's vessel was wrecked something in the nature of a (canvas?) cyclorama was evidently used, if we may rely on the following description by *The Illustrated London News* (19 July):

> The complete withdrawal of what are technically called the wings, and the substitution of a broad expanse of panoramic atmosphere extending over the whole area of the stage, is a new, bold and successful idea.

Nothing, unfortunately, is said about the lighting except that the 'struggling moonbeams gleam' and that 'slowly the tempest comes on and the lurid and darkened clouds thicken'.

Gas-lighting was a practical business, begotten of experience; modern lighting is the result first of much theoretical examination of the principles which should govern the art of stage decoration, and secondly of the technical work which has produced the apparatus designed to carry out these new ideas. In his attempt to work out the problems of stage setting for Wagnerian opera Adolphe Appia (1862–1928) not only propounded what have since been universally accepted as fundamental principles of stage design, but, as an integral part of his aesthetic theory, set forth with specific and practical illustrations the basic ideas concerning the nature and function of stage lighting which virtually govern all the best modern work (for an example of Appia's designs, see No. 97).

Envisaging a comprehensive artistic unity as the fundamental demand of a production, he rejected the painted scene in favour of the three-dimensional setting which is the only environment to which the three-dimensional actor can properly belong. To give both actor and setting their full plasticity, however, something other than the flat stage lighting of the end of the nineteenth century was required: if mass, form, and movement were to be self-expressive, to contribute their essential quality and meaning as a vital part of the drama, then shade as well as light was necessary: the light must behave as real light does. It is the unifying principle which links actor and setting in an artistic whole: consequently our emotional responses will be quickened—in both senses—by the light in which we are made to 'see': its colour, its stress, its comment will be in the full sense revelatory. Light, for Appia, is the visible counterpart of the music, interpreting to sensuous perception the dominant mood and following the pattern of the shift and play of feeling.

Appia did not invent apparatus, but the eighteen designs in *Die Musik und die Inscenierung* (1899) embodied his ideas so clearly and satisfactorily that they have enabled the theatre to put them into practice. Moreover, he pointed out that the movable arc lights of the then contemporary theatre provided a means for spotting or picking out the actor, emphasizing his importance, and giving him a shadow. Mobile lighting of this kind, breaking up the light and diversifying direction, intensity, and colour, has become the basis of modern interpretive dramatic lighting: atmosphere, suggestion, mood, and the stressing of the actor are so much the commonplaces of artistic direction today that the genius of Appia is honoured in theatre practice even by many who have no idea from whence the original stimulus derives.

An interesting practical contribution to modern stage lighting was made at the beginning of the twentieth century, when Mariano Fortuny (1871–1949) put into operation in about 1902 the system which bears his name. Because there are two kinds of light in nature—the direct rays of the sun, or of any other light-source, and the diffused general light which is reflected from the atmosphere and from light-coloured surfaces—he believed that the basic illumination of the stage, which made actors, objects, and settings visible, should be provided by reflected light. To give reflected light he 'invented' the sky-dome to act as reflector; the light itself was thrown by high-powered arcs on to bands of coloured silk which reflected it back on to the dome and on to the stage. For all the direct lighting needed spots were used. The softness of the reflected diffused light is very beautiful, but the amount of current consumed is prohibitive, and there are few sky-domes in use. Fortuny gave the theatre, however, the idea of the scope and beauty of indirect lighting, and the idea of the usefulness of the various kinds of reflecting surfaces that counterfeit what the nineteenth century called 'panoramic atmosphere' (see above), and which we call—loosely—the cyclorama. As used in Fortuny's own system it is the *Kuppelhorizont*, or true half-dome, made of silk or plaster: in its more usual form it is the semicircular plaster or canvas wall surrounding the greater portion of the stage—the *Rundhorizont*, or cyclorama properly so-called; and finally there is the flat plaster wall or plain canvas cloth which can be lighted in the same way to give distance and good sky effects, but cannot give space and vastness because it still needs masking (see also SCENERY, 6).

On the Continent the years 1900 to 1914 saw rapid technical and artistic advances in stage lighting, especially in Germany; England and America both lagged behind, though much of the progress made on the Continent was due to the influence of an Englishman, Edward Gordon Craig (1872–1966) (see No. 75), while in America David Belasco (1859–1931) made valuable experiments in the commercial theatre which solved specific lighting problems as they arose. His practical inventions and innovations gave to modern realistic spectacle some of its most beautiful early effects, and many years before the introduction of the Linnebach lantern for projecting from behind on to transparencies, Belasco, helped by a lucky accident (see Winter, op. cit.) achieved by somewhat similar methods the spectacular scene in *The Darling of the Gods* mentioned above, where the bodies of the dead were seen floating and drifting on the River of Souls.

In 1910 *The Stage Year Book* summed up the situation in the London theatre by the sweeping statement that 'on the legitimate stage, with such exceptions as His Majesty's and one or two others, all lighting details are left to the Stage Manager and the Electrician', while in 1913 an American critic, H. K. Moderwell, in *The Theatre of Today*, was equally severe on his own countrymen, and, praising the charm and beauty of the lighting of any well-executed German stage-setting, asserted that it was difficult to realize the secret of it because 'it seems to an American imagination so impossible that a stage should be other than glaring white, that one does not dream of looking for the explanation in the lighting'.

From crude and glaring lighting both countries were to emancipate themselves in the 1920s, but it was only in such things as the Reinhardt productions, or Granville-Barker's Shakespearian work, or the experiments of small non-commercial theatre units, that they had previously encountered anything which could be compared with good contemporary work in Germany. For the English theatre of his day Barker's lighting of his 1912 and 1914 Shakespearian productions was unusual, but his abolition of the floats and his use of front-of-house lighting was not simply an endorsement of fashionable Continental theory, but a practical solution of the problem of lighting the new acting areas created by the use of an apron over the orchestra pit and of a false proscenium which gave another plane between the stage proper and the apron. The description in *The Times* of 29 Sept. 1912 of his apparatus as 'search-lamps converging on the stage from the dress-circle' gives the measure of its novelty.

The fundamental principles governing the art of modern stage lighting were expounded by Appia, Craig, and others, and tried out on the Continent between 1900 and 1910. With the advent of such things as the Schwabe-Haseit system, the Linnebach projector, the G.K.P. projecting process, Wilfred's colour-organ, the pure-colour media of Munroe R. Pevear, and the immensely powerful lamps now used in the theatre, we are in the realm of scientific discovery and mechanical invention. Between them the theorists and the inventors have made modern stage lighting the most essential and the most sensitive of the mechanical means at the disposal of the theatre as a unifying and interpretive agent.

M. ST. CLARE BYRNE

2. MODERN STAGE LIGHTING IN ENGLAND. From the introduction of electricity into the Savoy, in 1881, and the use of the electric arc spotlight in place of the limelight, there was little progress, beyond the increased efficiency of the electric lamp itself, until 1919. The general lighting of the scenery and the acting area was provided by rows of lights, known as battens (border lights in the U.S.A.), up among the sky borders, by footlights, and by strips of lights up each side of the proscenium arch and the wings, consisting of coloured or varnished lamps; hand-fed arc spotlights and floodlights provided all the highlights and directional light that were deemed necessary.

The first revolutionary step came with the invention of the gas-filled electric lamp, which had, however, a serious drawback in that the temperature of the glass bulb was so high that the coloured lacquer or varnish would not remain on it beyond a few minutes. Other methods of obtaining coloured light had to be found, and so were evolved the magazine compartment battens and footlights, in which each lamp had its own compartment with colour-runners for frames containing glass or gelatine colour media.

It was in 1922 that methods were introduced for collecting as much as possible of the light given out by the lamp filament, and projecting it in the required direction. This was done by the use of scientifically designed reflectors. The advent of larger lamps of 500 and 1,000 watts led to the introduction of the high-powered flood lantern not only in the wings but hung among the sky borders for flooding backcloths and draperies.

About 1914 the introduction of a gas-filled lamp of high lumen (light) output, known as a projector lamp, was probably the most revolutionary step forward, and largely altered the whole technique of stage lighting. Previously all spotlighting had been by means of the hand-fed arc-lanterns mentioned above, each of which required an operator to 'feed' the carbons together. This naturally limited the positions in which the lanterns could be used. The projector lamp, however, had no need of an operator; it could be placed in any position and, being connected to a variable resistance known as a dimmer, its intensity could be varied at the wish of the producer. This incandescent spotlight quickly became the most important lighting unit on the British and American stages. It was aptly defined by Fuchs (*Stage Lighting*, 1929) as 'a piece of lighting mechanism used for lighting a small portion of the stage to a higher intensity than the remainder, and thus *unconsciously* focussing the attention of the audience to that part of the stage so lighted'. Its normal position on the stage was just upstage of the proscenium border and on the side walls of the proscenium, and its intelligent use provided the producer with a medium which rendered his whole production stereoscopic, causing flat scenery to appear three-dimensional and the characters prominent (but not too much so) in their surroundings.

From 1922 on there were many developments of this lighting unit. Originally it consisted of the lamp itself, the lens, and provision for moving the lamp towards or away from the lens to vary the beam; then came the introduction of reflectors of various types—optically worked mirrored glass, chromium plate, rhodium plate, etc.—together with stepped lenses and so on to increase the efficiency of the light output. Gradually it crept out into the auditorium so as to cover that area of the stage between the footlights, the spot-batten, and No. 1 batten, always a dark spot, from which actors are drawn unconsciously towards the footlights so that, illuminated only from below, their facial expressions become grotesque. To overcome this, spots were installed on the balcony fronts of theatres. At first, in order to reduce the distance from the stage, they were placed on the lowest circle, but as this is practically always level with the actors' faces, the result was not only to take all expression away from their features, but also to provide high and grotesque shadows on the backcloths. Removal of the spots to the second tier overcame these difficulties. The next problem was that of changing the colours in the lanterns so placed, which led to the development of remote control of the colour-frames by switch operation on the stage switchboard; actually electric magnets are attached to the lanterns.

These circle lanterns proved a big asset to the lighting of spectacular shows—revues, musical comedy, pantomime—and as these are mainly given in the bigger theatres, where the circle is some distance from the stage, increased efficiency was required. This led to the adoption of the lantern known as a mirror spot. This has a scientifically designed eight-inch-diameter optically-worked silvered glass reflector which projects an intense beam of light on a variable gate; this beam is focused by a six-inch diameter lens, in some cases a plain plano-convex and in others a stepped type. By means of the variable gate, rectangular spots of various sizes and shapes can be projected with an intensity of over double that obtained by the standard spotlight of the same size and wattage. In addition to the now traditional spot-batten, groups of these lanterns are used on 'boomerangs', steel barrels fixed to the stage floor and mounted upwards towards the fly floor. In straight plays these are usually mounted near the Prompt and O.P. corners, and may accommodate as many as twelve to fifteen spots in each.

In very large theatres the No. 1 spot-batten is apt to become difficult; in opera, for instance, it is sometimes necessary to move and reset the lanterns for each scene, and therefore a bridge is often provided, particularly in the big Continental opera-houses. The bridge should be, and often is, counter-weighted so that its height can be varied. The mobility of the bridge is allied in control with the 'perches' or ladder-type boomerangs, which can be moved on and off stage according to the width of the scene.

In the modern theatre there is a tendency to design a forward bridge out in the auditorium. An example of this can be seen at the London Coliseum. It is a very efficient method, and commends itself to the little playhouses such as those envisaged for civic centres, for example, where the circle or balcony, even if it exists, is usually too low.

Following spots, known also as 'the limes', are practically the sole remaining electric arc-lanterns used in the theatre, mostly in spectacular shows and in opera. In the modern theatre they are usually placed at the back of the gallery or top circle in a special chamber, and therefore the throw of light is frequently as far as 100 ft. The increase in the general lighting intensity of the acting area since the early 1920s has necessitated the introduction of the high-intensity mirror arc, which uses a carbon combination similar to the cinematograph projector; this, with the specially-designed reflector of mirrored glass and special lenses, has produced a most efficient lantern consuming about 100 amperes. It is fitted with various accessories to alter the shape and size of the beam, such as the 'barn-door' shutters which vary the light horizontally and vertically, and iris diaphragms which give a circular variation of the light so that it can be reduced to a pinpoint. The arc-lantern usually employs a direct-current (D.C.) supply which is obtained either by a motor generator or by a mercury arc-rectifier to convert the current from alternating (A.C.) to direct. The growth of alternating supply has led English designers to produce an arc-lantern that will operate satisfactorily on A.C. without the usual flicker.

In the early days of electric light a stage might be equipped with a colour circuit in a 'three- or four-colour scheme' which provided the basis of the colour effects obtained. Today the colour of the circuit merely differentiates one circuit from the other, since flexibility demands the grouping of the circuits into three or four sets independent of one another. The colour that is used is not fixed, but can be any one of the seventy hues obtainable, as desired by the producer. Nowadays the directional lighting units such as spots, which are not allied to any of the colour groups, are far in excess of the 'colour circuits' which are confined to foots, battens, and stage-floor connexions or dips (known as pockets in the U.S.A.).

There are numerous portable pieces of apparatus used in various parts of the stage, and mainly plugged into the dips, including strips for groundrow lighting which are, in England, similar to the footlights. There is also in the English theatre a lantern called a pageant which is somewhat similar to a small searchlight. It is used for sunbeams through a window, also in colour spectacles from a number of boomerangs; it has been used for front lighting from the auditorium, but has now somewhat fallen out of use (see below).

The cyclorama, though usually classed as scenery, is so closely allied with stage lighting that it must be considered here. It is best described as a perfectly plain screen with a uniform surface on to which coloured light is projected to produce skies of various hues, often with clouds, moving or stationary, thrown on to the cyclorama from optical projectors. It can also be used for the projecting of symbolic designs and shadows. If efficiently illuminated the cyclorama gives the playgoer the illusion of a natural sky, and a feeling of infinite space. The method of lighting is by means of banks of flood lanterns.

The use of the cyclorama on the Continent is practically universal. It stretches from the grid to the stage, and as it may be 90 ft. in height, and any scenery that has to be flied for storing must be above it, it therefore follows that the grid is frequently as high as 120 ft. Starting from the Prompt corner, the cyclorama passes round the stage near to the back wall, ending at the O.P. corner, thus forming half a cylinder. Most Continental cycloramas are made of canvas hanging from a track, and when not in use they can be rolled up in the Prompt and O.P. corners.

The British method is in plan either perfectly flat, or has curved ends to a radius of approximately 4 to 6 ft. In a playhouse with a definite policy, e.g. a good repertory theatre, it should be a permanent structure of hard cement (*not* plaster) which is treated with a white water-distemper. If temporary cycloramas of canvas have to be employed they should be attached to metal barrels at top and bottom and lashed to the stage with lacing to take up the slackness due to variations of temperature. With this type, borders will have to be used, but if their design is carefully considered they need not look unnatural. A cyclorama on these lines is more practicable than the Continental type described above, particularly if it is also the back wall of the stage, as it leaves the full acting area available for use.

The spot lanterns at the front-of-house, and the spot batten and perches will, when a cyclorama is used, illuminate adequately the acting area to within a certain distance of the cyclorama. It is essential that no portion of this light should strike the cyclorama, which should be confined to its own lighting. It is therefore necessary to provide some overhead directional lighting for the area directly in front of the cyclorama. The type of lantern used for this, both in England and on the Continent, was known as an acting-area lantern. The English model was so designed that the beam angle and the lamp cut-off are identical, generally 24°. A number of these lanterns were used, generally to cover most of the acting area. In the big spectacular shows such as those given at the London Palladium and Coliseum, as well as in pantomimes and musical comedies, they formed one of the main lighting units, but are no longer so much used (see below).

Projected scenic effects have been used in connexion with the cyclorama on the Continent by Strobach at Cologne, and by Messrs. Gayling, Kann, and Planer in Vienna. The latter is known as the G.K.P. system. In both methods the whole of the design is projected on to the big curved cycloramas from projectors fitted on a bridge over the proscenium arch. Optical effects such as clouds, snow, flames, and so on have long been in use on both cycloramas and ordinary scenery. They function in much the same way as a magic-lantern slide, and the mechanism for providing movement is either an electric motor or clockwork.

The stage switchboard is the brain of all stage lighting systems, and the electrical and mechanical contrivances which form the control unit must be carefully planned. They may be divided technically into two parts, the switching and fusing section, and the dimmer regulator. The latter is probably the most important point of the control, since it regulates the balance of stage lighting, and gives light and shade, life and realism, to the scenery and characters. The dimmer used in England is of the wire resistance type. It is relatively the least expensive, and satisfactory in every way where a fixed load has to be considered. On the Continent the reactance dimmer, of the tapped transformer type, has made much progress, while in the U.S.A. the direct current saturated choke finds favour. These last two are of course only operable when alternating current is available. In the average London theatre before 1940 the number of dimmers varied from eighty to two hundred. The mechanical operation of such a bank originally necessitated each individual dimmer handle being locked to shafting for gang control in such a way that it automatically released itself both at the top and bottom of its travel, but this method is now almost entirely superseded (see below). The collective operation of a number of shafts produced the 'Grand Master' control, where, by using bevels and 'spline' gears, the whole of the various dimmer shafts could be mechanically connected to the grand master wheel, each shaft being provided with gears for this purpose, so that it was possible for any shaft to be rotated in any direction irrespective of the direction in which its neighbours might be travelling.

An important development in control apparatus during the 1930s was the growth of complete remote control of the switches and the dimmers. The increase in the number of circuits to be controlled made the manually controlled switchboards in the larger theatres difficult to handle, and the various forms of remote control, whether operating mechanically by tracker wire, as in the German systems, or electrically, as in Britain and the U.S.A., have sought by reduction in size of the levers and switches to reduce in turn the size of the control panel, the object of such reduction being to bring all controls under the hands of one operator, and to enable the panel to be sited so as to give the operator a better view of the stage.

L. G. APPLEBEE†, *rev.*

It is interesting to note that the spotlight, as foreshadowed above, has now become the dominant instrument in stage lighting. Floodlights in the wide-angle sense seldom appear except to light the occasional cyclorama. Fixed narrow-beam flood-lights of the acting-area and pageant types have been replaced by Fresnel-type spotlights which allow a widely adjustable soft-edge beam. A very large number of the spotlights are to be found in the auditorium in order to provide illumination when the actors work downstage in close contact with the audience. These are important on an orthodox picture-frame stage but absolutely vital when, as often today, the stage projects largely into the auditorium (e.g. the Royal Shakespeare Theatre stages at Stratford-upon-Avon and at the Aldwych in London). Indeed, in the case of the open or arena stage and theatre-in-the-round where the stage is in the auditorium, obviously all the lighting must be situated there also. Spotlights of the mirror type with accurate beam control from an adjustable gate (known as ellipsoidals—the reflector shape—in the U.S.A.) become essential because light must be directed to the stage and to such part of the décor as may be significant at the time, and must not spill on, or dazzle, the audience seated on three or perhaps all four sides of it. For this, spotlights are essential, and thus the whole development of low-brightness fluorescent lamps which has so revolutionized lighting elsewhere has had no effect whatever in the theatre.

One factor that has effected a revolution in Britain in recent years is the need to reduce labour to a minimum in the manufacture of spotlighting in order to combat rising costs. To tool up for techniques of diecasting, pressing, etc., lighting units must be produced in thousands where short runs, numbered in tens, sufficed before the war. To reduce the number of types, each must be carefully designed to be versatile, and this is achieved by lens changes and attachments. In Britain the vast bulk of stage lighting is now based on two classes of spotlight, the mirror (known as the profile) spot already referred to, and the Fresnel soft-edge beam spot. Both of these are available in three sizes: 250/500 watt, 750/1,000 watt, and 1,000/2,000 watt.

The Fresnel lens spotlight is a development of the simple single-lens optical system originally used with arc lamp and limelight sources, and subsequently with projector lamps for the earlier spotlights (often referred to as focus lamps). The principle of the Fresnel lens is not new, but only comparatively recently has the price of the apparatus become low enough for its widespread use in Britain. It is a short-focus large-aperture (therefore very efficient) lens moulded as a flat plate with steps to avoid the bulk of glass which would otherwise be necessary. As the lamp is moved relative to the lens so the beam may vary in spread from 50° to 15° approximately. The nature of the lens, often assisted by a broken-up rear surface, is to give a soft-edged even beam. This beam provides a variable flood, though it can be confined to some extent by an arrangement of four hinged flaps on the front, known as a barn-door attachment. Fresnel spots are used to build up ill-defined pools of light on the acting area and the setting. They can flood-light an area of a cyclorama or other backing, particularly where the set is picked out only one part at a time. For general lighting of cycloramas or backcloths when they are required to form a visible backing to the whole of the stage, wide-angle flood-lights (fixed beam lanterns) of 500 or 1,000 watt are used, or even a couple of rows of the older type of magazine batten, each compartment of which has a 150-watt lamp. In Germany the large scale of their opera-house cycloramas makes fluorescent lighting essential.

In the theatre, depending on the scale of the enterprise, the various lanterns will be assembled to form an installation. Roughly speaking, profile spots are used for lighting from the front-of-house. Preferably, these are situated to the sides of the auditorium with beams crossed to light the opposite side of the stage and depressed through a vertical angle of approximately 45°. On the stage Fresnel spots are now the main basis with, where appropriate, floodlights for cloths, backings or cycloramas.

Spotlights should be controlled one to a circuit, but where two or more form a particular pattern of light they can be grouped. The number of circuits can be anything from 36, or even less, in a little theatre to 356, as at Covent Garden, the average for a professional theatre in Britain being just over 100. There are always many more dimmers to a European, especially German or British, installation than to an American one, for it is considered preferable here to instal a large number of smaller-wattage dimmer-channels and gain the necessary flexibility by grouping up the controls themselves. In the United States a control virtue is claimed for what was originally an economy measure which led to the purchase of a few large-wattage dimmers to which the many circuits could be 'patched' by plugging arrangements of one sort or another. Such an arrangement is said to be 'flexible', whereas, in fact, when it is used, the simplest lighting cannot be carried out without pre-planning, and unforeseen contingencies during rehearsal may require considerable reshuffling at the patch panel.

Stage-lighting installations can be divided, irrespective of size, into two classes, (i) the repertory, where a semi-permanent lighting layout has to be as complete as possible in order to comply with the demands of frequent changes of production; and (ii) the special, where in fact the electrical wiring and lighting control itself is often the only permanent feature in the theatre. This latter is the practice in London's West End, the lighting being designed and brought in for each production.

There has been, when planning or re-equipping a stage, an unfortunate tendency to lay out the control board and the electrical wiring to suit the style of lighting at the time of installation. Recently, however, an effort has been made to ensure that stage electrical installations provide the flexibility of a television studio, and thus there is a set of circuits identified as number 1 to number 120 or more on which any kind of lighting layout can be set up. Such a theatre is then safeguarded in respect of both fashion and technical changes in lighting. While on the subject, it is interesting to reflect that just as a complete change of lighting technique was represented by the change from floodlighting to spotlighting in the 1920s and 1930s, so too there has been a change in the spotlighting technique itself. It is remarkable to contrast the dozen or so spotlights (relatively inefficient into the bargain) used for the all-important lighting in Terence Gray's Cambridge Festival Theatre which opened in 1926 with the 300 or so used on 200 circuits for *My Fair Lady* at Drury Lane in 1958. While granting that this theatre is much larger, nevertheless mere proportion does not account for this great difference. Whereas the earlier spotlighting was clear-cut and direct, relying on one or two units for its effect, today a whole chorus of spotlights is brought to bear in a particular stage area. A spotlight today seldom plays a solo role, but forms part of an elaborate mosaic of what is, in effect, controlled floodlighting. Costs restrict this technique mainly to London's West End and New York's Broadway. The economic discipline elsewhere may be by no means a bad thing. The use of a large number of spotlights for one particular production must not be confused with repertory working. In this latter case, numbers multiply to avoid a lot of resetting and thereby reduce the labour needed. This need is at its most obvious in the daily change in an opera-house, or in a theatre playing in repertoire.

The theatre's unique requirement of electrical control by dimmers over its lighting is now shared with the television studio. The combined market has inspired considerable invention and development in recent years. The type of dimmer varies greatly, but even more important than the dimmers themselves is the grouping of them together to form a lighting control, for this is what converts a mere collection of circuits into an instrument of artistic expression.

Dimmers are electrical devices to vary the voltage supplied to the lamp, and several methods of doing this are in common use. The simplest takes the form of a variable resistance which can regulate the voltage in the circuit and so the light given by lamps fed therefrom. A resistance is a current device, and therefore the ability to dim smoothly from full light to off depends on the wattage of the load. Another, more elaborate, dimmer uses a tapped auto-transformer. This is a pure voltage regulator and is independent of load. The compromise in England has been to mix transformers and resistances, thereby keeping down the overall cost. Only circuits where variable load is really important will have the more expensive transformers. Resistance and transformer dimmers were formerly mounted on the back of the switchboards and operated directly by handles mounted in rows on shafting in front, as described above; but these methods have been almost completely superseded by remote-control systems. This is because the number of dimmers to an installation tends to be very large, and a direct-operated switchboard to control them becomes cumbersome. For remote control, resistances and transformers are provided with robot-operating arms which, by means of electro-magnetic clutches, connect each dimmer to be driven to raise lights or dim them. The speed is provided by a driving motor, which in effect replaces the master wheel of the direct-operated switchboard. Means are provided to determine the distance of dimmer travel from a remote miniature lever, the whole device being known to engineers as a servo-operated dimmer.

It is only in Britain, or in equipment exported from that country, that the full development of the possibilities of the electro-mechanical system is to be seen. The magnetic clutch was invented in 1929 by M. Mansell, and the first large installation was that for Covent Garden in 1934 (120 dimmers), replaced in 1964. In that case each clutch was under control from a two-way off switch (Raise, Lower, and Stop) with a position-indicator dial above. The master-shaft drives were manual, and the whole control tended to be slow in operation. To obtain a more flexible, playable quality, using the fingers rather than the hands, Frederick Bentham invented the Strand Lighting Console, in which a special Compton-organ console was used to control a similar but motorized dimmer bank. The principle here was to make use of the inertia inherent in a mechanical system, and thus only select circuits when some change was required to affect them. The selectors became organ-stop keys and the masters to operate (to dim, raise, switch or change colour, etc.) organ keyboards. Whereas in an organ when a stop is put off it ceases to sound, in the Lighting Console the light it represents ceases to change. Other organ devices, such as instantly adjustable combination pistons now known to the theatre as 'memories', were provided to assist the operator in picking out groups of lighting—very necessary when, as at the Coliseum or at Drury Lane, there are 216 circuits. It was originally intended that the lighting expert who lit the show should play the console, but in fact this has happened only in the case of lighting controls for television studios, where each production is for one night only. Elsewhere the effect of repeat performances, and the general economic climate, has prevented this. So a switchboard must be able to repeat precisely, night after night, a plot determined at rehearsals when the show was first lit.

More recently, the organ keyboards have been replaced by a series of dimmer levers to operate positioning servo-mechanisms, but the stop keys and 'memories' are retained. In London's West End this, known as Strand

System CD, is now the most commonly used.

Concurrent with the above inventions has been the development of dimmers which are all-electric and, except for the dimmer lever, have no moving parts at all. The simplest of these employs a coil of wire on an iron core (choke or reactor) wired in series with the lamp load, and designed to drop sufficient volts to take the light out. An additional coil is used to carry direct current from the remote-control lever. As more D.C. is applied, and the effect of the iron core is negatived, there is less volts-drop and more light. The control current is very small when compared to the load. The saturable reactor, as this device is called, was for some years the least expensive form of remote control, and was widely used in Britain in Little Theatres and other enterprises on the same scale. Other forms of dimmer have used Thyratron valves, and the most recent (1962) is the Silicon Controlled Rectifier (S.C.R.) now known as the Thyristor. Both these act, in effect, as ultra-fast switches, to chop more or less of the A.C. waveform and thereby provide dimming independent of load variation. The Thyristor dimmer is now the method preferred in Britain both for inexpensive control and for the more complex systems. However, whereas the electro-mechanical dimmer described earlier needs only to be energized to change, all forms of all-electric dimmers require to be constantly energized to hold any condition of light other than blackout. This leads to more complex control boards in which many repeat levers (preset) are provided to each dimmer. Thus a ten-preset control can store ten complete lighting changes, each to be brought in from a single master fader. The trouble here is that a ten-preset system for a hundred dimmers will have a thousand dimmer levers, to say nothing of accessory switches for grouping. Large installations breed large control desks, however miniature the levers, and the playable nature of the control is thus nullified by the multiplicity of miniature levers. The multi-preset system has been evolved in the U.S.A., where its main market is in the university and college theatres. In such installations large numbers of circuits are 'patched' to share relatively few dimmers. The ten-preset forty-eight dimmer system developed for Yale in 1947 can still be described as flexible; but the 996 circuits patched to 147 dimmers in the MacCormick Centre in Chicago are perhaps somewhat excessive. In Britain, where control development has mainly been confined to the West-End theatres, and in Germany, large numbers of dimmers without patching is the rule. Installations begin at a hundred dimmers, but since they can rise to two hundred, it is perhaps just as well that electro-mechanical systems have rendered multi-presets unnecessary. In the large German opera-houses, where all-electric dimmers are preferred, the control desks, with their elaborate facilities, tend to become very large. No existing British theatre could house such a system of control in the front-of-house (the position now preferred). Nevertheless, the Thyristor dimmer referred to above is so compact and convenient that Britain had to design a control desk to use it which would not involve sacrificing the undoubted control advantages of the electro-mechanical systems. This resulted in the apparatus known as Strand C/AE, installed at Covent Garden in 1964. Basically, two master faders, a red and a white, are used for each preset in conjunction with dimmer levers which can be made to light internally to display as red or white. Dimmers are selected on to the red either by hand or by 'memory' group action, and when raised on the red fader are parked automatically on the white fader. Thus, in the case of Covent Garden, although there are 960 dimmer levers, the operator has to concern himself only with those displaying white or red, and in particular the latter. The effect is to turn the large control, visually, into a small one, for the operator has his attention drawn only to the few controls active in the lighting change at the moment. Another important development is the duplicate control panel used from the stalls, as in the new Thyristor installation at Glyndebourne. This greatly assists in the conduct of lighting and other rehearsals.

The inconveniences of the multi-preset system have led to enthusiasm in the United States for the so-called infinite preset system which uses punched cards. There it has been adopted out of sheer necessity, but it has proved attractive for the working of 'true repertory' in Europe. The first really large system of this kind, using 180 magnetic amplifier dimmers, was installed in 1960 in the Swedish Dramatic Theatre in Stockholm. Strictly speaking, there is no limit to the facilities a switchboard can now be made to provide.

In Britain a control now exists in which lighting changes are instantly memorized on a magnetic drum and can be as instantly repeated in any order or modified. The system allows 300 lighting cues in respect of 300 dimmers to be stored at one time. The machine also punches its own tape record for future re-programming in theatres playing 'pure' repertory. The problem now is not what can be done technically, but where to draw the line financially. Otherwise large-scale expenditure might leave a theatre building with lavish equipment, and a budget inadequate for running costs. FREDERICK BENTHAM

(For illustrations of modern stage lighting, see Nos. 42, 45, 46, 47, and 113.)

3. STAGE LIGHTING IN THE UNITED STATES. Since the beginning of the use of electricity in the theatre the development of equipment has been influenced largely by the availability of new light sources. These in turn are influenced by the fact that the electrical systems in the U.S.A. operate for the most part at 110 volts; in England commonly at 220. Sources for each range are therefore not interchangeable. The higher voltage system also requires a third wire (ground; in England, earth) on each piece of portable apparatus for safety, and

requires larger filaments and bulbs (or the introduction of transformers and A.C. for low-voltage lamps). Low-voltage lamps are not used in the U.S.A. as extensively as they are in England. The compact ellipsoidal reflector spotlight (similar to, but smaller physically than, the English mirror spot, see above) has been made possible by the development of a T-12 (1½ in. diameter, tubular) lamp in a 500-watt biplane filament form, and recently even a 1,000-watt unit has been tested satisfactorily. This type of unit in its various forms (wide, 45°; medium, 30°; and narrow beams, 15°) is three to five times more powerful than the conventional plano-convex spotlight of equal wattage.

The Fresnel lens spotlight or step-lens spotlight seems to have had more development and use in the U.S.A. than in England. It is two to three times as powerful as the old plano-convex spotlight, and gives automatically a soft-edge beam. The soft-edge 'spill' or 'ghost' makes this instrument ('lantern' in England) useless for 'pin spot' or strictly localized 'spotlighting'.

The basic difference in type of equipment arises out of the 'portability' requirement for almost all instruments and even switchboards used in the 'legitimate' theatre in the U.S.A. A production carries with it not only actors, scenery, and properties, but all its lighting equipment. In England most theatres are fairly thoroughly equipped with permanent installations. Community, school, and motion-picture theatres and the opera-houses are the only theatres in the U.S.A. so equipped.

Remote colour control permitting the moving of one or more of four or five colour filters in front of or out of an instrument electrically from the switchboard is found only in the non-travelling equipment.

Perhaps because of hazards in handling, very little glass is used in American equipment. Alzak (electrolytically treated aluminium) is almost universally used for reflectors. It has a high reflection coefficient and can be spun readily into accurate reflector forms, so that it seems more practical to use than silvered glass. It is almost as efficient. Colour filters in the U.S.A. (for which cinemoid is extensively used in England) generally consist of cheap films of dyed gelatine. They can be had in many hues and tints. Although they become brittle and fragile with use and fade rather rapidly, they seem to have more general use than more expensive, more permanent colour filters, except in certain strip lights (battens in England) when the three primary colours in glass—red, green, and blue—are being used extensively.

There are several differences in method between English and American practice. In the U.S.A., with a few exceptions, the designer assumes complete responsibility for the ultimate visual effect on the stage. In England, this is the duty of the 'stage director' (or producer). In the U.S.A. the designer works closely with the electrician or in a few cases with the so-called lighting specialist. Another difference in which the English practice is similar to the Continental rather than the American lies in the use of so-called 'acting-area' units. These provide a narrow beam of high-intensity illumination directly down on the acting area. In some respects they take the place of border lights as they are used in the U.S.A. In others they provide much the same effect as the 'projectors'—narrow beam units—used for backlighting in musical shows. 'Acting-area lights' in the American theatre refer to the spotlights mounted 'out front', or on the bridge or first pipe, to light the actors from the front diagonal—not from directly overhead or from behind.

Front lighting in the U.S.A. is generally provided by ellipsoidal reflector spotlights mounted in the open on the front of the first balcony. The English method of using the second balcony gives a much better angle, but many theatres in the U.S.A. do not have second balconies.

While on the subject of 'frontlights' the arc 'follow spot' (English following spot) and 'flood' are invariably D.C. instruments. The A.C. arc such as is used in England has not had a satisfactory development in the U.S.A.

'Border lights' or 'X-rays' (battens in England) are used for much the same purpose in both countries, except that in England, apparently, acting-area lanterns are more often used to light the playing space, while battens and floods are used to light backcloths (backdrops in the U.S.A.). Border lights, in fact all three-colour striplights in use in the U.S.A., are generally equipped with compact etched Alzak reflectors, giving a narrow or medium beam spread. The introduction of the highly efficient reflector spot or flood lamp, with plain, coloured, or spread roundels (cover glasses), is meeting the need for more colour from a compact instrument. These lamps come in 150- and 300-watt sizes with spot or flood distribution. The shape of the bulb is roughly parabolic and about 5 inches in diameter so that it can be mounted in strips on 6-in. centres. These lamps are not yet available in voltages over 120.

The European tradition of large stages and considerable space given over to bridges and other lighting apparatus has made it possible to light cycloramas in England with efficient wide-angle floods mounted well downstage with no scenery cluttering the space between them and the cyclorama. This is seldom possible in the American theatre, where stages are not very deep. Cycloramas and backdrops are generally lighted by high-powered three-colour narrow beam striplights mounted close to the surface (not too smooth as a rule) at top and bottom. Where the English method has been used in the U.S.A. the results have generally been good.

The use of the high-powered Fresnel spotlight for sunlight, moonlight, and even backlighting restricts the use of the narrow beam projector (pageant lantern in England) to back-lighting or outdoor long-throw work.

The term 'batten' in the U.S.A. refers to the iron pipe on which lighting instruments (lanterns in England) and scenery are mounted. Ordinarily the horizontal pipe batten hung from steel ropes at the back of the proscenium, on which lighting equipment is mounted, is called simply 'first pipe'.

Control (switchboard) terminology and equipment vary considerably between the two countries. This is partly due to the two basic differences in operating voltage and portability.

The variable rheostat (wire resistance in England) is still the dimmer most used in the U.S.A. It is almost never used with remote motor operation because if that amount of money is to be spent either an auto-transformer (tapped transformer in England) with a motor or a tube (valve in England) reactor combination is used. These are all for permanent installations, which are the exception rather than the rule. In New York the Radio City Music Hall has an elaborate tube-reactor preset board (as the old Metropolitan had). In 1947 a simplified preset dimmer board was demonstrated at the Yale University Theatre. In this board there are no reactors. The tube itself is the dimmer, and there are ten presets with a manual 'fader'.

Since 1950 theatre lighting has become more important than ever as part of a professional production. A small group of designers have been active in carrying out the lighting of some of the more important productions of the period. *My Fair Lady* (1956) and *Camelot* (1961) were lighted by Abe Feder; *A Long Day's Journey into Night* (1956) by Tharon Musser; and *West Side Story* (1957) by Jean Rosenthal. These, with Peggy Clark, Leland Watson, Charles Elson, Klaus Holm, and a small group of others, are kept busy designing for the ballet and other projects, and constitute what appears to be a new professional body within the scene designers' union, since they devote themselves chiefly to the design of the lighting for theatrical productions.

The professional scene designer is, however, still generally expected to plan and carry out the lighting for the settings he designs. He is normally in charge of all visual effects on the stage, but may relinquish the design of the costumes and the lighting to specialists if he wishes. Many stage designers do the whole job: execute the settings, costumes, and lighting for the production. Professional theatre schools are giving training to designers in all three fields, so that more and more of those who come to Broadway as designers are equipped to do the lighting, the costumes, or the setting, or all three together.

The importance of lighting in the professional theatre is marked by increased budgets for lighting equipment, more rehearsal time, and the occasional employment of a lighting designer. Some of the large musical productions have used over 300 separate pieces of equipment and connected load of over 400 kilowatts. Not that quantity makes for better lighting; but it is an indication of greater dependence upon lighting to carry the visual and dramatic load of the production. Jo Mielziner, in his memorable production of *The Lark* (1955), designed a fixed setting with a translucent back-screen for projected or back-lighted effects—no other scenery. Scene changes were all done by lighting.

The new Vivian Beaumont repertory theatre in the Lincoln Center called for a flexible layout and control system to meet the exacting requirements of a different production every day. New methods imposed by special forms of staging, such as the Elizabethan apron at the Shakespearean Festival Theatre, Stratford, Ontario, the Loeb Theatre at Harvard, and the Kalita Humphrey Theatre at Dallas, have special architectural provisions for mounting equipment, and new forms of switchboards which reflect a greater dependence upon lighting than is characteristic of the more conventional proscenium theatre.

There has been a general improvement in equipment, although nothing as startling as the development which took place between the two world wars. New light sources—particularly the compact, efficient, and long-life reflector lamps—are being incorporated in instruments to give colourful washes of light with non-fading glass filters to cycloramas and backdrops. New filament forms, some low voltage, are making possible smaller yet more powerful spotlights. The new Quartzline lamp, with its tiny coiled filament and pencil-size Quartz bulb, promises a high-power near-point source for strip lights and broad surface floods. A fair selection of non-fading coloured reflector lamps are available for footlights, and border-lights which need no reflectors.

The electronic push-button age is gradually being recognized in the theatre. The silicon-controlled rectifier dimmer has been introduced, and has gone through its preliminary shakedown period in a number of installations. Century Lighting has installed a ninety-circuit ten-scene preset control in the great O'Keefe Auditorium in Toronto. Many television studios and community and college theatres have installed electronic boards of some sort since 1945. This indicates that the older type of resistance and auto-transformer dimmer boards are no longer considered adequate. Only in the professional theatre is the old piano box filled with resistance dimmers to be found. This condition will continue as long as the nucleus of rented theatres—mostly in New York—have only direct current.

The magnetic amplifier and the electronic tube dimmers of the 1950s will undoubtedly give way to the later compact silicon-controlled rectifier (S.C.R.) and it in turn may be replaced by newer and more useful control elements. So much has happened since the introduction of this unit that one hesitates to predict the future. One thing is certain: compact remote-control consoles, freeing the operator from tedious manipulations and giving him vision of the effects he is controlling, are now possible. Also, by remote control it is possible to perform master dims and fades that give truly dramatic mobile lighting, not the clumsy jerking effects of mechanical interlocking, with many hands trying to give a subtle effect of dim-out, dim-on, or blend, from one scene to the next, with hundreds of instruments involved.

The significant development in the realm of control is the multi-scene preset, a means of recording the dimmer readings of an infinite number of scenes, not just two or ten, but the scene set-up of the entire show, which might run through hundreds of separate lighting set-ups. The fading between scenes can also be automatically pre-determined, based on the artistic and dramatic tempo established in rehearsal. This feature can only be recommended whole-heartedly for the timing of the changes with a fountain display, or one with taped voices, as in the 'Son et Lumière' performances now popular in Europe. Where the live actor is concerned, the proportional fading of each light from one scene to the next should be timed by an operator who has been trained to have the timing sense of an actor. Mobile lighting in these circumstances can be a truly dramatic part of the performance.

There are several approaches to achieving multiple presetting beyond the conventional ten. Century Lighting, with George Izenour, has developed a punch-card system that can pick out thirty-two levels of illumination for each of any number of dimmer circuits up to eighty on each card, and by multiple cards fed into the machine subsequently can accommodate any practical number of dimmer ways. In order to be alert to variables in timing, mistakes, or any of the variations in a production due to human or unpredictable causes, the machine has a means of checking the reading for each light at any time. It can skip whole scenes, if the actor drops a cue. Generally, the fading from scene to scene is done manually by the lighting designer, who because of the compactness of the console is able to see all parts of the stage, and can follow the action just as if he were an actor in the production. The machine can feed the cue cards into position at the rate of two per second, which is faster than almost any sequence needs to be. The important aspect of the punch-card system is that it provides a fool-proof cue-sheet for the entire production. It guarantees the accurate setting of each dimmer reading for each scene, and is able to do it from performance to performance—an ideal arrangement for any repertory theatre where the same production is staged at frequent or long-spaced intervals.

Another system has what is called a show-card, consisting of small sliders—replicas of the control-face—mounted in a card, which can be inserted one after the other in one of three contact panels, each of which can be energized in turn by a fader to change the lighting from scene to scene, or to go back to a previous setting. This system is less expensive than the punch-card, but the cards are bulky, and each dimmer reading must be set by hand initially. Superior Electric has a similar system, using metal staples in portable cards to make the dimmer contact.

None of these systems has been in use very long yet, so that it is hard to say which will continue as a practical solution to the need for a fool-proof, fast, infinite-preset system. Although the number of lighting units used on any production, whether it be television, arena, or open staging, will be many and varied in type, we are looking forward to the ultimate control which can simplify these set-ups by giving regulation not only over intensity, but over colour and distribution as well. Where it is now necessary to use three or four colour circuits to get a practical range of tint and shade, and to use several instruments to cover a sequence of areas with the remote control over both colour direction and beam spread, the numbers of instruments may soon be reduced.

Another variation from the European approach to control, as practised in the United States, has to do with what is called 'patching'—the cross-connexion between lighting loads and dimmers like the early telephone switchboard with weighted cord lines, able to connect a number of trunk lines to any of several telephones. Inasmuch as there are many instruments hung, focussed, and connected, it is considered practical in the United States to gang groups working together, and to have only the number of dimmers in the switchboard for the particular instruments that are necessary for the separate readings and cues. Now that dimmers have multi-capacity, and are remotely controlled, the console, or operating face, also can be reasonably compact. The patching device with twenty, forty, or even ninety dimmer-controls can selectively cross-connect a group of instruments for cue-control to any group of dimmers. The philosophy in Europe dictates that every load circuit should be permanently connected to a specific dimmer. This means that 300 loads or circuits must be permanently connected to a corresponding 300 dimmers, and the large console must be operated by several men, because one operator can reach only a portion of the controls of a board such as this, which may be 20 to 30 feet long. Patching requires fewer dimmers, smaller consoles, and gives greater flexibility for organizing cue-groups, but it can prove a source of trouble where the operator seldom finds a particular circuit under control of the same dimmer from production to production or even from scene to scene.

Stage lighting in America is generally of a high order professionally, in spite of the criticism that too many instruments are used. The designer has been freed of many of the limitations of the past, and has achieved considerable stature as an artist in the theatre. With this new freedom and importance, experience will teach him how to simplify his layouts, and contribute more to the production with less equipment and greater confidence and dramatic effect than ever before. STANLEY MCCANDLESS†

LILLO, George (1693–1739), English dramatist, best remembered for his play *The Merchant*, usually known as *The London Merchant; or, the History of George Barnwell*, which was done at Drury Lane in 1731. Based on an old ballad, it shows how a good young man's passion for a bad woman leads him to murder his old uncle for money, the murderer and his accomplice being subsequently hanged. The play was immensely successful, being warmly praised by no less a person than Alexander Pope, and it became the fashion to act it for the apprentices at holiday times, particularly on Shrove Tuesday. It was frequently revived at the patent theatres, notably by Mrs. Siddons, and was known well enough to be the butt of several burlesques. It was also the play given by the Crummles family in *When Crummles Played* (1927), based by Nigel Playfair on *Nicholas Nickleby*. It had a great vogue on the Continent, and influenced the development of domestic tragedy, particularly in Germany through Lessing. The printed copy has a scene at the place of execution, with a noble speech by the hapless Barnwell, which is usually omitted in production, but was done at Bath in 1817. Lillo wrote several other plays and ballad operas, of which the most important was *The Fatal Curiosity* (1736), again based on an old ballad about a murder done in Cornwall. It was first produced at the Haymarket by Fielding, and was the play chosen by Mrs. Siddons for her benefit in 1797, with John Philip and Charles Kemble. It also had a great influence abroad, particularly on the so-called German 'fate-drama', and was the inspiration for Werner's *Der vierundzwanzigste Februar* (1810).

LIMELIGHT, see LIGHTING, 1 *c*.

LIMES, see LIGHTING, 2.

LINCOLN, which has a repertory company housed in a nineteenth-century theatre saved from demolition by the formation of the Lincoln Theatre Association, was the headquarters of the Lincoln circuit, which took in Grantham, Boston, Spalding, Peterborough, Huntingdon, Wisbech, and Newark-on-Trent. From 1802 to 1847 this was controlled by the Robertson family, to which T. W. Robertson the dramatist and the actress Dame Madge Kendal belonged. The first permanent theatre in Lincoln was built in about 1731 by Erasmus Audley in Drury Lane (so called after a local business man, and not after the London theatre). Two 'comedians' presumably connected with this theatre—Edward Maddesley and James Smith—are recorded as having been buried at St. Mary Magdalen's in 1740 and 1741 respectively.

In 1764 a new theatre was formed by the adaptation of some buildings in King's Arms Yard, nearer the centre of the city. This was managed up to about 1783 by William Herbert, who had also been manager since 1750 of the Drury Lane theatre. Lincoln Public Library, which has a large collection of playbills, has among them many announcing performances by 'Mr. Herbert's Company of Comedians'. A new theatre was built in King's Arms Yard in 1806. It was burned down in 1892, and a new one, substantially the same as the present building, arose on the same site, opening on 18 Dec. 1893 with *Charley's Aunt*.

LINCOLN CENTER FOR THE PERFORMING ARTS, a cultural complex of buildings planned for New York City on a fourteen-acre site bounded by West 62nd and 65th Streets and Columbus and Amsterdam Avenues. After many years of preliminary planning the Center was incorporated as a non-profit-making institution in 1956, and work began in 1959. The first building to be completed was the Philharmonic Hall, where the New York Philharmonic Orchestra gave its inaugural concert on 23 Sept. 1962. On 23 Apr. 1964 the New York State Theatre for ballet and operetta opened under Richard Rodgers with the New York City Ballet, and in the autumn of the following year there opened also the Library–Museum of the Performing Arts, which houses the theatre, dance, and music sections of the New York Public Library. On 21 Oct. 1965 the Vivian Beaumont Theatre gave its first production, with the Lincoln Center Repertory Company in Blau's translation of Bucher's *Dantons Tod*, followed during the season by the New York première of Sartre's *Sequestrés d'Altona* and Brecht's *Die Kaukäsische Kreidekreis*, also in translation, and Wycherley's *Country Wife*. In preparation for the opening of this theatre a company had been formed in 1963, under the direction of Elia Kazan and Robert Whitehead. Housed in a temporary building erected by the American National Theatre and Academy, and known as the Anta Washington Square Theatre, this opened on 23 Jan. 1964 with the world première of Arthur Miller's *After the Fall*, followed by a revival of O'Neill's *Marco Millions* and a new play by S. N. Behrman, *But for Whom Charlie*. The venture was not altogether a success, and after some disagreements Kazan and Whitehead withdrew, to be succeeded by Herbert Blau and Jules Irving from the San Francisco Actors' Workshop. The theatre in the Lincoln Center was designed by Eero Saarinen with the collaboration of the stage designer Jo Mielziner, and has a stage which can be adapted for proscenium-arch or semi-arena productions.

When completed, the Lincoln Center will also house the new Metropolitan Opera-House and the Julliard School of Music.

LINCOLN'S INN FIELDS THEATRE, London, also known as Lisle's Tennis-Court or the Duke's House. This playhouse bulks large in theatre history. It was originally a tennis-court, built in 1656 by Anne Tyler and James Hooker, and it was converted into a theatre by Sir William Davenant in 1661. It stood in Portugal Street, and was about 75 ft. in length and 30 ft. wide. It was the first theatre to have a proscenium arch and to employ scenery which was 'set' and 'struck'. The stage projected in apron form beyond the proscenium into the auditorium. There was a large scene room, and next door were Davenant's own lodgings, where his principal actresses, including Mrs. Davenport and Mrs. Saunderson (later Mrs. Betterton), also boarded. Davenant had taken his company over from Rhodes, and in addition to the young Betterton he had six actors who as juveniles had played women's parts, the best known being Ned Kynaston. But both Davenant and Killigrew were empowered by their charters to engage women to act in their theatres.

The theatre opened, probably on 28 June 1661, with the first part of *The Siege of Rhodes*. The second part was given on the following day, and the two parts were acted alternately for a fortnight, always in the afternoon. They were followed by *The Wits*, and on 28 Aug. the play was *Hamlet*, which Pepys saw, 'done with scenes very well, but above all Betterton did the prince's part beyond imagination'. This was the first scenic production of *Hamlet*. Among other plays *The Adventures of Five Hours* was a great success, and there was a revival of *Romeo and Juliet* played alternately 'tragical one day' in Shakespeare's version, and 'tragicomical another' in a new version by James Howard which preserved the lovers alive. Dryden, although he belonged to Drury Lane, wrote *Sir Martin Mar-All* for Lincoln's Inn Fields. The comedian Nokes made a great success in it.

Davenant was an excellent manager. He never delegated authority as did the more mercurial and easy-going Killigrew, but kept the reins in his own hands, and his theatre prospered. His death on 7 Apr. 1668 was a great blow to it, though he had already found it too small for him, and was erecting a new one (see DORSET GARDEN). His widow, with Harris and Betterton, carried on at Lincoln's Inn Fields Theatre until the new theatre was ready in 1671, and the old theatre reverted to its former status as a tennis-court, except for an interval in 1672–4 when Killigrew's company played there after the destruction by fire of the Theatre Royal in Bridges Street. In 1695 Betterton, now leading man at Drury Lane, after a dispute with Christopher Rich, returned to Lincoln's Inn Fields with Mrs. Barry and Mrs. Bracegirdle, and began a ten-years' tenancy with *Love for Love*. In 1705 Betterton and his company went to Vanbrugh's new theatre in the Hay (not the one we now know as the Haymarket Theatre), while Christopher Rich of Drury Lane, having lost his patent, planned to use the Lincoln's Inn Fields Theatre. He died before his work was completed, but the theatre was reopened on 18 Dec. 1714 by his son John with *The Recruiting Officer*. It was described as a very handsome house, the interior having mirrors along each side; the stage was excellent and the scenery new. John Rich, an illiterate man and a curious character, tried acting in tragedy but failed. He was, however, an excellent Harlequin, and made a big success at this theatre in 1717 with a pantomime called *Harlequin Executed*. The greatest event of Rich's career at Lincoln's Inn Fields was the production of *The Beggar's Opera* (1727–8), which took the town by storm.

In 1731, the theatre having fallen into decay, Rich started a subscription to build a new one in Bow Street, which eventually became Covent Garden Theatre. He left Lincoln's Inn Fields in 1732, and that was virtually the end of its career as a regular playhouse. In 1733–4 an Italian Opera Company under Porpora opened there in opposition to Handel at the King's (Haymarket). After that it was let for balls and concerts, and occasionally an actor, excluded from the two patent theatres, would try his luck there, as did Giffard for a short time when his theatre in Goodman's Fields was closed. It became in turn a barracks, an auction room, a china warehouse, and was pulled down in 1848.

LINCOLN'S MEN, a small company of actors, led by Laurence Dutton, who were in the service of the first Earl of Lincoln, and of his son, Lord Clinton, whose name they sometimes took. They appeared at Court before Queen Elizabeth I several times between 1572 and 1575, and were active in the provinces up to 1577, as was a later company of the same name from 1599 to 1610.

LINDBERG, AUGUST (1846–1916), Swedish actor-manager who toured widely in Scandinavia and did much to establish Ibsen's reputation. He was the first to play Oswald in *Ghosts*—which became a subject of controversy all over the North—and he also played Hamlet, Lear, Brand, Peer Gynt, Solness, and Borkman.

L. KATHLEEN MCFARLANE

LINDSAY, HOWARD (1889–1968), American actor, dramatist and producer, who collaborated with Russel Crouse (1893–1966) in a dramatization of Clarence Day's *Life with Father*. First produced in 1939, with Lindsay as Father, this set up a record with a seven-years' run in New York. It was also seen on tour, and in London, where it was less successful. Most of Lindsay's work was done in collaboration, and with Russel Crouse he was responsible for the Pulitzer Prize-winner, *State of the Union* (1945), and for the production of *Arsenic and Old Lace* (1941), which had a long run both in London and in New York.

LINE, the rope on which a piece of scenery is hung, and raised from or lowered to the stage.

LION COMIQUE, see LEYBOURNE, MUSIC-HALL and VANCE.

LISBON THEATRES, see PORTUGAL.

LISLE'S TENNIS-COURT, see LINCOLN'S INN FIELDS THEATRE.

LISTON, JOHN (1776–1846), English comedian, whose early life is somewhat obscure, though he is believed to have been an usher in a provincial school. He appears to have made an unsuccessful attempt to join the

Haymarket company in 1799, and then went into the provinces. He was at Weymouth in Nov. 1800, and subsequently at Newcastle-on-Tyne and at York, where he joined Stephen Kemble's company in succession to the elder Mathews, who said he was never known to smile. In private life he was nervous and melancholic, and much interested in the study of theology, but he had only to appear on the stage to set the audience laughing. He returned to London in 1805, and was seen at the Haymarket, under Colman, as Sheepface in *The Village Lawyer*. For the next thirty years he was one of the leading players of London. He excelled in farce, and his Paul Pry, dress and all, was imitated by Wright and later by Toole. He made the fortune of several managers and authors—Pocock, Dibdin, Hook—and was the first comic actor to command a salary greater than that of a tragedian. He occasionally aspired to play tragedy himself, but without success. Boaden said of him, 'He must be seen to be comprehended. Other actors labour to be comic, I see nothing like labour in Liston.' He retired in 1837.

LISTON, VICTOR (1838–1913), a favourite comedian of the early days of music-hall, who began his career at the Old Bower Saloon, in Stangate Street. For some time he worked the small halls and supper-rooms, such as the Cyder Cellars and the Coal Hole, until one night, acting as a deputy turn at the Philharmonic, Islington, his song 'Shabby Genteel' made such a sensation that he stayed for seven months, going afterwards to the Metropolitan, Collins's, and Evans's Supper Rooms, where the Prince of Wales (later Edward VII) brought the Duke and Duchess of Sutherland specially to hear him. Later in life he became a music-hall proprietor.

W. MACQUEEN-POPE†

LITTLE CATHERINE STREET THEATRE, LONDON, see ROYAL PANTHEON.

LITTLE CLUB, NEW YORK, see FORTY-FOURTH STREET THEATRE.

LITTLE DRURY LANE, LONDON, see OLYMPIC THEATRE, 1.

LITTLE THEATRE. 1. LONDON, in John Street, Adelphi. This was, as its name implies, one of London's smallest playhouses, holding only 350 people. There was no orchestra pit, and no pit or gallery, though a circle was added later, and an enclosure at the back, something like a jury box, was used for the cheaper seats. The theatre stood on the site of the old Coutts Bank, and the strong-rooms formed the dressing rooms. It was opened in Oct. 1910 by Gertrude Kingston with *Lysistrata*, in which she herself appeared. She proposed to do a new play every month, withholding the author's name until after production, but though Shaw's *Fanny's First Play* was put on anonymously, its run of 624 performances caused this scheme to be put aside. In 1922 the *Nine O'Clock Revue* was a successful innovation, and a season of Grand Guignol, with Sybil Thorndike, had a vogue, while later Herbert Farjeon staged some successful Little Revues. In 1927 the horrific *Dracula* was produced, followed by another 'horror' play, *Frankenstein*. In 1934 *Lady Precious Stream*, a traditional Chinese play translated and adapted by S. I. Hsiung, produced as part of Nancy Price's People's National Theatre Scheme, ran for 247 performances, and on revival for another 436. The Little Theatre was destroyed by enemy action on 16 Apr. 1941.

W. MACQUEEN-POPE†

2. NEW YORK, standing on West 44th St. between Broadway and Eighth Avenue. This was built by Winthrop Ames as a try-out theatre. It held only 300 people, though its capacity was later enlarged to 600, and it proved somewhat unprofitable. Ames opened it on 12 Mar. 1912 with *The Pigeon*, followed later in the year by *Anatol* with John Barrymore and Doris Kean, *Rutherford and Son*, *Prunella*, *The Philanderer*, and a revival of *Truth*, Guthrie McClintic appearing in the last in a small part. The Shuberts later took control of the theatre, which was enlarged and redecorated under their management, and produced among other things *The First Year* and *The Left Bank*, both successful. In 1935, the theatre was used as a broadcasting studio. *The New York Times* bought it in 1941, and used it for lectures and recitals, and at a later date for television. In Oct. 1963 it again became a theatre, reopening with Langston Hughes's adaptation of his own novel, *Tambourines to Glory*, as a 'gospel-singing' play. In 1964, when *The Subject Was Roses* was transferred from the Royale Theatre, the name of the Little Theatre was changed to the Winthrop Ames Theatre, in honour of its founder.

GEORGE FREEDLEY†

LITTLE THEATRE IN THE HAY, LONDON, see HAYMARKET THEATRE.

LITTLE THEATRE MOVEMENT, ENGLAND, see AMATEUR THEATRE IN GREAT BRITAIN; UNITED STATES OF AMERICA, 10.

LITTLE TICH (1868–1928), music-hall comedian, who was so named as a baby from his supposed likeness to the claimant in the famous Tichborne Case. His real name was Harry Relph. He first appeared as a child singer and performer on the tin whistle at Rosherville, near Gravesend, one of the last of London's pleasure grounds, and later appeared at London music-halls as a black-faced comedian. After a visit to America, where he found that his disguise was no longer fashionable, he discarded it and returned to England to play in pantomimes at Drury Lane, and in music-halls, where he proved an immense success. His impersonations, which ranged from grocers, blacksmiths, and sailors on leave, to fairy queens and Spanish dancers, usually ended, at least until his last years, with a dance in which he balanced on the tips of his preposterous boots, which were as long as he was high. He was very popular in Paris, where he appeared at a music-hall in the Rue St-Honoré, and was a friend of Toulouse-Lautrec, with whom he was often seen walking along the front at Dieppe or on Brighton pier.

LITTLEWOOD, Joan (1914–), English producer, founder and manager until 1961 of Theatre Workshop. Born in London, of working-class parents, she won a scholarship to the Royal Academy of Dramatic Art and did well there, though her training, combined with a naturally aggressive and experimental nature, turned her against what she regarded as the inanities of the normal West-End theatrical routine. Turning her back on the success which might have attended her in the commercial theatre, she went to Manchester, and while working there in radio founded with her husband Ewan McColl [Jimmy Miller] an amateur group, Theatre Union, which soon made a name for itself with unconventional productions, in halls and in the open air, of experimental plays. The group dispersed on the outbreak of war in 1939. It came together again in 1945, and in 1953 took over the lease of the Theatre Royal at Stratford, London. Here began a series of productions which made the company famous in London and on the Continent, where Paris was the first to acclaim its brilliance. Joan Littlewood, who is uncompromisingly left-wing but refuses to be labelled communist, works on a system which is entirely her own, though it may derive from Stanislavsky and Brecht, and was responsible for the success of such productions as *The Quare Fellow* (1956), *A Taste of Honey* (1958), *Fings Ain't Wot They Used T'Be* (1959), all of which were later transferred to the West End. This, which constantly drained her company and led to the danger of its integrity being lost in the blaze of publicity, drove her to leave Theatre Workshop in 1961, but she returned in 1963 to undertake the successful production of *Oh What a Lovely War!*, based on soldier-songs of the First World War, which was also transferred to the West End and later was successful on Broadway.

LITURGICAL DRAMA. It is an interesting and ironic fact that modern drama in Europe evolved from the services of that Church which had done so much to suppress the last vestiges of classical drama, and which has throughout the centuries battled with varying success against the manifestations of its secularized offspring. The dramatic instinct in man, driven underground by the ordinances of the Early Fathers, was bound to break out somewhere, and when one considers the drama inherent in Christianity it is not surprising that mimetic tendencies should early have shown themselves in the services of its cult. The celebration of the Mass was a highly dramatic spectacle, enhanced by ceremonial and symbolic ritual and the use of antiphonal singing; so were the services of Easter and Christmas and such specialized festivities as the dedication of a church or the enthronement of a bishop. Antiphonal singing, which may owe something to the influence of the Greek tragic chorus, lends itself readily to dialogue, and so has in it the germ of drama. As church services became more elaborate the earlier antiphons were supplemented by additional melodies, first sung to vowel sounds only (neumes), later to specially written texts, or tropes, many of which took on a dialogue form.

One of these tropes, from the Benedictine Abbey of St. Gallen, is for Easter, and follows closely the Gospel account of the interview between the Angel at the Tomb and the three Maries on Easter morning. It is known shortly as the *Quem quaeritis* (Whom seek ye?), and from it liturgical drama was born. At some point this trope got detached from its proper place at the beginning of the Easter Mass, either as an Introit trope or as a processional chant, and reappeared as a separate little scene at Matins on Easter morning, with four persons to act the parts of the women and the angel, and with a building, temporary or permanent, to represent the empty tomb (for the complete scenario see Chambers, *Mediaeval Stage*, ii, pp. 14–15). This symbolic representation of the sepulchre had already been used, says St. Ethelwold, 'for the strengthening of faith in the unlearned vulgar and in neophytes'. In it the Cross was laid on Good Friday, and removed before Easter morning. This ceremony ended in England with Elizabeth I (1559), and on the Continent was later fused with the Adoration of the Reserved Host on Maundy Thursday. It cannot be said at what date this little drama of the *Quem quaeritis* started, but it is certain that, aided perhaps by the interchange of ideas of the wandering scholars, it gave ever fuller expression to the dramatic instinct which had first prompted it. Anthems were added to the original trope, then proses, and finally metrical hymns took their place in the dialogue, the most important being the *Victimae paschali* written by Wipo of St. Gallen in 1125–50, which found its way into the scenario of the *Quem quaeritis* during the thirteenth century. There were now two scenes—the angel showing the empty sepulchre to the Maries, and they in turn announcing the Resurrection to the rest of the congregation. The *Victimae paschali* formed part of the second little scene, and new voices were introduced to represent the disciples. A third scene was added when the apostles John and Peter were shown going themselves to the sepulchre. This occurred probably at the end of the eleventh or beginning of the twelfth century, and in most churches brought the drama to a close; in a few a fourth scene or dramatic moment was added with the person of the Risen Christ and His dialogue with Mary Magdalene. An important step in dramatic evolution was the singing by the Maries of lyric laments as they approached the sepulchre. An interpolation (probably of the 13th or 14th century) with no scriptural basis was a short scene between the Maries and the Seller of Spices. But it is possible that this character, who is important in the vernacular religious drama of Germany, and who brings in the first hint of secularized humour, is a counter-influence on the late liturgical play of the vernacular drama which had by now developed from it.

Materials for a study of the evolution of the liturgical play are fragmentary, but it is found all over Europe. It seems to have been most common in Germany and France, Spain and Italy developing somewhat differently. Even in the early days some attempt at costume was made, with robes for women, angels, and apostles, and properties were used, such as a palm and wings for the angel, and a box for the spices. But the *Quem quaeritis* always remained part of the Liturgy, and the actors were priests, nuns, and choirboys. The dialogue was chanted, not spoken, and the hymns and proses were sung by the choir without the intervention of the congregation. The scene was immediately followed by the *Te Deum*, and so merged into Matins.

A further Easter play, called the *Peregrinus* and modelled perhaps on the above, was that which showed the Risen Christ with the disciples at Emmaus, with in some cases the addition of the three Maries and Doubting Thomas. This had its place at Vespers, and was performed in the church, as was a longer version, preserved at Tours, which blended the scene at the sepulchre, the *Quem quaeritis*, and the *Peregrinus* in one. Gradually the details coalesced and further ones were brought in, notably the Lamentations of those stationed by the Cross on Good Friday. This led to a drama on the Passion of Christ, distinct from that of the Resurrection, which extended from the preparations for the Last Supper to the burial of Christ. It was given only in a rudimentary form inside the church, mostly in dumb show with dialogue restricted to passages from the Vulgate, but it developed in importance when it moved to the market-place (see PASSION PLAY).

The services of Christmas gave scope for a drama of the Nativity, centring on the crib with Mary, Joseph, the ox and ass, shepherds, and angels. The practice of dressing a crib, which was the focal point of the Nativity play, has never ceased on the Continent, and has been widely re-adopted in England. But the Nativity play does not seem to have attained in liturgical drama the importance of the Easter play, and, with a further short scene dealing with Rachel and the massacre of the Innocents, was soon absorbed into an Epiphany play where the interest centred on the Wise Men and their gifts. The evolution of this play was probably complete by the end of the eleventh century. It began with the journey of the Magi, their visit to Jerusalem and interview with Herod, their meeting with the shepherds, the presentation of their gifts at the manger, their return home by a different route after a warning by an angel, Herod's rage at being outwitted, the massacre of the Innocents, and ended with the Flight into Egypt. Occasionally a further scene was added, showing the death of Herod and the return of the Holy Family from exile. Herod, so important in later secular plays on religious subjects, was from the first a noisy, blustering fellow, whence Hamlet's phrase 'to out-Herod Herod'. He was probably played by the 'king' chosen from among the minor clergy for the Feast of Fools, and may be an importation from extra-ecclesiastical gaieties at Christmastide. The textual evolution of the Epiphany play can be studied from collated fragments, and begins with antiphons and prose sentences based on Scripture only. The influence of the wandering scholars led later to the writing of new metrical texts with occasional tags from Sallust or Virgil, débris thrown up by the submerged classical learning and used by the Church for her own purposes.

Another Christmas play, and the most important for the future development of the drama, was based on a narrative sermon attributed to St. Augustine, and known as the Prophet play. This made use of the Old Testament prophets, as well as of Virgil and the Erythraean Sibyl, listing their prophecies concerning the coming of the Messiah. In the eleventh century it was converted into a metrical dramatic dialogue, in some cases enriched by the appearance of Balaam and his Ass, and the Three Children in the Fiery Furnace. The ass was probably another importation from the Feast of Fools, and its use may mark a determined effort by the Church to canalize the irrepressible licence of Christmas merry-making by incorporating into its own more orderly proceedings an undoubted element of buffoonery.

Apart from these Christmas and Easter plays, which grew up organically within the Church, and developed in accordance with certain rules and limitations, others exist on the same lines, deliberately written for performance in a church. The manuscript works of a wandering scholar, Hilarius, pupil of Abelard, contain three plays of this kind, a Miracle of St. Nicholas, the Raising of Lazarus, and a two-part play on Daniel, probably detached from the Prophet play. There are in addition a number of anonymous plays on these subjects, those dealing with St. Nicholas being particularly connected with the children's scholastic feast and the Boy Bishop. There are traces of other subjects—John the Baptist, Isaac and Rebecca, the Conversion of St. Paul—and a French play on the Wise and Foolish Virgins has, as many of these later plays had, speeches in the vernacular. An Advent play from Germany, *Antichristus*, demanded a number of actors, and much space, probably the nave of some great church. It is well written, dramatically conceived, and probably had some significance in church politics of the time. It introduces allegorical as well as biblical figures, and its date is about 1160. We are here far from the simplicity of the angel and the three Maries, and it is hard to avoid the suspicion that the amateur actors of early days have now been reinforced by those to whom acting was no novelty, no part of a ritual church service, but a means of livelihood—the lineal descendants of those *mimi* whom the Church had tried to suppress. Certainly the wandering scholars, as witness Hilarius, had some practice in the mimetic art and, having once written their plays, may have called upon their acquaintances among the travelling tumblers to eke out the shortcomings of the local clergy. The participants in local folk-plays, too, may have been pressed into service, to dance, to sing, to bear a part with experienced assurance. But all this is conjecture. What can be said with certainty is merely that liturgical drama, as it evolved from the simple antiphon of Easter or Christmas, was complete by the end of the thirteenth century, and that in its later development it necessarily ceased to be liturgical. Plays were given in churches, mostly in the vernacular, right up to the fifteenth century, and in isolated cases even later, but they were intermixed with, and influenced by, the secular plays of the market-place to such an extent that they can no longer be considered purely, or even, as time went on, partly, liturgical. Having given back the drama to Europe the Church again withdrew, and prepared to do battle with the theatre it had engendered. (For the later developments of the drama see the separate countries of Europe.)

The very successful revival, in a production by E. Martin Browne, of the twelfth-century Beauvais *Play of Daniel* in 1960 and 1963 has raised the question of the musical accompaniment to the liturgical play. Was the singing mainly unaccompanied, and if not, how many and what kind of instruments were used? Noah Greenberg, director of the New York Pro Musica society, which presented the play in New York and in a number of cathedrals in England and on the Continent, provided his company with an assortment of period instruments such as hurdy-gurdys, portable organs, cymbals, recorders; Dr. René Clemencic, for a Viennese production of the same play, was far more liberal and made provision for a string group, a wind group, and a percussion group, in addition to a portative organ. This led Dr. W. L. Smoldon, the foremost British authority on Liturgical Drama, to protest against over-elaboration, since he believes that for plays sung in Latin in the church—as opposed to the spoken vernacular plays given outside—the only accompaniment was provided by organ and chime-bells, both used sparingly.

Since the surviving texts, which have been extensively studied from the purely literary point of view, give only a simple line of melody for the singers, and musicians have only recently turned their attention to even these vestigial remains, the question is not likely to be solved easily or immediately. But at present there seems to be, in Dr. Smoldon's view, no certain evidence for the use of harmony, and only the scantiest for any instrumental accompaniment, whereas Dr. Clemencic argues that all the instruments he used were represented in the painting and sculpture of the period, in the hands of saints or angels, and were therefore, *ipso facto*, permissible in such a reconstruction, and that constant prohibitions by ecclesiastical authorities against the use of instruments in church proves how widespread the practice was. It does not, however, solve the problem of how many of the existing instruments were used at the same time. Dr. Inglis Gundry, musical director of the Sacred Music Drama Society (founded 1961), which has given presentations of six liturgical dramas in seven different churches, has some interesting things to say based on practical experience. Since actors must move during the play, and scenes be done in different parts of the building, and since all singers are no longer trained in the medieval tradition of unaccompanied chant nor are modern audiences conditioned to listening to it for long stretches at a time, it seems reasonable to adapt one's accompaniment to the acoustics of the church, the skill of the singers, and the degree of familiarity of the audience with the story, as long as it is in accordance with the style of the period and used with restraint. As Dr. Gundry wisely says: 'Actual performances in the Middle Ages may have been different in various churches, and at different periods, or on different occasions, some partially accompanied, some elaborately, some not at all.' And, he inquires, 'may not this be the reason why the accompaniment was . . . never written down?'

LITURGY, in Athens, a public service required of wealthy citizens. One such duty was the staging of a play (see CHOREGUS and GREECE). In Europe the liturgy, or form of worship, of the early Christian Church gave rise to the performance of plays in Latin, for which see LITURGICAL DRAMA, above.

LIVERIGHT, HORACE BRISBIN (1886–1933), American publisher who was also active in the theatre, being the first to take an interest in the plays of O'Neill. At 17 he had written a light opera which failed to reach the stage, and it was not until 1924 that he again made contact with the theatre, one of his outstanding ventures being the controversial modern-dress *Hamlet*. He was opposed to censorship and constantly in trouble with the authorities. Among his productions were *An American Tragedy* (1926), *Dracula* (1927), and *The Dagger and the Rose* (1927). In 1930 he went to Hollywood as adviser to Paramount Studios.

LIVERPOOL, which is the proud possessor of the oldest surviving repertory theatre in England, saw its first theatrical performances —in cockpits—in the early part of the eighteenth century. The Old Ropery Theatre, which existed in the 1740s, was a converted room, visited by Irish companies. In 1749–50 a theatre without boxes was built in Drury Lane, and was used by actors from the London theatres during the summer. Boxes were added in 1759, and a green-room and dressing-rooms provided in 1767. In 1772 a new theatre was built at a cost of £6,000; among its lessees were Joseph Younger and George Mattocks, husband of Isabella Hallam, whose father took the first company to the New World. In 1803 the theatre was rebuilt in horseshoe shape. It was adapted as a circus and later became a cold storage depot. In its heyday Liverpool had a theatre season which lasted practically all the year, and was independent of a circuit. It now has two theatres and a repertory theatre. In 1958 the New Shakespeare Theatre, formerly a music-hall, the Pigalle, was opened as a Theatre Club under the direction of Sam Wanamaker, but the venture failed after a year, and the building was subsequently destroyed by fire.

The Liverpool Repertory Theatre, now known as the Playhouse, was the third to be opened in Great Britain (the earlier ones were the Abbey, Dublin, and the Gaiety, Manchester) and the oldest to survive. It owes its inception to the success of an experimental season given at Kelly's Theatre, Paradise Street, in Feb. 1911, under the direction of Basil Dean. This showed that Liverpool wanted good theatre, and a scheme was set on foot to provide a permanent repertory company which should make the town independent of visiting companies from London. The Star Theatre in Williamson Square, home of lurid melodrama, was acquired and completely reconstructed. It opened on 11 Nov. 1911, since when it has closed only for short summer vacations. Because it has been almost entirely dependent on its box-office receipts, it has been unable to risk putting on many plays with a frankly limited appeal, but its policy is always to produce plays which are outstanding and which might not otherwise be seen in Liverpool. It does not cater for any definite class of audience, or for any one type of playgoer, and its productions range from the lightest of light comedies to such serious plays as Raynal's *The Unknown Warrior* or Susan Glaspell's *Inheritance*, which had its first English performance at the Playhouse. The encouragement given to new and young authors has been one of the theatre's special activities, and it is the only repertory theatre which has made a point of doing one-act plays. Every Christmas it stages a new play specially written for children. 'The Playhouse Circle', which met on alternate Sunday evenings, was for many years a valuable adjunct to the theatre's work. It had a membership of over nine hundred, and many notabilities spoke at its meetings. Another collateral activity, which owes its existence indirectly to the theatre, is the Shute Lectureship in the Art of the Theatre at the University of Liverpool, founded in 1923 by Colonel Sir John Shute, Chairman of the Playhouse directors.

The Playhouse has been a notable school of acting, of which St. John Ervine said, 'it has enriched English acting to a quite extraordinary extent, and I believe it is true to say that more of the best actors and actresses learned their job in Williamson Square than in any other part of the country'. Undeniably the theatre's success in the 1920s and 1930s, up to the outbreak of the Second World War, at which time it had just begun to triumph over its initial difficulties and even to show a profit, was due to the work and enthusiasm of William Armstrong, who was its director and resident producer from 1922 to 1944, and whose name is always associated with the Liverpool Rep. The Playhouse holds a unique place in the artistic life of Merseyside, enabling several thousand people a week to be 'decently entertained and often lifted above the grey atmosphere of this Northern city'.

WILLIAM ARMSTRONG†, *rev.*

LIVING NEWSPAPER, a stage production conceived in terms of the cinema, showing in short, swift-moving scenes problems of modern social life, and the methods of dealing with them. First evolved by the Federal Theatre in the United States, this technique was successfully used in England for adult education and propaganda in the armed forces during the Second World War.

LIVING THEATRE, THE, NEW YORK, an off-Broadway repertory company formed in 1947 by Julian Beck and his actress-wife Judith Malina to present new and experimental plays. They began their original and highly iconoclastic career at the Cherry Lane Theatre, where one of their first major productions was Gertrude Stein's *Dr. Faustus Lights the Lights* (1951), and they gained an enviable reputation for the production of plays by T. S. Eliot, Strindberg, Pirandello, Cocteau, and many others. In 1951 they moved to their own theatre at 530 Avenue of the Americas, where their most widely publicized production was Jack Gelber's *The Connection* (1959), which deals with the plight of dope addicts. In the summer of 1961 the Living Theatre made a highly successful visit to Europe, where they gained three first prizes at the Festival of the Théâtre des Nations, playing *The Connection* and William Carlos Williams's *Many Loves*, and afterwards touring Italy and Germany. On a second tour in 1962 they played Gelber's *The Apple* and Brecht's *In the Jungle of Cities.* On their return home they opened their 1962 season with an adaptation of Brecht's *Man Is Man*, based on his final version, which was prepared in 1953, thirty years after the original was written. Their theatre was closed, because of financial difficulties, in 1963, and in 1965 was operating in West Berlin.

GEORGE FREEDLEY†

LIVIUS ANDRONICUS, see ANDRONICUS.

LLOYD, MARIE (1870–1922), idol of the music-halls for many years. She was the daughter of a waiter at the old Grecian Saloon, and the eldest of eleven children, her real name being Matilda Alice Victoria Wood. She made her first appearance at the Royal Eagle Music Hall (as the Grecian was then called) in 1885, in an extra turn, billed as Bella Delmere, though it was not long before she discarded this for the name under which she became famous. She first made a hit at the Old Mo with Nellie Power's song 'The Boy I Love Sits up in the Gallery' and was then engaged for a year at the Oxford. Augustus Harris engaged her as 'principal girl' for his Drury Lane pantomime, where she appeared from 1891 to 1893. She was three times married: to Percy Courtney in 1887, from whom she was divorced in 1904, to Alec Hurley, the 'coster king', who died in 1913, and to Bernard Dillon the jockey. In spite of her success and popularity she had a hard life, which she faced with unassuming courage and unimpaired cheerfulness. In her work she was wittily improper, but never coarse or vulgar, and her humour lay less in her material than in her use of it. Though critics often railed, the public remained obstinately faithful. She appeared in all the leading music-halls of England, and in provincial and London pantomimes, and toured successfully in America, South Africa, and Australia. In 1920 her fiftieth birthday was celebrated by a special performance at the Bedford Music-Hall, and two years later she died, having continued on the stage until the last few days of her life. In her final years she was an almost legendary figure, and afterwards became the posthumous darling of Fleet Street. Her most famous songs were 'Oh, Mr. Porter!', 'My Old Man Said Follow the Van', and 'I'm One of the Ruins that Cromwell Knocked Abaht a Bit'. Of her six sisters, Alice (*d.* 1949) and Grace (1875–1961) appeared as the Lloyd Sisters, making their début at the Forresters' Music-Hall on 20 Feb. 1888. They continued to appear at music-halls and in pantomime until Grace's marriage to a well-known jockey, George Hyams. Alice then appeared as a solo turn in England and in America.

LOA, the name given to the prologue, or compliment to the audience, which preceded the early Spanish theatrical performance. It ranged from a short introductory monologue to a miniature drama having some bearing on the play which was to follow; in certain cases it was even inseparable from it. It need not be by the author of the main play, and Agustín de Rojas in his *El viaje entretenido* (1603) indicates that a strolling company would generally have a variety of *loas* which could be fitted to any play. In the seventeenth century, the *loa* appears to have been retained in the public theatres for the first performance only of a new company, although allegorical *loas sacramentales* were written for performance on Corpus Christi day as an introduction to an *auto*, and the praise of the audience continued to be an integral feature of Court performances.

LOCATELLI. (1) DOMENICO (1613–71), a player of the *commedia dell'arte*, who, as Trivellino, had a *zanni* part somewhat akin to Harlequin's. Indeed, he is sometimes believed to have played Harlequin. He spent many years in Paris, going there first about 1644, and again from 1653 till his death. His first wife, (2) LUISA GABRIELLI (*fl.* 1644–53), was also an actress, and went with her husband to Paris. They were playing in Modena together shortly before her death. Another Locatelli, (3) BASILEO (? –1650), was an amateur of the *commedia dell'arte* who collected and copied out over 100 *scenarii*, which are preserved in two manuscript volumes, dated 1618 and 1622, in the *Biblioteca Casanatense* in Rome.

LOFTUS, CISSIE [MARIE CECILIA] (1876–1943), English actress, the daughter of Marie Loftus, variety artist. She made her first appearance on the stage at the Oxford Music-Hall in 1893 and was immediately successful. In the same year she appeared at the Gaiety, and for some time oscillated between legitimate drama and the music-halls, where she gave a series of remarkable impersonations. She appeared in vaudeville in America in 1894, at the Lyceum, New York, in the following years, and later in light opera, with great success. She abandoned the music-hall for a time in 1900, and appeared in a number of straight plays with Mme Modjeska, Frohman, Sothern, and others. Irving brought her back from America to play Margaret (in *Faust*), Nerissa, and Jessica at the Lyceum. Later she appeared as Peter Pan, and as Nora in *A Doll's House*. She returned to the music-hall, both in England and America, and for many years alternated between both types and both countries, with equal success. An attractive, dark woman of great vivacity, she was a versatile and accomplished performer in both mediums.

W. MACQUEEN-POPE†

LOHENSTEIN, DANIEL CASPAR VON (1635–83), a dramatist in whom German baroque drama reached its height. Himself a scholar and a man of quiet abstemious life, his plays, which show much erudition, are nevertheless bloodthirsty melodramas couched in extravagant language, theatrical in the worst sense. It is not certain whether they were ever publicly performed, but as literary or 'closet' dramas they were read and acclaimed, since they fitted in with the prevailing taste for Gothic horrors. A new orientation in the direction of simplicity and realism caused them to be forgotten.

LONDON ACADEMY OF MUSIC AND DRAMATIC ART, THE, a training school for actors which has developed out of the London Academy of Music, founded in 1861 by Dr. T. H. Yorke-Trotter. Courses in elocution and speech-training were added to the curriculum under the supervision of the well-known reciter and producer Charles Fry, but it was not until Wilfred Foulis was appointed director of the school (which had moved from its original premises off Oxford Street to Queen's Gate Hall, where there was a small theatre) that the present name was adopted, and tuition extended to cover full-time acting classes and public examinations in acting.

After the Second World War, during which the Academy was evacuated to Hampton

Court with a skeleton staff, the present premises, Tower House, Cromwell Road, with a theatre in Logan Place, were opened, and in 1954 the well-known London actor and producer Michael Macowan took over, with Norman Ayrton as his assistant. Drastic changes were made in the curriculum with the object of improving the basic training, more attention was paid to singing and dancing as well as to straight acting, and in 1960 the two-year course was extended to three years.

In 1963 a new experimental theatre was opened in which the stage and auditorium were interchangeable and could be used for proscenium plays, for theatre-in-the-round, and for open-stage productions. This was used both by students during their training, and also by visiting companies, notably by Peter Brook with an improvisatory group in a series of exercises based on Artaud's 'Theatre of Cruelty'.

One of the most interesting features of the school's curriculum is the advanced course of one year intended for overseas students, most of whom have had some experience of theatre in their own countries. The training is based on Shakespeare, with excursions into Restoration and eighteenth-century comedy and such modern authors as Shaw, Fry, and Eliot. In 1966 Norman Aryton succeeded Michael Macowan as director of the school, which is usually known, from its initials, as Lamda.

LONDON CASINO, see PRINCE EDWARD THEATRE.

LONDON COLISEUM, see COLISEUM.

LONDON HIPPODROME, see HIPPODROME.

LONDON OPERA HOUSE, see STOLL.

LONDON PALLADIUM. This famous music-hall opened on 26 Dec. 1910 with a variety bill which included Martin-Harvey in a one-act play. Later it was used for revues, particularly those of de Courville (beginning with *Sky High* in 1925), and in the 1930s the theatre housed the Crazy Gang shows, ending in 1938 with *These Foolish Things*. During these years *Peter Pan* was seen annually until 1938. The theatre continues to flourish with variety, revue, and pantomime.

LONDON PAVILION, THE. This famous music-hall began as a 'song-and-supper-room' annexe to the Black Horse, the stable yard being roofed in for the purpose. On 23 Feb. 1861 it became a music-hall, where, among other well-known stars, The Great MacDermott sang in 1878 'We don't want to fight, but, by Jingo, if we do, We've got the ships, we've got the men and got the money too!'—whence the term Jingoism. The hall was demolished early in 1885, and a new Pavilion, whose façade is still standing, opened on 30 Nov. under the management of Edwin Villiers. In 1886 the separate tables in the old music-hall style were abolished, and normal theatre seating was installed. The interior was rebuilt in 1900, but continued to offer its patrons excellent music-hall fare, with as many as twenty 'turns' in an evening. In 1918 it became a theatre under Cochran, who staged revues and musical comedies there. In 1934 it was converted into a cinema.

W. MACQUEEN-POPE†, *rev.*

LONDON THEATRE STUDIO, see SAINT-DENIS, MICHEL.

LONG, JOHN LUTHER (1861–1927), American novelist, playwright, and librettist. The dramatic possibilities of his short story, *Madame Butterfly* (1898), attracted Belasco, who prepared a one-act stage version in which Blanche Bates scored a great success at the Herald Square Theatre in 1900. Puccini later used this as a basis for his opera, first performed in 1904. Long had very little to do with the dramatization of *Madame Butterfly*, but he later collaborated with Belasco on two other dramas, the enormously popular *The Darling of the Gods* (1902), a romantic melodrama set in ancient Japan, later produced by Beerbohm Tree at His Majesty's (1903), and *Adrea* (1905), a tragedy in which Mrs. Leslie Carter successfully played the title-role. Long wrote several other plays which, lacking Belasco's technical collaboration, were not successes, two opera librettos, and several novels, but to his lasting chagrin he was always known as the co-author of *Madame Butterfly*. ROBERT TRACY

LONGACRE THEATRE, NEW YORK, on 48th Street between Broadway and Eighth Avenue. This opened on 1 May 1913, mainly for farces and musical comedy, among which were interpolated some matinées of *Ghosts* and of that fine play, *The Hero*. Ethel Barrymore was first seen at the Longacre in 1922, in several good parts, while the end of 1925 saw the successful run of *The Butter and Egg Man*. In spite of fine acting by Constance Collier, Derrick de Marney, and Jessica Tandy, making her first appearance in New York, *The Matriarch* was a comparative failure, and *Overture*, though included by Burns Mantle in his ten best plays of the 1931-2 season, also had a short run. This was true too of *Wednesday's Child*, and of the *Noah* of Obey, with Pierre Fresnay as Noah. Several of Odets's plays were given at this theatre under the auspices of the Group Theatre. From 1944 to 1953 the theatre was used for broadcasting, but reopened with *Ladies of the Corridor*. In 1955 Lillian Hellman's adaptation of Anouilh's *The Lark* was presented with Julie Harris as Joan of Arc. Emlyn Williams was seen in his programme on Dylan Thomas, *A Boy Growing Up*, in 1957, and in 1961 Zero Mostel and Eli Wallach starred in Ionesco's *Rhinoceros*.

GEORGE FREEDLEY†

LONGEPIERRE, HILAIRE-BERNARD DE ROQUELEYNE (1659–1731), French dramatist, and the immediate successor of Racine in the history of French classical tragedy. From the great days of the genre he retains the form and to some extent the psychological conflict, as in his *Médée* (1694), and he gave an illusion of greatness before the final decadence of tragedy which was sufficiently strong for his contemporaries to rate him highly as a dramatist. In some places Longepierre is not unworthy of Racine, whose works inspired him to write for the stage. He was well educated and a student of antiquity, in the sense in which such study was understood at the time. In fact, he had everything of Racine but his genius, and his plays are forgotten.

LONGFORD, EDWARD ARTHUR HENRY PAKENHAM, 6th Earl of (1902–61), Irish playwright and theatre director, Chairman of the Dublin Gate Theatre, and founder of 'Longford Productions', his company alternating at the theatre with 'Gate Theatre Productions' (see IRELAND, 2) in plays by Shakespeare, Chekhov, Shaw, Molière, Sophocles, Euripides, Ibsen, Congreve, Sheridan, and translations from modern Continental dramatists. The best of Lord Longford's own plays was probably *Yahoo* (1933), which, with Hilton Edwards as Jonathan Swift, had a great success both in Dublin and in London, where the Longford company played seasons at the Westminster Theatre in 1935, 1936, and 1937. With his wife, Christine Patti Trew, who was up with him at Oxford, and who, like himself, spoke Gaelic, he translated several of the plays given by his company, notably the *Oresteia* of Aeschylus, the *Oedipus* of Sophocles, and the *Bacchae* of Euripides. He also translated *Tartuffe*, *Le Bourgeois gentilhomme*, and *Le Barbier de Séville*. Lady Longford, who wrote *Mr. Jiggins of Jigginstown* (1933), *Anything But the Truth* (1937), and *Sea Change* (1940), was also responsible for dramatizations of Jane Austen's *Pride and Prejudice*, Maria Edgeworth's *The Absentee*, and Sheridan Le Fanu's *The Watcher* and *The Avenger*.

LONSDALE [LEONARD], FREDERICK (1881–1954), English dramatist, whose best plays, written in the 1920s, are comedies of contemporary manners in the style of Maugham, but with less subtlety. Their amusing situations, adroitly handled in easy and effective dialogue, made them immediately popular, and *The Last of Mrs. Cheyney* (1925), an unusually effective crook-play, proved successful in revival in 1944. Of the others the most important are *Spring Cleaning* (1925), *On Approval* and *The High Road* (both 1927), and *Canaries Sometimes Sing* (1929), all of which gave scope for good, brittle, sophisticated acting. Lonsdale was also the librettist of *The Maid of the Mountains*, *Madame Pompadour*, and other musical comedies, and of a version of *Monsieur Beaucaire*, with music by Messager, done in 1919.

LOPE DE VEGA, see VEGA CARPIO, LOPE FÉLIX DE.

LÓPEZ DE AYALA, ADELARDO (1829–79), was, with Tamayo, the chief representative in Spanish drama of the transition from romanticism to realism. His historical drama, *Un hombre de estado* (1851), is still basically romantic, while his modern comedies, particularly *El tanto por ciento* (1861) and *Consuelo* (1878), criticize the materialistic tendencies of the age. The comedies have the complicated plots of *capa y espada* plays, but interest rates have taken the part of cloaks and swords. Virtue is finally triumphant and vice is vanquished in this Spanish bourgeois drama.

J. E. VAREY

LORAINE, ROBERT (1876–1935), English actor-manager, who made his first appearance on the stage in 1889, played with Tree and Alexander, and subsequently made a hit as D'Artagnan in *The Three Musketeers* (1899). After serving with distinction in the Boer War he went to America and made his first appearance there in *To Have and to Hold* (1901), returning to England to play Henry V. He was later associated with early productions of Shaw, playing John Tanner, Don Juan, and Bluntschli, the last with Lillah McCarthy, and opening his management of the Criterion in 1911 with a revival of *Man and Superman*, which he also took to America. During the First World War he made a great name for himself as an aviator, and was awarded the M.C. and D.S.O. for gallantry in action. His return to the stage in 1919 was made in the name part of *Cyrano de Bergerac*, which had a long run. Among his later parts were Deburau, the dual role of Rassendyl and Rudolf in a revival of *The Prisoner of Zenda*, the Nobleman in *The Man with a Load of Mischief* in its New York production, Adolph in *The Father*, and a number of Shakespeare parts, including Petruchio and Mercutio. He was essentially a romantic actor, but could subdue his flamboyance to such parts as John Tanner and Adolph. His life was written by his wife in 1938.

LORCA, FEDERICO GARCÍA, see GARCÍA LORCA, FEDERICO.

LORD ADMIRAL'S MEN, see ADMIRAL'S MEN.

LORD CHAMBERLAIN, see DRAMATIC CENSORSHIP.

LORD CHAMBERLAIN'S MEN, see CHAMBERLAIN'S MEN.

LORD HOWARD'S MEN, see ADMIRAL'S MEN.

LORD HUNSDON'S MEN, see CHAMBERLAIN'S MEN.

LORD OF MISRULE, see MISRULE.

LORD STRANGE'S MEN, see STRANGE'S MEN.

LORENZI, GIOVANNI BATTISTA (1721–1807), an Italian librettist and actor famed for his gift as an improviser. It is said that when Joseph II visited Naples he gave Lorenzi the outline of a plot on which he improvised a complete play, delighting the Emperor and his audience. Lorenzi also wrote fifteen comedies in Neapolitan dialect. Settembrini calls him the Neapolitan Aristophanes, and declares that he is worthy of a place by the side of Metastasio.

LOTAR, PETR (1910–), outstanding Czech actor, who trained under Max Reinhardt in Berlin and later appeared with Barnowsky and Piscator. In 1931, after appearing in Breslau, he returned to Czechoslovakia and worked for two years in the provincial theatres there. He was then appointed to the Municipal Theatre, Prague, where he produced a Czech version of *The Shoemaker's Holiday*, and appeared in such parts as Lysander, Orsino, Tybalt, Antony, and Jaques. He was on the committee of the Czech Actors' Association, and was one of the founders of a club directed towards the association and co-operation of Czech and German democratic artists. In May 1939 he emigrated to Switzerland, where his work as actor and producer introduced Swiss audiences to the standard works of modern Czech drama. Of his own plays, one, a picture of the Czech national struggle shown in individual destinies in the days of Munich, was an outstanding success in the Swiss theatrical season of 1945.

LOTTA, see CRABTREE, CHARLOTTE.

LOUTHERBOURG, PHILIP JAMES DE (1740–1812), a painter from Alsace, who worked for some time in Paris and Italy, making a special study of stage illusion and mechanics. Arriving in London in 1771, he met Garrick, who appointed him scenic director at Drury Lane, a position he also held under Sheridan after Garrick's retirement. He introduced a number of new devices, including the reproduction of fleeting effects on a landscape by the use of silk screens working on pivots before concentrated lights in the wings, and his cloud-effects were particularly admired. He introduced a series of head-lights or border battens behind the Drury Lane proscenium, which at once discouraged the actors from stepping too much outside the picture, and increased the importance of the scenery by the flood of illumination. His work was vivid and arresting, though his bizarre use of colour sometimes rendered it too glaring. But he was particularly successful in producing the illusion of fire, volcanoes, sun, moonlight, and cloud-effects, and invented strikingly effective devices for thunder, guns, wind, the lapping of waves, and the patter of hail and rain. He was the first to bring a breath of naturalism into the artificial scenic convention of the time, and paved the way for the realistic detail and local colour of Kemble. He is referred to by Mr. Puff in *The Critic*, for which he had executed a striking design of Tilbury Fort, and he was responsible for some excellent new transparent effects in a revival of *The Winter's Tale* in 1779. In the same year a visit to the Peak district resulted in some fine local scenery for a pantomime, including an act-drop of a romantic landscape which remained in use until the theatre was destroyed by fire. W. J. Lawrence cites this as the earliest example of the use of an act-drop or scenic curtain in western Europe. Shortly after preparing the scenery for *Robinson Crusoe* on its first appearance on the stage—the first act alone had eight changes—de Loutherbourg, who had been elected to the Royal Academy in 1781, withdrew from the theatre, mainly on account of a dispute over his salary, and devoted most of his time to a remarkable scenic exhibition, 'Eidophusikon'. Although he seldom worked for the stage after this, his influence can be traced as late as 1820, when Elliston, in a revival of *King Lear* at Drury Lane, tried to reproduce some of the powerful effects of the storm scene in 'Eidophusikon'. De Loutherbourg has been credited with the breaking up of the scene by the use of perspective, and with being the first stage designer in England to make use of set scenes with raking pieces. But the time was not yet ripe for much practicable scenery, and he was for the most part sparing in his resort to built-up work. It is mainly as Garrick's scene designer that he is remembered, and his fine work gave momentary popularity to many an otherwise unremarkable piece. (See No. 162.)

LOW COMEDIAN, a term applied to a music-hall or pantomime player who specializes in a broad, somewhat vulgar, type of humour; sometimes known as a 'Red-nosed Comedian' from the traditional use of a fiery nose to indicate habitual insobriety (see also STOCK COMPANY).

LOWIN, JOHN (1576–1653), one of the best known of the actors in Shakespeare's plays, and an important link between the Elizabethan and Restoration stages. He first appears as an actor in 1602, and a year later was one of the King's Men (the former Chamberlain's Men), with whom he remained until the closing of the theatres in 1642. He was often referred to as a big man, and played the parts of bluff soldiers and gruff villains. His Falstaff was much admired, as was his Volpone, and his Melantius in *The Maid's Tragedy*. He was probably Bosola in the first production of *The Duchess of Malfi* (1614), and played in several of Massinger's plays. He was one of the actors caught playing in the Cockpit during the Puritan interregnum, and Betterton is supposed to have been coached in his part of Henry VIII by Davenant on instructions from Lowin, 'who', says Downes in *Roscius Anglicanus*, 'had his Instructions from Mr. Shakespeare himself'. In his old age Lowin, who fell into dire poverty, kept an inn at Brentford.

LUCILLE LA VERNE THEATRE, NEW YORK, see PRINCESS THEATRE.

LUCY RUSHTON'S THEATRE, NEW YORK, see NEW YORK THEATRE, 1.

LUDLOW, NOAH MILLER (1795–1886), one of the pioneer actor-managers of the American theatre. In 1815 he was engaged by Samuel Drake to go to Kentucky and later founded his own company, with which in 1817 he gave the first English plays in New Orleans. He travelled extensively, with his own or other companies, often being the first actor to penetrate to some of the more remote regions in the South and West. Going to New York in 1828 to recruit actors for his company, he was induced to take over the old Chatham Theatre with Cooper, but failed to make it pay, and returned to St. Louis. From 1835 to 1853 he was in partnership with Sol Smith as the American Theatrical Commonwealth Company, and ran several theatres simultaneously in St. Louis, New Orleans, Mobile, and other cities, often engaging outstanding stars. He was himself an excellent actor, particularly in comedy, and the author of an entertaining volume of reminiscences, *Dramatic Life as I Found It.*

LUDWIG, OTTO (1813–65), German novelist and dramatist, contemporary of Hebbel, whom he resembles in his passage from realistic prose to verse. In his best play, *Der Erbförster* (1850), a study of bourgeois life, a painful realism gains the upper hand, while an apocryphal drama, *Die Makkabäer* (1852), is written in a more romantic style. Ludwig, who studied music under Mendelssohn, was an ardent admirer of Shakespeare.

LUGNÉ-POË, AURÉLIEN-FRANÇOIS (1869–1940), French actor and manager, who studied at the Conservatoire, where he was a pupil of Worms, and obtained the second prize for comedy. He appeared at the Théâtre Libre under Antoine, and at the Théâtre d'Art with Paul Fort. He later took over this theatre and developed it into the celebrated Théâtre de l'Œuvre. Here, from 1892 to 1929, he worked as director and chief actor, and was responsible for introducing the work of many modern playwrights, of whom the first was Maeterlinck with *Pelléas et Mélisande*, *L'Intruse*, *Intérieur*, and *Monna Vanna*. He also staged plays by Ibsen, Bjørnson, Strindberg, Hauptmann, D'Annunzio and Echegaray, and produced Wilde's *Salome*. In later years he was the first to bring into prominence the plays of Claudel, producing *L'Annonce faite à Marie* for the first time in 1912. He did much to encourage young playwrights, and at the same time helped forward the development of the modern French theatre by putting before it the best contemporary work of other countries. Himself an excellent actor, he was seen in London in 1908 in *Poil de Carotte*, and was for several seasons manager for Eleonora Duse.

LUNACHARSKY, ANATOLI VASILEVICH (1875–1933), first Commissar for Education in Soviet Russia, an able, cultured man, friend of Lenin, to whom the U.S.S.R. owes the preservation and renewed vigour of those Imperial theatrical institutions, notably the Moscow Art Theatre, which survived the October Revolution. When uninformed fervour would have swept them away, he protected them, and gave them the time and the money to find their feet in the new world. He was also responsible for the organization of the new Soviet theatres, which have sprung up in such vast numbers and made a name for themselves. He realized that the new audiences, many of whom had never been in a theatre before, would eventually demand new methods and new plays approximating to their own life. That he provided for. But he realized at the same time that the old plays, both Russian and European, were part of the heritage of the new world, and that to falsify or misinterpret them was to betray the people. This led to his exposition of the principles of Socialist Realism, which caused a reorientation of the Soviet theatre, a new respect for the classics, and a series of fresh, vivid, and important revivals (as well as productions of new plays) of which Popov's *Taming of the Shrew* in 1937 is the best example. Lunacharsky wrote a number of articles on the theatre, which were published in two volumes (in 1924 and 1926), in which his theories, and the attempts made to put them into practice, can be further studied. A third volume was published in 1936. He was also the author of several plays. In 1934 the State Institute of Theatre Arts in Moscow (see G.I.T.I.S.) was named after him.

LUNDEQUIST, GERDA (1871–1959), Swedish actress, nicknamed 'the Swedish Bernhardt' because of her beautiful voice and powerfully dramatic acting. She had a long and distinguished career on the Swedish stage, being outstanding in such parts as Lady Macbeth and Antigone.

LUNT. (1) ALFRED (1892–), American actor, who made his début in 1913, toured with Margaret Anglin and Mrs. Langtry, and in 1919 made a great success as Clarence in Booth Tarkington's play of that name. With his wife, the English actress (2) LYNN FONTANNE (1887–), he has built up a big reputation in London and New York in the playing of intimate modern comedy. Miss Fontanne made her first appearance in London in 1905, and was with Ellen Terry, Tree, Waller, and other actor-managers before she first went to New York in 1910. She had already had a distinguished career before, with her husband, she joined the company of the Theatre Guild from 1924 to 1929, and appeared with him in a succession of plays, including *The Guardsman*, *Arms and the Man*, *The Goat Song*, and *Pygmalion*. They were first seen together in London in *Caprice* in 1929, and among their later successes have been *Reunion in Vienna*, *Design for Living*, *Amphitryon 38* (see No. 101), and *Love in Idleness* (known in America as *O Mistress Mine*). The combination of these two excellent players produces acting of great subtlety and sophistication which is in itself sufficient to make a success even of flimsy material, and rises to great heights when they approach material worthy of their exceptional talents. In 1958 they appeared in Dürrenmatt's *The Visit* at the former Globe Theatre, New York (see GLOBE, 4), renamed in their honour the Lunt–Fontanne. They were also seen in this play in London for the opening of the new Royalty, which shortly afterwards became a cinema.

LUPINO, a vast family of English dancers, acrobats, pantomimists, and actors, who trace their descent from a line of Italian puppet-masters, one of whom came to England in the time of James I. His seventh descendant in direct succession had sixteen children, mostly on the stage, of whom two married into the family of Sara Lane, lessee of the old Britannia Theatre, one having children and grand-children on the stage. The eldest son, George, was the father of (1) BARRY (1882–1962), who made his first appearance on the stage as a baby, was for some years stock comedian at the Britannia, toured extensively, and was seen in pantomime and musical comedy. He was one of the finest exponents of the Dame in pantomime, and wrote the librettos of about fifty pantomimes himself. His two children were also on the stage. His brother (2) STANLEY (1893–1942), also on the stage as a child, was in variety with an acrobat troupe and in pantomime for many years at Drury Lane. He was also seen in revue and musical comedy, was the author of several plays and novels, and of a volume of reminiscences, *From the Stocks to the Stars* (1934), from which many of the above details are taken. His nephew, (3) HENRY GEORGE (1892–1959), took his great-aunt Sara's name of Lane, and was known as Lupino Lane. As Nipper Lane he made his first appearance on the stage at the age of 4, and as an adult toured extensively in variety. He was also seen in musical comedy, and in pantomime, and made a great hit as Bill Snibson in *Me and My Girl* (1937), in which he created the well-known dance 'The Lambeth Walk'. He also had a son on the stage, though some younger members of this illustrious family have made their names in films.

LUZÁN, IGNACIO (1702–54), Spanish man of letters, was the most important theorist of the Spanish neo-classical period. His *Poética*, published in 1737, showed the influence of the classical doctrines of the Italian Renaissance, under whose yoke of Aristotelian unities Luzán endeavoured to subjugate Spanish poetry and drama. Luzán mentions with admiration the sixteenth-century poetry of Garcilaso, Camoëns, the Argensola brothers, and Herrera. He regrets that the dramatists of the seventeenth century, Lope de Vega, Calderón, Solís, did not write according to the rules, for otherwise their work would have been the envy and admiration of other nations. The posthumous second edition of his *Poética* (1789) shows a certain mellowing of his views. The dramatist is free to follow his instincts, his whims, or to write for the delight of the common people, but in all periods enlightened writers will turn to the rules which are based on reason and authority. Despite the considerable interest in neo-classical theories and despite official encouragement, the new school had, by 1789, produced no dramatist of the first rank and only a handful of tolerable plays. J. E. VAREY

LYCEUM THEATRE. 1. LONDON, in Wellington Street, just off the Strand. The name of this theatre is indissolubly linked with that of Irving, who was there from 1871 to 1902, even though the actual building was largely rebuilt after his departure. There had been a theatre on this site for a very long time. In 1765 a hall called the Lyceum opened for concerts and exhibitions, and in 1794 this was converted into a theatre by Dr. Arnold. He was, however, unable to get a licence for it owing to the opposition of the patent theatres, and it was used as a circus, for Musical Glasses, panoramas, phantasmagoria, a school of elocution, and an unlicensed theatre where out-of-work actors could play for their own benefit. In 1802 Madame Tussaud gave the first exhibition in London of her famous waxworks at this hall. Finally, in 1809, after the destruction by fire of Drury Lane, the company moved into it, bringing their licence with them. When the new Drury Lane opened in 1812 under Samuel Arnold, he was able to retain the licence for the Lyceum for the summer months only, and used it for mixed entertainments of opera and plays. In 1816 the theatre was largely rebuilt, and in 1817 the stage was lit by gas, which had already been used for the auditorium at the Olympic in 1815. The new building opened on 15 June with two plays starring Fanny Kelly. It was not successful, though 1818 saw Mathews in his celebrated entertainment 'Mathews at Home', and 1820 saw the opening night of Planché's melodrama, *The Vampyre; or, the Bride of the Isles*. Mrs. Glover played Hamlet in 1821, T. P. Cooke appeared as the Monster in *Frankenstein* in 1823, Kean played a season in 1828, and in 1830 the theatre was burnt down.

On 12 July 1834 a new building, whose frontage still stands on Wellington Street, opened as the Royal Lyceum and English Opera House. This was the building in which Irving made his name. It started well, but had a chequered career until the passing of the Licensing Act of 1843 enabled it to go over to legitimate drama. The Keeleys ran it successfully from 1844 to 1847 with extravaganzas, dramatizations of Dickens, and the famous 'Caudle Curtain Lectures'. After they left, Madame Vestris and her husband, the younger Mathews, took over, and a series of brilliant productions followed, mostly of Planché's extravaganzas. In one of them, *The Isle of Jewels* (1849), Beverley, the scene-painter, introduced the first transformation scene in a London theatre. Unfortunately Vestris was extravagant and Mathews no business man; they went bankrupt, and Mathews was imprisoned for debt. A few days after his release Vestris died. The theatre then took in the company from Covent Garden, which had been burnt down, but little of note happened during the next fifteen years, except for seasons by Madame Céleste (1858–61) and Charles Fechter (1863–7). Then, in 1871, the American impresario Bateman took the theatre in order to present his three daughters, Kate,

Virginia, and Isabel, in a London season, engaging as his leading man the young Henry Irving. Seven years later Irving took control, and with Ellen Terry as his leading lady inaugurated a series of fine productions which made the Lyceum the most notable theatre in London (see IRVING, and Nos. 73, 79, 173). During his absences on tour his tenants included some of the most famous actors of the day. He and Ellen Terry made their last appearance in this theatre (though both continued to appear elsewhere) on 19 July 1902 in *The Merchant of Venice*, and after their departure the fortunes of the theatre declined. It was partly demolished early in 1904, and rebuilt as a music-hall, but later became famous as the home of melodrama under the Melville brothers, who took possession in 1910 and remained for thirty years. Their plays were mostly written by themselves, and they also produced an annual pantomime. Later the plays of Edgar Wallace were seen there. In 1939 the theatre was again scheduled for demolition, and six farewell performances of *Hamlet*, with John Gielgud, took place, closing on 1 July. The outbreak of the Second World War two months later led to the abandonment of the demolition scheme, and the theatre stood empty until 1945, when it became a dance hall. At Christmas 1963 matinees of a children's play, *Pinocchio*, were given in the building, but there seems little hope of its again becoming a live theatre.

W. MACQUEEN-POPE†, *rev.*

2. NEW YORK, the old Fourteenth Street Theatre, which had for some time been the Théâtre Français. Fechter took it over and named it after the London Lyceum, hoping to establish it as the American national theatre; this proved impracticable, and under its new name the theatre finally opened on 11 Sept. 1873 with an English company in a version of *Notre-Dame de Paris*. This had little success and the theatre was mainly devoted to light opera, though Adelaide Neilson appeared there in 1874 and Booth, at the height of his glory, in the season of 1876–7.

3. NEW YORK. The New Lyceum, on Fourth Avenue, was a small jewel-box of a theatre built by Steele Mackaye, which opened on Easter Monday, 6 Apr. 1885, with Robert B. Mantell and Viola Allen in a new play by Mackaye, *Dakola*. This was not a success, and Mackaye withdrew from management. The theatre was later taken over by Daniel Frohman, who had many brilliant successes there, and in 1902 it was pulled down.

4. NEW YORK, on 45th Street east of Broadway, one of New York's most glamorous playhouses. It was built by Daniel Frohman, who named it after his old theatre (see above), and opened on 2 Nov. 1903 with E. H. Sothern in *The Proud Prince*, previously seen at the Herald Square Theatre. It is one of the few New York theatres to have a green room, and in the fine apartments on the top floor Frohman lived and entertained for many years. The first new play produced there was *The Admirable Crichton*, with William Gillette, and later Charles Wyndham and his wife brought their London company for a season of eight weeks. Among later successes were *The Lion and the Mouse*, *Arsène Lupin*, and several plays by Somerset Maugham. Lenore Ulric made her reputation at this theatre in *The Heart of Wetona* (1916) and *Tiger Rose* (1917), as did Jeanne Eagels in *Daddies*, transferred from the Belasco. Further productions by Belasco, who had been Frohman's first stage manager at the new Lyceum, heralded Warfield's Shylock in 1923, and the season ended with Ethel Barrymore in the Players' revival of *The School for Scandal*. *Antony and Cleopatra*, in 1924, was not a success, in spite of the fine acting of Jane Cowl, and the theatre had to wait for an outstanding success until *Berkeley Square* came in 1929. Later successes at the Lyceum were *George Washington Slept Here*, *Junior Miss*, *The Late George Apley*, and *Born Yesterday*, while Saroyan's *The Beautiful People* had an artistic, though not a commercial, success at this theatre. Later productions included Odets's *The Country Girl* (1950), and three imported English plays, *Look Back in Anger* (1957), *A Taste of Honey* (1960), and *The Caretaker* (1961).

GEORGE FREEDLEY†

(See also BROUGHAM and WALLACK.)

LYCOPHRON (b. *c.* 324 B.C.), a learned Alexandrian poet, composer of tragedies, none of which survives. He was one of the original Pleiad (see GREECE, 7).

LYCOPODIUM FLASK, the name given to a blow-pipe of vegetable brimstone which added a white flame to the terrors of red fire in the conflagrations of melodrama.

LYLY, JOHN (*c.* 1554–1606), English dramatist, important as the first writer of sophisticated comedy, and for his use of prose in drama. He is perhaps best known for his novels, *Euphues: The Anatomy of Wit* (1579) and *Euphues and his England* (1580), whose peculiarly involved and allusive style gave rise to the expression 'euphuism'; but by his contemporaries he was regarded as an outstanding dramatist, and his elegant writing had a salutary effect on some of the more full-blooded dramatists of the day. Lyly, who was an accomplished courtier and several times a Member of Parliament, wrote almost exclusively for a courtly audience, who delighted in the grace and artificiality of his style, and in the many sly allusions to contemporary scandal with which his plays are seasoned. His first two plays, *Alexander and Campaspe* and *Sapho and Phao*, were given by the Children of Paul's and of the Chapel in 1584, at Blackfriars. His most important play, *Endimion, the Man in the Moon*, has been ascribed by Chambers to 1588, when it may have been acted by the children before the Court 'on Candlemas Day at night', possibly with a multiple setting. It was first published in 1591. Of his other plays, several were pastoral comedies on mythological subjects, of ephemeral interest. Two comedies,

Midas and *Mother Bombie*—the latter in the style of Terence—were given by the Children of Paul's, of whom Lyly was vice-master in about 1590, and a further comedy, *The Woman in the Moon*, may not have been acted. Lyly is also suspected of having had a hand in numerous other plays of the time, but nothing can be ascribed to him with any certainty. He outlived the popularity of his work, but may have had the satisfaction of knowing that he had materially helped to lay the foundations of the great age of Elizabethan drama.

LYNN, Ralph (1882–1962), English actor, whose career on the stage spanned more than fifty years. He specialized in 'silly ass' roles—with monocle, protruding teeth, a winning smile, and sweet though asinine reasonableness under the most trying circumstances. He was a great favourite with several generations of London playgoers, many of whom still remember nostalgically the long series of farces, which, though mainly given at the Aldwych, began at the Shaftesbury in 1922, with *Tons of Money*, and continued through another twelve plays, of which the most successful were *A Cuckoo in the Nest* (1925), *Rookery Nook* (1926), and *Thark* (1928). In all these Lynn was partnered by Leslie Henson, Tom Walls, Robertson Hare, Winifred Shotter, and Mary Brough. The team finally disbanded in 1933, and Lynn turned increasingly to film work. But he made another hit in 1944 with *Is Your Honeymoon Really Necessary?* which ran for two years. Having made his first appearance on the stage at Wigan in 1900, he made his last in London in 1958. He then continued to tour in some of his old successes with unimpaired vigour and success until shortly before his death.

LYRIC THEATRE. 1. London, in Shaftesbury Avenue. This opened on 17 Dec. 1888 with *Dorothy*, transferred from the Prince of Wales's. It was followed by light opera and burlesque, and in May 1893 Eleonora Duse made her first London appearance here. A great success was scored when on 4 Jan. 1896 Wilson Barrett produced *The Sign of the Cross*, with himself as Marcus Superbus. It ran for 435 performances, its religious theme bringing many people to the theatre who had never before entered one. Barrett afterwards produced *The Manxman*, *The Daughters of Babylon*, *Virginius*, and *Othello*. In 1897 Réjane appeared in a season of French plays, as did Sarah Bernhardt in 1898. They were both seen in *Frou-Frou*. Loie Fuller made a success in *Little Miss Nobody* (also 1898) and then came *Florodora*, Leslie Stuart's outstanding musical comedy which opened on 11 Nov. 1899 and ran for 455 performances. In 1902 Forbes-Robertson took the theatre, presenting *Mice and Men*, *Hamlet*, *Othello*, and *The Light that Failed*. Musical comedy came back the following year with *The Duchess of Dantzig*. Lewis Waller was at this theatre from 1906 to 1908 with such favourite plays as *Brigadier Gerard* and *Monsieur Beaucaire*, and in 1910 *The Chocolate Soldier* began its long run. Another long run was that of *The Girl in the Taxi* (1912). During the First World War *Romance*, with Owen Nares and Doris Keane, transferred from the Duke of York's and ran for a long time. After this came a series of successful plays, including *Lilac Time* (1922), *Autumn Crocus* (1931), *Dangerous Corner* (1932), *Reunion in Vienna* (1934), *Victoria Regina* on its first public appearance (1936), *Amphitryon 38* with the Lunts and *The Flashing Stream* (both 1938), *The Nutmeg Tree* (1941), *The Winslow Boy* (1946), *The Little Hut* (1950), and two long-running musicals, *Grab Me a Gondola* (1956) and *Irma la Douce* (1958).

2. London, in Hammersmith (a western suburb). This opened as the Lyric Hall in 1888 with a French marionette show, and two years later became a theatre, opening under the management of Cordingley with a triple bill—*The Waterman*, *His Last Legs*, and *Puck*, a shortened version of *A Midsummer Night's Dream*. The theatre had a chequered career, became a home of melodrama, was extensively rebuilt and opened with *A House of Lies* on 20 July 1895. It then had a resident stock company, and after further alterations in 1899 continued to draw a good local audience until the opening of the King's, Hammersmith, in 1902. After this it sank to the level of a flea-pit, until Nigel Playfair took it over in 1918, and made this remote and unknown theatre prosperous and fashionable, drawing large audiences from the West End and raising it far above local importance. The opening production on 24 Dec. 1918 was Milne's *Make-Believe*. In 1919, in spite of a railway strike, Playfair decided to take what all thought a great risk, and put on Drinkwater's chronicle play, *Abraham Lincoln*, which had been seen previously at the Birmingham Repertory Theatre. It opened for a fortnight and ran for 466 performances. A lovely revival of *The Beggar's Opera*, with décor by Lovat Fraser (see No. 174), began on 5 June 1920, and further productions were revivals of *The Way of the World* (1924) and *The Beaux' Stratagem* (1927), in both of which Edith Evans made a great success, *The Cherry Orchard* (1925), *The Importance of Being Earnest* (1930) in black and white (see No. 157), Bickerstaffe's 'Lionel and Clarissa' (1925) and 'Love in a Village' (1928), new light operas and revues, mostly by A.P. Herbert and Thomas Dunhill, of which the most successful was *Riverside Nights* (1926), and an adaptation of part of *Nicholas Nickleby* as *When Crummles Played* (1927). In Nov. 1925 Ellen Terry made her last appearance on the stage in Walter de la Mare's *Crossings*. Playfair left in 1933. In 1948 a revival of *Captain Brassbound's Conversion* with Flora Robson (see No. 175) was a success, as was Gielgud's repertory season in 1952–3 with *Venice Preserved*, *Richard II* with Scofield as Richard, and *The Way of the World*. Occasional productions of interest since then have been Wolfit in *The Master of Santiago* and *Malatesta* (1957),

Mortimer's *The Dock Brief* and Pinter's *The Birthday Party* (both 1958), and Theatre 59's *Brand* (1959). W. MACQUEEN-POPE†, *rev.*

3. NEW YORK, on 42nd Street. This opened on 12 Oct. 1903 with Richard Mansfield in *Old Heidelberg*. One of its earliest successes was *The Taming of the Shrew* with Ada Rehan and Otis Skinner, while in its second season Réjane and Novelli appeared with Italian companies. Plays by Sudermann, Hauptmann, and Ibsen were all seen at this theatre and, in 1907, Percy Mackaye's *Jeanne d'Arc*. *The Chocolate Soldier* was successful in 1909, scoring 296 performances, and two years later came the success of *The Deep Purple*. In Nov. 1911 Ibsen's *Lady from the Sea* had its first performance in America, while 1912 saw a revival of *Julius Caesar*. Among later productions the most important were probably the musical comedies produced by Ziegfeld, though in 1932 Vittorio Podrecca brought his musical marionettes, known as the Teatro dei Piccoli, to the Lyric for 129 performances. The theatre's last production, before it became a cinema, was a memorable Negro drama with music, *Run, Little Chillun*. GEORGE FREEDLEY†

(See also CRITERION THEATRE, 2.)

LYTTON, EDWARD GEORGE EARLE LYTTON BULWER-LYTTON, LORD (1803–73), primarily an English novelist, but important in the history of the theatre as the author of several plays. Of these the most successful was *The Lady of Lyons; or, Love and Pride* (1838), which was first done by Macready at Covent Garden, with Helen Faucit as Pauline. It was immensely popular and was many times revived, notably by the Charles Keans, by Phelps, by Wallack and by Laura Keene in New York, by Barry Sullivan, by Fechter, by the Kendals, and, in 1879, by Henry Irving with Ellen Terry. Its continued popularity led to a number of burlesques on the same theme. Though romantic and sentimental, it has a touching sincerity and wears well. Lytton essayed a more modern note in *Money* (1840), a serious comedy which seems to foreshadow the reforms of Robertson. It held the stage for many years, being given in 1911 at Drury Lane with an all-star cast for a Command Performance. Lytton's only other important play was *Richelieu* (1839), first done by Macready and again frequently revived, notably by Irving at the Lyceum no less than four times. Although Lytton's plays do not rank high in dramatic literature, he was almost the only dramatist of his day to write plays that have survived on the stage.

M

MacCARTHY, Desmond (1877–1952), English literary and dramatic critic who began to write on the theatre in 1904, when he joined the staff of *The Speaker*. In 1913 he moved to the *New Statesman*. He was also editor for some years of *Life and Letters*, and published four volumes of collected essays, of which the last, *Drama*, appeared in 1940, and amounted, in its representative selection, to a review of the London theatre for the past quarter of a century. He also wrote *The Court Theatre 1904–7*, published by A. H. Bullen in 1907. In 1951 he was knighted for services to literature and the drama. It was said of him after his death: 'His judgements, particularly of the early plays of Shaw, though quick, were shrewd, and so sound that they stand today as outstanding examples of dramatic literature.'

McCARTHY, Lillah (1875–1960), English actress who created several of Bernard Shaw's heroines, and was associated with the Vedrenne–Barker venture at the Court Theatre in the early years of the twentieth century. She made her first appearance on the stage in 1895 in A. E. Drinkwater's company, and later that year joined Ben Greet, playing leading roles in Shakespeare and other plays. She also played opposite Wilson Barrett, notably as Mercia in *The Sign of the Cross*, in which she made her first appearance in the United States, and remained in his company until 1904. She was with Tree when she first met Bernard Shaw, who became a great friend and ardent admirer, and for him she played, at the Court in 1905, Nora in a revival of *John Bull's Other Island* and Ann Whitefield in the first public performance of *Man and Superman*. She also played Gloria in *You Never Can Tell* and Jennifer Dubedat in *The Doctor's Dilemma*. In 1906 she married Granville-Barker, who was directing the Court season, and among other parts played for him Nan in *The Tragedy of Nan* and Dionysus in *The Bacchae* of Euripides. In 1911 she took over the management of the Little, where she produced *The Master Builder*, playing Hilda Wangel, and, for the first time, *Fanny's First Play*, playing Margaret Knox. In 1912 she was Jocasta in Martin-Harvey's production of *Oedipus Rex*, and in the same year Iphigenia in *Iphigenia in Tauris*. When Granville-Barker took over the Savoy for a season she played Hermione in *The Winter's Tale*, and Viola in *Twelfth Night*. After divorcing Barker in 1918 (she had gone with him to America in a repertory of Shakespeare, Shaw, and Greek tragedy, and there he met and wished to marry Helen Huntingdon, who became his second wife) she took over the Kingsway. Her marriage to Sir Frederick Keeble took her to live in Oxford, and she practically retired from the stage, but made a final appearance in London in Dec. 1932 in *Iphigenia in Tauris*, and at the Oxford Playhouse in 1935 appeared in *Boadicea*. In 1930 she published *My Life* and in 1933 a further volume of memoirs, *Myself and My Friends*.

McCLINTIC, Guthrie (1893–1961), American actor, producer, and director, who studied for the stage at the American Academy of Dramatic Arts, and made his first appearance in 1913, being seen in New York a year later. He was for a time a member of Jessie Bonstelle's stock company at Buffalo, and assistant stage director to Winthrop Ames at the Little Theatre, New York. He then went into management on his own account, and from 1921 (in which year he married the actress Katharine Cornell, whose career is dealt with under her own name) until his death he was active in the New York theatre. He directed many of the plays in which his wife starred, notably *The Green Hat*, which first brought him into prominence in 1925, *The Barretts of Wimpole Street* (1931), *Romeo and Juliet* (1934), and *Candida* (1937). In 1936 he directed John Gielgud's *Hamlet* on Broadway. He was also instrumental in presenting to New York in 1952 the company of the Greek National Theatre in *Electra* and *Oedipus Tyrannus*.

McCULLOUGH, John (1832–85), American actor, born in Ireland, but an emigrant to the United States at the age of 15. He was self-taught, and had to make his way by hard work and study, gaining his experience first with amateur clubs and later in stock and touring companies. In 1861 he was taken by Forrest to play second lead, and later went with him to San Francisco, where he ran the California Theatre in partnership with Lawrence Barrett, and by himself, until financial difficulties caused him to give up management in 1875. He then toured until forced by illness to retire, making his last appearance as Spartacus in *The Gladiator* in 1884. McCullough, who was physically a big man, and a forceful personality, was often seen in New York, and in 1881 made a brief appearance in London. He had a high reputation in his own line of old-fashioned tragedy, in melodrama, and as some of Shakespeare's heroes, though his Hamlet was not good. He was noble and heroic rather than subtle, but maintained a good standard, and was much respected by his fellow actors and by the public, which he served faithfully to the best of his ability.

MACDERMOTT, Norman (1890–), English producer, who, after some experience in the provinces, opened the Everyman Theatre, Hampstead, which he ran from 1920 to 1926 as an experimental and non-commercial theatre, producing many new and unknown English and foreign plays. His first production, on 15 Sept., was Benavente's *Los intereses creados* as *The Bonds of Interest*, and among his later plays several were transferred to the West End—Munro's *At Mrs. Beam's* and Sutton Vane's *Outward Bound* (both 1923), *The Mask and the Face* (1924), a translation of Chiarelli's *La maschera e il volto*, and Noël Coward's *The Vortex* (also 1924). He also revived eight of Shaw's plays. After leaving the Everyman, Macdermott continued to produce in London until 1936, his last important venture being O'Casey's *Within the Gates* at the Royalty. He is the author of several plays and adaptations of foreign plays, and of a book dealing with his management of the Everyman Theatre.

MACDERMOTT, THE GREAT (1845–1901), a music-hall singer of patriotic songs—'We don't want to fight' and 'True Blues, stand to your Guns'. He was originally a bricklayer and a sailor, named G. H. Farrell, and went on the stage as Gilbert Hastings, from his Christian names. He was actor, author, and stage-manager at the Grecian and Britannia before blossoming out on the halls as The Great Macdermott. He later became a music-hall agent and manager.

MACGOWAN, KENNETH (1888–1963), American theatre director, who was for some years a dramatic critic on Boston, Philadelphia, and New York newspapers, and was associated with *Theatre Arts* from 1919 to 1925. From 1923 to 1925 he shared with Robert Edmond Jones and Eugene O'Neill in the management of the Provincetown Playhouse, and from 1924 to 1926 was associated with the Greenwich Village Theatre, producing new and unusual plays, among them a number by O'Neill himself. In 1927 he briefly directed the Actors' Theatre, and later produced plays on Broadway. He was the author of several books on the theatre, including *The Theatre of Tomorrow* (1922), *Footlights Across America* (1929), *A Primer of Playwriting*, and, in collaboration with Robert Edmond Jones, *Continental Stagecraft* (1922).

MACKAY, CHARLES (*c.* 1785–1857), Scotland's first great comic actor. Born in Edinburgh, he began his career in theatres in the West of Scotland, and in 1818 joined the company of the Edinburgh Theatre Royal, where his first appearance attracted little attention. In Feb. 1819, however, he appeared as Bailie Nicol Jarvie in Pocock's version of Sir Walter Scott's *Rob Roy*. His performance created a sensation and he was hailed as a star. Thenceforth he specialized, and had his greatest successes, in Scots character parts, many of them in further adaptations of Scott's novels. He played Bailie Nicol Jarvie for more than thirty years. He died in Edinburgh in 1857 and is buried in the Calton Cemetery, a few hundred yards from the scene of his greatest triumphs.

MACKAYE. (1) JAMES MORRISON STEELE (1844–94), American theatre designer, pioneer and inventor, whom Winter called 'a wayward genius of poetic temperament, enthusiastic, impetuous, fond of experiment'. While in the army in 1862 he made an amateur appearance as Hamlet, but it was not until ten years later, after studying in London and Paris, that he appeared on the professional stage, playing Hamlet in London on 3 May 1873 and, on 21 July of the same year, in Manchester with Marion Terry, who was making her first stage appearance, as his Ophelia. Later he appeared in New York with a group of students whom he had trained in the methods of Delsarte. In order to carry out his ideas he remodelled the old Fifth Avenue Theatre, installing elaborate scenic apparatus, overhead and indirect stage lighting, and a double movable stage, and opened it in 1879 as the Madison Square Theatre. Here his best play, *Hazel Kirke*, was first put on, and ran for nearly two years, though owing to Mackaye's unbusinesslike methods he received very little money from it. It was frequently revived and was seen in London, where Mackaye's first plays, mainly adaptations and collaborations, had been done. Unable to continue working at the Madison Square Theatre, he went to the Lyceum on Fourth Avenue, installed electric lighting, and established there the first school of acting in New York, later known as the American Academy of Dramatic Art, which did much good work in training future generations of actors. Mackaye, who was thin, dark, nervous, and dynamic, was everything by turns—actor, dramatist, teacher, lecturer—and his erratic personality had a great influence on the trend of the American theatre. Shortly before his death from overwork and worry he had planned a vast playhouse for the Chicago World Fair, which was to have had a wonderful cyclorama and all the most modern Continental stage equipment. It was never built, but later theatre architects were indebted to its plans for the introduction of many new ideas and methods. Mackaye influenced the theatre of his time and after, more by what he thought, dreamed of, and fought for, than by what he actually achieved, and none of his plays has survived. His life-story is told in *Epoch*, by his son, (2) PERCY WALLACE (1875–1956), also a playwright, much of whose best work was done in poetic drama, in modern masques and spectacles, and in the writing of operatic libretti. His independence of spirit, as well as his ideals of a free theatre, led him away from the commercial theatre of his day, and he developed his ideas in several volumes of criticism, including *The Playhouse and the Play* (1909), *The Civic Theatre* (1912), and *Community Drama* (1917).

MACKINLAY, JEAN STERLING (1882–1958), see WILLIAMS, (ERNEST GEORGE) HARCOURT (2).

MACKLIN [M'LAUGHLIN], CHARLES (*c.* 1700–97), Irish actor, best remembered for having rescued Shylock from the crudities of the low comedian, to whom the part had been assigned since Restoration days. Macklin raised him to the status of a dignified and tragic figure, thus drawing from Pope the memorable couplet: 'This is the Jew, That Shakespeare drew.' The date of his birth is uncertain, and he was for a long time believed to have been 107 when he died, but recent research points to his having been born about 1700. He had a wild and restless boyhood, and in 1716 joined a company of strolling players. In 1720 he was with the Bath company, and five years later he was engaged by Rich for Lincoln's Inn Fields Theatre, but his natural delivery, in which he preceded Garrick's reforms, told against him in the high-toned tragedy of the day. He went back to the provinces and fairs, playing Harlequin at Sadler's Wells, and Clown when the part called for an actor and not, as later on, for a dancer. At this period of his life, about which little is known and much surmised, he was known as the Wild Irishman, a jovial boon companion, a famous fives-player, a great lover, boxer, and pedestrian. On 4 Dec. 1730 he appeared at Lincoln's Inn Fields in Fielding's *Coffee-House Politician*, a rewriting, with an entirely new act, of *Rape upon Rape*, previously seen at the Haymarket; he may still have been there when Rich left for Covent Garden in 1732. Macklin then went to Drury Lane under Fleetwood and played secondary parts, until in 1741 he persuaded the management to revive *The Merchant of Venice*, and became famous overnight for his Shylock. There is an excellent description of him in the part by the German critic Lichtenberg.

After this Macklin might have risen to even greater heights, but with advancing years he became extremely quarrelsome and jealous (in May 1735 he had killed another actor, Hallam, in a fight over a wig), and he moved constantly from one theatre to another. At the Haymarket he played Iago to Foote's Othello, and the Ghost and Grave-digger to his Hamlet. At Covent Garden, where he appeared intermittently from 1750 to 1789, he played Mercutio to Barry's Romeo, and also played Macbeth, discarding Garrick's scarlet coat and appearing for the first time in something approximating to the dress of a Highland chieftain. A good deal of his energy was expended off the stage. He was constantly engaged in litigation, often with his managers, he went bankrupt after opening a tavern, and he also founded a school, his serious but not very sensible lectures providing Foote with excellent material for burlesque at the Haymarket. Macklin also embarked on a speculation to build a theatre in Dublin, but soon quarrelled with his partners and withdrew. He was the author of a number of plays, of which two were excellent and survived well into the nineteenth century—*Love à la Mode* (1759), in which he himself played Sir Archy McSarcasm, and the famous comedy, *The Man of the World* (1781), which he based on one of his former farces, the two-act *The True-Born Scotsman*, given at Smock Alley, Dublin, in 1764. In this Macklin again played the chief character, Sir Pertinax McSycophant, though he was by then an old man. In 1788 his memory began to fail, but he still acted, and his last appearance on the stage was on 7 May 1789, when he attempted Shylock, but was unable to finish it. Neither a good tragedian, nor yet a good light comedian, he was at his best in his own plays and in parts like Scrub and Peachum, which required a rough vigour. He was a complex personality, of whom it was said that he had a 'rough mind and rougher manner', impatient of contradiction, dogmatic, a tyrant in the theatre, but of great critical acuity. He is variously represented as a disgustingly rude and obnoxious person, and as a man of great charm, quarrelling with other actors—notably Garrick and Quin—and managers and winning them back by a disarming apology. He was also an excellent teacher of acting, and a man of strict integrity, benevolence, and generosity. His energy was unbounded, but his restless disposition prevented him from making much mark on the theatre, and he lived always in the shadow of Garrick's greatness. He was twice married, first in 1739, his wife dying in 1758. His second wife survived him, but his children all died before him. One of them, a daughter (1749–87), was a pretty, respectable girl, and though not a good actress was much admired in breeches parts. Another, Maria (1732–81), apparently illegitimate, was also an actress, making her first appearance at Drury Lane in Dec. 1742 as the Duke of York in *Richard III*.

MACLEISH, ARCHIBALD (1892–), American poet and dramatist, who continued Maxwell Anderson's attempts to write plays in poetry adapted to the rhythms of everyday American speech. He has had a distinguished career as a poet and lecturer on poetry, and is the author of *Nobo-daddy* (1925), *Panic* (1935), and, his best play to date, *J.B.* (1958) (see No. 111). This, a retelling of the story of Job in modern terms, was seen in London in 1961. It has since been performed in many European countries. Though not wholly successful in portraying living people in terms of a cosmic myth, it nevertheless has moments of authentic tragedy; it was awarded the Pulitzer Prize for drama (MacLeish has twice been awarded the Pulitzer Prize for poetry).

MAC LIAMMÓIR, MICHEÁL (1899–), Irish actor, scenic artist, and playwright in both Gaelic and English. He was on the London stage as a child, as Alfred Willmore, making his début at the age of 12 in *The Goldfish*, and appearing under Tree at the Haymarket as Macduff's son and Oliver Twist. He also appeared several years running as John Darling in *Peter Pan*. He then studied art, exhibiting in various parts of Europe, travelled widely, became familiar with the theatrical art and literature of several countries, and finally brought to the Dublin stage his combination of gifts as director and scenic artist. In 1928, in combination with Hilton Edwards, he founded the Gate Theatre, Dublin; he also created and directed from 1928 to 1931 the Galway Theatre (Taibhdhearc na Gaillimhe). He produced, for An Comhar Drámuíochta, a long list of foreign classics in Irish (he himself being responsible for translations of Chekhov, Guitry, and Shaw), and a number of original Irish plays. Among his own plays the best known are *Diarmuid and Gráinne*, given both in English and Irish, *Ill Met by Moonlight*, seen in London in 1947, and *Where Stars Walk*. He is also the author of a theatrical autobiography, *All For Hecuba*. In 1960–1 he gave in London, in Dublin, and on tour, a virtuoso one-man performance, *The Importance of Being Oscar*, based on readings from Oscar Wilde's works. In 1962 he played Iago in the Dublin Festival production of *Othello*, and two years later was seen as Hitler in *The Roses are Real*.

McMASTER, Anew (1894–1962), Irish actor, who did valuable work outside London in keeping Shakespeare before the public. He first appeared on the stage in 1911 under Fred Terry, with whom he remained for three years. He was leading man to Peggy O'Neill in *Paddy the Next Best Thing* (1920), and in 1921 went to Australia, where among other parts he played Iago to the Othello of Oscar Asche. In 1925 he began his important work by founding a company to present Shakespeare on tour, managing, acting, and directing himself. He was outstanding as Shylock, Richard III, and Coriolanus. A tall handsome man, with an imperious face crowned, in his later years, by a fine head of white hair, he 'took the stage' with great dignity. Under Bridges-Adams he appeared at Stratford in 1933, playing Hamlet and Coriolanus, and in the following year he played for a season at the Chiswick Empire, later taking his company on a tour of the Near East. After the Second World War he was active in Ireland, and at the time of his death was preparing to play Othello at the Dublin Festival to the Iago of Micheál Mac Liammóir. His insistence on taking Shakespeare to less favoured localities meant that he was less well known in London than he deserved to be, but he was a hard-working, conscientious, and dedicated theatre-worker, devoted to Shakespeare, and more than competent in direction and acting, often under very difficult circumstances on tour.

MACNAMARA, Brinsley (1891–1963), Irish dramatist and novelist, whose real name was John Weldon. Born in Delvin, the son of a schoolteacher, he joined the Abbey Theatre company at the age of 17. His first play, *The Rebellion at Ballycullen*, was staged there in 1917. A series of successful plays followed, including *The Land for the People* (1920), *The Glorious Uncertainty* (1923), *Look at the Heffernans* (1926), *The Master* (1928) in which F. J. MacCormick gave a fine performance, and *Margaret Gillan* (1935), probably his best play. He became a director of the Abbey Theatre, but resigned after a disagreement over O'Casey's *Silver Tassie*, which he did not think good enough for production. He was also for a time drama critic of the *Irish Times*, and compiled a useful indexed guide to the plays produced at the Abbey.

MACOWAN, Michael (1906–), English actor and producer, son of the actor-dramatist Norman Macowan (1877–1961) whose plays included *The Blue Lagoon* (based on Stacpoole's novel, 1920), *The Infinite Shoeblack* (1929), and *Glorious Morning* (1938). From 1954 to 1966 Michael Macowan was head of the London Academy of Music and Dramatic Art, known as Lamda. Here he began by limiting the number of students to 60, and evolved for them his own system of training, providing them in 1963 with an excellent adaptable and experimental theatre. As a young actor he made his first appearance in 1925 in Charles Macdona's repertory season of Shaw, but in 1931 he abandoned acting for production, and his work has since been seen in many theatres, including the Old Vic and Stratford-upon-Avon. He was associated with the short-lived Old Vic Theatre School and produced some of Fry's early plays, as well as plays by Priestley and Charles Morgan. Even while at Lamda he continued to work in the commercial theatre, producing plays such as *The Potting Shed* (1958).

MACQUEEN-POPE, Walter James (1888–1960), English actor, manager, and theatre historian, who traced his ancestry back to Jane Pope of Drury Lane and further back to Morgan Pope, owner of the Bear Garden, Bankside, and to Thomas Pope, actor at Shakespeare's Globe. Though these claims were never fully substantiated, they gave him much pleasure and were seldom challenged. Certainly he deserved such an illustrious theatrical background, for his devotion to the London theatre (he ignored all others) was whole-hearted, and he devoted his life to furthering its affairs. He was business manager of many London theatres, beginning with the Queen's. In 1925 he became press representative at the Palladium, and he was for twenty-one years in charge of publicity at Drury Lane. From 1945 to his death he publicized the theatre he loved through innumerable books, lectures, and broadcasts. A lovable and stimulating companion, he excelled in communicating his sense of the glamour and excitement of Edwardian theatre-going, and his occasional inaccuracies were forgiven for the sake of the brilliant light he threw on personalities and events of the theatre during his lifetime. After his death a plaque to his memory was unveiled by Sir Donald Wolfit in St. Paul's, Covent Garden. He contributed a number of articles to the first edition of this Companion.

MACREADY, William Charles (1793–1873), English actor, and one of the finest tragedians of his own or any time. He was the son of a provincial actor-manager, and his father's financial difficulties caused him to leave Rugby, where he had already shown talent as an amateur actor and reciter, to go on the stage. He made his first appearance at Birmingham as Romeo in 1810, and then toured the provinces, playing Hamlet for the first time the following year at Newcastle. In 1816 he was engaged to appear at Covent Garden as Orestes in *The Distrest Mother*, and there and in the provinces he subsequently played in a number of poor plays, which did nothing to reconcile him to a profession he already disliked. By 1819, however, he was firmly established as Kean's rival, and continued to appear at both Covent Garden and Drury Lane in a variety of parts. He was good in *Rob Roy*, *Gambia*, and *Virginius*, but it was his Lear, Hamlet, and Macbeth which were universally acclaimed, causing Hazlitt to say of him that he was the best tragic actor of his remembrance, except Kean. His rivalry with the latter was later transferred to Edwin Forrest, culminating in the Astor Place riot in New York (1849), in which several people were killed. Macready was a man of ungovernable temper, and on one occasion he and Alfred Bunn, then manager of Drury Lane, came to blows. Macready was himself manager at various times of both the patent theatres, where he sought always to improve current methods of production by subordinating scenery and costume to the play as a whole. His managements were artistically, though not always financially, a success. In 1837 (in which year he played Othello—see No. 71) he appeared with Helen Faucit in several outstanding new plays, including Browning's *Strafford*, and a year later produced *The Lady of Lyons*, playing Claude Melnotte to Helen Faucit's Pauline. Their fine acting did much to ensure the success of the play and its subsequent reputation. Another of Bulwer Lytton's plays which gave Macready a fine part was *Richelieu* (1839), while among the new poetic plays which owed their appearance to his encouragement and initiative was Byron's *Two Foscari* (1838). Macready made his first appearance in America in 1826, and his last on the occasion of the riot mentioned above, and in 1828 was in Paris. He played an important part in the struggle to free the London stage from the monopoly of the patent theatres, and also worked to rescue Shakespeare's text from many of the Restoration emendations. A scrupulous and cultured man, enjoying the society of some of the greatest writers of the day, he nevertheless made many enemies, particularly by his constant disparagement of the profession which he adorned. Apart from the excellence of his acting, in which he was surpassed only by Garrick, and equalled only by Kean, he is important in theatre history for his efforts to encourage all that was best in the theatre of his day, and for his many reforms both of acting and of texts. He was the first English manager to insist on full rehearsals, particularly for supers and crowd-scenes. His diary gives a lively picture of the society in which he moved, and reveals the man himself with all his virtues and shortcomings. It was published in two volumes in 1875, edited by Sir Frederick Pollock, and later supplemented by a little volume by Lady Pollock, entitled *Macready as I knew him*, much of which deals with his life after his retirement at Sherborne and Cheltenham. Macready's last performance was given at Drury Lane, where he appeared as Macbeth on 26 Feb. 1851.

MACSWINEY, OWEN, see SWINEY.

MACHIAVELLI, NICCOLÒ DI BERNARDO DEI (1469–1527), Florentine statesman and political philosopher, whose most famous work is *Il Principe*. Exiled from the service of the Medicis on suspicion of conspiracy, he gave some of his time and genius to the theatre. The best of his comedies is undoubtedly *La Mandragola*, written between 1513 and 1520 in sharp, precise prose. It is a pungent criticism of Florentine society, and portrays the gradual betrayal of its lovely heroine by her credulous husband, her ardent but unscrupulous lover, and her scheming mother, aided by the evil machinations of the corrupt priest, Fra Timoteo. Its audiences delighted in it, savouring its wit and accepting its portrayal of a rotten society as true. In a translation by Ashley Dukes it was successfully given at the Mercury Theatre in London during 1940. It was also published in New York in 1927 in a translation by Stark Young. In 1965, in a modernized version by Carlo Terron, it was revived by Peppino de Filippo, who played Fra Timoteo, at the Sant' Erasmo in Milan, with great success.

MACHINE PLAY, a name given to those seventeenth-century French plays which made excessive use of mechanical contrivances, especially for flights, and of elaborate changes of scenery. The development of these spectacular entertainments coincided with the popularity of opera, and is linked with the work of Torelli. The subjects were usually taken from classical mythology, which allowed the use of a *deus ex machina*, and, unlike the classical tragedies of the day, they were not usually written in regular alexandrines. The first French play of this type was Corneille's *Andromède* (1650), and it reached its peak with Molière's *Amphitryon* (1668) and *Psyché* (1671). By far the greater number of 'machine' plays, though not the outstanding ones, were given at the Théâtre du Marais, which had a large and excellently equipped stage suitable for their presentation.

MACHINERY. Most theatre machines come into the following four categories:

(*a*) *Machines for Quick Changes*. These include *periaktoi* or prisms, pivots, trucks, trolleys, moving platforms, and turntable stages, on all of which scenery is mounted so that it can be moved into and out of sight quickly and easily (see BOAT TRUCKS). Derricks, levers, drums, rollers, and pulleys are for lifting out of sight, by means of ropes and wires, backcloths, frontcloths, set pieces, and the top parts of certain pieces of scenery so that they can be got rid of speedily (see CARRIAGE-AND-FRAME, DRUM-AND-SHAFT, TRICKWORK).

(*b*) *Machines for Supernatural Appearances.* These include tracks above the stage, suspended ropes, wires, spring coils, and iron rods, to which are attached persons, chariots, aeroplanes, etc., so that they can be held or transported in the air in view of the audience. Also included are traps, moving-stairs, and platforms on which persons or things may be placed so that they can travel across or descend below stage, either slowly or in an instant (see FLYING EFFECTS, GREECE, 6, TRAPS, TRICKWORK).

(*c*) *Machines for Controlling Light.* These include contrivances that attempt to imitate the colouring, brightening, and fading of light in nature or the imitations of lightning, fire, etc., also those for illuminating the actors for the simple purpose of making them visible to the audience in closed theatres (see LIGHTING, *passim*).

(*d*) *Machines for Imitating the Sounds and Effects of Nature,* such as waterfalls, snowstorms, thunder, storms at sea, etc. (see TRICKWORK).

Classical Greek tragedy of the fifth century B.C. used only one machine, the crane for carrying an actor, alone or in a chariot, through the air. To this the Hellenistic theatre added the *periaktoi* for quick changes of scenery, and possibly the *bronteion* to imitate thunder (for the *ekkyklema*, see GREECE, 6). Very little information is extant on the use of machinery in the Roman theatre, and it was not until the fourteenth century A.D. that machines became important. They were first used in performances of liturgical dramas in churches. The earliest ones were fairly simple, and the first elaborate one of which we have details was the 'Paradiso' of Filippo Brunelleschi (1377–1446). Invented for the representation of the Annunciation which took place annually in the church of S. Felice in Florence, it consisted of a 'nosegay' of singing cherubim suspended in a copper dome from the roof, which was lowered by crane to a stage. From it a young actor emerged, played his part as the Angel of the Annunciation, returned to the dome, and was swung up again to heaven. Brunelleschi's work was continued and improved upon by Francesco d'Angelo called Il Cecco (1447–88), who added clouds of cotton wool to hide the machinery of Christ's Ascension from the mountain into heaven. Later, painted canvas, shaped into clouds and mounted on battens, took the place of cotton wool and, as a screen for the mechanical working of any supernatural being, lasted until the end of the eighteenth century.

When liturgical drama fell out of favour and a revival of classical drama took its place, the *periaktoi* of Hellenistic times were rediscovered and improved on, chiefly by Bastiano da San Gallo (1481–1551). Originally prisms of wood turning on a central pivot, they had their three sides painted with different scenes which revolved to give a degree of localization to an otherwise unchanging architectural set. San Gallo increased the size of the *periaktoi*, placing them behind each other like wings on either side of the proscenium, and in order to achieve a greater number of scene changes he changed the painted canvas panels during the intervals.

When the theatre had been re-established in Renaissance Italy as a social force, those princes who had encouraged it vied with each other in the splendour of their entertainments, and the devising of new machines, or the adaptation of old ones, formed part of the day's work for the many architects and artists whom they employed, among them Mantegna, Leonardo da Vinci, Andrea del Sarto, Giulio Romano, and Cristoforo Gherardi. After 1600 theatre machinery developed with great rapidity, and the first book to be published on the subject, *Pratica de fabricar scene e machine ne' teatri* (1638), by Nicola Sabbattini (1574–1654), was already out of date. The achievements of Giovanni Lorenzo Bernini (1598–1680) in a theatre in Rome, as described by Richard Lascelles in his *Italian Voyage* (1670), show how far the actual use of machines had progressed beyond Sabbattini:

> Here I have seen upon the stage, Rivers swelling, and Boats rowing upon them; waters overflowing their banks and stage; men flying in the air, Serpents crawling upon the stage, Houses falling on the suddain, Temples and *Boscos* appearing, whole towns, known towns, starting up on a sudden with men walking in the streets, the Sun appearing and chasing away darkness, sugar plums fall upon the spectators' heads like Hail, Rubans flash in the ladies' faces like lightning, with a thousand like representations.

This Lascelles was a contemporary of the English scenic designer Inigo Jones (1573–1652), who, after a visit to Italy in about 1613–14, met Giulio Parigi (1590–1636), and took back to England much of what he had learned from him, using it for the adorning of Court masques.

One of the most famous spectacles of the seventeenth century was that given in the Farnese Theatre in Parma on 21 Dec. 1628 to celebrate the marriage of Ranuccio II and Margherita of Tuscany. For this twenty-one machines were specially constructed, and records exist of all of them. The climax of the evening, which opened with the appearance of Aurora from the sea on a chariot drawn by fiery steeds, was the entry of Neptune, rising from the 'waves' on stage. These were spiral columns made of wood and painted. Laid on their sides, parallel with the proscenium opening, and turned slowly, they gave a most beautiful effect. Water from tanks under the stage, pumped up the previous day in readiness, then welled up and overflowed through gullies into the auditorium, which had been made waterproof with lead sheeting to the height of about 3 ft. Then, through side doors, entered marine monsters and floating islands, worked by men hidden inside. On each of these sat warriors who fought until, at a given signal, they disappeared, and Venetian sailors, who were in charge of the proceedings, knocked away the plugs which stopped up the sluice-holes and the water ran away.

An important name in the history of theatre machinery is that of Giacomo Torelli (1608–78). Born in Fano, he studied architecture and mechanics, and took to the theatre. In 1640 he built the Teatro Novissimo in Venice, and there displayed his inventions, which were destined to be used in the European theatre for two hundred years at least; some of them are still in use. Among other things, he invented a method of changing scenery quickly by attaching the wings to frames mounted on carriages below the stage, so that all could be pulled forward by one turn on a central drum and run back again by the action of counterweights (see CARRIAGE-AND-FRAME). John Evelyn was in Venice in 1645 and saw some of Torelli's wonders. He wrote:

> We went to the opera where comedies and other plays are represented . . . with variety of scenes painted and contrived with no less art of perspective and machines for flying in the air, and other wonderful notions. . . . The scenes changed thirteen times. . . . This held us by the eyes and ears until two in the morning.

His achievements soon acquired for Torelli the nickname of 'il gran stregone', the great wizard. In 1645 he went to France and introduced machines and footlights into the French theatre. The French went machine-mad and Torelli grew rich. Through intrigue, however, he was sent from the country in 1660, his place being taken by Gaspare Vigarani (1586–1663), who, out of jealousy, destroyed all Torelli's machines but kept his designs. However, Torelli's innovations were not forgotten, for in 1772, when Diderot published his great *Encyclopédie* (*M*), under 'Machines du Théâtre' was a complete record of the theatre machinery of the day, all based on Torelli's ideas.

The tradition, passed on by Vigarani, was maintained by Jean Nicolas Servandony (1695–1766), and by numerous French machinists. But the vogue of the machine-play was passing, and in the nineteenth century matters got so bad that unskilled craftsmen were trying to manage machines over a hundred years old. Gustave Chougnet, writing about Rossini's opera 'Mosè in Egitto', produced in Naples in 1818, says:

> The scene of the darkness was another step onwards, and the whole work was much applauded, with the exception of the passage of the Red Sea, the representation of which was always laughed at, owing to the imperfection of the theatrical appliances already spoken of. At the resumption of the piece therefore, in the following Lent, Rossini added a chorus to divert attention from the wretched attempt to represent the dividing waves, and it is to the sins of the Neapolitan stage machinists that we owe the universally popular prayer 'Dal tuo stellato soglio'.

The triumph of bourgeois drama, with its domestic scenes, and the universal adoption of the box-set, followed by the popularity of the open stage and theatre-in-the-round, brought almost to an end the use of theatre machinery. It is now mainly employed for changing scenery behind a curtain, except for pantomime, ballet, and the occasional play, like Giraudoux's *Ondine*, which demands magical effects.

MACKNEY, E. W. (1835–1909), an old-time music-hall performer who began his career in the supper-rooms, and was one of the first stars of the old Canterbury under Morton, also the first black-faced singer, accompanying himself on the banjo. He was also no mean dancer. His most famous songs were 'The Whole Hog or None' and 'I Wish I were with Nancy', sung to the tune of 'Dixie'. Unlike so many of the old music-hall favourites, he was a careful man, and retired when well advanced in years to live on a small farm at Enfield. W. MACQUEEN-POPE†

MADÁCH, IMRE (1823–64), Hungarian dramatist, whose best play, twice translated into English as *The Tragedy of Man*, was *Az ember tragédiája* (1862). Conceived on a vast scale, somewhat on the lines of *Faust*, this deals with the struggle between the Devil and Adam for the possession of man's soul, and has won international recognition.

MADDERMARKET THEATRE, see AMATEUR THEATRE IN GREAT BRITAIN, 1 *d*, MONCK, and NORWICH.

MADISON SQUARE THEATRE, NEW YORK. This was originally the Fifth Avenue Hall, on the site of Daly's first Fifth Avenue Theatre, and was adapted and renovated by the great inventive genius of the New York stage, Steele Mackaye, who intended to run it on the lines of the Comédie-Française as a stock-company theatre with a picked repertory. The venture was a failure, but the theatre, which had opened on 23 Apr. 1879, was firmly established. With the Mallory brothers in command and Daniel Frohman as business manager, it opened again on 4 Feb. 1880 with *Hazel Kirke*, which scored 486 performances, the longest run on the New York stage up to that time. Viola Allen made her first appearance in New York at this theatre, in July 1882, and in the same year *Young Mrs. Winthrop*, one of the first good American plays, was staged there. Mansfield was seen at this theatre in several of his best parts, and in the season of 1889–90 produced *A Doll's House*, with Beatrice Cameron as Nora. On 15 Sept. 1891 it was taken over by Hoyt and Thomas and some years later was renamed Hoyt's Theatre, until on 1 Feb. 1905 its original name was restored. A year later *A Case of Arson*, by Heijermans, was produced there, and in Mar. 1908 the theatre finally closed.

GEORGE FREEDLEY†

MADRID THEATRES. The first public playing places in Madrid were the courtyards of houses, used by wandering companies of players. In 1572 a monopoly of such performances was granted to a charitable brotherhood, the Cofradía de la Pasión, which maintained the Hospital of the same name. This brotherhood was joined by another, the Cofradía de la Soledad, and from this date the fate of the theatres was closely linked to that of the hospitals. The two brotherhoods bought property which they converted into theatres, the Corral de la Cruz opening in 1579 and the Corral del Príncipe in 1582. Protected by the monopoly of the hospitals, these theatres were unchallenged until the eighteenth century. In the 1640s, however, a royal theatre was built in the Palace of Buen Retiro, and in the later part of the century it became the practice to allow public performances in the Coliseo del Buen Retiro. These performances did not infringe the hospitals' monopoly, as the lessees of the public theatres were given authority to lease the royal theatre for these occasions. Apart from the performances in the well-equipped Coliseo, plays were also staged in other parts of the Palace of Buen Retiro, as well as in the royal apartments and in the Salón Dorado of the old Alcázar. These were, however, all private performances.

In the early years of the eighteenth century the hospitals' monopoly was challenged by Italian players who established themselves in a temporary building near the Caños del Peral. In 1719 an opera-house, known as the Teatro de los Caños del Peral, was established there. The present Teatro Real occupies the same site and has always suffered from the rising damp which was to be expected in a building constructed over a natural spring. In 1963 it was announced that this, the largest and most unsatisfactory of the theatres of Madrid, long abandoned for practical reasons, was to be demolished. The middle years of the eighteenth century saw also the rebuilding of the original two theatres. The Coliseo, or Teatro de la Cruz, was rebuilt in 1743, and the Príncipe in 1744–5. The Coliseo del Buen Retiro was also refurbished.

In the early nineteenth century the Cruz, Príncipe, and Caños del Peral were augmented by little theatres opened during the Christmas period and Carnival for puppet shows and acrobatics, whilst rope-dancers, tumblers, and equestrian performers also appeared in the bullring. It was the middle years of the century which witnessed the sudden proliferation of theatrical life and the establishment of a score of new theatres. By the end of the century the most important theatres were the Real (built in 1818 on the site of the Caños del Peral), Español (built in 1806 on that of the Príncipe), Comedia, Zarzuela, Apolo, Príncipe Alfonso, Lara, Variedades, Eslava, Alhambra, Novedades, and Princesa. In the twentieth century the Eslava came into prominence during the management (1917–25) of Gregorio Martínez Sierra. Sierra introduced to the Madrid public the technical innovations of the twentieth-century European theatre, seen for the first time on the Spanish stage in Barcelona, and the visual impact of his productions on a public used to nineteenth-century scene-painting, lighting, and stage management was tremendous. Another feature of the 1920s was the growing importance of the private theatres. During the last years of the Republic and the beginning of the Civil War, García Lorca's La Barraca and Alejandro Casona's El Teatro del Pueblo, both itinerant companies, took the drama to the common people. The Civil War virtually destroyed the indigenous theatre, and only recently has work of any significance emerged. The productions of the Little Theatres (*teatros de cámara*) continue to be highly significant. J. E. VAREY

MAEDER, MRS. JAMES, see FISHER, CLARA.

MAETERLINCK, MAURICE (1862–1949), Belgian poet and dramatist, whose symbolic plays were a challenge to both the ephemeral and the realistic drama of his time. In them he showed his characters as the instruments of some hidden force, emanating from the unseen reality which lies all around us. This is particularly true of the two plays best known in English, *L'Oiseau bleu* (1909) and *Les Fiançailles* (1919), which as *The Blue Bird* and *The Betrothal* were given in London and New York. Some critics, however, consider *The Burgomaster of Stilemonde*, given in London in 1918, to be his best work. Among his other plays, many of which were first given in Paris by Lugné-Poë, *Pelléas et Mélisande* was played by Mrs. Patrick Campbell in both English and French, the latter with Sarah Bernhardt. For the English version in 1898 the incidental music was composed by Fauré, while Debussy later used the play as the basis of an opera. Maeterlinck, who was much praised in his early years for having brought poetry and enchantment back to the stage, collaborated in 1907 with Paul Dukas in a *conte-lyrique*, *Ariane et Barbe-Bleue*, which had a considerable success.

MAFFEI. (1) (FRANCESCO) SCIPIONE (1675–1755), Italian dramatist who in the early years of the eighteenth century tried to give Italy a tragic drama worthy of the name. In 1714 he published his tragedy *Merope*, which had been given the previous year both in Italy and at the Comédie-Italienne in Paris. It was much admired by Voltaire, who later essayed the same subject and dedicated his *Merope* to Maffei. Maffei also wrote a *Trattato de' teatri antichi e moderni*, and some comedies of little importance. He visited England, where his reputation as a man of letters assured him a warm welcome and an honorary Doctorate at Oxford. *Merope* was translated into English by Ayre in 1740. Scipione Maffei should not be confused with the later (2) ANDREA (1798–1885), who translated into Italian the plays of Schiller, Goethe's *Faust*, and Shakespeare's *Othello* and *The Tempest*.

MAGALHAES, DOMINGO JOSÉ GONÇALVES DE (1811–82), see SOUTH AMERICA, 2.

MAGNES, an early Athenian comic poet, mentioned by Aristophanes in the *Knights*. He won a victory in 472 B.C.

MAGNON, JEAN (1620–62), a mediocre French dramatist, of whom it was said, since he wrote with great facility, that his works were more easily written than read. But he deserves to be remembered, since his first play, *Artaxerce* (1644), was given by a small company which included Jean-Baptiste Poquelin, later the immortal Molière, whose friend Magnon remained all his life. He wrote seven more plays, and a vast encyclopaedia called *La Science universelle*. He was assassinated on the Pont-Neuf by the hired bravos of his wife's marquis-lover. He had a son who opened a theatre in Copenhagen where Molière's plays were given and had much influence on the development of the Scandinavian dramatist, Holberg.

MAINTENON, MADAME DE (*née* Françoise d'Aubigné) (1635–1719), second wife of Louis XIV, deserves mention here on two counts. As a young and penniless girl she became the wife of the novelist and dramatist Scarron, and had a salutary effect on some of his later plays, and on the conduct of his house and conversation; and in 1689, as virtual mistress of France, she induced Racine, after twelve years' silence, to write for the young ladies of her school at Saint-Cyr his beautiful poetic dramas *Esther* and *Athalie*. She herself also composed, for the same young ladies, a number of one-act sketches illustrating well-known proverbs, a genre much in vogue in society at this time and later made famous by Alfred de Musset. These, preserved in manuscript, were not published until 1829.

MAIRET, JEAN (1604–86), one of the most important of early French dramatists. He was well educated, and arrived in Paris with his first play, a tragicomedy entitled *Chryséide et Arimand*, in 1625. This he sold to a troupe of actors, and it later figured in the repertory of the Hôtel de Bourgogne and of Montdory's troupe. Mairet then entered the service of the Duke of Montmorency, where he came into contact with Théophile and Racan, whose plays were already well known to him. They had a great influence on his development and inspired his second play, a pastoral, given in 1626. Mairet was soon recognized as the leading dramatist of the day, and when his *Sophonisbe* (1634), the first French tragedy to be written in accordance with the unities, was a success, contemporary dramatists were ready to imitate him. In form and content *Sophonisbe* was a complete contrast to the tragicomedies and pastorals which had preceded it, and a forerunner of French classical tragedy. Unfortunately Mairet attacked Corneille bitterly in the quarrel over *Le Cid*, and the opprobrium this has brought him from later generations has tended to obscure his importance as a dramatist. In his own day he was as successful as, and even more highly thought of than, Corneille. He was attached as dramatist to Montdory's troupe for some years, but in 1640 he gave up writing for the stage and entered the diplomatic service.

MAISON DE MOLIÈRE, see COMÉDIE-FRANÇAISE.

MAJESTIC THEATRE, NEW YORK. 1. This theatre, on Columbus Circle, opened on 20 Jan. 1903 as the Cosmopolitan (built by Hearst) with a musical version of the famous children's book, *The Wizard of Oz*. This had a long run, and was followed by the equally successful *Babes in Toyland*. In 1911 the theatre was renamed the Park, reopening on 23 Oct. with Ina Claire in *The Quaker Girl*. Three years later Mrs. Patrick Campbell and Philip Merivale appeared there in *Pygmalion*, and a notable revival of *The Merry Wives of Windsor* was given in 1917 with Constance Collier. In the following year the Society of American Singers leased the theatre for a season of light opera, which included a long run of the seldom-seen *Ruddigore*. After some further plays and musicals the theatre was devoted to films and burlesque, until, in 1925, Florenz Ziegfeld took it over and renamed it the Cosmopolitan. It later housed Max Reinhardt's company. As the International it saw *Sing Out, Sweet Land* (1945), and was taken over by the Marquis of Cueva for his ballet. Mike Todd renamed it the Columbus Circle in 1945. In 1946 it housed the production of Maurice Evans's *G.I. Hamlet*. It later reverted to its name of International, and in June 1954 it was pulled down. The New York Coliseum (an exhibition hall) now occupies the site.

2. A second Majestic, on 44th Street, between Broadway and Eighth Avenue, opened on 28 Mar. 1927 with an ephemeral production which soon gave way to musical comedy, for which this theatre is eminently suitable. In 1928, in spite of fine acting by Leslie Faber and Madge Titheradge, *The Patriot* had only a short run. John Gielgud made his first appearance in New York in a minor part in this play. After several more failures, the theatre reverted to musical comedy and light opera, and in 1935 was taken over by Michael Chekhov and his Moscow Art Players for a series of Russian plays. Several thrillers were revived here, beginning with *The Bat*, but success was mainly achieved by musical plays, and in 1945 the Theatre Guild presented a musical version of *Liliom*, as *Carousel*, which had a long run. Other musicals which have been successful here include *South Pacific* (1949) and *The Music Man* (1957). In 1963 Gielgud's production of *The School for Scandal* met with acclaim.

GEORGE FREEDLEY†

MAKE-UP. Until the introduction of gas and electricity and the invention of grease-paint, make-up in the theatre is the history first and foremost of the use of disguise, and only to a very minor extent the history of the use of cosmetics. Even as drama antedates the theatre, so disguise antedates the drama, following so hard upon the first expressions of the mimetic instinct as to be indistinguishable from them in point of time. The face-painting of the primitive ritual dance, equally with its animal- and spirit-masks, is disguise; and in the classical theatre it was for purposes of disguise that Thespis painted his face with white lead coloured with cinnabar, before he invented the unpainted linen mask.

In the religious drama of medieval Europe similar conditions prevailed. Grotesque masks and animal heads were used for devils; and visors—that is, vizards or face-masks—are frequently mentioned in accounts and lists of properties. It is generally stated that white lead and gold paint were used for painting the face and hands for God or Christ, in spite of their injurious effects on the skin. In Jean Michel's *La Passion* (1490), when Jesus appears transfigured on Mount Tabor, he is clad all in white and has 'une face et des mains toute d'or bruny. Et ung gran soleil à rays par derrière.' It is unlikely that *face* and *mains* mean mask and gloves; 'face' is, indeed, sometimes used in English for a theatrical mask, and 'white gloves' for Christ are mentioned in some English accounts; but it is to be noted that in another French play, when gloves are wanted for God and the Holy Ghost, the word *gants* is used (see *Le Livre de Conduite du Régisseur . . . pour le Mystère de la Passion . . . à Mons en 1501*, ed. Gustave Cohen, 1925). How far this practice was usual the evidence does not show. Generalizations about the use of gilt paint would appear to derive from a few particular items, and especially, perhaps, from the famous example in Vasari's *Lives of the Painters*, where in the life of Jacopo di Pontormo he recounts how, in the carnival celebrations for the creation of Pope Leo X in 1513, 'a naked gilded child' represented the Golden Age, and adds that 'the gilt boy, the child of a baker who had been paid 10 crowns, died soon after of the effects'. Burckhardt (*Civilization of the Renaissance in Italy*) also cites another instance of a child being gilded from head to foot for celebrations in Rome in 1473. This use of gilt paint, however, for special effects in the elaborate Italian secular festivals does not necessarily derive from or even relate to the practices of the religious drama throughout Europe. Cennino Cennini instructs artists to temper their colours with egg, oil, or liquid varnish, if they should be required to paint performers' faces for plays or masquerades; but like all other writers who mention the subject he strongly condemns the use of paint for cosmetic purposes, and refuses to give any information on the subject (*Il Libro dell'Arte*, *c.* 1437, trans. by D. V. Thompson as *The Craftsman's Handbook*, 1923).

In some of the French plays the angels had their faces painted red, as if they were cherubim. One rubric has the stage-direction 'N.B. Warn a painter to go to Heaven to paint the face of Raphael red; and Raphael must have his face as entirely reddened as the painter can manage' (Cohen, *Le Théâtre en France au Moyen Âge*, i, 1928). This particular theological confusion—or theatrical licence—would appear to derive its sanction from literature rather than from medieval art. It is to be noted, for example, that in the Fouquet miniatures of the famous *Book of Hours* of Étienne Chevalier (1452–60; reproduced in *Verve*, Nos. 5–6, 1939) the seraphim are blue and the cherubim red, in Heaven; whereas the ordinary angels, adoring the Virgin and Child on earth, have flesh-coloured faces. In Dante, however, the angel of the sixth terrace of the *Purgatorio* is wholly red, face and all, 'e giammai non si videro in fornace vetri o metalli si lucenti e rossi' (and never in a furnace were glass or metals seen so glowing and red). In the *Paradiso* the visible angels of the Empyrean are all described, without distinction of hierarchy, as having 'le facce tutte . . . di fiamma viva' (their faces all of living flame); and it is possible that when the play representing Raphael as the angel at the tomb requires him to have a reddened face this is due not so much to a theatrical carelessness of theological detail as to an attempt to reproduce the 'face of living flame' of literary tradition.

Paint for beautifying the human face takes us to the history of cosmetics. Whether it is as old as the war-paint of the savage may be arguable; but it is certainly as old as Assyrian civilization (2250 B.C.). The Assyrian noblemen, who oiled and curled and dyed their beards and hair, also whitened their faces with white lead, and dyed their eyebrows and lashes black and darkened the edges of the lids with *stibium* (finely powdered antimony). Egypt anticipated the twentieth century in its use of green eye-shadow and henna-ed fingernails. Cleopatra darkened her lashes and eyebrows with *kohl*; Jezebel painted her face; and at the court of Nero men and women alike whitened the skin with white lead or chalk and rouged the cheeks. The Crusaders are generally saddled with the responsibility of introducing to their European women-folk the cosmetics of the harem, since when the West has used them continuously, although their respectability quotient has varied greatly from century to century and even decade to decade, both in different countries and in different classes of society. Literature abounds with references, mostly satiric in tone; and it is perhaps not altogether unfair to judge of the general effect by such names as 'Lady Stucco', and by Sir Benjamin Backbite's description of Mrs. Evergreen, in *The School for Scandal*: ''tis not that she paints so ill—but, when she has finished her face, she joins it on so badly to her neck that she looks like a mended statue, in which the connoisseur may see at once that the head's modern, though the trunk's antique.'

The colouring ingredients of all paints are the dry powders known as pigments, obtained from minerals, vegetables, animals, insects: as, for example, the ochres, oxides, and carbonate compounds of metals; the sepia of the cuttle-fish, the dried body of the cochineal insect; the madder and indigo blue of these plants. When used in this powder form paint has generally been considered harmful to the skin, particularly white and the chromes, owing to the amount of lead these contain. The powder can be applied dry, and can be rubbed into or dusted over the skin; or it can be painted on to the skin after being mixed with water or some other liquid. Apart from injurious effects, the chief drawback to a completely dry powder make-up is that it tends to run if its wearer gets hot or perspires. In the past, western European cosmetics have required little save the pigments which would provide the smooth white lily complexions, the rosy cheeks, and the cherry—or ruby—lips of popular fancy and song: together with blue for tracing veins, and kohl or antimony for eye make-up.

Theoretically the Elizabethan theatre had at its disposal the same cosmetic resources as the lady of fashion, who used paint freely, if not always with discretion, to judge by Hamlet's reference to painting 'an inch thick'. The actor could also have obtained any of the pigments then used by artists. It is worth noting, however, that none of the contemporary diatribes against the theatre mentions face-painting; and that Stephen Gosson (*Plays Confuted in Five Actions*, 1582), while explicitly condemning the wearing of women's apparel by boys, and their counterfeiting of women's gestures and passions, makes no allusion to face-painting, though the practice itself, as indulged in by women, is abundantly censured in contemporary literature and especially in the drama. Philip Stubbes (*Anatomy of Abuses*, 1583), who condemns boy-actors and face-painting, never couples them: it is 'the women of England, many of them, who use to colour their faces with certain oils, liquors, unguents and waters made to that end'; the boy-actors are 'trained up in filthy speeches, unnatural and unseemly gestures'. There is no positive evidence to show that the Elizabethan boy-actor, aged from 10 to 13, who played young women's parts in a theatre lit by daylight, either needed to make up or was actually made up. That it would be quite unnecessary for an ordinary healthy child is, indeed, borne out by a passage in Ellen Terry's *Memoirs* where, speaking of her son Gordon Craig, she describes 'Teddy', then aged 10 or 11, playing in *Eugene Aram*, as 'associated in my mind with one of the most beautiful sights upon the stage that I ever saw in my life . . . as he tied up the stage roses, his cheeks, untouched by rouge, put the reddest of them to shame'. And this, it must be remembered, was on the gas-lit, lime-lit Victorian stage, not in Shakespeare's theatre. Lacking similar evidence for the Elizabethan stage, we can only say that if the boy who played Olivia in *Twelfth Night* was indeed made up it must have been excellently done: crudely done, it would have wrecked the passage in I. v, where she unveils herself to Viola:

> *Olivia.* . . . we will draw the curtain and show you the picture . . . is't not well done?
> *Viola.* Excellently done, if God did all.
> *Olivia.* 'Tis in grain, sir; 'twill endure wind and weather.
> *Viola.* 'Tis beauty truly blent, whose red and white
> Nature's own sweet and cunning hand laid on . . .

On the evidence, in fact, it would appear that the Elizabethan actor, whether man or boy, did not use make-up except for purposes of disguise, even when—to us—the advantage of paint seems obvious and simple, as in the well-known reference in Dekker's *Guls Hornebooke* (1609): 'Present not yourself on the stage . . . until the quaking Prologue hath (by rubbing) got colour into his cheeks.' Friction, rather than paint, is indicated; though the latter is obviously the simpler method, if paint was easily available in the tiring-house for making up the boy players. Ghosts and murderers whitened their faces with chalk (see below); and we know that Negroes and Moors were represented with coal-black faces, hands, etc., for which the texts give ample evidence, as well as the *Titus Andronicus* sketch of 1595 (reproduced in *The Library*, v, 1925, and Nicoll's *Development of the Theatre*). That umber may have been used for certain characters in plays involving disguises is perhaps suggested by the reference in *The Wild Goose Chase* (III. i) when Mirabel, realizing that he has been taken in by De Gard disguised as a Lord of Savoy, exclaims, 'Now I remember him; All the whole cast on's face, though it were umber'd, And mask'd with patches.' Whether Celia in *As You Like It* actually followed up her own suggestion (I. iv) and with 'a kind of umber smirched her face' to counterfeit a peasant's sunburnt complexion, the text does not indicate. Red was obviously required for Bardolph's nose, unless we make what is on the whole the more likely assumption that a false nose was worn. Having regard to the force of tradition in the theatre it is quite likely that the practice of smearing Cassio's face with snuff to indicate his drunken condition in *Othello*, II. iii, is Elizabethan in origin, but there is no evidence of this. It was apparently still usual in the middle of the eighteenth century, and is commented on by Lloyd in his poem *The Actor* (1762):

> But Michael Cassio might be drunk enough,
> Though all his features were not grimed with snuff.

Evidence of the use of make-up in the sixteenth-century Italian theatre is to be found in the *Dialoghi in materialia rappresentazione scenica* of Leone di Somi (*c.* 1565). There is a complete translation in the 1937 edition of Nicoll's *Development of the Theatre* (App. B). When considering the actor's physical suitability for a part, di Somi does not trouble about the features, 'since so much can be done by the aid of make-up . . . simulating a scar, turning the cheeks pale or yellow, or rendering an appearance of vigour, ruddiness, weakness or darkness'. To enable a beardless actor to play an old man he would simply 'paint his chin to make him appear shaven, with a fringe of hair showing under his cap. I should give him a few touches with the make-up brush on his cheeks and forehead, and by so doing I should make him seem aged, decayed and wrinkled.' Apart from the references to long white beards and appropriate wigs, we have no evidence of a similar kind to satisfy our curiosity about the English boy-actors who impersonated old men or women. All that we know about Salathiel (or Salmon) Pavy, whose memory is preserved by Ben Jonson's epitaph, is that he was a very good-looking boy, 'the stage's jewel', who between the ages of 10 and 13 was able to *act* 'old men so duly, As sooth the Parcae thought him one, *He play'd so truly*'. It may not be significant, but it is certainly noticeable that what Jonson singles out for praise is the boy's power of acting, not his appearance.

The stage for which di Somi made up his actors was artificially illuminated. In general, the Elizabethan and Jacobean playhouses, including the so-called 'private' theatres, gave daylight performances. It was not, however, the advent of stage lighting which introduced make-up to the English theatre. Such evidence as there is, even if it does not prove, does strongly suggest that make-up for enhancing the natural appearance came in with the actress, and that in the English theatres of the seventeenth and early eighteenth centuries face-painting was confined to women, except in the case of young men called upon to play old men's parts. T. G.'s satiric poem, *The Playhouse* (1703), when describing the attire of the tragedy king makes no mention of make-up; but the tragedy queen is make-up and very little else:

> His royal consort next consults her glass,
> And out of twenty boxes culls a face.
> The whitening first her ghastly look besmears,
> All pale and wan the unfinished form appears,
> Till on her cheeks the blushing purple glows,
> And a false virgin modesty bestows:
> Her ruddy lips, the deep vermilion dyes,
> Length to her brows the pencil's touch supplies,
> And with black bending arches shades her eyes.

'Every look the pencil's art betrays', is T. G.'s criticism; and when her admirer goes behind the scenes 'He sees the blended colours melt with heat, And all the trickling beauty run with sweat'.

One of the most helpful and interesting pieces of evidence is provided by the Italian actor Riccoboni who saw the English comedian James Spiller play the part of an old man in *Crispin médecin*, somewhere about 1727 (see his *Historical Account of the Theatres in Europe*, 1738, trans. 1741). At first he refused to believe he was watching a young man of about 26: the impression given was that of an actor with at least forty years' experience:

> Had he only used a trembling and broken voice, and had only an extreme weakness possessed his body . . . I conceived it possible for a young actor, by the help of art, to imitate that debility of nature to such a pitch of exactness; but the wrinkles of his face, his sunk eyes, and his loose and yellow cheeks, the most certain marks of a great old age, were incontestable proofs.

Nevertheless, Riccoboni had to accept the truth,

> that the actor to fit himself for the part of the old man spent an hour in dressing himself, and that with the assistance of several pencils he disguised his face so nicely, and painted artificially a part of his eyebrows and eyelids, that at the distance of six paces it was impossible not to be deceived.

Apart from its intrinsic interest this comment has the further interest that it is the only one of its kind in Riccoboni's book. Coming from an Italian actor who knew the theatres of Europe it should allow us to presume a considerable degree of skill in the use of this kind of disguise make-up among English actors of the early eighteenth century. Further, it would seem to suggest either that the skill described by di Somi was unusual in the sixteenth century or else that the practice of the Italian theatre had degenerated or altered since his time. It would be rash, however, to claim too much credit for the English actor in general throughout the whole of the eighteenth century on the strength of this single tribute. It should be offset, for example, by the remarks of F. G. Waldron, the 1789 editor of Downes's *Roscius Anglicanus*, who adds the following note to the comment made by Downes in 1708 on the actor Benjamin Johnson's skill in 'the art of painting':

> I apprehend this means the painting of the face and marking it with dark lines to imitate the wrinkles of old age; a custom formerly carried to excess on the stage, though now a good deal disused: I have seen actors who were really older than the characters they were to represent mark their faces with black lines of Indian ink to such a degree that they appeared as if looking through a mask of wire. Mr. Garrick's skill in the necessary preparation of his face for the aged and venerable Lear and Lusignan was as remarkable as his performance of those characters was admirable.

It seems to be generally agreed that Garrick used make-up for the purposes of disguise with extreme skill. According to the French actor Noverre, even his friends sometimes failed to recognize him. Alongside of this we have persisting throughout the century the traditional and obviously crude disguises. Steele in 1709 (*Tatler*, 42), in his humorous inventory of theatrical properties, lists 'The complexion of a murderer in a bandbox, consisting of a large piece of burnt cork and a coal-black peruke'; and in 1784 we have T. Davies (*Dramatic Miscellanies*) describing Hippesley's make-up for the first murderer in *Macbeth*: 'his face was made pale with chalk, distinguished with large whiskers and a long black wig.' In *Humphry Clinker* (1771) Mrs. Tabitha Bramble reminds the actor Quin how she had once been 'vastly entertained with your playing the ghost of Gimlet at Drury Lane, when you rose up through the stage with a white face and red eyes and spoke of *quails upon the frightful porcupine*'.

Besides the murderer's complexion Steele lists 'a bale of red Spanish Wool'. Spanish Wool and the 'Spanish Paper' demanded by

Lady Wishfort in *The Way of the World* (III. i) were two of the popular forms of rouge; and though Steele's intention is satiric there is obviously critical significance in his use of the word 'bale'. Nor was he alone in his opinion of the crudity of the make-up of the average actress who painted to enhance her beauty. Anthony Aston, writing in 1741 in praise of Mrs. Barry (*Supplement to Life of Colley Cibber*), refers scathingly to 'the actresses of late times' who are afraid to move a muscle or show any change of facial expression 'lest they should crack the cerum, white-wash or other cosmetic trowelled on'. That an embellishing make-up was essential, however, appears to have been accepted throughout the century. The anonymous admirer who in 1753 wrote *A Letter to Miss Nossiter* comments that nature has been kind to this lady above all other actresses on the stage, in that 'she hath so fine a natural bloom that she is under no necessity of wearing paint'—a fact which he discovered because at her first entry, as Juliet, 'she grew pale as cambric, but, as she recovered, her colour returned beyond what art could counterfeit'. Incidentally, his concluding remark confirms Aston's suggestion that the normal make-up was a complete coating of paint which inhibited facial expression, so that mobility of countenance was something which called for special comment: 'This [i.e. the lack of make-up] is no small assistance to her *surprising expression*; for I observed several times afterwards her colour came and went as the passion required it.' Steele in *The Spectator* (No. 41, 1711) also describes the 'dead, uninformed countenances' of ladies who paint: 'the muscles of a real face sometimes swell with soft passion, sudden surprise, and are flushed with agreeable confusions.' Not so with the Picts, as he terms them, who have 'a fixed insensibility'. The same impression is echoed by Fanny Burney's Lord Orville (*Evelina*, 1778), who observes that the difference between natural and artificial colour is very easily discerned: 'that of nature is mottled, and varying; that of art *set*, and *too* smooth; it wants that animation, that glow, that *indescribable something*' which he sees in Evelina's complexion. The italics are his lordship's.

Apart from the would-be embellishing make-up, the balance of the evidence suggests that the eighteenth-century actress did not, like the actor, use paint for the purpose of disguise. When Peg Woffington 'actually painted her handsome face with wrinkles and crowsfeet to give effect to a play of Shakespeare's' this was sufficiently unusual to excite comment; and that Mrs. Pritchard, when playing Jane Shore, did not make up in character is obvious from a criticism in John Hill's book, *The Actor* (1750): 'Nothing could be so unnatural as to see that plump and rosy figure endeavour to present us with a view of the utmost want and starving.' Two of Colley Cibber's anecdotes are equally helpful to indicate the normal procedure of the actor. When he first began to act, he tells us in his *Apology*, his ambition to play the hero and the lover was soon snubbed on account of the insufficiency of his voice, his 'meagre person', and his 'dismal *pale* countenance'. That the obvious remedy of a straight male make-up was never at this time envisaged as a possibility is emphasized by his further description of his own appearance in *The Orphan*, on the day when his death had been reported in *Mist's Journal*. He had 'that very day just crawl'd out, after having been some weeks laid up by a fever', and 'the surprise of the audience at my unexpected appearance on the very day I had been dead in the news, *and the paleness of my looks*, seem'd to make it a doubt whether I was not the ghost of my real self departed.' On the other hand, when at the beginning of his career he set out to imitate Doggett's performance of Fondlewife in *The Old Bachelor*, he tells us he 'laid the tint of forty years more than my real age upon my features', and impressed the audience by the likeness.

One of the best-known anecdotes of the eighteenth-century stage, told by every historian of the theatre, about Barton Booth's first appearance in Dublin in the name-part of *Oroonoko*, throws interesting light not only upon the subject of Negro make-up but also upon the use of grease in connexion with theatrical make-up. According to W. R. Chetwood, for twenty years prompter at Drury Lane (*A General History of the Stage*, 1749), 'It being very warm weather, in his last scene of the play, as he waited to go on, he inadvertently wiped his face, that when he entered he had the appearance of a chimney-sweeper (his own words).' For the next performance, therefore, an actress

> fitted a crape to his face, with an opening proper for the mouth, and shaped in form for the nose; but in the first scene one part of the crape slipped off: 'And 'zounds', said he (he was a little apt to swear) 'I looked like a magpie! When I came off they lamp-blacked me for the rest of the night, that I was flayed before it could be got off again!'

Chetwood's own helpful footnote explains that the proper composition for blackening the face is 'ivory-black and pomatum, which is with some pains cleaned with fresh butter'.

It is clear from the many references, both precise and casual, in literature and in the literature of the subject, that the use of oils and fats and pomatums as preservatives and beautifiers of the skin is as old as the use of cosmetic pigments. It is also clear, from Chetwood's note, that the use of greasy substances in connexion with theatrical make-up is at least as old as the first half of the eighteenth century, if not considerably older. Nevertheless, the introduction of grease paints as we know them, and as a commercial product, belongs to the latter half of the nineteenth century. Until then, all make-up, whether used with grease or some liquid medium, was basically a powder make-up.

Apart from references in literature, the

earliest comprehensive account of the powder make-up as used in eighteenth-century society is that given in 1740 by Charles Lillie, perfumer, of Beaufort Buildings, in the Strand, in a manuscript embodying the results of his thirty years' business experience. His book, which was not actually published until 1822, is called *The British Perfumer, Snuff Manufacturer and Colourman's Guide.* It deals with every kind of cosmetic then in use and has a chapter (No. 51) on 'Paints, or Colours for the Face'. Carmine, which is the finest red colour, derives from cochineal, is safe to use, and comes from Germany; but there is also a cheap variety adulterated with vermilion and red lead, and definitely poisonous. The vermilion is made in England, and is chiefly used for wash balls. Dutch Pink is a yellow colour made from whitening or chalk, sold at 1*s.* a pound, and to be obtained—like yellow ochre and umber, powdered and sifted—at any colourman's shop. Ivory black is a black powder made from calcined ivory turnings. It is cheap, and so are white lead (ceruse), and flake white, which can also be had ready ground and powdered from the colourman.

Carmine he considers too high and glaring a colour for the complexion, 'notwithstanding the knowledge of which some ladies still continue to use it'. French Red is prepared from carmine in three shades: the palest is nearest to a flesh red. All these red powders are best put on with a fine camel-hair pencil. Spanish Wool is of several sorts, but that made in London by the Jews is by far the best, and is 'a bright pale red'. That which comes from Spain is a very dark red. It is made up in what he calls cakes (i.e. pads), 'which ought to be of the size and thickness of a crown piece'; and the best of them 'shine and glisten, between a green and a gold colour'. Spanish Papers, in which the colour is laid on the paper instead of tingeing the wool, are made up for carrying in the pocket-book. Chinese Wool, which comes from China, is made up in large round loose cakes about 3 in. in diameter, as loose as carded wool. The finest kind gives 'a most lovely and agreeable blush to the cheek'. Portuguese Dishes, containing red paint for the face, are of two sorts: the one made in Portugal is scarce, the paint 'being of a fine pale pink hue and very beautiful in its application to the face'. The other, made in London, is of a 'dirty muddy red colour: it passes very well, however, with those who never saw the Portuguese Dishes, or who wish to be cheaply beautified'. The genuine dishes are rough on the outside: the London imitation is smoothly glazed. Chinese Boxes of Colour are not easily obtained. They are beautifully painted and japanned, and each contains two dozen papers, and inside each of these there are three smaller papers. One contains black for the eyebrows: the second is a paper of fine green colour, which when fresh makes a very fine red for the face; and the third contains about half an ounce of white powder, prepared from real pearls, for giving an alabaster colour to the neck and parts of the face. The colours in the dishes and wools and green papers 'are commonly laid on by the tip of the little finger, previously wetted'. All have some gum in them, so are apt to leave a shine on the cheek, 'which too plainly shews that artificial beauty has been resorted to'. For whitening the skin he recommends Pearl Powder. The best is made from genuine powdered pearls, the next best from bismuth and starch! Camphorated and chemical wash balls, which make no lather and are manufactured specially for ladies, 'are wholly designed to leave whiteness on the hands and face'.

The earliest comprehensive account of the use of make-up in the English theatre is that given by Leman Thomas Rede in his manual for theatrical aspirants, *The Road to the Stage* (1827). It remained a popular handbook for at least fifty years, and Rede's make-up instructions were freely borrowed, with or without acknowledgements, by most manuals of acting.

Rede begins by stating that make-up is an essential part of a performer's duty, and points out that 'the late introduction of gas into our theatres has rendered a more powerful colouring than that formerly used decidedly necessary'. He recommends 'too little rather than too much colour', but reminds actors that 'when heated, colour will sink, and it may be well in the course of a long part to retouch the countenance'. All paint being injurious to the skin one should 'neutralize its pernicious qualities as much as possible'. Rouge he condemns as an 'ineffective colour' which 'seldom lies well on the face'. 'Chinese vermilion boiled in milk, and then suffered to dry, and afterwards mixed with about half the quantity of carmine, is decidedly the best colour an actor can use.' He does not agree with the popular idea that this colour is 'too powerful for a female face'.

His instructions make it evident that it was already an established theatrical method to apply the pigment over some kind of greasy base:

> previous to painting it is best to pass a napkin, with a little pomatum upon it, over the part to receive the colour, then touch the cheek with a little hair powder, which will set the colour, and then lay on the vermilion and carmine. A rabbit's foot is better than anything else for distributing the paint equally.

That individual actors, however, were experimenting along lines which were to lead them to grease paints proper, is obvious from his account of how

> the late Mr. Knight [1774–1826] used to cover his cheek with a thin coat of pomatum, and paint upon it, without rubbing the face dry; but this, which he effected cleverly, may be found difficult to perform: where it is necessary to have a powerful colour, as in Country Boys, Clowns, etc., it is decidedly the proper method.

Similarly, that grease or oil was also used to remove paint after the performance may be inferred from his notes on how to remove colour on the stage 'in any scene of fright or surprise'. If the face is turned away from the audience 'a greased napkin' can be employed: if in full view 'the thing can generally be sufficiently effected by oiling the inside of your gloves, and burying your face in your hands at the moment of accusation; colour adheres to oil immediately'.

Although he considers that 'to ladies it is of the utmost importance', Rede gives no instructions for female make-up; his reason being that 'ladies have generally sufficient knowledge of the arts of decking the human face divine'. Lining the face with the wrinkles of age, he asserts, is an art little understood on the English stage, although 'our Parisian neighbours are adepts'. For this purpose he recommends 'a round wire, like a black hair-pin', held in the smoke of a candle, as giving 'a finer and more distinct line than can be made by dipping it in Indian ink'. He condemns 'the common though slovenly habit' of making moustaches and whiskers with a burnt cork, which involves 'the danger of transferring your lip ornaments to the mouth of a lady if it be necessary in the scene to salute her'. A 'camel's hair pencil and Indian ink' will give 'a more correct imitation of nature', and if the brush is wetted in gum water the ink will not rub.

He has no instructions to give for eye make-up though he says that for situations such as Macbeth's return with the daggers after the murder of Duncan 'it is usual to whiten the face and blacken beneath the eyes, which gives them a hollow and sunken appearance'. He also describes the interesting trick-make-up work of 'a celebrated tragedian of the present day' when playing Richard III:

> [he] always removes his colour in the dreaming scene, and applies pomatum to his countenance, and then drops water upon his forehead; and this he effects whilst tossing and tumbling in the assumed throes of mental agony, [so that] on rushing to the front at 'Give me another horse—bind up my wounds' his countenance is an exemplification of the text—'Cold drops of sweat hang on my trembling limbs'.

He is instructive, too, on the subject of Othello's make-up:

> Othello used not in former days to sport a coloured countenance, but wore the same sables as Mungo in *The Padlock*; but this, as being destructive of the effect of the face, and preventing the possibility of the expression being noted, has become an obsolete custom. A tawny tinge is now the colour used for the gallant Moor, for Bajazet [in *Tamerlane*] and Zanga [in *The Revenge*]; Spanish brown [a red brown] is the best preparation.

Spanish brown should also be used for the Moor, Sadi, in *Barbarossa*, for Bulcazin in *The Mountaineers*, and Rolla in *Pizarro*; though it is very common, in these parts, 'especially for comic performers, to use only an extraordinary quantity of vermilion or carmine spread over the whole of the face'. Previous to using the Spanish brown

> the whole of the face should be rubbed with pomatum, or the colour will not adhere. Some persons mix the colouring with carmine, and, wetting it, apply it to the face, but I never saw this plan answer.

For genuine Negro parts the face, neck, and hands should be covered with a thin coat of pomatum,

> or, what is better, though more disagreeable, of lard; then burn a cork to powder, wet it with beer (which will fix the colouring matter), and apply it with a hare's foot or a cloth.... A strong colouring of carmine should be laid upon the face after the black, as otherwise the expression of countenance and eye will be destroyed.

Black gloves he rejects as 'unnatural', because the colour is too intense to represent the skin; and considers that the 'arms of black silk, often worn in Hassan [in *The Castle Spectre*] have a very bad effect; armings dyed with a strong infusion of Spanish annatto [an orange-red dye] look much more natural'.

T. H. Lacy's *Art of Acting* (1863) quotes Rede freely, with and without acknowledgement, both on make-up and on other subjects; but it is to be noticed that he insists on the importance of a dry, non-greasy surface: 'Every one, on entering the theatre at night, should wash his face, and after drying it thoroughly pass lightly a powder-puff over it. This is highly necessary to those whose skin is naturally greasy.' W. J. Sorrell, in *The Amateur's Handbook* (1866), supplements Rede and Lacy with a few specific hints, such as, that rouge should be placed well under the eyes to make them sparkle, that cold cream and a dry towel should be used to remove make-up, and that sepia should be used for lining for old age and for sinking the eyes by painting underneath the lower lids.

The first comprehensive manual, illustrated, and devoted only to make-up, is *How to 'Make-Up'. A Practical Guide to the Art of 'Making-Up', for Amateurs, etc.... By 'Haresfoot and Rouge'. Copyrighted 1877. London: Samuel French.* The anonymous author explains that it has been written 'not so much with the idea of offering advice to Professionals' as with that of instructing amateurs and beginners, and to supply a long-felt want. It lists all the articles required, both in the text and in an advertisement which prices them. They represent the full resources of the powder make-up box of the nineteenth century, and are as follows: Pearl and Violet Powder, Prepared Whiting and Fuller's Earth, Rouge and Dark or Ruddy Rouge, Carmine, Mongolian, Crayon d'Italie for the Veins, Eyebrow Pencil, Powdered Antimony, Prepared Burnt Cork, Émail Noir, Paste Powder, and Spirit Gum—all priced at 1*s.*: Chrome, Dutch Pink, Blue, Cosmétique, Joining Paste, Haresfoot, Powder Puff—all at 6*d.*: Burnt Umber, Indian Ink and Lining Brush, at 2*d.* Good soap, a sponge, and towels are the only things recommended for removing the make-up; and the author follows Lacy in refusing to allow a greasy base: 'it is absolutely necessary that the face should be *clean shaved and thoroughly washed*, as it is impossible to "Make-Up" well if the skin is at all greasy.'

The instructions are given under the following headings: Youth, Manhood, Maturity, Old Age, Death; Low Comedy and Character Parts; Sailors, Soldiers, and Countrymen; Clowns; Irish, Scots, Frenchmen; Germans; Americans; Jews; Complexions—Pale and Wan, Pale and Sallow, Dark and Olive; Creoles, Indians, Mulattoes, Negroes; Chinese; Eyebrows and Whiskers, Nose and Chin, Mouth and Teeth, Hands and Arms. The last two sections deal with 'The Ladies' and 'Statuary'.

For Youth, Manhood, and Ladies, the rouge is applied on a base of Pearl or Violet Powder, and with a fine camel's-hair brush a thin Burnt Umber line is painted under the lower eyelashes. A touch of rouge on the chin 'brightens and throws up the complexion'. The base for Maturity, Old Age, Low Comedy, Sailors, Soldiers, Countrymen, Irish, Scots, French, Germans, Americans, Jews, and Creoles is prepared fuller's earth. For Death and 'Pale and Wan' (e.g. Louis XI or Eugene Aram) the base is prepared whiting, as also for Clowns. That the powder, fuller's earth, and whiting bases were to some extent regarded as the equivalent of a modern grease base is evident from the directions for the Creole make-up, which conclude: 'Although it is not absolutely necessary to prepare the face first with Fuller's Earth, it is advisable to do so as the Mongolian is then more easily removed.' The only time grease is suggested is for Red Indians. Mongolian is advised as the chief ingredient, to give the characteristic rich tawny colour. One method is 'to mix it with beer or water and to apply it with a small piece of sponge, and when dry to add a strong colouring of Carmine to the cheeks. . . . The other, and by far the better plan, as it looks more natural and is much easier to wash off, is *first* to paint the line under the lower eyelashes, and any that may be required to indicate age, very strongly with Indian Ink; then to mix some of the Mongolian with a little Cold Cream and apply it well to the face, neck and throat, and finally to put a strong colouring of Carmine to the cheeks and to darken the eyebrows with Cosmetique.' For Othello 'a little of the Prepared Burnt Cork should be mixed with the Mongolian. The hands should be coloured to match the face, or a pair of Brown silk gloves may be worn.'

Under several of the headings special instructions are given for what are described as 'strongly-marked character parts'. If a strongly-marked Irishman, for example, is required, 'with a moderate-sized camel's hair brush paint the underpart of the eyebrows and well into the hollows of the eyes with Burnt Umber to give them a deep-set appearance. Then fix on a pair of heavy black eyebrows, low down over the eyes, to give them a "beetle-browed" appearance. . . . Lastly, put just a tinge of Rouge on the eyelids and under the eyes, and rub the upper lip, chin and throat well with Powdered Blue, so as to give them a dirty and unshaved appearance.' The writer does not approve of the exaggerated dress and make-up usually employed for Americans, but Slave Owners are classified as strongly marked and given a dark complexion with a slight tinge of Mongolian, also lines at the corners of the mouth with 'a downward tendency'. The make-up for ordinary Frenchmen 'differs very little from that of English characters of the same class, the foreign accent being the principal requirement'.

Detailed instructions are given for altering the shape of the nose for Low Comedy characters such as Bardolph and Blueskin, 'to give it that bloated, blotchy appearance so noticeable in drunkards'. A truly horrific illustration shows the exaggerated effect achieved. One method is 'to gum on to the end of the nose a piece of wool, press it down to the shape and size required, then powder it well with Rouge . . . the cheeks may also be enlarged in the same way. . . . Blotches, warts and pimples may be made by sticking on small pieces of wool and colouring them either red or brown.' The better way, however, is to use paste powder, mix it with water to the consistency of dough, and 'fix it to the nose with Spirit Gum', moulding it to the shape and size required, and powdering it with rouge. 'To impart to the nose the hooked appearance characteristic of the Jew, shade that portion of it just over the bridge, in between the eye-brows, slightly with Burnt Umber; also define very carefully the nostrils.' Mouth and teeth can also be altered. 'To give the mouth a one-sided appearance, for Costermongers, etc., paint a line upwards from one corner of the mouth, and another from the other corner downwards.' To 'stop-out' two or three front teeth for Old Men, Old Hags, Gipsies, or Witches, Émail Noir could be used then as now, and is described as 'undoubtedly an improvement upon the old-fashioned method of sticking on Cobbler's Wax'.

The 'Death' make-up is intended for such characters as Lear, Werner, Louis XI, and Mathias, and is carefully described. The prepared whiting base is powdered with a good colouring of Dutch pink: the hollows of the eyes, underneath the eyes, and under the brows, are darkened with powdered antimony, 'taking care, however, not to let any get on the eyelids'; and 'the hollows of the cheeks and temples, the throat, the chin, the upper lip (if no moustache be worn)' are similarly powdered, and a very slight touch of it given to the sides of the nose and in between the eyebrows. 'Put a little Chrome on the eyelids, nostrils, and down the front of the nose. Darken with Burnt Umber the hollow in the centre over the upper lip, also the hollows at the corners of the mouth. Put a little of the Powdered Blue on the lips in order to give them that ashy hue that is so noticeable in death, and paint the lines about the eyes, forehead and mouth, etc., according to the age of the character to be represented. Then powder the whole slightly with Pearl Powder. This "Make-Up", with the addition of a pair of Gray eyebrows and a Grizzly beard will also apply to the Ghost in *Hamlet.*'

Like *The Road to the Stage*, the various editions of 'Haresfoot and Rouge' have been more or less thumbed out of existence. But there is one copy known to the present writer which has been largely reset, and which contains an extra section entitled 'Grease Paints'. It has the original imprint, 'Copyrighted 1877', and may be a later issue printed in that year. In the absence of contradictory evidence the obvious inference is that during 1877 grease paints first made their appearance in this country as a successful commercial product. At the most we need allow only a four years' margin-for-error in date, as L. Leichner's, London, Ltd. (founded in 1928) possess sticks known to have been imported in 1881.

That these paints described by 'Haresfoot and Rouge', and specified as German in all the early advertisements, were indeed Leichner's products admits of no real doubt. Until the turn of the century the firm had no competitors, either here or in Europe. Between the 1820s and the 1870s individual actors had experimented with the grease-paint idea; and S. J. A. Fitzgerald (*How to Make-Up*, 1902) singles out Hermann Vezin in particular, quoting his own statement, 'I know I mixed a lot of colour with melted tallow in Philadelphia in 1857.' Grease paint as we know it, however, sold in round sticks, was the invention of Ludwig Leichner (1836–?), the Wagnerian opera singer. About 1865 Leichner was in touch with the University of Würzburg, and either undertook some study of chemistry, or was given by the faculty such information and help as he needed to enable him to work out the formula which resulted in the original Leichner grease paints. He and his wife manufactured them at home, and they were used by Leichner and his fellow singers until a growing professional demand led to the foundation in 1873 of the business enterprise which has since become world-famous, and which still uses the original formula.

The account given by 'Haresfoot and Rouge' in what may be called his second edition, revised (?) 1877, is the earliest description of grease paints as first used in the English theatre. Their introduction, he asserts, has very much simplified the art of making-up, and has rendered it more effective, compared with the old method. 'These paints impart a clearer and more lifelike appearance to the skin, the lights and shades . . . for old men and character parts being more easily graduated. . . . Being of a greasy nature they are to a great extent impervious to perspiration. This is in itself sufficient to recommend their use, especially for any very arduous character, as it enables the actor to go through his part without fear of his make-up being affected by his exertions. These paints are made by special machinery with chemically pure fat and purified colours free from lead. They will be found very soft to use, no hard rubbing or heating required in applying them.' A slight coating of cocoa butter, he says, should be used to prepare the skin: then, 'after removing a small portion of the foil, rub the paint on the cheeks and forehead, and then with the tips of the fingers smear the composition all over the face'. A 'liberal application' of the cocoa butter should be used to clean the face afterwards.

Only a general instruction is given: namely, to use the flesh tints in conjunction with the auxiliary colours, chrome, blue-black, red, and white. Each stick is numbered and described. No. 1 is 'the lightest flesh colour made', for ladies with delicate complexions; No. 1½ 'is also used by ladies, especially for chambermaid parts'. No. 2 can be used by ladies and gentlemen; No. 2½ is 'the most popular colour in use', invaluable for all youthful parts; No. 3 is 'a florid shade, very useful for character parts', and No. 3½ 'is somewhat darker, suitable for men of 30 to 35, being a little more sunburnt in appearance than No. 3'. No. 4 is the deepest flesh colour made, 'a dark, ruddy colour, suitable for soldiers, sailors, countrymen, etc.' No. 5 is a light yellow, used for old men; and No. 6, somewhat darker, can be used in conjunction with it. No. 7 is a brown, 'suitable for Mulattoes', and No. 8 a reddish brown for Indians. Chrome can be used with No. 7 for Chinamen. All these sticks are priced at 6*d.* Thin sticks, used for lining only, cost 4*d.* These numbers, still in use, are those originally given to the various colours by Leichner himself.

The instructions for using the liners are slightly more detailed. The black liner is intended for darkening the eyebrows and lids, also for 'very strong wrinkles'. Brown is 'more suitable for wrinkling the face where the characters are near the audience'. Lake is 'a new tint which has been lately introduced', has 'a very soft appearance when used for wrinkles, and is most effective and useful for blotches, etc., in drunken parts'. White is used 'for shading the wrinkles on the face, and for the high lights'. This is the only indication given anywhere in the book that the painting-in of high lights was an accepted part of make-up technique. Blue liners are to be used for the veins, and also for the eyes: 'a line made with this colour round the eyelashes, and a second line with the black will be found most effective.' 'An elegant tin case containing 14 of the most useful sticks' costs 7*s.*

From this time onwards the old-fashioned powder make-up was gradually superseded in the theatre by grease paint. That the powder had indeed been harmful and dangerous to use is asserted by all the authorities on cosmetics. Eugene Rimmel in his *Book of Perfumes* (1864) writes: 'Paints for the face I cannot conscientiously recommend. Rouge is innocuous in itself, being made of cochineal and safflower; but whites are often made of deadly poisons, such as cost poor Zelger his life a few months since.' This unfortunate Belgian opera singer died, according to *The*

Musical World (23 July 1864), after a long and painful illness caused by blood-poisoning which he had contracted three years before from using a new composition containing white lead to whiten his beard and moustaches when playing Walter in 'Guillaume Tell' at Covent Garden. A. J. Cooley (*The Toilet and Cosmetic Arts*, 1866) is equally emphatic, though he adorns his tale with a less fatal moral. Deprecating the use by fashionable women of the metallic compounds which give greater brilliance to the complexion, he lists pearl powder (subchloride of bismuth), pearl white, and hydrated oxide of bismuth as containing poisonous elements, and points out that these preparations are darkened by sulphuretted hydrogen fumes and the smoke given off by coal fires, so that 'there are many instances recorded, and I have known more than one myself, of a whole company being suddenly alarmed by the fair complexion of one of its belles being thus in part transformed into a sickly gray or black'.

It is perhaps curious, therefore, that the use of powder make-up, both for the stage and in social life, should have taken such an unconscionable time a-dying. As late as 1882 Gustave Garcia in *The Actor's Art* refers only to powder make-up, although he recommends 'cold cream instead of water for the mixing of colours: not only does it spread evenly on the face without patches, but the perspiration does not affect it, nor does the skin get so easily injured'. In 1883 Dutton Cook in *On the Stage* gives powder make-up advice only, and does not even mention the existence of grease paints. Powder make-up boxes were advertised by make-up manuals as late as 1902; and a powder make-up is still used by a few actors today. By 1890, however, grease paint had obviously established itself. C. H. Fox in *The Art of Make-Up* (1890) speaks of its 'almost universal adoption' during the last ten years, points out the many advantages it has 'over the powders formerly employed', and recommends it as not merely innocuous but even positively beneficial to the skin. His book is the first to give detailed instructions for grease-paint make-up, and he explains many points which were left obscure by 'Haresfoot and Rouge'. He deals clearly, for example, with high lights and shadows, pointing out that the former emphasize a feature while the latter make it less prominent: 'shadows and high lights should nearly always be used in conjunction', so that each heightens the other's effect. For high lights he recommends a flesh tint lighter than the ground colour: everything must be toned in, and 'no line, as such, should ever be left on the face'. For lining almost any colour except black can be used: crimson lake is the most popular. Cocoa butter or vaseline is recommended as the base, to be wiped off with a towel before the ground work is applied thinly and evenly, not forgetting the neck. 'The rouge: i.e. bright scarlet grease paint' is applied next after the ground colour. It must be smeared on the cheek bones and rubbed in, taking care not to leave a line. A touch of it on the chin and under the eyebrows is recommended. He favours white rather than a coloured powder, and recommends fuller's earth for elderly make-ups. He considers it is 'an open question how far expressions should be painted on the face; but as it is almost impossible that one expression can be required during a whole play it is advisable that, if painted at all, it should be done only so lightly as to help the face when it assumes that character. To do this it is necessary that the expression be assumed, and the lines so produced be painted in and toned down and the high lights added.'

By 1895 a wider range of colours could be obtained. To the sticks listed by 'Haresfoot and Rouge', *Lynn's Practical Hints on Making-Up* adds the following: No. 5½, for Chinese, Yankees, etc.; No. 6½, for Japanese; No. 8, now described as Armenian Bole, used for sinking the eyes, and with No. 5 for American Indians; No. 9, Dark Sunburnt, for old sailors and fishermen; No. 10, Brown, for Arabs, Negroes, Hindus; No. 11, Burnt Umber; No. 12, Black, for Ministrels, and with No. 10 for Negroes; No. 13, Red Brown; No. 14, Chocolate, for Mulattoes; No. 16, Dark Browns, for Indians; No. 20, White, for Clowns and Statuary. This particular manual recommends Mascaro for greying the moustache and eyebrows: defines *wig-paste* as 'another name for grease paint'; advises stumps instead of liners for broad work such as sinking the eyes, and vermilion for shading and enlarging the mouth; and lists both spirit-gum and wet-white, as well as nose-paste for building up the nose, cheeks, jaws, etc. It points out that make-up for electric light should not be as heavy as for gas, that more care is needed, and that all lines used for shading must be toned down by powdering. *Turner's Complete Guide to Theatrical Make-Up* (1898) gives both grease and powder instructions, and considers that for close effects the powder make-up is the better. He states that the powder is frequently used in conjunction with grease paints by professionals.

The instructions and hints given by the half-dozen or more books on make-up published between 1900 and 1920 vary little; but S. J. Adair Fitzgerald's *How to Make-Up* (1902) deserves special mention because it attempts the first concise sketch of the history of the subject. By 1926 Leichner's had added to the foregoing list of colours a No. 4½, Reddish Brown, No. 8a, Delicate Yellow, No. 8b, Deep Greenish Yellow, No. 15, Fiery Light Brown (for Greeks and Romans), an entire new range of fourteen 'Lit.' shades—among them, Lit. K, the modern 'fleshing' shade, a combination of Nos. 5 and 9; a range of three new shades for women, Star Girl, Star Lady, and Star Madam, described respectively as 'very delicate natural light-yellowish', 'yellowish pink for modern stage lighting', and 'warm yellowish shade for modern stage lighting'; also six 'special glaring shades' for revue, music-hall, and circus. By 1938 the *Leichner Handbook on Make-Up for Stage and Screen* listed a colour range of 54 sticks, 30 liners, 24 shades of eye-shadow, 15 shades of powder, 7 of water-black for darkening eyelashes, eyebrow pencils in 7 shades, and a range of 30 rouges—all these for theatrical use and distinguished from the special ranges which now cover film, colour-film, and television work. Grease paint is now packed in tubes and tins, but these have not superseded the ordinary sticks. Liquid make-up, applied with a sponge, is available in the same shades as the paints; and a recent innovation is the 'water-moist' make-up, greaseless, and packed in tubes. The descriptions of some of the colours now differ considerably from those attached to the same numbers at the beginning of the century. No. 5, for example, has become Ivory (used for groundwork), and No. 5½ is Dark Ivory (used for Hamlet); No. 6½ is Sallow Grey Brown, No. 10 is Dull Yellowish Brown (Spanish), and No. 11 Deep Dark Brown (African Native). Leichner's No. 13, Red Brown, for Mexicans in 1926, is now allotted to Old Fishermen, and a No. 13a has been added for Egyptians.

Modern grease paint, save in its cheaper forms, rules out for its fat base the lard or suet or tallow recommended for bases by Rede and other early writers and experimenters. Liquid or hard paraffin, beeswax, and almond- or peach-kernel oil are among the most favoured ingredients. Lanolin or white wax helps to give the necessary tackiness for powder. The dry base, with which the fat base and the pigment must be combined in suitable proportions, is generally made from precipitated chalk, kaolin, or zinc oxide. The pigment must be perfectly mixed with the dry base: this mixture is then added to the fat base and milled in a paint-mill. The liquid is then run into moulds, and the resultant sticks are wrapped in tinfoil or cellophane. In the Leichner process the grinding, milling, and mixing take as much as six weeks. Standard recipes for compounding typical paints are given by W. A. Poucher in *Perfumes, Cosmetics and Soaps* (4th ed., 1932). The flesh tints from Nos. 1 to 3 are compounded from reds and yellows: the other flesh numbers are obtained by adding one or other of the lakes (as, crimson or geranium) and adjusting the other tones. No. 3½, for example, known as 'slightly sunburnt', uses crimson lake, golden ochre, and burnt sienna. For blues, cobalt, chinese, and ultramarine are used: in the carmines, the deeper tints are obtained by the addition of scarlet and vermilion: rose tints combine red lake and madder lake.

In the modern commercial theatre the make-up that embellishes and the make-up that disguises are of equal importance. The first is the 'straight' make-up; the other is the 'character' make-up. The first aims at restoring natural colour by using paints that will stand up to the effects of artificial lighting as nature cannot, and at restoring natural line and features by emphasizing or bringing up the high lights, restoring 'natural' or accustomed shadows, and eliminating the 'unnatural'. The intensity and the quality and the colours of the artificial light, together with the methods used to concentrate it upon the acting area, are responsible for the effects which it is the business of make-up to conceal. Intensity destroys natural colour, and also natural light and shade, flattening the features and creating false lights and shadows. Normal daylight is reflected on to us: in the theatre light is generally directed on to the performer from floods, battens, spots, and floats (see LIGHTING). Under these conditions make-up is essential for the illusion of reality and 'naturalness'.

The actor's attitude to make-up has always varied. What is known in the profession as a 'Sadler's Wells make-up' could be encountered in the early years of the present century, and expresses perhaps not merely the economical mind but the grudging concession. All that is required for the Sadler's Wells make-up is a couple of tobacco tins, into which is scraped from the dressing-room walls white distemper and red or brown distemper: for shadow work one merely runs the finger along in the dust under the dressing-table shelf.

Now and again the individual refuses the aid of make-up entirely: the outstanding example is Eleonora Duse. Paul Schlenther, commenting on her first appearance in Berlin, describes how every emotion that stirred within her was reflected in her face, and considers that her whole bearing and figure were equally expressive. 'No living person has ever looked so like a corpse as Mme Duse in the character of Fedora feeling the effects of the poison in her body and in her soul. For these transformations she needs no external artifice, not even the artifice of paint, which she seems to despise. She achieves them solely through the force of her imagination.' Genius makes its own laws, in the theatre as elsewhere; but perhaps the wisest comment comes from Ellen Terry's *Memoirs*, in the passages where she discusses Henry Irving's use of make-up:

> Make-up was, indeed, always his servant, not his master. He knew its uselessness when not informed by the spirit. . . . Irving's Lesurques was different from his Dubosc because of the way he held his shoulders, because of his expression. . . . He used to come on the stage looking precisely like the Vandyke portraits [of Charles I], but not because he had been building up his face with wig-paste and similar atrocities. His make-up in this, as in other parts, was the process of *assisting subtly and surely the expression from within.*

Nevertheless, make-up is an art. Interest, practice, and experience should enable anyone to become genuinely competent; but as in most things to do with the theatre, there is flair or inspiration, and some people have it and some have not. Talk to actors on the subject, and watch them at work, and the difference between the artist and the practitioner will be obvious. Always, the individual who excels has his own little tricks and devices and secrets—

sometimes jealously guarded. He still makes his own experiments in mixing colours, trying new methods; aiming, nowadays, at the complete illusion of reality—the perfectly executed disguise of a character make-up, or the straight make-up which makes him look equally natural whether viewed from stalls or gallery. He may draw his inspiration from anything: from his own visualization of the person he presents; from a single item of make-up, such as a wig, which starts him off so that he gradually builds up a suitable and expressive countenance and bodily appearance; from a portrait once seen and perhaps half forgotten; from an impression seized upon in a glimpse of a casual passer-by; from a mere inquisitive delight in seeing what happens to his own face when he alters the shape of his jaw or the line or position of his eyebrows.

In itself both disguise and illusion, it is an essential element of 'theatre', ministering both to the realistic and to the 'larger-than-life' demands of theatrical art. The 'smell of the grease-paint' is almost a synonym for the glamour and attraction of the theatre; and it can even fascinate by 'twopence-coloured' methods, as anyone can testify who remembers the blatancy and crudity of much of the Victorian and Edwardian make-up as revealed by the view from a stage-box. Strong actinic lighting will always make it a necessity: strong lighting is an essential concession to size in the theatre, if the subtleties of facial expression are not to be lost. But there will always remain one thing which transcends the particular contribution of make-up and beats it at its own game, and that is the gift occasionally made by nature of a certain kind of face, figure, and personality which enables some players—not necessarily the greatest of their day—to assume as if by magic the very being and appearance of the character they present. There is the actor—great or mediocre—who is always himself: there is also the man or woman of whom we can say as Lamb does of Munden, 'There is one face of Farley, one of Knight . . . but Munden has none that you can properly pin down and call *his*. . . . He, and he alone, literally *makes faces*: applied to any other person, the phrase is a mere figure, denoting certain modifications of the human countenance. Out of some invisible wardrobe he dips for faces, as his friend Suett used for wigs, and fetches them out as easily.' It is not a gift that depends either upon a certain cast of feature or upon the shaping spirit of imagination at its most intense, though both have something to do with it. One cannot, by taking thought, add a cubit to one's stature, but the fortunate possessor of this true 'actor's face', though he will need the assistance of some straight make-up for modern conditions, has gone beyond the original disguise necessity which introduced make-up into the theatre. M. ST. CLARE BYRNE

MALAYA. Although the Malays delight in theatrical performances of any kind, the Malay drama has never reached a high standard, nor has it sprung from the natural genius of the people themselves, since it shows, almost invariably, traces of foreign origin. It developed from the dance, and for the most part is strictly bound by tradition and convention, being usually confined to representations of the classical Indian epics, particularly the Ramayana (see INDIA), which have been modified and adapted until they have become naturalized.

In the Peninsula the oldest form of theatrical entertainments are the *ma'yong* and other dance dramas of the ancient kingdom of Ligor. To students of the drama the *ma'yong* is chiefly significant as an example of primitive dramatic art which has been preserved almost intact through the ages.

The *ma'yong* is acted by a company of professional players, who tour the countryside, giving performances in the houses of the local rajahs or chiefs, or in the towns and villages for the general public. The stage is set in a palm-thatched shed, enclosed on three sides, the audience sitting or standing in the open air. There is no scenery, and the masks and costumes of the players are the only accessories. The company consists of four leading players, a few supernumeraries, and an orchestra of drums, gongs, a native flute, castanets, and a staccato instrument with a wooden keyboard.

Every company includes a *pawang*, the magician-priest who acts as the intermediary between gods and men. An invariable prelude to every performance are the prayers and invocations in which the *pawang* calls upon the god Siva to spare the actors and musicians, and implores the spirits of the countryside not to be incensed by the intrusion upon their domain.

The plots of the plays belong to a cycle of twelve stories akin to the Malay romances, with interludes of dancing and singing. A typical example is one in which the chief characters are a Malay noble and his henchman, a princess and her nurse. The hero (*pa'yong*) appears in princely dress: long wide trousers, silken waist-cloth, short, tight jacket, headdress with aigrette, coloured scarf flung over the left shoulder. He carries a kris, the wavy-bladed sword of Malaya, and a curious wand. On his fingers are tapering gold nail-protectors, and he has golden bracelets on his wrists and arms. Comic relief is supplied by his companion, a rough jester (*pĕran*) with whom he indulges in sallies of broad humour. To enhance his ridiculous aspect the clown wears a mask. He is naked to the waist and carries a wooden sword.

To this pair appears the princess (*ma'yong* or *putri*), dressed in a sarong of many colours, a close-fitting silken bodice, a tight girdle with jewelled buckle, and a long scarf trailing over one shoulder. She is decked with gold chains, earrings, bracelets and rings, and wears jewelled nail-protectors. She is attended by her aged nurse (played by a man), who is the feminine counterpart of the clown. Nurse and clown discuss betrothal negotiations, in a scene of low comedy dear to the Malay audience, this being followed by love passages, dancing, and singing by the two juvenile leads. The clown then provides the prince with a love potion to win the heart of the princess, but it results in her falling in love with the clown, while the nurse develops an embarrassing attachment to the prince. The prince, furious, belabours the clown, to the delight of the audience, but in the end all comes right, and the play closes with the princess's father bestowing his blessing upon the young couple.

Another theatrical performance which is of great antiquity is the shadow play, or *wayang kulit*, which had its origin in Java and is now common throughout the Peninsula and Siam (see PUPPETS and Nos. 126 and 128.).

Like the *ma'yong*, it is played in a shed, the fourth side consisting of a white cloth, behind which the player manipulates the traditional figures, cut from deer-skin (*kulit*) or cardboard, before a hanging lamp which throws the silhouettes upon the screen. When not in use the puppets are stuck into lengths of banana pith, to be ready for the showman's hand. Behind the screen with the showman is the compère, who relates the story, with which every member of the audience is familiar. Usually the Ramayana cycle, which lasts seven nights, is played in a form which has been handed down by word of mouth from one generation to another, with a mixture of local folklore in which traces of the old Indonesian beliefs are to be found. But the old Hindu tradition is paramount, and although the Malays are now followers of Islam, Mohammedanism has never influenced these shadow plays, except in the preliminary invocations (which are as invariable as those which precede the *ma'yong*), when the four archangels of the Koran may replace the ancient divinities.

The characters are easy for the audience to identify upon the screen. A profile with nose and receding forehead in an unbroken line is immediately recognized as one of the gods or heroes of old Java; a figure with a snub-nose and irregular features is a demon or evil spirit. As each appears the orchestra, consisting of drums and gongs and a clarinet (*sĕrunai*), plays its appropriate tune. The Malays' love of comedy is catered for by the two comic characters (*Sĕmar* and *Turas* or *Chĕmuris*), who keep up a running and irreverent commentary on the ways of gods and demons.

A purely modern form of entertainment, which has become increasingly popular in recent years, is the *bangsawan*, the equivalent of the modern musical comedy. It came to Malaya from India. It is almost entirely devoid of any literary value, but it gives the Malay actor scope for his undoubted powers of mimicry and sense of comedy. It is at its best when it introduces a realistic element by portraying coolies, peasants, rickshaw-pullers, and other country types, which the players burlesque to perfection. But while it is not faithful to classical tradition it has not yet cut adrift from romantic legend or produced original plays with local settings. The Malay impresario cares nothing for convention or criticism, but is concerned only with studying the predilections of his laughter-loving audience, so that in his hands *Hamlet* becomes a comedy in which the part of the ghost is played by a clown. OWEN RUTTER†

MALLESON, MILES (1888–1969), English actor, who in his later years excelled in the portrayal of testy and eccentric old gentlemen. Some of his best work was done in his own adaptations of Molière (*The Miser*, *Tartuffe*, *The Prodigious Snob*, *Sganarelle*, *The Slave of Truth*, *The Imaginary Invalid*) which, though not always sufficiently close to the original to satisfy the purists, nevertheless had the merit of bringing Molière to the English stage in actable modern versions which appealed to the average playgoer, and have proved invaluable to repertory and provincial theatres on the look-out for something fresh and amusing and yet classical. Malleson, who made his stage début at the Liverpool Repertory Theatre in 1911, soon became known as a good actor of Shakespeare—Aguecheek, Quince, Gobbo—and of Restoration comedy, the latter under Playfair at the Lyric, Hammersmith (Scrub in *The Beaux' Stratagem*, Wittol in *The Old Bachelor*), where he also played Filch in the long run of *The Beggar's Opera*. In Gielgud's season at the Haymarket in 1944–5 he played Foresight in *Love for Love* (which he had previously played for a year at the Phoenix), Polonius, Quince, and Castruccio (in *The Duchess of Malfi*). He was with the Old Vic for several seasons, being particularly admired as Justice Shallow and Sir Fretful Plagiary. He was also outstanding as Old Ekdal in *The Wild Duck* (1949). He returned to modern plays with Mr. Butterfly in *Rhinoceros* (1960). Apart from his Molière adaptations, he wrote a number of other plays, of which the best was probably *The Fanatics* (1927).

MALONE, EDMOND (1741–1812), English man of letters, and one of the first scholars to study and annotate the works of Shakespeare. Born in Ireland, he came as a young man to London, intending even then to devote himself to literary criticism. He became the friend of Dr. Johnson, and was the first to perceive and denounce the Shakespeare forgeries of young Ireland. In spite of the many new facts which have been brought to light by later research, and an entirely new orientation in the study of Shakespeare as a dramatist, Malone's works, which include a biography, a chronology of the plays, and a history of the Elizabethan stage, are still valuable. The Malone Society, formed in 1907 to further the study of early English drama by reprinting texts and documents, was named after him in recognition of his eminence in the world of theatrical scholarship.

MALVERN FESTIVAL. A desire to bring together, for a month in the summer in a holiday setting, some of those having a sincere interest in the theatre led Sir Barry Jackson to found the Malvern Festival in 1929. His idea was to put on a succession of the best English plays, old and new, and for this purpose he assembled a company of which actors from his Birmingham Repertory Theatre formed the nucleus, with distinguished players imported from outside for special parts. Sir Barry's long association with Bernard Shaw at Birmingham led him to devote the first year's programme entirely to his plays, with *The Apple Cart*, having its first English production, and revivals of *Back to Methuselah*, *Caesar and Cleopatra*, and *Heartbreak House*. Shaw became the patron-in-chief of the festival, and more than twenty of his plays were produced there, *Geneva* and *In Good King Charles's Golden Days* having their first productions in 1938 and 1939 respectively, while *Too True to be Good* (1932), *The Simpleton of the Unexpected Isles* (1935), and *Buoyant Billions* (1949) had their first English productions. Apart from Shaw, the festival ranged over four centuries of English drama, from the religious *Hickscorner* (*c.* 1513) and the early comedies *Ralph Roister Doister* and *Gammer Gurton's Needle* (see No. 100), through Heywood, Ben Jonson, Etherege, Dryden, Sheridan, Bulwer Lytton, Henry Arthur Jones, and Pinero, to new plays by Drinkwater, Bridie, Priestley, and others. At the end of the 1937 season Sir Barry withdrew, and the festival was then run by Roy Limbert, manager of the Malvern Theatre, in association with Sir Cedric Hardwicke. During the Second World War Limbert maintained a skeleton organization at Malvern, and he has since made several attempts to revive the festival, meeting with some success, particularly in 1966.

MALY THEATRE, Moscow. This theatre, whose name means 'small' (as opposed to *bolshoi*—big) was opened on 14 Oct. 1824, on the site of a merchant's house, with a company which had been in existence as a corporate body since 1806, and is thus the oldest theatre in Moscow. The original building is still standing, and the theatre is the only one in Moscow to keep the old-fashioned drop curtain.

With its unbroken history the Maly is, not surprisingly, a theatre of tradition, and has been an important element in the history of Russian theatrical culture. It was well said that 'in Moscow one went to college but studied at the Maly'. Though an official Imperial Theatre, it represented the more liberal sections of society, and gave expression to progressive ideas. This was particularly noticeable in the 1840s, when *The Inspector-General* and *Woe from Wit* (or *Wit Works Woe*) were first produced, with that fine actor Mikhail Shchepkin (1788–1863) as the Governor and as Famusov. Shchepkin, who worked in close collaboration with his authors, was the first exponent of realistic acting on the Russian stage, and trained his company in his own methods.

An actor of a different type, but quite as effective in his way, was Pavel Mochalov (1800–48), who excelled in the great classical and Shakespearian parts. His Hamlet was much admired, and he was the first to insist on translations of Shakespeare being made direct from English instead of from French. A true romantic, Mochalov relied on inspiration and intuition, rather than on study and observation, and his performances were consequently erratic.

In 1854 the Maly Theatre first produced a play by Ostrovsky, and so began a brilliant partnership which lasted till 1885. Nowhere else, even now, can finer interpretations of Ostrovsky's plays be seen. His influence on the theatre was enormous, and it was for a long time known as the House of Ostrovsky. The actor who first played many of the main roles, and who fought for the recognition of Ostrovsky's genius, was Prov Sadovsky (1818–72), who joined the company in 1839, and whose son and grandson were also members of it. The latter, also named Prov, became its Art Director and one of its outstanding actors—a close connexion of over one hundred years.

Other great names of the Maly are Alexander Lensky (1847–1908), who first introduced Ibsen to Russia, and Maria Yermolova (1853–1928), a fine tragedienne, who, in a difficult period of the theatre's existence, advocated a return to the classic plays of which she was so brilliant an interpreter. With the theatre she weathered the storm of the October Revolution and, after a few years of cautious experiment, the Maly took its rightful place in the theatrical life of Soviet Russia with the production of Trenev's *Lyubov Yarovaya* (first version, 1926). Since then it has given some fine performances of new plays on Soviet problems, among which are *Fighters*, *Skutarevski*, *In the Steppes of the Ukraine*, *Front*, and *Invasion*. It has also continued to produce the classics of Russia and Europe. Like all other Moscow theatres, the Maly was evacuated during the Second World War, but afterwards returned to its old home. One of the outstanding post-war productions was *Othello*, with the veteran actor Alexander Ostushev (1874–1953) as one of the finest Russian Othellos in living memory. Since then a number of new Soviet plays have been produced, among them Korneichuk's *Hawthorn Grove* and *Wings*, Sofronov's *The Moscow Character*, *Money*, and *Honesty*. The Maly Theatre is regarded as one of the guardians of tradition in the Russian theatre, but at the same time it has played a great part in the building up of a new tradition of socialist realism and has greatly influenced Soviet dramaturgy. Since 1950 it has been directed by Mikhail Ivanovich Tsaryov (1903–), who joined the company as an actor in 1937.

MANAGER, see PRODUCER.

MANCHESTER. This town, which is renowned in English theatre history for the establishment there of the first modern repertory company (see HORNIMAN), had its first theatre in 1753, in Marsden Street. An all-purpose building, it housed balls, concerts, cock-fighting, and soldiers, and in 1758 was first used for plays. It closed in 1775. It then became a cotton warehouse, and was pulled down in 1869. The most enterprising manager of this theatre was the peripatetic J. A. Whitley, whose company 'took in' Manchester on its way from Leeds to Worcester from about 1760 to 1775. The first Theatre Royal opened in 1775, under Younger of Liverpool. Among his actors was Mrs. Siddons, who had already made her first appearance, unsuccessfully, in London, her brother John Philip Kemble, who played (at 19) Othello to her Desdemona, and Mrs. Inchbald, later to achieve fame as a dramatist. In 1789 the theatre burned down. Rebuilt on the same site, and the same size, it reopened in 1790; but it soon proved too small, and in 1807 it closed, being replaced by a vast structure in Fountain Street which proved disastrous to its first manager, Macready.

It was in 1907 that Miss Horniman, who had already established a repertory theatre in Dublin—the Abbey—took over the old Gaiety in Manchester—now a cinema—and there established the first repertory theatre in England (see REPERTORY THEATRE). It opened on 7 Sept. 1908, and fifty years later a commemorative festival was held, during which four repertory companies appeared in London. In Manchester there was an exhibition of material relating to the theatre, and a revival of *Hindle Wakes* by the Library Theatre, a repertory company which was founded by the local authority in 1953, and is housed in a corporation-owned theatre. Manchester also has two large commercial theatres used by touring companies—the Opera House and the Palace.

MANCHESTER SCHOOL OF DRAMA, THE, a term somewhat loosely applied to the dramatists connected with Miss Horniman's repertory seasons at the Gaiety, Manchester, between 1907 and 1914. The term was apparently first used in the magazine of the Manchester Grammar School in Oct. 1909, and included, among others, Harold Brighouse, Stanley Houghton, and Allan Monkhouse, who all had their first, though not their most successful, plays produced at the Gaiety. In the context of the time, these plays were 'realistic', and formed part of the 'new drama' of the period before the First World War. They have been described as 'homely but luminous, hovering on the edge of the bleakly insignificant, but with a singular force of veracity and comic illumination'.

MANET, 'he remains', see STAGE DIRECTIONS.

MANHATTAN THEATRE, NEW YORK, on the west side of Broadway between 53rd and 54th Streets, a cathedral-like playhouse which, as Hammerstein's, opened on 30 Nov. 1927, and was used almost entirely for musical shows. In 1931 it was given its present name, but adhered to its musical policy, until in 1934, after a long period of idleness, it became a music-hall. This was not successful, and the theatre then remained empty until in 1936 the Federal Theatre Project took it over and opened with *American Holiday*, by E. L. and A. Barker. Shortly afterwards came T. S. Eliot's moving poetic drama, *Murder in the Cathedral*, for a limited run, and the theatre was then taken over for broadcasting. GEORGE FREEDLEY†

See also STANDARD THEATRE 2.

MANNERS. (1) JOHN HARTLEY (1870–1928), American dramatist, who was born in Ireland, made his first appearances on the stage in Australia, and up to 1902 was in London. There he appeared with Alexander, was Laertes to the Hamlet of Forbes-Robertson, and wrote his first play for Mrs. Langtry, playing in it himself. He went with her company to the United States, settled there, gave up acting, and between 1908 and 1928 was closely associated with the New York stage, writing more than thirty plays. The best known is *Peg o' My Heart* (1912), which was translated into several European languages, produced with great success in London, and was at one time being played by five touring companies at once through several seasons. Its success overshadowed all his other work, and he never achieved his ambition to become a serious modern playwright. The heroine of *Peg o' My Heart* was played by his wife, (2) LAURETTE TAYLOR (*née* COONEY) (1884–1946), an actress who made her first appearance on the stage as a child, and had a long and distinguished career before she was seen in New York and London as Peg, a part always associated with her. She was absent from the stage for some years, but in 1945 returned to give an outstanding performance as the Mother in *The Glass Menagerie*, which ran in New York for over a year.

MANNHEIM, a city with a rich theatrical life and one which is of prime importance in the history of the German stage. In the seventeenth century there are records of displays by tumblers and travelling players, but the regular theatrical history of the town begins in 1720, when the Court made Mannheim the seat of government. In the years 1737–41 a baroque theatre was built in the castle by Alessandro Galli da Bibiena, who also designed the scenery. In 1752 a Garten Theater was built at Schwetzingen, as well as a tiny open-air theatre. In 1778 the Baron von Dalberg became director of the National Theatre, and under him it became one of the foremost theatres in the country. After Ekhof's death in Gotha in that year Dalberg engaged his troupe for Mannheim, with Iffland at its head. Following the example of the Vienna Burgtheater, he introduced regular meetings at which the actors discussed questions of repertory and production, a national style of acting, and the establishment of an original German repertory. But Dalberg's greatest service to the German theatre was his support of the young Schiller, who was greatly encouraged by the reception given by the Mannheim audience to *Die Räuber* in 1781. Dalberg aimed at what is known today as ensemble playing. He wanted his productions to be a unified whole and not a series of individual performances. In the last decade of the eighteenth century the fortunes of the Mannheim theatre declined, and little was done until in 1884 J. Werther reopened the theatre, gathered together a new company and, in collaboration with Fritz Brand, planned a repertory based on the classics. The growth of interest in the theatre in the following years necessitated the building of the small Colosseum Theater (1898), which was intended for farce and popular drama, and the Modernes Theater (1901). The National Theatre was completely destroyed in 1943, but reopened in a temporary structure in 1945, and the post-war repertory has included plays by Sartre, Giraudoux, and Priestley, as well as classical German plays. DOROTHY MOORE

MANOEL THEATRE, MALTA, an eighteenth-century playhouse, one of the oldest in Europe, which was built by the Grand Master Antonio de Vilhena in 1731, and opened a year later with Maffei's *Merope*. It flourished for a century or more, with a nine-month programme every year of mixed opera and plays. Renamed the Royal Theatre by the British occupying powers, it continued pre-eminent until the building of the much larger Opera House, after which it sank into disrepute. In the 1950s steps were taken to restore it. It was bought by the Malta government, and in 1957 a committee was set up to rebuild and modernize it backstage while retaining the historic auditorium and façade. On 27 Dec. 1960 it reopened as the National Theatre of Malta, with a season by the Ballet Rambert.

MANSFIELD. (1) RICHARD (1854–1907), American actor, son of a prima donna and a London wine merchant. He was born in Berlin, educated in England and on the Continent, and after several attempts to earn a living in the London theatre went on tour in the English provinces in Gilbert and Sullivan, and re-appeared in London in some minor parts. In 1882 he went to New York and made his first appearance there at the Standard Theatre on 27 Sept., again in light opera. It was, however, as Baron Chevrial in *A Parisian Romance* (1883) at the Union Square Theatre under Palmer that he first made his name, though struggles and disappointments still lay before him. Among his outstanding parts were Prince Karl, the dual role of Dr. Jekyll and Mr. Hyde, Beau Brummell in a play specially written for him by Clyde Fitch, Cyrano de Bergerac, and Monsieur Beaucaire. He also played the leading parts in his own play of *Monsieur* (1887), the romantic tale of a French refugee who earns his living by teaching music, in his own dramatization of *The First Violin* (1898), and in his own version of *Don Juan* in 1891, which was not, however, a success. He gave a fine performance as Nero in another unsuccessful play, and as Napoleon in a series of episodes based on the latter's career. During a visit to London in 1889 he first played Richard III, and among his other Shakespearian parts were Shylock, Brutus in *Julius Caesar*, and Henry V, which he produced with much pageantry in New York in 1900, making a spectacular appearance in the interpolated procession after Agincourt, riding a white horse. Mansfield was essentially a romantic actor at a time when the modern problem play was coming to the fore. But though he had little sympathy with the new drama as a whole, he much admired Ibsen's poetic drama, and in his last season of 1906–7 gave the first production in English of *Peer Gynt*, with himself in the title-role. He also introduced Shaw to America, appearing as Bluntschli in *Arms and the Man* in 1894, and Dick Dudgeon in *The Devil's Disciple* in 1897. He married in 1892 (2) BEATRICE CAMERON (1868–1940), who had played several small parts before in 1886 she appeared with him in *Prince Karl*. She continued in his company, playing Nora in *A Doll's House* in 1889–90, the first time the play was given in English under that title in New York. After her marriage she played Raina and Judith Anderson in his productions of Shaw, and retired in 1898. Mansfield's career was something of a paradox. Though frequently successful, and a hard worker, he failed to achieve greatness. He was unpopular in London, and spent much of his time outside New York, where in spite of several attempts at management he never had a permanent theatre. He had a hasty temper and a bitter tongue, which, allied to an air of conscious superiority, helped to lessen his popularity.

MANSFIELD THEATRE, NEW YORK, on 47th Street between Broadway and 8th Avenue. This has a wide, shallow auditorium which allows a very considerable seating capacity and yet preserves the intimacy usually found only in the smaller playhouses. It opened on 15 Feb. 1926 with an ephemeral play, and the only event of artistic importance during its early years was a visit from the Habima Players in *The Dybbuk* and other works in their repertory. Some successful musical comedies under Lew Fields brought temporary prosperity to the house, which in 1930 saw *The Green Pastures*, directed by the author, with sets and costumes by Robert Edmond Jones. This had 640 performances, and was followed by another period of ill fortune. *Black Limelight* (1936) with Margaret Rawlings, which was an outstanding success in London, ran for two months. *Thunder Rock*, again a greater success in London than in New York, was also seen at the Mansfield, as was Ruth Gordon's nostalgic evocation of her early days, *Years Ago*. After a period of radio and television shows, the theatre was renamed the Brooks Atkinson, in honour of the American critic, who had just retired, and reopened with a revue in Sept. 1960. In 1961 *Come Blow*

Your Horn started a long run there, and in 1964 came Rolf Hochhuth's *The Deputy*.

GEORGE FREEDLEY†

MANTEAU D'ARLEQUIN (Cloak or Mantle of Harlequin), the French name for the draped curtain frame inside the proscenium arch (see INNER PROSCENIUM).

MANTELL, ROBERT BRUCE (1854–1928), American actor, born in Scotland, who made his first appearance on the stage in Belfast. Owing to family opposition to his chosen career, he called himself Robert Hudson, resuming his own name when in 1878 he went with Modjeska to the United States, playing Tybalt. He remained with her for some time, then returned to England and after several years of hard work and little recognition went back to America, this time for good. In 1884 he played opposite Fanny Davenport with some success, and two years later took his own company on tour. As a young man he was essentially a romantic actor, handsome and passionate, at his best in such plays as *The Corsican Brothers*, *The Marble Heart*, and *The Lady of Lyons*. When with the years romance left him, he became somewhat heavy and uninspired, but he remained popular outside New York, where his careful studies of the chief Shakespearian characters won him respectful admiration. He was four times married, usually to actresses who were his leading ladies.

MANTLE, ROBERT BURNS (1873–1948), American dramatic critic, known as 'the Dean of the Dramatic Critics' until his retirement in 1943. He was born in Watertown, New York, and in 1898 became dramatic editor of *The Denver Times*. Later he worked as Sunday editor of *The Chicago Tribune* and from 1922 until his retirement he was dramatic critic of *The New York Daily News*. He edited till his death an annual volume of *The Best Plays*, a series he inaugurated in 1919. Each volume contains a lengthy condensation of ten of the season's plays together with an index of every play produced in New York during the year, with the date of its opening, its cast, its director, the number of performances it achieved, and a brief account of its plot. This useful history of the latter-day American theatre has been supplemented by two more volumes—somewhat less complete—covering the years from the beginning of the century to 1919. Burns Mantle was also the author of *American Playwrights of To-day* and edited *A Treasury of the Theatre* with John Gassner.

THOMAS QUINN CURTISS

MANUEL, NIKLAS (1484–1530), a painter and poet of Berne, and a writer of anti-Catholic plays during the Reformation (see GERMANY, 2).

MANZINI, GIOVANNI (*fl.* fourteenth century), early Italian tragic dramatist (see ITALY, 1 *b* i).

MANZONI, ALESSANDRO (1785–1873), the famous Italian poet and novelist, author of *I promessi sposi*, wrote also two tragedies, *Il conte di carmagnola* (pub. 1820) and *Adelchi* (pub. 1822). Both are historically more accurate than romantic tragedies are wont to be, and both entirely disregard the unities, in accordance with the principle set forth by the author in his *Lettre sur les unités de temps et de lieu dans les tragédies* (1823). They are, however, somewhat frigid, and have not survived on the stage. They were written with the purpose of proving that dialogue need not be unnatural because it happens to be in verse, and to give the poet, particularly in the beautiful lyric choruses of *Adelchi*, 'a little corner where he can speak in his own person' (see ITALY, 3 *b*).

MARAIS, THÉÂTRE DU. Recent research places the opening of this theatre, one of the forerunners of the Comédie-Française, at 31 Dec. 1634, in a converted tennis-court in the rue Vieille-du-Temple, with a company under the great actor Montdory. This company had previously played at various sites in the town, and had given Corneille's first play, *Mélite*, its Paris première. Once established in the Marais, they continued to act Corneille's early comedies, and were responsible for the first production of *Le Cid* in 1636, Montdory playing the name-part. Having lost some of his best actors by a whim of Louis XIII, who sent them to join Bellerose at the rival theatre of the Hôtel de Bourgogne, Montdory took on the Barons, parents of the great actor Michel Baron. Among his other notable productions was Tristan's *Mariane* (in the same year as *Le Cid*) in which Montdory played Herod with great sound and fury, an effort which undoubtedly hastened his breakdown in health the following year.

After Montdory left the Marais it went through bad times. The best actors joined the rival company, to which Corneille also gave his new plays, and the remnants of a good company were forced to revert to the playing of old-fashioned crude popular farces. The one good thing that came to them at this time was the return of that excellent comedian, Jodelet, for whom Scarron, d'Ouville, and the younger Corneille wrote excellent farces. At a later date the Marais, which was a big theatre, specialized in spectacular performances with a good deal of the newly imported Italian machinery. But it never regained the place in public esteem which it had held under Montdory, in spite of the efforts of Floridor (who in any case soon left to go to the Hôtel de Bourgogne), of Laroque, and of the Du Parcs, who left Molière's company a year after his arrival in Paris to join the Marais, but returned to him in despair. The theatre struggled on with little pleasure and few profits—though it continued to receive a small subsidy from the State—until 1673, when the company was amalgamated with that of Molière, who had just died. The combined company, which by its later fusion with that of the Hôtel de Bourgogne became part of the Comédie-

Française, acted at the theatre in the rue Guénégaud which had been built for Lully's opera company, and the old Marais stage was abandoned.

MARBLE, DANFORTH (1810–49), American actor, famous for his Yankee characters. He was originally a silversmith, but was always interested in the theatre, and for some time played small parts in amateur societies. In 1831 he made his first appearance on the professional stage, and proved an excellent mimic of the Yankee dialect. He perfected this in four years' touring, until in 1836 he appeared, in a play specially written for him, as Sam Patch, always one of his most popular parts, particularly along the Mississippi and at the Bowery, New York. In 1844 he was received with enthusiasm in London and the provinces, and also visited Glasgow and Dublin, playing in such typical plays as *Jonathan in England* and *The People's Lawyer*, where full scope was given to his inimitable assumption of Yankee characteristics. He married the daughter of William Warren of Philadelphia, and died young at the height of his popularity.

MARBURY, ELIZABETH (1856–1933), an American theatrical agent who started her successful career by managing a theatrical performance for charity with such acumen that Daniel Frohman advised her to go into the business. This she did, her first client being Frances Hodgson Burnett, while she handled in America the plays of Victorien Sardou and, through him, of innumerable other French dramatists. She was twice decorated by the French government for her services to French literature. She was also Shaw's agent, and was instrumental in introducing Mansfield to his plays. Among her other clients were Oscar Wilde, Hall Caine, Somerset Maugham, Stanley Weyman, and Sir James Barrie. It is said that it was she who persuaded Barrie to enlarge the part of Babbie in *The Little Minister* so as to make it acceptable to Maude Adams, who scored such a success in the part. Miss Marbury also handled the plays of Rachel Crothers and Clyde Fitch, brought the Castles to New York, and in partnership with Lee Shubert produced intimate revues with music by Jerome Kern and costumes designed by herself. In 1903 she bought a house in Paris which became a noted rendezvous for all connected with art and letters, and in 1914 incorporated her business as the American Play Company. In 1923 she published an autobiography, *My Crystal Ball*.

MARCEAU, MARCEL (1923–), French actor, the finest modern exponent of mime, or, as he prefers to call it, mimodrama, the drama of silence, speaking directly to the mind and the emotions, without words. He originally studied decorative art, specializing in enamel work, but after being demobilized from the army in 1945 he joined Barrault's company, and soon attracted attention as Arlequin in *Baptiste*. In 1946 he abandoned conventional acting for the study of mime, basing his work on the character of the nineteenth-century French Pierrot, and evolving from this his own Bip, a white-faced clown with sailor trousers and striped jacket. In this part, which he first played at the tiny Théâtre de Poche in 1946, he has toured all over the world, accompanied by supporting players whom he has trained himself. Apart from his characterizations of Bip, he has evolved short pieces of concerted mime, like that based on Gogol's *The Overcoat*, and longer symbolic dramas like *The Mask-Maker*. With the aid of a screen, he has also contrived to appear almost simultaneously as two sharply contrasted characters—David and Goliath, or the Hunter and the Hunted.

MARINELLI, KARL (1744–1803), Austrian actor and impresario, founder of the Leopoldstädter Theater in Vienna. As a member of Mathias Menninger's Baden company from 1760, he played romantic leads without great distinction. In 1780 he obtained Imperial consent for the building of a new theatre in the Leopoldstadt which was opened in 1781. It was here that the traditional Viennese impromptu burlesque found a new home after its eviction from the Hofburgtheater; it was here that Johann Laroche established Kasperle (see AUSTRIA) as one of the great Viennese comic types; it was here, later, that Ignaz Schuster, Ferdinand Raimund, and Therese Krones first achieved fame. Marinelli, who in 1801 was raised to the nobility for his services to the theatre, was also a playwright who provided dramas and farces in the Viennese tradition and, in *Der Ungar in Wien* (1773), introduced a figure who became a stereotype of the *Volkskomödie* and, later, the operetta.

J. B. BEDNALL

MARIONETTE. A marionette is a rounded full-length puppet controlled from above the stage. Originally the control was by a simple rod or strong wire to the centre of the head; sometimes another rod would go to one hand, used for fighting with; sometimes a string would be attached to each hand or to each leg. Marionettes controlled in this way are inevitably very crude, but they can be quite effective in their own tradition; folk-puppet theatres presenting this type of marionette are still open throughout Sicily, performing a series of plays based on the legends of Charlemagne, Roland, and their battles with the infidels, the cycle sometimes taking months to complete. A similar medieval tradition is found in Belgium, where, at Liège, a local peasant type—Tchantchès—has been introduced as hero or chorus. In France there are several local heroes of the puppet stage—Jacques at Lille, Lafleur at Amiens—who figure throughout the repertory of popular legends in the marionette theatres.

A great technical advance was achieved when marionettes were manipulated entirely by strings; this allows far greater flexibility for body and head movements and is less distracting to the audience. This was perhaps first done for the intricate Italian Fantoccini, of the 1770s, but possibly not until a hundred years later by Thomas Holden. Today marionettes are almost invariably strung in this manner, and literary allusions to 'puppet wires' have no relation to actuality. An ordinary standard marionette has a string to each leg and arm, two to the head, one to each shoulder (which take the weight of the body) and one to the back: i.e. nine strings (actually fine thread) in all. An elaborate figure will have twice or three times this number. These are gathered together on a wooden 'crutch' or control, held in one hand by the manipulator, while with the other he plucks at whatever strings are required. Marionettes are usually made of wood, but lighter materials such as papiermâché are sometimes now used; their size varies from 12 in. to 18 in. for home use up to 2 ft. to 3 ft. for public performance. With the exercise of great skill and ingenuity marionettes can be made that will reproduce almost every human movement—though simple and technically crude puppets will often convey an equally dramatic effect (see also PUPPETS). GEORGE SPEAIGHT

MARIVAUX, PIERRE CARLET DE CHAMBLAIN DE (1688–1763), French dramatist, who began his literary career by writing a number of plays and novels, much influenced by Spain and completely forgotten. He was a friend of Fontenelle and La Motte, who helped to develop in him that peculiarly paradoxical and precious style later known as *marivaudage*, first reproachfully, later in admiration of its superb subtlety. Marivaux first made himself felt in the theatre in 1720, when his *Arlequin poli par l'amour* was given successfully at the Comédie-Italienne, and his *Annibal* less successfully at the Comédie-Française, in spite of the acting of Baron and Dufresne. Having lost all his money in an American investment, Marivaux for the next twenty years looked to the theatre for his main source of livelihood. He wrote chiefly for the Comédie-Italienne, and among the best of his plays given there were *La Surprise de l'amour* (1722), *La Double Inconstance* (1723), *Le Jeu de l'amour et du hasard* (1730), *Les Fausses Confidences* (1737), and *L'Épreuve* (1740). At the Comédie-Française several of his plays were given without much success, but the second *Surprise de l'amour* (1727), a totally different play from the first, and a much better one, was successful after a disastrous first night which nearly wrecked its career. Marivaux's best work for the Comédie-Française was *Le Legs* (1736), which was particularly successful when revived later by Molé and Mlle Contat. His last important play was *Le Préjugé vaincu* (1746), in which the actresses Jeanne Gaussin and Mlle Dangeville were so outstanding that the king increased their pensions forthwith. In his own day Marivaux had none of the preeminence accorded him at present. His work, which renounced the help of intrigue and conflict, substituting for them psychological and emotional action and reaction, stands a little apart from his time, which preferred the tearful comedies of La Chaussée. Unlike Molière, Marivaux confides his chief roles to women, and his plays are adapted to the needs of a sheltered, cultivated, subtle society such as developed just prior to the Revolution and crept back again in the following century, when Marivaux's plays were successfully revived and had much influence on Alfred de Musset, again a dramatist who was in advance of his time. The best of them continue to be revived, particularly when an actress like Madeleine Renaud is available to interpret Marivaux's heroines. In 1960 the Théâtre National Populaire revived *L'Heureux Stratagème*, which had not been seen since 1733. Few of Marivaux's plays have made an impact in English, since they are so subtle and difficult to translate.

MARK HELLINGER THEATRE, NEW YORK, see HOLLYWOOD THEATRE.

MARKISH, PERETZ (1895–1955), Russian-Jewish writer of plays on contemporary themes, produced at the Moscow State Jewish Theatre (see JEWISH DRAMA, 6).

MARLOWE, CHRISTOPHER (1564–93), playwright of the English Renaissance, and an important figure in the development of the Elizabethan stage. Son of a Canterbury shoemaker and educated at Cambridge, he had a tragically short life, being stabbed in a tavern brawl before his thirtieth birthday, possibly during a dispute over the bill, but equally probably by a planned assassination due to his secret-service activities. His murderer was Ingram Frizer, with Skeres and the spy Robert Poley as accessories. Marlowe's first play was *Tamburlaine the Great, Part I*, given probably in 1587 by the Admiral's Men with Edward Alleyn in the name-part. Written in flamboyant blank verse of great poetic beauty, it is a bold, passionate, and highly imaginative drama, which suffers from poor construction and the concentration of attention on the chief figure. A second part was given in the following year. Both were highly successful and had a great influence on Shakespeare, who no doubt saw them on his arrival in London a few years later, since they continued to be revived up to the closing of the theatres in 1642. They were followed by *The Tragical History of Dr. Faustus*, a treatment of the German medieval legend, which has survived in a fragmentary and much-mutilated condition. Though written and produced between 1589 and 1592, it was not printed until 1604, by which time the development of the Devil as a comic character had led to interpolation and excision and the use of prose summaries for parts of the original verse. Though retaining all the fine poetry of *Tamburlaine, Dr. Faustus* is more consistently dramatic than the earlier play and shows Marlowe's great advance in stage-craft. It is the generally accepted opinion that the comic scenes are not from his pen, but were added later by Bird and Rowley at the instigation of Henslowe. As originally planned, the play was a vast dramatic poem which had much in common with the Morality play, infused with the genius of the new age. It continued to be acted in its mangled version until well into the eighteenth century, and was the inspiration of Goethe's *Faust*. Marlowe's last plays were *The Jew of Malta* and *Edward II*, the first a study of a crafty scoundrel who eventually over-reaches himself, the second a chronicle play which marks the highest point of Marlowe's development as a dramatist, though lacking the fine lyricism of some of his earlier work. *The Jew of Malta*, which may have contributed something to Shakespeare's Shylock, was first produced in about 1590, but not printed until 1633, and here again the text has suffered considerable revision, probably at the hands of Thomas Heywood. It appears to have been the most popular of Marlowe's plays, and Edward Alleyn was much admired in its title-role. It was revived in London in 1922 by the Phoenix Society, and in 1964 in Canterbury for the 400th anniversary of Marlowe's birth. In 1965 it was played at Stratford-upon-Avon as a companion-piece to Shakespeare's *Merchant of Venice*. *Edward II*, acted in about 1591–2, was printed during its author's lifetime, and is consequently less corrupt than the other plays. It seems to have maintained its popularity for a few years and then fallen out of the repertory. It also was revived in 1923 by the Phoenix Society, in 1956 by Theatre Workshop, and in 1958 by the Marlowe Society.

Marlowe, who was acquainted with many of the leading men of his day, including Sir Walter Raleigh, was highly thought of as a scholar and poet, though often in danger of arrest through his atheistical and outspoken opinions. His death brought forth many expressions of regard and admiration from his fellow writers, and there is no doubt that his *Tamburlaine* gloriously inaugurated the first great age of English drama. He was a greater poet than dramatist, and by his use of blank verse for the expression of his heroes' mighty destinies he prepared the way for the fine tragedies of Shakespeare. Unable in the short time at his disposal to rise to great heights as a dramatist, he nevertheless stands at the threshold of Elizabethan drama, and did much to liberate it from the remnants of the medieval play and the Tudor Interlude. Marlowe's quatercentenary in 1964 was, ironically enough, overshadowed by that of Shakespeare in the same year, since some people think that after his supposed assassination he was in some way concealed, to return and write his later plays under Shakespeare's name.

MARLOWE, JULIA (1866–1950), American actress, whose real name was Sarah Frances Frost. Born in England, she was taken to the United States at the age of 4, and, as Fanny Brough, made her first appearance on the stage in a juvenile *H.M.S. Pinafore* company in 1878. After some years on tour and a prolonged period of study she appeared in 1887 as Parthenia in *Ingomar*, in which she made her first appearance in New York. She was immediately successful, and began a long career as a leading actress, being at her best in such parts as Juliet, Viola, Rosalind, Beatrice, and Portia. She was also good in standard comedy, playing Lydia Languish in *The Rivals* with Jefferson and Mrs. John Drew, Lady Teazle, Julia in *The Hunchback*, and Pauline in *The Lady of Lyons*. She married as her second husband E. H. Sothern, playing Juliet to his Romeo in 1904. Three years later she made her first appearance in London, being well received in a series of Shakespearian and other parts, though a production of *When Knighthood was in Flower* was not a success. She toured for some years with her husband in a Shakespearian repertory, playing Lady Macbeth for the first time in 1910. She retired for a time in 1915, but returned to play mainly in Shakespeare until her final retirement in 1924.

MARMONTEL, JEAN-FRANÇOIS (1723–99), French man of letters, who was befriended in his youth by Voltaire, and was an *habitué* of the Comédie-Française. He had achieved some reputation as a poet when his first play, *Denys le Tyran*, was produced in 1748. In the existing dearth of good plays this pale reflection of classical French tragedy was well received. Some of its success was no doubt due to the acting of Mlle Clairon, who later became the mistress of its author, and was persuaded by him in about 1753 to discard her declamatory style for more natural acting, to the ultimate benefit of the French stage. Marmontel continued to write, with some success, until the failure of his *Égyptus* (1753) turned him from the theatre. None of his plays remained in the repertory, and it is mainly as a critic that he is now remembered. In 1758 he became editor of the *Mercure de France*, in which his *Contes moraux* had been appearing, and widely extended its scope and influence. Marmontel may be regarded as the founder of French dramatic criticism in journalism, and, in memory of Voltaire's kindness to him, he was always indulgent to young authors. He also wrote a number of libretti for light operas, mainly in order to help the composer Grétry, and his only rival in this genre was Favart. In the quarrel between the adherents of Gluck and Piccinni he was strongly on the side of the latter, with whom he also collaborated several times. He lived in Paris until the downfall of the Monarchy, and then retired to live in the country, returning only once to sit as deputy in the *conseil des anciens*, a post he lost in the upheaval of 18 Fructidor.

MARS, Mlle [ANNE-FRANÇOISE-HIPPOLYTE] (1779–1847), French actress, younger daughter of the actor-dramatist Monvel [really Boutet] (1745–1812) by a provincial actress. She appeared on the stage as a child, with her elder sister, playing at Versailles and in Paris under Mlle Montansier, and in 1795 made her first appearance at the Comédie-Française, being befriended and tutored by Mlle Contat. Four years later she joined the reconstituted troupe, and began a long and successful career, though she had first to compete with several talented and beautiful actresses whose names are now forgotten. She was at her best in the comedies of Molière, but was also good in such dramas as Dumas's *Henri III et sa Cour* (1829) and Hugo's *Hernani* (1830). She retired in 1841, her last appearance being on 31 Mar. as Elmire in *Tartuffe* and Silvia in *Le Jeu de l'amour et du hasard.* A year later she was seen at her benefit night as Célimène in *Le Misanthrope* and Armande in *Les Femmes savantes.* A beautiful woman, with a lovely voice, she continued to play young parts until she was over 60. She was, however, extremely proud, and behaved very badly to Mme Dorval when the latter finally joined the Comédie-Française. Her father was a good actor, to whom Talma admitted he owed much. Of his rather ephemeral plays, a comedy entitled *L'Amour bourru* and a drama, *Les Victimes cloîtrées,* were the most successful. His elder daughter was also a good actress, overshadowed by the fame of her younger sister.

MARSTON, John (*c.* 1575–1634), English satirist and dramatist, son of an Italian mother, which may account for the influence of Italian literature discernible in his plays. He was at Oxford from 1602 to 1604 but refused to follow his father in the legal profession, and turned to literature. His theatrical career was compressed into some eight years, after which he renounced the stage and took holy orders. The immediate cause of his retirement seems to have been a play, now lost, in which he satirized James I, and for which he was sent to prison. He had narrowly escaped imprisonment for his share in *Eastward Ho!* (1605), where he appears to have been the chief offender, and only avoided the fate of his collaborators, Chapman and Jonson, by ignominious flight. In fact, the whole of Marston's theatrical career was stormy, owing in part to this satiric bent and self-consciousness, in part to his constant enmity with Jonson, whom he satirized in an early work, while Jonson retaliated by portraying Marston as Crispinus in *The Poetaster.* Marston wrote mainly for the children's companies, his Revenge tragedy, *Antonio and Mellida,* and its sequel, *Antonio's Revenge,* being done in 1599 by the Children of Paul's who may also have produced a comedy, *What You Will* (1601), and a tragedy on the subject of Sophonisba. Among the plays done by the Children at Blackfriars was Marston's most important work, *The Malcontent* (1604), a somewhat sombre tragicomedy in which a deposed prince comes in disguise to the court of his usurper and so tests the character and loyalty of his subjects. *Eastward Ho!* was revived at Drury Lane in 1751 as *The Prentices,* and in 1775 as *Old City Manners.* It is said to have inspired Hogarth's 'Industrious and Idle Prentices'. Marston is thought to have had a hand in the writing of *Troilus and Cressida* (see *Englische Studien,* vol. xxx, 1901, article by R. Boyle).

MARSTON, John Westland (1819–90), English critic and playwright, who went from Lincolnshire to London, where he was a friend of Macready and Kean. He wrote, in succession to Bulwer Lytton and Sheridan Knowles, a number of plays in the then outmoded tradition of poetic drama, but they had little vigour and were soon forgotten. Marston's main claim to remembrance rests on his dramatic criticism for the *Athenaeum,* and a book entitled *Our Recent Actors* (1888).

MARTIN BECK THEATRE, New York, on 45th Street west of 8th Avenue, the furthest west of all New York's legitimate playhouses. Built by the late Martin Beck of vaudeville fame, it opened on 11 Nov. 1924 with *Madame Pompadour,* and has since staged on an average a hit a year, many of them musical comedies. Among straight plays produced there have been *Spread Eagle* and *The Shannons of Broadway,* while the Theatre Guild used this house for their productions of *Wings over Europe,* finely directed by Mamoulian, *Red Rust,* done by the Theatre Guild Studio, later the Group Theatre, *The Apple Cart,* and *Hotel Universe* with Ruth Gordon. Two massive productions at this theatre were *Roar, China!* and *Miracle at Verdun.* In 1931 the Group Theatre produced *The House of Connelly,* and the Lunts followed in their highly successful *Reunion in Vienna.* Later productions included the Abbey Players, the D'Oyly Carte on their first visit to New York for forty years, *Yellow Jack* (1934), and Katharine Cornell in a repertory which included *Romeo and Juliet, The Barretts of Wimpole Street,* and *The Flowers of the Forest.* This theatre saw the first Critics' Prize play, *Winterset,* with Burgess Meredith, who again appeared there with Peggy Ashcroft in *High Tor.* Plays of interest in later years were *Watch on the Rhine,* again a Critics' Prize play, which set up a record run for the theatre, and *The Iceman Cometh,* with which O'Neill broke a long silence. In 1947 there was a production of *Antony and Cleopatra* by Guthrie McClintic (see No. 88). Subsequent productions included *The Teahouse of the August Moon* (1953), a revival of *Major Barbara* (1956), and a musical version of Voltaire's *Candide,* by Leonard Bernstein (libretto by Lillian Hellman). This last, though well-received, had only a short run. In 1963 another distinguished play, Brecht's *Mother Courage and her Children,* also had a short run, and was followed by *The Ballad of the Sad Café,* adapted by Albee from Carson McCullers's novella of the same name.

George Freedley†

MARTINELLI. (1) Drusiano (?–1606/8), actor of the *commedia dell'arte,* who was probably in England in 1577–8 with the first regular Italian company to cross the Channel. He appears in the actor-lists of several companies after this, but his reputation was overshadowed by that of his wife, (2) ANGELICA ALBERIGI (or Alberghini) (*fl.* 1580–94), a fine actress who at one time had her own company, and by that of his brother, (3) TRISTANO (*c.* 1557–1630), who was probably the first to play Arlecchino. He was originally with Pedrolino's company, the Confidenti, but appears to have been of a roving and somewhat quarrelsome disposition, and is found in many places with different companies. He was popular in Paris, where he went several times, and was much admired for his wit, specimens of which are preserved in his *Compositions de rhétorique de M. Don Arlequin* (1600).

MARTÍNEZ DE LA ROSA, FRANCISCO (1787–1862), an important figure in the Spanish theatre, since he combined the classicism of the eighteenth century with the new spirit of Romanticism, and may be considered the first Romantic dramatist of the new era. His early plays were written in a conventional style, but with his *Aben-Humeya* (first written in French and given in 1830 in Paris, where he was in exile) and *La conjuración de Venecia* (1834) he openly declared himself on the side of the Romantics. These are typical Romantic prose dramas, with heavy local colour, and a mingling of tragedy and comedy. In his true comedies, of which the best is *La niña en la casa y la madre en la máscara* (1821), he followed the traditions of Moratín the younger, still considered a master of comedy. After the death of Ferdinand VII, Martínez de la Rosa played an important part in the political life of Spain.

MARTÍNEZ SIERRA, GREGORIO (1881–1947), a modern Spanish dramatist, novelist, and poet. Sierra translated the plays of Rusiñol and Maeterlinck. His first original play was *La sombra del padre* (1909). *Cancíon de cuna* (1911) is well known to English audiences as *The Cradle Song* and reflects Maeterlinck's slow-moving but effective style. Sierra's own plays are indeed more notable for their delicacy and quiet humour than for action or excitement, but technically his work as a producer was most stimulating. During the years 1917–25 the Teatro Eslava came under his management and there he introduced the Madrid public to contemporary foreign dramatists in translation, and to the new techniques introduced into the peninsula by Adrià Gual. He also staged some plays by unknown or little-known Spanish dramatists, including the first play of Federico García Lorca. It is in this period of Sierra's career that he can be said to have made his most significant impact upon the Spanish theatre.

J. E. VAREY

MARTIN-HARVEY, SIR JOHN, see HARVEY, JOHN MARTIN.

MARTYN, EDWARD (1859–1924), one of the founders of the Irish Literary Theatre, which, as its second production, on 9 May 1899, performed his *The Heather Field*, a play which reveals him as a disciple of Ibsen and Strindberg. In 1900 his *Maeve*, a psychological drama on the clash between England and Ireland, was performed. Martyn, who was a wealthy man, was a generous benefactor to the Irish Literary Theatre during its short life, and appears to have financed its first season. In 1914, with Joseph Plunkett and Thomas MacDonagh, he founded the Irish Theatre in Hawkwicke Street, Dublin.

MARYLEBONE MUSIC-HALL, LONDON. This was originally the Rose of Normandy tavern (still standing) which had been the centre of a vanished pleasure-garden known as Marylebone Gardens. Sam Collins converted it into a music-hall, but it was not a success, and he gave up in 1861. His successor, R. Botting, ran it more successfully until well into the 1890s, when it finally closed.

W. MACQUEEN-POPE†

MARYLEBONE THEATRE, LONDON, see WEST LONDON THEATRE.

MASEFIELD, JOHN (1878–1967), English poet, novelist, and dramatist, who became Poet Laureate in 1930 in succession to Robert Bridges. He was awarded the Order of Merit in 1935 and the Hanseatic Shakespeare Prize of Hamburg University in 1938. Some of his best poetry is to be found in his plays, which combine the influence of the Greek tragic writers with the Japanese *Nō* play, the latter most strongly in *The Faithful* (1916). Although his plays have been successfully acted, they are extensions of the dramatic side of his poetic gifts, and he remained always more poet than playwright. He wrote several plays on biblical themes: *Good Friday* (1917), *The Trial of Jesus* (1926), and *A King's Daughter* (1928), based on the story of Jezebel. His other plays include *The Campden Wonder* (1907), on an unsolved murder mystery, *The Tragedy of Nan* (1908), *The Witch* (1910), adapted from a Norwegian tragedy and several times revived with success, and *Melloney Holtspur* (1923). He was also the author of *A Macbeth Production* (1945), in which he gave some stimulating advice to a group of ex-service men about to produce the play, and incidentally ranged over a wide field of historical and literary criticism.

MASQUE, or more correctly Mask. The former spelling, which comes from sixteenth-century France, was first used extensively by Ben Jonson, and modern scholarship is reverting to the original term. This, however, tends to lead to confusion with mask, meaning a cover or disguise for the face, originally known in English as a visor. Both meanings are closely connected, since the players in a masque, known as the maskers, either blackened their faces or wore visors.

The origin of the masque is lost in obscurity, but is undoubtedly connected with primitive religious rites and folk-ceremonies. In essence it is the silent irruption into a festival of disguised guests, bearing presents, who then join with their hosts in a ceremonial dance. The latter point is important, since even in its most elaborate literary form the masque was designed to lead up to a dance or masked ball where the spectators mingled with the actors, who in Court masques were usually amateurs of high rank.

The early English mask, known as a Disguising or Mummery, gave rise to a traditional folk-play (see MUMMING PLAY), and also to an elaborate Court spectacle as practised in Renaissance Italy, where, mainly under the influence of Lorenzo de' Medici, it had become a vehicle for song, dance, scenery, and machinery, one of its non-dramatic offshoots being the elaborate Trionfo, or Triumph. From Italy it passed to France, and at the Court of the French king gave rise to the simple *ballet de cour*, or the more spectacular *mascarade* (from which is derived masquerade); in the sixteenth century it came, under its new name, to Tudor England, where, forgetful of its humble origin and the original 'guisers', it brought the maskers to play before the king in lovely dresses, with all the appurtenances of scenery, machinery, and rich allegorical speech.

In Elizabethan times the masque provided an excellent means of complimenting the queen in her own palace, or entertaining her on her summer progresses through England. The speeches were written by poets and scholars, often anonymously, and the main interest centred on the costumes, scenery, songs, and dances. The masque reached its height under the Stuarts, and became a literary rather than a social force in the hands of Ben Jonson, who in 1603 succeeded Samuel Daniel as Court poet. With him was associated the scene-designer and architect Inigo Jones, and their collaboration, which began with the Twelfth Night masque of 1605, produced some excellent work. Unfortunately their aims were incompatible, since Jonson saw the masque as an opportunity for the speaking of fine poetry, while Jones regarded it as a chance for trying out the stage innovations of Italy. Eventually Jones won, and Jonson retired, his last masque being produced in 1634. One of his innovations was the anti-masque, which he first employed in 1609. It introduced a grotesque element in contrast to the masque proper, as Hell before Heaven, Shipwreck before Peace, and was also known as the false masque. The form ante-masque is also found, presumably in reference to the fact that it preceded the main masque. It was not entirely new, since the earlier masques made use of grotesque elements in dancing, known as the antic, whence the suggestion that Jonson's innovation should properly be known as the antic masque. Whatever its origin, Jonson seems to have been the first to name it and make conscious use of it.

The double masque was one in which two sets of performers appeared in different disguises, as Fishermen and Marketwomen, or Sailors and Countrymaids, as against the one disguise—Blackamoors, Wild Men, Shepherds, etc.—of the single and more usual masque. The later operatic development of the masque made an unfortunate division between the masque and the anti-masque, which tended to reduce the latter to farce and pantomime. It may be noted that Milton's *Comus*, though called a masque, is considered by some scholars to be a pastoral—of which there are other less notable examples—done privately and probably so labelled to distinguish it from the plays of the public stage.

Lacking a poet of the calibre of Jonson, and having to provide for the entry of Henrietta Maria and Charles I as performers instead of spectators, the later masques became merely spectacular shows of small literary value, much under the influence of French courtly entertainment, particularly the *ballet à entrée* and *ballet de cour*. This led to a greater stress on dancing, and, through Inigo Jones, on spectacle. Shirley, as Court poet, merely had to provide a scenario and some rather dull speeches. The Civil War put an end to the masque, and later revivals were only belated imitations. The masque has an important place in theatre history, partly because of its influence on ballet, opera, and pantomime, but mainly because, when the London theatres reopened in 1660, they took their inspiration, their scenery, and some of their actors and dramatists, from the Court masque. It cannot itself rank as drama, however, since it has practically no story, no action, no crisis, and no inevitable ending, but is merely an excuse for a compliment, a gift, and an entertainment. An earlier influence of the masque on the public theatre was brought about by the children who played in both and the adult actors who were sometimes brought into the Court entertainments to play parts that had proved beyond the powers of an amateur. Shakespeare shows the influence of the masque in such plays as *As You Like It*, *A Midsummer Night's Dream*, and particularly *The Tempest*, where all the accessories of the masque are described in pure poetry.

MASQUE THEATRE, New York, see JOHN GOLDEN THEATRE.

MASSEY, Charles (?–1625), an English actor, friend of Alleyn and of the actor-dramatist Samuel Rowley. He first appeared with the Admiral's Men in 1597, and remained with them during their successive renamings until his death. He was one of the actors who leased the Fortune Theatre from Alleyn in 1618, and he was a shareholder in the new Fortune (1622), where he was one of the chief members of the company. He was also a dramatist, since two plays by him, now lost, were given by the Admiral's Men in 1602–3.

MASSINGER, Philip (1583–1640), English dramatist, author of some forty plays, of which half are lost; the manuscripts of at least eight were destroyed by Warburton's cook, who used them to line pie-dishes. Of those that survive the most important is *A New Way to Pay Old Debts*, a satiric comedy which was first produced in about 1625. Allowed to lapse during the Restoration, it returned to the stage in the eighteenth century and has been constantly revived up to the present day. Sir Giles Overreach was a favourite part with many great actors, particularly Kean (see No. 165), who had an immense admiration for Massinger, and revived also his *Roman Actor* (1626). Among Massinger's other plays are the romantic dramas, *The Duke of Milan* (1620) and *The Great Duke of Florence* (1627), with its charming idyll between Giovanni and Lidia; the comedies, *The City Madam* (1632) and *The Guardian* (1633); and the tragicomedies, *The Bondman* (1623) and *The Renegado* (1624). *The Fatal Dowry* (1619) and *The Virgin Martyr* (1620) were written in collaboration, the first with Field, the second with Dekker, while Massinger had a hand in several of the plays ascribed to Beaumont and Fletcher, and may have worked with the latter on *Henry VIII* and possibly *Two Noble Kinsmen*. Massinger has received less attention than other dramatists of his day. Archer, in *The Old Drama and the New*, called him 'one of the best writers of the period', and ascribed his neglect to the absence of passages of lyric beauty in his plays, though his art as a dramatist is indisputable.

MASTER OF THE REVELS, an officer appointed under the Lord Chamberlain to supervise and pay for some particular entertainment at Court. He first appears in 1494, and was an intermittent official until 1545, when Sir Thomas Cawarden was appointed Master for life. He supervised the entertainments given for the coronation of Elizabeth I, and was succeeded on his death in 1559 by Sir Thomas Benger. The powers of the Master were somewhat restricted, as a good deal of the financing of plays, and work in connexion with them, appertained to other departments of the Royal Household. After the death of Benger in 1572 there was a period of confusion and no new appointment was made, the work, however, continuing smoothly under the permanent under-officials, particularly Thomas Blagrove, the clerk, who served the Revels Office for fifty-seven years. He had hoped to be given the Mastership, but in 1579 this went, probably through influence at Court, to Sir Edmund Tilney, who appears to have done very little work, though he retained his title until his death in 1610. He was not responsible for the masques given at the Court of James I, and seems to have been occupied only with the fittings and lighting. By decrees of 1581 and 1603, however, the Master of the Revels was made censor of plays, and drew acting fees for plays licensed for public performance. Tilney was succeeded by his nephew, Sir George Buck, who had been his deputy for some years, and on the death of Buck in 1622 the office passed to its most famous holder, Sir Henry Herbert. He held it until the closing of the theatres in 1642, and on the Restoration tried to uphold its importance, but was defeated by the patents granted to Killigrew and Davenant. Most of his powers were taken from him, but he retained his title, which passed on his death to Thomas Killigrew and then to the latter's son Charles. By the Licensing Act of 1737 the censorship of plays became the direct responsibility of the Lord Chamberlain, as it is today, and the old office, dating from Tudor times, was virtually extinct (see DRAMATIC CENSORSHIP and HERBERT, HENRY). For a detailed account of the Revels office in its palmy days, see Chambers, *Elizabethan Stage*, vol. i, ch. 3.

MASTERSINGERS, German musical and literary guilds which flourished in the larger towns, particularly in Nuremberg, in the fifteenth and sixteenth centuries. The activities of such a guild are portrayed in Wagner's opera 'Die Meistersinger von Nürnberg' (1868) (see GERMANY, 1).

MATHEWS. (1) CHARLES (1776–1835), English actor, who would perhaps be more accurately classified as an entertainer, since the best part of his work lay in his imitations and assumptions of different characters, particularly in his *At Homes*—a form peculiar to himself which has been described as 'a whole play in the person of one man'. The son of a bookseller, Mathews had from early childhood a most retentive memory and amazing powers of mimicry, coupled with an intense desire to go on the stage. This he eventually achieved, making his first appearances in Dublin in 1794. After some years in the provinces, spent mainly at York under Tate Wilkinson, during which time he married, lost his wife, and married as his second wife a young actress, he appeared in London at the Haymarket in 1803, and soon made a reputation as an eccentric comedian. Among his successes were Sir Fretful Plagiary, always one of his best parts, and Risk in *Love Laughs at Locksmiths*. In her biography of her husband Mrs. Mathews says, 'Risk may be recorded as his first great part, *written* for him; all characters besides, at least for many years, were in fact mere outlines left for him to fill up by dint of his genius. . . .' He later appeared at both Drury Lane and Covent Garden, and in addition to the many new parts which he created, estimated at about 400, he was seen as Falstaff, Sir Archy MacSarcasm, and Sir Peter Teazle. It was in 1808 that he first conceived the idea of the one-man entertainment with which his name is principally connected. It was originally a programme of comic songs linked together by descriptions of eccentric characters whom he had evolved, partly from observation, partly from intuition. During the years he performed his entertainments they gradually grew to be short plays, on the lines of *The Actor of All Work* (1817), which Colman wrote for him. This represents a country manager interviewing applicants for a place in his company, and gave Mathews an opportunity of portraying a bewildering series of totally dissimilar characters, and of showing his power of mimicry in an imitation of the French actor Talma. Among the most successful of the sketches which Mathews concocted himself were *The Trip to Paris*, *Mr. Mathews and his Youthful Days*, in which he gave an imitation of Macklin, and *The Trip to America*. He first visited the United States in 1822, making his first appearance in Baltimore, and playing in New York in his own sketches and in *The Heir-at-Law* and *The Road to Ruin*. He returned there in 1834, but was already in a precarious state of health and died at Liverpool on the return journey. He was for some years manager of the Adelphi with Yates, which involved him in some financial difficulties, and he suffered all his life from a nervous irritability and tendency to melancholy which happily had no effect upon his work. He was also somewhat lame as the result of a carriage accident, and had a horror of publicity. Sir Walter Scott, who was his warm admirer, said that his imitations were of the mind, and that, far more than a mimic, he was an accurate and philosophic observer of human nature, blessed with the rare talent of identifying himself intuitively with the minds of others. This helps to explain the extraordinary success of his entertainments, which he played in London and all over the provinces for more than twenty years. By his second wife he had one son, (2) CHARLES JAMES (1803–78), who was trained as an architect, and as a young man idled his time away pleasantly, travelling and occasionally appearing in amateur theatricals. He did not take to the stage professionally until 1835, when he replaced his father in the management of the Adelphi. This arrangement lasted only a short time, and he then went to the Olympic, making his appearance on 6 Nov. 1835 in his own play *The Humpbacked Lover*, and in a farce by Leman Rede, *The Old and Young Stager*, in which he played with Liston. Three years later he married Mme Vestris and with her went to New York, but they were not very well received at first. On their return to London they took over the management of Covent Garden, where they staged some fine productions, including *London Assurance* (1841) with Mathews as Dazzle, always one of his best parts. The venture was not, however, a success financially and hoping to recover their losses they moved to the Lyceum. This proved an even worse speculation and in the midst of their bankruptcy Mme Vestris died. Mathews continued to act, and made another visit to America, from which he returned with his second wife, an actress named Lizzie Davenport. With her help he extricated himself from his difficulties and embarked on a more successful, though less eventful, career which lasted until his death. He made several extended tours which took him to Australia and India, and remained to the end an elegant, light-hearted, and improvident creature. Tragedy and pathos were outside his range, but he was inimitable in such parts as Dazzle, Affable Hawk in *A Game of Speculation*, Plumper in *Cool as a Cucumber*, Puff, Flutter, and Young Wilding. 'With what ease,' says Coleman, 'what grace and distinction he carried his chapeau bras, took snuff, or fluttered his cambric.' Like his father he was a good mimic, and one of his most popular pieces was *Patter v. Clatter*, which he wrote himself and in which he played five parts. He also appeared with his second wife in an entertainment reminiscent of that of his father called *Mr. and Mrs. Mathews at Home*. He had not the solid gifts of the elder Mathews, but much charm and delicacy tempered his high spirits and made him, within certain limits, one of the best light comedians of the English stage. His reminiscences were edited with biographical notes by the younger Charles Dickens (see also VESTRIS, 1).

MATTHEWS, ALBERT EDWARD (1869–1960), English actor, son of William Matthews of the original Christy Minstrels, and grand-nephew of the clown Tom Matthews, who was a pupil of Grimaldi. He had a long and successful career on the stage, beginning as a call-boy at the Princess's Theatre in 1886, and continuing to act almost until the time of his death. He never appeared in Shakespeare or classical plays, which he rightly considered outside his range, but in his own line, though never a star, he was inimitable. He was a most meticulous worker, with a sure technique which enabled him to seem at his most careless when he was most in control. He excelled in farce, from the Pinero farces of his early years (*Dandy Dick*, *The Magistrate*) and such perennials as *The Private Secretary* and *Charley's Aunt*, through Algy Moncrieff in *The Importance of Being Earnest* up to his last creation, the Earl of Lister in *The Chiltern Hundreds* and *The Manor of Northstead*. In private life he was an eccentric of dry humour, refusing to take his success seriously and posing always as the bluff country gentleman. For a long time there was great uncertainty as to his age, as when he was a young man he made himself out to be older than he was, fearing to seem too young when applying for a part, and in old age he cut off a good ten years. But it now seems established that he was 90 at the time of his death (his birthday was on 22 Nov., and he died on 25 July). In 1951 he was awarded the O.B.E., and in 1953 he published his autobiography, *Matty*, by which name he was universally known and loved.

MATTHEWS, JAMES BRANDER (1852–1929), American theatre historian, playwright, and the first man to be appointed a professor of dramatic literature in the United States. With Laurence Hutton he edited *Actors and Actresses of Great Britain and the United States* in five volumes (1886), wrote widely on the history of the theatre, and had had several one-act plays produced, as well as collaborating in two full-length plays, when in 1892 he was appointed Professor of Literature at Columbia. From 1900 to 1924 he was Professor of Dramatic Literature, and by his writings and lectures had a great influence on the professional theatre, on the practice of dramatic criticism, and on the attitude of the general public. He had a wide knowledge of European drama, and a keen feeling for all that was best in the dramatic literature of his own and other countries. Among his own writings, which included several volumes of essays on New York, and an autobiography, *These Many Years* (1917), the most important were *The Development of the Drama* (1903), *Molière* (1910), *Shakespeare as a Playwright* (1913), and *Principles of Playmaking* (1919). Matthews was one of the founders of both the Authors' and the Players' Clubs. He was also an original member of the National Institute of Arts and Letters and its president for a year.

MATTOCKS, Mrs. Isabella (1746–1826), English actress, the youngest daughter of Lewis Hallam, senior. Left behind when the rest of the family went to the New World, she was brought up by an aunt who was an actress, and is believed to have been on the stage from the age of 5, playing small parts at Covent Garden. She made her adult début as Juliet in 1761, and a few years later married an actor named George Mattocks (*d.* 1804), who became manager of the theatre in Liverpool, where Mrs. Mattocks played in the summer, spending the winter seasons, until her retirement in 1808, at Covent Garden. She also appeared at the Haymarket, and in Portsmouth. She had no aptitude for tragedy, and no singing voice, but was excellent in comedy, particularly in pert chambermaids. Her last appearance was as Flora in *The Wonder: a Woman Keeps a Secret.*

MAUDE, Cyril Francis (1862–1951), English actor-manager of great charm and energy, who had a long and successful career on the stage. He came of a military family, and was intended for the army or the Church, but decided on the stage. He had had some initial training when ill-health forced him to leave England. He went first to Canada, and, after his recovery, to America, where he made his first appearance on the stage as the servant in *East Lynne*. This was at Denver, Colorado, in 1884. A year later he returned to London, appeared at the Criterion in 1886, and then went on tour. His first outstanding success was as the Duke of Courtland in *Racing* (1887) at the Grand, Islington. Subsequently he was with Wyndham at the Criterion, and with Mrs. Langtry at the Haymarket. He made a great success again in the part of Cayley Drummle in *The Second Mrs. Tanqueray* (1893), and a further period of good all-round acting finally brought him into management. With Frederick Harrison he took over the Haymarket in 1896 and remained there until 1905, during which time he was responsible for a number of excellent productions with a distinguished cast led by his wife, Winifred Emery. On leaving the Haymarket Maude became manager of the Avenue Theatre (later the Playhouse), which was badly damaged during alterations when in Dec. 1905 the roof of Charing Cross Station collapsed on it. However, he successfully reopened it in Jan. 1907, having in the interval appeared at the Waldorf and Duke of York's. During 1913–19 he made a number of tours of Canada and the U.S.A. and reappeared in London in 1919 in *Lord Richard in the Pantry*, with Connie Ediss as the Cook. He remained at the Playhouse until 1915. He continued to appear in a wide variety of parts until 1927, when he retired, returning some years later for a couple of plays, his last part being Don Geronimo in *Cabbages and Kings* (1933). Maude excelled in old-men parts, and his best performances were probably Bob Acres (1900), and Lord Ogleby in *The Clandestine Marriage* (1903). His Sir Peter Teazle (1900) was also outstanding. Among modern plays his greatest success was *Grumpy* (1914), but he could play other parts, as witness his performances in *The Little Minister* (1897) and *Toddles* (1906). He was also good as Eccles in *Caste* (1907), in *The Flag Lieutenant* (1908), one of the successes of his Playhouse management, and in *Rip Van Winkle* (1911). His son John became a famous lawyer and M.P., and he had two daughters one of whom, Margery, became a well-known actress. After the death of his first wife in 1924 he married again, and spent a long and happy retirement in Devon. He was commanded to appear both at Sandringham and at Balmoral, and was in several Command Performances in London. For many years he was President of the Royal Academy of Dramatic Art. On his 80th birthday, in 1942, he appeared at the Haymarket as Sir Peter Teazle in the quarrel scene, and also in a one-act sketch, in aid of the R.A.F. Benevolent Fund and the Actors' Orphanage.

MAUGHAM, William Somerset (1874–1965), English dramatist and novelist. Born in Paris, he was educated at King's School, Canterbury, and at Heidelberg University, and trained as a doctor at St. Thomas's Hospital. He was a novelist before he was a playwright and continued to write novels, short stories, travel books, and memoirs after abandoning the theatre. The height of his popularity as a dramatist was reached in 1908, when he created a theatrical record by having four original plays performed in London concurrently, and from 1907, three years after the production at the Avenue Theatre of his first play, *A Man of Honour*, till the early 1930s, he was prolific, fashionable, and popular. With *The Circle*, which has been described as an almost perfect 'serious' comedy, he made in 1921 what may be a permanent contribution to the theatre. Among the best-remembered of the pieces that entertained a large public over many years are *Lady Frederick* (1907), *The Land of Promise* (1914), *Caroline* (1916), *Our Betters* (New York 1917; London 1923), *Home and Beauty* (1919), *East of Suez* (1922), *The Letter* and *The Constant Wife* (both 1927), *The Sacred Flame* (1929), *The Breadwinner* (1930), and *Sheppey* (1933). Several of these have been successfully revived.

There is a finish, a neatness, an air of accomplishment about every work of Maugham's, whatever its subject-matter, which ensures for playgoers and readers alike a certain quality of pleasure. He could always revive the oldest of themes, relacquer it, and make it look as good as new. He achieved popularity without being good-natured, expansive, optimistic, romantic, or soothing. His humour was sardonic, tending to hard epigram: his attitude towards the virtues mistrustful; but he took care to give the public what he himself liked, a good story. There are some interesting details of his theatrical career in *The Summing Up*, published in 1938, and in *A Writer's Notebooks*. He was created a Companion of Honour in 1954.

A. V. COOKMAN†, *rev.*

MAURO FAMILY, see SCENERY, 3.

MAX, (ALEXANDRE) ÉDOUARD DE (1869–1925), French actor, a pupil of Worms at the Conservatoire, where he took first prizes for comedy and tragedy in 1891. He made his début at the Odéon, and was seen at a number of theatres in Paris, being already considered one of the foremost actors of the day when in 1915 he first appeared at the Comédie-Française, playing Nero in *Britannicus*. He had a short but glorious career there, dying of heart failure at the age of 56 after playing Orestes.

MAXINE ELLIOTT'S THEATRE, NEW YORK, on W. 39th Street between Broadway and 6th Avenue. This was built by the actress after whom it is named, and opened on 30 Dec. 1908. The first outstanding success there was *The Passing of the Third Floor Back*, which achieved 216 performances. A riot heralded the arrival of the Abbey Players from Dublin on 20 Nov. 1911 in a fine repertory of Irish plays. Doris Keane was seen in *Romance*, which later had a phenomenal run in London, while 1922 saw the 648 performances of *Rain*, based on a short story by Somerset Maugham. Another Maugham success at this theatre was *The Constant Wife*, with Ethel Barrymore and C. Aubrey Smith, which had 295 performances. *Coquette* (1927), with Helen Hayes, ran for nearly a year. Later Jane Cowl appeared at this theatre in *Twelfth Night*, and in the same season Judith Anderson scored a success in *As You Desire Me*. In 1934 Shumlin was responsible for the production of *The Children's Hour*, with Florence McGee as the child who causes all the trouble. This set a record for the theatre with 691 performances, and the building was then taken over by the Federal Theatre Project with *Horse Eats Hat* (a translation of *Le Chapeau de paille d'Italie*), and Orson Welles in *Dr. Faustus*. *Separate Rooms* began its long run at the Maxine Elliott's, which only had time for a short season of Ballet Jooss before it was taken over for broadcasting. Late in 1959 it was demolished.

GEORGE FREEDLEY†

MAYFAIR THEATRE, THE, LONDON, built inside the hotel of that name, opened on 17 June 1963 with Ralph Richardson and Barbara Jefford in a new translation of Pirandello's *Six Characters in Search of an Author*, which ran for about nine months. In a limited area the theatre succeeds in being well equipped and modern. It has a stage of good depth, and a well-raked auditorium, and is adaptable, as it can be used for theatre-in-the-round, arena or platform staging, or as a conventional proscenium-arch theatre. For the opening production the proscenium was not used and the play was given on a bare stage with exposed wings and a good deal of trick lighting intended to capture the different levels of the acting, shifting between illusion and reality.

MAYAKOVSKY, VLADIMIR VLADIMIROVICH (1894–1930), Soviet poet and dramatist, born in Georgia, the son of a forester. In 1908 he joined the Communist Party, and was twice arrested for underground activities, being also expelled from the School of Painting, where he was a student. He was helped and encouraged in his writing by David Burlak and Maxim Gorky, and in 1913 produced and acted in his first play, which was followed, after the Revolution which he had helped to bring about, by the first Soviet play, *Mystery-Bouffe*. This, which shows the Revolution spreading over the whole world, was produced in Moscow in 1918, and in a revised version in 1921. It was also given in German for the Third Congress of the Comintern. In 1929 Mayakovsky wrote *The Bed-Bug*, a satire portraying a Soviet world of the future in which a pre-Revolutionary bourgeois and a bed-bug alone survive from the old world, and depicting the struggles and conflicts that result from their efforts to acclimatize themselves. A year later came *The Baths*, a satire on the last remnants of bourgeois elements in Soviet life. Both these plays were produced by Meyerhold, and with their symbolic settings, robots, mechanics, and angularities, typify the drama of the period. *The Bed-Bug* was later revived by Taïrov at the Kamerny Theatre and by Meyerhold for Stanislavsky. A good deal of Mayakovsky's poetry, some of which has been translated into English, is semi-dramatic in form, and intended for public declamation. *The Bed-Bug* was given its first professional English production in Feb. 1962 at the Mermaid Theatre. It had previously been produced by the London University Drama Society. The Theatre of the Revolution was renamed the Mayakovsky in 1954 (see OKHLOPKOV).

MAYINGS, MAY-DAY PLAY, see FOLK FESTIVALS and ROBIN HOOD.

MAYNE, CLARICE (1886–1966), a music-hall singer of great charm and wit, and a famous Principal Boy. With her first husband, James W. Tate (1876–1922), the song-writer and composer, at the piano and billed with her as 'Clarice Mayne and That', she sang songs which became the rage of the day. Tate, whose first wife was Lottie Collins, died as the result of a chill caught at rehearsal, and some years later Clarice Mayne married Teddie Knox, of Nervo and Knox, the knockabout comedians.

W. MACQUEEN-POPE†

MAYNE, RUTHERFORD [really SAMUEL WADDELL] (1878–1967), Irish dramatist, associated with the Ulster Theatre. He began to write plays for it soon after its foundation in 1904 and remained throughout its career a strong supporter and its leading playwright. A few of his plays were first produced by the Abbey Theatre, Dublin, and many of them have had subsequent productions there or in London. He is concerned, like most Ulster dramatists, with what is individual and characteristic in the life of Northern Ireland, but plays such as *Red Turf* (1911) have a significance which is more than local, and the life of the peasant revealed there and the forces which bring about the tragedy are akin to similar ways of life and similar forces in other countries and other ages.

The plays of Rutherford Mayne are *The Turn of the Road* (1906), produced at the Ulster Theatre, Belfast; *The Drone* (1908), produced at the Ulster and Abbey Theatres, and in the U.S.A. in 1913; *The Troth* (London, 1908); *The Gomeril* (Independent Theatre, Dublin, 1909); *Captain of the Hosts* (Ulster, 1909); *Red Turf* (Abbey, 1911); *Evening* and *Neil Gallina* (both Ulster, 1912); *If* (Ulster, 1913); *Industry* (Ulster, 1915); *Phantoms* (Ulster, and Gaiety, Dublin, 1928); *Peter* (Abbey, 1930); and *Bridgehead* (Abbey, 1934). Certain of these have been translated into Dutch, Swedish, and Norwegian, and produced in those countries. UNA ELLIS-FERMOR†

MAZARINE FLOOR, see MEZZANINE.

MEDDOKS, MIKHAIL EGOROVICH [MICHAEL MADDOX] (1747–1825). The researches of the Russian theatre historian Eugene Ilyin have unearthed the following interesting facts. In 1767 a young Englishman arrived in St. Petersburg with a set of mechanical dolls which he exhibited with immediate success. Ten years later he turned up in Moscow, and was invited by Prince Ourusov to assist in the management of the private theatre which the Prince, like many Russian noblemen of the time, maintained in his household. Ourusov had a patent from the Imperial Court for the building of a theatre and a monopoly of dramatic performances for ten years, but this, after encountering many difficulties and losing his private theatre by fire in 1780, he ceded to Meddoks. With the help of the experience he had gained under Prince Ourusov, Meddoks first established a number of 'little' theatres in various places for the training of actors, and also visited the private theatres of Moscow and the great country estates to choose actors for his main company. This was housed in the excellent theatre which he built on Petrovsky Square (where the Bolshoi Theatre now stands), and which flourished until it too was destroyed by fire twenty-five years later. One unexpected result of Meddoks's visit to Russia was the adoption of the word 'Vauxhall', which he first gave to the amusement-gardens he opened in Moscow, in memory of the similar pleasure-garden in London. After their disappearance it remained in the language in its modern form as the word for a railway station. The name Maddox, first transmuted to Meddoks, later became Medok, and a direct male descendant of Maddox, bearing that name, was killed on the Russian front in the Second World War.

MEDICI. All the members of this famous Italian family were patrons of the arts, and extended their interest and protection to the theatre. Two of them were dramatists, (1) LORENZO (*c.* 1449–92), known as the Magnificent, author of a *sacra rappresentazione* on the lives of the saints John and Paul, produced in 1489, and patron of the humanist-dramatist Poliziano, and (2) LORENZINO DI PIER FRANCESCO (*fl.* early sixteenth century), one of the first Florentine writers of comedy, whose *Aridosia*, based on Plautus and Terence, was performed in 1536 with fine settings by San Gallo. Larivey later based his *Les Esprits* on this play.

MEDWALL, HENRY (*fl.* 1500), see ENGLAND, 2.

MEGGS, MRS. MARY (?–1691), known as Orange Moll, a well-known figure in the early days of the Restoration theatre. She was a widow, living in the parish of St. Paul, Covent Garden. On 10 Feb. 1662/3 the managers of the Theatre Royal, Bridges Street, granted her a licence for thirty-nine years to hawk oranges and other eatables in their theatre. For this privilege she paid £100 down and 6*s.* 8*d.* for every day the theatre was open, which seems to show that the business was a lucrative one. A contemporary description of the fatal fire which destroyed the theatre in 1672 says it started under the stairs 'where Orange Moll keeps her fruit'. Perhaps one of the lively orange-girls, of whom Nell Gwynn had been one, went searching for fresh supplies with a naked flame. Pepys refers to Orange Moll several times, and gleaned many items of theatrical scandal from her. She was involved in a dispute with the actress Rebecca Marshall, and towards the end of her life was frequently in trouble with the management of the theatre. In 1682 the companies of Drury Lane and Dorset Garden were amalgamated, and the joint management put in a new orange-woman. This led to endless disputes, and the matter was still unsettled when Orange Moll died.

MEI LAN-FANG (1894–1961), famous Chinese actor, son and grandson of actors, known for the excellence of his playing of female roles in Peking opera. He was trained for the stage from the age of 9 and at 14 made his first appearance in public. Between 1919 and 1935 he visited Japan, the United States, Europe, and Russia, where he enjoyed the friendship of Stanislavsky and Nemirovich-Danchenko. He was the first to combine the dramatic techniques of the five roles in Peking opera into which the *tan* or female character is divided—the *ching-yi* (married woman), *hua tan* (ingénue), *kuei men tan* (maiden), *tieh tan* (handmaiden), and *tao ma tan* (militant female). With Mei Lan-Fang's rise to fame in his early twenties the *tan* roles for the first time ousted the *lao-shêng*, or righteous elderly bearded male role, from its pre-eminent place. During the Civil War Mei Lan-Fang refused to appear on the stage, signifying his resolution by allowing his beard and moustaches to grow. In 1949, with the establishment of the Chinese People's Republic, he returned to Peking from Shanghai, and was appointed to various official posts, including the Presidency of the Research Institute of Chinese Drama. He then continued to act until 1959, and in 1958 celebrated his fiftieth anniversary on the stage (see No. 119).

MEILHAC, HENRI (1831–97), a prolific French dramatist, whose first play was done in 1855 at the Palais-Royal, for which theatre, and for the Gymnase, he wrote many comedies and vaudevilles. He collaborated with Halévy in writing libretti for Offenbach's light operas, and was for many years one of the outstanding figures of the French theatre. He had all the ephemeral gifts, and none of the durable ones, but he made a lot of people laugh, and his work epitomizes the witty and slightly cynical spirit of the Second Empire, summed up in his nickname of 'the Marivaux of the Boulevards'.

MEININGER COMPANY. George II, Duke of Saxe-Meiningen (1826–1914), who was passionately interested in the theatre, formed, with his morganatic wife Ellen Franz (1839–1923), formerly an actress, a private resident group of actors attached to his Court theatre. The Duke, who directed the plays himself, and also designed the costumes and scenery, was ably assisted by the actor Ludwig Chronegk, who joined him in 1866 and was responsible for the controlling and disciplining of the company, and for the actual carrying-out of the Duke's intentions. The innovations for which they later became famous, and which derived in part from the English contemporary theatre, had a great influence throughout Europe, and consisted mainly in the use of historically accurate scenery and costumes, and the setting of the chief actors within the scene, thus getting away from the formal grouping characteristic of, for example, the French stage at this time. They also revitalized the handling of crowd scenes. The crowd became a personage in the drama, every member an actor in his own right, yet the whole responding to the needs of the moment in a unifying thought. The Duke, whose first wife was a niece of Queen Victoria, often visited London, and was familiar with the methods of Charles Kean. He followed his example in dividing the supers into small groups, each with a competent actor at its head. These, even when, on tour, the supers were recruited locally, remained and gave coherence to the crowd. He worked out the relationship of the various groups to one another and to the set, and insisted that all gestures should be within the period of the play and related to the style of the time. By the use of steps and rostrums he kept the action moving on different levels. He also insisted that his star actors should from time to time play minor roles. Realizing the inadequacy of the conventional set, and again drawing his inspiration from England, he used the realistic box-set (see No. 69), and so moved from two-dimensional to three-dimensional scenery. It was unfortunate that he never sought to abolish stage waits and so give Shakespeare's plays in one continuous, rapid flow, but otherwise his reforms were excellent. In 1874 his company appeared for the first time outside its own town when it visited Berlin. In 1881 it came to London, appearing at Drury Lane in *Julius Caesar*, *Twelfth Night*, and *The Winter's Tale* (in German), as well as in a number of German and other classics. Although the critics were not unanimous in their praise, the reaction was on the whole favourable, and the critic of the *Athenaeum* went so far as to say 'so picturesque and so faultless' a performance of *Twelfth Night* had not been seen upon the modern stage (for a costume design for this production, see No. 151). He also praised the 'disposition of the supernumeraries when, as in the case of the oration of Mark Antony over the body of Caesar, strong and growing emotion has to be expressed'. In the following years the company visited thirty-eight cities, including Brussels (where the young Antoine saw it), Moscow, St. Petersburg, and Odessa. Stanislavsky saw the Meiningers in Moscow on their second visit there in 1890 (their first was in 1885). Thus the two men who were to become the greatest exponents of stage realism, at the Théâtre-Libre and the Moscow Art Theatre, both came under the Meininger influence, which through them spread far into the twentieth century.

MEISL, KARL (1775–1853), see AUSTRIA.

MELL, MAX (1882–), see AUSTRIA.

MELLON, MRS. ALFRED (*née* SARAH JANE WOOLGAR) (1824–1909), English actress, daughter of an actor who trained her himself and subsequently guided her whole career. She first appeared as a child prodigy in the provinces, and made her adult début in London on 9 Oct. 1843, appearing at the Adelphi under Webster, with whom she remained for many years. She was at that time known as 'Bella' Woolgar, from her playing of Bella Wilfer in *Our Mutual Friend*. Subsequently, having married a musician, she was known as Mrs. Alfred Mellon. She was for some time at the Lyceum under Dillon, and in 1867 became manager of the Adelphi. She remained on the stage until 1883, retiring as the result of an illness which continued to harass her until her death. Towards the end of her career she was somewhat outmoded in style and lost the favour of the audience, but at her best she was a most accomplished all-round actress. In Old Comedy she lacked dignity, but she had plenty of high spirits and piquancy and some elegance. She was much admired as Mrs. Vane in *Masks and Faces*, and in *The Flowers of the Forest*. She appeared in a number of dramatizations of Dickens's novels, playing at various times Dot, Tilly, and Bertha in *The Cricket on the Hearth*, Mercy in *Martin Chuzzlewit*, and Mrs. Cratchit, one of her best parts, in *A Christmas Carol*. She was Black-Eyed Susan to T. P. Cooke on his last appearance, and played Anne

Chute in the first production of *The Colleen Bawn*. In 1859 she was seen as Catherine Duval in *The Dead Heart*. Her daughter Mary was for some time on the stage.

MELLON, HARRIOT (1777–1837), English actress, who was with a strolling company at Stafford in 1795 when Sheridan saw her and engaged her for Drury Lane, where she remained until her retirement in 1815 on her marriage to the banker Mr. Coutts. She was at her best in the light impertinent chambermaids of comedy, in which parts Leigh Hunt much admired her. After her first husband's death she married the Duke of St. Albans, leaving the vast Coutts fortune to the daughter of Sir Francis Burdett, later the Baroness Burdett-Coutts, friend and patron of Sir Henry Irving.

MELMOTH, CHARLOTTE (1749–1823), a fine tragic actress, important in the annals of the early American stage. As a young girl she ran away from school with an actor named Courtney Melmoth, really Samuel Jackson Pratt (1749–1814), author of a monody, *Shadows of Shakespeare, or Shakespeare's Characters paying Homage to Garrick*. They soon separated, but she continued to use his name, and became well known on the Dublin, Edinburgh, and provincial stages. She was at Covent Garden in 1774, and at Drury Lane in 1776. In 1784–5 she was acting in Dublin. In 1793 she appeared in New York, and after giving recitations at concerts, appeared at the John Street Theatre with the American Company, as Euphrasia in *The Grecian Daughter*, a favourite part of Sarah Siddons. At one point she got into trouble with her New York audience for refusing to recite a patriotic epilogue, but her excellent acting, particularly as Lady Macbeth, which caused many more tragedies to be added to the repertory, made her a universal favourite. She was one of the leading actresses at the Park Theatre, New York, when it first opened, leaving it in 1802 after a quarrel with Dunlap. She returned, however, the following season, and stayed until after Dunlap's bankruptcy, when she went to the Chestnut Street Theatre in Philadelphia. She made her last appearance in New York in 1812, and later opened a school of English diction and elocution.

MELNOTTE, VIOLET (1852–1935), English actress and theatre manager. Born in Birmingham, she took her stage name from *The Lady of Lyons*. She made her first appearance in pantomime under Sefton Parry, and also played opposite the younger Mathews. In 1880 she appeared in London under Sir Charles Wyndham and was subsequently seen at the Globe and the Folly Theatres. After touring with the Kendals she returned to London and was seen in light opera. She started in management in 1885 at the Avenue (now the Playhouse) and Comedy Theatres, and among her productions at the latter were Clement Scott's *Sister Mary*, and *The Red Lamp* with Beerbohm Tree. Wishing to have her own theatre, she built one in St. Martin's Lane, then an unfashionable thoroughfare. Opened as the Trafalgar Square Theatre, the enterprise was at first unsuccessful, but later, as the Duke of York's, flourished, and was let for a long term to Charles Frohman. Eventually Miss Melnotte resumed control, and for some years ran it herself. She married Frank Wyatt (1852–1926) (the original Duke of Plaza Toro), outliving him and their son, Frank Gunning Wyatt (1890–1933), actor and dramatic critic. Known to everyone as 'Madam', she was a striking figure, dressed always in rather flamboyant mid-Victorian fashion, with, in later years, silver hair, a pale face, and ropes of pearls. She had no settled home, living sometimes at the Hotel Metropole, Brighton, and at other times at the Piccadilly Hotel, London. W. MACQUEEN-POPE†

MELODRAMA had a twin birth as contradictory musical terms round about 1780. In Germany it meant a passage in opera that was spoken to an orchestral accompaniment. In France *mélodrame* was applied to the device, invented some years earlier by Jean-Jacques Rousseau in his monologue 'Pygmalion', whereby music expressed a character's emotions when he was silent. There is no hint in 'Pygmalion' of the melodramatic spirit that Jean-Jacques made fashionable, but this influenced Schiller when he wrote *Die Räuber*, which set a character-pattern with falsely accused hero of noble birth, long-suffering heroine in captivity, tortured old age, and cold-blooded villain in usurped castle. This in turn influenced Mrs. Radcliffe, whose novels created a mountainous world infested by bandits, and under her influence 'Monk' Lewis wrote, besides the novel that gained him his nickname, a drama called *The Castle Spectre* which is *Die Räuber* minus all meaning. Captives in castles had an intemperate vogue in the theatre of London and Paris. The usual climax was for prison walls to fall in flames by means of a stage-carpenter's device of wooden blocks easily pulled away. What effect this had on the revolutionary mob may be vaguely surmised. The Bastille fell, and then continued to fall nightly at theatres in both capitals. *Die Räuber*, banned in England, was performed in Paris to shouts of 'Guerre aux châteaux!' But Mrs. Radcliffe prevailed over further endeavours to represent the triumph of liberty on the stage. When Napoleon ruled, the popular imagination was fed on tales of mystery and terror in her style. Newspaper feuilletons provided plots for lurid dramas; music between the dialogue gave them the new name of *mélodrame*. Guilbert de Pixerécourt wrote many; they had such power over audiences in the popular theatres that he was known as the Napoleon of the Boulevard. In the contemporary theatre he shaped and coloured a peculiarly picturesque country as the home of virtue triumphant (see No. 33.). Mountains with mills, rivers with little bridges, pine forests with wayside inns or humble cottages, and Gothic castles with dungeons, were its regular features.

In Germany, where Schiller was regretting his undergraduate outburst, Kotzebue—destined to be shot by an undergraduate of *Die Räuber* stamp—was writing popular plays that had a widespread vogue. *Menschenhass und Reue*, translated as *The Stranger*, a lasting success on the English stage, upset moral conventions by providing forgiveness for an erring wife—which was interpreted as the beating down of the barrier between comedy and tragedy. Similarly the heroine of *Die Sonnen-Jungfrau* (done as *Cora; or, the Virgin of the Sun*) married happily after breaking her vows. Kotzebue's sequel to this gave joy alike to Paris under the Terror and to England under the threat of invasion, for in Sheridan's adaptation of *Die Spanier in Peru, oder Rollas Tod*, as *Pizarro*, Peruvians expressed British sentiments of patriotic loyalty. What the Boulevard du Temple was to Paris, Lambeth was to London, and there Kotzebue's Peruvian romances and Mrs. Radcliffe's tales of mystery were dramatized as musical spectacles with songs, recitative, and the display of important statements (such as 'I swear to be thine') on notice-boards, to explain what was meant by the dumbshow. Cross, manager of the Royal Circus which later became famous as the Surrey, made such a stir with these that the Theatres Royal imitated his style in pieces labelled 'serious pantomime' or *ballet d'action* (see PANTOMIME, 5). His outstanding success was *Blackbeard the Pirate* (1798), a nautical drama with a Jolly Jack Tar for hero. This character can be traced to the singers, in costume, of sea songs at musick-houses in the early eighteenth century. The stage adopted the convention that he should land from a little boat, find somebody in need of protection, and rescue her, some years before Charles Dibdin's songs were composed. To Cross's dramas-without-dialogue the sailor-with-song was a ready-made hero, not only for dramas of the sea but for others in the Radcliffe manner. Thus true-blue adventure had already staked its claim on the popular stage before the first *mélodrame* was billed at Covent Garden on 13 November 1802 as *A Tale of Mystery*, by Thomas Holcroft. It was translated from Pixerécourt, whose name was not printed either on the playbills or in any published copy; all the many English melodramas adapted from his originals followed this example, so that he was unknown in England even when *The Dog of Montargis* (1814), vehicle for a dog star, was as celebrated as *Hamlet*. Theodore Hook likewise took the credit for *Tekeli* (1806). When Caigniez's *La Pie voleuse* came to London as *The Maid and the Magpie* (see Nos. 31 and 32), the original author's name was attached to one or two of the many translations. Some of the English plays of the 'twopence coloured' type may have plots of their own, notably Isaac Pocock's *The Miller and His Men* (1813), which is still acted today on Toy Theatre stages (see No. 67). Though Planché's *The Brigand* (1829) was the last of these banditti dramas to be written, they were constantly revived for many years.

Meanwhile Scott's poems and novels had inspired many melodramas that discarded Rousseau's musical device. The musick-houses and circuses which had used dumb-show as a means of avoiding the law had become burletta houses. According to the Lord Chamberlain's new ruling, a play which contained at least six songs could be classed as a burletta and be performed at these specially privileged places. Thomas Dibdin staged several of the Waverley Novels at the Surrey a week or two after publication. There was no 'insensibility to the absurd' in his work; his later plays, *Suil Dhuv the Coiner* (1828) and *The Banks of the Hudson* (1829), provide masterly evidence of the new spirit in the drama of democracy. Previously its stage villains had been cast in the maudlin Gothic mould; human devilry became spirited after supernatural melodramas had proved how acceptable unrepentant evil in the forms of Frankenstein's charnel-house monster, Flying Dutchmen, and Vampires, could be. But this was but one of many new tendencies. Another important one was manifest in *The Lear of Private Life*, adapted by Moncrieff at the Coburg in 1820 from a story by Mrs. Opie, which set a fashion for domestic dramas.

With *Fifteen Years of a Drunkard's Life* at the Coburg in 1828, Douglas Jerrold made his earnestness apparent even in the midst of absurdity. His early life in the Navy inspired the light-hearted *Black-Eyed Susan* (Surrey, 1829); the next year he wrote *The Mutiny at the Nore; or, British Sailors in 1797* (Pavilion, Coburg, and Queen's) as a protest against flogging. In *Martha Willis, the Servant Maid* (Pavilion, 1831) and *The Rent Day* (Drury Lane, 1832) Jerrold championed democracy before succumbing to the pseudo-Shakespearian mode, but the drama of revolt was continued by others until 1840. Adaptations of *Oliver Twist* and *Les Mystères de Paris* are also to be included in these stage-echoes of the clamour for reform.

That ardour subsided. Social injustice was to playgoers merely a passing phase in the subject of crime, which was of permanent interest. *Maria Marten; or, the Murder in the Red Barn* is proof of this. It became a classic of melodrama round about 1830. None of its immediate rivals won such enduring popularity, though Edward Fitzball, that industrious hack who quickly sensed every new fashion, won success at the Surrey in 1833 with *Jonathan Bradford; or, the Murder at the Roadside Inn.* The romance of crime had a temporary vogue; it began with Rob Roy, whose appearance on the stage caused Gilderoy to be transformed into a transpontine hero by William Barrymore, who also made a circus spectacle of Dick Turpin's ride to York. Harrison Ainsworth and Bulwer Lytton raised a crop of thieving gallants who swaggered before the footlights. All such cut-throats, plain or coloured, were outdone when Dibdin Pitt (trained to the stage by his father's half-brother, Thomas Dibdin) borrowed the plot of a penny dreadful for his play at the Britannia in 1847 about Sweeney Todd.

In the patriotic style there was no rivalling the grand military and equestrian dramas of Astley's (circus and theatre combined), near the south side of Westminster Bridge. Though critics protested against an excessive admiration for Napoleon, the battles fought on its stage and in its ring celebrated many British victories from Waterloo to the Far East. *The Dumb Man of Manchester*, played here in 1837, was a factory drama which exhibited the skill in dumbshow of Andrew Ducrow, the famous wire-walker and trick-rider who ruled over Astley's until it was burned down in 1841. In the new building the battles of the Crimea were represented while the war was in progress. But *Mazeppa; or, the Wild Horse of Tartary*, first equestrianized in 1831, was the regular stand-by of Astley's; Adah Isaacs Menken caused a stir there in the 1860s as one of the earliest and certainly the most notorious of many female Mazeppas.

The growth of the middle classes produced a new type of melodrama, notably at the Adelphi, where Buckstone became its chief exponent after making his name there in the democratic style with *Luke the Labourer* in 1826. For Mme Céleste he wrote *The Green Bushes* in 1845 and *The Flowers of the Forest* in 1847. They were sentimental and picturesque in contrast with the horrors of real life borrowed by the Surrey side from *Les Bohémiens de Paris*, which stirred the Boulevard in 1843. It changed from *The Scamps of London* to *London By Night*, then into *Under the Gaslight* in New York (1867), and next into *After Dark, A Tale of London Life*, and *London by Gaslight* (both 1868), while its influence less directly shaped dozens of other dramas where heroes were bound to the railroad before the oncoming express. When working class and middle class were thus divided, a distinct type of melodrama was needed for the upper classes. This also came from Paris. It began when Frédérick, disgusted with his part of Robert Macaire in *L'Auberge des Adrets*, changed old-fashioned villainy into wild burlesque. Playwrights who had no wish to be guyed had to become more sophisticated, and the Gallic drama was the result. *Pauline*, from a story by the elder Dumas, was played at the Théâtre Historique in 1850, and the next year at the Princess's, where Queen Victoria was seen to clutch the curtains of her box in terror as the heroine fell unsuspectingly into the clutches of a murderer with charming manners and merciless instincts. The Princess's, which was visited by Frédérick, came under the management of Charles Kean, whom the queen specially favoured. From the Historique he brought another drama based on Dumas, and staged it as *The Corsican Brothers*. He also played Charles Reade's version of *The Lyons Mail* and Boucicault's of *Louis XI*. These three subjects stayed in the loftiest repertoires of the nineteenth century, side by side with Shakespeare's masterpieces, which were acted in the same manner. A melodramatic Hamlet (Fechter's) was acclaimed.

There was no challenging the 'Gallic' hold over the upper classes. Like opera and ballet it had the hot-house atmosphere which the world of fashion liked. Rachel radiated it—and later Bernhardt, with the *femme fatale* of Dumas *fils*. When the Victorian novelists wrote for the stage (Dickens, Wilkie Collins, and Charles Reade) they had to be content with the middle-class audiences of Drury Lane, Olympic, and Adelphi, where they were outshone by Boucicault. After an attempt at Miltonic blank verse, he won youthful fame with that comedy of conventions, *London Assurance* (Covent Garden, 1841), though John Brougham claimed to be the author. Boucicault left for America, where he wrote and played several adaptations. Among these was *The Poor of New York*—seen on the Boulevard as *Les Pauvres de Paris*, at the Strand as *Pride and Poverty*, and at Sadler's Wells as *Islington; or, Life in the Streets*—which he presented in Liverpool as *The Poor of Liverpool*, and at the Princess's as *The Streets of London*. Out of Gerald Griffin's novel *The Collegians* (already dramatized) Boucicault made *The Colleen Bawn*, which was rapturously received at the Adelphi in 1860 as the first 'sensation' drama because of the realistic drownings and rescuings in the cave scene. Among the other plays he brought back from America was *The Octoroon; or, Life in Louisiana*, which had the burning and blowing-up of a steamship as its sensation. Since the author and his wife played the leading parts at the Adelphi, he had the power to insist on a percentage of the takings instead of a fixed fee and so instituted the royalty system. *Arrah-na-Pogue* (Dublin, 1864) and *The Shaughraun* (Drury Lane, 1875) were the best of the many plays he wrote before he was outmoded by two important changes in the development of melodrama.

The first of these was the triumph of the woman novelist. Mrs. Beecher Stowe was the forerunner, as Fitzball realized when he dramatized *Uncle Tom's Cabin* for Drury Lane in 1853. A version of *East Lynne*, acted at the Effingham, Whitechapel, in 1864, was followed by others until a theatrical boom occurred in Mrs. Henry Wood's novel in 1879. In the 1860s she had had a formidable rival in Miss Braddon, whose *Lady Audley's Secret* and *Aurora Floyd* were denounced for interesting audiences in the 'unhealthy' subject of bigamy. Boucicault shared this profitable obloquy by making a bad woman his principal character in *Formosa; or, the Railroad to Ruin* at Drury Lane in 1869. But the second change was more difficult to withstand: it doomed all melodramatists who lived on other people's plots. (But not before such piracy produced, in Tom Taylor's *The Ticket-of-Leave Man*, at the Olympic in 1863, the best melodrama of all.) New laws of copyright, which protected novelists and foreign playwrights, made 'adaptation' a difficult career.

After collaborating with Dickens in *No Thoroughfare* at the Adelphi in 1867, Wilkie Collins dramatized his own novels, which increased the vogue of detective dramas and murder mysteries. Paul Merritt's *The Golden Plough* at the Surrey in 1877 proved that the trick of puzzling an audience concerning the identity of a criminal was soon mastered. Fergus Hume's *The Mystery of a Hansom Cab* was dramatized at the Princess's in 1888. But these did not destroy the vogue of virtue triumphant which was upheld by Wilson Barrett at the Princess's in plays by George R. Sims (*The Lights o' London* and *Romany Rye*) and Hall Caine (*Ben-My-Chree*) and still more notably in *The Silver King*, by H. A. Jones and H. Herman in 1882, a drama on the old theme of falsely accused innocence (incidentally its novel idea of a hero who wrongly believed himself guilty had been used by 'Monk' Lewis in *Adelmorn the Outlaw*). Though acknowledged to be one of the best melodramas ever written, *The Silver King* came second as a source of financial profit to *The Sign of the Cross*, by Wilson Barrett, who acted it in America before its first performance in England at the Grand, Leeds, in 1895.

From the first night of *The Bells* at the Lyceum in 1871, Henry Irving maintained melodrama in the highest dramatic sphere by the side of Shakespeare. Some plays in his repertoire had descended from the Boulevard du Temple by way of Charles Kean and Fechter—*Robert Macaire*, *The Lyons Mail*, *Louis XI*, and *The Corsican Brothers*—and these were among his greatest achievements. Members of his company established melodrama in companies of their own. William Terriss upheld the prestige of the Adelphi drama with *The Bells of Haslemere* in 1887. Martin-Harvey found in *The Only Way*, one of many versions of *A Tale of Two Cities*, the foundation of his managerial career. Arthur Wing Pinero, using the language, ethics, and characterization of melodrama, wrote plays that were accepted as an up-to-date criticism of life. London's leading actor-managers at the opening of the twentieth century relied mainly on melodrama—Tree with *Captain Swift*, *Oliver Twist*, and *Trilby*; Alexander with *Old Heidelberg*, *If I were King*, and *The Prisoner of Zenda*.

Because the word had become a term of abuse as soon as it had been associated with 'popular' audiences, melodrama usually appeared under heavy disguises. Less trouble was taken at Drury Lane, where 'autumn dramas' for fifty years kept to plots of the falsely-accused-innocence type as an excuse for spirited scene-shifting to represent shipwrecks, railroad crashes, earthquakes and horse-racing. Walter and Frederick Melville, who took to writing melodramas for the masses after years of managerial experience, were franker still; their titles, such as *The Bad Girl of the Family*, *The Worst Woman in London*, and *The Ugliest Woman on Earth*, advertised their shock tactics. But twentieth-century melodrama, particularly at Drury Lane, strayed further and further from the fundamental idea of identifying virtue with poverty and simplicity; or perhaps the change was that 'poverty' now meant that heroes and heroines were reduced to the state of relying on a Derby winner to restore their fortunes. *Love on the Dole*, at the Garrick in 1935, was the true drama of democracy, and it discarded all the conventions of melodrama. These were employed *in toto* by Walter Reynolds (who played Virgil to Irving's Dante) in *Young England*, which was riotously received by busy mockers at theatre after theatre from 1934 onwards until withdrawn as a disturber of the peace. Virtue triumphant and crime exultant were jokes until the autumn of 1939. *Young England* was then revived; somehow it seemed rather less funny.

As a pair of contradictory technical terms 'melodrama' (what is spoken to music—the monologues of a *diseuse*, for example) and 'mélodrame' (music accompanying dumb-show, as in Planquette's 'Rip Van Winkle') are still in use, especially in France and Germany. M. WILLSON DISHER†

MELODRAMMA, a play with music, each being given equal importance, which evolved in eighteenth-century Italy from the earlier pastoral. The chief writers connected with it are Apostolo Zeno and Metastasio, whose libretti have since been used by innumerable operatic composers.

MELPOMENE, the Muse of Tragedy.

MELUCHA, see JEWISH DRAMA, 6, and MOSCOW STATE JEWISH THEATRE.

MELVILLE. (1) WALTER (1875–1937) and (2) FREDERICK (1876–1938), sons of Andrew Melville, actor and theatre proprietor, under whom they both started their careers in Birmingham. For twenty-five years they were joint proprietors of the Lyceum Theatre, London, where they made their own tradition of Lyceum pantomimes. Mostly written by Fred, they were elaborate, expensive productions in which comedy predominated. No matter how absurd the situations, or how anachronistic the clothes, they were consistently successful, and taxed the capacity of the Lyceum every Christmas. The two brothers, who were also partners in other enterprises—they built the Prince's Theatre—amassed great wealth, which they made no effort to spend. They both had simple tastes, wore shabby clothes—Walter, who usually wore a white tie, was slightly better dressed than Fred, whose suits were seldom of one piece—lived plainly, and followed no fashionable pursuits. They were simply and solely men of the theatre. Their enterprises flourished, except when they were not on speaking terms, when everything stopped until the dispute was over. They then communicated through their excellent and trusted manager, Bert Hammond, while continuing to occupy the same office at the Lyceum, one of the oldest rooms in the building, furnished in an early Victorian manner. In spite of occasional disagreements there was a great bond between them, and when attacked by outsiders they stood firm together. They were good people to work for, in spite of the tales told of their economies—Fred's particularly—and their staff remained with them for years. Both brothers were successful writers of highly coloured melodrama, simple, direct stories with virtue triumphant, much to the taste of the time. Walter was responsible for *The Worst Woman in London*, *The Girl Who Took the Wrong Turning*, *The Girl Who Wrecked his Home*, among others, and, with George Lauder, for *The Great World of London* (see No. 171). He was a silent man, more reserved than his brother, but with a curious sense of humour which manifested itself in odd practical jokes which he much enjoyed. Fred, who early in his career was an actor, wrote *Her Forbidden Marriage*, *The Ugliest Woman on Earth*, and *The Bad Girl of the Family*, all lurid, and all successful in their day.

W. MACQUEEN-POPE†

MENANDER (*c.* 342–292 B.C.), Greek dramatist, son of Diopeithes, and an Athenian poet of New Comedy (see GREECE, 2 *b*). For a time he studied philosophy with Theophrastus, pupil and successor of Aristotle. He was invited to the Court of Ptolemy I of Egypt, but preferred to remain in Athens. His comedies had an enormous reputation in antiquity; plays of his were closely imitated by Plautus and Terence; Caesar called Terence 'a half-Menander'; citations from his works are very numerous in later writers, and include a verse quoted by St. Paul, 'Evil communications corrupt good manners'. Until this century Menander was known only indirectly and in these fragments, but in 1905 a papyrus (now in Cairo) was discovered which contains considerable parts of four plays, with smaller fragments of a fifth; they are the *Heros*, the *Samia*, the *Epitrepontes*, and the *Perikeiromenê*. The last was translated in 1941, with conjectural restorations, by Professor Gilbert Murray under the title *The Rape of the Locks*. In 1945 he published, as *The Arbitration*, a similar reconstruction of the *Epitrepontes*.

Because, very largely, of the change in the political status and atmosphere of Athens, the comedy of Menander is utterly unlike that of Aristophanes a hundred years earlier. It is a delicate comedy of manners and of neat intrigue drawn against a background of bourgeois city-life; the exuberant fancy, burlesque, and lampooning of Old Comedy are entirely absent. In fact, Menander is much closer, in form, matter, and style, to the later, non-tragic drama of Euripides than he is to Aristophanes.

As the earlier 'tragedy' was not always 'tragic' (in our sense of the word), so New Comedy was not regularly 'comic'; it is drama with a romantic flavour that turns usually on such things as the ill-used maiden and the slave-foundling who proves to be well born. The 'romance' is chastened by close observation of contemporary life, and by a tone of urbane philosophizing—another link with Euripides. The whole is distinguished by extreme elegance of composition and style, and by delicate and sympathetic characterization. Old Comedy was essentially local and topical; this was the opposite. Menander therefore gave to the Roman dramatists what Aristophanes could never have given—excellent models and useful material. It is in Menander that we meet the originals of some of the stock figures of later comedy—the irascible old man, the young rake with a good heart, the officious slave—portrayed with great delicacy and liveliness (see Nos. 5, 11*a*).

A drama which dealt exclusively with the fortunes of private individuals obviously left no room for a chorus, which must in some sense represent the community. Accordingly, Menander's 'chorus' is nothing but a group of singers and dancers who provide breaks between the acts; sometimes they are dramatically explained away as a band of tipsy revellers. Their songs are quite irrelevant to the play; in the papyrus there is only a heading 'Something for Chorus'. H. D. F. KITTO

In 1957 another play, the *Dyskolos*, was discovered in Egypt by Professor Martin, Professor of Greek at Geneva University, in a papyrus codex believed to have been written in the third century A.D. This is now in the library of M. Bodmer at Cologny, near Geneva. It has been published with textual emendations and criticisms by Professor Martin, who is inclined to think, from a note prefixed to the text, that it was first performed in 317 B.C., and was therefore a youthful work, Menander being about 25 at the time. It was first performed in its recovered form at Geneva in June 1959, and a year later at Epidaurus. An English translation by Philip Vellacott, as *The Bad-Tempered Man, or the Misanthrope*, has been published, and was broadcast in 1959.

MENKEN, ADAH ISAACS (1835–68), American actress, whose real name was Dolores Adios Fuertes. Orphaned at 13, she became a dancer in her home town, New Orleans, with great success, and later decided to become an actress. The only part associated with her name is that of Mazeppa in a dramatization of Byron's poem, though she was not, as is often asserted, the first woman to play the part. This equestrian drama was first given at the Coburg, in London, in 1823, and continued to be popular during the next fifty years, though it was not until 1859 that a woman essayed the part of the hero. Menken played it in 1863 in California, then in New York, and in 1864 at Astley's in London (see No. 169). In 1856 she married John Isaacs Menken, and kept his name through subsequent matrimonial and other adventures. She appears to have exercised a fatal fascination over 'literary gentlemen', including Swinburne, Dickens, and the elder Dumas. She died in Paris, where she had first appeared in 1866. There are no records of her acting ability, and her theatrical reputation seems to rest entirely on the 'magnificent audacity' with which she displayed her person 'in a state of virtual nudity when she was bound to the back of the wild horse'.

MERCIER, Louis-Sébastien (1740–1814), French dramatist, and an exponent of the *drame bourgeois* initiated by Diderot. A well-educated and much-travelled man, he was well versed in the dramatic literature of Europe, especially Shakespeare and Lope de Vega, and his book, *Du Théâtre*, makes interesting reading. His own plays, in which he gives elaborate directions for scenery, were not very successful in France, but in translation they were welcomed in England, Italy, Holland, and particularly in Germany, where they were very popular on account of their unimpeachable morality and their declamatory style. The most characteristic is *La Brouette du vinaigrier* (1784), the story of a marriage arranged between a wealthy girl and the son of a working-class man which brought tears to the eyes of its audiences, as did the earlier *Jenneval* (1768)—an adaptation of *The London Merchant* in which the hero escapes punishment by a last-minute conversion. Mercier was an optimist who believed that right would prevail and he had scant sympathy with tragedies in which the hero is at the mercy of forces outside his own control. In pursuance of this theory he gave his translation of *Romeo and Juliet* a happy ending, and reduced *King Lear* to a tale of a bourgeois household quarrelling over the misdeeds of the servants. His plays possess unity, but not that conflict which is the essence of drama, and to quote one critic 'are no more interesting than the projects of a town councillor for municipal reform would be if dramatised'. It is interesting to note that this moral dramatist was a friend of the outcast Restif de la Bretonne, while of his fellow-authors, Beaumarchais was an adventurer, La Chaussée wrote *contes grivois* and Diderot equivocal novels. Yet they all posed as moralists. Mercier's political views were not looked on with favour before the Revolution, and he went to Switzerland to await the outburst which he boasted of having helped to prepare. He then returned and worked as a journalist. As a deputy he voted against the execution of Louis XVI in favour of a life sentence. He was later imprisoned, but, luckier than André Chénier, who was with him in prison, he was saved from the guillotine by the fall of Robespierre.

MERCURY THEATRE, London, at Notting Hill Gate. This was opened by Ashley Dukes in 1933. It is a small but well-equipped theatre which has produced some excellent plays, often considered 'non-commercial'. It was at the Mercury that *Murder in the Cathedral* was first seen in London. The Mercury is also the home of the Ballet Rambert, run under the direction of Mrs. Ashley Dukes (Marie Rambert).

For the Mercury Theatre, New York, see COMEDY THEATRE, 2.

MERMAID SOCIETY, The, a play-producing society founded by Philip Carr which in the 1900s produced an impressive list of Elizabethan plays, by Marlowe, Jonson, Webster, Ford, and others. It was also responsible for a production of *Comus* in the Botanical Gardens at Oxford in 1903, and of Jonson's masque, *A Hue and Cry after Cupid*, at Stratford-upon-Avon in 1904, in which Nigel Playfair appeared. Unfortunately information about the society is difficult to obtain, and some research into its work and influence is desirable.

MERMAID THEATRE, London. This was originally a private theatre designed by Michael Stringer and C. Walter Hodges for Bernard Miles, reproducing, in general terms, the main features of an Elizabethan stage. It was erected in a hall attached to Miles's house in St. John's Wood, and opened on 9 Sept. 1951 with a performance of 'Dido and Aeneas' in which Kirsten Flagstad sang Dido. This was followed a week later by *The Tempest*. In 1952 Middleton's *A Trick to Catch the Old One* was performed. In 1953—Coronation Year—the Mermaid was erected in the quadrangle of the Royal Exchange in the City of London, and performances were given of 'Dido and Aeneas', *As You Like It*, *Macbeth*, and *Eastward Ho!* On 17 Oct. 1956 the foundations of a new Mermaid Theatre, designed by Elidir Davies, destined to be opened to the public, were laid at Puddle Dock in Upper Thames Street, near Blackfriars Station, on a site where a theatre was begun in 1615 by Philip Rosseter, but left unfinished owing to opposition by the City Fathers. The Mermaid opened on 28 May 1959 with a musical version of Fielding's *Rape Upon Rape* as *Lock Up Your Daughters*, which had an immediate success and later moved to the West End for a long run at Her Majesty's. Subsequent productions at the Mermaid have been Brecht's *Galileo*, Ibsen's *John Gabriel Borkman*, some parts of the Wakefield Mystery plays, Shaw's *Androcles and the Lion*, and the Christmas productions for children, *Treasure Island*, *Emil and the Detectives*, and *Rockets on Ursa Major*. In 1965 *Left-Handed Liberty*, by John Arden, commemorated the 750th anniversary of Magna Carta. The theatre, which has a restaurant, and a foyer used for small theatrical exhibitions, is built inside a bombed warehouse, and has a bare open stage (see No. 42).

MERRY, Mrs., see BRUNTON (2).

MERRY ANDREW, see CLOWN.

MERSON, Billy (1881–1947), a music-hall performer whose best-known songs were 'The Spaniard that Blighted my Life' and 'The Good Ship Yakihickidula'. Born in Nottingham, he was apprenticed to engineering, but ran away to join a circus, where he clowned as Ping-Pong. With a partner he went on the halls as Trewella and Snakella. Deciding to change the name of their act, they picked on two names that would look good on the bills, and tossed up for them. The partner became Keith, while William Henry Thompson became Billy Merson. He soon became famous, his shortness, his physical strength, and his ability to do acrobatics, added to a pleasing voice and an attractive personality, bringing him to the fore. He later went into pantomime and revue, and then starred at Drury Lane as Hard-Boiled Herman in *Rose Marie* (1925), in which he later toured. He went into management at the Shaftesbury, presenting and playing in a musical comedy called *My Son John*, and also played in some of Edgar Wallace's plays. During the Second World War he did fine service entertaining the troops.

W. MACQUEEN-POPE†

MESSEL, OLIVER (1905–), English artist and stage designer, who has been responsible for some outstanding theatre décors. He first attracted attention with masks and costumes designed for Cochran's revues in the late 1920s, and was given the task of converting the Lyceum stage and auditorium into a cathedral for a revival of Reinhardt's *The Miracle* (1932). He has since worked unceasingly in every form of theatrical manifestation—opera, ballet, film, straight play—and among his notable décors have been those for *The Lady's Not For Burning* (see No. 107) in 1949, *Ring Round the Moon* (1950), *The Dark is Light Enough* (1954). He also designed the interior of Sekers's private theatre in Whitehaven. He has held several exhibitions of his designs, and is the author of *Stage Designs and Costumes* (1934). In 1958 he was appointed C.B.E. in recognition of his services to the art of the theatre.

MESSENIUS, JOHANNES (1579–1636), early Swedish dramatist, one of the first to take his subjects from Swedish history and saga. He planned a series of fifty plays on the former, of which only six survive (see SCANDINAVIA, 3 *a*).

METASTASIO [PIETRO ANTONIO DOMENICO TRAPASSI] (1698–1782), Italian poet, and author of a number of libretti for plays with music which have been constantly used by operatic composers (see OPERA). He was a child of exceptional abilities, and was adopted by the Abbé Gravina. For some years he delighted Roman audiences by his rapid improvisations, and he wrote his first tragedy, *Il Giustino*, when he was 14. In 1729 he was appointed Court Poet at Vienna, in succession to Apostolo Zeno, a position which he retained under Charles VI and Maria Theresa. He wrote much, his lyrical vein appearing to be inexhaustible. Of his numerous libretti the best are *L'Adriano* (1731), *La Clemenza di Tito* (which has probably been set by more composers than any other text), and *Attilio Regolo*. These last were both written in 1732. The first was given in 1734 in Vienna, but the *Attilio Regolo*, considered Metastasio's masterpiece, was not performed until 1750 in Dresden. Voltaire admired Metastasio above all his contemporaries except Racine and Addison, whom he considered alone worthy of being compared to the classics. Rousseau was also a great admirer of Metastasio, but Alfieri, not without reason, attacked his style, which he found lacking in force and virility (see ITALY, 3 *a*).

METHOD, THE, the name given to an introspective approach to acting which is based on Stanislavsky's system, or, as some opponents of the Method think, on a misunderstanding, or partial understanding only, of the system which he advocated for his own actors, as set out in his various publications and translated into English. The Method first came into prominence when it was embraced by the American Group Theatre during the 1930s, in protest against what they considered to be the externalized, stereotyped techniques then dominating the New York and London stages. Its current fame rests largely on the work of the Actors' Studio, founded in 1947 by Elia Kazan, Cheryl Crawford, and Robert Lewis, who were all members of the Group Theatre. They were later joined by Lee Strasberg, the present director of the Studio. According to its practitioners, the Method seeks to free an actor so that he can give a truthful interpretation in any kind of part, deriving his characterization from his personal experience in the same or a similar situation. He must 're-act' rather than 'act', 'be' and not 'do'. He must use his imagination to re-create an experience, but the motivation and emotion generated must be 'real' as opposed to 'acted'. Using this approach a scene may grow along wholly unexpected but nevertheless valid and dramatically effective lines.

Extreme opinions have been expressed for and against the Method, some of its critics maintaining that it makes the actor so self-absorbed that he forgets the needs of the audience. Others, viewing it more dispassionately, have pointed out that it is only one of many methods or techniques of acting, that it is no substitute for talent or training, and that to be truly successful it must enable the actor to communicate a valid characterization to the audience within the context of the play being performed. It should therefore be as applicable to the classics as to modern plays, though so far its most successful practitioners seem more at home in, say, Tennessee Williams than in Shakespeare. Method acting does not automatically preclude good diction and voice production or controlled body movement, and it seems probable that good Method actors are primarily good actors; the Method's reputation has suffered most from those of its adherents who are fundamentally not good actors, and who try to place the blame for their failure on the Method rather than on their own inability to use it as part of a broadly-based approach to the problems of acting techniques.

The Method was imported into England in 1956 by Al Mulock, but it was not enthusiastically received. As Darlington pointed out, any system is simply a convenient way of making actors work hard and concentrate on their job. A great stage director and teacher like Stanislavsky gets results by force of personality, and may then safely codify his system; but, once codified, it is open to misinterpretation, and in the hands of a mediocre teacher may do more harm than good. An American actress, Irene Dailey, who has taught the Method in the United States as well as in England, has some sensible things to say about it. She points out that it was intended to help actors to develop their latent potentialities to the utmost, and from there to go on and build up their technique. 'But some actors, having enjoyed the preliminary stages, have lost interest when it came to sheer hard work. Every budding actor reads *An Actor Prepares*, but few bother to read the sequel, which explains how to build up a performance after the preliminary work has been done.' She also expressed the opinion that English actors are Method actors anyway, without realizing it. Critics have countered with the proposition that though the Method may be applicable to the type of play Stanislavsky was mainly dealing with, it is inapplicable to Elizabethan drama, and even more so to Restoration comedy, for instance. Nor, to judge from the production of *Three Sisters* (by the Actors' Studio) in London in 1965, does it even suit Chekhov when performed in a new translation by American actors. From the audience's point of view the niceties of Method or non-Method acting are unimportant, and they are content to leave the means of production to the actor and director, provided the end-product is satisfactory.

METROPOLITAN, THE. This stood on the site of a famous old inn, the White Lion, which had had a concert-room built on to it in about 1836. As Turnham's, after its proprietor, it opened on 8 Dec. 1862 as a new-style music-hall, and was renamed the Metropolitan in 1864, after the building of the Edgware Road station on the Metropolitan railway line. It was not at first successful, but after Edwin Winder, who had made a success of the 'Old Mo' (see MIDDLESEX), took it over it had a prosperous history. Under successive managers it flourished until in 1887 it was demolished and rebuilt, the façade retaining part of the old inn (this disappeared in 1905). It opened on 22 Dec. with a brilliant bill which included Tom Costello, Fred Russell, and Kate Carney, and after the usual vicissitudes which attended the waning popularity of the music-halls, it became a television studio. It was finally demolished in 1964.

W. MACQUEEN-POPE†, *rev.*

METROPOLITAN CASINO, NEW YORK, see BROADWAY THEATRE, 3.

METROPOLITAN THEATRE, NEW YORK, originally Tripler Hall, and then used for opera. The original building was burnt down on 7 Jan. 1854, and a theatre was erected on the site for Henry Willard. This opened on 18 Sept. 1854 with a somewhat hackneyed bill, and by January of the next year had become a circus. It was still occasionally used for plays, and in Sept. 1855 Rachel appeared there with a French company in *Phèdre* and *Adrienne Lecouvreur*. On 27 Dec. the theatre reopened under Laura Keene, and, in spite of prejudice against a woman manager, it was progressing satisfactorily when, on a technical point of law, she lost her lease. She closed on 21 June 1856, and the theatre was bought by Burton, who remained there only two years. After his departure there was a short season of old comedies under Conway. For the later history of this theatre see WINTER GARDEN (2).

MEXICO, see SOUTH AMERICA, 1.

MEYERHOLD, VSEVOLOD EMILIEVICH (1874–?1943), Soviet Russian actor and producer who began his theatrical career as a student in the Musical–Dramatic School of the Moscow Philharmonic Society under Nemirovich-Danchenko, and in 1898 was invited to join the newly founded Moscow Art Theatre. Here he worked until 1902, when he left and went to the provinces, acting and producing in the Society of New Drama founded by himself. His theatrical activity was intense and many-sided; he was actor, producer, artistic director, theoretician, and pedagogue. In 1905 Stanislavsky invited him to take charge of productions at the newly organized Studio which was to be an experimental laboratory for the Moscow Art Theatre along the lines of the Symbolists. *La Mort de Tintagiles* was put into rehearsal, but was never shown to the public, and soon afterwards the Studio closed. From 1906 to 1907 Meyerhold was invited to produce at the Theatre of Vera Komisarjevskaya, where he was able to put into practice the symbolic or stylized method he had envisaged at the Moscow Art Theatre Studio. In effect this amounted to 'abstract' theatre, placing the human element, the actor, on a level with the other elements of production, thus reducing to nothing the actor's individual contribution to the ensemble, and making him merely a super-marionette in the hands of the producer—in fact, a realization of Gordon Craig's one-time ideal. This treatment of the actor led inevitably to a break with Komisarjevskaya, and Meyerhold left. He staged some brilliant productions at the Imperial Theatres in Petrograd—the Marinsky and the Alexandrinsky—and at the same time continued experimental work in his own Studio, where from 1913 to 1917 he continued, under the influence of the improvisation and stylized traditions of the *commedia dell'arte*, to work out his own methods. On the outbreak of the Revolution Meyerhold was the first artist of the theatre to offer his services to the new government, and in 1918 he became a member of the Bolshevik Party. Two years later he was appointed head of the Theatre Section of the People's Commissariat for Education, where he began a campaign to reorganize the theatre on Revolutionary lines. His views did not entirely coincide with those of the Soviet government, since he was all for the immediate revolutionizing of the still existing pre-Revolutionary theatres, whereas the Government, and Lunacharsky in particular, saw that the revolutionizing of a delicate organism, such as the Moscow Art Theatre, could not be done by decree, or by external change, but only by its absorption into the general stream of Soviet activity, strengthening what was healthy and rejecting what was decadent. This was the plan actually followed, which twenty years later left Meyerhold high and dry. Yet nothing can take away from the flaming enthusiasm, daring sincerity, and originality of his early work, for he was the first producer to put on a Soviet play—Mayakovsky's *Mystery-Bouffe* in 1918, reviving it in 1921 at his own theatre of the R.S.F.S.R., which later became the Theatre of Meyerhold. In his own Theatre Workshop Meyerhold continued his teaching, and developed his famous 'bio-mechanics' system of acting. He trained a number of people who have since played an important part in the development of the Soviet theatre, and up to 1924 was director of the Theatre of the Revolution, the first Moscow theatre to specialize in Soviet plays. He also influenced the school of Stanislavsky, particularly in the Vakhtangov Theatre. In 1934 the building of a theatre for him was begun, but it was never finished, for in 1936 he incurred the displeasure of the authorities for his production of *Camille* (in which his wife, Zinaida Raikh, played the leading role), and he was charged with having a pernicious 'foreign' influence on other theatre directors. His theatre was closed in 1938, but Stanislavsky invited him to produce at the Opera Theatre, where he revived Mayakovsky's *The Bed-Bug*. The date, place, and manner of his death, and that of his wife, are at present unknown (but see John Mason Brown's *As They Appear*, 1950), but his work for the theatre endures, and his reputation, since his official rehabilitation, stands high. He was essentially a producer's producer. He left behind him a quantity of written material, articles, notes for productions, and so on, which prove him to have been not only a great actor and producer, but a keen scholar with an original and creative mind. Two volumes of his writing are being prepared for publication, and it is hoped that a full biography will appear shortly.

MEZZANINE FLOOR. Albert Smith, in *The National History of the Ballet Girl*, says this, which he spells 'Mezzonine', is 'underneath the stage, halfway between the stage and nowhere, inhabited by those active spirits who send fairies and demons up and down the traps'. He says that it is also known in the theatre as the Mazarine floor.

MEZZETINO, a *zanni* or servant of the *commedia dell'arte*, with many of the characteristics of Brighella or Scapino, though more polished. Towards the end of the seventeenth century (*c.* 1682) the role was altered and elaborated by Angelo Costantini, who adopted red and white as the distinguishing mark of his costume, as opposed to the green and white stripes of Scapino. When, on the death of Dominique, he inherited that actor's role of Harlequin, he retained his name and costume. A later French Mezzetin was the actor Préville, of the Comédie-Française, who was painted by Van Loo in the part.

MICHAU, see JADOT.

MICKIEWICZ, ADAM (1798–1855), the outstanding poet of Poland, and the founder of the Romantic movement there. Born and educated in Vilna, he went into exile in 1829, and lived mainly in Paris, where in 1840 he became Professor of Slavonic Literature at the Collège de France. His finest dramatic work is the great romantic poem, *Forefathers' Eve*, which was composed in a fragmentary manner, Parts II and IV being published in 1823, Part III in 1832. The unfinished Part I was not published until after his death, which occurred in the Crimea while he was endeavouring to organize a Polish detachment there. It was first co-ordinated and staged by Wyspiański in 1901, and remains the most important work of the Polish poetic theatre.

MIDDLE COMEDY, see GREECE, 2 *b*.

MIDDLESEX, THE, a famous music-hall which stood in Drury Lane. It was originally a singing-room attached to a public-house named the Great Mogul, and even after its change of name was affectionately known as the 'Old Mo'. Winder made it into a music-hall and left to go to the Metropolitan. In 1872 it was rebuilt, and under Graydon became so popular that it had to be enlarged. Many famous music-hall stars made their début there, including Sam Collins singing 'Paddy's Wedding', and it claimed to be the first London hall at which Dan Leno appeared. It was also connected with the early days of Marie Lloyd. Just before the outbreak of the First World War, at a time when revue was paramount, it made a sensation with a series of French revues, the Ba-ta-ta-Clan. It was one of the last halls to have a Chairman. It was converted into a theatre by Stoll in 1918, reopening the following May (see WINTER GARDEN THEATRE).

W. MACQUEEN-POPE†, *rev.*

MIDDLESEX AMPHITHEATRE, see OLYMPIC THEATRE, I.

MIDDLETON, THOMAS (*c.* 1570–1627), English dramatist, who began his career as one of Henslowe's hack-writers. Nothing survives of his work at this period, except some trace of collaboration with those other industrious workers, Dekker, Drayton, Munday, and Greene. He collaborated with Dekker in *The Honest Whore* (1604) and *The Roaring Girl* (1610), and by himself wrote a number of plays of which the best was *A Trick to Catch the Old One* (1604–5), to which Massinger may be indebted for the idea of his *New Way to Pay Old Debts*. Others were *A Mad World, my Masters* (1606), and *Your Five Gallants* (1607), both comedies of London manners, acted by the Children's companies; *A Chaste Maid in Cheapside* (1611); *No Wit, no Help like a Woman's* (? 1613); *Women Beware Women* (1621), which was revived by the Royal Shakespeare Company at the Arts, London, in the summer of 1962, and shows the same mingling of fine poetry, melodramatic traits, and feminine psychology as the best of Middleton's other works; and the notorious political satire, *A Game at Chess* (1624). This dealt with the fruitless attempts which were being made to unite the royal houses of England and Spain, and, in spite of its popularity, Middleton was severely admonished for having written it and was perhaps imprisoned. Middleton's best work was done in collaboration with Rowley, particularly in *The Changeling* (1622), and he was also responsible for a number of masques and pageants now lost.

MIELZINER, Jo (1901–), American scenic designer, who was for a short time an actor. Since 1924 he has devoted himself entirely to scenic design, and has been responsible for many fine sets, among them those for Maxwell Anderson's *Winterset* (1935), John Gielgud's New York production of *Hamlet* (1936), and Arthur Miller's *Death of a Salesman* (1948; see No. 106) and *After the Fall* (1964) (see also UNITED STATES OF AMERICA, 11).

MIKHALKOV, SERGEI VLADIMIROVICH (1913–), Soviet poet and playwright, who writes mainly for children, seeking to encourage in his young audience the qualities of daring, honesty, friendliness, and comradeship. His clarity of thought, his simplicity, and the expressiveness of his language, together with the interesting themes which he chooses for his plays, have all contributed to his success. His best-known plays are *The Red Kerchief* (1947), *Ilya Golovin* (1949), and *Rocket* (1950), but he has also written *The Savages* (1958), a musical comedy done at the Yermolova Theatre, and *A Monument to Oneself* (1959), done at the Moscow Theatre of Satire.

BEATRICE KING†

MIKHOELS, SALOMON [SALOMON MIKHAILOVICH VOVSKY] (1890–1948), Jewish actor and producer, and from 1928 until his death head of the Moscow State Jewish Theatre. Born at Dvinsk, he was educated at the Kiev Commercial Institute, and then studied at Petrograd University from 1915 to 1918 with the intention of becoming a teacher of mathematics. He was one of the original members of the Jewish Theatre Studio formed in Leningrad by Granovsky in 1919, and first came into prominence two years later with a performance in Sholom Aleichem's *Agents*. He became the company's leading actor, and in 1928 took over the directorship from Granovsky. One of his finest performances was given as King Lear in Radlov's production in 1935.

E. HARRIS

MILES, BERNARD (1907–), English actor and director, founder of the Mermaid Theatre, first as a private playhouse in the Elizabethan manner, attached to his home in St. John's Wood, London and later as a public theatre at Blackfriars. Miles, who was for some years a teacher, made his first appearance on the stage in 1930. He spent many years as a general utility man in repertory companies, experience which was to stand him in good stead when he came to run his own theatre. He was for a time with the Late Joys at the Players', and in 1941 he toured with the Old Vic as Iago in *Othello*. He was with them again in 1947–8, playing Christopher Sly in *The Taming of the Shrew* and the Inquisitor in *St. Joan*. After founding the first Mermaid he appeared there as Caliban and Macbeth. At the second Mermaid, in the Royal Exchange, he produced and acted in *As You Like It*, *Macbeth* again, and *Eastward Ho!* Since the third Mermaid Theatre opened in May 1959 he has devoted his whole time to it, and has been seen, among other things, as Long John Silver and Galileo. He was appointed C.B.E. in 1953 for services to the theatre. In all his efforts to provide London with a new and experimental playhouse he has been ably assisted by his wife, Josephine Wilson, actress and sculptor, who worked under Malcolm Morley at the Everyman Theatre in Hampstead, and later toured Australia. It was during a season at the Sheffield Repertory Theatre in 1931 that she met and eventually married Bernard Miles. Since then her energies have been directed towards furthering her husband's plans and bringing up her children, but she has appeared in several Mermaid productions, notably as Lady Macbeth.

MILLAR, GERTIE (1879–1952), one of the most famous of the Gaiety Girls, a beautiful dancer, with a small but sweet voice, and a beautiful face and figure. Born in Bradford, the daughter of a mill-worker, she first appeared on the stage at the age of 13, playing the Girl Babe in a Manchester pantomime of *The Babes in the Wood*. In 1899 she was at the Grand, Fulham, as Dandini in *Cinderella*, and two years later she made her first appearance at the Gaiety in *The Toreador*, singing 'Keep Off the Grass'. She remained at the Gaiety until 1910 (except for a short appearance at the Hicks Theatre in 1908), during which time she married the composer Lionel Monckton, and made her first appearance in New York (in *The Girls of Gottenberg*, 1908). In 1910 she was seen at the Adelphi, as Prudence in *The Quaker Girl*, and in 1912 she was at Daly's as Lady Babbie in *Gipsy Love*. In 1914 she was in variety at the Coliseum, and she made her last appearance on the stage at the Prince of Wales's in 1918 in *Flora*. She then retired, marrying the 2nd Earl of Dudley after Monckton's death in 1924.

MILLER, ARTHUR (1915–), American dramatist, who while a student at Michigan University won three drama prizes, one of which, the Theatre Guild National Award of 1937, he shared with Tennessee Williams. On leaving the university he joined the Federal Theatre Project. His first play, *The Man Who Had All* *the Luck* (1944), ran for only five performances on Broadway, but in 1947 *All My Sons* had a long run and was given the Drama Critics' Award (see No. 105). It was produced in London (in 1948), as was *Death of a Salesman*, which on its production in New York in 1949 again gained the Critics' Award, and the Pulitzer Prize (see No. 106). Two further plays, *The Crucible* (1952) and *A View from the Bridge* (1955), consolidated Miller's position in the theatre as a first-rate craftsman, and a writer who is not afraid to tackle contemporary problems. His aim, in his own words, has been to present 'man as the creature of society, and at the same time as its creator'. *The Crucible* was done in London by the English Stage Company at the Court in 1956, and *A View from the Bridge* by the Watergate Theatre Club at the Comedy in the same year, during Miller's visit to England after his second marriage, to the film-star Marilyn Monroe, which ended in divorce. This marriage formed the subject of his play, *After the Fall*, directed by Elia Kazan as the first production of the new Lincoln Center Repertory Company, in a setting by Jo Mielziner, which opened on 23 Jan. 1964. Later in the same year *Incident at Vichy* was produced by Harold Clurman at the same theatre.

MILLER. (1) HENRY (1860–1926), American actor-manager, born in England, who was taken to Canada at an early age and at 15, after witnessing a performance of *Romeo and Juliet*, decided to go on the stage. He made his first appearance in Toronto and then went to New York, where, after touring with many leading actresses of the time, and with Boucicault, he became leading man of the Empire Theatre stock company. In 1899 he appeared as Sydney Carton in *The Only Way*, which had a long run, and in 1906 went into management, producing *The Great Divide* at the Princess Theatre. He was later seen in the same play in London. Among his other productions were *The Servant in the House* (1908) and *The Faith Healer* (1910), in both of which he himself played. In 1916 he opened his own theatre in New York (see HENRY MILLER'S THEATRE). He died during rehearsals for Dodd's *A Stranger in the House*. He married Bijou, the daughter of the actress Matilda Heron, and their son, (2) GILBERT HERON (1884–1969), became an actor and later a well-known theatre manager in London and New York, producing alone and in collaboration many outstanding plays, and fostering the exchange of new works across the Atlantic. He was lessee of the St. James's Theatre in London from 1918 until its demolition in 1958.

MIME (literally 'imitation' or 'representation').

1. GREEK. (*a*) *Popular*. The mime was originally a sketch of a dramatic, and often crudely realistic, kind (see below, the Latin mime).

(*b*) *Literary*. The popular mime had literary offshoots, some intended for dramatic performance, some not. Of these, the earliest seems to have been the Syracusan comedy of the early fifth century B.C., in which Epicharmus and Sophron were the most important figures. This comedy survives only in a few fragments and some doubtful traditions. It seems to have been a vigorous drama, and mythological burlesque seems to have been one of its sources of fun. It strongly influenced the slightly later Old Comedy of Athens, from which it differed in having no chorus and no political background. Sophron was associated especially with mime, and one purely literary development of this was the semi-dramatic dialogues of Plato. A still later development was the Alexandrian mime. Theocritus's *Women at the Festival of Adonis* (well translated by Matthew Arnold) is a good example of this, and is said to have been inspired by a mime of Sophron's on a similar subject. Herodas's mime is a rougher and more realistic form of the same genre.

H. D. F. KITTO

2. LATIN. (*a*) *Popular*. Of all the forms of dramatic entertainment known in classical times the mime was at once the most primitive and the most permanent. In its origins it cannot be classed as drama at all. All over the ancient world there were jugglers, acrobats, and public entertainers of all kinds, male and female, who displayed their skill in the market-places, at festivals, in private houses, or wherever and whenever they could secure patrons. Among these nameless mountebanks there were some with a special gift for mimicry. They could imitate with their voices the neighing of horses, the sound of thunder, and so forth; even more important was their command of gesture, an art carried to a high pitch in the ancient world, involving the active use of every limb (the *mimi* were often themselves acrobats) and great control of facial expression. Such improvised performances were especially popular among the Doric peoples of Greece. The social status of the performers was low, and the performance was of the simplest kind. A rough platform served to raise the actors above the heads of the crowd; on it (at least in later times) was set up a movable curtain, behind which the actors stood until their turn came. Then, parting the folds in the middle, they stepped into the public gaze. While they performed, a colleague might collect coppers from the spectators, as we see in an Egyptian illustration. Xenophon gives us an admirable description of a performance by a boy and girl, the property of a Syracusan dancing-master, who by means of dance, gesture, and words represented the love of Dionysus and Ariadne. This performance was given at a banquet in a private house, and one of the guests was Socrates. The girl was an acrobat as well as an actress, and had already impressed the company by her skill in the sword-dance. The social status of the performers is indicated by the dancing-master's admission that the boy is his concubine. Wide indeed was the gulf between such performers and the actors who, in mask and costume, appeared in the theatre of Dionysus to present the tragedies of

Euripides or the comedies of Menander. An element of indecency clung to the mime from the beginning; its aim was to amuse, no matter how. The mimes of Herodas (third century B.C.), which we still possess, are subtle, realistic, and sometimes sordid studies of certain social types, and were probably intended to be read, not acted.

Among the Dorians of Sicily and south Italy the mime was popular from an early period. Linguistic barriers were no hindrance to the art of gesture and facial expression; the simple requirements of the troupes of strolling *mimi* (a platform and a curtain) could be found anywhere. The contacts of Rome with Hellenism which arose out of the Pyrrhic War and the struggle for Sicily must have familiarized many Romans with the mime at a time when the literary drama of Rome had scarcely begun. Two years after the introduction of Greek drama to the Roman stage was founded the festival of Flora, which became a favourite occasion for the performance of mimes; the merry festival was riotously celebrated by the common folk, and licence went so far as to sanction the appearance of mime-actresses naked on the stage. The influence of mime on the development of Latin comedy must have been considerable; at any rate much of the jesting and buffoonery which Plautus introduced in his adaptations of Greek comedies would have been quite appropriate in the mime.

About this time the strolling companies of mimes ('birds of passage', as a Greek author calls them) were active all over the Graeco-Roman world. At its highest level the more elaborate form of mime, known as the 'hypothesis' and performed by a company, may have approached the level of drama, from which it differed chiefly in its preoccupation with character-drawing rather than plot, a necessary consequence of its more or less improvised nature. But we also hear of solo performers who prided themselves on being able to give the impression that they were several individuals in one. An epitaph found at Rome and dating from about the age of Sulla commemorates Eucharia, slave and later freedwoman of Licinia. Eucharia was a mime actress who had just achieved renown when she was cut down by death at the age of 14. The epitaph tells us that it is the record of a 'parent's love'.

We picture these small companies of strolling players, men, women, and children, setting up their simple curtain in some public place and giving their show. The manager (or manageress) took the leading role, to which the others were little more than foils; he was almost continuously present during the performance, and he kept the dialogue in his control, so that 'the second actor in the mime' was a phrase which denoted complete subservience. The distinctive costume was a hood (*ricinium*—whence the name *fabula riciniata* for mime) which could be drawn over the head or thrown back, a patchwork jacket, tights, and the phallus; the head was shaven, the feet were bare (hence the name *planipes* for the 'barefoot actor'). Perhaps only the *stupidus* or clown was so attired; the elegant philanderer of whom Ovid speaks must have been dressed as a man of fashion; a beautiful actress would appear in the most attractive and expensive clothes. The size of companies was perhaps not large; three actors are shown on a terracotta lamp from Athens as performers of *The Mother-in-law*, and Ovid speaks of a cast of three to take the roles of the foolish old husband, the erring wife, and the dandified lover.

The plots were simple, the endings often abrupt. A stock device was to show a character in a novel situation—a poor man suddenly become rich, for example. The riches might not last, and the ex-millionaire might have to disguise himself in his cloak and hurry off the stage. Abrupt endings of this kind were natural in what must have been fairly short pieces; Cicero tells us how, when the plot had reached a deadlock, someone would escape, the claqueurs would give the signal that the piece was over, and the drop-curtain would conceal the stage from view. So important was a curtain of some kind to the mime that we find Juvenal using the term 'curtain' as synonymous with 'mime'. The movable curtain (*siparium*) would serve as a back-cloth, and an actor appearing through its folds would be thought of as coming out of a doorway.

(*b*) *Literary*. In the age of Caesar the mime assumed literary importance. Decimus Laberius (106–43 B.C.) was the first Latin author to give the mime written form. As a respectable Roman knight he did not act in his own mimes; bitter then was the blow to his pride when, in his sixtieth year, he was compelled by Caesar to appear on the stage as the competitor of a young writer and actor of mimes, the ex-slave Publilius Syrus. We still possess the dignified and manly prologue which Laberius uttered on this occasion, with its significant warning to the dictator: 'Many he needs must fear whom many fear.' In all we possess 43 titles and about 140 lines or parts of lines from the works of Laberius. The fragments indicate that the mimes dealt with adultery and unnatural vice. The traditional fondness of the mime for biting topical allusions is illustrated by a reference to some governor who, like Verres, plundered his province; by an allusion to Caesar's supposed plan to legalize bigamy; and by a remark in the above-mentioned prologue: 'Roman citizens! We are losing our liberties!'

Publilius Syrus was, as his name implies, a native of Syria. He became famous as a writer and actor of mimes in the provincial towns of Italy; then, coming to Rome for the *ludi Caesaris* of 46 or 45 B.C., he challenged his rivals to extempore performances and vanquished them all, including Laberius. As we should expect in the case of pieces which seem to have been partly extempore, practically nothing is left of Publilius's mimes except the famous collection of maxims, made in the first century A.D., the high ethical standard of which surprised Seneca, who observes that they are worthy of tragedy rather than of mime.

(*c*) *Mime under the Roman Empire*. The

composition of mimes for reading aloud was one of the amusements of literary dilettanti in the time of the Roman Empire, and Pliny's versatile friend, Vergilius Romanus, wrote character studies for recital, modelled on the *mimiambi* of Herodas. But the mime which all but drove other forms of spoken drama from the theatre was sub-literary, unmetrical, and largely impromptu. No Latin mimes of this type have survived; but in the Oxyrhynchus Mime we possess a Greek mime of the second century A.D., containing six or seven short scenes, supposed to take place in front of a house, the door of which could conveniently be represented by the opening in the portable curtain. The leading actress plays the part of a faithless wife. Where the text begins (the opening lines are lost) we find her attempting to seduce Aesopus, one of her slaves. But he is in love with a fellow slave, Apollonia, and rejects his mistress's advances. She then orders the lovers to be taken away and left to die. A later scene shows the body of Aesopus being brought in; the other slaves pretend that he has thrown himself from a height (in reality they have drugged him for his own safety); his mistress mourns his death, but soon consoles herself with the company of another slave, Malacus, with whom she conspires to poison her husband, whose 'corpse' is presently brought in. Now comes the turning-point. The old man gets up and denounces his guilty wife and Malacus; they are led off to punishment, while Aesopus and Apollonia are found to be alive and well, and all ends happily. The dialogue is in prose; probably the actors—or at least the *archimima*, who has by far the most important role—felt free to expand it at will. The sordid theme and the startling indecency of the language seem to be characteristic of the mime in general.

In indecency the mime of Imperial times reached almost incredible depths. Not only was adultery a stock theme, but the Emperor Heliogabalus appears to have ordered its realistic performance on the stage. If the plot included an execution, it was possible, by substituting a condemned criminal for the actor, to give the spectators the thrill of seeing the execution performed in fact. However popular the actors, they were socially and morally the lowest of the low. It was natural that the Christian Church should set itself against the mime, and equally natural that the actors should retaliate by mocking Christian sacraments, much to the delight of the crowd. Gradually the Church got the upper hand. In the fifth century it succeeded in excommunicating all performers of mime, and in the sixth century Justinian closed the theatres. Yet the mime lived on. Its simple requirements could be supplied in any public place or private house, and in such settings it continued to entertain audiences who were now nominally Christian. Though forced to drop its habit of burlesquing the sacraments, it still scandalized the Fathers by its indecency and the immorality of its performers. Yet, as one of the last strongholds of paganism, the mime did not lack defenders. About A.D. 500 Choricius of Gaza wrote his 'apology for actors' (i.e. performers of mime), while the lovely actress Theodora, whose daring performances had delighted the public of Byzantium, only gave up the theatrical profession because she had captured the affections of Justinian himself and sat beside him on the Imperial throne.

How far the mime survived the fall of ancient civilization is doubtful. So simple a type of performance might arise independently at different ages and in different countries. Yet precisely because of its primitive character it is hard to be sure that the classical mime ever became wholly extinct in Europe. Certainly the Middle Ages had their *mimi*. In its latest phase the classical mime was the last representative of classical drama; its strolling performers had taken over all that was left of a great tradition. Somehow or other they may have handed on their craft to their successors of the Dark and Middle Ages, and so to modern times. When the darkness clears we see a new drama arising. Perhaps its performers were in some sense the descendants of the strolling companies of mime-actors who had entertained the Roman world. WILLIAM BEARE†

3. MODERN. Today the art of mime is arousing an ever-increasing interest both in the theatre and as an educational force. From the Roman period until the present day it has passed through varying degrees of popularity, reaching its height at the time of the *commedia dell'arte* of Italy in the sixteenth century, when a form of extempore comedy was in use in which the actors wore masks and employed the spoken word together with mime and gesture. The familiar figures of the harlequinade, which survived in a modified form until recent times, are based on the characters of the *commedia dell'arte*, and much of the traditional word-gesture of modern mime may be traced to the same source.

During the 1570s several troupes of *commedia dell'arte* players, among them the Gelosi and possibly the company of Alberto Ganassa, visited Paris, where they were well received and popularized the art of impromptu acting. France soon produced companies of her own, and mime took its place as an important feature of the French stage. It lingered on until the nineteenth century, when the famous three-act mime play, *L'Enfant prodigue*, was produced, in which we find the forerunner of the modern mime play.

Mime has again become a purely silent art, in which the actor conveys his meaning by gesture, movement, and expression, and must be able, within the limits of that art, so to convey every thought and emotion that his audience is never at any time conscious of the lack of the spoken word. As in the French mimes of the nineteenth century, so modern mime generally has a musical accompaniment (though this is not essential) which is co-ordinated with every movement and expression of the actor. Properties may be used, as in a spoken play, but it is more usual to leave them to the imagination of the audience stimulated, by the actor's art. Although the number of exponents of pure mime in England is at present small, the necessity for every actor to have a knowledge and understanding of the art is fully realized; mime has become an essential part of the training of every stage student, and is now to be found in the curriculum of all dramatic and ballet schools. The growing popularity of mime in the theatre is shown by its inclusion in many revues and variety entertainments, and by the tendency of present-day ballet to contain a far higher percentage of pure mime than was the case in the nineteenth century. The fact that mime is not without its following on the amateur stage, and that it has become an important feature in many a village entertainment, gives ample proof that it is gradually becoming understood and appreciated by a far wider public than if its performances were confined only to the professional stage. MARGARET RUBEL

A more general interest in mime was first aroused through the film-performance of Jean-Louis Barrault in *Les Enfants du Paradis*, and has grown sufficiently to provide a large and enthusiastic audience for Marcel Marceau, whose Bip is perhaps the greatest creation in modern mime. A younger exponent of the art is Samy Molcho, an Israeli who was first seen in London in Dec. 1962.

MINNEAPOLIS, see GUTHRIE, TYRONE.

MINOTIS, ALEXIS (1900–), outstanding Greek actor, whose Hamlet was much admired when the Greek National Theatre appeared in London in 1939. He has been responsible for the production of classical plays in the old theatre at Epidaurus, in many of which his wife Katina Paxinou, who played Electra in London in 1939, has starred. They also appeared together at the National Theatre in Athens in such plays as *Ghosts*. Among Minotis's finest parts is Richard III.

MINSTREL. 1. Minstrel was the generic name for the professional entertainer of the Middle Ages (see also FOLK-PLAY, GLEEMAN, WAIT), whose origin must be sought in the fusion of the Teutonic *scôp*, or bard, with the floating debris of the Roman theatre, particularly the *mimi*. This process went on obscurely from the sixth to the eleventh century, helped by the wandering scholars, who brought to the mixture a certain leaven of classical erudition (see GOLIARD). The minstrel emerges in the eleventh century, and flourished till the fourteenth. Dressed in bright clothes, with flat-heeled shoes, clean-shaven face, and short hair—legacies of Rome —and with his instrument on his back, he tramped, alone or in company, all over Europe, sure everywhere of a welcome from his audience, though often harassed by the hostility of the Church and the restrictions of petty officialdom. In spite of this, he enlivened the festivities of religious fraternities, and may have had some small share in the development of liturgical drama; he relieved the tedium of pilgrimages—it was only lack of a minstrel that set Chaucer's pilgrims story-telling—and frequented the market-place or the nobleman's hall with equal facility and success. There were different grades of minstrels, even before the formation of guilds, in France in 1321, in England in 1469. At the top of his profession was the accomplished poet and musician, permanently attached to a royal or noble household. Such were Blondel, the faithful servant of Richard Cœur de Lion, and Rahere, of Henry I. He and his like disappeared when the introduction of printing drew their audiences away to read romances. Next came the itinerant, but still respectable, bands of players whose repertory included some true drama, dialogued songs and debates, or rough farces in which it is tempting to see an echo of the farces of Imperial Rome. These made their contribution to literary drama in the *dits* and *fabliaux* of France and the English interludes, and continued into Elizabethan days and beyond. Lastly came the vast anonymous horde of little people—rope-walkers, acrobats, jugglers, conjurors, puppet-masters with crude wooden figures and some dramatic skill in their presentation, animal imitators and trainers—whose appeal was to the unlearned. They therefore survived the Renaissance, and the line continues down to the circus and music-hall performers of the present day.

2. The modern Minstrel Show is a form of entertainment which originated from the Negro patter songs of Jim Crow [T. D. Rice] and from his burlesques of Shakespeare and opera, to which Negro songs were added. From 1840 to 1880 the Minstrel Show was the most popular form of entertainment in the United States (see NEGRO IN THE AMERICAN THEATRE). It came to England in the 1840s and was essentially a family entertainment—as distinct from the music-hall, which was for adults only—and took place usually in a hall, notably in St. James's Hall, Piccadilly, and not in a theatre. The performers, originally, as in the United States, white men with blacked faces (whence the term Burnt-cork Minstrels), but later true Negroes, sat in a semicircle with their instruments, banjos, tambourines, one-stringed fiddles, bones, etc., singing their haunting, plaintive coon songs and sentimental ballads, varied by soft-shoe dances and outbursts of back-chat between the interlocutor and Bones—the latter a permanent feature, and the butt of the party. The jokes were very elementary and relied for much of their humour on repetition, and after a great vogue the Minstrels gradually disappeared. Some of the performers migrated to the music-hall stage (see CHIRGWIN and STRATTON), while the last remnants of the fashion lingered on at the seaside, where two or three strollers in traditional minstrel costume—tight striped trousers and waistcoat and tall white hat, or straw boater—would wander along the sands with a banjo. Among the most famous minstrel troupes were the Christy Minstrels, the Burgess and Moore, and the Mohawks. The original

formula of Burnt-cork Minstrels was successfully revived by B.B.C. Television in the 1940s with the Kentucky Minstrels, and in the 1960s with the Black and White Minstrels. The latter company was transferred to the Victoria Palace as a live show in 1962.

MIRACLE PLAY, see AUTO; ENGLAND, 1; FRANCE, 1; ITALY, 1 *a* ii; MYSTERY PLAY; SACRA RAPPRESENTAZIONE, and SPAIN, 1.

MIRANDA, FRANCISCO SÁ DE (1481–1558), see PORTUGAL.

MIRBEAU, OCTAVE (1848–1917), French dramatist, whose plays deal with contemporary problems, in the style of Henri Becque. Among them are *Les Mauvais Bergers* (1897), a study of the struggle between labour and capital, and his best play, *Les Affaires sont les affaires* (1903), a mordant satire on the big-business man who is a slave to his wealth.

MIRROR SPOT, see LIGHTING, 2.

MIRROR THEATRE, LONDON, see HOLBORN THEATRE.

MISRULE, ABBOT, KING, OR **LORD OF,** a special officer (*dominus festi*) appointed to oversee the Christmas entertainments at Court and elsewhere in England in the late fifteenth and early sixteenth centuries. In Scotland he was also known as the Abbot of Unreason. His appointment was temporary and must not be confused with the permanent office of Master of the Revels, a Court official who first appears under Henry VIII in charge of masques and other set entertainments. Lords of Misrule were common in the colleges of the universities, particularly at Merton and St. John's, Oxford, where appointments were made as late as 1577. They are also found in the Inns of Court, intermittently until the time of Charles II. It was at the Gray's Inn Christmas Revels of 1594 that Shakespeare's *Comedy of Errors* was first given. The Lord of Misrule is a direct descendant of the 'king' in the Feast of Fools, and the equivalent in adult circles of the Boy Bishop of the schools.

MISS KELLY'S THEATRE, LONDON, see ROYALTY THEATRE, 2.

MISTINGUETT [JEANNE BOURGEOIS] (1875–1956), French actress and dancer, the possessor of the reputedly most beautiful, and certainly most highly insured, legs in the entertainment world. She made her first appearances in music-hall, and in 1907 was seen in straight comedy, deserting it, however, to go to the Moulin-Rouge, of which she was for some years part-proprietor. With Maurice Chevalier as her partner, she appeared in some sensational dances at the Folies-Bergère. She was also seen at the Casino de Paris, where she first sang some of her most famous songs. In her early days she was an eccentric comedienne of great originality, specializing in the portrayal of low-class Parisian women, but later she became the acknowledged queen of revue, and her fabulous hats and dresses attracted as much attention as her songs and sketches. She made her only appearance in London in Dec. 1947 at the Casino Theatre. She wrote a volume of reminiscences, which appeared in an English translation by Hubert Griffiths in 1938.

MITCHELL, LANGDON ELWYN (1862–1933), American poet and playwright, who in 1899 dramatized *Vanity Fair* for Mrs. Fiske, as *Becky Sharp*. It was a great success and was frequently revived. His finest play, however, was *The New York Idea*, a satire on divorce which has been cited as the best social comedy of the American stage in the early twentieth century. It was first produced by Mrs. Fiske at the Lyric Theatre, New York, on 19 Nov. 1906, with a remarkable cast, and was translated into German (production by Reinhardt), Dutch, Swedish, and Hungarian. In the same year Mitchell translated *The Kreutzer Sonata* from the Yiddish of Jacob Gordin, and later dramatized *Pendennis* for John Drew. As a successful playwright, he was invited to lecture at the University of Pennsylvania, and in 1928 became the first Professor of Playwriting at that university. He always retained his interest in the professional stage, but his high standards led him to be very critical of his own efforts, and he left a number of unfinished plays in manuscript.

MITCHELL, MAGGIE [MARGARET JULIA] (1832–1918), American actress, who made her first appearance on the stage in 1851, joining two sisters already established in the profession. She danced and played boy parts at the Bowery, being particularly admired as Oliver Twist. She then went on tour, becoming extremely popular in the South, and in 1857 became leading lady of Burton's company. It was in 1860 that she first played her famous role of Fanchon in an adaptation of George Sand's novel, *La Petite Fadette*. She continued to play it for the next twenty years, remaining always the same small, winsome, sprite-like child, piquant and overflowing with vitality. Although she was good in other parts, notably Jane Eyre, Pauline, Mignon, and Parthenia, it was Fanchon that the public wanted and invariably got.

MITCHELL, WILLIAM (1798–1856), American manager, born in England, where he had acted and worked in the theatre for some fifteen years before in 1836 he went to New York. His American career began when in 1839 he took over the Olympic Theatre, previously considered unlucky, opened it with *High Life Below Stairs*, and embarked on a long series of triumphs, both as actor and manager, which made the Olympic one of the outstanding theatres of New York. He was excellent as Vincent Crummles, as Hamlet in a burlesque of that play, and in a burlesque of Fanny Elssler. But it was as a purveyor of light amusement that he won the heart of the New York public, and a contemporary reviewer said of him that his pieces 'however trifling in incident, have always been produced admirably. . . . He has contributed much to the enjoyment of the people of this city, and has always secured a company, which taken together, has been better than at any of the theatres.' He retired in 1850. (See also OLYMPIC THEATRE, 2.)

MOCHALOV, PAVEL STEPANOVICH (1800–48), a famous Russian tragedian, and leading exponent of the 'intuitive' school of acting. He was born in Moscow, and was the son of a leading actor there. He attended the private academy of the Teslikov brothers in Kostromov Province, where his family took refuge from the Napoleonic invasion, and made his début on the stage in 1817 with great success. His great roles were Hamlet and Lear, and the heroes of Schiller's *Die Räuber* and *Kabale und Liebe*. The critic Belinsky thought highly of him, and wrote a detailed description of his Hamlet. With great gifts of temperament and passion, Mochalov was antipathetic to any rational methods and relied entirely on the inspiration of the moment. He was consequently extremely uneven in his acting and in his effect on his audience. He later began to drink heavily, his talent weakened and his inspiration grew less, while he had no technique to fall back upon. His romantic quality was out of tune with the realistic tendency of the Russian theatre of the nineteenth century, and he deprecated the reforms of Shchepkin, but his influence nevertheless persisted for some time.

MODENA. (1) GIACOMO (1766–1841), Italian actor, who was for a long time in a travelling company, where he proved excellent in the comedies of Goldoni. He later turned to tragedy, and was the first to play the name-part in Alfieri's *Saul*, in which he also made his last appearance, David being played on that occasion by his son (2) GUSTAVO (1803–61). Like his father, the younger Modena was accounted one of the best Italian actors of his day. In 1824 he was with Salvatore Fabbrichesi (1760–1827), an actor-manager who founded the first resident company in Milan, and with whom the elder Modena had often acted. He made his first success as David, and later proved excellent in both comedy and romance. He had his own company for some years. During the Revolution he escaped to England, where he gave Dante recitals, but he returned to Milan in 1839 and again had his own company until 1846. Although not well known outside Italy, he was the tutor of Rossi and Novelli, both of whom toured Europe extensively. Though not handsome, the younger Modena had a fine figure and a nobly rugged and expressive face.

MODJESKA [MODRZEJEWSKA], HELENA (1840–1909), Polish actress, daughter of a musician named Opid. In 1860 she ran away from home with a mediocre actor named Gustave Zimajer, and together they joined a provincial company. It was then that she adopted the name by which she is best known, retaining it even after her second marriage (in 1868), to Charles Chłapowski, a Polish aristocrat. In this same year she was invited to join a resident company in Warsaw, where she remained for nearly ten years, proving herself a fine actress in tragedy and comedy, her repertory ranging from Shakespeare to the latest productions of Feuillet and Sardou. In 1876 she emigrated with her husband to California, where they met with little success, and lack of means soon caused her to desert the ranch for the stage. She played at the California Theatre, San Francisco, in 1877, and in spite of her poor command of the English language scored an immense success. She then toured extensively in the United States, England, and on the Continent, and was considered one of the leading actresses of her generation, a woman of great charm and power, at her best in tragedy or strong emotional parts. She retired from the stage in 1905 after a farewell performance at the Metropolitan Opera House, New York.

She was in England from 1880 to 1882, and again in 1890. Her ambition had always been to act Shakespeare in English in a London theatre, and to achieve this she first studied English for six months in San Francisco and then toured America for several years. Even when she finally came to London, she first appeared in *Maria Stuart*, *Adrienne Lecouvreur*, and *La Dame aux camélias* before venturing on Juliet, with Forbes-Robertson as Romeo (Mar., 1881). There were fourteen Shakespearian parts in her repertory of 260 roles, some of which she had already played in Warsaw. She was the most fervent admirer of Shakespeare, did much to extend the study of his work in Poland, and helped to spread knowledge of him in America by her appearances on tour and in New York. One of her finest moments was as Lady Macbeth in the sleep-walking scene.

MOHUN, MICHAEL (*c.* 1620–84), English actor, and, with Charles Hart, the leading man of Killigrew's company when it took possession of the Theatre Royal in 1662. He had been a boy-actor under Beeston, and was already playing adult parts before the closing of the theatres. He joined the Royalist army, became an officer, and then returned to the stage. His Iago was much admired, and he created many Restoration roles in tragedy and comedy, including Abdelmelech in *The Conquest of Granada*, and Mithridates in Lee's play of that name.

MOISSI, ALEXANDER (1880–1935), German actor, of Italian origin, who was engaged as a super at the Vienna Burgtheater, and played his first speaking part in German at Prague in 1902. He remained there, playing leading parts, until 1905, when he went to Berlin. There his fine presence, and above all his rich, musical, speaking voice, soon brought him into prominence. At the Deutsches Theater under Reinhardt he played Romeo, Hamlet, the Fool in *Lear*, Oberon, and Touchstone; Faust, Mephistopheles, Posa in *Don Carlos*, Oswald in *Ghosts*, Louis Dubedat in *The Doctor's*

Dilemma, and Marchbanks in *Candida*, as well as a number of less well-known parts. His Oedipus and Orestes in the Reinhardt productions in Vienna were exceptionally fine. In 1930 he came to London, playing Hamlet in W. V. Schlegel's translation at the Globe, while Gielgud's Hamlet in its entirety, from the Old Vic, was playing next door at the Queen's.

MOLÉ [MOLET], FRANÇOIS-RENÉ (1734–1802), French actor. Originally a notary's clerk, he engaged in amateur dramatics with such success that in 1754 he was allowed to appear at the Comédie-Française. He was considered promising, but was sent into the provinces to gain experience, returning at the beginning of 1760. Fleury says of him that he was the personification of youth, grace, and vivacity, so it is not surprising that he was received into the company to play young heroes and lovers. After a few successes, often in parts specially written for him, he became the idol of the public, and on the retirement of Grandval shared leading roles with Bellecour. He excelled in comedy, but was content to leave the great tragic roles to Larive. Yet, ironically enough, he was destined to be the first French Hamlet, in 1769, in the adaptation made by Ducis, which was, however, nothing like the original. The French public liked it, and Molé was considered good in the part. In later life he got fat, but lost nothing of his agility of mind or body. A contemporary said of him that his wit was so quick, and his fooling so excellent, that he was capable of playing a part he did not know, relying entirely on the prompter, without the audience realizing it. Some of his mannerisms had an unfortunate influence on his younger companions, especially in tragedy, to which he unconsciously brought the technique of comedy. He was an adherent of the Revolution, and was not imprisoned with the rest of the company in 1793, going instead to play revolutionary drama at the theatre of Mlle Montansier. When the Comédie-Française reopened he went back and remained there until his death. His wife was also an actress, doubling roles with the wife of Préville.

MOLIÈRE [JEAN-BAPTISTE POQUELIN] (1622–73), the greatest actor and dramatist of France, author of some of the finest comedies in the history of the theatre. He was the eldest son of a prosperous upholsterer of Paris attached to the service of the king. Little is known of his early years, though he is reported to have been an excellent mimic, and a great frequenter of theatres. He probably saw Belleville at the Hôtel de Bourgogne, while Montdory at the Marais introduced him to the tragedies of Corneille. He may also have watched the farce-players and barkers at the fairs or in the market-places amusing the crowds from their trestle-platforms. But nothing in his early life gave proof of that overmastering passion for the stage which later possessed him. In about 1631 he became a pupil at the Jesuit College of Clermont (later Louis-le-Grand), and left in 1639 a good scholar, particularly in Latin, and an omnivorous reader of poetry and plays. While at school he probably took part in the plays—mainly adaptations of Latin authors—and ballets which formed part of the Jesuit educational curriculum (see JESUIT DRAMA). Among Molière's fellow students was the young Prince de Conti, who much later became his patron, and it may have been at Clermont that he met Cyrano de Bergerac, a lifelong friend and champion, who is known to have followed the lectures of Gassendi.

On leaving the College young Poquelin, who was supposed to succeed his father, made a half-hearted attempt to study law, and in 1642 went to Narbonne in the suite of Louis XIII. This may have been a move designed to break up a somewhat undesirable friendship which he had formed with a family of actors, the Béjarts. If so, it was unsuccessful, for a year later the young man renounced his succession, and with the Béjarts and some of their actor-friends formed a small theatrical company, known as the Illustre-Théâtre, which took over and adapted a disused tennis-court. The driving force behind the enterprise was undoubtedly Madeleine Béjart, the eldest of the family, a woman of great attraction and talent, and already an experienced actress. Molière, as he had now become—no reason for the adoption of this particular name has yet been found—was merely an enthusiastic but untried aspirant, whose ambitions tended towards the playing of tragedy, for which he was physically and temperamentally unsuited. It has been surmised that he was at this time the lover of Madeleine, a relationship which was to have tragic repercussions in his later life.

The new company failed completely, and Molière was imprisoned for debt. The Illustre-Théâtre vanished overnight, without leaving a trace in contemporary gossip. Its scanty history has had to be pieced together from extant documents and later, often apocryphal, memoirs. But the young actors were not discouraged, and after some change of membership they set off for the provinces, remaining there from 1645 to 1658. These are the formative years of Molière's career, and must not be forgotten in the later blaze of glory in Paris. He achieved some distinction as an actor, and served his apprenticeship to play-writing by supplying the company, of which he soon became the virtual leader, with partly improvised farces in the style of the *commedia dell'arte*. They appear to have been successful, though little of them survives beyond some stray titles, and fragments used again in later plays. Little more is known of the company's wanderings than a list of the towns they can be proved to have visited, under the patronage successively of the Duc d'Épernon and the Prince de Conti. There was no doubt a great deal of hard work and some hardship, but a corresponding degree of happiness and freedom. The company was reputable, usually well lodged and well received, and, with the later accession to its strength of the veteran actor

Dufresne, of Gros-René, and of the two fine actresses Mlle du Parc and Mlle de Brie, capable of giving a good account of itself. These years in the provinces provided Molière with experience of men and of affairs, with a storehouse into which he dipped unendingly for his later plays, and with a nucleus of devoted friends and experienced actors who were to provide the backbone of his company in Paris. Above all they taught him to know, to love, and to laugh at human nature in all its frailty and stupidity.

So much spade-work was not to be wasted, as might so easily have happened. Helped by friends in high places, the company once more approached Paris, and on 24 Oct. 1658—a date memorable in French dramatic history—appeared in the Guard Room of the old Louvre before the 20-year-old Louis XIV. In the audience of notables and courtiers were also the actors of the Hôtel de Bourgogne, which at this time had almost a monopoly of acting in Paris. The new company chose for their first play Corneille's *Nicomède*, in which everyone present had probably seen and admired the bombastic and ranting Montfleury. Molière's quieter and more natural style of acting failed to impress them. For a moment the future of the little company, and of French drama itself, hung in the balance. Then Molière came forward, and in a charmingly modest little speech introduced a farce of his own, *Le Docteur amoureux*. It was an immediate success. Molière, only a passable tragedian, was revealed as a comic actor of great gifts, ably supported by a company which had played together for many years. The actors of the Hôtel de Bourgogne, secure in their pre-eminence in tragedy, put no obstacles in the way, and the King granted Molière permission to remain in Paris, sharing the Petit-Bourbon, and later the Palais-Royal, with the *commedia dell'arte* troupe under Scaramouche (Tiberio Fiorelli) already installed there. The relationship between the two groups was most cordial, and Molière was always ready to acknowledge how much he had learnt from the Italians, though at first he suffered from their popularity. They retained the right to play on the most lucrative days, Tuesdays and Sundays, leaving the rest of the week for the newcomers. Molière had to pay them a heavy rent and also adapt his plays to their fixed scenery—houses round a square. Much of the action had therefore to take place in the open air, even the signing of wills and consultations with doctors. Later, however, he was able to rebuild the Palais-Royal, with ample space for scenery and orchestra, and by then the Italians were paying him rent.

In spite of the failure of *Nicomède*, the company continued to appear in tragedies by Corneille, without success. In the last few weeks of the year Molière, in desperation, put on two plays of his own, *L'Étourdi, ou les contretemps* and *Le Dépit amoureux*. Both were successful, and drew the attention of the town to the merits of the struggling company. Meanwhile Molière, viewing the life of Paris with an acuteness sharpened by years of absence and experience, turned from the stock plots and time-worn artifices of the Old Comedy, and took a subject nearer at hand. The result was the one-act satire *Les Précieuses ridicules* (1658), which at one blow demolished the pretensions of the younger generation of the Hôtel de Rambouillet, and drew all Paris to laugh at their absurdities.

From now on Molière's life is that of his theatre. It led him into bitter controversies, and a struggle for freedom to attack social iniquities which ended only with his untimely death from overwork. On the other hand it gave him the devoted friendship of France's greatest men of letters, and the patronage of Louis XIV, without which he might have succumbed to the attacks of his enemies. This he paid for, however, in periods of feverish activity in connexion with Court festivities, for which he was in constant demand. His main function was the provision and production of a series of plays interspersed with music and dancing, for which Lully provided the music. The plays were given by Molière's company, while the notables of the Court, including the king himself, danced in the ballets.

The first of these Court entertainments was *Les Fâcheux*, in 1661. Two years later, at the king's command, came *L'Impromptu de Versailles*, a biting satire on the actors of the Hôtel de Bourgogne, who had sought to undermine Molière's influence at Court by attacking him not only in his professional but also in his private life. It was a vulnerable spot, for in Jan. 1662 Molière, so wise and balanced in his writing and in his conduct of business matters, had made a most injudicious marriage with the youngest sister of Madeleine, Armande Béjart, a spoilt child of 20, capricious, flirtatious, and entirely lacking in affection. The affair was complicated by the belief of most people, even Molière's friends, that Armande was the daughter, and not the sister, of Molière's former mistress, and Montfleury, in rage and jealousy, even went so far as to accuse Molière before the king of having married his own daughter. The royal reply to this accusation was the commissioning of *L'Impromptu de Versailles*, while Louis also stood godfather to Molière's first child, born in 1664, who died the same year. A second child, Esprit Magdeleine (1665–1723), was born before matters became so bad between the parents that Molière took himself off to Auteuil while Armande stayed in Paris, while a third child, a son, who lived only a few weeks, was born in 1672, after a reconciliation had been effected.

The old theatre of the Petit-Bourbon had seen only one more play by Molière, *Sganarelle, ou le cocu imaginaire* (1660), before it was demolished, and the company moved to Richelieu's theatre in the Palais-Royal, henceforth to be their permanent home. Here they opened in 1661 with Molière's one failure, a heroic drama entitled *Don Garcie de Navarre, ou le prince jaloux*. He redeemed himself in the eyes of his public by *L'École des maris* (1661), *L'École des femmes* (1662), and *La Critique de l'École des femmes* (1663), in which he justifies his use of comedy, and replies to his critics. It was in this play that Armande, who was to prove an excellent actress, made her first appearance, as Élise.

In 1664 Molière, who had already earlier in the year provided the Court with *Le Mariage forcé*, in which the king danced the part of a gipsy, was responsible for the six-days' entertainment at Versailles given under the collective title of *Les Plaisirs de l'île enchantée*, for which he hurriedly wrote *La Princesse d'Élide*. It was during these celebrations that Molière produced privately the first version of a play which was to cause him much distress—*Tartuffe*. This attack on hypocrisy roused against him the false *dévots* of Paris, who succeeded in getting the play suppressed for many years. Though frequently given in private houses, it was not seen on the public stage until 1667, and then in an altered version as *L'Imposteur*. Another play which roused almost as much opposition was *Don Juan, ou le festin de pierre*, given at the Palais-Royal in the same year as *L'Amour médecin* (1665). It was followed by *Le Misanthrope* and *Le Médecin malgré lui* in 1666 and by *Amphitryon* and *L'Avare*, both written at Auteuil, in 1668, while for the Court Molière provided *Le Sicilien, ou l'amour peintre* (1667) and *Georges Dandin, ou le mari confondu* (1668). These were first given at Versailles, while *Monsieur de Pourceaugnac* (1669) appeared at Chambord and *Les Amants magnifiques* (1670) at Saint-Germain, where Louis XIV, as Neptune and Apollo, made his last appearances as an actor.

The best known of the Court plays is *Le Bourgeois gentilhomme* (1670), written to provide the king with an entertainment *à la turque*, a genre much in vogue at the time. *Psyché*, a *tragédie-ballet* in which Corneille collaborated—written, tradition says, to make use of some scenery representing Hell which Louis hated to see lying idle—was also produced in 1671, as was the last play written for the Court, *La Comtesse d'Escarbagnas*.

The Court plays, shorn of some of their splendour, had also been given publicly at the Palais-Royal, which in 1671 was rebuilt and enlarged to take the scenery and machines of *Psyché*. In the same year Molière reverted to his earlier farcical manner in the light-hearted *Fourberies de Scapin*. In 1672 came another of the great satires, *Les Femmes savantes*, followed by *Le Malade imaginaire*, Molière's last play, in which he acted on the night of his death, 17 Feb. 1673.

Molière's great achievement was that by his own efforts he raised French comedy to the heights of French tragedy. When he finally settled in Paris tragedy was the only thing worth watching or acting in; all the rest was trifling, at its best good for an hour's amusement, at its worst left solely to the raucous tumblers and travelling mountebanks. Molière made comedy a polite entertainment, acceptable to the Court and to men of sense. He raised it from the domain of farce, and made it a vehicle of social satire, a supple, living organism capable of the nicest gradations of light and shade, able at once to divert and admonish. His plays are universal in their application, yet untranslatable. In transit, the wit evaporates and only a skeleton plot is left. This, however, will not deter people from trying to translate them—a fascinating occupation.

Molière was noted in his lifetime as an excellent actor in comedy—though not in tragedy—in spite of a slight impediment in his speech to which one soon became accustomed. He was a fine producer, both of his own and of other people's plays, and as a working dramatist knew how to suit his characters to his actors. Like Shakespeare, he took his plots where he pleased, and all through his works there are echoes of Greek, Latin, Italian, and Spanish comedies. Yet the result is unmistakably his own.

Molière should also be honoured for having encouraged the genius of Racine, whose first play, *La Thébaïde, ou les frères ennemis*, he produced at the Palais-Royal in 1664. When that ungrateful man, on a flimsy pretext, took his *Alexandre le Grand* (1666) from the Palais-Royal to the Hôtel de Bourgogne, and suborned Molière's star actress, Mlle du Parc, to act in it, Molière was so hurt by his behaviour that he never spoke to him again.

Although not easy for English audiences to understand, either in French or in translation, Molière has always been popular in England. His influence was very marked during the Restoration, and most dramatists borrowed freely from him, usually without acknowledgement. It would be impossible to enumerate all the plays based on his works: Dryden made use of *L'Étourdi* and *Amphitryon*, Shadwell of *L'Avare*, *Psyché*, and *Don Juan*, Wycherley of *L'École des femmes* and *Le Misanthrope*, Betterton of *Georges Dandin*. In 1671 Ravenscroft adapted *Le Bourgeois gentilhomme* as *Mamamouchi; or, the Citizen turned Gentleman*, and also made use of *Monsieur de Pourceaugnac* for his *Careless Lovers* (1672). In 1676 Otway made a translation of *Les Fourberies de Scapin* which was revived in London in 1959. In 1717 Cibber based his successful *The Non-Juror* on *Tartuffe*, and Fielding in 1732 translated *L'Avare* and *Le Médecin malgré lui*. Towards the end of the eighteenth century and during the nineteenth and early twentieth centuries, Molière was somewhat in eclipse, though translations were made of his complete works for readers—Baker and Miller (1739), Heron Wall (1879), Curtis Hidden Page (1926, with the French text also). Stage versions began again with Somerset Maugham's *Perfect Gentleman* (1913), Vera Beringer's *The Blue Stockings* (1915), and the adaptations made by Lady Gregory as *The Kiltartan Molière* in the 1920s. A fresh impetus to the acting of Molière in English was given by the very free versions of Miles Malleson in which he appeared himself in the 1950s. Other good and more scholarly, though perhaps less actable, versions have been made by George Graveley, and by John Wood, the latter in the Penguin Classics series. French companies visiting London generally include at least one Molière play in their repertory. The first to be seen were *Tartuffe*, *L'Étourdi*, and *Georges Dandin* in the season 1718–19. The tradition continues to the present day (for illustrations of Molière productions, see Nos. 24, 109).

MOLINA, TIRSO DE, see TIRSO DE MOLINA.

MOLNÁR [NEUMANN], FERENC (1878–1952), Hungarian dramatist, and one of the best known outside his own country. He studied law, became a journalist, and first attracted notice with some light-hearted farces, in which he exploited for the first time the humour of Hungarian town life. *The Devil*, a modern variation on the Faust theme, was the first of his plays to be done in England, France, Germany, and New York. In this last city it opened at two theatres on the same night—18 Aug. 1908—at the Belasco with George Arliss and at the Garden with Edwin Stevens. At the same time it was being played in German and Yiddish. *Liliom* (1909) was, however, his best-known play. A mixture of realism and fantasy, it failed in Budapest on its first production, but became a resounding success ten years later. It was given in New York in 1921 by the Theatre Guild, and as a musical, *Carousel*, it had a long run from 1945, and in London in 1950. A long series of comedies followed, none as successful, but all acceptable, the most charming being *The Glass Slipper*, a Cinderella story in which the prince is a middle-aged cabinet-maker. Molnár's sure technique and brilliant dialogue won him international admiration, and all his most important plays have been translated into English. Among them *The Guardsman*, done by the Theatre Guild in New York in 1924, provided a perfect vehicle for the Lunts. Others which were successful in English were *The Glass Slipper*, and *The Swan*. *Olympe* was given an arena-style production at the Cockpit Theatre in London in 1953, produced by Ann Jellicoe. Molnár became an American citizen in 1940. His widow, Lili Darvas, is still active in theatre and films in the United States.

MOMOS, see PORTUGAL and SPAIN.

MOMUS, the Greek god of ridicule, and by extension of clowns. The name was frequently used to denote a clown, as in Grimaldi's reference to himself as 'the once Merry Momus', and became attached to one of the figures in the harlequinade.

MONAKHOV, NIKOLAI FEDOROVICH (1875–1936), Russian actor whose career was mainly in the theatres of Leningrad (formerly St. Petersburg). He began in a café-chantant, singing satirical songs, and then played many roles in operetta. After seventeen years on the stage he joined the Free Theatre founded by Konstantin Mardjanov, where he had the opportunity of revealing his many-sided talent in straight drama, in opera, and as a compère. When the Free Theatre went bankrupt, Monakhov could have gone to the Moscow Art Theatre, but he preferred to return to operetta for another five years. The October Revolution gave him a great chance. He joined the newly founded Leningrad Theatre, and appeared as Philip II in *Don Carlos* with great success, continuing to play leading parts until his death.

MONCK, NUGENT (1877–1958), English actor and producer, a disciple of William Poel, and founder of the famous Maddermarket Theatre, Norwich. His career as an actor, which had taken him from London to Ireland and New York, was cut short by the First World War, and it was not until 1919 that he became producer to the amateur group known as the Norwich Players, which he had founded in 1911. For them he bought and reconstructed a dilapidated building, giving it an Elizabethan stage complete with apron, and seats for about 250 people. Here the company, still amateur, play one week in every month, and have given all thirty-seven plays associated with Shakespeare, numerous early and Elizabethan comedies, foreign and adapted plays, Greek tragedy, and the works of Shaw and other modern writers. The Maddermarket celebrated its silver jubilee in 1946. In 1953 the theatre was altered and enlarged. Up to 1952 productions were entirely controlled by Nugent Monck, who appeared himself in many of them. He also did a certain amount of theatrical work elsewhere, and was responsible for a number of pageants in and around Norwich. In 1946 he was awarded the O.B.E. and in 1958 made a C.B.E. in recognition of his work for the theatre. He was a Fellow of the Royal Academy of Music from 1935 until his death.

MONCRIEFF, WILLIAM (GEORGE) THOMAS (1794–1857), English dramatist and theatre manager, and a prolific writer of melodrama and burlesque for the minor theatres. There is little to distinguish him from a host of other scribblers of the time, except that he had a propensity for dramatizing novels before their authors had finished them, which drew down upon his head the wrath of Dickens, who had been one of the worst sufferers. He revenged himself, however, by depicting Moncrieff in *Nicholas Nickleby* as 'the literary gentleman ... who had dramatized 247 novels as fast as they had come out—some of them faster than they had come out—and who *was* a literary gentleman in consequence'. Moncrieff certainly had nearly 200 plays to his credit, of which *Tom and Jerry* (1821) was the most successful of the innumerable dramatizations of Egan's book, while *The Cataract of the Ganges* (1823) was given at Drury Lane with the added attraction of a real waterfall. The first of his Dickens adaptations was *Sam Weller; or, the Pickwickians* (1837). Moncrieff was manager of the Regency Theatre when it opened in

1810, and in 1819 was at the Coburg, where he staged innumerable melodramas of the most startling nature. In 1826 he produced the first plays given in Vauxhall Gardens, and had a short period in management at Astley's with equestrian drama.

MONKHOUSE, ALLAN (1858–1936), dramatic critic and dramatist, who was on the *Manchester Guardian* when Miss Horniman opened her repertory theatre at the Gaiety, Manchester. He not only welcomed and supported her enterprise in his columns, but wrote for her his first play—which was afterwards considered to be the first manifestation of the so-called Manchester School of Drama—*Reaping the Whirlwind*. This was produced in 1908, and was followed in 1911 by a full-length play, *Mary Broome*, which had a mixed reception, but was later transferred to London. Monkhouse's one-act, *Nothing Like Leather* (1913), was a satire on the Gaiety company, in which Miss Horniman appeared for a moment as herself, but, surprisingly enough, Monkhouse's best play was not produced until after the Gaiety company had been disbanded. This was *The Conquering Hero*, an anti-war play which in 1924 was seen at the Aldwych in London, where it had a shorter run than it deserved. It is the story of a soldier who goes unwillingly to war, finds humiliation in battle, and returns to the irony of a triumphal welcome. Nicholas Hannen gave a moving performance as the hero, Christopher Rokeby, in a play which anticipated *Journey's End*.

MONODRAMA (sometimes called Melodrama, on account of its musical accompaniment). This short solo piece for one actor or actress supported by silent figures or by choruses was popularized in Germany between 1775 and 1780 by the actor Brandes. The Duodrama, a similar compilation, had two speaking characters. Both types of entertainment, which were useful in filling out the triple bill then in vogue, frequently consisted of scenes extracted and adapted from longer dramas.

MONTAGUE, CHARLES EDWARD (1867–1928), English provincial journalist who was dramatic critic to the *Manchester Guardian* from 1890 to 1925. His artistic integrity was of the highest, and he always insisted that, to be of any worth at all, art must be individual. 'That is the truth of art, to be less true to facts without you than to yourself as stirred by facts. To find a glove-fit of words for your sense of "the glory and the freshness of a dream", to model the very form and pressure of an inward vision to the millionth of a hair's breadth.' Montague invariably followed his own precept. He turned an unclouded vision on to play or player and reported what he saw and felt with an honesty that permeated every line of his scrupulous writing.

Montague also wrote leading articles and novels, and collected some of his *Manchester Guardian* theatre criticism in a volume called *Dramatic Values* (1910). But it was his day-by-day dramatic criticism that not only complimented drama in the north by the attentions of a fine mind, but also set an example to his critical colleagues throughout the country.

T. C. KEMP†

MONTAGUE, HENRY JAMES (1844–78), American actor, whose real name was Mann. He appeared in London in the 1860s, and in 1870 opened the Vaudeville with James and Thorne. In 1874 he was seen at Wallack's, New York, where his good looks and well-bred air made him immensely popular with the audience. He was at his best in contemporary comedy—*Diplomacy*, *Caste*, *The Overland Route*—and for the whole of his short career was associated with Lester Wallack. It was probably his youthful assurance and personal magnetism that made him successful, and it was said of him that people liked him for himself, and not for his acting. His early death cut short a career which might not have lived up to the brilliance of its beginnings.

MONTALAND, CÉLINE (1843–91), French actress, child of provincial actors, who was on the stage from her early years. At the age of 7 she appeared at the Comédie-Française in children's parts, and was much admired. Going from there to the Palais-Royal, she continued to attract the public in childish parts specially written for her, and after a few years in the provinces and in Italy reappeared in Paris and made her adult début in 1860 in the famous fairy-tale play, *Pied de mouton*, at the Porte-Saint-Martin. She was also seen at the Gymnase, where one of her finest parts was the mother in a dramatization of Daudet's *Jack*. She toured Europe and Russia several times, and in 1888 became a member of the Comédie-Française, remaining there until her death.

MONTANSIER, MARGUERITE (*née* BRUNET) (1730–1820), French actress-manageress. She was orphaned at an early age, and was brought up in Paris by her mother's sister, from whom she took her stage-name. Beautiful and witty, she became the toast of the town, and having broken many hearts, suddenly lost her own to a young actor, Honoré Bourdon de Neuville (1736–1812). She decided to go on the stage, and helped by powerful friends took over the management of the theatre at Rouen. She was soon directing several others, with equal success, while Neuville, who was devoted to her, acted as her business manager. While in charge of the Versailles theatre, Mlle Montansier was presented to Marie Antoinette, who had a box there which she frequented incognita with the Princesse de Lamballe. The queen was charmed by the young actress's wit and gaiety, and made a favourite of her, even inviting her to play at Court. This she did successfully, though a strong provincial accent, which she never lost, kept her off the public stage in Paris. In 1777 she built a new theatre at Versailles, demolished in 1886, where many famous actors made their first appearances, since it was used to try out aspirants to the Comédie-Française. On the outbreak of the

Revolution Mlle Montansier went to Paris, where her salon became the rendezvous of all the world. It was there that Napoleon, then an officer in the artillery, first met Talma, and laid the foundations of a friendship which lasted for many years. Accused by Fabre d'Églantine of royalist sympathies, owing to her friendship with Marie Antoinette, Mlle Montansier was arrested, but was saved from the guillotine by the fall of Robespierre. She immediately married her faithful Neuville and took up the management of the theatre she had just opened at the Palais-Royal, opposite the Bibliothèque Nationale, giving it her own name. It was closed in 1806 and became a café, where its previous owner, now retired, was a constant visitor.

MONTCHRÉTIEN, Antoine de (*c.* 1575–1621), early French Renaissance dramatist, who serves as a link between Garnier and Corneille. Son of an apothecary, he was early orphaned, and after being educated by wealthy friends was intended for the army. Instead he became a playwright. By 1600 he had written several plays on classical themes which had been given by the company at the Hôtel de Bourgogne. At the height of his success he laid siege to and successfully captured a rich widow, and took the name of Vasteville. In 1605 he had the misfortune to kill a man in a duel, and fled to Holland, and then to England. James I, to whom he had dedicated his play on Mary, Queen of Scots, *L'Écossaise*, given at the Hôtel de Bourgogne in 1603, and incidentally one of the first French plays to deal with modern history, secured his pardon, and he returned to France in 1611. He then set up a factory for the manufacture of steel cutlery, and turned his attention to political economy. In 1621 he joined the Huguenots, and was killed by royalist soldiers while taking refuge in an inn. His plays are technically weak, but contain passages of great lyric beauty, and his choruses, like those of Garnier, are particularly fine, while the note of heroism which he so often sounded is similar to that of Corneille.

MONTDORY [Guillaume Desgilberts] (1594–1651), with Bellerose the first outstanding French actor, friend and interpreter of Corneille. He is first heard of in 1610, with a provincial company under the leadership of Lenoir, and probably remained with it until about 1622. After forming a company of his own, he again joined Lenoir and went with him to Paris in 1630, where he appeared in Corneille's first play, *Mélite*. This was probably given in a converted tennis-court near the Porte-Saint-Denis. It began quietly, but was soon an outstanding success, and the company, deciding to settle permanently in Paris, took over a tennis-court in the rue Vieille-du-Temple, known as the Marais. Just before they opened, Lenoir, his wife, and several other members of the company were drafted to the Hôtel de Bourgogne by Louis XIII, probably to annoy Richelieu, who had shown his preference for Montdory as opposed to Bellerose and the King's Players at the Hôtel de Bourgogne. This left Montdory in charge of the new theatre, which soon became a formidable rival to the established players and had all the dramatists of the day, with the exception of Rotrou, working for it. Montdory was a man of great business ability, and a fine actor in the old, declamatory style, and to him goes the honour of having produced *Le Cid* (1636), in which he played the hero, Rodrigue. Another of his great roles was Herod in *Mariamne* (1636), in which he was acting before Richelieu, always a hard taskmaster, when he was stricken with paralysis of the tongue. His enforced retirement from the stage was a great blow, particularly for those authors who had in hand plays intended for his company. He had twice built up and controlled a good company in the face of much hostility, and he evidently trained and directed his actors well. Among them were the parents of Michel Baron, the first leading man of the Comédie-Française. It was said of Montdory that he was the first French actor who had never played in farce. He was also something of a poet.

MONTFLEURY. (1) [Zacharie Jacob] (*c.* 1600–67), French actor, who was in the company at the Hôtel de Bourgogne in 1639, where he was second only in importance to Bellerose, and later the companion of Floridor. He has been variously described as a nobleman, page to the Duc de Guise, and as the child of the strolling players Fleury Jacob and Colombe Venier, and thus the nephew of Marie Venier, the first French actress to be known by name. He was an enormously fat man, with a loud voice and a pompous delivery which Molière satirized in *L'Impromptu de Versailles* (1663). Montfleury had previously accused Molière before the king of having married his own daughter by Madeleine Béjart, but the accusation was not taken seriously, and Louis XIV showed how little credence he attached to it by standing godfather to Molière's first child. By his contemporaries Montfleury was considered a fine tragic actor, and was much sought after by authors. He was, however, disliked by Cyrano de Bergerac, friend of Molière, who is said to have ordered him off the stage, an incident made use of by Rostand in his play on Cyrano. In 1647 the Hôtel de Bourgogne put on a tragedy by Montfleury, *La Mort d'Asdrubal*, in which he played the lead. He married an actress, and his son, (2) Antoine (1639–85), became a lawyer, but was also a well-known and successful dramatist. His first play was a one-act farce, but he came into prominence with a reply to Molière's *Impromptu de Versailles* in which he satirized the company at the Palais-Royal. This was followed by a number of farces and comedies, often written in imitation of those of Molière, whom Montfleury hoped to surpass. But his plays, though written with much vivacity, and showing shrewd traits of wit and observation, lack permanence, and soon dropped from the repertory. He was probably induced to write most of them in order to supply the actors at the Hôtel de Bourgogne with something on the lines of Molière's successes, and a number of them have titles somewhat similar to Molière's. Montfleury's one serious play, *Trasibule* (1663), has some resemblance to *Hamlet*, but he is unlikely to have been acquainted with Shakespeare at so early a date, and probably adapted the story from a French work based on Saxo Grammaticus, one of Shakespeare's sources for *Hamlet*. Montfleury married the daughter of the actor Floridor, and two of his sisters were also on the stage. The elder, (3) FRANÇOISE (*c.* 1640–1708), married an inveterate gambler, and became an actress to support herself. As Mlle d'Ennebault she proved an asset to the company at the Hôtel de Bourgogne, playing several of Racine's young heroines. Her daughter Anne married the actor Desmares, brother of Mlle Champmeslé. Montfleury's younger sister, (4) LOUISE (1649–1709), married a provincial actor who had been in the provinces with Dorimond, and went with him in 1670 to the Théâtre du Marais. With Mlle d'Ennebault they were both members of the newly formed Comédie-Française, the husband, a poor actor, retiring almost immediately, while the wife remained until the reorganization in 1685.

MONTHERLANT, HENRI DE (1896–), French novelist and dramatist, and one of the great classical stylists of the modern French theatre in the tradition of Corneille and Racine. His first play, *L'Exil*, was written in 1914 but was never produced in full (it was published in 1929, and a scene from it was performed in 1934). *Pasiphaé*, an episode from a longer, abandoned work entitled *Les Crétois*, was however produced in 1938, but Montherlant's considerable reputation was based primarily on his novels until he turned seriously to the theatre after the success of *La Reine Morte*, produced at the Comédie-Française in 1942. Although many of his plays have a religious context, Montherlant, unlike Claudel, is not really a Catholic writer: rather, his plays are about Catholics and Catholic problems, and he prefers to describe himself as a psychological dramatist. His plays contain very little external action, make ample use of the classical tirade, unfold in a sonorous prose which makes little concession to realism, and are concerned with the conflicts within the human soul: the struggle between love and religion (*Le Maître de Santiago*, 1948), sexual obsession (*Celles qu'on prend dans ses bras*, 1950), or spiritual agony (*La Ville dont le Prince est un Enfant*, 1951, unperformed). Montherlant is one of the few living dramatists whose works have been regularly performed by the Comédie-Française, and three of his most recent plays have been given their first performances at this theatre: *Port Royal* (1954), *Brocéliande* (1956), and *Le Cardinal d'Espagne* (1960). His other plays include *Fils de Personne* (1943), *Demain il fera jour* (1949), *Malatesta* (1950), and *Don Juan* (1958). The first of Montherlant's plays to be produced in England was *La Reine Morte* as *Queen After Death* (Dundee Repertory Theatre, 1952); but although Donald Wolfit produced both *Le Maître de Santiago* (as *The Master of Santiago*) and *Malatesta* at the Lyric Theatre, Hammersmith, in 1957, and *Queen After Death* was revived in 1961, the plays have had little success in English.

T. C. C. MILNE

MONTMÉNIL, see LE SAGE (2).

MOOCK, ARMANDO, see SOUTH AMERICA, 1.

MOODY, WILLIAM VAUGHN (1869–1910), American dramatist, whose work marks a great step forward in the development of the native American playwright. Poet, scholar, and educationist, Moody had been for many years actively engaged in teaching when he decided that his real vocation lay in the theatre. His first plays, in verse, were not produced, but in 1906 *The Great Divide*, originally known as *The Sabine Woman*, was given by Margaret Anglin and Henry Miller with great success. It was seen in London in 1909. It was followed by *The Faith Healer* (1909), a somewhat better play which lacked the popular appeal of *The Great Divide*, but had a modified success, and was later used as the basis for a film. Both these plays are written in a dignified and poetic style, and mark the entrance into the American scene of the serious social dramatist, still somewhat crude and melodramatic, but moving in the right direction, away from the importations of French farce and the revamping of sentimental novelettes. Moody's early death was a great loss to the American stage, and it was unfortunate that none of his long poetic plays was produced during his lifetime.

MOORE, EDWARD (1712–57), English dramatist, author of two plays in the prevailing sentimental mode, of which the first, *The Foundling* (1747), bridges the gap, says Nicoll in his *Eighteenth Century Drama*, between the works of Cibber and Steele and those of Cumberland and Mrs. Inchbald. Moore's second important play—his *Gil Blas*, given at Drury Lane in 1751, was merely a dramatization of incidents from Le Sage's book—was *The Gamester* (1753), partly written by Garrick, who put it on at Drury Lane. It is a further essay in the vein of domestic tragedy exploited earlier by Lillo in *The London Merchant*, and though not at first successful, it proved so in revival and was translated into French, having a marked influence on the *tragédie bourgeoise*.

MOORE, GEORGE (1852–1933), the famous novelist, was one of the original sponsors of the Irish Literary Theatre, and materially assisted its initial development. Born in Ireland, he spent many years in London and Paris, and in Paris particularly had learnt something of the theatre. When, early in 1899, plans were started in London for the production of the first two plays to be given by the Irish Literary Theatre—*The Countess Cathleen* and *The*

Heather Field—Moore helped to recruit the players and directed the rehearsals. He subsequently returned to Ireland for some years. In 1900 his own play, *The Bending of the Bough*, was performed by the Irish Literary Theatre (it was based on a play by Edward Martyn, another collaborator in the Movement), and considered rather dull by the critics. Moore then collaborated with Yeats in *Diarmuid and Grania*, which was produced in 1901—the first play of the movement to be taken directly from Irish legend. A distinguished cast, headed by Frank Benson, was imported to act in it, and Elgar wrote the incidental music. The notices were unfavourable and the reception lukewarm, and with the winding up of the Irish Literary Theatre and the arrival of the Fay brothers with a permanent company of Irish actors, Moore withdrew from the scene.

MOORE, JOSEPH (*fl.* first half of seventeenth century), an English actor who is first mentioned in 1611 as one of the chief men in the newly formed Lady Elizabeth's Company. After appearing at Court, and in several London playhouses, Moore lost several of his best men and took to the provinces, where he remained from 1615 to 1622. In 1617 he played before James I on his journey to Scotland, probably at some town in his usual circuit, and in 1622 he returned to the Cockpit in charge of a second Lady Elizabeth's Company—distinct from the previous company which had toured under that name, and certainly more prosperous—until their break-up during the plague in 1625. Moore then returned to the provinces, and was still acting in 1640.

MOORE, MARY (1862–1931), see WYNDHAM (2).

MORAL INTERLUDE, a short pedagogic drama of the sixteenth century, which has much of the character of a Morality play, but with more humour. Outstanding English examples are *Hickscorner*, produced anonymously in about 1513, and R. Wever's *Lusty Juventus* (*c.* 1550) (see also ENGLAND, 2).

MORALITY PLAY, a late medieval form of drama which aimed at instruction and moral teaching. Its characters are abstractions of vice and virtue, and the only trace of humour is provided by the Devil and the Old Vice, or buffoon. Played on a fixed stage, it was somewhat static and by modern standards dull. It has been said of Morality plays that 'their very name is like a yawn'. The only one to survive in performance is *Everyman*, originally written in Dutch in about 1495. This has been successfully given in English on the modern stage, and in German as part of the Salzburg Festival in an open-air production by Reinhardt. Historically the Morality play is important and marks a big step forward in the secularization of the vernacular drama all over Europe. One of the best English examples is Skelton's *Magnyfycence*, the only play by this great satirist which has survived (see also ENGLAND, 2).

MORATÍN, see FERNÁNDEZ DE MORATÍN.

MORATORIA, OROSMÁN (1859–98), see SOUTH AMERICA, 1.

MORDVINOV, NIKOLAI DMITRIEVICH (1901–1966), Soviet actor, who joined an amateur group while in the Red Army in 1918, and gave proof of great talent. In 1925 he became a professional actor, and was first at the Zavadsky Theatre, and, from 1936 to 1940, at the Gorky State Theatre in Rostov. Here his outstanding role was Petruchio in *The Taming of the Shrew*. In 1940 he went with a group of leading actors to the Mossoviet, where he greatly influenced the acting, especially of heroic roles. Among the parts he played were Ognev in Korneichuk's *Front*, Petrov in Sofronov's *In One Town*, Arbenin in Lermontov's *Masquerade*, Othello, and, in 1958, Lear. He also gave an outstandingly comic performance as the Cavaliere di Ripafratta in Goldoni's *La Locandiera*. BEATRICE KING

MOREAU LE JEUNE (1741–1814), see COSTUME, 7.

MOREHOUSE, WARD (1898–), American dramatic critic, born in Savannah, Georgia. While a student at North Georgia College he joined a professional Shakespeare reader on a southern tour. Afterwards he served as a reporter on *The Atlanta Journal*, and in 1919 went to New York. Morehouse could be recommended for his sheer readability, but that would be an injustice to his many other talents. He is an expert theatrical journalist and historian and the green-room interviewer *par excellence*. His love of the theatre and his interpretation of that love are in everything he writes about it. Long before he was appointed dramatic critic of *The New York Sun*, his column for that paper, 'Broadway After Dark', and his lively book of memoirs concerning the American theatre of the 1920s and 1930s, *Forty-Five Minutes After Eight*, revealed him as a delightful raconteur who caught with admirable cunning the tempo and rhythm of the Great White Way. Since the demise of *The New York Sun* he has written for the Newhouse syndicate, and his first-night reviews appear in papers throughout the United States. That generous understanding of actors and actresses, of directors and producers, and even of press-agents, which one finds in his reporting, never binds him when he takes up the critical pen, but if talent flashes for a moment in some small 'bit' role he will see it and welcome it with encouraging praise. Like most critics he has on occasion succumbed to the wiles of the theatre and turned dramatist, and like most of them with indifferent results. Among his plays are *Gentlemen of the Press* (1928) and *Miss Quis* (1937). He has also written a biography of George M. Cohan.

THOMAS QUINN CURTISS

MORETO Y CABAÑA, Agustin (1618–69), Spanish dramatist. He had not the force of his predecessors, Lope de Vega and Calderón, nor even of his contemporary Rojas, but his poetry is delicate and his wit elegant and subtle. He excelled in stagecraft, especially in the setting of plots with relevant contemporary details. His best plays are *El lindo Don Diego* and *El desdén con el desdén* (adapted by Molière in *La Princesse d'Élide*). In this charming piece the Countess Diana treats all her suitors with coldness but, piqued by the apparent indifference of the Count of Urgel, falls in love with him and finally marries him. A number of Moreto's plays were really re-writings of older themes from Lope, Tirso, and others, to suit the taste of the time, but they are none the less excellent, and in most cases exceed their originals in dramatic force and clarity. He excelled in the *comedia de figurón*, in which the chief character is a caricature of a particular trait in human nature rather than a portrait, while his inventive and engaging *graciosos* are particularly noteworthy.

MORGAN, Charles Langbridge (1894–1958), English novelist and essayist, who succeeded A. B. Walkley as dramatic critic of *The Times* in 1926, a position which he held until 1939, writing with discernment and distinction of literary style. His first play, *The Flashing Stream*, in which Margaret Rawlings made a great success, was produced in 1938 at the Lyric Theatre, where it ran for six months. It has for its theme mental absolutism—'the power to assimilate and have repose in an idea, as one of the conditions precedent to singleness of mind'. The writing is marked by the same fastidious care that distinguishes all this author's work, the characters are drawn with nervous vitality, and in the theatre the piece displayed a striking command of stage technique. A second play, *The River Line*, was first seen at the Edinburgh Festival in 1952, and later in London. It was followed by *The Burning Glass* in 1954. Morgan, whose work was much admired in France, was elected to the French Academy, and in 1949 was made an Officer of the Legion of Honour. He was the husband of the novelist Hilda Vaughan.

T. C. KEMP†, *rev.*

MÓRICZ, Zsigmond (1879–1942), Hungarian dramatist, author of a number of problem plays in which the Hungarian peasants are no longer idealized, as in Szigligeti's comedies, but sharply and realistically drawn.

MORLEY, Henry (1822–94), Professor of Literature at University College, London, whose varied work included a number of dramatic criticisms published in 1891 as *The Journal of a London Playgoer from 1851 to 1866*. Morley was also a member of the committee of a School of Dramatic Art opened with a view to raising the standard of acting and drama. He was much concerned with the relations between literature and the stage. The vogue for plays lifted entire from the French caused him much concern, and he pointed out the greater advantage of the English dramatists borrowing the Frenchmen's tools and using them to make their own plays.

T. C. KEMP†

MORLEY, Robert (1908–), English actor and dramatist, who made his first appearance on the stage in 1928, and was in Fagan's repertory company at Oxford. He was also a member of the Cambridge Festival Theatre under Norman Marshall. His first outstanding success was as Oscar Wilde at the Gate Theatre in 1936, and he was also remarkable as Alexandre Dumas in a short-lived play, *The Great Romancer*, a year later. Among his later successes have been Sheridan Whiteside in *The Man Who Came to Dinner* (1941), the Prince Regent in *The First Gentleman* (1945), Arnold Holt in his own play *Edward My Son* (1947) which he played in England, America, and Australia, Philip in *The Little Hut* (1950), and Hippo in *Hippo Dancing* (1954), which he adapted himself from André Roussin's play. In 1956 he made his first appearance in a musical play, as Panisse in *Fanny*, and in 1960 he played the Japanese Mr. Asano in *A Majority of One*. He is an uneven actor, who at his best is extremely good, and he is limited by his physical appearance—he is a burly man with a smooth bald head—to a somewhat narrow range of parts. He is, however, widely and deservedly popular, and brings a technical excellence and discrimination to all his parts, whether serious or comic. He was created C.B.E. in the New Year's Honours List in 1957 for services to the stage. He has also had a successful film career.

MORMON THEATRE ON THE AMERICAN FRONTIER. When the Mormons left New York and settled in Illinois, they had leisure to occupy themselves with education and cultural activities, in which from the beginning amateur acting played a large part. The first productions were given, with the encouragement of Joseph Smith, in the 'Fun House' in Nauvoo. Some time later George Adams, a Mormon missionary in Philadelphia, appeared on the stage there to earn money with which to pay for the hire of a hall. He was seen as Richmond to the Richard III of his brother-in-law Thomas A. Lyne, a professional actor who was converted and went to Nauvoo, where, in the Masonic Hall, he produced a number of plays, among them *Pizarro*, in which, in May and June 1844, Brigham Young played the High Priest. In the same year the Mormons began their move to Salt Lake City, and during their two-year march entertained themselves with sessions round the camp fires of singing, reciting, dancing, and brass-band contests. Once settled, they turned to theatre-building, and in 1848 erected the first Bowery for religious services and entertainments. The first play to be given there was *The Triumph of Innocence*. This temporary shelter was replaced in 1850 by a more permanent second Bowery, in which plays were acted during the winter, among them *Robert Macaire* and *The Stranger*. In Jan. 1853 the Social Hall—an all-purposes building for plays, balls, concerts, and banquets—opened, the first theatrical bill consisting of *Don Caesar de Bazan* and *The Irish Lion*. The theatre flourished in this building, where husbands and wives were encouraged to act together and children were admitted to the auditorium, until in 1859 Henry Bowring built a new playhouse, the first in the territory to bear the name Theatre, and organized the Mechanics' Dramatic Association, which put on such plays as *Luke the Labourer*, *The Honeymoon*, *The Gamester*, *Othello*, and a number of one-act farces. Bowring's success led to the erection of the large and beautiful Salt Lake Theatre, which opened on 6 Mar. 1862. It was copied from Drury Lane. Over the entrance to the green-room was placed a large bust of Shakespeare which the Mormons had carried with them in all their travels. It was in this theatre, demolished in 1928, that Brigham Young's daughters acted. A replica of it has been erected on the campus of the University of Utah, and this is used, as are several other halls, by local and visiting companies (see also PIONEER THEATRE).

MOROSCO THEATRE, NEW YORK, on 45th Street west of Broadway. It was built by the Shubert brothers, and named in honour of Oliver Morosco, a well-known West Coast producer, who was responsible for the initial attraction, *Canary Cottage*, which opened on 5 Feb. 1917. Important productions at this theatre were O'Neill's *Beyond the Horizon* and Bennett's *Sacred and Profane Love*, while in 1920 *The Bat* had a record run with 867 performances and set the fashion for mystery thrillers. A long series of negligible plays was followed by *The Firebrand*, a Renaissance romance in which Joseph Schildkraut scored a personal triumph. The Pulitzer Prize-winner *Craig's Wife* was seen here with Chrystal Herne and Josephine Hull, and had 289 performances, and Katharine Cornell was successful with *The Letter*. The Theatre Guild production of *Call It a Day* ran for six months, and an interesting experiment was Wilder's revision of *A Doll's House* with Ruth Gordon and Paul Lukas. Two English plays which found favour were *Bachelor Born* (done in London as *Housemaster*) and *Spring Meeting*, in which Jean Cadell returned to Broadway with Gladys Cooper and A. E. Matthews. Later successes at this theatre have been *Skylark*, *Old Acquaintance*, *Blithe Spirit*, and *The Voice of the Turtle*. Two plays which won the Pulitzer Prize and Drama Critics' Circle award were Miller's *Death of a Salesman* (1949; see No. 106) and Tennessee Williams's *Cat on a Hot Tin Roof* (1955). A later success was Gore Vidal's comedy on American political life, *The Best Man* (1960). GEORGE FREEDLEY†

MOROZOV, MIKHAIL NIKOLAEVICH (1897–1952), Russian Shakespearian scholar and for many years editor of the English-language newspaper *News*. He encouraged the production of Shakespeare's plays all over the U.S.S.R., and early in his career translated *All's Well That Ends Well* and *The Merry Wives of Windsor* (with Samuel Marshak). He also wrote a short book entitled *Shakespeare on the Soviet Stage*, with an introduction by Dover Wilson, and was a contributor to *Shakespeare Survey*.

MORRIS [MORRISON], CLARA (1846–1925), American actress, who was on the stage as a child, and after touring the provinces appeared at Daly's first Fifth Avenue Theatre, making an immense impression as Cora the Creole in his *Article 47*. She was seen in a large range of parts, and in spite of a strong accent and an extravagant, unrestrained manner was popular both in New York and on tour. Though not a good actress, she had an extraordinary power of moving an audience, and could always be relied on to fill the theatre whenever she appeared. Her emotional sweep and range was best seen in such parts as Camille, but she also essayed Lady Macbeth, Julia in *The Hunchback*, and a number of modern heroines. She appeared for some years under the management of Palmer, but in 1885 was compelled by ill health to retire from the stage, spending her time in the writing of short stories and novels. In 1904 she appeared once more in the theatre, playing in an all-star revival of *The Two Orphans*, and subsequently went into vaudeville.

MORRIS. (1) OWEN (*fl.* late 18th cent.), actor who was with the American Company from 1759 to 1790. He was apparently a good low comedian, at his best in the portrayal of humorous old men. Among his parts were Sir Oliver Surface, Dogberry, and Polonius, all of which he played for the first time in New York. His first wife, also an actress, who played Ophelia in the first New York production of *Hamlet*, was drowned in a ferry accident in New York in 1767. Morris had married again by 1773, and his new wife, who is only known as (2) MRS. OWEN MORRIS (1753–1826), figures in the playbills with him, becoming one of the outstanding actresses of the American Company. She played Charlotte in *The Contrast*, the first American comedy, and was also seen as Lady Teazle, Ophelia, and Beatrice. For some years she was the toast of New York, which she left after the season of 1789, with her husband, to join Wignell's new company at the Chestnut Street Theatre, Philadelphia. Here she was soon eclipsed by the lovely Mrs. Merry (see BRUNTON, 2), and on returning to New York with the company for a season in 1797 she was thought little of. She probably continued to act too long, and had in her heyday relied too much on her fine appearance and high spirits. She remained in Philadelphia until 1810, during which time her husband is believed to have died, and Odell (*Annals of the New York Stage*) thinks she may have been the Mrs. Morris who appeared at the Commonwealth Theatre in New York as late as 1815.

MORRIS (MORRICE) DANCE, an English dance popular at all village festivals. Different authorities derive it either from the Germanic sword-dance, or from the Morisco, or Moorish dance, the latter on account of the blackened faces of the dancers or their companions. Chambers, however, sees in this custom a relic of the old pagan rite of smearing the face with ash from the sacrificial fire. In the same way the fool who accompanies the dancers, with his bladder and cow's tail, would be a survival of the primitive worshipper in sacrificial costume. The dancers, usually six in number, wear bells on their legs, and carry handkerchiefs or short staves in their hands. The music is traditionally supplied by a pipe and tabor, or by bagpipes, though in recent times a fiddle has been used. With the dancers went the fool, the hobby-horse, and, at Maytime, a Jack-in-the-Green; sometimes a dragon and a Maid Marian. From its popularity at Maytime the Morris came to be associated with Robin Hood and his Merry Men. It was also an essential part of the mumming play. It can be traced all over England and Scotland, and reached the height of its popularity under Henry VIII, when it appeared at Court. Among the people it still survives, notably at Bampton in Oxfordshire, and in the early twentieth century it had a fostered revival under the auspices of the English Folk Dance Society. The Morris dance can be either stationary or processional, and both forms can be seen in the streets of Oxford on May morning.

MORTON, CHARLES (1819–1904), known as 'the father of the halls', opened the Canterbury, the first regular music-hall, in 1852, and the Oxford in 1861, and was called in at various times to retrieve the fortunes of the Tivoli, the London Pavilion, and other halls, which he did most successfully. He had a wonderful flair for picking his performers, and hardly ever had a failure. Although he was the favourite target of the puritan element at that time, Chevalier calls him, in his *Before I Forget*, 'a gentleman of experience and refinement', and says that under him the Pavilion came nearer the ideal variety theatre than any other in London. Although Morton appreciated and employed purveyors of hearty vulgarity, he was opposed to innuendo and salacity, and demanded a high standard of all his entertainers.

MORTON. (1) THOMAS (*c.* 1764–1838), English dramatist, famous for having created the character of Mrs. Grundy, who does not appear, but is frequently referred to, in his *Speed the Plough* (1800), as the embodiment of British respectability. The play is otherwise unimportant, being a sentimental comedy of a type popular at the time. Morton wrote several others in the same vein—*The Way to Get Married* (1796), *A Cure for the Heart-Ache* (1797), and *Secrets Worth Knowing* (1800). He was also the author of two spectacular melodramas, of an amusing comedy, *The School of Reform* (1805), frequently revived up to 1883, and of an historical play with music in which Macready played the hero, Henri IV. His *Children in the Wood* (1793) passed into the repertory of the Juvenile Drama. His son, (2) JOHN MADDISON (1811–91), was a prolific writer of farces, mainly taken from the French, which helped to build up the reputation of such comedians as Buckstone, Wright, Harley, the Keeleys, and others. One of the most popular was *Lend Me Five Shillings* (1846), while he wrote, first as *The Double-Bedded Room* and then as *Box and Cox* (1847), the farce on which Burnand and Sullivan based their musical farce, *Cox and Box* (1867).

MOSCOW ART THEATRE. This famous theatre, now dedicated to Maxim Gorky, is the best known of all Russian theatrical organizations outside Russia. It was founded in 1898 by Stanislavsky and Nemirovich-Danchenko, and its name is indissolubly linked with that of Chekhov, whose plays were first given there with success. Its original company was drawn partly from the amateur actors of the Society for Art and Literature, and partly from the graduates of the dramatic class of the Philharmonic Society, and it was a co-operative venture, issuing shares to its members. It was also supported financially by rich patrons of the bourgeois intelligentsia, among whom the most active was Sava Morozov.

The theatre opened with *Tsar Feodor Ivanovich* before an audience which was almost equally hostile and appreciative and much intrigued by the new 'naturalistic' style of acting. The seal was set on the success of the new enterprise when it gave, as its fifth production, Chekhov's *The Seagull*, which had previously been given without success at the Alexandrinsky Theatre. This was followed by *Uncle Vanya*, *Three Sisters* (see No. 95), and *The Cherry Orchard*. Stanislavsky's system of dramatic training, which is described in his books and has achieved world-wide fame as the Method, scored a signal triumph, and the Moscow Art Theatre, which in longevity ranks next to the Moscow Maly, soon had an unassailable reputation. It has indeed been a mirror of the times, and the ferment of society that led to the abortive Revolution of 1905 was reflected in its production of Gorky's great play of the underworld, *The Lower Depths*. His *Children of the Sun* was in the bill at the Moscow Art Theatre when the Revolution actually took place. The repertory in pre-Revolutionary days included also a number of European classics, but the only Shakespearian play to be produced at this time was *Julius Caesar*.

The failure of the 1905 Revolution produced a period of uncertainty and unrest, which was reflected by the Moscow Art Theatre's productions of mystic, pacifist, or merely superficial plays. The October Revolution caught the directors unaware, as Stanislavsky himself admitted, and had it not been for the support of Lenin—who said: 'If there is a theatre from the past which must be saved and preserved at whatever cost, it is of course the Moscow Art Theatre'—and the tolerance and foresight of Lunacharsky, this great institution might have been swept away, a loss not only to the Soviet theatre, but to those of Europe and America. Given time to find its feet in the new world, with which it was fundamentally in sympathy, though as yet a little disorientated, the Moscow Art Theatre company left Russia in 1922 for a long tour of Europe and America, fêted and applauded wherever it went. Back in Moscow in 1924 it tentatively tried out a Soviet play, *Pugachov* (1925), but with little success; *The Last of the Turbins*, which followed in 1926, was a step in the right direction, and the theatre finally resumed its leadership of the Russian stage with a fine production of *Armoured Train 14–69* (see No. 99). A play by Gorky, *Yegor Bulichev*, followed in 1934. After that the Moscow Art Theatre staged a number of interesting new plays, including *Platon Krechet* (1937), *Kremlin Chimes* (1942), *The Russian People*, and *Depth Prospecting* (both 1943). It continued its work on the classics, approaching and interpreting them in the spirit of realism combined with the most brilliant theatrical art. Some of the actors who appeared in the first productions—notably Ivan Moskvin, Vasili Kachalov, and Olga Knipper-Chekhova (the widow of Chekhov and a brilliant interpreter of his plays)—passed the rest of their careers with the company, while a gifted younger generation carried on the traditions of the theatre after their deaths.

The theatre, evacuated in 1941, returned two years later to Moscow and established a training institute in preparation for post-war development. The years that followed were difficult ones, as the theatre lost successively Nemirovich-Danchenko, Khmelev, Moskvin, Kachalov, and the designers Williams and Dmitrov. But they were eventually replaced from the ranks of the theatre's own pupils, and by 1956 the Moscow Art Theatre was once again pre-eminent. In 1958 and 1963 it paid visits to London, where productions of *The Cherry Orchard*, *Uncle Vanya*, and *Three Sisters* were immensely successful.

From the studios established for training and experiment by the Moscow Art Theatre a number of important individual groups have developed (see REALISTIC and VAKHTANGOV THEATRES). The First Studio was started in 1913 under the leadership of L. A. Sulerzhitsky (1872–1916), who worked on Stanislavsky's method. His most successful production was an adaptation of *The Cricket on the Hearth*. In 1924 the First Studio was reconstituted as the Moscow Art Theatre II, under the direction of Michael Chekhov, who opened with a production of *Hamlet* in which he himself played the title-role. For some years after the Revolution this theatre held aloof from Soviet Realism. Its productions, brilliant in form, masterly in technique, still remained foreign to the new life. The position improved after the departure of Michael Chekhov, who emigrated in 1927, and a number of classic and modern plays were produced with a high degree of realism and artistic excellence.

MOSCOW STATE JEWISH THEATRE, known in Yiddish as Melucha and in Russian as Goset. This was founded as the Jewish Theatre Studio in Leningrad in 1919 by Alexander Granovsky for the production of plays in Yiddish. After a visit to Vitebsk, it went to Moscow, where it was at first known as the Jewish Chamber (Kamerny) Theatre. Its first performance was given in the Chagall Hall, which seated only ninety people, and was devoted to short comedy sketches by Sholom Aleichem. The company became so popular that in 1922 it was able to move to the Romanov Hall, seating 500. It later had a theatre seating 766. In 1928 a European tour was undertaken, during which Granovsky resigned his directorship and was succeeded by his assistant and chief actor, Mikhoels, who had been one of the original members. In 1941 the theatre was evacuated to Tashkent, returning to Moscow in 1943. One of its finest productions was *King Lear* in 1935, directed by Radlov, with scenery by Tishler, in which Mikhoels was outstanding in the name-part. Post-war conditions, and the death of some of the leading actors (Mikhoels died in 1948), caused the company to be disbanded, but it was re-formed in 1962 under Vladimir Shvartser, and a production of Aleichem's *Tevye the Milkman* was seen in Moscow in Mar. 1963 after a tour of eleven cities in different republics. The company has as yet no permanent home, and works mainly on tour.

MOSES, MONTROSE JONAS (1878–1934), an American dramatic critic and editor of a number of anthologies of drama, both American and European. His works reflect the breadth of his interests and his scholarly knowledge of the history of the stage. They include a survey of famous actor-families in America published in 1906, a study of Ibsen, a life of the actor Edwin Forrest, and *The American Dramatist* (3rd ed., 1925), the last an interesting contribution to the history of the theatre in the United States. Moses also contributed a number of articles on the theatre to periodicals and encyclopaedias. In 1911 he married the daughter of the American dramatist, James A. Herne. She died in 1921, following the birth of a son.

MOSKVIN, IVAN MIKHAILOVICH (1874–1946), outstanding Russian actor, who, after the deaths of Stanislavsky and Nemirovich-Danchenko, became director of the Moscow Art Theatre. He studied for the stage under Nemirovich-Danchenko in the Moscow Philharmonic Society, which he joined in 1893, and then worked for two years in provincial theatres. He was a member of the Moscow Art Theatre from its foundation, and came immediately to the fore, playing the lead in its first production. Among his later roles were Luka in *The Lower Depths*, Nozdrev in *Dead Souls*, and Epihodov in *The Cherry Orchard*. He again appeared in this last play in the 1938 revival, together with others of the original cast, and had one of the leading roles in the play about Lenin, *Kremlin Chimes* (1942). Among his later roles were the merchant Pribitkov in Ostrovsky's *The Last Sacrifice*, and Belobrov in Kron's *Officer of the Fleet*.

MOSS, SIR EDWARD (1852–1912), an English showman who began life among booths and circuses, built 'Empires' in Edinburgh and elsewhere, and went to London in 1900, having joined forces with Stoll in Moss Empires Ltd. He built the Hippodrome and, having dissolved his partnership with Stoll, ran his own circuit. He was knighted for his services to the entertainment industry.

MOSSOP, HENRY (1729–74), Irish actor, who, despite much ability and good sense, so wrecked his life by his jealousy of Garrick that he finally died in poverty in a Chelsea garret, and was only saved from a pauper's funeral by the intervention of a condescending uncle. Mossop went to Drury Lane from Ireland, and proved himself good in tragedy, being at first an excellent ally to Garrick in his rivalry with Barry. He took over the parts of Quin, and was seen as Richard III, Zanga, Horatio to Garrick's Lothario, and Theseus to Mrs. Pritchard's Phaedra. He was also good as Macbeth, Othello, Wolsey, and Orestes. A foolish insistence on playing young-lover parts, to which he was quite unsuited, led to some failure and ridicule, and the hot-tempered actor visited his resentment on Garrick. He then left London and went back to Ireland, opening the Smock Alley Theatre in Dublin in 1761 in opposition to Barry and Woodward at the Crow Street Theatre. He was soon plunged into financial difficulties, which he aggravated by gambling and general dissipation, and at last, ruined in pocket and health, he crept back to London. Too proud to appeal to Garrick, and impatient of advice or correction, he was gradually deserted by all his friends and died of starvation.

MOSSOVIET THEATRE, Moscow. This theatre, which since 1940 has been under the direction of Yuri Zavadsky, was founded in 1923 as the Moscow Trades Unions' Theatre with the object of encouraging young playwrights to tackle Soviet and political themes. It specialized in producing topical plays to celebrate Soviet or other revolutionary anniversaries, and its earliest and best dramatist was Bill-Belotserkovsky, whose *Hurricane* (or *Storm*) was produced there in 1926. It lapsed somewhat from its high standards in later years, dabbling in formalism and realism, but after it had been reconstructed as the Theatre of the Moscow Soviet (or Council) it seemed to mature and become more theatrical in the best sense, and less a living newspaper. During the Second World War the theatre was evacuated. It returned to Moscow with a number of interesting productions to its credit, and a company strengthened by the inclusion of some experienced actors from elsewhere and some promising youngsters. In the same year a Mossoviet studio under Zavadsky was opened for the training of young pupils, the course to last three years. For some time the theatre suffered, like many others, from a dearth of good new plays, but in 1948 Surov's *The Insult* and Shteyn's *Law of Honour* were successful, as was Surov's *Dawn over Moscow* the following year. A revised version of *Storm*, directed by Zavadsky in 1951, showed a great advance, while the same producer's *Merry Wives of Windsor* in 1957 showed him at the height of his powers. It was awarded the Lenin Prize, as was his revival of Lermontov's *Masquerade* in 1965, with Khachaturian's music and décor and costumes by Boris Volkov. It was generally agreed at the time that the theatre had, with this successful production of Shakespeare's comedy, established its reputation, which was further enhanced in 1958 by a production of *King Lear* with Mordvinov in the title-role. The theatre continues to produce new Soviet plays also, among them *Dangerous Profession* (1960) by Solovyev, *In Summer the Sky is High* (1961) by Virta, and *Leningrad Prospect* (1962) by Shtock.

MOTION, a name given in the sixteenth and seventeenth centuries to the puppet-plays of the itinerant showmen. The earliest dealt with biblical subjects, and Shakespeare refers in *The Winter's Tale* to 'a motion of the Prodigal Son'. Later the range of subjects was extended, and episodes were used from medieval romance, mythology, and contemporary history.

MOULIN-ROUGE, PARIS, a well-known dance-hall which opened on 5 Oct. 1889, including in its boundary a large garden used for dancing and entertainment in the summer. A feature of the Moulin-Rouge has always been its cabaret show, and it was there that the can-can made its first appearance, the dancers in 1893 being Grille d'Égout, la Goulue, la Môme Fromage, and Nini-patte-en-l'air. Mistinguett was for some years part-proprietor of the Moulin-Rouge and frequently appeared there, as did most of the stars of variety and music-hall.

For the Moulin-Rouge, New York, see NEW YORK THEATRE, 2.

MOUNET. (1) JEAN SULLY (1841–1916), known as Mounet-Sully, a famous French actor who, after studying under Bressant at the Conservatoire, made his début at the Comédie-Française in 1872 as Oreste in *Andromaque*. His fine physique, beautifully modulated voice, and sombre, penetrating gaze, added to fiery, impetuous acting and great originality, soon brought him into prominence. His career was one of unclouded success, and he appeared in all the great tragic roles of the French classical repertory. He was also outstanding in the plays of Victor Hugo when they were finally given at the Comédie-Française. His younger brother, (2) PAUL (1847–1922), was trained as a doctor, but deserted his profession for the stage. He appeared at the Odéon, mainly in tragic roles, and went to the Comédie-Française in 1889, where, though not as great an actor as his brother, he was an important member of the company.

MOUNTFORT. (1) WILLIAM (1664–92), English actor and author of several comedies, including a harlequinade in the Italian manner, *The Life and Death of Dr. Faustus.* He specialized in 'fine gentleman' parts, where the dramatist's witty lines seemed to come spontaneously from his lips. He was an excellent Sparkish in *The Country Wife* and created the part of Sir Courtly Nice in Crowne's play of that name. He was brutally murdered at the instigation of a certain Captain Hill, who had been annoying Mrs. Bracegirdle and suspected Mountfort of being a successful rival in her affections. His early death was a great loss to the stage. Six years previously he had married a young actress, (2) SUSANNA PERCIVAL (1667–1703). Herself the daughter of an actor, she had been on the stage since she was a child. She was equally good in broad comedy or subtle satire, and her playing of Melantha, in Dryden's *Marriage à la Mode*, as described by Colley Cibber, must have been superb. She was a natural mimic, and in spite of her beauty was sufficiently free from vanity to don grotesque clothes or make-up when the part called for it. In her younger days she was much admired in male attire, and was persuaded to play Bayes in Buckingham's *The Rehearsal*, which she did 'with true coxcombly spirit!' Her second husband was the actor John Baptista Verbruggen, who died in 1708.

MOUNT VERNON GARDEN THEATRE, NEW YORK, a playhouse in a summer resort opened in 1800 by one Corre. At first it gave open-air performances three times a week, with actors from the winter stock companies, mainly of light comedy, interspersed with concerts, fireworks, al fresco entertainments, and the Placides in a tight-rope-walking exhibition. By 1802 it had reached the stage of giving good five-act comedies with practically the whole of the Park Theatre company, but this ambitious achievement led to its downfall, as the following summer the actors went to Albany, and the Mount Vernon Garden Theatre was closed.

MOWATT, ANNA CORA (*née* OGDEN) (1819–70), American author and actress, mainly remembered for her social comedy, *Fashion* (1845), which usually ranks as the best, if not the first, of the early satiric treatments of American life. It was first produced at the Park Theatre, under Simpson, and was successfully revived in 1924. Mrs. Mowatt, who had already been giving public readings, was encouraged by its reception to become an actress, which she did very successfully, making her début as Pauline in *The Lady of Lyons* in 1845. She had a season at Niblo's, and then formed her own company, with E. L. Davenport as her leading man, being seen with him in London in 1848–50. She made her last appearance at Niblo's in 1854, shortly after the appearance of her *Autobiography*, and lived in retirement with her second husband, a Mr. Ritchie, dying in London. She wrote other plays, as well as novels, short stories, and magazine articles, but *Fashion* is the only one that has survived in more than name. Quinn, in his *History of the American Drama*, says of her:

> Real as her contribution to our drama was, her influence upon our theatre was probably even greater. . . . She proved triumphantly that an American gentlewoman could succeed in it without the alteration of her own standard of life. She took into the profession her high heart, her utter refinement, her keen sense of social values, and her infinite capacity for effort, and her effect was a real and great one.

MULTIPLE SETTING, a term applied to the stage décor of the medieval play (known in France as *décor simultané* and in Germany as *Standort-* or *Simultanbühne*). This was an inheritance from the liturgical drama, with its numerous 'mansions' or 'houses' disposed about the church, thus enabling the actors to pass from one place to another without any break in the action, the spectators agreeing to ignore the 'houses' not in use. When the medieval play first moved from the church, the 'mansions' were disposed on three sides of an unlocalized *platea* or acting space, but by the sixteenth century, at any rate in France, they are found in a straight line, or on a very slight curve (see No. 15). In England the different scenes of a Mystery cycle were on perambulating pageants, and the multiple setting was not needed. It continued in France, and possibly in Germany, for a long time, and was still in use at the Hôtel de Bourgogne in Paris in the early seventeenth century. It is even possible that Corneille's early plays, done at the Marais, were staged in a multiple setting, which was finally routed by the development of the 'machine' play. The set scenes of the Renaissance stage in Italy were single composite backgrounds, and not multiple settings in the original sense, though the unlocalized acting space in front of the tragic or comic houses corresponds to the medieval *platea* (see Nos. 72, 73). The Elizabethan public stage, such as the Globe, did not employ the multiple setting, though something of the kind may have been used in the early days of the private, roofed, playhouse, and was certainly a feature of the elaborate Court masque up to the beginning of the seventeenth century.

MUMMING BIRDS, see KARNO, FRED.

MUMMING PLAY. The nature of any primitive folk drama in the British Isles is rather a subject for speculation than for detailed analysis, but there almost certainly existed, from primitive times, semi-dramatic funeral rites and certain ceremonies marking the different periods of the agricultural year. It seems possible that the old English mumming play has preserved traces of some such early spring festival.

The mumming play is still performed in a handful of English villages, usually at Christmas time, and in Northern Ireland, but seems to have died out in Scotland, where the hero was known as Galatian or Golashans. Up to the middle of the nineteenth century it was performed all over the country by rustic amateurs; although there were numerous local variants, and the text had in some places degenerated into jingling nonsense, there is a surprising uniformity in the plot and even in the wording of the text of the many versions that have been recovered from widely separated districts.

The main features of the plot are as follows: St. George introduces himself as a gallant Christian Knight and is challenged by the Turkish Knight. A terrific combat ensues, in which one of them is slain. A Doctor is then introduced, who recites a litany of the diseases he can cure, and eventually restores the stricken warrior to life. The performance concludes with a collection. Upon this framework were always superimposed a number of subsidiary stock characters, varying with the district—a Fool in cap and bells, Beelzebub, Father Christmas, and Jack Finney (or Johnny Jack) the Sweeper. The play is spoken throughout in rhyming couplets of which the following are a fair sample, both in their vigour and in a certain almost surrealist obscurity into which the original text has often slipped:

> I am King George, this noble Knight
> Came from foreign lands to fight
> To fight that fiery dragon who is so bold
> And cut him down with his blood cold.

Father Christmas has his own distinctive lines, which recur usually in some such form as this:

> In come I, old Father Christmas,
> Welcome or welcome not,
> I hope old Father Christmas
> Will never be forgot.

It will be seen that the central feature of the drama is the death and resurrection of one of the protagonists. By analogy with similar ceremonies throughout the world it is not entirely fanciful to see in this episode a relic of a spring festival in which the reawakening of the earth from the death of winter is enacted with human characters. Beyond this legitimate supposition it is not possible to go; there are no records of the enacting of any such ceremonies in England at any time, nor are there any indications of the performance of such a play during the Middle Ages. It is not until the close of the eighteenth century that contemporary references to the mumming play are to be found.

The general plot of the play as it has been preserved for us can hardly be earlier than the beginning of the seventeenth century. The legend of St. George and the Seven Champions of Christendom, upon which the play is apparently founded, was not popularized in England until the end of the sixteenth century; Richard Johnson's *Famous History of the Seaven Champions of Christendom* was first printed in 1596. During the succeeding centuries it took a prominent position in native folk-literature, and was the subject of numerous ballads, chap-books, drolls, and puppet-plays. This legend elaborates the Dragon story endlessly and introduces various single combats with heathen Champions. But there is no suggestion of any resurrection of a defeated warrior.

During the eighteenth century, for the first time, travelling troupes of barnstormers and portable fairground theatrical booths began to penetrate to the most remote country villages; and it is not unlikely that the village folk borrowed the most popular subject-matter and characters from the drolls and puppet-plays that they saw, and tried to emulate them for their own amusement and profit. The most likely theory of the origin of the mumming play is that the distorted version of the legend of St. George was grafted upon some ancient and otherwise unknown traditional game involving the death and restoration to life of a human character.

This theory does not entirely explain the fact that performances so very similar grew up in such widely separated areas of England, Ireland, and Scotland. If there was a common original it must have enjoyed an exceptional and widespread popularity; but the existence of it cannot be proved—it has entirely disappeared from human records. Yet the only alternative to the existence of a common origin is the acceptance of the mumming play as a remarkable product of mass telepathy.

Once established in its main outlines, the mumming play preserved its traditional form without fearing to shed old characters or take on new ones. St. George soon became King George, and the Napoleonic Wars, and even the First World War, left their mark. The texts were invariably handed down by word of mouth, growing more and more corrupt in the process; every Christmas time a group of mummers would go from house to house—much like carol-singers—giving their performance and taking their collection wherever they were welcomed. With the steady urbanization of the countryside the old custom, like many others, has nearly disappeared. Yet, quite apart from its historical interest, the mumming play possesses a rough dramatic vigour which is well worth preserving for its own sake.

The scanty information regarding the mummers' play which it has been possible to collect has been collated and commented on exhaustively by Sir E. K. Chambers in *The English Folk-Play* (1933), which also contains a 'normalized' text, to use the editor's own expression. This gives a fair idea of the general run of the play and the order of the incidents.

GEORGE SPEAIGHT

MUNCH, ANDREAS (1811–84), Norwegian dramatist (see SCANDINAVIA, 2 *a*).

MUNDAY, ANTHONY (*c.* 1553–1633), English actor and dramatist. He may have acted with the company of the Earl of Oxford, but was later active as a pamphleteer, ballad-maker, translator, and general literary hack. He wrote a good deal for Henslowe, mainly in collaboration, and much of his work is lost. With Chettle he was responsible for two plays on

Robin Hood, and with several others for the lost plays on Sir John Oldcastle. He also had some part in *Sir Thomas More*, as the manuscript is in his handwriting. Some of his *John a Kent and John a Cumber* (1594), done by the Admiral's Men, may have suggested to Shakespeare the comic scenes of Bottom and his companions in *A Midsummer Night's Dream*, which was probably acted by the rival company a year later.

MUNDEN, JOSEPH SHEPHERD (1758–1832), English comedian, who after a hard apprenticeship in the provinces was seen at Covent Garden in 1790, taking over the parts of John Edwin, who had just died. His first great original part was Old Dornton in *The Road to Ruin*, which raised him to the front rank. Liston and Quick thought him the finest living actor, and he was particularly good in drunken scenes, seeming to find some fresh 'business' every night. In repose he had a sedate look, but could make his features assume fantastic forms, and Lamb, who had an unbounded admiration for him, wrote of his face: 'Munden has none that you can properly pin down and call *his*. . . . If his name could be multiplied like his countenance, it might fill a play-bill. He, and he alone, literally *makes faces*. . . . Out of some invisible wardrobe he dips for faces. . . . In the grand grotesque of farce, Munden stands out as single and unaccompanied as Hogarth.' The breadth of his acting would scarcely be conceivable nowadays, and even in his own time he was censured for caricature. But his acting made the fortune of many a poor play, transforming its shadows into living realities. He remained at Covent Garden for over twenty years, and then went to Drury Lane, retiring in 1824, when, though he had amassed a good fortune, he lived sparingly, thus lending colour to former accusations of meanness.

MUNICH. From the sixteenth century onwards there was a rich and varied cultural and artistic life in Munich which was encouraged by the Bavarian Court. The Jesuits, who had arrived in 1560, were responsible for the first theatrical performances, which began with the plays of Jakob Bidermann in 1598. In 1651 the Komödienhaus on the Salvatorplatz was constructed, and functioned as a theatre until 1802. In 1662 this theatre was the scene of a magnificent baroque festival to celebrate the birth of an heir to the electoral throne. 'Fedra incoronata' was presented with every technical resource that the theatre could provide—gods and goddesses appeared on flying clouds, a thunderstorm darkened the theatre, and gave way to a light rain of sweetly scented water. From 1671 there was a permanent company of French actors in the theatre, and they remained there until the close of the eighteenth century saw the waning of French influence. In 1753 the Residenztheater opened, and in 1812 the Theater am Isartor, which soon became an important centre in the theatrical life of the city, was built. In 1854 Franz Dingelstedt was director of the Munich Theater, leaving it to go to Weimar. In 1865 the Theater am Gärtnerplatz was founded, and in 1908 the Künstlertheater, whose repertory included a wide variety of classical plays. The Gärtnerplatz Theater specialized in dialect plays for which it soon became famous throughout Germany. In 1895 Messthaler founded the Modernes Theater, where he tried to combat the inertia of the Court theatre by producing works by modern dramatists. Under the direction of Otto Falckenberg (1873–1947) the Kammerspiele (founded in 1911) flourished as a theatre of modern drama, and from 1914 until Falckenberg's death it was the most important theatre in Munich, thanks to the artistic sense, ability, and courage of its director, who was never afraid of encouraging young dramatists. He was the first to produce a play by Brecht (*Trommeln in der Nacht*, 1922), and even succeeded in preserving for his theatre a certain amount of independence during the Nazi régime. After the First World War the Hoftheater became the Bayrisches Staatstheater, and under the direction of Karl Zeiss (1920–4) gave the first performance of Brecht's *Im Dickicht der Städte* (1924). Die Arbeitsbühne, founded in 1919 by Eugen Felber, had a brief but glorious existence, closing its doors in 1921 for lack of funds. In 1943–4 both the Nationaltheater and the Residenztheater were destroyed by bombing, and when, after the war, opera and music took possession of the Prinzregententheater, drama found a home in the Theater am Brunnenhof, and the Kammerspiele resumed productions in the Schauspielhaus. In these post-war years the repertory included a wide variety of foreign plays which had been banned in the German theatre in the years 1933–43, by such writers as Wilder, Rattigan, Giraudoux, and Elmer Rice. In 1951 the Residenztheater was reopened and by 1963 much of the war damage to Munich theatres had been made good. DOROTHY MOORE

MUNK, KAJ (1898–1944), Danish priest and playwright, whose name sprang into prominence when he became a victim of Nazi aggression during the Second World War. From 1924 until his death—he was shot by the Nazis on 4 Jan. 1944—he was parish priest at Vedersø, and during the occupation, which he resisted unceasingly, published his banned sermons and his last and best-known play, *Niels Ebbesen* (1943), a stirring patriotic drama. He had previously been well known in Denmark for a number of historical and contemporary plays, of which the first, dealing with Herod, appeared in 1929. One of his earliest successes was *Cant* (1934), on Henry VIII and Anne Boleyn, but *Ordet* (1932), on a contemporary religious theme, is considered by some critics to be his best work. A play on the life of the Danish philosopher Georg Brandes had some success, while Munk had already shown his opposition to the Axis by *Sejren* (1936), dealing with Italian aggression in Abyssinia, and *Han Sidder ved Smeltediglen* (1938), dealing with Nazi anti-Semitism.

MURDOCH. (1) JAMES EDWARD (1811–93), an American actor, considered by many of his contemporaries the finest light comedian of his day. He was especially noted for his excellent elocution. He began his career at the Chestnut Street Theatre in Philadelphia, his birthplace, and played there with Fanny Kemble in 1833. He remained on the stage until 1858, appearing in England in 1856 in several of his best-known parts, in which he was well received. Jefferson, who played Moses to his Charles Surface in 1853, admired his acting immensely. In his *Autobiography* he says:

> [Murdoch] stood alone, and I do not remember any actor who excelled him in those parts that he seemed to make his own. . . . There was a manliness about his light comedy that gave it more dignity than the flippant style in which it was usually played. . . . It was the finish and picturesque style of Murdoch's acting that agreeably surprised the audience of the Haymarket Theater when he played there. . . . The public was unprepared to see comely old English manners so conspicuous in an American actor, and he gained its sympathy at once.

Among his other parts were Benedick, Orlando, Mercutio, Mirabell, and the Rover. On the outbreak of the Civil War in 1861, in which his only son was killed, Murdoch came out of his retirement to give readings and lectures to, and on behalf of, the wounded, the last being at the dramatic festival in Cincinnati in 1883, in which town he died. His nephew, (2) FRANK HITCHCOCK (? –1872), also an actor, was the author of an excellent frontier play, *Davy Crockett*, produced only a few weeks before his death. Frank Mayo made a success in the name-part, after a cool initial reception, and it was later played by his son Edwin.

MURPHY, ARTHUR (1727–1805), English actor and dramatist, who was encouraged by Samuel Foote to go on the stage, but was not a particularly good actor. He retired in 1756 and devoted all his energies to play-writing, beginning with four farces and continuing with an adaptation of one of Voltaire's plays as *The Orphan of China* (1759). Among his later tragedies the best were *The Grecian Daughter* (1772) and *Alzuma* (1773), while of his comedies, several of which were based on Molière and other French writers, the outstanding ones were *The Way to Keep Him* (1760), *All in the Wrong* (1761), *The School for Guardians* (1767), and *Know Your Own Mind* (1777). Murphy had little originality, but was an adept at choosing and combining the best elements of the work of others, and had his place in the revival of the comedy of manners which led up to *The School for Scandal*.

MURRAY, ALMA (1854–1945), English actress, outstanding in poetic drama and tragedy, whom Robert Browning described as 'the poetic actress without a rival' and a woman of genius. She made her first appearance at the Olympic on 8 Jan. 1870 in *The Princess*, and in 1879 appeared at the Lyceum with Irving. In 1884 she made her first appearance in poetic drama in a revival of Browning's *In a Balcony*, followed in 1885 by his *Colombe's Birthday*. It was, however, as Beatrice in the single performance of Shelley's *The Cenci* in 1888 that she scored a great personal triumph. Everyone who saw her performance was enthusiastic about it, and it was much regretted that the censor would not allow the play to be put on for a normal run. Alma Murray continued to play leading parts in many West End theatres, and was particularly admired as Mildred Tresham in *A Blot in the 'Scutcheon* when it was revived in 1888. She created the part of Raina in *Arms and the Man* (1894) when it was first presented by Florence Farr at the Avenue Theatre, a production which marks Shaw's first appearance at a commercial theatre. He produced the play himself, with the help of George R. Foss. She retired in 1915, after playing Mrs. Maylie in a dramatization of *Oliver Twist*.

MURRAY, SIR (GEORGE) GILBERT AIMÉ (1866–1957), great English classical scholar, poet, humanist, and philosopher, whose verse-translations of Greek plays, particularly of Euripides, held the stage for many years, and introduced a whole generation of playgoers to the living reality of Greek drama. Although Murray's somewhat free and occasionally facile renderings have now been discredited and in some cases superseded, they were in their time infinitely superior to anything heard previously, and are still cherished by those who owe to them their introduction to Greek drama. Among his translations of Euripides, the *Hippolytus*, the *Trojan Women*, the *Electra*, and the *Bacchae* were first produced at the Court Theatre in London between 1904 and 1908 with Lillah McCarthy in the leading parts. The *Medea* was first seen at the Savoy in 1907, the *Iphigenia in Tauris* at the Kingsway in 1912. The *Alcestis* and the *Rhesus* have not been professionally performed, though, like the others, they have often been done by amateurs, particularly in universities and colleges. Murray also translated Sophocles' *Oedipus Rex*, *Antigone*, *Alcestis*, and *Oedipus at Colonus* and Aeschylus's *Oresteia* (which was done by Reinhardt at Covent Garden with Martin-Harvey), and, of Aeschylus's other plays, the *Suppliant Women*, the *Prometheus Bound*, the *Persians*, and the *Seven Against Thebes*. He was perhaps less successful with Aeschylus than with Euripides, but his versions of Aristophanes' *Birds*, *Frogs*, and *Knights* were eminently actable, as were his reconstructions of Menander's *Perikeiromenê* as *The Rape of the Locks* and *Epitrepontes* as *The Arbitration*.

MURRAY, THOMAS CORNELIUS (1873–1959), Irish dramatist. His subjects were drawn from the peasant and farming life of his native county of Cork and were distinguished, even among Irish dramatic works, for sympathetic perception of the deeply religious and sometimes actually mystical quality in the minds of those peasants. Tragedy, or potential tragedy, was most natural to him; the strict realism of situation, the penetration into the minds of his characters, and the excellence of his dialogue—which seemed to bring the speech of living people on the stage—combined to give his work a quality which makes it still live today. Despite success in America and England, Murray's work never achieved the esteem it deserved. Yet his name is high on the list of important Abbey Theatre playwrights.

He made his name in *Birthright*, produced at the Abbey in 1910. This is a play of rivalry and family jealousy in which passion and concentration produce genuine tragedy. *Maurice Harte* (1912) is a remarkable play, not only for its theme, the conflict between spiritual honesty and family affection in the mind of a young peasant, but for the imaginative sympathy with which the characters are portrayed, the directness of the dialogue, the concentration and economy of material in its two acts, and the fineness of the resultant tragic balance. *The Briery Gap* (published in 1917 but not produced) is an exquisite brief tragedy; *Spring* (1918) is a one-act study of poverty and the greed engendered by it; *Aftermath* (1922) is a full-length tragedy on the theme of an arranged marriage; and *Autumn Fire* (1924), another tragedy of mis-mating, is probably the author's best work in the three-act form. *The Pipe in the Fields* (1927) is a fine, brief study of the sudden flowering of the mind of an artist. *The Blind Wolf* (1928), the first of Murray's plays which is not set in Ireland, is again a peasant tragedy. His last plays were *A Flutter of Wings* (1929), *Michaelmas Eve* (1932), *A Stag at Bay* (1934), *A Spot in the Sun* (1938), and *Illumination* (1939).

UNA ELLIS-FERMOR†, *rev.*

MURRAY, WALTER, see KEAN, THOMAS.

MUSE, of Comedy, Thalia; of Dancing, Terpsichore; of Tragedy, Melpomene.

MUSEUMS, THEATRE, see COLLECTIONS, THEATRE.

MUSICAL COMEDY, a popular type of light entertainment which derives from a fusion of burlesque and light opera, taking from the latter the tradition of a sketchy plot, songs arising from it, and concerted finales for each act. Burlesque provided topicality and an intermission of speciality sketches. The first English show to approximate to a musical comedy was *In Town* (1892), which George Edwardes transferred from the Prince of Wales's to his own Gaiety, following it with *The Shop Girl* (1894), and thus inaugurating the series of musical comedies connected with his name. From America, where the foundations of musical comedy had been laid by Tony Pastor, and by the great names of vaudeville, came the swift-moving and tuneful *Belle of New York* (1898), while England sent back to America such productions as *Florodora* (1899) and the English versions of Lehár's *The Merry Widow* (1907) and Oscar Straus's *The Chocolate Soldier* (1910). In both countries the talent of composers, librettists, comedians, and beautiful chorus-girls was poured out on a host of light-hearted frolics whose tunes are still sung.

The First World War brought about many changes, but the essentials of musical comedy remained. The chief differences lay in the importation of large spectacular effects and the increased efficiency of the chorus, which led to the accent being on dancing rather than singing. Among the highlights of this period were Friml's *Rose Marie* and Youmans's *No, No, Nanette!* (both 1925), Romberg's *The Student Prince* (1924) and *The Desert Song* (1927), and the outstanding *Showboat* (1928), based on the novel by Edna Ferber with music by Jerome Kern.

In England musical comedy then suffered something of a setback, attention being concentrated on spectacular or intimate revue, or on the big musical plays of Ivor Novello and Noël Coward, though *Bless the Bride* (1947), by A. P. Herbert and Vivian Ellis, foreshadowed the revival referred to below. In America the genre flourished, first with such song-and-dance satires as Gershwin's *Of Thee I Sing* (1932), and later with the musical metamorphosis of such plays as *Green Grow the Lilacs* and *Liliom* into *Oklahoma!* (1943) and *Carousel* (1945), which mingled good music, a strong plot, and professional ballet dancing in a way which marked a great advance on the earlier, somewhat haphazard, concoction of the typical musical comedy in its less stringent days. America marked this advance by dropping the 'comedy' connotation of the term and ticketing its productions simply as 'musicals'. The American musical today represents bigger 'business' than any other form of theatre, and is served by the most eminent producers, designers, and choreographers. If a musical is a success recordings of its songs sell in vast quantities; a film is made, touring companies are formed, it is produced in London with runs possibly as spectacular as those of *South Pacific* or *My Fair Lady* at Drury Lane; and it may well be taken into the repertory alongside the classical operettas at such houses as the Vienna Volksoper. Successful composer-and-librettist teams are Rodgers and Hart (*The Boys From Syracuse*, 1938, London 1963; *Pal Joey*, 1940); Rodgers and Hammerstein (*Oklahoma!* 1943, *Carousel*, 1945, *South Pacific*, 1949, *The King and I*, 1951, *Flower-Drum Song*, 1958, *The Sound of Music*, 1959); Lerner and Loewe (*Brigadoon*, 1947, *My Fair Lady*, 1956, *Camelot*, 1960). Other important composers are Cole Porter (*Anything Goes*, 1934, *Kiss Me, Kate!* 1943); Kurt Weill (*Lady in the Dark*, 1941); Leonard Bernstein (*On the Town*, 1944, *Wonderful Town*, 1953, *West Side Story*, 1957); and Irving Berlin (*Annie Get Your Gun*, 1946, *Call Me Madam*, 1950).

The success of Sandy Wilson's *The Boy Friend* (1953) and of Julian Slade's *Salad Days* (1954) re-established British musicals as an important part of the London (and subsequently New York) scene; they were followed by Lionel Bart's *Fings Ain't Wot They Used T'Be* (1959), *Oliver!* (1960) (see No. 113), and *Blitz!* (1962).

MUSIC BOX, New York, between Broadway and 8th Avenue, one of the most popular theatres in New York, which has had surprisingly few failures. A spacious and comfortable house, seating 1,000, it opened on 22 Sept. 1921 with a revue by Irving Berlin, which ran into several editions. Several other revues followed, as did *Once in a Lifetime*, one of the best farces yet written about Hollywood, and *Of Thee I Sing* (1932), the first musical show to win the Pulitzer Prize. Later successes have been *Dinner at Eight*, with Constance Collier as, recognizably, the late Maxine Elliott, *Of Mice and Men* (1937), winner of the Critics' Prize, the hilarious *Man Who Came to Dinner* (1939), based on the antics of the late Alexander Woollcott, and the charming *I Remember Mama* (1944). In 1949 came a musical play, Anderson's *Lost in the Stars* (music by Kurt Weill), but in recent years the theatre has been used primarily for straight plays such as *Picnic* (1953), *Separate Tables* (1956), *Rashomon* (1959), *A Far Country* (1961), and *Any Wednesday* (1964). GEORGE FREEDLEY†

MUSIC-HALL. When Victorian publicans shouted, 'This way, gents, to the music-hall', they meant the one on their own premises—tavern annexes which had developed into gilt-and-plush 'palaces' devoted to comic songs, varied with acrobatics, conjuring, juggling, and dancing. These temples or theatres of variety were always known as music-halls to the British people, and also to the French, though to the American such entertainments were first 'variety' then 'vaudeville' then 'vodeville' (see VAUDEVILLE, 2).

Music-halls of this type began at small taverns in the early eighteenth century. These begat musick-houses, such as Sadler's Wells, to whose programmes of song, dance, and acrobatics were added pageant and pantomime until they outshone the Theatres Royal, in defiance of the law to protect the stage monopoly. These law-breakers were law-makers; attempts to suppress them changed them into minor theatres. Meanwhile the old demand for wine-and-song was supplied by music clubs, which flourished everywhere in the time of the four Georges. All, whatever trade, class, or district they catered for, fostered the comic song. Their history is influenced by street-lighting, for while the age-long black-out still persisted men liked to find entertainment at the next street-corner. As gas-lighting spread they flocked to more glamorous haunts. Evans's Song-and-Supper Rooms at the King Street corner of Covent Garden were celebrated for midnight concerts in the 1840s, under 'Paddy' Green, an Adelphi actor (for later history, see PLAYERS' THEATRE). There was a choir with an academic repertory of part-songs, relieved by the long-winded burlesque ballads of Sam Cowell, now remembered more for 'Villikins and his Dinah' and 'The Rat-catcher's Daughter'. Sam was connected with another early supper-room—the William IV—and dodged an engagement there to go to the audition at the Canterbury which made him a 'star'.

Every tavern had its music-room. In laughter-loving Lambeth the Canterbury Arms was so thronged that Charles Morton, the publican, opened a special building with a stage as well as space for tables and chairs, and so became 'the father of the halls'. Throughout the 1850s many a publican bought the house, school, or chapel next door, and transformed it into 'the music-hall'. The process changed the volunteer entertainers of the tavern 'free-and-easy' into red-nosed comics and buffo vocalists. Urgent calls for 'turns' from all quarters—street-lighting had now improved—sent up earnings. In fashionable clothes the 'comic' blossomed into the 'lion comique', notably in the person of George Leybourne, the singer of 'Champagne Charlie'. Women performers had promptly decided that the halls were a suitable place for the display of their talents, and Charles Morton responded by engaging sopranos of note. When his taste reverted from the operatic to the domestic, the female 'serio-comic' appeared in the fleshings and spangles of burlesque to sing of menaced virtue one minute and washing-day the next. Sudden success set a feverish pace that killed. Few stars of those early days lived to be 50 years old. One generation of them vanished with Sam Cowell, who died in 1864, and another with George Leybourne twenty years later. Jenny Hill, 'the Vital Spark', whose brave spirit shone in all her studies of pathetic little cockneys, was consistently praised as the brightest star of all. She retired broken in health a few years before she died in 1896.

The halls themselves changed with the changing stars. The tavern annexe survived until its licence to serve alcohol was taken away. All links with the bar-parlour were broken, even in those halls which still had the parent 'pub' firmly embedded in the oft-enlarged façade. In the provinces 'Empires' were being run with twice-nightly programmes by two managers who joined forces to capture London and then split, Moss installing his headquarters at the Hippodrome and Stoll his at the Coliseum. 'Variety' now meant variety. Despite a protest from the theatres, recalling that which was made against the musick-houses over a century earlier, drama (legally confined to performances occupying not more than thirty minutes) was included in the bill when Sir Herbert Tree, Sir George Alexander, and Sarah Bernhardt consented to appear on the music-hall stage. To meet the competition of talking-films, novelties of many kinds, from a Wild West Rodeo to symphony orchestras and bouts of professional tennis or pugilism, were tried at the Coliseum. Still the menace of the 'talkies' was felt until George Black, a manager from the north, caught the taste of the music-hall public. He banded the best knockabout comedians together in a 'Crazy Gang' which acted in the foyer and auditorium as well as on the stage, and interrupted other acts as well as performing their own. They made the Palladium more popular than it had ever been before; but this was an isolated example. Where there had been many hundreds of music-halls in Great Britain, there were now only survivors here and there. Most of the others were cinemas; those that were still variety theatres went in mainly for revue. 'Non-stop' variety was tried at the Windmill, near Piccadilly Circus, where it continued despite the Second World War; and the music-hall comedian came annually into his own in that typically British institution, the Christmas pantomime. M. WILLSON DISHER†

Unlike the actor of the legitimate stage, the music-hall artist—or performer, as he called himself—was never blinded by the glamour of the West End. To him London was a 'date', just the same as Manchester, Liverpool, Leicester, or elsewhere, a place in which he would 'work' (not 'play', an as actor would say), and where he would give the same act in the same way, apart from any local 'gag' he might interpolate.

This difference between 'work' and 'play' was one of the great distinctions between the music-hall and the theatre. The music-hall performer was identical with his act. He had so many minutes allotted for his turn, and had to make good in that time. The 'stars' (with whom the word originated before it was annexed by the cinema) sang songs written to suit their own style. They had their individual make-up, which was their trade-mark—Robey his eyebrows, Harry Tate his moustache, Mark Sheridan his frock coat and bell-bottomed trousers tied round the knee, Eugene Stratton his black face, George Lashwood his faultless tailoring and air of Beau Brummell; Gus Elen, Alex Hurley, and Albert Chevalier shared the 'coster' roles, though Chevalier was the 'pearliest' of the Pearly Kings; George Formby, the plaintive dare-devil and would-be roysterer, who wasn't going home 'till a quarter past nine', exploited the Lancashire accent; R. G. Knowles never appeared without his opera hat, frock-coat, and white duck trousers; Wilkie Bard had his high forehead and deliberate air; Kate Carney her 'Arriet's feathers; Grock his fiddle; Harry Lauder his kilts and curly stick; Happy Fanny Fields her Dutch costume; and T. E. Dunville his tight-fitting black suit. Some, on the other hand, varied their attire. Dan Leno, in whatever guise he appeared, was always Dan Leno, while his pantomime partner, Herbert Campbell, was beloved for his bulky figure. Marie Lloyd was always Marie Lloyd, the epitome of Cockney London, and although Little Tich might represent a variety of characters from a jockey to a fireman, still his diminutive size was his greatest asset, and he seldom failed to complete his act without using his elongated boots for his famous dance. Chirgwin was the unalterable 'white-ey'd Kaffir', and relied almost wholly upon two songs, 'My Fiddle is My Sweetheart' and 'The Blind Boy', asking the audience in his queer falsetto voice: 'Which will you have, ladies and gempmuns, The Fiddler or the Blind 'Un?' They always wanted both. Harry Champion specialized in songs about food—'Boiled Beef and Carrots'—delivered at terrific speed, and ending with a 'breakdown' which was his own particular property. They even had their own posters, which were as individual as themselves, and T. E. Dunville would advise the patrons of, say, the Hackney Empire that 'I'm Sticking Here for a Week'.

The tremendous efficiency of it all proved that these people were specialists at their jobs. To watch Cinquevalli juggling was to see perfection in that particular art. There was the neatness of dapper Vesta Tilley, the supreme clowning of Grock, the perfect understanding and timing of Clarice Mayne and 'That' (Jas. W. Tate), the dainty appeal and daring of Ella Retford, the humour of Vesta Victoria. The same applied to the trapezists, the acrobats, the Risley acts, the trampolinists, and the dancers, who went to make up a music-hall 'bill'. They worked hard, often playing at three or four widely separated halls a night, even in the days before motor transport, and keeping to a strict time-table. At halls like the Tivoli, the Oxford, the London Pavilion, could habitually be seen a programme of some twenty 'star turns'. Much the same was true of the Holborn Empire, which kept the banner of variety flying up to the end, until it was practically destroyed by enemy action in 1941.

Two halls peculiar to London were the Alhambra and the Empire, where variety alternated with ballet. The Palace at Cambridge Circus, which began as the English Opera House, became one of the most successful of the Theatres of Varieties and it was there that music-hall received its accolade, when King George V commanded a performance in 1912. In 1904 the London Coliseum struck an individual note as a refined and respectable music-hall to which one could safely take children. But by then the whole of music-hall was growing anaemic, and was already losing its grip upon that full-bodied vulgar humour which has been part of the British national make-up since the days of Chaucer through those of Shakespeare and Dickens.

In its heyday the music-hall represented the type of entertainment most loved by the masses. It was gay, raffish, carefree. Its themes were fully understood and appreciated by the multitude, for they dealt with their own emotions, their own troubles, their own raw humour. The lodger, the mother-in-law, the brokers, the overdue rent, the kipper and bloater, the annual seaside holiday, beer, the state of being stony-broke; and by way of contrast, mother love, two hearts that beat as one, the old home with its apple-trees, its ivy-clad walls and its village bells—these were the music-hall's great stand-bys. It embraced, too, husbands both errant and hen-pecked—

wives, both domineering and downtrodden—unfaithful swains and lasses, Gay Paree and midnight revelry. And it was very sound on the subject of patriotism: it told the British people that they were the salt of the earth and could never be beaten, and it glorified the Red, White, and Blue. It gave the people songs they could join in singing, songs they could whistle and remember. And they remember them still. It may be said to have supplied this country with the folk-songs of an era. Nothing was restrained, nothing was sophisticated: it was all high spirits, and every day was a Bank Holiday. That was what the halls were like, the Oxford, the London Pavilion, the Metropolitan, the Tivoli, the Holborn Empire, the South London, the Canterbury in its varying phases, the Middlesex (the 'old Mo'); and, to much the same degree, Collins's, Deacon's, the Eagle, and the hundreds of outlying halls like the Bedford, the Granville (Walham Green), the Star (Bermondsey), the Queen's (Poplar), the Paragon, and the countless Empires and Hippodromes of the suburbs and provinces.

W. MACQUEEN-POPE†

MUSIC IN THE THEATRE, see INCIDENTAL MUSIC.

MUSICOS, see CAFÉ-CONCERT.

MUSSATO, ALBERTINO (1261–1329), the first Italian dramatist to write a tragedy, *Eccerinus*, dealing with a recent event of Italian history. Written in Latin in about 1315, it was probably never acted, but is important as showing the influence on the old religious drama of the classic form, particularly of Seneca (see ITALY, 1 *b* i).

MUSSET, (LOUIS-CHARLES) ALFRED DE (1810–57), French poet and novelist of the Romantic school, and the one man who might have fused the new drama with the classical tradition of the French theatre. But the failure of his first play, *La Nuit vénitienne* (1830), due partly to an unfortunate accident, partly to organized opposition, turned him from the stage, and he wrote his later plays to be read. Consequently he had no influence on the stage in his own day, and it was not until 1847 that *Un Caprice* was put on at the Comédie-Française. It was immediately successful, and was followed by *Il faut qu'une porte soit ouverte ou fermée* and *Il ne faut jurer de rien*. To a theatre under the dual influence of Scribe and Balzac, de Musset brought back the poetry and fantasy which it was in danger of losing. Excellent examples of de Musset's method, which he himself explained as a fusion of the romantic and classical traditions, are *Les Caprices de Marianne*, first given in 1851, and *On ne badine pas avec l'amour*, which was seen ten years later. His best work is undoubtedly to be found, however, in *Fantasio*, given in 1866, and *Lorenzaccio*, written in Venice in 1834, after his tragic liaison with George Sand. De Musset's plays, which show a mingling of eighteenth-century France, Italian Renaissance, Shakespeare, and Marivaux, may also be considered a source of Symbolism. They have atmosphere, but an unlocalized action, for which scenery is unnecessary. Being liberated, by the conditions of their composition, from the conventions of theatrical presentation, they represent a world in which anything can and does happen. De Musset was a wonderful painter of women, and more than any other writer of his time recognized the tragedy of unrequited love. His plays are not well known in England, but three of them —*Un Caprice*, *On ne badine pas avec l'amour*, and *Lorenzaccio*—have been seen in London both in French and in various translations. Sarah Bernhardt appeared in the last-named at the Adelphi, and as *Night's Candles* it was produced in 1933 by Ernest Milton, who played the title-role.

MYNNISCUS, a Greek tragic actor who played for Aeschylus.

MYSTERY PLAY, a medieval religious drama, which derives from the liturgical play, but differs from it in being spoken instead of sung, and being wholly or partly in the vernacular and not in Latin. It was also performed out of doors, either in front of the church, in the market square, or on perambulating pageants. The term is synonymous with Miracle play, now seldom used, and a more satisfactory name would be Bible-histories, since each play was really a cycle of plays, based on the Bible, from the Creation to the Second Coming, and on the lives of the saints. A different guild was responsible for the production of each self-contained section, and the plays were usually performed at Whitsuntide or on the feast of Corpus Christi. The few surviving English mystery plays are known by the names of the towns where they are believed to have been performed—the Chester, probably written by Ralph Higden from Latin and French sources, the Coventry, which contains the beautiful carol 'Lullay thou littel tiny child'; the Townley (or Wakefield), rougher in humour and containing the farcical 'Second Shepherd's Play' with Mak the sheep-stealer; and the York, the longest extant, with forty-eight plays and one fragment, of which the manuscript is in the British Museum. A new interest in this early manifestation of vernacular drama has led to revivals in modern versions of part of the York cycle at York in a version by Canon Purvis, first in 1951, and triennially since; of the Chester cycle in the Church of St. Peter-upon-Cornhill in 1951; and of some of the Wakefield cycle, first at Bretton Hall, Wakefield, and then at the Mermaid in 1961 in an adaptation by Martial Rose.

Similar plays are found in the Middle Ages all over Europe (Fr. *mystère*, Ger. *Mysterienspiel*, It. *sacra rappresentazione*, Sp. *auto sacramental*), and are dealt with under the separate countries.

N

NADIR, Moses (1885–1943), writer of Yiddish plays produced in New York by Maurice Schwartz (see JEWISH DRAMA, 6).

NAEVIUS, Gnaeus (*c.* 270–*c.* 199 B.C.), one of the most original of Latin writers, was the first successor of Andronicus in drama. In 235 B.C. he produced a play at the Ludi Romani, and he continued to bring out a series of translations from Greek tragedy and comedy (as well as two original plays on Roman historical subjects) until the end of the war with Hannibal. The surviving fragments show that in style he altogether surpassed his predecessor; we see in him a man of daring and energy, one who loved liberty and had a gift for social and political satire which was to cost him dear. Into his translations he infused a strong Roman element; it is not surprising that his chief dramatic work was in comedy. A celebrated piece of characterization is his description of a flirt in *The Girl from Tarentum*. The Roman historical play (see FABULA, 4. *Praetexta*) was his creation; the surviving fragments scarcely enable us to say more than that one of his two *praetextae* dealt with Romulus, the other with the victory won at Clastidium by Naevius's great contemporary, M. Claudius Marcellus, in 222 B.C. Naevius's turn for satire brought him into collision with the powerful family of the Metelli, and after undergoing a period of imprisonment he is said to have died an exile in Africa, about the end of the century.

WILLIAM BEARE†

NAHARRO, Bartolomé de Torres, see TORRES NAHARRO, BARTOLOMÉ DE.

NAOGEORG, see KIRCHMAYER, THOMAS.

NARES, Owen (1888–1943), English actor, and for many years one of the most popular matinée idols of London. He had great personal beauty, which at times obscured his very real gifts as an actor. On his mother's side he was the grandson of the famous scene-painter Beverley. He made his first appearance in 1908, after studying with Rosina Filippi, and was at the St. James's in 1910, where he appeared in *Old Heidelberg*. Among his later successes were Lord Monkhurst in *Milestones* (1912), Julian Beauclerc in *Diplomacy* (1913), Peter Ibbetson, and the dual role of the Bishop and Thomas Armstrong in *Romance* (both 1915). In 1923 he took over the management of the St. James's, where he appeared as Mark Sabre in a dramatization of *If Winter Comes*, in which he had previously been seen on tour, and in 1925 went to South Africa with a repertory which included *Romance* and *Diplomacy*. Of his later parts the most successful were Roger Hilton in *Call it a Day* (1935), Robert Carson in *Robert's Wife* (1937), in which he played opposite Edith Evans, and Max de Winter in *Rebecca* (1940). His sudden death at the early age of 55 was a great loss to the English stage, since the excellence of his later work had given indications of much depth and maturity, and he seemed about to draw on greater reserves of strength and authority than he had previously been credited with. He married an actress named Marie Polini, who died in 1960. Daughter of a theatre manager, she made her first appearance at the Lyric in 1896, and later toured in some of her husband's productions. She had two sons, of whom one, Geoffrey (1917–42), was an actor and stage-designer. He appeared with his father in *Call it a Day* (1935), and designed the sets for several London productions. His promising career was cut short by the Second World War, and he died on active service.

NARR, the Fool of the German Carnival play (see GERMANY, 1).

NASHE, Thomas (1567–1601), English pamphleteer, noted for his part in the Martin Marprelate controversy and for his attacks on Gabriel Harvey, which arose from his friendship with Lyly. He was also a friend and collaborator of Greene, and with Christopher Marlowe wrote *Dido, Queen of Carthage*, his earliest extant essay in dramatic form. In 1597 he was concerned with Jonson in the ill-fated *Isle of Dogs*, played at the Swan on Bankside, which sent the actors and Jonson, and possibly Nashe also, to prison on account of its supposedly seditious nature. This play is lost, and the only extant dramatic work of Nashe's is *Summer's Last Will and Testament* (1592–3), a mixture of comedy and masque designed for performance in the house of a nobleman, probably Archbishop Whitgift at Croydon. It was used as the basis of Constant Lambert's masque for orchestra, chorus, and baritone solo, first heard in 1936.

NASSAU STREET THEATRE, or, more properly, the Theatre in Nassau Street, was probably the first place used for professional stage plays in New York. It consisted of a large room in a house on Nassau Street where in 1750 Walter Murray and Thomas Kean brought their company from Philadelphia to play *Richard III* as rewritten by Colley Cibber, together with a repertory of tragedies and farces. In 1751 Robert Upton, probably an actor sent over from London by Lewis Hallam, gave a short and unsuccessful season, which included *Othello*, and in 1753 the elder Hallam, arriving from his tour of the Southern cities, caused the old theatre to be dismantled and a new one, known as the New Theatre, or Hallam's in Nassau Street, to be built. Here he and his famous company stayed for a long season, opening in the autumn with *The*

Conscious Lovers, and ending in March of the following year with *The Gamester*. After Hallam's departure the theatre was devoted to more mundane uses, and disappears from theatre history.

NATANSON, JACQUES (1901–), French dramatist, whose plays were produced at the Théâtre de l'Œuvre in the years following the First World War. He was an ironic and unsentimental portrayer of the contemporary scene in the 1920s, and two of his plays, *Le Greluchon délicat* (1925) and *Je t'attendrai* (1928) were given in translation in New York. A more serious and subtle play was *L'Été* (1934), the story of lost happiness between two wars.

NATHAN, GEORGE JEAN (1882–1958), American dramatic critic who was for many years a leading figure in the New York scene. He was born in Fort Wayne, Indiana, and educated at Cornell and the University of Bologna, Italy. In 1905 he joined the staff of *The New York Herald* and began his career as a dramatic critic there. It is doubtful whether any other individual has exercised a more important influence on the transformation of his native stage. When Nathan first went to work the American theatre was an intellectual wilderness. The works of Augustus Thomas and David Belasco cluttered the playhouses to the exclusion of almost everything else. Nathan fought for the drama of ideas in America, and in those days it was a fight against great odds. He introduced the modern plays of Europe—Ibsen, Shaw, Hauptmann, and Strindberg—and derided the contemporary American producers and playwrights. His most important discovery in the U.S.A. was Eugene O'Neill, whose early work he published in *The Smart Set*, a magazine he edited with H. L. Mencken. There, too, appeared James Joyce, Brieux, Wedekind, Molnár, Melchior, Lengyel, Lord Dunsany, Harold Brighouse and a host of others, all hitherto unknown to the general public. Thus the American audience as well as the American theatre slowly came to change its outlook, and by the end of the First World War the stage was ready for the modern drama, foreign and domestic. Later Nathan championed Sean O'Casey—he was largely responsible for the New York production of *Within the Gates*—and William Saroyan, whose first theatre effort, *My Heart's in the Highlands*, he praised enthusiastically when there was still much doubt as to its worth. He wrote over thirty books on the theatre and for many years an annual volume on each New York season. Among his best-known works are *The Critic and the Drama*, *Mr. George Jean Nathan Presents*, *The World in False Face*, *The Autobiography of an Attitude*, *The House of Satan*, *Art of the Night*, *The Intimate Notebooks of George Jean Nathan* (especially interesting for its portraits of O'Neill, Dreiser, Sinclair Lewis, and others), *Testament of a Critic*, and *Encyclopaedia of the Theatre*.

THOMAS QUINN CURTISS

NATION, THÉÂTRE DE LA, see COMÉDIE-FRANÇAISE.

NATIONAL OPERATIC AND DRAMATIC ASSOCIATION, see AMATEUR THEATRE IN GREAT BRITAIN.

NATIONAL THEATRE, LONDON. The lack of an exemplary theatre in London endowed by the State, or by private generosity, and so preserved from the changes and chances of profit and loss, was, from the time of David Garrick, a cause of sorrow and complaint on the part of almost every lover of the drama. In other European countries endowed theatres are the rule rather than the exception (e.g. Comédie-Française), but in England the Puritan interregnum shattered the old relationship between the stage and the Court, and at the Restoration the two patent theatres, and the Lord Chamberlain's subsidiary office as censor of plays, were the only relics that remained of State patronage. Bulwer Lytton, early in the nineteenth century, and later on Sir Henry Irving were both fervent supporters of the National Theatre idea; but it was left to a younger group of professional actor-managers, dramatists, and critics to take positive action for the preparation of a practical scheme. This group included such men as Sir Herbert Tree, Arthur Bourchier, George Bernard Shaw, William Archer, and Harley Granville-Barker. In 1910 the last two collaborated in a volume entitled *The National Theatre: A Scheme and Estimates*, which immediately became the recognized handbook of the movement. For a complete exposition of the theory and practice of National Theatre work, readers are referred to this book, and to its sequel, rewritten and brought up to date by Granville-Barker alone, and published in 1930.

At the time the National Theatre group was establishing itself, a separate movement was on foot to celebrate the coming tercentenary of the death of William Shakespeare, in 1916, by the erection of a monument to his memory in some central position in London. Articles in the *Daily News* and *Daily Chronicle* urged that the only appropriate monument to Shakespeare would be a National Theatre. A fusion of the two schemes was effected, and a single joint Committee was set up with the avowed object of founding a National Theatre which should include a statue of Shakespeare as a prominent feature of its architecture. Sir Israel Gollancz became the secretary of this 'Shakespeare Memorial National Theatre Committee', and the project was launched under the highest auspices in the social, literary, and theatre worlds at a public meeting at the Theatre Royal, Drury Lane, in the summer of 1908. The appeal for funds was headed by a donation of £70,000 from Sir Carl Meyer; propaganda on a national scale was started; and it seemed quite likely that the necessary funds would be collected in time to lay the foundation stone of the theatre in 1916 according to plan. The outbreak of war in 1914 involved the total suspension of the appeal;

but in 1919 the Committee started again with the prospect that the then ascendant Labour Party might agree to government support for an enterprise which seemed so consonant with their avowed programme of post-war social and cultural reform. But attention was soon deflected to more urgent problems, and it was not till 1930 that a direct approach was made to the Cabinet, in reply to which it was stated that no help from that quarter could be looked for until evidence was forthcoming of a demand for a National Theatre by the people as a whole. However immediately discouraging, this reply at least made it clear that the principle of State aid was accepted, and the Committee was encouraged to undertake a further propaganda effort. For the success of this they largely relied on the new interest in good theatre which had been conspicuous throughout the country since the end of the First World War. The Earl of Lytton was now chairman of the Committee, and Geoffrey Whitworth had been appointed secretary in succession to Sir Israel Gollancz.

Meanwhile, the sum subscribed up to 1914 had increased by compound interest and capital appreciation to a total of £150,000. In 1938 a site for the theatre facing the Victoria and Albert Museum in South Kensington was purchased; architectural designs for the theatre by Sir Edwin Lutyens and Cecil Masey were completed, and a new and nationwide appeal for funds was launched. By the summer of 1939 it appeared that the National Theatre was once again in process of realization. That a new war, more terrible even than the last, brought an end to these hopes for a second time was disheartening. But the faith of the Committee did not weaken. Dame Edith Lyttelton, who from the first had been one of its most active members, was appointed acting-chairman of the committee, and the war period was utilized in the preparation of plans for the ultimate completion of the scheme.

GEOFFREY WHITWORTH†

The coming of peace in 1945 enabled the Committee to consider an even more ambitious scheme. By arrangement with the London County Council the site at South Kensington was to be exchanged for a larger one in a central position on the South Bank of the Thames, and an amalgamation was made with the Old Vic, who were to provide the National Theatre with a basic company in due course. It seemed as if the National Theatre was at last within reach. In 1949 the Government passed an Act voting a grant of £1 million towards the cost of the building, and on Friday, 13 June 1951, Queen Elizabeth, deputizing for King George VI, laid the foundation stone of the new building on the South Bank. (This was the third ceremony of its kind. The first was in Gower Street, the second in South Kensington, where Bernard Shaw 'turned the first sod'.) The stone has now been removed, and is believed to be in front of the main entrance of the Royal Festival Hall, about 50 yards from its original position.

Although the stone had been laid, repeated appeals for the £1 million met with no response, no date having been laid down in the Act for its disbursement. Some years later an elaborate new scheme was introduced, which included Sadler's Wells and Stratford-upon-Avon, as well as the Old Vic, and envisaged the building of an opera-house as well as a theatre. Stratford eventually withdrew, and grave doubts were expressed as to the desirability of moving Sadler's Wells Opera to the South Bank. It was felt that the inclusion of opera in a scheme originally adumbrated for drama only might draw away both energy and money from the National Theatre. Nevertheless, plans went ahead. An announcement was made in the House of Commons on 3 July 1962, and in August of that year two boards were appointed by the Chancellor of the Exchequer, the National Theatre Board (Chairman, Lord Chandos), responsible for the creating and running of a National Theatre company of which Sir Laurence Olivier was appointed director, and the South Bank Theatre and Opera House Board (Chairman, Lord Cottesloe), responsible for planning and erecting the buildings. For the National Theatre an amphitheatre auditorium is now envisaged, with the addition of a proscenium theatre later on. Meanwhile the former Old Vic Theatre serves as the National Theatre's temporary home.

In addition to the £1 million voted by the Government for the new buildings, the Greater London Council will provide £1,300,000 towards the cost. There will also be available the moneys held in the Shakespeare Memorial Fund, and the proceeds of the sale of Sadler's Wells Theatre, which, it is feared, will be demolished and replaced by a block of offices. The Government and the Greater London Council will both make annual grants towards the running costs of both playhouses, the amounts varying according to the theatres' needs. If the Festival Hall, Concert Hall, National Film Theatre, National Theatre, and Sadler's Wells Opera House, which are to lie cheek by jowl on the South Bank, all start their performances at the same time, traffic congestion around the area is likely to be considerable.

For a theatre in London called the National see QUEEN'S THEATRE, 2.

For the People's National Theatre, see PRICE, NANCY.

NATIONAL THEATRE, NEW YORK. 1. Originally the Italian Opera House, this opened as a theatre in 1836 under Tom Flynn and H. E. Willard. It had a good season from 1837 to 1838, when it was under the management of J. W. Wallack. Its fine company, perfect stage management, and Wallack's eye for detail made it a serious rival to the Park, and in opposition to the latter's nickname of 'Old Drury' it was often referred to as 'Covent Garden'. John Vandenhoff was seen at the National under Wallack, and was the first great English actor who did *not* appear at the Park. In the same year W. E. Burton came from Philadelphia to make his first appearance in New York, being engaged for a further season in Feb. 1839. After Wallack's withdrawal, Hackett was seen in a season of his own plays, and Charlotte Cushman came as Lady Macbeth and a female Romeo. Apart from straight plays the theatre housed a number of operas and ballets, and some Negro minstrelsy. It was burnt down on 23 Sept. 1839. Rebuilt, it was again destroyed on 29 May 1841, after a somewhat uneventful period, in which the Vandenhoffs made their last appearance in New York. The theatre had not been a financial success, except under Wallack, and as the neighbourhood was unsalubrious it was never rebuilt.

2. On 41st Street between 7th and 8th Avenues. This opened on 1 Sept. 1921 with Sidney Howard's first play, *Swords*, which had only a short run. The first success of the new theatre, after an unsuccessful revival of *Trilby*, was *The Cat and the Canary*, a thriller which ran for nearly a year. Early in 1923 came *Will Shakespeare*, in a production by Winthrop Ames, with Katharine Cornell, Cornelia Otis Skinner, Otto Kruger, and Haidée Wright, while the end of the same year saw Walter Hampden in his popular revival of *Cyrano de Bergerac*. The next success was *The Trial of Mary Dugan* (1927) with 437 performances, while a record for the house was set up by *Grand Hotel* (1930) with 459 performances. This last play was produced by Herman Shumlin with décor by Aline Bernstein and a superb cast. The next play of any distinction was *Within the Gates* (1934), while two years later came a successful dramatization of *Ethan Frome*, with a cast which included Pauline Lord, Ruth Gordon, and Raymond Massey. The end of 1936 saw the success of Noël Coward's *To-night at 8.30*, with the author and Gertrude Lawrence. It was withdrawn at the height of its success because of Coward's other commitments. Later successes at this theatre were *The Little Foxes* (1939), with Tallulah Bankhead, and *The Corn is Green* (1940), in which Ethel Barrymore gave a fine performance as the elderly school-teacher. After structural alterations the theatre reopened on 11 Nov. 1941 with Maurice Evans in *Macbeth*, and in 1946 *Call Me Mister* began its long run. In 1959 the theatre was renamed the Billy Rose, after the well-known American impresario, who bought and redecorated it, opening with an all-star revival of *Heartbreak House*. In 1962 came Albee's controversial play, *Who's Afraid of Virginia Woolf?*, and in 1964 his *Tiny Alice*, with John Gielgud and Irene Worth.

For the New National Theatre, New York, see CHATHAM THEATRE, 2. GEORGE FREEDLEY†

NATIONAL THEATRE CONFERENCE, U.S.A. This non-profit-making theatre group arose out of a conference held in 1925 at the Carnegie Institute of Technology in Pittsburg. A further conference at Yale University two years later cemented the organization, which was formally founded in 1930 at the opening of the theatre of the State University of Iowa. In 1937 it was dissolved and reorganized under a grant from the Rockefeller Foundation. The membership consists mainly of university and community theatre directors, with a sprinkling of invited members who have contributed in some way to the good of the non-profit-making theatre in America.

NATURALISM, a movement in the theatre of the late nineteenth century which arose in revolt against the artificial theatricality of contemporary forms of playwriting and acting. The citadel had already been breached by the realism of Ibsen and his followers, but it was a selective realism. Naturalism discarded all compromise and came out strongly on the side of stark reality. The forerunner of the movement was probably Strindberg, with *Miss Julie*, and Zola raised it to the importance of a literary creed, with his demand for a 'slice of life'. His dramatization of his own novel *Thérèse Raquin* (1873) was the first consciously conceived naturalistic drama; but it was Becque, as author, and Antoine, as producer, who established naturalism in the theatre. The Théâtre Libre, as Antoine's new venture was called, had much influence in Europe. It led to the formation of Brahm's Freie Bühne in Germany, where naturalism found its most triumphant expression with such plays as *Die Familie Selicke* and the realistic dramas of Hauptmann and Schönherr, and to Grein's Independent Theatre in England, where Shaw was the apostle of the new movement, which, however, languished in uncongenial soil. In Russia, on the other hand, it flourished, and attained world recognition in the work of Stanislavsky and the Moscow Art Theatre, particularly with their production of Gorky's *The Lower Depths*. In Spain naturalism is represented by *La Malquerida*, and in America by the early works of O'Neill, by some facets of Maxwell Anderson's works, and by the dramatized novels of Steinbeck.

NAUMACHIA, at Rome, a mimic sea-fight of great splendour, staged in an arena flooded for the purpose—also the name given to an amphitheatre specially built for this purpose by Augustus on the right bank of the Tiber. Naumachiae, or water-pageants, were given in Italy at the time of the Renaissance (see MACHINERY). For English nineteenth-century aquatic spectacles see CIRCUS.

NAUTICAL DRAMA. A type of romantic melodrama popular in the late eighteenth and early nineteenth centuries, which had as its hero a 'Jolly Jack Tar', in lineal descent from the sailor-characters in the novels of Smollett (*Roderick Random*, 1748; *Peregrine Pickle*, 1751). An early nautical play was Smollett's own *The Reprisal; or, the Tars of Old England*, seen at Drury Lane in 1757. The Jack Tar was then further popularized by Charles Dibdin the elder (1745–1814) before being adopted by Fitzball and Jerrold, with the actor T. P. Cooke making his name as the sailor-hero of such dramas as *The Pilot* (1825), *Black-Eyed Susan* (1829), *My Poll and my Partner Joe* (1835). The character flourished on the Surrey side until well into the 1850s, but he was already burlesqued in Dickens's *Nicholas Nickleby* (1838), a joke which reached its culminating point in *H.M.S. Pinafore.* Nautical Drama should not be confused with Aquatic Drama, in which the water itself often seems to have played the hero's part.

NAZIMOVA, Alla (1879–1945), Russian actress, who received her training in Moscow, and in 1904 was leading lady of a St. Petersburg theatre. She toured Europe and America with a Russian company, and in 1906, having learnt English in less than six months, made her first appearance in an English-speaking part —Hedda Tesman—at the Princess's Theatre, New York, under the management of the Shuberts. She remained in America, where she was considered an outstanding exponent of Ibsen's heroines, and in 1910 took possession of the Nazimova Theatre (see THIRTY-NINTH STREET THEATRE), built and named for her by the Shuberts. She opened there with *Little Eyolf.* After some years in films she returned to the stage, playing with the Civic Repertory Theatre and the Theatre Guild in Ibsen, Chekhov, Turgeniev, and O'Neill. She was a superb actress, vibrant and passionate, and vividly sensitive to every subtlety of her many great roles.

NEGRO IN THE AMERICAN THEATRE. On the early American colonial stage Negro characters were rare, since the repertory came from England. The outstanding exceptions, Shakespeare's *Othello* and the African Prince in Thomas Southerne's *Oroonoko*, had little appeal for audiences of slave-holders. In 1799 the latter play was enlivened and made more congenial by a song 'The Gay Negro Boy' sung in black-face to banjo strumming. A popular comedy, *The Padlock* (1769), had a West Indian slave, Mungo, who was a singing, bibulous, profane clown of little authenticity. Played by Lewis Hallam, who supposedly sought realism, Mungo fathered a long line of comic Negroes in American drama. In *Robinson Crusoe and Harlequin Friday* (1786) and *The Buccaneers; or, the Discovery of Robinson Crusoe* (1817) the dialect imitated Defoe's pidgin-English instead of actual Negro speech.

Minor Negro characters appeared in *The Candidates* (written probably before the Revolutionary War), in *The Fall of British Tyranny* (1776), where slaves, released by the British, promise to kill their masters, and in *The Yorker's Stratagem* (1792), which shows a New Yorker marrying a West Indian mulatto. The Negro servant, serving chiefly for comic relief, appears first in *Triumphs of Love* (1795) and *The Politicians* (1797). This comic stereotype, which roughly resembles the stage Irishman in buffoonery, far-fetched dialect, and singing, ranges from William Dunlap's *A Trip to Niagara* (1830) to Anna Cora Mowatt's *Fashion* (1845).

Meanwhile another tradition was hardening. Songs in alleged Negro dialect were interspersed in *A New Way To Win Hearts* (1802), *The Battle of Lake Champlain* (1815), and *Tom and Jerry* (1820–1), which found a spot for gay singing and dancing even in a Charleston slave-market. In 1823 Edwin Forrest's black-faced acting in *The Tailor in Distress* was praised as the first realistic representation of the plantation Negro. Finding no white actress willing to blacken her face to play opposite him, Forrest had to hire an old Negro washer-woman, but this squeamishness of white actresses did not last very long. In the 1820s George Nichols popularized 'Zip Coon' and other songs and dances learned from Negroes in the Mississippi Delta, and George Washington Dixon impersonated Negroes in songs like 'Coal Black Rose', 'Long Tailed Blue', and in Negro burlettas. It became a rule to interpolate Negro songs in theatre programmes, whether farce or tragedy; they were sung by circus clowns, sometimes from the backs of cantering horses.

In 1828 along the Ohio River (whether in Louisville, Cincinnati, or Pittsburgh is not clear) Thomas 'Daddy' Rice imitated the singing and shuffling of a Negro 'hostler'. The skit was enthusiastically received. In 1833, as a new fillip to the act, 'Daddy' Rice dumped a four-year-old burnt-corked urchin from a bag on to the stage; this was Joseph Jefferson the third, who perfectly mimicked Rice's ungainly dancing. Rice was not content with single songs but wove them together; his organized *Bone Squash* is probably the first 'Ethiopian Opera'. Rice's phenomenal popularity called for imitation in the 1830s; P. T. Barnum featured Ethiopian breakdowns; the American Museum exhibited the Ethiopian Comic Statues; and a popular circus act was 'Jim Crow, Esquire, on Horseback'. In 1843 the first regular minstrel troupe, a quartet including Daniel Emmett, the composer of 'Dixie', appeared on the stage in gala costume, performing on the fiddle, banjo, bones, and tambourine, telling jokes and ending with a grand breakdown. Ethiopian minstrelsy was born.

Contemporary rivals, the Kentucky Minstrels, the Congo Melodists, and the Original Christy Minstrels, along with many others, swept the nation. It was for the Christys, who retired wealthy, that Stephen Foster wrote his best-known songs. The minstrel craze saw its heyday in the four decades from 1840 to 1880. Among the numerous companies that sprang up after the Civil War, McIntyre and Heath, the Al G. Fields Minstrels, Haverly's Mastodons, and Dan Bryant's Minstrels were among the best-known. At the end of the 1870s, companies attempted to whip up a waning demand by quantity of performers and extravaganza. From spontaneity the minstrel show descended into ritualized conventionality. The end of this peculiar American phenomenon (which was extremely popular in England also) came during the second decade of the twentieth century. Amateur companies, however, still perform ministrelsy, and its influence remains strong in vaudeville, films, and television.

The minstrel show consisted of three parts. At the rise of the curtain the black-faced company with a lone white-faced middleman stood in a semicircle. Then the middleman, 'Mister Interlocutor', ordered 'Gentlemen, be seated'. The interlocutor, painfully correct, 'father of all the foils in vaudeville', engaged in badinage with Mr. Bones and Mr. Tambo, the two endmen, who were the chief punsters and wisecrackers. Quips and conundrums, interpolated comic and sentimental songs, with a gay song by full chorus and a grand walk-around, filled out the first part. The second part was the 'olio', a variety bill of dances, vocal and instrumental music, and stump speeches, ending with a 'hoe-down dance' accompanied by singing and hand-clapping. The third part consisted of after-pieces—farces, comic opera, or burlesque—at first supposed to be based on Negro life; but later any short play was used (even *Box and Cox*).

Though black-face minstrelsy started out with rudimentary realism, it soon degenerated into fantastic artificiality. It must be remembered that Ethiopian minstrelsy was white masquerade; Negro performers were not allowed to appear in it until after the Civil War; it was composed by whites, acted and sung by whites in burnt cork, for white audiences. It succeeded in fixing one stereotype deeply in the American consciousness: the shiftless, lazy, improvident, loud-mouthed, flashily-dressed Negro, with kinky hair and large lips, over-addicted to the eating of watermelon and chicken (almost always purloined), the drinking of gin, the shooting of dice, and the twisting of language into ludicrous malformations. Life was a perennial joke or 'breakdown'. Black-face minstrelsy underestimated and misrepresented the American Negro in much the same way that the English drama treated the stage Irishman.

Though minstrelsy generally showed an easy-going, amusing way of life, occasionally a few sentimental plaints about the woes of slavery—e.g. 'Darling Nelly Gray' (1856)—were ventured in the North. The first anti-slavery protest entered legitimate drama with *The Gladiator* (1831). Though this play dealt with the uprising of slaves in ancient Rome, the author feared that if produced in a slave state he and the actors would be 'rewarded with the penitentiary'. Two little-known abolitionist melodramas, *The Captured Slave* and *The Branded Hand*, appeared in 1845, but are not known to have been acted.

For full use of anti-slavery protest the American stage, like American fiction, had to wait for the appearance of *Uncle Tom's Cabin* in 1852. Within six months of the enormous success of Mrs. Stowe's novel two adaptations were produced in New York. Opposed to the theatre on religious grounds and unprotected by copyright, Mrs. Stowe received no share of the large profits made from dramatizations of her book. She did, however, attend incognito a performance of the play in the fifth year of its amazing run. There were many adaptations; two versions appeared in Paris; in 1878 five London theatres presented the play concurrently. *Uncle Tom's Cabin* has been America's most popular play by far; from 1852 to 1931 it never left the American boards, and since then it has been revived, notably in Abbott's very free *Sweet River* (1936) (see also No. 168).

The best-known version of *Uncle Tom's Cabin* was by George L. Aiken, who heightened the sentimentality and melodrama. His treatment of Topsy lacked Mrs. Stowe's understanding and was close to black-face minstrelsy; Eliza's crossing the ice was theatrical sensationalism. Over the years the abolitionist edge of the material was dulled, and the treatment veered toward melodrama and farce. Harriet Beecher Stowe's second anti-slavery novel, *Dred*, was thrice dramatized in 1856, by C. W. Taylor, John Brougham, and H. J. Conway. Though *Dred* had many good points as a novel, none of the dramatizations succeeded. For all their great anti-slavery service, *Uncle Tom's Cabin* and, to a lesser degree, *Dred* have helped in the stereotyping of Negroes on the American stage. More than the novel, the widely popular *Uncle Tom* plays have been too persuasive in supporting the generalizations that impish, light-fingered Topsy and the ideally forgiving and submissive Uncle Tom are 'typical Negroes', and that it is only the mixed-blood Negroes who are, as a result of their biological inheritance, aggressive, intelligent, and willing to fight for freedom.

The same sort of 'tragic mulatto stereotype' is constant in other abolitionist dramas. In 1857 J. T. Trowbridge dramatized his novel *Neighbor Jackwood*, which dealt with a beautiful octoroon who escapes from Louisiana to Vermont and there marries her Yankee benefactor. The revelation of Northern dislike for the Fugitive Slave Law gives the play more reality than the idealized characterization. William Wells Brown, the Negro author and anti-slavery agent, wrote *Escape; or, a Leap For Freedom* (1858), the first play by an American Negro. It is not known to have been produced, but Brown gave readings of it to great applause. As a play it is inept and imitative; even the comic scenes are closer to black-face minstrelsy than Brown's own experiences of slavery should have allowed. The heroine is the octoroon beauty, by this time becoming a stage familiar. Dion Boucicault's *The Octoroon* (1859) is the most theatrical in the gallery of doomed mixed-blood heroines. Canny artificer that he was, Boucicault wrote a play calculated to give offence to neither North nor South in those critical years. Slavery is shown as kindly; the slaves are happy-go-lucky sleepyheads; only Zoe, the octoroon, is tragic because she cannot marry the white man she loves. Zoe is a strange mixture of abjectness, of pride in her white blood, of forgiveness equal to Uncle

Tom's, and of devotion to her dead white father who had failed to guarantee her freedom. Boucicault provided two separate endings so the audience could take their choice, and the play reaped great financial returns.

Ossawatomie Brown (1859), the first dramatization of the Harper's Ferry Raid, significantly portrayed John Brown's Negro comrades. But in the numerous plays of the Old South and the Civil War, Negro characters were generally inconsequential and almost interchangeable. *The Guerrillas* (1863) showed the faithful slave indignantly refusing freedom, revealing to the Richmond audience its wish rather than the pressing actuality. On the other hand, *For A Brother's Life* (1885) portrayed Negro refugees to the Union camps. Augustus Thomas's version of *Colonel Carter of Cartersville* (1892) conventionally stressed the mutual affection between master and slave, but unconventionally had a real Negro in the role of the faithful servant. The favourite tragic octoroon appeared in *The White Slave* (1882), which rivalled in popularity *The Octoroon*, and in *Captain Herne, U.S.A.* (1895). A much more convincing octoroon appeared the same year in Frank Mayo's dramatization of Mark Twain's *Pudd'nhead Wilson*, a mordant exposé of slavery. Winston Churchill's dramatization of *The Crisis* (1902) contained a vivid slave auction. *The New South* (1893), by J. R. Grismer and Clay Greene, showed something of the uneasy side of slave life. In this play James A. Herne played the part of a Negro murderer named Sampson. In *The Reverend Griffith Davenport* (1899), Herne's own play about slavery and the Civil War, Sampson is the name of a runaway Negro who takes his own life. Herne's view of the cruelties of slavery is soberly realistic. So is Steele Mackaye's dramatization of Albion Tourgee's *A Fool's Errand* (1881), a sympathetic treatment of the problems of the newly freed in a hostile South. In Thomas Dixon's *The Clansman* (1906), however, the Ku Klux Klan is glorified and Negroes are characterized as brutes whose emancipation was a grievous mistake.

As an answer to this kind of propaganda a Negro, Joseph S. Cotter, Sr., wrote *Caleb, The Degenerate* (1906), more of a tract than a play. In 1909 William Vaughn Moody portrayed in *The Faith Healer* something of the superstition, religious fervour, and eloquence of Negro folk-life. The height of the problem play of the period was *The Nigger* (1910). Using a popular framework Sheldon shows a politically ambitious hero suddenly discovering that he has Negro blood. After advancing to the governorship and finding himself unable to help Negroes, he confesses his race and pledges himself to its service. As a writer of advanced ideas, Sheldon said bolder things about lynching and miscegenation than had been heard on the American stage before him. *Pride of Race* (1916) by Michael Landman also dealt with miscegenation, but less convincingly.

The comic Negro was continued in the 1880s and 1890s in Edward Harrigan's *Mulligan* cycle of vaudeville sketches about Negro life, dealing with dialect-speaking Irishmen, Germans, and Negroes. Harrigan's *The Doyle Brothers* (1874) and *Pete* (1887) glorify the faithful old Negro servant, but his metropolitan characters have a rough realism. Negro entertainers now began to appear in black-face minstrelsy, using not only the same make-up as the whites but the same artificial pattern. Early companies were Lew Johnson's Plantation Company, the Georgia Minstrels, later Callender's Original Georgia Minstrels, and the Colored Hamtown Singers. Famous Negro Minstrels were Billy Kersands ('King Rastus'), Sam Lucas, and James Bland, the composer of 'Carry Me Back to Ol' Virginny', and 'In the Evening by the Moonlight'. The minstrel show gave apprenticeship to song-and-dance comedians who were later to make their names on Broadway.

In 1890 *The Creole Burlesquers* emerged from the minstrel pattern; John W. Isham's *The Octoroons* (1895) and *Oriental America* (1896) followed. Where the minstrel shows had been all-male, these shows glorified the Negro girl both in the chorus and as principals. *Black Patti's Troubadours* (1896) kept the minstrel form until the finale in which the splendid-voiced Black Patti sang operatic selections. In 1898, with Bob Cole's *A Trip To Coontown*, the first show to be produced and managed by Negroes, the Negro show arrived. Within a decade Negro shows such as *Clorindy*, *The Origin of the Cakewalk*, *Jes' Lak White Folks*, *The Policy Players*, *The Sons of Ham*, *In Dahomey*, *Bandana Land*, *The Red Moon*, and *The Darktown Follies* had been produced, and were definitely part of America's theatrical scene.

For about a decade Negro shows lost favour because of repetitiousness. In 1921 *Shuffle Along*, produced by Miller and Lyles, a really new black-face team, and Noble Sissle and Eubie Blake, masters of the jazz music that was taking New York by storm, started a long series of successes. Their high-spirited gaiety in dancing, jazzed-up music, fresher comedy, lavish costumes and sets, put a definite stamp on American entertainment. Some of the hits were *Liza* and *Running Wild* (both 1923), *From Dixie to Broadway* and *Chocolate Dandies* (both 1924), *Plantation Revue* (1925), Lew Leslie's annual *Blackbirds* (1927–30) and his *Brown Buddies* (1930), and *Rhapsody in Black* (1931). Florence Mills, Josephine Baker, Adelaide Hall, Ada Ward, Ethel Waters, Bill Robinson, and Johnny Hudgins were a few of the headliners.

The Negro musical show was part of America's discovery of Harlem, and that, of course, only on its gay and colourful side. Realistic drama of Negro folk-life, with Negroes as major characters, came first to Broadway with Ridgely Torrence's *Three Plays for a Negro Theatre* (1917). Influenced by the Abbey Theatre's folk plays of the Irish, Torrence recognized the dignity in the lives of his

NEGRO IN THE AMERICAN THEATRE

own characters. *The Rider of Dreams* is a gentle portrait of a music-loving wastrel and his severely-tried, hard-working wife; *Granny Maumee* is a harsh portrait of an old woman who bitterly remembers that a mob burned her son. *Simon the Cyrenian* told of the black Simon who bore Christ's cross for him to Calvary. The presentation of these plays was significant in American theatre history.

Similarly historic was *The Emperor Jones* (1920), produced by the Provincetown Players. O'Neill had already shown interest in Negroes in *The Moon of the Caribees* (1918), and in *The Dreamy Kid* (1919), a one-act tragedy of a young Negro gangster in Harlem. *The Emperor Jones* was something new on the American stage; Brutus Jones, crafty, bold, arrogant, and truculent, is far from the comic servant or naïve folk-type. Though social protest is absent, certain pressures upon Negro life (slavery, the chain-gang) are clearly portrayed. The atavism is debatable if Brutus Jones is intended to symbolize *the* Negro; but it is possible that Brutus is another instance of O'Neill's study of man, not of a particular race. The new techniques, the use of the throbbing tom-tom, the exotic setting, the monologues delivered so powerfully by Charles Gilpin, and later Paul Robeson, made theatre history. *The Emperor Jones* is remote from Negro experience in America. *All God's Chillun Got Wings* (1923) is a closer approach to the problem play. In this study of intermarriage and the tragic effects of race prejudice, O'Neill has selected an extreme case, with the Negro too selfless and inept, and the white girl too weak and stupid, for credence. Even so the play was threatened with riots.

In 1923 the Ethiopian Art Players, organized by Raymond O'Neil and Mrs. Sherwood Anderson, indicated lines that Negro performances were to take, producing a jazzed-up *Comedy of Errors*, a revival of *Salome*, and a folk-play, *The Chip Woman's Fortune*, by a Negro playwright, Willis Richardson. The one-act *Rackey* (1919) and *Goat Alley* (1922) presented something of the drab misery of Negro slums. There is more colour and music and knowledge of folk-life in *Roseanne* (1923), a sympathetic study of Southern church life. *Black Boy* (1926) chronicled the rise and fall of a Negro pugilist, but the presence of the newly discovered Paul Robeson in the lead could not save it. Another play dealing with the meaner aspects of life is *Lulu Belle* (1926), the melodrama of a Harlem harlot's progress, with Lenore Ulric in the title-role. David Belasco's realistic sets of Harlem were notable. In 1929 the Negro novelist, Wallace Thurman, collaborated with William Rapp on *Harlem*, a swiftly paced melodrama of the seamier aspects of life, seen from the inside. Its racketeers, gamblers, loose women, its murder and rent party could have been matched in life. *Singing the Blues* (1931), by John McGowan, continued the exploitation of the gaudier Harlem.

Greater respect for his material was shown by Em Jo Basshe in his *Earth* (1927), a lyrical drama of a conflict in the deep South between Christianity and voodooism, featured by weird music composed by Hall Johnson. This was a production of the New Playwrights' Theatre. Another of their productions was *Hoboken Blues* (1927), an expressionistic play combining realism and fantasy, vaudeville and tragedy. Subtitled *The Black Rip Van Winkle*, contrasting Harlem at the turn of the century and in the gaudy boom twenty-five years later, the play contained much sharp protest at the economic plight of the Negro. A 'native opera' was attempted in *Deep River* (1926), another short-lived experiment. More in the older tradition was *Showboat* (1927), one of America's most popular, most revived musicals. One of the high spots of this colourful melodrama of river life has always been the singing of 'Old Man River', first by Jules Bledsoe, then by Paul Robeson, and more recently by Kenneth Spencer.

Of all American playwrights, Paul Green has made most thorough use of Negro folk-life in drama. His one-act plays, better known to the outlying than to the Broadway theatres, range from *The No 'Count Boy* (1924), depicting a musical vagabond reminiscent of Synge's Playboy, to stark snapshots of life among Negro farmhands such as *The Hot Iron* (1926), *White Dresses* (1926), and *The End of the Row* (1926). Folk superstitions are dealt with amusingly in *The Man Who Died At Twelve O'Clock* (1925) and gruesomely in *Aunt Mahaly's Cabin* (1925). Green's honesty in dealing with subjects generally taboo in the South and his recognition of the harshness of Negro life are apparent in *In Abraham's Bosom* (1926), a play about the last century. Abraham McCranie, the Negro son of a slave-owner, dreams and labours to bring education to his needy people, but meets with distrust and dislike from other Negroes, even his own family, and with hostility from the whites. When a white mob breaks up a meeting that he has called he is tormented beyond endurance and kills his white half-brother after a bitter quarrel. The mob, already formed, comes to his house and shoots him down. *In Abraham's Bosom* was awarded the Pulitzer Prize for its imagination, sympathy, and power. In *The House of Connelly* (1931) the Negro characters are minor but well characterized. *Roll, Sweet Chariot* (1935), an acting version of *Potter's Field* (1931), is experimental, with speech, chant, and song alternating. It gives a fluent cross-section of the loose morality and violence of a Southern shanty-town. Green does not make this material something picturesque; his chain-gang scene is brutal and true; the general tone is depressing. There is more social protest in *Hymn to the Rising Sun* (1936), an ironic, forceful drama of the horror of Southern convict camps; both Negro and white convicts are victims of their sadism. Paul Green has stated that his plays are not meant to be 'generally representative of the Negro race', that he has been chiefly concerned with 'the more tragic and uneasy side of Negro life'. This he has conveyed with authentic knowledge and imaginative insight.

Rather than the tragic and uneasy phases, the exotic attracted Du Bose Heyward and Dorothy Heyward in *Porgy* (1927), dramatized from the former's novel. Cleon Throckmorton's elaborate sets of Catfish Row, a waterside slum of Charleston, were the background for an appealing story of primitive passion, hatred, murder, humour, superstition, faith, and sorrow. The crippled beggar Porgy and his doomed girl Bess were characterized with great sympathy. Rouben Mamoulian directed the production with a flair for the picturesque, especially in the wake and storm scenes. The same authors' *Mamba's Daughters* (1939), also adapted from a novel by Du Bose Heyward, is a more conventional tale of fierce devotion on the part of Mamba, a cunning grandmother, and Hagar, a slow-witted Amazon mother, both of them single-tracked in their determination to make something of Hagar's daughter. *Mamba's Daughters* was Ethel Waters's first appearance on the legitimate stage, and she was highly praised for the power and dignity with which she played Hagar. Du Bose Heyward's *Brass Ankle* (1931), the tragedy of a woman of Negro-Indian-white stock who bears a son who is a 'throw-back' to some unknown Negro ancestor, is unconvincing. In 1935 George Gershwin selected *Porgy* as the basis of the 'first American folk-opera', for which Ira Gershwin wrote many lyrics. Presented by the Theatre Guild in 1935 and revived in 1942, directed by Mamoulian, and introducing Todd Duncan and Anne Brown to the American stage, 'Porgy and Bess' has become one of America's best-loved and most influential entertainments.

One result of *Porgy's* success was the dramatization (1930) of the best-selling novel, *Scarlet Sister Mary*. Ethel Barrymore in black-face played the scarlet sister of the Negro plantation, but the play was a failure. Another skilful and informed writer about South Carolina Negroes, E. C. L. Adama, failed in *Potee's Gal* (1929), a play about the primitive life in the Congaree swamps. Marc Connelly, a comparative outsider, succeeded where these comparative insiders failed. *The Green Pastures* (1930) is derived from Roark Bradford's *Ol' Man Adam an' His Chillun*, a book of burlesques purporting to be a Negro preacher's version of the Bible. Connelly retained some of the burlesque, such as a God in frock-coat and fedora, smoking a ten-cent cigar, and walking the earth like 'a natural man'. But he infused much tenderness and great reverence into Bradford's farces, aided by Richard Harrison as 'de Lawd', by a cast that performed with simplicity and dignity, and by the well-placed spirituals beautifully sung by Hall Johnson's Choir. Inexactly termed 'an attempt to present certain aspects of a living religion in the terms of its believers', *The Green Pastures* would probably shock the Negro folk as sacrilegious, and is really Marc Connelly's version of what Roark Bradford said was a Negro preacher's version of religion. Still, the kindly perplexed father of his people is like the God of the spirituals. There are some charming vignettes of Negro folk-life on its less uneasy side, and the majestic scene of the exodus to the Promised Land, with the ragged crowds of the heavy-laden, their faces lit with hope and faith, marching to the swelling choruses of 'I'm Noways Weary', touches upon profound reality.

In 1933 a Negro playwright's version of folk religion appeared in *Run, Little Chillun*, the first successful play of Negro authorship on Broadway. Based, as was Basshe's *Earth*, on a conflict between Christianity and a pagan cult, *Run, Little Chillun* made full use of spectacle, the dance, and music. It inclined to the exotic and melodramatic, but unquestionably has the authenticity of the inside view. The church scenes especially were distinguished by moving realism, with superb musical effects. Kenneth Burke pointed out that *The Green Pastures* was 'essentially a white man's play . . . exploiting the old conception of the Negro (naïve, good-natured, easily put upon)', whereas *Run, Little Chillun* emphasizes 'an aspect of the Negro symbol with which our theatre-going public is not theatrically at home: the power side of the Negro'. Lacking the stagecraft of *The Green Pastures*, its best scenes had greater verisimilitude.

Black Souls (1932) was a well-intentioned play, using educated Negroes for propaganda purposes, but it lacked the force of reality. One of the strongest anti-lynching plays was *Never No More* (1932), written after the author, an ex-cotton-planter, had accidentally witnessed a Negro's being burned at the stake. There is more than horror in the play; sympathetic understanding marks the portrait of the Negro tenant family ruled over by the mother (admirably played by Rose McClendon). The burning of the scapegrace son while the family is barricaded in their cabin was a scene of almost intolerable tension. Another powerful social indictment of the same year was *Bloodstream*, which showed the brutality of Negro and white convict labour in the mines. In 1934 John Wexley dramatized the notorious Scottsboro case in *They Shall Not Die*, throwing light on the travesty of justice, the violence of the police system and the mobs, and the poverty and ignorance of both Negroes and whites. *Mulatto*, in the same year, is a mordant sensational account of an illicit relationship in the South, showing the hatred of a mulatto son for his white father. *White Man* (1936) was an unconvincing tragedy of the near-white.

The most successful play of radical protest was *Stevedore* (1934). The frame-up of a Negro organizer, who is accused of rape in order to check his militancy, is prevented when the concerted action of white and black dockhands turn back a mob. Lonnie Thompson, who is class- rather than race-conscious, the spunky Binnie, keeper of a lunch-room, and Blacksnake, a man full of fight, are new Negroes on the

NEGRO IN THE AMERICAN THEATRE

American stage. In 1937 *Marching Song* also presented Negro life and characters in terms of social analysis and protest. A large number of left-wing plays followed *Stevedore* in urging that Negroes must organize and fight for their rights and that white and Negro labour must unite their forces. One of the best of these, *A Mighty Wind A-Blowin'* (1936), urged the union of white and Negro sharecroppers. Of the New Theatre League's 'agit-prop' plays, one Negro hero was Angelo Herndon, who was jailed for leading a march of the unemployed in Atlanta. Another hero was John Henry, the champion steel-driver, whom both Herbert Kline, editor of *New Theatre*, and Frank Wells stressed as a working-class hero. In 1939 the commercial theatre presented Roark Bradford's *John Henry*, but even with Paul Robeson and Josh White in the cast the play failed. Bradford revealed little sympathy with the essential dignity of John Henry.

Wells's *John Henry* had to wait for the Federal Theatre to produce it. The Federal Theatre Project was fortunate in having as its director Hallie Flanagan, who wanted a theatre that would fearlessly present problems touching American life; she was also greatly interested in a Negro theatre. Federal Theatre did more for Negroes than give employment to the many unemployed Negro actors; it served as a needed apprenticeship in acting, playwriting, producing, and designing; and it brought the people into the theatre.

The plays produced in Harlem and in such cities as Boston, Hartford, Philadelphia, Newark, Chicago, Seattle, San Francisco, Los Angeles, and Birmingham, were of many sorts. The most popular was *The Haitian Macbeth* (1936), which with Jack Carter, Edna Thomas, and Canada Lee in the leading roles, directed by Orson Welles and John Houseman, and with tropical settings by Nat Karson, made theatre history. The witchcraft scenes in a Haitian jungle, the weird dances performed to frenzied drumming, set a type of adaptation of the classics that has prevailed. Somewhat in the same vein was *Haiti* (1938), a melodrama of the revolt of Toussaint L'Ouverture and Christophe against the French. *The Swing Mikado* by the Theatre Project of Chicago was the hit of 1939; the free swinging of Gilbert and Sullivan, the exotic stage settings, and the enthusiastic abandon of actors, singers, and dancers swept away even confirmed Savoyards. Other adaptations, of *Lysistrata*, *The Taming of the Shrew*, *Androcles and the Lion*, and *Noah*, met with less success. *The Emperor Jones*, *In Abraham's Bosom*, *Run, Little Chillun*, and *Stevedore* were revived by Project Units.

Of great importance were the plays of Negro authorship which but for the Federal Theatre Project might never have received a professional hearing. Noteworthy among these are Frank Wilson's two treatments of folk life, *Brother Mose* (which appeared briefly on Broadway in 1929) and *Walk Together, Chillun* (1936); also a dramatization of a detective novel of Harlem, *The Conjure Man Dies* (1936), and *The Trial of Dr. Beck*, *The Case of Philip Lawrence*, and *The Natural Man* (all 1937), another treatment of the John Henry myth. Especially marked by social realism were *Turpentine* (1936), which dealt with the hardships of labour in Florida swamps, and *Big White Fog* (1938), a play about the depression. *Battle Hymn* (1936) dramatized John Brown's historic thrust for freedom; *Sweet Land* (1937) showed the Negro's continuing struggle. In *How Long Brethren?* (1937) Tamiris and her group danced to Lawrence Gellert's 'Negro Songs of Protest' sung by a Negro chorus. In 1939, with a text by Carlton Moss, *Prelude to Swing*, a dramatic history of the development of Negro music, was presented by a dance unit, a choral group, and a swing orchestra. *Bassa Moona* (1936) brought the real African jungle dance-drama to Broadway.

The success of the Federal Theatre's *Swing Mikado* stimulated private producers to stage the *Hot Mikado* (1939), which was less primitive but smarter, and, with Bill Robinson stopping the show, more commercially successful. Riding the crest, *Swingin' The Dream* (1939) jazzed up *A Midsummer Night's Dream* with the swing artists Louis Armstrong and Maxine Sullivan in key roles, but the result was more of a stunt than a play. *Cabin in the Sky* (1940) capitalized somewhat on *The Green Pastures*. The acting of Ethel Waters, Rex Ingram, Dooley Wilson, Todd Duncan, and Katherine Dunham made for a long run, but the play was sentimental, amusing fantasy, not drama of Negro life. The all-Negro musical show continued in *Jump For Joy* (1940), *Harlem Cavalcade* (1942), *Blue Holiday*, and *Memphis Bound* (both 1945). The last two, though studded with famous stars, had only short runs. With a good story around which to build the singing and dancing, the all-Negro *Carmen Jones* (1943) was an immense success. This spectacle was adapted by Oscar Hammerstein from Bizet's 'Carmen' and gorgeously produced by Billy Rose. In contrast, the curiosity value of a *Lysistrata* played by a Negro cast in Gilbert Seldes's adaptation proved inadequate, but a later all-Negro success was *St. Louis Woman* (1946). The story of the love-life of a flashy jockey at the turn of the century, this was a gay, loud extravaganza with gorgeous costumes and striking sets. Katherine Dunham and her troupe have been popular in their performances of exotic, chiefly Caribbean, dancing in *Tropical Revue* (1944), *Carib Song* (1945), and *Bal Nègre* (1946). Haitian dancing by Josephine Premice, and African and American Negro dancing by Pearl Primus, have also been popular. From *Kykunkor* (1934) to *A Tale of Old Africa* (1946), Asadata Dafora has presented occasional African dance-dramas in New York, with full knowledge of and respect for his native traditions.

No earlier play explored Negro life with such tragic intensity as *Native Son* (1941). Staged and directed for maximum excitement, more melodramatic and less clarified than Richard Wright's novel, the drama was highly successful

NEGRO IN THE AMERICAN THEATRE

in its portrait of Bigger Thomas, trapped like a rat in his Chicago slum home, warped into a killer. Canada Lee's understanding creation of the role of Bigger had much to do with the play's gripping power. Candour and insight marked the dramatization of *Strange Fruit* (1945). Losing some of the novel's depth, the adaptation conveyed movingly the tragedy of a love affair between a young white Southerner and a Negro girl, as well as a most convincing cross-section of a Southern town. Critics were more pleased by *Deep Are The Roots* (1945), which skilfully handled modern problems. A Negro lieutenant, decorated in war, returns to his native South to devote himself to educating his people. The play displays frankly the forces opposed to Negro development in the South, the problem of intermarriage (discussed more openly than ever before), Southern liberalism, and the intelligent Negro's determination to achieve full citizenship. *Jeb* (1946) posed another problem of the veteran, that of unemployment. It was sincere and sympathetic, but lacked the excitement of *Deep Are the Roots. On Whitman Avenue* (1946) dramatized the problem of restricted housing in Northern cities. A Negro family's living in a white neighbourhood causes ugly violence. The play hits hard on a significant theme, and the self-respecting average middle-class Negro family was new on the American stage.

A recent trend of integration is observable on Broadway, particularly in musical comedy. More and more Negro performers have been 'folded into' supporting casts, rather than made to stand out as something particular, like Bert Williams in the *Ziegfeld Follies* and Ethel Waters in *As Thousands Cheer*. From the Federal Theatre *Sing For Your Supper* (1939) through *This Is The Army* (1942), *On The Town* (1944), and *Sing Out, Sweet Land* (1944) ('A salute to American Folk and Popular Music'), Negroes have been part and parcel of the shows. The height of this integration is seen in *Call Me Mister* (1946), a musical of the returning veteran, in *Bloomer Girl* (1944), and especially in *Finian's Rainbow* (1947), a sharp, original satire of racism with Negroes sharing in major and minor roles. In 1943 the late Thomas 'Fats' Waller and George Marion, a Negro and white team, produced successfully *Early to Bed*, but in 1946 the even more significant *Beggar's Holiday*, based on Gay's *Beggar's Opera*, resulted from uniting the talents of two Negroes: the composer Duke Ellington and the designer and co-producer Perry Watkins, with those of two whites: co-producer John R. Sheppard and lyric-writer John La Touche. The play was cast without regard to colour; the male lead was white, the female was Negro; the rest of the cast interracial. Broadway took kindly to the innovation. A few Negro actors, notably Canada Lee as Caliban in Margaret Webster's production of *The Tempest* (1945) and as Bosola in the revival of *The Duchess of Malfi* (1946), have been assigned roles hitherto closed to Negroes. In 1946 the Equity-Library Theatre presented a mixed cast in *Outward Bound*. A further instance of integration was the choice of Langston Hughes to do the lyrics to Kurt Weill's score for the musical production of Elmer Rice's *Street Scene* (1947).

In the early 1940s over one hundred plays on Broadway included Negro actors in roles numbering nearly a thousand. But serious drama of Negro life was rare, and the Negro playwright noticeably absent. Even the few plays that dealt realistically with Negro life were most often by white authors. Except for the short-lived Federal Theatre Project, the Negro playwright has been without experience in the professional theatre. He has turned to the tributary theatre—community, college, and semi-professional groups—to learn and practise his craft. American Negroes by and large see little of the theatre; below the Mason-Dixon line they are not allowed in the legitimate theatres, except infrequently in segregated sections. Negro stock companies played at the Pekin Theatre in Chicago and the Lincoln and the Lafayette Theatres in New York. These theatres, especially the Lafayette, introduced many outstanding performers to the legitimate stage, but their repertory consisted of the melodramatic standbys of Broadway. Early amateur groups in Washington, D.C., presented *Star of Ethiopia* (1913), a pageant of race progress, and *Rachel* (1920), a play denouncing race prejudice. The Negro Little Theatre movement, however, generally followed the lead of Alain Locke and Montgomery Gregory, founders of the Howard University Players, in exploring the drama of Negro folk-life, though some Negro amateur groups refuse to do plays of Negro life.

The most productive playwright for the thriving college theatres has been Randolph Edmonds, whose *Six Plays for a Negro Theatre* about historic Negroes or the folk take well with college audiences. His *In the Land of Cotton* (1942), showing the harshness of sharecropping life, was performed by the People's Community Theatre of New Orleans, directed by Thomas Richardson, who has organized several working-class theatres.

A product of collegiate drama, Abram Hill was a moving force in the establishment of the American Negro Theatre, the most firmly established semi-professional group. Hill's *On Strivers' Row* (1942), produced at the 135th Street Library Theatre, has taken well with the Harlem that is gaily satirized; Hill's dramatization of Len Zinberg's *Walk Hard, Talk Loud* (1944), a novel of the prize-fighting world, did not take so well. The American Negro Theatre's most signal success was its production of *Anna Lucasta* (1944). This play by Philip Yordan about a Polish family was adapted to Negro life and first presented in Harlem. The skill of the production warranted its removal down-town, where it had a phenomenal run, introducing such stars as Hilda Simms and Frederick O'Neal. It also had a long run in London. The American Negro

NEGRO IN THE AMERICAN THEATRE

Theatre has also produced Owen Dodson's *The Garden of Time*, a retelling of the Medea story. Dodson is the author of other poetic plays, *The Divine Comedy*, a play suggested by Father Divine's movement (produced at the Yale University Theatre, 1938), and *The Amistad*, a play on the historic mutiny. He has been influential in college drama and is a member of the Negro Playwrights' Company. Another member of the company is Theodore Ward, whose *Big White Fog* was one of the strongest of the Federal Theatre Project's plays, and whose *Our Lan'*, a play of social realism tried out in the spring of 1947, received Theatre Guild encouragement for a more thorough-going production in the fall.

In 1821, while white actors were smearing their faces with burnt cork to mimic Negroes, a Negro group, the African Company, led by James Hewlett, was performing Shakespeare in New York City. Shortly thereafter, Ira Aldridge, finding no opportunities for his acting abilities in America, went to Europe, where he became famous, particularly as Othello to Charles Kean's Iago. Negroes have since played Shakespeare, notably Edward Sterling Wright in *Othello* at the Lafayette Theatre in 1915, but generally in a Negro theatre before a Negro audience. About a century after Aldridge, Paul Robeson matched his triumph in a London performance of *Othello*, with Maurice Browne as Iago; and in 1943 Margaret Webster's magnificent production of *Othello*, with José Ferrer's Iago and Uta Hagen's Desdemona supporting Robeson's Othello, achieved the longest recorded run of consecutive performance of any Shakespearian play.

STERLING A. BROWN

Since 1948 the history of the Negro in the American theatre is a record of the attempts made by the Negro playwright to deal with materials generic to him. The Second World War exposed fully for many people the menace of the myth of racial superiority. Colonial peoples demanded freedom. Political, economic, and educational advancement became realities to the American Negro. His self-image was revised. He no longer saw himself as his hostile countrymen had seen him—as a servile, humorous, black beast. He was now a citizen of the world, who had contributed to its cultural and economic growth. These factors, in part, contributed to the changing attitudes towards the American Negro which permeated all avenues of American life. The theatre was no exception. Before 1945 only three Broadway playhouses did not follow the usual custom of selling Negroes seats on the aisle—a custom based on the belief that white people did not want black people climbing over them. In 1945 the Playwrights' Company (which included Maxwell Anderson, S. N. Behrman, Sidney Howard, Elmer Rice, and Robert E. Sherwood) issued a declaration of principles which considerably influenced the treatment of the Negro both on and off stage. This declared that members would, in future, deal specifically with the Negro in dramatic terms and would also encourage the use of Negro actors in roles that might be considered 'non-Negro'. Sidney Kingsley's *Detective Story* (1948) featured a Negro policeman, but made no reference to his colour, so that the part could equally well have been played by a white actor, an innovation later followed by Joseph Kramm in *The Shrike* (1952). Actors' Equity Association welcomed this innovation and urged its continuance. The Greenwich Mews Theatre, a professional off-Broadway playhouse, made such casting one of its policies. Such offerings as Shaw's *Widowers' Houses* and *Major Barbara*, Sheldon Stark's *Time of Storm*, and Les Pine's *Monday's Heroes* featured Negro actors in non-Negro roles. In these plays Negroes were seen as family members without reference to colour.

Broadway, however, continued to use the Negro only in specified roles. Carson McCullers's *The Member of the Wedding* (1950) starred Ethel Waters in a role that often suggested the old 'mammy' type. In the Maxwell Anderson–Kurt Weill musical, *Lost in the Stars* (1949)—based on Alan Paton's *Cry, the Beloved Country*—the black South Africans were portrayed by Negro actors. Joshua Logan's *The Wisteria Trees* (1950), an adaptation of Chekhov's *The Cherry Orchard*, utilized Negroes in peasant roles. Negro performers also appeared in specifically Negro parts in Lillian Hellman's *The Autumn Garden* (1951), Moss Hart's *The Climate of Eden* (1952), and Arthur Miller's *The Crucible* (1953). These ventures, however, proved disappointing to the majority of Negro theatre workers, among whom wide-spread unemployment existed. The American Negro Theatre, which had served as a vital training place for professionals, had disbanded. Many of its charter members joined three Harlem groups: the Harlem Showcase, the Committee for the Negro in the Arts, and the Elks Community Theatre. In Nov. 1950 representatives from the three new groups met with a number of Negro playwrights and a Council on the Harlem Theatre was set up. The Council noted in a resolution that the use of Negro actors in non-Negro roles offered limited employment to only a few actors. In addition, this practice neither encouraged nor assisted in disseminating the cultural contributions of the Negro people. The Council noted, too, that the commercial failure of Theodore Ward's *Our Lan'* (1947) after his initial off-Broadway success suggested that the Broadway theatre was prepared to tolerate the Negro, but did not want to deal with him in strong, dramatic terms. The failure of Dorothy Heyward's *Set My People Free* (1948) further confirmed this.

The Council declared that the serious play of Negro life met with repeated commercial failure because it was too often written from a 'white' point of view. Generally, plays involving Negroes had a 'good' white character helping black people out of trouble. The obvious implication, the Council noted, was

NEGRO IN THE AMERICAN THEATRE

that white theatregoers faced psychological barriers and could not identify readily with central sympathetic Negro characters. The Council urged the representative groups to produce plays by Negro writers, and to assist one another mutually in casting, producing, and promoting. The target was the off-Broadway area. A number of plays by Negroes appeared and benefitted from the co-operative action outlined by the Council. Among these were: Harold Holifield's *J. Toth* and *Cow in the Apartment*, Loften Mitchell's *The Bancroft Dynasty* and *The Cellar*, Gertrude Jeannette's *This Way Forward* and *Bolt from the Blue*, Julian Mayfield's *The Other Foot* and *A World Full of Men*, and Alice Childress's *Just A Little Simple*. These plays, written, directed and produced by Negroes, mostly appeared during the years 1950 and 1951.

In the midst of what Harlemites considered a cultural renaissance, the Apollo Theatre—a local vaudeville house—sponsored two shabby productions of 'white' plays with all-Negro casts, namely, *Detective Story* and *Rain*. Both were artistically and commercially disappointing, despite the appearance of Sidney Poitier in *Detective Story*. The Apollo Theatre owner stated publicly that Harlemites did not care for the drama. Representatives from the Harlem Theatre Council issued a statement, declaring: 'The owner of the Apollo has insulted the Negro people by bringing to this community two inferior pieces of little meaning to our lives. Ridiculous prices were charged and when we exercised the buyer's right, we were accused of lacking taste.'

The Apollo owner's charge, however, served as a catalytic agent for productions by Negro authors. On 15 Oct. 1951 William Branch's *A Medal for Willie* was presented by the Committee for the Negro in the Arts to Harlem audiences. The critics hailed the play, which posed in strong dramatic terms the question: Should the Negro fight and die abroad or should he take arms against the American Southland? In Sept. 1952 Ossie Davis's *Alice in Wonder* was presented at the Elks Community Theatre. This work was highly critical of the national government for withholding passports from unpopular group members. On 24 Sept. 1953 Louis Peterson's *Take A Giant Step* opened on Broadway to favourable notices. It was, however, commercially unsuccessful. *Mrs. Patterson*, by Charles Sebree and Greer Johnston, starring Eartha Kitt, suffered a similar fate.

The years 1950–2 witnessed another significant development. Large numbers of Negroes moved out of Harlem to Long Island, Brooklyn, the Bronx, and Westchester County. This move to the suburbs robbed the Harlem area of many theatre workers and playgoers and efforts to build a Negro theatre in Harlem came to a halt. The Negro theatre worker turned to the Greenwich Village area, where the off-Broadway theatre was thriving. On 24 Oct. 1954 William Branch's *In Splendid Error*, the story of Frederick Douglass and John Brown, was produced at the Greenwich Mews Theatre as was Alice Childress's *Trouble in Mind* (1955), which satirized the plight of the Negro in the theatre. Luther James then produced an all-Negro version of John Steinbeck's *Of Mice and Men*, and on 29 Mar. 1956 Earle Hyman appeared as *Mr. Johnson* on Broadway. Despite a remarkable performance by Mr. Hyman, the play failed.

The drive towards the production of plays written by Negroes brought three offerings to local stages during 1956 and 1957. Louis Peterson's *Take a Giant Step* was successfully revived off-Broadway; Loften Mitchell's *A Land Beyond the River* opened at the Greenwich Mews Theatre in Mar. 1957 and continued throughout the year; the Greenwich Mews management, witnessing the large number of Negro theatre parties, installed the folk-musical, *Simply Heavenly* by Langston Hughes and David Martin, in another off-Broadway theatre. This was successful and was subsequently transferred to Broadway. The actress Claudia McNeil was brought to the attention of theatregoers and from *Simply Heavenly* she joined the Broadway cast of Lorraine Hansberry's *A Raisin in the Sun*. This, directed by Lloyd Richards and starring Sidney Poitier, opened on 11 Mar. 1959. It was highly acclaimed, stimulated interest in the transference of Negro problems to the stage with Negro actors, and won the Critics' Circle award. It later had a successful run in London. These artistic and financial successes impressed producers, who suddenly appeared willing to take an option on a considerable number of works by Negro playwrights. A play by William Branch, an adaptation of Peter Abrahams's novel, *A Wreath for Udomo*, had a successful engagement in Cleveland, and in 1961 opened in London, where it had a hostile reception from the critics.

Off-Broadway was the scene of three successful ventures during 1961 and 1962. In May 1961 Jean Genêt's *The Blacks* opened to critical acclaim and had an unprecedentedly long run. It had an all-Negro cast, and was interpreted as a 'clown show', dealing with the contemporary upward climb of the coloured peoples. Its characters were projected as neither American Negroes nor as Africans, but as universal prototypes of Negroes. The play's biting satire lashed audiences nightly. Many white members of the audience commented that this play revealed the deep feelings of Negroes, and wondered if all Negroes might retaliate once the yoke of oppression was lifted.

In 1962 Errol John's *The Moon on a Rainbow Shawl*, winner of a play-competition sponsored by the London *Observer*, was also successful, as was *Fly Blackbirds*, a revue. The most discussed work of the season was, however, Ossie Davis's *Purlie Victorious*, in which the leading character, the Reverend Purlie Victorious Judson, is a satire on the Negro stereotype, bent on outwitting a white plantation owner by lying, cringing, cajoling, or direct action, and Gitlow, another character, is a clown, an 'Uncle Tom', in front of his white master, but a very different person among his own people. In showing this side of the stereotype—the character so long imposed on theatrical treatment of Negroes, and so bitterly resented by them, just as Irishmen resent being portrayed as drunken buffoons, and Jews as unscrupulous misers—Mr. Davis, with great dramatic skill, managed to make a valid social comment in biting dialogue, presented in humorous vein, without alienating the large number of white people who flocked to see his play.

During the 1963–4 season eight plays by Negro authors were professionally produced in New York. These were *Ballad for Bimshire*, a musical by Irving Burgie and Loften Mitchell in which Ossie Davis co-starred with Frederick O'Neal and Jimmy Randolph; *Tambourines to Glory* and *Jericho-Jimcrow*, both by Langston Hughes, the first based on his own novel of the same name; *The Funny House of a Negro*, by Adrienne Kennedy; *Walk in Darkness*, by William Hairston, again based on the author's novel; *Dutchman*, by Le Roi Jones, a one-act play presented off-Broadway as part of a double bill, which won the 'Obie', or Off-Broadway award for the year; *In White America*, by Martin Duberman, a dramatization of historical documents dealing with the Negro on the American continent between 1782 and 1962; and finally James Baldwin's *Blues for Mr. Charlie*, which was also seen in London during the 1965 World Theatre season in a production by the Actors' Studio which was not particularly well received, either by the public or by the author, who accused the actors of misinterpreting his work.

The hopes aroused by the production of so many works in one season were not fulfilled in the following year, when only three Negro plays reached the stage. These were *The Sign in Sidney Brustein's Window*, by Lorraine Hansberry, whose career was tragically cut short by her early death during the run of the play; *The Toilet* and *The Slave*, two one-act plays given in a double bill, by Le Roi Jones; and *The Amen Corner*, by James Baldwin. This also had a London production in 1965.

During this period Negro actors appeared in a number of non-Negro plays, among them Diana Sands in *The Owl and the Pussycat* and Harold Scott in *Incident at Vichy*. The New York Shakespeare Summer Festival had Robert Hooks as Henry V, and this company—like the Prospect Summer Theatre in Brooklyn—has steadily cast plays without regard to race. Significant too was the appearance of Sammy Davis, jr., in the musical version of Odets's *Golden Boy*, which proved extremely successful. LOFTEN MITCHELL

NEIGHBORHOOD PLAYHOUSE, NEW YORK, at 466 Grand Street. This theatre, which for the first five years of its life was occupied by amateurs, was built and endowed in 1915 by Alice and Irene Lewisohn. It later housed a professional company which performed the plays of Shaw, O'Neill, and others, and did a certain amount of experimental work in music and drama. It closed in 1927, but the organization became a corporation sponsoring occasional productions of interest, and in 1935, to mark its 20th anniversary, it presented at the Lyceum Theatre a Spanish play entitled *Bitter Oleander*.

NEILSON, (LILIAN) ADELAIDE (1846–80), English actress, child of a strolling player, really Elizabeth Ann Brown. Born in Leeds, she had an unhappy childhood, and in 1865 made her first appearance on the stage as Julia in *The Hunchback*, always one of her best and favourite parts. After several years in London and the provinces, where she was much admired in Shakespeare and other productions, including a number of dramatizations of Scott, she made her first visit to the United States in 1872, touring the country with a fine repertory. She became exceedingly popular, and had just returned from a second extended tour of that country when she died. Beloved and admired by the public and by members of her own profession, her early death was a great loss to the stage. A beautiful woman, with dark eyes and a most expressive countenance, she was considered to be at her best in the part of Juliet, though she was also much admired as Viola. She made an unhappy marriage, and divorced her husband in 1877.

NEILSON, JULIA, see TERRY (9).

NEMIROVICH-DANCHENKO, VLADIMIR IVANOVICH (1859–1943), co-founder and director of the famous Moscow Art Theatre, and one of the outstanding personalities of the Russian stage, both Imperial and Soviet. He studied at Moscow University, and during his student days was already writing dramatic criticism. He later wrote a number of novels and eleven plays, mostly conventional and successful comedies which were done at the Maly Theatre. In 1891 he was in charge of the Drama Course of the Moscow Philharmonic Society, and among his pupils were Moskvin, Olga Knipper, and Meyerhold. It was at this time that he first began to realize that all was not well with the Russian stage, and took advantage of his opportunities at the Maly to introduce reforms there, including more rehearsals and a less rigid style of acting.

In 1897 took place his meeting and discussion with Stanislavsky which resulted in the founding of the Moscow Art Theatre, to which he brought a number of his pupils. He was responsible for the literary quality of the theatre's repertory, as Stanislavsky was for the high standard of its acting, and it was he who persuaded Chekhov to allow a second production of *The Seagull* after its failure at the Alexandrinsky. He was personally responsible for a number of the theatre's most widely admired productions both classic and modern, and shortly before his death received a Stalin award for his work on the new play about Lenin, *Kremlin Chimes* (1942).

While the Moscow Art Theatre was touring abroad under Stanislavsky in the difficult days after the October Revolution, Nemirovich-Danchenko remained in the U.S.S.R. and founded a Musical Studio, now called after him, where he developed a new style and standard of production for opera and operetta, in which he proved that the methods of the Moscow Art Theatre could be applied with as much success to the operatic as to the dramatic stage. Nemirovich-Danchenko has written an account of the founding of the Moscow Art Theatre, and expounded his own philosophy of the drama, in his *My Life in the Russian Theatre* (1937).

NERO, Roman Emperor from A.D. 54 to 68, was a devotee of the theatre, and himself appeared frequently on the stage. Not only did he perform as a dancer in pantomime—thus we are told that he wished to 'dance' the role of Virgil's Turnus, and that he was moved by jealousy to put the pantomimus Paris to death —but his pride in his 'divine voice' led him to appear as a tragic actor in such parts as the Mad Hercules, the Blind Oedipus, the Matricide Orestes, even Canace in Travail. These were evidently scenes taken from tragedy or modelled on tragedy, and intended to be 'sung' by a single performer. On such occasions the emperor, like other actors, wore a mask to indicate his role; but the features of the mask were modelled on his own, or on those of his mistress for the time being. From his famous theatrical tour of Greece (A.D. 66–67) he returned with 1,808 triumphal crowns. Even his worst crimes do not seem to have shocked conservative opinion in Rome as much as these antics—a fact which illustrates the low status of professional entertainers, at any rate under the Empire. WILLIAM BEARE†

NERONI, BARTOLOMEO (*c.* 1500–71/3), builder of the Siena Theatre (see SCENERY, 2).

NESTROY, JOHANN NEPOMUK (1801–62), see AUSTRIA.

NETHERLANDS, THE. In common with other European nations the theatre of the Netherlands sprang from the services of the Church, which gave rise to a drama in the vernacular on religious themes (see LITURGICAL DRAMA). The earliest extant dramatic texts, however, are of four *abele spelen*, secular or ('serious') plays which probably formed part of the repertory of the Flemish troubadours towards the end of the fourteenth century. Three of these are based on themes of chivalry drawn from medieval romances. One of them, *Esmoreit*, has the same subject as Shakespeare's *The Winter's Tale*. The *Spel van Lanseloet van Denemerken*, a short lyric tragedy, which tells of the love of a young knight for a servant girl, is still acted, and has survived mainly owing to the warmth and humanity of its poetic diction. These *abele spelen*, of which the fourth survival is an allegory, *The Play of Winter and Summer*, were followed by short farces of daily life of which several survive. An open-air performance of one of these farces forms the subject of one of Pieter Bruegel's paintings (see No. 17).

By the fifteenth century the vernacular religious drama was in full spate all over the Netherlands. Two of a series of Flemish texts on the Seven Joys of Mary have survived, and from Breda a play of the Holy Sacrament. One of the early treasures of Dutch literature is the Miracle play *Mariken van Nimwegen*, which, with the Morality play, *Elckerlyc*, is frequently revived in the Netherlands. *Elckerlyc* was first printed in 1495. A Latin version, as *Homulus*, was published in 1536. An English version was reprinted three times in the sixteenth century, and a manuscript of this in the Library of Lincoln Cathedral served as the basis for the first English production by William Poel, in July 1901, given in a quadrangle at the Charterhouse. It was a beautiful production, and it started the vogue for the revival of early religious plays which culminated in Martin Browne's production of the York Mystery Plays fifty years later (see RELIGIOUS DRAMA). Poel revived it annually for several years, and in 1903 Ben Greet took it on two extensive tours of America. It is interesting to note that Reinhardt, who was later to produce Hofmannsthal's German version, *Jedermann*, with such spectacular effect in front of the Cathedral at Salzburg, was at the first performance at the Charterhouse. The play has been revived in Salzburg many times, and has also been performed frequently in England and America. It is revived in Delft in an open-air production as part of an annual Dutch festival. It is probably the best-known and best-loved play of the early religious repertory.

In the sixteenth century, theatrical art in the Netherlands was connected with the activities of the Chambers of Rhetoric, the first of which arose in the Flemish towns. These bodies of rhetoricians—Rederijkers—who busied themselves with literature, poetry, processions, and open-air fêtes, in which secular and religious themes were mingled, had a great liking for allegory, whether verbal or pictorial, and played an important part in the intellectual struggles of the sixteenth century. Some of their scenic designs recall the triumphal arch; they probably had some influence on the Elizabethan stage, and they served as background to *tableaux vivants*.

The Netherlands were fated to undergo so many political upheavals that steady development of the theatre was for a long time hardly possible. There were nevertheless by the beginning of the seventeenth century a number of dramatists, of whom Pieter Cornelisz Hooft (1581–1647) and Gerbrand Adriaensz Bredero (1585–1618) were the most important. Hooft was the author of a pastoral, *Granida*, dating from 1605, while Bredero, who shows traces of Spanish influence, wrote *De Spaanse Brabander* (1617), one of the most successful comedies of the time. It was, however, with the comedies for which they both owed something to Latin models (Bredero to Terence for *Moortje*, 1615; Hooft to Plautus for *Warenar*, 1616), and with their comic interludes and farces, that they produced a dramatic equivalent to the Dutch paintings of the seventeenth century. Their characters have the same vivacity and vitality as those of Jan Steen and Frans Hals, and also recall the masks of the *commedia dell'arte*. It was with these two dramatists that their friend, the poet Samuel Coster, founded in Amsterdam in 1617 the Nederduitse Academie, which gave rise to a true folk-art, sprung from the heart of the people. (The Low Countries had no regular Court theatre.) Twenty years later, after the amalgamation of the Chambers of Rhetoric, the architect Jacob van Campen (*c.* 1595–1657), inspired by Italian examples, built the first theatre in Amsterdam, the Schouwburg (see No. 25), which opened on 3 Jan. 1638 with *Gijsbrecht van Amstel*, an historical tragedy by Joost van den Vondel (1587–1679). This play, which interprets classical themes in the light of Christianity, is still revived at the beginning of each year. Its author remained the chief dramatist of the theatre during its heyday. His work has much in common with that of his great contemporary Rembrandt, and influenced both Milton (with his masterpiece *Lucifer*, 1654, which deals with the archangel's fall) and Gryphius. In *Maria Stuart* (1646) he took his subject from Scottish history, but most of his plays were drawn from Old Testament history. He had a great influence on the Jewish theatre which developed in Amsterdam in the first half of the seventeenth century (see JEWISH DRAMA, 3), and many of the Hebrew plays which were written at the time were based on Vondel.

By 1665, van Campen's *scena stabile* was out of date and it was remodelled by Jan Vos (1615–67), being rebuilt in the Italian style with elaborate machinery. A set of engravings done for the centenary celebrations in 1738 shows the different types of décor in the possession of the theatre, painted by such artists as Gérard de Lairesse, Jacob de Wit, and Cornelis Troost (see No. 26). Towards the end of the seventeenth century the actor Jan Baptist van Fornenbergh, who had founded a theatre at The Hague, undertook a series of tours across north and central Europe, as did Jacob van Rijndorp and Anthony Spatzier at the beginning of the eighteenth century. But in Amsterdam national drama was succumbing to the influence of French classical tragedy, which, while not wholly bad, did result in a lessening of creative force and originality. Only in comedy, under the influence of Molière, was good work done, particularly in the plays of Pieter Langendijk (1683–1756), of which several are still in the repertory.

French influence was again paramount in the eighteenth century, with the pathos and sentiment of the *tragédie bourgeoise*, and the antagonism between the severe style of the early- and the nervous melancholy scepticism of the late-eighteenth century led to a clash between the neo-classic actor Jan Punt and the pre-romantic Marten Corver. The latter was the first Dutch producer, and the author of some interesting essays on the theatre published in 1786.

In 1772 the Schouwburg in Amsterdam was burnt down, and a new theatre opened in 1774, a year after the building of the first theatre in Rotterdam. By the beginning of the nineteenth century the art of acting had made great strides, in spite of somewhat mediocre plays, thanks to such actors as Ward Bingley, Johannes Jelgerhuis, painter, costume-designer, and author of an important book on acting, Johannes Theodorus Majofsky, Andries Snoek, and the well-known Johanna Cornélia Ziesenis-Wattier. The Theatre Royal at The Hague opened in 1804, and, later, under the same name, became a municipal theatre. Playwriting improved towards 1870 with such authors as Jacob van Lennep and particularly Hendrik Jan Schimmel. Het Nederlands Toneel (1876–1932) brought together the best actors, among them the celebrated portrayer of Shylock, Louis Bouwmeester (1841–1925), and his sister Theo (1850–1939), who played the heroines of Dumas *fils* and Sardou. But it was not until the European theatre had been dominated by the doctrine of realism that the Netherlands produced a dramatist to take his place in the main stream of European drama. This was Herman Heijermans (1864–1924), who made himself the mouthpiece of the oppressed, and explored in his plays the miseries and inequalities of the contemporary scene. His best-known play, *Op Hoop van Zegen* (1900), dealing with the life of fisherfolk in a small port on the North Sea, was seen in London as *The Good Hope* in 1903, in a translation by Christopher St. John, with Ellen Terry as the old mother Kniertje. It was translated into other languages also and widely played. Two of his contemporaries, who showed perhaps more psychological subtlety, were Marcellus Emants and Josine Simons-Mees. The outstanding producers of this era were Willem Royaards (1867–1929), who brought poetry back to the stage with Vondel and Shakespeare, and Eduard Verkade (1878–1961), an intellectual leader much influenced by English drama, who first staged Shaw's *St. Joan* in Holland. His Hamlet, and his views on acting in general, had a great influence on his younger contemporaries.

The period between the two world wars was dominated by expressionism, and by anti-Fascist feeling which came to a head with the company directed by the dramatist August Defresne (1893–1962) and the actor Albert van Dalsum (1889–), both excellent producers. After the occupation they returned to the theatre with Shakespeare's tragedies and such modern authors as Sartre and Eliot. Herman Teirlinck (1879–1967), author of *De Vertraagde Film* (The Slow-Motion Film, 1922), headed a theatrical revival in Flanders, where the Vlaamse Volkstoneel (Flemish Folk Theatre) had a great success under Johan de Meester from 1924 to 1929.

Since 1945 the theatre in the Netherlands has been subsidized by the State and the municipalities. There are permanent companies in Amsterdam, The Hague, Rotterdam, and Arnhem, as well as some touring companies. Their repertory is international, from the Greeks to the latest works of Anouilh, Ionesco, and Brecht. Among new plays the most remarkable are those of the Flemish author, Hugo Claus (1929–), apostle of poetic realism. New theatres have been built, notably the new City Theatre in Tilburg, which opened on 3 Mar. 1961 with the world première of Fry's *Curtmantle*. There have recently been great improvements in the art of acting, in décor, and in the translations of classic plays. The standard of achievement in theatres for young people is constantly rising, as it is among amateur companies, and there has been much activity in religious drama in verse. At Arnhem and Maastricht new drama schools have been founded in addition to that of Amsterdam, which dates from 1874, and there is also in Amsterdam a most interesting Theatre Museum, which opened in 1959.

BEN ALBACH

NETHERSOLE, Olga Isabel (1863–1951), British actress and theatre manager. The daughter of a London solicitor, she made her first professional appearance as Lettice Vane in H. Hamilton's *Harvest* at the Theatre Royal, Brighton on 5 Mar. 1887. Her first London appearance at Islington in Oct. 1887 was followed by minor roles in London and the provinces until John Hare engaged her for the Garrick. There her portrayal of the betrayed country girl, Janet Preece, in Pinero's *The Profligate* (24 Apr. 1889), quickly brought her recognition as an actress of unusual emotional power. Another triumph followed when she replaced Mrs. Bernard-Beere as Floria in *La Tosca*. After an Australian tour (1890–1) she had a London success in Grundy's *A Fool's Paradise* (1892), and another as Countess Zicka in Sardou's *Diplomacy* (1893), in which she appeared with Hare, Forbes-Robertson, and the Bancrofts. She then took over the management of the Court Theatre, where she produced and acted in A. W. Gattie's *The Transgressor* (1894), the play in which she made her American début (Palmer's Theatre, New York, 15 Oct. 1894). For the next twenty years she was as popular in the United States as in England, and at least half her acting career was spent there. In America she shocked puritans by her intense and realistic portrayal of fallen women, and she became to the younger generation a symbol of the revolt against prudery. In 1900 the New York police arrested her for her alleged indecency as Fanny Legrand in Clyde Fitch's *Sapho*. Defended by the usually conservative critic William Winter, she was legally absolved of any violation of the immorality laws. Her chief roles during these years were the heroines' parts in *The Spanish Gypsy* (an adaptation of 'Carmen'), *Camille*, Sudermann's *Magda*, *The Second Mrs. Tanqueray*, *Adrienne Lecouvreur*, *Romeo and Juliet*, and *The Notorious Mrs. Ebbsmith*. In 1910 she created the title-role in Maeterlinck's *Mary Magdalene*. She also managed Her Majesty's (1898), the Adelphi (1902), and the Shaftesbury (1904). In 1907 she had a successful season in Paris at the Théâtre Bernhardt, where she acted some of the roles most closely identified with Bernhardt herself. She retired from the stage in 1914 and devoted herself to Red Cross work, and subsequently to the health of the poor. For these services she was created C.B.E. in 1936.

Dark and Latin in appearance, she was best known for her work in parts which demanded emotion and fire, and in which she could exhibit the notoriously passionate 'Nethersole kiss'. However, she was also excellent in light comedy and in such seriously analytic plays as Paul Hervieu's *The Labyrinth*.

ROBERT TRACY

NEUBER, Frederika Carolina (*née* Weissenborn) (1697–1760), one of the earliest and best-known of German actress-managers. After a childhood made unhappy by a tyrannical father she eloped at the age of 19 with a young clerk, Johann Neuber (1697–1759), whom she afterwards married, and with him joined the theatrical company of Spiegelberg, then acting in Weissenfels. Here, and with another company run by Haak, they remained for ten years, and at the end of that time formed a company of their own, with a patent which enabled them to play at the Leipzig fairs. 'Die Neuberin', as she was called, was at this time a fine actress, at the height of her powers. She was much admired in breeches parts, and had already attracted the notice of Gottsched, who planned to make use of her art in the reforming of the German theatre. She was quite willing to carry out his ideas, as she had herself formed the project of raising and purifying the standard of both acting and repertory, and in 1727 she started on the production of French classic tragedies and comedies adapted by Gottsched and his adherents. Ideally the old improvised comedy and the popular farces and harlequinades should have been entirely abolished, but this was not immediately possible, and proved a bone of contention between actors, reformers, and the public, which finally wrecked the whole enterprise. Carolina Neuber was a high-spirited woman, intolerant of restraint and criticism, and she was bound sooner or later to come into conflict with the rigid principles of Gottsched. The first break came when the company, in 1739, having learnt one translation of *Alzire*, refused to replace it with a new translation by Gottsched's wife, and even the famous enactment of Harlequin's banishment from the stage, though ostensibly a gesture in Gottsched's favour, was aimed more at the Neubers' rival, the old harlequin-player Müller, at that moment delighting Leipzig audiences, who found the regular plays of the new drama rather dull. Once she had broken with Gottsched, Carolina Neuber's star waned, and her fortunes rapidly declined. Some disastrous appearances at Hamburg, where she offended her audience by outspoken criticisms of their taste, were followed in 1740 by an unfortunate visit to Russia, curtailed by the death of the Empress. The company, however, and particularly the acting of its leading lady, had been favourably noticed, and left its imprint on the Russian theatre, then struggling into being. Returning to Leipzig, the Neubers found themselves ousted by a former associate, Schönemann, and further offended Gottsched by ridiculing his *Der sterbende Cato*. He had insisted on Roman dress for this, a sensible innovation but one too far in advance of his time, and Carolina Neuber retorted by dressing the actors in flesh-pink leggings. She also satirized her former patron in a curtain-raiser written by herself, now lost, in which he was depicted as a bat-winged censor. These sallies, however, and the comforting admiration of the young Lessing, could not retrieve her lost fortunes. The company broke up, but the Neubers struggled along until the outbreak of the Seven Years War, which reduced them to complete poverty, and they died within a year of each other.

Carolina Neuber's association with Gottsched, in spite of its unfortunate conclusion, is generally regarded as the turning-point in German theatre history, and the starting-point of modern German acting. She certainly did a great deal for her profession, training her actors and actresses well, ruling them with a firm hand, and insisting on regularity and order. She produced the plays Gottsched provided for her not for financial gain, since the old popular comedy would probably have been more profitable, but because she realized that the theatre had fallen on evil times artistically and believed in the superior qualities of the well-written, regular French classic play. Though her style of acting, which was pompous in tragedy and affected in comedy, later went out of fashion, it was in its day a vast improvement on the old clowning and farcical horseplay, and prepared the way for the subtle, natural style of Ekhof and Schröder. Her husband, of whom little is known, was evidently no actor, but he appears to have been a sensible man of business, quiet and modest, entirely devoted to his wife and an unfailing support through good times and bad. Both domestically and in their work they offered an example worthy of emulation to their colleagues, and were the first to bring about a relationship between the stage and men of letters which had hitherto seemed impossible.

NEUE FREIE VOLKSBÜHNE, BERLIN, see FREIE BÜHNE.

NEVILLE, (THOMAS) HENRY GARTSIDE (1837–1910), English actor, son of a theatre manager, and the twentieth child of a twentieth child (both by second marriages). He was on the stage as a boy, and as an adult made his début in the provinces in 1857. He was first seen in London at the Lyceum on 8 Oct. 1860, and on 2 May 1863 he appeared at the Olympic Theatre (which he later managed from 1873 to 1879) as Bob Brierly in *The Ticket-of-Leave Man*, always considered his finest part. A flamboyant and romantic actor, he was at his best in melodrama, particularly at Drury Lane, where he was seen in 1900, 1905, and 1906. He continued to act until shortly before his death.

NEW AMSTERDAM THEATRE, NEW YORK, on West 42nd Street, renowned as the home of the famed Ziegfeld Follies. It opened on 26 Oct. 1903 with Nat Goodwin in the Klaw and Erlanger production of *A Midsummer Night's Dream*, while later in the same year came the Drury Lane pantomime *Mother Goose*, which ran for three months. Among visiting stars who appeared at this theatre in its early years were Mrs. Patrick Campbell in *The Sorceress*, H. B. Irving and Dorothea Baird in *Paolo and Francesca*, and the Forbes-Robertsons in *Caesar and Cleopatra*. *Brewster's Millions* and *The Merry Widow* were both successful productions here, while the first of the Ziegfeld shows was seen in 1914. Two years later Tree came in *Henry VIII*, but the theatre was mainly occupied by musical comedy and revue until, in 1933, Eva Le Gallienne brought *Alice in Wonderland* and *The Cherry Orchard* from the Civic Repertory for a successful run. The last production at this theatre, which is now a cinema, was Walter Huston in *Othello* (1937), with sets by Robert Edmond Jones (see No. 87). GEORGE FREEDLEY†

NEW BOWERY THEATRE, NEW YORK, see BOWERY THEATRE, 2.

NEW BROADWAY THEATRE, NEW YORK, see DALY'S THEATRE, 1.

NEW CHATHAM THEATRE, NEW YORK, see CHATHAM THEATRE, 2.

NEW CHELSEA THEATRE, LONDON, see ROYAL COURT THEATRE, 1.

NEW COMEDY, see GREECE.

NEW ENGLISH OPERA HOUSE, LONDON, see ROYALTY THEATRE, 2.

NEW LYCEUM THEATRE, LONDON, see PANHARMONIUM.

NEW NATIONAL THEATRE, NEW YORK, see CHATHAM THEATRE, 2.

NEW ORLEANS, see PIONEER THEATRE IN THE UNITED STATES.

NEW OXFORD THEATRE, LONDON, see OXFORD MUSIC-HALL.

NEW PARK THEATRE, NEW YORK, on the site of the old Aquarium, opened 15 Oct. 1883. It was furnished with a good deal of material bought when Booth's Theatre was demolished, and began with a series of musical plays. It was then occupied for a short time by Belasco, and by the company from the Windsor Theatre (destroyed by fire), who imported mainly melodrama. On 11 Aug. 1884 little Minnie Maddern, later Mrs. Fiske, was seen in *Caprice*, and the theatre then became a museum, occasionally housing itinerant companies and light opera.

See also PARK THEATRE, 2.

NEW QUEEN'S THEATRE, LONDON, see ALBION THEATRE.

NEW ROYALTY THEATRE, LONDON, see ROYALTY THEATRE, 2.

NEW STRAND THEATRE, LONDON, see STRAND THEATRE, 1.

NEW THEATRE, LONDON, in St. Martin's Lane, built for Charles Wyndham, who opened it on 12 Mar. 1903 with a revival of *Rosemary*. Forbes-Robertson then transferred *The Light that Failed* from the Lyric, and after a visit from Mrs. Patrick Campbell, Wyndham took over again with revivals and new plays, and the theatre settled down to a consistently successful career. From 1905 to 1913 Fred Terry and Julia Neilson occupied it for a six months' annual season, and many of their most successful plays were first seen there, including *The Scarlet Pimpernel* in 1905. The theatre also housed an annual revival of *Peter Pan* under Dion Boucicault for several years. Among the outstanding productions have been *Grumpy* (1914), *Little Women* (1919), in which Katharine Cornell made her only London appearance, *Mr. Pim Passes By* (1920), and, in 1924, Shaw's *St. Joan* (see No. 98) with Sybil Thorndike. A year later came the long run of *The Constant Nymph*, which saw the first appearance of John Gielgud (as Lewis Dodd in succession to Noël Coward) at a theatre which was later to play an important part in his career. This began in 1933, when (after the famous black-and-white *Twelfth Night* of 1932) he appeared there in *Richard of Bordeaux*, which established him as a star, followed by *Hamlet* (1934), *Noah* and *Romeo and Juliet* (both 1935). He then left and among later productions at this theatre were *The Taming of the Shrew* (1937) (see No. 86), *Mourning Becomes Electra* (1938) and *Johnson over Jordan* (1939). After the bombing of the Old Vic and Sadler's Wells Theatres, the New became their companies' London headquarters, opening on 14 Jan. 1941, and many outstanding plays (see No. 103) and ballets were seen there. Sadler's Wells withdrew in 1944 and the Old Vic in 1950, in which year *The Cocktail Party* began a successful run. The theatre has since housed a series of excellent plays, including *Dear Charles* (1952) with Yvonne Arnaud, *I am a Camera* (1954), *Gigi* and *Under Milk Wood* (both 1956), the Australian play, *The Summer of the Seventeenth Doll* (1957), and *Make Me an Offer* from Theatre Workshop. In 1960 *Oliver!*, a musical based on *Oliver Twist*, began a run of several years (see No. 113). W. MACQUEEN-POPE†, *rev.*

For the New Theatre, New York, see CENTURY THEATRE.

NEW YORK THEATRE, NEW YORK. 1. Originally the Church of the Messiah, at 728 Broadway, this had been used for concerts and lectures before, on 23 Dec. 1865, Lucy Rushton, an actress of little ability but great personal charm, opened it as her own theatre, appearing with the veteran Charles Walcot in *The School for Scandal*, *The Lady of Lyons*, and *As You Like It*. On 3 Sept. 1866, renamed the New York, it opened under Mark Smith and Lewis Baker. It was here that Daly took his company after the destruction by fire of his first Fifth Avenue Theatre, remaining there the whole of 1873. After his departure the theatre was known as Fox's Broadway, and eventually became a home of variety as the Globe.

2. On Broadway between 44th and 45th Streets. Originally the Olympia Music-Hall, this was opened by Hammerstein on 25 Nov. 1895. Vaudeville of a superior kind flourished with such stars as Yvette Guilbert and diverse attractions which included midgets, aerial ballet, acrobats, and a Bal Champêtre in the roof-garden. On 24 Apr. 1899 the theatre was renamed the New York, and among the many successes staged there were a dramatization of *Mrs. Wiggs of the Cabbage Patch* (1906), several of George M. Cohan's plays, and the musical comedy *Naughty Marietta*. In 1912 the theatre was known as the Moulin-Rouge. It returned to vaudeville, films being added in 1915, and was finally pulled down in 1935. GEORGE FREEDLEY†

For the New York Theatre, Bowery, see BOWERY THEATRE, 1.

NEW YORKER THEATRE, NEW YORK. This opened as the Gallo in 1927, with Margaret Anglin in *Electra*, followed by the Abbey Players in *Juno and the Paycock*. On 12 May 1930, the theatre opened under its present name with a handsome production of Ibsen's rarely seen *The Vikings*, for which Thomas Wilfred created backgrounds of colour and light in moving patterns in the place of realistic scenery. These, however, proved somewhat distracting in performance, and tended to take attention off the actors. In 1932 a fine Spanish company under Fernando Díaz de Mendoza and María Guerrero occupied the theatre for five weeks in an impressive repertory which ranged from Lope de Vega to the Quintero Brothers. It was later devoted to music-hall and musical comedy, under various managements, including that of the Federal Music Project in 1937, but in 1939 it reverted to its present name. It is now used only for radio and television shows. GEORGE FREEDLEY†

NEW ZEALAND. Although New Zealand has as yet no professional theatre of her own, plays were staged in hotel saloons along the waterfronts of Auckland and Wellington as early as the 1840s and 1850s, and by the 1860s professional companies from England and the United States of America found it worth while to visit New Zealand on their way to and from Australia. All this activity was swept away by the advent of the cinema, and between the First and Second World Wars drama was kept alive by the amateurs while awaiting the return of the visiting professional. This began again in 1948 with the visit of the Old Vic company, led by Laurence Olivier and Vivien Leigh, and has continued with increased momentum ever since. In spite of this, the hopes for the foundation of a professional theatre in New Zealand do not as yet seem to have been realized.

There is, however, hardly a town of any size which does not support a flourishing amateur company, many of which are affiliated to the New Zealand branch of the British Drama League, founded in 1931 with much the same aims as the parent body (see AMATEUR THEATRE). This organization arranges one-act (or sometimes three-act) play festivals held in each of the nineteen areas into which the country is divided for the purpose, and the survivors of the elimination tests are eligible to compete at a national festival held alternately in the North and South Islands. The New Zealand B.D.L. also holds schools for actors for which tutors are brought from overseas, and has lately held similar schools for playwrights, with a playwriting competition. At one time it published volumes of one-act plays by New Zealanders. It has a central library with an information service, and there is also a Playwrights' Association which helps its members with their problems and provides a play-criticism service.

Many of the amateur companies are also members of the New Zealand Drama Council, founded in 1945, which serves as a clearing-house of information, particularly in connexion with the production of new European plays. It publishes a journal, *The New Zealand Theatre* (founded in 1948), and holds schools of drama. It also arranges for established groups to have the services of a professional producer for up to six weeks at a time, which has done much to raise the standard of acting all round, and provides specialized tuition, usually at week-end schools, for individuals. The Council is also trying to help the emergence of the New Zealand playwright, and advises on theatre building or conversion everywhere.

In 1952 Richard and Edith Campion, trained at the Old Vic School, returned to New Zealand and started the Players' Company. They gave their first production at the Wellington Opera House in May 1953, but operated mainly on tour. Among their productions were *A Midsummer Night's Dream*, *The Merchant of Venice*, *Pygmalion*, and, their last recorded production, in 1960, *A View from the Bridge*. After a promising start, the Players' Company ran into difficulties; it may be that the interest in amateur acting among young people told against them, and for the moment they have restricted their activities. In Dunedin, Patric Carey and his wife run the small Globe Theatre, where good performances of modern plays are given by amateurs.

NEWINGTON BUTTS, LONDON. It is not known whether a theatre was built at Newington, or whether plays were merely given in an inn-yard there, or in an enclosure in the open air; but there can be no doubt that it was a theatrical centre of some importance. This is proved by many references to it, and by an entry in Henslowe's diary, which states: 'in the name of God, Amen, beginning at Newington, my Lord Admiralle and my Lord Chamberlain's men, as followeth, 1594. . . .' Then follows an entry of receipts from various plays performed there by these companies, and of expenses incurred. Newington was an excellent place for a theatre, inasmuch as it was the equivalent on the south side of Finsbury Fields on the north, where the first theatres arose (see THEATRE, THE and CURTAIN), and was a place of public resort for archery and general recreation. In 1586 the Privy Council desired that the Lord Mayor of London should restrain and prohibit plays at the Theatre and other places about Newington. Howes, in his *Continuation to Stow's Annals* in 1631, gives a list of London's theatres 'besides one in former times at Newington Butts'. But there is no record or description of such a theatre, only clear evidence of plays being given there. The accepted site is now known as the Elephant and Castle.

NEWTON, JOHN (?–1625), English actor, who was with Prince Charles's Men. It is thought that he played the lean clown to Rowley's fat clown, since he is several times referred to as gaunt and 'spiny', and is noted as having played 'A Fasting-Day' in *The Inner Temple Masque* in 1619. He was evidently an important person in the company, representing, again with Rowley, Prince Charles's Men before the Privy Council when Heminge and Burbage represented the King's Men.

NIBLO'S GARDEN, NEW YORK, originally a summer resort opened by William Niblo at the corner of Broadway and Prince Street on the site of the Columbia Garden. Here, in 1828, he built a small Sans Souci Theatre, which was used in the summer for concerts and varied entertainments. The greatest attraction was the amazing performance of the Ravel troupe, a family of tight-rope acrobats and pantomimists who entertained New York for some thirty summers. The theatre was also used for plays, notably after the burning of the first Bowery and Wallack's National Theatres, and for the visits of such stars as Jefferson, Burton, Mrs. John Drew, and Mrs. Mowatt. On 18 Sept. 1846 the theatre was itself burnt down, and not rebuilt until 1849, when, on 30 July, a new theatre destined to be used the whole year round made a good start. It was improved and enlarged in 1853, and saw the last appearance in New York of Rachel two years later. Niblo finally retired in 1861, and under the management of Wheatley was produced *The Black Crook*, with which the name of Niblo's is indissolubly linked. This was a fantastic mixture of drama and spectacle, with wonderful scenery and transformations, for which the entire stage was remodelled, and with an amazing ballet of scantily clad dancers —it has been called New York's first 'leg-show'. Opening on 12 Sept. 1866, it ran for 475 performances, and was three times revived. It was followed by a similar melodrama-spectacle, *The White Fawn*, which was less successful. On 16 Nov. 1868 came Boucicault's elaborate mechanistic melodrama, as given at the Adelphi, London, *After Dark; or, London by Night*, followed by Lydia Thompson and her blondes, then at the height of their popularity in burlesque. The theatre which had housed so many fine plays and players was now given over to melodrama and spectacle, and to such popular performances as Lotta in *Heartsease* and Chanfrau in *Kit, the Arkansas Traveller*, until on 6 May 1872 it was again burnt down. Rebuilt, it opened on 30 Nov. with a ballet-extravaganza which ran for six months, and then housed another pantomime family, the Vokes. But its great days were nearly over, and it was now finding itself too far down-town for a front-rank theatre. After remaining closed for nearly a year, it reopened in 1876 as a combination house for the accommodation of visiting stars with their own companies, but it continued its tradition of scenic splendour, particularly in ballet and opera, until 1895, when it was demolished.

NICOLET, Jean-Baptiste (*c.* 1728–96), French acrobat and entertainer, son of a puppet-master, who played at the fairs of St-Germain and St-Laurent. In 1760 he had a booth on the Boulevard du Temple, which he soon transformed into a small permanent theatre, with a good troupe of acrobats and animal turns. His monkey, Turco, was well known as a clever performer on the tight-rope, and died of eating too many sugared almonds given him by female admirers. Nicolet himself played young lovers and harlequins when he replaced his puppets by living actors, and his theatre flourished in spite of the opposition of the Comédie-Française. In 1772 he was summoned to Court by Louis XV, who allowed him to call his theatre the Spectacle des Grands Danseurs du Roi, a title which it retained until 1792, when it became the Théâtre de la Gaîté. The freedom of the theatres under the Revolution allowed Nicolet to play the repertory of the Comédie-Française, which he did, choosing for preference the lighter pieces, until in 1795 he retired and his associate Ribié took over. Nicolet may be said to have started the Boulevard du Temple on its glorious career as the central point of Paris's minor theatres, many of which attained notoriety, particularly in melodrama, before Haussmann's rebuilding scheme swept them away in 1862.

NICOLL, Allardyce (1894–), a Scot, and an outstanding historian of the theatre, successively Professor of English Language and Literature in London and Birmingham Universities, and at one time head of the Department of Drama in Yale University, where he began a vast and comprehensive file of photographs of theatrical material from all over Europe which is constantly being enriched and forms a precious deposit of valuable material for the theatre research worker. Nicoll is the author of a number of useful and well-illustrated books on specialized aspects of the theatre, including *Masks, Mimes, and Miracles* and *Stuart Masques and the Renaissance Stage*, and of more popular works, such as *British Drama*, *The English Theatre*, and *Readings in British Drama*, intended for the use of young students and non-specialists. In 1946 he brought to a close, with the publication of his two-volume *Nineteenth Century Drama, 1850–1900*, a series of eight volumes, begun in 1923, covering the history of the English theatre from the Restoration, each period having an invaluable hand-list of plays arranged under dramatists. He is a lecturer and writer on Shakespeare, and annually convenes a meeting of Shakespearian experts at Stratford-upon-Avon during the Festival season.

NICOSTRATOS, a Greek tragic actor, famous for his skill in delivering messenger-speeches.

NIGGER MINSTRELS. This term, which is no longer acceptable (see minstrel, 2), was originally used in Great Britain, though not in the United States, with no derogatory meaning, but carried overtones, now lost, of affection and amusement, and was applied indifferently to the Burnt-cork Minstrels (white men with blackened faces) and the true Negro Minstrel troupes.

NOAH, Mordecai Manuel (1785–1851), early American playwright, author of several plays on national historical themes. His first effort, however, produced in Charleston in 1812, was a translation of Pixerécourt's most popular melodrama, *Le Pèlerin blanc* (1801). It was later given at Covent Garden, with alterations by John Kerr, and in its new form returned to New York, where it remained popular for many years. Noah's later plays were produced at the Park Theatre, and it was after the third night of *The Siege of Tripoli* (1820), now lost, that the theatre was destroyed by fire. In a later play, *The Grecian Captive* (1822), the hero and heroine made their entrances on an elephant and a camel respectively, a spectacular device due, no doubt, to the fertile brain of the manager, Stephen Price, who later imported real tigers into Drury Lane. Noah's plays are simply written, with a good deal of action and sustained interest, and with the aid of lavish scenery, transparencies, and illuminations they held the stage for many years. He had an active life in politics and journalism, and in the prefaces to his printed plays gives an amusing account of his experiences in the theatre, and of the difficulties of the native American playwright in competition with the established English drama. He was, however, a great admirer of the English theatre, and in

1820 proposed the health of Edmund Kean at a banquet given in New York in the latter's honour. There is an account of him in Dunlap's *History of the American Stage*.

NOBILI, LAUDIVIO DE' (*fl.* fifteenth century), early Italian dramatist, whose *De Captivitate ducis Jacobi* (1464), written in Latin, and probably never performed, shows an interesting mingling of Senecan tragedy and the *sacre rappresentazioni* (see ITALY, 1 *b* i).

NOISES OFF, a term embracing such effects as Rain, Wind, Thunder, Galloping Hooves, etc. (see TRICKWORK ON THE ENGLISH STAGE).

NOKES, JAMES (?–1696), English actor, and a member of Davenant's company at the Duke's House. He was a fine comedian, of whom Colley Cibber has left a masterly pen-portrait, and usually played foolish old husbands, and clumsy fops, as well as a few ridiculous old-lady parts. He could set audiences laughing by his mere looks, and indulged in such expressive dumb-show that, to quote Cibber, 'his silent perplexity (which would sometimes hold him several minutes) gave your imagination as full content as the most absurd thing he could say'. He and Anthony Leigh played much together and were excellent foils for each other. Nokes's best part, among many that he created in Restoration drama, seems to have been Sir Martin Mar-all in Dryden's comedy of that name, produced at Lincoln's Inn Fields in 1667. He amassed a considerable fortune and retired from the stage some years before his death. He is believed to have kept a toy-shop. His elder brother Robert, of whom little is known, was also in Davenant's company.

NŌ PLAY, see JAPAN.

NORA BAYES THEATRE, NEW YORK, see FORTY-FOURTH STREET THEATRE.

NORTON, THOMAS (1532–84), a member of the Inner Temple who, with Thomas Sackville, wrote *Gorboduc, or Ferrex and Porrex*, the first surviving example of regular Senecan tragedy in English dramatic literature. It was given on New Year's Day 1561–2 at an entertainment before Queen Elizabeth I in Inner Temple Hall. Written in blank verse throughout, it is divided into five acts, of which Norton apparently wrote the first three and Sackville the last two. In theme it resembles *King Lear*, with Gorboduc, king of Britain, dividing his kingdom between his two sons, who quarrel and are both killed.

NORWAY, see SCANDINAVIA, 2.

NORWICH, which is best known today for its amateur theatre, the Maddermarket (see MONCK, NUGENT), founded in 1910 for the performance of Elizabethan plays in contemporary style (a playhouse on Elizabethan lines was built in 1921), was the headquarters of the Norwich circuit company, which visited Ipswich, Bury, Colchester, Yarmouth, and many lesser Norfolk towns. Before the building of the first theatre in 1758 by Thomas Ivory on Assembly Plain, a number of taverns served as playing-places, among them the White Swan, which, though it was last used for entertainment in 1771, was not finally demolished until 1961. Ivory obtained a royal patent in 1768, and was succeeded by William Wilkins, who appointed a series of managers, including Brunton, to run the circuit. A new Theatre Royal was built in 1826 at the cost of £6,000 on a site adjoining the old one. The Norwich circuit broke up about 1852, and the next ten years saw the change-over from stock to touring companies typical of the provinces at this time. The Theatre Royal, enlarged in 1913, was burnt down in 1934, but reopened in 1935. It is now used for more than six months of the year as a cinema. The Hippodrome, which closed in 1960, was the last full-time professional theatre in Norwich. SYBIL ROSENFELD

NORWID, CYPRIAN KAMIL (1821–83), Polish romantic poet and painter. Born near Warsaw, he was exiled in 1842, and spent most of his life in Paris. Beginning with historical tragedies—*Wanda* and *Krakus* (both 1847)—in the manner of Słowacki, he wrote between 1862 and 1881 a number of deeply religious poetic plays. He also worked on a tragedy on Cleopatra which was never finished. Of his twenty-one plays, only three were published in his lifetime. Rediscovered in 1904, and first acted in 1908, Norwid is now considered one of the masters of Polish drama.

NORWORTH, JACK (1879–1959), an American comedian who first appeared in 'blackface', and then went into vaudeville. With his second wife, the singer Nora Bayes, whom he married in 1907, he formed a double act which was extremely successful in New York and London. In 1913 they were divorced, but both returned to London, Norworth in 1914, when he made a hit in revue, and Nora Bayes in the 1920s. Norworth returned to America in 1918, and opened a small intimate theatre (see BELMONT) under his own name, but it was not a success. He is best remembered as the singer of such tongue-twisters as 'Sister Susie' and 'Which Switch is the Switch, Miss, for Ipswich'. Among his own compositions the best loved is probably 'Shine On, Harvest Moon'.

NOVELLI, ERMETE (1851–1919), Italian actor, son of the prompter to a travelling company, who was connected with the stage from early infancy. He made his first appearance, however, at the age of 18, and was not at first successful; but perseverance, joined to his natural genius, soon made him the outstanding actor of the Italian stage in his day. A large man, weighing some eighteen stone, he was nevertheless light on his feet and quick in action, with a fine, expressive head and mobile features. He was excellent in comedy, which he at first played exclusively, but it was in tragedy that he made his reputation. He toured extensively, and after appearing in several European countries visited the United States, South America, and Egypt. His greatest roles were Othello, Lear, Shylock, Macbeth, and Hamlet; in the last he played the death-scene with brutal realism—indeed, from contemporary accounts his acting appears to have been exceedingly forceful and melodramatic—and it was said that in the scene with the ghost he seemed to impart to the audience the certainty of a visitation from another world, merely by the concentration of his whole attention upon the inexplicable phenomenon. Another part in which he excelled was the title-role in a translation of Aicard's *Le Père Lebonnard*, a play originally given at Antoine's Théâtre Libre, in which Novelli was acclaimed by the author and the French critics for the excellence of his acting. In 1900 he attempted to found a permanent theatre in Rome, as La Casa di Goldoni, but the enterprise failed through lack of public support and had to be abandoned.

NOVELLO [DAVIES], IVOR (1893–1951), actor-manager, dramatist, and composer, and one of the most consistently successful men of the London theatre. Born in Cardiff, he was the son of musical parents—his mother, Clara Novello Davies (*née* Davies), was a well-known choral conductor, and owed her Christian names to her father's admiration for the great singer, to whom she was not related, and who was not, as is sometimes stated, her godmother. Ivor Novello, as he called himself, showed from his earliest days facility and tunefulness in the composition of light music. During the First World War he was responsible for part of the score of several successful musical comedies, and also wrote 'Keep the Home Fires Burning', a popular song of the time, which was first sung at a National Sunday League Concert at the old Alhambra. His parents were for some time averse to his taking up the stage as a career, but on 3 Nov. 1921 he made his first appearance at the Ambassadors Theatre in *Deburau*. Three years later he wrote his first play, *The Rat*, in collaboration with Constance Collier, and appeared in it himself. Subsequently he wrote more than twenty plays, both comedies and musical comedies, playing in most of them himself, and, for the latter, composing also the musical score. Among his straight plays were *Symphony in Two Flats* (1929), *I Lived With You* (1932), and *We Proudly Present* (1947). He set up a record by being the author, composer, and leading man of four successive musical plays at Drury Lane from 1935 to 1945, where he also played *Henry V* in a spectacular revival in 1938. His work was distinguished by his complete understanding of the theatre, and of the needs of the entertainment world. W. MACQUEEN-POPE†, *rev.*

NOVELTY THEATRE, LONDON, see KINGSWAY THEATRE.

NOVIUS, see FABULA, 1. *Atellana.*

NURSERY, THE, a training school for young actors during the Restoration period. There may for a short time have been two Nurseries—the point is obscure—but the name generally refers to that set up by Killigrew in Hatton Garden, which some time in 1668 moved to the old theatre in Gibbon's Tennis-Court (see VERE STREET THEATRE). This disappeared in 1671, when Lady Davenant built a new Nursery in the Barbican. This flourished until at least 1682, when it is referred to in Dryden's *MacFlecknoe.*

O

OBERAMMERGAU, see PASSION PLAY.

OBEY, ANDRÉ (1892–), French dramatist, whose early plays were written for the Compagnie des Quinze (see COPEAU and SAINT-DENIS). He had already collaborated in one play when he joined them in 1929, and remained their titular dramatist for three years. During that time he wrote *Noé*—given in an English translation in 1935 at the New Theatre, with John Gielgud as Noah—*Le Viol de Lucrèce*, which was later used as the basis of an opera by Benjamin Britten, and *La Bataille de la Marne* (all 1931). All three plays were written and presented according to the ideas of Copeau, and the fine performances which the Compagnie des Quinze gave of them went far to prove the excellence of his method, even though he was no longer in control. *Noé* was remarkable for the liveliness of its beasts, while *Le Viol de Lucrèce* and *La Bataille de la Marne* made fine use of a modified Greek chorus.

OBRAZTSOV, SERGEI VLADIMIROVICH (1901–), outstanding puppet-master of Russia, where he runs the State Central Puppet Theatre. As a child he roamed the streets of Moscow with a home-made puppet, collecting kopecks from passers-by. At 17 he married, became an actor, toured Europe and America, and returned to Russia to devote all his time to puppetry. By 1937 he had a theatre of his own, employing 200 people, and he now has thousands of individual puppets. He was seen in London in 1953, and in America in 1963, where two items in his repertory were particularly admired—*An Unusual* (originally *A Usual*) *Concert*, which satirizes the mannerisms and mistakes of bad concert-platform performers, and *Aladdin and His Wonderful Lamp*. Obraztsov's puppet shows are intended mainly for adults, but appeal also to children.

O'CASEY, SEAN [JOHN CASEY] (1880–1964), is known primarily as the dramatist of the Dublin slums, for, though others had used this setting, his popularity was far greater, both in Ireland and England. He knew intimately the people of whom he wrote and the events of the years from 1915 to 1922 which formed the material of the three plays by which his name was made. His treatment is closely related to that of the Irish realists before him; grim, clear-cut, and satiric, his reading of life is yet at bottom that of a poet. He belongs to a class of writers rare in all literature and very rare in drama, the tragic satirists, in whom the comedy of satire points directly to tragic implications. In two plays he approaches greatness, in *Juno and the Paycock*, whose universality and balance have tragic quality, and in *The Plough and the Stars*, where the satiric use of antithesis gives form to the play and, as a result, carries it beyond photography of life into interpretation.

The first of O'Casey's plays to be produced was *The Shadow of a Gunman* (1923), a melodramatic story of the war in 1920 and its effects on the lives of a group of people in a Dublin tenement house. This anticipates, in its subject, setting, and some of its implicit commentary, the finer plays that followed; the men who talk, live, and die for ideas are contrasted with women who live and die for actualities. Already the method of revelation by antithesis that gives force to his later work is beginning to be seen. *Juno and the Paycock* (1924), a moving, realistic tragedy, set in 1922, with similar materials and some of the same antitheses, impressed both English and Irish audiences (though differently) and had, like its successor, great popularity in both countries. *The Plough and the Stars*, a play of the Easter Rising of 1916, which caused a riot in Dublin when it appeared in 1926, has been highly esteemed since in both countries, the two audiences differing somewhat in the nature of their misinterpretation. In *The Silver Tassie* (1928) he began to change his style and to abandon in part his setting; in the war scenes in France (Act II) satiric reaction is crossed by stylization and sometimes by what is virtually symbolism. *Within the Gates* (1933) is set in London and, remarkable though the play is in certain ways, it is doubtful whether the extension of stylization and symbolism has helped O'Casey to master his material or his thought. Moreover, he is no more successful in portraying the processes of the Cockney mind than an English dramatist would expect to be in tackling O'Casey's own Dubliners.

UNA ELLIS-FERMOR†

In *The Star Turns Red*, *Purple Dust* (both 1940), and *Oak Leaves and Lavender* (1946), O'Casey used symbolism and expressionistic devices to endorse the ideals represented by the Marxist heroes of these three plays. As exemplified by *Red Roses for Me* (1942), *Cock-a-Doodle Dandy* (1949), *The Bishop's Bonfire* (1955), *The Drums of Father Ned* (1958), *Behind the Green Curtains*, and *Figuro in the Night* (both 1961), the latest phase of his work contrasts the repressive forces of the clergy and the moneyed classes in modern Ireland with the yearnings of youth for artistic, sexual, and political freedom. Many episodes in his plays are drawn from the personal experiences recorded in his autobiographical volumes, *I Knock at the Door*, *Pictures in the Hallway*, *Drums under the Windows*, *Inishfallen Fare Thee Well*, *Rose and Crown*, and *Sunset and Evening Star* (1939 to 1951; in 2 vols., 1963). His dramatic criticism in *The Flying Wasp* (1937) and *The Green Crow* (1957) vigorously attacks the fourth-wall convention and commercialism in the English theatre. The production of *Cock-a-Doodle Dandy* at the Court Theatre in London in 1959 started a fresh wave of interest in O'Casey's later plays, and an O'Casey season at the Mermaid in 1962 included *Red Roses for Me* and the first London production of *Purple Dust*. In 1964 the Abbey players were seen in London in the World Theatre season at the Aldwych in *Juno and the Paycock* and *The Plough and the Stars*.

WILLIAM A. ARMSTRONG

OCTAVIA. The manuscripts of Seneca's plays include a drama of this name, dealing with the misfortunes of Nero's wife. Among the characters are Nero himself and Seneca. A prophecy describing in circumstantial language the death of Nero is strong evidence that the play was written after that event, and cannot therefore be the work of Seneca. As our only example of the *praetexta* (see FABULA, 4) the play has some interest, but in style and content it displays the faults of Seneca's own plays without his brilliance. WILLIAM BEARE†

ODÉON, THÉÂTRE ROYAL DE L', the second theatre of Paris, which ranks next to the Comédie-Française. It was opened in 1816 by Picard, and two years later destroyed by fire. Rebuilt, it was again managed by Picard until his retirement in 1821. Its repertory, of which Picard himself wrote the greater part, helped by such authors as Andrieux, consisted mainly of light opera, or comedies with music. It was not until Harel took over its management in 1829 that music was left to the Opéra and the Opéra-Comique, and the Odéon built up a classical and contemporary repertory which gave it the position it holds today under Jean-Louis Barrault (see also FRANCE).

ODETS, CLIFFORD (1906–63), American dramatist, and the most gifted of the American playwrights who developed a theatre of social protest during the 1930s. Born in Philadelphia, but growing up in New York, he tried his hand at writing, and became an actor after graduation from high school. After joining the Group Theatre in 1931, he participated in that organization's effort to create a theatre devoted to social realities and ensemble acting along the lines laid down by Stanislavsky and the Moscow Art Theatre. When the tensions of the depression period drove the Group and Odets far to the political left, he aroused world-wide attention with a long one-act taxicab-strike play, *Waiting for Lefty* (1935), consisting of union-meeting scenes and vignettes descriptive of personal conversions to radicalism. For the Broadway production, the author added another multi-scened one-acter, *Till the Day I Die* (1935), a drama of the anti-Nazi underground in Germany. Encouraged by his success, Odets refurbished an earlier written full-length drama, *Awake and Sing* (1935), about a financially embarrassed Jewish family's frustration and revolt. Notable for its realism, contrapuntal technique, and mingling of humour with explosive passion, the play brought Odets recognition as the most promising new American playwright. Although his next work, *Paradise Lost* (1935), dealing with the bankruptcy of a middle-class family, met with a tepid reception, he retrieved his reputation with *Golden Boy* (1937), the story of a sensitive Italian youth's deterioration after economic pressures turn him from music to professional prize-fighting. The author's star declined, however, after 1937. *Rocket to the Moon* (1938) failed as a social parable in spite of excellent characterization and considerable pathos. In *Night Music* (1940), an extravaganza expressing the struggles of disoriented youth, Odets dissipated his fire in too many directions. In *Clash by Night* (1941) he attempted to create political allegory out of the personal humiliations of an unemployed labourer, but the play emerged as a laboured domestic triangle. Each of these plays displayed a turbulent talent that had become turbid. In 1949 Odets produced a melodramatic indictment of the Hollywood film industry, *The Big Knife*, but he followed this assertive work with a sympathetic character-drama, *The Country Girl* (known in England as *Winter Journey*) (1950), in which Uta Hagen played the leading role, and with a retelling of the biblical story of Noah, *The Flowering Peach* (1954). He was twice married, his first wife, whom he married in 1936, being the Austrian actress Luise Rainer, and his second Bette Grayson, who predeceased him.

JOHN GASSNER†

OEHLENSCHLAEGER, ADAM GOTTLOB (1779–1850), Danish poet and dramatist, was born at Vesterbro in Denmark and as a young man came in contact with the theatre in Copenhagen, first (and temporarily) as an actor and then as a playwright. Poetry was his natural medium and he began early to write. His first attachments were to the *bürgerliche Trauerspiel* of Kotzebue and his German contemporaries, to Shakespeare, and to the Danish poet Johannes Ewald, to whom he was in some ways a successor. As his genius defined itself he became more deeply attached to the myths and history of Scandinavia, and in his hands the saga-play reaches a power which makes him the greatest influence in Danish drama except Holberg. At a comparatively early stage his art was influenced by the work of Schiller and by the study of Greek drama, but some of the finest of his plays fall at the beginning of his career—*Sanct Hans Aften-Spil* in 1802, *Aladdin* in 1804–5, and *Hakon Jarl* in 1807—though the steady development of thought and of the reading of character gives dramatic depth to his later plays that these have not. Of the plays of his maturity perhaps the most famous are *Hagbarth og Signe* (1815) and *Væringerne i Miklagård* (1827), both tragedies. Oehlenschlaeger's output in plays alone is very great, without reference to his lyric and narrative poetry. Between 1802 and 1845 he wrote some thirty-odd, which ranged from tragedy (most numerous) through lyric drama and dramatic idyll to comedy.

UNA ELLIS-FERMOR†

OENSLAGER, DONALD MITCHELL (1902–), American scene designer, a graduate of Harvard, where he worked under Professor Baker. In 1923 he went to Europe to study scenic production there, and on his return worked at the Provincetown Playhouse and the Greenwich Village Theatre. He has deep convictions about the purpose and function of a stage setting, and is a teacher as well as a decorator, being Professor of Scenic Design in the Yale Department of Drama. With Robert Edmond Jones, Lee Simonson, and Jo Mielziner, he may be said to have contributed to the creation of a new age of stagecraft in the United States, and he has left a permanent mark upon the contemporary theatre there. His first independent commission, in 1925, was for a ballet at the Neighborhood Playhouse, since when he has designed sets for many ballets and operas, and for a number of major drama productions, among them *Stage Door* (1936), *Of Mice and Men* (1937), *The Doctor's Dilemma* (1941) for Katharine Cornell, *Pygmalion* (1945) for Cedric Hardwicke, *Washington Square* (1947), *Peer Gynt* (1951), *Coriolanus* (1954), *Major Barbara* (1956), and *A Majority of One* (1959). He lectures and writes extensively on theatre design, is the author of *Scenery Then and Now* (1936), and has a large collection of theatre iconography.

ŒUVRE, THÉÂTRE DE L', see LUGNÉ-POË.

OFF-BROADWAY, a term used collectively of those theatres and plays which, being mainly experimental and non-commercial, are outside the orbit of the American commercial and centralized theatre, located on Broadway (the New York equivalent of London's West End). Several of these ventures have made theatrical history (see CIRCLE-IN-THE-SQUARE, CITY CENTER, LIVING THEATRE, NEIGHBORHOOD PLAYHOUSE, PHOENIX THEATRE, 2, PROVINCETOWN PLAYERS, THEATRE DE LYS).

OFF STAGE (towards, or beyond, the sides of the acting area), see STAGE DIRECTIONS.

OHEL (the Hebrew word for tent), the theatrical company of the Israel Jewish Labour Federation, with its headquarters in Tel Aviv. It was founded on 21 Apr. 1925 by Moshe Halevy (1895–) and is supported by the various institutions of the Labour Federation. It has a portable stage for touring the agricultural settlements, and since 1948 has extended its activities to immigrant camps in Israel. Halevy, who was one of the original members of Habima, and a pupil of Stanislavsky, organized a year's intensive training for the thirty students who first presented themselves, and on 24 May 1926 gave his first public performance in Tel Aviv with dramatizations of stories by Isaac Leib Peretz dealing with life in the Hassidic villages. The style of presentation was fresh and humorous, with scenery modelled on the designs of the Russian-Jewish artist Chagall. Ohel, which went on European tours in 1934 and 1950, and to Egypt in 1938, has specialized in comedy, and generally in realism suited to its audiences. Since 1926 it has produced some 150 plays, international, Jewish, and Israeli. E. HARRIS

OHIO ROSCIUS, see ALDRICH, LOUIS.

OHNET, GEORGES (1848–1918), French novelist and dramatist, some of whose plays were taken from his own books, notably the best-known, *Le Maître de forges*. This was given at the Gymnase in 1883 and ran for a year. It had been published the previous year as a novel, and in both forms was a success. Ohnet had a big popular following, but his work aroused a good deal of controversy and he was mercilessly treated by the critics, particularly Jules Lemaître, who condemned his false idealism and sentiment and the banality of his style, attributes which no doubt contributed to his enormous though short-lived success. The opinion of the critics finally prevailed, and the tide of fortune turned against Ohnet; nothing of his is now known except the play mentioned above, which as *The Ironmaster*, in an adaptation by Pinero, was given in London in 1884.

O'KEEFFE, JOHN (1747–1833), Irish dramatist, who wrote his first play at the age of 15, and was for twelve years a member of Mossop's stock company in Dublin. At 23 his eyesight began to fail and he eventually went blind. This kept him from the stage, but did not prevent his writing a number of plays, mainly farces and light operas, the latter containing many well-known songs. The most popular of these was *The Poor Soldier* (1783), which had a great vogue in America also, as did the comedy *Wild Oats* (1791), first seen at Covent Garden. Hazlitt called O'Keeffe 'the English Molière', but in view of the total disappearance of all his work from the stage, this comparison can hardly be justified. In 1826 he published *Recollections of the Life of John O'Keeffe written by Himself*.

OKHLOPKOV, NIKOLAI PAVLOVICH (1900–1967), Soviet actor and producer, a Siberian who first worked as a carpenter in his local theatre, studied the 'cello, and painted. In 1924 he put on his first production, a May-Day spectacle in the central square of his birthplace, Irkutsk, of which he was dramatist, producer, and chief actor. His stage was a central platform, and his audience formed part of his cast. Here can be found the root of that original style which he later developed more fully at the Realistic Theatre in Moscow. He was also influenced by the Mongol–Chinese conventions, the Japanese *kabuki*, and the highly stylized presentations of the Yakut theatre. During the early days of the October Revolution Okhlopkov was a follower of the theories of Mayakovsky. In 1925 he went to Moscow and studied under Meyerhold, and in 1932 became artistic director of the Realistic Theatre (formerly a Moscow Art Theatre Studio). Here he produced a number of plays —*Mother*, *The Iron Flood*, *Aristocrats*—setting up a different stage, or set of stages, for each, and drawing the spectators into the whirlpool of action. In all his productions, which aroused much interest and controversy, he developed in the theatre Eisenstein's theory of *montage*, the uninterrupted flow of action, as in Shakespeare and the Greek dramatists. His work was necessarily experimental, and had a somewhat limited appeal. As a result the Realistic Theatre was closed in 1938, and Okhlopkov went to the Vakhtangov Theatre, where his production of *Cyrano de Bergerac* was notable for the originality of its setting and interpretation. (For a detailed description of Okhlopkov's work at the Realistic Theatre see André van Gyseghem's *Theatre in Soviet Russia*, 1943.) In 1943 he became director of the Theatre of the Revolution, now the Mayakovsky, where he did a highly successful production of Fadeyev's *The Young Guard* (1947). Virta's epic of the battle of Stalingrad, *Great Days*, which followed, was severely criticized, but Okhlopkov recovered his reputation with Shteyn's *Law of Honour* (1948), and above all with a revival of Ostrovsky's *Fear* (1953) and with *Hamlet* (1954) (see No. 90). A production of *Hotel Astoria* (1956) as a musical comedy, in which the orchestra appeared on stage while the actors penetrated into the auditorium by means of a built-out causeway, again aroused controversy. Among later productions were Leonov's *Gardener in the Shade* (1957), Arbuzov's *Endless Distance* (1958), and Pogodin's *The Little Student* (1959). In 1961 Okhlopkov stated in an interview that he was still searching for a new intimacy in the theatre, an intimacy which would create full communication between actor and audience. As in his early days, he was also preoccupied with mass action in open-air spectacles given before many thousands of spectators. With the help of his musical director, Meyerovich, he made extensive use of music in his productions to enhance the mood of the play.

OLD BOWERY THEATRE, NEW YORK, see BOWERY THEATRE, 1.

OLD COMEDY, see GREECE. The term was used in the nineteenth century, particularly in America, to denote English comedy from Shakespeare to Sheridan.

OLDFIELD, ANNE [NANCE] (1683–1730), one of the most famous of English actresses, successor to Mrs. Bracegirdle. She was first induced to go on the stage by Farquhar, who heard her reading aloud and recommended her to Christopher Rich; but it was not until Cibber, struck by her playing of Leonora in *Sir Courtly Nice*, produced her as Lady Betty Modish in his own *Careless Husband* (1703) that she made much stir. From then onwards her career was one of unbroken triumph. She was particularly good as Sylvia in *The Recruiting Officer* (1706) and as Mrs. Sullen in *The Beaux' Stratagem* (1707), and was the first Jane Shore. This, and Calista in *The Fair Penitent*, were her best parts in tragedy. She played with much majesty and power, particularly in *Cato* (1713) and as Andromache in *The Distressed Mother* (1712), whose first night was nearly wrecked by the partisans of Mrs. Rogers, Oldfield's rival. She was, however, always reluctant to undertake tragedy, and preferred comedy, in which she excelled. Her Lady Townly in *The Provoked Husband* (1728) was particularly admired. She made her last appearance in Fielding's first play, *Love in Several Masques* (also 1728). She was buried in Westminster Abbey, near Congreve, and Savage, whom she had rescued from destitution, wrote her epitaph. On her tombstone her name is spelt Ann. Because of her having been twice 'under the protection of a gentleman' and leaving two illegitimate sons, she was not allowed a monument over her grave. She was for about eight or nine years—up to his death in 1712—the mistress of Arthur Mainwaring, who wrote several prologues and epilogues for her, and is said to have coached her in her parts. Beautiful in face and figure, she had a most distinctive speaking voice, and was the only English actress Voltaire could follow without effort.

OLD MAN—WOMAN, see STOCK COMPANY.

OLDMIXON, MRS. (*née* Georgina Sidus) (?–1835), an English singer who, as Miss George, was a favourite at the Haymarket and Covent Garden, London, before she became a member of Wignell's company at the Chestnut Street Theatre, Philadelphia, in May 1793. There she took the lead in light opera, and also appeared in straight plays. She gave a concert in New York in 1797 and in the following year became a member of Dunlap's company at the newly built Park Theatre, playing Mrs. Candour in *The School for Scandal*. She also played Ophelia, and appeared in *Inkle and Yarico*, in which she had been seen at the Haymarket in 1787. For some years she was away from the stage, during which time no doubt her seven children were born, but in 1806 she reappeared under Cooper, playing the Nurse in *Romeo and Juliet*, and other elderly parts, though her singing was as good as ever. She retired some time before 1813, and in later years appeared only on the concert platform. She was the daughter of an Oxford clergyman, and married a grandson of the John Oldmixon mentioned in *The Dunciad*. After leaving the stage she kept a seminary for young ladies.

OLD MO, THE, see MIDDLESEX, THE.

OLD VIC THEATRE, LONDON, in the Waterloo Road, famous for its Shakespeare productions. It was originally the Royal Coburg, named in honour of Prince Leopold and Princess Charlotte, who headed the list of subscribers, and its foundation-stone and other materials came from the old Savoy Palace, recently demolished to make way for the entrance to Waterloo Bridge. The architect was Rudolph Cabanel of Aachen, and building began in 1816. Progress was slow, however, until the following year, when John Glossop, stage-struck son of a wealthy merchant, advanced money for its completion and finally took over the management. The theatre opened on 11 May 1818 with a melodramatic spectacle, *Trial by Battle; or, Heaven Defend the Right*, based on a much-talked-of murder trial which had taken place a few weeks before. This was preceded by a harlequinade and followed by a ballet, and was written and produced by William Barrymore (who was not, as is so often stated, the ancestor of the American Barrymores). Owing to the state of the roads the rank and fashion of town were unwilling to risk the journey across the river, and the Coburg became a local house for melodrama of the most sensational kind, but the plays were apparently well-staged and many actors enshrined in the 'penny plain, tuppence coloured' toy-theatre sheets appeared there. The interior was handsomely decorated (see No. 35), one of the most interesting features being the famous curtain installed in 1820–1, which consisted of sixty-three pieces of looking-glass and reflected the whole house. Its weight put too great a strain on the roof, and it had to be removed.

In 1833 the theatre, in which Edmund Kean had appeared two years previously for a six-night engagement at £50 a night, was re-decorated, and reopened as the Royal Victoria with a revival of *Black-Eyed Susan*. It soon became affectionately known as the Old Vic, and gradually sank to the level of a Blood-Tub. The audience was as rough as the shows, and there were frequent accidents, in one of the worst of which, in 1858, sixteen people lost their lives as the result of a false alarm of fire. In 1871, after a period as a music-hall under J. A. Cave, the theatre was sold by auction and became the New Victoria Palace. It finally closed in the early part of 1880. Then Emma Cons, a social reformer and the first woman member of the L.C.C., bought the freehold and reopened the theatre on Boxing Day 1880 as a temperance amusement-hall, naming it the Royal Victoria Hall and Coffee Tavern. It was intended as a cheap and decent place for family entertainment at reasonable prices, and in spite of considerable misgivings it prospered. From 1881 to 1883 William Poel was manager, and the project was greatly helped by Samuel Morley, after whom Morley College, which occupied part of the building, was named. In 1900 the first opera was produced there ('The Bohemian Girl') and scenes from Shakespeare supplemented the usual vocal and orchestral concerts. In 1912 Emma Cons's niece, Lilian Baylis, who had been assisting her since 1898, took over the management, and in 1914 the first regular Shakespeare season was given. This was under the direction of Rosina Filippi and was successful enough to warrant further productions, in spite of the outbreak of war. Under Ben Greet and with the devoted co-operation of such actors as Lewis Casson and Sybil Thorndike, the theatre survived the war years and became the only permanent home of Shakespeare in London. In 1923 it celebrated the tercentenary of the publication of the First Folio by a performance of *Troilus and Cressida*, thus completing the cycle of all Shakespeare's plays under the management of Lilian Baylis. A succession of excellent actors and directors, among them Robert Atkins, Andrew Leigh, Tyrone Guthrie, John Gielgud, Laurence Olivier, Ralph Richardson, Alec Guinness, assured the success of the Old Vic far beyond the confines of its own territory, a success only momentarily checked by the death of Lilian Baylis in 1937. Among her outstanding contributions to the theatre of her time had been the appointment of Ninette de Valois as ballet-mistress, from which came eventually the revival of British ballet-dancing and the establishment of the Royal Ballet Company, and the reopening of Sadler's Wells, famous as the home of opera. The Old Vic was badly damaged by enemy action on 19 May 1941 and had to be closed, but its work was continued, on tour or at the New Theatre in London, and reached a high standard of excellence under the management of Laurence Olivier in the late 1940s. Meanwhile the damaged auditorium (see No. 36) was being used as a training centre for the actors of the Old Vic School, which opened in Jan. 1947 and closed in July 1952. Another brave venture which did not survive, mainly for financial reasons, was the Young Vic, a company formed at Christmas 1946 to play to children, which was disbanded in Aug. 1951. The loss of these much-regretted enterprises was a sad blow to the English theatre, in spite of the fact that Michel Saint-Denis, who had been in charge of the Old Vic School, went eventually to the Royal Shakespeare Theatre at Stratford-upon-Avon, and that George Devine, director of the Young Vic, became head of the English Stage Company at the Royal Court Theatre. In 1950 the theatre was repaired and redecorated, and it reopened on 14 Nov. 1950 with a performance of *Twelfth Night*. From 1953 to 1958 a 'five-year' plan under Michael Benthall resulted in the presentation of the thirty-six plays in the First Folio beginning with Richard Burton in *Hamlet* and ending with Gielgud, Edith Evans, and Harry Andrews in *Henry VIII*. An outstanding young actor of this period was John Neville. In 1963 the Old Vic closed with a performance of *Measure for Measure* on 15 June and the company disbanded. On 22 Oct. the building, which had so long housed an unofficial national theatre for the performance of Shakespeare and other classics, reopened after extensive alteration as the temporary home of the National Theatre company under the direction of Laurence Olivier. The first production was *Hamlet*, with Peter O'Toole in the title-role. Among subsequent productions were a number from the Chichester Festival Theatre

—*St. Joan, Uncle Vanya, The Royal Hunt of the Sun*; revivals—*The Recruiting Officer, Hobson's Choice, Hay Fever*—and some translations—*Andorra, Mother Courage.*

OLENIN, Boris Yulievich (1904–61), Russian actor, who at the time of his death in Moscow was a leading member of the Mossoviet Theatre company. He made his first appearance with the Moscow Art Theatre in 1925, and worked as actor and producer in a number of theatres in Moscow before joining the Mossoviet in 1941. One of his outstanding parts was the Unknown in Yuri Zavadsky's production of Lermontov's *Masquerade.* He was a leading member of the Soviet Actors' Union and the All-Russian Theatrical Society, and was highly esteemed for his work in the Soviet theatre.

OLIMPICO, Teatro, Vicenza, see architecture and No. 20.

OLIVIER, Sir Laurence Kerr (1907–) actor and producer, knighted in 1947 for his services to the theatre. He studied for the stage under Elsie Fogerty, and made his first appearance at Stratford in 1922, as Katharina in a schoolboy production of *The Taming of the Shrew.* From 1926 to 1928 he was with the Birmingham Repertory company, and in 1937, after a somewhat varied career, which ranged from many modern parts to an alternation of Romeo and Mercutio with John Gielgud at the New Theatre in 1935, he joined the Old Vic Theatre company, with which his reputation was chiefly made. A fine, virile actor and athlete, a good fencer and a somewhat robust elocutionist, he is excellent in strong romantic costume parts, to which his dark good looks give an added attraction. His Hamlet, which he played in its entirety at the Old Vic in 1937 and later at Elsinore, was a fine, vigorous piece of work in which, however, some of the subtler shades evaporated. His versatility may be judged by his playing on one evening Hotspur and Justice Shallow, on another Oedipus and Mr. Puff. In 1955 he appeared with the Royal Shakespeare Theatre company in an outstanding revival of *Titus Andronicus.* He has also proved himself a good exponent of modern drama in such parts as Archie Rice in *The Entertainer* (1957) and Berenger in *Rhinoceros* (1960). In 1961 he was appointed director of the Chichester Festival Theatre, and directed all three plays of the first season there in 1962, appearing also in *Uncle Vanya* and *The Broken Heart*, but not in *The Chances.* In the same year he was appointed director of the National Theatre, and while waiting for the building of the theatre on the South Bank took over the Old Vic. Here he produced the opening play, *Hamlet*, and again appeared in *Uncle Vanya*; he was also a most engaging Brazen in Farquhar's *The Recruiting Officer.* In 1964 he appeared for the first time as Othello. He continued to direct the Chichester Theatre until 1965, when he was succeeded by John Clements. In 1961 he married, as his third wife, the actress Joan Plowright, with whom he had appeared in several productions, notably *Rhinoceros.* He was first married to the actress Jill Esmond (daughter of H. V. Esmond and Decima Moore) by whom he had a son, and then to the actress Vivien Leigh. Both these marriages ended in divorce. He has appeared in a number of films, of which the finest were his own productions of *Henry V, Hamlet*, and *Richard III.* During the Second World War he served for a time in the Fleet Air Arm.

OLUFSEN, Otto Carl (1764–1827), Danish dramatist of the early nineteenth century (see scandinavia, 1 *a*).

OLYMPIA MUSIC-HALL, New York, see new york theatre, 2.

OLYMPIC PAVILION, London, see olympic theatre, 1.

OLYMPIC THEATRE. 1. London, built in 1805 on the site of a public house, the Queen of Bohemia, by Philip Astley, mostly of timber from the old French warship *Ville de Paris*, the deck being used for the stage. There was very little brickwork, and the roof was of tin. No trace of the theatre now remains, the Aldwych rebuilding having swept away all the streets thereabout.

The original Olympic was built in the shape of a tent and was known as Astley's Middlesex Amphitheatre. It opened in 1806 and soon proved a failure. In Apr. 1813 Elliston took over, giving Astley £2,800 for the building and an annuity of £20 a year for life. Astley died the following year.

The theatre was then known as the Olympic Pavilion. Elliston changed the name to Little Drury Lane and opened on 19 Apr. 1813. The patent theatres caused him to close, but in Dec. he managed to get a licence and reopened, going back to the old name. In 1818 he rebuilt the theatre and engaged a fine company, but left shortly after to become lessee of Drury Lane. In 1824, having ruined himself there, he sold the Olympic and all its contents to John Scott, builder of the Sans Pareil (see adelphi), who ran melodrama there. At the end of 1830 Mme Vestris became Scott's tenant and opened on 3 Jan. 1831 with a drama about Mary, Queen of Scots, with Miss Foote as the queen, and an extravaganza by Planché, called *Olympic Revels.* Her policy of low prices, and light entertainment beautifully staged and played, brought success and made the Olympic a front-rank theatre with a hall-mark of its own. In 1835 Charles J. Mathews first appeared there, and three years later he and Mme Vestris were married. They left the Olympic in 1839 to go to Covent Garden. The theatre led a precarious existence until it was burned down on 29 Mar. 1849; there was a strong suspicion of incendiarism. Watts, who had taken over in 1848, rebuilt it and opened it again the following year, but it was closed down when he was arrested for enormous defalcations and forgery. It was found that he had been running the theatre on the money of the Globe Insurance Company where he was employed as a clerk. After a time Farren, now an old man, moved in with a splendid company which included Mrs. Stirling, but he had no success, though during his tenancy Frederick Robson made his first appearance. Robson was managing the theatre in 1863 when *The Ticket-of-Leave Man* drew crowded houses.

Robson died in 1864 and Horace Wigan then leased the theatre and ran romantic plays, making a small 'Olympic drama' tradition, with himself, Henry Neville, and Kate Terry as the stars. After four years Webster succeeded him and produced *The Woman in White*. In 1871 Ada Cavendish became manageress. A large sum was spent on improvements, but the venture was not a success and, though Neville and many others tried their luck, in 1889 the theatre closed. Entirely rebuilt, enlarged, and redecorated, it was opened by Wilson Barrett in Dec. 1890, but it was never successful and finally closed in 1899.

W. MACQUEEN-POPE†, *rev.*

2. NEW YORK, a handsome theatre at 444 Broadway, on the site of the old Broadway Circus. This was built for H. E. Willard and W. R. Blake and opened on 13 Sept. 1837 with a mixed bill. It was not a success, and it passed through many hands before on 9 Dec. 1839 Mitchell started it on its glorious career as a house for light entertainment—burletta, burlesque, and extravaganza. As Mitchell's Olympic it flourished for over ten years, guying the productions at the big New York playhouses in a constant succession of light-hearted frolics. It even weathered the depression of 1842–3 which proved fatal to many other enterprises, and was the first theatre in New York to play a weekly matinée. Among its outstanding successes were *Hamlet Travestie*, a dramatization of part of *Nicholas Nickleby* with Mitchell as Vincent Crummles and La Petite Céleste as the Infant Phenomenon, burlesques of Fanny Elssler, of *Richard III* (with Mitchell as Richard, cad, and later driver, to Omnibus No. 3), of *London Assurance*, and of 'The Bohemian Girl', as *The Bohea-Man's Girl*. The season of 1847–8 saw Planché's *The Pride of the Market*, and Chanfrau in *A Glance at New York in 1848*, in which he played Mose, his famous fireman character. In 1849 the theatre was redecorated, but Mitchell was failing in health and took to importing stars. This policy was disastrous, and on 9 Mar. 1850 the Olympic closed abruptly, much to the distress of those who had for so long enjoyed the gaiety and beauty of its productions. After a short spell under Burton the theatre became a home of German drama and finally closed on 25 June 1851. A shop was later built on the site.

3. NEW YORK. On 8 Oct. 1863 Laura Keene's Theatre (see KEENE, LAURA) opened as the Olympic under Mrs. John Wood. Among the plays produced in her first season was an adaptation by Daly of Sardou's *Le Papillon*. This management also sponsored the first appearance in New York of Mrs. G. H. Gilbert, later a much-loved star and player of aristocratic dowagers under Daly. She played Sairey Gamp, hitherto considered a man's part. Mrs. Wood's last season was memorable for the début of G. F. Rowe, who appeared as Micawber and Silas Wegg in his own adaptations of Dickens. She had had no settled policy, however, and in 1866 was replaced by Leonard Grover, who presented Joseph Jefferson in Boucicault's version of *Rip Van Winkle*, which had already had some success in London. Later productions at this theatre, which was for some time used for opera, were *A Midsummer Night's Dream* with a panorama by Telbin of London, in which Cornelia Jefferson played Titania, Clara Fisher Peaseblossom, and G. W. L. Fox Bottom, and Fox's famous pantomime of *Humpty-Dumpty* with himself as Clown and Emily Rigl as Columbine. This opened on 10 Mar. 1868 and ran for a year. It was followed by another pantomime, by Daly's *Horizon*, with Agnes Ethel, and in 1872 the theatre became a home of variety. It finally closed on 17 Apr. 1880, and was demolished, shops being built on the site.

4. The New Olympic, New York. A hall built in 1856 on Broadway to house Buckley's Serenaders was taken over in the following year by Chanfrau, who intended to revive the mixed bills of Mitchell's Olympic. He was unsuccessful, and after a few weeks the theatre became a music-hall, as Buckley's Olympic.

The Anthony Street Theatre was opened in 1812 as the Olympic for one year. There was a circus known as the Olympic Arena in 1858, a short-lived Olympic on 8th Avenue in 1860, and an Olympic Music-Hall at 600 Broadway on the site of the old Alhambra, which functioned from 1860 to 1861. Wallack's old theatre was renamed the Olympic in 1862 under Fox (see BROADWAY THEATRE, 2).

OMBRES CHINOISES, see PUPPETS.

O'NEILL, ELIZA (1791–1872), a delightful actress, who made her first appearance on the stage in her birthplace, Drogheda, where her father was actor-manager of the local theatre. Going to Belfast and Dublin, she soon made a name for herself and in 1814 was engaged on Mathews's recommendation for Covent Garden. Her first appearance as Juliet was overwhelmingly successful and for five years she had a career of unbroken triumph, being particularly admired in comedy—her Lady Teazle was excellent—but appearing also in tragedy. Her reputation stood high, and her worst enemies could accuse her of nothing more than some meanness over money matters. On 13 July 1819 she made her last appearance on the stage as Mrs. Haller in *The Stranger*, and retired to marry Mr. (later Sir William) Becher. On her début she was looked on as the worthy successor of Mrs. Siddons, with less nobility perhaps, but greater sweetness and charm. A classical beauty, with a deep, clear voice, she was much admired by Hazlitt, and her early retirement was a great loss to the stage.

O'NEILL, EUGENE GLADSTONE (1888–1953), American playwright, born in New York City, son of the well-known romantic actor James O'Neill (1847–1920). His early education, which was of a fragmentary nature, was received at various private schools. He attended Princeton University for one year only, took various temporary business jobs, signed on as a seaman on several voyages to South America, South Africa, and elsewhere, and worked as a reporter on a newspaper in New London, Conn. After a few months' apprentice work there, his health broke down,

> my lungs [as he wrote in 1919] being affected, and I spent six months in a sanatorium thinking it over. It was in this enforced period of reflection that the urge to write first came to me. The next fall... I began my first play—*The Web*. In 1914–15 I was a student in Professor Baker's English 47 at Harvard. The summer of 1916 I spent at Provincetown. It was during that summer the Provincetown Players, who have made the original productions of nearly all my short plays in New York, were first organized.

Although O'Neill had written several one-act plays and a few long ones before 1920, it was not until that year that his first full-length play was professionally produced. This was *Beyond the Horizon*, a starkly effective study of character, laid in rural New England. It was clear, both to the public and to the critics, that the young author was not only a man who was deeply concerned with the more tragic aspects of life, but that he was a playwright of genuine talent and considerable skill. In spite of ill-health, which continued almost without interruption to the time of his death, he was able to devote a large part of his energies and thought to playwriting. By temperament a man who preferred privacy to public life, he apparently allowed nothing in the external world to interrupt his writing. *Beyond the Horizon* was followed almost immediately by productions of four other plays—a one-act *Exorcism*; *Diff'rent*, a grim bit of dramatic irony in two acts; *The Emperor Jones*, one of his best-known and most popular plays; and an early version of what was to become *Anna Christie*. The last-named (1921) tells the story of a young woman who is, presumably, 'purified' by the love of a man; its popularity was based largely on the romantic and external theatrical qualities of the acting and production. (In 1957 it was recast by George Abbott as a musical and opened as *New Girl in Town* at the Forty-Sixth Street Theatre.) In quick succession other O'Neill plays were brought to the stage—*Gold*, *The Straw*, and *The First Man*—each of them a failure with the playgoing public, yet each revealing new aspects of their author's persistent attempts to show life and character honestly and effectively. In 1922 came *The Hairy Ape*, a rather experimental symbolic work which stemmed, according to the author, from *The Emperor Jones* rather than from the work of the European Expressionists, which it in many ways resembles. In 1924 three new plays were produced—*Welded*, *All God's Chillun Got Wings*, and *Desire Under the Elms*. The first, a compact and rather bloodless study in marriage, was a quick failure; the second was a moving character study of a Negro and his white wife; the last was the most mature work he had yet written, again showing the dramatist's deep concern with the tortured soul of man under the stress of extreme passion. *The Great God Brown* (1926), which was preceded by the short-lived *The Fountain* (1925), a romantic, pseudo-historical play about Ponce de Leon and his quest for the Fountain of Youth, remains to this day one of the most tortuous and complicated of the O'Neill plays. It is a study of the multifarious inter-relationships that exist between a man and his family on the one hand, and a man and his soul (to put it simply) on the other. In the author's own somewhat long explanation of his play, in which he made extensive use of elaborate masks, he says that his 'background pattern of conflicting tides in the soul of Man' should always be 'mystically within and behind them, giving them a significance beyond themselves'. Though it had some success as a stage piece in the theatre, it is more interesting and significant as showing the direction of the author's thinking and his dissatisfaction with surface realism as a means of revealing character. *Marco Millions* (1928) was a more serene work than anything O'Neill had done so far. It is pleasantly ironic and full of comedy and romantic colour, even though it is also a bitter satire on the aggressive business man who has lost touch with beauty and the eternal verities. *Strange Interlude* (1928), a play in nine acts, almost twice the length of an ordinary stage piece, is a work of extraordinary power, and another of the O'Neill plays which, aided somewhat and somewhat confused by the copious use of asides and soliloquies, seeks to probe deep into the usually hidden motives of human character. It is a far cry from the earlier plays, and it shows, for all its digressions, an ever-increasing tendency on the author's part to explain the thoughts and emotional reactions of the characters. In this play and in certain others that followed it, O'Neill seems to have endeavoured to clarify his ideas on the soul of man and the destiny of the human race to the detriment of his art as a playwright. A consideration of his later work, however, will show that he never wholly neglected the maxim about the proper study of mankind, not did he ever allow himself to stray too far away from the fundamental ends of drama as a spectacle of human life. *Lazarus Laughed* (1928) is the author's most pronounced philosophical affirmation of his belief in humanity, a munificent spectacle, its scene laid in ancient Rome. It tells the story of the resurrection of Lazarus and his ultimate triumph over death. 'Fear is no more!' runs the refrain, 'Death is dead!' The play has never been professionally produced in the United States. In 1929 came *Dynamo*, an unsuccessful piece, originally planned as the first part of a trilogy on man's efforts to find a lasting faith. After its production O'Neill decided not to continue with the other two plays. Meantime he had been labouring at another trilogy, *Mourning Becomes Electra*. In many respects his most successful work, it was first seen in 1931. In this impressive tragic work we have a 'retelling of the tragic tale of Agamemnon and Clytemnestra, Orestes and Electra. . . . O'Neill has reconceived the old doctrine of Nemesis in terms of the more or less biological and psychological doctrine of cause and effect. . . . A Puritan has transgressed the moral code of his time and people . . . and the son of his victim turns upon the living representatives of his family in order to have revenge.' A nostalgic comedy, *Ah, Wilderness!* (1933), and a somewhat barren and over-intellectualized play about faith, *Days Without End* (1934), followed *Mourning Becomes Electra*; then for twelve years O'Neill retired from the theatre, refusing to allow any of his new work to be staged. But from 1934 until 1946 he did an enormous amount of writing, which included several plays that are parts of a series of nine interrelated plays, and three or four that do not belong to the cycle. In late 1946 *The Iceman Cometh* was seen in New York, where it enjoyed a long run and aroused a vast amount of critical comment. Like its later companion piece, *A Moon for the Misbegotten* (1947; London, 1960), it is partly expository drama and partly a philosophical disquisition on faith. Both plays are technically in the best O'Neill manner, and both are clearly the work of a man who from the very first determined, by the help of his extraordinary talent as a craftsman, to illuminate so far as possible the soul of modern man at odds both with his fellow men and with a world which has fallen far short of the dramatist's conception of what it should be.

BARRETT H. CLARK†

O'Neill was awarded the Nobel Prize for Literature in 1936. The Coronet Theatre in New York has now been renamed the Eugene O'Neill in his honour. Of his two posthumous plays, *Long Day's Journey Into Night* (written in 1941, published in 1956) was first seen in Sweden in 1956, and in New York later the same year; *A Touch of the Poet* in 1958. Most of O'Neill's plays have been produced in London: *Anna Christie* (1923), *The Emperor Jones* (1925), *Strange Interlude* and *Desire Under the Elms* (both 1931), *Mourning Becomes Electra*, with Laura Cowie and Beatrix Lehmann (1937) (it was revived in 1955), *Marco Millions* (1938), *Days Without End* (1943), and *Long Day's Journey into Night* (1958). In this Gwen Ffrangcon-Davies gave a fine performance as the Mother. *A Moon for the Misbegotten* was seen in 1960. In Nov. 1962 *More Stately Mansions* had its first performance at the Dramatic Theatre in Stockholm, in a version translated from the original manuscript by Dr. Karl Ragnar Gievow and cut from 10 to 5 hours' playing time.

O'NEILL, MAIRE, see ALLGOOD (2).

ON STAGE (in view of the audience, also toward the centre line), see STAGE DIRECTIONS.

O.P. (Opposite Prompt), see STAGE DIRECTIONS.

OPEN AIR THEATRE, LONDON, founded by Sydney Carroll in 1933, and run for a long time by Robert Atkins, is an enclosure in Regent's Park, suitable for the presentation of pastoral plays by Shakespeare and others. It is open during the summer months, and has given some excellent productions with well-known actors.

OPEN STAGE, a term used of productions given on a raised platform built against one wall of the auditorium, with the audience on three sides. This was sometimes known in England as 'arena' theatre, a term reserved in America for a central playing area with the audience on all four sides (see THEATRE-IN-THE-ROUND and No. 41). The open stage derives basically from the Elizabethan platform stage (see Nos. 22 and 23). It can be seen today in a number of new theatres, mainly outside London, on account of that city's fire regulations, which demand a safety curtain in a proscenium arch. It is the style used for productions at the Assembly Hall, Edinburgh, during the festival there; it was chosen for the Chichester Festival Theatre; and can be seen at the Stratford Shakespearean Festival Theatre, Stratford, Ontario (see No. 43). Most of the new adaptable all-purpose theatres now being built (including the Questors; see AMATEUR THEATRE) make provision for open-stage productions, which, like theatre-in-the-round, call for an adjustment of acting technique by those accustomed to the proscenium-arch theatre, and a new approach from the audience, since they involve new problems of interpretation, staging, setting, and lighting.

OPERA. A drama—usually one specially written for the purpose—set to music. The words, as in the earliest examples, may be sung throughout: in *arioso* (a flow of melody closely related to speech rhythms and inflexions, without the formal patterns of musical 'numbers'); or in musical numbers (arias, duets, etc.) introduced by recitatives (declamatory passages, usually with light accompaniment); or in a continuous flow of melody (*durchkomponiert*—see below, 11. WAGNER). The musical numbers may, however, be set in a framework of spoken dialogue (the term *opéra comique* implies spoken dialogue, and not necessarily comic subject-matter). Any combination of these, and also *melodrama* (words spoken to musical accompaniment) and *Sprechgesang* (something between speech and song), may occur within a single work.

Opera is the most elaborate and resourceful medium available to the dramatist. An actor who merely speaks, say, the line 'I see the mountain peaks before me' can hardly convey by his inflexion of it that he is at the same time thinking of the fair maiden he left in the valley below. But to communicate such an idea is a commonplace of opera. Even more complicated ideas present little difficulty: a tenor with orchestral accompaniment can in that single line let his audience know that he not only sees the mountain peaks, but anticipates meeting there a fearsome dragon who guards a magic ring which he must secure for the fair one in the valley below. A melodic phrase, a harmony, a rhythm, an instrumental colour—any and all of these may communicate 'mountain peaks', 'fear', 'dragon', 'magic ring', 'fair maiden'. A dramatist who uses music as well as words has, as it were, an invisible and simultaneous chorus to echo, amplify, contradict, or elaborate on the actual words which are being uttered, either as a chorus or as so many individuals. His resources are practically limitless: the experienced opera-goer is accustomed to pay attention not only to the words, but also to the melody, rhythms, harmony, orchestration, etc., each of which may make its distinct contribution to the complex communication. Similarly, an actor can remain silent while the orchestra makes explicit the course of an interior monologue. Or four actors can hold forth at once, and though the listener may not be able to follow each line in detail, if the four strands are sufficiently distinct in character he will be able to trace the progress of four separate emotions. (Four is about the limit; in larger ensembles the effect becomes generalized, or else—for example, in the 'Meistersinger' quintet or 'Lucia' sextet—some of the voices are definitely subsidiary.) Wagner brought the system of musical allusion to its highest point of development with his system of *Leitmotive* (musical 'tags' corresponding to persons, objects, or ideas which can be combined, developed, and transformed as the drama progresses); but the principles involved were implicit in opera from the first.

The main price demanded for such resourcefulness may readily be discovered by comparing the libretto of any opera based on Shakespeare with its original play: shortening and simplification is the rule, for music has its own time-scale and its own forms, and to match these to those of a play requires a compromise. The history of opera is one of a shifting balance between words and music, and music usually wins. The musical dramatist makes a servant of the verbal drama; rare are the cases where the principal means of communication is not the music. Gluck (see below, 4) was one of the 'reforming' composers who strove to restore dramatic content to what had become too completely a musical entertainment and to give new emphasis to the words. The musical historian Charles Burney (1726–1814) declared that Gluck was 'not only a friend of poetry, but a poet himself; and if he had language sufficient, of any other kind than that of sound, in which to express his ideas, I am certain he would be a great poet'. But Gluck's 'language' was music, and it is significant that it is of a passage in his 'Iphigénie en Aulide' (1774) that Einstein remarks: 'For the first time opera demonstrates its superiority over the spoken drama; for the first time the orchestra recognizes its function of saying things and evoking conceptions not to be expressed in words and stirring only in the subconscious of the soul.'

The other drawbacks are practical. Ideally the performers should be as good actors as they are singers. This sometimes happens. More often—and inevitably, since music is made to carry the main dramatic burden—for the sake of eloquent singing a standard of acting and production is accepted which would never pass in the 'straight' theatre. Another difficulty is translation: not only must the sense be rendered; it must be rendered in metres and inflexions which fit the musical phrase. This is so difficult, and can lead to such ludicrous results, that at London's principal opera-house today operas are habitually performed in foreign languages, even by English singers. In a *Spectator* paper of 1711 Addison wrote: 'There is no question but our great-Grand-children will be very curious to know the reason why their Forefathers used to sit together like an Audience of Foreigners in their own Country, and hear whole Plays acted before them in a Tongue which they did not understand.' Two and a half centuries later they continue to do so. They go to hear the music. ANDREW PORTER

1. ORIGINS. The 'heightening power' of music was brought to dramatic performances from earliest times, in the European liturgical drama. There were operatic elements in many stage productions long before opera proper came into being, for instance in the Italian pastorals of the Renaissance period, in the English Court masque or in the French *ballet-mascarade*. Yet, as the American music critic O. G. T. Sonneck has said, 'no historical subtleties will ever succeed in proving that opera really existed before the Florentine Camerata stumbled on it. All the undercurrents of their time might have been converging towards opera, yet of themselves they would not have led to opera without the new element of dramatic musical speech.' The Camerata was a group of Florentine noblemen, poets, and musicians. One of the objects of their gatherings was the revival, or imitation, of ancient Greek tragedy, which in their opinion had originally been for the greater part recited to music. It was from these literary experiments that accidentally, as it were, the first opera resulted, a short play on the subject of Daphne. It was written by Ottavio Rinuccini (1562–1621), set to music by Jacopo Peri (1561–1633), and produced at a Florentine palace during the Carnival of 1597–8. A second opera by the same authors followed in 1600, treating for the first time the myth of Orpheus and Eurydice which has remained a favourite operatic subject throughout the centuries. Peri's 'Euridice' music has been preserved, and so has a rival setting by Giulio Caccini (*c.* 1545–1618). Judging from

these early scores, it can be said that the music was definitely subordinate to the words (or libretto), and was intended to heighten and intensify the poetry rather than to achieve an importance of its own. Luckily for the future development of opera, the next composer to try his hand at the new genre was a musician of genius, Claudio Monteverdi (1567–1643), who realized its immense possibilities and in his 'Orfeo' (1607) produced a masterpiece which in the course of the centuries has lost nothing of its dramatic power and beauty.

In the first forty years of operatic history operas were written and produced, not with any regularity, but for special occasions only. The form developed on a broader and more popular basis from 1637, when the first opera-house was opened to the general public in Venice. This was followed by a dozen others in the course of the seventeenth century. There were regular opera seasons, and schools of composers, librettists, stage-painters, and singers came into being. Venetian operas were exported to other towns where in turn local theatres were built and local schools originated. Within a few decades opera was safely and permanently established all over Italy, having reached Naples in 1651 and Palermo in 1658.

Between 1637 and the close of the century 360 operas by 66 composers were produced at Venice alone. Their names are of merely antiquarian interest today, as are the names of the early librettists, adroit craftsmen who knew exactly what the public wanted—ingenious plots with a vivid historical background, the more complicated the better, with an invariably happy ending, generally achieved by a *deus ex machina*. Above all, these libretti were full of opportunities for the painter and the engineer to work their miracles. The seventeenth century was the great age of scenic art and stage machinery, and the richest effects and most startling inventions were reserved for opera.

The subjects of the earliest operas were myths and legends drawn from Homer, Virgil, and Ovid. The epic poems of Tasso and Ariosto were other sources of inspiration. The 'Sant' Alessio' (1632) of Stefano Landi (*c.* 1590–*c.* 1655), produced at the Barberini palace in Rome, was a landmark for three reasons. It dealt with an historical character, the fifth-century St. Alexis; it introduced comic scenes; and it made a clear distinction between recitative and 'number'. Monteverdi's 'Incoronazione di Poppea' (1642) was also founded on history, and from that time onwards history and romance yielded an inexhaustible supply of Greek and Roman, oriental and nordic, kings, queens, and generals and their followers, enemies, and slaves. The plots grew more complicated from year to year; in 1662 an opera on the subject of Hercules had 33 singing characters, and in 1671 one on Darius had 15 changes of scenery, all compressed into the customary three acts.

Towards the end of the seventeenth century the influence of the great French dramatists, Corneille and Racine, makes itself felt, particularly in the libretti of the first literary reformer of the operatic stage, Apostolo Zeno (1668–1750). He tried to bring some order into the confusion of the degenerate libretti of the period by observing to a certain extent the (French) Aristotelian unities of time, place, and action, by restricting the number of characters, and by suppressing the scenic extravagances. Zeno's reform became convention in the hands of his famous successor, Pietro Metastasio (1698–1782). No words of any man were ever set to music as often as his. He wrote only about thirty different libretti, but there were more than a thousand settings of them between 1724 and 1840. Practically every operatic composer of the eighteenth century used one or more of his libretti. His lyrics are of great poetic beauty, and attracted musicians like Handel, Gluck, and Mozart.

2. DEVELOPMENT. Italian opera first crossed the Alps as early as 1618. The first stopping-place was Vienna, which under the Emperor Leopold I became, next to Venice, the most important operatic centre of the seventeenth century. It was here that Lodovico Burnacini (1636–1707) worked, the greatest representative of stage baroque at its richest and most typical. From Vienna Italian opera spread to Munich, Dresden, and Hanover, and by 1750 there was no German Court without its Italian company, complete with composer, poet, painter, and singers. Nor was the foreign influence limited to Austria and Germany. Brussels, Amsterdam, and Warsaw had Italian opera before 1700; London and Madrid, Stockholm and Lisbon, Copenhagen and St. Petersburg followed in the eighteenth century.

3. FRANCE. A notable exception to this Italian cult was France, where in 1671 the Académie Royale des Opéras was inaugurated. Its first great composer and absolute musical ruler was Jean-Baptiste Lully (1632–87). His literary collaborator, Philippe Quinault (1635–88), holds a place of honour in French drama. Together they established a tradition which lasted for well over a hundred years. Under Lully's successors, particularly Jean-Philippe Rameau (1683–1764), French opera developed independently of Italian influence. Features of the *tragédie-lyrique* of this time are its frequent choruses and elaborate dances. A typical French product which came into vogue about 1700 was the *opéra-ballet*, divided into scenes, or *entrées*, with alternate singing and dancing, the whole loosely held together by a unifying theme (see BALLET and MOLIÈRE).

4. ITALY. In Italy meanwhile the centre of operatic activity had passed from Venice to Naples. Under the leadership of the great Alessandro Scarlatti (1660–1725) the southern capital had become the source which supplied the whole of Europe with an unending stream of gifted musicians, composers, instrumentalists, and, above all, singers. While Venetian opera at its worst had been a mere pretext for the antics of the scenic designer, Neapolitan opera tended more and more to be dominated completely by the voice. The 'spectacle for the

eye' turned into a 'concert in costume'. The positive achievements of the school of Naples (including the rise of comic opera) should not be underrated; but the final results of its influence upon serious opera proved disastrous.

Famous prima donnas and even more celebrated castrati singers (like Senesino and Farinelli) aroused a general adoration. In time, the superficial cult of the voice began to overshadow all other considerations. Composers were expected to provide constant opportunities for the star singers to show off their trills and graces. The librettist mattered least of all—if indeed there was one, for the greater part of Italian operas produced between 1720 and 1760 consisted of settings of existing dramas by Zeno, Metastasio, and a few others. Audiences paid scarcely any attention to the action, chatted through the recitatives, and waited for the arias, whose words they knew by heart. A new type of opera developed, called *pasticcio*—a pie—made up of favourite airs strung together on a thin thread of recitative by some local hack composer.

It was against these abuses that the reforms of Christoph Willibald Gluck (1714–87) were directed. His experiences as a travelling conductor must have shown him how far the opera of his time had deviated from the ideals once set forth by the Florentines and by Monteverdi. In the poet Ranieri da Calzabigi (1714–95) he found a congenial librettist, and 'Orfeo' (1762) was the first-fruit of their collaboration. The preface to the score of 'Alceste' (1767) embodies the principles of Gluck's musical-dramatic creed, the return to a pure and noble representation of character and sentiment regardless of sensual gratification, preferring, as it were, 'the Muses to the Sirens'. In 1774 Gluck went to Paris, where since the death of Rameau the Académie was without a musical leader, and his later works, especially 'Iphigénie en Tauride' (1779), gave a new impulse to French opera. Gluck's personal style could not easily be imitated, and there were no immediate repercussions; but slowly his ideas gained ground, and his influence is clearly discernible in the general high standard of opera in Paris, Vienna, and some Italian towns at the time of his death.

5. Comic Opera. After some isolated early instances, a steady development of comic opera is first observed in Naples at the beginning of the eighteenth century. For some time Neapolitan composers and playwrights had specialized in adapting Venetian opera to local taste by adding comic scenes which were placed at the ends of the acts. Though at first they were connected with the main plot, the tendency was to make them more and more independent, until at last they became little operas in themselves, called *intermezzi*, performed between the acts of the serious opera. More often than not they formed the most popular part of the evening's entertainment and were gradually introduced into other operas, or detached altogether. The most famous example is 'La Serva Padrona' (1733), with music by Giovanni Battista Pergolesi (1710–36), which soon became a stock piece for travelling companies.

The visit of a comic opera or *opera buffa* company to Paris in 1752 gave a decisive start to French *opéra comique*, which had itself developed from the *pièces en vaudevilles* (the equivalent of the English ballad opera, with spoken dialogue). Jean-Jacques Rousseau (1712–78) wrote his *intermède* 'Le Devin du village' (1752) in direct imitation of Italian intermezzi, and the success achieved by this little piece gave rise to a whole school of similar ones, written by such excellent dramatists as Charles-Simon Favart (1710–92), Louis Anseaume (1721–84), and Michel-Jean Sedaine (1719–97), and set to music by composers like François-André Philidor (1726–95) and André Grétry (1742–1813). In Italy, meanwhile, the intermezzi had grown into three-act comic operas, the popularity of which increased from year to year. The Venetian playwright Carlo Goldoni (1707–93) lifted the somewhat primitive Neapolitan types to a higher literary level, and his character-comedies attracted the best contemporary musicians. Giovanni Paisiello (1740–1816), who wrote on the Barber of Seville thirty years before Rossini, and Domenico Cimarosa (1749–1801), whose 'Matrimonio segreto' (1792) still holds the stage, were the most brilliant representatives of Italian *opera buffa* at the end of the eighteenth century.

6. England. The general attitude of England towards opera is commented on in *The Gentleman's Journal* for 1693: 'Operas abroad are plays where every word is sung; this is not rellished in England.' But before this time there had been some very original English solutions of the operatic problem. Davenant's *The Siege of Rhodes* (1656, music by Locke and others) is regarded by some authorities as the first English opera, and was called a 'representation by the art of prospective in scenes and the story sung in recitative musick'. Two little chamber operas, the 'Venus and Adonis' (*c.* 1684) of John Blow (1649–1708) and Purcell's 'Dido and Aeneas' (1689), show a perfection of style completely untouched by the influence of foreign models. Henry Purcell (1659–95) might have become the Lully of his country but for his untimely death, as is shown by the excellence of his other two important stage works, 'King Arthur' (1691) and 'The Fairy Queen' (1692).

The further history of English opera is a series of scattered attempts rather than a steady progression. This is partly due to the fact that in 1705 Italian opera was established in London, and that the overpowering personality of George Frideric Handel (1685–1759) and the bulk of his thirty-five Italian operas stood in the way of a parallel development of opera in English. An occasional success like the 'Artaxerxes' (1762) of Thomas Arne (1710–78) (on his own translation of Metastasio's libretto 'Artaserse') merely serves to emphasize the fact that England had no serious opera fit to compare with that of Italy and France.

7. Ballad Opera. An entirely novel contribution to the musical stage was Gay's *The Beggar's Opera* (1728), a play with music arranged by John Christopher Pepusch (1667–1752). This was the first and best example of the ballad opera, a play of popular and often topical character with spoken dialogue and a large number of songs fitted to existing tunes. After a few years of unbroken success the new genre disappeared as suddenly as it had sprung up; but traces of it remained in the English theatre in plays which contained a good deal of compiled music, as, for example, Sheridan's *The Duenna* (1775). Among dramatists who took an an active interest in the progress of English opera were many illustrious writers, from Dryden and Addison to Fielding, Garrick, and Sheridan.

8. Germany. Disregarding some isolated earlier attempts, German opera began in 1678, when the first public opera-house in Hamburg opened its doors. It was here that young Handel started on his operatic career. The prolific Reinhard Keiser (1674–1739) was the chief composer. After 1700 Italian airs began to creep into German opera, and from that time onwards there was a steady decline towards the *pasticcio* until in 1739 German opera was abandoned altogether and an Italian company took over. About 1750 the German *Singspiel* originated as a popular reaction against the absolute reign of the Italians; at the beginning it was little more than a play with incidental songs, in imitation of the English ballad opera and the French *opéra comique*. With Mozart's 'Die Entführung aus dem Serail' (1782) the genre reached its artistic peak; in a more elaborate form it was carried on well into the nineteenth century. Among the German dramatists interested in the *Singspiel* must be mentioned Goethe, who provided a few libretti for it.

9. Mozart. The various styles and tendencies of eighteenth-century opera came to a head in the work of Wolfgang Amadeus Mozart (1756–91). Mozart was not a revolutionary innovator. He did not break with tradition, he rather used what was good in it as a foundation upon which to build. His first opera on a large scale, 'Idomeneo' (1781), seems to fulfil Gluck's ideal in a new and youthful spirit, while 'La Clemenza di Tito' (1791; libretto by Metastasio) brings the history of the old-type Italian serious opera to a dignified conclusion. The somewhat feeble genre of the German *Singspiel* culminates in 'Die Entführung aus dem Serail' (1782), while the progress of Italian comic opera is crowned by the masterpieces of 'Le Nozze di Figaro' (1786) and 'Così fan tutte' (1790). 'Don Giovanni' (1787) stands by itself, a tragicomedy which has no parallel in musical drama, and 'Die Zauberflöte' (1791), though rooted in age-old traditions of the Viennese fair and puppet-shows, prophetically heralds the romantic opera of the future. The scope and variety of Mozart's work has never been surpassed, not even by Gluck, Wagner, or Verdi, who all reached twice Mozart's age, for like Purcell and Pergolesi, Mozart, 'beloved of the gods', died young.

10. Romantic Opera. The fifty years between the death of Mozart and the rise of Wagner may conveniently be labelled the age of Romantic opera, although the main stream is not always clearly visible among a number of tributary currents. Operatic fashions were now dictated from Paris. The French Revolution had given a startling impulse to opera, as to the theatre in general. There was no great master in Paris worthy to be called the successor of Gluck; but there were many talented composers and dramatists, men full of ideas and imagination who grasped the demands of the new era, Frenchmen as well as emigrated Italians like Luigi Cherubini (1760–1842), attracted by the vigorous musical life of the capital of the new republic. Dozens of new theatres were opened in Paris between 1791 and 1805, many of them devoted to opera in some form, and to them flocked a new public to whom the gods of mythology and the shepherds of Arcady meant nothing. They wanted to see full-blooded heroes, villains, and lovers, melodramatic stories and effects, exciting rescues from tyranny, noble bandit chiefs, haunted castles, and subterranean dungeons. The English 'Gothic' novels of Ann Radcliffe and 'Monk' Lewis exercised a strong influence on French revolutionary opera.

Napoleon severely restricted the number of theatres; the opera of his Empire is marked by a short revival of classicism, and by imperialistic works on a grandiose scale such as the 'Fernand Cortez' (1809) of Gasparo Spontini (1774–1851). This was the forerunner of what is now generally called French grand opera, by which is meant the lavish and spectacular operas of Daniel Auber (1782–1871) ('La Muette de Portici', 1828), Jacques Halévy (1799–1862) ('La Juive', 1835), and, most typical, Giacomo Meyerbeer (1791–1864) ('Les Huguenots', 1836). The finest of French grand operas, however, were written by Rossini (see below) after he settled in Paris: 'Moïse' (1827) (a reworking of an earlier Italian piece) and 'Guillaume Tell' (1829). The Romantic movement was carried on at the Opéra-Comique by a number of highly successful operas with spoken dialogue, of which 'La Dame blanche' (1825), by François Boieldieu (1775–1834), Auber's 'Fra Diavolo' (1839), and 'Zampa' (1831), by Ferdinand Hérold (1791–1833), are the best examples. On the literary side mention must be made of Eugène Scribe (1791–1861), a prolific and proficient dramatist. His libretti were coveted and set to music by the greatest composers of his time, and he helped to make French opera a model of theatrical effectiveness and accomplishment.

The different types of French opera were duly taken up and imitated in Germany and, to a lesser degree, in Italy and other countries. The solitary contribution of Ludwig van Beethoven (1770–1827) to the lyric stage, 'Fidelio' (1805), is, as far as the literary material is concerned, directly derived from a French source, a typical rescue-story set in an operatic Spain of an indefinite period, but filled with very real characters of the composer's own time, and expressing his personal feelings and ideals. For the first time in its history German opera gained general recognition with 'Der Freischütz' by Carl Maria von Weber (1786–1826). On its appearance in 1821 the work was hailed as the fulfilment of the old German desire for a national opera, and it has remained a favourite of the people ever since, with the strong popular appeal of its rural setting against a folk-lore background, its melodious freshness, and the highly dramatic scene in the Wolf's Glen. A more sombre, supernatural element is predominant in the operas of Heinrich Marschner (1795–1861) ('Der Vampyr', 1828, and 'Hans Heiling', 1833), which form the perfect historical link between Weber and the early Wagner.

Italian opera of this period is represented by the works of Gioacchino Rossini (1792–1868), Vincenzo Bellini (1801–1835), and Gaetano Donizetti (1797–1848), but it is only in a limited sense that the term 'romantic' can be applied to some of them, although the novels of Walter Scott were largely exploited by Italian librettists, as they were also in France and Germany. Then, as always, Italian opera was above all a singers' opera; opportunities for vocal display were as important as dramatic subtleties; Bellini told the librettist Carlo Pepoli to 'grave on his mind in adamantine letters' that in the opera the singing should carry all the expression. Rossini's florid and brilliant operas such as 'L'Italiana in Algeri' (1813) and 'La Cenerentola' (1817) took the world by storm, and after a period of neglect they are again in favour; his 'Barbiere di Siviglia' (1816) has always been popular. Donizetti's comic masterpieces, 'L'Elisir d'Amore' (1832) and 'Don Pasquale' (1843), together with his tragic 'Lucia di Lammermoor' (1835), remain in the repertory, as do Bellini's 'La Sonnambula' and 'Norma' (both 1831) and 'I Puritani' (1835). A revival of interest in the operas, both serious and comic, of these three men was a notable feature of the 1950s. The chief librettist of this time was Felice Romani (1788–1865) who, besides being a poet of distinction, had a flair for well-constructed plots and effective situations.

The most important English Romantic opera was the work of a foreigner, Weber's 'Oberon', produced at Covent Garden in 1826. An English school may be dated from the 'Mountain Sylph' (1834) of John Barnett (1802–90) and is best represented by 'The Bohemian Girl' (1843) by Michael William Balfe (1808–70), and 'Maritana' (1845) by William Vincent Wallace (1812–65), unpretentious works of popular appeal which were also successful on the Continent. Musically they speak the universal European language of their time, the Donizetti–Auber idiom. As in Germany, development was seriously hampered by the lack of good libretti, and the effusions of Edward Fitzball (1792–1873) and Alfred Bunn (1798–1860) helped largely to discredit English opera at home and abroad.

11. Wagner. The second half of the nineteenth century is dominated by the powerful personality of Richard Wagner (1813–83), and by his peculiar creation, the music-drama. There never was—and probably never will be—another opera composer whose work stood for fifty years and more in the centre of heated controversy everywhere, and who divided the whole musical world into two camps, ardent adherents and bitter enemies. As a result of his unceasing struggles, opera was at last taken seriously not only by opera-goers but by all musicians, as seriously as Handel's 'Messiah' or Beethoven's Ninth Symphony. Wagner never had to rely upon the whims of a literary collaborator; from the beginning he wrote the words as well as the scores of his music-dramas, a fact which may partly account for the perfect unity of thought and expression found in the best of them. His 'Rienzi' (1842) is an historical grand opera in the florid style of Meyerbeer, and the three operas that followed, 'Der fliegende Holländer' (1843), 'Tannhäuser' (1845), and 'Lohengrin' (1850), today appear as the natural outcome of the German Romantic movement. With 'Tristan und Isolde' (1865), still the most revolutionary work in the whole history of opera, Wagner completely breaks away from operatic traditions and conventions, to return to them again, at least in part, in 'Die Meistersinger von Nürnberg' (1868). The tetralogy of 'Der Ring des Nibelungen' ('Das Rheingold', 'Die Walküre', 'Siegfried', and 'Götterdämmerung', 1869–76) and the 'sacred festival play' of 'Parsifal' (1882) complete the list of his important operas. An early and uncharacteristic work, 'Das Liebesverbot', was based on Shakespeare's *Measure for Measure*.

The purely musical features of Wagner's reform (and there are many besides the famous *Leitmotiv*) do not here concern us. On the dramatic side may be mentioned the abandoning of the chorus (completely achieved only in parts of 'Der Ring des Nibelungen') and the abolishing of 'set numbers' by substituting a continuous flow of melody for the old alternation of recitative and air. Wagner dreamed of a *Gesamtkunstwerk*—a unity of all arts in the service of music-drama—and never have an artist's dreams come truer than his. In 1876 he built the Festspielhaus at Bayreuth, an opera-house devoted exclusively to his own works, where he controlled singers, conductors, instrumentalists, and scenic artists, chosen by himself and performing before an enthusiastic and faithful audience. He was his own composer, librettist, and producer, and the complicated machinery called for in many of his operas was contrived and executed according to his own plans. So was the scenery (but this was unfortunately one of the worst periods in the history of German art). At Bayreuth the composer's grandsons, Wieland (d. 1966) and Wolfgang, have developed a new kind of staging, with scenery either reduced to the barest essentials needed for the action, or to a few bold symbols of the inner meaning of the dramas. Wieland, in particular, is a producer and designer of genius. His methods have been widely imitated (not only in Wagner's operas).

Dozens of pompous and ambitious music-dramas, complete with heavy orchestration and elaborate *Leitmotive*, bear testimony to Wagner's overwhelming influence. They were soon forgotten, and of all the many German operas written in the shadow of the master there are perhaps only two which still live, 'Der Barbier von Bagdad' (1858) by Peter Cornelius (1824–74), and 'Hänsel und Gretel' (1893) by Engelbert Humperdinck (1854–1921). What survives of European operas composed between 1850 and 1900 are those works which were hardly influenced by Wagnerism or were written in conscious or unconscious revolt against it. There is certainly little of Wagner in the most successful French opera of the period, the 'Carmen' (1875) of Georges Bizet (1838–75), a colourful and passionate drama of love and jealousy which became the starting-point for the Italian school of *verismo*, best known through the 'Cavalleria Rusticana' (1890) of Pietro Mascagni (1865–1945) and the 'Pagliacci' (1892) of Ruggiero Leoncavallo (1858–1919). A typical French product of the nineteenth century is the *drame-lyrique*, represented by such works as 'Mignon' (1866), by Ambroise Thomas (1811–96) and 'Faust' (1859), by Charles Gounod (1818–93), culminating in the sentimental charm of 'Manon' (1884), by Jules Massenet (1842–1912). Mention should be made too of Hector Berlioz (1803–69), whose chief operatic work, 'Les Troyens' (1863), stands by itself, indebted, if to anyone, to the great Gluck.

12. Verdi. The most important contemporary of Wagner was the Italian Giuseppe Verdi (1813–1901), who succeeded in erecting, under the eyes of his German rival, an operatic kingdom of his own, not perhaps of the same unity and consistency, but no less impressive in its proportions and infinite variety. Verdi started his career about 1840 as a rival of Donizetti, but he was soon recognized as the greatest Italian master of the century. Many of his libretti were taken from literary works of a high standard—from Shakespeare, Schiller, Byron, Hugo—and the composer's letters show his keen interest and active co-operation in their shaping, down to the smallest detail. 'Macbeth' (1847), 'Rigoletto' (1851), and 'La Traviata' (1853) are perhaps the most significant works of Verdi's middle period. In 'Don Carlos' (1867) he paid tribute to France, while 'Aida' (1871) is a magnificent example of Italian grand opera, the splendour of which has never been surpassed. In his last operas, 'Otello' (1887) and 'Falstaff' (1893), Verdi reached truly Shakespearian depths of passion and heights of humour; in his librettist, the dramatist Arrigo Boito (1842–1918), Verdi found the perfect literary collaborator.

13. Slavonic Opera. It is at this period that East European opera comes to the fore for the first time. About the middle of the nineteenth century national schools of opera had sprung up in many countries, inspired by native poetry, folk-lore, and folk-music. While the Hungarian operas of Ferencz Erkel (1810–93) and the Polish operas of Stanisław Moniuszko (1819–72) are little known outside their own countries, Czechoslovakia scored an international success with 'The Bartered Bride' (1866) by Bedřich Smetana (1824–84), a simple tale of Bohemian peasant life produced a year later than Wagner's 'Tristan und Isolde', and as un-Tristan-like as possible. Smetana wrote many other successful operas, as did his younger contemporary, Antonín Dvořák (1841–1904) ('Rusalka', 1900). In Russia, after feeble attempts in the eighteenth century which came to nothing, a national school of opera started with 'A Life for the Tsar' (1836) (known also as 'Ivan Susanin'), by Mikhail Glinka (1804–57), and among the greatest achievements of Russian opera are 'Boris Godunov' (1874), by Modest Mussorgsky (1839–81), a stirring musical drama taken from Russian history, 'Eugene Onegin' (1879) and 'The Queen of Spades' (1890), by Peter Ilyich Tchaikowsky (1840–93) and the scores of Andrey Nikolaievich (Nikolay) Rimsky-Korsakov (1844–1908) and Alexander Borodin (1833–87), full of vivid oriental colouring. The chief sources of inspiration for many of these operas were the poems and plays of the great Russian poet, Alexander Pushkin (1799–1837).

14. Light Opera. Another manifestation of anti-Wagnerian reaction was the rise of light opera which began in Paris, where the *opéra bouffe* of Jacques Offenbach (1819–80) and his successors ousted *opéra comique* of the old style. Parallel movements in other countries gave rise to the Spanish *zarzuela*, the Viennese waltz operetta of Johann Strauss (1825–99), and the Savoy operas of Sir William Schwenck Gilbert (1836–1911) and Sir Arthur Sullivan (1842–1900), a model of collaboration between librettist and composer. After 1900 there came a general decline of all the lighter genres towards musical comedy and revue.

15. Modern Opera. Wagner, and Verdi in his last works, had shown the importance of the literary side of opera, which should be something more than a mere libretto. As few musicians were able to equal Wagner in this respect, or to find a second Boito, composers of the early twentieth century took to using existing dramas of high literary quality as they stood, a method which seems to have been first employed by the Russian composer Alexander Dargomizhsky (1813–69) in 1868, with 'The Stone Guest', based on Pushkin's play of that name. This was produced after the composer's death, in 1872. In 1905 Richard Strauss (1864–1949), the outstanding German opera composer after Wagner, set *Salome*, by Oscar Wilde (1856–1900), in a German translation (1905), and four years later *Elektra*, by Hugo von Hofmannsthal (1874–1929), thus inaugurating a collaboration which continued with 'Der Rosenkavalier' (1911), 'Ariadne auf Naxos' (1912), 'Die Frau ohne Schatten' (1919),

'Arabella' (1932), and other works. Claude Debussy (1862–1918) was attracted by the mystic symbolism of Maurice Maeterlinck (1862–1949) and in 'Pelléas et Mélisande' (1902) created the masterpiece of modern impressionistic French music; the same poet's *Ariane et Barbe-Bleue* was set by Paul Dukas (1865–1935) in 1907. In Italy, the plays of Gabriele D'Annunzio (1863–1938) were used by Ildebrando Pizzetti (1880–1968) and others, while one of the most influential operas of modern times, 'Wozzeck' (1925), by Alban Berg (1885–1935), is a setting of a play by Georg Büchner (1813–37) written in 1836. The modern opera composer with the greatest popular appeal, Giacomo Puccini (1858–1924), proceeded in the old manner, and had libretti written to order. The world success of 'La Bohème' (1896), 'Tosca' (1900), and 'Madama Butterfly' (1904) is partly due to the skill of his literary collaborators, Giuseppe Giacosa (1847–1906) and Luigi Illica (1857–1919). His 'Turandot' (1926), based on a play by Gozzi, was left unfinished and was completed by his pupil and friend, Franco Alfano (1876–1954).

After the First World War there was a great revival of interest in opera, and conditions were very favourable for young and progressive composers and for experiments of all kinds. National opera-houses were opened in all the new states of Europe from the Baltic to the Balkans, and international festivals at Salzburg, Baden-Baden, Florence, Glyndebourne, and elsewhere, fostered the cause of opera. Strauss and Debussy had shown that there were unthought-of possibilities of creating something new and successful even after Wagner and Verdi, and in about 1920 opera composers started a hectic search for ways that would lead beyond Strauss and Debussy to an opera of the future.

ALFRED LOEWENBERG†, *rev.*

The language of music was at this time progressing far faster than the comprehension of audiences, and it was only after the Second World War that some of the keyworks of the earlier period—such as the 'Erwartung' (1909) of Arnold Schoenberg (1874–1951), the 'Doktor Faust' (1924) of Ferruccio Busoni (1866–1924), Berg's 'Wozzeck', mentioned above, and his 'Lulu' (1934)—began to be heard with any frequency. In Germany, Richard Strauss continued to explore his romantic vein with a series of operas culminating in the Wagnerian 'Die Liebe der Danae' (1940) and in 'Capriccio' (1941), an 'eighteenth-century' conversation piece about the making of an opera and the relative importance of its words and music. His works (with the exception of 'Die schweigsame Frau', 1935, after Jonson's *Epicoene*, whose librettist was the Jewish author Stefan Zweig) were approved by the Nazis. So were those of Carl Orff (1895–), 'Carmina Burana' (1936), 'Der Mond' (1938), and, later, 'Antigonae' (1949), a musical declamation of Hölderlin's version of Sophocles; Orff's innovations in the direction of sophisticated simplicity present no difficulties of comprehension. The music of Paul Hindemith (1895–1963), on the other hand, was proscribed by the Nazis; his 'Mathis der Maler' (1934), like the later 'Harmonie der Welt' (1957), deals with the creative artist's relationship to society. Also banned were the erotic operas of Franz Schreker (1878–1934) ('Der ferne Klang', 1909), which for a time had enjoyed a great success. Schoenberg was driven into exile; his 'Moses und Aron' (1932), left incomplete, is nevertheless, for its two finished acts, considered one of the greatest operas of the century. Kurt Weill (1900–50) had also to flee. In his collaboration with the dramatist Bertolt Brecht, Weill established a pungent, powerful operatic form in which attractive 'songs' were put to a serious purpose (*Die Dreigroschenoper* (1928), a version of *The Beggar's Opera* set in Victorian London; 'Mahagonny', 1930).

Active suppression in Nazi-controlled Europe, and later the general dislocation caused by war, delayed Berg's, Schoenberg's, and Weill's innovations from making their full effect. But after the war German opera companies swiftly recovered, and since almost every town has its opera-house, novelties were much in demand. Hans Werner Henze (1926–) emerged in 'Boulevard Solitude' (1952), a modern version of the Manon story, as a composer who could put all the techniques, both new and traditional, at the service of a personal vision, and with 'König Hirsch' (1956, after Gozzi), 'Der Prinz von Homburg' (1959, after Kleist), and 'Elegy for Young Lovers' (1961, original libretto by W. H. Auden and C. Kallman), he has found a way of continuing the operatic mainstream.

Brecht, Weill, and even more Igor Stravinsky (1882–1971), were largely responsible for breaking down the traditional borders between opera, play, and ballet in favour of a new kind of mixed theatre, hard to classify or define, whose influence has extended alike to Covent Garden and to the Theatre Royal, Stratford, E. Stravinsky composed 'The Soldier's Tale' (1918), 'a story told, acted and danced', 'The Fox' (1922), a 'burlesque in song and dance', 'The Wedding' (1923), 'choreographic scenes with songs and music', and 'Oedipus Rex' (1927), an 'opera-oratorio'. All these broke new ground, while the neo-classical 'Rake's Progress' (1951), a recitative-and-aria opera in eighteenth-century form, reclaimed some old ground for the present day.

In England, despite occasional revivals of pieces by Gustav Holst (1874–1934) and Ralph Vaughan Williams (1872–1958), few operas of the century survive before 'Peter Grimes' (1945), by Benjamin Britten (1913–), which has been performed all over the world. Britten then turned to chamber opera ('The Rape of Lucretia' 1946; 'Albert Herring', 1947; 'The Turn of the Screw', 1955), and even his 'grand operas' ('Billy Budd', 1951; 'Gloriana', 1953; 'A Midsummer Night's Dream', 1960) have retained a 'chamber' quality. Though Britten's utterance is intensely personal, he works with an easily comprehended musical idiom. The 'Troilus and Cressida' (1954) of William Walton (1902–) is a romantic opera in conventional form. 'The Midsummer Marriage' (1952) and 'King Priam' (1962) of Michael Tippett (1905–) are romantic in a thoroughly unconventional way; the second is indeed an 'epic' work in both the usual and the Brechtian senses of the word. Many young English composers are engaged on operas, but, largely owing to the lack of opera-houses in their country, they miss the Germans' practical experience of the genre while working as coaches, conductors, or musical assistants, and hence their pieces often lack theatrical proficiency.

From Italy there is little to report since Puccini's contemporaries such as Umberto Giordano (1867–1949) ('Andrea Chénier', 1895) and Francesco Cilea (1866–1950) ('Adriana Lecouvreur', after Scribe's play, 1902) and their successors. The most efficient of these, Gian Carlo Menotti (1911–) has worked mainly in America; his 'Consul' (1950) swept the world for a while. Pizzetti remains esteemed rather than popular (his 'L'Assassinio nella Cattedrale', 1957, is a setting of T. S. Eliot's play in translation); Luigi Dallapiccola (1904–) in 'Volo di Notte' (1940) and 'Il Prigioniero' (1946) adopted a more advanced musical idiom. French operas since 'L'Heure Espagnole' (1911) and 'L'Enfant et les Sortilèges' (1925) by Maurice Ravel (1875–1937) have seldom left France for long; among recent ones the most travelled perhaps is 'Dialogues des Carmélites' (1955, after Bernanos's script) by Francis Poulenc (1899–1963). No American opera has yet proved readily exportable (but see MUSICAL COMEDY); in 'Vanessa' (1957) (libretto by Menotti) Samuel Barber (1910–) adopted the Strauss model; 'The Tender Land' (1954) by Aaron Copland (1900–) is a fairly recent—and Kurt Weill's 'Down in the Valley' (1948) an earlier—example of the 'folk operas' which are being written there.

In Czechoslovakia Leoš Janáček (1854–1928), proceeding from a theory of speech-inflexions, arrived at a music of international eloquence ('Jenůfa', 1903; 'Káťa Kabanová', 1921, after Ostrovsky's *The Storm*; 'The House of the Dead', 1928, after Dostoievsky). Spain must be mentioned for Manuel de Falla (1876–1946) and his 'La Vida Breve' (1913) and Hungary for Béla Bartók (1881–1945) and his 'Bluebeard's Castle' (1911). The leading Russian composer of the century was Sergei Prokofiev (1891–1953), who in his early works ('The Gambler', 1915, after Dostoievsky; 'The Love of Three Oranges', 1919, after Gozzi, revised by Meyerhold; 'The Fiery Angel', 1925, after Bryusov's novel) showed a natural genius for the theatre which survived, though in less fiery form, in the long 'War and Peace' (1942). Most operas behind the Iron Curtain—if one may generalize from the few examples which reach the West—seem determinedly nationalist, 'folksy' in musical idiom, patriotic in subject-matter, and conservative in style. 'Lady Macbeth of Mtsensk', by Dmitri Shostakovich (1906–), initially successful in 1934, was withdrawn after official disapproval; renamed 'Katerina Ismaïlova', and slightly revised, it was released again in the more tolerant climate of the 1960s, and again has been internationally successful.

No pattern emerges, though perhaps three strands may be discerned: (*a*) the 'traditional' composers, still working in the Puccini–Strauss vein (Walton, Menotti); (*b*) composers who have renewed the traditional operatic form with new musical idioms, along lines suggested in Berg's 'Wozzeck' (Britten, Henze); (*c*) the innovators—there are plenty of them, but no well-known names suggest themselves. For opera as a contemporary and developing form is not flourishing. Innovations are unwelcome. In the nineteenth century audiences wanted to hear the latest novelty; today they shun it; the best-known works of Puccini, Verdi, Wagner, and Mozart form the staple repertory. Once composers vied with each other to write pieces for famous performers; today new operas are seldom given with star casts; the leading singers (Maria Callas, Joan Sutherland), producers (Franco Zeffirelli, Luchino Visconti, Walter Felsenstein), and conductors (Herbert von Karajan), apply their talents to revivals of the classics. The large opera-houses have become, in the main, museums where both executants and audience are habituated to the familiar idioms of the past; in any case the new operatic styles of our day are seldom suited to large houses. The situation seems healthiest in Germany, where there is no sharp distinction between opera and 'straight theatre' audiences; in London, the association of National Theatre and National Opera planned for the South Bank is a hopeful pointer for the future.

ANDREW PORTER

OPERA COMIQUE, LONDON. This theatre stood in the East Strand, near the old Globe (see GLOBE THEATRE, 2). The two playhouses were back to back, and were known as the Rickety Twins. It was badly built and was probably erected in the hope of compensation when the expected improvements led to the replanning and rebuilding of the district around. It was entered by long narrow tunnels from three thoroughfares, and was frequently referred to as Theatre Royal, Tunnels. It was so draughty that the audience could not sit in comfort, and many of them caught cold. In case of fire its stairs would have occasioned much loss of life, but, like its companion the Globe, it was never burned down, for which playgoers of the time had much reason to be grateful. Its very name was a mistake, for the public did not take to a foreign title. It opened on 29 Oct. 1870 with a French company under Déjazet. In 1871 the Comédie-Française, driven from Paris by the Franco-Prussian war, played there under Gôt, their first appearance outside France since their foundation. In

1873 Ristori appeared, followed by Gilbert and Sullivan, whose partnership had started at the Gaiety in 1871 with *Thespis; or, the Gods Grown Old.* Several of their operettas had their premieres here, notably *Patience* before transferring to D'Oyly Carte's new theatre, the Savoy. In 1885 the theatre was reconstructed, but success eluded it, and the last production was seen there in 1899.

W. MACQUEEN-POPE†

OPERA HOUSE, NEW YORK, see GRAND OPERA HOUSE and NATIONAL THEATRE, NEW YORK, I.

OPITZ, MARTIN (1597–1639), German author of a short handbook of poetics which turned the attention of his contemporaries to the classics, France, and Italy, and so brought about a break with the native theatre tradition, replacing it with a somewhat lifeless academic literature. He himself translated a number of Seneca's plays, and some Italian plays, into stately but monotonous alexandrines.

OPORTO EXPERIMENTAL THEATRE, see PORTUGAL.

O.P. RIOTS, see COVENT GARDEN.

ORANGE MOLL, see MEGGS.

ORANGE STREET THEATRE, LONDON, in Chelsea, a private theatre used by amateurs about 1831.

ORATOR, the name given in the early French theatre to the actor—usually the most distinguished member of the company—who drew up the playbill, and at the end of each performance addressed the audience, telling them what play would be given next, offering a graceful compliment to any royal or eminent visitor, and giving out any notices of general theatrical interest. He was often called on to quell riots, or silence interrupters, and the position called for wit, courage, and good-humour as well as authority and prestige. Among the early actors who filled the position were Montdory, Floridor, Laroque, Molière, and his successor La Grange.

ORIENTAL THEATRE, LONDON, a music-hall in Poplar which became a theatre in 1867. It was later called the Albion, and was used for melodrama for some time. It then again became a music-hall, as the Queen's Palace of Varieties.

ORLENEV, PAVEL NIKOLAYEVICH (1869–1932), Russian actor. After studying at the Maly Theatre in Moscow, he made his début in 1886, and spent much of his early years in the provinces. He was at the Suvorinsky Theatre, St. Petersburg, from 1898 to 1902, where on 12 Oct. 1898 he played the title-role in Tolstoy's *Tsar Feodor Ivanovich* (the play which opened the Moscow Art two days later). This had been banned for some years, and Orlenev caused it to be banned again by appearing made up to resemble Nicholas II. In 1904 he and Alla Nazimova took a company to Europe and England, and then on to the United States, where they had a great artistic success. Actors and critics were impressed by the ensemble playing, and by the actors' naturalistic style. The visit undoubtedly created an interest in Russian drama and in the stagecraft of Stanislavsky, praised by Orlenev as his master. It was during this visit that *Tsar Feodor Ivanovich* and *The Seagull* were first seen in America. Unfortunately the season was not a financial success, and Orlenev went back to Russia, leaving Nazimova to begin her successful American career. He returned to New York in 1912, acting in Russian with an English-speaking company. After the Russian Revolution he toured the provinces, acting in factories and on collective farms. Nervous and undisciplined in private life, he was capable of remarkable control and intense emotion in his favourite roles, among which were Raskolnikov, Brand, and especially Oswald in *Ghosts*.

ROBERT TRACY

ORRERY, LORD (Roger Boyle, first Earl of Orrery) (1621–79), a Restoration nobleman and man of letters, to whom Dryden generously, though not perhaps accurately, gave the credit for first writing rhymed heroic drama. He started his career as a dramatist by writing some forgotten comedies, but adopted the heroic theme of 'love and honour' in his later and more successful plays, notably *Mustapha* (1665) and *The Black Prince* (1667). These, and one or two other plays by him, are useful in their printed versions on account of their detailed stage directions.

OSBORNE, JOHN (1929–), English dramatist who first came into prominence when his play, *Look Back in Anger*, was produced at the Royal Court Theatre by the English Stage Company. It was their first outstanding success, and the date of the first night, 8 May 1956, is something of a landmark in the modern theatre. Osborne, who was for some years an actor, making his first appearance in 1948, and remaining a member of the Royal Court company until 1957, has written a number of other plays, including *The Entertainer* (1957), in which Laurence Olivier gave an outstanding performance as the seedy music-hall artiste, Archie Rice. *Epitaph for George Dillon* (1958) and *The World of Paul Slickey* (1959) were less successful, but *Luther* (1961), which had its first production by the English Stage Company at the Théâtre des Nations in Paris, with Albert Finney in the name-part, again caused something of a stir. In 1962 Osborne was responsible for a double bill at the Royal Court, but none of these plays reached the standard of his first two, which have been translated and acted in cities all over the world. In 1964 *Inadmissible Evidence*, in which Nicol Williamson gave a fine performance, was a success. A year later *A Patriot for Me* was refused a licence by the Lord Chamberlain, and was therefore given a private production for members of the English Stage Society by Anthony Page. The chief part was played by a famous Swiss actor, Maximilian Schell, making his first appearance in England.

OSTLER, William (?–1614), a boy-actor with the Children of the Chapel Royal, who appeared in *The Poetaster* in 1601. As an adult he was taken on by the King's Men, with whom he appeared in *The Alchemist* and was the original Antonio in *The Duchess of Malfi*. His excellent reputation is attested by a contemporary epigram which calls him 'sole King of Actors'. He married the daughter of Heminge, joint editor of Shakespeare's plays, in 1611, and had shares in both the Globe and Blackfriars, which Heminge tried to acquire from his widow.

OSTROVSKY, Alexander Nikolaivich (1823–86), Russian dramatist, who was born in Moscow and studied law at the university. He left before qualifying, and spent the next five years as a clerk in the Moscow Juvenile and Commercial Courts. Both there, and at home —his father was a lawyer with many clients among business men—he was able to study the merchant class, and so gathered the material for his plays, realistic studies of corruption and sharp practice, which have earned him the title of 'the Balzac of the Muscovite merchant'. He first came into prominence in 1848 as the author of *The Bankrupt* (later renamed *It's All in the Family*), an outspoken commentary on the faked bankruptcy of certain commercial magnates which lost him his job. It was banned for thirteen years, but circulated in manuscript and through private readings. After this Ostrovsky wrote a number of historical plays, a fairy-play which served as the basis for the libretto of Rimsky-Korsakov's opera 'The Snow-Maiden', and finally the series of realistic contemporary satires by which he is best known. Some of these have been translated into English, a difficult task owing to the richness and local colouring of Ostrovsky's style. They include *Even a Wise Man Stumbles* (also known as *Enough Stupidity in Every Wise Man*), *Easy Money*, and *Wolves and Sheep*, published in 1944 in a translation by David Magarshack; the second of these is based on *The Taming of the Shrew*. But the best-known of Ostrovsky's plays outside his own country is *The Storm*, a study in religious intolerance.

Most of Ostrovsky's plays were produced at the Maly Theatre in Moscow, where he found a champion and ideal interpreter in the actor Prov Sadovsky. In return he championed the stage, and in 1882 wrote a memorandum on the People's Theatres, urging the establishment of a National Theatre. He also founded the Society of Russian Playwrights, and in 1885 was appointed manager of the Moscow Imperial Theatres.

A statue of Ostrovsky stands at the entrance to the Maly—just as Molière's bust stands at the entrance to the Comédie-Francaise—each man commemorated by the theatre he made so peculiarly his own and which is often called after him—the House of Ostrovsky, La Maison de Molière.

OTWAY, Thomas (1652–85), English dramatist, who was educated at Winchester and Oxford, and in 1670 made his first and last appearance on the stage in Aphra Behn's *The Forced Marriage*. Disappointed in his ambition to be an actor, he turned to playwriting, and in 1675 produced *Alcibiades*, a tragedy which provided Mrs. Barry with her first great part. Otway was madly in love with her, though she gave him no encouragement, and in 1678, after the production of *Don Carlos*, a tragedy in rhymed verse, and a comedy entitled *Friendship in Fashion*, he enlisted in the army and went to Holland. Back in London, he returned to playwriting, and produced his two finest tragedies, *The Orphan; or, the Unhappy Marriage* (1680), and *Venice Preserved; or, a Plot Discovered* (1682), in both of which Betterton and Mrs. Barry appeared. They have been often revived, and contain some of the finest poetry of the day. Otway has been called 'an Elizabethan born out of his time', and his best work certainly shows a greater depth and sincerity, coupled with fine writing, than any other writing of the period. He was highly esteemed by his contemporaries. One of his most successful plays was his translation of *Les Fourberies de Scapin*. This was given at Dorset Garden as an after-piece to his *Titus and Berenice* (1676) (based on Racine), which remained on the London stage until 1812, and was played even later at the minor theatres and in the provinces.

O.U.D.S, see OXFORD.

OUVILLE, Antoine le Metel d' (*c.* 1590–1656/77), French dramatist, elder brother of the abbé-dramatist Boisrobert. He lived for some time in Spain, and was the first to introduce Calderón to France. He led a profligate and irregular life, which is reflected in the subject-matter of his comedies. The most successful of these was *L'Esprit folet* (1638–9), an adaptation of Calderón's *Dama duende*. Molière may have drawn on d'Ouville's *Trahisons d'Arbiran* (1638) for some of *Tartuffe*.

OVERSKOU, Thomas (1798–1873), Danish dramatic critic and historian, also the author of a number of plays, of which the best-known is *Pak* (1845).

OWENS, John Edmond (1823–86), American actor, born in London, but taken to the United States at the age of 5. He went on the stage at 17, and had a slow start; but after some initial successes he became known as an eccentric comedian and as an outstanding interpreter of Yankee characters. His most famous part was that of Solon Shingle in *The People's Lawyer*, in which Dickens saw him in London in 1865. He was also good as Toodles, Dr. Pangloss, Caleb Plummer, Paul Pry, and Aminadab Sleek. In 1876 he played Perkyn Middlewick in *Our Boys*, and some years later joined the Madison Square stock company, where he played with Annie Russell. He retired in 1885. Owens is described by Joseph

Jefferson in his *Autobiography* as 'the handsomest low comedian I had ever seen. He had a neat, dapper little figure, and a face full of lively expression. His audience was with him from first to last, his effective style and great flow of animal spirits capturing them.' He relied for his effects on his comic personality, and was somewhat extravagant in his acting, his Yankees being stage-folk rather than portraits from life. He was, however, popular and amusing, and made many successful tours throughout the United States.

OXBERRY. (1) WILLIAM (1784–1824), English actor, editor, and publisher, the son of an auctioneer. He was apprenticed in youth to a printer enamoured of acting. With him and his friends Oxberry acted *Douglas* and other plays in a converted stable. Emboldened by this experience, he broke his indentures at 18, and took to the professional stage, appearing at Watford as Antonio in *The Merchant of Venice*. After a round of the provinces he married, came to London, and appeared unsuccessfully at Covent Garden under Kemble. His performance was harshly criticized in *The Monthly Mirror*, a paper which, by an ironic twist of fate, he later edited. Discouraged, Oxberry set off for Scotland, where he appeared mostly in tragedy. On his return to London he made spasmodic appearances in small parts at the Lyceum and Drury Lane, and starred in minor suburban theatres. He was for a short time (1821) manager of the Olympic, but without much success. Shortly before his death he took over the Craven's Head Chophouse near Drury Lane, where his powers of mimicry and his readiness to drink made him a popular host and a boon companion. In addition to his histrionic activities, he was also a publisher and printer, and was responsible for a number of volumes of theatrical interest. He gave his name to *Oxberry's Dramatic Biography*, published posthumously by his widow, probably with the assistance of her second husband, Leman Rede. Oxberry was the author of a farce, *The Actress of All Work* (1819), which was probably inspired by Colman's *Actor of All Work*, written for Mathews in 1817. This play, which has been wrongly attributed to Oxberry's son, a lad of 11 at the date of its composition, shows one actress in six different roles, and was a favourite with little Clara Fisher, the child prodigy. Oxberry was a tall man, fat in his later years, dark in complexion, with small and piercing eyes. Passionate and of a difficult temper, he was yet considered a good friend, though a mediocre actor. His portrait hangs in the Garrick Club. His son, (2) WILLIAM HENRY (1808–52), was also an actor, and was one of the company who went with Miss Smithson to Paris in 1833. He succeeded the Keeleys in the management of Covent Garden, after managing the Lyceum without success, and was later with Mme Vestris. He was also for a time manager of the Windsor theatre. A contemporary said of him: 'There were few theatres at which he was not seen.' In contrast to his father he was a very little man, a lively actor and dancer in burlesque, with a quaint manner; he is said never to have known his part on first nights. He wrote a number of plays, mostly adapted from the French, of which *Mateo Falcone* (1836) was the most successful. He also dabbled extensively in theatrical journalism, conducting in 1843–4 *Oxberry's Weekly Budget*, in which many melodramas otherwise unknown were first printed.

OXFORD. In common with other centres, Oxford probably had its performances of medieval religious plays, and the constant association of play-acting with education may have led to undergraduate performances of which no trace remains. The earliest record is of a liturgical play on St. Katherine done at Magdalen in about 1490. In the 1540s several colleges acted plays in Latin by Nicholas Grimald, one, *Troilus*, based on Chaucer. There seems to have been much less acting at Oxford than at Cambridge, but in 1566 Queen Elizabeth I was present at a production in Christ Church of *Palaemon and Arcyte*, also based on Chaucer (*The Knight's Tale*), by Richard Edwardes. A pack of hounds was introduced into the quad, a stage-effect which delighted the Queen. Unfortunately the performance was interrupted by the collapse of a temporary wall which killed three men. The Queen sent her personal chirurgeon to attend them, but to no avail, and bade the actors proceed (see John Nichols, *Progresses and Public Processions of Queen Elizabeth*, 1823). In 1567, a comedy was produced at Merton with the intriguing title of *Wylie Beguylie*. Unfortunately, as with most of the other plays of the time, the manuscript is lost. A later royal visit was that of Charles I in 1636.

All the plays noted so far were in the nature of academic exercises, and incursions of professional companies seem to have been discouraged, as in later years, though Strange's Men were seen in an inn-yard in 1590–1, the King's Men in a tennis-court in 1680, and Betterton's company was in Oxford in 1703. The eighteenth century was unfavourable to the development of dramatic talent, though there were occasional private theatricals and some quasi-official performances at Commemoration. It was not until the middle of the nineteenth century that the colleges began to form their own dramatic societies, Brasenose being first in the field. These have now become a regular feature of undergraduate life, but officially the theatre has as yet no place in the university curriculum, and there is no Department of Drama as at Bristol and Manchester. There is, however, a University Theatre (see below), administered by a body of Curators drawn from the men's colleges under the chairmanship of the President of Magdalen and leased by them to a professional resident company. This theatre is also used by amateur university and city societies, and by visiting professional companies, during which time the resident company goes on tour, either to other provincial cities or abroad.

The Playhouse, in Beaumont Street, which was built by Eric Dance and opened on 20 Oct. 1938 with Fagan's *And So To Bed*, replaced an earlier and most inconvenient theatre in the Woodstock Road, a converted Big Game Museum, known also as the Red Barn, where intermittently from Oct. 1923 to Nov. 1928 J. B. Fagan made theatre history with a company which included at various times, and in the early part of their career, such actors as Tyrone Guthrie, Raymond Massey, Flora Robson, Glen Byam Shaw, Athene Seyler, Robert Morley, John Gielgud, and Emlyn Williams, in a fine programme of English and Continental plays. The venture was, however, ill-supported and Fagan finally gave up the struggle. From 1930 to 1938 a company under Stanford Holme and, later, Eric Dance, managed to keep the theatre open, but the town preferred to rely for its entertainment on the touring companies which came to the commercial New Theatre in George Street.

The new Playhouse was the last provincial theatre to be built before the Second World War, and it was twenty-one years before the next, the Belgrade at Coventry, opened. It managed to survive the rigours of the war years, under the direction of Peter Ashmore, with such guest producers as Malcolm Morley, Christopher Fry, and Esmé Percy, but later audiences dwindled, and in spite of the efforts of Frank Shelley, who had succeeded Ashmore, financial stringency finally caused the theatre to close in 1956. It was at this point that, at the invitation of Frank Birkett (Treasurer of Oxford Playhouse Ltd.) and Nevill Coghill (a senior member of the university), Frank Hauser brought in his Meadow Players, and, opening on 1 Oct 1956 with Giraudoux's *Electra*, presented an impressive programme of new and classical plays. In 1961, as the result of a motion in Congregation put forward by Coghill, the University bought the remaining lease of the theatre, and confirmed Hauser and his company in their tenancy. In 1963, as the result of an appeal by the Curators which raised £60,000, the theatre was redecorated and enlarged, over a hundred seats being added to the circle. An adaptable forestage was provided in front of the proscenium opening, which can be used as part of the auditorium or as part of an open stage, or, for performances of opera and ballet, can be removed entirely, leaving an orchestra well. The refurbished theatre opened on 14 Jan. 1964 with a Molière trilogy in translation (*L'Ecole des Femmes*, *La Critique de l'Ecole des Femmes* and *L'Impromptu de Versailles*).

Apart from the college societies, the main amateur theatrical activity in Oxford was for a long time vested in the Oxford University Dramatic Society (O.U.D.S.), which has given many distinguished actors and producers to the professional stage. It was founded in 1885, mainly through the exertions of Arthur Bourchier, then an undergraduate at Christ Church, and his friends, among them W. L. Courtney and Cosmo Gordon Lang, future Archbishop of Canterbury and cousin of Matheson Lang. The first production, given in the Town Hall, was *Henry IV, Part I*, in which Bourchier played Hotspur, and Lang spoke the Prologue. The production was by Alan Mackinnon, who was responsible for all productions up to 1895 and also wrote a history of Oxford theatricals. Up to the outbreak of the First World War thirty-two productions were given, mainly of Shakespearian comedies, in winter in the New Theatre and, during the summer, in various college gardens. During the war the society was disbanded, but it started again in 1919, the first production being Hardy's *Dynasts*, which the author himself attended. The society then followed the former plan of indoor and outdoor productions, but with less emphasis on the comedies, and with occasional plays—for instance, *Hassan*—by authors other than Shakespeare. At all these performances the women's parts—female members of the university being debarred from participation—were played by professional actresses of the front rank, and a number of professional producers were also employed as an alternative to undergraduates. On the outbreak of the Second World War the society was again suspended, but a new society, known as the Friends of the O.U.D.S., was formed under the auspices of senior members, prominent among them Nevill Coghill, who produced six of the twelve productions from 1940 to 1947. Under his direction the Friends not only maintained a high standard but also succeeded in paying off outstanding debts and laying by funds for the future. Their last production was Ibsen's *The Pretenders*. Shortly afterwards the O.U.D.S. was re-formed under the presidency of Glynne Wickham, later Professor of Drama at Bristol University. A major change was that professional actresses were no longer engaged for the women's parts, which were played either by members of the women's colleges, or by members of other amateur groups. In June 1947 the reconstituted society gave its first production, *Love's Labour's Lost*, in Merton Gardens. In May 1948 *The Masque of Hope*, written by Coghill and produced by Wickham, was acted before Princess Elizabeth (later Elizabeth II) in University College. In 1950 the society, which had taken new premises above the old ones (given up in 1939), was forced to relinquish them owing to the rise in rents, and the character of the club has necessarily changed somewhat. Lack of social amenities seems, however, to have resulted in an intensification of purely dramatic activities, and the level of O.U.D.S. productions remains high. The archives of the O.U.D.S., consisting of programmes, photographs, and press-cuttings, have been deposited at the Bodleian, and there is an officer annually appointed as archivist to keep them up to date.

In Feb. 1936 Nevill Coghill founded a new society, the Oxford Experimental Theatre

Club, which, unlike the O.U.D.S., was designed to leave everything connected with the production of a play in the hands of undergraduates. It also chose to do plays which were not within the province of the older society—no Shakespeare, but neglected classics, new English or foreign plays, particularly of the *avant-garde*, and, where possible, plays by undergraduate members. The first production was Dryden's *All for Love* in 1936; other productions were Cocteau's *Marriage on the Eiffel Tower* and *The Infernal Machine*, Pirandello's *Naked* and *Six Characters in Search of an Author*, Jonson's *Silent Woman*, and Skelton's *Castle of Perseverance*, which had not been revived since the fifteenth century.

Finally, mention should be made of the Greek plays. The first was the *Agamemnon* of Aeschylus done in 1880 under the patronage of Dr. Jowett, then Master of Balliol, in Balliol Hall, with a back-scene designed by Burne-Jones. Among the actors were Frank Benson and W. L. Courtney. Later productions were the *Alcestis* in 1887, the *Frogs* in 1892, and the *Knights* in 1897. The tradition of a play in Greek continued until the 1930s, and many of the college societies performed also the translations of Greek dramas by Gilbert Murray.

OXFORD'S MEN. The first mention of a company of players under this name occurs as early as 1492, and in 1547 the players of the 16th Earl of Oxford caused a scandal by playing in Southwark while a dirge was being sung for Henry VIII at St. Saviour's. This company may have been disbanded in 1562, but later the 17th Earl, himself a playwright, became patron of the Earl of Warwick's Men, who in 1580 appeared under Oxford's name in Burbage's Theatre during the absence on tour of its usual players. They got into trouble for brawling, and were banished to the provinces, not appearing at Court until 1584, when John Lyly was with them. The company included a number of boys, who, with some of the Children of the Chapel and of Paul's, played at Blackfriars. It was eventually (1602) merged in that of Worcester.

OXFORD MUSIC-HALL, London, built by Charles Morton on the site of an old coaching house, the Boar and Castle, at the corner of Oxford Street and Tottenham Court Road. It opened on 26 Mar. 1861, with a bill which, like those at Morton's Canterbury, offered good music as well as comedians and slapstick. It was a large and well-lit hall, with a full-length mirror at the back of the stage which reflected the audience seated at separate tables, where they ate and drank. On 11 Feb. 1868 it burnt down, but reopened eighteen months later, much enlarged. In 1892 it was rebuilt and modernized, the foundation stone being laid by Charles Morton, its original founder. On its act drop was a painting of Magdalen College tower, and the same device was emblazoned on its programmes. It opened on 31 Jan. 1893, and became a most successful music-hall in the old style, retaining its tables and a bar where men could order a drink and stand to watch the turns. For a time it ran Saturday matinées at which, for 6*d*., all the old stars could be seen, and sometimes a new one, for George Robey and Harry Tate both made their first London appearances here. In 1917 it was taken over by Charles Cochran and made into a theatre, its first success being *The Better 'Ole*, a musical play by Bruce Bairnsfather, the famous war cartoonist. In 1921 it was rebuilt and modernized, and used for revues like *The League of Notions* and *Mayfair and Montmartre*. In 1926 it was demolished, and a restaurant built on the site.

W. Macqueen-Pope†, *rev.*

OZEROV, Vladislav Alexandrovich (1770-1816), Russian dramatist, who was educated at the Cadet College for the sons of the nobility, where he became interested in the theatre and in languages, particularly French. He held many military posts, and worked in the Forestry Department. In 1808 he retired without a pension, and spent the last years of his life in poverty in a village. His first play, written in 1798, was a failure, but some of his later ones, though written in a frigid classical style much influenced by the neo-classicism of France, achieved a certain popularity. He took his heroes from widely different ages and countries—Oedipus, Ossian, Dmitry—but subjected them all to the same treatment, and their foreign origin was manifest in the ease with which they were translated into German and French. Ozerov is almost forgotten now, but one of his patriotic plays, dealing with the fourteenth-century leader of the Russians against the Tartars, Dmitry of the Don, was revived in 1943 by the Kamerny Theatre.

P

PACUVIUS, Marcus (*c.* 220–130 B.C.), one of the leading dramatists of Rome, and the first to specialize in tragedy. We possess the titles of twelve tragedies and one *praetexta*; the fragments amount to about 400 lines. Pacuvius seems to have liked pathetic scenes, philosophical discussions, and complicated plots—ancient critics ranked him first in point of learning, Accius first in force—while his language, though sometimes awkward and obscure, shows pictorial power (he was a painter as well as a writer) and careful attention to sound-effects. Many of his plays enjoyed great popularity down to the end of the Republic. A canticum from his *Armorum Iudicium* was sung at the funeral of Julius Caesar; one of its lines was very apposite: 'To think that I saved the men who were to murder me!' Perhaps the most famous scene in Roman tragedy was the opening of Pacuvius's *Iliona*. The play dealt with Polydorus, youngest son of Priam, who was entrusted to the care of his sister Iliona, wife of Polymestor, King of Thrace. Iliona brought up Polydorus as her son, pretending to Polymestor that their child was Polydorus. On the fall of Troy Polymestor murdered the supposed Polydorus—really his own son. The play opened with the ghost of the murdered boy rising to implore his sleeping mother for burial. In the half-light of early morning the sleeping form of Iliona was discovered on the stage; presently the ghost made its appearance from a recess in the stage-floor. Unfortunately, on one occasion in the first century, Fufius, the actor playing the part of Iliona, had got drunk and really fallen asleep, thus failing to hear the ghost's appeal until the whole theatre took up the words: 'Mother, I cry to thee.' Another favourite scene, in the *Chryses*, showed Orestes and Pylades brought captive before Thoas; he wished to punish Orestes alone, and there was a generous rivalry between the two friends, each claiming to be Orestes—a passage which, as Cicero tells us, brought the spectators to their feet in applause. Cicero claims that in the final scene of the *Niptra* Pacuvius has improved on Sophocles; whereas Sophocles allowed the mortally wounded hero to express all his agony, Pacuvius makes him die with a Stoic self-control. WILLIAM BEARE†

PAGEANT. In medieval times the word referred to the cart on which a scene of a religious play was performed. This stage on wheels (for a late example see No. 19) consisted usually of two rooms, the lower one curtained off as a dressing-room, though it could on occasion be used to represent Hell. Later the name was transferred to the ambulating entertainments, not entirely religious, of which we retain a survival in the Lord Mayor's Show, and, when the dramatic part of the proceedings had lapsed, to the dumb-show tableaux, sometimes accompanied by explanatory verse. From this meaning of the word comes its modern connotation of 'a spectacular procession', as applied to the elaborate civic pageants so fashionable in England in the early 1900s. The first was that produced by Louis N. Parker at Sherborne in 1905, and it was followed by others at Warwick, Dover, York, Oxford, and many other places. These mingled short dramatic sketches with displays of dancing, songs, and processions to music, the whole having some bearing on the history of the locality. During the First World War several patriotic pageants were produced at London theatres, while Drury Lane celebrated its own history in *The Pageant of Drury Lane* (1918), again with Louis N. Parker as pageant-master.

A further extension of the medieval meaning is found in the pageants, or stationary stages, set up out of doors or inside to welcome royal or distinguished visitors, or to celebrate a marriage or an embassy. These were popular in Tudor and Elizabethan times, and on them were enacted entertainments of songs and speeches, with a dramatic interlude, usually allegorical, specially written for the occasion.

The word pageant was also applied to the elaborate structures of wood and painted canvas which were used in the Tudor masques. These were often ingenious machines, fixed or movable, designed and built at considerable expense for the purposes of a single night's entertainment (see MASQUE).

PAILLERON, Édouard (1834–99), French dramatist, author of a number of light comedies which show a penetrating analysis of contemporary society, and an equal disregard of the problems of social conduct so popular on the stage at that time. Pailleron may be said to provide the light-hearted pendant to the later work of the younger Dumas and of Henri Becque. His plays are comedies of character, but they do not belong to any school, and have little affinity with the earlier comedy to which this label is given. His first plays were performed under the Second Empire, but his best, of which *Le Monde où l'on s'ennuie* (1881) and *La Souris* (1887) were the most successful, belong to the Third Republic. The former, a satire on pedantry and intellectual preciosity, was extremely successful, and has been several times revived. Unfortunately Pailleron's work dates, and the excellence of the dialogue does little to compensate for the loss of interest inevitable with the passage of time. His last plays, which included *Cabotins* (1894), a study of false pretences, were less successful, and soon forgotten.

PAINT FRAME, a device, hung from the grid, which is suspended at the back of the stage in some older theatres to carry the canvas while the scene-painter is at work on it. Sometimes the painter works on the level of the fly-floor, and drops the frame by means of a winch to any required level; sometimes the frame is fixed and he works at it on a moving bridge raised and lowered by a winch.

PAKISTAN. In spite of a flourishing film industry and a fairly wide-spread radio network, Pakistan has at the time of writing (1966) no professional theatre, and drama is in the hands of enthusiastic and hard-working bands of amateurs mainly based on Karachi, though Lahore and Dacca, for long the great cultural centres of the country, also support amateur groups. It is only since the mid-1950s that modern theatre art has been taken seriously in Pakistan, and it is to be hoped that the gradual spread of amateur acting will, as in other countries, lead eventually to a full professional and national theatre.

In Karachi, where plays are given in English, Urdu, and Bengali, the initial impulse towards the creation of a national drama came from a German, Mrs. Sigrid Nyberg Kahle, wife of a diplomat. She collected round her a group of young theatre lovers, and put on several plays in English and in Urdu, the latter resulting in an increase in the number of Urdu playwrights. Among them are Syed Imtiaz Ali Taj, whose *Anarkali* was given by an amateur group in 1951, and whose *Kamra No. 5* is often revived; Khwaja Moinuddin, author of *Lal Qilay Say Lalukhait Tak* and *Taleem-e-Belaghan*; Asghar Butt, author of *Nathu Khairy*, produced by Hameed Wyne in 1959, with the radio artist Mahmood Ali in the chief part; and Anwer Enayatullah, basically a short-story writer, but author of a number of good plays for children.

Parallel with the emergence of dramatists has been the development of producers and particularly actors, both in their own language and in English. One of the latter, Zia Mohyeddin, has made a reputation for himself on the English stage, having played the leading part in the dramatization by Santha Rama Rau of Forster's *Passage to India* (1960).

PALACE THEATRE, LONDON, in Cambridge Circus, Shaftesbury Avenue. This opened under D'Oyly Carte as the Royal English Opera House on 31 Jan. 1891 with Sullivan's opera 'Ivanhoe'. This had 160 performances, but its successor, Messager's 'La Basoche', failed to attract the public, and after a visit by Sarah Bernhardt, Augustus Harris took over the theatre, renamed it the Palace Theatre of Varieties, and opened it as a music-hall in 1892. Charles Morton was called in to run it, and under him, and Alfred Butt, who succeeded him in 1904, it had a long and successful career. In 1911 the theatre took its present name, but continued to present variety bills and revues, the first being *The Passing Show* (1914), with Elsie Janis. In 1924 the Co-Optimists were there, and in the following year the musical comedy *No, No, Nanette!* began its long run. It was followed by a number of other successful musicals, until in the early 1930s the theatre was used for straight plays. It reverted to revue with a series of Cochran shows, and during the Second World War housed Cecily Courtneidge and Jack Hulbert in musical comedy. Among later successes were *Gay Rosalinda* (1945) and *Song of Norway* (1946); in 1949 there was a long run of Novello's *King's Rhapsody*. During the 1950s the Palace was used for a number of foreign companies—the T.N.P., the Renaud–Barrault, the Berliner Ensemble, Antonio—brought to London on the initiative of Peter Daubeny. *Flower Drum Song* (1960) had a long run, as did *The Sound of Music* (1961).

PALAIS-ROYAL, THÉÂTRE DU. The first theatre of this name in Paris was a small private playhouse in the home of Cardinal Richelieu, which he rebuilt at great expense in the last years of his life, importing all the newest stage machinery, with superb interior decoration. It was long and narrow, the floor rising in a series of shallow steps, with two balconies on each side, and held about 600 people. It was formally inaugurated on 14 Jan. 1641, with a spectacular performance of *Mirame*, in whose composition Richelieu is believed to have had a hand, though it was attributed to Desmarets. The splendid audience was headed by the king and queen, and admittance was restricted to the great nobles of the Court and their immediate families. After Richelieu's death in the following year the theatre, with all his other possessions, became the property of the king and was used intermittently for Court entertainments until 1660, when it was given to Molière in place of the demolished Petit-Bourbon. After some hasty repairs and redecoration it remained in use until 1670, when it was rebuilt and enlarged and once more equipped with new machinery necessary for spectacular productions of opera. It reopened with *Psyché* (1671), and Molière played there until the night of his death, 17 Feb. 1673, after a performance of *Le Malade imaginaire*. Lully, who held a monopoly of music in France, immediately claimed the Palais-Royal for his new Academy of Music, and it was so called until it was burnt down in 1763. Rebuilt, it was again destroyed by fire in 1781.

The whole area occupied by the Palais-Royal then underwent reconstruction by its owner, the Duc de Chartres, as a vast pleasure-garden, and several theatres were built there, most of which at some time called themselves Palais-Royal. One of them, which opened in 1790 as the Variétés-Amusantes, was later renamed the Théâtre de la République, and housed Talma and his companions during the Revolution. In 1799 it became the present Comédie-Française (see No. 33). Another Palais-Royal opened under Dormeuil in 1831 and saw, among other things, the first night of

Labiche's famous comedy, *Un Chapeau de paille d'Italie* (1851). In England the term 'Palais-Royal farce' was applied to the broad suggestiveness of such productions as *The Pink Dominos* (1877) and *The Girl from Maxim's* (1902).

PALAPRAT, JEAN DE BIGOT (1650–1721), French dramatist, of good family. He went to Paris in 1671 and became friendly with Molière and Dominique. He also made the acquaintance of Brueys, with whom he later collaborated in several plays for the Comédie-Française, in which the actor J. B. Raisin, a friend of both authors, played leading parts. They were successful at the time, but soon forgotten, as were the plays which Palaprat wrote on his own, or with Dominique, for the Italian actors. Palaprat was a witty and amusing companion, a true Gascon, and Étienne later wrote a play dealing with his friendship and collaboration with Brueys.

PALESTINE, see JEWISH DRAMA, 8.

PALLADIO, ANDREA (1518–80), Italian architect, whose surname was bestowed on him by his benefactor J. G. Trissino (from Pallas) and has in turn given its name to the Palladian style of architecture, based on the principles of antiquity as Palladio interpreted them in his work, and in his *Quattro libri dell'architettura*, published in Venice in 1570. This was translated into English with notes by Inigo Jones, who was a pupil and admirer of Palladio, and imported his ideas into England, influencing both the theatre and public architecture. Palladio built, among other things, the Teatro Olimpico, Vicenza (see No. 20), the most important theatre of the Italian Renaissance, which was finished by his pupil Scamozzi.

PALLADIUM, see LONDON PALLADIUM.

PALLENBERG, MAX (1877–1934), German actor, who worked for some time with Reinhardt, and proved himself a versatile and subtle comedian. He made his first appearance on the stage in 1895, and was later in Vienna and in Berlin, where in 1914 he was an outstanding member of the Deutsches Theater. He was excellent at improvisation and in broad comedy, but could also play more serious parts, as was proved by his performance of the barker in *Liliom*. He was the husband of the eminent Viennese comedienne, Fritzi Massary.

PALLIATA, see FABULA, 3.

PALMER, ALBERT MARSHMAN (1838–1905), American theatre manager, who controlled successively the Union Square Theatre, the Madison Square Theatre, and Wallack's old theatre, to which he gave his own name. He retired in 1896, and became manager for Richard Mansfield, who had made his first appearance under Palmer at the Union Square Theatre. Palmer, who was well educated and a man of much taste, sought to rival Daly and Wallack, and built up in each of his theatres a good, well-disciplined company. He did not, like Daly, create stars, but chose his actors wisely and set many on the road to fame. In his early years he followed Wallack's lead in producing imported plays, but later turned to new American works, producing *Hazel Kirke*, *Beau Brummell*, *Alabama*, and other native dramas, and encouraging such American playwrights as Augustus Thomas, Clyde Fitch, Bronson Howard, and William Gillette. In 1882 he was instrumental in founding the Actors' Fund. Palmer did a great deal for the American theatre, and his influence on staging, back-stage conditions, and the fostering of native talent was extremely beneficial.

PALMER. (1) JOHN (1728–68), known as 'Gentleman' Palmer, an English actor who died young after making a good reputation in small comic parts, like that of Brush in *The Clandestine Marriage*. He married in 1761 Hannah, the daughter of Mrs. Pritchard, who proved to be but an indifferent actress. A year after Palmer's death she married a merchant named Lloyd, retired from the stage, and died in 1781. John was an extremely vain man and would no doubt have hated to be confused, as he so often is, with the son of Robert Palmer, pit door-keeper at Drury Lane, whose name was also (2) JOHN (1742–98). The younger John made his first appearance at the Haymarket under Foote, and in 1767 was taken on by Garrick for Drury Lane. Here he succeeded to many of the parts of the elder John, and was the first to play Joseph Surface (see No. 30). Lamb, who has left a description of him in the part, said that when he appeared he was the hero of the play, a feat achieved in our own day by John Gielgud. He was also good as Falstaff and as Sir Toby Belch, and in such impudent parts as Captain Absolute, Young Wilding, and Dick Amlet. Tragedy was beyond him, and he rarely attempted it. Sheridan nicknamed him 'Plausible Jack', and he was as famous for his mendacity as for his acting. He built the Royalty Theatre in Wellclose Square, opening in 1787 with a fine company, Braham, aged 14, singing between the acts of the play. Palmer, who had no licence, was summonsed by the Patentees, but wriggled his way out of any unpleasantness and rejoined the Drury Lane company. He died on the stage, while acting in *The Stranger* at Liverpool.

The younger John Palmer had two brothers, (3) ROBERT (1754–1817), who played important parts at both Drury Lane and Covent Garden, and (4) WILLIAM (?–1797), who was for a short time at Covent Garden, but played mainly leading parts in Dublin. None of these actors appear to be related to the Robert Palmer mentioned in *The Dunciad*.

PALMO'S OPERA HOUSE, NEW YORK, see BURTON, W. E.

PALSGRAVE'S MEN, see ADMIRAL'S MEN.

PANHARMONIUM, LONDON. This stood in New Road, King's Cross. It was a strange-looking building with a small portico, built originally by Lanza, a teacher of singing, for musical entertainments and displays by his pupils. In 1832 Mrs. Fitzwilliam and Buckstone opened it as the Clarence Theatre, with the interior decorated to represent a Chinese pavilion. They soon left, and in 1838 it was known as the New Lyceum. Many obscure managers ran it, but it sank so low that box tickets to admit four were sold for 3*d*. So disreputable did it become that it was closed by order of the magistrates. In 1870 an attempt to reopen it ended in failure and it was heard of no more. W. MACQUEEN-POPE†

PANOPTICON, LONDON, see ALHAMBRA.

PANTALOON, the old man—later Columbine's father, guardian, or husband—in the harlequinade, where he is the butt of Clown's practical jokes. He comes from Pantalone, who, in the *commedia dell'arte*, was an elderly Venetian, a caricature of the city merchant, by turns avaricious, suspicious, amorous, and gullible (see Nos. 134, 140). In Elizabethan England the term was applicable to any old man—as witness Shakespeare's reference to 'the lean and slipper'd pantaloon, with spectacles on nose and pouch on side'.

PANTHEON, LONDON, in Oxford Street, built by James Wyatt. This opened on 28 Apr. 1772, and was designed as an indoor Ranelagh or Vauxhall. It was a popular place for balls, routs, and, above all, masquerades. In 1784 it became an opera-house, and in 1789 the Drury Lane company used it after their temporary home (during Sheridan's rebuilding of Drury Lane) at the Queen's, Haymarket, was burnt down. Wyatt was responsible for the necessary alterations. The Pantheon was itself burnt down in 1792, only the façade, so long a London landmark, remaining. Wyatt rebuilt it, but its day had passed. Various attractions were tried, and in 1812 Colonel Henry Fulke Greville, who ran an entertainment in the Argyll Rooms called 'The Pic Nics', opened it as the Pantheon Theatre in partnership with a wine merchant called Cundy. They lost £50,000 in just over a month. Greville retired, but Cundy tried to carry on, unsuccessfully, and in 1814 the building, with the rent in arrears, was put up for sale. The creditors sold everything, even stripping the paper from the walls. The theatre remained closed for many years, reopened as a bazaar, and was then used for over seventy years as the offices of Gilbeys, the wine merchants. It was pulled down in 1937.

W. MACQUEEN-POPE†, *rev.*

PANTOMIME has seven distinct meanings, confused by persistent efforts to read into the word *pantomimus* the associated idea of performance wholly in dumbshow. Until this error takes root early in the eighteenth century, pantomime in English literature means 'player of every part'. The various meanings can be classified as follows:

1. The Greek label for a type of actor peculiar to Imperial Rome. By means of a mask with three compartments, each carved to represent the face of a different person—Mars, Venus, and Vulcan, for example—he suggested by gesture alone all the characters in a fable, as well as birds or beasts, tempest, fire, or flood, to illustrate a narrative sung by the chorus (for further details see MIME, 2 and PANTOMIMUS).

2. Eighteenth-century ballets with subjects taken from classical mythology. Inspired by a knowledge of *pantomimus* derived from Lucian's *Dialogues* without reference to other sources, the Duchesse du Maine staged *ballets-pantomimes* at Sceaux in the belief that she was reviving an ancient art. 'The Loves of Mars and Venus' at Drury Lane in Mar. 1717 was billed as a 'New dramatic entertainment after the manner of the ancient pantomimes'.

3. Traditional Christmas entertainments of the British Empire, originating in the comic dances of Arlequins from the Paris fairs (see COMMEDIA DELL'ARTE and HARLEQUINADE). By 1715 rivalry in such entertainments between London's leading theatres had become keen. At Lincoln's Inn Fields John Rich, the manager, appeared under his stage name of Lun as Harlequin. Drury Lane devised more and more elaborate harlequinades, then tried 'The Loves of Mars and Venus', and a month later showed Harlequin as Perseus with Columbine as Andromeda in a ballet called 'The Shipwreck'. This confused the public who (despite a managerial protest that harlequinades were 'not in the least designed for an imitation of the ancient pantomimes, Harlequin, Scaramouche, Punch, and Pierrot being of the present Italian theatre') made 'pantomime' the label for their favourite after-piece. None can be acclaimed as the first of a species whose peculiarity is that it has been shaped less by authors than by audiences. Public approval caused the harlequinades (see No. 140) to lengthen until their style had to be varied to provide rest for the dancers. In *Tom Jones* Fielding describes how harlequinade and classic fable alternated incongruously, but this was one device among many. The story of Dr. Faustus was thus Italianized so that trick-scenery could be employed, and Jack Sheppard so that Harlequin could demonstrate that criminal's prison-breaking exploits. Usually Harlequin was a comic character, until he was romanticized as the lover of Columbine. Their elopement, with Pantaloon, as her father, in pursuit through scenes that reflected the tastes and topics of the day, became a steadfast pattern. But the opening scenes, where some immortal bestowed the magic wand upon Harlequin, had to be novel. Classic mythology went out of fashion at the turn of the eighteenth century, and tales from chapbooks gradually took its place. In the nineteenth century the opening was elaborated in cast and scenery until it took the form of the fashionable burlesques or extravaganzas—not in dumbshow—with actresses in the heroes'

parts (see PRINCIPAL BOY). Victorian pantomimes gradually softened the burlesque, especially when pantomime troupes of dancers, notably the Vokeses at Drury Lane, acted fairy-tales (see Nos. 142, 143) dramatized at such length that the pantomime ceased to be an after-piece, though preceded for some years by a one-act comedy. When Augustus Harris became manager of Drury Lane he prompted a music-hall invasion throughout the country, which replaced theatrical companies in pantomimes by casts of variety artists. This brought comic relief uppermost, but the glamour was ensured by restricting the choice of subject mainly to tales that had the seal of nursery approval upon them. These tales, after contact with a century of Christmas audiences, have been artfully adapted to the stage. *Cinderella* uses another of Perrault's stories (*Les Fées*) as a kind of prologue, and absorbs part of the plot of Rossini's unfairylike opera, 'La Cenerentola', with its character of Dandini for second boy. *The Babes in the Wood* has Robin Hood and his Merry Men to make happy the ending. *Red Riding Hood* for over a hundred years has had a demon wolf on two legs from a Paris opera instead of the ordinary wolf of Perrault's story. *Aladdin* is based on a burlesque by H. J. Byron in the 1860s which bestowed on the hero's mother (see DAME) the name of Widow Twankey at a time when tea-clippers raced home from the East with cargoes of twankay. *Robinson Crusoe* has a survivor in its villain, Will Atkins, of Pixerécourt's *mélodrame* about Crusoe's densely populated isle. *Mother Goose*, merely a name on Perrault's title-page and little more than a figure in the piece with this title in which Grimaldi played, is a modern pantomime written by J. Hickory Wood for Dan Leno at Drury Lane. *Blue Beard* persistently disguises itself as the 1002nd Arabian Nights' Entertainment, for though Perrault knew it to be a legend of France, the Christmas pantomime decided otherwise. Oliver Goldsmith's *Goody Two-Shoes* includes in its pantomime form Bo-Peep, Tommy Tucker, Little Boy Blue, and other nursery-rhyme children. Thus pantomime has added another chapter to folklore, although the incongruity of such plots as the background for acrobatics, topical songs, and patriotic tableaux is such that the word 'pantomime' (or more particularly the words 'a proper pantomime') signifies in colloquial English 'a state of confusion'.

4. Wordless Pierrot plays, first inspired by the performance of English pantomimes in Paris. Comparing Grimaldi's *Mother Goose* with the French version played at the Funambules by Deburau shows how such very dissimilar entertainments were once related. The Gallic mentality, trying to rationalize the monstrous hotch-potch of the visitors, had first to get rid of Clown. All these tricks and transformations were a nightmare, to be seen not through the eyes of the very spirit of them, but in the mind of the one who suffers them. For this Deburau invented a new Pierrot, not the clumsy half-wit of the Italians, but a wistful mourner in the light of the moon. 'Le Napoléon de la Pantomime' Banville called him when to devise a pantomime for the Funambules was the ambition of every Paris romantic. Through Deburau's son the line of French Pierrots continued until Séverin died in 1930. They rarely made so much stir abroad as when *L'Enfant prodigue*, with a girl to play Pierrot, was acted in all parts of the world during the 1890s.

5. Melodrama in dumbshow. In the eighteenth century stage monopolies both in England and France forbade dialogue except at Theatres Royal. Unlicensed theatres presented wordless spectacles, displays of pageantry which developed into tales of adventure with songs, recitatives, and notice-boards or scrolls to explain the plot in between battles or single combats. In London the popularity of such shows at Sadler's Wells and the Royal Circus caused Drury Lane and Covent Garden to engage special pantomime companies to act after-pieces in imitation of their humble rivals. The label was either *ballet d'action* or 'serious pantomime' (see MELODRAMA). These terms continued during the following period (early nineteenth century) when similar pieces had some scenes in dialogue and some 'in pantomime'. Brief wordless versions of famous melodramas were played by the troupe of Paul Martinetti (1851–1924) in the variety theatres of several countries. His pantomimes included *The Duel in the Snow* (from *The Corsican Brothers*) and *Robert Macaire*. These were highly popular on the halls in England at a time when the dramatic sketch with dialogue was still forbidden—last relic of the stage monopoly.

6. Acrobatic-cum-scenic spectacles. Circus troupes, bent on exhibiting their talents in world-wide theatrical tours under their own management, borrowed ideas from both the Grimaldi and the Deburau traditions while devising pantomimes of a type that became peculiarly their own. From the 1860s to the 1890s the Ravels and the Hanlon-Lees excited astonishment with their nightmare spectacles, and in Paris the theatrical species called *la féerie*, notably *Les Pilules du Diable* at the Châtelet, adapted such antics for Christmas festivities. The American pantomime of *Humpty-Dumpty*, in which Fox, the most celebrated of American clowns, toured throughout the United States, may perhaps be included in this category, although it was of an earlier date, and in its style unique.

7. A term variously employed to describe what is seen in acting or dancing. It is applied to passages in plays when ideas are silently conveyed; to expressive movements made by actors with arms, legs, or face when not speaking; to passages in ballet which cannot strictly be described as dancing; to expressive movements made by a ballet dancer's arms, face, or anatomical parts other than legs. The technique thus baldly stated is an important

characteristic of modern acting and modern ballet.

In order to dissociate themselves from popular entertainments, modern exponents of dumbshow describe their art as 'mime' (see MIME, 3), although it has nothing in common with the mimicry, or the performances based on that idea, of Ancient Rome.

M. WILLSON DISHER†

PANTOMIMUS, THE, was a performer whose art consisted in representation by means of rhythmical gesture alone. This form of entertainment, popular in Magna Graecia (it was called the 'Italian dance'), was brought into fashion at Rome during the reign of Augustus by Pylades of Cilicia and Bathyllus of Alexandria. As a form of art it took itself seriously; though passionate and often demoralizing, it was not coarse or farcical like the mime, its chief competitor for the favour of the theatre-going public throughout the period of the Roman Empire (see MIME, 2). The central figure was the masked dancer, usually a solo performer, who with steps, postures, and gestures of every kind represented in turn each of the characters of the story; thus if the theme was the love of Mars and Venus, he would show first the Sun bringing the bad news to Venus's husband Vulcan, then Vulcan setting the net to entrap the guilty pair, then the other gods coming, one by one, to survey the confusion of the lovers, then the embarrassed Venus and the alarmed Mars. Lucian assures us that a performer of Nero's time was able, when put on his mettle, to represent all this by gesture alone, without the aid of chorus or musical accompaniment, to the satisfaction of his critic. The dancer might on occasion have an assistant; thus we hear of a *pantomimus* who so overacted the part of the mad Ajax that not only did he tear the costume of one of the *scabillarii* and seize the flute of one of the musicians, but he dealt with it so violent a blow to Odysseus, who was standing beside him in a triumphant attitude, that only his head-dress saved him from fatal injury; finally Ajax descended from the stage and took his seat between two alarmed spectators, while the crowd applauded what they considered a supreme display of acting. The better performers were more restrained; thus when his pupil, Hylas, could think of no better way of representing 'great Agamemnon' than by standing on his toes, Pylades showed him a subtler method by merely assuming an air of reflection. Language and facial expression were alike denied to the actor by his mask with its closed mouthpiece; his most important instrument was his 'speaking hands'. The art of gesture was carried to heights beyond our comprehension; Lucian tells us of a visitor to Rome from the Pontus who, though he knew no Greek and was thus unable to follow the words of the chorus, found the gestures of the *pantomimus* so lucid that he wanted to take him home as an interpreter. It is clear, however, that many of the gestures employed were conventionalized; thus there were certain steps prescribed by tradition for Thyestes when in the act of eating his children.

The performance usually took place in the theatre; the *pantomimus* wore the costume of a tragic actor, a cloak and a silken tunic reaching to the feet. A graceful, supple figure was essential. The mask was dignified in expression; in contrast with the mask of tragedy, the mouth was closed. The performer might wear a different mask for each role; thus we hear of five masks being used for one pantomime. The musical instruments employed by the orchestra included flutes, pipes, cymbals, and trumpets. During the performance the chorus sang the libretto, usually in Greek. The time was given by the *scabillarii*, who wore under their sandals the *scabillum*, a box of wood or metal capable of emitting a clear note under pressure.

The subjects of the pantomime, according to Lucian, might include anything from Chaos to Cleopatra, i.e. any theme taken from mythology or past history. Anything, it would seem, could be set to music and adapted for dancing; Nero wished to 'dance' the Turnus of Virgil, and we hear of poems and even speeches being so treated; in general, however, the pantomime took its themes from tragedy. The favourite subject was love. The songs of the chorus, like the accompanying music, were usually of but small artistic merit, though well-known poets sometimes enriched themselves by writing libretti for pantomimes. Everything turned on the skill of the dancer. A single unrhythmical movement on his part would ruin the performance. His beauty and skill, his intoxicating gestures, and the seductive nature of the theme, were calculated to have a potent, indeed a disastrous, effect, especially on female spectators. St. Augustine regarded the pantomime as more dangerous to morals than the circus, and Zosimus, writing in the fifth century, traces the moral decline of the Roman Empire to the introduction of the pantomime. So great was its popularity that fights between the supporters of rival *pantomimi* became a menace to the public peace. The performers found their way into private houses; Ummidia Quadratilla owned a troupe of them, whose performances were shunned by her puritanical grandson. Seneca speaks of privately owned and pampered female performers. *Pantomimi* were legally *infames*, members of a dishonourable profession; sometimes their performances were banned by the government, and any immoral behaviour on their part might be visited with the severest punishment. Still they continued to flourish, particularly under such emperors as Nero, themselves interested in the theatre. Nero's favourite *pantomimus* was Paris, who was eventually put to death owing to the emperor's professional jealousy. Large fortunes were made by successful *pantomimi*, and the Emperor Marcus Aurelius had to fix a maximum fee for their performances. So great was the place which the pantomime occupied on the stage of Imperial times that the old word for actor, *histrio*, came to have the meaning of 'performer of pantomime'. WILLIAM BEARE†

PAPP, JOSEPH (1921–), see SHAKESPEARE, 4.

PARADE, see BOBÈCHE and FAIRS.

PARAGUAY, see SOUTH AMERICA, 1.

PARALLEL, the American equivalent of the English rostrum, or stage platform.

PARFAICT, two brothers, (1) FRANÇOIS (1698–1753) and (2) CLAUDE (1701–77), who collaborated in a number of works on French theatre history. Their chief publications were an *Histoire générale du théâtre français depuis son origine* (1745–9), in 15 volumes; *Mémoires pour servir à l'histoire des spectacles de la foire* (1743), in 2 volumes; *Histoire de l'ancien théâtre italien depuis son origine jusqu'à sa suppression en 1697* (1753); and *Dictionnaire des théâtres de Paris* (1756–67), in 7 volumes. Although painstaking, they were not always accurate and their judgement was sometimes at fault, but their work is valuable and full of information which cannot be found elsewhere. François was also something of a dramatist, but nothing of his dramatic work has survived.

PARIGI. (1) GIULIO (1590–1636) and (2) ALFONSO (?–1656), father and son, and among the first scenic designers to work for opera. Their designs were comparatively simple, compared with later developments, and correspond to the classical simplicity of the early Florentine scores. Giulio was a pupil of Buontalenti and became architect to the Duke of Tuscany. His work (see No. 60) served as a link between Buontalenti and Torelli, and had a profound influence on such foreign visitors to Florence as Furtenbach and Inigo Jones. Attention has been drawn to the similarity between some of the designs for 'Les Plaisirs de l'Île enchantée', done by Vigarani for Versailles in 1664, and those done for an Italian ballet in 1625, which seems to show that Vigarani was not so much of an innovator as had been thought, but was drawing on the riches of an art already well advanced at the beginning of the seventeenth century (see *Revue d'Histoire du Théâtre*, 1951, iv, p. 394).

PARIS. There were two popular Roman actors (pantomime dancers) of this name, of whom one was executed under Nero (A.D. 67), owing, it is said, to Nero's jealousy of his art, the other under Domitian (A.D. 83). For the second Paris the Roman poet Statius wrote the libretto of a pantomime, *Agave*, now lost.

PARKER, HENRY TAYLOR (1867–1934), an American critic of music and the drama, first on the New York *Globe*, and later, for thirty years, on the Boston *Transcript*, where his articles on both branches of art were remarkable for their integrity and scholarship. His energy and enthusiasm were alike admirable, and he had the gift of conveying to his reader a vivid picture of what he had himself seen or heard. His assessment of acting was based on a wide knowledge of the history and traditions of the American stage, and of the careers of individual actors. An individualist among the critics of his day, he was respected by theatre people and the general public alike.

PARKER, JOHN (1875–1952), English dramatic critic and theatrical journalist, who put all writers on the contemporary English theatre in his debt by editing *Who's Who in the Theatre*. This valuable publication appeared first in 1912, in succession to the editor's previous *Green Room Book*, and has since run through numerous editions, each of which has been carefully revised and brought up to date. It now contains more than 3,000 biographical entries, much useful information on performances of notable plays, and genealogical tables of famous theatrical families prepared by the late Dr. J. E. M. Bulloch. After Parker's death his son edited the 12th edition. The 13th, edited by Freda Gaye, in which some earlier sections were omitted, replaced them by such new features as the playbills of Stratford-upon-Avon and Stratford, Ontario; a short history of the repertory theatre in Great Britain; and a list of centres for theatre research.

PARKER, LOUIS NAPOLEON (1852–1944), English dramatist, author of over 100 plays and adaptations. He was for some time a music-master at Sherborne. The success of his early plays enabled him to resign in 1892, and he went to London to devote the rest of his long life to the theatre. Among his plays, the most successful were *Rosemary* (1896), *Pomander Walk* (1910), and *Disraeli* (1911), which had a long run in America. Parker was in great demand for the civic pageants so much in vogue in Edwardian England, and produced among others the pageants at Sherborne (1905), Warwick (1906), Dover (1908), and York (1909). During the First World War he produced several patriotic pageants in London, and was the author of *The Pageant of Drury Lane* (1918). His work is uneven and diffuse, at its best admirable, at its worst hack-work. The partitioning of his undoubted talents among varied interests was amusingly underlined by the title of his reminiscences, *Several of My Lives* (1928).

PARKER, P. C., see AUSTIN, CHARLES.

PARK LANE THEATRE, NEW YORK, see DALY'S THEATRE, 3.

PARK THEATRE. 1. NEW YORK, the first outstanding theatre of the United States, known as the 'Old Drury' of America. Built by Hallam and Hodgkinson, it was originally called the New Theatre, and was opened on 29 Jan. 1798 with *As You Like It*. Hodgkinson played Jaques and Hallam Touchstone, while the cast contained many of the members of the former John Street Theatre company. The second production, on 31 Jan., was *The School for Scandal* with the Hallams as Sir Peter and Lady Teazle, and Jefferson in his later famous part of Moses. Prosperity first came to the theatre with the engagement of Thomas Abthorpe Cooper, then only 21, and on the threshold of a brilliant career. He made his first appearance on 28 Feb. as Hamlet, and was soon accounted one of the finest actors yet seen in New York. In spite of a good company, however, and of the popularity of plays by Kotzebue, and by Dunlap, one of the managers of the theatre, the fortunes of the venture were constantly jeopardized by quarrels between the managers, until finally Dunlap took over entirely, engaging his former associates as salaried actors. His repertory was mainly modern, consisting of contemporary successes from London, translations from the Continent, and his own plays, though a few classics were given, including *Twelfth Night*, first seen in New York on 11 June 1804 (for a painting by Dunlap of a production probably given at the Park, see No. 163).

In spite of enthusiasm and hard work, Dunlap went bankrupt in 1805, and a year later the theatre was bought by Beekman and Astor, who installed Cooper as sole manager, with Dunlap as his salaried assistant. Still the theatre did not prosper; Cooper was not a good business man, and a new era was inaugurated in the autumn of 1808, when Stephen Price bought a controlling interest in the management. Neither an actor, like Cooper, nor a dramatist, like Dunlap, he was able to devote himself to management. Under him the first indigenous American drama, *The Indian Princess; or, La Belle Sauvage*, was given on 14 June 1809, with a success which was later repeated at Drury Lane. Price also engaged the young American actor, John Howard Payne, whose first play had been given at the Park when he was 14, and added the parents of Edgar Allan Poe to his stock company.

It was Price who inaugurated the policy of importing foreign stars, a policy directly responsible for the decline of the old stock company. The first great English actor to appear at the Park was George Frederick Cooke, who, in Nov. 1810, began an engagement which lasted for two seasons. He was successful at first, but his popularity declined as his habitual vice of drunkenness overcame him, and as the stock company was still good, stars were not really necessary; nor was it possible to import them during the war with England, from 1812 to 1815. It was not until 1818 that the stock system was abandoned, and the company was retained purely to support visiting stars. One of the greatest of these was Kean, who was booked to appear at the Park when, on 24 May 1820, it was totally destroyed by fire. The company moved to the old Anthony Street Theatre, and there Kean made his first appearance in New York. The Park was rebuilt, and opened on 1 Sept. 1821 for the era of its greatest prosperity and influence. Practically every actor of importance at the time, whether English, American, or Continental, appeared at the Park—the Keans, the Mathews, Charles and Fanny Kemble, the Wallacks, Hackett, the Keeleys, Buckstone, Forrest, Vandenhoff, and Cushman, to name only a few. This period saw also the emergence of the American playwright, and the theatre was no longer dependent on importations. In 1824 the success of the newly opened Chatham Theatre led to the introduction of vast spectacular shows like *The Cataract of the Ganges*, but the constant succession of guest artists helped the retention of Shakespearian and other classic plays in the repertory. In the autumn of 1827 the Park was first lit by gas, and two years later, during a bad financial panic, it was closed for a time, and given over to masquerades and lectures. It was redecorated in 1834, and again in 1837, when it was forced to contend with the rivalry of Wallack's National Theatre. This year saw the appearance of Jean Davenport, aged 11, believed to be the original of Dickens's Infant Phenomenon, in a range of parts which included Sir Peter Teazle, Young Norval, Richard III, Shylock, and Little Pickle. The theatre was now losing its monopoly of New York acting, and was becoming out of date, clinging to the old system of frequent changes of bill, with all its attendant evils of under-rehearsal and over-fatigue. On 20 Jan. 1840 Stephen Price, who had managed it for over thirty years with the assistance of Simpson, died suddenly, and the Park entered on a bad period. In June 1841 everything was put up for sale to pay the rent. The theatre was intermittently used as a circus and, in spite of a few flickers of its former brilliance, such as the three-weeks' run of Boucicault's first play, *London Assurance*, in Oct. 1841, and another visit by Macready in 1843, it became more and more of a liability. After the death of Simpson in 1848 the theatre was taken over by Hamblin, who ran it in conjunction with his own theatre, the Bowery; but, in spite of extensive rebuilding, he could not restore its lost glory, and on 16 Dec. 1848 it was burnt down, thus breaking the last link with the Hallams and the John Street Theatre and the coming of professional drama to the New World.

2. A second Park Theatre, on Broadway and 22nd Street, opened on 13 Apr. 1874, with Fechter in the last new part he was to create, in his own adaptation of a French play. This theatre had been intended for Boucicault, but after continuous litigation its real history began on 16 Sept. 1874, when John T. Raymond appeared there in his famous part of Colonel Sellers. Later successes were *The Mighty Dollar* with the Florences in 1875, and G. F. Rowe in his own play, *Brass*, in 1876. Henry E. Abbey, later manager of the Metropolitan Opera House, took over the new Park late in 1876, and started it on a prosperous career which lasted until, on 30 Oct. 1882, the day on which Lily Langtry was to have made her New York début there, the theatre was totally destroyed by fire and never rebuilt.

3. The first professional theatre established in Brooklyn, after nearly forty years of unsuccessful tentatives, was the Park, which opened on 14 Sept. 1863, and soon passed into

the hands of the Conways. They remained there until 1871, and established the theatre firmly in the affections of its audience, playing together with a good company, and frequently importing stars for short seasons. After their departure it languished for a while, but housed the Florences, Minnie Maddern in *Oliver Twist*, and, in the season of 1873–4, an amazing array of stars—Lester Wallack, Adelaide Neilson, Chanfrau, Owens, Sothern, and others. The theatre tended more and more to be merely a halting-place for travelling companies. In 1876 it fell a victim to the craze for variety and burlesque, but after the burning of the Brooklyn Theatre it regained its monopoly of acting and turned again to legitimate drama. It was the last theatre in New York to have a stock company supporting visiting stars (for a later Park Theatre in New York, see MAJESTIC THEATRE).

4. Scotland's first Little Theatre, founded in Glasgow in 1941 by John Stewart, and conducted on club lines, was named the Park. One production was given each month, and the usual run was for a fortnight. It closed in 1949. John Stewart then founded the Pitlochry Festival.

For the Park Theatre, Camden Town, London, see ALEXANDRA THEATRE, 2.

PASHENNAYA, VERA NIKOLAYEVNA (1887–1962), Soviet actress, who joined the Maly Theatre company in 1905 and remained there until 1922. She later went to the Moscow Art Theatre, and in 1941 was appointed to the Chair of Acting in the Shchepkin Theatre School, having been active in teaching since 1914. Her talent, which showed itself early, covered a wide range of parts, including Schiller's Maria Stuart, Emilia in *Othello*, and Tanya in Tolstoy's *Fruits of Enlightenment*. Her conception of Vassya Zheleznova in Gorky's play of that name was characterized by great depths of psychological insight. All her roles gave proof of dramatic force and inner concentration; her heroines were given powerful complex characters, energy, and a vivid and original inner life. In addition to acting and teaching she wrote many articles on the theatre and two well-known works on acting, *My work with my roles* (1934) and *An Actress in a Socialist Country* (1937). In 1955 she celebrated her jubilee as an actress. A year later she gave a memorable performance of Praskovya Sharabai in Sofronov's *Money*, produced by Babochkin at the Moscow Maly, and in 1962 was equally successful in the same author's *Honesty*. BEATRICE KING†

PASO, a term applied in Spain in the sixteenth century to a short comic interlude. The most famous writer of *pasos* was Lope de Rueda. The *paso* later developed into the *entremés* and the term is not found in this connexion after the end of the sixteenth century. J. E. VAREY

PASQUINO, one of the minor *zanni* or servant roles of the *commedia dell'arte*. The name is said to have been that of a cobbler in Rome, noted for his caustic wit. It was given to a mutilated statue dug up in 1501 near the palace of Cardinal Caraffa, when a tradition grew up of hanging satirical verses on it on St. Mark's Day, replies being attached to another statue known as Marforio. The name was adopted by the *commedia dell'arte* towards the end of the sixteenth century, and from there passed into French comedy as Pasquin, possibly through the actor Baron. It is found as the name of the valet in the plays of Destouches. In the French seventeenth-century theatre the expression 'the Pasquin of the company' designated the actor who played the satiric roles in Regnard and Dufresny. In the eighteenth century the word 'pasquin' or 'pasquinade' was applied in England to a lampoon, squib, or satiric piece, often political. Fielding used it as the title of his production at the Haymarket in 1736, and often signed himself Mr. Pasquin in his newspaper articles and letters. Political writers of the time frequently took the pseudonyms of Pasquino and Marforio.

PASS DOOR, a fireproof door placed in an inconspicuous part of the proscenium wall, leading from the auditorium to the side of the stage and so backstage. It is usually used only by those connected with the theatre, ordinary members of the audience penetrating behind the scenes by means of the Stage Door which opens on to the street.

PASSION PLAY. The secular development of the Passion Play was widespread throughout Western Europe, and led to a tradition of open-air pageant productions of the Good Friday story in many small towns and villages. Most of these died out during the fifteenth century, but helped by the Catholic counter-reformation in the following century a few were revived in Switzerland, Austria, and Germany. They continue spasmodically in a few remote villages in Germany, but the only one to become famous is that given decennially (from 1634) at Oberammergau, in Bavaria. A fusion of two Augsburg cycles, this was first performed during a visitation of plague, and remains entirely amateur, the villagers dividing the parts among themselves, and being responsible also for the production, scenery, and music.

PASTOR, TONY [ANTONIO] (1837–1908), American music-hall or 'vaudeville' manager. The son of a New York theatre violinist, he was born in Greenwich Village, and at the age of 9 was a popular singer at temperance meetings. He made his professional début at Barnum's in 1846 as an infant prodigy, and later travelled as a circus clown, gaining managerial experience by organizing concerts in the towns he visited. The author or part-author of some 2,000 songs, he was also active as a minstrel and ballad-singer. In Apr. 1861 he made his first appearance in variety at the famous American Theatre at 444 Broadway. At that time variety had sunk to a low level of obscenity and vulgarity. Pastor decided to make it respectable, and opened his first Opera House at 199–201 Broadway as 'The Great Family Resort' in June 1865 with a clean bill. The venture was a success, and in 1875 he moved to 585 Broadway, eventually settling in 1881 on 14th Street, where he remained until his death. It was here, on 24 Oct. 1881, that he presented the first performance of what came to be called vaudeville—a word Pastor himself always avoided, considering it 'sissy and Frenchy'. He left his Bowery and Broadway audience of labourers and artisans behind, and made a successful bid for the attention of high society, thus raising the variety show from the gutter and making it first respectable and then elegant. He is rightly considered the father of American vaudeville. Nat Goodwin, Lillian Russell, and Weber and Fields were among his protégés.

ROBERT TRACY

PASTORAL, a dramatic form which evolved in Italy from pastoral poetry, by way of the dramatic eclogue or rustic (shepherd) play. There had previously been some pastoral elements in drama, notably in Agostino Beccari's *Sacrificio* (1554), which was labelled a *favola pastorale*, but the first outstanding pastoral play was Tasso's *Aminta* (1573), a tale of rustic love written in fine poetry with superb choruses. It was followed by Guarini's *Il Pastor Fido*, published about 1590, but probably not performed before 1596–8. Both were translated and performed in France and England, and had a widespread influence, *Il Pastor Fido* being given several times after the Restoration, once in a version by Settle, and continuing to be revived up to 1809. The latest of many versions of *Aminta* was that prepared by Leigh Hunt in 1820.

These two plays mark the highest achievements of the genre, but the pastoral continued in favour in Italy for some time (see ITALY, 1 *b* ii). The first English play to be called a pastoral was Peele's *Arraignment of Paris* (1581), but Peele does not appear to have been influenced by either of the above as were, later, Lyly and Samuel Daniel. In 1608–9 Fletcher tried to give the English stage a native pastoral with *The Faithful Shepherdess*. It was a failure at first, but proved a success in revival, being full of poetry and invention. Pepys saw it in 1663, and called it 'a most simple thing, and yet much thronged after and often shown, but it is only for the scenes' sake, which is very fine indeed and worth seeing'. Jonson's *Sad Shepherd* was never finished, and it cannot be said that the pastoral ever became acclimatized in England, though it had some influence on the masque and so on Shakespeare. Dr. Greg, in *Pastoral Poetry and Pastoral Drama* (1906), claims that *Comus*, though called a masque, is essentially a pastoral, directly dependent upon previous pastoral works.

The pastoral bears no relation to real rustic life; it is entirely artificial, and must be judged accordingly. It cannot flourish at the same time as romantic drama, which may account for its slight success in England. It was more at home in France, where it inspired a number of authors, notably Hardy, who wrote one pastoral; Racan, whose *Bergeries* (1623), though placed in France, shows definite traces of Italian influence; and Théophile de Viau, whose *Pyrame* (1621) was publicly burnt, but for its author's faults, not its own. The pastoral disappeared from French dramatic literature in the mid-1630s, but not before it had served as a vehicle for the introduction of the unities in Mairet's *Silvanire* (1630).

PATENT THEATRES, the name given to the two chief theatres of London, Drury Lane and Covent Garden, which operate under Letters Patent, or Charters, given by Charles II in 1662 to Thomas Killigrew (for Drury Lane) and Sir William Davenant (for Lincoln's Inn Fields, whence it descended in 1732 via Dorset Garden to Covent Garden) for the establishment of two companies to be known as 'The King's Servants' and 'The Duke of York's Servants' respectively. The company at Drury Lane was technically part of the Royal Household, and some members of it were sworn in as Grooms of the Chamber, as Shakespeare and his fellows had been before them. They were given an allowance of scarlet cloth and gold lace for their liveries—which are still worn by the powdered footmen at both theatres. The charters, which in the course of the next two hundred years changed hands many times, fluctuating sharply in value, are still in existence, and form an integral part of the leases of the theatres. They render the two patent theatres independent of the Lord Chamberlain as licenser of theatre buildings, though not as licenser of plays. The monopoly established by Charles II, and reinforced by the Theatres Act of 1737, which forbade the acting of 'legitimate' drama elsewhere, was finally broken in 1843. The Haymarket has the courtesy title of Theatre Royal by virtue of a patent obtained by Samuel Foote for the summer months only. During the nineteenth century a proliferation of Theatres Royal all over the country caused the term to become nothing more than a generic title for a playhouse, since these theatres were licensed by the local magistrates and not directly by the Crown (see CENSORSHIP, COVENT GARDEN, DRURY LANE, FOOTE, SAMUEL, and HAYMARKET).

PAVILION, LONDON, in Whitechapel. This was opened by Wyatt and Farrel in 1829. Fanny Clifton (Mrs. Stirling) went there from the City Theatre and made her first success. The theatre was burned down in 1856 and rebuilt. Under the management of Morris Abrahams it was a very efficient house, catering largely for the big Jewish population of the neighbourhood. Isaac Cohen also gave good plays and pantomimes there, and many famous Jewish actors appeared at it. It was for a time a cinema, and then returned to Jewish drama. It was demolished early in the 1960s.

W. MACQUEEN-POPE†

PAVILION MUSIC-HALL, see LONDON PAVILION.

PAVILION THEATRE, LONDON, see WEST LONDON THEATRE; NEW YORK, see ANTHONY STREET THEATRE and CHATHAM THEATRE, I.

PAVY, SALATHIEL (or SALMON) (1590–1603), one of the Children of the Chapel, taken from his apprenticeship at ten years old to become an active member of the boys' company at the Blackfriars. He is best remembered for Ben Jonson's epitaph on his early death at the age of 13. He was apparently noted for his excellence in playing the parts of elderly men.

PAXINOU, KATINA [really CONSTANTOPOULOS] (1900–), outstanding Greek actress, wife of Alexis Minotis, under whose direction she has been seen in many of the great classical tragedies, particularly in the festivals at Epidaurus. Trained as a singer, she first appeared in opera in Athens, but in 1920 became an actress. In 1932 she joined the Greek National Theatre company, of which her husband is also a member, and appeared with it in London in 1939, where she played Gertrude in *Hamlet*, and Electra. In 1960 she also went with the company to New York, where she is well known. For the National Theatre she translated and produced many English and American plays, among them some of O'Neill's, and for many years she revived and played in *Ghosts*, Mrs. Alving being one of her finest parts. She has also played it in English, in London in 1940 and in New York in 1942, where she also appeared as Hedda Gabler.

PAYNE, BEN IDEN (1881–), English actor and director, best remembered for his work in connexion with Shakespeare. He made his first appearance on the stage with Benson's company in 1899, at Worcester, and appeared in London the following year in *Henry V*. He helped Miss Horniman to establish her repertory theatre in Manchester, appearing in many of the plays himself, and acting as her general manager from 1907 to 1911, when he left to organize similar ventures in other provincial towns. In 1913 he went to the United States, became art director of the Philadelphia Little Theatre and of the Chicago Little Theatre, and worked for some years for Charles Frohman. From 1919 to 1934 he was visiting Professor of Drama at the Carnegie Institute of Technology, and then returned to England to become director of the Shakespeare Memorial Theatre in succession to Bridges-Adams. He did eight years of good unostentatious work, labouring under a system which demanded that eight plays should be seen at the beginning of the season, and so putting a great strain on actors and directors alike, a system happily now modified. He nursed the theatre through the difficult first years of the Second World War, and in 1943 left to lecture in America for the Ministry of Information. He remained there to become visiting professor at several universities, finally settling at the University of Texas in 1946. He has been married twice, his first wife being the actress Mona Limerick [Mary Charlotte Louise Gadney]. Their daughter, Rosalind Iden, is also an actress, and the widow of Sir Donald Wolfit.

PAYNE, JOHN HOWARD (1791–1852), an American actor and dramatist, best known as the author of the lyric of 'Home, Sweet Home'. The music was by Henry Bishop, and the ballad was first sung in his opera 'Clari, the Maid of Milan' (for which Payne wrote the libretto) at Covent Garden, 8 May 1823. Detached from its context, it became a popular concert piece, and figured in the repertory of almost every outstanding singer. Payne was a precocious boy, whose first play was produced in New York when he was only 14. Three years later, in spite of parental opposition, he went on the stage, and made a great reputation in such parts as Young Norval, Romeo, Tancred, and Hamlet. After a successful début in New York, he toured the larger American cities, and in 1811 appeared at the Chestnut Street Theatre, Philadelphia (see No. 28), as Frederick in his own version of Kotzebue's *Das Kind der Liebe*. As *Lovers' Vows*, this had already been translated by Mrs. Inchbald, Benjamin Thompson, Anne Plumptre, and William Dunlap. Payne's version, based on the first two of these, is interesting, in the opinion of A. H. Quinn, as 'showing his methods of work, and also his sense of the theatrically effective'. Frederick always remained one of his favourite parts, in which he was much admired.

In spite of his early successes, or perhaps because of them, Payne later found it difficult to establish himself in New York. So in 1813 he sailed for England, and appeared at Drury Lane, and in the provinces, with great success. A visit to Paris brought him the friendship of Talma and the freedom of the Comédie-Française, and for many years Payne was engaged in the translation and adaptation of current French successes for the English stage. These were also performed in the United States, but in spite of continued success in both countries Payne received very little money for his work.

Among his many plays—he has been credited with some fifty or sixty—the best were probably *Brutus; or, the Fall of Tarquin*, a tragedy played by Edmund Kean in London in 1818 and in Paris in 1827, and *Charles II; or, the Merry Monarch* (1824), based on a play by Alexandre Duval and written in collaboration with Washington Irving, a lifelong friend. Payne was also responsible for *Therese; or, the Orphan of Geneva* (1821), for one of the many versions of *The Maid and the Magpie* (1815), and for translations of several of Pixerécourt's melodramas. He had little originality, but a good sense of the theatre and a deft touch in handling his material. His work undoubtedly had some influence on the course of American drama, in spite of his continued residence abroad. At one time he tried, unsuccessfully, to manage

Sadler's Wells Theatre, but only landed himself in prison for debt, and he was for a couple of years editor of a theatrical paper, *The Opera-Glass*. In 1842 he was appointed American Consul at Tunis, where he remained until his death.

PECKHAM. There was a theatre in Peckham High Street, and a local legend held that Nell Gwynn played there, though no proof of this can be found. The theatre was occasionally used for dramatic purposes up to 1822, the last time by Penley, a Drury Lane actor. It was finally converted into a school.

PEDROLINO, see PIERROT.

PEELE, GEORGE (*c.* 1558–*c.* 1597), English dramatist, of good family and well educated, but a shiftless, dissolute fellow, companion of Greene, Nashe, and Marlowe, who lived by his wits and by such small sums as he could earn at play-writing and play-acting. He wrote a good deal of miscellaneous verse, some pageants, and a number of plays, of which the best are *The Arraignment of Paris*, given at Court, probably in 1581, *David and Bethsabe* (*c.* 1587), *Edward I* (1591), which survives only in a mutilated form, and his best-known and most popular work, *The Old Wives' Tale*, written probably in 1590. This 'pleasant conceited comedie', as it is called on the title-page of the first edition (1595), is a mixture of high romance and English folk-tale, which was long dismissed by critics as negligible and pretentious nonsense. Bullen was the first to appreciate its qualities, in his edition of 1888, and it is now considered something of a landmark in the development of English comedy, bringing a new and more subtle strain of humour into the farce of earlier days. Peele had a fine command of language and was the author of some charming lyrics.

PEEP-SHOW. The art of theatrical production leaves no legacy to the future, and it is often extremely difficult for us to reconstruct the physical appearance of the stage of even the last few centuries. The actual stage scenery has almost always been destroyed, and ordinary pictorial views and designs tend to give a hopelessly romanticized impression of the intended effect. But, when the ordinary channels of information are unsatisfactory, it is sometimes found that surprisingly accurate representations of stage effects have been preserved in such unconsidered trifles as children's toys and rich men's playthings. Such was the nineteenth-century English Toy Theatre, and such was the Peep-show.

The essence of a peep-show is that it is a device in which one can view a perspective; it usually takes the form of a box, with a small eyepiece, inside which are arranged the receding elements of a perspective view; the scenes were sometimes painted on glass and illuminated from behind, in the manner of transparencies, but more usually consisted of a number of cut-out sheets of wood or cardboard. Some such device is said to have been constructed by Leon Battista Alberti in 1437; in the sixteenth and early seventeenth centuries we find some highly elaborate moving scenes incorporated in the horological automata of the period; these appear to be closely based on the pageants of the Renaissance stage, representing the stately processions of gods and goddesses in classical and mythological settings. Some examples of these stage models have been preserved in the Kunsthistorisches Museum at Vienna, and they provide an interesting record of the Court entertainments of the Renaissance period.

In the latter part of the seventeenth century dramatic spectacle was confined more and more behind the stage proscenium, and the peep-shows reflect this tendency by concentrating upon producing an effect of vast distances within the narrow framework of their wooden box; at the same time what had originated as a scientific toy for the educated rich became popularized as a public entertainment, a fairground side-show, and a children's plaything. While the eighteenth-century peep-shows throw a valuable light on the state of perspective scene-painting, their subjects tend to diverge from the theatrical tradition and to be concerned rather with the representation of famous views and historical events. An important innovation was the placing of a lens in the eyepiece. Throughout the eighteenth century a large variety of stage models, moving pictures, musical clocks, and other types of scenic automata—many of them constructed in Germany and Holland—were exhibited throughout England by Penkethman and other lesser showmen; unfortunately, none of these seems to have been preserved. Within living memory small peep-shows were still being exhibited in the streets; these usually consisted of a number of single pictures, depicting legendary or contemporary sensational events, that were lowered, one after the other, before the view of the spectator, while the showman kept up a running commentary upon them.

Although the public peep-shows have vanished, some of the children's peep-shows have been preserved; the most exquisite of these were those made at Augsburg by the brothers Engelbrecht at the beginning of the eighteenth century; they provide some charming examples of the contemporary art of perspective-drawing in the representation of baroque halls, formal gardens, and the country scene.

The juvenile peep-show is dealt with in Grober's *Children's Toys in Bygone Days*, and there is a detailed description of the Renaissance models by Dr. Wolfgang Born in *The Connoisseur* for February and April 1941.

GEORGE SPEAIGHT

PÉLISSIER, HARRY GABRIEL (1874–1913), English composer and entertainer, of French origin, and the first husband of Fay Compton. He was the originator of the famous Pélissier Follies, who began their career on the sands and promenades of English seaside resorts and then appeared at the Apollo Theatre, London, where they delighted packed audiences for many seasons. They wore ordinary pierrot costume, alternately black with white pompons and white with black pompons, against a drape of black and white curtains, and were compèred by Pélissier, who wrote a good deal of their material himself. Their show was one of the best things of its kind, with good music, topicality, wit, and observation, and it was never equalled, in spite of several efforts to employ the same formula.

W. MACQUEEN-POPE†

PELLESINI. (1) GIOVANNI (*c.* 1526–1612), an actor of the *commedia dell'arte*. By 1576 he evidently had a company of his own, but shortly afterwards he joined the Confidenti, and became their director, and the husband of their star actress, (2) VITTORIA PIISSIMI (*fl.* 1575–94), whom he may have married about 1582. He played as Pedrolino, a *zanni* role which is considered to be the origin of Pierrot.

PEMBERTON, THOMAS EDGAR (1849–1905), English dramatist and stage historian, most of whose work was done in connexion with the theatre in Birmingham, where he was head of an old-established firm of brass-founders. From 1882 to 1900 he was dramatic critic of the *Birmingham Daily Post*, and was on intimate terms with many of the leading actors of the day. His memoirs of Sothern, the Kendals, Robertson, Hare, Ellen Terry, and Wyndham were written from personal knowledge, and are therefore interesting, but have no literary distinction. Pemberton lectured frequently on the theatre, and was a governor of the Memorial Theatre, Stratford-upon-Avon. His plays, which have not survived on the stage, were done mainly in the provinces. He was also the author of a book on Dickens and the stage, and of a history of the Birmingham theatres.

PEMBROKE THEATRE, a theatre-in-the-round, seating 440, which flourished in the London suburb of Croydon from 1959 to 1962. Though not particularly commodious or accessible, it drew audiences from London and the surrounding countryside (though not from Croydon itself, according to its founder, Clement Scott-Gilbert), who were attracted by its experimental nature—it was the only professional arena theatre near London—and by the excellence of some of its productions, several of which, including a remarkable *Inherit the Wind*, were transferred to the West End. Other interesting productions were *Crime on Goat Island*, and two plays by Inge, *The Dark at the Top of the Stairs* and *A Loss of Roses*. The Pembroke opened at a time when Croydon had lost its last two live theatres—the Davis and the Grand—and during its short life did excellent work. In 1962 its premises were scheduled for demolition under a road-widening scheme, and the company, still under Scott-Gilbert, an American who had come to England to promote the cause of theatre-in-the-round, migrated to a new civic theatre named in honour of Dame Peggy Ashcroft, who was born in the borough.

PEMBROKE'S MEN, an Elizabethan theatrical company with which Shakespeare is assumed to have been connected in about 1592–3. It was under the patronage of the Earl of Pembroke, and was first mentioned in late 1592. Among the play-books which its actors parted with to the booksellers a year later were Marlowe's *Edward II*, *The Taming of a Shrew*, and *The True Tragedy of Richard Duke of York*. Shakespeare's *Taming of the Shrew* and *Richard III* may have been revisions for Pembroke's Men of the two last titles. The company's name is also on the title-page of *Titus Andronicus*, which Shakespeare had refashioned from *Titus and Vespasian* for Sussex's Men. The revised draft of parts 2 and 3 of *Henry VI* was also in their repertory, the first part (a rewriting of *The Contention of York and Lancaster*) belonging still to Strange's Men. Chambers thinks it possible that Shakespeare also wrote at this time, and for this company, a first draft of Henry VIII, now lost; but his connexion with the company ceased in 1594, when he joined the newly formed Chamberlain's Men. The company itself underwent an eclipse until 1597, when a group of players, calling themselves Pembroke's Men, but seemingly made up of Admiral's and Chamberlain's Men, leased the Swan from Langley. Here they got into trouble with the authorities for their production of Nashe's and Jonson's *Isle of Dogs*. The theatre was closed, and some of the actors, including Jonson, were put in prison. This disaster broke up the group, and most of its members returned to play with the Admiral's Men under Henslowe at the Rose. A few remained faithful to the Swan, and formed the nucleus of a new company of Pembroke's Men which appeared in provincial records under that name during the next few years, and at the Rose for a day or so in 1600. Their visit was apparently unsuccessful, and no further record of them is found. It is surmised that they joined Worcester's Men, a company formed shortly afterwards.

PENÇO DE LA VEGA, JOSEPH (1650–1703), author of the first printed Hebrew drama (see JEWISH DRAMA, 3).

PENKETHMAN, WILLIAM (?–1725), English comedian, whose name is also spelt Pinkethman. He had a booth at Bartholomew and other fairs, where he was very popular, being nicknamed Pinkey, or, more disdainfully, the 'Idol of the Rabble'. He also managed a theatre at Richmond and at one time travelled the country with peep-shows and scenic automata introduced from the Continent. His early years are obscure, but he is believed to have played small comic parts under Betterton as early as 1682. Montague Summers, however, thinks that his first part was Stitchum, a tailor, in *The Volunteers*, in 1692. He was a member of the Drury Lane company under Cibber, who wrote for him Don Lewis, in *Love Makes a Man*, and Trappanti in *She Would and She Would Not*. Doran says he was remarkable as a speaking Harlequin in such plays as *The Emperor of the Moon*, playing in a mask, and losing all his wit and piquancy when he discarded it. He took unpardonable liberties with author and audience, gagging and fooling with his part until even his admirers complained. He continued to act until a year before his death.

PENLEY, WILLIAM SYDNEY (1852–1912), English actor-manager who came of a theatrical family, and as a child was at the Chapel Royal and a chorister at Westminster Abbey. He made his first appearance on the stage at the old Court Theatre under Marie Litton on 26 Dec. 1871, in farce, and then toured in light and comic opera. He was for some years at the Strand, playing burlesque under Mrs. Swanborough; he appeared in Gilbert and Sullivan, and was with the Hanlon-Lees, going with them to America. The first outstanding success of his career came when he succeeded Tree in the title-role of *The Private Secretary* (1884), with which he has become so identified that he is often believed to have been the first to play the part. He appeared in it for two years, and in frequent revivals. He is also closely identified with the farce *Charley's Aunt* (1892), in which he played Lord Fancourt Babberley during its run of 1,466 performances, a record for the period. In 1900 he opened the Novelty Theatre as the Great Queen Street Theatre, appeared in revivals of his most successful parts, and retired in 1901. Much of his success as a comedian lay in his dry humour, his serious, rather pathetic, face, and the solemnity of his voice and manner contrasting with the farcical lines of his part.

PENN, WILLIAM (*c.* 1598–?), a boy-actor in 1609, when he appeared in *Epicoene*, and from 1616 to 1625 an adult member of the Prince's Men, whom he left to join the King's Men. He seems to have played small parts, usually of heavy fathers or dignified old men, and by 1629 he was a shareholder in the company. He was still with them in 1636, after which there is no further trace of him.

PENNA, LUÍZ CARLOS MARTINS (1815–48), see SOUTH AMERICA, 2.

PENNYCUICKE, ANDREW (1620–?), who published several plays when the theatres were shut under Cromwell, claimed to have been an actor and to have played in them himself. Though there is no evidence of this beyond his bare word, it is probable that he was one of Beeston's Boys at the Cockpit, and he may have been one of the actors who were found playing surreptitiously there and in the Red Bull.

PENNY GAFF, see GAFF.

PENNY PLAIN, TWOPENCE COLOURED. For the origin of this phrase, see TOY THEATRE.

PEOPLE'S NATIONAL THEATRE, see PRICE, NANCY.

PEOPLE'S THEATRE, NEWCASTLE, see AMATEUR THEATRE IN GREAT BRITAIN.

PEPPER'S GHOST, a device by which a ghost can be made to appear upon the stage, so called because it was perfected and patented, after several earlier attempts, by 'Professor' J. H. Pepper, a director of the Royal Polytechnic Institution in London, a place of popular scientific entertainment in the second half of the nineteenth century. It is based, roughly speaking, on the principle that a sheet of glass can be both reflective and transparent, so that a reflection of a figure can appear side by side with an actual performer on the stage. Something of the kind had been tried out previously, but it was Pepper who made it practicable in the ordinary theatre. The Ghost Illusion was first shown privately at the Polytechnic on 24 Dec. 1862, and then exhibited publicly with great success. Dickens used it in connexion with his readings of *The Haunted Man*. It was first used in the theatre—though it had appeared at many music-halls before that—on 6 Apr. 1863, at the Britannia, and several plays there were written specially to introduce it. But it was never widely adopted for the theatre, probably because it was difficult to place in position, and no speech was possible for the ghost. This would have made it impracticable for *The Corsican Brothers*, for instance, where the ghost speaks in the last act. The device did, however, enjoy a semi-dramatic life in the Ghost shows, based on popular melodramas, which toured the fairs until the early twentieth century.

PEPYS, SAMUEL (1633–1703), English diarist, and Secretary of the Navy Office, deserves mention here for the information given in his diary on the world of the theatre during the early years of the Restoration. Pepys, whose passion for the theatre was nearly as great as his love for music, kept a note of the plays he saw, recorded his impression of their actors, and related many stray items of backstage gossip imparted to him by one or other of his theatrical friends. To him we owe many illuminating glimpses of the green room, of the theatre under reconstruction, and of the rowdy talkative audiences of his day.

PERCY, ESMÉ SAVILLE (1887–1957), a distinguished English actor, particularly admired for his work in Shakespeare and Shaw. He escaped from his school in Brussels in order to study the art of acting under Bernhardt, whom he greatly admired, and on whom in his later years he gave several witty and affectionate talks, and made his first appearance on the stage at Nottingham in Benson's company in 1904. A year later he was seen in London as Romeo. After touring South Africa he rejoined Benson, and played a large number of leading Shakespearian parts on tour. In 1908 he appeared under Granville-Barker at the Court Theatre as Pentheus in the *Bacchae*, and then joined Miss Horniman's company in Manchester until 1911. After active service in the

First World War he remained with the army of occupation until 1923 in charge of entertainment, and produced over 140 plays for the troops. Back in London he joined Reandean as associate producer, and remained active in the London theatre until his sudden death, which occurred shortly before the first night of *The Making of Moo*, in which he was to have appeared. His greatest contribution to the theatre was probably his work for Shaw, who was a personal friend. He was a recognized authority on his plays, and the first to stage the Hell scene from *Man and Superman*. From 1924 to 1928 he was with Charles Macdona's Shaw company, and played a wide variety of leading parts—John Tanner, Androcles, Dubedat, Higgins, and King Magnus. In 1949 he was appointed president of the Shaw Society. He was an extremely versatile actor, and could play tragedy (Hamlet), comedy (Quince), pathos (Gaev), and bombast (Hotspur), with equal felicity. Among his later parts were Humpty Dumpty in 1947, and Matthew Skipps in *The Lady's Not For Burning* (1949), of which he was also co-producer. He had immense technical resources, a prodigious memory, an immensely flexible and sensitive voice, and an intelligence which illuminated all he did. He had a great affection for dogs, which even an accidental bite that cost him the sight of one eye could not impair, and after his death some of his friends placed a dogs' drinking fountain in Kensington Gardens as a tribute to his memory.

PERETZ, Isaac Leib (1852–1915), Jewish writer and lawyer. Born in Poland, he became secretary to the Warsaw Jewish community, and in 1876 published his first work, a volume of poems in Hebrew. Later, however, he turned to Yiddish as his medium. Similarly, in his philosophy—there is a definite struggle of ideas in Peretz—he changed from the rationalism of the Haskala (or Enlightenment) Movement to the symbolism and mysticism of Hassidism, which henceforth permeated his whole outlook. Some of his short stories dealing with life in Hassidic villages were dramatized and produced by Ohel on its first public appearance in Tel Aviv in 1926. His dramatic poem, *Night in the Old Market*, was dramatized by Granovsky and produced in 1925 at the Moscow State Jewish Theatre. E. HARRIS

PÉREZ GALDÓS, Benito (1843–1920), the greatest Spanish novelist of the nineteenth century. Galdós turned in the 1890s to the theatre which had fascinated him in his youth, staging adaptations of his novels and also original plays. Although the speech of the characters of his novels is vivid and revealing, his plays tend to be unconvincing and stilted, set as they are in the mould of the nineteenth century. He lacked a sure stage-sense and his plays remain essentially novels in dialogue. His themes are mainly taken from the psychological and social problems of modern life, and he shows the influence of both Ibsen and Zola. In *La loca de la casa* (1893), Galdós states the need for the reconciliation of those forces which in his early novels he had shown to be openly opposed to each other. Cruz and Victoria are mutually antagonistic, yet relentlessly drawn together, and their marriage symbolizes the union of the effete aristocracy and the revitalizing force of the lower classes, the union of materialism and compassion, and the union of reason and imagination. *Electra* (1901) was interpreted as being anti-clerical and therefore regarded as highly controversial, while *El abuelo* (1904), probably his best work for the stage, deals with the problem of heredity. J. E. VAREY

PERFECT CURE, The, see STEAD, J. H.

PERIAKTOI, see ACOUSTICS, 3, GREECE, 6, MACHINERY and ROME, 3.

PERKINS, Richard (?1585–1650), English actor, one of the Queen's Men, and probably the best known and most experienced of them. He is first heard of in 1602, when he appeared as one of Worcester's Men in a play by Heywood, with whom he remained friendly for many years. Heywood and Webster both praised his acting, and he seems to have had a large range of parts.

PERTH REPERTORY THEATRE, see SCOTLAND.

PERU, see SOUTH AMERICA, 1.

PERUZZI, Baldassare (1481–1537), Italian scenic designer, and the first to apply the science of perspective to theatrical scenery. His flat work was as convincing as built pieces. He was responsible for the scenery of Bibbiena's *Calandria* when it was given at Rome in 1507, the year after its first production (see SCENERY, 1).

PETIT-BOURBON, SALLE DU, the first Court theatre of France, in the long gallery of the palace of the Dukes of Bourbon. This had been falling into disrepair since the treachery of the Constable (who went over to the Spaniards in 1527) but was finally rescued and used for Court balls and ballets (see No. 18). It was a long, finely proportioned room, with a stage at one end, and the first recorded professional company to play on it was the *commedia dell'arte* troupe, the Gelosi, in May 1577, though they may have appeared there on an earlier visit. The stage was frequently used by visiting Italian companies after this, and in 1604 the famous Isabella Andreini played there for the last time, dying on the return journey to Italy. In 1645 Mazarin invited the great Italian scene-painter and machinist Torelli to supervise the production of the opera 'Orpheus and Euridice', given at the Petit-Bourbon two years later, and in 1658, when the theatre was again in the possession of a *commedia dell'arte* troupe under Tiberio Fiorillo, the famous Scaramouche, Molière's company, fresh from the provinces, was allowed to share it. For this privilege Molière paid a heavy rent, and was given the less profitable days for his appearances—Mondays, Wednesdays, Thursdays, and Saturdays—the Italians keeping the more lucrative Tuesdays and Sundays.

Molière opened on 2 Nov. 1658 with five plays of Corneille in succession, and not until the end of the month did he put on one of his own farces, *L'Étourdi*, followed by *Le Dépit amoureux*. The Petit-Bourbon saw also the first night of *Les Précieuses ridicules* and *Sganarelle, ou le cocu imaginaire* before it was suddenly scheduled for demolition by the Superintendent of the Royal Buildings in October 1660. Work was begun without reference to Molière—the Italians had departed before this—on some flimsy pretext, probably at the instigation of Molière's rivals and detractors, and the company, in full tide of success, found itself homeless. However, Louis XIV gave them Richelieu's disused theatre in the Palais-Royal, and the Petit-Bourbon disappeared. Molière took the boxes and fittings with him, but Vigarani, at that time Court architect and scene-painter, claimed Torelli's scenery and machinery for the Salle des Machines which he was building for the king in the Tuileries. When they had been handed over, he burnt them, hoping no doubt to destroy all traces of his admired predecessor, of whom he was extremely jealous.

PETRI, Olavus (1493–1552), Swedish humanist, usually credited with the authorship of the first Swedish play in the vernacular, *Tobiae Comedia*, published in 1550.

PHELPS, Samuel (1804–78), English actor and manager, and the first to run Sadler's Wells Theatre as the home of Shakespeare. He was originally a journalist, but after appearing with success in some amateur theatricals decided to make the stage his career. He toured the provinces for several years, particularly the northern cities on the York circuit, and made a great reputation as a tragedian, being engaged by Macready for Covent Garden. He first appeared in London, however, at the Haymarket under Webster in 1837, playing Shylock, Hamlet, Othello, and Richard III, repeating his Othello to Macready's Iago at Covent Garden. After the abolition of the patent monopoly in 1843 he took over Sadler's Wells Theatre, and did much to redeem the English stage from the triviality into which it had fallen, particularly in respect of poetic drama, by his fine and imaginative productions of Shakespeare. Among them the most important were *Macbeth* in 1844, and *Antony and Cleopatra* in 1849. His *Pericles, Prince of Tyre* in 1854 was the first performance of the play since Restoration times. By the time he retired in 1862 he had produced all Shakespeare's plays with the exception of *Henry VI*, *Titus Andronicus*, *Troilus and Cressida*, and *Richard II*, appearing in most of them himself. Though primarily a tragedian, he gave an excellent performance as Bottom, and was also much admired as Sir Pertinax McSycophant, giving a highly coloured but forcible rendering of the part. Lear and Othello were considered his best parts. His lovers were cold, and his delivery in love scenes tended to be harsh, though he revelled in the pathetic. After leaving Sadler's Wells he appeared in London and the provinces in Shakespeare and dramatizations of Sir Walter Scott's novels, in which he was much admired. He remained on the stage until almost the end of his life, his last appearance being as Cardinal Wolsey on 31 Mar. 1878 at the Aquarium Theatre under Miss Litton, at which time he was already in poor health. Phelps was a hard-working, conscientious actor, who made the theatre his life, and during his long period at Sadler's Wells needed all his fortitude and obstinacy to enable him to maintain a consistently high standard, often in the face of much opposition. His productions were remarkable for their scenic beauty, though he never succumbed to the prevailing desire for mere exhibition and pageantry. His work was continued by a number of young actors whom he had trained, and whose boast it later was that they had played Shakespeare at Sadler's Wells under Phelps.

PHERECRATES, an Athenian comic poet, slightly earlier than Aristophanes. He probably won his first victory in 437 B.C. In one of his plays, *The Savage*, referred to by Plato in the *Protagoras*, he poked fun at the idea of the Noble Savage, and suggested that even certain contemporary Athenians were preferable to him.

PHILADELPHIA, a town which from the beginning of American history has been closely connected with theatrical enterprise. A company under Kean and Murray acted *Cato* there in 1749, and it was the third town to be visited by the elder Hallam, in 1754. Douglass brought the American Company there in 1766, and built the first permanent theatre building in the United States (see SOUTHWARK THEATRE). This saw the production in 1766 of the first American play. Later theatres were the Chestnut Street (see No. 28), which opened in 1794, was burnt down in 1820 and again in 1856, and demolished in 1917, not having been used since 1905; the Walnut Street, which opened in 1811, and the Arch Street which, although it suffered severely, as did the other two theatres, from the theatre slump in 1829, had a brilliant season in 1831–2, mainly through the efforts of Edwin Forrest, whose brother was one of the managers. In contrast to its rivals it gave the preference to American actors in American plays, instead of relying on imported stars in their own repertory. The Arch Street Theatre became famous again under the management of Mrs. John Drew. It was not until the 1830s that Philadelphia lost its foremost position in the theatrical world, the lead passing to New York. This was mainly due to the intense rivalry between the theatres in the town, and the vicious system of importing foreign stars, which ruined all the managements. From then on Philadelphia supported stock companies, or visiting touring companies, and continued to enjoy good plays, but without regaining its former supremacy.

PHILEMON (*c.* 361–263 B.C.), an Athenian poet of the New Comedy, who was considered almost the equal of Menander. He was freely imitated by Roman comic poets. Plautus' *Mercator*, *Trinummus*, and *Mostellaria* are perhaps adaptations from Philemon.

PHILHARMONIC, LONDON, see GRAND THEATRE.

PHILIPE, GÉRARD (1922–59), French actor, whose early death deprived the European stage of one of its finest *jeunes premiers*. He studied at the Paris Conservatoire, and made his début in 1943 in Giraudoux's *Sodome et Gomorrhe*, which starred Edwige Feuillère. He first attracted attention in 1945, in the title-role of Camus's *Caligula*. In 1951, by which time he had made an outstanding reputation on both stage and screen, he joined Vilar's Théâtre National Populaire, and gave a superb performance as the hero of *Le Cid* (he was buried in the costume he wore for this part). He continued to act for the T.N.P. until his sudden death, and his fame and popularity did much to attract the young audience it sought and now commands. At the same time, continuity of work in this company, with its classical repertory and modern urgency of style, enabled Philipe to develop and enrich his talent as an actor, and also to try his hand at production. Among the plays in which he appeared for the T.N.P., in Paris, at the Avignon Festival, and in tours to Russia, the U.S.A., and Canada, were *Prinz Friedrich von Homburg* (1951), *Lorenzaccio* (1952), which he also produced, *Ruy Blas* and *Richard II* (both 1954). In 1958 and 1959 he appeared in *Les Caprices de Marianne* and *On ne badine pas avec l'amour*. He also played Eilif in the first French production of Brecht's *Mother Courage* (1951). He never acted in England, but was known there through his films. Off-stage he was unaffected, charming, a delightful conversationalist, happily married, and passionately interested in all aspects of the theatre. At the time of his death he was president of the French actors' union.

PHILIPPIN, see VILLIERS (1).

PHILIPS, AMBROSE (1674–1749), son of a draper in Shrewsbury, where he was educated, going on to Cambridge, a versifier and dramatist, a member of Addison's circle. His main claim to fame in the theatre is that he wrote one of the best pseudo-classical tragedies in English, *The Distrest Mother* (1712), an adaptation of Racine's *Andromaque* (1667). It is considered second only to Addison's *Cato* (1713). Fielding parodied it, not very successfully, in *The Covent Garden Tragedy* in 1732, thus proving its continued popularity. Philips also wrote two unremarkable plays, *The Briton* (1722) and *Humphrey, Duke of Gloucester* (1723). He was nicknamed Namby-Pamby (by Swift) for his poor verses, but fathered at least ten children.

PHILLIPS, AUGUSTINE (?–1605), one of the actors in Shakespeare's plays, who after playing with Strange's and the Admiral's Men, joined the Chamberlain's Men on its formation in 1594. In his will he left 30*s.* to Shakespeare, Condell, and Christopher Beeston respectively. He was one of the original shareholders in the Globe.

PHILLIPS, STEPHEN (1864–1915), English poet and dramatist, whose poetic drama *Paolo and Francesca*, when produced by Sir George Alexander at the St. James's Theatre in Mar. 1902, with the young Henry Ainley as Paolo and Evelyn Millard as Francesca, was such a success that it was thought to have inaugurated a new era of poetry in the English theatre. Phillips, who had been for a short time an actor in the company of his cousin, Frank Benson, had already achieved some success with *Herod* (1900) and *Ulysses* (Feb. 1902), both produced by Tree at Her Majesty's, but a later work, *Nero* (1906), also at Her Majesty's, failed to reach a like standard, and his early promise was not fulfilled.

PHILLPOTTS, EDEN (1862–1960), English dramatist and novelist, author of a number of light comedies of English rural life, of which the most successful was *The Farmer's Wife*. First seen at the Birmingham Repertory Theatre in 1916, it was revived in 1924 with Cedric Hardwicke as Churdles Ash. Transferred to the Court Theatre, London, it ran for over 1,300 performances and has several times been revived with success. Also produced at the Birmingham Repertory Theatre were *Devonshire Cream* (1924), *Jane's Legacy* (1925), and *Yellow Sands* (1926), in the last of which Phillpotts had the collaboration of his daughter Adelaide, also a novelist and dramatist in her own right. Kemp, in *The Birmingham Repertory Theatre*, contends that *Yellow Sands*, which was transferred to the Haymarket, London, successfully, is a better play than *The Farmer's Wife*. 'The plot is trim, tidy and probable; the characters are wholesome, and the wit springs easily from the situation.' He also adds: 'There has been no one quite so adept at staging a party as Phillpotts. Thirza Tapper's tea-party in *The Farmer's Wife* is, of course, the classic example of fun among the tea-cups; but *Jane's Legacy* has its own bright bout of celebration', while there is another grand 'do' in *Yellow Sands*, in which Jennifer Varwell assesses her relatives when the wine is in.

PHILOCLES. The writer of the Argument to the *Oedipus Tyrannus* of Sophocles says that the trilogy of which it formed part was placed second to a trilogy by Philocles 'whoever he was'. He was in fact a nephew of Aeschylus.

PHLYAX, the name given to a form of classical mime-play, which bridges the gap between the Athenian and Roman comedy. Much of it was probably improvised, and consisted of burlesques of earlier tragedies and comedies, with a liberal lacing of scenes of common daily life. Most of our knowledge of the *phlyakes* derives from vase paintings (see No. 12), which portray the characters and settings of the fourth century B.C. The form of stage depicted is important, for from it may have developed the salient forms of the Roman theatre, which differed so markedly from the Greek (see ARCHITECTURE, 2). The most primitive type consisted of roughly-hewn posts supporting a wooden platform. Later the posts appear to be joined by panels of wood with ornamental patterns, while later still the structure, though still not permanent, has a background for the actors which approximates to the Roman *scaenae frons*, with a practicable door and windows which were used in the course of the play.

PHOENIX SOCIETY, THE, was founded in 1919 under the auspices of the Stage Society for the adequate presentation of the plays of the older English dramatists. Little work of this kind had been seen in London since the productions of Philip Carr's Mermaid Theatre early in the twentieth century, and, Shakespeare alone excepted, the plays of the Elizabethan, Jacobean, and Restoration dramatists appeared to have fallen completely out of the theatrical repertory. The Stage Society began the work of revival in 1915, and continued annually to produce one Restoration comedy by Farquhar, Congreve, or Vanbrugh until 1919. The Phoenix was then constituted, and a committee of four appointed, to continue the work on a wider scale. In the six years of its existence, up to 1925, twenty-six plays were produced; the authors included Marlowe, Ben Jonson, Beaumont and Fletcher, Heywood, Ford, Dryden, Otway, Wycherley, and Congreve. From the beginning enthusiastic support was given by actors and actresses, many of them already of well-established reputation; two permanent adaptable sets were designed by the late Norman Wilkinson; and the productions were directed by Edith Craig (2) and Allan Wade (24). In 1923 a brilliant performance of Fletcher's *Faithful Shepherdess*, with special and elaborate scenes and dresses, was given in conjunction with Sir Thomas Beecham, who arranged and conducted the musical accompaniment.

There can be little doubt that the influence of these performances helped considerably to combat the indifference—in some cases the hostility—once shown to early English drama; several of the plays revived by the Phoenix have since been frequently and successfully acted on the public stage; and a large section of English drama, undeservedly neglected, has been enabled to prove in the theatre its continuing vitality.

PHOENIX THEATRE. 1. LONDON, on the Charing Cross Road and Phoenix Street, from which it takes its name. Built by Sydney L. Bernstein, it had Giles Gilbert Scott as one of its architects, and the décor was by Komisarjevsky. The theatre opened on 24 Sept. 1930 with the first night of Coward's *Private Lives*, in which the author himself appeared, with Gertrude Lawrence and Laurence Olivier, under the management of C. B. Cochran. Later successes by Coward were *To-night at 8.30* (1936), and *Quadrille* (1952) with the Lunts. In its early years the Phoenix had a chequered history, but it later housed a number of important plays, including Saint-Denis's productions of *The White Guard* and *Twelfth Night* (1938), Gielgud's revivals of *Love for Love* (1943) (see No. 102), *The Winter's Tale* (1951) and *Much Ado About Nothing* (1952), Rattigan's *Playbill* (1948) and *The Sleeping Prince* (1953), *The Skin of Our Teeth* (1945), Paul Scofield's *Hamlet* (1955), the long runs of *Roar Like a Dove* and *A Majority of One*, and, in 1961, Albert Finney in Osborne's *Luther*.

W. MACQUEEN-POPE†, *rev.*

2. NEW YORK. This theatre, formerly Maurice Schwartz's Yiddish Art Theatre on 2nd Avenue and 12th Street, was opened by T. Edward Hambleton and Norris Houghton on 1 Dec. 1953 as the Phoenix with Sidney Howard's *Madam, Will You Walk?* The managers envisaged a 'playhouse within the means of everyone where may be seen such new and old plays as are not likely to be produced elsewhere because of the pressures [of Broadway]. . . . We want this theatre to operate at the highest professional level of excellence, and to be as exhilarating for you who come to see us as for us who work in it.' Although they have done a few new plays, their repertory is mainly European. Noteworthy productions have been *Coriolanus*, *The Seagull*, *The Doctor's Dilemma*, *The Master Builder*, *Miss Julie*, and *A Month in the Country*. In 1961 the founders abandoned their huge old downtown playhouse and took over a smaller one, on East 74th Street, which almost immediately achieved critical success with Conway's *Who'll Save the Ploughboy?* and both critical and commercial success the following year with Kopit's *Oh Dad, Poor Dad, Momma's Hung You in the Closet and I'm Feeling So Sad*, which had previously had a short but unsuccessful run in London.

GEORGE FREEDLEY†

PHRYNICHUS. (1). A Greek tragic poet, slightly earlier than Aeschylus, who won victories in 512 and 476 B.C. He was fined for his *Capture of Miletus* (see GREECE, 5. Censorship), and wrote also another historical play, *Phoenician Women*, on the defeat of Xerxes. In his drama the chorus was more prominent and the actor less so than in Aeschylus. Aristophanes, more than half a century later, refers to Phrynichus's 'sweet lyrics' as being still very popular.

(2). An Athenian comic poet, contemporary with Aristophanes. He gained several victories, but little is known of his work.

H. D. F. KITTO

PIAF, EDITH [GIOVANNA EDITH GASSION] (1915–63), French singer and entertainer, daughter of the acrobat Jean Gassion. She had a hard and unhappy childhood, and at an early age supported herself by singing in the streets. However, once launched into cabaret and music-hall, she rapidly became a popular favourite, and something of a cult among a group of influential critics. Among the songs which she made famous were 'Mon légionnaire', 'La Vie en rose' of which she wrote both the words and the music, 'Le voyage du pauvre nègre', and 'Pour deux sous d'amour'. Her style was deceptively simple and nostalgic, but technically of great expertise and always highly personal. Although she was above all a singer, either alone or with a group—she made extensive tours of Europe and America with Les Compagnons de la Chanson, for instance—she appeared in a number of films, and was also seen in the theatre in *Le Bel Indifférent*, specially written for her by Cocteau, who died on the same day as she did, and *La P'tite Lili*. In 1958 she published a volume of autobiography, *Au Bal de la Chance*, of which an English translation appeared in 1965.

PICARD, Louis Baptiste (1769–1828), one of the few successful dramatists of France under Napoleon, a period singularly barren in good literature. Intended for the law, he was irresistibly drawn to the theatre, and became, like Molière, actor, author, and manager. He was always cheerful, and rode the storms of the Revolution, the Empire, and the Restoration with an unquenchable gaiety, flourishing under all of them. Napoleon found in him his ideal comic author, ready to amuse the public without touching on thorny questions of the day. Yet he had a caustic humour, which under more auspicious circumstances might have flowered into satire, and did not spare the newly rich and newly risen. He excelled in depicting bourgeois or provincial interiors, and was the originator of a mingling of light satiric prose comedy with music which proved immensely popular in its day. Indeed, one of his plays, *La Petite Ville* (1801), went to Vienna as *Die lustige Witwe* and so to England as *The Merry Widow*. He may be regarded as a transitional author, since his comedies bear out Beaumarchais's prophecy of a continued corruption of society, and yet are often moral and full of a naïve belief in the future. His published texts give careful directions for settings and costume, in which he aimed above all at pictorial effect, and he can be credited with the creation of one new character, the valet Deschamps. But most of his plays are forgotten, since he lacked a touch of genius to kindle his undoubted talents. He was the founder and for many years the manager of the Odéon, which ranks second in importance only to the Comédie-Française. He gave up acting in 1807 in order to qualify for admission to the French Academy and for the award of the Légion d'Honneur, which Napoleon himself did not dare give to an actor, not even to Talma. Among his plays *Médiocre et rampant* (1797), whose title comes from a speech by Figaro, is perhaps the best in its picture of contemporary society, while *Le Passé, le présent et l'avenir* (1791) pays tribute to the new ideas of his time. Far more amusing, however, is the lighthearted *Le Collatéral, ou la Diligence à Joigny* (1799) which with *La Vieille Tante* (1811) and *Les Deux Philibert* (1816) ranks among the best of Picard's work.

PICCADILLY THEATRE, London, in Denman Street. This opened on 27 Apr. 1928 with Evelyn Laye in a musical play, *Blue Eyes*, which transferred to Daly's to finish its long run. The Piccadilly was then used as a cinema for a time, but returned to live theatre and housed Bridie's *Sleeping Clergyman* (1933) with Robert Donat. The theatre then struck a bad patch, and was used for the transfer of long runs at reduced prices. After being closed for some time at the beginning of the Second World War, it reopened with Coward's *Blithe Spirit* (1941), and among later successes were Gielgud in *Macbeth* (1942), and the American musical *Panama Hattie* (1943). The building was then damaged by flying bombs, and reopened again in 1945. Productions since then include a musical version of *Jacobowsky and the Colonel* and of *Little Women* as *A Girl Called Jo* (both 1955), *Romanoff and Juliet* (1956), *The Rape of the Belt* (1957), *Toys in the Attic* (1960), and Edward Albee's *Who's Afraid of Virginia Woolf?* (1964).

W. MACQUEEN-POPE†, *rev.*

PICCOLO TEATRO DELLA CITTÀ DI MILANO, the first post-war permanent theatre to be set up in Italy. Founded in 1947 by the actor Paolo Grassi, with a municipal grant, it later received a State subsidy, and was the model for several other similar ventures in Rome, Turin, and elsewhere; but up till now it remains supreme in its field. It opened on 14 May with Gorky's *The Lower Depths*, produced by Giorgio Strehler, with Marcello Moretti, the famous Harlequin, in the cast. Since then it has built up a steadily increasing audience which includes many people who were not previously in the habit of going to the theatre, and it has toured extensively, visiting twenty-six countries and sixty-six Italian towns. Among its outstanding achievements has been its introduction of Brecht to Italian audiences. Apart from revivals of the classics—Shakespeare, Goldoni—it has presented a number of contemporary European and American plays, and also the work of new Italian playwrights.

PICCOLOMINI, Enea Silvio (1405–64), later Pope Pius II, was the author of a comedy, *Chrysis* (1444), written in Latin verse in imitation of Terence and Plautus. Unlike other comedies of the time, most of which were based on Italian student life and follies and owed little to classical models, *Chrysis* contains a number of characters who are recognizably Roman and derive from the *Asinaria* and the *Curculio* (see ITALY, 1 *b* iii).

PICKARD, Helena (1899–1959), English actress and theatre manager. She was the first wife of Cedric Hardwicke, by whom she had one son, Edward, also an actor. Fellow-students at the Royal Academy of Dramatic Art, and members of the Birmingham Repertory company in its early days, they were married during the London run of *The Farmer's Wife*, a play with which she was closely connected, playing Sophy Smerdon on its first production in Birmingham, Sibley Sweetland (in succession to Phyllis Shand) in London in 1924, and Thirza Tapper in the revival of 1947. Helena Pickard had a consistently successful, if not spectacular, stage career for over forty years, making her first appearance in Birmingham in 1915, and her last in a television play only a few days before her sudden death. In 1931 she took over for a year the management of the Grafton Theatre, with Beatrix Thomson, opening with *The Lilies of the Field*, in which she played Catherine. The theatre was then used for the trying out of new plays, but the venture was not a success and was abandoned. In 1936 she made her first appearance in New York in *The Country Wife*, and was subsequently seen there in *Time and the Conways* (1938) and *Flare Path* (1942). She toured Canada, lecturing and broadcasting, and returned to London to appear in a number of plays, including *Preserving Mr. Panmure* (1950) and *The Remarkable Mr. Pennypacker* (1955). Known as 'Pixie' to innumerable friends, she had a charming, witty, vivacious personality which captivated on stage and off.

PICKELHERRING, see REYNOLDS, ROBERT.

PIECE. This term originally covered any element of a scene, apart from the Drop and the Flat, including such things as Ground Rows and Set Pieces, and adjuncts like Cottage Pieces, Foot Pieces, and Set Waters.

PIERROT. The original of this famous character must be looked for in the *commedia dell'arte*, where he started life as Pedrolino, a *zanni* or servant role, of which Giovanni Pellesini was the earliest and best-known exponent. The character had in it something of Pulcinella (Punch), and one of its offshoots is the clown, hero of Leoncavallo's 'Pagliacci'. Although only one among many *zanni*, Pedrolino seems to have ranked high, judging by the place he occupies in the *scenarii* of Flaminio Scala, published in 1611. The credit for bringing this role into France, and transforming it into the earliest version of the French Pierrot, is usually given to an Italian actor named Giuseppe Giaratone, or Giratoni, who joined the Italian company in Paris about 1665. He accentuated Pierrot's simplicity and awkwardness, so important a feature of his later manifestations, and dressed him in the familiar costume, loose white garments with long sleeves, ruff, and large hat whose soft brim flapped round his whitened face. This, with some slight alterations, has remained his distinguishing garb ever since, but his character has been strangely altered. He soon made a place for himself in the affections of the French audience at the fairs, where, in company with other characters from the *commedia dell'arte*, he was played by some excellent actors. He might have remained but one good thing among many had it not been for the genius of Deburau, who made the character his own, and for twenty years, at the Funambules, acted nothing else. Without speaking a word, he mimed the *naïveté*, the clumsiness, the childish joys and sudden despairs of this comic yet often pathetic figure, which became almost legendary. Deburau, who drew the whole of Paris to his little theatre, and was praised by critics and fellow-actors alike, created, from the scattered offshoots of the *commedia dell'arte* Pedrolino, a character which lived in its own right, a French, indeed a Parisian, figure which retained little of its Italian origin beyond white clothes and its incurable, yet somehow appealing, stupidity. He was followed in the part by his son, and later by Paul Legrand at the Folies-Dramatiques (later Théâtre Déjazet), but Legrand made Pierrot less amusing and more sentimental, a trait which was later developed by a host of imitators until the robust country lad of early days had become a lackadaisical, love-sick youth pining away from unrequited love, and much addicted to singing mournful ballads under a full moon.

Meanwhile the Pierrot of Deburau had been given a new lease of life as the hero of the wordless play, *L'Enfant prodigue*, which was produced at the Cercle Funambulesque in 1890. Although Pierrot had come to England with pantomime, it was *L'Enfant prodigue* which established him in London, excellently mimed as it was at the Prince of Wales's Theatre in 1891 by Jane May, Zanfretta, Courtis, and others. The popularity of Pierrot brought the first English pierrot-troupe to Henley Regatta, under the genial management of Clifford Essex, and soon they had spread all over England, ousting the black-faced minstrels from the beaches and pier-pavilions of English seaside towns. Formed into 'concert parties', they toured the country, the girls in short frilly white frocks, the men in loose black or white suits, all enlivened by coloured buttons, ruffs, and ruffles. The men, following Deburau in this, covered Giratoni's bald head by a tightly stretched black handkerchief, knotted behind, and the floppy hat of Pedrolino was replaced by a dunce's cap, also ornamented with coloured buttons. In this costume, augmented on occasion by 'token' accessories, the various members of the company—singers, dancers, conjurors, comedians—went through their acts, and, ignoring the solitariness of their prototype, formed a gregarious 'Pierrot troupe'. The apotheosis of this form of entertainment, which has largely been replaced by the more sophisticated and individual agglomeration of turns known as revue, was reached by Pélissier's Follies, who, having conquered the provinces, came to London in the early

1900s and became a permanent feature of theatrical life there until their final break-up. A successful revival of the old Pierrot show, staged by the Co-Optimists under Davy Burnaby, enlivened London for several seasons in the 1920s. Present-day concert parties, which, despite competition from the cinema and radio, still figure among the attractions of the seaside in summer, have mostly discarded the Pierrot costume, though some smaller groups retain it, last vestige of a long tradition.

PIGEON-HOLE, a term applied to a box in a theatre auditorium framed by a small arched opening.

PIKE'S GRAND OPERA HOUSE, NEW YORK, see GRAND OPERA HOUSE.

PILGRIM PLAYERS. 1, see BIRMINGHAM REPERTORY THEATRE and JACKSON, SIR BARRY; 2, see BROWNE, E. MARTIN.

PINERO, SIR ARTHUR WING (1855–1934), English dramatist, son of a solicitor of Portuguese-Jewish descent (the family name was originally Pinheiro). Born in Islington, he left school at the age of 10, and was apprenticed to the law. The study of it he relieved with much amateur acting, and from it he presently escaped and obtained employment as an actor in the Edinburgh stock company, making his first appearance at the Theatre Royal, Edinburgh, on 22 June 1874. He was an actor for ten years, but only as a means to achieve his real purpose. On 6 Oct. 1877 he had his first play, *Two Hundred A Year*, produced at the Globe. Many minor pieces followed. With *The Money Spinner* in 1881 Pinero arrived at the St. James's. Popularity came with *The Magistrate* (1885), the first of the Court Theatre farces which became all the rage. It is often maintained still that in *The Magistrate*, *The Schoolmistress* (1886), *Dandy Dick* (1887), *The Cabinet Minister* (1890), and (in its rather more romantic way) *The Amazons* (1893), not only Pinero but also farce were at their best. *Sweet Lavender* (1888), a frank appeal to sentimentality, confirmed its author in prosperity.

With *The Profligate* (1889) Pinero made his first memorable venture into what was then considered the 'unpleasant' in drama. Not very important in itself, this piece at least hinted at possibilities in the author's development which were to be made clear when, at the end of May 1893, *The Second Mrs. Tanqueray* appeared at the St. James's and, with the assistance of Mrs. Patrick Campbell, startled the town. On the thought of the world at large it can have had no direct influence at all; but in a theatrical world so much and so long given over to farce, burlesque, and melodrama, Pinero's play was revolutionary. It was a serious English play with an idea—and it made money. *The Second Mrs. Tanqueray* had the effect of breaking down a host of fearful prejudices and clearing the intellectual air. During the next thirty years Pinero was regularly productive. *The Notorious Mrs. Ebbsmith* (1895) was Paula Tanqueray's successor. *Trelawny of the 'Wells'* enjoyed 135 performances from Jan. 1898. *The Gay Lord Quex* (1899), a brilliant piece of theatricalism, contained a third act which is perhaps the author's masterpiece of contrivance. With the turn of the century began a long succession of serious plays from *Iris* (1901) and *Letty* (1903) to *His House in Order* (1906) and *Mid-Channel* (1909). Of these *Iris* may be reasonably considered as Pinero's best study of a woman. In 1909, the year of the production of *Mid-Channel*, Pinero was knighted. His reputation was at its zenith. Thereafter his hold on the public slipped, and an attempt to renew it in *A Cold June* (1932), two years before his death, was a pathetic failure.

Pinero's thought moved easily in response to the currents of fashionable interest. He preached only to discover that London was already half-way to elegant conversion. He had a remarkable gift for setting a spark to polite controversy, but where he shocked his countrymen he shocked them within the range of their pleasure. Success was a necessary consequence, and when the fashion in which he had risen disappeared, a part of his reputation went with it. Though hailed as a disciple of Ibsen, he was, on the contrary, a successor to Scribe and Sardou, and the hope that later generations will rediscover his serious plays (his farces have been constantly revived, as has *Trelawny of the 'Wells'*) must rest on his magnificent powers of telling a story for the stage. Not even his tendency to stilted language in naturalistic scenes can spoil the eagerness of his audiences to know what is going to happen next.

A. V. COOKMAN†

PIN-RAIL, another name for the Fly-rail to which the lines are made fast.

PINTER, HAROLD (1930–), English actor and dramatist, who trained for the stage at the Central School in London, and for nine years acted in Ireland and in the English provinces as David Baron. His first play, the one-act *The Room*, was first produced by the Drama Department of the University of Bristol in 1957, and was later seen professionally in a double bill with *The Dumb-Waiter*. Pinter's first full-length play was *The Birthday Party* (1958), a tale of mystery and horror which followed naturally on his earlier works, though without their element of the supernatural. It was with *The Caretaker*, at the Arts Theatre in 1960 and later at the Duchess, that Pinter finally established himself as one of the outstanding younger playwrights. The play, which contained only three characters, dealt with the impossibility of communication between human beings. It was not successful in a French translation, but was played all over Germany, in India, Turkey, Belgrade, and New York. In 1962 the Royal Shakespeare company at the Aldwych, London, put on Pinter's one-act play, *The Collection*, in a double bill with Strindberg's *Playing with Fire* and in 1965 a new full-length play, *The Homecoming*. Pinter is also the author of revue sketches included in *One To Another* and

Pieces of Eight. It has been said of him that though his work is basically serious, even tragic, he displays a brisk sense of humour, the wit in his spare, exact dialogue being particularly lively and effective. He writes in the tradition of Beckett and Ionesco, but none the less with welcome originality.

PIONEER THEATRE IN THE UNITED STATES. Perhaps nowhere in the history of the theatre has man's instinctive craving for drama, whether as an outlet for self-expression or as a form of diversion, been more strikingly demonstrated than in the United States of the first half of the nineteenth century. Nowhere else is its vitality more significantly underlined. As far back as 1538, Spanish soldiers had staged plays in the territory now embraced in the states of Texas and New Mexico, but from these regions the drama had disappeared with the Spaniards. The eighteenth century had witnessed its rebirth on the continent, and seen it, gradually winning over tremendous odds, achieve an accepted place on the eastern seaboard. Then, after 1800, national expansion over the Allegheníes and down into the valley of the Mississippi gained in impetus and volume as a young people pushed with determination into the wilderness. The hardships and dangers they encountered have been recounted many times, but they were not great enough to extinguish the inborn passion for acting and the stage.

First came the military, who were giving plays at Fort Pitt, the Pittsburgh of to-day, as early as 1790, and on the site of present-day Detroit eight years later. Then, as the civilians moved in, there sprang up in one crude frontier settlement after another equally crude Roscian and Thespian societies, almost invariably wholly male in composition. The ebullient Kentuckians did not wait for the new century, but began their histrionic experiments in Lexington in 1799. By 1801 tyros were busy in Cincinnati, presenting O'Keeffe's *The Poor Soldier* 'between a ragged roof and sorry floor', as the dedicatory poem states. Pittsburgh was only two years behind with its civilian enthusiasts. In whatever the town, the amateurs held forth in any sort of room or hall they could press into service, and both acting and staging were of the roughest type. For the most part the pieces offered were trivial in quality, but occasionally, being ambitious, the would-be tragedians tried their hands at Shakespeare.

Close upon the heels of the amateurs came the professionals, sometimes, in ability and experience, scarcely distinguishable from their predecessors. In 1806 they invaded Pittsburgh. In 1812 came the Turners, Sophia, William, and their offspring. Sophia had played Montreal, and had even trod the boards of the famous Park Theatre in New York. Moreover, in their journeys they had picked up assorted satellites, including such veterans as Mrs. Giles Barrett and Thomas Caulfield, and also various novices who preferred the stage to less glamorous vocations. This little corps remained in Pittsburgh three years, and they turned their faces westward, spending two months in Cincinnati. It had been Turner's plan to cross the Ohio into Kentucky, where he had leased quarters in Frankfort, Lexington, and Louisville, but he had found himself dispossessed even before arriving on the scene.

In the same year, 1815, 'Old Sam' Drake (1772–1847), surrounded by his family and a few attendant outsiders, including Noah Miller Ludlow (1795–1886) and Frances Ann Denny (1798–1875) (later, as Mrs. Alex Drake, the tragedy queen of the West), accomplished a hazardous journey from Albany to Pittsburgh, and thence into Kentucky, where he occupied the buildings for which Turner had contracted, and put the drama on a permanent footing in the Blue Grass State. He did not, however, limit his activities to any restricted region, but travelled about from place to place, including Cincinnati, where in about 1826 his son and daughter-in-law, Mr. and Mrs. Alex Drake, assumed direction and delighted even so severe a critic as Mrs. Trollope. After Alex's death in 1830 his widow withdrew, leaving the field to James H. Caldwell (1793–1863), who set about raising the standards of audience behaviour. Such a reform was badly needed. If even in the 'Old Country' decorum had not yet wholly possessed the play-going public, little could be expected of these uncouth spectators on the mid-Western frontier. Like their Elizabethan forebears, they cracked and crunched nuts; they also chewed tobacco and spat—not always accurately. Men wore their hats, and there was much obstreperous by-play with the helpless actors. There was also the never-absent threat of a fight. Until these conditions were corrected, ladies were prone to stay away from the theatre unless their potential escorts were satisfied that they would not be disturbed.

Far to the south in New Orleans the drama had first asserted itself in 1791, when some French comedians had fled thither from a Negro revolt on the island of Santo Domingo. The English theatre was first introduced in 1806, in a tavern, but the roots did not grow deep, and, despite sporadic performances, it did not flourish before 1818, when Ludlow, then himself a mere beginner, brought his modest forces to the St. Philippe Street Theatre. In 1821 the lordly Caldwell assumed dominion, and made the Louisiana metropolis his kingdom. He opened the American Theatre in Camp Street, and later, in 1835, his great St. Charles, which gave the drama its first really worthy home in the South. But by this time the frontier was a long way from New Orleans, and its later fortunes do not come within the scope of this article.

While these events were taking place, itinerant companies were trying their luck in various communities in the south-eastern states, and on the banks of the Mississippi, notably at Natchez, Vicksburg, and St. Louis. The most important, theatrically, of the river towns was unquestionably St. Louis, twenty miles below the mouth of the Missouri. Here amateurs, as usual, blazed the trail when in 1815 they gave two plays in an abandoned log blacksmith's shop which served also as a courthouse, ballroom, and church. Thither headed Turner after disappointments farther east, but he did not arrive until Jan. 1818. After about six months he again moved on, abandoning the town to the amateurs until 1820, when Ludlow, with the Drakes hard upon his heels, landed on the water-front. St. Louis not proving large enough to support two companies at once, the rivals merged their forces, but even so, times being bad, business was unprofitable, and they departed. The same misfortune attended the Collins and Jones troupe in the fall. These companies used the Thespian Theatre, a frame structure erected by the amateurs, and this in turn gave way in 1826 to the notorious Salt House, a ventilation-proof hot-box fashioned from an abandoned warehouse, which held its own until 1837, when it went up in flames. On 3 July of that year Ludlow, together with his new partner, the celebrated comedian Sol Smith (1801–69), dedicated the New St. Louis Theatre, the handsomest 'Temple of the Muses' yet built west of the Mississippi (it actually had individual seats in the parquet). St. Louis now took its place as the theatrical capital of the West, a position it maintained until it was dethroned by Chicago after the Civil War.

Chicago had been late in falling into line. In fact, until 1830 or thereabouts, there had been no Chicago. Farther to the north-west in Feb. 1834, officers at Fort Crawford, now Prairie-du-Chien, Wisconsin, staged *Who Wants a Guinea?* Ten days later a company composed of four adults and a child essayed *The Woodman's Hut*, in an unfinished house in Galena, Illinois, with horses stabled below. In 1837 Chicago had its first taste of the theatre when two young actors, Isherwood and McKenzie, began giving plays in the dining-room of the Sauganash Hotel, in front of which quail still wandered. The following year McKenzie was joined by his brother-in-law, Joseph Jefferson II (1804–42), and a considerable segment of the family circle, including two young boys who were in time to attain wide fame as Rip Van Winkle; these were his step-son, Charles Burke (1822–54), and his celebrated son Joseph III (1829–1905). Failing to find the pot of gold at the foot of the rainbow in Chicago, the little group cheerfully set out for points south, and spent the next few years barn-storming in the hinterlands of the Mississippi and Missouri rivers, and so on down to Mobile on the Gulf, where Joseph II succumbed to yellow fever.

In 1847 John B. Rice (1809–74) raised the curtain of a new frame theatre in Chicago and welcomed an array of celebrities, but the frontier had by now moved away. Meanwhile, in Nauvoo, thirty miles to the south, the Mormons were diligently cultivating the tragic muse, the great Brigham Young himself playing a priest in *Pizarro* in 1844. But it was not, apparently, until 1851 that the future metropolis of St. Paul enjoyed its first taste of the drama, when George Holland (1791–1870) presented his company in a converted hall. A frame store served as the first playhouse in Omaha in 1857. Three years later the lovely Julia Dean (1830–68) (grand-daughter of 'Old Sam' Drake) took her bow in the dining-room of the Herndon House. Omaha prospered theatrically because it was on a direct route from East to West.

By Western standards it was not far from there to Denver, and there in 1859 a room in Apollo Hall saw Charles R. Thorne (1814–93) and his sons, also the later favourite Mike Dougherty (?–1865). Shortly after, the Thornes went their ways, but the local forces were greatly strengthened by the arrival of John S. Langrishe (1829–95) who, soon joining with his fellow Hibernian, the irresistible Mike, was taking the drama up into the mining gulches and the rowdy mountain hamlets, where human life was cheap and entertainment dear.

Though farther removed from the centres of civilization, Salt Lake City actually anticipated the Colorado communities. The Mormons had always relished play-acting, and soon after settling down in their distant Eden, they turned to their favourite amusement, putting on productions, first, in 1848, in a small building called 'the Bowery' and subsequently in the Social Hall, both men and women participating enthusiastically. Federal troops sent to keep an eye on them set up a canvas theatre at Camp Floyd on the shores of the great lake. Lacking the conventional materials for constructing scenery, the soldiers fell back on chalk and mustard for colouring materials. These make-shifts sufficed, but a carelessness in the matter of rehearsal almost proved the undoing of the military Thespians. Common love of the drama actually seems to have served to bind the watching army and the watched Mormons together, and ladies from Salt Lake sometimes acted at the camp. In 1860 Brigham Young, remembering the pleasure he had derived from his participation in *Pizarro* back in the Nauvoo days, ordered the construction of an imposing theatre, which was finally dedicated with solemn religious services in 1862 (see MORMON THEATRE).

Just as the Mormons welcomed all forms of dramatic entertainment, so the early settlers of the future great state of Texas opened their arms, and in the late 1830s both Houston and Matagordo had theatres before they had churches. Even during the turbulent days of the republic stars from the East made their way to the Texas towns.

Far to the west on the Pacific coast, as in the Colorado Rockies, the gold-seekers demanded their plays—and got them. The first California performances are thought to have been staged in a rough one-story building in Monterey shortly before 1850, about the same time that soldiers were demonstrating their histrionic mettle in Los Angeles, almost on the site of present-day Hollywood. By 1849 Sacramento had its Eagle Theatre, a flimsy structure of canvas and wood which is reputed to have cost the almost incredible sum of $75,000 and more. As in Colorado, admission was paid in gold dust, and when there was high water the spectators clambered up on the benches to keep their extremities dry. The year 1850 witnessed the opening of the first theatre in San Francisco, over a saloon. Soon thereafter building after building was put up and almost as speedily burned down. Yet, the proprietors never admitted defeat, and to California flocked the great and the near-great of the theatrical world, some of them to write their names large in the flamboyant history of the state. Outshining all others in brightness was that of the appealing child-actress Lotta Crabtree (1847–1924), whose mother took her from mining-camp to mining-camp, risking her limbs but guarding her morals. In a sense a child-actress Lotta always remained, and to this day her memory is cherished by the Golden Gate.

After the Civil War, the railroad united the East and the West, and, although for years the desperate Indians remained in places a deadly menace, the frontier soon disappeared. The recent wilderness was dotted with towns and villages, the inhabitants of which, like their pioneering forebears, demanded plays and players. Dion Boucicault (1822–90) fathered 'the Road', and the theatre had come to stay—until the movies rudely and crudely thrust it aside. Yet even today it is far from dead. The vitality which survived heat, cold, fire, and flood, impromptu stages, and often unspeakable acting, has not succumbed before the advances of cinema and radio. It has changed, adapted itself to new conditions, but died it has not (see also UNITED STATES OF AMERICA, 4).

W. G. B. CARSON

PIRANDELLO, LUIGI (1867–1936), Italian playwright. Sicilian by birth, but in no sense a regional artist, Pirandello, who began his literary career as a poet and philologist, was an established major novelist, short-story writer and critic before he achieved fame as a dramatist. Clearly, he must now be ranked above Goldoni as Italy's greatest man of the theatre; it is also plain that he is a dominant force in European drama of the 20th century, comparable in status and influence to Ibsen, Strindberg, and Chekhov. He inspired the *teatro grottesco* (see CHIARELLI) with his novel *Il fu Mattia Pascal* (1904), gave it an aesthetic with his critical volume, *L'umorismo* (1908; revised 1920), and superseded it with his own plays, some of which can be related to it thematically and formally, just as others take over and give life to concepts and practices associated with Futurism (see CHIARELLI). He is in the dramatic tradition which stems finally from the Greeks, absorbs the implications of Dante's *Divina Commedia,* and is freed from inhibiting classicism by Shakespeare (who, together with Ibsen, was Pirandello's most admired theatrical 'ancestor'). In method, in principle, and in temper, Pirandello is frequently and austerely classical: notably in *La giara* (1917), *Sei personaggi in cerca d'autore* (1921; drastically revised 1925), *Enrico IV* (1922), and *L'altro figlio* (1923). He owes something to Ariosto, much to Machiavelli. His concept of irony (*umorismo*) as transcendental farce derives from them, tempered by Verga's vision of humanity as a world of 'vanquished' individuals bound together in a religion of compassion. Popular criticism has typed him as the dramatist of the question mark. More correctly, he has pushed the frontiers of drama outwards by successfully bringing to the stage the preoccupations peculiar to our age. He understands, and debates with us—for all Pirandello's work is *argument* —man's despair at being unable to communicate, even with himself; he obliges his audience to participate in the experience of the multiple identity (and consequent nonentity) of every one of us; and he involves it in the progress of sentient man—self-discovery, self-evasion, self-construction, regeneration, and even destruction. He is in pursuit of the unattainable (often seen as the 'dream' virgin); equally, he stands out as the clear-sighted chronicler of an age of decay and fragmentation. He was the reverse of cerebral. He was respected by his actors as a born producer, and a comparison of the first and final texts of *Sei personaggi in cerca d'autore* shows how acute was his awareness of the demands of the theatre. He radically reformed the Italian straight theatre, giving it the strength to challenge the debilitating supremacy of opera. Central to his work is the trilogy made up of *Sei personaggi in cerca d'autore* (1921), *Ciascuno a suo modo* (1924), and *Questa sera si recita a soggetto* (1929). In the first he is concerned to establish the greater reality of a created character when compared with human beings who have not been transformed into legends by time, and to argue the nature of a work of art; in the second he asserts that art may have a truth superior to that proposed by life, and may therefore dictate a more appropriate pattern of conduct; in the third he postulates the dominance of an actor by the part he is playing. None of the plays, of course, is a bare examination of a thesis; all are intricate and sympathetic realizations of man caught in the trap of life. *Enrico IV* and *L'uomo dal fiore in bocca* are typical of Pirandello's new tragedy: intelligent man, having freed himself from the morass of the senses, emerges to the solitude of his self-imprisonment. His last play, *Non si sa come* (1934), may properly be ranked with *Enrico IV*. Other important works are: *Il giuoco delle parti* (1918), *Vestire gli ignudi* (1922), *Come tu mi vuoi* (1930), and *Quando si è qualcuno* (1933). In verse are the witty *Scamandro* (1909) and *La favola del figlio cambiato* (1933), which was set to music by Malipiero. Many of the plays have been translated into English by different hands, and acted in England and America.

FREDERICK MAY

Pirandello, who was awarded the Nobel Prize in 1934, had an unhappy life. His early years were overshadowed by the failure of his father's sulphur mines in 1896, but loss of money was nothing compared with the domestic unhappiness which resulted from his marriage in 1894. His wife, for some years afflicted by hysteria, developed a mental illness bordering on insanity, and from 1904 to 1919, when she entered a nursing home where she died in 1959, he cared for her himself. Doubtless the tragedy in his own home accounts for Pirandello's preoccupation with the mentally unbalanced. He had an abiding and practical love for the theatre; in 1925 he established his own theatre in Rome at the Teatro Odescalchi, and later undertook tours with his company in Europe and America.

In 1955 a Pirandello Society was founded in Leeds, closely linked with the university through the Department of Italian. It has produced or encouraged the production of many English versions of plays by Pirandello and other modern Italian dramatists, including Bracco, Giacosa, and Luongo (the principal Italian author of children's plays). There is also a Pirandello Society in America.

PIRON, Alexis (1689–1773), French dramatist. He was educated for the law, but the bankruptcy of his father sent him to seek his fortune in Paris. There he wrote farces for Francisque's Théâtre de la Foire, and overcame the difficulty of not employing more than one speaking actor, as enacted by the law of 1718, by a series of monologues, of which the first was *Arlequin Deucalion* (1722). Encouraged by his success, he sent a comedy, *L'École des pères*, to the Comédie-Française, where it was produced in 1728. It is an interesting mingling of the old and new theatre, for it stands on the threshold of the *comédie larmoyante*, though its author still holds to the theory that comedy should seek to amuse first, and only incidentally instruct. Piron's best work, and one of the outstanding comedies of the eighteenth century, was *La Métromanie* (1738), while of his tragedies *Gustave Wasa* (1734) remained in the repertory for some time. Piron was a gay and witty companion, who frequented the salon of Mme de Tencin, and was a friend of Rousseau. He suffered all his life from some scurrilous verses which he wrote in his youth; they turned up at the most inopportune moments, and finally lost him his seat in the French Academy.

PISCATOR, Erwin (1893–1966), German producer, disciple of Max Reinhardt. He is credited with having evolved the first 'epic' play, so initiating the style later developed for the Berliner Ensemble by Brecht, who collaborated with Piscator in the latter's outstanding production, at the Volksbühne in Berlin, where he worked from 1919 to 1930, of *Die Abenteuer des braven Soldaten Schweik* (1927), his own dramatization of a Czech novel. He also adapted for the Volksbühne Dreiser's *An American Tragedy*, Gogol's *Mother*, and Schiller's *Die Räuber*. It was characteristic of Piscator's method of work that he would arrange and ruthlessly alter texts of plays to suit his own theories. In his early days he made use of expressionist technique, and was one of the first to employ films and animated cartoons on the stage, to reinforce the argument of the play and speed up the action. Later it was said of him that he endeavoured to replace both naturalism and expressionism by an intellectual clarity which was not without its own emotion. His work had a big influence on the contemporary trend of play-production in Europe, which is only now becoming apparent. In 1933 Piscator left Germany and settled in America, where he became director of the Dramatic Workshop of the School for Social Research. In the 1940s the Workshop, which is now run on a more modest scale by Piscator's widow, Marie Ley, maintained two off-Broadway theatres, where, among other plays, it gave the first American production of Sartre's *Les Mouches*, and Robert Penn Warren's *All The King's Men*, based on his own novel and adapted in 'epic' style. From 1951 onwards Piscator returned occasionally to Berlin to direct plays, being responsible for *War and Peace* (his version of this was seen briefly in London in 1962, in a production by the Bristol Old Vic company, so providing the only chance of seeing Piscator's work in England, even at second-hand), *Dantons Tod*, *Requiem for a Nun*, all at the Schiller Theater, and *Death of a Salesman*, at the Theater am Kurfürstendamm. In 1962 Piscator took over this theatre, while awaiting the completion of a new Volksbühne, where he was to have settled permanently with his own company. His first production on his return was an amalgamation into a single play of Hauptmann's last four poetic plays on the House of Atreus, a feat which surprised and delighted those who had forgotten, or never known, his earlier work. In it he used with great dramatic effect a translucent stage lit from below, stylized settings which recalled the Japanese stage, screens with projections from the back, and symbolic orbs of red, black, and gold.

PISISTRATUS, tyrant of Athens, on and off, from 560 B.C. to his death in 528 B.C. He did much for the economic and cultural development of Athens. In particular he reorganized on a grand scale the festivals of Dionysus, instituting contests in dithyramb and in tragedy, this being the first official recognition of tragedy (see GREECE).

PISTOIA, Il, see CAMINELLI, ANTONIO and ITALY, I *b* i.

PIT, the name given to the ground floor of the theatre auditorium, generally excavated below ground level. In the early playhouses the stage and lower boxes were approximately at ground level, and the whole space sunk between these was called the pit, from the Elizabethan cockpit, used for cock-fighting. In the early nineteenth century the lower boxes were replaced by a raised circle, with the pit extending underneath; shortly after, the old rows of pit seats near the orchestra were replaced by the higher-priced stalls, and the name 'pit' was applied only to the more distant rows.

PITLOCHRY. The Pitlochry Festival Theatre owes its inception to Malvern, as it was during a visit to the Shaw festival there that Glasgow's Little Theatre enthusiast, John Stewart, founder of the Park Theatre, Glasgow, conceived the idea of building a 'theatre in the hills' for the presentation of a festival of plays in repertory. It was not, however, until 19 May 1951 that the theatre opened, and the first two seasons were given in a large marquee which housed a theatre with a fan-shaped auditorium and a stage with a very large proscenium opening, as well as excellent front-of-house amenities. This tent theatre was so happily designed that its features were retained in the more permanent structure built in 1953. Generally speaking, Pitlochry presents six plays running from April to the beginning of October. Usually there is at least one Scots play in the repertory, a work by a foreign author, a classic or near-classic, and a new play. Since John Stewart's untimely death in 1957 Kenneth Ireland has been the artistic director, and has adhered closely to the original play-pattern while extending the festival's scope to include concerts, art exhibitions, and lectures. Some very good performances, often of uncommon plays by such authors as Pirandello, Centlivre, Davenant, and Macklin, have graced the unusually spacious stage of this most interesting 'theatre in the hills'. J. F. ARNOTT

PITOËFF. (1) GEORGES (1885–1939), Russian actor who settled in Paris after the First World War and, with his wife (2) LUDMILLA (1896–1951), exerted a great influence on the French theatre up to the time of his death. Like Copeau, he believed that the French theatre, and indeed the theatre everywhere, was suffering from bankruptcy, both of ideas and of imagination. Pitoëff's attempt to remedy this state of affairs consisted in the presentation of the best work of foreign dramatists, as well as the plays of such innovators in the French theatre as Claudel, Cocteau, and Anouilh. The value of his work lay not only in the plays he presented, but in the subtle and entirely personal interpretation which he gave them. He had already had some experience of the theatre before he came to Paris, having for two years directed his own amateur company in St. Petersburg. After appearing in various theatres of Paris, including that of Copeau, he took his company to the Théâtre des Arts in 1924, and from there to the Mathurins. Much of his best work was done in these two theatres, particularly after 1934 when he finally settled at the Mathurins. There he proved himself a fine actor and a complete man of the theatre, adapting, translating, producing, and acting at one and the same time. Among the dramatists whom he popularized in Paris three particularly stand out—Shakespeare, Shaw, and Pirandello—and it was perhaps in Shakespeare that his genius found its fullest scope. He was nobly assisted in his task, which brought him much hard work and little money, by his wife, an excellent actress, who after her husband's death continued to direct the company, taking it on an extended tour of America and Canada. Among the many parts which she played to perfection were Nora in *A Doll's House*, Marthe in Claudel's *L'Échange*, and the hostess in Goldoni's *La Locandiera*. She was also extraordinarily moving as Shaw's St. Joan, which she played in London in a French translation, together with *La Dame aux camélias*, in 1930.

PITT, see DIBDIN.

PITTSBURGH, see PIONEER THEATRE IN THE U.S.A.

PIXERÉCOURT, (RENÉ-CHARLES) GUILBERT DE (1773–1844), French dramatist, called by his contemporaries 'the Corneille of Melodrama', of which he wrote more than fifty, ranging from fairy-tale plots to dramas of contemporary life in realistic settings. His early life, which no doubt influenced his writing, was as tormented and extravagant as that of any of his heroes. Seventeen when the Revolution broke out, he escaped to Coblenz, came back to serve in the Revolutionary army, was saved from the wrath of Robespierre by Carnot, and penniless, with a wife and child to support, he painted fans for a living for eighteen long months. He had already written sixteen plays, some of which had been accepted by various theatres but not yet produced, when in 1797 the Ambigu-Comique put on *Les Petits Auvergnats*. It was successful enough to warrant his abandoning the fans for ever, and the rest of his life was devoted to the theatre. Alone or in collaboration he wrote nearly 100 plays, and for thirty years provided the staple fare of the secondary theatres. The first of the long series of melodramas by which he is mainly remembered was *Victor, ou l'enfant de la forêt* (1798), and the most successful *Coelina, ou l'enfant de mystère* (1800), which was soon translated into German, English, and Dutch. Many of his later plays suffered from too much collaboration, but they made money, most of which he lost when the Théâtre de la Gaîté, of which he was a director, and where his best plays were given, was burnt down in 1835. This disaster, joined to the effects of a serious illness, ended his career, and he retired to Nancy to die a lingering death. He was an odd, tormented creature, who in his extraordinary plays seems to typify the Revolution, that mixture of ferocity and idealism, when blood and tears were shed with equal facility. Yet he had an appreciation of good literature, formed a fine library which he wept to see dispersed, and took his work very seriously, setting forth his credo in *Le Mélodrame* and *Dernières Réflexions sur le mélodrame*, being the first writer to use the word in its present sense (see MELODRAMA). He wrote quickly, but spent a long time over the production and scenery of his plays, for which he often invented new machinery and provided spectacular effects. He said himself: 'I write for those who cannot read', a large, enthusiastic, but unlettered public, whom he never failed, and whose counterpart today is catered for mainly by the films. Pixerécourt, who was the undisputed king of the lesser theatres, marked the extent of German influence in the early nineteenth-century theatre, and in his turn influenced the Romantic dramatists. Hugo and Dumas, among others, saw and enjoyed the melodramas of Pixerécourt, and their own plays are often only melodrama raised to a literary status by the beauties of style and lyric poetry. He also had a great influence in England, where the main characteristics of his theatre are preserved in the drawings of the Penny Plain, Twopence Coloured Toy Theatre. Constant controversy rages round the spelling of his name, which he himself seems to have spelt more often with one accent than with two. Custom is gradually enforcing the spelling Pixérécourt in spite of efforts to establish one accent only, in accordance with the original pronunciation.

PLABILISCHIKOV, Peter Alexeivich (1760–1812), Russian actor and dramatist, educated at Moscow University, where he first became interested in the theatre. On leaving the university he went to St. Petersburg and appeared in revivals of Sumarokov's plays. In 1779 he joined the Court theatre company, playing the roles of heroes and lovers to which his handsome appearance made him eminently suitable. He later became Inspector of Russian Theatres, and in 1793 returned to Moscow, where he was much admired. He wrote a number of plays, of which the historical tragedies are negligible; but those dealing with the everyday life of merchants and peasants are of greater interest, and may be considered the forerunners of social realistic comedy in Russia. A year before his death he was elected a member of the Society of Russian Writers at Moscow University.

PLACIDE, a family of actors, of whom the first, (1) Alexandre (? –1812), was rope dancer to the king of France. He left the Continent on the outbreak of the Revolution, was seen in Dublin, Bath, Bristol, and Norwich, and in 1791 landed at Charleston, U.S.A., where he gave a display of 'agility and pantomime' which he repeated in New York. He also danced in a ballet, danced a hornpipe, played a fiddle while on the tight-rope, and was seen to 'somerset backward and forward, over a table and chair'. At some point he married an actress, the daughter of Mrs. Pownall and James Wrighten, prompter at Drury Lane, who from 1793 to 1795 was a good leading actress and singer at the John Street Theatre, New York. They had a large family, of whom the eldest girl married William Rufus Blake, and with her two sisters was on the stage. Of the boys the younger became a popular comedian, while the other, (2) Henry (1799–1870), was the best-known of the family. As a child he appeared at the Anthony Street Theatre, New York, and in 1823 made his adult début at the Park in *The Heir-at-Law*. He remained there for many years, except for short tours to other American towns, and one somewhat unsuccessful appearance in London in 1841, and was later at Burton's. Like John Gilbert, he represented the best traditions of polished acting in Old Comedy, and was excellent in the role of the high-bred English gentleman, Sir Peter Teazle being one of his best parts. He was also good in eccentric humour, particularly in broken-English parts and in dialect, and in his youth was a good singer and farce-player.

PLANCHÉ, (Jean-Baptiste) Gustave (1808–57), French dramatic critic, mainly remembered for his attacks on the Romantics, by which he aroused the enmity of Victor Hugo. A clever man, but much embittered by early poverty, he became critic of the *Revue des Deux Mondes* in 1831, and his somewhat morose and sarcastic temperament was naturally antipathetic to the excesses of the young writers of the time. Later he became the friend of Alfred de Vigny, George Sand, and Balzac, who recognized the sincerity of his work and the justification, according to his own lights, of his strictures on their fellow writers.

PLANCHÉ, James Robinson (1796–1880), English dramatist, of Huguenot descent, who was interested in the theatre from an early age, and appeared with some success in amateur theatricals. He was a most prolific writer, mainly of burlesques, extravaganzas, and pantomimes, though he also wrote a few melodramas and comedies. His first play, a burlesque, was given at Drury Lane in 1818, and for the next few years he produced several plays a year, many of them being given at the Adelphi. He was associated with the Vestris–Mathews management at the Lyceum, and wrote for it what many considered his best work, *The Island of Jewels* (1849), for which the scene-painter Beverley produced some remarkable effects. Planché's adaptation of a French melodrama as *The Vampyre; or, the Bride of the Isles* (1820) first introduced to the English stage the so-called 'vampire' trap. Planché was a serious student of art, and designed and supervised the costumes for Charles Kemble's production of *King John* in 1823, the first to approximate to historical accuracy. He was also a good musician, and from 1826 to 1827 was musical director of Vauxhall Gardens. He wrote a quantity of libretti for opera, including Weber's 'Oberon', and English versions of 'William Tell' and 'The Magic Flute'. An unauthorized production of one of his plays led him to press for reform in the laws governing theatrical copyright, and it was mainly his efforts that led to the passing of the Act 3 William IV, c. 15 giving protection to dramatic authors. He published in 1834 a *History of British Costume* which long remained a standard work. Among his many interests he included the study of heraldry, and in his capacity as Rouge Croix Pursuivant of Arms and later Somerset Herald at the Heralds' College he several times went abroad to confer the Order of the Garter on foreign royalties. His work for the theatre seems strangely at variance with his more scholarly activities, but it was enormously successful. It appears to have no literary merit whatever, and divorced from its music and spectacular effects is quite unreadable. It depended largely on its staging and topicality, and taken as a whole provides an excellent picture of the English stage during sixty years. According to Sir St. Vincent Troubridge, much of Gilbert's libretti for the Savoy operas was based on or suggested by the texts of Planché's extravaganzas (see *Notes and Queries*, vols. 180, 181).

PLANCHON, Roger (1931–), French producer, actor, and playwright. When his first production (*Bottines, Collets Montés*, a burlesque, 1950) for an amateur group in Lyon won first prize in a local competition, the group turned professional and built their own 100-seat theatre, the Théâtre de la Comédie de Lyon, opened in 1952. By 1957, the company had staged twenty-eight productions, including the first performances of Adamov's *Le Professeur Taranne* and *Paolo Paoli* and Michel Vinaver's *Les Coréens*, and had achieved a considerable reputation as an avant-garde company with productions of Marlowe, Kyd, Shakespeare, Jonson, Calderón, Kleist, Vitrac, Ghelderode, and Ionesco. Planchon's productions at this time constituted, in effect, a conscious programme of investigation into stagecraft in which he experimented with techniques borrowed from every possible source, from the Elizabethan theatre to American gangster films and silent comedies. Under the influence first of Jean Vilar, and later of Bertolt Brecht (whose *Good Woman of Setzuan* he produced in 1954, and *Splendours and Miseries of the Third Reich* in 1956), Planchon evolved a bold, sweeping style which has done much to reinvigorate the presentation of classical plays, and to overcome the French predilection for the well-bred and orderly as represented by Racinian tragedy and the Comédie-Française. His increasing interest in epic styles led him to seek a larger theatre, and in 1957 the company moved to the 1,300-seat Théâtre de la Cité de Villeurbanne, in an industrial suburb of Lyon. Addressing themselves now to factory workers rather than the sophisticated theatre-goers of Lyon, the company ran a methodical campaign of meetings, discussions, publications, and exhibitions, and succeeded in attracting an entirely new audience. Planchon's opening production of *Henry IV Parts I and II* (in which he himself played Prince Hal) was followed by his own adaptation of Dumas's *The Three Musketeers* (brought to the Edinburgh Festival and the Piccadilly Theatre, London, in 1960, with Planchon as d'Artagnan), and Marivaux's *La Seconde Surprise de l'amour* (which caused considerable surprise and scandal, as Planchon cut through the traditional marivaudage to reveal a biting social satire). Visiting Paris in 1960 at the invitation of Jean-Louis Barrault, the company achieved a resounding success, and was awarded a government subsidy: the Théâtre de la Cité thus became the first national theatre in the French provinces. His subsequent productions have included Gogol's *Dead Souls* (adapted by Adamov), Marlowe's *Edward II* (adapted by Planchon), Brecht's *Schweik in the Second World War*, and his own first play, *La Remise*. T. C. C. MILNE

PLATO. (1) An Athenian comic poet, contemporary with Aristophanes. He gained several victories, but only a few fragments of his work survive. He is often referred to as Plato Comicus, to distinguish him from the philosopher.

(2) The philosopher (427–348 B.C.), of Athens, of highly aristocratic family. In his youth he composed tragedies and other forms of poetry, but on coming under the influence of Socrates and his rigorous intellectualism, he burnt his plays and devoted his life to philosophy and mathematics. However, a few of his epigrams survive, and are among the best in the Greek language.

The philosophical work that he published was put into a dialogue form which was a development of the mime (see MIME, 1 *b*). In the more abstruse works, and in most of the *Republic*, the dialogue is only nominal; elsewhere it is consistently dramatic, with occasional passages of astonishing vividness and power. The character-sketches of Euthyphro or Ion, or the opening scenes of the *Protagoras*, are good examples of Plato's dramatic skill; his mastery of ironic comedy is shown by his picture of the sophists in the *Euthydemus*; of tragedy by the scene of Socrates' death in the *Phaedo*.

Plato's theories of literature and drama have had immense influence. His 'inspirational' theory of poetry is the direct source of the idea of the *furor poeticus*—'the poet's eye in a fine frenzy rolling', through a sixteenth-century translation of Plato's *Ion*, which greatly influenced the French Pléiade. In other dialogues Plato is much less sympathetic to literature; his idea that a conception of 'the Good' can be reached only through the intellectual process of dialectic led him, apparently, to mistrust 'inspiration'; and in the *Republic*, and elsewhere, Plato would admit poetry into his ideal society only under a paralysing censorship. He objects in particular to drama because it appeals especially to the ignorant, seeks what is agreeable rather than what is good, and debilitates the community by appealing to emotions, not to reason, by representing characters as being overcome by their emotions, and by propagating blasphemous and impossible ideas about the deity (e.g. by repeating stories of strife between gods). There was also the more metaphysical objection, against art in general, that since it makes only a copy of sensible objects, themselves only a copy of 'reality', it is further from the truth even than the imperfect world of sense. These criticisms were important chiefly for the reply which they drew from Aristotle. H. D. F. KITTO

PLATT, the Elizabethan theatrical term for 'plot', which consisted of a prompter's outline of the action of a play, with division into acts, actors' entrances and exits, and other notes, drawn up and posted somewhere behind the scenes for the help and convenience of organizing calls and properties. It should not be confused with an author's synopsis, nor with the *scenarii* of the *commedia dell'arte*, which were used as the groundwork for improvisation. The 'platt' was a purely utilitarian device, of which a few stray specimens have been preserved among Henslowe's papers.

PLAUTUS, Roman playwright. The twenty-one plays (one of them a mere fragment) contained in his extant manuscripts must be the twenty-one selected by Varro as universally admitted to be authentic out of the 130 which had come by his time (first century B.C.) to be attributed to Plautus. The authenticity of the *Mercator* and the *Asinaria* may be questioned; but in general the plays which have come down to us possess a unity of style and display the qualities which Roman writers attribute to Plautus—command of language and metre, wit, high spirits, and indifference to form.

Neither Plautus's full name, nor the dates of his birth and death (which are usually given as *c.* 254/3 B.C.–184 B.C.), nor any details concerning his life, can be regarded as established. The prologues to his plays, our earliest documents, refer to him as 'Plautus'; whether the 'Maccus' who wrote the *Asinaria* and the 'Maccus (or Maccius) Titus' who wrote the *Mercator* are to be identified with each other and with him is difficult to say. A passage in the *Cistellaria* (*ll.* 197–202) speaks of the Hannibalic War as drawing to a close; and according to notes in the oldest extant manuscript the *Stichus* was produced in 200 and the *Pseudolus* in 191 B.C. The traditional account is scarcely wrong in saying that Plautus knew poverty and hardship, that he acquired a practical knowledge of the theatre at an early age, and that he depended for his livelihood on the success of his plays. These plays, the earliest complete works of Latin literature which we possess, are all free translations from Greek New Comedy. There is no evidence that Plautus deliberately remodelled the plots or characters given him by his Greek originals; what he did was to choose which plays he would like to translate and to infuse his translations with his own personality. He seems to have liked complicated plots, strongly marked characters, and scenes of love-making, revelry, trickery, and debauchery; he was himself able to supply song, repartee, jests, puns, and topical allusions, and to dilate on congenial topics, often with small regard for what was dramatically appropriate. The fate of Naevius was a warning to all dramatists to abstain from political and personal satire, but there seems to have been no absolute ban on indecency; several of Plautus's plays, such as the *Bacchides*, the *Pseudolus*, and the *Truculentus*, portray the life of the brothel; and the concluding scenes of the *Casina* (a favourite play with the public, to judge by its prologue, which was written for a revival performance) carry farce to outrageous lengths, while suggesting by their lack of form that they are largely the independent work of Plautus himself. There appears indeed to have been some reaction on the part of the public against the prevailing licence of comedy, for the prologue and epilogue to the *Captivi* boast of the high moral tone of that particular play. We note, too, that Plautus keeps his wit within bounds where the honour of a respectable woman is concerned.

Among the better-known plays the *Menaechmi* (source of Shakespeare's *Comedy of Errors*) and the *Amphitruo* deal with the complications caused by mistaken identity; the *Aulularia* shows us a poor old man, Euclio, not free from some traits of miserliness, who has been half-crazed by the discovery of a buried treasure; the *Mostellaria* or 'Ghost Story' displays the endless fertility of invention whereby, amid growing difficulties, the slave Tranio contrives to baffle his young master's father, unexpectedly returned from abroad; the *Rudens* tells of storm and shipwreck on the lonely shore of Libya, a treasure recovered from the sea, and a long-lost daughter restored to her parents; in the *Captivi* the noble courage and devotion of a slave enable his master to escape from captivity, while he himself eventually finds that his captor is his own father. Considering the limits imposed by New Comedy, the variety of plot in Plautus's plays is considerable; and, if we miss in him the subtle effects of Menander and Terence, we have instead a flow of wit and a vigour of language which explain his supreme popularity on the Roman stage. Within a few years of his death Plautus had become a classic; and even when his plays were ceasing or had long ceased to be acted they provided a source of merriment for generations of readers, from Cicero to St. Jerome. WILLIAM BEARE†

PLAY, a generic term applied to any work written to be acted, and covering such more limiting terms as tragedy, comedy, farce, drama, &c. It may range from a spirited exchange of backchat between two mountebanks in the market-place to a full-length work given in a special building—a theatre—with a cast of highly trained professional actors aided by all the appurtenances of lighting, costuming, and production. The one essential requisite is that it should be entirely or mainly spoken; if given without dialogue it ranks as mime or ballet, if all the dialogue is sung, as opera. Hybrid forms give rise to ballad opera, burletta, and musical comedy (for the use of music as an adjunct to a play, see INCIDENTAL MUSIC).

A play can be read, either alone or in company, but only fulfils its original intention when it is acted. The text may therefore be regarded as a skeleton, a dead thing to which the producer, actor, and audience must contribute before it can be brought to life. Although the fundamental principles of drama remain constant—action, conflict, unity of purpose, resolution—the form of a play may conform to certain conventions—five-act, three-act, unity of time and place, separation (or alternatively fusion) of tragedy and comedy—which vary from age to age, and even from country to country. The form, however, comes first, the rules afterwards, even with Aristotle. In the same way, although the art of acting is to some extent dependent on the type of play in favour at the moment, it has an independent life of its own, and at certain points in the history of the theatre there may be conflict between the text and its interpreters. Just as a bad play may succeed temporarily because of some topical allusion or contemporary fashion or because of superlative acting, so a good play may be temporarily eclipsed in its own day, and only appreciated in revival. Generally speaking, plays written to be read—Closet drama—remain outside the main stream of the theatre, though this theory is refuted by the success of Alfred de Musset's *Comédies et Proverbes* on the stage many years after they were written, and by the enormous influence on European drama of the tragedies of Seneca, which were probably not acted, but read aloud. The poetic drama of the nineteenth century, which from a purely literary point of view contains many fine things, has not yet proved successful in action. A change in theatrical fashion may bring it into prominence, but it seems likely that an inherent lack of dramatic impulse allied to too great a weight of pure poetry may always hinder its immediate effect on an audience (see POETIC DRAMA). The author alone cannot produce a play in the full sense of the word, and his work demands the co-operation of many other people, among whom he is merely the furnisher of the text. This aspect is lost sight of in our modern use of the word dramatist, but the earlier playwright, in its affinity with such words as wheelwright, reveals it clearly, and makes the author a fellow worker in the theatre with actor, producer, designer, stage-carpenter, and so on. Some of the finest of our plays have been written by men labouring under all the advantages and disadvantages of actual daily participation in the work of the theatre.

PLAYBILL, PROGRAMME (ENGLISH). The playbill, which is the earliest form of theatrical programme as we know it, occurs comparatively late in the history of dramatic art. What means of publicity were adopted by the Elizabethan players on Bankside are unknown, but it may be assumed that the managers relied mainly upon word of mouth and the services of what would now be called a 'barker'. It is possible that small 'bills' or tickets, giving only the name of the play and the theatre, like the one for 1692 reproduced in W. J. Lawrence's *Elizabethan Playhouse* (2nd series), may have been scattered in the gentry's coaches or delivered at their houses by hand, but that more elaborate announcements existed earlier than this has been proved by the discovery in 1951 of a playbill at the Public Record Office dating from 1672. This is for the Booth at Charing Cross, and is reproduced in *Theatre Notebook*, vol. 6. It was probably intended to be stuck up on walls near the theatre, and distributed to coffee-houses in the vicinity.

If one excepts an amateur playbill of 1681 for a performance at Kelso Grammar School, the earliest example from an established theatre, as opposed to a fair-booth, seems to be that of 22 Feb. 1687 for *A King and No King* at Drury Lane. This, like the few other specimens that survive from the late seventeenth and early eighteenth centuries (for a complete list up to 1718 see *Theatre Notebook*, vol. 17), is printed on roughish paper with the Royal Arms at the top and 'Vivat Rex' at the bottom, and dated. At first few details were given, but these were gradually expanded to include the names of the cast. As the text grows the Royal Arms disappear (see No. 166). Towards the end of the eighteenth century mention is made not only of the cast but of the stage decorator (e.g. de Loutherbourg, who worked for Garrick). The playbill was therefore by this time becoming the equivalent of the modern programme, but it still served as a theatre poster. The practice of dating and issuing it daily continued until about 1860 (see No. 167), when weekly or half-weekly changes occurred. Towards 1810 it grows larger, about foolscap size, and shortly afterwards it becomes a double sheet, in order to accommodate the elaborate descriptions of scenery and painters' names which the new triumphs of the landscape school (Telbin, Clarkson Stanfield, &c.) had made fashionable. The size of the playbill was soon about 19½ in. square folded in the middle. By 1850 it had grown to 26 in. × 17 in., and in 1856, during Charles Kean's management of the Princess's Theatre, to 20 in. × 30 in. folded in three, one column being devoted to lengthy dissertations on his Shakespearian productions. Pantomime characters of this period were also provided with descriptions of a humorous nature, consisting almost entirely of puns in the taste of the time.

The effect of these developments was to make the playbill extremely unwieldy for use as a theatre programme, and about 1850 the Olympic Theatre, London, began to issue small playbills on a quarto sheet about 12 in. × 9 in. as well as the larger bills. These smaller bills were printed on one side and folded in the middle, and were probably supplied to occupants of the more expensive seats without charge. Drury Lane soon followed, and the other theatres came slowly into line.

No use had yet been made of the theatre programme as a medium of advertisement, but in the 1860s the firm of Eugene Rimmel, 'Perfumers of London and Paris', began printing, by arrangement with the theatres, notepaper-size programmes with stamped paper-lace borders, some very elaborate. The fourth page of the programme was devoted to Rimmel's advertisement and the whole was perfumed. This practice continued until the 1880s, and the changes in the details of the advertisements often make it possible to date otherwise undated programmes.

In 1869 the St. James's Theatre, London, began to issue a kind of magazine programme called *Bill of the Play*. The second and third pages were filled with literary matter—notes on the theatre, the current production, &c.—while the fourth page provided a list of omnibus routes, cab fares from different parts of London, and Spiers and Pond's Refreshment Department charges. Similar details of transport facilities appeared on a few other theatre programmes in the 1870s, but the only other 'magazine' programme of the period was that issued by the Criterion Theatre under the title of *The Firefly*.

The same theatre, in the later 1870s, began to adorn its programmes with sketches of scenes from the play and actors in character. These appeared on the front and on the borders of the middle pages. All details of the play itself were now confined to the latter. The Haymarket Theatre followed a similar practice, but most other programmes were still very simple, consisting of a single sheet of notepaper with no advertisements. They were issued free, while the legend 'No fees or gratuities of any kind' gives a hint of a controversy which still agitates the theatre from time to time. At the Gaiety Theatre John Hollingshead was a no-fee enthusiast. He issued a four-sheet programme (9½ in. × 19 in.), which grew to eight sheets in the later 1870s, with pages 2, 3, 6, 7, and 8 devoted to advertisements. The fanciful design on the cover varied from year to year.

About 1880 thin cardboard programmes came into use, often printed in colour. The Savoy, which opened in 1881 and was the first theatre to be lighted solely by electricity, issued some very elaborate cardboard programmes, printed at first by Marcus Ward & Co., with complicated borders on gold, featuring electric bulbs as decorative motifs. Subsequently Savoy programmes showed coloured sketches of the characters in various Gilbert and Sullivan Savoy operas. Some of these are admirable examples of colour printing and must have been quite costly to produce. The Haymarket Theatre in the period 1886–96 provided cardboard programmes for stalls and dress-circle, paper ones for pit and gallery. These were adorned with a view of the façade of the theatre and a group from *The School for Scandal* as depicted on the drop-curtain.

In the 1880s appeared for the first time a type of programme which long lingered in provincial music-halls. This was the threefold card, each panel measuring about 8 in. × 3 in. These were originally printed by the Edwardes Menu Co. and had small advertisements on either side of the programme-matter and all over the two backs. These programmes, which cost 6*d.*, were used at nearly all the 'fee' theatres and continued in decreasing numbers until well into the twentieth century.

Irving at the Lyceum revived the practice of issuing a programme freshly dated for each performance. This began in the autumn of 1880 and continued for the greater part of his management. Augustin Daly followed the same practice at the various theatres in which his company appeared. After the uniformity of earlier programmes, those of the 1880s show astonishing variety. Sizes varied enormously, and almost every theatre had its own cover-design. The St. James's Theatre under Alexander used a Beefeater as a kind of symbolic mark. Tree at His Majesty's reproduced many of Charles Buchel's posters of himself. Some theatres showed views of the interior and exterior on the front cover. Aubrey Beardsley's poster design for the season at the Avenue Theatre in 1894 was reproduced in monochrome on the programme. At the Savoy in 1912 Granville-Barker made a similar use of Albert Rutherston's costume-designs for *The Winter's Tale* and of William Nicholson's for *Twelfth Night*.

After 1910 the 6 in. × 9 in. type of programme became common. Programmes were now usually issued by the refreshment contractors and this made for greater uniformity. After the First World War 'magazine' programmes on American lines were used by many theatres. These cost 6*d.* and contained a certain amount of light reading-matter or theatrical gossip. Other theatres issued a programme of as much as twenty pages with photographs of the performers, scenes from the play, and a very large number of advertisements, the actual programme-matter being confined to the middle sheet. The increasing commercialization of the theatre affected even the actual programme-matter. Whereas formerly only theatrical purveyors had been mentioned, credit was now given to dressmakers, milliners, and the suppliers of shoes, stockings, furniture, typewriters, cigarettes, and properties of all kinds. Programmes were then sold in all theatres at prices varying from 3*d.* to 6*d.* (Old Vic, 2*d.*) except on first nights, when they were usually presented free of charge. When paper restrictions came into force during the Second World War programmes were reduced to a single folded sheet, or were cut to a size of about 3 in. × 5½ in. The raising of the restrictions brought back the larger programme, but at an increased cost, usually a shilling. Although a cast-list and photographs and biographies of the actors are usually supplied, the bulk of the commercial programme consists of advertising. Efforts have been made, however, notably at the National Theatre, the Royal Shakespeare Theatre, and the Mermaid, to improve on this. At the first two (and also at the Aldwych, the London home of the Stratford company) a cast-list is provided free of charge, and only the accompanying booklet, containing interesting information about the play and its author, is charged for. A free programme was also issued originally at the Mayfair and Mermaid Theatres, but they are now charged for.

'Gala' programmes, usually printed on fringed silk or satin, form a class by themselves. The earliest known on silk is for 12 Oct. 1790 for a benefit night at the New Theatre, Brightelmston (i.e. Brighton). Other early silk programmes are those of the Mander and Mitchenson Collection (22 Feb. 1796, for the Haymarket) and Mr. Cecil Price of the University of Wales (10 Oct. 1796, for the Swansea Theatre). The practice of printing on silk continued into the twentieth century. In the late nineteenth century the programmes of the St. James's Theatre were printed in gold on cardboard for first nights, and for similar occasions. Irving had his printed on imitation vellum. Some of the programmes issued for performances of the Russian Ballet were artistic productions of a high order. These Gala programmes were often very expensive (5*s*.). Attempts to introduce a transparent programme which could be read when held up to the light were not very successful, for such a programme is necessarily confined to a single sheet (see also POSTERS, THEATRICAL).

GABRIELLE ENTHOVEN†, *rev.*

PLAYERS, THE, NEW YORK. This club was founded in 1888 on the lines of the Garrick Club in London, Edwin Booth, the first president, donating and endowing a house he had purchased for the purpose in Gramercy Park. He retained a suite of rooms in it, which are kept as he left them when he died there in 1893. The club has a large collection of theatrical relics, including jewellery and weapons owned by famous actors, paintings of American and foreign players, death-masks, and a fine library, which, under a charter from the Regents of New York State, was opened in 1957 to accredited public research as The Walter Hampden Memorial Library, named for the club's fourth president, who served twenty-seven years before his retirement in 1955. Ladies were formerly admitted to the premises only at an afternoon reception on Shakespeare's birthday, but since 1946 have been admitted to four annual Open Houses, featuring entertainments and refreshments. About four evenings a year (Pipe Nights) are given over to honouring members or distinguished guests in the arts or in public life. The club's first three presidents, Booth, Joseph Jefferson, and John Drew, died in office. Hampden, and Howard Lindsay, who succeeded him, both retired, Lindsay in 1965. He was succeeded by Dennis King.

ROBERT DOWNING

PLAYERS' CLUB, TORONTO, founded in 1913 as a university dramatic society. It gave its first performance in the hall of Victoria College, its repertory consisting mainly of established one-act plays, though occasional new Canadian short plays were given. Its first producer was the American-trained actor and director, Roy Mitchell, who in 1919 took the company to the newly opened Hart House Theatre, where they gave an interesting season of classical plays, accompanied by a programme of lectures and musical matinées. The organization of what was virtually an undergraduate society, however, was not adapted to the management of a permanent theatre with technical and financial problems, and on the emergence of the Board of Syndics, with nine members under the Chairmanship of Vincent Massey, the Players' Club withdrew and re-formed as a separate body. Among its later productions was an outstanding *Way of the World*. Sir Ernest Macmillan was for some years Director of Music for the club.

PLAYERS' THEATRE. A small studio theatre on the first floor at 6 New Compton Street opened in Jan. 1927 as Playroom Six. It was here that Peggy Ashcroft made her first London appearance, as Bessie in *One Day More* (May 1927). In Nov. 1929, on its removal to ground-floor premises, with John Fernald as producer, the club changed its name to the Players' Theatre. It moved again in Apr. 1934 to premises in 43 King Street, Covent Garden—the building which in Victorian times had housed Evans' (late Joy's) Song and Supper Rooms. It soon closed, but in Dec. 1936 it was reopened by Peter Ridgeway as the New Players' Theatre. It was here, in Dec. 1937, that Harold Scott produced the first Victorian cabaret, so inaugurating the entertainment that later became famous in London as Ridgeway's Late Joys. After Ridgeway's death in 1938, a mixture of plays and Victorian music-hall items continued to fill the bill until 1940, when, because of the blitz, the club, now directed by Leonard Sachs, and known simply as the Players' Theatre, moved to 13 Albemarle Street. In 1945 it acquired the premises under the arches of Charing Cross station which had originally been the Hungerford Music Hall, later known as Gatti's-under-the-Arches to distinguish it from Gatti's-over-the-Water (in Westminster Bridge Road). Here, under the direction of Don Gemmell, Reginald Woolley, and Gervase Farjeon, the theatre continues to run an old-time Victorian music-hall, with other entertainments which include an annual Victorian pantomime.

PLAYFAIR, SIR NIGEL (1874–1934), English actor, producer, and manager, who gained his early experience with the O.U.D.S. and other amateur societies. He was intended for the law, but in 1902 made his first appearance on the stage and later toured with Benson, and was in Shaw's plays at the Court Theatre. He also appeared in a number of Shakespearian parts at His Majesty's under Tree, and played Bottom in Granville-Barker's production of *A Midsummer Night's Dream* at the Savoy in 1912. In 1918 he took over the Lyric Theatre, Hammersmith, and remained there until 1932, making it one of the most popular and stimulating centres of theatrical activity. He produced there *Abraham Lincoln*, a revival of *The Beggar's Opera* with settings by Claude Lovat Fraser (see No. 174) which ran for nearly 1,500 performances, *Lionel and Clarissa*, *Riverside Nights*, an intimate revue by A. P. Herbert and others, *The Way of the World* and *The Beaux' Stratagem*, both with Edith Evans, a stylized black-and-white revival of *The Importance of Being Earnest*, with John Gielgud as Worthing, *When Crummles Played*, a burlesque of *The London Merchant* set in the theatrical background of *Nicholas Nickleby*, and numerous other plays old and new, in many of which he himself appeared. He was also responsible for the production of *The Insect Play*, given at the Regent in 1923, being part-author of the translation. He wrote an account of his Hammersmith management in *The Story of the Lyric Theatre, Hammersmith* (1925) and *Hammersmith Hoy* (1930). In 1928 he was knighted for his magnificent services to the English theatre.

PLAYHOUSE. 1. LONDON, at the Embankment end of Northumberland Avenue. This theatre was built by Sefton Parry as a speculation. It was for a time thought that the South Eastern Railway Co. would require the site for the extension of Charing Cross station, but they did without it, and the theatre, then known as the Avenue, opened on 11 Mar. 1882, with 'Madame Favart', the cast including Florence St. John, Fred Leslie, and Marius. After a series of light operas, George Alexander started his career as an actor-manager at this theatre with *Dr. Bill*. A year later Henry Arthur Jones's *The Crusaders* was a success, but the most important event of these early years was the production of Shaw's *Arms and the Man* in a season managed by Florence Farr and financed by Miss Horniman.

Mrs. Patrick Campbell and Forbes-Robertson were at the Avenue in 1899, and in the same year Charles Hawtrey staged one of the theatre's greatest successes, *A Message from Mars*, which opened on 22 Nov. and ran for 544 performances. In 1905 Cyril Maude, who had severed his partnership with Harrison at the Haymarket, took the Avenue, demolished and rebuilt it. On the night of 5 Dec. the roof of Charing Cross station collapsed and wrecked the new building. It was again rebuilt, and opened as the Playhouse on 28 Jan. 1907, with Cyril Maude in *Toddles*. He remained there until Sept. 1915, producing and playing in many successful plays, both new and revivals, together with his wife, Winifred Emery. He was succeeded, in 1917, by Gladys Cooper, who, with Frank Curzon until 1928, and later by herself, staged and appeared in many plays, including a distinguished revival of *The Second Mrs. Tanqueray*. After her departure in 1933 the theatre had no settled policy, though in the 1940s there were several interesting productions there, including a translation of a play by Simonov, *The Russians*, done by the Old Vic company, and Ustinov's early play, *Blow Your Own Trumpet*. The theatre became a B.B.C. Studio in 1951.

W. MACQUEEN-POPE†, *rev.*

2. NEW YORK, on 48th Street, between Broadway and 6th Avenue. This was built by William A. Brady, and opened on 15 Apr. 1911. It had its first success with *Bought and Paid For*, which ran up 431 performances, and in 1915–16 Grace George, wife of Brady, appeared there in a repertory which included *The Liars*, the first American performance of *Major Barbara*, and a revival of *Captain Brassbound's Conversion*. Later successful new plays were *For the Defence* (1919) and *The Wonderful Thing* (1920) with Jeanne Eagels, and in 1924 came *The Show-Off*, with a fine performance by Louis-Jean Bartels, which ran for 571 performances. The next important production was *The Road to Rome* (1927), followed by *Street Scene* (1929) in its original form. This gained the Pulitzer Prize, and is considered by many to be Elmer Rice's finest play. After a somewhat blank period the theatre had a further success with *Three Men on a Horse* (1935). *Yes, My Darling Daughter* (1937) had 405 performances, and was followed by several successful revivals, including *The Circle*, *Outward Bound*, and *Kind Lady*. In 1945 *The Glass Menagerie*, in which Laurette Taylor made her last appearance, as the Mother, began a long run at this theatre, and in 1959 Gibson's *The Miracle Worker*, with Anne Bancroft, was highly successful. It was demolished in 1968.

GEORGE FREEDLEY†

PLAYROOM SIX, see PLAYERS' THEATRE.

PLINGE, WALTER, a name used on English playbills to conceal a doubling of parts, particularly in a Shakespeare play (for the American equivalent, see SPELVIN, GEORGE). Sir St. Vincent Troubridge has kindly supplied the following note on his career. 'There are two versions of the origin of Walter Plinge, and though they differ somewhat, both connect him with drinking in the early and great days of the Benson Company. The more frequent version, which I have read in the memoirs of old Bensonians and heard from them in the 1920s, claims him as the landlord of a pub opposite or near the stage door of the Lyceum when Benson played his first season there in 1900. His geniality, good beer, and easy credit endeared him to the company, who thought he should be immortalized in print, and started using his name in the programme for their second and third appearances covered with crêpe hair.' Matheson Lang, in *Mr. Wu Looks Back* (pp. 207–8) gives the other version: 'Walter Plinge is a mystery. He has appeared not only in several of my plays, but also at the same time in casts of other productions in other London theatres.... The dreadful truth is simply this. During Benson's first London season there was, close to the stage-door of the theatre, a pleasant and cheery little bar to which members of the company would sometime "step aside". When an interval during rehearsals gave rise to such an opportunity, H. O. Nicholson invented a kind of code-word for this delectable stepping. As thus: "If you have time, Mr. Plinge is waiting to see you outside the stage-door." In other words that meant: "Have we time for a quick one?" It can readily be understood from this that Mr. Plinge became a very important and a very popular personage in the Benson Company. Where he got the name Walter I don't really know, but someone—I've got an idea it was Oscar Asche—had a brain-wave one day and used the name for a double on a programme. Thus Plinge grew into quite a popular actor of small parts.' The name was never, as with Spelvin in America, used for doll or animal actors, but still makes occasional appearances on London and provincial playbills.

PLOUGH (or PLOW) MONDAY, in English folk festivals the Monday after Twelfth Night. Fragmentary texts of a Plough Monday play have been recovered from the East Midlands, similar in character to the Christmas Mumming Play, with which it was probably associated. The main differences between the two are that the characters of the Plough Monday play are farm-hands and their like, not heroes, as in the Mumming Play, and the central incident, the death of one of the characters, is due to an accident and not to a fight. Both plays are probably survivals, later influenced by literary trends, of a primitive folk festival of Winter and Spring (see MUMMING PLAY).

PLOWRIGHT, JOAN (1929—), English actress, who studied at the Old Vic Theatre School, and made her first appearance at the Croydon Repertory Theatre in 1948. She was then with the Bristol Old Vic, and after touring with the Old Vic company in South Africa, she made her first appearance in London in July 1954, as Donna Clara in *The Duenna.* After a season in Nottingham she joined the company at the London Royal Court Theatre under Devine, who had been one of her teachers at the Old Vic School, and in Dec. 1956 she suddenly sprang into prominence with a superb performance of Margery Pinchwife in a revival of *The Country Wife.* She continued to play leading parts at the Court, among them the Old Woman in *The Chairs,* Jean Rice in *The Entertainer,* Beatie in *Roots,* and Daisy in *Rhinoceros.* She made her first appearance in New York in 1958 in an Ionesco double-bill of *The Chairs* and *The Lesson,* and also appeared there as Josephine in *A Taste of Honey* (1960). She is the third wife of Sir Laurence Olivier, and appeared in his first season at Chichester as Sonya in *Uncle Vanya* and Constantia in *The Chances* (1962). A born *comédienne,* able also to suggest an infinite pathos, she has already played a wide range of parts, and is equally at home with the bawds of Restoration comedy and the equivocal heroines of modern drama.

PLYMOUTH THEATRE, NEW YORK, on West 45th Street, opened on 10 Oct. 1917. Among the more interesting of the early productions here was *The Wild Duck* (1918), this being the first time the play had been given in New York in English. Nazimova starred in it, and also appeared in *Hedda Gabler* and *A Doll's House.* Later in the year John Barrymore appeared in a dramatization of Tolstoy's *Redemption,* entitled *The Living Corpse,* and, in 1919, in *The Jest,* with his brother Lionel. Among later successes the most memorable was *What Price Glory?* (1924), a realistic portrayal of war which, with a fine cast, ran for 433 performances. In 1925 came Winthrop Ames's delightful revivals of Gilbert and Sullivan, while later successes at this theatre include *Burlesque* (1927), which established Barbara Stanwyck as a star, *Counsellor-at-Law* (1931) with Paul Muni, *Tovarich* (1936), the Pulitzer Prize-winner *Abe Lincoln in Illinois* (1938), the anti-Nazi melodrama *Margin for Error* (1939), and the charming *Lute Song* (1946), an adaptation by Sidney Howard of a Chinese play in which Mary Martin gave a fine performance. More recently the theatre has housed such outstanding productions as *Don Juan in Hell* (1952), *Tiger at the Gates* (1955), *Chips with Everything* (1963), and Alec Guinness as Dylan Thomas in *Dylan* (1964).

GEORGE FREEDLEY†

POCKETS (the American name for Dips), see LIGHTING, 2.

POCOCK, ISAAC (1782–1835), English painter and dramatist, mainly remembered today for his melodrama, *The Miller and his Men* (1813), which, with its romantic scenery, strong situations, and incendiary denouement (see No. 67) proved most popular in the nineteenth-century Juvenile Drama, and is still occasionally revived in cardboard. Pocock was the author of several other popular melodramas—including one of the many versions of the thieving magpie story as *The Magpie, or the Maid?* (1815), another Toy Theatre favourite given at Covent Garden (see No. 32)—of a number of farces, written mainly at the beginning of his career, and of innumerable adaptations of Scott's novels. He has little originality, and is merely one of the many writers of the period whose work in a more literary age would have been relegated to the minor theatres. However, in the general poverty of play-writing at the time, he was usually accorded production at Covent Garden and Drury Lane, or at the very least at the Haymarket. It was Pocock's *Rob Roy Macgregor* (1818) that first brought Macready into prominence, while his farce *Hit or Miss* (1810) gave Mathews a capital part as Dick Cypher. Pocock was a pupil of Romney and a good artist, exhibiting several times at the Royal Academy.

PODESTÀ, JOSÉ J., see SOUTH AMERICA, 1.

POEL, WILLIAM (1852–1934), English actor and producer, son of William Pole. He changed his name in deference to his father's dislike of his chosen profession, and made his first appearance on the stage in 1876. His first production was an episode from *Don Quixote,* given at the King's Cross Theatre in 1880. For two years Poel was manager of the Old Vic, then a music-hall, and many of his early productions were adaptations made by himself from novels and stories. He was for many years general instructor to the Shakespeare Reading Society, for which he produced a number of plays, and it was with a donation from them, and one from Mr. Arthur Dillon, that in 1894 he founded the Elizabethan Stage Society, whose work had such an enormous influence on the staging and production of Shakespeare in the following century. The Society appeared in various halls and courtyards, and, on a stage modelled in accordance with Poel's idea of an Elizabethan stage (see No. 74), produced Shakespeare (beginning with *Twelfth Night* in 1895), Marlowe, Beaumont and Fletcher, Jonson, Middleton, Rowley and Ford, and a translation of *Everyman*, its first performance for 400 years. Much of the incidental music was written and played by Arnold Dolmetsch and his family, and the plays were given with the minimum of scenery and the maximum of poetic effect. Shaw, reviewing Poel's work, said:

> The more I see of these performances by the Elizabethan Stage Society, the more I am convinced that their method of presenting an Elizabethan play is not only the right method for that particular sort of play, but that any play performed on a platform amidst the audience gets closer home to its hearers than when it is presented as a picture framed by a proscenium.

The last production of the Elizabethan Stage Society was *Romeo and Juliet* in 1905. Financially the venture had not been a success, but artistically it vindicated Poel's theories, and stimulated others to experiment with simple settings and so free Shakespeare from the cumbersome trappings of the late nineteenth century. Poel continued to work in the theatre until his death, and was responsible for the revivals, under various auspices, of the old improvised *Hamlet* play of the English Comedians, *Fratricide Punished*, given for the first time in England at the Oxford Playhouse in 1924; of *Arden of Feversham* (1925); and of *David and Bethsabe* (1932) for the first time since 1599. He was President of the London Shakespeare League, and author of several plays and books on the theatre. An account of his life and work was written by Robert Speaight (1954).

POETIC DRAMA. The use of poetry for plays was constant in early times all over Europe, and continued for tragedy long after comedy had suffered the incursion of prose. From the prose comic scenes of Shakespeare, interpolated among some of his sublimest poetry, it was an easy step to the complete prose comedies of, for example, Dryden, who continued to use poetry for tragedy. But even the latter usage waned, and it finally became the fashion for all plays intended for the stage to be written throughout in prose, a fashion that was intensified in the late nineteenth and early twentieth centuries by the growing commercialism of the theatre, which effectively ousted the poet from the stage. In return, many poets conceived their dramatic works as pure poetry, often not intended for production. But some, uneasily aware of the unhappy gulf between what had originally been the component parts of a good play, tried to effect a reconciliation. The term 'poetic drama', which would at one time have been unnecessary, was then adopted to signalize their attempts to bring poetry back to the theatre as a living organism and is applied also to plays written in a deliberately 'poetic' manner, even if not in verse-form. ED.

In nineteenth-century England most of the leading poets, who usually lacked skill in playwriting, joined with star performers, such as Kean, Macready, and Irving, in presenting poetic drama of varying literary and dramatic merits. Byron's *Werner* (1830), Browning's *A Blot in the 'Scutcheon* (1843), Shelley's *The Cenci* (1886), and Tennyson's *Becket* (1893), were outstanding, but the rhetorical dramas of James Sheridan Knowles, and Sir Edward Bulwer-Lytton's *The Lady of Lyons* (1838) and *Richelieu* (1839), were more popular and more frequently performed. The plays of John Davidson, which contain excellent poetry, have gone unproduced, and it has been possible to perform (in 1914) only portions of Thomas Hardy's magnificent epic drama, *The Dynasts* (pub. 1904–8). Stephen Phillips, probably the most successful combination of poet and dramatist of his time, brought blank verse back into the commercial theatre of London for a brief period with his plays *Herod* (1900), *Ulysses*, and *Paolo and Francesca* (both 1902). But he was also the last of the poetic dramatists in the tradition of the nineteenth century, a time which had seen a gradual estrangement of poetic drama from the main body of plays written for the theatre.

About the turn of the century, poetic drama, under such diverse influences as the *Nō* plays of Japan, Ibsen (whose 'realism' is fundamentally that of a poet), and the writings of the French symbolist poets, took on a more experimental tone, and poetic dramatists were encouraged to think in terms of a theatre of their own. The leaders of the Irish literary revival, William Butler Yeats, John Millington Synge, and Lady Gregory, produced many plays of great poetic beauty and sound dramatic structure. In spite of such fine verse-plays as *The Land of Heart's Desire* (1894), *Cathleen Ni Houlihan* (1902), *The King's Threshold* (1903), and *Deirdre* (1906), they were, however, never able to establish the poetic theatre they had hoped for, but Yeats's integrity as a poet and dramatist raised the standards of poetic drama and deeply influenced his Irish and English contemporaries. Synge's plays, though written in prose, are the work of a true poet, as are those of O'Casey.

Among the English poetic dramas of the early twentieth century, John Masefield's *The Tragedy of Nan* (1908) (in poetic prose), John Drinkwater's *Rebellion* (1941). James

Elroy Flecker's *Hassan* (also 1923), and Gordon Bottomley's *King Lear's Wife* (1915) and *Gruach* (1923), were the most important. In the 1930s a number of poets, including T. S. Eliot, Stephen Spender, W. H. Auden, and Christopher Isherwood, broke away from the traditional verse play and laid new foundations for poetic drama with free verse, modern symbolism, satire, and social consciousness. Eliot's early plays, *Murder in the Cathedral* (1935) and *The Family Reunion* (1939), are notable for their fine poetry, and have been revived in the post-war period; *The Dog Beneath the Skin* (1936) and *The Ascent of F.6* (1937) by Auden and Isherwood, were valued in their day for their intellectual wit, penetrating satire, and social criticism, but have not yet been revived.

The first important American poetic dramatist, William Vaughn Moody, won his principal success with a prose play, *The Great Divide* (1906), but his work and teachings have influenced many, among them Josephine Preston Peabody and Percy MacKaye. Maxwell Anderson carried on a long and valiant fight to establish poetic drama in the American theatre with such plays as *Mary of Scotland* (1933), *Winterset* (1935), *Joan of Lorraine* (1946), but his poetry was not of the first rank and his dramatic construction frequently left something to be desired. Other American poets, notably E. E. Cummings, Edna St. Vincent Millay, Robinson Jeffers, Wallace Stevens, and Alfred Kreymborg, have written distinguished poetic dramas, but only a few of them have been widely produced. Their work is, for the most part, characterized by great freedom and individuality and considerable experiment.

As the cleavage between the poetic theatre and the commercial theatre has become more acute in the twentieth century, the production of poetic drama has had to depend mainly on university theatres, dramatic schools, and groups which have been formed specifically for that purpose. In England, the Mercury Theatre, which began in London in the 1930s, was exclusively devoted to the production of poetic drama, and its successful presentation in 1945 of Ronald Duncan's *This Way to the Tomb* and Anne Ridler's *The Shadow Factory* indicated that there was still an audience for poetic drama. Plays in verse, including *The Zeal of Thy House*, by Dorothy Sayers, and *Christ's Comet*, by Christopher Hassall, were written for production in the Chapter House of Canterbury Cathedral, as part of a revival of religious drama in England (see RELIGIOUS DRAMA). Poetic plays by Christopher Fry, including *A Phoenix Too Frequent* (1946), *The Lady's Not for Burning* (1949), and *The Dark is Light Enough* (1954), were successfully produced in London, New York, and elsewhere. Ten years after *The Family Reunion*, T. S. Eliot's *The Cocktail Party* was produced at the Edinburgh Festival and later in London and New York; it was followed by *The Confidential Clerk* (1954) and *The Elder Statesman* (1958). Dylan Thomas's *Under Milk Wood* (1953), written as a radio script in poetry, song, and prose, has had many stage readings and performances. But these were isolated phenomena and in spite of the sudden success of Fry's plays in the commercial theatre in the late 1940s and early 1950s English dramatists seem once again, as after Phillips's success, to have turned away from poetic drama.

Since the collapse of the Federal Theatre Project in the United States in 1939, the Poets Theatre, founded in 1951 in Cambridge, Mass., has been one of the most important agencies for the commissioning and production of poetic drama. Richard Eberhart, its founder and first president, has written *The Apparition* (1951) and *The Visionary Farms* (1952), both of which were well received. In 1958, Archibald MacLeish's *J.B.*, the story of a modern Job, enjoyed a long Broadway run (see No. 111); but although adaptations of poetic plays by Anouilh and Giraudoux have been conspicuous on Broadway, poetic drama has, during the past decades, become increasingly identified in the United States with the off-Broadway and experimental theatre. In this connection it is interesting to note that translations of plays by Samuel Beckett and Eugene Ionesco, which combine poetical quality, often of a high order, with surrealism, the world of dreams, and human despair, have had runs both on and off Broadway.

In the last century and a half poetic drama has developed from the traditional blank-verse pattern to the most experimental forms of poetry and prose. It has been at the heart of many important literary movements, notably French symbolism and the Irish literary renaissance, and never far from the frontiers of modern literature. The competition of the commercial theatre has been severe and the position of poetic drama in the modern theatre is not so assured as it deserves to be, but some dramatists still have faith in it as a medium of expression, and the future for poetic drama lies in the successful development of their art.

HERBERT CAHOON

POGODIN [STUKALOV], NIKOLAI FEDOROVICH (1900–1962), Soviet dramatist, who steadily consolidated his reputation, and became one of the outstanding figures of the Soviet stage. By profession a journalist, he entered the theatre in 1929, with a play which was rehearsed by the Moscow Art Theatre, but for some reason not performed. This was followed by *Tempo*, which shows a group of Soviet workers, helped by an American engineer, constructing a building in record time. This play, which is based on fact, and is hardly more than a 'documentary', was produced in 1930 at the Vakhtangov Theatre, and was translated into English by Irving Talmadge in *Six Soviet Plays* (1934). *Poem About an Axe*, which deals with the trials of a blacksmith who finds a new process for the manufacture of steel and then forgets how he did it, was produced by Popov at the Theatre of the Revolution in 1931, as was

My Friend in the following year. This, a more human and profound piece of work, paved the way for Pogodin's most famous play, *Aristocrats*, an extraordinary piece of stagecraft as well as an intensely moving human document. It deals with the regeneration of a gang of criminals engaged on the digging of a canal from the Baltic to the White Sea and also appeared in *Six Soviet Plays*, in a translation by Anthony Wixley. It was first produced at the Vakhtangov Theatre in 1934, and by Okhlopkov in the same year at the Realistic Theatre, while in 1937 it was seen at the Unity Theatre in London. But even in this play Pogodin had not yet succeeded in making his characters individuals rather than types, nor in evolving action credibly from within rather than imposing it from without. In these and other respects his next play, *The Man with the Gun*, a play about Lenin produced at the Vakhtangov Theatre in 1937, showed a great advance, which was maintained in his later plays, particularly in *Kremlin Chimes* (1942) and *The Third Pathétique* (1959), which completed his Lenin trilogy. In the last-named, produced at the Moscow Art Theatre, Smirnov won high praise for his portrayal of Lenin. Pogodin's war plays, *The Ferryboat Girl*, which deals with the defence of Stalingrad, and *Moscow Nights*, were also successful. After the war he wrote *Creation of Peace* (1947), dealing with demobilized and wounded soldiers, and *End of Summer* (1949), which was produced at the Yermolova Theatre. These upheld his reputation, but his next play, *Three of Us Went to Virgin Lands* (1949), was criticized as giving a one-sided view of his subject. In 1956 a new version of *Kremlin Chimes*, which was seen in London in 1964, was produced at the Moscow Art Theatre with immediate success, and was followed by *The Petrarch Sonnet* (1957), produced by Zotova at the Mayakovsky, and *Living Flowers* (1961), again at the Moscow Art Theatre.

POISSON, a family of actors who served the French stage during three generations. The first, (1) RAYMOND (*c.* 1630–90), known as Belleroche, was intended for the medical profession, but joined a provincial company in about 1650, and a few years later was at the Hôtel de Bourgogne, where his wife played the parts given up by Mlle Bellerose, wife of the famous tragedian. A big man, with an expressive face and a large mouth, Poisson was an excellent comic actor, in spite of a slight stutter, and was a favourite of Louis XIV, who liked both his acting and his companionship, and of Colbert, who stood godfather to one of his children. He took from Scarron's *Écolier de Salamanque* (1654) the character of the valet Crispin and made it peculiarly his own, introducing it into several of his plays and playing the part himself. His many light comedies have been forgotten, since they had none of the gaiety of his acting. One, however, is interesting—*Le Baron de la Crasse* (1663)—since it shows a strolling company performing before some local gentry, and its leader may be intended as a satirical portrait of Molière. Two of Poisson's daughters were on the stage and married actors (see DAUVILLIERS and LA TUILLERIE), while his second son, with an actress wife, was a member of a company maintained by the King of Poland. Of all his children, however, it was (2) PAUL (1658–1735) who best carried on the family tradition. He joined the Comédie-Française in 1688, playing his father's old parts, including Crispin, with the same stutter, and remained with the company until 1724, except for a short retirement between 1711 and 1715. He married (3) ANGÉLIQUE (1657–1756), actress daughter of du Croisy, who was on the stage at 13, and a member of the Comédie-Française from its foundation until she retired in 1694. Her sons, (4) PHILIPPE (1682–1743) and (5) FRANÇOIS ARNOULD (1696–1753), were both actors, though the elder disliked the life and retired in 1722. He was, like his grandfather, a dramatist, and wrote a number of comedies, of which the best was *L'Impromptu de campagne* (1733). François Arnould, on the contrary, ran away from the army to join a company of strolling players, and was admitted to the Comédie-Française against his father's wish. He was excellent in valets and heavy humorous characters, and he too inherited Raymond's stutter. His most admired role was Lafleur in *Le Glorieux*. His sister, (6) MADELEINE-ANGÉLIQUE (1684–1770), married a Spaniard named Le Gomez, and was the author of four tragedies, of which *Habis*, given at the Comédie-Française in 1714 and frequently revived, was the most successful.

POLAND. The origins of the theatre in Poland, as in all European countries, must be looked for in the liturgy of the Church (see LITURGICAL DRAMA). It was Jan Kochanowski (1530–84), the foremost Polish poet of the Renaissance, who gave Poland its first secular play of any importance (*The Dismissal of the Grecian Envoys*, 1578), but Moralities and popular farces continued to flourish until well into the seventeenth century. A typical example of the latter was P. Baryka's *A Peasant Made King* (1633).

The agricultural nature of the country, and the comparatively small size of the towns, favoured the activities of strolling companies rather than of permanent theatres (John Green's English Comedians visited Poland as early as 1607), but a Court theatre was opened in Warsaw in 1637, which for a time housed a resident Italian opera company. Italian and French plays were given, among them *Le Cid* (1662), *Andromaque* (1672), and *Le Bourgeois gentilhomme* (1687), as well as elaborate masques and an increasing number of Polish plays. Drama in schools flourished under the Jesuits and the Piarists (see JESUIT DRAMA).

The first public theatre, the Teatr Narodowy (National Theatre) (so called because the plays there were given in Polish), opened in Warsaw in 1765. In 1783 Wojciech Bogusławski (1757–

1829), who had joined the company five years earlier and was the first Polish actor to play Hamlet (in 1797), became its director, and in the next thirty years he laid the foundations of theatrical life throughout the country, financing, building, and directing theatres in a number of towns. He encouraged new playwrights, and he himself wrote and translated some sixty plays, of which *Cracovians and Mountaineers* (1794) was the most popular. Other important dramatists of this period were Franciszek Zabłocki (1754–1821), and Julian Niemcewicz (1757–1841).

In the nineteenth century the theatre became, for a country under foreign domination, both an instrument of national aspiration and a means of escape. The former was expressed by the Romantic poets—Adam Mickiewicz (1798–1855), Juliusz Słowacki (1809–49), Zygmunt Krasiński (1812–59) and Cyprian Kamil Norwid (1821–83)—followed by the writers of the Young Poland movement, of whom the Cracow poet Stanisław Wyspiański (1869–1907) was the most important, while comedy flourished with such writers as Aleksander Fredro (1793–1876) (whose *Life Annuity* was seen in London in the original in 1964), Michał Bałucki (1837–1901), Józef Bliziński (1827–93), and others. Later, drama became more concerned with social realities, and among the writers of this period were Aleksander Świętochowski (1849–1938), Gabriela Zapolska (1857–1921), Stanisław Przybyszewski (1868–1927), Tadeusz Rittner (1873–1921), J. A. Kisielewski (1876–1918), K. H. Rostworowski (1877–1937), and Włodzimierz Perzyński (1878–1930). An important dramatist was Stanisław Ignacy Witkiewicz [Witkacy] (1885–1939).

The efficiency of the theatres in the nineteenth century depended partly on the degree of freedom allowed to them. In Warsaw the theatres were nationalized after the 1830 rising, and Russian police officials were nominally in charge. The Teatr Narodowy, whose company had been giving performances in the Teatr Rozmaitości since 1829, was reorganized as the Warsaw State Theatre. In 1833 a new theatre, the Teatr Wielki, was opened, and the two former theatre buildings were abandoned, a new Teatr Rozmaitości being housed in the right wing of the vast new building. The companies in these new theatres maintained a high standard during the second half of the century with such outstanding actors as the great comedian Alojzy Żółkowski the younger (1814–89), Bołeslaw Leszczyński (1837–1916), Wincenty Rapacki (1841–1924), the internationally famous Helena Modjeska [Modrzejewska] (1840–1909), whose career is dealt with under her own name, and Mieczystaw Frenkiel (1859–1934). In Vilna, where Bogusławski had appeared in 1785, and established a theatre, performances in Polish were forbidden from 1864 to 1906. In Poznań, the main theatre centre of the Prussian part of Poland, a permanent theatre was not established until 1870, and then only a private one (Teatr Polski) was allowed. Conditions were more favourable in the Austrian part of the country. Bogusławski appeared in Lwów in 1780, and fourteen years later he settled there for five years and built a permanent theatre. He was succeeded by J. N. Kamiński (1777–1855), who reconstructed and reopened this theatre in 1809, and remained in management for twenty years. Two other theatres were built, one in 1842, the other, to replace it, in 1900. The latter reached a high standard under Koźmian from 1865 to 1888, under Pawlikowski, manager until 1906, and under Heller, who succeeded him until 1918. Cracow had its first permanent theatre in 1797. In 1893, when a second theatre (named in 1909 the Juliusz Słowacki) was opened, among the important directors there were Tadeusz Pawlikowski (1893–99), J. Kotarbiński (1899–1905), and Ludwik Solski [really SOSNOWSKI] (1905–13), and Cracow became for a time the chief theatre centre of Poland.

After the First World War the theatre in Poland was able to develop freely. One of its finest theatres was the Polski in Warsaw, which opened in 1913 under Arnold Szyfman (1882–1967), who directed it until shortly before his death. *The Apple Cart*, by Shaw, in a Polish translation by Florian Sobienowski as *Wielki Kram*, had its world première in this theatre on 14 June 1929 and two other Shaw plays their European premières, *Too True to be Good* in 1932, and *The Simpleton of the Unexpected Isles* in 1935. Also important was the Reduta Theatre, founded in Warsaw in 1919 by the eminent actor-producer Juliusz Osterwa (1885–1947). It later transferred to Vilna, and split into two sections, one playing in the city, the other touring the small towns of Eastern Poland. Also deserving of mention are the *avant-garde* theatre Ateneum, which was directed by the distinguished actor Stefan Jaracz (1883–1945), and the Bogusławski Theatre in Warsaw (built in 1901, directed from 1924–6 by Leon Schiller (1887–1954), a disciple of Craig, and probably the finest producer of his day in Poland, one of the founders of the modern theatre movement there). Another remarkable producer was Wilam Horzyca (1889–1959). Among the great actors of this period was Ludwik Solski (1855–1954) (see above), for many years *doyen* of the Polish stage. He retained his powers until the end of his long life, and was at his best in comedy, where his wit, dexterity, and perfect timing had full play.

The Second World War brought total destruction to the Polish theatre. All theatre buildings, archives, and libraries in Warsaw, as well as in many other cities, were destroyed by bombing or lost their equipment, and many eminent theatre men were killed or driven out of the country. But as soon as the war ended companies sprang up again, and theatres were rebuilt with official financial help. In 1949 all theatres were subjected to a central authority, which controlled their organization and repertory, but this was abolished in 1956, and replaced by decentralization, which gives each theatre a large measure of freedom in choice of repertory and manner of presentation. The number of new theatres has now passed the hundred mark. Some of them are among the best in the country, notably the Teatr Ludowy (People's Theatre) in the new town of Nowa Huta, directed by Krystyna Skuszanka and her husband Jerzy Krasowski, which opened in 1955 with *Cracovians and Mountaineers* in the pre-war production of Leon Schiller; the Teatr Dramatyczny in Warsaw, with Ludwik René as its principal producer; and Teatr Współczesny (the Contemporary Theatre) in Warsaw, founded by Erwin Axer, which brought to London in 1964 two short plays by the modern satirist Sławomir Mrożek (1930–), *Let's Have Fun* and *What a Lovely Dream!* There is no lack of talented actors and producers to staff all these new theatres, and though plays in the old traditions are still being written, some by dramatists who made their name before the war, the tendency to experimentation which has lately developed in all the arts finds its reflection also in dramatic writing. Décor is important, and among the outstanding scenic designers are W. Drabik, K. Frycz, A. Pronaszko, W. Daszewski, and J. Kosiński. Poland has many puppet theatres, and some children's theatres. Theatre criticism is particularly lively, and there are three periodicals specifically devoted to the theatre—*Dialog*, a monthly established in 1956; *Teatr*, a fortnightly established in 1946; and *Pamiętnik Teatralny*, a quarterly established in 1952 and devoted to articles on theatre history. Theatre workers everywhere are kept informed of events in Poland by the monthly bulletin published by the Polish Centre of the I.T.I. There are two theatre museums in Poland, one in Warsaw, and one in Cracow (see also JEWISH DRAMA, 5, and RUSSIA, 1).

POLITIS, PHOTOS (1890–1934), an outstanding man of the theatre, and the first director of the Greek National Theatre, founded in 1930. His premature death at the age of 44 was a great loss, as he had even in those few years imbued the company with his own high ideals, and begun the process, so ably continued by his successors, of integrating the gifts of individual actors into a harmonious whole, from which has resulted the excellent ensemble playing which has been particularly admired in classical revivals. Politis realized that the strength of Greece lay in her beginnings, and that any effort to revive a national theatre must start with a return to the roots. Hence his insistence on the importance of the classical repertory. But his alert and inquiring mind was open to all the influences of the modern theatre, and his productions were often experimental. He established the National Theatre on firm foundations, and his influence has been felt in all branches of Greek acting and production.

POLIZIANO, also POLITIAN [ANGELO AMBROGINI] (1454–91), early Italian dramatist, friend and protégé of Lorenzo de' Medici (the Magnificent) and the tutor of his two sons. His *La Favola d'Orfeo* was one of the first plays by an Italian to be written in the vernacular, and to make use of a classical-mythological, instead of a biblical, subject. Written in 1472, it was performed at the Court of Mantua on 18 July of that year, with music by Germi. In 1932 it was again used as a libretto (adapted by Corrado Pavolini) by Casella for an opera produced at the Teatro Goldoni on 6 Sept. In form the *Orfeo* resembles a *sacra rappresentazione*, but its content points forward to the imminent development of the secular forms of Renaissance drama, especially of the pastoral (see ITALY, 1).

POLLARD, THOMAS (*fl.* first half of seventeenth century), English actor, a comedian with the King's Men. He probably began his acting career as Shank's apprentice in the Palsgrave's Company in about 1610. By 1623, when he was already a member of, though not a shareholder in, the King's Company, he had achieved some eminence as a player of comic roles, and he added considerably to his reputation in later years. With the actor Bowyer he was accused of having embezzled the wardrobe and effects of the company on the closing of the theatres in 1642, but there may be an element of exaggeration in this, since Pollard was still *persona grata* with his old companions after this date, and with them signed the dedication of the Beaumont and Fletcher folio of 1647.

POLUS, the most famous Greek tragic actor of the fourth century B.C. (see GREECE, 4).

POMPONIUS, see FABULA, 1. *Atellana.*

PONSARD, FRANÇOIS (1814–67), French dramatist, whose somewhat frigid neo-classical plays came as a relief to a public wearied by the excesses of Romanticism. Ponsard, who was a lawyer by profession, was first attracted to the theatre by seeing the great actress Mlle Rachel at Lyon, where she appeared in a number of plays by Racine and Corneille, and his first play, *Lucrèce*, based directly on Livy and Corneille, ignored entirely the poetry and passion of the Romantic school. Given in 1843, the year which saw the failure of Hugo's *Les Burgraves*, it was an instantaneous success. Some of the credit for this must go to its actors, headed by Bocage and Mme Dorval, some to the reactions of an audience who found in its sobriety, says a contemporary critic, some dignity, some reticence, and much common sense, above all a subject and a style which they could understand and appreciate. Ponsard, who followed up this play with several other tragedies, thus found himself the champion of order and seemliness, in opposition to the licence of Romanticism, and the founder of what was known as *le théâtre du bon sens*. His most successful play, based on a contemporary theme, was *L'Honneur et l'argent* (1853), which opened to him the doors of the French Academy in 1855. He did not, however, enjoy writing these moralizing bourgeois plays, which were coming into fashion with Augier and the younger Dumas, and returned to his earlier methods in *Le Lion amoureux* (1866) and *Galilée* (1867). The first was successful, but the second aroused the opposition of the clerical party. It had not been intended for production, and the slowness of the action was not compensated for by the beauty of the verse. Ponsard, whose works are now completely forgotten, kept up a steady level of talented mediocrity, and his initial success was due more to the reaction against the Romantics than to his intrinsic merits. He wrote a charming idyll, *Horace et Lydie* (1850), for Mlle Rachel, who had refused to play the heroine in his *Charlotte Corday* earlier in the year, a part interpreted with much success by Mlle Judith.

PONTI, DIANA DA (*fl.* 1582–1605), an actress of the *commedia dell'arte*, known as Lavinia, who, after appearing with the Confidenti and possibly Gelosi troupes, had a company of her own, which may have been the Desiosi. She appeared in Lyon in 1601, and is last heard of at the head of a company under the patronage of the Duke of Mirandola in 1605. She played young lover parts.

POPE, JANE (1742–1818), English actress, who played as a child with Garrick, and made her first appearance as an adult on 27 Sept. 1759, as Corinna in *The Confederacy*. She was immediately successful, and soon succeeded Kitty Clive, playing hoydens, chambermaids, and pert ladies, with a brilliance that made Churchill in 1761 call her 'lively Pope'. She was the original Mrs. Candour in *The School for Scandal* and Tilburina in *The Critic*. She is sometimes confused with Mrs. Pope (formerly Miss Younge), a well-known actress who was playing Portia when Macklin made his last abortive attempt at Shylock at Covent Garden in 1789. She only relinquished young characters when age and obesity forced her to, and then proved herself equally good in elderly duenna parts, and in such roles as Mrs. Heidelberg. She retired in May 1808.

POPE, THOMAS (?–1604), one of the actors in Shakespeare's plays, and an original shareholder in the Globe and the Curtain. In 1586–7 he went with Kempe and other actors to Denmark and Germany, and joined the Chamberlain's Men on their formation in 1594. He is referred to as 'a clown' and may have played some of the parts created by Kempe.

POPOV, ALEXEI DMITREVICH (1892–1961), outstanding Soviet producer, who joined the Moscow Art Theatre in 1912 and worked there for six years. He then went to Kostroma to become director of a drama studio organized by local students, and under him the theatre achieved professional status. While there he produced plays, such as *The Cricket on the Hearth* and *The Devil's Disciple*, on which he had previously worked either in Moscow or independently. From 1923 to 1930 he worked at the Vakhtangov Theatre, where his six main productions played an important part in the development of the company. In 1931 he was invited to become artistic director of the Theatre of the Revolution, where his outstanding productions were *Poem about an Axe*, *My Friend*, and *Romeo and Juliet*. In 1936 he went to the Red Army Theatre in Moscow, where his production of *The Taming of the Shrew* in 1938 made theatre history. (For a detailed account of this see Joseph Macleod's *New Soviet Theatre*, 1943.) He also did there *Field-Marshal Suvorov* (1939), and a lavishly spectacular *Midsummer Night's Dream* (1940). During the Second World War he was evacuated with his company for which he again produced a number of plays, among them *Long, Long Ago* (1942) and the brilliant and topical *Stalingrad* (1944). Back in Moscow, he produced a number of new plays, and in 1951 won acclaim for his revival of *Revizor*, and also for his staging of the new version of Pogodin's *Kremlin Chimes* (1956) and the dramatization of Sholokhov's *Virgin Soil Upturned* (1957). He was one of the outstanding producers of the Soviet Union, and under his direction the theatre, now known as the Central Theatre of the Soviet Army, became one of the most exciting, as well as one of the most satisfying, theatres in the city, intellectually, artistically, and emotionally. A tall, strikingly handsome man, with the courtly manners of an earlier generation, he came to London in 1955, where with Samuel Marshak, the Russian translator of Burns, he attended the theatre conference which resulted in the foundation of the International Federation for Theatre Research. In 1959 he published a book on production. As a producer he was the opposite of Okhlopkov in that he first considered all the details of a production and then combined them into a whole, whereas Okhlopkov sees the whole first and then turns to consider the details.

PORTA, GIAMBATTISTA DELLA, see DELLA PORTA.

PORTABLE THEATRES, see ENGLISH FAIRGROUND AND PORTABLE THEATRES.

PORTER, HENRY (*fl.* 1596–9), English dramatist, mentioned by a contemporary as one of 'the best for comedy amongst us'; he worked for Henslowe, but of the several plays recorded in Henslowe's diary only one survives. This is *The Two Angry Women of Abingdon* (*c.* 1598), a comedy of English rural life which, says Lamb, is 'full of business, humour and merry malice'. Nothing is known of Porter's life, though he appears to have been at Oxford, and he can be identified equally well with any of the numerous Henry Porters listed there towards the end of the sixteenth century.

PORTER, MARY ANN (?–1765), English actress, who understudied Mrs. Barry, and later succeeded her in tragic parts. She had been on the stage as a child, and was a pupil of Betterton. In later life she was an ideal tragedy queen, tall, well-formed, with a deep, modulated voice which rendered her unsuitable for comedy. Barton Booth, who did not admire Anne Oldfield in tragedy, was in raptures over Mrs. Porter's Belvidera. In parts where passion predominated she seemed to be inspired with an enthusiastic ardour capable of raising the coldest spectator to animation. Yet, when grief and tenderness were called for, she was capable of the most affecting softness. Among her original parts were Hermione in *The Distrest Mother* and Alicia in *Jane Shore*. She made her first appearance at Lincoln's Inn Fields in 1699, and her last at Covent Garden in 1742. In private life she was a quiet, respectable person, and enjoyed a long retirement in the society of her friends.

PORTER'S HALL, London (or Rosseter's Blackfriars), a playhouse in the precincts of Blackfriars, erected by Philip Rosseter in 1615. Although authorized by royal patent dated 3 June, it was objected to by the residents, and on 26 Sept. work on the building was stopped by order of the Lord Chief Justice. It must, however, have advanced sufficiently for the accommodating of plays, for the Lady Elizabeth's and the Prince's Men appear to have acted there, and in Jan. 1617 another order was dispatched by the Privy Council for the suppression of the 'playhouse in the Blackfriars almost, if not fully, finished'.

PORTE-SAINT-MARTIN, THÉÂTRE DE LA, Paris. This theatre was built on its present site in 1781, after the burning of the Opéra, and housed the company of the latter until 1794. It was then used for various purposes and did not open again as a theatre until 1810, after which it was used exclusively for strong drama and spectacular works. In 1822 a company of English actors tried unsuccessfully to act *Othello* there. Later the plays of Delavigne and Hugo were given, as were the spectacular fairy-tale shows, *La Biche au bois* and *Pied de mouton*. It was at this theatre, under the management of Harel, that Frédérick made his first triumphant appearances with Mme Dorval. The building was destroyed by fire in 1871, but was rebuilt on the same site from the original plans, and continued its successful career.

PORTMAN THEATRE, London, see west london theatre.

PORTUGAL. Evidence of the nature, or even the existence, of medieval drama diminishes steadily as we move westwards across the Iberian peninsula: plentiful in Catalonia, fragmentary but suggestive in Castile, it is tantalizingly scarce in Portugal. The Latin liturgical play is represented by a solitary example, found in a fourteenth-century breviary at Coimbra: a Christmas shepherds' ceremony for performance at Lauds. In the vernacular, nothing remains to set beside the Castilian *Auto de los Reyes Magos*. Faced with this lack of direct evidence, some scholars have concluded that there was a thriving tradition, but that the plays were never written down or have since been lost; most, however, believe that religious drama never really took root in Portugal until the sixteenth century. There were, of course, symbolic representations (for example, the placing of the reserved sacrament, or of a cross, in a sepulchre on Good Friday), and in the 1470s the Archbishop of Oporto specifically permits 'some good and devout representation such as that of the Manger or the Three Kings or other similar subjects'. It does not, however, seem that such representations went beyond symbol and tableau.

Church legislation is naturally more concerned with prohibition than with exhortation, and from the thirteenth century we find a series of attempts, presumably unsuccessful, to prevent clergy from attending profane performances, to keep lewd *jogos* (games) outside the church precincts, and to prevent the use of ecclesiastical vestments for comic purposes. It is certain that there were burlesque sermons and parodic ceremonies, and likely that some rudimentary form of farce grew up; there is, unfortunately, no way of discovering the precise form that it took. The performers would normally be the *mimi* and *joculatores*, or wandering entertainers, so often condemned by the Church, but there are indications that priests also took part from time to time. The earliest performers known to us by name are Bonamis and Acompaniado (presumably professional rather than baptismal names), who are referred to in a document of 1193. Their performance is called an *arremedillum*, a term which appears to mean simply a comic or imitative act.

These popular entertainments appealed to all levels of society, but they later had to compete in Court circles with *momos* (mummers). Accounts of such performances appear in chronicles of the later fifteenth century, and the elaborate mummings of Christmas 1500 are fully described in a letter from the Spanish Ambassador in Lisbon. Classical, chivalresque and exotic scenes were represented with the help of rich costume and complex mechanism. There was little dramatic action and no dialogue, the element of pageantry being dominant throughout, but the mummers' technique can be traced in some of Gil Vicente's plays, and the mechanism evolved for such festivities was fruitfully used in later allegorical drama.

Another form not in itself dramatic but capable of dramatic development was the dialogue poem. In one form or another—the allegorical debate, the flyting—this was one of the most persistent and widespread of medieval European genres. The Galician–Portuguese *cancioneiros* (song-books) contain numerous poems of the thirteenth and fourteenth centuries in which the dialogue is vigorous and often scurrilous, and this tradition is continued and expanded in the vast *Cancioneiro Geral* (1516). Here, a few poets approach the ill-defined frontier that separates dialogue poems and true drama, and one poet, Anrique da

Mota, seems to have crossed it. Four of his dialogue works are extant, together with one in which he and Gil Vicente apparently collaborated with others. The keynote of Mota's work is satirical treatment of easily recognizable types, and the language that he puts into the mouth of a young Negress (similar language is used by a few other poets in the *Cancioneiro*) foreshadows the 'special languages' evolved by Vicente. There is no record of the staging of any of Mota's works, but some at least are easily stageable, and one of these, the 260-line *Farsa do Alfaiate* (composed between 1496 and 1506), may be earlier than any of Vicente's work.

The festivities of Christmas 1500, mentioned above, were preceded on Christmas Eve by music and 'shepherds, who came into the chapel dancing and singing "gloria in excelsis Deo"'. This suggests that the influence of Juan del Encina's religious eclogues was beginning to be felt in Portugal, and may well be connected with King Manuel's marriage to the Spanish princess, María. In June 1502 the queen gave birth to a son, and among the celebrations was a monologue by Gil Vicente (*c.* 1465–*c.* 1537), the *Auto da Visitação*. Despite its Portuguese title, this work, Vicente's first, is in Spanish; a type of Spanish, moreover, that is tinged by *sayagués*, the rustic dialect of the Salamanca region used by Encina and Lucas Fernández for the speech of their shepherds. Thus both in genre and in language, Vicente begins under the tutelage of Encina. It is not easy to trace his subsequent development, since the first collected edition of his plays, the 1562 *Copilaçam* prepared by his son Luís Vicente, puts them into categories that now seem unacceptable, and gives dates that are often suspect. Probably the best division of his work is a fivefold one: eclogues, moralities, farces, romantic plays, allegorical spectacles.

The eclogues, of which the *Auto pastoril castelhano* is a good example, are more highly developed than their prototype, the *Auto da Visitação*, and make good use of dialogue, but they are still obviously dependent on Encina. Gradually, however, a new form grew out of them: the morality, sharing some features with medieval European tradition (though there is no sign that this took root in Portugal), but owing most to Vicente's own powers of invention. The first step is taken in the *Auto da Fé* (1510). The *Auto dos Quatro Tempos* (*c.* 1511) is already half-way to the morality, and from it Vicente went on to his masterpieces in this form, the *Auto da Alma* and the trilogy of the *Barcas* (boats): *Barca do Inferno*, *Barca do Purgatório*, and *Barca da Glória*. These four works, composed within a short period (1517–*c.* 1519), combine the morality play with outspoken social comment, possible only because of Vicente's privileged position at Court. Where the eclogues needed only actors (tradition has it that the author was also the actor in the *Auto da Visitação*), the *Barcas* trilogy calls for fairly elaborate scenery, for which the mumming tradition was an obvious source of inspiration, though the Corpus Christi processions of Spain may also have contributed something. Vicente is unquestionably the greatest religious dramatist of this period in the Peninsula, and his moralities belong to the theatre of Spain as well as that of Portugal, both because some were written in Spanish and because his true successors are to be found in the Spanish writers of *autos sacramentales*.

Whereas in the morality Vicente had to rely on a Spanish tradition which he then transformed, his farces seem to have had behind them not only the sketches of Anrique da Mota, but indigenous popular entertainments. He was thus able to find his feet at once, and the *Auto da Índia* (1509) has great technical assurance. In this and in later works (*Farsa de Inês Pereira*, 1523, is among the best, and is unlike the others in having a clearly defined and unified plot) Vicente combines knockabout humour and pungent social satire. He evolves a series of 'special languages' for different racial and social groups, and his peasants learn to speak rustic Portuguese instead of *sayagués*. Here, as in the eclogues, the staging is simple: a dividing curtain would allow simultaneous scenes, and not much else would be needed. Vicente went on writing farces all his life, but from about 1520 his attention was mainly devoted to other forms. For a few years he experimented with romantic comedy: *Comédia Rubena* (1521) shows the amatory misfortunes and final triumph of the heroine; *Dom Duardos* (1522) and *Amadis de Gaula* (?1523) put chivalresque fiction on the stage in a convention owing much to Court mummings; and *Comédia do Viúvo* (1524) leans heavily on the figure of the disguised nobleman. This development of farce into comedy has been plausibly attributed to the influence of the *comedias a fantasía* (novelesque comedies) of Bartolomé de Torres Naharro, a Spaniard with an Italian background.

The morality and the romantic comedy were theatrically the most promising forms evolved by Vicente, but in the last twelve years of his life he turned chiefly to secular allegorical fantasies, leading away from the main paths that European drama was to follow in the sixteenth and seventeenth centuries, though not necessarily away from dramatic achievement—a recent critic has compared Vicente's final technique to that of Brecht. There are hints of this form as far back as the *Auto dos Quatro Tempos*, but the characteristic note of the last period is a blend of allegory, lyricism, uninhibited satire, and lavish staging. Sometimes there is an organic plot, as in *Auto da Feira* (*c.* 1526–8), sometimes the work is held together only by the visually dazzling allegorical framework, as in the *Frágua do Amor* (1524). The splendour and complexity of the stage devices used in these works is a direct outcome of the fifteenth-century Court mummings, and there is a striking similarity between the mummings of Christmas 1500 and the staging of the *Frágua do Amor*.

Vicente had always been a deviser of Court entertainments rather than a professional dramatist, and his later works merely accentuate this fact. They move away from the kind of drama that could take root outside the Court, and when the Court lost interest fairly soon after Vicente's death, the way of his successors was hard.

Post-Vicentine dramatists fall into two main groups, those who tried to follow the paths indicated by Vicente, and those who turned to classical and Renaissance models. The earliest figure of any importance in the former group is Afonso Álvares, a mulatto who is probably the originator of the hagiographic drama in Portugal. Vicente had written an 80-line Spanish playlet on St. Martin, but had never tried to develop the form. Álvares, commissioned by the Church, combined stories from the *Legenda Aurea* with comic elements taken from Vicente. His *Auto de Santo António* was performed in 1531, and three more of his plays survive. The blind Baltasar Días, living in Madeira, wrote plays of this and other types. Though Días's literary quality is poor, his work won and retained great popularity, especially by circulation in chap-books. António Ribeiro Chiado (?–1591), an unfrocked Franciscan who conducted a long and scurrilous controversy with Afonso Álvares, wrote sketches of Lisbon life, usually dispensing with a plot. He had a good eye for types of character and a good ear for dialogue. António Prestes (*fl. c.* 1565), highly regarded by his contemporaries and described by Manuel de Melo in the seventeenth century as the equal of Gil Vicente, has been condemned by most modern critics for his structural weakness and his obscurity of language. Seven plays are extant: six domestic comedies containing some attractive scenes, and an ambitious morality, *Auto da Ave Maria.* Of the three plays written by Luís Vaz de Camões (*c.* 1525–80), best known as the poet of the *Lusiads*, two have classical subjects, but all are treated in a non-classical manner deriving ultimately from Vicente. *Os Anfitriões*, based on the *Amphitruo* of Plautus, and *El-Rei Seleuco*, a story of royal love and self-sacrifice, were performed when Camões was in Lisbon as a young man. His best play, *Filodemo*, has a plot recalling that of chivalresque fiction, and its tone blends romance with realism. It is believed to have been performed in Goa before the Governor-General in about 1555, though it may have been written much earlier. An author who deserves mention rather for historical interest than for literary stature is Francisco da Costa (1533–91), who died in captivity in Morocco. During his long imprisonment he wrote many poems and seven plays on biblical or hagiographic subjects. Some at least were performed by the Christian captives, and they have survived in manuscript, the only examples of their kind; they have recently been published. In the closing years of the sixteenth century, Simão Machado composed two talented and original plays, successful modifications of the Vicentine tradition: an historical drama, *O Cerco de Diu*, and a pastoral comedy, *Comédia da Pastora Alfea.*

In conscious opposition to these dramatists is the classical tradition founded by Francisco de Sá de Miranda (1481–1558). Neither the work of Plautus and Terence nor the drama of Renaissance Italy had had any fundamental effect on the Portuguese theatre by the time Miranda returned, in 1526, from a stay of several years in Italy. In the preface to his first play, *Estrangeiros* (?1526), Miranda states his aims as a writer. Both this play and the later *Vilhalpandos* (?1538) are in prose, with divisions into act and scene; the plots are complex and the influence of both classical and Renaissance comedy is strongly marked. Despite some attempt to transpose this into Portuguese terms, the plays are on the whole unsuccessful, for where Vicente's aim was performance, Miranda's was literary correctness. Greater, but still limited, success was attained by António Ferreira (1528–69) with his two comedies, *Cioso* and *Bristo.* Ferreira's real achievement, however, is his authorship of the greatest Portuguese tragedy, *Castro.* Before Ferreira there had been a translation, via Spanish, of Sophocles' *Electra*; a fragmentary tragedy of *Cleópatra* by Miranda; and Latin plays written and performed in the College of Arts at Coimbra and the Jesuit College at Évora. This neo-Latin drama (whose best writer was Father Luís da Cruz, ?–1604) had, of course, very little appeal outside the universities and perhaps the Court, but Ferreira was able to draw on it and on the Latin plays of the Scottish humanist George Buchanan (1506–82), who came to Coimbra as professor in 1548; more important, he was able to acclimatize it in a way that seemed impossible with classical comedy. His subject was the tragic story of Inês de Castro, mistress of the heir to the throne, murdered at the king's command as an act of state policy; her murder wrecks the lives of her lover and of the king. Ferreira had no worthy successors, and *Castro* remained an isolated achievement. A third writer usually described as a classical dramatist is Jorge Ferreira de Vasconcelos (*c.* 1515–?), but his *Eufrosina*, inspired by *La Celestina*, is, like its source, a novel in dialogue rather than a play, designed for reading (or reading aloud) and not for acting. The same is true of Vasconcelos's other two works in this form.

During the sixteenth century the forces tending to widen the audience for the drama were counterbalanced by the forces tending to restrict drama in Portuguese. One of the main restrictive forces was the activity of the Inquisition, whose Indexes became increasingly comprehensive: the 1562 edition of Gil Vicente's works escaped unscathed, but the second edition (1586) was heavily censored, and the total loss of some chap-book plays may be due to this censorship. Inquisitorial activities and episcopal prohibitions also extended to theatrical performances. Another hampering factor was loss of interest by the Court before the drama had found firm support elsewhere. On the other hand, the number of outlets grew: by the last quarter of the century, the plays of Vicente's followers were being performed in the houses of the aristocracy and, if the subject was suitable, in churches and monasteries, while the universities and sometimes the aristocracy saw performances of classical drama. Chap-books circulated widely, though the publication in 1586 of the *Primeira parte dos Autos e Comédias portugueses* (twelve plays by Camões, Prestes, and others) was never completed by the promised later volumes. In 1580, Philip II of Spain became King of Portugal as well (the dual monarchy lasted until 1640), and Portuguese literature quickly declined to a subordinate position. Some Portuguese dramatists wrote only in Spanish, and the growing opportunities for the theatre were largely taken up by Spanish companies presenting Spanish plays; it has indeed been suggested that some Spanish dramatists wrote with half an eye on a Portuguese audience. The Spanish connexion was probably responsible for the beginnings of the commercial theatre. In 1588, King Philip forbade the performance of plays in Lisbon except with the permission of the Hospital de Todos os Santos, which was to receive a share of the profits (this monopoly lasted until 1743). Plays were performed in *pátios de comédias*, the equivalent of the *corrales* of Madrid (see SPAIN), originally mere open courtyards, later covered and made more comfortable. The oldest, the Pátio do Poço Borratém, was already in existence in 1588, and the most famous, the Pátio das Arcas, was established in 1594. Burned down in 1697 and rebuilt in 1700, it was finally destroyed by the earthquake of 1755. Other *pátios* were founded in the seventeenth century, and one of these, the Pátio dos Condes, attained great prosperity in the eighteenth century.

Seventeenth-century Portugal thus presents the paradox of flourishing theatrical performances and an indigenous drama that is almost dead. The only noteworthy play in Portuguese is *O Fidalgo Aprendiz* (*c.* 1646), by Francisco Manuel de Melo (1608–66). Melo here enriches the tradition of Vicentine comedy with classical, Italian and Spanish elements; his play is a possible source of Molière's *Bourgeois gentilhomme*, but despite its popularity and its merits it failed to revive the vernacular drama in Portugal. A vigorous tradition was to be found only in the Jesuit colleges, where elaborate spectacle was used for didactic ends (see JESUIT DRAMA). One of the most lavish productions was staged at the Colégio de Santo Antão in 1619 to celebrate the king's entry into Lisbon.

By 1700 the neo-Latin drama had died out, and there remained only the commercial theatre, where the dominant forms were Spanish plays and popular comedies of little merit. These were challenged early in the eighteenth century by the Italian opera, which increasingly replaced other dramatic forms, and by a new vogue for puppets (*bonecos* or *bonifrates*), which often parodied the opera. From this improbable combination arose the work of António José da Silva (1705–39). Born in Brazil of a Jewish family, he was brought to Portugal at the age of 8, became in his late twenties the most popular dramatist of the day, and was executed by the Inquisition on charges of doubtful validity. His plays, produced at the Teatro do Bairro Alto (where the first Portuguese company of professional actors was formed), are best described as operatic comedies; most of them, including *Vida do Grande D. Quixote* (1733), seem to have been puppet-plays, though *Guerras do Alecrim e da Mangerona* (1737), probably his best work, had human actors. His structure is weak, but there is excellent comedy of situation and of language (often provided by *graciosos*, comic servants taken over from the Spanish tradition), and vigorous social satire. Once again, a talented dramatist had no fit successors, though *O Falso Heroísmo* of António Dinis da Cruz e Silva (1731–99) combines humour and social criticism effectively. The influence of the Spanish drama gradually waned and, after controversy in the 1740s, that of France established a theoretical superiority; French plays were often performed, though the Portuguese drama scarcely benefited from this. In the second half of the century the Arcadian movement made an effort to work out a coherent dramatic theory. The leading figure here is Pedro António Correia Garção (1724–72), a good poet and critic. The attempts of Manuel de Figueiredo (1725–1801) to write neo-classical plays in accordance with Arcadian theories were, however, notably unsuccessful.

Where the Arcadians had failed, one man succeeded, though only temporarily: João Baptista de Almeida Garrett (1799–1854), the leading figure of Portuguese Romanticism. The first of his plays to be produced, in 1819, was *Lucrécia*. Garrett became involved in Liberal politics—his play *Catão* (1821) has clear political implications—and was an exile in England. After the Revolution of 1836 he was appointed Inspector-General of Theatres. He founded the Teatro Nacional (later the Teatro de D. Maria II) and the Conservatório, and determined to provide a repertoire of Portuguese plays himself, beginning with his first major dramatic work, *Um Auto de Gil Vicente* (1838), a love story in an historical setting. This is the starting-point of Romantic drama in Portugal (*Lucrécia* and *Catao* are neo-classical). Garrett's masterpiece is *Frei Luís de Sousa* (1843), a personal tragedy set in a time of national tragedy, the late sixteenth century. The characters and their situation are convincing, and their emotions are powerfully conveyed.

Garrett founded a National Theatre, but he could not found a tradition. His immediate followers were minor writers who absorbed only the superficial elements of his work, as in the historical dramas of Mendes Leal (1818–86). A long-term result of Garrett's work was that for over a century most of the leading Portuguese writers felt impelled to write at least one play. Some of these plays are bad, and the good ones are better read than staged. Among such authors are the poet and historian Alexandre Herculano (1810–77), the novelist Camilo Castelo Branco (1825–90), the essayist Oliveira Martins (1845–94), and the poets Eugénio de Castro (1869–1944), Mário de Sá-Carneiro (1890–1916), and Fernando Pessoa (1888–1935). The theatres of late nineteenth-century Lisbon were dominated by the well-made historical plays and polite comedies of João da Câmara (1852–1908), who could also be realistic in *Os Velhos* (1893) and a Maeterlinckian symbolist in *Meia Noite* (1900). Realistic scenes from modern life are found also in Marcelino Mesquita (1856–1919), and became the prevailing fashion with the foundation of the Teatro Livre (1904) and the success of Ramada Curto (1886–1961) and Alfredo Cortês (1880–1946). Raul Brandão (1867–1930) adds psychological insight in such works as *O Doido e a Morte* (1923).

The theatrical censorship imposed in the early 1930s suppressed morally and politically dangerous plays, and for a long time isolated Portugal from modern European developments in the theatre. The first signs of new life came in the late 1940s with a number of plays that, barred from the stage by their subject or its treatment, were aimed chiefly at the reader, while interest in theatrical technique was stimulated by the Teatro Estúdio do Salitre (founded 1946). These two currents have now converged, giving Portugal at least the promise of a vigorous modern drama. While the commercial theatres of Lisbon have on the whole presented safe mediocrity to dwindling audiences, the Teatro Experimental in Oporto (founded in 1953) has, while making many mistakes, been an invaluable outlet for the new drama. Plays have come from established poets such as Miguel Torga (1904–) and Jorge de Sena (1919–) and from a group of young dramatists. Some of the plays have been staged in Oporto (the censor sometimes intervening), some abroad, a few in the commercial theatre, while some still await performance. Among the most successful have been *O Vagabundo das Mãos de Ouro* (1961) by Romeu Correia (1917–) and *Felizmente há Luar* (1961), by Luís de Sttau Monteiro (1926–), the latter showing signs of Brecht's influence. The two leading figures are, however, Bernardo Santareno (1924–), a moralist who shows equal concern for ultimate problems and for the lives of ordinary people in *A Promessa* (1957) and *O Lugre* (1959); and Luís Francisco Rebello (1924–), who turned from early expressionist work to the social protest of plays like *O Dia Seguinte* (1953) and *Os Pássaros de Asas Cortadas* (1959), and who has become an outstanding dramatic critic.

The story of Portuguese drama is one of individual achievements (Vicente, Ferreira, da Silva, Garrett) and unfulfilled hopes. External reasons in the sixteenth century, simple lack of dramatic talent in the nineteenth, prevented the growth of a vigorous native tradition. Today Portugal faces the exciting prospect of a drama aware of social problems and of theatrical technique, interested in real people and real speech, open to European influences and to the country's past achievement. When the external conditions become more favourable, the hopes of the past may at last be fulfilled. (For a view of the interior of the San Carlos Theatre, Lisbon, see No. 45.)

ALAN DEYERMOND

PORTUGUESE-AMERICAN THEATRE, see SOUTH AMERICA, 2.

POSSART, ERNST VON (1841–1921), German actor and theatre manager, who made his first appearance on the stage at Breslau in 1860, where he played Iago. This began his apprenticeship to tragedy, of which he was a distinguished exponent in later years, some of his finest parts being Shylock, Franz Moor, Mephistopheles, Carlos in *Clavigo*, and Nathan the Wise in Lessing's play of that name. In 1864 von Possart was in Munich, where he became manager of the theatre in 1875, and Intendant General of the Royal Theatres in 1893. He was the founder of the Prinz Regent Theater, and of festivals in commemoration of Wagner and Mozart held between 1893 and 1905. In 1910 he appeared in New York in a repertory of distinguished plays, with much success. A fine-looking man, with an alert, intelligent face and flashing eyes, he was noted for the beauty of his voice and the dignity and ease of his movements. He adapted a number of plays for the German stage, including some of Shakespeare's.

POSTERS, THEATRICAL. If the poster may be defined as a temporary public announcement by means of letters or pictures, or both, it is at least as old as the Egypt of Ptolemy, for there is in existence a papyrus of about 150 B.C. giving details of two slaves escaped from the neighbourhood of Alexandria. The Greeks were in the habit of inscribing notices on whitewashed walls or on wooden boards. They used in addition a kind of rotating square column on the four faces of which inscriptions were either painted or engraved. It is probable that some of these inscriptions referred to theatrical performances.

Theatrical publicity was certainly known to the Romans, for considerable evidence has survived of the way in which the problem was handled in such a representative town as Pompeii. A so-called 'album' was discovered in the ruins in the early years of the nineteenth century. It consisted of a wall divided by pilasters with panels, and on these it was the custom to announce in red and black paint the details of gladiatorial shows and other attractions. It is believed not only that these advertisements had the names of the principal actors in large letters, in the modern manner, but that it was at least sometimes the custom to add a pictorial representation of one of the scenes of the play as well. At all events Pliny mentions a certain Calludes as excelling in this kind of painting.

There follows a long gap in the history of the poster. In the Dark Ages the times were too disturbed, and most people, even among the upper classes, illiterate. The Middle Ages made use not of posters but of heraldry and criers. It was not until the end of the fifteenth century that posters, used for political purposes, once more appeared. With the rise of the printing press their usage became of such importance that governments were forced to take notice of it, and to make stringent laws for its regulation. Official posters (e.g. royal proclamations) were among the first to have any pictorial content, usually merely the Royal Arms.

About the middle of the seventeenth century, in France, both the actors and the religious confraternities began to make use of posters. In England, according to Brewer's *Dictionary of Phrase and Fable*, before the Fire of London (1666) the posts which protected pedestrians in the street were used for affixing theatrical and other announcements, whence the name of 'posters'. But no specimen seems to have survived. The earliest English play-bill in the Enthoven Collection is for Drury Lane, 1718, and it is not pictorial (for earlier bills see PLAYBILL).

However, before this pictorial posters had been used, at least in France, for recruiting purposes. The illustrations were in woodcut, and were sometimes coloured by hand in a similar manner to the broadsheets of the period. The *Cabinet des Estampes* in Paris has also pictorial posters issued by troupes of acrobats in the early years of the eighteenth century. Woodcut continued to be the approved method of embellishing posters until the rise of commercial lithography in the first half of the nineteenth century.

In this development France took the lead, and some of the finest artists of the Romantic period produced posters, generally advertising books or periodicals, and for the most part in one tint only. Various attempts were made to add the colour which was felt to be necessary. Roucher tried to introduce the methods which had proved successful in the production of wallpapers, others reverted to the more primitive practice of stencilling. The honour of bringing the true colour-poster to perfection belongs to Jules Chéret.

Jules Chéret was born in 1836 in Paris, but he served his apprenticeship as a lithographer in England. In 1866, profiting by the introduction of machines making use of large lithographic stones, he launched out on his career as probably the most prolific poster-artist of all time. He produced nearly a thousand posters, all of them good and some of them masterpieces. Working for the most part directly on the stone, he was able, with the limited number of colours at his disposal, to produce the most diverse effects. He was an excellent draughtsman with a pronounced individual style, and the very narrowness of his range was an advantage in his work for the theatres, music-halls, and 'dancings' of Paris. From 1867, when he announced the appearance of Sarah Bernhardt in *La Biche au Bois*, to the end of the century, his gay and dancing figures called the passers-by to a perpetual carousal at the Folies-Bergère, at the Alcazar d'Hiver, at the Cirque Fernando, or the Moulin-Rouge.

His example inspired a host of others, some of whom, like the brothers Choubrac, followed him closely, while others, like Eugène Grasset and Mucha (see No. 170), struck out a line of their own. But the artist who took up the manner of Chéret and transformed it most completely was Toulouse-Lautrec. Other well-known French artists have designed posters—Forain, Willette, Valloton, Métivel, Anquetin, Bonnavel, Guillaume, and Steinlen—but, with the possible exception of the last, none has so completely fused his own personality with the theatrical poster as the artist who gave the world such masterpieces as 'Aristide Bruant dans son cabaret' (see No. 172), 'Jane Avril', and 'La Goulue — Moulin-Rouge'. Among the finest *affiches* of Steinlen may be mentioned his 'Yvette Guilbert' and his 'Mothu et Doria — Scènes Impressionnistes'. Posters—theatrical posters in particular—have never reached a higher standard than that attained on the Paris hoardings in the 1890s.

The first English theatrical poster of any note was designed by Fred Walker to advertise a dramatized version of *The Woman in White*, produced in 1871. This, however, was not a lithograph but a wood-engraving (for an earlier, somewhat crude, example, see No. 169). The Beggarstaff brothers (William Nicholson and James Pryde) were among the pioneers of the poster in England, and most of their work was done for the theatre. Their method was the highly original one of building up the design in cut-out layers of different shades of brown paper. Their work was commissioned by Irving for *Hamlet* and *Don Quixote* (see No. 173), and the original cut-out designs for these have been preserved.

English artists in general took longer to assimilate the lessons of Impressionism than their French colleagues, so that while the Frenchmen were already thinking in terms of flat colour and the balance of masses, the English had not yet shaken themselves free from the trammels of academic realism. So we find advertisers buying pictures (the classic example is Millais's 'Bubbles') and transforming them into advertisements by the simple process of adding a caption. However, in the mid-1890s posters by Aubrey Beardsley for the Avenue Theatre began to appear, and the admirable poster-artist Dudley Hardy produced simple and effective designs for a number of plays.

In any purely aesthetic evaluation the melodrama poster is usually left out of account, but it must be admitted that it loomed much larger on the hoardings of the last twenty-five years of the nineteenth century and the first decade of the twentieth than any other kind of theatrical advertisement. Its method was one of blatant realism turned to the service of situations highly coloured in both senses of the word. The lurid incident, the pathetic situation, the improving sentiment—these were the stock-in-trade of the designer, who was more concerned to move the emotions than to produce a work of art. For such plays as *It's Never Too Late To Mend*, *The Great World of London* (see No. 171), *The Silver King*, *Uncle Tom's Cabin* (with its almost unbroken run of eighty years), *East Lynne*, *The Streets of London*, and the Irish dramas of Dion Boucicault, immense numbers of posters were produced, for the most part designed by men whose names have faded into obscurity.

The traditions of the artistic poster were carried on in the early years of the twentieth century by Frank Brangwyn, Cecil Aldin, Phil May, John Hassall, Maurice Greiffenhagen, Will Owen, and others. Later some excellent theatrical posters were produced by Lovat Fraser (notably for *The Beggar's Opera*) (see No. 174), Aubrey Hammond, Doris and Anna Zinkeisen, Guy Kortright, Bert Thomas, Norman Wilkinson of Four Oaks, Thomas Derrick, M. H. Lawrence, Charles A. Buchel, Charles Mozley (see No. 175), and John Garside.

The poster all over the continent of Europe was much influenced by the French school of designers. In Germany artists of the calibre of Max Klinger and Franz Stück did not disdain to design for the hoardings, but for a whole generation advertising art in central Europe was dominated by the figure of Ludwig Hohlwein. The stimulus given to the German theatre by the work of Reinhardt was manifest also in the sphere of theatrical publicity. In Austria Emil Orlik produced some excellent posters. In Belgium the work of Meunier, V. Mignot, H. Cassiers, and Toussaint did much to improve prevailing standards. The Russian theatre had few poster-designers of note, but the Diaghilev Ballet employed first-rate artists not only for its costumes and décor, but for its public announcements. Some of the costume designs of Léon Bakst made excellent posters with hardly any change. The best Spanish posters are those advertising bull-fights. They are generally bold in conception and striking in colour, but their designers are, for the most part, anonymous (for a modern Rumanian theatre poster, see No. 176).

Before 1900 American posters, with the exception of some designs by Matt Morgan, were of the kind described above as advertising English melodrama (see No. 168). With the 1890s a new era began, Louis J. Mead and W. H. Bradley leading, for the most part with small decorative placards. Then such well-known artists as Maxfield Parrish, James Montgomery Flagg, Will Denslow, and Charles Dana Gibson took up the work, to be followed by Harrison Fisher, Norman Rockwell, Karl Johnson, McClelland Barclay, and others. Not all of these, however, worked exclusively or even chiefly for the theatre. Indeed, of recent years theatrical advertising has found it difficult to compete with the ampler funds of the vendors of other products. On a Paris hoarding of the 1890s most of the posters displayed were advertisements of theatres, music-halls, or some other kind of entertainment. Today most posters seem to advertise alcoholic beverages. Theatre managers are now compelled to content themselves with more modest displays, and there has therefore been a revival of something like the old playbill: a small announcement giving the name of the theatre and play, the principal actors, &c., adorned sometimes, but by no means always, by an appropriate design. This seems to be true of most countries, and so it may be said that the theatrical advertisement in poster form has come full circle and ended where it began, as a simple announcement affixed to a wall or post or column. With the advance of other methods of publicity (the name of the principal actors 'in lights', &c.) it seems unlikely that the ambitious theatrical poster will ever be revived in any quantity. As for quality, that can hardly surpass the standard reached in Paris in 1895.

JAMES LAVER

POTIER DES CAILLETIÈRES, CHARLES-GABRIEL (1774–1838), French actor, considered by Talma the greatest comedian of his day. Of good family, he was in the army during the Revolution, but in 1796 went to Paris and decided to adopt the stage as a profession. He was for some years in the provinces, and in May 1809 made his début at the Théâtre des Variétés. He was slow in making his way into popular favour, but once established he never lost his hold on the affection of the public. His last years were spent at the Palais-Royal, where he first appeared in 1831. His one fault was a weak voice, but this was offset by the subtlety and vivacity of his acting, which conveyed his meaning without words. He had two sons, of whom one was a good actor, though overshadowed by the memory of his father, and the author of a number of vaudevilles.

POTTER, MRS. JAMES BROWN- (*née* CORA URQUHART) (1859–1936), one of the first American society women to go on the stage. She was trained by David Belasco, though she never appeared under his management, being first seen as a professional, after innumerable amateur performances for charity, in London in 1886. With Kyrle Bellew as her leading man she toured Australia and the Far East, preceded by immense publicity, and returned to London in 1892. During the Boer War she raised large sums of money for war charities by her recitation of such poems as 'The Absent-Minded Beggar', and in 1904 became manager of the Savoy. Her venture was unsuccessful, and ended in bankruptcy, after which she went on tour, retiring from the stage in 1912.

POWELL, GEORGE (1668–1714), English actor, who between 1687 and the year of his premature death created many gallant and tragic roles. He was Bellamour in *The Old Bachelor* (1693) and the first to play Lothario in *The Fair Penitent* (1703), and, says Barton Baker, 'he wanted only sobriety and industry to have risen to be one of the finest actors of his time'. As it was, drink and brawling kept him back, and he was soon outdistanced by Wilks. He caused many disturbances in the theatre, was usually imperfect in his part and drunk on the stage, where, it is said, he made such violent love that Vanbrugh grew nervous for the actress. In spite of his debaucheries Christopher Rich tolerated him because, in his capacity as director of rehearsals, he kept the actors content on low salaries. He was the author of two tragedies given at Drury Lane, and of several comedies.

POWELL, MARTIN, a puppet showman who flourished between 1709 and 1715. He is first heard of in Bath in 1709. He moved to London in the winter of that year, and in Jan. 1710 was giving performances in a theatre in St. Martin's Lane. In the following year he was installed in the Little Piazza at Covent Garden, where he gave winter seasons of puppet-plays, alternating with summer seasons in Bath, until 1713. He also visited Bristol and Oxford, probably in the autumn. In 1714 he was at the Spring Garden in Charing Cross. George Speaight, who gives a detailed account of Powell's movements in *Studies in English Theatre History* (1952), believes that he died shortly before 1725, and that he probably toured Europe, and also wrote his own plays based on popular tales and ballads or on the Bible. This 'Shakespeare of the minor stage' is possibly the person referred to in Disher's *Clowns and Pantomimes* as 'Robert Powell, a showman popular in France, Germany, and Spain, as well as England'.

POWELL, WILLIAM (1735–69), English actor, a pupil and protégé of David Garrick at Drury Lane, where he was the first to play Lovewell in *The Clandestine Marriage* (1766). During Garrick's absence abroad in 1763–4 Powell played his parts, with great success, and later, tiring of a subordinate position, joined Colman and Harris as part-patentee of Covent Garden, where he played Honeywell in the first production of *The Good-Natured Man* (1768). He died suddenly, at the height of his success, 'having every perfection but experience', while in Bristol, where he was managing a theatre.

POWER. (1) TYRONE (1795–1841), Irish actor, son of a strolling player, who essayed both the army and the navy before he finally took to acting in 1815. For some years he played light comedy in the provinces and minor theatres of London, but made little mark in the theatrical world until in 1826 he was unexpectedly called upon to play a comic Irish role. This he did with such success that he succeeded to the stage Irishmen left vacant by the death of Charles Connor, and appeared at both the patent theatres and the Haymarket in such parts as Murtoch Delany, Dennis Brulgruddery, Lucius O'Trigger, Major O'Flaherty, and Dr. O'Toole. A handsome, high-spirited man with thick curling hair, a rich brogue, and a fine singing voice, he quickly became a favourite with the public. He also turned to authorship and produced a number of light comedies and farces—*St. Patrick's Eve* (1832), *Paddy Cary, the Boy of Clogheen* (1833), *O'Flannigan and the Fairies* (1836)—in which he appeared himself. His last appearance in London was made in 1840. He then left for America, where he had already made two visits and was much admired, and on the return journey was drowned in the sinking of s.s. *President*. His death was a great loss, both financially and artistically, to the English and Irish theatres, where he was always sure of packed houses. It was a sad coincidence that his friend and fellow actor, E. W. Elton, was also drowned two years later, in the wreck of the s.s. *Pegasus*. Power left a wife (*née* Anne Gilbert) and eight children, of whom only one, Maurice (? –1849), was on the stage; but another son, Harold, who married an actress and singer whose stage name was Ethel Levenu, was the father of (2) (FREDERICK) TYRONE EDMOND (1869–1931), whose stage career was mainly in America, where he was leading man for such actresses as Mrs. Fiske, Julia Marlowe, Mrs. Leslie Carter, and Henrietta Crossman. He was also a prominent member of Augustin Daly's company from 1890 to 1898, appearing with it in London, his birth-place, where he played also with Tree and Irving. In his later years he appeared mainly in Shakespearian parts. His son, (3) TYRONE (1914–58), had a distinguished career in films which overshadowed his work in the theatre. But he was for some years on the American stage, making his first appearance in New York as a page in *Hamlet*. Later parts were Fred in *Romance* (1934), with Leontovich; Benvolio in *Romeo and Juliet* (1935); de Poulengy in *Saint Joan* (1936), with Katharine Cornell; and Gettner in the New York production of *The Dark is Light Enough* (1955). In 1950 he was seen in London in *Mister Roberts*.

Harold's niece, Norah, was the mother of the distinguished theatre director Sir Tyrone Guthrie.

PRADON, JACQUES (1644–98), a French dramatist remembered only for his rivalry with Racine. Little is known of his early years, but he had some facility in verse-writing, and Racine's detractors, looking round for a figure-head, found in him just what they wanted. His *Phèdre* (1677) was applauded at the expense of Racine's, a verdict which has been reversed by posterity. Pradon's first play was *Pirame et Thisbé* (1674), done at the Hôtel de Bourgogne with some success, due again to the cabal against Racine. Pradon owes whatever posthumous fame he has achieved to the greatness of the enemies he roused against him, including the redoubtable Boileau, and so the names, at least, of his plays are remembered, though they are seldom read or acted.

PRAETEXTA, see FABULA, 4.

PRATINAS (*fl.* 496 B.C.) of Phlius, an important figure in pre-Aeschylean drama (see SATYR-DRAMA).

PREHAUSER, GOTTFRIED (1699–1769), see AUSTRIA.

PRESTON, THOMAS (*fl.* 1570), the unknown author of a popular early English tragicomedy, *Cambyses King of Persia*, written with bombastic eloquence, thus giving rise to Falstaff's remark that he must speak in passion, and would do it in 'King Cambyses' vein'. The play helps to mark the transition from the medieval Morality play to the Elizabethan historical drama. Its author, who may also have written the heroical romance, *Sir Clyomon and Sir Clamydes*, given at about the same time, and some broadsheet ballads, should not, according to Chambers, be confused with the academic Thomas Preston (1537–98) who was a Fellow of King's, Cambridge, and later Vice-Chancellor. In 1592 the latter, as Master of Trinity Hall, was one of a number of petitioners who asked for the banning of plays in Cambridge.

PRÉVILLE [PIERRE-LOUIS DUBUS] (1721–99), French actor, who was perhaps, after J. B. Raisin, the greatest comedian the Comédie-Française had yet known. He had an unhappy childhood, and was befriended by a wealthy man who put him into a lawyer's office and forbade him to go to the Comédie-Française, hoping thus to put an end to his hankerings after an actor's life. On the death of his benefactor, Dubus, as he then was, considered himself released from his promise, and went to see *Le Légataire universel*, with F.-A. Poisson as Crispin. He afterwards gave so masterly an imitation of Poisson that he was encouraged to join a company of provincial actors. He went to the Comédie-Française in 1753, replacing Poisson in comic roles. He was also excellent in Marivaux's plays, partnered by Mlle Dangeville. Of less than medium height, he had sharp features and expressive eyes. His only faults, in the eyes of his companions, were his hasty temper and his excessive devotion to the pleasures of the table. He made a great personal success as the six characters in one in a revival of Boursault's *Mercure galant*. He retired in 1786, and with his wife, also an actress at the Comédie-Française, went to live at Senlis, returning to the theatre for a short time in 1791.

PRICE, MAIRE [MAIRE NIC SHIUBHLAIGH, *née* MARIE WALKER] (?–1958), Irish actress, one of the founder-players of the Irish National Theatre, and a fine tragedienne in the early days of the Abbey Theatre. Her brother and two sisters were also early members of the Abbey company. She first joined Maude Gonne's club, the 'Daughters of Ireland', acting in the amateur group directed by Frank Fay, and then became a member of the Fays' Irish National Theatre, appearing as Delia Cahel in Yeats's *Cathleen Ni Houlihan* on its first production in 1902, and going with the company to the Abbey Theatre in 1904, where she played leading parts with the sisters Sara Allgood and Maire O'Neill. She was perhaps less versatile than they, and at her best in tragic roles, among them Nora Burke in Synge's *The Shadow of the Glen* (1903) and Moll Woods in O'Kelly's *The Shuiler's Child* (1910). She retired in 1917, and for many years produced plays for amateur drama festivals. She made a last appearance on the Dublin stage in 1947, in Lady Gregory's *Gaol Gate*, and in 1950, in collaboration with her nephew, she published a book about the renaissance of the Irish theatre entitled *The Splendid Years*.

PRICE, (LILIAN) NANCY BACHE (1880–1970), English actress and theatre manager, who first appeared on the stage with Benson's company, and in 1902 made a success as Calypso in *Ulysses*. Among her later parts were Olivia in *Twelfth Night*, Rosa Dartle in *Em'ly* (a dramatization of *David Copperfield*), and Hilda Gunning in *Letty*. She continued to enhance her reputation in a wide variety of parts, but it is as the founder and guiding spirit of the People's National Theatre that she is best remembered. This venture began in 1930 with a revival at the Fortune Theatre of *The Man from Blankley's*, and during the next few years Nancy Price was responsible for the production of over fifty plays, ranging from Euripides to Pirandello, and including *Alison's House*, *Lady Precious Stream*, and *Whiteoaks*, in which she played for two years the part of old Adeline Whiteoaks. These were all produced at the Little Theatre (destroyed by enemy action in 1941), which was for some years the headquarters of her People's National Theatre. She made her last appearance in *The Orange Orchard* in 1950. She was the author of a number of books on various open-air subjects, and of a volume of reminiscences, *Shadows on the Hill*, published in 1935. In 1950 she was appointed C.B.E. in recognition of her services to the theatre. She married the actor Charles Raymond Maude (1882–1943), grandson of Jenny Lind, who retired after the First World War.

PRICE, STEPHEN (1783–1840), the first outstanding American theatre manager who was neither an actor, like Hallam and Douglass, nor a playwright, like Dunlap. In 1808 he bought a share in the management of the Park Theatre, New York, and gradually assumed complete control. Odell, in his *Annals of the New York Stage*, calls him 'a theatrical speculator', since to him was due the constant importation of famous European actors, beginning with G. F. Cooke in 1810–11, which by 1840 had wrecked the old resident companies of the larger American towns. He spent a good deal of time in London between 1820 and 1839, engaging English and Continental actors and singers for America. Odell also likens him to Barnum in his love of spectacular and freakish effects—real horses and tigers on the stage, for example. It was this trait which caused many people to disapprove of his tenancy of London's Drury Lane in 1826–30. Price, whose whole theatrical career was closely bound up with that of the Park Theatre, died opportunely just as its fortunes were beginning to decline.

PRIESTLEY, JOHN BOYNTON (1894–), English dramatist, novelist, and critic. He was born at Bradford and educated there and at Trinity Hall, Cambridge. He served in the First World War with the Duke of Wellington's and the Devon Regiments. His writing career, beginning in 1918 with a volume of verse, *The Chapman of Rhymes*, brought him in 1931 to *The Good Companions*, a vastly successful novel which the author, in collaboration with Edward Knoblock, successfully dramatized. Any doubts of Priestley's innate theatrical capacity were soon set at rest. *The Roundabout* was quickly followed by *Dangerous Corner* (both 1931), perhaps the most ingenious play ever put together, and *Laburnum Grove* (1933) confirmed him as a successful dramatist. *Eden End* (1934) mingled gentle melancholy and rich humour in a rounded beauty which he has not since matched. Out of modern conceptions of time he succeeded in making two excellent plays, *Time and the Conways* and *I Have Been Here Before*, both written in 1937. A brief period of experimental work followed. In *Music At Night* (1938) and *Johnson Over Jordan* (1939) he sought with courage, skill, and sincerity to give modern drama a new depth, but the technical means he employed were not to the taste of the public, and he turned during the war to less ambitious comedies. It is possible that in his strenuous endeavour to entertain a public much in need of amusement he wrote too quickly, for he also did much miscellaneous writing and a famous series of broadcasts; nor did he forget that he was a novelist and an essayist. *They Came To A City* (1943) may be excepted from this generalization; it was an earnest political tract which the public absorbed with every sign of enjoyment.

Priestley has some affinities with H. G. Wells. So long as he is satisfied to draw from human character, especially Yorkshire character, its simple fun and pathos, his judgement of what the public wants is pretty nearly infallible. *When We Are Married* (1938), for instance, was a gorgeous farce with its roots firm in Yorkshire nature. He can enrich a good story with touches of shrewd, humorous, and sentimental observation. But there is a pertinacious reformer at work in his composition. He would be a politician and a dramatic innovator. As a political thinker he tends to over-simplify problems, and as a serious dramatist in search of new forms he would seem to prefer fresh combinations of dubious stage devices to some heightened form of speech through which his ambitions might be realized. Fortunately, there is no need at present to attempt a final estimate of a dramatist whose work is still capable of development in many different directions.

A. V. COOKMAN†

Since 1943 Priestley has written a number of plays, among them *An Inspector Calls* (1945), *The Linden Tree* (1947), *Mr. Kettle and Mrs. Moon* (1955), *The Glass Cage* (1957), and two plays in collaboration with his third wife Jacquetta Hawkes, a well-known archaeologist—*Dragon's Mouth* (1952) and *The White Countess* (1954). He has taken a great interest in international theatre. He acted as chairman of theatre conferences in Paris in 1947 and Prague in 1948, and of the British Theatre Conference in 1948, and was the first President of the British International Theatre Institute.

PRIME MINISTER OF MIRTH, see ROBEY, GEORGE.

PRINCE CHARLES'S MEN, usually known as the Prince's Men, a theatrical company formed in 1616 on the death of Henslowe by his son-in-law Alleyn from an amalgamation of the Lady Elizabeth's Men and the Duke of York's Men. Their first settled home was the Phoenix, where Beeston installed them after he had ousted the remnants of the Queen's Men, and here they enjoyed some measure of prosperity. In 1622 they were themselves ousted by the new Lady Elizabeth's Company, and went to the Curtain. The company broke up when Charles succeeded to the throne, and many of its important players transferred to the King's Men. In 1631 a new company was formed under the patronage of the young Prince Charles, and appeared at Salisbury Court. Just before the closing of the theatres the Prince's Men were connected with the Fortune, where one of their chief actors was Fowler, a player of 'conquering parts'.

PRINCE CHARLES THEATRE, LONDON, at the corner of Leicester Square and Lisle Street. The foundation stone was laid by Dame Flora Robson on 18 Dec. 1961, and it opened with a Canadian revue, *Clap Hands*, transferred from the Lyric, Hammersmith. Its manager, Alfred Esdaile, said of its general plan and décor—it is a conventional proscenium-arch theatre—that it was 'modern but not contemporary'. In 1964 it housed the Late Joys from the Players' Theatre—their first appearance for members of the public as opposed to their usual club-membership audience—and then became a cinema.

PRINCE EDWARD THEATRE, LONDON, in Old Compton Street, Soho. It opened in 1930 with *Rio Rita* under the management of Lee Ephraim. It did not prove very successful as a theatre, and its principal productions were musical comedies and revues, of which *Nippy* in 1930 was outstanding, as was a play based on the adventures of Sexton Blake. It then became a restaurant-cabaret, as the London Casino, where one dined or supped and watched a spectacular stage-show. After the outbreak of war in 1939 it became the Queensberry All-Services Club, but subsequently resumed operations as a theatre, with variety shows, spectacle, and pantomime. In 1954 it became a cinema.

W. MACQUEEN-POPE†

PRINCE HENRY'S MEN, see ADMIRAL'S MEN.

PRINCE OF WALES THEATRE, LONDON, in Coventry Street. This opened as the Prince's Theatre on 18 Jan. 1884, under Edgar Bruce, with a revival of Gilbert's *Palace of Truth*. In March a free adaptation of *A Doll's House*, called *Breaking a Butterfly*, was produced with Tree as Kronstad (renamed Dunkerley) and Miss Lingard as Nora. It was adversely criticized and withdrawn almost immediately. It was followed by *The Private Secretary*, with Tree as the Revd. Robert Spalding. It was not a success, but Hawtrey transferred it to the Globe, and with W. S. Penley in Tree's part it had a long run and was often revived. Lily Langtry was at the theatre in 1885, and in 1886 the name was changed to the Prince of Wales. The 'wordless' play, *L'Enfant Prodigue*, had a great success in 1891, superbly mimed by Jane May, Zanfretta, and others, and served to introduce Pierrot to London. The first musical comedy, *In Town*, was presented by George Edwardes in 1892 and a year later came *A Gaiety Girl*. *Gentleman Joe*, with Arthur Roberts in the title-role, had a long run in 1895, and in 1898 Mrs. Patrick Campbell and Forbes-Robertson were seen in *Pelleas and Melisande* and other plays. Marie Tempest, giving up musical comedy, appeared at this theatre in *English Nell* and *Peg Woffington* (both 1900) and *Becky Sharp* (1901), all adaptations from novels. Between 1903 and 1910 the theatre housed a succession of musical comedies, including *Miss Hook of Holland* (1907). Charles Hawtrey had several successful seasons in comedy up to 1918, when Charlot presented revue, interspersed with plays. One of the most successful was *The Blue Lagoon* (1920). Later successes were *Alibi* and *By Candlelight* (both 1928). During the 1930s the theatre was given over to non-stop revue, and in Jan. 1937 it was closed for rebuilding. The new theatre opened on 26 Oct. with revue again. It later saw Sid Field's London début in *Strike a New Note* (1943). He starred in *Piccadilly Hayride* (1946) and was seen here in the last part he played before his early death, in *Harvey* (1949). After a further period devoted to revue, *The World of Susie Wong* opened in 1959 and had a long run, as did *Come Blow Your Horn* (1962). W. MACQUEEN-POPE†, *rev.*

The name of the above theatre is also found as Prince of Wales', and Prince of Wales's.

The Scala, under the management of the Bancrofts, was known as the Prince of Wales's Theatre.

PRINCES THEATRE, LONDON, in Shaftesbury Avenue. This was built by Walter and Frederick Melville, who opened it on 26 Dec. 1911 with a transfer of *The Three Musketeers* from their Lyceum. Its early years were mainly devoted to 'Lyceum' melodramas, but it never had a settled policy, and its productions ranged from straight drama to pantomime, ballet, and opera. It was managed for a time by Seymour Hicks, by Cochran, and, intermittently from 1929 to 1946, by Firth Shephard. Successful early productions were *Monsieur Beaucaire* (1919), *Alf's Button* (1924), and *Funny Face* (1928), during whose run the theatre had to be closed because of a burst gas-main. Among the distinguished foreign visitors to the Princes during this period were Sarah Bernhardt (in *Daniel*, 1921), Diaghilev's Ballets Russes, and Sacha Guitry with Yvonne Printemps. Ian Hay's dramatizations of two Edgar Wallace stories, *The Frog* (1936) and *The Gusher* (1937), had long runs, as did *Wild Oats* (1938) and *Sitting Pretty* (1939). The theatre was badly blasted in 1940 and twice in 1941, but managed to stay open, and for a time housed the Sadler's Wells opera and ballet companies. After the war the main successes were Gilbert and Sullivan seasons, and there was also a long run of *His Excellency* (1950) with Eric Portman, and of two American musicals, *Pal Joey* (1954) and *Wonderful Town* (1955). In 1962 the theatre closed for renovation, and reopened on 28 Mar. 1963 as the Shaftesbury, with an American musical, *How To Succeed in Business Without Really Trying*. In its early days the theatre was known officially as the New Princes. The Prince of Wales Theatre in Coventry Street, London, was first named the Prince's, as was the St. James's for a short while. W. MACQUEEN-POPE†, *rev.*

PRINCESS THEATRE, NEW YORK, at 104 West 49th Street, one of the city's smallest and most perfect playhouses. Holding 299 people, it was built by F. Ray Comstock on the site of an old livery stable, and named for his old second-floor theatre on 29th Street. It opened on 14 Mar. 1913 with the Princess Players in one-act plays. The first outstanding production was a translation of Brieux's *Maternité* in 1915, while, after a series of musical comedies and intimate revues, the Princess saw in 1920–1 the Provincetown Players in several of their productions, including *The Emperor Jones*. In the same year Brock Pemberton produced *Six Characters in Search of an Author*, which ran for 17 weeks, while in 1922 came Maxwell Anderson's first New York production with *White Desert*, which speedily failed. In 1928 the theatre was renamed the Lucille La Verne, but after two productions reverted to its original name, only to change it for the Assembly in 1929. It then became a cinema, except for a short interval in 1937, when as the Labour Stage—after it had become the recreation centre of the International Ladies' Garment Workers Union—it staged a topical revue, *Pins and Needles*, which caught the fancy of the town and ran into three editions with 1,108 performances. GEORGE FREEDLEY†

PRINCESS'S THEATRE, LONDON. This was built by a silversmith named Hamlet, on the site of a building called the Queen's Bazaar, on the north side of Oxford Street, near the Circus. This was used for the sale of fancy and miscellaneous goods. It was destroyed by fire in 1829 and rebuilt to house exhibitions. Hamlet transformed it into a theatre and opened it on 30 Sept. 1840. Its reconstruction evidently took some time, since it had been named by permission after Queen Victoria before her accession. It was advertised as being 'fitted up in a style and splendour never before equalled in this country', and the first attractions were promenade concerts, for which the prices were 1*s.* and 2*s.* These were not very successful, and after further alteration the theatre reopened on 26 Dec. 1842 with Bellini's 'La Sonnambula' and other operas and light dramatic pieces. In 1843 Hamlet went bankrupt and Maddox took over. He staged several of Balfe's operas, and General Tom Thumb, the circus midget, also appeared. In 1845 Charlotte Cushman and Edwin Forrest made their London début there in a tragedy called *Fazio*. In 1850 Maddox gave up the theatre, which was taken over by Charles Kean, with Keeley as his partner for the first year. Kean's management was memorable, both for his productions of Shakespeare (see Nos. 72, 167) and for his success in transforming French drama into plays suited to English popular taste. Queen Victoria was so thrilled by *Pauline* that she clutched the curtain of her box in a convulsive grasp until the tense situation was over. *The Corsican Brothers* was a great personal success for Kean, as was *Louis XI*. In his *Henry VIII* limelight was used for the first time, and the burning of the palace in *Sardanapalus* was a great piece of realism. Here Ellen Terry, as a child, had her first engagement under Kean, who gave up the Princess's on 29 Aug. 1859, after appearing as Wolsey. In the following September Augustus Harris, father of the future manager of Drury Lane, took over, and engaged Henry Irving, then a stock actor at the Theatre Royal, Edinburgh. He failed, and returned to the provinces. In 1860 Harris brought Fechter to the Princess's, where his portrayal of Hamlet in what was then a novel fashion caused a sensation. In Oct. 1862 Harris retired and a Mr. Lindus took the theatre to please his wife, sustaining a heavy loss. George Vining was the next tenant, and he inaugurated the epoch of melodrama, for which the theatre became famous, with *The Huguenot Captain* (starring Adelaide Neilson), *The Streets of London*, including the thrilling fire scene, and *Arrah-Na-Pogue*. In Oct. 1865 *It's Never Too Late To Mend* began with a riotous first night, when the audience objected to the savagery of one of the scenes, showing a boy in prison being flogged. The critics railed against it, but the play ran for 148 nights and made a profit of £8,000. In the same year Kean gave a farewell season, dying three years later. Benjamin Webster succeeded Vining as manager in 1869, Chatterton joining him the following year and becoming sole manager in 1872. Chatterton ran seasons of Shakespeare, alternating Phelps with Creswick in an attempt to revive the glories of Kean's management, but he had to go back to melodrama, including *Lost in London* and *The Lancashire Lass*. In 1875 Joseph Jefferson revived *Rip Van Winkle* with great success, and in 1879 Charles Warner startled theatre-goers with his amazing performance as Coupeau in *Drink*. After a short and unsuccessful venture by Booth, Wilson Barrett, with Modjeska, took the theatre. His first success was *The Lights of London*, and on 16 Nov. 1882 came *The Silver King*, which ran for a year and became, perhaps, the classic example of melodrama. In 1886 Barrett left, and the importance of the theatre waned. The last successful play staged there was *The Fatal Wedding* in 1902. Shortly afterwards it was taken over by an American syndicate, but owing to difficulties with the lease, and considerable requirements in the way of alterations, it was never reopened but became a warehouse, and was demolished in 1931. W. MACQUEEN-POPE†

PRINCIPAL BOY, the chief character in the English pantomime—Aladdin, Dick Whittington, Idle Jack, Prince Charming, Prince Florizel, Robinson Crusoe—traditionally played by a woman. This custom appears to have originated in the playing of young boys' parts in opera by women singers (for example Cherubino in 'The Marriage of Figaro') and from the wide popularity of the 'breeches part'—the young male lover played by an actress, in the eighteenth century—together with the *travesti* fashion of the nineteenth century in burlesques and extravaganzas, which standardized the blonde wig, short tunic, fleshings, and high heels of the typical Principal Boy. Some authorities have sought to derive the custom from the fact that the pantomime may be looked on as a survival of the Roman Feast of Saturnalia, which took place approximately at what is now the Christmas season. One of its main features was the exchange of costume between the sexes, an example of topsy-turvydom which is well in the spirit of the modern pantomime, and intensified there by the fact that the Dame—the hero's mother—is usually played by a man. But again, in the eighteenth century comic female characters were played by men, and this may have led to the development of the Dame as the prerogative of the comedian. The Principal Boy was not firmly established until the 1880s, and it was Augustus Harris, at Drury Lane, who insisted on opulent curves, as with Harriet Vernon, a 'magnificent creature of ample figure'. Other Principal Boys were Nellie Stewart and Queenie Leighton. In the twentieth century the tradition was carried on, with less emphasis on curves, by such Principal Boys as Phyllis Neilson-Terry and Madge Elliott as Prince Charming, Marie Burke as Jack and Prince Charming, Fay Compton as Robin Hood (in *The Babes in the Wood*), Anne Ziegler as Prince Silverthistle (in *The Sleeping Beauty*), Jill Esmond as Prince Hal (in *Beauty and the Beast*) and Dorothy Ward as Dick Whittington. A later tendency towards realism even in pantomime was, however, responsible for the appearance of such actors as Patrick Waddington and Tommy Steele in roles hitherto reserved for actresses. With the general decline of pantomime, particularly in London, the species is dying out.

PRINTEMPS, YVONNE (1895–), French actress and singer, who made her first appearance in Paris in revue in June 1908. She was for some time at the Folies-Bergère, and also appeared at the Palais-Royal. In 1916 she made a great success as Suzanne in *Le Poilu*, and in the same year joined the company of Sacha Guitry, who became her first husband (after a divorce she married the actor Pierre Fresnay). She appeared with Guitry in a number of plays, being seen with him in London in 1920 in *Nono*. After several French plays, she played in English for the first time in *Conversation Piece* (1934), and was also seen in *O Mistress Mine* (1936). She made her first appearance in New York in 1926 as Mozart in the play of that name in which she had been seen in Paris the year previously. In 1937 she took over the Théâtre de la Michodière, and appeared there in a long succession of musical plays during the next twenty years. She has also had a successful career in films.

PRITCHARD, HANNAH (1711–68), English actress, who as Miss Vaughan made some reputation at the fairgrounds and around London. She married William Pritchard (?–1763), treasurer of Drury Lane, and had a short engagement at the Haymarket, going on to Drury Lane, where she was established some ten years before Garrick appeared. At first she played only in comedy, but in later years she turned to tragedy, and was a fine Lady Macbeth. She was also the first and only interpreter of Dr. Johnson's *Irene*. Her acting was somewhat mannered and old-fashioned, as she had been formed in the school of Quin, and she was not seen to advantage in artificial comedy. In later life, as Churchill does not fail to point out in *The Rosciad*, she became somewhat stout, but could still play young heroines with charm. She remained with Garrick until her retirement a few months before her death, appearing for the last time, as Lady Macbeth, on 25 Apr. 1768. Garrick was disconsolate, and determined never to play Macbeth again, a resolution which he broke only once, on 22 Sept. at the request of the King of Denmark, who was anxious to see him in the part. Doran said of Mrs. Pritchard:

> Her distinguishing qualities were natural expression, unembarrassed deportment, propriety of action, and an appropriateness of delivery which was the despair of all her contemporaries, for she took care of her consonants, and was so exact in her articulations, that, however voluble her enunciation, the audience never lost a syllable of it.

She was considered to have given more prominence than is usual to the part of Gertrude in *Hamlet*, and her Queen Katharine in *Henry VIII* was equally fine. She had a brother, Henry (?–1779), who played Falstaff at Covent Garden in 1734, and her daughter, who married the first John Palmer, was also on the stage for a time, retiring on her marriage.

PRIVATE THEATRES IN ENGLAND. The vogue for private theatricals in English high society in the second half of the eighteenth century, which reached its peak from 1770 to 1790, resulted in the building of several private theatres. Earlier, the few amateur dilettanti performances had taken place in rooms, an example of which can be seen in Hogarth's painting of a children's performance of Dryden's *Indian Emperor* in the house of John Conduitt, Master of the Mint, in 1731. The first specially erected theatre was built in 1766 for Sir Francis Delaval and the Duke of York in James Street, Westminster. It had a capacity of only fifty and was fitted up by Benjamin Wilson.

The most magnificent of these theatres, and one which could vie with the Continental Court theatres (see CELLE, ČESKÝ KRUMLOV, DROTTNINGHOLM, GRIPSHOLM), was erected for the Earl of Barrymore at Wargrave in 1789. Rectangular in shape, it had a capacity of 400, and contained two tiers of boxes and two stage boxes unusually placed over the orchestra well. It was provided with a series of work rooms and an adjoining salon for refreshments. After ruining its owner it was demolished in 1792.

The Margravine of Anspach built her theatre on the bank of the Thames at Brandenburgh House, Hammersmith, in 1793 and it was in use for theatricals until 1804. It was in castellated style and is said to have resembled the Bastille rather than a temple of the muses. An engraving of the interior shows a large central box and a parterre raised on a shallow platform after Continental models.

A theatre in a simpler style was converted from a kitchen for Sir Watkins Williams Wynn at Wynnstay, and was used for annual performances from 1771 to 1789. Other famous theatres were those at Blenheim Palace, 1787–9, converted from a greenhouse, and the Duke of Richmond's at Richmond House, London, constructed out of two rooms by Wyatt in 1787 to hold about 150 spectators. In an open-air theatre at Cliveden, still extant, 'Rule Britannia' was first sung in Thomson's masque, *Alfred*, in 1740.

Well-known scene-painters were sometimes employed in private theatres, for instance Thomas Greenwood at Richmond and Blenheim, Inigo Richards at Wynnstay, and Malton at Brandenburgh House. The wardrobe book of Wynnstay and the sale catalogue of Wargrave are evidence of the sumptuous décor employed in the performances. Professionals frequently acted with or coached the amateurs.

The Duke of Devonshire's private theatre at Chatsworth, dating from about 1830, is the oldest still in existence. Another theatre of the period was that at Burton Constable, Yorkshire, which functioned from 1830 to 1850. Among later Victorian private theatres may be mentioned a small one attached to Campden House, Kensington, in the 1860s; Capethorne Hall, Cheshire, 1870; the artist Herkomer's at

Bushey, and the singer Patti's at Craig y Nos, Wales, still extant. In the twentieth century Lord Bessborough gave annual productions for some years in his theatre at Stansted, and Lord Faringdon has a theatre, still in use, at Buscot Park. More recent private theatres have been used mainly for opera, the most famous being John Christie's at Glyndebourne. The latest private theatre is Nicholas Sekers' at Rosehill, Whitehaven, but both these last employ professional companies, are open to the general public, and charge for admission. SYBIL ROSENFELD

PROCTOR, FREDERICK FRANCIS (1851–1929), American manager, who made a good deal of money in vaudeville and built a number of theatres in New York, the first being the Twenty-Third Street Theatre, which opened on 5 May 1890 with *Shenandoah*, transferred from the Star Theatre. Later productions at this theatre were *All the Comforts of Home* and *Men and Women*. Proctor was first the rival and then the partner of that other vaudeville pioneer, B. F. Keith, and was known as the 'dean of vaudeville', being owner of a chain of music-halls.

PRODUCER. 1. In America, the man responsible for the financial side of play-production, for the buying of the play, the renting of the theatre, the engagement of actors and staff, and the handling of receipts. In England the American 'producer' is known as the manager.

2. In England the man responsible for the general interpretation of the play, and for the conduct of rehearsals, during which he guides and advises the actors, welding them into a corporate body. He has no responsibility for the financial or business side of the production, but only for its artistic and dramatic integration. In America the English 'producer' is known as the director—a term increasingly used in England also—on the Continent as the *régisseur*. It is only since the beginning of the twentieth century that play-production has become a separate profession, distinct from that of actor or author, and that the producer has achieved a paramount position in the theatre. In early days a play was directed by its author, who might also, like Molière, be the chief actor; the eighteenth-century 'star' produced his own play, as did the nineteenth-century actor-manager; often only new plays were rehearsed, merely to perfect lines and cues, and settle entrances and exits. A newcomer in an old play was left to learn his way about by trial and error, while a visiting star might walk through his lines with the principals of the stock company, and leave the lesser people to accommodate themselves to his acting during the actual performance. From a perusal of memoirs and letters, it seems as if many actors were engaged merely on recommendation or recitation—as Mrs. Jordan was by Tate Wilkinson at Leeds—and appeared on the stage with no previous rehearsal, trusting to the older members to carry them along until they found their feet. Study of one's lines was a personal matter, and in tragedy particularly—the chief preoccupation of the great actors of the past—each production was regarded as a series of bravura performances, with the star scoring 'points'. Comedy was approached somewhat differently, but even there co-ordination of the different parts of the play was left to the stage-manager (who was the prompter too), from whose humble functions the modern omnipotence of the producer takes its origin. Belasco, one of the first American producers, was in his early days stage-manager and prompter in San Francisco. Possibly the first producer (or director) in its modern sense was George, Duke of Saxe-Meiningen. Stanislavsky, the first great Russian producer, appeared in the plays he directed, which most modern producers do not. Among those producers who have achieved international fame are Max Reinhardt, Granville-Barker, Jacques Copeau, Meyerhold, Taïrov, Komisarjevsky, Tyrone Guthrie, Peter Brook, Jean-Louis Barrault, and Elia Kazan; and many more are famous in their own countries. The requirements of modern producers may be summed up in the words of Ivor Brown in *Parties of the Play*:

> They must know acting from within, and be perfectly acquainted with its technical difficulties and with the use of stage mechanism. . . . Their chief task is to take a detached view of the point which the author seeks to establish. . . . They must relate the word to the appearance, the idea to the atmosphere, the movement to the scene. They are working, accordingly, in terms of mind and of matter in order to fuse them in the service of the whole artistic conception. . . . Their implements are their own sensibility, the plasticity of others, and the mechanical equipment of the playhouse from its footlights to its 'floats'.

It has also been said that the ideal producer must be an actor, an artist, an architect, an electrician, an expert in geography, history, costume, accessories, and scenery, and have a thorough understanding of human nature—the last trait being the most essential.

PROFILING, an edging of ¼ in. board added to the straight edge of a flat, and cut to a required shape (see FLAT).

PROGRAMME, see PLAYBILL.

PROJECTED SCENERY, see LIGHTING, 1 and 2.

PROJECTOR LAMP, see LIGHTING, 2.

PROLETCULT THEATRE, Moscow, see TRADES UNIONS THEATRE.

PROLOGUE, an introductory poem or speech, which originally explained or commented on the action of the play which it preceded. It was first used by Euripides (see GREECE, 1 *c*), and later by the Elizabethans, who applied to it the name Chorus. Together with the epilogue, which closed the action, the prologue was extensively used during the

Restoration period, and survived well into the eighteenth century. It disappeared with the crowded bills of the nineteenth century, and is now used only on special occasions. At their best the prologue and epilogue were witty and sometimes scurrilous commentaries on the politics and social conditions of the day, written by outstanding men of the theatre, of whom Dryden and Garrick were the greatest, and spoken by the finest actors of the day.

PROMPT BOOK — BOX — CORNER — SIDE, see STAGE DIRECTIONS.

PROPS, the usual term for stage properties. It covers anything essential to the action of the play which does not come under the heading of costume, scenery, or furniture. Hand-props are those which an actor handles—letters, documents, revolvers, newspapers, knitting, snuff boxes, &c. These are given to him as he goes on stage, and taken from him as he comes off, and are not his personal responsibility. Other props—stuffed birds, food in general, dinner-plates, telephones—are placed on stage by the property man, who is responsible for all props under the direction of the stage manager. He has for storage a property room backstage, from which he is expected to produce at a moment's notice anything that may be required. He is also charged to prevent the removal from it of oddments by members of the company.

PROSCENIUM, the permanent, or semi-permanent, wall dividing, in the modern theatre, the auditorium from the stage. The opening in this wall frames the stage picture, and has the curtain, in all its variations (see CURTAIN) hanging in it. The word is classical in origin but has completely changed its meaning (see ARCHITECTURE), since it first meant the area in front of the stage, then that part of the stage which was in front of the curtain, and finally the surroundings of the stage, possibly by extension from the meaning in such compounds as 'proscenium door' (see ENGLISH PLAYHOUSE). In its heyday the proscenium, which has a long tradition behind it artistically, was a feature of considerable architectural complexity, forming an essential link between the auditorium and the scene. It is now often thought of only as a hindrance, particularly in the production of Shakespearian and modern epic plays, and the tendency is to abolish it where possible, in favour of the open stage, or of theatre-in-the-round (see FLEXIBLE STAGING). One obstacle which confronts the experimenters in the older London theatre buildings is the presence within the proscenium arch of the Safety Curtain called for by the G.L.C. Fire Regulations (see also FALSE PROS. and INNER PROSCENIUM).

PROSCENIUM DOORS, or Doors of Entrance, a feature of the English Restoration playhouse. They varied in number from one to three on each side of the forestage, continuing the façade of the lower box tier. They provided the usual means of entrance for an actor, and could be locked if necessary. They also had practicable knockers and bells. An actor leaving a room by one door was presumed to be entering another room when he returned by an adjacent door, even though the wings and back scene remained unchanged. The number of doors probably varied, not only at different theatres (six at the Theatre Royal, Bridges Street, four at Dorset Garden), but in the same theatre at different periods. It is also possible that in some late Restoration theatres the doors may have been, not in the proscenium, but in a specially built piece inside. By the early eighteenth century the doors were reduced to one each side, and by the beginning of the nineteenth they were used only by the actor 'taking a bow' after the play. Entering by one door, he crossed the stage, pausing halfway to bow (or curtsey, if an actress), and went out by the opposite door. They were then known as Call Doors (for some examples see Nos. 31, 32, 35; see also ACOUSTICS, 5). RICHARD SOUTHERN

PROTAGONIST. The Greek tragic poet was restricted to three actors (apparently; the point is disputed). These came to be known as Protagonist, Deuteragonist, Tritagonist: first, second, and third actor (from *agôn*, contest). When contests between actors were instituted (see GREECE, 3 *a*) only the protagonists came into question. In the early Aeschylean drama there was one preponderant part for the protagonist; later, this was not necessarily true. In Sophocles he must often have taken several roles, and the distinction between him and the deuteragonist was of little dramatic significance. H. D. F. KITTO

PROVINCETOWN PLAYERS, an experimental group of American actors and playwrights, founded in 1916 by Susan Glaspell, her husband, George Cram Cook, Eugene O'Neill, and Ida Rank, who spent a summer together in Provincetown in 1916. They gave plays by O'Neill (including his first to be staged, *Bound East for Cardiff*), Susan Glaspell, Edna St. Vincent Millay (*Aria da Capo*), and Langner, among others. The first productions of the group were seen at the Wharf Theatre, Provincetown, but they later moved to New York, to the Playwrights' Theatre in Greenwich Village. They ceased production in 1921. The Provincetown Playhouse was re-opened early in 1924 under the management of Kenneth Macgowan, Robert Edmond Jones, and Eugene O'Neill. It operated in conjunction with the Greenwich Village Theatre, which saw the first production of *Desire Under the Elms*, as well as of many foreign contemporary plays and some classical revivals such as *Love for Love*. Certain of the original workers among the Provincetown Players continued from 1925 to operate the Playhouse, and in 1929, after an unsuccessful move to the Garrick Theatre, they disbanded, having successfully fulfilled their avowed purpose of giving 'American playwrights a chance to work out their ideas in freedom'. Certainly their ardent experimentalism gave

O'Neill, probably America's greatest dramatist, the opportunities he needed for freedom of expression and an unhampered development. The Greenwich Village Theatre, after functioning for a further year as the Irish Theatre, was demolished in 1930.

PROVINCIAL THEATRES IN GREAT BRITAIN. 1. General Survey. (*a*) *Strolling Players up to 1700.* In medieval times the larger towns outside London had their own performances of plays based on the Bible (see ENGLAND and LITURGICAL DRAMA). These were the monopoly of the town guilds and were acted by local amateurs, both lay and clerical. For ephemeral amusement the people depended on wandering minstrels, tumblers, acrobats, and their own May-day games and Harvest revels. Elizabethan England had a fairly large body of strolling players, of whom little is known. London companies, under licence and permission from their patron, toured the country in the summer, or when plague drove the Court from town, and there may have been a number of unlicensed companies, living largely on their wits and liable at any time to be hauled up before the magistrates as rogues and vagabonds. The universities (see OXFORD and CAMBRIDGE) had their own academic exercises, which were not intended for the townspeople. There were at this time no theatre buildings outside London, and any touring company, however important, had to put up with an inn-yard or a makeshift arrangement in a barn, or at the best in a hall. Civil war no doubt laid as heavy a hand on provincial drama as on that of London, but immediately after the Restoration strolling companies began to operate once more in the provinces. It is impossible to estimate how many of them there were, or to what extent they covered the country. Records at Norwich reveal the existence of several companies, and elsewhere parish registers have entries relating to them. They travelled with Letters Patent from the King or licences from the Master of the Revels or the Lord Chamberlain, which they presented to the Mayor's court in order to obtain leave to play. It was difficult for the Mayor to refuse a licence, though at Norwich he got permission to curtail the stay of the players, and he frequently made it a condition that a benefit should be given for the poor, a custom that persisted in later years when an annual benefit for charity was usually given. Some companies—the Duke of Monmouth's, the Duke of Grafton's, and Lord Strange's—were still under the protection of noblemen, as they had been in Elizabethan times, and performances took place in inns, barns, and booths temporarily adapted or specially set up for the purpose.

(*b*) *The Circuit System and the First Theatres.* As more companies came into the field at the beginning of the eighteenth century they gradually adopted a number of towns in their district which they visited regularly. These formed what was known as their 'circuit'. This was not accomplished, however, without disputes between rival companies. The Duke of Norfolk's and the Duke of Grafton's Servants clashed at Norwich, and in Newcastle Herbert's and Keregan's companies produced rival performances of *The Beggar's Opera* on the same night. One town in the circuit naturally became the headquarters of the troupe, and between 1720 and 1730 companies began to be known by the name of their chief town instead of by that of their manager or patron. The circuit was arranged so that the larger towns could be visited during Race or Assizes week when they were full of people, while lesser towns and villages were visited biennially or occasionally. Towns were sometimes changed from one circuit to another; Beverley, for instance, changed hands three or four times.

The establishment of regular circuits naturally led to the building of the first provincial playhouses, since a company that was sure of acting once or twice a year in a town found that it was better to have its own specially erected building rather than to depend on inns, town halls, and other makeshifts. Among the earliest playhouses built in the provinces were those of Bath (1705), Jacob's Wells, Bristol (1729), York (1734), and Ipswich (1736).

(*c*) *Licensing Act, 1737.* The increased activities of the players met with a great deal of Puritan opposition. Power's company was twice chased away from Bristol, but fulminations against the players, issued from press and pulpit until well into the nineteenth century, resulted often in nothing but bigger audiences. The usual indictments were of the immorality of the plays, and of their ill effects on the workers who wasted time and money attending them. This opposition culminated in the passing of the Licensing Act of 1737, which at one blow abolished the right of all provincial companies to act for hire, gain, or reward, branded the players once again as rogues and vagabonds, and put them at the mercy of informers. The Bath and York theatres were closed down, though acting continued elsewhere in both towns; but in practice the Act made singularly little difference, though informers did sometimes cause the suspension of performances and the imprisonment of players. Justices still granted licences to play and performances continued unless information was lodged against the players. Several companies evaded the law by charging for entry to a concert and giving a play free in the interval; but many did not even trouble to do this, and simply took the risk of fine and imprisonment.

(*d*) *Sharing System.* All the companies in the first half of the eighteenth century worked on shares. After the expenses of the night had been paid, the profits, even down to the remains of the candles, were shared among all members of the company equally, except that the manager took four extra shares, known as dead shares, for his expenses in connexion with the scenery, the wardrobe, and so on.

Every night an account was made up and the money paid out, the youngest and least experienced member of the company receiving the same as the leading actors. This commonwealth system, though good in many ways, was open to abuse by unscrupulous managers, for the accumulation of important bills which the management owed, known as the stock debt, sometimes figured among the expenses though it had long since been paid off. Such abuses led to the system falling out of favour in the mid-century and being replaced by the payment of salaries. The actors, however, depended more on their benefits, of which they had one or more during the year, either single or shared, according to their importance, than on either their shares or their salaries. In the larger companies in the latter part of the century a benefit night for a popular favourite might bring in as much as £200–£300.

(*e*) *Strolling Companies.* Throughout the eighteenth and the beginning of the nineteenth centuries the established circuit companies were supplemented by many lesser troupes who played in haylofts, stables, and booths in the small towns and villages, and even sometimes intruded on the circuit towns. These troupes were generally very poor; they frequently fled from a town by night leaving their debts behind, and were as frequently left stranded by rascally managers who escaped with what cash there was. Such companies were continually changing personnel and were recruited from London pot-houses or from each other. They travelled on foot, sometimes with their scenery and properties on their backs, though the better of them had wagons. They sent ahead a player or two to take the town, i.e. to obtain a licence from the local justice, and on arrival the drum was beaten and playbills distributed. Their resources in scenery, properties, and wardrobe were often pitiful and their paucity of numbers necessitated doubling and trebling of parts. They also continued to work on the sharing system long after the circuit companies had abandoned it. But they did bring drama, however inadequately, to many places which otherwise would have been without it. A good idea of their life may be obtained from the autobiography of Mrs. Charlotte Charke, daughter of Colley Cibber, and the volumes of Ryley's *The Itinerant.*

(*f*) *Companies from London.* Some provincial towns depended wholly or largely for their entertainment on the visits of London actors during the long vacation. Troupes of minor players from both patent houses and minor theatres paid annual visits to Bristol, Canterbury, Liverpool, Birmingham, and other towns. With one such company in Ipswich Garrick made his first appearance on the stage.

(*g*) *The Provinces as Training Centres.* By the middle of the eighteenth century Bath, Norwich, and York had become the important centres in the provinces, and engagements there were eagerly sought after, as they were looked upon as stepping-stones to the London boards. Before the days of dramatic schools experience in the provinces was almost the only way in which an actor could learn his job; and the wide variety of plays and audiences that the circuit companies offered proved invaluable to him. A large proportion of the great actors and actresses of the latter half of the eighteenth and the early nineteenth centuries received their first chance on the stage, and years of training, in provincial companies. To give only a few examples: J. P. Kemble trained in Wolverhampton and York, Mrs. Siddons and Macready at Bath, Elizabeth Farren at Liverpool, G. F. Cooke at Manchester, Chester and Newcastle, Mrs. Jordan and Samuel Phelps at York, Elliston at Bath and York, Edmund Kean at Exeter, E. A. Sothern at Birmingham. Much of the credit for the fact that the eighteenth century was a period of great acting must go to the provincial theatres.

(*h*) *The Heyday of Provincial Theatres, 1750–1810.* The latter half of the eighteenth century saw many theatres arise all over England. The circuit companies flourished and commanded, first as learners and then as stars, most of the theatrical talent of the time. Seasons in the principal towns lasted two to four months, performances being given three or four times a week. Sometimes there was a second shorter season. Royal patents were granted to Bath and Norwich in 1768, York and Hull 1769, Liverpool 1771, Manchester 1775, Bristol 1778, and Newcastle 1788, thus legalizing the position of these theatres. Brighton, Windsor, and Richmond, Surrey, being places of royal residence, operated under licences from the Lord Chamberlain. In 1788 an Act was passed legalizing acting in the provinces by giving justices powers to license players for sixty days at one time. This gave a further stimulus to theatre-building: thus Samuel Butler opened six theatres in his Yorkshire circuit between 1788 and 1805, and Fisher eleven in his East Anglian one between 1809 and 1828. The chief circuit companies now concentrated on the larger centres and left the smaller towns and villages to lesser circuits, many of which were formed in this half-century. A list in *The Authentic Memoirs of the Green Room* (*c.* 1815) gives 25 main circuits in England and 3 in Wales; a fuller list of principal provincial managements in England and Wales in L. T. Rede's *Road to the Stage* (1827) gives a total of 41, a few of which were independent of circuits; and in addition 8 sharing companies are mentioned which mostly visited towns where the theatres had long been closed; these do not include companies which merely acted at fairs. Managers such as Tate Wilkinson of York, Watson of Cheltenham, Mrs. Baker of Canterbury, and James Augustus Whitley of Chester, became famous figures in the theatrical world of their period.

(*i*) *Theatres.* There were several ways in which money was raised to erect theatres, but usually it was done by subscription, the subscribers then being the proprietors of the theatre. Subscribers took shares of a certain sum on which they generally received interest as well as silver tokens admitting them to all performances. In other cases, viz. Ipswich, speculators built the theatre in return for a concession such as receipts from the gallery. Frequently, as at Doncaster and York, the theatre was built on ground leased from the corporation. The circuit manager then became lessee of the theatre for a term of years. The theatres were of widely differing size and cost: Liverpool cost £6,000, Huddersfield £2,400, Winchester only £1,000. The larger theatres such as Liverpool and Beaufort Square, Bath, held £300, the smaller ones anything from £40–£80. Sometimes the theatre was built after a London model, sometimes on an original plan. Bristol Theatre Royal claims to have the first semicircular auditorium, and subsequently other provincial playhouses were converted from square to horseshoe shape: Brighton in 1796, Liverpool in 1803, and York in 1822. Four Georgian theatres still survive as playhouses: that at Bristol, built in 1766 (see No. 27), is an example of a larger theatre of the time and retains some early machinery; that at Richmond, Yorks., dating from 1788, is small, rectangular in shape, and retains its proscenium; that at Margate, built in 1787, was remodelled in 1874; and that at Bury St. Edmunds, built by William Wilkins in 1819, was rehabilitated and reopened as a theatre in 1965. All are of great interest and value to the theatre historian. Other shells survive, notably at Cambridge and Dorchester (Dorset), but have been adapted as warehouses, chapels, auction-rooms, and the like.

(*j*) *Charges.* Prices of seats varied from 2*s.* to 3*s.* for boxes, later rising to 4*s.* and 5*s.*; pit 2*s.* or 2*s.* 6*d.*; upper boxes 1*s.* 6*d.* or 2*s.*; gallery 1*s.* or 1*s.* 6*d.*; upper gallery 6*d.* Seats on the stage were abolished as the century progressed, and stage boxes took their place. Half-price was usual except on first nights, on the visits of stars, and when expensive pantomimes were given. Manchester did not allow half-price. Many theatres also offered a subscription season for a certain number of nights, this being followed by a series of benefits.

(*k*) *Scenery.* The best companies had good resources. The initial layout on scenery for the Newcastle Theatre Royal in 1788 was £800, and Tate Wilkinson spent £500 on scenery at York in one season, 50 guineas on one scene. Wilkinson tells us that though he had treble the scenery of any other provincial theatre, his stage was too confined for many sliding scenes, and the drop scenes from fixtures could not be added to unless the work of the play were to be hindered. Thus pieces and pantomimes with a long scene-plot could not be properly staged, and an apartment often did duty for a farm-house, and prisons and chambers appeared with palace wings. The question of how the smaller theatres managed needs investigation. Most companies of importance had their own scene-painters, who were sometimes also responsible for house decorations. In the Norwich circuit the scene-painter was more highly paid than the actors. He prepared scenery for the whole tour at Norwich, but certain stock scenes were kept at each circuit theatre. London scene-painters were also employed, for instance Greenwood and Carver at Brighton, and Grieve and Capon at Bath. In smaller companies the scene-painter was also an actor. Local views were often introduced into drop scenes and act drops.

(*l*) *Lighting and Heating.* Tallow candles and oil-lamps were the means of illumination on the stage and in the auditorium until they were replaced by wax candles (Salisbury in 1777, Ipswich in 1787, Birmingham in 1795, Liverpool in 1800). Gas was used at Exeter in the same year that it was introduced into the London theatres (1817), but owing to explosions a reversion to candles took place shortly after. Other theatres which early adopted gas lighting were Brighton and Liverpool in 1818, Cheltenham in 1819, and York in 1822. Theatres were warmed by braziers or stoves, but there were many complaints of damp in winter and lack of ventilation in summer. Theatres frequently suffered destruction by fire: Birmingham and Manchester twice and Exeter three times.

(*m*) *Plays.* As in London, the main play was followed by an after-piece, sometimes by two or even occasionally three. In addition, with one or two exceptions such as Liverpool, there were interludes of singing, dancing, and recitation, so that performances lasted five hours or more. London successes appeared on the provincial stage a few weeks after their metropolitan presentation. Provincial managers did not wait for plays to be printed, but obtained copies by various direct or devious means. Sometimes the London manager was induced to lend the manuscript, sometimes agents were instructed to take copies at the play, or prompters were bribed to supply them. Garbled versions were often presented. Authors were paid no fees in the provinces until after the Act of 1842 (see COPYRIGHT). A few plays by local dramatists appeared at Manchester, Liverpool, York, Whitby, Worcester, and elsewhere; licences to act them were sometimes, but by no means always, obtained, as by law they had to be, from the Lord Chamberlain. Plays were rarely given more than two or three times during the season, but each new production was repeated at every town in the circuit. The companies had large repertories; Butler's company, for example, performed 100 plays and after-pieces during their year's travels. Taste in general followed London, though Wilkinson records that some successes from the capital failed in York and some London failures succeeded there.

(*n*) *Players.* The advantage to the actor of the circuit system was that he could reckon on employment all the year round, as the chief companies generally articled players for a term of months or years. Many of the strolling and some of the circuit companies were very much family affairs. Actors' children started to appear on the stage at the ages of 3 and 4, and Dickens's picture of the Crummles family in *Nicholas Nickleby* is hardly exaggerated. Typical weekly salaries at different periods are: York, 1736, 12*s*., 1785, £2; Richmond, Yorks., 1780, 15*s*.; Norwich 35*s*. to 2 guineas. At Exeter Kean received 2 guineas in 1811, and in 1821 the highest salary paid at Liverpool was £2. 10*s*. L. T. Rede (*op. cit.*) gives the average salaries of all the circuits, the lowest being 15*s*., the highest £5, and the majority varying from one guinea to £1. 10*s*. An actor in Bath or York could realize £400–£500 a year. The tragedian commanded the best salary and was considered the leading actor in the company. Actors were expected to supply a good part of their wardrobe, and actresses all of it. The starring system, whereby special actors and actresses were brought from London to play for a few nights or weeks, started in the 1790s. One or two theatres, as at York and Portsmouth, realized the danger to their stock players and at first refused to engage visitors. But the demand for stars grew rapidly and their prices rose accordingly. Thus Cooke was paid £20 a night in Bath in 1805. Soon the stars refused a salary and demanded half profits or even whole receipts. Kemble refused 30 guineas at York and by taking a share instead made £150. Even the lesser companies were compelled to engage stars for one or two nights, and the principal actors and actresses often returned as stars to play with the companies in which they had trained.

(*o*) *The Audience*. The audience, itself often noisy and ill behaved, demanded humility and acquiescence from the players. The manager had to give thanks on leave-taking and frequently to appear on the stage to apologize for various real or supposed shortcomings or misdemeanours. Riots were often the result of raised prices or other proceedings objectionable to the audience. Requests not to go behind the scenes were couched in begging terms. Bespeaks were granted by the gentry, military, freemasons, schools, race stewards, &c. Keen playgoers often undertook hazardous coach journeys in winter to see the play, and playbills used to advertise moonlight nights for their encouragement.

(*p*) *The Decline in the Nineteenth Century*. In the second and third decades of the nineteenth century the provincial theatres, like the London ones, showed a rapid decline. Audiences dwindled, managers went bankrupt, and theatres changed lessees with bewildering frequency. Many theatres ceased to function or stood empty for seasons at a time. Lesser circuits began to break up, Butler's of Richmond, Yorks., for instance, in 1822, Fisher's of Norfolk and Suffolk in 1844. Stock companies confined themselves to fewer theatres, and the lesser towns had either no drama at all or had to rely on occasional visits from scratch companies. Many reasons are adduced for the general decline: the rise of Methodist opposition, the unrest and uncertainty caused by the industrial revolution, the poverty of the drama and consequent craze for melodrama with expensive effects, the coming in of later dining hours. To these, as far as the provinces are concerned, may be added the bad effects of the starring system. The more stars, or 'auxiliaries' as they were called, that were brought at exorbitant fees from London the more the audiences demanded. They ceased to be satisfied with the efforts of the stock company, and the stock companies in turn declined in talent because of the poor rewards the provincial theatres now afforded. Once the principal theatres engaged stars of note to play leads they ceased to become the great schools of acting that they had been in the preceding century.

In 1843 an Act for Regulating the Theatres (see DRAMATIC CENSORSHIP) attempted to stimulate dramatic activity. The monopoly of the patent houses was finally ended; freedom was granted to all theatres to present legitimate drama, and all had a right to be licensed by the justices. Restrictions with regard to length of seasons were abolished, so that a stock company could stay in one theatre all the year round. This was a death-blow to many circuits, since the minor theatres, which had been functioning in most big towns as circuses, amphitheatres, music-halls, and the like, presenting only pantomimes and burlettas, could now obtain licences as regular theatres. As they were usually large buildings, holding 2,000–3,000 spectators, their competition proved a serious embarrassment to the old-established theatres.

(*q*) *Touring Companies*. Another factor hastened the end of the system of stock companies with or without circuits: this was the rise of the touring company. Already in the late 1820s the rage for foreign operas, which could not be satisfied by the stock companies, had led to the formation of opera companies which toured the country, performing for a week or two at each theatre. These were followed by English light opera companies playing either one opera or a series of operas. Some London theatre companies started to send their productions on tour, though often they relied on the local stock companies to fill the minor roles. Indeed, from 1850 to 1880 the two systems existed side by side, the stock companies being used to reinforce the travelling companies, as well as to give some performances on their own account, especially the Christmas pantomime, which had become an annual custom at most theatres by mid-century. The enormously increased facilities for travel afforded by the development of the railways, however, ensured the final triumph of the touring over the stock system. The circuits were finally broken up, and lessees were able to run theatres at different ends of the country. It was a bad day for the provincial stage when this happened, because all local and regional interests were lost, whilst touring companies provided no variety of experience for the actor. The provincial theatres ceased to be independent centres of theatrical life and by the 1880s relied almost entirely on the visits of weekly touring companies bringing their versions of the latest London successes. The few remaining stock companies ceased at about the same time. Thus, when the cinema entered the provincial field about 1910, the theatres rapidly succumbed. Many were converted to cinemas, with the result that large towns, often with long theatrical histories, ceased to have any theatre at all until the new repertory theatres began to supply the deficiency (see REPERTORY THEATRE MOVEMENT). These returned to something like the idea of a local resident stock company, but not generally to the nightly change of bill.

In 1948 local authorities were given permissive power to levy a rate up to 6*d*. for artistic and recreational purposes. Not one has fully implemented this power, and many have done nothing at all. The first theatre to be built and financed by a local authority was the Belgrade at Coventry (see BELGRADE THEATRE and No. 44), which opened in 1958. Several others, wholly or partly supported by the municipality, have followed (see CIVIC THEATRES). Repertory theatres have received subsidies from the Arts Council, local authorities, television companies, and charitable trusts. Although over 100 theatres have been closed or converted to other uses since 1956, several new ones have been built (Chichester, Guildford, Newcastle-on-Tyne, Nottingham). These are symptomatic of a distinct revival of theatrical life in the provinces which have also given a number of new playwrights to the English theatre. (See also BATH, BIRMINGHAM, BRIGHTON, BRISTOL, LINCOLN, LIVERPOOL, NORWICH, RICHMOND, 2 and YORK.) SYBIL ROSENFELD

PUBLILIUS SYRUS, see MIME, 2 *b*.

PUDDLE WHARF THEATRE, see MERMAID THEATRE, PORTER'S HALL, and ROSSETER, PHILIP.

PULCINELLA, one of the comic servants of the *commedia dell'arte* who may have originated with the actor 'Ciuccio' (Andrea Calcese). A hump-backed, doltish fellow, Pulcinella is regarded, by those who look for the origin of the Italian improvised comedy in the Atellan farces, as identical with the Maccus, or stupid servant, of Latin popular comedy. In his original Italian form he is regarded as typical of the Neapolitan district; as Polichinelle he stands to some for the quick wit of France; while as Punch (and Punchinello) he epitomizes English humour. His name first appears in the early seventeenth century, and the character, wherever it originated, was probably firmly established by Silvio Fiorillo, otherwise famous as Capitano Mattamoros. Pulcinella has no part in the English harlequinade, unless we consider that some of his characteristics may have passed to Clown, but, still in his Italian clothes, and with his humped back and hooked nose, he is the chief figure in the ubiquitous travelling puppet-booth (see PUNCH AND JUDY). In the opinion of competent critics, the popularity of Pulcinella, and the disproportionate attention paid to his buffoonery, was one of the main causes of the decline of the *commedia dell'arte* (see ITALY, 2).

PULITZER PRIZE FOR DRAMA, one of several literary awards established under the will of Joseph Pulitzer (1847–1911), given annually for the best 'original American play performed in New York'. It was first awarded in 1918, and it was three times awarded to Eugene O'Neill and Robert Sherwood respectively.

PUNCH AND JUDY. This old puppet-show, sometimes still to be seen in the streets and at the seaside, dates in its present form from about 1800. The familiar story is briefly as follows: Punch, a grotesque hunchback with hooked nose and chin and usually a protruding belly, is left to mind the baby while Judy, his wife, goes shopping. The baby begins to cry, ignores Punch's attempts to soothe it, and only screams louder when he chastises it; at last in anger and desperation Punch throws it out of the window. Judy returns, is furious with Punch, and belabours him with a stick; whereupon Punch seizes the stick, beats Judy senseless, and kills her. Then follow a number of encounters between Punch and various characters, most of whom he beats and kills—these usually include a Doctor, a Negro, and a Beadle. Eventually, however, Punch is captured and taken off to be hanged. At the last moment he tricks Jack Ketch, the hangman, persuading him to put his head into the noose, and then quickly pulling the rope. After his triumph over all human adversaries he is sometimes, however, frightened by the ghost of Judy, and then by the Devil, who arrives to carry him off; after a tremendous fight Punch usually emerges the victor, and hoists the lifeless body of the Devil upon his triumphant stick. Punch has a friendly companion in Joey, the Clown, and a scene is often introduced with a real live dog—Toby. Not the least remarkable aspect of this 'horrific' drama is that it invariably moves an audience to roars of laughter.

The origin of Punch is an obscure subject, about which it is tempting to romanticize; it is nevertheless not entirely fanciful to see his early prototype in the masked mimes of the popular Greek and Roman theatre; here we find grotesque figures, masked, sometimes with hooked noses, and padded absurdly or obscenely about their bodies (see No. 11a); their drama dealt with popular mythological stories and was enlivened with slapstick and buffoonery (see No. 12). Puppet-shows were popular at that period, and almost certainly reproduced the traditions of the mime. Throughout the obscurity of the Dark and Middle Ages it appears that this tradition, though suppressed by the Church, never entirely disappeared, and in the sixteenth century we find an essentially popular drama growing up in Italy, a drama of stock characters, improvised by masked figures, some of them grotesquely padded—the *commedia dell'arte* (see ITALY, 2). It is not impossible that this tradition was largely preserved through a thousand years in the puppet-shows.

Among the characters of the Italian comedy

was one Pulcinella—a sly comic servant, always getting into scrapes and cleverly escaping punishment; he invariably had a hooked nose and a hump-back, and was a great favourite in the district of Naples; but it was as a puppet that he gained his great success, for as a puppet his physical disfigurements could be comically exaggerated in a manner impossible to a living actor.

The Italian comedy spread all over Europe, and was firmly established in Paris; with it went the Italian puppet theatres, and in France Pulcinella became Polichinelle—a witty Gallic character destined to preside over the French puppet stage for 150 years. When, in 1660, the English Court returned to England, and King Charles II once again threw the theatres open to every kind of entertainment, the Italian puppets were not slow to take advantage of the fields that had been so fruitful earlier in the century; on 9 May Samuel Pepys, passing through Covent Garden, notes 'the Italian puppet-play of Signor Bologna which is very pretty, the best that ever I saw, and a great resort of gallants'. In 1962 the 300th anniversary of 'Mr. Punch' in England was celebrated by the unveiling of a plaque in the portico of St. Paul's Church, Covent Garden, and a service attended by some fifty Punch and Judy men, some with Toby dogs.

On 1666 Pepys again records seeing 'Polichinello, which pleases me mightly'.

England took 'Polichinello' to her heart, and soon anglicized him from 'Punchinello' to plain 'Punch'. But it was not only in name that he was translated; he retained all his physical grotesqueries, but was adopted as a ubiquitous English buffoon in every puppet-play of the period. At this time the old biblical stories that had been banished from the living theatre were still the staple fare on the puppet stage, and Punch was introduced as a vulgar 'farceur' into the Garden of Eden, Noah's Ark, or the Court of Solomon; he turned up unexpectedly in the story of Dick Whittington or of Doctor Faustus. This apparent incongruity was in effect no more than the traditional stage 'business' of the English clown; with the decline of the Morality plays, towards the end of the sixteenth century, the character of the Vice, who was accustomed to run through every play as a perpetual trouble-maker among the more virtuous characters, declined into a mere buffoon or clown, but continued to crop up as light relief throughout the whole body of Elizabethan drama; his distracting antics were gradually banished from the stage, but he found a home in the character of Punch upon the puppet stage—always a sure preserver of popular dramatic tradition.

Thus it will be seen that the character of Punch is derived partly from the early Mediterranean mimes through the Italian comedy, and partly from the tradition of the English medieval fool through the dramatic types of the Vice and the Clown; he has evolved into a character quite different from both Pulcinella and Polichinelle. Throughout the eighteenth century Punch continued as the chief and presiding character on the puppet stage; there was no such thing as a Punch play, but merely hundreds of biblical, legendary, and sometimes literary stories, in all of which Punch appeared; for a few years (1710–14) Punch's theatre in Covent Garden was the rage of the town, but long after the fashion had died away puppet-plays were still popular at fairs and country wakes among the ordinary common people. It was during these years that Punch's character was formed: he was a quarrelsome nuisance to the rest of the actors, he had a wife called Joan, who nagged him, and whom he beat, the Devil usually appeared at the end to take him away—and sometimes succeeded—and he spoke in a high squeak, formed by inserting a 'swazzle' or squeaker into the mouth of the speaker. He was the beloved favourite of the people.

Gradually, however, the popularity of an essentially Elizabethan stage technique began to fade, even on the puppet stage; Punch and Joan were often banished to a comic afterpiece, or entirely ousted by the new craze for Fantoccini, or Trick Figures, and the old fairground puppet-plays degenerated into a mere jumble of nonsensical and indecent absurdities. It was at this point, at the end of the eighteenth century, that Punch must have seemed on the verge of extinction.

To understand what happened now it is important to appreciate the distinction between the various types of puppet-show (see MARIONETTE and PUPPET). The early English puppet-shows were probably presented by hand- or glove-puppets; the puppet-play in Ben Jonson's *Bartholomew Fair* (1614) appears to be designed for this type of puppet. The Italian puppets brought over after the Restoration were probably marionettes, and it was undoubtedly as a marionette that Punch developed in England. English puppet-shows of the eighteenth century were almost invariably presented by marionettes. A marionette theatre, however, is difficult to transport—it requires at least a cart—and by the end of the eighteenth century Punch had declined so much in favour that it was no longer economically worth while to transport all the apparatus of a marionette theatre presenting Punch plays from one village or fair to another. Punch nearly died—but instead he became a hand-puppet. The old tradition had never been entirely lost, and hand-puppet booths, presenting short knock-about turns between Punch and Joan, or Punch and the Devil, had been set up outside fairground puppet theatres as a sort of 'trailer' for the full-length puppet-plays inside. Now Punch was relegated solely to the open-air hand-puppet booth; it was easily portable, for one man could carry it on his back, and present an entire show single-handed, with the indispensable aid of a mate to 'bottle' or collect the pennies from the audience. In this transformation Punch found a new lease of life.

It is important to realize that the form taken by the Punch and Judy show has been dictated far more by these practical and economic considerations than by any literary or symbolical fantasies of later commentators. The essential features of every hand-puppet show are that only two characters can appear at a time (unless there is more than one manipulator), that there is very little opportunity for elaborate staging effects, and that the gestures of the figures are extremely limited; it is, therefore, almost essential for a hand-puppet show to concentrate on fast, witty dialogue, or on broad and vulgar effects, with plenty of slapstick and fighting, which hand-puppets can do to perfection. That is precisely what the Punch and Judy show provides. Punch is on the stage the whole time, occupying the manipulator's right hand; on the left hand are introduced one after another a whole procession of lively characters, each to do battle and fall before Punch's furious assaults. The scheme of the play can be seen as a not unnatural development from the earlier Punch dramas, but the dialogue has been cut to the bone to suit the new medium, and there appears indeed little rhyme or reason in Punch's pugnacity; Judy—probably a corruption from the familiar 'Joaney'—hardly has time to show herself a shrew before she is slaughtered; Joey was introduced early in the nineteenth century in honour of Grimaldi, the famous clown; a doctor made his appearance soon after; a hangman was introduced to dispatch Punch, but was tricked into putting his head into his own noose; the beadle, now usually a policeman, is an obvious native growth; the combat with the Devil was a feature of the late Morality plays.

Throughout the nineteenth century Punch and Judy prospered, and Punch's squeak was familiar in the streets of London and throughout the countryside. From time to time new characters were added or old ones were transformed—'Shallaballah', an obscure Oriental, became Jim Crow the Negro minstrel; Mr. Jones, a respectable tradesman, appeared as the owner of Toby; a boxing match was introduced; but the main outlines of the story have remained exactly the same. Today Punch and Judy is not often seen in the streets, but it is not defunct; a survey carried out by *The World's Fair* showed that in recent years there were resident Punch and Judy shows at over sixty English and Welsh seaside towns; at the larger of these the showmen have to pay a rent for the right to perform, and rely on collecting throughout the season not only enough to cover that, but enough to keep themselves during the winter until Christmas time, when there are plenty of parties to be attended. There are probably about a hundred men in this country able to perform Punch and Judy; many of them belong to families who have been doing it for generations, but there have also recently been newcomers from the music-halls, and amateurs who have turned a hobby into a part-time source of income. Some of the work of these newcomers is excellent: Punch and Judy demands a strong and extremely adaptable voice, an ability to gag in the true *commedia dell'arte* tradition, perfect timing of minute finger-movements, and considerable physical toughness—the strain of holding one's arms above one's head for half an hour and of throwing one's body about during the fights is most exhausting.

Punch's continued existence in modern England is something of a miracle, but he is still popular, and is still genuinely funny, and there seems no reason why he should disappear now; the details of his drama may change in the future as they have done in the past, but the type seems to be immortal and the tradition is too strong to die.

The text of Punch and Judy was first taken down in 1827 by J. Payne Collier and published with illustrations by George Cruikshank. This text is not free from suspicion, and has probably been edited and 'improved' with literary emendations, but it has remained in print to this day. The early editions contained a 'History of Punch and Puppets' by Payne Collier that was certainly very good for its period, but can now be shown to contain some inaccuracies and inventions. There is a chapter on Punch, including the Payne Collier text, in *Popular Entertainments through the Ages* by Samuel McKechnie; Mayhew's *London Labour and the London Poor* (1851) contains a verbatim transcription of an actual mid-Victorian street performance, while a modern version of the story, played in Scotland by a travelling company, is given in George Baker's *Playing with Punch* (1944). For other accounts of Punch see P. T. Stead's *Mr. Punch* (1950) and George Speaight's *History of the English Puppet Theatre* (1955) (see also No. 141).

GEORGE SPEAIGHT

PUNCH AND JUDY THEATRE, New York, a delightful playhouse, holding only 300 people, situated on the north side of 49th Street. It opened on 10 Nov. 1914 with *The Marriage of Columbine*, and one of its first successes was a dramatization of *Treasure Island*. Charles Hopkins and his wife were identified with this theatre from its opening, and in 1926 it was renamed the Charles Hopkins and opened with *The Makropulos Secret*. A record for the house of 321 performances was set up by *Mrs. Moonlight*, while in 1928 a translation of Reynal's *Le Tombeau sous l'Arc de Triomphe* ran for a week. In 1932 the theatre became a cinema for the showing of special films.

GEORGE FREEDLEY†

PUNCH'S PLAYHOUSE, London, see STRAND THEATRE, I.

PUPPET. A puppet, strictly speaking, is any inanimate figure controlled by human agency. There are many different types of puppets, and in their long history they have been put to many different uses.

Probably their earliest appearance was in connexion with religious ceremonies or as a medium for popularizing religious legends; for the temples of Egypt and Greece statues were constructed that could incline their heads and make other movements under the direction of concealed controls; similar figures were known in the churches of medieval Europe; and among African tribes, idols have been found that could be secretly operated in the same manner. The dividing line between charlatanry and religious drama was, perhaps, sometimes finely drawn. To this day, in the Far East—China, Burma, the islands of Java and Bali—the traditional epics of Buddhist mythology are still performed by puppets, and the puppet-showman is venerated as a great popular educator. In Europe, in the Middle Ages, religious dramas performed by puppets developed from the Christmas crib plays and, especially in Italy, came to have an important part in the instruction and entertainment of the people.

With the disappearance of the living religious drama in Europe the puppet-shows still continued to present biblical stories, since they were the popular traditional stories of the common people. Even in England, plays like *The Creation of the World* or *The Court of Solomon* were performed by itinerant puppeteers almost to the beginning of the nineteenth century—250 years after they had been banished from the stage. The puppet-show was essentially the drama of the people and preserved, often for centuries, age-old dramatic types and popular legends; puppet-showmen were usually simple and unlearned men who earned a modest livelihood by enacting what their fathers had taught them.

Throughout Western Europe, up to the end of the nineteenth century, the travelling puppet theatres were regular visitors to country fairs and remote villages; their performances were usually crude and sometimes vulgar, but they carried the drama where even the strolling players never ventured. It was not only dramatic and literary traditions that were preserved by puppets—when Bohemia lay under Austrian domination the puppet-showmen played a great part in fortifying the national culture of the people as they travelled from village to village performing native Czech plays in their own language.

Perhaps not far removed from the religious puppet-show is the puppet designed to arouse wonder; at certain periods of its history the puppet has been admired for its mechanistic rather than its dramatic qualities; its movements have been regarded as a sort of conjuring trick, the secret of its construction jealously guarded, and great ingenuity has been displayed in devising clever and intricate effects. This aspect of puppetry was probably first highly developed in the Fantoccini of the late eighteenth century by those masters of puppetry, the Italians, and was soon absorbed into the English and other national traditons; in the nineteenth century this development was still further advanced by the clever English marionette showman, Thomas Holden, and in the twentieth century the brilliant Podrecca's Piccoli represented further advances in intricate articulation. Among the favourite tricks are the 'Dissecting Skeleton' whose bones gradually float apart and dance separately in the four corners of the stage and then reunite, and the 'Grand Turk' whose arms, legs, head, and finally trunk fly apart, each turning into a separate small figure.

Puppets have always been popular among the common people, but in their time they have also provided fashionable entertainment for high society. The Italian puppets that went to London soon after the Restoration were summoned to several command performances by Charles II; the famous Puppet Theatre under the Piazza in Covent Garden, under the direction of a brilliant dwarf, Martin Powell, was one of the most fashionable and successful entertainments of its day (1711–13); later in the same century the Italian puppets, presenting opera and Fantoccini, again took London by storm; the Prince of Wales himself was a subscriber at Carnevale's select Puppet Theatre in Savile Row in 1790. In eighteenth-century Italy there were many princes who patronized puppets in their private theatres—such as Cardinal Ottoboni, for whose theatre Filippo Juvarra (1685–1736) designed scenery (see No. 66) and Scarlatti wrote music. In Hungary in the 1770s there was an elaborate private puppet theatre belonging to Prince Esterházy, for which Haydn was commissioned to write several operettas.

The fashionable puppet-show, as might be expected, emancipated itself from the traditional legacies of the folk-puppet theatre, and developed in their place a sophisticated charm and a keen sense of satire. The puppet is indeed particularly well suited for mimicry and satire and has often been employed for that purpose. That twisted genius, Samuel Foote, used to introduce an act with puppets into his entertainments with the object of impersonating and mimicking popular actors of the period, and in 1773 produced an entire puppet-play at his theatre in the Haymarket as a satire on the popular taste in sentimental comedy. Charles Dibdin, another gifted eccentric of the English stage, erected his own puppet theatre at Exeter 'Change in 1775, and mocked at his contemporaries on its boards. Satire has flourished even more happily across the Channel than in England—so much so that the Roman puppet theatres were closed down in about 1850 by the state authorities because of their thinly disguised political references. In France, in the 1860s, a clever journalist, Lemercier de Neuville, developed a puppet-show whose political and literary allusions made it in great demand in the *salons*; in the same period Maurice Sand, at Nohant, diverted himself and his sister with a puppet theatre which, with its witty contemporary allusions, was designed to appeal essentially to their own literary circle.

The fortunes of the puppet-show waxed and waned through many centuries without anyone, at least in Europe, regarding it very seriously, or thinking of it as anything other than a crude entertainment or, at most, an amusing diversion. However, the closing years of the nineteenth and the early years of the twentieth centuries saw a marked revival, in which puppets were 'discovered' by the artists, and accorded a serious respect that they had never enjoyed before. In 1862 the 'Theatron Erotikon' in Paris was the scene of a series of puppet performances devised by a group of young artists who permitted a certain sophisticated impropriety to enliven their productions; the puppet-show has continued to exercise a great attraction upon many French writers and artists ever since. In England, Gordon Craig, with his emphasis on the actor's role as an 'uebermarionette', campaigned with enthusiasm for the puppet as a worthwhile artistic and dramatic medium. From these efforts came an artistic revival, which, while remaining largely an affair of the studio with a limited circle of devotees, nevertheless had its influence on the specifically 'entertainment' puppets. Among those who devoted themselves to the art of the puppet were Walter Simmonds, with a delightful one-man show, Olive Blackham, founder of the Roel Puppet Theatre, Margaret Hoyland, who worked with expressive paper figures, and Jan Bussell, who evolved a technique of puppet ballet. In France Marcel Temporal, Jacques Chesnais, and the Arc-en-Ciel group worked with intelligence and wit, usually with hand-puppets. In Germany, traditionally a great home of puppetry, Paul Brann founded the Munich Art-Puppet Theatre in the great tradition of South German woodcarving, and Harro Siegel gave delicate productions of opera.

One of the interesting developments of puppetry was its widespread adoption by schools as a handicraft subject. Educationalists welcomed the puppet-show as a means of self-expression and as a vehicle for instruction. It seemed likely that the practice of school puppetry, combining as it did the elements of formal instruction with manual dexterity both in the making and handling of puppets, would be extended, but it has in fact declined somewhat and is now not so widely used.

There are many different types of puppets, including the Hand- or Glove-Puppet, the Rod-Puppet, the Marionette, which are all rounded figures, and the flat puppets of the Shadow Show and the Toy Theatre. Of these the Hand-Puppet is best known in England (see PUNCH AND JUDY and No. 141; also No. 131). It has a firm head and hands with a loose open costume; the performer inserts his hand into the costume, with his first finger placed in the head and the second finger and thumb each in a hand; he stands behind a screen and holds the puppets above it. The head and hands of a hand-puppet are usually made of wood, but this has the disadvantage of being heavy, and they are sometimes now made of papier-mâché, which is very light and strong. The disadvantages of the hand-puppets are that the gestures of the figures are limited to the twitching of a man's fingers, and that one performer cannot introduce more than two characters at a time; the great advantages of hand-puppets are that they are quickly and simply made and very light and easy to carry about. The successful hand-puppet play concentrates on broad simple effects, witty dialogue, or knock-about comedy. Many of the popular national puppet characters are hand-puppets, carried in this form across Europe by wandering showmen. Such, apart from Punch and Judy in England, are: in France, Guignol, the type of the Lyonnais silkweaver, generous, bibulous, and witty; in Germany, Kasperl, a sly clever peasant type; in Russia, Petrushka, from the same stock as Punch; and in Italy, Pulcinella, the father of them all; even in China there is a family of hand-puppets not very dissimilar from the European breed. All these folk-puppet shows make a great point of beatings, terrific fights, and broad low comedy.

The satiric and literary puppet-shows that sprang up in France towards the end of the nineteenth century, the puppets of Edmond Duranty, Lemercier de Neuville, and Maurice Sand, were all hand-puppet shows. Among later exponents of the hand-puppet who developed shows on their own individualistic lines one might mention Walter Wilkinson in England, the author of several books describing his life as a travelling showman, and Nina Efimova in the U.S.S.R., who wrote a charming account of her work in *Adventures of a Russian Puppet Theatre*. The Continental-style theatre, allowing several manipulators to work together, permits considerably more ambitious productions than the one-man booth used for Punch and Judy.

The Rod-Puppet (see No. 129) is an extension of the hand-puppet, a full-length rounded figure, supported and manipulated by rods from below. Its movements are sometimes slow and limited, but the control is absolute, and broad gestures of rare beauty with the arms can be obtained. The most famous and beautiful rod-puppets are found in the island of Java (see No. 128); in Europe the only native tradition is in the Rhineland, but the puppets of Sergei Obraztsov, head of the Moscow State Central Puppet Theatre, are rod-puppets. In Paris, in the 1880s, Henri Signoret opened a puppet theatre with the intention of reviving the great plays of classical antiquity; the medium he adopted was figures controlled from below the stage by strings passing through their bodies and operated from a sort of keyboard. Later Gera Blattner in Paris experimented along the same lines. The most striking modern work with rod-puppets was achieved by Richard Teschner in Vienna; his stage was seen through a great golden framed convex lens, thus enlarging the figures and lending an air of mystery and enchantment to a highly polished performance.

The Marionette, which ranks in importance with the hand-puppet, is a rounded full-length puppet controlled from above the stage. Originally the control was by a simple rod or strong wire to the centre of the head; sometimes another rod would go to one hand, used for fighting; sometimes a string would be attached to each hand or to each leg. Marionettes controlled in this way are inevitably very crude, but they can be quite effective in their own tradition; folk-puppet theatres presenting this type of marionette are still open throughout Sicily, performing a series of plays based on the legends of Charlemagne, Roland, and their battles with the infidels, the cycle sometimes taking months to complete. A similar medieval tradition is found in Belgium, where, at Liège, a local peasant type—Tchantchès—figures as hero or chorus. In France there are several local heroes of the puppet stage—Jacques at Lille, Lafleur at Amiens—who figure throughout the repertory of popular legends in the marionette theatres.

A great technical advance was achieved when marionettes were manipulated entirely by strings (see No. 130); this allows far greater flexibility for body and head movements and is less distracting to the audience. This was perhaps first done by the intricate Italian Fantoccini of the 1770s, but possibly not until a hundred years later by Thomas Holden. One of the best-known examples of a marionette theatre is that at Salzburg, where delicate productions with an eighteenth-century Mozartian atmosphere have gained wide popularity. There is also the famous Teatro dei Piccoli of Vittorio Podrecca, with its brilliant Fantoccini and potted-opera programmes. Some of the marionettes in these theatres are most intricately strung, but the ordinary standard marionette has a string to each leg and arm, two to the head, one to each shoulder (which take the weight of the body) and one to the back: i.e. nine strings (actually fine thread) in all. An elaborate figure will have two or three times this number. These are gathered together on a wooden 'crutch' or control, held in one hand by the manipulator, while with the other he plucks at whatever strings are required. Marionettes are usually made of wood, but lighter materials such as papier-mâché are sometimes now used; their size varies from 12 in. to 18 in. for home use up to 2 ft. to 3 ft. for public performance. With the exercise of great skill and ingenuity marionettes can be made that will reproduce almost every human movement—though simple and technically crude puppets will often convey an equally dramatic effect.

The Shadow Show is a form of puppetry in which flat figures are passed between a strong light and a translucent screen; the audience, on the other side of the screen, sees their shadows, passing across it. Limited of necessity to a highly stylized convention, the shadow show has proved itself an artistic medium of rare and delicate charm (see Nos. 126 and 127).

The oldest form of shadow theatre is found in the Far East—particularly in China and the islands of Java and Bali, where there are still potent shadow-show traditions in which ancestor-worship and magic play their part. The grotesque Javanese figures are particularly striking. Gradually the shadow show spread westwards in a cruder and more decadent form; there are traces of it in Arabia, along the north coast of Africa, and in Anatolia (see TURKEY). From Turkey the shadow theatre was taken to Greece, where it took root and evolved into a native popular entertainment, in which a witty, vulgar Greek character appears in every play, invariably getting the better of all the unpopular characters.

Shadow shows of some kind must have existed in Western Europe from very early times—there is a complete shadow-show performance indicated in Ben Jonson's *Tale of a Tub* (1633)—but it was not till the second half of the eighteenth century that travellers returning from the East brought the Eastern shadow show with them and the 'Ombres Chinoises' sprang into popularity. In 1774 Dominique Séraphin established a Shadow Theatre at Versailles, which was extensively patronized by the Court, and in the next year Ambroise introduced this entertainment to England; the craze for 'Ombres Chinoises' did not last for very long, but in its time it was a constant attraction and must have been a pretty and clever entertainment; the plays seem to have consisted of amusing episodes rather than dramatic pieces—the great classic was *The Broken Bridge*, in which a traveller indulges in a pantomime argument with a workman on the other side of a river. This was first given by Séraphin after he moved to the Palais-Royal in 1784. His theatre there continued under his nephew (who succeeded him in 1799) until 1859, and was the delight of successive generations of Parisian children.

The 'Ombres Chinoises' were preserved in the English Galanty Show, which was often given in a Punch and Judy booth with a sheet stretched across the opening and lit by candles from inside. The old favourite of *The Broken Bridge* was still performed in the London streets up to the end of the nineteenth century, but the Galanty Show seems to have disappeared completely now.

Towards the end of the nineteenth century there was something of a revival of the shadow show in France; a group of artists and writers who gathered at the Chat Noir café in Montmartre, led by Henri Rivière and Caran d'Ache, combined during the 1880s and 1890s in presenting a series of shadow-show performances that became famous for their wit and artistry.

An interesting revival of the shadow-show technique was seen in the 1930s with the shadow films of Lotte Reiniger; their method of production varied slightly from the ordinary shadow technique: the figures, cut from tin and fully jointed, were laid upon a translucent 'table', brightly illuminated from below, and moved gradually while a 'stop camera' above recorded each position.

Shadow figures can be made of cardboard, but are much better constructed of tin (as in the Chat Noir and Galanty shows), of leather (as in Java and Bali), or of some coloured transparent material (as in China and Greece). There are several methods of manipulation:

1. By thin bamboo rods, held by the operator from below the screen, as in the Far East (see No. 126).
2. By rods held at right angles to the screen, as in Greece and Turkey (see No. 127).
3. By concealed strings or wires passing down behind the figures and operated from below, as in the Chat Noir and Galanty shows.

Figures that do not possess any actions of their own can be drawn across the screen from the sides. This is the method used in the Toy (or Model) Theatre, or Juvenile Drama, a form of children's entertainment popular on the Continent in the nineteenth century, particularly in Germany, Denmark, and Spain, where sheets of characters and scenery printed by colour lithography were sold with texts of plays specially written for children. In England, however, where Toy Theatres started earlier and had a great vogue, the plays were adapted from those given in the London theatres, and the sheets were sold either plain or hand-coloured. They were then stuck upon cardboard, coloured by hand, if plain, and cut out, and the scenery was mounted in grooves on and above the stage. The characters were pushed on and off stage on tin slides with long handles (unlike the Continental model stages, where the figures moved either in grooves cut in the stage-floor or were manipulated from above the stage), and were changed as often as necessary, several figures in different positions being used in a short scene (for a more detailed account of the English version, see TOY THEATRE; also No. 68).

There are several other less well-known types, notably the intricate and almost life-size Japanese puppets, held in full view of the audience by sometimes as many as three manipulators, and operated by small wires and levers concealed in their backs. Some of the finest Japanese dramatists of the eighteenth century composed plays for the puppet stage, which was closely linked with the popular *Kabuki* drama and recognized as an integral form of theatrical art (see JAPAN). The 'Cheeky Boys' and other dummies used by ventriloquists represent humbler examples of the same type of puppet.

Then there are 'Jigging Puppets' or 'Marionnettes à la planchette', consisting of one or two figures with a string passing horizontally through their breasts from an upright post to the performer's knee, and made to jig or dance about to the bagpipes or similar instrument. These were for many centuries a popular street entertainment.

One cannot do more than mention the Giant Figures carried in street processions, or the many different types of mechanical automata—the peep-show, the water theatres, the moving pictures, and so on. These may all be included in the sphere of puppetry, but, interesting and charming though they may often be, they belong rather to the non-dramatic aspect of the subject and lie outside the scope of the present volume. GEORGE SPEAIGHT

After the Second World War there was a great increase in the use of puppets, particularly in the Soviet bloc, as a means of education and propaganda, chiefly for children, but in some cases for adults also. In general the teaching was conveyed with great simplicity and directness, but lavish use was made of colour and music, and the stories were presented with pathos and humour. One of the great difficulties in the puppet theatre, as in all branches of children's theatre, is the shortage of good plays, particularly for the older children who are no longer satisfied with the fairy tales, nursery rhymes, and animal fables which delight the younger audiences.

In the Soviet Union and other Communist states the professional puppet theatres are state-aided, but, within the basic similarity of the pattern which evolved, national characteristics emerged and gave individuality to the productions, each country dealing with its particular problems in its own way and with due regard to the historical traditions of its own culture. What they have in common is the pattern of control, and the fact that all, or most of them, have their own theatre buildings, where they perform every day and from which they go on tour to factories, schools, and village halls over a wide area. Also, they employ their actors on a permanent basis, often as many as thirty people making up the company. Programmes are divided into two groups, one for children from 3 to 7, the other for children from 8 to 12, and the theatres work in close association with kindergartens and junior schools. It has been found that the use of puppet-plays can often help to resolve problems of adjustment and discipline among the smaller children, or stimulate the older ones to take an interest in school subjects in which they are weakest.

Although many of the early puppeteers were necessarily drawn from the ranks of enthusiastic amateurs, as there were not enough professionals to meet the increased demand, there are now a number of official courses in puppet-making and handling, often lasting up to three years, run by the Institutes of Drama and by dramatic schools, and it should eventually be possible to staff all the puppet theatres with trained graduates from these courses. This will not, of course, oust the amateur, who still flourishes. In Bulgaria, which with a population of about eight million, has eight permanent puppet theatres, a special Puppet Faculty was added to the Institute of Theatre Art in Sophia in 1962. In Czechoslovakia, where puppets did much to keep Czech theatre alive during the years of oppression (see CZECHOSLOVAKIA), puppet-theatres flourish—one of the best known being Jan Skupa's Marionette Theatre in Prague—and puppeteers are trained in the Dramatic Academies of Prague, Bratislava, and Brno. There are about fifteen puppet theatres for children; the first was established mainly through the efforts of the kindergarten teacher, Ludmilla Tesarova (1857–1936), and the plays, which are based on current events as well as on fairy tales, have as their chief character the puppet Kasparek. In Hungary (see No. 130) the first permanent puppet theatre dates from 1947. There are now about seven companies based on Budapest, which tour the country with a repertory of about twenty plays, some for the younger and some for the older children, some for town and some for rural audiences. The State Puppet Theatre, which was awarded a gold medal at the Second Puppet Festival in Bucharest in 1960, runs a three-year course for the training of puppeteers. In Poland, where conditions are much the same externally, the plays and productions have a decidedly Polish flavour, and are perhaps somewhat more sophisticated than elsewhere. There are also Polish puppet theatres for adults. In Rumania there has been an enormous development. The first puppet theatre was founded in 1949, and by 1960 there were twenty-three, mostly with their own theatres and staffs of about thirty to forty. The most important is the Tandarica in Bucharest, established in 1950, which employs a staff of ninety and has two stages, one for hand-puppets, the other for string-puppets (see Nos. 130, 176). Some of the theatres cater for minority audiences with productions in German and Hungarian. Special programmes are also given for adults. In Soviet Russia the various nationalities have their own puppet theatres, often with a long tradition behind them. Officially puppets, which are an acceptable leisure activity for adults, are also regarded as an educational art-form for children, with a large repertory embracing all age-groups. The famous State Central Puppet Theatre in Moscow, directed by Sergei Obraztsov, was set up in 1931. His work has since been seen and admired far beyond the confines of his own country. By 1965 rod- and string-puppets had almost entirely ousted hand-puppets in the professional puppet theatres, and to give additional movement mechanical aids, such as a spring, were fitted to the puppet's limbs. An interesting volume which gives detailed, illustrated instructions for the making of such puppets is *Sekrety Teatra Kukol* (*Secrets of the Puppet Theatre*), by A. Fedotov, published in Moscow in 1963.

In the Far East, particularly in China, the ancient traditions of puppetry have been adapted to modern needs, and many touring puppet companies, small and large, take entertainment and instruction to illiterate audiences in remote areas. In India, where the decline of traditional puppetry was most noticeable, a more sophisticated type of modern puppet theatre has evolved in the towns, and in 1959 an All-India Puppet Festival was organized in Udaipur by the Puppet Unit of the Lok Kala Mandal. But every state has its own folk-puppet personality, and care is being taken to preserve this and other individual features. The old leather shadow-puppets are still in use, as are rod- and string-puppets; among the latter are the famous Rajhastani puppets, legless, full-skirted wooden figures dressed in gay colours. Since 1952 the Calcutta Group of puppeteers has also been experimenting with hand-puppets. In Burma and Indonesia the approach to puppetry is still traditional, though in Burma a major change is seen in the appearance of a woman manager, Saya Lin, formerly a thing unknown. In Ceylon the ancient art of puppetry was stimulated by an academic conference held in 1956, which has had interesting results. Vietnam long retained its special form of the art, the Water Puppets, which performed on a raised stage moored in a lake, the audience sitting on the bank, and the manipulators, who might be men or women, working from boats hidden behind the stage.

There has been no comparable development of puppets in western Europe, except in Germany, which had a long tradition dating back to the twelfth century, and comprising the folk-puppets Hanswurst, and Kasper and Gretel, who approximate to the English Punch and Judy. In East Germany the state-controlled and state-aided pattern has imposed itself, but in West Germany the puppet theatres are mainly in private hands, though they may be supported by the municipality. Puppets in Germany are not considered solely as a form of entertainment for children, and there are a number of groups which cater for adults with a form of improvised and sophisticated satire.

In England there has been less activity than was at one time hoped, in spite of the foundation in 1925 of a British Puppet and Model Theatre Guild which publishes a quarterly journal and holds an exhibition every year. Among the few outstanding companies are the Hogarth Puppets, which were awarded a prize at the International Puppet Festival in 1960, and John Wright's Marionettes, which operate at the Angel Theatre, Islington, in North London. In North Wales a specially designed puppet theatre was opened by Eric Bramall. But the main use of puppets in Great Britain is still educational.

In Italy a Puppet Theatre was established in 1949 by Maria Signorelli at the University Theatre in Rome, which has had a great success. Her puppets, which have little in common with the original Pulcinella, though simple in design, are individuals, and the productions, which employ all the resources of modern science, are very elaborate, with extensive use of music and choreography.

In the United States puppets were slow to establish themselves, in spite of the small folk theatres which catered for the minority national groups. A few companies—among them those of Tony Sarg, Rufus Rose, Remo Bufano—toured with some success due to their technical skill and freshness of outlook, and at one time there was a vogue for a simplified cabaret-style puppet-show, of which the outstanding exponent was Bob Bromley, working with one figure at a time with no stage or scenery in a plain 'spot'. The cause of puppetry—which is served by an association known as the Puppeteers of America—received a distinct fillip in 1952, when the McPharlin family presented a magnificent collection of puppets (which now numbers over a thousand figures) together with an extensive library to the Detroit Institute of Arts. This resulted in the establishment of a Puppet Theatre there, to which leading American puppeteers are invited to present programmes both for children and for adults. BEATRICE KING

In 1929 the Union Internationale des Marionnettes was founded, and a year later a congress was held at Liège. The organization lapsed during the Second World War, but was re-founded in 1957, since when conferences and festivals have been held in various large cities every two years, with smaller gatherings in the intervening years.

PURDY'S NATIONAL THEATRE, NEW YORK, see CHATHAM THEATRE, 2.

PURIM PLAYS. The Jewish Festival of Purim on the 14th Adar (roughly early March), commemorating the events described in the Book of Esther, is a semi-religious holiday which acquired particular importance during the Jewish persecutions in the Middle Ages. Its secular character is attributed by some authorities to a Babylonian or Persian influence, and amusements of all kinds have always been associated with it. Purim plays appear to have been extemporized in France and Germany as early as the fourteenth century, but they take their origin mainly from the improvised songs and masquerades in which the mummers impersonated the characters of the Book of Esther under the influence of the Italian carnival. These masquerades were at first opposed by the religious authorities, but later tolerated as long as they did not overstep the bounds of decency.

The plays were mostly in one act. Costumes and style were fixed by tradition. Prose and verse were intermingled. All had songs, amusing interludes featuring comic rabbis, apothecaries, midwives, and devils, pantomimic dances, and a final chorus foretelling Israel's salvation. The dialogue was largely improvised, and based on such subjects as the story of Esther and Haman, the sale of Joseph by his brethren, the story of David and Goliath, and sometimes the life of Moses. These plots, which show one man fighting with God's help against overwhelming odds, could be adapted to local conditions within the traditional framework. Until recently they were still given in Eastern Europe in barns, stables, workshops, and in the house of the rich man of the village. Some idea of the dramatic possibilities of these primitive plays may be gathered from the account of one given as late as the end of the nineteenth century in Jerusalem, where life was still unaffected by the Jewish renaissance. The subject was the sale of Joseph. The scene was laid in front of the tomb of his mother Rachel—a well-known landmark in Jerusalem—represented by two chairs covered by a white cloth. Joseph, being led away into captivity, broke away from the slave-dealers and clung weeping to the tomb, from which his mother's voice was heard issuing, bidding him not to fear, for one day he would be a king in Egypt.

The Purim plays, which have had a considerable influence on the development of Jewish drama, took on a literary form in the early seventeenth century. Their technique was borrowed from the *commedia dell'arte*, the Capitano becoming Goliath or Haman, Pantalone Abraham or Jacob, Arlecchino Satan. Certain non-Jewish plays also had an influence on them; for English readers the most interesting are those done in Germany by the English Comedians, which included a version of *Esther and Haman* printed in the 1640 collection of their repertory. There was probably an English original of this, but if so it is lost. The popularity of the German version helped to raise the standard of Purim plays by making them studies in ambition. With the Hebrew revival in Holland and Italy comes a dramatization of the Book of Esther by Usque and de Graziano, which was produced at Ferrara in 1619, while at the end of the century Enriquez wrote a *Comedia famosa de Aman y Mordechai* (1699), also intended for general representation.

The first-known Purim play in Germany was a very poor *Ahasuerus* given at Frankfurt-am-Main in 1708. In the same city in 1712 Beerman von Limburg's play on the sale of Joseph proved so popular that it was printed, and produced as late as 1858 at Minsk. It appears to have been very spectacular in production, with fire, thunder, and other wonders. A point of interest is the appearance in it of the Pickelherring of the English Comedians, who henceforth becomes the traditional Purim clown. Another Purim play by Beerman dealt with David and Goliath, and, like the earlier one, proved so popular that Christians were forbidden by the authorities to attend it.

Purim plays became increasingly vulgar as time went on, and in 1720 the reaction set in with the production in Prague of a new play on Esther, shorn of much extraneous matter. This proved popular, and was reprinted for the third time at Amsterdam in 1774. The fight against vulgarity was continued energetically by the Haskala groups, which improved the Purim plays by relegating the comic figures to the background, and introducing a serious educational element. By the early nineteenth century the Purim plays were covering the whole range of drama, and with the founding by Goldfaden of a permanent Yiddish theatre which embodied in its productions much of the spirit and method of the Purim plays, their days were numbered. E. HARRIS

PURITAN INTERREGNUM. The Puritan opposition to the theatre, which had been growing steadily since the beginning of the seventeenth century, culminated in the closing of the theatres in 1642 by a Parliamentary Ordinance which stated that 'whereas public sports do not well agree with private calamities, nor public stage-plays with the seasons of humiliation . . . while these . . . do continue public stage-plays shall cease and be forborne'. It will be seen that public plays only were forbidden. There is no direct evidence that the Puritans as a whole were hostile to drama. Their objections to the public theatres were partly social, partly political, and only in extreme cases religious. Under the early Stuarts the London theatre, its plays, and its dramatists, had become increasingly attached to the Royalist cause, and the assembling of an audience at the playhouse provided excellent opportunities for subversive activities. Plays continued to be acted under the Commonwealth in schools—with the approbation of Cromwell himself—and possibly in private houses, and in 1656 Davenant was allowed to produce publicly his 'entertainment with music'—*The Siege of Rhodes*—now regarded as the first English opera. But for 18 years the professional actors were deprived of their means of livelihood, and their theatres stood derelict, many of them never to be used again. Some actors joined the army, some drifted into the provinces, some, like Andrew Cane, returned to earlier, half-forgotten trades. Only the boldest, or most desperate, tried to evade the ban. Evidence of surreptitious performances is given by records of the fining or imprisoning of the actors concerned. Among them were Richard Baxter, William Beeston, and Robert Cox, who took refuge in the Fortune, and in the smaller theatres, such as the Cockpit, Gibbon's Tennis-Court, and the Red Bull.

PUSHKIN, ALEXANDER SERGEIVICH (1799–1837), Russia's first and greatest national poet, born in Moscow. His father was a civil servant and his mother was descended from Peter the Great's famous Moor, Hannibal. Pushkin, whose uncle Vasily was a well-known poet, was educated privately, and at the age of 8, according to his brother, wrote little plays in French, which he acted with his sister. At 15 he included among his favourite writers the French dramatists, Molière, Racine, and Voltaire—and the Russians Ozerov and Fonvizin. But two of the greatest influences on him were Byron and Shakespeare. He valued the former for his progressive romanticism and his poetry of the rebel-hero, the latter for his superb characterization and the profundity of his philosophy. He once compared Shakespeare and Molière thus:

> Characters created by Shakespeare are not types of such and such a passion, or such and such a vice, as with Molière, but living beings, filled with many passions, many vices . . . Molière's miser is miserly and no more; Shakespeare's miser is miserly, keen-witted, vengeful, ambitious, sagacious.

It was under the influence of Shakespeare that Pushkin started work on his great drama *Boris Godunov*. He had already realized that Russia had no truly national drama, only an imitation of the neo-classic French school, and that it could only be created by returning to Russian themes and Russian folklore, and by making the Russian language a literary instrument fit to rank with the French and German languages for which it had been so often discarded in its own country. His association with the Decembrist revolutionaries shows that he realized also the social implications of his literary search for the soul of Russia.

It is evident from his letters and from fragments of unpublished works that Pushkin contemplated a series of dramatic works of which *Boris Godunov* alone was completed. It is notable in being the first Russian tragedy on a political theme—the relationship between a tyrant and his people—which, though set back in time, was actually a burning contemporary problem; and it does not rely on a love-intrigue. In other respects, too, it was revolutionary: it was broken up into scenes and episodes, it mingled poetry with prose, and made use of colloquial Russian speech. It was not published until six years after its completion in 1825, owing to trouble with the censorship, and was not seen on the stage for nearly fifty years, being given its first production in 1870. It became the basis of an opera by Mussorgsky, in which form it is usually seen nowadays.

Just before his death in a duel, Pushkin completed a series of one-act tragedies, little psychological portraits presented with great subtlety. One deals with Don Juan, one with the rivalry of Mozart and Salieri, and shows the latter, envious of Mozart's genius, poisoning him, while a third, depicting the character of a miser, owes something to Harpagon, but more to Shylock. With some unfinished scenes from Russian folklore and from the age of feudalism, this makes up the tale of Pushkin's work for the theatre. Though he is not primarily remembered as a dramatist—for his fine poems must take pride of place—and had little direct contact with the stage, the Russian theatre owes him a great debt, since it was he who first made Russian a literary language. There are theatres bearing his name in Moscow (see below) and in Leningrad (see ALEXANDRINSKY), and his works are quoted as often by Russians as Shakespeare's are by Englishmen.

PUSHKIN THEATRE, Moscow. This theatre, which has virtually taken the place of Taïrov's Kamerny, opened in 1951 under the directorship of Vasily Vasilyevich Vanin (1898–1951) after two years' preparation which included several provincial tours. Babochkin was responsible for most of its productions up to 1954, when Tumanov took over. The theatre has lived through several creative phases in its search for its own identity, and has not yet evolved a style of its own, but it has been responsible for some interesting productions, including *Krechinsky's Wedding* by A. V. Sukhov and *Stolen Happiness*, by I. Frank, both produced by Vanin shortly before his death, Ostrovsky's *At a Busy Place* (1952), Casona's *The Trees Die Standing* (1958), and Wilde's *The Importance of Being Earnest* (1957), produced by Petrov. BEATRICE KING†

PYLADES, a Roman pantomime actor (see PANTOMIMUS).

Q

'Q' THEATRE, Kew Bridge, see SUBURBAN THEATRES.

QUAGLIO, a family of artists, extending over several generations, many of whom worked for the theatre. They were of Italian origin, but late in the seventeenth century moved from Lake Como to Munich, where at least three generations were connected with the Court theatre, while a descendant was working at the Berlin Court theatre as late as 1891 (see SCENERY, 4).

QUARTERMAINE. (1) LEON (1876–1967), English actor, who made his first appearance on the stage at Sheffield in 1894. He was first seen in London in 1901, with Forbes-Robertson, and was a member of Granville-Barker's company at the St. James's in 1913, where he played in Shaw, Galsworthy, and Ibsen. He was a fine Shakespearian actor, and in later years his Banquo, John of Gaunt, Buckingham, and Cymbeline were memorable. He also gave a fine performance as the Nobleman's Man in *The Man with a Load of Mischief* (1925). He appeared many times in America with great success. He married as his second wife the actress Fay Compton, whose third husband he was, she being then the widow of Pélissier (*d.* 1913) and Lauri de Frece (*d.* 1921). His brother (2) CHARLES (1877–1958) was also an actor, whose later career was mainly in films. He was first seen in London in 1900, with Benson's company, and was for some years with Tree at His Majesty's. His first wife was the actress Madge Titheradge.

QUAYLE, (JOHN) ANTHONY (1913–), English actor and producer, who made his first appearance on the stage in 1931, at the 'Q' Theatre. In 1932 he joined the Old Vic company and played a variety of parts, going with it to Elsinore, playing Laertes, and subsequently toured the Continent and Egypt. He had already given proof of solid qualities, notably as Essex in *Elizabeth la Femme sans Homme*, and in his work with the Old Vic, when the Second World War interrupted his career. From 1939 to 1945 he served with the Royal Artillery, and from his experiences of guerrilla warfare in Albania came his first novel, *Eight Hours from England*, followed by *On Such a Night*. Meanwhile he had returned to the stage, where his acting revealed a maturity and breadth which proved that his war-service had in no way hindered, but rather had furthered, his artistic development. This was abundantly proved by his production in 1946 of *Crime and Punishment*, and by his work as actor and producer at the Stratford Memorial Theatre, of which he became director in 1948, in succession to Sir Barry Jackson. He retired from this post in 1956, after having appeared in a wide variety of leading parts, and appeared in London in *A View from the Bridge*. He then played Aaron in *Titus Andronicus* with Laurence Olivier as Titus, and gave a fine performance as James Tyrone in O'Neill's *A Long Day's Journey into Night* (1958). He was then seen in *Look After Lulu* (1959), *Chin-Chin* (1960) and as Dilke in *The Right Honourable Gentleman* (1964). He has also had a distinguished career in films. He married first the actress Hermione Hannen, and subsequently Dorothy Hyson, daughter of Dorothy Dickson. He was appointed C.B.E. in the Birthday Honours of 1952.

QUEEN ANNE'S MEN, a company—usually known as the Queen's Men—formed on the accession of James I, from the combination of Worcester's and Oxford's Men which had previously been at the Hope. They played at the Curtain, and among them in the beginning were Christopher Beeston, Richard Perkins, and Thomas Heywood. By 1609 they were playing also at the Red Bull, and seem to have had a successful career, both in London and in the provinces; but in 1616 internal dissension and the pressure of outward circumstances had combined to trouble them, and Beeston, who was their manager, moved them to his new playhouse, the Cockpit, or Phoenix. Their tenancy started off with a Shrove Tuesday riot of the London apprentices. This was a bad omen and they never prospered, it being left to the Prince's Men under Taylor to make a success of the new theatre. The Queen's Men broke up on the death of their patron, the best of them remaining at the Red Bull, the rest going into the provinces, while Beeston joined the Prince's Men, now his tenants at the Cockpit.

QUEEN ELIZABETH'S MEN, the most famous of London's theatrical companies in the 1580s–90s, was formed in 1583 by Tilney, acting under orders from Walsingham. Originally twelve in number, its members were appointed Grooms of the Chamber. Among them was the famous jester, Tarleton, favourite of Queen Elizabeth until he offended her with jokes against Raleigh and Leicester. The company made its first appearances at Court in December and in the following March, and then went on tour, returning to play, among other things, Tarleton's *Five Plays in One*, later revived as *The Seven Deadly Sins, Part I*. The death of Tarleton in 1588 was a great blow. The company was superseded by the Admiral's Men, to whom the dramatist Greene in 1591 sold *Orlando Furioso* after having previously sold it to the Queen's. He probably took advantage of the fact that the latter company was touring the provinces, and not in great favour in London. The last performance of the Queen's Men at Court was given in 1594, though they appeared at one of Henslowe's theatres later in the year, and from then onwards they dwindled away in the provinces, having sold their playbooks to Henslowe.

QUEEN HENRIETTA'S MEN, usually known as the Queen's Men, a theatrical company whose early origins are obscure. It was formed under Beeston some time in 1625, probably after the plague of that year had shut the theatres and disrupted the existing companies. The chief actors seem to have come from the late Queen Anne's Men and from the Lady Elizabeth's Men, among them Perkins, Bowyer, Turner, and Timothy Reade. They appear to have flourished, and among their successful plays were those which their official dramatist, James Shirley, wrote for them, some twenty, alone or in collaboration, from 1625 to 1636. They also appeared with great success before the Court in Heywood's masque, *Love's Mistress*, for which Inigo Jones designed some admirable scenery. They might have continued to flourish but for the plague of 1636 which closed the theatres. This gave Beeston the excuse to disband the company and form another, Beeston's Boys, which took over the Cockpit, while the Queen's Men were absorbed into other companies. Later a new Queen's company was formed, and played at Salisbury Court, its official dramatist being Richard Brome. Little more is known of its existence, which must have been somewhat precarious, and it disappeared at the final closing of the theatres in 1642.

QUEEN OF BOHEMIA'S MEN, see LADY ELIZABETH'S MEN.

QUEEN STREET THEATRE, LONDON, see KINGSWAY THEATRE.

QUEEN'S THEATRE, LONDON. 1. In the Haymarket. This theatre, named for Queen Anne, was built by Sir John Vanbrugh, who was hoping to profit from Rich's mismanagement of Drury Lane. With Congreve as manager, he installed Betterton and his company there, and the theatre opened on 9 Apr. 1705 with an opera, the prologue being spoken by Mrs. Bracegirdle. Although Vanbrugh's own comedy, *The Confederacy*, with Doggett, was a success in the autumn of the same year, so much money was lost altogether that Vanbrugh was glad to withdraw. He had let the theatre to Swiney, who decamped in 1711, leaving a load of debt. The theatre was really too big for drama, and became the first English opera-house. Just before Swiney left, Handel produced his 'Rinaldo' here with such success that he followed it with a series of similar works. On the death of Queen Anne the theatre was renamed the King's, and it was there that Handel produced 'Esther', the first oratorio to be heard in England. Opera continued to be the staple fare, Porpora succeeding Handel, until on 17 June 1789 the building was destroyed by fire (for another theatre on the same site, see HER MAJESTY'S).

2. In Long Acre, originally St. Martin's Hall, which was reconstructed as a theatre and opened on 24 Oct. 1867. Alfred Wigan was in charge, but the real manager was Henry Labouchère. The theatre had a short but lively existence. The first production was an adaptation of Charles Reade's novel, *White Lies*. Liston, afterwards of the Olympic, followed Wigan, and then came Ernest Clifton, who brought success. Mrs. Rousby made her London début there in 1869 in *The Fool's Revenge* and, helped by Tom Taylor, made a success.

There was always an excellent company at the Queen's, which for a time included Toole and Lionel Brough. Henry Irving played there, as did Charles Wyndham and Phelps, Ellen Terry, and Salvini, the last, in 1875, giving a fine performance as Othello. The theatre was well appointed with an excellently equipped stage, and in size it ranked next to Drury Lane. In 1879 it ceased to be a theatre, and was occupied by the Clerical Co-operative Stores. It now forms part of Odhams Press, and its outer walls still stand, while up to a short time ago the old direction signs were still to be seen inside the building. At one time it was known as the National Theatre.

3. In Shaftesbury Avenue, sister theatre to the Globe, which it adjoins. This was opened on 8 Oct. 1907 by J. E. Vedrenne with *The Sugar Bowl*. In 1908 a musical play, *The Belle of Brittany*, ran for 147 performances, and a year later H. B. Irving gave a season of revivals which included *The Bells* and *Robert Macaire*. In 1913 the theatre housed the fashionable tango teas, and in 1914 it had its first big success with *Potash and Perlmutter*, which ran for 665 performances. In 1919 Owen Nares, in association with Alfred Butt, became actor-manager of the Queen's and later appeared there in a revival of *The Little Minister*. Among the fine productions at this theatre were *And So To Bed* (1926), the Malvern Festival production of *The Apple Cart* (1929) with Edith Evans and Cedric Hardwicke, and Gielgud's *Hamlet* from the Old Vic (1930). The theatre then had a long series of good and successful plays, among them *The Barretts of Wimpole Street* (also 1930), *Evensong* (1932), *Short Story* (1935) with Marie Tempest and an excellent cast, and in 1937–8 Gielgud's season of *Richard II*, *The School for Scandal*, *Three Sisters*, and *The Merchant of Venice*, in all of which he appeared himself. He was also in *Dear Octopus* (1938), which was still running when the outbreak of the Second World War caused the theatres to close. It had reopened, and was housing the successful *Rebecca* with Owen Nares, when in 1940 it was hit by a bomb. It was derelict for nearly twenty years, but in July 1959 it reopened with Gielgud in his solo recital, *The Ages of Man*. Since then the theatre has again had a successful record, with such plays as *The Aspern Papers*, *The Tiger and the Horse* (both 1960), and the musical *Stop the World—I Want To Get Off* (1961).

QUESTORS THEATRE, EALING, LONDON, see AMATEUR THEATRE.

QUICK, JOHN (1748–1831), English actor, who as a boy of 14 joined a provincial company, and in 1767 was engaged for the Haymarket summer season by Foote. Here his good work caused him to be taken on at Covent Garden, where he was Postboy in *The Oxonian in Town*, and in *The Good-Natured Man*. He remained at Covent Garden for the rest of his career, except for occasional visits to the provinces and a brief managership of the King Street Theatre, Bristol. He had a vast repertory of comic parts, which ranged from Shallow and Polonius to the Clown in pantomime, through numerous rustics and comic servants. He inherited the roles of Ned Shuter and of Woodward, and was the original Tony Lumpkin and Bob Acres. He hankered after tragedy, and for his benefit in 1790 chose to appear as Richard III, only to be laughed off the stage. After that he remained faithful to comedy until his retirement in 1798, from which he occasionally emerged, being seen at the Lyceum in 1800. His last appearance was at the Haymarket as Don Felix in *The Wonder*, at a benefit for Mrs. Mattocks. A small, impetuous man, Quick was the favourite actor of George III, and his pleasant and somewhat chubby face was painted by Zoffany and others, in portraits which now hang in the Garrick Club, London.

QUICK-CHANGE ROOM, a small, closed recess opening off the stage, used by actors for changing their clothes when the time of their absence from the stage does not allow of a return to their dressing-rooms.

QUIN, JAMES (1693–1766), English actor, who made his first appearance at the Smock Alley Theatre in Dublin in 1712. Two years later he was playing small parts at Drury Lane, where he made a sudden success in the part of Bajazet in *Tamerlane* when the actor billed to play it was taken ill. In 1716 he went to Lincoln's Inn Fields Theatre, where he remained for fourteen years, appearing first as Hotspur, and then in a range of parts which included Othello, Lear, Falstaff, the Ghost in *Hamlet*, and Buckingham in *Richard III*. In 1732 he went to Covent Garden, and from there returned to Drury Lane, where he remained for several years, playing leading roles in tragedy. He was a declaimer rather than an actor, and almost the last representative of the school of Betterton, whose manner he may have caught from Booth. He was also a stickler for the old traditional costumes, and would not alter one detail. A portrait of him as Coriolanus, in Thomson's play (1748), shows him equipped with plumes, peruke, full spreading short skirt, and truncheon. Pope refers to 'Quin's high plume', as does Addison in *The Spectator*. But Quin's supremacy was soon to be challenged by the rising star of Garrick, of whom he said, 'if the young fellow is right, I and the rest of the players have been all wrong.' In 1751 he retired to Bath, having spent the last years of his career in constant rivalry with Garrick. A man of great gifts, he had had little formal education, and despised book-learning. Vain, obstinate, and quarrelsome, he was yet generous and warm-hearted, and was esteemed by some, notably Walpole, above Garrick. He was immortalized by Smollett in *Humphry Clinker*. His epitaph was written by Garrick, with whom he was reconciled in his last years.

QUINAULT, a family of French actors. The father and five children were all members of the Comédie-Française in the first half of the 18th century. The most famous was the second son (for whom see DUFRESNE), while of the three daughters the eldest, known as Mlle de Nesle, died young, and the youngest, known as Quinault la Cadette, shared soubrette roles with Mlle Dangeville.

QUINAULT, PHILIPPE (1635–88), French dramatist and librettist. The son of a baker, he became valet to Tristan l'Hermite, through whose influence his first play, *Les Rivales* (1653), was put into rehearsal at the Hôtel de Bourgogne as being by Tristan. When the actors discovered the truth, they wanted to halve the money that they were paying for the play, and the result of the negotiations was that the author was given a stipulated share in the receipts of each performance, and not, as hitherto, in those of the first few nights only. This has been cited by Fabian, Pill, and others as the origin of the royalty system, but the point is disputable. By 1666 Quinault had written sixteen plays, of which *La Mère coquette* (1665) was much praised by La Harpe. He was, however, maligned by Boileau, who found him insipid and sentimental, and much disliked by Racine. The last of his plays to profit from the advice of Tristan was *La Comédie sans comédie* (1655), which was a great success. Several of the characters in it bore the names of the actors playing the parts. Quinault later married a wealthy young widow, whom he had loved before her first marriage. She persuaded him to give up writing for the stage, which she considered a low pastime, but having been elected to the French Academy in 1670, he felt he ought to return to literature, so collaborated with Molière in the lyrics for *Psyché* (1671). He then contributed to 'Les Fêtes de l'Amour et de Bacchus', parts of which were written by Molière and de Benserade. This led to a meeting with Lully, composer of the music, and to a fruitful collaboration between the two. Quinault wrote a libretto for Lully every year, and his work was much admired by Louis XIV, who often, with royal condescension, suggested subjects for his pen. Such is the purifying power of music that his wife did not object to his engaging in such tasks. Quinault appeared to be at the height of his powers when he wrote what proved to be his last libretto, that for 'Armide'. The death of Lully and the influence of the religious ideas of the time then turned him finally against the stage. In the opinion of a contemporary critic, his verses were already music before Lully set them, in which respect he approached Racine, though with nothing of the latter's strength and passion.

QUINTERO, THE BROTHERS, see ÁLVAREZ QUINTERO.

R

RABINOVICH, Isaac Moiseivich (1894–1961), Russian stage designer, who was for many years leading designer of the Moscow State Jewish Theatre. Among his outstanding productions were *Uriel Acosta* at the Maly, and *Hamlet* at the Vakhtangov. He also designed for the Moscow Art Theatre and the Bolshoi.

RACAN, Honorat de Bueil, Marquis de (1589–1670), French dramatist who marks the entry into French dramatic literature of the poet and courtier. He was a page at Court, and as a boy frequented the theatre, where he much enjoyed the plays of Hardy. But his own play, a pastoral entitled *Les Bergeries*, given in 1620, is more influenced by the *Aminta* of Tasso and Guarini's *Pastor Fido* than by the ranting tragicomedies of Hardy. It was written in accordance with the unities and helped to popularize their vogue. It is weak in construction, but, under the influence of Malherbe, who was then working hard to purify and ennoble the French language, the author paid great attention to style, and the play contains some good lyric passages. Racan, who preferred the pleasures of the country to the pains of Court life, had an uneventful history, and died peacefully at an advanced age.

RACHEL [Élisa Félix] (1820–58), child of a poor Jewish family, and one of the greatest actresses France, or perhaps the world, has ever known. She had an unhappy childhood, but was given some instruction in verse-speaking by her father, in which her cousin Julie Bernat, later the actress Mlle Judith, also shared. After singing in the streets, she was befriended by Choron, who passed her on to Saint-Aulaire. She studied at the latter's dramatic school in the old Théâtre Molière, played an astonishing number of parts between the ages of 13 and 16, and made a reputation for herself as a most promising young actress. A course of study at the Conservatoire was cut short by her father, who was anxious to make money out of her undoubted gifts, and she was engaged by Poisson, manager of the Gymnase-Théâtre, where she appeared in the early part of 1837 in *La Vendéenne* by Dupont, based on a scene from Scott, an ephemeral play which would be forgotten but for Rachel's connexion with it. She was lucky enough to win the favourable opinion of Jules Janin, the powerful critic of the *Journal des Débats*. But she still had a lot to learn and Samson, himself a pupil of Talma, was willing to teach her. Coached by him, she entered the Comédie-Française in 1838, appearing as Camille in *Horace*. This and later parts brought her some success, but the public did not become fully aware of her until Janin had more than once eulogized her in the *Journal des Débats*. His enthusiasm for his 'discovery' was laughed at, but he was listened to, and encouraged by him Rachel revived the glories of French tragedy, which had been almost entirely neglected since the death of Talma. Phèdre was destined to be her greatest part, but she was excellent in all the great plays of Corneille and Racine, as well as in a number of modern plays, including a revival of *Marie Stuart* by Lebrun and the first production of *Adrienne Lecouvreur* (1849) by Scribe and Legouvé. But it was in classical roles that she excelled—Hermione, Roxane, Camille—and it was mainly in these that she appeared on tour, either in the French provinces, in Europe, going as far as Russia, in London, where she first appeared in 1841 with outstanding success, or in America, where, on her one visit in 1855, she finally aggravated her tubercular condition, the result of early hardships and later overwork, combined with a feverish succession of amorous intrigues. She died at the age of 38, leaving a great memory, and a tradition of tragic acting which has never been surpassed. Rachel's four sisters, Sophie (later known as Sarah) (1819–77), Adelaide (known as Lia) (1828–72), Rachel (known as Rebecca) (1829–54), and Mélanie Émilie (known as Dinah) (1836–1909), were all on the stage, as was also her brother Raphaël (1825–72).

RACINE, Jean (1639–99), French playwright and poet, with Corneille the greatest dramatist of the seventeenth century. Orphaned at the age of 4, he was brought up by his grandparents and his aunt Agnès, later Abbess of Port-Royal, where Racine was educated after a few years at the Collège de Beauvais. He was an excellent scholar, though somewhat undisciplined, an enthusiastic admirer of the Greek dramatists, and at 19 already a good poet. He soon escaped from the restraining influence of Port-Royal and the Jansenists, and led a free, though not particularly dissipated, life. His close friends at this time were La Fontaine, Boileau, and Molière, and it was the last who was instrumental in putting Racine's early work before the public, when in 1664 he produced *La Thébaïde, ou les frères ennemis*, at the Palais-Royal. It was moderately successful, and Molière was emboldened to accept another play by the same author.

Racine had already shown that he had little gratitude for those who helped him, and this was abundantly proved when he let the Hôtel de Bourgogne produce his second play, *Alexandre le Grand* (1665), a fortnight after Molière, thus causing the receipts at the Palais-Royal to drop perceptibly. The only excuse for this conduct was that the Hôtel de

Bourgogne had a greater reputation in tragedy than Molière's company, and Racine did indeed say that he was not satisfied with the Palais-Royal production. It is, however, believed that feminine intrigue was at the bottom of the affair, particularly as Mlle du Parc, a fine tragic actress and Racine's mistress, left Molière's company in order to play the lead in Racine's next play, *Andromaque*, produced at the Hôtel de Bourgogne in 1667, with Montfleury, Floridor, and Mlle Desœillets. After this double betrayal Molière never spoke to Racine again. The latter did not long enjoy his triumph, however, since Mlle du Parc died suddenly the following year. Many years later the infamous Catherine Voisin accused Racine of having poisoned her to make way for Mlle Champmeslé, who came from the Marais to play the part of Hermione during the illness of Mlle Desœillets. Champmeslé certainly became Racine's mistress, and was particularly associated with his later work, creating, among other parts, his Phèdre and Bérénice.

It was with the production of *Andromaque* that Racine achieved recognition as a great dramatist, rival of the ageing Corneille, and in some ways superior to him. He assisted in the production of his plays, and got many of his best stage-effects by declaiming his verses aloud as he wrote, and by studying the parts closely with the actors.

Andromaque, which was translated into English as *The Distrest Mother* by Ambrose Philips in 1712, when Anne Oldfield played the leading part, was followed by Racine's one comedy, *Les Plaideurs* (1668). It was originally intended for the Italian troupe, and was based to some extent on Aristophanes' *Wasps*, but on the departure of Scaramouche from Paris it was given at the Hôtel de Bourgogne. It was not successful at first, but after it had been applauded at Court its popularity was assured, and frequent revivals have intensified the regret that Racine did not again venture to compose a comedy. His next tragedy, *Britannicus* (1669), was not very successful, though it was much admired for its exquisite poetry, and the example of Nero is said by Boileau to have deterred Louis XIV from featuring himself further in Court ballets and entertainments. With his next play Racine once again found himself at odds with Corneille, for either by coincidence or design they were both working on the same subject, and the production of Racine's *Bérénice* (1670) took place a week before that of Corneille's *Tite et Bérénice* at Molière's theatre. Racine's was more generally applauded, and was followed by *Bajazet* (1672) and *Mithridate* (1673), oriental subjects treated in a completely French and contemporary style, a reproach often levelled at Racine. They enhanced his reputation, however, and assured his position as the leading tragic dramatist of his day.

For his next play he returned to Greek tragedy, a field which was at that time being exploited by two of his rivals, Thomas Corneille and Quinault. His *Iphigénie* (1674) was a brilliant success and it seemed likely that it would be followed by a succession of equally fine plays. But with his next composition Racine's career as a dramatist came to an abrupt end. He had made many enemies, and they, looking about for someone to set against him, since he seemed to have vanquished Corneille, hit on Pradon, a pleasant, mediocre, and sugary writer, who adapted his subjects to the sentiments of the time. When they discovered that Racine was writing *Phèdre*, they persuaded Pradon to compose a tragedy on the same theme. This he did, and to Racine's chagrin Pradon's play was slightly more successful than his when both were produced at the rival theatres in 1677.

This, and perhaps even more Racine's appointment by Louis XIV as historiographer-royal, caused him to give up the theatre. He married, had seven children, made his peace with Port-Royal, and turned his gifts to the studying and recording of contemporary French history. He retained his interest in the theatre, however, and at the request of Mme de Maintenon—who, it should be remembered, was once the wife of the dramatist Scarron—produced, for her school of young ladies at St-Cyr, the tender and poetic play, *Esther* (1689). It was given at the school with great success, but by Racine's express desire was not performed in public, and it had to wait for that until 1721, when Baron, Duclos, Dufresne, and Adrienne Lecouvreur appeared in it at the Comédie-Française. By then the vogue for biblical subjects was over, and the play failed. The beauty of the poetry did not compensate for the lack of action.

Esther was followed by an even finer play for the same purpose, *Athalie* (1691), which was given in a much simpler form than *Esther*, with no costumes and far less pomp. Perhaps some of the youthful actresses had had their heads turned by their previous success. It was given at the Comédie-Française in 1716, and has since proved to be one of Racine's most admired works.

Racine was not a particularly estimable character. He had a bitter wit, was ungrateful, cold-hearted, and bad-tempered; but as a dramatist, within the strictly defined limits of French classical tragedy, he was a master spirit. He was restricted by the conventions of his time, which forbade excess in any form, but the abounding vitality and passion of his characters, particularly of his women, seems all the greater for the limitations imposed on them. It may be said that the rules he chose to observe served only to enhance his genius, while his great poetic gifts saved his plays from monotony or rigidity. In his own field he has never been surpassed.

Up to the end of the seventeenth century only two of Racine's plays had been translated into English—*Andromaque*, by Crowne, and *Bérénice*, by Otway. These were both acted at Dorset Garden, in 1674 and 1676 respectively. His only comedy, *Les Plaideurs*, is, however, thought to have had some influence on Wycherley's *Plain Dealer*. In 1707 Edmund Smith produced the first translation of *Phèdre*, which as *Phaedra and Hippolitus* was acted at the Haymarket. Ambrose Philips's adaptation of *Andromaque* as *The Distrest Mother*, acted at Drury Lane in Mar. 1712 and frequently revived, had an immediate success, and it is thought that this persuaded the actors to embark on Addison's *Cato*, a play which, more than any other production of the time, shows the influence of French classical drama.

Ozell, the translator of *Le Cid*, also translated Racine, but there is no evidence that his *Britannicus*, *Alexander*, and *The Litigants* were ever acted. They were intended for a reading public, as were many later translations. Exceptions were Charles Johnson's *The Victim* (based on *Iphigénie*) (Drury Lane, 1713) and *The Sultaness* (based on *Bajazet*) (Drury Lane, 1716).

There is no modern translation of Racine's complete works, though there are several American translations of single plays. Masefield made adaptations of *Bérénice* and *Esther*, which have not been professionally produced. Four of Racine's plays were in the repertory of a French company which visited the Haymarket in Dec. 1721, and since then most visiting companies have included at least one of his plays in their programme—in May 1953 the Comédie-Française did *Britannicus*—but the only one which is at all familiar to London playgoers is *Phèdre*. It was in the 1721 programme, and has since been done in London by Rachel, Ristori, Bernhardt, and, in Mar. 1957, by Edwige Feuillère. On 17 Feb. 1958 Margaret Rawlings appeared at the Mahatma Gandhi Hall in her own version of this play.

RADIO CITY MUSIC HALL, NEW YORK, the largest theatre in the world. Situated in the Rockefeller Center, it opened in about 1932 with a galaxy of talent and a staff made up of well-known theatre personalities, including Robert Edmond Jones and Martha Graham. It closed almost immediately, to open again with a combined cinema and stage show which has proved extremely popular. New full-length films alternate with a programme of music-hall turns which for speed and precision would be hard to beat. Owing to its enormous size and superb equipment the theatre is eminently suitable for spectacular effects, to which the well-drilled chorus, known as the Rockettes, contributes in no small degree.

GEORGE FREEDLEY†

RADLOV, SERGEI YEVGENYEVICH (1892–1958), Soviet actor and producer, whose work was done mainly in Leningrad, where he started his theatrical career under Meyerhold. After a varied career during which he produced a number of plays and operas, he established his own theatre in Leningrad, where he staged *Ghosts*, *Romeo and Juliet*, and an excellent *Othello* (1935), a production which he repeated for the Moscow Maly Theatre. He also did an interesting production of *Hamlet*. His outstanding achievement, however, was his production of *King Lear* for the Moscow Jewish Theatre, with Mikhoels in the title-role. Although he did some good productions of Russian plays, among them Ostrovsky's *Dowerless Bride* (1940), he was pre-eminently a producer of Shakespeare, whom he studied deeply, pondered on, and wrote about. In this he was greatly helped by his wife, who translated the plays for him.

RAHERE (*d.* 1144), a jester attached to the service of Henry I, as a permanent member of the Royal Household. He amassed a large fortune by his wit, and used it to found the priory of St. Bartholomew at Smithfield, later the famous hospital. He entered the Church and became prebendary of St. Paul's in 1111 (see MINSTREL, 1).

RAIL, the piece of timber forming the top or bottom of a flat.

RAIMUND, FERDINAND [JAKOB RAIMANN] (1790–1836), Austrian playwright and actor, akin to Molière by the deep-seated melancholy beneath his wit. He first won popularity by his acting in farce, but despite the success of his folk-comedies at the Leopoldstädter Theater in Vienna, of which he became manager, he was more interested in tragedy, and had already shown signs of mental disturbance when he committed suicide in 1836. Among his best plays were *Das Mädchen aus der Feenwelt oder der Bauer als Millionär* (1826), which preaches, with the help of magical forces and a host of allegorical personages, the doctrine of contentment on small means, and *Der Alpenkönig und der Menschenfeind* (1828), in which a kindly mountain spirit cures a misanthropist by assuming his shape and character, while the misanthropist, disguised as his own brother-in-law, has to watch the havoc caused by his suspicions and ill will. Needless to say all ends happily (see also AUSTRIA). W. E. DELP

RAISIN, a family of French actors, consisting of (1) CATHERINE (1650–1701), (2) JACQUES (1653–1702), and (3) JEAN-BAPTISTE (1655–93). As children they were brought to the Foire Saint-Germain in 1662 by their father, an organist of Troyes, who mystified the crowd, and later the Court, with a mechanical spinet which proved on investigation to have Jean-Baptiste, aged 7, inside it. Louis XIV was so amused by the elder Raisin's ingenuity that he allowed him to form a company of child-actors under the patronage of the Dauphin. Among its members were Jean de Villiers, destined to be the husband of Catherine, whom he married in 1679, and Baron, who was later taken by Molière into his own company. After the death of the elder Raisin his widow took the children into the provinces. Jean-Baptiste came back to the Hôtel de Bourgogne in 1679, with his wife, (4) FRANÇOISE PITEL DE LONGCHAMP (1661–1721), known as Fanchon, who was related to the famous actress Mlle Beauval. They were both members of the original troupe of the Comédie-Française, and after her husband's death Fanchon became the mistress of the Dauphin, by whom she had two daughters. Jean-Baptiste was an excellent comedian, known as 'little Molière', but it was not until after the death of Rosimond in 1686 that he was given leading parts to play. His early death was much regretted. His elder brother joined the Comédie-Française four years after its foundation. He appeared mostly in tragedy, and was a tall, thin, solemn, reserved man, very different from Jean-Baptiste. He wrote some successful comedies, and also composed music for the theatre.

RAKE, see ARCHITECTURE and STAGE RAKE.

RAKING PIECE, a canvas-covered wooden frame with a sloping top edge, used as a small groundrow or to conceal a ramp on the stage.

RÁKOSI, JENÖ (1842–1929), Hungarian dramatist, and with Dóczy the leader of the neo-romantic drama of the late nineteenth century in Hungary, which forsook the popular realistic and social problems of the day for legend and fantasy.

RAMP, an inclined approach to a rostrum.

RANCH, HIERONYMUS JUSTESEN (1539–1607), early Danish dramatist (see SCANDINAVIA, 1 *a*).

RANDALL, HARRY (1860–1932), a music-hall performer who as a child played minor parts in pantomime, but left the stage and went into business. A few amateur appearances at Saturday-night shows brought him offers from the halls which he finally accepted, and he became one of the great names of music-hall and pantomime. He was a pillar of the famous pantomimes at the Grand, Islington, in which he appeared continuously, with only one break, from 1891 to 1901, playing both male and 'dame' parts. He appeared in Dan Leno's last Drury Lane pantomime, *Humpty-Dumpty*, and was a worthy successor to that great comedian, whose intimate friend he was.

RANKIN. (1) ARTHUR MCKEE (1841–1914), American actor, who had already had some experience as an amateur before in 1865 he made his first appearance on the professional stage at the Arch Street Theatre, Philadelphia, under Mrs. John Drew. Four years later he married (2) KITTY BLANCHARD (1847–1911), with whom he starred at the Union Square Theatre, and later in a series of long tours, mainly in somewhat crude melodrama. The most famous play in his repertory was *The Danites*, first given in 1877, and in London in 1880. He was for some time manager of the Third Avenue Theatre, New York. He later separated from his wife, and with Nance O'Neill as his leading lady toured all over the world, visiting London again in 1902. His three daughters all married well-known actors. Phyllis became Mrs. Harry Davenport, Doris Mrs. Lionel Barrymore, and Gladys Mrs. Sidney Drew.

RASTELL, JOHN (?–1536), brother-in-law of Sir Thomas More, and father-in-law, through the marriage of his daughter Elizabeth, of John Heywood, author of early English interludes, some of which were printed by John and his son, William Rastell. John Rastell is believed to have been the author of *Calisto and Meliboea*, an adaptation of part of de Rojas's *Celestina*, and of *The Dialogue of Gentleness and Nobility*, both of which were acted in his own garden at Finsbury in about 1527, and printed by him in the same year. He may also have been the author of an earlier interlude entitled *The Play of the Four Elements* (*c.* 1517).

RATTIGAN, TERENCE (1911–), English dramatist, whose first play, written in collaboration with Philip Heimann, was *First Episode* (1933). This was followed in 1936 by an immensely successful light comedy, *French Without Tears*, and in 1939 by *After The Dance*. Two plays in collaboration in 1940, *Follow My Leader* (with Anthony Maurice) and *Grey Farm* (with Hector Bolitho), were followed by *Flare Path* (1942), *While The Sun Shines* (1943), and *Love In Idleness* (1944). The last provided an excellent vehicle for the Lunts, who played in it in London, and also in America under the title of *O Mistress Mine*. Rattigan, who had hitherto been considered an astute purveyor of light entertainment, now began to show signs of a more serious purpose in *The Winslow Boy* (1946), the story of a father's fight to clear his young son of a charge of petty theft. This won for the author the Ellen Terry Award for the best play of the year, and in 1947 the New York Critics' Award for the best foreign play. *Playbill*, consisting of two plays, *Harlequinade* and *The Browning Version*, followed in 1948, and also received the Ellen Terry Award. *Adventure Story* (1949), with Paul Scofield as Alexander the Great, was an interesting failure, and with *Who Is Sylvia?* (1950) Rattigan appeared ready to return to his former vein of comedy. In 1952, however, he produced *The Deep Blue Sea*, an 'emotional drama' in which a charming middle-aged woman (played successively by Peggy Ashcroft, Celia Johnson, and Googie Withers) falls in love with a feckless, drunken, ex-R.A.F. fighter-pilot, and twice attempts suicide. The play, though well written and theatrically exciting, failed to come to grips with the central problem. An excursion into Ruritanian romance, *The Sleeping Prince*, in which Laurence Olivier and Vivien Leigh appeared, followed in 1953, in which year Rattigan published his *Collected Plays* in 2 vols., each with a long introduction by the author. It was then that he first used the term 'Aunt Edna' to indicate the ordinary unsophisticated playgoer who has no use for experimental *avant-garde* plays. This has since proved a useful shorthand word for the dramatic critic and an Aunt Sally for the progressives. Since then Rattigan has written *Separate Tables* (1954), a double bill in which Eric Portman and Margaret Leighton gave excellent performances, *Variations on a Theme* (1958), *Ross* (1960), which had a great success with Alec Guinness as T. E.

Lawrence, and a musical version of his own *French Without Tears* (also 1960), which lasted four nights.

RAUCOURT [FRANÇOISE-MARIE-ANTOINETTE-JOSÈPHE SAUCEROTTE] (1756–1815), a somewhat turbulent French actress, daughter of a provincial actor who had tried without success to join the Comédie-Française. Having profited by the lessons of Mlle Clairon, and gained experience in the provinces and abroad, she appeared at the Comédie-Française in 1771 with great success. She was excellent in stern, tragic parts, for which her queenly figure and deep voice were eminently suitable. Unfortunately she led a wild life, got into debt, lost the affection of the audience, and fled from Paris in 1776. Recalled by Marie-Antoinette, she returned and was with some difficulty reinstated at the theatre, where she immediately came into conflict with the all-powerful Mme Vestris. She also took a leading part in the troubles of the revolutionary period, when she opposed Talma's secession from the company, and was herself imprisoned with a number of her comrades.

RAVENSCROFT, EDWARD (*fl.* 1671–97), English dramatist, of whose life little is known. His career as a playwright was a long one, extending from *Mamamouchi; or, the Citizen turned Gentleman*—based on *Le Bourgeois gentilhomme*—in 1672 to *The Italian Husband* in 1697. His best work was done in farce, and it became a tradition to give his outrageous *The London Cuckolds* (1681) at both patent theatres on Lord Mayor's Day until Garrick stopped it at Drury Lane in 1751 and Covent Garden also dropped it a year later. It was revived in 1782 for the benefit night of Quick, and then disappeared for ever. Among Ravenscroft's other plays, which he took from many sources, were the comedies of *The Careless Lovers* (1673) (also based on Molière) and *The Wrangling Lovers* (1676), *Dame Dobson* (1683), and *The Anatomist; or, the Sham Doctor* (1696). He also wrote a Harlequin play based on *Les Fourberies de Scapin* which was forestalled by Otway's version, an English adaptation of the Latin play *Ignoramus*, and an 'improved' version of *Titus Andronicus*. Ravenscroft has achieved some notoriety on account of his quarrel with Dryden, but none of his plays survives on the stage.

RAYMOND, JOHN T. [really JOHN O'BRIEN] (1836–87), American actor, famous for his playing of Colonel Mulberry Sellers in a dramatization of Mark Twain's *The Gilded Age* (1874). He made his first appearance in 1853, and was immediately hailed as a fine comedian. He toured and worked in stock companies for some years, and in 1861 joined Laura Keene in New York, taking over the part of Asa Trenchard in *Our American Cousin* from Jefferson. He was also seen as Tony Lumpkin and Crabtree, with great success. In 1867 he went with Sothern to England, where his Asa Trenchard was well received; but his Colonel Sellers, which he did there in 1880, seven years after its first production, was a disappointment. Jefferson, who knew him well, preferred him in the part of Ichabod Crane (in a dramatization from Washington Irving's *Wolfert's Roost*), and said of his performance, 'It was quaint and strong; his love scene with Katrina was acted in the best spirit of comedy; the serio-comic expression that he threw into this woe-begone, love-sick swain was irresistibly droll.' Raymond, who was an able and energetic man and remained on the stage until his death, had a long imperturbable face, and a slow seriousness which made his comedy even more appealing. He was popular with the public and with his fellow actors, and once he was established as a star appeared mainly in plays by and about Americans, except for *The Magistrate*, in which he was excellent as Posket. His second wife was the daughter of the actress Rose Eytinge.

RAYNER'S NEW SUBSCRIPTION THEATRE IN THE STRAND, LONDON, see STRAND THEATRE, 1.

READE, CHARLES (1814–84), English novelist, who was also the author of a number of plays. Of these the best-known are *Masks and Faces* (1852), dealing with Garrick and Peg Woffington, which he wrote in collaboration with Tom Taylor, *The Courier of Lyons* (1854), which became famous as *The Lyons Mail*, and was revived by Irving and Sir John Martin-Harvey, and *It's Never Too Late To Mend* (also 1854). Among Reade's later plays the most outstanding was a version of Zola's *L'Assommoir* as *Drink* (1879), written in collaboration with Charles Warner. He also dramatized Tennyson's *Dora* in 1867. Reade was essentially a novelist, and his best work for the stage was done in collaboration with more theatrically minded men, or based on existing foreign plays. He also dramatized some of his own novels.

READE, TIMOTHY (*fl.* first half of seventeenth century), a comedian popular in London prior to the closing of the theatres in 1642. He probably began his career as a boy-actor in 1626, and later was at Salisbury Court with the King's Revels, rejoining the Queen's Men at a later date. From contemporary allusions it is evident that he was renowned as a dancer, and in 1641 *The Stage-Players' Complaint* was issued with the sub-title *In a Pleasant Dialogue between Cane of the Fortune and Reed of the Friers*, with a woodcut of two dancers, one of which was probably intended for Reade. The prologue to *The Careless Shepherdess* (1656) refers also to his fame as a comedian in the lines 'I never saw Rheade peeping through the Curtain, But ravishing joy enter'd into my heart.' Reade—'Tim Reade the Fool'—was one of the actors who tried to break the law by acting in 1647, but was stopped and apprehended, and Gayton later referred to him as 'the most incomparable mimicke upon the face of the Earth'.

REALISM, which may be accounted a modified form of naturalism, sought, at the end of the nineteenth century, to substitute for the well-made play, and the traditional declamatory acting of the period, dramas which should approximate in speech and situation to the social and domestic problems of every day, played by actors who rejected all artifice and spoke and moved naturally against scenery which reproduced with fidelity the usual surroundings of the people they represented. The movement began with Ibsen, and spread rapidly across Europe, upsetting the established theatre, and demanding the evolution of a new type of actor to interpret the new playwrights. Realism, with some extension to its grosser offshoot, naturalism, and some reaction as in symbolism and Impressionism, has dominated the serious stage of Europe and America in some form or another since the 1880s. In spite of a temporary poetic reaction after the Second World War, it invaded the London theatre again with the so-called 'kitchen-sink' drama, and can be detected in the manifestations of the Theatre of Cruelty and Theatre of the Absurd.

REALISTIC THEATRE, Moscow. This small theatre, also known as the Krasnya Presnya Theatre from the district in which it is situated, had its origin in a group of actors from the Moscow Art Theatre who in 1918 became a mobile unit touring local Working Clubs. In 1921 it was reorganized as the Fourth Studio of the Moscow Art Theatre, when its first production was *The Promised Land* by Somerset Maugham. This, and *The Brave Soldier Schweik*, were the only good productions of this early period, followed by *Cement*, the theatre's first Soviet play, in 1927. From the beginning of its activities the theatre was based on the methods of the Moscow Art Theatre, but the decisive change in its history came with the appointment in 1932 of Nikolai Okhlopkov as its artistic director. All his productions, which include *Razbeg*, *Mother*, *The Iron Flood*, and *Aristocrats*—the last being the one which made him virtually world-famous—called for an entire reconstruction of the playing space in the theatre, and the use of a cinema technique, with several stages in various parts of the auditorium, used simultaneously or in quick succession, while actors and audience mingled freely, the latter sometimes being called on to take part in the action of the play.

This experimental technique, while interesting and valuable, had necessarily a limited appeal and in 1938 the theatre was closed (see also OKHLOPKOV).

REBHUN, Paul (*c.* 1500–46), a German Protestant playwright, whose *Susanna* (1535), written under direct encouragement from Luther, shows in its multiple setting and division into five acts an interesting mingling of medievalism and humanism (see GERMANY, 2).

RECITAL THEATRE, New York, see DALY'S THEATRE, 3.

RED ARMY THEATRE, Moscow. This theatre, which has been renamed the Central Theatre of the Soviet Army, was founded in 1919, in a building holding about 900 spectators, as a permanent centre for the production of plays about the Red Army which might interest the public, and also for plays of any description which might be supposed to interest Soviet soldiers. In 1940 it moved into a vast new building with the exterior shape of a five-pointed star, containing a theatre and stage equipped with all the most modern devices obtainable and with a seating capacity of 2,000. The original staff was drawn from the small groups of amateur soldier-actors who had been catering for the amusement of their fellows since 1917. The first director was Yuri Zavadsky, followed by Alexei Popov, who rapidly became one of the outstanding producers of the U.S.S.R. A list of plays staged at this theatre would show a wide range, from Shakespeare to Pogodin, from the Napoleonic days of *Suvorov* (1939) to the actuality of *People of Stalingrad* (1944). During the Second World War the theatre was evacuated, but returned with an imposing list of productions. Not all were as successful as had been hoped, and the theatre's reputation suffered a little, but Popov's production of *The Broad Steppe*, by N. Vinnikov, in 1949 was highly praised as an excellent evocation of the war years. Another success was Vishnevsky's *The Unforgettable 1919th* (1952). Five years later Popov had another success with *Virgin Soil Upturned*, based on Sholokhov's novel. Since 1958 the repertory has included a number of foreign plays, among them *Mrs. Warren's Profession* and works by Čapek, Nazim Hikmet, Remarque, and de Filippo. But it has not neglected the new Soviet plays, and in 1961 and 1962 productions were seen of Pogodin's play on Chapaev, *It Will Never Tarnish*, and Shteyn's *A Game Without Rules*.

RED BULL THEATRE, London. There is a reference to the fact that part of the Red Bull fell down during the performance of a puppet-play in 1599; but it may then have been an inn, one of whose galleries collapsed under the strain of a large audience. The Red Bull playhouse was built about 1600 by Aaron Holland in Upper Street, St. John Street, Clerkenwell. It was occupied by the Queen's Men until 1617, and then by other companies. It was renovated and partly rebuilt in 1625, and may have been roofed in, either then or later; opinions are divided, Hotson claiming that it was always an open-air theatre, while W. J. Lawrence inclines to the view that it was roofed, anyhow by the Restoration period. Contemporary dramatists frequently sneered at it, and it appears to have been what is usually known in theatrical circles as a 'blood tub'. But it served to start on his theatrical career no less a person than Thomas Killigrew, for Pepys reports of him: 'He would go to the Red Bull and when the man cried to the boys "Who will go and be a devil and he shall see the play for nothing?" then he would go in and be a devil upon the stage and so get to see the plays.' This gives an insight into the type of play performed there

—hot and strong dramas, with plenty of devils and red fire, very popular with the people of the neighbourhood. When the theatres were closed under the Commonwealth, surreptitious shows and puppet-plays were sometimes given at the Red Bull, and at the Restoration a company under Michael Mohun acted there before moving to the renovated Cockpit. Killigrew was also there before he went to Vere Street, taking with him some of the best remaining actors in the Red Bull company. It was the depleted company that Pepys saw on 23 Mar. 1661:

> Out to the Red Bull . . . up to the tireing-room, where strange the confusion and disorder that there is among them in fitting themselves, especially here, where the clothes are very poor, and the actors but common fellows. At last into the pitt, where I think there was not above ten more than myself, and not one hundred in the whole house. And the play, which is called *All 's Lost by Lust*, poorly done; and with so much disorder, among others, that in the musique-room the boy that was to sing a song not singing it right, his master fell about his ears and beat him so that it put the whole house in an uprore.

The theatre fell into disuse soon afterwards, but was still standing in 1663. By 1665 it had vanished. W. MACQUEEN-POPE†, *rev.*

REDE. (1) (THOMAS) LEMAN TERTIUS (1799–1832), English actor, who in 1824 married the widow of Oxberry and was responsible for many publications under the latter's name, particularly the posthumous *Oxberry's Dramatic Biography*. Rede was also the author of *The Road to the Stage* (1827), a useful manual of acting, interesting for a study of the contemporary theatre (see MAKE-UP). He continued to act after his marriage and was seen at Sadler's Wells a fortnight before his death. His younger brother, (2) WILLIAM LEMAN (1802–47), was a prolific playwright, who began his career in 1823 with a version of *Sixteen String Jack* given at the Coburg Theatre. Among his many farces the best-known was *The Old and Young Stager* (1835), written for the début of the younger Mathews, in which he appeared at the Olympic with Liston as the Old Stager. Rede also wrote *The Peregrinations of Pickwick*, based on Dickens, and a burlesque of *Douglas* (both 1837), and was responsible for a number of dramas played at the minor theatres in London.

REDGRAVE. (1) Sir MICHAEL SCUDAMORE (1908–), English actor, knighted in 1959 for services to the theatre. The son and grandson of actors, he was for a time a schoolmaster, but in 1934 joined the Liverpool Repertory Theatre, where he remained for two years, playing a wide variety of parts and marrying a fellow member of the company, Rachel Kempson, who has since appeared with him in many plays. They were together at the Old Vic in 1936, where Redgrave, among other parts, played Mr. Horner in a revival of *The Country Wife*. In this, and in his Aguecheek in 1938, he displayed a gift for comedy which has been too rarely exploited. Since the Second World War, during which he served in the Royal Navy, he has been seen in a number of Shakespearian parts, for which he is well equipped, having a fine presence and a beautiful speaking voice. These include Hamlet at the Old Vic and at Elsinore, Macbeth, in which he made his first appearance in New York, Richard II, Prospero, Shylock, Antony, and Lear, all at Stratford-upon-Avon. In 1958 he was leading actor of the company which visited Leningrad and Moscow, playing Hamlet. He has also appeared in a number of modern plays, including *The Family Reunion* (1939), *The Duke in Darkness* (1942), *Uncle Harry* (1944), *Jacobowsky and the Colonel* (1945), *Tiger at the Gates* (1955), *A Touch of the Sun* (1958), *The Tiger and the Horse* (1960), and his own adaptation of *The Aspern Papers* (1959). Several of these he also directed. At the first Chichester Festival in 1962 he gave an outstanding performance as Uncle Vanya, which he repeated the following year in the National Theatre's first season at the Old Vic. At his best in nervous, intellectual parts which carry overtones of internal conflict, he suffered at the start of his career from the inhibitions induced by an academic background. But the effort of overcoming these has meant that in his later years he has become a finer actor, both on stage and screen (for he has also had a distinguished film career), than many who were more precociously successful. He is the author of *The Actor's Ways and Means* (1955), *Mask or Face* (1958), and *The Mountebank's Tale* (1959). In 1962 he was appointed director of the Yvonne Arnaud Theatre (the Guildford Repertory) Project. His elder daughter, (2) VANESSA (1937–), who trained at the Central School, has rapidly made a name for herself as one of our outstanding young actresses. She appeared with her father in *A Touch of the Sun* (1958), and *The Tiger and the Horse* (1960), and was with the Stratford-upon-Avon company in 1959 and 1962, where among other parts her Rosalind and Imogen were much admired. Her younger brother and sister, Corin and Lynn, are also on the stage, the latter having already given some excellent performances with the National Theatre company.

RED LION INN, see INNS USED AS THEATRES.

REFLECTORS, see LIGHTING, 2.

REGENCY THEATRE, LONDON, see SCALA THEATRE.

REGENT THEATRE, LONDON. This opened as the Euston Music-Hall, and became a regular theatre in 1922. Among its most interesting productions were *The Insect Play* (1923), and 'The Immortal Hour' (1931). It later became a cinema.

RÉGISSEUR, see PRODUCER.

REGNARD, JEAN-FRANÇOIS (1655–1709), French dramatist. He had an adventurous early life, for while on a journey he was captured by Algerian pirates and spent two years as a slave in Constantinople. Being ransomed, he travelled all over Europe, but at last settled in Paris, and put his undoubted talent for versification at the service of the Comédie-Italienne from 1688 to 1696, often in collaboration with Dufresny. From 1694 to 1708 he wrote also for the Comédie-Française. He ranks immediately after Molière as a writer of comedies. His first successful production at the Comédie-Française, where he made good use of the experience he had attained elsewhere, was *Attendez-moi sous l'orme* (1694). He followed it with several other comedies, the best being *Le Joueur* (1696) and *Le Légataire universel* (1708); the latter remained in the repertory of the Comédie-Française until the early twentieth century. Though Regnard had a great gift for devising comic situations, and wrote witty dialogue, he inevitably suffers by comparison with his illustrious predecessor, and his comedies have been labelled 'Molière caricatured' or 'Molière with all that makes him immortal omitted'. But it is interesting to note in Regnard's plays the gradual emergence of the valet as the central figure, forerunner of Figaro. Regnard's greatest fault is a weakness in character development, due to the introduction of circumstantial evidence in no way essential to the present traffic of the stage, a vice which got steadily worse during the eighteenth century, particularly in the moral *drame* of the period, and was still prevalent in the nineteenth century.

RÉGNIER [François-Joseph-Pierre Tousez] (1807–85), French actor, who studied painting and architecture and then went on the stage under his mother's maiden name. In 1831 he went to the Comédie-Française, and made a great success in a revival of *Le Mariage de Figaro*. He was soon in possession of all the leading classic parts of comedy, and was good in modern plays also, particularly *Gabrielle*, *L'Aventurière*, *La Joie fait peur*, and *Supplice d'une femme*. He retired in 1872, and was for some years a professor at the Conservatoire, where he trained a number of outstanding actors. He published a volume of memoirs and essays on the theatre and collaborated in two plays.

REHAN [Crehan], Ada (1860–1916), American actress, and for many years the leading lady of Augustin Daly's company. Born in Ireland, she went to the United States at the age of 5. Her elder sisters were on the stage, and she herself first played at the age of 13, with her brother-in-law, Oliver Byron, who was instrumental in getting her into a play which he had written, performed in Newark, N.J. She then joined Mrs. John Drew's company at the Arch Street Theatre, Philadelphia. It was there that, by a printer's error, she was first billed by the name she afterwards retained and made famous. She was with several stock companies, playing opposite famous stars of the day, and in 1879 was engaged by Daly for New York. Her first part on Broadway was in Daly's version of *L'Assommoir*, and when Daly first opened his own theatre she played Nelly Beers in *Love's Young Dream*. She became one of the best-loved actresses in New York and in London, where she made her first appearance in 1884 at Toole's. She was later seen at Daly's own theatre in London, of which she laid the corner-stone in 1891. Her most famous part, in a repertory which covered Shakespearian and classic comedies as well as adaptations of foreign farces, was probably Katharina in *The Taming of the Shrew*. She first played this in New York in 1887, when the Induction to the play was also given there for the first time. Other parts in which she was much admired were Lady Teazle and Rosalind. She was essentially a comedienne, at her best in parts of arch and somewhat artificial comedy, and that side of her art was developed by Daly to the exclusion of all others. This was unfortunate in that the turn of the century saw a new style of play which demanded a new style of acting, and made her, while still young, seem outmoded. The precision and sparkling technique of Old Comedy could not be adapted to the new drama. After Daly's death she continued to present plays of his former repertory, but with dwindling success, in spite of her attractive personality, and she made her last public appearance in May 1905. Her life had been entirely devoted to the theatre, and she never married.

REHEARSAL, see PRODUCER.

REINHARDT, Max [really Goldmann] (1873–1943), Austrian actor, manager, and outstanding producer of plays. After two years (1890–2) as a drama student in Vienna, during which time he appeared in a wide variety of parts at the Sulkowski Theatre and the Volkstheater in Rudesheim, he joined the resident company at the Salzburg theatre, and in the following year went to the Deutsches Theater in Berlin, where under the tuition of Otto Brahm he became noted as a masterly portrayer of old men. In 1903 he ceased to act, and devoted all his time to production. A new era in theatrical presentation was at hand, helped on by the work of such men as Taïrov and Craig. It was to involve the use of new mechanical devices, of new methods of lighting, of well-schooled crowd work as opposed to the star-actor system of the past. Reinhardt gathered together these multiple activities of the theatre, ably supported by keen young actors trained in his methods, and by equally zealous scenic, musical, and choreographic experts. It was his avowed intention to free the theatre from the shackles of literature, to set it on its own feet. Creative vision of a high order, infectious enthusiasm, and a gift for attracting devoted collaboration, enabled him to brush obstacles to one side. In order to create intimacy of contact between actors and audience, such as had existed in the days of ancient Greece, he projected the stage into the arena, into the midst of the spectators. Scenery he replaced by highly stylized architecture, using vertical lines where the actor required to be dwarfed, horizontal where his stature was to be magnified. By the use of rhythmic mass movement—and very few producers have equalled Reinhardt in the management of crowds—he sought to sweep the spectators into the very heart of the play. No place was too vast for him. He produced the *Oedipus Rex* in the Zirkus Schumann in Vienna in 1910, and in 1911 was brought to London by C. B. Cochran, first to present his wordless play *Sumurūn*, founded on *The Arabian Nights*, with his Berlin company, and then to produce *The Miracle* at Olympia. The following year saw his production of *Oedipus Rex*, with Martin-Harvey, at Covent Garden, and among other outstanding productions must be reckoned his *Midsummer Night's Dream*—which he also produced at Oxford (on Headington Hill) in 1933, and in Hollywood in 1934—*Macbeth*, *Julius Caesar*, *Agamemnon*, his season of plays in New York in 1927–8, his *Helen* in London in 1932, again under C. B. Cochran's management, and his numerous productions of light and comic opera. In 1920 Reinhardt founded the Salzburg Festival, where every year he staged in front of the Cathedral a lavish and exciting production of the old Morality play, *Jedermann*, adapted by von Hofmannsthal, and in the theatre a number of plays which included Goethe's *Faust*. He also ran the first school for the training of producers. It was inevitable that Reinhardt should be accused of vulgarizing the theatre, but it must not be forgotten that in addition to his vast spectacular shows in which he appealed to the multitude, in his smaller theatres, such as the Kammerspiele and the Kleines Theater, he staged intimate productions intended to appeal to the connoisseur, and gave to many masterpieces a subtly individualized atmosphere characterized by simple line and subdued lighting. When Hitler came into power in 1933 Reinhardt left Germany, and spent the rest of his life in America, where he continued to work until his death (see also SCENERY, 6 and No. 78).

RÉJANE [GABRIELLE-CHARLOTTE RÉJU] (1857–1920), famous French actress, who made her first appearance in 1875, at the Vaudeville, whose manager she afterwards married and divorced. She was soon recognized as a leading player of comedy and appeared at many Parisian theatres. She was frequently seen in London, making her first appearance there in 1894, and Shaw, in *Our Theatres in the Nineties*, while despising her choice of play, says of her acting 'it has the quick sensibility which is the really moving quality in fine comic acting, and it is perfectly honest and self-respecting in its impudence'. Few of her parts were memorable, with the exception of Madame Sans-Gêne, in which she was seen in New York in 1895, and she never ventured to approach the classics. But in her own line of light comedy she was unapproachable. In 1906 she opened her own theatre in Paris, and also took over the Royalty in London, intending to run it as a French repertory theatre. In 1909 she toured South Africa, and retired in 1915.

RELIGIOUS DRAMA IN GREAT BRITAIN AND AMERICA. Religion, which had, since the doctrinal controversies of the sixteenth and seventeenth centuries, been almost entirely avoided as the subject-matter of drama, began to re-enter the theatre around the beginning of the twentieth century. It did so from two directions. First, writers for the professional stage, following the lead given by Henry Arthur Jones in *Saints and Sinners* (1884), *The Tempter* (1893), and *Michael and his Lost Angel* (1896), began to include religion and the clergy in plays which aimed at giving a picture of contemporary life. The best known of these is probably Jerome K. Jerome's *The Passing of the Third Floor Back* (1908). A little later, the biblical 'spectacular' of which Wilson Barrett's *The Sign of the Cross* (1895) is typical, was found to be a profitable form of popular entertainment until the screen did it better with the mammoth films of the 1950s and 1960s.

In this early phase it was the setting and emotional appeal of the religious story that appeared on the stage, rather than the ideas from which it was derived. These were mainly introduced, as were so many others, by George Bernard Shaw, who in a series of plays from *The Devil's Disciple* (1897) to *Saint Joan* (1923) returned to religion, and particularly to Christian ideas—as in *Androcles and the Lion* (1913)—again and again, and for the first time gave them serious dramatic treatment. James Bridie followed with his unique brand of comedy through which some of the tales of the Apocrypha (*Tobias and the Angel*, 1930) and the Old Testament (*Jonah and the Whale*, 1932) took on new life, while in *Mr. Bolfry* (1943) he presented the classic religious conflict in an unexpected guise.

Meanwhile, religious drama was arising from another direction; the Church, which had before the Reformation encouraged plays both inside and outside church buildings, was offering hospitality to modern dramatists. Since the revival of *Everyman* by William Poel (who, ironically enough, was a firm agnostic, and staged the old play purely on account of its theatrical quality) in 1901, medieval scripts were being played, even though one of the pioneers, Nugent Monck of the Maddermarket, Norwich, was arrested on a charge of blasphemy. The death-blow was dealt to the puritan prejudice against religious drama by George Bell, then Dean of Canterbury, who invited John Masefield to write a play for Canterbury Cathedral. *The Coming of Christ* was presented there in 1928. Bell became Bishop of Chichester the next year, and promptly appointed E. Martin Browne as the first Director of Religious Drama for his diocese. Bell also became the first president of the Religious Drama Society of Great Britain, an interdenominational advisory body founded in 1929 by Sir Francis Younghusband and Mrs. Olive Stevenson.

Canterbury continued to provide the Church's most lively stage, and in 1935 T. S. Eliot wrote for it his masterpiece, *Murder in the Cathedral.* This became a big success in the commercial theatre, and so two streams of religious drama, from church and from theatre, found their confluence.

The annual Canterbury Festival produced more notable plays: before the war, Charles Williams's *Cranmer*, Dorothy L. Sayers's *The Zeal of Thy House* and *The Devil to Pay*, Christopher Hassall's *Christ's Comet*; in 1949 Christopher Fry's *Thor, With Angels.* This young author was also commissioned by the Religious Drama Society to write a church play for the Festival of Britain in 1951, and responded with *A Sleep of Prisoners.* The same festival was the occasion of the first full-scale revival of the York Cycle of Mystery plays, the only complete medieval cycle to survive, in its native city. This has become the central event of a triennial Festival of the Arts; and other cycles—Chester, Wakefield, the *Ludus Coventriae*—have also been revived. Coventry, most famous of all the late-medieval centres of religious drama, has made drama a part of the regular work of its new Cathedral. Plays are given every four to six weeks, either on the 'Nave Stage' in a side-wall of the Cathedral, or in the porch, or in the ruins of the bombed building. This is the most active programme of any single church, but many hundreds of churches of all denominations are producing religious plays. In the commercial theatre, plays of religion are now well established: the modern plays of T. S. Eliot, Graham Greene, Christopher Fry, have been successful; while within the Church, particularly under the aegis of the Religious Drama Society, authors like Philip Turner, R. H. Ward, Philip Lamb, James Brabazon, Norman Nicholson, Anne Ridler, present a challenging picture of Christianity.

The Religious Drama Society provides the focus and the clearing-house for this activity. Its library is the fullest on its subject and is run in connexion with an information service. Training for both adult and youth leaders culminates in an annual Summer Course. A number of Bishops and Church bodies use the Society as a court of reference upon the quality of plays, especially those to be produced in churches.

In America Fred Eastman, of Chicago, was writing religious plays as early as 1930, and the work of Dr. Harold Ehrensperger at Boston University, and of the annual summer Workshop at Green Lake, Wisconsin, has been established for many years. Canada has had a Christian Drama Council since 1954: and during the 1950s a very rapid and widespread development took place in the United States. At Union Theological Seminary, New York, a programme in Religious Drama was introduced as a curricular activity in 1956. This had E. Martin Browne and his wife Henzie Raeburn as Visiting Professor and Lecturer till 1962, when Robert E. Seaver, who had created it with them, assumed directorship of the programme as a course leading to a Master's degree in Religious Education. Many of the most significant of European religious plays have been introduced to the United States at Union Seminary, and a playwriting course under Tom F. Driver has encouraged the work of younger American playwrights.

This experiment was made possible by the Rockefeller Foundation. Other seminaries have followed according to their resources, and a number of touring companies have been established. Some parishes of various denominations have started play production with trained directors, and often travel their shows to the surrounding area. A well-thought-out plan has been implemented in the San Francisco area, where 'Bards' sends out literature for preparatory study before its production visits a parish. In the Boston area 'Bards East' has followed suit. It seems as if a nation-wide organization is not too far distant. Meanwhile, the special talent of the American theatre for musicals is being brought into play, notably in Robert Seaver's production of a Christian revue, *For Heaven's Sake.*

The Rockefeller Foundation also made possible the first international exchanges in religious drama. At Oxford in 1955 and at Royaumont near Paris in 1960 the Religious Drama Society of Great Britain acted as convenor for international conferences, at each of which some twenty countries of Europe, America, Australasia, and Asia were represented and performances were given in many styles and languages. Members took a special interest in the liturgical drama movement, under Dr. Olav Hartman, at Sigtuna, Sweden, the formation of a national society in Greece, and the Christian use of native dramatic traditions in Japan, India, Thailand, and Uganda. A small committee carries on the promotion of exchanges and the dissemination of scripts and information. E. MARTIN BROWNE

REMOTE CONTROL, see LIGHTING, 2.

RENAISSANCE, THÉÂTRE DE LA, PARIS. 1. The first theatre of this name was built by Aténor Joly, and opened on 8 Nov. 1838 with a licence for plays with and without music. This aroused the jealousy of both the Comédie-Française and the Opéra, who finally caused it to close in 1841, but not before it had done some good work. The actors were headed by Frédérick and Mme Dorval, and the first play they appeared in was *Ruy Blas.* Among later productions was a ballet in which Carlotta Grisi made her first appearance in Paris.

2. The second Renaissance opened in 1873, on the site cleared by the burning of the Théâtre de la Porte-Saint-Martin in 1871. It was a small theatre, and unwisely endeavoured to play strong drama. This soon gave way to light

operas, the most successful being those by Lecocq. Between 1884 and 1892 the theatre was in a bad way, passing through many hands, and finally it closed. Sarah Bernhardt, returning from a long tour abroad, took it over and made it successful, appearing there with the elder Guitry, de Max, and sometimes Coquelin. Among her successful productions there were *La Princesse lointaine*, *Magda*, *Lorenzaccio*, and revivals of *Phèdre* and *La Dame aux camélias* (see No. 70). The theatre was also leased to the companies of Duse and Novelli, and to the Spanish actress Maria Guerrero. Sarah Bernhardt later went to the Châtelet and the Renaissance became the Théâtre-Lyrique, playing musical shows only.

RENAUD, MADELEINE-LUCIE (1903–), French actress, wife of the actor-manager Jean-Louis Barrault, with whom she founded and has sustained a company which has greatly enriched the theatrical life not only of France but of every country in which it has appeared during its extensive tours abroad. She began her career at the Comédie-Française, where she made her mark as a player of Marivaux, and she was already an established star when Barrault joined the company. In 1943 she appeared under his direction in Claudel's *Soulier de satin*, and three years later became the leading actress of the Renaud-Barrault company, in which she played a wide range of parts, from Molière, Chekhov, de Musset, Racine, Fry, Giraudoux, Lope de Vega, and has been equally admirable in all. The beauty of her voice and person gave her an initial advantage to which years of hard work and technical mastery have given added embellishments, but it is above all the fine, mature intelligence which governs all her work which has made her outstanding, and even when she does not herself appear in the company's productions, as happens occasionally, one can sense her influence on them. It would be impossible to apportion between her and her husband the part of each in the company's success, since, as Barrault himself has said, their gifts are complementary, as was their training, she having proceeded by the direct classical route, he by the modern system of trial-and-error; but it is certain that she has participated actively in all that concerns the company's theatrical life. Her first husband was the actor Charles Grandval, by whom she had a son, Jean-Pierre, now a member of the Renaud-Barrault company.

REPERTORY (REPERTOIRE), the name used to indicate the total collection of plays which are in active production in a theatre in the same season, or which can be put on at short notice, each play taking its turn in a constantly changing programme. In earlier times, when audiences were small and mainly localized, all theatres, including those of England and America, had a large repertory of plays, and changed their bill practically every night. After its first performance a successful play would be retained in the permanent repertory; an unsuccessful one might be seen a few more times and then dropped. Later, in the nineteenth century, the influx of larger audiences and the improvement in transport facilities led to the establishment of the 'run', in which the same play is given a consecutive number of performances. At first these 'runs' were comparatively short, and depended more on the willingness of the leading actor—who was also in many cases the manager—to appear continually in the same part than on the desire of the audience to see him in it. But with the disappearance of the old-style actor-manager, and the rise in financial costs, plays began to run, in London and in New York, as long as the public was willing to come to them. This has led to a pernicious system under which one play can remain in a theatre, or a succession of theatres, over a period of years. Nor is it always the outstanding play which has the longest run. The lightweight comedy, with low running costs, or the spectacular musical, is more likely to achieve a long run—in some cases a very long run—than the more serious or more experimental play. In New York this has had the further result that a play, now a very costly enterprise, must be an immediate success, or be taken off. It can neither be nursed along for a few weeks to enable it to find its audience, nor can it join a tried repertory and be given a second showing. Consequently vital theatre is more likely to be found off-Broadway or in the theatres outside New York (see UNITED STATES OF AMERICA, 10) than on Broadway. In London the situation is not yet so extreme, but the tyranny of the long run has taken many theatres out of circulation. The Ambassadors has had only one play—*The Mousetrap*—since Nov. 25, 1952, the Whitehall had only four plays in over 12 years, while five American musicals accounted for nearly 12 years in the life of Drury Lane.

The long run is sometimes defended on the grounds that it provides financial security for the actor. But it may result in artistic stagnation, and it certainly enriches one author to the exclusion of others who might benefit financially, and above all artistically, from a quicker turnover in productions, a situation aggravated by the diminishing number of theatres. The Continental system, with its constantly changing repertory interpreted by a relatively stable company, offers the actor comparable security with a wider range of interpretation. On the debit side, the repertory system may lead to miscasting, stagnation, and complacency. An effort was made in the early twentieth century to import the Continental repertory system into England (see below, REPERTORY THEATRE MOVEMENT), but it was not successful except in the summer seasons at Stratford-upon-Avon, and led in the provinces to a system of weekly or fortnightly changes of bill to which the word 'repertory' is wrongly applied. A fresh attempt to play 'in repertoire' as it is now called, has been made, with apparent success, by the National Theatre at the Old Vic, and the

London company of the Royal Shakespeare Theatre at the Aldwych.

The word 'repertory' is also used sometimes of all the parts played by a particular actor, though he may have played some only once.

REPERTORY THEATRE MOVEMENT IN GREAT BRITAIN. The use of the word 'repertory' in this connexion has become something of a misnomer. It appears to have been the intention of the original sponsors of the Repertory Movement—which has become synonymous in the history of the English theatre with the efforts made by a few enlightened pioneers to replace the falsities of the nineteenth-century stage with the 'new drama' of Shaw and Ibsen—to establish the Continental system of 'true repertory', where several plays are performed during the week, with new ones in preparation. But on the one hand English theatres were no longer able to deal with such frequent changes of bill, and on the other the audience had become accustomed to a 'run', however short, and refused to cooperate. The consequence is that most so-called 'repertory' theatres in England produce one play for a week, a fortnight, or very occasionally three weeks. 'Weekly rep' is an excellent training-ground for young actors, and many famous players have graduated from it, though too long a stay may prove exhausting. The strain of rehearsing one play while acting in another and learning lines for a third, with the added tension of frequent first nights, can do much harm. On the other hand, acting in repertory makes for versatility and resourcefulness, is excellent for training the memory, and will soon give a young actor self-confidence. There is also, in the case of an established and successful repertory theatre, a special bond between actor and audience which no longer exists in the more transient world of the commercial West End.

It is impossible to name any one person as the sponsor of the Repertory Movement in England, but it owes much to the vision and courage of J. T. Grein, who in 1891, a significant date in English theatre history, launched the Independent Theatre, where the plays of Ibsen and Shaw were first presented. The Stage Society carried on Grein's work, but it was not until the memorable Vedrenne–Barker seasons at the Court Theatre from 1904 to 1907 that the word 'repertory' came into general use.

Other London repertory seasons which aroused interest were those run by Lena Ashwell at the Kingsway in 1907 and by Gertrude Kingston at the Little in 1910. But although all these experiments were of inestimable value to the movement in general, the real impetus, and the one later to bear most fruit in the provinces, was given by the activities of Miss Horniman, who started repertory theatres in Dublin in 1903 (see ABBEY THEATRE) and in Manchester in 1908 (see HORNIMAN).

In 1910 the American impresario Charles Frohman again attempted to acclimatize 'true repertory' in London, at the Duke of York's Theatre. But in spite of excellent actors and good plays the venture was not a success, the audiences being unwilling to accept frequent changes of bill.

Meanwhile, in Glasgow a repertory theatre was opened in 1909 under the skilful direction of Alfred Wareing, who was eager to make the city independent of the touring company from London. With a good company and a high standard of production the venture was just beginning to find its feet financially when the outbreak of the First World War caused it to close down (see SCOTLAND).

While the Manchester and Glasgow repertory theatres were still running, a new venture was started. This was the Liverpool repertory theatre, founded in 1911 and still functioning, being the longest-lived repertory theatre in Great Britain. It was the first theatre of the new movement to be founded and owned by a large number of small shareholders (see LIVERPOOL).

Two years later, in 1913, the Birmingham repertory theatre was opened, and under its founder and patron, Barry Jackson, attained an international reputation. It trained many young actors who later became famous, and gave many a dramatist his first audience. It was also owing to Barry Jackson's initiative that the Malvern Festival, devoted mainly to the plays of Shaw, was inaugurated, with a 'true repertory' based on a constant change of bill (see BIRMINGHAM).

It would be impossible to list all the repertory theatres established in Great Britain consequent on the success of the pioneer ventures, of which Birmingham and Liverpool still function. Some, like those at Windsor (established in 1938 by John Counsell, who still runs it), Guildford, Oldham, Nottingham, Derby, have been successful, others have sunk without trace. Very few have been both adventurous and successful. On the whole the regular audiences, which according to a survey made in 1959 amount to about 55 per cent. of the theatre's capacity, seem content with lightweight revivals of West-End successes and occasional new but uncontroversial plays. On the other hand, there have been many plays, first produced by a repertory company, which have then been transferred to London, with great financial benefit to the original sponsors. But this is a two-edged policy, since the theatre may at the same time suffer artistic impoverishment by the loss of its leading actors, who go to London with the play and do not return. This was the case with Theatre Workshop—which embodied some features of a so-called repertory theatre—and led to the departure of its director, Joan Littlewood, and its final closure, and it seems to add yet another hazard to the problems of the provincial theatre, which must at all times fight for survival. The English apathy with regard to the theatre which for so long prevented the establishment of a National Theatre in London extends also to the greater part of the provinces, where an apparent paradox is evident in that districts with no live theatre are said to be clamouring for it, while established theatres are poorly supported. In the late 1950s a decided decline in provincial audiences was commented on in the Arts Council Report (1958–9). One solution proposed was the establishment of a national 'grid', with provincial companies exchanging visits. Although this seems to be working well with Lincoln and its associated playhouses, the idea has not in general met with approval. With the building of some new theatres, however, the situation in the early 1960s appears to be improving, though the already chaotic situation over the use of the word 'repertory' is now made even more chaotic by the recent establishment of Civic Theatres. The two names are not interchangeable (see CIVIC THEATRE). There have also been complaints that the word 'repertory' has become associated with 'amateur'—though most repertory theatres are fully professional—or with a slipshod and unadventurous policy. But for want of a better word it must be used for the moment in its accepted meaning of a permanent company established in a theatre building, whether this belongs to a local authority, as at Nottingham, or to a university, as at Oxford, and appearing in the same play for one to three weeks, to distinguish such a theatre from the theatre housing touring companies for a week only, or from a London theatre where a run may last for years.

No article on repertory would be complete without a reference to the National Theatre and the Royal Shakespeare Theatre, which are the nearest approximations to a 'true' repertory theatre in England. Both, in fact, started with the 'true' repertory system, but in Stratford-upon-Avon plays are now introduced into the bill one at a time, and given a short run before being merged in a changing bill. There is thus a compromise between 'weekly rep' and 'true rep'. The same, to a lesser degree, is also true of the London home of the Stratford-upon-Avon company, the Aldwych, where the transfers and revivals of successes from earlier Stratford seasons mingle with new plays to produce something nearly akin to the Continental system. The Old Vic in its day maintained a repertory system within seasonal bounds, as does its successor the National Theatre company. The English Stage Company, at the Royal Court, was something of a hybrid, having both short runs and long, as well as transfers of successful plays to other theatres in London under the normal 'long run' system (see also REPERTORY, above).

WILLIAM ARMSTRONG†, *rev.*

REPUBLIC THEATRE, NEW YORK, on 42nd Street, west of Times Square. This was built by Oscar Hammerstein and opened on 27 Sept. 1900 with a play by James A. Herne, in which he appeared himself, with his two daughters, Mrs. Sol Smith, and the young Lionel Barrymore. Two years later the theatre was leased to David Belasco, given his name, and used for a number of his outstanding productions, including *The Darling of the Gods*, *Sweet Kitty Bellairs*, *The Music Master*, *Adrea*, *The Girl of the Golden West*, and *The Rose of the Rancho*. When Belasco's second theatre, the Stuyvesant, was renamed the Belasco, the Republic reverted to its original name. Among the distinguished actors who subsequently appeared there were Jane Cowl and Lou Tellegen, while successful plays included *Abie's Irish Rose*, transferred from the Fulton. The last play seen at the Republic, before it became a burlesque house and then a cinema named the Victory, was *Frankie and Johnny*, which opened on 25 Sept. 1930 and closed after 61 performances.

GEORGE FREEDLEY†

RÉPUBLIQUE, THÉÂTRE DE LA, see COMÉDIE-FRANÇAISE.

RETURN, a narrow flat set back in the walls of a box-set to produce a break.

REVEAL, a false thickness-piece used in a box-set to give solidity to the openings.

REVELS OFFICE, see MASTER OF THE REVELS.

REVERE, GIUSEPPE (1812–89), Italian poet and patriot, whose historical drama, *Lorenzino de' Medici*, had some success when produced in 1839. It was followed by a number of others, published in 1860. Though of interest from a literary and historic point of view, Revere's plays are not particularly well adapted for the stage.

REVOLVING STAGE, see JAPAN and SCENERY.

REVUE, a term of French origin, used to describe a survey, mainly satiric, of contemporary events, with songs, sketches, burlesques, monologues, and so on. No satisfactory English term has ever been found for this mixture, and the French continues in use. It is first found in Planché's *Recollections* (1872), where he says he was responsible for the first revue on the English stage with his *Success; or, a Hit if you Like It*, produced at the Adelphi in 1825. This was, however, a 'review' of the dramatic productions of the past season. The first real revue seen in England was *Under the Clock*, produced at the Court Theatre in 1893, and written by Seymour Hicks and Charles Brookfield.

A few years before the First World War what is now known as revue became very popular, and revues were produced at the Empire, the Alhambra, and the London Hippodrome. They were spectacular, with a smattering of topicality, but that, and the wit, was subdued by excessive spectacle, and they became parades of singing, dancing, and costume-display, with a few sketches thrown in. The names most closely associated with these productions were those of Albert de Courville at the London Hippodrome and of André Charlot at the Alhambra. Austen Hurgon took revue to the provinces through the music-halls, where it soon began to crowd out variety entertainment.

In 1914 Alfred Butt started a series of revues at the Palace Theatre, beginning with *The Passing Show*, which introduced Elsie Janis to England. Much of the revue music, and many of its artists, came from America, for at this period ragtime was popular, and *Hullo Ragtime!* (1912), produced by de Courville and starring Ethel Levey, was a typical example.

In America revue was inaugurated in 1907 by Florenz Ziegfeld, with his *Ziegfeld Follies* which ran through twenty-four editions. A later producer of American revue was George White, whose *Scandals*, inaugurated in 1919, became a regular annual feature of the New York stage.

At the Ambassadors Theatre in 1914 Cochran's *Odds and Ends* was a serious attempt at an intimate revue, which relied on cleverness and wit more than on dress and dancing. He followed it up with other shows at the Oxford, and then at the London Pavilion. So popular did revue become in the West End that certain managements presented it continuously from 2 p.m. till midnight. One theatre, the Windmill, made a special feature of this, and remained open right through the London Blitz of 1940–2, with a form of entertainment known as Revuedeville, and also as 'non-stop variety'.

English revue reached a high standard at the private Gate Theatre, and was just beginning to emerge from there when the Second World War broke out in 1939. Noël Coward did some excellent revues, but one of the best librettists of revue in England was undoubtedly the late Herbert Farjeon, whose Little Revues were a feature of London's theatrical life in the years immediately preceding the Second World War.

W. MACQUEEN-POPE†, *rev.*

During the Second World War the vogue for revue continued. Farjeon was again active in satisfying it, as was George Black with a series beginning in 1940 with *Apple Sauce*. Among other revues, mostly the mixture as before, were *New Faces* (1940) and *Rise Above It* (1941), both at the Comedy, and Robert Nesbitt's *Strike a New Note* (1943). The great success of this period, however, was *Sweet and Low* at the Ambassadors, with Hermione Gingold and Walter Crisham. First produced on 10 June 1943, this continued as *Sweeter and Lower* (1944) and *Sweetest and Lowest* (1946), in which Henry Kendall replaced Walter Crisham. In 1949 *Oranges and Lemons* had a success, first at the Lyric, Hammersmith, and then at the Globe, and Nesbitt continued to produce successfully. Revue became a feature of the little theatres like the Boltons, the New Lindsay, the Watergate, and the Irving, and in 1953 came *Airs on a Shoestring*, at the Royal Court, by Laurier Lister. This ran for two years, with Max Adrian, who had previously been in *Tuppence Coloured* and *Penny Plain*, and Moyra Fraser. These were all somewhat more sophisticated than the usual revue, but it was not until the advent in London of *Beyond the Fringe*, a Cambridge Footlights' production which was seen in Edinburgh on 10 May, 1961, that satire entered the field. This had a long run, first with the four original (and amateur) members of the cast, Peter Cook, Alan Bennett, Jonathan Miller, and Dudley Moore, and later, when they had gone as professionals to achieve an equal success in New York, with the professionals Joe Melia, Terence Brady, Robin Ray, and Bill Wallis. This type of revue influenced such productions as *The Royal Commission Revue* at the Mermaid (1964), and had wide-spread repercussions both in London and in New York. Meanwhile, the older style of revue continued to flourish with *Pieces of Eight*, *One Over the Eight*, and, in 1963, *Six of One*, with Dora Bryan, at the Adelphi. Somewhat apart from the general run of revue was the successful partnership of Michael Flanders and Donald Swann in *At the Drop of a Hat* (1956; N.Y. 1959) and *At the Drop of Another Hat* (1962; new edition, 1963). Some importations from overseas were the revues *Clap Hands* (1960) and *Les Feux-Follets* (1965) from Canada, and *Wait a Minim!* (1964) from South Africa.

REYNOLDS, FREDERICK (1764–1841), English dramatist, author of over 200 plays of which the most notorious was *The Caravan; or, the Driver and his Dog*. This netted him £350, a good sum for those days, and saved Drury Lane from disaster when it was first produced in 1803, mainly because of the appearance on the stage of a real dog, Carlos, who dived into a tank of water to save a child from drowning. Reynolds's first play was a translation of *Werther*, produced at Bath in 1785, but in the main his plays were either light comedies, like *How to Grow Rich* (1793), melodramas, or adaptations of Shakespeare as light operas. In 1827 he published an interesting volume of reminiscences, containing many side-lights on the contemporary stage, entitled *The Life and Times of Frederick Reynolds, Written by Himself*.

REYNOLDS, ROBERT (*fl.* 1610–40), English actor who was a Queen's Man but by 1616 had gone to Germany, where he was one of the popular English Comedians under Robert Browne and John Green, succeeding the latter as leader of the company. As a clown, Pickelherring, he made an enviable reputation on the Continent, where records of his appearances are found up to 1640.

RHINTHONICA, see FABULA, 5.

RHODES, JOHN (*c.* 1606–?), a London bookseller, said by Downes in *Roscius Anglicanus* to have been connected before the Commonwealth with Blackfriars Theatre, probably as wardrobe-keeper or prompter. At the Restoration he obtained a licence to reopen the Cockpit—of which he had become Keeper in 1644—with a small company of players, among whom were his young apprentices Thomas Betterton and Edward Kynaston. His licence was rendered null by the patent granted to Killigrew and Davenant, and his actors were taken over by them, Betterton becoming leading man in Davenant's company, and later the leading actor of his day. There was also a John Rhodes, presumably a different man, who was part-owner of the Fortune Playhouse in 1637.

RICCOBONI. (1) ANTONIO (*fl.* 1675–95), an actor of the *commedia dell'arte*, who played Pantalone, and was seen in this part in London when the Italian actors paid a visit there in 1679. His son, (2) LUIGI (*c.* 1675–1753), known as Lelio, was a fine actor, and was entrusted with the task of selecting and directing the Italian company which returned to Paris in 1716. With him were his wife and brother-in-law, who played the young lovers, Silvia, later the interpreter of Marivaux, and the Harlequin, Thomassin. He was also the author of several books on the theatre in French and Italian, of which one was published in an English translation in 1741. They form one of the main sources of our knowledge of the *commedia dell'arte*.

RICE [REIZENSTEIN], ELMER (1892–1967), American dramatist, born in New York. He studied and practised law, and became a successful writer with his first play, the melodrama *On Trial* (1914), the first American play to employ the flashback technique of the screen. It was followed by several other less successful efforts, and his first major contribution to the theatre was the expressionistic fantasy *The Adding Machine* (1923), which satirized the growing regimentation of man in the machine-age through the life and death of the arid book-keeper, Mr. Zero. Rice's next play, *Street Scene* (1929), won the Pulitzer Prize for its realistic chronicle of life in the slums. *The Left Bank* (1931) described expatriation from America as an ineffectual escape from materialism, and *Counsellor-at-Law* (also 1931) drew a realistic picture of the legal profession.

The depression of the 1930s inspired the polemical *We, the People* (1933), the Reichstag trial was paralleled in *Judgement Day* (1934), and conflicting American and Soviet ideologies formed the subject of the conversation-piece *Between Two Worlds* (1934). When these plays failed on Broadway their author retired from the theatre after venting his wrath on dramatic critics and composing a satire on the stage, *Not for Children*, published in 1935. He returned to Broadway in 1937 to write and direct for the Playwrights' Producing Company, which he helped to establish. He employed fantasy and recapitulated history in *American Landscape* (1938) to press a plea for racial tolerance and peace between capital and labour. He dispensed with preaching in the romantic *Two on an Island* (1940), but returned to the political scene with *Flight to the West* (also 1940), a fervent denunciation of the 'rational madness' of Nazism, punctuated with melodrama when a refugee tries to assassinate a German diplomat on a transatlantic clipper. *A New Life* (1942) presented a mild conflict between youthful idealism and social snobbery. Rice recaptured the success of his early plays with the fantasy *Dream Girl* (1945), in which a too imaginative girl encounters unexpected romance in reality, and there was much distinction in his operatic version of *Street Scene* (1947), to which Kurt Weill supplied the music. In 1958 Rice presented a modern psycho-analytical variation on the Hamlet theme in *Cue for Passion*, in which Diana Wynyard played the Gertrude-like character, Grace Nicholson. JOHN GASSNER†

RICE, JOHN (*c.* 1596–?), an Elizabethan boy-actor apprenticed to Heminge, who lent him to the Merchant Taylors' Company to deliver a speech before King James in 1607. In 1610 he appeared with Burbage in a water-pageant as Corinea, a nymph. He joined the King's Men, probably in succession to Nathan Field, in 1619, and remained with them some years. He is presumed to have taken Holy Orders, since Heminge in his will of 1630 leaves 20*s.* to 'John Rice, clerk, of St. Saviour's in Southwark'. Rice appears in the actor-list of Shakespeare's plays, and was in the original production of *The Duchess of Malfi*, playing the part of the Marquis of Pescara.

RICE, THOMAS DARTMOUTH (1808–60), an American vaudeville performer and Negro impersonator, known as Jim Crow, from the refrain of his most famous song. This, according to one account, was based on a song and shuffling dance done by an old Negro while grooming a horse, and Rice, having arranged it to his satisfaction, first gave it in 1828 while playing in Ludlow and Smith's Southern Theatre in Louisville, Kentucky, as an intermission between the acts of a play. It caught the public fancy, was published in several editions, and performed all over the United States. In 1833 Rice visited Washington, and there had as partner in his turn the 4-year-old Joseph Jefferson (1829–1905), later one of America's most famous actors. Dressed as a miniature Jim Crow—a ragged nondescript costume and a white hat, his face blacked with burnt cork—he was tumbled out of a sack at the conclusion of Rice's song, and performed the song and dance himself. In 1836 Rice appeared at the Surrey Theatre, London, and started the enormous vogue of minstrel shows in England. In spite of this, and of the burlesques into which he introduced old Negro songs, and which formed the basis of the later Ethiopian Operas, he never himself became part of a troupe, preferring to work alone. Rice was an eccentric man, and died in poverty. In 1837 he married an Englishwoman, but she and their children predeceased him.

RICH. (1) CHRISTOPHER (?–1714), a lawyer who in 1689 bought Charles Davenant's share of the Drury Lane patent, and by 1693 had got complete control of the theatre. He soon became known as a tyrant, a twister, and a mean man, and under his management the company went from bad to worse. Salaries were cut, expenses pared to the minimum, and Rich was constantly involved in lawsuits. In the end Betterton, with most of the better actors, broke away and formed his own company, leaving Rich to carry on with a mediocre group of players. He was finally forced out of management, and took over the deserted theatre in Lincoln's Inn Fields. He died before it was ready, but his son, (2) JOHN (*c.* 1692–1761), managed it, and was responsible for the production there of *The Beggar's Opera* in 1728. Developing the ideas of Weaver, who was the first to introduce the Continental form of pantomime into England from France, John made it immensely popular, and, as Lun, played Harlequin himself with great success, though he was quite illiterate. He produced a pantomime annually from 1717 to 1760. His own masterpiece in acting was probably 'Harlequin Hatched from an Egg by the Sun' in *Harlequin Sorcerer* at Tottenham Court Fair in 1741. Rich had three wives, the third being the actress Priscilla Wilford, whom he married in 1744. Her stage name was Stevens (see COVENT GARDEN, DRURY LANE, LINCOLN'S INN FIELDS THEATRE and PANTOMIME, 3).

RICHARDSON, SIR RALPH DAVID (1902–), English actor, knighted in 1947 for his services to the stage, which he has served well since his first appearance in 1921 at the Little Theatre, Brighton, as Lorenzo in *The Merchant of Venice.* He was with the Birmingham repertory company in 1926, and later appeared in London in several plays by Priestley, giving an exceptionally fine performance in *Johnson over Jordan* (1939). He first played at the Old Vic, where his reputation was chiefly made, in the season of 1930, and on the reopening of Sadler's Wells a year later he played Sir Toby Belch in the initial production of *Twelfth Night.* During further seasons with the Old Vic he played a wide variety of parts, ranging from Petruchio to Bottom, and also appeared several times at the Malvern Festival. After some years in the Fleet Air Arm during the Second World War, he returned to the Old Vic, being much admired as Peer Gynt and Sir John Falstaff. In 1952 he played Prospero and Volpone at the Royal Shakespeare Theatre, and returned to the Old Vic in 1956 to give a fine performance as Timon. An unselfish and unspectacular actor, he brings to all his parts the same integrity of purpose, and his work in Shakespeare and other classics has not prevented him from being a subtle interpreter of modern parts, notably in *The Heiress* (1949), *Home at Seven* (1950), *Flowering Cherry* (1957), and *The Complaisant Lover* (1959).

RICHELIEU, ARMAND-JEAN DU PLESSIS DE, CARDINAL (1585–1642), famous statesman, and for many years virtual ruler of France. He did a great deal for the theatre, and by his patronage of the actor Montdory, whom he often summoned to play before him, helped to establish a permanent professional theatre in Paris and to raise the status of the actor. He had strong leanings towards dramatic authorship, and wrote a number of plays in collaboration with a committee of five—Corneille, Rotrou, Boisrobert, Colletet, and Claude de l'Étoile. They were not very successful, and Corneille resigned after helping with two, having incurred the Cardinal's wrath by making a trifling alteration to his part of the plot. Richelieu built a very well-equipped theatre in his palace, which later, as the Palais-Royal, became famous under Molière. It was opened on 14 Jan. 1641, in the presence of the king and queen and a brilliant audience, with a production of *Mirame,* attributed to Desmarets, but partly the work of Richelieu himself. The new machinery and splendid settings, which heralded the later vogue for such accessories in opera, were received with admiration and applause, but the play had nothing like the ovation given to works by Corneille and other authors in the less splendidly equipped public theatres, and is now forgotten. Richelieu is mainly remembered in theatrical history for his association with Corneille, whom he alternately befriended and rebuked, as in the famous quarrel over *Le Cid.*

RICHEPIN, JEAN (1849–1926), French poet and dramatist, a brilliant but undisciplined man, who was for a short time an actor. He is perhaps best known for his novels and poetry, and like them his plays, of which the first was *L'Étoile* (1873), are somewhat marred by an insistent morbidity. They represent, nevertheless, an important part of his work, and include *Nana Sahib* (1883), *Monsieur Scapin* (1886), *Le Filibustier* (1888), *Par la glaive* (1892), *Le Chien de garde* (1898), and *Don Quichotte* (1905). They were mostly given at the Comédie-Française, though *Le Chemineau* (1897), having been accepted there subject to correction, was taken by the author to the Odéon, and had an immense success. Richepin also wrote words for music by Massenet and Georges.

RICHMOND HILL THEATRE, NEW YORK. This opened on 14 Nov. 1831, in the converted house of Aaron Burr, with *The Road to Ruin.* It had a good company under able management, and was probably intended to give scope to the talents of Mrs. Duff, who played there for two seasons, mainly in revivals. The theatre had the temerity to stage *The Hunchback* on the same night as the Park Theatre, 18 June 1832, and was prospering when it was closed on account of plague, which claimed one of its best actors, Woodhull. It then housed Italian opera, sponsored by Lorenzo da Ponte (1749–1838), Mozart's librettist and Professor of Italian at Columbia University. In 1836 Mrs. Hamblin opened it for a couple of seasons, and the famous comedian James E. Murdoch made there his first appearance in New York, while later Miss Nelson took it over and made a hit in *The Mountain Sylph.* For a few seasons it opened as the Tivoli Gardens, and from 1845 to 1848 was again advertised as the Richmond Theatre, but mainly housed circus and variety. It then disappears from theatrical records.

RICHMOND THEATRE. 1. LONDON, opened on 15 June 1765 and pulled down in 1880. It was quite an important playhouse, and many great actors appeared there. The elder Mathews, as a stage-struck youth, paid 7½ guineas to be allowed to play Richard III. Dibdin appeared there, and so did Edmund Kean, who died in the house next door. Helen Faucit made her début there in 1833. The present theatre on the Green was built in 1899, and has had an interesting, though not spectacular, history, being used mainly for revivals, and try-outs of new plays, many of which have subsequently found their way to the West End. A still earlier theatre, on Richmond Hill, opened in June 1730 and closed in Oct. 1769. It was finally demolished about 1826.

W. MACQUEEN-POPE†, *rev.*

2. YORKSHIRE. This theatre is one of the only four surviving eighteenth-century playhouses in England (the others are in Bristol, Bury St. Edmunds, and Margate). It is a small theatre, with a rectangular auditorium, and is unique in having preserved its original proscenium. It was built by Samuel Butler the elder on Corporation ground, and opened in 1788. The Richmond circuit included Harrogate, Beverley, Northallerton, Whitby, Kendal, and Ulverston. After Butler's death in 1812 his widow, who was a member of the Jefferson family, ran the circuit until her son, Samuel Butler, was old enough to take over in 1821. Soon after it started to break up, and Butler's connexion with the Richmond Theatre ended in 1830. For a few years it was rented for short seasons to visiting managers, and in 1848 it was converted into a wine cellar and auction room, the sunk pit being boarded over. In 1943 the unrestored building was used for a performance in commemoration of the 850th anniversary of the enfranchisement of the borough. A Trust was formed in 1960 to restore and redecorate it, which was done at a cost of £17,000, and in 1962 it was re-opened as a theatre. It is used occasionally for performances.

SYBIL ROSENFELD

RICINIATA, see FABULA, 6 and MIME, 2.

RICKETTS, CHARLES (1866–1931), see COSTUME, 10 and No. 98.

RING, THE, an octagonal structure, originally a chapel, which stood in Blackfriars Road, London, about 500 yards from Blackfriars Bridge. Built in 1783, it later became a well-known boxing-ring, and sprang into temporary theatrical fame when in 1936–7 Robert Atkins used it for some of the earliest theatre-in-the-round productions in England, producing there on 29 Nov. *Henry V* with Hubert Gregg as the King, on 17 Jan. *Much Ado About Nothing* with Jack Hawkins as Benedick, and on 14 March *The Merry Wives of Windsor* with Roy Byford as Falstaff and Irene and Violet Vanbrugh as Mistress Page and Mistress Ford. It then sank back into obscurity, and was demolished some time after the Second World War. It has been confused with the Rotunda, an occasional theatre and music-hall which stood near by on the corner of Stamford Street.

RISE AND SINK, a method of effecting a Transformation Scene (see TRICKWORK ON THE ENGLISH STAGE).

RISTORI, ADELAIDE (1822–1906), Italian actress, celebrated far beyond the confines of her native country, particularly as a player of tragic parts. The daughter of actors, she was on the stage as a child, and at 14 gave a successful interpretation of the part of Francesca da Rimini in Silvio Pellico's version of the play. At 18 she played for the first time a part which she made peculiarly her own—Maria Stuart in Schiller's tragedy. She retired from the stage for a short time on marriage, but returned and in 1855 went to Paris, where, after a somewhat quiet début, she soon became an outstanding figure and a serious rival to Rachel. From Paris she went to England, Spain, and the United States, where she first appeared in 1866, and then toured the country with great success. In 1882 she was seen in London as Lady Macbeth and was much praised by the critics. Mrs. Kendal, in a characteristic remark, said of her that she was a greater actress than Sarah Bernhardt because she had no sex-appeal. She retired in 1885, and three years later published her memoirs, which provide an interesting account of her life, and a penetrating study of her approach to her art.

RITTERDRAMA, an offshoot of the *Sturm und Drang* drama, which followed Goethe's *Götz von Berlichingen* (1773) and Klinger's *Otto* (1774). It might perhaps be translated as 'feudal' drama. In it the valour and doughty independence of the medieval knights was shown amidst battle scenes, jousting, and pageantry, often with a marked vein of Bavarian local patriotism. Among the authors of such plays were Josef August von Törring (1753–1826), Bavarian Minister of State, with *Kasper der Thorringer* (publ. 1785) and *Agnes Bernauerin* (1780), and Joseph Marius Babo (1756–1822), for some time director of the Court theatre in Munich, with *Otto von Wittelsbach* (1782). Like the *Sturm und Drang* drama, the *Ritterdrama* is written in prose, is irregular in form, and has as its theme strong passions and a contempt for conventions. These plays did much to foster the taste for romantic and medieval settings kindled by *Götz von Berlichingen*, and it is significant that Schiller's *Die Räuber* was given in sixteenth-century costume. Reactionary influences caused the *Ritterdrama* to be banned from the Munich stage, but its vogue continued elsewhere, notably in Austria, where Karl Friedrich Hensler (1761–1825) fused this type of drama with the native operatic fairy-tale in *Das Donauweibchen* (1797).

RITZ THEATRE, NEW YORK, on 48th Street west of Broadway. This opened on 21 Mar. 1921 with Clara Eames in Drinkwater's *Mary Stuart*. It was a failure, as was his *Robert*

E. Lee. In 1922 came *It Is the Law*, and in 1924 a successful production of *Outward Bound*. A year later Winthrop Ames produced *Old English*, with George Arliss, which ran for 183 performances, while later in the same year *The Man with a Load of Mischief*, with Ruth Chatterton and Robert Loraine, had a short run. A series of failures was broken in 1927 by the 27-weeks' run of *Excess Baggage*, a comedy on the heartbreaks of vaudeville, while in the autumn of 1932 Ruth Draper gave a three-weeks' season of monologues. In 1937 the theatre was taken over by the Federal Theatre Project, which presented there Arthur Arent's Living Newspaper *Power* for 118 performances. A year later *Murder in the Cathedral* was given 21 performances, and after a Federal Theatre production of *Pinocchio* the theatre became a cinema. It is now used for radio and television shows. GEORGE FREEDLEY†

RIVAS, DUQUE DE, see SAAVEDRA, ÁNGEL DE.

R.K.O. CENTRE, and **R.K.O. ROXY**, NEW YORK, see CENTRE THEATRE.

ROBERTS, ARTHUR (1852–1933), one of the earliest of music-hall comedians and, unlike many others, neither red-nosed nor shabby. At 19 he sang in tavern entertainments, and all through the 1870s he appeared on the halls, where his first successful song was 'If I Was Only Long Enough, a Soldier I Would Be'. In 1880 he first appeared in pantomime, under Harris at Drury Lane, and later appeared as immaculate guardsmen and men-about-town in burlesques and musical comedies. In the first of these, *In Town*, as Captain Coddington, he set a fashion in male headgear. He celebrated his jubilee in 1924, and later appeared in London and the provinces in 'The Veterans of Variety'. He was a great gagster. It was not necessary to write him a part; he did that for himself, and altered it every night.

W. MACQUEEN-POPE†

ROBERTSON, THOMAS WILLIAM (1829–71), English dramatist, eldest of the twenty-two children of an actor. Several of his brothers and sisters were on the stage, the most famous being the youngest girl, Madge (see KENDAL). Robertson himself acted as a child, and after some years' schooling went as an adult actor to Lincoln where the Robertson family had for many years been in control of the theatres on the Lincoln circuit. Here he made himself generally useful, painting scenery, writing songs and plays, and acting small parts. He was in fact trained in the old school which he was later to destroy, a process which can be studied, with reservations, in Pinero's *Trelawny of the 'Wells'* (1898). Yet his earliest plays were in no way remarkable. He wrote them quickly and sold them cheaply to Lacy, the theatrical publisher, and his first success was achieved with *David Garrick* (1864), based on a French play and written for Sothern. Though built up very largely on the old formulae and abounding in 'type' characters, the printed copy of this play, with its elaborate directions for realistic scenery and costume, and its wealth of stage directions, is a definite pointer in the direction which Robertson was to take almost immediately with such plays as *Society* (1865), *Ours* (1866), *Caste* (1867), *Play* (1868), and *School* (1869). Their monosyllabic titles alone come as a refreshing change after the flowery nomenclature of earlier and even contemporary plays. They were all given at the Prince of Wales's Theatre (the old Queen's, later the Scala) where the success of *Society* established the reputation not only of the author but of the newly formed Bancroft management. With these plays Robertson founded what has been called 'the cup-and-saucer drama'—that is, the drama of the realistic, contemporary, domestic interior. His rooms were recognizable, his dialogue credible, his plots, though they now seem somewhat artificial, were true to his time and an immense advance on anything that had gone before. *Caste* in particular still holds the stage, and some of the others would revive well.

Robertson, who was a robust and convivial creature, with red hair and beard and a brilliant flow of conversation, directed his own plays, and has sometimes been accounted the first of the modern producers. Years of hard work and continual rebuffs embittered him, but with the coming of success his naturally sweet temper reasserted itself, and he was able to enjoy a few years of fame before his tragically early death at the height of his career. He had, however, left a permanent mark on the theatre of his time, and the work of many modern dramatists is adumbrated in his early efforts at realism.

ROBESON, PAUL (1898–), American Negro actor and singer, who abandoned a legal career for the stage, where he first appeared in 1921. A year later he was seen in England, playing opposite Mrs. Patrick Campbell in *The Voodoo*, and on his return to New York created a great sensation by his performances with the Provincetown Players in O'Neill's plays, particularly as Brutus in *The Emperor Jones*. It was his singing of 'Ole Man River' in *Showboat* that first revealed the haunting quality of his superb bass voice, and for many years afterwards he toured Europe and America with a programme of Negro spirituals. He returned to the stage in 1930, when he was seen in London in *Othello*, which, when revived in 1943 in New York, achieved the longest recorded run of any Shakespearian play. Robeson has appeared in a number of films, and is the subject of a biography, written by his wife, and published in 1930. He returned to London, after a long absence, in 1958, in which year he published *Here I Stand*, a plain statement of his life and beliefs, which has aroused controversy in America and elsewhere, as did his visit to Russia in 1963. He has done excellent work in furthering the interests of the Negro people, and is one of the best-known artists of our time, being highly-gifted, sincere, and courageous.

ROBEY, Sir George (1869–1954), one of the most successful and popular comedians of the English music-halls, nicknamed 'the Prime Minister of Mirth'. He made his first appearance at the Aquarium in 1891, and after a trial at the Oxford in the same year was engaged for most of the leading halls of London and the provinces. Apart from popular songs, he was very successful in a series of humorous caricatures and sketches, and in 1916 he appeared for the first time in revue as Lucius Bing in *The Bing Boys Are Here*, following it with *The Bing Boys on Broadway*. Other ventures which displayed his amazing versatility were Dame Trot in *Jack and the Beanstalk* (1921), Menelaus in *Helen!* (1932), and Falstaff in *Henry IV, Part I* (1935). He was for some years manager of the Prince's Theatre, where he put on his own revue, *Bits and Pieces* (1927), in which he subsequently toured. Robey's humour was robust, and he appeared to consist largely of a bowler hat and two enormous eyebrows. He was an excellent painter, exhibiting at the Academy and at the Royal Institute of Painters in Water Colours, a writer—his first book was published in 1908—a violin-maker, a cricketer, and a student of Egyptology. In 1919 he was created a C.B.E. for his efforts in raising over £11,000 by concerts given for the French Red Cross, and shortly before his death he was knighted for his services to the stage and to charity.

ROBIN HOOD, an English legendary hero, whose name first appears in *Piers Plowman* (1377). He typifies the chivalrous outlaw from oppression, champion of the poor against the tyranny of the rich. Though his story may have some basis in fact, it is impossible to identify him with any historical personage, though an Elizabethan playwright, Anthony Munday, made him the exiled Earl of Huntingdon. Since he is always dressed in green, he may be a survival of the Wood-man, or Jack-in-the-Green, of the early pagan spring festivities, or he may have been imported by minstrels from France (see ADAM DE LA HALLE, *Le Jeu de Robin et Marion*). By the end of the fifteenth century he and his familiar retinue of Maid Marian, Little John, Friar Tuck, and the Merry Men, with their accompanying Morris Dance, were inseparable from the May-Day revels, and the protagonists of many a rustic drama. These, however, cannot be considered folk plays, as were the Mumming and Plough Monday plays, since they were written by minstrels. The May-Day festivities found their way to Court, where they became mixed up with allegory and pseudo-classicism. Henry VIII, in particular, enjoyed many splendid Mayings, including one in which he was entertained by Robin Hood to venison in a bower. After that their popularity waned, and they were finally suppressed by the Puritans. The story of Robin Hood and his Merry Men has been a favourite subject for nineteenth- and twentieth-century pantomime.

ROBINS, Elizabeth (1862–1952), American actress, who passed the greater part of her professional life in England, and was prominently identified with the introduction of Ibsen to the London stage. She made her first appearance, however, with the Boston Museum stock company in 1885, and remained with them for some years, afterwards touring with Booth and Barrett. She was first seen in London in 1889, and in June of that year appeared as Martha Bernick in *The Pillars of Society*. A visit to Norway had awakened her interest in Ibsen, and in 1891 she played Mrs. Linden in *A Doll's House* and the title-role in *Hedda Gabler*, in which she gave a remarkable performance. Two years later she played Hilda in *The Master Builder*, Rebecca West in *Rosmersholm*, and Agnes in *Brand*. *Little Eyolf* followed in 1896 and *John Gabriel Borkman* in 1897. She held the stage rights of most of these plays, and was responsible, sometimes in conjunction with such advanced groups as the Independent Theatre, for their initial productions. She was seen also in a wide variety of other parts, notably as Mariana in Echegaray's play of that name. She then retired, apart from a brief return to the stage as Lucrezia in *Paolo and Francesca* (1902), and devoted herself to literature, publishing a number of novels and two volumes of theatrical reminiscences.

ROBINSON, (Esmé Stuart) Lennox (1886–1958), Irish actor, playwright, theatre director, and dramatic critic, who was closely connected with the modern Irish drama from the time his first play, *The Clancy Name*, appeared at the Abbey Theatre, Dublin, in 1908, until his death, at which time he was still a director of the theatre, having joined it as a producer in 1910. In his early plays—*Harvest* (1910), *Patriots* (1912), *The Dreamers* (1913)—he presented aspects of Irish life which had not been touched on by Yeats, Lady Gregory, or Synge, and treated political and patriotic themes as matter for tragedy, with no danger of weakening into sentimentalism. His comedy, *The White-Headed Boy* (1916), was much appreciated in Ireland, England, and America, and has remained popular in all three countries. In these plays, and in *Crabbed Youth and Age* (1922), his skill as a structural craftsman, and as a creator of character in the style of the comedy of manners, was manifest, and it never faltered in its development.

In *The Big House* (1926) Robinson showed that he was abreast of the age and its problems, and was the first man in Ireland to write a play on the changing order of its civilization—a theme touched on also by Yeats, notably in his last play, *Purgatory*. In *The Far-Off Hills* (1928) and in *Church Street* (1934) he returned to that comedy in which his most precise work had been done, achieving in *Church Street* not only a fine and skilful piece of dramatic structure, but a tragicomedy or 'mingled drama' whose satire was genial and whose ironies were tragic. His later works included *Give a Dog* (1928), *Ever the Twain* (1929), *All's*

Over Then? (1932), *Is Life Worth Living?* (also known as *Drama at Inish*) (1933), *When Lovely Woman* (1936), *Killycreggs in Twilight* (1937), *Bird's Nest* (1938), *Forget Me Not* (1941), and *The Lucky Finger* (1948). His contribution to dramatic history and criticism includes *The Irish Theatre* (1939), a collection of lectures given by him and other leaders of this theatre in 1938, and *Curtain Up* (1941). After fire had destroyed the Abbey in 1951, he published *A History of the Abbey Theatre.*

UNA ELLIS-FERMOR†, *rev.*

ROBINSON, MARY (*née* DARBY) (1758–1800), English actress who, after a short career on the stage, left it to become the mistress of the Prince Regent, making her last appearance on 31 May 1780 as Eliza in Lady Craven's *The Miniature Picture.* Her finest part was Perdita in *The Winter's Tale,* which she first played on 20 Nov. 1779 at Drury Lane, and it is by that name that she is best known. She was the spoiled child of a spendthrift, and at 16 made an unhappy marriage with a dissolute young man, with whom she shortly afterwards went to prison for debt. She was coached for her first appearance, as Juliet, by Garrick, and appeared at Drury Lane in 1776, her success being already assured by her reputation for beauty and profligacy. Yet some critics saw in her the makings of a fine actress, better suited to heavy tragedy than to the light, girlish parts she usually played. After her short-lived affair with the Regent, for which she was much pitied and considered the less blamable of the two, she would probably have returned to the theatre; but she was strongly advised not to, and a severe attack of rheumatic fever left her, at 24, too helpless to do so. She spent the rest of her life wandering from one spa to another, seeking relief, and supporting herself by writing poems and novels, now forgotten.

ROBINSON, RICHARD (?–1648), English actor, who appears in the actor-list of Shakespeare's plays. He was probably a boy-actor at the Blackfriars, and was certainly one of the King's Men from 1611 onwards. As a young lad he played women's parts, and was much praised by Ben Jonson. Later he witnessed Burbage's will and possibly married his widow, which has inclined some to think that he may have been apprenticed to Burbage. He signed the dedication of the Beaumont and Fletcher folio in 1647.

ROBSON, FLORA (1902–), English actress, created D.B.E. in the Birthday Honours, 1960, for her services to the stage. After a season with Ben Greet, she joined Fagan's company at the Playhouse, Oxford, and in 1924 left the stage for four years. Since her return she has steadily consolidated her position as an outstanding player of modern parts demanding controlled nervous tension, among them Abbie Putnam in *Desire Under the Elms,* Mary Paterson in *The Anatomist* (both 1931), Eva in *For Services Rendered* (1932), Margaret Hayden in *Message for Margaret* (1946), Alicia in *Black Chiffon* (1949), Miss Giddens in *The Innocents* (1952), Janet in *The House by the Lake* (1956), and Miss Tina in *The Aspern Papers* (1959). She joined the Old Vic company in 1933, playing a wide variety of parts, and was much admired as Paulina in *The Winter's Tale* (1951). Her talent for comedy, which has not been given much scope recently, showed itself in *Captain Brassbound's Conversion* (1948) (see No. 175), and in her earlier Gwendolen Fairfax and Mrs Foresight. In 1962 a modernized repertory theatre named after her was opened at Newcastle-upon-Tyne, and she appeared there as guest artist in a revival of *The Corn is Green.*

ROBSON, FREDERICK (1821–64), English actor, whose real name was Thomas Robson Brownbill. He was apprenticed to an engraver, but made a number of appearances in amateur companies before deserting his trade for the stage. After several engagements in the provinces he appeared at the Grecian in 1844, and became famous as a singer of popular ballads. In 1850 he went to Dublin, but returned to become one of the mainstays of burlesque at the Olympic, of which he later became joint manager with Emden. He was very short and ugly, but an actor of great power, and was affectionately known as 'the great little Robson'. Among his most popular parts were Jacob Earwig in *Boots at the Swan* (1842), Jim Baggs in a revival of *The Wandering Minstrel* (1853), Daddy Hardacre in the play of that name (1857), and Sampson Burr in *The Porter's Knot* (1858). Robson died at the early age of 43, a victim of intemperance.

ROBSON, STUART [HENRY ROBSON STUART] (1836–1903), American comedian, whose odd voice and quaint personality provided his stock-in-trade for over fifty years of acting. He began as a boy of 16, and after ten years with leading stock companies went to Laura Keene's Theatre in New York as principal comedian. He also spent some years with Mrs. John Drew at the Arch Street Theatre in Philadelphia and with Warren in Boston. In 1873 he was seen in London, and shortly afterwards he began a long association with Crane, playing with him in light farce, in *The Henrietta,* which was specially written for them, and as one of the two Dromios in *The Comedy of Errors*; he was also Falstaff to Crane's Slender. In 1889 the two parted amicably, and Robson produced several new plays, dying suddenly while on tour shortly after celebrating his stage jubilee.

RODE, HELGE (1870–1937), Danish dramatist (see SCANDINAVIA, 1 *a*).

ROD-PUPPET, see PUPPET and Nos. 126–9.

ROGERS, WILLIAM PENN ADAIR (1879–1935), American comedian, better known as Will Rogers. He had Red Indian blood in him and spent his youth on the range, later, after a good though erratic education, becoming a cowboy. In 1902 he joined a Wild West circus in the Argentine, being billed as the Cherokee Kid. After a tour in Australia he returned to the States to appear at the St. Louis Exhibition. In 1905 he made his first appearance in New York, where he soon became very popular, joking informally with his audience. He appeared in musical comedy for the first time in 1912, and rapidly became a star on Broadway, reaching the height of success when he appeared in several editions of Ziegfeld's *Follies*. His personality was more important than his material, and his wisecracks were quoted everywhere. In the 1920s the stage lost him to Hollywood, and he also became a newspaper correspondent, a lecturer, and a radio commentator. An enthusiast about flying, he was killed on a flight with the aviator Wiley Post. In contrast to the exotic background of his Broadway shows and the publicity accorded to his every movement, his domestic life, with a devoted wife and three children, was quiet and happy.

ROJAS, FERNANDO DE, see CELESTINA, LA.

ROJAS ZORRILLA, FRANCISCO DE (1607–48), Spanish dramatist, author of many plays, of which the best known is *Del rey abajo, ninguno* (otherwise known as *García del Castañar* or *El labrador más honrado*). In common with many other Golden Age dramatists, Rojas utilizes in this play three main themes: personal honour, the contrast between life at Court and life in the country, and the relationship between the social classes. *Del rey abajo, ninguno* is distinguished by the strong contrast between the peaceful countryside and the vicious and formal Court. Rojas's comedies, in which the *gracioso*, or clown, is often the chief personage, are distinguished by wit and neatness of versification. The best known is *Entre bobos anda el juego*. Rojas was also the author of a number of *autos sacramentales*.

J. E. VAREY

ROLL-OUT, a loose flap of canvas at the bottom of a piece of scenery, which enables an actor to appear suddenly on the stage by rolling through it and springing quickly to his feet.

ROMAGNESI, a family of actors belonging to the *commedia dell'arte*. Little is known of the father, (1) NICCOLÒ (?–1660), beyond his stage name, Orazio, and the fact that he married (2) BRIGIDA BIANCHI (1613–*c.* 1703), the daughter of a player and herself a good actress, known as Aurelia. Her son, (3) MARC' ANTONIO (*c.* 1633–1706), first appeared in young lover parts, and later as the Pedant-Doctor. He must at some time have appeared in London, since his wife died there in 1675. Two of his sons were actors, one, (4) Carlo VIRGILIO (1670–1708), known as Leandro, making his début at the Théâtre-Italien in Paris in 1694, and remaining there until the theatre was closed. He was accounted a fine player of young lovers.

ROMAINS, JULES [really LOUIS-HENRI-JEAN FARIGOULE] (1885–), French poet and novelist, was also an outstanding dramatist. His first play, *L'Armée dans la ville*, was produced by Antoine, but it was not until after the First World War that Romains began his close association with the theatre through his friendship with Cocteau and Copeau. He worked for a time at the Vieux-Colombier, where his *Cromedeyre-le-Vieil* was produced in 1920. But it was Jouvet who produced and played in his three successful farces, *M. le Trouhadec saisi par la débauche*, *Knock, ou le Triomphe de la Médecine* (both 1923), and *Le Mariage de M. le Trouhadec* (1925). The second of these, a satire on the medical profession and the credulity of human beings, is probably Romains's best-known play. As *Dr. Knock* it was translated by Granville-Barker, and successfully produced in London in 1926 and in New York in 1928. Romains's later plays included *Jean le Maufranc* (1926) which was initially unsuccessful but, rewritten as *Musse ou l'École de l'hypocrisie*, offered Dullin a fine part in 1926, *Le Dictateur* (also 1926), which was most successful outside France, an excellent adaptation of *Volpone* (1928), *Boën, ou la Possession des Biens* (1930), in which Gémier made one of his last appearances, and *Donogoo* (1931). Romains then concentrated on his vast panoramic novel, *Les Hommes de Bonne Volonté*, and, except for some one-act plays, and *L'An Mil*, produced by Dullin in 1947, wrote no more for the theatre. But a revival of *Donogoo* at the Comédie-Française in 1951 proved a great success, as did *M. le Trouhadec saisi par la débauche*, and the one-act *Amédée et les Messieurs en rang* in 1956. *Volpone* was successfully revived by Barrault at the Marigny in 1955, with himself as Mosca and Ledoux as Volpone.

ROMANELLI OF MANTUA, SAMUEL (1757–1814), writer of plays in Hebrew, into which language he translated Metastasio and other Italian authors (see JEWISH DRAMA, 3).

ROMANI, FELICE (1788–1865), Italian poet, a writer of great charm and distinction, who wrote some excellent libretti for Italian operas. Two of these are from Shakespeare, whom he probably knew only through the French adaptations of Ducis—*Hamlet* for Mercadante (1822), and *Romeo and Juliet*, which was set by Vaccai in 1825 and by Bellini in 1830. Perhaps his best, and certainly his best-known, work was done for Bellini's 'La Sonnambula' (1831).

ROMANTIC COMEDY, see COMEDY.

ROMASHOV, BORIS SERGEIVICH (1895–1958), Soviet dramatist, whose first play, *Meringue Pie*, a satire on the pretensions of bourgeois elements in Soviet society, was produced in 1925. Among his later plays, which were mainly melodramas based on episodes of the Civil War, were *The End of Krivorilsky* (1927), which was revived in Leningrad in 1957, *The Fiery Bridge* (1929), and *Fighters* (1934). This last, which is perhaps his most important work, dealt with the Red Army in peacetime, and the clash between private and public interests among the officers. In 1942 a play dealing with the defence of Moscow, *Shine, Stars!*, was put on at the Sverdlovsk Theatre less than a year after the events it deals with took place. Its theme is the courage of a young student galvanized by war into a man of action, and it proved immensely popular. In 1947 *A Great Force*, which depicted the conflict between conservative and progressive scientists, was staged at the Maly Theatre by N. V. Petrov and K. A. Zubov.

ROME. 1. FROM THE ORIGINS TO THE END OF THE REPUBLICAN PERIOD. Roman drama was produced by a succession of writers who strove to adapt Greek originals to the native taste for rhetoric, spectacle, and sensationalism, and also for buffoonery, homely wit, and biting repartee. Livy tells us that out of a blend of the primitive 'Fescennine Verses', or interchanges of jest by clowns at harvest and other festivals, with music and dance imported from Etruria, there grew a 'medley' (*satura*) which we may perhaps liken to the music-hall entertainment of Edwardian days. The advance to true drama was made by Livius Andronicus, who in 240 B.C. produced at the public games a Greek play in translation. From then till the end of the Republic Greek tragedies and comedies in translation continued to be produced in Rome. Attempts at original composition consisted of a very few plays on Roman historical themes (see FABULA, 4), and a considerable number of comedies on middle-class or humble life in Italy (see FABULA, 9), but such pieces were probably slight. We have no reason for attributing to any Latin writer the invention of plot or character on a grand scale. The Roman crowd, who were also the electorate, wanted entertainment. The State and the magistrates were anxious to satisfy them and to pay those who could supply the entertainment; the easy and obvious method of translating Greek plays for public performance provided a livelihood for Latin writers in days when there was as yet no reading public in Rome. In general the method adopted was to select a Greek play hitherto untranslated, and to render it freely into Latin, introducing modifications in detail which aimed at pleasing the audience, such as the expression of Roman sentiments in Roman rhetorical style or the addition, in comedy, of jests and topical allusions, however incongruous with their context. Only in the case of Terence can we discern a conscious artistic impulse to improve on the Greek model; in general we may say that the creation of plot and character was neither aimed at by the Roman dramatists nor expected of them by their audience. They were neither men of independent means nor (usually, at any rate) slaves, but hard-working folk, dependent for a livelihood on their pens, and organized, along with the scribes, into a trade guild, the *collegium poetarum*.

Dramatic performances formed part of the entertainment provided free to the public at the games. The actors had to compete with rival attractions such as boxing or rope-dancing; even after the play had begun, a rumour that better fare was to be found elsewhere might cause the spectators to desert in a body. The authorities, however anxious to please the public, were alive to the danger of allowing so large a body of people to hear any utterance on the stage which might reflect on the government or on members of the governing classes; political and personal allusions were therefore in general banned, though it would have been difficult to prevent the actors and the audience from occasionally finding a topical reference in the words of an old play (thus a line in honour of 'Tullius', i.e. Servius Tullius the king, was on one occasion taken by the audience as referring to their own contemporary, M. Tullius Cicero). With moral and religious matters the censorship was less concerned; the *Amphitruo* of Plautus shows the gods Jupiter and Mercury as heartless deceivers, and it is precisely those plays of Plautus and Terence which we know to have been particularly popular (the *Casina* and the *Eunuchus*) which strike us as being the most improper works of their authors. But Plautus's boast in the prologue and epilogue to the *Captivi* that this play is of a higher moral tone than most Greek comedies suggests that Roman public taste itself might impose limits on the dramatist's freedom; in general our extant Latin comedies are fairly free from indecency.

To judge from the prologues, admission to the games was open to all—citizens and slaves, matrons and courtesans, even nurses and their squalling charges. Performances began in the morning; a play could be got through by lunch time. All performances were in the open air. At first there was no permanent theatre; the simple buildings required—the stage and behind it the scene-building—could be put up where required. We have several references in the prologues and plays to a seated audience; no doubt tiers of wooden scaffolding could be erected for a performance and taken down afterwards. What the spectators saw was an open stage with behind it a building, the front wall of which was pierced by three doors. The stage itself represented the open street running from the centre of the town to the harbour or country, or the space in front of a palace, a cottage, or other building. Our modern stage convention allows us to see what is happening inside a house; the spectators of a Roman comedy were in the position of people standing in the public street and observing what was taking place in front of two or three houses which fronted on that street. Interior scenes and changes of setting within the course of a play were unknown. The absence of a front curtain during the period when our extant comedies were written made it necessary to begin and end each play with an empty stage. Act-division, interludes, and intervals were unknown; on one occasion only do we hear of a solo by the *tibicen* (player on double pipes) to cover the momentary absence of the chief actor.

Every care was taken that the audience should follow the plot and realize the significance of each means of entrance and the identity of each character. The characters in comedy were types rather than individuals—old gentlemen, usually rather close-fisted, young gentlemen, usually extravagant and spineless, intriguing slaves, jealous wives, boastful captains, treacherous pimps—and custom prescribed the appropriate costume, wig, and mask for each of these types. Unmarried women of the respectable classes were excluded by Greek convention from appearing in public, except at religious or other festivals; consequently the unmarried heroines of Greek New Comedy and its Latin derivatives are something below respectability—courtesans, or maidens who have by some misfortune been separated from their parents and brought up in humble circumstances. A common form of plot shows a young gentleman in love with a slave-girl and anxious to raise the money for her purchase; if marriage is to be the outcome, it must be shown in the course of the play that the girl is not only chaste but the long-lost child of respectable parents. In general the plots of comedy turn on intrigues, attempts to raise money, and swindling and deception of many kinds.

The use of costumes and masks (see No. 13) (Terence uses *persona*, mask, in the sense of 'character') enabled small companies of five or six actors to perform almost any play by doubling of parts. The leading actor might himself be the producer. Such leading actors might rise to fame and fortune; the careers of Ambivius Turpio, in the second century B.C., and of Cicero's contemporaries, Aesopus and Roscius, seem to prove that the theatrical profession was not yet regarded as in itself degrading. We hear nothing of slaves appearing on the stage until Cicero's day, when Roscius trained a slave named Panurgus for the stage.

Much of what in the Greek originals had been spoken was in the Latin adaptations recited by the actors in various metres to a musical accompaniment supplied by a *tibicen*, who was also capable of covering up a gap in the performance by supplying a solo. On one occasion the *tibicen* is given a drink, and while he is drinking the metre necessarily becomes that of unaccompanied speech, the iambic trimeter. On the other hand, the chorus of fifth-century Greek tragedies was in the Latin adaptations probably represented by a single speaker, attended perhaps by mutes, who appeared on the stage with the other actors. Actors complained of the strain on their voices; indeed, when we consider that they were performing in the open air before large audiences and amid considerable noise, we see that strength of voice must have been one of an actor's chief qualifications.

As for the production of plays, it seems that the authorities responsible for the public games would commission a producer to procure a good play and arrange for its performance. Although revivals of old and successful plays were not unknown, the attraction of novelty would naturally suggest, at least during the productive period of Latin drama, the purchase of a newly written work from its author. The author probably sold his manuscript outright to the producer, who also paid the company, hired the costumes from the *choregus*, and in general took all business details on his shoulders, hoping to reap a profit from the sum handed him by the magistrates or other persons responsible for the giving of the games. Somehow the manuscripts of plays managed to survive to later generations, sometimes with modifications, such as the addition of an alternative final scene, which indicate the hand of a later producer; but even the archaic plays of Livius Andronicus, which can hardly have enjoyed much popularity on the stage, survived, perhaps as school texts, to the time of Cicero, who read them and pronounced them not worth a second reading. Such a manuscript would naturally include the prologue if there was one—or prologues, if the play had been given a revival performance; the author's name would appear on the title-page, and notes of opening or later performances might also be included. From such information scholars of a later generation seem to have derived their accounts of theatrical activities and their biographical information with regard to the early dramatists. It is only too clear that the records were soon confused; there was much dispute as to which were the genuine plays of Plautus, and no means of settling such a controversy, while the tendency to fill in biographical details from inference and even imagination is indicated by the discrepancies in the 'Life' of Terence. The safest basis for the study of Latin drama is the text of the plays and prologues.

Though tragedy seems to have attracted fewer writers than comedy, the popularity and influence of the leading tragic writers appear to have been great. In general they seem to have selected as models the more melodramatic of the Greek originals. Exciting plots, flamboyant characters, gruesome scenes, violent rhetoric were more attractive to the Roman crowd than the qualities for which we chiefly prize our extant Greek tragedies. By comparing the fragments we can see how Roman translators modified their originals to suit national taste. In substance there was probably little alteration; the changes were in matters of style and detail, the chief feature being the development of rhetoric at the expense of truth and naturalness. In comedy the free-and-easy methods of the early writers appear to have been succeeded by greater fidelity to the Greek originals; but that something was felt to be lost thereby is suggested by the contemporary development of the comedy of Italian manners (see FABULA, 9). By the end of the second century B.C. Turpilius, the last writer of comedy for the stage, was dead, while Accius, the last writer of tragedy, died some fifteen or twenty years later.

From about the time of Sulla we notice new developments. While old plays are still produced (actors such as Aesopus in tragedy and

Roscius in comedy made large fortunes), we gather on the whole that new plays were not being written for the stage. The writing of tragedy and comedy appears now to be regarded as a purely literary affair and is practised by persons of the governing class, e.g. Julius Caesar Strabo and Quintus Cicero; such writers seem to have composed original plays, not translations. While the theatres become more splendid, the standard of theatrical entertainment seems to sink; rustic farce (see FABULA, 1) and mime enjoy increasing popularity, and even the revivals of old plays are marred by tasteless extravagance of production. The introduction of the drop-curtain makes possible elaborate scenic effects and quick changes of setting. A divorce sets in between drama and the stage; Cicero seems to think of drama as something to be read, while theatrical performances are for him little more than a vulgar form of popular entertainment.

2. THE EMPIRE. Many plays were written during the Empire, and theatres arose in Europe, Asia, and Africa; but these plays and these theatres had little or nothing to do with each other. As public taste had been found to prefer mime and pantomime (see MIME, 2, and PANTOMIMUS), the stage was almost monopolized by these light performances, though we have a few references to the revival of old plays. The tragedies and comedies now written are independent compositions intended to be read aloud among friends. The tragedies ascribed to Seneca, including the *praetexta*, *Octavia*, are examples of this Closet drama; though full of clever rhetoric, they are clearly not designed for the stage, and were probably never performed. As the only examples of Latin tragedy to reach the modern world, they were destined nevertheless to exercise great influence on the drama of the Renaissance.

3. THE ROMAN THEATRE AND STAGE. Unlike the Greek theatre, the central feature of the Roman theatre was from the first not the orchestra but the raised stage, on which all the performers appeared. As every seat had to command a view of the stage, the *cavea*, or portion occupied by the seating, could not exceed semicircular form. The orchestra, immediately in front of the stage, was unused except to accommodate distinguished spectators. As in the Greek theatre, the scene-building behind the stage (the *scaenae frons*, taken over from Hellenistic usage) must from early times have been used both as the back-scene and as the actors' dressing-room. The spectators sat on tiers of wooden benches (*spectacula*) supported by scaffolding, or on the ground below; we see a similar arrangement in an Etruscan tomb-painting. The whole structure was a temporary affair during the productive period of Latin drama. There was at this time no curtain; the back-scene, with its regulation three doors, was open to view throughout the play. Characters could enter from any one of the house-doors, each of which might represent a different house in the play, or from the side-entrances in the wings; the side-entrance to the spectators' right denoted the near distance, that to their left the further distance. Thus, if the scene was laid in a town, a character going off to the spectators' right was supposed to be going to the forum; if he went off to their left he might, according to circumstances, be supposed to be on his way to the country or the harbour. Near the side-entrances, and illustrating their significance at the moment, stood the *periaktoi*. These seem to have been two revolving stands, carrying on each of their three sides pictures indicating the scenery in the neighbourhood, e.g. the harbour, the country, the market-place. Thus, when an actor was leaving for the harbour, the *periaktos* near the 'harbour' entrance might revolve to show, for example, the picture of a ship.

If for some reason it was necessary to move a character from one house to another, or to the forum or harbour, without bringing him on the stage, which represented the street, he was supposed to use the back door and the *angiportum*, an imaginary street running behind the houses. Of scenery, other than the front wall of the scene-building and the *periaktoi*, there was little or none; interior scenes could not be represented; all action had necessarily to take place in front of the houses shown in the background. If a banquet was to be shown, the tables and couches had to be brought on the stage for the purpose and taken indoors again at the end of the scene. The rocks of the *Rudens* (*l.* 206) were probably left to the imagination. The stage-building had a practicable roof. References to scenery which could be 'drawn' or 'turned' are impossible to explain in view of our lack of information.

In the first century B.C. theatres and scenery grew more elaborate; finally, in 55 B.C. Pompey built the first stone theatre in the Campus Martius. In 13 B.C. Cornelius Balbus built another theatre, while the theatre of Marcellus, also erected in the reign of Augustus, is still in existence. In fulfilment of the Roman policy of keeping the crowd entertained, theatres were erected all over the Empire; splendid examples are still to be seen at Orange, in the south of France, at Aspendus, in Asia Minor, and at Sabratha and Leptis Magna (see No. 8) in North Africa. In Britain the theatre at Verulamium (St. Albans) (see No. 9) is of the 'cock-pit' type designed for gladiatorial and animal combats as well as for stage-shows; that at Canterbury (see Sheppard S. Frere's *Roman Canterbury*, 1961) was also of this type when first erected in the late first century A.D., but the second theatre, built in the early third century, was a large masonry structure similar to those in the South of France and North Africa. There are also traces of a Roman theatre at Gosbeck's Farm outside Colchester. As many of these theatres were erected on sites where there was no natural slope to carry the tiers of seats, these were supported by masonry, through which passages led from outside to the orchestra or to a corridor at the top of the auditorium; thence, by means of flights of steps, each spectator could find his way to his place, assisted, perhaps, by the picture, name, and number on his ticket, of which numerous examples are extant. Meanwhile the *aulaeum* or drop-curtain, first mentioned by Cicero, had come into use. It was lowered at the beginning of the performance into a recess under the stage and raised at the end to conceal the stage from view. It seems that it was not until the second century A.D. that the curtain came to be operated in the modern manner, being raised to reveal and lowered to conceal the stage. We see in Apuleius, *Metamorphoses*, x. 29–34, how behind the curtain an elaborate scene could be built up on the stage, and trapdoors made possible the rapid removal of unwanted scenery and pieces of stage furniture. Over the stage was a wooden roof, protecting actors and scenery from the weather. The vast auditorium was also protected by means of coloured linen awnings attached to masts fixed in the enclosing wall. For the further comfort of spectators cooling artificial showers were sometimes provided, as we see in a public notice in Pompeii, which shows, incidentally, that the Romans knew the uses of the theatrical poster. In these vast, splendid, and luxurious theatres were staged the trivial shows of Imperial Rome, which, however magnificent, catered, it must be confessed, for a debased public taste.

The acoustics of ancient theatres were excellent, as we can discover if we visit the extant remains. Vitruvius points out how important it is that every syllable spoken by the actor should be audible even in the furthest seats. Elsewhere he says that singers would turn towards the doors in the scene-building (*valvas scenae*) to get improved resonance. Evidently the doors were still of wood in his day, though the rest of the scene-building was now built of stone. Theatres built of wood (i.e. with a wooden scene-building) are superior acoustically to those built of stone, and do not, he says, need *echeia*. The use of these latter is in any case very obscure (see ACOUSTICS, 3). The statement that the mask (*persona*) increased the sound of the voice is based on nothing more than a false etymology; a cork or linen mask could not serve as a megaphone (see also ARCHITECTURE, 2).

WILLIAM BEARE†

4. DECADENCE AND DESTRUCTION. To the other disintegrating factors working against the serious theatre in Imperial Rome was added the constant hostility of the Christian Church. No Christian could be an actor, under pain of excommunication, and all priests and devout persons refrained from attendance at theatrical performances of any kind. Tertullian in *De Spectaculis* urged the Christian to look for spectacle to the services of the Church, not perhaps foreseeing that he would later be taken literally. As far back as the Code of Theodosius, A.D. 435, public performances were forbidden on Sundays, a prohibition which still holds good in England, and in the sixth century the theatres in Europe were finally closed, the much-harassed actors being forced to rely on private hospitality or take to the road. In Constantinople the rules were relaxed, possibly at the instance of the Empress Theodora, herself, according to contemporary gossip, an actress, and the government still considered the provision of actors and public performances as being among its duties. The theatre in the East perished in the Saracen invasions of the seventh and eighth centuries (but see BYZANTINE THEATRE). In the West, in spite of a continued interest in drama as literature, an interest which St. Augustine in *Civitate Dei* upholds as a means of education, the theatre as organized entertainment vanished under the onslaught of the barbarians, who despised it. The last reference to it is in A.D. 533.

From then until the tenth century there was nothing but an undercurrent of itinerant mimes and acrobats (see MIME, 2 and MINSTREL, 1), while the Church quietly absorbed pagan rites (see FOLK PLAY and MUMMING PLAY) into its own ritual, and unconsciously prepared the way for a revival of the theatre it had tried to suppress (see LITURGICAL DRAMA and the separate countries of Europe).

RONDIRIS, DIMITRIOS (1899–), Greek producer, who was for many years director of the Greek National Theatre. He also founded the Festival of the Arts at Athens, now an annual event, and the great revivals of classical plays given in the old theatre at Epidaurus. He has been throughout his life a pioneer in the modern production of the old Greek repertory. He is now director of the Piraikon Theatre in the Piraeus, where he continues his work on the staging of classical plays.

ROOKE, IRENE (1878–1958), English actress, closely associated at the beginning of the century with the 'new' drama. She began her career in the orthodox way, touring in Shakespeare under Ben Greet, making her first London appearance as Ophelia to the Hamlet of Gordon Craig in 1897, and playing in *Quality Street* (1902). Her first association with the progressive drama of the time came when she played Mrs. Jones, the charwoman, in Galsworthy's *The Silver Box*, at the Court Theatre under Granville-Barker in 1906. She played leading parts in six other plays by Galsworthy—*The Eldest Son*, *The Fugitive*, *Strife*, *The Mob*, *Windows*, *Old English*. She also appeared in several of Shaw's plays, and was for a time a member of Miss Horniman's repertory company in Manchester. Her best-remembered part was perhaps the hero's mother in Drinkwater's *Oliver Cromwell* (1923). She retired in 1928, after playing at the Everyman with her second husband, the actor Milton Rosmer (her first was Francis Greppo), under the management of Malcolm Morley.

ROPE HOUSE, the name given to a theatre which follows the traditional practice of raising scenery by hand-lines from a fly-floor, as against the modern counterweight system; also known as a hand-worked house, since the power used is purely manual. In this system the piece of scenery to be flown is hung by means of a set of lines, generally three in number, and known as the long, short, and centre lines respectively, which ascend to pass over three pulley blocks in the grid. The lines are then taken to a triple head-block at the side of the stage, and their ends descend together to be made fast to a cleat on the fly rail, or pin rail, which is the railing along the fly-gallery edge (see STAGE). Borders and ceilings are also flown like cloths, and, at need, almost any other element of a stage set. Even a complete box-set may be battened together, with property furniture attached to its walls, and the whole flown entire on a number of sets of lines. RICHARD SOUTHERN

RORKE, KATE (1866–1945), English actress, a member of an old theatrical family. She made her first appearance at the Court Theatre under the management of Sir John Hare in 1878 as one of the school-children in *Olivia*, and in 1880 was engaged by Wyndham for the Criterion, where she remained for a considerable time, playing in a great variety of parts and growing in experience and popularity. In 1885 she made a great success as Lucy Preston in *The Silver Shield*. In 1889 she returned to Hare as his leading lady, and during her six years with him gave some fine performances, including Mrs. Goldfinch in *A Pair of Spectacles* (1890). A handsome and imposing woman, she was leading lady for many of the outstanding actor-managers of the day, including Tree, with whom she went to America, Alexander, Waller, and others. In 1906 she was appointed Professor of Dramatic Art at the Guildhall School of Music, and there trained a number of young players who afterwards became famous. As time went on she made fewer appearances on the professional stage, although she occasionally took part in gala performances. In 1917 she appeared in her old part when *A Pair of Spectacles* was revived at the New Theatre and Wyndham's. For many years she had her own school of acting, and was accounted one of the best instructors in dramatic art of her day.

W. MACQUEEN-POPE†

ROSCIUS, QUINTUS (?–62 B.C.), Roman comic actor, and the most famous of his day, liked and admired by Cicero, who delivered on his behalf the speech *Pro Roscio Comoedo*. Roscius's success was the result of careful study; he thought out and practised every gesture before employing it on the stage. He was awarded a gold ring, the symbol of equestrian rank, by the dictator Sulla. Pliny tells us that his yearly takings amounted to fifty million sesterces (half a million pounds in our money).

WILLIAM BEARE†

For the American Roscius, see ALDRIDGE, IRA; for the Dublin, or Hibernian, Roscius, see BROOKE, G. V.; for the Ohio Roscius, see ALDRICH, LOUIS; for the Scottish Roscius, see JOHNSTON, H. E.; for the Young American Roscius, see COWELL (2); for the Young Roscius, see BETTY, WILLIAM.

ROSE, CLARKSON [really ARTHUR] (1890–1968), English actor and manager. He made his first appearance on the stage in 1908, in the provinces, and was at the Liverpool Repertory Theatre from 1911 to 1915. He then came to London as Captain Phoenix in *Trelawny of the 'Wells'*, was with the Birmingham Repertory Theatre, toured with a Shakespeare company, and was in pantomime and revues. From 1921 until his death he devoted himself to his summer revue *Twinkle*, and to annual appearances as Dame in pantomime all over England. He was the author of two volumes of reminiscences, *With a Twinkle in My Eye* and *Beside the Seaside*, and wrote the greater part of the material in his own revues.

ROSE TAVERN, see WILL'S COFFEE HOUSE.

ROSE THEATRE, LONDON. This owed its name to the fact that it stood in what had been a rose garden. It was built by one James Grigges, carpenter, for Henslowe and his partner, John Cholmley, citizen and grocer of London, and was probably opened at Michaelmas 1587. It is not known what company first played there, but five years later, after extensive repairs and alterations, Lord Strange's Men were there, followed by other companies, until in 1594 the Admiral's Men settled there and stayed till their transfer in 1600 to the Fortune. It was at this theatre that Alleyn made his great reputation, and it is probable that Shakespeare's *Henry VI, Part I*, was given there. From Henslowe's accounts it can be inferred that the theatre was of wood and plaster on a brick foundation, partly thatched, and octagonal in shape. After 1600 various companies occupied the theatre until in 1605 Henslowe's lease ran out, and the building was deserted. It was pulled down some time before 1606.

ROSENBLÜT, HANS (*fl.* fifteenth century), a writer of German popular farces, who lived in Nuremberg and was probably a Mastersinger, like his contemporary Hans Folz (see GERMANY, 1).

ROSIMOND [CLAUDE LA ROZE] (*c.* 1640–86), a French actor who, after playing in the provinces and joining the Théâtre du Marais in 1668, was invited by the remnants of Molière's company to join them after the latter's death. This he did, playing as his first part Molière's role in *Le Malade imaginaire*. He was already known as a dramatist, and it may have been his double reputation that induced La Grange and his companions to look on him as a successor to Molière. If so, he proved a disappointment, as he produced only one more play, and that not a very successful one. He was an educated man, something of a scholar, and he had one of the finest libraries of plays in Paris. He was said to have been very intemperate and to have died of drink, but this was denied by Mlle

Desmares, who had acted with him. His comedies were often revived during his lifetime, but are now forgotten. His play about Don Juan was the source of Shadwell's *The Libertine* (1675).

ROSSETER, PHILIP (*c.* 1575–1623), English musician, friend of Campion, who left him all his property with the wish that it had been more. Rosseter became involved in theatrical affairs when he obtained a patent, with other musicians, to train the Children of the Revels. He was later associated in management with Henslowe, and was a lessee of Whitefriars. In 1615 he began to build a new playhouse in Blackfriars, known as Porter's Hall or Puddle Wharf Theatre (on the site of the present Mermaid Theatre), but it was never finished, for the civic authorities succeeded in having its licence taken away. After this Rosseter retired from the theatre, but continued as royal lutanist until his death.

ROSSI, ERNESTO FORTUNATO GIOVANNI MARIA (1827–96), Italian actor, at his best in tragedy. He was early enamoured of the stage, and at the age of 10 formed a company of children which played with some success in private houses. At 18 he made his début on the professional stage of Leghorn, his birthplace, in the troupe of Calloud. He later joined the company of Gustave Modena, and in 1852 was acting with the great Italian actress, Adelaide Ristori, with whom he went to Paris in 1855. He quickly proved himself a fine interpreter of the Italian classic tragedies, and of Shakespeare, being the first Italian actor to play *Othello* (1856), in the blank-verse translation by Carcano, following it with *Hamlet* in an early version by Rusconi. He was also good as Lear. He travelled widely, being much admired in Paris and Germany, and died while returning from a successful season in St. Petersburg. His method of interpreting Shakespeare was not, however, acceptable in England or America. In 1886 and 1888 he published two volumes of theatrical memoirs, and also translated *Julius Caesar* into Italian.

ROSSO DI SAN SECONDO, PIER MARIA (1887–1956), Italian playwright, the most lyrical of the dramatists of the *teatro grottesco* and (though Chiarelli is historically the *caposcuola*) possibly the most important, because deeply probing and subtle, exponent of the form. His symbolism is immediately dramatic, and his fables are universal and timeless in their application. The recurrent themes of his plays are the reality/illusion conflict, the dream/waking identity, the possibility of discovery and regeneration of self, and (echoing the Vichian analysis of Pirandello, his friend and mentor) man's finally poetic nature. He demonstrates the continuing validity of archetypal myths as everyday experience, constantly refashioning (in particular) that of Persephone. Central to his work (and his best-known drama) is *Marionette, che passione!* (1918), a sensitive and compassionate confrontation of man's despair and the world's crisis. His major plays (with *Marionette, che passione!*) are probably *La bella addormentata* (1919), *Una cosa di carne* (1924), and *Il ratto di Proserpina* (1954—but completed in 1933, due to be staged in 1940, broadcast in 1953). Popular were *La scala* (1926) and *Tra vestiti che ballano* (1927). Some of Rosso's plays have been seen in England and America, but he is as yet little known there. FREDERICK MAY

ROSTAND, EDMOND (1868–1918), French romantic dramatist, whose colourful poetic plays came as a relief after the drab realities of the naturalistic school. Born in Marseille, he was a true son of the south, and his plays are full of colour and movement, with a saving grace of humour which usually redeems their sentimentality. His first play was a delicious satire on the aspirations of young lovers, *Les Romanesques* (1894), which was followed by the more serious but infinitely tender and lyrical *Princesse lointaine* (1895). A biblical play, *La Samaritaine* (1897), was less successful, but in *Cyrano de Bergerac* (1898), written for the elder Coquelin, Rostand achieved a wonderful fusion of romantic *bravura*, lyric love, and theatrical craftsmanship which has made this play a perennial favourite, both in France and in America and England, where something of its quality survives even in a pedestrian translation. A later play, *L'Aiglon* (1900), in which Sarah Bernhardt played the ill-fated son of Napoleon, had less vigour, but appealed by its pathetic evocation of fallen grandeur and the frank sentimentality of its theme. Rostand's last complete play—he died at 49 after years of ill health—was *Chantecler* (1910), which, though not as popular as his earlier works, is by some critics accounted his best, as it is certainly his most profound. The verse is masterly, and the allegory unfolds effortlessly on two planes of consciousness, the beast's and man's. A further play, *La Dernière Nuit de Don Juan*, was left unfinished, but indicates how much Rostand's undoubted talent might have matured had he been given longer in which to perfect it. The two plays by which he is best known are obviously youthful works, frankly romantic and sentimental, but they appealed to a public wearied by naturalism and somewhat disconcerted by symbolism. Their influence has not been obvious, nor has Rostand had many followers, but he made a valiant attempt to break through the meshes of the 'useful' and 'realistic' theatre and recapture the glamour and poetry of an earlier age.

ROSTRUM, any platform, from a small dais for a throne to a vast battlement, placed on the stage. It is usually made with a removable top and hinged sides, to fold flat for packing. It is reached by steps or a ramp, and quitted offstage by 'lead-off' steps. A rostrum-front is a canvas-covered flat placed to conceal the front of the platform.

ROSWITHA, see HROSWITHA.

ROTROU, Jean de (1609–50), French dramatist, and next to Corneille the best and most important of his day. He was only 19 when he had two plays produced at the Hôtel de Bourgogne, where he may have succeeded Hardy as official dramatist to the troupe. His work shows some originality and a true feeling for the theatre, and his popularity may be gauged from the fact that he had four plays given in Paris in 1636, the year of Corneille's *Le Cid.* More than thirty of his works survive, some of them the best examples extant of the popular tragicomedy of the time. Rotrou was much interested in Spanish literature, and translated one of Lope de Vega's plays as *La Bague de l'oubli* (1629), important as being the first extant French play to be based on one from Spain. It was also the first French comedy, as distinct from farce. Rotrou was the author of one of the numerous versions of the story of Amphitryon, which, as *Les Sosies,* is considered his best play. His *Venceslas* (1647), a tragedy based on a play by Francisco de Rojas, was sold to pay a gambling debt, and long remained in the repertory of the French theatre, providing an excellent part in Ladislas for such actors as Baron, Lekain, and Talma. Its first interpreter was probably Montfleury. Rotrou was a man of great charm and nobility of character, which endeared him even to his rivals. He loved Paris, but remained faithful to his native town of Dreux, where he held important municipal offices. He died during a plague in the city, having refused to relinquish his post and seek safety elsewhere.

ROTUNDA, The, a hall in Blackfriars Road, London, at the corner of Stamford Street. It has sometimes been confused with the Ring, which was on the opposite side of the road about 500 yards away. Variety performances were given at the Rotunda as early as 1829, and in 1833 it opened for a few years as the Globe Theatre; but its history was undistinguished. It was later used for boxing, and as a music-hall, during which time Dan Leno's parents appeared there as duettists and dancers. The hall was closed after an illegal cockfight, and became an ironmongery warehouse. Traces of its theatrical past were still discernible, but it was demolished in about 1945, and a large modern building now occupies the site.

ROUSSEAU, Jean-Baptiste (1671–1741), French man of letters who wrote some comedies before being banished from France for the publishing of libellous verse. They were given at the Comédie-Française with some success. He also translated Machiavelli's *Mandragola,* and based a play on Ben Jonson's *Epicoene.* These two plays were apparently never acted. Rousseau was also responsible for the libretti of two operas.

ROUSSEAU, Jean-Jacques (1712–78), French philosopher and man of letters. He was the author of two light operas, of which 'Le Devin du village', containing many simple and charming songs, was a great success. Paradoxically—though perhaps it may be accounted for by his quarrel with Diderot—Rousseau in his *Lettre à d'Alembert contre les spectacles* (1758) opposed the favourite eighteenth-century view that the stage can be used for political and moral teaching, and declared that, being only intended for amusement, it is harmful and useless and should be suppressed. Incidentally, this may also have been meant as an attack on Voltaire, whose passion for the theatre was well known. Yet, though no dramatist himself, Rousseau is important through the influence of his ideas on the drama, as well as on French and European literature in general.

ROWE, George Fawcett (1834–89), American actor, who made his first appearance in New York, at the Olympic, in 1866, billed as 'from the London and Australian theatres'. Little is known of his early years, but he became popular in America, and for some time played young lovers, to which his fair, handsome, boyish face and elegant figure were eminently suited. In 1872 he made a great success as Digby Grant—Irving's part—in Albery's *Two Roses,* and later toured extensively in character parts. Among his best performances were Micawber in *Little Em'ly,* Waifton Stray in *Brass,* and Hawkeye in *Leatherstocking,* Rowe's own adaptation of *The Last of the Mohicans.* He was also responsible for the adaptation of Feuillet's *Sphinx* (1875), in which Clara Morris gave a powerful and horrifying performance.

ROWE, Nicholas (1674–1718), English dramatist of the Augustan age, and one of the few to display any real dramatic power. Of his seven tragedies, the early ones were written in a somewhat frigid neo-classic style, but his masterpieces, *The Fair Penitent* (1703) (based on Massinger's *The Fatal Dowry*) and *The Tragedy of Jane Shore* (1714), have genuinely moving and poetic passages, and both were frequently revived, Mrs. Siddons being particularly good in the parts first played by Mrs. Barry and Anne Oldfield respectively. Rowe, who was in love with the unresponsive Mrs. Bracegirdle, was also the author of *Tamerlane* (1701), in which Betterton was outstanding in the name-part, of *The Tragedy of Lady Jane Grey* (1715), and of one unsuccessful comedy. He was made Poet Laureate in 1715, published a translation of Lucan which was much admired by Dr. Johnson, and edited Shakespeare's plays in 1709, adding stage directions, act- and scene-divisions, and working to make the text less corrupt. He was not a great dramatist; he had many talents and a feeling for the theatre, but, either through his own weakness or because of the general decline of tragedy at the time, he failed to infuse into his work any vitality. The only one of his plays which has been revived in recent times is *Jane Shore* (see No. 32).

ROWLEY, Samuel (?–1624), English actor and dramatist, who is credited with having had a hand in a number of plays which preceded, and possibly provided material for, some of Shakespeare's, including *The Taming of a Shrew*. His only extant play is a chronicle drama on the life of Henry VIII, acted in 1603 by the Admiral's Men, *When You See Me, You Know Me*. He is believed to have revised Marlowe's *Dr. Faustus* for Henslowe in 1602, mainly by adding some comic passages. A number of lost plays were given by the Palsgrave's Men in 1623–4, of whom Rowley, an actor of some repute, was a member, having joined the company in 1597 when it was known as the Admiral's, and remained with it under successive changes of patron.

ROWLEY, William (*c.* 1585–*c.* 1637), English actor and dramatist, whose best work was done in collaboration with Middleton, notably in *The Changeling* (1622). Of his own plays the most important is *All's Lost by Lust* (1622), in which he himself played the clown. He had previously played the fat clown, Plumporridge, in *The Inner Temple Masque* in 1619, as a foil to John Newton's thin clown, and was the fat bishop in Middleton's *A Game at Chess* (1624). Otherwise little is known of him, though he was at one time credited with collaboration with no less a person than Shakespeare in *The Birth of Merlin*. This, however, is now discredited, and Dekker, Middleton, Beaumont, and Fletcher have been suggested in the place of Shakespeare.

ROYAL ACADEMY OF DRAMATIC ART, a stage training school in London, founded by Tree in 1904 at His Majesty's Theatre. It was moved a year later to Gower Street, its permanent home, and under the strict but kindly rule of its first principal, Sir Kenneth Barnes, grew steadily in size and reputation. In 1921 a theatre with a full-sized stage was built on ground adjoining the Gower Street premises but fronting Malet Street, and in 1931 a more commodious building replaced the original houses in Gower Street. This also contained a small theatre; it was seriously damaged by blast in Apr. 1941, when the larger theatre was completely destroyed. This was replaced by the present Vanbrugh Theatre in 1952. On his death Bernard Shaw, who was for a long time on the Council of the Academy, bequeathed to it part of his estate, from which the institution has benefited greatly, mainly owing to the royalties derived from the phenomenal success of *Pygmalion* in its musical version, *My Fair Lady*, on stage and screen. In 1955 Barnes retired, and was succeeded by John Fernald, who remained as principal until 1965.

ROYAL ALFRED THEATRE, London, see west london theatre.

ROYAL BOROUGH THEATRE, London, in Tooley Street. This was used between 1834 and 1836, and then pulled down, as the land on which it stood was required by a railway company.

ROYAL CIRCUS, London, see surrey theatre.

ROYAL COURT THEATRE, London. 1. The first theatre of this name was on the south side of Sloane Square, and opened as the New Chelsea on 16 Apr. 1870, under the management of Morgan and Oliver, with cheap prices and a mixture of stage-shows and music-hall. It was a badly transformed Nonconformist chapel, and had no success at all, in spite of changing its name to the Belgravia, until Marie Litton took it over, reconstructed and redecorated it, and reopened it as the Royal Court on 25 Jan. 1871 with *Randall's Thumb*, by W. S. Gilbert, who provided further successes with *The Wedding March* and *The Happy Land* (both 1873). In the last of these he burlesqued contemporary politicians so mercilessly that the Lord Chamberlain intervened, and the actors' make-up had to be altered. In 1875 Hare became manager of the Royal Court, bringing with him the Kendals, John Clayton, Henry Kemble, and a good company, and produced a number of successful plays. Wilson Barrett took over in 1879, and a year later Modjeska made her first appearance in London there, with Barrett as her leading man. In 1885 a company which included Marion Terry, Mrs. John Wood, and Brandon Thomas achieved a success with a series of farces by Pinero, beginning with *The Magistrate*, followed by *The Schoolmistress* (1886), and *Dandy Dick* (1887). These were truly English in spirit and not adapted from the French or German, as most farces were at the time. The theatre now had to be demolished to make way for improvements, and it closed on 22 July 1887.

2. A new theatre was built on the east side of the square, which opened on 24 Sept. 1888 under the joint managership of Mrs. John Wood and Arthur Chudleigh with Grundy's *Mamma!* It was for a time less successful than the old theatre in spite of the popularity of Pinero's new farce, *The Cabinet Minister* (1890), but on 20 Jan. 1898 came the first night of *Trelawny of the 'Wells'*, which scored an immediate success. A later success was Martin-Harvey's production of *A Cigarette-Maker's Romance* (1901). A brilliant partnership began in 1904, when J. E. Vedrenne and Granville-Barker took the theatre and produced there a remarkable series of plays, both new and revivals, ranging from Shakespeare to Shaw, Galsworthy, Barker, and St. John Hankin. This memorable season ran until 1907, and its influence on the English theatre was incalculable. Barker and Vedrenne then moved to the Savoy Theatre, and Somerset Maugham's *Lady Frederick* (also 1907) filled the Royal Court to capacity. After that its fortunes suffered a decline, until after the First World War J. B. Fagan took over the management and did some excellent productions, including Shakespeare and Shaw, whose *Heartbreak House* (1921) had its first production here. In 1924 Barry Jackson brought his Birmingham Repertory Theatre company to the Court, opening with the five parts of *Back to Methuselah*, followed by the

long-running *The Farmer's Wife*. In 1928 he returned with productions of *Macbeth* (see No. 81) and *The Taming of the Shrew*, both in modern dress. After three seasons of Shaw plays by the Macdona Players the theatre closed in 1932, and was used as a cinema. It was extensively damaged in Nov. 1940 when Sloane Square station was bombed, and was not reopened until 1952. Four years later the English Stage Company under George Devine took over and added a further glorious page to the theatre's history with productions of new and controversial plays, which included Osborne's *Look Back in Anger* (1956) and *The Entertainer* (1957), and Arden's *Serjeant Musgrave's Dance* (1959; see No. 112). These had an immense influence on the general trend of English playwriting and production, and drew a predominantly young and enthusiastic audience. The theatre closed for reconstruction in Feb. 1964, and the company moved to the Queen's, returning to the Royal Court later in the same year. Among their subsequent productions were John Osborne's *Inadmissible Evidence* (1964) and *A Patriot for Me* (1965), Brecht's *Happy End* (also 1965), and a revival of the Ben Travers farce, *A Cuckoo in the Nest* (1964).

W. MACQUEEN-POPE†, *rev.*

ROYAL ENGLISH OPERA HOUSE, LONDON, see PALACE THEATRE.

ROYAL GROVE, LONDON, see ASTLEY'S AMPHITHEATRE.

ROYAL ITALIAN OPERA HOUSE, LONDON, see QUEEN'S THEATRE, 1.

ROYAL KENT THEATRE, LONDON. This stood in High Street, South Kensington, between 1834 and 1840. It held only about 250 people, but had a Royal Entrance down a back court, though there is no evidence that it was ever used. Brown, a well-known comedian of the time, played there, as did Wyatt, brother of G. A. Sala. It was at the Royal Kent that Bunn saw Denvil and engaged him to play Manfred at Drury Lane. The theatre took its name from the Duke of Kent, who gave it his patronage.

ROYAL MANOR HOUSE THEATRE, LONDON, stood in the King's Road, Chelsea, from 1838 to about 1841. It was for a time under the management of E. L. Blanchard, but otherwise little is known about it.

ROYAL PANTHEON THEATRE, LONDON. This was a small nineteenth-century playhouse in Catherine Street, Strand, known also as Jessop's Hall and the Little Catherine Street Theatre. It was used chiefly by amateurs, many of whom afterwards became professionals. It was possible here, as at other minor theatres, such as the King's Cross, to purchase the privilege of playing principal parts. Henry Neville is said to have appeared at this theatre in his early days, and Mrs. Sumbel Wells, a well-known actress, gave imitations of Mrs. Siddons there. The site of the theatre was incorporated in the Aldwych rebuilding scheme. Its exact location is uncertain, but it stood somewhere near the second Gaiety Theatre.

ROYAL STANDARD THEATRE, LONDON, see STANDARD THEATRE, 1.

ROYAL STANGATE THEATRE, LONDON, see BOWER SALOON.

ROYAL VICTORIA HALL, LONDON, see OLD VIC.

ROYALE THEATRE, NEW YORK. Built by the Chanins on West 45th Street, this opened on 11 Jan. 1927 with a musical comedy, followed by further musical shows, and by Winthrop Ames's productions of Gilbert and Sullivan. In 1928 came Mae West in *Diamond Lil*, which ran for nearly a year, and in 1933 *Both Your Houses*, a Pulitzer Prize-winner sponsored by the Theatre Guild. The controversial *They Shall Not Die*, based on the Scottsboro case, with a distinguished cast and settings by Lee Simonson, was seen at this theatre in 1934, while in the autumn of the same year the theatre was renamed the Golden, and presented a series of moderately successful comedies. From 1936 to 1940 it was used for broadcasting, but then returned to drama under its old name. Successful productions there include *The Lady's Not For Burning* (1950), *The Matchmaker* (1955), the revue *La Plume de ma Tante* (1958), and *The Night of the Iguana* (1961). GEORGE FREEDLEY†

ROYALTY. The custom of paying a dramatist a royalty, or small percentage of the receipts, for every night his play is performed is of comparatively recent origin. In Elizabethan times plays were either bought outright, as can be seen from Henslowe's accounts, or formed, as with Shakespeare, part of the stock-in-trade of the co-operative society of which the author was a member, and from which he drew moneys under various headings. For the printing of plays the publisher sometimes, though not always, paid a small sum down, but the practice of printing the text of plays was not encouraged, as they could then be played freely by companies other than that to which the manuscript belonged. Conditions under the Restoration were much the same, in that the dramatist received very little for his work, and that only at the whim of the management. The system of patronage was universal, and a needy author—it should be remembered that many Restoration dramatists were men of substance or had other, less chancy, sources of income—might be given the entire profits of a benefit night; but it was not until the second half of the eighteenth century that a playwright could expect to live on the proceeds of his works. Thus, for instance, Dr. Johnson and Oliver Goldsmith were given the proceeds of the third, sixth, and ninth nights of *Irene* (1748) and *The Good-Natured Man* (1768) respectively. From scattered references in the period it seems that the third night was traditionally the author's night. With only two or three playhouses, a small audience, and consequently a continual change of bill, many plays failed to achieve even three nights. Towards the end of the eighteenth century—by which time Beaumarchais had established the royalty system in France—a return was made to the custom of buying plays outright, Morton receiving a thousand pounds for one of his comedies, and Mrs. Inchbald eight hundred for *Wives as they Were, and Maids as they Are* (1797). By this time reputable publishers were also willing to pay several hundred pounds for the right to publish a play, a custom by this time almost universal, and this, in spite of piracies, added considerably to a dramatist's income.

With the nineteenth century the prestige, and consequently the money-value, of the dramatist declined sharply. The lightest farces and musical pieces earned the most money, and even that was very little when mounting costs and the expense of the star system involved managers in heavier outlays. This led to an enormous amount of hack-work at pitiable prices, and may help to explain the constant stream of thefts, plagiarisms, and adaptations from French and German sources which flooded the English stage at its worst period.

The first movement to secure proper recognition of authorship was made by Planché, and it was due mainly to his efforts that the Copyright Bill of 1832 was passed, and the Dramatic Authors' Society formed. This, however, only gave protection to plays written after 1833, and the copyright of plays printed before that date remained the property of the publisher and not the author. It was also extremely difficult to collect acting fees from provincial managements and from America, and cases are on record of actors attending a theatre, memorizing a play, and reproducing it without payment (see FLORENCE and HOLCROFT).

Apparently the first English dramatist to receive a royalty, or at any rate a definite share in the profits irrespective of what they might be, was Boucicault, who had for some years been receiving roughly £100 down for each new play, and in 1860 suggested to Webster that for his next play, in which he and his wife were as usual appearing in the leading parts, he should, as author, be given a fixed percentage of the takings. The play in question was either *The Colleen Bawn* or *The Octoroon*—accounts vary; but the new method netted Boucicault some £10,000, and the more astute of his fellow authors were quick to follow his example. The American critic, William Winter, says that the first play in America to be paid for on this system was Belasco's *Valerie* (1886), written for Lester Wallack, but as the author received a flat rate of 250 dollars a week, that was not a royalty in the generally accepted sense—though a great advance on the £2 or £3 a night that some authors in England were still accepting at this time. By degrees the standard rate of royalty became 5 to 10 per cent., rising perhaps to 20 per cent. in the case of established dramatists, while piracy was finally checked by the International Copyright Agreement of 1887 and the American Copyright Bill of 1891. These made it possible for the author to enjoy the additional income derived from publication without at the same time losing his acting fees.

ROYALTY THEATRE, LONDON. 1. On 20 Dec. 1785 the foundation-stone of a new theatre, to be called the Royalty, was laid in Well Street, Wellclose Square, in East London. Under the management of John Palmer, an actor from Drury Lane, and the elder Bannister, it opened on 20 June 1787, with *As You Like It* and *Miss in her Teens*. Palmer had tried to evade the Licensing Act of 1737 by obtaining a licence from the Governor of the Tower of London, in whose precincts the theatre stood, and the magistrates of the Tower Hamlets, but the patent theatres took proceedings, and although the first night passed off with nothing more than a minor riot, the theatre was then closed and Palmer arrested. He was ordered to produce his licence, and in the meantime the theatre reopened with burlesque and pantomime, for which no licence was necessary. Released on bail, Palmer made another fruitless effort to obtain a licence, and then returned to Drury Lane. Several managers tried to make a success of the Royalty, including the elder Macready, but it led a precarious existence. In 1813 another Palmer, not John, changed its name to the East London, but it was no more successful than before, and in 1826 it was burnt down. Rebuilt, it reopened on 25 Feb. 1828 as the Royal Brunswick, but it was so badly constructed that three days later it collapsed while the company was rehearsing *Guy Mannering*, killing fifteen people and injuring twenty.

2. Miss Fanny Kelly (Charles Lamb's 'Barbara S——') built a small theatre in Dean Street, Soho, which she used in conjunction with a school of acting. It opened on 25 May 1840 with a drama called *Summer and Winter*, but the newly installed stage-machinery, worked by a horse, proved so noisy that it had to be removed. Miss Kelly struggled on for ten years, but in the end had to give up, and a new management opened the theatre as the New English Opera House, perhaps the most ominous title that can be given to a London playhouse. After a further period as the Royal Soho, it was taken over by Mrs. Selby, who, like Miss Kelly, ran a school of acting, and in 1861 became the New Royalty. It was used for performances by Mrs. Selby's pupils, one of whom, Ada Cavendish, became a well-known actress. Ellen Terry played half a dozen parts at the Royalty, as did David James. Charles Wyndham made his London début there in 1862, Adelaide Neilson in 1865, playing Juliet with immediate success. Among the plays staged there after it became a regular theatre were *Trial by Jury* (1875), *Ghosts* (1891), *Charley's Aunt* and *Widowers' Houses* (both 1892), the latter produced privately by the Independent Theatre. In 1900 Mrs. Patrick Campbell redecorated the theatre, and with herself as actress-manageress staged a number of revivals, including *Magda* and *Pelleas and Melisande*. She also gave the first

English production of Bjørnson's *Beyond Human Power* (1901). Some years later Vedrenne, who had done splendid work with Granville-Barker at the Royal Court, took over the theatre, and, with Dennis Eadie as his leading man, put on a series of plays which included *Milestones* (1912) and *The Man Who Stayed at Home* (1914). Among the young actors who appeared under Vedrenne were Owen Nares and Gladys Cooper. Later productions included *The Vortex* (1924), the first London production of *Juno and the Paycock* (1925), and the successful farce, *While Parents Sleep* (1932), by Anthony Kimmins. After this the theatre had no settled policy, and it closed in 1939. It was severely damaged during the Second World War and was eventually pulled down. A block of offices called Royalty House was then built on the site. W. MACQUEEN-POPE†, *rev.*

3. A small theatre enclosed in an office block which arose on the site of the former Stoll Theatre in Kingsway. It was the first new West End theatre to be built since the Saville in 1931, and it opened on 23 June 1960 with the Lunts in Dürrenmatt's *The Visit*. Early in 1961 it became a cinema.

RUCELLAI, GIOVANNI (1475–1525), Italian dramatist of the Renaissance, whose *Oreste* (*c.* 1514) and *Rosmunda* (1516) are tragedies constructed on the Greek model, as laid down by Trissino. The second is taken from Gothic history, while the first, on a classical theme, seems to owe something to the *Iphigenia in Tauris* of Euripides.

RUEDA, LOPE DE (*c.* 1505–65), Spain's first actor-manager and popular dramatist. A goldsmith by trade, he forsook his workshop for the theatre, performing in public square and primitive courtyard theatre, as well as in palaces and great houses. He wrote mostly in prose, and his plays are strongly influenced by the Italian *commedia dell'arte*. His dialogue is natural, easy, and idiomatic, with a strong sense of the ridiculous and a happy satirizing of the manners of his day. His main purpose was to amuse, and in this he seems to have succeeded admirably. Cervantes speaks of him as 'a brilliant actor and a man of sound sense'. He was the originator of the *paso*, or comic interlude, of which the best is *Las aceitunas*. Rueda's comedies stem from Italian originals, *Los engañados* being drawn from the same Italian source as Shakespeare's *Twelfth Night*. His two prose pastoral plays and the verse-play *Cuestión de amor* reflect the growing interest in the pastoral genre, and were presumably written for presentation before Court audiences. The latter play was renowned for the skilful way in which the author resolved the complications of his plot. Witty and entertaining, Rueda had a great influence on the nascent Spanish theatre. J. E. VAREY

RUGGERI, RUGGERO (1871–1953), Italian actor, who made his first appearance in 1888, after studying singing. He had a long and active career, but his formative years were from 1891 to 1899, and he retained until the end his taste for strong dramatic and romantic acting. He was an excellent Iago, a fine, if somewhat old-fashioned, Hamlet, and in 1904 scored an outstanding success in *Figlia di Iorio*. He was for some years leading man of Pirandello's company, where his finest part was Enrico IV (in which he appeared in London shortly before his death), and he played opposite most of the Italian actresses of the time, particularly Emma Gramatica. In his later years he disliked the trend of the modern theatre, and was particularly unreceptive to Brecht, preferring, among the modern dramatists, T. S. Eliot.

RUGGLE, GEORGE (1575–1622), a scholar of Cambridge who in 1615 wrote a satire on the lawyers, *Ignoramus*, partly in English and partly in Latin. This was seen by James I on a visit to the town, and so pleased him that he made another visit to see it again a week later. The play is based to a great extent on the *Trappolaria* (1596) of Della Porta, but the chief part is a satire of the then Cambridge recorder, Francis Brackyn. Ruggle is believed to have written two other comedies played at the university.

RUÍZ DE ALARCÓN Y MENDOZA, JUAN (*c.* 1581–1639), Mexican-born dramatist of the Golden Age, contemporary and bitter enemy of Lope de Vega, alienated from many of his contemporaries by their ridicule of his physical deformities. Less prolific than other dramatists of his time, he excelled in ingenious and economical plot construction and in the clever contrasting of well-selected characters. Many of his plays are openly didactic. *La verdad sospechosa*, the source of Corneille's *Le Menteur*, deals with a young man much given to lying, and the central premise, that truth is suspect in the mouth of a habitual liar, is ingeniously and amusingly demonstrated. Lies and deceptions are piled one upon the other until at length truth is no longer recognizable as truth. The play is presented in neat, sober verse, and the characterization is adequate. Alarcón's plays never appear to have been as popular in Spain as they proved to be in other countries, the French dramatists being particularly enamoured of his plots, for his plays approached more closely to French standards of taste than those of any other seventeenth-century Spanish dramatist. J. E. VAREY

RUMANIA. The Rumanians fell more or less under Turkish rule during the sixteenth century, and were not entirely free until 1878. As a result, cultural development was impeded, though less seriously than elsewhere in the Balkans, for Rumania, bordering on Russia, Poland, and the Hapsburg dominions, was exposed to some degree of influence from both the Slavic East and the European West. Up to the nineteenth century Western influences predominated, partly because of the weakness of Russia during this period, but chiefly because in Transylvania, with its

Rumanian population, the Hapsburg rulers carried on an extensive campaign which stressed the Roman and Romance elements in Rumania for religious and political reasons, while the Catholic Church was active in introducing French and Italian culture. Consequently Transylvania, though politically separated from the rest of Rumania until 1920, served as a cultural bridge between the Rumanians and western Europe.

The first theatrical performance in Rumanian was given in Transylvania in 1782 ('Achille in Sciro', with Metastasio's libretto translated by Iordache Slătineau); but an indigenous drama had begun to appear among the Rumanian peasants by the middle of the eighteenth century. In addition to the mimetic dances common to the Balkans, Nativity plays developed, probably under the influence of the School Drama of Poland and Kiev. These represent a late flowering of the medieval Mystery play. Later in the century they acquired comic epilogues in the form of puppet-shows satirizing rural types and political issues, which probably reached Rumania from the Ukraine. In the seventeenth century the Courts of the princes at Jassy, the capital of Moldavia, and Bucharest, the capital of Wallachia, were often visited by strolling troupes of actors *en route* to Poland or Russia. There are records of several such visits to the Court of Vasile Lupu (Prince of Moldavia, 1634–54), and by the eighteenth century they were quite common. About 1787 there were two resident dramatic companies at Bucharest, one French and one German; an Italian company acted at Jassy for a time, about 1800, a Russian company in 1809–12, and in 1813 there was an Italian *commedia dell'arte* troupe at Bucharest. These foreign companies created a strong interest in drama among the upper classes, and Princess Ralu, the daughter of Prince Ioan Caragea of Wallachia (reigned 1812–18), rebuilt a ballroom in Bucharest to provide a permanent theatre.

A more potent influence was that of the Hetairists, or pro-Greek Society of Friends, founded in Bucharest in about 1780. A dramatic movement began at their Greek school there, the students acting in the plays of Greek and French authors under the direction of Costache Aristia (1799–1840), a Greek who had been trained in the tradition of Talma. The plays acted were usually nationalistic and anti-despotic. A similar repertory was presented at the Greek school in Jassy and at the French schools directed by *émigrés*. The Hetairists were suppressed in 1821, but not before their schools had introduced acting and stagecraft to Rumania.

In 1815 a Rumanian theatre opened at Oraviţa, in Transylvania. The following year Gheorghe Asachi (1788–1869) recruited an amateur company at Jassy, and in about 1836 he founded a Philharmonic-Dramatic Society, where singing, acting, and declamation were taught.

It was at Jassy also that the first National Theatre opened in 1840, under C. Negruzzi (1808–69), M. Kogălniceanu (1817–91), and Vasile Alecsandri (1821–90). Alecsandri, who began by adapting Scribe and Labiche, soon emerged as the first important Rumanian dramatist. His original works include a large number of farces, a three-act comedy, *Iórgu dela Sadagúra* (1844), which presents the conflict between the new generation of Westernizers and their fathers, several comedies which record the adventures of Chirita, a provincial lady, and *Boiéri şi ciocói* (1872). Two verse-plays on Horace and Ovid inaugurated the use of Roman subjects, later very popular among Rumanian playwrights, who searched for a glorious national past to celebrate, and patriotically made much of their supposed descent from Roman colonists.

This early theatrical activity at Jassy was paralleled in Bucharest, where Iancu Văcărescu (1791–1863) and Ion Eliáde Răduléscu (1802–72) presented Euripides' *Hecuba* and Molière's *L'Avare* in Rumanian in 1819. Rădulescu later helped to found, in 1833, the Societatea Filarmonica at Bucharest, organized, like Asachi's society, mentioned above, to teach acting and encourage the growth of a national drama. The society's emphasis on social and revolutionary drama caused its suppression in 1837, but by training both actors and audience it had laid the foundations of a Rumanian theatre. Thanks to its work a fine permanent theatre which opened in Bucharest on 31 Dec. 1852 became the National Theatre two years later.

In the 1830s and 1840s a school of Rumanian dramatists began to appear, including Costache Faca (1800–45), whose *Franţuzítele* (1833) preserves in its dialogue the curious half-French, half-Rumanian argot spoken by the Francophiles of the day, Costache Bălăcescu (1800–80), and Cezar Boliac (1813–81). A more important dramatist was Bogdan Hasdéu (1838–1907), author of several historical plays; but the most important Rumanian dramatist was probably Ion Luca Caragiale (1852–1912), son and nephew of actors, who is best known for two comedies, *O noápte furtunoása* (1878), which deals with foolish marital jealousy, and *O scrisoáre pierdută* (1884), a satiric comedy about a provincial electoral campaign which the modern Rumanian theatre stages as a work of social criticism. Caragiale is now considered a forerunner of socialist realism, and the National Theatre has been renamed in his honour.

In 1877 the National Opera and the National Theatre were united into the Rumanian Society of Drama and Acting, which encouraged native dramatists and also gave Rumanians a chance to acquaint themselves with foreign masterpieces. The National Theatre flourished under such directors as Prince Ion Ghica (1877–81), who presented a number of Shakespeare's plays in Rumanian. Among actors Mihail Pascaly and Grigore Manolescu, both successful Hamlets, were outstanding, while Aristiza Romanescu was notable as Ophelia. The new drama of Ibsen and Sudermann, and the new stage-craft of Antoine and Stanislavsky, came to the National Theatre during the directorships of Alexándru Davilá (1905–8, 1912–14) and Pompiliu Eliade (1908–11). Davila also promoted the new ideas during his directorship of the Modern Theatre (1909–11), the first private theatre in Rumania.

The romantic drama continued to flourish for some time, however, notably in the work of Bárbu Stefănéscu (1858–1918), who wrote under the name of Delavráncea. His best-known drama is an historical trilogy dealing with the careers of the fifteenth-century Stephen the Great of Moldavia (1457–1504), his son, and his nephew. A. Davila (1862–1929) who helped to introduce the naturalistic drama to Rumania also wrote *Vláicu Vádă* (1902), a romantic historical drama in the style of Hugo with occasional populist overtones: one character speaks for 'the people', and the hero is full of the sentiments of 1848.

Symbolism entered Rumanian drama with the works of Victor Eftímiu (1889–) and Adrian Maníu (1891–), who combined the styles of Maeterlinck and the later Ibsen with the traditions of Rumanian folklore. Lucian Blaga 1895–1961) also employed symbolism in his *Zamolxe* (1922), a 'pagan mystery', while his *Avrám Iáncu* (1934) is an historical play about the hero of the Transylvanian revolt against Hungary in 1848. Zaharía Bârsán (1878–1948), an actor and, from 1919 to 1939, director of the Rumanian theatre at Cluj, was another symbolist playwright, best known for *Trandafíri róşii* (1915), a Wildean tale of a prince, a princess, a poet, and a rose. Other important playwrights included George Diamandy (1867–1917) and Victor Ion Popa (1895–1946), also known as a director. Notable also among theatre directors were Paul Gusty and Soare Z. Soare, a follower of Reinhardt, while actors of the time included Aristide Demetriad; Ion Manolescu; Tony Bulandra (1881–1943); his wife, Lucia (1873–1961); Maria Filotti (1891–), a fine comedienne; Agepsina Macri Eftimiu (1890–1961), (wife of Victor), successful as Lady Macbeth, Antigone, and Ophelia; and many others.

In 1944 the National Theatre was destroyed by a German bomb, but it has since been rebuilt. Since the occupation and the establishment of a Communist state the theatre has become an important instrument of propaganda, and has prospered accordingly. Under the monarchy, drama was found only at the National Theatres in Bucharest, in Jassy, Craiova, and Cluj, and in a few private theatres. This system has now been extended to include thirty-six state theatres in the provinces. In Bucharest the National Theatre is supplemented by a Municipal Theatre, a Theatre of the Workers, the Theatre of the Army, the Theatre of Youth, a children's theatre, and the Jewish State Theatre.

A number of new playwrights have appeared since the war, but their work is mostly propaganda. Among them are Horia Lovinescu, Aurel Baranga, Mihail Davidoglu, Lucia Demetrius, and Alexandru Mirodan. Historical dramas continue to appear, among them Camil Petrescu's *Bălcescu*, which deals with a Rumanian revolutionary leader of 1848; Laurentiu Fulga's *Ion Vodă cel cumplit* and A. Kiritescu's curious trilogy *Borgia, Nunta din Perugia*, and *Michelangelo*. ROBERT TRACY

RUNDHORIZONT, see LIGHTING, 1 *d*.

RUSHTON, LUCY (1844–?), see NEW YORK THEATRE, 1.

RUSSELL, ANNA (1911–), a solo entertainer, trained as a singer, who uses her fine voice and wide knowledge of her art to prick the bubble of musical pretentiousness. She can hit off to a nicety the subtle differences between the folk-songs of various nations, provide words and music of a do-it-yourself Gilbert-and-Sullivan, teach, with illustrations and mime, the mastery of any instrument, and poke gentle fun at Shakespeare 'adapters' with an 'Amletto' in the style of Verdi. She was probably the first to point out, in a lecture on Wagner's Ring Cycle, that Sieglinde was the first woman Siegfried had ever met who was not his aunt. In 1962 this intrepid soloist ventured to appear in a play, which toured for some weeks but failed to reach London, much to the relief of most of her admirers, who welcomed her back in her usual programme, enlivened by a Wagneresque account of her temporary aberration.

RUSSELL, ANNIE (1864–1936), American actress, who was on the stage as a child and after touring South America and the West Indies in a juvenile opera company, returned to New York to make a big success in the name-part of *Esmeralda* (1881). At the height of her subsequent popularity she was forced to retire from the stage through illness, but in 1894 she returned, playing in a number of new plays, among them *Sue*, in which she was also seen in London for the first time in 1898. On a subsequent visit in 1905 she appeared at the Court Theatre under the Vedrenne–Barker management as the heroine of *Major Barbara*. She had essayed several Shakespearian parts before, in 1912, she organized an Old English Comedy company, for which she played Kate Hardcastle, Beatrice, and Lydia Languish, later appearing as Lady Teazle in a revival of *The School for Scandal*. She retired in 1918.

RUSSELL, FRED [really THOMAS FREDERICK PARNELL] (1862–1957), a ventriloquist, known as 'the Father of Variety' because of the part he played in the founding of the Variety Artists' Federation, of which he became President at the age of 90. In 1906 he also founded and edited *The Performer*, the Federation's official organ, which ceased publication only a month before his death. At the age of 20 he was already well known as an amateur performer, though a journalist by career, when he made his first professional appearance under Charles Morton at the Palace. He changed his name because of its political associations at the time and, with his doll 'Coster Joe', soon became a top-liner throughout England, sometimes working with 10 to 15 dolls. He also undertook extensive tours of Australia, New Zealand, South Africa, America, and Ceylon. He retained his full faculties to the end of his life, and in Jan. 1952 appeared in a music-hall programme on television. He was a member of the Grand Order of Water Rats from its foundation, and in 1903 became King Rat. He was appointed O.B.E. in 1948. At a dinner given by the Water Rats to celebrate his 90th birthday, he made a most dignified and impressive speech. Some fourteen members of his family were connected with variety, among them one of his four sons, Val Parnell, for fourteen years associated with Moss Empires.

RUSSELL, LILLIAN (1861–1922), American actress and singer, whose real name was Helen Louise Leonard. A beautiful woman, both in face and figure, with a vivid and flamboyant personality, she made her first appearance at Tony Pastor's Theatre, in 1881, soon made a name for herself in burlesque and light opera, and was nicknamed 'the American Beauty'. She was four times married.

RUSSELL, SOL SMITH (1848–1902), American actor, who was on the stage at the age of 12. He was for a time in Daly's company, and also toured America with a company of his own, one of his most successful productions being *A Poor Relation* (1888). He was also good in *A Bachelor's Romance*, by Martha Morton.

RUSSIA. 1. PRE-SOVIET. Compared with the rest of Europe the Russian theatre made a late start. This was mainly due to the hostility of the Church and later to the iron hand of absolutism, to which must be added the illiteracy of the bulk of the population and the neglect of the Russian language among the nobility. The early history of the establishment of the theatre in Russia is mainly that of a struggle against competition from imported and experienced foreign companies, usually German or French. These companies, few of which remained for any length of time, were supported by the authorities, who considered, no doubt correctly, that a stable national theatre would prove too great a threat to their security.

Nevertheless, the records show that as far back as the eleventh century there were wandering troupes—the Skomorokhak—which performed at fairs, weddings, holiday gatherings of all kinds, and at carnivals and such religious festivals as Christmas and Easter. These troupes included a variety of entertainers—clowns, buffoons, puppet-masters, jugglers, acrobats, ballad-singers—and they were often accompanied by performing animals, particularly bears. Varying their programme to suit their audience, they played musical instruments, tumbled, danced, sang, and declaimed folk-ballads and folk-tales which often served as vehicles for indirect criticism of current abuses.

These nomadic troupes never received from Church or State the support which might have enabled them to produce a stable theatre, and although as time went on they no doubt developed their skill and enlarged their repertory, they existed always on sufferance. In the fourteenth century indifference turned to intolerance, and they were driven out of Muscovy—the then comparatively small area actually ruled by the Moscow Dukes. They never disappeared completely, however, as they eventually settled in villages to the north of the territory, across the border, where their descendants kept alive, by oral traditions handed on from one generation to another, with all the embellishments and falsifications which this entailed, a popular form of entertainment, consisting mainly of mime-plays and farces in which the Russian puppet-theatre played a big part. In the sixteenth and seventeenth centuries the strolling players again took to the road and became a familiar and welcome sight at fairs and village festivals.

There is little information available regarding Tsarist amusements at this time, but it seems likely that during the period of reaction under Boris Godunov (1598–1605) there were none, while the 'time of the troubles' after his death left little leisure for play-acting. With the establishment of the first Romanov, however, in 1613, the country recovered a little, and a 'House of Amusement' was built by royal command. Since 'amusement' in this context was practically synonymous with 'theatre', and since the Russian strolling players were still considered suitable for popular entertainment only, the chief actors at this first Russian theatre were probably experienced foreigners, perhaps Germans. It is, however, significant that at the wedding celebrations of the Tsar in 1626 the traditional church choir was replaced by a company of Russian strolling players, and this example was followed by the leading nobles of the Court. Thus, by an ironic twist of fortune, those who had been forced out of Muscovy into the remote countryside now found themselves installed in the palace of the Tsar and the great houses of his nobles. Their triumph, however, was short-lived, for in 1648 a decree of the Tsar Alexis (1645–76), then in a reactionary mood, forbade all types of worldly amusement, ordered all musical instruments and other theatrical properties to be broken up and burnt, and anyone found making use of them to be severely punished. The strolling players once more disappeared, temporarily, from the scene, and at Alexis's wedding the traditional church choir replaced secular music and play-acting. Meanwhile, away from the Court, School Drama, as elsewhere in Europe, was coming into being. The 'time of the troubles' had brought Russia into conflict with the West, particularly with the Jesuits. It was necessary for the Russian Church to defend itself and its dogmas, and, for this, education and training in theology were essential. In 1633 the first Russian theological academy was founded on the lines of existing Jesuit schools in Europe. The Jesuits had long used the theatre as a means of instruction and propaganda (see JESUIT DRAMA), and Russian churchmen realized that they must do the same. So began the development of written plays on biblical and historical themes, many of them adapted from Polish plays, but with interpolated scenes of daily life. Later, as the students themselves took over the responsibility for dramatic entertainment, farce, always a potent social weapon, crept into the repertory, and, in response to an increasing demand, new plays by Russian authors made their appearance. One of the earliest-known writers of Russian School Drama was Simeon Polotsky (1629–80), who in 1664 became tutor to the Tsar's sons, and produced two plays, of which one, based on the story of the prodigal son, shows a great advance in characterization and dramatic action on the purely scholastic exercises which had preceded it.

It was now that the secular theatre again made its appearance at the Russian Court. The Tsar, reversing his former attitude towards the theatre under the influence of his journeys in Poland and his Anglophile second wife, Natalia Naryshkina, and seeking to bring to his surroundings some of the brilliance that characterized the contemporary European Courts, realized that for this a flourishing Court Theatre was indicated. A play was planned as part of the celebrations for the birth of a son (later Peter the Great) in 1672, and an envoy was sent abroad to recruit actors. He was, however, unsuccessful, and in this quandary the Court officials looked to the free German quarter of Moscow, where plays had not been banned, and where, as early as 1664, the English Ambassador of Charles II had been present at the performance of a comedy. It was from this source that the authorities procured the services of the German priest, Johann Gottfried Gregory (1631–75), who brought a number of German students to act at Court (see GREGORY), and in 1673 was put in charge of a theatre school for the training of Russian actors. Two years later, when Gregory died, the school was flourishing, and continued its work under Gregory's assistant, Georg Huebner. He, however, proved unacceptable to the authorities, probably because of his enlightened ideas, and he was quickly replaced by Stepan Chizinsky, a former teacher in a theological college and the author of two plays, now lost. A year later, on the death of Alexis, the theatre was closed and the company disbanded. When, under Peter the Great, a more liberal atmosphere again prevailed, all the work had to be done afresh. An Hungarian puppet-master resident at the Court, Ivan Splavsky, was sent from Moscow to Dantzig to hire actors. He returned with a company led by Johann Kunst, described as 'an eminent master of theatrical science'. Peter the Great, who intended to use drama more for political purposes than for amusement, built a theatre for his new company in the Red Square, Moscow—the first public theatre in Russia—and issued a decree ordering everyone, particularly foreigners, to attend. To make this easier he arranged that on days when performances were given the city gates should remain open until 9 p.m. and no toll should be levied. The price of admission was the equivalent of a few pence, and according to contemporary records the average attendance was 124, though during the summer festivities it rose to as many as 400.

Unfortunately Kunst died less than a year after his arrival, and although his work was carried on by members of his company, the venture was not a success and was abandoned, partly for financial reasons, in 1707. Drama, together with spectacular ballet and opera, became once more the prerogative of Court circles, the Tsar's sister having her own private theatre, for which she herself wrote a number of plays. Some of these, based on old Russian legends, were later included in the repertory of the wandering troupes which still existed in the countryside, and of the students and apprentices who gave intermittent performances in improvised theatres and in the public squares.

Meanwhile, the School Drama continued to flourish quietly, and there are records of several plays, which dealt allegorically with the political events of the time, mainly for the purpose of eulogizing Peter the Great and aiding his reforms. One important writer of religious plays was St. Dmitri of Rostov, most of whose works were based on earlier Jesuit School Dramas (see DMITRI). It seemed as if a national theatre might arise out of the School Drama, particularly when in 1705 Feofan Prokopovich (1681–1736), an ardent supporter of the Tsar, produced a tragicomedy in the theatre in the Red Square, based on a Russian historical theme. This shows the efforts of a Prince of Kiev to reform his kingdom after his adoption of Christianity. The three heathen priests who oppose him are thinly veiled caricatures of contemporary Russian clergy. This play, which is quite unlike anything that preceded it, shows some psychological insight, and is written in a style which is, for its period, brilliantly realistic. Prokopovich's experiment was destined to fail, however, and although a new spirit was later manifest in School Drama when it began to introduce into its productions a larger proportion of comic and peasant scenes, the dead weight of authority, the popularity of foreign actors, and the too-rigidly moral and educational purpose behind it, combined to stifle its aspirations. After a last splendid offering of panegyric plays for the coronation of the Empress Elizaveta Petrovna in 1742, Russian School Drama disappeared. But it had not been without its uses. Some of its comic interludes remained in the repertory of the popular puppet-theatres, and, more important still, it had taught its practitioners something of the technique of writing and staging plays. In this way it made an important contribution to the later Russian drama.

The time was now coming when the Russian theatre as a social force could no longer be suppressed. The impetus towards a national theatre was given by the plays of Alexei Petrovich Sumarokov (1718–77), who may be accounted the first Russian dramatist. He was a member of the Society of Lovers of Russian Literature, founded in connexion with the Cadet College opened in 1732 for the education of the sons of the nobility. Though intended as a military academy, its curriculum included training in a number of cultural subjects such as poetics, declamation, deportment, music, and dancing. The students were thus admirably fitted to assist in Court festivities, and it was they who played in Sumarokov's first tragedy, *Khorev*, which was performed in 1749. He wrote nine tragedies in all, seven of them dealing with Russian history. They were all in the neo-classical style first introduced into Russia by the company of Caroline Neuber, which in 1740 replaced an Italian *commedia dell'arte* company at Court, and then popularized by a French company which remained in Russia for fifteen years, during which time French became the fashionable language of the nobility, completely ousting German. Sumarokov's work is distinguished by economy of expression; he uses few characters, and the epic speeches of his heroes have great dramatic intensity. He fought hard to establish a truly national theatre and to purge Russian literary speech of gallicisms. He was more successful in his second objective than his first, but it was undoubtedly due to his plays that a final and successful effort was made to achieve a professional and stable Russian theatre. The cadets, who had acquitted themselves well enough in *Khorev* and other plays by Sumarokov when summoned to Court occasionally to play before the Empress, could not be expected to sustain the burden of constant acting, neither could the Court singers whom the Empress sent to the college with the specific intention of having them trained as actors. Luckily there was in Yaroslavl an amateur company, headed by two brothers named Volkov, which since 1750 had been giving excellent performances, mainly of adapted School Dramas. This was brought to the notice of the Empress, and the company was summoned to play before her. Feodor Grigoryevich Volkov (1729–63) and his brother Grigori, with Ivan Afanasyevich Dmitrevsky (1733–1821) and other members of the company, were chosen to go to the Cadet College for training, and were later seen at Court in a performance of Sumarokov's *Sinav and Truvor* (1755). Others joined the company, as did some actresses, and by 1757 they were receiving a subsidy, negligible compared to that given to the French company, but at least a sign of official recognition, and of their professional status. The cadets ceased to appear in plays except for their own amusement, and the acting of Russian plays, or of plays translated into Russian, was left to the established company headed by Volkov. The repertory was naturally restricted, and the main influences were those of the French *comédie larmoyante* and the German realistic bourgeois tragedy. There were also a number of comedies and light operas, many based on idealized scenes of village life, which, superficial, charming, and tuneful as they were, served to pass the time, as did the plays of the Empress Catherine herself—comedies based on Russian folklore and fairytales, or historical scenes in the style of Shakespeare, which show a break with the neo-classical tradition. Almost the only dramatist of importance in this lighter vein, after Sumarokov, was Denis Ivanovich Fonvizin (1744–92), whose play, *The Minor*, first produced in 1782, was considered by Gorky to be his best and still remains popular in present-day repertories.

Mention should be made here, however, of the development of the so-called 'serf' theatres towards the end of the eighteenth century, for it is from them that the Russian acting tradition comes, however much it may have been influenced by foreign players. It became the custom for the landed gentry living on their vast country estates to provide entertainment for relations and friends who came to stay for days or even weeks, as Konstantin tries to do in *The Seagull*. Beginning with an individual musician, or some dancers, amateur groups developed, many of the best actors being serfs on the estate, and it was from among these that some of the finest actors of the rapidly expanding Russian professional theatre were eventually drawn. Parallel with this development went a progressively critical and realistic tendency in drama and theatre criticism, the former dealing seriously with social problems and the rights of the individual. Apart from Sumarokov and Fonvizin mentioned above, there were also such playwrights as Nikolai Ivanovich Novikov (1744–1816), author of the outspoken and biting satires *The Drone* and *The Painter*, and Alexander Nikolaievich Radishchev (1749–1802), who provided opportunities for the realistic character-acting which in one form or another has remained a feature of the Russian tradition.

Before the end of the nineteenth century Russia was to produce a body of dramatic literature second to none in Europe, and actors whose traditions were to be an inspiration in the theatre everywhere. But little of this was apparent in the early years, when the only Russian dramatist of importance, among the many translators or imitators of French plays, was Vladislav Alexandrovich Ozerov (1770–1816) whose heroes, from Oedipus to Ossian, were all cast in the same sublime mould. Modern problems and the detail of contemporary life had as yet no place on the official Russian stage, which was completely under the control of the Secret Police, even to the choice of play and allotting of roles.

There were at this time two theatres in St. Petersburg—the Bolshoi (or large), used mainly for ballet and opera, and the Maly (or little), used for drama. These should not be confused with the Moscow theatres of the same name, which still flourish, nor is there any connexion—a confusion which has arisen in some English minds—between the words Bolshoi and Bolshevik. The Bolshoi in Moscow was burnt down at the time of the Napoleonic invasion, rebuilt in 1824 and substantially altered after a disastrous fire in 1853 (see Nos. 34, 54). Also in 1824, the Moscow Maly, founded in 1806, moved into its present building (see MALY). In St. Petersburg a third theatre was opened by the dramatist-prince, Alexander Alexandrovich Shakhovsky (1777–1846), as the Youth Theatre, for the performance of light comedies, mainly by the graduates of the Imperial theatre school.

Two popular but otherwise unimportant dramatists who emerged in the first half of the nineteenth century were Nestov Vasilyevich Kukolnik (1809–68) and Nicholas Alekseyevich Polevoy (1796–1846). The former began his career in 1833 with a play on the life of Tasso, but had his first great success with a patriotic drama dealing with the accession of the first Romanov. This encouraged him to continue in the same strain, and he turned out a number of plays which gave all the characters the opportunity of asserting their loyalty to the existing régime. Polevoy was a merchant of Siberia who became a literary critic, and in his journal dared to criticize the plays of Kukolnik. As a result the paper was suppressed, and Polevoy turned his attention to the writing of plays instead. His first patriotic drama was produced in 1837.

Apart from these patriotic plays, which earned the approbation of Nicholas I, the staple theatrical fare was melodrama, both home-made and imported, which was tolerated because it provided, in the words of a later critic, 'an emotional lightning-conductor which grounded the energy of social protest'. All that was necessary, in the case of imported melodrama, was to make it safe. How this was done is shown by the handling of a dramatization of *Notre-Dame de Paris*, where the Antwerp Town Hall was substituted for the Paris cathedral, the clerical characters became laymen, and the dissolute young rake was transformed into a moral and Platonic lover. It is hardly surprising that in spite of the Tsar's efforts to suppress unfavourable criticism, such men as the redoubtable Vissarion Grigorievich Belinsky (1811–48) savagely attacked the plays, the authors, and the actors. The Tsar, tired of trying to muzzle him, at last ordered his arrest and exile, but Belinsky cheated him at the last moment by dying of consumption just before the police came for him.

The plays may have been bad, but there were already outstanding Russian actors to appear in them. The traditions begun by Volkov and his associates were worthily upheld, first by the great actor Mikhail Semenovich Shchepkin (1788–1863), friend of Gogol, Pushkin, and others, the creator of the part of Famusov in *Woe from Wit*, founder of a dramatic school, and the man who first raised the status of the actor in Russia from serfdom to freedom; and then by two very different men—Pavel Stepanovich Mochalov (1800–48), an emotional, romantic actor, who raised melodrama to the heights, but, according to Belinsky, was at his best in Hamlet, to which he imparted less melancholy than usual, replacing it by strength and energy; and Vasily Andreyevich Karatygin (1802–53), endowed by nature with an expressive face and a fine voice and figure which made him the ideal exponent of the heroes of neo-classic tragedy. He appeared mainly at the imposing Alexandrinsky Theatre in St. Petersburg, built in 1832, whereas Mochalov was at the Maly in Moscow, where Shchepkin had made his first appearance outside the provinces in 1822. By this time the serf-theatres mentioned above were in decline. As many of the nobility grew poorer they transported their private companies to the nearest town and opened public theatres with the idea of making money. Other companies were taken over by rich merchants as a commercial proposition. But all these theatres came under the jurisdiction of the Secret Police, and could produce only plays permitted by the authorities. Their standards of acting were not high, good actors being soon drawn away to Moscow or St. Petersburg. There was a great deal of fustian, and a reliance on stereotyped tricks to arouse laughter or bring applause which meant death to any realism in character or situation. Apart from the popularity of melodrama and frigid tragedy, there was the growing appeal of vaudeville, imported from France in about 1840. Intended purely for entertainment, devoid of all suspicion of social criticism, it was tolerated by the authorities, and made little demand upon the acting powers of the company, since it consisted mainly of singing, dancing, and witty dialogue. Its kindly satire, its ability to poke fun at individuals without giving offence, its high spirits and tuneful background, made an instant appeal to the Russians, who soon adopted it as their own. Eminent writers, even the great Pushkin, did not disdain to write for it. One dissident voice, however, was that of Gogol, who maintained that vaudeville was the ruin of Russian acting, and never forgave the actor at the Alexandrinsky Theatre who played Khlestakov in *Revizor* (*The Inspector-General*) as a vaudeville character. Belinsky too protested against 'the transplanting of this obviously French plant on to Russian soil', maintaining that it had no affinity with the Russian language nor with the strivings of the Russian actor towards reality. This did not prevent authors and composers from writing vaudevilles, or actors, who considered them good training, from playing in them.

It would seem impossible for a free national drama to flourish in such an atmosphere. Yet, in spite of all difficulties, the nineteenth century, from the defeat of Napoleon in 1812, saw the emergence of the great dramatists of Imperial Russia—Pushkin, Tolstoy, Gogol, Turgeniev, Chekhov, and Gorky.

The reasons for this are not far to seek. The Napoleonic invasion had raised the people to heights of patriotism previously undreamed of, and proved a vital inspiration to many writers. Since literature was now becoming of importance to the state, it must obviously be written in Russian. Even the nobility woke up to the emergence of a national consciousness, and the first great writer to use Russian as a literary medium—Alexander Sergeivich Pushkin (1799–1837)—was universally acclaimed. It is impossible to exaggerate his influence on Russian literature as a whole, and on the theatre in particular. His works, important in themselves, proved also a storehouse of plots on which his contemporaries and successors drew for the themes of their operas and dramas. Both he and his contemporary Mikhail Yurevich Lermontov (1814–41), author of *Masquerade* (written 1835; produced 1852 in a cut version, 1864 in full), represented the lesser nobility who had suffered under the oppression of the Court and the higher bureaucratic circles, and were closely in sympathy with the aspirations of the people. Their plays—tragedies in verse—were implicit criticisms of the life of the aristocracy, which, in the same period, Alexander Sergeivich Griboyedov (1795–1829) was satirizing in his comedies. His most famous play is *Goré ot Ooma* (published 1833), usually known as *Woe from Wit*, though it also has a dozen other titles in translation, among them *Wit Works Woe* and *The Disadvantages of Being Clever*. It depicts the moral corruption of the ruling class, and the stupidity of the politician, and is the first social play in Russian drama, organically linked with the literature of the Decembrist revolt of 1825, in which Pushkin also may have been implicated.

For the first time Russian dramatists were writing about living people, and were concerned to write the truth about the existing order. Had these authors lived longer, they might have had an even greater influence on the course of Russian drama. As it was, they all died young. But they had prepared the way, and it was left to Nikolai Vasilievich Gogol (1809–52) and his friend Shchepkin to effect the reform of the Russian stage.

Although Gogol was only in his early forties when he died he had written two long plays and a number of short ones, which, in their pointed criticism and their truthful delineation of a corrupt society, pointed the way for future dramatists. His *Revizor* (1836; also known as *The Government Inspector* and *The Inspector-General*) was produced, surprisingly enough, at the Alexandrinsky Theatre in the presence of the Tsar Nicholas I, with Shchepkin as the Mayor. Although some people affected to regard it as an unimportant farce, it was so bitterly attacked in responsible quarters that Gogol left Russia, not to return until 1848.

This period of reaction, which followed the Decembrist revolt of 1825, was ended by the accession in 1855 of Alexander II, on the whole the most liberal of the Tsars. Under him the nobility began to give place to an emerging bourgeoisie, from which arose an intelligentsia (many of them recruited from the ranks of the lesser nobility) supported by the wealthy merchants, who were for the most part of humble origin, and felt themselves despised by the more reactionary among the aristocracy. The changes in social life which this entailed were reflected in the theatre in the works of Alexander Nikolaivich Ostrovsky (1823–86), prolific author of a number of realistic middle-class comedies, whose themes embraced practically the whole of contemporary Russian life and society. During more than forty years of dramatic activity he had over fifty plays produced, of which some half a dozen have been translated into English. Parallel with this new realistic drama came a reform in the staging of plays. Ostrovsky's first play, produced in 1853, startled the audience by its simple and photographically exact presentation. For the first time a heroine appeared in a cotton frock, with naturally smooth hair. Before this silk dresses and French hairdressing had been obligatory. Shchepkin, who was the moving spirit behind these reforms, was helped by some of the younger actors, notably Alexander Martynov (1816–60) and Prov Sadovsky (1818–72), though some of the others, unable to adapt themselves, remained hostile. Ostrovsky took a practical interest in the reforms, and participated actively in the running of the Moscow Maly Theatre, which is now dedicated to his memory as the House of Ostrovsky.

In spite of the advances that were made at this time, and in spite of the occasional excellence of such a play as *A Month in the Country*, by Ivan Sergeivich Turgeniev (1818–83) (first produced in 1861, many years after it was written) the Russian theatre had a long way to go before it could deal adequately with the work of one of Russia's greatest dramatists, and the best known outside Russia—Anton Pavlovich Chekhov (1860–1904). One important event was the visit of the Meininger company to Russia in the 1880s, another the plays of Leo Nikolaivich Tolstoy (1828–1910). He first turned to the theatre in 1856, but his finest plays, *The Power of Darkness* (1886) and *The Fruits of Enlightenment* (1889), are contemporary with Chekhov's early plays. These were one-act comedies which, like Chekhov's first full-length play, *Ivanov* (1887), were performed in small theatres without much success. It was the failure of the Alexandrinsky Theatre to come to terms with *The Seagull* in 1896 which made plain the incompetence of the old Imperial theatre, and showed the need for a new approach to acting and production, based on truth and realism. Luckily this was to come almost at once, fostered by the establishment in 1898 of the famous Moscow Art Theatre under Vladimir Ivanovich Nemirovich-Danchenko (1859–1943) and Konstantin Sergeivich Alexeyev (1865–1938), better known as Stanislavsky. Here Chekhov and other writers of the European naturalistic movement found their ideal interpreters. The history of the Moscow Art

Theatre, of its actors and its authors, has been plentifully documented (see BIBLIOGRAPHY: RUSSIA; also CHEKHOV, MOSCOW ART THEATRE and STANISLAVSKY) and it continues to flourish. Its influence has been enormous, not only in Europe, where it has paid many visits to capital cities, but in America (see METHOD, THE). Like the last outstanding dramatist to appear before the Revolution of 1917 changed the face of Russia almost beyond recognition—Alexei Maximovich Pyeshkov (1868–1936), better known as Maxim Gorky—the Moscow Art Theatre helped to form a bridge between the old and the new, carrying forward into the Soviet theatre the fruits of many years of unremitting labour and reform. It was at the Moscow Art Theatre that the first two plays of Gorky were produced, *The Philistines* and *The Lower Depths*, both in 1902. Prophet of the Revolution, and one of its builders, Gorky represented the new power in the theatre—the proletariat. The plays which he wrote after the 1905 revolution were not produced until after 1917, when he came into his own. A later play, and one of his best, *Yegor Bulychev*, was done in 1934 by the Moscow Art Theatre. Though not as well known outside Russia as Chekhov, he is perhaps more truly representative of the Russia which prepared and carried through a great social revolution.

2. SOVIET THEATRE. The nineteenth century and the earliest years of the twentieth saw the emergence and establishment of a national Russian theatre. It had produced the great names listed above, one of which at least, Chekhov's, has since transcended all frontiers. It may be said that the theatre (at its best in the Moscow Art Theatre, the Imperial opera, and the Imperial ballet), which the monarchy either encouraged by patronage or allowed to develop without too much interference, was the outstanding product of the last years of the old régime.

The new régime had the intelligence to take over the best of what it inherited, and immensely to foster its extension. The mere physical development of the stage under Soviet rule is enormous. Before the outbreak of the Second World War there were nearly 800 professional theatres in the Soviet Union, of which 410 staged plays in non-Russian languages. The present Georgian Republic, for example, which in 1913 had three theatres, in 1938 had forty-eight. And the same rapid expansion is to be found in all the provinces, apart from the big increase in the number of theatres in the capital cities. To these must be added the children's theatres, a factor of great importance in the training of the younger generation (see CHILDREN'S THEATRE). Outside the vast professional theatre there are again innumerable amateur groups, tens of thousands of them, mostly attached to farms, factories, and other institutions. They are equipped with stages, and receive invaluable help and encouragement from the professional actors and producers. Each amateur group is usually adopted by a professional theatre, in Moscow or elsewhere, and special facilities are given for the training of promising youngsters, who often graduate from these amateur groups to the professional stage.

This vast expansion of the theatre, reaching into regions where no stage play had probably ever penetrated before, could not have been achieved without sympathetic encouragement, and above all practical assistance, from the new government. Indeed, the Bolshevik treatment of the theatre is probably one of the brightest spots in its history, and those who, in the first flush of victory, would have swept away the Moscow Art Theatre with other pre-Soviet organizations were properly rebuked when Lunacharsky, first Commissar for Education, gave it generous support. He made it financially independent, and allowed it time to readjust itself to the new régime—a forbearance which has been amply repaid by the fine work it has done since it regained its balance in about 1924–7. Among other theatres inherited and absorbed by Soviet Russia mention must be made of the Alexandrinsky and the Theatres for the People in Petrograd (formerly St. Petersburg, later Leningrad), and of the Maly, the Kamerny, and the various offshoots of the Moscow Art Theatre in Moscow.

To the inherited theatres, which in spite of trained actors and a seasoned repertory started anew with the handicap of being out of touch with the new audiences, were now added innumerable new theatres. These, though in sympathy with their audiences, and intended partly as instruments of education in the new social order, were on their side handicapped by the lack of highly trained theatre men, and by a dearth of plays suitable for their purpose, a dearth which developments in Soviet dramatic art before 1939 were going some way to remedy. The first steps were necessarily tentative and experimental, and a beginning was made by assisting various groups from the former bourgeois artistic intelligentsia, some of which had already attempted a minor reorganization, as in the short-lived Theatre of Artistic Drama and Theatre of Tragedy.

It would be impossible to enumerate all the theatres which sprang into being as a result of the rapid uprising, under active government encouragement, of the Russian love of and aptitude for the drama. Some have since changed their names, some have closed. The most important of the present-day theatres in Moscow and Leningrad are dealt with under their own names. Theatres which produce only ballet and opera, such as the Bolshoi in Moscow and the Kirov (formerly the Marinsky) in Leningrad, are somewhat outside the scope of this book. It has also been necessary to omit a number of small studio theatres, which nevertheless do good work, and the whole gamut of light, ephemeral entertainments, music-hall, musical comedy, circus, &c., which flourish all over the U.S.S.R., but on which information is not easily obtainable.

The theatre in the Soviet Union comes under

the aegis of the Theatre Board of the Ministry of Culture, assisted by the Theatrical Society of each particular republic. This might be expected to lead to uniformity, but in reality this has not happened, since, within the limits imposed by state control, each theatre has full responsibility for its productions and all matters relating thereto. Tradition has played a large part in shaping the destiny of each particular theatre. Thus the Moscow Art Theatre continues the tradition of Stanislavsky and Nemirovich-Danchenko. Okhlopkov created his own tradition, and though he has modified his earlier experimental style his aim is still to 'create an intimacy between actors and audience'. He still uses the auditorium as an extension of the stage, and sometimes mixes actors and audience. He would like to have a vast open-air arena, completely circular, with the actors in the centre. He also has plans for completely mobile theatres which would go by train.

In Leningrad, where many of the directors and actors have been trained by the Stanislavsky method, the theatres have a more restrained and disciplined character, each with its own individual stamp. The theatres of the different nationalities express very strongly their national characteristics; the Ukrainians have vivaciousness, the Georgians a powerful emotional energy and a plasticity of movement, the Armenians a dreamy fantasy.

Until 1948 the Soviet theatre was, as in most European countries, subsidized by the state, but this was discontinued, except in the case of childrens' theatres. The greatly improved economic condition of the people, and greater efficiency in the running of theatres, made it possible for them to become self-supporting economically. The effect of this, both on plays and production and on the standard of acting, has been altogether beneficial. Theatre buildings are now the liability of the company occupying them. Some belong to city councils, trade-unions, and other organizations, and can be rented by a company for an extremely low figure. Provision of backstage amenities is governed by labour regulations, and in new theatres these are outstanding. In addition to the latest technical equipment, there are excellent dressing rooms and rehearsal rooms, lounges, rest rooms, &c. A theatre also has special financial privileges, and its income is exempt from tax.

The keynote of the actor's life in the U.S.S.R. is security and permanence. Students receive their training free, and may in addition be given free living accommodation and a monetary grant for other expenses. On finishing their training they join a permanent company, attached to a particular theatre, where they may perhaps remain for the rest of their working lives. There is no question of engaging actors who may happen to be free in order to present a certain play, nor of disbanding the company at the end of the run; indeed, there are no 'runs' in the English sense, since each theatre plays in repertoire, and presents a number of different plays each season, varying the programme nightly.

The close association of actor and theatre makes for excellent team-work, the building up of a 'house' tradition, and a smooth running in every detail, obtainable only by the constant working together of actor, producer, and staff. Employment in the theatre is governed by the same labour laws as in other trades or professions, with some specific regulations called for by the peculiarities of theatrical life. The number of performances given by each individual actor is laid down as roughly between eight and twenty-two a month, according to the role. For anything over the maximum, the actor receives extra pay. Rehearsals are held daily from 10 a.m. to 2 p.m., or 11 a.m. to 3 p.m. with a short break. There is a minimum of one month's paid holiday, and actors qualify for reduced rates at many holiday homes and sanatoria. Salaries are fixed in accordance with training, qualifications, experience, and standard of work. There are a number of refresher courses for producers, which, for Leningrad and Moscow producers, do not involve absence from work. For provincial producers special seminars are held, during which they are given full pay and travelling and living allowances. Producers and leading actors are often sent on visits to other theatres, in Moscow, Leningrad, and other capital cities of the U.S.S.R., or even abroad. This gives them the opportunity of broadening their own conception of theatre, and of helping to widen the horizons of the group they visit, in the course of long personal discussions and participation in all activities connected with the theatre.

The head of the permanent company in each theatre is the director, who has an over-all responsibility, but is chiefly concerned with the artistic side of the work. A deputy director looks after the practical side, including advertising, sale of tickets, and so on. A chief producer oversees the actual production of each play. The larger theatres have a council, on which, in addition to the above, sit leading actors, representatives of the younger actors, the designer, stage-manager, and sometimes the lighting expert and the chief engineer. The council discusses plans for the repertory, and all questions dealing with allocations of work to producers and actors. The final decision, however, rests with the director. There are also regular conferences during the preparation of each new production at every stage of the work. After each first night a meeting of all concerned is held in the theatre, to discuss the production. In this way every member of the company feels that he has a responsibility towards the play. As Zavadsky, director of the Mossoviet Theatre, has said: 'The theatre is a collective art, and everything must be subordinated to what takes place on the stage.' He demands strict artistic discipline, and agrees with the generally accepted view that there are no insignificant parts in a play. Even the members of the crowd are important. 'The value of an actor is determined not by the importance of his part, but by the quality of its execution.' The rules of the Mossoviet Theatre, which are those of the majority of other theatres also, are: daily training by all, close contact with the audience by means of joint conferences, constant mingling with workers from other walks of life, and, it should be noted, mastery of Marxist-Leninist theory. In the training of Soviet actors political understanding plays almost as large a part as theatre work. The long list of rules ends with: 'The work of this theatre is experimental in character. It must become a laboratory for the creation of Soviet plays.'

In its early years the dearth of contemporary dramatists was one of the weak spots in the Soviet theatre, and accounted for the many revivals of Russian and European classics. The lack of good dramatists was understandable. Actors, producers, and technicians could be found among the men of the Revolution. Some had been in, but not of, the old régime, and after a quick adjustment were able to lead and train younger men. They were essentially men of action. For the writer, the thinker, adjustment was harder. Gorky was the only dramatist to ride out the storm he had helped to raise. The new plays of the post-Revolution period, inspired by the Proletcult (proletarian culture) movement, were inevitably instruments of propaganda rather than works of art. To encourage and support the emerging communist régime, the Soviet hero was shown as a man without faults, while the villain (usually a member of the bourgeoisie or of an enemy nation) had no redeeming features. This period is marked by the emergence of formalism, which in 1936 gave way to socialist realism. Though still occasionally met with, formalism is no longer important in the Soviet theatre, and it had little effect on the best of the early dramatists —Bulgakov, whose *Days of the Turbins* (1926) was seen in London in 1938 as *The White Guard*; Ivanov, whose *Armoured Train 14–69* (1927) (see No. 99) was perhaps the first outstanding Soviet play; Afinogenov, author of *Fear* (1931) and *Distant Point* (1934); and Simonov, author of *The Russians* (1942), done in London by the Old Vic company in the following year. Others, not so well known outside Russia, were Trenev, Pogodin, and Korneichuk. Since 1956 there has been a much larger output of contemporary plays, some of which, like V. Rozov's *In Search of Joy*, have been performed in over fifty theatres, but criticism of and dissatisfaction with modern Soviet playwriting still continues. Dramatists are accused of dealing in trivialities, whereas serious drama should be concerned with the conflicts and problems of man in his environment. A recent survey of theatre-going in the Soviet Union, conducted by a monthly theatre journal by means of a questionnaire, led to the conclusion that theatre-goers, while woefully ignorant of such details as who played which part, or of the work of the younger dramatists, or of dramatists in other republics, were agreed that the role of the Soviet theatre was actively to aid the 'bringing-up of the new man for a communist society'.

The most interesting of the new plays were considered to be: *The Irkutsk Story*, by Arbuzov; *Factory Girl*, by Volodin; *Colleagues*, by Aksenov and Stabatov; *More Dangerous than an Enemy*, by Ayl and Rakov; *My Friend Kolka*, by Khmelik; *Ocean*, by A. Shteyn; and *Leningrad Prospect*, by Shtock. It is interesting to note that among the first twenty plays selected there was not one classic. This was attributed to old-fashioned production, which tended to turn them into museum pieces, and to the reactions of the older critics, whose condemnation of 'modern' methods applied to Ostrovsky or Chekhov discourages the experimental producer. Among the actors who were frequently mentioned were B. Belokurov (1904–) as Alyosha in *Earth*, by Virta; A. Georgyevskaya (1914–) as Potapova in *Battle on the Road*, by Nikolayeva; and Nikolai Dmitrievich Mordvinov (1901–66) as Zabrodin in *Leningrad Prospect*, by Shtock.

Until 1954 plays were allocated to theatres by a now defunct Arts Council. This centralized method of forming a repertory no doubt hindered the development of Soviet plays of good quality, and the classics became too preponderant. It is now possible for the theatre director to choose his own play and to work on it with the dramatist, thus often improving its quality. With adequate financial resources it is even possible for a theatre to employ its own dramatist. Although open to abuses, this system has its advantages, in that the director and company can collaborate with the dramatist in the final version of the play.

It was in 1931 that the Lunacharsky State Institute of Theatre Art (see G.I.T.I.S.) extended its training facilities to actors of the non-Russian-speaking republics of the U.S.S.R. The groups founded then were known as National Theatre Workshops, and the first fully trained graduates came from them in 1936. Five years later four National Studios were founded—Turkmenian, Tadzhik, Kirghiz, and Adygei. For the first time audiences in these regions were able to hear plays by such authors as Shakespeare, Molière, Goldoni, and Beaumarchais, as well as Russian plays, in their own languages. Now most of the nationalities which make up the Soviet Union have a studio for training actors in Moscow or Leningrad, and some are beginning to set up similar training schools in their own capitals. It is impossible to deal here with the theatres of all the National Republics of the Soviet Union, but a number of them have a most interesting history, and are rapidly developing their own theatrical culture.

ARMENIA, which under the Tsarist government had no theatre at all, now has twenty-four, which, in addition to the works of such local playwrights as Deremik Demirchyan, produce the plays of Russians and Europeans. In 1939 an Armenian Theatre Company was invited to perform in Moscow. AZERBAIJAN, which already possessed a fine playwright in the nineteenth-century Ilya Elvin Akhundov, has a vigorous theatrical life. Plays are given by different groups in Armenian, Russian, and Turkish, and in 1938 the State Dramatic Theatre produced *Macbeth*. There are also a number of local playwrights. BYELORUSSIA had a long tradition of acting, and was particularly notable for its puppet-theatre (for adults), Bataleika, which flourished from the sixteenth century on. The first professional theatre was established in 1907, two of its best playwrights being Yanko Kupala and Yakub Kolass, after whom two important modern theatres have been named, in Minsk and Vitebsk respectively. After the Revolution there was a great expansion, until in 1941 there were twenty-three theatres. During the Nazi occupation these were destroyed, but the companies had been evacuated; on the cessation of hostilities they returned, and there are once again a dozen flourishing theatres, with plans for many more. GEORGIA also has had a long theatre history and plays were widely used throughout its history in the struggle against foreign domination. The closer contact with Russia which developed in the nineteenth century led to the temporary establishment of a professional theatre, much helped by Griboyedov, who lived for a long time in Tbilisi (formerly Tiflis). Later, the leaders of the Georgian theatre were closely associated with the Russian theatre, one of them, Abashidze, having been a student at the Maly Theatre in Moscow. In 1921 the Rustavelli Theatre in Tbilisi opened, and inaugurated a time of rapid development, the key man being K. A. Mardjhanishvilli, who was responsible for the training of a whole generation of Georgian actors and playwrights. By 1960 there were twenty theatres in Georgia, of which all but three perform in Georgian. The repertory is international, but acting, which has been much influenced by Stanislavsky, shows the national characteristics of vigour and depth of feeling, and also great beauty of movement, a result of a basic training in ballet. Georgian stage design has also been outstanding, shaped in large measure by the gifted artist Guimrekelli (1889–1945). In UZBEKISTAN there was from very early times a flourishing tradition of circus, puppets, shadow-shows, and singers of folk-ballads, while the nomadic tribes had their own primitive musical instruments. To the rich heritage of song and dance has now been added the repertory of the Western theatre and of the great Russian masters, without, however, swamping the national characteristics. It would take too long to recount in detail the development of the theatre in Uzbekistan, which, in its essentials, has followed the pattern set by other regions since 1917. It must suffice to mention here the honoured names of Tamara Petrosiants and Kari Yakubov, and the Khamza Theatre, one of the leading playhouses, which opened in Tashkent in 1920. In 1924 it sent a group of actors to be trained in the Uzbek Studio in Moscow. It was for a time located in Samarkand, but in 1929 it returned to Tashkent, now the official capital, and was given the name of the Uzbek poet Khamza. Finally, a word may be said about the theatre in YAKUTIA, a vast, sparsely populated region of which much lies beyond the Arctic Circle. It has about twenty national groups, each with its own language and customs. Illiteracy was wide-spread, and efforts which were made spasmodically from 1905 onwards to found a national theatre failed. But in 1920 a theatre was set up with Russian actors, performing plays of political propaganda, which were taken long distances to remote groups. During the difficult years the theatre nearly foundered, but it was saved by some heroic and ingenious methods, one among them being the acceptance in 1922, of firewood for heating the building (wood being one of the commodities in short supply) as part-payment of a ticket for a performance. Barley and other provisions were also accepted and distributed to the starving population. With the coming of better times a Yakut State National Theatre was established, with G. M. Turalyssov as its director, and within a year Yakut plays were being given. In 1932 more than twenty students were sent to Moscow to be trained, and today Yakutia has a flourishing theatre where plays by local authors are given in the venacular, as well as plays by Russian dramatists and translations of European classics.

Thus, by the united efforts of all the nationalities of the U.S.S.R., a Soviet theatre is being built up which, differing as to its outward form and language according to the region which it serves, is national in form and socialist in content. A noticeable development in the Russian theatre since 1963 has been the emergence of a younger generation of directors, bringing with them greater freedom of expression and a more genuinely creative approach, and the encouragement of experimental studios, which as they mature become established theatres, challenging the older methods and traditions.

It would be impossible to end this article without saying something about scenic design, which in Russia has always been remarkable for its variety and vitality, covering in its time all styles of stage-setting, from conventional operatic decoration to naturalistic representation, from modernized baroque to abstract constructivism. Before the Revolution stage design fell into two categories—the symbolic and impressionistic, exemplified by the work of Mstislav Dobujinsky (1875–1957) and Alexandre Benois (1870–1960), and the naturalism of the early Moscow Art Theatre, where Stanislavsky's chief designer was Victor Simov (1858–1935) (see Nos. 95 and 99). In the period immediately following the Revolution the reaction from both types of stage design led to constructivism. The pioneer of this method was Meyerhold, whose pre-Soviet designer had been Alexander Golovin (1863–1930). (see No. 155). There followed collaboration with Shestakov, Popova, Shlepanov, and Rodchenko to clear away the 'rubbish' which cluttered the stage. Wings, borders, painted drops were swept away and replaced by revolving wheels, ladders, lifts, stairs, and stands. The theatre became a factory, with actors as workers and the performance as a process of production. This was an excellent symbolic gesture, but it went too far. The new, alive, untutored audiences crowding the theatres for the first time wanted colour and evocative settings. So contructivism went; but it had served its purpose, and from it modern designers have learned to consider the sociological angle of the play, an essential part of Soviet production and design, while retaining from the pre-Revolutionary theatre, with its stylized presentation of a given epoch, the richness of colour and line.

The designers' quest for the architectural image has led to such different manifestations as the stylized architectural settings of Rabinovich and V. Beyer, the architectural constructivism of some of V. Ryndin's settings, the rich romantic architecture of Tishler, and the satirical romanticism of Nikolai Akimov, and of Levin. The conflict between Akimov's romantic and sceptical tendencies was most noticeable in his production of *Hamlet* at the Vakhtangov Theatre in 1932. Levin has many fine designs to his credit, particularly in opera, but he is so many-sided that it would be difficult to assign him to any particular school. His work is to be found everywhere, from grand opera to music-hall, and some of his designs, particularly those for the Maly Theatre production of Gorky's *Enemies* in 1933, were strongly naturalistic. This influence is also paramount in the work of Vladimir Vladimirovich Dmitriev (1900–48) who was responsible for the décor of Gorky's last plays when they were done at the Vakhtangov Theatre.

Architectural theatre design was carried to its apotheosis in the work of Y. Stoffer (1906–51) for Okhlopkov at the Realistic Theatre, where the whole auditorium was taken as the stage space in which the scene is set, each production involving a totally different arrangement of seating and view-points for the audience. This method was brilliantly successful in the productions of *Mother*, *The Iron Flood*, and *Razbeg*. Another outstanding scenic designer was N. A. Shifrin (1892–1959), one of whose fine settings for Popov's production of *The Taming of the Shrew* in 1938 was reproduced at the Soviet Theatre Exhibition in London in 1946. Throughout the play the use of tapestries combined with solid furniture gave a vivid and evocative picture of a mingled Elizabethan and Italian Renaissance scene. Shifrin designed equally lovely settings for Popov's production of *A Midsummer Night's Dream* in 1940, and later some realistic décor, from sketches made on the spot, for a play by a Red Army soldier on the siege of Stalingrad.

Other outstanding artists also made their name in the theatre, among them Peter Vladimirovich Williams (1902–47), who created some most original settings for *The Pickwick Club*, done at the Moscow Art Theatre in 1934, with full use of backcloths (this play was a wonderfully alive dramatization of the novel, satisfying even to an English lover of Dickens); V. Basov (1901–46), whose settings for such productions as *Romeo and Juliet* and *Othello*, the latter at the Maly, showed him to be an artist on a monumental scale; and V. Favorsky (1889–1964), who enchanted his audiences with his first stage designs (for *Twelfth Night*), which made use of an architectural synthesis of the Renaissance with a painted backcloth panorama.

The period immediately after the Second World War was one of hesitation, of playing for safety, almost of inhibition of creative experience. Only Okhlopkov went his own way, encouraging his stage designers to be original and daring, so that their sets would not only drive home the message of the play but also arouse the audience to greater receptivity. His spherical architectural structure with a roof which slides down to form walls, which in their turn move apart to show designs that change according to the angle of turn of the amphitheatre, added to the imaginative use of light, gives the stage designer immense scope for experimentation.

Williams's death in 1947 was a great loss to the stage. In *Ivan the Terrible* (1946), he rejected external displays of sumptuousness and grandeur, and used instead a simple and severe wooden structure which served to bring out the harsh spirit of the time. One of his last décors was for Virta's *Great Days* (1947), where he used light and colour to emphasize the author's directness.

An equally great loss was the death a year later of Dmitriev, whose approach to stage design showed great versatility. For the Moscow Art Theatre's production of Ostrovsky's *The Last Sacrifice* in 1944 his designs concentrated the audience's attention on the deep psychological content of the play, while for Virta's *Our Daily Bread* (1947) he produced a modern collective-farm landscape showing a power-station, endless fields, and a river. In Act III the dark garden, lit by the gold of autumn leaves and the gay costumes of the actors, while the lighted window of the house betokened the feverish atmosphere within, was acclaimed by all as a masterpiece. Dmitriev's last designs were done for a production of 'The Bartered Bride', but he did not live to see them on the stage.

Shifrin continued active in the theatre until his death in 1959. In the 1940s he was criticized for his exaggerated theatricality, and for his excess of naturalism. But in spite of ill-health, his work continued to develop, and his designs for *Virgin Soil Upturned* (1957) won universal acclaim. Here he showed the vastness of the land stretching away to the endless steppes, and, with such poetic and yet almost tangible effects as the soft outline of poplars numbed by the cold, and lonely branches on the horizon under a lofty sky, the slow yielding of winter to spring and hopefulness. In light comedies, such as *The Merry Wives of Windsor* (1957), at the Mossoviet, he used folk art, with its clear graphic drawing and rich colouring, very successfully.

Among stage designers today Vadim Fyodorovich Ryndin (1902–) holds a high place. He combines the use of built scenery on stage with film projection to give a sense of space, as in *The Fate of a Man*, where the interior scene is expanded by an exterior projected on to the back and sides of the stage. He maintains that this extension of the scenic image stimulates the imagination of the spectator and involves him in creative activity. In 1953 Ryndin became chief stage designer at the Bolshoi Theatre (for an example of his work see No. 90).

Two designers who often work in collaboration are M. Kashintsev and A. Kaikhel, whose work is receiving growing appreciation. For *The Apple of Discord* (1962) at the Satire Theatre they used a small revolving stage which as it turned produced various scenic combinations. Instead of a backdrop they used a screen on to which they projected vast pictures of clouds, birds, apples, &c. This had the effect of confining Koval, the leading character, within a small space, and so arousing the sympathy of the audience for him even while they laughed at his plight.

Ivan Sevastyanov, a pupil of Favorsky and Dmitriev, who went to Novosibirsk from the Art School in Saratov in 1952, has already begun to make a name for himself. He employs massive architectural forms for solidity, and makes imaginative use of colour and lighting to emphasize emotion. His sets are remarkable for their economy of detail, and for the way in which they help to reveal the character of the actor.

Another young designer, who studied at the Surkov Art Institute until 1956, Margarita Moukasseyeva, shows a great gift for symbolic design which rouses the imagination of the spectator and makes him aware of the reality of the play. She is not only a stage designer but a painter with a great liking for applied art, which enriches her work for the theatre and helps her in her search for new and beautiful forms.

V. V. Ivanov is another very promising designer. His settings for *The Wreck of the Squadron* admirably expressed the spirit of the revolutionary events dealt with by the dramatist, and created the impression of space allied to simplicity by the use of a vast sea horizon above the spacious deck of a ship which extended into the orchestra pit. Two other young designers who deserve mention are Bossulayev and Tishler.

It is impossible, in the space available here, to deal with the numerous artists and designers of the National Republics of the Union whose work, in general, shows an equal variety of styles, to which is added the richness of their national traditions. The Ukrainian theatre, for example, had two great scenic artists in Vahim Meller and Anatol Petritsky. The former worked chiefly in the Berezil theatre, most of its designs being by himself or his pupils. At first a constructivist, Meller in his later work achieved a synthesis of architecture, painting, and sculpture, with striking results. Petritsky, an artist of temperamental brilliance, sonorous colouring, and entrancing fancy, specialized in designs for opera. He also worked in Moscow, where he did some dynamic settings for Dikie at the Trades Union Theatre.

Among the newcomers the Georgian, Irakli Gamrekeli, has already won a leading position. He is greatly influenced by the landscape of his native land, and his designs convey the feeling of its spaciousness, its strength, and its romance. He is much addicted to the use of architectural forms and to strong colours. Byelorussia has a number of promising stage designers, among them V. G. Miller, and I. M. Ushakova. Armenia has M. S. Saryan and A. O. Mirzoyan.

The tendency in the Russian theatre for several years now has been to get away from the naturalistic set and to encourage creative individuality. This has sometimes led to controversy, as for instance over Zakhava's production of *Hamlet* in 1958. Contrary to the usual practice, Zakhava approached the play from the pictorial angle, and devoted most of his attention to the lighting, and particularly to the sky, which in some scenes changed colour, from clear pale blue to stormy black, thus, in his own words, 'producing a spectacle that would speak of the eternal disquiet of the human spirit and its ceaseless striving for truth, goodness, and beauty'.

BEATRICE KING†, *rev.*

RUTEBEUF (*c.* 1230–*c.* 1285), a medieval minstrel who, with Adam de la Halle and Jean Bodel, stands at the beginning of French secular drama. Very little is known of his life; he was always poor and never very successful, though he ranked slightly above some of the humbler brethren in the hierarchy of minstrels, since at one time he possessed a horse. He married a plain, elderly wife, and though uneducated and of humble birth, his skill as a rhymer and singer made him a welcome guest in the halls of the feudal barons. His most important play was *Le Miracle de Théophile*, which in the 1930s was revived by Gustave Cohen's students at the Sorbonne, who took from it their name of 'Les Théophiliens'.

RUTHERFORD, MARGARET (1892–1972), English actress, in the great tradition of English eccentrics and star personalities. She made a late entry on the stage, being in her early thirties when a small legacy enabled her to give up her job of teaching elocution and the piano. She made her first appearance at the Old Vic in 1925, under Robert Atkins, and subsequently played several small parts, but without achieving much success. The turning point in her career came when in 1938 she was engaged to play the likeable, formidable, and extremely eccentric Bijou Furze in *Spring*

Meeting. She was immediately recognized as an outstanding comedienne, and played Miss Prism in *The Importance of Being Earnest* in the following year. Among her outstanding parts were Madame Arcati in *Blithe Spirit* (1941); Miss Whitchurch in *The Happiest Days of Your Life* (1948); Madame Desmortes (in a bath-chair) in *Ring Round the Moon* (1950); Lady Wishfort in *The Way of the World* (1953), giving a masterly impression of the 'old peeled wall'; Minerva Goody in *Farewell, Farewell Eugene* (1959); and Bijou again in the sequel to *Spring Meeting, Dazzling Prospect* (1961). At her best in comedy, she could nevertheless play pathos and also inject a certain sinister element into some of her personifications of elderly and unpredictable old ladies. Her husband, Stringer Davis, appeared with her in a number of London productions, and also on her numerous and wide-ranging tours.

RUZZANTE, see BEOLCO and ITALY, 2.

RYAN, LACY (1694–1760), an English actor of great talent, almost amounting to genius, who lacked physical advantages and the help of careful training. He first appeared as Seyton to Betterton's Macbeth, in a full-bottomed wig, and was Marcus in the original production of *Cato* (1713). He had a steady, uneventful career, mostly at Covent Garden, where he played big Shakespearian roles in opposition to Garrick at Drury Lane, with little success. It is said that Garrick went to see his Richard III, intending to scoff, but was astonished and moved by the genius and power which he saw striving to make itself felt through the burden of bad training, uncouth gestures, and slovenly figure. Ryan continued to play youthful lovers and heroes until his death, and was all his life a friend of the actor Quin, whom he had befriended in early days.

RYER, PIERRE DU (*c*. 1600–58), French dramatist, who though well educated and the holder of several important positions, was always handicapped by poverty, and relied for his living on hackwork translations of Greek and Latin authors. He wrote a number of plays, of which the earliest were tragicomedies in the style of Hardy, three being given in the year 1628–9. They were spectacular, calling for elaborate staging in the old-fashioned simultaneous style, and ignored the unities of time and place. Several comedies followed, containing good parts for the comedian Gros-Guillaume, of which the best was *Les Vendanges de Suresne* (1633), and then, under the influence of Mairet's *Sophonisbé* (1634), du Ryer turned his attention to tragedy. The most successful of several tragedies, which included some on biblical subjects, was *Scévole* (1644). This remained in the repertory of the Comédie-Française for over 100 years, and was one of the plays given by Molière's short-lived Illustre-Théâtre. In the opinion of competent critics, du Ryer did more than anyone, except Mairet and Corneille, to establish French classical tragedy, though his range was wide, and included also pastorals like *Clitophan et Leucippe* (1629), which survives only in manuscript. Most of du Ryer's plays were given by the company at the Hôtel de Bourgogne.

S

SÁ DE MIRANDA, Francisco de (1485–1558), Portuguese dramatist, was approximately contemporaneous with that other pillar of the Portuguese theatre, Gil Vicente, but he contributed very different talents and achievements to the theatrical history of his country. Born in Coimbra of a noble family, a friend of kings, he was an austere and learned man who loved the classic forms of poetry and drama. These he had observed and practised during extensive travels in Italy; he brought them back as his great gift to Portugal. His two comedies, *Estrangeiros* and *Vilhalpandos* (probably written between 1528 and 1538), are foundation stones of the classic theatre in his country. In contrast with the plays of Gil Vicente, these were shaped logically and divided neatly into acts and scenes, with some attention to the three unities, and bearing echoes of the classic theatres of Greece and Rome. Sá de Miranda also wrote at least one tragedy, *Cleopatra*, but no more than a dozen verses of it remain. His plays, like his poetry, helped to give Portugal's theatre a solid sense of form which was lacking in the greater genius of Gil Vicente (see also PORTUGAL).

MILDRED ADAMS

SAAVEDRA, Ángel de, Duque de Rivas (1791–1865), one of the foremost Spanish Romantic writers. Exiled in Malta, he was encouraged by Hookham Frere to write the ballad sequence of *El moro expósito* (1834). Later, in France, under the influence of Victor Hugo, Rivas abandoned his former neo-classical style of playwriting and composed *Don Álvaro, o la fuerza de sino*. In 1835 this play received its first performance in Madrid and has been acclaimed as the great triumph of Spanish Romanticism, the *Hernani* of the Madrid stage. Although this claim is somewhat exaggerated, Rivas's play had undoubtedly a great effect in the political and literary atmosphere then prevailing, representing, as Larra said of Romanticism in general, 'liberty in literature'. Apart from the fine sweep of his emotions, Rivas's play is noteworthy for the use of local colour and the careful attention to detail in his stage sets. It provided Piave with the libretto of Verdi's opera 'La Forza del destino' (1862). Rivas's later plays reveal the loss of the first fine frenzy, and are costume drama after the fashion of Dumas.

J. E. VAREY

SABBATTINI, Nicola (1574–1654), Italian architect, designer of the Teatro del Sole in Pesaro, and author of a treatise on stage designing, *Pratica di fabricar scene e machine ne' teatri* (1638) (see LIGHTING, 1 *a*).

SABBIONETA THEATRE, see SCENERY, 2 and No. 21.

SACHS, Hans (1494–1576), German dramatist and Mastersinger, a cobbler by profession, whose main dramatic activity began about 1518. Immensely proud of his facility, he turned out long tragedies and comedies, and short brisk Carnival plays. His range is enormous: the Bible, legend, history, the classics, and the vast store of popular anecdote furnished him with material. His subjects are treated without the faintest historical perspective, sense of poetry, or tragic depth, and were merely used to serve his purpose of moral betterment. Most of the tragedies, such as *Die mörderisch Königin Clitimestra* or *Der Hörnen Sewfriedt*, strike the modern reader as travesties, but the comedies—that is, plays with a happy ending, though not necessarily humorous—are more successful. In *Die ungleichen Kinder Eve* the Lord pays a friendly visit to the cottage of Adam and Eve, and examines their progeny—six good and six bad—in the Lutheran Catechism (Sachs was one of the first poets of his day to support Luther), dealing out appropriate rewards and punishments.

Sachs's fame rests chiefly on his Carnival plays, of which he wrote about 200, notable for their vivid folk-pictures and homespun humour. He may be said to have turned the horseplay of Shrovetide into a folk-play in simple form. Comparison with his sources shows that he did not aim at originality, but deft omissions and additions, and many telling touches, reveal his power of characterization and a sense of dramatic economy. The dialogue is often very natural and the rough and ready verse is not unpleasing. Sachs, who is the hero of Wagner's opera 'Die Meistersinger von Nürnberg', united in himself the healthiest tendencies of past and present, combining *naïveté* with shrewdness, humanity, and a glorious gift of laughter. W. E. DELP

SACKVILLE, Thomas, first Earl of Dorset (1536–1608), English lawyer and politician, Lord Treasurer under Elizabeth I and James I. In 1561 he collaborated with his fellow student Thomas Norton in the writing of the first regular Senecan English tragedy in blank verse, *Gorboduc, or Ferrex and Porrex*. This was given before Queen Elizabeth I on New Year's Day in the hall of the Inner Temple. He also contributed, to the second edition of *A Mirror for Magistrates* (1563), the *Induction* and *The Complaint of Buckingham*, the only contributions having any literary merit. (For the actor Sackville, see ENGLISH COMEDIANS.)

SACRA RAPPRESENTAZIONE, the fifteenth-century religious play of Italy, comparable in many respects with the *auto* of Spain and the Mystery play of France and England, for which modern criticism has now coined the generic name of 'Bible-histories'. As elsewhere, the Italian religious drama began in the church, but migrated to the market-place, where the original solemnity of the Bible story was gradually enlivened by humorous and contemporary elements, and by material imported from the lives of the saints (see ITALY, 1 *a* ii).

SADLER'S WELLS THEATRE, LONDON. The discovery of a medicinal spring in the grounds of a Mr. Sadler in the year 1683–4 led to the establishment of a popular pleasure-garden there, which became known as Sadler's Wells. Entertainments of a varied nature were given, and Sadler, in partnership with a dancing-master named Forcer, erected a wooden 'Musick House' with a platform to serve as a stage. Sadler's Wells then stood in open country, and though it seems to have been a well-conducted place as a rule, a murder was committed there in 1712, when a naval lieutenant was killed by a lawyer 'near the organ loft'.

Sadler apparently retired in 1699 in favour of one Miles, who with Forcer ran the place as Miles's Musick House. He died in 1724 and Forcer in 1730. The son of the latter, a barrister, carried on the place, again called Sadler's Wells, and added musical interludes, the first stage performances on record there. The Princesses Amelia and Caroline visited it in 1735. In 1746 Rosoman, a local builder (after whom a nearby street is now named), took over the Wells, which had rather lost its reputation, and restored its good name. In 1753 he engaged a regular company and the old Musick House became a theatre. In 1855 the Rural Calendar refers to it, saying: 'this theatre—for such it now is—is now so well regulated, under the present manager, that a better company is not anywhere to be met with.' *The Tempest*—possibly in Dryden's version—was performed there in 1764. In 1765 Rosoman demolished the old wooden building and raised a stone theatre at a cost of £4,225, the whole thing being completed in seven weeks. It opened with a mixed bill on 8 Apr., and Rosoman continued to run it successfully until his retirement in 1772. He was succeeded by Tom King, a Drury Lane actor and the original Sir Peter Teazle. He ran the place well, and it was under him that the future great clown Joseph Grimaldi appeared as a 'sprite' in 1781, being then not quite three years old. He continued to appear at the theatre until 1805. Associated with the management at this time were the husband of Sarah Siddons, the elder Charles Dibdin, and two of his sons. In 1801 a small boy named Master Carey appeared at the theatre. He afterwards became the great Edmund Kean. Other successes were made by a troupe of performing dogs in 1783, Miss Romanzini, better known as Mrs. Bland, in 1786, and Master Abraham, later the tenor Braham, in 1788. In 1804, under Dibdin, a large tank was installed on the stage, filled with water from the New River, and Sadler's Wells became the home of Aquatic Drama. The first of these was *The Siege of Gibraltar*, complete with naval bombardment. The vogue for these spectacles continued for some years, during which time the house was known as the Aquatic Theatre.

In 1807 a false alarm of fire caused a panic in the theatre; twenty-three people were killed and many injured. In 1818 Grimaldi took over and sustained a heavy loss. He made his farewell appearance at Sadler's Wells on 17 Mar. 1828, broken in health and fortune. Tom Mathews succeeded him as clown.

For the next fifteen years there was nothing much of interest at the Wells, until in 1844 it was let to Samuel Phelps and Mrs. Warner. They opened with *Macbeth* on 27 May 1844. Mrs. Warner retired two years later, but Phelps, with Greenwood, made theatre history with his productions of Shakespeare and classical dramas. His production of *Pericles* in 1854 was the first since its appearance as *Marina* (in an adaptation by George Lillo) at Covent Garden in 1738. He retired in 1862, and the glory of Sadler's Wells, which had been one of the foremost theatres of London, faded. Morton Price and Miss Lucette gave light entertainments there, and Robert Edgar ran it for six years with his wife, Miss Mariott, a noted female Hamlet, as its leading lady; but it soon became a skating-rink and a venue for prize-fights, and in 1878 it was closed as a dangerous structure.

In 1879 Mrs. Bateman, on leaving the Lyceum, reconstructed the interior, and, opening on 9 Oct., tried to revive the glories of the past. After her death in 1881 her daughter Isabel carried on for a while. But the theatre never attained the heights reached under Phelps, and sank to be a house of indifferent twice-nightly shows. For a long time it was derelict. In 1893 it became a music-hall under George Belmont, and later it was used as a cinema. It finally closed in 1906. A project to reopen it in 1921 came to nothing. Then, in 1927, Lilian Baylis conceived the idea of making it a North London pendant to the Old Vic in South London. A new theatre rose on the site, and opened on 6 Jan. 1931 with the Old Vic company in *Twelfth Night*, John Gielgud playing Malvolio and Dorothy Green, Viola. The plan of alternating plays and operas at both theatres was soon dropped, and the Old Vic remained the home of Shakespeare until it closed in 1963, to become the temporary home of the National Theatre company. The ballet company from the Old Vic, under Ninette de Valois, moved to North London to become the Sadler's Wells and later the Royal (Covent Garden) Ballet company, sharing the theatre with the Sadler's Wells Opera company. Fine work was done by both companies until the theatre closed in 1940. It was later damaged by enemy action, and did not reopen until 1945, when a performance of Britten's opera 'Peter Grimes' was given on 7 June. After the departure of the ballet company to Covent Garden the opera company carried on alone, though the theatre was sometimes used for visiting companies. The Moscow Art Theatre was there in 1958. When the new theatre buildings on the South Bank are completed, the opera company will move to a new home there, and it is not known yet what will become of Sadler's Wells. W. MACQUEEN-POPE†, *rev.*

SADOVSKY [really YERMILOV], PROV MIKHAILOVICH (1818–72), one of the best of early Russian actors. He was born in Moscow, and educated for the stage by a well-known provincial actor, Sadovsky, a relative on his mother's side, from whom the young Yermilov took his professional name. He appeared on the provincial stage, in Tula, at the age of 14, and in 1839 went to Moscow and joined the company of the Imperial Maly Theatre. He occupied a modest place at first, but came to the fore in Ostrovsky's plays, of whose comic roles he proved to be the ideal interpreter, as Shchepkin was of Gogol's. With Sadovsky it may be said that the internal psychological development of the character was at one with the external, life-like presentation. It was due largely to Sadovsky's championship that Ostrovsky's plays were first done and then kept in the repertory until they received due recognition from the public. Unlike the earlier actors, Kachalov and Mochalov, Sadovsky followed Shchepkin in a realistic approach to his art.

Sadovsky's son and daughter-in-law were also members of the Maly company, and his grandson, also named Prov, is still with the theatre, thus maintaining a family connexion which dates back over a century.

SAFETY CURTAIN, an iron or fireproof sheet which falls in front of the ordinary curtain of a proscenium-arch theatre, and is designed to separate the stage and auditorium in the event of fire. By law it must be lowered once at every performance and this is generally done during an interval. The earliest reference to this device, which is sometimes nicknamed 'the Iron', occurs at Drury Lane in 1794.

SAINETE, a term found in Spain in the late seventeenth century, applied in the eighteenth to the *entremés*, the comic interlude usually played between the acts of a full-length play. The best eighteenth-century *sainetes* are those of Ramón de la Cruz, their racy speech and satirical view of society forming a welcome relief from the stereotyped and usually lifeless neo-classical dramas, and from the extravaganzas of the school of Comella. This note of social criticism may be said, in general terms, to distinguish the *sainete* from the *entremés*. Modern descendants of the *sainete* are to be found in the comic playlets of the *género chico* and in the work of such twentieth-century dramatists as Arniches and the brothers Quintero. J. E. VAREY

SAINT-DENIS, MICHEL (1897–1971), French actor and producer. He began his career under Jacques Copeau at the Vieux-Colombier, where he was stage-manager and assistant producer, and went with him to Burgundy when he founded his theatre school there. He then went with the company on tour throughout the Continent and to England, and in 1930 founded the Compagnie des Quinze, for whom he produced *Noé*, *Le Viol de Lucrèce*, and *Bataille de la Marne*, all by Obey, as well as other plays, appearing in all of them himself. The company achieved a great reputation, but was finally disbanded, and in 1936 Saint-Denis, who had already produced *Noah* (in English) (1935) and *The Witch of Edmonton* (1936) in London, founded the London Theatre Studio for the training of young actors. Several public performances were later given, and the work of the school had already made an interesting contribution to the English theatre, when the outbreak of war in 1939 caused it to close down. Meanwhile, Saint-Denis had done several more productions, including *Macbeth* (1937), *Three Sisters* and *The White Guard* (both 1938), and *The Marriage of Blood* (1939), to all of which he brought the same fastidious intellect, clarity of vision, and refusal to be bound by tradition which had marked the productions of the Compagnie des Quinze. After the Second World War he became head of the short-lived Old Vic School, and on its demise returned to France to become head of the Centre Dramatique de l'Est based on Strasbourg. Appointed artistic adviser to the Lincoln Center Project in New York in 1962, he is also general artistic adviser to the Royal Shakespeare Theatre. In 1960 he published an interesting book entitled *Theatre: The Rediscovery of Style*, which contained an admirable chapter on training for the stage, and one on the duties of the director and designer.

ST. JAMES THEATRE, NEW YORK, on 44th Street and 8th Avenue. This opened as Erlanger's on 26 Sept. 1927. It was intended as a house for musical and spectacular shows, and received its present name in 1932. Among its early productions was an all-star revival of *She Stoops to Conquer* with Mrs. Leslie Carter as Mrs. Hardcastle, followed after two weeks by a revival of *Diplomacy*. In 1929 Mrs. Fiske made one of her last stage appearances in the highly amusing *Ladies of the Jury*, while a year later came *Jew Süss*, followed by light opera until 1932. A return to straight drama was made with *Lost Horizon* (1934), but the house reverted to musical shows, with some success, until in 1937 critics and public alike acclaimed Margaret Webster's production of *Richard II*, with Maurice Evans in the name-part. The same combination was responsible for *Hamlet* in 1938 and for *Henry IV, Part I*, with Evans as Falstaff, in 1939. The following year saw Helen Hayes and Maurice Evans in *Twelfth Night*, produced under the auspices of the Theatre Guild, and the poignant *Native Son*, in which Canada Lee gave a fine performance. The theatre was for a long time occupied by the Theatre Guild's production of *Oklahoma!*, a musical play based on *Green Grow the Lilacs*, which opened in 1943. Other highly successful productions have been *Where's*

Charley? (1948), a musical based on the old farce, *Charley's Aunt*; *The King and I* (1951), in which Gertrude Lawrence made her last appearance on the stage; *Becket* (1960); and *Luther* (1963), in which Albert Finney made a successful Broadway début. This last named moved in 1964 to the Lunt–Fontanne to make way for a musical, *Hello, Dolly!*, based on Thornton Wilder's *The Matchmaker*.

GEORGE FREEDLEY†

ST. JAMES'S THEATRE, LONDON, in King Street. Designed by Samuel Beazley, this theatre was built for the singer John Braham, who invested in it all his life savings. It opened on 14 Dec. 1835 with an 'operatic burlesque', *Agnes Sorel*, followed by two short farces; but in spite of a rapid succession of new plays Braham lost money steadily, and early in 1836 sublet the theatre to a French company. He returned in the autumn, and among his productions were two by Dickens—his first dramatic work, the two-act farce *The Strange Gentleman*, and a ballad-opera, *The Village Coquettes*. In 1838 an adaptation by another hand of *Oliver Twist*, which was still appearing in parts, was booed on its first night and not revived. Braham, having lost all his money, left the St. James's and it was taken over by Bunn, but the only things that made money were wild beast shows and, in 1840, a German company which profited by the fashion for all things German due to the marriage of Queen Victoria to Prince Albert, in whose honour the theatre was renamed the Prince's. When Bunn went bankrupt at Drury Lane, the St. James's closed too, to reopen under its old name in 1842. Its manager for the next twelve years was John Mitchell, who relied almost entirely on imported French companies, Rachel appearing under him in 1846, 1850, 1853 and, for the last time in England, in 1855. During Mitchell's tenancy Queen Victoria was a frequent visitor to the theatre, and continued to patronize it intermittently after his departure, her last visit being on 7 Feb. 1861 to see an English version of *Adrienne Lecouvreur*, in which she had seen Rachel in 1853. It was Mitchell who brought to England Bateman, later Irving's manager at the Lyceum, with his two talented children, Kate and Ellen. Mitchell, having lost a good deal of money, gave up in 1854, and managements came and went. Toole appeared in his first regular London engagement in 1854; Braham's son Augustus tried his fortunes with an opera company in 1859; Louisa Herbert, later to become manageress of the theatre, thrilled the town in *Lady Audley's Secret* in 1863; Gilbert's first play, an operatic burlesque entitled *Dulcamara; or, the Little Duck and the Great Quack*, was staged under Miss Herbert in 1866, and in the same year Irving made his second London appearance in a season which ran from Oct. to the following June. Mrs. Wood, later manageress of the Royal Court, managed the theatre from 1869 to 1876, but she was in America for part of the time, and imported managements came and went with varying success. In 1879 Hare and the Kendals took over, and the theatre at last had a settled policy, which brought a modicum of success. Among their productions were some early plays by Pinero, who was later to figure prominently in the history of the St. James's, and they also engaged the young George Alexander who, after Hare's departure in 1888 and a further period of short-lived managements, took over the theatre himself and inaugurated the most brilliant period in its history. He opened on 31 Jan. 1891 with a transfer of *Sunlight and Shadow* from the Avenue Theatre, and remained at the St. James's until his death. Among his outstanding productions were *Lady Windermere's Fan* (1892), *The Second Mrs. Tanqueray* (1893), in which Mrs. Patrick Campbell made a sensation, *The Importance of Being Earnest* (1895), *The Prisoner of Zenda* (1896), *Paolo and Francesca* (1902), which introduced Henry Ainley to London, *Old Heidelberg* (1903), *His House in Order* (1906), and *The Passing of the Third Floor Back* (1908), with Forbes-Robertson. The last play in which Alexander appeared was *The Aristocrat* (1917). After his death in 1918 Gilbert Miller, the American impresario, took over, and the theatre was subject to a succession of managements. Among successful productions were *The Green Goddess* (1923), with George Arliss, *The Last of Mrs. Cheyney* (1925), produced by Gerald du Maurier with Gladys Cooper, *Michael and Mary* (1930), with Herbert Marshall and Edna Best, an adaptation of *Prenez garde à la peinture* as *The late Christopher Bean* (1933), with Cedric Hardwicke and Edith Evans, a dramatization of *Pride and Prejudice* (1936) with scenery by Rex Whistler, and a fine revival of *A Month in the Country* (1943) in a new version by Emlyn Williams, with Michael Redgrave as Rakitin. The theatre suffered some damage from enemy action, but remained in use, and in 1945 saw the production by Emlyn Williams of his own *Wind of Heaven*, in which he also appeared. A distinguished failure in 1949 was Rattigan's *Adventure Story*, in which Paul Scofield gave an excellent performance as Alexander. In 1950 Laurence Olivier took over, appearing in *Venus Observed* and, with Vivien Leigh, in Shaw's *Caesar and Cleopatra* alternating with Shakespeare's *Antony and Cleopatra*, in celebration of the 1951 Festival of Britain. In the same year the St. James's returned to an old tradition when it housed the French company of Madeleine Renaud and Jean-Louis Barrault in a season which included Salacrou's *Les Nuits de la colère*, and Edwige Feuillère in Claudel's *Partage de midi*. In 1953 there was an Italian season with Ruggero Ruggeri in Pirandello, and a three-weeks' visit from the Comédie-Française. In 1954 *Separate Tables* had a successful run, but the theatre remained empty for long periods, and after a final spate of unmemorable plays, and in spite of energetic protests from the theatrical profession and the play-going public, it finally closed on 27 July 1957. It was then demolished and a block of offices was built on the site. W. MACQUEEN-POPE†, *rev.*

ST. LOUIS, see PIONEER THEATRE IN THE U.S.A.

ST. MARTIN'S THEATRE, LONDON, in West Street, St. Martin's Lane, a small, intimate theatre which opened on 23 Nov. 1916 with C. B. Cochran's production of *Houp La!* This was followed by Brieux's *Damaged Goods*, which created something of a sensation. In 1917 Seymour Hicks appeared in *Sleeping Partners*, and three years later Alec L. Rea took over. The Reandean and Reandco managements, of which he was chairman, then produced a series of plays, many of them by new authors. Among them were *The Skin Game* (1920), *A Bill of Divorcement* (1921), with Meggie Albanesi, *Loyalties* (1922), *Berkeley Square* (1926), *The White Château* (1927), considered by some critics to be the best play yet written about the First World War, *Strange Orchestra* (1932), the first modern play to be produced by John Gielgud, and *The Wind and the Rain* (1933). In 1938 Priestley's Yorkshire comedy, *When We Are Married*, produced by Basil Dean, had a successful run. During the Second World War, and for some years afterwards, the theatre had no settled policy, and short runs came and went, though *The Shop at Sly Corner* (1945), *Penny Plain* (1951), with Joyce Grenfell, *The Rainmaker* (1956), and two plays by Hugh and Margaret Williams, *Plaintiff in a Pretty Hat* (1957) and *The Grass is Greener* (1958), did well.

In the foyer of the theatre is a plaque in memory of Meggie Albanesi, the young actress whose early death was a great loss to the stage, and who made her earliest successes at the St. Martin's Theatre.

W. MACQUEEN-POPE†, *rev.*

SAINTE-BEUVE, CHARLES-AUGUSTIN (1804–69), one of the greatest of French critics, who from 1848, after a short excursion into politics, settled down peaceably to write an essay every Monday for one of several journals. These were later collected and published in a series of volumes—*Causeries du lundi*, *Nouveaux lundis*, *Premiers lundis*—which provide a panorama of the French theatre during his lifetime. As a young man he wrote his first article on Victor Hugo, who became his friend and initiated him into the delights of Romanticism, which he first encouraged but later criticized with much acrimony. He also wrote plays and novels, but finally gave up creative work and became, as he said himself, 'merely a spectator, an analyst'. He was a friend of the actor Molé, and little that went on in the theatre escaped him. He wrote well and fluently, though rather too much, and besides his Monday articles was responsible for many books of theatrical and literary criticism.

ŚAKUNTALĀ, see INDIA.

SALACROU, ARMAND (1899–), French dramatist, whose finest, but perhaps least characteristic, play is *Les Nuits de la colère*, which deals with the German occupation of France during the Second World War. Superbly acted by Barrault and his company, this was first seen at the Marigny in 1946, and in London during the visit of Barrault in 1951. It was broadcast by the B.B.C. as *Men of Wrath*, but has not yet been seen on the stage in English. Unlike Anouilh and Sartre, Salacrou has not yet made contact with the English public, though performances have been given, mainly by student groups, of *L'Archipel Lenoir*, *L'Inconnue d'Arras*, and *Une Femme libre*. The Arts Theatre produced a translation of *Histoire de rire* as *No Laughing Matter* (by Lucienne Hill) in Jan. 1957. Salacrou's other plays include *Un Homme comme les autres*, *La Terre est ronde*, *Les Fiancés du Havre* and *Comme les Chardons*. During the season of 1946–7 three of Salacrou's plays were running simultaneously in Paris. Several of them have been translated into Italian. Detailed studies of his work were written in 1947 by José van den Esch, and in 1951 by Serge Radine.

SALISBURY COURT, LONDON, the last theatre built in London before the Civil War. It was erected in 1629 by Richard Gunnell and William Blagrove at a cost of one thousand pounds. It stood on part of the site of Dorset House, where Salisbury Square, Fleet Street, now stands. It was a 'private' theatre, with a roof; built of brick, it occupied a piece of ground 140 ft. × 40 ft. It was in the possession of the King's Revels from 1629 to 1631, of Prince Charles's Men, 1631 to 1635, of the Queen's Men, 1637 to 1642. During the Commonwealth surreptitious performances were given there, but the interior fittings were destroyed by soldiers in Mar. 1649. William Beeston restored it in 1660, and Rhodes's company played there, as did Davenant's before he built his own theatre near by. In 1661 George Jolly was there, and Beeston himself had a company there from 1663 to 1664. It was burned down in the Great Fire of London, 1666. W. MACQUEEN-POPE†

SALLE DES MACHINES, a small but well-equipped theatre in the Tuileries, built by Vigarani in 1660 to house the spectacular shows given in honour of the marriage of Louis XIV. It continued in use for many years for Court entertainment, and was later under the control of the artist and scenic designer Jean Bérain. It was, however, under Servandony that it reached the height of its splendour, many magnificent spectacles being given there with his designs and machinery.

SALTICA, see FABULA, 7.

SALTIKOV-SHCHEDRIN, MIKHAIL EVGRAFOVICH (1826–89), one of the most brilliant satirists in Russian literature, and the author of one outstanding play, *The Death of Pazukhin*, published during his lifetime, but not performed until 1901. It was revived by the Moscow Art Theatre in 1914, and done by them in New York in 1924. Another, *Shadows*, was found among his papers and first produced in 1914. Both plays reveal the rottenness and corruption of the Tsarist society of the time, a theme to which Saltikov-Shchedrin returned again and again in his other writings. Many of these were subsequently dramatized, though they, and his so-called 'Dramatic Essays', written in dialogue form, were not intended for the stage.

SALT LAKE CITY, see MORMON THEATRE and PIONEER THEATRE IN THE U.S.A.

SALVINI, TOMMASO (1829–1916), Italian actor, child of actors, who was on the stage at 14, appearing with much success in the comedies of Goldoni. In 1847 he joined the company of Adelaide Ristori, then just beginning her successful career, and with her made his first success in tragedy. His life was a succession of triumphs, and he was known all over Europe and America, visiting England frequently, and the U.S.A. five times between 1873 and 1889. On one visit he played Othello to the Iago of Edwin Booth. Othello was always his finest part, and he sensibly refused to play it more than four times a week. He was also good as Macbeth and as King Lear, and in the plays of Alfieri. Among modern parts his best was Conrad in Giacometti's *La morte civile* (1861). He retired in 1890, but in 1902 returned to the stage to take part in the celebrations in Rome in honour of Adelaide Ristori's 80th birthday. He published a volume of memoirs, part of which appeared in English as *Leaves from the Autobiography of Tommaso Salvini* (1893). His son Alessandro (1861–96) was also an actor, and had some success in the United States, while his nephew Guido (1893–1965) was a theatrical designer and director who did much to popularize Pirandello in Italy, and also made many attempts, without success, to found a permanent company in Rome.

SAM H. HARRIS THEATRE, NEW YORK, on the south side of 42nd Street between Broadway and 8th Avenue. This opened on 7 May 1914 and was originally a cinema, as it is today. In between it saw the production of several successful plays, including *On Trial*, *Justice*, and *The Greeks Had a Word For It*, while in 1922 John Barrymore, under the direction of Arthur Hopkins, played Hamlet 101 times, thus breaking by one performance Booth's former record for the part. The theatre reverted to films on 18 Mar. 1933.

GEORGE FREEDLEY†

SAMSON, JOSEPH-ISIDORE (1793–1871), French actor, who entered the Conservatoire at 16, and subsequently spent several years in the provinces. In 1819 he appeared in Paris at the opening of the new Odéon theatre, and made such a good impression that the manager, Picard, retained him as leading man until 1826, when the Comédie-Française claimed his services. There he found himself overshadowed by several older actors, and resigned in order to go to the Palais-Royal. After a few years he returned to the Comédie-Française, where he remained for the rest of his career, making his first success as Bertrand de Rantzau in 1833. In 1843 he became Doyen of the company, and retired in 1863. A handsome man, with a fine profile and a mass of curly hair, he was accounted a good actor, but it is as the teacher of Rachel that he is chiefly remembered. It was his influence that enabled her, at 15, to enter the Conservatoire, and though her father soon took her away in order that she might earn money by acting, she returned to Samson for private lessons. By instructing her in the classical tradition, which he had himself received from Talma, Samson contributed not a little to the revival of French tragedy with which Rachel is associated. He is said to have been one of the finest teachers of acting ever known at the Conservatoire, where he remained on the staff until his death, and many of his pupils became famous. He was also the author of a number of comedies.

SAM S. SHUBERT THEATRE, NEW YORK, see SHUBERT.

SÁNCHEZ, FLORENCIO (1875–1910), see SOUTH AMERICA, 1.

SANDERSON, MARY (?–1712), see BETTERTON (2).

SANDFORD, SAMUEL (*fl.* 1660–99), Restoration actor, a member of Davenant's company at Dorset Garden, and a master of facial expression. He specialized in somewhat wicked characters, and Charles II called him 'the best Villain in the world'.

SAN FRANCISCO, see PIONEER THEATRE IN THE U.S.A.

SAN GALLO, BASTIANO DA (1481–1551), see MACHINERY.

SANGER'S AMPHITHEATRE, LONDON, see ASTLEY'S.

SANQUIRICO, ALESSANDRO (1780–1849), see SCENERY, 4.

SANS PAREIL, LONDON, see ADELPHI THEATRE, 1.

SANS SOUCI, LONDON, a small theatre built by Charles Dibdin at the corner of Leicester Place, Leicester Square, in 1796. Here he appeared in his one-man 'Table Entertainments', of which he was author, composer, narrator, singer, and accompanist, until 1805, when he sold it. Edmund Kean, as a boy, gave acrobatic performances there. Although described as 'an elegant little theatre', it was too small for any save special shows, and became a place for amateur entertainments and benefits. In 1832 it was given over to vaudeville, and in 1834 a French company occupied it. After that it was disused and was pulled down in 1898.

W. MACQUEEN-POPE†

For the Sans Souci, New York, see NIBLO'S GARDEN.

SANSKRIT DRAMA, see INDIA, 1.

SANTURINI, FRANCESCO (1627–82), see SCENERY, 3.

SARAT, AGNAN (?–1613), French provincial actor, who in 1578 took a company to Paris and leased the theatre of the Hôtel de Bourgogne from the Confraternity of the Passion. After a short stay he disappeared again into the provinces, and in 1600 returned to Paris as chief comedian in the company of Valleran-Lecomte, with whom he remained until his death.

SARCEY, FRANCISQUE (1827–99), French dramatic critic, who had an immense following, and by his numerous writings and lecture-tours could make or break a dramatist. Himself convinced of the rightness of his opinion, he could convince his audience, and knew how to gain their confidence from the beginning. He personified for the polyglot audiences that flocked to hear him all over Europe the fat, jolly, gesticulating Frenchman whose common sense one could trust. Many of his dramatic judgements—which were not always reliable, since he distrusted originality in any form—were reprinted in his books, notably *Comédiens et comédiennes* (1878) and *Quarante ans de Théâtre* (1900).

SARDOU, VICTORIEN (1831–1908), French dramatist, and one of the most uniformly successful of his day. Like Scribe, whose successor he was, Sardou wrote copiously on a number of subjects, with expert craftsmanship and superficial brilliance. His first successful play was a comedy, *Les Pattes de mouche* (1860), done in London as *A Scrap of Paper*, but he was equally at home in historical drama, of which the best known is probably *Madame Sans-Gêne* (1893), in melodrama—*Fédora* (1882) and *La Tosca* (1887), later used by Puccini for his opera—and in social drama. Of the last, his *Dora* (1877) and *Divorçons* (1880) are typical. The former, as *Diplomacy*, in a translation by Clement Scott, was for a long time popular with London audiences. Many of Sardou's plays were written for Sarah Bernhardt, to whom they owed much of their success. Sardou, who brought everything to a commonplace level, and judged a play solely as a vehicle for a popular success, has been the cockshy of many critics. Shaw, who disliked everything he stood for, coined the word Sardoodledom to epitomize his 'well-made' play, while Henry James called him 'that supremely clever contriver'. Yet he had great gifts theatrically, and his characters lack only life—but it is a fatal lack.

SAROYAN, WILLIAM (1908–   ), American writer whose plays are marked by improvisatory exuberance and rhapsodic celebration of the common man. He was born of Armenian parents in Fresno, California. After a little schooling, he sold newspapers, carried telegrams, worked in a vineyard, and started writing short stories, first attracting attention with *The Daring Young Man on the Flying Trapeze* (1934). The first of his plays to be produced the long one-act *My Heart's in the Highlands* (1939), was a tender treatment of a poet's struggle to maintain his integrity in a materialistic world. The carefree spirit of the play affirmed its author's faith in man's ability to triumph over bleak reality. Saroyan's next rhapsody, *The Time of Your Life* (1939) (awarded the Pulitzer Prize and the Drama Critics' Award), assembled a motley group of characters whose hungers were counterpointed by a sense of comradeship and assertions of their individuality. Hovering over them was a disenchanted man who dispensed encouragement and money to them on the principle that 'in the time of your life, live—so that in that good time there shall be no ugliness or death for yourself or for any life your life touches'. Less successful but also suffused with sympathy for delicate and frustrated souls were *Love's Old Sweet Song* (1940), which treated the awakening of a genteel spinster by a salesman of bottled panaceas, and *The Beautiful People* (1941), which celebrated the spiritual beauty of a sensitive girl and her shiftless father. The lynching of an innocent tramp was the theme of a distinguished one-act play *Hello Out There* (1942), and an irrepressible young writer's conflict with a ruthless Hollywood mogul was the subject of *Get Away, Old Man* (1943). Saroyan wrote a number of other elusive professionally-unproduced plays, which suffered from chaotic dramaturgy and failed to win support. After some efforts to recover his prestige, he finally prevailed with a touching extravaganza, *The Cave Dwellers* (1957). In 1960 *Sam the Highest Jumper of Them All*, an improvization which was good in patches, was seen in a production by Joan Littlewood at London's Theatre Workshop.

JOHN GASSNER†

SARTHOU, JACQUES (1920–   ), French actor and producer, who made his first appearances singing in night clubs and, after being imprisoned by the Germans during the Second World War, toured the provinces. At 25 he appeared in Vilar's production of *Murder in the Cathedral* at the Vieux-Colombier. He had already written some plays and it was as a playwright that he founded the Association des Jeunes Auteurs Dramatiques. In 1952 he formed a company to bring theatre to the working-class suburbs of Paris, based on the Théâtre de l'Île-de-France. This also performs in summer in the provinces, and has founded several conservatoires of dramatic art in such suburbs as Colombes and Noisy-le-Sec. In 1958 a Centre Culturel Intercommunal was formed, with a total of twenty out of the eighty in the Département de la Seine, and it is hoped that a 700-seat portable auditorium designed by Jacques Bosson, to be known as the Théâtre Ambulant, will soon be opened by Sarthou's company. He is also trying to establish an acting centre in Haute Provence, in the village of Vesc, where he is training a group of young theatre workers who, incidentally, are building their own theatre. In 1961 a Festival of Kremlin-Bicêtre was given in the predominantly working-class south-eastern suburbs of Paris. Among the plays given were Giraudoux's *Supplément au voyage de Cook*, Hugo's *Marie Tudor*, and a triple bill of Molière, de Musset, and Marivaux, all directed by Jean Puyberneau.

SARTRE, JEAN-PAUL (1905–), one of the most controversial of modern French playwrights, and the one who, with Anouilh, has become best-known abroad. His philosophy of existentialism, which he has propagated not only in his plays but in novels and essays, became extremely popular with young people everywhere in the late 1940s, in the mood engendered by the Second World War. His first play, *Les Mouches*, dealt with the legend of Orestes, and was translated into English as *The Flies*; it was followed by *Huis-clos* (*Vicious Circle* or *No Exit*), *Morts sans sépulture* (*Men Without Shadows*), *La Putain respectueuse* (the English title, *The Respectable Prostitute*, is a mistranslation, and would be better rendered *The Respectful Prostitute*, since the woman of the title betrays her coloured lover through a craven respect for the dictates of society), *Les Mains sales* (*Crime Passionnel* or *Red Gloves*—Sartre seems to suffer from alternative titles in English)—and *Le Diable et le Bon Dieu*, which has not yet (1966) been seen in England, though a manuscript translation is in circulation. In 1956 Unity Theatre gave the first English production of *Nekrassov*, in which Robert Helpmann later played the lead at the Royal Court, and Sartre's latest play, *Altona*, was seen in London in 1961. Sartre's plays pose the problem of liberty, with the conclusion that each person must find his or her own solution.

SATYR-DRAMA. The Greek tragic poet had to present four plays at one performance—three tragedies (whether a connected trilogy or not) and a satyr-play. This was a burlesque, in which a hero of myth, often a hero from the trilogy, was introduced in some ludicrous situation, and always in association with a chorus of satyrs. Satyrs, or Sileni, were conceived as creatures of the wild, half-human, half-animal; their stage-costume was indecent, and gave them the ears and tail of a horse.

The origin of this surprising association of tragedy and the satyr-drama is not clear. Aristotle speaks of tragedy 'developing out of the satyric, with its short plots and ludicrous diction'; some modern scholars, naturally, find this difficult to believe. Certainly the dramatic form of the satyr-drama resembled that of tragedy—definite episodes were separated, or linked, by choral odes; and the metre was the metre of tragedy, not of comedy—but this may be due to imitation. The characteristics of the satyr-drama were rude action, vigorous dancing, boisterous fun, and indecency in speech and gesture.

Arion is said to have been the first to make the satyr-revel metrical in form; elsewhere Pratinas, a century later, is said to have been the 'first to write satyr-plays'. It seems that the satyr-play must have formed part of the tragic contest when that was instituted by Pisistratus at the festival of Dionysus; though the connexion between satyrs and Dionysus is not clear either. Pratinas and Aeschylus were regarded as the great masters of the satyr-drama. One satyr-play survives entire, the *Cyclops* of Euripides; another in part, the *Ichneutae* of Sophocles. During the fifth century there was at least a partial modification of the tradition, inasmuch as Euripides' *Alcestis*, a tragicomedy, was presented in lieu of a satyr-play.

There is no connexion whatever between satyric drama and satire, or between it and any form of Greek comedy. H. D. F. KITTO

SAURIN, BERNARD-JOSEPH (1706–81), French dramatist, originally a lawyer. A pension from a wealthy friend enabled him at 40 to retire and devote himself entirely to literature, for which he had a great aptitude. He was the author of a successful tragedy, *Spartacus* (1760), of a comedy, *Les Mœurs du temps* (1759), and of a *drame bourgeois*, *Béverlei* (1768), based on Moore's *The Gamester*. It was probably taken from Diderot's translation of the latter, for there is no evidence that Saurin knew English, and represents the most serious of several attempts to introduce contemporary English drama to France. But Saurin omits much of the melodrama, and concentrates on the pathetic situation of Béverlei's family, including Tomi, his infant son. Of all Saurin's plays it is the most interesting to read nowadays. Of the rest, the actors, says Clairon, who played in it, had great hopes of *Blanche et Guiscard* (1763), but it was disappointingly received. This, too, is based on an English play, Thomson's *Tancred and Sigismunda*, given at Drury Lane in 1745.

SAVILLE THEATRE, LONDON, in Shaftesbury Avenue. This opened on 8 Oct. 1931 under the management of Jack Waller with *For the Love of Mike*, a musical play which proved successful. It was followed by further musical plays, including a musical version of *Ambrose Applejohn's Adventure*, which starred Bobby Howes, entitled *He Wanted Adventure* (1933). *Jill Darling!*, starring Frances Day, was successful in 1934, and the theatre continued to house musical comedy and revue until the end of 1938, when it turned to straight plays with Shaw's *Geneva*, and, later, a transfer of *Johnson Over Jordan*. The theatre was damaged by enemy action in 1940–1, but was hastily repaired and carried on, mainly with musicals and light comedy, until in 1955 John Clements took over and inaugurated a fine series of revivals which continued until 1957 and included Ibsen, Shaw, and Chekhov. Later productions of note were *A Touch of the Sun*, with Michael Redgrave and his daughter Vanessa, *Expresso Bongo* (both 1958), Evelyn Laye in *The Amorous Prawn* (1960), Ustinov's *Photo*

Finish (1962), and Harry Secombe in a musical, *Pickwick* (1963). W. MACQUEEN-POPE†, *rev.*

SAVOY THEATRE. 1. LONDON, built and opened by D'Oyly Carte in Oct. 1881 with *Patience*, transferred from the Opera Comique. With its delicate colouring, quilted silk curtain, and electric lighting, it struck a new note in theatres. Here were staged the Gilbert and Sullivan light operas, and all, including those which first appeared at the Royalty or the Opera Comique, are now labelled with the name of the Savoy. After a long series of successes, and some failures, which included the last collaboration between Gilbert and Sullivan, *The Grand Duke* (1896), the reign of light opera came to an end with *Merrie England* (1901) and *The Princess of Kensington* (1903). Later Harley Granville-Barker came from the Royal Court Theatre, and did some notable Shaw and Shakespeare productions (see No. 77). In 1910 H. B. Irving took over the Savoy, and from then until his death in 1919 he appeared there in many plays, including *Hamlet*. It was at this theatre that the children's play, *Where the Rainbow Ends*, was first given in 1911. It was revived annually for many years, though not at the Savoy, and in 1954 and 1955 was seen at the Festival Hall. Later successes at the Savoy included *Paddy the Next Best Thing* (1920), *The Young Idea* (1923), by Nöel Coward (whose *Sail Away* was to come there in 1962), *Young Woodley* (1928), and *Journey's End* (1929). When this last play closed in Dec. the theatre was rebuilt and redecorated, and opened again on 21 Oct. 1929 with a revival of *The Gondoliers*, the first Gilbert and Sullivan since 1909. Further revivals of Savoy operas followed, and proved popular, but during the latter 1930s the theatre was used mainly for transfers. In 1941 *The Man Who Came To Dinner* had a long run, as did *My Sister Eileen* (1943) and *Life With Father* (1947). Later successes were *The Gazebo* (1960) and *The Masters* (1963). W. MACQUEEN-POPE†, *rev.*

2. NEW YORK. This theatre opened as Schley's Music-Hall in Feb. 1900, playing only vaudeville, and in October of the same year changed its name and policy. It housed a number of musical shows, and transfers of successful plays from other theatres, but had a somewhat uneventful history and eventually became a cinema. GEORGE FREEDLEY†

SAXE-MEININGEN, see MEININGER COMPANY.

SCALA, FLAMINIO (*fl.* 1600–21), an important figure of the *commedia dell'arte*, known as Flavio. He was concerned with the second group of Confidenti, and more occupied with their business management, of which his letters reveal many interesting details, than with acting. He was the author of a collection of *scenarii* printed in 1611.

SCALA THEATRE, LONDON. In 1772 the musician Francis Pasquali built a concert room in Tottenham Street, Tottenham Court Road, which after a successful career, during which it was known as the King's Concert Rooms, was bought and enlarged by the committee for the Concerts of Antient Music, whose performances were patronized by George III. In 1802 it became the headquarters of a private theatrical club known as the Pic-Nics, whose success earned them the hostility of the patent theatres. In 1808 they were replaced by a circus, which was not successful. The hall then closed, but reopened as a theatre on 23 Apr. 1810 with *Love In a Village*. It had been bought by John Paul, a gunsmith in the Strand, to gratify his wife's theatrical ambitions. These brought him to the Bankruptcy Court, and in Dec. 1814 the building was sold to Harry Beverley, father of the well-known scene-painter, who opened it as the Regency Theatre. It struggled on for six years, and after falling into decay was refurbished and opened again as the West London under Brunton, father of the actress Elizabeth, later Mrs. Yates, who starred in a number of his productions. The famous actor Frédérick appeared with a French company in 1826, but the theatre was constantly in trouble with the patent theatres, and closed until 1831. As the Queen's, or alternatively the Fitzroy, it had a chequered career, until under the scenic artist, C. L. James it sank to lurid melodrama, and became known as the Dust Hole. In 1865 Marie Wilton took it over. Completely redecorated, and renamed, by permission, the Prince of Wales's, it opened in the presence of the future Edward VII and was immediately successful. It was here that T. W. Robertson's epoch-making 'cup-and-saucer' dramas were first produced, beginning with *Society* in 1865; other important productions were *Masks and Faces* (1875) and *Diplomacy* (1878). Marie Wilton's leading man was Squire Bancroft, whom she later married, and together they built up an excellent company in which many well-known actors of the period, including Ellen Terry, Robertson's sister Madge and her husband W. H. Kendal, and John Hare, were happy to appear. By the time the Bancrofts left to go to the Haymarket, the despised Dust Hole had become a fashionable theatre. Their last production was a revival of *Ours*, which closed on 24 Feb. 1880. Edgar Bruce then took over and presented Genevieve Ward in a revival of *Forget-Me-Not* and other plays, in some of which she was partnered by the young Beerbohm Tree. In 1882 the theatre was condemned as structurally unsound, and was closed for repairs. Owing to a long-drawn-out dispute, it did not reopen until 1905, being used for part of the time as a Salvation Army hostel. In 1903 it was bought by a wealthy surgeon, Dr. Distin Maddick, who had happy memories of early playgoing there, and completely rebuilt, only the portico entrance of the old theatre being left to serve as the stage-door entrance. Renamed the Scala, it opened on 23 Sept. 1905 under the management of Forbes-Robertson with *The Conqueror*, in which his wife, Gertrude Elliott played a leading part. Unfortunately the theatre was not a success, and was often empty. It was used spasmodically for films and for special matinées. It housed dancers, puppets, amateur productions, Gilbert and Sullivan, and, during the 1930s, Ralph Reader's *Gang Show*. It was slightly damaged by enemy action in 1940–1, but remained usable and in 1943 was the headquarters of the U.S. Army Theatre Unit. Apart from an annual revival of *Peter Pan* at Christmas, the theatre was used mainly by amateurs until it was demolished in 1970.

W. MACQUEEN-POPE†, *rev.*

SCAMMACCA, ORTENSIO (1562–1648), an Italian Jesuit, author of nearly fifty plays on sacred or moral themes, intended ostensibly for the edification of the faithful, but containing a good deal of sensational matter, eked out with love intrigues, and interlarded with piety. The religious element is, however, preponderant, and even in plays drawn from classical sources angels and devils make their appearance, while women, contrary to the usual practice of Jesuit drama, are given important parts.

SCAMOZZI, VINCENZO (1552–1616), Italian architect, pupil of the great Palladio, whose Teatro Olimpico at Vicenza he finished after his master's death (see No. 20). He was also responsible for the building of the Sabbionetta theatre (see No. 21; also ARCHITECTURE, 4 and SCENERY, 2).

SCANDINAVIA. Of the four Scandinavian countries, each of which has produced a remarkable literature, only Denmark has what might be termed a typical European dramatic history, beginning, like England, France, Germany, and Italy, with medieval religious drama and the later School Drama, or its equivalent, and thereafter producing plays, now predominantly native, now influenced in varying degrees by the great movements of general European literary history: seventeenth-century classicism, Romanticism, and so forth. Like the other European literatures, it has had periods predominantly dramatic or marked by the emergence of great dramatists, alternating with others relatively unproductive in this field, but since the seventeenth century it has never for long been entirely sterile. In this way it may be said to conform to the broad pattern of European drama, possessing, like other literatures, though not necessarily in the same order as any other, its systole and diastole.

But the dramatic history of each of the other countries is, in one way or another, peculiar to itself. Iceland, even in the great saga period (approximately thirteenth century), produced no drama, though often showing a strong underlying dramatic instinct; not until the late nineteenth and early twentieth centuries did a drama begin to grow up under the stimulus of the rest of Scandinavia, Europe, and America (see ICELAND). Norway, whose literary history in every branch is affected by the union with Denmark in the late fourteenth century and the gradual substitution of the Danish for the native language, produced indeed, in the eighteenth and early nineteenth centuries, dramatists whose spirit, and sometimes subject-matter, was essentially Norwegian, but who wrote in Danish and were partially assimilated into Danish literature. Its great native contributions to drama did not come until the second half of the nineteenth century, with Bjørnson and Ibsen. Then, at one stroke, by the work of Ibsen, it produced the most potent influence in European drama for what is now nearly a century. A glance over Norwegian literature, however, makes it clear that the genius of the nation has always been, potentially if not actually, dramatic, and that the leading place it has taken in European drama since the rise of Ibsen has not been accidental. The history of Swedish drama has been completely different again from the other three. Here, on the contrary, it would seem that the genius of the race was not essentially dramatic. All the facilities for drama have been there, as they were in Denmark and the rest of Europe, from the sixteenth century, and there has in fact been a continuous stream of dramatists. But most of them were either imitators of Danish, German, French, or English playwrights, or poets who, engaging more happily in some other form of literary expression, found there their distinction and international reputation. Not until the coming of Strindberg at the end of the nineteenth century did Sweden, in spite of its advantages, produce a dramatist who, *as* a dramatist, had even a limited reputation outside Scandinavia.

1. DENMARK. (*a*) *Drama.* The history of Danish drama begins in the sixteenth century, where the presence of relatively late medieval forms suggests that there had been, to some extent, an earlier drama also. No records remain to indicate a body of Danish drama comparable with that of England, France, and Holland in the thirteenth, fourteenth, and fifteenth centuries, and only the School Drama of Christiern Hansen (?–post 1545) (*Den Utro Hustru* and *Dorothiae Komedie*), and of Hieronymus Justesen Ranch (1539–1607), and the anonymous *Ludus de Sancto Kanuto Duce* (1530), survive to indicate varying degrees of independence in the use of native sources. Most important of these are perhaps Ranch's *Kong Salomons Hylding* (1584), *Karrig Niding* (1598), and *Samsons Fængsel* (1599). The absence of vernacular plays throughout the seventeenth century (a fact remarked upon by Holberg himself), coupled with the tradition of producing French and German plays in the Copenhagen theatres in the early eighteenth century, suggests that, with the disappearance of the ecclesiastical and scholastic Latin or vernacular School Drama, dramatic writing ceased for a time in Denmark. It was re-created at one stroke by Holberg.

Ludvig Holberg (1684–1754), though a Norwegian by birth, worked in Copenhagen and was the first dramatist to use the Danish language. He had a strong influence upon Danish drama, setting an example of realistic comedy combining the technique of the classics and of Molière that was the more important in that Danish literature was soon afterwards exposed to strong German influences. Without the steadying effects of Holberg's authority in native comedy, Danish poets and dramatists, who assimilated the influence of Klopstock and the 'bardic' German poetry that the Norwegians resisted, might have postponed the development of a native Danish drama.

Johannes Ewald (1743–81) was the first to experience this sympathy with contemporary German inspiration and to carry it over into drama. He followed Holberg in so far as he wrote in Danish, but in little else. One of Denmark's great lyric poets, he wrote its first tragedies, beginning with the dramatic poem, *Adam og Eva* (pub. 1769), and passing on to drama proper with *Rolf Krage* (1770) and *Balders Død* (1774). His genius gradually freed itself from the German influence and in *Fiskerne* in 1778 his power as a dramatic poet and native dramatist produced the finest of his works. This and two fragments that his early death left unfinished show tendencies and potentialities so far unknown in Europe.

At the death of Ewald, Denmark was on the verge of the *Guldalderen* (the Golden Age) in which her poets were from time to time dramatists and her dramatists poets. Ole Samsøe with the *Dyveke* (1796) marks the end of the eighteenth century, and the nineteenth opens with the works of Otto Carl Olufsen (1764–1827), whose *Gulddaasen* (1793) was probably the best comedy since Holberg, and Peder Andreas Heiberg (1758–1841), leading on to the astonishing succession of Oehlenschlaeger, J. L. Heiberg, Hertz, and Hauch.

Adam Oehlenschlaeger (1779–1850) is generally considered to have had a greater influence upon Danish drama than any other writer except Holberg, and it was an influence that balanced Holberg's. He was a writer of tragedies upon native themes, some of them historical or legendary, but essentially northern, a romantic whose romanticism led on from the later work of Ewald, converting rather than counteracting the German influences of the eighteenth century. At a period when the energies of Norwegians were necessarily preoccupied with establishing their Constitution and their nationality, Danish nationalism was rich in imaginative, poetic, and dramatic expression. Oehlenschlaeger's most characteristic plays are *St. Hans Aften-Spil* (1802), *Hakon Jarl* (1807), *Baldur hin Gode* (1808), and *Helge* (1814).

Johan Ludvig Heiberg (1791–1860) was a writer of a wholly different kind, whose popular romantic dramas gradually took precedence over the tragedy of Oehlenschlaeger. His gifts were varied, extending to realistic comedy on one side and strongly influential literary criticism upon the other. His familiarity with Paris and Parisian culture was of no little value at this period of Denmark's dramatic history. Between 1847 and 1854 his directorship of the National Theatre gave him yet another sphere of influence. Characteristic of his romantic plays are *Elverhøj* (1828) and *Fata Morgana* (1838), and of his comedies and satires *En Sjæl efter Døden* (1841) and *Nøddeknækkerne* (1845). At the other extreme are his vaudevilles, realistic comedies with songs on topical Danish themes, though on French models.

The sentimental drama of Bernhard Severin Ingemann (1789–1862) had great popularity and he sometimes threw the work of Oehlenschlaeger into the shade in the affections of the Danish public by his national, historical novels. He was a prolific writer, perhaps best remembered as a dramatist by his *Sulamith og Salomon* (1839).

Henrik Hertz (1798–1870), who was of Jewish parentage, wrote chiefly comedies, realistic or romantic, but he is remembered also for at least one romantic national drama and two tragedies. He also made a notable excursion into criticism in sympathy with J. L. Heiberg. His most characteristic comedies are, perhaps, *Herr Burchardt og hans Familie* and *Flyttedager* (both 1827). These were followed until 1836 by other comedies, including *Sparekassen*, and in 1837 by *Svend Dyrings Hus*, a national drama drawn from folk-tales, and the famous *Kong Renes Datter* (1843), which was widely translated. The tragedy *Ninon* (1848) and the romantic comedy *Tonietta* (1849) represent the work of his middle years. From the later plays may be mentioned *Et Offer* (1854), *En Kurmethode* (1861), and *Tre Dage i Padua* (1869), his last play.

Thomas Overskou (1798–1873), the dramatic critic and historian, also left a number of plays, of which *Pak* (1845) is probably the best known.

From the middle of the century onwards come the tragedies and historical dramas of Johannes Carsten Hauch (1790–1872), of which the best known is probably *Marsk Stig* (1850). He, with Jens Christian Hostrup (1818–92), bridges the gulf between the dramatists of the Golden Age and the group in the later nineteenth century forming part of the movement that originated with Georg Brandes (1842–1927). This eminent critic swayed literary opinion in Denmark and far beyond, and was one of the first, as he is still the best, of the supporters of Ibsen.

Earliest of this circle to leave a considerable mark was Holger Drachmann (1846–1908), poet and lyric dramatist, who was at the end of the century the most popular playwright of Denmark. Best known of his plays are, perhaps, *Der var en Gang* (1885), *Vølund Smed* (1894), *Brav Karl* (1898) in which he made his name, *Gurre* (1899), *Halfred Vandraadeskjald* (1900), and *Det Grönne Haab*. His strength was in the poetic and lyrical quality of his dramas rather than in their structure and form.

With Edvard Brandes (1847–1931) and Otto Benzon (1856–1927) the characteristic modern drama sets in, analytical and critical of contemporary society as that of Norway, France, and England also became, as soon as the influence of

Bjørnson and Ibsen was felt. Edvard Brandes' *Et Besøg* (1882) and Benzon's *En Skandale* (1884) show the tendency clearly.

From the late nineteenth century to the present day the Danish drama may be roughly divided into two phases, that of the period before the 1930s and that of the 1930s onwards. The early twentieth century was a period of fertility; there were few major dramatists but a number of plays of some distinction. The most familiar names are those of Einar Christiansen, Sven Lange, Henri Nathansen (the dramatist of Jewish problems), Olaf Hansen, and, outstanding among their contemporaries, Hjalmar Bergström, Gustav Wied, and Helge Rode.

Helge Rode (1870–1937) is a poetic dramatist of religious and national problems, whose plays are less well known outside Scandinavia than those of Bergström and Wied. Hjalmar Bergström (1868–1914) is a dramatist of social problems closely related to Ibsen's tradition, whose best-known plays are, perhaps, *Lyngaard & Co.* (1905), *Karen Bornemann* (1907), and *Dame-Te* (1910). Gustav Wied (1858–1914) is a highly original novelist and dramatist with close affiliations, this time, to Strindberg. He began his dramatic career with a series of small satirical plays distinguished by their wit and the quality of their dialogue. His best-known play is probably *Ranke Viljer* (1906), translated into English as *2×2 = 5*.

Two outstanding dramatists of later years were Kaj Munk and Kjeld Abell.

Kaj Munk (1898–1944) represents a drama unlike that of his immediate forerunners, a theatre of action and not of psychological dissection. Many of his plays are historical, *En Idealist* (1928), *Cant* (1934), *De Udvalgte* (1933), *Sejren* (1936), *Pilatus* (1937), and finally *Niels Ebbesen* (1943), the play by which his name is best known, by reason of the associations which surround it. Notable among his non-historical plays are *I Brændingen* (1929), *Ordet* (1932), which will probably prove to be his greatest play, and *Han Sidder ved Smeltediglen* (1938).

Kjeld Abell (1902–1961) was a brilliant man of the theatre who wrote some extremely interesting plays. Best known, perhaps, in Denmark and elsewhere, are *Melodien, der blev væk* (1935), a lyrical play done in England as *The Melody that got Lost*, and the more serious *Anna Sophie Hedvig* (1939), a play whose ideological implications link with the work of Kaj Munk and the Norwegian writer Nordahl Grieg (see NORWAY).

UNA ELLIS-FERMOR†

(*b*) *Theatre.* The first step towards the development of a truly Danish theatre was taken in the time of Ludvig Holberg, when in 1722 Denmark's first permanent theatre for the production of plays in the language of the country was established in Copenhagen. Previous to this, the drama in Denmark had been almost exclusively in the hands of foreign travelling companies. One of the first productions was Holberg's *Den Politiske Kandestøber* (1722). This theatre succumbed to puritanical opposition after only three years; but in 1748 it was re-established on a new site by King Frederik V, with Holberg as literary consultant. In 1772 it became the Kongelige Teater (the Royal Theatre); the building itself was renovated in 1773–4, and it continued under the control of the Court until 1849, when it passed to the Ministry of Culture. In 1874 it acquired new premises, and from 1876 until 1894 was directed by E. Fallesen, who made a speciality of presenting the plays of Ibsen and Bjørnson. Apart from the Royal Theatre, Copenhagen has several other first-class theatres, including the Dagmarteater, Casinoteater, Folketeater and Det Nye Teater. Provincial theatres of high standing include those of Odense and Aarhus; and the Royal Theatre also regularly sends a travelling company round the provinces.

The end of the nineteenth century and the beginning of the twentieth witnessed a great blossoming of theatrical talent in Denmark. Among the distinguished players one might mention Betty Hennings and the brothers Emil and Olaf Poulsen in the first wave, followed by Johannes Poulsen, Else Skouboe, Eyvind Johan-Svendsen, Bodil Ipsen, Clara Pontoppidan, Poul Reumert, Holger Gabrielsen (also a distinguished producer), Berthe Qvistgaard, Bodil Kjer, Henrik Bentzon, Ingeborg Brams, Ebbe Rode, and Mogens Wieth (1919–62), who died in London shortly before he was to have appeared with the Old Vic company in *Othello*. L. KATHLEEN MCFARLANE

Denmark was one of the first countries to translate and act the plays of Shakespeare. The famous Danish actor, Peter Foersom, who died in 1817, made a number of versions, beginning with *Hamlet* in 1813, in which he himself played the title-role. In 1873 Edward Lembcke translated all the plays except *Titus Andronicus* and *Pericles*. His versions are still used in the theatre. Valdemar Osterberg published a number of more literary translations with excellent introductions and notes, intended mainly for reading. The best of the nineteenth-century Danish actors in Shakespeare was probably the great comedian Olaf Poulsen, whose Falstaff and Bottom were famous. In the early twentieth century the theatre historian, manager, and actor Karl Mantzius arranged an approximation of an Elizabethan stage in the Royal Theatre, Copenhagen, and appeared there as Richard III, Lear, Shylock, Aguecheek, and Mark Antony in *Julius Caesar*. From 1926 to 1937 Poulsen's nephew, Johannes Poulsen, also appeared in a number of Shakespearian parts, and contributed to something of a revolution in Danish ideas of the plays. Before and after the Second World War a *Hamlet* festival took place at Elsinore, with companies from different countries appearing in the play. From England came Olivier, Gielgud, and Redgrave and, among Continental actors, Gustaf Gründgens from Germany. ED.

2. NORWAY. (*a*) *Drama.* As has been said

above, the drama of Norway is bound up with that of Denmark—in fact until the separation of 1814, and in effect for some years longer. There is some evidence that Norway had a share in the School Drama of the late sixteenth century, probably in the form of plays in Norse and Latin mixed; there would appear to have been no other regular theatrical activity apart from that afforded by Denmark. A fresh development is indicated by the opening of the theatre in Christiania in 1837 (its predecessor having been burnt in 1835), but its personnel remained Danish for some years. The first national theatre (Den Nationale Scene) was created at Bergen by the initiative of Ole Borneman Bull (1810–80), the musician, and opened only in 1850. The early years of Norwegian dramatic history are thus somewhat confused, as it is difficult to say to what extent the three earliest dramatists, Holberg, Brun, and Wessel, can be regarded as Norwegian, seeing that they owed to Copenhagen their theatrical education, the production of their plays, and their audiences. A measure of acclimatization is inevitable, since the nature of an audience and the traditions of a theatre have a powerful shaping influence upon the work of a dramatist. It has, however, seemed best to regard them here as Norwegian, and the significant history of that drama may therefore be said to begin in 1721.

In that year Ludvig Holberg became director of the Danish theatre in Copenhagen (doubling the post with that of Professor of Metaphysics in the university), and began to write plays in Danish, or Dano-Norwegian, the language of the educated classes throughout the *Tvillingrikene* (the 'twin-kingdoms'). Hitherto the Danish theatre had produced only plays in French or German, but for the next six years Holberg poured out comedies written not only in the native language but about native types, Danish or Norwegian or both. He was a scholar who knew his Aristophanes, his Plautus, his Terence, but above all his Molière and his *commedia dell'arte*. But he was primarily a comic genius who, while using the technique and forms of the great comedy-writers of the past, drew his material from what lay at hand. The Danish people saw for the first time their customs, habits, and civilization presented in the mirror of comedy, the Danish and Norwegian literatures (as yet unseparated) were founded, the native language acclimatized, if only temporarily, upon the stage, and for this, as much as for his activities as a historian and a philosopher, the early eighteenth century in Denmark and Norway is known as 'The Age of Holberg'. His first play, *Den Politiske Kandestøber* (1722), and the later *Erasmus Montanus* (1723) are among the best known.

After Holberg the output flags. The lead in drama passes from Norway to Denmark with the work of Ewald, but among the Norwegian writers resident in Copenhagen and forming Det Norske Selskab (The Norwegian Club) some were dramatists, if only to the extent of one remarkable play. Nordahl Brun (1745–1816) produced in 1772 a tragedy, *Zarine*, in the fashionable French tradition, and a little later *Einer Tambeskielver*, an early example of the patriotic saga-dramas popular for the next hundred years. *Zarine* was one of those plays which call for parody, and it got it. A parody by Johan Wessel (1742–85), *Kjærlighed uden Strømper*, a brilliant mock-tragedy, destroyed not only *Zarine*, but the outworn tradition it represented. Wessel was a comedy-writer of Holberg's own kind, but he wrote very little more: *Lykken bedre end Forstanden* (1776) is perhaps the best known.

Nor did the period that followed present any activity comparable with Holberg's. During the next half century some of Norway's most distinguished poets from time to time wrote plays and, more fortunate than their contemporaries in England, had their plays produced. But, coinciding with the Golden Age in Denmark, it is a barren period. The energies of the nation appear to have been absorbed in the political efforts leading up to and following the creation of the Constitution and the separation from Denmark in 1814.

Henrik Bjerregaard (1792–1842) produced a musical play, *Fjeldeventyret* (1824), which was native in material and setting, and Henrik Arnold Wergeland (1808–45), though it was not his medium, wrote several plays. Of these, the first was *Irreparabile Tempus* (1828) and the finest *Venetianerne* (1841); he wrote also some plays, such as *The Campbells* (1837), on English subjects. Andreas Munch (1811–84), son of Johan Storm Munch, again turned sometimes from verse to playwriting, contributing *Kong Sverres Ungdom*, the prize-winning play of 1838, an English-history play, *Lord William Russell* (1857), which was the subject of much discussion, and the unfortunate *Hertug Skule* which, appearing in 1864, was immediately eclipsed by Ibsen's *Kongsemnerne*. Finally, the great linguist and philologist Ivar Aasen (1813–96) produced *Ervingen*, a popular musical play, in 1855 (one of its songs, 'Millom bakkar og berg', being the most popular national song even today).

But in that year Henrik Johan Ibsen (1828–1906) had already written his earliest plays and Bjørnstjerne Bjørnson (1832–1910) was just beginning. Between them these two dramatists revolutionized Norwegian thought, literature, and language, and carried the dramatic reputation of the country ahead of that of any other in Europe. Bjørnson's work in drama was less than Ibsen's both in quantity and in power, but he carried great weight in his own day because of his further reputation as a novelist and song-writer, and his immense popularity as a political leader. Ibsen's influence upon Norwegian civilization is occasionally lost sight of only because the world has been primarily concerned with estimating his influence upon the world's. Bjørnson's early historical plays and Ibsen's great poetic dramas, *Brand* (1866) and *Peer Gynt* (1867), stirred the national imagination, and Ibsen's astounded Europe. Bjørnson's realistic and contemporary analyses and condemnation of the errors of society, culminating in *En Handske* in 1883, in part preceded Ibsen's similar but graver and more profound studies of social evils. Both brought some salutary shocks and disturbance to the complacency of the society they condemned and, at least in Ibsen's case, to many similar societies outside Norway. When Ibsen died in 1906 Scandinavian drama was established among the great dramatic literatures of history.

The modern period has produced until recently no outstanding figures except Heiberg and Kinck, though again, men of great reputation as novelists or poets have from time to time written plays. Jonas Lie is known for *Lystige Koner* (1894), a social comedy, and *Lindelin* (1897); Alexander Kielland for *Paa Hjemveien* (1878), a comedy on business morality, *Hans Majestats Foged* and *Det Hele er Ingenting* (both 1880), *Bettys Formynder* (1887), a study of modern women, and *Professoren* (1888), on the conflict between the old and the new worlds in university life; Arne Garborg for *Uforsonlige* (1888) and *Læraren* (1896); Knut Hamsun for a number of plays, some of them comparable with his novels, of which the best-known are, perhaps, the trilogy *Ved Rikets Port* (1895), *Livets Spil* (1896), and *Aftenrøde* (1898). To these may be added *Livet Ivold* and the eight-act dramatic poem *Munken Vendt* (1903).

Gunnar Heiberg (1857–1929) is, however, essentially a dramatist, a writer of great skill and originality, often satiric and often showing some affinity with Ibsen's last phase. His *Tante Ulrikke* appeared in 1884, *Kong Midas* in 1890, and the two plays by which he is best known, *Balkonen* and *Kjærlighedens Tragedie*, iu 1894 and 1904. To these may be added *Det Store Lod* (1895), *Folkeraadet* (1897), *Harald Svans Mor* (1899), *Kjærlighed til Næsten* (1902), *Jeg vil verge mit Land* (1912) and *Paradesengen* (1913).

Another fine dramatic artist is Hans Kinck (1865–1926), whose *Driftekaren*, a play on the theme of the erratic emergence of genius, with its sequel *Paa Rindalslægret* (1925), is sometimes compared with *Peer Gynt*. His plays on Italian themes are, in addition, works of learning: *Agilulf den Vise* (1906), *Den Sidste Gjest* (1910), *Mot Karneval* and *Paa Ekrenes Gaard* (both 1913). To the early years of this century belong also the works of Peter Egge; Hans Aanrud—*Storken* (1895), *Höit til hest* (1901), *Hanen* (1906); Gabriel Scott—*Himmeluret* (1905), and *Babelstaarn* (1910); Hans Wiers-Jenssen—*Anne Pedersdotter* (1908); Gabriel Finne; Sigurd Ibsen; Anders Stiloff; Nils Collett Vogt; Johan Bojer; Vilhelm Krag—*Baldevins Bryllup* (1900). Outstanding slightly later was Nils Kjær (1870–1924), with satirical comedy and the drama of contemporary political and religious problems: *Regnskabets dag* (1902), *Mimosas Hjemkomst* (1907), *Det lykkelige Valg* (1913), and *For Træet er det Haab* (1917). Here, too, should be mentioned the Landsmaal writer, Vetle Vislie.

The most notable names in Norwegian drama of the immediate past are Helge Krog (1889–1962) and Nordahl Grieg (1902–43); the difference between them is considerable and obvious. Krog was an acute and subtle psychologist whose perception of the undertones of human relations remained his chief characteristic whatever material he used and whatever the mood of his play. His dialogue had the skill and fineness of finish associated with certain schools of modern French dramatists. Some of his most remarkable plays are *Det store Vi* (1919), *Jarlshus* (1923), *På Solsiden* (1927), *Blåpapiret* (1928), *Konkylien* (1929), *Underveis* (1931), *Treklang* (1933), and, perhaps the most notable of all, *Opbrud* (1936).

Nordahl Grieg, whose death in action in 1943 robbed Norway and Europe of one of their most promising younger dramatists, was a writer of power and of passionate thought, an experimenter in material and technique whose final form had hardly declared itself. His two most notable plays made a strong impression both in Scandinavia and abroad; the first, *Vår Aere og Vår Makt* (1935), was an anti-war play of overwhelming force and originality, and the second, *Nederlaget* (1936), was a tragedy of the Paris Commune which has become famous far beyond Scandinavia, and influenced Brecht in his writing of *Die Tage der Kommune*. His earlier plays were *En Ung Mands Kjærlighet* and *Barabbas* (both 1927), and *Atlanterhavet* (1932), to which should be added *Men imorgen* (1936).

UNA ELLIS-FERMOR†

(*b*) *Theatre*. It was not until the beginning of the nineteenth century that a serious interest in the theatre began to show itself in Norway. Before this time, a theatrical company (founded in 1770) had existed in Christiania (later Oslo), in which Bernt Anker and Envold de Falsen had been the moving spirits; but it was only in 1800 and 1802 that the first theatres were built in Bergen and Christiania respectively. In 1827, the first public theatre was opened in Christiania by J. P. Stromberg; this burned down, and in 1837 was replaced by the Christiania Teater, of which however the control and the repertoire were predominantly Danish. It was not until much later in the century that the Danish dominance in the theatres of Norway was finally overcome. The first attempt to establish a genuinely Norwegian theatrical tradition was made by the poet and dramatist Henrik Wergeland in the 1830s; in 1850 a theatre with Norwegian actors and producers was founded in Bergen by Ole Bull, and in 1825 a Norsk Teater began operating in Christiania; the former of these theatres was forced by financial difficulties to close down in 1863, and did not reopen until 1876, whilst the latter theatre lasted as an independent institution only until 1863, when it was merged with the capital's other and more Danishly inclined theatre, the Christiania Teater. Both Ibsen and Bjørnson held appointments at these Bergen and

Christiania theatres, and it was here they learned their craft. The most talented players of this age were Laura Gundersen and Johannes Brun. In 1884, the dramatist Gunnar Heiberg followed the example of Ibsen and Bjørnson by accepting appointments first in Bergen and then in Christiania. With the building of the present Nationalteater in Christiania in 1899, and the establishment of a company there under the direction of Bjørn Bjørnson (1859–1942), son of the dramatist, the theatre finally became firmly established in Norway. This resulted in the emergence of many distinguished actors and actresses, the most illustrious being Johanne Dybwad (1867–1950), famous not only in Scandinavia generally, but also in England, Germany, and France for her performances in the roles of Ibsen's heroines. In 1913 the Norske Teater, intended for the performance of plays in *nynorsk*, was added to the metropolitan theatres, and in 1929 the Nye Teater was started, at which Lillebil Ibsen was a brilliant leading lady and Gyda Christensen an outstanding director. The Riksteater, a state travelling company, was formed in 1948 under the direction of Frits von der Lippe, with Ingolf Rogde as its leading actor; this company gives performances all over the country in local theatres and halls, and also occasionally performs abroad. The capital's most recent theatre is the Folketeater, which opened in 1952 under the direction of Hans Jacob Nilsen, the present director being Jens Gundersen, and its leading players Else Heiberg, Ola Isene, and Per Sunderland. Among Norway's leading players in recent times should be mentioned Stein Grieg Halvorsen, Knut Wigert, Liv Strømstad, Wenche Foss, Helen Brinchmann, Agnes Mowinkel, Gerda Grieg, Tore Segelcke, Aase Bye, Hans Jacob Nilsen, Tordis Maurstad, Lars Tvinde, Per Aabel, and Olafr Havrevold; and among producers the names of Knut Tomasen and Tormod Skagestad. The Nationalteater, Norske Teater, and Folketeater in Oslo are all subsidized, as are also the Riksteater and the provincial theatres in Bergen, Trondheim, and Stavanger. In 1953 a State Drama School was founded, offering a three-year, full-time course in the arts of the theatre.

L. KATHLEEN McFARLANE

3. SWEDEN. (*a*) *Drama.* Although Swedish drama has a history of nearly equal length with Dano-Norwegian, there is a marked contrast in the significance of its contribution; until the work of Strindberg appeared no Swedish dramatist had reached European fame and exerted an influence upon European drama. The history of Swedish drama is, then, on the one hand, a succession of reflections of the prevailing tendencies in European drama—Italian, French, Dutch, English, German, Danish, and Norwegian—mirrored in the work of writers who were often skilled dramatists but of no great original genius and, on the other hand, a record of single, often remarkable, plays written by poets whose chief claim to fame rests upon their work in other forms. It would then, until the coming of Strindberg, appear to be the history of a race distinguished in other branches of literature but lacking any powerful dramatic tendency. Nor can this be entirely explained away by the presence of easily accessible drama in the neighbouring countries, for the history of Danish drama shows, in the early nineteenth century, the victory of a powerful native instinct over a vogue for translation and adaptation. The submission to such vogues which governed, for example, the English theatre from the middle of the eighteenth century until nearly the close of the nineteenth seems, in the case of Sweden, to have had a duration of nearly three hundred years.

The presence of the early School Drama, or Reformation Bible-play, suggests that Sweden had already some dramatic tradition in the mid-sixteenth century and had made some contribution to the medieval drama proper in which many literatures of Europe shared. But, as in the case of Denmark, there appears to be no record of those earlier phases which played a considerable, if not impressive, part in the history of English and of French drama. As it is, the history of Swedish drama begins with the vernacular *Tobiae Comedia* (pub. 1550), generally attributed to the humanist Olavus Petri (1493–1552). Unlike Denmark, Sweden has an almost continuous, if not particularly distinguished, series of vernacular plays from that point onwards, though when the School Drama dies down in the early seventeenth century, there is little to record until we find the work of the first foreign imitators in the middle of that century.

To the early School Drama proper belong such plays as *Josephi Historia* (pub. 1601) and *Dawidhs Historia* (pub. 1604), but modifications soon begin to set in. As in England and France at an earlier date, native comedy begins to mingle with the religious material and to fuse with the imitations of classical drama which soon appear. Johannes Messenius (1579–1636) and his followers begin to draw their material from Swedish saga and history, using dialogue as the vehicle for secular instead of sacred history. Messenius intended to cover Swedish history in 50 plays, but six only are extant, of which *Disa* (1611) is the first. In similar tradition are Nikolaus Holgeri Catonius with *Troijenborg* (1632), sometimes reckoned the best play of the period, and Andreas Johannis Prytz with *Olof Skottkonung* (1620) and other chronicle plays, all with a religious trend. In *Judas Redivivus* (1614), Jacobus Rondeletius produced a 'Christian tragicomedy' with more dramatic power, especially in its comic parts. All this, though imitative and perhaps on the whole more notable for quantity than quality, seems about to lead on to a healthy, native drama. Yet, when the work of this group ceases nothing rises to take its place, and the coming of foreign influences in the middle of the century found no native stock strong enough to resist them. Except for Urban Hiärne (1641–1724), who belatedly carries the School Drama to its climax in the famous and popular *Rosimunda* (1665), the native drama is left to the university circles, while the Court patronizes the new French masque and the imitations of it in Swedish by Georg Stiernhielm (1598–1672): *Then fångne Cupido* (1649) and *Parnassus Triumphans* (1651).

By the beginning of the last decade Swedish actors were established in Stockholm but this in no way loosened the hold of the classical French drama, which carried over into the eighteenth century the traditions of seventeenth-century France and led to heavy Voltairian tragedies, and comedies (with rather more vitality) after Molière.

Olof Dalin (1708–63) is the most eminent writer of the mid-eighteenth century in Sweden, a man of genius who from time to time also wrote plays, showing the influence of French tragedy, of Molière and Holberg in comedy, and of his English contemporaries, Addison, Pope, and Swift in general. His *Brynhilda* (1738) was the first Swedish tragedy of pure French classical derivation, and his comedy, *Den afundsjuke*, of the same year, points to Molière and Holberg. Genuine comedy, sometimes nearer to Holberg than to the English or French tradition, was contributed by Carl Gyllenborg (1679–1746), whose *Den Svenska sprätthöken* opened the Royal Swedish Theatre in 1737, and by R. G. Modée (1698–1752), who presented bourgeois comedy material in classical form. Erik Wrangel (1686–1765) produced between 1739 and 1748 two tragedies and one comedy. There were also a number of translations of foreign plays, among them some of Holberg's.

The influence of King Gustav III (1746–92) upon the drama of the latter part of the eighteenth century was very strong. He encouraged dramatists, supported the National Theatre at Stockholm (opened in 1773), and himself wrote or collaborated in plays for Court performances. He gathered about him a group of playwrights: Carl Israel Hallman (1732–1800); Johan Henrik Kellgren (1751–95), who between 1780 and 1788 had some share in a number of historical plays; Carl Gustaf Leopold (1756–1829), with his Scandinavian legendary themes; Gudmund Jöran Adlerbeth (1751–1818), with his imitations of Racine and Voltaire at the turn of the century; Olof Kexél (1748–96), with his comedies of French and English derivation; and Carl Envallsson (1756–1806), who parodied the classical form with his *Iphigenie den andra* in 1800. In all this abundance there was little independence. In content, theme, or form (or in all of them) the French influence still held.

But even in the Romantic period that follows there is little emancipation in the drama and there are fewer dramatists. In Sweden, as in England, there is little drama worthy of note in the early nineteenth century except that written by poets who were primarily concerned with other kinds of literature. The Swedish poets, however, unlike their English contemporaries, had every encouragement to write drama, and the work of Atterbom and Stagnelius thus reached the stage.

Per Daniel Amadeus Atterbom (1790–1835) produced in the dramatic form what is often considered his masterpiece, *Lycksalighetens Ö* (1824), but wrote no other plays. The highly original plays of Erik Johann Stagnelius (1793–1823) are, similarly, the work of a poet who was not primarily a dramatist: *Martyrerna* (1821); *Bacchanterna* (1822); and *Thorsten Fiskare* and *Sigurd Ring*, produced posthumously. To the next period belong the historical dramas of Bernhard von Beskow (1796–1868), beginning to show the influence of Schiller, and the dramatic work of Carl Jonas Love Almqvist (1793–1866).

Between this period and the coming of Strindberg in the late nineteenth century stand the names of Blanche, Børjessen, Dahlgren, and Jolin. August Theodore Blanche (1811–68) acclimatized in his comedies the art of J. L. Heiberg and Scribe; of some thirty-six plays may be mentioned *Positivhataren* (1843); *Magister Bläckstadius* (1844); *Rika Morbror* (1845); *Hittebarnet* (1847); *En Tragedi i Vimmerby* (1848). Johan Børjessen (1790–1866) wrote romantic drama influenced by his interpretation of Shakespeare, recently made accessible in K. A. Hagberg's translation. Fredrik August Dahlgren (1816–95), who also shows the influence of Shakespeare (as well as of Calderón), produced at least one popular play, his peasant play *Vermländingarne* (1846).

By the late nineteenth century the influence of Ibsen and Bjørnson was growing strong, and was soon modified and then reinforced in Sweden by the work of Strindberg in the 1880s. To this period of Swedish drama belong the names of Agrell, Leffler, Ahlgren, and Hedberg, though the later work of Hedberg continues into the twentieth century. Alfhild Agrell (1849–1923) is remembered chiefly by the impression made by her *Räddad* in 1882. Closer still to the influence of Ibsen is perhaps the work of Anne Charlotte Leffler (1849–92). Her *Sanna kvinnor* (1883) was followed by *Hur man gör godt* (1885), and in 1891 by three more comedies. Ernst Ahlgren [Victoria Benedictsson] (1849–88) is known by one play, *Final* (1885). The early work of Tor Hedberg (1862–1931) has close associations with Ibsen: *En Tvekamp* (1892); *Nattrocken* (1893); *Judas* (1895); *Gerhard Grim* (1897); *Guld och gröna skogar* (1903). His later work belongs to the twentieth century, but a few plays may be mentioned here: *Johan Ulfstjerna* (1907); his most notable play, *Karlavagnen* (1910); and *Perseus och vidundret* (1917).

August Strindberg (1849–1912) brought vitality into Swedish drama, though his themes sometimes provoked hostility as great as that raised by Ibsen's in Norway. In him Swedish drama ceased to be imitative and offered instead an art whose originality, in both matter and form, has inspired a succession of imitators, acknowledged and unacknowledged. Strindberg's name is remembered abroad for the realistic plays of the first half of his career and for the sometimes mystical impressionist drama of the second half. To these, for Sweden, must be added the fifteen major dramas on Swedish history, the popularity of which recalls the fact that the story of Swedish secular drama begins with a group of native history plays.

Since Strindberg's day he has been regarded as a classic in Sweden (and abroad). His work as a dramatist and man of the theatre may be said to have led first to the raising of the famous Swedish theatres to the position they still hold among the connoisseurs of theatrical art in Europe, and then to a tendency to imitation among the Swedish dramatists of the early twentieth century. This in turn gave place to a drama of some originality which holds considerable promise for the future.

From the beginning of this century to the outbreak of the First World War, Swedish drama is best represented by the later plays of Strindberg, the earlier plays of Per Hallström (1866–1960), the later work of Tor Hedberg, and such plays as *Elna Hall* (1917), by Ernst Didring (1868–1931), which had international success. Per Hallström is remembered chiefly as a poet and story-writer; his plays, beginning with *Grefven af Antwerpen* (1899), are dramas and tragedies on classical or Swedish history.

In the period between the wars a group of dramatists came to the fore, the most notable of whom were Hjalmar Bergman (1883–1931) and Pär Lagerkvist (1891–). Bergman, who is also famous as a novelist, is closely linked with Strindberg both by theme and mood and by his constant and often fruitful experimentation in dramatic form and technique. His earlier work (until about 1925) generally took the form of subtle, psychological tragedy; his later, no less experimental, was almost entirely high comedy. Pär Lagerkvist represents the group of still more recent Swedish playwrights who are concerned with the problems of modern life, political, economic, and psychological. Even more than Bergman, he derives from Strindberg in mood, theme, and technique, but his work is far from being merely derivative and it is chiefly with Strindberg's last phase that he is associated. The most representative of his early plays is *Himlens hemlighet* (1919), which shows a powerful imagination at work upon an interpretation of life whose despair is almost unalleviated. His later work, though still essentially tragic, admits a certain resolution of the tragic elements, or at least an indication of a balancing, redemptive element. This remarkable dramatist is also distinguished by the elliptical, suggestive form of his dialogue, which appears at times to have some relation to the corresponding technique of the French dramatist, J.-J. Bernard.

Mention should also be made of a number of other Swedish dramatists, most of whom can be represented by one or two plays only: Runar Schildt by *Galgamannen* (1922); Vilhelm Moberg by *Hustrun* (1929) and *Våld* (1932); Ragnar Josephson by *Kanske en diktare* (1932); Rudolf Värnlund by *Den heliga familjen* and *Vägen till Kanaan* (both 1932), and *Modern och stjärnan* (1940); Sigfrid Siwertz by *En hederlig man* and *Skönhet* (both 1933); Herbert Grevenius by *Första maj* and *Som folk är mest* (both 1935); Karl Ragnar Gierow by *Varulven* (1941).

To these should be added the names of Lars-Levi Laestadius, Rüne Lindström, Sven Stolpe, and Marika Stjernstedt.

UNA ELLIS-FERMOR†

(*b*) *Theatre*. The first attempt to found a genuinely national theatre in Sweden—as distinct from the School Drama of the sixteenth century, played in Latin, and the performances of foreign travelling companies in the seventeenth and eighteenth centuries—was not made until the latter part of the eighteenth century. A Royal Theatre had in fact been opened in 1737, but performances by Swedish nationals were still a rare occurrence. A Royal Swedish Opera was begun in 1782, and the Royal Swedish Dramatic Theatre in 1788, with help and financial support from King Gustav III. The present building of this theatre, the Kungliga Dramatiska Teater, dates in part from 1898 (for opera), and in part from 1908 (for drama); in 1960 it was extensively modernized, and an intimate studio theatre added. Other theatres in Sweden which enjoy financial support from public funds include the Stockholm Municipal Theatre (built in 1960), two theatres in Gothenburg, and others in Uppsala, Hälsingborg, Linköping-Norrköping, and Malmö (see No. 40). Commercial theatres in Stockholm include the Svenska Teater (burnt down in 1925 and rebuilt), and the Intima Teater, founded in 1907 by Strindberg and Falck, for which Strindberg wrote specially a number of his so-called 'chamber plays', including *The Ghost Sonata*. There is also the Riksteater, a touring company founded in 1930. Since very early days, Sweden has run lotteries to help to subsidize her theatres. A drama school has existed since 1787, attached to the Dramatiska Teater. Among the leading players of Sweden of this century up to the Second World War were Anders de Wahl, Ivan Hedquist, Gosta Ekman, Lars Hansson, Harriet Bosse (Strindberg's third wife), Gerda Lundequist, Pauline Brunius, Bengt Ekerot, Tore Teje, and Inga Tidblad; among the producers, Per Lindberg, Olaf Molander, Alf Sjöberg, and Ingmar Bergman are the outstanding names. In more recent years the Dramatiska Teater in Stockholm, under the direction of Karl Ragnar Gierow, has attracted considerable interest by its first performances of a number of posthumous O'Neill plays; and the municipal theatres of Gothenburg and Malmö have also attracted attention from far beyond the boundaries of Sweden.

L. KATHLEEN MCFARLANE

SCAPINO, one of the *zanni* or servant roles of the *commedia dell'arte*. Like Brighella, he is crafty and unprincipled, but in moments of danger he does not belie his name, which means 'to run off' or 'to escape'. The first actor to play him was Francesco Gabrielli, a prominent member of the Confidenti, and one of a company which went with the younger Andreini to Paris in 1624. He made the part an important one, but it dwindled later, until with Molière Scapino passed into French comedy as a quick-witted and unscrupulous valet, as in *Les Fourberies de Scapin.*

SCARAMUCCIA, a character of the *commedia dell'arte* which is classed with the *zanni* roles (see ITALY, 2 and No. 137), but considered by some to have approximated more to the blustering braggart soldier. The actor most closely associated with the part, though he may not actually have created it, was Tiberio Fiorillo, a magnificent actor who won fame all over Italy before proceeding to Paris, where at one time his company shared the Petit-Bourbon with Molière. He returned to Italy intermittently, but from 1661 the greater part of his time was spent in Paris. He went several times to England. The life of Scaramouche was written, rather inaccurately, by his companion Mezzetin [Angelo Costantini], and he was one of the *commedia dell'arte* actors who had the greatest influence on Molière and so on the development of the French theatre.

SCARRON, PAUL (1610–60), French playwright and novelist. He had an unhappy childhood, and after a visit to Rome began to study for the Church. He was quite unsuited to it, and soon began to lead a riotous life. A foolish adventure led to his being crippled by rheumatism at the age of 30. Unable to move, he was forced to rely on his pen for a livelihood. He turned his attention to the theatre, and wrote a number of witty though slightly scabrous farces, of which the first two, *Jodelet, ou le maître-valet* (1643) and *Jodelet souffleté* (1645), were acted by the comedian of that name at the Théâtre du Marais. They were followed by others, all equally successful, some of them based on Spanish plays to which Scarron added a good deal of his own, modernizing the originals. Meanwhile, Scarron's house had become the rendezvous of the literary figures—including Corneille—whom he amused with his wit, mocking at the world as he mocked at his own infirmities. In 1652 he married the beautiful but penniless orphan, Françoise d'Aubigné, who as Mme de Maintenon was destined to be the second wife of Louis XIV and the virtual ruler of France. Meanwhile, Scarron continued to write for the theatre. His *Don Japhet d'Arménie* (1647) had been extremely successful, and was later to be frequently revived by Molière. *L'Écolier de Salamanque* (1654) was barefacedly plagiarized by Boisrobert; but Scarron was revenged, for Boisrobert's version is forgotten, while that of Scarron is remembered, particularly on account of the valet Crispin, played for so long by the actor-family Poisson. Scarron, whose interest in Spanish literature has already been noted, may have taken from *La viaje entretenido* of de Rojas the idea of his great novel, *Le Roman comique* (1651), which depicts the adventures and miseries of a band of strolling players, for whose leader, Leandro, the provincial actor-manager Filandre is believed to have served as a model.

SCENARIO. This word, which is now used mainly for the script of a motion picture, or for a synopsis of the action of a musical play, was originally applied to the skeleton plots of the *commedia dell'arte,* replacing some time in the early eighteenth century the older word *soggetto.* These are not such synopses as might be drawn up by an author for his written drama, nor should they be confused with the Elizabethan 'platts', chiefly charts of entrances and exits and properties drawn up for the convenience of the prompter. They are theatrical documents, prepared for the use of the professional companies either by their leader or most gifted member, or by enthusiastic amateur admirers of the *commedia dell'arte* style. They consist of a scene-by-scene résumé of the action, together with some notes on locality and special effects. Their informal elasticity allowed the insertion of extraneous 'business' according to the discretion or ability of the company or player presenting them (see ITALY, 2).

SCENE BAY, or dock, rooms opening off the stage proper, and used for the storing of scenery.

SCENERY. 1. ORIGINS. Scenery is a comparatively recent invention in the history of the theatre. The drama of ancient Greece was played before a background which gradually became more elaborate until in Roman times it had become a grandiose architectural façade, the *scaenae frons* (see No. 10). But if we except the *periaktoi,* or revolving prisms, of Hellenistic and Roman times, and a few slight stage furnishings like rocks and thrones, the ancient world knew nothing of what we should call stage scenery.

The same is true of the medieval period. Sacred drama had begun to be played inside the churches by the tenth century. Soon it moved outside, and the west front of a cathedral provided a 'permanent setting' more splendid than anything even the Romans had imagined. Then, as drama grew steadily more profane, performances were given in town squares and market-places, and special structures had to be built to represent the various scenes. But these 'houses', as they were called, were more in the nature of 'properties' than of scenery. Even when there was an effort, towards the end of the medieval period, to group the 'houses' on one raised platform or stage, no attempt was made to present a coherent or unified stage-picture. The 'simultaneous setting' had Heaven in one corner, Hell-Mouth in the other, and, in between, Pilate's House, or Golgotha (see No. 15).

2. RENAISSANCE. The unification of the stage

picture was the work of the princely Courts of the Renaissance, and it is no accident that stage scenery and the new Absolutism arose at the same time. In Italy, throughout the fifteenth century, the New Learning had resulted in a growing interest in the classical drama. Plautus was revived by the Roman Academy towards the end of the century, and in 1486 by Ercole d'Este at Ferrara. Humanists and princes combined to see that plays should be as 'classical' as learning could make them and that they should form part of Court festivities. Many such festivities took place in the open air, but there was what might be called a natural tendency to move indoors, and in 1491, also at Ferrara, a play was performed in a closed room. In these circumstances there was no room for the old methods, the stage-picture was unified perforce, and an attempt was made to make the space available seem larger by the use of perspective painting. This perspective painting, rendered possible by the researches of artists and scholars during the second half of the fifteenth century, was perhaps originally intended merely to enlarge the apparent size of the room. The greatest artists of the period, Leonardo da Vinci, Raphael, Bramante, were employed in the decoration of princely fêtes. Of these the last-named might almost be called a specialist in using perspective for this purpose; he had done so with great effect as early as 1480, in the sacristy of San Satiro in Milan and in the church itself. It was probably under his influence that Baldassare Peruzzi (1481–1537) applied the newly perfected science to the deliberate construction of theatrical decoration.

In this project he was helped by the spread of the influence of the architectural writings of Vitruvius (*fl.* 70–15 B.C.). This precious legacy from the ancient world had been discovered in manuscript at St. Gallen in 1414 and published in 1484 but it was not until 1511 that the first illustrated edition appeared, and not until 1521 that the work was first translated into Italian. Some of the scenery which Peruzzi designed for Pope Leo X and Pope Clement VII is described by Vasari, who also records that 'he began a book on the antiquities of Rome, with a commentary on Vitruvius'. His notes and drawings were utilized by his pupil Sebastiano Serlio (1475–1554) in the preparation of his great work *De Architettura*, the part of which dealing with perspective appeared in 1545. Serlio wrote with the banqueting-hall of a prince in mind, and he described three kinds of stage sets for different dramatic genres (see Nos. 56, 57, 58.) The 'houses' of his sets were arranged on both sides of a street receding at right angles from the front of the stage, and were two-sided and carefully foreshortened.

In 1560 Bartolomeo Neroni (*c.* 1500–71/3) built a theatre in Siena in a great hall behind the Palace of the Senate (that is, he erected a proscenium in a building already existing), and he provided it with scenery on the Serlio model. An engraving of this has fortunately been preserved.

Other influences, however, were at work, and there were those who strove for theatres more completely faithful to the Roman model, that is, consisting of a semicircle of ascending seats and, at the back of the stage, an elaborate, permanent architectural façade. The Teatro Olimpico at Vicenza was begun, it is said, by the great Andrea Palladio (1518–80) in 1580, but as he died in the same year the work was entrusted to Vincenzo Scamozzi (1552–1616), who completed it in 1584 (see No. 20). It is probable that the three arches in the architectural façade were originally closed either by doors or by painted cloths, but Scamozzi had the brilliant idea of building behind each arch a street of houses diminishing in perspective. Five scenic runways (one for each of the archways and one for each of the side doors) were added by him on the occasion of the visit of the Empress Maria of Austria in 1585.

The passion for plays in the second half of the sixteenth century could not be confined to those who were able or willing to have special theatres erected. Performances continued to be given in the halls of palaces, converted for the purpose, and among the most important of these were the Florentine *Intermezzi* of 1589.

These were of such importance in theatrical history that they are worth considering in some detail. The festivals in honour of the marriage of the Grand Duke Ferdinand I of Tuscany lasted throughout May 1589, and included masquerades, animal-hunts, a Naumachia, or water-pageant, on the Arno, and three comedies. These comedies were enlivened by *intermezzi* or interludes, a series of spectacular pantomimes *sul gusto antico* interspersed with madrigals, the seed from which the whole of opera took its origin. We are not concerned, however, with their importance in the history of music (for which see OPERA) but only with the manner of their presentation. The machinist and designer was Bernardo Buontalenti (1536–1608), called delle Girandole, i.e. of the Fireworks. He entered the service of the Medici family in 1547 and for nearly sixty years was laying out palaces, villas, fortresses, and gardens, as well as presiding over all Grand Ducal festivities, constructing theatrical machinery, arranging firework displays, and ordering funeral ceremonies. He was in fact a typical 'architect' of the period, including in his scope everything from stage costume to military engineering. Both drawings and engravings of his work for the *Intermezzi* of 1589 have been preserved and are among the most important early documents of scenic history (see No. 59).

There is some dispute as to whether the side-pieces shown in his sets are true theatrical 'wings', i.e. whether they were flat pieces of painted canvas stretched on wooden frames and able to slide in and out when it was desired to change the scene. Buontalenti is usually considered to have worked with *telari*, that is, three-sided revolving prisms constructed in supposed imitation of the classical *periaktoi*, but whether this be so or not, the scenery he devised created immense interest, as can be seen from the number of contemporary accounts, and became the ancestor of a long progeny.

His pupils were Giulio Parigi (1590–1636) and Agostino Migliori (*fl.* 1610). The former was in charge of the Florentine festivities of 1606, 1608, and 1615, and we are fortunate in having representations of these in the engravings of Canta-Gallina, Stefano della Bella, and Callot. Jacques Callot (1592–1635) was himself a designer at the Court of Tuscany until 1622, and when he went to Nancy he carried the seed with him and devised *entrées* in the Florentine manner. A contemporary of Parigi was Josef Furtenbach (1591–1667), who in 1641 was responsible for the building of a theatre in Ulm, with a stage on the Italian principle of *telari*. He also produced a work on architecture which included some valuable engravings of stage settings. But from our point of view the most interesting scenic designer of this time was Inigo Jones (1573–1652). He paid several visits to Italy in the early years of the seventeenth century, and the influence of contemporary Italian designers on his work is beyond question.

He was fortunate in that James I shared the passion of other European princes for courtly festivities, especially for the masque, which gave Jones his opportunity. As elsewhere, stage scenery in England was confined to the Court. The public theatres still used the bare apron stage derived from the medieval tradition, and the most prodigious dramatic achievement of all time was just drawing to its close unaided by any scenic illusion whatever. At the most Shakespeare had only the curtained alcove at the back of the stage which might by any stretch of imagination rank as 'scenery'. He was compelled to put the scenery into the language of the play, and the world is the richer for it. Yet it is tempting to speculate what use he might have made of the new art of theatrical decoration if it had become known in England twenty years or so earlier.

A large number of drawings by Inigo Jones for the scenery and costume (see Nos. 61, 144) of Court masques has fortunately been preserved at Chatsworth, and these, together with the texts by Ben Jonson and others, provide a complete enough picture of performances at Whitehall under James I and Charles I. What we find is a simplified version of the Italian system, Jones never using more than four wings on each side. It is probable that his influence would have spread to the public theatres, but the outbreak of the Civil War put an end to developments and it is not until after the Restoration that the story can be resumed.

3. Seventeenth Century. Meanwhile the new art of opera, with its inevitable elaboration of scenery, was spreading from Florence all over Italy. Magnificent musical plays were mounted at Milan and at Viterbo. In Parma the Teatro Farnese was inaugurated towards the end of 1618 and provided with a complete system of wings. Perhaps these were invented by Giambattista Aleotti (1546–1636), the architect of the theatre, perhaps by his pupil Giacomo Torelli (1608–78), but whoever devised them, they were to have an enormous influence on the development of the theatre, and to last, unmodified in their essential principles, until the end of the nineteenth century.

In Rome the fury for opera knew no bounds, a future Pope writing some of the libretti. The powerful Barberini family built an immense theatre capable of holding 3,000 spectators, furnished it with complicated machinery, and employed artists like Giovanni Lorenzo Bernini (1598–1680) to design the décor. The opera of 'Sant'Alessio' was performed there in 1634 in the presence of Alexander Charles of Poland and afterwards published with engravings showing the principal scenes. Such illustrated commemorative volumes became increasingly frequent as the century progressed, and are the source from which much of the history of the *settecento* theatre has been compiled.

Torelli (see No. 62) was one of the first, if not *the* first, of the professional scene-painters who were nothing else. He was called 'il gran stregone', the great wizard, of the theatre, and he spread the system which he had learned at Parma through the princely houses of Italy, all of whom wished to be in the fashion and have a theatre of their own. It was at Venice, however, that his influence was felt with most far-reaching effect, for it was there that commercial opera with spectators paying for their seats took its rise. The first public performance of opera took place at Venice in the San Cassiano Theatre in 1637. In general the commercial theatre offered a simplified version of the new stagecraft, a mere perspective of columns or pilasters with a changing background. An exception was the Teatro Novissimo, and Torelli acted as decorator there from 1641 until 1645. A large number of commemorative volumes which have come down to us make it easy to form an estimate of his style and methods.

In 1645 Cardinal Mazarin invited Torelli to Paris, and an engraving by Stefano della Bella shows the scene which he devised for un opera produced at the Petit-Bourbon in 1647. Although some of the Paris theatres, such as the theatre in the Hôtel de Bourgogne, clung to a kind of permanent setting with doors in an architectural façade, the Italian system made rapid headway, and when Torelli returned to Italy in 1662 his work was carried on in France by his followers and pupils, the architect Amanadini (*fl.* 1660) and the machine-master Gaspare Vigarani (1586–1663). It was the latter who constructed the Salle des Machines in the Tuileries, which was to reach the height of its fame in the next century under the celebrated Servandony (see below).

In England, as we have noted, there was a gap in theatrical development during the Puritan domination, but even before Cromwell's death tentative efforts were made to revive the drama, played this time not on the old, bare Elizabethan stage, but with all the elaboration of the new technique. The influence of the Shakespearian theatre persisted in the survival of the apron stage, with the proscenium arch placed behind it. Professor Allardyce Nicoll has acutely suggested that 'just as in Italy the scene space developed out of the *periaktoi*, set within the archways, so in England the scenic part of the stage developed from that room in which Shakespeare had shown Ferdinand and Miranda playing their amorous game of chess'. But the development was arrested, as it were, halfway, and until well on into the eighteenth century much of the action still took place on the projecting apron.

English audiences had their first taste of opera when Davenant in May 1656 produced *The Siege of Rhodes*, a play with music by Locke (now considered the first English opera). It was first given privately at Rutland House in Aldersgate and later at the Cockpit or Phoenix. Davenant entrusted the décor to John Webb (1611–72), the kinsman and pupil of Inigo Jones, and, as might be expected, his designs show a direct descent from the scenery of the Jacobean and Caroline masques, modified to some extent by the new wave of Italian influence. After the Restoration the new London theatres adopted the Italian system, Dorset Garden leading the way (see No. 63). But it was long before England had anything to rival the work of the great Continental designers. There are, however, in the Victoria and Albert Museum, some very interesting designs by Sir James Thornhill (1675–1734) for performances in the early years of the eighteenth century.

The influence of the Italians was not only maintained by foreign artists who studied their work, but by the actual migration of the Italian scenic painters themselves. In the second half of the seventeenth century the rage for Italian opera spread all over Europe, and every prince and princeling wanted to make it a part of his Court festivities. Reference has already been made to developments in France. In Germany, the end of the Thirty Years' War was followed by a period of recovery. In 1652 a theatre was built in Vienna by Giovanni Burnacini (?–1656), who designed the scenery also. When he died he was succeeded by his son Lodovico Ottavio Burnacini (1636–1707), who became a great favourite of the Emperor Leopold I. Munich saw its first opera in 1654, 'La Ninfa ritrosa', with decorations by Francesco Santurini (1627–82). He was succeeded by Domenico (*fl.* 1685–1710) and Gasparo (*fl.* 1662–86), sons of Francesco Mauro. The Mauri later migrated to Dresden. They were among the first of the great Italian families of scenic artists. There were five brothers, of whom three were decorators and two machinists, and they made their enormous reputation first in Venice. They passed to Piacenza, to Parma, and thence to wider fields beyond the Alps; and it was while they were at Parma that they were assisted by a young beginner who was to be the founder of a still more famous dynasty of decorators. Ferdinando Galli da Bibiena (1657–1743) and his brother Francesco (1659–1739) were orphaned at an early age. They showed a talent for theatrical design from their earliest years, and we find Ferdinando, at the age of 28, installed at Parma as 'primario pittore ed architetto'. After devising many princely fêtes there he was called to Barcelona for the wedding of Charles and Elizabeth, afterwards Emperor and Empress. They invited him to Vienna, where he remained for the greater part of his life. Many of his original drawings have been preserved, and he is credited with a revolution in the art of theatrical design by his discovery of the diagonal perspective setting. Like Francesco, he ended his career as a teacher of the art of scene-painting at Bologna. He had four sons, who all followed in his footsteps; Giuseppe (1696–1757) was the most important and prolific of them. He assisted his father in Barcelona and Vienna, decorated his first opera in 1716, worked at Prague, Dresden, Munich, Breslau, and Graz, and was responsible, with his son Carlo (1728–87), for the decoration of the Opera House at Bayreuth. Carlo, while still a youth, entered the service of the Margrave of Bayreuth, and later worked in Italy, France, Holland, Flanders, England (about 1763), and perhaps in Russia. In three generations the Galli da Bibiena family had spread the principles and practice of baroque theatre décor over the whole continent (see BIBIENA and No. 64).

An almost parallel career was followed by the Galliari, a Piedmontese artist family. Like the Galli, two of a family of brothers left orphans at an early age set up as scene-painters and became the originators of the school of theatrical decoration which had its centre at Turin and Milan. Bernardino Galliari (1707–94) worked at both places before being summoned to Innsbruck, where, with his brother Fabrizio (1709–90), he was entrusted with the decorations for royal festivals. It would be tedious to enumerate all the places where he worked; but in 1772 he was summoned to Berlin by Frederick the Great, and there, with the aid of his nephew Giovanni (1746–1818), he designed six scenes and a curtain for the Royal Opera House. Another nephew, Gasparo (1760–1818), was also a scenic artist.

4. EIGHTEENTH CENTURY. By this time the whole character of theatrical decoration had changed. The elaborate architectural backgrounds of the baroque had yielded on the one hand to a more classical style and on the other to the growing interest in landscape. Fabrizio Galliari himself, although he had specialized in the diagonal perspective invented by Ferdinando Galli and carried to its ultimate extreme by Giuseppe Galli, was one of the first to introduce romantic naturalistic landscape into the architectural stage picture.

Neo-classicism had long been evident in

real architecture; indeed, there is a sense in which the whole movement inaugurated by Ferdinando Galli was a deliberate turning away from the formal tendencies of Palladian classicism and symmetry. The influence of the ultra-baroque persisted longer in the theatre than elsewhere, but towards the middle of the eighteenth century the fight was joined again. The reaction against the baroque style in the theatre began in Paris, and even Germany, which had hitherto been completely under Italian masters, now began to yield to the influence of the French. One of the most influential of these was Jean Nicolas Servandony (1695–1766), who in the early part of his career as a scenic artist called himself Servandoni, and made out that he was a Florentine. He was actually born at Lyons, but had studied in Italy. After much decorative work in Portugal and France, he assumed control of the Salle des Machines at the Tuileries and mounted a whole series of magnificent spectacles. Later he worked at Dresden, Vienna, and other cities in central Europe. He even went to London. He represented the neo-classical impulse which was soon to be supreme and, after the death of the last Galli da Bibiena, to be plainly manifested in the work of such later Italian artists at foreign Courts as the Quaglio brothers, Lorenzo (1730–1804) and Giuseppe (1747–1828), Paolo Landriani (1770–1838), and Alessandro Sanquirico (1780–1849).

England, which had escaped by its isolation both the splendours and the excesses of the baroque theatre, was not much influenced by neo-classicism in stage decoration. But the idea, which had persisted since the middle of the sixteenth century, that a stage setting must inevitably be architectural, was abandoned, and the new enthusiasm for romantic landscape rapidly gained ground. One of its first exponents was the Strasbourg artist Philip James de Loutherbourg (1735–1810), who came to England in 1771 and was soon afterwards employed to design the scenery for Drury Lane. Even if some of his *maquettes* had not been preserved, his well-known paintings would give a sufficient idea of his romantic tendencies. Most of his work was done for the pantomimes and 'entertainments' which, under Garrick's management, varied the theatrical fare provided for the audiences of Drury Lane; and by his invention of transparent scenery — moonshine, fire, volcanoes—and by 'cut-out' scenery he did much to increase the attractiveness of the stage-picture.

The neo-Gothic enthusiasm entered the English theatre some twenty years later with the romantic architectural settings of William Capon (1757–1827). For J. P. Kemble's revivals of Shakespeare he devised a number of flats and backcloths based upon authentic documents, and so began the progress towards antiquarian 'correctness'. Not only Shakespeare but the new school of historical drama represented by such a play as George Colman's *The Iron Chest* offered scope for his talents, and his work and that of de Loutherbourg provided the basis for the development of English scenic design during the first half of the nineteenth century.

5. Nineteenth Century. Spectacular equestrian shows were very popular in the early 1800s, and Astley's playhouse gave an opportunity for the talents of John Henderson Grieve (1770–1845) and other members of his family. Indeed it may be said that the Grieve family, like the Galli da Bibiena family of a century before, dominated scene-painting for nearly a hundred years. Thomas Grieve (1799–1882) and William Grieve (1800–44) carried the family tradition through a second generation, and Thomas's son through a third. Another great name in scene-painting was that of Clarkson Stanfield (1793–1867), whose somewhat histrionic talent was less at home in his innumerable landscape-paintings than on the stage of a theatre. So popular did his work become that the playbills of the period display his name in larger type than the name of the principal actor.

The antiquarian tendency inaugurated by Capon was carried still further in the Kemble productions of the 1820s, and to its logical or illogical conclusion in the series of Shakespeare revivals put on by Charles Kean at the Princess's Theatre in the 1850s. The principal artists employed were T. Grieve, F. Lloyds, H. Cuthbert, I. Dayes (see No. 72), and William Telbin (1813–73). The last-named was the founder of a scene-painting family which persisted into the twentieth century. The second half of the century showed little change in the methods of presentation, and under Irving at the Lyceum we find that Hawes Craven (1837–1910) (see No. 79) employed the same transparencies, cut-out scenes, &c. which de Loutherbourg had used a hundred years before. Irving also employed Telbin's son William (1846–1931) (see No. 73).

But by the time the nineteenth century had reached its final quarter the theatrical traditions inherited from the baroque and romantic periods were in full decay. For spectacular pieces—pantomimes and the like—the cut-cloth, or series of cut-cloths, had been developed to such excess that the stage-picture resembled lace-work, or a cut-paper valentine. In serious plays audiences were growing dissatisfied with the artificial conventions of walls of rooms which were no walls, but a row of flats, of doors, windows, and even furniture, painted on stretched canvas. There was a cry for realism, in tune with the contemporary realism of painting and literature, and realism was in its turn the first essential of reform. Interiors were in future to be represented by the box-set (see No. 70) with three solid walls and a ceiling; furniture and accessories, sometimes even food, were to be real.

6. The Modern Period. It was in 1887 that Antoine founded the Théâtre Libre in Paris in order, as he and his supporters firmly believed, to apply the principles of stage naturalism in all their completeness. As he was a producer of

genius he actually did much more than this, for he used the scenery and stage properties to reinforce the mood of a play in a way which had never been attempted before. Perhaps Antoine himself, with his passion for real meat, real fountains, and the like, never realized the force of some of his *mises-en-scène*, and as his repertoire was wilfully limited to the works of the new naturalistic school of drama he was deprived of plays which might have lent themselves to his innovations.

The reaction against realism came from the group of young writers and artists known as the *Symbolistes*, who, led by Paul Fort, attacked the Théâtre Libre for its search for the exact and for giving no help to authors of fantasy and imagination. Fort founded the Théâtre Mixte which, after two performances, became the Théâtre d'Art, and in his manifesto enunciated many of the principles which were later to become the commonplaces of the modernist school. Scenery was to be simplified, evocative rather than descriptive; there was to be frank stylization, complete harmony between scenery and costume, and the absolute abandonment of the perspective backcloth. Among the painters who joined in the battle against naturalism and painted decorations for the Théâtre d'Art were Vuillard, Bonnard, Maurice Denis, Odilon Redon, and K. X. Roussel.

The works of some new dramatists, especially Maeterlinck, were sufficiently imaginative to give scope to the new method, and in 1892, when the Théâtre d'Art had become the Théâtre de l'Œuvre, Lugné-Poë, collaborating with Camille Mauclair and Édouard Vuillard, presented *Pelléas et Mélisande* at the Bouffes-Parisiens. The great Konstantin Stanislavsky (1863–1938) was present at this performance, and afterwards admitted how much he owed to the decorations by Vogler, and to all the experimental work which was being carried out in Paris towards the end of the last century.

Shortly afterwards Stanislavsky returned to Russia, and in 1897 founded the Art Theatre of Moscow. His object was the reform of the Russian stage, but he began by proclaiming the gospel of naturalism according to Antoine, and by striving to emulate the realistic effects of the Meininger company which, under Chronegk, had visited Moscow only a few years before. In fact, naturalism was pushed to an extreme, an attempt being made to reproduce actual conditions of life, with all its accumulated detail, and in particular its merging of the principal characters of a drama in the mass of the participants. The abolition of the 'star' system, and the rehearsing of crowds to a point never before attempted, was perhaps Stanislavsky's greatest individual contribution to the new movement. By the very perfection of their technique the actors in his theatre transcended realism and evolved a kind of symbolic rhythm which was to prove a perfect instrument for the presentation of the plays of Chekhov.

Meanwhile, a French-speaking Swiss, Adolphe Appia (1862–1928), had, in 1899, published his epoch-making work on the reform of staging, *Die Musik und die Inscenierung*. Some years before he had issued a smaller work dealing with Wagner's operas, moved thereto by the unsatisfactory nature of the scenery at Bayreuth. His aesthetic sense was offended in particular by the glaring contrast between the flatness of the scenery and the inevitable three dimensions of the actor. Appia declared that the essentials of good stage-presentation were, first, a plastic scene which would give the actors' attitudes and movements all their value, and, second, lighting which would emphasize instead of destroying the solidity of the human form. His suggested designs for Wagner, Shakespeare, etc., which were marked by an extreme simplicity and by the use of dramatic lighting, had an immense influence on the future of stage décor (see No. 97).

It was, of course, the invention of electric lighting and its adaptation to stage purposes which made Appia's ideas practicable. Gas had made it possible to use light not only for illumination but for effect, but electricity opened up a much wider range of possibilities. By the Fortuny system which was worked out in Germany at the beginning of the twentieth century it became possible to obtain a uniform illumination approximating to real daylight. The essence of the system was the reflection of light from bands of coloured silk and its diffusion thence on to a sky-dome or cyclorama occupying the back of the stage. The original Fortuny system of illumination has been largely abandoned, but the sky-dome has remained as one of the most potent devices for attaining complete scenic illusion. Fortuny's sky-dome of silk which could be shut up like a carriage-hood and transported from one theatre to another has been replaced in many theatres, chiefly in Germany and America, by the sky-dome of plaster which, no longer semicircular (for that blocked the side entrances to the stage), takes the form of a flattened shell, bending inwards sharply at the top and at the sides. Whitewashed plaster makes an admirable surface for light to play upon, and the effect seen from the front of the stage is of infinite distance, open sky. Its more realistic possibilities have been worked out in the Swedish Ars system which permits photographs of real clouds to be projected upon the artificial sky. But it is also capable of more imaginative use. (See also LIGHTING, 1 *d*.)

Simultaneously with improvements in lighting came other mechanical contrivances which placed new power in the hands of the producers, for good or ill. Chief among these was the revolving stage, installed in 1896 by Lautenschläger at Munich. This enabled three or even more settings to exist at the same time on the revolve and to be moved into view of the audience in turn. The scenery itself could be of the most solid type, although of course considerable ingenuity was needed to fit the various scenes into segments of the circle. This raised so many difficulties in practice that an attempt was made to avoid them by the invention of sliding stages, rising and falling stages, and the like. One of the most elaborate was installed in the Théâtre Pigalle in Paris in the late 1920s. But the living actor should beware of too much machinery. It is merely the end of a logical process that the Théâtre Pigalle is now a cinema.

Such developments were the very opposite of those envisaged by a prophet like Appia, and there were others who sought the salvation of stagecraft not in an ever-increasing elaboration but in a drastic simplicity. A leading place among these was taken by Edward Gordon Craig (1872–1966) (see No. 75), whose influence has been out of all proportion to the number of his actual productions. His writings are a permanent inspiration to all workers in the theatre, but his actual system resolved itself into a series of large screens, with a limited number of movable features such as flights of steps, and with these he endeavoured to build up an imaginative stage-picture with no concessions to realism at all. His production of *Hamlet* at the Moscow Art Theatre in 1912 is still capable of arousing controversy, but his ideas have undoubtedly had a large progeny. But before dealing with these and with other attempts to escape from the tyranny of the picture-stage it is necessary to say something of one of the most extraordinary outbursts of creative activity that the modern theatre has known.

While all these tendencies had been taking shape, scene-painting had not entirely vanished even from progressive stages; indeed it had reached a new and wonderful flowering in the Russian Ballet, or, as it should be called to distinguish it from the traditional ballet which remained in Russia, the Diaghilev Ballet. It sprang from a painters' movement, a group of young St. Petersburg painters inspired by Wronbel to attempt the complete transformation of the art of scenic design. Serge Diaghilev (1872–1929), with his gift for organization, collected them under the banner of his review, *Mir Iskousstva*, or *The World of Art*. The members of this group, of which the most famous were Léon Bakst (1866–1924) and Alexandre Benois (1870–1960), practised a kind of mannered archaism which proved particularly suited to the decoration of ballet. In opposition to them was a Moscow group, more in touch with such Parisian movements as Cubism, and these artists also were enlisted in Diaghilev's service. The most famous names were Larionov, Goncharova, and Barthe, and it was in succession to their work that it seemed natural and logical to Diaghilev to call in the services of French painters like Picasso and Derain.

These developments, however, were still in the future when the Diaghilev Ballet burst like a bombshell upon the Paris of 1909. Its triumph in France and in England are matters of history, but its influence on stage design was perhaps less than on the arts in general. From the point of view of stage décor, indeed, Bakst and Benois were not the beginning of anything; they were the flowering of an age-long process. The Russian Ballet was the gorgeous sunset of scene-painting. In its glorious career it reflected every changing phase of painting, but (except for late attempts by Diaghilev to make use of some of the developments of the post-Revolutionary Russian theatre) it did not reflect the history of the contemporary theatre in its effort to break away from the old traditions of presentation.

Craig, in his desire for artistic unity in presentation, had dreamed of a theatre entirely controlled by one man; a super-man at once author, producer, decorator, and costumier. For the actor himself he preferred to substitute the 'Über-marionnette'. Extreme as this notion was, it was in tune with the rise of the producer during the first decade of the twentieth century to a commanding and almost dictatorial position in the theatre. Such a producer, or *régisseur*, animating the whole enterprise, had Diaghilev been. An even more typical figure was Max Reinhardt (1873–1943)—more typical and more important for our purpose, because he summed up in his career nearly all the developments of the contemporary theatre, and his extensive travels made his influence world-wide.

He was the complete eclectic, changing his manner completely in accordance with the mood of the play. His choice of play ranged from the most realistic to the most imaginative, and his presentations varied no less. He used the revolving stage, the semi-permanent setting, simultaneous settings, runways, flights of steps. Refusing to be confined within the framework of the proscenium arch, his productions spilled over into the orchestra and then out of the theatre altogether, into the circus, the public hall, the street, and finally back into the church from which the modern European theatre had emerged. In 1910 he produced *Oedipus Rex* in the Zirkus Schumann in Vienna. His most famous production, *The Miracle*, was staged at Olympia in London in 1911. After the First World War he found even wider opportunities, and at Salzburg turned, as it were, the whole city into a stage, setting *Jedermann* in front of the façade of the cathedral. In Vienna the authorities turned over to him the old ballroom in the Hofburg, where he erected a formalized permanent setting, harmonizing with the character of the room, and staged upon it plays by Goethe, Calderón, and Beaumarchais. There for a quarter of a century he dominated the stage of central Europe and summed up every vital impulse of the theatre, with the exception of some of the Parisian developments of the early 1920s. His activity continued until the advent of the Nazi régime when he went to America, where he died.

In the years immediately following the

First World War the dominant aesthetic movement in Germany was known as Expressionism. So far as scenic design was concerned this reduced itself to an attempt to 'make the décor act'. This meant on the one hand a drastic simplification of scenery—playing *Richard III*, for example, on a single flight of blood-red steps—and on the other the twisting of the shapes of inanimate objects to emphasize the mood of a play. Curiously enough, the most complete example of this was not in a play, but in a film, the famous *Cabinet of Dr. Caligari*. In Russia Evreinov's theory of 'monodrama' took up the same theme, and the Dutch director Herman Rosse experimented in the theatre with animated backgrounds, some of them projected by a cinematograph machine. The designs of the American designer Robert Edmond Jones (1887–1954) for *Macbeth* in 1921 showed lopsided cardboard archways as crazily insecure as the fortunes of the hero whose mood they reflected and emphasized (for an example of his work, see No. 87). In the same year another American designer, Norman Bel Geddes (1893–1958), schemed to build in Madison Square Gardens a gigantic theatre specially for the production of Dante's *Divine Comedy*, with a kind of permanent setting for Heaven, Hell, and Purgatory; but this ambitious project was never realized.

In England the theatre remained for the most part indifferent to Continental and American developments. The designs of artists like Charles Ricketts (1866–1931) broke no new ground, magnificent as some of them were (see No. 98), but Lovat Fraser (1890–1921), had he lived, might have inaugurated a movement of far-reaching significance. His famous designs for *The Beggar's Opera* made use of a very simple semi-permanent setting which could be either indoors or out by the expedient of changing two small painted panels. It should not be forgotten, however, that one of Reinhardt's most revolutionary productions was ordered for, and produced in, London by Charles B. Cochran—*The Miracle* at Olympia. In general the English theatre remained faithful to realism and the box-set, and the large number of good stage-designers who existed found little scope for their talents.

France produced no stage director with the sweep and variety of Reinhardt or Diaghilev, but important developments took place in the French theatre in the years immediately before and after the First World War. The scenic traditions of the Russian Ballet were carried on by the Ballets Suédois, by Comte Étienne de Beaumont's Soirées de Paris, and to a lesser extent by Jacques Rouché, who took over the direction of the Théâtre d'Art in 1910 and employed such artists as Dethomas, Drésa and Dunoyer de Segonzac. But the most interesting of the *régisseurs* were those who strove to get away from the whole tradition of the painted scene. The greatest of these was Jacques Copeau (1878–1949), who at the Vieux-Colombier arranged, in a very small space, a permanent setting in which the classics could be played in a new (or a very old) way. Later Copeau went round the country with a troupe of actors—les Copiaus—who played, in barns and market-places, pieces written by themselves or improvised on the spot. We are back in the world of the medieval theatre and the *commedia dell'arte*, where the actor is paramount, and have parted company with the whole question of scenic design.

Charles Dullin (1885–1949) founded the Théâtre de l'Atelier in 1921 and two years later began production in a regular theatre in Montmartre. His décors were extremely simple, formed for the most part of easily movable screens. The special flavour of a scene was less a matter of scenic design than of costume and manner of playing, but Dullin sought also by a modified constructivism to allow the actors three dimensions to move in instead of only two.

Louis Jouvet (1887–1951), a great actor as well as producer, learned much from Copeau, but struck out on his own original lines. He believed that there could be no rebirth of the theatre without rebuilding it from the beginning. In his actual productions at the Comédie des Champs-Élysées he strove for an extreme simplicity, a scene in which the décors were merely indicated without any attempt at illusion. A later worker at the same theatre was Gaston Baty (1885–1952). He asked of his actors a minimum of gesture and emphasis. His décors also were simple, but he strove to make each detail significant, bearing a part in the action. At the Théâtre des Arts, and particularly at the Mathurins, Georges Pitoëff (1896–1939), a Russian actor who settled in Paris, had many successes, of which the most notable was Shaw's *Saint Joan*, but his characteristic style was seen most clearly in a play like *Les Ratés*, with its division of the scene into a series of compartments, like the 'houses' of the medieval stage.

In Russia itself the Revolution left Stanislavsky in charge of the Art Theatre of Moscow, but there were some who had studied under him who were dissatisfied with the methods of realism. Chief among these was Vsevolod Meyerhold (1874–?1943). He wished to restore the primacy of the actor, and at the same time to abolish the 'mystic gulf' which had for so long separated the actor from his audience. Hence a frank theatricality, with the action spilling over among the spectators and drawing them into the communion of the represented drama. In revolt against any kind of realism he thrust the scene-painter out of the theatre, and reduced scenery to a few scaffoldings on a bare stage. An even more drastic exponent of constructivism was Alexander Taïrov (1885–1950) of the Moscow Kamerny Theatre. After the Revolution, academic art was swept away and artists of the advanced school found scope for their talents not only in the actual theatre but in organizing popular manifestations, military reviews, and open-air fêtes. The destruction and disorder everywhere apparent gave birth to constructivism, which was partly the result of a natural desire to stabilize life, and partly an echo of the theories of the futurists with all their admiration for the bare lines of the machine. Constructivism for Taïrov developed into a system of stage scaffolding with the various actions of the play taking place at different levels, up flights of wooden steps, across ladders, or on little jutting platforms far above the stage. Decoration was reduced to the frankly symbolic, to an almost mathematical abstraction. For certain modern plays, especially those which are assumed to take place in a workshop or factory, constructivism was very effective, but it was hardly a universal formula and was soon abandoned by its chief exponents. In Rabinovitch's sets for the Moscow Art Theatre production of the *Lysistrata* of Aristophanes the scenery was simplified almost to the point of abstraction, but did suggest Greek architecture in a non-naturalistic way. Within recent years the Russian theatre would appear to have swung back to a kind of stylized realism and even to a certain romanticizing tendency when dealing with plays of the past. Certainly the almost fanatical extravagances of the early years of Soviet rule have been abandoned.

Throughout Europe the period of fundamental innovation ended with the 1920s. The 1930s were, almost from the first, overshadowed by the threat of coming war and few new and vital experiments were made. But England at last began to catch up with Continental developments. The increased interest in opera and ballet opened a whole new field of which advantage was taken by William Chappell, Roger Furse, and Leslie Hurry. After the Second World War the rise of a new, non-realistic drama gave scope to such designers as Edmund Delaney, Sophie Fedorovitch, Osbert Lancaster, Michael Ayrton, Alan Barlow, Cecil Beaton, Feliks Topolski, and John Piper. Other artists who have done excellent work for the theatre in England during recent years include John Gower Parks (1905–55), James Bailey, Nicholas Georgiadis, Peter Goffin, Felix Kelly, Tanya Moiseiwitch (see No. 89), Lila de Nobili, Reece Pemberton (see No. 103), Osborne Robinson, Leonard Rosoman, Loudon Sainthill, Hugh Stevenson, Franco Zeffirelli, Sean Kenny (see No. 113) and Jocelyn Herbert (see No. 112).

London had the opportunity of seeing the work of a number of foreign artists. Peter Brook's production of *Salomé* had scenes and costumes by Salvador Dali, while the American Jo Mielziner mounted a *A Streetcar Named Desire*. The last-named is one of the most successful stage designers in America (see No. 106). Another veteran is Boris Aronson (see No. 111), while interesting work has been done by Oliver Smith, Harry Horner, Horace Armstead, Stewart Chaney, Nat Karson, Millia Davenport, James Reynolds, Aline Bernstein (see No. 82), Simon Lissim, Claude Bragdon, and Raoul Pene du Bois.

A marked feature of the French stage has been the willingness of directors to employ as scenic artists those who have already made their reputation as easel painters, e.g. Fernand Léger and Christian Bérard (see No. 104). Some directors and authors like Gaston Baty, Jouvet, and Jean Cocteau have designed their own sets and costumes. Among the professional stage designers may be mentioned Félix Labisse, Jean-Victor Hugo, André Barsacq, J. D. Malclès, Gischia, Jean Mercure, Georges Vitely, Pierre Valde, Jacques Fabbri, and Georges Wakhevitch (see No. 110).

It was for a long time difficult to discover what was happening behind the Iron Curtain, but an exhibition at the Festival Hall in London in 1956 showed the work of a number of Soviet stage designers who would otherwise have been unknown to the West, among them V. Simonov (see Nos. 95 and 99), Peter Williams (1902–47), and G. Epishin, who designed 'The Snow Maiden' for the London Festival Ballet in 1961 (see also RUSSIA). The opening of the new opera-house in Leipzig gave opportunities for such East German artists as Eleanor Kleiber and Erika Simmank.

In recent years there have been several interesting developments both in Europe and America. A new enthusiasm for platform stages of all kinds and for theatre-in-the-round seemed for a time to threaten the very existence of scene-*painting* as such. Recently, however, there seem to be signs of a reaction, due to a realization that the plays of such masters as Ibsen and Chekhov were intended to be presented inside the proscenium arch and that they lose something of their intimacy on open stages. At least it can be said that the stage designer and director of the future will not be confined to any single manner of presentation. He will be able to choose the frank rhetoric of the platform stage, the built-up box-set of realism, or any degree of abstraction and stylization. The art of scenic design has, as it were, come full circle: all styles are possible, and the only question the artist has to ask himself is which of these is most in harmony with the mood and message of the play.

JAMES LAVER

SCHIKANEDER, EMANUEL [really JOHANN JOSEF] (1751–1812). The son of a lackey from Straubing, Schikaneder became a minor actor at Augsburg in 1773 before moving to Innsbruck in 1776. He married the actress Eleonore Ardtin, and in 1788 became director of the Moser company, of which they were both members. He was a man of fine figure with a good bass voice, and excelled in both serious and comic roles in plays ranging from the classics (he was a noted Hamlet) to popular farce and the *Singspiel*. He was a supporter of the German opera of Gluck, Haydn, and, above all, Mozart, whom he first met at Salzburg in 1780. Schikaneder was favoured by the Emperor Joseph II, and produced *Singspiele* (which the latter was especially eager to promote) at the Kärntnertor Theater in

1784–5. From 1785–6 he was at the Hofburgtheater. After a period away from Vienna, he returned in 1789 and obtained Imperial consent for the erection of a new theatre near the Glacis, but was not able to complete this project until 1801, when his Theater an der Wien was opened. This represented the climax of his career. In 1791 the collaboration with Mozart for which he is now chiefly remembered had resulted in 'Die Zauberflöte', in which he himself created the part of Papageno, a character who sums up, as indeed does the whole opera, the traditions and motifs of the Viennese popular theatre. As well as being an actor, Schikaneder was also the greatest impresario of his age, noted for the lavish spectacle with which he presented a long series of romantic dramas of the age of chivalry, many of them from his own pen. After 1801 Schikaneder's fortunes declined, and he died poor and insane. J. B. BEDNALL

SCHILLER, JOHANN CHRISTOPH FRIEDRICH VON (1759–1805), German dramatist and poet, who ranks as one of the chief playwrights of Germany. He was the son of an army surgeon, and after receiving a good education at the school founded by the Duke of Württemberg for the sons of his officers, he was himself destined for the medical profession. Literature, however, was his passion, and he was only 22 when his first play, *Die Räuber*, was accepted by Dalberg for production, after the action had been relegated to the safe distance of the sixteenth century. The play, which deals with the hostility of two brothers, was an outburst of pent-up resentment, and thrilled the younger generation. Schiller, who was now an army doctor, twice attended performances without leave of absence. A severe reprimand and a fortnight's imprisonment left him smarting and resentful, and in 1782 he took refuge in Mannheim. He was not unkindly received, though his uncouth manners were at variance with his new surroundings, and his relationship with Dalberg, who appointed him author and stage-manager to the Mannheim theatre, was cordial. In spite of this, and of the success of *Kabale und Liebe* in 1784, Schiller, who was living in Mannheim under an assumed name, found life difficult. He was heavily in debt, and might have starved had not a kindly friend, Frau von Wolzogen, offered him her country cottage as a refuge. He was also befriended by Charlotte von Kalb, one of the many cultured women of the period who sought in literary patronage compensation for a marriage of convenience. Her influence may be traced in *Don Carlos* (1787), Schiller's first attempt at historical tragedy in the grand style. While he was engaged on it he went to Leipzig, where he first met Gottfried Körner, one of his admirers, who became a lifelong friend. Under Körner's influence Schiller made Posa, the friend who lays down his life in a vain effort to save Don Carlos, the champion of religious tolerance, prepared to carry his ideals into the presence of Philip II himself.

This play, which was produced in 1787, marks the transition to Schiller's later style, though twelve years were to elapse before another play came from his pen. Meanwhile he married and was appointed unsalaried professor of history at Jena, eking out his meagre income from students' fees by historical essays and the editorship of *Thalia*, in which he and Körner published the results of their aesthetic discussions. The two main works of this period were historical, *Die Geschichte des Abfalls der vereinigten Niederlande*, written before he went to Jena, and *Die Geschichte des dreißigjährigen Kriegs*.

The intensive study necessary for this latter work provided him with the material for his great trilogy of *Wallenstein*, which was finally completed in 1799, and translated into English by Coleridge in the following year. He was by this time, after a period of rest and recuperation from illness, which he spent mainly in an intensive study of Kant, settled in Weimar, where he enjoyed the friendship and collaboration of Goethe in pursuit of their common goal—an ordered, self-disciplined, and seemly society—and in the denunciation of mediocrity and low aims. Nothing now remained but the delimitating in *Naive und sentimentalische Dichtung* of his own reflective poetic temperament from Goethe's spontaneous genius before he strode forward from achievement to achievement until his regrettably early death from tuberculosis in 1805.

These last few years saw the appearance of *Maria Stuart* (1800), of *Die Jungfrau von Orleans* (1801), of *Die Braut von Messina* (1803), and of Schiller's last play, *Wilhelm Tell* (1804) (for a detailed discussion of these, see GERMANY, 4). W. E. DELP

SCHILLER, LEON (1887–1954), Polish theatre director. Born in Cracow, he lived for some time in Paris, where he became a disciple of Gordon Craig, later collaborating with him in *The Mask* (1908–9) and organizing the first exhibition of Craig's drawings in Warsaw in 1913. After studying music in Vienna, he became director of the Teatr Polski in Warsaw. At the Reduta Theatre between 1924 and 1926 he staged a number of early Polish liturgical dramas, and then directed the Bogusławski Theatre. Here his productions of Shakespeare, Wyspiański, and particularly of Krasiński's *The Undivine Comedy* (1926), were particularly remarked. Like Wyspiański, he envisaged the 'total theatre' to which everything—acting, music, scenery, lighting—contributed, and which was above all a theatre of ideas. His political affiliations with the Left finally led to the closing of his theatre, but he continued the struggle elsewhere, in Łódź, Lwów, and again in Warsaw. One of his most remarkable productions was *Roar, China!* by Tretiakov, but he also remained faithful to the romantic Polish repertory, producing Mickiewicz's *Forefathers' Eve* in several towns between 1932 and 1934, and at Sofia, in Bulgarian, in 1937. By this time his style was becoming simpler and more supple, and tending towards neo-realism, and he had already had a great influence on the younger generation of directors and scene-designers through his work at the Institute of the Art of the Theatre, where many years later he was to work again, and to found the theatre journal, *Pamiętnik Teatralny*. Interned at Auschwitz, he was released in 1941, and since the Germans had closed all the Polish theatres, he produced secretly, in a convent near Warsaw, the old Polish liturgical dramas. In 1944 he founded a Polish theatre in Germany, and later took it to Łódź, where his last important production was *The Tempest* (1947). He left there in 1949 and returned for a year to the Teatr Polski in Warsaw. In spite of some reaction against his influence, he left a decisive mark on the Polish theatre. In 1961 a collection of his writings on the theatre was published under the title of *Teatr Ogromny*.

SCHLEGEL. (1) JOHANN ELIAS VON (1719–49), German dramatist, author of some good comedies, and of tragedies, some of which are historical. He received his literary training from Gottsched in Leipzig, but though his own plays are conservative in style, and he employs the alexandrine line in tragedy, he soon emancipated himself from Gottsched's yoke in thought and in aesthetic judgement, a process which was helped by his appointment to Copenhagen, where a more liberal atmosphere prevailed. His objective valuation of the drama of different nations, and his views on the relation of art and nature, are well in advance of his time. He was, however, destined to be eclipsed by Lessing's more trenchant mind and greater forcefulness of expression. His nephew, (2) AUGUST WILHELM (1767–1845), is remembered more as a sensitive and discerning critic of enormous range, and a highly talented translator of Shakespeare, Dante, Cervantes, and Calderón, than as a creative artist, though he wrote some sixteen plays. He had little originality, but avoided the extravagances of his fellow Romantics. In his famous lectures given at Vienna, *Über dramatische Kunst und Literatur*, published from 1809 to 1811, he was the first to trace the development of drama in all nations. W. E. DELP

SCHLEY'S MUSIC-HALL, NEW YORK, see SAVOY THEATRE, 2.

SCHNITZLER, ARTHUR (1862–1931), Austrian dramatist, a doctor by profession, who brought to his plays something of the dispassionate attitude of the consulting-room. His first work for the theatre, and the one which is usually associated with his name, was *Anatol*, a series of sketches of an irresponsible gallant. This was written in 1890, and was followed in 1894 by the darker side of the picture in *Liebelei*, where the working-class girl kills herself on learning of the death of the young aristocrat who had been merely trifling with her. Among his later plays are *Der grüne Kakadu* (1899), a one-act play on the French Revolution in which Schnitzler handles with a sure touch the change from irresponsible make-believe to grim reality, *Der einsame Weg* (1904), a sensitive play of delicate half-lights, *Der Ruf des Lebens* (1905), and *Professor Bernhardi* (1912), his one contribution to the problem-play, in which he views from all angles the repercussions of an anti-Semitic incident in a Viennese hospital (see also AUSTRIA).

SCHOOL DRAMA, a term applied to the academic, educational type of play which developed under the influence of the humanists, and is found in the early dramatic literature of all European countries. Written by scholars for performance by schoolboys, as part of their educational curriculum, they were originally all in Latin, a tradition which persisted longest in the Jesuit colleges (see JESUIT DRAMA). A Shrewsbury School ordinance of 1577–8, No. 21, enacted that 'every Thursday the scholars of the highest form . . . shall for exercise declaim and play one act of a comedy', presumably in Latin. Elsewhere they tended quickly to slip into the vernacular, and had some influence on the development of the non-academic, popular, and later professional drama. There was a great deal of dramatic activity in English schools and colleges in the first half of the sixteenth century, and the first two regular English comedies—*Ralph Roister Doister* and *Gammer Gurton's Needle*—were given at Eton (or possibly Westminster), and at Christ's College, Cambridge, respectively. (For further information on SCHOOL DRAMA, see the separate countries of Europe.) The tradition of an annual school play has been revived in many public and other schools. Bradfield does a Greek play in the original in an open-air theatre annually. Harrow productions of Shakespeare in an approximation to an Elizabethan theatre made some stir under Ronald Watkins in the 1950s, Sloane School gave a long series of excellent productions under the headmastership of Guy Boas, as did Bryanston under Coade. The only surviving tradition of a Latin play in modern times was at Westminster (see WESTMINSTER PLAY) though plays in Greek are occasionally given at Oxford and Cambridge.

SCHÖNHERR, KARL (1867–1943), see AUSTRIA.

SCHÖNEMANN, JOHANN FRIEDRICH (1704–82), German actor, originally a harlequin in a travelling troupe. He later joined the company of Caroline Neuber, where he acted a variety of parts, and was particularly admired in the valets of French comedy. He married an actress, Anna Rachel Weigler, and after the Neubers' break with Gottsched and their departure for Russia he formed his own company in 1740 and took Caroline Neuber's place in Leipzig. Into this new company he took Sophie Schröder, Ekhof, and Ackermann, all destined to play so large a part in the theatrical development of Germany. Schönemann, who was 36 when he formed his company, was at first an able and astute leader, though he lacked the idealism which had inspired the young Caroline Neuber. He continued to act well in comedy, but was less successful in tragedy, retaining to the end the stiff and pompous declamatory style evolved by Gottsched and Caroline Neuber. Later he became completely immersed in his hobby of horse-dealing and left the company to Ekhof, and, when financial ruin could no longer be avoided, he abandoned his profession entirely and retired into private life.

SCHREYVOGEL, Josef (1768–1832), manager of the Vienna Burgtheater during its most successful period. He first became involved in theatrical matters in 1802, and by 1814 was in charge of the choice, casting, and production of plays at the Burgtheater. He continued in this position, in spite of financial and other difficulties, introducing many excellent and much-needed reforms, until he was finally dismissed in 1832 for outspokenness unpalatable to his employers. Among the authors he encouraged and produced, often in the face of opposition from the censor, was Grillparzer, while he was instrumental in bringing to the Burgtheater Heinrich Anschutz, who became one of the leading actors of Vienna. Schreyvogel's own plays are now forgotten.

SCHRÖDER, Friedrich Ludwig (1744–1816), the greatest name in German theatrical annals, a fine actor and the first to introduce Shakespeare to Germany. He was the son of Sophie Schröder (see ACKERMANN, 2) by her first marriage, and grew up in the theatrical company of her second husband, Konrad Ackermann. He was acting at three years old, and had a hard, unhappy childhood, which is described in his biography by his friend F. L. W. Meyer. On the outbreak of war in 1756 the Ackermann company left Königsberg, where Schröder was then at school, and he was unaccountably left behind. He lived in the deserted theatre, which he occasionally was able to let to wandering companies, and earned his living somehow. From his tenants he learnt acrobatics and dancing, and at 13 was befriended by an English rope-dancer and acrobat, Michael Stuart, and his charming Danish wife. A year or two later, after a hazardous journey on foot, he succeeded in rejoining the Ackermanns in Switzerland. He worked with the company, but was contemptuous of acting, which he thought a puerile occupation compared to the rigours of tumbling.

The turning-point of his career came when Ekhof, then at the height of his powers, joined the company. Schröder, though outwardly as contemptuous and ill-mannered as usual, saw at last what acting could be, and for the five years that Ekhof remained with them he studied him closely, deepening and purifying his own art in the process. Conscious of his growing mastery, he manœuvred Ekhof into such a difficult position that the older man retreated, leaving his young rival—he was then about 25—a clear field. During the Ackermanns' occupation of the new National Theatre at Hamburg Schröder was much admired, particularly in the parts of the quick-witted, light-heeled valets of French comedy, but when a new management was installed he declined to remain under it, and joined a popular but somewhat inferior travelling company run by Joseph von Kurz, which continued to give the old improvised comedy. Here he remained for a year, with little profit to himself, and then returned to Hamburg, where, the successive managements having failed, and Ackermann being now too old and indolent to take over, the young Schröder grasped the reins of management with a firm hand. He married in 1773 a young actress named Christine Hart (? –1829), who made him an excellent wife, and though the financial side of the company was still under the control of his mother, now a widow, he took complete responsibility for the artistic side. He seemed to grow up overnight, and to his excellent qualities as a brilliant actor he added those of astute manager and inspiring producer. At the head of a brilliant company, which included his two half-sisters, Dorothea and Charlotte Ackermann, he was in the forefront of the new movement in Germany. His first independent production was *Emilia Galotti*; he encouraged the *Sturm und Drang* writers, and was the first producer of Goethe's play *Götz von Berlichingen*, in which he abolished the last remnants of French costume—powdered wigs and lace ruffles—not only reforming the costumes and scenery, but directing the new approach to acting necessitated by the new type of play.

The chief enterprise with which Schröder's name is imperishably linked, however, is the introduction of Shakespeare to the German stage. He was known on the printed page to all the ardent youngsters of the new generation, but they had not had an opportunity of seeing him acted. Even now, they saw him only in the adapted versions made by Schröder himself, where Hamlet survived, as did Cordelia, but even so each production was a revelation, and probably as much as audiences could have stomached at the time. The series started in 1776 with *Hamlet*, in which Brockmann played the name-part and Schröder the Ghost (he later played Laertes, the Grave-digger, and Hamlet), and by 1780 eleven plays had been given, of which *Othello* was a failure and *King Lear* an outstanding success.

With this pioneer work Schröder also combined the production of a more conservative repertory, including the once popular but now forgotten plays and monodramas of Brandes, ballets, and even light musical pieces. He continued to dance himself till 1778, the year in which he did Lear, and made the rest of the company do the same. He worked his actors hard—indeed, he was considered to have caused the death by overwork and worry of his gifted half-sister Charlotte—but he taught them the value of application, of steady consistent progress, and of team-work. The first phase of Schröder's Hamburg management, which brought him in nothing financially, since his mother kept the profits and gave him a beggarly salary, was perhaps the most glorious of his career. It ended when friction between himself and the company caused him to go with his wife to Vienna, where he remained for four years as an honoured guest-artist of the Burgtheater. This period contributed little to his own development, but he left a mark on the Viennese stage. Under his influence it quietened down considerably and lost much of its pompous ranting in tragedy and its old-fashioned foolery in comedy. Indeed, Schröder may be said to have laid the foundations of the subtle and refined ensemble playing of the Vienna Burgtheater company which was later to become their distinguishing mark.

Back in Hamburg in 1786 Schröder took over the theatre again, and raised it from the slough of despond into which a series of incompetent managements had plunged it. For twelve years he kept it orderly and prosperous, and at the head of the theatrical world in Germany. It was a less glorious period than his previous one. His ideals had flagged a little, and the stage that should have seen the triumphs of the mature Goethe and Schiller was given over to the trivialities of Kotzebue and Iffland. But it was a prosperous time, and at 54, having achieved financial independence, Schröder gave up the stage entirely, buying a country estate in Holstein where he spent the rest of his life in intellectual activity and honourable retirement. It is interesting to note, in passing, that Schröder and his sister figure in Goethe's *Wilhelm Meister* as Serlo and Aurelie.

SCHUCH, Franz (*c.* 1716–64), German harlequin-player, leader of a company of travelling actors to which the great actor Ekhof belonged for a short time after he left Schönemann. Brandes, a poor actor and a prolific dramatist, who afterwards obtained some success, had his first stable engagement with Schuch, and describes him in his memoirs as a fine comedian and improviser, homely without descending to triviality, humorous without vulgarity. He was a shrewd businessman, and much esteemed by his company and by the audiences of the towns where he played. Lessing thought highly of him, and attended his performances whenever possible. After his death his three sons, who had inherited some of his talents but not the probity of his character, undertook the management of the troupe, which they soon reduced to bankruptcy. It was then taken over by Döbbelin, who had previously been a member of the company, and established by him in Berlin, where it prospered.

SCHUSTER, Ignaz (1779–1835), Austrian actor, one of the most popular comic figures in the Viennese popular theatre during the Congress period. Born in Vienna, Schuster, who was small and deformed, was trained as a singer, and from 1798 to 1806 was a member of the Schottenkloster choir. After a period with Karl Marinelli's Baden company, he joined the Leopoldstädter company in 1801 and remained with it until his death. From 1805 onwards he appeared in local *Singspiele*, particularly in Joachim Perinet's adaptations of works by Philipp Hafner. Schuster gradually came to the fore in small comic parts, but did not achieve fame until 1813, when he created the part of Chrysostomus Staberl the umbrella-maker in Adolf Bäuerle's *Die Bürger in Wien* (see AUSTRIA). Thereafter he was the hero of innumerable *Staberliaden*, many of them written by Karl Carl, and gradually replaced Anton Hasenhut in popular favour. He was never a rival of Ferdinand Raimund, however, whose melancholy irony provided an effective contrast to his own essentially sunny and self-confident humour. J. B. BEDNALL

SCHWARTZ, Maurice (1889–1960), Jewish actor and producer. Born in the Ukraine, he was to have gone to America with his family in 1899, but owing to some misunderstanding over the steamship passages he was left behind in England. There he lived by his wits, working in a rag factory, doing odd jobs in the Yiddish theatre in London, and singing in a synagogue choir. Two years later his family traced him and took him to New York. In 1905 he joined the Delancey Street Dramatic Club, where his first appearance earned him a job in a Baltimore theatre. After several years in Yiddish theatres there and in Cincinnati, Chicago, and Philadelphia, he joined David Kessler's company in New York. In 1912 he produced his first play, a translation from the English, following it a year later with an original play. In 1918 he became a partner in the Irving Place Theatre, where, after a short period of management on his own elsewhere, he opened his Jewish Art Theatre. This was successful, and in 1924 he embarked on a tour of Europe. On his return to New York Schwartz moved his theatre to Broadway, hoping to attract assimilated Jewry. The result was disappointing, and he returned to Second Avenue, traditional New York home of the Yiddish theatre. He then toured the Argentine, visited Palestine, where he worked with Ohel, and appeared in films. His repertory was extensive, including both Jewish and other classics, and he encouraged the development of many Yiddish playwrights by his careful productions of their early plays. In 1959 Schwartz went to Israel in order to establish a Yiddish company there, but died after producing only one play, Singer's *Yoshe Kalb*. E. HARRIS

SCISSOR CROSS, see STAGE DIRECTIONS.

SCISSOR STAGE, see BOAT TRUCK.

SCOFIELD, Paul (1922–), English actor who, after appearing in a variety of parts in a students' repertory company, and on tour during the Second World War, joined the Birmingham Rep in 1945. Here he scored a great success as the Bastard in *King John*, and in the following year moved to Stratford-upon-Avon with Sir Barry Jackson, who had been appointed director of the Memorial Theatre. There he remained until 1948, as a fantastical Don Armado in Peter Brook's production of *Love's Labour's Lost*, an endearing Clown in *The Winter's Tale*, a suavely ironic Lucio in *Measure for Measure*, a fiery Mercutio, a wistful Aguecheek, and a Hamlet whose excellences had to struggle against unbecoming Victorian trappings. This part he played again, in more favourable circumstances, in 1955, first in London and then at the Moscow Art Theatre, in the first English company to appear in Russia since the Revolution. For this, and for his services to the stage, he was appointed C.B.E. in the New Year Honours of 1956. In the intervening years he had been seen in a wide variety of parts, to each of which he brought some new facet of his many-sided personality. He was Tegeus-Chromis in *A Phoenix Too Frequent* at the Arts Theatre (1946), Alexander in Rattigan's ill-fated historical pageant, *Adventure Story* (1949), and made a great impression as the twin brothers Hugo and Frederic in *Ring Round the Moon* (1950), which ran for two years. One of his few modern parts was Sturgess in *The River Line* (1952), and he also played the drunken priest in *The Power and the Glory* (1956). One of his finest performances was as Pierre in *Venice Preserved* in 1953 at the Lyric, Hammersmith, where he had previously been seen as the foppish Witwoud in *The Way of the World*. He was also outstanding as Sir Thomas More in *A Man For All Seasons* (1960). In 1962 he appeared with the Royal Shakespeare company as Lear, in which he also appeared in London and on tour to great critical acclaim all over Europe and America. With his strongly moulded face, his curious voice, sometimes harsh, sometimes bell-like, but always arresting, and his astonishing versatility, Scofield is an actor who escapes classification, but has already proved himself a power in the English-speaking theatre.

SCOTLAND. The seemingly belated appearance of a Scottish drama was really a revival after early arrested growth, for in the fifteenth and sixteenth centuries Moralities and festival pageants flourished in Scotland as elsewhere, though Sir David Lindsay's *Ane Pleasant Satyre of the Thrie Estaitis* (produced at Cupar in 1552 and revived during the Edinburgh Festival of 1948) is the only example to survive. Indeed, the Scottish Renaissance seemed at one time to be tending towards the theatre though, once more, only one play of the period survives, the comedy *Philotus*. The country's turbulent history, in which the clash of individuals had free play, and the natural humour of the people, offered a fitting soil for the drama, while dramatic imagination shone richly in the great ballads. But a Scots parallel to the Elizabethan stage did not develop, the green shoots being blighted by the civil and religious strife of the seventeenth century and by the removal of the Court to London in 1603. Drama did not begin to flourish again in Scotland until the second half of the eighteenth century, and it was not until the 1920s that her native authors concerned themselves at all seriously with the writing of plays in the vernacular, or in English on Scottish themes for production on a Scottish stage. Satire, fantasy, humour, and a taste for the macabre—these elements in Lindsay's Morality and in the non-dramatic writings of the Makars have, however, found free expression in the plays of a modern Scottish dramatist like Bridie, thus suggesting that the roots of the modern Scottish dramatic movement are embedded deeply in the past.

From the close of the sixteenth until the opening of the twentieth century there were, however, some Scottish playwrights, including William Clark, Sir Thomas St Serfe, David Crawford, James Thomson, Archibald McLaren, Joanna Baillie, and John Galt. The most prominent of the manifestations of indigenous drama in Scotland was the tragedy *Douglas*, by John Home. This laborious work was produced in 1756 in the 'Concert Hall', Canongate, Edinburgh. A happier essay was Allan Ramsay's *Gentle Shepherd*, published in 1725, but which, being written in Scots, had to wait over a quarter of a century for a professional production, the Edinburgh Company being recruited from England. In 1736 Ramsay had ventured to build a theatre in one of the closes of the Scottish capital, but it was immediately closed under the Licensing Act, an English measure. Towards the end of the eighteenth century the theatre fared a little better, existing more or less regularly in both Edinburgh and Glasgow, and spreading to the other principal cities and towns, while throughout the nineteenth century it flourished. Day bills issued between 1815 and 1817 by the Theatre Royal, Edinburgh, and the Theatre Royal, Glasgow, reveal the existence of a stirring theatrical life. Stock companies played Shakespeare and the eighteenth-century classics regularly, and introduced new comedies and farces every week. Itinerant stars from the London stage—Kean, the Kembles, and others—paid regular visits, while distinguished actors like Charles Mackay (*c.* 1785–1857) could spend their whole professional careers in Scotland. Dramatic versions of Sir Walter Scott's novels were popular. *Guy Mannering* (published in 1815) appeared on the stage in Glasgow and Edinburgh in 1817. Many of the melodramas and romances produced have a Scottish flavour, and a popular 'grand Scottish National Pantomime' entitled *Oscar and Malvina* drew inspiration from Macpherson's *Ossian*. Among other pantomimes were *Sawney Bean's Cave* and *The Falls of Clyde*. *Deacon Brodie* (1880), by R. L. Stevenson and W. E. Henley, and the early plays of Barrie, were heralds of the distinctly Scottish drama that was to rise in the twentieth century (see also EDINBURGH and GLASGOW).

The latter half of the nineteenth century saw the stock company replaced by the English touring company, but Scotland made a fresh contribution to the theatre in the five years 1909–14, when the repertory movement that followed the impact of Ibsen made its way north of the Border, inspiring the Glasgow Repertory Theatre, which during its five seasons brought together some of the most brilliant actors and actresses of a generation, and produced plays by prominent English and Continental dramatists, as well as a few Scottish plays, the most notable being John Ferguson's *Campbell of Kilmohr*, a one-act tragedy of exceptional merit. Though the company, according to the declared policy of its founder, Alfred Wareing, was to be 'peculiarly adapted for the production of plays national in character', in fact it was more English than Scottish.

The outbreak of the war in 1914 forced the Glasgow Repertory Theatre to close down. Its work in fostering Scots drama was not forgotten, however, and what remained of its funds (about £400) was transferred to the St. Andrew Society, which used the money to launch the movement that produced the Scottish National Players. This body of active and talented actors, mainly amateur, formed between 1921 and 1936 the chief focal point of native Scots drama. It soon ceased to be part of the St. Andrew Society and functioned independently. In Jan. 1922 the Scottish National Theatre Society was formed to support it. Its aims were to develop Scottish drama, to found a Scottish National Theatre, and to encourage the taste of the public for good drama of any type. These aims were only partially fulfilled. The society never acquired a theatre building of its own, and the development of a school of Scottish dramatists proceeded very slowly. The movement unfortunately failed to establish in Glasgow a Scottish counterpart of the Abbey Theatre in Dublin, mainly owing to the absence of financial backing, the prevalence of economic depression, the industrialization of the modern Lowland Scot, and the magnetic force of the London stage, which drew away producers and players, and was the Mecca of the best dramatists. Nevertheless the Scottish National players shaped a number of excellent actors and produced the works of over thirty Scottish dramatists, in addition to many plays by Shakespeare, Shaw, Chekhov, Sierra, and others.

When the energies of the Scottish National players flagged in the 1930s a new company of Glasgow amateurs, the Curtain Theatre, became the pioneering vehicle for the production of new plays in the vernacular. In the meantime various theatrical ventures of a repertory nature appeared on the Scottish scene, presenting mostly English plays. The Masque Theatre, the Brandon-Thomas players, the Howard and Wyndham players, and the Wilson Barrett company, conducted seasons of varying length with a fair amount of success in Glasgow and Edinburgh. From 1935 onwards a repertory theatre in Perth, directed by David Steuart and Marjorie Dence, ploughed a gallant furrow, producing plays by authors old and new, and in the summer of 1939 the first Scottish Theatre Festival was successfully launched there, at which the plays presented were Chekhov's *Three Sisters*, Bridie's *The Golden Legend of Shults* (a first performance), Shaw's *Caesar and Cleopatra*, and Shakespeare's *Romeo and Juliet*. In 1947 the management of the theatre was broadened by the formation of a Board of Directors.

The Dundee Repertory Theatre was founded in 1939. In the past the commercial play was prominent in its programmes, but it has now embarked on a more adventurous policy. In 1961, with the aid of a grant from Scottish Television and a guarantee from the Arts Council, a first play was commissioned from a young Scottish writer, Clifford Hanley. In 1963 the theatre was extensively redecorated by Richard Buckle, but was burnt down. Within four months, performances were resumed in a disused church converted to a theatre. The Perth, and in the past the Dundee, companies have undertaken much touring in Scotland; both have given command performances at Balmoral and have appeared at the Edinburgh Festival.

The work of the Curtain for the creation of a Scottish drama was taken up by the Rutherglen Repertory Theatre and the Glasgow Unity Theatre; then by the Glasgow Citizens' Theatre, started by James Bridie in 1943, and the Edinburgh Gateway Theatre, which opened in 1946. The first Edinburgh Festival in 1947 presented no Scottish drama; but at the second, *The Three Estates* was a revelation of the riches of Scottish acting and of the Scots tongue. 1951 saw the addition of a fifth Scottish repertory company with the establishment of the Pitlochry Festival Theatre. In 1963 the Traverse Theatre Club opened its small theatre in the Royal Mile in Edinburgh, and soon became internationally known for its policy of presenting new plays. The Gateway Theatre gave its final performance at the Edinburgh Festival of 1965, handing over to the Edinburgh Civic Theatre Trust. No account of the contemporary situation in Scotland would be complete without a mention of the tiny but picturesque Byre Theatre in St. Andrews.

Much of this development is to be credited to the Scottish Committee of the Arts Council. The repertory theatres receive grants towards their running costs, and a creative policy is supported by means of bonuses for approved plays and new drama schemes. The Scottish Committee also arranges tours. The New Scottish Touring Theatre has undertaken a dozen annual tours of the highlands and islands. The civic authorities in Glasgow, Edinburgh, and Dundee have also given substantial financial support. A stimulus was given in 1950 by the establishment in Glasgow (with James Bridie as prime mover) of a College of Dramatic Art within the Royal Scottish Academy of Music. The University of Glasgow is responsible for part of the teaching; and the B.B.C. and Citizens' Theatre also assist. The accommodation of the College includes the Athenaeum Theatre, and, since 1962, a closed-circuit television studio.

The changed status of the drama in Scotland can be seen in the career of James Bridie, a change which he did much to bring about. It was the Glasgow Repertory Theatre which helped to lead his talents towards the theatre, and it was the Scottish National Players who first produced one of his plays; but to achieve his full development as a playwright he had to turn to the resources, artistic and financial, of the English theatre. The later playwrights Robert Kemp and Robert McLellan had an alternative to the road to England and chose to write for the Scottish theatre, even if this has meant writing for a smaller audience. Their work illustrates another choice which confronts the Scottish playwright, that between English, and Scots or 'Lallans'. (The third alternative, Gaelic, need not be discussed here; there is an interesting Gaelic drama of modern origin, but the audience for it is relatively small.) The clash of English and Scottish cultures has provided a theme for several of their plays, the classic example being Kemp's *The Other Dear Charmer*. In *Let Wives Tak Tent* Kemp has achieved a better translation of Molière than would be possible in contemporary English; a similar claim can be made for Douglas Young's translations of Aristophanes. The full-blooded comedy of McLellan's *Toom Byres*, or the blend of humour and romance in Alexander Reid's *The World's Wonder*, depend on the resources of Lallans. It may be thought, however, that too high a proportion of recent Scots plays are set in the past, even when the past is as dramatic as Scotland's; and that the riches of Lallans have lured the successors of Bridie and the Unity playwrights away from the play of contemporary life.

The Community Drama Movement (see AMATEUR DRAMA) has flourished successfully in Scotland, and led to the composition of a large body of one-act plays in the vernacular, among which Joe Corrie's may be given pride of place. It has also popularized the drama in both rural and urban Scotland, and helped to keep the theatre active in a period dominated by the cinema. J. F. ARNOTT

SCOTT, CLEMENT WILLIAM (1841–1904), English dramatic critic, on the *Daily Telegraph* from 1872 until within a few years of his death. He wrote several plays under the pseudonyms 'John Doe' and 'Saville Rowe' and often in collaboration with B. C. Stephenson. Some of these were translations from Sardou, of which *Diplomacy* (1878), from *Dora*, was the most notable. He was the editor of *The Theatre*, a monthly magazine devoted to the drama, which ran from 1877 to 1897.

As a dramatic critic Scott was in the forefront of the Old Guard that put up a determined resistance to the new drama. He was at the opposite pole of contemporary criticism from William Archer, whose translations of Ibsen's plays caused such distress to Scott when they were performed in London. Scott's well-known attack on *Ghosts* was marked by that obstinate refusal to look at anything outside conventional morality which tinged his whole outlook on the theatre.

When Scott published *From 'The Bells' to 'King Arthur'*, a critical record of first-night productions at the Lyceum Theatre from 1871 to 1895, Bernard Shaw reviewed the book and wrote of the author:

> Mr. Clement Scott is not the first of our great dramatic critics but he is the first of the great dramatic reporters . . . the main secret of his popularity is that he is, above all, a sympathetic critic . . . an average young university graduate would hang himself sooner than wear his heart on his sleeve before the world as Mr. Scott does, and that is just why the average young university graduate never interests anyone in his critical remarks. . . . Mr. Scott is not a thinker: whatever question you raise with him you must raise as a question of conduct, which is a matter of feeling, and not of creed, which is a matter of intellectual order . . . the drama which asserts and argues will never be tolerated by him . . .

This was borne out by Scott's assessment of Ibsen's *Ghosts* as 'a wretched, deplorable, loathsome history, as all must admit. It might have been a tragedy had it been handled by a man of genius. Handled by an egotist and a bungler, it is only a deplorably dull play.' T. C. KEMP†

SCOTTISH COMEDIANS. These come in two, occasionally overlapping, types—the drolls, who create one comic *persona* and present it in every situation, and the character comedians, who offer studies of widely-recognized characters, such as village doctors, dance-hall queens, Kirk elders, marine engineers, and so on. Widely held to be the greatest of the drolls was Tommy Lorne (born Hugh Corcoran in a Glasgow slum), who until his early death in 1934 had reigned for a decade or two in the Glasgow Princess's and Theatre Royal pantomimes. His Dame, a working-class woman indomitable against a world that was both menacing and incomprehensible, was an individual and idolized creation. Lorne was succeeded at the Princess's by George West, a clown who maintained the Grimaldi tradition in make-up and fantastic costume; others in this tradition were Dave Willis and the late Tommy Morgan. Today, the mantle rests on the shoulders of Rikki Fulton, lean, toothy, and with the true droll's flair for comic 'business'.

The character comedian is primarily an actor with the comic talent, and his character studies at their best are acutely observed and solidly created. Will Fyffe, once a 'fit-up' actor, was the greatest of them, and they are best represented today by Duncan Macrae and Stanley Baxter, both of whom went to the pantomime and revue stage from the Glasgow Citizens' Theatre.

The Scottish minstrels, as exemplified once by Sir Harry Lauder and now by Andy Stewart, are essentially singers rather than true comedians, content to raise chuckles rather than belly-laughs. But all of them have some streak of the daft eccentricity, the pawky and sentimental humours, which seethe beneath the stolid Scots exterior, and which is revealed most strongly in the country's addiction to pantomime.

SCOTTISH COMMUNITY DRAMA ASSOCIATION, see AMATEUR THEATRE IN GREAT BRITAIN.

SCOTTISH NATIONAL PLAYERS, THE, made their first appearance under the auspices of the St. Andrew Society of Glasgow in a hall in that city in Jan. 1921, presenting three new Scottish one-act plays. A similar programme followed three months later, and towards the end of the year they presented two new full-length plays in the Athenaeum Theatre, Glasgow. They now ceased to be the responsibility of the St. Andrew Society, coming under a newly-formed body, the Scottish National Theatre Society; when the society was wound up in 1934, the Players continued independently, their last productions (after a war-time interruption), being in 1948.

Although the movement did not succeed in its aim of creating a Scottish Abbey Theatre, never acquiring a permanent home or establishing a fully professional company, it did call into being a body of plays reflecting many aspects of Scottish life by over thirty authors, including Gordon Bottomley, John Brandane, James Bridie, Donald Carswell, Joe Corrie, John Ferguson, Neil Gunn, and Robert Kemp. During the golden years from 1921 to 1931 the Players produced seventy-one new plays. In 1926 and 1927 their producer was Tyrone Guthrie. Many excellent actors were trained by the Players; some found their way to London and New York, others contributed their experience to the Glasgow Citizens' Theatre and the Gateway Theatre in Edinburgh.

J. F. ARNOTT

SCOTTISH ROSCIUS, see JOHNSTON, H. E.

SCRIBE, (AUGUSTIN) EUGÈNE (1791–1861), French dramatist, the originator and exponent of the 'well-made play'. A prolific writer, he was responsible, alone or in collaboration, for more than 400 plays, comprising tragedies, comedies, vaudevilles, and libretti for light opera. His collaborators, of whom Legouvé, Dupin, Delavigne, Mélesville, and Saintine are the best known, all brought much to the common stock, but the stagecraft was Scribe's. Yet his early plays, which began in 1810 with a protest against Romanticism, were failures, and it was not until 1815 that he achieved fame with *Une Nuit de la Garde Nationale*. Some years later the first night of *Un Verre d'eau* (1820) occasioned a stormy scene at the Comédie-Française, as it saw the first appearance of a young actress whose success was unpalatable to Mlle Mars. The most successful of Scribe's plays, and the one best remembered, was *Adrienne Lecouvreur* (1849), written in collaboration with Legouvé, who in 1874 wrote Scribe's biography. The play, though incorrect historically, provided a fine part for Rachel, and later for Sarah Bernhardt. In translation it was played by Mme Ristori, Mme Modjeska, Helen Faucit, and many others.

Scribe's popularity has not guaranteed him against almost complete oblivion. His plays, which in their banality and pettiness reflect very faithfully the bourgeois epoch of the Restoration and the Monarchy of July, are constructed with the utmost neatness and economy, a relief to his middle-class audiences after the incoherence of the Revolution and the excesses of the Romantics. They are still interesting as examples of dramatic construction, though seldom revived nowadays. He had no depth, no delicacy of perception. But though he was not a literary figure, though his language was poor, and though he has not created a single figure, with the possible exception of Adrienne Lecouvreur, who has remained in theatrical memory, he was an excellent craftsman. He had an uncanny flair for theatrical effect, and was unrivalled in judging what would appeal to an audience at any given moment. He wrote successfully for a number of theatres for more than thirty years, and his example weighed heavily on the European theatre for long after his death. Indeed, he was blamed for all the shortcomings of the dramatists who succeeded him, and in France his influence was strong on Labiche and Sardou. His much-sought-after libretti helped to make French romantic opera a model of theatrical effectiveness.

SCRUTO, a device used in effecting a Transformation Scene (see TRICKWORK ON THE ENGLISH STAGE).

SCUDÉRY, GEORGES DE (1601–67), French author, brother of the famous Madeleine de Scudéry, *précieuse* and novelist, with whom he collaborated in the well-known romantic novel, *L'Astrée*. Georges was in the French Guards in his youth, and always retained a soldierly bearing and a touch of the gentleman-adventurer. His first play was produced in 1630, and during the next thirteen years he wrote some sixteen more, mostly tragicomedies. He played a leading part in the attack on *Le Cid*, probably in order to conciliate his patron Richelieu, who at one time, by way of indirect reproach to Corneille, made much of him. He was annoyed at not being one of the five dramatists chosen to write Richelieu's plays, but consoled by his election as a foundation member of the French Academy, an honour which he had done little to deserve. His plays are now forgotten. One of them, *Le Trompeur puni* (1631), was done at the Cockpit in London by Floridor's company in 1635.

SEDAINE, Michel-Jean (1719–97), French dramatist, who, owing to the early death of his father, was forced to leave school and work as a stone-cutter. He was befriended by the painter David and by the architect Buron (whose kindness he was later to repay by adopting Buron's grandson) and rapidly made good the deficiencies in his education. Finding himself endowed with a facility for writing amusing lyric verse, he turned out a number of excellent libretti for light operas, with music by Grétry, Philidor, Monsigny, and others. His 'On ne s'avise jamais de tout' (1761) was the last light opera given at the Théâtre de la Foire Saint-Laurent before it was closed at the request of the Comédie-Italienne, who then amalgamated with it to form the Opéra-Comique. One of Sedaine's most successful libretti was 'Le Roi et le Fermier', based, probably by way of Collé's *La Partie de chasse d'Henri IV*, on Dodsley's *King and the Miller*. Sedaine's most important work, however, and the one by which he is best remembered, is *Le Philosophe sans le savoir* (1765), a *drame bourgeois* written under the influence of Diderot and interpreting his dramatic theories better than their originator could do in his own plays. It shows little imagination, but has a lively wit and delicately drawn characters, and is the only play of its type to have remained in the repertory. Sedaine became a member of the French Academy in 1789.

SEDLEY, Sir Charles (*c.* 1639–1701), Restoration dramatist, wit, and man of letters, friend of Rochester and Etherege. He wrote several plays, of which the best are *The Mulberry-Garden* (1668), a comedy of contemporary manners which owes something to Molière's *École des maris* and something to Etherege's *Comical Revenge* (1664), and the lively but licentious *Bellamira; or, the Mistress* (1687), based on the *Eunuchus* of Terence. Sedley was also the author of a dull tragedy on the subject of Antony and Cleopatra, written in imitation of Dryden's heroic drama.

SEDLEY-SMITH, William Henry (1806–72), an American actor, born in Wales, who at 14 ran away from home to escape the unkindness of his step-father, and joined a company of strolling players, adding Smith to his real name of Sedley. He toured the English provinces for some years, and in 1827 went to America, making his first appearance at the Walnut Street Theatre, Philadelphia, as Jeremy Diddler in *Raising the Wind*. A year later he was seen in Boston, where he became extremely popular. He managed the Boston Museum from 1836 to 1860, during which time he also appeared in New York, being first seen there in a number of Shakespeare plays in 1840. He made his last appearance in Boston in 1869 and then went to San Francisco, where he became manager of the California Theatre until his death, and was able to be of service to the young David Belasco. Winter, in his life of the latter, says of Sedley-Smith: 'Robust, rosy, stately, with a rich, ringing voice, a merry laugh, and a free and noble courtesy of demeanour . . . he played all parts well, and in some he was superlatively excellent.' Among the latter Winter mentions Sir Oliver Surface, Old Dornton, and the Stranger. He was also good as Edgar and Laertes, in which parts he often supported Junius Brutus Booth. Sedley-Smith married a charming actress, by whom he had one daughter, Mary, later the wife of Sol Smith. With the possible assistance of an unnamed 'gentleman' Sedley-Smith wrote *The Drunkard; or, the Fallen Saved*, a temperance tract turned into melodrama, which achieved an astonishing success. It was first performed in Boston in 1844, and was the first American play to run for nearly 200 performances (in New York, under Barnum in 1850). Often revived, it opened in Los Angeles in 1933 (at about the time prohibition ended) and ran for twenty-six years (9,477 performances).

SELWYN THEATRE, New York, on the north side of 42nd Street. This theatre opened on 2 Oct. 1918 and one of the most successful plays staged there was *The Royal Family* (1927), a saga of the Drew and Barrymore families, seen in England as *Theatre Royal. Battling Butler*, with Charles Ruggles, was seen here, as was *The Constant Nymph*, while *Wake Up and Dream* introduced Jessie Matthews to the New York stage, in company with Tilly Losch and Jack Buchanan. The last outstanding event in the theatre's history was a series of six matinées of *Electra* with Blanche Yurka and Mrs. Patrick Campbell, after which it became a cinema. George Freedley†

SEMENOVA, Ekaterina Semenovna (1786–1849), famous Russian actress. The daughter of a serf and of a teacher in the St. Petersburg Cadet Corps, she was sent to the Theatre School in St. Petersburg at the age of ten, and studied under Dmitrevsky. She made her first appearance in 1803, and came to the fore in the tragedies of Ozerov. Later she played the heroines of Racine, Shakespeare, and Schiller. Having had little education she could not work out her roles unaided, and was coached first by Prince Shakhovsky, the dramatist, and Head of the Repertory of the Alexandrinsky Theatre, and then by Gnedich, the famous poet and translator of the *Iliad*. She made a great impression on her contemporaries by her beauty and her lovely contralto voice. Pushkin dedicated some of his poems to her, and wrote of her with ecstasy in his essay on the Russian theatre. According to him she had no peer on the Russian stage, though her acting lacked continuity, and was marred by gusts of emotion. She was much influenced by the visit of Mlle George to Moscow, and retired from the stage for a time in order to ameliorate her acting style by study. In 1823 she reappeared successfully in *Phèdre*. Two years later she married a Senator Prince, and played only in the private theatres of Moscow and St. Petersburg. She has been called the Russian Mrs. Siddons.

SEMPER, GOTTFRIED (1803–79), German theatre architect, designer of the Dresden Opera House. He was connected with Wagner in the planning of a Festival Theatre for Munich, which was never built, but of which many features were incorporated later into the Festspielhaus at Bayreuth. The story of his relations with Wagner and Bayreuth has been told by his son, who was also an architect (see also Ernest Newman's *Life of Wagner*, Vol. iii, Ch. 17).

SENECA, LUCIUS ANNAEUS (*c.* 4 B.C.–A.D. 65), Roman dramatist, philosopher, satirist, statesman, the tutor and later the victim of Nero. Under his name we have nine Latin tragedies: *Hercules* (*Furens*), *Phoenissae* (or *Thebais*), *Troades, Medea, Phaedra* (or *Hippolytus*), *Oedipus, Agamemnon, Thyestes, Hercules* (*Oetaeus*). Some manuscripts add the *Octavia*, a Roman historical play dealing with the unfortunate wife of Nero. Of these plays the *Octavia* at any rate can hardly be the work of Seneca: it brings Seneca on the stage as a character, it refers to Nero in terms which would never have been permitted during the emperor's lifetime, and it contains a prophetic passage describing his death too circumstantial to have been written by one who died three years before him. The authenticity of the other nine plays is generally accepted by modern scholars; their style, their Stoic outlook, and their occasional touches of humane sentiment and moral elevation are paralleled in Seneca's other writings, and Quintilian quotes part of a line from the *Medea* as Seneca's. As our only extant Latin tragedies, and the only dramas of any kind which have come down to us from the Roman Empire, these plays have great historical importance, and their influence on the development of drama in modern times has been profound.

As a dramatist Seneca seems to owe little to the old dramatists of the Republic, whose style he would probably have despised. His plays are not translations from the Greek but independent works, though based on Greek models. His metres are strictly quantitative, unlike the non-dipodic metres of the Republican dramatists, yet at the same time quite unlike the metres of Greek drama. Seneca's plays differ from anything bequeathed to us by the stage of earlier times, whether Greek or Roman; and one reason for the difference is that his plays were designed not for the stage but for reading, especially dramatic reading to a select audience —the so-called *recitatio*. There are scenes in Seneca which could not be staged: Hercules shoots down his wife and children, the dismembered body of Hippolytus is pieced together by his sorrowing father, Medea kills her son and flings his body down to his father from the palace roof. We do not see the actors coming and going as in a real play: characters speak, then relapse into silence, and we cannot always be sure whether a character not actually speaking is conceived of as present or absent. Objects which in a real play would be visible to all are strangely ignored: thus though Phaedra kills herself under her husband's eyes, he makes no reference to her action, and does not deign to notice her corpse until the very end of the play. The pervading atmosphere is not that of a stage-play, in which the dramatist must visualize every scene and every movement, but that of a *recitatio*, where the speaker takes now one part, now another, and where he can ignore everything but the idea or emotion which the author desires to have expressed at the moment. Character-drawing is too crude to be convincing: Hercules will of course utter heroic sentiments, Ulysses will be crafty, and so on; but all the characters speak with the overstrained voice of the reciter. It is the nature of the *recitatio* to aim at immediate, often merely verbal, effects; plot and character tend to be subordinated to the constant search for smart and surprising turns of speech, for hyperbole and epigram. The grand object seems to be to startle the audience into applause by novel excesses in emotion or expression. The pleasure we as readers may derive from even the best passages is qualified by our apprehension of suddenly meeting with some absurd conceit or some wearisome display of learning.

It is evident that Seneca departed widely from his Greek models, and that his alterations were usually for the worse: compare, for example, his *Oedipus* with the *Oedipus Tyrannus* of Sophocles, or his *Phaedra* with the *Hippolytus* of Euripides. Nevertheless it would be unfair to deny the dramatic power of many scenes in such plays as the *Medea* and the *Troades*, or the beauty of many choral passages. There is perhaps some dramatic quality even in the atmosphere of gloom and horror, of treachery, brutality, and witchcraft, which pervades these plays, and which is itself to some extent a reflection of the times in which Seneca lived. After all, when Seneca writes of the fears and suspicions of Court life, the instability of power, the anxieties of princes and the crimes to which tyranny can lead, or the courage and inward peace which can sustain a man in direst peril and in the pangs of death, that is something more than mere literary reminiscence and commonplace.

For the Renaissance Seneca was the model writer of tragedy. He wrote in Latin, and his language could be understood; his plays were regularly constructed in five acts, according to the Horatian precept; they dealt with emotions and catastrophes which, if they seem to us overdrawn, were universally intelligible; even his rant and rhetoric appealed to the prevailing taste. His rattling line-by-line interchange of dialogue, his chorus, his tyrants, ghosts, and witches, his corpse-strewn stage, all reappear in Elizabethan drama. In 1551–2 his *Troades* was performed at Trinity College, Cambridge. Shakespeare's *Titus Andronicus* is a gruesome example of Senecan influence, while in his *Richard III* we see the splendid effects which Senecan material can be made to yield when employed by dramatic genius.

WILLIAM BEARE†

SENTIMENTAL COMEDY, see COMEDY.

SERLIO, SEBASTIANO (1475–1554), Italian painter and architect, who after working for many years on theatrical problems produced a treatise on architecture, of which the part dealing with perspective in the theatre appeared in 1545. An English edition, *The Second Book of Architecture*, was published in 1611 (see LIGHTING, 1*a* and SCENERY, 2; also Nos. 56, 57, 58).

SERVANDONY, JEAN-NICOLAS (1695–1766), a French scenic artist, born in Lyon, who was one of the first to react against the baroque style. After working in various parts of Europe, and particularly in Italy, he settled in Paris and took over the control of the Salle des Machines in the Tuileries. There he produced some interesting work, which influenced the stage designing of Italy and Germany. He was in London in 1749, and married there. In an effort to appear Italian, as was fashionable among scenic artists at the time, he changed the spelling of his name to Servandoni (see also COSTUME, 7 and SCENERY, 4).

SET. This word has developed far from its original meaning, and has now became a noun covering any 'set' of pieces arranged to make a stage scene. Originally the word was used only in 'set scene'—that is, a scene set up in concealment because of the complication of its parts and revealed as a discovery at the opening of a front scene, as against the flat scene whose two simple parts slide on or off the stage in view of the audience (see FLAT). This was the customary procedure in the English theatre up to the time of Irving, and it is not too much to say that a nice mixture of flat scene and set scene was one of the most important formative elements in English drama. It allowed the speedy transition from scene to scene so essential to a drama based on the unique Elizabethan tradition, and at the same time allowed of peak moments of grandiose scenic depth, and multiplane elaboration, that permitted the fantasy of the theatre to have full play. With time the elaboration of the set scene grew, and by early Victorian times it was a serious matter, involving much built stuff as well as painted. A specially contrived short front scene, known as the Carpenter's Scene and devised by the playwright to permit the building of an elaborate set behind, was developed as a makeshift device, but soon proved inadequate, and, with Irving, visible scene-change finally died, a curtain being dropped to conceal the scene-shifting during an interval. The flat scene was no longer used, and the set scene became general, till now all scenes may be labelled 'sets', while the term 'setting' has become the general name for the whole theatrical art of designing and staging the scenery of a play.

RICHARD SOUTHERN

SET PIECE. 1. Scenery of canvas stretched on a wooden frame cut to the silhouette of, for example, a house or a fountain (see FLAT).

2. The solid three-dimensional elements of full scenery (see BUILT STUFF).

SET SCENE, see FLAT and SET.

SET WATERS, a series of groundrows set one behind the other to represent a lake, river, or sea, and by their arrangement capable of permitting the passage of a stage boat between them.

SETTLE, ELKANAH (1648–1724), a Restoration dramatist now chiefly remembered for his quarrel with Dryden, who considered his popularity at Court endangered by the success of his rival's bombastic dramas. Settle figures as Doeg in *Absalom and Achitophel.* He began his career by staging drolls at the fairs but, fired by the favourable reception given to Dryden's *Conquest of Granada,* he put on, with the help of Rochester, Dryden's bitter enemy, an equally elaborate and heroic *Empress of Morocco* (1671). This, with Betterton in the cast, was well enough received to warrant the publication of the text embellished with most valuable scenic illustrations—perhaps the first play to be so published (see No. 63). It was also parodied in a farce by Doggett. Settle wrote a number of other plays, but never again achieved such a success. In the last years of his life he returned to Bartholomew Fair, where he wrote and acted in drolls at Mrs. Minn's (or Myn's) booth. It is also recorded that he played a dragon in green leather at Bartholomew Fair.

SEYLER, ABEL (1730–1801), a merchant of Hamburg, who fell in love with the actress Sophie Hensel, took her part in her quarrels with Ackermann, and eventually became manager of the Hamburg theatre. He might have proved successful but for the intrigues and hot temper of Sophie Hensel, whom he married and took on tour in her own company. Ekhof was with them for a time, and took over the management of the company when it was faced with financial ruin, which caused Sophie to retire in high dudgeon to Vienna. She soon returned, however, and she and Seyler started a new company with varying success. In 1779 Seyler was invited by Dalberg to take over the management of the new Mannheim theatre, but there again his wife's ungovernable temper and jealous disposition caused their dismissal, and forced them to resume their travels. He remained faithful to her in spite of her faults, which must have caused him much suffering, and on her death found a little peace in the hospitable house of Schröder at Holstein.

SEYLER, ATHENE (1889–), English actress, appointed C.B.E. in the Birthday Honours of 1958 in recognition of her fifty years on the London stage. She studied at the Royal Academy of Dramatic Art, gaining the Gold Medal in 1908, and becoming, in 1950, the first former pupil to be appointed President of the Council. She made her début in London in 1909, and has had a steady, unspectacular but eminently successful career, continually widening her range, improving and polishing her admirable technique, and in every way doing honour to her profession. In 1920 she appeared for the first time in Restoration comedy, playing Melantha in *Marriage à la Mode*, and was equally successful as Mrs. Frail in *Love for Love* (1921) and Lady Fidget in *The Country Wife* (1924). Also in 1920 she first appeared in Shakespeare, as Rosalind in *As You Like It*. She has appeared in many Shakespeare parts, and in plays by Wilde, Maugham, Shaw, and Rattigan, as well as in such light comedies as *Breath of Spring* (1958). In 1961 she appeared as Mrs. Caution in *The Gentleman Dancing Master* at the Pembroke, Croydon, and in 1962 as an Old Bawd in *The Chances* at the first Chichester Theatre Festival, with unimpaired wit and vitality. A born comedienne, she is also an inspired teacher, and her *Craft of Comedy*, published in 1944, which she wrote in collaboration with Stephen Haggard, is an essential handbook for all aspiring actors.

SEYMOUR [really CUNNINGHAM]. (1) JAMES (1823–64), a comedian, born in Belfast, who began his stage career in Ireland as a boy. From 1840 to 1864 he was well known in the United States as an interpreter of stage Irishmen. He married an American actress, Lydia Eliza Griffith (1832–97). Their only son, (2) WILLIAM GORMAN (1855–1933), made his first appearance on the stage at the age of 2, and at 7 played the Duke of York to Lawrence Barrett's Richard III. He continued to play children's parts with most of the stars of the day, and in 1869, while call-boy at Booth's Theatre, played François to Edwin Booth's Richelieu and the Player Queen to his Hamlet. He was Henrick in the run of 149 consecutive performances of *Rip Van Winkle* with Jefferson, and in 1871 he joined the stock company at the Globe Theatre, Boston, appearing with Edwin Forrest at his final performance. From 1875 until his retirement in 1927 he continued to act, and was also manager of a number of theatres, being general stage director for Charles Frohman and the Empire Theatre, New York, from 1901 to 1919. He married May Davenport, daughter of E. L. Davenport and sister of Fanny (see DAVENPORT, 4), and of their five children three went on the stage. After his death his library was presented to Princeton University to form the nucleus of a William Seymour Theatre Collection.

SHADOW SHOW, see PUPPET.

SHADWELL, THOMAS (*c.* 1642–92), Restoration dramatist, whose best comedies, *Epsom Wells* (1672), *The Squire of Alsatia* (1688), and *Bury Fair* (1689), give interesting though somewhat scurrilous pictures of contemporary manners. His first play, *The Sullen Lovers; or, the Impertinents* (1668), was based on Molière's *Les Fâcheux*, but on the whole Shadwell was more indebted to Jonson, whose disciple he claimed to be. Indeed, it was his devotion to Jonson that led to his quarrel with Dryden, whom he succeeded as Poet Laureate. Shadwell has been much criticized for his adaptations of Shakespeare, particularly for his version of *The Tempest* as 'The Enchanted Island' (1674) in operatic form, following the example of Davenant and Dryden. Here everything was subordinated to the machinery and scenery, as in his own opera 'Psyche', which cost Dorset Garden £800 in scenery alone. Shadwell, who disliked and satirized the heroic tragedy of Dryden as well as the early Restoration comedies, was a competent dramatist whose plays were most successful in his own day, though they no longer bear revival, mainly owing to their coarse and topical humour. Nicoll says of him: 'Many might laugh at his idiosyncrasies, his love of beer, and his habit of declaring that his plays were written in unconscionably brief spaces of time, but for all that he remains one of the chief of the comic dramatists outside of the school of manners'. He married an actress, Anne Gibbs, who was in Davenant's first company. She outlived him, and published posthumously his last comedy, which was given in 1692, and was rated below some of his earlier work.

SHAFTESBURY THEATRE, LONDON, the first playhouse to be built in Shaftesbury Avenue. It opened in 1888 under the direction of Miss Wallis, who had played leading parts at many London theatres. The first production was *As You Like It*, with Forbes-Robertson as Orlando to Miss Wallis's Rosalind, followed by *The Lady of Lyons*. The season was a failure, but E. S. Willard had more success with *The Middleman* (1889) and *Judah* (1890). There was a season of Italian opera in 1891, when Lago introduced 'Cavalleria Rusticana' to London. Miss Wallis reappeared, without success, and later Letty Lind, a beautiful dancer, drew the town. In 1896 £15,000 was lost over comic opera. In the following year a dramatized version of Marie Corelli's *The Sorrows of Satan* was produced with Lewis Waller in the lead, but it was not until 1898 that the Shaftesbury had its first real success, when *The Belle of New York*, produced there on 12 Apr., ran for 697 performances. It revolutionized musical comedy as then known, and introduced Edna May to London. Later Fred Terry and Julia Neilson had one of their few failures at the Shaftesbury, with a play called *For Sword or Song*. In 1903 a musical play, *In Dahomey*, with a complete Negro cast, was a success. The theatre, after many vicissitudes, had another success in *The Arcadians* (1909), under the direction of Robert Courtneidge. In 1933 Werner Krauss, an eminent German actor, appeared at the Shaftesbury at a time when political feeling ran high, and there was a disturbance in the theatre on the first night. On 17 Apr. 1941 the building was completely demolished by enemy action.

W. MACQUEEN-POPE†

In Mar. 1963 the Princes, in Shaftesbury Avenue, was redecorated and reopened as the Shaftesbury (see PRINCES THEATRE).

SHAKESPEARE. 1. LIFE AND WORKS. William Shakespeare (1564–1616), first son and third child of John Shakespeare, a glover yeoman of Stratford-upon-Avon, and his wife, Mary Arden, a minor heiress of Wilmcote, was christened on 26 Apr. 1564; tradition asserts that his birthday was 23 Apr., St. George's Day. Presumably the boy attended the grammar school of his native town, but the first record of his activities is that of his marriage, evidently a hasty one, to a lady whom extant documents almost certainly (but not positively) identify as Anne Hathaway of Shottery. The wedding took place about the end of Nov. 1582; a daughter, Susanna, was born in May 1583, and twins followed in 1585. Another gap in our knowledge extends from this time until 1592, when a pamphlet written by the dying Robert Greene shows Shakespeare evidently well established in London as actor and dramatist. There is a story that he left Stratford because of a deer-stealing escapade at Charlecote; another tale asserts that he served as a schoolmaster in the country; it is possible that he was the William Shakeshafte (a variant of 'Shakespeare' used by the poet's grandfather) who has been recorded as a player in the service of a Lancashire gentleman, Alexander Houghton of Lea. Whatever his activities, during those years he must have added to his education and gained experience of life in circles higher than his own domestic surroundings. From this time contemporary documents yield us more information. In 1593 and 1594 he dedicated his poems *Venus and Adonis* and *The Rape of Lucrece* to the Earl of Southampton, in terms that suggest familiarity, and by the beginning of 1595 he had evidently become a 'sharer' in the Lord Chamberlain's company. Evidence of his rise in the world appears in his father's successful application in 1596 to the Heralds' College for a coat of arms, and by the poet's purchase in 1597 of the large house known as New Place, in Stratford. Other documents show him, in 1596, associated with Francis Langley, builder of the Swan Theatre, in a complicated quarrel involving William Gardiner, a Justice of the Peace in London, and at the same time concerned with Stratford interests (the only extant letter addressed to him is from his fellow townsman Richard Quiney, in 1598). About that time he was resident at St. Helens, Bishopsgate, but by 1599 he had moved to the Liberty of the Clink, and in 1604 was a lodger in the house of Christopher Mountjoy in Cripplegate. In 1610 he seems to have taken up residence at New Place, although his presence in London during the summer of 1612, the spring of 1613, and the winter of 1614, together with his purchase of some Blackfriars property in 1613, demonstrates his continued association with the metropolis. His will, signed on 25 Mar. 1616, preceded his death (23 Apr.) by about a month; tradition says he died after a too convivial evening with Drayton and Jonson. He was buried in the chancel of Stratford church.

There are other documents, but these mainly concern business transactions at Stratford, and do not add much to our knowledge of the man. The record of his life can, however, be expanded both by relating his literary work to those meagre facts, and by cautiously making use of traditional material. The prefatory matter to the First Folio shows how highly he was esteemed by his fellow actors and by his great contemporary, Ben Jonson: tradition speaks, with probable truth, of royal esteem as well. There must be a personal story behind the sonnets, and with that story the puzzling narrative of *Willobie his Avisa* (1594) is likely to be connected. It has been recorded that he 'died a Papist', and this suggestion is not without some vague corroborative evidence.

Bare factual information, however, and legends regarding his adventures fade into insignificance when we confront the extraordinary range of his poetic achievement. He came just at the right moment to make full and fresh use of the teeming drama of his time, finding a novel and flexible stage apt for his purposes, and an eager audience representative of all classes in the community to encourage and inspire. The man and the time were in harmonious conjunction. Starting to write probably about 1590, he contributed at least thirty-six plays to the theatre. Of these, sixteen were printed in quarto during his lifetime, but, apart from the fact that some are obviously bad texts, surreptitiously obtained, the publishing conditions of the age make it probable that he himself did not read the proofs. In 1623 Heminge and Condell of the King's Men, the company to which he had belonged, issued the entire body of his dramatic work in folio form; this volume presents the only texts of another twenty plays, and is probably the most important single volume in the entire history of literature. Arranging the contents under the headings of Comedies, Histories, and Tragedies, the editors of the Folio give no indication of the dates of composition of the separate items, but from a careful scrutiny of such external evidence as exists, and from 'internal' tests (the quality of the blank verse, use of prose and rhyme, &c.), most scholars are agreed, at least in general terms, concerning their chronology—although the problem is complicated by the fact that some editors find evidence of different layers of textual strata in individual plays: thus, for example, Professor J. Dover Wilson believes that *A Midsummer Night's Dream* was originally written in 1592, revised in 1594, and again revised four years later. Any attempt to date the dramas exactly must, therefore, be hazardous and uncertain.

One thing seems certain, that Shakespeare started his career by penning, unaided or in collaboration, an historical tetralogy consisting of the three parts of *Henry VI* and *Richard III*. In all probability Parts II and III of *Henry VI* came first in 1591, followed by Part I in 1592 and by *Richard III* in 1593. The great Elizabethan actor Burbage won fame in the role of Richard, and *Richard III* was still being performed in 1633, as a record of a Court performance shows. The success of these plays no doubt urged Shakespeare to write his *King*

John, probably based on an older two-part dramatization of that monarch's reign. This tragedy stands alone, but shortly afterwards, about 1595, another historical tetralogy was started with *Richard II*, which, during the Essex conspiracy in 1601, won notoriety because of its abdication scene; it was still in the Globe repertory in 1631, and from the year 1607 comes an interesting record of its popularity, when it was produced on the high seas by sailors in the fleet of William Keeling. The two parts of *Henry IV* (probably about 1597 or 1598) carry on the story of Henry Bolingbroke and introduce a richly contrasting comic element with the character of Falstaff (originally named Oldcastle), while the general theme is rounded off with *Henry V* (probably 1598). With this play Shakespeare closed his career as a writer of histories, save for the late *Henry VIII*, produced in the summer of 1613, in which he is believed by many scholars to have collaborated with the young Fletcher.

Early in his career he started to try his hand at comedy, experimenting during the early 1590s in gay satire (*Love's Labour's Lost*), in the style of Plautus (*The Comedy of Errors*), and in that of Ariosto (*The Taming of the Shrew*). One has the impression here of a young dramatist unsure of his orientation, yet all these plays are skilful and succeeded in holding the stage. The first was revived in 1605 and was still being played in 1631; the second, which is known to have been acted at Gray's Inn in 1594, was revived in 1604; a quarto of the third, issued in 1631, indicates that it was still in the playhouse repertory, and a Court performance is recorded in 1633. In *The Two Gentlemen of Verona* the lack of assurance persists, although here a definite approach is made towards the comedy of humour, and immediately afterwards, probably between 1595 and 1599, this kind of comic drama finds rich and lyrical expression in *A Midsummer Night's Dream*, *Much Ado About Nothing*, *As You Like It*, and *Twelfth Night*. Little is known concerning the stage-history of these plays. *A Midsummer Night's Dream* was given a Court performance in 1604; *Twelfth Night* was acted at the Middle Temple in 1602, was given at Court in 1618 and 1623, and was still popular in 1640. Some time following the production of *Henry IV* comes *The Merry Wives of Windsor*, an aberration in this series; probably tradition is right in saying it was written at the command of Queen Elizabeth, who wanted to see Falstaff in love. It was revived at Court in 1604 and 1638. In *The Merchant of Venice* a break in the almost perfect balance observable in the other comedies is patent, and this leads to a couple of so-called 'dark comedies'—*All's Well that Ends Well* and *Measure for Measure* (given at Court in 1604), in which the romantic material is strained almost to breaking. With these may be associated the cynically bitter *Troilus and Cressida*, which possibly was acted not on the public stage but privately.

These were composed at the same time as Shakespeare was reaching towards the deepest expression of tragic concepts. Already at the very beginning of his career he must have had some part (but how great is questionable) in *Titus Andronicus*, a play which, despite or because of its bloodiness, seems to have remained popular with less critical audiences. Again, in the midst of his lyrical comedies, the dramatist made a second, but a false, attempt at creating the tragic spirit—*Romeo and Juliet* (about 1595), evidently a popular play although there are no definite records of early performances. Then came the great series of tragedies and Roman plays. *Julius Caesar*, which was seen by a visitor to London in 1599, was probably the first, but the final *Hamlet* must have come very soon after. *Othello* may have been new when it was presented at Court in 1604; it was evidently very popular. Performances are recorded in 1610, 1629, 1635, and there were Court productions in 1612 and 1636. Burbage acted Othello and Taylor Iago. *King Lear* must have followed not many months later; it appeared at Court in 1606, and about the same time came *Macbeth*, which, tied in theme with *Julius Caesar*, clearly addresses itself to a Jacobean Court. The classical subject-matter of *Julius Caesar* is paralleled in *Antony and Cleopatra*, in *Coriolanus*, and in the almost hysterical *Timon of Athens* (all probably about 1607 or 1608).

In *King Lear* Shakespeare had turned to ancient British history, and the atmosphere of this play is reproduced, albeit with a changed tone, in *Cymbeline*. Seen by Forman in 1611, it was written probably about 1610; there was a revival at Court in 1634. Another play seen in 1611 by Forman, *The Winter's Tale*, is similar in spirit, darker than the early comedies of humour and including incidents reminiscent of the tragedies, yet ending with solemn happiness. Evidently popular, it had Court productions in 1611, 1613, 1618, 1619, 1624, and 1634. *The Tempest*, gravest and serenest of all the dramas, was presented at Court in 1611 and in the following year.

To Shakespeare have been attributed, in whole or in part, several other dramas. His hand in *Pericles*, which had been printed as his in 1609, and which was added to the Third Folio of 1664, has generally been accepted, and recent scholarship suggests that we may actually have some pages of his own writing in the manuscript of *Sir Thomas More*. Less likely, although still possible, is his participation in *Edward III* (printed in 1596), and in *The Two Noble Kinsmen*, which was printed in 1634 as by him and Fletcher.

Of his non-dramatic work, *Venus and Adonis* was (carefully) printed in 1593, and *The Rape of Lucrece* in 1594; the *Sonnets* were first printed in 1609, with a dedication to 'Mr. W. H.' over which a lively, acrimonious, but inconclusive controversy has raged for many years. Some of his work appeared in *The Passionate Pilgrim* (1599) and in *Love's Martyr* (1601).

Although there is some reason for believing that a few of Shakespeare's plays were originally written for private or for Court performance, his strength rests in the fact that he was essentially a 'public' dramatist, addressing himself to the demands of a widely representative audience, eager to listen to rich poetic utterance, keenly interested in human character, and apt to welcome both the delicacy of the romantic comedy and the rigours of tragedy. There is little known concerning the contemporary production of his dramas, but sufficient information concerning the Elizabethan stage is extant to give us a general impression of the methods used in their presentation. The absence of scenery helps to explain the strong emphasis on poetic utterance; for the Elizabethans the visual appeal lay in the rich costumes worn by the actors, which threw stress on the persons speaking rather than on dumb, inanimate properties. Here was an opportunity for the dramatist to reveal an essential reality that has kept his plays vivid over three centuries. Again and again commentators have spoken of Shakespeare as a 'child of nature', or as one who vied with nature in his creative power, and possibly there is no other author who so harmoniously and with such ease reveals the basic power of the great playwright—the power at once to create the characters of his imagination and to enter into them. Transcendence and immanence are the two bases of his genius, and it is the presence of these qualities that explains the prime paradox—that Shakespeare himself belongs in a sphere beyond our grasp even while we have the impression of knowing him intimately; it likewise explains that peculiar irony which is the characteristic feature both of his comedy and his tragedy. This quality is, of course, dependent upon the nature of his own literary genius, yet one cannot too firmly assert that for its expression in these plays the Elizabethan theatre and the contemporary audience were definitely responsible. ALLARDYCE NICOLL

2. PRODUCTION IN ENGLISH. Although some of Shakespeare's plays remained continuously in the repertory of the English theatre, from the Restoration until the end of the nineteenth century few people had an opportunity of seeing them in their original form. For this the change in theatre building and theatrical technique was partly responsible, but the main onus lay on those who, while professing their admiration for Shakespeare, deliberately altered his texts to make them conform to the requirements of a new age. During the Commonwealth his comedies were pillaged to provide short entertainments or drolls, like that of 'Bottom the Weaver', taken from *A Midsummer Night's Dream*. There was every excuse for this, in the precarious state of the theatre at that time, since a full-length production would have had little chance of survival. But there was no excuse for later remodellings except that, to a small sophisticated audience much under the influence of French classical tragedy, Shakespeare was a barbarian, whose occasional poetic beauties entitled him to some consideration, but whose work stood in need of purification and revision.

It was in this spirit that the Restoration and early eighteenth-century theatre approached Shakespeare. Davenant embellished *Macbeth* with singing and dancing; his 'singing witches' were to last until 1847. *Romeo and Juliet* was given a happy ending. Neither play was revived in its proper form until 1744. *The Tempest* formed the basis of an opera by Shadwell, *A Midsummer Night's Dream* provided a libretto for Purcell, and Lacy the actor made a new version of *The Taming of the Shrew*.

If Davenant was the first of Shakespeare's adapters, Nahum Tate was undoubtedly the worst. In 1681 he rewrote *King Lear*, omitting the Fool, who was not seen again until 1838, and keeping Cordelia alive in order that she might marry her lover, Edgar. He also tackled *Richard II* and *Coriolanus*, but with less success. An adaptation which survived even longer than Tate's *Lear* was the *Richard III* of Colley Cibber. First given in 1700, it proved immensely popular, and provided an excellent part for a tragic actor, containing as it did passages from *Henry IV*, *Henry V*, *Henry VI*, and *Richard II*, as well as a good deal of Cibber's own invention. Equally popular were the various versions of other plays, by Tate, Cibber, Shadwell, and later Garrick. For this great actor, though in some ways he tried to prune back the excrescences of the Restoration texts, and produced *Antony and Cleopatra* for the first time since 1660, retained Cibber's *Richard III*, allowed Macbeth to die on the stage, and Juliet to awake before the death of Romeo. He even made short versions of four of the comedies, and his *Katherine and Petruchio* (1756) held the stage until Ben Webster revived *The Taming of the Shrew* at the Haymarket in 1844. It is, however, Garrick's tampering with *Hamlet*, and his omission of the Grave-diggers, that marks the end of this phase in Shakespearian production. The tide had already begun to turn slowly in favour of the original texts, and in 1741 Macklin had rescued Shylock, in the so-called *Jew of Venice*, from the hands of the low comedian, and by his interpretation of the part caused Pope to exclaim: 'This is the Jew, That Shakespeare drew.' It was a long time before actors and producers scrupulously respected the text, and Kemble still thought it necessary to cut, combine, and edit each play before producing it. He did, however, try to follow the lead, again given by Macklin, who in 1773 had dressed Macbeth in Highland costume, in reforming the costuming of Shakespeare's plays. His Othello was still a scarlet-coated general, his Richard III wore silk knee-breeches, and Lear defied the storm in a flowered dressing-gown. But, helped by his sister Sarah Siddons, who was the first to discard the hoops, flounces, and enormous headgear of tragic heroines, he made an effort to combine picturesqueness with accuracy, and his Coriolanus wore what in contemporary thought approximated to a Roman costume. The *Examiner* scoffed at his innovations, but they bore fruit in Charles Kemble's *King John*, staged in

Mar. 1823 with historically accurate costumes designed by Planché.

The battle for a fairly accurate text was almost won by this time, and Kean had taken a step in the right direction on 10 Feb. 1826 when he restored the original ending to *King Lear*. Helped by the patience and research of scholars, and by the criticisms of such men as Coleridge and Hazlitt, the original plays were gradually emerging from the accretions of more than a century's rewriting. Madame Vestris and the younger Mathews revived *Love's Labour's Lost* and *A Midsummer Night's Dream* in 1839–40 with the original text, and the freedom of the theatres in 1843 enabled Phelps to embark on his fine series of productions at Sadler's Wells from 1844 to 1862, while Charles Kean staged his equally remarkable Shakespeare seasons at the Princess's.

Shakespeare was now presented in a reasonably correct form, but he suffered a new distortion at the hands of his admirers by their emphasis on detail, scenery, and pageantry. The archaeological correctness—which apparently led also to dullness—of Charles Kemble heralded the magnificent spectacles of Macready at Covent Garden from 1837 to 1843. He should be credited with having restored the Fool to Lear, though played by a woman, and with having revived *The Tempest* without Dryden's interpolations, which included a male counterpart of Miranda. But he helped forward the smothering process, which continued at the Princess's, and reached its height at the Haymarket and His Majesty's under Tree, and at the Lyceum under Irving. Phelps, who in 1845 restored a male Fool, and in 1847 put on *Macbeth* without Locke's singing witches, as well as reviving *The Winter's Tale*, was more concerned with the text than with the scenery, which was pleasantly sober and unobtrusive. But elsewhere the newly restored text was in danger of disappearing under the elaboration of detail, while the action of the play, designed for an untrammelled stage, was constantly held up by the necessity for elaborate scene-changes.

It was the publication in 1888 of de Witt's drawing of the Swan Theatre (see No. 22) which first turned men's minds to the possibility of reproducing not only the text of Shakespeare's plays but also the physical conditions in which they were first seen. The main interest had already switched from the problem of the text to the problem of interpretation. This became even more important as the producer gained the upper hand in the theatre. To this was added the problem of providing a building suitable for Shakespeare, an approximation to the original Elizabethan stage. This was first tackled by William Poel, with his early productions of Shakespeare and the later founding of the Elizabethan Stage Society, and by Nugent Monck with the Maddermarket at Norwich. Robert Atkins's productions at the Ring, Blackfriars, made an effort to solve the difficulties by presenting Shakespeare-in-the-round. After the Second World War the stages at Stratford-upon-Avon and the Old Vic crept out beyond the proscenium arch, which Stratford finally abolished altogether. These and other tentatives, including the Mermaid Theatre in St. John's Wood, London, and the open stage at the Shakespearean Festival Theatre, Stratford, Ontario (see No. 43) showed that Shakespeare cannot adequately be presented in the proscenium-arch theatre. But the actual form of stage best suited to his plays is still a matter of dispute, and in view of the divergent opinions on the actual form of his original stage (see ENGLISH PLAYHOUSE) it seems as if it will not soon be settled.

Even in the proscenium-arch theatre, however, efforts have been made to present the plays more simply and coherently, allowing the action to flow unchecked for as long as possible. One of the landmarks in the history of Shakespearian production was undoubtedly Granville-Barker's season at the Savoy in 1912; another was the introduction in 1914 of the first season of Shakespeare at the Victoria Theatre in the Waterloo Road (see OLD VIC), where the pioneer work of Lilian Baylis did more for Shakespeare *vis-à-vis* the general public than the lavish but intermittent spectacles of the West End theatres. The plays continue to suffer from experiments destined to 'bring them alive' or 'modernize' them—from Barry Jackson's modern-dress *Hamlet* to the fantastications of Komisarjevsky or the elaborations of Reinhardt. In more recent times there have been a *Lear* with Japanese décor, a *Hamlet* set in Victorian times, a *Romeo and Juliet* in modern Italian style by Zeffirelli. But, with all its divergencies and aberrations, the main trend since 1900 has been the simplification of the background, either by a permanent set, a bare stage, or symbolic settings, and a consequent insistence on the importance of the text, the free flow of the verse, and the unhampered action of the plot. A happy combination of scholarly research and theatrical experience seems the best method of dealing with the many problems that inevitably arise in producing plays written in haste, printed without the author's supervision, and designed for a vanished playhouse—plays, moreover, which have suffered from the over-zealous attentions of erudite editors on the one hand and the mutilations of hack-writers or 'star' actors on the other.

In America the first productions of Shakespeare were given by visiting English actors, and the situation was therefore much the same as in contemporary England. For instance, the first recorded play, *Richard III*, acted in New York City on 5 Mar. 1750 by Kean and Murray's company at their Nassau Street Theatre, was in Colley Cibber's version. There is little information available on the texts of subsequent productions, but it is reasonable to suppose that they were substantially those current in the English theatre at the time. Although there was not, as in Europe, a language barrier or a preconceived notion of classical writing to be overcome, there were moral difficulties. Even Shakespeare's reputation was not always sufficient to overcome deep-rooted prejudices against play-going, and *Othello* was first introduced to Boston as 'a Moral Dialogue against the Sin of Jealousy'. Probably more people in the eighteenth century were reading Shakespeare as a poet than seeing him as a playwright. Although the Eastern cities had opportunities of seeing the full-length plays in theatres modelled on contemporary English lines (see No. 28), in the West it was the lecturers, elocutionists, entertainers, and showboat companies who first popularized Shakespeare, in isolated scenes and speeches. It may be said that from the earliest times Shakespeare played a large part in the emergent culture of the pioneer peoples.

After the first fifty years it is difficult to disentangle the imported productions of Shakespeare from those of the young but vigorous American theatre. Cooper and Wallack, who both appeared in Shakespeare early in their respective careers, were typical of the new generation of actors who, though born in England, spent the latter and greater part of their working lives in America. The honour of being the first native-born actor to play leading roles in Shakespeare must probably go to John Howard Payne, who as a youth of about seventeen played Hamlet and Romeo in 1809, but the greatest was undoubtedly Edwin Booth, whose Hamlet in 1864 was generally admired. The nineteenth-century personality-cult of the 'star' actor and the insistence on elaborate trappings was as prevalent in America as in England, and was reinforced by the many tours undertaken by such London companies as Charles Kean's and later Irving's.

The twentieth century saw, as in England, the gradual liberation of the play from over-decoration, with the simplified settings of Robert Edmond Jones and Norman Bel Geddes, and the new approach to a purified text. This was reinforced by a phenomenon peculiar to America—the invasion of the world of the theatre by the universities, which did not take place in England until much later. The proliferation of university theatres attached to departments whose syllabuses lead to a degree in drama (see UNITED STATES OF AMERICA, 10) has not been without its dangers, but it has led to much scholarly work on the problems of Shakespeare and the Elizabethan theatre in general, and to a wider spread of interest in and productions of Shakespeare than would have been the case otherwise. This is particularly fortunate since the commercial theatre on Broadway has not on the whole been enthusiastic about Shakespeare's plays. With no tradition of Shakespearian acting, with the same handicap as in London of unsuitable theatres, and with no pressing demand from the audience, managers have found them expensive to stage and uncertain in their box-office returns. There have been exceptions, but these have mostly been due to the efforts of an individual—John Barrymore, Eva le Gallienne, Orson Welles, Maurice Evans, Margaret Webster, Joseph Papp. It is therefore the universities who have had to bear the main burden of keeping Shakespeare alive on the American stage, either by incorporating his plays in the repertory of a community theatre, or by organizing festivals devoted solely to his works. The establishment of the Shakespeare Festival at Stratford, Conn. (see below, 4) may do much to consolidate the position of Shakespeare in the American theatre, where he is often 'more honoured in the breach than the observance'. The main dangers of academic Shakespeare are pedantry in the presentation (which can easily become tiresome) and immaturity in the actors. But a healthy spirit of experiment—as in the Texan *Midsummer Night's Dream* and *Much Ado About Nothing*—may do much to redress the balance. It certainly seems as if the future of Shakespeare in the United States lies rather with the community and the off-Broadway theatres than with the commercial theatre.

3. PRODUCTION IN TRANSLATION. During the first quarter of the seventeenth century the English Comedians, travelling on the Continent, included in their repertory cut versions of some of Shakespeare's plays. Traces of his influence have been detected in some early Polish and Hungarian plays, and it may have been through seeing the English Comedians that Heinrich Julius wrote his comedies in Shakespearian style, which were acted on a stage in his castle of Wolfenbüttel believed to have been designed on the model of an Elizabethan theatre. But these were isolated manifestations, and it is probably true to say that Shakespeare's name, and his works, remained virtually unknown outside England until well into the eighteenth century, when Voltaire first drew attention to him in the *Lettres philosophiques* (1734), and for a long time the prevalent opinion of his plays was that of the contemporary English theatre—that he was an undisciplined genius whose faults might be forgiven, but whose influence on young dramatists was to be deplored. Even his first admirer in Germany, Herder, had no wish to see him on the stage. Nor were the early translations such as to alter the general outlook. A frigid version of *Julius Caesar* in 1741, by C. W. von Borck, written in alexandrines; a prose summary of a number of his plays in French by Laplace, with dull verse renderings of some of the more important poetic scenes; a bowdlerized version in German prose by Wieland—none of these had any success. The first translation to be widely read was that in fairly faithful prose by Le Tourneur, published in 1776–82. This was the only one known to Italy, where it was warmly defended by Dr. Johnson's friend Baretti, until Leoni's Italian versions in 1819–22; it was read by Manzoni, the first Italian to be profoundly influenced by Shakespeare, and it provided Ducis, who knew no English, with the basis of the first French stage versions used by Molé at the Comédie-Française between 1769 and

1792. These were tailored to fit the unities, so that Desdemona, for instance, was wooed, wedded, and murdered in the space of a day, while *Hamlet*, *Romeo and Juliet*, and *King Lear*, were provided with happy endings on the lines of the English adaptations mentioned above.

In Germany Lessing's *Hamburgische Dramaturgie* (1767–9) first drew the general attention to Shakespeare, but it was the great actor Schröder who put him on the stage. The success of *Götz von Berlichingen* in 1773 had breached the fortress of classicism, and in 1776—the year of Le Tourneur's first French translations—Schröder ventured to produce *Hamlet* in Hamburg. It was an adapted *Hamlet*, but even so it proved something of a shock to his audience, though when they had recovered from the Ghost they broke into applause. Thus encouraged, Schröder put on *Othello*, which was a failure, *The Merchant of Venice*, and *Measure for Measure*, which had a cool reception, and finally, in 1778, *King Lear*, which was an unqualified success. This encouraged other German towns to take the plunge, particularly after Schröder had taken his productions to Berlin, Mannheim, and elsewhere, and new translations were provided by J. J. Eschenburg in his Mannheim Shakespeare (1775–8) and by A. W. Schlegel, whose seventeen plays were somewhat closer to the original, though still bowdlerized. Schlegel was completed later by Tieck and others, and republished with revisions and additions by F. Gundolf in 1908. In passing it may be noted that good acting-versions of the main plays were provided between 1869 and 1871 by Emil Devrient.

The struggle to acclimatize Shakespeare in Germany is pictured in the first part of Goethe's novel *Wilhelm Meisters Lehrjahre*. The incomplete early version points to a climax in which *Hamlet* in its entirety was to have been performed on a regenerated German stage, the hero by this time having come to stand for the young idealist of Goethe's generation. In a discussion with Serlo, who represents Schröder, and his companions, Wilhelm gives the first consistent reading of Hamlet's character—'a costly vessel in which an oak-tree has been planted'. Even in the later version, where Wilhelm yields to Serlo's demand for a compromise, the adapting is mild compared with what the play suffered at Schröder's hands. But, like Ducis, the latter knew how much his audience could stand, and was careful to give them no more. That was reserved for a more enlightened future, which would, however, have had no chance if Schröder had not blazed a trail. Once introduced into Germany Shakespeare prospered until he was finally claimed as 'unser' Shakespeare. His genius was thought akin to that of the Teutons. In the Romance countries he fared somewhat otherwise. In France the rising tide of Romanticism swept him into favour, and the visit of an English company, which included Charles Kemble and Miss Smithson, to Paris in 1827 set the seal on his reputation. In 1839 came a new translation by Laroche with an introduction by Dumas *père*, and from 1856 to 1867 a translation of the complete works by Victor Hugo. As knowledge of Shakespeare spread and his influence was more profoundly felt, earlier translations were found to be inadequate. In Italy he established himself more slowly. Rusconi's *Hamlet* did not appear until 1839 and Carcano's standard translation was not begun until 1843. This, in blank verse, was finally completed in 1882. The great actor Gustavo Modena could not reconcile his audience to *Othello* in 1843, and the first Italian to succeed in the role was his pupil Ernesto Rossi, in 1856. He was also good as Hamlet, Macbeth, Lear, Coriolanus, Shylock, and Romeo, while Salvini triumphed as Othello, and Adelaide Ristori as Lady Macbeth. These were all tragic roles, and although Zacconi and Ermete Novelli made a success of Petruchio, and a fine production of *A Midsummer Night's Dream* with Mendelssohn's music was given in Rome in 1910, it still seems as if the tragic aspect of Shakespeare's genius appeals more to the Latin races than his comic spirit—witness the success of the 1947 version of *Hamlet* in French, by André Gide, interpreted by Jean-Louis Barrault.

In Spain, where the exuberance of the Golden Age, and its close proximity in time to Elizabethan drama, might have led one to expect some interest in Shakespeare, little was heard of him until well into the nineteenth century, nor have any of the great actors there popularized him on the stage. The first translations, and those most acted, were based on Ducis. In the 1870s Jaime Clark and Guillermo Macpherson both undertook translations from the original, but neither of them completed their task. The only complete version so far is that of Luis Astrana Marin, which he began in 1920 and finished in 1950. There are also two series of translations into Catalan, one by C. A. Jordana (1930), the other, in course of publication, by Josep Maria de Sagarra. These, and other Spanish translations, are used in South America, except in Brazil, where Portuguese versions, mainly from the French, are current. In 1948 the University of Coimbra began the publication of a complete series of translations, but Shakespeare does not seem to have become popular on the Portuguese stage.

The first Greek translator was Demetrios Bikelas, whose versions, made between 1876 and 1884, were acted in Athens. In 1949 a start was made on a complete edition under the auspices of the British Council in Athens.

Interest in Shakespeare was not, however, confined to the above countries. It is probably true to say that today there is practically no country in the world where some, at least, of his plays have not been done in translation. He has influenced the theatres not only of Europe and America, but of the Far East. The desire to read him in the original, or to translate and adapt him for their own stages, has led many people to learn English. In fact, it may be said that England has had no more powerful ambassador than Shakespeare. It would be impossible to list all the translations of his plays. Many of the earliest were intended for reading only. Others were made for the stage by actors who appeared in them themselves, like the professional Peter Foersom in Denmark in the early nineteenth century, or the scholarly amateur Dr. Tsubouchi in Japan in the 1920s. Some were adapted to local conditions, like the Zulu *Macbeth* of 1961, or the early Chinese versions.

The first translations in central Europe were made from German versions. But from about the middle of the nineteenth century onwards new versions direct from the original were made, often by distinguished poets, as was the case in Hungary, where as early as 1864 a complete translation of all the plays was made by a group of poets and writers under the auspices of the Kisfaludy Society, though some of the plays had already been translated by Mihály Vörösmarty (1800–55). In Poland, where the great actress Modjeska appeared in many Shakespearian parts before playing them in English in America and England, the first direct translation was of *Hamlet* in 1840. New versions by a group of three Polish poets appeared in 1911–13. There is a plan on foot to make new stage versions of all the plays in the Serbo-Croat language. The first Macedonian translations appeared in 1949. The Yugoslav theatre director Branka Gavelo has recently made some new versions which he directed and played in himself. The playwright Ivan Cankar made a number of Slovene versions, while versions in Czech were made by Vrchlický in the early years of the twentieth century; to these have been added the new acting-versions of Emil Saudek. Fan Noli, a noted politician who died in 1965, translated a number of the plays into Albanian.

There are excellent versions of most of the plays in Norwegian, by H. Rytter (1932). The first Swedish versions were made in 1847–51 by Carl August Hagberg, and Per Hallström's magnificent versions, on which he worked for many years, appeared in the 1920s and 1930s. In 1873 Edvard Lembcke published Danish versions of all the plays except *Titus Andronicus* and *Pericles*. In Finland Shakespeare is done in both official languages, Finnish and Swedish; he has already figured in the repertory of the Iceland National Theatre, founded in 1950. In Belgium, which also has a double-language theatre, French and Flemish versions are found. The first play done in Flemish was *Romeo and Juliet* in 1884, with the actor Jan Dilis as Romeo. In the same year he appeared as Hamlet, after a visit to England to study Irving's interpretation. In 1929 a new version of *The Merry Wives of Windsor*, with settings resembling Flemish paintings, was given, with Jos Gevers as a recognizably Flemish-type Falstaff. But the translations generally used in the Flemish theatre are those of the Dutch author L. A. J. Burgersdijk, first published in 1885. In the 1940s these were revised and modernized by F. de Backer and G. A. Dudok. They are used in the Netherlands also, as are the Dutch versions of A. S. Kok.

In Russia adaptations of Shakespeare in the eighteenth century bore little resemblance to the originals. Among them was Catherine the Great's adaptation of *The Merry Wives of Windsor* as *What It is Like to Have Linen In A Basket* (1786). Nineteenth-century versions were usually made from the French or German—the first to be acted was *Richard III* (1833), with Bryansky as Richard. In the latter part of the century, however, several translations from the original were staged. In Soviet Russia eighteen of Shakespeare's plays, in new translations, are in the permanent repertory of the main theatres, the most popular being *Hamlet*. An interesting production of *King Lear* was done in 1935 by the State Jewish Theatre with Mikhoels in the lead, and in 1937 A. D. Popov produced a remarkable *Taming of the Shrew*. The plays have been translated into seventeen of the languages of the U.S.S.R., and an annual Shakespeare Conference is held at which scholars, producers, actors, and critics meet to discuss and plan productions of the plays. Shakespeare has also appeared on the Jewish stage, in Hebrew as early as 1874 (*Othello*), and in Yiddish—in Goldfaden's *The Two Kune Lemels*, a version of *Romeo and Juliet*—in 1880. None of the plays has been performed in Ladino, but two, *The Comedy of Errors* and *Romeo and Juliet*, formed the basis of novels in that language.

In India Shakespeare was used for a long time as a medium of teaching English, and many early performances were given by students. The first versions in the vernacular may have been in Marathi, as a *Comedy of Errors* was in the repertory of a Marathi touring company in 1843. In 1850 Parsi actors performed an adaptation of *The Taming of the Shrew* in Gujarati. There are also versions of some of the plays in Tamil, Bengali, and Kannada. A version of *Othello* in Marathi, as *Jhumjararava*, by Govind Ballal Dewal, in which he appeared in the name-part, was very popular, and was widely acted. The hero was a South Indian Maratha adventurer, and the heroine a fair high-class Hindu maiden.[1]

Although the most important translations of Shakespeare into Japanese are those by Dr. Tsubouchi already referred to, which were completed in 1928, an earlier attempt to acclimatize him was made by Oto Kawakami, the founder and leader of a new school of acting in Japan. With his wife, Sada Yacco, he appeared in *Hamlet* and *Othello*, with the scene set in Japan and the actors wearing contemporary Japanese costume. Hamlet, for instance, became Toshimaru and Ophelia Orive. Kawakami took his company to London and the United States in the early 1900s, where their productions aroused much interest.

[1] It is sad to have to record that Shakespeare is no longer performed in any Indian-language theatre, but he may come back into favour one day.

The many immigrant groups in the United States were able to attend performances of Shakespeare in their own languages given either by their own amateur groups or by visiting stars from Europe.

The quatercentenary celebrations of 1964 produced a vast new crop of translations, which must be added to the above. There is, for instance, to be a new Swedish translation of all the plays, and in the Daghestan Autonomous Republic plays are to be staged in the Avar, Darghen, and Lezghin languages (for a series of illustrations showing Shakespeare productions in Europe and the United States, see Nos. 71–94).

4. Shakespeare Festivals. The main festivals of Shakespeare plays by professional companies are given in the three Stratfords, in England (see STRATFORD-UPON-AVON), Canada, and the United States. At Stratford, Ontario, a Shakespeare Festival takes place annually from late June until mid-September. It owes its inception to a native of the town, Tom Patterson, whose enthusiasm led to the formation of a committee, which invited Tanya Moiseiwitsch to design and Tyrone Guthrie to direct the first theatre and its productions. At first the building was no more than a huge tent with an approximation to an Elizabethan open stage. Here in 1953 the Festival was inaugurated with *Richard III* and *All's Well That End's Well*, with Alec Guinness and Irene Worth. In 1957 a permanent structure replaced the original tent, though the architect, Robert Fairfield, was able to retain the original stage, and also the style of the pillars. The conical roof, locked by thirty-four girders which meet at the centre like wheel spokes, is without visible means of support. This means no obstructing pillars in the auditorium, which sweeps in a full semicircle round the stage; although the building holds over 2,000 people, no one of them is further than seventy feet from the stage. This makes for an Elizabethan intimacy between players and audience. The stage, which is lit from above, has a deep practicable trap, and at the back is a triangular balcony, supported on slender columns, which is a permanent fixture. The whole of the stage area, with its doors and extra entrances through the audience, is designed to facilitate that swift succession of scenes which is the essence of modern productions of Shakespeare. In 1955 Guthrie handed over the directorship of the theatre to Michael Langham, who continued the policy of maintaining a permanent Canadian company with visiting stars. In 1956 the company from Stratford, Ontario, appeared at the Edinburgh Festival in *Henry V*, with French-speaking actors in the French parts, and Fridolin [Gratien Gelinas] as the French King. They played on a permanent platform stage in the Assembly Hall, resembling as nearly as possible their Canadian stage. The first Canadian actor to star at Stratford, Ontario, was Christopher Plummer, who has since been seen with the Royal Shakespeare company in Stratford-upon-Avon and London, in *Richard III* and *Becket*. In 1959 Douglas Campbell and Frances Hyland, both Canadians, starred in *Othello*, which was directed by Jean Gascon, founder of Montreal's Théâtre du Nouveau Monde. The Stratford theatre is not used exclusively for Shakespeare, but has also housed *Cyrano de Bergerac*, *The Gondoliers*, produced by Guthrie, and a series of concerts (see No. 43).

The Shakespeare Festival at Stratford, Connecticut, resulted from the initiative and energy of Lawrence Langner. The building, designed by Edwin Howard, stands on the banks of the Housatonic River, and seeks to combine modern and traditional forms into a flexible, functional whole. The theatre opened on 12 July 1955, with two plays in repertory, *Julius Caesar* and *The Tempest*. The following year it expanded its programme to include three productions and a longer run, and while still depending on a few stars to head each production, the authorities began to gather the nucleus of a permanent company and to arrange for a longer period of employment for them. After the second Festival season a limited winter engagement was undertaken at the Phoenix Theatre, New York, for two of the three summer productions, and after the 1957 season a touring company in *Much Ado About Nothing*, led by Katharine Hepburn, who had starred in the summer production, visited six major cities of the U.S.A. In 1959 the theatre began to present a special pre-season programme for students only, and the success of these spring engagements has grown each year. Though it receives no financial support from the Government, the Festival company was honoured in 1961 when several of its members were invited to the White House to present scenes from past productions.

The American Shakespeare Festival Theatre, to give it its full title, also ran an acting academy directed by Helen Menken. She died in 1966, and the educational side of the Theatre's work is the concern of the Shakespeare Institute, University of Bridgeport, under Allan Lewis.

Two professional open-air festivals are those in Central Park, New York City, and Regent's Park, London. Shakespeare-in-the-Park, as it is affectionately known to the thousands who have witnessed free performances of Shakespeare in Central Park, was founded by Joseph Papp, whose energy and tenacity has enabled him to fight and win the many battles which have punctuated the festival's existence. With no charge for admission, financial problems have constantly beset the organization, and there have been stormy legal proceedings involving the company's right to use public park facilities. Papp's first productions of free Shakespeare were given in 1954, in a church hall. Two years later, with the blessing of the City authorities, he presented *Julius Caesar* and *The Taming of the Shrew* on a portable stage mounted on a truck to capacity audiences in the East River Park amphitheatre. The plays were well received by the critics, and the work of the director, Stuart Vaughan, was highly praised. In 1957 the City offered Papp the use of a site in Central Park, where *Romeo and Juliet*, *Macbeth*, and *Two Gentlemen of Verona* were given to large and enthusiastic audiences. Since then productions have been given in the Park in summer and in a theatre in winter, and have also been sent on tour to different secondary schools in the City. The future looked considerably brighter when in 1962 a new Festival Theatre, financed by private and public donations, was built on the old site. This open-air auditorium has a semi-arena stage with good lighting and amplification facilities, dressing rooms, and an audience area planned for excellent sight-lines and acoustics. The summer season of 1962 opened here with *The Merchant of Venice*, in which Shylock was played by George C. Scott, an actor who first came into prominence with his Richard III in the 1957 Festival season, and who has since starred on Broadway.

The Open-Air Theatre in Regent's Park, though not entirely limited to Shakespeare, is best known for productions of his plays which, given favourable climatic conditions, can be most enjoyable. Unfortunately many have been ruined by rain and cold winds, and forced to retire to a somewhat hampering marquee. Plays in Regent's Park were first given from 1900 onwards by Ben Greet and his Woodland Players, but it was not until Sydney Carroll in 1932 tried the experiment of giving some afternoon performances of *Twelfth Night*, which was then on the bill at the New Theatre, that the idea of a permanent theatre attracted official attention. Since 1933, with the exception of the years of and immediately after the Second World War, plays have been given in a natural woodland setting, with the addition of lighting and amplifiers and an occasional piece of built scenery. Many distinguished players have appeared in Regent's Park, and from 1933 to 1935 Ben Greet returned as Master of the Greensward. But the man most closely associated with the development of the enterprise was Robert Atkins, who produced the first *Twelfth Night*, playing Sir Toby Belch, and later produced and acted in many of the plays.

An annual summer festival is held in Balboa Park, San Diego, California, where three plays, preceded by traditional sixteenth-century festivities with actors in Elizabethan costume, are given in the Old Globe Theatre. This was designed by Thomas Wood Stevens for the 1935–6 California Pacific International Exposition, and was based on contemporary ideas of the structure of the original London playhouse, some of which, of course, have since been modified by the results of intensive research. After the Exposition the theatre, which seats 400, was used by the San Diego Community Theatre for old and modern plays. In 1949 B. Iden Payne inaugurated the first Shakespeare Festival, run in conjunction with a Workshop course sponsored by the San Diego State College. The company was then wholly amateur and local, but in 1954 it was decided to present Shakespeare in repertory, using student actors and technicians from colleges and drama schools throughout the country. The system was further modified in 1958 to allow professional actors to fill the major roles, while minor parts continued to be played by scholarship students recruited for the company through funds supplied by local patrons.

One of the oldest amateur festivals is the one at Ashland, Oregon, which was founded in 1935. Plays were first given by college students in a frame structure with no roof, a former domed Chautauqua building. This was damaged by fire in 1940, and the festival was suspended until 1947, when a new stage was built, and professional actors were engaged for the first time. Five or six plays are given during the Festival, which is held during the summer vacation. Attached to the theatre is an Institute of Renaissance Studies.

An important festival, devoted entirely to *Hamlet*, was for a time a feature of the Danish summer theatre scene. A different country was asked to send a company each year to perform the play at Elsinore, in the courtyard of Kronberg Castle. The Old Vic inaugurated the scheme in 1937 with Laurence Olivier as Hamlet. In 1938 there was a German company headed by Gründgens, and in 1939 another English company under John Gielgud. After the Second World War efforts were made to revive the festival. Swedish, Norwegian, Finnish, American, and Irish Hamlets were seen, and Michael Redgrave appeared with a third English company in 1950. The venture now seems to have been abandoned.

Performances of *Hamlet* are also one of the highlights of the Summer Festival at Dubrovnik, and it is interesting to note that the Municipal Theatre in Istanbul begins its season each year with a performance of a play by Shakespeare.

All the above are now professional undertakings, but there are innumerable amateur festivals, of which the most important is probably the one held in London in the week nearest to Shakespeare's birthday, 23 Apr., when the Southwark Borough Council (a district which has close ties with Shakespeare) sponsors a series of amateur productions, by college or other societies, one of which takes place in the yard of the George Inn, Southwark, a site which approximates as nearly as possible to the public playing-place of London actors before the building of Burbage's Theatre in 1576 (see INNS USED AS THEATRES).

SHAKESPEARE THEATRE, LONDON, in Curtain Road. There exist scarcely any records of this early nineteenth-century theatre, which seems at one time to have been given over to feats of horsemanship. Grimaldi played there once. Later it became a house for legitimate drama. It may have stood on the site of the Standard Theatre.

SHAKHOVSKY, ALEXANDER ALEXANDROVICH (1777–1846), Russian dramatist, author of many plays, mainly comedies, though he also wrote a few tragedies. He is regarded as the founder of the Court vaudeville. Born near Smolensk, he was privately educated, and joined the army, retiring with the rank of staff-captain. In 1795 his first comedy was given at the Hermitage Theatre, of which he later became a director. His work there was interrupted by the Napoleonic invasion, during which time he led a troop of civilian volunteers against the French, but was resumed in 1819. A quarrel with the director, Prince Tyuafyakin, led to his dismissal, but in 1824 he was back once more, taking part in production and administration. In 1808 he founded and edited a theatrical journal, and built the third theatre in St. Petersburg, the Youth Theatre, for light comedy, played mainly by graduates of the Government Theatrical School.

SHANK, John (?–1636), English actor, who appears in the actor-list of Shakespeare's plays, and whose name is found in many different spellings. He apparently began his career with the Queen's Men, but no record of this beyond his own asseveration has been found. He was, however, a member of the King's Men, joining them either shortly before, or at the time of, the death of Armin, whose position as chief clown he inherited. He was a comedian, well thought of as a singer and dancer of jigs, and appears to have been very popular with his audience, and though the written lines of his roles are often few, it seems that he was allowed considerable licence in gagging. From the number of boy-apprentices with whom his name is connected, and from the fact that so many people were buried from his house in Cripplegate, it has been inferred that one of his functions in the company was the training of apprentices, who lodged with him. He had a son John, also an actor, who played at the Fortune. The latter led a dissolute life, and was court-martialled in 1642 for cowardice while fighting on the Parliamentary side in the Civil War.

SHARER, the name given to a member of an Elizabethan theatrical company who owned a share in the wardrobe and playbooks, as distinct from the apprentice or hired man. If he had also a share in the actual playhouse building, he was known as a 'housekeeper' as well.

SHARING SYSTEM, see PROVINCIAL THEATRES, 1 *d*.

SHARPE, Richard (*c.* 1602–32), an excellent actor with the King's Men, who from 1625 until his early death played the parts of romantic young heroes. Since he is known to have played the name-part in *The Duchess of Malfi* and to have been acting several years previous to that, it is evident that he started his career as a young boy and quickly gave proof of much ability. His other women-roles are not known, but he is conjectured to have played queens and haughty young women. It was probably Sharpe who ran up a bill with young Condell for 41*s.* 10*d.* for stockings.

SHATTERELL. There were two actors of this name, Edward and Robert, who may have been father and son, but more likely brothers. Edward was evidently the elder, since he is found among the actors on the Continent after the closing of the theatres, and must therefore have had some experience of acting before 1642. He was also one of those who contrived to put on surreptitious plays at the Red Bull as early as 1654, where he is found again in Mohun's company immediately on the Restoration. Robert was one of Beeston's Boys at the Cockpit, may have served in the army during the Civil War, and with Edward joined Killigrew's first company. Edward disappears from the records soon after this, but Robert flourished, and was evidently a man of substance, since he was one of those who could afford to build themselves houses near the new Drury Lane in 1663. He remained with Killigrew until his death, which took place some time shortly before 1684.

SHAW, George Bernard (1856–1950), dramatist, critic, and writer on public affairs, born in Dublin, son of George Carr Shaw (a pensioned sinecure-office-holder of the Four Courts) and Lucinda Elizabeth (Gurly) Shaw. The impecunious ways of her husband led Mrs. Shaw to adopt a career as vocalist and teacher of singing, and it was from this circumstance that G.B.S. obtained the early knowledge and love of classical music which qualified him later to become a music critic in London. Following a sketchy formal education which began at the Wesleyan Connexional School in Dublin, he started work in his early teens as a land-agent's office-boy at 18*s.* a month and became cashier when 16. In the spring of 1876, having risen to a salary of £84 a year, he migrated to London, where he worked for a few months with the Edison Telephone Company. During the next nine years he earned a total of £6 (for an article, a patent-medicine advertisement, and a set of verses), his keep being provided by his mother. Between 1879 and 1883 he wrote five unsuccessful novels (all of which have since been included in his collected works) and made himself an effective speaker on political and other subjects, joining the Fabian Society in 1884.

Through William Archer, Shaw became a book-reviewer for the *Pall Mall Gazette* and art critic on *The World* (he had qualified for this by haunting the Dublin National Gallery in boyhood), and gradually extended his journalistic connexions. From 1888 to 1890 he wrote music criticism for the *Star* (using the pseudonym Corno di Bassetto), and then until 1894 for *The World*. Admirable though his music articles were, their quality was surpassed by that of the dramatic criticism he contributed to the *Saturday Review* between Jan. 1895 and May 1898. These essays on plays and players (later reissued as *Our Theatres in the Nineties*), as fresh and invigorating more than half a century later as at the time they were written, set a new standard in English theatre criticism.

Though Shaw professed no love of the stage, he quickly recognized its value as a platform for the transmission of ideas of social and political reform to which he had dedicated himself. He also became an ardent disciple of Ibsen, whose works in translation were at that time bringing a stimulating breath of reality into the stale atmosphere of a drama which had been for many generations remote from life outside the theatre. Bernard Shaw therefore turned to the writing of plays, and *Widowers' Houses* (begun in 1885) opened in 1892 his long career as the most notable dramatist of his time. This first play was produced on 9 Dec. at the Royalty Theatre by J. T. Grein as part of his Independent Theatre venture. *Arms and the Man* was played at the Avenue Theatre on 21 Apr. 1894, but *The Philanderer* and *Mrs. Warren's Profession* had been written in the previous year. The last-named play did not reach the stage before 1902, when it was produced privately by the Stage Society, the Censor's ban on public performances being maintained until the 1920s. These early dramatic works caused Shaw to be regarded in many quarters as subversive, since he was attacking vested interests and bringing into the light social evils considered unfit for open discussion. He had embarked upon a crusade designed to introduce to the stage subjects—such as slum landlordism, prostitution, war, religion, family disturbances, health, economics—previously confined to political meetings, the courts, or the pulpit. Deliberately turning his back upon the variations and vagaries of sex attraction, the stock material of a vast majority of plays, Shaw aimed at the minds of playgoers instead of at their emotions and physical sensations. He wanted 'a pit of philosophers', not merely a theatre full of folk seeking meretricious titillating entertainment. Thought, not action, was therefore the staple of the Shavian theatre; but, as several generations of playgoers came to learn and to acknowledge with gratitude and enthusiasm, thought salted with humour and talk enlivened with wit and eloquence provide a more rewarding type of entertainment than any that the modern stage had previously offered.

When the early antagonism to Shaw died down and cooler judgement replaced it, the two main charges laid against him were that he had no sense of human character and could create nothing but mouthpieces for the utterance of his own views, and that he was nothing but a destructive critic. Time has already answered the first of those charges, for plays do not survive on 'views'. The second charge could only be sustained if audiences and readers were held to be under no obligation to draw plain and, indeed, inescapable inferences from the material before them.

The popularity of Shaw's work dates from the Court Theatre repertory season under the management of H. Granville-Barker and J. E. Vedrenne, 1904–7, during which 701 performances were given of 11 of his plays. His since-familiar leading idea of the Life Force as the governing factor in human affairs was first embodied in dramatic form in *Man and Superman* (1903). In the author's opinion the masterpiece among his nearly fifty plays is *Back to Methuselah* (1921), though this opinion is not widely shared. In film versions, based upon faithful transcriptions of the original text, *Pygmalion*, *Major Barbara*, and *Caesar and Cleopatra* reached millions who do not frequent the theatre. It is difficult to assess the relative popularity of the other plays, most of which have been performed throughout the world in many languages. In England *Saint Joan*, first produced in 1924 with Sybil Thorndike as St. Joan (see No. 98), probably outstrips the rest in general favour, with *Candida*, *Arms and the Man*, *The Doctor's Dilemma*, and *You Never Can Tell* following. *Heartbreak House* stands in high esteem with critical judges.

Shaw gave careful attention to the presentation of his plays in print. In typographical layout he set a revolutionary high standard which others followed, and his detailed stage-directions amount to a commentary which greatly assists the reader to visualize the author's intentions for the actors. As a producer at rehearsals Shaw earned praise and respect from the players.

The famous Prefaces to the plays form an independent branch of the author's writings and are largely responsible for his reputation as one of the great masters of English prose. A book demanding special mention is *Ellen Terry and Bernard Shaw: A Correspondence* (1931), which on both sides is rich in graces and virtues impossible to characterize in measured terms. Shaw's major critical writings include *The Quintessence of Ibsenism* (1891; revised 1913) and *The Perfect Wagnerite* (1898; 3rd ed., enlarged, 1913). A. C. WARD

SHAW, GLEN(CAIRN) ALEXANDER BYAM (1904–), English actor and stage director, who made his first appearance in 1923, and was seen in London two years later as Yasha in *The Cherry Orchard*. He gained experience in Fagan's company at the Playhouse, Oxford, and continued to act, both in England and America, until the outbreak of the Second World War in 1939, his last appearance on the stage being as Horatio to the Hamlet of John Gielgud at the Lyceum and at Elsinore. After the war he returned to the theatre, not as an actor, but as a director, and was associated with the short-lived Old Vic School. He produced several modern plays before being appointed co-director, with Anthony Quayle, of the Shakespeare Memorial Theatre in 1953, becoming sole director in 1956. He directed a number of plays, including the four tragedies, during his stay in Stratford, in several of which his wife Angela Baddeley appeared (see No. 92). He resigned in 1960 and was succeeded by Peter Hall. After leaving Stratford he produced *Ross*, with Alec Guinness as Lawrence of Arabia, and in 1962 he was appointed Director of Productions (a new post) at Sadler's Wells Opera. He was created C.B.E. in 1954. A sensitive, unassuming, but devoted theatre man, he has profited, in directing plays, from his own experience as an actor, and brings to his work sound scholarship, infinite sympathy, and a genuine understanding of and liking for his fellow-workers.

SHAW, Robert Gould, see harvard.

SHCHEPKIN, Mikhail Semenovich (1788–1863), one of the greatest of Russian actors, born in Kursk Province, the son of a serf. He had his first reading lessons from a baker's wife and a priest, and then entered the county school. His interest in the theatre was aroused when he accidentally witnessed a play in a nobleman's private theatre, and at school he played in one of Sumarokov's comedies. In 1802 he was sent back to Kursk to attend the provincial public school. He was an excellent scholar and a great reader. Through a school-friend he became acquainted with Bafsov, owner of the Kursk theatre, where he was allowed to prompt, and copy music. He also appeared in private theatricals with some success. At fifteen he finished school, and being a serf could go no further. During the next year or two he appeared in public performances during the summer, and in private shows in Kursk during the winter. In Nov. 1805 a benefit performance for the actress Lykova was given. The leading actor got drunk and could not appear, and Shchepkin offered his services. He gave a brilliant performance, and was rewarded with some good roles, though until 1808 he worked mainly as an understudy. In that year he joined the troupe to play comic roles, and remained until the company was dissolved in 1816. He was then invited to join the Stein and Kalinovsky troupe in Kharkov, and went with them at the invitation of Prince Repin to play in Poltava, where he met the actor Uragov. In 1818 a movement, inaugurated by Prince Repin, was set on foot to purchase Shchepkin's freedom from his owner Volkenstein; and shortly after his liberation the manager of the Moscow Maly Theatre invited him to join the Imperial company. He made his début in Nov. 1822 in Zagoskin's *Gospodin Bogatonov; or, a Provincial in the Capital.* He was already an accomplished actor, but Moscow offered him great opportunities which he was not slow to take advantage of. From 1825 to 1828 he played in St. Petersburg. Griboyedov's *Woe from Wit* and Gogol's *Inspector-General* provided him with some fine roles, and he was at his best during the 1840s. After that he declined and his acting lost its grip, though that does not detract from his great influence on the Russian theatre. He was a convinced and militant realistic actor, and the Russian critic Belinsky saw in his work a synthesis of Mochalov's passion and Karatygin's technical perfection, which demanded of its exponent a perpetual observation of life and its truthful presentation on the stage. Shchepkin's greatest roles were in the comic characters of Shakespeare, Schiller, and Gogol. He created from the varied tendencies of his time a school of acting which realized itself in the plays of Ostrovsky, Chekhov, and Gorky. Encouraged by Pushkin, Shchepkin wrote his autobiographical notebooks, which are of great artistic and theatrical interest.

SHCHUKIN, Boris Vasilievich (1894–1939), Soviet actor whose early death robbed the Russian stage of one of its outstanding figures. He was for twenty years at the Vakhtangov Theatre, where he played leading roles. In his last years he gave some exceptionally fine performances, notably in the title-role of *Yegor Bulichev*, in Afinogenov's *Distant Point*, and as Lenin, whom he was the first actor to impersonate. Joseph Macleod, in *The New Soviet Theatre*, wrote of him that, as befitted a man so essentially of the theatre, 'if he did not die in harness, he very nearly did—in bed, reading Diderot's *Paradoxe sur le comédien*'. After his death the street in which he lived was renamed in his honour.

SHELDON, Edward Brewster (1886–1946), American dramatist, and one of the first to graduate from Baker's '47 Workshop'. His first play, *Salvation Nell* (1908), was produced when he was only 22, and, with Mrs. Fiske as the heroine and her husband as director, proved a great success. Sheldon was immediately hailed as the rising hope of the American theatre, and as the leader of the new school of realistic writers. His next play, *The Nigger* (1909), was a theatrical but courageous handling of the Negro problem, while *The Boss* (1911) was a study of modern industrial conditions. But all Sheldon's serious work was overshadowed by the success of his popular romantic play, *Romance* (1913), which, with Doris Keane as the Italian opera singer who attracts the young idealistic clergyman, had a long run both in New York and London. It made an immense emotional appeal to audiences all over the world, and was translated into French and other languages. Handicapped by serious illness, Sheldon did most of his later work in collaboration, and also translated and adapted anonymously a number of popular successes. Summing up his work, Quinn in his *History of American Drama* says of him:

> He is the celebrator of the aspiration of those who strive to lift themselves out of circumstances or a mode of life to something higher, and his sympathy is always with them, even if they are doomed to disappointment from the beginning.... In this general attitude of sympathy with the aspiring soul, Sheldon points forward to Eugene O'Neill. But as in O'Neill the poet dominates the dramatist, so in Sheldon the playwright limits or at least defines the poet's power.

SHELLEY, Percy Bysshe (1792–1822), famous English Romantic poet, and author of several plays in poetry, of which the best known is *The Cenci*. Published in 1819, this was first acted by the Shelley Society in 1886, and has been several times revived and broadcast; it is, however, pure poetry but poor drama, being confused in action and somewhat too dependent upon Shakespeare, and it is unlikely to find a permanent place even in the repertory of poetic drama on the stage.

SHEPHERD, Edward (*c.* 1670–1747), English architect, designer of Shepherd Market, Mayfair, and of the first theatre built in Covent Garden in 1732.

SHERIDAN, Mark (? –1917), a music-hall comedian, whose speciality was Cockney songs with rousing choruses, often descriptive of seaside delights. One which is still sung was 'I do like to be beside the seaside'. He was at his best in the 1890s, but during the First World War—whose soldiers marched to his rousing 'Here we are again'—he was beset by melancholy. While appearing in a pantomime in Glasgow he became convinced that his powers were failing, and he committed suicide. His dress was distinctive and unvaried. He wore a top hat, a frock coat, bell-bottomed trousers fastened round the knee with a strap in imitation of the old-time navvies, big boots, and carried a cane. W. MACQUEEN-POPE†

SHERIDAN, Richard Brinsley (1751–1816), English dramatist, theatre manager, and politician, whose best play, *The School for Scandal*, stands as the masterpiece of the English comedy of manners, with all the wit, but none of the licentiousness, of the Restoration comedy from which it derives. Sheridan, who was the son of an actor and of an authoress—his mother, Mrs. Frances Sheridan (1724–66), wrote both plays and novels—was born in Dublin, educated at Harrow, and intended for the law. But at 21 he made a romantic marriage with the daughter of the singer and composer Linley, and two years later his first play, *The Rivals*, was produced at Covent Garden. This was followed by a farce, *St. Patrick's Day; or, the Scheming Lieutenant*, and a comic opera, 'The Duenna', all given in 1775. In 1776 Sheridan bought Garrick's share in Drury Lane and rebuilt the theatre in 1794. He remained there until its destruction by fire in 1809, always in financial difficulties. His later plays, all produced at Drury Lane, include *A Trip to Scarborough*, altered from Vanbrugh's *The Relapse*, and the famous *School for Scandal* (both 1777), with Mrs. Abington as the first Lady Teazle (see No. 30); *The Critic; or, a Tragedy Rehearsed* (1779), the best of the many burlesques stemming from Buckingham's *The Rehearsal*, and the only one to have been constantly revived; and, many years later, when Sheridan had practically deserted the theatre for politics, *Pizarro* (1799), an adaptation of a popular drama by Kotzebue. He was also part-author of several entertainments, and wrote the pantomime of *Robinson Crusoe* for Drury Lane in Jan. 1781, as an after-piece to *The Winter's Tale*, as well as three new spectacular scenes for a revival of *Harlequin Fortunatus* in 1780. Sheridan is said by Oulton to have appeared as Harlequin for one night, but there is no proof of this. He certainly exploited to the full the popular taste for spectacle and pantomime, helped by Noverre and de Loutherbourg, and *The Critic*, for example, was produced with remarkable scenic effects and lavish costumes. His management of Drury Lane was marked by a succession of quarrels with the managers of the smaller theatres—Astley's, Sadler's Wells, the new Royalty—whose success alarmed him, and with his co-partners, Linley and Ford, he was several times successful in embroiling his rivals with the authorities, though he failed to retain the monopoly he was striving for. The pressure of the unlicensed theatres was too great. Sheridan became a Member of Parliament in 1780, rose rapidly in his new profession, and made some remarkable speeches at the trial of Warren Hastings. But his last years were unhappy, and he never recovered from the destruction of Drury Lane, though he endeavoured to bear the blow with equanimity. He died in 1816 and was buried in Westminster Abbey.

SHERIDAN, William Edward (1840–87), American actor, with a virile and forceful personality and a fine resonant voice. He made his first successes in Philadelphia, and in the last years of his brief career was extremely popular in San Francisco, where he first appeared in 1880. Among his best parts were Louis XI, Othello, and Shylock, and he was also good in *A New Way to Pay Old Debts* and *The Lyons Mail*. During the Civil War he was a captain in the Union Army, returning to the stage afterwards, when he appeared at Niblo's Garden as the first American Beamish McCoul in *Arrah-na-Pogue*. His first wife dying in 1872, he married Louise Davenport, and with her embarked on a long tour of Australia, where he died.

SHERLOCK, William (*fl.* first half of seventeenth century), English actor, probably the keeper of Beeston's Cockpit from its opening in 1616 until he was succeeded by John Rhodes some time between 1637 and 1644. He was a Queen's Man from 1625 until the closing of the theatres in 1642, and was transferred with them in 1637 to Salisbury Court. From his extant list of parts it is obvious that he played both comic and villainous parts, though he was stronger as a comedian.

SHERRIFF, Robert Cedric (1896–), English dramatist and novelist, who became widely known with his war-play, *Journey's End* (1928), which gives a realistic and yet emotionally moving picture of the reactions of a small group of men in a dug-out just before an attack. It was the first play dealing with the First World War to achieve success, and its phenomenal popularity came as a surprise even to those who had ventured to back their faith in it. First produced on a Sunday night by the Stage Society, it was brought to the commercial theatre by Maurice Browne, whom it established as a manager and producer, and ran for two years, the all-male cast including such actors as Colin Clive, Maurice Evans, and Robert Speaight. Translated and played all over the world, and frequently revived by amateur societies, it remains one of the few plays dealing with modern warfare to be both artistically and theatrically acceptable. Sherriff also wrote a comedy on village cricket, *Badger's Green* (1930); a play on Napoleon's last years, *St. Helena* (1935); *Miss Mabel* (1948); *Home at Seven* (1950), in which Sir Ralph Richardson gave an impressive study of amnesia; and *A Shred of Evidence* (1960). A musical entitled *Johnny the Priest* (also 1960) was based on Sherriff's earlier play, *The Telescope.*

SHERWOOD, Robert Emmet (1896–1955), American dramatist, who distinguished himself as a writer of both comedy and plays of social and political content. He was born in New Rochelle, near New York, and graduated from Harvard in 1918. After seeing service in the First World War and writing for periodicals, Sherwood scored a success with his first play, *The Road to Rome* (1927), a satirical treatment of Hannibal's march which deflated military glory. *The Love Nest* (also 1927) was a trivial dramatization of a Ring Lardner short story, and *The Queen's Husband* (1928) drew a moderately amusing portrait of a henpecked king. The melodrama *Waterloo Bridge* (1930) was more successful in London than in New York, and *This is New York* (also 1930), a melodrama of blackmail and scandal, was a total failure. Sherwood's next effort, however, was the brilliant high comedy *Reunion in Vienna* (1931), which revived the embers of a pre-war romance between a dashing Hapsburg archduke and the wife of a psycho-analyst who is hoist with his own petard of intellectual complacency.

With *The Petrified Forest* (1935) and the almost simultaneously written *Acropolis* (a well-regarded failure in London, never professionally produced in America) Sherwood addressed himself to the deteriorating world situation. He drew a parallel between the decline of Periclean civilization and the rising tide of Fascism in *Acropolis*, and composed an allegory on intellectual bankruptcy in the melodrama *The Petrified Forest*, which recounted the disintegration and virtual suicide of a young writer. Sherwood's pessimism grew darker in the ironic Pulitzer Prize-winner *Idiot's Delight* (1936), in which he foretold a second world war and postulated further bankruptcy for Western civilization. *Tovarich* (also 1936), from the French of Jacques Deval, was only a pleasant detour for Sherwood, who next wrote the stirring democratic affirmation *Abe Lincoln in Illinois* (1938). This chronicle paralleled contemporary political struggles with those of the past and characterized Abraham Lincoln as a man of peace who entered the political arena reluctantly. *There Shall Be No Night* (1941), written in response to the invasion of Finland, showed a pacifistic scientist choosing war as a preferable alternative to slavery. At about this time Sherwood himself entered upon a life of action as a friend of Franklin D. Roosevelt and as a leading interventionist prior to Pearl Harbour, writing no new plays until *The Rugged Path* (1945), a rather disjointed account of an idealistic journalist's conflict with his isolationist family and his death on a Pacific Island. Sherwood's last play, *Small War on Murray Hill* (produced in 1957), was a mild romantic comedy about the American Revolution.

JOHN GASSNER†

SHIELS, George (1886–1949), one of the most popular and versatile playwrights of Ireland, esteemed alike in the North and in the South for his serious as for his humorous work. He had a range of experience that was somewhat uncommon and he drew upon a wide knowledge of character and social relations in both parts of Ireland and in America. His treatment of this material is realistic without bitterness or harshness, humorous or fanciful without becoming farcical, and sympathetic without forfeiting that humour or the satire into which it merges.

He was first known by his comedies, humorous and satirical pictures of contemporary life, one of which, *Bedmates* (1921), made his name. Among the most popular of them were *Paul Twyning* (1922), *Professor Tim* (1925), and *The New Gossoon* (1930). But his serious plays, such as *The Passing Day* (1936) and *The Rugged Path* (1940), show clearly that he was not limited to comedy; the second of these had an unprecedented run at the Abbey Theatre.

UNA ELLIS-FERMOR†

SHIRLEY, James (1596–1666), the leading dramatist of London when the Puritans shut the playhouses in 1642. He survived the Commonwealth, only to die of exposure during the Great Fire of London. A university man, he took orders in the Church of England, but became a Roman Catholic and a schoolmaster, and wrote some forty plays, most of which have survived in print, though not on the stage. These include tragedies like *The Maid's Revenge* (1626); *The Traitor* (1631), Shirley's most powerful play, a horror-and-revenge tragedy into which he imported a masque of the Lusts and Furies; *Love's Cruelty* (1631); and *The Cardinal* (1641), of which Wilson in Vol. VI of the *Cambridge History of English Literature* says, '[It] brings to a fitting close the tremendous file of English tragedy'. Shirley's best work, however, was done in comedy, in which he provides a link between Jonson and the Restoration. This is particularly true of *The Lady of Pleasure* (1635), in which, it has been said, 'the cool and calculated intrigue of Aretina is thoroughly typical of the degradation of love in the seventeenth-century comedy of manners'. Other comedies by Shirley are *The Witty Fair One* (1628), *Hyde Park* (1632), *The Gamester* (1633), which was later adapted by Garrick, and *The Sisters* (1642). A promptbook of this last, dating from the early years of the Restoration, supplies some interesting stage-directions, and is now in the library of Sion College. Shirley was popular in the early days of the Restoration, no less than eight of his plays being revived, including *The Cardinal*, which Pepys saw in 1667.

SHOP, theatrical slang for engagement. To be out of a shop, or 'resting', means to be unemployed.

SHOWBOAT, the name given to the floating theatres of the great North American rivers of the West, particularly the Mississippi and the Ohio, which represent an early and most successful attempt to bring drama to the pioneer settlements. It is not known who first built a showboat, or at what date. In fact, the entire history of the floating theatre, being mainly preserved by oral tradition, is confused and obscure, and has gathered about itself such an accretion of legend that it is difficult to disentangle the facts. But from the earliest pioneering days boats were thick on the rivers, for trade, for freight, and for less legitimate purposes such as gambling and drinking, and it would require little ingenuity to transform a keel-boat or a raft into a passable theatre. Doubtless many of the early itinerant companies of the West moored their boats to the bank and built on deck a rough cabin to shelter and enclose the players. The first recorded instance of this, however, dates from 1817, when that intrepid pioneer player, Noah Miller Ludlow (1795–1866), took his company along the Cumberland river to the Mississippi in a flat-boat with a shelter at one end. In general, however, Ludlow played on land, even if he moved by water, and it is William Chapman (1764–1839), formerly an actor in London and New York, who has the honour of heading the list of showboat managers. Ludlow, in his memoirs, has left a description of Chapman's showboat, as he saw it in about 1831. He describes the structure as being 'a large flat-boat with a rude kind of house built upon it, having a ridge-roof, above which projected a staff with a flag attached, upon which was plainly visible the word Theatre'. The interior was apparently long and narrow, with a shallow stage at one end and benches in front across the width of the boat, the whole lighted by guttering candles. Here the Chapman family, consisting of husband and wife and five children, a group large enough to dispense with outside help, played one-night stands along the rivers wherever a sizeable settlement made it feasible. The average entrance fee was about 50 cents, and the staple fare strong melodrama or fairy-tale plays, ranging from *The Stranger* to *Cinderella*. There are some interesting references to the Chapmans in the memoirs of Tyrone Power (1795–1841), one of which deserves to be quoted: 'Chapman's practice is to have a building suitable to his views erected upon a raft at some point high up the Mississippi, or one of its tributaries, whence he takes his departure early in the fall, with scenery, dresses, and decorations, all prepared for representation. At each village or large plantation he hoists banner and blows trumpet and few who love a play suffer his ark to pass the door, since they know it is to return no more until the next year; for, however easy may prove the downward course of the drama's temple, to retrograde, upwards, is quite beyond its power. . . . When the Mississippi theatre reaches New Orleans, it is abandoned and sold for firewood; the manager and troop returning in a steamer to build a new one.' The use of trumpet and flag suggests an interesting parallel with the practice of the Elizabethan theatre (see ENGLISH PLAYHOUSE). Later, showboats made use of steam-tugs for the journey up river, coming in time to own their own steamships as an integral part of the outfit.

After Chapman's death his widow sold the showboat to that other pioneer player, Sol Smith (1801–69), who lost it in the following year in a collision. It is not known what happened to Chapman's children, though they probably remained on the stage, and one of his sons may have been the Henry Chapman (1822–65), well known as an actor, whose two daughters, Blanche and Ella, both handsome and proficient actresses, appeared in burlesque for many years on tour. Ella also visited England, making her début there in 1876 and later appearing in pantomime at the Grand, Islington, and at Her Majesty's Theatre.

Another showboat captain of the early days was Henry Butler (dates unknown), an old theatre manager who took a combined museum and playhouse up and down the Erie Canal from about 1836 until his death, showing stuffed animals and waxworks by day, and at night, since he had a good sailor-actor in Jack Turner, playing such nautical dramas as *Black-Eyed Susan*.

A showboat about which a certain amount of information is available is the Floating Circus Palace of Spaulding and Rodgers. Built in Cincinnati in 1851, it was shorter and wider than the river steamboats of the time, and was intended for elaborate, usually equestrian, shows. It had a central arena with several tiers of benches, capable of accommodating a large audience, kitchens, dressing-rooms, stables, and living-quarters. In addition to circus, vaudeville, and minstrel acts, concerts, and a museum, the Floating Circus Palace also gave dramatic performances. Its history coincides with the heyday of the showboats, which increased in numbers and popularity until the outbreak of war in 1861 drove them off the river, never again to return in such numbers.

The spirit of showmanship survived, however, and in 1878 a Captain A. B. French (? –1902) took his *New Sensation* along the Mississippi. He had to live down a good deal of prejudice, but the high moral tone of his productions, and the good behaviour of his small company, soon won favour, and the showboat was again considered respectable. Captain French's wife was the first woman to hold a pilot's licence in those waters, and the only one to hold both that and master's papers.

At one time she and her husband ran two showboats, piloting one each.

A formidable rival to French was Captain E. A. Price (dates unknown), owner of the *Water Queen*, built in 1885. This had a stage nineteen feet across, lit by oil, a good stock of scenery, a company of some fifty persons, and that indispensable adjunct to all showboats, a steam calliope. After a long and honourable career as a showboat it became a floating dance-hall in Tennessee, and in 1935 was used in the filming of Edna Ferber's *Showboat*. This excellent, though fictionalized, account of life on a floating theatre was the first to bring the Mississippi showboat prominently before the general public, and had a well-deserved success as novel, play, and film.

Incidentally, another river-boat which figured in a film was the sidewheeler *Kate Adams*, built in 1898, the third of her line, which in 1926 appeared as *La Belle Revere* in *Uncle Tom's Cabin*. She was later burnt to the waterline.

Among the many other showboat managers of the time was Captain E. E. Eisenbarth (dates unknown), owner of the first boat to bear the name *Cotton Blossom*. This was capable of seating a large audience, and on a stage twenty feet by eleven feet presented a three-hour entertainment of straight solid drama, usually popular melodrama, though in 1904 Eisenbarth made showboat history by producing *Faust*. The *Cotton Blossom* was one of the first showboats to be lit by electricity. The name persisted, and a later *Cotton Blossom* was owned by Captain Otto Hitner, who produced adaptations of such novels as *The Little Shepherd of Kingdom Come*, made by his wife.

It was in 1907 that a famous showboat personality, Captain Billy Bryant, author of the fascinating book, *Children of Ol' Man River* (1936), first entered the profession, when his father launched *The Princess* with a programme featuring himself and his family. Among the early productions of the Bryant family were a somewhat unusual version of *Hamlet* and such popular melodramas as *East Lynne*. By 1918 the Bryants were able to build their own boats, on which they gave successful revivals of many good old melodramas—*Jesse James*, *From Rags to Riches*, *Bertha the Sewing-Machine Girl*, *The Bird in the Gilded Cage*, and, most popular of all, *Ten Nights in a Bar Room*. Vaudeville, interspersed with songs and magic lantern shows, filled up the intervals, while Captain Billy's own speeches before and after the show became famous. A typical one was printed in *The New York Times* for 12 Oct. 1930.

Another well-known showboat family is the Menkes, four brothers who in 1917 bought French's *New Sensation* from Price, who had purchased it from French's widow in 1902. They kept the old name, though the boat has been several times replaced, and in 1922–3, under Captain J. W. Menke, it made a trip lasting a year and covering 5,000 miles. Other boats owned by the Menkes were *Golden Rod* and *Hollywood* (which, with their headquarters at St. Louis, are still operating), *Wonderland*, *Sunny South*, and *Floating Hippodrome*. Their repertory was again melodrama, including such favourites as *The Trail of the Lonesome Pine*, though in the late 1920s they made an innovation by presenting a musical comedy.

In the years before the slump of 1929 a number of new managements made their appearance on the water—the *Majestic* under Nico and Reynolds, the *America*, the *River Maid*, another *Princess*, a new *Water Queen* under Captain Roy Hyatt—mostly offering melodrama and variety; but they were hard hit by the economic depression, and for some time Menke's *Golden Rod* and Bryant's *Showboat* were the only ones still functioning. Things picked up again later, however, and in 1940 Ben Lucien Burman, in his book on the Mississippi, *Big River to Cross*, was able to mention five by name as still working, as well as many other smaller and less well-known ones on distant waters. That the structure of the showboat had altered little with the years can be seen by his description of it as

> resembling an old-time packet whose owner, in a fit of anger, has knocked off both the smokestacks and the pilot house; moored behind is a small steamboat, to move it on its journeyings. . . . At one end (of the vessel) is the stage, its wings piled high with scenes of ruined castles or a dusty, lamp-lit street corner of Old Chicago; the curtain depicts a bridge over some precipitous valley high in the Alps, or a horde of white-robed men and women fleeing terror-struck from the flames of Vesuvius. . . . At the side of the curtain is a hole, through which the proprietor can peep unobserved and count the audience in the seats before him; when he has mentally translated the spectators into money that seems sufficient for the evening, he smiles with content and gives the orchestra the signal to begin. . . . The plays on the larger boats are either melodrama or musical spectacles, the melodramas being acted in burlesque fashion when the boat is anchored at the wharf of a metropolis, but losing all such artificial quality the moment the vessel points its prow toward the wilderness. Always their programs are broken with vaudeville: a Swiss bell ringer: a musician who can play Dixie on the flute as he swings from a horizontal bar: an artist who can draw a picture of the President in red, white, and blue chalk upside down, and balance a huge American flag on his right shoe during the entire creation of the masterpiece.
>
> These talented vaudevillians are performers in the main drama as well. For an actor on a showboat is nothing if not versatile. He must play the cornet in the orchestra . . . when the drama begins he must portray the bearded father. . . . He must sell popcorn and ice cream cones during the first intermission, and stop to play an accordion solo; when the play begins again, he must enact the hind-end of a horse. . . . He must do a tap dance; play the piano strings with a nail as though it were a harp; ride roller skates on a barrel; and one minute before the final curtain be thrown to his death to the Indians waiting in triumph at the foot of Grand Canyon.
>
> The actors on the showboats are of infinite variety. Some are carnival troupers, dancers and acrobats, come from the tents of the sideshows; some are country boys and girls, lured by the glamor of the theater from the cornfields . . . some

are professional actors, like those in the old stock companies, weary of trouping in one night stands and the vagaries of the metropolis. The smaller boats are family affairs, a man and his wife, with any roving performer they may chance upon in their travels.

The life of the showboat player is hard and hazardous, but it has the charm of individualism and the unexpected, and will not be corralled into the classification of the modern theatre. Found nowhere but in the United States, it represents, in all its aspects, a survival of the old and colourful pioneering days in the Golden West.

SHTEYN, ALEXANDER PETROVICH (1906–), Soviet dramatist, who was born in Samarkand and studied at Leningrad University. He began his literary career in 1929, and has written a number of successful plays, among them *The Law of Honour* (1949), dealing with Soviet scientists; *The Admiral's Flag* (1950), about the leader of the Russian fleet, Ushakov; *A Personal Affair* (1954), which deals with the different ways in which people adapted themselves to the new régime; and *Prologue* (1955), which portrays the heroic days of 1905–7. In 1956 his *Hotel Astoria* was produced by Okhlopkov. *The Ocean* was seen in Leningrad in 1961 and *A Game Without Rules* in Moscow in 1962. BEATRICE KING†

SHUBERT. (1) LEE (1875–1953), (2) SAM S. (1876–1905), and (3) JACOB J. (1880–1963), American theatre managers and producers. After varied experience in theatre business they formed the Shubert Theatre Corporation, which controlled the major part of the theatres in New York and the principal cities of the U.S. In 1950 the government brought an action against the corporation for their monopoly of the legitimate theatre, and six years later J. J., the sole surviving brother, sold twelve of the corporation's playhouses. The Shuberts established themselves in London in the 1920s, but withdrew in 1931. They had their offices on the upper floors of the Sam S. Shubert Theatre on 44th Street, which opened on 2 Oct. 1913 (named by the survivors in memory of their dead brother) with Forbes-Robertson in *Hamlet*. The first American play to be seen there was *A Thousand Years Ago* (1914). The theatre housed mainly musical comedy, but among its straight successes were *Copperhead* (1918) with Lionel Barrymore, *And So To Bed* (1927) with Yvonne Arnaud, and *Dodsworth* (1934). Elisabeth Bergner made her Broadway début there in *Escape Me Never*, under the auspices of the Theatre Guild, who were also responsible for the appearance of the Lunts in *Idiot's Delight* and *Amphitryon 38*. It was at this theatre that *Bloomer Girl* opened on 5 Oct. 1944, running until 27 Apr. 1946. Later productions were *Paint Your Wagon* (1951), *Take Me Along* (1959), a musical based on O'Neill's *Ah, Wilderness*, *Stop the World, I Want to Get Off* (1962), starring Anthony Newley, part-author of the show, with Leslie Bricusse, and Newley's *The Roar of the Greasepaint, the Smell of the Crowd* (1965), starring also Cyril Ritchard. GEORGE FREEDLEY†

SHUSHERIN, YAKOV EMELYANOVICH (1753–1813), one of the most prominent actors of the early Russian theatre. Born in Moscow, where regular dramatic performances started about 1756, he became infatuated with the stage and joined the Moscow troupe of M. E. Meddoks about 1770. Later he studied for a time under Dmitrevsky. In 1785 he had a great success as Iarbas, the jealous rival of Aeneas in the classical tragedy *Dido*, by Y. B. Knyazhin (1742–91), an imitator of Racine and Voltaire. He went to St. Petersburg in 1786, where he played the title-role in Sumarokov's *Dmitri the Impostor* and Count Appiani in Lessing's tragedy *Emilia Galotti*, two of his best roles, and became a favourite of Catherine the Great after appearing successfully in her comedy, *The Disconcerted Family*, and her chronicle play, *The Early Rule of Oleg*. From 1791 to 1800 he again acted in Moscow, and then returned to St. Petersburg. Shusherin survived the transition from the classical to the sentimental style and was especially popular in the fashionable *comédie larmoyante*. His talents were suited to the pathetic rather than the heroic, and after 1800 he was very successful in Gnedich's adaptation of *King Lear*, as Oedipus in Ozerov's *Oedipus in Athens*, and as Philoctetes. He retired from the stage about 1811. ROBERT TRACY

SHUTER, EDWARD (NED) (1728–76), English actor, of whom Doran said:

> There are few comic actors who have had such command over the muscles of the face as Shuter. He could do what he liked with them, and vary the laughter as he worked the muscles. Not that he depended on grimace; that was only the ally of his humour, and both were impulsive—as the man was, by nature; he often stirred the house with mirth, by saying something better than the author had put down for him.

Shuter, whose portrait was painted by Zoffany, made his first appearance on the stage at Richmond in 1744, and his last as Scrub in *The Beaux' Stratagem* at the Haymarket on 23 Sept. 1776, five weeks before his death. In June 1746 he played Osric and the Third Witch to Garrick's Hamlet and Macbeth, and during his long and arduous professional life he created a number of parts, among them Justice Woodcock, Druggett, Old Hardcastle, and Sir Anthony Absolute.

SHWARTZ, EVGENYI LVOVICH (1896–1961), Soviet writer, whose work was first published in 1925. His best-known plays are adaptations of fairytales for children (*Red Riding Hood*, 1937; *The Snow Queen*, 1938) in which he was careful to stress the ultimate triumph of high moral principles over dishonesty and deceit. In 1956 his last play, a satirical fairy-tale entitled *An Ordinary Miracle*, was produced by Akimov at the Leningrad Comedy Theatre. BEATRICE KING†

SIDDONS, SARAH (1755–1831), the greatest tragic actress of the English stage. She was the eldest of the twelve children of Roger Kemble, a Midland actor-manager, and spent her childhood travelling in his company. At 18 she married William Siddons, also a member of the company, and together they appeared in the provinces, Sarah first showing her mettle at Cheltenham. A tentative appearance at Drury Lane under Garrick in 1775 was a failure, and she returned to the provinces, playing at York under Tate Wilkinson and at Bath under John Palmer. A second attempt in London in 1782 was more successful, and Mrs. Siddons was instantly acclaimed a tragic actress without equal, a position she maintained until the end of her career. She began, however, at the zenith of her powers and unlike her great brother, John Philip Kemble, did not improve with age. Among her early parts were Isabella in *The Fatal Marriage*, Belvidera in *Venice Preserved*, and Jane Shore, while she was later outstanding as Constance in *King John*, Zara in *The Mourning Bride*, and above all as Lady Macbeth, the part in which she made her farewell appearance on 29 June 1812. She returned to the stage on 9 June 1819 as Lady Randolph in *Douglas* for the benefit of her younger brother Charles and his wife, but she was only a shadow of her former self. Macready called it 'the last flicker of a dying flame'. But at her best there was no one to touch her, and contemporary critics were unanimous in their praise of her beauty, tenderness, and nobility. Hazlitt said of her: 'Power was seated on her brow; passion emanated from her breast as from a shrine. She was tragedy personified.... To have seen Mrs. Siddons was an event in everyone's life'; and after her retirement he wrote: 'Who shall make tragedy stand once more with its feet upon the earth, and its head above the stars, weeping tears and blood?' A superbly built and extremely dignified woman, with a rich resonant voice and great amplitude of gesture, Mrs. Siddons wisely left comedy alone, and appeared almost exclusively in tragic and heroic parts. She was not much liked behind the scenes, being unapproachable and avaricious, and she had a great dislike of publicity which led her to be somewhat uncivil to her admirers. Yet her intelligence and her good judgement made her the friend of such men as Dr. Johnson and Horace Walpole, while Reynolds, Lawrence, and Gainsborough delighted in painting her, the first immortalizing her beauty as the Tragic Muse. Towards the end of her career she became somewhat stout, and her acting was considered monotonous and outmoded. She was also extremely prudish, even in her youth, and jibbed at the breeches in Rosalind, appearing in a costume which was that neither of a man nor of a woman, and extremely unbecoming. In any case she was poor in the part, and seldom played it. Yet, her brother once referred to her as 'one of the best comic singers of the day', though as no record exists of her having appeared before the public in that role, one can only surmise that she unbent in private. She had seven children. Four girls died in infancy. Of the surviving two sons and one daughter, a son, Henry (1775–1815), was for a long time connected with the Edinburgh Theatre, but was accounted a poor actor (see KEMBLE and No. 164).

SIERRA, GREGORIO MARTÍNEZ, see MARTÍNEZ SIERRA.

SILL IRONS, flat strips of metal used as strengthening pieces across the bottom of openings in flats.

SILVA, ANTÓNIO JOSÉ DA, see PORTUGAL and SOUTH AMERICA.

SIMON [SIMEON], JOSEPH (1594–1671), see JESUIT DRAMA.

SIMONOV, KONSTANTIN MIKHAILOVICH (1915–), Soviet dramatist, whose first play, *The Russian People*, dealing with the impact of war on a group of civilians and soldiers near the front line, was produced in 1942 and frequently revived. It was given in London in 1943 as *The Russians* by the Old Vic company. His next play, *A Fellow from Our Town* (also 1942), was awarded a prize, while a third, *Wait for Me* (1943) (the title is taken from one of Simonov's own poems), was played all over the U.S.S.R. and established his reputation, a reputation which continued to grow with each subsequent work from his pen. In 1947 a dramatization of his novel *The Russian Question* was successfully staged, as was *Friends and Enemies* in 1949. Among his later plays are *A Foreign Shadow* (1950), the comedy *A Good Name* (1953), *The Story of a Love* (1954), done by Akimov in Leningrad, and *The Fourth*, seen in Moscow in 1961.

SIMONOV, REUBEN NIKOLAIVICH (1899–1968), Soviet actor and producer, who has made a name for himself as a serious and original worker in the theatre. He began his career during the First World War at the Chaliapin Studio, which was much influenced by the Moscow Art Theatre, and in 1920 joined that theatre's Fourth Studio, later to become the Vakhtangov Theatre. His first production was *Intervention* (1933), with settings by Rabinovich. He was also one of the producers of the first play given by the Uzbek National Theatre, and in 1931 he organized a group of students, trained by himself in the methods of Stanislavsky and Vakhtangov, which later became a State theatre. Among its notable productions was a dramatization of Sholokhov's novel, *Virgin Soil Upturned*. Simonov was a good producer of opera, and an excellent actor, one of his best parts being Cyrano de Bergerac. Outstanding among his productions in the 1950s were Pogodin's *Missouri Valse* (1950) at the Vakhtangov, Sofronov's *In Our Time* (1952), and Gorky's *Foma Gordeyev* (1956), a brilliant piece of work. (For a description of Simonov at work, see Norris Houghton's *Moscow Rehearsals*, published in 1936.)

SIMONSON, LEE (1888–1967), American theatrical designer, author of *The Stage is Set*

(1932) and of a volume of memoirs, *Part of a Lifetime* (1943). His first work for the theatre was done in connexion with the Washington Square Players, and he later became one of the founders and directors of the Theatre Guild, for whose productions much of his finest work was done. He was also director of the International Exhibition of Theatre Art held in New York in 1934, and was for many years a director of the American National Theatre and Academy and of the Museum of Costume Art in New York (see also UNITED STATES, 11).

SIMOV, VICTOR ANDREYEVICH (1858–1935), Russian theatrical designer, who, after studying at the Moscow School of Art, and working as a painter, lithographer, and designer for a private opera group, joined the Moscow Art Theatre on its foundation in 1898, and spent most of his life in its service. He was closely concerned with the producer in creating the style and atmosphere, as well as the outward aspect, of each play, endeavouring in his work to bring out all aspects of the playwright's conception, and re-creating the social, material, and psychological setting, with due consideration for the personalities of the individual actors. In Stanislavsky's own words, Simov 'became the founding father of a new concept of stage décor'. He was responsible for the décor of Chekhov's plays on their first production, in which his gifts found their fullest expression (*The Seagull*, 1898; *Uncle Vanya*, 1899; *Three Sisters*, 1901 (see No. 95); *The Cherry Orchard*, 1904), and also for such important productions as *Tsar Feodor Ivanovich* (1898), *The Lower Depths* (1902), *Julius Caesar* (1903), and *The Living Corpse* (1911). He then left the Moscow Art Theatre for a while, and designed for the Free Theatre, the Maly, and the Stanislavsky Operatic Theatre Studio. He also worked for the cinema. In 1925 he returned to the Moscow Art Theatre, and was responsible for the settings of *Armoured Train 14–69* (1927) (see No. 99) and *Dead Souls* (1932).

SIMPSON, EDMUND SHAW (1784–1848), American actor and manager, who made his first appearances in 1806 in the English provinces, and was playing in Dublin when Cooper and Price engaged him for the Park Theatre, New York. He made his first appearance there in Oct. 1809, and remained for thirty-eight years, being possibly the most important man to come into the American theatre since Cooper. He played Richmond to the Richard III of Kean, Cooke, and the elder Booth, and remained a prime favourite with the audience until 1833, when he retired from the stage because of lameness caused by an accident. He had been appointed acting manager of the theatre in 1812, and Price's partner in 1815, and had kept the theatre running well, in spite of the disastrous fire of 1820, mainly by importing English stars and encouraging the fashion for Italian opera. He continued in management after his retirement from acting, and in 1837, by which time the prestige of the Park was on the wane, he became sole lessee. He struggled to maintain his former position in the theatrical world, but his theatre was in a bad state of repair and his methods out of date. In 1848 he surrendered it to Hamblin, manager of the Bowery, against an annuity, and died almost immediately. He was held in high esteem by his public, both for his long and devoted service to the theatre and for his brave struggle against adversity in his declining years.

SINCLAIR, ARTHUR (1883–1951), Irish actor, husband of Maire O'Neill, who made his first appearance on the stage in Yeats's *On Baile's Strand* (1904) with the Irish National Theatre Society, and was with the Abbey Theatre, Dublin, until 1916, playing in all the notable productions of that time. He then formed his own company and toured Ireland and England, subsequently appearing in variety theatres in Irish sketches. He built up a great reputation as an Irish comedian, some of his finest parts being Flaherty in *The Playboy of the Western World*, John Duffy in *The White-Headed Boy*, in which he toured America and Australia, Boyle in *Juno and the Paycock*, Fluther Good in *The Plough and the Stars*, Shields in *The Shadow of a Gunman*, and James in *Spring Meeting*. He was also seen as Christopher Sly in *The Taming of the Shrew* and as Smee in *Peter Pan*.

SKELTON, JOHN (*c.* 1460–1529), see ENGLAND, 2.

SKINNER. (1) OTIS (1858–1942), American actor, best remembered for his performance as Hajj in the oriental fantasy *Kismet* (1911), which he appeared in for two years and frequently revived on tour. He had, however, had a long and distinguished career before this, making his first appearance on the stage in Philadelphia in 1877, and in New York at Niblo's Garden in 1879. After some years with Booth and Lawrence Barrett, he joined Augustin Daly and with him made his first appearance in London, where he was again seen in 1890 as Romeo. For two years he toured with Modjeska, playing such parts as Orlando, Benedick, and Major Schubert in *Magda*, and with Joseph Jefferson played Young Absolute in *The Rivals*. Among his later successes were *His Grace de Grammont* (1894), in which his wife, Maud Durbin, played opposite him as Mistress Hamilton, *The Honour of the Family* (1907), *Your Humble Servant* (1910) and *Mr. Antonio* (1916), the last two written for him by Booth Tarkington. In 1926 he appeared as Falstaff in *Henry IV, Part I* and two years later as the same character in *The Merry Wives of Windsor*. Among his last appearances were Shylock, with Maude Adams, and Thersites in *Troilus and Cressida*. He wrote several volumes of reminiscences, including *Footlights and Spotlights* (1924) and *The Last Tragedian* (1939). His daughter, (2) CORNELIA OTIS (1902–), is celebrated as a diseuse, and has toured extensively in solo performances all over the United States and in London. She was trained for the stage by Jacques Copeau, and made her first appearance in her father's company in 1921. She is the author of a number of entertaining books, including a volume of reminiscences of Continental travel, *Our Hearts Were Young and Gay*.

SKY-DOME, see LIGHTING, 1 *d* and SCENERY, 6.

SLIPS, a name used in the late eighteenth and early nineteenth centuries to designate the ends or near-stage extremities of the upper tiers of seats in the theatre.

SLOMAN, CHARLES (1808–70), a performer in the early music-halls, and the original of Young Nadab in Thackeray's *The Newcomes*. He is best remembered for his doggerel verses improvised on subjects given him by members of the audience, or on the appearance and dress of those in front of him, but he was also a writer of songs, both comic and serious, for himself and for other music-hall performers, including Sam Cowell and Ross. He was at the height of his fame in the 1840s but fell on hard times. One of his last engagements was as Chairman of the Middlesex Music-Hall in Drury Lane, and he died soon after, a pauper, in the Strand Workhouse.

SLOTE (or SLOAT), a device for raising a long narrow piece of scenery—a groundrow, for example—from below to stage level. It could also be used for carrying an actor up or down from the stage. From references in a prompt-book of *Comus* now in the Folger Shakespeare Library, made for Charles Kean from Macready's prompt-book of the same play, it appears that the slote was standard equipment at Drury Lane in 1843. There are elaborate stage-directions in *The Orange Girl* (Surrey, 1864) for the conveyance of the heroine by a slote from a height downwards to a trap. In a letter to the *Era Almanack* of 1887 Irving says: 'the slote in *Faust* struck me on the head, instead of carrying me up into the flies above.' In describing this accident in his *Life of Irving*, Brereton uses the word slide. A variant of the slote may therefore have been the Corsican Trap (see TRAP). To allow free passage to the slote the floor-board above it was divided vertically, each half dropping and being pulled to the side of the stage by ropes, thus leaving a cut in the stage floor. On occasion a cloth might be attached to the base of a groundrow and be drawn up from its rolled position in a Slote Box below by means of lines from the grid. It would thus unroll as the groundrow rose in the air during a transformation scene. With two slote sets in each of three sections of the stage, the elements of six separate scenes could be raised from below the stage.

SLOVAK THEATRE, see CZECHOSLOVAKIA.

SŁOWACKI, JULIUSZ (1809–49), Polish poet and playwright, who was exiled in 1831 and lived mainly in Paris. He wrote more than thirty plays, of which several remained unfinished. The first production of any of his plays took place in 1847, in Budapest, in a Hungarian translation, but they have been acted in Polish since 1851, and were all finally seen on the stage by 1908. It was not, however, until 1918 that they became part of the national repertory. His first plays were naïvely romantic, as in *Mazeppa* (1833), but he matured quickly, and his *Balladyna* (1834) and *Lilla Weneda* (1840)—based on early legends—show an astonishing perfection. His masterpieces are usually considered to be *Kordian* (1833), a poetic tragedy, *Fantazy* (1843), a comedy, and above all his last tragedies, *The Silver Dream of Salomé* (also 1843) and *Samuel Zborowski* (1844). Słowacki, who is considered the founder of Polish tragedy, died in exile, but in 1927 his body was conveyed to Cracow and buried in the royal vault there, because, it was said, 'he was the equal of kings'.

SLY, WILLIAM (?–1608), English actor, who appears in the actor-list of Shakespeare's plays. He was connected with the theatre from about 1590, when his name appears in the cast of *Seven Deadly Sins, Part II*, and he joined the Chamberlain's Men on its formation in 1594. He was not one of the original shareholders of the Globe, but became one at some time, since he mentions it in his will, and he also had a seventh share in the Blackfriars, later taken over by Richard Burbage.

SMITH, ALBERT (1816–60), an interesting but somewhat forgotten figure of literary and theatrical London in the mid-nineteenth century, whose novels are very like those of Dickens. He dramatized several of the latter's works for the stage, and also produced some original but forgotten plays of his own. His main claim to fame lay in his one-man entertainments, of which the first was *The Overland Mail*, given in 1850. This was an amusing and no doubt exaggerated account of a recent trip to India, interspersed with topical songs and stories, and illustrated by scenery specially painted for the occasion by the famous scene-painter, William Beverley. It proved such a success that Smith followed it with *The Ascent of Mont Blanc*, given at the Egyptian Hall, Piccadilly, again with scenery by Beverley, who had accompanied Smith to Switzerland to gather material for the display, and by a similar 'lecture' on China. During the run of the last he married Mary, actress daughter of the Keeleys, leaving her a widow in less than a year. His death was caused by his insistence on giving his lecture in spite of a sharp attack of bronchitis, which turned to pneumonia. For the last ten years of his life he had enjoyed enormous popularity. His simple entertainment, whose charm lay as much in its spontaneity and wit as in the actual material, was reckoned among the things to be visited in London, and was frequently patronized by Queen Victoria and the royal children. Smith was also a prolific journalist, and a contributor to *Punch* for many years.

SMITH, Edward Tyrrell (1804–77), English theatre manager, was the son of an admiral. He became a policeman, an auctioneer, and finally the most reckless theatrical speculator of his day. In 1850 he took over the Marylebone Music-Hall, and later rented Drury Lane, then in very low water, for £3,000, and opened it in 1852 with *Uncle Tom's Cabin* and one of Blanchard's pantomimes. He also bought the Panopticon in Leicester Square, renamed it the Alhambra, and reopened it in 1858 as a circus, after having disposed of all the scientific paraphernalia with which it was filled, and sold the famous organ to St. Paul's Cathedral. He exhibited Sayers and Heenan there, and then ran it as a music-hall. Smith was an amazing man, to whom nothing came amiss. At Drury Lane he had Gustavus Brooke, the younger Mathews, and operatic singers. He mixed opera with drama and with Shakespeare, he introduced Chinese conjurors and a 'Human Fly' who crawled about the ceiling. He presented Rachel, the tragedienne, and followed her with a circus. He was lessee of Her Majesty's for Italian opera, of the Lyceum, of Astley's, and of the Surrey. He was the proprietor of Highbury Barn, and of the Regent Music-Hall, Westminster; he was also landlord of the Radnor Tavern in Chancery Lane, a wine merchant, a picture dealer, a land agent, a bill discounter, and a newspaper proprietor. In the multitude of activities there was no wisdom, and he eventually ruined himself. In his day he was a noted character, and in spite of his many follies he made friends everywhere and kept them. He was also the first to inaugurate the morning performance, which under Hollingshead became the modern afternoon matinée.

W. MACQUEEN-POPE†

SMITH, Richard Penn (1799–1854), American dramatist, one of the leading members of the Philadelphia group, and a lawyer by profession. He was the author of some twenty plays, of which fifteen were acted. They are of all types, ranging from farce to romantic tragedy, and represent the transition in the American theatre from the play imported or inspired by Europe and the true native production of later years. Most of his comedies were adaptations from the French, while his romantic plays were mainly based on incidents of American history. What is believed to be his finest piece of work, a tragedy entitled *Caius Marius*, has not survived. It was produced by Edwin Forrest in 1831, with himself in the title-role, and proved extremely successful. It was possibly Forrest's aversion to the printing of plays in which he appeared that caused it to be lost. Another interesting play, also lost, was *The Actress of Padua* (1836), which was based on Hugo's *Angelo*, one of the first echoes of French Romanticism in American theatrical history. It was revived by Charlotte Cushman in the early 1850s, and was seen in New York as late as 1873, probably with some alterations by John Brougham, to whom the play has been attributed.

SMITH. (1) Solomon Franklin (1801–69), a pioneer of the American theatre on the frontier, usually known as Sol Smith. He had a hard childhood, and at 16 ran away from his brother's shop, where he was employed, in the hope of becoming an actor. He was forced to return for a while, but eventually achieved his ambition, travelling with the Drakes and other itinerant companies, and eking out a livelihood by spasmodic journalism. By 1823 he had got together a company of his own, but marriage and financial difficulties caused him to look about for a more stable position, and in 1827 he and his wife, a singer, joined the company of J. H. Caldwell, with which they visited St. Louis and other Mississippi towns. Smith eventually went into partnership with Noah Ludlow. The combination prospered and dominated the St. Louis stage until 1851, building there the first permanent theatre west of the Mississippi. Smith, who appeared as a star at the Park Theatre, New York, under Simpson, and in Philadelphia under the management of Wemyss, was at his best in low comedy, particularly in such parts as Mawworm in *The Hypocrite*. He was a man of upright character, popular, and much respected, and published three books on the theatre, the last, *Theatrical Management in the West and South* (1868), being a combination of the two earlier ones. In 1853 he dissolved his partnership with Ludlow and became a lawyer. Two of his sons were on the stage, (2) Marcus (1829–74), better known as Mark, making his first appearance as a child in his father's theatre, and then going to New York, where he was a member of Burton's until it closed. He excelled in the portrayal of the English gentleman of old comedy, and was with Wallack's from 1862 to 1863. In London, under Mrs. John Wood, he made a good impression, and returned to New York to play his last part at Union Square Theatre in *One Hundred Years Old*, in which he made a great hit. His daughter became an opera singer.

SMITH, William (? –1696), English actor, friend of Betterton, a tall, handsome man who was the original player of Pierre and Chamont in Otway's famous tragedies, and also of Sir Fopling Flutter and Scandal. He became embroiled behind the scenes with a nobleman, who struck him and was severely reprimanded by Charles II for doing so; upon which a party of gentlemen combined to drive Smith from the stage by their hisses and cat-calls. Being a wealthy man, he retired and lived quietly, but later returned to the theatre, and died while playing in *Cyrus the Great*.

SMITH, William (1730–1819), English actor, known as 'Gentleman Smith', on account of his elegant figure, fine manners, and handsome face. Sent down from Cambridge, he took to the stage, and after being coached by Spranger Barry he made his first appearance at Covent Garden on 1 Jan. 1753. He remained there until 1774, and then went to Drury Lane, where he was the first to play Charles Surface (see No. 30). He was also Mrs. Siddons's first Macbeth, and alternated Hamlet and Richard III with Garrick, whom he greatly admired, though his own style was more that of Quin. He was in possession of most of the big tragic parts when John Philip Kemble came to Drury Lane in 1783, and kept them until his retirement in 1788. He then went to Bury St. Edmunds and spent his time hunting and attending race-meetings, though he appeared once more in his famous part of Charles Surface in 1798 for the benefit of his friend King, the original Sir Peter Teazle. In an age which expected its actors to turn their hands to anything from tragedy to pantomime—Garrick himself is said to have played Harlequin—Smith's proudest boast was that he had never blackened his face, never played in a farce, and never ascended through a trap-door. He would also never consent to appear at the theatre on a Monday during the hunting season, as he was a zealous rider to hounds.

SMITHSON, HARRIET CONSTANCE (1800–54), an English actress who made her first appearance in London in 1818 as Letitia Hardy in *The Belle's Stratagem* at Drury Lane. She then played Lady Anne and Desdemona to the Richard III and Othello of Edmund Kean, and was seen also at Covent Garden and the Haymarket, returning to Drury Lane in 1822 as Countess Wilhelm in *Adeline*. Little is known of her early days, but she seems to have been a promising but not particularly well-known actress when in 1827 she went with Charles Kemble to Paris, and was received with acclamation. A year later she was there with Macready. Her Desdemona and Ophelia excited enormous enthusiasm, and the young Romantics of the day covered her with adulation, even Janin declaring that she had revealed Shakespeare to France, and had made his tragedies the prerogative of the actress, thus forestalling Rachel, who called her many years later 'a poor woman to whom I am much indebted'. Her fame was short-lived, as she soon afterwards made an ill-judged and unhappy marriage with Berlioz, the French composer, and retired from the stage.

SMOCK ALLEY THEATRE, see DUBLIN.

SOCIALIST REALISM, the name given to the theatrical method and approach expounded in Soviet Russia by Lunacharsky, on the lines laid down by Lenin, and carried out, often with excellent and unexpected results, by the producers of the U.S.S.R. Apparently the term was first used in 1932, as a protest against the dry, formalist productions of such men as Meyerhold and Taïrov. It reasserted the importance of the individual and summed up the work of the theatre as 'a representation which must not be untrue, either to present-day facts or to the facts of the past; but it must express that truth in such terms that the worker-audience of today gets a perspective of either the socialism it is helping to build, or of the factors of the past out of which that socialism has come.' In other words, it makes the theatre an instrument for the education of the masses in Communism. This affects not only the producer's attitude to the classics, but also the playwright's, as the personal problems of his characters are increasingly bound up with their general surroundings, and with the forces which led to, or arise from, the upheaval of 1917. Although the externals of Socialist Realism, of which Gorky is considered to be the founder (with *Mother* and *Enemies*) and Mayakovsky the first brilliant theatrical exponent, have changed with changing conditions in the Soviet Union, its basic approach to the problems of theatrical creation and interpretation remain the same.

SOCIÉTÉ JOYEUSE, see FRANCE, I.

SOCIETY FOR THEATRE RESEARCH, THE, was founded in 1948, after a meeting held at the Old Vic (see No. 36) on 15 June, which brought together all those interested in the problems of theatre history and the preservation of ephemeral and other material relating to the theatre. The society holds monthly meetings during the winter, with an occasional summer meeting, at which lectures, with discussion, are given on specific points of theatrical history (including ballet and opera). Members receive an illustrated quarterly, *Theatre Notebook*, and an annual publication, as well as occasional pamphlets, and are entitled to use the library which the society is gradually building up from gifts and purchases. The preservation of theatres, of source material on the theatre, and of photographic records, is encouraged, and the society aims at establishing local groups in the large provincial towns, the most successful so far being that in Manchester. In the summer of 1955 the society held in London the first international conference on theatre history, attended by representatives of twenty-two countries, which resulted in the formation of the International Federation for Theatre Research. The first president of the society was Mrs. Gabrielle Enthoven, who was succeeded on her death in 1950 by Professor Edward J. Dent. When he died in 1957 Professor Allardyce Nicoll took his place, with Dame Edith Evans as vice-president. The society administers an annual prize for diction, awarded to a drama student in memory of William Poel. Among the recipients have been Jeremy Brett, John Stride, and Judi Dench.

In 1956 an American Society for Theatre Research was founded by Professor A. M. Nagler and Alan Downer. Unlike most national theatre societies, it is concerned not only with American theatre, but with all aspects of theatre studies which may interest its members. It holds an annual meeting in New York, and publishes an occasional newsletter (three or four times a year) and an annual volume of essays, *Theatre Survey*. In 1957 it undertook two major projects—an index to the illustrations in Odell's *Annals of the New*

York Stage, and a *Dictionary of American Drama*.

SOCK, from the Latin *soccus*, referring to the light, soft shoe worn by the comic actor, in contrast to the heavy boot of the tragedian (see COTHURNUS and BUSKIN). By extension, the word is used to denote comedy. Milton uses it in this sense in *L'Allegro*: 'Then to the well-trod stage anon, If Jonson's learned sock be on.'

SOFRONOV, ANATOL VLADIMIROVICH (1911–), Soviet dramatist, who was born in Minsk and began his literary career while working in a factory. His plays include *In One Town* (1946) and *The Moscow Character* (1948), which were both awarded Stalin prizes; *Beketov's Career* (1949), *Impossible to Live Otherwise* (1952), and *A Man in Retirement* (1957). These all deal with topical social problems in the daily working life of the Soviet people. *Honesty* (1962), in which Pashennaya gave a memorable performance as the heroine Praskovya Ivanovna, deals realistically with the problems of co-operative farming.

BEATRICE KING†

SOGGETTO, the earlier name for the *scenario* of the *commedia dell'arte*, which was also known as *commedia a soggetto* (see ITALY, 2).

SOLDENE, EMILY (1840–1912), a music-hall performer who first appeared as Miss Fitzhenry at the Canterbury, where she sang in the excerpts from opera which Morton made such a feature of his programmes there. When he opened the Oxford she appeared there also, and became the leading lady of the light opera and opera-bouffe company at the old Philharmonic (later the Grand) Theatre, Islington. She scored many successes there, and the Prince of Wales (afterwards Edward VII) went frequently to see her, as did many West-End playgoers. She accompanied Morton to America when he took his light opera company there, but retired on marriage and went to live in Australia. She published in 1897 a volume of reminiscences giving much interesting information on the stage and music-hall of her time. W. MACQUEEN-POPE†

SOMI, LEONE EBREO DI (1527–92), see JEWISH DRAMA, 3, LIGHTING, 1 *a* and MAKE-UP.

SONNENFELS, JOSEF VON (1733–1817), see AUSTRIA.

SOPHOCLES (496–406 B.C.), Greek dramatist, son of Sophillus, was born of good family at Colonus, near Athens. As a boy he was celebrated for the beauty of his voice and figure, and took part in a boys' dance which celebrated the victory of Salamis (480 B.C.). (Aeschylus fought in the battle, and a neat but inaccurate tradition caused Euripides to be born on the day of the battle—four years too late.) Sophocles is said to have written over a hundred plays; seven are extant, as well as substantial parts of a not very amusing satyr-play, the *Ichneutae* (Trackers), and many fragments. He won eighteen victories, the first—over Aeschylus—in 468. He is said to have won the second prize very often, and never to have been third. The extant plays are: *Ajax* (*c.* 450 B.C.), *Antigone* (*c.* 442), *Trachiniae*, *Oedipus Rex* (? *c.* 425), *Electra*, *Philoctetes* (409), and *Oedipus Coloneus* (posthumous).

Aeschylus represents the heroic period of Athenian democracy, Sophocles its triumphant maturity. The first part of his active life coincided with the Periclean Age, in which Sophocles was a distinguished and congenial figure. In 440 he was elected (for the year) to the high military and administrative post of *Strat-êgos* (General), and apparently on at least one other occasion held public office. He lived through the greater part of the long struggle with Sparta, dying, in his native Colonus, a few months after Euripides, and just before the final defeat of Athens in the Peloponnesian War. Cicero is the earliest authority for the story that, towards the end of his long life, Sophocles was brought into court by his sons on the charge of being incapacitated by old age from managing his affairs; and that, having read to the jury an ode from the play which he was composing, the *Oedipus Coloneus*, he was triumphantly acquitted. The truth of the story is doubted, but it does seem that Sophocles did at least complete this remarkable play at the age of 90 or thereabouts. All the ancient references to him agree in giving a picture of a serene, distinguished, and greatly loved figure.

This serenity pervades his drama; but it is a serenity that comes from the triumph over suffering, not from its avoidance. Few things in drama are more poignant than Sophocles' tragic climaxes. Sophocles approached drama in a very different spirit from Aeschylus, and therefore modified the form considerably (see GREECE, 1 *b*). In addition to this, he developed a poetic style which, while always beautiful and dignified, was amazingly supple, reflecting character and emotion with a subtlety approached, in Greek, only by Plato; outside Greek, by nobody. These new complexities and delicacies were used by Sophocles with a logic and an economy which make him as powerful a dramatist as any.

Aristotle's analysis of tragedy is based, in the main, on the Sophoclean drama, since he regarded this as the mature form of tragedy, and therefore neglected others (e.g. the Aeschylean). H. D. F. KITTO

SOPHRON of Syracuse, a writer of mimes (see MIME, 1 *b*).

SORANO, DANIEL (1920–62), French actor, considered one of the finest comedians of his generation. His intelligence and his amazing powers of self-discipline enabled him to pass easily from the farcical characters and comic valets of classical comedy to the dramatic and tragic personages of modern times, all his parts being undertaken in a spirit of profound humility. A warm voice, eloquent gestures, spontaneity, vivacity, exceptional bodily control, a face of extraordinary mobility, enabled him to make apparent the slightest movements of the soul. He began his stage career with the Grenier de Toulouse in 1942, with whom he played in Paris, where he made a great impression with his Scapin (in *Les Fourberies de Scapin*) and in an adaptation of Plautus's *Carthaginians*. In 1952 he became a member of the Théâtre National Populaire, where his most notable roles were Sganarelle in *Don Juan*, Arlequin in *Le Triomphe de l'Amour*, Don César de Bazan in *Ruy Blas*, Figaro in *Le Mariage de Figaro*, Mascarille in *L'Étourdi*, Argan in *Le Malade imaginaire*, and L'Aumônier in *Mère Courage*. He was an excellent interpreter of Shakespeare and the Elizabethans, particularly fine as Richard III, Biondello in *The Taming of the Shrew* (in the production by the Grenier de Toulouse), and the Porter in *Macbeth*. He also appeared in Ford's *'Tis Pity She's a Whore* under the direction of Visconti. His last role was Shylock for the Compagnie Renaud–Barrault, a powerful and sober interpretation.

SORGE, Reinhard Johannes (1892–1916), German poet, who began as a disciple of Nietzsche, and fell, a devout Catholic, in the First World War. His most important play, *Der Bettler* (written in 1912, but not performed until 1917), was a drama of social protest written in an expressionist style. It foreshadows the revolt of the young generation against the old, and the striving for a higher spiritual orientation, two of the most insistent themes of the expressionist movement. His later plays are expressions of religious ecstasy.

SORMA [Zaremba], Agnes (1865–1927), German actress, who was on the stage as a child, and in 1883 was engaged for the newly founded Deutsches Theater, where she soon became popular in young girls' parts. As her powers developed, however, she began to be recognized as an outstanding actress, some of her first successes being scored in revivals of Grillparzer's works, particularly *Weh dem, der lügt!* in which she played opposite Joseph Kainz. She was also seen as Juliet, Ophelia, and Desdemona, and later as Nora, a part which she continued to play for many years, notably on a visit to Paris, and on an extended tour of Europe. She also made her first appearance in New York in that part, appearing at the Irving Place Theatre in Apr. 1897 with a German company. She was a distinguished interpreter of the heroines of Sudermann and Hauptmann, and, in lighter vein, was successful as the Hostess in *La Locandiera*. A beautiful woman, with dark hair and eyes, and a charming smile, she was for many years the best-known actress of Germany, and from 1904 to 1908 worked under Max Reinhardt in Berlin.

SOTHERN. (1) Edward Askew (1826–81), English actor who made his name in New York, as Lord Dundreary in *Our American Cousin* (1858), a part which he practically created, and with which he is always associated. He first appeared on the stage in the English provinces under his real name, Douglas Stewart, and then went to Boston, where he was not a success, being considered by a contemporary critic 'under-taught and over-praised'. After some years on tour he joined Lester Wallack's company in New York as Sothern, the name by which he was known thereafter. Jefferson, who played in the original production of *Our American Cousin*, says in his *Autobiography* that Sothern had at first little opinion of the small part he had been offered by Laura Keene, 'and as the dismal lines of Dundreary were read, he glanced over at me with a forlorn expression, as much as to say "I am cast for that dreadful part", little dreaming that the character of the imbecile lord would turn out to be the stepping-stone of his fortune'. Jefferson then goes on to describe how, during the first weeks of the run, Sothern began to introduce 'extravagant business' into his part. This went down well, and by the end of a month he was the equal of any other character; at the end of the run he was the whole play. He was equally successful in London in 1861, where long side-whiskers as he wore them became known as 'dundrearies'. The play became almost a series of monologues, and several other sketches were written round Sothern's creation. Another of Sothern's great parts was *Brother Sam*, which Jefferson, and also Clement Scott, thought even better than his Dundreary. Sothern had ambitions toward the playing of romantic drama, but though parts of his *David Garrick* (1864) were excellent, Scott says 'his love scene that ends the play acted as a soporific on many of us'. *A Crushed Tragedian* (1874), in which he played the part of an old actor, was also a failure in London, though well received in New York. Sothern was essentially an eccentric comedian, and it was in that line that he did his best and most memorable work. He had three sons on the stage, of whom (2) Edward Hugh (1859–1933) inherited the major share of his father's talent and charm. Educated in England, he intended to take up painting, but heredity led him to the stage. He started slowly, toured with McCullough in the United States, and in 1883 became leading man of Frohman's Lyceum company, where he remained until 1898. A light comedian and a charming romantic hero in cloak-and-sword plays like *The Prisoner of Zenda*, he was immensely popular, both in New York and on tour. He was seen as Hamlet in 1900, and later opened the new Lyceum in New York with *The Proud Prince*. For some years he headed a Shakespearian repertory company with Julia Marlowe, who became his second wife in 1911. After her retirement in 1924 he continued to appear intermittently, being last seen in 1927. He devoted much of his later years to public readings and lectures and wrote his autobiography as *The Melancholy Tale of 'Me'* (1916). A small but dignified man, with a handsome, sensitive face, he was the ideal romantic hero of the late nineteenth century, and although by hard work he achieved some success in tragedy, his real talent lay in light comedy and romance. He was good as Malvolio, and several times revived his father's old part of Lord Dundreary.

SOTIE, the topical and satirical play of medieval France, whose best-known author is Pierre Gringore, the *mère-sotte* or chief fool of the Parisian *enfants sans souci*. The *sotie* was not a farce, though they had elements in common, and was often inspired by political or religious intrigue. It was intended for amusement only, and is not to be compared with the Mystery or Morality play, to which it often served as a curtain-raiser. The actors, or *sots* (fools), wore the traditional fool's costume, dunce's cap, short jacket, tights, and bells on their legs. Modern research inclines to the idea that the *soties* were acted not only by such amateur associations as the *enfants sans souci* and the *clercs de la basoche*, but by semi-professional and more or less permanent companies, somewhat in the tradition of the *commedia dell'arte*, each with its own repertory. The point is, however, still obscure, and needs further elucidation. There are a number of extant texts, of which the Recueil Trepperel is the most representative.

SOUND EFFECTS, see TRICKWORK ON THE ENGLISH STAGE.

SOUTH AFRICA. When Captain Cook visited the Cape of Good Hope in 1771 he remarked: 'There are no public entertainments.' However, towards the end of the century this deficiency was made good, first by French troops stationed in Cape Town and, after 1795, by the British occupying garrison. The African Theatre, in Hottentot Square, was opened in 1801, and until, in 1839, it was closed by a wave of puritanism, it saw many amateur performances in English, Dutch, French, and German, and even occasional appearances by voyaging professionals from England. By 1843 puritanism had subsided sufficiently to permit the conversion of two wine stores into little theatres, and when Sefton Parry, the English theatrical manager, opened the Drawing-Room Theatre on 13 July 1855, he inaugurated a system—a professional management with a semi-professional company—which is occasionally found in South Africa still.

The Diamond Rush of the 1860s brought with it a number of theatrical adventurers, notably Captain Disney Roebuck (*c*. 1821–85), who from 1873 provided Cape Town with regular entertainment; with the Gold Rush of the 1880s came real prosperity, a much inflated population, and an endless variety of theatrical activity. Excellent theatres were built in Cape Town (the Opera House, 1893, the Tivoli, 1903), Johannesburg (the Standard, 1891, the Globe (later the Empire), 1892, the Gaiety, 1893, His Majesty's, 1903), Pretoria, Durban, Port Elizabeth, Bloemfontein, Kimberley, Grahamstown, and other smaller towns; almost every great player of the time came out to appear in them. The central figure during this period was Leonard Rayne, (1869–1925), lessee of many of the theatres, who, besides importing overseas artists, had his own company and, with his wife, Freda Godfrey, played leading roles. After his death the South African theatre suffered the decline then common to all theatres. Many of the old buildings were converted into cinemas, others were torn down. However, this decline was accompanied by the rise of the amateur theatre movement, and by the emergence of the Afrikaans professional theatre. A Hollander, Paul de Groot (1882–1942), led the first company to tour in this language in 1926. He was followed by many others, including André Huguenet, the Hanekoms, Wena Naude, Pikkie Uys, and Anton Ackermann. During the 1930s and 1940s they toured continuously throughout the country, giving European plays in translation and simple, somewhat melodramatic and sentimental, works by the many folk-dramatists who arose to satisfy their needs. The emergence of an Afrikaans literature was not paralleled by that of an English; the amateur companies performed West End and Broadway popular fare, with considerable personal success, and the two leading groups, the Cape Town Repertory Theatre Society, founded in 1921, and the Johannesburg Rep, founded in 1927, built their own theatres. In Cape Town the Drama Department of the university has presented in its Little Theatre (founded in 1931) an international repertory of the classics. Formerly based on this theatre, the University Ballet has, since 1965, become a fully professional touring company.

The war years, 1939–45, saw a brilliant renaissance of the English-speaking professional theatre, opera, and ballet. The company formed by Gwen Ffrangcon-Davies and Marda Vanne gave, from 1941 to 1946, seasons of distinction in the larger towns. Since the war their standard has been maintained by other companies, notably by Brian Brooke, who has established theatres in Cape Town (1946–56) and Johannesburg (1955), and presents continuous seasons of repertory.

To correlate South Africa's diverse theatrical activities, and to improve the standard of the touring companies, the government was approached to subsidize a parent group, and in 1947 the National Theatre Organization was instituted. With headquarters in Pretoria, under the direction of P. P. Breytenbach, this body suffered various vicissitudes until it was splintered into provincial groups, one for each of the four provinces, known as Councils of Performing Arts, and embracing activities wider than drama alone. Numerous companies, playing in both official languages, tour all the large and most of the small towns, and on occasion South-West Africa and Rhodesia, successfully presenting work of quality where often none was known before. Local writing, particularly by Afrikaans dramatists, has been encouraged, and played before an audience constantly more enthusiastic, more discerning, and, latterly, more willing to accept home-grown plays. This is particularly true of the English-speaking audience. More sophisticated, yet suffering from a sense of colonial inferiority, they preferred for a long time the foreign, and more proficient, import.

Afrikaans dramatists, however, found ready acceptance of their plays, which, in naïve and romantic terms, epitomized the nationalist aspirations of some sections of the Afrikaner people. Once these aspirations had found political and social assurance in the post-1948 triumphs of a nationalist government, the need for the old soap-operas fell away. The result has been a more sophisticated, if less theatrical, approach to the theatre.

A further result has been the emergence of a most articulate group of South Africans writing in English. Intensely aware of the racial tensions splintering the country, they have created an extensive literature. Plays such as *Try for White*, by Basil Warner, and *Kimberley Train*, by Lewis Sowden, have excited wide interest and sympathy, as have the plays of Athol Fugard, particularly *The Bloodknot* (1961), a play for two characters, brothers, one white, one black, which was also seen in London in 1963, with Ian Bannen as the white brother and Zaikes Mokae as the black.

Fortunately this literary development enjoyed dramatic scope because of the parallel growth of small professional companies performing in, and touring between, the larger cities. New theatres have been built—although too often in the small towns where they were least needed. In Johannesburg itself, at least twelve little makeshift theatres have been fitted up. In 1962 a fine new civic theatre was completed.

This period of social disturbance has been constantly underlined by the nascent nationalisms of non-white South Africans.

Since the latter part of the nineteenth century, Cape Town has been the scene of colourful 'Coon Carnivals', growing spontaneously from the musical exuberance of the Cape Coloureds and Malays. From the 1930s some of this talent was, with sympathetic white assistance, corralled into a cultural welfare group, Eoan. Although of amateur status, the Eoan Opera Group has become the liveliest operatic company in the country. It makes annual tours, and presents the established favourites of the Italian opera repertory.

A somewhat similar pattern has resulted from the urbanization of primitive African tribal music and dance. The vitalities, inherent in these elements, produced numerous bands of black, heavily Americanized, professional entertainers. By the end of the 1950s some of of these had, again with white guidance, been recruited into the theatre. Of a number of plays and musicals the most successful was *King Kong* (book and lyrics by Harry Bloom; production by Leon Gluckman; music by Todd Matshikiza). First produced in Johannesburg in 1959, the piece, somewhat rewritten and with a full black cast, was transferred to London in 1961, and was seen at the Princes Theatre. VICTOR GLASSTONE

SOUTH AMERICA. For the purposes of this article the term South America is stretched to cover all territory south of the Rio Grande river, which is to say that it includes Central America and Mexico. Strictly speaking, that takes in the theatres of twenty nations, speaking four European languages and many native dialects, but in reality only a few of these have a native theatre of any real importance.

Those characteristics of the theatre in South America which distinguish it from that in other nations of European extraction can be understood only in the light of the continent's history and of the Spanish and Portuguese who, invading at the start of the sixteenth century, brought with them not only new languages and a new religion, but also what was then the most brilliant theatre tradition in Europe. They found among Indian tribes native to the new land a dramatic tradition expressed in terms of religious ceremonial. This skill and this custom were utilized by the priests who came with the soldiers; they changed the content of dramatic recital to that prescribed in Catholic pastorals and Miracle plays. Hardly was the conquest completed when the plays of Lope de Vega, Juan de Encina, and Gil Vicente, which had been popular at home, were imported to the new land.

These two double roots of the South American theatre, the native and the European, the lay and the religious, have continued to flourish through four centuries and a half, sometimes blooming separately and sometimes intertwined. To them should be added, particularly in the case of Brazil and Cuba, a racial heritage out of Africa which is only now being studied. Their influence extends throughout the continent, and sometimes shows itself in strange ways. When Mozart's 'Magic Flute' was presented in Mexico City not long ago the arias and choruses were sung in German, but the recitative was in Mexican Spanish; the scene in the temple was set and costumed as in an Aztec temple. The Mexican audience found nothing peculiar in the mixture. In the same spirit, Indians in various villages enliven holiday festivals with pageants presenting the fifteenth-century Spanish struggle between the Moors and the Christians—a struggle still fresh to their conquerors when they reached America, and impressed on the primitive Indian mind with such force that though it took place in an alien land it has become a Mexican folk-theme.

A third root of continuing importance is the colonial attitude of dependence and uncertainty imposed by four centuries of European rule exercised by viceroys governing on the order of distant kings. At times this still shows itself in an immaturity of workmanship and a lack of confidence which hamper dramatic development of the first order.

1. Spanish America. The theatre in those parts of South America conquered by the

Spaniards developed earlier and with more abundance than in Portuguese-settled Brazil. The Spaniards took Mexico in 1521, and in 1538 put on their first recorded performance in the European manner. They had a 'House of Comedies' in Mexico City by 1597—only twenty years after the first permanent theatre was established in Madrid itself. In Peru the earliest touring company arrived in 1599. In Chile, thirty-four years later, on 11 Sept. 1633, 'comedies were presented by captains, sergeants major, scribes and nobles' on a stage a span and a half high.

Meanwhile the priests, using Miracle plays as vehicles for teaching Indian converts in monastery schools the content as well as the speech and the ways of the conquering religion, trained them to present *pasos*, *entremeses*, and *entradas a Jerusalén*. The natural result, among a natively dramatic people, was the emergence of Indian versions of the *nacimiento* and the *pastorela*, which in some instances became native village festivals with the chief roles handed down by inheritance.

Not much from the sixteenth and seventeenth centuries has survived intact excepting plays which had been imported from Europe. Three plays by Lope de Vega are said to have been translated into Quechua (a native dialect), but there are few records of a Quechuan play surviving in Spanish other than the famous historical echo *Ollantay*, thought for years to be a vestige from pre-Spanish days. It was written in the eighteenth century and performed in 1780 before Tupac Amaru, the last great Inca rebel against Spanish rule. It was shortly afterwards banned by the ruling Spanish Viceroy, and therefore a few copies were carefully guarded. It has been translated into many tongues.

Three early playwrights represent the best of that first period. Juan Ruíz de Alarcón (*c.* 1581–1639) was born in Mexico and is eagerly claimed there, but he went to Madrid at an early age, and there made his reputation as one of Lope de Vega's competitors (see SPAIN). Fernán González de Eslava (*fl.* 1566–1700) was a Spaniard who made a dramatic career in Mexico; he is seldom read by anyone except scholars, to whom he is important because he preserved in his plays the popular speech of the time. A more famous playwright, and one authentically Mexican, is the poetess Sor Juana Inés de la Cruz, born Juana Inés de Asbaje y Ramírez de Cantillana (1651–95). Known to her admiring compatriots as 'the tenth Muse', she was rich, learned, determined, and beautiful; she seems to have been a distracting influence in high circles, and no convent could silence her pen. Her fame as poet and playwright survives.

Of eighteenth-century plays two are occasionally revived, the disputed Inca romance *Ollantay* and *Siripo*, written in 1789 by Manuel J. Labardén of Argentina. The first concerns the love of a minor chieftain for the daughter of an Inca chief and, while written in Quechua, is Spanish in form and situation. The second is the melodramatic story of Lucía Miranda, a heroine of the colonizing period. In both instances the subject-matter is South American, but the manner of writing and of development is European. That balance continues.

The nineteenth century brought independence from Spain, and a breaking apart of the old vice-royalties into smaller units, self-governing within and competitive without. The cultural influences that had centred in vice-regal capitals persisted, but with independence came an effort on the part of the small proportion of cultured people to create national literatures which should be expressive of national ideals and free from the repressive effect of royal edicts issued at long distance. During the nineteenth century they sought to escape from the hampering influence of Spain; during the twentieth they are trying to escape from the crippling effect of the colonial mentality.

Of the score of South American countries which owe their heritage to Spain, there is hardly one which fails to honour a favourite playwright. For foreign students, however, those whose fame extends beyond the borders of their own countries hold most interest. The modern theatre in South America (meaning by that the theatre which shows the influence of the Ibsen revolution) has flourished with most promise in Argentina, Chile, and Mexico. In Argentina it began in 1884, when José J. Podestà, a circus clown turned impresario, took one of the famous gaucho legends and acted it out for a country audience. The gauchos were the cowboys of the great South American plains, and dear to all Argentinians. The South American theatre had found its first native source, and one that continues to be active to this day. *Juan Moreira* (1884) was the name of that first gaucho play, and it was full of blood, thunder, and galloping hooves down the centre aisle. *Calandria* (written in 1896), by Martíniano Leguizamón (1858–1935), a dramatist with literary pretensions, was the next step, but still rough. *Juan Soldão*, by Orosmán Moratoria (1859–98), had its gallopings better timed and placed, and now ranks as the most famous of the gaucho plays.

Late in the nineteenth century echoes of Ibsen, coming out of Spain by way of Echegaray, began to appear in Buenos Aires. The gauchos grew older, acquired sons and problems—and playwrights to deal with them in the new manner. *M'Hijo el Dotor* (1903), written by Florencio Sánchez (1875–1910), a Montevideo newspaper man and the most famous playwright of the region, deals with a gaucho's son who takes to city ways and his old gaucho father who understands neither the son's ambitions nor his weaknesses. Sánchez was followed by Ernesto Herrera (1887–1917), whose biographer considers him the equal as well as the disciple of the older man. He explored further into social problems which had no gaucho heritage, and his plays picture early twentieth-century society, especially in the lower strata.

The Argentine theatre was for years the most hospitable and most fruitful in South America, but its creative originality is just beginning to recover from the suppressive influence of the Perón dictatorship, which ruled in Argentina from 1944 to 1955. Native drama is still weak, but translations from England, Europe, and the United States are in great demand, while touring companies bring European plays for huge immigrant audiences. The large English colony in Buenos Aires supports an amateur group.

The centre of theatrical life is of course Buenos Aires. Since 1955, and as a protest against the decline of the professional theatre, amateur companies called 'independent theatres' have sprung up in the outskirts of the great capital and in provincial cities. Some of these resemble the *carpas* of Mexico, some are connected with universities, some, with leftist connexions, serve the purposes of propaganda rather than of art.

Ideally, all this activity should result in new playwrights of stature, but the older men still hold sway. Thanks to a law passed in 1910 which gives playwrights an unusually large share of royalties, author-managers flourish in Argentina. These include Leonidas Barletta, creator and manager of the once famous Teatro del Pueblo, which offered good plays to workers at a low price. (This theatre still functions, but less brilliantly than in earlier days.) Samuel Eichelbaum, most famous as a playwright, has also taken his turn at managing. A. Cunill Cabanellas was the first director of the short-lived National Comedy Theatre. Lola Membrives, now wealthy and mostly retired from active appearances, was long Argentina's leading star. No one has yet taken her place.

The most famous modern Argentine playwright, Samuel Eichelbaum, (1894–   ) is an all-purpose theatre man, having been a critic as well as an author, a manager, and a producer. Like so many artists, he lost favour when social protest became suspect by the government, but in these freer days he has recently reappeared. His best-known plays are *Un Hogar*, *Un Tal Servando Gómez*, and *Un Guapo del 900*. He follows in the tradition of Florencio Sánchez and Ernesto Herrera, with more attention to psychological complications than was attempted by his predecessors. Carlos Gorostiza, author of the famous *El Puente*, is still active, but younger men now vie for the places formerly occupied by the late Armando Discepolo with *Relojero*, the late Rodolfo Gonzales Pacheco, famous, with the late Pedro E. Pico, for such plays as *Que La Agarre Quien Quiera*, and the Spaniard, the late Alejandro Casona, who added to the Buenos Aires theatre circles a lustre that went beyond continental limits. His *Los Arboles Mueren de Pie* was played for three seasons, both in Buenos Aires and in Paris. *La Dama de Alba* is a favourite with theatre schools.

With Argentina's theatre in the doldrums, honours in the south have passed to Chile, which since 1941 has developed a vigorous theatre life, with a programme of education which trains actors, playwrights, scenic artists, and producers for the professional as well as the amateur stage. Its headquarters are in Santiago, but its influence spreads to other cities—Concepción, for instance, has a flourishing theatre—and from time to time goes beyond the national boundaries.

Given the long theatrical history of Chile, with two older playwrights who are known throughout the Spanish-speaking world, Antonio Acevedo Hernández and Armando Moock, this new energy had a good base, to which the famous Spanish actress Margarita Xirgu, who left Spain in the 1930s and founded a drama school in Santiago, added the element of foreign actor-training. Her work at this school, which was later absorbed into that of the Teatro Nacional, had an important influence.

The two institutions which have been foremost in this theatrical development are the Instituto del Teatro de la Universidad de Chile, and the Teatro de Ensayo (Experimental Theatre) de la Universidad Católica. The first, which is at present directed by Augustin Siré and works in the Teatro Antonio Varas, was founded in 1941 by Pedro de la Barra and has started many well-known Chilean dramatists on their careers through its annual competition for new plays. Among prize-winning entries have been *Mama Rosa*, by Fernando Debesa; *Parejas de Trapo*, by Egon Wolf; *El Camino Más Largo*, by Asunción Requeña; and *Animas de Día Claro*, by Alejandro Sieveking. The Teatro de Ensayo, housed in the Teatro Camilo Henríquez, was founded in 1943 by Pedro Mortheiru and Fernando Debesa, and has also done excellent work. Among its productions of important Chilean plays have been *Versos de Ciego*, by Luis A. Heiremans, whose death in 1964 at the early age of 36 was a great loss; *Deja que los Perros Ladren*, by Sergio Vodanovic; and *La Pérgola de las Flores*, a long-running musical by Isidora Aguirre and Francisco Flores. These three plays were taken to Paris and Madrid on a European tour in 1961 by a company which included Ana González, Silvia Piñeiro, Justo Ugarte, and Mario Montilles.

An important independent theatrical group which functions in Santiago is that known as Ictus. It specializes in *avant-garde* theatre, and has presented the plays of a remarkable dramatist Jorge Díaz, author of *El Velero en la Botella*. All these theatres, and many others throughout South America, are aided by the activities of the Latin-American branch of the International Theatre Institute, which helps them to break through the isolationism which was for so long a drag on their work, and enables them to test productions against and match experiences with those of their peers in other lands.

Mexico's theatre is also hospitable, also fruitful, and has certain spontaneous and popular qualities which make its activities important both to the participants and to the audiences. On the literary plane, it enlists poets and writers of high quality. Few of them stay with the theatre long; conditions are difficult and remuneration insufficient. The very successful playwright Rudolfo Usigli left the theatre for diplomacy; Celestino Gorostiza, who was director of Mexico's Department of Fine Arts in the 1930s, has resigned; Xavier Villaurutia is dead. Such men wrote for experimental groups, or for famous actresses, rather than for the general stage. Their plays—e.g. *La Hiedra* of Villaurutia, or *Noche de Estío* of Usigli—were in the tradition made famous by Europe's *avant-garde*. In their places one now sees Emilio Carballido with *La Zona Intermedia*, Sergio Magaña with *Moctezuma Segundo*, and the poet Salvador Novo, who has long been interested in all aspects of the theatre.

Professional companies in Mexico devote themselves mostly to revivals of popular Spanish pieces, or to translations and adaptations of plays which have proved their drawing power in Europe or the United States. Between them and the literary playwrights flourishes a mutual scorn. The former must please an audience hungry for novelty, and this means a repertory schedule calling for a new play every week. The company meets on Monday to plan the next week's programme. They may have a new play in hand, adapt an old one, or find a new way of presenting an individual speciality of an individual actor. In such circumstances a playwright who is not present gets short shrift. Performances are put together with more haste than finish, and producers seldom have time or money for fine décor or brilliant costumes.

Mexico's important contributions to the theatre are the popular *carpas* in cities and the Indian pageants in towns. The *carpa* is a tent on a street corner or a vacant lot in which players working along *commedia dell'arte* lines put on two *tandas*, or revues, for a small entrance fee. Their material is topical, their plots are sketched, their lines improvised according to the mood and the news of the day. Out of the *carpas* has come a procession of clowns, still led by the famous Cantinflas who, on stage and screen, has made all America laugh. The growing size and sophistication of Mexico City has made these street players less evident there than they used to be, but they still hold an important place as popular commentators.

The Indian ceremonial pageants are the fruit of four and a half centuries of Indian persistence under Spanish rule and influence. The dances of the *concheros* at San Miguel de Allende, for example, celebrate Christ's conquest of the savage Otomites. Some villages tell the story of Cortés and the Indian girl Malinche, others send troupes to the shrine of the Virgin of Guadalupe to put on feast-day pageants in her honour.

The first recorded theatrical performance in Cuba took place some time in 1598, with a production of a Morality play, *Los Buenos en el Cielo y los Malos en el Suelo*, by Spanish settlers. In the early eighteenth century the first play of the Cuban writer Santiago Pita y Borroto, *El Principo Jardinero o Fingido Cloridano*, was produced, but it was not until 1776 that the first theatre—the Coliseo, later known as the Principal—was opened in Havana. In the early nineteenth century Francisco Covarrubias inaugurated a popular theatre which made use of local material and music, and formed a parallel stream to the imported theatre, which was largely influenced by European taste and achievements. Both streams of theatre flourished during the whole of the nineteenth century, and a number of local playwrights provided a varied repertory in which comedy predominated. By the beginning of the twentieth century, however, the initial impulse had spent itself, and apart from the plays of José A. Ramos little good work was being done. It is interesting to note that his *Tembladera*, first produced in 1917, had a successful revival in 1959.

In the 1940s and early 1950s Cuba created an Academia Dramática in the Escuela Libre de Habana, and a Teatro Universitaria, both of which did excellent work. Luis Baralt was the island's most distinguished producer. But here, as happened in Argentina, the dictator's hand has fallen heavily, and under Castro the theatre has become merely one more vehicle for propaganda.

Argentina's neighbour, Uruguay, home of the famous nineteenth-century playwrights Florencio Sañchez and Ernesto Herrera, is still popular among theatre people for audiences both enthusiastic and discriminating. Colombia has had a trio of dramatists famous in this century—Antonio Alvarez Lleras, Alejandro Mesa Nicholls, and Luis Enrique Osorio—whose plays show colour and originality. Bolivia has a famous playwright, Mario Flores, whose reputation was won in Argentina. Paraguay's most celebrated playwriting is unexportable, being written not in Spanish but in a native Indian dialect called Guaraní which is widely spoken. Julio Correa, playwright, actor, and director, organized the Elenco Teatral Guaraní in Asunción, and makes it the headquarters for his highly original and locally popular drama. Peru likes plays that celebrate its pre-Spanish Inca culture. In 1941 a spectacle called *Inca Takay*, which included war and religious dances, native songs and recitations, went on tour. Famous in theatre history as the scene of the escapades of the eighteenth-century actress La Perrichola (enshrined in Offenbach's opera 'La Périchole'), Peru has both modern plays and Indian ceremonials that pre-date the Spanish conquest.

Of Latin-American stars, Fernando Soler, Maria Teresa Montoya, who has her own theatre in Monterey, and the clown Cantinflas make their home in Mexico and their fame throughout the continent. Argentina still boasts Lola Membrives, though in semi-retirement.

Chile is creating a group of young stars who, having recently taken three Chilean plays on a European tour, are on their way to more than local fame. In many of these countries there lingers an almost Elizabethan tradition of the theatrical way of life, in which participants can turn their hands to any tasks. In Mexico, Luís G. Basurto is still playwright, impresario, and director. In Chile, Agustín Siré is versatile and inventive, as was Luis A. Hieremans. In Brazil (see below), Alfredo Mesquita writes, directs, teaches, and provides steady inspiration and encouragement.

Theatre buildings throughout the continent tell of a people's pride in supplanting kings and emperors who were patrons of the stage and counted a magnificent opera-house as a ruler's proper jewel. The cities are proud of their theatres. Rio de Janeiro in Brazil, Santiago in Chile, Lima in Peru, have municipal theatres, elaborately baroque, where performances are given under municipal patronage. The Teatro Municipal in Rio, and the famous Teatro Colón which is the official state theatre in Buenos Aires, are primarily opera-houses built for big spectacles; the new Teatro San Martín in Buenos Aires, with its three stages, is more versatile. The cities have in addition several big commercial theatres. The official theatre in Mexico City is the Palacio de Bellas Artes, begun in 1904 by the dictator Porfirio Diaz; built of marble, it was opened in 1934. It has elaborate stage machinery but its resources are seldom put to full use.

2. BRAZIL. The Brazilian theatre, stemming distantly from the Portuguese, has in recent years advanced beyond its somewhat frail heritage and come into the main stream of modern theatrical activity. Brazil is the only South American country which has a royal past of its own and a theatre once under direct royal patronage. Freed in the nineteenth century from Portuguese rule by the royal rebel, Prince Pedro, whose father, João VI, had fled to the colony in 1807 when Napoleon invaded the Iberian peninsula, it was proclaimed an independent empire by Pedro in 1822, and it continued so under the control of the Bragança family until 1889, when it became a republic.

With this background one might assume that, just as the American theatre claims the English Shakespeare as its parent, so the Brazilian theatre would claim the Portuguese geniuses Gil Vicente (*c.* 1465–*c.* 1539) and Sá de Miranda (1481–1558). But the Portuguese language has undergone such changes in Brazil that classic Portuguese plays are said to need considerable modification in order to be understood by modern Brazilian audiences. Theatre schools read them, but they are not generally played.

Brazil's own first theatre genius was António José da Silva (1705–39) known as O Judeu (The Jew). He was born in Rio, but taken to Lisbon at the age of 8, where his extraordinary dramatic talent developed throughout a short and stormy life; in the end he was spectacularly murdered by the Inquisition. Both countries now claim him as their greatest playwright. Witty and malicious, he satirized the false and precious life of the eighteenth century, to the delight of audiences and the annoyance of officials. A hundred years later his married life and tragic fate formed the theme of Brazil's first national play, *António José* (1838), written by the romantic poet Domingo José Gonçalves de Magalhães (1811–82). His plays still form part of the teaching material of theatre schools.

Brazil's first playhouse was built in the eighteenth century in Ouro Preto, then the capital. Another burst of splendour, not so early, resulted in the famous opera-house of Manaus. In Rio de Janeiro, the baroque Royal Theatre of St. John was the gift of King João VI of Portugal, when he went there in 1807. For eleven years it welcomed drama imported from Europe; then it burned down, and was replaced by the Royal Theatre of St. Peter, which in turn was destroyed in 1926, about the time when the baroque opera-house, now called the Teatro Municipal, was erected.

Three new theatres testify that the nation's interest in drama has not waned. Bahia (Salvador) is finishing a handsome theatre complex, where audiences can sit out of doors as well as in. Rio has built a small theatre on the edge of the bay in connexion with its Museo Municipal, and the national government is erecting a double theatre within a single spectacular building in the new capital, Brasilia. This Teatro Nacional is planned with two auditoriums, one large and one small, having stages back to back which can be so manipulated as to throw the two theatres into one vast auditorium having a central stage and seating 2,000 people. Now a grey concrete skeleton, this ambitious project is to be plated with white marble. Its date of completion is uncertain.

The first major dramatist to write on Brazilian themes was Luíz Carlos Martins Penna (1815–48). His work consists of some nineteen comedies, of which *O Juiz de Paz na Roca* is considered Brazil's first national comedy; he also wrote seven dramas, and one tragi-farce in three acts, *O Noviço*, which is perhaps the most famous of his plays; all of them picture the life of the period with wit and grace.

With Martins Penna stands the novelist José Mariniano de Alencar (1829–77), who wrote eight plays of a moralizing nature as well as the famous novel *O Guaraní*, which has been made into a play. His *O Demonio Familiar* (1864) was readapted for the modern stage by Viriato Correa and put on by Procopio Ferreira, actor-producer, in Rio de Janeiro; it is still played. There is also Joaquín José da França Junior (1838–90), who wrote gay comedies, of which the most successful are *Tres Candidatos*, the satire *As Doutoras*, *Como se faz um Diputado*, and *O Ministerio Caiu*. Arthur Azevedo, whose centenary was observed in 1955, wrote his first play at the age of 9, and left some two hundred others (including a number of translations) as a legacy to his country. His *Uma Vespera de Reis* was revived in a published version in São Paulo in 1955. A more recent success was the revival of *Maembembe* in Rio in 1959. There is also a volume of plays extant by the famous novelist Machado de Assis (1839–1908).

Today's theatre in Brazil has famous actor-producers, including Procopio Ferreira, who has for many years revived native classics, imported European drama, and played modern local comedies. Ageing, he now plays mostly in the provinces. Brazilian audiences are hospitable and fun-loving, native farces are plentiful and popular, student groups in several cities are actively feeding new blood and new ideas into the professional theatre. Former President Vargas's ambitious plan (approved in 1943 and furnished with the equivalent of seven and a half million American dollars) for the 'cultural uplift of our national theatre' left behind a Comedia Brasileira, and a Children's Theatre. Later governments have continued to pay homage and subsidies to the theatre in the European manner. At present the Serviço Nacional de Teatro operates under the Ministerio de Educaçao e Cultura.

Today's theatre in Brazil has two lively and competitive centres, Rio de Janeiro and São Paulo, each with several professional companies and at least one good theatre school. There are also theatres and schools of note in Bahia, Recife, Pernambuco, Pôrto Alegre, Belo Horizonte, and Belém. Since 1945, due in part to the educative influence of such theatre schools, a number of playwrights have begun to concern themselves with social problems. Gianfresco Guarnieri with *A Semente*, Dias Gomes with *O Pagador de Promessas*, Augusto Boal and Oduvaldo Vianna Filhio are among the best of these. Jorge Andrade, with *Pedreiras das Almas* and the lighter *O Telescopio*, has great talent. The famous *Deus Lhe Pague* of Joraçy Camargo, written some years ago, but still valid, treats social protest in a lighter vein. Edgard Rocha da Miranda has won fame with *Não so Eu* and *E Noreste Soplo*. The latter was also produced in London and New York, as *When the Wind Blows*. Rocha da Miranda and Guilhermo Figuereido, who already has more than a dozen plays to his credit (including *Maria del Ponte*, which is scheduled both for Bulgaria and the United States), are active in many aspects of the drama.

Theatrical activity in Brazil owes both stimulus and substance to Alfredo Mesquita, playwright, producer, and leader for thirteen years of the Escola de Arte Dramatica de São Paulo. Himself a theatre man in the best sense of the phrase, he has also been active in promoting theatrical interests through the famous Bienal das Artes Plasticas de Teatro, held every two years. It was started in connexion with the biennial exposition of painting and sculpture in the Museu de Arte Moderna, but is now independent. His school has helped to develop at least one fine actress, Cacilda Becker, who has her own theatre in São Paulo, along with Maria della Costa and Nydia Licia, who have their own companies.

Thus far Brazil is rich in acting talent, but lacking in enough producers and directors of equivalent ability. Sergio Cardoso is also an actor; Franco Zampari founded the Teatro Brasileiro de Comedia. Ziembinski, who is a Pole, Adolfo Celli and Gianni Ratto, who are Italians, Augusto Boal, José Renato, Atunes Filho, and Flavio Rangel rank among the best of the directors; the names show the importance of immigrant influence in the Brazilian theatre picture (see also CHILDREN'S THEATRE).

MILDRED ADAMS

SOUTH LONDON, THE, one of the earliest music-halls, founded after the Canterbury and Weston's (see HOLBORN EMPIRE). Built and decorated in imitation of a Roman villa, it stood on the site of a Roman Catholic chapel, and opened on 30 Dec. 1860 with E. W. Mackney in the bill. In 1869 it was burnt down, but quickly rebuilt and reopened. Five years later it was taken over by an enterprising manager, J. J. Poole, who produced excellent spectacles and ballets there. Among his discoveries was Connie Gilchrist. It was at this hall that Fred Coyne made his last appearance and Florrie Forde her first. One of its Chairmen was 'Baron' Courtney. It was badly damaged by enemy action during the Second World War and has since been demolished.

SOUTH STREET THEATRE, see SOUTHWARK THEATRE.

SOUTHERNE, THOMAS (1660–1746), English dramatist, friend of Dryden (for whose plays he wrote a number of prologues and epilogues) and of Mrs. Aphra Behn, two of his plays, *The Fatal Marriage; or, the Innocent Adultery* (1694) and *Oroonoko* (1695), being based on her novels. These are both tragedies, as was his first play, *The Loyal Brother; or, the Persian Prince* (1682). These show a mingling of heroic and sentimental drama which was not without influence on the development of eighteenth-century tragedy as typified in Rowe. Southerne was also the author of three comedies of manners which enjoyed much success when they were first produced. They contain some witty scenes, but are weak in construction and overloaded with unnecessary detail. It was on Southerne's advice that Colley Cibber's first play was produced at Drury Lane in 1696.

SOUTHWARK THEATRE, PHILADELPHIA, the first permanent theatre in America. Built in 1766 by Douglass, manager of the American Company, it was a rough brick and wood structure, painted red, its stage lit by oil. From its position it was sometimes called the South Street Theatre. During its first season, which opened on 12 Nov. with *The Provoked Husband* and *Thomas and Sally*, it saw the production of *The Prince of Parthia*, the first American play to be produced professionally in America. During the War of Independence the theatre was closed, but after the departure of the British was reopened for a short time in the autumn of 1778. In 1784 the younger Hallam and John Henry, who had assumed the management of the American Company, returned to the Southwark before proceeding to New York, and the building continued to be used for theatrical purposes until in 1821 it was partly destroyed by fire. Rebuilt and used as a distillery, it was not finally demolished until 1912.

SOVIET THEATRE, see RUSSIA, 2.

SOYA, CARL ERIK (1896–), Danish dramatist. His earliest plays, *Parasitterne* (1929) and *Den leende jomfru* (1930), are naturalistic in style and cynical in tone. *Hvem er jeg?* (1931) is coloured by Freudian symbolism, whilst *Vogelfeder*, *Umbabumba*, and *Chas* are wickedly satirical. His plays of the 1940s—the tetralogy *Brudstykker af et mønster* (1940), *To tråde* (1943), and *30 års henstand* (1944), together with the concluding farce, *Frit valg* (1948)—deal generally with the problem of human guilt. L. KATHLEEN MCFARLANE

SPAIN. 1. THE ORIGINS. Spain, a favoured province of the Roman Empire, possessed many theatres and circuses, and, after the fall of imperial power, the repeated condemnations by Church Councils of charioteer (*auriga*) and actor (*pantomimus*) suggest that they continued in use for many years. Nevertheless the most significant evidence of dramatic activity during the first centuries of the Christian era concerns the pagan rites and festivals, many containing dramatic elements, which also earned the condemnation of the ecclesiastical authorities. During the first centuries A.D. the Church stood firm against all theatrical representation; that her condemnations were of little avail is shown by their frequent repetition. But a more powerful weapon lay ready for use. An attempt was made to convert pagan song and ritual dance to Christian purposes by the introduction of mime and dance into the ceremonies of the Church. Enthusiasm easily turns into excess, and by 627 the third Council of Toledo was condemning the use of dances and lewd songs in the churches, to the prejudice of the divine nature of the services and to the inconvenience of the clergy. That the pagan spectacles continued is not surprising; they had the vital force of a popular form of art, degenerate, but still appealing to the masses. But in the south of Spain they were to be eliminated, as far as we can judge, by the invasion of the Moors in 711. And in the north-east the growth of the power of the Church, and the added wealth and attraction of its festivals, gradually sapped the strength of the old traditions, emasculated them, until all that survived was the lighting of ceremonial fires, the burning of precious objects, and rustic rites and dances, whose origins were unknown to those who performed them.

2. MEDIEVAL. It was in the north-east of the peninsula, then, that the liturgical drama first developed. Its immediate origin lies in the singing of tropes, a practice which is said to have made its appearance in the early part of the ninth century, and which may be defined as a deliberate amplification of a passage in the authorized liturgical text. The trope gradually becomes detached from its context and eventually develops into an authentic playlet (see LITURGICAL DRAMA). In Catalonia the Latin Easter play was widespread, and many examples of the *Peregrinus* and *Planctus* have been identified. At Christmas and Whitsun lavish spectacles were staged in the cathedral of Valencia. Whilst actors wearing masks performed and sang on scaffolds set on the floor of the cathedral, mechanical doves flew down from the vaulting, heavens constructed in the roof of the church opened, and there descended platforms in the shape of clouds or globes bearing angels, saints, and statues of the Virgin Mary. A peculiarly Spanish theme is that of the Assumption of the Virgin Mary. Various versions are known, the most famous being the still extant performance at Elche. In this play, which lasts two days (14 and 15 Aug.) and utilizes three separate *aracelis*, or cloud-machines, we have a sixteenth-century crystallization of a play which is probably much earlier in origin, a theatrical performance which is today unquestionably unique.

From the ninth to the eleventh centuries much of Castile remained under Moorish domination and thus was relatively untouched by the developments in the north-east; for this reason, little evidence has survived of the liturgical play in Castile. Nevertheless, it is in Toledo that the *Auto de los Reyes Magos* appears, a fragment of a play in the vernacular dealing with the journey of the Magi and usually ascribed to the twelfth century. It has been argued that this play may be evidence of the introduction from France of such plays, already in a vernacular state, following upon the replacement of the old Hispanic liturgy (or Mozarabic rite) by the Roman towards the end of the eleventh century.

It is to the foregoing types of performance that Alfonso X (1252–84) mainly refers in the oft-quoted passage from the laws of the *Siete partidas*: in churches under the direct control of archbishops, bishops, or their representatives, but not in small towns or villages, the Nativity and Easter plays may be performed, plays which would present the Scriptural happenings as a physical reality and turn the hearts of men to devotion and good works. But the clergy are to refrain from bringing their cloth into disrepute, and the laity are prohibited from wearing religious habits for the same reason.

A struggle was thus taking place between the desire to save the churches from irreligious pollution, and the desire to instruct and enlighten their congregations, appealing to them through their dramatic sensibilities. The establishment of the Corpus Christi procession in Spain in the first half of the fourteenth century allowed these two aims to be simultaneously pursued: priest and layman could exercise their dramatic ingenuity to the full, but their efforts were excluded for the most part from the churches. The form taken by the procession was influenced by the *juglares*, the wandering players of all kinds, of high and low degree, who had come into prominence during the preceding three centuries. Many other existing dramatic forms—processional floats, counterfeit figures, devils, mock savages, and mimic battles—were incorporated into this, the chief procession of the Church, a statement of faith, ostentatious and magnificent, parading in Spain not only before Christians, but before Jews and Moors. In the early references to the procession it is this feeling of religious fervour that predominates. The procession of 1408 passed through the streets of Valencia 'praising the name of God and revering and honouring as best they might the Lord God manifest in the sacrament'. But gradually the religious fervour died, its place being taken by a more worldly and satirical attitude; the spectacular began to appeal for its own sake. The Church, however, was alive to the danger, and the procession was thoroughly reformed by the provisions of the Council of Trent which, in 1551, declared that the Corpus Christi procession should proceed from a cathedral and that the town council should be in charge of the entire festivity. The many enactments of succeeding years show that the Church of Spain was fully alive to the abuses current in the representations which took place both within and without its churches.

The officials at royal Courts who were responsible for regal displays and courtly entertainments soon saw the possibilities of adapting this religious pomp for their own purposes. Elements of the Corpus Christi procession, notably the counterfeit animals, were borrowed and used to grace coronations; the heaven filled with stars, and the clouds which descended from it, were used to greet royal visitors at a city gate. Counterfeit figures filled with fireworks gradually developed into representations in their own right. It was through these entertainments, in all probability, that the people of Spain enjoyed their closest contact with the Renaissance of classical learning, as Perseus and Andromeda, Hercules and the Titans, sailed across the night sky in every great city of Spain, fought out pitched battles in the principal squares, or graced river pageants and water spectacles. The seventeenth century was to see the ideas of the Counter-Reformation mirrored in these same pyrotechnical representations.

The same period saw the tourney develop from a display of prowess at arms to a semi-dramatic entertainment. The introduction of fire-arms had largely defeated the original purpose of the tourney, and gradually the spectacular element increased in importance, display coming to be valued for its own sake. As the chivalresque novel increased in popularity during the sixteenth century, it became usual to introduce some features of this literary genre into the tourney. Often the joust was in earnest, and the novelesque element was used as a backcloth, the participants being rewarded according to their deserts by a human being impersonating a figure from a chivalresque novel. Again, the challenge of a real tourney might echo literary language. Occasionally whole episodes from a book of chivalry were consciously enacted in what may best be described as a pageant play. These entertainments, together with the *entrameses* (French *entremets*) of the court banquet, mummings (*momos*), masquings, processions, and masquerades, formed the principal diversions of the Courts of Spain during the period which saw the birth of the Court theatre.

3. The Renaissance. The Court theatre which comes into being at the end of the fifteenth century reflects both the religious performances of its day and the secular inspiration of the Renaissance. Gómez Manrique (*c.* 1412–*c.* 1490) conflates in his *Representación del nacimiento* the courtly mumming and the Nativity play, and the gifts presented to the new-born Child in a manner reminiscent of the mumming are nevertheless the symbols of the Passion. In a secular mumming written for the birth of his nephew, Manrique introduced speeches by the seven Virtues, whilst in a festivity presented at the Court of Queen Isabella at Arévalo in 1467, the nine Muses descended from Helicon, each bestowing upon the infant Prince Alfonso a particular gift or quality.

It is the secular plays of Juan del Encina (*c.* 1468–*c.* 1529) that most clearly show Renaissance influence. His religious plays were intended for performance at the court of the Duke of Alba, and develop elements of the liturgical plays. In the second of the two short plays dealing with the Nativity the four disputing shepherds represent the four Evangelists, and the play is a blending of the *Officium pastorum* and the Gospels. In these plays and in his Easter plays, Encina introduces charming lyrics. At the same time his *Vigilia de la enamorada muerta* recalls the farced representations of the day of the Innocents. The shepherds of the Christmas plays speak in a dialect normally termed *sayagués*. The subject matter of his secular plays belongs to the Renaissance, extolling the power of love and contrasting unfavourably life at Court with the simple pleasures of the country, but dramatically they show little advance. The *Égloga de Plácida y Vitoriano* is the most highly developed, although even here there is no concentration on a single theme. The tropes had developed into playlets by the interpolation of additional material, and, when playwrights turned to secular themes, they still thought it necessary or effective to introduce extraneous matter into the main development of the plot. Lucas Fernández (*c.* 1474–1542), like Encina, was born in Salamanca. His religious plays are self-conscious developments of the liturgical playlets, bearing the stamp of the individual, whilst in his secular plays comic shepherds speak a rustic language and are affected by the *mal du siècle*, love, which bears the responsibility for much confusion and entangled situations.

Gil Vicente (*c.* 1465–*c.* 1537) is a shadowy figure. Writing for a Castilian Queen at the Court of Portugal, he is equally at home in Castilian and Portuguese. His simpler religious plays are very similar in subject to those of Encina: the shepherds, the arrival of the angel, the songs and the adoration. The *Auto dos quatro tempos* adds an element of pageantry derived from Court festivities, for the four disputing shepherds do not represent the four Evangelists, as with Encina, but the four seasons. The *Auto da Sibila Cassandra* shows further advance, a plot being integrated into the Christmas play and the Sibyl seen both as a simple country lass and as the pagan prophetess foretelling Christ's coming. The *Auto da alma* is a highly developed Morality, whilst the outstanding trilogy of the *Barcas* lifts the somewhat pedestrian Dance of Death into the realms of drama and presents it with the complex staging of the Court pageants, themselves influenced by processional floats and neo-classical triumphs. The secular plays show the same influences, particularly in those which, like *La fragua de amor*, are on the border-line of ballet and opera, whilst in *Dom Duardos* and in *Amadís de Gaula* Vicente dramatizes chivalresque episodes. Indeed, in the plays of Encina and Vicente we find already well developed two of the three main themes of the seventeenth-century Court theatre: the pastoral and the chivalresque. The later sixteenth century was to add the third, the mythological.

The year 1500 saw also the first extant edition of *La Celestina*, a prose work which, although it cannot be classed as a play, nevertheless exerted considerable influence on the development of the drama, particularly through the comparative realism and raciness of its prose dialogue.

Bartolomé de Torres Naharro (?–*c.* 1524) published his collected works in 1517 under the title *Propalladia*. Here again we find a static Christmas play, with an *introito* (prologue), a dialogue between two Spanish pilgrims, and an *Adición* which ends with a farced version of the *Ave maris stella*. The *Comedia Trofea*, performed at Rome in 1514, is a development of the disguising. In the prologue to his work, Torres Naharro distinguishes between the *comedia a noticia* and the *comedia a fantasía*, terms which may be rendered as realistic and novelesque plays. Of the former category, two plays have survived, the *Comedia soldadesca*, dealing with a braggart recruiting-officer, and the *Comedia tinellaria*, which presents a multilingual picture of low life below stairs in a great house. The second genre is represented by various plays, of which the most notable is the *Comedia Himenea* (showing the influence of *La Celestina*), creating a relationship between master and man which was to be developed by seventeenth-century dramatists and revolving around a conflict between love and honour. These latter plays are Italianate, a feature also of the plays of Lope de Rueda (*c.* 1505–65), an artisan turned actor-manager who performed with his company in religious festivities, at the Courts of the great, and in public squares. Cervantes has left us a well-known passage describing the bare stage of one of these latter performances, with rough and ready costumes and décor. The plots of Rueda's longer plays are complex and recall *Gl'ingannati*, on which his *Comedia de los engañados* is based. His pastoral plays present similar complicated situations. Rueda's fame rests more securely on the *pasos*, the short farcical interludes which exploit simple situations, practical jokes, or the outwitting of the trickster. Racy and popular, they still have considerable vitality.

4. The Establishment of the Professional Theatre. Rueda appears to have come early into contact with Italian *commedia dell'arte* players performing in Spain. The influence of these troupes, particularly that of Ganassa, on the development of the Spanish theatre was considerable. Ganassa was responsible for structural changes in the early commercial theatres, and it may well be that the typical composition of the Spanish commercial troupe of the late sixteenth and seventeenth centuries owes much to the appearance of these polished professionals in Spain at the precise moment when commercial theatres were being established throughout the peninsula (see ITALY, 2).

Another influence which cannot be ignored is that of the neo-classical dramatists. Scholars translated classical plays or wrote in imitation of them: Hernán Pérez de Oliva (*c.* 1494–1533), who made free translations of Sophocles, Euripides, and Plautus; Pedro Simón Abril (*c.* 1530–*c.* 1595), who translated Terence; Lupercio Leonardo de Argensola (1559–1613), who wrote neo-classical tragedies, *Isabela*, *Filís*, and *Alejandra*. But the humanists have little importance in the development of the commercial theatre. A far more potent influence is to be found in the Senecan tragedies of Juan de la Cueva (*c.* 1550–*c.* 1610). Writing for the commercial theatre of Seville, Cueva puts upon the stage the tyrant prince, the revengeful ghost, the Fates and Furies, and those scenes of violence and gore which typify the imitations of Seneca. Cueva also turned to Spanish legend, to the chronicles and ballads recounting the deeds of Bernardo el Carpio, the Infantes de Lara, and King Sancho. He is indeed the first dramatist to exploit this vein, but, in his versions, the chronicle stifles the ballad. Other dramatists of the period include Juan de Timoneda (?–1583), actor and bookseller as well as dramatist, whose greatest strength lies in the clarity of his exposition; Andrés Rey de Artieda (1549–1613), a dramatist of the school of Valencia, who first utilized the theme of *Los amantes de Teruel*; and Cristóbal de Virués (*c.* 1550–*c.* 1610), another Valencian, and a neo-classical writer.

SPAIN

Ten plays have survived from the pen of Miguel de Cervantes Saavedra (1547–1616), together with eight *entremeses*. In four of his plays Cervantes attempts to combine a sub-plot based on his own experiences as a slave in Algiers with a novelesque main plot: his endeavour is to combine truth and fiction (*mezclar/verdades con fabulosos intentos*). This attempt to combine in one play the *comedia a fantasía* and the *comedia a noticia* results in failure, the elements being unfortunately incompatible. More successful is *El cerco de Numancia*, dealing with the heroic resistance of that Spanish city faced with all the might of Rome. The *entremeses*, a type of interlude which shows considerable development from the simpler *paso*, are highly suited to their task of keeping the interest of a volatile audience between the acts of a full-length play, and in their speech, vigour, humour, deft characterization, and spontaneity, they show themselves to be light theatre at its best.

The dramatic careers of Cueva and Cervantes saw the establishment of the commercial theatres of the great towns of Spain. In Madrid the first playing places were unregulated, the actors hiring a *corral* or courtyard around which the typical town-house of the period was built. In 1572 a monopoly of stage performances in Madrid was granted to a charitable brotherhood which maintained the Hospital de la Pasión. This monopoly was later extended to include other Hospitals and provided a stout bulwark during the seventeenth century against the moralists who from time to time endeavoured to close the public theatres. The Hospitals purchased properties in 1579 and 1582 and there established the two *corrales de comedias*, the Corral de la Cruz and Corral del Príncipe, which continued to monopolize public entertainments in Madrid until the beginning of the eighteenth century. The theatres were leased to speculators in the early years of the seventeenth century, and from 1615 came under the jurisdiction of the town council.

Documentary evidence, drawings, and the stage directions of plays inform us that in both these theatres the stage projected into the auditorium. The audience stood in the courtyard (*patio*), were seated on benches (*bancos*), on a raised platform along the sides of the theatre (*gradas*), in boxes (*aposentos*) which occupied the ground floor and first storey of the three sides of the theatre, or crowded into the attics (*desvanes*) above the boxes. Facing the stage on the first floor was the separate gallery for women (*cazuela*) and above it the box of the municipality. Across the façade behind the projecting stage ran a balcony which was used to represent city walls, a tower, or a balcony (*lo alto del teatro*); staircases allowed access to this balcony from the open stage. At stage level were entrances at either side of the stage and windows, and inner scenes could be revealed or 'discoveries' made by the drawing back of the curtains at the rear of the platform stage. The theatrical machinery was simple, and consisted for the most part of trap-doors and a cloud-machine lowered from the attics (*desván de las tramoyas*) to the stage below. Courtyard theatres basically similar in design were built in all the chief cities of Spain, Seville being distinguished by its Coliseo of 1631, which was oval in shape and roofed in. To these theatres came professional troupes, the actors bound by yearly contracts to the manager (*autor de comedias*), who himself contracted with the lessee of the theatre (*arrendador*) or municipality to give a stated number of performances. These contracts always stress the need for novelty in the repertoire, the audience's appetite for new plays being insatiable. The manager usually bought his plays outright from the dramatist, who then had no further financial interest. In all the great cities the audience consisted largely of tradespeople, servants, soldiers, the bourgeoisie, the professional classes, and the nobility. The actors certainly played also in small towns and villages, but the plays, it is important to remember, were written for an urban audience.

5. The Golden Age of the Professional Theatre. *Como las paga el vulgo*, said Lope de Vega, mock-modestly, *es justo/hablarles en necio para darles gusto*. Since the common people pay for the plays, it is only fitting that one should speak down to them to give them pleasure—or, in modern terms, the dramatist writing for the audience of the *corrales* must always keep in mind box-office values. This, however, does not mean to say that the plays of Lope de Vega (1562–1635), despite his enormous output, are necessarily trivial, but rather that the values which they stress are those commonly held in his day. Lope claimed to have written 1,500 plays: religious, historical, mythological, novelesque, pastoral, and plays of intrigue. He concerns himself often with the relationship between the social classes in an idealized society, consisting only of king, nobles, and commoners (and thus omitting from the social structure the majority of his audience); with the contrast between life in the hard and vicious capital, and the tranquil peace of an idealized countryside (a theme particularly suited to an audience composed largely of first- and second-generation town-dwellers); and with the theme of honour. All these themes reflect contemporary preoccupations, the theme of the idealized society with its benevolent king as the fount of God's justice being particularly relevant at a period when the king was fast losing political power and Spain its sense of purpose. Furthermore, all these themes can be stated in terms of a struggle between harmony and disorder, between the harmony intended by God at the Creation, and the disharmony brought about by sin, by the unbridled appetites of man.

Lope writes in freely flowing verse, adapting his verse form to the subject matter, avoiding irrelevancies and building up to a tense climax at the very end of the play. His plays are plays of straight lines, of clear-cut divisions between main and sub-plots. In *Fuenteovejuna*, for instance, although main and sub-plot can be seen to be aspects of one single theme—the disorder caused by one lustful and ambitious noble—the action alternates rapidly between them. Lope's plays are energetic, vital. But this surface vitality must not blind us to the fact that they are a simplification of reality, the imposing of a clear, ordered pattern on the muddle which is life. The gentleman in an honour-play knows at once where his duty lies. If his honour is threatened or sullied, he has no doubts, shows no half-hearted lack of resolution; rather do we find quick resolve and a prompt dispatch. Life is not so simple. But this simplification of reality does not mean that the plays themselves are shallow. Their simplifications are, indeed, a criticism of their times.

Professor A. A. Parker, in a masterly analysis, has isolated five general principles which underlie the seventeenth-century *comedia*:

(1) the primacy of action over character drawing; (2) the primacy of theme over action, with the consequent irrelevance of realistic verisimilitude; (3) dramatic unity in the theme and not in the action; (4) the subordination of the theme to a moral purpose through the principle of poetic justice, which is not exemplified only by the death of the wrong-doer; and (5) the elucidation of the moral purpose by means of dramatic causality.

The new critical approach embodied in Professor Parker's analysis has enabled us to look at the *comedia* with fresh eyes, to seek not 'characterization', in the sense of the nineteenth-century critic, but, through the action, a theme which displays dramatic unity and has a moral purpose effected through the principle of poetic justice. As Professor Parker shows, this new approach may be applied to the work of any dramatist of the seventeenth century, although, of course, it will be found that individual dramatists modify the general principles to suit their purposes and tastes.

Among Lope's contemporaries are Guillén de Castro y Bellvís (1569–1631), a dramatist of the school of Valencia, remembered for his plays based on ballads, and particularly for *Las mocedades del Cid* and *Las hazañas del Cid*, dealing with the exploits of the national hero. Antonio Mira de Amescua (*c.* 1574–1644) is best known for *El esclavo del demonio*. Luis Vélez de Guevara (1579–1644) follows Lope de Vega in the effective introduction of popular songs into his plays, and in *Reinar después de morir* creates a delicately tender evocation of the sombre legend of the unfortunate Inés de Castro. Juan Ruíz de Alarcón y Mendoza (*c.* 1581–1639), a Mexican by birth, was a cripple, at odds with most of the leading literary figures of the day. His plays castigate the faults of society, the best known being *Las paredes oyen* and *La verdad sospechosa*. The economy of structure of these ingeniously constructed plays later commended them to French taste. Tirso de Molina [pseudonym of Fray Gabriel Téllez, *c.* 1571–1648] will always be remembered for *El burlador de Sevilla*, the first and in many ways the most successful version of the Don Juan theme, a play in which divine justice overcomes the gay deceiver and which teaches the audience that it is never too early to repent. The heroines of Téllez's plays are especially notable, from the redoutable queen of *La prudencia en la mujer* to the volatile, ingenious young women on whom depends the machinery of his plays of intrigue.

Francisco de Rojas Zorrilla (1607–48) belongs to the next generation of dramatists. *Del rey abajo, ninguno* is a fine example of the later development of the honour-play, the initial situation being complicated by the apparent intervention of the king, and presented to the audience neatly and with effective use of imagery. Juan Pérez de Montalbán (1602–38) wrote several plays based on the lives of saints, a popular genre; he also essayed historical themes. Agustín Moreto (1618–69) is especially notable for his witty comedies of intrigue, and particularly for his comic servants, the *graciosos*, never at a loss for an ingenious idea, who come to dominate their masters and mistresses and thus foreshadow Beaumarchais's Figaro. All these dramatists wrote copiously, and it is not surprising that many of their productions are refashionings of previous plays (*refundiciones*), a practice which was, of course, recognized, and carried with it no suggestion of plagiarism. Each generation rewrote its favourite plays to suit the changing taste of the time. Many of these dramatists also turned their attention to the minor theatrical forms, the *entremeses*, *bailes*, *jácaras*, and *loas*. Foremost among the *entremesistas* is Luis Quiñones de Benavente (*c.* 1589–1651), his plays being a series of ingenious variations on various well-established subjects. Nor should we forget the minor entertainers, the acrobats, jugglers, and puppet-players, who had a monopoly of the public theatres during Lent, when the performance of plays was prohibited.

Pedro Calderón de la Barca (1600–81) was not as prolific a dramatist as Lope de Vega, but nevertheless some two hundred of his dramatic pieces have survived. His plays were written in the early 1620s, that is to say, some forty years after Lope de Vega began to write for the Spanish stage. His most famous *comedias* date from the period 1625–40; during these years he also wrote *autos sacramentales* and in the late 1630s Court plays destined for the newly built palace of Buen Retiro. From 1638 to 1642 Calderón took part in various military campaigns. For many years during the period 1644–51 the commercial theatres were closed, partly as a result of Court mourning, and partly because of the attacks of reformers. Calderón wrote little during these years, and in 1651 he was ordained priest. From that date until his death in 1681 his dramatic output was confined to Court plays and to *autos sacramentales.* Calderón was a master craftsman, at home with the mythological play of spectacle performed on the ornamental waters of Buen Retiro or in the Coliseo, its up-to-date theatre; with the equally elaborate machinery of the *auto sacramental*; with the religious and moral themes of such *comedias* as *La vida es sueño*, *La devoción de la cruz*, and *El mágico prodigioso*; with the intricacies of such plays of intrigue as *La dama duende* or *Casa con dos puertas mala es de guardar*; or with the plays which develop and comment upon the honour theme, such as *El médico de su honra*, *El pintor de su deshonra*, and *A secreto agravio, secreta venganza.* In all Calderón's plays the dramatist's ideas are transmitted not only through the relationship between the characters, through the actors' speeches, significant actions, dress, and gestures, through the highly developed use of the stage and of impressive machinery, but also through the images which parallel or subtly contradict the surface movement of the play. Calderón's plays are highly organized; the dramatist is always firmly in control of his medium. The sub-plot becomes an aspect of the main plot, and the *gracioso* as much as the hero and heroine serves to illustrate the moral lesson implicit in the play. With Calderón no character is superfluous, no action irrelevant, no detail extraneous.

6. THE AUTO SACRAMENTAL. Calderón's genius is particularly evident in his development of the *auto sacramental.* The *auto* of the seventeenth century is a dramatic homage paid to the Eucharist at the feast of Corpus Christi, a symbolic representation which may deal with the Eucharist itself or with biblical or hagiographic themes. Originally performed on a scaffold before the church where the Host was displayed for adoration, these plays came in Madrid to be presented on three carts set in line ahead, the outer two housing elaborate machinery in tower-like constructions, and the centre cart forming a flat playing-space (for a cart of this type see No. 19). A typical early *auto* is Lope de Vega's *La adúltera perdonada* in which the husband (Christ) calls for the punishment of his erring wife (the Soul). On one cart a globe opens to reveal Justice aloft, and sentence of death is pronounced, but before it can be put into effect the second cart opens to reveal the Church seated on a throne resting on the back of a dragon (heresy), and the Church successfully intervenes on behalf of the Soul. Another master of the *auto* in the first part of the seventeenth century is the unjustly neglected José de Valdivielso (*c.* 1560–1638), an excellent poet, skilful in his use of costume, action, machinery, and song to underline the allegory. *Autos sacramentales* were performed in all the great cities of Spain, in slightly different playing conditions. Up to 1645 four were presented each year in Madrid, two by each of two companies of professional actors. There were no performances in 1646; from 1647, the number of plays produced each year was reduced to two, and four carts bearing machinery were employed for each play in place of two. This change meant that the plays had to be performed on specially constructed scaffolds around which the carts were disposed (a method of production occasionally employed in earlier years for special performances), but it also allowed the dramatist much greater scope. The balanced effect of the two pairs of carts appealed to the logical mind of Calderón, and all his four-cart plays make considerable use of antithetical balance. From 1651 until his death in 1681, Calderón wrote two *autos* each year for performance in the capital. Many of his plays can be understood on more than one level. *La cena de Baltasar*, for instance, can be interpreted as a dramatic account of the Old Testament story, as an allegory of God's judgement on humanity, or as a representation of the forces at work in Belshazzar's soul. In this last view of the play, all the characters are in truth elements of Belshazzar himself, and he is the sole protagonist. These various interpretations are made possible not only through the speeches of the characters, but through the actions, dress, and movements of the actors and the complex and elaborately painted machinery. The *auto sacramental* of the seventeenth century is, to use Calderón's own terms, a sermon in verse, theology put upon the stage (*Sermones/puestos en verso, en idea/representable, cuestiones/de la Sacra Teología . . .*), and it is only when the plays have been visually re-created in performance that their import can be clearly seen and their didactic purpose fully realized.

7. THE COURT THEATRE. The Court theatres of the seventeenth century also employed elaborate machinery. No permanent theatre was available until the late 1630s, when the elaborate and up-to-date Coliseo of the palace of Buen Retiro came into use. Up to that date, *comedias* had been presented by the commercial troupes in the private apartments of king and queen in the Alcázar, or in its magnificantly decorated Salón Dorado. Special structures were also built for lavish performances, such as the theatre constructed in 1622 by the Italian architect and engineer, Julius Caesar Fontana, for the Conde de Villamediana's *La gloria de Niquea*, which employed visible scene-changes. A similar theatre was built in 1629 for Lope de Vega's *La selva sin amor*, a pastoral eclogue set to music, the machinery being designed by another Italian, Cosmo Lotti. Italian designers indeed dominated the Court theatres of Spain during the first half of the century, but after 1650 Spanish architects and artists, such as José Caudi, began to work for the royal theatres. The second half of the century saw also the rise of the *zarzuela*, a short opera usually on a mythological theme. The genre takes its name from the palace of La Zarzuela, where Calderón's *El golfo de las sirenas* was first performed in 1657. These elaborate Court plays combine elements taken from the spectacles of Italian Courts with contemporary

staging techniques: the use of perspective in scene design, concealed lighting, a concealed orchestra, and transformations which take place before the eyes of the audience. They offer a type of spectacle distinct from that of the *comedia*, the latter appealing by reason of the ingenuity and novelty of its plot, the former by reason of the lavishness of its spectacular production.

It can indeed be argued that the relative growth of importance of the Court theatre in the last decades of the seventeenth century is one of the causes of the decline of the commercial stage. Such dramatists as Francisco Antonio de Bances Candamo (*c.* 1662–1709) wrote elaborate Court plays with political implications, and such productions were unsuitable, both as regards subject-matter and staging techniques, for performance in the public theatres. From 1680 onwards the commercial theatre rapidly declined, and, after the death of Calderón, no new *autos sacramentales* of any literary distinction were written.

8. The Eighteenth Century. The eighteenth century opened inauspiciously for the Spanish theatre. The new dynasty imported Italian players and broke the long monopoly of the two *corrales de comedias* of the capital, whilst the economic effects of the War of the Spanish Succession were disastrous. The typical Court entertainment of the eighteenth century is the Italian opera, and the successive theatres constructed on the site of the Caños del Peral were all intended primarily for the performances of opera. In the course of the reign of Philip V, the Coliseo of Buen Retiro was refurbished according to the stipulations of Farinelli, summoned to Spain by the Bourbon monarch. The old *corrales* continued in use until 1743 (Corral de la Cruz) and 1744–5 (Corral del Príncipe), when they were replaced by modern structures better adapted to the demands of the day. Both the new theatres were typical eighteenth-century designs, with horse-shoe amphitheatres, heavy prosceniums, and perspective scenery. Up to the middle of the century the stock-in-trade of the commercial theatres continued to be *refundiciones* of seventeenth-century *comedias*. Representative dramatists are Antonio de Zamora (*c.* 1664–1728), whose work includes a version of the Don Juan legend, *No hay deuda que no se pague y Convidado de piedra*, and José de Cañizares (1676–1750), a dramatist best known for his complicated and boisterous farces, such as *El dómine Lucas*. Both of these plays are *refundiciones* and, although a detailed examination reveals considerable change of emphasis, still recognizable as seventeenth-century *comedias*.

French influence on the Spanish theatre was noticeable in the last decades of the seventeenth century, and the accession of a Bourbon king naturally stimulated the interest in French literature, although the immediate effect on the Madrid stage was, as we have seen, to encourage Italian opera. Neo-classical theories began to be expounded, but the era of neo-classical influence cannot be said to begin in earnest until 1737, the year of the publication of the *Poética* of Ignacio Luzán (1702–54). Luzán admires the poets of Spain's sixteenth century, but deplores the inability of the dramatists of the following century to write according to the rules. His definitions of poetry, tragedy, comedy, and epic follow closely the Aristotelian tradition, stressing the didactic purpose of art, its *utilidad*. A familiarity with the theory of *peripecia* and *agnición* and a desire to perfect nature were not sufficient, however, to produce good plays, as Nicolás Fernández de Moratín (1737–80) demonstrated in his lifeless comedies and dull tragedies. One of the few effective neo-classical tragedies in Spain is the *Raquel* of Vincente García de la Huerta (1734–87), a play very reminiscent of a seventeenth-century tragicomedy and owing its success in all likelihood to Huerta's probably unconscious concessions to popular taste. An official attempt to encourage the writing of neo-classical plays was launched in 1784 to celebrate the birth of twin princes and the Peace of Paris. The prizewinners were *Las bodas de Camacho*, by the poet Juan Meléndez Valdés (1754-1817), and *Los menestrales*, by Cándido María Trigueros (1736–*c.* 1801), both worthy but heavy comedies. The high-water mark of the neo-classical movement in Spain is often taken to be the banning, in 1765, of the *autos sacramentales*, after considerable controversy. It is clear that the *autos* were out of tune with the new age, both technically and in the treatment of their subject matter. The finest neo-classical dramatist is Leandro Fernández de Moratín (1760–1828), whose plays, particularly *El café* and *El sí de las niñas*, are still alive. *El café* upholds good sense in the theatre and attacks the extravagances of such playwrights as Luciano Francisco Comella (1751–1812).

It must not be imagined that classical plays were all that the eighteenth-century theatre had to offer. *Refundiciones* still appeared on the boards, together with such new genres as the *melólogo* (dramatic monologue or dialogue set to music), and the *escena muda* (a short piece played in silence with musical accompaniment). The *zarzuela* developed, in the hands of Ramón de la Cruz (1731–94), into musical *folklorismo*, although its popularity did not survive competition from the improved Italian opera of the last years of the century. Ramón de la Cruz is best known for his racy, lively, satirical sketches, the *sainetes*. 'I write,' he said, 'and truth dictates' (*Yo escribo, y la verdad me dicta*). In these popular pieces can be seen the trend towards a more realistic portrayal of life which is one of the features of the Romantic drama and was to find its culmination in the realistic and naturalistic novels and plays of the second half of the nineteenth century.

9. Romanticism and Realism. Neo-classicism never recovered from the French invasion of Spain during the Napoleonic wars. If

Luzán's *Poética* of 1737 can be said to mark the beginning of its influence in Spain, the publication in 1827 of another *Poética*, that of Francisco Martínez de la Rosa (1787–1862), may be said to signal its close. Martínez de la Rosa, one of the last writers to defend neo-classicism, is already much influenced by Romanticism. Spanish Romanticism is essentially an alien growth, nurtured in France and England by the Liberal exiles of the 1820s and brought back to Spain with the return to power of the Liberals in 1835. Playwrights like Mariano José de Larra (1803–37) struggle to put the new wine into old bottles: his *Macías* is essentially a Romantic hero in a neo-classical strait-jacket. The first frenzy of fine rhetorical denunciations of destiny, as in the *Don Álvaro* of the Duque de Rivas (1791–1865) and *El trovador* of Juan Eugenio Hartzenbusch (1806–80), gives way to the lachrymose appeal of *Los amantes de Teruel* of Antonio García Gutiérrez (1813–84). The only play of the period which still survives in the repertoire of the modern theatre is the *Don Juan Tenorio* of José Zorrilla (1817–93), still played each year on All Saints' Day, a version in which the hero is sentimentalized and where his defiance of God is finally overcome. At the end of the play, Don Juan's soul is received into Heaven, an apotheosis which symbolizes the fate of Romanticism in Spain.

Almost as significant as the Romantic plays of the 1830s are the bourgeois comedies of such writers as Manuel Bretón de los Herreros (1796–1873). His satirical pieces are facile and never very deep, but in many ways Bretón is a much more accurate thermometer of public taste than either Moratín or Zorrilla. In the second half of the century the bourgeois drama predominates. Adelardo López de Ayala (1829–79) and Manuel Tamayo y Baus (1829–98) delight in social criticism and didactic pieces which stress the deplorably materialistic tendencies of the age. José Echegaray e Izaguirre (1832–1916) wrote for a middle-class audience. His plays lack the colour, exoticism, and vitality of Romantic drama at its best, although in many ways the contrived situations, dramatic revelations, and high-flown style can be classified as neo-Romantic. Antonio Vico, the foremost actor of the time, exhibited his over-emphatic style of acting in many of these pieces. Typical are *O locura o santidad* (1877) and *El hijo de don Juan* (1892), the latter a somewhat pale shadow of Ibsen's *Ghosts*. The influence of the Norwegian dramatist was undoubtedly important at this period. The best realistic dramatist of the late nineteenth century is Benito Pérez Galdós (1843–1920). As in his novels, the characters of his plays stand for points of view, but are convincing characters at the same time. In *La loca de la casa* (1893), for instance, the class struggle, the economic struggle, the conflict between good and evil and between man and woman, are seen as different facets of the relationship between the hero and the heroine, and the message of the play is the necessity for a union between the different polarities which they represent, for out of this union will be born the new Spain. The weakest aspect of the plays of Galdós is undoubtedly their dialogue, a surprising defect in a writer who, as a novelist, excels in the self-revelation of a character through monologue and dialogue. Also important for their social themes are the thesis plays of Joaquín Dicenta (1863–1917).

The year 1894 may be said to mark a turning point in the history of the Spanish theatre. María Guerrero displaces Antonio Vico as the most influential actor of the period. The same year saw the first performance of *La verbena de la Paloma*, by Ricardo de la Vega (1839–1910), a *zarzuela* (the term now being applied to a light musical play reminiscent of the Gilbert and Sullivan operettas), and the high-water mark of the *género chico*, as the less pretentious type of theatrical entertainment came to be called. Typical also are the short pieces of Carlos Arniches (1866–1943), putting the people of Madrid upon the stage in sketches which are the lineal descendants of the *entremeses* and *sainetes* of previous centuries. 1894 saw also the first performance of the first play of Jacinto Benavente (1866–1954). Benavente's first popular success was *Gente conocida*, a social satire staged in 1894. He reacted against the predominant realism, and in such plays as *La noche del sábado* (1903) suggests that will and energy can overcome reality, reflecting thus the non-rational philosophies of the day.

The last years of the nineteenth century saw also a renaissance of the Catalan drama, and Barcelona under the *modernistes* became an important centre of theatrical experiment and foreign influence. Santiago Rusiñol (1861–1931) reacted against the materialism of bourgeois society; Adrià Gual (1872–1943), under the influence of Maeterlinck, breaks with rhetorical drama, experiments with symbolism and aims at the establishment of a national theatre, and, in his own Teatre Intim, sets new artistic standards for scene design, hitherto neglected in Spain. Meanwhile Ángel Guimerà (1847–1924) excels in naturalistic drama. *Terra baixa* (1896) studies primitive sexual passions and dissects the cruelty of ignorance.

10. THE TWENTIETH CENTURY. The influence of Gual was not immediately felt in Madrid, and it was not until the second decade of the new century that the young designers he had shaped and trained triumphed in the capital. But the early years saw various reactions in Madrid against the dominant realistic drama. The Andalusian plays of the Quintero brothers, simple in ethics and sparkling in impact, apparently spontaneous and fresh even if basically false, do at least open a window and let fresh air into the stuffy atmosphere of an Echegaray study. Jacinto Grau (1877–1958), in *El Conde Alarcos* (1907), suggests the overwhelming power of demoniacal love, a deep relentless force which humbles mankind to the status of a puppet. Gregorio Martínez Sierra (1881–1947), in *Canción de cuna* (1911),

suggests another facet of the influence of Maeterlinck: his play is concerned with the everyday, but the *comedia del vivir cotidiano*, rather than *le tragique quotidien.* A significant indication of the revolt from realism is the revival of interest in puppetry, a popular theatrical form still alive in Spain (see also PUPPETS). The artists who frequented Els Quatre Gats, the Barcelona café of the turn of the century, were entertained by popular puppets and an artistic shadow-show, the latter a reminiscence of the shadow theatres of the cafés of Montmartre, notably Le Chat Noir. Such writers as Santiago Rusiñol and Benavente turned for inspiration to the puppet theatre, the latter in *Los intereses creados* (1907), an excellent modern version of the farces of the *commedia dell'arte.* Benavente and Ramón María del Valle-Inclán (1866–1936) both wrote highly sophisticated plays for children's theatres, and Valle-Inclán makes excellent use of the puppet metaphor in *La marquesa Rosalinda* (1913), a graceful satire of his own exquisite style.

The new theatre was to see its culmination in the years 1917–25, when Martínez Sierra took over the management of the Teatro Eslava. Although the Eslava was small and not particularly well equipped, Sierra, the Spanish Lugné-Poë, presented a large range of extremely varied works: classical and modern, indigenous and foreign, poetic theatre, children's plays, pantomime, and *autos.* The unifying force was Sierra's artistic vision. His productions were much influenced by the visits of the Ballets Russes, and the influence was reciprocal, for it was on the basis of Sierra's theatrical version of Pedro Antonio de Alarcón's novel, *El sombrero de tres picos*, that Manuel de Falla wrote the music for the ballet 'Le Tricorne' (1919) at the request of Diaghilev. A typical production was that of *El pavo real* of Eduardo Marquina (1879–1946), a stylized Eastern fable with magnificent scenery by Fontanals. Sierra's principal designers were Fontanals, Rafael Barradas, and Sigfredo Burmann, the latter a pupil of Max Reinhardt. His leading actress was Catalina Bárcena. Sierra introduced contemporary techniques in lighting, acting, and scene-painting. During his management of the Eslava the Spanish theatre was finally europeanized and the theatre-going public re-educated.

Cipriano Rivas Cherif (1891–), a pupil of Gordon Craig, was, like Sierra, an advocate of the *reteatralización* of the theatre. His original company, El Caracol, founded in 1928, presented the first surrealist plays seen on the Spanish stage. Cherif also produced *Sombras de ensueño* by Miguel de Unamuno (1864–1936). In 1928 Cherif was appointed artistic director of the Teatro Español, and, in collaboration with the director of the company and leading actress, Margarita Xirgu, set up an influential theatre study group, the Teatro Escuela de Arte. The most popular dramatists of the day were Arniches, Pedro Muñoz Seca (1881–1936) (the inventor of the *astracanàda*, a clever sketch depending for its success on word play and situation), and the Quintero brothers. The brothers Antonio and Manuel Machado put upon the stage their poetical evocations of Andalusia, and Azorín [pseudonym of José Martínez Ruiz, 1873–1967] analysed personal problems in his plays of discussion.

In the early 1920s Valle-Inclán turned from gentle satire to savage caricature. His *esperpentos* are a deliberate defamation of Spanish society and traditional values, an attack on humbug and sham. In the political atmosphere of the 1920s such plays could not be publicly performed, and the important private theatres and theatre clubs of the period had often a political as well as an artistic purpose. El Mirlo Blanco, the theatre of the brothers Baroja, staged plays by Valle-Inclán; El Club Anfistora played both Lope de Vega and Lorca. With the coming into power of the Third Republic in 1931, various *teatros proletarios* were formed with the intention of taking drama to the people. The Republic also subsidized two travelling theatres, La Barraca, under the direction of Federico García Lorca and Eduardo Ugarte, which presented classical plays (with the one exception of a theatrical adaptation by García Lorca of a ballad sequence by Antonio Machado); and El Teatro del Pueblo, under the direction of the dramatist Alejandro Casona (1900–65). Casona's own plays have been called *teatro de evasión*, but are rather thesis plays presented in terms of fantasy; he does not attempt to ignore moral responsibilities.

Among the plays presented by Sierra during his management of the Eslava was the first play of Federico García Lorca (1898–1936), an insect play entitled *El maleficio de la mariposa* (1920). Lorca's fame rests most securely on his three great tragedies, *Bodas de sangre* (1933), *Yerma* (1934), and *La casa de Bernarda Alba* (1936). Lorca's career was cut short by the Civil War. A few days after its outbreak he was murdered in Granada. Another victim of the Civil War was Miguel Hernández (1910–1942), who died in prison. His *El labrador de más aire* echoes Lorca's tragedies, but is weaker in conception and poetic force.

The Civil War of 1936–39 brought to a sudden halt a resurgence in the Spanish theatre of solid achievement and high promise. The atmosphere of the years immediately after the war was not conducive to a rebirth of artistic endeavour, and all the arts were slow to recover from the national disaster. Casona, Rafael Alberti (1902–), Pedro Salinas (1892–1951), had left Spain. Immediately after the war, the dramatists who enjoyed the greatest success had all begun their careers before 1936: José María Pemán (1898–), José López Rubio (1903–), Enrique Jardiel Poncela (1901–52), and, above all, Benavente, who continued to write copiously until his death. It was not until the mid-1940s that new dramatists came to the fore. Victor Ruiz Iriarte (1912–) followed at first in the steps of Casona. The first success of Antonio Buero Vallejo (1916–) was *Historia de una escalera* (1949). Alfonso Sastre (1926–) has written *Escuadra hacia la muerte*, *La mordaza*, *El cuervo*, and other moving tragedies. Miguel Mihura (1906–), a satirical dramatist, can combine rich humour with tenderness. In *Maribel y la extraña familia* he exploits a theme which would have delighted Pirandello or Unamuno, but avoids, however, their set seriousness.

The most interesting experiments are to be found in theatre clubs and little theatres. Few classics are staged, and the commercial theatres have relied largely on translations of foreign successes. Nevertheless, as has been demonstrated, the Spanish theatre has in the past absorbed many foreign influences, combining them with indigenous themes and techniques to form a drama which, whilst European, has been truly and deeply Spanish.

J. E. VAREY

SPANISH-AMERICAN THEATRE, see SOUTH AMERICA, 1.

SPECTACLE THEATRES, the name given to the early ornate playhouses of which only Italy has been able to preserve any sixteenth- and seventeenth-century examples. These are Palladio's Teatro Olimpico in Vicenza (see No. 20), Scamozzi's Court Theatre at Sabbioneta (see No. 21), and Aleotti's Teatro Farnese at Parma. This last was partially destroyed by bombing, but is in process of restoration. All these theatres, and many like them which no longer exist, were sumptuously decorated and had finely equipped stages which could deal with the most elaborate settings and machinery (see ARCHITECTURE).

SPECTATORY, see AUDITORIUM.

SPEECH. The appeal of drama is both visual and auditive. Its sound-element, like that of poetry, consists of significant words, both logical and emotional in their appeal. Speech may be considered the most vital element in drama, and the actor's speech is the chief factor in expressing the dramatist's conception of character, particularly in the absence of stage directions, an innovation not generally employed until the first half of the nineteenth century. The dramatist's lines must reach our ear with the exact shade of intonation, of emphasis, and of phrasing required by him. His dialogue and spoken descriptions must convey all we need to know of the two elements of dramatic conflict, character and circumstance.

Speech times the action of a play, and must be timed to suit that action. It is the principal factor in establishing the illusion of time. The author writes the play, but is dependent on those who are trained as actors, and who are the living medium of its representation, for its presentation to the public. The dramatist may, like Shakespeare, have left no stage directions but those implicit in the text, or, like Shaw, he may have left a continuous commentary in the form of directions which make his plays as readable as a novel. In either case the actor must mould his speech to the action, and time his action to the speech, as a dancer moulds himself to the rhythm of his music.

The history of dramatic representation makes this clear. Greek drama originated in a ritual-dance, set to choric words. Its earliest form was a narrative commentary on the dance action. The first great progressive step was the introduction of dialogue, probably antiphonal in character, between the chorus and an actor. In comedy this took a more impromptu and jesting form. The distinction between choric and dramatic delivery may not at first have been clearly marked. Choral lyrics were in the nature of chanted odes illustrated by vivid ritual and mimetic action. There were a number of lyric forms, all with their prescribed ritual character, the very perfection of their traditional form giving significant variety to the scheme of choric action in each different play. The need to blend, and also to contrast, with this ritual measure necessitated a contrasting uniformity in the dramatic passages. This was at first marked by long soliloquy or narrative passages. But with the advent, under Aeschylus, of the second actor, dialogue proper begins, and contrasted character plays its part.

The huge theatres of Athens or Epidaurus imposed a measured delivery, orchestral and lyric in character, and it is interesting to note that the site chosen for a Greek theatre, and its form of construction, gave almost perfect acoustics. The seats rose from the orchestra tier after tier to a huge wall of rock; the actor, standing below, at the central point of the orchestra or against the sounding-board of the wall that hid the *skênê*, can, even in the ruined theatres left us today, make every word audible while his speech maintains its rhythmic character (see ACOUSTICS, 2, and ARCHITECTURE, 1). We know that the Greek audiences were most critical of rhythm and stress, as in the French theatre of 1900.

As we pass from the *Prometheus* to the *Oresteia* and on to the *Iphigenia in Taurus* of Euripides, we see clearly the steady growth in characterization as the actors gained in power of execution, and as the audience demanded a greater reality in the acting. The action develops through the dialogue, and the contrasting character of speech in each person is shown by choice of words, and by the vivid cut-and-thrust of the dialogue. All that was at one time implied by the term 'classic' is foreign to the wild incoherent cries of the Furies, though they never lose their rhythmic pattern, or to the poignant suspense and change of mood in the recognition of Orestes, and the flight of the brother and sister from Thoas's vengeance. Every tradition and comment which has come down to us points to a high, even unique, standard of speech in the Greek theatre. Action, in our sense of the word, was very limited for the tragic actor; the chorus was the orchestration of the play. Without programmes or books of the words, audibility and intelligibility must have demanded unending study.

This is stressed by the comparative rarity of the dramatic festivals, and the high estimation in which great interpreters of drama were held.

All this goes to prove that the two great arts of speech and of plastic rhythm in movement must have transcended any modern achievement. It implies a harmony of author and executant, and demands the technical skill of perfect verse-writing and of diction which is as definite and finished as a musical performance.

To come to modern times, Italian drama was essentially a 'mime' drama, that is, a drama of gesture and action in which only stock characters were employed. The Latin tradition of the Renaissance produced certain splendid plots, but character, and therefore speech, had no free play. Poetry took over the task, and the glorious enrichment of our mother tongue, which culminated in the Authorized Version of the Bible (1611), prepared the way for the miracle of speech which we call Elizabethan drama. The discovery by Marlowe of the perfect vehicle for dramatic speech—blank verse—was the result of many earlier lyric experiments, and of the revival of classical learning. In blank verse we have a line where every verse stress is a sense stress. The stresses must recur at regular intervals of time, but they may be divided by a varying number of unstressed syllables, and the number of the stresses themselves may vary from line to line. The manner of writing, and speaking, this great metric unit varies with every shade of character. Compare Rosalind's 'measure' with that of Beatrice, Hamlet's with Prospero's, Henry V's with Antony's. Then again, it is adjusted to suit the individual actor. Hamlet's 'rant' was made to fit Burbage like a glove; the acquisition of a singing clown gave rise to the lyrics of *Twelfth Night*. Young men trained to impersonate women, with voices which had been carefully safeguarded from too harsh a break, played the Queen in *Hamlet*, Lady Macbeth, Cleopatra. In one magnificent scene the whole technical theory of acting and speech in the theatre is tabulated for us by a dramatist who is himself an actor (see *Hamlet*, Act III, Scene ii). Shakespeare was no university dramatist unable to endure vigour and breadth of delivery. His impeccable ear carries him on from prose to blank verse, from blank verse to couplet, from couplet to lyric. His young lover can speak a sonnet almost unperceived, his clown can jingle his mockery. Lady Macbeth can find a music so incredible in its significance that she can stand motionless almost throughout her part and chain us to her words. Shakespeare's greatest music coincides with his greatest freedom of metric form. Yet he can give Caliban blank verse and Ariel a form of lyric music unique in our literature. Here again in the Elizabethan theatre we have an hour of perfect achievement; master dramatists, a public all lovers of their language and its triumphs, and a theatrical tradition still fresh and vigorous, which one supreme genius rules for over twenty years. This music reaches us only at second hand, and our theatrical tradition was sacrificed to Puritan intransigence. When the theatre revived in 1660 it followed a magnificent, but alien, tradition, that of French diction as created by Molière, together with the formal music of Corneille and Racine. A Court where manners ruled gave us the supreme comedy of manners. The stuff itself was not so great, but the technique of its utterance achieved perfection, and the country it served had the intelligence to see in perfectly spoken drama the one supreme school of a nation's speech. Hence the foundation of the Comédie-Française (1680), and for lack of any such living school of speech in this country we still bear the reproach of speaking our own language worse than any other nation speaks theirs.

Simplicity is Molière's ideal. His comedy is full of sharply defined contrasted character-drawing. His people spoke to their audience in the language of their own day. Like Shakespeare, he mocks the pedant, the *précieux*, with fanciful vocabulary and stilted diction; like him he derides heroic rant, and even more than Shakespeare he demands contrasted team-work in people who are almost all of one social standing and period. Next to the scene in *Hamlet* referred to above, Molière's *Impromptu de Versailles* is the finest lesson to actors ever written, finer than *The Critic* because the end to be achieved is perfection, not the parodying of theatrical faults.

Something of Molière's quality of speech is translated into our own Restoration comedy, particularly in the case of Mirabell and Millamant (*The Way of the World*). Sheridan and his lovely Linley have behind them the great school of song, in which she excelled. The dialogue of *The Rivals* and *The School for Scandal*, and also of *She Stoops to Conquer*, demands diction, not to be confused with the monstrous horror of 'elocution' which was to descend on the untrained, uneducated players of the early nineteenth century, with their perpetual swinging between exaggerated melodrama and stereotyped comedy. The cause of this plague is not far to seek; there were no new plays of contemporary value. Opera had absorbed the interest of the fashionable world, and the evangelical dislike of the theatre closed the door to many lines of dramatic activity. The star actor counted his eccentricities of speech as an asset, and up to the 1860s there was no real sense of style in dialogue. Even then a trifling realism disfigured the real value of the 'cup-and-saucer' comedy. Scenery, production, lighting, crowd effects, costume—these were the standbys of great nineteenth-century revivals. Realism was a matter of *mise en scène* and construction rather than of dialogue. Irving, the greatest tragedian of his time, maintained, until almost the end of his career, an artificial eccentricity of speech which was the delight of the caricaturist. The women did better, but worked on the principle of imitation only. Stage delivery was not human delivery. The reaction to realism suffered from the low standard of everyday speaking, and only with the close of the nineteenth century did saner and more rhythmic standards of utterance return. The Vedrenne–Barker management, with Shaw as its teacher, showed the final swing of the pendulum. Modern players, particularly the women, are fine interpreters of verse, and as good comedians, probably, as England has ever known. Modern speech is, however, threatened by the distortion of the microphone and by the gradual extinction of the art of singing, and no effort should be spared in keeping up the present high standard.

What makes up the equipment of the good speaker? Not an artificial and imitative production, but a diction which physiologically, phonologically, and aesthetically represents the most perfect functional action of which he is individually capable. The true stage voice is a voice physiologically faultless, allied to a mind which can take in accurately before attempting to give out.

The question of speech training for the stage is a big one, but a brief analysis of the elements needed for success may be helpful. Speech includes vocabulary, pronunciation, articulation, utterance, and significant phrasing by stress, pause, and pitch.

Vocabulary may be defined as a knowledge of words and the custom of using them with the most perfect sense of their accepted significance. It is the actor's lifelong study, since he must possess an historical as well as a contemporary knowledge of his own language, and a quick capacity for the acquisition of certain foreign words and idioms.

Pronunciation is based on phonetic standard and customary use. It includes the quick recognition of vowel quality and of syllabic stress. The noun 're′cord' and the verb 'recor′d', for instance, are distinguished by a change of stress, and a modification of the quality of the first vowel sound. Historically, Hamlet should substitute the verbal for the substantive pronunciation in the phrase 'I'll wipe away all trivial fond recor′ds'.

Articulation is the muscular action of jaw, lips, and tongue in framing the rhythm of speech. Its characteristics are lightness, precision, and unconscious control. A speaker may select the correct combination for the word 'thermometer', and stress the word correctly. Defective dentition may confer the knighthood of 'Sir Nometer' on the word, or a bad cold in the head reduce it to 'Der-bo-be-tah'. Good articulation is a matter of physical training.

Utterance implies the addition of vocal tone to the perfect articulatory action. It calls for the co-ordination of breath, phonation, resonation, and pitch variety, with the previous qualities of speech listed above. Above all, it aims at a perfect co-ordination of sound and significance which in the actor must become altogether automatic. Its standard is not a matter of opinion but of physiological correctness and aesthetic perfection.

Phrasing links all the preceding qualities into the significant expression of a complete thought: a sentence, affirmative or interrogative; a command, or a plea; a parenthesis or a contradiction. Every line of the actor's part requires this knowledge and the power of instantly imitating a given reading from the producer, or in response to a comrade's line. It is the basis of all team-work in speech. The unending study of rhythmic speech in great prose or verse is the basis of the whole achievement. The aim is unconscious automatic perfection.

The success of the performer depends on his capacity, first, for receiving sound-impressions and translating them into sense, and, secondly, for giving out such impressions with original significance even though the words themselves are none of his choosing and convey a meaning foreign to his character and mood. The French stage is our master in all that concerns this great art, which is called the Art of Diction. Behind the actor's success lies always the combination of imagination and technique. The question of emotional self-transformation or technical skill at the time of performance is a purely personal one. It may vary during the repetitions of a long run, or according to the mental philosophy of a Coquelin or a Kean, but one thing is certain: speech is fundamentally a technical matter, a question of perfect motor action placed at the service of the mind. Passion will no more render a hideous phonation endurable than extra acceleration will improve the running of a motor-car with a flat tyre.

What is it then to speak badly? It is to use an impoverished vocabulary eked out with slang and an utterance depending on custom and on phonetic standard, not on phonological principles and the practice of great poets. The nature of good speech is like that of all good art. It is not a mimicry of any artificial standard. It is a perfect fitting of our physiological instrument for significant and emotional and aesthetic uses. It is not an artificial constancy of pronunciation. It is no great matter whether you say I-ther or EE-ther; what excoriates the listener's ear is the yapping nasal whine of something for which our alphabet has no symbol, a tight-shut nasal 'Oiver'.

Our national art is the drama. Our national inheritance is the greatest and most widespread language man has ever spoken. Every Englishman should know, and practise his knowledge of, these facts. ELSIE FOGERTY†

SPELVIN, George, a fictitious stage name used in the cast-lists of American theatrical productions. It is first found in New York in 1886, in Charles A. Gardiner's play, *Karl the Peddler*. Spelvin's usefulness as a playbill identity to cover doubling persisted through the managements of George C. Tyler and William Collier, Sr. The latter, with his partner, Charles Reed, even gave him credit for gags used in a comedy, *Hoss and Hoss* (1895). He appeared in almost all the plays of Winchell Smith, and the late John Golden carried the tradition into the contemporary theatre. It is estimated that George Spelvin or his relatives (for several variations of the

Christian name have been used) have figured in more than 10,000 Broadway performances since George's début. The name has also been applied, theatrically, to dead bodies, dolls substituting for babes in arms, and animal actors. *Theatre Arts* magazine has sporadically featured a critic of the critics who masquerades under Spelvin's name (for the English equivalent of Spelvin, see PLINGE).

ROBERT DOWNING

SPENCER, GABRIEL (?–1598), an Elizabethan actor often described by his first name only. He was a member of the Admiral's Company at the time of his death, and was killed by Ben Jonson during a duel in Hoxton Fields on 22 Sept., having himself two years previously killed his opponent in a duel.

SPENCER, JOHN (?), one of the best known of the English Comedians on the Continent, where he first appears in 1605. He continued to tour the Netherlands and Germany until 1623, and was known evidently as a clown, taking for his pseudonym the name Hans Stockfisch, analogous to the Pickelherring of Robert Reynolds.

SPERONI, SPERONE (1500-88), Italian dramatist, whose *Canace* (1543) is considered the most horrible of the many bloodthirsty tragedies of this period. Dealing with incestuous love, and ending with a pile of corpses, it caused fierce controversy when it was first performed at Padua (see ITALY, 1 *b* i).

SPIEGELBERG, CHRISTIAN (?–1732), a German actor-manager, who first acted under Velten, and later assumed the leadership of a young company which toured extensively, from Scandinavia, across Europe, to Russia. It was with this company that the famous German actress, Caroline Neuber, made her first appearance.

SPOTBLOCK, a pulley block set in the grid for a special purpose, such as the suspension of a chandelier.

SPOTLIGHT, see LIGHTING, 2.

STAGE. 1. The space in which the actors appear before the audience is the stage. In its simplest form this may be only a cleared area with the audience standing or sitting all round, indoors or out, with or without a raised platform; in its most complicated—as in the proscenium theatre—it is an elaborate structure with a raked stage floor, surmounted by a fly-floor and a grid, with a cellar underneath to house the machinery needed for working traps and mechanical scene-changing. In this case the boards of the stage floor will be removable to permit the passage of actors and props from the cellar. An intermediate form of stage is the high platform built against a permanent wall-structure, with a cellar underneath. This may or may not have an enclosed space above for the provision of simple scenic effects. The spaces adjacent to the stage proper, used by actors and stage staff, form the backstage area. In the Restoration theatre that part of the stage floor which was in front of the proscenium arch was known as the apron, or forestage.

2. The word stage is also used of the whole ensemble of acting and theatre production as in 'the history of the English stage', excluding the texts of the plays, which belong to dramatic literature. To be 'on the stage' is to be an actor; to be 'on stage' is to appear in the scene then being played; off-stage refers to a position close to the stage, but invisible, though not inaudible, to the audience.

STAGE BRACE, an extensible rod which supports a flat, or piece, being hooked to the back of the flat at one end and attached to the floor by a stage screw, or weighted by a braceweight, at the other end. A variant, composed of a right-angled triangle of wood hinged to the flat, opened out and weighted, is known as a French Brace.

STAGE-CLOTH, see CLOTH.

STAGE DIRECTIONS, or notes added to the script of a play to convey information about its performance not already explicit in the dialogue itself. Generally speaking, they are concerned with (*a*) the actor's movements, (*b*) the scenery or stage effects.

Stage directions concerning the actor's movements are, in the English theatre, based on two important peculiarities: they are all relative to the position of an actor facing the audience—right and left are therefore reversed from the spectator's point of view—and they all date from the period when the stage was raked, or sloped upwards, towards the back. Thus, movement towards the audience is said to be Down-stage, and a movement away from the audience is Up-stage. (A derivative use of the latter word arises in stage slang when any haughty behaviour is said to be 'up-stage'.)

The simplest examples of stage directions relating to the actor's movements are such single words as 'enters', 'sits', 'stands', 'turns'. To these may be added two instructions whose grammar is hallowed by tradition, and in the latter of which a very interesting convention is recalled—they are *Exit* and *Manet*. *Exit* ('he goes out', originally *Exeat*, 'let him go out') has today become an English word in its own right, inflected by theatrical people as a normal verb; hence, 'you exit here', 'he exits', 'they exit', and so forth are now common usage, while *Exeunt* has become pedantic save in the conventional phrase *Exeunt omnes*, and *Exeant* is almost unknown. The antithesis, *Manet* ('he remains'), is far less commonly seen, but it was used as far back at least as 1698 to indicate the remaining of a character on the stage while the others went off—especially at the end of a scene, when it implied that the player remained through the visible change of scenery and proceeded with the action directly the following scene was in place, thus carrying on the flow of the play without a break.

Directions may also indicate change of position on the stage—for instance, the word

'Crosses', which is an instruction to the player to go across the stage, either for practical reasons, so as to reach a given object, or for technical reasons, so as to provide a break in a passage otherwise without action. A 'Scissor Cross' is the crossing of two characters from opposite directions simultaneously and (unless arranged as an intentional effect) is regarded as an ugly move significant of clumsy technique.

It is when actual direction of movement is indicated that the two conventional peculiarities of English usage become apparent. The acting area of the stage is supposed to be divided approximately into nine main zones, three situated Down-stage (that is, in front), three Up-stage (that is, at the back), and three across the centre between the other two. The zones are called (front) Down Left, Down Centre, and Down Right; (back) Up Left, Up Centre, and Up Right; (middle) Left, Centre, and Right. Further subdivisions are indicated around the centre zone by Up Left Centre, Down Left Centre, and similarly for the right side. Three further terms relating to the back-wall of the scene are Centre Back, Left and Right Centre Back. All these terms are usually abbreviated to initials when writing. Lateral movements to or from the centre line of the stage are described as movements On or Off respectively, the extent of the movement being generally qualified by an adverb; thus, while 'to go off' is equivalent to *Exit*, 'to go off a little' is limited to partial withdrawal to the side.

Movement round an object is, according to the conventional usage, expressed in terms of height, alluding to the old sloping stage. Thus an actor is not told to go 'behind' or 'in front of' a table, but 'above' it or 'below' it. Such an apparently odd form of direction becomes justified in considering a movement round, say, a sofa, when it will be seen that 'Go in front of the sofa' is an equivocal instruction if the sofa has its back to the audience.

A further variety of stage directions is found in melodrama and earlier plays, where such terms as R.U.E. and L.2.E. are found. These relate to the times when all side-walls of scenes were composed of separate wings, and the Entrance was the passage between one wing and its neighbour. Thus R.U.E. signifies Right Upper Entrance, and L.2.E. Left Second Entrance—the first entrance being that between the proscenium wing and the first wing of the scene proper. A further, and earlier, variant of this method of terminology (found as far back as 1748) was to indicate an entrance, or the position of a piece of scenery, as 'in the second [&c.] grooves'; this signified that the piece of scenery slid in, and was supported by, those particular grooves, or that the entrance took place immediately behind them. In 1887, moreover, it was possible to say that a backcloth hung 'in the 3rd grooves', though that backcloth had nothing to do with the grooves save that, in this particular case, it hung in the space between the third and fourth sets.

Any note on stage directions must include mention of the two curious and apparently redundant terms Prompt Side and Opposite Prompt. Rarely in actual stage conversation is the former term ever alluded to by initials, while its opposite is as rarely alluded to in full. But in writing, P.S. and O.P. are generally used. This applies only to the English-speaking theatre, where the Prompt Side is usually accepted as the stage left, and O.P. as the stage right (though in some theatres the prompter's corner is found on the right). The Prompt Corner, in the British theatre, is a desk against the inner side of the proscenium wall where the prompter installs his Prompt Book (a copy of the play, generally interleaved, and carrying the full directions and warnings necessary to the management of the production), and where a board of switches for signals, communicating to various parts of the theatre, is generally situated. Among the signals is the Bar Bell to warn patrons in the bars and foyers of the approaching end of an interval. On the Continent the Prompter's Box is usually sunk beneath a coved hood in the centre of the footlights. Hence in English theatres presenting opera the central prompter's box is sometimes seen.

Stage directions covering scenery are, today, generally self-explanatory descriptions of the layout and appearance of the stage for the scene in question, and offer little for special comment beyond the conventions for describing positions explained above. The history of stage directions does, however, contain some special expressions. In Elizabethan and Restoration plays the location of the scene is often not specified, and was, in fact, frequently not held as of great importance; in the earlier period the location of a scene was the stage, and there was little serious attempt to make the stage look like, or mean, some other place. This attitude remained to some extent after the introduction of scenery, but, though actual location was still sometimes not specified (or limited to, say, 'Don Diego's House', without indication of any particular room, or even whether exterior or interior), a new direction was now needed indicating what happened at the scene-change, though how the scene appeared might be left to the presenter. Thus we read 'The scene draws' or 'draws off', indicating that the two flats of the back-scene were opened to disclose the next scene. Or we have 'The scene draws over' or 'closes in' (the latter term used in a poetic sense even as late as 1892 when all reference to its original significance had passed). Further, we have what is so frequently misunderstood, the simple 'The scene closes' and 'The scene opens'; such directions referred to the actual movement of the scenery.

Many technical directions have crept unintended into published plays based on original prompter's scripts. These are often of high interest to students. In Theobald's *The Perfidious Brothers* published in 1715 and acted at Lincoln's Inn Fields a year later, the initials U.D.P.S., M.D.O.P., and L.D.P.S. (indicating Upper, Middle, or Lower Doors on Prompt or Opposite Prompt Sides) show the use of six proscenium doors in the early eighteenth-century playhouse.

A further development in the form of stage directions, but one chiefly intended to facilitate the wider reading of plays by the general public, came about the end of the nineteenth century. Ibsen's descriptions of the appearance of the details of his scenes and his characters were full and careful. Bernard Shaw went even further in this direction in his printed plays, and Granville-Barker, Barrie, and others all tended to change the stage direction from a technical thing to a readable thing, designed to refer less and less to the means of the stage itself, but to define more and more the effects those means must achieve. RICHARD SOUTHERN

STAGE DIRECTOR, see PRODUCER, 2.

STAGE DOOR. This, situated at the back or side of the theatre, provides the link between the street and the stage. Through it pass the actors and stage hands, and authorized visitors, to gain the dressing-rooms, rehearsal-rooms, and various offices. Access to these, and to the business offices, can also be obtained via the front entrance of the theatre. Immediately inside the stage door is the cubicle, usually with a glass front, of the stage-door keeper (more properly designated the hall keeper), a permanent and important member of the theatre staff. It is his business to check the arrival and departure of all who frequent the theatre, to prevent unauthorized persons from entering, to receive and transmit telephone and other messages. He keeps a jealously guarded list of the home addresses and telephone numbers of actors in the current show, not to be divulged except under extreme pressure, receives their letters and parcels, and occasionally executes commissions for them. A good stage-door keeper is a valuable adjunct to any theatre, and often the staunch friend and ally of the actor, particularly of the leading players, protecting them from the curiosity of 'fans', who gather outside the stage door after the performance to see the actors leave, and to obtain autographs. Just inside the stage door is the Call Board or Notice Board on which calls for rehearsal and all important information for the company is posted, including the dreaded 'Notice' informing them of the end of the play's run. In Elizabethan times the Stage door—or Tiring House door—was the only entrance to the theatre except for the main front entrance, and was used by those members of the audience who had seats on the stage.

STAGE EFFECTS, see MACHINERY and TRICKWORK ON THE ENGLISH STAGE.

STAGE-KEEPER, a functionary of the Elizabethan theatre who was responsible for the sweeping and clearing of the acting space, and probably for other odd jobs.

STAGE LIGHTING, see LIGHTING.

STAGE PROPERTIES, see PROPS.

STAGE RAKE, the slope of the stage floor from the back to the footlights. This had once a definite purpose in that it aided the illusion of scenes painted in perspective. With the passing of such scenes it ceased to have any practical purpose, since, contrary to traditional belief, it did not give the dancer a better basis for a leap, nor did it make the actors up-stage more visible to the audience. This is better done by grouping them on rostrums at least a foot higher than the group in front. The raked stage, which has a long and traditional history, is limited in practice to a slope of 4 per cent., and was often as small as 1½ per cent. It had serious disadvantages in the setting of scenery, as pieces set diagonally could not join neatly to squarely vertical neighbours; also the side-flats of a box-set needed fox wedges under the base of each to compensate for the slope, or else they had to be built out of true with sloping bottom rails, and ceased to be interchangeable. Moreover, any setting of pieces on a boat truck became dangerous, since the truck might run off on its own down the incline. The modern practice is to have a flat stage floor, and to rake the floor of the auditorium (see ARCHITECTURE).

STAGE SETTING, a term sometimes used to define the arrangement of a stage (with curtains, &c.) in such a way as to provide a general background suitable for any play, as distinct from scenery, which is suitable for one play or part of a play only (see SET).

STAGE SOCIETY, THE INCORPORATED, LONDON. This was founded in 1899 for the production of plays of artistic merit which stood very little chance of performance in a commercial theatre. These were to be given with a West End cast at a West End theatre for one, or at the most two, performances. One consequence of this policy was that productions were, of necessity, given on Sunday nights, since only then were West End theatres available. This led to a police raid on the Royalty Theatre on 26 Nov. 1899, when the Society's first production took place there. This was Shaw's *You Never Can Tell*, incidentally the first performance of this play.

The original group of sponsors, which included Frederick Whelen, William Sharp (Fiona Macleod), W. Lee Mathews, Sydney Olivier (afterwards Lord Olivier), Hector Thomas, and H. A. Hertz, were enthusiasts for the theatre and dissatisfied with its condition at that time, but they had little professional connexion with it, and it may be that much of their success was attributable to that fact. They were amateurs in the best sense. How firmly they adhered to their original admirable intentions may be seen by the list of the society's productions, which number more than 200. It includes the first production in England of a number of Shaw's plays, as well as of plays by such foreign dramatists as Hauptmann, Gorky, Gogol, Wedekind, Kaiser,

Pirandello, J. J. Bernard, Afinogenov, Cocteau, and Odets.

In 1930 the then Council of the Stage Society considered that its work was done, owing to the emergence of such groups as the Gate Theatre, and suggested that it should be wound up. The proposal was defeated by an overwhelming majority, and a leading article in *The Times* for 2 Dec. 1930 said: 'The Stage Society has by its own excellence created for itself a trust which cannot lightly be abandoned.' With the outbreak of the Second World War in 1939 the society fell into abeyance and was not revived. Much of its later work was done under the aegis of W. S. Kennedy, who was elected to the council in 1907 and served it in various capacities until 1938. It is interesting to note that the Stage Society was the first body to sponsor plays on Sunday since the days of Charles I, and that the Vedrenne–Barker management at the Court Theatre may be said to have arisen out of its activities. In 1927 the Stage Society was amalgamated with the Three Hundred Club, also a Sunday play-producing society, founded in 1924 by Phyllis Bell, wife of Geoffrey Whitworth, which produced some interesting modern plays, including van Druten's *Young Woodley*, Ackerley's *Prisoners of War*, and D. H. Lawrence's *David*.

STAGE SWITCHBOARD, see LIGHTING, 2.

STAGG, CHARLES and his wife MARY (*fl.* early eighteenth century), actors and teachers of dancing, who in 1718 were in possession of a theatre built by a merchant in Williamsburg. Nothing is known of their activities, but after the death of Charles in 1735 his widow was in charge of dancing assemblies in the same town. There is a possibility that the Staggs may have prepared and produced a play given in 1718 before the Governor of Virginia. Their names figure in the earliest records of professional entertainment in the New World.

STAGNELIUS, ERIK JOHANN (1793–1823), Swedish poet, author of a number of poetic plays staged in Stockholm (see SCANDINAVIA, 3 *a*).

STAIRCASE-SIDE, see FLAT.

STALL, the name given in the modern theatre to the individual seats between the stage front and the pit, those nearest the stage being known as Orchestra Stalls. They first appeared in the 1830s to 1840s, after the raising of the first circle had allowed the pit to extend further back, and are considered by most people to be the best seats in the house, an honour claimed by some, however, for the central seats of the front row of the Dress Circle. The Stalls are, with the exception of Boxes, the most expensive seats in the theatre. They were at one time called by their French name of *fauteuils*, which was then taken by extension to mean the whole area of stalls, including the Orchestra Stalls. In some theatres the term Balcony Stalls was applied to the front rows of the Dress Circle.

RICHARD SOUTHERN

STANDARD THEATRE. 1. LONDON, in Shoreditch. This theatre opened in 1835 as the Royal Standard and in 1837, when its records begin, was under the management of Johnson and Lee. They remodelled it in 1845 and called it the New Standard. It was up for sale in 1849, and was taken over by John Douglass, who, like Nelson Lee, had been a showman. After his death it was run by his sons. It was burned down in 1866 and rebuilt on a larger scale, reopening in 1868 as the Standard. It had a good stock company, and was the first of the north-east suburban theatres to attract visiting stars from the West End. This gave it a position of some importance and drew good audiences. It was one of the largest theatres in London, and while Richard Douglass was in charge its pantomimes rivalled those of Drury Lane and the neighbouring Hoxton Britannia. The Melville family, afterwards connected for so long with the Lyceum, ran it successfully for a considerable period, a feature of their management being the annual visit of the J. W. Turner Opera Company. The growth of other suburban theatres eventually robbed the Standard of its audiences and, like so many others of its kind, it became a cinema. It was destroyed by enemy action in 1940–1 (for a poster of a production at this theatre see No. 171).

W. MACQUEEN-POPE†

For the Royal Standard, Pimlico, London, see VICTORIA PALACE.

2. NEW YORK. This opened as the Eagle on 18 Oct. 1875, and had a prosperous career as a home of variety and light entertainment. Renamed the Standard, it witnessed on 15 Jan. 1879 the first production in New York of *H.M.S. Pinafore*, which had a sensational success. It ran for 175 nights, and was soon being played everywhere. An unsuccessful season in 1880 had for its only success Annie Pixley as M'liss in Bret Harte's play, and shortly afterwards the theatre changed hands at a very low price. *Patience*, beginning on 22 Sept. 1881, ran for a whole season, as did *Iolanthe* in the following year. On 14 Dec. 1883 the theatre was destroyed by fire, but it was rebuilt and reopened on 23 Dec. 1884, again as a home of light opera. In 1897, renamed the Manhattan, it opened again as a playhouse with *What Happened to Jones*. It became a cinema a few years later, and in 1909 was demolished to make way for a department store, Gimbel's, which still stands on the site.

STANFIELD, CLARKSON (1793–1867), English scenic artist, son of an actor and author. He was for some years in the Merchant Navy, and first painted scenery for the Royalty Theatre in Wellclose Square. In 1831 he worked in the Theatre Royal, Edinburgh, and returned to London to become scenic director at the Coburg and eventually at Drury Lane. By 1834 he had exhibited with such success at the Royal Academy that he gave up scene-painting as a profession, though he did some work for Macready's pantomime in 1837 and again in 1842. He was also a friend of Charles Dickens, for whose private production of *The Frozen Deep* at Tavistock House he painted the backcloth. His last theatrical work was a drop-scene for the New Adelphi which he painted for his friend Ben Webster in 1858.

STANISLAVSKY, KONSTANTIN SERGEIVICH (1863–1938), Russian actor, producer, and teacher, whose real name was Alexeyev. He began by acting in amateur productions at his own home and elsewhere. With a growing interest in the professional theatre he observed and analysed the great actors of the time—Salvini, Rossi, Yermolova, Sadovsky, Lensky—attended a theatrical school, and finally began a more systematic course of study under F. P. Komisarjevsky (father of Vera and Theodore and himself a dramatist and producer). He played in vaudeville, operetta, drama, and comedy, and was at one time prepared to embark on an operatic career. In all these ways he revealed his passion for work, his profound self-criticism, and his rare quality for systematizing and generalizing his experience. In 1888, together with the elder Komisarjevsky and Fedotov (son of a well-known actor), he founded the Society of Literature and Art, whose aim was to bring together workers from all spheres of art for the systematic presentation of good plays. At first Stanislavsky was an actor in the amateur group of the society, later he became its producer. In 1891 he produced for the first time on the Russian stage Tolstoy's *The Fruits of Enlightenment*, and a dramatization of Dostoievsky's *Sela Stepanchikov*. These brought him to the notice of the public; his further productions brought him fame.

At this period Stanislavsky was working mainly under the influence of the Meininger company, famous on the Continent for its historically exact décor and costumes and for the elaborate detail of its productions, especially in crowd scenes. From it he took the striving for historical truth, the superb method of producing crowd scenes, and the smooth running of the whole. He rejected its somewhat declamatory style of acting, seeking rather simplicity and truth. In 1898 he and Nemirovich-Danchenko jointly founded the Moscow Art Theatre, with which their names are indissolubly linked. This created a new epoch in the development of Russian, and indeed of world, theatre art. In its first productions (Tolstoy's *Tsar Feodor Ivanovich*, 1898; Ostrovsky's *Snow Maiden*, 1900; Tolstoy's *Power of Darkness*, 1902; Shakespeare's *Julius Caesar*, 1903) Stanislavsky continued and developed the ideas he had expounded for the Society of Literature and Art. Away with all theatricality, all pompous, stereotyped mannerisms; the stage and the actor must give the complete illusion of reality. Thus the Moscow Art Theatre became the home of theatrical naturalism.

Among Stanislavsky's greatest achievements were the productions of Chekhov's plays, *The Seagull* in 1898, *Uncle Vanya* in 1899, *Three Sisters* in 1901 (see No. 95), and *The Cherry Orchard* in 1904. These mark a further stage in the development of Stanislavsky's style, the accent being transferred from the external to the internal, from the truth of history, manners, and customs to the truth of feelings, moods, and expressions. He produced the plays as lyric dramas, underlining the emotional elements with music, and showing how Chekhov's apparently passive dialogue demands great subtlety, and a psychological internal development of the role with great simplicity of external expression.

During the years of upheaval leading to the uprising of 1905 Stanislavsky produced the plays of that 'stormy petrel of the Revolution', Maxim Gorky, including *The Lower Depths*. In the years of reaction (1905–16) he turned to the Symbolists—Maeterlinck and Andreyev—and aestheticized, stylized productions. Under the Soviet régime, after an initial period of adjustment, he continued his work as a fine producer of both old and new plays (see MOSCOW ART THEATRE and No. 99). He was himself a superb character actor, and through long and persistent practice he raised his technique to a high pitch of perfection. His temperament was deep, powerful, but controlled. Among his best roles were Astrov in *Uncle Vanya*, Vershinin in *Three Sisters*, Gayev in *The Cherry Orchard*, Dr. Stockmann in *An Enemy of the People*, and Rakitin in *A Month in the Country*. In later years, owing to ill health, he gave up acting, but continued to work as a producer and teacher. He left a record of his ideas and methods in his books, *My Life in Art* (1924) and *An Actor Prepares* (1926), and in two works published posthumously, *Stanislavsky Rehearses Othello* (1948) and *Building a Character* (1950) (see METHOD, THE).

STAR THEATRE, NEW YORK. This was Lester Wallack's second theatre, and when he left it became the home of plays in German until 23 Mar. 1882, when it opened as the Star, taking the place of Booth's. It was at this theatre on 29 Oct. 1883 that Irving made his first appearance in New York, appearing with Ellen Terry and his Lyceum company under the management of Henry E. Abbey. He confined himself to modern plays, not wishing to challenge Booth in Shakespeare, and his staging, lighting, and acting proved a revelation to New York audiences. Later visitors to the Star were Booth himself, Modjeska in Barrymore's *Nadjezda*, John McCullough on his farewell visit to New York, Mary Anderson, returning after two years in London, Bernhardt in her most popular parts, and Wilson Barrett.

STARKE, JOHANNE CHRISTIANE (1731–1809), a fine tragic and emotional German actress, who became the leading lady of Koch's company at Leipzig. Her only rival in her own line was Sophie Hensel, but the latter's evil temper and intriguing nature often lost her the sympathy of the audience, whereas Johanne Starke retained her friends, on stage and off. She was excellent as Miss Sara Sampson in Lessing's play of that name, and later played older, maternal and lachrymose roles to perfection. When her tragic style became somewhat outmoded she turned to comedy, and was a great success as comic elderly women. She played for a time under Ekhof at Gotha, and went with the company to Mannheim after his death.

STEAD, JAMES HENRY (?–1886), a music-hall performer who achieved fame with one song from which he took his nickname 'The Perfect Cure'. It was written by a song-writer named Tom Perry, and Stead first sang it at Weston's Music-Hall (afterwards the Holborn Empire). All through the 1870s it created a furore, not so much on account of the song, perhaps, as of the curious dance which accompanied it. Dressed in a suit with very broad stripes running down it, his pale face painted with red cheeks like a Dutch doll and adorned with a small moustache and imperial, the whole surmounted by a clown's hat, Stead bounded up and down all the time he was singing, with his hands held tightly by his side. He is said to have made as many as sixteen hundred leaps at each performance. He never found another song to equal 'The Perfect Cure', and when its vogue waned he fell on bad times, and died in poverty in an attic in Seven Dials.

W. MACQUEEN-POPE†

STEELE, SIR RICHARD (1672–1729), English soldier, politician, essayist, pamphleteer, and incidentally dramatist, in which capacity he was one of the first to temper the licentiousness of the Restoration drama with sentimental moralizing. His work for the theatre falls into two periods, the first covering his three early comedies, *The Funeral* (1701), a satire on the fashionable parade of grief, *The Lying Lover* (1703), an amusing trifle spoiled by a priggish last act, and *The Tender Husband* (1705), which, like its predecessors, had only a short run and a moderate success. Steele then turned his energies to *The Tatler* and *The Spectator*, though remaining in close touch with the theatrical world, particularly Drury Lane, and it was not until 1722 that he produced his last, and most important, play, *The Conscious Lovers*, a sentimentalized adaptation of Terence's *Andria*, marked throughout by a high moral tone and given under Colley Cibber's supervision with an excellent cast which included Booth, Wilks, and Mrs. Oldfield. It was a great success, and was immediately translated into German and French, exercising an immense influence on the current European drift towards *la comédie larmoyante*. Steele was the founder and editor of the first English theatrical paper, *The Theatre*, which appeared twice a week from 1719 to 1720.

STEINBECK, JOHN (1902–68), American writer, best known as a novelist, who qualified as a playwright with dramatizations of his short published novels *Of Mice and Men* and *The Moon Is Down*, which were already dramatic both in structure and in dialogue. Born in Salinas, California, of German and Irish descent, Steinbeck worked as an itinerant farm-hand in his youth, and later as foreman on a ranch and as a chemist in a sugar refinery. After some desultory education at Leland Stanford University he worked as a manual labourer and as a reporter in New York. Returning to California, he began to write the novels that won him a reputation without assuring him a livelihood until he published *Of Mice and Men*. The play taken from that novel was produced in 1937 and won the Drama Critics' Prize in 1938 for its realistic picture of itinerant labour and the tragic story of a feeble-minded farm-hand. Steinbeck's second play, *The Moon Is Down* (1942), which was more favourably received in Europe than in New York, dramatized the occupation of a peaceful town by the Germans, and its resistance movement.

JOHN GASSNER†

STERNHEIM, CARL (1878–1943), German dramatist, whose bitter anti-bourgeois satires have caused him to be likened to Molière and Wycherley. The son of a banker, he took delight in flaying the snobbery and petty-mindedness of his immediate circle. His plays deal with social climbers, newly enriched millionaires, weak-kneed would-be gallants, and financial jugglers. His biting humour, enhanced by his telegraphic style, reminiscent of the expressionists, struck a new note in the German theatre of his time, and he ranks as one of the few modern German dramatists to succeed in comedy. Among his plays the most successful were *Die Hose* (1911), *Bürger Schippel* (1912), *Der Snob* (1913), *Tabula Rasa* (1916), *Libussa* and *Der Nebbich* (both 1922). A revival of *Der Snob* was the first play to be produced in Berlin after the defeat of the Nazis in 1945. Sternheim's last play was *Oscar Wilde* (1925). In 1962 a translation by Eric Bentley of *Die Hose* as *The Knickers* was brought to London in the repertory of the Margate Stage Company.

STEVENSON, WILLIAM (?–1575), a Fellow of Christ's College, Cambridge, who is believed to have been the author of *Gammer Gurton's Needle*, a play which, with Udall's *Ralph Roister Doister*, stands at the beginning of English comedy. No definite date can be assigned for its performance, but it was probably given at Cambridge between 1552 and 1563. It was printed in 1575, the year of Stevenson's death, and may be identical with a play referred to as *Diccon the Bedlam*, the name of the chief character in *Gammer Gurton's Needle*. This play has also been attributed, with little likelihood, to Dr. John Still, Bishop of Bath and Wells in 1593, and to Dr. John Bridges, who is mentioned as its author in the *Martin Marprelate* tracts. It is possible that Bridges may have assisted Stevenson in the composition of the play, since he is known to have been a prolific writer of verse and a noted wit; or he may have revised it for a later performance. Although structurally the play conforms to the classic type, its material is native English, and one of its characters, Hodge, has given his name to the conventional English farm labourer.

STEWART, JOHN, see PITLOCHRY and SCOTLAND.

STICHOMYTHIA, a type of dialogue employed occasionally in Greek classical drama, in which two characters speak single lines of verse alternately during passages of emotional tension or forceful disputation. The device has been likened to 'alternate strokes of hammers on the anvil'. It has been used in English drama, notably in Shakespeare's *Richard III* (e.g. Act I, Scene ii, lines 193–203), and the clipped prose dialogue in some of the plays of the 1920s (Noël Coward's among them) may be thought to derive, however remotely and indirectly, from the Greek practice. It is, however, essentially a poetic device, and its effectiveness even in verse drama depends upon a carefully limited employment. It is sometimes referred to as 'cut-and-parry' or 'cut-and-thrust' dialogue.

STIERNHIELM, GEORG (1598–1672), Swedish dramatist, author of a number of imitations of contemporary French masques, much patronized by the Court.

STILE, the vertical side-piece of a flat.

STILL, JOHN, see STEVENSON, WILLIAM.

STIRLING. (1) FANNY [really MARY ANNE KEHL] (1815–95), English actress, who made her first appearance at the East London in 1829 as Fanny Clifton. Here she met and married an actor (2) EDWARD STIRLING [really LAMBERT] (1809–94), who had made his first appearance on the stage in 1828. He wrote some 200 plays, many of them based on the novels of Dickens, and produced either at the Lyceum or at the Adelphi, of which he was stage-manager with Frederick Yates. He was also the author of a volume of reminiscences published in 1881. His wife appeared under his management at the Adelphi, and had a successful career in soubrette and comedy roles, though she was not good in Shakespeare or in tragedy. In later years her acting was thought somewhat extravagant, but she was one of the last exponents of the grand style in comedy. Peg Woffington in *Masks and Faces* supplied her with one of her best parts, while in her later years she had no equal as Mrs. Malaprop, Mrs. Candour, and Juliet's Nurse. In 1870 she retired from the stage, but gave recitals and taught elocution. On her husband's death she married again, becoming Lady Gregory, but died a year later.

STOCK COMPANY, a theatrical troupe which was regularly attached to a particular theatre or group of theatres, operating on a true repertory basis with a nightly change of bill. The term seems to have come into use about the mid-nineteenth century, probably in order to distinguish a regular, resident company from a touring one. The system was, however, in existence long before that, and the name would have been applicable to the companies attached to the patent theatres in London from the Restoration onwards, and to the eighteenth-century circuit companies in the provinces. The early nineteenth-century theatres in New York, Boston, Philadelphia, and other centres in the United States, were also occupied by stock companies, which, as in England, found themselves threatened by the establishment of the long run, and, in the provinces, by the competition of the touring companies. By 1880 the touring company, assisted by cheap and easy railway transport, had triumphed, and the stock companies had practically ceased to exist. The last of the old stock companies in London was that of Irving at the Lyceum. They had been excellent training grounds for young actors, giving them variety of acting experience together with some permanence and security. Something of the same function is now performed by the repertory companies, but their weekly or fortnightly change of bill gives a less wide range of parts, with practically no repetition. (The Nottingham Playhouse, with its nightly change of bill, is an exception.) A revival of the stock company playing in repertoire was instituted by the Royal Shakespeare company at the Aldwych in 1961, and by the National Theatre company at the Old Vic in 1963. The state-subsidized theatres of the Continent, such as the Comédie-Française and the theatres of Soviet Russia, approximate to the old stock company, but the enormous increase in the size of the potential audience has made the constant change of bill unnecessary and uneconomic, added to which the modern audience has come to rely on a continuous run and tends to be bewildered by the true repertory system. An attempt to establish something of the kind in New York has not yet proved successful.

The old stock company was formed of a group of actors each of whom undertook some special line of business. The Tragedian, who was also the leading man, took such parts as Hamlet and Macbeth—though he also appeared in comedy. The Old Man played Sir Anthony Absolute and Sir Peter Teazle, and was a person of consequence. The Old Woman took Juliet's Nurse. The Heavy Father or Heavy Lead was a term which came into use about 1830 to describe tyrants and villains in tragedy and melodrama; while the Heavy Woman played the more mature parts in tragedy, such as Lady Macbeth, or Emilia in *Othello*. The Juvenile Lead was the young lover and hero, and the Juvenile Tragedian took on Macduff or Laertes, often combining such parts with light comedy roles. The Low Comedian played leading comic parts of a broad, farcical, or clownish type, and was usually apportioned minor roles in tragedy, while the Walking Lady or Gentleman played secondary parts in comedy, such as Careless in *The School for Scandal*. These roles were usually given to beginners and the salary was low. General Utility played minor roles in any and every type of play—'to have the most to do—the least notice of doing it—and receive the lowest salary' was how Leman Rede described it in *The Road to the Stage* (1827). A Super, or Supernumerary, was an actor or actress who was engaged merely to walk on in a particular play in addition to the regular company, and had nothing to say. Such persons were often not paid at all. Among other members of a stock company were such specialists as the Leading or First Singer, or Vocalist, the Principal Dancer, the Singing Chambermaid, the Countryman and the Singing Countryman (see also PROVINCIAL THEATRES). SYBIL ROSENFELD

STOCKFISCH, see SPENCER, JOHN.

STOLL, SIR OSWALD (1866–1942), English theatre manager, an Australian of Irish parentage, whose real name was Gray. He took his stepfather's name, however, and gained his first theatrical experience at the Star Music Hall in Cardiff under his mother's management. He then joined forces with Moss and built Empires all over the provinces; but when they came to London the original Empire in Leicester Square was not for sale, so Moss built the Hippodrome and Stoll the Coliseum. When first opened the latter gave four shows a day, which did much to change the old-style music-hall show into Variety. Stoll made the Coliseum a respectable place, with more music than comedy, and cleaned up Variety, refusing to allow any comedian to use an expletive, however mild. He controlled the Stoll circuit and gave his name to the Stoll Theatre, formerly the London Opera House (see below). In 1919 Stoll was knighted, not only for his services to the stage, but for his benevolent works and his War Seals Foundation during the First World War. He sometimes wrote songs, among them one for Vesta Tilley which was a great success. W. MACQUEEN-POPE†

STOLL THEATRE, LONDON. This theatre, which stood in Kingsway, near the junction with the Aldwych, was built partly on the site of Gibbon's Tennis-Court (see VERE STREET THEATRE). It was opened on 13 Nov. 1911 by Oscar Hammerstein I as the London Opera House with Nouguès's opera 'Quo Vadis?'. It had only a short operatic career, since it was in competition with Covent Garden, and Hammerstein soon gave up the struggle. The theatre staged revue and pantomime, but was often closed for long periods. It was eventually acquired by Sir Oswald Stoll, who gave it his own name and turned it into a cinema, with complete success. It did not return to use as a theatre until 1941, when revue and pantomime were seen there, followed by revivals of famous musical comedies. In 1947 Tom Arnold used the vast stage for Ice Shows. In 1951 it became the headquarters of the Festival Ballet under Markova and Dolin. Gershwin's 'Porgy and Bess' had its first London production at the Stoll in 1952, Ingrid Bergman made her first appearance in London in Honegger's 'Joan of Arc at the Stake' in 1954. The last play seen at the theatre was *Titus Andronicus* with Laurence Olivier and Vivien Leigh, fresh from a triumphant European tour. It closed on 4 Aug. 1957 and an office block containing a small theatre was built on the site (see ROYALTY 3). W. MACQUEEN-POPE†, *rev.*

STONE, JOHN AUGUSTUS (1801–34), American dramatist, author of *Metamora*, one of the first plays to be based on American history. This was awarded a prize by Forrest for 'the best tragedy, in five acts, of which the hero, or principal character, shall be an original of this country'. It was given in New York in 1829, and was a great success, being revived as late as 1887. After playing in it for some years Forrest commissioned Bird to rewrite it, but as no complete manuscript of either version exists, it is not possible to say how much Bird altered it. Stone, who was a mediocre actor, wrote also a number of romantic historical plays which have not survived. Disappointed as actor and author, he committed suicide, according to Wood, by throwing himself into the river at Philadelphia.

STORER, see HENRY, JOHN.

STORM AND STRESS, see STURM UND DRANG.

STRAND LIGHT CONSOLE, see LIGHTING, 2.

STRAND THEATRE, LONDON. 1. In 1831 Benjamin Lionel Rayner, a celebrated Yorkshire comedian, acquired a building which from 1803 to 1828 had housed panoramas. In seven weeks he transformed it into a theatre and opened it on 25 Jan. 1832, as Rayner's New Subscription Theatre in the Strand. It was decorated in white, gold, and silver, and, as it had no licence, tickets were sold off the premises at 4*s*., 3*s*., and 2*s*. There was no gallery. At this time the last battles between the unlicensed houses and the patent theatres were being waged, and the opening attraction at the new theatre was a skit on the situation, called *Professionals Puzzled; or, Struggles at Starting*. There was also a special little play for Mrs. Waylett, the star actress, and Rayner appeared in one of his former successes, *The Miller's Maid*. A few weeks after the opening Mrs. Waylett took sole charge, and in Nov. 1832 the theatre closed down. It reopened in February of the following year, when Fanny Kelly gave a monologue entertainment, and in October Wrench and Russell tried drama there. But the patent theatres caused it to be closed. In 1834 Mrs. Waylett tried again, resorting to every expedient to evade the patent laws, such as free admission on the purchase of an ounce of lozenges for 4*s*. A real Red Indian chief and his squaw appeared, as did Mrs. Nisbett, while the greatest success was Gilbert à Becket's burlesque of *Manfred*. But in 1835 the theatre was again closed at the behest of the patent houses. At last, in 1836, it was put on the same footing as the Olympic and the Adelphi, and on 1 May Douglas Jerrold and James Hammond reopened it. The partnership did not last long, but Hammond remained until 1839. A gallery had been added to the theatre, holding 800 people at 1*s*. 6*d*. each. Dickens's novels in dramatic form were played there, notably *Pickwick Papers* under the title of *Sam Weller*, and *Nicholas Nickleby*; but the dramatic fare was always reinforced by extravaganza.

In 1841 a conjuror named Jacobs took the theatre. The Keeleys starred there, and Mrs. Stirling appeared in *Aline* (1843). Fox Cooper took over in 1847, followed by Oxberry and Edward Hooper in rapid succession. From 1848 to 1850 William Farren took command. Under him Mrs. Stirling appeared as Olivia in *The Vicar of Wakefield*—Farren playing Dr. Primrose and Mrs. Glover making her last stage appearance as Mrs. Primrose. William Copeland of Liverpool was the next tenant. He renamed the theatre Punch's Playhouse, but though he engaged good actors he lasted only two seasons. After a varied career, during which the theatre sank very low, W. H. Swanborough, in Feb. 1858, started a scheme which seemed certain to fail. He starred his sister in H. J. Byron's burlesques, and success came their way. *Fra Diavolo*, *The Miller and His Men*, *The Lady of Lyons* were all popular and the public flocked to see the Swanborough shows, with a cast that also included James Thorne, Edward Terry, Miss Raynham, Mrs. Raymond, and Marie Wilton (afterwards Lady Bancroft). The last of the Swanborough burlesques was given in 1872. In 1882 the theatre was condemned, rebuilt, and reopened. A period of failure followed. Swanborough died, and J. S. Clarke became lessee, with a notable season of old English comedies. In the early 1890s Willie Edouin took the theatre, and had some success, particularly with *Niobe* (1892) and a revival of *Our Flat* (1894). When *Niobe* was revived in 1895 it became the fashion for wedding-parties to visit it, no one ever found out why! Written by the Paulton brothers, this extravaganza, which starred Beatrice Lamb and Harry Paulton, had already had a success in America, and in Liverpool, where it was first produced. It was followed by a series of farces, and in 1901 came the long-running musical play, *The Chinese Honeymoon*. The theatre was demolished in 1905, and the site is now covered by the Aldwych Underground station.

2. The present Strand Theatre opened on 22 May 1905 as the Waldorf, under the direction of the Shubert brothers of New York, with Italian opera. Duse then played a season there, appearing in an Italian version of *The Second Mrs. Tanqueray*, and Tree transferred *Oliver Twist* from His Majesty's when the proscenium arch of the latter developed a crack. After the destruction of the Avenue Theatre, Cyril Maude made the Strand his headquarters, remaining until 1907. A season by E. H. Sothern and Julia Marlowe followed, which included several Shakespeare plays and their successful production of *When Knighthood was in Flower* (1907), and two years later the theatre took its present name. In 1911 it was bought by an American manager F. C. Whitney, who named it after himself, but his venture was not a success, and in 1913 it reverted to being the Strand, under Louis Meyer, whose first outstanding success was Matheson Lang's *Mr. Wu* (1913). In 1915 Fred Terry and Julia Neilson occupied the theatre with new plays and revivals of their old successes, including *The Scarlet Pimpernel*. The building was slightly damaged during the Zeppelin raids, but continued in use. It was later controlled by Arthur Bourchier, who between 1919 and 1923 staged a number of successful plays, among them *At the Villa Rose* (1920), *A Safety Match* (1921), and a dramatization of *Treasure Island* (1922) which was revived annually for several years. It was at this theatre that in 1923 O'Neill's *Anna Christie* was seen for the first time in London. Another American play which had a success here was *Broadway* (1926). From 1930 to 1934 the theatre was run with great success by Leslie Henson and Firth Shepherd, their partnership being inaugurated with *It's a Boy*. In 1935 a dramatization of *1066 and All That* had a successful run. A period of steady success followed, and in 1940, at the height of the blitz, Donald Wolfit kept the theatre open with midday productions of Shakespeare. On 8 Oct. 1940 the building was badly blasted. The dressing-rooms were damaged, and the actors had to scramble over débris to reach the stage, but the performance then taking place was continued, though some costumes had to be dug out of the ruins and hastily brushed down. The theatre was finally repaired, and among later successes there have been *Arsenic and Old Lace* (1942), *Sailor Beware!* (1955), which established Peggy Mount as a star, the revue *For Adults Only* (1958), and two plays based by Ronald Miller on novels by C. P. Snow, *The Affair* (1961) and *The New Men* (1962).

W. MACQUEEN-POPE†, *rev.*

For the Strand Musick-Hall, see GAIETY, 1.

STRANGE'S MEN, an Elizabethan theatre company, presumed to be the first by which Shakespeare was employed, either as actor and playwright, or as playwright only, in 1592. The company had been in existence before this, playing mainly in the provinces. At the same time a company called the Earl of Derby's Men, under the patronage of Lord Strange's father, was also in existence, a duplication which has caused some confusion. Both companies were at Court in 1582,

Strange's Men being referred to as 'tumblers'. Their chief actor was a John Symons, who joined the Queen's Men in 1588, while the rest of Strange's Men amalgamated with the Admiral's Men at the Theatre under James Burbage, with Edward Alleyn as their chief actor. After quarrelling with Burbage, they left the Theatre and went together to the Rose, Henslowe's new playhouse, where the joint company played sometimes under one name, sometimes under the other, though Alleyn always kept his personal status as an Admiral's Man. In Court records the company is invariably referred to as Strange's, as it is also in Henslowe's diary during their six weeks' season in 1592. It was at this time that Shakespeare probably wrote for them, or perhaps rewrote from an older play, the first part of his *Henry VI*, and he may, in the following year, have written for them *The Comedy of Errors* under the title of *The Jealous Comedy*. Among their other plays were *Titus and Vespasian*, which later became *Titus Andronicus* for Sussex's Men, and *A Knack to know a Knave*, while the older plays in their repertory included *The Jew of Malta*, *Orlando Furioso*, and *Friar Bacon and Friar Bungay*, as well as a number of plays now lost. The company, which separated itself from the Admiral's in 1594, included Kempe, Heminge (later the friend and editor of Shakespeare), Pope, and Phillips. On the death of their patron in 1594 (he had succeeded his father as Earl of Derby only six months before), and on the general reshuffling of the companies which took place with the formation of the Chamberlain's Men in that year, the company vanished into the provinces, to reappear at Court in 1599–1600. The last mention of them is at Islington in 1618.

STRANITZKY, Joseph Anton (1676–1726), originator of the comic figure Hanswurst (see austria). There is an amusing account in Lady Mary Wortley Montagu's letters of a visit she paid to one of Hanswurst's performances in 1716.

STRATFORD-UPON-AVON, in Warwickshire, England. This Midland town, the birthplace of Shakespeare in 1564, is the scene of a yearly festival devoted to his works given at the Shakespeare Memorial Theatre, which in 1961 changed its name to the Royal Shakespeare. This festival, which now opens in April with a repertory of six to eight plays, has been growing and developing slowly, persistently, and always unpredictably, since it was established in the 1860s. It would never have been possible without a great deal of that generosity of spirit which Shakespeare's name is able to evoke not only in men of the theatre but in the theatre's patrons; and the patrons of Stratford have belonged to many different races.

The famous Jubilee of 1769 turned the town into a stage—for Garrick; and its feasting and fireworks, its commemorative odes and masquerades, were perhaps the beginning of Stratford as a centre of Bardolatry. The origins of the festival come much later. The notion of celebrating the tercentenary of Shakespeare's birthday with the performance of a play on 23 Apr. emanated from Stratford in 1861, and, despite lack of enthusiasm and some discouraging opposition from London, was carried into effect three years later. Its moving spirit was E. F. Flower; and it was his son, Charles Edward Flower, who first conceived the idea of a permanent memorial theatre. A committee was formed, but the first result of its activities was a renewal of London's hostility to Stratford's claim to have a special interest in its son. C. E. Flower, ignoring metropolitan gibes, issued a national appeal for £20,000. The response was generally poor, and the greater part of the money came from his own purse. He also presented the Governors of the theatre with the riverside site (see No. 50). So that it was in 1879 that the festival as we know it today began. *Much Ado About Nothing* was the first play to be performed. Barry Sullivan was Benedick, and Helen Faucit came out of her retirement to play Beatrice. So delighted was Sullivan by the triumph of his first festival that he returned the following year. It was through the influence of Sullivan that Edward Compton took over the festival plays for 1881, and he also returned the following year. The festival tradition had been established. Young Frank Benson came in 1886, and remained in control of the spring and summer festivals for the next thirty years. He produced every play in the Folio except *Titus Andronicus* and *Troilus and Cressida*. He made theatre history by giving festival audiences an uncut version of *Hamlet* in 1899. In the same year Sarah Bernhardt was seen in the part, in French, at a Saturday matinée. Benson's local popularity was so great that the whole town turned out to welcome him at the station, and he was drawn to his hotel in a carriage from which the horses had been taken. The Bensonians created an atmosphere of athleticism and conviviality which still lingers about the festival.

The year 1925 had a character of its own. A Royal Charter was granted to the Memorial Theatre, and the festival made a profit for the first time in its forty-six years of life. On Saturday, 6 Mar. 1926 the theatre—something of a Victorian monstrosity—was destroyed by fire. The festival was due to open in six weeks' time. A local fund of £1,600 was raised almost overnight, a cinema was converted into a theatre, and for the next six seasons W. Bridges-Adams, who had succeeded Sir Frank Benson in 1919, contrived in spite of all difficulties to please visitors with swift and well-balanced productions. More than half of the large sum required to build a new theatre was raised in America, and both there and in this country it was again a Flower—this time Sir Archibald, who died in 1950 and was succeeded as chairman of the governors by his son, Colonel Fordham Flower—who was the moving spirit of the appeal. The new theatre, designed by Elizabeth Scott (see No. 51), was opened by the then Prince of Wales (later the

Duke of Windsor) on 23 Apr. 1932, when a performance of *Henry IV*, *Parts I* and *II* was given. A. V. COOKMAN†, *rev.*

During the ensuing years some interesting productions were seen there, notably by Komisarjevsky. Bridges-Adams, having seen the new theatre firmly established, and the season extended into September, resigned in 1934, and was succeeded by Ben Iden Payne, under whom the standard of verse-speaking notably improved. He also introduced the policy of allowing lesser dramatists a hearing on Shakespeare's stage—Jonson, for the tercentenary of his death, in 1937, Goldsmith in 1940, Sheridan several years running. This continued until 1946, since when Shakespeare has reigned supreme.

When war broke out in 1939 the theatre closed with two weeks of the season still to run, but it reopened as usual in 1940. In spite of wartime difficulties, a full programme was maintained, first under Iden Payne, and then under Milton Rosmer and Robert Atkins, both of whom did sterling work. Manpower and material were 'in short supply', but audiences were large, though somewhat uncritical. With the coming of peace Sir Barry Jackson was appointed director (1946), and instituted a number of reforms, the most far-reaching being that which spaced out the first nights over the whole season, instead of cramming them all into the first fortnight. This allowed adequate time for rehearsals and lessened the strain on the actors. He also continued the policy, which had served him so well at Birmingham, of choosing his leading actors for their promise rather than their reputation, and in his first season introduced Scofield as actor and Peter Brook as director. In 1948 Helpmann came to play King John, Shylock, and Hamlet in alternation with Scofield. Meanwhile the neglect of the war years was remedied, backstage repairs and cleaning were undertaken, and the theatre workshops were enlarged and refitted under Nancy Burman, the productions manager, all scenery being built and painted and costumes made there. It was thus a vigorous and newly furbished theatre that Anthony Quayle took over in 1948 (see No. 89). Established stars were now willing to leave London for Stratford, and a series of brilliant productions followed, with Peggy Ashcroft, Diana Wynyard, Godfrey Tearle, and John Gielgud in leading parts. In 1949 the company went to Australia, in 1950 to Germany.

During the winter of 1950–1 the interior of the theatre was extensively altered and redecorated. A front curtain was dispensed with, and a semi-permanent set behind an extended forestage greeted the audience for the 1951 season, which opened with Michael Redgrave as Richard II. He also played Hotspur and Prospero, while Richard Burton played Prince Hal (in *Henry IV*) and Henry V. In 1953 Glen Byam Shaw joined Quayle as co-director, taking over alone in 1956. Two companies were now formed, one to play at Stratford, the other to tour. Australia was visited again in 1952–3, Canada and the United States in 1953–4. In 1958–9 the company visited Russia, and with the appointment in 1960 of Peter Hall as director (later joined by Peter Brook and Michel Saint-Denis) greater expansion was undertaken, signalized in 1963 by the production of a sequence of history plays as *The Wars of the Roses*. The Aldwych Theatre became the London home of a Stratford company, opening on 15 Dec. 1960 with *The Duchess of Malfi*, followed by a judicious mingling of old and new plays in repertory, some of them transferred from Stratford, others being seen only in London. Among the early productions were Giraudoux's *Ondine*, Anouilh's *Becket*, Brecht's *Caucasian Chalk Circle*, Fry's *Curtmantle*, and, from Stratford, *Twelfth Night*, *The Taming of the Shrew*, *As You Like It*, and *Troilus and Cressida*. Meanwhile the Arts Theatre was taken temporarily to serve for experimental work, five new plays and two revivals being presented. Of these the best was undoubtedly Middleton's *Women Beware Women*, a baleful Jacobean tragedy to which the company did full justice. Unfortunately the venture proved too costly to continue without a subsidy, and had to be abandoned after six months. Plans were afoot in 1965 to build a theatre in the Barbican development area of the City of London to serve as a permanent London home for the Royal Shakespeare company. It was estimated that it would cost nearly £1½ million and be ready by 1970.

Stratford interest in Shakespeare is not confined to the theatre. In addition to the library and picture-gallery, which escaped the fire and have been incorporated into the new theatre, the Shakespeare Birthplace Trust has been steadily extending its facilities over the years, and in 1961 embarked on an ambitious project, the building of a library and study centre, opened in Apr. 1964. Mason Croft, once the home of Marie Corelli, is now the Institute of Shakespeare Studies. Sponsored by the University of Birmingham, it grew out of the lectures and conferences arranged there by the British Council from 1947 onwards, and opened in 1951 under Professor Allardyce Nicoll. The British Council offices are housed in Hall's Croft, home of Shakespeare's daughter after her marriage to Dr. Hall, which serves as a festival club and maintains a useful information service for visitors (for STRATFORD, ONTARIO, CANADA, and STRATFORD, CONNECTICUT, U.S.A. and other Shakespeare Festival centres, see SHAKESPEARE, 4) (see also Nos. 89, 91, 92, 160, 161).

STRATTON, EUGENE (1861-1918), an American Negro impersonator who, like Chirgwin, became a well-known music-hall star. He was born in Buffalo, U.S.A., his real name being Eugene Augustus Ruhlmann. At the age of 17, after some experience as a solo turn, he joined the Haverly Minstrels, with whom he went to London in 1880. He was for many years with the Moore and Burgess Minstrels. When their popularity began to wane he took to the music-hall stage, making his first appearance at the Royal Holborn in 1892. As a white-faced performer he was not successful, but on resuming his Negro make-up he made an instant appeal and became the outstanding black-face performer of the halls, particularly when he sang 'Lily of Laguna' and other coon songs by Leslie Stuart—wistful ballads to which he whistled a refrain while dancing on a darkened, spotlighted stage in soft shoes, a noiseless, moving shadow. He retired in 1914, making his last appearance at the Queen's, Poplar.

STREATER [STREETER], ROBERT (1624–80), English painter, who was responsible for the decorations of the Sheldonian Theatre, Oxford. He was said to excel in architectural and decorative paintings on a large scale, especially those in which perspective and a knowledge of foreshortening were required. Evelyn, in his diary for 9 Feb. 1671, says he saw 'at White-hall Theatre' 'the famous play call'd *The Siege of Granada* two days acted successively; there were indeed very glorious scenes and perspectives, the worke of Mr. Streater, who well understands it'.

STRINDBERG, (JOHAN) AUGUST (1849–1912), Swedish dramatist, author of some fifty-odd plays (as well as poems, novels, stories, and autobiographical works) besides being a proficient scholar in several unrelated branches of knowledge. His genius was of that passionate and sensitive kind which is driven to, though not satisfied by, never-resting mental activity and exploration. His life, and the consequent matter of his plays, was divided by the crisis thus brought on in his middle years (about 1895–7). His earlier plays, after the experimental stage usual to young dramatists, are first historical and then realistic. These latter offer a reading of life whose implications denounce, not so much the accidental corruption of society already analysed by his Norwegian predecessors, Bjørnson and Ibsen, as certain of the basic tendencies of human nature. The later plays, from 1898 onwards, are either, again, historical (histories now of some power and originality) or attempts to reveal, in expressionist forms of which he was often the first master, the unexplored areas, the inarticulate impulses and processes, of the human mind. In many of these it would seem that a genuine mystical experience lies behind the implications of the play and that a resolution of the earlier problems has been found. On the strictly technical side his genius is now less fertile than it is in the discovery of subject and theme. The variety and abundance of his technical invention and theatrical devices is astounding. Much of the structural virtuosity later fashionable in Europe and America was, in fact, either anticipated by Strindberg or actually derived from him (consciously or unconsciously) by playwrights who have merely dotted his 'i's' and crossed his 't's'. He is one of the most difficult of modern dramatists to measure, for the raw force and copiousness of his genius still dazzles the judgement. He has been both over- and under-estimated, now being regarded as the equal of Ibsen (which, if only for lack of artistic wholeness, he could not be) and now merely as a brilliant theatre-man, remarkable only for novelty of theme and form.

His principal plays may be grouped roughly in the following way. The early plays, including the first group of histories, fall between 1870 and 1882, from *Fritänkaren* to *Lycko-Pers Resa*. A sharp change, already anticipated in his fiction, enters his dramatic work with *Fadren* (1887), which, with *Fröken Julie* (1888) and its famous preface, contains the clear revelation of Strindberg's growing pre-occupation with sin, crime, and abnormality, and his reading of human nature in terms of these. The dramatic technique of these plays and the corresponding comments in the preface also mark an advance in power and definition. Other plays of this second phase, some of which have been widely produced, show also some interesting experiments in length, ranging from the full play to brief studies such as *Den Starkare* (1890), with only one speaking part. This period includes two plays in German which were later translated into Swedish, *Das Band* (1892) and *Das Spiel mit dem Feuer* (1893).

The main division in Strindberg's work, in thought and technique, may perhaps best be made at this point. For the plays that follow in 1899, such as *Advent* on the one hand and *Brott och Brott* on the other, reveal, in their widely different styles, the presence of those governing conceptions of spiritual reality which are apparent during the remaining ten years of Strindberg's work. The plays of this last period include *Till Damaskus I* and *II* (1898); *Gustaf Vasa*, the first of his fifteen major historical plays, and *Erik XIV* (both 1899); *Gustaf Adolf* (1900); *Päsk*, *Midsommar*, *Dödsdansen I* and *II*, and *Carl XII* (all 1901); *Ett Drömspel* (1902); *Kristina*, *Gustaf III*, and *Näktergalen i Wittenberg* (all 1903); *Till Damaskus III* (1904); *Spöksonaten* (1907); and, his last play, *Stora Landsvägen* (1909).

UNA ELLIS-FERMOR†, *rev.*

In 1907 Strindberg, together with August Falck, founded the Intima Teatern in Stockholm for the production of his own plays. He married in 1901, as his third wife, the actress Harriet Bosse. This, like his earlier marriages, ended in divorce. She survived him by fifty years, dying in 1962. Although Strindberg has not achieved in the English-speakng theatre the place accorded to Ibsen, most of his plays have been translated and a number produced, and his influence can be traced in a number of contemporary playwrights. His best-known plays in English are *The Father* and *Miss Julie*, and possibly *The Spook* (or *Ghost*) *Sonata*. The first was produced in London in 1927 with Robert Loraine and Dorothy Dix, in 1949 with Michael Redgrave and Freda Jackson, and, in a new translation by Michael Meyer, in 1964 with Trevor Howard and Joyce Redman. *Miss Julie* was first seen in 1927 in a private production by the Stage Society, and publicly in 1935 with Rosalinde Fuller as Miss Julie. Diane Cilento played the name-part in 1960, and Maggie Smith in 1965, at the Chichester Festival, with Albert Finney as Jean. It had, however, been translated into French and played at Antoine's Théâtre Libre as early as 1893, in which year *Fordringsägare* was seen in Berlin. In America the Provincetown Players first performed *The Spook Sonata* in 1924 and *The Dream Play* in 1926, and both productions had a great influence on the development of O'Neill.

STURM UND DRANG, the name given to a phase of eighteenth-century German literature and drama which carried to its furthest consequences the doctrine of the rights of the individual as preached by the protagonists of enlightenment. The writers of this movement espoused Rousseau's doctrine of a return to nature, but they meant by that something far more elemental than Rousseau had intended. In drama Shakespeare was their idol. Characteristic themes appear again and again in their work, among them the Faust legend, treated by Goethe and Klinger, and the tragedy of the unmarried mother executed for the murder of her child while her seducer goes free. This latter was an injustice which weighed heavily on the conscience of these young writers, and it was treated by H. L. Wagner in *Die Kindesmörderin* and by Lenz in *Die Soldaten* (both 1776), as well as by Goethe in his *Faust*. Other subjects were the hostile brothers, incompatible natures fettered by malignant fate in a close relationship and in love with the same woman—Klinger's *Die Zwillinge* (1776) and Schiller's *Die Räuber* (1781)—and the overmastering power of love, hurling even honourable natures into crime—Müller's *Genoveva* and again Goethe's *Faust*. The movement had repercussions all over Europe, and its influence can be clearly seen in the late eighteenth- and early nineteenth-century melodrama of England. Of its progenitors Goethe and Schiller went on to greater things; Klinger, from one of whose plays the movement took its name, lapsed into mediocrity; Lenz wrote no more.

W. E. DELP

STUYVESANT THEATRE, New York, see BELASCO.

SUBURBAN THEATRES, LONDON. All through the 1890s and the early 1900s there was a great deal of theatrical activity in the London suburbs, and many theatres were built. The best known, with their dates of opening, are:

Balham, The Duchess, 1899; The Bedford, 1896 (demolished 1968); The Brixton (destroyed by enemy action, 1940), 1896; Camberwell, The Metropole, 1894; Camden Town, The Camden, 1900; Clapham, The Shakespeare, 1896; Crouch End Opera House, 1897; The Dalston, 1898; Deptford, The Broadway, 1897; Fulham, The Grand, 1897; Hammersmith, The King's, 1902 (demolished 1964); Holloway, The Marlborough, 1903; The Kennington, 1898; The Kilburn, 1895; Notting Hill Gate, The Coronet, 1898; Peckham, The Crown, 1898; Poplar, The Prince's, 1905; Rotherhithe, The Terriss, 1899; Stoke Newington, The Alexandra, 1897; Stratford, The Borough, 1896, The Theatre Royal (still a theatre), 1884; Woolwich, The Grand, 1900.

These theatres were used solely for the visits of touring companies and for an annual pantomime. Some later became repertory theatres, some music-halls, but the majority are now cinemas or demolished. There was a small theatre called the Parkhurst at the junction of Holloway Road and Camden Road, which has now vanished. There was a large theatre inside the Crystal Palace, and there is also one inside the Alexandra Palace, which was rebuilt in 1922, but it remained in use for a short time only. It is now used by the B.B.C. in connexion with television.

More recent suburban theatres are those at Wimbledon, opened in 1910, at Lewisham (The Hippodrome), opened in 1912, at Golders Green (The Hippodrome), opened in 1913 as a music-hall, and as a theatre in 1923, and at Streatham (Streatham Hill), opened in 1929. These last were very successful with touring companies and shows before and immediately after London production, and with annual pantomimes. The Intimate Theatre, Palmers Green, opened by John Clements in 1935, did excellent work as a repertory theatre whose new plays were sometimes transferred to the West End. The 'Q' Theatre at Kew Bridge, opened on 26 Dec. 1924 by J. and D. De Leon, was also used for try-outs and revivals (see also LYRIC, 2).

W. MACQUEEN-POPE†

SUCKLING, Sir John (1609–42), English poet, and the author of several plays done by the King's Men. The best known, *Aglaura* (1638), contains the lyric 'Why so pale and wan, fair lover?'

SUDAKOV, Ilya Yakovleivich (1890–1969), Soviet actor and producer, who received his training at the Moscow Art Theatre, and was one of the founders of the Second Studio, where he first tackled production. When the studio was merged with the Moscow Art Theatre he continued to direct, first under Stanislavsky and Nemirovich-Danchenko and then independently, without, however, ceasing to act. He taught in a number of theatre schools, and in 1933 became artistic director of the Maly, where some of his best productions were *Uriel Acosta* (1940), with sets by Rabinovich, *Front* by Korneichuk, and *Invasion* by Leonov. He then worked in several theatres, and spent a year at the Yanka Kupala Theatre in Minsk. His work had a great influence on other producers. Among his post-war productions were *Uncle Vanya* (1947), with Kedrov and Litovtsev, *Our Daily Bread*

(1948), Afinogenev's *Mother of Her Children* (1954), and Alexei Tolstoy's *The Road to Calvary* (1957). In 1959 he became director of the Gogol Theatre.

SUDERMANN, Hermann (1857–1928), German dramatist, a writer of the realistic era whose first play, *Die Ehre*, was given at the Lessing theatre (founded by Oskar Blumenthal in 1888) in 1889, the same year as Hauptmann's *Vor Sonnenaufgang* at the Freie Bühne. Sudermann became the outstanding exponent of German middle-class drama, and helped to make a facile form of naturalism acceptable to the general public. He was much influenced by Ibsen, as may be seen by his *Das Glück im Winkel* (1895) and *Johannisfeuer* (1900); and even his historical plays, *Johannes* (1898) and *Die drei Reiherfedern* (1898), have an obstinately modern and naturalistic atmosphere. The play by which he is best remembered, however, is *Die Heimat* (1893), known in England and America as *Magda*, which combines the theatrical effectiveness of the 'well-made' play with the social significance of Magda, the 'new woman'.

SŪDRAKA, see INDIA.

SUE, Eugène (1804–57), French dramatist, who trained as a naval surgeon and was present at the battle of Navarino in 1827. After running through a fortune and getting involved in several scandals, he wrote a series of novels which had a great and unexpected success and were immediately adapted for the stage. They had little literary quality, but all the ingredients for popularity, being full of bloodshed, horrors, and melodramatic events. Among them were *Les Mystères de Paris*, which was translated into English and had a great influence, and *Le Juif errant*, a version of the Wandering Jew legend which gained wide popularity.

SUETT, Richard (1755–1805), English comedian, commonly known as Dicky Suett. As a boy he sang in the choir at St. Paul's, and made his first appearance at Drury Lane in 1780, when he was considered extremely comical, though with a little too much gag and grimace. He was at his best in the fools of Shakespeare, which seemed to have been specially written for him. Lamb, who called him the Robin Goodfellow of the stage, said: 'They have all the true Suett stamp, a loose and shambling gait and a slippery tongue.' Off the stage he was somewhat melancholic, a tall, thin, ungainly man much given to solemn practical jokes and outrageous puns. He was a heavy drinker, which doubtless hastened his death.

SUKHOVO-KOBYLIN, Alexander Vasileivich (1817–1903), Russian dramatist, whose whole life was overshadowed by the death of his mistress, whom he was suspected of having murdered. He had already started to write a play, *Krechinsky's Wedding*, before this tragic event, and during the time he spent in jail—the case dragged on for many years—he finished it, averring that many of the best scenes had been written in prison. It was finally staged at the Moscow Maly Theatre in 1855. Its subject, like that of his two other plays—one written in 1862 and performed at the Alexandrinsky twenty years later, and the other written in 1868 and staged in 1900 in the Theatre of the Literary Society—was the decay of the patriarchial life of old Russia, the breaking-up of the great country estates, the decadence of the nobility, and the growing power of a corrupt bureaucracy. Although Sukhovo-Kobylin truly asserted that he was not a revolutionary, he was regarded as a dangerous man and his plays were banned by the censor. He was a great friend and admirer of Gogol, whose influence is seen in the character of Krechinsky. Sukhovo-Kobylin was also much influenced by that other great satirist of the time, Saltikov-Shchedrin. Worn out by his struggles with the censorship, Sukhovo-Kobylin finally gave up the theatre for philosophy, and retired to France, where he died.

SULLAVAN, Margaret (1911–60), an American actress who began her stage career at Cape Cod, Massachusetts, in 1928. She first appeared in New York in 1931, playing Teddy Simpson in *A Modern Virgin* at the Booth Theatre. In 1933 she took over the leading role of Paula Jordan in *Dinner at Eight*. After several years in films she returned to the stage to play Sally Middleton in John Van Druten's *The Voice of the Turtle* (1943), which many consider her greatest triumph, utilizing fully both her husky 'cello' voice and the candour and unaffected charm of her acting style. It was in this part that she first appeared in London in 1947 at the Piccadilly Theatre. Later appearances included Hester Collyer in *The Deep Blue Sea* (1952) and Sabrina Fairchild in *Sabrina Fair* (1953). She died during a pre-Broadway tour of *Sweet Love Remember'd*.

SULLIVAN, (Thomas) Barry (1821–91), Irish actor, who joined a touring company after seeing Macready act, and played for some years in Ireland, mainly in Cork. From 1841 to 1852 he was seen in the English provinces and in Scotland, where he managed a theatre in Aberdeen for three years. He then made his first appearance in London in 1853 as Hamlet under Buckstone at the Haymarket, and achieved sufficient recognition to warrant a season at Sadler's Wells with Phelps. In the autumn of 1858 he went to New York and at the Broadway Theatre was seen in a wide range of leading parts. He also toured extensively, being exceedingly well received in San Francisco. He made a long visit to Australia, and returned to England to play Benedick to Helen Faucit's Beatrice for the inaugural performance of the Shakespeare Memorial Theatre in 1879. After this he was seldom seen in London, but continued to be popular in the provinces and Ireland. He made his last appearance on the stage in 1887 as Richard III in Liverpool. He was never a really first-class actor, but his vigorous action and forcible delivery made him a success in tragedy with less sophisticated audiences, for whom he kept alive the good old traditions of Shakespearian acting. His sturdy build and face much pitted with small-pox, as well as his natural roughness, rendered him unsuited to comic or romantic parts, which he wisely did not attempt.

SUMAROKOV, ALEXEI PETROVICH (1718–77), the first Russian dramatist. He was born in Finland, of an old and noble family, and at 14 entered the newly founded Cadet College for the education of the sons of the nobility. Here his natural talent for elocution and his love of literature led him to join the Society of Lovers of Russian Literature, of which he was one of the first members. On leaving the college he worked in various government departments, but continued his literary avocations, and in 1749 his first play, a tragedy, *Khorev*, was acted by the cadets, as were the plays which followed. He wrote in the neo-classical style which had been imported into Russia from Germany and France, but took his subjects from Russian history, and endeavoured to refine and purify the Russian literary language. He took an active part in the organization of the Cadet College amateur dramatic performances, and when the Yaroslavl actors arrived in St. Petersburg it was largely owing to his efforts that the leading actors were admitted to the College for training, and afterwards allowed to organize the first professional Russian company. In 1756 Sumarokov was appointed head of the Russian (as distinct from the Italian and French) Theatre in St. Petersburg, and three years later he founded a journal in which to air his literary and dramatic opinions, and wage war against his numerous detractors. In 1761 his liberal outspokenness caused him to be dismissed from office, and thereafter he confined himself to literature. He moved in theatrical circles in Moscow, but the Court banned his plays, which may nevertheless be regarded as the starting-point of a native Russian drama.

SUMMERS, THE REV. (ALPHONSUS JOSEPH-MARY AUGUSTUS) MONTAGUE (1880–1946), English critic and theatre historian. He wrote widely upon Restoration drama and in 1919 founded the Phoenix, a society for the production of old plays. He also edited the plays of Congreve, Wycherley, Otway, Shadwell, and Dryden. His *Bibliography of Restoration Drama* is a valuable compilation, covering a period on which he was one of the foremost authorities. At the time of his death he was working on nineteenth-century melodrama, and had just completed the writing of his autobiography.

T. C. KEMP†

SUPER, SUPERNUMERARY, see STOCK COMPANY. The term is still in use for soldiers, crowds, servants, who are essential to a play but have no lines to speak.

SURREY MUSIC-HALL, THE, LONDON. This hall, originally attached to The Grapes public house in Southwark Bridge Road, became a music-hall in the 1840s. The famous Vokes family appeared there, as did many stars in their early days. When the Surrey Gardens were opened it changed its name to the Winchester, which it remained until its demolition in 1878. At one time it was owned by W. B. Fair. W. MACQUEEN-POPE†, *rev.*

SURREY THEATRE, LONDON. In 1771 an equestrian performer named Charles Hughes opened a riding-school and exhibition in opposition to Philip Astley. Some years later he and Charles Dibdin built, at the cost of £15,000, an amphitheatre near the Obelisk in Blackfriars Road, and opened it in 1782 as the Royal Circus. It was here that the equestrian drama, made famous by Astley, really started. The Royal Circus had a very troubled existence and was burned down in 1805. Rebuilt in 1806, it continued its previous course, until in 1809 Elliston, the Great Lessee, converted it into a theatre (see No. 49). He renamed it the Surrey, and it kept the name permanently from 1819 onwards. To evade the patent act, he put a ballet into all the plays, which included *Macbeth*, *Hamlet*, and *The Beaux' Stratagem*. In 1814 he gave up, and the building became a circus again until in 1816 Thomas Dibdin reopened it. He failed in 1823 and the theatre sank very low. Elliston took it over again in 1827, when he left Drury Lane. Douglas Jerrold, then a struggling young playwright, brought him *Black-Eyed Susan*, which he accepted at once. T. P. Cooke was engaged for it at £60 a week and a 'half clear' benefit every sixth week, and it was produced on 8 June 1829. It drew all London, and on the 300th night the theatre was illuminated. The author, who wrote many more plays for the Surrey, received no more than £70 as remuneration for a successful run of 400 nights.

Elliston made his last appearance at the theatre on 24 June 1831, and died a fortnight later. Osbaldiston then took over, and among other things produced *Jonathan Bradford; or, the Murder at the Roadside Inn*, a poor play which ran successfully for 260 nights. It had a novel stage-set divided into four, with four actions going on simultaneously.

Osbaldiston was succeeded by Davidge, a miserly man, and then by Bunn, from Drury Lane, who essayed opera. In 1848 'Dick' Shepherd, the originator of the rough-and-tumble melodrama now associated with the Surrey, took over, with Osbaldiston back as his partner. This soon ended, however, and Creswick, a fine legitimate actor, joined Shepherd, who was broad and vulgar. Yet their association was successful and lasted, with a short break, from 1848 to 1869. In 1865 the theatre was again burned down and rebuilt. Nothing of importance then took place until 1881, when George Conquest, actor, playwright, and pantomimist, took over. He ran sensational dramas, many of them written by himself, which proved very much to the taste of his patrons, and every Christmas he put on a fine pantomime. The house flourished until his death in 1901. It declined after this and became a cinema from 1920 to 1924, with a brief season of opera. Several attempts were made to reopen it, but there were too many restrictions in the lease and it became derelict. Eventually the land was purchased by the Royal Ophthalmic Hospital, and the building was pulled down in 1937.

W. MACQUEEN-POPE†

SUSARION, of Megara, is said to have 'invented the comic chorus' (i.e. made it other than a simple improvisation) in Icaria, Attica, between 580 and 560 B.C.

SUSIE, see TOBY, 2.

SUSSEX'S MEN, a company of players with whom Shakespeare may have been connected for a short time. They were attached to the service of three Earls of Sussex in succession, from 1569 to about 1618. They first appeared at Court in 1572, when their patron became Chamberlain, and for a time were referred to as the Chamberlain's Men, not to be confused with the later brilliant company of the Chamberlain's Men which emerges in 1594. They appeared in many provincial towns, and made periodic visits to London. On one of these, in 1594, they played for six weeks under Henslowe at the Rose, and their one new play was *Titus Andronicus*, revised for them from an earlier play, which had belonged to Pembroke's Men, by the hand of Shakespeare. They may have had in their repertory at this time other plays by Shakespeare, and they also appeared in *The Jew of Malta*, the property of Henslowe, in *God Speed the Plough*, and in *Friar Bacon and Friar Bungay*.

SWAN THEATRE, LONDON. The actual date of the building and opening of the Swan is uncertain, but it was probably about 1596. It was a Bankside theatre standing in Paris (or Parish) Garden, near the Bear Gardens, a popular place of resort. It was consequently well situated for its purpose, and had the advantage of being near several landing-stairs for boats bringing visitors from the north bank of the Thames. It was built by Francis Langley, a substantial and respectable citizen of London. He was in favour at Court, but this did not prevent his having trouble over his projected theatre; in 1594 the Lord Mayor addressed a complaint to the Lord Treasurer, begging that the building of this playhouse might be stopped, on account of the evils arising therefrom. This may have delayed Langley, but did not prevent him from carrying out his design. The theatre arose, and probably took its name from the great number of swans which then frequented the river and its banks near by.

Although the Swan had by no means a glorious career, a good deal is known about it. It served Henslowe as a model for the Hope Theatre, and is frequently mentioned in his diary. John de Witt, of Utrecht, not only visited the Swan while on a visit to London, but wrote a description and made a sketch of it.

> Of all the theatres, however, the largest and most distinguished is that whereof the sign is a Swan . . . since it contains 3,000 persons, and is built of a concrete of flint stones (which greatly abound in Britain) and supported by wooden columns painted in such exact imitation of marble that it might deceive even the most cunning. Since its form seems to approach that of a Roman structure, I have depicted it above.

We have only a copy of De Witt's drawing (see No. 22), which shows three galleries, the stage with a play in progress on the apron (but not the 'heavens' above the stage, i.e. the canopy over the players), the flag flying, and a man blowing a trumpet. The flint-and-mortar work probably filled up the spaces between the wooden pillars, for the theatre was essentially a wooden building on a brick foundation. De Witt has been criticized for his estimate of 3,000 spectators, which has been regarded as a slip of the pen for 300. H. B. Wheatley, however, estimated the capacity of the galleries at 2,000, while the contemporary theatre, the Fortune, is thought to have held well over that number.

The Swan does not seem to have housed a permanent company, and was as much in demand for sports, fencing and so on, as for plays. There was trouble in 1597 over the production of *The Isle of Dogs*, a seditious comedy by Nashe and Jonson, which led to a temporary closing of all theatres, and imprisonment for the actors and Jonson (Nashe managed to escape). In 1598 Robert Wilson challenged all comers to a contest of wit and extempore versification, a popular form of entertainment at that time, and defeated them all. In 1600 Peter Bromville, an expert fencer, exhibited his skill, while two years later, during a bout of fencing, a man called Dun was thrust in the eye and killed. In the same year Richard Vennar announced a spectacular show called *England's Joy*, to be played at the Swan by gifted amateurs, but after taking the money at the door he decamped, while the infuriated audience wreaked vengeance on the theatre. Vennar was caught and punished. *A Chaste Maid in Cheapside* (1611) was produced at the Swan, but after that few plays seem to have been given there. The last mention of the theatre is found in a pamphlet issued in 1632 (*Holland's Leaguer*), which, after referring to the Globe and the Hope, says 'the last . . . was now fallen to decay, and like a dying Swanne, hanging downe her head, seemed to sing her owne dierge'.

W. MACQUEEN-POPE†

SWANN, DONALD IBRAHIM (1923–), English composer, song-writer, and entertainer, who has appeared with Michael Flanders, his contemporary at school and at Oxford, in a two-man entertainment, *At the Drop of a Hat* (1956), for which he wrote the music and Flanders the lyrics and dialogue. This outstanding production, which ran for over two years at the Fortune Theatre in London, and was then seen in New York and on extensive world tours, was followed by *At the Drop of Another Hat* (1965) at the Haymarket, in which the same formula was again successfully exploited. Although much of Swann's music was written for Flanders's lyrics, he has also set many other writers, among them Shakespeare and a number of modern Greeks (he is fluent in several languages). He has also written a quantity of modern church music, an opera, 'Perelandia', and music for radio, notably for Henry Reed's *Emily Butter*.

SWANSTON, ELIARD or HILLIARD [he himself spells it Eyllaerdt] (?–1651), a prominent actor with the King's Men from 1624 to the closing of the theatres in 1642. He had been an actor at least two years previously to 1624, and took a prominent part, not only in the acting, but in the management of the company, being associated with Lowin and Taylor in business affairs. He played a variety of roles—Othello, Bussy d'Ambois, and various villains, including Richard III. During the Civil War he turned Parliamentarian, in contrast to most of the other actors, who remained staunchly Royalist, and became a jeweller. Shadwell refers to his reputation in *The Virtuoso* when Snarl says: 'I . . . have seen . . . Swanstead: Oh a brave roaring Fellow! Would make the house shake again.'

SWEDEN, see SCANDINAVIA, 3.

SWINEY, OWEN (*c.* 1675–1754), Irish actor and manager, who in his youth may have been in the army. In about 1700 he was at Drury Lane, where for a time he acted as right-hand man to Christopher Rich. In 1705 he joined with Cibber and others in an attempt to break Rich's stranglehold over his actors by leasing Vanbrugh's old theatre in the Haymarket, where he produced *The Beaux' Stratagem* with Anne Oldfield as Mrs. Sullen. This brought him into conflict with the licensing laws, and he was forbidden to do plays. He was for a time able to stave off ruin by pandering to the popular taste for opera, but after an unsuccessful attempt to run Drury Lane in partnership with Wilks, Doggett, and Cibber, from which he was ousted by William Collier, he was forced to leave England to escape his creditors. He went to Venice, and remained in exile from 1710 to 1730. On his return he called himself MacSwiney, by which name he is sometimes known. He became the friend and patron of Peg Woffington, to whom he imparted the traditions of Anne Oldfield, and on his death he left her all his property.

SWITZERLAND. The masked ceremonies and other mime plays still found in almost every part of Switzerland derive from the original drama of the Celts and ancient Germans. The primitive plays, which have survived in the district of Berne, in the German-speaking section of Valais, and in the Rhaeto-Romanic Grisons, go back to the even older magic rituals of the hunting play, and the processions of the Magi and of St. Nicholas betray a heathen origin in a Christian setting. It was during the Roman occupation that Switzerland first took its place in the historical framework of the European theatre. Under Tiberius (A.D. 14–37) the first Roman theatre was built at Augusta Raurica (Kaiseraugst bei Basel), and the first amphitheatre at Vindonissa (Windisch bei Brugg). There were also amphitheatres at Octodurus (Martigny), at the foot of the Great St. Bernard, at Aventicum (Avenches), the captial of Helvetia, and at the Roman settlement on the narrow peninsula near Berne, the arena of which was discovered in 1960. A new theatre was built about A.D. 150 in Basle on the site of the first theatre; its ruins are today among the most imposing of those north of the Alps. As was also the case with the contemporary theatre at Aventicum, the theatre formed a single entity with the temple, and comprised a vast festival area.

The first dramatic manifestations of the Middle Ages were closely connected with, and arose from, the liturgy of the Christian Church, as is shown in illustrated documents in the Benedictine Abbey of St. Gallen which date from the tenth and eleventh centuries, and which are vital for our study of the period (see LITURGICAL DRAMA), and in the semi-dramatic *Ordinarium Sedunense* of the church of St. Valeria in Sion, composed in the thirteenth century. The employment of mimicry and gesticulation can be inferred from an Easter celebration in the monastery of Einsiedeln during the twelfth century, where the progress of the Apostles to the Sepulchre already possesses certain comic features. An Epiphany celebration of the same period displays even more elaborate features. It seems likely that the first Mystery plays in the vernacular also originated in Switzerland. The Easter play at Muri is first recorded about 1250; it is the only contribution to religious drama in the Germanic tongue made by the aristocratic poetry of chivalry, and was performed in a simultaneous setting in front of the church. The so-called Christmas play of St. Gallen dates from about 1300, and possibly belongs also to Muri. It too is remarkable for its solemn and aristocratic character. The oldest known Swiss Mystery play in French is a comprehensive Epiphany play performed in Neuchâtel, which has remarkably poetic pastoral scenes. A *Mystère de Saint Bernard de Menthon*, first written down in 1453, shows affinities with the dialect and customs of the Valais. Possibly the most important Mystery play in Switzerland before the Reformation was the Rheinau play of the Last Judgement, printed in 1487. It is one of the best texts in the German language, and obviously influenced similar plays at Donaueschingen, Copenhagen, and Berlin. The Passion plays of Donaueschingen and Villingen, however, derive from an early Lucerne play, as does the later famous

Lucerne Passion play, which in the last years of the sixteenth century assumed great importance under the direction of Renward Cysat. The large number of documents relating to his productions, which are still extant, rank among the most important for the history of the later medieval theatre, and from them it has been possible to reconstruct the original stage setting. Mystery plays received a fresh impulse during the sixteenth century from other Catholic areas, for example, from Freiburg, where the Epiphany plays, dating from 1433, were produced with ever-increasing splendour, and continued up to the end of the eighteenth century, unlike the Lucerne play, which was last performed in 1616. Even in places like Basle, Berne, Biel, Geneva, Lausanne, and Zürich, which had gone over to the Reformed faith, there were still traces of the Mystery plays. Carnival plays too attained their peak of activity in the sixteenth century. Pamphilius Gengenbach, a printer in Basle, was the author of the moralizing Carnival play *Die zehn Alter der Welt* (1515), the first drama of any importance in the German language in the sixteenth century, and also the first to appear in print. The Carnival play was also used in the service of the new learning even before the Reformation, as is shown, for instance, by the works of Niklaus Manuel of Berne (1485–1530), the most important Swiss dramatist of the sixteenth century (see also GERMANY, 2).

In 1512 the first known *Tellspiel* (based on the exploits of the legendary hero of fourteenth-century Switzerland) was performed at Altdorf; in 1545 a new version was made by the prolific dramatist Jacob Ruf, and it has been constantly performed ever since, while the original subject of the legend has passed into world literature. Finally, the School Drama of the humanists flourished throughout Switzerland. Even Ulrich Zwingli (1485–1531), the great reformer, took part in it, since he wrote incidental music for a production of Aristophanes' *Plutus*, while Calvin's disciple, Théodore de Bèze (1519–1605), wrote, among other things, a play, *Abraham sacrifiant* (1550). Unfortunately the new puritanical slant given to Protestantism in Geneva and Zürich, which found expression in the sumptuary laws of Geneva, 1617, and in the condemnatory tract, *Bedenken von Comoedien* (1624), by Johann Jakob Breitinger, head of the church in Zürich, put an end to all theatrical activity, though School Drama survived in reformed Berne, and the Cathedral there was sometimes used for performances, as, for instance, in 1692, when an allegorical play which inveighed against the persecution of the Hugenots by Louis XIV led to a protest from the French envoy. Shortly after the middle of the seventeenth century there was a manifestation of folk-drama in the reformed city of St. Gallen, stimulated by the dramatic pageants of the Catholic monastery there, in which Josua Wetter, writer of popular plays and much under the influence of Gryphius, was particularly prominent. In Catholic Switzerland the drama of the Jesuit schools in Lucerne, Freiburg, Solothurn, Brigue, Porrentruy, and Sion (see JESUIT DRAMA) also influenced the growth of native folk-drama, mainly through the work of their former pupils. This reached its height not only in the religious plays of the pilgrims at Einsiedeln, but also in the patriotic plays like those given in the small town of Zug, where in 1672 the *Eidgenössisches Contrafeth der Jungfrauen Helvetiae*, which provided a cross-section of Swiss history, was given on an open-air stage with five acting areas. With its baroque overtones, this play, which lasted for two days, shows some affinity with the English drama of Shakespeare's time.

But all local drama was soon swept aside by the influx of foreign travelling companies which took place from the end of the sixteenth century. More than 230 such troupes are known by name up to 1800, mainly of German, Austrian, and French origin, but also of isolated Italian and English. Their repertory consisted of plays, ballad operas, pantomimes, puppet-plays, and shadow-shows. They pitched their booths in the open air, or set up stages in warehouses and tennis-courts. A permanent stage was at their disposal in Baden from 1673, in Lucerne from 1741, in Solothurn from 1755. During the Age of Enlightenment society in the larger towns delighted in theatrical performances. Voltaire himself roused the enthusiasm of French Switzerland for the theatre, first at Les Délices, outside Geneva, and then at Mon Repos, between Lausanne and Ouchy. The first performance of his *Tancred*, played by a company composed for the most part of members of Geneva families, took place in 1760 in Tournay near Geneva. Geneva also provided the Comédie-Française with its first Swiss professional actor in the person of Jean Rivaz (1728–1804), known as Aufresne, and built its first permanent theatre for foreign visitors in 1783. In German Switzerland the company of Konrad Ernst Ackermann (1710–71), which operated with great success in 1758–60, was the principal source of inspiration. The architect Niklaus Sprüngli, a pupil of Blondel and Servandony, built for the Grande Société in Berne an 'Hôtel de Musique', one of the finest of the old Swiss theatres, though it was not used for plays until 1798. Abel Seyler (1730–1801), who was born in Liestal (Basle), not only helped to found the first German National Theatre in Hamburg, but later became director of the Court theatres of Hanover, Weimar, and Gotha.

The Age of Enlightenment also led to a new appraisal of Swiss folk-drama, in so far as it was not expressly religious in character. The so-called Helvetic movement, which sought to achieve a comprehensive political and cultural revival in Switzerland, rightly regarded the theatre as one of the best instruments for its purpose, and as early as 1758 Jean-Jacques Rousseau in Geneva was sponsoring a national open-air theatre based on classical models. Johann Georg Sulzer, of

Zürich, inaugurated Swiss dramatic criticism with his *Allgemeinen Theorie der Schönen Künste* (1771–4), in which, for the national festival plays, he argued in favour of sweeping movements of chorus and ballet on an enormous open-air stage. There was also, towards the end of the eighteenth century, a revival of the *Tellspiele* in German Switzerland, while in French Switzerland the traditional wine-harvest festival in Vevey developed into a Play of the Four Seasons, with mime, ballet, and music; this was produced for the first time in 1797 in the market-square, and was revived five times in the nineteenth century, with ever-increasing elaboration. It continues to be given at intervals.

Although in the eighteenth century there had already been an increasing demand for the establishment of a Swiss National Theatre with a permanent professional company of Swiss actors, and the nineteenth century brought a certain measure of consolidation into the Swiss theatre, nevertheless the acting companies still consisted mainly of foreigners, with Germans and French predominating, up to 1833. Regular theatre seasons in Berne date from 1800, in St. Gallen from 1805. Lausanne had its first permanent theatre in 1804, Basle and Zürich in 1834, Biel in 1842, and Chur in 1861. New theatres were erected in Lucerne in 1839, in St. Gallen in 1857, in Basle in 1873, in Geneva in 1879, and in Zürich in 1891. The municipal theatre in Berne, which had been spasmodically supported by the authorities since the early years of the nineteenth century, began to receive a regular subsidy in 1837; Zürich in 1856, Basle in 1859. The repertory, which included operas as well as plays, and the operettas fashionable in Paris and Vienna, was more or less in line with that of the smaller theatres of Germany, France, and Austria, though foreign producers put on more classical works than they would probably have done at home, and they also responded occasionally to the demands of the local audience for a Swiss play. As there was no censorship, works which were forbidden in neighbouring countries could be staged, and the first public performance of Ibsen's *Ghosts*, for example, took place in the municipal theatre in Berne.

While this international activity was taking place in the indoor theatres, the characteristic Swiss folk-drama was being performed in the open air, all classes participating under the direction of schoolmasters and poets, physicians and clergymen. The favourite play was Schiller's *Wilhelm Tell*; sometimes the whole landscape would be incorporated into the production, and players and audience alike moved from one stage to another, as at the final performance in 1882 of the Passion Play at Lumbrein in Grisons. Festival plays performed by thousands of players and singers on vast stages before audiences of tens of thousands made a spectacle unique in Europe. In 1886 a three-tier stage of steps and platforms was erected on the battlefield of Sempach for the performance of the dramatic cantata, *Siegesfeier der Freiheit*. This started a long series of historical festival plays, whose progressive advance in staging attracted attention far beyond Switzerland. It was to them that the outstanding theatrical personality of Switzerland, Adolphe Appia (1862–1928), owed much of his inspiration, as well as to French symbolism. He is the real founder of modern theatre production, and in 1895 and 1899 produced two important works in which he laid down the foundations of his theories: *La mise en scène du drame Wagnérien* and *Die Musik und die Inszenierung* (for an example of his work see No. 97).

With the twentieth century the theatres of Switzerland became important centres of European culture. Oskar Eberle (1902–56) achieved an international reputation in the 1930s with his *avant-garde* productions of the Lucerne Passion play, Calderón's *El gran teatro del mundo*, in the square in front of the church of Einsiedeln, and the official festival play of the Swiss national exhibition in Zürich in 1939. He also produced Cäsar von Arx's *Bundesfeierspiel* at Schnyz in 1941, the Festival play at Vevey in 1955, for which a vast wood and concrete open-air theatre was specially built, and in 1956 was responsible for the *Tellspiel* at Altdorf, which had been performed regularly since 1899. In French Switzerland, Emile Jaques-Dalcroze (1865–1951), who worked with Appia, achieved recognition as a producer, as did René Morax, who with his brother Jean directed the Festival play at Vevey in 1905, for which he wrote a new libretto. He also built in 1908 at Mezières, near Lausanne, a festival theatre on new architectural and scenic lines, the Théâtre du Jorat, which became the centre of theatrical activity in western Switzerland. Among many interesting productions there were Gluck's 'Orfeo' in 1911, as well as the premières of Honegger's 'Roi David' and 'Judith' in 1921 and 1925 respectively.

It was, however, the influx of political and cultural refugees from the totalitarian states which, from the late 1930s, gave the Swiss theatre its present outstanding international status. One of the first results was the foundation of the famous art theatre Cabaret Cornichon in 1933, and it was responsible also for the broadening of the repertory, which was most apparent in the Zürich Schauspielhaus, directed since 1938 by Oskar Wälterlin (1895–1961), successor of the famous Alfred Reucker (1868–1958), under whom the first performance of 'Parsifal' outside Bayreuth was given in 1913. Before the end of the Second World War the Swiss-German theatre was the only one in the German-language zone which could make its voice heard, and even when the war was over the Zürich Schauspielhaus, where Brecht's epoch-making *Mutter Courage und ihre Kinder* had its first production in 1941, retained its position as one of the principal playhouses in Europe. *Avant-garde* theatres opened in Berne (the Ateliertheater), in Basle (the Komoedie), in Lausanne (the Théâtre des Faux-Nez), in Geneva (the Théâtre de Carouge). A new generation of scenic artists came into being as a result, and made a decided impact at international theatre exhibitions. Further dramatic activity also attracted attention with Cäsar von Arx and Alfred Gehri, Max Frisch and Friedrich Dürrenmatt, of whom the last two have become well known in English translations. An official Swiss School of Drama was opened in Zürich in 1945; in addition to drama, opera, and ballet classes, it has also a section devoted to amateur popular drama. The Swiss Gesellschaft für Theaterkultur has since 1927 concerned itself with the encouragement of theatrical activities in theory and practice by lectures and exhibitions, publications, and the collecting and classification of Swiss theatrical archives, deposited in the Swiss National Library since 1945, and by the presentation annually since 1958 of the Hans Reinhart ring to the best actor in Switzerland. Since 1947 the universities of Berne and Zürich have also added courses of drama to their official syllabuses. EDMUND STADLER

SYMBOLISM IN THE THEATRE. Symbols have been used on the stage since the earliest times. Much of Elizabethan 'stage furniture' was symbolic, as, a throne for a Court, a tent for a battlefield, a tree for a forest. Symbolic elements are found in Chekhov, and in the later plays of Ibsen and Strindberg. But symbolism as a conscious art-form, conceived as a reaction against realism, came into the theatre with Maeterlinck, writing under the influence of Mallarmé and Verlaine. His characters have no personality of their own, but are symbols of the poet's inner life. This aspect was intensified in Yeats's early plays in verse. Other dramatists to come under the influence of symbolism include Andreyev and Evreinov in Russia, Hugo von Hofmannsthal and the later Hauptmann (with *Die versunkene Glocke*) in Germany, Synge (*The Well of the Saints*) and O'Casey (*Within the Gates*) in Ireland, and O'Neill in the United States.

SYNDICATE, see THEATRICAL SYNDICATE.

SYNGE, (EDMUND) JOHN MILLINGTON (1871–1909), Irish dramatist, and with Yeats a leading figure in the Irish Dramatic Movement (see IRELAND). Unlike Yeats, whose reputation rests equally upon his poetry, his drama, and his imaginative prose, Synge is remembered primarily as a dramatist. In him the expression of poetic imagination took an inevitable dramatic form. Although he died prematurely, while his art was still developing rapidly and continuously, he left enough in his six plays not only to show the unmistakable quality of his poetic and dramatic power, but to establish him as the greatest of modern Irish dramatists. His control of dramatic structure—whether in comedy or tragedy—is firm and powerful; his revelation of the characters and processes of mind of a subtle and imaginative peasantry is sure and penetrating; his language, and especially his imagery, is rich, live, and essentially poetic. The two prose works, *The Aran Islands* and *In Wicklow and West Kerry*, form a background to the plays and reflect, like them, an intent preoccupation with nature and with the minds and lives of Irish peasants in close and living contact with nature.

Yeats, meeting Synge in Paris, and divining the nature of his genius before he himself had done so, induced him to go back to Ireland and settle in the far west, among those peasants whose ways of life and speech gave him the material of most of his plays. His first, *In the Shadow of the Glen* (1903), begins the series of grave, original studies of Irish character and thought which from time to time drew upon Synge the hostility of his audiences, but are now appreciated wherever Irish drama is played. *Riders to the Sea* followed in 1904, a one-act tragedy whose brevity and economy of form and intensity and simplicity of passion make it one of the finest, if not the finest, of all modern short plays. *The Well of the Saints* (1905) is a comedy in which poetic beauty is mingled with underlying irony that is potentially tragic. *The Tinker's Wedding*, which may have been written earlier than these, was not produced; the theme would have made it unsuitable, but its comedy, drawn from the life of the roads, is richer and more jovial than any other that Synge wrote. The climax of his achievement in the comedy of bitter, ironic, yet imaginative realism comes with *The Playboy of the Western World*. The keen and unsparing (though sympathetic) portraiture in this play raised riots in the Abbey in 1907, and again among certain Irish patriots in America in 1911. But it has long been accepted as Synge's finest work; his power is here seen at its full capacity, as it could not be in the later but unfinished *Deirdre*. This last play, which turns back to the ancient legends of Ireland for its subject, while still characteristic of Synge in its language and imagery, is nobly planned and all but greatly carried out.

UNA ELLIS-FERMOR†

T

TABARIN [ANTOINE GIRARD] (?–1626), a popular figure in the streets of Paris for many years. Nothing is known of his birth or early years, but in about 1618 he set up a booth on the Pont-Neuf with his brother Philippe, better known as the quack-doctor, Mondor. Here, and in the Place Dauphine, Tabarin and a few companions, among whom was his wife Francisquine, would mount their trestle-platform and put the holiday crowd into a good humour before Mondor began the serious business of the day, selling his nostrums and boluses. Most of his material Tabarin wrote himself, or rather sketched out in the style of the *commedia dell'arte* scenarii, and from 1622 to 1632 a number of small volumes, entitled *Les Subtilités tabariniques*, were published, containing his farces, puns, jokes, and monologues. There is reason to believe that he was much influenced by the Italian actors who so often played in Paris, and from them he took the 'sack-beating' joke which Molière later borrowed for *Les Fourberies de Scapin* (1671). Tabarin himself never trod the boards of the legitimate theatre, but his fame long outlasted him, both La Fontaine and Boileau mentioning him years after his death, while his name passed into everyday speech (*faire le tabarin* = play the fool). It survives today in the name of a dance-hall in Montmartre.

TABERNARIA, see FABULA, 8 and 9.

TABS (short for Tableau Curtain), used originally of an act-drop which parted and rose sideways towards the outer top corners, and by extension to any front curtain, or, mistakenly, to curtain settings on the stage.

TADEMA, SIR LAWRENCE ALMA- (1836–1912), English artist, of Dutch origin, who worked for Irving and Tree, designing for the first the costumes and scenery of *Cymbeline* (1896) and *Coriolanus* (1901), and for the second *Hypatia* (1893) and *Julius Caesar* (1898).

TAGORE, RABINDRANATH (1861–1941), see INDIA, 4.

TAILS, see BORDER.

TAÏROV, ALEXANDER YAKOVLEVICH (1885–1950), Soviet producer, who in 1914 founded the Kamerny Theatre, with which he remained associated until his death, together with his wife, Alice Koonen (1889–), one of the outstanding actresses of the Soviet stage, who played many of the leading parts in her husband's productions. Taïrov survived the stormy aftermath of the Revolution, but his production of a contemporary play, *The Optimistic Tragedy*, in 1934 was severely criticized on the grounds that he was out of touch with the new audiences. The theatre was taken over by a committee, and Taïrov was constrained to work under supervision. Today that production is considered to be one of the most important of the period, and it is generally agreed that a revival of it by Tovstonogov at the Pushkin Theatre, Leningrad, in 1957 owed much to Taïrov. He returned to favour with his production of *Madame Bovary* in 1939, and his theatre served to introduce many modern Western authors to Russia, among them Shaw and O'Neill. In 1947 two productions, *Life in the Citadel*, dealing with events in a small Estonian town in 1941, and Ostrovsky's *Guiltless, Guilty*, won high praise. Theatre critics today acknowledge the importance of Taïrov's work, and pay tribute to his mastery of stage technique.

TALFOURD, SIR THOMAS NOON (1795–1854), English lawyer and man of letters, best known in the theatre for his tragedies, *Ion* (1836), *The Athenian Captive* (1838), and *Glencoe* (1840). The first, finely acted by Macready, was a success on its production at Covent Garden, and belongs to the small group of poetic plays with which the more literary-minded authors of the day sought to re-establish poetry on the stage. A classic and somewhat frigid production, it is modelled on the lines of French tragedy, with careful observance of the unities and a somewhat uninspired flow of blank verse. The two later plays were also written for Macready, but were eventually produced at the Haymarket, with less success than *Ion*, which was several times revived up to 1850. Talfourd wrote a good deal of dramatic criticism, and was the literary executor of Lamb, whose works he edited after the latter's death, as he did the posthumous publications of Hazlitt. He supported the rights of authorship in the agitation over the Copyright Bill, and was an intimate friend of Dickens and Bulwer-Lytton, the first dedicating to him *The Pickwick Papers* and the second *The Lady of Lyons*.

TALMA, FRANÇOIS-JOSEPH (1763–1826), French actor, who, though born in Paris, spent some of his early years in England. Returning there as a young man to study under his father, a fashionable dentist, he spent all his time in amateur theatricals. His acting, and his English, were so good that he was offered work at one of the patent theatres, but his father sent him back to Paris. There he became an assiduous playgoer, and eventually went to the École Royale de Déclamation (founded in 1786), where his tutors were Molé, who was also a personal friend, Fleury, and Dugazon. He made his début at the

Comédie-Française on 21 Nov. 1787 in Voltaire's *Mahomet*. Handsome, with a fine presence and voice, he was an excellent speaker of verse. He had played only small parts when on 4 Nov. 1789 he took over the part of Charles IX in a play by Marie-Joseph Chénier which had been refused by the older actors because of its political implications. Talma, immediately acclaimed as the successor to Lekain, declaimed the revolutionary speeches in *Charles IX* with such fervour that there were stormy scenes in the theatre, the older actors refusing to appear with him, while the audience, particularly Mirabeau, and the younger actors, supported him. The theatre was then closed, and with Dugazon, Madame Vestris, Grandmesnil, and Monvel, Talma moved to the Théâtre de la République (the present Comédie-Française), where he played Le Cid and other classical roles, and several of Shakespeare's tragic parts in Ducis's translations. One of his greatest successes was in a revival in 1806 of *Manlius Capitolinus*. Under the influence of the painter David, Talma made many reforms in the costuming of plays, and was the first French actor to play Roman parts in a toga instead of contemporary dress. He also reformed theatrical speech, suppressing the exaggerations of the declamatory style, and allowing the sense rather than the metre to dictate the pauses. In 1799 Napoleon, who was a great admirer of Talma, reconstituted the Comédie-Française on a firm footing, drawing up a detailed code for its administration. He also took Talma to Erfurt in 1803, where he played before an audience which contained five crowned heads.

Talma, whose influence on the French theatre was altogether salutary, was almost more successful in his later years than in his youth. He sometimes played in comedy, but preferred tragedy, at which he excelled. In 1817 he visited London, appearing with Mlle George at Covent Garden in extracts from his best parts, and he attended Kemble's farewell performance and banquet. He remained on the stage until shortly before his death with no lessening of his powers, and made his last appearance on 3 June 1826 in a poor play by Delaville, *Charles VI*, which he made successful by his acting. He died four months later. He left some interesting reflections on the art of acting, which were published as a preface to the memoirs of Lekain, whom he much admired.

Talma's first wife, several years older than himself, was (Louise) Julie Careau (1756–1805), a famous *demi-mondaine* and a Girondist. They married in 1791, had three sons who died in infancy, and were divorced in 1801. Talma then married his mistress, the actress Caroline Vanhove (1771–1860), daughter of an actor at the Comédie-Française, and herself a member of the company from 1785 to 1810. Her memoirs and her *Études sur la vie théâtrale* contain some passages on Talma, whom she left in 1814, after learning that Bazue, then his mistress, by whom he already had three daughters, had borne him a son. Talma was also for a time the lover of Pauline Bonaparte. Madame de Stael admired him greatly, and immortalized him in her book, *De L'Allemagne*, published in 1810.

TAMAYO Y BAUS, MANUEL (1829–98), Spanish dramatist, with Lopez de Ayala the chief representative of the transition period from romanticism to realism. Under his own name, and also as Joaquín Estébanez, he wrote a number of plays, some historical, like *La locura de amor* (1855), which shows the queen Doña Juana driven mad by jealousy of her husband, others dealing with modern domestic and social problems, like *Lo positivo* (1862), which deals with the conflict between sentiment and interest. One of Tamayo's most interesting plays is *Un drama nuevo* (1867), written in simple, powerful prose, in which Shakespeare appears, and in which Yorick, the central figure, kills on the stage, during a mock fight, his supposed rival in love.

TARKINGTON, (NEWTON) BOOTH (1869–1946), American novelist, and author of a number of plays, of which the best known is the romantic costume drama, *Monsieur Beaucaire* (1901). This was based in collaboration on his own novel, but was spoilt artistically by the substitution of a conventionally happy ending for the ironic ending implicit in the novel. It was nevertheless very successful in America, with Richard Mansfield in the name-part, and also in London, where it later provided the material for a musical play with a score by Messager. Among Tarkington's other plays were two for Otis Skinner, *Your Humble Servant* (1909) and *Mr. Antonio* (1916), a charming comedy of youth entitled *Clarence* (1919), and a social drama on the theme of snobbery, *Tweedles* (1923), which failed in production. Tarkington appears to have taken his plays far less seriously than his novels, and produced little of permanent value for the stage.

TARLETON, RICHARD (?–1588), the most famous of Elizabethan clowns, probably the original of Yorick 'the king's jester', as described by Hamlet, and the 'pleasant Willy' of Spenser's *The Tears of the Muses*, 'with whom all joy and jolly merriment Is also deaded'. A drawing of him preserved in a manuscript in the British Museum and reproduced in *Tarleton's Jests* (a posthumous work) shows that he was short and broad, with a large, flat face, curly hair, a wavy moustache, and a small starveling beard. Tarleton himself tells us that he had a flat nose and a squint, a peculiarity well brought out in a second portrait of him discovered by W. J. Lawrence in 1920. His usual clown's dress was a russet suit and buttoned cap, with short boots strapped at the ankle, as commonly worn by rustics at this time. A leather money-bag hung from a belt at his waist, and he is depicted playing on a tabor and pipe. He was one of the Queen's

Men, and though few of his original parts are definitely known, he is believed to have been the Mouse in *Mucedorus*, possibly Bullethrumble in *Selimus*, and conjecturally Pedringano in *The Spanish Tragedy*. A great deal of his clowning was probably extempore, and Shakespeare may have had him in mind when he said 'Let those that play your clowns speak no more than is set down for them', and also Marlowe, when he railed at 'clownage' in the prologue to *Tamburlaine*. W. J. Lawrence, in a penetrating study *On the underrated genius of Dick Tarleton*, ascribes to Shakespeare's desire to organize the gagging Clown such richly comic parts as Launce, Speed, Bottom, and Dogberry, and the Grave-digger in *Hamlet*. There can be no doubt that the genius of Tarleton led to a persistent mingling of tragedy and farce in early Elizabethan plays; but his great *tour de force* was the Jig—'dear delight of the Elizabethan multitude'—a farce in rhyme, sung and danced to a series of popular tunes. The music for some of Tarleton's jigs has been preserved, but the only libretto, *Tarltons Jigge of a horse loade of Fooles* (*c.* 1579), is considered by Chambers and others to be one of Collier's forgeries. Tarleton is, however, known to have written for the Queen's Men a composite play, now lost, entitled *The Seven Deadly Sins*, in two parts, the first containing five short plays, the second three. The plot, or outline, of the second part has been preserved in manuscript, and was for some time thought to be a scenario for an improvised play after the manner of the Italian *commedia dell'arte*. It seems now to be accepted, however, that this plot (or 'platt', as it is sometimes called) was merely a helpful indication of the sequence of events for the use of the actors and prompter. A number of books published under Tarleton's name after his death are probably spurious, the authors having annexed his name to ensure their sales. His popularity may be judged from the number of taverns named after him, of which one, *The Tabour and Pipe Man*, with a sign-board taken from *Tarleton's Jests*, still stood in the Borough two hundred years after his death, while the action of *Cuck-queans and Cuckolds Errant* (1601) takes place in the Tarlton Inn, Colchester. Tarleton himself at some time had an eating-house in Paternoster Row.

TASSO, Torquato (1544–95), famous Italian poet, whose play *Torrismondo* (pub. 1587) is a mingling of tragedy and romance. Though classic in form, it deals in romantic fashion with the love of Torrismondo for Rosmonda, who turns out to be his sister, and whom he has married on behalf of a friend. Thus proved traitor and incestuous, Torrismondo dies, fulfilling the prophecy that his sister would cause his death. Tasso was also the author of a pastoral, *L'Aminta* (1573), which, with Guarini's *Pastor Fido* (1598), stands at the head of a long line of similar plays, their influence spreading all over Europe (see ITALY, 1 *b* and PASTORAL).

TATE, Harry (1872–1940), a comedian of the music-halls, best remembered for his series of sketches on golfing, motoring, fishing, and so on. He made his first appearance at the Oxford in 1895, though he had previously done a good deal of work as an entertainer at concerts. He took his stage name from the firm of Henry Tate & Sons, Sugar Refiners, by whom he was at one time employed, his real name being Ronald Macdonald Hutchison. He appeared in the earliest revues at the London Hippodrome, but returned to the music-halls, and in 1935 played the King in *The Sleeping Beauty* pantomime, in which Nellie Wallace appeared as the Witch.

TATE, Nahum (1652–1715), a poor poet and worse playwright, who collaborated with Dryden in the second part of *Absalom and Achitophel* and with Nicholas Brady in a metrical version of the Psalms. His plays were mainly adaptations, and he is chiefly remembered for his tamperings with Shakespeare—in *King Lear* he makes Cordelia survive to marry Edgar—and for his mention by Pope in *The Dunciad*.

TAVISTOCK HOUSE THEATRE, a perfectly fitted and well-appointed private theatre in the London residence of Charles Dickens, where amateur performances were frequently given (see DICKENS).

TAVISTOCK LITTLE THEATRE, see AMATEUR THEATRE IN GREAT BRITAIN.

TAYLOR, Joseph (*c.* 1585–1652), English actor, with Lowin the chief business manager of the King's Men after the death of Condell and Heminge. He joined the company in 1619, at which date he was already a well-known actor, and took over many of Burbage's parts. He also appeared as the handsome young lovers, or the handsome dashing villains, in the plays of Beaumont and Fletcher. The third edition of *The Faithful Shepherdess*, which was acted at Court on Twelfth Night, contains a eulogy of Taylor, presumably for his acting in, and his production of, the play. Some of the costumes used were given to Taylor by the Queen 'the year before of her owne pastorall'. Taylor was one of the actors caught playing in the Cockpit when it was raided by Commonwealth soldiers, and Downes, writing during the Restoration, says that Davenant had seen Taylor act Hamlet, in which he had been coached by Shakespeare. This is unlikely, since Shakespeare was dead before Taylor joined the King's Men, but he may well have seen Burbage, the original player of the part, and modelled his performance on that. He is certainly said to have played it 'incomparably well', and also to have been good as Ferdinand in *The Duchess of Malfi*, another of Burbage's parts, as Iago, as Truewit in *Epicoene*, and as Face in *The Alchemist*. His name long remained synonymous with good acting.

TAYLOR, Laurette (1884–1946), see MANNERS (2).

TAYLOR, TOM (1817–80), English dramatist and editor of *Punch.* He was for some years Professor of English at London University, but from 1850 to 1871 was a civil servant in the Health Department. From his youth he was attracted to the theatre, and in 1844, his first year in London, had a play produced by the Keeleys at the Lyceum. He continued to write copiously until two years before his death, and was one of the most popular dramatists of his day. His chief successes were scored in domestic drama, though he also attempted plays on historical themes. He had little dramatic genius, and borrowed his material freely from various sources; but his excellent stagecraft and his skilful handling of contemporary themes make him always interesting, and in some respects a forerunner of the reforms of Robertson. Among his plays, which number over seventy, the best-known are *To Parents and Guardians* (1846); *Masks and Faces* (1852), a comedy on the life of Peg Woffington written in collaboration with Charles Reade and frequently revived; *Still Waters Run Deep* (1855), a play based on a French novel and remarkable in its time for its frank discussion of sex; *Our American Cousin* (1858), first done in New York and noteworthy because of the appearance in it of Sothern as Lord Dundreary, a part which he enlarged until it practically swamped the play; *The Overland Route* (1860); *The Ticket-of-Leave Man* (1863), a melodrama on a contemporary theme of low life which had much influence on such later works as *The Silver King*; and finally two plays written in collaboration, *New Men and Old Acres* (1869) and *Arkwright's Wife* (1873). Taylor was himself an enthusiastic amateur actor, playing at Tavistock House in Dickens's private theatre and being one of the leading members of the Canterbury Old Stagers. A genial, though sometimes irascible, man, he was extremely popular in London literary society, and an excellent journalist. There are some interesting glimpses of him in Ellen Terry's *Story of My Life.*

TCHEHOV, TCHEKHOV, see CHEKHOV.

TEARLE. (1) (GEORGE) OSMOND (1852–1901), English actor, who made his début at Liverpool on 26 Mar. 1869 and two years later appeared at Warrington as Hamlet, a part he subsequently played many times. After six years in the provinces he appeared in London and soon formed his own company, with which he toured. On 30 Sept. 1880 he joined the stock company at Wallack's, New York, making his first appearance there as Jaques, and later alternated between London and New York. In 1888 he organized a Shakespearian company which appeared with much success at Stratford-upon-Avon, and proved an invaluable training-ground for young actors. He was himself a fine Shakespearian actor, combining excellent elocution with a natural elegance and dignity. He had a high reputation in the provinces, and made his last appearance on the stage at Carlisle in 1901, dying a week later. His second wife was the daughter of the American actor F. B. Conway (see CONWAY, 4) and both their sons were on the stage, (2) GODFREY (1884–1953) making his first appearance in his father's company, and remaining with him until his death. He then had a long and illustrious career on the London stage, and in films, one of his outstanding parts being Commander Edward Ferrers in *The Flashing Stream* (1938). He was also good as Othello, as Hamlet, and as Antony. He was knighted in the Birthday Honours of 1951 for services to the stage.

TEASER (a term used in America for the proscenium border), see INNER PROSCENIUM.

TEATRO POR HORAS, see GÉNERO CHICO.

TELARI, see SCENERY, 2.

TELBIN, a family of English scene-painters, of whom (1) WILLIAM (1813–73) worked at Drury Lane under Macready in 1840. He had previously been connected with several provincial theatres, and was later at Covent Garden and at the Lyceum. His son (2) WILLIAM LEWIS (1846–1931) was at Manchester Theatre Royal for many years, and later in London, where in 1902, after a visit to Italy, he designed the settings and costumes for Alexander's production of *Paolo and Francesca* at the St. James's Theatre. He also worked for Irving at the Lyceum (see No. 73). Two sisters of the elder Telbin were on the stage in New York.

TEMPEST, MARIE [MARY SUSAN ETHERINGTON] (1864–1942), English actress, who in 1937 was created D.B.E. in recognition of her services to the stage. She was trained as a singer, and her first appearances were made in light opera and musical comedy. It was not until 1899 that she forsook music for straight acting, subsequently appearing only in comedy. Her first successes were made as Nell Gwynn, Peg Woffington, and Becky Sharp, and as Kitty in *The Marriage of Kitty*, in which she appeared during her engagement at the Duke of York's under Frohman. She subsequently revived this several times, in London and New York, and also on an extensive tour which took her all over the world. On her return she continued to appear in modern comedy, and soon became noted for her playing of charming and elegant middle-aged women—Judith Bliss in *Hay Fever*, Olivia in *Mr. Pim Passes By*, the title-role in *The First Mrs. Fraser*, and Fanny Cavendish in *Theatre Royal.* In 1935 she celebrated her stage jubilee with a matinée at Drury Lane in the presence of King George V and Queen Mary, the proceeds going to endow a ward for the theatrical profession in St. George's Hospital. She continued to act until her death, and retained to the end her elegant appearance, enhanced by an excellent taste in dress, and the subtlety and sureness of her superb technique.

TENNIS-COURT THEATRES. Both in Paris and in London in the mid-seventeenth century, tennis-courts were converted into theatres. Among the most famous were the Illustre-Théâtre (1644), where Molière first acted in Paris, and, in London, Killigrew's Vere Street Theatre (1660) and Davenant's Lincoln's Inn Fields Theatre (1661). They were used only for a short time, and their conversion into theatres must have entailed no more alteration than could have been easily removed to allow them to revert to their original use. The rectangular shape of the tennis-court auditorium, which approximated more to the private than the public Elizabethan theatre auditorium, may have influenced the eventual shape of the Restoration theatre, just as the boxes round the pit may have developed partly from the 'pent-house' or covered way which ran along one side and one end of the court itself. But lacking precise contemporary details of the method and work involved in such a conversion, no definite conclusion can be arrived at.

TENNYSON, ALFRED, LORD (1809–92), Poet Laureate after the death of Wordsworth. Though not gifted dramatically nor very much in touch with the contemporary stage, he nevertheless contributed to the poetic drama of his day. His first play, *Queen Mary* (1876), a somewhat frigid tragedy in blank verse on Elizabethan lines, was adapted and produced by Irving, as were *The Cup* (1881), with Ellen Terry as Camma, and *Becket* (1893), the last being considered by many the finest achievement of Irving's career. Of Tennyson's other plays in verse *The Falcon*, based on an episode in the Decameron, was given at the St. James's by the Kendals in 1879, *The Promise of May* (1882), a drama of modern village life, was unsuccessful at the Globe, and *The Foresters* (1892), with music by Sullivan, was seen at the Lyceum. A play on Harold was published in Tennyson's lifetime but not performed until Apr. 1928, when it was given by the Birmingham Repertory company at the Court Theatre, London, with Laurence Olivier as Harold; Robert Speaight, Ralph Richardson, and Gwen Ffrangcon-Davies were also in the cast. Like many other writers of his day, Tennyson failed to amalgamate fine poetry and good theatre, and the success of *Becket* was mainly due to the beauty and compelling power of Irving's interpretation. It has not been revived since his death.

TERENCE (*c.* 190–159 B.C.), Roman dramatist. We possess six plays by Publius Terentius Afer, produced between the years 166 and 160 B.C. From the prologues prefixed to these plays scholars of later ages attempted to reconstruct the life of the author, but their results were conflicting and should be treated with reserve. All Terence's prologues were written to meet the criticisms of his enemies. They said that he accepted literary help from his noble friends, that his plays were not accurate versions of his originals, and that he sometimes introduced scenes or characters from plays which had already been translated by other Roman dramatists. Terence's replies are evasive, but we can see that he endeavoured to improve on his Greek originals, thereby displaying an originality which we find in no other Roman writer of tragedy or comedy. Evidently he had his own artistic standards. He held that a play should explain itself, and ought not to require an explanatory prologue; on more than one occasion he altered monologue into dialogue to secure a more dramatic effect; he says that he added to Menander's *Eunuchus* two characters, the Captain and the Parasite, from another play by Menander; possibly he merely means that he added to the characters certain touches taken from the corresponding characters in the *Colax*; in the *Andria* he added a second lover who wishes to marry the girl destined by the parents as the bride of Pamphilus, who is himself in love with a girl of humble family. Everywhere in Terence we find contrasts of character; thus, for example, in the *Adelphi*, between Demea, the strict father, and his genial bachelor brother Micio; again there is a contrast between Demea's two sons, the headstrong if generous Aeschinus and the timid Ctesipho. Throughout his plays we find an atmosphere of culture and refinement, not unnatural in the works of a writer who had some contact with the aristocracy. The contrast with Plautus is complete; there are few jokes and no buffoonery or topical allusions or irrelevancy; we find ourselves in a world which is not strikingly Greek or Roman, but independent of place and time. When Terence added Charinus to the *Andria* he introduced a situation not to be paralleled in Greek comedy —a young gentleman in love with a young lady of his own station. The oriental seclusion of young ladies in Athens, as reflected in comedy, made it practically impossible for a young man to meet any young woman of his own class. The greater freedom of women in Rome made it possible to develop the love-interest in literature on almost modern lines.

That Terence had his difficulties with the public as well as with his critics is shown by the two failures of the *Hecyra*. The turbulent Roman audience was only too ready to leave the theatre if bored, and seek the entertainment presented by rope-dancers and gladiators. We can well understand Julius Caesar's criticism that Terence lacked *vis comica*. Nevertheless he achieved success, even during his short career as a dramatist; and after his death the polish of his style made him one of the favourite Roman authors. Terence's interest was, above all things, in humanity at large; the fine and famous remark of one of his characters, 'I am a human being and think all human affairs my concern', is true of Terence himself, and gives his work an abiding charm. In the schools of the Middle Ages the plays of Terence were read and acted. In the tenth century the nun Hroswitha wrote the well-known plays in which she tried to imitate Terence's style while improving on his morality. At the Renaissance his works were translated into several languages, and his influence was particularly marked in France. WILLIAM BEARE†

TERPSICHORE, the Muse of Dancing.

TERRISS. (1) William [really WILLIAM CHARLES JAMES LEWIN] (1847–97), English actor, known affectionately by the British public as 'Breezy Bill' and 'No. 1, Adelphi Terriss', since his best work was done at the Adelphi Theatre. In his early days he was a sailor, but, irked by the monotony, he left; nor did medicine and engineering, both suggested careers, attract him. He looked for excitement, action, and rapid movement, and found them on the stage. His first professional appearance —he had been an enthusiastic amateur—was made in Birmingham in 1867, and was by no means successful. Nothing daunted, he applied to Bancroft and was engaged. Still he made no mark, and with his wife, Amy Fellowes, also an actress, he emigrated to the Falkland Islands, where he bred sheep and broke-in wild horses. Eventually he returned to England, tried the stage again—as Doricourt in *The Belle's Stratagem*—and this time was successful. One of his first big successes was as Nicholas Nickleby at the Adelphi, but he made his name as Squire Thornhill in *Olivia* at the Court Theatre in 1878, playing opposite Ellen Terry. Later he played Romeo to Adelaide Neilson's Juliet, and in 1880 he joined Irving at the Lyceum, where he remained for some time. He was one of the few actors who were not afraid to stand up to the great actor-manager. But he is best remembered as the hero of a famous series of melodramas at the Adelphi. His charm and gusto delighted the audience, and the success of such plays as *Harbour Lights*, *The Girl I Left Behind Me*, and *One of the Best* (which Bernard Shaw reviewed under the heading of 'One of the Worst') owed much to his handsome, debonair presence and vigorous acting. He was one of the most popular actors of his time, as he was also one of the kindest and most generous of men, and his untimely assassination by a madman in 1897 outside the Adelphi Theatre was a great grief to his numerous admirers, and a loss to the English stage. A theatre at Rotherhithe, which opened in 1899, was named after him. His daughter (2) ELLALINE (1871–1971), who was born during her parents' stay in the Falkland Islands, married Seymour Hicks, a partnership which proved ideal both on and off stage. She made her first appearance under Tree at the Haymarket in 1888, and had a long and varied career, appearing with her husband in many of his own plays, including *Bluebell in Fairyland*, first produced in 1901 and many times revived. One of her outstanding appearances was as Phoebe Throssel in *Quality Street* (1902). She accompanied her husband on tour, both in straight plays and on the music-halls, and went with him to France in 1914 to give concerts to the troops, and in the 1920s to Australia and Canada. She made her last appearance on the stage in *The Miracle Man* (1935). In 1928 she published a volume of reminiscences (see also HICKS).

TERRY, a family of English actors which has given many illustrious players to the stage. The first was (1) BENJAMIN (1818–96), son of an innkeeper at Portsmouth, a handsome man with a fine voice, gifts which he has transmitted to his descendants through several generations. Some of their good looks and excellent elocution may also have come from his wife, (2) SARAH BALLARD (1817–92), the daughter of a Portsmouth builder, who adopted her husband's profession and as Miss Yerret proved herself a good actress. Of their eleven children two died in infancy, the rest were connected with the stage, three sons in business or managerial capacities. The eldest daughter, (3) KATE (1844–1924), was on the stage as a child, and at eight years of age went to London to play Prince Arthur in Charles Kean's production of *King John* at the Princess's. She remained there until the Keans left that theatre, playing also Cordelia. She then went to the Bristol stock company, returned to London to play Ophelia to Fechter's Hamlet, appeared in several of Tom Taylor's plays, and seemed to be heading for a brilliant career when in 1867 she left the stage on her marriage to Arthur Lewis. Of her four daughters, one, also Kate, became the mother of Val and John Gielgud, while another, (4) MABEL GWYNEDD TERRY-LEWIS (1872–1957), went on the stage, making her first appearance on 17 Jan. 1895 with John Hare in *A Pair of Spectacles*. She retired on her marriage in 1905, but lost her husband during the First World War, and returned to the theatre in 1920, playing in *The Grain of Mustard Seed* at the Ambassadors. Her retirement had in no way impaired her excellence, and she immediately embarked on a long and successful career.

The most distinguished member of the Terry family was Benjamin's second daughter, (5) ELLEN ALICE (1847–1928), who made her first appearance on the stage at the Princess's Theatre as Mamillius in *The Winter's Tale* at the age of 9 (see No. 167). She too remained with the Keans until their retirement in 1859, and in the summer of that and succeeding years toured with her sister Kate in *A Drawing-Room Entertainment*, in which they each played several parts in some small sketches. Ellen joined the Bristol stock company and later returned to London to appear at the Haymarket. It was while acting there that she left the stage to marry the painter G. F. Watts, an ill-judged union which soon came to an end. Returning to the theatre for a short while, she again left it, this time for six years, during which time her two children were born (see CRAIG, EDITH and EDWARD GORDON, and GODWIN, E. W.). When she reappeared as Philippa in *The Wandering Heir*, at the insistence of the author, Charles Reade, to replace Mrs. John Wood, she was as brilliant as ever, and the long rest seemed only to have increased the excellence of her acting. This was particularly noticeable in Portia, which she played at the Prince of Wales's under the management of the Bancrofts. She remained with them for a year, and then went to the Court Theatre under Hare, playing one of her few 'original' parts—Olivia in an adaptation of *The Vicar of Wakefield*. It was during the run of this play that Ellen Terry married her second husband, Charles Kelly, who died in 1885.

In 1878 Irving, who had recently begun his tenancy of the Lyceum, engaged Ellen Terry as his leading lady, thus inaugurating a partnership which became one of the glories of the English stage. It lasted until 1902, and ranged over a wide field, including a good deal of Shakespeare, revivals of modern plays like *The Lady of Lyons* and *Robert Macaire*, and plays specially written for Irving, *Charles I*, *Becket*, and *The Bells*. Ellen Terry accompanied Irving on his American tours, and subsequently toured there under the management of Charles Frohman. After leaving the Lyceum she became manager of the Imperial Theatre, where she produced *The Vikings* and *Much Ado About Nothing*, with sets designed by her son Gordon Craig, and then appeared in two new plays, *The Good Hope*, by Heijermans, and Barrie's *Alice Sit-By-The-Fire*. In 1906 she celebrated her stage jubilee with a mammoth matinée at Drury Lane at which all the stage personalities of the day assisted, as well as 23 members of her own family. She was at this time appearing at the Court Theatre in *Captain Brassbound's Conversion*. In 1907 she married as her third husband James Carew [Usselman], and appeared rarely on the stage. Instead she toured America and Australia, giving lectures on Shakespeare, four of which were published in 1931, proving once again how excellent was her critical faculty and how masterly her handling of the written word. These qualities had already appeared in her autobiography, published in 1908 (republished with notes and an additional section by Christopher St. John in 1933), and can be seen in her correspondence with Bernard Shaw, published in 1931. Throughout her career she was an inspiration to those who played with her, and Matheson Lang, who once played Benedick to her Beatrice—which many considered her finest part—said that he learnt more of the real art of acting from that experience than from all the work of the seven years before. It is difficult to convey any impression of her luminosity and joyousness. She was not at her best in tragedy, though some critics thought her Lady Macbeth very fine, and she never played Rosalind, which seemed above all other parts to have been written for her. But as Beatrice, as Olivia, as Portia, as Lilian in *New Men and Old Acres*, as Lady Teazle, as Desdemona, as Viola, as Cordelia, and in a hundred other parts, she played with a freshness and vitality which gave life to the dullest moment. She was created D.B.E. in 1925.

Two more Terry sisters were on the stage, (6) MARION (1852–1930), who made her first appearance as Ophelia in Tom Taylor's version of *Hamlet*, and (7) FLORENCE (FLOSS) (1854–96), who also made her first appearance as a child in one of Tom Taylor's plays. She played Nerissa to Ellen's Portia, and was much admired in her elder sister's part of Olivia, which she played on tour. She was apparently a young actress of great promise, but left the stage on her marriage in 1882. Her daughter, Olive, and granddaughter followed the family tradition. Marion continued her career as an able and attractive actress, playing, among many other parts, Dorothy in *Dan'l Druce, Blacksmith* (1876), and the young ladies of T. W. Robertson's comedies. She went with the Bancrofts to the Haymarket and later, with Alexander at the St. James's, was the first Mrs. Erlynne in *Lady Windermere's Fan*. She also played in some of H. A. Jones's plays, and was the original Susan Throssel of *Quality Street*. She was not often seen in Shakespeare, though on occasion she deputized for her sister Ellen, and was at her best in light comedy. Her last appearance on the stage was as the Princess in *Our Betters* in 1923, after which she retired on account of ill health. It was said of her by a critic in her young days that she represented the type of woman whom all good Englishmen love.

The youngest child of Benjamin and Sarah was (8) FRED (1863–1933), a handsome, romantic actor, who made his first appearance on the stage at the Haymarket under the Bancrofts in 1880. In 1884 he played Sebastian to his sister Ellen's Viola at the Lyceum, and was an immediate success. He is mainly remembered for his performance as Sir Percy Blakeney in *The Scarlet Pimpernel*, which he frequently revived, but he was also much admired in *Sweet Nell of Old Drury*, *Dorothy o' the Hall*, *Matt o' Merrymount*, and *Henry of Navarre*. In these and many other productions he played with his wife (9) JULIA EMILIE NEILSON (1868–1957), who was a student at the Royal Academy of Music and went on the stage on the advice of Gilbert, playing Cynisca to Mary Anderson's Galatea at the Lyceum, 21 Mar. 1888. She later appeared as Galatea, and was in *Broken Hearts* and *The Wicked World* at the Savoy. After touring with Tree she returned with him to the Haymarket, where she remained for five years, making an outstanding success as Drusilla Ives in *The Dancing Girl* and as Hester Worsley in *A Woman of No Importance*. It was here that she first met her future husband, whom she describes in her memoirs as 'tall, taller than I; handsome as a picture; ardent about the theatre. He had all the gay charm of his already famous family, beautifully courteous manners and a passion for hard work.' She appeared for a short time under other managements, notably as Princess Flavia in *The Prisoner of Zenda*, but from 1900 to 1930 she and her husband toured or played in London with their own company. They were ideally suited, and though some may have thought her a finer player than her husband it was truly said in his obituary notice that 'the public which only remembers him as the actor-manager . . . playing a strictly limited type of role, have really no conception of what a sound all-round actor Fred Terry really was'. After his death Julia was seen with Seymour Hicks in *Vintage Wine* (1934). She celebrated her stage jubilee in 1938, and after some years in retirement made a final appearance in 1944, playing Lady Ruthven in *The Widow of Forty*. Her son and daughter were both on the stage, (10) Dennis (1895–1932) making his first appearance at Drury Lane as a page in the 1906 celebrations of his aunt Ellen Terry's jubilee. As Derrick Dennis he played a wide variety of parts up to the outbreak of the First World War in 1914. Invalided out of the army in 1917, he returned to the stage, and shortly after married an actress, Mary Glynne [really Aitkin] (1898–1954), by whom he had two daughters, Hazel and Monica, of whom the former also became an actress. Dennis and his wife were on tour in South Africa when he died suddenly of pneumonia. His sister, (11) Phyllis (1892–), made her first appearance in *Henry of Navarre* (1909) under her father's management, and later was much admired as Viola. She has appeared in a number of Shakespeare productions, both in England and in America (see No. 8o), toured in vaudeville, and played Principal Boy in pantomime. It was under her management that her young cousin, John Gielgud, made his first professional appearance.

Two nieces of Ellen Terry, (12) Minnie (1882–1964) and (13) Beatrice (1890–), daughters of her brother Charles, were also on the stage. Beatrice went to America in 1916 and had a distinguished career there, making her last appearance in New York in 1938. Minnie, who married the distinguished actor Edmund Gwenn (1875–1959), played mainly on the London stage and retired in 1923. Both sisters were on the stage as small children, Minnie at 3 playing in *Frou-Frou* (1885), and Beatrice at the same age appearing as the Baby in *Olivia* (1893) with Irving and Ellen Terry.

TERRY, Daniel (1789–1829), English actor, friend of Sir Walter Scott, several of whose novels he dramatized for Covent Garden, where they were given with elaborate scenery, and music by Bishop. Terry, who was no relation to the above family as far as is known, was trained as an architect, and later applied his knowledge to the designing of Abbotsford, but in 1803 he joined a company in Sheffield under the father of Macready. Two years later he was with Stephen Kemble, and then went to Edinburgh with Henry Siddons. A good-looking man, with a fine voice and a sensitive, alert face, he made his first appearance in London at the Haymarket in 1812, playing the fop, Lord Ogleby, in *The Clandestine Marriage*. From 1813 to 1822 he was a member of the Covent Garden company, and went to Edinburgh in 1815 to support Mrs. Siddons in her farewell engagement there. He was also seen at Drury Lane. In 1825, in partnership with Frederick Yates, he took over the Adelphi, but the venture was not a financial success, and Terry soon retired. He was at his best in character parts, particularly those of old men, or in strong emotional drama, but he had little tenderness or subtlety, and seldom attempted young lovers or the serious gentlemen of old comedy.

TERRY, Edward O'Connor (1844–1912), English actor and manager, not connected with any of the actors listed above. He made his first appearances in amateur theatricals, and in 1863 appeared in several provincial towns, notably in the Isle of Man, with a touring company which included the young Henry Irving. He then went to Belfast, where he supported a number of visiting stars. He was first remarked for his playing of such Shakespearian parts as Touchstone and Dogberry at Manchester under Calvert, and was seen in London, at the Surrey, in 1867. A year later he played the First Grave-digger at the Lyceum, and then spent several years with Mrs. Swanborough at the Strand, playing in burlesque and light comedy. This led to his engagement by Hollingshead for the Gaiety, where from 1876 he was a member of the famous 'Gaiety Quartet' with Nellie Farren, Kate Vaughan, and Edward Royce. In 1887 he opened his own theatre in the Strand. It was built on the site of a famous supper-room and music-hall called the Coal Hole. Terry gave it his own name, and opened with *The Churchwarden* and *The Woman Hater* on Oct. 17. His first success at this short-lived theatre was *Sweet Lavender*, produced there on 21 Mar. 1888 with himself as Dick Phenyl —his best part. It ran for 684 performances, and its author, Pinero, had a further play produced at Terry's—*The Times* (1891)— as well as a revival of *In Chancery* (1892). Terry's Theatre later became a cinema and was pulled down during the rebuilding of the Strand in 1923. In 1904, Terry, who toured extensively in Australia, South Africa, and America, married as his second wife the widow of Sir Augustus Harris. Though not an outstanding actor, he was a good eccentric comedian, and a careful and conscientious manager.

THADDÄDL, see AUSTRIA.

THALIA, the Muse of Comedy.

THALIA, New York, see BOWERY THEATRE, 1.

THEATRE, The, the first—and most appropriately named—playhouse to be erected in London, was built by James Burbage, who on 13 Apr. 1576 obtained a twenty-one years' lease of houses and land situated between Finsbury Fields and the public road from Bishopsgate to Shoreditch Church. The site became Holywell Lane, Shoreditch, at the south-west corner of the Fields. It was a definite article of the lease that a playhouse should be erected on the land. Burbage took his father-in-law,

John Braynes, into partnership, and they built a circular wooden building, without a roof, for theatrical and other entertainments. It cost between £600 and £700; the actual sum advanced by Braynes was one thousand marks, roughly about £660. Burbage was his own architect and builder. The actual dimensions are not known, but the building was apparently commodious, with scaffolding for galleries and what would now be described as boxes. It opened in the autumn of 1576. Admission was one penny for standing room on the ground, and a second penny for admission to the galleries; for a further penny one could obtain a stool, or what was described as 'a quiet standing'.

The history of the Theatre is stormy. The Corporation of the City of London strongly disapproved of plays and players, and consequently of this innovation of playhouses, and kept up a continual persecution. But the public evidently flocked there, for the authorities and the preachers of the day complained constantly of the crowds which resorted to the playhouse. Burbage was made to pay an extra £10 in rent 'in respect of the great profit and commoditie which he had made and in time to come was further likely to make out of the Theatre'. That profit, however, seems problematical.

The Theatre did not have a very distinguished dramatic career. Its chief use for a while, and at intervals throughout its existence, was for exhibitions and competitions of sword-play, fencing, quarterstaff, and athletic exercises. But naturally Burbage used it for the company with which he was connected, the Earl of Leicester's Men: Warwick's Men played there too. The Queen's Men and other players were there in 1583–91. Strange's and the Admiral's Men played there in 1590–1, and then the Chamberlain's Men, the most distinguished company of the time, which Burbage and the best of Leicester's Men had joined. Plays performed there include the lost and anonymous *Blacksmith's Daughter* and *The History of Caesar and Pompey*, *Cataline's Conspiracies*, probably the original *Hamlet* on which Shakespeare based his play, and *Dr. Faustus*, during a performance of which the theatre cracked, to the alarm of the audience. Tarleton and Kempe also performed 'jigges and drolls' there.

In spite of the claim that he was doing good business, Burbage found it hard to pay the higher rent for which he was always being pressed, and also the interest on the original loan. The City Corporation, too, made things difficult for him, and when in 1597 Giles Allen, the ground landlord, declared that he intended to end the lease, Burbage's sons, Richard and Cuthbert, who had succeeded their father, now dead, took advantage of a clause which enabled them to remove from the site 'all such buildings and other things as should be builded'. They pulled down the Theatre, transported the timber and material across the river to Bankside, and used them to build the famous Globe. W. MACQUEEN-POPE†

THEATRE ACOUSTICS, see ACOUSTICS.

THEATRE ARCHITECTURE, see ARCHITECTURE.

THEATRE ARTS, an American magazine of international interest, which monthly surveyed the theatre all over the world in essays, reviews, and photographs. Founded in Detroit in Nov. 1916, as a quarterly under the name of *Theatre Arts Magazine*, its first editor was Sheldon Cheney. From the beginning the magazine set itself a high standard, which was consistently maintained under the subsequent editorships of Edith J. R. Isaacs and Rosamond Gilder. It was also responsible for the publication of a number of important theatrical books, and of portfolios of stage designs (see also ISAACS, EDITH J. R.). In Feb. 1948 it was amalgamated with *The Stage*, and under a new management and editor continued to appear monthly until Jan. 1964, when it finally ceased publication.

THEATRE COLLECTIONS, see COLLECTIONS.

THÉÂTRE D'ART, PARIS, see LUGNÉ-POË; **DE L'ATELIER,** PARIS, see DULLIN; **DE L'ŒUVRE,** PARIS, see LUGNÉ-POË.

THEATRE DE LYS, NEW YORK, on Christopher Street in Greenwich Village. This off-Broadway playhouse, run by Lucille Lortel, housed for six years, from 1955 to 1961, *The Threepenny Opera*, Marc Blitzstein's English adaptation of *Die Dreigroschenoper*, by Brecht, with music by Kurt Weill, which was itself based on Gay's *The Beggar's Opera.* This was followed by George Tabori's compilation of Brecht items known as *Brecht on Brecht* (1962), which also had a long run. One of the outstanding features of the theatre has been its Matinée Series, run for the American National Theatre and Academy by Lucille Lortel, in which established actors experiment with new forms and techniques. *Brecht on Brecht* began in this way in 1961. Among the performers in this series, in works by O'Neill, Thurber, Giraudoux, Marlowe, and Kafka, have been Peggy Wood, Helen Hayes, Eva Le Gallienne, Siobhan McKenna, Sybil Thorndike, and Lewis Casson.

THÉÂTRE DE MADAME, PARIS, see GYMNASE-DRAMATIQUE.

THÉÂTRE DES NATIONS, PARIS. This International Festival, held annually in Paris, arose out of the establishment in 1954, by A. M. Julien, of an experimental early summer season of plays by foreign companies specially imported for the purpose. This proved so successful that after two further seasons it was officially established in 1957, with sixteen different companies, acting in nine languages, succeeding each other at the Théâtre Sarah-Bernhardt from March to July. Every year an increasing number of foreign companies takes part, and the range covers every type of theatrical entertainment—classical, neo-classical, and modern drama; opera, ballet, dance-drama, and the exotic and unclassifiable companies from the Far East—the Peking Opera, the Korean Opera, the Japanese *Nō* and *kabuki*, the Ceylon dancers. Some of the pleasure of this festival lies in seeing great acting ensembles interpreting the masterpieces of their own dramatic heritage—the Old Vic in Shakespeare, the Moscow Art Theatre in Chekhov, the Berliner Ensemble in Brecht, the Italians in Goldoni and Pirandello, the Americans in O'Neill—there can by now be hardly a country in the world which has not contributed something of its own theatre to the international repertory. But there is also the added interest of seeing works from one country interpreted by another—Molière by Canadians and Moroccans, Sartre by Germans, Brecht by Israelis. Nothing could be more instructive, and at the same time more conducive to understanding of and research into international theatre, than this confrontation within narrow limits of time and space of different, often extreme, styles of acting and presentation.

The Théâtre des Nations, which brings together theatre-lovers and theatre-workers from all over the world, does not confine itself to the provision of plays only. It has its own journal, *Rendezvous des Théâtres du Monde*, now known as *Théâtre: drame, musique, danse*, which appears eleven times a year, and whose original title still serves as a device for the enterprise as a whole; it invites distinguished lecturers on theatrical subjects to address the members of its club, which has many thousands of French and foreign members, and encourages discussion on points of interest; it organizes conferences on specific subjects, whose conclusions are published in volume form; it has founded an International Association of Theatre Technicians and one of Dramatic Critics; and every year it widens the horizons of actors and audience alike with new importations from all over the world. In 1960 A. M. Julien, who was appointed Director of the Réunion des Théâtres Lyriques Nationaux, handed over the direction of the Théâtre des Nations to Claude Planson, who has worked for it since its inception.

THÉÂTRE-FRANÇAIS, PARIS, see COMÉDIE-FRANÇAISE.

THEATRE GUILD, NEW YORK, a membership society for the presentation of distinguished and non-commercial American and foreign plays, which made its first public appearance in 1919 with *The Bonds of Interest*. Its second production, which scored an unexpected success, was *John Ferguson*, since when the Theatre Guild has been the means of introducing many notable plays and players to America. Its influence, in its early years particularly, was very great, and although success later modified its original programme somewhat, it maintains its high standard and its preference for what is new and unusual in the world's theatre. The precursor of the Theatre Guild was the group known as the Washington Square Players, which was formed in 1914 under Edward Goodman, began productions in 1915, and moved from the Bandbox to the Comedy Theatre in 1916. It presented a programme of non-commercial plays with some success. Katharine Cornell made one of her earliest appearances with this group. The first productions of the Theatre Guild were given at the Garrick, and in 1925 the society built its own playhouse (see GUILD THEATRE).

THEATRE-IN-THE-ROUND, a form of play presentation in which the audience is seated all round the acting area, usually in raked tiers, since otherwise they are not all able to see the stage easily. If, however, this is a raised platform, it is possible to accommodate the spectators on the flat. In present practice this form of theatre is inexpensive, since it can be set up in any convenient hall, and lends itself to experiment by those who are rebelling against the so-called tyranny of the proscenium arch. The idea is not new. It has been shown that a number of medieval productions, notably in Cornwall, were given in open-air emplacements with the audience on a raised bank encompassing the actors. Indoors, the Christmas Mumming play must often have found itself developing in a closed circle of spectators. There is so much informality in the set-up, and it leads to so close a rapport between actor and audience, that it may be ideal for a certain type of play, more particularly one which depends on intimacy and not spectacle for its appeal. But this very intimacy may prove disconcerting both to actor and to audience, who both need to become accustomed to the distractions inherent in a closed circle, through which the actors must pass to reach the stage.

Modern theatre-in-the-round first came into prominence in Russia, where in the 1930s Okhlopkov in his Realistic Theatre produced a number of Soviet plays on stages set up in the central area with the audience pressing close on all sides, and sometimes being drawn into the action. At the same time, in England, Robert Atkins was producing Shakespeare in The Ring (a boxing-ring) at Blackfriars, an interesting experiment which seemed, however, to have no immediate impact. It was in America, particularly in the rapidly expanding world of university drama, that theatre-in-the-round flourished. Robert Edmond Jones had already, in 1920, prepared drawings for a centrally-staged production of *The Cenci*, thus antedating Okhlopkov, but the project was never realized. Nor was his theatre-in-the-round design of 1930 actually used, but it may have influenced the building at the University of Washington in Seattle in 1940 of Glenn Hughes's Penthouse Theatre (see No. 41), which had an elliptical acting area and auditorium contained within a circular foyer, the space between them on two sides being used for prop rooms and a lighting control booth.

Outside the universities the most important American exponent of this type of production was undoubtedly Margo Jones, whose work at Dallas she has herself chronicled in a volume published in 1951. Such theatres as Circle-in-the-Square have made theatre-in-the-round familiar to off-Broadway playgoers, and in 1961 the first specifically designed playhouse of this type was built in Washington, D.C. Seating 750, it has a square acting area, with on each side a steep tier of eight rows of seats with an aisle and private boxes behind. The first row is raised slightly above stage level and set back behind a low rail. This has the advantage of putting it outside the area covered by the stage lighting, and so does away with one of the main distractions of this type of production, the awareness of the audience immediately opposite. This theatre, designed by Harry Weese, was taken over by a company which had previously been playing in-the-round in a converted brewery known familiarly as the 'Old Vat'. It opened with Brecht's *Caucasian Chalk Circle* in a version by John Holmstrom, which enjoyed a successful four-weeks' run.

In England the main exponent of theatre-in-the-round has been Stephen Joseph, whose work in Scarborough and the surrounding district has proved the value of this type of production in places which might otherwise not be able to support living theatre, and for whose company the old Victoria Theatre, Stoke-on-Trent, was reopened in 1962 as a permanent winter theatre-in-the-round. His wide choice of play has also enabled playgoers to judge of the suitability of central staging for works of various periods and styles. Londoners have on several occasions had the opportunity of seeing his company on visits to the Mahatma Gandhi Hall. Otherwise their only chance of estimating theatre-in-the-round was at the short-lived but exciting Pembroke Theatre in Croydon. A number of new theatres, both professional and amateur, are being built with adaptable stages which can be used, among other things, for theatre-in-the-round.

An unfortunate confusion of name has arisen over these new techniques in staging. Theatre-in-the-round is self-explanatory, as is the seldom-used 'central staging'. But in America the term 'arena' has also, and, one would think, quite properly, been applied to such staging. The Washington theatre referred to above is officially the Arena Stage. But in England the term has been used of the platform, or open stage, which has the audience on three sides only, as in the Elizabethan public theatre, and now at Chichester, in the Assembly Theatre in Edinburgh, at Stratford, Ontario (see No. 43) and in the travelling Arena Theatre of John English. There is also the so-called 'open-end' stage at the Mermaid, Puddle Dock, which has seats in straight rows facing the stage only, but does away with all barriers between actors and audience (see No. 42). These, and many other varieties of staging, seem to prove that any form of production will succeed, provided the play and the actors are good enough in themselves to hold the audience's attention.

THÉÂTRE-ITALIEN, PARIS, see COMÉDIE-ITALIENNE.

THEATRE LIBRARY ASSOCIATION, an organization founded in 1937 by H. M. Lydenberg, then head of the New York Public Library, at the suggestion of George Freedley, with the intention of fostering the preservation of theatrical books, pamphlets, playbills, programmes, relics, and ephemera, by the exchange of material and ideas between private and public collectors all over the world. Since May 1940 the Association has published a *Broadside* three times a year on theatre work, research in progress, and the location of theatrical material, and from 1942 to 1960 it also issued a *Theatre Annual*.

THÉÂTRE LIBRE, PARIS, see ANTOINE.

THEATRE MACHINERY, see MACHINERY and TRICKWORK ON THE ENGLISH STAGE.

THÉÂTRE MIXTE, PARIS, see THÉÂTRE DE L'ŒUVRE.

THEATRE MUSIC, see INCIDENTAL MUSIC.

THÉÂTRE NATIONAL POPULAIRE. In 1920 Firmin Gémier sought to establish in France a popular theatre which should appeal to, and be supported by, the masses. After a chequered career, this enterprise found itself in 1937 in the Palais de Chaillot, with a newly built theatre seating 2,700 spectators, a stage 70 feet deep and a proscenium opening 80 feet wide. It languished from lack of funds and audiences, until in 1951 Jean Vilar became its director. He removed the footlights and batten lights from the theatre, and extended the forestage into the audience, thus providing a flexible stage for experimental productions. He inaugurated in Nov. 1951, with the 'Week-end de Suresnes', a series of suburban performances in large halls, where, for a small inclusive fee, the public was offered two plays, a lecture or discussion with the actors, a concert, two meals, and a dance. As well as these and other activities in Paris, the T.N.P., as it is usually called, plays at the Avignon Festival (founded by Vilar) and tours France and other countries. It was seen at Edinburgh in 1953 and in London in April 1956. Subsidized by the State, it is bound to give at least 150 performances in and around Paris every year, and must keep its prices low. Otherwise the director is free to choose his plays and his company, which consists of some eighteen to twenty-five actors, on a yearly contract. Under Vilar's able direction the T.N.P. flourished, and became the most important theatrical enterprise in France. In 1963 Jean Vilar resigned, and was succeeded by Georges Wilson, an actor who first appeared with the T.N.P. in *Lorenzaccio* (with Gérard Philipe) in 1952. He later did a number of productions, and was responsible for staging *L'Illusion comique*, a little-known comedy by Corneille with which he opened his first season.

THEATRE OF COMEDY, Leningrad, see akimov.

THEATRE OF CRUELTY, see artaud, a.

THEATRE OF DRAMA, Moscow, see theatre of the revolution.

THEATRE OF THE BALTIC FLEET. In 1930 an amateur dramatic group formed of sailors from the Baltic Fleet, which was based on Leningrad, began giving concerts on board ship and in Baltic ports. By degrees its members achieved professional status, and it was reinforced by professional actors conscripted into the Navy. In 1934 A. V. Pergament, a Leningrad producer, became its director, and its repertory ranged from Russian classics to plays specially written for it, mainly about the sea. It continued to perform during the Second World War, suffering many casualties, and was in Leningrad during the siege, when a new topical play, *To Meet the Squadron*, was performed (1942). It also continued to give concerts and revues. In 1943 Vishnevsky wrote for it *At the Walls of Leningrad* and, in collaboration with Kron and Azarov, a musical play, *Wide Spreads the Sea*, dealing with the siege of Leningrad. This group is now fully professional, with a permanent base at Fleet headquarters. Most of its performances are intended for naval audiences, and plays on naval and military subjects predominate in its repertory, though classics and modern plays on civilian life are occasionally performed.

THEATRE OF THE REVOLUTION, Moscow. This theatre, which in 1945 was amalgamated with the Moscow Theatre of Drama, and in 1954 was renamed the Mayakovsky, was directed by Okhlopkov from 1943 until his death in 1967. It was founded in 1922 as an organ of propaganda, and under Meyerhold produced a series of new plays, mostly dealing with problems of the day. Popov, later to rank so high in the history of the Soviet theatre, became its director in 1930, and an immediate deepening of serious purpose was apparent. An earlier manifestation of this had been seen in *The Man with the Portfolio* (1928), produced by Dikie, but it was strengthened by such productions as *Poem About an Axe*, *My Friend*, and *Joy Street*. Under Popov the theatre also tackled *Romeo and Juliet* with such success that it has remained in the repertory ever since. During the Second World War the theatre was evacuated, but returned under Okhlopkov with a programme of new and interesting plays, some of which provoked criticism. Okhlopkov's audiences could always be sure of being interested and stimulated, but controversy raged over his production of *Hamlet* in 1954 (see No. 90) and even of *Mother Courage* in 1960, in spite of the fine performances of Y. S. Glizer and M. M. Shtrankh which made the play an outstanding success. Among Okhlopkov's other production's were Fadeyev's *The Young Guard* and Virta's *Great Days* (both 1947), *Glory* (1954), by V. Gusev, Finn's *The Beginning of Life* (1958), and *Vassilyi Terkin* (1961), based on Tvardovsky's poem of the same name (see also okhlopkov).

THEATRE ORCHESTRA, see incidental music.

THEATRE PRESERVATION IN GREAT BRITAIN. By the beginning of the 1960s more than half the theatres which were functioning in 1939 had been demolished or taken over for other purposes. Many buildings of great historical interest had disappeared, and a number of towns found themselves with no live theatre at all, or with a sole survivor seriously threatened. To meet this situation local Theatre Preservation Societies and others are pressing local authorities to use more fully the powers vested in them for the preservation of theatre buildings.

Under Clause 29 of the 1947 Town and Country Planning Act, the local Planning Authority can, by means of a building preservation order, restrict the demolition, alteration, or extension of any building of special architectural or historical interest, and for their guidance the Minister of Housing and Local Government under Clause 30 of the same Act has compiled a schedule of such buildings. But so far as theatres are concerned the effect has been slight. Only fifteen buildings have been scheduled, and of these only three—Drury Lane, Covent Garden, and the Haymarket—are classified as Grade I, that is as buildings whose preservation is considered a matter of national concern. Buildings in Grade II are protected only to the extent that the developer of the site must give the local authority two months' notice of his intentions. This did not save the Theatre Royal, Leicester, or the Lyceum, Newport, as the time is too short for emergency action if the local authority has not already a considered policy on theatre buildings. Buildings in Grade III are merely listed.

To assist him in scheduling buildings the Minister appointed an Advisory Committee, but since its interests were mainly architectural and historical, it was not suitable for dealing with theatres. A voluntary Theatres' Advisory Council representative of all aspects of the theatre, capable of offering expert guidance to local authorities, was therefore set up in 1962.

Of greater importance than scheduling is the legal provision that any 'development' which makes a material change in the use of any building requires the prior permission of the local authorities. To guide potential developers the authority can designate on the Town Development Plan the proper use of sites in specific areas. The Finsbury Park Empire was saved in this way, since the site was in a designated residential area. To designate the centre of a town as an 'amenity area' is an even more positive help. In its 'amenity' area of theatreland, the G.L.C. requires that a theatre, if demolished, should be replaced by another building for use as a theatre.

The main limitations to the present exercise of the above powers are threefold. First, the developer has the right of appeal to the Minister. But recent cases suggest that a sympathetic view of theatre needs is now being taken by the Minister's inspectors, who conduct the public inquiries arising out of appeals. The judgement after the 1962 inquiry into the position of the New Theatre, Cardiff, stated:

> The financial loss which has resulted from the theatre's use is evidence of a lack of need from a purely commercial point of view . . . but there are other aspects which need to be considered. . . . There is a strong case for preserving the New Theatre as a live theatre, to ensure the equitable distribution of art and culture.

In the second place, there is a serious loophole in the legal provisions, as planning permission is not required for works which affect only the interior of a building unless there is a 'change of use'. In accordance with the 1950 Order which regulated this matter, a theatre building may be saved, but its interior could be used as 'a cinema, a music-hall, a dance-hall, a skating rink, a swimming bath, a Turkish or other vapour foam bath, or gymnasium or for indoor games.' Under the 1965 Order a separate 'use class' was provided for theatres, music-halls, and cinemas.

Finally, theatre preservation may involve a less profitable use of a site, and the local authority may therefore be faced with the possibility of having to provide financial support. Powers to incur expenditure in providing 'civic entertainment' are contained in the 1948 Local Government Act, and a number of 'civic' theatres have come into existence in this way. But hesitancy about the spending of public money may mean inadequate preservation, particularly where it inhibits a policy which might, for example, lead to the replacing of an obsolete theatre by a modern one (see also CIVIC THEATRE). WILLIAM KENDALL

THEATRE ROYAL, BRIDGES STREET, see DRURY LANE; HOLBORN, see CONNAUGHT THEATRE; MARYLEBONE, see WEST LONDON THEATRE; STRAND, see STRAND THEATRE, 1; STRATFORD, LONDON, see THEATRE WORKSHOP; WESTMINSTER, see ASTLEY'S AMPHITHEATRE. Many provincial theatres were given the name Theatre Royal when they obtained a licence.

THEATRE SCENERY, see SCENERY.

THEATRE WORKSHOP, a company founded in Kendal in 1945 by a group of actors who, according to their manifesto, were 'dissatisfied with the commercial theatre on artistic grounds' and on 'social and political grounds'. Some of the original members of Theatre Workshop had worked together in the North of England before 1939, among them Joan Littlewood, who became producer and director of the new group, and Gerald Raffles, who took over the administration. For seven years the company toured Great Britain and Europe, seldom remaining more than a few weeks in the same place. It had no financial backing or official support, and all income was shared equally among the members. In 1953 they took over the derelict Theatre Royal at Stratford, London (Chaucer's Stratford-atte-Bowe)—which first opened on 17 Dec. 1884—and after repairing and redecorating the interior themselves, they opened in February with a production of *Twelfth Night* which, like all subsequent productions, ran for five weeks. The company was invited by the French organizers to represent Great Britain at the Paris International Theatre Festivals in 1955 and 1956, playing *Arden of Feversham* and *Volpone* on the first occasion, and *The Good Soldier Schweik* (in an English adaptation by Ewan McColl, a member of the company and Joan Littlewood's husband) on the second. On both occasions they were highly praised. They also visited Zürich, Belgrade, and Moscow, where they appeared in the Moscow Art Theatre, filling it to capacity. One of their most interesting and controversial productions was *Richard II*. Left-wing, and indeed almost communist in their ideology, they sought always to revivify the English theatre by a fresh approach to established texts, or by the commissioning of working-class plays, many of which were subsequently transferred to West-End theatres. The first of these was Brendan Behan's *The Quare Fellow*, a play on prison life (1956). Others were *A Taste of Honey* and *The Hostage* (both 1958) and *Fings Ain't Wot They Used T'Be* (1959). In 1961 Joan Littlewood, finding that this commercial success was endangering her ideals, and that constant transfers of complete casts to London theatres drained her resources, left the company to work elsewhere. After a period of inactivity, it started up again under Gerald Raffles, and in 1963 Joan Littlewood returned to produce *Oh, What a Lovely War!*, which was subsequently transferred to Wyndham's. In Aug. 1964 the company finally disbanded and the theatre was taken over by a new company. It opened on 17 Sept. 1964 with Max Frisch's *Count Oederland*, and has since done interesting work.

THEATRICAL COMMONWEALTH. 1. The name taken by a group of disgruntled actors in Philadelphia in 1812, who tried unsuccessfully to start a profit-sharing company of their own, in opposition to the established theatres.

2. A group of actors who seceded from the Park Theatre, New York, in the autumn of 1813, and set up for themselves in a converted circus on Broadway. The company included Holman and his daughter, Gilfert, later Holman's son-in-law, Leigh, Wareing, Mrs.

Twaits, and Mrs. Goldson. Twaits was the manager, and the company gave some good plays—an excellent *School for Scandal*, and good productions of *The Rivals* and *As You Like It*. Emboldened by their popularity, the rebels had the temerity to put on *The Virgin of the Sun* on the same night as the Park, with some success. The theatre closed in Dec. 1813 on the death of Mrs. Twaits, and the company finally disbanded in Jan. 1814, several of the actors returning to the Park.

THEATRICAL SYNDICATE, an association of American businessmen in the theatre, formed in 1896, which included the firm of Klaw and Erlanger, Charles Frohman, Al Hayman, Sam Nixon [Samuel F. Nirdlinger], and J. Fred Zimmerman. For about sixteen years they controlled most of the theatres of New York and many of those in other big towns, and gradually exerted a stranglehold over the entertainment life of the country. They were powerful enough to harm those who opposed their monopoly, forcing Mrs. Fiske to play in second-rate theatres on tour, and Sarah Bernhardt to appear in a tent. Both, with Belasco, helped in the end to break the syndicate, whose original good intentions of organizing the theatre and preventing exploitation and wastage had been overlaid by a desire to make money without reference to aesthetic values, and a determined elimination of healthy competition.

THEODORUS, a Greek tragic actor of the fourth century B.C.

THEOGNIS, a Greek tragic poet who, according to Aristophanes, was so frigid that when his play was produced in Athens the rivers froze in Thrace.

THÉOPHILE DE VIAU (1590–1626), French dramatist, author of *Pirame et Thisbé*, a pastoral given in 1621. It was most successful, and helped to establish the vogue of the unities. It was revived at Court in 1627 with Mlle de Rambouillet as Pyramus. With his contemporary the Marquis de Racan, Théophile marks the entry into French drama of the poet and courtier, but unlike his companion he had a stormy life. He was suspected of being —as a Huguenot and a *libertin*—part-author of *Le Parnasse satirique*, and therefore exiled. Though he later returned to France and became a Catholic, he was again accused of atheism and immorality, and condemned to be burnt at the stake. Escaping this fate, he was banished, and died shortly afterwards at the home of his friend and benefactor Montmorency.

THEORIC FUND, a grant of two obols distributed to the poorer citizens of Athens to enable them to pay for admission to the theatre at the Dionysiac festivals. It was introduced in the time of Pericles, suppressed during the Peloponnesian War, and revived by the demagogue Agyrrhius in 394 B.C., when it was raised to one drachma a head. It was finally abolished by the intervention of Demosthenes after Chaeronea.

THESPIS, of Icaria, in Attica, a Greek poet who has good claims to be considered the founder of drama, since he was the first to use an actor in his plays, in addition to the chorus and its leader. He won the prize at the first tragic contest in Athens, *c.* 534 B C. Titles only of his plays are preserved, and even these may not be genuine. H. D. F. KITTO

Tradition has it that Thespis took his actors round in a cart, which formed their stage (cf. Horace, *Ars Poetica*, and Dryden's prologue to Lee's *Sophonisba*). The adjective Thespian has come to be used of actors and acting in general, and often figures in the names of amateur companies, while 'the Thespian art' is journalese for the art of acting.

THIRTY-NINTH STREET THEATRE, NEW YORK. This had a short but brilliant career as a playhouse. It was opened by the Shuberts on 18 Apr. 1910 as the Nazimova, with that actress in the first New York production of *Little Eyolf*, which ran for six weeks. A year later, rechristened, it opened again with *Green Stockings*, and later saw Charles Quartermaine and Madge Titheradge in *A Butterfly on the Wheel*. Towards the end of 1912 Annie Russell conducted a repertory season of English classics at this theatre, and a year later John Barrymore appeared there in the Harvard Prize Play, *Believe Me, Xantippe*. In 1919 Walter Hampden appeared as Hamlet, and the theatre continued to flourish until 1925, when it was pulled down. An office building now stands on the site. GEORGE FREEDLEY†

THOMAS, AUGUSTUS (1857–1934), American dramatist, whose numerous plays are mainly based on themes of American life and thought. He was associated as a young man with an amateur dramatic club in St. Louis, his birthplace, both as actor and author, and a sketch, *Editha's Burglar*, written for production by the club, was later rewritten as a full-length play and produced in 1889 with Maurice Barrymore in the role of the burglar. Thomas succeeded Boucicault as adapter of foreign plays at the Madison Square Theatre under Palmer, but his first popular success, an original drama entitled *Alabama* (1891), enabled him to resign and devote his time to his own work. Among his later plays were several others based on a definite locality—*In Mizzoura* (1893), *Arizona* (1899), *Colorado* (1901), and *Rio Grande* (1916). His best play was *The Copperhead* (1918), in which Lionel Barrymore made a hit as Milt Shanks. An interest in hypnotism and faith-healing was shown in *The Witching Hour* (1907), *Harvest Moon* (1909), and *As a Man Thinks* (1911), but on the whole Thomas's plays are not profound, and provided entertainment of a kind acceptable to his audience. He probably wrote too much and too unevenly, but he is of significance in the development of the modern

American play by his consistent use of native material. In 1922 he published his autobiography under the title of *The Print of My Remembrance*.

THOMAS, WALTER BRANDON (1856–1914), English actor, playwright, and song writer, best remembered for his farce *Charley's Aunt*, which has been seen in London almost every year since its first production at the Royalty on 21 Dec. 1892, when it ran for four years with W. S. Penley in the title-role. In later revivals Thomas played the part himself. It was filmed, has been seen as a musical, *Where's Charley?* (which was successful in New York in 1948, but not in London ten years later), and has figured in the repertory of almost every amateur and provincial theatre, as well as being played all over the world in English and in innumerable translations. At one time it was running simultaneously in 48 theatres in 22 languages, among them Afrikaans, Chinese, Esperanto, Gaelic, Russian, and Zulu. Thomas, who wrote other plays, but never again with such success, made his stage début, after some amateur experience, with the Kendals at the Court Theatre in 1879, and was with them at St. James's until 1885. He also appeared on the halls in coon songs which he wrote himself.

THOMPSON, JOHN (?–1634), English actor, who was with the King's Men for some years as their leading boy-player. In about 1621 he played the Cardinal's mistress in *The Duchess of Malfi*, and for the next ten years continued to appear as a woman, mostly in queenly or haughty parts, sometimes as a regal villainess. Since several of his roles comprised songs, it is reasonable to suppose that he was something of a singer. He does not appear to have fulfilled as an adult player the promise of his youth, but since he only lived for a short time after attaining male roles, it is probable that he lacked time and opportunity to show what he could do. He was closely associated with the actor Shank, and may have been apprenticed to him.

THOMPSON, LYDIA (1836–1908), English actress, who was first a dancer, appearing at His Majesty's in 1852, and then went into burlesque, with which her name is chiefly connected. She became well known in the provinces, and in 1868 took a troupe of golden-haired English beauties to the United States, where she remained six years, joining forces with Willie Edouin and introducing burlesque to America. She also went to Australia and India, and on returning to England in 1874 alternated between there and New York until her death. From 1886 to 1888 she was manageress of the Strand Theatre, London, and made her last appearance at the Imperial in 1904.

THOMSON, JAMES (1700–48), English poet, author of the long poem *The Seasons*, and possibly of 'Rule Britannia', which first appeared in his masque of *Alfred* (1740). He was celebrated in his own day for some forgotten tragedies on classical lines: *Sophonisba* (1730); *Agamemnon* (1738), in which the Cibbers and Quin appeared, though with little success; *Tancred and Sigismunda* (1745), possibly his best work, in which, says Allardyce Nicoll in *Eighteenth Century Drama*, 'while the treatment is classical to a degree, the theme shows clearly Thomson's move from the duller realms of pseudo-classicism to the spacier realms of romantic enthusiasm'; and *Coriolanus* (1749), given posthumously, again with Quin, and a failure. Thomson's only other play, *Edward and Eleonora*, which deals classically with the romantic theme later treated by Scott in *The Talisman*, was banned by the censor and not produced. Thomson was one of the best dramatists of his day, in the opinion of Pope and others, but the permanent eclipse of his theatrical work shows to what a low ebb the English theatre had fallen at this time in its endeavours to ape the stately measures of French classical tragedy.

THORNDIKE. (1) DAME (AGNES) SYBIL (1882–), English actress, widow of Sir Lewis Casson, whom she married in 1908. In 1931 she was created D.B.E. for her services to the English theatre. She began her career under Ben Greet, touring with him in England and the United States, and was leading lady for several seasons at Miss Horniman's Repertory Theatre in Manchester, where she laid the foundations of her later career, Shaw calling her even then his ideal Candida. From 1914 to 1918 she was at the Old Vic, where she played not only a long series of Shakespearian and other heroines, but also such parts as Prince Hal, Puck, Launcelot Gobbo, the Fool in *King Lear*, and Ferdinand in *The Tempest*. She returned to the Vic many times, and during the Second World War toured mining towns and villages with an Old Vic company as Lady Macbeth, Candida, and Medea. Among the outstanding performances of her long and distinguished career have been Hecuba in *The Trojan Women* (1920), Joan of Arc in Shaw's *Saint Joan* (1924), and the elderly schoolmistress, Miss Moffat, in *The Corn is Green* (1938). To celebrate her golden wedding she appeared with her husband (see CASSON) in *Eighty in the Shade* (1958), a play specially written for them by Clemence Dane. In 1962 they both appeared at the first Chichester Theatre Festival, as the Nurse and 'Woffles' in *Uncle Vanya*, and in 1964 she was seen in a new comedy, *The Reluctant Peer*. Her versatility has been shown by her appearances in Grand Guignol, in modern comedy, in Greek tragedy, in poetic drama, and in English and foreign classics. Her biography was written in 1929 by her brother, (2) (ARTHUR) RUSSELL (1885–), with whom she collaborated in a life of Lilian Baylis. Like his sister, Russell Thorndike, actor, dramatist, and novelist, has been associated with Ben Greet and the Old Vic, where he was leading man for several seasons. He was also with Matheson Lang, and was a member of Miss Horniman's company in Manchester. One of his finest performances was given in the title-role of his own play, *Dr. Syn* (1925). He was also much admired as Smee in many productions of *Peter Pan*. His best Shakespearian parts were Caliban, Touchstone, Launcelot Gobbo, Sly, Pistol, and Pandarus. His younger sister, (3) EILEEN (1891–1953), was also an actress, making her first appearance at the Court Theatre in 1909. From 1912 to 1917 she was at the Liverpool Repertory Theatre, but retired from the stage on her marriage, and did not act again until 1930. Among her later parts were Katharine in *Henry VIII*, Viola, the Queen in *Hamlet*, and an outstanding Charlotte in *The Brontës of Haworth* (1932). She was also good as the Nurse in *Romeo and Juliet* and as Mrs. Hawkins in *Treasure Island*. She made her last appearance on the stage at the Arts Theatre in 1950 in a revival of *The Mask and the Face*, playing Teresa. From 1933 to 1939 she was principal of the Embassy School of Acting, and was also connected with the Central School of Speech Training.

THORNE. (1) CHARLES ROBERT, senior (*c.* 1814–93), American actor, son of a New York merchant, who made his first appearance on the stage at the Park Theatre in 1829. A year later he starred at the Bowery, where he met and married (2) ANN MARIA MESTAYER (? –1881), member of a famous circus family. He appeared with her at many theatres and was for some time manager of the Chatham, but though his work was good he had no settled policy, and contributed little to the development of the American stage. He toured extensively, and managed theatres in several large towns, notably San Francisco. Of his five children the best known was (3) CHARLES ROBERT, junior (1840–83), who as a child toured with his parents, and in 1860 was with Jefferson in New York, where he played in the latter's revival of *Our American Cousin* at Laura Keene's Theatre. He was later in Boston, but his career really began when in 1871 he joined the Union Square Theatre under Palmer, where he was for many years immensely popular as the dashing young heroes of melodrama. A good-looking, athletic, and attractive person, not over-intelligent, he represented the ideal romantic hero of the time. In 1874 he was seen in London with some success. He made his last appearance in 1883 in *The Corsican Brothers*, but was forced to retire from the cast owing to illness, and died soon afterwards.

THORNE, SARAH (1837–99), English actress and theatre manager, who for many years ran the stock company at the Theatre Royal, Margate, where she trained a number of young players, including Louis Calvert, Granville-Barker, and Violet and Irene Vanbrugh. She came of good theatrical stock, her father being Richard Samuel Thorne, a provincial actor-manager. Of her seven brothers and sisters, who all went on the stage, the best known is (2) THOMAS (1841–1918), for many years actor-manager at the Vaudeville, where with David James he presented and played in *Our Boys*. This ran for several years and made fortunes for its author, H. J. Byron, and the two partners. Sarah's son (3) GEORGE (1856–1922) was also an actor, and made his first appearance at his mother's theatre at the age of two. He toured India, and played Grossmith's parts in D'Oyly Carte's principal touring company. In addition he wrote a number of burlesques and pantomimes and adapted several of Dickens's novels for the stage. W. MACQUEEN-POPE†

THREE HUNDRED CLUB, LONDON, see STAGE SOCIETY.

THROWLINE, a cord used to join the flats forming a wall, as in a box-set (see FLAT).

THUNDER. The noise of thunder is usually produced off-stage by the shaking of a suspended iron sheet known as the Thunder Sheet. An earlier, Georgian, device was the Thunder Run, consisting of two long, inclined, wooden troughs down which iron balls were rolled past releasing-doors, to produce an effect whose sound not only came from overhead but whose reverberations shook the building with a trembling as awful as the true peals of Jove himself. For an account of the existing Thunder Run at the Theatre Royal, Bristol (see No. 27), see an illustrated article by Richard Southern in *The Architectural Review* for May 1944.

TIE-BARS, metal strap-hooks, linking the upright posts under a raked stage.

TIECK, LUDWIG (1773–1853), German romantic poet and playwright, whose early plays were fairy-tales treated in a vein of Aristophanic satire. Among these were *Der gestiefelte Kater* (1797), *Ritter Blaubart* (1797), and *Die verkehrte Welt* (1798). His wit and his mental acrobatics are often engaging, but they tend to pall as the absence of any positive standard becomes apparent. He followed his short plays in prose with long, often very long, verse dramas such as the *Leben und Tod der heiligen Genoveva* (1799) and *Kaiser Oktavianus* (1804). In 1824 Tieck was appointed director of the Dresden Court theatre, where he insisted on clear diction and simplified staging. He became an influential critic, and his writings on the theatre, afterwards collected as *Dramaturgische Blätter* (1826), reveal him as a man of insight and taste, but without the moral force of a great reformer. His interest in the Elizabethan age is reflected in his novels, *Dichterleben* (1826) and, with echoes of *Wilhelm Meister*, in *Der junge Tischlermeister* (1836), and also in his translations of Ben Jonson. His daughter Dorothea completed Schlegel's translations of Shakespeare, whose reputation in Germany she and her father did much to further.

TILLEY, VESTA (1864–1952), a famous music-hall performer, at her best in male impersonations. Her real name was Matilda Alice Powles, and her father was on the stage as Harry Ball, being later Chairman of Gloucester

Music-Hall, and manager of St. George's Hall, Nottingham. It was here that she first appeared at the age of 3½, billed as 'The Great Little Tilley'. She made her first appearance in male attire at the age of 5 in Birmingham, as 'The Pocket Sim Reeves'. In 1873 she made her first appearance in London, playing three halls a night—the Canterbury, Lusby's, and Marylebone, adding the name of Vesta to her pet-name of Tilley. At 13 she appeared in pantomime as Robinson Crusoe in Portsmouth, and later was Principal Boy in many pantomimes in London and the provinces, including Drury Lane, where she appeared for the first time in 1880 under Harris. But her real home was the music-hall, and among the songs she made famous were 'Burlington Bertie', 'Jolly Good Luck to the Girl who Loves a Soldier', 'The Army of To-day's All Right', 'Six Days Leave', 'Following in Father's Footsteps', and 'The Piccadilly Johnny with the Little Glass Eye'. She was known for many years as the London Idol, and was sadly missed when she retired from the stage after a final appearance at the Coliseum in 1920. In 1890 she married Walter de Frece, who was knighted in 1919 and died in 1935.

TILNEY, Sir Edmund, see MASTER OF THE REVELS.

TIMES SQUARE THEATRE, New York, on the north side of West 42nd Street. This was opened by the Selwyns on 30 Sept. 1920 with *The Mirage*, which ran for 192 performances. Several musical plays were followed by *The Fool*, and by a short-lived version of *Pelleas and Melisande* with Jane Cowl. Two later successes were André Charlot's *Revue*, with a large cast of London favourites, and *Gentlemen Prefer Blondes*, while *Front Page* occupied the season of 1928–9 with 199 performances. In Jan. 1931 came Coward's *Private Lives*, with the author, Gertrude Lawrence, Jill Esmond, and Laurence Olivier; in spite of changes in the cast, it ran for 256 performances. The last play at this theatre, which then became a cinema, was *Forsaking All Others*, which introduced Tallulah Bankhead to Broadway. GEORGE FREEDLEY†

TIREMAN, the Elizabethan equivalent of the modern Wardrobe Master (or Mistress). Chambers sums up his duties as follows: He 'fitted the dresses and the beards, furnished stools, and in the private theatres took charge of the lights'.

TIRSO DE MOLINA (*c.* 1571–1648), a Spanish ecclesiastic whose real name was Fray Gabriel Téllez. His secular works include novels and a large number of plays, of which more than eighty are extant, though he claimed to have written 400. Their technique derives from that of his near-contemporary Lope de Vega, whom he much admired, but the technique is modified by Tirso's greater interest in the psychology of his characters. He was particularly good at drawing women, at their wittiest and most intelligent in such comedies as *Don Gil de las calzas verdes* and *El vergonzoso en palacio*. His historical play, *La prudencia en la mujer*, gives an excellent portrait of the heroic Queen María, and points a moral for Spanish politics of the 1620s. Tirso also wrote a number of religious plays, including *autos sacramentales* and biblical plays, and he is probably the author of *El condenado por desconfiado*, which dramatizes the theological sin of despair and the power of grace through faith. His most famous work is *El burlador de Sevilla y Convidado de piedra*, the first of many plays based on the legend of Don Juan, later developed in contrasting ways by Molière, Mozart, Zorrilla, Shaw, and others. A. A. Parker's statement that Spanish dramatists of the seventeenth century subordinate character to action and action to theme is true of Tirso as well as of others, yet even so he allows character a more important place than do his contemporaries, and for this reason he has been considered the Spanish dramatist with most affinity to Shakespeare. After a period of temporary eclipse, he now takes his place in the front rank with Lope de Vega and Calderón.

J. E. VAREY

TITINIUS, see FABULA, 9. *Togata*.

TIVOLI, The, one of London's most famous music-halls. It stood in the Strand when that thoroughfare was a great centre of amusement and night-life, and was erected in 1890 on the site of a beer-hall of the same name. At first it was unsuccessful, but when Charles Morton was called in to run it, it picked up and as the 'Tiv' became a popular resort. It closed in 1914, and a cinema was built on the site in 1923, which in its turn was pulled down in 1957.

TIVOLI GARDENS, New York, see RICHMOND HILL THEATRE.

TOBY. 1. The dog of the Punch and Judy show. He joined Punch after the latter had become established in England, and has no connexion with the *commedia dell'arte*; nor does he figure in the harlequinade, though Clown is sometimes accompanied by a mongrel puppy. In early Punch and Judy shows there was sometimes a puppet-dog, but there is no evidence that he was called Toby. The name seems to have come into use with the introduction of a live dog, somewhere between 1820 and 1850, possibly because the first dog to be employed was already so called. It has also been suggested that the name has some connexion with Tobit or Tobias, a favourite subject for a seventeenth-century puppet-show, where Tobias and the angel are accompanied by a dog. Toby is usually a small, quick-witted, mongrel terrier. Wearing a ruff round his neck, he sits on the sill of the puppet-booth window, taking little part in the action, though he may be fondled by Punch in a momont of lachrymose sentimentality, or incited to bite the heads off some of Punch's enemies, not excepting the baby. In the end he usually seizes Punch by the nose, and is killed. After the show he goes round among the audience, with whom he is a firm favourite, collecting pennies in a little bag which he holds in his mouth. ED.

2. A stock character in the folk theatre of the United States, a bucolic comedy juvenile leading man in provincial repertory companies of the Mississippi Valley and the Great South-West. Most travelling dramatic tent-shows, playing one-week stands in rural communities, feature a Toby-comedian, and he is also popular aboard the remaining showboats on the inland American waters. Deriving from the *commedia dell'arte*, the Shakespeare clown, the conventional stage 'silly boy', and the Yankee comedian, Toby is the only standard character in the American theatre who is permitted to improvise within the framework of his background. He represents the country bumpkin triumphant over evil (usually personified as 'city slickers'). With a freckled face and a blacked-out front tooth, he wears a rumpled red wig, battered hat, calico shirt, baggy jeans, and large ill-fitting boots or shoes. He first emerged in the 1900s, and Frederick R. Wilson, member of a touring tent-show company known as Horace Murphy's Comedians, was the first of a long line of actors to specialize in Toby roles; plays have been specially written for him, and Broadway successes have been plagiarized with titles and plots altered to include Toby as the chief character. Toby-comedy includes generous use of the topical 'ad-lib', and expert use of such theatrical gymnastics as the pratt-fall, glides, splits, and rubber-legs. Toby sometimes leaves the stage during the play and conducts his fooling in the audience. It is traditional in revivals of *Uncle Tom's Cabin* for the Toby-comedian of the troupe to don black-face and a gunnysack costume to impersonate Topsy. Toby frequently has a feminine counterpart in the company, the granddaughter of the old-time 'rough soubrette', by the name of Susie. Although there are still a number of small-time Toby shows in remote areas, the last of any importance, with a tradition of continuity, closed in Wapello, Iowa, on 1 Oct. 1962, after nearly fifty years under its managers Mr. and Mrs. Neil Schaffner, who played Toby and Susie. ROBERT DOWNING

TOGATA, see FABULA, 9.

TOGGLE RAIL, a wooden bar across the back of a canvas flat, used to strengthen it and to counteract the drawing power of size paint as it dries (see FLAT).

TOLLER, ERNST (1893–1939), German dramatist, and one of the best and most mature writers of the expressionist school. His first play, *Wandlung* (1918), written during his imprisonment as a pacifist, is a plea for tolerance and the abolition of war. Three years later came his best-known work, *Masse-Mensch* (1921), followed by *Die Maschinenstürmer* (1922), which deals with the Luddite riots of 1815 in England, and was done in London by the Stage Society as *The Machine Wreckers*. It is less expressionist in technique than *Masse-Mensch*, and less pessimistic, since Toller, in the person of his hero, Jim Cobbett, foreshadows the day when the rebellious workers will be an organized and stable body of intelligent men. But Toller's later plays, which failed to reach the heights of his earlier work, were progressively less hopeful in tone as he watched the domestic tragedy of Germany unfold itself, and the man who had been imprisoned for his part in the communist rising of 1919 left Germany in 1933 to become a British subject. He went to America, lecturing and advising on drama, and committed suicide in the summer of 1939.

TOLSTOY, ALEXEI KONSTANTINOVICH (1817–75), Russian diplomat, friend of Alexander II, who was born in St. Petersburg of a noble family, and held many important posts. He was the author of a number of poems, and of a fine historical trilogy, containing excellent crowd scenes and written with much semi-oriental imagery, in which he idealized old feudal Russia. They are *The Death of Ivan the Terrible*, *Tsar Feodor Ivanovich*, and *Tsar Boris*. Written between 1866 and 1870, they were banned by the censor, who finally allowed the second to be put on as the opening production of the Moscow Art Theatre in 1898. Later the complete trilogy was given.

TOLSTOY, ALEXEI NIKOLAIVICH (1882–1945), one of the outstanding writers of early Soviet Russia, whose first work was published under the Imperial régime, in 1908. Member of an aristocratic family, he received a good education, and devoted himself to literature. His first play was written after the October Revolution, and showed its influence reaching out even to Mars. Later works included a trilogy on Peter I, based on his own novel, and another historical trilogy on Ivan the Terrible, of which the first part, dealing with Ivan's youth and marriage, was produced by the Maly in 1943, and the second part, dealing with Ivan's struggles to unite Russia, by the Moscow Art Theatre later in the same year. Among plays on a modern theme an outstanding one was *The Road to Victory* (1939), dealing with an episode of the Revolution in which both Stalin and Lenin appear.

TOLSTOY, LEO NIKOLAIVICH (1828–1910), one of the great names in Russian literature and social history, the bulk of whose work lies outside the theatre. He was first encouraged to try his hand at playwriting in the 1850s, under the influence of Turgeniev and Ostrovsky, and started some comedies which, however, remained unfinished. It was not until 1886 that he once more turned to the theatre, and by then his whole philosophy of life had undergone a change. Under the influence of M. V. Lentovsky, director of one of the Moscow People's Theatres, who was looking for plays dealing with the life of the people—a subject few fashionable authors cared to touch at that time—Tolstoy wrote *The Power of Darkness*, possibly the most forceful peasant play ever written. The material for it came from real life, since the main outline was taken from a criminal case heard at Tula. In the hands of such an artist as Tolstoy the sordid tale of crime became a stark naturalistic document, comparable with Hauptmann's *Vor Sonnenaufgang*, and as such was for many years banned by the censor. It was first acted abroad, in Paris, and then in Berlin. In it Tolstoy revealed to what depths of degradation the 'idiocy of village life' could reduce human beings, until their most ordinary instincts were perverted and grew unnatural.

His second play, *The Fruits of Enlightenment*, which was also begun in 1886, arose out of a visit to a spiritualist séance. Published in 1891 and produced at the Moscow Maly Theatre in the following year, this satirizes the parasitic life of the country gentry, their preoccupation with trifles, their exploitation of the poverty-stricken peasants, and the latter's growing resentment. It is one of the world's classics, and rings as true today as when it was written. In presentation it is probably possible to give it greater truth today than at its first production, since the Imperial Theatres were ill equipped to enact the peasant characters, which even the Moscow Art Theatre could not at first fully develop.

Tolstoy's last plays were both unfinished, and bring into the theatre the theory of 'passive resistance' which he was developing in his other work at the time. *Redemption* (or *The Living Corpse*, as it is sometimes called) is a problem play centring upon the conflict between the Christian doctrine of self-sacrifice and the marriage laws of the State. It made a great impression when it was first seen in Europe, and Lenin, in his analysis of Tolstoy's work, said 'it is a wonderfully powerful, direct and truthful protest against social lies and hypocrisy'. It was produced by the Moscow Art Theatre in 1911.

The Light that Shines in Darkness was Tolstoy's last work for the theatre, and its final act exists only in outline. In it he tried to sum up all his hopes, experiences, and opinions on life. Here again he uses the method of parallel conflict, in which the useless life of the wealthy Sarintsev family alternates with that of the poverty-stricken, overworked, and helpless peasants.

Two of Tolstoy's novels, *Resurrection* and *Anna Karenina*, were also dramatized and produced with great success at the Moscow Art Theatre and elsewhere.

TOOLE, JOHN LAURENCE (1830–1906), English actor and theatre manager. Born in London, where his father was Toastmaster to the East India Company, he was for a short time, like Garrick, clerk to a wine-merchant, but success in amateur theatricals, notably as Jacob Earwig in *Boots at the Swan*, turned his thoughts to the stage. Encouraged by Dickens, he joined Dillon's company in Dublin in 1852 as a low comedian, and two years later made a fleeting appearance in London, returning to establish himself, after further experience in the provinces, in 1856. He was seen at the Lyceum as Fanfaronade in *Belphegor*, in which Marie Wilton, later Lady Bancroft, also made her first appearance in London. On the recommendation of Dickens, Toole was engaged by Ben Webster for the New Adelphi in 1858, and remained there nine years. Among his successful parts were Bob Cratchit in *A Christmas Carol* (1859) and Caleb Plummer in *Dot* (1862), Boucicault's dramatization of *The Cricket on the Hearth*. In this he combined humour with a pathos which showed how well he might have played serious character parts; but the public preferred him in farce. He was for many years a close friend of Irving, with whom he first played at the Queen's, Long Acre, in 1857, and subsequently on tour. In 1869 he began a long association with Hollingshead at the Gaiety, being excellent in burlesque and *opéra bouffe*, and in 1879 he went into management at the Charing Cross Theatre with a good resident stock company, giving it his own name in 1882. The most important production of his last years was Barrie's first play, a farce entitled *Walker, London* (1892). He habitually toured the provinces in summer with a good company, gaining thereby much profit and reputation. Crippled by gout, he left the stage in 1895, when his theatre was pulled down, and retired to Brighton, where he died. He made one appearance in New York, in 1874, at Wallack's, but was not very successful, his humour being too cockneyfied for the Americans. Clement Scott called him 'one of the kindest and most genial men who ever drew breath. . . . No one acted with more spirit or enjoyed so thoroughly the mere pleasure of acting.' He was much respected in his profession, and always on good terms with his audience, being particularly good at end-of-performance speeches.

TOOLE'S THEATRE, LONDON, in King William Street, Charing Cross. This was originally the Polygraphic Hall, where Woodin gave monologue entertainments. In 1869 it became a small theatre, known as the Charing Cross, but nothing of any importance happened there until J. S. Clarke revived *The Rivals* in 1872, himself playing Bob Acres with Mrs. Stirling as Mrs. Malaprop, her first appearance in this, her best, part. Alexander Henderson became manager in 1876, and renamed the theatre the Folly. His wife, Lydia Thompson, starred under him in burlesque. In 1878 the theatre had a tremendous success with Violet Cameron and Shiel Barry in Planquette's 'Les Cloches de Corneville'.

In 1879 Toole took over, and three years later gave the theatre his own name. Pinero's early comedy, *Imprudence*, was produced there in 1881, followed by *Boys and Girls*. Both failed, but burlesques by H. J. Byron were successful. Daly's company made their first London appearance at Toole's in 1884, and in 1892 Barrie's first play, *Walker, London*, began a successful run. Toole had enlarged and improved the theatre, but it never held more than 900 people. His last production there was *Thoroughbred*, in Feb. 1895. It closed in the same year, the land having been acquired for an extension of the Charing Cross Hospital.

W. MACQUEEN-POPE†

TOOLEY, NICHOLAS (*c.* 1575–1623), English actor whose real name was Wilkinson. He was with the King's Men from about 1605 to his death and was an intimate friend of the Burbage family. He may indeed have been apprenticed to Richard, whose will he witnessed, and he was lodging in Cuthbert Burbage's house at the time of his death. It is not known with any certainty what roles he played, except for that of Forobosco in *The Duchess of Malfi* (1614). His name appears in the actor-list of Shakespeare's plays.

TOP DROP, another name for Border.

TORELLI, GIACOMO (1608–78), the first professional scene-painter who was not primarily an artist. He was working at the Teatro Novissimo in Venice in 1641–3, where, it is said, the magical effects of his stage mechanisms gave rise to a suspicion that he was in league with the devil. He thereupon went to Paris, remaining there from 1645 until 1662. In 1650 he devised some fine scenic effects for Corneille's spectacle-play *Andromède*, given at Molière's first theatre, the Petit-Bourbon, which Torelli had refurbished backstage. He was above all a practical man of the theatre, and made many important innovations in the setting and designing of scenery, being the first inventor of a device for moving several sets of wings on to the stage simultaneously. His achievements earned him the nickname of 'il gran stregone' (the great wizard, or magician), but much of the work he did in Paris was destroyed by his rival Vigarani (see SCENERY, 2 and No. 62).

TORMENTOR, a term originally applied to a sliding extension of the proscenium wing, now to the fixed narrow flat, covered in black velvet, which has replaced it.

TORRES NAHARRO, BARTOLOMÉ DE (?–*c.* 1524), with Encina and Vicente, one of the leading Spanish dramatists of the early part of the sixteenth century. Little is known of his life, but from 1513 he was in Rome, where most of his plays appear to have been written. His collected works appeared in 1517 under the title of *Propalladia*. The important prologue distinguishes between two types of play, the *comedia a noticia* and the *comedia a fantasía*, terms which may be said to correspond to realistic and novelesque genres. Of the former type two examples have survived, the *Comedia soldadesca*, dealing with a braggart Spanish Captain, and the *Comedia tinellaria*, depicting life in the servants' hall of an Italian palace. The best-known example of Torres Naharro's novelesque plays is the *Comedia Himenea*, where the relationship between master and man and the theme of the conflict of love and honour both foreshadow the plays of Lope de Vega.

J. E. VAREY

TOTTENHAM STREET THEATRE, LONDON, see SCALA THEATRE.

TOURING COMPANY, see PROVINCIAL THEATRES, I.

TOURNEUR, CYRIL (1575–1626), English dramatist, of whose life very little is known, though he was connected with the Cecils and may have been used by them on secret missions abroad. In the year before his death he was secretary to the council of war at Cadiz under Sir Edward Cecil. Two extant plays are doubtfully assigned to him, *The Revenger's Tragedy*, published in 1607 and probably played a year or two previously, and *The Atheist's Tragedy*, published in 1611 and probably written in 1606, since echoes of *King Lear* have been noted in it. The manuscript of a further play, *The Nobleman*, was destroyed by Warburton's cook.

TOVSTONOGOV, GEORGYI ALEXANDROVICH (1915–   ), Soviet producer, who began his theatrical career in 1935 in the Russian theatre in Tbilisi, and in 1949 became director of the Lenkom in Leningrad. He was already regarded as one of the most promising of the younger producers, and his services were in demand everywhere. In 1956 he became chief producer at the Gorky Bolshoi Dramatic Theatre, where one of his most successful productions was *The Ocean* (1941) by Shteyn. He has a very individual style, and often prefaces his productions with a prologue intended to put the audience in the right mood for what is to follow. *When the Acacia Blooms*, a comedy, was preceded by a witty conversation between two elegant actors; *Sixth Floor*, a tragedy, opened with one dim lamp in a dreary corridor; Dostoievsky's *The Idiot* was prefaced by the showing of a vast facsimile of the original title-page of the novel; in *The Irkutsk Story* the hero, seated at the top of rising tiers of seats, struck chords on a piano. Tovstonogov's experiments may not always succeed, but whatever he does is worth watching, being full of life and vigour and showing a fresh approach not only to new plays but also to revivals of the classics.

BEATRICE KING†

TOWERS, SAMUEL, see AGGAS, ROBERT.

TOWNELEY CYCLE, see ENGLAND, I and MYSTERY PLAY.

TOWSE, JOHN RANKEN (1845–1927), American dramatic critic, who was born near London and educated at Cambridge. In 1869 he went to the United States and became a journalist, working for *The New York Post*. Five years later he was appointed dramatic critic of that paper, a post he held until his retirement in 1927. Imbued with the traditions of Drury Lane, the Haymarket, and Sadler's Wells, he remained ever faithful to the theatre of his youth. Ibsen and Shaw he held in slight esteem and on many matters he saw eye to eye with William Winter. But Towse had a more judicial temper and never descended to abuse. On his retirement, however, he denounced the modern theatre as destitute of morality. Apart from his newspaper work he has left a volume of theatrical memoirs, *Sixty Years of the Theatre*, in which he recalls the golden age of Augustin Daly, Salvini, Samuel Phelps, Modjeska, Adelaide Neilson, and Edwin Booth. THOMAS QUINN CURTISS

TOY THEATRE. One of the most delightful of the many charming ephemeral publications of the nineteenth century in England was the 'Juvenile Drama'—a sort of miniature edition of the contemporary theatre. In the year 1811 a Mr. William West, who kept a small stationer's shop in Exeter Street, off the Strand, was publishing sheets of theatrical characters copied from the latest productions at Covent Garden, Drury Lane, and the minor theatres; each plate of figures contained about eight small drawings depicting the various characters in their most dramatic moments. Soon scenery, consisting of back drops and side wings, was also included. Considerable care was apparently taken to make an accurate copy of the details of costume and scenery, and even the faces of the actors were sometimes faithfully reproduced. Each play consisted of some ten or twenty sheets, usually sold at a 'penny plain, or twopence coloured'. The colouring was done by hand in bold, vivid hues that are as fresh today as when they were first applied.

These sheets may have originated from those sold by French theatrical agencies for the benefit of provincial and foreign managements. They were probably first intended as some form of theatrical souvenir, but the idea proved immensely popular and was very soon adapted as a children's plaything; between the years 1815 and 1835 the Juvenile Drama seems to have been quite a thriving industry, with some fifty different publishers engaged in it; as soon as a new production at any of the theatres showed signs of popularity it was quickly issued in a toy-theatre version. As the trade came to cater more and more for children the fine quality of the early engraving and colouring began to fall off, but several publishers continued to produce new plays in the original style until the 1850s and even later.

In the second half of the nineteenth century toy-theatre plays were sometimes given away with boys' magazines, or cheaply printed on a single sheet and sold for a penny; but the genuine Juvenile Drama never quite disappeared, and is still obtainable today. As late as 1932 there were two shops in the Hoxton district of London, kept by Webb and Pollock, where these old plays were still printed and sold; both these men are now dead, but Pollock's shop has been transferred to No. 1, Scala Street, under new management, and toy-theatre material is still available there.

The Juvenile Drama is of unique interest, as it has preserved with astonishing fidelity the appearance of the early nineteenth-century theatre and even the gestures and mannerisms of its actors. Here is recorded the theatre of J. P. Kemble, Edmund Kean, Madame Vestris, Liston, and Grimaldi; the productions, not only of the patent theatres, but of the Surrey, the Olympic, Astley's Amphitheatre, and other minor theatres; plays like *The Miller and his Men*, *George Barnwell*, *The Corsican Brothers*, with a total repertory of some three hundred melodramas and pantomimes in all the bright colours and heroic gestures of their first performance (see No. 67).

Among the best publishers of toy-theatre plays were West, Jameson, Hodgson, Skelt, Green, Park, and Webb. There are good collections in the Print Room of the British Museum, in the Enthoven Collection at the Victoria and Albert Museum, and at the London Museum; the history of the subject is recorded in *Juvenile Drama*, by George Speaight (1947), and in *Penny Plain, Twopence Coloured*, by A. E. Wilson (1932); while in an essay under this latter title (1884) Robert Louis Stevenson paid a graceful tribute to the charm of the Juvenile Drama.

(For a note on the Continental Toy Theatre, see PUPPETS.) GEORGE SPEAIGHT

TRABEATA, see FABULA, 9 and 10.

TRADES UNIONS THEATRE, Moscow. This theatre, which is affiliated to the Central Council of the Trades Unions of the U.S.S.R., was created in 1932 from the Proletcult Theatre, started after the October Revolution by Sergei Eisenstein. A pupil of Meyerhold, Eisenstein (who later belonged entirely to the cinema) turned his stage into a circus ring and staged shows of which no trace remains except in the heightened apprehension of the audiences which came freshly to them. After Eisenstein left, the Proletcult Theatre passed through many vicissitudes until it received its new name at the same time as a new director, Alexei Dikie. His first production, *Sailors of Cattaro*, showed that he had combined with his Moscow Art Theatre training a modicum of the Proletcult Theatre's formalism, an amalgam which determined the future line of the theatre's development. Another interesting production at this theatre was *Nonsense*, of which André van Gyseghem gives a detailed description in his *Theatre in Soviet Russia*. Later productions were less successful, and in 1936 the theatre was closed (see also DIKIE).

TRAFALGAR SQUARE THEATRE, LONDON, see DUKE OF YORK'S THEATRE.

TRAGEDY, a term applied to plays dealing in an elevated, poetic style with the grandeur and misery of man in his loftier aspects, as the plaything of fate and yet superior to it. The word is of Greek origin, and Greek tragedy, as written by Aeschylus, Euripides, and Sophocles, set a standard for world drama that has never yet been surpassed (see GREECE, 1). Rome knew only the tragedies of Seneca, written to be read and not acted, which had nevertheless a remarkable influence on European tragedy through the translations of the humanists. On the Continent Italian tragedy, derived directly from the Greek, developed early, but had to wait for its finest expression in the plays of Alfieri in the eighteenth century. Both France and England took to tragedy by way of Seneca, but the latter mingled with it less learning and more romance. Marlowe and Shakespeare in England and Calderón in Spain remained impervious to the French classical tragedy, which reigned supreme elsewhere until the Romantic Revival. Its greatest exponents were Corneille and Racine, who constructed their plays according to the French interpretation of Aristotle's *Poetics*, but with a touch of genius denied to their successors. It was the letter and not the spirit of French tragedy that was imported into England after the Restoration, and resulted in such plays as Addison's *Cato*, while in Germany Gottsched, aided by the actress Caroline Neuber, endeavoured to impose it on the somewhat chaotic German theatre. In neither country did it become acclimatized, nor was Luzán more successful in Spain. Germany had to wait for Schiller and Goethe before she could claim to have produced any great playwrights, while the English and Spanish genius had already shown its true bent with the plays of Lope de Vega and Shakespeare. The influence of the latter spread over Europe in the last years of the eighteenth century, and so helped to produce the highly coloured tragedies of the Romantic Revival.

An effort to apply the formula of classical tragedy to the misfortunes of the domestic interior was made in the eighteenth century, resulting in such plays as those of Lillo in England, Lessing in Germany, and Mercier in France. These, however, cannot be classified as true tragedy, and are known as *tragédie bourgeoise* or domestic tragedy. Nor can the realistic dramas of Ibsen and his disciples rank as tragedy, though their implications are often tragic enough. In the narrow theatrical sense of the word, tragedy demands a cast of princes and demi-gods, an unfamiliar background—exotic, romantic, or imaginary—and a sense of detachment whose effect is heightened by the use of verse or rhetorical prose. The modern revival of poetic drama was closely allied with a renewal of interest in the tragic aspects of life. Efforts were made to tame tragedy and bring it within the family circle, but it is interesting to note that T. S. Eliot's *Murder in the Cathedral*, dealing with politics in high places, was successful, while the same author's domestic tragedy, *The Family Reunion*, which contains some equally fine poetry, failed.

An offshoot of pure tragedy is the tragicomedy, a play dealing with a story inherently tragic, and having an unhappy end, which yet contains certain elements of comedy. Under such a definition some critics have classified *Hamlet* as a tragicomedy, but the perfect example of the type is *Le Cid*, while the most prolific writer of tragicomedies was undoubtedly Corneille's predecessor, Alexandre Hardy.

The Tragedy of Revenge was the name given to those Elizabethan plays of which Kyd's *Spanish Tragedy* (*c.* 1589) was the first. Dealing with bloody deeds which demand retribution, their motto was 'an eye for an eye and a tooth for a tooth', and their sublimity could easily turn to melodrama; and indeed in a cruder form the revenge motif underlay many of the melodramas of the nineteenth century. In the range of Shakespeare's plays *Titus Andronicus* may be considered the lowest form of the Revenge Tragedy, *Hamlet* its perfect flowering. Under the same heading come the great tragedies of Webster, those of Tourneur, and such plays as *Bussy d'Ambois* and *The Changeling*.

The playing of tragedy makes great demands on the actor, who must have a stately presence—Garrick notwithstanding—fine features, and a resonant and perfectly controlled voice. The stately alexandrine of French tragedy developed a somewhat static style of acting, with slow impressive gestures, which was carried into England after the Restoration and was exemplified by Quin.

TRAGIC CARPET, a green baize stage cloth, spread before the performance of a tragedy to prevent the corpses from soiling their clothes on the dusty boards. It may originally have been a permanent covering, though early references to green cloth coverings seem to refer to the benches in the auditorium rather than to the stage itself. By the end of the seventeenth century its appearance was invariably restricted to and heralded the performance of tragedy. It continued in use into the nineteenth century, and is frequently referred to in theatrical letters and memoirs.

TRAMPOLINE, the apparatus resembling a spring mattress upon which acrobats bounce. It usually has a gymnast's horizontal bar at either end. The word comes from *tremplin*, the wedge-shaped springboard used by acrobats of many generations. In the announcements of Philip Astley, father of the circus, it was anglicized as tramplin and then trampline.

M. WILLSON DISHER†

TRANSFORMATION SCENE, TRANSPARENCY, see TRICK-WORK ON THE ENGLISH STAGE.

TRANSPONTINE MELODRAMA, a term applied, usually in genial derision, to a type of crude and extravagantly sensational play staged in the mid-nineteenth century in London theatres 'across the bridges' (i.e. on the south side of the Thames) such as the Surrey Theatre and the Old Vic. By extension the term was later attached to such plays wherever performed.

TRAP, a device by which scenery or actors can be projected on to the stage from below. It is used for transformation scenes, mostly in pantomime, and for ghostly apparitions. In the older stage floor the traps are arranged according to a traditional pattern. Behind and nearest to the curtain are the Corner Traps, used to raise a single standing figure. They are square openings, placed symmetrically, and about two feet across. To accommodate them the joists are cut and specially framed with a trap door constructed in a variety of ways. Sometimes it is a mere square of boards, battened out. Sometimes it is an arrangement of thin strips, hinged together or mounted on a flexible backing, and capable of sliding like a roll-top desk. Sometimes the door is taken away altogether and replaced for the occasion by a closure of a special type, to allow of a sudden appearance as if by magic. Of such, the most famous is the Star Trap, which projects an actor on to the stage at great speed, and is used for the arrival of the Demon King. It consists of a circular opening filled by a series of triangle-like segments of wood, fitted radially, and hinged to the circumference of the opening with leather; as the figure shoots through, the flaps open like a crown, and immediately fall again as the player passes. In other examples, a diaphragm of rubber is used with a slit across it; or bristles are attached radiating inwards from the edge of the circular opening, to be pressed aside as the player ascends, returning at once to their original position. This is known as a Bristle Trap (see also CORSICAN TRAP, below).

The commonest method of getting rid of a trap door is, however, by means of the Slider system. In this the door section itself is supported at one edge on a fillet in the joist below, and at the opposite edge by a lever, which, when vertical, takes the weight of the door and holds it in position. When the lever is pulled, the edge of the door drops a couple of inches, and its sides come to rest in a pair of sloping grooves cut in the face of the side frames of the opening. These sloping ways are continued under the stage floor so that the whole trapdoor can be slid along them till it is completely concealed under the stage, leaving the opening free. The trap platform is then raised with the figure on it, and itself becomes the filling to the aperture, till the trap is again lowered, and the original door slid back, and, by its lever, lifted to a flush position.

Beyond the corner traps comes a similar, but larger, single trap, centrally placed. This is the Grave Trap. It may be 6 ft. long and 3 ft. wide. It has a platform below, which can be raised or lowered, and its traditional use is in the grave scene in *Hamlet* (whence its name), though it was pressed into service on many other occasions. Again, many varieties of ingenious development are to be found for the mechanism of the trap. Sometimes it opens by the dropping of a pair of longitudinal flaps, counterweighted by levers to close again at need, and it may have a cushioned trough below to break a player's leap-down. Sometimes the door is so arranged that by the dropping of a pair of bars the sections of the floor descend severally on to a sloping timber cut like the stringer of a stair, thus forming a flight of steps. Most frequently, the mechanism is in the form of a counterweighted platform, like a larger edition of the footlight trap.

A similar, but square, trap is more rarely found, also central, and further up-stage, called the Cauldron Trap. This owes its name to the cauldron scene in *Macbeth*.

The mechanism of the traps which worked in conjunction with the particular openings is varied in detail, but they mostly consist of a rigidly built platform on strong legs which slides up and down between four uprights, or corner posts. In a few smaller traps the platform slides between two posts only, which are grooved down the inner face to take two projections from the sides of the platform.

From the framework of the platform itself, ropes are led up to pulleys at the head of the uprights, and over these to some sort of counterweight. In the large and slower-moving traps the counterweight approximately balances the trap and its load, and the rising movement is achieved by means of a hand winch on the mezzanine floor, actuating a rope passing to a drum-and-shaft system below the trap, which is connected with the trap itself by further ropes wound in the opposite direction. In a small, fast-moving trap, such as a Star Trap, the arrangement is a little different; the weight of the trap, with the figure it is to carry, is heavily over-counterweighted, and the trap itself retained in position by a lever. Upon the turn of the lever, the counterweights rapidly fall and the trap leaps up. It is clear that some considerable shock is likely to be sustained when the swiftly rising platform reaches the limit of its travel, and has to be checked sharply at the level of the stage. Several methods of lessening the shock are used. One of the simplest and most ingenious is that in which the counterweight consists of a series, or chain, of iron balls, each about nine inches in diameter, hung one below another. At the beginning of the run this chain of balls falls swiftly through the air, exerting all its dead weight on the movement of the trap. But the length of the 'chain' is so adjusted that towards the latter part of the run the first of the balls has reached the limit of its descent and come to rest on a ledge, or floor. Its weight is thus deducted from the motive power exerted upon the trap; in a fraction of a second the next ball in the chain has come to rest, and then the next, and so forth, until, when the summit of the ascent is nearly reached, all the counterweight balls are 'dead' upon the floor, and the trap is travelling for the last few inches practically on its momentum alone. Though described in some detail here, the whole action is in practice so quick as to be over in a moment. The player is shot through the opening, but the platform comes to rest in its position with far less of a shock than if the full counterweight force had been equally exerted through the whole length of its run.

Most traps can be dismantled and moved to another position or substituted for one of a different type as need arises. A Grave Trap may, for instance, be removed and its place taken by a pair of traps of the type usually seen in a Corner Trap; or a special aperture may be cut in the stage beside an existing Corner Trap to allow of the placing of a duplicate mechanism close beside it. The use of such a double trap was for the substitution of characters to suggest the magic transformation of a person. The two adjacent platforms were so geared that one rose as the other fell. Upon his cue, the player on the stage moved to his position upon the platform of the first trap, now raised and appearing as part of the stage floor, while his partner in the change stood ready waiting upon the other trap, lowered to its starting position. At the crucial moment a diversion was caused, or a cloak waved in front of the figure on the stage; the traps were released, one fell and, simultaneously, the other rose. In a second, a different figure stepped from a part of the stage floor so near the original spot as to be indistinguishable from it. To complete the effect, the trapdoor of the second opening was arranged to flap over, or slide, into a new position covering the aperture left by the descent of the first trap, all as part of the one concerted movement.

One of the most ingenious trap mechanisms was that devised for the apparition in *The Corsican Brothers* (1852), which had to appear out of the earth so slowly that it was not possible to rely on the quickness of action which deceives the eye to conceal the working of the trick. It was therefore necessary that no square opening, or aperture of any sort, should appear round the ghost as he was rising; and, most difficult of all, the figure did not rise steadily at one fixed spot, but appeared to drift slowly across the full width of the stage.

The brilliant solution of this problem, in which skilled and judicious use was made of the existing possibilities of stage mechanism, became known as the Corsican Trap, or Ghost Glide. Its mechanism was as follows: first, the slider fillings were removed from a complete cut, leaving a long, narrow aperture across the full width of the stage. Into this a new filling was fitted, capable of sliding, not in two pieces to either side, but in one piece to one side only. (One method of accommodating such a long piece under the floor of a very much narrower wing-space would be to build it on the system of a roll-top desk, and coil it up under the stage as it drew off to the side.) To the far extremity of this sliding floor the trapdoor itself was fitted, to be drawn along with it, and beyond that a further, and similar, length of filling was attached. This was drawn from under the opposite side of the stage and pulled across to cover the aperture that would otherwise have been left behind the travelling trap as it followed the first slider off-stage.

Below this cut an inclined railway was built to accommodate a small truck, upon which stood the ghost. The truck rose from a point some six feet below stage at the beginning of its travel to the level of the stage itself at the end of it. It was drawn by a line working simultaneously with that drawing the trapdoor and its attached sliders across the stage, so that the truck was continuously under the trap but rose nearer and nearer to it as the travel proceeded.

The final ingenuity was the construction of a trapdoor which would allow the figure to pass slowly through the stage floor, without, at any time, there being visible the shape of an aperture. For this the Bristle Trap was used. The aperture of the trap-opening was lined with a fringe of inward projecting bristles which were coloured to resemble the stage cloth. The player's body pushed these aside as he rose, and they immediately returned to their position when the pressure was released. No aperture was ever perceptible and the ghost did indeed appear to rise through the stage. So popular did the effect become that a Corsican Trap was installed in 1858 even at the little Theatre Royal, Ipswich (see also SLOTE; for the Vamp Trap, which could be in the stage floor or in a piece of scenery, see TRICKWORK ON THE ENGLISH STAGE). RICHARD SOUTHERN

TREE, Ellen (1806–80), see KEAN (3).

TREE. (1) Sir Herbert Draper Beerbohm (1853–1917), English actor-manager, the second son of Julius Ewald Beerbohm and Constance Draper, and the half-brother of Max Beerbohm. His father, a naturalized British subject, was of German, Dutch, and Lithuanian extraction. Herbert was educated first at a school at Frant, in Kent, and afterwards at Schnepfenthal College, Thuringia. He became at the age of 17 a clerk in the city office of his father, who was a grain merchant. Soon afterwards he began to be known as an amateur actor, and in 1878 he went on the stage professionally. His chief successes in the early eighties were his impersonations of the Revd. Robert Spalding in *The Private Secretary*, and of Macari in *Called Back*. In Apr. 1887 he became manager of the Comedy Theatre, where he produced *The Red Lamp*. Later in that year he took over the management of the Haymarket Theatre. Among his productions were *Captain Swift* (1888), *The Merry Wives of Windsor* (1889), *The Dancing Girl* (1891), *Hamlet* (1892), *A Woman of No Importance* (1893), and *Trilby* (1895), the most resounding of his successes. He built Her Majesty's Theatre, which was completed early in 1897, opening with *The Seats of the Mighty*. (During the reigns of Edward VII, George V, and George VI this theatre was known as His Majesty's, reverting to its original name on the accession of Elizabeth II.)

In this theatre Tree carried on the sumptuously illustrative Lyceum tradition of Shakespearian production (see Nos. 75, 76), lavishing upon largely visual interpretation all the resources of a generously imaginative romantic mind, and achieving effects of magnificence much to the taste of the day. 'It was the whole tradition that was wrong,' declared a contemporary critic, 'not the way he carried it out.' Between 1888 and 1914 Tree produced eighteen of Shakespeare's plays, and once at least, in *Richard II*, he succeeded in reinforcing and exhibiting, not merely supplementing by ingenious 'business', the author's imagination. Interspersed with these were such pieces as *Herod* (1900), *The Last of the Dandies* (1901), *Ulysses* (1902), *The Darling of the Gods* (1903), *Colonel Newcome* (1906), *Faust* (1908), *Drake* (1912), *Pygmalion* and *David Copperfield* (both 1914). Tree was knighted in 1909. His versatility found outlet in lecturing and in authorship. He wrote three books: *An Essay on the Imaginative Faculty* (1893), *Thoughts and Afterthoughts* (1913), and *Nothing Matters* (1917). He also founded, in 1904, a drama school (see ROYAL ACADEMY OF DRAMATIC ART).

Tree was a romantic actor, delighting in grandiose effects and in the representation of eccentric characters in which his own imagination had freest play. When he was not interested in some aspect of a play he had the amateur's fault of 'walking through' the supposedly dull passages. He often chose parts outside his temperamental and physical range. His tragic acting lacked fundamental force. Yet when all his limitations and waywardness are taken into account he must still be reckoned a romantic actor of erratic brilliance and a fine character actor. Connoisseurs would discover, even in his extravagances, redeemingly delicate strokes of characterization, thrown off as by a sudden impulse.

In 1883 Tree married (2) HELEN MAUD HOLT (1863–1937), a highly intelligent young woman who had been educated at Queen's College, London, where she read classics and took part in performances of Greek plays. Her marriage proved the starting-point of a distinguished stage career, and in the next 50 years she was seen in a great variety of parts. She excelled in comedy, playing in Shakespeare, Sheridan, Shaw, and Barrie, among others. Her earliest success was at the Court Theatre in 1883, as Hester Gould in *The Millionaire*. She appeared in the following year as the heroine of her husband's one-act play, *Six and Eightpence*. In 1887 she joined him at the Haymarket and acted with him in *The Red Lamp*. Other parts followed, and in 1897 she was Madame de Cournal in *The Seats of the Mighty* at the opening of Her Majesty's Theatre. As hostess and as leading lady, she shared Herbert Tree's reign, and played in most of the lavish productions which gave his theatre its special place in the theatrical history of the time. Soon after the South African war broke out in 1899 she handed over to the War Fund £1,700 in three weeks, her salary for reciting Kipling's 'Absent-Minded Beggar'. In 1902 she assumed for a while the direction of Wyndham's Theatre. After Tree's death she continued to be a familiar figure on the London stage. At the age of 70 she played Mistress Quickly at His Majesty's. Her last part was the Duchess of Stroud in *Our Own Lives* at the Ambassadors' in 1935.

Of the three daughters of Sir Herbert and Lady Tree, the eldest, (3) VIOLA (1884–1938), followed in the family tradition and in 1904 made her first appearance at the Theatre Royal, Edinburgh, playing Viola in her father's production of *Twelfth Night*. During the next four years she was frequently seen in Shakespeare at His Majesty's, and in 1906 appeared in *The Winter's Tale* as Perdita to the Hermione of Ellen Terry. It was in 1908 that she began seriously to study singing, and in 1910 she sang Eurydice to the Orpheus of Marie Brema in Gluck's opera with some success. The stage, however, regained her interest, and she appeared in a variety of parts till shortly before her death. She was a woman whose gifts far exceeded her ambitions. She wrote with ease and vivacity and published several books. In 1912 she married the dramatic critic Alan Parsons. Her son David also became an actor. A. V. COOKMAN†, *rev.*

TREMONT THEATRE, see BOSTON.

TRENEV, KONSTANTIN ANDREIVICH (1884–1945), Soviet dramatist, son of a peasant, who by great efforts, after a poverty-stricken childhood, became a school-teacher and editor of a Ukrainian newspaper. He soon began to write, and his first volume of short stories was published in 1914. After the Revolution he turned to the theatre, and his first play, dealing with an eighteenth-century peasant insurrection, was staged by the Moscow Art Theatre in 1925. This was the theatre's first attempt at a Soviet play, and was not particularly successful, but it served to establish Trenev as a playwright, a position which he strengthened in the following year when the Maly Theatre produced the first version of his *Lyubov Yarovaya*. This, in a second, much altered form, with five acts instead of four, was one of the outstanding productions of the Moscow Art Theatre in 1937, and was awarded a Stalin Prize in 1940. It tells the story of an intelligent and progressive school-teacher, who is an active Revolutionary, but whose husband has joined the White Russians. Finally she is forced to choose between love and loyalty, and betrays her husband. This play, which abounds in excellent characterizations, with the sailor Shvandya and the peasant-soldier Pikalov typifying old and new Russia, proved popular all over the U.S.S.R., and is still acted today. Trenev's best play, however, was probably *On the Banks of the Neva*, also produced in 1937. In 1941, on the eve of the Soviet Union's entry into the Second World War, he produced *Anna Luchinina*. A year later came *Meeting Halfway*, and in 1944 *The General*, in which Field-Marshal Kutuzov (1745–1813) plays a leading part. A study of Trenev's work was published in 1956.

TRETYAKOV, SERGEI MIKHAILOVICH (1892–1939), one of the earliest Soviet dramatists, whose best-known play, *Roar, China!*, was produced by Meyerhold in 1926. Though somewhat elementary and melodramatic, and written for propaganda purposes, it is a vivid historical document, presenting with intense conviction the conflict between Chinese coolies and foreign imperialists.

TREVELYAN, HILDA [TUCKER] (1880–1959), English actress, who played Wendy in the first production of *Peter Pan* in 1904, and continued to play it in many subsequent revivals.

She also starred in Barrie's *What Every Woman Knows* (1908) with great success, and appeared in several of his other plays, including *Alice Sit-By-The-Fire* (1905) and *The Admirable Crichton* (1908). She made her first appearance on the stage in 1889 as one of the children in *The Silver King*, but returned to school and did not appear again until 1894, when she toured in musical comedy. She also played Avonia Bunn in *Trelawny of the 'Wells'* many times, and Lady Babbie in *The Little Minister*, though she was not the first to create these parts. In 1912 she took over the management of the Vaudeville Theatre with Edmund Gwenn, but the venture was not a success and she returned to the stage. Her next success was in *A Kiss for Cinderella* (1916). In 1926 she played in *Mary Rose*, taking over from Mary Jerrold, and was also in the long run of *Housemaster*. She made her last appearance on the stage in 1939. She was the wife of the author Sydney Blow.

TRIBUTARY THEATRE, U.S.A., see UNITED STATES OF AMERICA, 10.

TRICKWORK ON THE ENGLISH STAGE. It was in their tricks, with the high skill they demanded from the carpenter and the acrobatic actor, that the English actors were, in the nineteenth century, acknowledged leaders of the world. Perhaps less attention than it deserves has in the past been paid at home to the startling brilliance achieved by English trickwork, though several admiring and almost envious references were made to it on the Continent.

Tricks may involve scenery, or supply an accompanying 'effect' to a scene, or may involve the person of the player himself, and depend not on their working alone but on the skill and brilliant timing of the man or woman who takes part in them.

Tricks with scenery generally involve some change in its appearance, either wholly or in part. Methods for effecting such changes were many, but possibly the most widely used was that of Falling Flaps. An account of 1803 mentions 'those double flat scenes, which are also used to produce instantaneous changes. The whole scene being covered with pieces of canvas, framed and moving upon hinges, one side [of each of these hinged flaps] is painted to represent a certain scene, and the other to represent one totally different.' Before the working of the trick, these flaps are all 'elevated above the joints', that is to say each flap is raised and presents its obverse face to the audience, making, with its fellows, a complete picture. 'The contrivances for moving them are very various. In general, however, they are kept in the elevated situation by catches, which being suddenly relieved, they fall by their own weight', presenting the reverse face to the audience, and displaying thus the painting of a completely different subject.

An interesting example of such a system of flaps is to be found in the Victorian toy-theatre sheets. Here the sheets for certain back scenes bear the legend 'Trick Scene', and close inspection will show that across part of the design are one or more rows of dotted lines. On a separate sheet of 'Tricks' one or more smaller pieces correspond with the scene and fit in the area marked by the dotted lines. The piece, or pieces, are to be cut out, hinged in position on the back-scene sheet, and worked to effect the trick change in exactly the same way as the framed canvas flaps mentioned above.

Such a system is generally applied only to part of a scene, as for instance to one shop front out of a row of shops in a street scene. For the magic transformation of the whole scene other methods are available, and the skilled development of these led to the great erstwhile feature of every pantomime, the Transformation Scene. In later years much of the transformation has been effected by gauze cloths, and by straightforward flying of cloths, but the Rise and Sink was once an effective variant, in which the upper part of the scene detached itself from the lower and ascended to the low grid (which was formerly not high enough to allow the flying of more than half a back scene at most), while the lower part, framed out and possibly with a profiled upper edge, descended into the cellar upon sloats. The Fan Effect was also sometimes employed, where sectors of the back scene, pivoted centrally at the foot of the scene, sank sideways upon each other like a pair of collapsing fans.

Again, a quick transition of scene might be achieved by dividing the back scene into a series of vertical strips, each of which was wound on its own vertical roller. The set of rollers is stationed across the stage like a row of columns, with another scene visible behind as a backcloth. Upon the change, lines from the top and bottom of each roller are pulled sideways, and the new scene is drawn out from the 'columns' to fill the intercolumnar spaces, hiding the view behind, and presenting, in a flash, a new scene.

Scruto may also be employed. Scruto is the name given to a surface made by attaching a number of narrow strips of thin wood side by side on a canvas backing, so as to form a continuous flexible sheet, like the cover of a roll-top desk. Upon the scruto a subject may be painted and the whole attached to a scene so as to roll down or up, at cue, and replace the old painting with a new.

The intricacies of inventiveness by which these methods may be applied and developed are amazing. One extension of the Falling Flap method, for instance, was used to transform a set piece instantaneously before the eyes of the audience, at a touch, maybe, of Harlequin's baton. In its simplest form, the set piece—a small one, let us say, representing a square bale labelled 'Shag Tobacco'—possesses half its subject painted on the normal surface, but the other half is on one face of a hinged flap, turning, in this case, vertically. On the action of a simple trick-line, this flap is swung over, like the page of a book, to lie over the first portion of the piece, so discovering the remaining portion and the reverse face of the hinged flap. Hereon is painted perhaps a large cabbage with a watering-can beside it—the quality of the tobacco is revealed in its source.

But this is not all. When one withdraws a letter from an envelope, it may be a small sheet folded once; the act of opening the letter is then the simple pivoting of a 'flap'. But the letter may be large, and folded not once, but again. Now, upon pulling it open, it exhibits in effect not only a turning flap, but also a couple of rising flaps within, which must spring up before the whole sheet is revealed. So in trick set pieces a series of separate flaps may all be spring-hinged together to lie compactly flat when folded, but upon release all fly out to present not only a totally different painted subject but one which considerably exceeds the original piece in size, so augmenting the wonder of the trick. The complication of a large *châssis à développement*, as the French so well call this type of set piece, is illustrated in a cut in Moynet's *L'Envers du Théâtre* (1873).

Possibly an early reference to such a trick-piece in England lies in an item to be found in the Covent Garden Inventory of 1743 (now in the British Museum), where, under the heading *Painted Pieces in Great Room* is listed a 'front of garden that changes to house'; or again in the inventory of scenery at the Crow Street Theatre, Dublin, 1776, where we find a 'changeable flat in Mercury Harlequin'.

Associated with such tricks are the 'effects' of sounds—that of a body falling into water after a leap behind a sea row (accompanied maybe with the 'splash' of a flung-up shower of rice); that of the Glass Crash, where a quantity of broken glass and china is flung from one bucket into another; that of the Thunder Sheet, where a suspended iron sheet is vigorously shaken to produce the sound of the rolling of a storm; that of the Wind Machine, where a ribbed drum is revolved against a sheet of silk, or other material, producing a variable singing note admirably suggestive of howling wind; and there are many others, some detailed in A. Rose's *Stage Effects*, in A. E. Peterson's articles on 'Stage Effects and Noises Off' included in *Theatre and Stage* (1934), or Frank Napier's *Noises Off* (1936). Georgian thunder was, however, frequently produced by the far better method of a Thunder Run—two long inclined wooden troughs, down which iron balls were rolled.

Possibly one of the most effective visual tricks is the Transparency. Here part or all of the back-scene is painted, not upon canvas, but upon linen or calico, and executed, not in opaque size-paint, but in transparent dye. The appearance of the painting is normal when lit from the front, but as lights are brought up behind, the subject fades or becomes supplemented by further painting on the back of the linen, until the whole effect is changed, and a normal building, for instance, appears given over to the ravages of fire, or a quiet country landscape blossoms into the glow of a lurid sunset. Any features of the former scene required to remain in dark silhouette after the change are, of course, executed in opaque paint.

From these beginnings the resources of tricks develop to the most advanced and closely guarded secrets of first-class conjuring, passing on the way such fascinating phantoms as Pepper's Ghost, or those of Young and Poole—perfectly transparent actors, capable of moving to any part of the stage, and of being stabbed or walked-through with impunity. Such an effect is based on the principle of reflection, the image of an actor walking in the orchestra-well appearing up a sheet of glass suspended at a critical angle in, or near, the proscenium opening, together with a judicious balancing of lights. Many applications of tricks to the theatre are to be found in two French books, wherein much English procedure is described, namely Georges Moynet's *Trucs et Décors* (1893), and A. de Vaulabelle and Ch. Hémardinquer's *La Science au Théâtre*. It is perhaps significant of the wide influence of English trick-work that one of the most frequently mentioned traps in these two books is the *trappe anglaise*.

But the final apotheosis of the trick, where the highest art of the theatre in this direction is reached, comes with the union of actor and effect—where the trick is the combination of brilliant timing and acrobatic skill in the player with the sureness and ingenuity of the experienced stage-carpenter.

The humblest example of this union, in bare simplicity, is the Roll-out, a mere flap of loose canvas left at the bottom of a piece of scenery, through which a player can suddenly roll from behind, and leap to his feet on the scene. After this comes the famous Vamp Trap, consisting of two spring-leaves, either in the stage or in the scenery, through which the body of an actor can pass like a spirit through a solid. The name is stated by J. R. Planché to be derived from the title of his melodrama *The Vampire; or, the Bride of the Isles*, produced at the Lyceum (then called the English Opera House) in 1820.

The Leap is the supreme test of the trick player. In essence, it is no more than an acrobat's jumping through a trap in the scenery; but by the skilful interplaying of a group of highly trained players, and the clever multiplication and placing of types of traps, it can produce a notable piece of theatre, and one able to occupy on its own merits a place in a programme. Such was the Dumb Ballet, of which acts like *Fun in a Bakehouse* or *Ki Ko Kookeeree* are examples. A diagrammatic plot of the latter remains in the form of a coloured sketch of the scene, with hinged flaps, made to be forwarded each week to the stage manager of the next house to inform him of the practicalities of the show. In the sketch are seen at least eight varieties of trap, all to be used in dazzling succession as the flashing troupe went through their evolutions in the

Victorian back-yard they took as their setting. Mr. A. E. Peterson, present owner of this drawing, states that the act visited, among other places, the Adelphi Theatre, Liverpool, about 1871.

Many names in English stage history are associated with such trickwork, from 'Don Jumpedo', who jumped 'down his own throat', through the immortal Grimaldi, and along the line of the Lupinos and that of the Conquests, till international and almost royal eminence was achieved by the staggering 'entortillationists', exhibiting 'zampillerostation' and countless other acts, who were known as the Hanlon-Lees.

These men brought trickwork, leaps, and tumbling to the height of an art, and to an eminence recognized throughout the world as peculiarly English. RICHARD SOUTHERN

TRIGG, WILLIAM (*fl.* first half of seventeenth century), a boy-actor in the King's Company, who played women's parts from about 1626 to 1632. He was probably one of Shank's apprentices, and by 1636 he had graduated to adult parts, and was a hired man. He may have joined Beeston's Boys at about this time, and is still found with them in 1639. There is a possibility that during the Civil War he started as a royalist but turned parliamentarian; this, however, is not certain. The date of his death is unknown, but he was still alive in 1652. He does not appear to have returned to his old profession after the Restoration.

TRISSINO, GIAN GIORGIO (1478–1550), Italian dramatist whose *Sofonisba* shows the first direct contact with Greek drama during the Renaissance. This tragedy, whose material is taken from Livy and remodelled on the familiar lines of Greek tragedy, was published in 1515 and many times reprinted before its first production at Vicenza in 1524. Somewhat lifeless and uninteresting in itself, it is important in its implications, since it marked out the way of rigid adherence to Greek models for future writers of Italian tragedy.

TRISTAN L'HERMITE, FRANÇOIS (1601–55), French dramatist, considered by his contemporaries a formidable rival to Corneille. He had a stormy youth, as having killed a man in a duel he was forced to fly to England. He then started out for Spain, but in passing through Poitiers he met and was befriended by Scévole de Sainte-Marthe, generous and learned patron of literature, who found him work and secured the king's pardon for him. Tristan was thus enabled to return to Paris, and in 1636 his first play, *Mariamne*, was given at the Théâtre du Marais with almost unprecedented success, largely due to the acting of Montdory as Herod, with Mlle de Villiers as his leading lady. The play, taken from various sources, including one by Hardy, held the boards for nearly 100 years. Corneille is said to have praised its last act. Encouraged by this initial success, Tristan continued to write plays, but none of them equalled his first, and all are forgotten. Two were in the repertory of Molière's short-lived Illustre-Théâtre. Tristan was a great gambler and often in debt, but he was generous and kind-hearted, and a good friend. The dramatist Quinault was in his youth befriended by Tristan, who left him a large sum of money in his will.

TRITAGONIST, see PROTAGONIST.

TROUNCER, CECIL (1898–1953), one of the finest character actors of his day. He made his first appearance on the stage in 1920 and was seen in London a year later. He had a consistently successful career, and never failed to give a good, equable performance. He worked at the Old Vic for several years, and toured in Shakespeare with Robert Atkins. He also went to South Africa with the Macdona players in a Shaw repertory. He had a warm rich voice and a most sympathetic personality, being equally good in stylized comedy and pathos. Two of his best parts were Newton in Shaw's *In Good King Charles's Golden Days*, which he played at Malvern in 1939 and subsequently in London, and Menenius in *Coriolanus* at the Old Vic the year before. Although never a 'star', he typifies the gifted, hardworking, and dedicated actor who is the backbone of the theatre, in England and elsewhere.

TRUCKS, low platforms on castors, to take previously arranged scenery on and off the stage. Also called Boat Trucks.

TUCCIO, STEFANO (1540–97), see JESUIT DRAMA.

TUKE, SIR SAMUEL (?–1674), a gentleman at the Court of Charles II, who, on the suggestion of the king, wrote *The Adventures of Five Hours*, a tragicomedy adapted from Calderón, which was given at Lincoln's Inn Fields on 8 Jan. 1663. It was seen by Pepys, who praised it rather extravagantly, and also spoke of his liking for the author, in spite of his evident conceit. This was Tuke's only venture into playwriting, the rest of his time being spent in attendance on, and secret missions for, Charles II, who held him in high favour because of his support of the royalist party during the Civil War, when he fought at Marston Moor, and in Paris during the Commonwealth.

TUMANOV [TUMANISHVILI], JOSEPH MIKHAILOVICH (1905–), Soviet producer, born in Georgia, and from 1928 to 1932 a pupil and then a colleague of Stanislavsky, on whom he lectured in London in 1963, on the occasion of the Stanislavsky centenary celebrations. He has been director of a number of theatres in Moscow, and is at present a professor at the Moscow Institute of Dramatic Art. During his directorship of the Pushkin Theatre (1953–61) he produced, among other things, a dramatization of *Little Dorrit* (1953) and a translation of Ewen MacColl's *The Train Can Stop* (1954).

TUMBLER, a loose roller inside a rolled-up cloth (see DROP).

TURGENIEV, IVAN SERGEIVICH (1818–83), Russian novelist and dramatist, whose best-known play is *A Month in the Country.* He belonged to a wealthy land-owning family, but had an unhappy childhood. After private lessons from French and German tutors he entered Moscow University, where he soon turned to literature, translating Shakespeare, and writing poems and articles. He was sent to Berlin University to finish his education, and in 1843 published his first play, a romantic swashbuckling drama set in Spain. In the same year he met Belinsky, the great Russian critic, who had an important influence on his development. His second play, a satirical comedy in the style of Gogol's *Inspector-General,* was published in 1846. Entitled *Penniless; or, Scenes from the Life of a Young Nobleman,* its leading character is a gentleman adventurer who sums up the theme of the play in its last words: 'You have passed, golden times, you have gone, noble breed.' Two years later he wrote a one-act comedy in the style of Alfred de Musset's *Comédies et Proverbes, Where It's Thin, It Breaks,* and in 1847 a play intended for the benefit night of the actor Shchepkin. This, however, was banned by the censor, and did not appear in print until 1857. It finally reached the stage in 1861. Meanwhile Turgeniev had written another play for Shchepkin, a delicate and touching comedy entitled *The Bachelor.* Written with one eye on the censor, this inoffensive trifle shows an elderly man and his young ward deceived and disappointed by the girl's fiancé, the bachelor's protégé, who turns out to be a hypocrite and a coward. The role of the old man gave Shchepkin, and later Martynov and Karatygin, an excellent opportunity to show their talents. It was produced and published in 1849, and was followed by *The Boarder,* a further study of unhappy old age, and by a lively comedy dealing with a partition of land between brother and sister (according to the old Russian custom) and the quarrels that ensue.

In 1850 Turgeniev wrote his masterpiece for the theatre, *A Month in the Country,* originally entitled *The Student.* It was prematurely announced for publication, but the censors held it up for five years, and it was not staged until 1872. It is important as the first psychological drama in the Russian theatre. It did not fit into the acknowledged genres of 'comedy of manners' or 'comedy of characters', and was considered, even by its author, a 'novel in dramatic form'. In it Turgeniev proves himself to be the forerunner of Chekhov, in that he shifted the dramatic action from external to internal conflict. A similar shifting of interest was taking place in all European literature, and Turgeniev might have pursued the matter even further had not his battles with the censorship, and his subsequent imprisonment and exile, caused him to give up writing plays and to concentrate on short stories. His last play was a light comedy of no great significance. He certainly had no opinion of himself as a dramatist, and intended his plays mainly for reading. But his insight and inner realism could not fail to make them effective in performance when they were staged and interpreted as they should be—a feat which has only become possible in recent years. *A Month in the Country* has become popular in the repertory of the European theatre, particularly in Great Britain, where it has had several important productions. It was first seen at the Royalty in 1926, and was revived in 1936 and 1937. In Constance Garnett's translation it was done by the Old Vic company at the New Theatre in 1949, with Michael Redgrave as Rakitin, a part he had previously played at the St. James's in 1943, in an adaptation by Emlyn Williams. It was with this adaptation that he opened the Yvonne Arnaud Theatre at Guildford in 1965, Ingrid Bergmann playing Natalie.

TURKEY. 1. TRADITIONAL. Several influences combined to produce the Turkish theatre and dance-drama, among them the rituals of the *shamans* of the Uralo-Altaic group from which the Turkish nation takes its origin, and the culture of the Anatolian peninsula, the bridge between Asia and Europe which the Turks have occupied for so long and which has seen the passage of so many migrant civilizations.

The influence of Islam, whose faith the Turks adopted, has been largely negative, since the essence of theatrical art is impersonation, which is repugnant to Islam. Yet in practice dramatic representations have been allowed, mainly for religious purposes, and the ban has been mainly on anything calculated to belittle educational, legal, or religious institutions.

Turkey's imperial expansion westward from the fifteenth to the nineteenth centuries brought her into contact with the culture of the countries over which she ruled, and this doubtless contributed elements of organized entertainment to what is now recognized as the theatre and dance of Anatolian Turkey. In the absence of precise records, nothing much can be said of the Turkish theatre from the twelfth to the fourteenth centuries, though no doubt the entertainers normally in attendance on medieval rulers would have been in evidence at the Court. An early description of a Turkish dramatic performance, in which an actor impersonated the Byzantine Emperor Alexius, lying on a sofa during an illness, with doctors and attendants bustling about, can be found in the epic prose-poem, the *Alexiad,* an account of the period 1069–1118, written by the Emperor's eldest daughter, Anna Comnena (1083–1148).

During the Ottoman period any important event, such as the birth of a prince, a royal marriage, a conquest, or the arrival of a foreign ambassador, provided the opportunity for public festivities, which sometimes lasted as long as forty days and forty nights. These festivities included not only processions, fireworks, equestrian games, and hunting, but also dancing, music, recitals of poetry, and performances by jugglers, mountebanks, and buffoons. Here, as in Renaissance Italy, the chief forms of festal display were processions and shows, which might include a magnificent parade of masked figures on foot or in chariots —animals, giants, dragons—artificial islands, or ships which seemed to float, moved by men concealed within them, spectacular mock fights between Turks and Christians, with the Turks always the victors. From the fifteenth century onwards Tahtakale was a fairground and centre of entertainment in Istanbul. All in all, the early public festivities included almost everything that was later to be found in the circus, and each type of entertainer had his separate designation. It is probable that in the intervals between the great city festivals for which they were engaged, these performers would travel from one village to another giving shows where they could. All were organized into Guilds or Colleges, according to their activities, with different degrees of elaboration in the several localities according to their traditions and their ethnic groups. In Turkey, drama was brought before the public in three ways—by storytellers, by puppets (either rounded marionettes or flat shadow-show figures), and by live actors. Imitation (called *taklit*) and mimicry of dialectic peculiarities are common to all three forms, and the plot always revolves round certain stock characters, easily recognized by the audience because of their unvarying costume and their introductory music. There are, in fact, no true plays, in the modern sense of written scripts, but only scenarios giving a bare outline of plot and action. The storyteller, puppeteer, or actor memorized a number of stock phrases, usually in rhymed couplets, expressive of the colourful everyday life and language of their time. They relied very little on properties, and hardly at all on scenery. Women's parts were played by men. The plays, which were performed in public squares, in coffee-shops, in inn yards, or in private houses, had little or no consecutive action, depending for their comic effect on lively slapstick and monologues or dialogue involving puns, repartee, misunderstandings, crude practical jokes, *double entente*, and interpolated quips. Longer speeches were delivered according to clearly formulated rules of intonation. Performances were freely interspersed with songs and dances.

The simplest form of Turkish theatre is the dramatically presented story told by a single speaker, the Meddah (literally praise-giver), a clever mimic who can portray, by gesture and change of voice, more than one person. Apart from that, he relies mainly on two props, a cudgel and a kerchief wrapped round his neck.

The shadow show (*hayali zıl*), performed indoors, has always been one of the great delights of the Turkish people (for a description of the technique, see PUPPET; see also No. 127). The chief characters of the Turkish shadow show are Karagöz, who represents the ordinary Turk, of any trade or profession, and Hacıvat, who represents the false, pretentious, affected Turk. The greater part of the play consists of dialogues between them, but they are supported by a number of minor characters, who are simple caricatures of different races, professions, and human defects. There were in Turkey many kinds of puppets including *el kuklasi* (hand-puppets), *ipli kukla* (string-puppets), *iskemla kuklasi* (jigging puppets), and *dev kukla* (giant puppets or effigies). There was also a form of puppet show—*kukla*—which is often mistaken for the Karagöz play. The early *kukla* player, the *kuklabaz* or *suretbaz*, had an assistant who mingled with the audience and carried on a conversation with a puppet alone on the stage who addressed the public. The chief characters of this puppet play are *Ihtiyar* (the old man) and *Ibiş* (his servant) who correspond to Karagöz and Hacıvat in the shadow show, though they are not so well defined. The plots of the *kukla* were borrowed from popular tales and legends and even from the plays of the live actors, *Orta Oyunu*.

The *Orta Oyunu*, or middle play, to which in characters, plots, and atmosphere the Karagöz bears a strong resemblance, with the substitution of puppets for live actors, was preceded by some rudiments of dramatic art in the impromptu farces, where animal mimicry played an important part (the deer was the principal character, or the camel), which can still be seen in parts of Anatolia. There were also performances in the open, acceptable to a street-corner audience, in which the onlookers took part, and in which a prearranged comic situation was worked out with considerable improvisation. The actors, impersonating such officials as the watchman, the tax-collector, or the fortune-hunter, might play practical jokes on the shopkeepers or owners with the object of obtaining money from them.

As time went on these farces, whether they were called *Kol Oyunu* (company play) or *Meydan Oyunu* (public-square play) or even *Taklit Oyunu* (mimicry play) were all absorbed into the *Orta Oyunu* (middle play), which bears some resemblance to the *commedia dell'arte* or the Latin mime play. The characters represent the various peoples inhabiting Turkey and the actors imitate their dialects while depicting their occupations and professions in daily life. Their 'stage' is an open space round which the audience stands or sits (the raised platform sometimes appears, as the result of Western influence). In some cases a low railing marks off the actors' enclosure, but there is no curtain or dressing room, and the actors get ready and sit waiting with the orchestra for their cues in full view of the audience. Stage scenery consists of a large screen to represent a house and a smaller one to represent a shop. The imagination of the audience has to supply the rest. Near the stage area, beside the main entrance to it, sits the orchestra. Each actor has his own music and introduces himself with a short song or dance. The chief character is Pişekâr, who opens the play and rarely leaves the stage. When he does, he sits among the spectators. He wears bright colours—red trousers, a yellow gown and a variegated nightcap—and carries a cudgel with which he sometimes hits the other actors. The secondary character is Kavuklu, 'the man with the large wadded hat'. He is the comic character and his dialogues with Pişekâr form the main part of the play. Among the supporting characters the most important is Zenne (the woman), played by a man. A subsidiary actor may play several parts, changing his costume with his character. Each play consists of two parts, one the dialogue between Pişekâr and Kavuklu, the other, the play proper, in which the actors impersonate the different types found in Turkey (see No. 115).

2. MODERN. The history of the evolution of the modern Turkish theatre and of the adoption of Western drama can conveniently be divided into two periods. From the early nineteenth century to 1923 the Levantines brought the contemporary theatre to educated Turkish audiences and held it up as a model. Public performances began in about 1839, under Abdül Mecit I, by which time Istanbul had two amphitheatres, a theatre for Italian opera, and a theatre for Turkish improvised plays. Modern Turkish drama began in 1859, when a comedy by Ibrahim Şinasi was published, *Şair Evlenmesi*. In one act, it makes fun of the inconveniences and embarrassments which may arise from the conventionally 'arranged' marriage. There is, however, evidence that plays had been written earlier. After 1859 Turkish drama developed rapidly, with the help of Armenian actors, actresses, and managers. Among the important playwrights were Racaizade Ekrem, Namık Kemal, Ali Bey, Ahmet Mithat Efendi, Ahmet Vefik Paşa, and Ebüzziya Tevfik. Parallel with this development some of the actors from the *Orta Oyunu* theatre, seeking to evade the stranglehold of the theatre manager's patent which covered only the legitimate theatre 'with a prompter', started putting on plays 'without a prompter'. These were impromptu performances in which a general outline was filled out with improvised incidents taken from local events or newspaper reports, or even street gossip. This form of theatre was known as *Tulûat Tiyatrosu*. In 1913–14 the Mayor of Istanbul, Cemil Paşa (Topuzlu) invited Antoine, then director of the Paris Odéon, to come and organize a permanent municipal theatre and drama school in the city. This is still in existence, and today runs four theatres and an opera house.

The establishment of the Republic of Turkey in 1923, and the reforms of 1925–8, began a new era in the cultural development of the country. Dramatic art received official support and Western theatre became an integral part of Turkish life, the state assuming full responsibility for the actors' training and professional career. A State Conservatory (Devlet Konservatuari) was established in Ankara in 1936, by Paul Hindemith, with a dramatic section for the training of actors, dancers, and singers under Carl Ebert. There is also a ballet-school, founded and supervised by Dame Ninette de Valois. All training is free, and takes five years, after which the students become salaried members of the various State companies. Two-thirds of the plays produced are from world drama (see No. 93), the rest are by Turkish playwrights (see No. 116), who are being encouraged in their activities by the payment of substantial royalties on their plays, and the sole use of one State theatre. There is also a department of drama, with a degree course, in Ankara University. During the last few years Turkish playwriting has undergone great changes. Among the young playwrights of distinction are Turgut Özakman, Refik Erduran, Cahit Atay, Haldun Taner, Orhan Aśena (see No. 116), Hidayet Sayın, and Güngör Dilmen, and although there is as yet no characteristically Turkish dramatic literature, this may come, particularly in view of the opening of permanent theatres in the cities and the taking of first-rate theatrical productions into remote areas. METIN AND

TURLUPIN [HENRI LEGRAND] (*c.* 1587–1637), a player of farcical comedy at the Hôtel de Bourgogne, where he was partnered by Gaultier-Garguille and Gros-Guillaume. Tradition has it that they were all three originally bakers, and evolved their comic turns when throwing flour at each other. They probably all three played at the Paris fairs before joining a professional company, which Turlupin did after his companions, in 1615. He excelled in broad comedy, playing roguish valets, and with the rest of the company figures as himself in *La Comédie des comédiens* (1633), by Gougenot. As Belleville he also played serious parts, but it is as a farce-player that he is best remembered. His wife, Marie Durand, was anxious to go on the stage. This he would not permit, but after his death, being left with five small children, she married another actor, d'Orgemont, who succeeded Montdory at the Théâtre du Marais, and became an actress.

TURNER, ANTHONY (?), English actor, who is first found at the Cockpit in 1622. He remained there with the Queen's Men for the next fifteen years, but was evidently not one of the leading men. The parts in which he is known to have appeared include that of an old man. In 1637 he was one of those who remained in Beeston's new company at the Cockpit, and he seems then to have become slightly more important. He was arrested in 1659 for playing illegally at the Red Bull, and was evidently one of the more active theatrical law-breakers under the Commonwealth, in company with Edward Shatterell.

TURPILIUS, see ROME and FABULA, 3. *Palliata*.

TURPIO, AMBIVIUS, a Roman actor-producer of the second century B.C. (see ROME, I and CAECILIUS STATIUS).

TWAITS, WILLIAM (?–1814), a low comedian who was appearing with some success under the elder Macready in Birmingham and Sheffield when Wood engaged him for the Philadelphia theatre. He played there opposite Jefferson, and in 1805 made his first appearance in New York at a benefit night for Dunlap, who describes him as short, with stiff carroty hair, a mobile and expressive face, and a powerful asthmatic voice which he used with great comic effect. He was at his best in farce and broad comedy, and in accordance with the tradition of the day he appeared as Polonius. He was also seen as Richard III, and, somewhat incongruously, as Mercutio. More suited to his peculiar talents were the parts of the First Grave-digger, Dogberry, Launcelot Gobbo, and Goldfinch in *The Road to Ruin*, all of which he played under Cooper's management at the Park Theatre, New York. In 1813 Twaits was one of the recalcitrant players who formed the Theatrical Commonwealth, which played in the old circus on Broadway. He withdrew on the death at the end of the year of Mrs. Twaits, one of the lovely Westray sisters, previously known on the stage as Mrs. Villiers, and shortly before his own death appeared at the newly opened Anthony Street Theatre.

TWOPENNY GAFF, see GAFF.

TYLER, ROYALL (1757–1826), author of the first American comedy, *The Contrast*. Born in Boston, he graduated from Harvard, served in the army, and was then admitted to the Bar. While in New York he made the acquaintance of Thomas Wignell, at that time the leading comedian of the American Company, and it was probably due to his interest and influence that *The Contrast* was produced at the John Street Theatre on 16 Apr. 1787. In return for his help Tyler gave Wignell the copyright of the play, which was published in 1790 with George Washington heading the list of subscribers. The play, which is a light comedy in the style of *The School for Scandal*, was a success and was several times revived, though when given in Tyler's birthplace it had, like *Othello*, to be disguised as a 'Moral Lecture in Five Parts'. It was revived in 1917 at Philadelphia under the supervision of Otis Skinner. Tyler wrote several other plays, some of which are lost, but never again achieved the excellence of his first.

U

UDALL, Nicholas (1505–56), English scholar, headmaster in turn of Eton and Westminster and the author of *Ralph Roister Doister*, the earliest-known English comedy. Written while he was at Eton for performance by the boys in place of the usual Latin comedy, it was probably performed there between 1534 and 1541, though efforts have been made to connect it with Udall's headmastership at Westminster and date it 1552. In any case, it was not printed until about 1566–7. This comedy, the first play in English to deserve that name, is much influenced by Terence and Plautus, and turns on the efforts of a vainglorious fool to win the heart and hand of a wealthy London widow, egged on by the parasite Merygreeke, and finally thwarted by Gawin Goodluck, the lucky suitor. Although Udall is known to have written several other plays, as well as dialogues and pageants for Court festivities, where he was connected with the Revels Office under Mary Tudor, they are lost, or survive only in fragmentary form. Udall is sometimes credited with the authorship of *Thersites*, an interlude acted at Court in 1537 which A. W. Pollard considers to be the work of John Heywood.

UKRAINE, see russia.

ULSTER GROUP THEATRE, see ireland, 4.

UNAMUNO, Miguel de (1864–1936), Spanish philosopher, essayist, and novelist, author of a number of plays which present various facets of his thought. *Soledad* (1921) is concerned with loneliness and the theme of life as make-believe, a theme to which Unamuno returned in *Sombras de ensueño* (1926). *El otro* (1926) dramatizes the Cain–Abel relationship, and *El hermano Juan* (1929) is Unamuno's typically personal contribution to the development of the Don Juan theme, stressing also the relationship between character and author in a manner reminiscent of Pirandello. His eleven plays were written for performance, and of the eleven, nine were staged. They are not, however, truly successful stage plays, and the most popular Unamuno play has been the adaptation of his short story, *Nada menos que todo un hombre*, made by Julio de Hoyos. j. e. varey

UNDERHILL, Cave (*c.* 1634–*c.* 1710), an actor of the Restoration period well equipped by nature for the playing of boobies and lumpish louts, such as Clodpate in *Epsom Wells*, Lolpoop in *The Squire of Alsatia*, Drydrubb in *The Maid's Last Prayer*, and Sir Sampson in *Love for Love*. He was also much admired as the Grave-digger in *Hamlet*, and it was in this part that he made his last appearance shortly before he died, at a benefit performance given at the instigation of *The Tatler*. Colley Cibber, in his *Apology*, has left an excellent portrait of Underhill, who was esteemed one of the best actors of his day.

UNDERWOOD, John (*c.* 1590–1624), a boy-actor at the Blackfriars, where he appeared in *Cynthia's Revels* and *The Poetaster*. As an adult actor he joined the King's Men, and from 1608 to his death played with them regularly, though his only known role is that of Delio in *The Duchess of Malfi*. It has been conjectured that he played juvenile leads, princes, gallants, and libertines. He owned shares in the Blackfriars, Globe, and Curtain Theatres.

UNICORN THEATRE, Abingdon, near Oxford, a private venture founded in 1953 with the object of converting the medieval Checker Hall (once part of Abingdon Abbey) into a miniature Elizabethan theatre. Within the framework of stone walls and timbered roof a gaily painted façade has been erected with gallery, inner stage, and apron. There is seating for just over a hundred. Each summer the Unicorn Theatre Club sponsors a season of drama, opera, chamber music, and poetry, the plays ranging from Shakespeare to Eliot and Fry, the opera group specializing in Handel. Productions are mainly by local amateur clubs, including college groups from Oxford.

UNION SQUARE THEATRE, New York, on the south side of Union Square. This opened as a variety hall on 11 Sept. 1871. Among the initial attractions were the Vokes family—Jessie, Victoria, Rosina, Fred, and Fawdon—in their pantomime-spectacle *The Belles of the Kitchen*. On 1 June 1872 A. M. Palmer took over, and for ten years made the theatre one of the finest in New York. Many of the best actors in the United States appeared there, and its stock company was remarkable. Among its outstanding productions were *Agnes*, which ran for 100 nights, Mark Smith in *One Hundred Years Old*, Charlotte Thompson in *Jane Eyre*, and Clara Morris in *Camille*. *The Two Orphans*, produced in Dec. 1874, made a fortune for Palmer and a star of Kate Claxton. Maude Granger and W. H. Gillette both made their first appearances in New York under Palmer, while Stoddart, who played at the Union Square Theatre in 1875–6, remained with the stock company until it was disbanded in 1885, and then went to Madison Square with Palmer. The last play done under Palmer's management was *A Parisian Romance* (1883), which saw the début of Richard Mansfield in a small part that made him famous overnight. The theatre then opened under new management, but the stock company, though somewhat depleted by death and withdrawals, continued to function, being almost the last to resist the combination houses. After it was disbanded the theatre was used by travelling stars until in Feb. 1888 it was burnt down. It was rebuilt but never regained its former brilliance, and was mostly devoted to continuous vaudeville, under various names. It later became a burlesque house and then a cinema, and in 1936 it was demolished.

UNION THEATRE, New York, see chatham theatre, 2.

UNITED STATES OF AMERICA. The history of the theatre in the United States of America is complex—complex because of the vast geographical extent of the country and because of its gradual settlement and growth during the eighteenth and nineteenth centuries. To appreciate the way in which the stage has developed there, it is best to think of it as divided into a number of clearly marked, yet interrelated, sections. First comes the colonial period, ending about the year 1775; from the establishment of the new nation up to about 1820 is a period when theatre-lovers, proud of their independence, endeavour to set up a national playhouse; rapid progress is evident in the period 1820–70, and still more during the thirty years (1870–1900) to the close of the century, when the American stage draws well abreast of the European in technical skill, if not in dramatic artistry; thereafter comes an age of interesting experiment (1900–30), with the modern period seeing the fruits of many earlier efforts.

1. The Colonial Theatre: From the beginning to 1776. Long before any English plays were presented in the New World, what is now Latin America and the west coast of the United States had witnessed performances, directly or indirectly sponsored by the Catholic Church, which carried back in spirit to medieval times. From the year 1538, for example, comes a record of the production in Mexico, on the traditional Corpus Christi Day (the Thursday after Trinity Sunday), of a series of religious plays—*La Anunciación de la Natividad de San Juan Bautista hecha a su padre Zacarias*, *La Anunciación de Nuestra Señora*, *La Visitación de Nuestra Señora a Santa Isabel*, and *La Natividad de San Juan*. The following year yields a *Conquista de Rodas*, succeeded by a *Conquista de Jerusalén*. As early as 1598 there was a performance in New Mexico of 'an original play on a subject connected with the conquest of New Mexico', while professional Spanish actors were presenting dramas in the New World colonies by the beginning of the seventeenth century. From far off to the northward, too, comes a record of early dramatic activity: in 1606 a masque in French was performed, in honour of the Sieur de Poutrincourt, at Port Royal in Acadia (see also south america).

While the ancient religious plays were still to be found in the eighteen-thirties and while the early productions (whether religious or secular) unquestionably succeeded in leaving some sporadic traces behind them, it is not from this source that the theatre known as 'American' fundamentally springs. From England, not Spain or France—from Shakespeare, not from Lope de Vega—stems the American playhouse.

This American playhouse, however, starts late. The initial attempts to establish an English-speaking community in the New World were made in the first decade of the seventeenth century—just in time to find an imaginative echo in Shakespeare's *Tempest*: but it was a long time before the uneasy conditions of life in the struggling colonies allowed for such luxuries as attendance at plays. A few sparse records from this century hint that the drama was not entirely unknown and that, in the more leisured and latitudinarian South at least, men were dreaming of reproducing in their new homes the theatrical delights they had left behind them in London: even in the very home of austere Puritanism, Increase Mather had, to his vivid alarm, heard in 1687 'much discourse of beginning Stage-Plays in New England'. At the same time, although it is certain that some men were thinking of these things, it is equally certain that, whatever occasional and surreptitious endeavours may have been made in this way, nothing was attempted beyond one or two amateur—and no doubt woefully crude—productions.

The distinction of being the first professional actor to exhibit his talents to the colonists must, it seems, go to the eccentric and not over-respectable Tony Aston (*fl.* first half of eighteenth century), who apparently found his way in 1703 to 'Charles-Town', South Carolina, and, a few months later, to New York. Since he had no company with him, we are bound to assume that any performances he gave were in the nature of monologues and readings only. He was, however, the swallow heralding a coming summer, and it is significant that between 1699 and 1702 a certain Richard Hunter, otherwise unknown, asked for a licence to act plays in New York (which then had a population of scarcely 4,000). Another decade had barely passed when Williamsburg, Virginia, had a playhouse built in its midst; here a certain Charles Stagg, with his wife Mary, presented a few dramas. Thereafter accounts of stage performances begin to come from many localities. In the 1730s Charleston, South Carolina, had its Dock Street Theatre, and audiences there were able, from time to time, to see such Restoration tragedies as *The Orphan* and such almost contemporary comedies as *The Recruiting Officer*—although, without a doubt, in the most primitive of surroundings. If we may judge of these early playhouses by their successors on the frontier, they consisted simply of a plain wooden hut, with a platform at one end concealed by a frayed front curtain; scenery was nothing more than some paper wings, while dingy illumination came from a meagre array of smoking candles.

By the middle of the century, circumstances of life along the eastern coast had become such as to warrant the appearance of professional companies more stable, and presumably much more competent, than those which tentatively

UNITED STATES OF AMERICA

preceded them. In 1750 what had been but villages were becoming towns; road travel was less hazardous; the industry of the original settlers had produced a small but active leisured society. The time was ripe for the formal introduction of the theatre to America.

All through the period immediately following this date we hear of increasing dramatic effort, associated rather with Philadelphia and the South than with New York. It was in Philadelphia that a company led by Thomas Kean and Walter Murray constructed a playhouse in 1749 out of a warehouse; after presenting an interesting repertory (including *Richard III*) they formed the 'Virginia Company of Comedians', playing at Williamsburg, Annapolis, and elsewhere in that vicinity. A few years later, in 1752, Williamsburg welcomed another company, newly arrived from England, headed by the elder Lewis Hallam (1714–56) and consisting of twelve persons in all—the first theatrical group especially dispatched from London to America and now recognized as responsible for establishing the professional theatre, in a form not too far removed from contemporary English standards, in the colonies. During the 1750s, this company, later headed by David Douglass (?–1786), contributed much to the youthful American theatre. They introduced many plays not hitherto presented (*King Lear*, for example, *Romeo and Juliet*, *Hamlet*, and *The Merchant of Venice*); they were active, too, in the building of new theatres, among which were the Southwark, or South Street, in Philadelphia (1766) and the John Street in New York (1767). The latter, a wooden house, had two rows of boxes, a pit, and a gallery; proscenium doors with boxes above them flanked the stage. In 1785 this theatre was repainted 'at a vast expense, beautified and illuminated in a style to vie with European splendour'. (Preceding this house were New York's first Nassau Street Theatre (1750), Hallam's Nassau Street Theatre (1753), Cruger's Wharf Theatre (1758), and the Chapel (or Beekman) Street Theatre (1761)—all short-lived and of minor importance.)

By the time the Revolutionary War had drawn men's thoughts to things other than the theatre, the playhouse had established a hold, weak perhaps but nevertheless tenacious, on the imagination of the States. Nothing can demonstrate this better than the fact that in 1777 the John Street Theatre, renamed the Theatre Royal, was used by British soldiers anxious to display their acting talents, and that in the following year (1778) Addison's *Cato* was performed, in the other camp, at Valley Forge before a 'splendid audience' which included George Washington himself.

2. THE BEGINNING OF THE AMERICAN THEATRE: 1776–1820. Just at first, after winning success in the war, some of the infant States tried to prohibit the playhouse, but soon professional acting was proceeding on a still more extended scale. Lewis Hallam junior (1740–1808) returned from Jamaica (whither he had gone during the disturbances) in 1784, and the following year, by entering into partnership with John Henry (1738–94), broadened the scope of what was already known as the American Company. This group, with the comedian Thomas Wignell (1753–1803) and the second Mrs. Owen Morris (1753–1826), won considerable fame, was honoured by Washington, and maintained for several years a virtual monopoly over New York, Philadelphia, Baltimore, and Annapolis. It had the distinction of producing in 1787 Royall Tyler's *The Contrast*, the first native comedy written for professionals, and of attracting some English actors (of minor eminence at least) to American shores.

By the close of the century rivals began to appear, for the rapidly growing cities were now such as could provide audiences for more than one histrionic troupe. Under the inspiration of Wignell, who had seceded from the American Company in 1791, a new body of actors, which included Mrs. Oldmixon (?–1835/6), Thomas Jefferson (1732–1807), James Fennell (1766–1816), Mrs. Merry (1769–1808), and later young Thomas Cooper (1776–1849), started performances in 1794 in Philadelphia, at a new house, the Chestnut Street Theatre. Built on the model of the Theatre Royal at Bath (see Nos. 27, 28), this playhouse, seating 2,000 persons, with its Corinthian columns outside and its well-equipped stage, marked a definite milestone in the progress of the American theatre. We are now in the transition period between two ages. More attention is being paid to scenic effects, and the standard of acting is rising; comfort is creeping in for the audience, and the better-class patrons can enjoy reserved seats in the boxes: yet manners remain rough, notices respectfully requesting the spectators 'not to spit in the stove', managers finding it difficult to prevent those in the gallery from throwing 'apples, nuts, bottles, and glasses on the stage and into the orchestra'. On the one hand we hear of the engagement of competent scene-painters; on the other, of 'dirty pieces of canvas' serving to represent a landscape, and of backcloths showing a street 'while the side-scenes represent a wood'. Success attended the Wignell company: soon it spread its activities southward beyond Philadelphia and was responsible for the erection of other theatres at Baltimore (1794) and Washington (1800).

Meanwhile, signs were evident that rising New York was about to challenge the supremacy of Philadelphia. Four years after the opening of the Chestnut Street Theatre, the Park Theatre in New York was opened (1798), and this was immediately hailed as marking another distinct advance in theatre architecture. A stone building, it had three tiers of boxes, a gallery and a pit; the seating capacity was about 2,000. Here William Dunlap (1766–1839), whose drama, *The Father; or, American Shandyism*, had been first produced at the John Street Theatre in 1789 and who, in 1796,

UNITED STATES OF AMERICA

became associated with the American Company, pursued a chequered career until 1805, distraught by quarrels and jealousies among his actors but winning fame by his own plays and some success by his exploitation of the mediocre, but then highly esteemed, dramatic talents of the German playwright Kotzebue (for a painting of one of his productions, see No. 163).

In 1805 Dunlap's efforts to keep the Park Theatre going ended in failure: the house was sold to John Jacob Astor and John K. Beekman, who put in charge of it the well-established actor Thomas Cooper. A sum of $15,000 was laid out in the embellishment of the interior; new actors were engaged, notably the eccentric comedian William Twaits (?–1814); 'stars' were called in for short seasons (thus denting, if not shattering, the structure of the old stock companies); and once more a landmark in theatre history was reached when John Howard Payne (1791–1852), who had appeared at the Park as Young Norval in 1809, reversed the theatrical flow by travelling to England in 1813 and acting at Drury Lane. The American theatre was beginning to come of age.

If Payne went to England (and there later thrilled all good sentimental hearts by his lyric for 'Home, Sweet Home'), excited American audiences hailed the arrival of George Frederick Cooke (1756–1812), the most brilliant tragedian that the States had so far seen, but one whom intemperance rendered hopelessly unreliable. In 1810 he played at the Park, and thereafter, until his death two years later, visited various cities, leaving behind him many memories of his Richard III and other famous roles. Not long after (in 1820) appeared the equally brilliant and equally unreliable Edmund Kean (1787–1833).

The old Park Theatre was burned to the ground in 1820, and a new Park, with improved lighting facilities and other advances on its predecessor, opened the following season. Already this house had set New York as the leader of the American cities in dramatic affairs. The fact that in 180 it was taken over by the first theatre manager, Stephen Price (1783–1840), indicates the position it had gained. Commercially active, this Price, according to the English manager Alfred Bunn, 'lured away to the shores of America every performer of any distinction (and what is of equal importance—utility) whom gold could tempt, or speculation seduce'. The new Park seated 2,500 persons, and boasted of 'patent' oil lamps hung in three chandeliers, each containing thirty-five lights—a wonder to the age. For long, Philadelphia struggled to maintain its rivalry, but the traditions of 'Broadway'—if not as yet on Broadway itself—were surely being formed.

At the same time, as we leave this period of growth and concentration of power, it is important to note that, while the influence of the South began to decline, the force of events was carrying the stage into the puritanical North. There, at first, plays had to be disguised as moral lectures and theatres as exhibition rooms, but Boston's 'New Exhibition Room' (1792) was nothing but a playhouse. Under the irrepressible enthusiasm of Joseph Harper, Boston, Providence, and Newport were initiated into the mysteries of the stage. How rapidly circumstances were changing is shown by the erection, despite the still strong Puritan bias, of the Federal Street Theatre in Boston (1794), followed two years later by the Haymarket. The former was constructed of brick, with a stage opening of 31 feet; some improvements were introduced in 1798 when it had to be rebuilt after a disastrous fire. Elsewhere, to the west, Albany, which had welcomed a visit by Hallam's company in 1769, got its first permanent theatre—the brick-built, 'neat and commodious' Green Street Theatre—in 1812.

3. The Rise of New York: 1820–70. For a short time the new Park Theatre of New York dominated theatrical life in America. Here Junius Brutus Booth (1796–1852), Kean's rival, made his New York début in 1821, after a few initial performances at Richmond, Virginia; here in 1822 appeared the elder Mathews (1776–1835), whose particular style in comedy was so highly acclaimed on both sides of the Atlantic.

Soon, however, conditions altered. New York had crushed the rivalry of Philadelphia, but the city had grown sufficiently large to produce rivalry within its own boundaries. In 1824 the Chatham Garden Theatre was opened with a distinguished company that included Joseph Jefferson (1774–1832), as well as the founder of a great theatrical dynasty, Henry Wallack (1790–1870). Graciously planned, it retained the useful old forestage which was so rapidly disappearing in England, together with the proscenium doors (also vanishing relics of the past) set in a framework that is almost reminiscent of the Elizabethan stage. Two years later the Lafayette Theatre was introduced to the public: recognized as one of 'the most splendid theatres in the Union', it was particularly well equipped for those equestrian and aquatic shows which made such an appeal to contemporaries. Although it vanished in a fire a few years later, already in 1826 still another playhouse, the Bowery, had appeared on the scene. This theatre, with a name destined to evoke many fond memories, was a classic structure holding nearly 3,500 persons, with a huge stage lit by the new medium of gas. (Gas lighting had been introduced at the Chestnut Street Theatre in Philadelphia ten years before, and at the Camp Street Theatre in New Orleans two years before its use for theatrical purposes in New York.) Fire took its toll of this house also (1828), but ninety days after its destruction a new Bowery, with a stage 84 feet deep and considerable improvements in the auditorium, took its place. When this likewise was destroyed in a conflagration in 1836, a third Bowery appeared (1837). This lasted for only a year (fire, again) and a fourth Bowery was built in 1839. In 1845, after still another fire, a fifth Bowery was opened; this pursued a fairly successful, but chequered, career into the present century (see No. 52).

From the 1830s onward theatrical development was swift. In 1835 came the Franklin Theatre, a small house holding only six hundred spectators. Two years previously New York acquired its first Italian Opera House. (Another, Palmo's, was opened in 1844, and a third, the Astor Place Opera House, in 1847; the theatre of the Academy of Music, with an audience capacity of 4,600, was constructed in 1854, enduring till the Metropolitan appeared in 1883. It was pulled down in 1926.) In 1836 the Opera House ceased to fulfil its original purpose and the following year came under the management of James William Wallack (1791–1864) as the National Theatre: here a formidable company, including many distinguished players, won considerable fame until its destruction by fire three years later. Although this house thus suffered from the prevailing menace, its place was taken by the New Chatham Theatre (otherwise called the New National). At the same time appeared the Olympic Theatre, where, between 1839 and 1850, the comedian William Mitchell (1798–1856) entertained audiences with burlesques, farces, and adaptations of Dickens's novels. In 1850 John Brougham (1810–80), already well known on the English stage, built the Lyceum on Broadway. A few years before this, Palmo's Opera House was transformed into Burton's Theatre (1848): here, and in other houses with which he was associated, William Evans Burton (1804–60) presented productions more ambitious than any so far seen in America. Brougham's Lyceum became, in 1852, Wallack's Lyceum, and what Burton had achieved found a fitting rival. The company assembled here was probably more brilliant than any in the past and it established a tradition which was carried on to a New Lyceum (1861) and which endured until 1882 under the famous actor Lester Wallack (1820–88). It was with this theatre that Dion Boucicault (1822–90), a stormy petrel in theatres on both sides of the Atlantic, was closely associated. Still another highly popular playhouse was that of Laura Keene (1826–73), opened in 1856, also situated on Broadway—a theatre distinguished by many triumphs, not least of which was the production of *Our American Cousin*, with Edward Askew Sothern (1826–81) and Joseph Jefferson III (1829–1905) (best remembered for his Rip Van Winkle of 1859) in the cast. Just at the end of the period came Booth's Theatre on Sixth Avenue (1869). Erected at a great cost, with a capacity of 1,800, this house possessed special facilities for scenic effects; the wide stage could be made to sink, and hydraulic rams were introduced for the handling of the sets. It was the home of Edwin Booth (1833–93), an outstanding actor, son of Junius Brutus Booth (1796–1852), and brother of that John Wilkes Booth (1839–65) who assassinated Abraham Lincoln in 1865 during a performance of *Our American Cousin* at Ford's Theatre in Washington. The same year that Booth's was opened, a new era was being ushered in by the opening of the Fifth Avenue Theatre (originally built in 1867), soon to be under the management of Augustin Daly (1838–99): in this playhouse standards of production were set which surpassed even the notable and worthy efforts of its predecessors.

As the very names given to the theatres indicate, these fifty years from 1820 to 1870 were a period of star actors and managers. They formed a period, too, when the stages of the United States and of England, despite many attempts to establish a native American tradition, became as one. In early years it had been mainly the minor London players who hazarded the long and then exhausting journey across the Atlantic, but now, following the visits of Cooke and Kean, almost all the actors prominent on London's boards arranged American tours. W. C. Macready (1793–1873) arrived in 1826, Charles Kean (1811–68) in 1830, Charles Kemble (1775–1854) in 1832.

While this is true, there is evident another paradoxical truth. The New York stage during this time was not simply an echo of London's: in tragedy and in comedy alike an individual style was being born among American players. James Henry Hackett (1800–71) was the perfect Yankee. Edwin Forrest (1806–72) rose slowly to become the most representative American actor of his age, one who introduced a peculiar style of his own and who was instrumental in encouraging much native dramatic talent. In 1835 the great Charlotte Cushman (1816–76) came before the public, while Mrs. John Drew (Louisa Lane) (1820–97), whose long stage career extended from her appearance as a crying baby at twelve months old to the very last years of the nineteenth century, almost provided in herself a history of the American playhouse.

4. The Opening of the Frontier: 1820–70. While New York, notwithstanding its close association with London, was thus beginning to strike an individual note, other parts of the United States, from proud and genteel Boston to the furthest of rough frontiers, were awakening theatrically. The famous 'Boston Museum' was opened in 1841 and was destined to prove of some considerable significance in the future; in 1854 a new Federal Street Theatre, with an auditorium seating 3,000 persons and with an excellent stage, showed that the capital of Massachusetts was in process of forgetting the austerity of the Pilgrim Fathers.

Meanwhile, a great stirring was to be felt everywhere in the South and West of the Alleghenies. Already in 1791 a group of French actors had appeared in New Orleans, and soon the city boasted a St. Pierre Theatre (1807), a St. Philippe (1808), and an Orleans (1809). A few years later, in 1817–18, Noah Miller Ludlow (1795–1886), later to win much repute in the circuits, brought his American Theatrical

Commonwealth Company to this largely French-speaking town, and his initial success there led to the building of the American Theatre by James H. Caldwell (1793–1863) in 1822. Caldwell rapidly assumed almost complete power in the district. Anxious to introduce the latest improvements to his southern audiences, he was one of the first in America to install gas lighting in a theatre, while in the St. Charles Theatre (1835), erected at a cost of $350,000, he gave New Orleans what was then the most magnificent playhouse in the States.

During these years his predecessor, Ludlow, had been active elsewhere. To St. Louis he carried a company in 1820; four years later he constructed a small brick theatre at Mobile. For some time he was associated with Joshua Collins and William Jones (who built in 1820 the important Columbia Street Theatre at Cincinnati), but later joined his fortunes with the picturesque Sol Smith (1801–69), a stage-struck farmer's son who, with many vicissitudes, played a significant part in opening up the theatre in the West. Their united efforts were responsible for the erection (1837) of a new theatre in St. Louis, a large three-tiered building with a capacity of 1,500. Here they maintained a local monopoly until in 1851 John Bates opened another theatre, which in turn was followed by the Varieties (1852), the People's (1852), and the Olympic (1866).

All over the speedily growing States the record was similar. A theatre had already been established at Washington in 1800, but this must have been but a humble affair. By 1835 Washington possessed, in the National Theatre, an adequate playhouse, with a stage 68 feet by 71; in 1862 this was followed by Ford's, where Lincoln met his end. The first performances at Indianapolis, in the West, were given in 1823; thirty years later, in 1858, that city had, in the Metropolitan, a theatre seating 1,500 persons, while a couple of decades after that date it claimed that its Opera House (1875) was 'the best arranged theatre in the United States'. During the early years of the century Chicago was nothing but a village: even towards the end of the 1830s it had no stage save an improvised affair set up in an hotel dining-room. By 1847, however, the time had arrived for the construction of a permanent theatre, and from then on progress was rapid. A fine playhouse was built in the rising city in 1857 (McVicker's Theatre), and others followed both before and after the disastrous fire of 1871. Crosby's Opera House (1865) cost $600,000, and in 1889 the Auditorium was reputed to be the largest theatrical building in America (see PIONEER THEATRE).

In the Far West, San Francisco experienced similar theatrical development during the fifties: the Mormon State of Utah rejoiced, by 1862, in the possession of its handsome Salt Lake Theatre; while up and down the wide Mississippi the showboats—calliopes screaming, bands blaring, flags flying—splashed their colourful way. (see MORMON THEATRE and SHOWBOAT).

Whereas in 1800 there were no more than 150 professional actors in the United States performing in a bare handful of theatres, by 1885 over 3,500 towns, with a total of more than 5,000 theatres, were witnessing dramatic productions, and much of this growth took place during the period (1820–70) in question.

5. THE BEGINNING OF NATIVE AMERICAN DRAMA: 1820–70. During all this time English plays, classic and contemporary, formed the main bill of fare, both in New York's star theatres and in the rude theatres of the frontier. Signs, however, were not lacking, both in New York and in the newly explored theatrical territory, that a native drama was in the making. Far back in 1767 Thomas Godfrey's (1736–63) *Prince of Parthia* had started the ball rolling, while *The Contrast* of Royall Tyler (1757–1826) in 1787 had made comic use of local types. Slightly later came the plays of William Dunlap, the first American professional dramatist. In 1808 the Chestnut Street Theatre in Philadelphia saw the first acted drama by an American author on an Indian theme—*The Indian Princess*, by James Nelson Barker (1784–1858); this play, presented in 1820 at Drury Lane as *Pocahontas; or, the Indian Princess*, appears also to have been the first American dramatic work produced, after performance in the New World, on a London stage. John Howard Payne carried native playwriting a stage further, as did Robert Montgomery Bird (1806–54) and George Henry Boker (1823–90), whose *Francesca da Rimini* (1855), still remembered, is one of the best poetic plays written in English during the course of the century.

Nearly all these plays, however, despite the utilization in many of American scenes and characters, were dominated by English models, and although some are worthy of note, little was provided in them of an individual spirit. In less literary realms, on the other hand, new possibilities were being discovered. When T. D. Rice (1808–60) in 1828 listened to an old Negro outside the theatre at Louisville, persuaded him to repeat the song he was singing, and later, in black-face, reproduced the song—'Jump Jim Crow'—in a native play, he was responsible for starting the vogue of the Minstrel Show. In little more than a decade—1842—the famous Christy Minstrels had been formed and something entirely fresh had been given to the stage. The minstrel shows may have been a travesty of the Negro song-and-dance (see NEGRO IN THE AMERICAN THEATRE) from which they took their being, but other entertainers too were beginning to forget the classic, romantic, melodramatic, sentimental, dramatic traditions and were listening to the actual forms of speech used by persons around them. In the earliest plays introducing Red Indian characters, they communicated their noble thoughts in bombastic classic or romantic style: when Boucicault introduced into *The Octoroon* (1859) a Red Indian who merely grunted, he carried his contemporaries from an old world into a new.

6. The Triumph of Realism: 1870–1900. In 1869 the opening of Daly's Fifth Avenue Theatre was a landmark greater than any in the past. Daly was a theatrical genius, a man who had at once the ability to engage the best talent of his time and the personality to exert a very definite influence upon those, no matter how talented, with whom he worked. Under his direction appeared a company of brilliant players, and, when one considers that to their contributions were added the results of his own meticulous and sensitive direction, it is not surprising to find that he moved on from success to success, opening a second Daly's Theatre in 1879, taking his actors to London in 1884, and completing the eastward trend by setting up a Daly's Theatre there in 1893. The care he took with his rehearsals is now proverbial: almost legendary are the stars of his cast—John Drew, Jr. (1853–1927), Adelaide Neilson (1848–80), Maurice Barrymore (1847–1905), and others. Nor was his inspiration confined entirely to the practical work of the stage: it was Daly who introduced to New York audiences *Saratoga* (1870), by Bronson Howard (1842–1908), a play which firmly placed this forerunner of the modern American dramatists in the theatrical firmament.

Despite the excellence of his directorship, sharp rivalry was given to Daly's, between 1872 and 1883, by the Union Square Theatre under the management of Albert Marshman Palmer (*c.* 1840–1905), a man of vastly different calibre but one who had the skill (some said, the luck) to make use of the services of others more gifted than himself.

Theatre after theatre sprang up during this time. The 14th Street Theatre (which had been opened originally in 1866 as the Théâtre Français) appeared in 1870, came under the management of Laura Keene in 1871, and two years later, after extensive alterations, became the Lyceum, under Fechter. Increasing sums of money were put into these buildings. The Park of 1874 cost $100,000, Wallack's in 1882 cost $250,000, and so on to Oscar Hammerstein's Manhattan Theatre (1892), the foyer of which was said to be equalled only by the great opera-houses of Paris and Vienna. The New Park (1883), the Bijou Opera House (1880, renamed the Bijou Theatre in 1883), the Lyceum (1885), the Broadway (1888), the Garrick (1890), the Empire (1893), the American (1893), Hammerstein's Olympia (rechristened the Lyric, 1895)—these and others gave to New York a theatrical world fit to be compared with that of any other metropolis.

In some respects New York went beyond the other capitals, for among her new theatres was one, the Madison Square Theatre (1879), which was the marvel of its time, introducing stage equipment of the kind which later brought fame to the theatres of Germany. With justification a newspaper of the time declared that 'anyone in doubt that New York is rapidly becoming the theatre centre of the world must have been convinced of it at the opening of the new Madison Square Theatre'. The seats were more commodiously arranged than in any other house; air-conditioning provided freshness to the auditorium; the balconies, no longer in the old horseshoe form, were 'broken into three flowing bays, like Moorish archways laid horizontally', with lower boxes 'like moresque pavilions—octagonal in form, guarded by lattices of carved wood, embossed with old ivory and gold'. Revolutionary as was the auditorium, it was the stage that caused the greatest wonder. The orchestra was set, not below the stage, but above the proscenium arch, in a recess which could be concealed by curtains, while beyond the arch there was a 'double elevator stage' by means of which sets could be prepared above or below that which was being shown to the audience and raised or lowered, when necessary, into position. The inventor of all these wonders was Steele MacKaye (1844–94), dramatist, visionary, actor, and manager. From his fertile brain flowed idea after idea for the improvement of theatres. The double stage was one, but from him came also such devices, simple and grandiose, as the folding theatre seat, the 'curtain of light' to take the place of the ordinary drop-curtain, the cloud-machine, the sliding stage, and the proscenium adjuster (altering the size of the stage opening). For the Lyceum (1885) he introduced electric light and gave to the auditorium a delicacy of form and colouring well in accord with the latest views of the aesthetes, while in the Spectatorium, designed for the Chicago World Fair of 1893, he planned a 'house for spectacles' far beyond the dreams of any contemporary.

This was a time of great actors, American and other. Robert Mantell (1854–1928), William Gillette (1855–1937), Richard Mansfield (1857–1907), Mrs. Fiske (1865–1932), Julia Marlowe (1866–1950), Maude Adams (1872–1953), Ethel Barrymore (1879–1959) played during these years on the same stages as saw Henry Irving (1838–1905), Benoît Coquelin (1841–1909), Sarah Bernhardt (1845–1923), Ellen Terry (1847–1928), and Mrs. Patrick Campbell (1865–1940). It was a time, too, when new methods of directing came to supersede the old. Daly had set fresh standards and the age found its most characteristic producer in the realist David Belasco (1859–1931). Those in charge of the theatre had become tired of the artificialities of the past and their dreams were set on achieving more and more of an approximation to the actual: the qualities essential to the cinema were being exploited in those years when the cinema had not as yet been born. For the achievement of this realism Steele MacKaye invented new devices; for it Belasco trained his actors; for it the new playwrights penned their dramas. As yet the American drama did not acknowledge the hard austerity of Ibsen, but even though the plays of the time seem now to be unduly sentimental, and reminiscent of the melodramatic form against which they reacted, it is possible to see how the path was being made smooth for the future. Augustus Thomas (1859–1934), whose first great success was *Alabama* (1891)—a study of North and South

UNITED STATES OF AMERICA

after the Civil War—and who contributed many later dramas to the stage, introduced New York audiences to the 'play of ideas'. American history and contemporary social life were exploited in the interesting works of Clyde Fitch (1865–1909). Realistic observation of native types gives distinction to the writings of James A. Herne (1839–1901), whose *Margaret Fleming* (1890) is still remembered. Perhaps these men did not accomplish much, but, poor as most of their plays now seem to us, it is clearly evident that collectively they were evolving a style characteristically American.

To a large extent the promise of this age was vitiated at the very close of the century by the arising of a new force in the theatre—the theatrical trust. The stars and the acting managers had, it is true, dealt a serious blow to the old stock-company tradition, but the fact that these men were creatively concerned with practising the art of the stage gave their work a liveliness and vigour which cannot come from a playhouse dominated by commercial interests. The first Theatrical Syndicate, under Sam Nixon, Fred Zimmerman, Al Hayman, Charles Frohman, Marc Klaw, and Abraham Erlanger, was formed in 1896 and gradually extended its control not only over New York but over the entire country. Belasco and others fought bitterly to preserve their independence, but it was obvious that the concentration of power in the hands of business men was destined to triumph. The days of the actor-manager, like the days of the stock company, were over.

7. THE GROWTH OF A NEW THEATRE: 1900–30. In 1900 there were no less than forty-three theatres in New York, and still the building of playhouses continued apace. Abbey's Theatre, which was opened by Henry Irving and Ellen Terry in 1893, became, after alterations, the Knickerbocker in 1896. Oscar Hammerstein (1847–1919) constructed the Republic in 1900: this became the Belasco two years later. The Savoy appeared as Schley's Music-Hall in 1900, while another variety house, the Gotham, came into being in 1901. The year following saw the erection of the handsome Majestic; Daniel Frohman's Lyceum was opened in 1903, and Hammerstein's gorgeous Manhattan Opera House, constructed at a cost of $2,000,000, in 1906. One after another they came—the Gaiety and the Stuyvesant (the present Belasco) (1907), the Maxine Elliott (1908), the New (1909), the Globe (1910), the Winter Garden (1912), the Cort (1912), the Booth (1913), the Longacre (1913), the Henry Miller (1918), the Music Box (1921), the Earl Carroll (1922), the Imperial (1923), the Guild (1924). And these are the names of only a few among the important buildings constructed during the first quarter of the century. By 1926 New York had sixty-eight playhouses in active use; two years later there were eighty.

Significant things were happening during these decades. The commercialism which had taken such a hold of the stage in the last years of the nineteenth century and the first years of the twentieth was now being fought with other weapons than Belasco had used. In New York the attempt of Winthrop Ames (1871–1937) to re-establish repertory at the New Theatre in 1909 failed, but other efforts in that direction were to prove more fortunate. In 1915 and 1916 two groups were formed, destined to wield considerable influence on the playwrights of the age: one of these was the Washington Square Players who, after preliminary performances at the Bandbox, moved to the Comedy, moved on to the Garrick and formed the Theatre Guild; the second was the Provincetown Players, closely identified with the introduction to the American public of the early plays of O'Neill—indeed, when this body was reconstituted in 1924, that dramatist shared with Robert Edmond Jones (1887–1954) and Kenneth Macgowan (1888–1963) the task of directing it. Less concerned with producing the work of living American authors but nevertheless of considerable importance in bringing the new drama to the attention of playgoers was another venture of 1915—the Neighborhood Playhouse, sponsored by Alice and Irene Lewisohn; while in 1926 came Eva Le Gallienne's (1899–   ) experiments at the Civic Repertory.

A new generation of actors was arising, a new generation of producers and scene-designers. Above all, there was arising a new generation of playwrights. The century opens with the work of a number of authors, among whom were William Vaughn Moody (1869–1910) (whose *The Great Divide* appeared in 1906) and Edward Sheldon (1886–1946) (creator of *Romance*, 1913), able craftsmen, inheritors of the late nineteenth-century tradition, adding to that tradition something characteristic of their own but in no wise striking out fresh dramatic paths. By the middle of the second decade the Provincetown Players were presenting some one-act plays by a young writer, Eugene O'Neill (1888–1953), whose entire approach to the theatre was revolutionary. Hailed at first only by a small group of enthusiasts, O'Neill startled large numbers of his contemporaries in the 1920s by his daring in *Beyond the Horizon* and *The Emperor Jones* (both 1920), *The Hairy Ape* (1922), *All God's Chillun Got Wings* and *Desire Under the Elms* (both 1924), *The Great God Brown* (1926), *Marco Millions* and *Lazarus Laughed* (both 1927). His *Strange Interlude*, with its deliberate use of the 'aside' expanded into fundamental dialogue, came in 1928; the 1930s saw the tense *Mourning Becomes Electra* (1931) and the nostalgic *Ah, Wilderness!* (1933); the 1940s, *The Iceman Cometh* (1946) and *A Moon for the Misbegotten* (1947).

In O'Neill the American theatre recognized a master, and he did more than any of his predecessors to bring the world to a realization of the existence in the New World of a self-conscious independent stage. It is possible that now, looking back on his works in the perspective of time, we are forced to acknowledge that they do not possess to the fullest degree those excellences which once we thought were there.

All too clearly we see now that O'Neill has missed the heights of genius by his lack of that infinite capacity for taking pains which is the hall-mark of the supreme artist; as clearly do we see that, during the period of his stormy apprenticeship, he did not train himself sufficiently as a master of words—so that in most of his plays scenes of crisis and emotional intensity cry out for a peerless expression which he is incapable of producing. Yet the fact remains that in O'Neill the American theatre came to own one of the world's most dominating dramatic figures, a man who, potentially if not in actual realization, may stand on the same exalted level as the most disinguished masters of past eras.

And with O'Neill arrived a whole school of other writers who, in contradistinction to the dramatist-craftsmen of preceding years, aimed at high artistry in their works. Sidney Howard (1891–1939) enlarged the scope of the realistic play in *They Knew What They Wanted* (1924), *The Silver Cord* (1926), and *Yellow Jack* (1934). In the last of these, indeed, he showed that his talent was capable of embracing much more than domestic issues, and of utilizing dramatic conventions beyond those of the naturalistic stage. In Robert Sherwood (1896–1955) the theatre welcomed an author of rich qualities who passed from the gently sceptical and ironically comic effects of *The Road to Rome* (1927) and *Reunion in Vienna* (1931) to serious reflection on the very fundamentals of our modern civilization (*The Petrified Forest*, 1934; *Idiot's Delight*, 1936). To Broadway, Elmer Rice (1892–1967) brought an inventive mind and a vigorous willingness to experiment; his expressionistic *The Adding Machine* appeared in 1923, his ultra-naturalistic *Street Scene* in 1929. The first play of Maxwell Anderson (1888–1959), *White Desert*, came in 1923, to be followed by the vastly successful *What Price Glory?* (1924), written in collaboration with Laurence Stallings (1894–1968), which, although it did not by any means indicate what this author was later to do in the field of poetic drama, at once revealed the presence of a young playwright of worth. In these years, too, were presented the vigorous *Hell Bent for Heaven* (1924) by Hatcher Hughes (1883–1945) and the experimental *Processional* (1925) by John Howard Lawson (1895–).

No less active were the scene-designers. Norman Bel Geddes (1893–1958) and Robert Edmond Jones (for an example of his work, see No. 87), although both practical men, had visions of grandeur for the theatre which carried it far from the ideals of Belasco. For long identified with the Theatre Guild, Lee Simonson (1888–1967) (see No. 101), without aiming at the majesty of conception which inspired Geddes and Jones, contributed to the New York stage a long series of fresh and imaginative settings, all characteristic yet widely varied in their technique. In the work of these men the theatre was displaying its willingness to harmonize with the achievements of the new playwrights.

UNITED STATES OF AMERICA

8. The Nineteen-Thirties. During the 1930s the theatre in the United States seemed to be progressing yet further, to be moving towards the realization of things as yet but dimly dreamed of. There was an electric tension on Broadway and beyond. The Federal Theatre Project appeared to many to have within it the makings of a national dramatic movement; theatres of the Left, such as the Theatre Union and the Group Theatre, brought new vigour to the stage; in the ordinary commercial playhouses audiences were being amused or moved by a series of dramas which, excellent in themselves, were thought by many to betoken still greater things in the future.

These were the days when Maxwell Anderson seemed about to usher in a great era of poetic drama—*Winterset* (1935) following *Mary of Scotland* (1933), *High Tor* (1937) following *Winterset*. Archibald MacLeish (1892–), in *Panic* (1935), turned from lyrical poetry to the theatre. At the same time the skilful and mellowed comedies of Sam Behrman (1893–), *Biography* (1932) and *End of Summer* (1936), evoked a gracious spirit, lost for a moment in *No Time for Comedy* (1939) and recaptured in *Jacobowsky and the Colonel* (1943). Philip Barry (1896–1949), less skilful and more inclined towards sentiment yet gifted with a fine ear for word values, presented then his *Hotel Universe* (1930), *The Animal Kingdom* (1932), and *Philadelphia Story* (1939). The atmosphere of Gilbert and Sullivan, made modern and mordant, seemed to be reborn in *Of Thee I Sing* (1931), in which George Kaufman (1889–1961) collaborated with Morrie Ryskind (1895–). Collaborating later with Moss Hart (1904–1961), Kaufman was thought to have established in *You Can't Take It With You* (1936) a fresh kind of American comedy-farce, a form which was also enriched by the fantastic *Three Men on a Horse* (1936) by George Abbott (1887–). Marc Connelly (1891–) came forward with his sensitive dramatic treatment of Negro religion, *The Green Pastures* (1930); Paul Green (1894–) with his imaginative *House of Connelly* (1931); Clare Boothe (1903–) with her viciously (and perhaps superficially) witty *The Women* (1936); Lillian Hellman (1905–) with her incisive *Children's Hour* (1934) and *Little Foxes* (1939); John Steinbeck (1902–68) with his psychopathic study *Of Mice and Men* (1937). From the Leftist theatre came the angry *They Shall Not Die* (1934) of John Wexley (1902–), and the melodramatic *Stevedore* (1934) of Paul Peters (1908–)—above all, the *Waiting for Lefty* (1935) of Clifford Odets (1906–63), to be followed by his *Awake and Sing* (1935), *Golden Boy* (1937), and *Rocket to the Moon* (1938).

It was a glorious decade, yet in retrospect it seems, one must regretfully admit, a little tarnished. Even by the end of these ten years the hopes for the future were by no means so roseate as they had been at its start. In particular, it could be observed that, with the exception of Clifford Odets (who soon deserted Broadway for Hollywood), no young playwright of any real outstanding potentialities had risen to carry on the torch from the men of the older generation—O'Neill, Anderson, Rice, Behrman, Sherwood. It was as though, instead of keeping forces in reserve, the American theatre had, within this brief space of time, expended all its strength. The Federal Theatre Project came, bringing with it such memorable productions as that of the Negro *Macbeth*, and went—condemned by its unfortunate foundation as a relief measure—to leave behind it few permanent relics. The theatres of the Left faded away. There seemed to be real justification for the judicial summing-up made in 1939 by a distinguished American critic, Joseph Wood Krutch, of the century's achievements in drama:

> The fact remains that no playwright who has emerged since 1918, not even O'Neill, has produced an impact even remotely comparable to that produced by Ibsen or Shaw. Nor does the surviving corpus of dramatic writing seem to justify entirely the sense which one has had from year to year that excellent plays were being produced in considerable number. Too many of these plays seem to have fulfilled their function of keeping alive a vital and interesting theatre without actually achieving any permanent place in dramatic literature. The 'best play of the year' has very often owed its popularity to some novelty of theme or dramatic method which seemed exceptionally interesting at the moment but which failed to remain so for very long, and some of these 'best plays' have already been almost completely forgotten.

ALLARDYCE NICOLL

9. THE MODERN PERIOD. During the Second World War the American theatre was generally flourishing, but mostly with trivial farces, melodramas, and musical entertainments. A few of these in late 1939 did, however, rise above mediocrity—notably, the period comedy *Life with Father*, by Howard Lindsay and Russel Crouse; the character satire *The Man Who Came to Dinner*, by George S. Kaufman and Moss Hart; James Thurber and Elliott Nugent's satire on American academic life *The Male Animal*. Subsequently, comedies of distinction became rare. In 1941 Joseph Kesselring's comic melodrama, *Arsenic and Old Lace*, won great success, and in 1943 came the one noteworthy war-time romantic comedy, John van Druten's *The Voice of the Turtle*, a penetrative and ingeniously written three-character play. In 1944 came Mary Chase's *Harvey*, a *tour de force* of comic invention revolving around a lovable alcoholic who fancies an imaginary six-foot rabbit, 'Harvey', for his friend, and even makes his psychiatrist believe in its existence. Frank Fay (1897–1961) made the bibulous hero one of the best-known roles in the modern American theatre. At about the close of the war the stage also acquired effective comedies of political and sociological importance in *State of the Union* (1945) by Howard Lindsay and Russel Crouse, and *Born Yesterday* (1946) by Garson Kanin.

Serious drama seemed tame by comparison with the momentous events of the war period excitingly reported in the press and vividly represented on the screen by documentary and fictional motion pictures. At the same time, the public wanted compensatory light entertainment from the theatre, which was disposed to provide it after the failure of many serious but humdrum efforts to express the conflict of ideologies. An early casualty of the period was the famous Group Theatre, which had led the American theatre in the expression of social tensions and ideas. Only one new playwright made an impression at the beginning of the Second World War, when William Saroyan (1908–), first known as a writer of bizarre short stories during the 1930s, wrote a long one-act fantasia on the pathos and nobility of the common man, *My Heart's in the Highlands*, which the Group Theatre produced early in 1939. Next, in the fall of the same year, the Theatre Guild produced, jointly with Eddie Dowling, an odd mélange, *The Time of Your Life*, an original representation of inchoate life in a run-down San Francisco saloon and of confusion in society. Several other plays produced in the early years of the decade (*Love's Old Sweet Song*, *The Beautiful People*, *Jim Dandy*, *Across the Board of Tomorrow Morning*, and *Get Away, Old Man*) expressed Saroyan's defiant optimism and generous disposition to mingle toughness and tender-mindedness, commonplaceness and romance, realism and fantasy. He also wrote a superb one-act drama about the lynching of a young tramp, *Hello, Out There!*, which had a number of productions after 1941. But Saroyan's work became increasingly disorganized and by 1943 his vogue seemed over. He made an impression on Broadway again only when his *Cave Dwellers* was produced in the late 1950s.

American playwrights tried to respond to the war with numerous anti-Nazi and patriotic plays. Less than a dozen of these rose above stereotyped characters and situations. In Apr. 1941 Lillian Hellman gave the theatre a prophecy of America's involvement (within eight months) in the war, *Watch on the Rhine*, which combined moving family drama with spy melodrama. One of the earliest and certainly the most imaginative of war-inspired dramas was Thornton Wilder's fantasia on human history, *The Skin of Our Teeth* (1942), a telescopic representation of man's frequent state of crisis from the Ice Age to the present time. Sidney Kingsley contributed an historical drama *The Patriots* (1943), that derived a lesson in national unity from the formative years of the American republic. Several other plays proved provocative, especially *Tomorrow the World* (1943), a study of a Nazified child in a tolerant American milieu, by James Gow and Arnaud D'Usseau, and Elmer Rice's discussion-drama *Flight to the West* (1940), in which the playwright charged Nazi-ism with 'rational madness' in contrast to democracy's 'irrational sanity'.

After 1944 a promising revival of the American drama began to be observed. It was marked by O'Neill's brief return to the theatre with a weighty pessimistic work, *The Iceman*

Cometh (1946), revolving round the hopelessness of the human condition and man's dependency on sustaining illusions, and an even darker play, *A Moon for the Misbegotten* (1947), a compassionate treatment of a grotesquely large girl and her hopelessly damned alcoholic lover, which was withdrawn while on tour and brought to Broadway only a decade later. After O'Neill's death in 1953 his widow authorized the posthumous production of two other plays, the autobiographical *Long Day's Journey into Night* (1955) and the first play of an abandoned cycle about the history of an American family, *A Touch of the Poet* (1958). Although both plays were bleak studies of failure, and somewhat laboured, they were impressively penetrating.

Two important new playwrights also appeared on the horizon after 1944, Tennessee Williams (1914–), with the semi-autobiographical play *The Glass Menagerie* (1944–5), and Arthur Miller (1915–), with his attack on a *laissez-faire* philosophy of life, *All My Sons* (1947) (see No. 105). Williams followed *The Glass Menagerie* in 1947 with *A Streetcar Named Desire*, the semi-clinical tragedy of a former Southern belle driven to drink and madness by her misfortunes; Miller, in 1949, with *Death of a Salesman* (see No. 106), a semi-expressionistic account of the failure of a victim of success-worship, which the young author intended as a 'tragedy of the common man'. In 1950 these authors were joined by another talented writer, William Inge (1913–), whose drama of an alcoholic gentleman and his slatternly lower-class wife, *Come Back, Little Sheba*, was genuinely moving. In the 1950s Inge increased his reputation with several other rueful plays about simple people's frustration and confusion, *Picnic* (1953), *Bus Stop* (1955), and *The Dark at the Top of the Stairs* (1957). Tennessee Williams enlarged his career with several other plays, but without greatly altering his theme of psychological bankruptcy or his semi-poetic, semi-naturalistic style, verging on sensationalism. Notable among his later, generally successful, productions were the chronicle of a fastidiously moral young woman's deterioration, *Summer and Smoke* (1948); the folksy comedy of a Sicilian widow, *The Rose Tattoo* (1951); and the powerful character-drama *Cat on a Hot Tin Roof* (1955). With the Broadway productions of these and other plays, including *A Streetcar Named Desire* and *Death of a Salesman*, Elia Kazan became the leading American stage director; and the dynamic qualities of these and other plays were sometimes credited to Kazan even more than to their authors. Miller continued to widen the scope of his work with his Salem witch-trial tragedy, *The Crucible*, which appeared on Broadway in 1953 and carried an unmistakable protest against mass hysteria and persecution of opinion; and this play, which appeared to be inspired by the vogue of Senator Joseph McCarthy's anti-liberalism in American political life, was followed by another effort to base tragedy on the passions of characters of low degree, *A View from the Bridge* (1955), patterned after classical tragedy although the background was the New York waterfront.

Other new authors continued to arrive on Broadway, the most gifted being Robert Anderson, best known for his boarding-school drama *Tea and Sympathy* (1953); Paddy Chayefsky, who succeeded with an affecting romance between a young woman and an elderly man, *Middle of the Night* (1956), and with a Jewish folk comedy, *The Tenth Man* (1959); William Gibson, who won popularity with his two-character love comedy *Two for the Seesaw* (1957) and his Helen Keller drama, *The Miracle Worker* (1959); and Arthur Laurents, whose first produced play, *Home of the Brave* (1945), an attack on religious intolerance in the form of a spare psychological drama dealing with a soldier's psychosis, was the most powerful of his contributions. Laurents continued to experiment with psychological drama (*A Clearing in the Woods*, 1957), and contributed the 'book', or libretto, to the musical drama *West Side Story* (1957), one of the most successful products of the American musical theatre. This work, along with a number of other musical productions, such as the Hammerstein–Rodgers collaborations starting in 1943 with *Oklahoma!* (the others included *Carousel*, *South Pacific*, and *The King and I*) and the Lerner and Loewe adaptation of *Pygmalion* as a musical under the title of *My Fair Lady* (1956), gave the post-war American theatre its most distinctive and most profitable product.

Individual plays that had an impact on individual seasons were Lillian Hellman's Chekhovian study of failure, *The Autumn Garden* (1951), and her somewhat scattered but powerful tragedy of possessiveness, *Toys in the Attic* (1960). Carson McCullers contributed a sensitive drama of a girl's adolescence in a small Southern town, *The Member of the Wedding* (1950), and Sidney Kingsley an effective anti-totalitarian drama, *Darkness at Noon* (1951), based on Arthur Koestler's famous political novel. Lorraine Hansberry's drama of Negro life and its tensions, *Raisin in the Sun* (1959), was an unusually successful social drama. John van Druten's dramatization of Christopher Isherwood's Berlin stories about the coming of Nazi-ism, *I am a Camera* (1951), and Herman Wouk's war-play, *The Caine Mutiny Court-Martial* (1954), treated the recent past with discernment, as did John Patrick's charming comedy about the American occupation of Okinawa, *The Teahouse of the August Moon* (1953), and the internationally acclaimed dramatization of *The Diary of Anne Frank* (1955) by Frances Goodrich and Albert Hackett.

Comedies of little significance but lively spirit such as Jan de Hartog's *The Fourposter*, George Axelrod's *The Seven Year Itch*, and Thornton Wilder's *The Matchmaker* (1954) flourished at the same time both in the professional and the amateur theatre, but did not overshadow the effort to achieve significant dramatic art. Unsuccessful but provocative experiments in dramatic form, such as Tennessee Williams's *Camino Real* (1953) and *Orpheus Descending* (1957), continued to appear on Broadway. Meanwhile the off-Broadway movement, operating in small theatres at low cost, had by 1960 brought to public notice such new American playwrights as Edward Albee, who arrested attention with an intense short drama, *The Zoo Story*, Jack Gelber, who became known for his play about drug addicts, *The Connection*, and Jack Richardson, who turned out a pithy anti-heroic treatment of the Oresteian theme in *The Prodigal*. Often experimental in production, employing central staging, and most effective in reviving older plays, the off-Broadway theatre did much to alleviate a condition of aridity that periodically overcame the Broadway theatre. Theatrical enterprise had numerous and costly failures. By 1960 it was evident that the American professional theatre was in serious economic and artistic straits. Off-Broadway stage productions and a handful of meritorious Broadway plays each season alone saved the American drama from a state of total paralysis and gave occasion for minor gratifications and some optimism for the future, until Edward Albee, with *Who's Afraid of Virginia Woolf?* (1962) and, to a lesser extent, with *Tiny Alice* (1964), provided Broadway with some intense writing, while Arthur Miller produced a somewhat inchoate autobiographical drama, *After the Fall*, and an affecting, if rather static, anti-Nazi play, *Incident at Vichy* (both 1964).

JOHN GASSNER†

10. THE THEATRE OUTSIDE NEW YORK. The American movement known for a time as 'The Tributary' or 'Nationwide Theatre'—terms no longer in use—is active throughout the fifty United States, in myriad forms and with a wide range of qualities. No new major playhouses have been built on Broadway since 1932, but more than fifty were built as college, university and community theatres during the 1950s alone. A more recent one is the Tyrone Guthrie Theatre in Minneapolis, completed in 1963. Vitality and promise in regional theatre still continue to flourish.

The date usually given for the start of the Little Theatre movement in the United States is 1900, when a theatre was built for the Hull House players in Chicago. G. P. Baker's '47 Workshop', which started at Harvard University in 1912, marks the first systematic introduction of theatre into higher education. Now community theatres (they are no longer called Little Theatres), producing one play a year, as well as those presenting a highly efficient and effective season of six to eight plays, are countless. Estimates run from 20,000 to 65,000 for local theatres of all descriptions. Three to six thousand do three plays or more a year in a permanent building. One play agency has a mailing list for five thousand theatre groups, another has from six to seven thousand. The American Educational Theatre Association, in its directory of American college theatres (1960) reports that 308 colleges and universities offer a 'major' (or final honours course) in theatre and, in addition, 293 offer a 'minor' (or subsidiary course).

The Department of Dramatic Arts at Pittsburgh's Carnegie Institute of Technology was founded in 1914; Frederick Koch (1877–1944) started the Carolina Playmakers in 1918 at the University of North Carolina; and the Yale Theatre of 1926 was the first of the large university playhouses, followed by the Cleveland (see No. 53). During the 1930s and 1940s, academic playhouses were built for the State University of Iowa (1934), Stanford University (1937), Amherst College (1938), Indiana University (1940), William College (1941), and the University of Washington (1940) (the Penthouse, for theatre-in-the-round; see No. 41). Now campuses all over the country are replacing makeshift quarters with various forms of theatre buildings.

The civic theatre had its inception with the building of Le Petit Théâtre de Vieux Carré in New Orleans in 1919. This was followed by the opening of the Pasadena Playhouse in 1925 and the Goodman Theatre in Chicago in the same year. Others, in places widely apart, such as Texas, Nebraska, and Indiana, were, like the Palo Alto Community Playhouse in California, part of a cultural civic centre. Most of these were amateur, with a professional managing-director. Frederick McConnell, at the Cleveland Playhouse, had a remarkable success using both amateurs and professionals. On a grant from the Ford Foundation, the Cleveland Playhouse developed over a period of three years a touring company which created audiences in outlying regions. In 1955 Stratford, Connecticut, found itself with a theatre, the American Shakespeare Festival theatre on the Housatonic River. The Oregon Shakespeare Festival in Ashland, Oregon, was founded in 1935.

There have been several attempts to organize the 'local theatre', the term suggested by Kenneth Macgowan in his *Footlights Across America* (1929). Currently the most promising effort is the American Community Theatre Association (A.C.T.A.) organized as a division of the American Educational Theatre Association. The Theatre Communications Group in New York City represents and serves regional professional companies.

Those concerned with both university and community theatre are conscious of their mission, which is to decentralize the theatre and to offer vocational training as well as avocational opportunities for the promising talent to be found among the 190 million people in all parts of the country. They offer a repertory of old and new plays which interest contemporary audiences, of all possible differences in background and taste, who seek entertainment in the theatre. The contribution from the best of these various educational and community theatres has been considerable, though perhaps not yet up to expectations.

Since 1958, however, a further development has arisen out of a new and extremely promising relationship between the university and the professional theatre. Without seeking to replace student drama, the new plan supplements university productions with professional companies playing on or near the campus, often as a university extension course intended mainly for adults. Since the summer of 1959 John Houseman and the Theatre Group at the University of California at Los Angeles have produced plays with professional companies on the campus. Now a site has been offered to them by the university, a major grant has been made by the Ford Foundation, and leading members of the professional theatre community have undertaken to raise funds for a building for the Theatre Group. Frank Whiting and his staff at the University of Minnesota worked closely with Tyrone Guthrie to open a theatre there in 1963, with a resident repertory company supplemented by advanced drama students (see GUTHRIE, TYRONE). Robert Schnitzer has inaugurated the University of Michigan Professional Theatre Programme by engaging the Association of Producing Artists; Alan Downer at Princeton experimented with the use of professionals in the McCarter Theatre; Father Gilbert V. Hartke at Catholic University has developed a variation of his own for talented graduates at the Olney Playhouse. These efforts have proved that a good professional company can flourish under university auspices, and can perhaps offer the talented student an intermediate status on the way towards the professional theatre. It is possible that the 'Tributary Theatre', which Edith J. Isaacs dreamed of and wrote about in *Theatre Arts* (when that journal was hers, until 1948), may prove to be the means of carrying the theatre outside New York to a fulfilment which will enrich the whole of the American theatre. At the moment, however, most playwrights—especially the unacted—will continue to refuse all offers for production except from Broadway and, perhaps, off-Broadway. It is, however, significant that in 1965 the American Playwrights' Theater, formed by professional and university theatre men, released a new play, *The Days Between*, by Robert Anderson, for fifty productions during the year outside New York. The première at the Dallas Theatre Centre in May received extensive notice, particularly on Broadway, which had had an option on the play, but let it go. Although this is only a first step, it seems to show that an alternative to a Broadway production now exists, even for an established playwright. The effort that is being made to relate the university theatre department to a professional company playing on the campus and offering to the newcomer, as well as to the professional theatre at large, a chance to act, design, write, and manage, opens up a vast field of possibilities. Other developments of local theatre are to be found in current efforts to establish an inexpensive form of touring with 'bus-and-truck' companies; and some local groups are eyeing the new 'giant market centres', which constitute a central crossroads for the local community, have ample room for parking at night, and offer adaptable space for a small theatre.

In the nationwide theatre people will continue to write potboilers for their own pleasure, but the local theatres which, like the Actors' Workshop in San Francisco, the Alley Theatre in Houston, the Arena Theatre in Washington D.C., and the Dallas Playhouse, may grow and develop towards professional standards, introduce latent talents that will enliven the theatre and contribute serious and stimulating work in all regions of the country.

Organizations like the American National Theatre and Academy (A.N.T.A.), chartered by Congress in 1936, the National Theatre Conference, and the American Educational Theatre Association (A.E.T.A.), with its 4,000 members, support nationwide growth, help to bring theatre workers together, and encourage the raising of standards and more effective production all over the country.

Although little has yet come of it, talk continues in Congress of support for the arts. A half-dozen or so bills have been presented (e.g. Humphrey and Javits in the Senate; Thompson, Fogarty, and Lindsay in the House). The State of New York has already passed a bill to support the arts, and other states are now introducing their own proposals. A bill to establish a United States Arts Foundation, roughly comparable to the National Science Foundation, was unexpectedly recommended by a vote of the Educational and Labour Committee of the House in Sept. 1962. Scientists like Dr. Glenn Seaborg, Nobel Prize Winner and Chairman of the Atomic Energy Commission, have pointed out that the vast sums given to scientists for defence is understandable, but that these moneys have left the arts and the humanities out of balance and at starvation level—through no fault of scientist, artist, or scholar. This is untenable in a healthy society, the scientists say, and they recommend a balancing-out of support for the arts and humanities in American life. This, coupled with the growing interest of some of the large foundations in the arts, may offer local theatres in the United States unparalleled opportunities to experiment and expand during the 1960s. As an earnest of this intent, the Ford Foundation in Oct. 1962 gave more than six million dollars in grants to local theatres outside New York.

What the future will bring is uncertain, but if effective efforts are made in the direction of experiment, designed to help the professional theatre as well as the community and educational theatre, creating both audiences and actors, the years ahead may well bring a theatre that was born barely two hundred years ago—and yet is the inheritor of all the conditions that created Shakespeare—truly before the world as inspirer and leader. At the moment a sense of direction is in the air, but it has not yet determined its course. Technically the American theatre—amateur and profession-

UNITED STATES OF AMERICA

al alike—is well abreast, and in many respects well ahead, of theatre in other lands; what is still uncertain, despite its truly great achievements, is what it wishes to do spiritually with its technical skill. JACK MORRISON

(See also NEGRO IN THE AMERICAN THEATRE, PIONEER THEATRE, and American actors, dramatists, and theatres, under their own names.)

11. EARLY SCENIC DESIGN. Scenic design in the United States, originally known as 'the new stagecraft', has become a recognized, artistic profession and an integral part of theatrical production. A designer's name appears on every programme directly under that of the play's director, in recognition of the fact that the designer is considered an essential collaborator in interpreting a script. As such, he (or she) is expected to provide not only a background that is pictorially effective, but one that can, by its arrangement of playing areas and the emphasis of its lighting, sustain dramatic action, reflect the mood, and heighten the emotional values of a performance. Very few settings seen in the course of a theatrical season fail to do so. American designers as a group display great versatility, maintain a high level of taste, technical skill in both plan and execution, and, as frequently as playwrights provide the opportunity, fantasy and imagination.

The development of scenic design in the American theatre began shortly before the First World War and was directly influenced and inspired by its previous development in Europe: the doctrines and designs of Gordon Craig, Adolphe Appia's theory of stage lighting and the drawings with which he illustrated it, the work of Emil Orlik and Ernst Stern for Max Reinhardt's first repertory seasons in Berlin, Linnebach's at Dresden, the productions of the Moscow Art Theatre, and those of other Continental stages. A pioneer volume by an American critic, H. K. Motherwell, *The Theatre of To-day* (1914), illustrated and analysed the successive innovations in style and technique of European productions. The *Theatre Arts* magazine, founded in 1916 by Sheldon Cheney, provided up to 1964 a valuable focus for critical discussion of stage designs and direction both in America and abroad. The first experiments in the simplification and stylization of stage settings as well as atmospheric lighting were in part a revolt against traditional scene-painting, but also part of an insurgent movement in the American theatre directed against stereotyped methods of acting, stage direction, and conventional subject-matter. The new stagecraft appeared, within the course of a few years, in Little, semi-amateur, or experimental theatres which were recruiting new audiences for modern playwrights, such as the Washington Square players, the Neighborhood Playhouse, and the Provincetown players, who staged the early plays of Eugene O'Neill; on the operatic stage, in musical revues and ballets, as well as on the professional stage, centred in New York City and known as 'Broadway'.

Among the first stylized settings were those of Sam Hume (1913) at the Arts and Crafts Theatre in Detroit, based on rearrangements of simplified architectural units. Robert Edmond Jones (see No. 87) was the first designer to make a successful professional début with his setting and costumes for *The Man Who Married a Dumb Wife*, as part of Granville-Barker's repertory season (1915), when New York audiences also saw Norman Wilkinson's festooned forest for *A Midsummer Night's Dream*, and its gilded fairies. Jones's setting was almost poster-like in its decorative simplification, the silver grey of a house front, the black accent of its door and window, without any suggestion of medieval ornament or architectural detail, and the brilliant contrast of the women's costumes of clear yellow and orange with their towering hennins and exaggerated trains; it was accepted as a manifesto of 'the new movement'. But Jones presently achieved a more subtle, dramatic, and romantic chiaroscuro both in stage lighting and three-dimensional composition (after designing a ballet for Nijinsky, 'Till Eulenspiegel') in a series of notable productions directed by Arthur Hopkins that included *Redemption*, *The Jest* (*La cena delle beffe*), *Richard III*, and *Hamlet* with John Barrymore. These productions had the dignity and simplicity, almost austerity, of composition, the balance of large masses and simplified architectural form, which remained characteristic of all Jones's subsequent work.

Lee Simonson (see No. 101), who had served his apprenticeship with the Washington Square Players, established his reputation at the Theatre Guild—founded in 1919—with *The Faithful*, *Power of Darkness*, *Liliom*, *Heartbreak House*, *Back to Methuselah*, *Peer Gynt*, and *Marco Millions*. Joseph Urban, Viennese architect and decorator (see No. 80), who had demonstrated the values of Continental stagecraft in a series of operatic settings for the Boston Opera Company in 1913, achieved nationwide popularity with his investiture of the *Ziegfeld Follies*, a lavish annual revue 'glorifying the American Girl'. Among Norman Bel Geddes's first designs were those for the operas 'Shanewis' and 'La Nave', a musical comedy, and a revue. His most spectacular production was *The Miracle*, when he replaced a conventional gilded proscenium with the soaring, full-scale apse of a cathedral for Max Reinhardt's presentation of that medieval pageant. His most typical work, besides his projects for *King Lear* and *The Divine Comedy*, were his settings for *Lazarus Laughed*, *Hamlet*, and *Lysistrata*, architectonic units of plinths, ramps, and terraced levels, so-called 'abstract settings', the plastic forms used being an integral part of the total patterns of movement of the actors and the variations in emphasis of the stage lighting.

This first group of designers was speedily followed by another, most of whose members are still active in the theatre today. These, with some of their more important productions, are: Cleon Throckmorton (*The Hairy Ape*, *The*

Emperor Jones, All God's Chillun Got Wings); Aline Bernstein (*The Little Clay Cart, The Dybbuk, Romeo and Juliet* (see No. 82), *Grand Hotel*); Raymond Sovey (*St. Joan, Wings over Europe*); Woodman Thompson (*What Price Glory?, Beggar on Horseback, Iolanthe*); James Reynolds and Albert Johnson, in the field of musical revues; Mordecai Gorelik (see No. 105) (*Processional* and the Group Theatre's repertory); Jo Mielziner (see No. 106) (*The Guardsman, Street Scene, Romeo and Juliet, Hamlet* (for John Gielgud), *Saint Joan, The Barretts of Wimpole Street, The Glass Menagerie*, the ballet 'Pillar of Fire', and numerous musical comedies); Donald Oenslager (*The Doctor's Dilemma, Pygmalion*, and the operas 'Tristan and Isolde', 'Salome', and 'Abduction from the Seraglio'); Stewart Chaney (see No. 159) (*Life with Father, The Voice of the Turtle, Hamlet* (for Leslie Howard), *The Winter's Tale, The Merry Wives of Windsor*); and later Howard Bay (*One-Third of a Nation, Carmen Jones*); Cecil Smith, ballets and musical comedies; and Lemuel Ayres (*Oklahoma!*).

The above list can serve only as an indication of the work of American scenic artists, many of whom have designed from fifty to a hundred productions or more, the most successful from ten to twenty or more productions a season. Their designs have been widely reproduced, including excellent photographs of many settings as lighted in performance. A verbal description being inadequate, the interested reader is referred to the illustrations in the volumes listed under TECHNICAL BOOKS in the *Select List of Theatre Books* (p. 1031).

In general, the work of American designers displays a great variety of method and style, ranging from realism to decorative simplification and formalization. This is in part the consequence of the conditions under which the American theatre operates. There are virtually no permanent companies or endowed playhouses as in Europe; every production is financed as a separate enterprise, the director as well as the cast recruited for each play. Designers in America rarely have the opportunity of working consecutively with a director, such as Copeau, Meyerhold, or Taïrov, who has developed a single method of production. Realism remains as vital and predominant a form of expression for American playwrights as for the American novelists; contemporary poets have not developed an effective dramatic form; revivals of classic or poetic drama are still infrequent. Nevertheless Jones, in his barroom for O'Neill's *The Iceman Cometh*, displayed, in naturalistic terms, subtlety and artistry in conveying an atmosphere of forlorn despair; *Liliom* and *Winterset* were imbued with poetic intensity and a certain degree of tragic grandeur. And many period settings underline the satiric interest of a script or, as lighted, dramatize its emotional force (see LIGHTING). LEE SIMONSON†

UNION OF SOVIET SOCIALIST REPUBLICS, see RUSSIA.

UNITI, THE, a *commedia dell'arte* company which has caused much discussion, since it is possible that the word refers not to a distinct company, as did the words Gelosi and Confidenti, for example, but means a combined troupe of actors from different companies formed for a special occasion. Because of this some critics consider the Uniti to be part of the history of the Gelosi, some of the Confidenti. Whatever the facts, it remains certain that a company under that name was directed by Drusiano Martinelli and his wife Angelica in 1584, and for some years afterwards. A company calling itself the Uniti is noted in 1614, but this may have been a temporary amalgamation. Among its members were Silvio Fiorillo and his son.

UNITIES, THE THREE, of Time, Place, and Action, see ARISTOTLE, DRAMATIC CRITICISM, and FRANCE.

UNITY THEATRE, GLASGOW. This theatre was formed in 1941 by the war-time amalgamation of four amateur companies, the Transport, the Clarion, the Jewish Institute, and the Workers' Theatre, and rapidly achieved more than local fame for able productions and catholic choice of play. Its first production was *Major Operation*, by the Scottish novelist James Barke. In the summer of 1945 the company presented *The Lower Depths* in London and received high commendation. In 1946 Unity, while retaining an amateur wing, formed a full-time professional group. It began with *Starched Aprons*, a hospital play by Ena Lamont Stewart, but its biggest success was with *The Gorbals Story*, a study of life in an overcrowded slum, written by Robert MacLeish and produced by Robert Mitchell, a mixture of broad comedy and pathos reminiscent of early O'Casey. This play was revived many times, toured all over Britain, taken into the West End briefly (its arrival coincided with a heat wave), and was eventually filmed. Lack of a permanent home and theatre of its own was, however, Unity's eventual downfall, and by the early 1950s it had ceased to be an effective force. (For UNITY THEATRE, London, see AMATEUR THEATRE)

UNIVERSITY DEPARTMENTS OF DRAMA IN GREAT BRITAIN. One of the most striking developments of recent years has been the gradual acceptance of the theatre (apart from dramatic literature) as a subject suitable for academic study. This has resulted in the foundation at Bristol and Manchester Universities of Departments of Drama on the lines of those found in American universities (see UNITED STATES OF AMERICA, 10).

The Bristol Department of Drama was established within the Faculty of Arts of Bristol University in the 1946–7 session. The syllabus covers the history of drama from classical to modern times, and the three-year course, combined with other subjects, leads eventually to the degree of Bachelor of Arts. Instruction is also given on the practical side of the theatre, for which purpose a drama studio, designed by Richard Southern, was opened in Feb. 1951. Built in a disused squash-rackets court, the studio provides a lecture-room which can be transformed into a picture-frame theatre, an open-stage theatre, or an arena theatre. It was financed by part of a grant from the Rockefeller Foundation, which has also helped to equip the library, and provides each year a visiting lecturer, usually a person of eminence in the theatre, such as Michael Redgrave (1952) or Hugh Hunt (1953). The Department provides facilities for post-graduate study and for research work leading to the degree of M.A. and Ph.D., and works in close association with the Bristol Old Vic. Its present head is Professor Glynne Wickham.

The Department of Drama at Manchester was established in the session of 1961–2 as the result of a generous grant made to the university by Granada Television Network Ltd. Its object is to provide a liberal education through the study of the theatre, both in theory and practice. It offers a three-year course in drama, combined with other subjects, or a four-year course in drama and a foreign language, leading to the degree of Bachelor of Arts. There are also facilities for post-graduate work. Practical work is undertaken in the university theatre (opened in 1965 by Dame Sybil Thorndike) and in a studio attached to the Whitworth Art Gallery. In addition to this students are expected to attend a two-weeks' vacation course in practical theatre work. The present head of the department is Professor Hugh Hunt. In 1962 Stephen Joseph was appointed to the first Fellowship in Drama, a post combining research with teaching and production.

Although (in 1965) these were the only Departments of Drama in Great Britain, all universities undertake some dramatic activities, though these are extra-curricular. In Oxford the university owns and administers the Playhouse, which is used for amateur productions as well as by a professional company. Reading, typical of most universities, has a flourishing dramatic society, which took part in the open-air Festival at Stratford-upon-Avon in 1959, as did Queen's University, Belfast. In 1960 the Nuffield Foundation made a large grant to Southampton University to build and equip the Nuffield Theatre, which opened on 2 Mar. 1964. This was designed by Basil Spence, with Dr. Richard Southern, now Southampton's Director of Drama, as theatrical adviser. A multi-purpose building, it has been deliberately designed to look like a ship. Performances at this theatre will be open to the public.

There is at Liverpool University a Shute Lectureship in the Art of the Theatre, founded in 1923 by the chairman of the board of directors of the Liverpool Playhouse, Colonel Sir John Shute, with the laudable desire to bring together more closely academic and professional theatrical interests, as has since been done at Birmingham also.

UNIVERSITY THEATRE, U.S.A., see UNITED STATES OF AMERICA, 10.

UPSTAGE, the acting area furthest from the audience (see STAGE DIRECTIONS).

URBAN, JOSEPH (1872–1933), architect and stage designer, born in Vienna, where he worked for many years before going to Boston in 1911–12 to design sets for the opera there. He was also in New York, where he designed settings for the *Ziegfeld Follies*, the Metropolitan, and James K. Hackett's Shakespearian productions. He built the Ziegfeld Theatre in New York, with its egg-shaped interior, and introduced much of the new Continental stagecraft to American theatre-audiences, making use of broad masses of colour and novel lighting effects on costume and scenery (for an example of his work, see No. 80).

USIGLI, RODOLFO, see SOUTH AMERICA, 1.

U.S.S.R., see RUSSIA.

USTINOV, PETER ALEXANDER (1921–), English actor, dramatist, and producer, who through his mother Nadia is the grand-nephew of Alexandre Benois, the stage-designer. His best work has a fantastic fairy-tale quality which nevertheless contains a hard core of commonsense and a shrewd perception of the problems of life today, in their international rather than their insular aspect. He combines these same qualities in his acting, joined to a great gift of mimicry. Trained under Saint-Denis at the London Theatre Studio, he made his first appearance in London in Aug. 1939, at the Players' Late Joys, in his own sketches, and was memorable as the ageing opera-singer, Madame Liselotte Beethoven-Finck. After some miscellaneous experiences in repertory, revue, and straight plays, in and around London, during which time his first play, a translation of Sarment's *Le Pêcheur d'ombres* as *Fishing for Shadows* (1940), was done at the Threshold Theatre, he joined the army. He returned to the stage in June 1946, playing Petrovitch in Rodney Ackland's adaptation of *Crime and Punishment*. In 1948 he appeared in his own adaptation of Ingmar Bergman's *Hets* (*Frenzy*), and in the following year produced and acted in Linklater's *Love in Albania*. Since then he has appeared mainly in his own plays, which include *House of Regrets* (1942), *Blow Your Own Trumpet* (1943), *The Banbury Nose* (1944), *The Tragedy of Good Intentions* (1945), *The Indifferent Shepherd* (1948), *The Moment of Truth* (1951), and *No Sign of the Dove* (1953). His first popular success in London was *The Love of Four Colonels* (1951), followed by the equally successful *Romanoff and Juliet* (1956), in both of which he gave excellent performances. In 1962 he achieved a further success with his portrayal of the 80-year-old hero of his own play, *Photo Finish*, which was translated into German and Dutch and played simultaneously in four towns. Ustinov was appointed one of the directors of the new Northampton Civic Playhouse in 1963.

UTILITY, see STOCK COMPANY.

UZBEKISTAN, see RUSSIA.

V

VADSTENA, a small town in Sweden which has, in the middle of a row of early nineteenth-century houses, a small private theatre. This was built in 1826, and the last professional production was given there in 1878. Its origin, architect, and original owner are unknown. The theatre is still in working order, and is occasionally used for amateur performances.

VAKHTANGOV, EUGENE V. (1883–1922), Soviet Russian actor and producer, and founder of the theatre in Moscow which now bears his name. As a young man he joined the Moscow Art Theatre, and became the devoted pupil and friend of Stanislavsky. In 1914 he was put in charge of a studio attached to the theatre, which made a great success with a production of *Macbeth*, with Vakhtangov, a fine, sensitive actor, in the title-role. In 1920 the company was reorganized as the Third Studio, and under its dynamic young leader began to break away from the parent theatre. While the latter still limited itself to naturalism, and was striving towards the complete illusion of reality, Vakhtangov made the widest possible use of theatre-forms, though he never allowed form, as such, to overpower the production as a whole, and always sought for an ensemble which would correspond to the basic idea of the play under consideration. It was in his constant striving for truth that he developed that unsurpassed use of the grotesque which is so typical of his work. The culminating point of his career was his production of *Turandot*, which he did not live to see. It has remained in the repertory of the theatre ever since, exactly as he conceived it. In the same year (1922) his brilliant production of *The Dybbuk* was given at the Habima Theatre (see JEWISH DRAMA), another offshoot of the Moscow Art Theatre founded by Vakhtangov.

Since his death the Vakhtangov Theatre, under the management of his widow, has continued to do good and stimulating work, still under the inspiration of his short but glorious leadership. The first Soviet play was given in 1924, and was followed by such contemporary works as *Yegor Bulichev* and *Aristocrats*. In 1932 Akimov's production of an unorthodox *Hamlet* aroused a storm of protest, and was withdrawn, but not before it had focused the attention of the theatrical world on this vital young theatre, which has had in its company men of the calibre of Okhlopkov, and the late Boris Shchukin, who made a great impression as Bulichev, and as Lenin in *The Man with the Gun*.

During the early part of the Second World War the theatre was evacuated to Omsk, and returned to find its premises damaged by bombs. Repairs were put in hand, and the building was found to have suffered no permanent damage. Zakhava, Remizova, and Ruben Simonov worked together to raise the standard of acting once more and a successful production of Gorky's *Foma Gordeyev* in 1956 proved that the theatre still merited its great reputation. It continues to draw a regular and devoted audience. Among its later productions have been Arbuzov's *City at Dawn* (1957), *Hamlet*, with Astangov in the title-role, Dostoievsky's *The Idiot* (both 1958), Pushkin's *A Little Tragedy* (1959), produced by Simonov, and Arbuzov's *Midnight* (1960).

VALERIO, see BENDINELLI.

VALLE-INCLÁN, RAMÓN MARÍA DEL (1866–1936), Spanish novelist and poet, author of a number of plays and of novels in dialogue. *El yermo de las almas* (1908) is a realistic play, but more typical of Valle's writings before 1918 is the *Farsa infantil de la cabeza del dragón* (1909), a sophisticated and mannered children's play with a satirical content. *Cuento de abril* (1910) and *Voces de gesta* (1912) are verse plays, the latter dealing with the Carlist wars, a favourite theme of Valle. *El embrujado* (1913) is a sinister, tense play of vice and poverty, but *La marquesa Rosalinda* (1913) shows once again the obverse side of Valle's writing, satirizing the exquisite. In the plays written after the First World War the satirical vein predominates: in the *Farsa y licencia de la reina castiza* (1920), which censures the court of Isabel II; in *Divinas palabras* (1920), a tragedy of poverty in primitive Galicia; in *Luces de Bohemia* (1924), a biting attack on Madrid society at the turn of the century. In this latter play Valle attempts to define the *esperpento*, a term applied to *Los cuernos de don Friolera* (1921) and *La hija del capitán*. The *esperpento* holds up to ridicule the shams and evasions of contemporary society, warping and twisting the characters into parodies of heroic figures. The puppet plays an important part in Valle's work and proves a suitable vehicle for his mockery. His plays, brilliant in their use of language, are currently enjoying a long overdue revival.

J. E. VAREY

VALLERAN-LECOMTE (*fl.* 1590–*c.* 1613), early French actor-manager, who is first heard of at Bordeaux in 1592. Shortly afterwards he had his own company, with Marie Venier, wife and daughter of actors and the first French actress to be known by name, as his leading lady. As author for his company he engaged the prolific Alexandre Hardy, often considered the first professional dramatist of France, and by the early years of the seventeenth century was established intermittently at the Hôtel de Bourgogne as the tenant of the Confraternity of the Passion. The old actor, Agnan Sarat, who more than twenty years before had brought his own company to Paris, was Valleran-Lecomte's chief comedian, and remained with him until his death in 1613, Valleran-Lecomte himself dying or retiring shortly afterwards. Little is known of Valleran-Lecomte's acting, though he appears to have been good in farcical parts as well as in serious plays, and it is interesting to note that when the company first came to Paris he took the entrance-money at the door himself—or so says Tallemant des Réaux in his *Historiettes*.

VAMP TRAP, a device to enable the body of an actor to pass through a solid piece of scenery. It takes its name from Planché's melodrama *The Vampire* (1820), where it was first, or most extensively, used (see TRICKWORK ON THE ENGLISH STAGE).

VANBRUGH, SIR JOHN (1664–1726), English dramatist and architect, in which latter capacity he was responsible for Blenheim Palace, Castle Howard, the Clarendon Building, Oxford (with Hawksmoor), and the Queen's Theatre in the Haymarket (not to be confused with the present Haymarket), which was also known as the King's, and the Opera House. It was built to house Betterton's company, and three of Vanbrugh's own plays were given there, including *The Confederacy* (1705), a comedy based on Dancourt's *Les Bourgeoises à la mode*. He was responsible for several other translations, of Dancourt, Boursault, Molière, and a Spanish play, but his best work undoubtedly went into *The Relapse; or, Virtue in Danger* (1696), a sequel to and parody of Cibber's *Love's Last Shift*, produced the previous year, and *The Provoked Wife* (1697), written, according to tradition, while Vanbrugh was imprisoned in Paris for some unspecified offence, the two countries being then at war. The unequal quality of Vanbrugh's work, and the comparative smallness of his output, are due to the fact that the theatre was to him merely a spare-time amusement, though he often proves himself a master dramatist. His last two plays were much castigated by Jeremy Collier in his diatribe against the stage, and Vanbrugh was moved to reply to his accusations. But as his fame as an architect grew he left the theatre, and his last play, originally called *A Journey to London*, was left unfinished at his death. It was completed and produced by Colley Cibber in 1728 as *The Provoked Husband*. Vanbrugh, who had the Restoration traits of coarseness, pungent wit, and cynicism, has perhaps been underrated as a dramatist, and holds an important place in the evolution of English comedy. 'He helped', says Professor Thaler, 'to extend the range of the comedy of manners . . . and he packs into his best plays much solid food for thoughtful laughter.' It should be noted that *The Relapse* was later adapted for a more prudish stage by Sheridan as *A Trip to Scarborough* (1777), but in its original form had a long run at the Phoenix Theatre, London, in 1947–8.

VANBRUGH. (1) VIOLET AUGUSTA MARY (1867–1942), a distinguished English actress, daughter of the Rev. Prebendary Reginald Barnes of Exeter. She made her first appearance at Toole's Theatre, London (now demolished), in burlesque, in 1886, and in 1888 joined the stock company at Margate, where she first appeared as Ophelia. Under the capable management of Sarah Thorne she perfected herself in her chosen profession, and later joined the Kendals, accompanying them to America. On her return she was engaged by Irving, making her appearance as Anne Boleyn in *Henry VIII* with great success, and understudying Ellen Terry. In 1894 she married the actor-manager Arthur Bourchier, and appeared at the Royalty as his leading lady, playing a great number of parts, always with distinction, polish, and versatility. Indeed, much of the success of her husband's ventures then and later at the Garrick and on tour may be said to have been due to her talent and popularity. With Tree at His Majesty's she was a fine Queen Katharine (*Henry VIII*) and Lady Macbeth, and her later appearances included an outstanding performance in *Thunder in the Air* at the Duke of York's in 1928. She celebrated her golden jubilee in 1937 shortly after appearing as Mistress Ford in *The Merry Wives of Windsor* at the Ring, Blackfriars, and in the Open Air Theatre, Regent's Park. Tall and distinguished looking, she was a fine actress, much loved and respected in her profession. Her sister, (2) IRENE (1872–1949), who married the younger Dion Boucicault, was also trained by Sarah Thorne, and made her first appearance at the Theatre Royal, Margate, as Phoebe in *As You Like It* in 1888. The same year saw her début at the old Globe in London, where she played the White Queen in *Alice in Wonderland*. She then gained experience under various managements, with Tree at the Haymarket, with Alexander at the St. James's, where she played Ellean in *The Second Mrs. Tanqueray* (1893) and Gwendolen Fairfax in *The Importance of Being Earnest* (1895), and with Hare at the old Globe. It was there that she scored her first great success, as Sophie Fullgarney in *The Gay Lord Quex* (1899). She became the outstanding interpreter of Pinero's heroines, and her Letty in 1903 and her Nina Jesson in *His House in Order* (1906) were memorable performances. At the Duke of York's under Charles Frohman she appeared in *The Admirable Crichton* (1902), and then and later proved herself a perfect player of Barrie parts. Among the portraits with which she enriched the English stage her Rose Trelawny in *Trelawny of the 'Wells'* (1898) and Norah Marsh (in *The Land of Promise*, 1914) should not be forgotten. She celebrated her golden jubilee in 1938 by a matinée at His Majesty's, and in 1941 was created D.B.E. Dark, with wonderfully expressive eyes, she was an actress of great charm, and represented all that was best in the acting of her generation.

W. MACQUEEN-POPE†

The Vanbrugh Theatre at the Royal

Academy of Dramatic Art, used mainly for student shows before invited audiences, was so named in honour of Violet and Irene by their brother, Sir Kenneth Barnes, for nearly fifty years Director of the Academy.

VAN CAMPEN, JACOB (*c.* 1590–1657), Dutch architect, builder of the first theatre in Amsterdam in 1637, on the lines of Palladio's Teatro Olimpico in Vicenza (see ARCHITECTURE, 4 and Nos. 20, 25).

VAN DRUTEN, JOHN (1901–57), dramatist, of Dutch extraction, born in London, where his first plays were produced, but later an American citizen. He first came into prominence with *Young Woodley* (1928), a slight but charming study of adolescence which was unaccountably banned by the censor and produced by the Stage Society as a protest. When the ban was removed, it was seen in London and had a long run. It was also successful in New York. Van Druten's later plays, which are mainly light comedies, include *After All* (1929), a study of family relationships, *London Wall*, a comedy of office life, and *There's Always Juliet* (both 1931), which contains one of the few successful efforts by an Englishman to portray an American girl. His gift for the delineation of women was further shown in *The Distaff Side* (1933), in which Sybil Thorndike gave a moving performance as the mother, and *Old Acquaintance* (1940), a study of two disparate women writers which was successful on both sides of the Atlantic. *The Voice of the Turtle* (1943), a war-time comedy which had a long run in New York, was coldly received in London, where the philanderings of its three characters seemed trivial and pointless. Van Druten was also responsible for several dramatizations and translations, sometimes in collaboration, and in 1938 published a volume of reminiscences, *The Way to the Present.* In 1954 he achieved success both in London and New York with *Bell, Book and Candle*, an amusing comedy on witchcraft. He directed a number of plays, among them several of the above, and the London production of *The King and I* (1953).

VAN DEN VONDEL, JOOST (1587–1679), see the NETHERLANDS and JEWISH DRAMA, 3 (also No. 25).

VANCE, THE GREAT (1839–88), a music-hall 'lion comique', friend and rival of Leybourne. He was employed in a solicitor's office in Lincoln's Inn, but forsook it for the halls, and became best known for his comic cockney songs in the style of Sam Cowell, such as 'The Chickaleery Bloke'. Inspired by the success of Leybourne's 'Champagne Charlie' he countered with the praises of Clicquot, and between them they went through the whole wine-list. Vance, whose real name was Alfred Peck Stevens, was also a fine singer of moral 'motto' songs, such as 'Act on the Square, Boys'. He died during an appearance at the Sun, Knightsbridge, on Boxing Day.

VANDENHOFF. (1) JOHN (1790–1861), English actor, who made his first appearance on the stage in 1808, and spent many years in the provinces. He was for some time in Bath, and from 1815 to 1820 was a favourite with audiences in Liverpool, Manchester, and other big towns. He was also much liked in Edinburgh, particularly as Coriolanus. In 1820 he was seen at Covent Garden as Lear, following it with other leading parts, being much admired as Iago. He remained in London about eighteen years, and in 1834 played Hamlet at the Haymarket, going to Drury Lane in 1838. In spite of a good voice and features and a certain manly dignity, he failed to reach a commanding position, being somewhat deficient in pathos and passion, and from 1839 onwards was mainly seen in the provinces. His son, (2) GEORGE (1813–85), made his first appearance in 1839 at Covent Garden, where among other parts he played Mercutio in Mme Vestris's production of *Romeo and Juliet.* In 1842 he went to New York and made his début at the Park as Hamlet. A tour which followed brought him friends and financial success, and he decided to remain in the United States. From 1843 to 1853 he taught elocution and gave poetry readings, and appeared on the stage in New York and elsewhere, being at one time leading man at the Chestnut Street Theatre, Philadelphia, and at Palmo's Opera House. In 1845 he staged an English translation of Sophocles' *Antigone*, with music by Mendelssohn, on a stage approximating to the contemporary idea of a Greek theatre. He returned to London in 1853 and was seen as Hamlet, but he had little liking for his profession and retired in 1856. He was then called to the bar, but continued to give poetry readings, and in 1860 published his reminiscences as *Leaves from an Actor's Notebook.* A tall, scholarly man of good sense and good breeding, but somewhat aloof, he made a final appearance on the stage with Geneviève Ward in 1878, playing Wolsey, and Gloster in *Jane Shore.* His sister, (3) CHARLOTTE ELIZABETH (1818–60), a small, fair, gentle woman, was an excellent actress in parts requiring delicacy and pathos. She made her first appearance in 1836 as Juliet, and among her later parts were Cordelia, Julia, and Pauline. She was the first to play Lydia in *The Love Chase* (1837) and Parthenia in *Ingomar* (1851), and was much admired as Antigone and Alcestis in translations from the Greek.

VANDERBILT THEATRE, NEW YORK, a modest but handsome playhouse on the south side of 48th Street, east of Broadway. It opened on 2 Nov. 1921 with Pauline Lord and a fine cast in *Anna Christie*, which was a success with critics and public alike. Later productions were less successful, though *Lazybones*, with George Abbott, ran for ten weeks in 1924, and *Mulatto* (1935) had 373 performances. But *See Naples and Die, Days to Come*, and a revival of *London Assurance*, proved unacceptable to the public. The last play of any importance at this theatre, which in 1939 was taken over for broadcasting, was an all-star revival of *The Importance of Being Earnest*. It was demolished in 1954. GEORGE FREEDLEY†

VARIETY. When the music-halls were rebuilt, in their era of prosperity, so as to exclude the individual supper-tables, the resulting entertainment lost much of the free-and-easy sparkle of the old days and a good deal of the boisterous element, both on the stage and among the audience, and was more properly known as 'variety', while the buildings themselves were called Theatres of Variety. For the former unbroken succession of single turns was substituted the twice-nightly programme, first instituted by Maurice de Frece at the Alhambra, Liverpool; ballets and spectacular shows were imported, and the whole elaborate set-up was far removed from the original idea of music-hall. The old name clung, however, side by side with the new, and the history of this form of entertainment will be found under MUSIC-HALL, and, for America, under VAUDEVILLE, 2.

VARIUS RUFUS, Lucius (*c.* 74–14 B.C.), the friend of Virgil and Horace, and author of a lost tragedy, *Thyestes*, which was given in 29 B.C. at the games in celebration of the victory of Actium. The author is said to have received the equivalent of £8,000 for it from Augustus, and Quintilian said that in his opinion it was as good as any Greek tragedy.

VAUDEVILLE, a name of French origin, applied to plays of a light or satiric nature, interspersed with songs; later a form of light or comic opera. In the United States the term has become synonymous with the English music-hall, and is now often used in England with that sense.

1. Vaudeville, which has undergone several changes of form and meaning, may have originated in the fifteenth century, when a workman in Normandy, named Olivier Basselin, composed satiric couplets on popular airs, directed against the English invaders. These became popular throughout the region where he lived and took their name from it—chansons du Vau (or Val) de Vire—songs of the valley of Vire. Another writer of these early couplets was Jean le Houx. Or the word may derive from 'voix de villes'—song of the city streets. By 1674 it had already received its present form, and Boileau in his *Art Poétique*, published in that year, describes it as a satiric and often political ballad. It passed into theatrical parlance by way of the little theatres of the Paris fairs, where, owing to the monopoly of the Comédie-Française, plays could only be given in dumb-show, with interpolated choruses on well-known tunes, often parodying the productions of the legitimate theatre. These *pièces en vaudevilles*, as they were called, were the staple fare of the Opéra-Comique, and were written by such men as Piron, Collé, Le Sage, Fuzelier, Favart, Autreau—to name only the best known—and corresponded roughly to the English ballad opera. Their popularity paved the way for the immense vogue of light opera in the Paris of the mid-nineteenth century, catered for by the prolific Scribe and his many collaborators and rivals—Mélèsville, Désaugiers, Ancelot, Mazères, Dumersan, Théaulon, the Cogniard brothers, and many more. When these vaudevilles lost their popularity the use of the word was restricted to the variety stage, whence its present meaning in America. ED.

2. VAUDEVILLE IN AMERICA (for England see MUSIC-HALL). In Apr. 1861 Tony Pastor (1837–1908), who had been working in the theatre from the age of 9, made his first appearance in variety, which was then at a low ebb, a feature of the beerhalls which existed mainly for the benefit of heavy drinkers and prostitutes. Pastor was an astute showman, and he reasoned, wisely, that if he cleaned up his bills he could double his audience by attracting respectable women patrons and their escorts. After a long struggle to raise the standard of variety by providing 'clean' entertainment in a succession of New York theatres, he finally settled on 14th Street, where, on 24 Oct. 1881, he gave a show of what later came to be called vaudeville. For his opening night he presented eight contrasting acts—comedy, acrobatic, song, and dance—headed by Ella Wesner, a male impersonator of the dandies of the day, who also sang English music-hall songs. To Pastor's delight the theatre was filled with a good mixed audience of respectable men and women, and the box-office revenue was gratifying. But he never realized that he had set a pattern for family entertainment. It has been said that Benjamin Franklin Keith (1846–1914) and his subsequent partners, Edward Franklin Albee (1857–1930) and Frederick Francis Proctor (1851–1929), were the first to take vaudeville out of the beerhalls. But this is not wholly borne out by the facts. Pastor's 'clean' entertainments were offered years before Keith entered this branch of theatrical business.

The transition from the lusty variety acts of early days to the 'refined' vaudeville of the 1890s and 1900s was welcomed by seasoned performers, who enjoyed working in the spacious theatres built by the new managers. They relished their comfortable dressing-rooms, the new scenery, good furniture, and props. Better still, the more responsive audiences attracted by this burnished type of vaudeville spurred them on in their efforts to entertain, and a new theatrical presentation, of impact, subtlety, neatness, and realism, was developed.

New sketches, written to a specific 'punch' formula (all acts were limited to twenty minutes or less), replaced the blowzy after-pieces of the 1870s, and they looked fine in the bright settings provided. Realistic mountings intensified dramatic portrayals, and animal acts improved out of all recognition in fresh landscapes of light wood with cut borders. Trainers replaced their black suits and top hats by hunting or riding costume, and also put smart uniforms on their assistants. Mechanical improvements made for better magic, musical, and spectacular numbers. And there was also more employment, for the managers increased their bills to ten, twelve, sometimes fifteen, acts. A new technique in comedy, drama, and novelty acts came out of all this. Elaborate gestures, distorted facial expressions, the unlovely prattfall, were curbed—noticeable improvements over the excessive slapstick methods of comics in pre-Pastor times. An example of the new technique was the act of James J. Morton (1862–1933) and Maude Ravel. This was one of the funniest acts of the mid-1890s, and the team played the circuits for years. Morton's smooth delivery, the economy of his art, was astonishing. The audiences of the 1870s, accustomed to bladder clouts and stuffed clubs, would have looked askance at Morton's cadaverous, expressionless countenance as he presented his material. He would make heart-scalding attempts to help Maude with her songs—earnest, futile efforts that never accomplished anything except to throw his audience into unbuttoned laughter.

Another development was the headline system. The more intelligent audiences of later vaudeville began to rate their favourites, and the managers responded with top billing and increased salaries for performers with box-office appeal. This led to the abuse of 'name' billing. A 'name' act was just that. What other appeal in vaudeville had Sarah Bernhardt, Emma Calvé, Lily Langtry, or Mrs. Patrick Campbell? But to the true vaudeville artist soaring salaries gave incentive to create new styles. Burlesque or 'nut' acts—Collins and Hart, or Duffy and Sweeney, are incomparable examples—were popular. For vaudeville was America in motley, the national relaxation. It was a dig in the nation's ribs, its brassy assurance nothing but a mask for an emotional simplicity, a beguiling sincerity, that was often as naïve as a circus.

Here one recalls some of the great names that graced vaudeville in its halcyon days—roughly a thirty-year span from the mid-1890s to 1925, when the popularity of films, especially of the talkies which followed in 1927, led to its decline. Among them were Charlie Case (1858–1916), Joe Jackson (?–1942), Joe Cook (1890–1959), Ed Wynn (1886–1966), Bert Williams (1873–1922), W. C. Fields (1879–1946), Frank Tinney (1878–1940), Bill Robinson (1878–1949), the Howards, Eugene (1880–1965) and Willie (1883–1949), Eddie Cantor (1893–1964), Lou Holtz (1898–1966), and Jimmy Durante (1893–). Their feminine foils in acclaim were Nora Bayes (1880–1928), Eva Tanguay (1878–1947), Elsie Janis (1889–1956), Irene Franklin (1876–1941), Cissie Loftus (1876–1943), Marie Cahill (1874–1933), Fay Templeton (1865–1939)—the snows, alas, of yesteryear. There were outstanding teams, too, but the single artist predominated as the headliner. There is not space to discuss the merits of each of these performers whom we salute for their effortless pleasantries—indeed, much of their art is indescribable. But two selected at random—a monologist and a silent act—admirably illustrate the flourishing art of vaudeville. The first is Charlie Case, whose quiet monologue was one of the most entrancing acts in the vaudeville of the 1900s. His unassuming presentation, the while he twiddled the piece of string that was his only prop and without which he could not go on, shrank him to a parity with the little man in his audience. In a land of racial conflict no one remembered he was a Negro. He was your true comic, likeably sad; winning, never bargaining for, favour. For pathos is akin to comedy, and sympathy a spur to tearful laughter. All this was part of Case's art. A part too of Joe Jackson's. His bicycling tramp was the acme of pantomime. In fright wig and red nose he accomplished by eye-work, by his slightest gesture, by his furrowed, quizzical brow, by an awkwardness born of grace, the poignancy that Case conveyed in words—a magnificent intimate act was this of Jackson's.

No doubt the insistence of the managers on clean acts provoked a delicacy and restraint that made for subtlety. The force of restriction is a powerful challenge. Yet all the performers mentioned, especially the women, owed a debt to the English and French artists of the halls. Their invasion of the American vaudeville theatres was an incalculable influence for good. These splendid performers—Sir Harry Lauder (1870–1950), Albert Chevalier (1861–1923), Marie Lloyd (1870–1922), Yvette Guilbert (1866–1944), Vesta Victoria (1873–1951), Vesta Tilley (1864–1952), Wilkie Bard (1874–1944)—accented sophistication, satire, characterization. They employed the *mot*, were alive to their pitch of acceptance, and played up, not down, to American audiences; a superb illustration of the universal quality of art.

The life of American vaudeville was incredibly brief—fifty-odd years from Pastor's experiment to the closing in 1932 of Broadway's Palace Theatre as a two-a-day. The precise reasons for its demise are difficult to assess. But films and radio played their part in ousting it, and many of its patrons now find their entertainment in television.

DOUGLAS GILBERT†, *rev.*

VAUDEVILLE THEATRE, LONDON, in the Strand, built for a triumvirate consisting of three of the most popular actors of the day, H. J. Montague, David James, and Thomas Thorne. It opened on 16 Apr. 1870 with *For Love or Money*, and had its first success shortly afterwards with Albery's *Two Roses*, which introduced to the London public a young actor named Henry Irving, playing Digby Grant. Montague left in 1871, but the next success, *Our Boys* (1875) by H. J. Byron, had both James and Thorne in the cast, and ran for four years. After a further period of success with straight plays, the theatre was devoted to farces, of which one, *Confusion* (1883), ran for a year. James had left the previous year, but Thorne continued in management until 1892. Among his later successes were *Saints and Sinners* (1884), which caused some controversy because of its use of biblical quotations, and a series of productions starring Cyril Maude. In 1891 the theatre was closed for reconstruction, and a new frontage, which still stands, was added. Later in the year this theatre saw the first performances in England, for matinées only, of Ibsen's *Rosmersholm* and *Hedda Gabler*. In the latter production Elizabeth Robins made a great success as Hedda. From 1900 to 1906 Seymour Hicks and his wife Ellaline Terriss appeared in a series of long runs under the management of Charles Frohman. Among their productions were *Bluebell in Fairyland* (1901), a Christmas entertainment which was revived annually for many years; *Quality Street* (1902); and several musical comedies, including *The Belle of Mayfair* (1906). Charles Hawtrey then appeared at the theatre in comedy, and in 1915 it became the home of Charlot's revues. These continued until 1925, when the theatre was again closed for reconstruction, the interior being completely altered and redecorated. In its new guise the theatre opened on 23 Feb. 1926, again with revue, which continued with great success until 1937. After this the theatre went through a difficult phase, but in 1938 Robert Morley had a success with his *Goodness, How Sad!* Subsequent successes were *No Medals* (1944), *The Chiltern Hundreds* (1947), and the record-breaking *Salad Days* (1954), which finally closed in 1960. Later in that year *The Bride Comes Back* had a good run.

W. MACQUEEN-POPE†, *rev.*

VAUDEVILLE, THÉÂTRE DU, PARIS. This was opened on 2 Jan. 1792 by the actors who were forced to leave the Comédie-Italienne when its licence was renewed for musical plays only. The company was headed by Rozières, and was frequently in trouble for the topical and political allusions found in its productions by the vigilance of the censor. It eventually fell back on the safety of semi-historical pieces, based on anecdotes of heroic figures, and in 1838 was burnt down. The company moved to the Théâtre des Nouveautés, where plays by Dumas *fils* and others were given with some success, but the theatre fell on bad times and was frequently closed. In 1868 the present building was opened, under the old name, and has since had a steady, though somewhat uneventful, career.

VAUGHAN, KATE [CATHERINE CANDELIN] (*c.* 1852–1903), English comedy actress, child of a theatre musician. She was trained as a dancer by Mrs. Conquest and with a sister made her début in the music-halls in 1870. For some years she continued her career as a dancer, inaugurating a new school of skirt dancing, and also played in burlesque; from 1876 to 1883 she was a member of the famous Gaiety quartet, with Nellie Farren, Edward Terry, and Royce. She then abandoned dancing, and was seen only in standard comedy, playing Lydia Languish, Miss Hardcastle, Peg Woffington, and Lady Teazle during her tenancy of the Opéra Comique in 1887. With H. B. Conway she organized a company to tour the provinces in these and similar parts, and scored a great hit as Peggy in *The Country Girl*.

VAUXHALL, a place of entertainment in London, originally known as Spring Gardens, Foxhall, which opened in 1660, and was frequented by Pepys. Writing of it in 1700 Tom Brown said: 'In the close walks the most experienced mothers have often lost themselves in looking for their daughters.' During the eighteenth century it was used extensively for concerts, glee-singing, fireworks, and occasional spectacular dramatic shows. It figures in many memoirs of the period, and in Fanny Burney's *Evelina* (1779). In the early nineteenth century it was known as the Royal Gardens, Vauxhall, and a mimic battle of Waterloo was staged there, as were some of Bishop's operettas. It first opened during the day in 1836, and was lit by gas-lamps in 1849. It was described by Dickens, and was often in trouble owing to rioting and disorders, which finally led to its closing in 1859, the site being built over, though the name persists.

There was a Vauxhall in New York in the early part of the nineteenth century, which had a small open-air theatre for summer shows. This was burnt down in 1808, but the gardens long remained a favourite resort, and several seasons of plays were given there in the 1840s (see also MEDDOKS).

VEDRENNE, JOHN E. (1867–1930), English theatre manager, best remembered for his association with Granville-Barker at the Court Theatre from 1904 to 1907, and at the Savoy later in 1907, during which time they presented a number of outstanding plays, including some of Shaw's for the first time. Vedrenne, who was originally in commerce, became a concert agent and business-manager for several theatres, and was associated with such stars as Benson, Forbes-Robertson, Lewis Waller, and Dennis Eadie.

VEGA, VENTURA DE LA (1807–65), Spanish dramatist and, with Espronceda, the pupil of Alberto Lista. His best-known play is *El hombre del mundo* (1845), a bourgeois drama in verse in the tradition of Moratín. His other dramatic works include an unsuccessful historical drama, *Don Fernando el de Antequera*, a tragedy, *La muerte de César* (1865), various comedies, and translations from the French.

J. E. VAREY

VEGA CARPIO, LOPE FELIX DE (1562–1635), famous Spanish playwright and the most prolific dramatist of all time; he himself claimed to have written 1,500 plays, though the actual number of extant texts is about 470. Lope also wrote novels and much excellent non-dramatic verse. His prodigious output has caused the quality of his work to be underrated, and has tended to deter critics from attempting a serious valuation of his plays. Recent criticism has, however, turned again to the 'monster of Nature', as he was called in his own day, and his work is now in process of revaluation.

Lope de Vega found the professional theatre in its infancy. His first plays date from the period of the early *corrales de comedias* of Madrid, and Lope's first great claim to fame is the key part he played in the crystallization of the *comedia*. The formula which he evolved in the last decade of the sixteenth century remained largely unchanged for a hundred years. His *Arte nuevo de hacer comedias* (*c.* 1609) is an interesting, if ironical, exposition of his views on the writing of plays, written with one eye on classical precedent but based securely on practical experience.

Critics have endeavoured to cope with Lope's enormous output by dividing his plays into various categories: religious, mythological, pastoral, historical, novelesque, and plays of social comment. Nevertheless it is more important to stress the unity of his dramatic production. Lope's world is that of a Spanish Catholic—he himself took orders in 1614—of the reigns of Philip II, Philip III, and Philip IV. Society is viewed in an idealized light, and the multiple social distinctions of the day are reduced to three clear-cut divisions: king, nobles, and commoners, the last usually peasants. The kingdom is governed by the king as God's vice-regent, dispensing God's justice and in this way maintaining the natural harmony intended by the Creator. The harmony of society is thus seen as a reflection of the harmony of the universe, and the correlation between God's creation and the actions and thoughts of individual men is maintained in Lope's plays by poetic images which set man against the background of the universe, linking microcosm to macrocosm.

> Within this universal structure [as R. D. F. Pring-Mill has pointed out], human motivation is governed by three things: the theory of the four 'humours' (so prominent in Elizabethan drama); the systematic conceptions of Catholic moral theology (basically Thomist), exemplified both by the values which are admired and by the way in which the conduct of those who reject them is analysed in terms of weakness and passion, and condemned for misuse of their free will; and, lastly, by the highly stylized code of honour.

It is against this universal background that such plays as *Fuenteovejuna*, *El mejor alcalde el rey* and *Peribáñez y el Comendador de Ocaña* should be considered. *Fuenteovejuna* deals with the rising of a village against a brutal lord; shorn of its sub-plot—the rising of that same lord against his king—the play can be, and has been, interpreted in terms of the class-struggle. Main- and sub-plot are, however, interdependent and both are essential to the true understanding of this and similar plays. As recent criticism has demonstrated, Lope's position is conservative rather than revolutionary: the brutal overlord is removed because he disrupts the harmony of society, failing in his duties to the king above him as well as to the commoners beneath him. It is for this reason that he must be removed, and not merely because of his tyrannous repression of the villagers of Fuenteovejuna. This and other similar historical dramas of Lope have suffered from an attempt to interpret them according to the ideas of a later age.

The plays dealing with honour have suffered in a similar way. Lope's handling of this theme is diverse. In the early *Los comendadores de Córdoba*, the outraged husband, discovering that he is openly and publicly dishonoured, takes open, public, and bloody revenge. In the mature *El castigo sin venganza*, the duke secures his public position and at the same time revenges himself upon his bastard son and adulterous wife who have caused the loss of his honour. His public reputation is saved, since his revenge is secret, and, with it, the honour of the state, but this secret revenge entails the killing of the only two persons he has loved. The subtlety of the play consists in Lope's demonstration that this state of affairs is the direct consequence of the duke's own licentiousness. The theme of honour is more than a barbaric convention.

Lope also wrote for the entertainment of the Court, usually plays with a mythological or pastoral plot. *La selva sin amor* is a particularly interesting work, being partly set to music and thus a forerunner of the later *zarzuela*, or operetta. Lope has himself left a description of its elaborate machinery, the work of an Italian designer, Cosmo Lotti. Equally spectacular were the *autos sacramentales*, the dramatic performances which celebrated the day of Corpus Christi. Lope's dramatic career saw the establishment of the *auto* played on three carts, the centre being the main playing-space, and the outer carts bearing complicated machinery. His *autos* have not the lyrical beauty of those of Valdivielso nor the subtle symbolism of the works of Calderón, but they present their theme simply, forcibly, and dramatically, and show an excellent grasp of technique.

Lope de Vega can rightly be held to be the consolidator, if not the founder, of the commercial theatre in Spain. His *autos* were written during the period when this important genre was being developed, and his Court plays make use of the most up-to-date machinery and scenic effects. Lope's verse is neat, ingenious, and superbly lyrical. His great achievement was to establish, popularize, and develop an art-form which exactly suited the audiences of the great towns of sixteenth- and seventeenth-century Spain, an art-form which, while an undoubted commercial success, was also a great artistic achievement.

J. E. VAREY

VELTEN, JOHANNES (1640–92), German actor, a man of culture who studied at the universities of Wittenberg and Leipzig, but deserted science for the stage. There is a theatrical tradition that he was attracted to acting by taking part in an undergraduate production of Corneille's *Polyeucte*, but Mantzius points out that this is presumed to have taken place in 1669, when Velten was long past the age of an undergraduate and indeed had probably been a member of Carl Andreas Paulsen's troupe for some years. Here he remained, touring in the usual heterogeneous repertory of the time, to which he added translations of some of Molière's plays, and, in 1686, a version of *Hamlet* as *Der bestrafte Brüdermord*. In 1678, having married the daughter of an actor, he took over the company himself and managed it until his death, when it was carried on by his wife, Catharina Elizabeth Velten. Under different names, and with many fluctuations of fortune, this company held together until in 1771, after passing through the hands of Caroline Neuber, Schönemann, Koch, and Ackermann, it came under the leadership of Schröder.

VENICE THEATRE, New York, see century theatre, 2.

VENIER [Vernier], Marie (*fl.* 1590–1619), the first French actress to be known by name. She was the daughter of Pierre Venier, a provincial actor-manager who established himself at the Foire St-Germain in 1600, and later played at the Hôtel d'Argent on payment of a daily levy to the Confraternity of the Passion, holders of the monopoly of acting in Paris. At that time Marie Venier, with her husband Laporte, also an actor, was at the Hôtel de Bourgogne with Valleran-Lecomte, with whom she had probably already appeared in the provinces. According to contemporary accounts Marie Venier was a beautiful and accomplished actress, at her best as tragedy queens.

VENNE, Lottie (1852–1928), English actress, best known for her work in burlesque under Ada Swanborough at the Strand Theatre, where she played from 1873 to 1877. She then turned to straight comedy, and was seen in *The Young Mrs. Winthrop* (1884), *The Magistrate* (1885), and other plays, though she continued intermittently to appear in musical comedy and farce. She was an excellent mimic, and her imitations of Marion Terry in *Lady Windermere's Fan* and of Lady Tree in *Hamlet* made the fortune of Brookfield's travesty, *The Poet and the Puppets* (1892). A fine-looking woman, high-spirited and good-humoured, she had the good sense to take over in later years the parts of saucy matrons in the place of her earlier soubrette roles, and thus retained the affection of her public and the respect of the critics. Her son and daughter were both on the stage, the latter being the wife of the actor James Welch.

VERBRUGGEN, Mrs., see mountfort (2).

VERE STREET THEATRE, London, originally a tennis-court built in 1634, and belonging to, or named after, a man called Gibbon; it stood in Clare Market. The out-of-work actors played there after the closing of the theatres, but were betrayed by one of the company, whom a contemporary calls 'an ill Beest . . . causing the poor actors to be routed by the soldiery'. In 1656 Davenant gave one of his entertainments with music and dancing there. In 1660 Killigrew converted it into a theatre, opening with *Henry IV, Part I*, on 8 Nov., and used it while he got ready to build Drury Lane. As he had a Royal Charter and his company was the King's, Vere Street has been regarded by some as the first Theatre Royal; but that title properly belongs to Drury Lane, to which Killigrew moved in 1663. Vere Street, under George Jolly, was then used as a Nursery, or training-school for young actors, by both Killigrew and Davenant (who later had his own school) until 1671. From 1675 to 1682 it was a Nonconformist meeting-house. It became a carpenter's shop, and a slaughterhouse, and was finally destroyed by fire in 1809. On its site was built another playhouse—the Stoll Theatre (London Opera House), demolished in 1957. W. MACQUEEN-POPE†

VERGA, Giovanni (1840–1922), Italian playwright. Principally a novelist and short-story writer, Verga's output as a dramatist was relatively slight. He was, however, the only completely successful writer of tragedy in the Italian theatre between Alfieri and Pirandello, a *verist*, not by formula, but by conviction, and his portraits of Sicilian life were unflinching confrontations of the grey desperation with which it is instinct. His 'vanquished' characters have much in common with Hardy's Tess and Jude. *Cavalleria rusticana* (1884), a dramatization of one of his own short stories which later provided the libretto for Mascagni's opera, is a sparse and swiftly moving example of Verga's power to fuse two interlinked personal tragedies, the tragedy of a community and the tragedy of a religious man. With no other play did he enjoy such popular favour, but *La lupa* (1896), a most perceptive study of female sexuality and man's rank fear of it, and *La caccia al lupo* (1901), where he succeeds in transmuting the melodrama of jealousy into the poignancy of inescapable aloneness, are comparable achievements. There is no complete edition of Verga's plays, though a one-volume *Teatro*, published in 1952, is a valuable beginning, in which is emphasized, for instance, the overlooked excellence of *In portineria* (1885), a play set—untypically—outside Sicily, and *Dal tuo al mio* (1903), a terse and evocative analysis of the the clash between two classes of society. Only recently have critics come to appreciate the extent of Verga's achievement in dramatic literature, and to discern the unequivocal poetry informing his dramas. He was, in fact, the sole authentic exponent of *verism*, and freed the Italian theatre for the alert comprehension of Pirandello. FREDERICK MAY

VERGERIO, Pier Paolo (1370–1444), an early Italian dramatist, author of *Paulus*, the first extant Italian comedy (since one believed to have been written earlier by Petrarch is lost). Written in Latin, probably at Bologna in 1389, where Vergerio was a student, it is a study of contemporary university life, a satiric, licentious comedy which owes little to the classics, though it has some superficial resemblance to the comedies of Terence (see ITALY, 1 *b*).

VERNEUIL, see LA GRANGE (3).

VERSAILLES. Although there was a good deal of theatrical entertainment at Versailles under Louis XIV, there was no permanent theatre there. Plays were given on temporary stages erected indoors (see No. 24) or in the gardens. It was not until 1768 that Louis XV instructed his chief architect, Ange-Jacques Gabriel (1698–1782), to design and build a theatre in the north wing of the château. The first oval, as opposed to rectangular, theatre in France, it was built of wood, much of it painted to resemble marble. The decorations were by Augustin Pajou, the painted ceiling by Louis-Jacques Durameau. The stage was almost as large as that of the Paris Opéra and well supplied with machinery by Arnoult. The floor of the auditorium could be raised to stage level to form a large room for balls and banquets. Lighting was provided by crystal chandeliers whose candles had to be renewed three times during the course of the evening. The theatre was first used on 16 May 1770 for a banquet in honour of the marriage of the future Louis XVI to Marie-Antoinette. The first plays to be given were Racine's *Athalie*, on 23 May, with Mlle Clairon in the title-role, and, on 20 June, Voltaire's *Tancrède*. During the Revolution the theatre served for a time as the meeting place of the Versailles branch of the Jacobins. When in 1837 Louis-Philippe made Versailles into a museum of French military history, the theatre was redecorated by Frédéric Nepveu in red velvet, and the chandeliers were replaced by oil-lamps. It was used for a gala performance after the formal opening of the museum on 10 June, when Mlle Mars and the company from the Comédie-Française performed *Le Misanthrope*. It was then used occasionally for concerts and on 18 August 1855 for a banquet in honour of Queen Victoria. In 1871 it was taken over by the Assembly, who met there under Grévy during the Commune. A floor was laid over the pit, and everything above it was painted brown. This fortunately preserved the decorations below, and when in 1952 restoration began on the château, the theatre too was restored to its pristine glory in the original colours of dark blue, pale blue, and gold. It was even found possible to replace the original material on the seats, made from the old patterns by the firm which had supplied it in 1768. The restoration was completed in time for an official visit by Elizabeth II on 9 April 1957, when a theatrical and musical entertainment was given. The theatre is still occasionally used for concerts, operas, and plays.

VERULAMIUM. The Roman theatre in this second-century city (now St. Albans) was for a long time the only one known in Britain (traces of others have now been found at Canterbury and near Colchester). It was probably built between A.D. 140 and 150, and had a completely circular orchestra, with seating round two-thirds of it, and a small stage building in the remaining space. It would therefore have been unsuitable for the normal dramatic performances of the time, which demanded a semicircular orchestra and a high raised stage with an elaborate architectural background (see No. 8). As two of the theatres in northern France which resemble that at Verulamium have dens for wild beasts, it seems likely that it was used mainly for sport, particularly cock-fighting. The orchestra would have served also for mimes and dancing, and the stage for small-scale entertainments. In A.D. 200 the stage was enlarged, possibly to allow for the positioning of a slot into which a curtain could be lowered, and at the end of the third century, after a period of disuse, the theatre was rebuilt with modifications. The auditorium was extended at the expense of the orchestra, the floor levels were raised, and a triumphal arch was built spanning Watling Street. It was finally abandoned at the end of the fourth century, and the site used as a municipal rubbish-dump. It was excavated in 1847, and, more scientifically, in 1934 by Dr. Kathleen Kenyon (see No. 9).

VESTRIS [VESTRI]. This great family of French ballet-dancers (who originally came from Italy) is connected with the history of the English theatre through the work of Auguste Vestris (1770–1842) at the King's Theatre during the Handel season of 1791, and through the marriage of his son Armand (1788–1825), also a dancer, with the 16-year-old granddaughter of the engraver Bartolozzi, (1) LUCIA ELIZABETTA (or Lucy Eliza) (1797–1856), whom he deserted in 1820. As Mme Vestris, she had a distinguished career on the London stage. She was an excellent singer and might have made a career in grand opera, but preferred to limit herself to lighter entertainment. A fascinating woman, with large lustrous eyes and dark hair, she was at her best in burlesque, or in the fashionable ladies of high comedy. She made her first success in the title-role of Moncrieff's *Giovanni in London* (1817), a burlesque of Mozart's 'Don Giovanni'. She played in Paris for several years, with such success that she was able to return to London on her own terms, playing alternately at Covent Garden and Drury Lane. In 1830 she took over the Olympic, with a strong cast which included Liston, Maria Foote (soon to become the Countess of Harrington), the Glovers, the Blands, and two members of the Vining family. The theatre opened with *Olympic Revels*, by Planché, who furnished Mme Vestris with a succession of farces and burlesques both at this theatre and later at the Lyceum. During her tenancy of the Olympic she engaged Charles Mathews the younger, marrying him in 1838, and the rest of her career ran parallel to his (see MATHEWS, 2). She was an excellent manageress, known as 'Madame' to her company, whom she ruled with a rod of iron, and effected many reforms in theatre management. She also made many improvements in theatrical scenery and effects and had good taste in costume, being one of the first to use historically correct details, thus anticipating Charles Kean and the Bancrofts. She was responsible for the introduction of real, as opposed to fake, properties and in Nov. 1832 introduced the box-set, complete with ceiling.

Angelo Vestris, who went to Paris from Italy in 1747, married a French actress, (2) FRANÇOISE GOURGAUD (1743–1804). She was the daughter of a provincial actor, her brother and sister being members of the Comédie-Française (see DUGAZON). She herself made her début there in 1768, and though not an outstanding actress, she had some success. She engaged in constant quarrels with her rival, Marie Blanche Sainval, whose début at the Comédie-Française she managed by her intrigues to get retarded for several years. An indiscretion on the part of Sainval later caused her to be exiled, and Mme Vestris was blamed. It took her some time to regain the favour of the public. On the outbreak of the Revolution she left the stage, but returned and continued to act until just before her death. She created a number of tragic heroines, and was much admired by Voltaire in his *Irène* (1778). She was also good as Catherine de Médicis in *Charles IX* (1789), and in the death scene of *Gabrielle de Vergi* (1772). She was not tall, but was very dignified, and owed much to the teaching of Lekain. In later years the passionate temper of her acting became much modified, and Janin said of her, 'Toute froide et toute blanche, cette femme avait du feu dans les yeux et pas de sang dans ses veines.' She was a great admirer of the work of Marie-Joseph Chénier, and managed to secrete a copy of his *Timoléon* when he had been ordered by the censor to destroy it.

VEZIN. (1) HERMANN (1829–1910), English actor, born in the U.S.A., who came to England in 1850 and made his first appearance on the stage at York. After further experience in the provinces and two years in America, he took the Surrey Theatre, London, and appeared there in a fine series of classic parts. Phelps then engaged him for Sadler's Wells, and by 1861 he was recognized as an outstanding actor in both comedy and tragedy, being excellent as Macbeth, Othello, Jaques, Sir Peter Teazle, and Dr. Primrose, which he was the first to play. He also appeared as Iago to the Othello of John McCullough, and was with Irving at the Lyceum, making his last appearance under Tree on 7 Apr. 1909. A scholarly, intellectual man, of small stature, with clear-cut features, a dignified bearing, and a very lovely voice, he lacked only warmth and personal magnetism. In 1863 he married an Australian actress, (2) JANE ELIZABETH THOMSON (1827–1902), formerly the wife of the American actor, Charles Young. She was on the stage as a child, and was an admirable actress, with much romantic fervour and a sweet voice. She made her first appearance in England in 1857, at Sadler's Wells, and from 1858 to 1875 she had few rivals as an exponent of Shakespearian and poetic drama.

VICE, see FOOL.

VICENTE, GIL (*c.* 1465–*c.* 1537), Portuguese Court dramatist and deviser of entertainments under King Manuel I and King John III. A leading goldsmith of the time, maker of the famous Belem monstrance, was also called Gil Vicente, and goldsmith and dramatist may have been the same man. Forty-four of Vicente's works survive, seventeen in Portuguese, eleven in Spanish, and sixteen using both languages, though all have Portuguese titles. His use of Spanish, and perhaps his early dependence on Spanish literary models, is explained by the Spanish origin of several Portuguese queens. Vicente's first work was performed at the Alcáçova Palace in Lisbon, in June 1502, to commemorate the birth of an heir to the throne. He developed the Morality play, wrote many farces and a group of romantic comedies, and in his last period devised brilliant allegorical spectacles. His social criticism is strong, and in 1531 his intervention probably prevented a massacre of converted Jews. Almost single-handed, Vicente created the Portuguese drama, and he has also an important place in the dramatic history of Spain. ALAN DEYERMOND

VICTORIA PALACE, LONDON, opposite Victoria Station. This was for many years a music-hall, having formerly been the Royal Standard, Pimlico. In 1911 it was rebuilt and renamed, and from 1921 to 1929 it housed an annual Christmas play, *The Windmill Man*, with Bert Coote as the chief character, a mad gardener. Otherwise it continued to function as a music-hall and a home of revue until in 1934 it became a theatre with a most curious production, Reynolds's *Young England*, which, although meant to be a serious patriotic play, was treated with ridicule, and drew vast crowds who came to laugh, jeer, and interrupt the performance. It went to various other theatres, including Daly's, where a riot occurred which endangered the theatre's licence. In 1935 Seymour Hicks took over the Victoria and produced there *The Miracle Man*, following it with revivals of some of his former successes, including *The Man in Dress Clothes*. In 1937 Lupino Lane succeeded him, and on 16 Dec. presented a musical play called *Me and My Girl* which ran for 1,065 performances up to the temporary closing of the theatres on the outbreak of the Second World War. It was later revived. From 1947 to 1962 the theatre was the home of the Crazy Gang, which under Jack Hylton's management starred in a succession of shows from *Knights of Madness* to the final *Young in Heart*, in which they appeared together for the last time. It later housed the B.B.C. television show, *The Black and White Minstrels.*

W. MACQUEEN-POPE†, *rev.*

VICTORIA THEATRE, LONDON, see OLD VIC; NEW YORK, see GAIETY, 3.

VIENNA, see AUSTRIA.

VIERTEL, BERTHOLD (1885–1954), Austrian theatre director, who was born in Vienna and began his career there as a producer at the Volksbühne. Later he went to the Dresden State Theatre, and eventually became director of 'Die Truppe' in Berlin. In 1938 he emigrated to Hollywood, but returned to Vienna in 1945 and produced at the Burgtheater until his death. He was a keen advocate of the interpretation of the classics for modern times, a subject on which he lectured in London in 1939.

DOROTHY MOORE

VIEUX-COLOMBIER, THÉÂTRE DU, PARIS, see COPEAU.

VIGARANI. (1) GASPARE (1586–1663), Italian stage-designer and machinist, inventor of many new stage tricks and superb effects. He was working in Modena when in 1659 he was called to Paris by Mazarin to supervise the entertainments to be given in honour of Louis XIV's approaching marriage. For these he built the Salle des Machines in the Tuileries, and designed its stage machinery. As Molière's first theatre, in the Petit-Bourbon, was then being demolished, Vigarani claimed the scenery and machinery for use in his new theatre, and burnt it all, probably in the hope of destroying the work of his rival Torelli. After his death his son, (2) CARLO, who had been working with him, was responsible for the mechanics of *Les Plaisirs de l'île enchantée*, an entertainment given at Versailles with the collaboration of Molière and Lully. He became a naturalized Frenchman, lived in an apartment in the Louvre, and was frequently employed by Lully for operatic spectacles. His dates are uncertain; he was still alive in 1693 and his widow, a Frenchwoman, in 1716.

VÍGSZÍNHÁZ THEATRE, see HUNGARY.

VILAR, JEAN (1912–71), French actor and producer, who in 1951 was appointed head of the Théâtre National Populaire (T.N.P.). As a boy he showed great musical talent, but while studying in Paris in 1932 he attended a rehearsal of Dullin's production of *Richard III* at the Atelier, and decided to make the stage his career. He worked as Dullin's stage-manager for some years, playing also small parts, and after serving in the army during the Second World War joined a company of young actors, La Roulotte, which toured the provinces. In 1943 he was seen in Paris in Synge's *The Well of the Saints*, and then took over the Théâtre de Poche, which seats only about a hundred persons. In 1945 he produced, first at the Vieux-Colombier and later in front of the Abbey of Bec-Hellouin, T. S. Eliot's *Murder in the Cathedral*, with himself as Becket. This aroused great interest, and in 1947 Vilar was asked to organize a dramatic open-air summer festival at Avignon, which became an annual event (see AVIGNON). Its success led to Vilar's appointment to the Théâtre National Populaire, whose vast theatre in the Palais de Chaillot, though not in the open air, presented many of the same problems as those at Avignon. With his productions Vilar endeavoured to bring the theatre to the vast mass of people in the suburbs, and to young people who were unable to afford the prices of seats in the established Parisian theatres. His ideas were always controversial, and few theatrical enterprises have been as much written about and discussed as the Théâtre National Populaire. But it was expensive to run, and in 1962 Vilar announced his resignation as a protest against the inadequate financial support given to it by the French Government. He was succeeded by Georges Wilson, who had worked with him for many years, both in Paris and at Avignon.

Vilar, who was an excellent actor as well as a masterly and inspiring producer, appeared in many of his own productions, notably as Macbeth, Don Juan, Ruy Blas, Richard II, and as the Gangster in *Arturo Ui.* He was also seen in 1951 as Heinrich in Sartre's *Le Diable et le Bon Dieu*, and he played Oedipe with the company of Jean-Louis Barrault and Madeleine Renaud. A spare, ascetic-looking man, he could on stage appear amazingly handsome, and his voice had great sonority and emotional overtones. His view of the theatre as a great educational and spiritual force gave a certain gravity to all he did, but his influence on the French theatre was wholly good. At the time of his death he was a freelance producer of opera and plays, both in France and abroad.

VILLAURUTIA, XAVIER, see SOUTH AMERICA, 1.

VILLIERS. (1) CLAUDE DESCHAMPS DE (1600–81), French actor and author of several plays, including farces and a version of Don Juan which may have had some influence on Molière. He played in farce himself as Philippin, his name being often given to the character he was to portray. He was a member of a company formed in 1624 which included Lenoir and Montdory, and with his second wife, (2) MARGUERITE BÉGUET (?–1670), was with them again when they came to Paris in 1630. Husband and wife remained at the Théâtre du Marais until the retirement of Montdory, when they went to the Hôtel de Bourgogne. Both were excellent actors, and the wife is best remembered for having been the first to play the part of Chimène in *Le Cid* (1636). De Villiers is caricatured in Molière's *Impromptu de Versailles* (1664), together with the rest of the company of the Hôtel de Bourgogne. He retired from the stage on the death of his wife, who had not acted since about 1664. (3) JEAN DE VILLIERS (1648–1701), who as a child appeared with the Raisin children in the Troupe du Dauphin, and was a member of the Comédie-Française from

1679 to 1680, was possibly related to the above. He was better in comedy than in tragedy, and was much admired in the part of a ridiculous marquis. He married Catherine Raisin, who gave up the stage on her marriage in 1679. Their son and daughter were both actors.

VILLIERS, GEORGE, Duke of Buckingham, see BUCKINGHAM.

VILNA TROUPE. This company was founded at Vilna in 1916 by David Hermann (1876–1930) as the Union of Yiddish Dramatic Artists (called Fado, from the initials of the original name), with the intention of continuing Peretz Hirschbein's reform of the Yiddish stage. The first production was Sholom Asch's *Landsleute*, which was immediately successful. The company attracted the attention of Jewish intellectuals in the German Army of Occupation, and in 1917, partly on their advice, moved to Warsaw, where Hermann scored an immense success with his production, a month after the author's death, of Ansky's *The Dybbuk*, in Yiddish. This was taken on tour to Berlin, London, and New York. Returning to Warsaw in 1924 the company found that they had lost their theatre, and at the end of the year they moved to Vienna. There they split up, one section going to America, where it joined forces with Maurice Schwartz, the other, led by Hermann, going to Rumania. This latter group returned to Warsaw in 1927 and remained there until Hermann's death. The repertory of the Vilna Troupe was at first fairly extensive, and included a number of Yiddish classics, but later it became associated with and entirely dependent on a single play, *The Dybbuk*, a limitation which probably accounts for its decline. E. HARRIS

VINCENT, MARY ANN (*née* FARLOW) (1818–87), American actress, born in England, where she joined a provincial company and married an actor named Vincent. She went with her husband in 1846 to act at the National Theatre, Boston, where he died shortly afterwards. She continued to act as Mrs. J. R. Vincent, and in 1852 joined the stock company at the Boston Museum, staying there thirty-five years, first as its leading comedienne and later in duenna and old-lady parts. She was exceedingly popular, and a great personality, being described as a 'jolly, chubby little figure, with a pleasant voice, kindhearted, fond of animals and children'. At her jubilee in 1885 she appeared in two of her finest roles, Mrs. Hardcastle and Mrs. Malaprop. The Vincent Memorial Hospital in Boston was founded in her memory.

VIRGINIA COMPANY OF COMEDIANS, the name given by Walter Murray and Thomas Kean to the troupe with which they toured the southern cities of America in 1753, in opposition to that of the elder Hallam.

VIRTA, NIKOLAI YEVGENIEVICH (1906–), Soviet novelist and dramatist. In 1923 he left his remote village to become a journalist, in which capacity he worked on the editorial staffs of several provincial papers. The experience of these early years provided material for his first novel, *Loneliness*, published in 1935, which was well received. His later works, however, were subjected to severe criticism, particularly his comedy, *Soldiers' Wives* (1942), and this had a profound effect on him. His later plays, which include *Great Days*, based on the siege of Stalingrad, *Our Daily Bread* (both 1947), *The Doomed Conspiracy* (1948), *The Destruction of Pompeyev* (1953), *Endless Distance* (1957), and *In Summer the Sky is High* (1961), were successful, and showed his increasing mastery of his medium. His characters are portrayed with all their vices and virtues, and he brings out with great skill the various phases of the struggle between the reactionaries and the progressive peasants under communist leadership. His plays have been translated into many languages of the U.S.S.R. and also performed in other communist countries. BEATRICE KING†

VIŚĀKHADATTA, see INDIA.

VISCONTI, LUCHINO (1906–), Italian producer and scene designer. Son of a noble family, he was well educated with a view to embarking on the musical profession, but as a young man went to Paris and became involved in film-production. Although much of his early work was in films, he produced plays in Milan in 1937, and in 1945 was responsible for the introduction of a number of European dramatists in translation into the repertory of the Teatro Eliseo in Rome, where in 1948 he staged *As You Like It* in Italian as *Rosalinda*. In 1946, in which year he produced Beaumarchais's *Mariage de Figaro*, he joined the Morelli-Stoppa company. He worked with Zeffirelli on *Troilus and Cressida* in Florence, and also on *A Streetcar Named Desire*. Latterly his main work has again been in films.

VISHNEVSKY, VSEVOLOD VITALEVICH (1900–51), Soviet dramatist, of whom it was said that 'the fanaticism of the revolution sings through his plays'. After three plays dealing with the Civil War, he wrote *The Optimistic Tragedy*, which was produced with great success by Taïrov at the Kamerny Theatre in 1934. It dealt with the work and final death in battle of a woman commissar with the Red Fleet during the early days of the Soviet régime. The part of the heroine was played by Taïrov's wife, Alice Koonen. The play was published in *Four Soviet Plays* (1937) in a translation by H. G. Scott and Robert S. Carr. In 1943, after several productions which did not equal the success of *The Optimistic Tragedy*, he collaborated with Alexander Kron, author of *Depth Prospecting*, and Alexander Azarov, in a musical play, *Wide Spreads the Sea*, and also wrote *At the Walls of Leningrad*. Both these plays were produced at the Baltic Fleet Theatre, and were well received. In 1949 his last play, *The Unforgettable 1919*, was produced with great success. Both this and

The Optimistic Tragedy remain in the repertory.

VITAL SPARK, THE, see HILL, JENNY.

VITRAC, ROGER (1899–1952), French poet and playwright who was associated with Antonin Artaud in the founding of the Théâtre Alfred Jarry in 1927, and was deeply influenced by Artaud's theories. It was at this theatre that Vitrac's first two plays were performed under Artaud's direction: *Les Mystères de l'amour*, as part of the opening programme in 1927, and *Victor ou les Enfants au pouvoir* as its fourth and last production in 1928. *Les Mystères de l'amour*, which evokes the amorous and sadistic fantasies of a pair of lovers, is probably one of the most successful attempts to write a play on the surrealist principle of automatic writing. In *Victor ou les Enfants au pouvoir*, however, Vitrac moved away from pure surrealism (though elements always remained in his writing), and constructed his play along the lines of a farcical domestic comedy. He used parody of language and its clichés, monstrous characters (the 9-year-old child who is fully grown both mentally and physically), farcical incident (the lady visitor who cannot stop breaking wind), and tragi-comic dénouement (the child's choice of death as the only alternative to growing up into the adult world), in a manner which clearly foreshadows the work of Ionesco and his imitators. *Victor* was successfully revived in 1946 by Michel de Ré, and again in 1962 in a production by Jean Anouilh and Roland Pietri, and was seen in London in translation at the Aldwych in 1964, but Vitrac's other plays have been unjustly neglected, notably *Le Coup de Trafalgar* (1934), *Les Demoiselles du large* (1938), and *Le Loup-garou* (1940). T. C. C. MILNE

VITRUVIUS POLLIO, MARCUS (*fl.* 70–15 B.C.), the Roman author of a treatise in ten books, *De Architectura*, which deals among other things with theatre construction, illustrated by diagrams. Discovered in manuscript at St. Gallen in 1414, it was printed in 1511 and translated into Italian in 1521. It had a great influence on the building of Renaissance theatres (see also ACOUSTICS, ARCHITECTURE, and SCENERY).

VIVIAN BEAUMONT THEATRE, see LINCOLN CENTER.

VOKES, a family of English pantomimists, popular in England and America, consisting of (1) FREDERICK MORTIMER (1846–88), (2) JESSIE CATHERINE BIDDULPH (1851–84), (3) VICTORIA (1853–94), and (4) ROSINA (1854–94). Children of a theatrical costumier in business at 19 Henrietta Street, London, they played child parts on the legitimate stage, and first appeared as a family group at Edinburgh in 1861, their numbers augmented by (5) WALTER FAWDON (?–1904), who also took the name of Vokes. They toured for some years, and in 1865 appeared at the Lyceum in *Humpty-Dumpty*. From 1869 to 1879 they were the mainstay of the Drury Lane pantomime, where, says Disher in *Clowns and Pantomimes*, '[the Vokes] set the claims of the fairy-tale high and made an attempt to keep the humour within its limits'. They were also seen at the Adelphi and elsewhere in two amusing burlesque and pantomimic sketches, *The Belles of the Kitchen* and *A Bunch of Berries*, and made their first appearance in America in the latter in 1871. The first member of the family to break away was Rosina, 'the pick of the bunch' according to a contemporary critic. Her place was taken by Fred's wife, Bella, daughter of 'Pony' Moore of Minstrelsy fame, while Rosina married the composer Cecil Clay, and after some years in retirement went back to the stage. In 1885 she took a light comedy and burlesque company to the United States and Canada, and became a great favourite there. The family group broke up finally on the death of Jessie.

VOLKOV, FEODOR GRIGORYEVICH (1729–63), a Russian actor of great talent, and one of the founders of the Russian national theatre. He was the son of a merchant, and was born in Kostroma. He organized an amateur theatre in Yaroslavl which gave performances in the houses of the merchants, and in Jan. 1752 was summoned with his troupe to St. Petersburg, where he gave a private performance before the Court. In 1754 Volkov, with Dmitrevsky, and other members of his company, was sent to the Cadet College for the sons of the nobility, where he was trained as an actor and received in addition a good general education. He appeared at Court again in 1755, and in August of the following year joined what may be regarded as the first professional Russian theatrical company, organized by the dramatist Sumarokov. Volkov became its leading actor and Sumarokov's chief assistant. At first the company was hampered by lack of money, but its productions soon attracted the attention of those Court circles later responsible for the overthrow of Peter III and the accession of Catherine the Great. Volkov and his brother Grigori, who was also an actor, took part in the revolt, and were rewarded with Court offices. Fedor Volkov also organized the celebrations in honour of Catherine's coronation in Moscow, and it was there, while directing a street masquerade entitled *The Triumph of Minerva*, that he caught cold and died.

VOLKOV [ZIMNYUKOV], LEONID ANDREYEVICH (1893–), Soviet actor and producer, who studied at the Vakhtangov Theatre Studio, and soon showed a talent for the most varied characterization. At the Moscow Art Theatre, which he joined in 1943, he has played such parts as Simyonov-Pishchik in *The Cherry Orchard* and Ferapont in *Three Sisters*, and he has also had wide experience as a producer, being director of the Theatre of Young Spectators from 1930 to 1934, and of the Central Children's Theatre in Moscow from 1943 to 1948, where his production of Gabbé's

The City of Masters (1946) was outstanding. Between 1954 and 1960 he produced three of Ostrovsky's plays at the Moscow Maly. He has been a professor at the Moscow Art Theatre since 1952. BEATRICE KING†

VOLTAIRE [FRANÇOIS MARIE AROUET] (1694–1778), has an important place in the history of the theatre, the only aspect of his many-sided activity which need concern us here. Before his visit to England in 1726, a turning-point in his life, he had written one good tragedy, *Œdipe* (1718), which was successful enough to be parodied by Dominique at the Théâtre-Italien, and two mediocre ones, *Artémire* (1720) and *Mariamne* (1724). The latter promised well, but failed when a joke from the pit as Adrienne Lecouvreur drank poison set the audience laughing. A few months later Voltaire, who had by this time adopted the name by which he is known, an anagram of Arouet l(e) i(eune), rewrote it, and it was then successful. The first-fruits of his visit to England, during which he discovered Shakespeare, and appreciated him as far as was possible for a Frenchman raised in an entirely different tradition, were *Brutus* (1730), inspired by *Julius Caesar*, and *Zaïre* (1732), which owes something to *Othello*. The latter was extremely successful and ranks with the later *Mérope* as Voltaire's best play. In the same year as his famous *Lettres philosophiques* appeared *Adélaïde du Guesclin* (1734), which failed after two performances. It also was rewritten and given eighteen years later as *Amélie, ou le Duc de Foix* with some success, while in yet another thirteen years, under its original title, and in its original form, it was extremely successful, a reversal of fortune which afforded Voltaire much amusement. This constant remodelling of old plays, of which *Mariamne* and *Mérope* are further examples, shows Voltaire's continual preoccupation with the theatre, a passion which remained with him all his life, and to which he owed many of his happiest hours. He was an indefatigable promoter of theatrical performances, himself no mean actor, and he built several private theatres, having the money to indulge so expensive a taste. The best of these was at Ferney, his last home. Meanwhile *Mérope* (1743), written for Mlle Dumesnil, and the first French play at which the audience called for the author, had been preceded by *La Mort de César* (1735), *Alzire* and *L'Enfant prodigue* (both 1736)—the last pure eighteenth-century *drame*, with comedy and tragedy mingling, a practice Voltaire later condemned—and *Mahomet, ou le fanatisme* (1742), first given at Lille by La Noue, who successfully played the name-part in Paris. By this time Voltaire's enemies had opposed to him as France's greatest dramatist the aged writer of tragedies, Crébillon. Voltaire's reply to that was to take the subjects of six of Crébillon's plays—though not his best—and write on them himself. The first, *Sémiramis*, was given in 1748, and Voltaire himself later admitted that it contributed to the continued decline of French classical tragedy by its lavish use of spectacular effects. But it had one important consequence, since its crowd scenes and spectacular effects led the author to insist on the removal of the audience from the stage, a reform long overdue which finally took place in 1759.

Voltaire's next play, *Nanine* (1749), based on Richardson's *Pamela*, is again a *drame*, and well illustrates the dangers of an excess of sensibility. It was followed by *Oreste* (1749) and *Rome sauvée* (1750). From this period dates Voltaire's friendship with the great actor Lekain, who made his début in a revival of *Brutus* at the Comédie-Française in 1750. Soon after, Voltaire left France for the Court of Frederick the Great, and several years elapsed before his next play was seen in Paris. This was *L'Orphelin de la Chine* (1755), followed by *Tancrède* (1760), Voltaire's last good play, for six further tragedies are negligible, though one, *Irène* (1778), deserves a passing mention, since it was to see it (arriving at the moment of Lekain's funeral) that Voltaire made his last journey to Paris, dying there in a moment of triumph, for the audience applauded the author, if not the play. Of four comedies written in this last period one, *L'Écossaise* (1760), owed its success to its satire, while *Le Droit du seigneur* (1762) failed completely. The others were only given on the less exacting stage of Ferney.

Voltaire was not a great dramatist, nor a great poet, but his plays show a breadth of treatment and force of description hardly surpassed in his own day. He had the gift of attracting and interesting his audience, and if his works are now never revived, the fault lies in his facility, which led him to write too carelessly and too much, and in the fact that he lived in an age of transition, reflecting its momentary preoccupations. He considered himself a traditionalist, yet contributed not a little to the decay of French tragedy. The form of his best plays is seventeenth century, the contents eighteenth. Many of his later works were marred by the introduction of philosophical propaganda, as in *Les Guèbres*, which was never acted. He inaugurated the romantic melodrama that was to flourish in the early nineteenth century, and to him, rather than to the Romantics, goes the honour of having first introduced local colour into the theatre. By slackening the rigid form of tragedy to something more acceptable to the larger but less educated audience for which he was writing he drove tragedy a step further on the road which led to melodrama, *drame bourgeois,* and *opéra-comique*.

W

WADE, Allan (1881–1954), English actor, manager, and producer. He was one of the four original founders of the Phoenix Society and responsible for the productions of nearly all the plays staged by it. He made his first appearance on the stage in 1904, and shortly afterwards was with Frank Benson, leaving him in 1906 to become assistant to Granville-Barker at the Court Theatre, where he was instrumental in arranging the first visit of the Abbey players in 1909. Most of his work was done as play-reader and producer for various managements, but he appeared in a number of plays both in London and New York, and in 1935 he was appointed adjudicator in the Canadian Dominion Drama Festival. Author of a *Bibliography of W. B. Yeats* (1908), he was also responsible for the translations, done by the Stage Society, of *Intermezzo* (1934) and *The Infernal Machine* (1935).

WAGGON STAGE, see BOAT TRUCK.

WAGNER, Richard (1813–83), see GERMANY, 5 and OPERA, 11.

WAITS. Originally night watchmen in medieval palaces, castles, and walled towns, who indicated the hour by playing upon some musical instrument, waits later became musicians in the service of a noble person and eventually of a town, functioning as a town band. It is not always easy to distinguish the early waits from the minstrels, but it seems likely that the former were resident, the latter itinerant; also the waits appear to have had some formal musical training. They come into the history of the theatre because from the early sixteenth century they are found performing any music called for by a play. They are mentioned several times in Elizabethan plays, and in London were probably hired by the theatres from the corporation when needed, to supplement the musicians among the actors. They varied in number from four to nine, and wore the livery of the noble house or town to which they were accredited. They were paid a nominal wage and received extra money from private individuals or theatres which hired them. They were not finally disbanded until the early nineteenth century.

WAKEFIELD CYCLE, see ENGLAND, 1 and MYSTERY PLAY.

WAKHEVITCH, Georges (1907–), a stage-designer, born in Odessa, whose work has lain entirely in the French theatre. He studied architecture and painting in Paris, and began his career by designing for the cinema. He brought to the theatre a wide knowledge of both the technical and theoretical aspects of design (he is himself responsible for all working plans and oversees the construction of his sets), and has not hesitated to mingle built and painted scenery. His first work in the theatre was for Lugné-Poë at the Théâtre de l'Œuvre, and he then designed for the Rideau Gris of Marseilles, where his *Macbeth* was particularly admired. He has since worked extensively for the ballet and opera in Paris, and has been responsible for the décor, among other plays, of *L'Invitation au Château* at the Théâtre de l'Atelier, of *Donogoo* and *L'Annonce faite à Marie* (1955) at the Comédie-Française (see No. 110), and of *L'Échange* for the Renaud–Barrault company.

WALCOT. (1) Charles Melton (1816–68), American actor, born in London, where he trained as an architect, going in 1837 to the United States. His handsome person and fine voice turned his thoughts to the stage, as did his marriage to an actress in New York. He made his first appearance in 1842, and was for many years connected with Mitchell's famous Olympic, both as an eccentric comedian and as a dramatist, writing a number of topical burlesques which have not survived, but which were popular in their day. From 1852 to 1859 he was one of the leading members of Wallack's company, where he played such parts as Charles Surface and Bob Acres. He had an alert, intelligent face with a high domed forehead, which was inherited by his son, (2) Charles Melton (1840–1921); but whereas the father had side-whiskers and in his later years looked like a venerable clergyman, the son wore a moustache and the jovial expression of a genial British squire. The latter first went on the stage as Brown, but later resumed his own name, and in 1863 married (3) Isabella Nickinson (1847–1906), an accomplished actress who was for many years with him at the Walnut Street Theatre, Philadelphia. They then joined Daniel Frohman's stock company at the Lyceum, where from 1887 onwards they appeared in comic or dignified elderly parts in most of the Lyceum successes. Walcot, who like his wife was beloved by the public and his fellow actors alike, bridged the gap between the old romantic actors and the newer realism, and brought to the modern Lyceum plays an intelligent interest combined with the authority of the old school of comedy.

WALDIS, Burkhart (*fl.* sixteenth century), at one time a monk, later author of a virulent anti-Catholic play in support of the Reformation given at Riga (see GERMANY, 2).

WALDORF THEATRE, New York, on the south side of 50th Street, between Sixth and Seventh Avenues. This opened on 20 Oct. 1926 and had its first hit with a musical comedy in the following year, while in 1929 and 1930 it was used for the Little Theatre Tournament.

In 1930 also came Leo Bulgakov's production of *The Lower Depths* as *At the Bottom*, which had seventy-two performances, and was followed by five performances of *The Seagull*. A revival of *An American Tragedy* in 1931 ran for seventeen weeks, and *Dangerous Corner* in 1933 was the last production at this theatre, which became a cinema, and was later demolished. GEORGE FREEDLEY†

For the Waldorf Theatre, London, see STRAND THEATRE, 2.

WALES. There is in Wales, with its strong musical tradition, a flourishing National Opera Company, which gives annual seasons of about eight weeks, and has several times appeared very successfully in London. But in spite of the debt which the English theatre as a whole owes to Welsh players and playwrights, there is in Wales itself no longstanding theatrical tradition, and until recently there was little interest in the provision of professional drama. The larger towns have always had some opportunities for theatre-going, usually provided by visiting companies in West-End successes, or by local amateur groups which, particularly if they play in Welsh, are given financial assistance by the Arts Council. But Swansea was the only city to support a resident professional company. In 1962 the Welsh Committee of the Arts Council established a permanent Welsh Theatre Company under Warren Jenkins with the idea of providing plays both in English and in Welsh throughout the country. This company is based mainly on Cardiff, where it has rehearsal rooms, a wardrobe, workshops, and offices; its Welsh-speaking actors are, however, based on Bangor under Wilbert Lloyd Roberts, the Welsh-language producer. The Welsh Theatre Company made its first tour in the year it was founded, with Bolt's *A Man for All Seasons*, produced by Jenkins in a set designed by Richard Lake. In 1965 it appeared in Cardiff in a repertory of four plays, the opening production on 9 June being Gwyn Thomas's *Jackie the Jumper*, previously seen in London at the Royal Court Theatre. A year later Warren Jenkins was appointed director of the Belgrade Theatre, Coventry, and was succeeded by Gareth Morgan.

Although the company continues to send out successful tours of plays in English and Welsh, it has difficulty in building up an audience in Cardiff itself, owing to the lack of a suitable theatre—the New Theatre is too big for its purpose. The possibility of building a Welsh National Theatre in Cardiff has therefore been under discussion for some time. A design by Elidir Davies, architect of the Mermaid Theatre, London, for a large open-air theatre, together with a small indoor one seating about 700, had unfortunately to be abandoned, but a site has now been allocated by the Cardiff Corporation for a National Theatre, again to a design by Davies, and there are also plans for the building of a theatre in Bangor in conjunction with the University College of North Wales. Meanwhile the company hopes to acquire a mobile theatre which will operate at certain times of the year on the National Theatre site while the bulding is being erected, and during the rest of the year will visit seven or eight centres throughout the Principality.

WALKLEY, ALFRED BINGHAM (1855–1926), English dramatic critic, on *The Times* from 1900 to 1926. Previously he had written criticisms for the *Speaker*, the *National Observer*, and the *Star*. He republished a volume of his earlier criticisms as *Playhouse Impressions* (1892); and selections from his *The Times* criticisms as *Drama and Life* (1907), *Pastiche and Prejudice* (1921), *More Prejudice* (1923), and *Still More Prejudice* (1925).

Walkley in an essay on criticism wrote: 'Your critic is a sedentary person with a literary bias. His instinct is to bring to the play the calm lotus-eating mind with which he day-dreams over a book in his library. To this frame of mind the boisterous flesh-and-blood element of the actor comes as a rude distraction.' No working theatre critic could live up to the letter of this declaration, yet it gives some indication of Walkley's critical quality. His criticisms were more literary than theatrical. He devoted more of his space to the play than to the players: although he was always critical of what he called 'coterie criticism'.

Walkley was a cultured and conscientious writer who took himself and his duties seriously. He wrote as well as the theatre of his time demanded; and this, in view of the productive period in which he worked, is high praise. In 1903 he delivered three lectures on dramatic criticism at the Royal Institution. These were published in the same year, and they sum up Walkley's outlook on the profession to which he brought distinction. T. C. KEMP†

WALLACE, (RICHARD) EDGAR HORATIO (1875–1932), English journalist, novelist, and playwright, son of a touring actor who took West End successes into the provinces, and grandson of the Alice Marriott who was a well-known theatre manager and actress and a noted female Hamlet. He was the first to make a speciality of detective drama. Many of his plays were based on his own books, the twentieth-century equivalent of Mrs. Radcliffe's 'horror' novels. Among the most successful were *The Ringer* (1926), *The Terror* (1927), *The Squeaker* (1928), *The Flying Squad* (1929), *On the Spot* and *Smoky Cell* (both 1930), and *The Case of the Frightened Lady* (1931). Wallace showed extraordinary perfection of detail, narrative skill, and inside knowledge of police methods and criminal psychology, the fruit of his apprenticeship as a crime reporter.

WALLACE, NELLIE (1870–1948), one of the greatest women comedians of the English music-halls. She first appeared at Birmingham in 1888 as a clog-dancer, and later toured as one of the three Sisters Wallace. Then followed a long apprenticeship of touring in various plays before she returned to the halls as a single turn. She also appeared in revue, and in pantomime, notably as the Wicked Witch Carabosse in *The Sleeping Beauty* at the Vaudeville in 1935. One of her most famous songs was 'I Lost Georgie in Trafalgar Square'. Nellie Wallace was a mistress of the grotesque, and one of the few successful women Dames in pantomime. In private life she was Mrs. Eleanor Jane Liddy. Her husband and her only child, a daughter, predeceased her.

WALLACK, a family of actors, of English origin, important in connexion with the development of the theatre in New York. The first, (1) HENRY JOHN (1790–1870), was born in London, where his parents were leading players at Astley's Amphitheatre, and later at the Surrey. There young Wallack, with his brother and sisters, made his first appearance at an early age. In 1819 he was engaged to go to the United States, making his début at Baltimore, and first playing in New York at the Anthony Street Theatre, where he was seen in tragedy and heroic drama. In 1824 he was leading man of the Chatham Theatre company, but he later returned to London, and was for some years at Covent Garden, returning to New York in 1837 to manage the first National Theatre, and in 1847 playing Sir Peter Teazle at the Broadway. He was later manager of the Theatre Royal, Manchester, and he made his last appearance on the stage as Falstaff in 1858. One of his sisters, as Mrs. Stanley, was popular at the Coburg Theatre, London, the other married an actor named Pincott, and was the mother of Leonora, later Mrs. Alfred Wigan. His brother, (2) JAMES WILLIAM (1794–1864), also made his early appearances in London, and was for several years at Drury Lane, playing such parts as Laertes, Young Absolute, Joseph Surface, Richmond, Faulconbridge, and Iago. In 1818 he made his first appearance in New York, and proved himself an actor of the school of Kemble. He was extremely handsome, with a distinguished bearing, dark hair and eyes, fine features, a rich, sonorous voice, and great vitality. He divided his time between England and the United States, and was said to have crossed the Atlantic thirty-five times. In 1837 he took over the management of the National Theatre, New York, with his elder brother as stage-manager, and when two years later it burnt down he went first to Niblo's Garden, and then on tour. He made his last appearance in London in 1851, and in the following year opened Brougham's old Lyceum, New York, as Wallack's. Elegantly redecorated, well equipped, and furnished with a good stock company in a repertory of Shakespeare and standard comedies, with some modern plays, it flourished for ten years. Wallack himself made his last stage appearance there in 1859, but continued in management, opening a new theatre on Broadway and 13th Street in 1861. His inaugural speech marked his last public appearance, and three years later he died, leaving the traditions he had established to be carried on by his nephew, (3) JAMES WILLIAM (1818–73), and two nieces, Fanny and Julia, and by his son, (4) JOHN JOHNSTONE (1819–88), known as Lester. James served his apprenticeship under his father and uncle, being at Covent Garden with the former, and in 1837 joined the latter's company at the National, where he rose from walking gentleman to leading juvenile. A man of rugged physique, with a deep powerful voice, he was at his best in tragedy and strong sombre drama—Macbeth, Othello, Iago, Richard III. Fagin, in a dramatization of *Oliver Twist* (1867), was one of his finest parts, and at Booth's in 1872–3 he played Mathias in *The Bells* most terrifyingly. He was not at home in comedy, except for Jaques and Mercutio. In 1865 he was a member of Wallack's stock company under his cousin John, who made his first appearances on the stage in the English provinces, first as Allan Field, later as John Lester, retaining the Lester when he eventually resumed the surname of Wallack. He was for some time in Dublin, and in 1845 played at Manchester with Helen Faucit and Charlotte Cushman. He then made his first appearance in New York at the Broadway, presented himself and his cousin in his own adaptation of *The Three Musketeers*, and in 1850 was with Burton at the Chambers Street Theatre, where he proved excellent as Aguecheek and Charles Surface. He was stage-manager for his father when the latter took over Brougham's Lyceum, and played a wide range of parts, comic and romantic. He was the real manager of the new Wallack's even before his father's death. Under him the theatre flourished until 1881, but kept to its former policy of staging mainly English plays, becoming as much identified in New York with Robertson's comedies as the Bancrofts were in London. Shakespeare, however, lapsed somewhat, Lester appearing as Benedick in 1867–8, and doing nothing further until *As You Like It* in 1880. Among the new plays produced there was Lester's own dramatization of a novel, *Rosedale* (1863), in which he gave a fine performance for many years as the hero, Elliot Grey. From about 1870 Wallack's began to feel the competition of Booth's and Daly's theatres, but it continued on its well-bred and somewhat old-fashioned way, and was still capable of attracting such players as young H. L. Montague and Rose Coghlan, and of being redecorated in 1880 in red and gold. A year later it closed (for its later history see STAR THEATRE), and on 4 Jan. 1882 a new Wallack's opened on Broadway and Thirtieth Street with yet another revival of *The School for Scandal*. Mrs. Langtry, who was to have made her New York début at the Park on the day it was burnt down, went to Wallack's instead, and a year later melodrama, in the person of *The Silver King*, made its appearance at the home of old comedy, which was sinking fast. In 1887 Lester transferred the lease to other hands, allowing them to retain the old name, and the last stock season was given under Abbey in 1888, in which year Lester died. His memoirs were published a year later. The theatre was then leased by Palmer, but reverted to its original name in 1896 and finally closed in 1915 in a last blaze of glory with Granville-Barker's productions there of *A Midsummer Night's Dream*, *Androcles and the Lion*, and other plays. It was then demolished.

A Wallack Theatre, which flourished from 1924 until it became a cinema in 1931, was originally opened as the Lew Fields in 1904, and renamed the Hackett in 1906, James K. Hackett appearing there in 1908 in a revival of *The Prisoner of Zenda*. The same year saw the production of *Salvation Nell*, with Mrs. Fiske, and in 1911 the theatre again changed its name, this time to Harris. One of its most successful productions was *Dulcy* (1921), with Lynn Fontanne, while a year later the Theatre Guild gave twenty-four performances of *From Morn to Midnight* there.

WALLER, EMMA (1820–99), American actress, who with her husband went to New York from London, and there became one of the leading players of the day. She made her first appearance at the Walnut Street Theatre as Ophelia to her husband's Hamlet in Oct. 1857, was seen in New York the following year, and from then until her retirement in 1878 played leading roles all over the United States. A tall, stately woman, with an interesting and expressive face, she was good as Lady Macbeth, as Queen Margaret in Cibber's version of *Richard III*, which she played with Edwin Booth, as Meg Merrilies, and as Julia in *The Hunchback*. She also, in the fashion of the time, played Hamlet and Iago. After her retirement she continued to give readings in public, and was also a teacher of elocution.

WALLER. (1) LEWIS [really WILLIAM WALLER LEWIS] (1860–1915), English actor-manager, and one of the outstanding romantic actors of his day. Born in Spain, of English parents, he was an enthusiastic amateur before he went on the professional stage, making his first appearance at Toole's Theatre in 1883. During a long and varied career he appeared in a number of famous romantic parts, including Monsieur Beaucaire—perhaps the supreme example of his talent—Brigadier Gerard, and D'Artagnan. A robust and dynamic actor, with a magnificent voice, he was at his best in costume parts, and particularly in Shakespeare. His Brutus, his Faulconbridge, and particularly his Henry V, were memorable. He was one of the first so-called matinée idols, but entirely without conceit, and the hysteria of his more fervid supporters was a cause of much embarrassment to him. In modern-dress comedy he did not appear to such advantage, and *An Ideal Husband*, with which he first went into management at the Haymarket in 1895, was not a suitable medium for his particular gifts. He has, somewhat unkindly, been called 'the high-priest of dignified tushery', a two-edged tribute which has at least the merit of conceding something more than flamboyance and spectacle to his romantic productions. He married an actress, (2) FLORENCE WEST (1862–1912), sister-in-law of the dramatic critic Clement Scott, who appeared with her husband in many of his outstanding successes, notably as Miladi in *The Three Musketeers*.

W. MACQUEEN-POPE†

WALNUT STREET THEATRE, PHILADELPHIA. Built as a circus in 1809, this was first used as a playhouse in 1811, when it entered into competition with the successful and well-established Chestnut Street Theatre. It is still in use, and is the oldest playhouse in the United States. It flourished until 1829, when intense rivalry between the various managements in the city brought about the bankruptcy of them all. From then onwards it had a good stock company, which supported visiting stars, but contributed little to the development of American theatrical life, whose centre moved to New York.

WALTER, EUGENE (1874–1941), American dramatist, whose early plays, though somewhat melodramatic, seemed to point the way towards a more realistic and sober approach to social problems. The best of them were *Paid in Full* (1908) and *The Easiest Way* (1909). A later play, *Fine Feathers* (1913), was good also, but less successful. Unfortunately Walter failed to live up to his early promise, and his last plays are negligible. Among them were dramatizations of two popular novels by John Fox, Jr., *The Trail of the Lonesome Pine* (1912) and *The Little Shepherd of Kingdom Come* (1916). He was also the author of a handbook on dramatic technique, entitled *How to Write a Play* (1925).

WARD, DOROTHY (1890–), English actress, best known for her annual appearance as Principal Boy in pantomime, though her career has embraced, as she herself has said, 'everything but Shakespeare'. She made her first appearance in 1905, in Birmingham, and was seen in London a year later in *The Dairymaids*. Her first outstanding success was made as Louise in *The Cinema Star* (1914), and in New York she was widely acclaimed as Phoebe in *Quality Street* (1921). She first appeared in pantomime in 1924, her favourite parts being Jack in *Jack and the Beanstalk* and Dick Whittington. Her husband, Shaun Glenville [really Browne] (1884–1968), son of the manageress of the Abbey Theatre, Dublin, and himself a noted comedian and music-hall artist, has appeared with her in many pantomimes as the Dame (Dame Trot, Cook in *Dick Whittington*, Mrs. Crusoe, etc.). He first appeared on the stage as a babe in arms, and had a consistently successful career both on the halls and in the theatre, making a perfect foil to the pink-and-white golden-haired English beauty of his wife in her broadbrimmed hat, tights, and short tunic, in which she proved herself a worthy successor to those first principal boys, Harriet Vernon, Nellie Stewart, and Queenie Leighton.

WARD [Buchanan], Fannie (1872–1952), an American actress who was said to have 'discovered the secret of eternal youth'. Born in St. Louis, she made her first appearance on the stage at the Broadway, New York, as Cupid in *Pippino* in 1890. She then played successfully in a series of light comedies, and in 1894 made her first appearance in London as Eva Tudor in *The Shop Girl* at the Gaiety. She had only one line to say—'Watch my wink!'—specially written in for her by George Edwardes, but it was enough. Her beauty and charm made an instant impression, and she remained in London until 1906, appearing with undiminished success in a series of light and musical comedies. On her return to New York she was seen at Wallack's as Rita Forrest in *A Marriage of Reason* (1907), and in the same year she returned to London in one of her greatest successes, Nance in *In the Bishop's Carriage*. From then onwards she pursued her career in London and New York, occasionally touring, and in the late 1920s she was at the Coliseum in London, 'looking', as one critic said 'sixteen and admitting to 60'.

WARD, (Lucy) Geneviève Teresa (1838–1922), an American actress equally well known in England, and, in her earlier career, as an opera singer under the name of Mme Guerrabella. While on tour in Cuba she lost her singing voice, as a result of diphtheria and overwork, and became an actress, making her début as Lady Macbeth in Manchester in 1873. The following year she appeared in London, where she achieved success in a wide variety of roles, which included Antigone, Mrs. Haller, Belvidera, Portia, and Emilia in *Othello*. A fine linguist, she played Lady Macbeth in French at the Porte-Saint-Martin in Paris, and after further appearances in London was first seen as an actress in New York in 1878. A year later she produced under her own management in London the famous *Forget-Me-Not*, which proved such a success that she played it all over the world. Playing opposite her in the original production was the young Johnston Forbes-Robertson as Sir Horace Welby. After her last visit to the United States in 1891 she joined Irving at the Lyceum, playing Queen Eleanor in *Becket*, Queen Katharine in *Henry VIII*, and Queen Margaret in *Richard III*. From 1900 onwards she played more rarely, but was seen several times with Benson's company, and in 1920 played Volumnia at the Old Vic. She made her last appearance with Benson's company, playing Queen Margaret in *Richard III*. A tall, commanding woman, with aquiline features, she bore some resemblance in her youth to Adelaide Ristori, with whom she was often compared. She was created D.B.E. in 1921.

WARDE, Frederick Barkham (1851–1935), an American actor and lecturer on Shakespeare and the drama. He was intended for the law, but in 1867 joined a small touring company, and after several years in stock companies, where he played with such stars as Irving and Adelaide Neilson, he went to Booth's Theatre, New York, making an immediate success. He remained there for three years, playing in Shakespeare with McCullough, Booth, and Charlotte Cushman, and then toured with Janauschek and the Lingards. In 1881 he began a long career of starring in his own company, mainly in Shakespeare and such old favourites as *Virginius*, *The Gladiator*, and *The Lady of Lyons*, since he was unable to find any modern plays to his taste. He did not appear on the stage after 1919, though he made several films of Shakespeare and classical novels. In 1907 he began lecturing, and in 1913 published *The Fools of Shakespeare*. He was also the author of a charming book of reminiscences, *Fifty Years of Make-Believe* (1920). He was a scholarly man, and received an Hon. D.Litt. from the University of Southern California for his services to literature.

WARFIELD, David (1866–1951), American actor, associated at the height of his fame with David Belasco. Warfield was a programme-seller and later an usher at the San Francisco theatre—where Belasco incidentally spent many of his early years—and in 1888 joined a travelling company, playing Melter Moss in *The Ticket-of-Leave Man*. This failed after a week, and he went into variety, appearing in New York in 1890 in vaudeville and musical comedy. He was Karl in the original production of *The Belle of New York*, and later spent three years in a burlesque company. He was adept at presenting the New York East Side Jew of his day, and had already given proof of fine qualities in his acting when in 1901 Belasco starred him in *The Auctioneer*. This was an instantaneous success and had a long run, but it was as the gentle, pathetic, self-sacrificing Anton von Barwig in *The Music Master* (1904) that Warfield set the seal on his growing reputation. He played nothing else, in New York and on tour, for three years. Among his later successes were Wes Bigelow in *A Grand Army Man* (1907), and the title-roles in *The Return of Peter Grimm* (1911) and *Vanderdecken* (1915). He was also seen as Shylock in Belasco's 1922 production of *The Merchant of Venice*. He retired from the stage two years later.

WARNER, Charles (1846–1909), English actor, son of an actor named James Lickfold who was in Phelps's company at Sadler's Wells. Here the son made his first appearance at the age of 15, but was then put to study with an architect. The theatre soon drew him back, and he left home to play in the provinces under the name of Warner, which he later retained. He was first seen in London in 1864 as Paris in *Romeo and Juliet*. A year later he played Iago and Romeo at the West London and in 1869 Steerforth in *Little Em'ly*. Two years later he succeeded Irving as Jingle, and then toured with Adelaide Neilson. He was the first Charles Middlewick in *Our Boys* (1875), but, though good in comedy, he was at his best in melodrama, playing at the Adelphi for many years. His finest part was Coupeau in *Drink* (1879), an adaptation of Zola's *L'Assommoir* in which he collaborated with Charles Reade. He made his last appearance under Tree, playing Leontes to the Hermione of Ellen Terry in *The Winter's Tale* in 1906. He then went to America, where he committed suicide. Two of his children were on the stage.

WARREN. (1) WILLIAM (1767–1832), American actor, of English birth, who made his early appearances in the English provinces, where he was at one time in the same company as Thomas Jefferson. In 1788 Warren was with Tate Wilkinson, and played in support of Sarah Siddons. His real career began, however, when in 1796 he was invited by Wignell to join his Philadelphia company, and there, except for a number of short visits to New York, the rest of his life was passed. He succeeded Wignell as manager of the Chestnut Street Theatre, in partnership with William Wood, and it was under them that the great American actor Edwin Forrest made his first appearance, as Young Norval. Warren was a fine actor of old men, Sir Anthony Absolute, Old Dornton, Sir Toby Belch, Falstaff, and Sir Peter Teazle being accounted his best parts. He had a long and successful career, somewhat saddened towards the end by financial reverses and domestic sorrows, and retired in 1829, making a final farewell appearance the year before his death. He was three times married. His first wife, Ann, was an actress, daughter of the actor William Powell; his second the famous actress Mrs. Merry (Anne Brunton) whom he married in 1806 as her third husband. On her death in 1808 he married the sister-in-law of the first Joseph Jefferson. His six children were all connected with the theatre, his four daughters marrying actors or managers, and one son being himself a manager and the father-in-law of the third Joseph Jefferson. The best known was (2) WILLIAM (1812–88), who spent most of his professional life at the Boston Museum. He made his first appearance at the Arch Street Theatre, Philadelphia, shortly after his father's death, as Young Norval. He then toured for some years, and was a member of several good stock companies. He was seldom seen in New York, and only once in England, in 1845. He began his long association with the Boston Museum in 1847, and remained there over forty years, becoming one of the leading citizens of the town. In his early days he acted a wide variety of parts, but later specialized in comedy, being particularly admired as Touchstone, Polonius, Bob Acres, and Sir Peter Teazle. He appeared also in a number of new plays, which his excellent acting often redeemed from mediocrity. In 1882 he celebrated his jubilee, playing Dr. Pangloss and Sir Peter Teazle, and in 1883 retired after playing Old Eccles in *Caste*, to spend the rest of his life pleasantly and happily in the company of his many friends. He was never married. It was said of him that 'his acting seems the fine flower of careful culture, as well as the free outcome of a large intelligence and native genius'.

WASHINGTON SQUARE PLAYERS, founded in 1914 by a group which included Edward Goodman, Philip Moeller, Helen Westley, and Lawrence Langner. They opened in Feb. 1915 at the Bandbox Theatre, New York, in a programme of one-act plays, some of them specially written for the occasion. In 1916 they first presented full-length plays, beginning with Maeterlinck's *Aglavaine* and Chekhov's *The Seagull*. In the same year they moved to the Comedy Theatre, and again did mainly one-act plays. Some exceptions were Andreyev's *Life of Man*, Ibsen's *Ghosts*, Langner's *Family Exit*, Miles Malleson's *Youth*, and Shaw's *Mrs. Warren's Profession*. In 1917 they did O'Neill's one-act play *In the Zone*, and in 1918 Elmer Rice's *Home of the Free*. Lee Simonson worked for this group, and Katharine Cornell made her first professional appearances with them. They disbanded in 1918.

WASHINGTON SQUARE THEATRE, NEW YORK, at 40 West 4th Street, a shed-like, corrugated-steel building which was completed in Dec. 1963 and opened on 23 Jan 1964 with the world première of Arthur Miller's *After the Fall*, directed by Elia Kazan. This was the first major playhouse to be opened in New York for many years. Financed by the American National Theatre Association, it was erected on ground loaned by New York University and became the temporary home of the Repertory Theatre of Lincoln Center. Miller's play was followed by a revival of O'Neill's *Marco Millions*, directed by José Quintero, and a new play by S. N. Behrman, *But For Whom Charlie*, also directed by Kazan. Jo Mielziner, who designed this temporary theatre, is also responsible for the design of the company's permanent home, the Vivian Beaumont Theater in the Lincoln Center for the Performing Arts.

WATER RATS, THE GRAND ORDER OF, a British association of members of the music-hall profession which originated in 1889 from an up-river (Thames) party to celebrate the successes of the Water Rat, a racing pony. Joe Elvin was a prime mover in the formation of the Society. Its present name was adopted in 1890, the objects being Philanthropy, Conviviality, and Social Intercourse. It has raised large sums for needy artistes and for public charities.

WATERS, ETHEL (1900–), American Negro actress and singer, who began her stage career in 1917, singing in night-clubs and vaudeville. She made her first appearance on Broadway in 1927 at Daly's Theatre, in *Africana*, an all-Negro revue, and in 1933 she appeared with Clifton Webb and Marilyn Miller in Irving Berlin's *As Thousands Cheer*. Her first dramatic role was Hagar in *Mamba's Daughters* (1939), in which she proved herself an actress of the front rank. Subsequent Broadway appearances, as Petunia in *Cabin in the Sky*

(1940) and Berenice in *The Member of the Wedding* (1950), enhanced her reputation. She has also given many solo performances, among them *At Home with Ethel Waters* (1953), in which she sang many of the songs she had helped to make famous, including 'Dinah', 'Stormy Weather', and 'Am I Blue?'. Her autobiography was published in 1951.

WATTS, Jr., RICHARD (1898–), American dramatic critic, who was born in Parkersburg, West Virginia, and attended Columbia University. He was a reporter on *The Brooklyn Eagle* in 1922 and in 1924 joined *The Herald-Tribune* as film critic. He was one of the first Americans to write seriously of the films, and his work in that field has historical as well as critical value. In 1936 he became *The Herald-Tribune* dramatic critic, though prior to that he had acted as assistant dramatic critic to the late Percy Hammond in addition to writing on the cinema. During the Second World War he served in China and in Ireland, and then became dramatic critic of *The New York Post.* THOMAS QUINN CURTISS

WEAVER (WEVER), JOHN (1673–1760), a Drury Lane dancing-master to whom we owe the introduction to the English stage of the harlequinade, from which the later pantomime developed. He brought over from France 'scenical dancing' or 'Italian Night Scenes', stories in mime with no speech. He was himself the author of several pantomime scenarios, and of a *History of Mimes and Pantomimes* published in 1728. Acting on his ideas, John Rich developed the pantomime and took it a stage further, but Weaver must be given credit as the pioneer in this form of entertainment.

WEBB, JOHN (1611–72), English artist. He was a pupil of Inigo Jones, and was employed by Davenant to design and paint scenery for his productions, beginning with *The Siege of Rhodes.* For this Webb prepared landscapes showing the general layout of the town and harbour, based probably on actual engravings of the scene. In the epilogue to *The World in the Moon* Settle emphasizes the native origin of his elaborate scenery, in contrast to the French fashion of the time, with his play on the scene-painter's name, ''Tis all home-spun Cloth; All from an English Web'.

WEBER AND FIELDS, an American comedy team consisting of JOSEPH WEBER (1867–1942) and (1) LEW FIELDS (1867–1941). Sons of poor Jewish immigrants, they entered into partnership at the age of 9, appearing at dime museums and beer gardens in and around New York in burnt-cork minstrelsy. They soon discarded this in favour of a 'knock-about Dutch act', which included jokes and dialogue in comically mangled English. Much of their subsequent work was a variation of this basic formula, which combined slapstick clowning with the immigrant's difficulties with the English language. Their sketches were really little plays with two traditional characters, Fields always appearing as Myer—tall, thin, tricky—and Weber as Mike—short, squat, guileless. Both wore padded suits, and often shallow derbies. In 1885 they established their own company, writing and acting in burlesques of the serious drama of the day (*Cyranose, Quo Vass Iss?*). These anticipated the 'revues' of the 1920s with their sketchy plots, their 'turns', and their big ensemble numbers. In 1895 they opened the former Broadway Music-Hall as Weber and Fields', remaining there until 1904. After that their careers diverged, though they were seen together again in 1912 in *Hokey-Pokey* (see FORTY-FOURTH STREET THEATRE). Weber retired from acting in 1918, but continued to direct plays for another ten years, among them *The Squaw Man's Girl of the Golden West*, a burlesque of Puccini's opera. Fields opened his own theatre, and later took over the Herald Square, producing and acting in a number of musical comedies. He was on the stage until 1929, and did his last production a year later. Three of his children have been active in the theatre. His son, (2) JOSEPH (1895–), collaborated with Jerome Chodorov in several plays, including the successful *My Sister Eileen* (1940), *Wonderful Town* (1953), and *Anniversary Waltz* (1954), and with Anita Loos in *Gentlemen Prefer Blondes* (1949). In 1958 he directed *Flower-Drum Song* in New York, and later in London, where he had also been responsible for the London production of *Anniversary Waltz.* His brother, (3) HERBERT (1897–1958), in collaboration with their sister Dorothy, was responsible for the libretti of such successful musicals as *Mexican Hayride* (1944) and *Annie Get Your Gun* (1946). ROBERT TRACY

WEBSTER. (1) BENJAMIN NOTTINGHAM (1797–1882), English actor, manager, and dramatist, descended from a long line of theatrical and musical people. He had numerous brothers and half-brothers, all of whom were connected with the stage, one of them, Frederick (1802–78), being stage-manager at the Haymarket for many years. Frederick's grandchild, Florence Ann (1860–99), who was an actress and dancer, married George Lupino. Ben himself was first a dancer, playing Harlequin and Pantaloon in the provinces and at Drury Lane. He then took to broad comedy, proving himself a useful actor, and was with Mme Vestris at the Olympic. In 1837 he became lessee of the Haymarket, which he managed for sixteen years, engaging all the best actors of the day and putting on many notable plays, in which he himself frequently appeared. In 1844 he took over the Adelphi as well, and was associated with Mme Céleste, and with Dion Boucicault, collaborating with the latter in two plays. He made an adaptation of *The Cricket on the Hearth* in which he appeared with great success as John Peerybingle, but his finest part was Triplet in *Masks and Faces*, which he produced at both the Haymarket and the Adelphi in 1852. He opened the New Adelphi in 1859, and continued in management until his retirement in

1874. He retained his faculties to the end, and some of his latest parts were outstanding. In his own line as a character actor he was unsurpassed in his own day, but he had little liking for farce, in spite of having written a number of successful ones, and tempered his comedy with a somewhat grim humour. Two of his children were on the stage, and his namesake, by profession a barrister, wrote a number of plays, mainly melodramatic, none of which has survived. The first Ben's grandson, (2) BENJAMIN (1864–1947), who had three sisters on the stage, was intended for his father's profession, the law, but deserted it for the theatre. He made his first appearances with Hare and Kendal, and was subsequently with Irving at the Lyceum and on tour in the United States. He was also in the companies of Alexander, Ellen Terry, and Boucicault, and appeared in the plays of Shaw, Shakespeare, Pinero, Barrie, and others, as well as *Richard of Bordeaux* and *Mr. Pim Passes By*. On the outbreak of war in 1939 he went to America, where his reputation stood as high as in England, and remained there till his death, making his last appearance on Broadway as Montague in *Romeo and Juliet* with Laurence Olivier and Vivien Leigh. In 1892 he married (3) MAY WHITTY (1865–1948), who made her first appearance at the Court Theatre, Liverpool, in 1881. She was for a year with Irving at the Lyceum, and made her first visit to America, where she subsequently made many appearances, in his company in 1895. She was for many years an outstanding figure of both the London and New York theatre worlds, and in 1918 was made Dame Commander of the British Empire for charitable work in connexion with the First World War. She and her husband both had distinguished careers in films also. Their daughter, (4) MARGARET (1905–), known as Peggy, was on the stage for some years, making her first appearance in 1917, and her adult début in 1924 with Sybil Thorndike in *The Trojan Women*. She was a member of Fagan's Oxford Repertory company, toured with Ben Greet, and was with the Old Vic from 1929 to 1930. In 1936 she went to New York and, while continuing to act, made an outstanding reputation as a director, particularly of Shakespeare. Out of her experiences she wrote *Shakespeare Without Tears* (1942), which was revised and reissued in England in 1956 as *Shakespeare Today*. Her production of *Othello* in New York in 1943, in which she played Emilia, broke all records for a Shakespearian play there with 295 consecutive performances. From 1948 to 1950 she toured the United States with a Shakespearian company, and later produced opera at the Metropolitan Opera House. Since the Second World War she has produced several plays in London, and worked at the Old Vic before it closed, and at Stratford-upon-Avon. In 1964 she gave a short season at the Arts Theatre in a solo performance based on the life and works of the Brontë sisters. She has made numerous lecture tours in the United States, and supervised the Shakespearian productions at the New York World's Fair in 1939.

WEBSTER, JOHN (*c.* 1580–1634), English dramatist, whose fame rests almost entirely on two plays, *The White Devil* (1612) and *The Duchess of Malfi* (1614). Both are founded on Italian *novelle* and are passionate dramas of love and political intrigue in Renaissance Italy, compounded of crude horror and sublime poetry. Indeed, in the latter respect Webster approached Shakespeare more nearly than any of his contemporaries, and both these plays have held the stage down to the present day. They provide scope for great acting and fine settings, and in the category of poetic drama remained unsurpassed by any later work, except that of Otway, until a new conception of tragedy was imported into European literature by Ibsen. Webster's other work is of little importance. Apart from *Appius and Virginia* (*c.* 1608) and *The Devil's Law Case* (1623), his other plays, including some now lost, were written in collaboration, chiefly with Dekker. It has been suggested that Webster had a hand in Tourneur's *Revenger's Tragedy*, but there is no proof of this. Practically nothing is known of his life, and Chambers has surmised that he may have come late to play-writing and previously have been an actor, possibly the John Webster who appears among the English Comedians in Germany under Browne in 1596.

WEDEKIND, FRANK (1864–1918), German dramatist and actor, who, after working as a journalist, and secretary to a circus, appeared in cabaret in songs which he had written and composed. He then joined Carl Heine's company at the Krystal Palast in Leipzig, and began to write. His plays, which show the influence of Hauptmann and the new realistic school of drama, nevertheless in their fantasy and symbolism point the way towards expressionism. In fierce revolt against the secrecy imposed on adolescents in sex matters, and as a stern critic of 'middle-class morality', he wrote *Die junge Welt* (1890), and *Frühlings Erwachen* (1891), first performed in 1906, both dealing with the problems of youth, while in *Erdgeist* (1895) and its sequel *Die Büchse der Pandora* (1903), used by Alban Berg for his unfinished opera 'Lulu' (1937), he portrays sex in its most raw and lustful aspects. Here, and in later plays, his sex-ridden males and females, his gentlemen crooks, as in *Der Marquis von Keith* (1900), and his grotesque yet vital cranks, as in *Hidalla* (1904), typify the feverish spirit of the years before 1914. The first of Wedekind's plays to be seen in London was the one-act *Der Kammersänger*, produced by the Stage Society in 1907. In 1931 the Sunday Theatre Club did *Spring's Awakening*, which, as *Spring Awakening*, had its first public production at the Royal Court Theatre in 1965. Sub-titled 'a children's tragedy', it analyses the situation of two 14-year-olds who pay with their lives for the moral dishonesty of their tyrannical parents.

Wedekind's plays, which so shocked their audiences on their first production, seem now, in an atmosphere of relaxed morals and increasing juvenile delinquency, less shocking perhaps, but still valid, and revivals of them are becoming more frequent in Germany. In 1963 the Schillertheater in Berlin revived *Der Marquis von Keith*.

WEIMAR. In 1757 the Duchess Anna Amalia became regent of Weimar, and her Court developed into one of the most important centres of artistic culture in Germany. There was already a small theatre in Weimar at this time (built in 1696) where groups of visiting players occasionally performed, and to this theatre the Duchess summoned Seyler's company, with Karl Ekhof, in 1772; but the enterprise was abandoned three years later when the theatre was destroyed. As there was no money to rebuild it immediately, the Duchess established a temporary theatre in one wing of the castle, and here a troupe of professional actors continued to present plays, operettas, and farces. Gradually the standard of performance became so low that the company was dismissed, and a group of amateurs took their place. It was at this moment that Goethe arrived in Weimar, and soon found himself acting as an unofficial 'Maître des Plaisirs'. There were at the time three amateur groups in the town; the first, which Goethe directed, was made up of courtiers, and favoured French comedy; the second, recruited by F. J. Bertuch (1747–1820) from the bourgeoisie, specialized in German plays; the third was a group of young people who acted fairy-tales and children's plays. These various groups soon left the temporary stage in the castle and went first to the house of Anton Hauptmann, then to a room in the castle at Ettersburg, and finally to a new playhouse built in 1780. From 1773 to 1783 Goethe was closely associated with all the amateur theatricals at Court, producing pageants for royal and other occasions, also plays, acting in comedy and tragedy, always finding himself hampered by lack of money and the irresponsible attitude of his amateur company. In 1779 he played Orestes to Corona Schroeter's Iphigenie in his own play of that name. By 1781 the Court was beginning to lose interest in amateur theatricals, but in Jan. 1784 a new Court theatre opened with a professional company under Bellomo, and in 1791 the direction of this theatre passed to Goethe. He brought to it his former experience in the amateur theatre and, though he had never been a professional actor, was able to direct those who were, and so became the first modern stage director. Some actors from Bellomo's company were retained, among them the celebrated Christiane Neumann, and the company was enriched by guest artists like Schröder and Iffland. Goethe wanted to establish a company capable of exploiting the educational possibilities of the theatre, and in this he received the support and sympathy of Schiller, who shared his vision. The outstanding feature of the Weimar theatre in this period was the rapid succession of plays by Schiller—*Wallenstein*, *Maria Stuart*, *Die Jungfrau von Orleans*, *Die Braut von Messina*, *Wilhelm Tell*—in which dramatic appeal was combined with literary quality. Goethe's interest in acting was stimulated by Iffland's performances in 1796 and 1797, and he tried to extend the range of parts of which his troupe was capable by coaching and instruction. Some critics found the Weimar actors stiff and unwieldy, but admitted that crowds were skilfully handled. In 1798 the theatre was renovated, and from 1799 to 1805 Goethe and Schiller were jointly responsible for its direction. The repertory included the works of both poets, also plays by Calderón, Lessing, Voltaire (*Mahomet* and *Tancred* in Goethe's translation), and Shakespeare. After Schiller's death in 1805 Goethe once more became sole head of the theatre, which he continued to direct until 1817. The conviction that he had already done his best work for the theatre, combined with the lack of interest shown by the actors, and their many intrigues, made his departure easy. The golden age of the Weimar theatre ended with his death in 1832. The building was burnt down in 1826 and rebuilt, had a chequered history and finally came under the direction of Liszt (1848–58). 'Tannhäuser' and 'Lohengrin' were both performed there and the repertory was enriched by the works of dramatists of the new German school. In 1857 Dingelstedt came to Weimar from Munich and produced all Shakespeare's historical plays and, in 1861, Hebbel's *Nibelungen*. After the Second World War the theatre was rebuilt, reopening in 1948. Among important post-war productions have been the first performance of *Doktor Eisenbart* by A. Böckmann (1954), and *Marika Weiden* by Karl-Rudi Griesbach, which last was written to celebrate the eleventh anniversary of the German Democratic Republic.

DOROTHY MOORE

WEISE. (1) CHRISTIAN (1642–1708), German dramatist, headmaster of a school at Zittau, where he wrote and produced a number of long plays, on subjects taken from many and varied sources. He made good use of the Narr, or fool, to point the moral, and in contrast to the exuberant, ranting verse of Lohenstein and his imitators used a plain, dry, prose style which he coached his boys to speak clearly and simply. He should not be confused with (2) CHRISTIAN FELIX WEISSE (1726–1804), friend and contemporary of the young Lessing, with whom Weisse collaborated in translating a number of French and English plays for Caroline Neuber's company.

WEITER, AISIG (1878–1919), Russian-Jewish writer of plays on contemporary themes, produced at the Moscow State Jewish Theatre.

WELL, the lower part of the cellar beneath the stage (see STAGE, 1). The orchestra well for the accommodation of the theatre musicians is in front of and below the stage itself.

WELLES, Orson (1915–), American actor and director, a forceful and controversial personality who has had a stormy and spectacular career both in the theatre and in films. He made his first appearance in Dublin in 1931, as the Duke of Württemberg in *Jew Süss*, and worked with the Abbey and Gate Theatres before going back to America, where he was born. He played Mercutio, Marchbanks, and Octavius Barrett on tour with Katharine Cornell in 1933–4, and then organized the Woodstock Theatre Festival in Illinois. He continued to act, and in 1936 became director of the Negro People's Theatre, where he was responsible for a Negro version of *Macbeth*. A year later he was appointed a director of the Federal Theatre project, and did a number of productions at the Maxine Elliott Theatre before leaving to found the Mercury Theatre, with John Houseman. Here he directed and played in a controversial but enormously successful modern-dress revival of *Julius Caesar*. Even more controversial was his famous broadcast *The War of the Worlds* in 1938, which caused a panic in the United States. He made his first appearance in London as Othello in 1951, and in 1955 was seen there again in his own version of *Moby Dick*. He was responsible for the décor and production of Ionesco's *Rhinoceros* at the Royal Court Theatre, with Olivier in the lead, in 1960.

WEMYSS, Francis Courtney (1797–1859), English actor and manager, who spent most of his professional life in the United States. He made his first appearances in the English provinces, and in 1821 was seen in London, where he was engaged for the Chestnut Street Theatre company. He made his début there the following year with such fine actors as Warren, Wood, Henry Wallack, and the elder Jefferson, and in 1824 made his first appearance in New York. He was a good actor, but not of the first rank, playing mainly small parts in revivals. He was Duncan to Macready's Macbeth on the occasion of the Astor Place Opera House riot. Nor was he more successful as a manager, though he was at various times in charge of the Chestnut Street Theatre, Barnum's American Museum, and theatres in many big American cities. In spite of his shortcomings, he has a high place in the history of the American theatre, which he served devotedly till the end of his life with impeccable taste and integrity. He was the author of a most entertaining autobiography, *Twenty-Six Years of the Life of an Actor and Manager* (1847), and also edited the Philadelphia series of standard plays, published as *The Acting American Theatre*, with fine frontispieces of American actors by Neagle. A pleasant, cultured, and courtly man, he was extremely popular in America, but never ceased to be regarded as an Englishman. He helped to found and administer the Theatrical Fund.

WERFEL, Franz (1890–1945), Austrian novelist and dramatist, whose trilogy, *Der Spiegelmensch* (1920), is an interesting resumption of the Faust-Mephistopheles theme. This symbolic drama was followed by two historical plays, which had some success, *Juarez und Maximilian* (1924) and *Paulus unter den Juden* (1926). A chronicle-play dealing with the history of Jewry, *The Eternal Road* (1936), though elaborately staged and produced by Max Reinhardt in New York, was little more than a pageant. Werfel's most original contribution to the theatre, however, was his adaptation of his novel, *Bocksgesang* (1921) (known in English as *The Goat Song*), in which the crazy brutality of man in rebellion is symbolized by the monster, half-goat, half-man, who leads a peasants' revolt in the eighteenth century. He is eventually killed, but not before he has passed on his heritage of cruelty and bestiality to his child by a young nobleman's wife.

WERGELAND, Henrik Arnold (1808–45), Norwegian poet and dramatist, best known for his epic poem, *Skabelsen, Mennesket og Mesias*. He also wrote a number of plays. The earliest of these were farces (written under a pen-name) and were later followed by plays written under the influence of Shakespeare: *Sinclars Død* (1828): a comedy, *Opium* (1831); and *Irreparabile Tempus* (1828). In his later plays there is less of this influence and more of Wergeland's own fertile, fantastic, and sometimes apocalyptic imagination. *Den indiske Cholera*, *Barnemordersken*, and *De sidste Kloge*, ranging from tragedy to farce, all belong to 1834; two more political farces followed in 1837, and then *Campbellerne*, the cause of a controversy better known than the play. To the last group, written after 1839, belong some more political farces, the drama *Venetianerne* (1841), and the posthumously produced *Søkadetterne iland*.

UNA ELLIS-FERMOR†

WERNER, Friedrich Ludwig Zacharias (1768–1823), author of the one-act tragedy, *Der vierundzwanzigste Februar* (1810), which established the so-called Fate Drama in Germany. He was a poet and mystic who became a Roman Catholic priest in Vienna, where he was renowned for his preaching. His plays, which include *Das Kreuz an der Ostsee* (1806), *Martin Luther* (1807), and *Kunigunde, die Heilige* (1815), bear a strong religious imprint, and mingle scenes of telling realism with weird fantasies. They were among the few German romantic verse-dramas to obtain success on the stage.

WESKER, Arnold (1932–), English dramatist, prominent in what has been called 'kitchen-sink' drama. His first play, *Chicken Soup with Barley*, was done at the Belgrade, Coventry, and brought to London by the company, being seen at the Royal Court in July 1958. It later formed part of the trilogy of which *Roots* and *I'm Talking About Jerusalem* (1959; 1960) were the other components. Joan Plowright appeared as Beatie in *Roots* with great success, both in Coventry and in London, at the Royal Court. Wesker was given the Evening Standard

Award of 1960 for the most promising British playwright. He has also written *The Kitchen* (1959), based on his experiences as a pastry-cook, *Chips With Everything* (1962), a study of life in the R.A.F., which later had a great success in New York, *Their Very Own and Golden City* (originally entitled *Congress*), which was awarded a Marzotto prize in 1964, and *The Four Seasons* (1965), in which Diane Cilento and Alan Bates played the only two characters (see also CENTRE 42).

WESSEL, JOHAN (1742–85), Norwegian dramatist (see SCANDINAVIA, 2 *a*).

WEST, FLORENCE (1862–1913), see WALLER (2).

WEST LONDON THEATRE. In 1832 this theatre opened as the Pavilion. It was an unlicensed theatre for crude melodrama and comic songs. In 1835 it was renamed the Portman Theatre, and two years later was pulled down and rebuilt. The new theatre, known as the Marylebone, opened on 13 Nov. 1837. It continued to offer the same fare as before, and was closed several times. In 1842 it was again largely rebuilt and given the name of the Theatre Royal, Marylebone. Under the direction of John Douglass it knew a period of prosperity, playing popular melodrama and pantomime. Douglass retired in 1847, and the theatre was taken over by Mrs. Warner, the Drury Lane actress who had recently been with Phelps at Sadler's Wells. She failed, as also did E. T. Smith and J. W. Wallack, her successors. In 1858 it was taken over by Joseph Cave, who had appeared there as a boy. He remained for some years, and in 1864 the old house was rebuilt and enlarged, being renamed the Royal Alfred in 1866, when an effort was made to provide better entertainment. Charles Harcourt brought Henrietta Hodson and the company from the Queen's Theatre, Long Acre, there, but in 1870 it reverted to its old name of the Marylebone, and to melodrama. Towards the end of the nineteenth century it was again rebuilt and renamed the West London, still remaining faithful to melodrama. It became a cinema in 1932 and was damaged by enemy action in 1941. It was then used as a warehouse. While being finally demolished in 1962 it was destroyed by fire. Its history has been written in two booklets by Malcolm Morley. W. MACQUEEN-POPE†, *rev.*

The Scala was at one time (1820) known as the West London.

WESTERN. (1) (PAULINE) LUCILLE (1843–77), and (2) HELEN (1844–68), American actresses, daughters of a comedian and of his actress-wife, who by a second marriage after his death became Mrs. Jane English, the name by which she is usually known. The children toured with their mother and step-father in a mixed entertainment which gave plenty of scope for their precocious talents in acting and dancing. Helen died before she could become well known as an adult actress, but Lucille was noted for her playing of strong emotional parts in such plays as *East Lynne, Camille, Masks and Faces,* and *The Stranger.* One of her finest performances was given as Nancy in a dramatization of *Oliver Twist,* with E. L. Davenport as Bill Sikes and the younger J. W. Wallack as Fagin. She died at the height of her career.

WESTMINSTER PLAY, LONDON. It is now generally recognized that the contribution made to the early history of the English stage by the older schools and universities, and by the companies of boy players, was a considerable one. For a time, and mainly owing to the patronage of Queen Elizabeth and King James I, the acting of plays both in English and Latin by the 'little eyases', as Hamlet called them, had a considerable vogue, and their popularity was such that they were viewed with dislike by the recognized adult companies. Apart from the plays produced by the Children of the Chapel Royal and by the Children of Paul's, there are records of theatrical performances during the sixteenth century by the boys of Eton, Winchester, Westminster, Shrewsbury, St. Paul's, and other schools, and by the undergraduates of Oxford and Cambridge. In the first years of the seventeenth century their popularity began to wane, and in the twentieth century the annual Latin Play at Westminster School alone survived, and preserved a more or less unbroken tradition from the sixteenth century.

Some confusion has, however, resulted from the fact that those who have written on the early history of the Westminster Play have failed to realize that there were three distinct 'sets' of boys at Westminster who presented plays. First the Queen's or King's Scholars, who are invariably referred to in the records as 'the Children of the grammar school'. They acted an annual play, usually at Christmas, and always in Latin, and this is the ancestor of the modern Westminster Play. It has always been acted by the boys who are in 'College'. Secondly, there were the Town Boys or Oppidans, as distinct from the Scholars, who from time to time acted a play in English. This was known as the Town Boys' Play and was probably always an unofficial production. Lastly, there were the Choir Boys of Westminster, who were a separate school with their own schoolmaster. They are always referred to in sixteenth-century records as 'the Children of Westminster' and their plays were invariably in English and suitable to their education and upbringing.

The origin of the Westminster Play is probably to be found in the Christmas ceremonies connected with the election of the Boy Bishop in medieval times, but there is definite evidence to show that the acting of plays by Terence and Seneca was introduced at Westminster during the headmastership of Dr. Alexander Nowell (1543–55), who has a further claim to fame both as the writer of the Shorter Catechism and as the inventor of bottled beer. When the school was re-founded by Queen Elizabeth in 1560 a clause was inserted in the Statutes enjoining the annual presentation of a Latin play by the Scholars on the grounds of the advantages to be derived by them from a habit of correct action and pronunciation. The Latin Play thereby became an annual event. Several of the bills of expenses for these plays have been preserved among the muniments of Westminster Abbey (see L. E. Tanner, *Westminster School*, pp. 123–6, and Motter, pp. 272–4, where they are printed). It was perhaps natural that Terence and Plautus should hold the stage, but occasionally performances were given of plays by other authors. The most interesting of these was, probably, the performance of the *Sapientia Salomonis* given in the College Hall in January 1566 in the presence of Queen Elizabeth and the Princess Cecilia of Sweden. The Queen had also been present two years before at the performance of the *Miles Gloriosus* when the exertions of the youthful actors were such that xijd. had to be expended 'for buttered beere for ye children being horse'. All these performances took place in the ancient and still existing College Hall, formerly the Abbot's Dining Hall. The Play was given every Christmastide until the outbreak of the Civil War in 1642.

It is a curious fact that there is no further record of the Play until sixty years later, when it reappears in 1704 apparently as a well-established annual event. The missing period covers most of the long headmastership (1638–95) of the famous Dr. Richard Busby (1605–95). He was himself, however, no enemy to acting, for as an undergraduate he had acted in *The Royal Slave* (1636) before the King and Queen at Christ Church, Oxford, with such success that he had contemplated taking up the stage as a profession. It is probable that the Play was in fact revived at the Restoration, for James Russell, writing as a Westminster boy (*c.* 1660–6), states that the boys 'are to act a play very shortly', and it is recorded that Barton Booth, who was at the School from 1689 to 1698, received his 'first encouragement in acting from his Master . . . Dr. Busby at the rehearsals of a Latin play acted at that school'. At any rate in 1704 the *Amphitruo* was acted complete with Prologue and Epilogue, and in this form and from that date the records are continuous. 'At first the Epilogue was a monologue; in due course it became a dialogue, and it has finally developed into a witty and scholarly satire in Latin on contemporary events, in which all the characters [in the Play] play a part and appear in modern dress. The Prologue, on the other hand, has tended more and more to become a serious review of the events of the past school year. To the student of the last centuries the Prologues and Epilogues of the Westminster Play are an invaluable storehouse of allusions, and not infrequently preserve the memory of events or words of topical interest which would otherwise have passed into oblivion.' (L.E. Tanner, *Westminster School*, p. 61.)

The cycle of plays has always included the *Adelphi*, *Andria*, and *Phormio*, but the fourth play has varied. The *Eunuchus* was acted until 1860, when the *Trinummus* of Plautus took its place. In 1907 the *Eunuchus* was revived as the *Famulus*, but in 1926 it gave place to a revival of the *Rudens*, which now appears to have established itself in the cycle.

The Play was originally acted in the College Hall. After the Restoration it was transferred to the Old Dormitory of the King's Scholars in Dean's Yard. In 1730 it was again transferred to the New Dormitory in Little Dean's Yard and continued to be acted there until 1938. In May 1941 the Dormitory was gutted by an incendiary bomb.

Apart from the usual 'properties' there is evidence that in the sixteenth century there was some attempt at providing scenery. In 1565, for instance, a painter was paid for 'drawing the cytee and temple of Jerusalem and for paynting towres' for the *Sapientia Salomonis*. This may, perhaps, have been exceptional, and in general no doubt the Hall with its 'screens' and musicians' gallery provided a simple and adequate setting. In the eighteenth century a back-scene representing Covent Garden was considered sufficient, but in 1758 'Athenian' Stuart devised a more suitable classical background. This 'impossible mountain with a temple perched on the top of it', lit by a chandelier which 'with glittering improbability' hung from the skies in the middle of the stage, remained until 1858, when Professor C. R. Cockerell, R.A., an Old Westminster, designed a drop-scene representing the Bay of Salamis and a back-scene of Athens and the Acropolis. These exceedingly beautiful scenes, painted by Fenton, Phelps's scene-painter, remained in use until 1938, though a special back-scene was designed for the revival of the *Rudens*.

In early days the dresses of the actors were hired from the Office of the Revels and thousands of pins seem to have been required to make them fit the children. No doubt they were glad to take what they could get without much regard to suitability. Those playing unusual parts, such as the Furies in the *Mostellaria*, had special clothes made for them. In the eighteenth century, following the convention of the time, the actors appeared more or less in the ordinary dress of the period, and it was not felt to be incongruous if Choerea appeared in the full uniform of the Guards, or Davus in the livery of an eighteenth-century footman. It was not until 1839 that classical costumes were introduced; but the older convention survived in the Epilogue, where the actors wore the modern dress appropriate to their parts. The Prologue was always spoken in front of the curtain by the Captain in knee-breeches, buckled shoes, evening dress, gown, and bands.

Other stage traditions may also be noticed—some of which survived only on the Westminster stage. The auditorium was divided into separate 'pits'—Seniors, Masters, Ladies, etc. The Dean presided on the second night, and the senior or most distinguished Old Westminster present, on the third and last night. At the conclusion of the Epilogue they called for the 'Cap'—an ancient custom suggestive of the hunting-field rather than the theatre. The audience passed through the King's and other 'Bars' (i.e. Toll Bars) to their seats. The boys were seated in the 'Gods' under the control of two 'Gods' Monitors' who, by waving their tanning-canes at traditional places in the text, ensured that applause was not withheld.

Not the least important part of the Play was the audience, which in distinction found no parallel elsewhere. Not only was the Play the annual meeting-place for Westminsters of all generations, but ambassadors, statesmen, judges, and bishops were usually numbered in the audience, and indeed there were but few who had held high place in Church or State during the last two hundred and fifty years who were not at some time present. We have noted the visits of Queen Elizabeth. In 1800 the Prince Regent was present, and in 1834 King William IV attended a performance of the *Eunuchus*. The Prince Consort came more than once and brought the young Prince of Wales. In 1937, King George VI and Queen Elizabeth attended a performance of the *Adelphi*, and, in accordance with ancient custom when members of the royal family are present, were escorted by King's Scholars bearing torches as they crossed the Yard to the Dormitory.

The remodelling of the Dormitory, as a result of the damage inflicted on it in 1941, has meant that it is no longer possible to act the Plays there with all the ancient customs described above. But of recent years annual performances have taken place in modern dress in the open air, during the summer term, and this seems to be opening a new chapter in the history of the Westminster Play (see also ACOUSTICS, 5).

LAWRENCE E. TANNER

WESTMINSTER THEATRE, LONDON. 1. This was built by an undertaker named Gale in 1832 on the site now covered by the Wesleyan Central Hall. T. D. Davenport, reputed to have been the original of Dickens's Vincent Crummles, was its first manager. Dibdin Pitt and John Douglass followed. The theatre never obtained a licence in the four years of its existence, but William Davidge, Joseph Raynor, and Munyard, all of whom eventually achieved fame, appeared there.

2. The present Westminster Theatre in Palace Street, near Victoria Station, opened on 7 Oct. 1931 with Bridie's *The Anatomist*, in which Henry Ainley played the title-role. The theatre was under the direction of Anmer Hall [A. B. Horne] until 1938, during which time he presented a wide selection of English and foreign plays, among them *Six Characters in Search of an Author* (1932), *Waste* (1936), *Mourning Becomes Electra* (1937), and *The Zeal of Thy House* (1938). The Dublin Gate also gave several seasons at the Westminster. When Hall left, the theatre was taken over by the London Mask Theatre under J. B. Priestley, with Michael Macowan as producer. This group was still in occupation when the outbreak of war caused the closing of all London theatres, and it was the first to reopen, with Priestley's own play, *Music at Night*.

Successful productions since then have included *Distant Point* (1941), *Mr. Bolfry* (1943), *The Cure for Love* (1945), *Message for Margaret* (1946), and *Black Chiffon* (1949). Seasons were given by Wolfit, Donat, Atkins, and the Oxford Group, which eventually acquired the theatre for the production of Moral Rearmament plays, and so removed it from the commercial highway. The last successes there before the new régime were *Dial M for Murder* (1952), *Carrington V.C.* (1953), and, the last, *Any Other Business* (1958).

WESTON, THOMAS (1737–76), an English actor, whose father was head cook to George II. He joined a strolling company, and thinking himself a tragedian, played Richard III abominably. He found his true vocation in comedy, and after playing in Shuter's and Yates's booths at Bartholomew Fair, he was engaged for small parts at the Haymarket. Foote thought highly of his comic talents, and wrote for him the part of Jerry Sneak in *The Mayor of Garret* (1763). He went also to Drury Lane, alternating seasons at both theatres, being considered second to none in comedy, and surpassing even Garrick in the part of Abel Drugger. The German critic Lichtenberg has left a fine description of his playing of Scrub in *The Beaux' Stratagem*, and of his acting in general. He was somewhat dissipated, constantly in debt, and finally died of drink.

WESTRAY, a family of actresses, consisting of a mother, Mrs. Anthony Westray (?–1836) and three beautiful daughters, who were all at the Park Theatre, New York. The mother had married as her second husband at Devizes in 1792 an actor named John Simpson, and four years later the whole family went to America, where the husband died in 1801. Of the three girls, Ellen became Mrs. John Darley, and after twenty years in New York joined her sister Juliana, wife of W. B. Wood, at Philadelphia, where she was extremely successful. The third sister, Elizabeth, married the comedian Twaits.

WHARF THEATRE, NEW YORK, see CRUGER'S WHARF THEATRE.

WHEATLEY. (1) FREDERICK (?–1836), an Irish entertainer who in 1803 appeared with much success at the Park Theatre, New York, and spent the rest of his life on the American stage. He married (2) SARAH ROSS (1790–1872), who made her début at the Park in 1805 and was for many years an outstanding actress of comic elderly women, including Mrs. Malaprop and Juliet's Nurse. Her son, (3) WILLIAM (1816–76), made his début at the Park at the age of ten, playing a juvenile role with

Macready, whom he then accompanied on tour. He was for several years the chief player of children's parts at the Park, and after careful schooling made his adult début there in 1834. A hard worker, an excellent actor, and a good manager, he was at Niblo's Garden from 1862 to 1868, where his greatest achievement was the production of the spectacular ballet-extravaganza, *The Black Crook* (1866). Its success netted him a fortune, on which he retired. Of his two sisters, Julia was a singer, but (4) EMMA (1822–54) was a highly accomplished and popular actress. Frederick had also a brother Samuel on the stage, whose wife, a Mrs. Williams from London, was at the Park at the same time as Sarah and later went to Boston.

WHELAN, ALBERT (1875–1961), a music-hall comedian, who was the first to use a signature tune ('Lustige Brüder'). He was born in Melbourne, and first appeared as a red-nosed comedian in a mining camp. Back in Melbourne, he joined the company of *The Belle of New York*, in which he subsequently played in England. In 1901 he appeared at the Empire, Leicester Square, and all other principal halls. A clever performer, he never altered his style. His whistled entrance tune, his immaculate evening dress, his tall hat, his stick, his white gloves, and his wrist-watch were unchanged. But his songs were always new and entertaining.

WHITE-EYED KAFFIR, THE, see CHIRGWIN, G. H.

WHITEFRIARS THEATRE, LONDON. This seems to have been the refectory hall of the Whitefriars monastery, situated on ground in and around where Bouverie Street and adjoining thoroughfares stand today. Some stones of the old monastery can still be seen incorporated in the offices of the *News of the World*. The hall was adapted for use as a 'private' theatre, on the lines of the first Blackfriars Theatre, by Thomas Woodford and Michael Drayton in 1606, though it may have been used earlier. Its dimensions were about 35×85 ft. It was used by the Children of the King's Revels from 1608 to 1609; by the Queen's Revels, 1609–13; by the Lady Elizabeth's Men, 1613–14; and possibly by the Prince's Men thereafter. It was still in use in 1621, but its later history is obscure. Pepys, in his diary for 1660, records a visit there to see Massinger's *The Bondman*, one of his favourite plays, but he may have meant Salisbury Court, which replaced it in 1629, and with which it is sometimes confused.

W. MACQUEEN-POPE†

WHITEHALL THEATRE, LONDON, built on the site of the historic Old Ship Tavern, is a small, intimate, modern playhouse. It was opened on 29 Sept. 1930 by Walter Hackett with his own play, *The Way to Treat a Woman*, transferred from the Duke of York's. He and his wife, Marion Lorne, controlled the theatre until 1934, he writing the plays and she acting in them. Subsequent productions included *Viceroy Sarah* and *Anthony and Anna* (both 1935). After the outbreak of war the theatre housed non-stop revue with Phyllis Dixey, who remained until 1944, when *Worm's Eye View* began its long run. In 1950 the theatre was taken over by Brian Rix, who has since staged there a series of farces rivalling the pre-war popularity of the old Aldwych farces. These—*Reluctant Heroes* (1950), *Dry Rot* (1954), *Simple Spymen* (1958), *One for the Pot* (1961), and *Chase Me Comrade!* (1964)—sufficed to keep the theatre open without a break, running three or more years each, usually with the same leading actors, including Brian Rix himself.

WHITING, JOHN (1917–63), English dramatist and actor, who first came into prominence with *A Penny for a Song*, produced at the Haymarket in 1951. This won good opinions from the press and the actors, but failed with the public. Rewritten and much improved, it was put on again in their repertory season at the Aldwych by the Royal Shakespeare company, who also staged his *The Devils*(1961), based on Aldous Huxley's *The Devils of Loudon*. Whiting, who died as his reputation in England was beginning to equal that which he had achieved on the Continent, particularly in Germany, was also the author of *Saint's Day* (1951), *Marching Song* (1954), and translations of Anouilh's *Madame de ...* and *Voyageur sans bagage* (both 1959). He was for some time drama critic of *The London Magazine*. After his death a play, *Conditions of Agreement*, was found among his papers and given its first performance at the Bristol Old Vic in 1965.

WHITNEY THEATRE, LONDON, see STRAND THEATRE, 2.

WHITTLE, CHARLES R. (?–1947), a music-hall performer from the North, singer of a dozen songs with the word 'girl' in the title, of which the best was 'The Girl in the Clogs and Shawl'. The most popular of his songs, however, was 'Let's All Go Down the Strand'.

WHITTY, DAME MAY (1865–1948), see WEBSTER (3).

WHITWORTH, GEOFFREY (1883–1951), founder of the British Drama League (see AMATEUR THEATRE IN GREAT BRITAIN), which he directed from its inception in 1919 until 1948. He was also active in the cause of the National Theatre, which formed the subject of two of his books—*The Theatre of My Heart* (1930) and *The Making of a National Theatre* (1951). On 13 July 1951, two months before his death, he saw his work begin to bear fruit when Her Majesty Queen Elizabeth laid the foundation-stone of a National Theatre on the South Bank of the Thames. Whitworth was for many years on the Executive Committee of Governors of the Shakespeare Memorial Theatre, Stratford-upon-Avon, and a member of the Critics' Circle. Although his work lay mainly with amateurs, it was of considerable benefit to the English theatre as a whole. His wife, Phyllis, started in 1924 the Three Hundred Club for the production of distinguished but non-commercial plays. These included *David* by D. H. Lawrence and Van Druten's *Young Woodley*. In 1927 the Club amalgamated with the Stage Society.

WIED, GUSTAV (1858–1914), Danish dramatist, best known outside his own country by his satiric comedy *Ranke Viljer* (1906), which, as *2 × 2 = 5*, had a great success in Germany in 1908, and later in New York, where it was given in 1928 at the Civic Repertory Theatre.

WIETH, MOGENS (?–1962), Danish actor, who had been engaged to play Othello and Peer Gynt with the Old Vic company, and had just started rehearsals when he died suddenly in London. He occupied a unique position in the Danish theatre, where in the early days of the Second World War he established himself as a classical actor before he was 21. Among his outstanding parts were Peer Gynt, the Narrator in Stravinsky's 'The Soldier's Tale', Jack Worthing in *The Importance of Being Earnest* and Higgins in *My Fair Lady*. In 1948, during the celebrations held for the 200th anniversary of the Royal Danish Theatre in Copenhagen, he played ten leading parts in eighteen days. He was invited to appear in London after attaining wide popularity through his films. He had six languages at his command, and was a man of great integrity, humility, and generosity, as well as being technically and artistically a fine actor.

WIGNELL, THOMAS (1753–1803), American actor, of English extraction. He was a cousin of the younger Hallam, by whom he was induced in 1774 to join the American Company, in which he quickly became leading man. He was instrumental in getting the first American comedy, Tyler's *The Contrast*, put on in New York in 1787, and in 1789 he spoke the prologue to, and played the comic doctor in, William Dunlap's play, *The Father; or, American Shandyism*. He was much admired by Washington, who attended his benefit night at the John Street Theatre in Nov. 1789. Shortly afterwards Wignell left New York and went to England, where he recruited a company to play at the new Chestnut Street Theatre in Philadelphia. Among its members were James Fennell, Mrs. Merry, Mrs. Oldmixon, and the Morrises, whom Wignell had brought with him from New York. The theatre was designed on the lines of the Theatre Royal, Bath (see Nos. 27, 28) and saw a number of distinguished performances under Wignell and his successors, Warren and Wood. In 1797 Wignell took his company to New York for a season, playing in Ricketts's Circus. It was considered superior to the American Company, but Wignell soon returned to Philadelphia, and never again essayed New York, remaining at the Chestnut Street Theatre till his death. Seven weeks before he died he married his leading lady, Mrs. Anne Merry, who later became the wife of William Warren.

WILDE, OSCAR FINGAL O'FLAHERTIE WILLS (1854–1900), Irish wit and dramatist. Educated in Dublin, he then went to Oxford, where he won the Newdigate Prize for English Verse, and, in spite of a reputation for idleness, took a First Class degree in Classics. He was the leader of a new aesthetic cult, satirized in *Patience*, where he figures as Bunthorne. In 1882 he went on a lecture tour in the United States, and had a play, *Vera*, produced in New York. It was not a success, and for some years he confined himself to the writing of novels, poems, and short tales, though a blank-verse tragedy, *The Duchess of Padua*, was also seen in New York in 1891. It was, however, with his light comedies that Wilde ultimately achieved fame on the stage—*Lady Windermere's Fan* (1892), *A Woman of No Importance* (1893), *An Ideal Husband* (1895), and finally, his most characteristic play, *The Importance of Being Earnest* (1895). In this he discarded his former vein of sentiment, which he knew to be false and a concession to the times, and returned to the pure formula of Congreve. Though all his plays have been revived, *The Importance of Being Earnest* wears best and has proved the most successful. Few comedies of the English stage have as much wit, elegance, and theatrical dexterity. His poetic play, *Salome*, was banned in England, but produced in Paris by Sarah Bernhardt in 1894, and later set to music by Richard Strauss, since when it has occasionally been revived in England. In 1895 Wilde was sentenced to two years' imprisonment with hard labour on conviction for a moral offence, and afterwards went to Paris, where, broken in health and fortune, he soon died. His life was made the subject of a play by Leslie and Sewell Stokes, given in London in 1936. He was married, and had two sons.

WILDENBRUCH, ERNST VON (1845–1909), German dramatist, who paid tribute to the new unity of Germany under the Hohenzollerns in his historical dramas, *Die Karolinger* (1882), *Die Quitzows* (1888), and *Heinrich und Heinrichs Geschlecht* (1896), which earned him the approbation of Kaiser Wilhelm II. His one realistic play, *Die Haubenlerche* (1890), was written under the influence of the new spirit of naturalism. He also wrote a play on Christopher Marlowe. His style is lively but platitudinous, with frequent repetitions of important statements, and his characters are without psychological depth. He has been termed a 'belated Romanticist', and was a capable rather than an inspired playwright.

WILDER, THORNTON NIVEN (1897–), American novelist and dramatist, whose most important work for the theatre has been done in his two stimulating and provocative plays, *Our Town* (1938), a picture of a small American community, and *The Skin of Our Teeth* (1942), a survey of man's hairbreadth escape from disaster through the ages, both of which have been awarded the annual Pulitzer Prize. The latter provided, in Sabina, an excellent part for Tallulah Bankhead in New York and Vivien

Leigh in London, where Laurence Olivier was responsible for its production. Among Wilder's earlier works for the theatre were *The Trumpet Shall Sound*, a play about the American Civil War done by students of the American Laboratory Theatre in 1927, a translation of Obey's *Lucrèce* for Katharine Cornell in 1932, a new version of *A Doll's House* for Ruth Gordon in 1937, and an adaptation of one of Nestroy's farces (*Einen Jux will er sich machen*, based on *A Day Well Spent*, by John Oxenford) as *The Merchant of Yonkers* (1938). Rewritten and retitled *The Matchmaker*, this was seen at the Edinburgh Festival in 1954, with Ruth Gordon and Eileen Herlie in a production by Tyrone Guthrie, and later at the Haymarket in London. In 1965, as a musical entitled *Hello, Dolly!*, it had a spectacular success. Wilder's *Life in the Sun*, on the legend of Alcestis, was commissioned by Guthrie for the 1955 Festival, and produced in the Assembly Hall there, but was not wholly successful, being rather three one-act plays, of which the second was the best, than a coherent whole. *Three Plays for Bleecker Street* opened at the Circle-in-the-Square in 1962. Wilder is an original and unconventional dramatist, who arouses controversy, but whose work forms a permanent contribution to the American stage.

WILDGANS, ANTON (1881–1932), see AUSTRIA.

WILKINSON, NORMAN (1882–1934), English artist, designer of some of the most beautiful settings and costumes seen in the English theatre, particularly in the years immediately before the First World War. His first work was done for Charles Frohman at the Duke of York's in 1910, but he sprang into prominence with his costumes and scenery for Granville-Barker's Shakespeare season at the Savoy, *A Midsummer Night's Dream* being particularly memorable, with its gilded fairies and 'magical iridescent forest'. His permanent set for *Twelfth Night* (1912) was also much admired (see No. 77). In the same year he designed the costumes and settings for a production of Euripides' *Iphigenia in Tauris*. He was with Playfair at the Lyric, Hammersmith, worked for C. B. Cochran and for the Phoenix and Stage Societies, and in 1932 designed *A Midsummer Night's Dream* for the Memorial Theatre at Stratford-upon-Avon, of which he was a Governor. To distinguish him from a marine artist of the same name he was usually referred to as Norman Wilkinson of Four Oaks.

WILKINSON, TATE (1739–1803), English actor and provincial theatre manager whose passion for the theatre led him, though of good family, to adopt the stage as a profession. He was given a small part by Shuter and then recommended to Garrick, who engaged him for Drury Lane. He became well known for his imitations of living actors, and Peg Woffington, offended by his mimicry of her, tried to keep him out of the theatre. They later became friends, however, and it was on his arm that she left the stage after her last appearance in 1757. Wilkinson played only minor parts until Foote, liking his imitations, took him to Dublin, where he was most successful. He failed, however, to rouse much enthusiasm in a London audience, and eventually took himself off to the provinces. After some restless years he took over the York circuit, which included also Hull and Leeds, and conducted it for about 30 years with conspicuous success. Many well-known actors, among them Mrs. Jordan, Kemble, Fawcett, Suett, Emery, and the elder Mathews, 'owed their first advancement to his discrimination'. As he grew older he became very eccentric, and the elder Mathews used to do a charming monologue in imitation of him, Foote, after a violent but short-lived quarrel. satirized him as Shift in *The Minor* (1760). In spite of his many foibles he was much loved and respected, and his death was greatly regretted. He left an interesting account of his life in his *Memoirs* (1790) and *The Wandering Patentee* (1795).

WILKS, ROBERT (1665–1732), a gifted English actor, good in tragedy but better in comedy, who to the end of his life could play young men. He was first engaged by Christopher Rich for Drury Lane, on the recommendation of Betterton, and after a season in Ireland returned to play the parts of Mountfort, who had just been assassinated. He became very popular with the public and with his fellow actors, but on being appointed joint manager of Drury Lane he found himself constantly at odds with the parsimonious Doggett, who eventually retired in favour of Booth. Wilks was the first to play the fine gentlemen of Cibber's plays and the heroes of Farquhar, his most famous part being Sir Harry Wildair. In tragedy he was at his best in the portrayal of manly sorrow, as in Macduff, when he always drew tears from his audience. He was also good as Hamlet. He was a conscientious, hard-working actor, but his fiery temper often led him into trouble, and caused several of the company to migrate to Lincoln's Inn Fields Theatre.

WILLARD. (1) EDWARD SMITH (1853–1915), English actor, chiefly remembered for his villains in contemporary melodrama. He made his first appearance on the stage at Weymouth in 1869, and remained in the provinces, except for a short engagement at Covent Garden in 1875, until 1881, in which year he first came prominently before the public as Clifford Armytage in *The Lights o' London*. His reputation was enhanced by his Captain Skinner in *The Silver King* (1882), and he remained with Wilson Barrett until 1886, playing in all the latter's subsequent productions. Among Willard's later successes were *Jim the Penman* (1886) at the Haymarket, and Jem Dalton in a revival of *The Ticket-of-Leave Man* at the Olympic in 1888. In the following year he went into management at the Shaftesbury, where he produced among other things *The Middleman* (1889), himself playing Cyrus Blenkarn. He then went to America with such success that he returned there annually for some years, touring the United States and Canada with a repertory of successful plays. Among them was *The Professor's Love Story* (1894) in which he made a great hit, thus proving, what his earlier performances in *Arkwright's Wife* and as Tom Pinch had made apparent, that he could handle tenderness and emotion with the same skill as villainy. He retired from the stage in 1906.

(2) His nephew, EDMUND (1884–1956), who acted for some time under the name of Vassal Vaughan, made his début under his uncle's management at the Tremont Theatre, Boston, in 1900. He made his first appearance in London in 1903, and after touring for many years in the provinces, he played a series of Shakespeare parts at Stratford in 1920 and 1921. He was at his best in strong dramatic parts, Macbeth, Othello, Jones in *The Silver Box*, Lopakhin in *The Cherry Orchard*, Matvei in *Distant Point*. One of his last and finest parts was the sinister Jonathan Brewster in the long run of *Arsenic and Old Lace* (1946).

WILLIAM STREET THEATRE, NEW YORK, used, probably by amateurs, in 1790 for entertainments and comedies. Among the plays produced there were *The Miller of Mansfield* and *George Barnwell*, and Dunlap's farce, *The Soldier's Return*. There was also a pantomime of Robinson Crusoe with a display of transparencies and Italian Shades, or shadow shows.

WILLIAMS, BARNEY (1823–76), American actor, who with his wife (Maria Pray, the sister of Mrs. W. J. Florence) toured the United States, mainly in Irish comedies. They were both seen in London in 1855 in *Rory O'More*, and remained for four years, returning to New York to continue their Irish impersonations, which became a tradition in the theatre. Williams was for two years manager of Wallack's old theatre, which he rechristened the Broadway, but soon found that touring was both pleasanter and more profitable, and once more took to the road. He made his first appearance in 1836 and his last in 1875, and to the end remained not so much an actor as an entertainer, a much-loved, jovial, rollicking, drinking, stage Irishman on the boards and off.

WILLIAMS, BRANSBY [BRANSBY WILLIAM PHAREZ] (1870–1961), a top-line music-hall performer who for many years specialized in the presentation of characters from Dickens and Shakespeare, musical monologues, and imitations of famous actors. He had made many appearances as an enthusiastic amateur, in the intervals of tea-tasting in Mincing Lane, before, encouraged by William Terriss, he joined a provincial stock company, playing a variety of parts which laid the foundation of his excellent technique. He deserted the theatre for the music-hall in 1896, making his first appearance as an impersonator at the London, Shoreditch. Shortly afterwards he deputized at short notice for Dan Leno at the Tivoli with such success that he was immediately engaged on his own account, and he soon became one of the most popular entertainers of his day, both in England and America. In 1904 he was commanded to Sandringham to play before King Edward VII. He was a fine low comedian in pantomime, and in his later years a star of radio. Among his most famous recitations (to music) were Milton Hayes's 'The Green Eye of the Little Yellow God' and 'The Whitest Man I Know'. He appeared in Irving's double part of Lesurques and Dubosc in *The Lyons Mail*, and also as Micawber and Peggotty in *David Copperfield*. At Birmingham in 1923 he even essayed Hamlet. Towards the end of his long professional life he appeared with great success on television. In 1954 he published a volume of reminiscences.

WILLIAMS, EGBERT AUSTIN (*c.* 1876–1922), Negro comedian, usually known as Bert Williams, who came from the Bahamas as a child and later joined a minstrel troupe. In 1895 he teamed up with George Walker, also a Negro comedian, and their vaudeville act was successfully produced at Koster and Bial's, New York, in the following year, after some time spent on tour in perfecting it. By 1903 Williams was in a position to produce an all-Negro musical comedy, *In Dahomey*, which was given with much success in New York and London. It was followed by several others, but after the death of his partner in 1909 Williams gave up management and went as leading comedian to the Ziegfeld Follies, writing his own material. Off-stage he was a tall, serious, and scholarly man, light in colour, but for his performances he blacked himself and portrayed the shuffling, shiftless nigger of tradition. He had great gifts, and might, had circumstances permitted, have become a great actor. In his chosen line he did excellent work, and was a pioneer for his race in the American theatre.

WILLIAMS. (1) (ERNEST GEORGE) HARCOURT (1880–1957), English actor and producer, who at the end of 1947 celebrated his stage jubilee while appearing as William the Waiter in a revival of *You Never Can Tell*. He made his first appearance in Belfast with Benson, after studying for the stage under Kate Bateman (Mrs. Crowe), and with the same company first appeared in London in 1900. He was associated with a number of leading actors, including Kate Rorke, Ellen Terry, H. B. Irving, whom he accompanied to America, and George Alexander, and was seen in many interesting new plays, including those of Ibsen, Shaw, and Granville-Barker. His career was interrupted by the First World War, but in 1919 he was seen in *Abraham Lincoln*, and later appeared as the Player King in John Barrymore's *Hamlet*. From 1929 to 1934 he was producer at the Old Vic, where his innovations in Shakespearian production were first criticized and later hailed as epoch-making, based as they were upon the ideas advanced by Granville-Barker in his *Prefaces to Shakespeare*, and Williams's own love of and feeling for the swiftness and splendour of Elizabethan verse. He also introduced Shaw into the repertory, a precedent not often followed. In 1937 he gave a fine performance as William of Sens in *The Zeal of Thy House*, which he also produced, and some years later returned to the Old Vic company, with which he visited New York in 1946. In 1935 he published a volume of reminiscences, *Four Years at the Old Vic*. In 1908 he married the distinguished actress (2) JEAN STERLING MACKINLAY (1882–1958), who studied for the stage with Dame Geneviève Ward, made her first appearance in 1901 with Benson, and was later with both Hare and Alexander. She was prominently associated with the movement for a Children's Theatre in England and for twenty-seven years staged a unique series of children's matinées at Christmas-time.

WILLIAMS, (GEORGE) EMLYN (1905–), Welsh actor, dramatist, and producer. He was a member of the O.U.D.S. while at Oxford, and in 1927 made his first appearance on the professional stage in *And So To Bed*. Among his early (and otherwise unsuccessful) plays was an adaptation of *Prenez garde à la peinture* as *The Late Christopher Bean* (1933) which ran for over a year with Edith Evans as Gwenny; but his first outstanding success, both as actor and author, was scored with *Night Must Fall* (1935), both in London and in New York. Among other excellent performances which he has given are Angelo in *Measure for Measure* at the Old Vic in 1937, and Sir Robert Morton in *The Winslow Boy* in 1946. In 1962 he successfully took over the part of Sir Thomas More in the American production of *A Man For All Seasons*, following Paul Scofield. He became widely known for his impersonation of Dickens in a 'one-man reading' from the latter's works, first seen in 1951, in which he toured the world, and also for *A Boy Growing Up* (1955), a reading from the works of his fellow-countryman, Dylan Thomas. Some of his best work on the stage has been done in his own plays, some of which he produced. Among them are *Spring 1600* (1934); *He Was Born Gay* (1937) (which, as one critic put it, unfortunately 'died young'); *The Corn Is Green* (1938), perhaps his best and certainly his most popular play, in which he played the young Welsh miner with Sybil Thorndike as the schoolteacher, Miss Moffat; *The Light of Heart* (1940); *The Morning Star* (1941); *The Druid's Rest* (1944); *The Wind of Heaven* (1945); *Someone Waiting* (1953); and, his last to date, *Beth* (1958). In 1961 he published an autobiography, *George*, a finely written, moving account of his youth up to his first appearance on the stage, which ranks with Moss Hart's *Act One* as one of the best theatrical autobiographies of modern times.

WILLIAMS, 'TENNESSEE' [THOMAS LANIER] (1914–), American playwright, whose outspoken plays have caused much controversy, particularly in England and Ireland, where he has found himself banned and booed. It has been said of him that he writes of the worst human frailties and excesses as if he shared them, and, being a bad hater, finds himself reluctant to condemn them, a combination the 'moral man' finds it hard to forgive.

Born in Columbus, Mississippi, and brought up in St. Louis, he had a hard youth, working in a factory and as a waiter during the years of depression. He nevertheless managed to finish his university education, and in 1939 was awarded a Theatre Guild prize for four one-act plays entitled *American Blues*. After this auspicious start it was a bitter disappointment when his first full-length play, *Battle of Angels* (1940), failed to reach Broadway after being seen on tour. However, with his next play, *The Glass Menagerie*, he achieved success both in New York, in 1945, where Laurette Taylor made her last appearance as the Mother, and in London in 1948, where Helen Hayes played the part. Meanwhile, working feverishly in the grip of what he thought was a mortal illness, he produced *A Streetcar Named Desire* (1947), a savage, passionate play in which Jessica Tandy and Marlon Brando gave outstanding performances. In London, in 1949, Vivien Leigh and Bonar Colleano played their parts, the former giving a remarkable performance as the sex-starved drug-crazy Blanche du Bois. This play was awarded the Pulitzer Prize.

Williams's later plays, which have all eventually reached London, though usually after a time-lag has softened their initial impact, include *Summer and Smoke* (1948); *The Rose Tattoo* (1950) (closed by the police in Dublin); *Camino Real* (1953), an unsuccessful essay in symbolism based on *Don Quixote*; *Cat on a Hot Tin Roof* (1955), which was also awarded the Pulitzer Prize, but was banned by the Lord Chamberlain in England, where the Watergate Club performed it for its members only; *Orpheus Descending* (1957); *Garden District* (1958); *Sweet Bird of Youth* and *Period of Adjustment* (both 1959). The latter had a successful run in London in 1961. In 1962 *The Night of the Iguana*, with Margaret Leighton, was seen on Broadway, and briefly, with a different cast, at the Arts Theatre in London. In 1965 it was produced at the Ashcroft, Croydon, and later at the Savoy, with Sian Phillips, who gave an outstanding performance as Hannah Jelkes, and Donald Eccles as her grandfather, Nonno.

WILLIAMSBURG, VIRGINIA, U.S.A., one of the first towns in the New World to witness theatrical performances. In 1736 *Cato* was given there, probably by a group of amateurs, also *The Busybody* and, at a slightly later date, *The Drummer; or, the Haunted House*. It was at Williamsburg that Hallam's (professional) company first played on their arrival from England, opening on 15 Sept. 1752 with *The Merchant of Venice* and *The Alchemist*.

WILLIS, NATHANIEL PARKER (1806–67), early American drama critic and playwright, who wrote among other things a successful melodrama, *Tortesa the Usurer*, for James W. Wallack.

WILL'S COFFEE HOUSE, also known as the Rose Tavern, was situated at No. 1, Bow Street, Covent Garden, on the west side, at the corner of Russell Street. It was kept by one Will Unwin, and here the Restoration wits resorted after the play, to praise or damn it. They mainly congregated in a room on the first floor. There are many references in contemporary literature to this famous tavern.

WILSON, Francis (1854–1935), an American actor, who at 14 appeared in a black-face song-and-dance act which toured successfully for many years. He then worked on the staff of the Chestnut Street Theatre, Philadelphia, and subsequently appeared in a number of plays, mainly musical. It was not, however, until his appearance as Cadeaux in *Erminie* (based on *Robert Macaire*) at the Casino, 10 May 1886, that he made money and reputation. From then until 1904 he appeared in a succession of musical comedies, finally turning to straight comedy with a play by Clyde Fitch. In 1907 he appeared in *When Knights were Bold*, following it with his own play, *The Bachelor's Baby*, which ran for three years and earned him a fortune. In 1913 Wilson was elected President of the newly formed Actors' Equity Association, resigning in 1921, when he also left the stage, except for a few sporadic appearances on special occasions. An ardent book-collector, particularly of Boothiana, he wrote several volumes of reminiscences, and books on J. W. Booth and on his friends Eugene Field and Joseph Jefferson.

WILSON, John (1585–? 1641), a member of Shakespeare's company who has been confused with the eminent lutanist and Oxford Professor of Music of the same name. He was evidently a musician, since a stage direction of *Much Ado About Nothing* puts 'Jacke Wilson' for Balthasar. He must therefore have been the original singer of 'Sigh no more, Ladies'. He may have been concerned in a performance of *A Midsummer Night's Dream*, played in 1631 on a Sunday, which gave much offence to the Puritans; but this may have been the other John Wilson, or even another actor and lute-player, Henry Wilson.

WILSON, Robert (?–*c.* 1600), an Elizabethan actor and playwright, who was very well thought of in his own day and referred to as a rare man 'for a quicke, delicate, refined, extemporall witt'. He was originally one of Leicester's Men, and joined the Queen's Men in about 1583. On the breaking-up of this company during the plague of 1592–3 Wilson probably gave up acting and devoted himself to playwriting, mainly for Henslowe's Admiral's Men, and to extemporizing, a favourite Elizabethan pastime in which he is noted as having indulged at the Swan on Bankside.

WILTON, Marie (1839–1921), see BANCROFT.

WIND MACHINE, a device used off-stage to reproduce the stormy howling of wind (see TRICKWORK ON THE ENGLISH STAGE).

WINDMILL THEATRE, London. This one-tier intimate playhouse, originally a cinema, was in Great Windmill Street (so called because a windmill stood there during the seventeenth and eighteenth centuries), off Shaftesbury Avenue. It opened on 22 June 1931 with a play called *Inquest*, but the venture was not a success, and early in the following year Mrs. Laura Henderson, the owner of the theatre, and her manager, Vivian Van Damm, tried the experiment of continuous variety, which had already proved popular in Paris. The idea caught on. Performances ran from 2.30 to 11 p.m.; the Windmill Girls became a feature of London life; and many famous comedians, among them Jimmy Edwards, Harry Secombe, Eric Barker, and Tony Hancock, made their first successes on the small stage of the Windmill. It was the only theatre to remain open during the bombing of London in 1940–2, and adopted as its slogan 'We never closed'. After the death of Vivian Van Damm in 1960 the theatre continued for a time along the same lines, but finally closed on 31 Oct. 1964. The history of the Windmill was told by Vivian Van Damm in *To-night and Every Night* (1954). It is now a cinema.

WINDSOR THEATRE, New York, see FORTY-EIGHTH STREET THEATRE.

WING, a canvas-covered flat placed at the side of the stage, either facing or obliquely towards the audience, used in conjunction with a backcloth to mask-in the side of the set. There may be anything from one to eight wings on each side of the stage. Their use has been largely superseded by the closed-in box-set, except in pantomime and spectacular musical shows and in exteriors. To be 'in the wings' means to be standing in the space behind the wings, out of sight of the audience; here actors normally await their cues.

WINTER, William (1836–1917), American dramatic critic whose conservative attitude towards innovators and new tendencies in the theatre made him the transatlantic counterpart of the London critic, Clement Scott. They adopted a closely similar attitude to the stage, and their tastes and preferences in relation to acting—especially Shakespearian acting—were almost identical. Both indulged in sentimental eulogy of popular players of their time; both consistently upheld the view that conventional morality must take precedence in any conflict with aesthetic principle; and both struggled stubbornly but in vain against the insurgence of realism in modern drama. In retrospect, however, Scott can be seen to have had merits not possessed by Winter, who is unlikely—despite his contemporary prominence and repute—to be remembered in the history of criticism except, possibly, as the last champion of provincial puritanism in the theatre.

Born in Gloucester, Massachusetts, and educated at Harvard, he descended upon New York in 1859 as literary editor of *The Saturday Press*. Two years later he became dramatic critic of *The Albion* and in 1865 went to work for *The New York Tribune*, where he served as dramatic critic until 1909. His reign was a long and severe one, and his enormous success —he was the most conspicuous figure in American dramatic criticism of the period— was due solely to the mentality of his readers. During his long career he rarely committed himself to an opinion at variance with that of the great majority of his readers, who were not concerned with the fundamental tenets of sound criticism. He was undisguisedly antagonistic to foreign visiting performers—the English excepted—and his notices of Eleonora Duse, Sarah Bernhardt, and Réjane were disfigured by violent irrelevancies concerning their private lives. He denounced both Ibsen and Shaw. 'The slimy mush of Ibsen', he wrote, 'and the lunacy of Maeterlinck are made to trickle into the public mind and turn the public stomach.' And again: 'There is more true drama in Wills's *Olivia*, Young's *Jim the Penman*, Thomas's *Witching Hour*, and McLellan's *Leah Kleschna* than there is in a round dozen of the works of Ibsen.'

After his retirement from *The Tribune*, he continued to write, contributing to *Harper's Weekly* and other periodicals. He also wrote biographies of Henry Irving, Joseph Jefferson, Edwin Booth, Ada Rehan, Tyrone Power, sr., Richard Mansfield, and David Belasco. There is much valuable information in these books but, unfortunately, they are composed in such a pompous style that they make almost intolerable reading. Another book, *Other Days*, is a backward glance at the actors of an earlier generation. THOMAS QUINN CURTISS

WINTER GARDEN THEATRE. 1. LONDON, in Drury Lane, adapted from the Middlesex Music-Hall. It opened on 20 May 1919 under George Grossmith and Edward Laurillard with Leslie Henson in *Kissing Time*, transferred from the Gaiety. Leslie Henson appeared in further successes until he left in 1926, as did George Grossmith, Dorothy Dickson, and Heather Thatcher. An outstanding success in 1927 was *The Vagabond King*, a musical version of *If I Were King*, with music by Friml. During the 1930s little of note happened, and the theatre was often closed. In 1944 it was slightly damaged by blast, but it was still usable, and in 1946 *No Room at the Inn*, which dealt with the wartime evacuation of children from danger areas during the Second World War, began a long run. In 1952 Alec Clunes transferred the Arts Club company to this theatre, but without much success. Subsequently *Hotel Paradiso* (1956), with Alec Guinness, was a hit, and in 1959, after a Christmas production of *Alice in Wonderland*, the theatre closed. It was demolished in 1965.

2. NEW YORK, originally the Metropolitan. This theatre was managed by Burton in his last years. After some vicissitudes it opened as the Winter Garden on 14 Sept. 1859 with a good company under Dion Boucicault. The first production was *Dot*, Boucicault's dramatization of *The Cricket on the Hearth*, with Joseph Jefferson as Caleb Plummer and Agnes Robertson as Dot. They later played Newman Noggs and Smike in *Nicholas Nickleby*, but Boucicault's own plays occupied most of the first season. An interesting production at this theatre was that of Joseph Jefferson's early version of *Rip Van Winkle*, while the appearance in quick succession of John Sleeper Clarke, Charlotte Cushman, Edwin Booth, Sothern, and the Florences, proved how completely the United States could depend on her own great actors, and no longer needed to import them from Europe. It was at the Winter Garden that the three Booths appeared on 25 Nov. 1864 in *Julius Caesar*, a performance given to raise money for the Shakespeare statue in Central Park. Edwin played Brutus, Junius Brutus played Cassius, and John Wilkes played Antony. This was the second and final appearance in New York of Lincoln's assassin. *Julius Caesar* was followed by Edwin Booth's run of *Hamlet* for 100 performances, a record not broken until John Barrymore and John Gielgud both surpassed it; and it was at this theatre that Edwin Booth appeared in public for the first time after Lincoln's murder, to be greeted by an enthusiastic audience. They were again assembling to see Booth as Romeo when, on 23 Mar. 1867, this historic old theatre was burnt down. It was not rebuilt.

3. NEW YORK, on the site of the American Horse Exchange, 50th Street. This theatre was opened by the Shuberts on 20 Mar. 1911 with a musical show, since when it has had a glamorous and eventful life. It has been mainly given over to musical comedies and revues, including that in which Gaby Deslys made her first appearance in New York in 1911, and to the various editions of *The Passing Show*. Most of the outstanding personalities of the vaudeville stage have appeared at the Winter Garden, including Mistinguett, Al Jolson, Ed Wynn, Eddie Cantor, Bert Lahr, and many others. For some years it was a cinema but returned to live drama in 1933. In recent years it has housed musicals like *Wonderful Town* (1953) with Rosalind Russell, Mary Martin in *Peter Pan* (1954), and *West Side Story* (1957).

WINTHROP AMES THEATRE, NEW YORK, see LITTLE THEATRE, 2.

WOFFINGTON, PEG [MARGARET] (*c.* 1714–60), celebrated English actress. Born in Dublin, the daughter of a bricklayer who died when she was very young, she was befriended and educated by the famous rope-dancer Madame Violante, and at 10 was playing Polly and other parts in a children's company. She was then engaged at the Smock Alley Theatre, Dublin, where she appeared in a wide range of parts, including old ladies, Ophelia, and her later famous breeches part, Sir Harry Wildair in

Farquhar's *The Constant Couple*, in which she was first seen in Apr. 1740. She was immediately engaged by Rich for Covent Garden, and as Sir Harry became the toast of the town. She was the only one who could act the part with the spirit and elegance of the original, Wilks, and for a long while no male actor dared attempt to rival her. She had a fine figure, vivacious features, and flashing dark eyes, and her one defect was her harsh voice, which, though she managed to subdue it, rendered her unfit for tragedy. But her high-born ladies—Millamant, Lady Townly, Lady Betty Modish—her women of spirit and elegance, her homely humorous females, were all excellent. Her company was sought as much by men of sense as by the fops, for she had a good wit and charmed them by her conversation. She was known as the most beautiful and least vain woman of her day, but her good nature did not extend to her fellow actresses, and she was constantly at odds with Kitty Clive, Mrs. Cibber, and George Ann Bellamy, whom she is said to have driven from the stage and wounded with a dagger in a fit of rage. She was for some years the mistress of Garrick, who wrote to her the charming song 'My Lovely Peggy', and played opposite him both in London and Dublin before going to Covent Garden. The last male part she created was Lothario, and the last original part Lady Randolph in *Douglas*, playing opposite Barry as Young Norval. She made her last appearance on the stage as Rosalind in *As You Like It* on 3 May 1757, being taken ill at the beginning of the epilogue. She lingered on for three years, and gave herself to good works and repentance for her former life, endowing almshouses at Teddington in expiation of the past. She is the subject of the play *Masks and Faces* (1852), written by Charles Reade and Tom Taylor, on which Reade later based his novel, *Peg Woffington*. Peg's younger sister Mary, known as Polly, was also on the stage for a short time, but left it to make a brilliant marriage with Robert, second son of the Earl of Cholmondeley.

WOLFENBÜTTEL, a town in Germany, the residence until the mid-eighteenth century of the Dukes of Brunswick. Here, as early as the end of the sixteenth century, the reigning Duke, Heinrich Julius (1564–1613), no doubt under the influence of his second wife, the Danish Princess Elizabeth, had in his service a troupe of professional actors, consisting mainly of English players under Thomas Sackville. It appears from the extant Court records that Sackville was for many years in contact with Heinrich Julius, and no doubt acted in the plays which he wrote in 1593 and 1594. Although the Duke no doubt adopted some of the stage conventions of the English Comedians, the influence on his plays of the Elizabethan dramatists, and particularly of Shakespeare, has perhaps been somewhat over-rated. A careful analysis by Willi Flemming of the eleven extant dramas seems rather to show that the Duke must be regarded as a transitional figure between the sixteenth century and the baroque period. This is particularly evident in the fact that about half the plays call for a multiple set in the old tradition, while the others are set in a single scene. Unfortunately we have no evidence for the place and style of presentation of these plays in the castle, and this phase of the Court's theatrical activity soon came to an end because of the Duke's increasing political commitments. It was not until the second half of the seventeenth century that Wolfenbüttel entered upon a second period of theatrical activity, this time under the influence of France. Duke Anton Ulrich (1633–1714), who loved pomp and display, and was himself a gifted author and writer of opera libretti, took into his service a number of French actors and dancers, as well as Italian singers and musicians, and in 1688 built a theatre on the west side of the castle which was reputed to hold 2,500 spectators, and to be most lavishly decorated inside. His most famous creation, the *château* at Salzdahlum near Wolfenbüttel, modelled on Marly, also had an indoor stage and an open-air garden theatre.

WOLFIT [WOOLFITT], SIR DONALD (1902–68), English actor-manager, whose career was spent mainly in the service of Shakespeare. He made his first appearance in York, walking on in *The Merchant of Venice* in Sept. 1920. After touring with Fred Terry, he appeared in London in Nov. 1924 as Phirous in *The Wandering Jew*. He was at the Old Vic from 1929 to 1930, toured Canada as Robert Browning in *The Barretts of Wimpole Street* during 1931–2, and in 1933 was Thomas Mowbray in *Richard of Bordeaux*. He was at Stratford-upon-Avon in 1936, and in the following year formed his own company, touring extensively in a Shakespearian repertory, with which he also appeared for a season at the Kingsway in 1940. During the Battle of Britain he gave over a hundred lunch-time performances of scenes from Shakespeare, which were much appreciated by those whom the war and the black-out would otherwise have deprived of theatre. He continued to tour in Shakespeare and other classics, two of his best performances being as Volpone and as Sir Giles Overreach (in *A New Way to Pay Old Debts*). He was excellent at the Old Vic in 1951 as Tamburlaine, and as Lord Ogleby in *The Clandestine Marriage*. In 1957 he appeared at the Lyric, Hammersmith, in two plays by Montherlant, *The Master of Santiago* and *Malatesta*. He was the author of an autobiography, *First Interval*, and in the 1957 Birthday Honours he was knighted for his services to the English stage, and to Shakespeare in particular. He married Rosalind, the daughter of Iden Payne, who appeared as his leading lady in Shakespeare and other productions.

WOLHEIM, LOUIS ROBERT (1881–1931), American stage and screen actor, who had been a teacher of mathematics and a mining engineer before, in 1922, he appeared with the Provincetown Players in *The Hairy Ape* as a very realistic and brawny stoker. He then appeared at the Plymouth Theatre, New York, as the brutally aggressive Flagg in *What Price Glory?*, and from then onwards his career was entirely in the films. A tall, heavily built man, he had been a fine athlete in his youth, and had a broken nose which gave him the truly tough appearance necessary for his parts, though in private life he was gentle and scholarly.

WONDERLAND, London, see effingham saloon.

WOOD, Mrs. John (*née* Matilda Charlotte Vining) (1831–1915), actress and manageress well known in England and the United States. Member of a big theatrical family, she was first cousin to Mrs. E. L. Davenport. Born in Liverpool, she made her first appearance at Brighton as a child, and had already built up a good reputation in the English provinces when in 1854 she went to America. Widowed in 1863, she took over the Olympic, New York, later to be made famous by Mitchell, and ran it successfully for three years, leaving to make her first appearance on the London stage in 1866 as Miss Miggs in *Barnaby Rudge*. She appeared frequently in London and New York, and was from 1869 to 1877 manageress of the St. James's Theatre, London, where she was highly respected by her company and popular with the public, and from 1888 to 1891 of the New Royal Court. A woman of liberal views, she spared no expense in the conduct of her affairs, and ruled her actors firmly but kindly. Clement Scott, who had a great admiration for her, said of her in 1899:

> In a certain line of character she stood alone . . . I have seldom seen an actress so brimming over with fun, with such a keen sense of a ludicrous situation, or one who has that remarkable gift of being able to get her nature and individuality over the footlights. . . . She brings to her work . . . training and experience; she possesses all the glow and style of the old school, with the polish, nature, and finesse of the new.

WOOD, William Burke (1779–1861), the first American-born actor to hold a high place in the American theatre. With Warren he was for many years manager of the Chestnut Street Theatre, Philadelphia (see No. 28), and a diary which he kept from 1810 to 1833 contains much of interest on the history of the early American theatre. The list of plays given each season shows a marked preponderance of Shakespeare and of plays imported from England, but in later years more native offerings crept in. Wood's predilection for the English classics may have been due to his own admirable playing of polished comedy, but he was also good in the lighter parts of tragedy. He married Juliana Westray, who with her two sisters had been at the Park Theatre, New York. She appeared for many years under her husband's management, and was extremely popular and a good actress.

WOOD'S BROADWAY THEATRE, New York, see bijou theatre, 3.

WOOD'S MUSEUM, New York, see daly's theatre, 1.

WOODWARD, Harry (1717–77), an English comedian, who was with Garrick at Drury Lane, and wrote a number of pantomimes for him, basing them on the fairytales which later became so popular for this purpose. He played Harlequin himself, and was accounted a fine performer, being a nimble dancer and a master of expressive gestures. Educated at the Merchant Taylors' School, Woodward made his first appearance on the stage on 2 Jan. 1729 in a performance of *The Beggar's Opera* given by a children's company known as the Lilliputians, playing three small parts. A year later he was engaged by Rich for Covent Garden, where he was known as Lun Junior. He went to Drury Lane in 1738 and remained there for twenty years. Apart from his Harlequin, he was also considered excellent in such parts as Mercutio, Bobadil, Touchstone, Marplot, Captain Absolute (which he was the first to play), and Petruchio, with Kitty Clive as Katharina. In 1758 he went to Dublin and engaged with Macklin (who soon withdrew) and Barry in the management of the Crow Street Theatre, in which they ruined themselves and Mossop, their rival at Smock Alley. Returning to London in 1763, Woodward went back to Covent Garden, but the vogue for harlequinades was passing, and he turned his talents to burlesque and topical skits. He remained on the stage until his death and was perhaps the last of the great Harlequins, since in the early nineteenth century Grimaldi made Clown the central figure of the pantomime.

WOODWORTH, Samuel (1785–1842), early American dramatist, whose best play is *The Widow's Son* (1825), based on an actual incident in the War of Independence, and first given at the Park Theatre in New York. Woodworth, who was also a journalist, and collaborated with another American dramatist, John Howard Payne, in the editing of a Boston newspaper, wrote two domestic dramas in the European tradition, *The Deed of Gift* (1822) and *The Forest Rose* (1825). The latter, which had a musical accompaniment, contains the popular Yankee character Jonathan Ploughboy, which provided Henry Placide and Dan Marble with fine opportunities in comedy. The play was also given successfully in London. Woodworth's other plays are of less importance, but one of them, based on an incident in the life of Lafayette, was played before the latter on his visit to New York in 1824.

WOOLGAR, Sarah Jane (Bella), see mellon, mrs. alfred.

WOOLLCOTT, Alexander (1887–1943), American dramatic critic, who will probably be better remembered as the prototype of Sheridan Whiteside in the Kaufman-Hart farce, *The Man Who Came to Dinner*. He was born in Phalanx, New Jersey, and attended Hamilton College. Some years before the First World War he went to New York and worked as a police reporter on *The New York Times*. Later he graduated to the drama department and in 1914—when only twenty-seven—he was made dramatic critic. During the war he served as an enlisted man in the A.E.F. for two years, including one on the editorial council of the service paper, *Stars and Stripes*. In 1919 he returned as dramatic critic for *The New York Times*. In 1922 he went to *The New York Herald* and the following year was transferred to *The Sun*. From 1925 to 1928 he was dramatic critic for *The New York World*, but after 1928 he retired from active newspaper reviewing and devoted himself to broadcasting, lecture tours, and the writing of magazine articles.

Woollcott's judgements were capricious in the extreme. It has been said that he had every aptitude for literature except a taste for the first-rate. His critical opinions were certainly extravagant. Unqualifiedly he nominated Charlie Chaplin as 'the greatest living actor' and *The Skin of Our Teeth* as 'head and shoulders above anything else ever written for our stage'. On the other hand, he found some of Eugene O'Neill's work (*Strange Interlude* and *Mourning Becomes Electra*) completely worthless and seems to have missed much of importance that came before him during his reviewing years. Actually he was more interested in players than in plays. He wrote the lives of Mrs. Fiske, Irving Berlin, Charlie Chaplin, and the Marx Brothers, and discoursed—in print and over the radio—on Maude Adams, Helen Hayes, Maxine Elliott, Ruth Gordon, and Katharine Cornell.

A fat, owlish man, both sharp-tongued and sentimental, he cut a colourful figure on the Broadway of his period. His idiosyncrasies, foibles, and *bons mots* have been recorded by many of his contemporaries, and Samuel Hopkins Adams has written an informative and full-length biography of him. Woollcott's criticism was of the ephemeral variety, but he wrote in a bright manner and with a shrewd understanding of popular taste. He turned playwright on two occasions, collaborating with George Kaufman on *The Channel Road* (1929) and *The Dark Tower* (1932), and actor on three—*Brief Moment*, *Wine of Choice*, and in the road company of *The Man Who Came to Dinner*.

His books include *The Command Is Forward*, *Mr. Dickens Goes to the Play*, *Enchanted Aisles*, *Going to Pieces*, *While Rome Burns*, *Long, Long Ago*, and *As You Were*.

THOMAS QUINN CURTISS

WORMS, Gustave-Hippolyte (1836–1910), French actor, who studied under Beauvallet and in 1858 made his début at the Comédie-Française, playing young lovers in comedy and tragedy. He soon proved himself a good actor but, tired of the internal politics which hindered his reception as a member of the company, he left it to go to Russia, where he spent several successful and profitable years. Back in Paris in 1877, he was to have gone to the Gymnase, but the Comédie-Française, recognizing their mistake in letting him go, asked him to return. This he did, making a great success as Don Carlos, with Mounet-Sully as Hernani, and Sarah Bernhardt as Doña Sol. Zola, who admired his intelligence and his artistic integrity, said that he gave the monologue in his part so well, and so calmly, that all the applause was for him, and 'the realist beat the romantic on his own ground'. Dumas *fils*, in several of whose plays Worms appeared, said his voice 'was the voice of honour itself', and he was at his best in heroic parts or in the gentlemanly heroes of old comedy. For many years he was a professor at the Conservatoire.

WREN, Sir Christopher (1631–1723), English architect, designer of St. Paul's Cathedral and the Sheldonian Theatre, Oxford, and of the 1672 Drury Lane Theatre (see ARCHITECTURE and No. 30).

WYCHERLEY, William (1640–1716), Restoration dramatist, whose comedies, though coarse and often frankly indecent, show so much strength and savagery in attacking the vices of the day that their author has been labelled 'a moralist at heart'. Educated in France and at Oxford, Wycherley was to some extent influenced by Molière, but he transmuted his borrowings by his own particular genius, and his style has an individuality seldom found in other writers of the time. His first play, which brought him the patronage of the Duchess of Cleveland, was *Love in a Wood; or, St. James's Park* (1671), followed by *The Gentleman Dancing-Master* (1672), based on Calderón and the least characteristic of Wycherley's plays. His best-known work is *The Country Wife* (1674–5), in which the comedy hinges upon the efforts of a jealous husband to keep his young but naturally wanton country wife from the temptations of London life, which she takes to only too easily. It was revived several times and in 1766 was adapted by Garrick as *The Country Girl* and produced at Drury Lane. The part of the heroine was a favourite with Mrs. Jordan, who played it inimitably, though she might have shone even more in the original version. This was not seen in London again until revived in 1924 by the Phoenix Society, with a fine cast. The play was later seen at the Old Vic. Wycherley's last play, considered by many critics to be his finest work, was *The Plain Dealer* (1676), which Dryden called 'one of the best, most general and most useful satires that has ever been presented on the English Theatre'. This view has been often disputed, and Wycherley's morality called in question, but the play was certainly successful in its own day, and its author was dubbed 'Manly' Wycherley from the name of its hero, with whose outspoken and misanthropic bent he doubtless had much sympathy. It was frequently revived up to the turn of the century, and in 1925 was given in London by the Renaissance Society. Wycherley, who contracted a secret marriage with the widowed Countess of Drogheda, which brought him into disfavour with Charles II and later landed him in prison for debt, was somewhat unhappy in his later years, but was cheered by the friendship of the young Alexander Pope, who revised many of his poems.

WYLIE, Julian (1878–1934), English theatre manager, whose real name was Samuelson. He was born in Southport and proud of being a Lancastrian. He showed a leaning towards the theatre and showmanship from his earliest youth, and Barnum himself was anxious to adopt him. Having built up a big connexion in Manchester as an agent, he went to London, married, and started out to conquer the metropolis with a pound lent him by his wife, to whom he was all his life devoted—and she to him. His business grew, and he added to it an 'ideas department', advising the artistes he represented how best to use their talents and build up their acts. He was himself a very accomplished illusionist and invented a 'talking head', which, without any body attached, answered questions put to it by the audience. In addition to his mastery of stage magic he was well versed in theatre mechanics, and was probably one of the best technical producers of his day. When pantomime was at a low ebb, he rescued it, producing some magnificent specimens in the true tradition. He became the unchallenged Pantomime King of his time, and one of his proudest moments was when he produced *The Sleeping Beauty* at Drury Lane in Dec. 1929, after the traditional home of pantomime had been without one for ten years. Although pantomime was his chief concern, he will be remembered also for his production of *Mr. Cinders* (1929) and *The Good Companions* (1931). Under a brusque exterior which covered his shyness, he had a kind and gentle nature, and he adored children. This was probably the reason for his success with pantomime, for he never really grew up. His love and enthusiasm for the theatre, and his capacity for work in its service, were boundless. He died suddenly while producing his second Drury Lane pantomime.

W. MACQUEEN-POPE†

WYNDHAM. (1) Sir Charles (1837–1919), son of a surgeon named Culverwell, was one of the finest of English actor-managers, whose long and brilliant career covers the story of an epoch. He trained as a doctor in London, Dublin, and Germany, qualifying as a surgeon, but was an enthusiastic amateur actor, and made several appearances in private theatricals as Charles Wyndham (he adopted the name legally in 1886). In 1862 he made his professional début at the Royalty in a company which included Ellen Terry and W. H. Kendal. When the theatre closed after four months Wyndham decided to resume the practice of medicine, but not in England. He went to the United States, where the Civil War was at its height, and enlisted in the Federal Army. He twice resigned in order to appear on the stage, first with Grover in Washington, where he was Osric to John Wilkes Booth's Hamlet (in Apr. 1863), and secondly with Mrs. John Wood at the Olympic, New York, where he played Thomas Brown in *Pocahontas* (Oct. 1863). Both ventures ended in disaster, and he re-enlisted. His war service ended in 1864, and he returned to London with his wife and family. After appearing in Manchester in a farce written by himself, he returned to the Royalty and embarked on a series of performances of Shakespearian and other parts. This gave him a varied experience that proved useful later on. Venturing into management without much success, he returned to America and remained there for some years, becoming known as an excellent light comedian. From 1871 to 1873 he led the Wyndham Comedy Company on an extended tour of the Middle West, and in 1883 took his London company on a further tour, the first completely English venture to visit California and the West. Meanwhile he had made a success in England with *Brighton*, which he subsequently took to the Criterion, thus inaugurating an association with that theatre which was to last the rest of his life. He made it one of the foremost playhouses of London, and also built and managed the New Theatre and Wyndham's, making them equally successful. A tall, handsome man, with a mobile expressive face and a distinguished presence, he had a voice which, though at times a little husky, had great charm. A fine light comedian, he could play serious roles also, and in dramatic scenes, such as his deadly cross-examination of Felicia Hindmarsh in *Mrs. Dane's Defence* (1900), he had few equals. His judgement and his productions were alike impeccable. He delighted in roles where, in the last act, he had a long speech which put everything and everyone to rights, and in the delivery of it he was superb. Among his roles the greatest was perhaps that of David Garrick, in Tom Robertson's play, which he made peculiarly his own. He was also outstanding in *The Case of Rebellious Susan* (1894), *Rosemary* (1896), *The Liars* (1897) and *The Mollusc* (1907), to name but a few. He was knighted in 1902, and few actors have better deserved the honour, for he did much for the stage. He married as his second wife (2) Mary Moore (1862–1931), widow of the playwright James Albery. A fine actress, she remained under Wyndham's management, playing leading roles with him, until his death, when she continued in the management of his theatres. She made her first appearance on the stage at the Gaiety, under John Hollingshead, but gave up acting on her first marriage, not returning to the theatre until 1881, when she first appeared (as

Miss M. Mortimer) under Wyndham. She was outstanding in his revival of *David Garrick* (1886), in which she played Ida Ingot, and in that and other roles had few equals. Her performance in *The Mollusc*, which contained only four characters, and in which she, as leading lady, scarcely stirred from a settee, was a *tour de force*. A woman of great beauty and charm, she retained her energy, her business acumen, and her quick intelligence to the end. After her death her son (see ALBERY, 2) and Sir Charles's by his first wife, (3) HOWARD (1865–1947), who had long been associated with his father's theatres, took joint control of them, and produced a number of successful new plays and revivals.

WYNDHAM'S THEATRE, LONDON, in Charing Cross Road. This was built by Charles Wyndham, and opened on 16 Nov. 1899 with a revival of *David Garrick*, in which Wyndham and his wife Mary Moore had already appeared with great success. A number of successes followed, among them *Mrs. Dane's Defence* (1900), in which Wyndham and Lena Ashwell gave remarkable performances, and *Glittering Gloria* (1903), with James Welch and a bulldog in the leading parts. Frank Curzon, who took over the management in 1902, scored a success with *Mrs. Gorringe's Necklace* and also with *When Knights were Bold* (1907). Two years later a play by Guy du Maurier dealing with the invasion of England, under the title of *An Englishman's House*, caused a sensation, and materially increased the recruiting for the newly established Territorial Army. In 1910 Gerald du Maurier joined Curzon, and their joint management scored a number of successes, among them *A Kiss for Cinderella* (1916), *Dear Brutus* (1917), *Bulldog Drummond* (1921), and *The Ringer* (1926) by Edgar Wallace, who was for a time manager of the theatre. Six of his plays had their first productions there, the last, *The Green Pack*, in 1932, on the night before Wallace's death in Hollywood. Howard Wyndham and Bronson Albery took over the theatre and inaugurated a long series of successful productions, among them *George and Margaret* (1937), *Quiet Wedding* (1938) and its sequel, *Quiet Week-End* (1941), both revived in 1944. Among post-war successes have been *Deep Are the Roots* (1947), *Daphne Laureola* (1949), in which Edith Evans gave a fine performance, Ustinov's *Love of Four Colonels* (1951), in which he played a leading part himself, and four transfers from Theatre Workshop—*A Taste of Honey* and *The Hostage* in 1959, *Sparrers Can't Sing* in 1961, and *Oh, What a Lovely War!* in 1963.

WYNYARD, DIANA [DOROTHY ISOBEL COX] (1906–64), English actress of great personal beauty and charm, who appeared with equal success in a great variety of Shakespearian and modern parts. She made her first appearance in London in 1925, and then went on tour. From 1927 to 1929 she was with the Liverpool Repertory Theatre, where she laid the foundations of her future outstanding career. After a visit to New York in 1932, she returned to London to make a great success as Charlotte Brontë in Clemence Dane's *Wild Decembers* (1933) and in 1939 played Gilda in Noël Coward's *Design for Living*—a part originally played in New York by Lynn Fontanne. After the Second World War she spent two years (1948 and 1949) at the Stratford Memorial Theatre, where her Desdemona, Beatrice, and Queen Katharine, among many other parts, were much admired, and then toured Australia with the Stratford company. She also appeared in Moscow as Gertrude in *Hamlet*, with Paul Scofield. She was, however, always ready to appear in new plays, and was seen in Whiting's *Marching Song* (1954), Hellman's *The Bad Seed* (1955) and *Toys in the Attic* (1960), and Tennessee Williams's *Camino Real* (1957). She was created C.B.E. for her services to the English stage in the New Year Honours, 1953.

WYSPIAŃSKI, STANISŁAW (1869–1907), Polish poet and playwright, who was also a producer and scene designer. Born in Cracow, he grew up in the shadow of Mickiewicz and Słowacki, whose plays were often performed there. He studied painting for three years in Paris, and then returned to Cracow for the rest of his life, writing and producing his own poetic plays, which are based on national themes interwoven with classical symbolism. The best are probably *The Wedding* (1901), *Akropolis* (1903), and *November Night* (1904), which deals with the Polish insurrection of 1830. Some of his works were translated into English in 1933. Considered as the successor of Mickiewicz, he was the first to co-ordinate and stage the latter's vast poetic drama, *Forefathers' Eve*, in 1901. He made many innovations in stagecraft, and in revolt against the fashionable 'well-made play' he envisaged a form of 'total theatre' which included a new architectural concept of theatre building. Unfortunately his early death prevented the realization of his plans, but he had a great influence on his successors in the Polish theatre, notably on Leon Schiller.

Y

YABLOCHKINA, Alexandra Alexandrovna (1868–1964), famous Russian actress, daughter of an actor and theatre director, manager of the Tbilisi Theatre and stage director at the Alexandrinsky Theatre in St. Petersburg. She was on the stage at the age of 6, and in 1888 made her adult début at the Maly, where she remained until her death, playing Miss Crawley in *Vanity Fair* at the age of 94. During her long career she appeared in a vast range of parts that included Ophelia, Cordelia, Desdemona, the heroines of Wilde and Galsworthy, and in Russian plays from Griboyedov and Gorky to Romashov and Korneichuk. She devoted much of her time under the Tsarist régime to theatrical charities, and was chairman of the All-Russian Theatrical Society from 1916 to her death.

YAKOVLEV, Alexei Semenovich (1773–1817), Russian actor, a member of the St. Petersburg Imperial Theatre company. He was a member of a merchant family and had practically no education. His parents died when he was young, and all schooling ended when at 13 he was set to work in a wine-merchant's shop. In 1793, under the influence of the playwright Perepechin, he wrote his first play, and was persuaded by the actor Dmitrevsky to go on the stage, where he made his first appearance in 1794 as Oskold in *Semina*. Helped by his excellent presence and powerful voice, and by the counsels of Dmitrevsky, he was soon playing leading roles. His acting was mainly intuitive, and his temperament rebelled against craftsmanship and technical detail. His performances were therefore very unequal, but he had some perceptions of greatness, and tried to initiate reforms which were later carried out by Shchepkin. He was a heavy drinker, and at one time tried to commit suicide, subsequently leaving the stage for a while. On his return the public welcomed him back warmly, but his talent was declining. In Oct. 1817 he played Othello, and was carried from the stage in a state of collapse, dying shortly afterwards.

YALE. This American university had theatrical performances in its very early days, since in 1771 an annual series of plays was inaugurated to which the students invited their friends. The performance, held in the early summer and accompanied by a garden party, was usually given at a large house in the town. Among the plays performed were *The Conscious Lovers*, *The Beaux' Stratagem*, and in 1785 an original play, *The Mercenary Match* written by one Bidwell, an undergraduate in his senior year. There has been for many years an amateur dramatic society for the students, and in 1925 the official Drama Department was inaugurated, with an excellent little experimental theatre built and endowed by Edward Harkness, of which Professor George Baker, fresh from the triumphs of his playwriting course and '47 Workshop' at Harvard, was the first director. The curriculum comprises an elaborate post-graduate course, and gives instruction in design, lighting, costuming, and production, as well as the opportunity of writing plays for subsequent production. There is also in the university library a Theater Collection which houses among other things a vast dossier of photographs of theatrical material collected from all over Europe. This was begun under the supervision of Professor Allardyce Nicoll during his term of office as head of the Drama Department, and is constantly being added to.

YANSHIN, Mikhail Mikhailovich (1902–), Soviet actor and producer, who became a member of the Moscow Art Theatre in 1924. From his early days he gave proof of great talent, one of his most successful roles being Lariossik in Bulgakov's *Days of the Turbins* (1926), in which he showed warmth, intimacy, and a subtle sense of humour. Among his later outstanding classic parts were Gradoboyev in Ostrovsky's *Warm Heart*, Telyegin in *Uncle Vanya*, and Sir Peter Teazle in *The School for Scandal*. Behind the clumsy, comical exterior of many of his character parts lay hidden a great strength of character and a feeling for personal dignity. He was artistic director of the Gypsy Theatre from 1937 to 1941, and in 1950 became chief producer at the Stanislavsky Theatre in Moscow, where under his direction many new Soviet plays were produced, including *Griboyedov* (1951) by Yermolinsky, *Beauteous Maidens* (1952) by Simukov, and *The Dreaming Forest* (1955) by Shcheglov.

YATES. (1) Frederick Henry (1795–1842), English actor, friend of the elder Mathews, with whom—Yates being then in the army—he played to the troops of the Duke of Wellington near Cambrai. Mathews persuaded him to go on the stage, and he was first seen in Edinburgh, where it is said 'precocity and consummate self-confidence enabled him to play leading parts in Shakespeare with distinction'. In 1818 he went to London, where he was Iago to the Othello of Charles Mayne Young, and in the following year Falstaff to Macready's Hotspur. Having no pretensions to be anything but a useful actor, he played everything that was offered to him, and always well, but he eventually deserted tragedy for comedy, where his real talent lay. In 1825, with Daniel Terry, he took over the Adelphi and gave a series of melodramas, farces, and burlesques, being joined on Terry's death in 1829 by his old friend Mathews. Some of the best authors of the day wrote for him, and he himself was excellent in such parts as Fagin, Mantalini, and Miss Miggs. In his company, besides T. P. Cooke, Rice, and the low comedian Wright, was his wife, Elizabeth Brunton, niece of the famous Mrs. Merry. She was an excellent actress, and mother of (2) EDMUND (1832–94), a well-known journalist, friend of Albert Smith and Clement Scott, and the author of a number of light ephemeral plays. It was in a dramatization of one of his novels as *A Millionaire* (1883) that Lady Tree made her first big success.

YATES. (1) RICHARD (1706–96), English comedian, accounted in his day almost as good a speaking Harlequin as the famous Woodward. He was with Giffard's company when Garrick made his first appearance there, and was the first to play Sir Oliver Surface. His style in comedy was modelled on that of Doggett, and he was a careful and conscientious actor, seldom resorting to trickery. He was excellent in all Shakespeare's fools, and was considered the only actor of the time to have a just notion of how to play them. In all characters of low humour he was unsurpassed, but fine gentlemen and serious comedy lay outside his range. His second wife, (2) MARY ANN GRAHAM (1728–87) (his first wife died in 1753), was a fine tragic actress. Coached by her husband, Garrick, and Murphy, she made her first appearance at Drury Lane in 1754, and was at first unnoticed, owing to the ascendancy of Mrs. Cibber. On the latter's death, however, she was considered the finest exponent of classical heroines in eighteenth-century tragedy, to which her dignified presence and powerful, though monotonous, voice were eminently suitable. She was somewhat frigid in her deportment, and of little use in the portrayal of tenderness, pathos, or comedy. She made her last appearance on the stage in 1785, at a benefit for George Ann Bellamy.

YEATS, WILLIAM BUTLER (1865–1939), Irish poet and dramatist, and a founder of the Irish Dramatic Movement at the end of the nineteenth century (see IRELAND). It was to his determination and foresight that it owed its beginning, and it was his courage, his eloquence, and his acute business intelligence that combined with Lady Gregory's work to keep it alive through the first precarious years. It was his criticism that defined and guided it; it was his name that gave it distinction when little else was known of it.

Yeats's early plays, *The Land of Heart's Desire* (1894), *The Countess Cathleen* (1899), and *The Shadowy Waters* (1897–1906), are poetic plays which appeal to the innate imagination of their audiences; their themes are remote; the experience they present, though universal, is not revealed in terms of actual, contemporary life. They thus separate clearly from the contemporary European tradition in serious drama, which was based on that of Ibsen's middle plays. The next three, *The Hour Glass* (1903, 1912), *The King's Threshold* (1903), and *The Unicorn from the Stars* (1907), are, dramatically and poetically, an advance. The thought and the poetry are deepened and clarified, but the plays are also more dramatic. The first is virtually a modern morality, the third a bold piece of speculative thinking, and both are based on a similar mystical experience; in *The King's Threshold* the function of poetry and of the poet is the major theme. During, or just after, this period come the two brief peasant plays, *Cathleen Ni Houlihan* and *The Pot of Broth* (1902), and those based on the heroic legends of Ireland, *On Baile's Strand* (1904), *Deirdre* (1906 seq.), and *The Green Helmet* (1908). The 'Four Plays for Dancers' follow in 1916 and 1917: *At The Hawk's Well*, *The Only Jealousy of Emer* (1916), *The Dreaming of the Bones*, and *Calvary* (1917). In these, extreme simplicity of design and setting is matched by brevity of expression and severity of thought. In the latest plays of all, this plainness and severity, characteristic also of his poetry after 1916, reaches fulfilment, and the underlying thought makes stricter demands than ever upon the intelligence and imagination of the audience. Perhaps most characteristic of these are the last two, *The Words upon the Window Pane* (1934) and *Purgatory* (1938).

Yeats's work, whether in prose or verse, was essentially poetic, and he was unexcelled in his own time by any other poetic dramatist writing in English. UNA ELLIS-FERMOR†

YERMOLOVA, MARIA NIKOLAIEVNA (1853–1928), tragic actress of pre- and post-Revolutionary Russia, whom Stanislavsky considered the greatest actress he had ever known, not excepting Duse. She was the daughter of the prompter at the Maly Theatre, and, after attending a theatre school, made her début there as Emilia Galotti in 1870. She approached this, and her other leading roles, in a new way, making her heroines active, independent members of society, in contrast to the passive, unreal presentations of the past. She was outstanding in such plays as *Maria Stuart*, *Die Jungfrau von Orleans*, *Phèdre*, *La Estrella de Sevilla*, and *Macbeth*. On the occasion of her benefit in 1876 she chose to appear in Lope de Vega's *Fuenteovejuna*, in which she scored such a success with the more liberal-minded among her audience that it was promptly banned. Yermolova was in no whit disconcerted by the October Revolution, which her large humanity and progressive liberalism rather welcomed, and her fifty years on the stage were celebrated in 1920 with full honours and the title of People's Artist of the Republic, which may be compared with the English D.B.E. In 1930 the students of the Maly Theatre named a studio in her honour. This became the Yermolova Theatre in 1937, after its fusion with the Khmelev Studio. Khmelev himself became its director, and its first production was Gorky's *Children of the Sun*. In the following year Bill-Belotserkovsky's *Storm* and Ostrovsky's *Poor Bride* were seen, and

Khmelev then scored a great triumph with an outstanding production of *As You Like It*. Among later productions one of the most interesting was *Far From Stalingrad*, a war play by Surov, who also wrote *Dawn over Moscow*, which was less successful, being criticized for the poverty of its psychological content. Productions in recent years have ranged from the sombre tragedy of *Crime and Punishment* (1956) to Mikhalkov's gay vaudeville, *The Savages* (1958). In 1962 Shatrin produced Shteyn's *A Game Without Rules*.

YEVREINOV, Nikolai, see evreinov.

YIDDISH ART THEATRE, New York, see jewish drama, 6.

YIDDISH DRAMA, see jewish drama.

YORK. The first theatre in York was adapted from a tennis-court for Keregan's company in 1734. Previously his and other companies had acted at the Merchant Taylors' Hall, Banks's Cockpit, and elsewhere. From 1732 the season was on a subscription basis, and the company was one of the first to be a salaried instead of a sharing one. The second theatre was built by Joseph Baker, adjoining the site of the present Theatre Royal. Baker erected another and larger theatre in 1765. In the same year Tate Wilkinson, most famous of provincial managers, succeeded him, and under his régime many famous actors and actresses were trained. Hull, Leeds, Doncaster, Wakefield, Pontefract, and other towns were in the York circuit. Wilkinson died in 1803 and was succeeded by his son John Wilkinson, who later sub-let to a succession of lessees. The theatre was remodelled in 1822, the cost being defrayed by subscription. Further improvements were made in 1835. J. L. Pritchard, Henry Beverley, W. S. Thorne, and John Coleman were the lessees from 1848 to 1878. Coleman employed famous authors to write plays and pantomimes for his circuit, but eventually went bankrupt. The theatre was reconstructed in 1875 and 1880 and rebuilt in 1901. Waddington's stock company was given up about 1880 in favour of touring companies. The Theatre Royal is now used by a repertory company.

York came back into theatrical history with the revival of the York Mystery plays in 1951 and subsequently every three years.

SYBIL ROSENFELD

YOUNG, Charles (?–1874), American actor, about whom very little information is available. He was born in Australia, and managed a theatre in Hobart. He appears to have been eccentric and undisciplined, though erratically good in tragedy. He was for a short time the husband of Mrs. Duff, though the marriage was never consummated, and he was also the first husband of Jane Elizabeth Thomson, later well known on the London stage as Mrs. Hermann Vezin.

YOUNG, Charles Mayne (1777–1856), celebrated English actor, and one of the finest disciples of the Kemble school of acting. The son of a doctor, he was well educated, but owing to financial and other difficulties had to support his mother at an early age. He became a clerk, but amateur theatricals gave him a taste for the stage, and in 1798, as Mr. Green, he made his début at Liverpool. From there he went to Manchester and Edinburgh, and became an intimate friend of Sir Walter Scott. Two years later he married a young actress who had recently appeared at the Haymarket as Juliet with much success. She died in childbirth the following year, her son becoming a clergyman and author of a life of his father, who never married again. It was through the good offices of the elder Mathews, always his close friend, that Young was first seen in London in 1807, playing Hamlet at the Haymarket with much success, Mathews appearing with him as Polonius. Both actors appeared in the same parts when Young took his farewell of the stage in May 1832, with Macready as the Ghost. During his years in the London theatre he proved himself a sterling actor and an ornament to his profession. He played with John Philip Kemble, Mrs. Siddons, Macready, and Miss O'Neill, and in 1822 was with Kean at Drury Lane. The only new part of any importance which he created was Rienzi, but he was good both in tragedy and comedy, as Falstaff, Macheath, McSycophant, Falkland, Cassius, Iago, the Stranger, Hamlet, and Macbeth. Equable in temper, with a steady confidence in and knowledge of his own powers, he was welcomed everywhere, and in private life was a delightful companion, enjoying his long retirement to the full.

YOUNG, Stark (1881–1963), American dramatic critic, who was born in Como, Mississippi, and attended the universities of Mississippi and Columbia. Afterwards he was an instructor in English at the University of Texas and at Amherst College. In 1921 he joined the editorial staff of *The New Republic*. During the season of 1924–5 he was also dramatic critic of *The New York Times*. Stark Young was one of the best critics of acting in America and wrote brilliantly of the many foreign artists who came before him: the Moscow Art Company, Mei Lan-Fang, Duse, Bernhardt. He also wrote several plays, and directed productions of Lenormand's *Failures* and O'Neill's *Welded*. An expert linguist, he translated Chekhov's *The Seagull* (1939) and plays from Spanish and Italian. One of his novels, *So Red the Rose* (1934), a nostalgic picture of the ante-bellum South, achieved great success and was subsequently made into a film.

THOMAS QUINN CURTISS

YOUNG ROSCIUS, see betty.

YOUTH THEATRE, an organization founded in 1956 by Michael Croft—a master at Alleyn's School, Dulwich, who had, among other things, been an actor—for the production of Shakespeare by a selected cast of schoolboys. Drawn originally from Alleyn's and Dulwich

College, these came later from schools all over London and sometimes from far beyond. The first production, at Toynbee Hall, was *Henry V*. Since then the company, freshly recruited each summer, has appeared at the Edinburgh Festival (in *Troilus and Cressida*), at the Queen's Theatre, London (in *Hamlet*), at Sadler's Wells (again in *Henry V* and *Julius Caesar*), and at the National Theatre (the Old Vic) in *Anthony and Cleopatra* and *Troilus and Cressida*. It has also toured on the Continent. The plays have all been directed by Michael Croft, and in spite of constant financial anxiety, and the lack of central premises, the loosely knit and entirely amateur organization continues to flourish. Girls are now admitted to play the women's parts, and a certain continuity is provided by allowing youngsters to return each year until they reach the age of 21. A special production of *Hamlet* in the autumn of 1962 for presentation in provincial schools under the auspices of Wesker's Centre 42 was seen in London the following year.

YUGOSLAVIA. The early history of the theatre in Yugoslavia is similar to that of other European countries. After the Graeco-Roman period (some of whose theatres still exist, in a semi-ruined state, and are occasionally used for performances), liturgical drama evolved, and gave way to folk-plays of the indigenous peoples and Mystery plays in the vernacular. In the sixteenth and seventeenth centuries Jesuit drama flourished, and in the seventeenth and eighteenth centuries there were numerous visits from French and German companies. In spite of oppression and occupation, national theatres gradually took root, but it was not until 1918 that they were firmly established. Even today it is not possible to speak of a 'Yugoslav' theatre, for plays are given not only in the languages of the three main groups—Serbo-Croat, Slovene, and Macedonian—but also, since 1945, in the minority languages. Nor is there any one town in the country which enjoys pre-eminence in the theatre, as Paris does, or London. There is an active theatrical life in many towns—Belgrade, Zagreb, Ljubljana, Novi Sad, Skopje, Dubrovnik, Split.

There is one interesting early document still extant in this part of Europe—a Croat play-text in a Codex of 1492 which is perhaps the earliest prompt-book, with its text in black and its stage directions in red; otherwise written documents appear to date from 1721 (a Passion play in Slovene by a priest, Father Romuald) and 1733 (an historical tragedy in Serbian). The play of 1721 has its scene-headings in Latin, and its stage-directions in German. The latter was adapted and published in 1798 by Jovan Raič.

Secular Renaissance plays in the Croat language were given in Dubrovnik from 1527 onwards, among them pastorals on classical themes and farces of everyday life. A hundred years later Jesuit pupils were acting in Slovene in Ljubljana, and in 1736 students acted in Serbian at Carlowitz, which then formed part of Austro-Hungary. But these early tentatives were only scattered manifestations of the theatrical impulse. It was not until the nineteenth century that determined efforts were made to establish national theatres. A performance in Slovene was given at Ljubljana in 1789, but the turmoil of the Napoleonic wars prevented further developments. Performances in the Croat language were given in Zagreb in 1840, in a theatre built some years earlier. The actors (from Novi Sad) formed the first professional indigenous company, based on an amateur group founded in 1838 by 'the father of the Serbian theatre', Joakim Vujič (1772–1847), who also organized a Court theatre for the ruling prince, Miloš, at Kragujevac in 1843. The Novi Sad actors were in Belgrade in 1841–2, but in the absence of a theatre had to act in a converted hall in the Customs House. The first workers' theatre was established in Idrija in 1850. Plays in Slovene were given for the mining community there, in a theatre dating from 1796. This still stands, though it is now a cinema, and is the second oldest theatre building in the country—the oldest, dating from 1610 to 1612, being on the island of Hvar.

The theatre in Zagreb became a national institution with a state subsidy in 1861, and Croatian drama developed rapidly under Dmitrije Demetar (1811–72) and J. Frajdenrajh. In 1869 the present Serbian National Theatre in Belgrade opened (it has been rebuilt and modernized after damage in two world wars), and in Ljubljana, where efforts had been made since 1876 to found a permanent Slovene company, a building was finally erected and opened in 1892. In all three centres plays were given, often under difficulties, while opera and operetta flourished.

The years between the two world wars were also difficult, with centralization in Belgrade causing financial hardships in the other two centres, Zagreb and Ljubljana. There was also the censorship to contend with. But an appreciable improvement in standards of acting and production was noticeable, and the repertory was widened to include such European authors as Shaw, Ibsen, and Pirandello. Among the outstanding national dramatists whose works figured in the repertory were Jovan Sterija Popovič (1806–56), Ivo Vojnovič (1858–1928), Branislav Nušič (1863–1938), and Ivan Cankar (1876–1918). The most important theatre director of this period was undoubtedly Branko Gavella (1885–1962), who first appeared in 1914 in Zagreb, and who worked in all the theatres of Yugoslavia as well as in several towns abroad—Sofia, Prague, Milan, and others. In the 1930s Bojan Stupica did excellent work, and was often referred to as the 'Yugoslav Reinhardt' for the diversity and *éclat* of his productions.

In 1941 all theatrical life came to a standstill with the German invasion, but after the liberation companies of young actors were quickly formed, and played before soldier audiences and in the liberated towns. As in many other countries at this time, there was a sudden rapid expansion in theatrical activity and Yugoslavia, which in 1939 had twelve professional theatres, in 1949 had sixty-six. Many of these were in industrial towns and in remote places which had previously had no drama. In Macedonia, for instance, where plays were sporadically given between 1918 and 1941, there are now six theatres giving plays in Macedonian. The most important are in Skopje, where the most active producer is D. Kjostarov, a pupil of Pavlov, from Stanislavsky's company.

A Hungarian theatre was founded at Subotica in 1945. There is another at Bačka Topola, a Shiptar theatre at Priština, an Italian at Rijeka, a Rumanian at Vršac, and a Turkish at Skopje.

Although there is intense theatrical activity in many provincial towns, whose companies often tour the surrounding countryside, the chief centres are still Belgrade, Zagreb, and Ljubljana. In Zagreb the Croat National Theatre tends to stage works, whether classical or modern, which require space and large casts—Shaw's *St. Joan*, for instance, or Brecht's *Caucasian Chalk Circle*. In 1953 a group of young actors took over the small theatre attached to the National Theatre, and founded there, under Mladen Skiljan, pupil of Gavella, the Zagreb Dramatic Theatre, which has been responsible for such interesting productions as *Jovadin* (a transference into eighteenth-century Dubrovnik of Molière's *Monsieur de Pourceaugnac*), and Anouilh's *Antigone*, produced by Kosta Spaič, also a pupil of Gavella, who in 1955 worked at the Nottingham Playhouse as guest producer. This group has also put on new plays by Yugoslav authors, but, like so many countries, Yugoslavia is short of good new dramatists, and relies mainly on translations and revivals. The Comedy Theatre, Zagreb, specializes in light operetta and comedy, and the town has also a children's puppet theatre. Belgrade's National Theatre is still in its 1869 building; there is also the Comedy, which specializes in light comedy and musical shows, and the Yugoslav Dramatic Theatre, which, founded with a company drawn from all over the country, achieved great success in Paris in 1954 with a production of Marin Držic's *Dundo Maroje*. In 1956 it staged the first Irish play to be seen in Yugoslavia, O'Casey's *The Plough and the Stars*, produced by Miroslav Belovič, who was also responsible for an interesting production of Gogol's *Wedding*. The Belgrade Dramatic Theatre, which was originally formed by a group of young actors fresh from their training school, toured Yugoslavia in 1952 and inspired minor theatrical revolutions in many of the towns which it visited.

In Slovenia, as in other parts of the country, amateur societies have played a large part in the maintaining and diffusing of theatrical life, and in 1957 a new Cultural Centre which opened at Trbovlje, about 30 miles from Ljubljana, contained a small theatre, seating about 500, which is used by local amateur groups, and sometimes by visiting professionals.

An important feature of theatrical life in Yugoslavia is the annual Dubrovnik Festival of the Arts, which takes place every summer. It began in 1950, and draws on companies from all over the country, as well as some visiting artists. Most of the productions are given in the open air—Fort Revelin, Gradac Park, and Fort Lovrijenac, where a fine *Hamlet* was seen in a production by Dr. Branko Fotez, with Jovan Miličevič as Hamlet, and a practically uncut text. Other classics, like *Phèdre*, have also been given, and some modern Yugoslav plays (*Aretaeus* by Miroslav Krleža), as well as plays from the modern European and American repertory.

There are several experimental theatres in Yugoslavia, and at Ljubljana and Belgrade theatre-in-the-round flourishes, with productions of such *avant-garde* authors as Ionesco and Beckett, and the latest plays of the young Yugoslav dramatists.

Z

ZACCONI, Ermete (1857–1948), Italian actor, child of strolling players, who made his first appearance on the stage at the age of 7. After many years on tour, during which he perfected his art without attracting much attention, he became, in 1884, leading man in a company run by Giovanni Emanuel. He was soon recognized as one of the outstanding actors of the Italian stage, equalled only by Novelli, and was able to found and direct his own company. He was the first Italian actor to put on *Ghosts*, playing Oswald Alving himself, and with Duse was instrumental in reconciling the Italian public to Ibsen's plays. He produced translations of plays by Tolstoy, Hauptmann, and Strindberg, and also appeared in a number of Italian plays and in the great roles of Shakespeare. In 1899 he played with Duse in *La Gioconda* and Dumas's *Le Demi-monde*, but with small success, and they separated to tour each with his own company. He penetrated as far as Russia, being well received, and was also seen in Austria and Germany. He was accounted a most versatile actor, equally at home in old and modern plays, and in tragic and comic parts, being particularly good as Hamlet, and as the name-part in Testoni's *Il Cardinale Lambertini* (1905), a comedy of intrigue based on the life of a seventeenth-century cardinal of Bologna.

ZAKHAVA, Boris Evgenevich (1896–), Soviet actor and producer, pupil and close collaborator of Vakhtangov, participating with him in many of his productions, notably the famous *Turandot*, in which he played Timur. After the death of Vakhtangov, Zakhava produced independently many plays by Ostrovsky, Leonov, Schiller, Gorky, and others, of which the most important was *Yegor Bulichev* in 1935. He continued to act, however, and worked for two years in Meyerhold's theatre in order to study his methods. Among his later productions, which were sometimes controversial, were *Hamlet* and Dostoievsky's *The Idiot* (both 1958). He is the author of several books in which he expounds and develops the methods of Stanislavsky and Vakhtangov, and of a number of articles on the problems of dramatic production.

ZANGWILL, Israel (1864–1926), Jewish author and philanthropist, who established his literary reputation with a fine novel, *The Children of the Ghetto* (1892). He also wrote some plays, of which *The Melting Pot*, a study of Jewish immigrant life in the United States, was the most important. First produced in New York in 1908, it was a great success, and was several times revived, being first seen in London in 1914.

ZANY, the anglicized form of the Italian *zanni*, a term which covers all the male servant masks of the *commedia dell'arte*. Among them were the prototypes of the English Harlequin (Arlecchino) and Punch (Pulcinella), who have changed greatly in appearance and function; and Scapin, Scaramouche, and Pasquin, who are perhaps more famous in these French forms than in the Italian—Scapino, Scaramuccia, and Pasquino. The lovesick French Pierrot and the English Pierrot of concert-parties are also distantly derived from a zany, Pedrolino. In Elizabethan times the word, which is now rarely used in England, though still current in parts of America, always conveyed the idea of a 'clumsy imitator'.

ZARZUELA, Spanish musical play or operetta. The name comes from the Palacio de la Zarzuela, a hunting-lodge in the woods of El Pardo, not far from Madrid, and was first applied to two-act plays in which was intercalated a large proportion of music. From the days of Gil Vicente, music had formed a part of any theatrical performance, and both Lope de Vega and Calderón used songs to comment upon the action of their plays. More immediate forerunners of the *zarzuela* are Lope de Vega's *La selva sin amor* (1629), Calderón's two-act version of *El jardín de Falerina*, and Gabriel Bocángel y Unzueta's *El nuevo Olimpo* (1648), into all of which a large proportion of music is introduced. The first true *zarzuela* is Calderón's *El laurel de Apolo*, performed in 1658 in the Coliseo of the Palace of Buen Retiro, having been transferred there from La Zarzuela. *La púrpura de la rosa* (1660) and *Celos aún del aire matan* (1660), both by Calderón, are entirely sung and therefore are closer to the Italian opera than most *zarzuelas*. The music of most of these plays has been lost, but in 1933 José Subirá published that of the first act of *Celos aún del aire matan*, and in 1945 Luís de Freitas Blanco discovered that of the second act in a Portuguese library. Recently much of the music has been identified for Juan Vélez de Guevara's *Los celos hacen estrellas*. From 1660 onwards Calderón, Diamante, Zamora, the Conde de Clavijo, and Bances Candamo, among other writers, produced libretti for many of these plays, their mythological or heroic plot subtly flattering their royal audiences and revealing their purpose as courtly entertainment. The best composer is Juan Hidalgo, and with him can be named Sebastián Durón and Antonio de Literes.

In the eighteenth century the *zarzuela* suffered from competition with the Italian opera, but was revitalized by Ramón de la Cruz, who introduced new plots drawn from popular customs. The first of these is *Las segadoras de Vallecas*. The popularity of

Ramón de la Cruz's *zarzuelas* was immense, but after his death Italian opera companies ousted the native form, and the *zarzuela* suffered a second eclipse which was to last until the second half of the nineteenth century. In 1851 Barbieri staged *Jugar con fuego*, in three acts instead of the traditional two. This *zarzuela grande*, as it was called, was very successful, and in 1856 a Teatro de la Zarzuela was opened in Madrid. The best known modern *zarzuelas* are *La Gran Vía* (Felipe Pérez, Chueca, and Valverde); *Agua, azucarillos y aguardiente* (Ramos, Carrión, and Chueca); *La Revoltosa* (López Silva, Fernández Shaw, and Chapí); and, best-loved of all, *La verbena de la Paloma* (Ricardo de la Vega and Bretón). The second half of the nineteenth century was the golden age of the modern *zarzuela*, although the form persisted in popularity well into the twentieth century and still exists, in a form strongly influenced by foreign revues and musicals. J. E. VAREY

ZAVADSKY, YURI ALEXEIVICH (1894–), Soviet actor and producer, who began his career in 1916 as a pupil of Vakhtangov, in whose famous last production, *Turandot*, he appeared. In 1924 he opened his own studio with a group of young actors, several of whom joined him later on when he was appointed director of the Gorky State Theatre in Rostov. His early productions, among which were *On ne badine pas avec l'amour* and a highly praised *The Devil's Disciple*, showed the influence of Stanislavsky and Vakhtangov, but he soon evolved a personal style, combining lyricism with excellent stagecraft, and giving a larger place than usual to music. He was with the Mossoviet Theatre in 1940, but returned to Rostov during the Second World War, where he produced *Lyubov Yarovaya*, Trenev's *On the Banks of the Neva*, Gorky's *Enemies* and *The Philistines*, and *Othello*. Back at the Mossoviet after the war, his productions included *The Brandenburg Gate* (1946) with Chislyakov, Surov's *Dawn over Moscow* (1950), for which he had music and songs specially composed, a revival of Bill-Belotserkovsky's *Storm* (1953) with Stradomsky, who also appeared in *A Turkish Tale* (1957), by Nazim Hikmet, and Virta's *Endless Distance*. Zavadsky contributed not a little to the forward movement of the Soviet theatre during 1953–6, and holds a high position in theatre life today, many distinguished young actors having been his pupils. He has twice been awarded the Lenin Prize—in 1947 for a production of *The Merry Wives of Windsor*, and in 1965 for a revival of Lermontov's *Masquerade*.

ZEFFIRELLI, FRANCO (1923–), Italian producer and scene designer, who first came into prominence with his sets for Visconti's productions of *Troilus and Cressida* and *Three Sisters*. His first production of opera was Rossini's 'La Cenerentola' for La Scala in 1953. His work has since been seen at Covent Garden and the Metropolitan, and in many other opera-houses throughout the world. Although mainly known for his work in opera, he has produced a number of plays, notably *Romeo and Juliet* at the Old Vic in 1960 with John Stride and Judi Dench, and *Othello* at the Royal Shakespeare in 1961 with John Gielgud and Dorothy Tutin.

ZENO, APOSTOLO (1668–1750), for many years Court poet at Vienna, the predecessor there of Metastasio, and like him a writer of libretti for *melodramma*, plays where words and music have equal weight. These have since been used by numerous composers as operatic libretti. He had his first resounding success in 1695, when *Gl'Inganni felici*, with music by Carlo Francesco Pollardo (1653–1722), was first performed at the Teatro Sant'Angelo in Venice. A later *Lucio Vero* (1700), with music by the same composer, was also successful, and has been set by about twenty composers since. Zeno produced a drama every year for the Court at Vienna, some of them in collaboration with Pariati. Most of his subjects were taken from classical history and mythology (see ITALY 3 *a*).

ZIEGFELD, FLORENZ (1867–1932), American theatre manager, son of the President of the Chicago Musical College. He originated and perfected the American theatrical revue in a series of productions called the *Ziegfeld Follies*, which began in 1907 and ran for twenty-four consecutive editions under the caption 'An American Institution'. He borrowed his pattern largely from the Folies-Bergère, Paris, basing the emphasis on beautiful girls, scenic invention, comic sketches, and noteworthy vaudeville specialities. His name connotated prodigality in both his theatrical and his personal life. He spent thousands on production numbers which he discarded after a first night. He outbid other managers for stars whose services he wanted, and when he travelled it was in luxurious style with a retinue of attendants—chauffeurs, secretaries, and a valet. His slogan, 'Glorifying the American Girl', resulted in making the Ziegfeld girl symbolize perfect American beauty for more than three decades. His standard of female perfection was adopted largely by the early motion pictures, many of whose first stars were Ziegfeld girls, including Olive Thomas, Mae Murray, Marion Davies, Irene Dunne, Martha Mansfield, and Paulette Goddard.

Engagement in a Ziegfeld production was counted a primary theatrical honour because of the producer's superb taste and critical selectivity. He was a star-maker and a discoverer of talent, chiefly responsible for bringing into prominence such famous stars of the stage, screen, and radio as Fannie Brice, W. C. Fields, Eddie Cantor, and Bert Williams. Among the artists, national and international, who played under his aegis were Anna Held, Maurice Chevalier, Fred and Adele Astaire, Lupino Lane, Billie Burke, Nora Bayes, Marilyn Miller, Sophie Tucker, and Evelyn Laye. Among those associated with him in his productions were Joseph Urban, scenic artist; Victor Herbert, Irving Berlin, Sigmund Romberg, George Gershwin, and Richard Rodgers, composers; J. P. McEvoy, Irving Caesar, Ring Lardner, William Anthony McGuire, and Oscar Hammerstein II, librettists and lyricists. His productions included, in addition to the Follies, *The Red Feather*, *The Comic Supplement*, *Kid Boots*, *Sally*, *Showboat*—one of the finest musical comedies in the history of the American stage—and numerous straight plays. Ziegfeld's second wife (the first was Anna Held) was Billie Burke (1885–1970), who made her stage début in London and went to America to be John Drew's leading lady. She became one of the most popular comediennes of the American stage, and later appeared extensively in films and on the radio. She wrote a volume of reminiscences, *With a Feather on My Nose* (1949). The life of Ziegfeld was the subject of a film by M.G.M.

BERNARD SOBEL†

ZIEGFELD THEATRE, New York. This opened on 2 Feb. 1927, and was one of the handsomest playhouses in the city, superbly designed by Joseph Urban to provide more than adequate backstage space, a handsome auditorium, and a fine, stark exterior. Its life was a short one, for the great American showman for whom it was built and named was nearly at the end of his career, but he saw several successes there before he died in 1932. Among them were *Rio Rita*, the opening attraction, *Showboat*, *Bitter Sweet*, and the *Ziegfeld Follies* of 1931. In 1932 the theatre became a cinema, but on 7 Dec. 1944 it was reopened as a theatre by Billy Rose, with Beatrice Lillie in *Seven Lively Arts*. Carol Channing appeared as Lorelei Lee in the musical version of *Gentlemen Prefer Blondes* (1949), and the theatre also housed a revival of 'Porgy and Bess' (1953). From 1955 to 1963 it was used for television, but returned to live production with an evening of songs and sketches starring Maurice Chevalier; in 1963 *Foxy*, starring Bert Lahr, was seen there. The building was demolished in 1967.

ZIEGLER, Clara (1844–1909), German actress, who from 1867 to 1868 was in Leipzig, and later went to Munich for some years as guest artist. A beautiful woman, with a particularly lovely voice, she was at her best in such parts as Joan of Arc, Penthesilea, and Medea; she also, in the tradition of her day, played Romeo. She was the author of several plays, and on her death left her house and library to the city of Munich as a theatre museum, together with money for the maintenance there of a theatre collection. The idea of such a museum first came to her in 1892, when visiting the International Music and Theatre Exhibition in Vienna, and it was formally opened in 1910. Its curator for many years was the famous German theatre historian, Franz Rapp. Several other collections have been added to the original deposit, and in 1932 extra space for display was acquired elsewhere, the house being used for the books and catalogues, and such special treasures as the first film made by UFA and unique records of broadcast plays.

ZILAHY, Lajos (1891–), Hungarian dramatist, author of a number of plays dealing realistically with the social problems of the post-1914 period.

ZOFFANY, John (1733/5–1810), a painter, of Bohemian extraction, who in 1758 settled in London and remained there until his death. Among his works were many theatrical portraits, particularly of David Garrick—as Abel Drugger, as Jaffier (with Mrs. Cibber), as Macbeth (with Mrs. Pritchard), as Sir John Brute and so on. He also painted Samuel Foote, Shuter, King, and other actors, either singly or in groups from a particular play, as for example King and Mrs. Baddeley in *The Clandestine Marriage*, and a scene from *Love in a Village*. Many of his paintings are in the possession of the Garrick Club.

ZOLA, Émile (1840–1902), French novelist and dramatist, leader of the naturalistic school. He much disliked the facile, optimistic plays of Scribe and his followers, and thought that a play should be a 'slice of life', thrown on the stage without embellishment or artifice. His own plays, particularly *Thérèse Raquin* (1873), which he dramatized from his novel of that name, carry out this theory, which he developed at greater length in his critical articles, later republished in two volumes as *Le Naturalisme au théâtre* and *Nos Auteurs dramatiques*. The second volume castigates the major dramatists of the time, of whom Zola had a very poor opinion, and is less interesting than the first, in which he deals mainly with his own ideas of reform. It is as a novelist that Zola is chiefly remembered, but he had an important influence on the development of the French, and through that of the European, theatre of his day and afterwards. His novel, *L'Assommoir*, was dramatized by Busnach and Gastineau, and in an English version as *Drink*, by Charles Reade and Charles Warner (who played Coupeau with great success), it had a long run in London in 1879. It was subsequently revived several times. Other versions, by different hands (Lacy, Callender, Banks) were less successful.

ZORRILLA, Francisco de Rojas, see rojas zorrilla.

ZORRILLA Y MORAL, José (1817–93), poetic dramatist of the Romantic movement in Spain. His most famous play is the extraordinarily popular *Don Juan Tenorio* (1844), which added yet another version to the numerous interpretations of the Don Juan legend. It is still traditionally performed annually on All Saints' Day (1 Nov.). Zorrilla also wrote comedies, tragedies, and historical plays. Of the last the best known are *El puñal del Godo* (1842); *El zapatero y el Rey*, written in two parts (1840 and 1841), of which the second is the more successful; and *Traidor, inconfeso y mártir* (1849), on the life of a pretender to the Crown of Portugal. Zorrilla is also the author of many *romances*, verse legends, which are among the foremost literary productions of Spanish Romanticism.

ZUCKMAYER, CARL (1896–), German dramatist. After serving in the First World War, Zuckmayer drifted from one job to another, and was for a time an assistant producer in a provincial theatre. His first plays, *Am Kreuzweg* (1920) and *Pankraz erwacht* (1925), were unsuccessful, barely surviving their first performances. In writing them Zuckmayer had been deeply influenced by the Impressionist movement. He now abandoned this for the new realistic drama, and his comedy, *Der fröhliche Weinberg* (1925), had an enthusiastic reception in Berlin. It was followed by *Schinderhannes* (1927), based on a popular national figure of the Napoleonic wars, a kind of Robin Hood who robbed the rich to give to the poor and was finally executed in Mainz; *Katharina Knie* (1929), set in a circus; *Kakadu Kakada* (1930), a play for children; and *Der Hauptmann von Köpenick* (1931), which was destined to become one of his best-known works. Based on an actual incident, it shows a local shoemaker, disguised as an officer, achieving his ends because of the Prussian habit of obedience to a uniformed figure. Under the guise of satire, it was an outspoken attack on the revival of militarism which was a feature of the final phase of the Weimar Republic.

After the rise of Hitler, Zuckmayer went to Austria, where he produced *Der Schelm von Bergen* (1934) and *Bellman* (1938), both based on historical themes. The latter was revived in Germany in 1953 as *Ulla Winblad.* He then moved on to the United States, where he achieved his greatest success with *Des Teufels General* (1946), a play with a Nazi background which, as *The Devil's General,* was seen in London in 1953. Among his later plays, none of which has achieved a comparable success, have been *Barbara Blomberg* (1949), *Der Gesang im Feuerofen* (1950), set in France under the German occupation, *Das kalte Licht* (1956), based on the case of Dr. Fuchs, and *Die Uhr schlägt eins* (1961). DOROTHY MOORE

SELECT LIST OF THEATRE BOOKS

Compiled by D. M. MOORE

Librarian, Westfield College (University of London)

THE list of theatre books which follows has been compiled for the general reader who may wish to pursue further the study of some subject in the main text which has aroused his interest. It is not intended as an exhaustive bibliography of world theatre, and for the most part contains only those works which are in print or fairly easily obtainable through libraries. A few out-of-print books have been included, but only where nothing else covers the subject adequately.

The basis of the list is that published in earlier editions of *The Oxford Companion to the Theatre*, and certain sections, such as that on *Jesuit Drama*, originally compiled by Professor Edna Purdie, reappear unaltered. Throughout, an attempt has been made to give the most recent edition or reprint of a book.

As in the earlier editions, books are entered once only, and cross-references have been made where necessary from one section to another. The longer bibliographies have been divided chronologically, the general works in each section being arranged in one alphabetical sequence under the name of the author or editor; this section is followed by memoirs and biographies listed alphabetically under the name of the subject.

D. M. M.

Abbreviations: B. = Bibliography
ed. = editor, edition
enl. = enlarged
ill. = illustrations
n.d. = no date
repr. = reprint
rev. = revised
tr. = translated, translation

GENERAL WORKS

1. *Reference Works*

W. D. ADAMS: *A dictionary of the drama, a guide to the plays, playwrights, players, and playhouses of the United Kingdom and America.* Vol. 1: A–G (no more published). London and Philadelphia, 1904.

B. M. BAKER: *The theatre and allied arts, a guide to books dealing with the history, criticism and technic of the drama and theatre and related arts and crafts.* New York, 1952.

A. BOUCHARD: *La langue théâtrale, vocabulaire historique, descriptif et anecdotique des termes et des choses du théâtre.* Paris, 1878.

H. BOUCHOT: *Catalogue de dessins relatifs à l'histoire du théâtre conservés au Département des Estamples de la Bibliothèque Nationale.* Paris, 1896.

W. P. BOWMAN and R. H. BALL: *Theatre language, a dictionary of terms in English of the drama and stage from medieval to modern times.* New York, 1961.

British Drama League: *The player's library, the catalogue of the Library.* London, 1950. First supplement, 1951. Second supplement, 1954. Third supplement (with a catalogue of plays in French), 1956.

Ch. BRUNET: *Table des pièces de théâtre décrites dans le catalogue de la bibliothèque de M. de Soleinne.* Paris, 1914.

Dictionnaire des hommes de théâtre français contemporains. Vol. 1, Paris, 1957– . (In progress.)

Enciclopedia dello spettacolo. Ill., 9 vols. and appendix, Rome, 1954–64.

Encyclopédie du théâtre contemporain, 1850–1950. Ill., 2 vols., Paris, 1957–9.

W. G. FAY: *A short glossary of theatrical terms.* London, 1930.

I. K. FLETCHER: *British theatre 1530–1900, catalogue of an exhibition at the National Book League, October 1950.* London, 1950.

R. GILDER: *A theatre library, a bibliography of 100 books relating to the theatre.* New York, 1932.

—— and G. FREEDLEY: *Theatre collections in libraries and museums, an international handbook.* New York, 1936.

W. A. GRANVILLE: *A dictionary of theatrical terms.* London, 1952.

Green Room Book, or Who's Who on the Stage (later *Who's Who in the Theatre*)*: an annual bibliographical record of the dramatic, musical, and variety world.* Ill., London, 1906–11.

L. A. HALL: *Catalogue of dramatic portraits in the theatre collection of the Harvard College Library.* 4 vols., Harvard U.P., 1930–4.

J. F. KERSLAKE (ed.): *Catalogue of theatrical portraits in London public collections.* London, 1961.

H. KINDERMANN: *Theatergeschichte Europas.* Ill., Vienna, 1957– . (In progress, 7 vols. already published.)

A. LOEWENBERG (ed.): *The theatre of the British Isles, excluding London, a bibliography.* London, 1950.

R. W. LOWE: *A bibliographical account of English theatrical literature from the earliest times to the present day.* London, 1888.

P. A. MERBACH: *Bibliographie für Theatergeschichte, 1905–10.* Berlin, 1913.

A. POUGIN: *Dictionnaire historique et pittoresque du théâtre et des arts qui s'y rattachent.* Ill., Paris, 1885.

K. RAE and R. SOUTHERN (eds.): *An international vocabulary of technical theatre terms in 8 languages (American, Dutch, English, French, German, Italian, Spanish, Swedish).* London, 1959.

A. RONDEL: *Catalogue analytique sommaire de la Collection théâtrale Rondel*, suivi d'un *Guide pratique à travers la bibliographie théâtrale et d'une chronologie des ouvrages d'information et de critique théâtrales.* Paris, 1932. B.

B. SOBEL (ed.): *The theatre handbook and digest of plays.* New York, 1940. B.

R. STALLINGS and P. MYERS: *A guide to theatre reading.* New York, 1949.

A. VEINSTEIN (ed.): *Bibliothèques et musées des arts du spectacle dans le monde.* Paris, 1960.

Who's Who in the Theatre, a bibliographical record of the contemporary stage. 14th (Jubilee) ed., London, 1967.

2. *General History and Drama*

G. ALTMAN and others: *Theater pictorial.* Ill., Berkeley (Calif.), 1953.

V. ARPE: *Bildgeschichte des Theaters.* Ill., Cologne, 1962.

R. H. BALL: *The amazing career of Sir Giles Overreach.* Ill., Princeton and London, 1939. B.

A. BATES (ed.): *The drama.* 22 vols., London, 1913.

A. BOLL: *Théâtre, spectacles et fêtes populaires dans l'histoire.* Ill., Paris, n.d.

D. C. BOUGHNER: *The braggart in Renaissance comedy.* Minnesota U.P. and London, 1954. B.

O. G. BROCKETT: *The theatre, an introduction.* Ill., New York and London, 1964. B.

S. W. CHENEY: *The theatre, 3000 years of drama, acting and stagecraft.* Ill., enl. ed., London and New York, 1959. B.

L. DUBECH and others: *Histoire générale illustrée du théâtre.* Ill., 5 vols., Paris, 1931–4.

U. M. ELLIS-FERMOR: *The frontiers of drama.* 2nd ed., with an introduction by A. Nicoll and a bibliography by H. Brooks. London, 1964. B.

G. FREEDLEY and J. A. REEVES: *A history of the theatre.* Ill., New York, 1941. B.

B. GASCOIGNE: *World theatre.* Ill., London, 1968. B.

J. GASSNER: *Masters of the drama.* New York, 1940. B.

L. GHÉON: *The art of the theatre.* New York, 1962.

R. GILDER: *Enter the actress, the first women in the theatre.* Ill., repr., New York, 1959.

H. GRANVILLE-BARKER: *The use of the drama.* London, 1946.

Sir TYRONE GUTHRIE: *In various directions, a view of theatre.* Ill., New York, 1965, London, 1966.

P. HARTNOLL: *A concise history of the theatre.* Ill., London and New York, 1968. B.

G. HUGHES: *The story of the theatre, a short history of theatrical art from the beginning to the present day.* Ill., London and New York, 1928. B.

B. HUNNINGHER: *The origin of the theater, an essay.* Repr., New York, 1961.

K. MACGOWAN and W. MELNITZ: *The living stage, a history of world theater.* Ill., New York, 1955. B.

B. MATTHEWS and L. HUTTON (eds.): *Actors and actresses of Great Britain and the United States from the days of David Garrick to the present time.* Ill., 5 vols., New York, 1886.

L. MOUSSINAC: *Le théâtre des origines à nos jours.* Ill., Paris, 1957.

A. M. NAGLER: *A source-book in theatrical history.* Ill., New York and London, 1959. B.

A. NICOLL: *The development of the theatre, a study of theatrical art from the beginnings to the present day.* Ill., 4th ed., London, 1958. B.

—— *The theatre and dramatic theory.* London, 1962.

—— *World drama from Aeschylus to Anouilh.* Ill., London, 1949.

C. NIESSEN: *Handbuch der Theaterwissenschaft.* Ill., Emsdetten, 1949– . (In progress.)

H. ORMSBEE: *Backstage with actors, from the time of Shakespeare to the present day.* Ill., New York, 1938.

T. PRIDEAUX: *World theatre in pictures.* Ill., Philadelphia, 1953.

D. C. STUART: *The development of dramatic art.* New York, 1928. B.

J. L. STYAN: *The elements of drama.* Repr., Cambridge, 1963. B.

—— *The dramatic experience.* Ill., Cambridge, 1965. B.

E. Welsford: *The fool, his social and literary history.* Ill., London, 1935. B.

N. S. Wilson: *European drama.* London, 1937. B.

3. *Modern Drama*

J. A. Andrews and O. Trilling (eds.): *International theatre.* London, 1949.

E. Bentley: *In search of theatre.* Ill., New York, 1953, London, 1955.

B. Blau: *The impossible theatre, a manifesto.* Ill., New York, 1964, London, 1965.

J. M. Brown: *The modern theatre in revolt.* New York, 1929. B.

R. Brustein: *The theatre of revolt, an approach to the modern drama.* New York, 1965.

H. Carter: *The new spirit in the European theatre, 1914–1924, a comparative study of the changes effected by the war and revolutions.* Ill., London and New York, 1925.

F. W. Chandler: *Modern continental playwrights.* New York, 1931. B.

S. W. Cheney: *The art theater, its character as differentiated from the commercial theater, its ideals and organization . . .* Ill., rev. and enl. ed., New York, 1924.

—— *The New movement in the theatre.* Ill., New York, 1914.

B. H. Clark: *A study of the modern drama, a handbook for the study and appreciation of typical plays, European, English and American, of the last three-quarters of a century.* Rev. ed., New York, 1938. B.

—— and G. Freedley (eds.): *A history of modern drama.* New York, 1947. B.

T. H. Dickinson: *An outline of contemporary drama.* Boston, 1927. B.

—— (ed.): *The theatre in a changing Europe.* Ill., London and New York, 1937.

M. Dietrich: *Das moderne Drama — Strömungen, Gestalten, Motiven.* Stuttgart, 1961. B.

'Encore' reader: a chronicle of the new drama (1956–63), ed. by C. Marowitz, T. Milne, O. Hale. Ill., London, 1965.

H. Flanagan: *Shifting scenes of the modern European theatre.* Ill., New York, 1928.

J. Gassner: *The theatre in our times.* New York, 1954.

I. Goldberg: *The drama of transition.* Cincinnati, 1922.

M. Gorelik: *New theatres for old.* Ill., London, 1947. B.

J. Guerrero Zamora: *Historia del teatro contemporáneo.* Ill., 3 vols., Barcelona, 1960–2.

A. Henderson: *European dramatists.* Ill., rev. ed., New York, 1926.

M. Kesting: *Das epische Theater, zum Struktur des modernen Dramas.* Stuttgart, 1959.

T. Komisarjevsky: *Myself and the theatre.* Ill., London, 1929.

M. Lamm: *Modern drama.* Oxford, 1952.

K. Macgowan: *The theatre of tomorrow.* Ill., New York, 1922. B.

S. Melchinger: *The concise encyclopedia of modern drama . . .* Ill., London, 1966. B.

A. I. Miller: *The independent theatre in Europe, 1887 to the present.* New York, 1931. B.

H. K. Moderwell: *The theatre of today.* Ill., new ed., London and New York, 1927.

W. L. Phelps: *The twentieth century theatre, observations on the contemporary English and American stage.* New York, 1918.

G. Ruberti: *Il teatro contemporaneo in Europa.* Bologna, 1921.

J. L. Styan: *The dark comedy, the development of modern comic tragedy.* Cambridge, 1962.

R. Williams: *Drama from Ibsen to Eliot.* London, 1952.

(Consult also the files of *The Mask*, ed. Gordon Craig, Florence, 1908–29; and *Theatre Arts*, New York, Nov. 1916–Jan. 1964.

TECHNICAL BOOKS

1. *General Stagecraft, including Scenery*

V. Adix: *Theatre scenecraft for the backstage technician and artist.* Ill., Univ. of Utah, 1936.

M.-A. Allevy: *La mise en scène en France dans la première moitié du XIXe siècle.* Ill., Paris, 1938. B.

R. Alloi: *Esempi di arredamenti, architettura e decorazioni d'oggi di tutto il mondo.* Ill., Milan, 1958.

American Federation of Arts: *The ideal theatre, 8 concepts, an exhibition of designs and models . . .* Ill., New York, 1962, London, 1965.

D. Amiel and H. Fescourt (eds.): *Les spectacles à travers les âges.* Ill., 3 vols., Paris, 1931–2.

C. Antonetti: *Notes sur la mise en scène à l'usage des jeunes acteurs.* Ill., Paris, 1950.

A. Appia: *La mise en scène du drame wagnérien.* Paris, 1895.

—— *Die Musik und die Inscenierung.* Ill. Munich, 1899.

—— *The work of living art and man's the measure of all things,* ed. B. Hewitt. Miami U.P., 1960.

D. Bablet: *Le décor de théatre de 1870 à 1914.* Ill., Paris, 1965.

G. BAPST: *Essai sur l'histoire du théâtre, la mise en scène, le décor, le costume, l'architecture, l'éclairage, l'hygiène.* Ill., Paris, 1893.

P. W. BARBER: *The scene technician's handbook.* Ill., New Haven, 1928.

P. BAX: *Stage management.* Ill., London, 1936. B.

A. BOLL: *La décoration théâtrale, conseils aux amateurs.* Ill., Paris, 1958.

W. P. BOYLE: *Central and flexible staging.* Ill., Berkeley and London, 1956.

H. BURRIS-MEYER and E. C. COLE: *Scenery for the theatre, the organization, processes, materials, and techniques used to set the stage.* Repr., London and Boston, 1946. B.

C. CANFIELD: *The craft of play directing.* Ill., New York, 1963.

K. ČAPEK: *How a play is produced.* Ill., London, 1928.

L. CELLER: *Les décors, les costumes et la mise en scène au XVIIe siècle, 1615–80.* Paris, 1869.

S. W. CHENEY: *Stage decoration.* Ill., London and New York, 1928.

R. COGNIAT: *Cinquante ans de spectacle en France, décorateurs de théâtre.* Ill., Paris, 1956.

T. COLE and H. K. CHINOY (eds.): *Directing the play, a sourcebook of stagecraft.* Ill., New York and London, 1953. B.

—— *Directors on directing, a source book of the modern theatre.* Ill., new ed., New York, 1963, London, 1964. B.

H. CONWAY: *Stage Properties.* Ill., London, 1960.

E. G. CRAIG: *Designs for the theatre.* Ill., London, 1948.

—— *On the art of the theatre.* Ill., reissue, London and New York, 1956.

—— *Scene.* Ill., London and New York, 1923.

E. CROFT-MURRAY: *John Devoto, a baroque scene painter.* Ill., London, 1953.

L. DAMERON: *Bibliography of stage settings.* Baltimore, 1936.

V. E. D'AMICO: *Theater art.* Ill., Peoria (Illinois), 1931. B.

Décor de théâtre dans le monde depuis 1935, préface de J. Cocteau. Ill., Brussels, 1956.

N. DECUGIS and S. REYMOND: *Le décor de théâtre en France du moyen âge à 1925.* Ill., Paris, 1953. B.

S. W. DEIERKAUF-HOLSBOER: *L'histoire de la mise en scène dans le théâtre à Paris de 1600 à 1673.* Paris, 1960.

S. DHOMME: *La mise en scène contemporaine d'A. Antoine à B. Brecht.* Ill., Paris, 1959.

J. E. DIETRICH: *Play direction.* Ill., New York, 1953, London, 1955.

G. FERRARI: *La scenografia.* Ill., Milan, 1902. B.

O. FISCHEL: *Das moderne Bühnenbild.* Ill., Berlin, 1923.

M. FISHMAN: *Play production, methods and practice.* Ill., London, 1965. B.

D. FITZKEE: *Professional scenery construction.* Ill., San Francisco, 1930.

G. FRETTE: *Stage design, 1909–54.* Ill., London, 1956.

W. R. FUERST and S. J. HUME: *Twentieth century stage decoration.* Ill., 2 vols., London, 1928. B.

M. GALLAWAY: *The décor in the theater.* Ill., New York and London, 1963.

W. B. GAMBLE: *The development of scenic art and stage machinery (a bibliography).* Rev. ed., New York, 1928.

J. GASSNER and P. BARBER: *Producing the play.* New ed., New York, 1953.

A.-C. GERVAIS: *Propos sur la mise en scène.* Ill., Paris, 1943.

P. GOFFIN: *The art and science of stage management.* London, 1953.

H. GOUHIER: *L'essence du théâtre.* Paris, 1943.

—— *L'œuvre théâtrale.* Paris, 1958.

J. GREGOR: *Monumenta scenica, Denkmäler des Theaters.* 12 portfolios, Vienna, 1925–30.

—— *Weltgeschichte des Theaters.* Ill., Zürich, 1933. B.

—— *Wiener szenische Kunst.* Ill., 2 vols., Vienna, 1924–5.

R. HAINAUX and Y. BONNAT (eds.): *Stage design throughout the world since 1935.* Ill., London, 1957.

—— *Stage design throughout the world since 1950.* Ill., London, 1964.

H. C. HEFFNER and others: *Modern theatre practice.* London, 1961.

H. HELVENSTON: *Scenery, a manual of scene design.* Ill., Stanford U.P., 1931.

H. HUNT: *The director in the theatre.* London, 1954.

—— *The live theatre, an introduction to the history and practice of the stage.* Ill., London, 1962.

J. JACQUOT (ed.): *Réalisme et poésie au théâtre.* Paris, 1960.

—— and A. VEINSTEIN (eds.): *La mise en scène des œuvres du passé.* Ill., Paris, 1957.

L. A. JONES: *Scenic design and model building.* Ill., Boston (Mass.), 1939.

R. E. JONES: *Drawings for the theatre.* Ill., New York, 1925.

S. JOSEPH (ed.): *Adaptable theatres.* Ill., London, 1962.

—— *Theatre-in-the-round.* Ill., London, 1955.

L. JOUVET: *Écoute, mon ami.* Ill., Paris, 1952.

G. R. KERNODLE: *From art to theatre, form and convention in the Renaissance.* Ill., Chicago, 1943. B.

T. KOMISARJEVSKY and L. SIMONSON: *Settings and costumes of the modern stage.* Ill., London and New York, 1933.

F. KRANICH: *Bühnentechnik der Gegenwart.* Ill., 2 vols., Berlin, 1929–33. B.

S. LOEWY: *Deutsche Theaterkunst von Goethe bis Reinhardt, mit einem Anhang, Das alte Wiener Volkstheater.* Vienna, 1923.

K. MACGOWAN and R. E. JONES: *Continental stagecraft.* Ill., New York, 1922.

V. MARIANI: *Storia della scenografia italiana.* Ill., Florence, 1930. B.

N. MARSHALL: *The producer and the play.* Ill., rev. and enl. ed., London, 1962.

A. H. MAYOR: *The Bibiena family.* Ill., New York, 1945.

—— and others: *Tempi e aspetti della scenografia.* Ill., Turin, 1954.

J. MIELZINER: *Designing for the theatre.* Ill., New York, 1965.

L. MOUSSINAC: *The new movement in the theatre, a survey of recent developments in Europe and America.* Ill., London, 1931. B.

—— *Traité de la mise en scène.* Ill., Paris, 1956.

H. NELMS: *Play production.* London, 1958.

C. NIESSEN: *Das Bühnenbild, ein kulturgeschichtlicher Atlas.* Bonn, 1924–7.

D. OENSLAGER: *Scenery then and now.* Ill., New York, 1936.

W. O. PARKER and H. K. SMITH: *Scene design and stage lighting.* Ill., London, 1963.

H. PARMELIN: *Cinq peintres et le théâtre — décors et costumes de Léger, Coutaud, Gischia, Labisse, Pignon.* Ill., Paris, 1956.

M. PELLEGRINI: *Scenotecnica scenografia.* Ill., Florence, 1948.

H. PHILIPPI: *Stagecraft and scene design.* Ill., Boston (Mass.), 1953.

G. POLTI: *The thirty-six dramatic situations,* tr. L. Ray. Repr., Boston (Mass.), 1948.

C. POUPEYE: *La mise en scène théâtrale d'aujourd'hui.* Ill., Brussels, 1927. B.

C. RICCI: *La scenografia italiana.* Ill., Milan, 1930. B.

N. SABBATINI: *Pratica di fabricar scene e machine ne' teatri, con aggiunti documenti inediti e disegni originali,* a cura di E. Povoledo. Ill., Rome, 1955.

M. SAINT-DENIS: *Theatre, the rediscovery of style.* Ill., London, 1960.

J. SCHOLZ (ed.): *Baroque and romantic stage design.* Ill., New York, 1955. B.

O. SCHUBERTH: *Das Bühnenbild, Geschichte, Gestalt, Technik.* Ill., Munich, 1955. B.

S. SELDEN: *The stage in action.* Ill., New York, 1941, London, 1962.

—— and H. D. SELLMAN: *Stage scenery and lighting.* Ill., new ed., New York, 1959, London, 1964.

G. SHERINGHAM and J. LAVER (eds.): *Design in the theatre.* Ill., London, 1927. B.

W. D. SIEVERS: *Directing for the theatre.* 2nd ed., Brown (W. C.), 1965.

L. SIEVERT: *Lebendiges Theater, 3 Jahrzehnte deutscher Theaterkunst.* Ill., Munich, 1944.

L. SIMONSON: *The art of scenic design.* Ill., New York and London, 1950.

——*The stage is set.* Ill., New York, 1932. B.

P. SONREL: *Traité de scénographie.* Ill., repr., Paris, 1956. B.

R. SOUTHERN: *Changeable scenery, its origin and development in the British theatre.* Ill., London, 1952.

—— *The medieval theatre in the round.* Ill., London, 1957.

—— *The open stage and the modern theatre in research and practice.* Ill., London, 1953.

—— *Stage-setting for amateurs and professionals.* Ill., 2nd. ed., London, 1964. B.

E. STERN: *My life, my stage.* Ill., London, 1951.

UNESCO: *Décors de théâtre dans le monde depuis 1935.* Ill., Paris, 1956.

A. N. VARDAC: *Stage to screen, theatrical method from Garrick to Griffith.* Ill., Harvard U.P. and London, 1949.

A. VEINSTEIN: *La mise en scène théâtrale et sa condition esthétique.* Paris, 1955.

G. WHITWORTH: *Theatre in action.* Ill., London and New York, 1938.

D. ZINKEISEN: *Designing for the stage.* Ill., repr., London, 1948.

W. ZNAMENACEK: *Kulissen, Bühne und Bild.* Ill., Augsburg, n.d.

P. ZUCKER: *Die Theaterdekoration des Barock.* Ill., Berlin, 1925. B.

—— *Die Theaterdekoration des Klassizismus.* Ill., Berlin, 1927. B.

(*See also* AMATEUR THEATRE.)

2. *Architecture and Acoustics*

J. C. ADAMS: *The Globe playhouse, its design and equipment.* Ill., 2nd ed., London, 1963.

S. BELL, N. MARSHALL, and R. SOUTHERN: *Essentials of stage planning.* Ill., London, 1949. B.

P. CORRY: *Planning the stage.* Ill., London, 1961.

C. DALY and G. DAVIOUD: *Architecture contemporaine — les théâtres de la Place du Châtelet . . .* Ill., Paris, n.d.

J. FABRIS: *Instruction in der teatralischen Architectur und Mechanique,* ed. T. Krogh. Ill., Copenhagen, 1930.

M. HAMMITZSCH: *Der moderne Theaterbau: der höfische Theaterbau, der Anfang der modernen Theaterbaukunst, ihre Entwicklung und Betätigung zur Zeit der Renaissance, des Barock und des Rokoko.* Ill., Berlin, 1906. B.

C. W. HODGES: *The Globe restored.* Ill., London, 1953.

HOME OFFICE: *Manual of safety requirements in theatres and other places of public entertainment.* Reissue, London, 1949.

L. HOTSON: *Shakespeare's wooden O.* Ill., London, 1959.

E. J. R. ISAACS (ed.): *Architecture for the new theatre.* Ill., New York, 1935.

S. JOSEPH (ed.): *Actor and architect.* Ill., Manchester, 1964.

—— *Planning for new forms of theatre.* Ill., 3rd ed. rev. and enl., London, 1966.

E. B. KINSILA: *Modern theatre construction.* Ill., New York, 1917.

R. LEACROFT: *Civic theatre design.* Ill., London, 1949.

H. LECLERC: *Les origines italiennes de l'architecture théâtrale moderne.* Ill., Paris, 1946. B.

LONDON (GREATER LONDON COUNCIL): *Places of public entertainment, technical regulations.* London, 1966.

G. K. LOUKOMSKI: *Les théâtres anciens et modernes.* Ill., Paris, 1934.

A. S. MELOY: *Theatres and motion picture houses, a practical treatise on the proper planning and construction of such buildings...* Ill., New York, 1916.

H. B. MEYER and E. C. COLE: *Theatres and auditoriums.* Ill., New York, 1949.

A. M. NAGLER: *Shakespeare's stage.* Yale and London, 1960. B.

NEW YORK PUBLIC LIBRARY: *Contemporary theatre architecture.* New York, 1965.

F. PAWLEY: *Theatre architecture, a brief bibliography.* New York, 1932.

I. PICHEL: *Modern theatres.* Ill., New York, 1925. B.

A. C. RAMELLI: *Edifici per gli spettacoli.* Ill., 3rd augmented ed., Milan, 1956.

P. E. SABINE: *Acoustics and architecture.* Ill., London and New York, 1932. B.

R. W. SEXTON and B. F. BETTS: *American theatres of today.* Ill., 2 vols., New York, 1927–30.

P. M. SHAND: *Modern theatres and cinemas.* Ill., London, 1930.

I. SMITH: *Shakespeare's Globe playhouse.* Ill., New York and London, 1956.

—— *Shakespeare's Blackfriars playhouse, its history and its design.* Ill., New York, 1965, London, 1966. B.

R. SOUTHERN: *The Georgian playhouse.* Ill., London, 1948.

—— *Proscenium and sight lines, a complete system of scenery planning.* Ill., 2nd ed., London, 1964.

—— *The seven ages of the theatre.* Ill., London, 1962. B.

J. URBAN: *Theatres.* Ill., New York, 1930.

E. WERNER and H. GUSSMANN: *Theatergebäude — Geschichtliche Entwicklung — Technik des Theaterbaus.* Ill., 2 vols., Berlin, 1954.

3. *Costume*

L. BARTON: *Historic costume for the stage.* Ill., repr., London and Boston (Mass.), 1949. B.

M. VON BOEHN: *Das Bühnenkostüm in Altertum, Mittelalter und Neuzeit.* Ill., Berlin, 1921. B.

I. BROOKE: *Costume in Greek classic drama.* Ill., London, 1962.

—— *English children's costume since 1775.* Ill., London, 1930.

—— and J. LAVER: *English costume of the nineteenth century.* Ill., London, 1929.

W. BRUHN and M. TILKE: *A pictorial history of costume.* Ill., London, 1955.

M. CONTINI: *Fashion from ancient Egypt to the present day,* ed. J. Laver. Ill., London, 1965.

M. DAVENPORT: *The book of costume.* Ill., 2 vols., New York, 1948, London, 1954.

M. FERNALD and E. SHENTON: *Costume design and making.* Ill., London, 1958.

J. GREGOR: *Das Bühnenkostüm in historischer, ästhetischer und psychologischer Analyse.* Ill., Zürich, 1925.

H. H. HENSEN: *Costume cavalcade.* Ill., London, 1956. B.

A. JULLIEN: *Histoire du costume au théâtre depuis les origines du théâtre en France jusqu'à nos jours.* Ill., Paris, 1880.

F. M. KELLY: *Shakespearian costume for stage and screen.* Ill., London, 1938. B.

—— and R. SCHWABE: *Historic costume, a chronicle of fashion in western Europe, 1490–1790.* Ill., 2nd ed., London, 1929.

—— *A short history of costume and armour, chiefly in England, 1066–1800.* Ill., London, 1931.

C. KÖHLER: *A history of costume,* ed. and augmented by E. von Sichart. Ill., London, 1928. B.

T. KOMISARJEVSKY: *The costume of the theatre.* Ill., London, 1931.

J. LAVER: *Drama, its costume and décor.* Ill., London, 1951. B.

—— *Costume in the theatre.* Ill., London, 1964. B.

—— (ed.): *Costume of the Western world. Vol. 3: The Tudors to Louis XIII.* Ill., London, 1951.

R. LEVI PISETZKY: *Storia del costume in Italia.* Ill., Milan, 1965– . (In progress.)

M. C. LINTHICUM: *Costume in the drama of Shakespeare and his contemporaries.* Ill., Oxford and New York, 1936. B.

M. LISTER: *Stage costume.* Ill., London, 1954.

M. LUKEŠ: *Costume on the stage, a book of costume designs.* Ill., Prague, 1962.

K. MANN: *Peasant costume in Europe.* Ill., London, 1931.

I. MONRO and D. COOK (eds.): *Costume index.* New York, 1937.

MOTLEY (pseud.): *Designing and making stage costumes.* Ill., London, 1964.

J. R. PLANCHÉ: *A cyclopaedia of costume or, dictionary of dress.* Ill., 2 vols., London, 1879.

B. PRISK: *Stage costume handbook.* Ill., New York, 1966.

G. SHERINGHAM and R. B. MORRISON (eds.): *Robes of Thespis, costume designs by modern artists.* Ill., London, 1928.

N. TRUMAN: *Historic costuming.* Ill., London, 1936.

F. P. WALKUP: *Dressing the part, a history of costume for the theatre.* Ill., London, 1959. B.

R. T. WILCOX: *Five centuries of American costume.* Ill., New York, 1963, London, 1966. B.

A. B. YOUNG: *Stage costuming.* Ill., New York, 1927. B.

4. *Lighting*

F. BENTHAM: *Stage lighting.* Ill., 2nd ed., London, 1955.

P. CORRY: *Lighting the stage.* Ill., 3rd ed., London, 1962. B.

A. VON ENGEL: *Bühnenbeleuchtung, Entwicklung und neuester Stand der lichttechnischen Einrichtungen an Theaterbühnen.* Ill., Leipzig, 1926. B.

T. FUCHS: *Stage lighting.* Ill., London and Boston, 1929. B.

L. HARTMANN: *Theatre lighting, a manual of the stage switchboard.* Ill., London and New York, 1930. B.

W. J. LAWRENCE: *Early English stage- and theatre-lighting, 1580–1800.* Ill., London, 1927. (Stage Year Book.)

M. LUCKIESCH: *Lighting art, its practice and possibilities.* Ill., New York, 1917.

S. R. MCCANDLESS: *Glossary of stage lighting.* 5th ed., New Haven, 1941.

—— *A method of lighting the stage.* Ill., 3rd ed., New York, 1947.

—— *A syllabus of stage lighting.* New Haven, 1931.

W. P. MAYCOCK: *Electric wiring, fittings, switches, and lamps.* 6th ed. rev. by P. Kemp, London, 1928.

A. L. POWELL: *Lighting of theatres and auditoriums.* Ill., New York, 1923.

—— and A. RODGERS: *Lighting for the non-professional stage production.* Ill., New York, 1931.

C. H. RIDGE: *Stage lighting.* Ill., Cambridge, 1928. B.

—— and F. S. ALDRED: *Stage lighting, principles and practice.* Ill., London, 1935.

R. G. WILLIAMS: *The technique of stage lighting.* Ill., 2nd ed., London, 1958.

(*See also* AMATEUR THEATRE.)

5. *Machinery*

D. DIDEROT and J. LE ROND D'ALEMBERT: *Encyclopédie dictionnaire raisonné des sciences, des arts et des métiers: recueil de planches sur . . . les arts méchaniques avec leur explication.* 9ᵉ livraison ou 10ᵉ volume: *Machines de théâtre.* Ill., Paris, 1772.

M. J. MOYNET: *L'envers du théâtre, machines et décorations.* Ill., 3rd ed., Paris, 1888.

—— *La machinerie théâtrale, trucs et décors, explication raisonnée de tous les moyens employés pour produire les illusions théâtrales.* Ill., Paris, 1895.

F. NAPIER: *Noises off, a handbook of sound effects.* Ill., London, 1936.

A. ROSE: *Stage effects, how to make and work them.* Ill., London and New York, 1928.

A. DE VAULABELLE and CH. HÉMARDINQUER: *La science au théâtre.* Ill., Paris, 1908.

6. *Scene-painting*

R. FORMAN: *Scene painting.* Ill., London, 1950.

A. S. GILLETTE: *Stage scenery.* London, 1960.

L. A. JONES: *Painting scenery.* Ill., Boston, 1935.

S. JOSEPH: *Scene painting and design.* Ill., London, 1964. B.

F. LLOYDS: *Practical guide to scene-painting and painting in distemper.* Ill., London, 1875.

H. MELVILL: *Designing and painting scenery for the theatre.* London, 1948.

V. POLUNIN: *The continental method of scene-painting,* ed. by C. W. Beaumont. Ill., London, 1927.

A. ROSE: *Scenes for scene-painters, a practical handbook.* Ill., London, 1925.

ACOUSTICS

See TECHNICAL BOOKS, 2

AFRICA

1. *North Africa*

G. CAPUTO: *Il teatro di Sabratha e l'architettura teatrale africana.* Ill., Rome, 1950.

2. *South Africa*

P. W. LAIDLER: *The annals of the Cape stage.* Ill., Edinburgh, 1926.

O. RACSTER: *Curtain up, the story of Cape theatre.* Ill., London, 1951.

3. *West Africa*

W. SOYINKA: *Five plays.* London, 1965.

AMATEUR THEATRE

G. Boas: *Shakespeare and the young actor.* Ill., London, 1955.

J. Brandon-Thomas: *Practical stagecraft for amateurs,* ed. by D. C. Keir. Ill., London, 1936.

W. Campbell: *Amateur acting and play production.* Ill., New York, 1931.

P. Corry: *Amateur theatrecraft.* Ill., London, 1961.

——*Stage planning and equipment for multi-purpose halls.* Ill., London, 1949.

L. Crump: *Directing for the amateur stage.* Ill., New York, 1935.

H. Downs (ed.): *Theatre and stage, a modern guide to the performance of all classes of amateur dramatic, operatic, and theatrical works.* Ill., 2 vols., 2nd ed., London, 1951.

W. G. Elliott (ed.): *Amateur clubs and actors.* Ill., London, 1898.

W. J. Friederich and J. H. Frazer: *Scenery design for the amateur stage.* Ill., New York and London, 1951.

W. P. Halstead: *Stage management for the amateur stage, with an index to the standard works on stagecraft and stage lighting.* Ill., London and New York, 1938. B.

P. Hamilton: *Amateur stage handbook.* London, 1957.

N. Lambourne: *Dressing the play.* Ill., London, 1953. B.

—— *Staging the play.* Ill., London, 1956. B.

F. Mackenzie: *The amateur actor.* 2nd ed., rev. and enl., London, 1936. B.

A. Mackinnon: *The Oxford amateurs, a short history of theatricals at the university.* Ill., London, 1910.

C. Mill: *Make-up for the amateur.* Ill., London, 1955. B.

J. Morris: *Amateur stage make-up.* Ill., London, 1958.

A. Nelson-Smith: *The business side of the amateur theatre.* London, 1953.

C. S. Parsons: *Amateur stage-management and production.* Ill., London, 1931.

N. Pilbeam: *Acting on the amateur stage.* Ill., London, 1953.

E. D. Schonberger: *Play production for amateurs.* Ill., New York, 1938.

G.B. Siks and H. B. Dunnington: *Children's theatre and creative dramatics.* Washington, 1965.

(*See also* U.S.A., *and* PROVINCIAL AND REPERTORY THEATRES.)

AMERICA

See CANADA, SOUTH AMERICA, *and* U.S.A.

ARCHITECTURE

See TECHNICAL BOOKS, 2

ARGENTINE

See SOUTH AMERICA, 2

ART OF ACTING

W. Archer: *Masks or faces?* Repr., New York, 1957.

H. d'Aubignac: *La pratique du théâtre.* New ed., Algiers and Paris, 1927.

S. D. Balukhaty (ed.): *'The Seagull' produced by Stanislavsky.* Ill., London, 1952.

J.-L. Barrault: *Reflections on the theatre.* Ill., London, 1951.

—— *The theatre,* trs. J. Chiari. New York, 1961.

S. Bernhardt: *The art of the theatre.* London, 1924.

A. Bernier: *Théorie de l'art du comédien ou manuel théâtral.* Paris, 1826. B.

J. Blunt: *The composite art of acting.* Ill., New York and London, 1966.

R. Boleslavsky: *Acting, the first six lessons.* New York, 1933, London, 1950.

H. Bosworth: *Technique in dramatic art.* Ill., rev. ed., New York, 1934.

L. Calvert: *Problems of the actor.* London and New York, 1918.

S. W. Carroll: *Acting for the stage.* 3rd ed., London, 1949.

T. Cole (ed.): *Acting, a handbook of the Stanislavsky method.* Ill., London, rev. ed., 1955.

—— and H. K. Chinoy (eds.): *Actors on acting, an anthology with introduction and biographical notices.* New York, 1949, London, 1952. B.

C. B. Coquelin: *The art of the actor.* New ed., London, 1955.

L. Crauford: *Acting, its theory and practice, with illustrative examples of players past and present.* London, 1930.

D. Diderot: *Paradoxe sur le comédien, avec les opinions de M. Achard, J.-L. Barrault, J. Copeau, Ch. Dullin.* Paris, 1958.

—— *The paradox of acting,* tr. by W. H. Pollock, introd. by H. Irving. London, 1883, repr., New York, 1957.

G. Dobbelaere and P. Saragoussi: *Techniques of expression.* Ill., London, 1966.

Ch. Dullin: *Souvenirs de travail d'un acteur, souvenirs personnels sur sa vocation théâtrale et exposé de sa méthode de travail.* Paris, 1946.

C. Edwards: *The Stanislavsky heritage.* Ill., New York, 1965, London, 1966. B.

L. Funke and J. E. Booth: *Actors talk about acting.* London, 1962.

G. Garcia: *The actor's art, a practical treatise on stage declamation, public speaking and deportment.* Ill., 2nd ed., London, 1888.

R. Gilder: *John Gielgud's Hamlet, a record of performance.* Ill., London, 1937.

N. A. Gorchakov: *Stanislavsky directs.* New York and London, 1955.

J. H. Hackett: *Edmund Kean's performance as King Richard III recorded,* ed. by A. S. Downer. London, 1959.

B. L. Joseph: *Acting Shakespeare.* London, 1960.

—— *Elizabethan acting.* Ill., 2nd ed., London, 1964.

—— *The tragic actor.* Ill., London, 1959.

L. Jouvet: *Le comédien désincarné.* Paris, 1954.

—— *Réflexions du comédien.* Paris, 1952.

G. H. Lewes: *On actors and the art of acting.* 2nd ed., London, 1875.

R. Lewis: *Method—or madness?* London, 1960.

C. J. McGaw: *Acting is believing.* 2nd ed., New York, 1966.

B. Matthews (ed.): *Papers on acting.* New York, 1958.

I. Mawer: *The art of mime.* Ill., 5th ed., London, 1960.

M. Redgrave: *The actor's ways and means.* Ill., London, 1953.

—— *Mask or face, reflections in an actor's mirror.* Ill., London, 1958.

S. Selden: *A player's handbook, the theory and practice of acting.* Ill., New York, 1934. B.

R. Speaight: *Acting, its idea and tradition.* London, 1939. B.

K. Stanislavsky: *An actor prepares.* London and New York, 1936.

—— *Building a character.* Ill., London and New York, 1950.

—— *Creating a role.* New York and London, 1963.

—— *The Stanislavski system, the professional training of an actor.* Rev. and enl. ed. of *An actor's training,* New York, 1965, London, 1966. B.

L. H. Strasberg: *Strasberg at the Actors Studio, tape-recorded sessions.* Ill., New York, 1965, London, 1966.

F. C. Strickland: *The technique of acting.* Ill., New York, 1956.

B. A. Talladoire: *Commentaires sur la mimique et l'expression corporelle du comédien.* Montpellier, 1951.

F. J. Talma: *On the actor's art,* preface by H. Irving. London, 1883.

J. C. Turner: *Voice and speech in the theatre.* 2nd ed., London, 1956.

J. Wildeblood and P. Brinson: *The polite world, a guide to English manners and deportment from the 13th to the 19th century.* Ill., London, 1965.

(*See also* DRAMATIC CRITICISM, *and* MAKE-UP.)

AUSTRALIA

1. *General*

J. B. Fowler: *Stars in my backyard, a survey of the Australian stage.* Ill., Ilfracombe (Devon), n.d.

P. McGuire, B. Arnott and F. M. McGuire: *The Australian theatre.* Ill., London, 1948.

Meanjin Quarterly, No. 19: *Theatre and drama.* Ill., Melbourne, 1964.

2. *Drama, Theatre*

I. Brodsky: *Sydney takes the stage.* Ill., Sydney, 1964.

F. Clune: *Dig, drama of central Australia.* Sydney, 1937.

L. Rees, *Towards an Australian drama.* Ill., Sydney and London, 1953.

J. Tucker: *Jemmy Green in Australia,* ed. C. Roderick. Sydney and London, 1955.

3. *Actors, Dramatists, etc.*

A. Bagot: *Coppin the great, father of the Australian theatre.* Ill., Melbourne and London, 1965. B.

H. Porter: *Stars of Australian stage and screen.* Ill., London and Adelaide, 1965.

N. Stewart: *My life story.* Sydney, 1923.

L. Wright: *The Jack Davey story.* Sydney, 1961.

AUSTRIA

1. *General*

J. GREGOR: *Geschichte des oesterreichischen Theaters.* Vienna, 1948.

H. KINDERMANN: *Das Theater der Barockzeit.* Salzburg, 1959.

—— and M. DIETRICH: *300 Jahre österreichisches Bühnenbild.* Ill., Vienna, 1959.

J. NADLER: *Literaturgeschichte Oesterreichs.* Salzburg, 1951.

J. W. NAGL and J. ZEIDLER (eds.): *Deutsch-Oesterreichische Literaturgeschichte.* Ill., 4 vols., Vienna, 1898–1937.

O. ROMMEL: *Die Alt-Wiener Volkskomödie.* Ill., Vienna, 1952.

A. VON WEILEN: *Geschichte des Wiener Theaterwesens von den ältesten Zeiten bis zu den Anfängen der Hoftheater: die Theater Wiens.* 2 vols., Vienna, 1894–9.

2. *Drama, Theatre*

K. ADEL: *Das Jesuitendrama in Österreich.* Vienna, 1957.

K. HOLL: *Geschichte des deutschen Lustspiels.* Ill., Leipzig, 1923. B.

J. MEISSNER: *Die englischen Komödianten zur Zeit Shakespeares in Oesterreich.* 1884. (Beiträge zur Geschichte der deutschen Literatur . . . in Oesterreich, IV.)

R. PAYER VON THURN (ed.): *Wiener Haupt- und Staatsaktionen.* Vienna, 1908–10.

A. BAUER: *Das Theater in der Josefstadt.* Vienna, 1957.

—— *150 Jahre Theater an der Wien.* Vienna, 1952.

R. HOLZER: *Die Wiener Vorstadtbühnen, Alexander Girardi und das Theater an der Wien.* Vienna, 1951.

BURGTHEATER: *175 Jahre Burgtheater, 1776–1951, fortgeführt bis Sommer 1954.* Ill., Vienna, 1955.

H. KINDERMANN: *Das Burgtheater.* Vienna, 1939.

R. LOTHAR: *Das Wiener Burgtheater.* Ill., new ed., Vienna, 1934.

3. *Actors, Dramatists, etc.*

O. M. FONTANA: *Wiener Schauspieler.* Vienna, 1948.

H. IHERING: *Von Josef Kainz bis Paula Wessely.* Heidelberg, 1942.

L. KOESSLER: *Ludwig Anzengruber.* Paris, 1943.

D. ASLAN: *Ein Lebensbericht über Raoul Aslan.* Ill., Vienna, 1953.

B. GLOSSY and G. BERGER: *Josefine Gallmeyer, Wiens grösste Volksschauspielerin.* Ill., Vienna, n.d.

A. BURKHARD: *Franz Grillparzer in England und Amerika.* Vienna, 1961.

N. FUERST: *Grillparzer auf der Bühne.* Ill., Vienna, 1958.

U. HELMENSDORFER: *Grillparzers Bühnenkunst, Studien.* Bern, 1960. B.

J. NADLER: *Franz Grillparzer.* Vaduz, 1948.

F. NAUMANN: *Grillparzer, das dichterische Werk.* Zürich, 1956.

G. POLLAK: *Franz Grillparzer and the Austrian drama.* Ill., New York, 1907.

H. HAMMELMANN: *Hugo von Hofmannsthal.* London, 1957.

E. HEDERER: *Hugo von Hofmannsthal.* Frankfurt-on-Main, 1960.

K.-J. KRÜGER: *Hugo von Hofmannsthal und Richard Strauss.* Berlin, 1935.

K. J. NAEF: *Hugo von Hofmannsthal, Wesen und Werk.* Zürich, 1938.

E. PIRCHAN: *Therese Krones, die Theaterkönigin Altwiens.* Ill., Vienna, 1942.

O. F. DE BATTAGLIA: *Johann Nestroy.* Munich, 1962.

H. KINDERMANN: *Ferdinand Raimund.* Vienna, 1940.

H. CARTER: *The theatre of Max Reinhardt.* Ill., London, 1914.

H. HERALD: *Max Reinhardt, Bildnis eines Theatermannes.* Hamburg, 1953.

F. HORCH: *Die Spielpläne Max Reinhardts, 1905–30.* Munich, 1930.

S. JACOBSOHN: *Max Reinhardt.* Ill., Berlin, 1910.

H. ROTHE: *Max Reinhardt, 25 Jahre deutsches Theater.* Ill., Munich, 1930.

O. M. SAYLER (ed.): *Max Reinhardt and his theatre.* Ill., New York, 1924.

E. STERN and H. HERALD (eds.): *Reinhardt und seine Bühne, Bilder von der Arbeit des deutschen Theaters.* Ill., Berlin, 1918.

S. LIPTZIN: *Arthur Schnitzler.* New York, 1932.

A. KAHANE: *Die Thimigs, Theater als Schicksal einer Familie.* Ill., Leipzig, 1930.

Hugo Thimig erzählt von seinem Leben und dem Theater seiner Zeit, Briefe und Tagebuchnotizen, ausgewählt von F. Hadamowsky. Ill., Graz, 1962. B.

(*See also* RELIGIOUS DRAMA, DRAMATIC CRITICISM, *and* SHAKESPEARE.)

AUTOS SACRAMENTALES

See RELIGIOUS DRAMA, *and* SPAIN

BELGIUM

1. *General*

J. BITHELL: *Contemporary Belgian literature.* London and New York, 1915. B.

G. DOUTREPONT: *Histoire illustrée de la littérature française en Belgique.* Ill., Brussels, 1939. B.

A. DUPONT: *Répertoire dramatique belge.* 2 vols., Liège, 1884.

F. FABER: *Histoire du théâtre français en Belgique depuis son origine jusqu'à nos jours d'après des documents inédits.* Brussels and Paris, 1878–80.

M. GAUCHEZ: *Histoire des lettres françaises de Belgique des origines à nos jours.* Brussels, 1922. B.

H. LIEBRECHT: *Histoire du théâtre français en Belgique aux 17ᵉ et 18ᵉ siècles.* Paris, 1923.

2. *Drama, Theatre*

J. ISNARDON: *Le théâtre de La Monnaie depuis sa fondation jusqu'à nos jours.* Ill., Brussels, 1890.

S. LILAR: *60 ans de théâtre belge.* Ill., Brussels, 1952.

L. RENIEU: *Histoire des théâtres de Bruxelles depuis leur origine jusqu'à ce jour.* Ill., 2 vols., Paris, 1928.

P. CLAYES: *Histoire du théâtre à Gand.* Ill., 2 vols., Ghent, 1892.

3. *Actors, Dramatists, etc.*

J. BITHELL: *Life and writings of Maurice Maeterlinck.* London and New York, 1913. B.

U. TAYLOR: *Maurice Maeterlinck, a critical study.* London, 1914.

D. HALLS: *Maurice Maeterlinck, a study of his life and thought.* Ill., Oxford, 1960. B.

BIBLE-HISTORIES

See RELIGIOUS DRAMA, ENGLAND, *and* FRANCE

BOLIVIA

See SOUTH AMERICA, 3

BRAZIL

See SOUTH AMERICA, 4

BURLESQUE

See POPULAR ENTERTAINMENT, 1 and 2

BURMA

See EASTERN THEATRE, 1 and 2

CANADA

1. *General*

G. BELLERIVE: *Nos auteurs dramatiques.* Quebec, 1933.

—— 'Le théâtre canadien'. *Le Canada Français*, Apr. and Sept. 1933.)

J. BÉRAUD: *350 ans de théâtre au Canada français.* Ill., Ottawa, 1958.

R. HARVEY: *Curtain time.* Boston (Mass.), 1949.

H. N. HILLEBRAND: *Edmund Kean.* New York, 1933.

L. HOULE: *L'histoire du théâtre au Canada.* Montreal, 1945.

J. D. LOGAN and D. G. FRENCH: *Highways of Canadian literature.* Toronto, 1924.

V. B. RHODENIZER: *A handbook of Canadian literature.* Ottawa, 1930.

ROYAL COMMISSION ON NATIONAL DEVELOPMENT IN THE ARTS, LETTERS, AND SCIENCES: *Report.* Ottawa, 1951.

—— *Studies.* Ottawa, 1951.

2. *Drama, Theatre*

F. GRAHAM: *Histrionic Montreal.* Montreal, 1902.

H. MARCEL: *Le théâtre à Montréal.* Paris, 1911.

T. GUTHRIE, R. DAVIES, G. MACDONALD: *Twice have the trumpets sounded, a record of the Stratford Shakespearean Festival in Canada.* Ill., Stratford (Ont.), 1954.

3. *Actors, Dramatists, etc.*

E. ALBANI: *40 years of song.* London, 1911.

E. H. SOTHERN: *My remembrances.* London, 1917.

CHILE

See SOUTH AMERICA, 5

CHINA

See EASTERN THEATRE, 1, 4

CIRCUS

C. BEATTY: *Facing the big cats, my world of lions and tigers.* Ill., New York and London, 1965.

B. B. BURLEIGH: *Circus.* Ill., London, 1937.

J. S. CLARKE: *Circus parade, a pictorial review of the circus.* Ill., London, 1936.

R. CROFT-COOKE and W. S. MEADMORE: *The sawdust ring.* Ill., London, 1951.

M. W. DISHER: *Fairs, circuses and music halls.* Ill., London, 1942.

—— *Greatest show on earth.* Ill., London, 1937.

J. and A. DURANT: *Pictorial history of the American circus.* Ill., New York, 1957.

W. D. EDMONDS: *Chad Hanna.* London, 1940.

C. P. FOX: *A ticket to the circus, a pictorial history of the Incredible Ringlings.* Ill., Seattle, 1959.

T. FROST: *Circus life and circus celebrities.* London, 1875.

S. GASCH: *El circo por dentro.* Ill., Barcelona, 1961.

C. KEITH: *Circus and amusement (equestrian, dramatic and musical) in all nations.* Derby, 1879.

A. H. KOBER: *Circus nights and circus days, extracts from the diary of a circus man.* Ill., London, 1928.

J. LLOYD: *My circus life.* London, 1925.

F. A. LORD: *Little Big Top.* Ill., London and Sydney, 1965.

R. MANNING-SANDERS: *The English circus.* Ill., London, 1952.

J. PRÉVERT: *Le cirque d'Izis.* Ill., Monte Carlo, 1965.

Lady ELEANOR SMITH: *British circus life.* Ill., London, 1948.

H. THÉTARD: *La merveilleuse histoire du cirque.* Ill., Paris, 1947.

R. TOOLE-STOTT: *Circus and allied arts, a world bibliography, 1500–1959.* Ill., 3 vols., Derby, 1958–62.

—— *A bibliography of books on the circus in England from 1773–1964.* Derby, 1964.

Sir GEORGE TYRWHITT-DRAKE: *The English circus and fair ground.* Ill., London, 1946.

M. R. WERNER: *Barnum.* Ill., New York, 1923. B.

COLUMBIA

See SOUTH AMERICA, 6

COMEDY

See TRAGEDY, *and* COMEDY, 2

COMMEDIA DELL'ARTE

M. APOLLONIO: *Storia della commedia dell'arte.* Milan, 1930. B.

G. ATTINGER: *L'esprit de la commedia dell'arte dans le théâtre français.* Paris, 1950.

A. BASCHET: *Les comédiens italiens à la cour de France sous Charles IX, Henri III, Henri IV et Louis XIII.* Paris, 1882.

C. W. BEAUMONT: *The history of Harlequin.* Ill., London, 1926. B.

E. CAMPARDON: *Les comédiens du roi de la troupe italienne pendant les deux derniers siècles.* 2 vols., Paris, 1880.

X. DE COURVILLE: *Un apôtre de l'art du théâtre au XVIIIe siècle, Luigi Riccoboni dit Lélio (1676–1753).* Ill., 4 vols., Paris, 1943–58. B.

P.-L. DUCHARTRE: *La commedia dell'arte et ses enfants.* Ill., repr., rev. and augmented, Paris, 1955. B.

—— *The Italian comedy, the improvisation, scenarios, lives, attributes, portraits and masks of the illustrious characters of the commedia dell'arte.* Ill., London and New York, 1929. B.

K. M. LEA: *Italian popular comedy, a study in the commedia dell'arte, 1560–1620.* 2 vols., repr., Oxford, 1963. B.

C. MIC: *La commedia dell'arte, ou, le théâtre des comédiens italiens des XVIe, XVIIe et XVIIIe siècles.* Ill., Paris, 1927. B.

F. NICOLINI: *Vita di Arlecchino.* Ill., Milan, 1958.

A. NICOLL: *The world of Harlequin, a critical study of the commedia dell'arte.* Ill., Cambridge, 1963. B.

T. NIKLAUS: *Harlequin phoenix, or the rise and fall of a Bergamask rogue.* Ill., London, 1956. B.

V. PANDOLFI (ed.): *La commedia dell'arte, storia e testi.* 4 vols., Florence, 1957.

F. and C. PARFAICT: *Histoire de l'ancien théâtre italien depuis son origine en France jusqu'à sa suppression en l'année 1697.* Paris, 1753.

E. PETRACCONE: *La commedia dell'arte, storia, tecnica, scenari.* Naples, 1927.

L. RICCOBONI: *Nuovo teatro italiano, che contiene le commedie stampate e recitate dal S. L. Riccoboni, detto Lelio.* 3 vols., Paris, 1733.

M. SAND: *The history of the harlequinade.* Ill., 2 vols., London, 1915.

I. A. SCHWARTZ: *The commedia dell'arte and its influence on French comedy in the 17th century.* Paris, 1933. B.

K. G. SIMON: *Pantomime, Ursprung, Wesen, Möglichkeiten.* Ill., Munich, 1960.

W. SMITH: *The commedia dell'arte, a study in Italian popular comedy.* Ill., New York, 1912. B.

—— *Italian actors of the Renaissance.* Ill., New York, 1930.

S. THÉRAULT: *La commedia dell'arte vue à travers le Zibaldone de Pérouse.* Ill., Paris, 1965.

(*See also* FRANCE, *and* ITALY.)

COMMUNITY THEATRE

See AMATEUR THEATRE, PROVINCIAL AND REPERTORY THEATRES, REGIONAL AND PIONEER THEATRE, *and* U.S.A.

COSTUME

See TECHNICAL BOOKS, 1 and 3

DENMARK

See SCANDINAVIA, 2

DRAMATIC CRITICISM

J. AGATE (ed.): *The English dramatic critics, 1660–1932, an anthology.* London, 1932.

—— *These were actors, extracts from a newspaper cuttings book, 1811–33.* Ill., London, 1943.

—— *Those were the nights, an anthology of criticism, 1880–1906.* Ill., London, 1946.

H. J. CHAYTOR: *Dramatic theory in Spain, extracts from literature before and during the Golden Age.* Cambridge, 1925.

B. H. CLARK: *European theories of the drama, with a supplement on the American drama: an anthology of dramatic theory and criticism from Aristotle to the present day, in a series of selected texts, with commentaries, biographies and bibliographies.* New York, 1947. B. Rev. ed. H. Popkin, 1965.

H. CLURMAN: *Lies like truth, theatre reviews and essays.* New York, 1958.

H. DOWNS: *The critic in the theatre.* London, 1953.

C. H. GRAY: *Theatrical criticism in London to 1795.* New York, 1931. B.

C. HAMILTON: *The theory of the theatre and other principles of dramatic criticism.* Rev. ed., New York, 1939.

W. HAZLITT: *Liber amoris and Dramatic criticisms,* with an essay of introduction by Charles Morgan. London, 1948.

—— *Hazlitt on theatre,* ed. W. Archer and R. Lowe. London, 1957.

A. WHITLEY: *Hazlitt and the theater.* 1955. (Univ. of Texas Studies in English, xxxiv.)

H. HOBSON: *Verdict at midnight, 60 years of dramatic criticism.* London, 1952.

LEIGH HUNT: *Dramatic criticism, 1808–31,* ed. L. H. and C. W. Houtchens. New York, 1949, London, 1950.

H. JAMES: *The scenic art, notes on acting and the drama, 1872–1901.* London, 1949.

E. JOURDAIN: *Dramatic theory and practice in France, 1690–1808.* London, 1921.

—— *The drama in Europe in theory and practice.* London, 1924. B.

S. R. LITTLEWOOD: *Dramatic criticism.* New and enl. ed., London, 1952. B.

M. MCCARTHY: *Sights and Spectacles, 1937–1958.* London, 1959.

M. J. MOSES and J. M. BROWN (eds.): *The American theatre as seen by its critics, 1752–1934.* New York, 1934.

A. NICOLL: *The theatre and dramatic theory.* London, 1962.

SEAN O'CASEY: *The green crow (1930–1957).* London, 1957.

C. RICE: *The London theatre in the eighteen-thirties.* London, 1950.

A. Ridler (ed.): *Shakespeare criticism, 1919–35.* London, 1936.

—— *Shakespeare criticism, 1935–1960.* London, 1963.

J. G. Robertson: *Lessing's dramatic theory, being an introduction to, and a commentary on his 'Hamburgische Dramaturgie'.* Cambridge, 1939. B.

G. Saintsbury: *A history of criticism and literary taste in Europe from the earliest times to the present day.* 3 vols., London, 1900–4.

G. B. Shaw: *Dramatic criticism (1895–8).* New York, 1962.

—— *On theatre*, ed. E. J. West. New York, 1962.

—— *Plays and players, essays on the theatre*, selected by A. C. Ward. London, 1952.

D. N. Smith (ed.): *Shakespeare criticism, a selection.* New ed., London, 1946.

F. Sper: *The periodical press of London, theatrical and literary (excluding the daily newspaper), 1800–30.* Boston (Mass.) and London, 1937.

K. Tynan: *Curtains (1950–1960).* London, 1961.

—— *He that plays the king, a view of the theatre.* London, 1950.

A. C. Ward (ed.): *Specimens of English dramatic criticism, 17th–20th centuries.* London, 1945.

S. Young: *Immortal shadows, a book of dramatic criticism (1922–1947).* New York, 1948.

EASTERN EUROPE

1. *Bulgaria*

Le centième anniversaire du théâtre bulgare. Ill., Sofia, 1956.

2. *Czechoslovakia*

Ročenka Kruhů Solistů Městských Divadel Pražských (Yearbooks of the Municipal Theatre in Prague). Ill., 17 vols., Prague, 1924–40.

Instituto teatral: *La escenografia checoslovaca 1914–1959.* Ill., São Paulo, n.d.

3. *Poland*

E. Csato: *The Polish theatre.* Ill., Warsaw, 1963.

A. Grodzicki and R. Szydłowski: *Theatre in modern Poland.* Warsaw, 1963.

E. Misiołek: *Bibliographie théâtrale polonaise, 1944–1964.* Warsaw, 1965.

R. Nowicki: *Theatre schools in Poland.* Warsaw, 1962.

4. *Rumania*

G. Oprescu (ed.): *Istoria teatrului în România.* Ill., Bucharest, 1965– . B. (In progress.)

5. *Yugoslavia*

S. Batušić and M. Nikolić: *The theatre in Yugoslavia.* Ill., Belgrade, 1955.

EASTERN THEATRE

I. FAR EAST

1. *General*

F. Bowers: *Theatre in the East.* Ill., New York and London, 1956. B.

2. *Burma*

M. H. Aung: *Burmese drama, a study with translations of Burmese plays.* 2nd ed., London, 1937.

U. P. Ni: *'Konmara Pya Zat', an example of popular Burmese drama in the 19th-century*, translated . . . by H. Pe. London, 1952.

K. Sein (pseud.) and J. A. Withey: *The great Po Sein, a chronicle of the Burmese theatre.* Ill., Bloomington, 1965, London, 1966. B.

3. *Ceylon*

E. R. Sarathchandra: *The Sinhalese folk play and the modern stage.* Ill., Colombo, 1953.

4. *China*

L. C. Arlington: *The Chinese drama from the earliest times until to-day, a panoramic study of the art in China, tracing its origin and describing its actors (in both male and female rôles), their costumes and make-up, superstitions and stage slang, the accompanying music and musical instruments, concluding with synopses of 30 Chinese plays.* Ill., Shanghai, 1930. B.

K. Buss: *Studies in the Chinese drama.* Ill., rev. ed., New York, 1930.

J. Chen: *The Chinese theatre.* Ill., London, 1949.

H. A. Giles: *A history of Chinese literature.* Rev. ed., London and New York, 1931. B.

R. F. Johnson: *The Chinese drama.* Ill., Shanghai, 1921.

C. Poupeye: *Le théâtre chinois.* Ill., Paris, 1933. B.

A. C. Scott: *The classical theatre of China.* Ill., London, 1957. B.

H. W. Wells: *The classical drama of the orient (China and Japan).* Bombay and London, 1965.

A. E. Zucker: *The Chinese theater.* Ill., Boston (Mass.) and London, 1925. B.

C. S. L. Zung: *Secrets of the Chinese drama, a complete explanatory guide to actions and symbols as seen in the performance of Chinese dramas.* Ill., London and Shanghai, 1937.

5. *India and Pakistan*

M. R. ANAND: *The Indian theatre.* Ill., London, 1950.

A. BAUSANI: *Storia delle letterature del Pakistan.* Milan, 1958.

S. BENEGAL: *A panorama of theatre in India.* Bombay, 1969.

B. GARGI: *The theatre in India.* New York, 1962.

H. H. GOWEN: *A history of Indian literature from Vedic times to the present day.* London and New York, 1931. B.

P. GUHA-THAKURTA: *The Bengali drama, its origin and development.* London, 1930. B.

H. N. DAS GUPTA: *The Indian stage.* 2 vols., Calcutta, 1938.

G. JACOB, H. JENSEN, H. LOSCH (eds.): *Das indische Schattentheater.* Ill., Stuttgart, 1931.

R. V. JAGIRDAR: *Drama in Sanskrit literature.* Bombay, n.d.

A. B. KEITH: *The Sanskrit drama in its origin, development, theory and practice.* Oxford and New York, 1924.

S. KONOW: *Das indische Drama.* Berlin, 1920.

A. A. MACDONELL: *A history of Sanskrit literature.* London, 1913. B.

D. R. MANKAD: *The types of Sanskrit drama.* Karachi, n.d.

J. C. MATHUR: *Drama in rural India.* Ill., Bombay and London, 1964. B.

M. SADIQ: *A history of Urdu literature.* London, 1964.

—— *20th century Urdu literature.* London, 1965.

R. B. SAKSENA: *A history of Urdu literature* Allahabad, 1927.

M. SCHUYLER, Jr.: *A bibliography of the Sanskrit drama, with an introductory sketch of the dramatic literature of India.* New York, 1906.

H. W. WELLS: *The classical drama of India.* Bombay and London, n.d.

—— (ed.): *Six Sanskrit plays in English translation.* Ill., Bombay and London, 1964.

H. H. WILSON, V. RAGHVAN etc.: *The theatre of the Hindus.* London, 1956.

R. K. YAJNIK: *The Indian theatre, its origins and its later developments under European influence, with special reference to Western India.* London and New York, 1933.

6. *Japan*

J. T. ARAKI: *The ballad-drama of medieval Japan.* Ill., Berkeley (Calif.) and London, 1965.

P. ARNOLD: *Le théâtre japonais.* Ill., Paris, 1957.

W. G. ASTON: *A history of Japanese literature.* London, new ed., New York, 1933. B.

A. BEAUJARD: *Le théâtre comique des japonais, introduction à l'étude des Kyôghén.* Paris, 1937. B.

A. BÉNAZET: *Le théâtre au Japon, ses rapports avec les cultes locaux.* Ill., Paris, 1901. B.

F. BOWERS: *Japanese theatre.* Ill., New York and London, 1956.

O. EDWARDS: *Japanese plays and playfellows.* Ill., London, 1901.

E. ERNST: *The Kabuki theatre.* Ill., London, 1956.

Z. KINKAID: *Kabuki, the popular stage of Japan.* Ill., New York, 1925.

F. A. LOMBARD: *An outline history of the Japanese drama.* Ill., London and New York, 1929. B.

A. MAYBON: *Le théâtre japonais.* Ill., Paris, 1935.

A. MIYAMORI: *Masterpieces of Chikamatsu, the Japanese Shakespeare.* New York, 1960.

M. PIPER: *Das japanische Theater, ein Spiegel des Volkes.* Ill., Frankfurt-on-Main, 1937.

G. RENONDEAU: *Le nô.* Tokyo, 1954.

A. C. SCOTT: *The Kabuki theatre of Japan.* Ill., London, 1955, New York, 1966. B.

M. C. STOPES and J. SAKURAI: *Plays of old Japan: the 'Nō', together with translations of the dramas.* Ill., London, 1913. B.

K. TOYOTAKA: *Japanese music and drama in the Meiji era.* Tokyo, 1957.

A. D. WALEY: *The Nō plays of Japan.* Ill., new ed., London, 1950. B.

II. MIDDLE EAST

J. M. LANDAU: *Studies in the Arab theatre and cinema.* Ill., Pennsylvania and Oxford, 1958.

V. COTTAS: *Le théâtre à Byzance.* Paris, 1931. B.

A. C. MAHR: *The Cyprus Passion Cycle.* Ill., Notre Dame (Indiana), 1947.

G. J. THEOCHARIDIS: *Beiträge zur Geschichte des byzantinischen Profantheaters im IV. und V. Jahrhundert.* Munich and Thessaloniki, 1940.

M. AND: *A history of theatre and popular entertainment in Turkey.* Ill., Ankara, 1963.

—— *Dances of Anatolian Turkey.* Ill., New York, 1959.

N. M. MARTINOVITCH: *The Turkish theatre.* Ill., New York, 1933.

ELIZABETHAN PLAYHOUSE

See ENGLAND, *and* SHAKESPEARE

ENGLAND

1. *Reference Works*

DOBSON'S *Theatre year book 1948*. London, 1949.

H. DOWNS (ed.): *Theatre and stage*. Ill., 2 vols., 2nd ed., London, 1951.

G. ENTHOVEN: *Studies in English theatre history, in memory of Gabrielle Enthoven*. London, 1952.

W. W. GREG: *A bibliography of the English printed drama to the Restoration*. Ill., 4 vols., London, 1939–59.

A. HARBAGE: *Annals of English drama, 975–1700*, revised by S. Schoenbaum. London, 1964.

E. NUNGEZER: *A dictionary of actors and of other persons associated with the public representation of plays in England before 1642*. Yale and Oxford, 1929. B.

Stage Cyclopaedia, a bibliography of plays, ed. R. Clarence. London, 1909.

Theatre Notebook, a quarterly of notes and research. Ill., London, 1945– . (In progress.)

2. *Drama, Theatre*

D. E. BAKER, I. REED, S. JONES: *Biographia Dramatica, or, a companion to the playhouse*. 3 vols., London, 1812.

H. B. BAKER: *Our old actors*. Rev. ed., London, 1881.

—— *History of the London stage and its famous players, 1576–1903*. London, 1904.

W. BRIDGES-ADAMS: *The irresistible theatre*. Ill., 2 vols., repr., London, 1964. B.

E. J. BURTON: *The British theatre, 1100–1900, its repertory and practice*. Ill., London, 1960.

W. CLEMEN: *English tragedy before Shakespeare, the development of dramatic speech*. London, 1961.

A. CLUNES: *The British theatre*. Ill., London, 1964.

D. COOK: *Hours with the players*. London, 1883.

W. A. DARLINGTON: *The actor and his audience (studies of Burbage, Betterton, Garrick, Siddons, Kean, Irving)*. Ill., London, 1949.

J. DORAN: *Annals of the English stage from Thomas Betterton to Edmund Kean*, edited and revised by R. W. Lowe. Ill., 3 vols., London, 1888.

J. DOWNES: *Roscius Anglicanus, or an historical view of the English stage from 1660 to 1706*. Repr., with notes by M. Summers, London, 1930.

T. GILLILAND: *The dramatic mirror . . . including a biographical and critical account of . . . the most distinguished performers from the days of Shakespeare to 1807, and a history of the country theatres in England, Ireland, and Scotland*. Ill., 2 vols., London, 1808.

W. HAZLITT: *On the theatre*, ed. W. Archer and R. Lowe. London, 1958.

—— *A view of the English stage*. (*see* Complete works, ed. P. P. Howe. Vol. 5.) London, 1930.

S. JOSEPH: *The story of the playhouse in England*. Ill., London, 1963.

E. MALONE: *An historical account of the rise and progress of the English stage, and of the economy and usage of our ancient theatres and of the original actors in Shakespeare's plays*. (*See* vol. 2 of Malone's edition of Shakespeare, London, 1790.)

R. MANDER and J. MITCHENSON: *A picture history of British theatre*. Ill., London, 1957.

A. NICOLL: *The English theatre, a short history*. Ill., London, 1936. B.

—— *A history of English drama, 1660–1900*. 6 vols., Cambridge, 1952–9. (Vol. 6 contains *Short-title ABC catalogue of plays produced or printed in England from 1660–1900*).

G. SAMPSON: *The concise Cambridge history of English literature*. 2nd ed. with a new chapter on 'The age of T. S. Eliot', by R. C. Churchill. Cambridge, 1961.

R. F. SHARP: *A short history of the English stage from its beginnings to 1908*. London and New York, 1909.

J. SPEED: *The theatre of the empire of Great Britaine*. Facsimile of 1st ed. of 1611, by J. Arlott. 2 vols., London, 1953.

A. THALER: *Shakespere to Sheridan, a book about the theatre of yesterday and to-day*. Ill., Harvard and Oxford, 1922.

G. WICKHAM: *Early English stages, 1300–1660*. Ill., London, Vol. I, 1959; Vol. II, Pt. 1, 1963. (In progress.)

W. J. WIMSATT (ed.): *English stage comedy*. New York and London, 1955.

3. *Elizabethan Period*

J. Q. ADAMS: *Shakespearean playhouses, a history of English theatres from the beginning to the Restoration*. Ill., Boston, 1917.

W. A. ARMSTRONG: *The Elizabethan private theatres, facts and problems*. Ill., London, 1958.

M. C. BRADBROOK: *The rise of the common player, a study of actor and society in Shakespeare's England*. London, 1962.

O. M. BUSBY: *Studies in the development of the fool in the Elizabethan drama*. London, 1923.

E. K. CHAMBERS: *The Elizabethan stage*. Ill., 4 vols., repr., Oxford, 1951. B.

—— *The English folk-play*. Oxford, 1933.

D. M. BEVINGTON: *From mankind to Marlowe, growth of structure in the popular drama of Tudor England*. Harvard and London, 1962.

T. W. CRAIK: *The Tudor interlude, stage, costume, and acting*. Ill., Leicester, 1958. B.

F. G. FLEAY: *A biographical chronicle of the English drama, 1559–1642.* 2 vols., repr., London, 1962.

W. W. GREG: *Dramatic documents from the Elizabethan playhouses, stage plots, actors' parts, prompt books, reproductions and transcripts.* Ill., Oxford, 1931.

—— *Pastoral poetry and pastoral drama, a literary inquiry, with special reference to the pre-Restoration stage in England.* London, 1906. B.

P. HENSLOWE: *Diary*, ed. with supplementary material . . . by R. A. Foakes and R. T. Rickert. Ill., Cambridge, 1961.

W. J. LAWRENCE: *The Elizabethan playhouse and other studies.* Ill., 2 vols., Stratford-upon-Avon and New York, 1912–13. B.

—— *Old theatre days and ways.* Ill., London, 1935.

—— *The physical conditions of the Elizabethan public playhouse.* Ill., Harvard, 1927.

—— *Pre-Restoration stage studies.* Ill., Harvard, 1927.

—— *Speeding up Shakespeare, studies of the bygone theatre and drama.* Ill., London, 1937.

—— *Those nut-cracking Elizabethans, studies of the early theatre and drama.* Ill., London, 1935.

D. MEHL: *The Elizabethan dumb show, a dramatic convention.* London, 1965. B.

T. H. V. MOTTER: *The school drama in England.* Ill., London, 1929.

C. T. PROUTY (ed.): *Studies in the Elizabethan theatre.* Hamder (Conn.), 1961.

(*See also* RELIGIOUS DRAMA.)

A. W. REED: *Early Tudor drama—Medwall, the Rastells, Heywood and the More circle.* Ill., London, 1926.

P. SIMPSON: *Studies in Elizabethan drama.* Oxford, 1955.

C. W. WALLACE: *The evolution of the English drama up to Shakespeare, with a history of the first Blackfriars Theatre, a survey based upon original records now for the first time collected and published.* Berlin, 1912.

G. L. HOSKING: *The life and times of Edward Alleyn.* Ill., London, 1952.

E. M. WAITH: *The pattern of tragicomedy in Beaumont and Fletcher.* Yale and London, 1952.

L. C. KNIGHTS: *Drama and society in the age of Jonson.* London, 1937. B.

J. PALMER: *Ben Jonson.* Ill., London and New York, 1934.

F. S. BOAS: *Marlowe and his circle, a biographical survey.* Ill., London, 1929.

—— *Christopher Marlowe, a biographical and critical study.* Ill., repr., with supplementary note, Oxford, 1953.

M. ECCLES: *Christopher Marlowe in London.* Harvard, 1934.

U. M. ELLIS-FERMOR: *Christopher Marlowe.* London, 1927.

P. HENDERSON: *And morning in his eyes, a book about Christopher Marlowe.* Ill., London, 1937. B.

L. HOTSON: *The death of Christopher Marlowe.* Ill., Harvard and London, 1925.

H. T. LEVIN: *Christopher Marlowe, the overreacher.* London, 1965. B.

(*See also* SHAKESPEARE.)

4. *Seventeenth and Eighteenth Centuries*

G. E. BENTLEY: *The Jacobean and Caroline stage.* Vols. 1–2: Dramatic companies and players. Vols. 3–5: Plays and playwrights. 5 vols., Oxford, 1941–56. B.

U. M. ELLIS-FERMOR: *The Jacobean drama, an interpretation.* Ill., rev. and repr., London, 1965. B.

STRATFORD-UPON-AVON STUDIES, 1: *Jacobean theatre.* London, 1960.

(*See also* MASQUE.)

E. BOSWELL: *The Restoration court stage, 1660–1702, with a particular account of the production of 'Calisto'.* Ill., Harvard, 1932. B.

P. FITZGERALD: *A new history of the English stage from the Restoration to the liberty of the theatres in connection with the Patent Houses.* 2 vols., London, 1882.

J. GENEST: *Some account of the English stage, from the Restoration in 1660 to 1830.* 10 vols., Bath, 1832.

L. HOTSON: *The Commonwealth and Restoration stage.* Ill., reissue, Cambridge (Mass.) and Oxford, 1964.

L. HUGHES: *A century of farce . . . from the Restoration to the middle of the 18th century.* Princeton and London, 1956. B.

H. W. LANIER: *The first English actresses from the initial appearance of women on the stage in 1660 till 1700.* Ill., New York, 1930.

London Stage, 1660–1800, a calendar of plays . . . together with casts . . . and contemporary comment. Carbondale (Illinois), 1960– . (In progress.)

J. J. LYNCH: *Box, pit and gallery, stage and society in Johnson's London.* Ill., Berkeley (Calif.) and Cambridge, 1953.

H. W. PEDICORD: *The theatrical public in the time of Garrick.* New York, 1954. B.

R. R. REED: *Bedlam on the Jacobean stage.* Harvard and London, 1952. B.

S. ROSENFELD: *Foreign theatrical companies in Great Britain in the 17th and 18th centuries.* London, 1955.

D. F. SMITH: *Plays about the theatre in England, 1671–1737.* Ill., Oxford, 1936.

J. H. SMITH: *The gay couple in Restoration comedy*. Harvard and London, 1948.

A. C. SPRAGUE: *Beaumont and Fletcher on the Restoration stage*. Ill., Harvard and Oxford, 1926. B.

Sir RICHARD STEELE: *The theatre 1720*, ed. by J. Loftis. Oxford, 1962.

STRATFORD-UPON-AVON STUDIES, 6: *Restoration theatre*. London, 1960.

M. SUMMERS: *The playhouse of Pepys, a description of the drama produced in the years 1660–82*. Ill., London, 1935.

—— *The Restoration theatre, an account of the staging of plays in the Restoration theatre*. Ill., London and New York, 1934.

A. N. WILEY: *Rare prologues and epilogues, 1642–1700*. Ill., London, 1939.

J. W. BOWYER: *The celebrated Mrs. Centlivre*. Ill., London, 1953. B.

R. H. BAKER: *Mr. Cibber of Drury Lane*. New York, 1939. B.

C. CIBBER: *An apology for the life of Colley Cibber, with an historical view of the stage during his own time*. New ed., with supplement and notes by R. W. Lowe. Ill., 2 vols., London, 1889.

E. L. AVERY: *Congreve's plays on the 18th century stage*. Oxford, 1951.

J. C. HODGES: *William Congreve, the man, a biography from new sources*. Ill., New York, 1944. B.

D. C. TAYLOR: *William Congreve*. Oxford, 1931.

C. DIBDIN (the younger): *Memoirs*, ed. by G. Speaight. London, 1956.

W. CONNELY: *Young George Farquhar*. Ill., London and New York, 1949.

W. A. DARLINGTON: *Sheridan*. London, 1933.

K. FOSS: *Here lies Richard Brinsley Sheridan*. New York, 1940.

L. GIBBS: *Sheridan*. London, 1947.

W. S. SICHEL: *Sheridan*. Ill., 2 vols., Boston (Mass.), 1909. B.

W. CONNELY: *Brawny Wycherley*. London and New York, 1930.

E. R. PAGE: *George Colman the elder, essayist, dramatist and theatrical manager, 1732–94*. New York, 1935. B.

W. DUNLAP: *Memoirs of George Frederick Cooke, late of the Theatre Royal, Covent Garden*. 2 vols., London, 1813.

W. COOKE: *Memoirs of Samuel Foote, with a collection of his genuine bon-mots, anecdotes, opinions, etc., mostly original* ... 3 vols., London, 1805.

D. GARRICK: *The diary, a record of his memorable trip to Paris in 1751*. Ill., London and New York, 1928.

—— *The letters*, ed. by D. M. Little and G. M. Kahrl. Ill., 3 vols., London, 1964.

M. BARTON: *Garrick*. Ill., London, 1948. B.

K. A. BURNIM: *David Garrick, director*. Pittsburgh, 1961.

T. DAVIES: *Memoirs of the life of David Garrick, interspersed with characters and anecdotes of his theatrical contemporaries, the whole forming a history of the stage which included a period of 36 years*. 2 vols., London, 1780.

P. FITZGERALD: *Life of David Garrick, from original family papers and numerous published and unpublished sources*. 2 vols., new and rev. ed., London, 1899.

F. A. HEDGCOCK: *A cosmopolitan actor, David Garrick and his French friends*. Ill., London, 1912. B.

A. MURPHY: *Life of David Garrick*. 2 vols., London, 1801.

C. OMAN: *David Garrick, a new biography*. Ill., London, 1958.

E. P. STEIN: *David Garrick, dramatist*. Ill., New York, 1938. B.

C. L. LEWES: *Memoirs, containing anecdotes of the English and Scottish stages, during a period of 40 years*. 4 vols., London, 1805.

W. W. APPLETON: *Charles Macklin, an actor's life*. Ill., Harvard and London, 1961.

W. COOKE: *Memoirs of Charles Macklin, comedian, with the dramatic characters, manners, anecdotes, etc. of the age in which he lived, and a chronological list of all the parts played by him, forming an history of the stage during almost the whole of the last century*. London, 1804.

J. T. KIRKMAN: *Memoirs of the life of Charles Macklin, Esq*. 2 vols., London, 1799.

T. SNAGGE: *Recollections of occurrences, memoirs*, with an introduction by H. Hobson. London, 1951.

A. M. TAYLOR: *Next to Shakespeare, Otway ... on the London stage*. Ill., Duke U.P., 1950. B.

J. C. LUCEY: *Lovely Peggy, the life and times of Margaret Woffington*. Ill., London, 1952.

5. *Eighteenth and Nineteenth Centuries*

C. F. ARMSTRONG: *A century of great actors, 1750–1850*. London, 1912.

A. BUNN: *The stage, both before and behind the curtain, from observations taken on the spot*. 3 vols., London, 1840.

E. FITZBALL: *35 years of a dramatic author's life*. 2 vols., London, 1859.

T. HOLCROFT: *Life written by himself*, continued ... from his diary ... by W. Hazlitt, and now newly ed. ... by E. Colby. Ill., 2 vols., London, 1925.

C. MATHEWS: *Memoirs*, ed. by Mrs. Mathews. Ill., 4 vols., London, 1838–9.

H. SIMPSON and C. BROWN: *A century of famous actresses, 1750–1850*. London, 1913.

E. B. WATSON: *Sheridan to Robertson, a study of the 19th century London stage.* Ill., Harvard, 1926. B.

F. FLEETWOOD: *Conquest, the story of a theatre family.* Ill., London, 1953. B.

G. RAYMOND: *The life and enterprises of Robert William Elliston, comedian.* London, 1857.

B. FOTHERGILL: *Mrs. Jordan, portrait of an actress.* Ill., London, 1965.

M. W. DISHER: *Mad genius, a biography of Edmund Kean.* Ill., London, 1950.

F. W. HAWKINS: *The life of Edmund Kean, from published and original sources.* 2 vols., London, 1869.

H. M. HILLIBRAND: *Edmund Kean.* New York, 1933.

J. F. MOLLOY: *The life and adventures of Edmund Kean, tragedian, 1787–1833.* 2 vols., London, 1888.

G. PLAYFAIR: *Kean.* Ill., London, 1939.

J. W. COLE: *The life and theatrical times of Charles Kean.* 2 vols., London, 1859.

H. BAKER: *John Philip Kemble, the actor in his theatre.* Harvard and London, 1942. B.

J. BOADEN: *Memoirs of the life of John Philip Kemble, including a history of the stage from the time of Garrick to the present day.* 2 vols., London, 1825.

P. FITZGERALD: *The Kembles.* 2 vols., London, 1871.

(*For* FANNY KEMBLE *see* U.S.A.)

W. C. MACREADY: *Reminiscences and selections from his diaries and letters,* ed. by Sir F. Pollock. 2 vols., London, 1875.

W. ARCHER: *W. C. Macready.* London, 1890.

Lady POLLOCK: *Macready as I knew him.* London, 1885.

C. H. SHATTUCK (ed.): *Bulwer and Macready, a chronicle of the early Victorian theatre.* Ill., Urbana (Illinois), 1958.

J. C. TREWIN: *Mr. Macready, a 19th-century tragedian and his theatre.* Ill., London, 1955. B.

J. COLEMAN: *Memoirs of Samuel Phelps.* London, 1886.

W. M. PHELPS and J. FORBES-ROBERTSON: *The life and life-work of Samuel Phelps.* Ill., London, 1886.

J. BOADEN: *Memoirs of Mrs. Siddons, interspersed with anecdotes of authors and actors.* Ill., repr., London, 1893.

T. CAMPBELL: *Life of Mrs. Siddons.* 2 vols., London, 1834.

Y. FFRENCH: *Mrs. Siddons, tragic actress.* Ill., London, 1936. B.

Mrs. C. PARSONS: *The incomparable Siddons.* Ill., London, 1909. B.

W. ARCHER: *English dramatists of today.* London, 1882.

F. J. H. DARTON: *Vincent Crummles, his theatre and his times, with an historical introductory note and appendixes.* Ill., London, 1926.

S. DESMOND: *London nights of long ago.* Ill., London, 1927.

C. DICKENS (ed.): *The life of Charles J. Mathews.* Ill., 2 vols., London, 1879.

M. W. DISHER: *Blood and thunder, mid-Victorian melodrama and its origins.* Ill., London, 1949.

—— *Melodrama, plots that thrilled.* Ill., London, 1955.

H. MORLEY: *The journal of a London playgoer from 1851 to 1866.* London, 1891.

H. C. NEWTON: *Crime and the drama, or dark deeds dramatized.* Ill., London, 1927.

H. PEARSON: *The last actor-managers.* Ill., London, 1956.

E. REYNOLDS: *Early Victorian drama, 1830–70.* Cambridge, 1936. B.

G. ROWELL: *The Victorian theatre, a survey.* Ill., London, 1956. B.

C. SCOTT: *The drama of yesterday and today.* Ill., 2 vols., London, 1899.

Sir SQUIRE *and Lady* BANCROFT: *Mr. and Mrs. Bancroft on and off the stage.* 2 vols., London, 1888.

(*For* DION BOUCICAULT *see* U.S.A.)

E. G. CRAIG: *Henry Irving.* Ill., London, 1930.

C. HIATT: *Henry Irving, a record and review.* Ill., London, 1899.

L. IRVING: *Henry Irving, the actor and his world.* Ill., London, 1951. B.

H. A. SAINTSBURY and C. PALMER (eds.): *We saw him act, a symposium on the art of Sir Henry Irving.* Ill., London, 1939.

C. SCOTT: *From 'The Bells' to 'King Arthur', a critical record of the first-night productions at the Lyceum Theatre from 1871 to 1895.* Ill., London, 1897.

B. STOKER: *Personal reminiscences of Henry Irving.* Ill., 2 vols., London, 1906.

R. A. CORDELL: *Henry Arthur Jones and the modern drama.* New York, 1932.

D. A. JONES: *The life and letters of Henry Arthur Jones.* Ill., London, 1930; in an American edition as *Taking the curtain call.* New York, 1930.

J. M. D. HARDWICK: *Emigrant in motley, the journey of Charles and Ellen Kean in Australia and America, as told in their unpublished letters.* Ill., London, 1954.

T. E. PEMBERTON: *The Kendals.* Ill., London, 1900.

H. FYFE: *Sir Arthur Pinero's plays and players.* Ill., London, 1930.

T. E. PEMBERTON: *The life and writings of T. W. Robertson.* Ill., London, 1893.

E. Robins: *Theatre and friendship (correspondence with Henry James)*. Ill., London and New York, 1932.

G. B. Shaw: *Dramatic opinions and essays, 1894–8*, ed. by J. Huneker. 2 vols., new ed., New York, 1962.

—— *Our theatres in the nineties, criticisms contributed . . . to the 'Saturday Review' from January 1895 to May 1898*. 3 vols., London, 1931.

—— *Plays and players, essays on the theatre*, selected with an introduction by A. C. Ward. London, 1952.

—— *Shaw on theatre*, ed. by E. J. West. London, 1960.

—— *Bernard Shaw and Mrs. Patrick Campbell: their correspondence*, ed. by A. Dent. London, 1954.

M. Colbourne: *The real Bernard Shaw*. Ill., London, 1949.

R. Mander and J. Mitchenson: *Theatrical companion to the plays of Shaw*. Ill., London, 1955.

M. Meisel: *Shaw and the 19th century theater*. Princeton and London, 1963. B.

H. Pearson: *Bernard Shaw, his life and personality*. Ill., London, 1942; in an American edition as *G.B.S., a full-length portrait*. New York, 1942. B.

A. C. Ward: *Bernard Shaw*. Ill., London, 1951. B.

E. Stirling: *Old Drury Lane, 50 years' recollections of author, actor, and manager*. 2 vols., London, 1881.

E. Terry: *The story of my life*. Ill., London, 1908. Reprinted as *Memoirs*, with . . . notes and biographical chapters by E. Craig and C. St. John. London, 1933.

E. Terry and B. Shaw: *A correspondence*, ed. by C. St. John. Ill., new ed., London, 1949.

E. G. Craig: *Ellen Terry and her secret self*. Ill., London, n.d. [1931].

C. Hiatt: *Ellen Terry and her impersonations*. Ill., London, 1898.

T. E. Pemberton: *Ellen Terry and her sisters*. Ill., London, 1902.

C. St. John: *Ellen Terry*. Ill., London, 1907.

M. Steen: *A pride of Terrys*. Ill., London, 1962.

M. Beerbohm (ed.): *Herbert Beerbohm Tree, some memories of him and his art*. Ill., London, 1920.

H. Pearson: *Beerbohm Tree, his life and laughter*. Ill., London, 1956.

A. Gide: *Oscar Wilde, a study*. London, 1905.

H. Pearson: *The life of Oscar Wilde*. Ill., London, 1946; in an American edition as *Oscar Wilde, his life and wit*. New York, 1946. B.

A. Ransome: *Oscar Wilde*. London, 1912.

6. *Twentieth Century*

J. Agate: *A short view of the English stage, 1900–26*. London, 1926.

W. Archer: *The old drama and the new*. London and Boston, 1923.

Sir George Arthur: *From Phelps to Gielgud, reminiscences of the stage through 65 years*. Ill., London, 1936.

Sir Kenneth Barnes: *Welcome, good friends, an autobiography*. London, 1958.

M. Beerbohm: *Around theatres, 1898–1910*. 2 vols., new ed., London and New York, 1953.

G. W. Bishop: *My betters*. Ill., London, 1957.

T. H. Dickinson: *The contemporary drama of England*. Rev. ed., Boston (Mass.) and London, 1931. B.

P. Godfrey: *Backstage, a survey of the contemporary English theatre from behind the scenes*. Ill., London, 1933.

J. T. Grein: *The new world of the theatre, 1923–4*. London, 1924.

A. Hare: *The Georgian theatre in Wessex*. Ill., London, 1958.

L. Hudson: *The English stage, 1850–1950*. Ill., London, 1951.

N. Marshall: *The other theatre*. Ill., London, 1947.

E. Reynolds: *Modern English drama*. Ill., London, 1949.

Royal Shakespeare Theatre Company, *1960–1963*. Ill., London, 1964.

R. Speaight: *William Poel and the Elizabethan revival*. Ill., London, 1954.

Stratford-upon-Avon Studies, 4: *Contemporary theatre*. London, 1962.

G. Weales: *Religion in modern English drama*. Pennsylvania and London, 1961.

A. Williamson: *Theatre of two decades*. Ill., London, 1951.

A. E. Wilson: *Edwardian theatre*. Ill., London, 1952.

W. A. Darlington: *J. M. Barrie*. London, 1938.

J. A. Roy: *James Matthew Barrie*. New York, 1938.

J. C. Trewin: *Benson and the Bensonians*. Ill., London, 1960.

A. Dent: *Mrs. Patrick Campbell*. London, 1961.

W. Bannister: *James Bridie and his theatre*. London, 1955.

R. Mander and J. Mitchenson: *Theatrical companion to Noël Coward*. Ill., London, 1957.

E. G. Craig: *Index to the story of my days, 1872–1907*. London, 1957.

—— *On the art of the theatre*. Ill., reissue, London, 1956.

SELECT LIST OF THEATRE BOOKS

D. BABLET: *Edward Gordon Craig.* Ill., Paris, 1962.

E. ROSE: *Gordon Craig and the theatre, a record and an interpretation.* Ill., London and New York, 1931. B.

A. DUKES: *The scene is changed.* London, 1942.

M. M. MORGAN: *A drama of political man, a study in the plays of Harley Granville-Barker.* London, 1961.

C. PURDOM: *Harley Granville-Barker.* London, 1955.

N. SCHOONDERWOERD: *J. T. Grein, ambassador of the theatre, 1862–1935, a study in Anglo-Continental relations.* Assen, 1963. B.

W. F. ISAAC, *Ben Greet and the Old Vic, a biography.* Ill., London, 1965. B.

R. MANDER and J. MITCHENSON: *Theatrical companion to Maugham.* Ill., London, 1955.

C. HASSALL: *Notes on the verse drama.* Ill., London, 1948. (The Masque, No. 6.)

R. PEACOCK: *The poet in the theatre.* London and New York, 1946.

P. THOULESS: *Modern poetic drama.* Oxford, 1934. B.

C. H. SMITH: *T. S. Eliot's dramatic theory and practice, from 'Sweeney Agonistes' to 'The Elder Statesman'.* Oxford and Princeton, 1963.

Consult also the files of *The Era*, 1881–1939, and *Era Almanacks*; *Play Pictorial*, 1902–40, and *Theatre World*, 1925–65; *Plays and Players*, 1952– ; *The Stage*, 1908–, and *The Theatre*, ed. Clement Scott, 1877–97.

ENGLISH COMEDIANS

See AUSTRIA, ENGLAND, GERMANY, *and* SHAKESPEARE

FAIRS AND FAIRGROUNDS

See CIRCUS, *and* POPULAR ENTERTAINMENT

FRANCE

1. *General*

G. BATY and R. CHAVANCE: *Vie de l'art théâtral des origines à nos jours.* Ill., Paris, 1952.

G. CAIN: *Anciens théâtres de Paris: le boulevard du Temple, les théâtres du boulevard.* Ill., Paris, 1906.

S. CHAPPUZEAU: *Le théâtre françois divisé en trois livres où il est traité (1) De l'usage de la comédie (2) Des autheurs qui soutiennent le théâtre (3) De la conduite des comédiens.* 3 vols., Paris, 1674.

M. DESCOTES: *Le public de théâtre et son histoire.* Paris, 1964. B.

V. HALLAYS-DABOT: *Histoire de la censure théâtrale en France.* Paris, 1862.

J. JANIN: *Histoire de la littérature dramatique.* Ill., 6 vols., Paris, 1853–8.

G. LANSON: *Manuel bibliographique de la littérature française moderne, 1500–1900.* 4 vols., Paris, 1909–12.

V. LEATHERS: *British entertainers in France.* Toronto and Oxford, 1960. B.

E. LINTILHAC: *Histoire générale du théâtre en France.* 5 vols., Paris, 1904–10. B.

C. and F. PARFAICT: *Histoire du théâtre françois depuis son origine jusqu'à présent.* 15 vols., Amsterdam and Paris, 1735–49.

B. DUSSANE: *Reines de théâtre, 1633–1941.* 13ᵉ éd., Lyons, 1946.

L. LACOUR: *Les premières actrices françaises.* Ill., Paris, 1921.

H. LYONNET: *Dictionnaire des comédiens français.* 2 vols., Geneva, 1911–12.

A. POUGIN: *Acteurs et actrices d'autrefois, histoire anecdotique des théâtres à Paris depuis 300 ans.* Ill., Paris, 1896.

P. VAN TIEGHEM: *Technique du théâtre: les grands comédiens (1400–1900), les grands acteurs contemporains.* Paris, 1960.

C. VARLET DE LA GRANGE: *Registre (1658–1685).* Paris, 1876.

H. C. LANCASTER: *The Comédie-Française, 1701–74, plays, actors, spectators, finances.* Philadelphia, 1951.

G. MONVAL: *Liste des sociétaires de la Comédie-Française, 1658–1900.* Paris, 1900.

J. VALMY-BAYSSE: *Naissance et vie de la Comédie-Française.* Ill., Paris, 1945. B.

J. VILAR: *De la tradition théâtrale.* Paris, 1955.

W. L. WILEY: *The early public theatre in France.* Harvard, 1961.

2. *Middle Ages—Sixteenth Century*

G. COHEN: *Le théâtre en France au moyen âge.* Ill., 2 vols., Paris, 1931. B.

M. DELCOURT: *La tradition des comiques anciens en France avant Molière.* Liège, 1934.

D. ROATEN: *Structural forms in the French theater, 1500–1700.* Ill., Pennsylvania and London, 1960.

3. *Seventeenth Century*

H. C. LANCASTER: *A history of French dramatic literature, 1610–1700.* 9 vols., Baltimore and Paris, 1929–42. B.

H. C. Lancaster (ed.): *Le mémoire de Mahelot, Laurent et d'autres décorateurs de l'Hôtel de Bourgogne et de la Comédie-Française au XVII*e *siècle.* Ill., Paris, 1920.

T. E. Lawrenson: *The French stage in the 17th century, a study in the advent of the Italian order.* Ill., Manchester, 1957. B.

J. Lough: *Paris theatre audiences in the 17th and 18th centuries.* Ill., London, 1957. B.

P. Mélèse: *Le théâtre et le public à Paris sous Louis XIV, 1659–1715.* Ill., Paris, 1934. B.

G. Montgrédien: *La vie quotidienne des comédiens au temps de Molière.* Paris, 1966.

—— *Dictionnaire biographique des comédiens français du 17*e *siècle, suivi d'un inventaire des troupes (1590–1710).* Paris, 1961.

—— *Les grands comédiens du 17*e *siècle.* Paris, 1927.

P. Corneille: *Writings on the theatre,* ed. by H. T. Bernwell. London, 1965. B.

M. Descotes: *Les grands rôles du théâtre de Corneille.* Paris, 1962.

—— *Les grands rôles du théâtre de Molière.* Paris, 1960.

L. Gossman: *Men and masks, a study of Molière.* Baltimore, 1963.

M. Jurgens and F. Maxfield-Miller: *100 ans de recherches sur Molière, sur sa famille et sur les comédiens de sa troupe.* Paris, 1963.

D. B. W. Lewis: *Molière, the comic mask.* London, 1959.

M. Descotes: *Les grands rôles du théâtre de Jean Racine.* Paris, 1957.

R. Picard: *La carrière de Jean Racine.* Paris, 1958.

E. Vinaver: *Racine and poetic tragedy.* Manchester, 1955.

4. *Eighteenth Century*

M. Aghion: *Le théâtre à Paris au XVIII*e *siècle.* Ill., Paris, 1926.

D. Diderot: *Writings on the theatre,* ed. F. C. Green. Cambridge, 1936.
(*See also* ART OF ACTING)

M. Fuchs: *La vie théâtrale en province au XVIII*e *siècle.* Ill., Paris, 1933.

H. C. Lancaster: *French tragedy in the time of Louis XV and Voltaire, 1715–44.* 2 vols., Baltimore and London, 1950. B.

—— *French tragedy in the reign of Louis XVI and the early years of the French Revolution, 1774–92.* Baltimore and London, 1953. B.

—— *Sunset: a history of Parisian drama in the last years of Louis XIV, 1701–15.* Baltimore and Paris, 1945.

E. Melcher: *Stage realism in France between Diderot and Antoine.* Bryn Mawr, 1928. B.

L. S. Mercier: *Du théâtre.* Amsterdam, 1773.

L. de Loménie: *Beaumarchais et son temps, études sur la société en France au XVIII*e *siècle, d'après des documents inédits.* 2 vols., 4e éd., revue et corrigée, Paris, 1880.

Mlle Clairon: *Mémoires et réflexions sur l'art dramatique.* Paris, 1799.

E. de Goncourt: *Mlle Clairon d'après ses correspondances et les rapports de police du temps.* Paris, 1927.

D. Diderot: *Entretiens avec Dorval.* Paris, 1875.

H.-L. Lekain: *Mémoires, suivis d'une correspondance inédite.* Paris, 1801.

M.-S. Burnet: *Marc-Antoine Legrand, acteur et auteur comique (1673–1728).* Paris, 1938. B.

J.-J. Olivier: *Voltaire et les comédiens interprètes de son théâtre.* Paris, 1899.

5. *Nineteenth Century*

J.-A. Barbey d'Aurevilly: *Le théâtre contemporain.* 4 vols., Paris, 1888–96.

C.-M. des Granges: *La comédie et les mœurs sous la Restauration et la monarchie de juillet (1815–48).* Paris, 1904.

D. O. Evans: *Le théâtre pendant la période romantique (1827–50).* Paris, 1925.

G. P. Ihrig: *Heroines in French drama of the Romantic period, 1829–48.* New York, 1950. B.

L.-H. Lecomte: *Histoire des théâtres de Paris (1847–1911).* 8 vols., new ed., Paris, 1900–12.

J. Lemaître: *Theatrical impressions.* London, 1924.

J. Marsan: *Théâtre d'hier et d'aujourd'hui.* Paris, 1926.

B. Matthews: *The theatres of Paris.* Ill., London and New York, 1880.

L.-H. Lecomte: *Une comédienne au XIX*e *siècle, Virginie Béjazet, étude biographique et critique d'après des documents inédits.* Paris, 1892.

J. Janin: *Deburau, histoire du théâtre à quatre sous.* Paris, 1881.

F. Febvre: *Journal d'un comédien (1850–94).* Ill., 2 vols., Paris, 1896.

R. Baldick: *The life and times of Frédérick Lemaître.* Ill., London, 1959.

R. de Beauvoir: *Mémoires de Mlle Mars.* 2 vols., Paris, 1849.

W. G. Hartog: *G. de Pixerécourt.* Paris, 1913.

J. Agate: *Rachel.* London, 1928. B.

L. Barthou: *Rachel.* Ill., Paris, 1926.

J. Janin: *Rachel et la tragédie.* Ill., Paris, 1859.

J. Richardson: *Rachel.* Ill., London, 1956. B.

N. G. Arvin: *Eugène Scribe and the French theatre, 1815–60.* Harvard, 1924. B.

H. F. Collins: *Talma, a biography of an actor.* Ill., London, 1964. B.

A. DUMAS: *Mémoires de Talma.* 4 vols., Paris, 1852–4.

(*See also* ART OF ACTING.)

6. *Twentieth Century*

M. BEIGBEDER: *Le théâtre en France depuis la libération.* Ill., Paris, 1959.

H. BORDEAUX: *La vie au théâtre.* 5 vols., Paris, 1910–21.

P. BRISSON: *Le théâtre des années folles (1919–40).* Ill., Geneva, 1943.

R. CARDINNE-PETIT: *Les secrets de la Comédie-Française (1936–1945).* Ill., Paris, 1958.

É. CHAMPION: *La Comédie-Française.* 5 vols., Paris, 1927–37.

L. CHANCEREL: *Petite histoire de l'art et des artistes — le théâtre et les comédiens.* Ill., Paris, n.d.

J. CHIARI: *The contemporary French theatre—the flight from Naturalism.* London, 1958.

R. COURSAGET and M. GAUTHIER: *Cent ans de théâtre par la photographie, comédiens et comédiennes d'hier.* Ill., Paris, 1949.

A. CURTIS: *New developments in the French theatre, a critical introduction to the plays of J.-P. Sartre, Simone de Beauvoir, Albert Camus and Jean Anouilh.* Ill., London, 1948. (The Masque, No. 8.)

É. DECROUX: *Paroles sur le mime.* Ill., Paris, 1963.

L. DUBECH: *Le théâtre 1918–23, la critique.* Paris, 1925.

W. FOWLIE: *Dionysius in Paris.* London, 1961.

D. I. GROSSVOGEL: *20th century drama.* Repr., New York, 1961. B.

H. HOBSON: *The French theatre of today, an English view.* London, 1953.

J. HORT: *Les théâtres du Cartel et leurs animateurs, Pitoëff, Baty, Jouvet, Dullin.* Ill., Geneva, 1944.

J. JACQUOT (ed.): *Le théâtre tragique, études de G. Antoine &c.* Paris, 1962.

R. E. JONES: *The alienated hero in modern French drama.* Univ. of Georgia Press, 1962.

L. C. PRONKO: *Avant-garde, the experimental theatre in France.* Ill., Berkeley (Calif.), 1962, Cambridge, 1963. B.

S. A. RHODES: *The contemporary French theatre.* New York, 1942. B.

K. ROURE: *A theater in your head.* New York, 1960.

A. VEINSTEIN: *Du Théâtre Libre au théâtre de Louis Jouvet: les théâtres d'art à travers leurs périodiques (1887–1934).* Ill., Paris, 1955.

E. O. MARSH: *Jean Anouilh, poet of Pierrot and Pantaloon.* Ill., London, 1953.

A. ANTOINE: *Le théâtre.* 2 vols., Paris, 1932–3.

A.-P. ANTOINE: *Antoine, père et fils, souvenirs du Paris littéraire et théâtral, 1900–39.* Ill., Paris, 1962.

S. M. WAXMAN: *Antoine and the Théâtre Libre.* Cambridge (Mass.), 1926. B.

A. ARTAUD: *Œuvres complètes.* Vol. 1, Paris, 1956– . (In progress.)

J. HORT: *Antonin Artaud, le suicidé de la société.* Geneva, 1960.

G. BATY: *Rideau baissé.* Paris, 1949.

R. COHN: *Samuel Beckett, the comic gamut.* New Brunswick, 1962.

A. CAMUS: *Méditation sur le théâtre et la vie.* Liège, 1961.

S. BERNHARDT: *Mémoires: ma double vie.* 2 vols., Paris, 1923.

M. AGATE: *Madame Sarah.* London, 1945.

M. BARING: *Sarah Bernhardt.* London, 1933.

L. BERNHARDT: *Sarah Bernhardt, ma grand'-mère.* Ill., Paris, 1947. In an English tr., London, 1949.

A. CASTELOT: *Sarah Bernhardt.* Ill., Paris, 1961.

R. HAHN: *Sarah Bernhardt, impressions.* Ill., London, 1932.

J. RICHARDSON: *Sarah Bernhardt.* Ill., London, 1959. B.

A. W. ROW: *Sarah the divine, the biography of Sarah Bernhardt.* Ill., New York, 1957.

J. CHIARI: *The poetic drama of Paul Claudel.* New York and London, 1954. B.

R. FARABET: *Le jeu de l'acteur dans le théâtre de Claudel.* Paris, 1960.

M. CROSLAND: *Jean Cocteau.* Ill., London, 1955. B.

N. OXENHANDLER: *Scandal and parade, a study of the theatre of Jean Cocteau.* London, 1958.

F. ANDERS: *Jacques Copeau et le Cartel des Quatre.* Paris, 1959. B.

A. ARNOUX: *Charles Dullin, portrait brisé, documents biographiques et iconographiques. . . .* Ill., Paris, 1951.

J. C. MCLAREN: *The theatre of André Gide.* Oxford, 1953. B.

E. IONESCO: *Notes et contre-notes.* Paris, 1962.

L. JOUVET: *Notes et documents sur Louis Jouvet (1887–1951).* Ill., Paris, 1952.

B. L. KNAPP: *Louis Jouvet, man of the theatre.* Ill., Oxford and New York, 1957.

J. ROBICHEZ: *Le symbolisme au théâtre (Lugné-Poë et les débuts de l'Œuvre).* Paris, 1957.

—— *Lugné-Poë.* Ill., Paris, 1955.

S. CHEVALLEY: *Henry de Montherlant, homme de théâtre . . .* Paris, 1960.

M. PAGNOL: *The time of secrets.* New York and London, 1962.

C. ANTONA-TRAVERSI: *Réjane.* Paris, 1930.

M. W. CRANSTON: *Jean-Paul Sartre.* New York and London, 1962.

A. WARNOD: *Yves-Bonnat.* Ill., Paris, 1954.

(*See also* ART OF ACTING, RELIGIOUS DRAMA, COMMEDIA DELL'ARTE, DRAMATIC CRITICISM, *and* SHAKESPEARE.)

GERMANY

1. *Drama, Theatre: General, including Nineteenth Century*

E. DEVRIENT: *Geschichte der deutschen Schauspielkunst.* 5 vols., new ed. rev. by W. Stuhlfeld, Berlin, 1929.

H. KNUDSEN: *Deutsche Theatergeschichte.* Stuttgart, 1959.

B. Q. MORGAN: *A critical bibliography of German literature in English translation, 1481–1927. Supplement, 1928–35.* Stanford, 1939.

J. G. ROBERTSON: *A history of German literature.* 3rd ed. rev. and enlarged by E. Purdie. Edinburgh, 1959. B.

G. SCHWANBECK: *Bibliographie der deutschsprachigen Hochschulschriften zur Theaterwissenschaft von 1885 bis 1952.* Berlin, 1956.

B. VON WIESE (ed.): *Das deutsche Drama, vom Barock bis zur Gegenwart: Interpretationen.* 2 vols., 2nd ed., Düsseldorf, 1960.

H. C. HOLDSCHMIDT: *Der Jude auf dem Theater des deutschen Mittelalters.* Emsdetten (Westf.), 1935.

E. E. MASON: *Prolog, Epilog und Zwischenrede im deutschen Schauspiel des Mittelalters.* Affoltern am Albis, 1949. B.

W. F. MICHAEL: *Frühformen der deutschen Bühne.* Ill., Berlin, 1963. B.

V. MICHELS: *Studien über die ältesten deutschen Fastnachtspiele.* 2 vols., 2nd ed., Düsseldorf, 1960.

M. J. RUDWIN: *The origin of the German carnival comedy.* New York, 1920. B.

B. AIKIN-SNEATH: *Comedy in Germany in the first half of the 18th century.* Ill., Oxford, 1936. B.

F. GÜTTINGER: *Die romantische Komödie und das deutsche Lustspiel.* Frauenfeld, 1939 (1940). B.

K. HOLL: *Geschichte des deutschen Lustspiels.* Ill., Leipzig, 1923. B.

W. H. BRUFORD: *Theatre, drama and audience in Goethe's Germany.* London, 1950. B.

H. KINDERMANN: *Theatergeschichte der Goethezeit.* Ill., Vienna, 1948. B.

M. MARTERSTEIG: *Das deutsche Theater im 19. Jahrhundert.* Leipzig, 1904. B.

R. PEACOCK: *Goethe's major plays.* Manchester, 1959.

W. SPEMANN: *Goldenes Buch des Theaters.* Ill., Berlin, 1902.

J. BAB: *Deutsche Schauspieler.* Berlin, 1908.

M. JACOBS (ed.): *Deutsche Schauspielkunst, Zeugnisse zur Bühnengeschichte klassischer Rollen.* Ill., Berlin, 1954.

K. LEMMER: *Deutsche Schauspieler der Gegenwart.* Ill., Berlin, 1955.

2. *Actors, Dramatists, etc.*

J. C. BRANDES: *Meine Lebensgeschichte,* ed. P. A. Merbach. Ill., Berlin, 1924; in a French translation as *Mémoires de Brandes, auteur et comédien allemand.* 2 vols., Paris, 1823.

J. A. CHRIST: *Schauspielerleben im 18. Jahrhundert.* Ill., Leipzig, 1912.

H. FETTING: *Conrad Ekhoff, ein Schauspieler des 18. Jahrhundert.* Ill., Berlin, 1954.

B. LITZMANN: *Der grosse Schröder.* Ill., Berlin, 1904.

H. SIEVERS: *Hebbels „Maria Magdalene" auf der Bühne, ein Beitrag zur Bühnengeschichte Hebbels.* Berlin, 1933.

R. MARCH: *Heinrich von Kleist.* London, 1954. B.

H. B. GARLAND: *Lessing, the founder of modern German literature.* London, 1962.

—— *Schiller.* New York, 1950.

S. SCHACHT: *Schillers Wallenstein auf den Berliner Bühnen.* Oldenburg, 1929.

E. L. STAHL: *Friedrich Schiller's drama, theory and practice.* Oxford, 1954. B.

3. *20th Century: Drama, Theatre*

J. BAB: *Das Theater der Gegenwart, Geschichte der dramatischen Bühne seit 1870.* Ill., Leipzig, 1928. B.

J. BITHELL: *Modern German literature, 1880–1938.* Ill., London, 1939. B.

E. FEISE: *Fifty years of German drama, a bibliography of modern German drama, 1880–1930, based on the Loewenberg Collection in the Johns Hopkins University Library.* Baltimore, 1941.

E. FRANZEN: *Formen des modernen Dramas, von der Illusionsbühne zum Anti-Theater.* Munich, 1961.

H. F. GARTEN: *Modern German drama.* London, 1959. B.

R. GEISSLER: *Zur Interpretation des modernen Dramas: Brecht—Dürrenmatt—Frisch.* 2nd ed., Frankfurt-on-Main, n.d.

4. *Twentieth Century: Actors, Dramatists, etc.*

B. BRECHT: *Brecht on theatre, the development of an aesthetic,* tr. by J. Willett. Ill., London, 1964.

—— *The Messingkauf dialogues,* tr. by J. Willett. London, 1965.

—— *Schriften zum Theater, 1918–1956.* Repr., London, 1963.

—— *Theaterarbeit: 6 Aufführungen des Berliner Ensembles,* ed. by H. Weigl. Ill., London, 1962.

M. ESSLIN: *Brecht, a choice of evils.* London, 1959.

J. WILLETT: *The theatre of Bertolt Brecht, a study from eight aspects.* Ill., London, 1959. B.

G. HAUPTMANN: *Die Kunst des Dramas — über Schauspiel und Theater.* Frankfurt-on-Main, 1963.

H. F. GARTEN: *Hauptmann.* London, 1954. B.

5. *Theatres*

C. SCHÄFFER and C. HARTMANN: *Die königlichen Theater in Berlin — statistische Rückblick vom 5 Dec. 1786 bis 31 Dec. 1885.* Ill., Berlin, 1886.

M. SCHLESINGER: *Geschichte des Breslauer Theater.* Bd. 1. 1522–1841. Berlin, 1898. [No more published.]

R. PRÖLSS: *Geschichte des Hoftheaters zu Dresden, von seinen Anfängen bis zum Jahre 1862.* Dresden, 1878.

E. KILIAN (ed.): *Beiträge zur Geschichte des Karlsruher Hoftheaters unter E. Devrient.* Karlsruhe, 1893.

E. L. STAHL: *Das Mannheimer Nationaltheater, ein Jahrhundert deutscher Theaterkultur im Reich.* Ill., Mannheim, 1929.

M. GRUBE: *Geschichte der Meininger.* Ill., Berlin, 1926.

G. FUCHS: *Revolution in the theatre: conclusions concerning the Munich Artists' Theatre,* condensed and adapted by C. C. Kuhn. Ill., Cornell and Oxford, 1959.

M. LITTMAN: *Die königlichen Hoftheater in Stuttgart.* Ill., Darmstadt, 1912.

O. SCHLEMMER, L. MOHOLY-NAGY, and F. MOLNÁR: *The theater of the Bauhaus,* ed. by W. Gropius. Ill., Middletown (Conn.), 1961.

GREECE AND ROME

1. *General*

J. T. ALLEN: *Stage antiquities of the Greeks and Romans and their influence.* Ill., London and New York, 1927. B.

P. D. ARNOTT: *An introduction to the Greek theatre.* Repr., London, 1961.

M. BIEBER: *The history of the Greek and Roman theater.* Ill., 2nd ed., rev. and enlarged, Princeton, 1961. B.

H. D. F. KITTO: *Classical drama and its influence.* Essays presented to H. D. F. Kitto, London, 1965.

A. N. MODONA: *Gli edifici teatrali greci e romani.* Ill., Florence, 1960.

M. VALSA: *Le théâtre grec moderne 1478–c. 1950.* Berlin, 1960.

VITRUVIUS: *On architecture,* book 5. Ill., 2 vols., London, 1955.

E. CAPPS: *Vitruvius and the Greek stage.* Chicago, 1893.

2. *Greece*

P. ARNOTT: *Greek scenic conventions.* Oxford, 1962.

R. C. FLICKINGER: *The Greek theater and its drama.* Ill., 4th ed., Chicago and Cambridge, 1936. B.

A. E. HAIGH: *The Attic theatre: a description of the stage and theatre of the Athenians and of the dramatic performances at Athens.* Ill., 3rd ed. rev. and ed. by A. W. Pickard-Cambridge. Oxford, 1907.

H. D. F. KITTO: *Form and meaning in drama, a study of six Greek plays and Hamlet.* New ed., London, 1959.

F. L. LUCAS: *Greek drama for everyman.* London, 1954.

A. W. PICKARD-CAMBRIDGE: *The theatre of Dionysus in Athens.* Ill., Oxford, 1946. B.

—— *The dramatic festivals of Athens.* Ill., Oxford, 1953. B.

—— *Dithyramb, tragedy and comedy.* 2nd ed. rev. by T. B. L. Webster. Oxford, 1962.

J. A. SYMONDS: *Studies of the Greek poets.* 2 vols., new ed., London, 1920.

T. B. L. WEBSTER: *Greek theatre production.* Ill., London, 1956.

3. *Aristotle*

ARISTOTLE: *On the art of poetry,* a revised text with critical introduction, translation, and commentary by I. Bywater. Oxford, 1909.

—— *Art of poetry, a Greek view of poetry and drama,* with an introduction and explanations by W. H. Fyfe. Oxford, 1940.

—— *On the art of fiction, an English translation of Aristotle's 'Poetics',* with an introductory essay and ... notes by L. J. Potts. Cambridge, 1953. B.

—— *Theory of poetry and fine art,* with a critical text and translation of the *Poetics* [by] S. H. Butcher ... 4th ed., New York, 1951.

G. F. ELSE: *Aristotle's 'Poetics', the argument.* Cambridge (Mass.), 1957. B.

A. H. HOUSE: *Aristotle's 'Poetics',* revised, with a preface by C. Hardie. London, 1956. B.

A. S. OWEN: *Aristotle on the art of poetry, an analytic commentary and notes, being a companion to the translation by I. Bywater.* Oxford, 1931.

4. *Comedy—Aristophanes and Menander*

F. M. CORNFORD: *The origin of Attic comedy.* London, 1914.

P. E. LEGRAND: *New Greek comedy,* tr. by J. Loeb. New York, 1917.

K. LEVER: *The art of Greek comedy.* London, 1956.

G. NORWOOD: *Greek comedy*. 2nd ed., New York and London, 1964.

T. B. L. WEBSTER: *Studies in later Greek comedy*. Ill., Manchester, 1953.

L. E. LORD: *Aristophanes, his plays and his influence*. Boston, 1925. B.

V. L. EHRENBERG: *The people of Aristophanes, a sociology of old Attic comedy*. Ill., 2nd ed. rev. and enl., Oxford, 1951.

G. MURRAY: *Aristophanes, a study*. Oxford, 1933.

T. B. L. WEBSTER: *Studies in Menander*. Manchester, 1950.

5. *Tragedy—Aeschylus, Euripides, and Sophocles*

H. H. BACON: *Barbarians in Greek tragedy*. New Haven, 1961. B.

A. E. HAIGH: *The tragic drama of the Greeks*. Ill., Oxford, 1896.

H. D. F. KITTO: *Greek tragedy, a literary study*. 3rd ed., London, 1961.

A. LESKY: *Greek tragedy*, tr. by H. A. Frankfort. London, 1965.

A. C. MAHR: *The origin of the Greek tragic form, a study in the early theatre in Attica*. Ill., New York, 1938. B.

G. NORWOOD: *Greek tragedy*. 4th ed., London and New York, 1953.

J. T. SHEPPARD: *Greek tragedy*. Ill., Cambridge, 1920.

—— *Aeschylus and Sophocles, their work and influence*. Ill., London and New York, 1927. B.

G. MURRAY: *Aeschylus, the creator of tragedy*. Oxford, 1940.

H. W. SMYTH: *Aeschylean tragedy*. Berkeley (Calif.) and Cambridge, 1924.

P. DECHARME: *Euripides and the spirit of his dramas*, tr. by J. Loeb. New York, 1906.

L. H. G. GREENWOOD: *Aspects of Euripidean tragedy*. London, 1953.

G. M. A. GRUBE: *The drama of Euripides*. Repr. London, 1961. B.

F. L. LUCAS: *Euripides and his influence*. London, 1928. B.

G. MURRAY: *Euripides and his age*. 2nd ed., London and New York, 1946.

G. NORWOOD: *Essays in Euripidean drama*. London, 1954.

A. RIVIER: *Essai sur le tragique d'Euripide*. Lausanne, 1944. B.

G. ZUNTZ: *The political plays of Euripides*. Manchester, 1955.

C. M. BOWRA: *Sophoclean tragedy*. Oxford, 1944.

F. J. H. LETTERS: *Life and work of Sophocles*. London, 1953.

A. J. M. WALDOCK: *Sophocles the dramatist*. Cambridge, 1951. B.

T. B. L. WEBSTER: *An introduction to Sophocles*. Oxford, 1936.

6. *Rome—Plautus, Terence, and Seneca*

W. BEARE: *The Roman stage*. Ill., 3rd ed. rev., London, 1964. B.

T. A. DOREY and D. R. DUDLEY (eds.): *Roman drama*. London, 1965. (Incl. essay on Westminster School Latin plays since 1945.)

G. E. DUCKWORTH: *The nature of Roman comedy*. Ill., Princeton and London, 1952. B.

H. N. FOWLER: *A history of Roman literature*. Oxford and New York, 1932.

W. W. FOWLER: *The Roman festivals of the period of the Republic*. London, 1899.

J. A. HANSON: *Roman theater-temples*. Ill., Princeton and London, 1959.

PLAUTUS: *Three plays*, tr. with an introduction by F. A. Wright and H. L. Rogers. New York, 1925.

F. LEO: *Plautinische Forschungen zur Kritik und Geschichte der Komödie*. 2nd ed., Berlin, 1912.

J. W. CUNLIFFE: *The influence of Seneca on Elizabethan tragedy*. London and New York, 1893.

L. HERRMAN: *Le théâtre de Sénèque*. Paris, 1924. B.

F. L. LUCAS: *Seneca and Elizabethan tragedy*. Cambridge and New York, 1922.

C. W. MENDELL: *Our Seneca*. London and New York, 1941.

J. ANDRIEU: *Étude critique sur les sigles de personnages et les rubriques de scène dans les anciennes éditions de Térence*. Paris, 1940. B.

G. NORWOOD: *The art of Terence*. Oxford, 1923.

HEBREW DRAMA

See JEWISH DRAMA

HOLLAND

See NETHERLANDS

INDIA

See EASTERN THEATRE, I, 5

IRELAND

1. *Drama, Theatre*

W. S. CLARK: *The early Irish stage, the beginnings to 1900.* Ill., Oxford, 1955.

—— *The Irish stage in the county towns, 1720–1800.* Ill., Oxford, 1965.

S. GWYNN: *Irish literature and drama in the English language, a short history.* London, 1936.

R. HITCHCOCK: *Historical view of the Irish stage.* 2 vols., Dublin, 1788–94.

P. KAVANAGH: *The Irish theatre, being a history of the drama in Ireland from the earliest period up to the present day.* Ill., Tralee, 1946. B.

E. BOYD: *Ireland's literary Renaissance.* New ed., London and New York, 1923. B.

—— *The contemporary drama of Ireland.* Dublin and New York, 1918. B.

U. M. ELLIS-FERMOR: *The Irish dramatic movement.* 2nd ed., London, 1954. B.

A. E. MALONE: *The Irish drama, 1896–1928.* London and New York, 1929.

L. ROBINSON (ed.): *The Irish theatre, lectures delivered during the Abbey Theatre Festival held in Dublin in August 1938.* London, 1939. B.

C. WEYGANDT: *Irish plays and playwrights.* Ill., London and Boston, 1913.

J. F. MOLLOY: *The romance of the Irish stage, with pictures of the Irish capital in the 18th century.* 2 vols., Dublin, 1897.

La T. STOCKWELL: *Dublin theatres and theatre customs, 1637–1820.* Ill., Kingport (Tenn.), 1938. B.

D. BYRNE: *The story of Ireland's National Theatre, the Abbey Theatre, Dublin.* Ill., Dublin, 1929.

G. FAY: *The Abbey Theatre.* Ill., London, 1958.

L. ROBINSON: *Ireland's Abbey Theatre, a history, 1899–1951.* Ill., London, 1951.

M. NICSHIUBHLAIGH: *The splendid years, story of the Irish National theatre as told to Edward Kenny.* Dublin, 1955.

A. SIMPSON: *Beckett and Behan and a theatre in Dublin* [The Pike Theatre]. Ill., London, 1962.

R. M. LEVEY and J. O'RORKE: *Annals of the Theatre Royal, Dublin, from its opening in 1821 to its destruction by fire, 1880, with occasional notes and observations.* Dublin, 1880.

2. *Actors, Dramatists, etc.*

W. G. FAY and C. CARSWELL: *The Fays of the Abbey Theatre, an autobiographical record.* Ill., London and New York, 1935.

AUGUSTA, LADY GREGORY: *Journals, 1916–1930.* London, 1946.

—— *Our Irish theatre.* London and New York, 1913.

E. COXHEAD: *Lady Gregory.* London, 1961.

M. MACLIAMMOIR: *All for Hecuba, an Irish theatrical autobiography.* Ill., London, 1946.

S. O'CASEY: *Autobiography.* 2 vols., London, 1963–4.

F. BICKLEY: *J. M. Synge and the Irish dramatic movement.* London and New York, 1912. B.

M. BOURGEOIS: *John Millington Synge and the Irish theatre.* Ill., London, 1913. B.

D. CORKERY: *Synge and Anglo-Irish literature, a study.* Dublin and London, 1931. B.

P. P. HOWE: *J. M. Synge, a critical study.* London, 1912. B.

F. L. LUCAS: *The drama of Chekhov, Synge, Yeats, and Pirandello.* Ill., London, 1963.

W. B. YEATS: *Autobiography.* London and New York, 1938.

J. M. HONE: *Yeats.* 2nd ed., London, 1962.

H. S. KRANS: *W. B. Yeats and the Irish literary revival.* New York, 1904. B.

L. E. NATHAN: *The tragic drama of W. B. Yeats, figures in a dance.* New York, 1965.

P. URE: *Yeats the playwright, a commentary on construction and theme in the major plays.* London, 1963.

(*See also* ENGLAND.)

ITALY

1. *Drama, Theatre*

G. ANTONINI: *Il teatro contemporaneo in Italia.* Milan, 1927.

M. APOLLONIO: *Storia del teatro italiano.* Florence, 1940.

R. BACCHELLI and R. LONGHI: *Teatro e immagini del settecento italiano.* Ill., Turin, 1954.

A. BELLONI: *Il seicento,* cap. 5, *Il teatro.* Milan, 1947. B.

E. BERTANA: *La tragedia.* 3rd ed., Milan, 1929. B.

Cinquant'anni di teatro in Italia, testi di R. Assunto, G. Bellonci, etc. Ill., Rome, 1954.

G. COSTETTI: *Il teatro italiano nel 1800.* Turin, 1901.

B. CROCE: *La letteratura della nuova Italia.* 6 vols., Bari, 1921–40. B.

—— *I teatri di Napoli dal rinascimento alla fine del secolo decimottavo.* New ed., Bari, 1916.

L. Fassò (ed.): *Teatro del seicento.* Milan, 1956.

J. S. Kennard: *The Italian theatre.* Ill., 2 vols. New York, 1932. B.

H. Lyonnet: *Le théâtre en Italie.* Ill., Paris, 1900.

L. MacClintock: *The contemporary drama of Italy.* Boston, 1920. B.

A. McLeod: *Plays and players in modern Italy.* Ill., London, 1912.

A. M. Nagler: *Theatre festivals of the Medici, 1539–1637.* Ill., Yale U.P., 1964.

L. Rasi: *I comici italiani, biografia, bibliografia, iconografia.* 2 vols., Florence, 1897–1905.

L. Riccoboni: *Histoire du théâtre italien depuis la décadence de la comédie latine, avec un catalogue des tragédies et comédies italiennes imprimées depuis l'an 1500 jusqu'à l'an 1660 et une dissertation sur la tragédie moderne.* 2 vols., enl. ed., Paris, 1730.

G. and C. Salvioli: *Bibliografia universale del teatro drammatico italiano.* Venice, 1894–1903.

I. Sanesi: *La commedia.* 2 vols., Milan, 1911–35.

A. Tilgher: *Studi sul teatro contemporaneo.* 3rd ed., Rome, 1928.

—— *La scena e la vita, nuovi studi sul teatro contemporaneo.* Rome, 1925.

L. Tonelli: *L'evoluzione del teatro contemporaneo in Italia.* Palermo, 1913.

—— *Il teatro italiano dalle origini ai giorni nostri.* Milan, 1924.

J. C. Walker: *Historical memoir on Italian tragedy.* Ill., London, 1799.

2. *Actors, Dramatists, etc.*

E. A. Rheinhardt: *The life of Eleonora Duse.* Ill., London, 1930. B.

E. Schneider: *Eleonora Duse, souvenirs, notes et documents.* Paris, 1925. B.

O. Signorelli: *Eleonora Duse.* Ill., London, 1959.

A. Symons: *Eleonora Duse.* London, 1926.

C. Goldoni: *Memoirs,* tr. from the French by J. Black, ed. A. W. Drake. London, 1926.

H. C. Chatfield-Taylor: *Goldoni, a biography.* Ill., London and New York, 1914. B.

C. Gozzi: *Memoirs,* tr. by J. A. Symonds. Ill., 2 vols., London, 1890. B.

W. Starkie: *Luigi Pirandello, 1867–1936.* 3rd ed., rev. and enl., Berkeley (Calif.) and London, 1965. B.

D. Vittorini: *The drama of Luigi Pirandello.* Philadelphia, 1935. B.

T. Salvini: *Leaves from the autobiography.* London and New York, 1893.

(*See also* COMMEDIA DELL'ARTE, *and* SHAKESPEARE.)

JAPAN

See EASTERN THEATRE, 1, 6

JESUIT DRAMA

A. and A. Backer and C. Sommervogel: *Bibliothèque de la Compagnie de Jésus: bibliographie.* Brussels and Paris, 1890 ff.

P. Bahlmann: *Jesuiten-Dramen der niederrheinischen Ordensprovinz.* Leipzig, 1896.

L. van der Boogerd: *Het Jezuïetendrama in de Nederlanden.* Groningen, 1961.

E. Boysse: *Le théâtre des Jésuites.* Paris, 1880.

F. Colagrosso: *Saverio Bettinelli e il teatro gesuitico.* 2nd ed., Florence, 1901.

B. Duhr, S.J.: *Geschichte der Jesuiten in den Ländern deutscher Zunge.* Freiburg in B., 1907.

A. P. Farrell: *The Jesuit code of liberal education, development and scope of the 'Ratio studiorum'.* Ill., Milwaukee, 1938. B.

L. Ferrari: 'Appunti sul teatro tragico dei Gesuiti in Italia'. (See *Rassegna Bibliografica della Letteratura italiana,* vii, 1899.)

W. Flemming: *Geschichte des Jesuitentheaters in den Ländern deutscher Zunge.* Berlin, 1923.

J. García Soriano: 'El teatro de colegio en España'. (See *Boletín de la Real Academia Española,* xiv, 1927; xv, 1928; xvi, 1929.)

L. V. Gofflot: *Le théâtre au Collège du moyen âge à nos jours.* Ill., Paris, 1907. B.

J. Jouvancy, S.J.: *Magistris Scholarum inferiorum Societatis Jesu de ratione discendi et docendi.* Florence, 1703.

F. Lang, S.J.: *Dissertatio de actione scenica, cum figuris eandem explicantibus, et observationibus quibusdam de arte comica.* Ill., Munich, 1727.

W. H. McCabe: *An introduction to the early Jesuit theatre.* Cambridge, 1929.

C. F. Menestrier, S.J.: *Des ballets anciens et modernes.* Paris, 1682.

J. Müller, S.J.: *Das Jesuitendrama in den Ländern deutscher Zunge vom Anfang (1555) bis zum Hochbarock (1665).* 2 vols., Augsburg, 1930.

G. M. Pachtler, S.J. (ed.): *Ratio studiorum et institutiones scholasticae Societatis Jesu.* 2 vols., Berlin, 1887. (*See* Monumenta Germaniae paedagogica, ed. Kehrbach, vols. 2, 5.)

C. Rahlenbeck: 'Le théatre des Jésuites en Belgique (1540–1640)'. (See *Revue de Belgique*, lx.) Brussels, 1888.

W. Richter: 'Paderborner Jesuitendramen von 1592–1770. (See *Mitteilungen der Gesellschaft für deutsche Erziehungs- und Schulgeschichte*, iv.) Berlin, 1894.

B. Soldati: *Il Collegio Mamertino e le origini del teatro gesuitico.* Turin, 1906. (Contains text of S. Tuccio's *Juditha*, 1564.)

J. Zeidler: *Studien und Beiträge zur Geschichte der Jesuitenkomödie und des Klosterdramas.* Hamburg and Leipzig, 1891.

JEWISH THEATRE AND DRAMA

E. D. Coleman: *Plays of Jewish interest on the American stage, 1752–1821.* Baltimore, 1934.

—— *Habimah, Hebrew theatre of Palestine.* Ill., Tel Aviv, 1937. (Available in French, German, Hebrew, Yiddish.)

H. Freeden: *Jüdisches Theater in Nazideutschland.* Tübingen, n.d.

Jewish Encyclopaedia, a descriptive record of the history, religion, literature, and customs of the Jewish people from the earliest times to the present day. Ill., 12 vols., London and New York, 1901.

M. J. Landa: *The Jew in drama.* London, 1926.

D. S. Lifson: *The Yiddish theatre in America.* Ill., New York and London, 1965. B.

A. A. Roback: *The story of Yiddish literature.* Ill., New York, 1940. B.

M. Waxman: *A history of Jewish literature.* Ill., 5 vols., London and New York, 1961.

JUVENILE DRAMA

See POPULAR ENTERTAINMENT, 5

KABUKI, KYÔGÉN

See EASTERN THEATRE, 1, 6

LIGHTING

See TECHNICAL BOOKS, 1 and 4

LITTLE THEATRE

See AMATEUR THEATRE, PROVINCIAL AND REPERTORY THEATRES, *and* REGIONAL AND PIONEER THEATRE

LONDON THEATRES

R. Mander and J. Mitchenson: *The theatres of London.* Ill., 2nd ed. rev., London, 1963.

T. F. Ordish: *Early London theatres (in the fields).* Ill., reissue, London, 1899.

E. Sherson: *London's lost theatres of the 19th century, with notes on plays and players seen there.* Ill., London, 1925.

Theatre World Annual: A pictorial review of West End productions with a record of plays and players. London, 1950– (In progress.)

A. E. Wilson: *East End entertainment.* Ill., London, 1954.

F. Barker: *The house that Stoll built* [Coliseum Theatre]. Ill., London, 1957.

D. MacCarthy: *The Court Theatre, 1904–7, a commentary and criticism.* London, 1907.

H. Saxe-Wyndham: *The annals of Covent Garden, from 1732–1897.* Ill., 2 vols., London, 1906.

D. Shawe-Taylor: *Covent Garden.* Ill., London, 1948.

T. E. Pemberton: *The Criterion Theatre 1875–1903.* Ill., London, 1903.

D. Forbes-Winslow: *Daly's, the biography of a theatre.* Ill., London, 1944.

D. MacMillan (ed.): *Drury Lane calendar 1747–76, compiled from the playbills.* Oxford, 1938.

W. Macqueen-Pope: *Theatre Royal Drury Lane.* Ill., London, 1945.

J. Hollingshead: *Gaiety chronicles.* Ill., London, 1898.

J. HOLLINGSHEAD: *'Good old Gaiety', an historiette and remembrance.* Ill., London, 1903.

W. MACQUEEN-POPE: *Gaiety, theatre of enchantment.* Ill., London, 1949.

—— *Haymarket, theatre of perfection.* Ill., London, 1948.

C. MAUDE: *The Haymarket Theatre, some records and reminiscences.* Ill., London, 1903.

J. HOLLINGSHEAD: *The story of Leicester Square.* Ill., London, 1892.

—— *A Lyceum historiette.* Nassau Press, 1899.

A. E. WILSON: *The Lyceum.* Ill., London, 1952.

N. PLAYFAIR: *The story of the Lyric Theatre, Hammersmith.* Ill., London, 1925.

J. BOOTH: *A century of theatre history, 1816–1916: the Old Vic.* Ill., London, 1917.

E. J. DENT: *A theatre for everybody, the story of the Old Vic and Sadler's Wells.* Ill., London, 1945. B.

C. HAMILTON and L. BAYLIS: *The Old Vic.* Ill., London, 1926.

H. WILLIAMS: *Four years at the Old Vic, 1929–33.* Ill., London, 1935.

—— *Vic-Wells, the work of Lilian Baylis.* Ill., London, 1938.

A. WILLIAMSON: *Old Vic drama, a twelve years' study of plays and players.* Ill., London, 1948.

M. MORLEY: *The Royal West London Theatre.* London, 1962.

D. ARUNDELL: *The Story of Sadler's Wells, 1683–1964.* Ill., London, 1965.

B. DUNCAN: *The St. James's Theatre, 1835–1957.* Ill., London, 1964.

A. E. W. MASON: *Sir George Alexander and the St. James's Theatre.* Ill., London, 1935.

(*See also* ENGLAND.)

MACHINERY

See TECHNICAL BOOKS, 1 *and* 5

MAKE-UP

J. F. BAIRD: *Make-up, a manual for the use of actors, amateur and professional.* Ill., London and New York, 1930.

G. BAISSE and J. ROBIN: *Maquillages et perruques au théâtre.* Ill., Paris, 1954.

T. W. BAMFORD: *Practical make-up for the stage.* Ill., 2nd ed. rev., London, 1965.

A. BRACHART: *L'art de se maquiller et de se grimer.* Ill., Paris, 1912.

R. CORSON: *Stage makeup.* Ill., London, 1961.

R. G. LISZT: *The last word in make-up.* Ill., London and New York, 1939.

C. MORTON: *The art of theatrical make-up.* Ill., London, 1909.

C. S. PARSONS: *A guide to theatrical make-up.* Ill., London, 1932.

H. S. REDGROVE and G. A. FOAN: *Paints, powders and patches, a handbook of make-up.* Ill., London, 1930.

S. STRENKOVSKY: *The art of make-up.* Ill., New York, 1937, London, 1960. B.

E. WARD: *A book of make-up.* Ill., London, 1930.

N. E. B. WOLTERS: *Modern make-up for stage and screen.* Ill., London, 1935.

(*See also* ART OF ACTING.)

MARIONETTES

See POPULAR ENTERTAINMENT, 5

MASQUE

L. B. CAMPBELL: *Scenes and machines on the English stage during the Renaissance, a classical revival.* Ill., repr., New York and Cambridge, 1960.

W. W. GREG: *A list of masques, pageants, etc.* (*See* ENGLAND: W. W. GREG: *A bibliography of the English printed drama to the Restoration.* Ill., 4 vols., London, 1939–59.)

I. JONES: *Designs for masques and plays at court, a descriptive catalogue of drawings for scenery and costumes*, introduction and notes by P. Simpson and E. F. Bell. Oxford, 1924.

J. A. GOTCH: *Inigo Jones.* Ill., London, 1928.

A. NICOLL: *Stuart masques and the Renaissance stage.* Ill., London, 1937.

S. ORGEL: *The Jonsonian masque.* Ill., Cambridge (Mass.), 1965.

P. REYHER: *Les masques anglais (1512–1640).* Paris, 1909. B.

M. S. STEELE: *Plays and masques at court during the reigns of Elizabeth, James and Charles.* Yale and Oxford, 1926. B.

M. SULLIVAN: *The court masques of James I.* Ill., New York, 1913.

E. WELSFORD: *The court masque, a study in the relationship between poetry and the Revels.* Ill., Cambridge and New York, 1927.

(*See also* ENGLAND.)

MEXICO

See SOUTH AMERICA, 8

MINSTRELSY

See ENGLAND, NEGRO IN THE THEATRE, POPULAR ENTERTAINMENT, 3, *and* U.S.A.

MUSIC-HALL

See POPULAR ENTERTAINMENT, 2

NEGRO IN THE THEATRE

F. W. BOND: *The Negro and the drama.* Washington, 1940. B.

S. A. BROWN: *Negro poetry and drama.* Washington, 1937. B.

F. P. GAINES: *The Southern plantation.* New York, 1925. B.

E. J. R. ISAACS: *The Negro in the American theatre.* Ill., New York, 1947.

J. W. JOHNSON: *Black Manhattan.* Ill., New York, 1930.

H. LAWSON: *The Negro in American drama (bibliography of contemporary Negro drama).* Ill., Urbana, 1939.

H. MARSHALL and M. STOCK: *Ira Aldridge—the Negro tragedian.* Ill., London, 1958. B.

(*See also* POPULAR ENTERTAINMENT, 3, *and* U.S.A.)

THE NETHERLANDS

B. ALBACH: *Helden, draken en comedianten, het nederlandse tooneelleven voor, in en na de franse tijd.* Ill., Amsterdam, 1956. B.

—— *Jan Punt en Marten Corver: nederlandsch tooneelleven in de 18e eeuw.* Ill., Amsterdam, 1946.

J. FRANSEN: *Les comédiens français en Hollande aux 17e et 18e siècles.* Paris, 1925.

G. A. GILLHOFF: *The Royal Dutch Theatre at The Hague, 1804–76.* The Hague, 1938. B.

H. JUNKERS: *Niederländische Schauspieler und niederländisches Schauspiel im 17. und 18. Jahrhundert in Deutschland.* The Hague, 1936.

F. PRINCE: *André Antoine et le renouveau du théâtre hollandais (1880–1900).* Amsterdam, 1941. B.

NŌ PLAYS

See EASTERN THEATRE, 1, 6

NORWAY

See SCANDINAVIA, 3

PANTOMIME

See COMMEDIA DELL'ARTE, *and* POPULAR ENTERTAINMENT, 4

PIONEER THEATRE, U.S.A.

See REGIONAL AND PIONEER THEATRE

POETIC DRAMA

See ENGLAND

POPULAR ENTERTAINMENT

1. *General*

N. M. Bernardin: *La comédie italienne en France et les théâtres de la Foire et du Boulevard (1570–1791).* Ill., Paris, 1902.

E. Campardon: *Les spectacles de la foire — théâtres, acteurs, sauteurs ... depuis 1595 jusqu'à 1791.* 2 vols., Paris, 1877.

L. Celler: *Les types populaires au théâtre, étude dramatique, les valets au théâtre (Polichinelle, Arlequin, Jocrisse, R. Macaire).* Paris, 1870.

V. Fournel: *Les spectacles populaires et les artistes des rues.* Paris, 1863.

—— *Le vieux Paris, fêtes, jeux et spectacles.* Ill., Tours, 1887.

F. Fried: *A pictorial history of the carousel.* Ill., New York, 1964, London, 1965. B.

T. Frost: *The old showmen, and the old London fairs.* London, 1874.

J. Grant: 'Penny Theatres' (from *Sketches in London,* 1838). Ill., London, 1952.

H. Le Roux: *Les jeux du cirque et la vie foraine.* Ill., Paris, 1889.

S. McKechnie: *Popular entertainments through the ages.* Ill., London, 1931.

G. J. Nathan: *The popular theatre.* New York, 1918.

A. Nicoll: *Masks, mimes and miracles, studies in the popular theatre.* Ill., London and New York, 1931.

C. and F. Parfaict: *Mémoires pour servir à l'histoire des spectacles de la foire.* 2 vols. in 1, Paris, 1743.

S. Rosenfeld: *The theatre of the London fairs in the 18th century.* Ill., Cambridge, 1960. B.

2. *Burlesque, Music-Hall, Variety, Vaudeville*

W. D. Adams: *A book of burlesque, sketches of English stage travestie and parody.* London, 1891.

W. H. ('Billy') Boardman: *Vaudeville days,* ed. by D. Whitelaw. Ill., London, 1935.

D. C. Calthrop: *Music-Hall nights.* Ill., London, 1925.

V. C. Clinton-Baddeley: *The burlesque tradition in the English theatre after 1660.* Ill., London, 1952. B.

—— *All right on the night.* Ill., London, 1954.

J. Damase: *Les folies du Music-Hall — histoire du Music-Hall à Paris de 1914 à nos jours.* Ill., Paris, 1962.

M. W. Disher: *Winkles and champagne, comedies and tragedies of the music-hall.* Ill., London, 1938.

S. T. Felstead: *Stars who made the Halls, a hundred years of English humour, harmony, and hilarity.* Ill., London, 1946.

P. Fitzgerald: *Music-Hall land.* Ill., London, 1891.

D. Gilbert: *American vaudeville, its life and times.* Ill., New York, 1940.

—— *Lost chords, a social history of American popular songs.* New York, 1942.

A. Haddon: *The story of the music-hall.* Ill., London, 1935.

Jacques-Charles: *Cent ans de Music-Hall.* Ill., Paris, 1956.

G. Le Roy: *Music-Hall stars of the nineties.* Ill., London, 1952.

R. Mander and J. Mitchenson: *British Music-Hall, a story in pictures.* Ill., London, 1965.

W. H. Morton and H. C. Newton (eds.): *Sixty years' stage service, being a record of the life of Charles Morton, 'The Father of the Halls'.* Ill., London, 1905.

H. C. Newton: *Idols of the 'Halls', being my music-hall memories.* Ill., London, 1928.

E. Renton: *The vaudeville theatre, building, operation, management.* New York, 1918.

C. Rose: *Red plush and greasepaint, a memory of the music-hall ... from the 90s to the 60s.* London, 1964.

H. Scott: *The early doors, origins of the music-hall.* Ill., London, 1948. B.

E. Short: *Fifty years of vaudeville, 1894–1945.* Ill., London, 1946.

B. Sobel: *Burleycue.* Ill., New York, 1931.

—— *A pictorial history of burlesque.* Ill., New York, 1956.

C. D. Stuart and A. J. Park: *The variety stage: a history of the music-hall from the earliest period to the present time.* London, 1895.

3. *Minstrels*

L. Hutton: *Curiosities of the American stage.* Ill., New York, 1891.

D. Paskman and S. Spaeth: *'Gentlemen, be seated!' A parade of the old-time minstrels, profusely illustrated from old prints and photographs and with complete music for voice and piano.* Garden City, New York, 1928.

H. Reynolds: *Minstrel memories, the story of burnt cork minstrelsy in Great Britain from 1836 to 1927.* Ill., London, 1928.

E. LeR. Rice: *Monarchs of minstrelsy, from 'Daddy' Rice to date.* Ill., New York, 1911.

C. Wittke: *Tambo and bones, a history of the American minstrel stage.* Durham (N.C.), 1930. B.

4. *Pantomime*

C. Aubert: *The art of pantomime.* Ill., London, 1927.

R. J. Broadbent: *A history of pantomime.* London, 1901.

V. C. Clinton-Baddeley: *Some pantomime pedigrees.* London, 1964.

M. W. Disher: *Clowns and pantomimes.* Ill., London, 1925.

L. Wagner: *The pantomimes and all about them.* London, *c.* 1881.

A. E. Wilson: *Christmas pantomime, the story of an English institution.* Ill., London, 1934; in an American ed. as *King Panto*, New York, 1935. B.

—— *Pantomime pageant, a procession of Harlequins, clowns, comedians, principal boys, &c.* Ill., London and New York, 1946.

—— *The story of pantomime.* Ill., London, 1949.

T. Rémy: *Jean-Gaspard Deburau.* Ill., Paris, 1954.

C. Dickens (ed.): *Memoirs of Joseph Grimaldi.* Ill., London, 1838.

R. Findlater: *Grimaldi, king of clowns.* Ill., London, 1955. B.

5. *Puppets, Marionettes, Punch and Judy, Toy Theatre*

M. Batchelder: *The puppet theatre handbook.* Ill., London, 1948. B.

—— *Rod puppets and the human theatre.* Ill., New York, 1947. B.

G. Baty: *Trois p'tits tours et puis s'en vont . . . les théâtres forains de marionnettes à fils et leur répertoire (1800–1890).* Ill., Paris, n.d.

—— and R. Chavance: *Histoire des marionnettes.* Paris, 1959.

C. Beaumont: *Puppets and puppetry.* Ill., London and New York, 1958.

S. Benegal (ed.): *Puppet theatre round the world.* Ill., Delhi, 1960.

H. Binyon: *Puppetry today.* Ill., London, 1966. B.

M. von Boehn: *Dolls and puppets*, tr. by J. Nicoll. Ill., London, 1932. B.

J. Chesnais: *Histoire générale des marionnettes.* Ill., Paris, 1947. B.

J. P. Collier: *Punch and Judy.* Ill., London, 1828.

N. Efimova: *Adventures of a Russian puppet theatre.* Ill., Birmingham (Mich.), 1935.

A.-C. Gervais: *Marionnettes et marionnettistes de France.* Ill., Paris, 1947. B.

G. Jacob: *Geschichte des Schattentheaters im Morgen- und Abendland.* Ill., Hanover, 1925.

J. M. Jones: *Glove puppetry.* Ill., new ed., Leicester, 1965.

H. H. Joseph: *A book of marionettes.* Ill., New York, 1920.

Karagöz, son histoire, ses personnages, son esprit mystique et satirique. Ill., Istanbul, 1951.

D. Keene: *Bunraku, the art of the Japanese puppet theatre.* Ill., Tokyo and London, 1965. B.

E. Kolár: *The puppet theatre in Czechoslovakia.* Ill., Prague, 1955.

J. B. Laglaise: *Pantins et marionnettes.* Paris, 1900.

P. McPharlin: *The puppet theatre in America.* Ill., New York, 1949.

É. Maindron: *Marionnettes et guignols, les poupées agissantes et parlantes à travers les âges.* Ill., Paris, n.d.

T. Menzel: *Meddah, Schattentheater und Orta Ojuna.* Prague, 1941.

H. Netzle: *Das süddeutsche Wander-Marionettentheater.* Ill., Munich, 1938. B.

S. Obraztsov: *The Chinese puppet theatre.* Ill., London, 1961.

H. Pascar: *Mon théâtre à Moscou (histoire d'un théâtre pour enfants).* Ill., Paris, 1930.

H. Ritter: *Karagöz.* Ill., 3 vols., Hanover, 1924, Leipzig, 1941, Wiesbaden, 1953.

G. Speaight: *A history of the English puppet theatre.* Ill., London, 1955. B.

—— *Juvenile drama, the history of the English toy theatre.* Ill., London, 1946.

O. Spies: *Türkisches Puppentheater.* Ill., Emsdetten (Westf.), 1959.

P. J. Stead: *Mr. Punch.* Ill., London, 1950.

J. E. Varey: *Historia de los títeres en España (desde sus orígenes hasta mediados del siglo XVIII).* Ill., Madrid, 1957. B.

A. E. Wilson: *Penny plain, twopence coloured, a history of the juvenile drama.* Ill., London and New York, 1932.

(*See also* CIRCUS, COMMEDIA DELL'ARTE, FRANCE, NEGRO IN THE THEATRE, *and* SPAIN.)

PORTUGAL

A. F. G. Bell: *Portuguese bibliography.* New York and Oxford, 1922.

—— *Portuguese literature.* Oxford, 1922.

T. Braga: *História do teatro português.* 4 vols., Oporto, 1870–1.

H. Cidade: *Luís de Camões: os autos e o teatro do seu tempo.* Lisbon, 1956.

C.-H. Frèches: *Le théâtre néo-latin au Portugal, 1550–1745.* Lisbon, 1964.

L. F. Rebello: *Teatro português.* Lisbon, 1959– . (In progress.)

I. S. Révah (ed.): *Bulletin d'histoire du théâtre portugais.* 5 vols., Lisbon, 1950–4.

A. Crabbé Rocha: *O teatro de Garrett.* 2nd ed., Coimbra, n.d.

A. J. Saraiva and O. Lopes: *História da literatura portuguesa.* 3rd ed., Oporto, 1961.

L. Stegagno-Picchio: *Storia del teatro portoghese.* Rome, 1964.

T. P. Waldron: *Introduction to* Gil Vicente, *Tragicomedia de Amadís de Gaula.* Manchester, 1959.

(*See also* religious drama, *and* dramatic criticism.)

PROVINCIAL AND REPERTORY THEATRES (including SCOTLAND AND WALES)

1. *General*

H. Browne: *Pilgrim story: The Pilgrim Players, 1939–43,* with a chapter on the organisation by E. Martin Browne. Ill., London, 1945.

C. Chisholm: *Repertory, an outline of the modern theatre movement, production, plays, management.* Ill., London, 1934. B.

B. Dean: *The repertory theatre.* Liverpool, 1911.

E. Elder: *Travelling players, the story of the Arts League of Service.* Ill., London, 1939.

P. P. Howe: *The repertory theatre, a record and a criticism.* London, 1910.

A. Loewenberg (ed.): *A bibliography of the theatres of the British Isles (excluding London).* London, 1950.

S. Rosenfeld: *Strolling players and drama in the provinces, 1660–1765.* Ill., Cambridge, 1939.

S. W. Ryley: *The itinerant, or memoirs of an actor.* 6 vols., London, 1808.

T. Wilkinson: *Memoirs of his own life.* 4 vols., York, 1790.

2. *English Towns*

B. S. Penley: *The Bath stage, a history of dramatic representations in Bath.* Ill., London and Bath, 1892.

M. F. K. Fraser: *Alexandra Theatre, the story of a popular playhouse.* Ill., Birmingham, 1950.

T. C. Kemp: *The Birmingham Repertory Theatre, the playhouse and the man.* Ill., 2nd ed. rev., Birmingham, 1948.

B. Matthews: *A history of the Birmingham Repertory Theatre.* Ill., London, 1924.

J. C. Trewin: *The Birmingham Repertory Theatre, 1913–1963.* Ill., London, 1963.

P. P. Rodway and L. R. Slingsby: *Philip Rodway and a tale of two theatres.* Ill., Birmingham, 1934.

J. E. Cunningham: *Theatre Royal* [Birmingham]. Ill., London, 1950.

M. T. Odell: *Mr. Trotter of Worthing and the Brighton theatre, 1814–1819.* Ill., Worthing, 1944.

H. C. Porter: *The history of the theatres of Brighton from 1774 to 1885.* Brighton, 1886.

M. E. Board: *The story of the Bristol stage, 1490–1925.* London, 1926.

G. R. Powell: *The Bristol stage, its story,* [*1586–1918*]. Bristol, 1919.

K. Barker: *The Theatre Royal, Bristol, the first seventy years.* Bristol, 1962.

—— *The Theatre Royal, Bristol, decline and rebirth, 1834–1943.* Bristol, 1966.

G. T. Watts: *Theatrical Bristol.* Bristol, 1915.

F. W. Steer: *The Chichester theatre.* Ill., Chichester, 1957.

W. Cotton: *The story of the drama in Exeter during its best period, 1787–1823, with Reminiscences of Edmund Kean.* Ill., London and Exeter, 1887.

T. Sheppard: *Evolution of the drama in Hull and district.* Ill., Hull, 1927.

R. J. Broadbent: *Annals of the Liverpool stage from the earliest period to the present time, together with some account of the theatres and music-halls in Bootle and Birkenhead.* Ill., Liverpool, 1908.

G. Wyndham Goldie: *The Liverpool Repertory Theatre, 1911–34.* Ill., Liverpool, 1935.

J. L. Hodgkinson and R. Pogson: *The early Manchester theatre.* London, 1960.

R. Pogson: *Miss Horniman and the Gaiety Theatre, Manchester.* Ill., London, 1952.

H. Oswald: *The Theatres Royal in Newcastle-upon-Tyne, desultory papers relating to the drama and its homes in that place.* Ill., Newcastle, 1936.

R. King: *North Shields theatres, a history of the theatres at North Shields and the adjoining village of Tynemouth, from 1765, including an account of the travelling booths.* Ill., Gateshead, 1948. B.

L. Warwick: *Death of a theatre, a history of the New Theatre, Northampton.* Ill., Northampton, 1960.

A. Dyas: *Adventure in repertory (Northampton Repertory Theatre, 1927–48).* Ill., Northampton, 1948.

T. L. G. Burley: *Playhouses and players of East Anglia.* Ill., Norwich, 1928.

S. Rosenfeld: 'The players in Norwich, 1669–1709, 1710–1750', *Review of English Studies* xii, Apr. and July 1936.

R. H. Mottram: *The Maddermarket Theatre.* Norwich, 1929.

—— *The Norwich Players.* Ill., Norwich, 1936.

B. Harcourt: *Theatre Royal, Norwich, the chronicles of an old playhouse.* Norwich, 1903.

T. A. Seed (ed.): *The Sheffield Repertory Theatre, a history.* Ill., Sheffield, 1959.

M. C. Day and J. C. Trewin: *The Shakespeare Memorial Theatre.* Ill., London, 1932.

R. Ellis: *The Shakespeare Memorial Theatre.* Ill., London, 1948. B.

W. Senior: *The old Wakefield theatre.* Wakefield, 1894.

D. Farquhar: *The history of Wallasey theatre.* Wallasey, 1950.

M. T. Odell: *The old theatre, Worthing, 1807–55.* Ill., Worthing, 1938.

—— *More about the old theatre, Worthing, its plays, players and playbills, its proprietor and his playhouses.* Ill., Worthing, 1945.

—— *Some playbills of the old theatre, Worthing.* Ill., Worthing, 1953.

T. Wilkinson: *The wandering patentee, or a history of the Yorkshire theatre from 1770 to the present day.* 4 vols., York, 1795.

Scotland

W. Baynham: *The Glasgow stage.* Glasgow, 1892.

Citizens' Theatre, Glasgow: *A conspectus to mark the Citizens' twenty-first anniversary as a living theatre.* Ill., Glasgow, 1964.

J. C. Dibdin: *The annals of the Edinburgh stage with an account of the rise and progress of dramatic writing in Scotland.* Ill., Edinburgh, 1888.

Edinburgh Gateway Company: *The twelve seasons of the Edinburgh Gateway Company, 1953–1965.* Ill., Edinburgh, 1965.

J. Jackson: *The history of the Scottish stage, the whole interspersed with memoirs of his own life.* Edinburgh, 1793.

R. Lawson: *The story of the Scots stage.* Ill., Paisley, 1917.

A. J. Mill: *Medieval plays in Scotland.* St. Andrews, 1927.

S. W. Ryley: *The itinerant in Scotland.* 3 vols., London, 1827.

Wales

C. Price: *The English theatre in Wales in the 18th and early 19th centuries.* Ill., Cardiff, 1948. B.

PUNCH AND JUDY, PUPPETS

See POPULAR ENTERTAINMENT, 5

REGIONAL AND PIONEER THEATRE, U.S.A.

H. P. Phelps: *Players of a century, a record of the Albany stage.* Rev. ed., Albany, 1890.

W. W. Clapp, Jr.: *A record of the Boston stage.* Boston, 1853.

C. McGlinchee: *The first decade of the Boston Museum.* Ill., Boston, 1940. B.

K. Ryan: *Old Boston Museum days.* Ill., Boston, 1915.

E. Tompkins and Q. Kelby: *The history of the Boston Theatre, 1854–1901.* Ill., Boston, 1908.

G. R. MacMinn: *The theater of the golden era in California.* Ill., Caldwell (Idaho), 1941. B.

C. Rourke: *Troupers of the Gold Coast, or the rise of Lotta Crabtree.* Ill., New York, 1928.

W. S. Hoole: *The ante-bellum Charleston theatre.* Ill., Alabama U.P., 1946. B.

E. Willis: *The Charleston stage in the 18th century.* Ill., Columbia (S.C.), 1924. B.

H. C. K. Naeseth: *The Swedish theatre of Chicago, 1868–1950.* Ill., Rock Island (Illinois), 1951. B.

M. Schoberlin: *From candles to footlights, a biography of the Pike's Peak theatre, 1859 to 1876.* Ill., Denver, 1941. B.

J. S. Schick: *The early theatre in Eastern Iowa, cultural beginnings and the rise of the theatre in Davenport and Eastern Iowa, 1836–1863.* Ill., Chicago, 1939. B.

R. D. James: *Old Drury of Philadelphia, a history of the Philadelphia stage, 1800–1835.* Ill., Philadelphia, 1932.

T. C. Pollock: *The Philadelphia theatre in the 18th century, together with the 'Day Book' of the same period.* Philadelphia, 1933. B.

A. H. Wilson: *A history of the Philadelphia theatre, 1835–1855.* Philadelphia, 1935. B.

W. B. Wood: *Personal recollections of the stage, embracing notices of actors, authors and auditors during a period of forty years.* Philadelphia, 1855.

C. Blake: *An historical account of the Providence stage.* Ill., Providence (R.I.), 1868.

G. O. Willard: *History of the Providence stage, 1762–1891.* Providence (R.I.), 1891.

W. G. B. Carson: *The theatre on the frontier, the early years of the St. Louis stage.* Ill., Chicago, 1932. B.

N. M. Ludlow: *Dramatic life as I found it.* St. Louis, 1880.

S. Smith: *Theatrical management in the West and South for thirty years.* Ill., New York, 1868.

M. E. Henderson: *History of the theatre in Salt Lake City.* Ill., Evanston (Illinois), 1934. B.

E. N. Gagey: *Annals of the San Francisco stage.* Ill., New York and London, 1950. B.

C. E. Willson: *Mimes and mines, a historical study of the theatre in Tombstone.* Tucson (Ariz.), 1935.

A. Hunter and J. H. Polkinhorn: *The new National Theater, Washington, D.C., a record of 50 years.* Ill., Washington, 1885.

(*See also* U.S.A.)

RELIGIOUS DRAMA

A. d'Ancona: *Origini del teatro in Italia, studi sulle sacre rappresentazioni.* 2 vols., Florence, 1877.

K. L. Bates: *The English religious drama.* London and New York, 1893. B.

E. K. Chambers: *The mediaeval stage.* 2 vols., repr., Oxford and New York, 1954. B.

S. W. Clarke: *The miracle play in England, an account of the early religious drama.* Ill., London, 1897. B.

G. Cohen: *Histoire de la mise en scène dans le théâtre religieux français du moyen âge.* 3rd. ed. rev. and augmented, Paris, 1951. B.

—— *Le livre de conduite du régisseur et le compte des dépenses pour le Mystère de la Passion joué à Mons en 1501.* Paris, 1925.

—— *Le théâtre en France au moyen âge.* 1. *Le théâtre religieux.* Ill., Paris, 1928. B.

H. Craig: *English religious drama of the middle ages.* Oxford, 1955. B.

G. Frank: *The medieval French drama.* Oxford, 1954. B.

A. Franklin: *Seven miracle plays.* Oxford, 1963.

K. Langosch: *Geistliche Spiele, lateinische Dramen des Mittelalters.* Basle, 1957.

A. A. Parker: *The allegorical drama of Calderón, an introduction to the autos sacramentales.* Oxford, 1943.

A. W. Pollard: *English miracle plays, moralities and interludes.* Ill., 8th ed., Oxford, 1927.

M. J. Rudwin: *Historical and bibliographical survey of the German religious drama.* Pittsburgh, 1924.

C. J. Stratman (ed.): *Bibliography of medieval drama.* Berkeley (Calif.) and London, 1955.

P. R. Vincent: *The 'Jeu de saint Nicolas' of Jean Bodel of Arras, a literary analysis.* Oxford, 1955.

K. Young: *The drama of the medieval Church.* Ill., 2 vols., Oxford, 1933. B.

(*See also* the general histories of ENGLAND, FRANCE, GERMANY, ITALY, *and* SPAIN.)

REPERTORY THEATRES

See PROVINCIAL AND REPERTORY THEATRES

ROME

See GREECE AND ROME, 1 *and* 6

RUMANIA

See EASTERN EUROPE, 4

RUSSIA

1. *Drama, Theatre*

A. Bakshy: *The path of the modern Russian stage, and other essays.* Ill., London, 1916.

H. Carter: *The new theatre and cinema of Soviet Russia, being an analysis and synthesis of the unified theatre produced in Russia by the 1917 Revolution, and an account of its growth and development from 1917 to the present day.* Ill., London and New York, 1924.

—— *The new spirit in the Russian theatre, 1917–28.* Ill., London and New York, 1929.

A. P. Coleman: *Humour in the Russian comedy from Catherine to Gogol.* New York, 1925. B.

H. W. L. Dana: *Handbook on Soviet drama.* New York, 1938. B.

—— *Drama in wartime Russia.* Ill., New York, 1943.

N. Evreinoff: *Histoire du théâtre russe.* Paris, 1947.

R. Fülöp-Miller and J. Gregor: *The Russian theatre, its character and history, with especial reference to the revolutionary period.* Ill., London and Philadelphia, 1930.

N. A. Gorchakov: *The theater in Soviet Russia.* Ill., Columbia and London, 1958.

M. Hayward and L. Labedz (eds.): *Literature and revolution in Soviet Russia, 1917–62, a symposium.* London, 1963.

N. Houghton: *Moscow rehearsals.* Ill., New York, 1936.

T. Komisarjevsky: *Moscow theatres.* Ill., Moscow, 1959.

J. G. MacLeod: *Actors across the Volga.* Ill., London, 1946.

—— *The new Soviet theatre.* Ill., London, 1943.

P. A. Markov: *The Soviet theatre.* Ill., London, 1934.

P.-L. Mignon: *Le théâtre en U.R.S.S. — avec le T.N.P. à Moscou et à Léningrad.* Ill., Paris, 1957.

J. Patouillet: *Le théâtre des mœurs russes des origines à Ostrovski (1672–1750).* Paris, 1912.

O. M. Sayler: *Inside the Moscow Art Theatre.* Ill., New York, 1925.

—— *The Russian theatre.* Ill., rev. and enlarged ed., New York, 1923.

M. Slonim: *From Chekhov to the Revolution: Russian literature, 1900–1917.* New York, 1962.

—— *Modern Russian literature: from Chekhov to the present.* New York and Oxford, 1953.

—— *An outline of Russian literature.* London, 1958. B.

—— *Russian theater.* Ill., London, 1963.

A. van Gyseghem: *Theatre in Soviet Russia.* Ill., London, 1943.

B. V. Vareke: *A history of the Russian theatre.* New York, 1951.

L. Wiener: *The contemporary drama of Russia.* Boston, 1924. B.

(*See also* ART OF ACTING, POPULAR ENTERTAINMENT, 4, *and* SHAKESPEARE.)

2. *Actors, Dramatists, etc.*

W. H. Bruford: *Chekhov.* London, 1957.

W. Gerhardi: *Anton Chekhov, a critical study.* London, 1923.

R. F. Hingley: *Chekhov.* Ill., London, 1950. B.

D. Magarshack: *Chekhov.* Ill., London, 1952. B.

J. Lavrin: *Nikolai Gogol.* London, 1952.

—— *Gogol.* London, 1925. B.

—— *Lermontov.* Cambridge, 1959.

V. Nemirovich-Danchenko: *My life in the Russian theatre.* Ill., London and Boston (Mass.), 1936.

K. Stanislavsky: *My life in art.* Ill., new ed., London, 1962.

—— *Stanislavski's legacy, comments on 'Some aspects of an actor's art and life'*, ed. and tr. by E. R. Hapgood. London, 1959.

—— *Stanislavsky on the art of the stage*, tr. by D. Magarshack. Ill., new and rev. ed., London, 1961.

(*See also* ART OF ACTING.)

D. Magarshack: *Stanislavsky.* Ill., London, 1953.

—— *Turgenev.* Ill., London, 1954. B.

SACRE RAPPRESENTAZIONI

See RELIGIOUS DRAMA, *and* ITALY

SCANDINAVIA

1. *General*

F. BLANKNER (ed.): *The history of the Scandinavian literatures.* New York, 1938. B.

E. L. BREDSDORFF, B. MORTENSEN and R. POPPERWELL: *Introduction to Scandinavian literature from the earliest time to our day.* Copenhagen and Cambridge, 1951.

E. GOSSE: *Northern studies.* London, 1890.

E. SPRINCHORN (ed.): *The genius of the Scandinavian theater.* New York and London, 1965. B.

H. G. TOPSÖE-JENSEN: *Scandinavian literature from Brandes to our day.* Ill., New York, 1939. B.

2. *Denmark*

T. KROGH: *Christian VII's franske hofaktører paa Hofteatret ved Christiansborg: saertryk for medlemmerne af selskabet for dansk teaterhistorie.* Copenhagen, 1947.

—— *Skuespilleren i det 18de aarhundrede, belyst gennem danske kilder.* Copenhagen, 1948.

J. NEIIENDAM: *Hofteatret rundt: skaebner og typer i Teatermuseet, en introduktion.* Christiansborg, 1952. (Short summary in English at end.)

T. OVERSKOU: *Den danske skueplads.* 4 vols., Copenhagen, 1854–62.

C. S. PETERSEN and V. ANDERSEN: *Illustreret dansk litteraturhistorie.* Ill., vol. 4., Copenhagen, 1925. B.

3. *Norway and Ibsen*

F. BULL: *Fra Holberg til Nordahl Brun, studier til norskaandshistorie.* Christiania, 1916.

——, F. PAASCHE and A. H. WINSNES: *Norsk litteraturhistorie.* Ill., vol. 4, 1–2, Christiania, 1937. B.

I. GRØNDAHL and O. RAKNES: *Chapters in Norwegian literature.* London, 1923.

T. JORGENSON: *History of Norwegian literature.* New York, 1933.

A. H. WINSNES: *Det norske selskab, 1772–1812.* Christiania, 1924, B.

M. C. BRADBROOK: *Ibsen the Norwegian, a revaluation.* Repr., London, 1948.

B. W. DOWNS: *Ibsen, the intellectual background.* Cambridge, 1946.

I. ten E. FIRKINS: *Henrik Ibsen, a bibliography of criticism and biography.* New York, 1921.

H. GREGERSEN: *Ibsen and Spain, a study in comparative drama.* Harvard U.P., 1936. B.

O. HELLER: *Henrik Ibsen, plays and problems.* Boston, 1912.

J. LAVRIN: *Ibsen and his creation, a psycho-critical study.* London, 1921.

—— *Ibsen, an approach.* London, 1950.

F. L. LUCAS: *The drama of Ibsen and Strindberg.* Ill., London, 1962.

J. W. MCFARLANE: *Ibsen and the temper of Norwegian literature.* London, 1960.

M. J. MOSES: *Henrik Ibsen, the man and his plays.* New ed., New York, 1920. B.

J. NORTHAM: *Ibsen's dramatic method, a study of the prose dramas.* London, 1953. B.

G. B. SHAW: *The quintessence of Ibsenism.* New ed., London and New York, 1913.

P. F. D. TENNANT: *Ibsen's dramatic technique.* Ill., Cambridge, 1948. B.

H. J. WEIGAND: *The modern Ibsen, a reconsideration.* New York, 1925.

A. E. ZUCKER: *Ibsen the Master Builder.* Ill., New York, 1929. B.

4. *Sweden and Strindberg*

A. GUSTAFSON: *A history of Swedish literature.* Ill., Minnesota and London, 1961.

G. HILLESTRÖM: *Le théâtre et la danse en Suède,* traduit par M. Cazaux. Ill., Stockholm, 1951.

E. WIKLAND: *Elizabethan players in Sweden, 1591–92, facts and problems.* Stockholm, 1962.

A. BEIJER: *Court theatres of Drottningholm and Gripsholm.* Ill., Malmö, 1933.

G. HILLESTRÖM: *The Drottningholm theatre, past and present.* Ill., Stockholm, 1956.

J. BULMAN: *Strindberg and Shakespeare, Shakespeare's influence on Strindberg's historical drama.* London, 1933. B.

E. HEDÉN: *Strindberg, en ledtråd vid studiet av hans verk.* Rev. ed., Stockholm, 1926. In a German tr. as *Strindberg, Leben und Dichtung.* Munich, 1921.

M. LAMM: *August Strindberg.* 2 vols., Stockholm, 1940–2.

V. T. MCGILL: *August Strindberg, the bedeviled Viking.* Ill., New York, 1930. B.

B. M. E. MORTENSEN and B. W. DOWNS: *Strindberg, an introduction to his life and work.* Cambridge, 1949. B.

E. SPRIGGE: *The strange life of August Strindberg.* London, 1949. B.

V. THOMPSON: *Strindberg and his plays.* New York, 1921.

SCENERY, SCENE-PAINTING

See TECHNICAL BOOKS, 1 *and* 6

SHADOW SHOW

See EASTERN THEATRE, 1, 5

WILLIAM SHAKESPEARE (1564–1616)

W. SHAKESPEARE: *Works, recorded by the Marlowe Society and professional players, under the direction of George Rylands.* Argo Records Company, 1957–64.

BRITISH MUSEUM: *Shakespeare,* an excerpt from the General Catalogue of Printed Books. London, 1964.

W. EBISCH and L. L. SCHUCKING: *A Shakespeare bibliography.* Oxford, 1931. *Supplement, 1930–5.* Oxford, 1937.

H. GRANVILLE-BARKER and G. B. HARRISON: (eds.): *A companion to Shakespeare studies.* Cambridge, 1934. B.

F. E. HALLIDAY: *A Shakespeare companion, 1564–1964.* Rev. ed., London, 1964. B.

Shakespeare Survey. Ill., London, 1948– . (In progress.)

P. ALEXANDER: *Shakespeare.* Oxford, 1964. B.

I. BROWN: *Shakespeare.* London, new ed. rev. and abr., 1964.

—— *How Shakespeare spent the day.* London, 1963.

E. K. CHAMBERS: *William Shakespeare, a study of facts and problems.* Ill., 2 vols., Oxford, 1930. B.

M. CHUTE: *Shakespeare of London.* New York and London, 1951. B.

M. ECCLES: *Shakespeare in Warwickshire.* Wisconsin, 1961.

C. L. BARBER: *Shakespeare's festive comedy, a study of dramatic form and its relation to social customs.* Princeton U.P., 1959.

B. BECKERMAN: *Shakespeare at the Globe, 1599–1609.* New York and London, 1962.

S. L. BETHELL: *Shakespeare and the popular dramatic tradition.* London, 1944.

A. C. BRADLEY: *Shakespearean tragedy.* 2nd ed., London, 1905.

J. R. BROWN: *Shakespeare and his comedies.* Repr., London, 1962.

H. B. CHARLTON: *Shakespearian comedy.* London and New York, 4th ed., repr., 1959.

—— *Shakespearian tragedy.* Repr., Cambridge, 1961.

M. M. CHARNEY: *Shakespeare's Roman plays.* Cambridge (Mass.) and London, 1961.

S. T. COLERIDGE: *Essays and lectures on Shakespeare.* London, 1849.

—— *Shakespearean criticism, 1849,* ed. T. M. Raysor. 2 vols., new ed., London, 1960.

B. EVANS: *Shakespeare's comedies.* Repr., London, 1961.

H. FARJEON: *The Shakespearean scene [1913–1944].* London, 1949.

G. GORDON: *Shakespearian comedy, and other studies.* London and New York, 1944.

H. GRANVILLE-BARKER: *Prefaces to Shakespeare.* Ill., 4 vols., repr., London, 1963.

F. E. HALLIDAY: *Shakespeare and his critics.* Ill., London, 1949. B.

—— *Shakespeare, a pictorial autobiography.* Ill., 2nd ed., London, 1964.

P. HARTNOLL (ed.): *Shakespeare in music.* London, 1964.

W. HAZLITT: *Characters of Shakespeare.* London, 1916.

H. HUNT: *Old Vic prefaces, Shakespeare and the producer.* London, 1954.

S. JOHNSON: *Johnson on Shakespeare, essays and notes,* selected by Sir Walter Raleigh. Repr., London, 1952.

J. KOTT: *Shakespeare our contemporary,* tr. by B. Taborski, preface by Peter Brook. London, 1964.

E. A. LAMBORN and G. B. HARRISON: *Shakespeare, the man and his stage.* Ill., London, 1923.

L. MARDER: *His exits and his entrances . . . Shakespeare's reputation.* London, 1964. B.

G. C. D. ODELL: *Shakespeare, from Betterton to Irving.* Ill., 2 vols., repr., London, 1963.

J. PALMER: *Comic and political characters of Shakespeare.* London, 1963.

E. TERRY: *Four lectures on Shakespeare.* London, 1932.

C. E. L. WINGATE: *Shakespeare's heroes on the stage.* Ill., New York, 1896.

—— *Shakespeare's heroines on the stage.* Ill., New York, 1895.

C. DE BANKE: *Shakespearean stage production, then and now, a manual for the scholar-player.* Ill., New York and London, 1953. B.

N. COGHILL: *Shakespeare's professional skills.* Cambridge, 1964.

G. CROSSE: *Shakespearean playgoing, 1890–1953.* London, 1953.

A. HARBAGE: *Theatre for Shakespeare.* Toronto U.P. and London, 1955.

C. W. HODGES: *Shakespeare's theatre.* Ill., London, 1964.

C. B. HOGAN: *Shakespeare in the theatre, a*

record of performances in London, 1701–1800. 2 vols., New York and Oxford, 1952–7.

L. HOTSON: *The first night of 'Twelfth Night'.* New York and London, 1954.

T. C. KEMP and J. C. TREWIN: *The Stratford Festival.* Ill., Birmingham, 1953.

G. W. KNIGHT: *Shakespearian production.* Ill., 3rd. ed., London, 1964.

T. LELYVELD: *Shylock on the stage.* Ill., London, 1961.

R. MANDER and J. MITCHENSON: *Hamlet through the ages, a pictorial record from 1709.* Ill., London, 1952.

W. M. MERCHANT: *Shakespeare and the artist: artist, illustrator, and designer as interpreters of the text.* Ill., London, 1959.

A. M. NAGLER: *Shakespeare's stage,* tr. R. Manheim. Yale U.P. and London, 1964. B.

A. I. PERRY WOOD: *The stage history of Shakespeare's 'King Richard the Third'.* New York, 1909. B.

W. POEL: *Shakespeare in the theatre.* London, 1913.

C. B. PURDOM: *Producing Shakespeare.* London, 1950.

M. ROSENBERG: *The masks of Othello.* Berkeley (Calif.) and London, 1964.

A. C. SPRAGUE: *Shakespearian players and performances.* Ill., Harvard and London, 1954.

—— *Shakespeare's histories, plays for the stage.* London, 1964.

K. STANISLAVSKY: *Stanislavsky produces Othello.* Ill., London and New York, 1948.

STRATFORD-UPON-AVON STUDIES, 5: *Hamlet.* Ill., London, 1963.

A. H. THORNDIKE: *Shakespeare's theater.* Ill., New York, 1916. B.

J. C. TREWIN: *Shakespeare on the English stage, 1900–64, a survey of productions.* Ill., London, 1964. B.

J. WAIN: *The living world of Shakespeare, a playgoer's guide.* London, 1964.

M. WEBSTER: *Shakespeare today.* London, 1957.

T. BALDWIN: *The organization and personnel of the Shakespearean company.* Princeton U.P., 1927.

W. R. DAVIES: *Shakespeare's boy actors.* Ill., London, 1939.

A. HARBAGE: *Shakespeare's audience.* Columbia U.P., 1941. B.

M. HOLMES: *Shakespeare's public.* Ill., London, 1960.

A. C. SPRAGUE: *Shakespeare and the audience, a study in exposition.* Harvard U.P., 1935.

—— *Shakespeare and the actors, the stage business in his plays, 1660–1905.* Ill., Harvard and London, 1944.

—— *The stage business in Shakespeare's plays, a postscript.* London, 1954.

—— *The doubling of parts in Shakespeare's plays.* London, 1966.

E. C. DUNN: *Shakespeare in America.* New York, 1939.

J. POKORNY: *Shakespeare in Czechoslovakia.* Ill., Prague, 1955.

C. M. HAINES: *Shakespeare in France.* London, 1925.

J.-J. JUSSERAND: *Shakespeare in France under the ancien régime.* Ill., London, 1899.

A. COHN: *Shakespeare in Germany in the 16th and 17th centuries, an account of English actors in Germany and the Netherlands and of plays performed by them during the same period.* London, 1865.

L. COLLISON-MORLEY: *Shakespeare in Italy.* Ill., Stratford-upon-Avon, 1916. B.

J. CALINA: *Shakespeare in Poland.* London, 1923.

M. M. MOROZOV: *Shakespeare on the Soviet stage.* Ill., London, 1947.

V. POPOVIĆ: *Shakespeare in Serbia.* London, 1928.

(*See also* ENGLAND, DRAMATIC CRITICISM, PROVINCIAL AND REPERTORY THEATRES, *and* SCANDINAVIA, 4.)

SOUTH AFRICA

See AFRICA, 2.

SOUTH AMERICA

1. *General*

E. ANDERSON IMBERT: *Historia de la literatura hispanoamericana.* 2 vols., Mexico City, 1954–61. B.

J. J. ARROM: *El teatro de Hispanoamérica en la época colonial.* Ill., Havana, 1956.

C. V. AUBRUN: *Histoire des lettres hispano-américaines.* Paris, 1954. B.

R. BAZIN: *Histoire de la littérature américaine de langue espagnole.* Paris, 1953. B.

J. DE M. DE CARVALHO (ed.): *Panorama das literaturas das Américas, de 1900 à actualidade.* 4 vols., New Lisbon (Angola), 1958–65.

—— *Spanish-American literature, a history,* tr. by J. V. Falconieri. Detroit, 1963.

A. COESTER: *The literary history of Spanish America.* New ed., New York, 1938. B.

A. J. DARNET DE FERREYRA: *Historia de la literatura americana y argentina, con su correspondiente antología.* 15th ed., 1950.

I. GOLDBERG: *Studies in Spanish American literature.* New York, 1920.

—— *Behind Spanish American footlights.* U. of Texas, 1966.

P. HENRÍQUEZ UREÑA: *Literary currents in Hispanic America.* Harvard U.P. and London, 1945. B.

W. K. JONES: 'Latin-American drama, a reading list', *Books abroad*, xvii, no. 1, London, 1943. B.

R. LAZO: *Historia de la literatura hispano-americana, el periodo colonial, 1492–1780.* Mexico City, 1965. B.

L. A. SÁNCHEZ: *Escritores representativos de America.* 2 vols., Madrid, 1957.

— *Historia de la literatura americana.* Santiago de Chile, 1937. B.

A. TORRES-RIOSECO: *Aspects of Spanish-American literature.* Seattle, 1963. B.

—— *Ensayos sobre literatura latino-americana*, 2 vols. Berkeley (Calif.), 1953–8.

—— *The epic of Latin-American literature.* Repr., Berkeley (Calif.), 1961. B.

2. *Argentine*

E. CARILLA: *Estudios de literatura argentina (siglo XX).* Tucuman, 1961.

R. ROJAS: *Historia de la literatura argentina.* Ill., 9 vols., 4th ed., Buenos Aires, 1960.

R. RICHARDSON: *Florencio Sánchez and the Argentine theatre.* New York, 1933. B.

E. H. BIERSTADT: *Three plays of the Argentine.* New York, 1920.

3. *Bolivia*

E. FINOT: *Historia de la literatura boliviana.* Ill., Mexico City, 1943.

4. *Brazil*

R. DE CARVALHO: *Pequena história da literatura brasileira.* Ill., 6th ed., Rio de Janeiro, 1937. B.

I. GOLDBERG: *Brazilian literature.* New York, 1922. B.

A. MOTTA: *História da literatura brasileira.* São Paulo, 1930.

J. OSORIO DE CASTRO E OLIVEIRA: *Historia breve de la literatura brasileña.* Brazil, 1958.

M. DA PAIXÃO: *O teatro no Brasil.* Rio de Janeiro, 1936.

J. M. TOPETE: *A working bibliography of Brazilian literature.* Brazil, 1957.

E. VERISSIMO: *Brazilian literature, an outline.* New York, 1945. B.

5. *Chile*

D. AMUNÁTEGUI Y SOLAY: *Las letras chileñas.* New ed., Santiago de Chile, 1934.

A. DE MARÍA Y CAMPOS: *Breve historia del teatro en Chile y su vida taurómaca.* Mexico City, 1940.

A. TORRES-RIOSECO: *Breve historia de la literatura chileña.* Mexico City, 1956.

6. *Colombia*

G. OTERO MUÑOZ: *Resumen de historia de la literatura colombiana.* Ill., 3rd ed., Bogotá, 1940.

7. *Cuba*

N. GONZALEZ FREIRE: *Teatro cubano (1927–61).* Ill., Havana, 1962. B.

8. *Mexico*

A. DE MARÍA Y CAMPOS: *Memoria de teatro — crónicas (1943–1945).* Mexico City, 1946. B.

—— *Archivo de teatro — crónicas de enero a diciembre de 1946.* Mexico City, 1947. B.

A. MAGAÑA ESQUÍVEL: *Imagen del teatro.* Ill., Mexico City, 1940. B.

R. USIGLI: *Méjico en el teatro.* Mexico City, 1932. B.

9. *Uruguay*

A. ZUM FELDE: *Proceso intelectual de Uruguay y crítica de su literatura.* Montevideo, 1941.

10. *Venezuela*

J. J. CHURIÓN: *El teatro en Caracas.* Caracas, 1924.

SOVIET THEATRE

See RUSSIA

SPAIN

J. ALENDA Y MIRA: *Relaciones de solemnidades y fiestas públicas en España.* Madrid, 1903. B.

C. A. DE LA BARRERA Y LEIRADO: *Catálogo bibliográfico y biográfico del teatro antiguo español.* Madrid, 1860. B.

E. COTARELO Y MORI: *Bibliografía de las controversias sobre la licitud del teatro en España.* Madrid, 1904. B.

A. F. VON SCHACK: *Geschichte der dramatischen Literatur und Kunst in Spanien.* 3 vols.,

Berlin, 1845–6. Spanish transl., 5 vols., Madrid, 1885–7.

A. VALBUENA PRAT: *Historia del teatro español.* Ill., Barcelona, 1956.

J. E. VAREY: *Historia de los títeres en España (desde sus orígenes hasta mediados del siglo XVIII).* Ill., Madrid, 1957. B.

J. SÁNCHEZ ARJONA: *Noticias referentes a los anales del teatro en Sevilla desde Lope de Rueda hasta fines del siglo XVII.* Seville, 1898.

L. LAMARCA: *El teatro en Valencia desde su origen hasta nuestros días.* Valencia, 1840.

H. MÉRIMÉE: *L'art dramatique à Valencia.* Toulouse, 1913. B.

—— *Spectacles et comédiens à Valencia, 1580–1630.* Toulouse and Paris, 1913.

N. ALONSO CORTÉS: *El teatro en Valladolid.* Madrid, 1923.

J. P. W. CRAWFORD: *The Spanish pastoral drama.* Philadelphia, 1915.

—— *Spanish drama before Lope de Vega.* Rev. ed., London and Philadelphia, 1937. B.

R. B. DONOVAN: *The liturgical drama in medieval Spain.* Toronto, 1958. B.

W. H. SHOEMAKER: *The multiple stage in Spain during the 15th and 16th centuries.* Princeton U.P., 1935. B.

R. B. WILLIAMS: *The staging of plays in the Spanish peninsula prior to 1555.* Iowa U.P., 1935. B.

C. BRAVO-VILLASANTE: *La mujer vestida de hombre en el teatro español (siglos 16–17).* Madrid, 1955. B.

J.-L. FLECNIAKOWSKA: *La formation de l'«auto» religieux en Espagne avant Calderón (1550–1635).* Montpellier, 1961. B.

A. A. PARKER: *The approach to the Spanish drama of the Golden Age.* Repr., London, 1964.

C. PÉREZ PASTOR: *Nuevos datos acerca del histrionismo español en los siglos XVI y XVII.* Madrid, 1901.

—— *Nuevos datos ...* 2a serie. Bordeaux, 1914.

H. A. RENNERT: *The Spanish stage in the time of Lope de Vega, with an alphabetical list of Spanish actors and actresses, 1560–1680.* New York, 1909. Repr. (but without list of actors), 1964.

R. SEPÚLVEDA: *El Corral de la Pacheca.* Ill., Madrid, 1888.

N. D. SHERGOLD and J. E. VAREY: *Los autos sacramentales en Madrid en la época de Calderón, 1637–1681, estudio y documentos.* Ill., Madrid, 1961. B.

B. W. WARDROPPER: *Introducción al teatro religioso del siglo de oro: (la evolución del auto sacramental, 1500–1648).* Madrid, 1953. B.

E. ASENIO: *Itinerario del entremés desde Lope de Rueda a Quiñones de Benavente.* Madrid, 1965.

S. G. MORLEY and C. BRUERTON: *The chronology of Lope de Vega's 'comedias'.* New York and London, 1940. B.

H. A. RENNERT: *The life of Lope de Vega (1562–1635).* Repr., New York, 1937.

E. COTARELO Y MORI: *Ensayo sobre la vida y obras de D. Pedro Calderón de la Barca.* Ill., Madrid, 1924.

A. A. PARKER: *The allegorical drama of Calderón.* Oxford, 1943.

A. E. SLOMAN: *The dramatic craftsmanship of Calderón.* Oxford, 1958. B.

B. W. WARDROPPER: *Critical essays on the theatre of Calderón.* New York, 1965.

E. COTARELO Y MORI: *Don Francisco de Rojas Zorrilla, noticias biográficas y bibliográficas.* Madrid, 1911.

R. R. MACCURDY: *Francisco de Rojas Zorrilla and the tragedy.* Albuquerque, 1958.

J. A. COOK: *Neo-classic drama in Spain, theory and practice.* Dallas, 1959.

E. COTARELO Y MORI: *Don Ramón de la Cruz y sus obras.* Madrid, 1899.

—— *Iriarte y su época.* Madrid, 1897.

F. CURET: *El arte dramático en el resurgir de Cataluña.* Barcelona, n.d.

E. A. PEERS: *A history of the Romantic movement in Spain.* 2 vols., Cambridge, 1940. B.

F. GARCÍA PAVÓN: *El teatro social en España (1895–1962).* Ill., Madrid, 1962.

J. CASALDUERO: *Vida y obra de Galdós (1843–1920).* Madrid, 1951. B.

D. POYÁN DÍAZ: *Enrique Gaspar, medio siglo de teatro español.* 2 vols., Madrid, 1957.

J. P. BOREL: *Théâtre de l'impossible, essai sur une des dimensions fondamentales du théâtre espagnol au XXe siècle.* Neufchâtel, 1963.

A. GAUL: *Mitja vida de teatre, memòries.* Ill., Barcelona, 1960.

G. MARTÍNEZ SIERRA: *Un teatro de arte en España, 1917–1925.* Ill., Madrid, 1925.

G. TORRENTE BALLESTER: *Teatro español contemporáneo.* Ill., Madrid, 1957.

R. LIMA: *The theatre of García Lorca.* New York, 1963. B.

R. G. SÁNCHEZ: *García Lorca, estudio sobre su teatro.* Madrid, 1950.

I. SÁNCHEZ ESTEVAN: *Jacinto Benavente y su teatro.* Ill., Barcelona, 1954.

STAGECRAFT

See TECHNICAL BOOKS, *and* AMATEUR THEATRE

SWEDEN

See SCANDINAVIA, 4

TOY THEATRE

See POPULAR ENTERTAINMENT, 5

SWITZERLAND

P. PÖRTNER: *Experiment Theater, Chronik und Dokumente.* Ill., Zürich, 1960.

J. U. SAXER: *Gottfried Kellers Bemühungen um das Theater.* Zürich, 1957.

H. WYSS: *Der Narr im schweizerischen Drama des 16. Jahrhunderts.* Bern, 1959. B.

A. HUGUENIN: *Le théâtre de Lausanne dès sa fondation en 1871 jusqu'à nos jours.* Ill., 3rd ed. rev. and augmented, Lausanne, 1933.

ZÜRICH: *Theater in Zürich: 125 Jahre Stadttheater,* herausgegeben von der Theater AG Zürich. Ill., Zürich, 1959.

G. FREI: *Das Zürcher Stadttheater unter der Direktion Alfred Reucker, 1901-1921.* Zürich, 1951.

G. KUMMER: *Beiträge zur Geschichte des Zürcher Aktientheaters, 1843–1890.* Zürich, 1938.

G. SCHOOP: *Das Zürcher Schauspielhaus im zweiten Weltkrieg.* Ill., Zürich, 1957.

TRAGEDY AND COMEDY

1. *Tragedy*

W. M. DIXON: *Tragedy.* 3rd ed., London, 1929.

F. L. LUCAS: *Tragedy in relation to Aristotle's 'Poetics'.* London, 1927.

C. E. VAUGHAN: *Types of tragic drama.* London, 1908.

(*See also* ENGLAND, FRANCE, GREECE AND ROME, ITALY, *and* SHAKESPEARE.)

2. *Comedy*

C. HOY: *The hyacinth room: an investigation into the nature of comedy, tragedy, and tragicomedy.* London, 1964.

J. PALMER: *Comedy.* London, 1914.

—— *The comedy of manners.* Ill., London, 1913. B.

H. ten E. PERRY: *Masters of dramatic comedy and their social themes.* Harvard U.P., 1939. B.

A. SEYLER and S. HAGGARD: *The craft of comedy, a correspondence.* 2nd ed. rev., London, 1958.

W. SMITH: *The nature of comedy.* Boston, 1930. B.

(*See also* ENGLAND, FRANCE, GREECE AND ROME, ITALY, RUSSIA, SHAKESPEARE, *and* SPAIN.)

TURKEY

See EASTERN THEATRE, II

URUGUAY

See SOUTH AMERICA, 9

U.S.A.

1. *Drama, Theatre: General and including Nineteenth Century*

J. ANDERSON: *The American theatre.* Ill., New York, 1938. B.

B. BLAKE: *The awakening of the American theatre.* Ill., New York, 1935.

D. BLUM: *Great stars of the American stage, a pictorial record.* Ill., New York, 1952.

T. A. BROWN: *History of the American stage.* Ill., New York, 1870.

—— *A history of the New York stage from the first performance in 1732 to 1901.* 3 vols., New York, 1903.

O. S. COAD and E. MIMS, Jr.: *The American stage.* Ill., New Haven, 1929. (*See* The Pageant of America, xiv.)

W. DUNLAP: *History of the American theatre.* 2 vols., London, 1833.

D. EWEN: *The complete book of the American theatre.* Ill., London, 1959.

M. FELHEIM: *The theater of Augustin Daly, an account of the late 19th century American stage.* Ill., Harvard and Oxford, 1956.

P. GRAHAM: *Showboats, the history of an American institution.* Ill., Austin (Texas), 1951. B.

J. GREGOR and R. FÜLÖP-MILLER: *Das amerikanische Theater und Kino.* Ill., Zürich, 1931.

D. C. HASKELL: *List of American dramas in the New York Public Library.* New York, 1916.

B. HEWITT: *Theatre U.S.A., 1668–1957.* Ill., New York, 1959.

F. P. HILL: *American plays printed 1714–1830, a bibliographical record.* Palo Alto (Calif.), 1934.

A. HORNBLOW: *A history of the theatre in America from its beginnings to the present time.* Ill., 2 vols., Philadelphia, 1919.

F. E. MCKAY and C. E. L. WINGATE: *Famous American actors of to-day.* Ill., 2 vols., New York, 1896.

M. G. MAYORGA: *A short history of the American drama, commentaries on plays prior to 1920.* Ill., New York, 1932. B.

M. J. MOSES: *The American dramatist.* Ill., rev. ed., Boston, 1925. B.

—— *Famous actor families in America.* Ill., New York, 1906. B.

G. C. D. ODELL: *Annals of the New York stage.* Ill., 15 vols., New York, 1927–49.

A. H. QUINN: *A history of the American drama.* 2 vols., New York and London, 1923–37.

W. RIGDON (ed.): *The biographical encyclopaedia and who's who of the American theatre.* New York, 1966.

L. C. STRANG: *Famous actresses of the day.* Ill., repr., Boston, 1906.

—— *Players and plays of the last quarter century.* 2 vols., Boston, 1903.

O. WEGELIN: *Early American plays, 1714–1830.* Rev. ed., New York, 1905.

W. WINTER: *The American stage of to-day, biographies and photographs of leading actors and actresses.* Ill., New York, 1910.

—— *The wallet of time, containing personal, biographical, and critical reminiscences of the American theatre.* Ill., 2 vols., New York, 1913.

2. *Actors, Dramatists, etc.*

E. S. BRADLEY: *George Henry Baker, poet and patriot.* Philadelphia, 1927. B.

J. M. FARRAR: *Mary Anderson . . . her life and professional career.* London, 1884.

W. WINTER: *The stage life of Mary Anderson.* New York, 1886.

W. P. KINNE: *George Pierce Baker and the American theatre.* Ill., New York, 1954. B.

W. WINTER: *The life of David Belasco.* Ill., 2 vols., New York, 1920.

C. FOUST: *Life and dramatic works of Robert Montgomery Bird.* Philadelphia, 1919.

A. B. CLARKE: *The elder and the younger Booth.* Ill., London and Cambridge (Mass.), 1882.

L. HUTTON: *Edwin Booth.* Ill., New York, 1893.

S. KIMMEL: *The mad Booths of Maryland.* Ill., New York, 1940. B.

E. RUGGLES: *Prince of players—Edwin Booth.* London, 1953.

W. WINTER: *Life and art of Edwin Booth.* Ill., London and New York, 1893.

T. WALSH: *The career of Dion Boucicault.* New York, 1915.

J. COWELL: *Thirty years passed among the players in England and America.* New York, 1844.

M. W. DISHER (ed.): *The Cowells in America, being the diary of Mrs. Sam Cowell, 1860–61.* Ill., London, 1934.

(*For* LOTTA CRABTREE, *see* REGIONAL AND PIONEER THEATRE.)

E. A. DITHMAR: *The life of Augustin Daly.* New York, 1917.

(*See also* ENGLAND, *and* LONDON THEATRES.)

O. S. COAD: *William Dunlap, a study of his life and works, and of his place in contemporary culture.* Ill., New York, 1917. B.

O. WEGELIN: *A bibliographical checklist of the plays and miscellaneous writings of William Dunlap, 1766–1839.* New York, 1916.

A. BELL: *The Clyde Fitch I knew.* New York, 1909.

M. J. MOSES and V. GERSON: *Clyde Fitch and his letters.* Boston, 1924.

W. R. ALGER: *The life of Edwin Forrest.* Ill., 2 vols., Philadelphia, 1877.

L. BARRETT: *Edwin Forrest.* Ill., London and Cambridge (Mass.), 1882.

G. HARRISON: *Edwin Forrest, the actor and the man.* Ill., Brooklyn, 1889. B.

J. REES: *The life of Edwin Forrest.* Philadelphia, 1874.

D. FROHMAN: *Memories of a manager, reminiscences of the old Lyceum and of some players of the last quarter century.* Ill., London, 1911.

—— *Daniel Frohman presents.* New York, 1935.

J. JEFFERSON: *'Rip Van Winkle': an autobiography*, ed. A. S. Downer. Ill., London and Cambridge (Mass.), 1964.

W. WINTER: *The Jeffersons.* Ill., London and Cambridge (Mass.), 1881.

—— *The life and art of Joseph Jefferson.* Ill., New York, 1894.

M. ARMSTRONG: *Fanny Kemble, a passionate Victorian.* Ill., London and New York, 1938.

D. DE B. BOBBÉ: *Fanny Kemble.* Ill., London and New York, 1932. B.

L. S. DRIVER: *Fanny Kemble.* Ill., Chapel Hill (N.C.), 1933. B.

F. KEMBLE (*Mrs.* Frances Anne Butler): *Journal.* 2 vols., London and Philadelphia, 1835.

M. B. LEAVITT: *Fifty years in theatrical management.* Ill., New York, 1912.

(*For* NOAH LUDLOW, *see* REGIONAL AND PIONEER THEATRE.)

P. MACKAYE: *The life of Steele MacKaye.* Ill., 2 vols., New York, 1927. B.

P. WILSTACH: *Richard Mansfield, the man and the actor.* Ill., London and New York, 1908. B.

W. WINTER: *Life and art of Richard Mansfield.* 2 vols., New York, 1910.

H. MODJEWSKA: *Memories and impressions.* London, 1910.

J. T. ALTEMUS. *Helena Modjewska.* Ill., New York, 1883.

M. COLLINS: *The story of Helen Modjewska.* Ill., London, 1883.

D. D. HENRY: *William Vaughn Moody, a study.* Boston (Mass.), 1934.

Mrs. A. C. MOWATT: *Autobiography of an actress, or eight years on the stage.* Boston (Mass), 1854.

J. H. PAYNE: *Memoirs.* London, 1815.

R. P. CHILES: *John Howard Payne.* New York, 1930.

G. HARRISON: *The life and writings of John Howard Payne.* Philadelphia, 1885.

(*For* SOL SMITH, *see* REGIONAL AND PIONEER THEATRE.)

A. THOMAS: *The print of my remembrance.* New York, 1922.

L. WALLACK: *Memories of fifty years.* Ill., New York, 1889.

F. C. WEMYSS: *Twenty-six years of the life of an actor and manager.* Glasgow, 1848.

3. *Twentieth Century: Drama, Theatre*

D. BLUM: *A pictorial history of the American theatre, 1900–50.* Ill., New York, 1950.

J. M. BROWN: *The American theatre as it is to-day.* New York, 1930.

R. BURTON: *The new American drama.* New York, 1913.

T. H. DICKINSON: *Playwrights of the new American theater.* New York, 1924.

A. S. DOWNER: *Fifty years of American drama, 1900–50.* Chicago, 1951.

W. P. EATON: *Plays and players, leaves from a critic's scrapbook.* Ill., Cincinnati, 1916.

—— *The Theatre Guild, the first ten years.* Ill., New York, 1929.

E. FLEXNER: *American playwrights, 1918-38: the theatre retreats from reality.* New York, 1938.

N. HAPGOOD: *The stage in America, 1897–1900.* New York, 1901.

M. JONES: *Theatre-in-the-round.* Ill., New York, 1951. B.

J. W. KRUTCH: *The American drama since 1918.* New York, 1939.

B. MANTLE: *American playwrights of to-day.* New York, 1926.

B. MARTIN: *Modern American drama and stage.* Ill., London, 1943.

J. S. PRICE: *The off-Broadway theater.* New York, 1962.

J. V. REED: *The curtain falls.* New York, 1935.

O. M. SAYLER: *Our American theatre: important productions on the American stage, 1908–23.* Ill., New York, 1923.

F. SPER: *From native roots, a study of American folk drama.* Ill., Idaho, 1948.

THEATRE WORLD, *a pictorial and statistical record of the American theatre*, ed. D. Blum. Ill., New York, 1944/5– . (In progress.)

4. *Twentieth Century: Actors, Dramatists, etc.*

B. H. CLARK: *Maxwell Anderson, the man and his work.* New York, 1933. B.

H. ALPERT: *The Barrymores.* Ill., London, 1965.

E. BARRYMORE: *Memories.* Ill., London, 1955.

J. BARRYMORE: *Confessions of an actor.* Indianapolis, 1926.

G. FOWLER: *Goodnight, sweet Prince (the life and times of John Barrymore).* Ill., New York, 1944, repr. London, 1966.

M. D. ZABEL: *The art of Ruth Draper.* Ill., London, 1960.

D. ALEXANDER: *The tempering of Eugene O'Neill.* New York, 1962.

O. CARGILL, N. B. FAGIN and W. J. FISHER (eds.): *Eugene O'Neill and his plays, a survey of his life and works.* New York, 1961, London, 1962. B.

B. H. CLARK: *Eugene O'Neill, the man and his plays.* Rev. version repr., London and New York, 1947. B.

—— *A bibliography of the works of Eugene O'Neill.* New York, 1931.

H. DEUTSCH and S. HANAU: *The Provincetown, a story of the theatre.* Ill., New York, 1931.

E. A. ENGEL: *The haunted heroes of Eugene O'Neill.* Harvard U.P. and London, 1953.

D. FALK: *Eugene O'Neill and the tragic tension, an interpretive study of the plays.* New Brunswick (N.J.), 1958.

A. and B. GELB: *O'Neill.* Ill., New York and London, 1962.

R. D. SKINNER: *Eugene O'Neill, a poet's quest.* New York, 1935.

S. K. WINTHER: *Eugene O'Neill, a critical study.* Rev. ed., New York, 1961.

5. *Nation-wide Theatre*

H. FLANAGAN: *Arena (the Federal Theatre).* Ill., New York, 1940. B.

W. WHITMAN: *Bread and circuses, a study of Federal Theatre.* London and New York, 1937. B.

H. CLURMAN: *The fervent years, the story of the Group Theatre and the thirties.* New York, 1945, London, 1949.

—— *Lies like truth, a collection of theatrical reviews.* New York, 1958.

L. LANGNER: *The magic curtain.* Ill., New York and London, 1952.

A. G. ARVOLD: *The little country theatre.* Ill., New York, 1922. B.

L. BURLEIGH: *The community theatre in theory and practice.* Ill., Boston, 1917. B.

A. DEAN: *Little Theatre organization and management for community, university, and school, including a history of the amateur in drama.* London and New York, 1926.

C. J. DE GOVEIA: *Community playhouse.* Ill., New York, 1923. B.

T. H. DICKINSON: *The insurgent theatre: organisation and management of the non-commercial theatre.* New York, 1917.

N. HOUGHTON: *Advance from Broadway.* New York, 1941.

A. MCCLEERY and C. GLICK: *Curtains going up.* Ill., New York, 1939. B.

K. MACGOWAN: *Footlights across America: towards a national theater.* Ill., New York, 1929. B.

C. A. PERRY: *The work of the Little Theatres.* New York, 1933. B.

(*See also* CIRCUS, DRAMATIC CRITICISM, ENGLAND, NEGRO IN THE THEATRE, POPULAR ENTERTAINMENT, REGIONAL AND PIONEER THEATRE.)

VARIETY, VAUDEVILLE

See POPULAR ENTERTAINMENT, 2

VENEZUELA

See SOUTH AMERICA, 10

WEST INDIES

R. WRIGHT: *Revels in Jamaica, 1682–1838: plays and players of a century, tumblers and conjurers, etc.* Ill., New York, 1937.

YIDDISH DRAMA

See JEWISH DRAMA

YUGOSLAVIA

See EASTERN EUROPE, 5

NOTES ON THE ILLUSTRATIONS

Nos. 1–7. GREECE

No. 1. Theatre at Epidaurus, which, though it dates only from about the mid-4th century B.C., shows the circular orchestra characteristic of earlier theatres (but see ARCHITECTURE, 1). This theatre is now used regularly in the summer for the performance of revivals of Greek classical plays (see EPIDAURUS). (From Pickard-Cambridge, *The Theatre of Dionysus in Athens*, 1946. Photo: Messbildsanstalt.)

No. 2. Theatre at Priene in Asia Minor, built in the second half of the 4th century B.C., with modified semicircular orchestra and more elaborate stage buildings. (From Pickard-Cambridge, op. cit. Print supplied by the Clarendon Press, Oxford.)

Nos. 3 and 4. Marble representation of a male tragic mask (in the possession of Professor Sir John Beazley, Oxford) and a female tragic mask from Athens, 4th–5th century A.D. (Agora, S. 1144). For the use of masks in Greek plays, see GREECE, 6.

No. 5. Menander with masks. A terracotta panel in the Lateran Museum, Rome, which is thought to show Menander in his studio with the masks of three of his chief characters—the young man, the maiden, and the angry father (see MENANDER). The standing female holding something now lost is either the Muse of Comedy, or Menander's mistress Glykera. (Print supplied by the Mansell Collection. Photo: Anderson, Rome.)

No. 6. Iphigenia in Tauris. A vase-painting (volute krater from Ruvo) showing Iphigenia, with an elderly attendant, speaking to the seated Orestes, with Pylades standing behind. Above are Apollo and Artemis. This is not necessarily a scene taken directly from the theatre, but is probably based on Euripides. (From Pickard-Cambridge, op. cit. Photo: Bruckmann, Munich.)

No. 7. The Revenge of Medea. Vase-painting (volute krater from Canosa). These scenes are based on the Medea legend, as used by Euripides and other dramatists, but do not necessarily represent theatrical aspects of any one play. The death of Creusa, for instance, shown in the central episode, would have been narrated, not acted. Above are Herakles, Athene, and the Dioscuri. (From Pickard-Cambridge, op. cit. Photo: Bruckmann, Munich.)

Nos. 8–13. ROME

No. 8. Theatre at Leptis Magna, with semicircular orchestra and elaborate architectural background (see ROME, 3). This theatre, built on the site of an early Phoenician cemetery, was paid for by a wealthy citizen, Annobal Rufus, and dedicated in A.D. 1–2. The front steps, and the altar in the middle of them, were given by Titus Claudius Sestius in A.D. 91–92. The *scaenae frons*, of three superimposed orders, originally, presumably, of limestone, was replaced by Corinthian columns of marble in the reign of Antoninus Pius (A.D. 138–61). Behind the stage area can still be seen the trench for the curtain which concealed the *scaenae frons*, when necessary, but not the acting area. Behind it is an irregular quadrilateral portico (*porticus post scaenum*) with Corinthian columns of grey granite and marble-panelled walls. (See D. E. L. Haynes, *The Antiquities of Tripolitania*. Photo: Victor Glasstone.)

No. 9. Theatre at Verulamium (St. Albans), the best-preserved in Britain, which differs in several respects from the normal Roman theatre (see No. 8). For a brief description of it, see VERULAMIUM. (See also the official guide, *The Roman Theatre of Verulamium*, by Kathleen M. Kenyon and Sheppard S. Frere. Photo: Aerofilms, Ltd.)

No. 10. A tragic scene. This terracotta relief, is from the monument of P. Numitorius Hilarus (last part of 1st century A.D.). It is probably from *Astyanax*, by Accius, based on Sophocles, and shows Odysseus demanding the surrender of the child Astyanax by his mother Andromache. Two slaves stand by. Note the richly ornate *scaenae frons* and, in spite of the Roman costumes and setting, the persistence of the later Greek type of mask with the high *onkos* (see No. 3). (Museo delle Terme, Rome.)

No. 11. Actors. (*a*) An Etruscan terracotta statuette, probably, judging by the half-hidden money-bag, a thieving slave (the head shows a typical slave-mask) in an adaptation of a Greek New Comedy, possibly, but not necessarily, by Menander. (Reproduced by courtesy of the British Museum, where the figure can be seen.)

(*b*) The so-called 'Rieti' statuette (ivory), a late Roman work (probably 2nd century A.D.), thought by Professor Bieber to represent an elderly female character. The costume, a long blue robe with yellow decorations, is Roman, not Greek. The supports at the base are not, as was once supposed, examples of the *kothurnos* or high tragic boot, but pegs to fix the statuette (now in the Petit Palais, Paris) to its base. (Print supplied by Professor Sir John Beazley.)

No. 12. A comic scene. A *phlyax* painting now in the British Museum, illustrating the type of mythological burlesque popular in Southern Italy in the 4th century B.C. (see PHLYAX). Jupiter mounts a ladder towards his lady-love, while Mercury stands by with a torch and a decorated casket, probably containing a present. (Print supplied by the late Professor William Beare, Bristol.)

No. 13. Actor with mask. A wall-painting from Pompeii, now in the National Museum, Naples; a copy of a votive tablet of the end of the 4th or early 3rd century B.C. The seated actor has evidently been playing the part of a tragic hero, and has just removed his mask, which, with its high *onkos*, can be seen on the table. (Print supplied by the Mansell Collection. Photo: Anderson, Rome.)

Nos. 14–19
EARLY EUROPEAN DRAMA

No. 14. A Renaissance stage intended for the production of a play by Terence, from the Trechsel edition of Terence's works published in Lyon in 1493. The classical revivals in this type of indoor theatre were intended for a learned audience. For a description of this particular stage, see ARCHITECTURE, 4. (Photo: Victoria and Albert Museum, London. Crown copyright.)

No. 15. A religious drama, *Le Martyre de Sainte Apolline*, *c.* 1460, from a miniature by Jean Fouquet (1415–83) now in the Condé Museum, Chantilly. Plays of this type, given in the open air, were intended for an unsophisticated audience, and continued the tradition of the religious plays formerly given in churches (see LITURGICAL DRAMA). The illustration shows a raised platform stage, static (as opposed to the perambulating pageant shown in No. 19), with simultaneous décor. Heaven is on the actors' right, Hell on the left (see also No. 16). The figure on the spectators' right, with wand and book, may be the producer taking a rehearsal or, alternatively, directing the play (and the musicians) during the performance. (Photo: Giraudon.)

No. 16. Hell-mouth, from the West Door of Bourges Cathedral. It seems probable that the inspiration for this may have come from stage representations of Hell-mouth, of which one example can be seen in the right-hand top half of No. 15. (Print supplied by the Victoria and Albert Museum, London. Photo: Bruckmann, Munich.)

No. 17. A secular comedy. A Dutch open-air platform stage in the 16th century, part of a painting by Pieter Breugel (*c.* 1525–69). This type of stage, easily set up (like the earlier *phlyakes* stage of No. 12), must have been in common use by strolling players all over Europe, and in a more elaborate form served also for performances by *commedia dell'arte* troupes. Its informality, and the plays performed on it—usually short farces of daily life—by a handful of actors, are in marked contrast to the elaboration of the pageants (see No. 19) and the formality of the contemporary Court entertainment (see No. 18). (From a photo in the Oskar Fischel Collection, Victoria and Albert Museum, London. The original is in a private collection, Du Croy, Belgium.)

No. 18. A Court performance in Paris, the 'Ballet comique de la Reine', performed in the Salle du Petit Bourbon on 15 Oct. 1581 in honour of the marriage of the Duc de Joyeuse with the Queen's sister. The illustration shows the simultaneous setting (inherited from the religious plays, see No. 15), which consists of Pan's grotto on the right, a wood on the left, with Circe's palace and garden at the back. There was also, according to the libretto, a 'cloud' (not shown here) which descended from the roof bearing Mercury with a message from Jupiter, evidently based on Brunelleschi's 'Paradiso' (see MACHINERY). Circe can be seen on the stage at the back, Pan in the grotto, with a nymph in the branches, and two nymphs in the wood. The actor in the centre of the bare space which later served for the ballet, in which members of the royal family took part, is the 'Gentilhomme', the only human being in the play—the others being Tritons, divinities of various kinds, and animals. For a detailed description of this performance, important in the history of ballet and of stage scenery, see *Theatre Research / Recherches Théâtrales*, vol. iii, no. 2, 1961, article by Hélène Leclerc. (See also BALLET.) (Print taken from the libretto of the ballet in the Bibliothèque d'Art et d'Archéologie. Photo: M. Rigal.)

No. 19. A Pageant Stage. The Cart of the Nativity, from the Triumph of Isabella, 1615. From a painting by Van Alsloot, now in the Victoria and Albert Museum, London. This shows a perambulating stage of the type commonly used in England up to the mid-16th century for the presentation of scenes from Biblical plays. Although the static, built-up stage (see No. 15) was more usual on the Continent, pageants continued in use there for religious scenes much later than in England, where they were taken over for secular processions and triumphs, the last survival being the 'floats' used annually in London in November for the Lord Mayor's procession. (From Hugh Hunt's *The Live Theatre*. Photo: Victoria and Albert Museum, London. Crown copyright.)

Nos. 20–44. THEATRE INTERIORS

(See also Nos. 56–70, STAGE SETTINGS; Nos. 71–94, SETTINGS FOR SHAKESPEARE; Nos. 95–114, SOME MODERN SETTINGS, and Nos. 116, 117, 120, 121–5, 140, 142–3, 162–5.)

No. 20. The Teatro Olimpico, Vicenza. This superb theatre, which is still standing, was designed by Andrea Palladio (1518–80) and completed after his death by Scamozzi, architect of the Sabbionetta Theatre (see No. 21). It opened on 3 Mar. 1585 with an Italian translation of Sophocles' *Oedipus Rex* (for a description of this first production, see Leo Schrade, *La Représentation d'Édipo Tiranno au Teatro Olimpico*, 1960). The Teatro Olimpico was the last of the Renaissance academic theatres (see ARCHITECTURE, 4) of which the Terence-stage (see No. 14) was perhaps the first, and its *scaenae frons* is reminiscent of the great Roman theatres (see No. 8). (Photo: L. Chiovato, Vicenza.)

No. 21. The theatre at Sabbionetta, a small playhouse, built about 1588 by Vincenzo Scamozzi (1552–1616), who was responsible for finishing Palladio's Teatro Olimpico (see No. 20). In its general features it looks forward to the later Italian opera-house rather than back to the Renaissance stage. (From Bulley, *Art and Everyman*, vol. i, 1951. Photo: R. Sop. dell'Arte, Verona.)

No. 22. The Swan Theatre, London. A copy by Arend van Buchell, in his commonplace book, of a drawing made by a Dutch visitor to London, Johann de Witt, in 1596. This is the only extant representation of an Elizabethan theatre which has so far been discovered, and it has been a fruitful source of controversy. In its general features the interior of the theatre seems to support the theory that the main influence behind its construction was the English inn-yard used by the players before the building of Burbage's Theatre in 1576 (see ENGLISH PLAYHOUSE, 1). There may, however, have been other sources of inspiration, including the temporary platform stages erected for ceremonial occasions and the Dutch Rederijker and other Continental stages (for a detailed discussion of these points, see Glynne Wickham, *Early English Stages*). For a possible Renaissance, rather than Tudor, derivation, see *Theatre Notebook*, vol. xi, p. 57, where Richard Southern argues that the columns described in the note accompanying the drawing were painted to represent marble, and therefore approximated to the columns of the Teatro Olimpico (see No. 20). Two puzzling features of the de Witt drawing are the absence of an inner stage and the presence of people in the gallery behind the stage. The first has been explained away by assuming that de Witt made his drawing from the topmost gallery, and was therefore rather vague about details under the stage roof. The second has given rise to the theory that the drawing was done during a rehearsal and the people are therefore actors waiting to go on, or persons otherwise connected with the theatre (see *Theatre Notebook*, vol. x, p. 80—but see also No. 23). (Print supplied by the Victoria and Albert Museum, London.)

No. 23. A Commonwealth stage, London; the title-page of Francis Kirkman's *The Wits; or, Sport upon Sport* (1672), with a composite drawing showing the kind of improvised stage which may have been used when the theatres were officially closed from 1642 to 1660, and not, as was previously thought, the stage of the Red Bull playhouse. According to Mander and Mitchenson, however (in *A Picture History of the British Theatre*, 1957), W. J. Lawrence was of the opinion that it might represent the stage of the Vere Street Theatre. The characters represented on stage are from the 'drolls' or short plays printed in the volume: Sir John Falstaff and the Hostess, from Shakespeare's *Henry IV* (1597); Clause, from Fletcher's *The Beggar's Bush* (1622); the French dancing-master, from the droll of that name based on *The Variety* (1639), by William Cavendish, Duke of Newcastle; the Changeling, from Middleton and Rowley's play of that name (also 1622); and the Simpleton, from a droll entitled *Simpleton, the Smith*, written and acted by Robert Cox, here shown in the part. The man emerging from the curtains at the back may be Kirkman himself, or the presenter of the entertainment. The presence of spectators in the gallery behind the stage seems to confirm de Witt's drawing of a similarly occupied gallery behind the stage of the Swan Theatre (see No. 22). This drawing is also interesting as giving evidence of the use of chandeliers for lighting the stage, and for the first recorded use of footlights in the London theatre (see LIGHTING, 1). (Print supplied by the Victoria and Albert Museum, London.)

No. 24. A Court performance before Louis XIV at Versailles, 1674. This contemporary engraving by Le Pautre (1617–82) shows a scene from *Le Malade imaginaire* by Molière (1622–73), first produced in 1673. Argan, created by Molière, is probably being played by Rosimond. It makes an interesting comparison with No. 18. The stage has been enlarged, and the action confined within a picture-frame proscenium arch. Chandeliers light the stage and spectators (see also No. 23). The orchestra-pit cuts off the audience from the action, but there is still a large empty space in front of the king, which may later have been used for dancing. (Print supplied by the Victoria and Albert Museum, London.)

No. 25. The Schouwburg in Amsterdam, built on the Keizergracht (Emperor's Canal) in 1637 by Jacob van Campen (*c.* 1590–1657). This was the first permanent theatre building in the Netherlands. It opened on 3 Jan. 1638 with *Gijsbrecht van Amstel*, a tragedy by Joost van den Vondel (1587–1689). The permanent architectural setting shows the influence of Palladio's Teatro Olimpico (see No. 20) as well as of the Rederijker stage and of the temporary stages set up for triumphs, royal entries, etc. The galleries on each side of the stage may have been used by musicians when the play called for musical accompaniment. (For a note on this theatre, see ARCHITECTURE, 4.) (From an engraving of 1658 by S. Savry. Print supplied by the Victoria and Albert Museum, London.)

No. 26. The Schouwburg in Amsterdam, as it appeared after extensive remodelling in 1665 by Jan Vos (1615–67). Van Campen's *scena stabile* (see No. 25) has been replaced by a contemporary-style Italian proscenium arch flanked by statues, with an orchestra-pit in front of the stage, and painted canvas scenery. This engraving, one of a series done for the centenary celebrations in 1738, shows an exterior scene (designer unknown) for a farce, *Het verliefde Brechtje*, by P. W. van Haps. The theatre shown here was burnt down in 1772, and replaced by a new theatre on the Leidseplein, which opened in 1774 and was itself burnt down in 1890. (Print from the Richard Southern Collection.)

No. 27. The Theatre Royal, Bristol, built in King Street in 1766. The architect was John Paty. This theatre is the oldest theatre in Great Britain still in use by a regular permanent company. It was also the first theatre to be state-aided, when in 1943 it was restored and reopened as the Bristol Old Vic with the help of a grant from the Council for the Encouragement of Music and the Arts (later the Arts Council). It is a typical Georgian theatre, with a tier of boxes directly flanking the pit. (Print from the Richard Southern Collection. Photo: Baynard Press.)

No. 28. The Chestnut Street Theatre, Philadelphia, U.S.A., built in 1793 on the plans of the Theatre Royal, Bristol (see No. 27). This theatre, which again shows the typically Georgian arrangement of large forestage, proscenium doors, and boxes directly round the pit, remained standing until 1940. (From an engraving in the *New York Magazine*, Apr. 1794, reproduced in Altman, Freud, Macgowan, and Melnitz, *Theater Pictorial*, 1953. Print supplied by the Harvard Theater Collection.)

No. 29. Drottningholm Court Theatre, Sweden, near Stockholm, built in 1766, the same year as the Theatre Royal, Bristol (see No. 27). Now used as a theatre museum, it still has its original flat wings and painted backdrops, its stage machinery, and many of its original props and costumes. Occasional performances are given here on ceremonial occasions. (For a description of this theatre, see DROTTNINGHOLM THEATRE; compare also No. 65, built at about the same time.) (Photo: C. G. Rosenberg.)

No. 30. The Theatre Royal, Drury Lane, London, designed by Sir Christopher Wren (1632–1723), erected in 1672 and extensively altered by the Adam brothers in 1775. Characteristic of the period are the painted backcloth and wings, the large forestage, and the boxes directly flanking it. This engraving of 1778 shows the Screen Scene in the first production of *The School for Scandal*, by R. B. Sheridan (1751–1816), on 8 May 1777, with Tom King and Mrs. Abington as Sir Peter and Lady Teazle, and John Palmer and William Smith as Joseph and Charles Surface. For the playbill of the second performance, see No. 166; for an American painting of the same scene, see No. 163; for Covent Garden at roughly the same period, see No. 140. (Print supplied by the Victoria and Albert Museum, London.)

No. 31. The Theatre Royal, Drury Lane, London, in 1815, after the rebuilding in 1791–4 by Henry Holland (1746–1806). This building was burnt down in 1809. The illustration is taken from a folding plate in *The Stage*, vol. iii. 1, 16 Sept. 1815. The play in progress on stage is *The Magpie; or, the Maid of Palaiseau*, by Thomas Dibdin (1771–1841), one of the many adaptations of Caigniez's *La pie voleuse*. (Print from the Richard Southern Collection.)

No. 32. The Theatre Royal, Covent Garden, London, built after the burning down of the old theatre in 1808. The new building, designed by Richard Smirke (1781–1867), opened on 18 Sept. 1809 with *Macbeth*. This illustration is also from *The Stage*, iii. 6, 21 Oct. 1815. The play may be Pocock's version of *La pie voleuse, The Magpie, or the Maid* (see also No. 31)—the prison scene—or a scene from a revival of *Jane Shore*, by Nicholas Rowe (1674–1716), first produced in 1714, which provided Mrs. Siddons with one of her favourite and most successful parts. (Print from the Richard Southern Collection.)

No. 33. The Comédie-Française, Paris. Designed by Victor Louis (1731–1802) (for a note on its construction, see ARCHITECTURE, 6), this theatre opened in 1790 as the Variétés-Amusantes. After some internal reconstruction, during which the stage was much enlarged, as shown here, it reopened on 30 May 1799 as the Théâtre-Français. The illustration shows a scene from one of the popular melodramas of the day, perhaps from *Cœlina, ou l'Enfant de mystère*, by Guilbert de Pixerécourt (1773–1844), first produced in 1800 at the Ambigu-Comique and frequently revived. On 8 Mar. 1900 this theatre was burnt down. A new theatre was built on the same site, opening on 29 Dec.; the interior was remodelled in 1935, reopening on 30 Oct. (From the archives of the Comédie-Française. Photo: M. Rigal.)

No. 34. The Bolshoi Theatre, Moscow. First built in 1824 by I. O. Bove on plans made earlier by A. A. Mikhailov, this theatre was badly damaged by fire in 1853. It was rebuilt, with a much enlarged stage and an ornately decorated auditorium, and reopened in 1856, since when it has remained substantially the same (for an exterior view, see No. 54). In this photograph, taken during the 1950s, a festival of folk-art from one of the Soviet Republics is taking place. (Print supplied by the Society for Cultural Relations with the U.S.S.R., London.)

No. 35. The Royal Coburg, London, later famous as the Old Vic (see No. 36) and as the first home of the British National Theatre. Designed by Rudolph Cabanel, it opened on 11 May 1818 (Whit Monday) with a Harlequinade, a melodrama, and a grand Asiatic ballet. The illustration, an engraving by Stow, after Schnebbelie, shows the first-night audience, with, on stage, the final tableau of the melodramatic spectacle, *Trial by Battle; or, Heaven Defend the Right*, by William Barrymore (1758–1830), manager of the theatre. (From the Enthoven Collection, Victoria and Albert Museum, London.)

No. 36. The Old Vic, London, in Nov. 1948, showing the interior patched up after bomb damage. It was then being used as a practice theatre by the Old Vic School. It was here that the inaugural meeting of the Society for Theatre Research took place on 15 June 1948 (for the full history of this famous theatre, see OLD VIC). (Print from the Richard Southern Collection. Photo: A. F. Kersting.)

Nos. 37 and 38. The Burgtheater, on the Franzensring, Vienna. The first theatre on this site, which replaced the former theatre on the Michaelerplatz, and opened on 14 Oct. 1888, was burnt down in a bombing raid on 12 Apr. 1945. Rebuilt on substantially the same plan, but with a modern interior and excellent backstage equipment, it opened again on 15 Oct. 1955 with a revival of *König Ottokars Glück und Ende*, by Franz Grillparzer (1791–1872). (No. 37 is from Hennings, *Zweimal Burgtheater*, 1955; No. 38 was specially photographed for this book, as a pendant to No. 37. Both photos: Alpenland, for the Austrian National Library.)

No. 39. The Grosses Schauspielhaus, Berlin. This theatre, designed by Hans Poelzig for Max Reinhardt (1873–1943), opened on 29 Nov. 1919 with Reinhardt's production of the *Oresteia* (for a note on its construction, see ARCHITECTURE, 7). (From the Oskar Fischel Collection, Victoria and Albert Museum, London.)

No. 40. The Stadsteater, Malmö, Sweden. This has close affinities with the Grosses Schauspielhaus (see No. 39), whose architect was one of the committee which chose its design as the winner in a competition. Although the design was chosen in the 1930s, the building was not completed until 1944, opening on 23 Sept. The back curtains can be drawn, providing more stage space, and there is also a proscenium arch, which can be lowered when needed. The seating capacity is 1,700, but can be reduced by sliding walls to 400. The influence of this building can be seen in the Shakespearean Festival Theatre at Stratford, Ontario, Canada (see No. 43) and in the Chichester Festival Theatre. For a note on it, see ARCHITECTURE, 7. (From the Richard Southern Collection. Photo: Jarke.)

No. 41. The Penthouse Theatre, built by Glenn Hughes for the School of Drama, University of Washington, Seattle, U.S.A. A 1940 example of 'arena' theatre, or 'theatre-in-the-round', which attempted to break the tyranny of the proscenium arch by placing the audience all round the actors, a return to primitive practice (for an early English example, see CORNISH ROUNDS. See also THEATRE-IN-THE-ROUND). (Photograph supplied by Glenn Hughes.)

No. 42. The Mermaid Theatre, London. Designed by Elidir Davies for Bernard Miles, this theatre opened on 28 May 1959 with *Lock Up Your Daughters*, a musical version of Fielding's *Rape Upon Rape* (1730). The original walls of the bombed warehouse in which the theatre was built (see MERMAID THEATRE) can be seen on the left. The theatre has an open stage, a raked auditorium, and overhead and side lighting visible to the audience. The stage shows Giles Fletcher's set for the first production in England of *The Andersonville Trial* (1961), by Saul Levitt. Lighting by David Kaye. (Photo: Strand Electric.)

No. 43. The Shakespearean Festival Theatre at Stratford, Ontario, Canada (architect, Robert Fairfield, of Toronto). This theatre, which replaced an earlier, temporary, tent-like building, erected in 1952, opened in 1957. It shows traces of the influence of such theatres as the Grosses Schauspielhaus, Berlin, and the Stadsteater, Malmö (see Nos. 39 and 40, also ARCHITECTURE, 7). The open stage, with the audience on three sides, has eight acting levels and a central trapdoor. It was designed by Tanya Moiseiwitsch, in association with Tyrone Guthrie for the original theatre, and modified, in association with Brian Jackson, for the season of 1961–2 (see CANADA, 2, and SHAKESPEARE, 4). (Photo: Peter Smith.)

No. 44. The Belgrade Theatre, Coventry, England's first civic theatre, which opened on 27 March 1958 with *Half in Earnest*, a musical version of *The Importance of Being Earnest*, by Oscar Wilde (1854–1900). This photograph, taken during the run of John Osborne's *Luther*, shows the set designed by Christopher Morley, a basic standing structure with flown pieces (see also BELGRADE THEATRE). (Photo: Richard Sadler.)

Nos. 45–47. THEATRE LIGHTING

No. 45. The San Carlos, Lisbon, showing the modern lighting equipment installed there in 1942, and also, through the proscenium arch, the lighted auditorium with its central Royal Box. (Photo: Strand Electric.)

No. 46. Drury Lane, London, showing the new lighting installed in 1948, during the run of *Oklahoma!* (see also Nos. 30, 31). (Photo: Strand Electric.)

No. 47. Her Majesty's Theatre, London, showing the lighting installed for *Bye Bye Birdie* in 1961. For a general description of modern lighting as seen above, see LIGHTING, 2. These illustrations all show lighting units installed in a proscenium-arch theatre, hidden from the audience. For lighting in the modern open-stage theatre, visible to the audience, see Nos. 41, 42, and 113. For the lighting of stage and audience by chandeliers, see Nos. 23, 24, 25, and 26; also, for a central lantern, No. 63; for an early use of footlights, No. 23; also Lighting, *passim*. (Photo: Strand Electric.)

Nos. 48–55. THEATRE EXTERIORS

No. 48. The Globe Playhouse, London. A detail from Visscher's 'View of London', 1616. For an Elizabethan theatre interior, see No. 22; see also GLOBE THEATRE, 1. (From a print in the Guildhall Library, London. Photo: John Freeman.)

No. 49. The Surrey Theatre, London, home of transpontine melodrama, in 1814. For an interior of about the same period, see No. 35; see also SURREY THEATRE. (From the Richard Southern Collection.)

No. 50. The Shakespeare Memorial Theatre at Stratford-upon-Avon—the first theatre. This opened on 23 Apr. 1879 with *Much Ado About Nothing*, Barry Sullivan and Helen Faucit playing Benedick and Beatrice. It was burnt down on 6 Mar. 1926. For the new theatre, see No. 51; see also STRATFORD-UPON-AVON. (From the Shakespeare Memorial Theatre Collection.)

No. 51. The Royal Shakespeare Theatre, Stratford-upon-Avon—the second theatre (for the first, see No. 50). Until 1961 this also was known as the Shakespeare Memorial Theatre. Designed by Elizabeth Scott, it opened on 23 Apr. 1932 with *Henry IV*, Part I being played in the afternoon and Part II in the evening. Randle Ayrton, who as Leontes had spoken the last words from the old stage, spoke the opening lines as King Henry IV. Roy Byford played Falstaff and Gyles Isham Prince Hal. For stage settings in this theatre, see Nos. 89, 91, and 92; for costume designs, see Nos. 160 and 161. (Photo: Angus McBean.)

No. 52. The Bowery Theatre, New York, in 1859. This was the fifth Bowery, all on the same site. The earlier ones were burnt down in 1828, 1836, 1838, and 1845. The building shown here was several times renovated, and finally destroyed by fire in 1929. See BOWERY THEATRE, 1. (Illustration from the Harvard Theater Collection.)

No. 53. The Cleveland Playhouse, Ohio, U.S.A., designed by Philip Lindsley Small, 1927. A typical example of the American University Theatre as it developed in the 1920s and 1930s, under the influence of the central-European theatre-centre, of which Stuttgart (1912), designed by Max Littmann (1862–1931), provided a good example. (See ARCHITECTURE, 7.) (Photo: Miller-Ertler Studios.)

No. 54. The Bolshoi Theatre, Moscow, in 1856. For further details, and an illustration of the present-day interior of this theatre, see No. 34. (Print supplied by the Society for Cultural Relations with the U.S.S.R., London.)

No. 55. The Bolshoi Theatre, Minsk, a typical Russian theatre building of the 1940s. (Print supplied by the Society for Cultural Relations with the U.S.S.R., London.)

Nos. 56–70. STAGE SETTINGS

(For other examples, see Nos. 71–94, SETTINGS FOR SHAKESPEARE, and Nos. 95–114, SOME MODERN SETTINGS; also Nos. 116, 140, 143, 162–5.)

Nos. 56–58. The three basic sets—Satiric, Comic, and Tragic—given by Sebastiano Serlio (1475–1554) in his Book II of *De Architettura*, published in 1545. This was based largely on Vitruvius (see SCENERY, 2). An English translation of it was published in 1611, from which these illustrations are taken. Serlio's influence can be discerned in many of the illustrations which follow (see also LIGHTING, 1.) (Photo: British Museum.)

No. 59. A setting after Bernardo Buontalenti (1536–1608) for the Florentine Intermezzi of 1589. This particular design was for the third Intermezzo, *Il Combattimento pitico d'Apollo*, and was engraved by Agostino Carracci (see SCENERY, 2). (From the original in the Victoria and Albert Museum, London.)

No. 60. A setting by Giulio Parigi (1590–1636) for a Florentine Intermezzo, *c.* 1620: The Ship of Amerigo Vespucci. Parigi was a pupil of Buontalenti (see No. 59). (From the original in the Corsini Gallery, Rome. Photo: Lazzari.)

No. 61. A setting by Inigo Jones (1573–1652), probably for the first scene of *Coelum Britannicum* (1634), a Court masque by Thomas Carew (*c.* 1595–1639?). Jones, who introduced Italian scenery into England, studied on the Continent. He designed sets and costumes (see No. 144) for a number of Court masques, and many of his designs have been preserved in the Duke of Devonshire's Collection at Chatsworth (see also JONES, Inigo, and SCENERY, 2). (Reproduced by permission of the Trustees of the Chatsworth Settlement.)

No. 62. A setting by Giacomo Torelli di Fano (1608–78) for the Courtyard of a Palace, dating from *c.* 1660, and probably intended for a classical tragedy acted in Paris, though there is no proof that it was ever used. (From the original in the Corsini Gallery, Rome. Photo: Lazzari.)

No. 63. Dorset Garden London, William Davenant's second Restoration Theatre, which opened on 9 Nov. 1671 with a revival of *Sir Martin Mar-All*, by John Dryden (1613–1700), first produced in 1667. The illustration, one of a series by William Dolle for the 1673 edition of *The Empress of Morocco*, by Elkaneh Settle (1648–1724), shows the heavily ornate proscenium arch with the music-room over the stage (above the Royal Arms), and also indicates the size of the forestage with its proscenium doors, typical of the Restoration theatre (see DORSET GARDEN THEATRE, and ENGLISH PLAYHOUSE). (Print supplied by the Victoria and Albert Museum, London. Crown copyright.)

No. 64. An unidentified setting, now in the Victoria and Albert Museum, London, by one of the Galli-Bibiena family, dating from about 1690. It is a good example of the Bibienas's *scena d'angolo*, or diagonal perspective setting, which had a widespread influence (see No. 66) and is in marked contrast to the earlier central perspective of Nos. 20 and 25, for instance. (See also BIBIENA, and SCENERY, 3.) (Print supplied by the Victoria and Albert Museum, London. Crown copyright.)

No. 65. Český Krumlov, Czechoslovakia. The stage of this 18th-century theatre (for its history see ČESKÝ KRUMLOV) still has a number of fine sets of its original scenery, probably the oldest surviving in Europe. The street scene, in the angled perspective introduced by the Bibienas (see No. 64), was painted by J. Wetschela and L. Merkla, probably in 1766–7. (For another Court Theatre contemporary with Český Krumlov, see DROTTNINGHOLM and No. 29.) (Photo: C. Šild.)

No. 66. A design by Filippo Juvarra (1676–1736), from a collection of his designs now in the Victoria and Albert Museum, London, executed somewhere between 1708 and 1712 for Cardinal Ottoboni's puppet-theatre in the Cancellaria Palace, Rome (see *Theatre Research/Recherches Théâtrales*, vol. i. 2, pp. 5–10). The small sketch in the lower right-hand corner is a floor-plan showing how the wings were to be placed. The influence of the Bibienas's *scena d'angolo* is plainly visible (see No. 64). This setting may have been designed for Act II, Scene 3 of the opera 'Il Teodosia', by Adami, produced in 1711 (for a tentative identification, see *The Ohio State University Theater Collection Bulletin*, no. 11, 1964). (Print supplied by the Victoria and Albert Museum, London. Crown copyright.)

No. 67. An early 19th-century setting, as shown in Park's Juvenile Drama sheet, for one of the most famous scenes in early English melodrama—the blowing-up of Grindoff's mill in *The Miller and his Men*, by Isaac Pocock (1782–1835), first performed at Covent Garden, London, on 21 Oct. 1813. (From the George Speaight Theatre Collection.)

No. 68. A design by Karl Friedrich Schinkel (1781–1841) for a production of *Die Jungfrau von Orleans*, by Friedrich von Schiller (1759–1805), at the Court Theatre in Berlin, 1817. (From a collection of lithographs showing stage settings by Schinkel, pub. Berlin 1819. Reproduced in Bamber Gascoigne's *World Theatre*, 1968, p. 240. Print kindly loaned by Mr. Gascoigne.)

No. 69. A setting by George II, Duke of Saxe-Meiningen (1826–1914) for Act II (Marwood's bedroom) of *Miss Sara Sampson* (first produced in 1755), by G. E. Lessing (1729–81). The design dates from about 1884, and shows a realistic box-set with solid detail scenery and practicable door. (See MEININGER COMPANY, and SCENERY, 6; also, for a costume design by George II, No. 151; for an early English box-set, No. 71.) (From Max Grube, *Geschichte der Meininger*, 1925. Photo: Meininger Kunstsammlungen.)

No. 70. Late 19th-century setting for a provincial revival in 1893 of *The Grip of Iron*, by Arthur Shirley (based on *Les Étrangleurs de Paris*), first performed at the Surrey Theatre on 17 Oct. 1887. The apotheosis of realism, typical of the period, and soon to be challenged by the simplicity of William Poel (No. 74) and the imagination of Gordon Craig (No. 75). (From *The Magazine of Art*. Photo: Common Ground.)

Nos. 71–94
SETTINGS FOR SHAKESPEARE

(These are of European and American productions only, and are arranged chronologically, with, where possible, a note of date, designer, theatre, chief actor or producer, and cross-references to other settings or costume designs for the same play, or by the same designer.)

No. 71. *Othello*, 1837. Setting—the Senate House—by George Scharf (1788–1860) for Macready, Covent Garden, London, 16 Oct. (see also No. 87). (From Scharf's *Recollections . . .*, 1839. Photo: Common Ground.)

No. 72. *Macbeth*, 1853. Setting for the Banqueting Hall in the Palace, by I. Dayes (*fl.* 1850–60) for Charles Kean, Princess's Theatre, London, 14 Feb. This shows the banquet in progress, with Banquo's ghost—an effect obtained by setting an actor in a hollow pillar with an opening concealed by a gauze which could be illuminated at the appropriate moment (see also Nos. 75, 81). (From the original water-colour drawing in the Enthoven Theatre Collection, Victoria and Albert Museum, London. Crown copyright.)

No. 73. *Romeo and Juliet*, 1882. Setting—Juliet's Tomb—by William Telbin (1845–1931) for Irving, Lyceum, London, 8 Mar. (see also Nos. 82, 162). (From *The Illustrated London News*, Enthoven Theatre Collection, Victoria and Albert Museum, London.)

No. 74. *Hamlet*, 1900. Permanent set by William Poel (1852–1934) for his production at the Carpenters' Hall, London. This was formerly thought to be the 1881 production at St. George's Hall, but research by Messrs. Mander and Mitchenson and the Enthoven Theatre Collection establishes it as 1900 (see also Nos. 79, 90). (Enthoven Theatre Collection, Victoria and Albert Museum, London. Photo: Wykeham.)

No. 75. *Macbeth*, 1908. Setting for Act II, designed by Gordon Craig for Beerbohm Tree at Her Majesty's Theatre, London, but not used. Tree preferred the designs of Joseph Harker, whose realistic style is well seen in No. 76 (see also Nos. 72, 81, 161). (Reproduced in Janet Leeper's *Edward Gordon Craig: Designs for the Theatre* (King Penguin), 1948. Copyright, Edward Gordon Craig.)

No. 76. *Henry VIII*, 1910. Setting for the scene of Buckingham's farewell speech, by Joseph Harker (1855–1927), for Tree, Her Majesty's Theatre, London, 1 Sept. (see also Nos. 84, 89, 164). (Photo: Messrs. Newton and *The Daily Mirror*.)

No. 77. *Twelfth Night*, 1912. Permanent setting by Norman Wilkinson of Four Oaks

(1882–1934) for Granville-Barker's production, Savoy Theatre, London, 15 Nov. (see also Nos. 80, 151). (Photo: Messrs. Newton and *The Daily Mirror*.)

No. 78. *Henry IV, Part I*, 1912. Setting by Ernest Stern (1876–1954) for Max Reinhardt's production, Deutsches Theater, Berlin, 12 Oct. (Print supplied by the Harvard Theater Collection.)

No. 79. *Hamlet*, 1913. Setting for the last scene by Hawes Craven (Henry Hawes Craven Green) (1837–1910), designed for Irving at the Lyceum in 1878 and here used by Forbes-Robertson, Drury Lane, London, 22 Mar. (see also Nos. 74, 90). (Photo: Messrs. Newton and *The Daily Mirror*.)

No. 80. *Twelfth Night*, 1914. Setting by Joseph Urban (1872–1933) for the production in which Phyllis Neilson-Terry, as Viola, made her American début, Liberty Theatre, New York, 23 Nov. (see also Nos. 77, 151). (From Altman *et al.*, op. cit., Kenneth Macgowan Collection.)

No. 81. *Macbeth*, 1928. Setting by Paul Shelving for Barry Jackson's production in modern dress, Royal Court, London, 6 Feb. (see also Nos. 72, 75, 151). (Print supplied by the Enthoven Theatre Collection, Victoria and Albert Museum, London. Photo: Lenare.)

No. 82. *Romeo and Juliet*, 1930. Setting of the Tomb Scene by Aline Bernstein (1882–1935) for Eva Le Gallienne's production, Civic Repertory Theatre, New York, 21 Apr. (see also Nos. 73, 162). (Print supplied by the Harvard Theater Collection.)

No. 83. *The Merchant of Venice*, 1931. Setting for the Court Scene by Antonin Heythum for Karel Dostal's production of a Czech translation by Bohumil Stepanek, 16 Jan. First produced at the Narodni Divadlo (National Theatre), Prague, this was later transferred to the Stavovske Divadlo (State Theatre), the building in which the first performance of Mozart's 'Don Giovanni' was given on 29 Oct. 1787. It is now known as the Tylovo Divadlo (Tyl Theatre). In Dostal's production Shylock was played by Vaclav Vydra (1876–1953) (see also No. 158 and, for another production of Shakespeare at the Tyl Theatre, No. 94). (Print supplied by the Harvard Theater Collection.)

No. 84. *Henry VIII*, 1931. Terence Gray's permanent simplified setting with different acting levels, for his own production at the Festival Theatre, Cambridge, Feb. (see also Nos. 76, 89, 164). (From a photograph in the possession of Norman Marshall.)

No. 85. *The Tempest*, 1934. Setting by Knut Ström for the opening production at the Municipal Theatre, Gothenburg, Sweden, 29 Sept. (Print supplied by the Harvard Theater Collection.)

No. 86. *The Taming of the Shrew*, 1937. Permanent set by Doris Zinkeisen for a production at the New Theatre, London, 23 Mar., with Edith Evans and Leslie Banks as Katharina and Petruchio. (From the designer's original model in the Victoria and Albert Museum, London.)

No. 87. *Othello*, 1937. Setting by Robert Edmond Jones (1887–1954) for a production at the New Amsterdam Theatre, New York, 6 Jan. with Walter Huston as Othello (see also No. 71). (Print supplied by the Harvard Theater Collection.)

No. 88. *Antony and Cleopatra*, 1947. Setting by Leo Kerz (1912–) for Guthrie M'Clintic's production, Martin Beck Theatre, New York, 26 Nov. (From Altman *et al.*, op. cit. Photo: Vandamm.)

No. 89. *Henry VIII*, 1949. Permanent set by Tanya Moiseiwitsch (1914–) for Tyrone Guthrie's production at the Shakespeare Memorial Theatre, Stratford-upon-Avon, 15 July (see also Nos. 76, 84, 164). (From the Shakespeare Memorial Theatre Collection.)

No. 90. *Hamlet*, 1954. Setting by V. Ryndin for Okhlopkov's production, Mayakovsky Theatre, Moscow, 18 Dec. (see also Nos. 74, 79). (Print supplied by the Society for Cultural Relations with the U.S.S.R., London.)

No. 91. *King Lear*, 1955. Setting by Isamu Noguchi for George Devine's production at the Shakespeare Memorial Theatre, Stratford-upon-Avon, with John Gielgud as Lear. This photograph was taken on tour (see also No. 93). (From the Shakespeare Memorial Theatre Collection.)

No. 92. *The Merry Wives of Windsor*, 1955. Setting by Motley for Glen Byam Shaw's production at the Shakespeare Memorial Theatre, Stratford-upon-Avon, 12 July (see also No. 94). (Photo: Angus McBean.)

No. 93. *King Lear*, 1959. Setting by Ulrich Damrau for a production at the State Theatre, Ankara, by Cüney Gökcer, who played Lear (see also No. 91). (Print supplied by Metin And. Photo: Osman Darcan.)

No. 94. *The Merry Wives of Windsor*, 1962. Setting—the Garter Inn—by Oldřich Šimáček (1919–) for Jaromír Pleskot's production of E. A. Saudek's translation at the Tyl Theatre, Prague, showing Frantisek Filipovský as the Host and Jan Piveč as Falstaff (see also No. 92, and, for another Shakespeare production at this theatre, No. 83). (Photo: Dr. Jar. Svoboda.)

Nos. 95–11

SOME MODERN SETTINGS, 1901–61

(See also Nos. 75–94, SETTINGS FOR SHAKESPEARE.)

No. 95. *Three Sisters*, 1901. Part of the setting by V. Simov (1858–1935) for Act IV of Stanislavsky's production at the Moscow Art Theatre, 31 Jan., showing Olga Knipper (later

Chekhov's wife) as Masha, Maria Germanova as Olga, Vera Baranovskaya as Irina (for another design by the same artist, see No. 99). (Print supplied by the Society for Cultural Relations with the U.S.S.R., London.)

No. 96. *Rosmersholm*, 1906. Setting for a production at the Norwegian National Theatre, Oslo, with Eleonora Duse as Rebecca West (for other Ibsen settings, see Nos. 97, 103). (Photo: L. Szacinski.)

No. 97. *Little Eyolf*, 1924. A setting by Adolphe Appia (1862–1928) for Act II of Ibsen's play, consisting of tree trunks, a curtain, and a simple bench and table. (From the original in the Appia Archives, Swiss Theatre Collection, Bern.)

No. 98. *St. Joan*, 1924. Setting by Charles Ricketts (1866–1931) for the Epilogue in the first production of Shaw's play by Lewis Casson, New Theatre, London, 26 Mar. (From the original in the Walker Art Gallery, Liverpool. Reproduced by permission of the owners of the copyright of the late Charles Ricketts.)

No. 99. *Armoured Train 14–69*, 1927. Setting by V. Simon (1858–1935) for Stanislavsky's production of Ivanov's play at the Moscow Art Theatre, 8 Nov. (for another design by this artist, see No. 95). (Print supplied by the Society for Cultural Relations with the U.S.S.R., London.)

No. 100. *Gammer Gurton's Needle*, 1933. Permanent set by Paul Shelving for Barry Jackson's production of this 16th-century anonymous farce (first produced *c.* 1560) at the Malvern Festival (for another design by this artist, see No. 81). (Print kindly loaned by the late Sir Barry Jackson.)

No. 101. *Amphitryon 38*, 1937. Setting by Lee Simonson (1888–1967) for Act I of the Theatre Guild production of S. N. Berhman's comedy, with Lynn Fontanne and Alfred Lunt, New York, 1 Nov. (From Altman *et al.*, op. cit. Photo: Vandamm.)

No. 102. *Love for Love*, 1943. Setting by Rex Whistler (1905–44) for Gielgud's revival of Congreve's comedy (first produced 1695) at the Phoenix Theatre, London, 8 Apr. (From a positive transparency in the possession of Sir John Gielgud, reproduced by permission of the executors of the late Rex Whistler.)

No. 103. *Peer Gynt*, 1944. Setting by Reece Pemberton for the Old Vic Company's revival of Ibsen's play, produced by Tyrone Guthrie, New Theatre, London, 31 Aug. (for other Ibsen settings, see Nos. 96, 97). (Photo: John Vickers.)

No. 104. *La Folle de Chaillot*, 1945. Setting by Christian Bérard (1902–49) for Act III of Jouvet's production of Giraudoux's play, Athénée, Paris, 19 Dec. (Photo: Lipnitzki.)

No. 105. *All My Sons*, 1947. Setting by Mordecai Gorelik (1899–   ) for Elia Kazan's production of Arthur Miller's play, Coronet Theatre, New York, 29 Jan. (for the setting of another play by Miller, see No. 106). (From Altman *et al.*, op. cit.)

No. 106. *Death of a Salesman*, 1948. Composite set by Jo Mielziner (1901–   ) for Elia Kazan's production of Arthur Miller's play, Morosco Theatre, New York, 10 Feb. (for the setting of another play by Miller, see No. 105). (From Altman *et al.*, op. cit.)

No. 107. *The Lady's Not for Burning*, 1949. Permanent set by Oliver Messel (1905–   ) for Gielgud's production of Christopher Fry's play, Globe Theatre, London, 11 May. (Photo: Angus McBean.)

No. 108. *Mutter Courage und ihre Kinder*, 1949. The Berliner Ensemble in Brecht's play, with his wife, Helene Weigel, as Mother Courage, Peter Leihbroch as Scheiber, and Erwin Geschonneck as Feld Kaplan. (Photo supplied by the Berliner Ensemble.)

No. 109. *Le Bourgeois gentilhomme*, 1952. Permanent set by Suzanne Lalique for a revival of Molière's comedy at the Comédie-Française, Paris (for a costume design for this play, see No. 154; for an illustration of another play by Molière, see No. 24). (Photo: Lipnitzki.)

No. 110. *L'Annonce faite à Marie*, 1955. Setting by Georges Wakhevitch for Act II in a revival of Claudel's play, Comédie-Française, Paris, 17 Feb. (Photo: Lipnitzki.)

No. 111. *J.B.*, 1959. Permanent set by Boris Aronson (1900–   ) for the first production of Archibald MacLeish's play, based on the story of Job, Anta Theatre, New York, 11 Dec. (Photo: Robert Galbraith, reproduced by permission of Boris Aronson.)

No. 112. *Serjeant Musgrave's Dance*, 1959. Setting by Jocelyn Herbert for Act III, Scene 1, of the first production by the English Stage Company of John Arden's play, Royal Court Theatre, London, 22 Oct. (Photo supplied by the English Stage Company.)

No. 113. *Oliver!*, 1960. Design by Sean Kenny for Lionel Bart's adaptation of Dickens's *Oliver Twist*, New Theatre, London, 30 June. Lighting by John Wyckham. (Photo: Strand Electric, London.)

No. 114. *Enrico IV*, 1961. Setting by Mario Chiari for a revival of Pirandello's historical play, produced by Orazio Costa, Piccolo Teatro della Città di Milano. (Photo: Pozzetti.)

Nos. 115–116. TURKEY

No. 115. A painting of an early 20th-century performance of an *Orta Oyunu*, or traditional Turkish open-air play, now in the Istanbul Municipal Museum. The artist, Muazzez, was also an *Orta Oyunu* actor. For a description of such plays, see TURKEY. (Print supplied by Metin And. Photo: Ara Güler.)

No. 116. A modern Turkish play, Orhan Aśena's *Hurrem Sultan*, produced at the State Theatre, Ankara, in 1959. Setting by Refik Eren. (Print supplied by Metin And. Photo: Osman Darcan.)

Nos. 117–125

FAR EASTERN THEATRES—CHINA, JAPAN, INDIA

No. 117. A performance in Pekin in 1935. The Fu Lien Chêng company in *Yü Chou Fêng* (see CHINA, 1.) (Print supplied by Harold Acton.)

No. 118. The Monkey God. Hon Yung-K'uei as Sun Wu-K'ung (the Monkey God) in *An T'ien Hui*. (Print supplied by Harold Acton.)

No. 119. The famous Mei Lan-Fang (1895–1961), the only Chinese actor so far to make an impact on the outside world, in one of his female impersonations. (Print supplied by Harold Acton.)

No. 120. A Kabuki stage. A colour-print by Utagawa Toyokuni of the Nakamura-za in 1798 (see JAPAN, 1). (From Zoe Kincaid, *Kabuki*, 1925.)

No. 121. A Nō stage. The Onishi Ryotaro in Osaka in the early 1920s (see JAPAN, 1). (From Kincaid, op. cit.)

No. 122. A modern play, Tokyo, 1959. *Chidori*, by Chikao Tanaka (1905–), produced at the Actors' Theatre (Haiyūza-Gekijo) in Tokyo, with Etzuko Ichihara as the heroine, Chidori, and Eijiro Tono as her father (see JAPAN, 2). (Print supplied by Toshio Kawataki.)

No. 123. Modern Kabuki. *Kanjinchō* at the Kabuki-za Theatre in Tokyo in 1960. Koshiro VIII as Benkei, Danjūrō XI as Togashi. A revival in a modern style of one of the most representative classical Japanese plays, first performed in 1840. (Print supplied by Toshio Kawataki.)

No. 124. A modern Indian dance-drama, in Ahmedabad, 1959. A village fight, from *Chando shi shyamalo* (*The Moon Is Dark*), by Pannalal Patel. (Photo: Tryambak Patel.)

No. 125. A classical Sanskrit play, Madras, 1961. A revival of the *Abhinjnana Sakuntalam* of Kalidasa. A scene from Act IV, where the heroine Sakuntala takes leave of the forest, the deer, and the trees, and of her foster-father and friends. Performance by the Sanskrita Ranga, Madras, at the All-India Kalidasa Festival, Ujjain, in Nov. It was adjudged the best production of the Festival, and was performed again at the Madras Music Academy in Jan. 1962. (Photo supplied by Dr. Suresh Awasthi.)

Nos. 126–131

SHADOW-SHOW AND PUPPETS

No. 126. A Javanese shadow-show; flat figures, jointed, handled from below (compare with No. 127), but basically a form of rod-puppet (see Nos. 128 and 129). For a description of the Shadow-show, see PUPPETS. (From the Richard Southern Collection. Photo: Dr. Edward Burton MacDowell.)

No. 127. A Turkish shadow-show. Flat figures moved directly by rods (compare with No. 126). This is a recent photograph, as an electric bulb has replaced the old oil-lamp. The initials on the rods indicate the names of the characters, Karagöz (K) and Hacıvat (H) (see TURKEY, 1). (Print supplied by Metin And. Photo: Ara Güler.)

No. 128. Old Javanese rod-puppets. Unlike the flat shadow-show puppets, these are rounded and dressed, and are not jointed (see PUPPETS; also No. 129). (From the originals in the Horniman Museum, London.)

No. 129. Modern Russian rod-puppets. A scene from *The Devil's Mill*. The heroine, Katsa, meets the Devil (see also No. 128). (Print supplied by the Society for Cultural Relations with the U.S.S.R., London.)

No. 130. Modern Rumanian string-puppets (see PUPPETS). A scene from a children's play, *A Purse with two Copper Coins*, by Viorica Filiporie, based on a fairytale by Ton Creanga. Directed by Magareta Vieleuscu, puppets designed and made by Ella Concorici. The play produced at the Tăndărică Puppet Theatre (see also No. 176). (Print supplied by Mrs. Beatrice King.)

No. 131. Modern Hungarian glove-puppets. These are substantially the same as the English Punch-and-Judy puppets (see PUPPETS and No. 141). This illustration shows a puppet-play for children, *Hero John*, produced at the Szeged Puppet Theatre, Budapest. The hero, John, with his stepmother and Nellie. (Photo: B. Tóth.)

Nos. 132–139

COMMEDIA DELL'ARTE

Nos. 132–139. Characters from the Italian *commedia dell'arte* (see COSTUME, 6 and ITALY, 2) through 19th-century eyes. These drawings, based on the original engravings of Jacques Callot (1592/3–1635), were done for his book, *Masques et Bouffons* (Paris, 1860), by Maurice Sand, who did much to further a revival of interest in the old Italian improvised comedy. They show the persistence of certain masks—among them Nos. 134, 135, and 139, which as Pantaloon, Harlequin, and Columbine are still well known, and No. 136, which has been transmuted into an operatic clown.

No. 132. La Ballerina. The dancer of the company, since Columbine was originally a maid-servant and not, as in the later English Harlequinade, a dancer (see No. 140). She played no part in the development of the plot, and was a decorative accessory only. There is no evidence here of any influence from the ballerina of the Romantic Ballet, unless it be the slight touch of the gipsy in the hair-style. The tambourine is from Callot's engraving.

No. 133. Coviello. A character who appears in several early prints and engravings of the *commedia dell'arte* troupes, but who has no distinct personality, though he is one of the best known to students of iconography, owing to Callot's excellent engraving of him on which this drawing is based. He was probably a Neapolitan, and occasionally appeared as a doctor, a merchant, or a gentleman, but he was usually a servant, playing with Pulcinella—better known today as Punch. Coviello himself has disappeared.

No. 134. Pantalone. A Venetian nobleman, who appears in various guises—as an old father, or a silly guardian, or the doting husband of a young wife. His costume is traditional, and varied little during the centuries—a tight-fitting red suit, Turkish slippers, a long, black, sleeved coat, and a soft brimless cap. Shakespeare refers to him (in Jaques's 'Seven Ages of Man' speech in *As You Like It*) as 'the lean and slippered pantaloon, with spectacles on nose and pouch on side'.

No. 135. Harlequino. Although Harlequin is, with Punch, the most famous of all the *commedia dell'arte* masks, he began as Arlecchino, one of the many *zanni* or servant roles, together with Pedrolino, Pulcinella, Scapino, Mezzetino, Scaramuccia, and many others. But while they seemed to merge into one another, several coalescing to form Pierrot, for instance, or Scaramuccia, Harlequin took on, from early times, a distinct personality, and with him the ragged costume common to all the *zanni* became a patchwork coat of many colours. The patches were already stylized by the beginning of the 17th century, as they are shown here in Sand's drawing. Soon they became the regular diamonds or triangles of red, blue, and green cloth which can be seen in No. 140. With this close-fitting garment, well suited to the acrobatics in which Harlequin was to indulge in the English Harlequinade (see Nos. 140, 149) went a little round hat, black slippers and white socks, a black mask, and a magic *bat* or wand with which he gave the signal for the transformation scene in pantomime.

No. 136. Pagliaccio. This character, whose name is found in early *commedia dell'arte* lists, and has become well known through Leoncavallo's opera, was one of the *zanni* or servant roles to which Coviello and Arlecchino also belonged. But no early illustration of him has been found, and here he seems to be a figment of Sand's imagination. His loose white costume is that of Pierrot as he developed in France from Pedrolino, with the characteristic long sleeves, big buttons, frill, and tall hat.

No. 137. Scaramuccia. Since his name means 'little skirmisher', this character must evidently have been originally one of the Captains, together with Mattamoros and Spezzafer (see No. 138). But he is later found among the *zanni*, and with his fellow-servant Scapino (gallicized as Scapin) he figures largely in 17th- and 18th-century French comedy as Scaramouche. The most famous player of the part was Fiorelli, the subject of Angelo Costantini's *La Vie de Scaramouche* (Paris, 1695), and the master of Molière. Sand has here turned him into a mixture of soldier and musician.

No. 138. Il Capitano Spezzafer. One of the braggart soldiers of the *commedia dell'arte*; their names were innumerable, but their characters all much alike. Based on the Spanish soldier of the 15th century, the Captain wore a plumed hat, a ruff, a short military cloak, dark breeches and boots, and always a sword. He had enormous black mustachios, and sometimes a beard. Originally a serious character, he became a caricature, a boaster, bully, booby, beggar, and a coward. He may descend from the Miles Gloriosus of Plautus; and may have been the prototype of Shakespeare's Ancient Pistol.

No. 139. Colombine. The most famous of the many maid-servants of the *commedia dell'arte*. Originally a rough, even vulgar, character, she gradually became quieter and more refined, until in 1683, when the part was first played by Catarina Biancolelli in Paris, she emerged as the confidant, almost the equal, of the heroine, with nothing but a small lace apron, seen here, to remind us of her earlier position. From this it was a short step to the lover of Harlequin and the dancing Columbine of the English pantomime (see No. 140).

Nos. 140–143

HARLEQUINADE, PUNCH, PANTOMIME

No. 140. A Harlequinade at Covent Garden, London, *c.* 1770. This shows the large fore-stage with proscenium doors and stage boxes (for Drury Lane at the same period, see No. 30), and a set consisting of wings and backcloth painted in angled perspective (the Bibienas's *scena d'angolo*, see No. 64). On stage, characters from the *commedia dell'arte*, already recognizably transmuted into their English form—Harlequin (see No. 135) and Columbine (see No. 139) escaping from their pursuer, probably Pantaloon (see No. 134), who lost his long coat shortly after his arrival in London in the 'Italian night scenes', and is seen tripping over a *zanni*, or servant, who is well on his way to becoming the purely English Clown (see HARLEQUINADE, and PANTOMIME, 3). (From the Mander and Mitchenson Collection.)

No. 141. A Punch and Judy booth, *c.* 1870. The portable puppet-theatre, with a long history stretching back into medieval times, and perhaps beyond. On stage, the puppet Punch, directly descended from Pulcinella of the *commedia dell'arte*, via the French Polichinelle, and the live dog Toby. On the right-hand side the showman's partner, mate, or 'bottler', whose job it was to gather a crowd with his music and patter, to exchange some dialogue with Punch, and to take up the collection. He is beating a drum, slung on a leather strap over his right shoulder, and playing the panpipes which are fastened in position by a stock round his neck. Invisible behind the curtain is the showman himself, manipulating Punch (see PUNCH AND JUDY, and TOBY). This cutting from a newspaper is entitled 'A Professional Dog'. (From the George Speaight Collection.)

No. 142. *Dick Whittington and his Cat*, 1852. A scene from a pantomime by T. L. Greenwood at Sadler's Wells, 27 Dec. The sub-title of the piece, *Old Dame Fortune and Harlequin Lord Mayor of London*, shows the tenuous connexion with the *commedia dell'arte* via Harlequin, but this was soon to be lost (see PANTOMIME, 3). (From *The Illustrated London News*, 1 Jan. 1853. Mander and Mitchenson Collection.)

No. 143. *Puss in Boots*, 1887. The pantomime, already established as an annual Christmas entertainment by this time, has become less grotesque (see No. 142), and provides occasion for elaborate costuming, crowd scenes, stage sets, and specialized turns, enlarging the fairytale opening and pushing a vestigial Harlequinade to the final moments of the last act. In this pantomime written by E. L. Blanchard for Drury Lane (he had previously written one on the same theme for the Crystal Palace, 1873), the scenery and costumes were designed by Wilhelm (see No. 152). (From *The Graphic*, 7 Jan. 1888. Enthoven Theatre Collection, Victoria and Albert Museum, London.)

Nos. 144–161
SOME COSTUME DESIGNS, 1609–1949

(For further details, see COSTUME, *passim*.)

No. 144. Design by Inigo Jones (1573–1652) for Penthesilea in Ben Jonson's *Masque of Queens*, 1609, given before the Court at Whitehall on Oct. 2 (for a scene design by the same artist, see No. 61). (From the Collection of the Duke of Devonshire, reproduced by permission of the Trustees of the Chatsworth Settlement.)

No. 145. Design by Stefano della Bella (1610–64) for a masque costume. (From the original in the Victoria and Albert Museum, London.)

No. 146. Design by Henri Gissey (1621–73) for a grotesque male costume representing Music. (From the original in the Victoria and Albert Museum, London.)

No. 147. Design by the elder Jean Bérain (1637–1711) for a female costume, probably for Hermione in Lully's 'Cadmus et Hermione', 1673. (From the original in the Victoria and Albert Museum, London.)

No. 148. Design by Lodovico Burnacini (1636–1707) for a male masque costume, probably a Red Indian warrior. (From the original in the Victoria and Albert Museum, London.)

No. 149. Engraving by Claude Gillot (1673–1722), 'La révérence d'Arlequin', 1695 (for other illustrations of Harlequin, see Nos. 135, 140). (From the Victoria and Albert Museum, London.)

No. 150. Design by J. R. Planché (1796–1880) for Constance in Charles Kemble's production of *King John*, Covent Garden, London, 3 Mar. 1823. This was the first time in England that a play had been set and dressed with some regard to historical accuracy, and led to the later work along the same lines of Charles Kean. (From Planché's *Costumes of Shakespeare's 'King John'* . . . , 1823–5. British Museum, London.)

No. 151. Design by George II, Duke of Saxe-Meiningen (1826–1914) for Junker Bleichenwang (Sir Andrew Aguecheek) in the Meininger production of *Was ihr wollt* (*Twelfth Night*), *c.* 1874 (for a scene design by the same hand, see No. 69; for other *Twelfth Night* sets, see Nos. 77, 80). The Meiningers were for a long time considered to have brought historical accuracy in costume, as well as other innovations, into the English theatre during their visits to London, but exhaustive research by, among others, Miss M. St. Clare Byrne has established the precedence of Kemble, Macready, and Kean in this respect (see Byrne, 'Charles Kean and the Meininger Myth', *Theatre Research / Recherches Théâtrales*, vol. vi, no. 3, 1964, and 'What we said about the Meiningers in 1881', *Essays and Studies*, 1965). (From Max Grube, *Geschichte der Meininger*, 1925.)

No. 152. Design by Wilhelm (William John Charles Pitcher, 1859–1925) for Touchstone in Robert Courtneidge's production of *As You Like It*, Princess's Theatre, Manchester, between 1896 and 1903. A fantasticated adaptation of the traditional costume of the Court jester (see also No. 143 for other designs by Wilhelm; No. 156 for another design for the same play). (From the original in the Victoria and Albert Museum, London.)

No. 153. Design by Albert Rutherston (1881–1953) for Hermione in Granville-Barker's production of *The Winter's Tale*, Savoy Theatre, London, 21 Sept. 1912 (see also No. 167). (From the original in the Victoria and Albert Museum, London.)

No. 154. Design by Ernest Stern (1876–1954) for Reinhardt's production of *Der Bürger als Edelmann* (*Le Bourgeois gentilhomme*), Stuttgart, 24 Oct. 1912 (see also Nos. 78 and 158 for other Reinhardt productions; No. 109 for another production of Molière's play). (From the original in the Victoria and Albert Museum, London.)

No. 155. Design by Alexander Golovin

(1863–?1930) for Meyerhold's production of Lermontov's *Maskerad*, Alexandrinsky, St. Petersburg (now Leningrad), 25 Feb. 1917. (From a volume of Golovin's designs for this production, costumes and sets, published Moscow, 1946.)

No. 156. Design by Claude Lovat Fraser (1890–1921) for a Court Lady in Nigel Playfair's production of *As You Like It*, Lyric, Hammersmith, 21 Apr. 1920 (see also Nos. 152, 174). (From the original in the possession of the artist's widow.)

No. 157. Design by Michael Weight (1906–) for Lady Bracknell in Nigel Playfair's black-and-white production of Wilde's *The Importance of Being Earnest*, Lyric, Hammersmith, 7 July 1930. (From the original in the Victoria and Albert Museum, London.)

No. 158. Design by Titina Rota for the Duke of Aragon in Max Reinhardt's production of *The Merchant of Venice*, Venice, 1934 (see also Nos. 78, 83, 154). (From *Theatre Arts Prints*, vol. iii.)

No. 159. Design by Stewart Chaney (1910–) for Julia in Esmé Church's production of Sheridan's *The Rivals*, Old Vic, 6 Dec. 1938. (From *Theatre Arts Monthly*, Oct. 1938.)

No. 160. Design by Mariano Andreu for Benedick (played by Anthony Quayle in 1949, John Gielgud in 1950) in Gielgud's production of *Much Ado About Nothing*, Shakespeare Memorial Theatre, Stratford-upon-Avon, 19 Apr. 1949. (Shakespeare Memorial Theatre Collection.)

No. 161. Design by Roger Furse (1903–) for Macbeth in Glen Byam Shaw's production of *Macbeth*, Shakespeare Memorial Theatre, Stratford-upon-Avon, 7 June, 1949 (see also Nos. 72, 75, 81). (Shakespeare Memorial Theatre Collection.)

Nos. 162–165

SOME THEATRICAL PAINTINGS

No. 162. *Romeo and Juliet*, 1765. An engraving by S. F. Ravenet, after a painting by Benjamin West; Garrick and Mrs. Bellamy in the Tomb Scene, a cut-out in the style of de Loutherbourg with a Gothic backcloth. This shows Juliet waking before the death of Romeo, in the version used by Garrick (and possibly before him), which held the stage until the time of Macready. It was this version which Berlioz saw in Paris during Charles Kemble's 1827 season, with Harriet Smithson as Juliet, and followed in his choral symphony (see *Shakespeare in Music*, ed. Hartnoll, pp. 192–5). (For a description of this engraving, see M. St. C. Byrne, *Catalogue of an Exhibition of Shakespearean Production . . .*, 1947, item 33; see also Nos. 73, 82.) (Photo: R. B. Fleming.)

No. 163. *The School for Scandal*, *c.* 1802. The Screen Scene, from a painting by William Dunlap (1766–1839), now in the Harvard Theater Collection, showing Joseph Jefferson, John Hodgkinson, Mrs. Whitlock, and Joseph Tyler as Sir Peter, Charles Surface, Lady Teazle, and Joseph Surface respectively, probably at the Park Theatre, New York (for the same scene in the first English production of 1777, see No. 30; for the original playbill, see No. 166). (From the Harvard Theater Collection.)

No. 164. *Henry VIII*, 1817. The Trial Scene (also known as 'The Kemble Family'), a mezzotint by George Clint, after a painting by Henry Harlow. A composite group, showing Mrs. Siddons as Queen Katharine with her brothers John Philip, Charles, and Stephen Kemble as Wolsey, Cromwell, and Henry VIII. Although they all appeared in these parts at different times at Covent Garden and elsewhere, there is as yet no definite evidence that they all played them at the same time anywhere. The scenery depicted is probably a stock set by William Capon (1767–1827), designed for Kemble at Drury Lane in 1794, lost in the fire of 1809, and remade from the old designs for Kemble at Covent Garden. (See M. St. C. Byrne, op. cit., item 49; also W. Moelwyn Merchant, *Shakespeare and the Artist*, 1959, pp. 200–6; also Nos. 76, 84, 89.) (Print supplied by the Enthoven Theatre Collection, Victoria and Albert Museum, London.)

No. 165. *A New Way to Pay Old Debts*, *c.* 1816. A painting by George Clint, now in the Garrick Club, London, showing Edmund Kean as Sir Giles Overreach in a revival of Massinger's play (first performed *c.* 1625), which opened at Drury Lane, London, on 12 Jan. 1816. (Reproduced by permission of the Garrick Club, from a print supplied by Messrs. Longmans, Green & Co.)

Nos. 166–176

PLAYBILLS AND POSTERS, 1777–1957

No. 166. Playbill for the second performance of Sheridan's *The School for Scandal*, Drury Lane, London, 9 May 1777 (see also Nos. 30, 163). (From the Enthoven Theatre Collection, Victoria and Albert Museum, London.)

No. 167. Playbill for Charles Kean's revival of *The Winter's Tale*, Princess's Theatre, London, 28 Apr. 1856. It was in this production that Ellen Terry, aged 9, made her first appearance on the stage, playing Mamillius. Her father and sister Kate were also playing small parts (see also No. 153). (From the Enthoven Theatre Collection, Victoria and Albert Museum, London.)

No. 168. Playbill for *Uncle Tom's Cabin*, 10 Oct. 1859, at the Pine Street Theatre, Troy, N.Y., U.S.A. Probably the most famous of all American melodramas, this was based on the novel by Harriet Beecher Stowe, published in 1852. For a note on it, see NEGRO IN THE AMERICAN THEATRE. (From the Harvard Theater Collection.)

No. 169. Poster for *Mazeppa*, 7 Nov. 1864, at Astley's Amphitheatre, London; the best known of the many 'hippodramatic spectacles' put on by purveyors of melodrama. Based on Byron's poem, it was first seen (in a version by H. M. Milner) at the Coburg (later the Old Vic) in 1823. It moved to Astley's in 1831. Adah Isaacs Menken first played the part of Mazeppa in 1863 in America, and it is the only one to be associated with her name. She caused a pleasurable scandal by her appearance, apparently naked, but in reality in flesh-coloured tights and singlet, bound to the back of a galloping horse. (From the Enthoven Theatre Collection, Victoria and Albert Museum, London.)

No. 170. Two posters for productions in 1896 by Sarah Bernhardt at the Théâtre de la Renaissance, Paris, which she managed from 1893 to 1898. Both are by Alphonse [Alfons Maria] Mucha (1860–1939). Born in Austro-Hungary, he spent most of his working life in Paris, and was a leading exponent of the *art nouveau* style of the 1890s, of which these posters are excellent examples. Seven feet long, they were printed in two halves and then pasted together. The join can be clearly seen in (*a*) *La Dame aux Camélias*. This famous play by Dumas *fils*, first produced in 1852, provided Bernhardt with one of her most popular successes. She was first seen as Marguérite Gautier, its consumptive prostitute heroine, in America in 1880. A year later she played it at the Gaiety Theatre in London, and not until 1882 did she venture to play it in Paris, with her young husband, Ambroise Aristide Damala, as Armand. (Victoria and Albert Museum. Crown copyright.) (*b*) *Lorenzaccio*. This was the first performance of Alfred de Musset's poetic tragedy, written in Venice in 1834. It was 'adapted' for contemporary playgoers by Armand d'Artois, and though it was hailed by the French critics as a masterpiece, and Bernhardt's acting in it as 'incomparably sublime', it fared less well in London, where Shaw, who disliked Bernhardt, dismissed it as 'a new pretext for the old exhibition'. In 1933 a translation of the play, as *Night's Candles*, by May Agate (billed as Grant Yates), who had seen Bernhardt in the part in 1912, was staged at the Shilling Theatre, Fulham, and later at the Queen's on Shaftesbury Avenue, with Ernest Milton in the name part. (Print supplied by the Victoria and Albert Museum, London. Reprinted by kind permission of the Grosvenor Gallery, London.)

No. 171. Poster for a revival of *The Great World of London*, 3 Apr. 1899, at the Standard Theatre, Shoreditch. This highly coloured topical melodrama, which does not appear to have been published (the manuscript is in the Lord Chamberlain's Office in London), was written by one of the managers of the Standard, Walter Melville, in collaboration with George Lander. It had been successful enough on its first production, also at the Standard, 31 Oct. 1898, to warrant a revival. The poster, which, unlike the earlier playbills (see Nos. 166, 167), is entirely pictorial, has no artistic merit whatsoever, but manages to convey a good deal of information and excitement, and was exactly suited to the large and unsophisticated audience to which it was addressed. (For contemporary posters of artistic merit, see Nos. 170, 172–6.) (From the Enthoven Theatre Collection, Victoria and Albert Museum, London.)

No. 172. Poster by Toulouse-Lautrec (Henri Raymond de Toulouse-Lautrec-Monfa) (1864–1901), 1893, to advertise the cabaret show of Aristide Bruant. (Victoria and Albert Museum, London.)

No. 173. Poster by the Beggarstaff Brothers (William Nicholson, 1872–1949, and James Pryde, 1866–1941) for Irving's production of *Don Quixote*, Lyceum, London, 4 May 1895. The play, based by W. G. Wills on an incident in Cervantes's novel, was not a success, though Irving, who, according to Kate Terry's daughter, looked 'like a Doré engraving (the perfect White Knight of Lewis Carroll's *Alice*)', received an ovation when he appeared in it on Saturday, 25 May, the day on which the news of his knighthood (the first conferred on an actor) was made public. It was never revived. The poster, for which Irving paid the artists £100, was never used on the hoardings for which it was intended; but, reproduced in a number of art journals, it had a great influence on poster design. (From the original cut-out design now in the Victoria and Albert Museum, London.)

No. 174. Poster by Claude Lovat Fraser (1890–1921) for Nigel Playfair's revival of *The Beggar's Opera*, Lyric, Hammersmith, 5 June 1920. One of the best, and probably the best known, of all London theatrical posters (for a costume design by this artist, see No. 156). (From the Victoria and Albert Museum, London.)

No. 175. Poster by Charles Mozley for a revival of Shaw's *Captain Brassbound's Conversion*, Lyric, Hammersmith, 13 Oct. 1948. (From the Mander and Mitchenson Collection. Reproduced by permission of Tennent Productions Ltd.)

No. 176. A modern poster from Rumania for a puppet-play, *Harlequin's Millions*, at the Tăndărică Theatre (see also No. 130). Boldly designed and executed in black and two clear colours, this combines words with a simple pictorial design in balanced proportions. (Poster supplied by Mrs. Beatrice King.)

1. Theatre at Epidaurus

2. Theatre at Priene

3. Marble mask (male)

4. Marble mask (female)

5. Menander with masks

6. Iphigenia in Tauris

7. The Revenge of Medea

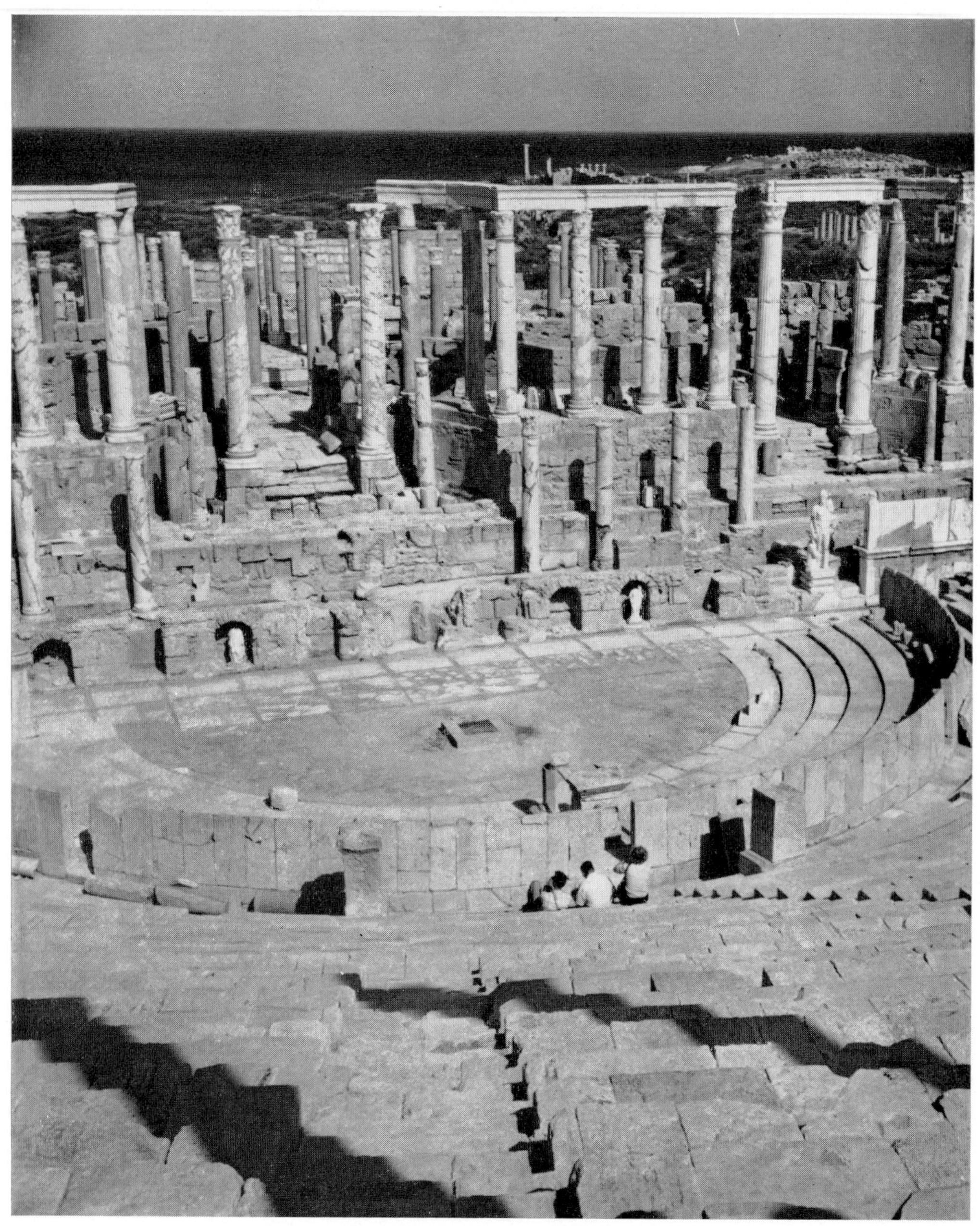

8. Theatre at Leptis Magna

9. Theatre at Verulamium (St. Albans)

10. A tragic scene

(*a*) Terracotta

(*b*) Ivory

11. Actors

12. A comic scene

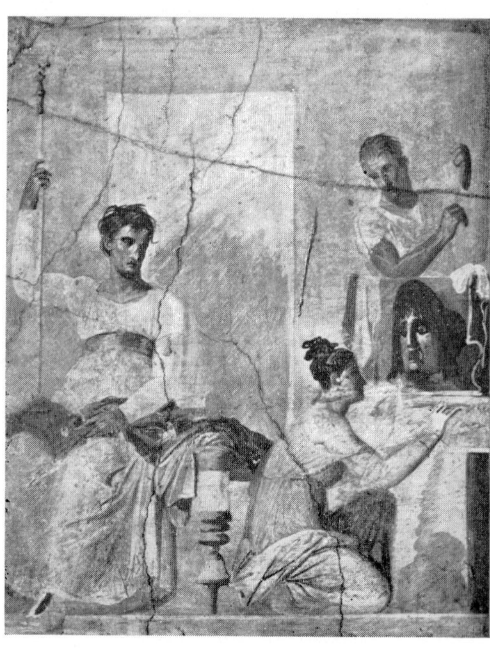

13. Actor with mask

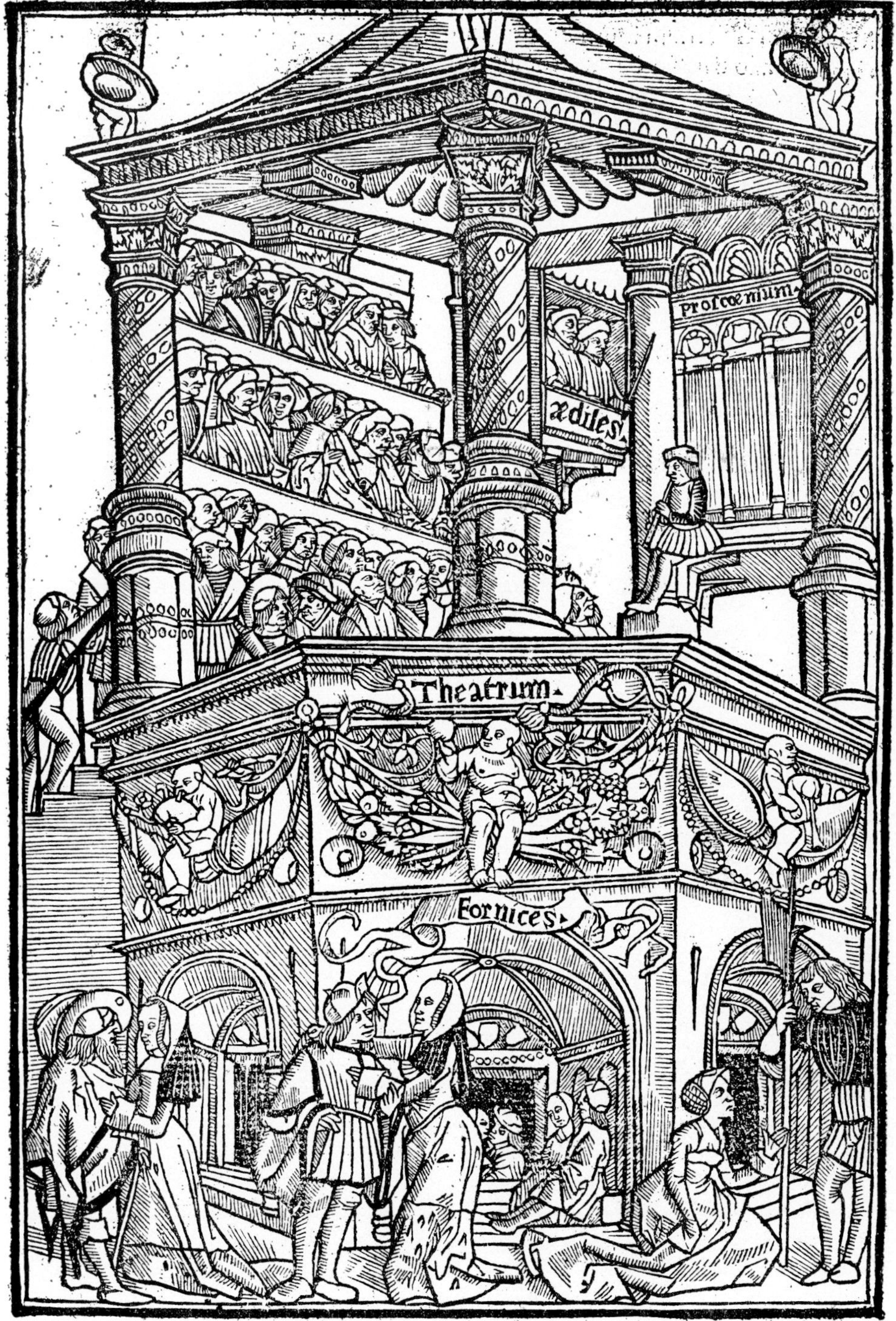

14. A Renaissance Terence-Stage, 1493

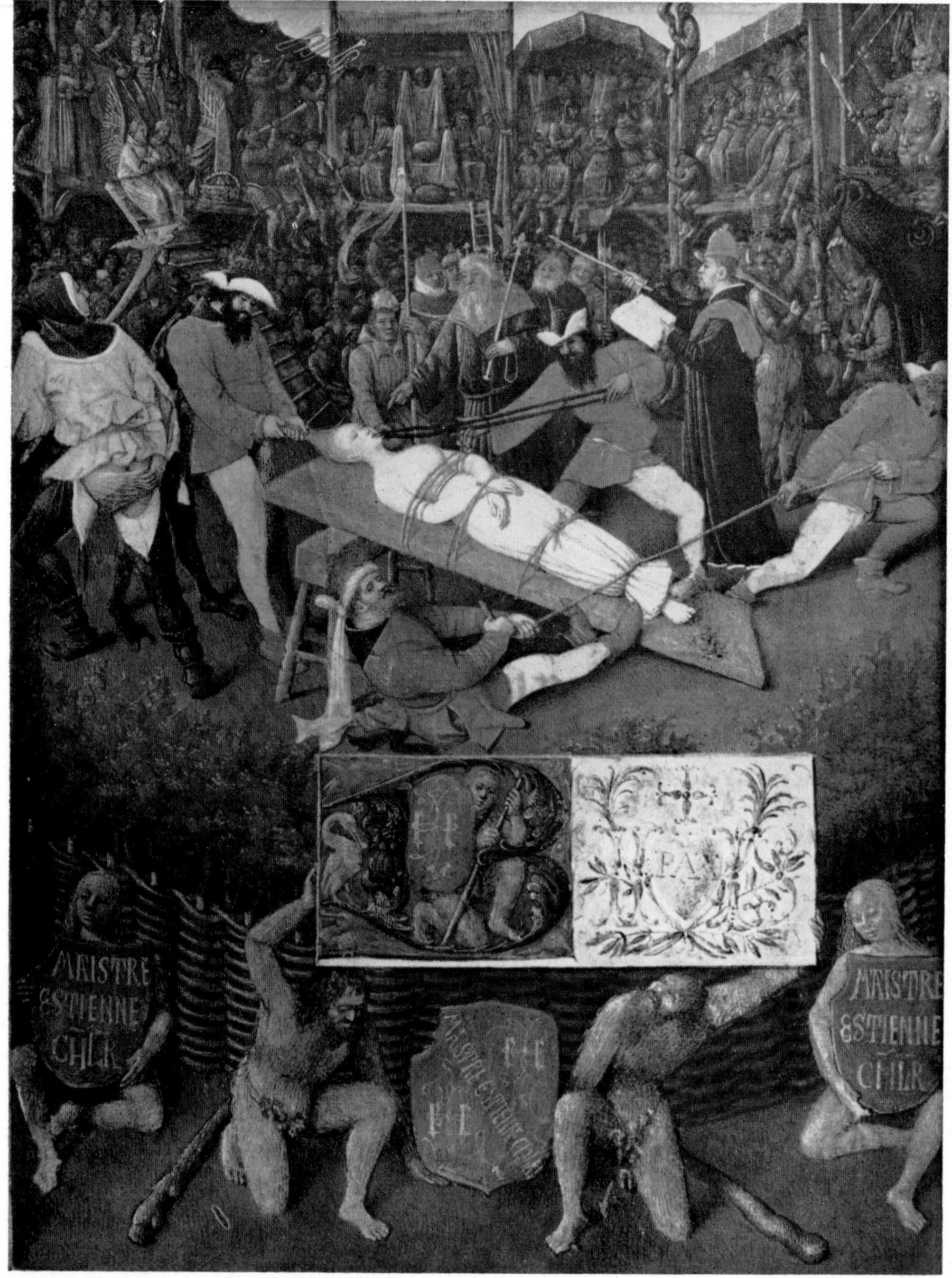

15. A religious drama, *c.* 1460

16. Hell-mouth

17. A secular comedy, 16th century

18. A Court performance in Paris, 1581

19. A Pageant of the Nativity, 1615

20. Teatro Olimpico, Vicenza, 1585

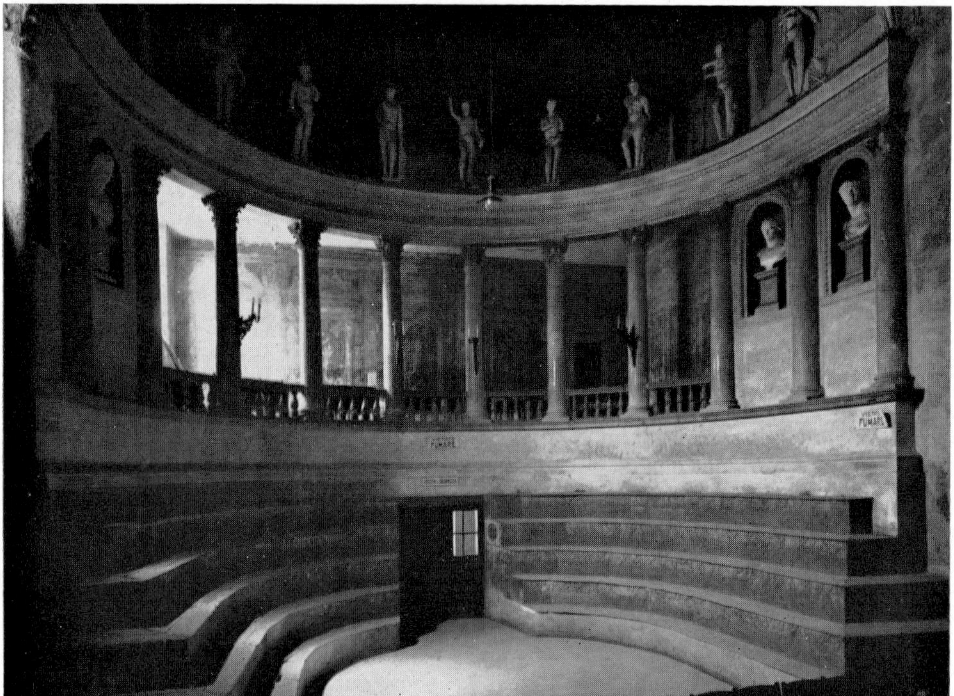

21. Theatre at Sabbionetta, 1588

22. The Swan Theatre, London, 1596

23. A Commonwealth stage, London, *c.* 1650

24. A Court performance at Versailles, 1674

25. The first Schouwburg, Amsterdam, 1637

26. The rebuilt Schouwburg, Amsterdam, 1738

27. Theatre Royal, Bristol, 1766

28. Chestnut Street Theatre, Philadelphia, 1791

29. Drottningholm Court Theatre, Sweden, 1766

30. Drury Lane, London, 1777

31. Drury Lane, London, 1815

32. Covent Garden, London, 1815

33. The Comédie-Française, Paris, 1808

34. The Bolshoi Theatre, Moscow, 1856

35. The Royal Coburg, London, 1818

36. The Old Vic, London, 1948

37. The old Burgtheater, Vienna, 1888

38. The new Burgtheater, Vienna, 1955

39. The Grosses Schauspielhaus, Berlin, 1919

40. The Stadsteater, Malmö, Sweden, 1944

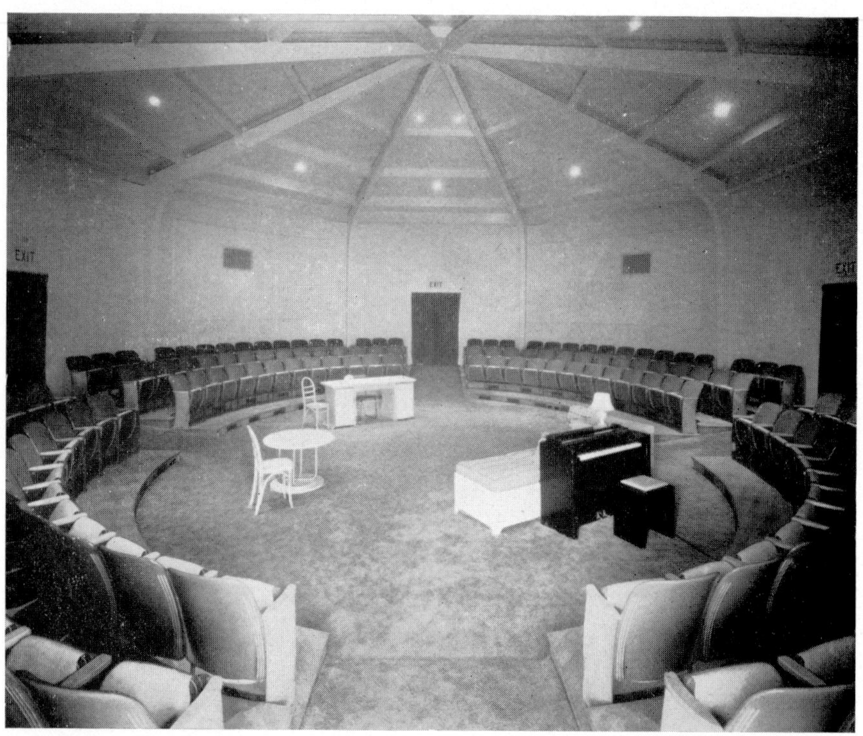

41. The Penthouse Theatre, University of Washington, Seattle, 1940

42. The Mermaid Theatre, London, 1959

43. The Shakespearean Festival Theatre, Stratford, Ontario, 1957

44. The Belgrade Theatre, Coventry, 1958

45. The San Carlos, Lisbon, 1942

46. Drury Lane, London, 1948

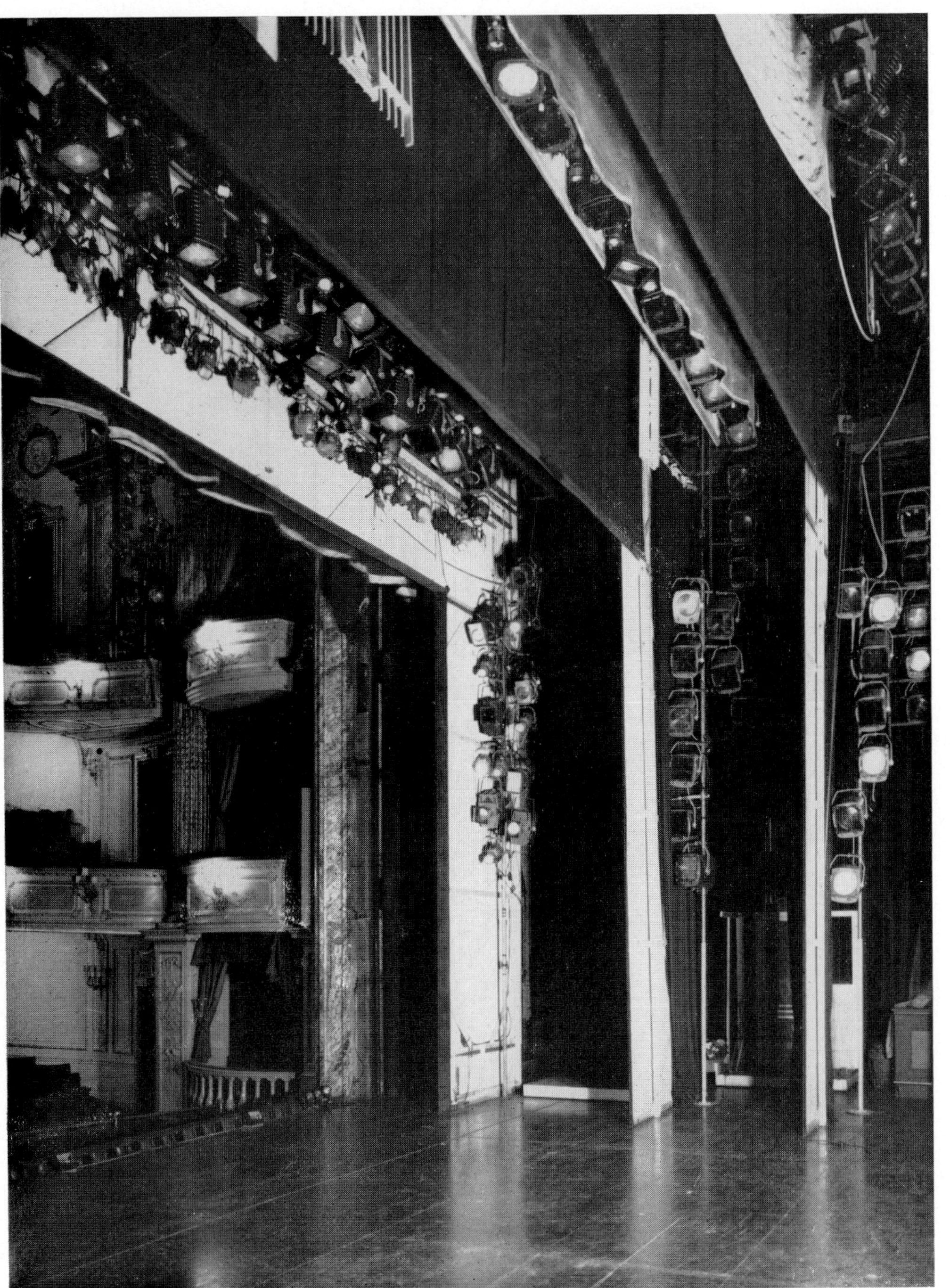

47. Her Majesty's Theatre, London, 1961

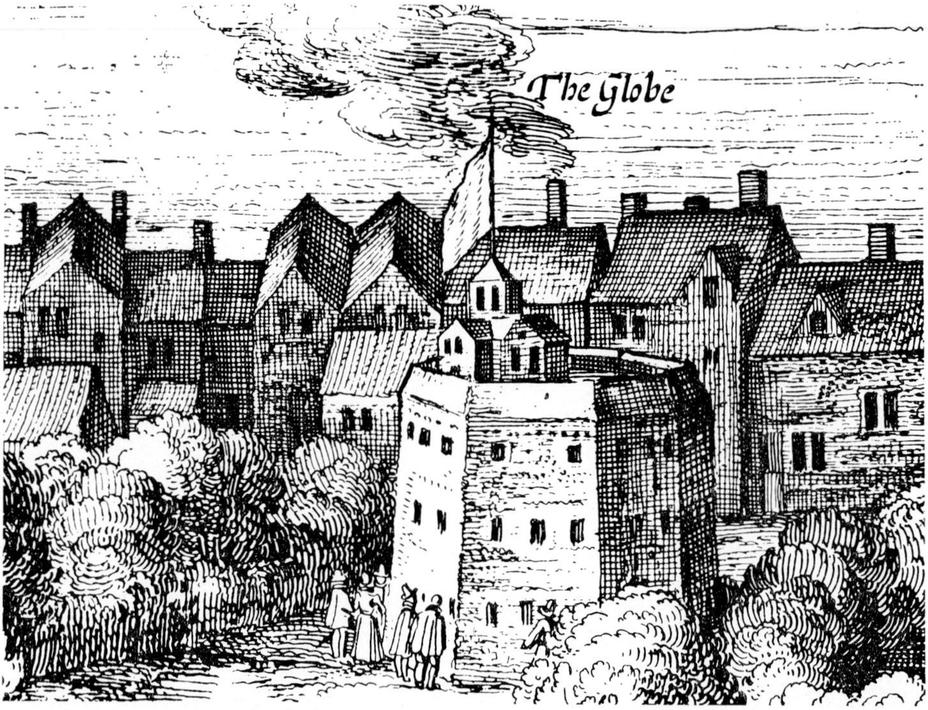

48. The Globe Playhouse, London, 1616

49. The Surrey Theatre, London, 1814

50. The old theatre at Stratford-upon-Avon, 1879

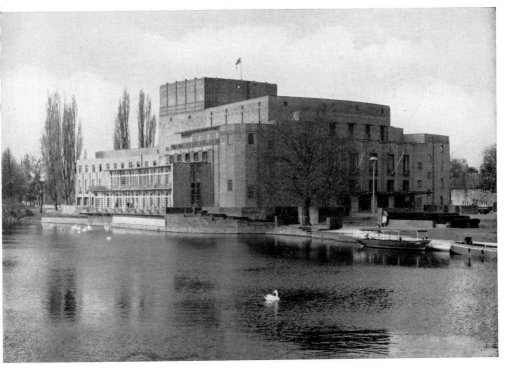

51. The new theatre at Stratford-upon-Avon, 1932

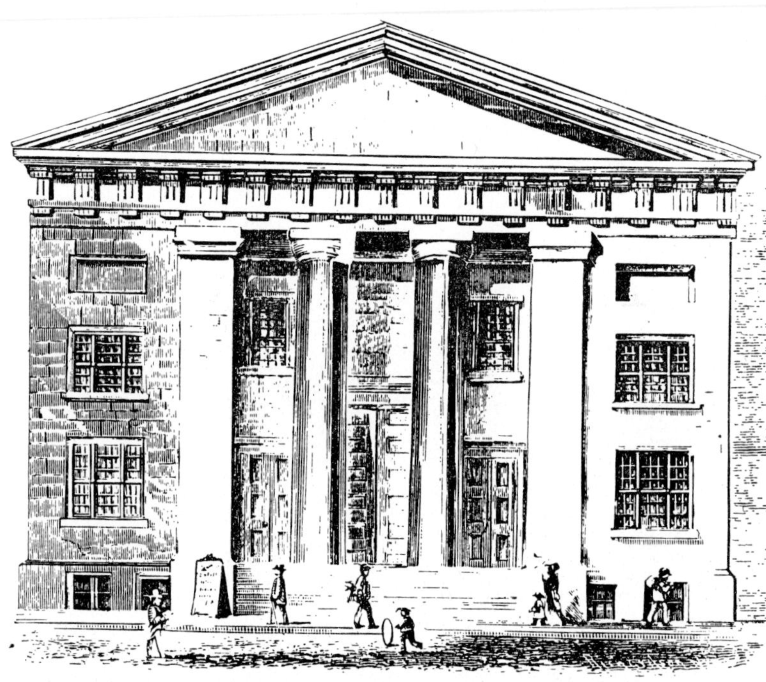

52. The Bowery Theatre, New York, 1859

53. The Cleveland Playhouse, Ohio, 1927

54. The Bolshoi Theatre, Moscow, 1856

55. The Bolshoi Theatre, Minsk, *c*. 1953

56. Satyric Scene

57. Comic Scene

58. Tragic Scene

Serlio, 1545

59. Buontalenti, 1589

60. Parigi, *c.* 1620

61. Inigo Jones, 1634

62. Torelli, *c.* 1660

63. Dorset Garden Theatre, London, 1673

64. Galli-Bibiena family, *c.* 1690

65. Český Krumlov, Czechoslovakia, *c.* 1766

66. Juvarra, *c*. 1711

67. English melodrama, 1813

68. Schinkel, 1867

69. George, Duke of Saxe-Meiningen, *c.* 1884

70. English provinces, 1893

71. *Othello*, 1837

72. *Macbeth*, 1853

73. *Romeo and Juliet*, 1882

74. *Hamlet*, 1900

75. *Macbeth*, 1908

76. *Henry VIII*, 1910

77. *Twelfth Night*, 1912

78. *Henry IV, Part I*, 1912

79. *Hamlet*, 1913

80. *Twelfth Night*, 1914

81. *Macbeth*, 1928

82. *Romeo and Juliet*, 1930

83. *The Merchant of Venice*, 1931

84. *Henry VIII*, 1931

85. *The Tempest*, 1934

86. *The Taming of the Shrew*, 1937

87. *Othello*, 1937

88. *Antony and Cleopatra*, 1947

89. *Henry VIII*, 1949

90 *Hamlet*, 1954

91. *King Lear*, 1955

92. *The Merry Wives of Windsor*, 1955

93. *King Lear*, 1959

94. *The Merry Wives of Windsor*, 1962

95. *Three Sisters*, 1901

96. *Rosmersholm*, 1906

97. *Little Eyolf*, 1924

98. *St. Joan*, 1924

99. *Armoured Train 14–69*, 1927

100. *Gammer Gurton's Needle*, 1933

101. *Amphitryon 38*, 1937

102. *Love for Love*, 1943

103. *Peer Gynt*, 1944

104. *La Folle de Chaillot*, 1945

105. *All My Sons*, 1947

106. *Death of a Salesman*, 1948

107. *The Lady's Not for Burning*, 1949

108. *Mutter Courage und ihre Kinder*, 1949

109. *Le Bourgeois gentilhomme*, 1952

110. *L'Annonce faite à Marie*, 1955

111. *J.B.*, 1959

112. *Serjeant Musgrave's Dance*, 1959

113. *Oliver!*, 1960

114. *Enrico IV*, 1961

115. An open-air street performance

116. A modern play, Ankara, 1959

117. A performance in Pekin, 1935

118. The Monkey God

119. Mei Lan-Fang

120. A Kabuki stage, 1798

121. A Nō stage, *c*. 1922

122. A modern play, Tokyo, 1959

123. Modern Kabuki, 1960

124. A modern dance-drama, 1959

125. A classical play, 1961

126. A Javanese shadow-show

127. A Turkish shadow-show

128. Old Javanese rod-puppets

129. Modern Russian rod-puppets

130. Modern Rumanian string-puppets

131. Modern Hungarian glove-puppets

132. La Ballerina

133. Coviello

134. Pantalone

135. Harlequino

136. Pagliaccio

137. Scaramuccia

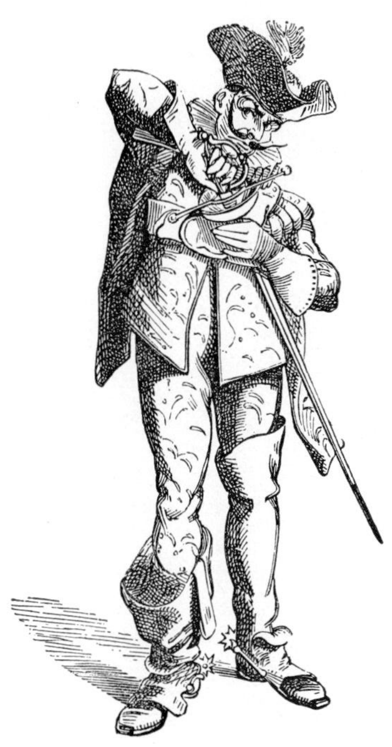

138. Il Capitano Spezzafer

139. Colombine

140. A Harlequinade at Covent Garden, London, *c.* 1770

141. A Punch and Judy booth, London, *c.* 1870

142. *Dick Whittington and his Cat*, Sadler's Wells, London, 1852

143. *Puss in Boots*, Drury Lane, London, 1887

SOME COSTUME DESIGNS

144. Inigo Jones

145. Della Bella

146. Gissey

147. Bérain

148. Burnacini

149. Gillot

150. Planché

151. Meininger

152. Wilhelm

SOME COSTUME DESIGNS

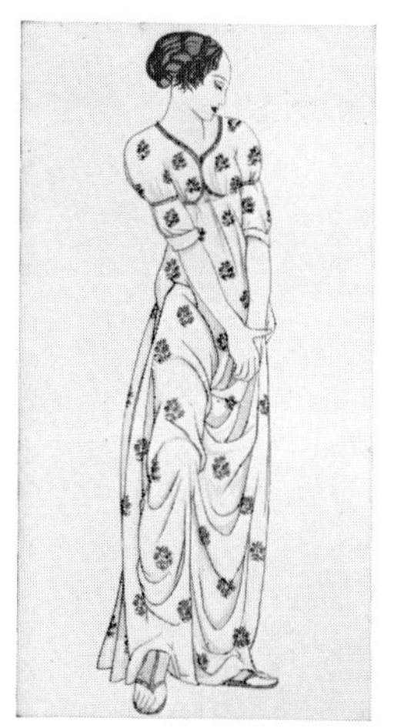

153. Albert Rutherston

154. Ernest Stern

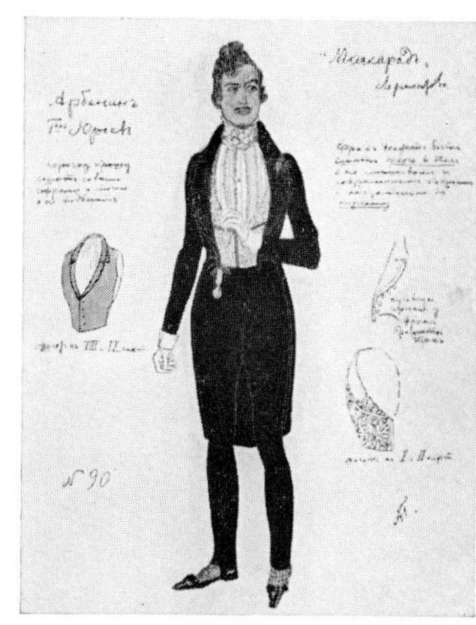

155. Alexander Golovin

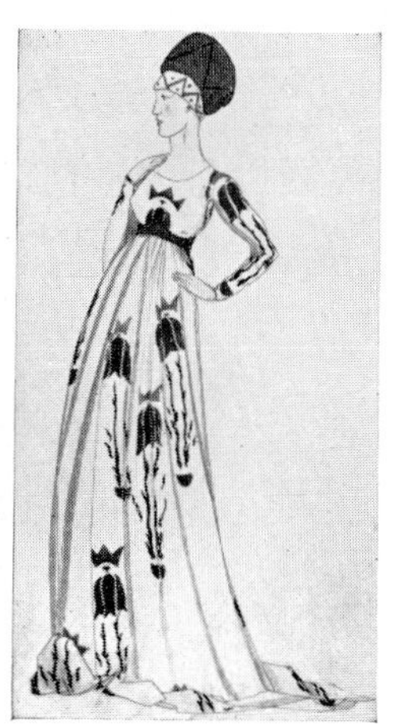

156. Lovat Fraser

157. Michael Weight

158. Titina Rota

159. Stewart Chaney

160. Mariano Andreu

161. Roger Furse

162. *Romeo and Juliet*, 1765

163. *The School for Scandal*, c. 1802

164. *Henry VIII*, 1817

165. *A New Way to Pay Old Debts*, *c.* 1816

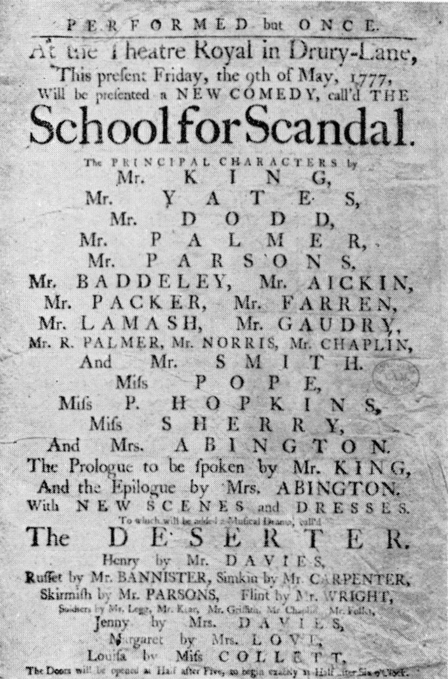

166. 1777

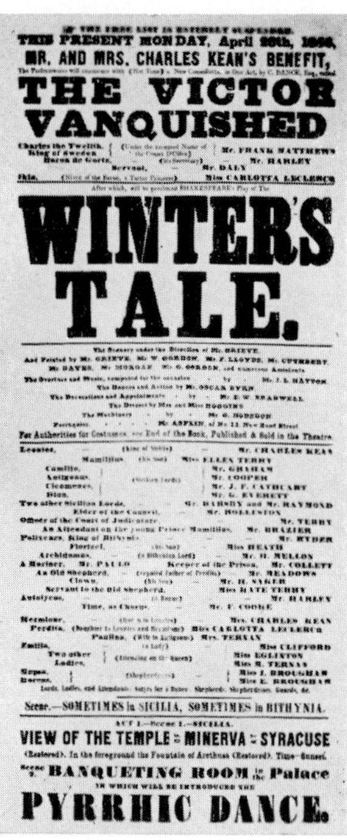

167. 1856

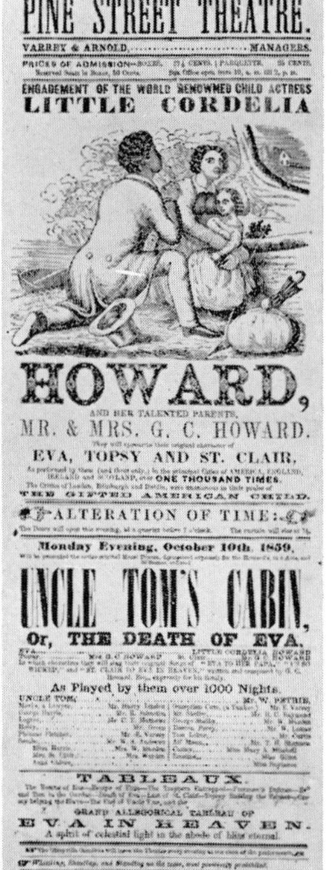

168. 1859

169. 1864

(*a*)

(*b*)

170. 1896

STANDARD THEATRE, BISHOPSGATE and SHOREDITCH EASTER MONDAY AT 2 & 7.45
APRIL 3rd, and During the Week.
GRAND REVIVAL
THE GREAT WORLD OF LONDON
BY GEORGE LANDER & WALTER MELVILLE
SHADOWED.
THE RAILWAY MURDER.
"CORNERED!"
THE VERDICT.
13
DAVID ALLEN & SONS
HARROW

171. 1899

172. 1893

173. 1895

174. 1920

175. 1948

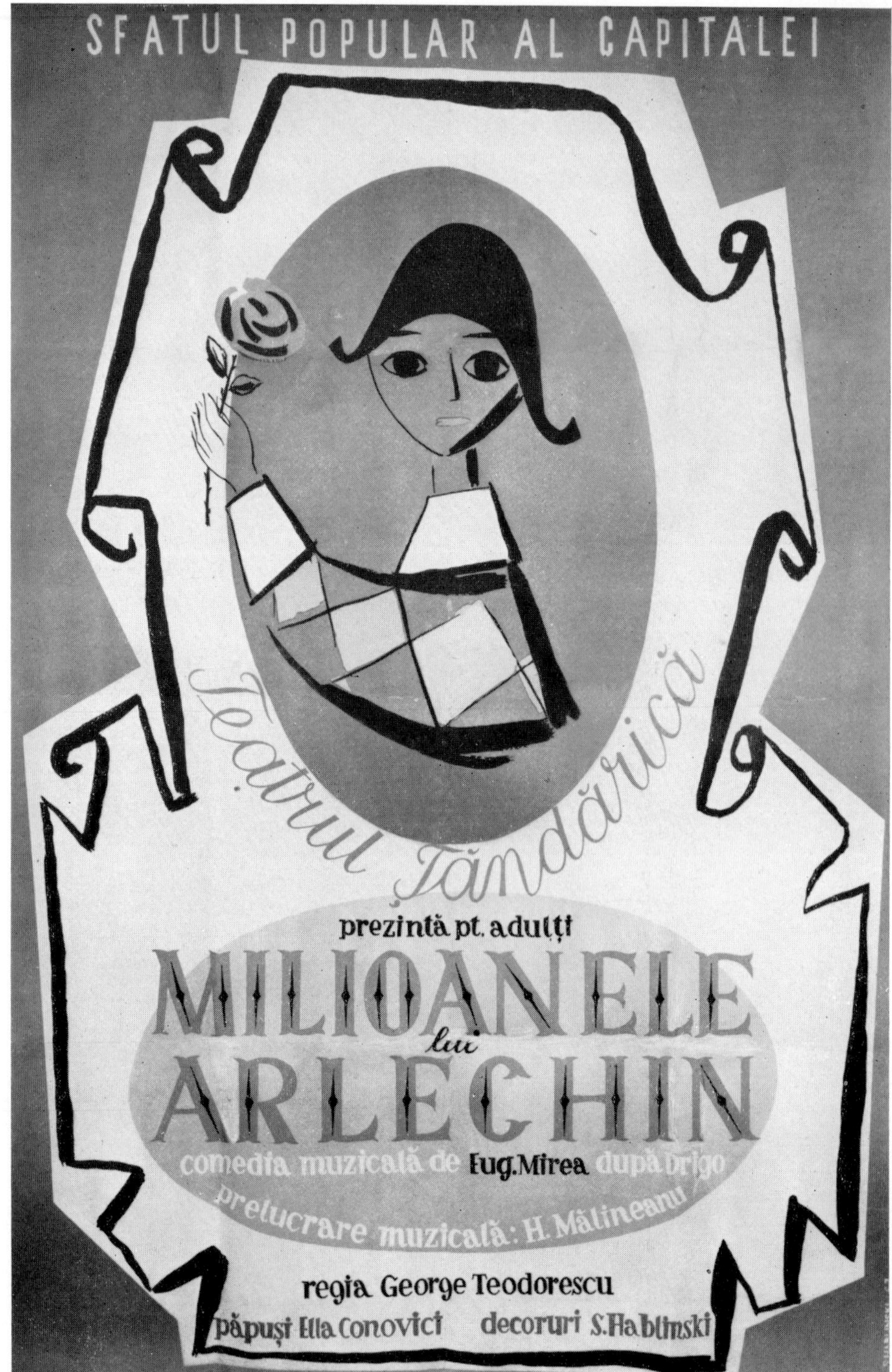
SFATUL POPULAR AL CAPITALEI
Teatrul Țăndărică
prezintă pt. adulți
MILIOANELE
lui
ARLECHIN
comedia muzicală de Eug. Mirea după Drigo
prelucrare muzicală: H. Mălineanu
regia George Teodorescu
păpuși Ella Conovici
decoruri S. Hablinski

176. 1957